Lipo Wang   Ke Chen   Yew Soon Ong (Eds.)

Advances in Natural Computation

First International Conference, ICNC 2005
Changsha, China, August 27-29, 2005
Proceedings, Part III

 Springer

Volume Editors

Lipo Wang
Nanyang Technological University
School of Electrical and Electronic Engineering
Block S1, 50 Nanyang Avenue, Singapore 639798
E-mail: elpwang@ntu.edu.sg

Ke Chen
University of Manchester
School of Informatics
P.O. Box 88, Sackville St., Manchester M6O 1QD, UK
E-mail: k.chen@manchester.ac.uk

Yew Soon Ong
Nanyang Technological University
School of Computer Engineering
Blk N4, 2b-39, Nanyang Avenue, Singapore 639798
E-mail: asysong@ntu.edu.sg

Library of Congress Control Number: Applied for

CR Subject Classification (1998): F.1, F.2, I.2, G.2, I.4, I.5, J.3, J.4

ISSN   0302-9743
ISBN-10   3-540-28320-X Springer Berlin Heidelberg New York
ISBN-13   978-3-540-28320-1 Springer Berlin Heidelberg New York

This work is subject to copyright. All rights are reserved, whether the whole or part of the material is concerned, specifically the rights of translation, reprinting, re-use of illustrations, recitation, broadcasting, reproduction on microfilms or in any other way, and storage in data banks. Duplication of this publication or parts thereof is permitted only under the provisions of the German Copyright Law of September 9, 1965, in its current version, and permission for use must always be obtained from Springer. Violations are liable to prosecution under the German Copyright Law.

Springer is a part of Springer Science+Business Media

springeronline.com

© Springer-Verlag Berlin Heidelberg 2005
Printed in Germany

Typesetting: Camera-ready by author, data conversion by Scientific Publishing Services, Chennai, India
Printed on acid-free paper   SPIN: 11539902   06/3142   5 4 3 2 1 0

Lecture Notes in Computer Science 3612

Commenced Publication in 1973
Founding and Former Series Editors:
Gerhard Goos, Juris Hartmanis, and Jan van Leeuwen

Editorial Board

David Hutchison
 Lancaster University, UK
Takeo Kanade
 Carnegie Mellon University, Pittsburgh, PA, USA
Josef Kittler
 University of Surrey, Guildford, UK
Jon M. Kleinberg
 Cornell University, Ithaca, NY, USA
Friedemann Mattern
 ETH Zurich, Switzerland
John C. Mitchell
 Stanford University, CA, USA
Moni Naor
 Weizmann Institute of Science, Rehovot, Israel
Oscar Nierstrasz
 University of Bern, Switzerland
C. Pandu Rangan
 Indian Institute of Technology, Madras, India
Bernhard Steffen
 University of Dortmund, Germany
Madhu Sudan
 Massachusetts Institute of Technology, MA, USA
Demetri Terzopoulos
 New York University, NY, USA
Doug Tygar
 University of California, Berkeley, CA, USA
Moshe Y. Vardi
 Rice University, Houston, TX, USA
Gerhard Weikum
 Max-Planck Institute of Computer Science, Saarbruecken, Germany

Preface

This book and its sister volumes, i.e., LNCS vols. 3610, 3611, and 3612, are the proceedings of the 1st International Conference on Natural Computation (ICNC 2005), jointly held with the 2nd International Conference on Fuzzy Systems and Knowledge Discovery (FSKD 2005, LNAI vols. 3613 and 3614) from 27 to 29 August 2005 in Changsha, Hunan, China. In its budding run, ICNC 2005 successfully attracted 1887 submissions from 32 countries/regions (the joint ICNC-FSKD 2005 received 3136 submissions). After rigorous reviews, 502 high-quality papers, i.e., 313 long papers and 189 short papers, were included in the ICNC 2005 proceedings, representing an acceptance rate of 26.6%.

The ICNC-FSKD 2005 featured the most up-to-date research results in computational algorithms inspired from nature, including biological, ecological, and physical systems. It is an exciting and emerging interdisciplinary area in which a wide range of techniques and methods are being studied for dealing with large, complex, and dynamic problems. The joint conferences also promoted cross-fertilization over these exciting and yet closely-related areas, which had a significant impact on the advancement of these important technologies. Specific areas included neural computation, quantum computation, evolutionary computation, DNA computation, chemical computation, information processing in cells and tissues, molecular computation, computation with words, fuzzy computation, granular computation, artificial life, swarm intelligence, ants colonies, artificial immune systems, etc., with innovative applications to knowledge discovery, finance, operations research, and more. In addition to the large number of submitted papers, we were blessed with the presence of four renowned keynote speakers and several distinguished panelists.

On behalf of the Organizing Committee, we thank Xiangtan University for sponsorship, and the IEEE Circuits and Systems Society, the IEEE Computational Intelligence Society, and the IEEE Control Systems Society for technical co-sponsorship. We are grateful for the technical cooperation from the International Neural Network Society, the European Neural Network Society, the Chinese Association for Artificial Intelligence, the Japanese Neural Network Society, the International Fuzzy Systems Association, the Asia-Pacific Neural Network Assembly, the Fuzzy Mathematics and Systems Association of China, and the Hunan Computer Federation. We thank the members of the Organizing Committee, the Advisory Board, and the Program Committee for their hard work in the past 18 months. We wish to express our heartfelt appreciation to the keynote and panel speakers, special session organizers, session chairs, reviewers, and student helpers. Our special thanks go to the publisher, Springer, for publishing the ICNC 2005 proceedings as three volumes of the Lecture Notes in Computer Science series (and the FSKD 2005 proceedings as two volumes of the Lecture Notes in Artificial Intelligence series). Finally, we thank all the authors and participants for their great contributions that made this conference possible and all the hard work worthwhile.

August 2005

Lipo Wang
Ke Chen
Yew Soon Ong

Organization

ICNC 2005 was organized by Xiangtan University and technically co-sponsored by the IEEE Circuits and Systems Society, the IEEE Computational Intelligence Society, and the IEEE Control Systems Society, in cooperation with the International Neural Network Society, the European Neural Network Society, the Chinese Association for Artificial Intelligence, the Japanese Neural Network Society, the International Fuzzy Systems Association, the Asia-Pacific Neural Network Assembly, the Fuzzy Mathematics and Systems Association of China, and the Hunan Computer Federation.

Organizing Committee

Honorary Conference Chairs	Shun-ichi Amari, Japan
	Lotfi A. Zadeh, USA
General Chair	He-An Luo, China
General Co-chairs	Lipo Wang, Singapore
	Yunqing Huang, China
Program Chairs	Ke Chen, UK
	Yew Soon Ong, Singapore
Local Arrangements Chairs	Renren Liu, China
	Xieping Gao, China
Proceedings Chair	Fen Xiao, China
Publicity Chair	Hepu Deng, Australia
Sponsorship/Exhibits Chairs	Shaoping Ling, China
	Geok See Ng, Singapore
Webmasters	Linai Kuang, China
	Yanyu Liu, China

Advisory Board

Toshio Fukuda, Japan
Kunihiko Fukushima, Japan
Tom Gedeon, Australia
Aike Guo, China
Zhenya He, China
Janusz Kacprzyk, Poland
Nikola Kasabov, New Zealand
John A. Keane, UK
Soo-Young Lee, Korea
Erkki Oja, Finland
Nikhil R. Pal, India

Witold Pedrycz, Canada
Jose C. Principe, USA
Harold Szu, USA
Shiro Usui, Japan
Xindong Wu, USA
Lei Xu, Hong Kong
Xin Yao, UK
Syozo Yasui, Japan
Bo Zhang, China
Yixin Zhong, China
Jacek M. Zurada, USA

Program Committee

Shigeo Abe, Japan
Kazuyuki Aihara, Japan
Davide Anguita, Italy
Abdesselam Bouzerdoum, Australia
Gavin Brown, UK
Laiwan Chan, Hong Kong
Sheng Chen, UK
Shu-Heng Chen, Taiwan
YanQiu Chen, China
Vladimir Cherkassky, USA
Sung-Bae Cho, Korea
Sungzoon Cho, Korea
Vic Ciesielski, Australia
Keshav Dahal, UK
Kalyanmoy Deb, India
Emilio Del-Moral-Hernandez, Brazil
Andries Engelbrecht, South Africa
Tomoki Fukai, Japan
Lance Fung, Australia
Takeshi Furuhashi, Japan
Hiroshi Furutani, Japan
John Q. Gan, UK
Wen Gao, China
Peter Geczy, Japan
Fanji Gu, China
Zeng-Guang Hou, Canada
Chenyi Hu, USA
Masumi Ishikawa, Japan
Robert John, UK
Mohamed Kamel, Canada
Yoshiki Kashimori, Japan
Samuel Kaski, Finland
Andy Keane, UK
Graham Kendall, UK
Jong-Hwan Kim, Korea
JungWon Kim, UK
Irwin King, Hong Kong
Natalio Krasnogor, UK
Vincent C.S. Lee, Australia
Stan Z. Li, China
XiaoLi Li, UK
Yangmin Li, Macau
Derong Liu, USA

Jian-Qin Liu, Japan
Bao-Liang Lu, China
Simon Lucas, UK
Frederic Maire, Australia
Jacek Mandziuk, Poland
Satoshi Matsuda, Japan
Masakazu Matsugu, Japan
Bob McKay, Australia
Ali A. Minai, USA
Hiromi Miyajima, Japan
Pedja Neskovic, USA
Richard Neville, UK
Tohru Nitta, Japan
Yusuke Nojima, Japan
Takashi Omori, Japan
M. Palaniswami, Australia
Andrew P. Paplinski, Australia
Asim Roy, USA
Bernhard Sendhoff, Germany
Qiang Shen, UK
Jang-Kyoo Shin, Korea
Leslie Smith, UK
Andy Song, Australia
Lambert Spannenburg, Sweden
Mingui Sun, USA
Johan Suykens, Belgium
Hideyuki Takagi, Japan
Kay Chen Tan, Singapore
Kiyoshi Tanaka, Japan
Seow Kiam Tian, Singapore
Peter Tino, UK
Kar-Ann Toh, Singapore
Yasuhiro Tsujimura, Japan
Ganesh Kumar Venayagamoorthy, USA
Brijesh Verma, Australia
Ray Walshe, Ireland
Jun Wang, Hong Kong
Rubin Wang, China
Xizhao Wang, China
Sumio Watanabe, Japan
Stefan Wermter, UK
Kok Wai Wong, Australia

Hong Yan, Hong Kong
Ron Yang, UK
Daniel Yeung, Hong Kong
Ali M.S. Zalzala, UK
Xiaojun Zeng, UK

David Zhang, Hong Kong
Huaguang Zhang, China
Liming Zhang, China
Qiangfu Zhao, Japan

Special Sessions Organizers

Ke Chen, UK
Gary Egan, Australia
Masami Hagiya, Japan
Tai-hoon Kim, Korea
Yangmin Li, Macau
Osamu Ono, Japan
Gwi-Tae Park, Korea
John A. Rose, Japan
Xingming Sun, China

Ying Tan, Hong Kong
Peter Tino, UK
Shiro Usui, Japan
Rubin Wang, China
Keming Xie, China
Xiaolan Zhang, USA
Liang Zhao, Brazil
Henghui Zou, USA
Hengming Zou, China

Reviewers

Ajith Abraham
Wensen An
Yisheng An
Jiancong Bai
Gurvinder Baicher
Xiaojuan Ban
Yukun Bao
Helio Barbosa
Zafer Bingul
Liefeng Bo
Yin Bo
Gavin Brown
Nan Bu
Erhan Butun
Chunhong Cao
Huai-Hu Cao
Qixin Cao
Yijia Cao
Yuan-Da Cao
Yuhui Cao
Yigang Cen
Chunlei Chai

Li Chai
Ping-Teng Chang
Kwokwing Chau
Ailing Chen
Chen-Tung Chen
Enqing Chen
Fangjiong Chen
Houjin Chen
Jiah-Shing Chen
Jing Chen
Jingchun Chen
Junying Chen
Li Chen
Shenglei Chen
Wei Chen
Wenbin Chen
Xi Chen
Xiyuan Chen
Xuhui Chen
Yuehui Chen
Zhen-Cheng Chen
Zhong Chen

Jian Cheng
Il-Ahn Cheong
Yiu-Ming Cheung
Yongwha Chung
Lingli Cui
Jian-Hua Dai
Chuangyin Dang
Xiaolong Deng
Hongkai Ding
Zhan Ding
Chao-Jun Dong
Guangbo Dong
Jie Dong
Sheqin Dong
Shoubin Dong
Wenyong Dong
Feng Du
Hai-Feng Du
Yanping Du
Shukai Duan
Metin Ertunc
Liu Fan

Gang Fang
Hui Fang
Chen Feng
Guiyu Feng
Jian Feng
Peng Fu
Yongfeng Fu
Yuli Fu
Naohiro Fukumura
Haichang Gao
Haihua Gao
Zong Geem
Emin Germen
Ling Gong
Maoguo Gong
Tao Gong
Weiguo Gong
Danying Gu
Qiu Guan
Salyh Günet
Dongwei Guo
Tian-Tai Guo
Xinchen Guo
Xiu Ping Guo
Yi'nan Guo
Mohamed Hamada
Jianchao Han
Lixin Han
Soowhan Han
Xiaozhuo Han
Fei Hao
Jingsong He
Jun He
Liqiang He
Xiaoxian He
Xiping He
Yi He
Zhaoshui He
Xingchen Heng
Chao-Fu Hong
Chi-I Hsu
Chunhua Hu
Hai Hu
Hongying Hu
Hua Hu

Jianming Hu
Li Kun Hu
Tao Hu
Ye Hu
Bingqiang Huang
Gaoming Huang
Min Huang
Yanwen Huang
Yilun Huang
Siu Cheung Hui
Changha Hwang
Jun-Cheol Jeon
Hyuncheol Jeong
Guangrong Ji
Mingxing Jia
Sen Jia
Zhuang Jian
Chunhong Jiang
Dongxiang Jiang
Jijiao Jiang
Minghui Jiang
Mingyan Jiang
Quanyuan Jiang
Li Cheng Jiao
Liu Jie
Wuyin Jin
Xu Jin
Ling Jing
Peng Jing
Xing-Jian Jing
Tao Jun
Hosang Jung
Jo Nam Jung
Venu K Murthy
Jaeho Kang
Kyung-Woo Kang
Ali Karci
Hyun-Sung Kim
Jongmin Kim
Jongweon Kim
Kee-Won Kim
Myung Won Kim
Wonil Kim
Heeyong Kwon
Xiang-Wei Lai

Dongwoo Lee
Kwangeui Lee
Seonghoon Lee
Seunggwan Lee
Kaiyou Lei
Xiongguo Lei
Soo Kar Leow
Anping Li
Boyu Li
Cheng Li
Dahu Li
Guanghui Li
Guoyou Li
Hongyan Li
Huanqin Li
Jianhua Li
Jie Li
Jing Li
Kangshun Li
Qiangwei Li
Qian-Mu Li
Qingyong Li
Ruonan Li
Shouju Li
Xiaobin Li
Xihai Li
Xinchun Li
Xiumei Li
Xuming Li
Ye Li
Ying Li
Yongjie Li
Yuangui Li
Yun Li
Yunfeng Li
Yong Li
Bojian Liang
Jiuzhen Liang
Xiao Liang
Yanchun Liang
Yixiong Liang
Guanglan Liao
Yingxin Liao
Sehun Lim
Tong Ming Lim

Jianning Lin
Ling Lin
Pan Lin
Qiu-Hua Lin
Zhi-Ling Lin
Zhou Ling
Benyong Liu
Bing Liu
Bingjie Liu
Dang-Hui Liu
Feng Liu
Hehui Liu
Huayong Liu
Jianchang Liu
Jing Liu
Jun Liu
Lifang Liu
Linlan Liu
Meiqin Liu
Miao Liu
Qicheng Liu
Ruochen Liu
Tianming Liu
Weidong Liu
Xianghui Liu
Xiaoqun Liu
Yong-Lin Liu
Zheng Liu
Zhi Liu
Jianchang Lu
Jun Lu
Xiaobo Lu
Yinan Lu
Dehan Luo
Guiming Luo
Juan Luo
Qiang Lv
Srinivas M.B.
Changshe Ma
Weimin Ma
Wenping Ma
Xuan Ma
Michiharu Maeda
Bertrand Maillet
Toshihiko Matsuka

Hongling Meng
Kehua Miao
Teijun Miao
Shi Min
Hongwei Mo
Dhinaharan Nagamalai
Atulya Nagar
Mi Young Nam
Rongrong Ni
Rui Nian
Ben Niu
Qun Niu
Sun-Kuk Noh
Linlin Ou
Mayumi Oyama-Higa
Cuneyt Oysu
A. Alper Ozalp
Ping-Feng Pai
Li Pan
Tinglong Pan
Zhiming Pan
Xiaohong Pang
Francesco Pappalardo
Hyun-Soo Park
Yongjin Park
Xiaomei Pei
Jun Peng
Wen Peng
Yan Peng
Yuqing Peng
Zeng Peng
Zhenrui Peng
Zhongbo Peng
Daoying Pi
Fangzhong Qi
Tang Qi
Rong Qian
Xiaoyan Qian
Xueming Qian
Baohua Qiang
Bin Qin
Zhengjun Qiu
Wentai Qu
Yunhua Rao
Sundaram Ravi

Phillkyu Rhee
Lili Rong
Fuhua Shang
Ronghua Shang
Zichang Shangguan
Dayong Shen
Xisheng Shen
Daming Shi
Xiaolong Shi
Zhiping Shi
Noritaka Shigei
Jooyong Shim
Dongkyoo Shin
Yongyi Shou
Yang Shu
Valceres Slva
Daniel Smutek
Haiyan Song
Jiaxing Song
Jingyan Song
Wenbin Song
Xiao-Yu Song
Yan Yan Song
Tieming Su
Xiaohong Su
P.N. Suganthan
Guangzhong Sun
Huali Sun
Shiliang Sun
Wei Sun
Yuqiu Sun
Zhanquan Sun
Jin Tang
Jing Tang
Suqin Tang
Zhiqiang Tang
Zhang Tao
Hissam Tawfik
Hakan Temeltas
Nipon Theera-Umpon
Mei Tian
Chung-Li Tseng
Ibrahim Turkoglu
Juan Velasquez
Bin Wang

Chao-Xue Wang
Chaoyong Wang
Deji Wang
Dingcheng Wang
Gi-Nam Wang
Guojiang Wang
Hong Wang
Hongbo Wang
Hong-Gang Wang
Jigang Wang
Lin Wang
Ling Wang
Min Wang
Qingquan Wang
Shangfei Wang
Shaowei Wang
Teng Wang
Weihong Wang
Xin Wang
Xinyu Wang
Yan Wang
Yanbin Wang
Yaonan Wang
Yen-Nien Wang
Yong-Xian Wang
Zhanshan Wang
Zheng-You Wang
Zhurong Wang
Wang Wei
Xun-Kai Wei
Chunguo Wu
Fei Wu
Ji Wu
Qiongshui Wu
Qiuxuan Wu
Sitao Wu
Wei Wu
Yanwen Wu
Ying Wu
Chen Xi
Shi-Hong Xia
Guangming Xian
Binglei Xie
Li Xie
Tao Xie

Shengwu Xiong
Zhangliang Xiong
Chunlin Xu
Jianhua Xu
Jinhua Xu
Junqin Xu
Li Xu
Lin Xu
Shuxiang Xu
Xianyun Xu
Xin Xu
Xu Xu
Xue-Song Xu
Zhiwei Xu
Yiliang Xu
Jianping Xuan
Yaofeng Xue
Yuncan Xue
Hui Yan
Qiao Yan
Xiaohong Yan
Bo Yang
Chunyan Yang
Feng Yang
Guifang Yang
Guoqqing Yang
Guowei Yang
Huihua Yang
Jianwei Yang
Jing Yang
Li-Ying Yang
Qingyun Yang
Xiaohua Yang
Xiaowei Yang
Xuhua Yang
Yingchun Yang
Zhihui Yang
Jingtao Yao
Her-Terng Yau
Chaoqun Ye
He Yi
Ling-Zhi Yi
Li Yin
Rupo Yin
Liang Ying

Chen Yong
Eun-Jun Yoon
Xinge You
Changjie Yu
Fei Yu
Fusheng Yu
Guoyan Yu
Lean Yu
Mian-Shui Yu
Qingjun Yu
Shiwen Yu
Xinjie Yu
Mingwei Yuan
Shenfang Yuan
Xun Yue
Wu Yun
Yeboon Yun
Jin Zeng
C.H. Zhang
Changjiang Zhang
Chunkai Zhang
Da-Peng Zhang
Defu Zhang
Fan Zhang
Fengyue Zhang
Hong Zhang
Hong-Bin Zhang
Ji Zhang
Jiang Zhang
Li Zhang
Liyan Zhang
Li-Yong Zhang
Min Zhang
Ming-Jie Zhang
Rubo Zhang
Ruo-Ying Zhang
Weidong Zhang
Wei-Guo Zhang
Wen Zhang
Xiufeng Zhang
Yangsen Zhang
Yifei Zhang
Yong-Dong Zhang
Yue-Jie Zhang
Yunkai Zhang

Yuntao Zhang
Zhenya Zhang
Hai Zhao
Jian Zhao
Jianxun Zhao
Jianye Zhao
Lianwei Zhao
Lina Zhao
Wencang Zhao
Xingming Zhao
Xuelong Zhao
Yinliang Zhao
Zhidong Zhao

Tiejun Zhao
Liu Zhen
Guibin Zheng
Shiqin Zheng
Yihui Zheng
Weicai Zhong
Zhou Zhong
Dongming Zhou
Gengui Zhou
Hongjun Zhou
Lifang Zhou
Wengang Zhou
Yuren Zhou

Zhiheng Zhou
Zongtan Zhou
Chengzhi Zhu
En Zhu
Li Zhu
Wen Zhu
Yaoqin Zhu
Xiaobin Zou
Xiaobo Zou
Zhenyu Zou
Wenming Zuo

* The term after a name may represent either a country or a region.

Table of Contents – Part III

Evolutionary Methodology

Multi-focus Image Fusion Based on SOFM Neural Networks and Evolution Strategies
Yan Wu, Chongyang Liu, Guisheng Liao 1

Creative Design by Chance Based Interactive Evolutionary Computation
Chao-Fu Hong, Hsiao-Fang Yang, Mu-Hua Lin 11

Design of the Agent-Based Genetic Algorithm
Honggang Wang, Jianchao Zeng, Yubin Xu 22

Drawing Undirected Graphs with Genetic Algorithms
Qing-Guo Zhang, Hua-Yong Liu, Wei Zhang, Ya-Jun Guo 28

A Novel Type of Niching Methods Based on Steady-State Genetic Algorithm
Minqiang Li, Jisong Kou 37

Simulated Annealing Genetic Algorithm for Surface Intersection
Min Tang, Jin-xiang Dong 48

A Web Personalized Service Based on Dual GAs
Zhengyu Zhu, Qihong Xie, Xinghuan Chen, Qingsheng Zhu 57

A Diversity Metric for Multi-objective Evolutionary Algorithms
Xu-yong Li, Jin-hua Zheng, Juan Xue 68

An Immune Partheno-Genetic Algorithm for Winner Determination in Combinatorial Auctions
JianCong Bai, HuiYou Chang, Yang Yi 74

A Novel Genetic Algorithm Based on Cure Mechanism of Traditional Chinese Medicine
Chao-Xue Wang, Du-Wu Cui, Lei Wang, Zhu-Rong Wang 86

An Adaptive GA Based on Information Entropy
Yu Sun, Chun-lian Li, Ai-guo Wang, Jia Zhu, Xi-cheng Wang 93

A Genetic Algorithm of High-Throughput and Low-Jitter Scheduling for Input-Queued Switches
Yaohui Jin, Jingjing Zhang, Weisheng Hu 102

Mutation Matrix in Evolutionary Computation: An Application to Resource Allocation Problem
Jian Zhang, Kwok Yip Szeto 112

Dependent-Chance Programming Model for Stochastic Network Bottleneck Capacity Expansion Based on Neural Network and Genetic Algorithm
Yun Wu, Jian Zhou, Jun Yang 120

Gray-Encoded Hybrid Accelerating Genetic Algorithm for Global Optimization of Water Environmental Model
Xiaohua Yang, Zhifeng Yang, Zhenyao Shen, Guihua Lu 129

Hybrid Chromosome Genetic Algorithm for Generalized Traveling Salesman Problems
Han Huang, Xiaowei Yang, Zhifeng Hao, Chunguo Wu, Yanchun Liang, Xi Zhao 137

A New Approach Belonging to EDAs: Quantum-Inspired Genetic Algorithm with Only One Chromosome
Shude Zhou, Zengqi Sun 141

A Fast Fingerprint Matching Approach in Medicare Identity Verification Based on GAs
Qingquan Wang, Lili Rong 151

Using Viruses to Improve GAs
Francesco Pappalardo 161

A Genetic Algorithm for Solving Fuzzy Resource-Constrained Project Scheduling
Hong Wang, Dan Lin, Minqiang Li 171

A Hybrid Genetic Algorithm and Application to the Crosstalk Aware Track Assignment Problem
Yici Cai, Bin Liu, Xiong Yan, Qiang Zhou, Xianlong Hong 181

A Genetic Algorithm for Solving Resource-Constrained Project Scheduling Problem
Hong Wang, Dan Lin, Minqiang Li 185

Evolutionary Algorithm Based on Overlapped Gene Expression
Jing Peng, Chang-jie Tang, Jing Zhang, Chang-an Yuan 194

Evolving Case-Based Reasoning with Genetic Algorithm in Wholesaler's Returning Book Forecasting
Pei-Chann Chang, Yen-Wen Wang, Ching-Jung Ting, Chien-Yuan Lai, Chen-Hao Liu 205

A Novel Immune Quantum-Inspired Genetic Algorithm
Ying Li, Yanning Zhang, Yinglei Cheng, Xiaoyue Jiang, Rongchun Zhao 215

A Hierarchical Approach for Incremental Floorplan Based on Genetic Algorithms
Yongpan Liu, Huazhong Yang, Rong Luo, Hui Wang 219

A Task Duplication Based Scheduling Algorithm on GA in Grid Computing Systems
Jianning Lin, Huizhong Wu 225

Analysis of a Genetic Model with Finite Populations
Alberto Bertoni, Paola Campadelli, Roberto Posenato 235

Missing Values Imputation for a Clustering Genetic Algorithm
Eduardo R. Hruschka, Estevam R. Hruschka Jr., Nelson F.F. Ebecken 245

A New Organizational Nonlinear Genetic Algorithm for Numerical Optimization
Zhihua Cui, Jianchao Zeng 255

Hybrid Genetic Algorithm for the Flexible Job-Shop Problem Under Maintenance Constraints
Nozha Zribi, Pierre Borne 259

A Genetic Algorithm with Elite Crossover and Dynastic Change Strategies
Yuanpai Zhou, Ray P.S. Han 269

A Game-Theoretic Approach for Designing Mixed Mutation Strategies
Jun He, Xin Yao 279

FIR Frequency Sampling Filters Design Based on Adaptive Particle Swarm Optimization Algorithm
Wanping Huang, Lifang Zhou, Jixin Qian, Longhua Ma 289

A Hybrid Macroevolutionary Algorithm
Jihui Zhang, Junqin Xu 299

Evolutionary Granular Computing Model and Applications
Jiang Zhang, Xuewei Li 309

Application of Genetic Programming for Fine Tuning PID Controller Parameters Designed Through Ziegler-Nichols Technique
Gustavo Maia de Almeida, Valceres Vieira Rocha e Silva, Erivelton Geraldo Nepomuceno, Ryuichi Yokoyama 313

Applying Genetic Programming to Evolve Learned Rules for Network Anomaly Detection
Chuanhuan Yin, Shengfeng Tian, Houkuan Huang, Jun He 323

A Pattern Combination Based Approach to Two-Dimensional Cutting Stock Problem
Jinming Wan, Yadong Wu, Hongwei Dai 332

Fractal and Dynamical Language Methods to Construct Phylogenetic Tree Based on Protein Sequences from Complete Genomes
Zu-Guo Yu, Vo Anh, Li-Quan Zhou 337

Evolutionary Hardware Architecture for Division in Elliptic Curve Cryptosystems over $GF(2^n)$
Jun-Cheol Jeon, Kee-Won Kim, Kee-Young Yoo 348

An Evolvable Hardware System Under Varying Illumination Environment
In Ja Jeon, Phill Kyu Rhee 356

An Evolvable Hardware Chip for Image Enhancement in Surface Roughness Estimation
M. Rajaram Narayanan, S. Gowri, S. Ravi 361

Evolutionary Agents for n-Queen Problems
Weicai Zhong, Jing Liu, Licheng Jiao 366

Fictitious Play and Price-Deviation-Adjust Learning in Electricity Market
Xiaoyang Zhou, Li Feng, Xiuming Dong, Jincheng Shang 374

Automatic Discovery of Subgoals for Sequential Decision Problems Using Potential Fields
Huanwen Chen, Changming Yin, Lijuan Xie 384

Improving Multiobjective Evolutionary Algorithm by Adaptive Fitness
and Space Division
    Yuping Wang, Chuangyin Dang 392

IFMOA: Immune Forgetting Multiobjective Optimization
Algorithm
    Bin Lu, Licheng Jiao, Haifeng Du, Maoguo Gong 399

Genetic Algorithm for Multi-objective Optimization Using GDEA
    Yeboon Yun, Min Yoon, Hirotaka Nakayama 409

Quantum Computing

A Quantum-Inspired Genetic Algorithm for Scheduling Problems
    Ling Wang, Hao Wu, Da-zhong Zheng 417

Consensus Control for Networks of Dynamic Agents via Active
Switching Topology
    Guangming Xie, Long Wang 424

Quantum Search in Structured Database
    Yuguo He, Jigui Sun 434

Swarm Intelligence and Intelligent Agents

A Fuzzy Trust Model for Multi-agent System
    Guangzhu Chen, Zhishu Li, Zhihong Cheng, Zijiang Zhao,
    Haifeng Yan 444

Adaptive Particle Swarm Optimization for Reactive Power and Voltage
Control in Power Systems
    Wen Zhang, Yutian Liu 449

A Dynamic Task Scheduling Approach Based on Wasp Algorithm in
Grid Environment
    Hui-Xian Li, Chun-Tian Cheng 453

A Novel Ant Colony Based QoS-Aware Routing Algorithm for MANETs
    Lianggui Liu, Guangzeng Feng 457

A Differential Evolutionary Particle Swarm Optimization with
Controller
    Jianchao Zeng, Zhihua Cui, Lifang Wang 467

A Mountain Clustering Based on Improved PSO Algorithm
  Hong-yuan Shen, Xiao-qi Peng, Jun-nian Wang, Zhi-kun Hu 477

Multi-agent Pursuit-Evasion Algorithm Based on Contract Net
Interaction Protocol
  Ying-Chun Chen, Huan Qi, Shan-Shan Wang 482

Image Compression Method Using Improved PSO Vector Quantization
  Qian Chen, Jiangang Yang, Jin Gou 490

Swarm Intelligence Clustering Algorithm
Based on Attractor
  Qingyong Li, Zhiping Shi, Jun Shi, Zhongzhi Shi 496

An Agent-Based Soft Computing Society with Application in the
Management of Establishment of Hydraulic Fracture in Oil Field
  Fu hua Shang, Xiao feng Li, Jian Xu 505

Two Sub-swarms Particle Swarm Optimization Algorithm
  Guochu Chen, Jinshou Yu 515

A Mobile Agent-Based P2P Autonomous Security Hole Discovery
System
  Ji Zheng, Xin Wang, Xiangyang Xue, C.K. Toh 525

A Modified Clustering Algorithm Based on Swarm Intelligence
  Lei Zhang, Qixin Cao, Jay Lee 535

Parameter Selection of Quantum-Behaved Particle Swarm Optimization
  Jun Sun, Wenbo Xu, Jing Liu 543

An Emotional Particle Swarm Optimization Algorithm
  Yang Ge, Zhang Rubo 553

Multi-model Function Optimization by a New Hybrid Nonlinear
Simplex Search and Particle Swarm Algorithm
  Fang Wang, Yuhui Qiu, Naiqin Feng 562

Adaptive XCSM for Perceptual Aliasing Problems
  Shumei Liu, Tomoharu Nagao 566

Discrete Particle Swarm Optimization (DPSO) Algorithm for
Permutation Flowshop Scheduling to Minimize Makespan
  K. Rameshkumar, R.K. Suresh, K.M. Mohanasundaram 572

Unified Particle Swarm Optimization for Solving Constrained
Engineering Optimization Problems
    K.E. Parsopoulos, M.N. Vrahatis 582

A Modified Particle Swarm Optimizer for Tracking Dynamic Systems
    Xuanping Zhang, Yuping Du, Zheng Qin, Guoqiang Qin, Jiang Lu .. 592

Particle Swarm Optimization for Bipartite Subgraph Problem: A Case
Study
    Dan Zhang, Zeng-Zhi Li, Hong Song, Tao Zhan 602

On the Role of Risk Preference in Survivability
    Shu-Heng Chen, Ya-Chi Huang 612

An Agent-Based Holonic Architecture for Reconfigurable Manufacturing
Systems
    Fang Wang, Zeng-Guang Hou, De Xu, Min Tan 622

Mobile Robot Navigation Using Particle Swarm Optimization and
Adaptive NN
    Yangmin Li, Xin Chen 628

Collision-Free Path Planning for Mobile Robots Using Chaotic Particle
Swarm Optimization
    Qiang Zhao, Shaoze Yan 632

Natural Computation Applications: Bioinformatics and Bio-medical Engineering

Analysis of Toy Model for Protein Folding Based on Particle Swarm
Optimization Algorithm
    Juan Liu, Longhui Wang, Lianlian He, Feng Shi 636

Selective Two-Channel Linear Descriptors for Studying Dynamic
Interaction of Brain Regions
    Xiao-mei Pei, Jin Xu, Chong-xun Zheng, Guang-yu Bin 646

A Computational Pixelization Model Based on Selective Attention for
Artificial Visual Prosthesis
    Ruonan Li, Xudong Zhang, Guangshu Hu 654

Mosaicing the Retinal Fundus Images: A Robust Registration Technique
Based Approach
    Xinge You, Bin Fang, Yuan Yan Tang 663

Typing Aberrance in Signal Transduction
  M. Zhang, G.Q. Li, Y.X. Fu, Z.Z. Zhang, L. He 668

Local Search for the Maximum Parsimony Problem
  Adrien Goëffon, Jean-Michel Richer, Jin-Kao Hao 678

Natural Computation Applications: Robotics and Intelligent Control

Optimization of Centralized Power Control by Genetic Algorithm in a DS-CDMA Cellular System
  J. Zhou, H. Kikuchi, S. Sasaki, H. Luo 684

Cascade AdaBoost Classifiers with Stage Features Optimization for Cellular Phone Embedded Face Detection System
  Xusheng Tang, Zongying Ou, Tieming Su, Pengfei Zhao 688

Proper Output Feedback H_∞ Control for Descriptor Systems: A Convex Optimization Approach
  Lei Guo, Keyou Zhao, Chunbo Feng 698

Planning Optimal Trajectories for Mobile Robots Using an Evolutionary Method with Fuzzy Components
  Serkan Aydin, Hakan Temeltas 703

Hexagon-Based Q-Learning for Object Search with Multiple Robots
  Han-Ul Yoon, Kwee-Bo Sim 713

Adaptive Inverse Control of an Omni-Directional Mobile Robot
  Yuming Zhang, Qixin Cao, Shouhong Miao 723

Other Applications of Natural Computation

A Closed Loop Algorithms Based on Chaos Theory for Global Optimization
  Xinglong Zhu, Hongguang Wang, Mingyang Zhao, Jiping Zhou 727

Harmony Search for Generalized Orienteering Problem: Best Touring in China
  Zong Woo Geem, Chung-Li Tseng, Yongjin Park 741

Harmony Search in Water Pump Switching Problem
  Zong Woo Geem 751

A Selfish Non-atomic Routing Algorithm Based on Game Theory
Jun Tao, Ye Liu, Qingliang Wu 761

Clone Selection Based Multicast Routing Algorithm
Cuiqin Hou, Licheng Jiao, Maoguo Gong, Bin Lu 768

A Genetic Algorithm-Based Routing Service for Simulation Grid
Wei Wu, Hai Huang, Zhong Zhou, Zhongshu Liu 772

Clustering Problem Using Adaptive Genetic Algorithm
Qingzhan Chen, Jianghong Han, Yungang Lai, Wenxiu He, Keji Mao 782

FCACO: Fuzzy Classification Rules Mining Algorithm with Ant Colony Optimization
Bilal Alatas, Erhan Akin 787

Goal-Directed Portfolio Insurance
Jiah-Shing Chen, Benjamin Penyang Liao 798

A Genetic Algorithm for Solving Portfolio Optimization Problems with Transaction Costs and Minimum Transaction Lots
Dan Lin, Xiaoming Li, Minqiang Li 808

Financial Performance Prediction Using Constraint-Based Evolutionary Classification Tree (CECT) Approach
Chi-I Hsu, Yuan Lin Hsu, Pei Lun Hsu 812

A Genetic Algorithm with Chromosome-Repairing Technique for Polygonal Approximation of Digital Curves
Bin Wang, Yan Qiu Chen 822

Fault Feature Selection Based on Modified Binary PSO with Mutation and Its Application in Chemical Process Fault Diagnosis
Ling Wang, Jinshou Yu 832

Genetic Algorithms for Thyroid Gland Ultrasound Image Feature Reduction
Ludvík Tesař, Daniel Smutek, Jan Jiskra 841

Improving Nearest Neighbor Classification with Simulated Gravitational Collapse
Chen Wang, Yan Qiu Chen 845

Evolutionary Computation and Rough Set-Based Hybrid Approach to
Rule Generation
  Lin Shang, Qiong Wan, Zhi-Hong Zhao, Shi-Fu Chen 855

Assessing the Performance of Several Fitness Functions in a Genetic
Algorithm for Nonlinear Separation of Sources
  F. Rojas, C.G. Puntonet, J.M. Górriz, O. Valenzuela 863

A Robust Soft Decision Mixture Model for Image Segmentation
  Pan Lin, Feng Zhang, ChongXun Zheng, Yong Yang, Yimin Hou ... 873

A Comparative Study of Finite Word Length Coefficient Optimization
of FIR Digital Filters
  Gurvinder S. Baicher, Meinwen Taylor, Hefin Rowlands 877

A Novel Genetic Algorithm for Variable Partition of Dual Memory
Bank DSPs
  Dan Zhang, Zeng-Zhi Li, Hai Wang, Tao Zhan 883

Bi-phase Encoded Waveform Design to Deal with the Range
Ambiguities for Sparse Space-Based Radar Systems
  Hai-hong Tao, Tao Su, Gui-sheng Liao 893

Analytic Model for Network Viruses
  Lansheng Han, Hui Liu, Baffour Kojo Asiedu 903

Ant Colony Optimization Algorithms for Scheduling the Mixed Model
Assembly Lines
  Xin-yu Sun, Lin-yan Sun 911

Adaptive and Robust Design for PID Controller Based on Ant System
Algorithm
  Guanzheng Tan, Qingdong Zeng, Shengjun He, Guangchao Cai 915

Job-Shop Scheduling Based on Multiagent Evolutionary Algorithm
  Weicai Zhong, Jing Liu, Licheng Jiao 925

Texture Surface Inspection: An Artificial Immune Approach
  Hong Zheng, Li Pan 934

Intelligent Mosaics Algorithm of Overlapping Images
  Yan Zhang, Wenhui Li, Yu Meng, Haixu Chen, Tong Wang 938

Adaptive Simulated Annealing for Standard Cell Placement
  Guofang Nan, Minqiang Li, Dan Lin, Jisong Kou 943

Application of Particle Swarm Optimization Algorithm on Robust PID Controller Tuning
Jun Zhao, Tianpeng Li, Jixin Qian 948

A Natural Language Watermarking Based on Chinese Syntax
Yuling Liu, Xingming Sun, Yong Wu 958

A Steganographic Scheme in Digital Images Using Information of Neighboring Pixels
Young-Ran Park, Hyun-Ho Kang, Sang-Uk Shin, Ki-Ryong Kwon ... 962

Noun-Verb Based Technique of Text Watermarking Using Recursive Decent Semantic Net Parsers
Xingming Sun, Alex Jessey Asiimwe 968

A Novel Watermarking Scheme Based on Independent Component Analysis
Haifeng Li, Shuxun Wang, Weiwei Song, Quan Wen 972

On Sequence Synchronization Analysis Against Chaos Based Spread Spectrum Image Steganography
Guangjie Liu, Jinwei Wang, Yuewei Dai, Zhiquan Wang 976

Microstructure Evolution of the K4169 Superalloy Blade Based on Cellular Automaton Simulation
Xin Yan, Zhilong Zhao, Weidong Yan, Lin Liu 980

Mobile Robot Navigation Based on Multisensory Fusion
Weimin Ge, Zuoliang Cao 984

Self-surviving IT Systems
Hengming Zou, Leilei Bao 988

PDE-Based Intrusion Forecast
Hengming Zou, Henghui Zou 996

A Solution to Ragged Dimension Problem in OLAP
Lin Yuan, Hengming Zou, Zhanhuai Li 1001

Hardware Implementations of Natural Computation

A Convolutional Neural Network VLSI Architecture Using Sorting Model for Reducing Multiply-and-Accumulation Operations
Osamu Nomura, Takashi Morie, Masakazu Matsugu, Atsushi Iwata 1006

A 32-Bit Binary Floating Point Neuro-Chip
  Keerthi Laal Kala, M.B. Srinivas 1015

Improved Blocks for CMOS Analog Neuro-fuzzy Network
  Weizhi Wang, Dongming Jin 1022

A Design on the Vector Processor of 2048point MDCT/IMDCT for MPEG-2 AAC
  Dae-Sung Ku, Jung-Hyun Yun, Jong-Bin Kim 1032

Neuron Operation Using Controlled Chaotic Instabilities in Brillouin-Active Fiber Based Neural Network in Smart Structures
  Yong-Kab Kim, Jinsu Kim, Soonja Lim, Dong-Hyun Kim 1044

Parallel Genetic Algorithms on Programmable Graphics Hardware
  Qizhi Yu, Chongcheng Chen, Zhigeng Pan 1051

Fuzzy Neural Systems and Soft Computing

A Neuro-fuzzy Approach to Part Fitup Fault Control During Resistance Spot Welding Using Servo Gun
  Y.S. Zhang, G.L Chen 1060

Automatic Separate Algorithm of Vein and Artery for Auto-Segmentation Liver-Vessel from Abdominal MDCT Image Using Morphological Filtering
  Chun-Ja Park, Eun-kyung Cho, Young-hee Kwon, Moon-sung Park, Jong-won Park 1069

Run-Time Fuzzy Optimization of IEEE 802.11 Wireless LANs Performance
  Young-Joong Kim, Myo-Taeg Lim 1079

TLCD Semi-active Control Methodology of Fuzzy Neural Network for Eccentric Buildings
  Hong-Nan Li, Qiao Jin, Gangbing Song, Guo-Xin Wang 1089

Use of Adaptive Learning Radial Basis Function Network in Real-Time Motion Tracking of a Robot Manipulator
  Dongwon Kim, Sung-Hoe Huh, Sam-Jun Seo, Gwi-Tae Park 1099

Obstacle Avoidance for Redundant Nonholonomic Mobile Modular Manipulators via Neural Fuzzy Approaches
  Yangmin Li, Yugang Liu 1109

Invasive Connectionist Evolution
  Paulito P. Palmes, Shiro Usui 1119

Applying Advanced Fuzzy Cellular Neural Network AFCNN to
Segmentation of Serial CT Liver Images
  Shitong Wang, Duan Fu, Min Xu, Dewen Hu 1128

New Algorithms of Neural Fuzzy Relation Systems with Min-implication
Composition
  Yanbin Luo, K. Palaniappan, Yongming Li 1132

Neural Networks Combination by Fuzzy Integral in Clinical
Electromyography
  Hongbo Xie, Hai Huang, Zhizhong Wang 1142

Long-Term Prediction of Discharges in Manwan Hydropower Using
Adaptive-Network-Based Fuzzy Inference Systems Models
  Chun-Tian Cheng, Jian-Yi Lin, Ying-Guang Sun, Kwokwing Chau .. 1152

Vector Controlled Permanent Magnet Synchronous Motor Drive with
Adaptive Fuzzy Neural Network Controller
  Xianqing Cao, Jianguang Zhu, Renyuan Tang 1162

Use of Fuzzy Neural Networks with Grey Relations in Fuzzy Rules
Partition Optimization
  Hui-Chen Chang, Yau-Tarng Juang 1172

A Weighted Fuzzy Min-Max Neural Network and Its Application to
Feature Analysis
  Ho-Joon Kim, Hyun-Seung Yang 1178

A Physiological Fuzzy Neural Network
  Kwang-Baek Kim, Hae-Ryong Bea, Chang-Suk Kim 1182

Cluster-Based Self-organizing Neuro-fuzzy System with Hybrid
Learning Approach for Function Approximation
  *Chunshien Li, Kuo-Hsiang Cheng, Chih-Ming Chen,
  Jin-Long Chen* 1186

Fuzzy Output Support Vector Machines for Classification
  Zongxia Xie, Qinghua Hu, Daren Yu 1190

Credit Rating Analysis with AFS Fuzzy Logic
  Xiaodong Liu, Wanquan Liu 1198

A Neural-Fuzzy Based Inferential Sensor for Improving the Control of Boilers in Space Heating Systems
Zaiyi Liao 1205

A Hybrid Neuro-fuzzy Approach for Spinal Force Evaluation in Manual Materials Handling Tasks
Yanfeng Hou, Jacek M. Zurada, Waldemar Karwowski, William S. Marras 1216

Medicine Composition Analysis Based on PCA and SVM
Chaoyong Wang, Chunguo Wu, Yanchun Liang 1226

Swarm Double-Tabu Search
Wanhui Wen, Guangyuan Liu 1231

A Meta-heuristic Algorithm for the Strip Rectangular Packing Problem
Defu Zhang, Yanjuan Liu, Shengda Chen, Xiaogang Xie 1235

Music Composition Using Genetic Algorithms (GA) and Multilayer Perceptrons (MLP)
Hüseyin Göksu, Paul Pigg, Vikas Dixit 1242

On the Categorizing of Simply Separable Relations in Partial Four-Valued Logic
Renren Liu, Zhiwei Gong, Fen Xu 1251

Equivalence of Classification and Regression Under Support Vector Machine Theory
Chunguo Wu, Yanchun Liang, Xiaowei Yang, Zhifeng Hao 1257

Fuzzy Description of Topological Relations I: A Unified Fuzzy 9-Intersection Model
Shihong Du, Qiming Qin, Qiao Wang, Bin Li 1261

Fuzzy Description of Topological Relations II: Computation Methods and Examples
Shihong Du, Qiao Wang, Qiming Qin, Yipeng Yang 1274

Modeling and Cost Analysis of Nested Software Rejuvenation Policy
Jing You, Jian Xu, Xue-long Zhao, Feng-yu Liu 1280

A Fuzzy Multi-criteria Decision Making Model for the Selection of the Distribution Center
Hsuan-Shih Lee 1290

Refinement of Clustering Solutions Using a Multi-label Voting
Algorithm for Neuro-fuzzy Ensembles
    Shuai Zhang, Daniel Neagu, Catalin Balescu 1300

Comparison of Meta-heuristic Hybrid Approaches for Two Dimensional
Non-guillotine Rectangular Cutting Problems
    Alev Soke, Zafer Bingul 1304

A Hybrid Immune Evolutionary Computation Based on Immunity and
Clonal Selection for Concurrent Mapping and Localization
    Meiyi Li, Zixing Cai, Yuexiang Shi, Pingan Gao 1308

Author Index 1313

Table of Contents – Part I

Neural Network Learning Algorithms

A Novel Learning Algorithm for Wavelet Neural Networks
  Min Huang, Baotong Cui 1

Using Unscented Kalman Filter for Training the Minimal Resource Allocation Neural Network
  Ye Zhang, Yiqiang Wu, Wenquan Zhang, Yi Zheng 8

The Improved CMAC Model and Learning Result Analysis
  Daqi Zhu, Min Kong, YonQing Yang 15

A New Smooth Support Vector Regression Based on ϵ-Insensitive Logistic Loss Function
  Yang Hui-zhong, Shao Xin-guang, Ding Feng 25

Neural Network Classifier Based on the Features of Multi-lead ECG
  Mozhiwen, Feng Jun, Qiu Yazhu, Shu Lan 33

A New Learning Algorithm for Diagonal Recurrent Neural Network
  Deng Xiaolong, Xie Jianying, Guo Weizhong, Liu Jun 44

Study of On-Line Weighted Least Squares Support Vector Machines
  Xiangjun Wen, Xiaoming Xu, Yunze Cai 51

Globally Exponential Stability Analysis and Estimation of the Exponential Convergence Rate for Neural Networks with Multiple Time Varying Delays
  Huaguang Zhang, Zhanshan Wang 61

Locally Determining the Number of Neighbors in the k-Nearest Neighbor Rule Based on Statistical Confidence
  Jigang Wang, Predrag Neskovic, Leon N. Cooper 71

Fuzzy Self-organizing Map Neural Network Using Kernel PCA and the Application
  Qiang Lv, Jin-shou Yu 81

An Evolved Recurrent Neural Network and Its Application
  Chunkai Zhang, Hong Hu 91

Self-organized Locally Linear Embedding for Nonlinear Dimensionality
Reduction
    Jian Xiao, Zongtan Zhou, Dewen Hu, Junsong Yin, Shuang Chen ...   101

Active Learning for Probabilistic Neural Networks
    Bülent Bolat, Tülay Yıldırım   110

Adaptive Training of Radial Basis Function Networks Using Particle
Swarm Optimization Algorithm
    Hongkai Ding, Yunshi Xiao, Jiguang Yue   119

A Game-Theoretic Approach to Competitive Learning in
Self-Organizing Maps
    Joseph Herbert, JingTao Yao   129

A Novel Intrusions Detection Method Based on HMM Embedded
Neural Network
    Weijin Jiang, Yusheng Xu, Yuhui Xu   139

Generate Different Neural Networks by Negative Correlation Learning
    Yong Liu   149

New Training Method and Optimal Structure of Backpropagation
Networks
    Songyot Sureerattanan, Nidapan Sureerattanan   157

Learning Outliers to Refine a Corpus for Chinese Webpage
Categorization
    Dingsheng Luo, Xinhao Wang, Xihong Wu, Huisheng Chi   167

Bio-kernel Self-organizing Map for HIV Drug Resistance Classification
    Zheng Rong Yang, Natasha Young   179

A New Learning Algorithm Based on Lever Principle
    Xiaoguang He, Jie Tian, Xin Yang   187

An Effective Method to Improve Convergence for Sequential Blind
Source Separation
    L. Yuan, Enfang. Sang, W. Wang, J.A. Chambers   199

A Novel LDA Approach for High-Dimensional Data
    Guiyu Feng, Dewen Hu, Ming Li, Zongtan Zhou   209

Research and Design of Distributed Neural Networks with Chip
Training Algorithm
    Bo Yang, Ya-dong Wang, Xiao-hong Su   213

Support Vector Regression with Smoothing Property
Zhixia Yang, Nong Wang, Ling Jing 217

A Fast SMO Training Algorithm for Support Vector Regression
*Haoran Zhang, Xiaodong Wang, Changjiang Zhang,
Xiuling Xu* 221

Rival Penalized Fuzzy Competitive Learning Algorithm
Xiyang Yang, Fusheng Yu 225

A New Predictive Vector Quantization Method Using a Smaller Codebook
Min Shi, Shengli Xie 229

Performance Improvement of Fuzzy RBF Networks
Kwang-Baek Kim, Dong-Un Lee, Kwee-Bo Sim 237

Neural Network Architectures

Universal Approach to Study Delayed Dynamical Systems
Tianping Chen 245

Long-Range Connections Based Small-World Network and Its Synchronizability
Liu Jie, Lu Jun-an 254

Double Synaptic Weight Neuron Theory and Its Application
Wang Shou-jue, Chen Xu, Qin Hong, Li Weijun, Bian Yi 264

Comparative Study of Chaotic Neural Networks with Different Models of Chaotic Noise
Huidang Zhang, Yuyao He 273

A Learning Model in Qubit Neuron According to Quantum Circuit
Michiharu Maeda, Masaya Suenaga, Hiromi Miyajima 283

An Algorithm for Pruning Redundant Modules in Min-Max Modular Network with GZC Function
Jing Li, Bao-Liang Lu, Michinori Ichikawa 293

A General Procedure for Combining Binary Classifiers and Its Performance Analysis
Hai Zhao, Bao-Liang Lu 303

A Modular Structure of Auto-encoder for the Integration of Different Kinds of Information
  Naohiro Fukumura, Keitaro Wakaki, Yoji Uno 313

Adaptive and Competitive Committee Machine Architecture
  Jian Yang, Siwei Luo 322

An ART2/RBF Hybrid Neural Networks Research
  Xuhua Yang, Yunbing Wei, Qiu Guan, Wanliang Wang, Shengyong Chen 332

Complex Number Procedure Neural Networks
  Liang Jiuzhen, Han Jianmin 336

Urban Traffic Signal Timing Optimization Based on Multi-layer Chaos Neural Networks Involving Feedback
  Chaojun Dong, Zhiyong Liu, Zulian Qiu 340

Research on a Direct Adaptive Neural Network Control Method of Nonlinear Systems
  Weijin Jiang, Yusheng Xu, Yuhui Xu 345

Improving the Resultant Quality of Kohonen's Self Organizing Map Using Stiffness Factor
  Emin Germen 353

A Novel Orthonormal Wavelet Network for Function Learning
  Xieping Gao, Jun Zhang 358

Fuzzy Back-Propagation Network for PCB Sales Forecasting
  Pei-Chann Chang, Yen-Wen Wang, Chen-Hao Liu 364

An Evolutionary Artificial Neural Networks Approach for BF Hot Metal Silicon Content Prediction
  Zhao Min, Liu Xiang-guan, Luo Shi-hua 374

Application of Chaotic Neural Model Based on Olfactory System on Pattern Recognitions
  Guang Li, Zhenguo Lou, Le Wang, Xu Li, Walter J. Freeman 378

Double Robustness Analysis for Determining Optimal Feedforward Neural Network Architecture
  Lean Yu, Kin Keung Lai, Shouyang Wang 382

Stochastic Robust Stability Analysis for Markovian Jump Neural Networks with Time Delay
Li Xie 386

Neurodynamics

Observation of Crises and Bifurcations in the Hodgkin-Huxley Neuron Model
Wuyin Jin, Qian Lin, Yaobing Wei, Ying Wu 390

An Application of Pattern Recognition Based on Optimized RBF-DDA Neural Networks
Guoyou Li, Huiguang Li, Min Dong, Changping Sun, Tihua Wu 397

Global Exponential Stability of Cellular Neural Networks with Time-Varying Delays
Qiang Zhang, Dongsheng Zhou, Haijun Wang, Xiaopeng Wei 405

Effect of Noises on Two-Layer Hodgkin-Huxley Neuronal Network
Jun Liu, Zhengguo Lou, Guang Li 411

Adaptive Co-ordinate Transformation Based on a Spike Timing-Dependent Plasticity Learning Paradigm
QingXiang Wu, T.M. McGinnity, L.P Maguire, A. Belatreche, B. Glackin 420

Modeling of Short-Term Synaptic Plasticity Using Dynamic Synapses
Biswa Sengupta 429

A Chaotic Model of Hippocampus-Neocortex
Takashi Kuremoto, Tsuyoshi Eto, Kunikazu Kobayashi, Masanao Obayashi 439

Stochastic Neuron Model with Dynamic Synapses and Evolution Equation of Its Density Function
Wentao Huang, Licheng Jiao, Yuelei Xu, Maoguo Gong 449

Learning Algorithm for Spiking Neural Networks
Hesham H. Amin, Robert H. Fujii 456

Exponential Convergence of Delayed Neural Networks
Xiaoping Xue 466

A Neural Network for Constrained Saddle Point Problems: An
Approximation Approach
    Xisheng Shen, Shiji Song, Lixin Cheng 470

Implementing Fuzzy Reasoning by IAF Neurons
    Zhijie Wang, Hong Fan 476

A Method for Quantifying Temporal and Spatial Patterns of Spike Trains
    Shi-min Wang, Qi-Shao Lu, Ying Du 480

A Stochastic Nonlinear Evolution Model and Dynamic Neural Coding
on Spontaneous Behavior of Large-Scale Neuronal Population
    Rubin Wang, Wei Yu 490

Study on Circle Maps Mechanism of Neural Spikes Sequence
    Zhang Hong, Fang Lu-ping, Tong Qin-ye 499

Synchronous Behaviors of Hindmarsh-Rose Neurons with Chemical
Coupling
    Ying Wu, Jianxue Xu, Mi He 508

Statistical Neural Network Models and Support Vector Machines

A Simple Quantile Regression via Support Vector Machine
    Changha Hwang, Jooyong Shim 512

Doubly Regularized Kernel Regression with Heteroscedastic Censored
Data
    Jooyong Shim, Changha Hwang 521

Support Vector Based Prototype Selection Method for Nearest
Neighbor Rules
    Yuangui Li, Zhonghui Hu, Yunze Cai, Weidong Zhang 528

A Prediction Interval Estimation Method for KMSE
    Changha Hwang, Kyung Ha Seok, Daehyeon Cho 536

An Information-Geometrical Approach to Constructing Kernel in
Support Vector Regression Machines
    Wensen An, Yanguang Sun 546

Training Data Selection for Support Vector Machines
    Jigang Wang, Predrag Neskovic, Leon N. Cooper 554

Model Selection for Regularized Least-Squares Classification
  Hui-Hua Yang, Xing-Yu Wang, Yong Wang, Hai-Hua Gao 565

Modelling of Chaotic Systems with Recurrent Least Squares Support
Vector Machines Combined with Reconstructed Embedding Phase Space
  Zheng Xiang, Taiyi Zhang, Jiancheng Sun 573

Least-Squares Wavelet Kernel Method for Regression Estimation
  Xiangjun Wen, Xiaoming Xu, Yunze Cai 582

Fuzzy Support Vector Machines Based on λ—Cut
  Shengwu Xiong, Hongbing Liu, Xiaoxiao Niu 592

Mixtures of Kernels for SVM Modeling
  Yan-fei Zhu, Lian-fang Tian, Zong-yuan Mao, Li Wei 601

A Novel Parallel Reduced Support Vector Machine
  Fangfang Wu, Yinliang Zhao, Zefei Jiang 608

Recurrent Support Vector Machines in Reliability Prediction
  *Wei-Chiang Hong, Ping-Feng Pai, Chen-Tung Chen,
  Ping-Teng Chang* 619

A Modified SMO Algorithm for SVM Regression and Its Application in
Quality Prediction of HP-LDPE
  Hengping Zhao, Jinshou Yu 630

Gait Recognition via Independent Component Analysis Based on
Support Vector Machine and Neural Network
  Erhu Zhang, Jiwen Lu, Ganglong Duan 640

Uncertainty Support Vector Method for Ordinal Regression
  Liu Guangli, Sun Ruizhi, Gao Wanlin 650

An Incremental Learning Method Based on SVM for Online Sketchy
Shape Recognition
  Zhengxing Sun, Lisha Zhang, Enyi Tang 655

Eigenspectra Versus Eigenfaces: Classification with a Kernel-Based
Nonlinear Representor
  Benyong Liu, Jing Zhang 660

Blind Extraction of Singularly Mixed Source Signals
  Zhigang Zeng, Chaojin Fu 664

Application of Support Vector Machines in Predicting Employee Turnover Based on Job Performance
  *Wei-Chiang Hong, Ping-Feng Pai, Yu-Ying Huang,
  Shun-Lin Yang* 668

Palmprint Recognition Based on Unsupervised Subspace Analysis
  Guiyu Feng, Dewen Hu, Ming Li, Zongtan Zhou 675

A New Alpha Seeding Method for Support Vector Machine Training
  Du Feng, Wenkang Shi, Huawei Guo, Liangzhou Chen 679

Multiple Acoustic Sources Location Based on Blind Source Separation
  Gaoming Huang, Luxi Yang, Zhenya He 683

Short-Term Load Forecasting Based on Self-organizing Map and Support Vector Machine
  Zhejing Bao, Daoying Pi, Youxian Sun 688

A Multi-class Classifying Algorithm Based on Nonlinear Dimensionality Reduction and Support Vector Machines
  Lukui Shi, Qing Wu, Xueqin Shen, Pilian He 692

A VSC Scheme for Linear MIMO Systems Based on SVM
  Zhang Yibo, Yang Chunjie, Pi Daoying, Sun Youxian 696

Global Convergence of FastICA: Theoretical Analysis and Practical Considerations
  Gang Wang, Xin Xu, Dewen Hu 700

SVM Based Nonparametric Model Identification and Dynamic Model Control
  Weimin Zhong, Daoying Pi, Youxian Sun 706

Learning SVM Kernel with Semi-definite Programming
  Shuzhong Yang, Siwei Luo 710

Weighted On-Line SVM Regression Algorithm and Its Application
  Hui Wang, Daoying Pi, Youxian Sun 716

Other Topics in Neural Network Models

Convergence of an Online Gradient Method for BP Neural Networks with Stochastic Inputs
  Zhengxue Li, Wei Wu, Guorui Feng, Huifang Lu 720

A Constructive Algorithm for Wavelet Neural Networks
  Jinhua Xu, Daniel W.C. Ho 730

Stochastic High-Order Hopfield Neural Networks
  Yi Shen, Guoying Zhao, Minghui Jiang, Shigeng Hu 740

Predicting with Confidence - An Improved Dynamic Cell Structure
  Yan Liu, Bojan Cukic, Michael Jiang, Zhiwei Xu 750

An Efficient Score Function Generation Algorithm with Information Maximization
  Woong Myung Kim, Hyon Soo Lee 760

A New Criterion on Exponential Stability of a Class of Discrete Cellular Neural Networks with Time Delay
  Fei Hao, Long Wang, Tianguang Chu 769

A Novel Local Connection Neural Network
  Shuang Cong, Guodong Li, Yisong Zheng 773

An Unsupervised Cooperative Pattern Recognition Model to Identify Anomalous Massive SNMP Data Sending
  Álvaro Herrero, Emilio Corchado, José Manuel Sáiz 778

A Fast Nonseparable Wavelet Neural Network for Function Approximation
  Jun Zhang, Xieping Gao, Chunhong Cao, Fen Xiao 783

A Visual Cortex Domain Model for Illusory Contour Figures
  Keongho Hong, Eunhwa Jeong 789

Cognitive Science

ANN Ensemble Online Learning Strategy in 3D Object Cognition and Recognition Based on Similarity
  Rui Nian, Guangrong Ji, Wencang Zhao, Chen Feng 793

Design and Implementation of the Individualized Intelligent Teachable Agent
  Sung-il Kim, Sung-Hyun Yun, Dong-Seong Choi, Mi-sun Yoon, Yeon-hee So, Myung-jin Lee, Won-sik Kim, Sun-young Lee, Su-Young Hwang, Cheon-woo Han, Woo-Gul Lee, Karam Lim 797

Comparison of Complexity and Regularity of ERP Recordings Between Single and Dual Tasks Using Sample Entropy Algorithm
Tao Zhang, Xiaojun Tang, Zhuo Yang 806

Representation of a Physio-psychological Index Through Constellation Graphs
Oyama-Higa Mayumi, Tiejun Miao 811

Neural Network Based Emotion Estimation Using Heart Rate Variability and Skin Resistance
Sun K. Yoo, Chung K. Lee, Youn J. Park, Nam H. Kim, Byung C. Lee, Kee S. Jeong 818

Modeling Belief, Capability and Promise for Cognitive Agents - A Modal Logic Approach
Xinyu Zhao, Zuoquan Lin 825

PENCIL: A Framework for Expressing Free-Hand Sketching in 3D
Zhan Ding, Sanyuan Zhang, Wei Peng, Xiuzi Ye, Huaqiang Hu 835

Blocking Artifacts Measurement Based on the Human Visual System
Zhi-Heng Zhou, Sheng-Li Xie 839

A Computation Model of Korean Lexical Processing
Hyungwook Yim, Heuseok Lim, Kinam Park, Kichun Nam 844

Neuroanatomical Analysis for Onomatopoeia and Phainomime Words: fMRI Study
Jong-Hye Han, Wonil Choi, Yongmin Chang, Ok-Ran Jeong, Kichun Nam 850

Cooperative Aspects of Selective Attention
KangWoo Lee 855

Selective Attention Guided Perceptual Grouping Model
Qi Zou, Siwei Luo, Jianyu Li 867

Visual Search for Object Features
Predrag Neskovic, Leon N. Cooper 877

Agent Based Decision Support System Using Reinforcement Learning Under Emergency Circumstances
Devinder Thapa, In-Sung Jung, Gi-Nam Wang 888

Dynamic Inputs and Attraction Force Analysis for Visual Invariance
and Transformation Estimation
  Tomás Maul, Sapiyan Baba, Azwina Yusof 893

Task-Oriented Sparse Coding Model for Pattern Classification
  Qingyong Li, Dacheng Lin, Zhongzhi Shi 903

Robust Face Recognition from One Training Sample per Person
  Weihong Deng, Jiani Hu, Jun Guo 915

Chinese Word Sense Disambiguation Using HowNet
  Yuntao Zhang, Ling Gong, Yongcheng Wang 925

Modeling Human Learning as Context Dependent Knowledge Utility
Optimization
  Toshihiko Matsuka 933

Automatic Text Summarization Based on Lexical Chains
  Yanmin Chen, Xiaolong Wang, Yi Guan 947

A General fMRI LINEAR Convolution Model Based Dynamic
Characteristic
  Hong Yuan, Hong Li, Zhijie Zhang, Jiang Qiu 952

Neuroscience Informatics, Bioinformatics, and Bio-medical Engineering

A KNN-Based Learning Method for Biology Species Categorization
  Yan Dang, Yulei Zhang, Dongmo Zhang, Liping Zhao 956

Application of Emerging Patterns for Multi-source Bio-Data
Classification and Analysis
  Hye-Sung Yoon, Sang-Ho Lee, Ju Han Kim 965

Nonlinear Kernel MSE Methods for Cancer Classification
  L. Shen, E.C. Tan 975

Fusing Face and Fingerprint for Identity Authentication by SVM
  Chunhong Jiang, Guangda Su 985

A New Algorithm of Multi-modality Medical Image Fusion Based on
Pulse-Coupled Neural Networks
  Wei Li, Xue-feng Zhu 995

Cleavage Site Analysis Using Rule Extraction from Neural
Networks
  Yeun-Jin Cho, Hyeoncheol Kim 1002

Prediction Rule Generation of MHC Class I Binding Peptides Using
ANN and GA
  Yeon-Jin Cho, Hyeoncheol Kim, Heung-Bum Oh 1009

Combined Kernel Function Approach in SVM for Diagnosis of Cancer
  Ha-Nam Nguyen, Syng-Yup Ohn, Jaehyun Park,
  Kyu-Sik Park 1017

Automatic Liver Segmentation of Contrast Enhanced CT Images Based
on Histogram Processing
  Kyung-Sik Seo, Hyung-Bum Kim, Taesu Park, Pan-Koo Kim,
  Jong-An Park 1027

An Improved Adaptive RBF Network for Classification of Left and
Right Hand Motor Imagery Tasks
  Xiao-mei Pei, Jin Xu, Chong-xun Zheng, Guang-yu Bin 1031

Similarity Analysis of DNA Sequences Based on the Relative Entropy
  Wenlu Yang, Xiongjun Pi, Liqing Zhang 1035

Can Circulating Matrix Metalloproteinases Be Predictors of Breast
Cancer? A Neural Network Modeling Study
  H. Hu, S.B. Somiari, J. Copper, R.D. Everly, C. Heckman,
  R. Jordan, R. Somiari, J. Hooke, C.D. Shriver, M.N. Liebman 1039

Blind Clustering of DNA Fragments Based on Kullback-Leibler
Divergence
  Xiongjun Pi, Wenlu Yang, Liqing Zhang 1043

Prediction of Protein Subcellular Locations Using Support Vector
Machines
  Na-na Li, Xiao-hui Niu, Feng Shi, Xue-yan Li 1047

Neuroinformatics Research in China- Current Status and Future
Research Activities
  Guang Li, Jing Zhang, Faji Gu, Ling Yin, Yiyuan Tang,
  Xiaowei Tang 1052

Australian Neuroinformatics Research – Grid Computing and
e-Research
  G.F. Egan, W. Liu, W-S. Soh, D. Hang 1057

Current Status and Future Research Activities in Clinical
Neuroinformatics: Singaporean Perspective
    Wieslaw L. Nowinski 1065

Japanese Neuroinformatics Research: Current Status and Future
Research Program of J-Node
    Shiro Usui 1074

Neural Network Applications: Communications and Computer Networks

Optimal TDMA Frame Scheduling in Broadcasting Packet Radio
Networks Using a Gradual Noisy Chaotic Neural Network
    Haixiang Shi, Lipo Wang 1080

A Fast Online SVM Algorithm for Variable-Step CDMA Power Control
    Yu Zhao, Hongsheng Xi, Zilei Wang 1090

Fourth-Order Cumulants and Neural Network Approach for Robust
Blind Channel Equalization
    Soowhan Han, Kwangeui Lee, Jongkeuk Lee,
    Fredric M. Ham 1100

Equalization of a Wireless ATM Channel with Simplified Complex
Bilinear Recurrent Neural Network
    Dong-Chul Park, Duc-Hoai Nguyen, Sang Jeen Hong,
    Yunsik Lee 1113

A Novel Remote User Authentication Scheme Using Interacting Neural
Network
    Tieming Chen, Jiamei Cai 1117

Genetic Algorithm Simulated Annealing Based Clustering Strategy in
MANET
    Xu Li 1121

Neural Network Applications: Expert System and Informatics

A Gradual Training Algorithm of Incremental Support Vector Machine
Learning
    Jian-Pei Zhang, Zhong-Wei Li, Jing Yang, Yuan Li 1132

An Improved Method of Feature Selection Based on Concept Attributes in Text Classification
  Shasha Liao, Minghu Jiang 1140

Research on the Decision Method for Enterprise Information Investment Based on IA-BP Network
  Xiao-Ke Yan, Hai-Dong Yang, He-Jun Wang, Fei-Qi Deng 1150

Process Control and Management of Etching Process Using Data Mining with Quality Indexes
  Hyeon Bae, Sungshin Kim, Kwang Bang Woo 1160

Automatic Knowledge Configuration by Reticular Activating System
  JeongYon Shim 1170

An Improved Information Retrieval Method and Input Device Using Gloves for Wearable Computers
  Jeong-Hoon Shin, Kwang-Seok Hong 1179

Research on Design and Implementation of the Artificial Intelligence Agent for Smart Home Based on Support Vector Machine
  Jonghwa Choi, Dongkyoo Shin, Dongil Shin 1185

A Self-organized Network for Data Clustering
  Liang Zhao, Antonio P.G. Damiance Jr., Andre C.P.L.F. Carvalho 1189

A General Criterion of Synchronization Stability in Ensembles of Coupled Systems and Its Application
  Qing-Yun Wang, Qi-Shao Lu, Hai-Xia Wang 1199

Complexity of Linear Cellular Automata over $\mathbb{Z}_m$
  Xiaogang Jin, Weihong Wang 1209

Neural Network Applications: Financial Engineering

Applications of Genetic Algorithm for Artificial Neural Network Model Discovery and Performance Surface Optimization in Finance
  Serge Hayward 1214

Mining Data by Query-Based Error-Propagation
  Liang-Bin Lai, Ray-I Chang, Jen-Shaing Kouh 1224

The Application of Structured Feedforward Neural Networks to the
Modelling of the Daily Series of Currency in Circulation
  Marek Hlaváček, Josef Čada, František Hakl 1234

Time Delay Neural Networks and Genetic Algorithms for Detecting
Temporal Patterns in Stock Markets
  Hyun-jung Kim, Kyung-shik Shin, Kyungdo Park 1247

The Prediction of the Financial Time Series Based on Correlation
Dimension
  Chen Feng, Guangrong Ji, Wencang Zhao, Rui Nian 1256

Gradient-Based FCM and a Neural Network for Clustering of
Incomplete Data
  Dong-Chul Park 1266

Toward Global Optimization of ANN Supported by Instance Selection
for Financial Forecasting
  Sehun Lim 1270

Other Applications of Natural Computations

FranksTree: A Genetic Programming Approach to Evolve Derived
Bracketed L-Systems
  Danilo Mattos Bonfim, Leandro Nunes de Castro 1275

Data Clustering with a Neuro-immune Network
  *Helder Knidel, Leandro Nunes de Castro,
  Fernando J. Von Zuben* 1279

Author Index 1289

Table of Contents – Part II

Neural Network Applications: Pattern Recognition and Diagnostics

Monitoring of Tool Wear Using Feature Vector Selection and Linear Regression
Zhong Chen, XianMing Zhang 1

Image Synthesis and Face Recognition Based on 3D Face Model and Illumination Model
Dang-hui Liu, Lan-sun Shen, Kin-man Lam 7

Head-and-Shoulder Detection in Varying Pose
Yi Sun, Yan Wang, Yinghao He, Yong Hua 12

Principal Component Neural Networks Based Intrusion Feature Extraction and Detection Using SVM
Hai-Hua Gao, Hui-Hua Yang, Xing-Yu Wang 21

GA-Driven LDA in KPCA Space for Facial Expression Recognition
Qijun Zhao, Hongtao Lu 28

A New ART Neural Networks for Remote Sensing Image Classification
AnFei Liu, BiCheng Li, Gang Chen, Xianfei Zhang 37

Modified Color Co-occurrence Matrix for Image Retrieval
Min Hyuk Chang, Jae Young Pyun, Muhammad Bilal Ahmad, Jong Hoon Chun, Jong An Park 43

A Novel Data Fusion Scheme for Offline Chinese Signature Verification
Wen-ming Zuo, Ming Qi 51

A Multiple Eigenspaces Constructing Method and Its Application to Face Recognition
Wu-Jun Li, Bin Luo, Chong-Jun Wang, Xiang-Ping Zhong, Zhao-Qian Chen 55

Quality Estimation of Fingerprint Image Based on Neural Network
En Zhu, Jianping Yin, Chunfeng Hu, Guomin Zhang 65

Face Recognition Based on PCA/KPCA Plus CCA
Yunhui He, Li Zhao, Cairong Zou 71

Texture Segmentation Using Intensified Fuzzy Kohonen Clustering Network
  Dong Liu, Yinggan Tang, Xinping Guan 75

Application of Support Vector Machines in Reciprocating Compressor Valve Fault Diagnosis
  Quanmin Ren, Xiaojiang Ma, Gang Miao 81

The Implementation of the Emotion Recognition from Speech and Facial Expression System
  Chang-Hyun Park, Kwang-Sub Byun, Kwee-Bo Sim 85

Kernel PCA Based Network Intrusion Feature Extraction and Detection Using SVM
  Hai-Hua Gao, Hui-Hua Yang, Xing-Yu Wang 89

Leak Detection in Transport Pipelines Using Enhanced Independent Component Analysis and Support Vector Machines
  Zhengwei Zhang, Hao Ye, Guizeng Wang, Jie Yang 95

Line-Based PCA and LDA Approaches for Face Recognition
  Vo Dinh Minh Nhat, Sungyoung Lee 101

Comparative Study on Recognition of Transportation Under Real and UE Status
  Jingxin Dong, Jianping Wu, Yuanfeng Zhou 105

Adaptive Eye Location Using FuzzyART
  Jo Nam Jung, Mi Young Nam, Phill Kyu Rhee 109

Face Recognition Using Gabor Features and Support Vector Machines
  Yunfeng Li, Zongying Ou, Guoqiang Wang 119

Wavelet Method Combining BP Networks and Time Series ARMA Modeling for Data Mining Forecasting
  Weimin Tong, Yijun Li 123

On-line Training of Neural Network for Color Image Segmentation
  Yi Fang, Chen Pan, Li Liu 135

Short-Term Prediction on Parameter-Varying Systems by Multiwavelets Neural Network
  Fen Xiao, Xieping Gao, Chunhong Cao, Jun Zhang 139

VICARED: A Neural Network Based System for the Detection of
Electrical Disturbances in Real Time
*Iñigo Monedero, Carlos León, Jorge Ropero, José Manuel Elena,
Juan C. Montaño* 147

Speech Recognition by Integrating Audio, Visual and Contextual
Features Based on Neural Networks
Myung Won Kim, Joung Woo Ryu, Eun Ju Kim 155

A Novel Pattern Classification Method for Multivariate EMG Signals
Using Neural Network
Nan Bu, Jun Arita, Toshio Tsuji 165

Data Fusion for Fault Diagnosis Using Dempster-Shafer Theory Based
Multi-class SVMs
Zhonghui Hu, Yunze Cai, Ye Li, Yuangui Li, Xiaoming Xu 175

Modelling of Rolling and Aging Processes in Copper Alloy by
Levenberg-Marquardt BP Algorithm
Juanhua Su, Hejun Li, Qiming Dong, Ping Liu 185

Neural Network Applications: Robotics and Intelligent Control

An Adaptive Control for AC Servo System Using Recurrent Fuzzy
Neural Network
Wei Sun, Yaonan Wang 190

PSO-Based Model Predictive Control for Nonlinear Processes
Xihuai Wang, Jianmei Xiao 196

Low Cost Implementation of Artificial Neural Network Based Space
Vector Modulation
Tarık Erfidan, Erhan Butun 204

A Novel Multispectral Imaging Analysis Method for White Blood Cell
Detection
*Hongbo Zhang, Libo Zeng, Hengyu Ke, Hong Zheng,
Qiongshui Wu* 210

Intelligent Optimal Control in Rare-Earth Countercurrent Extraction
Process *via* Soft-Sensor
Hui Yang, Chunyan Yang, Chonghui Song, Tianyou Chai 214

Three Dimensional Gesture Recognition Using Modified Matching Algorithm
  Hwan-Seok Yang, Jong-Min Kim, Seoung-Kyu Park 224

Direct Adaptive Control for a Class of Uncertain Nonlinear Systems Using Neural Networks
  Tingliang Hu, Jihong Zhu, Chunhua Hu, Zengqi Sun 234

Neural Network Based Feedback Scheduler for Networked Control System with Flexible Workload
  Feng Xia, Shanbin Li, Youxian Sun 242

Humanoid Walking Gait Optimization Using GA-Based Neural Network
  Zhe Tang, Changjiu Zhou, Zengqi Sun 252

Adaptive Neural Network Internal Model Control for Tilt Rotor Aircraft Platform
  Changjie Yu, Jihong Zhu, Zengqi Sun 262

Novel Leaning Feed-Forward Controller for Accurate Robot Trajectory Tracking
  D. Bi, G.L. Wang, J. Zhang, Q. Xue 266

Adaptive Neural Network Control for Multi-fingered Robot Hand Manipulation in the Constrained Environment
  Gang Chen, Shuqing Wang, Jianming Zhang 270

Control of a Giant Swing Robot Using a Neural Oscillator
  Kiyotoshi Matsuoka, Norifumi Ohyama, Atsushi Watanabe, Masataka Ooshima 274

Neural Network Indirect Adaptive Sliding Mode Tracking Control for a Class of Nonlinear Interconnected Systems
  Yanxin Zhang, Xiaofan Wang 283

Sequential Support Vector Machine Control of Nonlinear Systems via Lyapunov Function Derivative Estimation
  Zonghai Sun, Youxian Sun, Yongqiang Wang 292

An Adaptive Control Using Multiple Neural Networks for the Position Control in Hydraulic Servo System
  Yuan Kang, Ming-Hui Chua, Yuan-Liang Liu, Chuan-Wei Chang, Shu-Yen Chien 296

Neural Network Applications: Signal Processing and Multi-media

Exon Structure Analysis via PCA and ICA of Short-Time Fourier Transform
  Changha Hwang, David Chiu, Insuk Sohn 306

Nonlinear Adaptive Blind Source Separation Based on Kernel Function
  Feng Liu, Cao Zhexin, Qiang Zhi, Shaoqian Li, Min Liang 316

Hybrid Intelligent Forecasting Model Based on Empirical Mode Decomposition, Support Vector Regression and Adaptive Linear Neural Network
  Zhengjia He, Qiao Hu, Yanyang Zi, Zhousuo Zhang, Xuefeng Chen 324

A Real Time Color Gamut Mapping Method Using a Neural Network
  Hak-Sung Lee, Dongil Han 328

Adaptive Identification of Chaotic Systems and Its Applications in Chaotic Communications
  Jiuchao Feng 332

A Time-Series Decomposed Model of Network Traffic
  Cheng Guang, Gong Jian, Ding Wei 338

A Novel Wavelet Watermark Algorithm Based on Neural Network Image Scramble
  Jian Zhao, Qin Zhao, Ming-quan Zhou, Jianshou Pan 346

A Hybrid Model for Forecasting Aquatic Products Short-Term Price Integrated Wavelet Neural Network with Genetic Algorithm
  Tao Hu, Xiaoshuan Zhang, Yunxian Hou, Weisong Mu, Zetian Fu 352

A Multiple Vector Quantization Approach to Image Compression
  Noritaka Shigei, Hiromi Miyajima, Michiharu Maeda 361

Segmentation of SAR Image Using Mixture Multiscale ARMA Network
  Haixia Xu, Zheng Tian, Fan Meng 371

Brain Activity Analysis of Rat Based on Electroencephalogram Complexity Under General Anesthesia
  Jin Xu, Chongxun Zheng, Xueliang Liu, Xiaomei Pei, Guixia Jing 376

Post-nonlinear Blind Source Separation Using Wavelet Neural Networks and Particle Swarm Optimization
Ying Gao, Shengli Xie 386

An MRF-ICA Based Algorithm for Image Separation
Sen Jia, Yuntao Qian 391

Multi-view Face Recognition with Min-Max Modular SVMs
Zhi-Gang Fan, Bao-Liang Lu 396

Texture Segmentation Using Neural Networks and Multi-scale Wavelet Features
Tae Hyung Kim, Il Kyu Eom, Yoo Shin Kim 400

An In-depth Comparison on FastICA, CuBICA and IC-FastICA
Bin Wang, Wenkai Lu 410

Characteristics of Equinumber Principle for Adaptive Vector Quantization
Michiharu Maeda, Noritaka Shigei, Hiromi Miyajima 415

ANFIS Based Dynamic Model Compensator for Tracking and GPS Navigation Applications
Dah-Jing Jwo, Zong-Ming Chen 425

Dynamic Background Discrimination with a Recurrent Network
Jieyu Zhao 432

Gender Recognition Using a Min-Max Modular Support Vector Machine
Hui-Cheng Lian, Bao-Liang Lu, Erina Takikawa, Satoshi Hosoi 438

An Application of Support Vector Regression on Narrow-Band Interference Suppression in Spread Spectrum Systems
Qing Yang, Shengli Xie 442

A Natural Modification of Autocorrelation Based Video Watermarking Scheme Using ICA for Better Geometric Attack Robustness
Seong-Whan Kim, Hyun Jin Park, HyunSeong Sung 451

Research of Blind Deconvolution Algorithm Based on High-Order Statistics and Quantum Inspired GA
Jun-an Yang, Bin Zhao, Zhongfu Ye 461

Differential Demodulation of OFDM Based on SOM
Xuming Li, Lenan Wu 468

Efficient Time Series Matching Based on HMTS Algorithm
Min Zhang, Ying Tan 476

3D Polar-Radius Invariant Moments and Structure Moment Invariants
Zongmin Li, Yuanzhen Zhang, Kunpeng Hou, Hua Li.............. 483

A Fast Searching Algorithm of Symmetrical Period Modulation Pattern Based on Accumulative Transformation Technique
FuHua Fan, Ying Tan 493

A Granular Analysis Method in Signal Processing
Lunwen Wang, Ying Tan, Ling Zhang 501

Other Neural Networks Applications

Adaptive Leakage Suppression Based on Recurrent Wavelet Neural Network
Zhangliang Xiong, Xiangquan Shi 508

New Multi-server Password Authentication Scheme Using Neural Networks
Eun-Jun Yoon, Kee-Young Yoo 512

Time Domain Substructural Post-earthquake Damage Diagnosis Methodology with Neural Networks
Bin Xu 520

Conceptual Modeling with Neural Network for Giftedness Identification and Education
Kwang Hyuk Im, Tae Hyun Kim, SungMin Bae, Sang Chan Park ... 530

Online Discovery of Quantitative Model for Web Service Management
Jing Chen, Xiao-chuan Yin, Shui-ping Zhang..................... 539

Judgment of Static Life and Death in Computer Go Using String Graph
Hyun-Soo Park, Kyung-Woo Kang, Hang-Joon Kim 543

Research on Artificial Intelligence Character Based Physics Engine in 3D Car Game
Jonghwa Choi, Dongkyoo Shin, Jinsung Choi, Dongil Shin 552

Document Clustering Based on Nonnegative Sparse Matrix Factorization
C.F. Yang, Mao Ye, Jing Zhao 557

Prediction Modeling for Ingot Manufacturing Process Utilizing Data
Mining Roadmap Including Dynamic Polynomial Neural Network and
Bootstrap Method
  Hyeon Bae, Sungshin Kim, Kwang Bang Woo 564

Implicit Rating – A Case Study
  Song Wang, Xiu Li, Wenhuang Liu 574

Application of Grey Majorized Model in Tunnel Surrounding Rock
Displacement Forecasting
  Xiaohong Li, Yu Zhao, Xiaoguang Jin, Yiyu Lu, Xinfei Wang 584

NN-Based Damage Detection in Multilayer Composites
  Zhi Wei, Xiaomin Hu, Muhui Fan, Jun Zhang, D. Bi 592

Application of Support Vector Machine and Similar Day Method for
Load Forecasting
  Xunming Li, Changyin Sun, Dengcai Gong 602

Particle Swarm Optimization Neural Network and Its Application in
Soft-Sensing Modeling
  Guochu Chen, Jinshou Yu 610

Solution of the Inverse Electromagnetic Problem of Spontaneous
Potential (SP) by Very Fast Simulated Reannealing (VFSR)
  Hüseyin Göksu, Mehmet Ali Kaya, Ali Kökçe 618

Using SOFM to Improve Web Site Text Content
  *Sebastián A. Ríos, Juan D. Velásquez, Eduardo S. Vera,
  Hiroshi Yasuda, Terumasa Aoki* 622

Online Support Vector Regression for System Identification
  Zhenhua Yu, Xiao Fu, Yinglu Li 627

Optimization of PTA Crystallization Process Based on Fuzzy GMDH
Networks and Differential Evolutionary Algorithm
  Wenli Du, Feng Qian 631

An Application of Support Vector Machines for Customer Churn
Analysis: Credit Card Case
  Sun Kim, Kyung-shik Shin, Kyungdo Park 636

e-NOSE Response Classification of Sewage Odors by Neural Networks
and Fuzzy Clustering
  Güleda Önkal-Engin, Ibrahim Demir, Seref N. Engin 648

Using a Random Subspace Predictor to Integrate Spatial and Temporal
Information for Traffic Flow Forecasting
  Shiliang Sun, Changshui Zhang 652

Boosting Input/Output Hidden Markov Models for Sequence
Classification
  Ke Chen 656

Learning Beyond Finite Memory in Recurrent Networks of Spiking
Neurons
  Peter Tiňo, Ashley Mills.. 666

On Non-Markovian Topographic Organization of Receptive Fields in
Recursive Self-organizing Map
  Peter Tiňo, Igor Farkaš 676

Evolutionary Learning

Quantum Reinforcement Learning
  Daoyi Dong, Chunlin Chen, Zonghai Chen 686

Characterization of Evaluation Metrics in Topical Web Crawling Based
on Genetic Algorithm
  Tao Peng, Wanli Zuo, Yilin Liu 690

A Novel Quantum Swarm Evolutionary Algorithm for Solving 0-1
Knapsack Problem
  Yan Wang, Xiao-Yue Feng, Yan-Xin Huang, Wen-Gang Zhou,
  Yan-Chun Liang, Chun-Guang Zhou 698

An Evolutionary System and Its Application to Automatic Image
Segmentation
  Yun Wen Chen, Yan Qiu Chen 705

Incorporating Web Intelligence into Website Evolution
  Jang Hee Lee, Gye Hang Hong 710

Evolution of the CPG with Sensory Feedback for Bipedal Locomotion
  Sooyol Ok, DuckSool Kim 714

Immunity-Based Genetic Algorithm for Classification Rule Discovery
  Ziqiang Wang, Dexian Zhang..................................... 727

Dynamical Proportion Portfolio Insurance with Genetic Programming
  Jiah-Shing Chen, Chia-Lan Chang 735

Evolution of Reactive Rules in Multi Player Computer Games Based on Imitation
Steffen Priesterjahn, Oliver Kramer, Alexander Weimer, Andreas Goebels 744

Combining Classifiers with Particle Swarms
Li-ying Yang, Zheng Qin 756

Adaptive Normalization Based Highly Efficient Face Recognition Under Uneven Environments
Phill Kyu Rhee, InJa Jeon, EunSung Jeong 764

Artificial Immune Systems

A New Detector Set Generating Algorithm in the Negative Selection Model
Xinhua Ren, Xiufeng Zhang, Yuanyuan Li 774

Intrusion Detection Based on ART and Artificial Immune Network Clustering
Fang Liu, Lin Bai, Licheng Jiao 780

Nature-Inspired Computations Using an Evolving Multi-set of Agents
E.V. Krishnamurthy, V.K. Murthy 784

Adaptive Immune Algorithm for Solving Job-Shop Scheduling Problem
Xinli Xu, Wanliang Wang, Qiu Guan 795

A Weather Forecast System Based on Artificial Immune System
Chunlin Xu, Tao Li, Xuemei Huang, Yaping Jiang 800

A New Model of Immune-Based Network Surveillance and Dynamic Computer Forensics
Tao Li, Juling Ding, Xiaojie Liu, Pin Yang 804

A Two-Phase Clustering Algorithm Based on Artificial Immune Network
Jiang Zhong, Zhong-Fu Wu, Kai-Gui Wu, Ling Ou, Zheng-Zhou Zhu, Ying Zhou 814

Immune Algorithm for Qos Multicast Routing
Ziqiang Wang, Dexian Zhang 822

IFCPA: Immune Forgetting Clonal Programming Algorithm for Large Parameter Optimization Problems
Maoguo Gong, Licheng Jiao, Haifeng Du, Bin Lu, Wentao Huang .. 826

A New Classification Method for Breast Cancer Diagnosis: Feature
Selection Artificial Immune Recognition System (FS-AIRS)
  Kemal Polat, Seral Sahan, Halife Kodaz, Salih Günes 830

Artificial Immune Strategies Improve the Security of Data Storage
  Lei Wang, Yinling Nie, Weike Nie, Licheng Jiao 839

Artificial Immune System for Associative Classification
  Tien Dung Do, Siu Cheung Hui, Alvis C.M. Fong 849

Artificial Immune Algorithm Based Obstacle Avoiding Path Planning
of Mobile Robots
  Yen-Nien Wang, Hao-Hsuan Hsu, Chun-Cheng Lin 859

An Adaptive Hybrid Immune Genetic Algorithm for Maximum Cut
Problem
  Hong Song, Dan Zhang, Ji Liu 863

Algorithms of Non-self Detector by Negative Selection Principle in
Artificial Immune System
  Ying Tan, Zhenhe Guo 867

An Algorithm Based on Antibody Immunodominance for TSP
  Chong Hou, Haifeng Du, Licheng Jiao 876

Flow Shop Scheduling Problems Under Uncertainty Based on Fuzzy
Cut-Set
  Zhenhao Xu, Xingsheng Gu 880

An Optimization Method Based on Chaotic Immune Evolutionary
Algorithm
  Yong Chen, Xiyue Huang 890

An Improved Immune Algorithm and Its Evaluation of Optimization
Efficiency
  Chengzhi Zhu, Bo Zhao, Bin Ye, Yijia Cao 895

Simultaneous Feature Selection and Parameters Optimization for SVM
by Immune Clonal Algorithm
  Xiangrong Zhang, Licheng Jiao 905

Optimizing the Distributed Network Monitoring Model with Bounded
Bandwidth and Delay Constraints by Genetic Algorithm
  *Xianghui Liu, Jianping Yin, Zhiping Cai, Xueyuan Huang,
  Shiming Chen* 913

Modeling and Optimal for Vacuum Annealing Furnace Based on
Wavelet Neural Networks with Adaptive Immune Genetic Algorithm
   Xiaobin Li, Ding Liu 922

Lamarckian Polyclonal Programming Algorithm for Global Numerical
Optimization
   Wuhong He, Haifeng Du, Licheng Jiao, Jing Li 931

Coevolutionary Genetic Algorithms to Simulate the Immune System's
Gene Libraries Evolution
   Grazziela P. Figueredo, Luis A.V. de Carvalho,
   Helio J.C. Barbosa 941

Clone Mind Evolution Algorithm
   Gang Xie, Xinying Xu, Keming Xie, Zehua Chen 945

The Application of IMEA in Nonlinearity Correction of VCO Frequency
Modulation
   Gaowei Yan, Jun Xie, Keming Xie 951

A Quick Optimizing Multi-variables Method with Complex Target
Function Based on the Principle of Artificial Immunology
   Gang Zhang, Keming Xie, Hongbo Guo, Zhefeng Zhao 957

Evolutionary Theory

Operator Dynamics in Molecular Biology
   Tsuyoshi Kato 963

Analysis of Complete Convergence for Genetic Algorithm with Immune
Memory
   Shiqin Zheng, Kongyu Yang, Xiufeng Wang 978

New Operators for Faster Convergence and Better Solution Quality in
Modified Genetic Algorithm
   Pei-Chann Chang, Yen-Wen Wang, Chen-Hao Liu 983

Fuzzy Programming for Multiobjective Fuzzy Job Shop Scheduling
with Alternative Machines Through Genetic Algorithms
   Fu-ming Li, Yun-long Zhu, Chao-wan Yin, Xiao-yu Song 992

The Study of Special Encoding in Genetic Algorithms and a Sufficient
Convergence Condition of GAs
   Bo Yin, Zhiqiang Wei, Qingchun Meng 1005

The Convergence of a Multi-objective Evolutionary Algorithm Based on Grids
Yuren Zhou, Jun He 1015

Influence of Finite Population Size – Extinction of Favorable Schemata
Hiroshi Furutani, Makoto Sakamoto, Susumu Katayama 1025

A Theoretical Model and Convergence Analysis of Memetic Evolutionary Algorithms
Xin Xu, Han-gen He 1035

New Quality Measures for Multiobjective Programming
Hong-yun Meng, Xiao-hua Zhang, San-yang Liu 1044

An Orthogonal Dynamic Evolutionary Algorithm with Niches
*Sanyou Zeng, Deyou Tang, Lishan Kang, Shuzhen Yao,
Lixin Ding* 1049

Fitness Sharing Genetic Algorithm with Self-adaptive Annealing Peaks Radii Control Method
Xinjie Yu 1064

A Novel Clustering Fitness Sharing Genetic Algorithm
Xinjie Yu 1072

Cooperative Co-evolutionary Differential Evolution for Function Optimization
Yan-jun Shi, Hong-fei Teng, Zi-qiang Li 1080

Optimal Design for Urban Mass Transit Network Based on Evolutionary Algorithms
Jianming Hu, Xi Shi, Jingyan Song, Yangsheng Xu 1089

A Method for Solving Nonlinear Programming Models with All Fuzzy Coefficients Based on Genetic Algorithm
Yexin Song, Yingchun Chen, Xiaoping Wu 1101

An Evolutionary Algorithm Based on Stochastic Weighted Learning for Constrained Optimization
Jun Ye, Xiande Liu, Lu Han 1105

A Multi-cluster Grid Enabled Evolution Framework for Aerodynamic Airfoil Design Optimization
*Hee-Khiang Ng, Dudy Lim, Yew-Soon Ong, Bu-Sung Lee,
Lars Freund, Shuja Parvez, Bernhard Sendhoff* 1112

A Search Algorithm for Global Optimisation
  S. Chen, X.X. Wang, C.J. Harris 1122

Selection, Space and Diversity: What Can Biological Speciation Tell Us About the Evolution of Modularity?
  Suzanne Sadedin 1131

On Evolutionary Optimization of Large Problems Using Small Populations
  Yaochu Jin, Markus Olhofer, Bernhard Sendhoff 1145

Membrane, Molecular, and DNA Computing

Reaction-Driven Membrane Systems
  Luca Bianco, Federico Fontana, Vincenzo Manca 1155

A Genetic Algorithm Based Method for Molecular Docking
  Chun-lian Li, Yu Sun, Dong-yun Long, Xi-cheng Wang 1159

A New Encoding Scheme to Improve the Performance of Protein Structural Class Prediction
  Zhen-Hui Zhang, Zheng-Hua Wang, Yong-Xian Wang 1164

DNA Computing Approach to Construction of Semantic Model
  Yusei Tsuboi, Zuwairie Ibrahim, Nobuyuki Kasai, Osamu Ono 1174

DNA Computing for Complex Scheduling Problem
  Mohd Saufee Muhammad, Zuwairie Ibrahim, Satomi Ueda,
  Osamu Ono, Marzuki Khalid 1182

On Designing DNA Databases for the Storage and Retrieval of Digital Signals
  Sotirios A. Tsaftaris, Aggelos K. Katsaggelos 1192

Composite Module Analyst: Tool for Prediction of DNA Transcription Regulation. Testing on Simulated Data
  Tatiana Konovalova, Tagir Valeev, Evgeny Cheremushkin,
  Alexander Kel 1202

Simulation and Visualization for DNA Computing in Microreactors
  Danny van Noort, Yuan Hong, Joseph Ibershoff,
  Jerzy W. Jaromczyk 1206

Ants Colony

A Novel Ant Clustering Algorithm with Digraph
  Ling Chen, Li Tu, Hongjian Chen 1218

Ant Colony Search Algorithms for Optimal Packing Problem
  Wen Peng, Ruofeng Tong, Min Tang, Jinxiang Dong 1229

Adaptive Parallel Ant Colony Algorithm
  Ling Chen, Chunfang Zhang 1239

Hierarchical Image Segmentation Using Ant Colony and Chemical
Computing Approach
  Pooyan Khajehpour, Caro Lucas, Babak N. Araabi 1250

Optimization of Container Load Sequencing by a Hybrid of Ant Colony
Optimization and Tabu Search
  Yong Hwan Lee, Jaeho Kang, Kwang Ryel Ryu, Kap Hwan Kim 1259

A Novel Ant Colony System Based on Minimum 1-Tree and Hybrid
Mutation for TSP
  Chao-Xue Wang, Du-Wu Cui, Zhu-Rong Wang, Duo Chen 1269

Author Index 1279

Multi-focus Image Fusion Based on SOFM Neural Networks and Evolution Strategies*

Yan Wu[1,2], Chongyang Liu[2], and Guisheng Liao[1]

[1] National Key Laboratory of Radar Signal Processing, Xidian University,
710071 Xi'an, Shaanxi, P.R. China
[2] School of Electronics Engineering, Xidian University,
710071 Xi'an, Shaanxi, P.R. China
ywu@mail.xidian.edu.cn

Abstract. A new method is proposed for merging two spatially registered images with diverse focus in this paper. It is based on multi-resolution wavelet decomposition, Self-Organizing Feature Map (SOFM) neural networks and evolution strategies (ES). A normalized feature image, which represents the local region clarity difference of the corresponding spatial location of two source images, is extracted by wavelet transform without down-sampling. The feature image is clustered by SOFM learning algorithm and every pixel pair in source images is classified into a certain class which indicates different clarity differences. To each pixel pairs in different classes, we use different fusion factors to merge them respectively, these fusion factors are determined by evolution strategies to achieve the best fusion performance. Experimental results show that the proposed method outperforms the wavelet transform (WT) method.

1 Introduction

In recent years, image fusion has been widely applied to many areas such as computer vision, automatic target recognition, remote sensing and medical image processing, etc. It can be defined as the process of combining two or more different source images from the same scene into one new image with extend information content by a certain algorithm [1-2].

As commonly known, optical lenses suffer from a limited depth of focus. If one object in the scene is focus, another one will be out of focus. A possible way to alleviate this problem is by multi-focus image fusion, in which the auto-focus merged image can be formed by combining several images with different focus points in the same scene under the same imaging conditions. This fused image will then hopefully contain all the relevant objects in focus.

The primitive image fusion scheme is to take the average of the source images pixel by pixel. However, this often leads to undesired side effects such as reduced

---

* Foundation item: Postdoctoral Science Foundation of China (J63104020156) and National Defence Foundation (51431020204DZ0101).

contrast. In recent years, various methods based on multi-scale transforms have been proposed, including the Laplacian pyramid, the gradient pyramid and the ratio-of-low-pass pyramid etc [3–5]. More recently, some papers introduced the Wavelet Transform (WT) method [6–9] which is superior to the previous pyramid-based methods. The fused image of this method was obtained by performing an inverse wavelet transform using the fused wavelet coefficients derived by the area-based maximum selection rules. Because of its orthogonality symmetry and compact support, WT method can achieve better image fusion performance than pyramid-based methods, but they do suffer from the ringing effect in the fused image. Since wavelet transform is actually a high-pass or low-pass filtering process, a little edge information is lost in the reconstructed image.

In this paper, a new multi-focus image fusion method is proposed. It is based on multi-resolution wavelet decomposition, SOFM neural networks and evolution strategies. In this method, the multi-scale and multi-directional information of redundant WT coefficients is fully used in calculating the feature image, and the number of clusters is determined by the number of peaks of its histogram. Based on this feature image, SOFM networks are adopted to partition the regions according to clarity difference, and different optimal fusion factors determined by ES are applied in fusing the pixel pairs in different areas to achieve the best fusion performance. Experimental results show that the proposed method outperforms the WT method. The following sections of this paper are organized as follows: the proposed fusion scheme will be described in Section 2. Experimental results will be presented in Second 3, and some concluding remarks are given in the last section.

2 Multifocus Image Fusion Based on SOFM Neural Networks and Evolution Strategies

In the wavelet decomposition of images, assuming that an original image is $A_1 f$, $A_1 f$ is completely represented by one approximate image at resolution 2^{-J} and $3J$ detail images. (J is decomposition level, $-J \leq j \leq -1, J \geq 0$)

$$\left(A_{2^{-J}} f, \left(D_{2^j}^1 f\right)_{-J \leq j \leq -1}, \left(D_{2^j}^2 f\right)_{-J \leq j \leq -1}, \left(D_{2^j}^3 f\right)_{-J \leq j \leq -1}\right) \tag{1}$$

where $A_{2^j} f$ corresponds to the lowest frequencies, $D_{2^j}^1 f$ gives the vertical high frequencies, $D_{2^j}^2 f$ gives the horizontal high frequencies, $D_{2^j}^3 f$ is the high frequencies in the diagonal directions. The details are referred in reference[10].

2.1 Feature Extraction

Experimental results show that the WT sub-images (WT coefficients) produced by wavelet transform at resolution level 1~3 have contained most of the high frequency information in multi-focus source images. When the wavelet transform is used to decompose the source images, down-sampling is not adopted in order to keep the WT coefficients being in the same size as the source images, in this way, the wavelet coefficients are redundant, this is helpful to image fusion.

Let two source images with diverse focus be f_A, f_B. After decomposing f_A、f_B into 3 levels by redundant WT transform, high frequency coefficients are added for further calculation. Assuming Df_A, Df_B to be the sum of high frequency information of each source image, Df_A, Df_B can be defined as:

$$Df(n,m) = \sum_{-3 \le j \le -1} \left[|D_{2^j}^1 f(n,m)| + |D_{2^j}^2 f(n,m)| + |D_{2^j}^3 f(n,m)| \right] \quad (2)$$

In the sum of high frequency coefficients, the local regional energy E_A and E_B from two multi-focus images are respectively expressed as:

$$E(n,m) = \sum_{n' \in l, m' \in k} [Df(n+n', m+m')]^2 \quad (3)$$

where $E(n,m)$ denotes the energy sum in a local region with the center of (n,m); l、k is the size of local region (such as 3×3,5×5,7×7 ,etc); n' and m' are changed in regions l and k, then the feature image $E_f g(n,m)$ is defined as:

$$E_f g(n,m) = E_A(n,m) / (E_A(n,m) + E_B(n,m)) \quad (4)$$

It reflects the regional clarity difference of two source images f_A and f_B in a local region centered in (n,m). In the areas where f_A is clearer than f_B, the values of $E_A(n,m)$ are much more larger than $E_B(n,m)$, so the values of $E_f g(n,m)$ are close to 1, contrarily, in the areas where f_B is clearer than f_A, the values of $E_f g(n,m)$ are close to 0, and in the areas where f_A and f_B have a similar clarity, the values of $E_f g(n,m)$ vary slightly in a range centered at 0.5. Here, $E_f g(n,m)$ has the same size as source images. It's easy to find corresponding relations between $E_f g(n,m)$ and two source multi-focus images in the spatial and frequency domain.

2.2 Classification of Pixels Using SOFM Neural Networks

According to the analysis above, the clarity differences in source images correspond with different normalized gray values in $E_f g(n,m)$, and the histogram of $E_f g(n,m)$ indicates 3 peaks with centers close to 0, 0.5 and 1 (It is showed in Fig.1). The 3 peaks correspond to 3 kinds of areas with dissimilar clarity differences in source images. Therefore, classifying pixels in source images based on clarity difference could be achieved by classifying pixels in $E_f g(n,m)$ based on the normalized gray values.

In this paper, Kohonen's Self-Organizing Feature Map (SOFM) neural networks are adopted as a classifier for $E_f g(n,m)$ [11]. The SOFM neural network is one of the most popular neural network models based on unsupervised and competitive learning. It consists of two layers of processing units which provides a topology preserving mapping from the high dimensional space to a plane. The basic idea of this type of self-organizing neural network is that the signal representations are automatically mapped onto a set of outputs in such a manner that the response can preserve the same neighbourhood on the topology of the map. Therefore, the network can automatically form a correct topological map of features of observable events. In other words, SOFM can adapt to the training data in such a way that a high-dimensional-input space is reflected to a 2-dimensional grid on the generated Kohonen-map. By preserving the neighbourhood on the topology of the map, structures of the input space can be discovered by exploring the feature map. As the 1-D input pattern $E_f g(n,m)$ is expected to be clustered into $c = 3$ (here, c is the number of classification), 1-D networks is employed to accomplish this task. It has one input neuron and 3 output neurons which (the output neurons) are assembled in a 1-D array, and each one has a topological neighbourhood, choosing the size of the neighbourhood properly, clustering result could be most close to our expectation, this is the best convenience Kohonen networks taking to us. The input neuron is fully connected to output neuron j by synaptic weights $w_j, j = 1, \cdots, c$. Each neuron has as many input connections as the number of attributes to be used in the classification. After training, these synaptic weights will be equivalent to the inputs representing the centroid coordinates of each cluster. So the 1-D training vectors are the value of the normalized gray scale of the pixels in $E_f g(n,m)$. Networks of this kind use a competitive-learning algorithm, which can be summarized as:

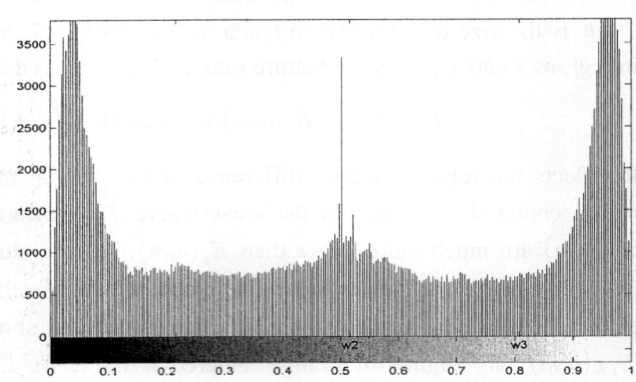

Fig. 1. Histogram of $E_f g(n,m)$

Step1. Initialize the weight vectors $w_j, j = 1, \cdots, c$ of the network; initialize the learning parameter: define topological neighbourhood function; set $k = 0$.

Step2. Check the termination condition. If false, continue; else quit.

Step3. For each training vector x, perform the steps from 4 through 7

Step4. Compute the best match of a weight vector with the input

$$q(x) = \min_{1 \leq j \leq c} \|x - w_j\|^2 \tag{5}$$

Step5. For all units in the specified neighbourhood $j \in N_q(k)$ (where q is the winning neuron), update the weight vectors according to

$$w_j(k+1) = \begin{cases} w_j(k) + \eta(k)[x(k) - w_j(k)] & \text{if} \quad j \in N_q(k) \\ w_j(k) & \text{if} \quad j \notin N_q(k) \end{cases} \tag{6}$$

where $0 < \eta(k) < 1$ (is the learning rate parameter).

Step6. Adjust the learning rate parameter.

Step7. Reduce the learning rate parameter appropriately.
Step8. Set $k = k+1$; then go to step2, repeat this process until a terminate condition is satisfied.

2.3 Fusion Rule

As showed in Fig1, after clustered by SOFM neural networks in $E_f g(n,m)$, there are three kinds of areas with dissimilar clarity difference, their normalized gray value centers are $\omega_1, \omega_2, \omega_3$. ($\omega_1, \omega_2, \omega_3$ are synaptic weights of one dimensional SOFM networks). To obtain the best fusion performance, we apply different fusion factors to the pixels of the source image in different kinds of areas. Once the fusion factors $\alpha_A(n,m)$ ($\alpha_A(n,m) \in [0,1]$) are assigned for the pixels in source image f_A, fusion factors $\alpha_B(n,m)$ for the pixels in source image f_B will be $\alpha_B(n,m) = 1 - \alpha_A(n,m)$. In the areas where f_B is much more clear than f_A, $E_f g(n,m)$ is less than ω_1, we assign 0 as the fusion factor for f_A, therefore, the fusion factor for f_B will be 1. In the areas where f_A is much more clear than f_B, $E_f g(n,m)$ is larger than ω_3, we assign 1 as the fusion factor for f_A, and the fusion factor for f_B will be 0. In the areas where the pixel feature values in $E_f g(n,m)$ equal to $\omega_1, \omega_2, \omega_3$, we assign $\alpha_1, \alpha_2, \alpha_3$ $\alpha_j \in [0,1], (j = 1 \sim 3)$ as their fusion factors of f_A (how to determine $\alpha_1, \alpha_2, \alpha_3$ will be discussed later). In this fusion algorithm, the three fusion factors $\alpha_1, \alpha_2, \alpha_3$ are not only meaningful to the pixels whose feature values equal to ω_1, ω_2 or ω_3, but also have an important effect on the other pixels whose feature values vary in the range between ω_1 and ω_3. In the areas where f_A and f_B have a similar clarity, the values of $E_f g(n,m)$ just vary between ω_1 and ω_3, and ω_2 is approximately close to the center of ω_1 and ω_3, for the pixels in this area, fusion factors will be $\sum_{j=1}^{3}\left[\alpha_j \times \left(d_j^{-1} / \sum_{i=1}^{3} d_i^{-1}\right)\right]$, Here, $d_j = \|E_f g(n,m) - \omega_j\|^2$, ($\omega_1 < E_f g(n,m) < \omega_3$), is the Euclidean distance between the pixel gray values in $E_f g(n,m)$ and $\omega_j, (j = 1,2,3)$. In this way, every pixel pair in source images could obtain a suitable fusion factor of their own. For the pixel with coordinate (n,m) in source image f_A, its fusion factor $\alpha_A(n,m)$ could be summarized as:

$$\alpha_A(n,m) = \begin{cases} 0 & E_f g(n,m) < \omega_1 \\ 1 & E_f g(n,m) > \omega_3 \\ \alpha_j & E_f g(n,m) = \omega_j, j = 1,2,3 \\ \sum_{j=1}^{3}\left[\alpha_j \times \left(d_j^{-1} / \sum_{i=1}^{3} d_i^{-1}\right)\right] & \omega_1 < E_f g(n,m) < \omega_3 \end{cases} \quad (7)$$

Let f_M be the fused image, f_M is expressed as

$$f_M(n,m) = \alpha_A(n,m) \times f_A(n,m) + \alpha_B(n,m) \times f_B(n,m) \qquad (8)$$

2.4 Determination of Fusion Factors $\alpha_1, \alpha_2, \alpha_3$ by Evolution Strategies

2.4.1 Fitness Function

How do we choose fusion factors $\alpha_1, \alpha_2, \alpha_3$ on the range [0,1] of $\alpha_A(n,m)$ to obtain the optimal fusion image? Here, we adopt evolution strategies(ES) method, which is suitable to optimize real functions.

The searching process of ES depends on a fitness function. In the problem of multi-focus image fusion, the fitness function should indicate the character that the fused image can simultaneously maximumly conserve the high frequency information in the two source images. Cross entropy measure method is adopted in this paper. The cross entropy measure of images X and Y is

$$CE_{X,Y} = \sum_{i=0}^{L-1} p_{Xi} \log \frac{p_{Xi}(X)}{p_{Yi}(Y)} \qquad (9)$$

where L denotes the total number of gray scales of an image, p_i is the ratio of the number of the pixels with the gray scale i to the total number of the pixels in an image.

Since different sets of $\alpha_1, \alpha_2, \alpha_3$ correspond to different fused images, the fitness function of fused images can be regarded as the fitness function of each set of $\alpha_1, \alpha_2, \alpha_3$. The fitness function of fused images is defined as

$$\begin{cases} F(f_M) = \sqrt{(CE^2_{f_A,f_M} + CE^2_{f_B,f_M})/2} \\ s.t. \quad |E(f_M) - E(f)| \leq \varepsilon \end{cases} \qquad (10)$$

where $E(\cdot)$ is the mean average value of an image, and $E(f) = E(f_A) = E(f_B)$, ε is the permitted error range of average values.

In definition (10), $CE^2_{f_A,f_M}$ and $CE^2_{f_B,f_M}$ are considered synthetically, namely total cross entropy. It synthesizes the differences between the fused image and two source images, which are all in the permitted range of mean value. The iterative process above is going in the direction of decreasing the fitness function, the iterative optimization process of ES will find the most wanted set of $\alpha_1, \alpha_2, \alpha_3$, whose fitness is highest in a population.

2.4.2 Evolution Strategies (ES)

The operating objects of ES is a population consisted by the feasible solutions of the problem. The individual in the population is defined as a real vector $A = (\alpha_1, \alpha_2, \alpha_3)$. The fitness of each individual can be measured by a fitness function. The goal of solving a problem is to find the individual $A\cdot = (\alpha_1^*, \alpha_2^*, \alpha_3^*)$ whose fitness is highest in the population, and it obtains the least fitness function value of the fused image. The processes of ES are as follows:

(1) Produce initial father population $\{A_i, i = 1,2,\cdots,\mu\}$ with individual numbers μ. The values of each individual distribute randomly on in the interval [0,1].

(2) Mutation: producing offspring individuals, $A_i^j = A_i + N(0, \delta_j^2)$, $i = 1,2,\cdots,\mu$, $j = 1,2,\cdots,\lambda$, where $N(0, \delta^2)$ denotes Gaussian noise with mean value of 0 and deviation of δ^2. The deviation of the noise can be constant or changing with time [12]. By mutation, each individual in the father population can produce λ offspring individuals.
(3) Selection: using certain choosing method to compose new father population with μ individuals, whose fitness function values are the least in the $\mu + \mu\lambda$ individuals
(4) Repeat steps (2) and (3) until the fitness function can meet the requirement or reach the maximum running degree. The highest fitness individual in the final population will be the result.

3 Fusion Experiment and Discussion

The fusion experiment has been done in two sets of multi-focus images. The test images are showed in Figs. 2(a), 2(b) and 3(a), 3(b), their sizes are 480×640 and 512×512 respectively, they contain several objects in different distances to the camera, and only one object in each image is in focus. Using the fusion techniques we can make clear all the objects in the fused images. The fused images of WT method and the proposed method (using bior3.7 wavelet and level=3) are shown respectively in Figs.2(c), 2(d) and Figs. 3(c), 3(d). From the obtained results, we find that the fused images of the proposed method are of more richer in detail information than those of the WT method.

The fusion experiment has been done in two sets of multi-focus images. The test images are showed in Figs. 2(a), 2(b) and 3(a), 3(b), their sizes are 480×640 and 512×512 respectively, they contain several objects in different distances to the camera, and only one object in each image is in focus. Using the fusion techniques we can make clear all the objects in the fused images. The fused images of WT method and the proposed method (using bior3.7 wavelet and level=3) are shown respectively in Figs.2(c), 2(d) and Figs. 3(c), 3(d). From the obtained results, we find that the fused images of the proposed method are of more richer in detail information than those of the WT method.

Performance of fusion results is evaluated by the total cross entropy measure and spatial frequency. Total cross entropy measure has already been shown in Eq.(9). Spatial frequency is directly related to image clarity [13]. It is used to measure the overall activity level of an image. For an $N \times M$ image Z, whose gray value at pixel position (n, m) is denoted by $Z(n, m)$, its spatial frequency is defined as:

$$SZ = \sqrt{RZ^2 + CZ^2} \qquad (11)$$

where RZ and CZ are the row frequency

$$RZ = \sqrt{\frac{1}{NM} \sum_{n=1}^{N} \sum_{m=2}^{M} (Z(n,m) - Z(n, m-1))^2} \qquad (12)$$

and column frequency

$$CZ = \sqrt{\frac{1}{NM} \sum_{m=1}^{M} \sum_{n=2}^{N} (Z(n,m) - Z(n-1,m))^2} \qquad (13)$$

Table 1 shows the evaluation of the two sets of multi-focus images. Compared with the WT method, we find that the spatial frequency values of the results obtained by the proposed method is large and the total cross entropy is small. It indicates that the fusion results obtained by our method have higher clarity and less difference with the two source images. Looking carefully, we can find that the detail of the fused images of the proposed method is much clearer than those of the WT method.

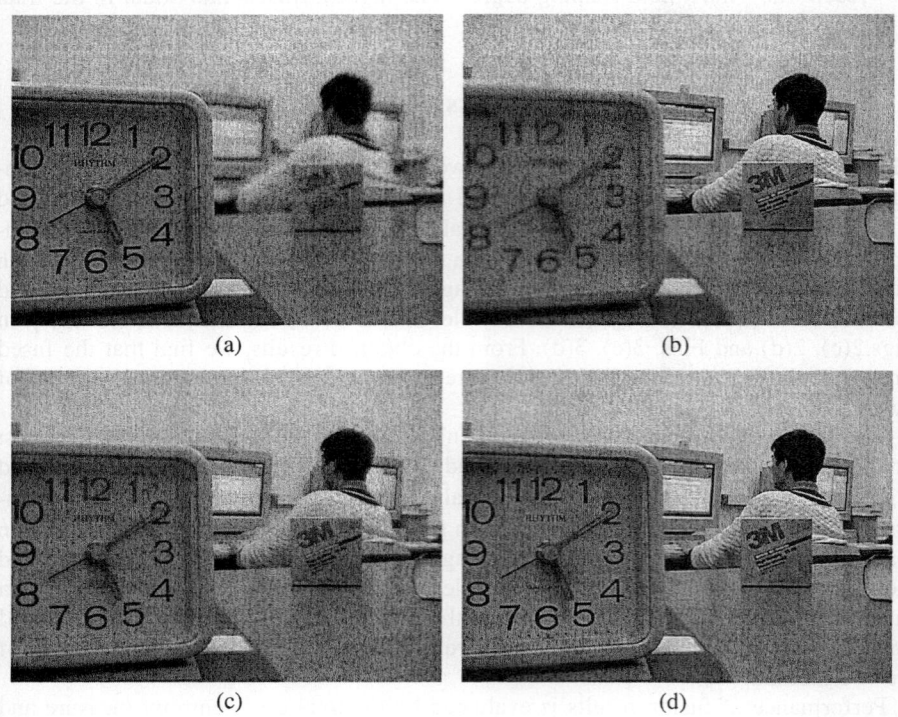

Fig. 2. Fusion results of Lab images. (a) Lab1 (focus on the clock); (b) Lab2 (focus on the student); (c) Fused image by WT method; (d) Fused image by the proposed method.

Table 1. Total cross entropy and spatial frequency of fusion results obtained by WT method and the proposed method

	Lab images		Clock images	
	W T method	The poposed method	W T method	The proposed method
Total cross entropy	0.6393	0.0144	0.1853	0.0195
Spatial frequency	31.7464	39.4748	31.0757	34.5398

Fig. 3. Fusion results of Clock images. (a) Clock1 (focus on the right part); (b) Clock2 (focus on the left part); (c) Fused image by WT method; (d) Fused image by the proposed method.

4 Conclusion

A pixel level multi-focus image fusion method based on multi-resolution wavelet decomposition, SOFM neural networks and evolution strategies has been proposed in this paper. The advantage of this method is that the multi-direction and multi-scale information of wavelet decomposition without down-sampling are fully used to extract normalized feature image, but inverse wavelet transform process is avoided by adopting SOFM neural networks to partition the regions according to clarity difference and evolution strategies to determine optimal fusion factors.The experimental results show that the proposed method can keep the edge information of two spatially registered images to utmost extent and also achieve better fusion performance than WT method.

References

1. Van Genderen J.L. Pohl, C. Image fusion: Issues, techniques and applications. Intelligent Image Fusion, Proceedings EARSeL Workshop, Strasbourg, France, 1994, pp.18-26.
2. Hall, D.L., Mathematical Techniques in Multi-sensor Data Fusion. Boston, Artech House,1992, pp.20-59.
3. Burt, P.T., Andelson, E.H., The Laplacian pyramid as a compact image code. IEEE Trans.on Commum 1983,31(4), pp. 532-540.
4. Burt, P.J., Kolczynski, R.j. Enhanced image capture though fusion. In:Proc.4th Internat.Conf. on Computer Vision, Berlin, Germany, 1993.pp.173-182.
5. Toet, A., van Ruyven, L.J., Valeton, J.M., Merging thermal and visual images by a contrast pyramid. Opt.Engrg.28(7),789-792.
6. Li,H., Manjunath, B.S., Mitra,S.K., Multisensor image fusion using the wavelet transform. Graphical Models Image Processing 1995,57(3),235-245.
7. Koren, I., Laine, A., Taylor, F., Image fusion using steerable dyadic wavelet. In:Proc. Internat. Conf.on Image Processing,Washington,USA,pp.232-235.
8. Yocky, D. A. Image merging and data fusion by means of the discrete two-dimensional wavelet transform. J. Opt. Soc. Am. A:Image Sci. Vision ,1995,12(9),pp.1834- 1841.
9. Zhang, Z., Blum, R S. A categorization of multiscale-decomposition-based image fusion schemes with a performance study for a digital camera application. Proc.IEEE, 1999,87(8) pp. 1315-1326.
10. Mallat, S.G. A theory for multiresolution signal decomposition: the wavelet representation. IEEE Transactions on Pattern Analysis and Machina Intelligence, 1989,11(7)pp. 674-693.
11. Kohonen.Self-organized Formation of Feature Maps. Cybem.Syst.Recognit.,Learn,1984:3-12
12. Fogel, D.B. Fogel, L.J., An introduction to simulated evolutionary optimization. IEEE Trans. on Neural Networks, 1994, 5(1),pp. 3-14.
13. Shutao Li, James T. Kwok, Yaonan Wang, Multi-focus image fusion using artificial neural networks, Pattern Recognition Letters 2002,23 pp.985–997.

Creative Design by Chance Based Interactive Evolutionary Computation

Chao-Fu Hong[1], Hsiao-Fang Yang[2], and Mu-Hua Lin[2]

[1] Associate Proffessor, Department of Information Management,
Altheia University, 32 Chen-Li Street,
Tamsui, Taipei, Taiwan 251
cfhong@email.au.edu.tw
[2] Graduate School of Management Sciences, Altheia University
32 Chen-Li Street, Tamsui, Taipei, Taiwan 251
fa925711@email.au.edu.tw, fa925710@email.au.edu.tw

Abstract. Kotler and Trias De Bes (2003) at Lateral Marketing defined the creativity: each cluster had its own concepts, when a new need was generated and the designer could not find a solution from his own clusters, therefore he had a gap to overcome. This gap was as the original of creativity. If he wants to solve this problem, chose a new important concept for beginning was the only way he could do. This phenomenon was called the laterally transmitting. Then according to the designer's subjective to choose the concept and connected other cluster to generate or enter a new cluster. This kind designing process could generate a creative product. But it also brought a new problem, there had many concepts in conceptual space, how to decide an effectiveness concept and extents it to create a good product. Here we combined Watt's (2003) Small World model and Ohsawa and McBurney (2003) Chance Discovery Model to decide the creative probability and decreased the searching path length. Finally, we integrated the choosing mechanism and recombination mechanism into our chance based IEC (CBIEC) model. And we applied on the cell phone design. After the experiment we analyzed the interactive data found the choosing mechanism could bring the effective creativity and the recombination mechanism could quickly search as we expected the short-cut effect. Beside these results we also directly investigated the subjective of designer found our CBIEC model also better than the IGA (interactive genetic algorithms, Caldwell and Johnston, 1991).

Keywords: lateral marketing, chance discovery, small-world, interactive evolutionary computation (IEC), value-focused thinking (VFT).

1 Introduction

In recent years what the creativity was, it was one of the hot researching topics, and the Kotler and Trias De Bes at 2003 in their lateral marketing had already defined it. When the new need as the creating purpose or the new environment was happened, then the product would be modified to suit it. It meant the laterally marketing was not only a new marketing but also made a good product for consumer. Unfortunately, the Kotler and Trias De Bes only propose the conceptual model, did not supply the operating model. Here we believed only the dynamic and interactive evolutionary model had a chance to include the laterally transmitting and vertical transmitting in same process as Fig.1.

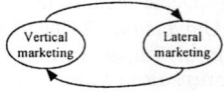

Fig. 1. A dynamic model of lateral marketing and vertical marketing

Because in the interactive process the system was not only gave the designer stimulating information to drive him defined the creativity, but also let the designer could design a creative product in his mind. Therefore the system must give the choosing and recombining power to the designer, let him could try to do the laterally transmitting. Then the creative designing problem became how to help the designer decided in which concept could effectively help him found a new creativity and recombining the concepts to build a creative product. Fortunately, Ohsawa and McBurney (2003) proposed the concept of Chance Discovery: analyzed whole network and found the key terms was used to calculate the probability of key terms to connect other cluster. The whole processed as building the random graph. Finally, according to these probabilities discovered the important key term and it as the chance. Therefore, in this study we believed that the designer's intention could drive him understanding every key term and chose the important key term to builds the new creative product in his mind. But this method lacks experiment's results to evidence that it can quickly reach. At 2003 the Watts's Small World model evidenced about 5-7 times could solve the problem.

From Fig.2 we found the Small World's area, in there connected any two points only needed a few path length. This was because the clusters were overlapping each other and the components also connected each other as an affiliation network.

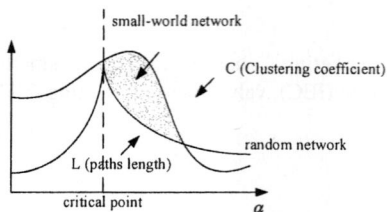

Fig. 2. Compare paths length (L) with clustering coefficient (C). The area between the two curves is small-world network. (Watts, 2003).

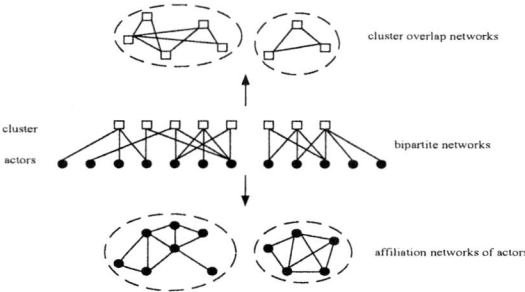

Fig. 3. Affiliation networks (Watts, 2003)

As in Fig.3, analyzing the movies and actors data, could find their relationship as bipartite networks, and this network was divided two separating networks, one was the affiliation networks for actors and the other was the cluster overlap networks. If we wanted to find any actor from a special actor, the first thing was that we must identify this actor's attribute to separate the possible cluster from the cluster overlap network. Then we also were according to the actor's affiliation networks to analyze which cluster had high probability, and this algorithm could small down the searching area. That is why the small world searching mechanism could quickly find the other actor.

But how to define the designing space, the Keeney (1992), firstly he analyzed the problem then defined the objective space. Finally according to the value network assembled the context space. The Corner, Buchanan and Henig (2000) at their dynamic system also used the same method, from the VFT (value-focused thinking) decided the alternative, and AFT (alternative-focused thinking) would stimulate the designer to find the creating value and modify his VFT. And all of them believed that the brainstorming was a useful method to build the complete problem space.

From above discussed we found some important mechanisms, one was the choosing mechanism in which was not only a kind of the lateral transmitting, but also was a starting point for the creating design. The other was that the recombination mechanism based on the chance discovery decided the important key term and recombined with good product as a shot-cut in designing process.

2 Methodology of CBIEC Model

From the Kotler and Trias De Bes at 2003 in the lateral marketing had clearly defined what the creativity was. Because the designer had his personal need to generate a new creating purpose or a new product. Therefore, our model supplied the choosing mechanism and recombination mechanism for the designer. The choosing mechanism was that according to his preference decided what component was the designer wanted. Then he would choose a new component as the chance of laterally transmitting. And the recombination mechanism was the power that the designer how to assemble the new component with the best chromosome as the anchor to make a creative product.

2.1 The Choosing Mechanism

Because the CBIEC model has two kinds of choosing mechanism, first is the designer based on his value network to estimates the product and chooses the elitism chromosomes b. It likes Ohsawa's (Llorà, et al., 2004a; Llorà, et al., 2004b; Ohsawa, Benson and Yachida, 1998; Ohsawa, 1999) model identifies the term, the system will according to Eq. 1 lock set b as the anchor,.

$$b = \frac{CS_c}{\sum_{i=1}^{p} CS_i} \qquad (1)$$

CS_c the score is given by the designer for c^{th} chromosome, and p is the population size.

Secondary choosing mechanism is only the CBIEC model has. When the designer changes his purpose, secondary choosing mechanism supplies the limited products (the population size is 6.) for him to decide his preferable direction. Because this operation according to the designer's subjective, it can help the designer to discover the chance: our model allows him has a choosing power to select his favorite component's a. He will use the component's a links to another cluster, then the a also as the chance to accomplish his idea and the a will be the chance to makes a creative product. The choosing mechanism is shown on following figure 4.

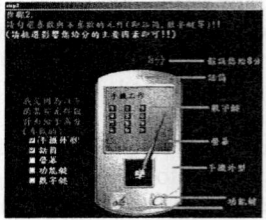

Fig. 4. Choice mechanism

It also points out that the choosing mechanism likes a chance which can connect another cluster. And this works as the laterally transmitting, the designer can start here to do the new design. Therefore, our system must supply the components selecting operation for designer as above figure 4. And we adopt the concept of shot-cut in Small World, it follows Eq.2 to calculate the linking probability to every creative direction. And according to these probabilities chooses the direction as a chance to start the new design.

$$a = \frac{SG_{ks}}{\sum_{i=1}^{g} SG_{kg}} \qquad (2)$$

The a is the probability for entering the shot-cut in Small World. The SG_{ks} is the g level on k attribute.

2.2 The Recombination Mechanism

Passed through the choosing mechanism, the recombination mechanism can connect the elite allele a with the anchor b to generate a creative product ab. In our CBIEC model the new product is following the designer prefer the a and the b, then the probability to connects the ab is higher then the a connects other components. It is called the triadic closure (Watts, 2003).

$$CBIEC = a_t + b_t \qquad (3)$$

The a_t is the set a on t^{th} generation and it is selected by designer at the secondary choosing mechanism. And the b_t is the anchor b at t^{th} generation and it is generated by evolutionary process.

2.3 The Operation of CBIEC

The following example shows the operation of CBIEC, and the cell phone's chromosome is shown on table 1. At primary generation the chromosome is generated by randomness.

Table 1. The cell phone's chromosome

faceplate				handset				screen				function key				number key			
1	2	...	18	1	2	3	4	1	2	3	4	1	2	3	4	1	2	3	4

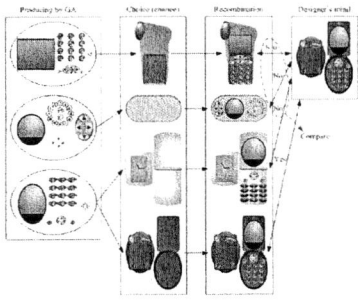

Fig. 5. Process of operation

The designer estimated all cell phones and according to Eq.1 the system could find the important components b is shown on the left of Fig.5. When other faceplates appear and some of there (a) are also selected by designer (Eq.2) as shown on second column in Fig.5. Then the system according to Eq.3 recombines the a with the b to generate the better product ab. The better products will be shown on next generation as the third column in Fig.5. Finally, the designer chooses a best product. The whole operation likes a kind of the communicating process talks with the mind in designer.

3 Experiment Design

The purpose of this experiment was that recombined IEC with chance to guide the designer found his wanted creativity. Therefore, we developed a CBIEC system to help the designer created his favorite cell phone. But before developed this design system, we had surveyed all cell phone in the market and found the cell phone could be composed by five parts as the faceplate, handset, screen, function key and number key.

Therefore in our experiment the faceplate has 18 types, the handset has 4 types, the screen has 4 types, the function's key has 4 types and the number's key has 4 types. And the variables of IGA are shown on Table2.

Table 2. Component's design

Items	Context
Coding	Real coding
Population size	6
Crossover rate	0.65
Mutation rate	0.01

We had held two fields for creative design; the first time we invited the professors and college's students, the second time we invited the high school's teachers. These schools are all in north Taiwan. We had collected 40 samples and the recovery rate was 77.5% (valid data divided all samples).

4 Experiment Result and Discussion

In these experiments we wanted to evidence two things: the a was the chance and it could link other clusters as the short-cut path in Small World, the other was analyzing the chance process to see it could induce the creativity or not. Therefore, in this section firstly we used the case to subjectively explain the chance how to work in designing problem. Secondly, the Ohsawa's Chance Discovery model was used to observe the performance of our model to find the chance. Finally, we directly investigated that the designer could feel the CBIEC supplied the chance for him in designing process.

4.1 Case Study

Here we have two kinds of case.

Case 1:
At primary the designer cumulated what components was he wanted, it liked cumulating the anchor b and let the b did not easily disappear on evolving process. The other part the a was generated by randomness, at the creative design was depended on good and creative a helped him enter another cluster as the short-cut in

Small World: imaged which *a* connected with *b* could become the creative product *ab*. The products *ab* were shown on right side of Fig.6. Then we compared every generation's *ab*, found the change of product between the generations was not smoothing, it seemed jumping into other cluster. And compared the *ab*'s score with the *b*'s score, the results were shown on table 3. It showed the *ab*'s score was better than the *b*'s score.

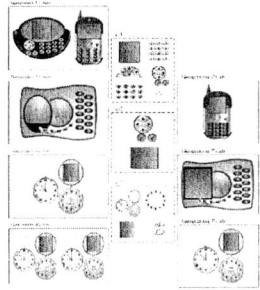

Fig. 6. The CBIEC evolving process

Table 3. Result of b and a scores

generation	b	a	Accomplishment (1-(g-(b+a))/g)
1	0	4	0.8
2	2	2	0.8
3	1	4	1
g: allele's size,			

Case 2:
In this case the designer at the choosing mechanism selected some components *a* to assemble the product *ab*, but the *ab*'s score was not higher than *b*'s score, it seemed that the *ab* did not clearly response the designer's wanted. But when the anchor *b* was locked by designer then *ab*'s score could be higher than *b*'s score and quickly reached his wanted.

These cases all evidenced that the *a* could help the designer selected useful components as the anchor *b* and according to *a* connected another cluster as the short-cut in the Small World, then recombined the *a* with *b* to make the creative *ab*. Beside this, our model according to *a* linked the other cluster as the lateral transmitting, it meant the *ab* also obeyed the creativity of Kotler's definition.

Table 4. ab's and b's score of case 2

generation	ab score	b score	generation	ab score	b score
2	6	6	8	5	4
4	3	5	9	9(ab=b)	
5	3	7	10	10	8
7	5	4			

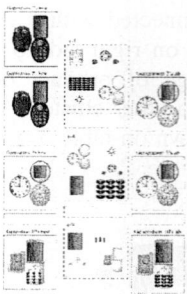

Fig. 7. Evolutional process

4.2 The Performance of Chance Process

Here we used the evolving data and the random graph method to building the evolutionary key graph. Because the first generation the all chromosomes were generated by random, and we used the score to separate the cluster. Then we could see there were 5 clusters (1, 2, 3, 4, and 5) in Fig. 8 and some components were linked to two or three cluster. There seemed that these components were more important then other only belong to the one cluster and we called these components as the key terms. And Followed the CBIEC process to generate the secondary offspring, we could find the some key terms were still strongly connected the higher score's cluster to become an anchor in the evolutionary. And this phenomenon was not usually passed through a few generation could observing it. At last we used key graph to show all data, and clearly found a strong anchor was at the central of graph and it also was accepted by many cluster. This result demonstrated that the anchor was as our model defined, it could increase the converging speed and our model also could lock the anchor in evolutionary.

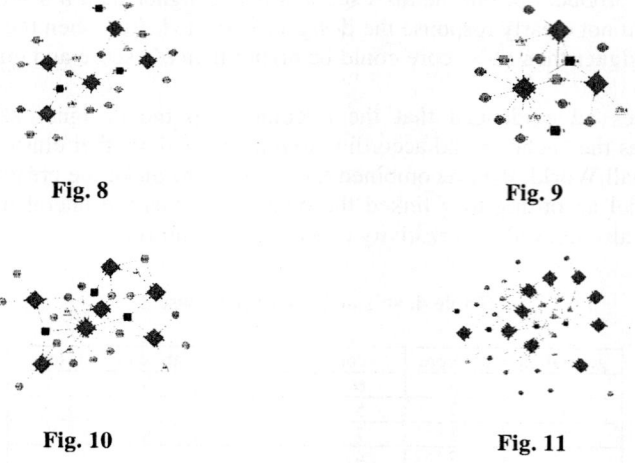

Fig. 8 Fig. 9

Fig. 10 Fig. 11

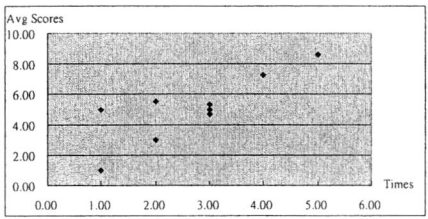

Fig. 12

In our model also defined the *a* as the chance: from the key graph we could find the pink circles were around the cluster, but there did not like the anchor were linked almost all clusters, only a few clusters were linked to them. From the Osawa's model the chance were defined as following:

It must have some cluster on the key graph.

Some individual key terms and some of these key terms have linked to few clusters.

These few key term is called the chance, there also as the *a* in our model.

We followed the above algorithm and the importance in the design to calculate the individual key terms, the faceplate 14 was the most important key term, and the result was shown on Figure 12.

$$x = Sum(Times)$$

$$y = Avg(f_i)$$

The x axis is the selecting frequency of the component and the y axis is the average score of the component. This result also demonstrated our secondary choosing mechanism was the chance maker.

Then the recombination mechanism in our model was depended the Eq.3, the first, we compared the virtual product *ab* with the best chromosome, the result also was shown on table 6 and the virtual *ab* was significantly better than the best chromosome, the mean were 8.11 and 6.64. It could demonstrate our recombination mechanism as we expected it could jump to the creative area as the designer's wanted.

Table 6. t test between ab and b

Method	N	Mean	Sig.
ab	15	8.11	0.008<0.05
the best chromosome	12	6.64	

4.3 Investigate the Chance in Designer's Mind

In this section we wanted to directly evidence one thing: the designer cold feel that the secondary choosing and the recombination by CBIEC could help him to make a creative product.

Table 7. t test of evolution times

		N	Mean	Sig. (2-tailed)
Evolution times	IGA	16	10.00	0.308
	CBIEC	15	6.67	

At first the t-test was used to compare the speed of convergence of CBIEC and IGA, there were not significant difference, but the CBIEC was still faster than IGA.

And table 8 was directly asked the designer: secondary choosing mechanism could help him chose a creative *a* and entered another cluster as the short-cut in Small World to design the favorite *ab*. The result was that at the 95% confidence about 79.7% designer agreed it.

Table 8. t test of question

Question	Test Value = 3.986
	Sig. (2-tailed)
Choosing mechanism could help him create the favorite cell phone	0.047

Table 9. t test of question

	QUESTION	METHOD	N	Mean	Sig. (2-tailed)
6	Cell phone is your need	IGA	16	3.69	0.088
		CBIEC	15	4.07	
7	It is a creative cell phone	IGA	16	3.56	0.127
		CBIEC	15	4.13	
9	Do you like	IGA	16	3.56	0.090
		CBIEC	15	4.00	
11	It worth to buy	IGA	16	3.88	0.841
		CBIEC	15	3.93	
14	Easily operate	IGA	16	3.63	0.112
		CBIEC	15	4.00	
16	Next generation your feasible cell phone will be disappeared	IGA	16	2.50	0.061
		CBIEC	15	1.93	
17	System know what you need	IGA	16	3.81	0.242
		CBIEC	15	4.13	
18	The cell phone usually is not your want	IGA	16	2.63	0.103
		CBIEC	15	2.07	

Recombined the *a* with *b* to assemble the creative *ab* at the CBIEC, it increased the communication with the designer in designing process. But IEC lacked the chance process and the recombination, the designer only waited the evolutionary process to generate the new product for him to estimate the cell phone. Therefore the question 16 was significant. At the question 17 and 18 were asked designer: the *ab* was as same as the design on his mind and the results were near significant. The above analysis results also evidenced our chance process was useful to help the designer communicated with himself and designed what product was he wanted. The question 6 and 7 were used to ask the designer that this product had creativity. They also agreed our model could help them to design a creative product. Finally, the question 9 and 11 were investigated they would purchase this product. We could see they had a high intention to buy it. Of course the CBIEC was higher than the IGA. These analysis results also agreed the chance process was useful method to help the designer to accomplish his design.

5 Conclusion

How to increase the ability of communication between the designer and IEC and that is the only way can help the designer to do the creative design. In our model the designer has the choosing and the recombination power to guide the evolutionary direction. It could quickly make a creative product as he imaged in his mind. The results of statistics analysis evidenced our model could help the designer to design a creative product. We also followed the Osawa's method to check the secondary choosing, the a was the key term on the key graph and the a also had the weak links between the two clusters. This result supported that the a was the chance.

References

1. Caldwell, C. and Johnston, V. S. (1991), Tracking a criminal suspect through 'face-space' with a genetic algorithm, in Proceedings of the Fourth International Conference on Genetic Algorithms, Morgan Kaufmann, San Mateo, California, pp.416-421.
2. Corner, J., Buchanan, J., and Henig, M. (2000), A dynamic model for structuring decision problems, 35th Annual Meeting of ORSNZ, 10.
3. Keeney, R. L. (1992), Value Focused Thinking. Harvard University Press, Cambridge, MA.
4. Kotler, P., and Trias De Bes, F. (2003), Lateral Marketing: New Techniques for Finding Breakthrough Ideas, John Wiley & Sons Inc.
5. Llorà, X., Goldberg, D. E., Ohsawa, Y., Ohnishi, K., Tamura, H., Washida, Y., and Yoshikawa, M. (2004a), Chances and Marketing: On-line Conversation Analysis for Creative Scenario Discussion, First European Workshop on Chance Discovery (EWCD'2004), pp.152-161, Valencia, Spain.
6. Llorà, X., Matsumura, N., Goldberg, D. E., Ohsawa, Y., Ohnishi, K., and Gonzales, A. (2004b), Discovering Chance Scenarios using Small-World KeyGraphs and Evolutionary Computation, First European Workshop on Chance Discovery (EWCD'2004), pp.51-61, Valencia, Spain.
7. Ohsawa, Y. (1999), Get timely files from visualized structure of your working history, Knowledge-Based Intelligent Information Engineering Systems, pp.546-549.
8. Ohsawa, Y. and McBurney, P. (Eds.) (2003), Chance Discovery, Advanced Information Processing, Springer-Verlag.
9. Ohsawa, Y., Benson, N. E. and Yachida, M. (1998), KeyGraph: Automatic indexing by co-occurrence graph based on building construction metaphor, Proceedings of Advanced Digital Library Conference.
10. Watts, D. J. (2003), Six Degrees: The Science of a Connected Age, New York: W.W. Norton & Company.

Design of the Agent-Based Genetic Algorithm

Honggang Wang, Jianchao Zeng, and Yubin Xu

Division of system simulation and application,
Taiyuan university of science & technology, 030024, Shanxi, China
wanghg@public.ty.sx.cn

Abstract. In the standard GA, the individual has no intelligence and must act upon some rules established by a programmer in advance, such as various genetic operator. The result is to make the evolutionary process to be trapped into the local optimization of the objective function. In order to solve this problem, through studying the structure of an agent and selection operator, the paper designs a new genetic algorithm based on agent, called AGA (Agent-based Genetic Algorithm). At the premise of giving the definition of the outer environment where an agent lives and of an agent's belief, this paper gives some rules on how an agent selects one agent to cross their genes and some rules on how to solve competition. In addition, a communication method based on blackboard is presented to solve the communication among the agent society. Finally, the paper gives the structure of AGA and the simulation result for a multi-peak function, which demonstrates the validity of the AGA.

1 Introduction

Genetic algorithm (GA) is a stochastic optimization methods inspired by the biological mechanisms of evolution and heredity, which were first developed by Holland in the 1960s[1]. From the view of society, the principle of genetic algorithm (GA) is an evolutionary process of a society including lots of individuals. Each individual has a fitness, which values the performance of an individual. If an agent has a higher fitness value than the other agents, it can enter into next generation with higher probability[2]. In recent years, GA have been widely used in various fields, for example, global numerical optimization, combinatorial optimization, machine learning, and many other engineering problems[3~4]. But in the Canonical GA, each individual has no autonomy, and can't select another individual at his will to cross their genes.

Agent is an important subject in the field of distributed artificial intelligence and has been widely used in other branches of computer science. Reference [5] considered an agent as a physical or virtual entity that essentially has four properties: 1) It is able to live and act in the environment. 2) It is able to sense its local environment. 3) It is driven by certain purposes. 4) It has some reactive behaviors. These properties show that an agent has his own autonomy and he can do something at his will. But the ability of an agent is limited for solving complex problem, so we must use lots of agents (Agent society).

Considering that GA has many individuals but each individual has no autonomy and agent has autonomy, this paper integrates GA with agent and designs a new algorithm, called AGA (Agent -Based Genetic Algorithm). In this algorithm, each individual is recognized as an agent and the set of individuals is recognized as an agent society.

The rest of this paper is organized as follows: Section 2 describes the structure of an agent including the definition of belief and environment. Sections 3 gives the competition rules and the communication method based on the blackboard. Section 4 describes the structure of AGA. Section 5 shows the simulation result, for solving the global numerical optimization. Finally, conclusions are presented in Section 6.

2 Structure of the Agent for GA

Each agent corresponds to an individual in GA population, which intelligence is exhibited through it's belief, desire and intention. According to the real situation, the structures of the agent for GA is designed based on the BDI model presented by Bratman, illustrated as Fig. 1.

Each agent has two properties: name and performance value. The name property is an agent's ID and unique. The performance value evaluates the agent, the more higher the value is, the more better the agent is. The performance value corresponds to the fitness value in GA. In this paper, an agent's property is described by a 2-tuple: $<ID, v>$.

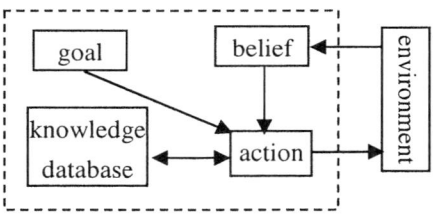

Fig. 1. The Structure of the agent for GA

The set of all agents's property forms the environment in which an agent lives. Assume the population has n agents and the property of the agent i is $P_i = <ID_i, v_i>$, then the environment can be defined as below:

Def 1: The environemt is defined as a n-tuple: $<p_1, p_2, \cdots, p_n>$.

For GA, an agent's goal is to prompt his performance value through cooperating with other agents or competing with other agents. In section 3, competition rules will be discussed in detail.

In the semantic, an agent's belief states corresponds to the extent to which he can determine what world he is in. In a given world, the belief state determines the set of worlds that the agent considers possible. For AGA, the belief state determines the set of agents with which he maybe cross his gene. In traditional GA, two individuals are selected randomly and cross their genes. But in nature, it's unpractical. For example, a man and a woman can't hold a marriage if they are not familiar with each other. For AGA, the right of selection is left to agent. The belief is defined as below:

Def 2: Assume the performance value of an agent i is v_i, the belief states B_i of an agent i is defined as :

$$B_i = \{j \mid |v_i - v_j|/v_i < \alpha, 0 < \alpha \leq 1, j \text{ is an agent}\} \tag{1}$$

In Equation (1), α is a selection factor. The more bigger α is, the more broader the range of selection is. From equation (1), we can know that if an agent has higher performance value than the other agents, he has more candidates to select than the other agents. It is beneficial for an agent with high performance to propagate his gene.

The knowledge database stores the knowledge on how to select another agent to exchange their genes. The knowledge is described by "if-then" rules. For AGA, there are some rules as below:

1) if $B_i = \emptyset$, then select nothing;
2) if ($B_i \neq \emptyset$) $\wedge$ (j is the best) $\wedge$ ($j \in B_i$), then select j;
3) if j has been selected by another agent, then select the second best in B_i;
4) if the best and the second best has been selected by other agents, then selects an agent from the rest in B_i;
5) if all agents in B_i have been selected by the other agents, then selects nothing;

For AGA, an agent has five actions: *select, cross, calculate, mutate* and *percept*. The five actions are defined as below:

select(j): means that an agent selects the agent which ID is j;

cross(j): means that an agent crosses his gene with the agent which ID is j;

calculate( ): means that an agent computes his performance value;

mutate( ): means that an agent changes one bit in his gene with probability p_m;

percept( ): means that an agent percepts the outer environment;

The quantity of the action an agent has corresponds to it's ability. From the five actions, we can know that an agent can percept the outer environment, select an agent, cross his gene with an agent he selected and compute his performance value.

3 Competition Rules and Communication Method

To improve his performance value, an agent must select another agent to cross their genes. During the process of selection, there exist competition. For example, when an agent is selected by at least two agents, the competition emerges. For solving this conflict, we can establish some rules in advance.

Let's suppose that $\alpha_1, \alpha_2, \cdots$ and α_m selects β at the same time, where α_1, $\alpha_2, \cdots, \alpha_m$ and β are agent. We left the selection right to agent β and set four rules as below:

1) if $\alpha_i \notin B_i (i = 1, 2, \cdots, m)$, then β selects the best agent in $\{\alpha_1, \alpha_2, \cdots, \alpha_m\}$;
2) if only $\alpha_i \in B$, then β selects α_i;

3) if $\alpha_{i1}, \alpha_{i2}, \cdots, \alpha_{ik} \in B$, then β selects the best agent in $\{\alpha_{i1}, \alpha_{i2}, \cdots, \alpha_{ik}\}$;

4) if $\alpha_{i1}, \alpha_{i2}, \cdots, \alpha_{ik} \in B$ and $v_{i1} = v_{i2} = \cdots = v_{ik}$, then β selects an agent randomly.

The first descirbes that if $\alpha_i (1 \leq i \leq m)$ doesn't belong to his belief state B, he selects the best agent in $\{\alpha_1, \alpha_2, \cdots, \alpha_m\}$. This is similar to the situation when some young boys propose to a young girl, the young girl can select the best young boy if she has not an ideal person in her mind. The second is similar to that if only a young boy within the boys proposing to her is her ideal young boy, the young girl selects the young boy. The third describes that if a young girl has many ideal young boys, she selects the best. The fourth describes that if a young girl has many ideal young boys and these young boys are similar good, she randomly selects one from these young boys.

To simplify communication among these agents in AGA, this paper presents a communication method based on blackboard. As described in section 2, the environment is a n-tuple. After an agent has finished computing his performance value, he must wirte down his ID and performance on the blackboard. In reality, the process of an agent doing action *percept()* is the process of an agent reading the information in the blackboard. Because the method is simple, it is not discussed here any more.

4 Structure of AGA

Based on the above description, the structure of AGA can be described as below:

```
Program AGA
Begin
    // p_c, p_m are reproduction probability and mutation
    //probability respectly
    initialize the variance p_c, p_m, α;
    generate the initial population p(k); k =0;
    each agent does action calculate;
    repeat
      each agent does action percept;
      each agent does action select and cross;
      each agent does action mutate;
      operate the reproduction operator on population p(k) to
generate population p(k+1); k:=k+1;
    until convergence condition is satisfied;
End.
```

In AGA, the reproduction operator and the cross operator adopt the common operator[1].

5 Simulation

Considering the below optimization problem:

$$\min \quad f = \frac{x_1^2 + x_2^2}{2} - \cos(2\pi x_1)\cos(2\pi x_2)$$

The function is multi-peak function with 40,000 local mini value in [-10, 10] and gets the global mini value at (0,0). It's graph in XOZ plane illustrated as Fig.2.

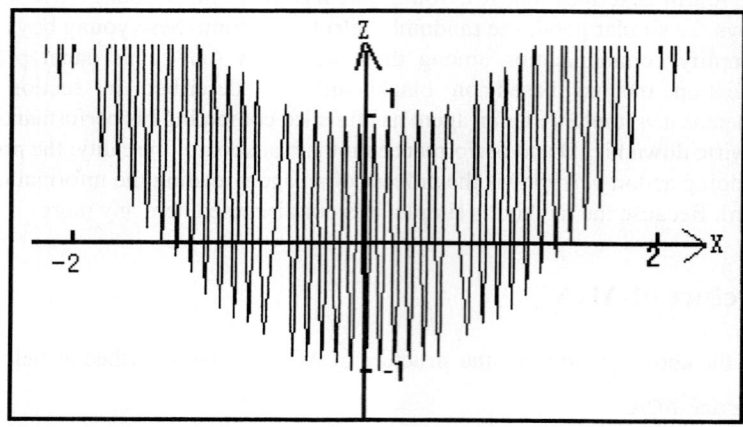

Fig. 2. The graph of the function f in XOZ plane

In the process of simulation, we adopt binary coding, the search space is $\{(x_1, x_2) | -10 \leq x_1, x_2 \leq 10\}$, the size of the population is 10, the length of the string is 16, $p_c = 0.7$, $p_m = 0.1$,and ☐. The simulation result is listed as Table 1.

From the simulation result, we can know that the probability of AGA convergencing to global optimization is higher than the SGA(Standard Genetic Algorithm).

Table 1. The simulation result

GA	No	The steps of mean convergence	The number of convergencing to global solution	The convergencing probability
SGA	1	85.23	37	88.33%
	2	82.22	41	85.00%
AGA	1	57.10	53	90.00%
	2	55.12	50	98.33%

6 Conclusion

Based on agent, a new genetic algorithm, AGA, has been proposed in this paper. Through integrating the GA with agent, this paper designs the structure of an agent for genetic algorithm, gives the definition of belief, action and environment. To solve the competition among agents, some rules are given. The simulation result shows that this algorithm can converge to global optimization solution with higher probability than SGA(Standard Genetic Algorithm). Comparing with SGA, an individual in AGA has autonomy.

References

1. J. H. Holland, Adaptation in Nature and Artificial System. Cambridge, MA: MIT Press, 1992.
2. Gunter Rudolph, Convergence Analysis of Canonical Genetic Algorithms, IEEE Transaction On Neural Networks, 1994, 5(4): 96—101
3. J. Liu, Y. Y. Tang, and Y. C. Cao, An evolutionary autonomous agents approach to image feature extraction, IEEE Trans. Evol. Comput, 1997, Vol.1, pp: 141–158, Feb.
4. Y.W. Leung and Y.Wang, An orthogonal genetic algorithm with quantization for global numerical optimization, IEEE Trans. Evol. Comput., vol. 5, pp. 41–53, Feb. 2001.
5. S. Russell and P. Norvig, Artificial Intelligence: A Modern Approach. Englewood Cliffs, NJ: Prentice-Hall, 1995.
6. J. Ferber, Multi-Agent Systems: An Introduction to Distributed Artificial Intelligence. New York: Addison-Wesley, 1999.

Drawing Undirected Graphs with Genetic Algorithms

Qing-Guo Zhang, Hua-Yong Liu, Wei Zhang, and Ya-Jun Guo

Department of Computer Science, Central China Normal University, Wuhan 430079, China
qgzhang@mail.ccnu.edu.cn

Abstract. This paper proposes an improved genetic algorithm for producing aesthetically pleasing drawings of general undirected graphs. Previous undirected graph drawing algorithms draw large cycles with no chords as concave polygons. In order to overcome such disadvantage, the genetic algorithm in this paper designs a new mutation operator single-vertex- neighborhood mutation and adds a component aiming at symmetric drawings to the fitness function, and it can draw such type graphs as convex polygons. The improved algorithm is of following advantages: The method is simple and it is easy to be implemented, and the drawings produced by the algorithm are beautiful, and also it is flexible in that the relative weights of the criteria can be altered. The experiment results show that the drawings of graphs produced by our algorithm are more beautiful than those produced by simple genetic algorithms, the original spring algorithm and the algorithm in bibliography [4].

1 Introduction

A number of data presentation problems involve the drawing of a graph on a limited two-dimensional surface, like a sheet of paper or a computer screen. Examples include circuit schematics, algorithm animation and software engineering. In almost all data presentation applications, the usefulness of a drawing of a graph depends on its readability, that is, the capability of conveying the meaning of the diagram quickly and clearly. Readability issues are expressed by means of aesthetics, which can be formulated as optimization goals for the drawing algorithms. Many aesthetic criteria can be conceived of and the generally accepted ones include:

(1) Uniform spatial distribution of the vertices.
(2) To minimize the total edge length on the precondition that the distance between any two vertices is no less than the given minimum value.
(3) Uniform edge length.
(4) To maximize the smallest angle between edges incident on the same vertex.
(5) The angles between edges incident on the same vertex should be as uniform as possible.
(6) Minimum number of edge crossings.
(7) To exhibit any existing symmetric feature.

While these criteria are useful measures of aesthetic properties of graphs, this is not an exhaustive list and there are other measures that can be used [1].

L. Wang, K. Chen, and Y.S. Ong (Eds.): ICNC 2005, LNCS 3612, pp. 28–36, 2005.
© Springer-Verlag Berlin Heidelberg 2005

It is not easy to locate the vertices of a general undirected graph so that it conforms to aesthetically pleasing principles of layout. There are many different strategies that can be used to draw a general undirected graph. One method is to use the spring model algorithm [2]. The algorithm likens a graph to a mechanical collection of rings (the vertices) and connecting springs (the edges). Two connected rings are attracted to each other or repelled by each other according to their distance and the properties of the connecting spring. A state with minimal energy in the springs corresponds to a nice drawing of the underlying graph. However, the spring method is likely to be trapped by local optima and thus obtains very poor drawings. Another method is to use simulated annealing algorithm [3]. Davidson and Harel have used the algorithm to draw undirected graphs. This algorithm produces drawings that are comparable to those generated by the spring model algorithm. However, the algorithm does not produce conventional looking figures for a large cycle with no chords. While this is normally drawn as a large circle, this algorithm tends to draw the cycle curled around itself and thus obtains a concave polygon but not a convex one. And also the simulated annealing algorithm is likely to be trapped by local optima and thus obtains very poor drawings. Eloranta and Mäkinen [4] present a GA for drawing graphs with vertices over a grid and use several operators but remark on the lack of a good crossover operator. And also the algorithm draws a large cycle with no chords curled around itself.

A graph $G=(V, E)$ is formed by a set of vertices V and a set of edges E. It may be represented in different styles according to the purposes of the presentation. We are interested here in producing aesthetically-pleasing 2D pictures of undirected graphs. Vertices will be drawn as points in the plane inside a rectangular frame and edges will be drawn as straight-line segments connecting the points corresponding to the end vertices of the edges. So the problem of graph drawing reduces to finding the coordinates of such points. This paper concentrates on constructing the straight-line drawings of general undirected graphs with genetic algorithms. The algorithm has the following four advantages:

(1) The figures drawn by the algorithm are beautiful.
(2) it can draw large cycles with no chords as convex polygons.
(3) It is simple and it is easy to be implemented.
(4) It is flexible in that the relative weights of the criteria can be altered.

2 The Genetic Algorithm for Drawing Undirected Graph

The most important thing of solving graph drawing problems with genetic algorithms is to design fitness functions according to the adopted aesthetic criteria. The fitness function is given in section 2.2, and the various elements of the algorithm are illustrated in the following subsections.

2.1 Encoding

Let $G=(V, E)$ be a finite, undirected, simple graph. Let $n=|V|$ denote the number of vertices of G, and let $m=|E|$ denote the number of edges of G. Suppose the vertices sequence of a graph G is $v_1, v_2, \cdots, v_n$, and the coordinates assigned to them are $(x_1, y_1), (x_2, y_2), \cdots, (x_n, y_n)$, respectively. The algorithm uses a real number vector $(x_1, y_1, x_2, y_2, \cdots, x_n, y_n)$ with the length of 2n to denote the solution to the problem. In order to draw graphs inside a rectangular frame in the plane, we add the following constraints:

$$a \leq x_i \leq b, \quad c \leq y_i \leq d$$

2.2 Fitness Function

The algorithm designs the following fitness function according to the aesthetic criteria (1)–(7), which are stated in Section 1. The fitness function is interpreted as follows:

$$f = \frac{w_1}{\sum_{i=1}^{n}\sum_{j=i+1}^{n}\frac{1}{d_{ij}^2}} + \frac{w_2}{\sum_{(v_i,v_j) \in E} d_{ij}^2} + \frac{w_3}{\sum_{(v_i,v_j) \in E}\frac{(d_{ij} - ideal\_edgelength)^2}{m}} +$$

$$\frac{w_4}{\sum_{\substack{i=1 \\ (v_i,v_j) \in E \\ (v_i,v_k) \in E}}^{n}\frac{1}{(\angle p_j p_i p_k)^2}} + \frac{w_5}{\sum_{\substack{i=1 \\ (v_i,v_j) \in E \\ (v_i,v_k) \in E}}^{n}\frac{(\angle p_j p_i p_k - \frac{2\pi}{deg\,ree(p_i)})^2}{deg\,ree(p_i)}} + \quad (1)$$

$$\frac{w_6}{\sum_{\substack{(v_i,v_j) \in E \\ (v_k,v_l) \in E}} Cross(\overline{p_i p_j}, \overline{p_k p_l}) + 1} + \frac{w_7}{\sum_{i=1}^{n}\frac{1}{d_{ic}^2}} + \frac{w_8}{\sum_{i=1}^{n}\frac{(d_{ic} - \frac{1}{n}\sum_{i=1}^{n}d_{ic})^2}{n}}.$$

p_i is the position vector of vertex v_i, d_{ij} is the Euclidean distance between points p_i and p_j and d_{ic} is that between point p_i and the center of the rectangular frame. The first and the second terms make the points distributed evenly and minimize the total edge length of graph G. The value of the first term will decrease if the points in the plane get too close, while that of the second term will decrease if the points get too far. In the third term, $ideal\_edgelength = \sqrt{s/n}$ is the desired edge length, where $s = (d-c)(b-a)$ is the area of the rectangular frame in the plane. The length of each individual edge will be as close as possible to the parameter ideal_edgelength because of the third term, and thus be uniform. $\angle p_j p_i p_k$ in the fourth and the fifth term is the angle between edges incident on the point p_i, degree(p_i) in the fifth term is the vertex degree of point p_i. $Cross(\overline{p_i p_j}, \overline{p_k p_l})$ in the sixth term is defined as formula (2). It can be calculated by means of analytic geometry according to the coordinates of end points of the two straight- line segments $\overline{p_i p_j}$ and $\overline{p_k p_l}$. The seventh and the eighth terms make drawings symmetric if such feature exists. w_i is the weight of criteria and it is a constant. They control the relative importance of the seven criteria and compensate for their different numerical magnitudes. The drawings produced by the algorithm can widely vary by modifying these constants.

$$Cross(\overline{p_i p_j}, \overline{p_k p_l}) = \begin{cases} 0 & \text{If straight-line segments } \overline{p_i p_j} \text{ and } \overline{p_k p_l} \text{ don't intersect}. \\ 1 & \text{If straight-line segments } \overline{p_i p_j} \text{ and } \overline{p_k p_l} \text{ intersect}. \\ \infty & \text{If straight-line segments } \overline{p_i p_j} \text{ and } \overline{p_k p_l} \text{ overlap}. \end{cases} \quad (2)$$

2.3 Selection

In order to avoid premature convergence, we perform a sigma proportional transformation on each individual's fitness value [5], i.e., for the fitness value f(i) of the i-th individual, at first we apply the following formula to f(i) to transform it into ExpVal(i):

$$ExpVal(i) = \begin{cases} 1 + (f(i) - f(t))/2\sigma(t), & \text{if } \sigma(t) > 0. \\ 1, & \text{if } \sigma(t) = 0. \end{cases} \quad (3)$$

where f(t) is the average fitness value of the t-th generation population, and $\sigma(t)$ is the standard deviation of the t-th generation population. After such transformation, the algorithm then uses elitist fitness proportionate selection mechanism for ExpVal(i) to select chromosomes for reproduction. The best individual in the population is always passed on unchanged to the next generation, without undergoing crossover or mutation.

2.4 The Design of Genetic Operator

The algorithm has three types of genetic operations: crossover, mutation and inversion. The crossover operator is defined as follows: The *single-point crossover* generates two new graph layouts by randomly selecting one vertex and exchanging the corresponding coordinates between the parent graphs. The mutation operators are applied sequential and independently from crossover. They are defined as follows:

The *non-uniform mutation*[6] – If S=(v_1, v_2,...,v_{2n}) is a chromosome and the element v_k is selected for this mutation (the domain of v_k is [a_k, b_k]), the result is a vector $S' = (v_1, v_2, ..., v_{k-1}, v'_k, ..., v_{2n})$, with $k \in 1, ..., 2n$, and

$$v'_k = \begin{cases} v_k + \Delta(t, b_k - v_k), & \text{if } c = 0, \\ v_k - \Delta(t, v_k - a_k), & \text{if } c = 1, \end{cases} \quad (4)$$

Where c is a random number that may have a value of zero or one, and the function $\Delta(t, y)$ returns a value in the range [0, y] such that the probability of $\Delta(t, y)$ being close to 0 increases as t increases:

$$\Delta(t, y) = y(1 - r^{(1-t/T)^\lambda}) \quad (5)$$

where r is a random number in the interval[0, 1], t is the current generation number, T is the maximum number of generations, and λ is a parameter chosen by the user, which determines the degree of dependency with the number of iterations. This property causes this operator to make an uniform search in the initial space when t is small, and a very local one in later stages.

The *single-vertex-neighborhood mutation*-choose a random vertex and move it to a random point in the circle of decreasing radius around the vertex's original location. Suppose that vertex $v_i(x_i,y_i)$ is chosen for mutation, then the new coordinates (x'_i, y'_i) of v_i are defined as follows:

$$\begin{cases} x'_i = x_i + r\cos\theta \\ y'_i = y_i + r\sin\theta \end{cases} \quad (6)$$

where radius r=ideal_edgelength*(1-t/T); $\theta \in [0, 2\pi]$ is an angle randomly produced; The meanings of t, T and ideal_edgelength are the same as above. As can be seen, the radius r is decreasing as the algorithm proceeds.

The last genetic operation is inversion. Inversion works by randomly selecting two inversion points within a chromosome and inverting the order of genes between the inversion points, but remembering the gene's meaning or functionality. If

$$S=(v_1,\ldots,v_i,\ldots,v_j,\ldots,v_{2n})$$

is the parent vector and the two inversion points are i and j, then the offspring vector will be

$$S'=(v_1,\ldots,v_{i-1},v_j,v_{j-1},\ldots,v_{i+1},v_i,\ldots,v_{2n})$$

In order to avoid swapping x-coordinates for y-coordinates, we add the following constraint:

$$(j-i) \bmod 2 = 0$$

2.5 Determining the Termination Condition of the Algorithm

The termination condition is just a check whether the algorithm has run for a fixed number of generations.

3 Experimental Results and Analysis

The algorithm described above was implemented and run on a PC with Celeron 1.7 GHz CPU, 128MB RAM. The experimental parameters values are shown as table 1. The simple genetic algorithm and our algorithm were applied respectively to six test graphs with the number of vertices ranging from 4 to 28. For each class of graphs, the two algorithms were run 20 times, respectively. Table 2 shows the mean fitness value of the two algorithms. As can be seen, our algorithm is much better than the simple genetic algorithm under the same condition. The experimental results are shown as figures 1-8. Figure 1 shows three different outputs of three different algorithms for the same cycle. Figure 1 (a) is the output of the algorithm in bibliography [3]; Figure 1 (b) is that of the algorithm in bibliography [4]; Figure 1 (c) is that of our algorithm. Clearly, Figure 1 (c) is the best because it is a convex polygon while the other two are concave polygons.

Figure 2 (a) shows a rectangular grid input graph with random locations for the vertices. Figure 2 (b) is the output of the simple genetic algorithm. Figure 2 (c) is that of our algorithm. Figure 2 (c) took 14.000547 seconds using 675 generation. As can be seen, the drawing produced by our algorithm is more beautiful than that produced by the simple genetic algorithm under the same condition.

Table 1. The parameters value of experiment

Parameters	Parameters value
Population size	30
Generation count	1000
Crossover probability	0.75
Mutation probability	0.25
Inversion probability	0.20

Table 2. Compare our algorithm with the simple genetic algorithm

Number of vertices	Simple GA	GA in this paper
4	0.106244	0.236976
7	0.106602	0.224305
11	0.104997	0.215806
16	0.103219	0.222807
25	0.062136	0.200684
28	0.054096	0.200018

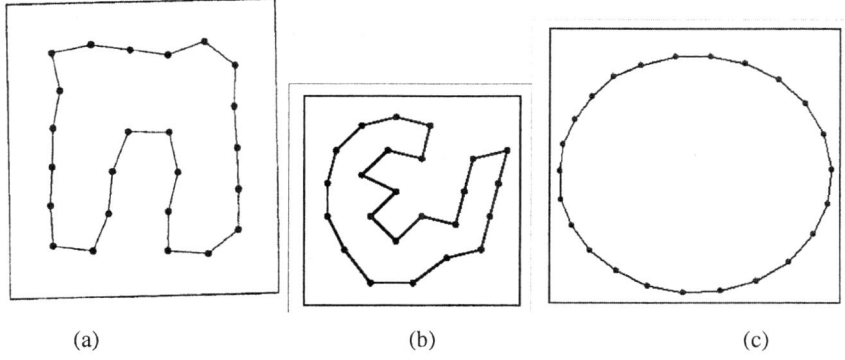

(a)   (b)   (c)

Fig. 1. Three different outputs of three different algorithms for the same cycle

Figure 3 shows two different layouts of the same graph with bridges. Figure 3 (a) is the layout produced by the original spring algorithm[2]; Figure 3 (b) is the layout produced by our algorithm. Clearly, Figure 3 (b) is better than Figure 3 (a) for the uniform edge length.

Figure 4 shows two different drawing of the same graph produced by two different algorithms. Figure 4 (a) is the drawing produced by the algorithm in bibliography [4]; Figure 4 (b) is that produced by our algorithm. Clearly, Figure 4 (b) is better than Figure 4 (a) because Figure 4 (b) has no crossing.

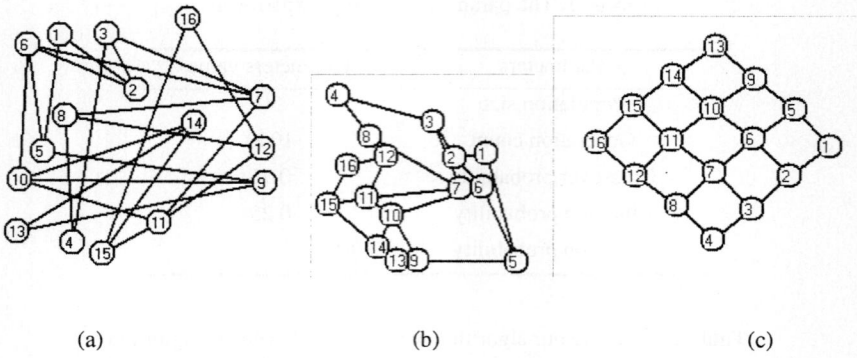

Fig. 2. A random input and the corresponding outputs of simple genetic algorithm and our algorithm

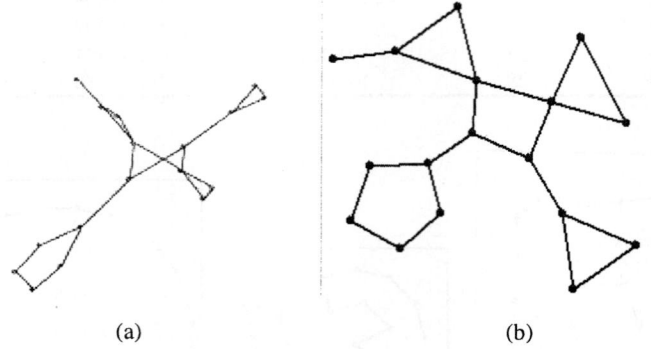

Fig. 3. Two different layouts of the same graph with bridges

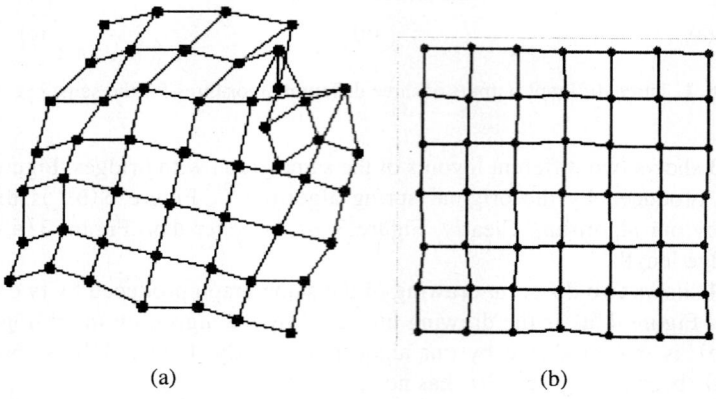

Fig. 4. Two different outputs of two different algorithms for the same graph

Figure 5 is an output for a tree. Figure 6 is an output for a disconnected graph. Figure 7 (a) shows an output for a rectangular grid graph with 25 vertices and 40 edges. Figure 7 (b) is an output for a triangular grid graph with 15 vertices and 30 edges. Figure 8 is other sample outputs of our algorithm.

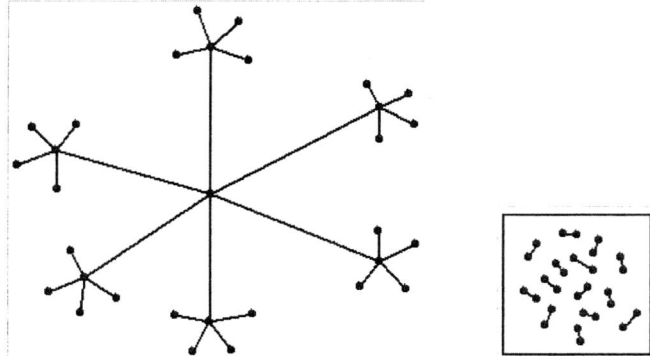

Fig. 5. An output for a tree   **Fig. 6.** An output for a disconnected graph

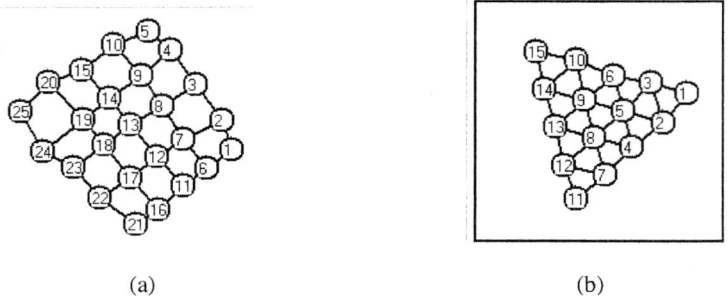

(a)   (b)

Fig. 7. Outputs for two grid graphs

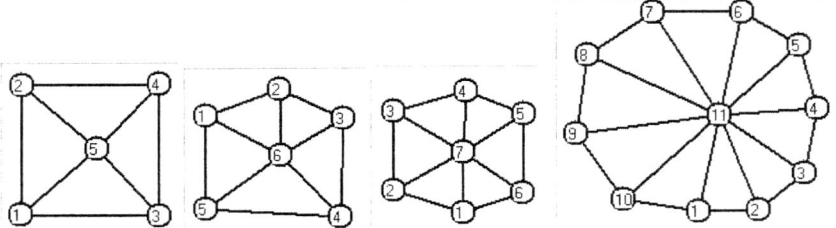

Fig. 8. Simple examples

4 Conclusions and Further Work

This paper has proposed an algorithm for producing aesthetically pleasing drawings of general undirected graphs. The primary advantage of our algorithm is that it can draw large cycles with no chords as convex polygons. This overcomes the disadvantage of previous undirected graph drawing algorithms drawing such type graphs as concave polygons. In addition, it is flexible in that the relative weights of the criteria can be altered. The experiment results show that the figures drawn by our algorithm are beautiful. The weakness of our algorithm is speed (like all that use GAs). The future research, based on bibliography [7], is the evolution (by a GA) of an ideal set of weights for the criteria - reflecting the aesthetic preferences of the user - by learning from examples. Those weights would then be used by the GA to layout graphs which will hopefully be more likely to please such users.

References

1. Tamassia, R., Di Battista, G., Batini, C.: Automatic graph drawing and readability of diagrams. IEEE Transactions on Systems, Man and Cybernetics, Vol. 18, no.1, (1988) 61-79
2. Eades, P.: A Heuristic for Graph Drawing. Congressus Numerantium, 42 (1984) 149-160
3. Davidson, R., Harel, D.: Drawing Graphs Nicely Using Simulated Annealing. ACM Transac-
4. tions on Graphics, Vol. 15, no.4, (1996)301-331
5. Eloranta, T., Mäkinen, E.: TimGA - a genetic algorithm for drawing undirected graphs. Tech-
6. nical report, Department of Computer Science, University of Tampere , December (1996)
7. Tanese, R.: Distributed Genetic Algorithms for Function Optimization. Unpublished doctoral dissertation, University of Michigan, Ann Arbor, MI.(1989)
8. Michalewicz, Z.: Genetic Algorithms + Data Structures = Evolution Programs. 3rd edition. Springer-Verlag, Berlin Heidelberg New York (1996)
9. T.Masui.: Evolutionary learning of graph layout constraints from examples. In Proceedings of the ACM Symposium on User Interface Software and Technology (UIST'94). ACM Press, November (1994) 103-108

A Novel Type of Niching Methods Based on Steady-State Genetic Algorithm

Minqiang Li and Jisong Kou

School of Management, Tianjin University,
Tianjin 300072, P.R. China
mqli@tju.edu.cn
jskou@tiancai.com.cn

Abstract. In this paper, a novel niching approach to solve the multimodal function optimization problems is proposed. We firstly analyze and compare the characteristics and behaviors of a variety of niching methods as the fitness sharing, the crowding and deterministic crowding, the restricted mating, and the island model GA with regard to the competition, exploration & exploitation, genetic drift, and the ability to locate and maintain niches. Then we put forward the idea that the local competition of individuals is crucial to realize the distribution equilibria among niches of the optimization functions, and two types of niching methods, q-nearest neighbor replacement and parental neighbor replacement, are formulated by adopting special replacement policies in the setting of the SSGA. Finally, we use a set of test functions to illustrate the efficacy and efficiency of the proposed methods and the DC scheme based on the SSGA.

1 Introduction

The standard genetic algorithms (GA), or the generalized evolutionary algorithms (EA), will converge to only one optimum of an optimization function when it is implemented based on single population and fitness-based selection [1],[2],[3],[4]. The final population is usually consisted of the copies of a local optimum, even if the initial population is sampled uniformly in the feasible solution space of the optimization problem. There will appear the phenomenon of genetic drift when the GA is used to solve the multimodal function optimization problems.

The multimodal fitness landscape of the GA in solving multimodal optimization problems, multi-objective function optimization, and in simulating complex and adaptive systems [2],[3] corresponds to the physical environment including many niches with high fitness that are occupied by locally evolved species through the specialized adaptation. In order to evolve a population that will converge to the all or most of the optima of an optimization problem, the niching technology has been proposed to extend the standard GA to realize the formation and maintenance of different solutions of local optima by reducing the effects of genetic drift, preserving the diversity of population, and promoting the exploitation of different optima.

In this paper, we firstly analyze the main aims of niching technology, and compare the characteristics of various niching methods and their affections on the behavior of the GA in Section 2. Then, we propose a new type of explicit niching methods based on steady-state GA (SSGA) by using special replacement policy in Section 3, which is suitable for all styles of multimodal functions. Section 4 reports the experimental results of the proposed methods on a set of typical multi-modal functions, and investigates the dynamic behavior of these methods. In Section 5, we conclude our research and point out some directions for the future work.

2 Niching Methods and Comparisons

By simulating the mechanics of natural coevolution, the niching GA tries to implement simultaneous exploration and exploitation of a number of different environmental niches for multimodal problems. A niche represents a local optimum and its attraction basin in the multimodal function [4],[5],[6]. Whatever the niching mechanism is, the final population should be distributed spatially among all or most of the niches. If a finite population is viewed as a resource, it should be shared among all niches, which means that local optima could only be exploited by a subpopulation of genetically similar individuals or by using limited resource (called a species).

In the evolution process of a niching GA, different species adapt to occupy different niches (called local adaptation), and all of the subpopulations reach gradually the equilibria, which is preserved afterwards. We tend to divide the equilibria of population distribution for single-population GA or multi-populations GA into two types: fitness dependent distribution and niche-size (attraction basin) dependent distribution. In the former case, the number of individuals adapting to a niche is proportional to the fitness of the niche, such as the fitness sharing method. The speciation niching as restricted mating belongs to the latter case.

We considers four styles of niching technologies [1],[3],[4],[5],[6],[7],[8]: the fitness sharing (FS) proposed by Goldberg and Richardson in 1987, the crowding technique introduced by De Jong in 1975 and the deterministic crowding (DC) suggested by Mahfoud, the restricted mating, and the island model GA. There are many varieties of niching methods for solving real-world problems.

2.1 Analyses and Comparisons

We adopt a set of indexes to analyze different niching methods based on the their characteristics and evolution behaviors, see Table 1. Although the selection operation is one of the main determinants for genetic drift, it is only when the selection operation is implemented on the total population that the GA is able to have a high exploration performance, and doesn't depend on the initial population. Similarly, the replacement is another main determinant for genetic drift. When both or only the replacement is global, the competition among individuals will be global that will cause definitely the genetic drift in population.

By adopting special sharing scheme, the fitness sharing method carries out global selection and local replacement, so that the individuals only compete with the ones in the same niche, and locates and maintains all or the most of niches within an enough large population. Since the crowding holds a global selection through random selection and pairing, and CF individuals are also selected randomly from the entire population, so the individuals will compete globally. The DC uses two rounds of tournaments to decide the replacement, and the competition domain is between the local and the global, so that there still exists the phenomena of genetic drift to some extent.

Table 1. Comparisons of the characteristics and behaviors of niching methods

Indexes	Niching methods			
	Fitness sharing	Crowding and DC	Restricted mating	Island model GA
a. Genetic operations:				
Selection	Global	Global	Local	Local
Replacement	Local	Global-Local	Global-Local	Global
Competition	Local	Global-Local	Global-Local	Global-Local
b. Performances:				
Exploration	High	High	Low	Intermediate
Exploitation	Intermediate	Low	High	High
Genetic drift	No	Yes	Yes	Yes
Locating niches	High	High	Low	Intermediate
Maintaining niches	High	Intermediate	Intermediate	Intermediate
c. Control parameters	Niching radius	CF/No	Dissimilarity threshold	Migration policy
d. Dependence:				
Problems dependent	Yes	No	Yes	No
Initial population dependent	No	No	Yes	Yes

The restricted mating scheme employs local selection by checking the similarity of individuals, but mutation could also produce aliens that belong to other niches, so that there is still the possibility for genetic drift. Besides, the restriction policy also restricts the power of exploration for locating niches, and the distribution of individuals among niches is related to the initial sampling.

The migration policy in the island model GA is good for exploration, but may also lead to the replacement of a subpopulation by intruders. Its capability for locating and maintaining niches are intermediate. The punctuate equilibria are dependent to some extent on the initial sampling and the implementation of migration policy.

The fitness sharing method and the restricted mating require prior information of target problems to choose proper threshold parameters.

3 A Novel Replacement Policy for Niching

The local competition of individuals is crucial to the forming and maintaining of multiple niches in a population, or in other word, the localization of individual competition is the basis for the coevolution of multiple species in limited resources [6]. In order to gain the capability of exploration by crossover operation, the selection operation should be implemented globally. Therefore, the replacement constitutes an important platform to carry out the niching mechanism.

Considering the single-population GA, we adopt the style of steady-state GA (SSGA) [3, p207 in vol.1] for designing and testing niching methods. By referring to the crowding method [1],[3],[5], we select randomly two individuals to pair, and only one of the offspring is retained to proceed for replacement. For simplicity in argumentation, we present the algorithm for real-code representation.

Suppose that P denotes population, $P = \{a_1, a_2, \ldots, a_N\}$, where the population size is N and is kept constant during the total evolution process. An individual $a_i = (a_{i,1}, a_{i,2}, \ldots, a_{i,m})^T$ is a vector of m-dimension variables in a real and continuous optimization function, $a_k \in [a_k^{\min}, a_k^{\max}]$. Two individuals $a_i = (a_{i,1}, a_{i,2}, \ldots, a_{i,m})^T$, $a_j = (a_{j,1}, a_{j,2}, \ldots, a_{j,m})^T$ produce a child $a' = (a'_1, a'_2, \ldots, a'_m)^T$ by the whole arithmetic recombination operation,

$$a'_k = (1-\alpha_k)a_{i,k} + \alpha_k a_{j,k}, \quad i = 1,2,\ldots,N \tag{1}$$

where $\alpha_k \in [0,1]$ is a randomly generated number for each dimension of the variable vector. Then we mutate a' to get $a'' = (a''_1, a''_2, \ldots, a''_m)^T$ by two styles of mutation.

Gaussian mutation:

$$a''_k = \min\{a_k^{\max}, \max\{a_k^{\min}, a'_k + \beta_k\}\}, \quad k = 1,2,\ldots,m \tag{2a}$$

where $\beta_k \sim N(0,\sigma)$ is randomly generated ($\sigma = 1$ for default).

Uniform matation:

$$a''_k = \beta_k, \quad k = 1,2,\ldots,m \tag{2b}$$

where $\beta_k \in [a_k^{\min}, a_k^{\max}]$ is uniformly generated on $[a_k^{\min}, a_k^{\max}]$.

3.1 q-Nearest Neighbor Replacement Policy (q-NNR)

In order to preserve local competition, we should consider how to insert the only offspring a'' into the population P, or which individual in P is selected to be replaced. In contrast to drawing CF individuals randomly from population in the crowding scheme, we tend to select similar ones to a'' by the phenotypic distance.

The Euclidean distance is employed to measure the similarity between a'' and elements in P:

$$d(a'', a_i) = \|a'' - a_i\| = \sqrt{\sum_{k=1}^{m}(a''_k - a_{i,k})^2}, \quad a_i \in P \tag{3}$$

so that we get $\{d(a'', a_i) \mid i = 1,2,\ldots,N\}$, which is further sorted ascendingly to get the population set as $P' = \{a_1, a_2, \ldots, a_N\}$. Formerly ranked q individuals in P' are drawn as the q-nearest individuals set: $P'' = \{a_1, a_2, \ldots, a_q\}$ ($P'' \subseteq P'$, $q \ll N$). Suppose that

$a^* = \{a_j \mid f(a_j) \le f(a_i), a_i, a_j \in P''; i, j = 1, 2, \ldots, q; i \ne j\}$, and if $f(a'') > f(a^*)$, then a^* will be replaced by a''.

The parameter q is problem independent, and it only relates to the efficacy and efficiency of the niching method. When q is set as a big integer, the replacement policy will cover a larger region of the space, and there will be a higher probability for the genetic drift. If $q = N$ (the worst deletion scheme in SSGA [3]), the global competition will happen.

A simple algorithm for the q-NNR niching SSGA is outlined as below.

```
procedure q-NNR_SSGA
    T_max  - the maximum individuals to generated
    N  - the population size
    p_c, p_m  - rates for crossover and mutation operations
    q  - the size for individual neighbor
    initialize: P(0)
    for t=1 to T_max do
        selection: a_i, a_j ∈ P(t), a_i ≠ a_j
        crossover: a' ← crossover(a_i, a_j)
        mutation: a'' ← mutate(a')
        calculate: {d(a'', a_i) | i = 1, 2, ..., N}
        sort: P' = {a_1, a_2, ..., a_N}
        get: P'' = {a_1, a_2, ..., a_q}, q nearest neighbor set
        find: a* = {a_j | f(a_j) ≤ f(a_i), a_i, a_j ∈ P''; i, j = 1, 2, ..., q; i ≠ j}
        if f(a'') > f(a*) then
            replace: a* ← a''
        end if
        P(t+1) ← P(t)
    end for
        output { P(T_max) }
end (procedure)
```

The q-NNR makes the replacement policy totally local although the selection operation is global. Hence, the number of individuals adapted to a niche is proportional to the size of its attraction basin.

3.2 Parental Neighbor Replacement Policy (PNR)

The parental neighbor replacement policy employs a parent-related method to calculate the neighbor of an offspring. Suppose that a'' is produced by a_i, a_j, and $d(a'', a_i) < d(a'', a_j)$, which means that then a'' is more similar to a_i. Then a'' and a_i are used to calculate the neighbor of a'' as below.

Ball neighbor set (BN-set):

$$P'' = \{a_j \mid d(a_{centroid}, a_j) \le r, a_j \in P\},\quad (4a)$$

where $a_{centroid} = (a''+a_i)/2$, $r = d(a'',a_i)/2$.

Ellipsoid neighbor set (EN-set):

$$P'' = \{a_j \mid d(a'', a_j) + d(a_i, a_j) \le r, a_j \in P\},\quad (4b)$$

where $r = \gamma d(a'',a_i)$, $\gamma \in [1,2]$. If γ is too great, $P'' = P$.

Then we find $a^* = \{a_j \mid f(a_j) \le f(a_i), a_i, a_j \in P''; i,j = 1,2,\ldots,q; i \ne j\}$, and if $f(a'') > f(a^*)$, insert a'' into the population to replace a^*.

The characteristics of the proposed niching schemes based on two types of replacement policies are shown in Table 2.

Table 2. Characteristics of the proposed niching methods

Indexes	Niching methods based on neighbor replacement policies		
	q-NNR	BN-set PNR	EN-set PNR
a. Genetic operations:			
Selection	Global	Global	Global
Replacement	Local	Global-Local	Global-Local
Competition	Local	Global-Local	Global-Local
b. Performances:			
Exploration	High	High	High
Exploitation	Intermediate	High	Intermediate
Genetic drift	No	Yes	Yes
Locating niches	High	High	High
Maintaining niches	High	Intermediate	Intermediate
c. Control parameters	q	No	γ
d. Dependence:			
Problems dependent	No	No	No
Initial population dependent	No	No	No

Since two parents are selected randomly from the population, the selection operation is global, so that the replacement based on either the BE-set or the EN-set is not totally local. There will appear some degree of the genetic drift because of the parental competition, but the algorithm of the SSGA by using the BE-set or the EN-set niching method is much more time efficient.

4 Experimental Studies

In this section, we attempt to examine the performance of the proposed niching methods on a set of test multimodal functions, and compare it to that of the DC niching scheme in the setting of SSGA. Experiments are reported with adopting different control parameters for the proposed niching mechanism.

The population size is set as $N=400$ so as to reduce the stochastic error caused by genetic operations. The rates for crossover and mutation are $p_c = 1.0, p_m = 1/m = 0.5$, the maximum number of individuals generated is fixed as $T_{max} = 10,000$. We have $q = 9$ and $\gamma = 1.10$ for calculating the q-nearest neighbor set and the ellipsoid neighbor set.

4.1 Function 1

A bimodal function is defined by combining two Gaussian functions in a variety of ways as below:

$$\max f(x) = \max\{\exp(-\|x-\mu_1\|^2/\delta_1^2), \alpha\exp(-\|x-\mu_2\|^2/\delta_2^2)\}, \ x \in R^2 \quad (5)$$

where μ_1, μ_2 and δ_1, δ_2 are the centroid and width parameters, and can be used to adjust the overlapping of the two peaks or niches. α is employed to change the comparative heights of the two peaks. $x \in [0,12] \times [0,12]$ is used in experiments.

When $\delta_1 = \delta_2$ and $\alpha = 1$, the two peaks are equal in height and have separate and equal attraction basins (called uniform competition niches). When $\delta_1 \ll \delta_2$ and $\exp(-\|x-\mu_1\|^2/\delta_1^2) > \alpha\exp(-\|x-\mu_2\|^2/\delta_2^2)$, the two niches form a style of deception (called deceptive niches). When $\delta_1 < \delta_2$ and $\exp(-\|x-\mu_1\|^2/\delta_1^2) < \alpha\exp(-\|x-\mu_2\|^2/\delta_2^2)$, the two niches compete unequally for resources (called non-uniform competition niches). Further, if $\delta_1 \ll \delta_2$, and $\|\mu_1 - \mu_2\|$ is small, we will say that the niche formed by $\{\mu_1, \delta_1\}$ is parasitized on the niche formed by $\{\mu_2, \delta_2\}$ (called host and parasite niches).

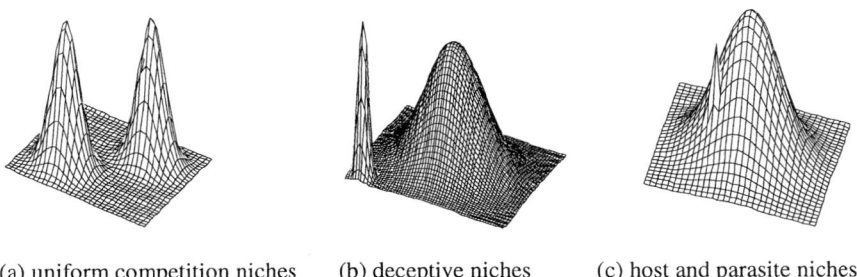

(a) uniform competition niches   (b) deceptive niches   (c) host and parasite niches

Fig. 1. Three cases of niches for Function 1

The individual numbers adapted to all niches is used to measure the results of locating and maintaining niches. The efficiency of a niching method is denoted by the sum of the deviation of individuals in different niches in the final population as:

$$dev = \sum_{i=1}^{N_{niches}} \sum_{j=1}^{N_{ind,i}} \| a_j - \bar{a}_i \|, \tag{6}$$

where N_{niches} is the number of niches, $\bar{a}_i$ is the mean vector of the ith niche that covers $N_{ind,i}$ individuals.

The experiments for each case are implemented 10 times, and the initial population are randomly generated each run. The averaged performance of different niching methods based on the SSGA is listed in Table 3.

Table 3. Averaged performance of different niching methods on the function 1

Cases	Niching methods			
	q-NNR	BN-set PNR	EN-set PNR	DC
a. $\{\mu_1 = 3.5, \delta_1 = 1.5; \mu_2 = 8.5, \delta_2 = 1.5; \alpha = 1.0\}$				
Individuals distribution (%)*	{50.4,49.6}	{50.0,50.0}	{50.2,49.7}	{47.5,52.5}
Sum of deviation	93.77	65.17	43.22	42.94
b. $\{\mu_1 = 1.0, \delta_1 = 0.5; \mu_2 = 6.0, \delta_2 = 3.0; \alpha = 0.8\}$				
Individuals distribution (%)*	{2.5,97.5}	{1.8,98.2}	{1.4,98.6}	{0.9,99.1}
Sum of deviation	63.91	19.47	10.42	7.57
c. $\{\mu_1 = 4.0, \delta_1 = 0.5; \mu_2 = 6.0, \delta_2 = 3.0; \alpha = 1.2\}$				
Individuals distribution (%)*	{1.13,98.9}	{0.3,99.7}	{0.4,99.6}	{0,100}
Sum of deviation	61.13	12.09	8.02	11.90

* the proportion of individuals adapted to niches.

The above table shows that all of the niching methods work well on case (a) of the function 1. For cases (b), the q-NNR niching locates and maintains more individuals in the niche $\{\mu_1 = 1.0, \delta_1 = 0.5\}$ though it has a quite small attraction basin. For cases (c), the q-NNR niching is still able to locate and maintain individuals in the niche $\{\mu_1 = 4.0, \delta_1 = 0.5\}$ even if it is parasitized on a bigger niche. The BN-set PNR niching, EN-set PNR niching, and DC niching are much more efficient in implementation, but there appear salient genetic drift in cases (b) and (c).

4.2 Function 2

The second function is a special two dimensional sin function as below:

$$\max f(x,y) = (1+\alpha\sqrt{x}) \times (\sin x \times \sin y)^2, \ x \in [1, 6\pi], y \in [1, \pi] \tag{7}$$

where α is a parameter to control the comparative heights of the six niches.

All experiments are run 10 times with random initial populations. The averaged performance is recorded in Table 4.

The results on function 2 illustrate that the BN-set PNR niching, EN-set PNR niching, and DC niching are not able to maintain the individuals in the niches with lower heights, and the genetic drift is very common in their evolution processes. However, the q-NNR niching scheme does quite well in maintaining a stable distribution of all individuals. Further, specific experiments are carried out for the q-NNR niching on function 2 with various values of q (see Table 5).

The number of q is an important factor to the coevolution process of SSGA with q-NNR niching scheme. As q gets greater (but is still smaller than population size), only a few of individuals are redistributed to higher niches, and the genetic drift is not apparent for a large population. But the q-NNR niching SSGA with a greater value of q is much more efficient for the local adaptation of individuals by the deviation index. But if q is too great as $q \geq 100$, the individuals would be redistributed.

Table 4. Averaged performance of different niching methods on the function 2

Case($\alpha = 1.0$)	Niching methods			
	q-NNR	BN-set PNR	EN-set PNR	DC
Individuals distribution (%)* Sum of deviation	{14.6,15.37, 16.42, 17.15, 17.74,18.73} 52.68	{0,1.28, 1.20, 22.55,30.88, 34.10} 43.89	{0, 0, 7.0, 20.63, 34.43, 37.95} 39.34	{0,0.15,4.23, 20.8,35.67, 39.15} 44.83

* peak coordinates of the six niches: { $(\pi/2,\pi/2),(3\pi/2,\pi/2),(5\pi/2,\pi/2),(7\pi/2,\pi/2),(9\pi/2,\pi/2),(1\pi/2,\pi/2)$ }.

Table 5. Performance of the q-NNR niching methods on the function 2

Case($\alpha = 1.0$)	q-NNR niching methods				
	$q = 1$	$q = 9$	$q = 50$	$q = 100$	$q = 200$
Individuals distribution (%) Sum of deviation	{15.5,15.5, 16.3,16.7, 17.5, 18.5} 233.88	{14.6,15.4, 16.4,17.2, 17.7,18.7} 52.68	{14.5,15.6, 16.0,16.9, 17.9,19.1} 26.59	{0,0,25.0, 25.0, 25.0, 25.0} 24.88	{0,0,0,0, 50.0,50.0} 47.60

4.3 Schaffer Function

The Schaffer function is a symmetric multimodal function with concentric torus ridges of different heights. We modify it a little as follows:

$$\min f(x_1, x_2) = 0.5 + (\sin^2 \sqrt{x_1^2 + x_2^2} - 0.5) \big/ [1 + \alpha \times (x_1^2 + x_2^2)]^2, \quad x_1, x_2 \in [-10,10] \quad (8)$$

where α is used to regulate the function shape, and we take $\alpha = 0.01$ in experiments. The niches formed in this function consist of a set of concentric torus ridges.

The origin (0,0) is the global optimum with $f(0,0) = 0$ and denoted as $niche_0$. The four torus ridges that locate at $\sqrt{x_1^2 + x_2^2} = \{\pi, 2\pi, 3\pi, 4\pi\}$ form the local optima denoetd as $\{niche_\pi, niche_{2\pi}, niche_{3\pi}, niche_{4\pi}\}$. The origin (0,0) and the four torus ridges constitute the five niches of the Schaffer function.

The experiments results are displayed in Table 6. The q-NNR niching is able to locate and maintain the special type of niches in the Schaffer function, and it is also efficient for exploitation and local adaptation. The DC scheme performs well in locating all niches, but it is not good at local adaptation of individuals and there is still the genetic drift towards the niches with greater fitness. Both the BN-set PNR and the EN-set PNR don't output good results since there appears notable genetic drift in the coevolution processes.

Table 6. Averaged performance of different niching methods on the Schaffer function

Index	Niching methods			
	q-NNR	BN-set PNR	EN-set PNR	DC
Individuals distribution (%)*	{2.05, 15.8, 30.38, 41.6, 10.18}	{5.53, 80.65, 13.82, 0, 0}	{5.95, 94.05, 0, 0, 0}	{2.83, 47.63, 27.95, 17.82, 3.78}

* five niches are ranked as { $niche_0, niche_\pi, niche_{2\pi}, niche_{3\pi}, niche_{4\pi}$ }

5 Conclusions

Two types of niching methods, q-nearest neighbor replacement and parental neighbor replacement, are designed by adopting special replacement policies in the setting of the SSGA. The experimental results obtained on a set of test functions illustrate the characteristics and behavior of the proposed methods and the DC scheme based on the SSGA, and prove that the q-NNR niching method is an effective tool for solving the multimodal function optimization problems. In future researches, we attempt to consider the incorporation of the q-NNR, BN-set and EN-set niching methods with the fitness sharing so as to dynamically calculate a set of non-uniform niching radii. Meanwhile, we will apply tentatively these methods to the rule learning tasks and the multi-objective optimization tasks.

Acknowledgements: The research reported here is supported by the National Science Foundation of China (Grant No.70171002, No. 69974026).

References

1. Goldberg, D. E. (ed.): Genetic algorithms in search, optimization and machine learning. New York: Addison-Wesley Publishing Company (1989)
2. Holland, J. H. (ed.): Adaptation in natural and artificial systems: An introductory analysis with applications to biology, control, and artificial intelligence. 2nd edition. Cambridge, MA: MIT Press (1992)
3. Bäck, T., Fogel, D. B., and Michalewicz, Z. (eds.): Evolutionary Computation. Bristol and Philadelphia, Institute of Physics Publishing (2000)
4. Eiben, A. E., and Smith, J. E. (eds.): Introduction to Evolutionary Computing. Berlin Heidelberg: Springer-Verlag (2003)

5. Mahfoud, S. W.: Niching methods for genetic algorithms, IlliGAL report No.95001, University of Illinois at Urbana-Champaign (1995)
6. Horn, J.: The nature of niching: genetic algorithms and the evolution of optimal, cooperative populations. A Dissertation from the University of Illinois at Urbana-Champaign (1997)
7. Sareni, B., and Krähenbühl, L.: Fitness sharing and niching methods revisited. IEEE Transactions On Evolutionary Computation, vol. 2, no.3, Sept. (1998) 97–106
8. Cioppa, A. D., Stefano, C. De, and Marcelli, A.: On the role of population size and niche radius in fitness sharing. IEEE Transactions on Evolutionary Computation, vol. 8, no. 6, Dec. (2004) 580-592

Simulated Annealing Genetic Algorithm for Surface Intersection

Min Tang and Jin-xiang Dong

State Key Laboratory of CAD&CG, Zhejiang University,
Hangzhou, 310027, China
{tang_m, djx}@zju.edu.cn

Abstract. The paper integrated genetic algorithm and marching method into a novel algorithm to solve the surface intersection problem. By combining genetic algorithm with local searching method the efficiency of evolution is greatly improved. By fully utilizing the global searching ability and instinct attribute for parallel computation of genetic algorithm and the local rapid convergence of marching method, the algorithm can compute the intersection robustly and generate correct topology of intersection curves. The details of the new algorithm are discussed here. The algorithm have been implemented in a prototype system named TigerSurf based on Windows/NT platform, and a soundly result is gotten from test datum.

1 Introduction

In recent years, there are a lot of literatures discussing the topic on calculating the intersection between two surfaces. They can be classified into analysis method, lattice method, tracing method, implicit function method, and sub-division method. The implicit function method is limited to CAD systems which support the implicit representation of surfaces, the other methods can be used in general surface intersection problem, but all of them have the delicate problem for tolerance setting [1].

Recently genetic algorithm has become a hot-spot in the field of AI, and has been applied successfully in the fields of machine learning, engineering optimizing, job scheduling, image processing, etc.

Applying a genetic algorithm involves the following steps [2]:

1. Choosing a space of "potential answers" for one's problem;
2. Determining an appropriate measure of "fitness" on this space;
3. Defining appropriate genetic operators on this space, for instance crossover and mutation operators.

The algorithm itself then involves iterating generations in a population of potential answers, at each stage selecting certain population elements, and using these selected elements to generate new elements according to the genetic operators. The trick is in the selection process: in order to provide an intuitive simulation of the biological process of evolution by natural selection, measures must be taken to ensure that, on the whole, the "fittest" elements are chosen to reproduce.

Genetic algorithm has the benefit for global searching, and will not be trapped in the rapid descending direction introduced by local minima. And with its intrinsic parallelism, the calculation speed can be easily improved by distribute computation methods.

Recently genetic algorithms have attracted attention as a powerful tool for optimization problems. Also, in the computer vision community a growing number of applications of these techniques can be seen. [3] used a genetic algorithm for registration of 3D images in a medical application. Cross and Hancock [4] reported fast convergence with a genetic search based on Hamming distance. [5] applied genetic algorithm for free-form surface matching. However, to the best of our knowledge no earlier use of genetic algorithms for intersecting free-form surfaces can be found in the literature. In this paper we will present a new algorithm applied to this problem.

Due to the lack of efficiency of "pure" genetic algorithm, local search methods based on heuristic information and field related knowledge are used to improve it. Surface/surface intersection calculating occurs frequently in the field of geometric modeling. Conventional method such as marching method has the advantages of accurate, efficient and robust in non-degenerate conditions. So we designed a algorithm to combine the global search ability of genetic algorithm and local rapid convergence of marching method.

2 Simulated Annealing Genetic Algorithm (SAGA)

As a technique to solve massive optimization problem, simulated annealing algorithm has received the attention of many researchers. The main idea of it is an analogy to the growth of single crystals from a molten metal while it cool down slowly.

Simulated annealing algorithms jump over the local minima using Metropolis rule, and will eventually converge to the optimization. When the algorithm has no knowledge about the objective space which has been detected, it's hard to decide which area is more possible to contain optimal result. To be more efficient and smart, simulated annealing algorithm should get knowledge of objective space from the searching process. This knowledge is collected by evolution process of genetic algorithm. The combination of these two methods called SAGA (simulated annealing genetic algorithm).

3 SSI Based on SAGA

The marching method for SSI comprises three primary phases: hunting (start point), tracing, and sorting. The hunting phase provides starting point for stepping on the intersection curve. It should locate all branches of the intersection curve and prevent multiple copies of the same sequence of points during marching phase. The commonly used hunting methods include hodographs methods, subdivision techniques, and algebraic methods. The marching methods make use of curvature analysis or power series expansions about each point of the intersection curve to control the step. The sorting phase orders the sequences of points into meaningful branches of the intersection curve. When the points on the intersection curve can be found sequentially, this sorting is trivial.

Simulated annealing algorithms jump over the local minima using Metropolis rule, and will eventually converge to the optimization. When the algorithm has no knowledge about the objective space which has been detected, it's hard to decide which area is more possible to contain optimal result. To be more efficient and smart, simulated annealing algorithm should get knowledge of objective space from the searching process. This knowledge is collected by evolution process of genetic algorithm. The combination of these two methods called SAGA (simulated annealing genetic algorithm).

4 Crossover Operation

Crossover operation can generate new individuals, and make new search in objective space. The new individuals inherit chromosome information from their procreators, and are usually different to them. The procreators (two points) in crossover operation are in the neighborhood of an intersection point. The crossover operator will determine the offset of parameters on surface domain to generate new individuals with the property that they are (probably) closer to the intersection than their procreators. It should also be simple to be efficient. We introduce an auxiliary plane and calculate an intersection point on this plane and tangential planes of the intersecting surfaces as the first approximate values for the parameters.

Given two points P and Q on each surface, we define two tangent planes: F_p at P and F_q at Q. We defines a plane F_n which passes through P and is orthogonal both to the planes F_p and F_q. On the plane F_n, we define the unit vectors i_n and j_n. i_n is the unit normal of plane F_p, and j_n is in the direction of the intersection line of the planes F_n and F_p. Then the normal of F_n is $K_n = i_n \times j_n$ (Fig. 1). If the points P and Q are represented by r(s, t) and s(u, v), we have the following relations:

$$(s(u,v)+\delta u \cdot s_u + \delta v \cdot s_v) \cdot i_n = h$$
$$(r(s,t)+\delta s \cdot r_s + \delta t \cdot r_t) \cdot j_n = (s(u,v)+\delta u \cdot s_u + \delta v \cdot s_v) \cdot j_n \quad (1)$$
$$(r(s,t)+\delta s \cdot r_s + \delta t \cdot r_t) \cdot k_n = (s(u,v)+\delta u \cdot s_u + \delta v \cdot s_v) \cdot k_n = h_n$$

Here h and h_n are distances from the origin to the planes F_p and F_n. Solving the equations, the intersection point of the three planes is determined as the increments of the parameters: δt, δs, δu, and δv. The new individuals P and Q can calculated by update the parameters as r(s+ δ s, t+ δ t) and s(u+ δ u, v+ δ v).

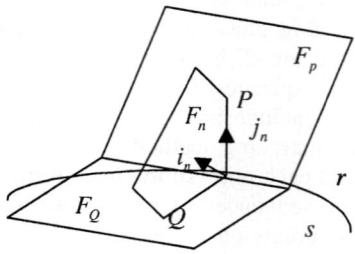

Fig. 1. Intersection of three planes

5 Strategy for Local Tracing

Given a set of initial intersection points and their normalized tangent vectors, the tracing process can be proceeded. The strategy for local tracing determinates the topology of intersection branches. Incorrect step direction or size may lead to erroneous results. Tracing in the tangent direction, along a circle, and along a parabola are some solutions presented in the literature. Most solutions use curvature-dependent step size for Tracing. Here we used a simple but efficient tracing method presented in [6]. For the given neighboring intersection points P and Q, and with their respective tangent vectors $\vec{u}$ and $\vec{v}$, an approximate osculating circle at Q is constructed as follows (Fig. 2):

Center (C) : The intersection of three planes: the plane that contains P and has $\vec{u}$ as normal vector; the plane that contains Q and has $\vec{v}$ as normal vector; and the plane that contains Q and has a normal $\vec{u} \times \vec{v}$.

Radius (R) : The distance between C and Q.

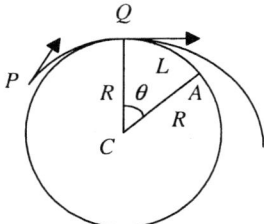

Fig. 2. Tracing along circular step

The step size can be easily computed from the approximated osculating circle. To assure that marching step adjusts automatically to the changes in the curvature of the intersection curve branch, the next approximated point to intersection curve A is calculated by extending Q with distance L.

We would like to stress that the class/style files and the template should not be manipulated and that the guidelines regarding font sizes and format should be adhered to. This is to ensure that the end product is as homogeneous as possible.

6 Convergence Proof

In this section we will give the proof for the convergence of the SSI algorithm.

Given two surfaces F and G, $F = f(D)$, $G = g(D)$, here f and g are all twice differentiable functions, $f, g : D \rightarrow R^3$. Without loss of generality, we assume that D is the unit parametric domain: $[0,1] \times [0,1]$.

We use the notation L_n for the current population L in the n iteration, and individual set $P_n = \{\phi(x) : (x, \phi) \in L_n\}$. Without the local tracing strategy, and not considering the crossover operation and mutation operation, the convergence of the algorithm can be proved [7].

Lemma: Let C be the intersection point set of f, g, and set $h_1 = 0$, Then the algorithm above without local tracing procedure and only using reproduction operation, either stops after a finite number of steps or yields a sequence $(P_n)_{n \in N}$ of sets of points with the property

$$\lim_{n \to \infty} (\max_{p \in P_n} \min_{x \in C} \|p - x\|_1) = 0. \qquad (2)$$

Proof: Clearly the algorithm terminates if $C = \Phi$. Now assume $C \neq \Phi$. In contrast to (2), suppose that there exist $\varepsilon > 0$, $p_n \in P_n$ ($n \in N$) satisfying

$$\min_{x \in C} \|p_n - x\|_1 \geq \varepsilon, \text{ for all } n \in N. \qquad (3)$$

Without loss of generality (otherwise we consider a subsequence of p_n) we may assume that

$p_n = \phi(x_n)$, $x_n \in D$, $\phi \in \{f, g\}$, independent of n;

And there exist $x^* = \lim_{n \to \infty} x_n$, $p^* = \lim_{n \to \infty} p_n$.

Then obviously

$$\min_{x \in C} \|p^* - x\|_1 \geq \varepsilon \qquad (4)$$

holds. Choose $\tilde{\phi} \in \{f, g\}$ such that $\{\phi, \tilde{\phi}\} = \{f, g\}$.

Because of the reproduction operator there exists a sequence $(y_n)_{n \in N}$ such that $(y_n, \tilde{\phi}) \in L_n$ and $\lim_{n \to \infty} \|\phi(x_n) - \tilde{\phi}(y_n)\|_1 = 0$. Consequently $\lim_{n \to \infty} \tilde{\phi}(y_n) = p^*$.

Since D is compact, (y_n) has an accumulation point y^*. Therefore

$$p^* = \phi(x^*) = \tilde{\phi}(y^*) \in C \qquad (5)$$

This contradicts with (4).

7 Implementation and Results

We have implemented the algorithm above in a prototype system named TigerSurf, which has been build on Windows/NT platform by C/C++. The surface intersection algorithm is a part of a Boolean operation of sculptured solids. The following are some examples made in TigerSurf for testing of the surface intersection algorithm.

7.1 Surface-Surface Intersection I——Multi-branch with Open Loops

The following is an example for calculating the intersection between two cubic Bezier surfaces. The intersection curves of surfaces B and C are 4 open loops (branches) in their parametric domain. Fig. 3(a) shows the 1st generation with $h_0 = 1/n$ and $n = 100$. Fig. 3(b) shows the 2nd generation evolved from the 1st generation, with

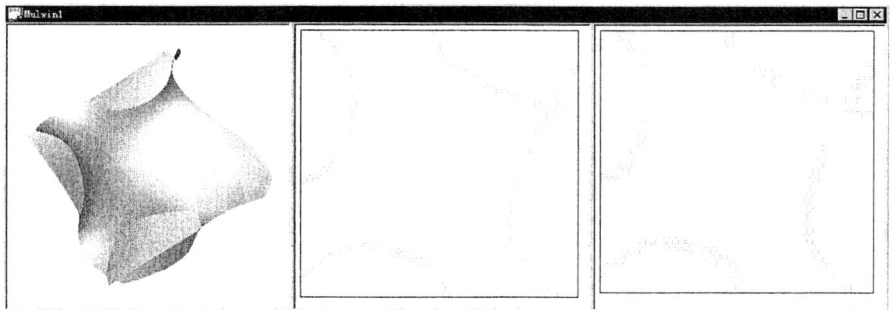

(a) 1st generation, with $h_0 = 1/n$ and $n = 100$

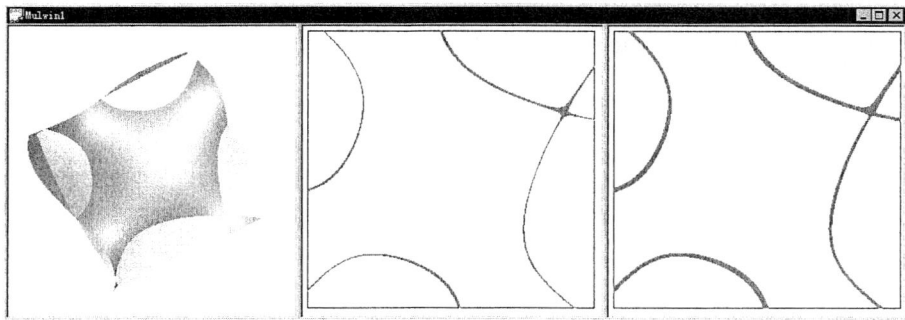

(b) 2nd generation, with $h_1 = h_0/3$

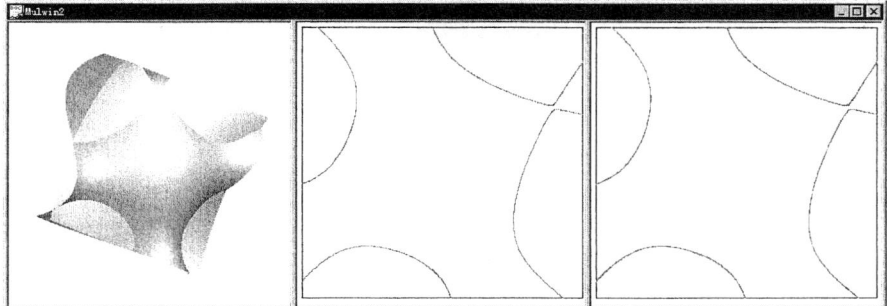

(c) 4 branches of intersection curve traced from the 2nd generation

Fig. 3. Process for calculating intersection of surfaces B and C

$h_1 = h_0/3$, Fig. 3(c) shows the intersection curves gotten by local tracing method from the 2nd generation.

7.2 Surface-Surface Intersection II——Inner Loop

The intersection curve of surface D and E is a close loop in their parametric domain. Fig. 4(a) shows the 1st generation with $h_0 = 1/n$ and $n = 100$, Fig. 4(b) shows the

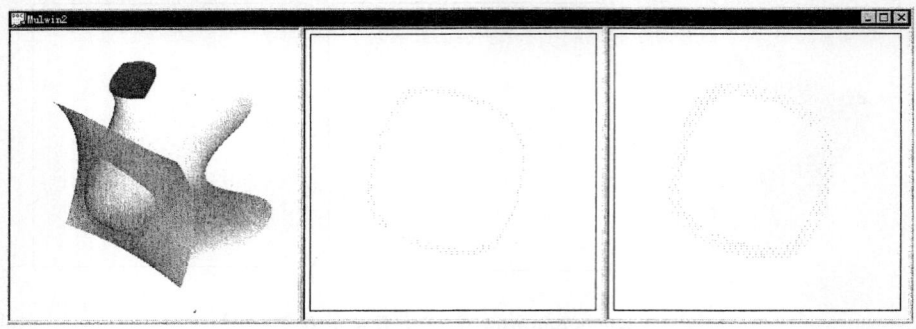

(a) 1st generation, $h_0 = 1/n$, $n = 100$.

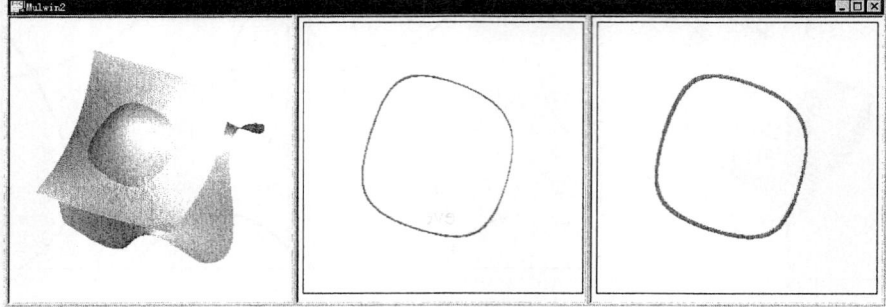

(b) 2nd generation, $h_1 = h_0/3$ .t

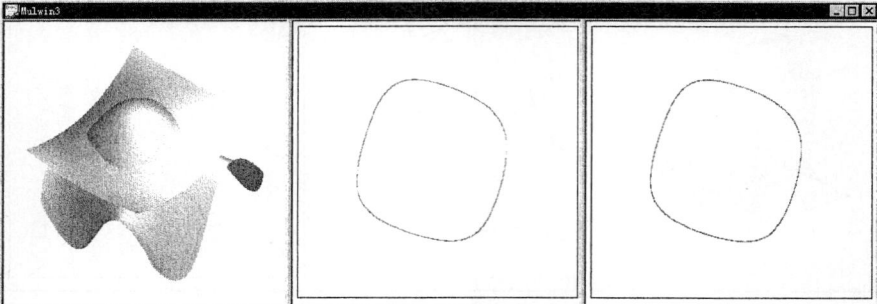

(c) The intersection loop traced from 2nd generation

Fig. 4. Process for calculating intersection of surface D and E

2nd generation evolved from the 1st generation with $h_1 = h_0/3$, Fig. 4(c) shows the intersection curve traced from the 2nd generation.

Although the two examples are calculating intersection for bicubic Bezier surfaces, our algorithm does not have any limitation on the surface type. It is designed for general parametric surface/surface intersection. Fig. 5 shows an example for intersecting two general parametric surfaces.

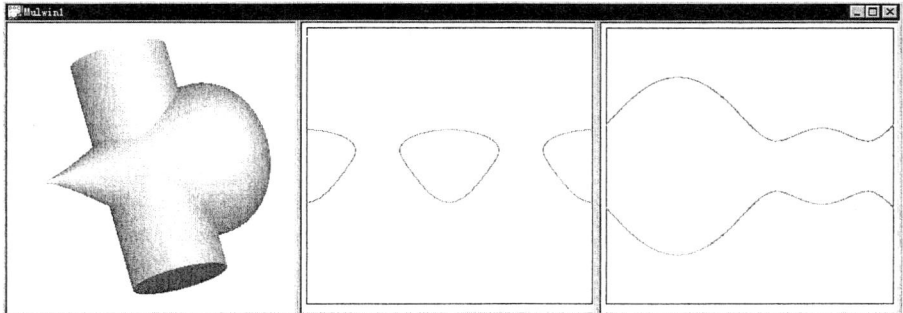

Fig. 5. Intersection of two general parametric surfaces

8 Conclusion

In this paper, the authors present a new surface intersection algorithm by applying simulated annealing genetic algorithm in the field of geometric modeling. By combining the knowledge of conventional surface/surface intersection methods, we can use local tracing strategy into the pure simulated annealing genetic algorithm. So the rapid convergence of the algorithm can be achieved. With the global searching ability and rapid convergence, we designed a practical algorithm for calculation of the intersection between general surfaces robustly and efficiently.

Degenerate cases are the situation a practical algorithm must face. There are three types of degenerate cases that may occur: singularities, osculate patches, and overlapping patches. In most algorithms, degenerate cases will lead to failure or aborting. More recent research can get form [8].

References

1. Granine, T.A., Klein IV, F.W.: A new approach to the surface intersection problem, Computer Aided Geometric Design, (1997) 14:111-134.
2. David, G.: Genetic Algorithms for Search, Optimization and Machine Learning. Addison-Wesley NY, (1988)
3. Jacq, J.-J., Roux, C.: Registration of 3D images by genetic optimization, Pattern Recognition, 16(8), (1995) 823-856

4. Cross, A., Hancock, E.: Genetic search for structural matching, In Proc. of 4th European Conference on Computer Vision, Volume 1064 of Lecture Notes in Computer Science, Cambridge, United Kingdom, Apr. 1996, Springer Verlag, New York, (1996) 514-525
5. Brunstrom, K., Stoddart, A.J.: Genetic algorithms for free-form surface matching, Technical Report ISRN KTH/NA/P--95/19—SE, Dept. Of Numerical Analysis and Computing Science, KTH(Royal Institute of Technology), Oct. (1995)
6. Wu, S.T., Andrade, L.N.: Marching along a regular surface/surface intersection with circular steps, Computer Aided Geometric Design, Vol. 16, (1999) 249-268
7. Mullenheim, G.: On determining start points for a surface/surface intersection algorithm, Computer Aided Geometric Design, 8, (1991) 401-408
8. Farouki, R.T., Hass, J., Sederberg, T.W.: Linear perturbation methods for topologically-consistent representation of free-form surface intersections, NSF/DARPA CARGO Project Report, May (2003)

A Web Personalized Service Based on Dual GAs

Zhengyu Zhu, Qihong Xie, Xinghuan Chen, and Qingsheng Zhu

Computer College of Chongqing University, Chongqing 400044, P.R. China
zhengyu_zhu@yahoo.com, eric119@163.com,
bigseahuan@163.com, qszhu@cuq.edu.cn

Abstract. In this paper, a different Web personalized service (PS) based on dual genetic algorithms (Dual GAs) has been presented. Firstly, to distinguish the importance of each keyword to a user, we have introduced a new concept called influence-gene and a user profile model $UP=(I, C)$, which includes not only the user's keyword-weights vector I but also a user's influence-genes vector C. Secondly, based on C, we have introduced a w-cosine similarity, which is an improver of the traditional *cosine* similarity. Finally, we have discussed how to design our Dual GAs to automatically discover and adjust the UP. The comparison tests show that the Dual GAs can discover the user profile more accurately and improve the precision of information recommendation.

1 Introduction

Bowman et al. said in 1994 that at least 99% of the available data was of no interest to at least 99% of the users. The functional absence of most of the current IR (information retrieval) systems can be framed as: 1) *Lack of filtering*: A user looking for some topic on Internet retrieves too much information. 2) *Lack of ranking of retrieved documents*: The system provides no qualitative distinction between the documents. 3) *Lack of support of relevance feedback*: The user cannot tell his subjective evaluation of the relevance of the document. 4) *Lack of personalization*: There is a need of personal systems that serve the specific interest of the users and build users' profiles. 5) *Lack of adaptation*: The system should notice when the user changes interests [1].

To improve or enhance the functionality of IR, various methods of Web personalized service (PS) based on natural computation have been introduced into IR, such as Data Mining [2], Machine Learning [3], Software Agent [4][5], Statistical Theory [6], Rough Set [7], Neural Network [8] and GA (genetic algorithm) [9][22]. PSs can help users to find information with potential value for their needs and now play a very important role in the research of IR.

The document spaces derived from the PS applications are spaces of large dimensions. Since GAs have a proven efficiency in exploring large complex spaces, PS now seems to be a major field of application of GAs to IR [1][10–16].

Cordón et al. [9] pointed out that the design of user profile for a PS was limited by the lack of personalization in the representation of the user's needs. An important issue in this situation was the construction of user profile that maintained previously retrieved information associated with previous user's needs.

In this paper, we will firstly suggest a different framework of PS by introducing a new user profile model and our new Dual-GAs, secondly explain how to use the Dual-GAs to automatically discover and adjust the user profile according to the user's relevance feedback, and finally give some experiments to show its efficiency.

2 A New Framework of PS

2.1 User Profile Model

The vector space model (VSM) given by Salton & McGill [17] is one of the most widely used models in PS applications [18]. In VSM, a Web page can be represented with an *n*-dimensional keyword-weights vector $d=(x_1, x_2, ..., x_n)$. Here x_i represents the weight of the *i*th keyword t_i (i=1, 2, .., n) and commonly is calculated by *TF*IDF* method. In a traditional user profile model, a user interest can be described with an *n*-dimensional keyword-weights vector $I=(w_1, w_2, ..., w_n)$.

We know the fact that, when describing a user interest and calculating the relevance of a Web page with it, some keywords may contain more important meanings and may play a more important role than the other keywords for the user. But in traditional PS, when calculating the relevance between a Web page *d* and the user profile *I* by *cosine* similarity, the importance of these keywords can only be partly reflected in its user profile *I* through its keyword-weights, but is not reflected in the keyword-weights vector *d* of the Web page, since TF*IDF method just concerns the frequency of a keyword but not their importance to the user. The frequency of a keyword and its importance are two different concepts.

In our PS, we have introduced a new concept called influence-genes of keywords and a new user profile model *UP=(I, C)*, which not only includes the keyword-weights vector *I* but also includes an influence-genes vector $C=(c_1, c_2, ..., c_n)$ (see Section 3.2). Furthermore, based on *C*, we have defined a new *w-cosine* similarity as bellow, which is an improver for the traditional *cosine* similarity.

$$Cos_c(I,d) = \frac{\sum_{i=1}^{n}((w_i * c_i) * (x_i * c_i))}{\sqrt{\sum_{i=1}^{n}(w_i * c_i)^2 * \sum_{i=1}^{n}(x_i * c_i)^2}} \quad (1)$$

2.2 Framework

The framework of our PS is shown in Fig.1. It uses the new *w-cosine* similarity and the Dual GAs (FSG and SGA). The Dual GAs is designed for automatically discovering and adjusting the user profile according to user's relevance feedback.

To describe the relevance level of a Web page, we have introduced the concept of UIL (user interest level) in our PS. For any irrelevant page d, its *UIL(d)* is 0. For a relevant page, its *UIL(d)* is a real number in [0, 1] corresponding to the interest level of the user on it. The main procedure of our PS can be described as follows.

Step1. (Initialization) S_{input} =NULL, C=(1,1,...,1), and $I=P_0$. P_0 is an interest page given by user (or retrieved by system according to some keywords given by user).

Step2. (Step2-Step7: repeating body) With $UP=(I, C)$, Web Site recommends the top-σ new pages by w-*cosine* similarity (ranking the values in a descending order).

Step3. The σ pages are browsed by user and the relevance feedback, the interest page set $S_{interest}$ among them and their UILs, are determined by one of the two ways: 1) *Directly given by user;* 2) *Automatically calculated by system.* As in [23], we use the user's average reading time β to calculate the *UIL* of each page. Suppose d_{read} is the reading time of page d. If d_{read}<β, then *UIL(d)*=0, else *UIL(d)*=min(d_{read},2β)/2β.

Step4. According to $S_{interest}$, S_{input} will be updated by selecting σ pages with better (bigger) UILs from S_{input} and $S_{interest}$. If S_{input} has not been changed, go to Step8.

Step5. With the new S_{input}, FGA on Client will discover a new I (See Section 3.1).

Step6. With the *UILs* of all the pages in S_{input}, SGA on Client will discover a new C (See Section 3.2).

Step7. Let $UP:=(I, C)$, then return to Step2.

Step8. (Termination) If all the current top-σ pages are irrelevant pages, the procedure will be ended, else return to step2. #

In our PS, Dual GAs plays a very important role and will be discussed below.

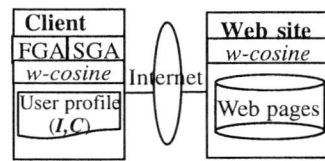

Fig. 1. The framework of our PS

3 Dual GAs

To discover and adjust the user profile $UP=(I, C)$, we have designed the Dual GAs: the first genetic algorithm (FGA) and the second genetic algorithm (SGA).

3.1 FGA

It is used to automatically discover and adjust I in UP with the interest pages in S_{input}.

1) Representation

There is only one chromosome in the population **P** for any generation. The chromosome W_0 in the initial population **P** can be formed as below,

$W_0=(w_1', w_2', ..., w_n')$
$w_i'=(MAX_i+MIN_i)/2$ i=1,2,...,n,

where *n* is the total number of keywords, MIN_i and MAX_i denotes respectively the minimum value and maximum value of the *i*th weights among all the vectors in S_{input}.

For any generation, the chromosome in **P** is always a keyword-weights vector with each gene representing a keyword's weight. By applying its genetic operators, FGA will adjust each gene to a felicitous value so that the chromosome in the final generation can represent accurately the user interest implicated in S_{input}.

2) Fitness Function

For any generation, the fitness value of a chromosome $W=(w_1, w_2, ..., w_n)$ in **P** is defined by the formula (*The bigger the fitness value is, the better the chromosome is.*),

$$f_{FGA}(W) = \sum_{i=1}^{m} Cos(W, d_i) \qquad (2)$$

where $m=|S_{input}|$ is the number of the vectors in S_{input}, each $d_i=(x_1, x_2, \ldots, x_i, \ldots, x_n)$ is in S_{input}, and *Cos* is the traditional *cosine* similarity in VSM and defined by,

$$Cos(W, d_i) = \frac{\sum_{i=1}^{n} w_i * x_i}{\sqrt{\sum_{i=1}^{n} w_i^2 * \sum_{i=1}^{n} x_i^2}} \qquad (3)$$

3) Genetic Operators

FGA has only two mutation genetic operators, *weight-adjusting* and *keyword-adjusting*. They will be executed randomly with fixed probabilities *m1* and *m2* such that *m1+m2*=1. The parameters can be adjusted by experiments.

- *Weight-adjusting mutation*

It is used to adjust the weight of each gene in the chromosome. It can generate an offspring from its parent, the only one chromosome in the current population **P**.

Firstly, produce randomly an integer i in (1, 2, ..., n). Secondly, produce randomly a real number w_i' between MIN_i and MAX_i. And finally, from the parent,

$$W=(w_1, w_2, \ldots, w_{i-1}, \mathbf{w_i}, w_{i+1}, \ldots, w_n),$$

an offspring can be generated as below,

$$W'=(w_1, w_2, \ldots, w_{i-1}, \mathbf{w_i'}, w_{i+1}, \ldots, w_n).$$

- *Keyword-adjusting mutation*

It is used to adjust the keywords in the chromosome, by adding a keyword into it or removing a keyword off from it. It can generate an offspring from its parent, the only one chromosome in the current population **P**.

First, produce randomly an integer i in (1, 2, ..., n) and then from the parent,

$$W=(w_1, w_2, \ldots, w_{i-1}, \mathbf{w_i}, w_{i+1}, \ldots, w_n),$$

an offspring can be generated as below by executing a reversal operation,

$$W'=(w_1, w_2, \ldots, w_{i-1}, \mathbf{w_i'}, w_{i+1}, \ldots, w_n),$$

where w_i' will be $(MAX_i + MIN_i)/2$ if $w_i=0$, otherwise 0.

4) Selection

After an offspring having been generated from its parent, the fitness function f_{FGA} will be used to select a chromosome to form the next generation.

For both *weight-adjusting* mutation and *keyword-adjusting* mutation, between the new offspring and its parent, the chromosome with bigger fitness value will become the only one chromosome in the next generation.

5) Convergence and Solution

In FGA, after the initial population is formed, next generation will be created repeatedly by using the two genetic operators. The fitness values of the parent and its offspring will be calculated and selective pressure applied. The weak perish and the strong survive. The process is applied iteratively.

FGA can be terminated in these cases: if the fitness value of the chromosome in current population is changed no more or very little (always less than a threshold) during a given iterative number, or if it has run a given iterative number θ.

After the termination, the chromosome in the last generation is the weighted-keywords vector I of the current user profile $UP=(I, C)$.

3.2 SGA

As did in many other papers, FGA does not distinguish the roles of different keywords when finding the user's interest. But as we have pointed out in Section 2.1, some keywords may have more important meanings than the others for a user. So the concept of influence-genes vector C has been introduced in our PS. Here, we will discuss how to determine and adjust C. It is the main task of SGA.

López-Pujalte et al.(2003) indicated that with respect to the fitness functions the best results were given by those that take into account not just which documents are retrieved, but also the order in which they are retrieved. Using the different *UIL*s of all the interest pages in S_{input}, SGA can automatically determine and adjust the influence-gene of each keyword and form the C for the user.

1) Chromosome and Population

For any generation, its population **P** has only one chromosome $C=(c_1, c_2, ..., c_n)$, and each gene c_i is always a positive integer (i=1, 2, ..., n). The chromosome in initial population **P** is set to $C_0=(1,1, ...,1)$.

2) Fitness Function

With the different *UIL(di)* of the interest page $d_i=(x_1, x_2, ..., x_i, ..., x_n)$ in S_{input}, the fitness value of the chromosome $C=(c_1, c_2, ..., c_n)$ is defined as below,

$$f_{SGA}(C) = \sum_{i=1}^{m} \left| Cos_c(I, d_i) - UIL(d_i) \right| \qquad (4)$$

(The smaller the fitness value is, the better the chromosome is.), where Cos_c is given by formula (1), $m=|S_{input}|$, and I is the weighted-keywords vector in current UP.

3) Genetic Operator

SGA has only one mutation genetic operator. It is used to adjust the values of the genes in the chromosome. It can generate an offspring from its parent, the only one chromosome in current population.

Firstly, produce randomly an integer i in (1, 2, ..., n), and a binary number $\mu = 0$ or 1. Then, from the parent,

$$C=(c_1, c_2, ..., c_{i-1}, c_i, c_{i+1}, ..., c_n),$$

an offspring C' can be generated as bellow.

If $\mu=1$, do the following two steps repeatedly ("Adding continuously").

  Step 1. $C'=(c_1, c_2, ..., c_{i-1}, c_i+1, c_{i+1}, ..., c_n)$.
  Step2. If $f_{SGA}(C') < f_{SGA}(C)$, then let $C := C'$ and go to Step1, else stop.

If $\mu=0$ and $c_i=1$, then do nothing and $C' = C$.

If μ=0 and c_i>1, do the following two steps repeatedly ("Reducing continuously").

Step1. C'=(c_1, c_2, ..., c_{i-1}, c_i-1, c_{i+1}, ..., c_n).
Step2. If $f_{SGA}(C')$<$f_{SGA}(C)$ and c_i>2, then let C:= C' and go to Step1, else stop.

4) Convergence and Solution
The convergence of SGA is almost the same as FGA and has been omitted. After the termination, the chromosome in the last generation is the influence-genes vector C of the current user profile UP=(I, C).

4 Experiments

4.1 Preparation

To form our test collection *Yahoo900*, we have selected 1100 Web pages from the Web site of Yahoo (http://dir.yahoo.com/Computers_and_Internet/). *Yahoo900* includes 11 classes with each class containing 100 pages. The 11 classes are Games (GM), Data Formats (DF), Multimedia (MM), Operating Systems (OS), Security and Encryption (SE), Cad, Databases (DB), Storage (ST), Protocol (PT). Grid (GD), Unified Modeling Language (UML).

VSM has been used to describe these Web pages. For the efficiency of extracting the keywords and forming the weights, a Dictionary K and a technique of *Characteristic Phrases* have also been used.

From [19], we know that a document can be described approximately only with its partial contents, called *Characteristic Phrases*. In our experiments, for each page, we select the first two paragraphs, the last paragraph, all the titles and subtitles, as well as all the italics or bold words as its Characteristic Phrases.

The Dictionary K=(t_1, t_2, ..., t_n), where n=1962 is the total number of keywords, has been formed by firstly extracting all the words from the Characteristic Phrases of all the 1100 pages, secondly removing all the stop-words, which appear in more than four of the eleven classes, and lastly stemming the rest of the words manually.

We use *TF*IDF* method to calculate the keyword-weight vectors for all the Web pages based on their Characteristic Phrases. As was done in López-Pujalte et al.'s experiments [12], in our experiments, we also use the *Residual Collection* method given by Salton [20], in which all the documents previously seen by the user (whether it is relevant or not) will be removed from the test collection.

4.2 Experiments and Results

In a PS, the method of forming its user profile plays an important role. In the PS, which uses a GA to form its user profile, the design of the GA's fitness function is very important. To test the efficiency of our new user profile model and Dual GAs, three different types of tests have been carried out. From López-Pujalte et al.'s experiments [12], we can see that the Fitness8 in [12], which was derived from the Horng & Yeh's GA method [21] could get a very good result in information retrieval with relevance feedback and can be seen as a representation of the current GA applications in IR.

In our experiments, we have compared our Dual GAs with Fitness8 and Fitness8'. Here Fitness8' is almost the same as Fitness8. The only difference is its similarity measure. Fitness8 used the *inner-product* similarity as was done by Horng & Yeh [21], but Fitness8' used the *cosine* similarity as was done by López-Pujalte et al. [12].

In our experiments, the parameter σ is set to 10. The probabilities of running the two mutation operators of FGA are $m1$=0.6 and $m2$=0.4. The iterative numbers θs of FGA and SGA are 5000 and 1000 respectively.

1) Test1: Efficiency of Information Recommendation

Based on the framework in Section 2.2, but using Fitness8 and Fitness8' respectively to discover and adjust the traditional user profiles I, and using our Dual GAs to discover and adjust the user profile with new model $UP=(I, C)$, we run the PS to compare them. For each class, and for each of the three methods, we run the PS three times. From each class, and at each time, the page P_0 used by our Dual GAs is selected randomly from the class. The test results are shown in Table 1. Here "avg" means "average".

Table 1. Comparison of information recommendation

Class	Fitness8		Fitness8'		Dual GAs	
	Recall(%)	Precision(%)	Recall(%)	Precision(%)	Recall(%)	Precision(%)
Cad-avg	54.5	79.6	52.0	86.6	80.3	77.0
SE-avg	53.2	73.6	48.8	67.9	98.2	60.2
ST-avg	35.5	66.4	36.3	68.5	73.5	48.7
GM-avg	55.4	83.3	54.0	87.2	71.8	69.9
GD-avg	64.0	94.9	51.8	86.4	88.3	81.1
UML-avg	86.0	97.8	80.2	97.9	61.6	79.5
All-avg	**58.1**	**82.6**	**53.9**	**82.4**	**79.0**	**69.4**

Table1 shows that our Dual GAs can recommend more relevant pages to the user than Fitness8 and Fitness8', improving average recall to 36% and 46.6% respectively with the sacrifice of average precision 19% and 18.7% respectively.

2) Test2 and Test 3: Accuracy of Adjusting User Profile

To test the accuracy of our Dual GAs in adjusting the user profile by using relevance feedback, two comparison tests among Fitness8, Fitness8' and our Dual GAs have been carried out. By inputting 10 (or 15) relevant pages and 20 irrelevant pages to each of the three GA methods, in one-off information recommendation, we calculate respectively their recalls and precisions in two popular ways, *RthP measure* and *R-P measure*.

Test 2 is for *RthP measure* (From high to low, the |R|th similarity value is chosen for the threshold, and then the precision ratio is calculated. Here |R|=100 is the total number of relevant pages of each class) and its result is shown in Table 2. Test 3 is for *R-P measure* (For recall thresholds at 0.1, 0.2, ..., 1.0, find as many documents as are retrieved for the query, and calculate respectively the precision ratio of the points where the threshold is achieved) and its result is shown in Table 3 and Fig. 2.

Table 2. The test with RthP measure

Class	Fitness8		Fitness8'		Dual GAs	
	Recall(%)	Precision(%)	Recall(%)	Precision(%)	Recall(%)	Precision(%)
GM-avg	43.0	38.7	59.6	53.7	64.8	58.3
SE-avg	11.5	10.3	12.6	11.3	45.6	41.0
MM-avg	28.6	25.7	40.7	36.7	49.7	44.7
Cad-avg	34.2	30.7	17.0	15.3	44.4	40.0
OS-avg	33.3	30.0	20.4	18.3	49.6	44.7
ST-avg	11.5	10.3	12.6	11.3	40.0	36.0
PT-avg	14.8	13.3	13.3	12.0	25.6	23.0
DB-avg	43.0	38.7	49.6	44.7	43.0	38.7
DF-avg	17.8	16.0	14.4	13.0	31.9	28.7
GD-avg	21.0	19.0	28.2	25.0	53.0	48.0
UML-avg	21.0	19.0	2.2	2.0	60.7	55.0
All-avg	**25.4**	**22.9**	**24.6**	**22.1**	**46.2**	**41.6**

Table 3. The test with R-P measure

	Class		Recall									
			0.1	0.2	0.3	0.4	0.5	0.6	0.7	0.8	0.9	1.0
Precision	GM-avg	Fitness8	0.185	0.213	0.245	0.258	0.260	0.262	0.208	0.185	0.153	0.107
		Fitness8'	0.825	0.863	0.849	0.699	0.556	0.417	0.337	0.229	0.164	0.110
		Dual GAs	0.881	0.841	0.874	0.737	0.390	0.311	0.191	0.177	0.162	0.120
	SE-avg	Fitness8	0.140	0.119	0.126	0.130	0.176	0.129	0.131	0.131	0.127	0.110
		Fitness8'	0.213	0.181	0.181	0.162	0.167	0.152	0.137	0.128	0.120	0.106
		Dual GAs	0.419	0.433	0.455	0.473	0.344	0.336	0.327	0.282	0.163	0.158
	Cad-avg	Fitness8	0.202	0.138	0.113	0.104	0.101	0.103	0.099	0.102	0.105	0.105
		Fitness8'	0.565	0.514	0.470	0.400	0.337	0.316	0.261	0.215	0.176	0.122
		Dual GAs	1.000	0.982	0.838	0.602	0.430	0.165	0.160	0.164	0.161	0.140
	ST-avg	Fitness8	0.214	0.210	0.197	0.173	0.174	0.155	0.148	0.137	0.114	0.102
		Fitness8'	0.180	0.213	0.193	0.191	0.161	0.146	0.133	0.116	0.111	0.105
		Dual GAs	0.838	0.698	0.546	0.503	0.486	0.453	0.439	0.367	0.175	0.103
	MM-avg	Fitness8	0.277	0.205	0.188	0.174	0.177	0.177	0.166	0.158	0.145	0.114
		Fitness8'	0.806	0.700	0.597	0.497	0.345	0.302	0.251	0.213	0.164	0.116
		Dual GAs	0.454	0.438	0.479	0.423	0.348	0.265	0.205	0.169	0.138	0.108
	DF-avg	Fitness8	0.245	0.181	0.174	0.148	0.155	0.152	0.132	0.124	0.113	0.105
		Fitness8'	0.265	0.192	0.160	0.139	0.122	0.100	0.100	0.099	0.100	0.104
		Dual GAs	0.640	0.383	0.286	0.205	0.186	0.160	0.157	0.139	0.128	0.108
	OS-avg	Fitness8	0.685	0.367	0.141	0.132	0.123	0.111	0.112	0.109	0.106	0.105
		Fitness8'	0.740	0.359	0.192	0.156	0.122	0.111	0.107	0.098	0.101	0.104
		Dual GAs	0.645	0.553	0.387	0.312	0.298	0.272	0.211	0.199	0.178	0.105
	DB-avg	Fitness8	0.245	0.308	0.349	0.346	0.258	0.229	0.201	0.172	0.152	0.117
		Fitness8'	0.416	0.446	0.427	0.366	0.271	0.243	0.208	0.165	0.135	0.108
		Dual GAs	0.524	0.366	0.257	0.255	0.211	0.205	0.201	0.188	0.146	0.103
	PT-avg	Fitness8	0.822	0.490	0.318	0.204	0.158	0.134	0.122	0.114	0.114	0.113
		Fitness8'	0.419	0.358	0.241	0.197	0.185	0.123	0.113	0.107	0.110	0.107
		Dual GAs	0.939	0.762	0.633	0.521	0.428	0.363	0.303	0.265	0.192	0.105
	GD-avg	Fitness8	0.231	0.184	0.166	0.150	0.151	0.145	0.138	0.132	0.121	0.107
		Fitness8'	0.517	0.476	0.420	0.363	0.281	0.255	0.215	0.181	0.150	0.114
		Dual GAs	0.764	0.706	0.621	0.509	0.421	0.294	0.268	0.233	0.158	0.117
	UML-avg	Fitness8	0.392	0.285	0.221	0.209	0.179	0.164	0.148	0.135	0.124	0.109
		Fitness8'	0.473	0.332	0.260	0.220	0.172	0.151	0.138	0.121	0.112	0.105
		Dual GAs	0.603	0.434	0.310	0.257	0.232	0.212	0.190	0.175	0.151	0.105
	All-avg	**Fitness8**	**0.331**	**0.245**	**0.203**	**0.184**	**0.174**	**0.160**	**0.146**	**0.136**	**0.125**	**0.109**
		Fitness8'	**0.493**	**0.421**	**0.363**	**0.308**	**0.247**	**0.211**	**0.182**	**0.152**	**0.131**	**0.109**
		Dual GAs	**0.701**	**0.600**	**0.517**	**0.436**	**0.343**	**0.276**	**0.241**	**0.214**	**0.159**	**0.116**

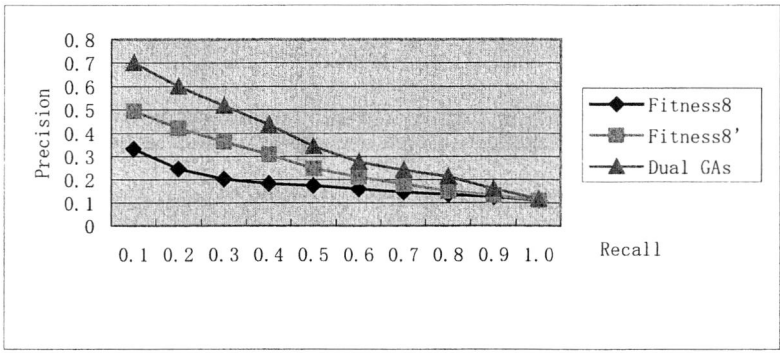

Fig. 2. The Graph of the test with R-P measure

The user profile discovered by our Dual GAs is accurate and its effect is remarkable. Table 2 shows that, compared with fitness8, our GA improves the recall and precision averagely to 81.9% and 81.7% respectively, and compared with fitness8', our GA improves the recall and precision averagely to 87.8% and 88.2% respectively. Table 3 and Fig. 2 also show that our GA is better than fitness8 and fitness8'.

5 Conclusions

The special suitability of GAs to the exploration of very large dimensional vector spaces has led to their being progressively applied to IR. The robustness of GAs has been demonstrated in this field [16].

In this paper, we have presented a different framework of PS. Firstly, by thinking that some keywords may play a more important role than the others for the user, we have introduced a new user profile model *UP*=(*I*, *C*), which includes not only the keyword-weights vector *I* but also an influence-genes vector *C*. Furthermore, with the influence-genes vector *C*, we have presented a new similarity measure *w-cosine*, which is an improver for the traditional *cosine* similarity.

Secondly, we have presented the design of our Dual-GAs, FGA and SGA, which can accurately discover and adjust the user profile *UP* according to the user's relevance feedback.

Finally, we have done three experiments on a *Yahoo900* collection to compare our GA with some other GAs. The results show that our GA can discover the user profile more accurately and improve the precision of information recommendation.

Acknowledgment

The project of Chongqing University Fund (2003A33) and the Sustentation Fund of Chongqing University for key teachers partially support this research.

Since September 2004, Zhengyu Zhu has been working as an academic visitor at the School of Computer Science of the University of Birmingham, UK. He would like to express his gratitude to Professor Xin Yao for providing him with some insights in Evolutionary Computation methods in the research.

References

1. Martín-Bautista, M.J., Larsen, H. Vila, M.A.: A Fuzzy Genetic Algorithm Approach to An Adaptive Information Retrieval Agent. Journal of the American Society for Information Science, 50(9) (1999) 760-771
2. Li, Y. F., Zhong, N.: Web Mining Model and Its Applications for Information Gathering. Knowledge-Based Systems, 17 (2004) 207–217
3. Bloedorn, E., Mani, I.: Using NLP for Machine Learning of User Profile. Intelligent Data Analysis, 2 (1998) 3-18
4. Liu, B., Wang, H., Feng, A.: Applying information agent in open bookmark service. Advances in Engineering Softare, 32 (2001) 519-525
5. Yang, C. C., Chung, A: Intelligent infomediary for web financial information. Decision Support Systems, 38 (2004) 65– 80
6. Fan, W., Gordon, M. D., Pathak, P.: Effective profiling of consumer information retrieval needs: a unified framework and emPSical comparison. Decision Support Systems. In Press, 2004
7. Li, Y., Zhang, C., Swan, J. R.: An information filtering model on the Web and its application in Job Agent. Knowledge-Based Systems, 13 (2000) 285-296
8. Mostafa, J., Lam, W.: Automatic classification using supervised learning in a medical document filtering application. Information Processing and Management, 36 (2000) 415-444
9. Cordón, O., Herrera-Viedma, E., López-Pujalte, C., Luque, M., Zarco, C.: A review on the application of evolutionary omputation to information retrieval. International Journal of Approximate Reasoning, 34 (2003) 241-264
10. López-Pujalte, C., Guerrero-Bote, V. P., Moya-Anegón, F. D.: Genetic algorithms in relevance feedback: a second test and new contributions. Information Processing and Management, 39 (2003) 669-687
11. Ho, M. H., Cheng, M.C., Chang, Y.S., Yuan, S. M.: A GA-BASED DYNAMIC PERSONALIZED FILTERING FOR INTERNET SEARCH SERVICE ON MULTI-SERACH ENGINE. Canadian Conference on Electrical and Computer Engineering, v 1 (2001) 271-276
12. López-Pujalte, C., Guerrero-Bote, V. P., Moya-Anegón, F. D.: A test of genetic algorithms in relevance feedback. Information Processing and Management, 38 (2002) 793-805
13. Vallim, M. S., Adán-Coello, J. M.: An Agent for Web Information Dissemination Based on a Genetic Algorithm. IEEE 2003
14. Leroy, G., Lally, A. M., Chen, H.: The Use of Dynamic Contexts to Improve Casual Internet Searching. ACM Transactions on Information Systems, 21(3), July (2003) 229–253
15. Martín-Bautista, M. J., Vila, M. A., Sánchez, D., Larsen, H L.: Fuzzy Genes: Improving the Effectiveness of Information Retrieval. IEEE (2000)
16. Trotman, A.: Choosing document structure weights. Information Processing and Management, 41(2), March (2003) 243-264
17. Salton, G., McGill, M.H.: Introduction to Modern Information Retrieval, McGraw-Hill (1983)

18. Baeza-Yates, R., Ribeiro-Neto, B.: Modern information retrieval. Essex, UK: Addison-Wesley (1999)
19. Bruce, K., Chad, B.: The Infofinder Agent: Learning User Interests through Heuristic Phrase Extraction. IEEE EXPERT, 12(5) (1997) 22−27
20. Salton,G., Buckley, C.: Improving retrieval performance by relevance feedback. Journal of the American Society for Information Science, 41(4) (1990) 288-297
21. Horng, J.T., Yeh, C.C.: Applying genetic algorithms to query optimization in document retrieval. Information Processing and Management, 36 (2000) 737-759
22. Eiben, A. E., Smith, J. E.: Introduction to Evolutionary Computing. Published by Springer, Berlin (2003)
23. Liang, T. P., Lai, H. J.: Discovering User Interests from Web Browsing Behavior: An Application to Internet News Services. Proceeding of the 35th Annual Hawaii International Conference on System Sciences (HICSS-35'02) IEEE (2002).

A Diversity Metric for Multi-objective Evolutionary Algorithms

Xu-yong Li, Jin-hua Zheng, and Juan Xue

The College of Information Engineering, Xiangtan University, Xiangtan 411105 China

Abstract. In the research of MOEA (Multi-Objective Evolutionary Algorithm), many algorithms for multi-objective optimization have been proposed. Diversity of the solutions is an important measure, and it is also significant how to evaluate the diversity of an MOEA. In this paper, the clustering algorithm based on the distance between individuals is discussed, and a diversity metric based on clustering is also proposed. Applying this metric, we compare several popular multi-objective evolutionary algorithms. It is shown by experimental results that the method proposed in this paper performs well, especially helps to provide a comparative evaluation of two or more MOEAs.

1 Introduction

In recent years, various Multi-Objective Evolutionary Algorithms (MOEAs) are available, in which different techniques are employed to try to find the best approximations. Therefore, the questions arise of how to evaluate the performance of different MOEAs. The representative metrics can be classified into two groups: some metrics focused on comparing the observed Pareto optimal set with its true Pareto optimal set and others are used to assess the diversity of the observed Pareto optimal set.

There are several techniques being used to assess the diversity of the observed Pareto optimal set. Such as: i) the approach is based on the distance to assess the performance of diversity by calculating the deviation from each solution point to the average distance; ii) the approach based on Shannon's Entropy is implemented by calculating the density function that is the sum of all influence function of its neighborhood. However, the output results are not as good as desired for the existing performance metrics, and some of them may even be misleading for some given problems.

In this paper, a clustering method based on the distance between individuals is discussed. It is shown by experimental results that the method can be correctly used to evaluate the diversity of different MOEAs.

2 The Diversity Metric Based on Clustering

2.1 Algorithm Description

The diversity metric proposed in this paper is based on the clustering: initially we regard every individual in the solution as a subclass. Then choose the two subclasses between which the centroid distance is the minimal, finally combine the two subclass if the centroid distance is smaller than D (D is the comparability of individuals).

The algorithm is presented as follows:

[1] Initialize cluster set C, let every subclass of C include one individual in NDSet:
$$C = \{\{p_1\},\{p_2\},\cdots,\{p_n\}\} \quad p_i \in NDSet \quad i = 1, 2, \cdots, n$$
n is the size of $NDSet$.

The centroid (o_i) of every subclass is the only individual in the subclass.

[2] Calculate the centroid distance between any two subclasses:
$$d(o_i, o_j) = \|o_i - o_j\|, \quad o_i, o_j \in C$$
Where $\|o_i - o_j\|$ is the distance between o_i and o_j.

[3] Choose two new clusters c_i and c_j which have minimal centroid distance in current C: $c_i, c_j : dist = \min\{d(o_i, o_j) | o_i, o_j \in C\}$

[4] If $dist > D$, then jump to [7]; where D is the given parameter.

combine c_i and c_j to cluster c_k: $C = C \setminus \{c_i, c_j\} \cup \{c_i \cup c_j\}$

[5] Find the centroid of subclass c_k:
$$d(p) = \{\sum d(p,q) | p, q \in c_k, p \neq q\}$$
$$o_k = \{p | \min(d(p)), p \in c_k\}$$

[6] Calculate the centroid distance between c_k ($c_k = c_i \cup c_j$) and any other subclass of C: $d(o_k, o_l) = \|o_k - o_l\|$
where o_k, o_l is the centroid of c_k and c_l respectively, $c_k, c_l \in C$ and $c_k \neq c_l$. Then go to [3].

[7] Calculate the number of the subclasses of C, then the diversity equals to the number divided by the size of NDSet, End

From the analysis of above paragraphs, we know the maximum diversity achievable is 1.000 and the larger the diversity measure the better is the distribution.

2.2 Parameter Setting

The value of D proposed in step 4 is given beforehand. Ideally, if the distance between the individuals in solution is almost the same, we choose the distance between the individuals as the value of D, which means the ideal condition. A too small value of D will make any distribution to have the maximum diversity measure of 1.000, whereas a very large value of D will make every distribution to have a small diversity measure. So we apply this method to get the value of D: first we choose the solution of the evolutionary algorithms that need to be evaluated, then for every algorithms' solution, we calculate the minimal distance between the individuals and choose the biggest one from the those minimal distance values as the value of D.

But the convergence of every algorithm is different, if directly calculating the minimal distance of the individuals, the minimal distance of the poor convergent algorithm must be bigger, and it will affect the choice of D. So we should project Pareto-optimal solutions on a suitable reference plane before calculating the minimal distance of the individuals, and at the same time keep the distribution of the solution.

If the true Pareto optimal front of the test problem is known, we consider the true Pareto optimal front as the reference plane; if it is unknown, we choose the suitable plane that is parallel with the solution plane as the reference plane. For example, the figure 1 illustrates the solution of SPEA2, and figure 2 illustrates the projective solution of SPEA2. (The three-objective test problem is DTLZ1, and the true Pareto optimal front is x+y+z=1).

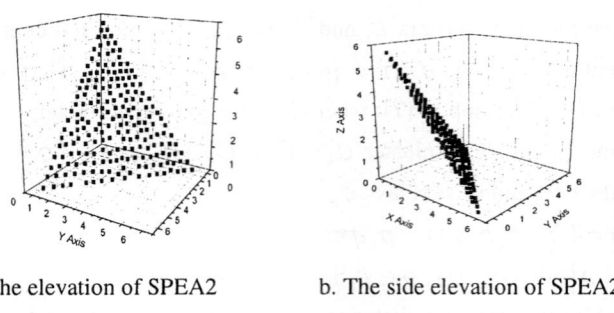

a. The elevation of SPEA2　　　　b. The side elevation of SPEA2

Fig. 1. The solution of SPEA2 on DTLZ1

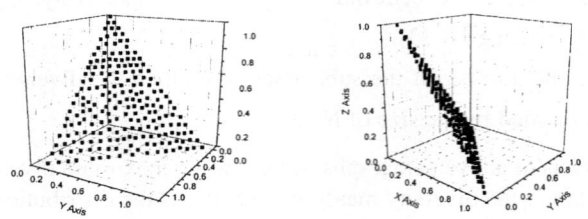

a. The elevation of projected SPEA2　　　b. The side elevation of projected SPEA2

Fig. 2. The projected solution of SPEA2 on DTLZ1

From Figure 1 with Figure 2, the solution of SPEA2 is projected on the reference plane (x+y+z=1) , but the distribution of the solution is almost unchanged.

3 Experiment

We apply the evaluation method proposed in this paper to evaluate the popular algorithms PESA2[1], NSGA2[2] and SPEA2[6].

We test our method with two test problems that presented by Deb [3]: DLTZ1 and DLTZ3. In DLTZ1, the objective function values lie on the linear hyper-plane. The difficulty in DLTZ1 is to converge to the hyper-plane. The search space contains (11^k-1) local Pareto optimal fronts, and each of which can attract the search procedure of a MOGA. In DLTZ3, there are (3^k-1) local Pareto optimal fronts and one global Pareto optimal front in the search space, and all local Pareto optimal fronts are parallel to the global Pareto optimal front.

3.1 Experimental Parameter

Table 1 shows the parameters of algorithms for 2, 3, 4, 6 and 8 objectives:

Table 1. Parameter setting scheme

Objectives (M)	2	3	4	6	8
Population size	200	200	250	300	500
Generations	200	250	300	400	600

Crossover probability: 0.8
Mutation probability: $1/len$, where len is the length of the chromosome.
Selection: Tournament selection

3.2 Experimental Results

We use the metric proposed in this paper to compare three algorithms in diversity.

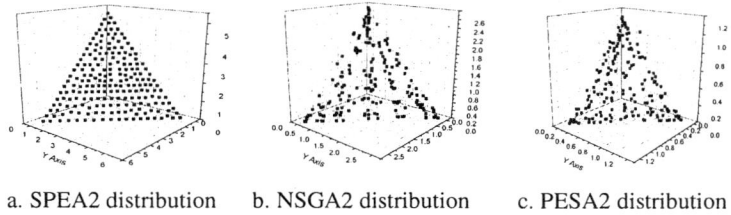

a. SPEA2 distribution   b. NSGA2 distribution   c. PESA2 distribution

Fig. 3. Three algorithms distribution for the three-objective DTLZ1

Obviously Figure 3 and Figure 4 show that SPEA2 attains the best distribution, followed by NSGA2 and then PESA2. The experimental results of Table 2 and Table 3 show the performance metric based on clustering can correctly evaluate the diversity of three algorithms. But the results of Deb's metric show the diversity of SPEA2 is worse than NSAG2 on highly dimensional objective space (3,4,6,8) of test problems.

Compared with the metric for diversity presented by Deb [4], the metric based on clustering can evaluate the evolutionary algorithms exactly.

Table 2. Diversity on DTLZ1

M	Diversity metric of clustering			Diversity metric of Deb		
	SPEA2	NSGA2	PESA2	SPEA2	NSGA2	PESA2
2	0.99550	0.75240	0.72550	0.92641	0.75362	0.83630
3	0.97560	0.49750	0.51743	0.59491	0.69837	0.59746
4	0.98720	0.44297	0.47100	0.49025	0.60297	0.50100
6	0.94336	0.37207	0.40503	0.50439	0.51207	0.55503
8	0.99470	0.45756	0.40432	0.41504	0.59653	0.33964

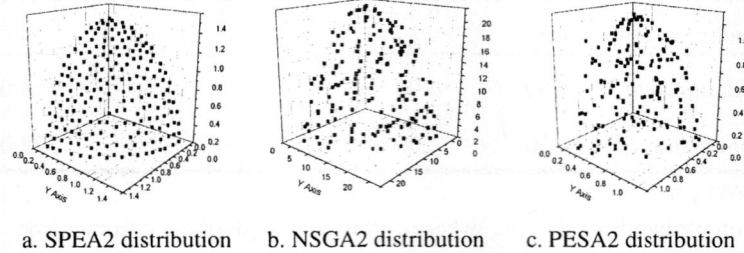

a. SPEA2 distribution   b. NSGA2 distribution   c. PESA2 distribution

Fig. 4. Three algorithms distribution for the three-objective DTLZ3

Table 3. Diversity on DTLZ3

M	Diversity metric of clustering			Diversity metric of Deb		
	SPEA2	NSGA2	PESA2	SPEA2	NSGA2	PESA2
2	0.97240	0.74650	0.73240	0.81368	0.74303	0.76550
3	0.99845	0.49532	0.47546	0.62813	0.72467	0.54601
4	0.98148	0.40454	0.48274	0.59034	0.69712	0.53318
6	0.96529	0.36007	0.44563	0.51595	0.47534	0.40752
8	0.96354	0.49843	0.43164	0.45580	0.51287	0.47165

4 Conclusion

With the development of evolutionary algorithms, many multi-objective algorithms are proposed, but there are not recognized performance metrics that can correctly evaluate the diversity of algorithms. In this paper, we proposed the metric based on clustering. It is proved by experiments that the method can evaluate the diversity of algorithms more exactly, but the method can only be used to compare the algorithms and not to evaluate one separate algorithm.

References

1. Corne, D.W., Jerram, N.R., Knowles, J.D., and Oates, M.J.: PESA-II: Region-based Selection in Evolutionary Multi-objective Optimization. In Proceedings of the Genetic and Evolutionary Computation Conference (GECCO-2001).(2001) 283-290.
2. Deb K., Agrawal S., Pratap A., & Meyarivan T.: A Fast Elitist Non-Dominated Sorting Genetic Algorithm for Multi-Objective Optimization: NSGA-II. KanGAL Report No. 200001(2000).
3. K. Deb, L. Thiele, M. Laumanns, and E. Zitzler.: Scalable Test Problems for Evolutionary Multi-Objective Optimization. KanGAL Report No. 2001001(2001).
4. K. Deb and Sachin Jain.: Running Performance Metrics for Evolutionary Multi-Objective Optimization. KanGAL Report No. 2002004(2002)
5. K. Deb, Mohan, M. and Mishra, S.: A Fast Multi-objective Evolutionary Algorithm for Finding Well-Spread Pareto-Optimal Solutions. KanGAL Report No. 2003002 (2003).
6. E. Zitzler., M. Laumanns, and L. Thiele.: SPEA2: Improving the Strength Pareto Evolutionary Algorithm for Multiobjective Optimization. EUROGEN 2001 - Evolutionary Methods for Design, Optimisation and Control with Applications to Industrial Problems, September 2001.
7. ZHENG jin-hua, SHI zhong-zhi, XIE yong.: A Fast Multi-objective Genetic Algorithm Based on Clustering .Journal of computer research and development(Chinese).(2004)

An Immune Partheno-Genetic Algorithm for Winner Determination in Combinatorial Auctions

JianCong Bai, HuiYou Chang, and Yang Yi

Department of Computer Science, Sun Yat-sen University, GuangZhou, 510275, PRC
bjcsnake@yahoo.com.cn

Abstract. Combinatorial auctions are efficient mechanisms for allocating resource in complex marketplace. Winner determination, which is NP-complete, is the core problem in combinatorial auctions. This paper proposes an immune partheno-genetic algorithm (IPGA) for solving this problem. Firstly, a zero-one programming model is built for the winner determination problem with XOR-bids and OR-bids. Then, steps of constructing three partheno-genetic operators and an immune operator are introduced. In the immune operation, new heuristics are designed for vaccines selection and vaccination. Simulation results show that the IPGA achieves good performance in large size problems and the immune operator can improve the searching ability and increase the converging speed greatly.

1 Introduction

Auctions are dynamic and efficient mechanisms for allocating items (goods, resources, services, etc.) in complex marketplace. And they provide a foundation for mediation and brokering in a variety of task and resource allocation problems, for example, bandwidth auctions, auctions for take-off and landing slots in an airport, purchase and supply management and so on [1], [2], [3]. With the popularity of e-Business continuing to rise, auctions become new ways for fully automated electronic negotiation in multiple parties. Combinatorial auctions allow that bidders can bid on combinations of items in multi-item auctions. However, basic combinatorial auctions may generate inefficient allocations of resources when bidders demand bundles of complementary resource, i.e. "I want A or B either, but I don't want A and B both". So, XOR-bids and OR-bids are added in combinatorial auctions to help bidders expressing their general preference more exactly [4], [5]. XOR-Bids and OR-Bids allow bidders to submit additive or exclusive bids over collection of combinations. In the former case, the bidder can express his preference exactly by submitting XOR-bids as "(A) XOR (B)".

In combinatorial auctions, finding the revenue maximizing set of winning bids is the first difficult challenge, called winner determination problem (WDP). And it is well known that the WDP is a complex computational problem and NP-complete [6]. Much of recent research on solving the WDP has been carried out by different approaches such as optimization, intelligent search and heuristics [7]. Sandholm developed Branch-on-Items and Branch-on-Bids algorithms for solving the WDP and gained significant popularity [5], [8]. Mito and Fujita proposed three heuristic bid-ordering schemes for solving the WDP [9]. Leyton-Brown, Shoham and Tennenholtz researched and developed a method for the WDP in multi-unit combinatorial auctions [10]. Gonen and Lehmann also applied the branch-and-bound procedure to solve the WDP as an IP problem in multi-unit combinatorial auctions [11].

For solving the WDP, we propose an immune partheno-genetic algorithm (IPGA). The IPGA is a genetic algorithm that has three partheno-genetic operators [12] and an immune operator [13], [14]. The IPGA repeals crossover operators and implements the functions of crossover and mutation by partheno-genetic operators. The immune operator is based on the theory of immunity in biology. And it operates as injecting the good vaccine into a solution and remove the bad one, so as to improve the revenue. It can increase the converging speed and make the improvement of the searching ability.

In this paper, Section 2 describes the WDP with XOR-bids and OR-bids. Section 3 introduces our algorithm IPGA in detail, including steps of constructing three partheno-genetic operators, procedure of vaccine selection and vaccination, heuristics for evaluating the bids to be good or not. In section 4, we test our algorithm in execution time, the percentage of producing the optimal solution and the least generations of finding the optimal solution. Finally, we present our conclusions.

2 Problem Description

Let $M = \{1, 2, ..., m\}$ be the set of items to be auctioned, and $A = \{1, 2, ..., n\}$ be the set of bidders to participate in the combinatorial auction. Each bidder i can submit XOR-bids or OR-bids but can't submit XOR-bids and OR-bids at the same time. XOR-bids and OR-bids are both a set of bids, as $B_i^{type} = \{b_i^1, ..., b_i^j\}$. Let $|B_i^{type}|$ be the number of bids in B_i^{type}. XOR-bids allow no more than one of the bids in XOR-bids to be accepted. OR-bids allow one or more of the bids in OR-bids to be accepted. For example, $B_i^{XOR} = \{b_i^1, b_i^2, b_i^3\}$ indicates that bidder i wants at most one of b_i^1, b_i^2, b_i^3 to be won. And $B_i^{OR} = \{b_i^1, b_i^2, b_i^3\}$ indicates that bidder i wants one or more, even all of them to be won. Bid b_i^j is a tuple, $b_i^j = (s_i^j, p_i^j)$, and indicates bidder i offer price p_i^j for item combination s_i^j.

Assume that there is one seller (or several sellers acting in concert) and multiple bidders, and only one unit of each item is available in the auction. The objective is to maximize the seller's revenue. The model of WDP with XOR-Bids and OR-bids is as follows:

$$\text{WDP: } \max \sum_{i=1}^{n} \sum_{j=1}^{|B_i^{type}|} p_i^j x_i^j \tag{1}$$

$$\text{s.t. } \forall k \in M : \sum_{s_i^j | k \in s_i^j} x_i^j \leq 1 \tag{2}$$

$$\sum_{j=1}^{|B_i^{type}|} x_i^j \leq 1 \quad type = XOR, \ i = 1, 2, \ldots, n \tag{3}$$

$$x_i^j = 0, 1 \quad i = 1, 2, \ldots, n, \ j = 1, 2, \ldots, |B_i^{type}| \tag{4}$$

Because single unit of each item is available, to any item k, only one bid can be won in all bids that contain item k. Therefore, Equation (2) ensures that each item will be allocated no more than once. Equation (3) ensures that no more than one bid in XOR-Bids can be won.

3 Immune Partheno-Genetic Algorithm

The WDP is a combinatorial optimization problem. And genetic algorithm (GA) is capable of solving combination optimization problems, such as traveling salesman problem, flow-shop problem and so on [15], [16]. In combinatorial optimization problems, GA often uses ordinal strings, and that make the implementation intuitionistic and convenient. But the crossover operation for ordinal strings is complex, GA has to use special crossover operators such as PMX, OX and CX [17], instead of general crossover operators, and that may cause immature convergence phenomenon. Therefore, a partheno-genetic algorithm (PGA) is proposed, and it use partheno-genetic algorithm operators to implement the function of crossover and mutation, and restrain the immature convergence phenomenon. In our algorithm IPGA, there are three particular partheno-genetic operators: SWAP, REVERSE, INSERT [18]. These partheno-genetic operators are easy to be carried out and they don't require the initial population to be varied.

In a complicated problem, there are many basic and obvious characteristics or knowledge. However, in basic GA, crossover and mutation operators usually lack the capability of utilizing these characteristics and knowledge. When using the PGA for solving the WDP, partheno-genetic operators may neglect the assistant function of these characteristics or knowledge. And the loss due to the negligence is sometimes considerable. Therefore we add an immune operator in our algorithm, and then the PGA becomes the IPGA. The immune operator utilizes the information of bids for seeking the ways or patterns of finding the optimal solution. By using the immune operator, the IPGA refrains the degenerative phenomena arising from the evolutionary process, improves the searching ability, and increases the converging speed greatly.

Before the main algorithm IPGA running, all bids should be preprocessed to find out noncompetitive bids and noncompetitive tuples of bids. Noncompetitive bids will be discarded directly and noncompetitive tuples of bids will be excluded in the searching process. We preprocess XOR-bids and OR-bids with particular methods, which were also develop by us [18].

To convenience the implementation, we use dummy bids [5] to make sure that each allocation includes all items. When an allocation includes a dummy bid that indicates the auctioneer keep the item from the dummy bid.

3.1 Chromosome Generation

In the IPGA, the natural number string is used as the gene representation. A chromosome represents an allocation. The length of chromosome is alterable. The fitness is the sum price of the bids in the allocation.

After preprocessing, number all survival bids and let B_{sur} be the set of the survival bids except dummy bids, $B_{sur} = \{b_1, b_2, \ldots \ldots b_n\}$. Let M be the set of all items, U be the set of allocated items and X be the set of bids in an allocation. The procedure of chromosome generation is as follows:

Step 1. Generate a random sequence Q on B_{sur}.

Step 2. Take the first bid b_{head} from Q; add b_{head} into X and add the items of b_{head} into U.

Step 3. If it comes to the end of Q, go to **Step6**; otherwise take the next bid b_{next} from Q in turn.

Step 4. If b_{next} doesn't meet equations (2) and (3) in the WDP model, go to **Step3**; else continue.

Step 5. Add the bid b_{next} into X and add the items of b_{next} into U. if U equals M, go to **Step 7**, else go to **Step3**.

Step 6. If U doesn't equal M, add the dummy bids into X until U equals M, which only contains the unallocated items; else continue.

Step 7. Output X as a chromosome.

3.2 Partheno-Genetic Operators

In genetic operation, three partheno-genetic operators work on Q. They change the order of bids in Q and generate the new chromosome from the new Q. When the length of Q is long, these partheno-genetic operators need to work on Q multiple times. The procedures of three partheno-genetic operators are stated as follows.

- **SWAP Operator**

    Step 1. Select two bids from Q randomly.

    Step 2. Swap the position of these two bids and generate a new array Q'.

    Step 3. Generate a new chromosome from Q'.

- **REVERSE Operator**

    Step 1. Select a sub-array from Q randomly.

    Step 2. Reverse the positions of these bids in the sub-array and generate a new array Q'.

    Step 3. Generate a new chromosome from Q'.

- **INSERT Operator**
  Step 1. Select a sub-array from Q randomly.
  Step 2. Move the last bid in the sub-array to the head position of this sub-array, and shift all other bids in the sub-array backwards, and generate a new array Q'.
  Step 3. Generate a new chromosome from Q'.

  For example, $Q = (b_3, b_1, b_5, b_2, b_6, b_4)$, random positions in Q are 2 and 5. In SWAP operator, new array $Q' = (b_3, b_6, b_5, b_2, b_1, b_4)$; In RRVERSE operator, new array $Q' = (b_3, b_6, b_2, b_5, b_1, b_4)$; In INSERT operator, new array $Q' = (b_3, b_6, b_1, b_5, b_2, b_4)$.

3.3 Heuristics for Bids Evaluation

In chromosome generation, bids in Q are selected one by one, so the order of bids decides the probability that a bid may be accepted in an allocation. The bid in the front of Q has more chance than the bid in the back. To find out the optimal allocation, intuitively, good bids should be placed in the front of Q, and bad bids should be moved backward. Price is a direct way for evaluating the bid to be good or not. In practice, the bid with high price often has many items, which may destroy many other bids' opportunity. So, we developed some new heuristics for evaluating the bids.

Heuristic h_{bavg} Bid's average contribution: the price of the bid divided by the number of the items in that bid. Formally,

$$h_{bavg}(b_i^j) = \frac{p_i^j}{|s_i^j|} \qquad (5)$$

Heuristic h_{iavg} Item's average contribution: the average of all the bids' h_{bavg}, which involves the item. Formally,

$$h_{iavg}(k) = \frac{\sum_{k \in s_i^j} h_{bavg}(b_i^j)}{|\{b_i^j | k \in s_i^j\}|} \qquad (6)$$

Heuristic h_{imax} Item's maximal contribution: the maximum of all the bids' h_{bavg}, which involves the item. Formally,

$$h_{i\max}(k) = \max\{h_{bavg}(b_i^j) | k \in s_i^j\} \qquad (7)$$

Heuristic h_{nh} Within a bid, the number of particular items that have their h_{iavg} less than the h_{bavg} of the bid, formally,

$$h_{nh}(b_i^j) = |\{k | h_{bavg}(b_i^j) > h_{iavg}(k), k \in s_i^j\}| \qquad (8)$$

Heuristic h_{nl} Within a bid, the number of particular items that have their h_{iavg} greater than the h_{bavg} of the bid, formally,

$$h_{nl}(b_i^j) = \left|\{k \mid h_{bavg}(b_i^j) < h_{iavg}(k), k \in s_i^j\}\right| \tag{9}$$

Heuristic h_{nm} Within a bid, the number of particular items that have their h_{imax} equal the h_{bavg} of the bid, formally,

$$h_{nm}(b_i^j) = \left|\{k \mid h_{bavg}(b_i^j) = h_{i\max}(k), k \in s_i^j\}\right| \tag{10}$$

When b_i^j contain item k and $h_{bavg}(b_i^j) > h_{iavg}(k)$, that indicates bid b_i^j can contribute more revenue than average on item k, then item k in bid b_i^j is a good item. If $h_{bavg}(b_i^j) < h_{iavg}(k)$, that indicates item k in bid b_i^j is a bad one. When a bid contains more good items, we evaluated the bid better. In the same way, we evaluate the bid worse when it contains more bad items. We don't evaluate the bid by the price but the number of good items and bad items. Obviously, heuristics h_{nl}, h_{nh} and h_{nm} show the number of good items and bad items of each bid. Therefore, they are key functions for evaluating bids and applied in the immune operator.

3.4 Immune Operator

In the IPGA, an immune operator is composed of two operations: vaccination and immune test. These two operations base on reasonable selecting vaccines. The operation of selecting vaccines is selecting the good bids as vaccines from all preprocessed bids. The operation of vaccination is injecting vaccines into the individuals for raising the fitness; and that of immune test is testing the effect of vaccination for preventing the deterioration.

- **Selecting Vaccine**

After preprocessing, vaccines are selected in survival bids except dummy bids. And each item has its own vaccine list. A bid can be selected as a vaccine as long as it satisfies one of these two conditions: 1) $h_{nm} > 0$; 2) the value of h_{nh} divided by the number of items in that bid is greater than 0.8. When a bid is selected as a vaccine, it will be added in all its items' vaccine list. For example, bids [({1, 2}, $5)] and [({2, 3}, $6)] are selected as vaccines, then they will be added in item 1, 2, 3's vaccine lists.

- **Vaccination**

The operation of vaccination is removing the worst bid from current allocation and accepting the corresponding bid (vaccine), then generating a better allocation. After preprocessing, let B_{sur} be the set of all survival bids except dummy bids, X be the current allocation, Q be the random array on B_{sur}, F be the set of unallocated items, and set F empty initially. The procedure of vaccination is as follows:

Step 1. Calculate h_{nl} for all bids in X.

Step 2. If all bids' h_{nl} equal zero, exit; otherwise select the bid with max h_{nl} as the worst bid b_{wst} (if multiple bids have the same max h_{nl}, select the one with lowest price).

Step 3. Remove b_{wst} and all dummy bids from X; add their items into F.

Step 4. Search in all unallocated items' vaccine lists for finding the bids that meet equations (2) and (3) in the WDP model. In these bids, select the bid with max h_{bavg} as the best bid b_{bst}.

Step 5. If b_{bst} exists, swap b_{bst} and b_{wst} in Q; else move b_{wst} to the end of Q.

Step 6. Generate a new allocation from the new Q, and output it as a vaccinated chromosome.

If the bids' order in Q is changed too much, the new allocation may be much different from the old one, and that may destroy the effect of vaccination. So we only select one bid as the worst bid and one bid as the best bid in vaccination. When the problem size is large, the worst bid b_{wst} often use up many items. The operation of removing b_{wst} and dummy bids from the current allocation will release the opportunities for other bids, which are behind b_{wst} in Q. After swapping b_{bst} and b_{wst} in Q, a new allocation is generated from the new Q. Because b_{wst} is removed, b_{bst} and other bids are accepted, the new allocation has great chance to obtain more revenue and has more probability to be the optimal allocation. If b_{bst} can't be found out, the operation, moving b_{wst} to the end of Q, equals removing b_{wst} from the current allocation and give chances to other bids. The operations of vaccination reflect the criterion of our strategy: Good bids should have more chance to be accepted in the allocation than bad bids.

- **Immune Tests**

After vaccination, the vaccinated chromosome needs immune test. If the fitness of the vaccinated chromosome is smaller than that of the original one, which means that degeneration has happened in the process of vaccination, instead of the vaccinated chromosome, the unvaccinated chromosome will participate in the next competition.

3.5 Immune Partheno-Genetic Algorithm Procedure

After all works have been introduced as above, the procedure of the IPGA for the WDP is as follows:

Step 1. Set the global parameter: the number of generations NG, the size of population size PS, probabilities of three partheno-genetic operators P_s, P_r and P_i, the probability of vaccination P_v.

Step 2. Preprocess all bids.

Step 3. Construct vaccine lists on each item.

Step 4. Produce initial random population.

Step 5. If the stopping criterion is satisfied, go to **Step9**; else continue.

Step 6. Perform three partheno-genetic operations on the kth generation A_k and obtain the results B_k.

Step 7. Perform vaccination and immune test on B_k and obtain the results C_k.

Step 8. Perform the roulette wheel proportional selection and quintessence selecting strategy on C_k, and obtain the next generation A_{k+1}, then go to **Step5**.

Step 9. Output the solution and stop.

There are two stop criterions: 1) stopping at the maximum number of generations; 2) the best fitness keeping no change in specific generations. The quintessence selecting strategy is that replace the random one chromosome in current generation by the best one in the pre-generation.

4 Experimental Results

To determine the efficiency of the algorithm, we run experiments on a general-purpose PC (CPU: 2.4GHZ Pentium IV; Memory: 1024MB; OS: Windows 2000). The algorithm is programmed in C language and run on Random bid distributions: For each bid, pick the number of items randomly from 1, 2, ..., m. Randomly choose that many items without replacement. Pick a random integer price from [1, 1000]. When all the bids are produced, we assign them to the bidders randomly and set bidders submitting XOR-bids or OR-bids randomly. The bidders can bid any item combination. Same bids cannot belong to the same bidder. XOR-bids must contain at least two bids.

In the following experiments, the comparison of execution time between the IPGA and the BOI+ algorithm shows how fast the IPGA is in large size problems. And we compare the percentage of producing the optimal solution between the IPGA and the PGA, and show the effect of the immune operator. At last, some instance results show the setting of global parameters in the IPGA. The BOI+ algorithm is derived form the algorithm BOI presented by Sandholm [5], and it use a different heuristic $h(F)$, which is also designed by Sandholm [8]. Using this heuristic, the BOI+ algorithm can get more accurate upper bound on the optimal revenue and search faster.

4.1 Execution Time

The BOI+ algorithm seeks the optimal solution in a tree [5] and doesn't stop until it finishes searching the whole tree. The execution time of it relies on the number of nodes in the tree. When the problem size becomes large, the number of nodes will increase explosively. Although using the heuristic can prune great many nodes in the tree, the execution time of the BOI+ algorithm still increase greatly.

Fig. 1 shows that in the small or middle problem size, the searching speeds of the BOI+ algorithm and the IPGA are differential not very. When the problem size becomes large, the execution time of the BOI+ algorithm increases greatly and nonlinearly. However the execution time of the IPGA increase steadily and almost linearly. Each point in the Fig 1 represents an average over 10 problem instances.

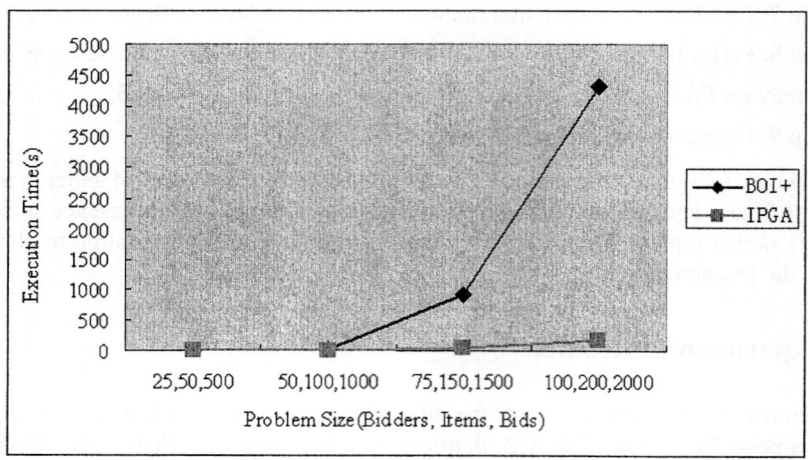

Fig. 1. Execution time of BOI+ and IPGA

4.2 Best Rate and Best Generation

In Fig.2 and Fig.3, the best rate means the percentage of producing the optimal solution. And the best rate of each problem instance is test by 100 running with different random seeds. The value of the best rate in histogram is an average over 10 problem instances. The best generation means the least generations of finding the optimal solution. And the value of best generation in histogram is also an average over 10 problem instances.

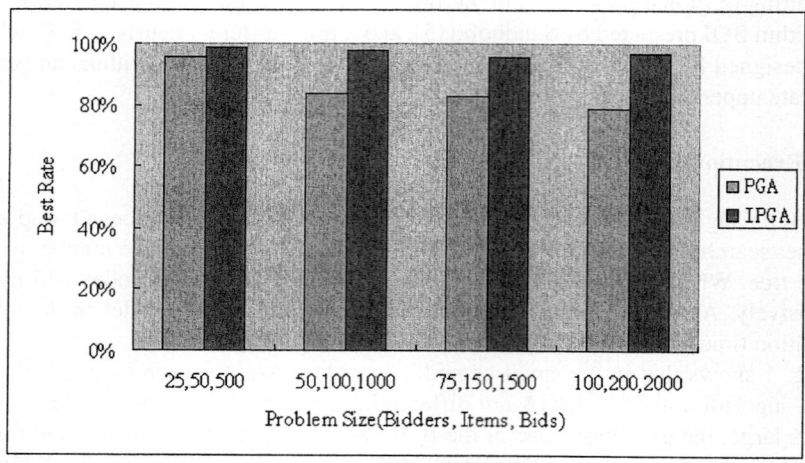

Fig. 2. Best rate of PGA and IPGA

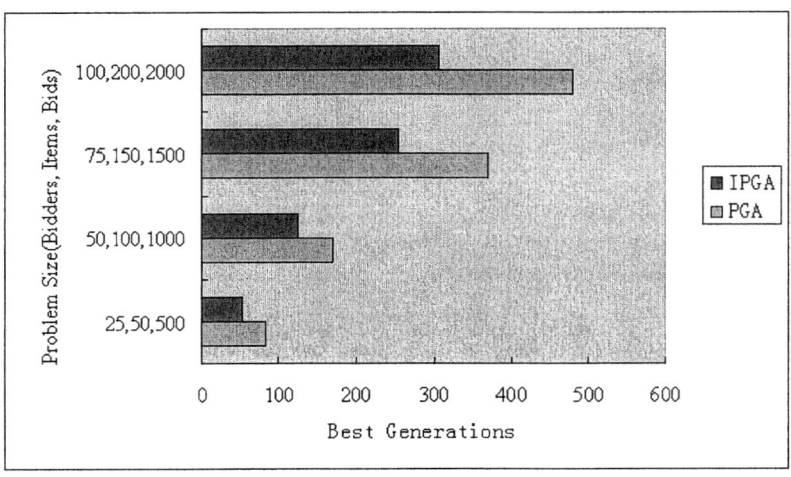

Fig. 3. Best generation of PGA and IPGA

Fig.2 shows that the immune operator improves the percentage of producing optimal solution efficiently. In the four kinds of different size problems, the best rate of the IPGA is higher 13%~18% than that of the PGA. In the four kinds of different size problems, the best rates of the IPGA are all higher than 95%.

Fig.3 shows that the IPGA find the optimal solution earlier than the PGA. In the four kinds of different size problems, the best generation of the IPGA is less 26%~37% than that of the PGA.

4.3 Parameters Setting

Table 1 shows different parameters setting in the IPGA for different problem sizes. For achieving high percentage of producing optimal solution in large size problems, we can enlarge the size of initial population, enhance the probabilities of INSERT operator and REVERSE operator, and the probability of the vaccination.

Table 1. Some instance results of IPGA

Problem Size	Parameters $PS/NG/P_r/P_i/P_s/P_v$	MAX Revenue	Average Revenue	Time (s)	Best Rate
25/50/500	50/1000/0.3/0.3/0.2/0.3	11684	11684	1.3	100%
50/100/1000	100/1000/0.3/0.3/0.2/0.3	18934	18931	8.6	99%
50/400/1000	300/4000/0.5/0.5/0.3/0.4	8957	8953	158	98%
75/150/1500	200/2000/0.4/0.4/0.2/0.3	22237	22235	49	96%
100/200/2000	300/4000/0.5/0.5/0.3/0.4	19010	19008	185	99%

5 Conclusion and Analysis

In this paper, we study the winner determination problem with XOR-bids and OR-bids in combinatorial auctions, and propose the immune partheno-genetic algorithm for solving the WDP. The IPGA has the advantage of GA, partheno-genetic operator and immune operator. The IPGA has the GA's characteristics of easier application, greater robustness, and better parallel processing than many classical methods of optimization. Using partheno-genetic operators, the IPGA avoid the complicated crossover operation and restrains the immature convergence phenomenon. Using the immune operator, the IPGA is capable of alleviating the degeneration phenomenon and greatly increasing the converging speed. Genetic operations of IPGA are simple and don't require their initial population to be varied. Different from heuristics in [5], [8], [19], we develop three new heuristics h_{nh}, h_{nl}, h_{nm} for evaluating the bids and apply them in vaccine selection and vaccination. With these heuristics, the IPGA utilizes the assistant function of the prior knowledge. It is well known that the WDP can be formulated as a multi-dimensional knapsack problem (MDKP) [7], [19]. In the further, we will try to apply the IPGA for the MDKP and make more research on that.

Acknowledgement

The authors would like to thank the referees for useful comments, which help to improve the paper. This paper is partially supported by National Science Foundation of GuangDong Province (031539) of People's Republic of China and GuangZhou High-Tech Program (TJ-rERP (GK0204105-2)).

References

1. McAfee, R.P. and McMillan, J.: Analyzing the airwaves auction. Journal Economic Perspectives, 1996, 10 (1): 159-175
2. Rassenti, S.J., Smith, V.L., Bulfin, R.L. A combinatorial auction mechanism for airport time slot allocation. Bell Journal of Economics, 1982, 13: 402-417
3. Hartley, J.L., Lane, M.D., Hong, Y. An exploration of the adoption of e-auctions in supply management. Engineering Management, IEEE Transactions on, 2004, 51 (2): 153-161
4. Parkes, D.C.: iBundle: An Efficient Ascending Price Bundle Auction. ACM Conference on Electronic Commence (EC99), 1999, 148-157
5. Sandholm, T.: Algorithm for optimal winner determination in combinatorial auctions. Artificial Intelligence, 2002, 135(1-2): 1-54
6. Rothkopf, M.H., Pekec, A., Harstad, R.M.: Computationally manageable combinatorial auctions. Management Science, 1998, 44(8): 1131-1147
7. Xia, M., Koehler, G.J., Whinston, A.B.: Pricing combinatorial auctions. European Journal of Operational Research, 2004, 154(1): 251-270
8. Sandholmm, T., Suri, S.: BOB: Improved winner determination in combinatorial auctions and generalizations. Artificial Intelligence, 2003, 145(1-2): 33-58
9. Mito, M., Fujita, S.: On heuristics for solving winner determination problem in combinatorial auctions. Proceedings of IAT2003, 2003: 25-31

10. Leyton-Brown, K., Tennenholtz, M., Shoham, Y.: An algorithm for multi-unit combinatorial auctions. Proceedings of the National Conference on Artificial Intelligence (AAAI), Austin, TX, 2000.
11. Gonen, R., Lehmann, D.: Optimal Solutions for Multi-Unit Combinatorial Auctions: Branch and Bound Heuristics. Proceedings of the 2nd ACM conference on electronic commerce, 2000
12. Li, M.J., Tong, T.S.: A partheno-genetic algorithm and analysis on its global convergence. ACTA AUTOMATICA SINICA, 1999, 25(1): 68-72
13. Jiao, L.C., Wang, L.: A novel genetic algorithm based on immunity. Systems, Man and Cybernetics, Part A, IEEE Transactions on, 2000, 30(5): 552-561
14. Wang, L., Pan, J., Jiao, L.C.: The immune programming. Chinese Journal of Computers (in Chinese), 2000, 23(8): 806-812
15. Li, M.J., Tong, T.S.: An improved partheno-genetic algorithm for traveling salesman problem. Proceedings of the 4th World Congress on Intelligent Control and Automation, 2002, 4: 3000-3004
16. Li, S.G., Wu, Z.M., Pang, X.H.: Hybrid partheno-genetic algorithm and its application in flow-shop problem. Journal of Systems Engineering and Electronics, 2004, 15(1): 19-24
17. Larranaga, P., Kuijpers, C.M.H., Murga, R.H., Yurramendi, Y.: Learning Bayesian network structures by searching for the best ordering with genetic algorithms. Systems, Man and Cybernetics, Part A, IEEE Transactions on, 1996, 26(4): 487-493
18. Bai, J.C., Chang, H.Y., Yi, Y.: A partheno-genetic algorithm for optimal winner determination in combinatorial auctions. Proceedings of 2004 International Conference on Machine Learning and Cybernetics, 2004, 1: 553-557
19. Nandy, M., A Mahanti, A.: An improved search technique for optimal winner determination in combinatorial auctions. Proceedings of the 37th Annual Hawaii International Conference, 2004: 63-72

A Novel Genetic Algorithm Based on Cure Mechanism of Traditional Chinese Medicine

Chao-Xue Wang, Du-Wu Cui, Lei Wang, and Zhu-Rong Wang

School of Computer Science and Engineering,
Xi'an University of Technology, Xi'an 710048, China
Wbllw@126.com, cuidw@xaut.edu.cn

Abstract. Enlightened by traditional Chinese medicine theory, a novel genetic algorithm (CMGA), which applies two types of treatment methods of "bu" and "xie" and dialectical treatment principle of traditional Chinese medicine theory to canonical GA, is proposed. The core of CMGA lies on constructing a cure operator, which is dynamically assembled with "bu" operation that replaces normal genes with eugenic genes and "xie" operation that replaces abnormal genes with normal genes. The main idea underlying CMGA is to give full play to the role of guidance function of knowledge to the evolutionary process through the cure operator. The simulation test of TSP shows that CMGA can restrain the degeneration and premature convergence phenomenon effectively during the evolutionary process while greatly increasing the convergence speed.

1 Introduction

In genetic algorithm (GA), because crossover and mutation operator search for new individuals randomly during the whole process, there exists the degeneration of offspring unavoidably, and the searching led by selection operator is comparatively slow and is often trapped in the local optimal area. Therefore canonical GA has the phenomena of low converging speed, being premature readily. One of the reasons causing such shortage is that canonical GA neglects the assistant function of knowledge as its universality. According to the NFL theory [1], if GA is guided by the related knowledge the matching between GA and the problem will be closer, then the performance of GA can be surely improved [2,3,4].

It is a perpetual theme in the research field of evolutionary algorithms and even intelligent computation to get inspiration from life sciences, and both the immune algorithm and the neural network from Western medicine are successful examples. While the traditional Chinese medicine, which is as important as the Western medicine, has a different theory, it should also be helpful to this research.

Inspired by traditional Chinese medicine theory, a novel genetic algorithm (CMGA) is introduced. The core of CMGA lies on constructing a cure operator, which consists of "bu" operation that replaces normal genes with eugenic genes and "xie" operation that replaces abnormal genes with normal genes. This algorithm's contents and the cure operator's construction and mechanism are introduced. To validate CMGA, simulation tests of TSP are performed. Lastly conclusions are given.

2 A Novel Genetic Algorithm Based on Cure Mechanism of Traditional Chinese Medicine

The fitness of individuals in GA can be considered as the index of health in iatrology, by which the higher fitness values indicate the strong and the lower fitness values indicate the weak. The process of population evolution in GA is similar to the process of the on-going improvement of human being's health condition. The treatment methods and mechanism adopted by human being to improve health level enlighten us to employ the similar ones to improve the fitness of the individuals in GA.

According to traditional Chinese medicine theory, treatment should combine "bu" with "xie". The "bu" is to supply the lacking nutritional ingredient, while the "xie" is to clear the harmful materials [5]. But they are not completely separate, and they often involve each other. When a doctor makes a therapeutic schedule, the orders, times, proportions and contents of the "bu" and "xie" should be arrange according to the principle of differentiation of symptoms and signs. Only used appropriately, can they achieve the goal of curing diseases and increasing people's health level.

Based on the consideration above, a novel genetic algorithm based on cure mechanism of traditional Chinese medicine (CMGA) is presented. Its flowchart is shown in Fig.1. The concepts involved in CMGA can be defined as follows.

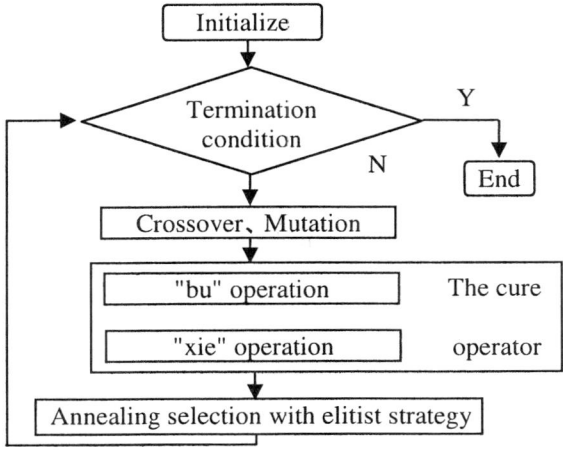

Fig. 1. The flow chart of CMGA

Definition 1. Eugenic genes: the genes or chromosomal fragment to be included in the global optimal individual at a higher probability that can be viewed as a pattern with a comparative higher fitness.

Definition 2. Abnormal genes: the genes or chromosomal fragment to be impossibly included in the global optimal individual at a higher probability that can be viewed as a pattern with a much lower fitness.

Definition 3. Normal genes: the genes or chromosomal fragment whose fitness is between abnormal genes' fitness and eugenic genes' fitness.

Definition 4. "Bu" operation: replacing normal genes in the individual with eugenic genes.

Definition 5. "Xie" operation: replacing abnormal genes in the individual with normal genes.

The selection operator in CMGA is annealing selection with elitist strategy. Because the cure operator has no side effect to the convergence of CMGA, CMGA converges to the global optimal solution at the probability 1 [6, 7]. After the cure operator is finished, an individual P_i ($0 \le i \le N$) in the present offspring $P=(P_1,\ldots,P_N)$ is selected to join in the new population with the probability below:

$$P(p_i) = e^{f(p_i)/T_k} / \sum_{i=1}^{N} e^{f(p_i)/T_k} \qquad (1)$$

where $f(P_i)$ is the fitness of the individual P_i, $T_k = \ln(T_0/k+1)$ is the temperature series approaching 0, k is the evolutionary generations, T_0 is the initial annealing temperature. Meantime, the best individual found in each generation is maintained.

3 The Construction and Mechanism of Cure Operator

The core of CMGA is the construction of cure operator. First, we must obtain eugenic genes and abnormal genes, which are sometimes more than one type respectively, according to prior knowledge or posterior knowledge. Secondly, the detailed methods of "bu" operation and "xie" operation can be fixed on. Lastly we can make the implementing scheme of cure operator.

In order to obtain eugenic genes according to prior knowledge, first a detailed analysis is carried out on the pending problem, and meanwhile, as many basic characteristics information of the problem as possible ought to be found. It is necessary to note that the characteristics information of the pending problem mainly relates to superior individual, for example the ingredients making up of superior individual. Secondly, the characteristics information is abstracted to be a schema. Finally eugenic genes are made of the schema.

On the basis of a detailed analysis carried out on the pending problem, abnormal genes can be obtained from comparing superior individual with inferior individual and finding out their differences. If we have found some schemas included in the inferior individual and definitely not included in the superior individual, these schemas become the basis of identifying abnormal genes. Usually an individual generated randomly is an inferior individual at high probability, thus we can get inferior individual by this way. If we don't know superior individual, we can reduce the dimension of pending problem and make it become a simple problem, which can be solved by a simple algorithm, then we can find out superior individual.

Different from the above-mentioned methods of obtaining eugenic genes and abnormal genes according to prior knowledge before population evolution, another method is to obtain and update them according to posterior knowledge from individuals produced during the evolutionary process.

When we make the implementing scheme of cure operator, we should fix on the execution time and probability, the order and proportion of "bu" and "xie" operation, and so on according to the information obtained during evolutionary process and the characteristic of pending problem.

In essence, eugenic genes and abnormal genes are a kind of expression form of knowledge, and the cure operator, which can accelerate population to flee from the infeasible areas of search space while accelerating population to move towards the promising areas of search space, is a kind of method to give full play to the role of guidance function of knowledge to evolution process. The correct selection of eugenic genes and abnormal genes has important influence on efficiency of CMGA and is the basis and guaranty on which the effect of the cure operator can be exerted.

4 Simulations

Five TSP instances from TSPLIB are used in our experiments. The size of population is the total number of cities. The source code is written in C++ and run on a PC (Pentium4 2.4GHz, 256 MB memory) with Windows 2000. In order to make the coding easy and clear, we take the permutation of the order of visiting the cities for the coding of TSP and regard the following equation as the fitness function:

$$f(p_i) = (100 \times L^*) \div w(p_i) \quad L^* = k \times \sqrt{n \times R} \qquad (2)$$

where L^* denotes the approximate length of the shortest tour of TSP, n is the number of cities, k is a low bound of Held-Karp as an experiential value and varies with n, R means the side length of the smallest square which can contain all the cities, and P_i is the current tour, $w(P_i)$ is the length of tour P_i [8, 9].

4.1 The Construction of Cure Operator

In "bu" operation, eugenic genes are obtained according to posterior knowledge. First, a chromosomal fragment that consists of k continuous cities ($2<k<n/2$, n is the total number of cities) is randomly and continuously selected in the current best individual. Secondly, find out all chromosomal fragments that contain the k same cities with the same start city and end city from population's individuals and compare their path lengths, then the chromosomal fragment G_k whose path length is the shortest is identified as eugenic genes. Lastly, replace the individual's chromosomal fragment that contains the same cities with the same start city and end city as G_k with G_k.

In "xie" operation, abnormal genes are obtained according to prior knowledge. First we find out superior and inferior individual to a simple TSP. Next we can discover that there are no crossed edges in superior individual and there are crossed edges in inferior one and the length of the inferior one is reduced after its crossed edges are removed. Thus, two crossed edges in an individual are identified as abnormal genes. Lastly a cross can be removed from an individual by reversing the sub path between the two cities that belong to two crossed edges and aren't linked. In addition, because the original city order of an individual is changed after a reversal is completed, the process of removing crosses of every two edges in an individual must be repeated for sufficient times so that all the crosses in this individual can be removed completely.

The implementing scheme of cure operator is described as follows. Since individuals created randomly often have many crossed edges, "xie" operation should be applied to the whole population in the first generation. From the second generation, "xie" operation is mainly used for removing crossed edges in individuals created by crossover and mutation operation, which will gradually decrease along with increment of population's fitness, so the probability of "xie" operation should gradually decrease along with evolutionary process. With respect to "bu" operation, it should begin to be applied after there are many superior individuals in population, and the probability of "bu" operation should increases with evolutionary process. By tests, the probability of "xie" and "bu" operation should be from 0.8 to 0.2 and from 0.2 to 0.8 respectively.

4.2 The Crossover Operator and Mutation Operator

PMX (Partially-Mapped Crossover) [10] is used in crossover, whose probability is from *0.6* to *0.8*. The combination of shift operation and swap operation is used in mutation, whose probability is from 0.2 to 0.6. In shift operation, a series (of random length) of cities are picked and then shifted a random amount of cities forward (or backward). In swap operation, two cities from an individual are picked randomly and then their positions are switched. The times of shift operation and swap operation in one mutation is based on the diversity of population.

4.3 The Results of Simulation

A comparison of the variation of fitness with iteration for eil75 among GA, IGA [2] and CMGA is shown in Fig.2 (the sub graph (a) and sub graph (b) of Fig.2 are directly taken from [2]). CMGA finds the global optimal tour with the length 542.31 after 33 generations while IGA finds the local optimal tour with the length 549.18 after 960 and GA finds it after 3550. It can be seen from Fig.2 that CMGA not only

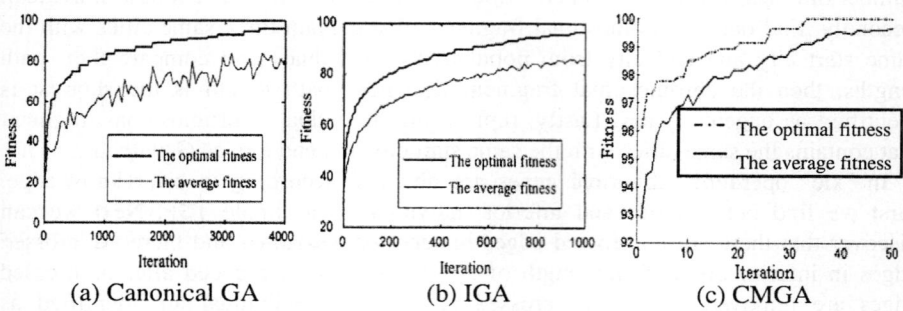

Fig. 2. A comparison of the variation of fitness with iteration among GA, IGA, CMGA

restrains the degenerate phenomenon effectively during the evolutionary process as IGA but also has the faster converging speed than GA and IGA.

With the basic parameter fixed, eil51, Kroa100, ch150 and d198 are solved with canonical GA and CMGA respectively. The experimental results are shown in Table 1, from which we can find that CMGA finds the global optimal tour of the four TSP while canonical GA only finds the local optimal tour. In the meantime, CMGA has the faster convergence speed and the shorter convergence time than canonical GA.

Table 1. A comparison of experimental results between anonical GA and CMGA

Name	CMGA optimal length	GA optimal length	CMGA best convergence time(s)	GA best convergence time(s)	CMGA best convergence generation	GA best convergence generation
eil51	428.87	429.53	0.15	3.95	20	936
kroa100	21285	21311	1.93	40.28	36	1809
ch150	6530.9	6535	7.04	90.74	87	2818
dl98	15809	15851	46.78	642.14	140	6859

5 Conclusions

A novel genetic algorithm based on cure mechanism (CMGA), which is inspired by the theory of traditional Chinese medicine, is proposed. The simulation of TSP shows CMGA is not only feasible but also valid and is helpful to alleviating the degeneration and premature convergence phenomenon in canonical GA while greatly increasing the convergence speed. The success of CMGA makes us believe that it is a new and promising research way to get inspiration from traditional Chinese medicine theory in the research field of evolutionary algorithms and even intelligent computation. In the future, we will keep on with the research work along this way.

References

1. Wolpert, D. H., Macready, W. G.: No Free Lunch Theorems for Optimization. IEEE Trans on Evolutionary Computation (1997) 1 (1) 67–82
2. Jiao, L.C., Wang, L.: A Novel Genetic Algorithm Based on Immunity. IEEE Transactions on Systems, Man, and Cybernetics, Part A: Systems and Humans (2000) 30(5) 552–561
3. Tang, M.: Knowledge-based genetic algorithm for layer assignment. In: Australian Computer Science Communications, IEEE Computer Society Press (2001) 23(1) 184–190
4. Yang, H., Kang, L.S., Chen, Y.P.: A Gene-Based Genetic Algorithm for TSP. Chinese Journal of Computers (2003) 26(12) 1753–1758 (in Chinese)
5. Liu X.: Various theories about traditional Chinese medicine. People's Medical Publishing House, Bei Jing (2001.8) (in Chinese)

6. Zhang, J.S., Xu, Z.B., Liang, Y.: Whole Annealing Genetic Algorithm and the Sufficient and Necessary Condition of its Convergence. Science In China (Series E) (1997) 27(2) 154–164 (in Chinese)
7. Rudolph, G.: Convergence analysis of canonical genetic algorithms. IEEE Trans on Neural Networks (1994) 5(1) 96–101
8. Held, M., Karp, R.M.: The Traveling Salesman Problem and Minimum Spanning Trees. Operation Research 18 (1970) 1138–1162
9. Held, M., Karp, R.M.: The Traveling Salesman Problem and Minimum Spanning Trees: Part II. Mathematical Programming 1 (1971) 6–25
10. Goldberg, D.E., Lingle, R.: Alleles, loci and the traveling salesman problem. In: Proceedings of the International Conference on Genetic Algorithms (1985) 154–159

An Adaptive GA Based on Information Entropy

Yu Sun[1], Chun-lian Li[2], Ai-guo Wang[1], Jia Zhu[2], and Xi-cheng Wang[3]

[1] Institute of Special Education, Changchun University, Changchun 130022, China
[2] School of Computer Science and Technology, Changchun University,
Changchun 130022, China
[3] Department of Computer Science and Engineering,
Dalian University of Technology, Dalian 116023, China
sunyu7473@sina.com

Abstract. An adaptive genetic algorithm based on information entropy is presented in this paper. Unlike traditionally approach, the proposed AGA let the crossover- and mutation- rate optimized by GA itself and user need not confirm the concrete values of the two parameters. Hence, it greatly decreases the workload for iterative debugging the corresponding parameters. As a modified algorithm, this AGA has the following holistic characters: (1) the quasi-exact penalty function is developed to solve nonlinear programming (NLP) problems with equality and inequality constraints, (2) entropy-based searching technique with narrowing down space is taken to speed up the convergence, (3) a specific strategy of reserving the most fitness member with evolutionary historic information is effectively used to approximate the solution of the nonlinear programming problems to the global optimization, (4) A new adaptive strategy is employed to overcome the difficulty in confirming the genetic parameters, (5) a new iteration scheme is used in conjunction with multi-population genetic strategy to terminate the evolution procedure appropriately. Numerical examples and the performance test show that the proposed method has good accuracy and efficiency.

1 Introduction

Genetic Algorithm (GA), initiated by Holland [1], is one of the most important evolutionary computation techniques. The principal advantages of the genetic algorithms reside in the fact that no sensitivity analysis is required and global optimal solution can be obtained. It has philosophical basis in Darwin's theory of survival of the fittest. As a global optimization technique, it has been successfully applied in a series of optimal design problems. However, it still has some defects such as that the premature convergence cannot always get the optimal solution, some parameters are difficult to confirm appropriately, etc. All these hindered GA from more popularity.

A new adaptive GA is presented in this paper to solve the above problems. Firstly, the adaptive genetic evolutionary model is constructed, which can be applied in the constraint optimization problems. Then, the information entropy-based genetic algorithm built on entropy-based searching technique developed in prior work [2,3] is described in detail. In the proposed method, the probability of both crossover and mutation need not to be confirmed, the only work is to limit them to a reasonable range according to the references in any GA books. Besides, an entropy-based searching technique with multi-population and the quasi-exact penalty function are used to ensure rapid and steady convergence, and use a specific strategy of reserving the most fitness member with evolutionary historic information to obtain the global solution. Numerical examples and performance test are given to demonstrate the efficiency of the proposed algorithm.

2 Adaptive Genetic Evolutionary Model Design

General GA used fix genetic operators, so the confirming of some genetic parameters is more difficult than others. Besides, in prophase and anaphase of evolution, the specialties are different. Hence, the genetic operators should be dynamic during the process of evolution. Otherwise, it will prone to cause premature convergence. Let the genetic operators varied appropriately in different evolutionary phase is the pursuit of AGA (Adaptive Genetic Algorithm). When the coding method is decided, the crossover- and mutation- rate play an important role in the algorithm convergence. More and more AGA emerged under all sorts of methods in the last few decades [4-6], most of them take the modus operandi that set one or two additional coefficient(s) which varied abbey some rule. In this paper, the author attempt to put aside the traditional approach and let the crossover- and mutation- rate evolving together with the variables of the optimization problem. Hence, as for the general constrained non-linear programming problem:

$$\begin{aligned} \min \quad & f(\mathbf{x}) \\ s.t. \quad & g_i(\mathbf{x}) \le 0, \quad i = 1, 2, \cdots, m \end{aligned} \quad (1)$$

The following transaction can be done

$$\begin{aligned} \mathbf{d} &= \left\{ \mathbf{x}^T, p_c, p_m \right\}^T \\ q &= m + 4 \end{aligned} \quad (2)$$

So, problem (1) can be transformed into:

$$\begin{aligned} \min \quad & f(\mathbf{d}) \\ s.t. \quad & g_j(\mathbf{d}) \le 0, \quad j = 1, 2, \cdots q \end{aligned} \quad (3)$$

where $f(\mathbf{x})$ is the objective function of original optimization problem, $\mathbf{x} = \{x_1, x_2, \cdots, x_n\}^T$ is a vector of n design variables, $g_i(\mathbf{x})$ ($i=1,2,\cdots,m$) are the constraint functions, p_c is the crossover rate and p_m is the mutation rate, after transformation, $\mathbf{d} = \{x_1, x_2, \cdots, x_n, p_c, p_m\}^T$, $g_j(\mathbf{d})(j=m+1,\cdots,m+4)$ are constraints derived from the upper and lower limits of p_c and p_m.

The soul idea is that user need not give the concrete values to p_c and p_m, but let them evolve with other design variables within a reasonable design space. The initial space of p_c and p_m can be easily decided according to the range given by every GA related book. With the procedure going on, p_c and p_m will be optimized towards its optimal solution respectively together with other design variables. At the end, they all get its optimum value.

Problem (3) is transformed into the following model by means of the aggregate function method [7]:

$$\min \quad f(\mathbf{d})$$
$$s.t. \quad g_\psi(\mathbf{d}) = (1/\psi)\ln \sum_{i=1}^{q} \exp(\psi g_i(\mathbf{d})) \leq 0 \qquad (4)$$

Problem (4) can be solved by using quasi-exact penalty function [8]:

$$\varphi_\psi(\mathbf{d}) = f(\mathbf{d}) + (\alpha/\psi)\ln\left\{1 + \sum_{i=1}^{q} \exp(\psi g_i(\mathbf{d}))\right\} \qquad (5)$$

the parameter ψ can be chosen in the range $10^3 - 10^5$ and $\alpha > 0$ is penalty factor. Fitness function of GA by means of equation (5) may be written as:

$$\max \quad F(\mathbf{d}) = C - \varphi_\psi(\mathbf{d}) \qquad (6)$$

where C is a large positive number to make sure that F >0. Equation (6) is the evolutionary model of the proposed AGA.

3 Information Entropy-Based Searching Technique

The proposed GA is a multi-population algorithm in conjunction with an entropy-based searching technique with narrowing down the searching space to ensure rapid and steady convergence.

3.1 Narrowing Coefficients of Searched Space for the Multi-population Evolution

The proposed GA begins from generating arbitrarily M populations with all the same searching space, i.e. initial design space. If $F_j(\mathbf{d})$ ($j = 1, \cdots, M$) represent that the best value of the fitness function occurs in the jth population, then we need to maximum $F_j(\mathbf{d})$ ($j = 1, \cdots, M$) by means of a genetic search, i.e. to solve the following optimum problem:

$$\min \quad -F_j(\mathbf{d}), \quad j = 1, 2, \cdots, m \qquad (7)$$

It is difficult to solve optimization problem (7) completely, and it is not necessary to do so when using the genetic algorithm with narrowing of the search space. We need only to get efficient narrowing coefficients for the searched space. By information entropy principle [9], an entropy based-optimization model can be constructed as follows:

$$\begin{cases} \min \ -\sum_{j=1}^{m} p_j F_j(\mathbf{d}) \\ \min \ H = -\sum_{j=1}^{m} p_j \ln(p_j) \\ s.t. \ \sum_{j=1}^{m} p_j = 1, \ p_j \in [0,1] \end{cases} \quad (8)$$

where H is the information entropy, p_j is here defined as a probability that the optimal solution of the problem (7) occurs in the population j. In discussing the relationship between problems (7) and (8) the following theorem is introduced.

Theorem 1. The optimization problem (7) and (8) both have the same optimal solution.

Proof. Suppose that $\mathbf{d}^*$ and $\mathbf{p}^* = \{p_1^*, p_2^*, \cdots, p_m^*\}$ are the optimal solution of problem (8), so that

$$\min \ H^* = -\sum_{j=1}^{m} p_j^* \ln(p_j^*) = p_l^* \ln(1) = 0 \quad (9)$$

where $p_l^* = 1$, $p_i^* = 0$ for $i \neq l$, i.e. the optimal solution of the problem (7) occurs in the population l. Hence

$$\min \ -\sum_{j=1}^{m} p_j F_j(\mathbf{d}^*) = \min \ - F_l(\mathbf{d}^*) \quad (10)$$

Obviously, $\mathbf{d}^*$ and $\mathbf{p}^*$ are also the optimal solution of problem (7). It can be similarly proved that the optimal solution of problem (7) is also the optimal solution of problem (8), and the proof is completed.

By means of the weighted coefficient method for solving multi-objective optimization, problem (8) can be transformed into a single objective optimization problem as follows:

$$\min \ -(1-\beta)\sum_{j=1}^{m} p_j F_j(\mathbf{d}) - \beta \sum_{j=1}^{m} \left(p_j \ln p_j \right)$$
$$s.t. \ \sum_{j=1}^{m} p_j = 1, \ p_j \geq 0, \ j = 1, 2, \cdots, m \quad (11)$$

where $\beta \geq 0$ is weight coefficient. The Lagrange augmented function of problem (11) is

$$L_H(\mathbf{d}, \mathbf{p}, \beta, \eta) = -(1-\beta)\sum_{j=1}^{m} p_j F_j(\mathbf{d}) \tag{12}$$

$$-\beta\sum_{j=1}^{m}(p_j \ln p_j) + \eta\left(\sum_{j=1}^{m} p_j - 1\right)$$

where η is Lagrange multiplier. The stationary conditions of L_H with respect to $\mathbf{p}, \eta$ and $\mathbf{d}$ give

$$\ln p_j = [(\beta-1)/\beta] F_j(\mathbf{d}) + \eta/\beta - 1 \tag{13}$$

$$\sum_{j=1}^{m} p_j = 1$$

$$(1-\beta)\sum_{j=1}^{m} p_j \cdot [\partial F_j(\mathbf{d})/\partial d_i] = 0 \tag{14}$$

$$i = 1, 2, \cdots, N$$

The solution of equation (13) is

$$p_j^* = \exp(\gamma F_j(\mathbf{d})) / \sum_{j=1}^{m} \exp(\gamma F_j(\mathbf{d})) \tag{15}$$

in which

$$\gamma = (\beta-1)/\beta \tag{16}$$

is called as quasi-weight coefficient. The $(1-p_j)$ can be used as the coefficients of narrowing searching space in the modified genetic algorithm. When the optimal solution occurs in the lth population, then $(1-p_j^*) = 0$, and its searching space is not narrowing.

3.2 Information-Entropy-Based Searching Technique

Design space is defined as initial searching space $D(0)$. M populations with N members are generated in the given space. After a few generations are independently evolved in each population (only two generations in this paper), Searching space of each population except for the worst one is narrowed according to the following equations:

$$D(K) = (1-p_j)D(K-1)$$

$$\underline{d}_i(K) = \max\left\{\left[d_i^*(K) - 0.5(1-p_j)D(K)\right], \underline{d}_i(0)\right\} \tag{17}$$

$$\overline{d}_i(K) = \min\left\{\left[d_i^*(K) - 0.5(1-p_j)D(K)\right], \overline{d}_i(0)\right\}$$

where $\underline{d}_i(K)$ and $\overline{d}_i(K)$ are the modified lower and upper limits of ith design variable at Kth iteration, respectively. $d_i^*(K)$ is the value of design variable i of the best member in the population j. The searching space of worst population remains as the initial design space to ensure that the algorithm will not lose the boundary solutions.

4 Implementation of Proposed AGA

4.1 Genetic Operators

The proposed AGA begins with generating arbitrarily M populations in which N strings corresponding to N possible solutions respectively, and here the strings are expressed in binary code. During the process of selection, an integer-decimal method is taken. Crossover allows string to exchange the characteristics among themselves and create new designs. In this paper, we use the two-point rule. Crossover is executed by first selecting two mating parents from two different populations, and selected randomly two cutting sites, then swap 0s and 1s of the strings between cutting sites of mating pairs according to crossover rate Pc. Mutation with a probability Pm is another operator. It is used to protect against the loss of some useful genetic information, and may help design to get out of local optimization solution. The process of mutation is to select simply a few strings from the population according to probability Pm and change the value of 0s or 1s on each chosen string in terms of some rule. A uniform mutation is employed in this paper. Both Pc and Pm are needless to be valued because of the adaptive scheme.

It is reasonable to find the global solution to the numerical optimization problems with a few decades and some times even several hundreds generations. So a lot of historic information will be generated during the evolutionary process. Among them, we considered most is the elitist of all the populations in each generation. In this paper, the information of the best individual is recorded first in the former generation, then compare with the best one of current generation, and the absolute excellent individual up to now is stored in the contemporary as the elitist. Iterate this process in every generation till the convergence is reached. The final elitist is the solution to the optimization problem.

4.2 Genetic Process

Computer program for entropy-based AGA with multi-population consists of the following steps:

Step 1. Deal with the constraints derived from Pc and Pm

Step 2. Give the initial design space $D(0) = [\underline{\mathbf{d}}(0), \overline{\mathbf{d}}(0)]$ and parameters. Generate M populations with given space $D(0)$

Step 3. Perform GA with elitist maintaining processes introduced in section 4.1 a few generations (only one generation in this paper)

Step 4. Perform the entropy-based searching process with narrowing down space, see equations (17)

Step 5. Check convergence: if the searching space in the best population has been reduced to a very small area (a given tolerance), then stop; else go to step 3.

5 Examples

In this section, two examples used in paper [3] with equality and inequality constraints are given to clarify the efficiency and accuracy of the proposed AGA (see tab.1). All of them are solved with the parameters: number of populations $M=4$, population size $N=10$, control parameters:

$$\psi = 10^3, \alpha = 1.2 \times 10^5.$$

Crossover rate Pc is controlled within [0.1, 0.99] and mutation rate Pm within [0.0001, 0.1];

Tab.1 lists the numerical examples, Fig.1-2 show the evolution history of genetic design. Tab.2 gives the optimization result using the proposed method. In order to test the performance of the adaptive strategy presented in this paper, a test on example 1 is done, tab.3 gives the result.

Table 1. Numerical examples

Example 1	max s.t.	$f(x) = -x_1^2 - x_2^2 - 2x_3^2 - x_4^2 + 5x_1 + 5x_2 + 21x_3 - 7x_4$ $x_1^2 + x_2^2 + x_3^2 + x_4^2 + x_1 - x_2 + x_3 - x_4 \leq 8$ $x_1^2 + 2x_2^2 + x_3^2 + 2x_4^2 - x_1 - x_4 \leq 10$ $2x_1^2 + x_2^2 + x_3^2 + 2x_1 - x_2 - x_4 = 5$
Example 2	max s.t.	$f(x) = -(x_1 - 3)^2 - (x_2 - 2)^2$ $x_1^2 + x_2^2 \geq 5$ $x_1 + 2x_2 = 4$ $x_1, x_2 \geq 0$

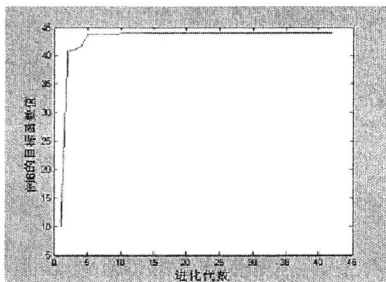 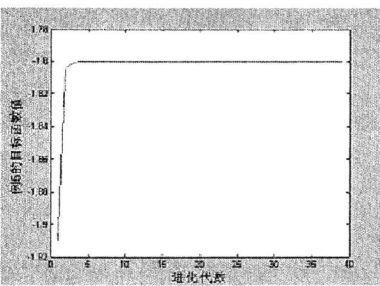

Fig. 1. The genetic evolution procedure of the optimization for example 1

Fig. 2. The genetic evolution procedure of the optimization for example 2

Table 2. Numerical examples

Example	Example 1	Example 2
Theoretical solution	$f(0, 1, 2, -1) = 44$	$f(2.4, 0.8) = -1.8$
This paper	$f(-0.00427, 0.984036, 2.007537, -0.994)$ $= 43.998357$	$f(2.4, 0.8) = -1.8$
Generations(g/G)*	10/42	3/25
Time-needed (s)	0.27	0.15

*g/G: shows that the algorithm evolved G generations and at the gth generation get the optimal solution.

Table 3. The performace test for the proposed algorithm without parameter adaptive

Run times	Pc	Pm	g	G	Time(s)
1	0.6325	0.0027	14	47	0.33
2	0.4346	0.0331	9	42	0.28
3	0.7592	0.0001	12	44	0.30
4	0.2587	0.0932	11	41	0.27
5	0.4870	0.0689	8	40	0.26
6	0.8734	0.0260	13	42	0.28
7	0.6825	0.0603	12	41	0.27
8	0.1387	0.0089	17	49	0.34
9	0.3497	0.0831	16	46	0.32
10	0.9832	0.0053	15	43	0.29

6 Conclusion

An adaptive multi-population genetic algorithm based on information entropy is presented in this paper for nonlinear programming. This method employs an entropy-based searching technique with narrowing down space of multi-population. The adaptive strategy can bring convenience to users by decreasing the parameter debugging workload. Instead of confirming the value of crossover- and mutation-rate, only the ranges are needed and which can easily be set according to basic GA principle. The efficiency of adaptive strategy is demonstrated by the test result listed in tab.3. Numerical examples show that the proposed AGA is accurate and efficient when dealing constrained non-linear programming problem.

Acknowledgments

The authors gratefully acknowledge financial support for this work from the National Natural Science Foundation(10272030) and the Subsidized by the Special Funds for Major State Basic Research Project (G1999032805) of China.

References

1. D. E. Goldberg, Genetic Algorithms in Search, Optimization & Machine Learning, Reading, Addison Wesley, 1989
2. Li chun-lian, Wang Xi-cheng, Zhao Jin-cheng, et al. An Information Entropy-based Multi-population Genetic Algorithm. Journal of Dalian University of Technology, vol.44(4):589-593, 2004(in Chinese)
3. Li chun-lian, Wang Xi-cheng, Zhao Jin-cheng, et al. An Entropy-based Multi-population GeneticAlgorithm: I. The basic principles, Proc. of Third International Conference on Machine Learning and Cybernetics, 1805-1810, 2004.
4. Yuan Xiao-hui, Cao-Ling, Xia Liang-zheng. Adaptive genetic algorithm with the criterion of premature convergence. Journal of Southeast University, vol.19(1):40-43
5. Shisanu Tongchim, Prabhas Chongstitvatana. Parallel genetic algorithm with parameter adaptation. Information Processing Letters 82:47-54, 2002
6. Jiang Rui, Luo Yupin, Hu Dongcheng, et al. An adaptive genetic algorithm based on population entropy estimating. Journal of Tsinghua University(Sci & Tech), vol.42(3): 358-361, 2002
7. Li,Xingsi. An aggregate function method for nonlinear program. Science in China, series A, vol34:1467-1473, 1991
8. Li, Xing-si. A quasi-exact penalty function method for nonlinear program [J]. Chinese Science Bulletin, 36,1451-1453 , 1991
9. Elements of information theory, New York: Wiley, 1991

A Genetic Algorithm of High-Throughput and Low-Jitter Scheduling for Input-Queued Switches

Yaohui Jin, Jingjing Zhang, and Weisheng Hu

State Key Lab of Advanced Optical Communication System and Network,
Shanghai Jiao Tong University, Shanghai 200030, China
{jinyh, zjj, wshu}@sjtu.edu.cn

Abstract. This paper presents a novel genetic algorithm (GA) for the scheduling problem of input-Queued switch, which can be applied in various networks besides the design of high speed routers. The scheduler should satisfy quality of service (QoS) constraints such as throughput and jitter. Solving the scheduling problem for the input-Queued switches can be divided into two steps: Firstly, decomposing the given rate matrix into a sum of permutation matrices with their corresponding weights; secondly, allocating the permutation matrices in one scheduling period based on their weights. It has been proved that scheduling problem in input-Queued switch with throughput and jitter constraints is NP-complete. The main contribution of this paper is a GA based algorithm to solve this NP-complete problem. We devise chromosome codes, fitness function, crossover and mutation operations for this specific problem. Experimental results show that our GA provides better performances in terms of throughput and jitter than a greedy heuristic.

1 Introduction

Input-Queued crossbar switch fabric with virtual output queues and fixed size cells has been widely employed in the design of high speed routers. The scheduler has to find matching from input to output ports and then configure switches based on the matching. In addition to high speed routers, such scheduler can be applied in various networks, for examples, ATM switches [1], satellite switched TDMA [2], time-slotted FDMA, packet-switched WDM passive optical networks [3], and slotted-WDM ring networks [4].

There have been many studies on optimal schedule algorithm, which can be typically divided into two categories. One is based on request-grant-accept mechanism [5], [6], [7], in which request-grant-accept process between input ports and output ports is operated at the beginning of every time slot or frame. The other one is based on matrix decomposition [3], [8], [9]. Given a traffic demand matrix in one period of time, the scheduler decomposes it into a sum of weighted permutation matrices. Then these matrices are allocated evenly in a schedule table according to their weights.

In the scheduling problem for input-queued switches, two main objects should be considered. The first objective is to obtain high throughput. Throughput is inversely proportional to the required bandwidth that is the sum of all the decomposition weights.

The second objective is to minimize the scheduling jitter, which is defined as the difference between maximum and minimum scheduling intervals in the schedule table.

In this paper, we focus on the matrix decomposition approach for the following reasons: firstly, it does not need to perform matching in every time slot or frame if the traffic pattern changes infrequently, and hence the signaling overhead and the transmission delay are decreased; secondly, it can obtain higher throughput since the traffic matrix is demand accumulation in one period of time; thirdly, it can provide fairness more easily among the input ports, and then assure lower jitter.

C. S. Chang *et al.* proposed minimum-bandwidth Birkhoff Von-Neumann decomposition [9]. However it does not take into account of jitter. I. Keslassy *et al.* formulated the problem to an integer linear programming (ILP) model by adding a low jitter (LJ) constraint and also proposed a greedy algorithm for the LJ ILP which is proved a NP-complete problem [8] [10].

We propose to use a novel generic algorithm (GA) for the scheduling problem with both throughput and jitter constraints. GA is a random search and optimization method, which is based on natural selection theory and genetic mechanism of the living beings. It has been used to solve many scheduling problems such as job-shop scheduling [11], and broadcast scheduling in packet radio networks [12]. Here we extend the chromosome codes into two dimensions in GA by setting them to be a list of schedules (permutation matrices), which is different from conventional GA whose chromosome is a vector. We also devise corresponding crossover and mutation operations for these chromosomes. Experimental results show that GA could improve 5% throughput and reduce 15% jitter compared to greedy algorithm.

The rest of the paper is organized as follows. Firstly, we present the problem formulation and review the related works. In section III we describe our genetic algorithm in terms of coding method, fitness function, crossover, as well as mutation. Then, simulation results that show the performance of our designed algorithm will be presented in section IV. The last section V provides some conclusion remarks.

2 Problem Formulation

The input-Queued switch requires that a port cannot send or receive two or more packets simultaneously. We use a permutation matrix $\mathbf{P}$ to describe the configuration of an input-Queued switch in one time slot. Given a traffic demand matrix $\mathbf{T}$, whose element T_{ij} denotes the number of slots that port i needs to send to port j, it can be decomposed into a sum of weighted permutation matrices. Mathematically,

$$\mathbf{T} \leq \sum_k c_k \mathbf{P}_k \tag{1}$$

$$\sum_{i=1}^{N} p_{i,j}^k \leq 1 \quad \forall j,k \tag{2}$$

$$\sum_{j=1}^{N} p_{i,j}^k \leq 1 \quad \forall i,k \tag{3}$$

$$p_{i,j}^k \in \{0,1\} \quad \forall i,j,k \tag{4}$$

where N is the size of switch fabric and c_k is the coefficient of the decomposed matrix $\mathbf{P}^k$. Constraints (2) (3) (4) ensure that $\mathbf{P}^k$ is a permutation matrix or partial permutation matrix if there is an all zero column or row. The required bandwidth B is defined as the sum of c_k:

$$B = \sum_k c_k \tag{5}$$

Obviously, we need to minimize B to obtain high throughput. For the sake of simplicity, we use a schedule vector **s** to denote permutation matrix **P**:

$$\mathbf{s}_i = \begin{cases} 0 & p_{ij} = 0 \\ j & p_{ij} = 1 \end{cases} \tag{6}$$

After decomposition, these schedule vectors (permutation matrices) are allocated into schedule table **s** according to their coefficients. Note that, the decomposition process may introduce redundant scheduling when the real traffic demand matrix is less than the sum of weighted permutation matrices. Finally, the redundant scheduling elements should be removed.

Birkhoff Von-Neumann theorem can be briefly explained as such: Any doubly stochastic matrix can be written as a convex combination of permutation matrices. If the original traffic demand matrix is not doubly stochastic, it has to construct a doubly stochastic matrix that is not less than the original matrix. BV decomposition, which is not NP complete, provides a lower bound of the required bandwidth [9]. . However, it results in unpredictable jitter because it allows the repeated configuration elements in different permutation matrices. The subsequent allocation process only considers the decomposition weights. Below is an example of BV decomposition:

$$T = \begin{bmatrix} 1 & 1 & 1 \\ 1 & 1 & 1 \\ 1 & 2 & 1 \end{bmatrix} \leqslant \begin{bmatrix} 1 & 0 & 0 \\ 0 & 1 & 0 \\ 0 & 0 & 1 \end{bmatrix} + \begin{bmatrix} 0 & 1 & 0 \\ 0 & 0 & 1 \\ 1 & 0 & 0 \end{bmatrix} + \begin{bmatrix} 1 & 0 & 0 \\ 0 & 0 & 1 \\ 0 & 1 & 0 \end{bmatrix} + \begin{bmatrix} 0 & 0 & 1 \\ 1 & 0 & 0 \\ 0 & 1 & 0 \end{bmatrix}$$

The minimum required bandwidth is 4. Its corresponding scheduling table is shown in S_{BV}. The average jitter of S_{BV} is 0.22.

$$S_{BV} = \begin{bmatrix} 1 & 2 & 0 & 3 \\ 2 & 3 & 0 & 1 \\ 3 & 1 & 2 & 2 \end{bmatrix}$$

As we describe in the introduction, the LJ ILP model added a constraint that any two permutation matrices cannot have the same configuration elements [8].

$$\sum_k p_{i,j}^k \leq 1 \quad \forall i,j \tag{7}$$

The object function is also to minimize the sum of c_k. The greedy heuristic is to find the matching for the maximum traffic demand elements first, and then eliminate them from the traffic demand. The decomposition is completed after several iterations. Note that greedy heuristic does not require that the traffic matrix is doubly stochastic. Below is an example of greedy LJ (GLJ) decomposition:

$$T = \begin{bmatrix} 1 & 1 & 1 \\ 1 & 1 & 1 \\ 1 & 2 & 1 \end{bmatrix} \leqslant 2 \begin{bmatrix} 1 & 0 & 0 \\ 0 & 0 & 1 \\ 0 & 1 & 0 \end{bmatrix} + \begin{bmatrix} 0 & 0 & 0 \\ 0 & 1 & 0 \\ 0 & 0 & 1 \end{bmatrix} + \begin{bmatrix} 0 & 0 & 1 \\ 0 & 0 & 0 \\ 1 & 0 & 0 \end{bmatrix} + \begin{bmatrix} 0 & 1 & 0 \\ 1 & 0 & 0 \\ 0 & 0 & 0 \end{bmatrix}$$

The minimum required bandwidth is 5, which is greater than BV decomposition. Its corresponding scheduling table is shown in the following S_{GLJ}. The average jitter of S_{GLJ} is 0.11, which is much less than that of S_{BV}.

$$S_{GLJ} = \begin{bmatrix} 1 & 0 & 0 & 3 & 2 \\ 3 & 2 & 0 & 0 & 1 \\ 2 & 3 & 2 & 1 & 0 \end{bmatrix}$$

3 Genetic Algorithm

In practice, GA is iterative search process as shown in Fig.1. G and M are generation number and maximal generation in the evolution process respectively. In each generation, fitter individuals survive with greater probability and weak ones are more likely to be eliminated. As long as we choose proper evaluation function and gene operation the population will converge to an optimal or near optimal result eventually. We then describe each step in detail.

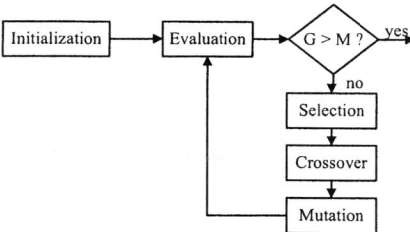

Fig. 1. Flow chart of genetic algorithm

3.1 Coding and Initialization

Generally, the candidate solution is encoded as a binary bit string, which is called chromosome. In our problem, an individual chromosome is composed of several scheduling vectors (permutation matrices).

The purpose of initialization is to produce individuals of the first generation which constitute the beginning searching space. The steps are as follows:

1. According to traffic matrix **T**, produce a permutation matrix **P** randomly. The position of nonzero element in **P** should consist with that in **T**. Then put the elements in **T** whose position in **P** is 1 into a set R;

2. Search for the maximal value in R and denoted it as the weight of **P**. Then eliminate the elements in R from **T**;
3. Repeat the above two steps until **T** is reduced to 0.

Note that, the initial populations for evolutionary process are generated randomly without any heuristic. But the length of a chromosome may be variable because the number of matrices is not fixed in each randomly decomposition.

3.2 Fitness Function and Selection

The object function of LJ ILP is to minimize the required bandwidth. So individuals with smaller bandwidth requirement are much easier to survive. We define a fitness function as follows:

$$Fit(i) = \frac{1}{B(i) - B_{min} + 1} \qquad (8)$$

$B(i)$ is the required bandwidth for an individual chromosome. B_{min} is the minimal value of all the required bandwidth in one generation. The above fitness function enables that the fitter individuals can be selected with greater probability. The range of $Fit(i)$ is from 0 to 1. Finally, a traditional tournament selection policy is employed according to the fitness function.

3.3 Crossover

As the order of these alleles in our chromosome is of no significance, we adopt uniform crossover to enable any combination of alleles be exchanged with another individual. Considering the character of our coding method, we modify the traditional uniform crossover operation which is divided into the following five steps:

Step1. Randomly generate two bit strings for two parent chromosomes respectively. The length of the bit string is equal to the length of its corresponding chromosome. For example, given two parent chromosomes $\mathcal{A}$ and $\mathcal{B}$,

$$\mathcal{A} = \begin{bmatrix} 3 & 1 & 2 & 0 \\ 2 & 0 & 1 & 3 \\ 1 & 3 & 0 & 2 \end{bmatrix} \quad \mathcal{B} = \begin{bmatrix} 3 & 2 & 1 \\ 2 & 1 & 3 \\ 1 & 3 & 2 \end{bmatrix}$$

Allele lengths of them are 4 and 3 respectively. Bit strings 0100 and 101 are then randomly generated for them.

Step2. Rearrange two individuals by moving the alleles sharing the same position with value one in its bit string to the end and those corresponding to zero to the front. We still take the above chromosomes and bit strings for example.

$$\mathcal{A} = \begin{bmatrix} 3 & 2 & 0 & 1 \\ 2 & 1 & 3 & 0 \\ 1 & 0 & 2 & 3 \end{bmatrix} \quad \mathcal{B} = \begin{bmatrix} 2 & 3 & 1 \\ 1 & 2 & 3 \\ 3 & 1 & 2 \end{bmatrix}$$

The second allele of $\mathcal{A}$, the first and third alleles of $\mathcal{B}$ are moved to the end of $\mathcal{A}$ and $\mathcal{B}$. Note that such movement does not produce new genes because of the first character of our coding. However, the uniform crossover with unequal chromosome length is reduced to one-point crossover by doing so.

Step3. Exchange the front alleles that correspond to zero in the bit string to create two new chromosomes. For the above two chromosomes, the first three alleles of $\mathcal{A}$ exchange with the first allele of $\mathcal{B}$.

$$\mathcal{A} = \begin{bmatrix} 3 & 2 & 0 & | & 1 \\ 2 & 1 & 3 & | & 0 \\ 1 & 0 & 2 & | & 3 \end{bmatrix} \Longrightarrow \mathcal{A}' = \begin{bmatrix} 2 & 1 \\ 1 & 0 \\ 3 & 3 \end{bmatrix}$$

$$\mathcal{B} = \begin{bmatrix} 2 & | & 3 & 1 \\ 1 & | & 2 & 3 \\ 3 & | & 1 & 2 \end{bmatrix} \Longrightarrow \mathcal{B}' = \begin{bmatrix} 3 & 2 & 0 & 3 & 1 \\ 2 & 1 & 3 & 2 & 3 \\ 1 & 0 & 2 & 1 & 2 \end{bmatrix}$$

It can be seen that these two new individuals do not satisfy constraints (1) (7).

Step4. Check whether scheduling for any nonzero traffic demand exists in the new chromosome. If the traffic demand is scheduled more than once, delete the redundant scheduling. If the nonzero traffic demand is not scheduled at all, search for feasible free spaces in the chromosome which satisfy conflict free condition after being added. If there does not exist such feasible free space. Append a new allele in the end of the chromosome to schedule this traffic demand.

For example, In chromosome $\mathcal{A}'$, $\mathcal{A}'_{3,2}$ is redundant scheduling and has to be deleted. And two new alleles should be appended to meet the traffic demand. After this step, two new valid chromosomes are obtained.

$$\mathcal{A}' = \begin{bmatrix} 2 & 1 & 3 & 0 \\ 1 & 2 & 0 & 3 \\ 0 & 3 & 1 & 2 \end{bmatrix} \quad \mathcal{B}' = \begin{bmatrix} 0 & 2 & 0 & 3 & 1 \\ 0 & 1 & 0 & 2 & 3 \\ 3 & 0 & 0 & 1 & 2 \end{bmatrix}$$

However, the above chromosomes may not be optimal with the shortest length. For example, in chromosome $\mathcal{B}'$, the third allele are all zero. Also note that the first and the second alleles can be combined together without violating constraints (1) (7) which we called degenerating process.

Step5. Delete zero alleles and degenerate alleles to obtain optimal chromosome. However, not all chromosomes are needed to be degenerated. For example, $\mathcal{A}'$ is an optimal one already. But chromosome $\mathcal{B}'$ is optimized after this step.

$$\mathcal{B}' = \begin{bmatrix} 2 & 3 & 1 \\ 1 & 2 & 3 \\ 3 & 1 & 2 \end{bmatrix}$$

Finally, crossover operation may break good patterns of parents to produce undesirable individuals and such broken pattern require a lot of energy to recover. We compare the sons and their parents, the sons are conserved only if they are fitter than their parents.

3.4 Mutation

In our mutation operation, we randomly select two schedule vectors in a chromosome and then try to exchange elements in the same two positions (rows) of the schedule vector until both new schedule vectors correspond to permutation matrices. We use the final chromosome C in the above paragraph to explain our mutation operation. We choose schedule vectors c_1 and c_2. If we exchange row 1 and 2, the new schedule vectors are:

$$\begin{bmatrix}1\\0\\3\end{bmatrix}\Leftrightarrow\begin{bmatrix}3\\2\\1\end{bmatrix}\Longrightarrow\begin{bmatrix}3\\2\\3\end{bmatrix}\begin{bmatrix}1\\0\\1\end{bmatrix}$$

The two new schedule vectors do not correspond to permutation matrices. So the mutation failed. Then we try to exchange row 1 and 3, the new schedule vectors are

$$\begin{bmatrix}1\\0\\3\end{bmatrix}\Leftrightarrow\begin{bmatrix}3\\2\\1\end{bmatrix}\Longrightarrow\begin{bmatrix}3\\0\\1\end{bmatrix}\begin{bmatrix}1\\2\\3\end{bmatrix}$$

The two new schedule vectors correspond to permutation matrices.

4 Simulation Results and Discussion

Firstly, we still take the above traffic matrix T for example. Our GA obtains the optimal decomposition:

$$T=\begin{bmatrix}1&1&1\\1&1&1\\1&2&1\end{bmatrix}\leqslant\begin{bmatrix}1&0&0\\0&1&0\\0&0&1\end{bmatrix}+2\begin{bmatrix}0&0&1\\1&0&0\\0&1&0\end{bmatrix}+\begin{bmatrix}0&1&0\\0&0&1\\1&0&0\end{bmatrix}$$

The required bandwidth is 4, which is the same as BV. The corresponding scheduling table is

$$S_{GA}=\begin{bmatrix}1&3&2&0\\2&1&3&0\\3&2&1&2\end{bmatrix}$$

Its average jitter is 0. Indeed, GA improves the jitter performance significantly.

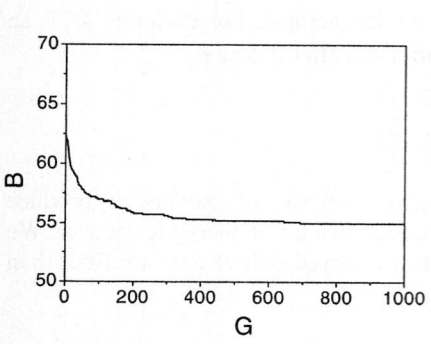

Fig. 2. Bandwidth requirement

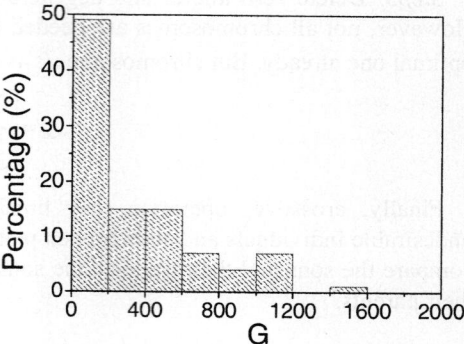

Fig. 3. Generation numbers

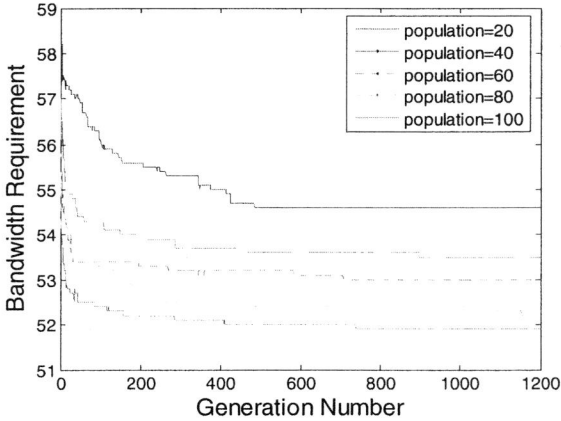

Fig. 4. Bandwidth requirement performance with different population size

In the following experiments we choose cross probability to be 0.5, mutation probability to be 0.1, N=8, and the population size to be 20, the traffic demand is generated randomly with that for every connection pair distributing uniformly from 0 to 10, individuals of the first generation is generated without any heuristic.

In Fig.2, we show a typical example in which the required bandwidth B improves over the generations number G. Fig. 3 shows the distribution of generation numbers where optimal (or near optimal) results appear in 100 experiments. Here traffic demands are generated randomly in each simulation.

With the optimal or near optimal results, generation numbers vary because of the random operation of the initialization, crossover, and mutation. Fig.3 shows that nearly half of the optimal or near optimal results can be obtained within 200 generations.

In the above figure 4, we vary individual number in a generation from 20 to 100. It shows that the larger the population size, the faster bandwidth requirement reduces. And smaller bandwidth requirement can be obtained for larger population size when maximal generation is fixed. When the individual number is small, the chromosome codes are not as diversity as that with large one. Thus it's more likely to jump into local optimal point and difficult to find a fitter individual. On the contrary, when the individual number is large, chances for searching a better individual are increased a lot.

In Fig.5 and Fig.6, the traffic demand matrices are generated randomly with their elements uniformly distributed between 0 and L. The value of L determines maximum traffic load. The maximal generation number is 2000. That means the iterative searching carries on for 2000 times. Such experiments were conducted 20 times for a single L.

In Fig.5, we compare the required bandwidth of BV, GLJ and GA.. BV provides minimal bandwidth for a given traffic. Because of the additional constraint (5), GLJ algorithm and GA based algorithm require some extra bandwidth. It can be seen that little extra bandwidth is needed for GA based algorithm and it provides about 5% improvement on throughput compared to greedy algorithm. We can conclude that our designed algorithm does help to find better solutions although the optimal solutions and lower bounds of the problem are unknown.

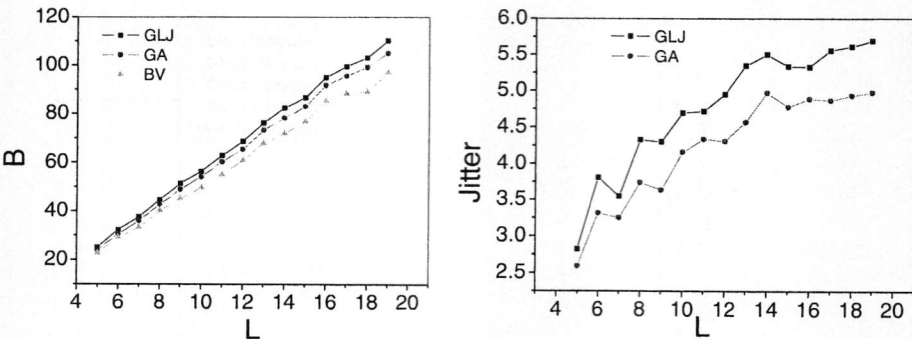

Fig. 5. Comparison of required bandwidth

Fig. 6. Comparison of jitter

Fig.6 is comparison of jitter between GLJ and GA based algorithm. Here we do not compare it with BV because jitter of it is extremely large compared to GA and GLJ. The total number of scheduling slots needed by GA based algorithm is less than that of GLJ. So for a single connection, the traffic is transmitted nearly uniformly in a shorter scheduling period. Correspondingly, jitter is reduced in general. GA can achieve an average of 15% jitter reduction compared with GLJ.

5 Conclusion

In this paper we studied low jitter scheduling for input-queued switch. Scheduling taking both jitter and bandwidth into account was proved NP-hard before and we proposed an optimization method based on GA to achieve optimal result or near optimal one. Firstly we use a list of permutation matrices to code our solution candidate which is different from conventional codes. Because of the various constraints of our codes, crossover and mutation operators should be specially designed. A modified uniform crossover is adopted for this specific problem owning to the order independence of the alleles and unfixed length of the chromosome. Problem specific mutation is designed as well. Finally, we perform simulations based on our novel genetic algorithm and shows how the fitness function improves generation after generation. Comparison of our GA with BV and GLJ were done to show good performances in terms of jitter and throughput.

Acknowledgement. This work was supported in part by National Natural Science Foundation of China.

References

1. Li, S., Ansari, N.: Scheduling Input-queued ATM Switches with QoS Features, Computer Communications and Networks, Proceedings. 7th International Conference on (1998) 107–112
2. Balas, E., Landweer, P.R.: Traffic Assignment in Communication Satellites, Operations Research Letters (1983), Vol.2, 141-147

3. Jin, Y., Su, Y., Zhang, J., Hu, W., et al.: Scheduling in a Packet-switched WDM PON with Reduced Delay and Low-Jitter Performance, ECOC (2004), WeP140
4. Jelger, C.S., Elmirghani, J.M.H.: Photonic Packet WDM Ring Networks Architecture and Performance, IEEE communication magazine (2002) Vol. 40, No. 11, 110-115
5. Kumar, S., Kumar, A.: On Implementation of Scheduling Algorithms in High Speed Input Queuing Cell Switches, Proceedings of IEEE ICC (2003) Vol. 1 152-157.
6. Spencer, M. J., Summerfield, M. A.: WRAP: A Medium Access Control Protocol for Wavelength-Routed Passive Optical Networks, Journal of Lightwave Technology (2000) Vol.18, 1657-1675
7. Kim, Y. H., Chao, Jonathan,: Performance of Exhaustive Matching Algorithms for Input-Queued Switches, Proceedings of IEEE ICC (2003) Vol.3, 1817-1822
8. Keslassy, I., Kodialam, M., Lakshman, T.V., Stiliadis, D.: On Guaranteed Smooth Scheduling For Input-Queued Switches, Proceedings of IEEE INFOCOM (2003) Vol.2, 1384-1394
9. Chang, C.S., Chen, J.W., Huang, H.Y.: Birkhoff-Von Neumann Input Buffered Crossbar Switches, Proceedings of IEEE INFOCOM (2000) 1614-1623
10. Rendl, F., On the Complexity of Decomposing Matrices Arising in Satellite Communication, *Operations Research Letters* (1985), Vol. 4, 5-8
11. Jensen, M.T.: Generating Robust and Flexible Job Shop Schedules Using Genetic Algorithms, IEEE Transactions on Evolutionary Computation (2003) Vol.7, 275 - 288
12. Chakraborty, G., Hirano, Y.: Genetic Algorithm for Broadcast Scheduling in Packet Radio Networks, Proceedings of IEEE Evolutionary Computation (1998) 183 – 188

Mutation Matrix in Evolutionary Computation: An Application to Resource Allocation Problem

Jian Zhang[1,2] and Kwok Yip Szeto[2,*]

[1] Department of Mathematics,
[2] Department of Physics, Hong Kong University of Science and Technology,
Clear Water Bay, Hong Kong SAR, China
phszeto@ust.hk

Abstract. A new approach to evolutionary computation with mutation only is developed by the introduction of the mutation matrix. The method of construction of the mutation matrix is problem independent and the selection mechanism is achieved implicitly by individualized and locus specific mutation probability based on the information on locus statistics and fitness of the population, and traditional genetic algorithm with selection and mutation can be treated a special case. The mutation matrix is parameter free and adaptive as the mutation probability is time dependent, and captures the accumulated information in the past generations. Three methodologies, mutation by row, mutation by column, and mutation by mixing row and column are introduced and tested on the resource allocation problem of the zero/one knapsack problem, showing high efficiency in speed and high quality of solution compared to other traditional methods.

1 Introduction

The fruitful use of genetic algorithms [1][2] usually requires intelligent choices of parameters, such as the criterion for the selection mechanism. One may need to use different percentage of the population for survival for different problems. Indeed, even for the same problem, the percentage of survivors in the evolution process should be time dependent to achieve a more effective convergence. This observation has been addressed in the work of adaptive parameter control in solving the financial knapsack problem [3]. In this paper, we like to address a novel way to do the selection process by the introduction of a mutation matrix, which is time dependent but problem *independent*.

In traditional simple genetic algorithm, the mutation/crossover operators are processed on the chromosome indiscriminately over the loci. The loci statistics is never employed. The recent work of Ma and Szeto [4] on Locus Oriented Adaptive Genetic Algorithm (LOAGA) has demonstrated the importance of the locus specific mutation rate in solving the zero/one knapsack problem. Their idea is inspired by the research of short tandem-repeat (STR) polymorphism [5], which shows evidence of very different mutation rate at different loci in Human's

---

* Corresponding author.

DNA. In this paper, we will generalize their method and further demonstrate the advantage of using the information on the loci statistics on mutation operator. Since genetic algorithm usually involves additional genetic operators such as crossover, it is difficult to include them together with the mutation operator for a clear comparison. Therefore, we focus on the development of a simple genetic algorithm with mutation only.

2 Mutation Matrix for Traditional Genetic Algorithm

We consider a population of N chromosomes, each encoded by L bits to form a $N \times L$ matrix $A(t)$ for the population at a given time t. The ith row indexes the chromosome which fitness f_i is of rank i, while the jth column indexes the jth locus for the entire population. Our ordering of the rows ensures that $f_i \geq f_k$ if $i \leq k$. We perform mutation on A to explore the solution space and exploit fit chromosomes through selection. Traditionally we divide N chromosomes into three groups: (1) Survivors who are the fit ones, forming the first $N_1 = c_1 \times N$ rows of the population matrix $A(t+1)$ and $0 < c_1 < 1$ is the fraction that survive. (2) N_2 children of the fit ones are formed by replacing the next $N_2 = c_2 \times N < N - N_1$ rows in the $A(t+1)$. The fraction c_1 and c_2 are model parameters to be specified. The children are usually generated from the fit parents (the first N_1 rows) by mutation and/or crossover. (3) the remaining $N - N_1 - N_2$ rows are the randomly generated chromosomes to ensure the diversity of the population so that the genetic algorithm continuously explores the solution space. We can merge all these three steps into one single operation by defining a $N \times L$ mutation matrix $M(t)$, with matrix element M_{ij} defined as the probability of mutation for the A_{ij}. In traditional genetic algorithm, we will have $M_{ij} = 0$ for the first N_1 rows, $M_{ij} = m$ for the next N_2 rows,(this constant $0 \leq m \leq 1$ is a pre-assigned mutation rate) and $M_{ij} = 1$ for the last $N - N_1 - N_2$ rows. In our new method, this matrix M is time dependent.

3 Row and Column Mutation Probability

To begin we first consider the case of mutation on a fit chromosome. We expect to mutate only a few loci so that it keeps most information unchanged. This corresponds to "exploitation" of the features of fit chromosomes. On the other hand, when an unfit chromosome undergoes mutation, it should change many of its loci in order to explore more regions of the solution space. This corresponds to "exploration". Under this principle, we should use a non-uniform and adaptive mutation structure for M instead of the rigid format of the traditional genetic algorithm. We require that M_{ij} should be a monotonic increasing function of the row index i since we order the population in descending order of fitness. This ordering of rows (chromosomes) by fitness effectively selects the survivors, the children by mutation, and the randomly generated chromosomes. In the next section, we will discuss the properties of the columns in the mutation matrix, when we incorporate locus statistics in our locus oriented adaptive genetic algorithm.

In order to formulate a general method for mutation that is problem *independent*, one must use information that is accessible in all kinds of problems. One such candidate is the fitness distribution function of the population. In any genetic algorithm, the course of evolution inevitably accumulates a fitness profile of the population, which we now use for our construction of mutation matrix. Intuitively, good chromosomes should have lower mutation rate than bad ones. We can simply increase the mutation rate linearly for chromosomes of increasing rank, or decreasing fitness so as to get row mutation probability $\alpha_i = \frac{i-1}{N-1}$. A more sophisticated choice is to use the cumulative distribution function $C(f)$ of fitness profile $P(f)$. Since $C(f)$ represents the fraction of the population with fitness value less than or equal to f, it is a monotonic increasing function of f with $C(f_{max}) = 1$ and $C(f_{min}) = 0$. We thus can choose $\alpha_i = 1 - C(f_i)$, which is monotonic increasing function of the row index i. As $C(f_i)$ evolves with time, our α_i becomes adaptive. In either case, we have a ranking mechanism for the chromosome so that the selection process of rows for mutation is automatic.

Next, we must decide on the choice of loci for mutation. We define p_{jX} as the locus mutation probability of changing to X at locus j. (X stands for either 0 or 1 for binary encoding). In the original LOAGA method[4], this is computed simply by counting how many 0 or 1 at locus j inside the population. The information about the chromosome to which this particular 0 or 1 belongs is not used. This loss of information can be remedied by giving more weight to the information provided by fit chromosomes, since fit chromosome contains more important information than unfit ones. We thus redefine the locus mutation probability of changing to a X at locus j as p_{jX} by

$$p_{jX} = \frac{\sum_{i=1}^{N}(N+1-i) \times \delta_{ij}(X)}{\sum_{m=1}^{N} m} \quad (1)$$

where i is the rank of the chromosome in the population. $\delta_{ij}(X)$ is 1 if the ith chromosome has a X at locus j, and zero otherwise. The factor in the denominator is for normalization. For example, if the first half of the population after ranking all have 0 at locus j and the second half have 1 at locus j. According to the original LOAGA method[4], we get $p_{j0} = 0.5$, while our modification yields

$$p_{j0} = \frac{\sum_{k=N/2}^{N} k}{\sum_{k'=1}^{N} k'}$$

which is bigger than 0.5. This is a more reasonable choice for p_{j0} than 0.5, since we place more emphasis on the statistics provided by the first half of the population, which are of higher fitness and all have 0. In this example, we see how we incorporate information from fitness statistics on locus mutation probability. We now compute the column mutation rate p_j using

$$p_j = \frac{1 - |p_{j_1} - \frac{1}{2}| - |p_{j_0} - \frac{1}{2}|}{\sum_k p_k}. \quad (2)$$

For example, if 0 and 1 are randomly distributed, then $p_{j_0} = p_{j_1} = 0.5$. In this case, we have no information about the locus so we mutate it, and $p_j = 1$.

On the other hand, in the extreme cases of $p_{j_0} = 1 - p_{j_1} = 0$, or 1, we have definitive information and we do not mutate this column, and $p_j = 0$.

3.1 Mutation Only Genetic Algorithm: MOGA

First we should remind ourselves that p_{j_X} contain information of both locus and individual. To select the column of the mutation matrix, we first compute the locus mutation probability p_{j_X} for each column j and then the corresponding column mutation probability p_j. We can then write our general form of the mutation matrix element as $M_{ij} = \alpha_i \times p_j$. Now we observe that there are two ways to apply M on the population. We can first decide which row (chromosome) to mutate and then which column (locus) to mutate, we call this particular method the *Mutation Only Genetic Algorithm by Row* or abbreviated as MOGAR. Alternatively, we can first select the column and then the row to mutate, and we call this the *Mutation Only Genetic Algorithm by Column* or abbreviated as MOGAC. This MOGAC is a new kind of mutation and we like to see if it can work just like traditional GA, which is a special kind of MOGAR.

For MOGAR, we go through the population matrix $A(t)$ by row first. We first arrange the locus mutation probability, $p_j(t)$, in descending order. The, for a given row i, we generate a random number x. If $x < \alpha_i(t)$, then we perform mutation on this row, otherwise we proceed to the next row and $A_{i,j}(t+1) = A_{i,j}(t)$, $,j = 1, ..., L$. If row i is to be mutated, we determine the set $R(i)$ of loci in row i to be changed by choosing the loci with the $p_j(t)$ in descending order, till we obtain $K(i) = \alpha_i \times L$ members. Once the set $R(i)$ is constructed, mutation will be performed on these columns of the ith row of the $A(t)$ matrix to obtain the matrix elements $A_{i,j}(t+1), j = 1, ..., L$. We then go through all N rows. In one generation, we need to sort N fitness, L probabilities $p_j(t)$, and generate N random numbers for the rows. After we obtained $A(t+1)$, we recompute the $\alpha_i(t+1)$ and $p_j(t+1)$ in the mutation matrix $M(t+1)$.

For MOGAC, the operation is similar to MOGAR mathematically. For a given column j, we generate a random number y and if $y < p_j(t)$, we perform mutation on this column, otherwise we proceed to the next column and $A_{i,j}(t+1) = A_{i,j}(t)$, $,i = 1, ..., N$. If column j is to be mutated, we determine the set $S(i)$ of rows in column j to be changed by choosing the rows with the $\alpha_i(t)$ in descending order, till we obtain $W(j) = p_j(t) \times N$ members. Since A is assumed to be row ordered by fitness, we simply need to choose the $N, N-1, ..., N-W(j)+1$ rows to have the jth column in these row mutated to obtain the matrix elements $A_{i,j}(t+1), i = 1, ..., N$. In one generation, we sort a N fitness values, compute L probabilities p_j and generate L random numbers for the columns.

3.2 Mutation Only Genetic Algorithm with Mixing MOGAM

In our Mutation Only Genetic Algorithm by Row and by Column, we do not need to introduce any parameter for selection or preset our mutation probability. Our MOGAR or MOGAC is entirely determined by the information accumulated in the fitness distribution and the locus statistics. We find that each MOGA method has its own advantages and disadvantages. For MOGAR, we have a well-defined mutation probability for the entire population throughout the evolution, since our row mutation rate is α_i. Once we choose a row to mutate, we must sweep through the L loci to decide on the mutation of each bit. This generally leads to slower speed compared to MOGAC. In MOGAC, $p_{jx} \simeq 0.5$ for all j in the first few generations, resulting in mutation of most entries in A. This rapid mutation allows a fast collection of statistics initially. In MOGAC, the column information provides more adaptive power, as our p_{jx} contains both the row and column information, resulting in higher speed in application. While faster, MOGAC also runs the risk of early convergence to local optimum, which is a serious problem for genetic algorithm. Indeed, when MOGAC converges to a local optimal solution, $p_{jx} \simeq 0$ for all j and the population stops evolving. When this happens, mutation by row will help as MOGAR always produce mutation in each generation: some unfit chromosomes always mutate. This forces the population to explore the global solution region continuously. The conclusion is that MOGA by column will speed up convergence and place emphasis on "exploitation", while MOGA by row will be slower but keeps on evolving and place emphasis on "exploration". A natural approach is to mix MOGAR with MOGAC, so that we can statistically exploit and explore to achieve better performance. We abbreviate this mutation only genetic algorithm with mixing row and column mutation as MOGAM, or *Mutation Only Genetic Algorithm with Mixing*. For illustrative purpose, we simply use MOGA by row and by column alternatively in our test example of the zero/one knapsack problem in the next section. We should note that the method of mixing should be problem dependent and in a separate paper, we further develop MOGAM into quasi-parallel genetic algorithm [6].

4 Application to the Zero/One Knapsack Problem

The model problem to test our ideas on MOGA is the Knapsack problem, considered a difficult problem for traditional genetic algorithm [7]. In the early version of our ideas on mutation matrix [4], we find that LOAGA outperforms dynamic programming which is the usual method for Knapsack problem. Now, we use LOAGA as our new benchmark and compare it with our MOGAR, MOGAC, and MOGAM

First we define the 0/1 Knapsack Problem [8]. Given L items, each has its own profit P_k, weight w_k and the the total capacity limit is c. The objective is to select a subset of L items to place in the knapsack so as to maximize the profit, while its total weight does not exceed the capacity limit. Mathematically, we need to choose the set $(x_1, x_2, ..., x_L)$ so as to maximize F given by $F = \sum_{k=1}^{L} P_k \times x_k$ subjected to the constraint $\sum_{k=1}^{L} w_k \times x_k \leq c$. Here $x_j = 0$, or 1. Applications of this class of problem often appear in economic problem, such as the problem of resource allocation[8], and logistic problem like airline cargo. Several commonly used methods to find the exact solution of the zero/one knapsack are branch and bound, depth-first with bound, and dynamic programming[8]. Here we simply want to use this problem to compare our MOGA with the Locus Oriented

Adaptive Genetic Algorithm, which is better than dynamic programming[4]. We consider a particular knapsack problem with size $L = 150$ items, $c = 4000$, $P_k \in [0, 1000]$, and $w_k \in [0, 100]$. In all test we use the same population size $N = 100$. For knapsack problem, we follow [4] and use two tricks, *"Punishment"* and *"Repairing"*, in solving the constraint problem. *"Punishment"* reduces the fitness when the constraint is violated, *"Repairing"* modifies the chromosome (adding/deleting items) until the constraint is satisfied. We will use a method called Greedy Repair. If a chromosome violates the constraint (total weight is over the constraint in the Knapsack), the repair scheme will remove the least p/w ratio selected items from the knapsack until the constraint is satisfied. When the constraint is satisfied, and if some empty space remains, Greedy Repair will tried to fill the knapsack "as full as possible" under constraint by picking up the unselected item and fill then in the knapsack in descending order of p/w. The repair stops once the constraint is violated. This scheme can repair all chromosomes into local optimal solution in Hamming space. Finally we should state that unlike MOGA, the selection mechanism in LOAGA must be specified. Here we use the adaptive selection as discussed in [3]. Chromosome will be selected if its fitness is greater than $f(max) - 0.5\kappa(f(max) - f(min))$, where κ is a constant between 0.5-0.6. The details of this method can be found in [4].

5 Result and Comparison

We compare LOAGA with three kinds of evolutionary computation using mutation matrix (MOGAR, MOGAC, and MOGAM) in two perspectives. The first one concerns the quality of the solution in terms of the best values (maximum

Table 1. Best Value of the Four Methods in Solving a Knapsack Problem

Example 1	Row	Column	Mix	LOAGA
50 generations	56243	59540	59481	60451
100 generations	58017	60526	60519	60500
200 generations	59144	60719	60719	60500
500 generations	60469	60719	60719	60500
1000 generations	60635	60719	60719	60549
Example 2	Row	Column	Mix	LOAGA
50 generations	59193	63808	63315	64696
100 generations	61783	64764	64270	64711
200 generations	62482	64802	64821	64711
500 generations	64782	64814	64821	64711
1000 generations	64782	64814	64821	64711
Example 3	Row	Column	Mix	LOAGA
50 generations	61455	64840	65368	66411
100 generations	63779	66113	66583	66729
200 generations	64171	66721	66738	66729
500 generations	66289	66738	66738	66729
1000 generations	66738	66738	66738	66729

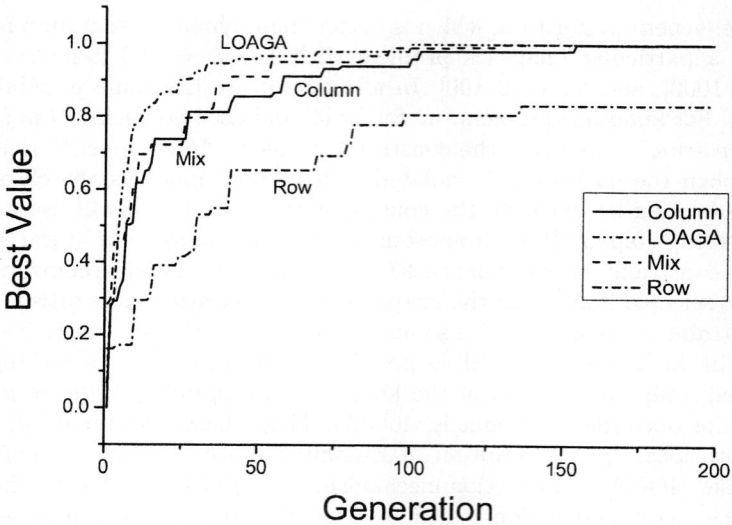

Fig. 1. Shows the performance of four different methods in solving a randomknapsack problem

of the knapsack). In table 1 we show the best values after 1000 generations for these four algorithms.

We see that all MOGA produce better results than LOAGA, as our MOGA programs handle the early convergence problem more satisfactorily. Although LOAGA uses adaptive selection to avoid early convergence problem, it requires extra parameter which needs adjustment to improve its performance. On the other hand, our MOGA methods are parameter free, as everything we use is based on information accumulated in the evolving population.

The second features for comparison is the speed to solution. In [4] we have already seen how LOAGA greatly improve the performance in solving knapsack problems. It shows high convergent rate with 91% successful rate in solving knapsack problem with $N = 500$ items. In Fig.1, we compare the convergence to a solution of LOAGA with three MOGA programs. As expected, MOGAR converges slower than the other algorithms, while MOGAM and LOAGA have similar rate of convergence. This indicates that our MOGA programs can produce better results at a speed comparable to LOAGA.

6 Conclusion

In conclusion, we see that mutation matrix provides a new method of evolutionary computation. Traditional genetic algorithm can be treated as a special case in our formalism. We show that the mutation matrix can be found in a problem independent manner and we achieve selection implicitly by individualized and locus specific mutation probability. Furthermore, mutation matrix is parameter free (no need to specify c_1 and c_2) and adaptive. Our formulation of mutation only genetic algorithm by row, by column or by mixing row and column have been tested. They are more reliable in quality of solution and comparable in speed to LOAGA. which has been shown to be better than the standard method of dynamic programming for the knapsack problem [4].

Acknowledgement

K.Y. Szeto acknowledges the support of CERG grant HKUST6157-01P and 603203.

References

1. Holland, J.: Adaptation in natural and artificial systems. Ann Arbor, MI: University of Michigan.
2. D.E. Goldberg: Genetic algorithms in Search, Optimization, and Machine Learning, Addison-Wesley, Reading, Massachusetts(1989).
3. Kwok Yip Szeto and Man Hon Lo: An Application of Adaptive Genetic Algorithm in Financial Knapsack Problem, *The 17th International Conference on Industrial & Engineering Applications of Artificial Intelligence & Expert Systems*, Ed Bob Orchard, Chunsheng Yang, and Moonis Ali, May 17-20, 2004, LNAI3029 Publication by Springer Verlag 2004.pp1220-1227.
4. Chun Wai Ma and Kwok Yip Szeto, *Locus Oriented Adaptive Genetic Algorithm: Application to Zero/One Knapsack Problem*, Proceeding of The 5th International Conference on Recent Advances in Soft Computing, RASC2004 Nottingham, UK. p.410-415, 2004.
5. Bernd Brinkmann et.al, Mutation Rate in Human Microsatellites: Influence of the Structure and Length of the Tandem Repeat, Am. J. Hum. Genet.62-1408-1415 (1998).
6. Kwok Yip Szeto and Jiang Rui: A quasi-parallel realization of the Investment Frontier in Computer Resource Allocation Using Simple Genetic Algorithm on a Single Computer. *Lecture Notes in Computer Science, LNCS 2367, Applied Parallel Computing , Advanced Scientific Computing , 6th International Conference, PARA 2002, Espoo, Finland, June 15-18, 2002*. Proceedings, PARA2002, pp.116-126. Springer-Verlag.
7. V. Gordon, A. Bohm, and D. Whitley: A Note on the Performance of Genetic Algorithms on Zero-One Knapsack Problems.*Proceedings of the 9th Symposium on Applied Computing (SAC'94), Genetic Algorithms and Combinatorial Optimization.*, Phoenix, Az, pp 194-195(1994).
8. Hans Kellerer, Ulrich Pferschy and David Pisinger: Knapsack Problem, Springer, 22-26.

Dependent-Chance Programming Model for Stochastic Network Bottleneck Capacity Expansion Based on Neural Network and Genetic Algorithm

Yun Wu[1,3], Jian Zhou[2], and Jun Yang[3]

[1] College of Management, Wuhan University of Technology,
Postfach 430077, Wuhan ,Hubei, China
wuyun1974@hotmail.com
[2] Department of Computer Sciences, University of Angers, France
zhoujian@hotmail.com
[3] College of Management, Huazhong University of Science and Technology,
Postfach 430077, Wuhan, Hubei, China
martineyang@163.com

Abstract. This paper considers how to increase the capacities of the elements in a set E efficiently so that probability of the total cost for the increment of capacity can be under an upper limit to maximum extent while the final expansion capacity of a given family F of subsets of E is with a given limit bound. The paper supposes the cost w is a stochastic variable according to some distribution. Network bottleneck capacity expansion problem with stochastic cost is originally formulated as Dependent-chance programming model according to some criteria. For solving the stochastic model efficiently, network bottleneck capacity algorithm, stochastic simulation, neural network(NN) and genetic algorithm(GA) are integrated to produce a hybrid intelligent algorithm. Finally a numerical example is presented.

1 Introduction

As we know, during the past years, many experts did relevant researches in the fields of network expansion. Ravindra K.Ahuja and James B.Orlin [1] studied a lot about network flows and network flow model, and they figured out an algorithm for the maximum flows problem with constrained conditions. O.Berman [2] worked over weight problem of decreasing a given tree edge to cut down weight of minimal tree, and proved a strongly polynomial algorithm for this problem. S.O.Krumke [3] presented two improved network flow models, and put forward heuristic algorithm to resolve some network improvement problems. Zhang,J and Yang,C[4] also showed us a strongly polynomial algorithm for a particular network expansion problem. Based on Zhang,J's research, Yang Chao, etc.[5]took budgets and bottleneck capacity restrictions into consideration, and gave a strongly polynomial algorithm for this kind of network expansion problems. Internally, Wang Hongguo,etc.[6-7] solved capacity expansion problems of undirected network and directed network by extending Yang Chao's network bottleneck model, and the concept of fixed expansion was brought forward. In the process of network expansion, Yang Xiaoguang [8] introduced several normal form problems, constructed a network model subtly to figure out network optimization problem, and offered a relevant arithmetic to deal with it. Whereas, restrictions exist in all the above researches about the determined network bottleneck capacity expansion problems for many uncertainty factors in reality, such as, uncertainty of needs, expansion costs, uncertainty of accomplishment time, etc. Charnes&Cooper[9] first studied dependent-chance models, they put forward second type stochastic programming. Most marked feature was that dependent-chance constrained condition must satisfy the believed area. After that, more researchers began to study these problems. Based on work of Charnes&Cooper ,Liu B[10] gave an arithmetic for dependent-chance programming. K.IWAMURA[11] introduces this dependant-chance programming to the field of integer programming ,and he gave heuristic arithmetic to solve it. upon that, H.Ishii and Nishida [12] introduced a new problem about stochastic bottleneck capacity expansion, afterwards,H.katagiri, H.Hishii [13] discussed a chance-constrained model of bottleneck spanning tree in terms of fuzzy stochastic edge weights. Based on the above algorithms, Hideki Katagiri and Masatoshi Sakawa[14] explored necessary probability and evaluation problems in fuzzy stochastic bottleneck spanning tree problem. Internally, Liu Baoding, etc. [15] employed genetic algorithm to solve orientation problem in network optimization problem efficiently. All the work will be appreciated.

In this paper, based on the above research fruits, no researchers have introduced the dependant-chance programming to network bottleneck capacity expansion problem. For solving stochastic model more efficiently, a strongly polynomial algorithm of network , neural network(NN) and genetic algorithm(GA) are integrated to produce a hybrid intelligent algorithm. Finally, a numerical example is presented.

2 Network Bottleneck Capacity Expansion Model with Stochastic Unit Expansion Cost

Let $G(V, E, C)$ be an undirected network structure, which is composed of vertices set $V = \{v_1, v_2, v_3, \cdots, v_n\}$ and edge set $E = \{e_1, e_2, e_3, \cdots, e_m\} \in V * V$. Every edge has an original edge capacity c_i. Let original network capacity vector be $C = \{c_1, c_2, c_3, \cdots, c_m\}$, let unit expansion cost on every edge be w_i, and let expansion cost vector W be a stochastic vector, which meets definite distribution function. Spanning tree $T = T(N, S)$ is a part of network graph, which meets the following terms:

(1) T and G have the same vertices;
(2) |S|= n -1 shows the force of set S, that is, the number of edges;
(3) T is connected graph.

Define the capacity of a spanning tree T of network $G(V, E, C)$ be $cap(T, C)$, which is the bottleneck capacity for every edge in T, i.e.

$$cap(T, C) = MIN\{c_i \mid e_i \in T, T \in G(V, E, C)\} \tag{1}$$

We use $T^*(C)$ to show the maximum capacity tree of network $G(V,E,C)$, i.e.

$$cap(T^*,C) = \underset{T}{MAX}\{cap(T,C)\} \qquad (2)$$

The beforehand problem of this paper is how to expand original capacity vector C to minimize the total expansion cost while the capacity $cap(T^*,C)$ of maximum expansion tree of expanded network $G(V,E,\underline{C})$ meets definite condition and scopes.

$$H(r) = \{\underline{C} \mid \underline{C} \geq C, cap(T^*, \underline{C}) \geq r\} \qquad (3)$$

2.1 Problem 1

Given r_0, how to expand C to $\underline{C}$ to minimize expansion cost $(\underline{C}-C)^T W$, and $cap(T^*,\underline{C}) \geq r_0$, problem 1 equals the following problem:

$$\min(\underline{C} - C)^T W$$
$$s.t.$$
$$\underline{C} \in H(r0) \qquad (4)$$

According to the above analysis, we introduce probability statistics concept, and induce the dependent-chance programming model of network bottleneck capacity expansion with stochastic unit expansion cost, the core idea of this dependent-chance model is to maximize probability of random issue and optimize the value of objective function in uncertain conditions, and get reasonable optimized value in reality.

When unit expansion cost vector $W = \{w_1, w_2, w_3, \cdots, w_m\}$ is stochastic variable, the total expansion cost $COST(\underline{C} \mid W, C) = \min(\underline{C}-C)^T W$ is also a stochastic variable. The problem we consider here is to let probability of the total cost for the increment of capacity can be under an upper limit to maximum extent In this section, we offer a new idea to set up a general dependent-chance model of network bottleneck capacity expansion with stochastic unit expansion cost as follows:

$$\max \Pr\{W \in \Omega \mid COST(\underline{C} \mid W, C) \leq M\}$$
$$s.t. \begin{cases} \underline{C} \geq C \\ cap(T,\underline{C}) \geq r0 \end{cases} \qquad (5)$$

or

$$\max \Pr\{W \in \Omega \mid COST(\underline{C} \mid W, C) \leq M\}$$
$$s.t.$$
$$\underline{C} \in Hr(r0) \qquad (6)$$

In the above formulas, we define stochastic variable $W = \{w_1, w_2, w_3, \cdots, w_m\}$ in the probability space $(\Omega, \Lambda, \Pr)$. From the beforehand problem analysis, we could shift to the essential problem in problem 2.

2.2 Problem 2

Thus, the ultimate problem of this paper is: considering stochastic unit expansion cost, how to expand original capacity vector C to maximize the probability that $COST(\underline{C}|W,C)$ is less than M which is a given expansion cost and minimize the value of the total expansion cost while the capacity $cap(T^*, C)$ of maximum expansion tree of expanded network $G(V, E, C)$ satisfies definite condition and scopes. A child problem of bottleneck capacity is included in dependent-chance model of problem 2, $COST(\underline{C}|W,C) = \min(\underline{C} - C)^T W$ i.e. problem 1, once choose a value in the probability space (Ω, Λ, Pr), stochastic variable W will become a determined value $\underline{w}$. In Yang Chao [4-5], strongly polynomial algorithm has been brought forward for this determined problem. In the next section, we will discuss the general algorithm for this problem.

3 Hybrid Intelligent Algorithm for Stochastic Network Bottleneck Capacity Expansion

3.1 Calculate Uncertainty Function

From the above thought, we could work out the algorithm for this dependent-chance model. First of all, we design a stochastic simulation algorithm to get the value of uncertainty function.

$$U(\underline{C}) \to \max \Pr\{W \in \Omega \mid COST(\underline{C}|W,C) \leq M\} \tag{7}$$

Steps:

(1) Let $N' = 0$;
(2) We need get definitive value of $\underline{w}$ from stochastic variable W, which produced from probability Pr in Ω;
(3) Employ definitive network bottleneck capacity expansion algorithm, which is designed by Yang Chao [4-5], to calculate problem 1. the algorithm is also a child problem of stochastic dependent-chance programming model. We show optimized solution for the child problem as c;
(4) If $c \leq M$, than $N' \leftarrow N' + c$;
(5) Repeat step 2 to step 4 N times, N is a prodigious circulation times;
(6) Back to N'/N.

3.2 Approximate Uncertain Function by Neural Network

NNs are inspired by the current understanding of biological NNs. The most popular and useful NN architecture is multilayer feedforward NN, which is widely used for pattern classification and functional approximation ,in this paper , NNs are used to approximate uncertain functions. When we solve models (5) or (6) by GA, the process of stochastic simulations to compute $U(\underline{C})$, will be repeated for thousands of times , which means large computations, so NNs are trained to approximate these uncertain function, which reduce the computations and speed up the solution process greatly. After making a set of input-output data for uncertain function U(C) by stochastic simulations ,we train an NN to approximate the uncertain function by the back propagation algorithm according to the training data.

In detail, in order to get training data , firstly , we take the steps which follow the section 3.1 to approximate the uncertain function U(C). we can get N training data according to repeating the process of stochastic simulation for N times. We let $N \geq \frac{32W}{\varepsilon} \ln \frac{32W}{\varepsilon}$ (or simply , $N \geq \frac{W}{\varepsilon}$) ,see [16], here, W is the sum of edges and nods of neural network, ε is the rate of misjudgment (let $\varepsilon = 2\%$) 。We use the back propagation algorithm to approximate the uncertain function U(C) . as everyone knows, the propagation ability of the neural network that has two hidden layers is better than the neural network that has one hidden layer. But for our bottleneck capacity network expansion problem, the neural network that has one hidden layer is enough to approximate any uncertain function.。in this paper, we just use the feedforward neural network which has one input layer ,one hidden layer and one input layer. Support the input layer has m input nodes, output layer has n output nodes and hidden layer has p hidden nodes. In the section 4 numeral example, we let m=5(the num of decision variable wi) , n=1(the num of uncertain function) . The hidden nodes p can be calculated by pruning algorithm [17]。 The purpose of the training process is to find the neural network 's best weight ω to minimize the value of error function

$$Err(\omega) = \frac{1}{2} \sum_{i=1}^{N} \| F(w_i, \omega) - u_i \|^2 \qquad (8)$$

here $F(W, \omega)$ is the output function of neural network.

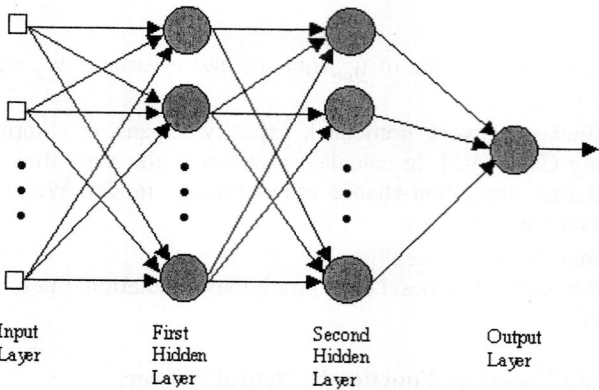

Fig. 1. Neural network

3.3 Hybrid Intelligent Algorithm

In order to solve the problem of network bottleneck capacity expansion, we combine network bottleneck capacity algorithm, stochastic simulation ,neural network and

genetic algorithm to produce a hybrid intelligent algorithm, which will reduce calculation work and manage large-scale problems.
Steps:

(1) Generate training input-out data for uncertain function by stochastic simulations
(2) Train neural networks to approximate the uncertain function according to the generated training data.
(3) Initialize chromosomes $V_k = (\underline{C}^k) = (c_1^k, c_2^k, c_3^k, ..., c_m^k)$,
$k = 1, 2, 3, \cdots, pop\_size$, check the feasible region $\underline{C} \in H(r_0)$ where the trained neural network will be used
(4) Calculate every chromosome's target value $U^k(\underline{C}^k)$ $k = 1, 2, 3, \cdots, pop\_size$ by the trained neural network. This algorithm includes Yang Chao [4-7]'s strongly polynomial algorithm for determined network bottleneck capacity expansion and employs to solve the problem 1;
(5) Calculate every chromosome's fitness extent, the evaluation function is:
$Eval(V_k) = \alpha(1-\alpha)^{k-1}$ $k = 1, 2, 3, \cdots, pop\_size$ $\alpha \in (0.1)$, α is a parameter in genetic algorithm.
Rearrange chromosomes $v_1, v_2, v_3, \cdots, v_n$ pop_size, in accordance with the different evaluation values, from good to poor in sequence;
(6) Confirm next generation by circumvolving roulette wheel pop_size time, according to the fitness extent. Finally, we obtain a new chromosome, and we use v_k, $k = 1, 2, 3, \cdots, pop\_size$ to denote it;
(7) Define Pc as the probability of intercross operation, and update chromosomes v_k, $k = 1, 2, 3, \cdots, pop\_size$ by intercross operation. In order to confirm father generations in the intercross operation process, we should repeat the following process from i=1 to pop_size: produce a stochastic number r from [0,1], if $r < Pc$, chose v_i as one father generation. Use $v_1', v_2', v_3', \cdots$ to denote the above chosen father generations, and divide this group of father generations into pairs like: $(v_1', v_2'), (v_3', v_4'), (v_5', v_6'), \cdots$. For example, in the pair of (v_1', v_2'), at first, we produce stochastic number c from (0, 1), and then produce two offspring X, Y through intercross operation between v_1', v_2', according to the formula as follows:

$$X = cV_1' + (1-c)V_2', Y = cV_2' + (1-c)V_1'$$

If these two children chromosomes belong to the feasible region $\underline{C} \in H(r_0)$, we could use them to substitute their parents. If not, we have to give up these two children chromosomes, and repeat intercross operation until the children chromosomes meets the feasible region $\underline{C} \in H(r_0)$. Finally, new chromosomes v_k, $k = 1, 2, 3, \cdots, pop\_size$ come into being;
(8) Renew chromosomes through variation operation. As the above step, firstly, define a parameter Pm as the probability of variation, and repeat the following process from i=1 to pop_size: produce a stochastic number r from [0,1], if $r < Pc$,

chose v_i as one father generation and operate relevant variation in the selected father generation $V' = (c_1, c_2, c_3, ... c_m)$. Then, we chose a variation direction d at random in the space R^n, if $X = V' + Md$ doesn't belong to the feasible region $\underline{C} \in H(r_0)$, we suppose M as a stochastic number from 0 to M, and M is a given big integer, then a new child chromosome will be produced. Size up whether the new child chromosome meets the feasible region, if not, repeats the process until it belongs to the feasible region $\underline{C} \in H(r_0)$. We substitute the satisfied child chromosome for the father chromosome, and at last we gain a group of new chromosomes v_k, $k = 1, 2, 3, \cdots, pop\_size$;

(9) Repeat step 2 to step 6 in terms of the given circulation times;

(10) The best chromosome $V^* = (c^*_1, c^*_2, c^*_3, ... c^*_m) = C^*$ is the optimum solution for network bottleneck capacity expansion model with stochastic unit expansion cost.

4 A Numerical Example

Here we calculate a simple numerical example, the network graph is as follows:

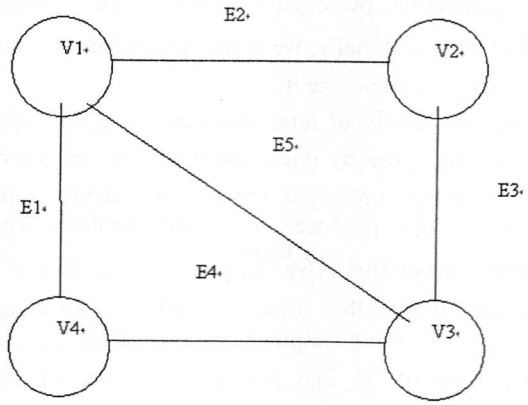

Fig. 2. Network graph

Table 1. Parameter value list in network graph

Edge of graph (E)	(E1)	(E2)	(E3)	(E4)	(E5)
Original capacity C	c1=20	c2=30	c3=40	c4=50	c5=80
Unit expansion cost W	w1→ N(280,400)	w2→ N(100,225)	w3→ N(152,64)	w4→ N(160,900)	w5→ N(167,49)

Let $r_0 = 75$ $\alpha = 0.9$, M=8600, $C^* = \{c_1^*, c_2^*, c_3^*, c_4^*, c_5^*\}$ be the optimum solution of expansion; $COST^*$ is the optimum solution of expansion cost; prob* is max probability, Error%=(Prob*-prob*$_{min}$)/prob*$_{min}$, Vi= wi($\underline{c}^*_i$ –ci) NNerror is average error rate of neural network

$$\max \Pr\{W \in \Omega \mid COST(\underline{C} \mid W, C) \leq 8600\}$$
$$s.t. \qquad (9)$$
$$\underline{C} \in Hr(75)$$

Table 2. The list of results

	popsize	Pc	Pm	α	gen	NNerror	V1	V2	V3	V4	V5	Prob*	Error%
1	30	0.2	0.1	0.07	600	0.023	0	4545	0	4025	0	93.5	0.322
2	30	0.2	0.1	0.07	600	0.028	0	4365	0	3900	0	94.8	1.717
3	30	0.3	0.2	0.05	600	0.019	0	4365	0	3925	0	96.2	3.219
4	30	0.3	0.2	0.10	600	0.032	0	4365	0	4025	0	95.7	2.682
5	40	0.1	0.3	0.11	600	0.016	0	4500	0	4050	0	93.2	0

The hybrid intelligent algorithm is run with 5000 cycle in simulations and 5000 training sample for NNs and 600 generations in GA, Different environment parameters of GA are taken, and corresponding solutions are give in table2, where 'prob' is the maximal probability. Similarly, we run the hybrid intelligent algorithm for 7 times with different parameters of GA on the basis of equivalent generations. In order to measure the differentia between these results,' error', I.e. the percent error, is calculated and given in table2. From these computational results, we see that the maximal percent error does not exceed4.292% when different parameters are chosen. Therefore the hybrid intelligent algorithm is also robust to the parameter settings and effective to solve model (9).

5 Conclusions

The paper first introduces dependent-chance model to network bottleneck capacity expansion problem. For solving the stochastic model efficiently, network bottleneck capacity algorithm, stochastic simulation, neural network and genetic algorithm are integrated to produce a hybrid intelligent algorithm.

Acknowledgement

This research work is funded by National Nature & Science Funds (Project Fund Code: 70271027). The authors appreciate it and all other people who have helped us.

References

1. Ahuja R.K,Magnanti T.L,Orlin J.B.: Network Flows. Englewood Cliffs, NJ: Prentice-Hall(1993)
2. Averbakh I, Berman O,Punnen AP .: Constrained Matroidal Bottleneck Problem. Discrete Applied Mathematics 63 (1995) 201-14
3. Krumke,S.O , Marthe ,M.V.,Ravi,R., and Ravi, S.S.: Approximation Algorithms for Certain Network Improvement, Journal of Combinatorial Optimization, 2(1998),257-288
4. Zhang,J., Yang,C., Lin, Y.: A Class of Bottleneck Expansion Problems , Computer and Operational Research, 124(2000),77-88
5. Yang,C., Liu,J.: A Capacity Expansion Problem with Budget Constraint and Bottleneck Limitation , Acta Mathematica Scientia , 22(2002),207-212
6. Wang Hongguo, Ma Shaohan: Capacity Expansion Problem on Undirected Network, Journal of Shangdong University, 35(2000),418–424
7. Wang Hongguo, Ma Shaohan: Capacity Expansion Problem on Directed Network, Application Mathematics Journal of Chinese University, 16(2001) 471-473
8. X.G.Yang, J.Z.Zhang: A Network Improvement Problem under Different Norms. Computational Optimization and Applications.27 (2004) 305-319
9. Charnes, A.,&Cooper, W.W: Management Models and Industrial Applications of Linear Programming , Englewood Cliffs , NJ: Prentice-Hall (1961)
10. Liu B : Dependent-Chance Programming : a class of stochastic programming. Computers& Mathematics with Applications 34(1997)89-104
11. 11K.IWAMURA, B.Liu: Dependent-Chance Integer Programming Applied to Capital Budgeting, Journal of the Operations Research Society of Japan, 42(1999) 117-127.
12. Ryan SM: Capacity Expansion for Random Exponential Demand Growth. Working Paper No.00-109, Industrial and Manufacturing Systems Engineering, Iowa State University, Ames, IA, August 2000.
13. H.Katagiri, H.Ishii: Chance Constrained Bottleneck Spanning Tree Problem with Fuzzy Random Edge Costs, Journal of the Operations Research Society of Japan 43 (2000) 128-137
14. H.Katagiri, Masatoshi Sakawa, Hiroaki Ishii: Fuzzy Random Bottleneck Spanning Tree Problem Using Possibility and Necessity Measures, European Journal of Operational Research 152 (2004) 88-95
15. Liu B: Uncertain Programming. New York : wiley(1999)
16. Venkatech S.: Computation and Learning in the Context of Neural Network Capacity, Neural Networks for Perception 2 (1992) 173-327
17. Castellano G.,Fanelli A.M, Pelillo M.: An Iterative Pruning Algorithm for FeedForward Neural Networks, IEEE Transactions on Neural Network 8 (1997) 519-537.

Gray-Encoded Hybrid Accelerating Genetic Algorithm for Global Optimization of Water Environmental Model

Xiaohua Yang[1], Zhifeng Yang[1], Zhenyao Shen[1], and Guihua Lu[2]

[1] State Key Laboratory of Water Environment Simulation,
Beijing Normal University, Beijing 100875, China
ylx1h1@sohu.com
[2] College of Water Resources and Environment, Hohai University, Nanjing 210098, China
lugh@hhu.edu.cn

Abstract. This improved algorithm, Gray-encoded hybrid accelerating genetic algorithm (GHAGA), is presented to reduce computational amount and to improve the computational accuracy for the global optimization of water environmental models. The hybrid method combines two algorithms, which are the Gray-encoded genetic algorithm and Hooke-Jeeves algorithm. With the shrinking of searching range, the method gradually directs to optimal result with the excellent individuals obtained by Gray genetic algorithm embedding the Hooke-Jeeves searching operator. The convergence and global optimization of the new genetic algorithm are analyzed. Its global convergence rate is 100%, and the computational velocity is fast for five test functions. And it is efficient for the global optimization in the practical water environmental model on wastewater treatment.

1 Introduction

The algorithms for global optimization are of increasing importance in modern environmental models. Many environmental models consist of a large number of parameters. The global optimization to the parameters of complicated models is intractable. The particular challenge is that an algorithm may be trapped in the local extreme point of an objective function when the dimension is high and there are numerous local optima. In the above case, the traditional optimization methods may not obtain the global optimization efficiently. Genetic algorithm (GA) is a kind of heuristic searching algorithm based on the mechanics of natural selection and natural genetics. The global solutions can be found for both linear and nonlinear formulations. The work on genetic algorithm was done by Holland [1]. The detailed genetic algorithm and its implementation were given by Goldberg [2]. De Jong [3] showed that the standard binary-encoded GA (SGA) could constitute an interesting alternative to perform the global optimization of a function depending on several continuous variables [4]. The genetic algorithm and its extensions are powerful in their search for the global optimum [5-6]. GA has been applied in many fields [7-12]. However, the computational amount is very large and premature convergence phenomena exist in SGA. To reduce computational amount and improve the computational precision, the binary-encoded accelerating genetic algorithm (BAGA), real-encoded genetic algorithm (RGA) and integer-encoded genetic algorithm were developed [13-16]. However, these genetic algorithms cannot be effectively applied for continuous variable global optimizations in nonlinear environmental models. The Hamming distance between two closest integers in binary code is very large. For instance, integers 127 and 128 are expressed by the 01111111 and 10000000 in binary code, respectively. All of the codes must be changed if we turn 127 into 128 in binary code. This operation reduces the efficiency of the genetic algorithms. This phenomenon is termed the 'Hamming cliff'. To overcome these difficulties relating to binary encoding for continuous variable optimizations, the standard binary-encoded GA was improved with Gray encoding [4, 12, 17]. For the Gray-encoded genetic algorithm (GGA), the integers 127 and 128 are expressed by the 01000000 and 11000000. It was found that this algorithm still needs a large amount of computation. So GGA should be developed. In this paper, a Gray-encoded hybrid accelerating genetic algorithm (GHAGA) is presented to improve the computational efficiency. This approach will apply to five nonlinear functions and one practical environmental model on the least-cost of wastewater treatment, and the results show that it is efficient and robust.

2 The Steps of GHAGA

Consider the following water environmental optimization problem:

$$\min f(x_1, x_2, \cdots, x_{n_p})$$
$$\text{s.t. } a_j \leq x_j \leq b_j \text{ , for } j=1,2,\ldots,n_p \quad (1)$$

where $x = \{x_j, j = 1,2,\ldots,n_p\}$, x_j is an environmental variable to be optimized, f is an objective function and $f \geq 0$.

And the steps of GHAGA are given as follows.

Step 1. Gray encoding.
Suppose Gray encoding length is e in every variable, the jth environmental variable range is the interval $[a_j, b_j]$, and then each interval is divided into $2^e - 1$ sub-intervals:

$$x_j = a_j + I_j \cdot c_j \quad (2)$$

where the length of sub- interval of the jth variable $c_j = (b_j - a_j)/(2^e - 1)$ is constant. The Gray code array of the jth variable is denoted by the grid points of $\{d(j,k) | k = 1,2,\ldots,e\}$ [12]:

$$I_j = \sum_{m=1}^{e} (\bigoplus_{k=m}^{e} d(j,k)) \cdot 2^{m-1} \quad (3)$$

where ⊕ denotes the operator of addition modulo 2 on $\{0,1\}$. GHAGA's process operates on a population of individuals (also called Gray code array, strings or chromosomes). Each individual represents a potential solution.

Step 2. Generating initial father population.
Initially, the chromosomes are generated at random in Gray-encoded genetic algorithm, and n-chromosomes in father population are:

$$I_j(i) = \text{int}(u(j,i) \cdot 2^e) \text{ for } j=1,2,...,n_p; i=1,2,...,n \quad (4)$$

where $u(j,i)$ is uniformity random number, $u(j,i) \in [0,1]$, $I_j(i)$ is a searching location, int ( ) is an integer function. From Eq.(3), the n-corresponding chromosomes are $d(j,k,i)$ for $j=1,2,...,n_p; k=1,2,...,e; i=1,2,...,n$. To homogeneously cover the whole solution space and to avoid the risk of having too much individuals in the same region, a large uniformity random population are selected in this algorithm.

Step 3. Fitness evaluation.
The fitness function $F(i)$ of ith chromosome for the optimization is defined as follows:

$$F(i) = \frac{1}{[f(i)]^2 + 0.1} \quad (5)$$

Step 4. Reproduction.
Compute the reproduction probability $p_r(i)$ of a certain chromosome with Equation (6).

$$p_r(i) = F(i) / \sum_{j=1}^{n} F(j) \quad (6)$$

Such two groups of n-chromosomes are selected by the above probabilities.

Step 5. Two-point crossover.

Perform crossover on each chromosome pair according to probability p_c to generate two offspring. For two-point crossover, two crossing points are randomly chosen. Crossover the two chromosomes, save the new chromosome and delete the parents from the population. Loop this step until all the parent chromosomes are computed with crossover. In order to enhance the diversity of population, the crossing probability is set as $p_c \geq 0.5$.

Step 6. Two-point mutation.
In this paper, two-point mutation is adopted. And a new offspring can be computed by a mutating probability p_m. The operator has the capability not only to exploration, but also exploitation. Thus the operator can improve the computational efficiency [12].

Step 7. Hooke-Jeeves evolution.
The Hooke-Jeeves algorithm is a useful, local descent algorithm, which does not make use of the objective function derivatives [18]. The best point in the previous phase becomes a new initial solution in the Hooke-Jeeves algorithm, and then a new best point is obtained by this Hooke-Jeeves algorithm. The new best point inside the offspring will be inserted to replace the worst one in the previous phase. Repeat step3 to step 7 until the evolution times Q or termination criteria is met.

Step 8. Accelerating cycle.
The variable ranges of n_s-excellent individuals obtained by Q-times of the Hooke-Jeeves evolution become the new ranges of the variables, and then the whole process return to step 1.

Step 9. Stop computation.
The computation process is over until the objective function value gets to an expected value, or algorithm running times gets to the design T times. Herein, the most excellent chromosome currently is the optimum solution of GHAGA.

The GHAGA is convergent [12]. The global optimization of the GHAGA is not only accurate but also stable. Let the Hooke-Jeeves evolution times be Q, the number of excellent individuals be n_s, the number of optimized variable be n_p and the times of accelerating evolution be T, the probability p_0 of excellent individuals surround the optimum point is $p_0 = (1 - 2^{-Q \cdot n_s})^{n_p \cdot T}$. The GHAGA is global convergence with probability $p_0 = 1.000$ when $Q=2$, $n_s = 10$, $n_p = 5$, $T=5$; $Q=2$, $n_s = 20$, $n_p = 5$, $T=5$; $Q=3$, $n_s = 10$, $n_p = 10$, $T=10$; $Q=5$, $n_s = 20$, $n_p = 15$, $T=15$; $Q=5$, $n_s = 20$, $n_p = 15$, $T=15$, etc.

3 Experiment

3.1 Criteria

Three main criteria, the relative error, the absolute error and the total computation number, for the objective functions, are very important when trying to determine the performances of an algorithm: convergence, speed and robustness [4]. The parameters of the GHAGA are selected as follows: The length $e = 10$, population size $n = 300$, the number of excellent individuals $n_s = 10$, the times of Hooke-Jeeves evolution Q=5, the crossover probability $p_c = 1.0$, the mutation probability $p_m = 0.5$, and the times of Hooke-Jeeves searching $m \leq 300$.

The global optimization of five test functions [4] is accomplished by using the following methods: standard binary-encoded GA (SGA), improved Gray-encoded genetic algorithm (IGGA) [4] and GHAGA. To compare with the global optimization ability of the above algorithms objectively, the absolute error or relative error in neighbor generations will be less than or equal 10^{-2}, and the less than or equal 18,000 computations of the objective functions are done, and one of the three termination criteria is used for ensuring the optimization precision and avoiding algorithm invalidation.

3.2 Experiment and Result

To test our GHAGA, five analytical test functions, F2 (1 variables), Branin (2 variables), Hartman1 (3 variables), Shekel1 (4 variables) and Brown1 (20 variables), were used. This set of classical test functions, were often used [4,16]. Because of the stochastic nature of GAs, the discussion of results derived from one single execution of the algorithm is meaningless [16]. So all results reported in this section are obtained by averaging the results from 100 executions per function. The computation results of the five nonlinear test functions are given in Tables 1~2 with the SGA, IGGA [4] and GHAGA. It is obviously observed that the GHAGA is the best one both in accuracy (see minimum found in Table 1) and in efficiency (see success rate and number of evaluation of the functions in Table 2) compared with existing algorithms. The results given in Table 2 show that the global optimum is reached since the ratio of success is equal to 100% for the five tested functions with GHAGA, and the 'Hamming cliff' phenomena are avoided in GHAGA.

Table 1. The minimum found with the SGA, IGGA(Andre et al., 2001) and GHAGA

Name of the functions	Number of variables	Theoretical minimum	Minimum found with different methods		
			SGA	IGGA	GHAGA
F2	1	-12.03125	-12.03120	-12.03120	-12.03123
Branin	2	0.39789	0.39789	0.39791	0.39789
Hartman1	3	-3.86278	-3.86249	-3.86114	-3.86277
Shekel1	4	-10.15320	-10.13490	-10.14866	-10.15209
Brown1	20	2	43.62810	8.55162	1.99877

Table 2. Results with the SGA, IGGA(Andre et al., 2001) and the GHAGA

Name of the functions	Number of evaluation of the functions for minimizing objective functions			Success rate %		
	SGA	IGGA	GHAGA	SGA	IGGA	GHAGA
F2	5347	744	300	100	100	100
Branin	8125	2040	305	81	100	100
Hartman1	1993	1680	319	94	100	100
Shekel1	7495	36388	390	1	97	100
Brown1	6844	128644	312	0	0	100

4 Application

Example. Consider the least-cost treatment of wastewater as an environmental optimization model to satisfy

$$\min F = 696.744 x_1^{1.962} + 10586.71 x_1^{5.9898} + 63.927 x_2^{1.8815} + 9054.54 x_2^{5.9898} +$$
$$375.658 x_3^{2.9972} + 57.428 x_3^{1.8731} + 5200.91 x_3^{5.9898} + 113.471 x_4^{1.8815} + \quad (7)$$
$$223.825 x_4^5 + 23.626 x_4^{4.8344} + 5431.427 x_4^{5.9898} + 3982$$

$$\text{s.t.} \quad g_1 = 20.475(1-x_1) - 22.194 \le 0,$$
$$g_2 = 17.037(1-x_1) + 12.998(1-x_2) - 23.505 \le 0,$$
$$g_3 = 15.660(1-x_1) + 11.942(1-x_2) + 8.822(1-x_3) - 24.031 \le 0, \quad (8)$$
$$g_4 = 14.229(1-x_1) + 10.855(1-x_2) + 8.026(1-x_3) + 21.965(1-x_4) - 24.576 \le 0,$$
$$0 \le x_1, x_2, x_3, x_4 \le 0.9,$$

where, x_i is the sewage treatment rate at the ith discharge point, F is total daily cost of treatment.

We consider the following objective function:

$$f = F + \sum_{i=1}^{4} h_i(g_i) \quad (9)$$

$$\text{and } h_i(g_i) = \begin{cases} 0 & \text{when} \quad g_i \le 0 \\ 10^5 & \text{otherwise} \end{cases} \quad (10)$$

where $h_i(g_i)$ is a penalty function.

The least objective function f is 5060.95($) with GHAGA, and x_1 =0.4884, x_2 =0.5058, x_3 =0.5062, x_4 = 0.6372. For the GHAGA, the evaluation number T is 11. For real-encoded genetic algorithm (RGA), the evolution number T is 1000, the least objective function f is 5076.28 ($). For the Hooke-Jeeves algorithm (HJA), the least objective function f is 5228.27($) of 100 independent runs. And for fuzzy nonlinear optimization method [20], the least objective function f is 5063.10 ($). Our GHAGA can overcome some Hamming-cliff phenomena in existing genetic algorithms, and the result is satisfied both in efficiency and accuracy for practical wastewater treatment model.

5 Conclusion

In this paper, a new method, GHAGA is proposed to solve water environmental optimal problem. Because the steps of Gray-encoding, Hooke-Jeeves hybrid searching operator and accelerating cycle are used, the efficiency and accuracy of the new algorithm are very high compared to existing algorithms. The corresponding convergence and global optimization ability are analyzed. This algorithm overcomes some Hamming-cliff phenomena in existing genetic methods, it has been applied to five nonlinear test functions and one practical wastewater treatment model, and the results are encouraging.

Acknowledgement

This work was supported by Foundation items: National Key Project for Basic Research (Grant No. 2003CB415204) and the Ministry of Science and Technology of China (Grant No. 2004BA611B020401).

References

1. Holland, J.H.: Adaptation in Natural and Artificial Systems. University of Michigan (1975)
2. Goldberg, D, E.: Genetic Algorithms: Search, Optimization and Machine Learning. Addison-Wesley (1989)
3. Jong, D.: An Analysis of the Behavior of a Class of Genetic Adaptive Systems. Ph.D. Dissertation, University of Michigan, Ann Arbor, MI.,USA (1975)
4. Andre, J., Siarry, P., Dognon, T.: An Improvement of the Standard Genetic Algorithm Fighting Premature Convergence in Continuous Optimization. Advances in Engineering Software. 32, (2001)49-60
5. Harrouni, K. El., Ouazar, D., Walters, G.A., Cheng, A. H.-D.: Groundwater Optimization and Parameter Estimation by Genetic Algorithm and Dual Reciprocity Boundary Element Method, Engineering Analysis with Boundary Elements, Vol.18, (1997) 287-296
6. Leung, Y. W., Wang, Y. P.: An Orthogonal Genetic Algorithm with Quantization for Global Numerical Optimization, IEEE Trans, On Evolutionary Computation. 5(1), (2001) 41-53
7. Wang Q. J.: Using Genetic Algorithms to Optimize Model Parameters, Environmental Modeling & Software, Vol.12, (1997)27-34
8. Cheng, C.T., Ou, C.P., Chun, K. W.: Combining a Fuzzy Optimal Model with a Genetic Algorithm to Solve Multiobjective Rainfall-runoff Model Calibration, Journal of Hydrology,Vol.268, (2002)72-86
9. Chau, K.W.: A Two-stage Dynamic Model on Allocation of Construction Facilities with Genetic Algorithm, Automation in Construction, Vol.13, (2004) 481-490
10. Yang, X. H.: Study on Parameter Optimization Algorithm and its Application in Hydrological Model. Ph.D. Dissertation, School of Water Resources and Environment, Hohai University, Nanjing, China(2002)
11. Yang X.H.,Yang Z. F., Shen Z.Y., et al.: A Multi-Objective Decision-Making Ideal Interval Method for Comprehensive Assessment on Water Resource Renewability. SCIENCE IN CHINA, Series E, Vol.47, Supp. I, (2004)8
12. Yang X.H., Yang Z.F., Lu G.H., Li J.Q.: A Gray-encoded, Hybrid-Accelerated, Genetic Algorithm for Global Optimizations in Dynamical Systems. Communications in Nonlinear Science and Numerical Simulation. 10(4), (2005)355-363

13. Jin, J. L., Ding, J.: Genetic Algorithm and Its Applications to Water Science. Sichuan: Sichuan University. (2000)
14. Janikow, C. Z., Michalewicz, Z.: An Experimental Comparison of Binary and Floating Point Representation in Genetic Algorithms. Proceedings of the Fourth International Conference on Genetic Algorithms, San Francisco, (1991)31-36
15. Renders, J. M., Flasse, S. P.: Hybrid Methods Using Genetic Algorithms for Global Optimization. IEEE Trans Systems, Man Cybernetics—Part B: Cybernetics. 26(2), (1996)243-258
16. Bessaou, M., Siarry, P.: A New Tool in Electrostatics Using a Really-coded Multipopulation Genetic Algorithm Tuned Through Analytical Test Problem. Advances in Engineering Software. 32, (2001) 363-374
17. Ming Z., Shudong S.: Genetic Algorithms: Theory and Applications, Beijing, Defence Industry Press. (2001)
18. Hooke, R., Jeeves, T. A. (1961). "Direct Search" Solution of Numerical and Statistical Problems. J. Ass. Comput. Mach.. 8, 212-229.
19. Anderssen, R. S., Jennings, L.S., Ryan, D. M.: Optimization. University of Queensland. (1972)
20. Xiong Deqi, Chen Shouyu, Ren Jie.: Fuzzy Nonlinear Programming Model for Water Environmental Pollution System. Journal of Hydraulic Engineering,12,(1994)22

Hybrid Chromosome Genetic Algorithm for Generalized Traveling Salesman Problems

Han Huang[1], Xiaowei Yang[2,*], Zhifeng Hao[2], Chunguo Wu[3],
Yanchun Liang[3], and Xi Zhao[2]

[1] College of Computer Science and Engineering,
South China University of Technology, Guangzhou 510640, P.R. China
[2] College of Mathematical Science, South China University of Technology,
Guangzhou 510640, P.R. China, Tel.: 86-20-88374044
xwyang@scut.edu.cn
[3] College of Computer Science and Technology, Jilin University,
Changchun 130012, P.R. China

Abstract. Generalized Traveling Salesman Problem (GTSP) is one of the challenging combinatorial optimization problems in a lot of applications. In general, GTSP is more complex than Traveling Salesman Problem (TSP). In this paper, a novel hybrid chromosome genetic algorithm (HCGA), in which the hybrid binary and integer codes are adopted, is proposed as an improvement of generalized chromosome genetic algorithm (GCGA). In order to examine the effectiveness of HCGA, 16 benchmark problems are simulated. The experimental results show that HCGA can perform better than GCGA does in solving GTSP.

1 Introduction

GTSP[1-3] has been first introduced in the context of computer record balancing and visit sequencing through welfare agencies. Other application fields of GTSP include: agent service brokering problem[4], covering tour problem, material flow system design, post-box collection, stochastic vehicle, arc routing and so on[5].

The GTSP can be described as the problem of seeking a special Hamiltonian cycle with the lowest cost in a completely weighted graph[6]. Let $G = (V, E, W)$ be a completely weighted graph, in which $V = \{v_1, v_2, ..., v_n\} (n \geq 3)$, $E = \{e_{ij} | v_i, v_j \in V\}$, and $W = \{w_{ij} | w_{ij} \geq 0 \text{ and } w_{ii} = 0, \forall i, j \in N(n)\}$ are vertex set, edge set and cost set, respectively. The vertex set V is partitioned into m possibly intersecting groups $V_1, V_2, ..., V_m$ with $|V_j| \geq 1$ and $V = \bigcup_j^m V_j$. The special Hamiltonian cycle is required to pass through all of the groups, but not all of the vertices. At present, there are two kinds of GTSP[5,7]: (1) the cycle passes exactly one vertex in each group and (2) the cycle passes at least one vertex in each group. In this paper, only the first case is discussed and called as GTSP for the sake of convenience.

---

* Corresponding author.

In the previous, simple dynamic programming methods were proposed to solve GTSP[1-3]. Laporte[8,9] used integer programming to solve the instances with 104 vertexes. Fischetti *et al*[10,11] applied branch-and-cut algorithm to solve the GTSP with 442 vertexes. Renaud and Boctor[12] designed a composite heuristic algorithm for GTSP. And some studies on GTSP focused on how to change GTSP into TSP[13-15]. Unfortunately, these methods could only be used to solve small GTSP problems for its low efficiency.

Recently, a generalized chromosome genetic algorithm (GCGA), which could be considered as the best solving algorithm for GTSP, was proposed by Wu *et al*[6]. However, GCGA cannot solve the GTSP instances with large groups very well due to the limits of the generalized chromosome setting and crossover strategy, which can be proved by the analysis of chromosome schema. In this paper, a hybrid chromosome genetic algorithm (HCGA) is designed to improve the performance of GCGA.

2 Hybrid Chromosome Genetic Algorithm for GTSP

In this section, a novel algorithm named hybrid chromosome genetic algorithm (HCGA) is given. There are also two parts in the new chromosome of HCGA: head part formed by binary numbers and body part, which is the same as generalized Chromosome of GCGA[6] (refer to Fig. 1).

Fig. 1. Hybrid Chromosome

Let $H = \{h \mid h = [h(1), h(2), ..., h(\hat{m})], h(i) = [a_1, a_2, ..., a_{N_i}]\}$
$(a_j \in \{0,1\}, 1 \le j \le N_i, N_i = [\log_2 |V_i|], i \le \hat{m})$

The coding for the head of hybrid chromosome can be described in the following:

$h = [h(1), h(2), ..., h(\hat{m})] \xrightarrow{coding} [h(1) \bmod |V_1|, h(2) \bmod |V_2|, ..., h(\hat{m}) \bmod |V_{\hat{m}}|]$

In the crossover strategy of HCGA, $h_x \otimes h_y \to (h'_x, h'_y)$ is changed into $h_x \otimes h_y \to (h'_1, h'_2)$ and $b_x \otimes b_y \to (b'_x, b'_y)$ is the same as that in GCGA, where

$h'_1 = [h_x(1)$ **and** $h_y(1), h_x(2)$ **and** $h_y(2), ..., h_x(\hat{m})$ **and** $h_y(\hat{m})]$

$h'_2 = [h_x(1)$ **or** $h_y(1), h_x(2)$ **or** $h_y(2), ..., h_x(\hat{m})$ **or** $h_y(\hat{m})]$

The mutation for the head of the hybrid chromosome is designed as follows:

M: $h = [h(1), h(2), ..., h(i), ..., h(\hat{m})] \xrightarrow{i} h = [h(1), h(2), ..., \textbf{not } h(i), ..., h(\hat{m})]$.

3 Computational Results

In this section, some benchmark problems are computed by HCGA. These instances can be obtained from TSPLIB library[16]. To test GTSP algorithms, Fischetti et al.[7] provided a partition algorithm to convert the instances used in TSP to those which could be used in GTSP.

In our experiments, we take the population size as 100, maximal generation as 200, crossover probability as 0.5, and mutation probability as 0.09. All of the instances are computed by HCGA and GCGA[6] five times on a PC with 1.2 GHz processor and 256 MB SDR memory, and the results are shown in Table 1.

Table 1. Comparisons of results for benchmark test problems

Problem\five runs	HCGA Max	HCGA Min	HCGA Average	GCGA Min	GCGA Average	HCGA Time(s)	GCGA Time(s)
30KROA150	11018	11018	11018	11018	11022	0.35	4.84
30KROB150	12195	12195	12195	12196	12314	0.89	4.31
31PR152	51573	51573	51573	51586	53376	0.60	4.95
32U159	22664	22664	22664	22664	22685	0.99	5.51
40KROA200	13408	13408	13408	13408	13617	1.76	6.10
40KROB200	13124	13113	13119	13120	13352	8.00	6.78
45TS225	68576	68340	68432	68340	68789	19.01	8.40
46PR226	64007	64007	64007	64007	64574	0.58	11.33
53GIL262	1011	1011	1011	1011	1057	41.20	10.11
53PR264	29546	29546	29546	29549	29791	3.07	14.51
60PR299	22647	22631	22638	22638	22996	68.63	11.18
64LIN318	21028	20788	20914	20977	22115	18.34	16.81
80RD400	6534	6456	6498	6465	6604	17.43	7.67
84FL417	9664	9663	9663	9663	9725	19.42	20.90
88PR439	60956	60184	60558	61273	62674	10.87	6.89
89PCB442	21987	21768	21860	21978	22634	31.80	13.77

From Table 1, one can see that HCGA can obtain much shorter GTSP cycles than GCGA does in all of the examples. The reason is that the crossover operator of HCGA is more powerful in searching GTSP cycles than that of GCGA. In some larger problems, the computational effort of HCGA is more than that of GCGA because the search range of HCGA is larger than that of GCGA.

4 Discussions and Conclusions

GCGA was considered as the best evolutionary algorithm for solving GTSP. However, for the setting of the generalized chromosome and its crossover, it is easy for GCGA to fall into local extremum. In order to improve the solution of GTSP, a hybrid chromosome genetic algorithm (HCGA) is designed with the new crossover and mutation operators. The experimental results show that HCGA has a wider search space than GCGA, and can overcome some disadvantages of GCGA.

Acknowledgements

This work has been supported by the National Natural Science Foundation of China (60433020, 10471045), Natural Science Foundation of Guangdong Province (970472, 000463, 04020079), Excellent Young Teachers Program of Ministry of Education of China, Fok Ying Tong Education Foundation (91005), Guangdong Key Laboratory of Computer Network Foundation (No.CN200403), Natural Science Foundation of South China University of Technology (E512199, D76010) and Key Laboratory of Information Science & Engineering of Railway/Beijing Area Major Laboratory of Advanced Information Science & Network Technology (TDXX0506).

References

1. Henry-Labordere, A.L.: The record balancing problem: A dynamic programming solution of a generalized traveling salesman problem, RAIRO B. 2 (1969) 43-49
2. Saksena, J.P.: Mathematical model of scheduling clients through welfare agencies, CORS Journal. 8 (1970) 185-200
3. Srivastava, S.S.S., Kumar, R.C.G., Sen, P.: Generalized traveling salesman problem through n sets of nodes, CORS Journal. 7 (1969) 97-101
4. Easwaran, M., Pitt, J., Poslad, S.: The agent service brokering problem as a generalized travelling salesman problem, Proceedings of the Third Annual Conference on Autononlous Agents, Seattle WA USA. (1999) 414-415
5. Laporte, G., Asef-Vaziri, A., Sriskandarajah, C.: Some applications of the generalized traveling salesman problem, J. Oper. Res. Soc. 47 (1996) 1461–1467
6. Wu, C.G., Liang, Y.C., Lee, H.P., Lu, C.: Generalized chromosome genetic algorithm for generalized traveling salesman problems and its applications for machining, Physical Review E. 70 (2004) 016701
7. Fischetti, M., Salazar, J.J., Toth, P.: Branch-and-cut algorithm for the symmetric generalized traveling salesman problem, Operations Research. 45(3) (1997) 378-394
8. Laporte, G., Nobert, Y.: Generalized traveling salesman through n sets of nodes: an integer programming approach, INFOR. 21 (1983) 61–75
9. Laporte, G., Mercure, H., Nobert, Y.: Generalized traveling salesman problem through n sets of nodes: the asymmetrical cases, Discrete Appl. Math. 18 (1987) 185–197
10. Fischetti, M., Salazar, J.J., Toth, P.: A branch-and-cut algorithm for the symmetric generalized traveling salesman problem, Working paper, University of Bologna (1993)
11. Fischetti, M., Salazar, J.J., Toth, P.: The symmetric generalized traveling salesman polytope, Networks. 26 (1995) 113–123
12. Renaud, J., Boctor, F.F.: An efficient composite heuristic for the symmetric generalized traveling salesman problem, European Journal of Operational Research. 108 (1998) 571-584
13. Noon, C.E., Bean, J.C.: An efficient transformation of the generalized traveling salesman problem, INFOR. 31 (1993) 39–44
14. Lien, Y., Ma, E., Wah, B.W.S.: Transformation of the generalized traveling salesman problem into the standard traveling salesman problem, Information Science. 74 (1993) 177–189
15. Dimitrijevic, V., Saric, Z.: An efficient transformation of the generalized traveling salesman problem into the traveling salesman problem on digraphs, Information Science. 102 (1997) 105–110
16. Reinelt, G.: TSPLIB. A traveling salesman problem library, ORSA Journal on Computing. 3(4) (1991) 376-384

A New Approach Belonging to EDAs: Quantum-Inspired Genetic Algorithm with Only One Chromosome

Shude Zhou and Zengqi Sun

State Key Lab of Intelligence Technology and System, Department of Computer Science
and Technology, Tsinghua University, Beijing, 100084, China
zsd03@mails.tsinghua.edu.cn

Abstract. The paper proposed a novel quantum-inspired genetic algorithm with only one chromosome, which we called Single-Chromosome Quantum Genetic algorithm (SCQGA). In SCQGA, by bringing the information representation in quantum computing into the algorithm, only one quantum chromosome (QC) is used to represent all possible states of the entire population. A novel quantum evolution method without using conventional genetic operators such as crossover operator and mutation operator is proposed, in which according to the best individuals generated by QC we adjust the quantum probability amplitude with quantum rotation gates so that the QC can produce more promising individuals with higher probability in the next generation. The paper indicated that SCQGA is a new approach belonging to estimation of distribution algorithms (EDAs). Experiments on solving a class of combinatorial optimization problems show that SCQGA performs better than conventional genetic algorithm.

1 Introduction

The dramatic advantages of quantum computing inspire people with the new idea: using the quantum information representation and the quantum information processing mode to improve the performance of conventional intelligent algorithms. The work about combining the quantum computing and artificial intelligence includes the study of quantum neural network, quantum evolution computing, quantum fuzzy set and so on. For example, Matsui et al. proposed a qubit neuron model in which a neural state is described by quantum superposition [1], Gopathy Purushothaman et al. built an inherent fuzzy quantum neural network in which multilevel active function is used in hidden-layer neurons [2], Ajit Narayanan et al. introduced a novel evolutionary computing method where concepts and principles of quantum mechanics are used to inform and inspire more efficient evolutionary computing methods [3]. And other related work can refer to [4], [5], [6].

This paper proposed a novel genetic algorithm—single-chromosome quantum genetic algorithm (SCQGA). In SCQGA, relying upon the quantum effects of superposition, we use only one quantum chromosome (QC) to represent all possible states of the entire population and explore the relationship between QC and conventional population. A novel quantum evolution method without using conventional genetic operators such as crossover operator and mutation operator is proposed, in which according to the best individuals generated by QC we adjust the quantum probability amplitude with quantum rotation gates so that the QC can produce more promising individuals with higher probability in the next generation. And, the SCQGA is in fact a new approach belonging to estimation of distribution algorithms (EDAs) and the relationship between EDAs and SCQGA is investigated in the research.

The outline of the work is as follows. In section 2, the background provides the rough description about quantum-inspired genetic algorithm and EDAs. In section 3, the details of the novel SCQGA are introduced. The connection between SCQGA and EDAs is discussed in section 4. In section 5, experimental analyses are given to show that the presented algorithm outperforms conventional genetic algorithm (CGA). At last, the conclusions and future work are given in section 6.

2 Background

2.1 Quantum-Inspired Genetic Algorithms

The work of merging quantum computing and evolutionary computing has been done by several researchers and it can be classified into two branches: to quantum computer and to classical electronic computer. In the literature, most of the studies are faced to quantum computer, such as Bart's quantum evolutionary programming [7], Martin Lukac's evolving quantum circuits using genetic algorithm [8], Hugo de Garis's using quantum evolution algorithm to accomplish a quantum neural network model [9]. Here, we focus on work related to classical electronic computer.

The most important work to classical computer was done by Han et al. [10]. They proposed a quantum evolutionary algorithm which is used to solve combinational problem on classical electronic computer. In their model, the idea of the encoding of chromosome using quantum bit and evolving the population by quantum rotation gate was first proposed. Instead of binary, numeric, or symbolic representation, a Q-bit is defined as the smallest unit of information and a Q-bit individual as a string of Q-bits is introduced. The SCQGA proposed in Section 3 is based on the Han et al.'s previous work. However, the novel quantum concepts in SCQGA, the novel evolution method with only one chromosome and the characters that can be cast to the framework of EDAs are very different from Han et al.'s algorithm.

2.2 Estimation of Distribution Algorithms

Recently, estimation of distribution algorithms (EDAs) have become one of the fastest growing techniques within genetic and evolutionary computation [18]. EDAs are fundamentally different form the traditional evolutionary algorithms. The central engine of evolution in EDAs is the estimation of distribution mode which creates new populations by employing probability model of the solution space. There is no traditional crossover or mutation operator in EDAs. Instead, they explicitly extract global statistical information from the population and build a posterior probability distribution model of promising solutions. Based on the extracted information, new solutions are sampled from the model and construct the next generation of solutions. As the process repeats, the promising solutions are generated.

One of the main issues in EDAs is how to estimate the accurate distribution that can capture the structure of the given problem. There are many kinds of EDAs, for example, population-based incremental learning (PBIL) [12], univariate marginal distribution algorithm (UMDA) [13], mutual information maximization for input clustering (MIMIC) [14], compact Genetic Algorithm (cGA) [15], factorized distribution algorithm (FDA) [16], Bayesian optimization algorithm (BOA) [17, 18] and so on. These methods have been studied in the last decade and exhibit good performance in solving search problems. Detailed discussion on EDAs can refer to a well-crafted book [18].

3 SCQGA

3.1 Information Representation in SCQGA

It is known that 0-1 bit string is usually used in conventional genetic algorithm to represent a chromosome, and the population can be represented by a number of such chromosomes. However, in SCQGA, based on the quantum effects of superposition, a string of quantum bits is used to represent a chromosome and the population can be represented by only one such special chromosome.

Def 1: *Quantum Gene (QG)* is the smallest information unit in SCQGA, which can be coded as a quantum bit.

QG is represented as a pair of numbers $\begin{pmatrix} \alpha \\ \beta \end{pmatrix}$, which can be also written as $|\psi\rangle = \alpha|0\rangle + \beta|1\rangle$, where α and β are the probability amplitudes associated with the $|0\rangle$ state and the $|1\rangle$ state such that $\alpha^2 + \beta^2 = 1$ and the values α^2 and β^2 represent the probability of seeing a conventional gene state 0 and 1 respectively when the quantum gene is measured [11]. Thus, a QG can be represented as the linear superposition of the two conventional binary genes (0 and 1).

Def 2: *Quantum chromosome (QC)* is a string of QGs.

For example, an n-length QC q can be written as

$$q = \begin{pmatrix} \alpha_1 & \alpha_2 & \cdots & \alpha_i & \cdots & \alpha_n \\ \beta_1 & \beta_2 & \cdots & \beta_i & \cdots & \beta_n \end{pmatrix}, \qquad (1)$$

where $\begin{pmatrix} \alpha_i \\ \beta_i \end{pmatrix}$ is a QG, $i = 1, \cdots, n$, and n is the length of the chromosome. In fact, the QC is the linear superposition of all possible conventional chromosomes. In CGA, an n-length chromosome must be in one of the 2^n situations. However, in SCQGA, an n-length QC can be in all the 2^n situations at the same time:

$$|q\rangle = a_0|00\cdots00\rangle + a_1|00\cdots01\rangle + \cdots + a_{2^n-2}|11\cdots10\rangle + a_{2^n-1}|11\cdots11\rangle, \qquad (2)$$

where a_i represents the quantum probability amplitude, a_i^2 is the probability of seeing the i-th conventional chromosome, $i = 1 \cdots 2^n$.

Def 3: *Quantum population (QP)* comprises *only one* QC.

In CGA, the population is composed of a number of chromosomes. Usually, the more chromosomes a population has, the more diversity it can achieve. The efficiency of the algorithm depends on the size of population in some way. It is impossible to use the population with only one chromosome to accomplish the optimization computation. However, it works if the QC is used. As described in Def 2, a QC can represent all the possible conventional chromosomes at the same time. So, only one QC is enough to construct the whole population. The distribution of the different individuals is indicated by the probability amplitude of the QC. The more the probability amplitude is, the more chance the corresponding individual have to appear. The diversity is not decreased at all, and even increased in fact. The QP will be transformed to conventional population while the fitness is evaluated.

3.2 SCQGA

The main process of SCQGA is similar to CGA. However, because of the novel information representation, the detailed method is very different. The procedure of SCQGA is shown as follows:

1. Initiate the QC;
2. Generate conventional population by collapsing method applied to the QC;
3. Calculate the fitness value of every individual in the conventional population. If the termination condition is achieved, then stop the algorithm;
4. Change the QC by quantum evolution method, and go to Step2.

Step1 is the initiation stage. First of all, parameters such as the length of QC n, the size of conventional population generated by QC N, the evolution rate and the termination condition are given according to the practical problem. And then the QC can be represented as:

$$q = \begin{pmatrix} \alpha_1 & \alpha_2 & \cdots & \alpha_i & \cdots & \alpha_n \\ \beta_1 & \beta_2 & & \beta_i & & \beta_n \end{pmatrix}, \tag{3}$$

where $\alpha_j = \frac{1}{\sqrt{2}}, \beta_j = \frac{1}{\sqrt{2}}$ $j = 1\cdots n$ so that every QG has the same probability amplitude at the beginning. Thus, the QC can represent the entire population and every possible individual is guaranteed to have the same probability to appear in the conventional population.

In Step2, the conventional population is generated so that the evolution of the QC can be evaluated in Step3. The QC is the superposition of conventional chromosomes, and it collapses to one conventional chromosome by calculating the probability of every QG. To every QG $\begin{pmatrix} \alpha_i \\ \beta_i \end{pmatrix}$, it has the probability of α_i^2 to collapse to conventional gene 0 and β_i^2 to collapse to 1[11]. A random number $\lambda \in [0,1]$ is generated first. Then it collapses to 0 if $\alpha_i^2 > \lambda$; otherwise it collapses to 1. The collapsing method is applied to every QG and a conventional chromosome is generated. The conventional population can be obtained by repeating the process N times.

In Step3, the fitness value is calculated for every chromosome generated in Step2. The termination condition is the same as that in conventional method.

Step4 is the key step which determines the performance of SCQGA. The QP is evolved by changing the probability amplitude of the QG using quantum rotation gate instead of using conventional genetic operations such as selection, crossover and mutation operations. The main idea is that the QP evolves toward more promising population by changing the probability amplitude of every gene in chromosome, so that the good individual has the high probability to appear in the next generation.

In quantum computing, the probability amplitude can be changed by altering the quantum phase θ to $\theta + \Delta\theta$ using quantum rotation gate [11]:

$$U(\Delta\theta) = \begin{pmatrix} \cos(\Delta\theta) & -\sin(\Delta\theta) \\ \sin(\Delta\theta) & \cos(\Delta\theta) \end{pmatrix}. \tag{4}$$

In order to change the QC, proper quantum rotation gates has to be constructed and is applied to QGs, and a QG is evolved as:

$$\begin{pmatrix} \alpha_{new} \\ \beta_{new} \end{pmatrix} = \begin{pmatrix} \cos(\Delta\theta) & -\sin(\Delta\theta) \\ \sin(\Delta\theta) & \cos(\Delta\theta) \end{pmatrix} \begin{pmatrix} \alpha_{old} \\ \beta_{old} \end{pmatrix}. \tag{5}$$

Now the key problem is how to construct proper quantum rotation gate. The idea for the construction of the rotation gate is to make the changing of the entire population (quantum chromosome) to the direction of the best individual, and to make the excellent individual have greater chance to appear in the next generation. A lookup table method is introduced below.

1. AVE is a 0-1 string which is the average representation of the QC. For QC
$q = \begin{pmatrix} \alpha_1 & \alpha_2 & \alpha_3 & \dots & \alpha_n \\ \beta_1 & \beta_2 & \beta_3 & \beta_n \end{pmatrix}$, if $\alpha_j^2 \geq 0.5$, then $AVE_j = 0$, otherwise $AVE_j = 1$, $j = 1 \cdots n$.

2. According to Step3, choose the best chromosome in the conventional population, written as $BEST$, which is also a 0-1 string;

3. Look up table 1 to get the proper $\Delta\theta$ and constructing the quantum rotation gate for every gene. $BEST_j$ and AVE_j refer to the j-th gene in $BEST$ and AVE respectively. The parameter a is a positive parameter which determine the evolving rate, $j = 1 \cdots n$.

Table 1. Lookup table of $\Delta\theta$

$BEST_j$	AVE_j	$\Delta\theta$
1	1	0
1	0	a
0	0	0
0	1	$-a$

The overall evolution process in SCQGA can be illustrated in the figure below. The solutions are generated according to conventional population which is constructed by collapsing methods applied to quantum population, and then quantum population is updated using quantum rotation gates. As the process repeats, the optimal or near-optimal solutions can be obtained.

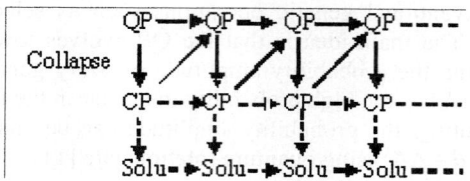

Fig. 1. Evolution process of SCQGA. QP: Quantum Population, CP: Conventional Population generated by collapsing method, Solu: Solutions

4 Connection Between SCQGA and EDAs

The SCQGA is a novel algorithm inspired from quantum computation, but this section shows that it is in fact a new-type approach in EDAs. EDAs attempt to solve optimization problems by repeating the following two steps:
1. Candidate solutions are generated using probabilistic model.
2. The probabilistic model is updated by evaluating the candidate solutions, so that the promising solutions will be generated with greater probability.

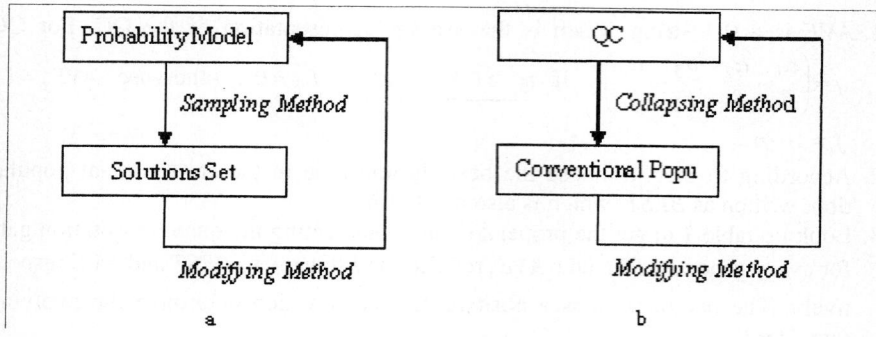

Fig. 2. Schematic description of EDAs and SCQGA. In EDAs (a), candidate solutions are sampled according to probability model, and then the probability model is rebuilt based on the extracted global statistical information from the population. In SCQGA (b), the QC is cast to probability model and the collapsing method is the corresponding the sampling method, so the process of SCQGA can be cast into the framework of EDAs.

The schematic description of EDAs is illustrated in Fig.2.a. Solution set is constructed according to the probability distribution, and then the probability distribution of the selected set of solutions is estimated and updated. The process is repeated until the termination criteria are met. Obviously, we can cast SCQGA into the framework of EDAs. As described in section 3, in SCQGA, QC is used to model the probability distribution, and using quantum collapsing method to generate conventional populations, and then, after evaluating the individuals in conventional population the QC is modified by quantum rotation gates. The schematic description is shown in the below Fig.2.b. So we can say that, the novel SCQGA is an approach in EDAs.

5 Experimental Analyses

In this part, experiments on knapsack problems are carried out to verify the performance of the novel SCQGA and empirical analyses will show that SCQGA outperforms conventional GA.

Knapsack problem is a well-known combinational optimization problem which belongs to NP-hard problem. Knapsack problems with 10, 50 and 100 items are used to evaluate the performance of the novel algorithm. The experimental data are generated randomly. The parameters of the algorithms are set in table 2 and we run the algorithms 30 times respectively.

The statistical comparisons between the quantum and conventional genetic algorithm in handling 10-item, 50-item and 100-item knapsack problem are demonstrated in table 3. It is found that the SCQGA performs much better than the conventional algorithm in solving the knapsack problem.

Table 2. The parameters setting of SCQGA and CGA. PS: population size; MG: maximum number of generations; ER: evolution rate; PAR: probability amplitude range; CP: crossover probability; MP: mutation probability.

Problem	SCQGA/CGA		SCQGA		CGA	
	PS	MG	ER	PAR	CP	MP
10-item	20	100	$\pi/36$	$[\pi/20,\ 9\pi/20]$	0.8	0.05
50-item	100	1000				
100-item	100	1000				

Table 3. The performance comparison of SCQGA and CGA in solving knapsack problem. To each problem, both algorithms run 30 times and performance can be compared by "Best Solution", "Worst Solution", "Average Solution" and "Success Rate". The success rate is defined as: success rate=the times of getting "Best Solution"/30.

Problem	Algorithm	Best Solution	Worst Solution	Ave Solution	Success Rate
10-item	SCQGA	51.9798	51.9798	51.9798	100.00%
	CGA	51.9798	39.226	49.0781	30.00%
50-item	SCQGA	1082.41	1079.50	1082.13	90.00%
	CGA	1082.41	1039.23	1068.72	3.33%
100-item	SCQGA	3976.43	3950.94	3965.71	16.70%
	CGA	3852.21	3644.41	3769.84	0.00%

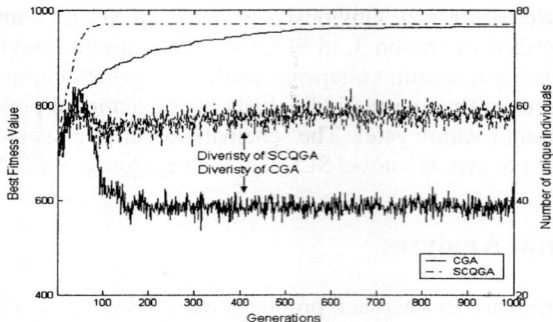

Fig. 3. The evolution process of SCQGA and CGA over 30 runs in solving 50-item knapsack problem. The smooth lines are the fitness variation process and the rough lines indicate the variation of number of individuals with unique fitness.

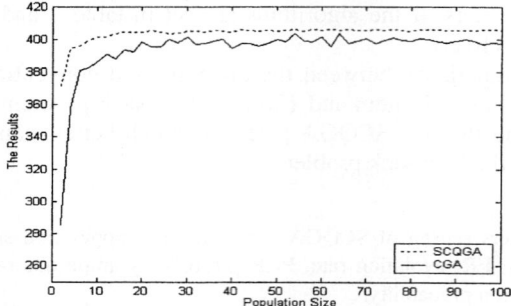

Fig. 4. The best results achieved by SCQGA and CGA averaged 10 runs with different population sizes

Fig.3. illustrates the evolutionary process of the two algorithms in solving the 50-item knapsack problem. The fitness variations show that SCQGA converges more quickly and achieves better solutions than CGA. The population diversity is an important factor that determines the performance of genetic algorithm. The number of individuals with unique fitness is used to measure the population diversity. It is found that SCQGA produces more unique individual than conventional method and we find that QGA produces total 86402 different individuals in the 1000 generations while CGA produces only 35251. The conclusion is that SCQGA maintains the diversity of population much better than CGA, which is the main reason of achieving better performance. The SCQGA makes a good balance between exploiting the best solution and exploring the search space.

To further examine the superiority of SCQGA, we set population size from 2 to 100. Given different population sizes, the SCQGA and CGA are used to optimize the 30-item knapsack problem. The best results they can achieved averaged 10 runs are shown in Fig.4. It can be concluded that SCQGA outperforms CGA for different population sizes obviously. This experiment also shows that even with small population, SCQGA can achieve good performance steadily.

6 Conclusions and Future Work

In this paper we present a novel genetic algorithm—SCQGA, in which relying upon the quantum effects of superposition, we use only one QC to represent all possible states of the entire population. A novel quantum evolution method without using conventional genetic operators is proposed. And SCQGA is cast into the framework of EDAs. To verify the performance of SCQGA, experiments are carried out on knapsack problems and the results show that SCQGA outperforms the conventional genetic algorithm. Though the performance of SCQGA and Han et al.'s algorithm [10] are almost the same in experiments (detailed empirical results were not shown because of the page limit), the novel quantum concepts in SCQGA, the novel evolution method with only one chromosome and the characters that can be cast to the framework of EDAs are very different from Han et al.'s algorithm [10].

SCQGA is our first attempt to combine quantum computing and genetic algorithm and it has some advantages over CGA. However, the model proposed in the paper is very simple. A great deal of research needs to do to increase the effectiveness of the algorithm. The comparison of SCQGA and other methods in EDAs should be further studied. In the research, we indicated that SCQGA is in fact a new approach in EDAs. Experimental and theoretical comparison with EDAs should be further investigated. Theoretical analysis of SCQGA isn't given in this paper. Proving the convergence of the algorithm, analyzing why SCQGA outperforms theoretically and giving mathematic explanation of the dynamic characters of SCQGA are also our next work.

Acknowledgement

This work was funded by the National Key Project for Basic Research of China (Grant No: G2002cb312205). We thank anonymous readers for their valuable comments.

References

1. Nobuyuki, M., Masato, T., Haruhiko, N.: Learning performance of neuron model based on quantum superposition. In: Proceedings of the 2000 IEEE International Workshop on Robot and Human Interactive Communication, Osaka, Japan, IEEE Press (2000)
2. Gopathy, P., Nicolaos, B. K.: Quantum Neural Networks (QNN's): Inherently Fuzzy Feedforward Neural Networks. IEEE Transactions on Neural Network, Vol. 8 (1997) 679-693
3. Narayanan, A., Moore, M.: Quantum-inspired genetic algorithms. In: Proceedings of IEEE international Conference on Evolutionary Computation, Piscataway, NJ: IEEE Press (1996) 61-66
4. Ventura, D., Tony M.: An Artificial Neuron with Quantum Mechanical Properties. In: Proceedings of the International Conference on Artificial Neural Networks and Genetic Algorithms, Norwich, England (1997)
5. Kak, S.: Quantum neural computing. Advances in Imaging and Electron Physics, Vol.94 (1995) 259-313
6. Davide, A., Sandro R., Fabio R., Rodolfo Z.: Quantum optimization for training support vector machines. Neural Networks, Vol.16 (2003) 763-770

7. Rylander, B., Terry, S., James, F., Jim A.: Quantum Evolutionary Programming. In: Proceedings of the Genetic and Evolutionary Computation Conference (2001) 1005–1011
8. Martin, L., Perkowski, M.: Evolving quantum circuits using genetic algorithm. In: Proceedings of the 2002 NASA/DoD Conference on Evolvable Hardware (2002)
9. Hugo, de G., et al.: Quantum versus evolutionary systems: total versus sampled search. In: Proceedings of the 5th International Conference on Evolvable Systems (2003) 457–466
10. Kuk-Hyun, H., Jong-Hwan, K.: Quantum-Inspired Evolutionary Algorithm for a Class of Combinatorial Optimization. IEEE transactions on evolutionary computation, Vol.6 (2002) 580–593
11. Eleanor, R., Wolfgang, P.: An Introduction to Quantum Computing for Non-Physicists. ACM Computing Surveys, Vol.32 (2000) 300–335
12. Baluja, S.: Population-Based Incremental Learning: A Method for Integrating Genetic Search Based function Optimization and Competitive Learning. Carnegie Mellon Univ., Pittsburgh, PA, Tech. Rep. (1994)
13. Mühlenbein, H.: The equation for response to selection and its use for prediction. Evolutionary Computation, Vol.5 (1998) 303–346
14. Jeremy, S. De Bonet, et al.: MIMIC: Finding optima by estimating probability densities. Advances in Neural Information Processing Systems, Vol.9 (1997) 424–431
15. Harik, G. R., Lobo, F. G., Goldberg, D. E.: The compact genetic algorithm. In: Proceedings of the IEEE Conference on Evolutionary Computation, IEEE press (1998) 523–528
16. Mühlenbein, H., Mahnig, T.: The Factorized Distribution Algorithm for additively decomposed functions. In: Proceedings of the 1999 Congress on Evolutionary Computation, IEEE press (2003) 752–759
17. Pelikan, M., Goldberg, D.E., Cantú-paz, E.: Linkage Problem, Distribution Estimation and Bayesian Networks. Evolutionary Computation, Vol.8 (2000) 311–340
18. Pedro, L., Jose, A.L.: Estimation of dstribution algorithm: A new tool for evolutionary compuation. Kluwer Academic Publishers (2002)

A Fast Fingerprint Matching Approach in Medicare Identity Verification Based on GAs

Qingquan Wang and Lili Rong

Institute of Systems Engineering, Dalian University of Technology, Dalian, 116024, China
dlwqq@hotmail.com, llrong@dlut.edu.cn

Abstract. This paper presents an approach to the problem of the identity verification speed by means of fingerprint pattern recognition in the Medicare real-time settlement system. This study aims to speed up the fingerprint feature transmission by greatly reducing the space of feature, and improve fingerprint matching speed under a comparative matching precision. To solve the problem, we take several aspects into consideration: reducing the space of one minutiae point occupied, abandoning the global feature to reduce the feature space, depending on the definition of minutiae point's direction and restriction of transformation for precision, and controlling the number of evolutionary species by searching the optimization parameters. The experiment results indicate that this approach manages to speed up the transmission and matching effectively, and therefore prove to be suitable for the Medicare identity verification.

1 Introduction

The real-time identity verification is a significant part of Medicare, because it not only guarantees the security of Medicare fund in case of an illegitimate loss, but also is indispensable to medical supervision. However, the identity verification in domestic Medicare is carried out through IC card. It is insecure because whether the patient is real or not depends on the eyeballing ability of hospital operators; while checking verification by Medicare controllers is a spot test. For the speciality of Medicare real-time settlement system, a biologic verification method, which is controlled by Medicare itself, should be adopted. According to the market research, Medicare governors deem that the fingerprint recognition is economical and practical compared with other methods, and also capable of being popularized in the Medicare.

However, it is a big problem to apply the technology of fingerprint recognition on Medicare, because the transmission occupies almost the whole finite bandwidth. It is very valuable for some hospitals, especially rural hospitals, since so many Medicare patients should get their identities verified at the same time. The speed of fingerprint matching, especially the speed of transmission, needs improving.

Therefore, to solve the problem of verification speed effectively, two factors---the size of fingerprint feature and the relationship between the speed of fingerprint matching and precision, should be taken into consideration in this research.

Many algorithms of fingerprint matching have been put forward. For instance, Ranade and Ro Senfeld present laxity algorithms for point matching [1]; Ratkovic presents a more special model of fingerprint features [2]; Sparrow.M.K [3] and A.K.Hrechak [4] present fingerprint feature matching based on structural information. In fact, the matching problem in this paper is a point matching based on comparing methods [5]. Since current methods are usually based on traditional searching strategies; the fingerprint feature usually includes global features for a better matching precision, like center point and pattern section; and it is hard to compress the size of feature more. Genetic algorithms, as a fresh theory and method, have been taken as an alternative to obtain a solution of hard optimization problems [6] [7] fit with the parallel processes, and can guarantee the global optimization in the searching process.

We solve the problem of speed with a set of methods: reducing the space of one minutiae point occupied; abandoning global features to compress the feature saved and transmitted; depending on the definition of direction and the restriction of transformation to guarantee a comparative precision of matching; controlling the number of species by searching for the best solution of genetic algorithms' parameters for a faster evolutionary speed. In addition, we adopt the method of simulative input fingerprint data, which is processed from database to test the matching precision.

2 The Definition and Storage of Fingerprint Feature

Controlling the size of fingerprint feature effectively can effectively save the required time of transmission and fingerprint matching. We abandon global features(such as ridge lines quantity, pattern section, center point, and ridge lines shape) except the minutiae points, save the size of space by reducing x-coordinate and y-coordinate range, and guarantee the matching precision through the definition of minutiae point.

The definition of minutiae point's type, which refers to that of FBI [8], according to ridge lines, includes two kinds: end point and forked point, other points can be combined by these two. Each point can have 16 directions shown in Figure 1.

The angle of consecutive direction is 22.5°; there are 32 kinds of minutiae points that we can apply in the matching process. So one minutiae point is a vector, which includes 4 elements (x-coordinate, y-coordinate, direction, type), presented with

$$P = \{(x_1^p, y_1^p, r_1^p, t_1^p), (x_2^p, y_2^p, r_2^p, t_2^p), \cdots\cdots, (x_m^p, y_m^p, r_m^p, t_m^p)\}. \quad (1)$$

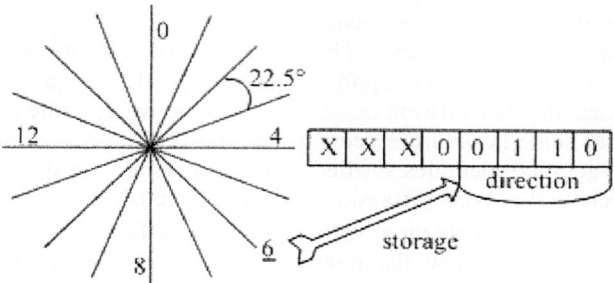

Fig. 1. Sketch Map of Minutiae Point's Direction and Storage

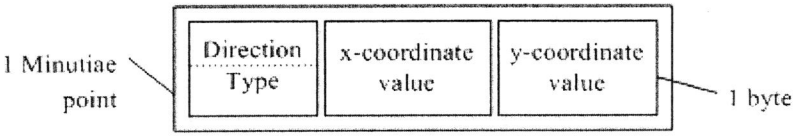

Fig. 2. Sketch Map for Minutiae Point Storage

A minutiae point occupies three bytes for storage. Two bytes of them are used to save the value of x-coordinate and y-coordinate respectively, and the third one is used to save the direction and type of minutiae points. Since the number of minutiae points obtained from input equipment is about 20 to 60, the size of one minutiae feature is controlled within about 60 to 180 bytes, while other methods use the size of 0.3K to 1K bytes. The sketch map storage of minutiae point is shown in Figure 2.

After the minutiae extraction, the feature is saved in the database as the ID for identity verification. But it cannot be completely identical with the feature inputted because of the inaccuracy of displacement and rotation (the zoom can be ignored). Therefore, the main problem of fingerprint matching is that the adjustment of the two features depends on the optimal solution of transformation through search strategies.

3 The Algorithms of Fingerprint Matching

For the fingerprint matching, the most important thing is how to improve the methods for decreasing computation and maintain an acceptable matching precision. As we have discussed above, because the dependence of global features is ignored, the features cannot be matched by traditional methods. Instead, the point matching, based on the underlying principles, is adopted:

1. After finding a corresponding point for each minutiae point from another feature in the fixed border upon region, a pre-matching couple, the gene, is created. The process is called pre-matching.
2. Two pre-matching couples are randomly selected to create an individual, and some individuals are used to create an original species.
3. An excellent individual whose fitness value is above a predefined threshold through selection, crossover and mutation operators is pricked off.

Basing on the summary of genetic algorithms by Michalewicz [9] and analysis by Yao, X. [10] [11], Four presented steps to analyze the matching as following.

3.1 The Gene Expression of Solution

The first thing is to encode a solution from a phenotype to the genotype. Because the expression of the features is based on the minutiae points, a vector of real-valued numbers encodes each individual in this paper, and it can avoid the illegality of solutions and represent a feasible solution only, and vice versa.

Generally speaking, center and trigonal points are used as the benchmark of displacement and rotation. If two couples of correct matching points were found to replace the center and trigonal point, the transformation between two features can be solved. If two features have no relative displacement and rotation or very little inaccuracy under a predefined threshold, the matching problem is to compare only minutiae points on types and directions. Two couples of minutiae points, used for displacement and rotation, are two genes of one chromosome, as is shown in Figure 3.

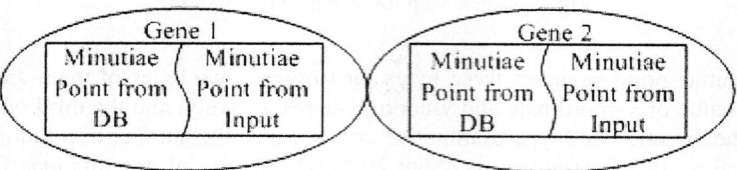

Fig. 3. Sketch Map of Individual's Chromosome

3.2 The Creation of Original Species

After encoding the chromosome, the original species should be created. Two discretional couples of points can be a transformation. One of them is called pre-matching couple. All of these pre-matching couples make up the gene space.

If there are 50 minutiae points, the total of pre-matching couples will be

$$C_{50}^1 \cdot C_{50}^1 = 2500 , \qquad (2)$$

which is the whole combination of a fingerprint feature. This kind of pre-matching couples is redundant and inefficient, so the whole gene space should be reduced. Displacement and rotation should be controlled in a certain range through normative fingerprint input, just as a door will be opened only when you insert the right key and turn it in the correct direction. Here there is a 22.5° for rotation threshold and 0.5cm for displacement threshold.

We need to find the same or similar type minutiae point R (existent or not) in a certain range of point P, and the features of these two points are presented as

$$P = (x^p, y^p, r^p, t^p), \ R = (x^r, y^r, r^r, t^r). \qquad (3)$$

And if point P and point R are pre-matched successfully, several rules of

$$\begin{cases} |x^p - x^r| \le x\text{threshold} \\ |y^p - y^r| \le y\text{threshold} \\ t^p = t^r \\ abs(\mod(r^p,16) - \mod(r^r,16)) \le 1 \ \ (or = 15) \end{cases} \qquad (4)$$

have to be observed for pre-matching. The pre-matching couples are saved to a two-dimension array. And rows, which express genes, constitute the gene space.

An individual can be created by two different genes, and the individual will solve the problem and also a transformation for two features. The population size is 30 in the original species and it remains the same in the evolutionary process.

3.3 Fitness Function for Individuals

This problem is in the field optimization, so we compute the value in the phenotype. Let F_d be the feature points saved in database, F_i the feature points inputted, let

$$I = (a,b,c,d), \qquad (5)$$

the individual selected, so fitness function has the transformation of the displacement and rotation shown in Figure 4, and returns the value of matching point quantity.

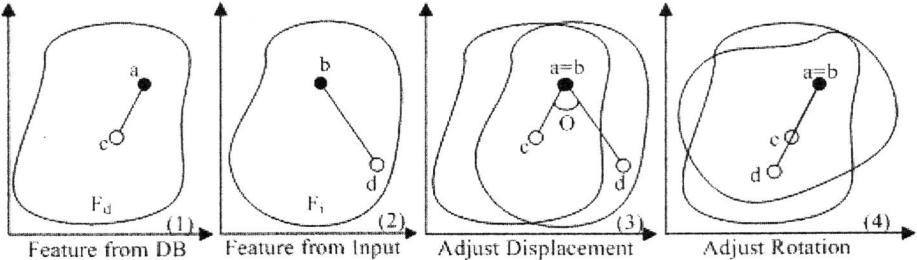

Fig. 4. Sketch Map of Displacement and Rotation Adjustment

However, this fitness function should compute each individual in each species; it will have the more computation, which increases with geometric series along with the evolutionary process. And the flow of fitness function is shown in the Figure 5.

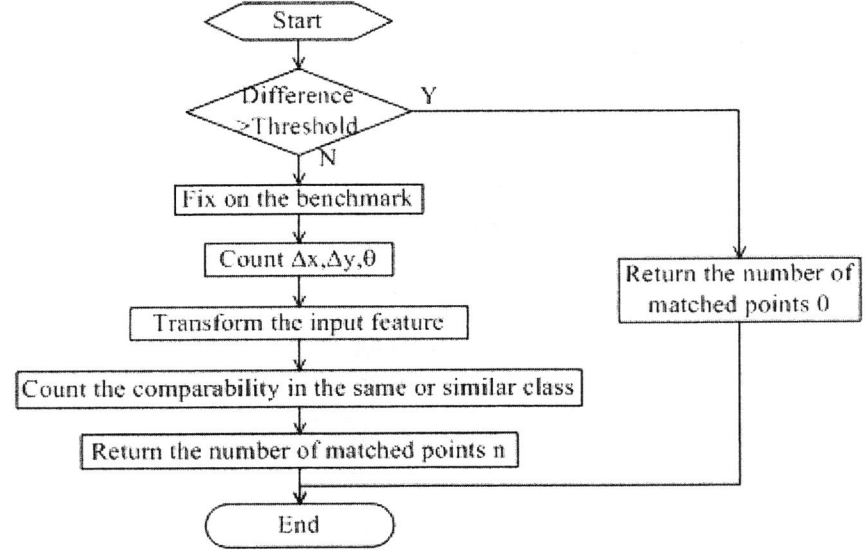

Fig. 5. Flow of Fitness Function

Before evaluating an individual in the phenotype, deterministic methods are used in the genotype to count the fitness value firstly, and it can save about 70% runtime of fitness function through experiments. That is the distance (*D*) (between two points, which are in the same feature) of *(a,c)* and *(b,d)* in the Figure 4. If matching result is accurate, *D(a,c)* and *D(b,d)* should be equal or margin under a predefined threshold.

3.4 Operators in Evolutionary Process and Parameters

A single individual with a certain acceptable fitness value cannot necessarily be found in the original species, so preferable species needs effective genetic operators. Here we emphasize exploration more than exploitation, because what we need is not a global optimal solution, but a local feasible solution above a predefined threshold, and we compare this notion to mountain climbing shown in Figure 6.

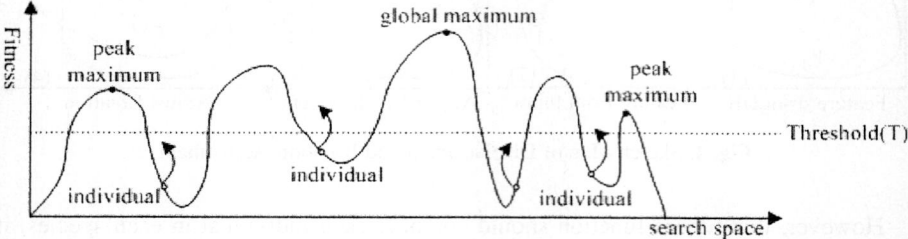

Fig. 6. Sketch Map of Mountain Climbing

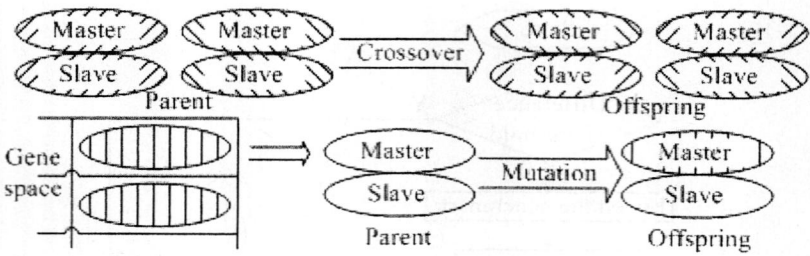

Fig. 7. Sketch Map of Crossover and Mutation

What we care is the first one who climb above the *T*, not the mountain which he climbs and whether it is the highest one. If an individual's fitness value is above *T* (=0.25), and the maximum number of species is above 20, the evolutionary process should be terminated. The crossover and mutation operators are shown in Figure 7.

However, how we can guarantee a fast convergence speed, and evolve a preferable offspring based on its parents' excellent quality?

Emphasizing on exploration, we mainly use crossover and mutation operators as the primary operators to search a preferable solution out of existing species, and selection operators is subordination. It is proved that the time of the first satisfactory individual's appearance will be prolonged along with the increased selection rate.

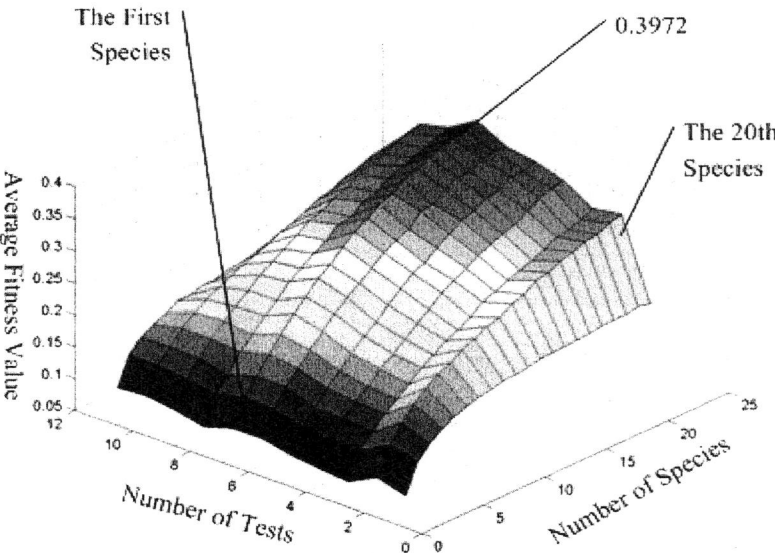

Fig. 8. Results of Average Convergence Speed by Changing Proportion

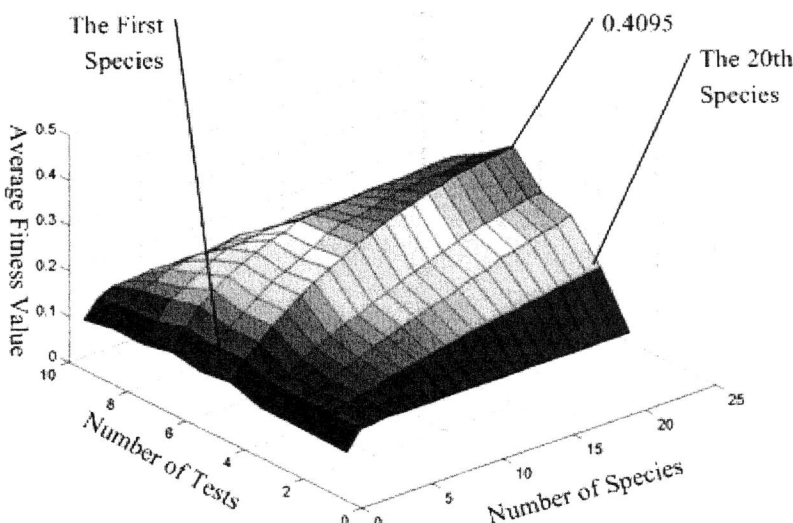

Fig. 9. Results of Average Convergence Speed by Changing Mutation and Crossover Rate

There are two steps to get a fast convergence speed and ensure the excellent quality as well through parameter selection. First fix the crossover and mutation rate, change the proportion of these two genes in the evolutionary process, according to the Table 1. And then, fixing the proportion, crossover and rotation rate are changed according to the Table 1. Therefore we can obtain the relationship among the number of species, master's proportion (or crossover and mutation rate), and average fitness value.

We can come to the conclusion from both the experiment results and the three-dimensional map in Figure 8. It is the fastest convergence speed when the master's proportion is 0.6 and the slave's proportion is 0.4. And then, the relationship among the number of species, mutation rate and fitness value is shown in Figure 9.

According to the results, the best mutation rate is 0.4 and the crossover rate is 0.5. The relationship of fixing proportion is shown in Figure 9 throught 10000 specimens.

Table 1. Variational Parameters in Experiments

No	Primary proportion	Slave proportion	No	Mutation Rate	Crossover Rate
1	0.0	1.0	1	0.0	0.9
2	0.1	0.9	2	0.1	0.8
3	0.2	0.8	3	0.2	0.7
4	0.3	0.7	4	0.3	0.6
5	0.4	0.6	5	0.4	0.5
6	0.5	0.5	6	0.5	0.4
7	0.6	0.4	7	0.6	0.3
8	0.7	0.3	8	0.7	0.2
9	0.8	0.2	9	0.8	0.1
10	0.9	0.1	10	0.9	0.0
11	1.0	0.0			

Table 2. Results of FAR Test

ANFD	ANFS	ANLP	ANAN	APT (ms)	ACT (ms)	AET (ms)	AMT (ms)	FAR (%)
40.250	42.643	11.700	14.093	6.957	0.383	3.621	10.961	0.10
40.040	42.442	11.615	14.016	6.876	0.380	3.661	10.917	0.10
39.981	42.369	11.599	13.987	6.812	0.386	3.574	10.772	0.10
40.101	42.520	11.603	14.022	6.836	0.377	3.311	10.523	0.07
39.817	42.160	11.596	13.939	6.785	0.359	3.465	10.608	0.12
39.825	42.270	11.503	13.948	6.760	0.363	3.715	10.838	0.12
40.138	42.484	11.708	14.055	6.754	0.402	3.631	10.787	0.08
40.050	42.499	11.559	14.009	6.929	0.397	3.659	10.985	0.10
40.026	42.532	11.492	13.997	6.933	0.362	3.702	10.997	0.11
40.218	42.643	11.670	14.095	6.875	0.353	3.652	10.880	0.12

Table 3. Results of FRR Test

ANFD	ASIP	APL	ANP	APT (ms)	ACT (ms)	AET (ms)	AMT (ms)	FRR (%)
39.967	42.477	11.522	13.989	6.787	0.398	188.745	195.930	0.00
39.819	42.453	11.649	14.026	6.742	0.374	187.966	195.081	0.00
39.925	42.654	11.628	14.081	6.860	0.362	188.113	195.334	0.00
39.974	42.482	11.524	14.003	6.702	0.388	188.823	195.913	0.00
39.813	42.300	11.601	13.972	6.695	0.374	187.630	194.699	0.00
39.792	42.330	11.524	13.988	6.810	0.382	188.861	196.053	0.00
39.939	42.550	11.790	14.081	6.804	0.373	189.454	196.631	0.00
40.024	42.267	11.665	13.983	6.857	0.366	189.348	196.571	0.00
40.044	42.397	11.536	13.999	6.776	0.370	189.382	196.528	0.01
40.146	42.352	11.492	13.969	6.852	0.389	189.889	197.130	0.00

4 Experimental Results

Generally, two criterions, False Reject Rate (FRR) and False Accept Rate (FAR), are used to evaluate the precision of matching. Using these two criterions on the identity verification on Medicare, FRR means the rate of regarding a real Medicare patient as a pretender, and FAR means the rate of regarding a pretender as a real one. These two criterions are contradictory but unified, and cannot be absolutely perfect values at the same time. So for the identity verification of Medicare, because the wrong result on a real Medicare patient can be remedied through artificial check, a lesser FAR and a comparatively bigger acceptable FRR are needed.

Except for the FRR and FAR, There are also two criterions of the matching speed, Average Success Matching Time (ASMT) and Average Unsuccessful Matching Time (AUMT), added specially in this paper. The reason is that these two terminate conditions determine the different number of species in the evolutionary process.

10000 specimens are selected randomly from fingerprint feature database, and we carry through a simulative fingerprint features input. There are 10 times matching test for FRR, and 10 times for FAR in a common computer. The results are shown in Table 2 and Table 3. And the abbreviation of experiments in Table1 and Table 2, ANFD, ANFS, ANLP, ANAN, APT, ACT, AET, AMT, express Average Number of Features in Database, Average Number of Features in Simulative-test, Average Number of Lost Points, Average Number of Added Noise, Average Pre-matching Time, Average Creating origin species Time, Average Evolution Time, Average Matching Time respectively.

According to the experimental data, FRR is about 0.1%, and ASMT in FRR test is about 10.827 ms; FAR is smaller than 0.01% and AUMT in FAR test is about 195.987 ms.

5 Conclusions

In this paper, we have increased the speed of transmission to a great extent, because of reducing the size of fingerprint feature. Compared to other methods, the size of a feature is reduced from 0.3K~1K bytes to 60~180 bytes, saving about 80% space of storage and transmission time. It also increases the matching speed effectively by searching the best parameters of genetic algorithms under an acceptable precision through the definition of minutiae points.

This paper takes the Medicare identity verification as the research background, the speed of identity verification as the main objective; and tries to improve the definition of features and the matching methods as well. According to the experiment results, these methods are valuable more in the practical sense, suitable for the domestic Medicare system, and relieve the workload of medical controller considerately. The matching time in experiments has satisfied the needs of Medicare real-time settle system on the whole.

References

1. Sanjay, Ranade, Azriel, Rosenfeld.: Point pattern matching by relaxation. Pattern Recognition. Vol. 12. (1980) 269~275
2. Ratkovic, J.P.: Increasing efficiency in the criminal justice system: the use of new technology for criminal verification and latent print processing. The Rand Corporation, California. (1980)
3. Sparrow, M K, Sparrow, P J.: A topological approach to the matching of single fingerprints: development of algorithms for use on rolled impressions. National Bureau of Standards Special Publication, Washington, DC. (1985)
4. Hrechak, A K, Mchugh, J A.: Automated fingerprint recognition using structural matching. Pattern Recognition. Vol. 23. (1990) 893~904
5. Skea, D., Barrodale, I., Kuwahara, R., Poeckert, R.: A Control Point Matching Algorithm. Pattern Recognition. Vol. 26. (1993)
6. Suganthan, P.N.: Structural pattern recognition using genetic algorithms. Pattern Recognition. Vol. 35. (2002) 1883~1893
7. Jun, H., Yao, X.: Drift analysis and average time complexity of evolutionary algorithms. Artificial Intelligence. (2001) 57~85
8. Jain, A., Hong, Lin., Bolle, R.: Online Fingerprint Verification. Pattern Analysis and Machine Intelligence. Vol. 19. (1997)
9. Michalewicz, Z.: Genetic Algorithm + Data Structure = Evolution Programs. 3rd edition. Springer-Verlag, New York (1996)
10. Yao, X.: Evolutionary computation comes of age. Journal of Cognitive Systems Research. (1999) 59-64
11. Yao, X.: Evolutionary Computation: Theory and Applications. World Scientific, Singapore (1999)

Using Viruses to Improve GAs

Francesco Pappalardo

Faculty of Pharmacy and Dept. of Mathematics & Computer Science,
University of Catania, Italy
francesco@dmi.unict.it

Abstract. In this paper, we will introduce an evolutionary algorithm for finding approximate solutions to the Weighted Minimum Hitting Set Problem. The proposed genetic algorithm, denoted by HEAT-V, makes use of a newly defined concept of virus. We will test its performance against a well known and efficient greedy algorithm, and on several families of sets.

1 Introduction

The *Weighted Minimum Hitting Set Problem (WMHSP)* and the standard *Minimum Hitting Set Problem (MHSP)*, are combinatorial problems of great interest for many applications. Although, these problems lend themselves quite naturally to an evolutionary approach, to our knowledge, there are no significant results of evolutionary algorithms applied to either the WMHSP or the MHSP, except for the results contained in [3].

We will now formally introduce the optimization problem and recall that the corresponding decision problem is $\mathcal{NP}$-complete [6].

- **Instance**: A finite set U, with $\mid U \mid = m$; a collection of sets $\mathcal{C} = \{S_1, \ldots, S_n\}$ such that $S_i \subseteq U \ \forall i = \{1, \ldots, n\}$. A weight function $w : U \to \Re^+$.
- **Solution**: A hitting set for $\mathcal{C}$, that is to say $H \subseteq U$ such that $H \cap S_i \neq \emptyset$, $\forall i = 1, \ldots, n$.
- **Optimal Solution**: a hitting set H such that $w(H) = \sum_{s \in H} w(s)$ is minimal.

The above definition is very general and, by simply putting $w(s) = 1, \ \forall s \in U$, we obtain the standard definition of the Minimum Hitting Set problem.
Theoretical results show that:

- the problem can be approximated within $1 + \ln m$ [7];
- it cannot be approximated within $c \ln m$, for some $c > 0$ [13];
- moreover [4], optimal solutions cannot be approximated within $(1 - \epsilon) \ln m$ $\forall \ \epsilon > 0$, unless $\mathcal{NP} \subset \mathcal{DTIME}(m^{\log \log m})$.
- Finally, in [2], is proven that it is not possible to approximate *Set Cover*, which is simply a *dual* problem of MHSP, with a ratio of $c \log m$, $\forall c < 1/4$ unless $\mathcal{NP} \subset \mathcal{DTIME}(m^{\text{poly} \log m})$; furthermore, if $c < 1/8$ it would be $\mathcal{NP} \subset \mathcal{DTIME}(m^{\log \log m})$.

1.1 Set and Minimum Vertex Cover

Minimum Vertex Cover (MVCP) can be used in many practical applications, especially in matching problems. We will now show a triangular reduction, *Set Cover (SCP)* → *Minimum Vertex Cover* → *Minimum Hitting Set*, which is computationally easy, e.g. quadratic. As a consequence, an approximation algorithm for the MHSP can be easily used for SCP and MVCP.

Let us formally define the combinatorial problems.

Minimum Vertex Cover

- **Instance MVCP**: A graph $G = (V, E)$, where $V = \{1, \ldots, n\}$ is the set of vertices and $E = \{e_1, \ldots, e_m\} \subseteq V \times V$ is the set of edges.
- **Solution**: A subset $V' \subseteq V$ such that $\forall (i,j) \in E : i \in V' \vee j \in V'$.
- **Optimal solution**: A vertex cover V' of minimal cardinality.

To E we can also associate a matrix A, called adjacency matrix, whose values a_{ij} are defined as

$$a_{ij} = \begin{cases} 1 \text{ if } (i,j) \in E \\ 0 \text{ otherwise} \end{cases}$$

Set Cover

- **Instance SCP**: A set X, with $|X| = m$; a collection $\mathcal{D} = \{Z_1, \ldots, Z_n\}$ such that $Z_i \subseteq X \ \forall i = \{1, \ldots, n\}$.
- **Solution**: A set cover for D, i.e. a collection $D' = \{Z_1, \ldots, Z_k\} \subseteq D$ such that $\bigcup_{i=1}^{k} Z_i = X$.
- **Optimal solution**: A cover D' of minimal cardinality.

Reductions. We can reduce $MVCP \to SCP$ by putting $X = E$ and $D = E^*$, where $E^* = \{E_i^* : i = 1, \ldots, m\}$ and for all i $E_i^* = \{(i,j) : (i,j) \in E \text{ for some } j \in V\}$. Therefore, E^* is the collection of all the sets representing, for every vertex, the collection of edges that have it as an endpoint.

We can reduce $SCP \to MHSP$ by putting $U = D$ and $\mathcal{C} = \{T_1, \ldots, T_n\}$ where $T_i = \{A \in D : a_i \in A\}$.

We can easily reduce directly $MVCP \to MHSP$, by putting $U = V$ and $\mathcal{C} = V^*$ with $V^* = \{V_1, \ldots, V_m\}$, where, for all $h = 1, \ldots, m$ V_h is the set of the two endpoints of the edge e_h.

It is easy to check that the above shown reductions take $O(|V + E|)$ time.

1.2 Evolutionary Algorithms and $\mathcal{NP}$-Complete Problems

Evolutionary algorithms have been applied with satisfactory results to a very long list of hard combinatorial problems. A complete description or enumeration of such results is, per se, a hard problem. We will cite here just few interesting examples and stress the fact that no evolutionary algorithm exists for the MHSP. EA's have been applied to SAT, 3SAT [1]; TSP [9,10]; Graph Coloring [5].

2 The Description of Our Algorithm

Our evolutionary approach and the resulting genetic algorithm, denoted by HEAT-V, is based on the idea of a *mutant virus*, which somehow acts as a non-purely random mutation operator.

Each chromosome in the population is a binary string of fixed length (see below for details). The selection operator is *tournament selection* and the selected individuals mate with probability $p = 1$. Reproduction uses uniform crossover (however this does not involve the virus part as we will describe later).

Elitism is used on three specific elements (not necessarily distinct) of the population:

- best fitness element;
- hitting set of smaller cardinality;
- hitting set of smaller weight.

2.1 Virus Description

Chromosomes contain some extra genes, specifically $2 + \lceil \log |U| \rceil$. These genes represent the genetic patrimony of the *virus*. As a consequence, the total length of a chromosome is $|U| + 2 + \lceil \log |U| \rceil$. We have

- The extra $\lceil \log |U| \rceil$ bits uniquely identify one of the first $|U|$ loci of the chromosome. If $|U|$ is not a power of 2, the above bits identify, as well, positions past the first $|U|$ bits. In such cases, the virus will have no effect. The virus is characterized by two behavioral phases, positive and negative, and it switches between them dynamically, specifically whenever the population has gotten used to the *disease,* that is to say when no improvements are generated after a specific number of generations. If the virus hits the individual, with probability one half, it is decided whether it will act selectively or generally.
  - If it acts selectively, the position identified by the $\lceil \log |U| \rceil$ and another randomly chosen are hit by the virus. That means, that if the virus is acting positively [resp. negatively] the gene with smaller weight (of the chosen two) is put to one [resp. the gene with higher weight of the chosen two, is put to zero].
  - If it acts generally, the position identified by the $\lceil \log |U| \rceil$ extra bits is put to one if the virus acts positively and zero otherwise.
- Viruses will hit an individual if the remaining two extra bits, control bits, have both value 1.
  Thus, chromosomes can be partitioned into three groups:
  - healthy (control bits are both 0);
  - disease carrier (control bits have different values);
  - sick (control bits are both 1).

However, all individuals, including healthy ones, carry in their genes the virus. Two disease carrier chosen for reproduction, will produce a sick offspring with probability 1/4.

During the first generation, the virus bits are randomly generated with a uniform distribution. Control bits are instead put to 1 with a probability p_{v1} that has to be set. In all cited tests, we did set $p_{v1} = 1/10$.

Virus reproduction is slightly different than uniform crossover.

Basically, in the case that the virus bits differ in one location, offspring are given a random value (in the uniform crossover, such a case would imply that one offspring will get the value 1 and the other the value 0).

Control bits have also their specific reproduction procedure. If c_1, c_2 are the offspring control bits and c_{11}, c_{12} are the first parent control bits, while c_{21}, c_{22} are the second parent control bits, we choose randomy $c_1 \in \{c_{11}, c_{12}\}$ and $c_2 \in \{c_{21}, c_{22}\}$. Then, with probability p_{v2}, we set first child control bit to 1 if control bits are both 0.

In all cited tests, we did set $p_{v2} = 1/10$.

2.2 The Fitness Functions

We will now describe the three fitness functions we used to test our algorithm.

Fitness 1: Algorithm HEAT-V1 The fitness function $f_1 : \mathcal{P} \to \Re^+$ that HEAT-V1 tries to <u>maximize</u> is defined as follows:

$$f_1(c) = \begin{cases} \rho \times n + \alpha + \frac{w(U)}{w(c)} & \text{if } c \text{ is not a} \\ & \text{hitting set for } \mathcal{C} \\ n + \alpha + \frac{w(U)}{w(c)} & \text{if } c \text{ is a} \\ & \text{hitting set for } \mathcal{C} \\ 0.0 & \text{if } w(c) = 0 \end{cases}$$

where $c \subseteq U$, $\rho = |U|$, $\alpha = \rho - |c|$, $w(U) = \sum_{u \in U} w(u)$, and in general $w(c) = \sum_{u \in c} w(u)$ and $\mathcal{P}$ is the population set. Intuitively, this is a two-phase fitness function. If the chromosome is not a hitting set its fitness function increases very rapidly when new elements are added to it. If it is a hitting set, the fitness increases when the cardinality of c decreases.

Fitness 2: Algorithm HEAT-V2 The fitness function $f_2 : \mathcal{P} \to \mathcal{N} \setminus \{0\}$ that HEAT-V2 tries to <u>minimize</u> is defined as follows:

$$f_2(c) = w(c) + w(\mathcal{L}_{c,M})$$

where

$\mathcal{L}_{c,M} = \{e : (\exists K \subseteq U) \text{ s.t. } K \cap c = \emptyset \land e \in K \land w(e) = \max\{w(e') : e' \in K\}\}$. Intuitively, f_2 is computed by adding to the weight of a chromosome, the maximum weight of elements of sets which c does not hit. In some sense, f_2 acts as a large upper-bound to the fitness function of any chromosome that could become a hitting set by including c.

Fitness 3: Algorithm HEAT-V3 The fitness function $f_3 : \mathcal{P} \to \mathcal{N} \setminus \{0\}$ that HEAT-V3 tries to <u>minimize</u> is defined as follows:

$$f_3(c) = w(c) + w(\mathcal{L}_{c,m}')$$

where $\mathcal{L}_{c,m} = \{e : (\exists K \subseteq U) \text{ s.t. } K \cap c = \emptyset \wedge e \in K \wedge w(e) = \min\{w(e') : e' \in K\}\}$. Intuitively, f_3 is computed by adding to the weight of a chromosome, the minimum weight of elements of sets which c does not hit. Thus, f_3 acts as a strict upper-bound to the fitness function of any chromosome that could become a hitting set by including c.

2.3 Comments on the Obtained Results

The first two fitness functions are equivalent from a quality point of view, i.e. the corresponding algorithms find the same minimal hitting sets. However, fitness 2 gives more stability since HEAT-V2 finds the best result in all the runs, whereas HEAT-V1 only 50% of the time. On the other hand, HEAT-V1 converges more rapidly than HEAT-V2.

HEAT-V3, which uses the third function, is less stable than the other two algorithms, yet in 33% of the cases, it produces better solutions.

Note also, that HEAT-WV is a variation of HEAT-V where no viruses are used but instead we use the mutation operator with probability $1/\mid U \mid$.

3 Computational Results

We compared HEAT-V to a greedy algorithm which is a very well known and quite efficient approximation algorithm. Such an algorithm approximates the optimal solution to a factor of $O(\ln m)$. In [14], ratio factor is improved to $\ln m - \ln\ln m + \theta(1)$, and, basically, no known polynomial algorithm can have a better performance [4].

Basically, the procedure greedy chooses at every step the element that maximizes the ratio between the number of hit sets (among the remaining ones) and its weight. The hit sets are eliminated.

HEAT-V was also compared to the results in [3], where an extension of the MHSP was studied. In such an extension, denoted by T-constrained, the problem is to find hitting set of minimal cardinality with the highest number of elements belonging to a given set $T \subseteq U$.

It is easy to see how the T-constrained version of the MHSP can be mapped into the WMHSP by assigning a small weight to the elements of T and a large weight to the elements outside of T. In our experiments we chose $w(t) = 1$, $\forall t \in T$ and $w(s) = 10$, $\forall s \notin T$.

Many tests were performed. For each test HEAT-V was tested three times. The population contained 200 individuals and each test ran for 500 generations.

3.1 Tests on Guaranteed Hitting Set Families

We have generated family of subsets of a universe U that have hitting sets of guaranteed cardinality.

For our experiments, we randomly created three test collections

(50) $|U| = 50$, and $|C| = 50000$ where for each subset, each element of U belongs to it with probability $\frac{1}{4}$;
(100) $|U| = 100$, and $|C| = 100000$ where for each subset, each element of U belongs to it with probability $\frac{1}{8}$;
(200) $|U| = 200$, and $|C| = 200000$ where for each subset, each element of U belongs to it with probability $\frac{1}{16}$.

Table 1 shows the results obtained by HEAT-V3. $w(G)$ stands for the weight of the guaranteed MHS. Note that we created two tests series (A and B) for each of the collections described above.

Table 1. $w(H)$ for guaranteed WMHS

TEST	$w(G)$	GREEDY	HEAT-V3	HEAT-WV
50A	115	194	115	115
50B	102	129	102	102
100A	501	837	501	584
100B	537	793	537	626
200A	2054	3094	2054	2552
200B	428	668	428	623

3.2 Results on T-MHSP

In table 2 we show the results obtained by HEAT-V3 on the T-constrained MHSP. In this case, $|T| = 10$, whereas $|U| = 100$ and $|C| = 100000$. To randomly generate the elements of C, we proceed as follows:

- We fixed two integer interval parameters $[a_1, \ldots, a_2]$ and $[b_1, \ldots, b_2]$.
- For each element $C \in C$ and for each bit in C,
  - we draw randomly two numbers $a' \in [a_1, \ldots, a_2]$ and $b' \in [b_1, \ldots, b_2]$.
  - If $a' < b'$ the bit is given the value 1 otherwise is given the value 0.

The test set $T - 100$ is characterized by the intervals $[0, \ldots, 9]$ and $[1, \ldots, 10]$. What is the probability that $a' < b'$? The event space is made of the 100 possible pairs of values $[a', b']$. Of these 100 pairs, the ones for which $a' < b'$ are exactly 55. Thus, with probability $\frac{55}{100}$ a bit is set to 1. Any set in C will therefore have a little over one half of its bits equal to 1.

We compare HEAT-V3 with the Greedy Algorithm above described and, a simpler algorithm proposed in [3].

3.3 Results on Papadimitriou and Steiglitz Regular Graphs

We also checked HEAT-V against *vertex cover*, which can be easily reduced to MHSP. In particular, we used the regular graphs proposed by Papadimitriou and Steiglitz (PS-rg) [12] built so that the classical greedy strategy fails. Such

Table 2. Results for T-MSHP

TEST SUITE	Algorithm	$\|H\|$	$\in T$
T-100	GREEDY	51	100%
T-100	HEAT-V3	49	100%
T-100	HEAT-WV	51	80%
T-100	CEC-2002 Alg.	49	60%

a greedy strategy chooses at every step the uncovered vertex with the highest degree, i.e. the highest number of edges incident to it. PS-rg's can be seen as 3-level graphs. Formally, every graph $G(V,E)$ has $n = 3k+4$ vertices, $k \geq 1$; $k+2$ in the first level, $k+2$ as well in the second level, but exactly k vertices in the third level. Every vertex in the third level is connected by an edge to every vertex of the second level. Every vertex in the second level is connected to one and only one vertex of the first level. Therefore a PS-rg graph has exactly $3k+4$ vertices and $k(k+3)+2$ edges. In figure 1 we see a PS-rg of degree $k = 3$. It

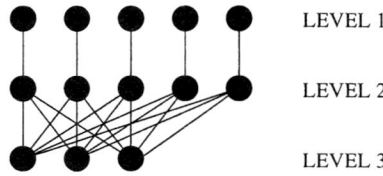

Fig. 1. PS-rg with $k = 3$

is easy to see that for PS-rg's an optimal cover is given by the vertices of the second level. Thus the cardinality of the optimal cover is $k+2$.

The greedy strategy instead, would choose the vertices of level 3, because they are the highest degree vertices, and then, to produce a cover, would choose the vertices of level 1. Obtaining a cover of cardinality $2k+2$.

In [8], the authors present a genetic algorithm for the minimum vertex cover, which reaches the optimal solution in 2/3 of the experiments on PS-rg's with degree $k = 32$ e $k = 66$.

3.4 PS-rg's Minimal Cover as MHSP

An instance of the minimum vertex cover for a PS-rg reduces to an instance of MHSP as follows:

- U is given by V, i.e. the number of elements of the universe is equal to the number of vertices in the graph.
- C is given by E, i.e. the number of sets is equal to the number of edges and each set has exactly two elements, corresponding to the two endpoints of the edge.

Table 3. | H | results on regular graphs with $k = 32, k = 66, k = 100$

Graph	GREEDY	HEAT-V3
PS-32	66	34
PS-66	134	68
PS-100	202	102

For the PS-rg in figure 1, the corresponding instance of MHSP would then be:
- $U = \{1, 2, \ldots, 13\}$
- Assuming that the level 1 vertices correspond to elements 1 to 5, second level to elements 6 to 10 and third level vertices to elements 11 to 13, the sets of the collection are:
  - $\{1, 6\}, \{2, 7\}, \{3, 8\}, \{4, 9\}, \{5, 10\}$, and
  - $\{i, 6\}, \{i, 7\}, \{i, 8\}, \{i, 9\}, \{i, 10\}$, for $i = 11, 12, 13$.

The Minimum hitting set is obviously given by the subset $\{6, 7, 8, 9, 10\}$.

Surprisingly, the best approximation algorithm for the MVCP is said to be the randomized algorithm [11]. It can be proven, that such an algorithm guarantees a cover which at most has twice the cardinality of the minimal cover.

We ran HEAT-V with PS-rg's of degrees $k = 32, k = 66, k = 100$. In table 3, we show the obtained results. HEAT-V always finds the optimal solution, whereas only 66% of the cases are claimed in [8]. We also ran our algorithm with an instance of degree $k = 100$. HEAT-V1 was not able to find the optimal in this case, whereas HEAT-V2 and HEAT-V3 found the optimal solution. For simplicity, we show just the results for HEAT-V3.

3.5 Results on Randomly Generated Subsets

We ran many tests on randomly generated families, changing the cardinality of U, of $\mathcal{C}$, and the range for the weights. We can distinguish two major test suites:

- TEST100: $| U | = 100, | \mathcal{C} | = 100000, w(u_i) \in \{1, \ldots, 50\}$.
- TEST200: $| U | = 200, | \mathcal{C} | = 200000, w(u_i) \in \{1, \ldots, 100\}$.

Elements are randomly assigned to subsets, using three different probability values: A: $p = \frac{55}{100}$, B: $p = \frac{45}{100}$, and C: $p = \frac{65}{100}$.

Table 4. $w(H)$ results for the **GREEDY** and **HEAT-V** algorithms

TEST	GREEDY	HEAT-V1	HEAT-V3	HEAT-WV
100A	870	849	796	1193
100B	1084	995	967	1160
100C	111	109	105	181
200A	1134	1107	1073	1895
200B	992	973	955	1872
200C	153	146	138	312

In all, we have six different test suites, 100A, 100B, 100C and 200A, 200B, 200C. Weights are randomly generated in the set interval. In table 4 we have the weight of the hitting sets produced by the greedy algorithm and by **HEAT-V**. The table clearly shows that HEAT-V3 always obtains the best results.

3.6 Comparing Various Crossover

We have compared various types of crossover operators with virus. We used six new tests. Tests "A" have low density, that is there are about 30% of "1". Tests "B" have high density, that is there are about 70% of "1". "G" stands for greedy approach; "OPC" for one-point crossover; "TPC" for two-point crossover; "UFC" for uniform crossover. The last three columns show result with the same crossover operators but with virus. How we can see from table 5, the virus strategy always enhances results.

Table 5. $w(H)$ with various crossover

TEST	G	OPC	TPC	UFC	VOPC	VTPC	VUFC
30A	334	317	309	309	305	291	281
30B	43	43	43	41	41	41	39
40A	357	353	352	352	352	350	346
40B	62	62	62	62	61	61	61
50A	415	415	414	414	410	407	404
50B	70	70	70	70	65	65	65

4 Future Work and Conclusions

We have presented an evolutionary algorithm which makes use of extra bits of data, called virus bits, and we have studied its performance on the Weighted Minimum Hitting Set Problem. The obtained algorithm turns out to be flexible and efficient in finding approximate solutions even for variations of the studied problem. It does not require any a-priori knowledge about the problem instance and it does not use any reduction techniques. Hence, we were able to test its performance even on different problems such as the Minimum Vertex Cover Problem.

One of the major novelties of HEAT-V, is the usage of a *virus*, which acts as a non purely mutation operator. Computationally, its usage has no meaningful extra costs.

HEAT-V was tested on a large set of test cases, and, compared with the best known greedy algorithm, it obtained better results in 100% of the cases. It also wins against the same algorithm that makes use of the mutation operator, but not the viruses.

Acknowledgments

F.P. acknowledges partial support from University of Catania research grant and MIUR (PRIN 2004: *Problemi matematici delle teorie cinetiche*). Part of this work has been done while F.P. is research fellow of the Faculty of Pharmacy of Universiy of Catania.

References

1. Bäck, T., Eiben, A., Vink, M.: A superior evolutionary algorithm for 3-SAT. Proceedings of the 7th Annual Conference on Evolutionary Programming (1998) 125–136
2. Bellare, M., Goldwasser, S., Lund, G., Russel, A.: Efficient probabilistically checkable proofs and applications to approximations. Proceedings of the 25th Annual ACM Symposium on Theory of Computing (1993) 294–304
3. Cutello, V., Mastriani, E., Pappalardo, F.: An evolutionary algorithm for the T-constrained variation of the Minimum Hitting Set Problem. Proceedings of 2002 IEEE Congress on Evolutionary Computation (CEC2002) **1** (2002) 366–371
4. Feige, U.: A threshold of $\log n$ for approximating set cover. Journal of ACM **45** (1998) 634–652
5. Galinier, P.: Hybrid Evolutionary Algorithms for Graph Coloring. Journal of Combinatorial Optimization, **3(4)** (1999) 379–397
6. Garey, M.R., Johnson, D.S.: Computers and Intractability: A guide to the theory of NP-completeness. W. H. Freeman and Company eds. (1979)
7. Johnson, D.S.: Approximation algorithms for combinatorial problems. J. Comput. System Sci. **1** (1974) 256–278
8. Khuri, S., Bäck, T.: An Evolutionary Heuristic for the Minimum Vertex Cover Problem. Proc. of the KI-94 Workshop (1994)
9. Laguna, M., Moscato, P.: On Genetic Crossover Operators for Relative Order Preservation. C3P Report 778, Algoritmos Geneticos, Chapter 3, Optimizacion Heuristica y Redes Neuronales, edited by B. A. Diaz, Ed. Paraninfo, Madrid, Espanya (1996)
10. Manner, R., Manderick, B.: Genetic Operators, the Fitness Landscape and the Traveling Salesman Problem. Parallel Problem Solving from Nature-PPSN 2 eds. (1992) 219–228
11. Papadimitriou, C.H.: Computational Complexity. Addison Wesley, Reading, MA (1994)
12. Papadimitriou, C.H., Steiglitz, K.: Combinatorial Optimization. Prentice Hall, (1982) 407–408
13. Raz, R., Safra, S.: A sub-constant error-probability low-degree test, and sub-constant error-probability PCP characterization of NP. Proceedings of the 29th Ann. ACM Symp. on Theory of Computation (1997) 475–484
14. Slavik, P.: A tight analysis of the greedy algorithm for set cover. Proceedings of 28th ACM Symposium on Theory of Comp. (1996) 435–439

A Genetic Algorithm for Solving Fuzzy Resource-Constrained Project Scheduling

Hong Wang[1,2], Dan Lin[1], and Minqiang Li[2]

[1] Department of Mathematics of the Science, Tianjin University,
Tianjin 300072, China,
{wanghong, Dlin}@tju.edu.cn
[2] Institute of System Engineering, Tianjin University,
Tianjin 300072, China
mqli@tju.edu.cn

Abstract. This paper studies the resource-constrained project scheduling problem with fuzzy activity duration and fuzzy deadline. On the basis of the concept of schedule robustness for fuzzy deadline and fuzzy project makespan, we seek for a schedule that maximizes the schedule robustness. First, An efficient genetic algorithm (GA) based on activity list representation is proposed for solving this problem, the performance of our GA and GA based on the priority value representation is compared. Second, we study the impact for the two different weak comparison rules (integral value method, distance method) in the performance of GA. The computational experiment shows that the performance of the proposed GA is better than GA appearing in the literature, there is no significant difference between the two weak comparison rules on the Performance of the algorithm.

1 Introduction

The resource-constrained project scheduling problem (RCPSP) is to schedule the activities such that precedence and resource constraints are satisfied while optimizing some managerial objective. Applications can be found in diverse industries, especially in make-to-order and small batch production such as construction engineering, software development, ships and planes etc. There are some recent papers that summarize researches for this problem [1,2].

During project execution, however, project activities are subject to considerable uncertainty that may lead to numerous schedule disruptions. So we should consider this uncertainty in any realistic RCPSP approach. One of the major uncertainty is activity duration that may be difficult to predict accurately at the project early stage because a project is usually unique and "open-ended". There are two major approaches to handle uncertainty: stochastic and fuzzy. The latter one is especially well suited to handle such vague information [3, 4].

There are some papers concerned with fuzzy RCPSP [5,6,7,8,9]. Hapke and Slowinski [5,6] transformed the non-deterministic problem into a deterministic problem that was then solved using known deterministic procedures. Hapke and Slowinski [7] extended the priority rule based serial and parallel scheduling schemes [2] to deal with fuzzy parameters and applied 12 dispatching rules to solve this problem. Pan [8] applied GA based on the priority value representation for solving the problem under the objective of minimizing the fuzzy makespan. Wang [9] presented a fuzzy beam search approach for this problem under the objective of minimizing the schedule risk. Wang [10] described a genetic algorithm based on the priority value representation for solving the problem with the objective of maximizing the schedule robustness.

In this paper, in order to model actual scheduling situation more suitably, we study RCPSP incorporating fuzzy activity duration and fuzzy deadline (FRCPSP). On the basis of the concept of schedule robustness for fuzzy deadline and fuzzy project makespan, we seek for a schedule that maximizes the schedule robustness. First, An efficient genetic algorithm based on activity list representation is proposed for solving the FRCPSP, we compare the performance of our GA and GA based on the priority value representation proposed in [8,10]. Second, we study the impact for the two different weak comparison rules (integral value method, distance method) on the performance of the genetic algorithm.

The paper is organized as follows. The second section presents some introductory material: uncertainty modeling using fuzzy sets, and weak and strong comparison rules of fuzzy numbers. The FRCPSP is described in Section 3. Section 4 presents the new GA to the FRCPSP. In section 5 we describe the result obtained by experiment. In the final section general conclusions are made.

2 Basic Concepts and Definitions

2.1 Representation of Fuzzy Activity Duration and Project Deadline

Activity duration and project deadline can be characterized by six-point fuzzy numbers for computational efficiency [4]. For example, activity duration can be denoted as follows: $\tilde{P} = (\underline{p}^\varepsilon, \underline{p}^\lambda, \underline{p}, \overline{p}, \overline{p}^\lambda, \overline{p}^\varepsilon)$ (see Fig. 1 (A)). Where $\varepsilon, \lambda, 1$ are three prominent membership levels at which the manager is able to express possible values of activity duration which will be realized. The values within the range $[\underline{p}, \overline{p}]$ are the most certain activity duration and the value outsides the range $[\underline{p}^\varepsilon, \overline{p}^\varepsilon]$ are the least possible ones. The values within $[\underline{p}^\lambda, \overline{p}^\lambda]$ have good chances to be realized.

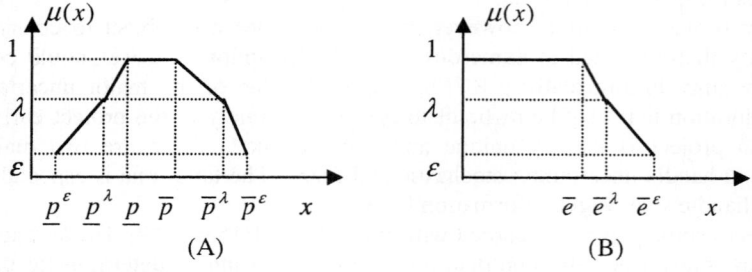

Fig. 1. (A) Fuzzy activity duration; (B) Fuzzy project deadline

Project deadline can be denoted by $\tilde{E}=(0,0,0,\bar{e},\bar{e}^\lambda,\bar{e}^\varepsilon)$ (see Fig. 1 (B)), if the makespan of the project is not greater than $\bar{e}$, then the project manager is completely satisfied. However, if the makespan is later than $\bar{e}$, then the degree of satisfaction decreases. When the makespan is equal to $\bar{e}^\lambda$, it is still acceptable and when the makespan is latter than $\bar{e}^\varepsilon$, the degree of satisfaction is zero.

2.2 Comparison of Fuzzy Numbers

Generally, the different fuzzy numbers $\tilde{A}$ and $\tilde{B}$ can overlap in two different ways:

(1) The values of both lower and upper bounds of any α-level set of $\tilde{B}$ are greater than those of $\tilde{A}$ (see Fig. 2(A)). That is, if $\max(\tilde{A},\tilde{B})=\tilde{B}$, we will say that $\tilde{B}$ is strongly greater than or equal to $\tilde{A}$. This relation is denoted by $\tilde{B} >>= \tilde{A}$. The rule determining $\tilde{B} >>= \tilde{A}$ is called the strong comparison rule (SCR).
(2) Fig. 2(B) presents another case of two overlapping fuzzy numbers. In such a case, it is proposed to apply the weaker comparison rule (WCR). This paper introduces two WCRs, due to their discriminating ability and easy computation.

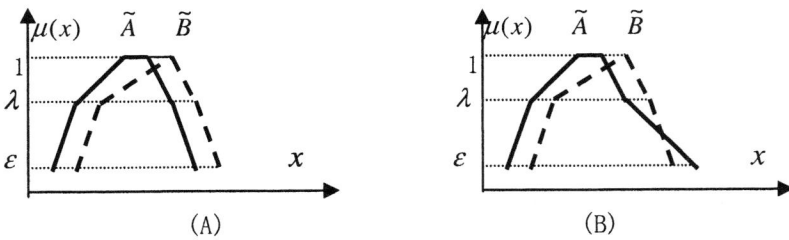

Fig. 2. Overlapping two fuzzy numbers

Distance Approach. Cheng [11] developed a distance approach for fuzzy number comparisons based on the calculation of the distance from original point to the centroid point $(\bar{x}_0, \bar{y}_0)$. Suppose that ε is equal to 0, Formula of calculating the centroid point for $\tilde{A}=(\underline{a}^\varepsilon, \underline{a}^\lambda, \underline{a}, \bar{a}, \bar{a}^\lambda, \bar{a}^\varepsilon)$ can be simplified as:

$$\bar{x}_0 = \frac{(\bar{a}^{\lambda 2} - \underline{a}^{\lambda 2}) + \lambda(\bar{a}^{\varepsilon 2} - \underline{a}^{\varepsilon 2} - \underline{a}^\varepsilon \underline{a}^\lambda + \bar{a}^\varepsilon \bar{a}^\lambda) + (\lambda-1)(\underline{a}^\lambda \underline{a} + \underline{a}^2 - \bar{a}^2 - \bar{a}\bar{a}^\lambda)}{3[(\bar{a}^\lambda - \underline{a} + \bar{a} - \underline{a}^\lambda) + \lambda(\bar{a}^\varepsilon + \underline{a} - \underline{a}^\varepsilon - \bar{a})]} \quad (1)$$

$$\bar{y}_0 = \frac{\lambda^2(\underline{a}^\varepsilon + \bar{a}^\varepsilon) + (1+\lambda)(\underline{a}^\lambda + \bar{a}^\lambda) + (2-\lambda-\lambda^2)(\underline{a}+\bar{a})}{3[\lambda(\underline{a}^\varepsilon + \bar{a}^\varepsilon) + (1-\lambda)(\underline{a}+\bar{a}) + (\underline{a}^\lambda + \bar{a}^\lambda)]} \quad (2)$$

$$R(\tilde{A}) = \sqrt{(\bar{x}_0)^2 + (\bar{y}_0)^2} \quad (3)$$

For two fuzzy numbers $\tilde{A}$ and $\tilde{B}$, if $R(\tilde{A}) > R(\tilde{B})$, then $\tilde{A} > \tilde{B}$.

Integral Value Approach. Liou and Wang [12] proposed the integral value approach described as follows. Given a fuzzy number $\tilde{A}$, $g_{\tilde{A}}^L(y)$ and $g_{\tilde{A}}^R(y)$ are denoted as the inverse functions of the left and right membership function of $\tilde{A}$ respectively. The left integral value and the right integral value of $\tilde{A}$ are defined as follows:

$$I_L(\tilde{A}) = \int_\varepsilon^1 g_{\tilde{A}}^L(y)\,dy \ . \tag{4}$$

$$I_R(\tilde{A}) = \int_\varepsilon^1 g_{\tilde{A}}^R(y)\,dy \ . \tag{5}$$

Then the total integral value of $\tilde{A}$ is defined as the weighted sum of $I_L(\tilde{A})$ and $I_R(\tilde{A})$:

$$I_T(\tilde{A},\beta) = \beta \times I_L(\tilde{A}) + (1-\beta) \times I_R(\tilde{A}) \ . \tag{6}$$

where $\beta \in [0,1]$ is the index of optimism and is determined by the attitude of manager.

As $\varepsilon = 0$, $\beta = 0.5$, for simplifying the computation, formula (9) can be rewritten for six-point fuzzy number $\tilde{A} = (\underline{a}^\varepsilon, \underline{a}^\lambda, \underline{a}, \overline{a}, \overline{a}^\lambda, \overline{a}^\varepsilon)$:

$$I_T(\tilde{A},0.5) = \frac{1}{4}[\underline{a}^\lambda + \underline{a} + \overline{a}^\lambda + \overline{a} + \lambda(\underline{a}^\varepsilon + \overline{a}^\varepsilon - \underline{a} - \overline{a})] \ . \tag{7}$$

For two fuzzy numbers $\tilde{A}$ and $\tilde{B}$, if $I_T(\tilde{A},\beta) > I_T(\tilde{B},\beta)$, then $\tilde{A} > \tilde{B}$.

3 Problem Description

FRCPSP can be defined as follow. A single project consists of J activities where each activity has to be processed in order to complete the project. The activities are interrelated by two kinds of constraints. First, precedence constraints force activity j not to be started before all its immediate predecessor activities have been finished. Second, performing the activities requires resources with limited capacities. We have R renewable resources. The duration of activities j $(j=1,2,...,J)$ is the fuzzy number $\tilde{P}_j$. Pre-emption of activities is not allowed. In each period of its executed time $t=1,2,...,\tilde{P}_j$, activity j requires l_{jr} units of resource r $(r=1,2,...,R)$. Resource r has a limited capacity of l_r^M at any point in time.

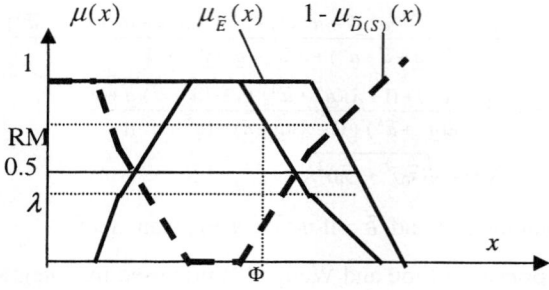

Fig. 3. The robustness measure $RM(S)$

A Genetic Algorithm for Solving Fuzzy Resource-Constrained Project Scheduling 175

The objective is to determine the schedule with the maximum schedule robustness; i.e. to select the schedule with the best worst-case performance. Let $\tilde{D}(s)$ be the fuzzy makespan of a project schedule s, characterized by the membership function $\mu_{\tilde{D}(s)}$, and $\tilde{E}$ be a deadline of the project, the robustness measure is defined:

$$RM(s) = \inf \max(1 - \mu_{\tilde{D}(s)}(x), \mu_{\tilde{E}}(x)) \ . \tag{8}$$

Fig. 3 shows that RM is determined by the intersections of $1 - \mu_{\tilde{D}(s)}(x)$ and $\mu_{\tilde{E}}(x)$. According to the obtained RM, the plausible project duration, from the pessimistic perspective, is defined as the maximum value of the α-level set of $\tilde{D}(s)$ (see Fig. 3):

$$\Phi = \max \left\{ x \big| \mu_{\tilde{D}(s)}(x) \geq RM(s) \right\} \ . \tag{9}$$

4 Genetic Algorithm

4.1 Solutions Encoding

The solution is encoded as a precedence feasible list of the activities. Each activity can appear in the list at any position after all its predecessors. Fig. 4 illustrates the activity list representation for a project with J activities. We would schedule the activities, one by one, in the order given by the list, so when an activity is going to be scheduled, all its predecessors have already been scheduled.

1	2	5	......	i	......	J

Fig. 4. Activity list

4.2 Decoding Procedure

An activity list is transformed into a schedule by a decoding procedure called the fuzzy parallel scheduling procedure [7]. The procedure is described as follows.
Denote

$\tilde{t}$ current time
CS   completed set that stores the activities that have been scheduled and completed
DS   decision set that stores the unscheduled activities which are available for scheduling with respect to precedence constraints
AS   activity set that stores the activities in progress
$S\tilde{T}_j$ the fuzzy start time of activity j
$F\tilde{T}_j$ the fuzzy finish time of activity j
π_r the left-over capacity of resource r

```
program  fuzzy parallel scheduling procedure
  begin
    ĩ := 0,  DS := φ,  CS := φ,  AS := {1},  π̃_r := l_r^M  r = 1,2,...,R;
    repeat
      Compose DS
      Repeat
        select activity j* in DS with the least position in
        activity list;
        update  DS := DS \ {j*};
        if  l_{jr} ≤ π̃_r ,  r = 1,2,...,R  then
          assign the start time of activity j*:  S̃T_{j*} := ĩ;
          assign the finish time of activity j*
          update resource availability: π̃_r := π̃_r − l_{rj*} , and AS;
      until  DS = φ
      select the earliest completed activity i*;
      determine current time:  ĩ := max{ĩ, F̃T_{i*}};
      Update resource availability: π̃_r := π̃_r + l_{ri*} , AS , and CS;
    Until number of activities in CS = J
  end
```

4.3 Initial Population

In order to initialize initial population, we employ a regret based biased random sampling procedure with Minimum Job Slack (MINSLK) as the selection rule proposed in [2]. This method can ensure the good initial solutions.

4.4 Selection

The expected value model is employed as the selection mechanism. The objective is converted into fitness function as:

$$f(i) = 1 + 10 \times F(i) \qquad (10)$$

where $f(i)$ is the fitness value of i individual, and $F(i)$ is the RM of i individual. The number of expected copies of each individual N_i is given by the probability of selecting that individual p_i, multiplied by the population size. Each individual is allocated samples according to the integer part of N_i, and the fractional parts are treated as probabilities of obtaining another copy with roulette wheel mechanism.

$$p_i = f(i) / \sum_{i=1}^{pop\_size} f(i) \qquad (11)$$

$$N_i = p_i \times pop\_size \qquad (12)$$

4.5 Crossover

Assume that two individuals of the current population have been selected for crossover as mother and a father

$$M = \{\lambda_1^M, \lambda_2^M, ..., \lambda_J^M, S/P^M, F/B^M\}, \quad F = \{\lambda_1^F, \lambda_2^F, ..., \lambda_J^F, S/P^F, F/B^F\}.$$

Now two children individuals have to be constructed as a daughter and a son:

$$D = \{\lambda_1^D, \lambda_2^D, ..., \lambda_J^D, S/P^D, F/B^D\}, \quad S = \{\lambda_1^S, \lambda_2^S, ..., \lambda_J^S, S/P^S, F/B^S\}.$$

In this paper, the one-point crossover of activity list is used. We draw a random integer r with $0 < r < J$ as crossover-point, daughter D is first considered and defined as follows: (a) the positions $i = 1,2,...,r$ in D are taken from the mother, that is $\lambda_i^D = \lambda_i^M$, $i = 1,2,...,r$. (b) the positions $i = r+1,...,J$ in D are taken from the father. However, the activities that have already been taken from the mother may not be considered again. We obtain $\lambda_i^D = \lambda_k^F$, $k = \min\{k \mid \lambda_k^F \notin \{\lambda_1^D, \lambda_2^D, ..., \lambda_{i-1}^D\} k = 1,2,...,J\}$, $i = r+1,...,J$.

As proven by Hartmann [2], this crossover strategy constructs precedence feasible solutions, given that the parents' activity lists are precedence feasible as well.

The generation of the son D is similar to the daughter D, but the positions $i = 1,2,...,r$ of the son S are taken from the father and the remaining positions are determined by the mother.

4.6 Mutation

For each activity with a probability of p_m, a new position is "randomly" chosen. In order to generate precedence feasible solution, this new position must be higher than any of its predecessors and lower than any of its successors. Then, this activity is inserted in the new position.

5 Computational Experiment

Computational experiments are conducted in two aspects: (1) compare the performance of our GA based on activity list representation and GA based on the priority value representation suggested in the literature [8,10]; (2) study the impact of two different weak comparison rules (integral value method, distance method) in the performance of the two genetic algorithm. So we design 4 different algorithms: activity list representation + integral value WRC, activity list representation + distance WRC, priority value representation + integral value WRC, priority value representation +distance WCR. The proposed algorithms have been coded in C++ language under the Windows XP operating system. The experiments have been performed on a PC (1CPU, Intel P4 2.0GHz, 512MB RAM, 60GB Hard Disk).

5.1 Test Design

The instance job301305 from the project scheduling problem library (PSPLIB) [13] has been used. This instance contains 32 activities and four renewable resource types, and the availability of resources is (17,18,20,18) in each period. Due to all the benchmarking problems created from PSPLIB are deterministic, we randomly fuzzify this instance data and called fuzzyjob301305. According to activity duration P_i and optimal makespan 67of instance job301305, six numbers used to define the fuzzy activity duration $\tilde{P}_i$ are randomly generated from the interval $(0.8 \times P_i, 1.2 \times P_i)$ and ranked in ascending order. The fuzzy deadline is (0,0,0,67,73.3,80.4). We assume that $\varepsilon = 0$, $\lambda = 0.5$, $\beta = 0.5$.

5.2 Computational Results

In this paper the parameters for performing genetic algorithms are set as follows: population size is 20, number of generations is 100, crossover probability is 0.8, and mutation probability is 0.1. Each procedure is randomly repeated 30 times.

Table 1 displays the best solution, average solution, and standard deviation (SD) of RM for the four different algorithms. In this table we can clearly observe that the GAs that make use of activity list representation give better results than priority rule based procedures.

A T-test has been conducted to compare the performance of the two GAs based on different representations, and investigate the impact of the two different WCRs (integral value method, distance method) on the performance of the make use of activity list representation give better results than priority rule based procedures.

A T-test has been conducted to compare the performance of the two GAs based on different representations, and to investigate the impact of the two different weak comparison rules (integral value method, distance method) on the performance of the GAs. The statistic used in the T-test:

$$t = \frac{\overline{X}_1 - \overline{X}_2}{\sqrt{(n_1-1)S_1^2 + (n_2-1)S_2^2}} \sqrt{\frac{n_1 n_2 (n_1 + n_2 - 2)}{n_1 + n_2}}.$$

where n_1 and n_2 are the number of samples, $\overline{X}_1$ and $\overline{X}_2$ are the mean value of samples, and S_1 and S_2 are the standard deviation of samples.

Table 1. Best solution, average solution, standard deviation of RM

Algorithm	Best	Average	SD
Priority Value+Distance WRC	0.5316	0.4833	0.0295
Priority Value+Integral Value WRC	0.5598	0.4907	0.0334
Activity List+Distance WRC	0.6264	0.5818	0.018
Activity List+Integral Value WRC	0.6165	0.5751	0.0172

The t value between the performance of activity list representation + distance WRC and priority value representation + distance WRC is 16.3091, the t value between the performance of activity list representation + integral value WRC and priority value representation + integral value WRC is 12.3049. Overall, The performance of GA based on activity list representation is statistically significantly better than GA based on priority value representation at the 95% confidence level ($t_{0.95}(58) = 2$).

The t value between the performance of priority value representation + distance WRC and priority value representation + integral value WRC is 0.9506, while the t value between the performance of activity list representation + distance WRC and activity list representation + integral value WRC is 1.3992. Overall, the difference between distance and integral value WCR is not statistically significant at the 95% confidence level ($t_{0.95}(58) = 2$).

Summing up, there is no difference between the two weak comparison rules on the performance of the algorithm statistically. But the activity list representation report statistically better results than the priority value representation.

The fuzzy project makespan and the plausible project duration of the schedule which RM is best for four different algorithms is shown in table 2.

Table 3 gives the fuzzy schedule which RM is best for the algorithm that makes use of the activity list representation and integral value WCR.

The proposed robust scheduling approach also can assist project managers in resource allocation decision to avoid the risk of late project. For example, Table 4 shows the sensitivity analysis of resource availability to the schedule robustness and the plausible project makespan. Project managers may consider increasing additional two units the first resource, if he/she feels that the risk of late project is high under the current resource availability $l^M = (17,18,20,18)$.

Table 2. Fuzzy project makespan and plausible project duration Φ

Algorithm	Fuzzy project makespan	Φ
Priority Value+ Distance	(57,59.5,62.9,66.7,73.1,75.9)	72.7
Priority Value+ Integral Value	(56.5,59.2,63.4,68.1,72.3,74.9)	71.8
Activity List+ Distance	(55.5,58.1,62,66.4,71.4,73.8)	70.1
Activity List+ Integral Value	(55.5,58.1,62,66.4,71.4,73.8)	69.9

Table 3. Sensitivity analysis of resource availability to schedule performance

Resource availability	Fuzzy project makespan	RM	Φ
(17,18,20,18)	(56.5,59.4,62.1,65.5,71.3,74.9)	0.6165	69.9
(19,18,20,18)	(54.3,56.5,59.4,63.9,69.5,71.3)	0.7471	66.7
(17,20,20,18)	(54.9,58,61.8,65.2,70.5,72.9)	0.6758	68.6
(17,18,22,18)	(54.5,57.9,61.2,65.3,70.2,73.5)	0.6750	68.5
(17,18,20,20)	(54.1,57.4,60.4,65.7,69.9,71.8)	0.7209	68.0

6 Conclusions

This paper studies the resource-constrained project scheduling problem with fuzzy duration and fuzzy deadline. On the basis of the concept of schedule robustness for fuzzy deadline and fuzzy project makespan, we seek for a schedule that maximizes the schedule robustness. First, An efficient genetic algorithm (GA) based on activity list representation is proposed for solving this problem, we compare the performance of our GA and GA based on the priority value representation. Second, we study the impact for the two different weak comparison rules (integral value method, distance method) in the performance of the GA. The computational experiment shows that the performance of the proposed GA is better than GA appearing in the literature, and there is no significant difference between the two weak comparison rules on the performance of the algorithm.

Acknowledgments

The research reported here is supported by the National Science Foundation of China (Grant No.70171002, No.70301005).

References

1. Demeulemeester, E.L., Herroelen, W.S.: Project Scheduling: A Research Handbook. Kluwer Academic Publishers, Boston Dordrecht London (2002)
2. Hartmann, S.: Project Scheduling Under Limited Resources: Models, Methods and Applications. Springer-Verlag, Berlin (1999)
3. Lootsma, F.A.: Stochastic and Fuzzy PERT. European Journal of Operational Research, Vol. 43 (1989) 174-183
4. Fortemps, P.: Jobshop Scheduling with Imprecise Durations: A Fuzzy Approach. IEEE Transactions on Fuzzy Systems, Vol. 5 (1997) 557–569
5. Hapke, M., Slowinski, R.: A DSS for Resource-Constrained Project Scheduling under Uncertainty. Decision Systems, Vol.2 (1993) 111-128
6. Hapke, M., Jaszkiewicz, A., Slowinski, R.: Fuzzy Project Scheduling System for Software Development. Fuzzy Sets and Systems, Vol. 21 (1994) 101-117
7. Hapke, M., Slowinski, R.: Fuzzy Priority Heuristics for Project Scheduling. Fuzzy Sets and Systems, Vol. 83 (1996) 291-299
8. Pan, H., Yeh, C.-H.: Fuzzy Project Scheduling. The IEEE International Conference on Fuzzy Systems, (2003) 755-760
9. Wang, J.: A Fuzzy Project Scheduling Approach to Minimize Schedule Risk for Product Development. Fuzzy Sets and Systems, Vol. 127 (2002) 99-116
10. Wang J.: A Fuzzy Robust Scheduling Approach for Product Development Projects. European Journal of Operational Research, Vol. 152 (2004) 180-194
11. Cheng, C-H.: New Approach for Ranking Fuzzy Numbers by Distance Method. Fuzzy Sets and Systems, Vol. 95 (1998) 307-317
12. Liou, T.-S., Wang, M.-J.: Ranking Fuzzy Numbers with Integral Value. Fuzzy Sets and Systems, Vol. 50 (1992) 247-255
13. Kolish, R., Sprecher, A.: PSPLIB−A Project Scheduling Problem Library. European Journal of Operational Research, Vol. 96 (1996) 205-216

A Hybrid Genetic Algorithm and Application to the Crosstalk Aware Track Assignment Problem*

Yici Cai[1,2], Bin Liu[2], Xiong Yan[1], Qiang Zhou[2], and Xianlong Hong[2]

[1] Department of Computer Science,
University of Science and Technology of China, Hefei, China
[2] Department of Computer Science and Technology,
Tsinghua University, Beijing, China
liubin00@mails.tsinghua.edu.cn

Abstract. This paper presents a genetic algorithm hybridized with a constructive procedure and reports its application on the crosstalk aware track assignment problem. In this algorithm, only dominating elements are encoded as chromosomes, on which genetic operators work to explore the solution space, while other elements are determined using constructive method. With proper dominating elements identification, the proposed approach essentially searches a much smaller space without trivial operations, efficiently generating competitive solutions with an effective constructive procedure. Experimental results on a set of industrial instances and ISPD98 benchmarks show that the proposed algorithm reduces both capacitive and inductive coupling in acceptable running time. It is probable that the proposed approach provides a practical way for the application of genetic algorithm on large scale engineering problems.

1 Introduction

Genetic algorithms (GAs) have shown great effectiveness in solution space exploration, and can be applied to a wide range of problems. However, classical GAs often suffer from slow convergence and a tremendous number of potential solutions, many of which are apparently inferior or even infeasible, have to be evaluated before a satisfactory solution can be reached. Researchers have proposed some hybrid schemes for GA by incorporating GAs with local search procedures, like hill-climbing [1], simulated annealing [2], tabu search [3]. These approaches are helpful, but when when applied to large scale problems, especially some engineering applications in which solution evaluation is highly time-consuming, local search procedures will probably either take much time to perturb the solution on some insignificant elements and achieve trivial improvements or lounges in a huge neighboring search space, making such methods unaffordable.

---

* This work is supported by the National Hi-Tech Research & Development (863) Program of China: 2005AA1Z1230 and the National Natural Science Foundation of China (NSFC) 60476014 and the Seed fund of Tsinghua University.

This paper introduces a GA hybridized with a constructive procedure, inspired by the observation that a good solution contains some *dominating elements* for many problems. Dominating elements are factors that can give a partial solution and shape the complete solution in the sense that other elements can be determined without much effort for a satisfactory solution under given dominating elements. Therefore, chromosomes can be encoded with only dominating elements for the genetic operations with little loss of solution quality. The search space much reduced, more efforts can be made to avoid prematurity and to improve solution quality. Moreover, the partial solution given by dominating elements are usually less likely to be infeasible, and thus the search efficiency is increased.

Crosstalk aware track assignment problem is a NP hard problem which emerges from VLSI design and has gained great interests in the EDA community. We have applied the proposed hybrid genetic algorithm to this problem, and experimental results have demonstrated the effectiveness of our approach.

2 GA Hybridized with a Constructive Procedure

Consider a general optimization problem,

$$\min f(x) \qquad (1)$$

Suppose we can find a *transformation function* $p : x = p(x_1, x_2)$, and a *completing procedure* $g : x_2 = g(x_1)$ so that $\forall x, f(p(x_1, x_2)) \leq f(p(x_1, x))$. In such circumstance, we have the following theorem.

Theorem 1. *If f has a minimum point $f(x^*)$ and the completing procedure g is optimal, there exists some x_1^*, so that*

$$f(x_1^*, g(x_1^*)) = f(x^*)$$

Theorem 1 tells that the search procedure can work in a reduced dimensional space with at least one global optimum not lost. This makes it possible for faster search process with satisfactory solution quality, which motivates the technique referred to as **reduced dimensional search**.

In practice, dominating elements are selected based on the power of the completing procedure with a tradeoff between solution quality and running time. In the reduced search space, couplings between the variables are usually hard to determine, and often little information can be explicitly used to guide the search process, which encourages the use of genetic algorithms due to their effectiveness in solution space exploration and convergence towards a good solution. We here propose to use genetic algorithm to search the reduced solution space while use constructive procedure to complete the solution. The reason why a constructive procedure may give high-quality solutions is that after the dominating elements are settled, other elements tend to be local, without complicated entanglements – possibly the problem or completing the solution is convex and separable, making it dispensable to perform a local search.

3 Application to Crosstalk Aware Track Assignment

The crosstalk aware track assignment assigns each wire segment onto a track, so that the undesired coupling effects (crosstalk) between neighboring wires *sensitive* with each other are minimized. The problem can be described as: given a set of segments S and a set of tracks T, find an assignment $f : S \to T$, so that total crosstalk between sensitive wires are minimized, under the constraint that no two overlapping segments are assigned to the same track.

A straightforward encoding scheme is used in our algorithm. A potential solution is represented with an array c, with c_i being the index of the track s_i is assigned to. On selecting dominating elements, some empirical rules (relating to wire length, the severity of potential coupling, etc.) are adopted to decide the significance value of a segment.

The initial dominating elements can possibly exclude some very critical segments relating to the detailed configuration of the segments. In order to grasp the dominating elements more accurately and flexibly, we allow adaptive update of the significance values during the evolution process. Each time after a number of populations are evaluated, the average coupling contributed by each segment is evaluated. The significance values are recalculated taking account of both the original significance and the average coupling the segment suffers. Dominating elements are then redetermined accordingly.

After dominating elements have been settled, all remaining segments form a priority queue. Each time, the segment with highest priority is assigned and removed from the queue. Every possible track for Segment s is evaluated with the cost of the partial solution, and the one with least crosstalk is adopted. The main difficulties of such a constructive procedure are that the quality of the final solution depends greatly on the order in which segments are processed, and that it is not easy to find a good order before the procedure begins. Here we adopt a *dynamic priority* strategy to avoid the undesired effects caused by sequential manner.

An unprocessed segment must be in one of the following statuses:

1. The segment is assignable on no track;
2. The segment is assignable on only one track;
3. The segment has more than one tracks to choose from, and the solution with least cost is much better than other solutions;
4. The segment has more than one tracks to choose from, and the best solution is not remarkably better than the second best one.

Apparently, segments in Status 2 or 3 should take the priority over ones in Status 4. We define the dynamic priority as follows,

$$pri(s) = \begin{cases} 0 & \text{, s in Status 1} \\ \infty & \text{, s in Status 2} \\ L(s_i) + \kappa \times (cost_{m2} - cost_m) & \text{, s in Status 3 or 4} \end{cases}$$

Here $cost_{m2}$ and $cost_m$ is the second minimum cost and the minimum cost for the segment.

4 Experimental Results

The proposed algorithm has been implemented in C++ on a SUN v880 workstation with 8 CPU and 4GB memory. Five criterions are used to measure the results: number of failed segments, capacitively/inductively coupled segment pairs, total capacitive/inductive coupling length. Results are listed in Table 1 and compared to those of a previous graph-based algorithm [4]. It is clear that

Table 1. Result Comparison: ours / [4]

name	failed	c_num	c_len	l_num	l_len	time (s)
biu	0/0	0/12	0/24	36/52	59/80	1/0.5
gdc	3/3	712/856	3156/4572	16908/18800	180588/221108	4806/118
ibm01	3/2	28/100	64/212	9728/13024	31940/43564	13336/677
ibm02	5/7	34/64	73/140	34902/41136	97110/128988	15930/996

the proposed algorithm finds better layout with less crosstalk than the previous algorithm.

5 Conclusion

We have proposed a new hybrid genetic algorithm for large scale optimization problems. With effective constructive procedure based on problem specific knowledge, the proposed algorithm takes advantage of genetic algorithm to better explore the solution space and perform global optimization. Application of the algorithm in crosstalk aware track assignment problem has shown encouraging results: the algorithm is able to reduce both capacitive coupling and inductive coupling notably compared to [4] within acceptable running time.

References

1. K. Katayama, H. Sakamoto and H. Narihisa, The efficiency of hybrid mutation genetic algorithm for the travelling salesman problem, *Mathematical and Computer Modelling*, vol. 31, no. 10-12, 2000, pp.197-203
2. L. Wang and D. Zheng, An effective hybrid optimization strategy for job-shop scheduling problems, *Comuters and Operations Research*, vol. 28, no. 6, May, 2001, pp.585-596
3. F. Glover, J.P. Kelly and M. Laguna, Genetic algorithms and tabu search: hybrids for optimization, *Computers and Operations Research*, vol. 22, no. 1, January, 1995, pp.111-134
4. Y. Cai, B. Liu, Q. Zhou and X. Hong, Integrated routing resource assignment for Crosstalk minimization, *Proc. the 2005 IEEE International Symposium on Circuits and Systems*, to appear.

A Genetic Algorithm for Solving Resource-Constrained Project Scheduling Problem

Hong Wang[1,2], Dan Lin[1], and Minqiang Li[2]

[1] Department of Mathematics of the Science, Tinjin University,
Tianjin 300072, China
{wanghong, dlin}@tju.edu.cn
[2] Institute of System Engineering, Tianjin University,
Tianjin 300072, China
mqli@tju.edu.cn

Abstract. Genetic Algorithm (GA) is an effective method for solving the classical resource-constrained project scheduling problem. In this paper we propose a new GA approach to solve this problem. Our approach employs a new representation for solutions that is an activity list with two additional genes. The first, called serial-parallel scheduling generation scheme gene (S/P gene), determines which of the two decoding procedures is used to computer a schedule for the activity list. The second, called forward-backward gene (F/B gene), indicates the direction in which the activity list is scheduled. The two genes determine the decoding procedure and decoding direction for the related activity list simultaneously. This allows the GA to adapt itself to a problem instance. The performance evaluation done on the 156 benchmark instances shows that our GA yields better results than the other two GAs which make use of the activity list representation and the activity list with S/P gene representation respectively. It is applicable developing self-adapting GA for the related optimization problems.

1 Introduction

The resource-constrained project scheduling problem (RCPSP) is to schedule the activities such that precedence and resource constraints are satisfied while optimizing some managerial objective, such as minimization of project makespan, project cost. Applications can be found in various industries, especially in make-to-order and small batch production such as construction engineering, software development, ships and planes etc. The models in this field are rich, and many well-known optimization problems are special cases, for instance job shop and flow shop scheduling.

The RCPSP has attracted many researchers [1,2]. The methods suggested can be classified into two categories: exact methods and heuristic methods. Since the RCPSP is known to be NP-hard, the exact methods are able to optimize small sized projects usually with less than 60 activities. For larger and more complex instances, heuristic methods can provide the best trade-off between performance and ease of implementation. Heuristics for the RCPSP can be classified into four methodologies: (1) priority rules based scheduling. (2) truncated branch and bound. (3) disjunctive arcs concepts. (4) metaheuristic techniques.

Many metaheuristics such as genetic algorithm (GA) [3,4,5,6], simulated annealing (SA) [7,8], and tabu search (TS) [9] are the latest generation of heuristic algorithms and have been applied to solve the RCPSP. The studies show that SA and GA significantly outperform all other heuristics, while GA performs best on the large projects [10].

It is crucial for the success of a GA to design a representation and decoding procedure for the solution. Hartmann [4] proposes a genetic algorithm that makes use of the so-called activity list representation for the RCPSP. Computational experiment shows that this GA outperforms GAs based on other representations. In this GA the serial scheduling generation scheme (SGS) [11] is used as the decoding procedure.

Hartmann [5] points out that not only the serial but also the parallel SGS can be adopted as the decoding procedure for the activity list representation. In fact, the parallel SGS can be easily applied to activity list: in each step, we simply choose the activity from the eligible set that has the lowest index in the activity list. While, an activity list, with different decoding procedures, may be transformed into different schedule, with possibly different makespan. So Hartmann proposes an extended representation to encode activity list with an additional gene, called serial-parallel SGS gene (S/P gene), which determines which of the two decoding procedures is used to transform the related activity list into a schedule. As with all genes in GA, this one is also subject to the genetic operations as crossover, mutation, and selection. Therefore, the SGS individuals leading to better results will survive while the others will probably die over the generations. This enables the GA to adapt itself dynamically to each instance. This method is called the mechanism of self-adaptation of GA.

Further, Alcaraz and Maroto [6] proposes a mechanism of self-adaptation as well. They use a new representation that is activity list with an additional gene, called forward- backward gene (F/B gene), which determines the direction in which the activity list is scheduled. This representation is based on the fact that an activity list may be transformed into different scheduling with possibly different makespan in a forward/backward way [12,13]. An extensive computational experiment shows that the algorithms proposed in the works of Hartmann [5] and Alcaraz and Maroto [6] outperform the other heuristic algorithms.

This paper tries to propose a new GA for the RCPSP that builds upon the self-adapting GA used in [5,6]. We design a new representation for the solutions that is activity list with two additional genes. The first, called serial-parallel SGS gene (S/P gene), determines which of the two decoding procedures is used to computer a schedule for the activity list. The second, called forward-backward gene (F/B gene), indicates the direction in which the activity list is scheduled. The two genes determine the decoding procedure and decoding direction for the related activity list simultaneously. 156 benchmark instances are used to evaluate the efficiency of this method.

This paper is organized as follows. After the introduction and problem description in section 2, Section 3 presents a new self-adapting GA to the RCPSP. In section 4 we describe the result obtained in the performance evaluation and analyze the behavior of the self-adapting GA. In the final section general conclusions are made.

2 Resource-Constrained Project Scheduling Problem

A single project consists of J activities that are processed in order to complete the project. The fictitious activities 0 and J correspond to the 'project start' and to the 'project end' respectively. The activities are interrelated by two types of constraints. First, precedence constraints force activity j not to be started before all its immediate predecessor activities have been finished. Second, performing the activities requires resources with limited capacities. We have K renewable resources. The duration or processing time of activities j ($j=1,2,...,J$) is p_j. Pre-emption of activities is not allowed. In each period of its execution time $t=1,2,...,p_j$, activity j requires r_{jk} units of resource k ($k=1,2,...,K$), and we have p_j=0 and r_{jk}=0 for the project start and end activities. Resource k has a limited capacity of R_k in any period. The values of r_{jk}, p_j, R_k are assumed to be non-negative and integer.

The objective is to determine the starting time of each activity, so that the project makespan is minimized, while both the precedence and the resource constraints are satisfied.

3 Genetic Algorithm

The GA, introduced by Holland, serves as a heuristic meta-strategy to solve hard optimization. It starts with an initial population generated by taking into account the representation of the solutions employed. We assume that the initial population contains *pop_size* individuals where *pop_size* is an even integer. After computing the fitness values of all individuals, the selection operation makes a number of copies of each individual, depending on its fitness. Then, the individual copies are mated at random and each pair undergoes crossover operation to produce offsprings. Finally, some offsprings of the population are mutated to become the next generation. The algorithm stops if a prespecified number of generations is evolved.

3.1 Solutions Encoding

Activity List Representation. The solution is encoded as a precedence feasible list of the activities. Each activity can appear in the list in any position after all its predecessors. In Fig. 1 (A), we can observe the activity list representation for a project with J activities. An activity list is transformed into a schedule by a decoding procedure that is called the serial/parallel schedule generation scheme (SGS). The parallel SGS proposed by Hartmann [5] is employed. We would schedule the activities, one by one, in the order given by the list, so when an activity is going to be scheduled, all its predecessors have already been scheduled (forward scheduling).

Activity List Representation with Decoding Procedure. The solution is encoded as an activity list with an additional gene, called serial/parallel SGS gene (S/P gene), which determines the SGS type to be used in decoding procedure for the related activity list. In Fig. 1 (B), when S/P gene is '1', the decoding procedure is serial SGS; otherwise, '0' means that the decoding procedure is parallel SGS.

Activity List Representation with Decoding Procedure and Decoding Direction. The solution is encoded as an activity list and two additional genes. The first, called serial-parallel SGS gene (S/P gene), determines which of the two decoding procedures is used to computer a schedule for the activity list. The second, called forward-backward gene (F/B gene), indicates in which of the forward and backward directions the related activity list is scheduled. In Fig. 1 (C), when F/B gene is '1' the scheduling direction is forward; otherwise; '0' means that the scheduling direction is backward. The two genes determine the decoding procedure and decoding direction for the related activity list simultaneously.

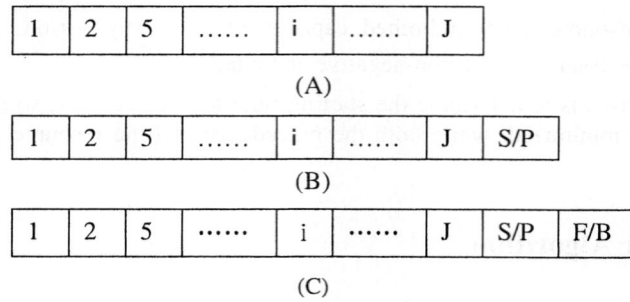

Fig. 1. (A) Activity list representation. (B) Activity list representation with decoding procedure. (C) Activity list representation with decoding procedure and decoding direction.

3.2 Initial Population

In order to initialize initial population containing pop_size individuals as described above, we will consider the construction of an activity list and the selection of the S/P and F/B genes respectively.

Construction of Activity List. To generate an activity list as described in section 3.1, we employ a regret based biased random sampling procedure with Minimum Job Slack (MINSLK) as the selection rule proposed in [11]. This method can ensure the good initial solutions.

S/P Gene. For each individual we select each of the two SGS types with a probability of $p = 0.5$.

F/B Gene. For each individual we first construct the related schedule applying forward scheduling with the SGS specified in the S/P gene. Then, the backward scheduling is applied, regardless of the schedule generated by the forward scheduling. If the forward scheduling obtains a better makespan, then the F/B gene is set to '1', otherwise it is set to '0'.

3.3 Selection

Selection is an artificial version of the natural phenomenon called the survival of the fittest. We implement the expected value model as the selection mechanism.

To generate the next generation, all individuals are evaluated by the fitness function and only fit individuals are chosen as parents. By the principle of GA, the fitter individuals should have a higher fitness value. In the project scheduling, the objective is to minimize the project makespan that is converted into fitness function as:

$$f(i) = F_{\max} - F(i) + 1. \tag{1}$$

where $f(i)$ is the fitness value of i individual, $F_{\max}$ is the maximum makespan of the current population, and $F(i)$ is the makespan of i individual.

The expected value model tries to reduce the stochastic errors associated with roulette wheel selection. The number of expected copies of each individual N_i is given by the probability of selecting that individual p_i, multiplied by the population size. Each individual is allocated samples according to the integer part of N_i, and the fractional parts are treated as probabilities of obtaining another copy with roulette wheel mechanism.

$$p_i = f(i) / \sum_{i=1}^{pop\_size} f(i). \tag{2}$$

$$N_i = p_i \times pop\_size. \tag{3}$$

3.4 Crossover

Assume that two individuals of the current population have been selected for crossover as mother and a father

$$M = \{\lambda_1^M, \lambda_2^M, ..., \lambda_J^M, S/P^M, F/B^M\}, \quad F = \{\lambda_1^F, \lambda_2^F, ..., \lambda_J^F, S/P^F, F/B^F\}.$$

Now two children individuals have to be constructed as a daughter and a son:

$$D = \{\lambda_1^D, \lambda_2^D, ..., \lambda_J^D, S/P^D, F/B^D\}, \quad S = \{\lambda_1^S, \lambda_2^S, ..., \lambda_J^S, S/P^S, F/B^S\}.$$

One-Point Crossover of Activity List. We draw a random integer r with $0 < r < J$ as crossover-point, daughter D is first considered and defined as follows: (a) the positions $i = 1, 2, ..., r$ in D are taken from the mother, that is $\lambda_i^D = \lambda_i^M$, $i = 1, 2, ..., r$. (b) the positions $i = r+1, ..., J$ in D are taken from the father. However, the activities that have already been taken from the mother may not be considered again. We obtain

$$\lambda_i^D = \lambda_k^F, \quad k = \min\{k \mid \lambda_k^F \notin \{\lambda_1^D, \lambda_2^D, ..., \lambda_{i-1}^D\}, k = 1, 2, ..., J\}, \quad i = r+1, ..., J.$$

As proven by Hartmann [4], this crossover strategy constructs precedence feasible solutions, given that the parents' activity lists are precedence feasible as well.

The generation of the son S is similar to the daughter D, but the positions $i = 1, 2, ..., r$ of the son S are taken from the father and the remaining positions are determined by the mother.

Forward-Backward Crossover of Activity List. This crossover technique is suited to the activity list representation with decoding procedure and decoding direction proposed in this paper. The last gene determines the way in which the crossover is performed.

First we draw a random integer r with $0 < r < J$ as crossover-point. If the mother's scheduling direction is forward, the generation of daughter is similar to the above definition. Otherwise, if the mother's scheduling direction is backward, the positions

$i = r+1,...,J$ in D are directly taken from the mother. That is $\lambda_i^D = \lambda_i^M$, $i = r+1,...,J$. The positions $i = 1,2,...,r$ in D are taken from the father. However, the activities that have already been taken from the mother may not be considered again. We obtain

$$\lambda_i^D = \lambda_k^F, \quad k = \max\{k | \lambda_k^F \notin \{\lambda_{i+1}^D, \lambda_{i+2}^D,...,\lambda_J^D\} k = 1,2,...,J\}, \quad i = r, r-1,...,1.$$

The generation of the son S is similar to the daughter D, but the way in which the son S is generated is determined by the father's F/B gene.

Selection of the S/P and F/B Gene. The daughter's S/P and F/B genes are taken from the mother. The son inherits the S/P and F/B genes from the father.

3.5 Mutation

For each activity with a probability of p_m, a new position is "randomly" chosen. In order to generate precedence feasible solution, this new position must be higher than any of its predecessors and lower than any of its successors. Then, this activity is inserted in the new position.

The S/P and F/B genes change with a probability of p_m. If S/P gene is '1', we set S/P gene to '0'. Otherwise, if S/P gene is '0', we set S/P gene to '1'. That is, by mutation operations, the serial SGS is replaced by the parallel one in the current individual and vice versa. If F/B gene is '1', we set F/B gene to '0'. Otherwise, if F/B gene is '0', we set F/B gene to '1'. That is, by mutation operations, the forward scheduling is replaced by the backward scheduling in the current individual and vice versa.

4 Computational Experiment

4.1 Test Design

In this section, we will study the performance of the GAs based on three different representations that are activity list representation, activity list representation with S/P gene, and activity list representation with S/P gene and F/B gene. These three GAs are described as follows. The first, called S-GA, employs the activity list representation, the serial SGS as decoding procedure, forward scheduling, expected value model, one-point crossover of activity list, and insert mutation. The second, called SP-GA, employs the activity list representation with S/P gene, the decoding procedure determined by the S/P gene, forward scheduling, expected value model, one-point crossover of activity list, and insert mutation. The third, called FBSP-GA, employs the activity list representation with S/P and F/B genes proposed by us, the decoding procedure and decoding direction determined by S/P and F/B genes, expected value model, forward-backward one-point crossover, and insert mutation. The above three algorithms have been coded in C++ language on a PC (1CPU, Intel P4 2.0GHz, 512MB RAM, 60GB Hard Disk) under the Windows XP operating system.

We have employed the 156 instances of the three standard sets in RCPSP library (PSPLIB) of Kolisch and Sprecher as test instances [14]. In the PSPLIB the first two sets contain 480 instances with four resource types as well as J=30 and J=60 activities (J30 and J60) respectively. The third one consists of 600 instances with J=120 activities (J120) and four resource types. The full factorial design with the three independent variable parameters network complexity (NC), resource factor (RF), and resource strength (RS) is used. For J30 and J60, the levels of the parameters are NC={1.5, 1.8, 2.1}, RF={0.25, 0.5, 0.75, 1}, and RS={0.2, 0.5, 0.7, 1}. For J120 the levels of the parameters are NC={1.5, 1.8, 2.1}, RF={0.25, 0.5, 0.75, 1}, and RS={0.1, 0.2, 0.3, 0.4, 0.5}. Each combination of the variable parameters contains 10 instances. We randomly select an instance from each combination. That is, select 48,48,60 instances from the three sets described above, respectively.

4.2 Computational Results

For each problem, the minimum makespan is taken from 10 random runs for each GA, in this paper the parameters for performing genetic algorithms are set as follows: population size is 50, number of generations is 100, crossover probability is 0.8, and mutation probability is 0.05.

Comparison of the Three GAs. Table 1 displays the average deviations from the optimal makespan for J30, and the average deviations from the upper bound for J60 and J120, obtained by the three GAs described above. As for some instances with J60 and J120 the optimal solutions are not known. The uppers of J60 and J120 are frequently updated in the library PSPLIB. The results of table 1 are based on the uppers reported there in October 2004.

The results show that the FBSP_GA and SP_GA lead to the better results than the S_GA for J120, the one with the best performance is FBSP_GA. For J60, the S_GA give better results than the SP_GA and FBSP_GA, and the SP_GA and FBSP_GA give almost identical results. For J30, the FBSP_GA yields the best results. Additional, in the table 1 we can observe that there are no significant differences among the performances of the three GAs for J30 and J60. Taking one with another, the performance of FBSP_GA outperforms the other two GAs.

Table 1. Average deviations from the optimal solution for J30 and from the upper bound for J60 and J120

Algorithm	J30	J60	J120
S_GA	0.208	1.097	4.648
SP_GA	0.204	1.165	4.103
FBSP_GA	0.165	1.167	3.989

Influence of Problem Parameters. Table 2 displays that distribution of four scheduling ways in the best solution found by the FBSP_GA for the three sets. Note: for some instances the best solution is found with different scheduling ways, for example, the optimal solution of the instance job300807 in J30 can obtained with three different scheduling ways that are SF, PF, and PB. In the table 2 we can observe that SF is more than the other three scheduling ways for J30, for J60 SF and PF are almost equal, and SF and PF more than SB and PB, for J120 PF is most among the four scheduling ways.

Table 2. Distribution of four scheduling ways in the best solution found by the FBSP_GA

Instance set	SF*	SB*	PF*	PB*
J30	71%	40%	46%	52%
J60	63%	21%	58%	27%
J120	27%	8%	53%	18%

SF: Serial SGS and forward scheduling; SB: Serial SGS and backward; PF: Parallel SGS and forward scheduling; PB: Parallel SGS and backward scheduling

Table 3. Distribution of SGS in the best solution found by the FBSP_GA w.r.t resource strength

SGS	RS=0.2	RS=0.5	RS=0.7	RS=1.0
Serial	2	8	11	12
Parallel	10	6	7	12

Table 3 gives the distribution of the SGS in the best solution found by the FBSP_GA for four different levels of the resource strength RS of J60. We can see that the resource strength has an impact on the SGS selection. For RS=1, the problems are resource-nonconsrained, each SGS can find an optimal solution. In case of low resource strength (RS=0.2), the parallel SGS leads to more best solutions than the serial one. In the case of more resource strength (RS=0.7), the best solutions contain the serial SGS more than the parallel one.

Summing up, it is a promising approach to include both decoding procedure and decoding direction into individual, and let GA select the more successful decoding way for the related activity list----as done in our self-adapting GA.

5 Conclusions

In this paper we consider the resource-constrained project scheduling problem with makespan minimization as objective. We propose a new GA approach to solve this problem. Our approach makes use of a new representation for solutions that is an activity list with two additional genes. The first, called serial-parallel SGS gene (S/P gene), determines which of the two decoding procedures is used to computer a schedule for the activity list. The second, called forward-backward gene (F/B gene), indicates the direction in which the activity list is scheduled. The two genes determine the decoding procedure and decoding direction for the related activity list simultaneously. This allows the GA to adapt itself to problem instance solved. In order to evaluate our approach, we compare it to the two GAs of Hartmann that employ the activity list and a activity list with S/P gene, respectively. Computational experiments show that our approach outperforms the other two GAs described above. This is due to the fact that our approach can enable each of individual to adapt itself to select the decoding way during the genetic search. It is applicable to develop self-adapting GA for the related optimization problems.

Acknowledgments

The research reported here is supported by the National Science Foundation of China (Grant No.70171002, No.70301005).

References

1. Demeulemeester, E.L., Herroelen, W.S.: Project Scheduling: A Research Handbook, Kluwer Academic Publishers, Boston Dordrecht London, (2002)
2. Hartmann, S.: Project Scheduling under Limited Resources: Models, Methods and Applications. Springer-verlag, Berlin, (1999)
3. Alcaraz, J., Maroto, C.: A Robust Genetic Algorithm for Resource Allocation in Project Scheduling. Annals of Operations Research, Vol. 102 (2001) 83-109
4. Hartmann, S.: A Competitive Genetic Algorithm for Resource-Constrained Project Scheduling. Naval Research Logistics, Vol. 45 (1998) 733-750
5. Hartmann, S.: A Self-Adapting Genetic Algorithm for Project Scheduling under Resource Constraints. Naval Research Logistics, Vol. 49 (2002) 433-448
6. Lee, J.-K., Kim, Y.-D.: Search Heuristics for Resource Constrained Project Scheduling. Journal of the Operational Research Society, Vol. 47 (1996) 678-689
7. Boctor, F. F.: Resource-Constrained Project Scheduling by Simulated Annealing. International Journal in Production Research, Vol. 34, No. 8 (1996) 2335-2351
8. Bouleimen, K., Lecocq, H.: A New Efficient Simulated Annealing Algorithm for the Resource-Constrained Project Scheduling Problem and Its Multiple Mode Version. European Journal of Operational Research, Vol. 149 (2003) 268-281
9. Thomas, P R., Salhi, S.: A Tabu Search Approach for the Resource Constrained Project Scheduling Problem. Journal of Heuristics, Vol. 4 (1998) 123-139
10. Hartmann, S., Kolisch, R.: Experimental Evaluation of State-of-The-Art Heuristics for the Resource-Constrained Project Scheduling Problem. European Journal of Operational Research, Vol. 127 (2000) 394-407
11. Kolisch, R.: Serial and Parallel Resource-Constrained Project Scheduling Methods Revisited: Theory and Computation. European Journal of Operational Research, Vol. 90 (1996) 320-333
12. Li, K., Willis, R.: An Iterative Scheduling Technique for Resource-Constrained Project Scheduling. European Journal of Operational Research, Vol. 56 (1992) 370-379
13. Özdamar, L., Ulusoy, G.: A Note on An Iterative Forward/ Backward Scheduling Technique with Reference to a Procedure by Li and Willis. European Journal of Operational Research, Vol. 89 (1996) 400-407
14. Kolish, R., Sprecher, A.: PSPLIB—A Project Scheduling Problem Library. European Journal of Operational Research, Vol. 96 (1996) 205-216

Evolutionary Algorithm Based on Overlapped Gene Expression*

Jing Peng[1,2], Chang-jie Tang[1], Jing Zhang[3], and Chang-an Yuan[1]

[1] School of computer Science and Engineering, Sichuan University, Chengdu 610065, China
{pengjing, tangchangjie, yuanchangan}@cs.scu.edu.cn
[2] Science and Technology Department, Chengdu Public Security Bureau, Chengdu 610017, China
[3] Chengdu Jiuheyuan Industry Company, Chengdu 610015, China

Abstract. Inspired by the overlap gene expression in biological study, this paper proposes a novel evolutionary algorithm-EAOGE i.e. Evolutionary Algorithm based on Overlapped Gene Expression. Different from existing works, EAOGE suggests a new expression structure of genes with probabilities of overlapped expression for some segments. The main contributions are: (1) Proposing a novel model and an algorithm of gene expression while borrowing some ideas from artificial immunity algorithm; (2) Analyzing the expressing space and encode characteristic of the new model; (3) The extensive experiments in function finding shows that new model is 2.8~9.7 times faster than usual GEP method, and in higher-degree polynomial function finding, the success rate of EAOGE is over 10 times than usual GEP.

1 Introduction

To solve complicated problems such as polynomial function finding, Cramer proposed GP (Genetic Programming) [1,2]. However, GP is too complicated in encoding and it is relatively slow. Ferreira, C combined the advantages of GA and GP, and proposed Gene Expression Programming (GEP) with speed 100-60000 times faster than GA or GP [3-9].

Enlightened by the phenom5ena of overlapped gene [10], this paper proposes a novel evolutionary algorithm, i.e. Evolutionary Algorithm based on Overlapped Gene Expression (EAOGE). Compared with other evolutionary algorithms, EAOGE has the advantages as follows:

1). Individual consists of several genes and gene segments can be overlapped under certain conditions. 2). By the segments' overlapping, EAOGE is efficiency in space.3). It is not needed to restrict the content of gene or chromosome. Both GP and GEP have to restrict the form5ats of gene in some ways such as constraints on the type and length of gene head and tail in GEP. Experiments show that under same condition, the velocity of EAOGE is 2.8 to 9.7 times of GEP. 4). The capability to discover higher-degree polynomial function is high. Compared with GEP, EAOGE greatly increases the success rate in polynomial function finding.

---

* This paper was supported by Grant of National Science Foundation of China (60073046), Sichuan Major Science and Technology Project (04SG1640).

2 Definitions and Encoding Methods

2.1 Definition

GA, GP, GEP and EAOGE are algorithms of simulating biological genetic evolution; several concepts about genetic computing are borrowed from biology, such as gene, genotype, phenotype, chromosome, individual, and population. The formal descriptions are as follows:

Definition 1 (Gene). Gene G is a quintuple: (E, T, F, Op, S), where E is genotype; T (Terminal set) is gene terminal character set; F (Function set) is gene function set; Op (Operator set) is gene genetic operator set, such as mutation operator, transition operator and root transition operator; S (Score) is the fitness score which gene gets from certain data set.

Definition 2 (Chromosome). Chromosome is a tetrad: C = (G, T, L, Op, S), where G is gene set; T (Terminal set) is gene terminal character set; L is connection operator of gene in chromosome; Op is the chromosome genetic operator set, and

$$Op = Op_c \cup (Op_{g1} \cup Op_{g2} \cup \cdots \cup Op_{gn}, n = length(C(G)))$$

Note that, Op_c is an operator which operates for multi-gene in the chromosome, such as one-point recombination operator, multi-points recombination operator, gene recombination operator, and gene transition operator. Op_{gi} (i=1... length(C(G))) is each gene operator in chromosome, usually, it assumes $Op_{g1}=Op_{g2}=...=Op_{gn}$ (where n=length(C(G))), i.e. all genes in chromosome take same genetic operators. S stands for chromosome fitness score.

Example 1: Let C1=({G1, G2, G3},'ab','*', Op, 0.7). It demonstrates that chromosome consist of 3 genes, the terminal character set of chromosome is (a, b), gene connection operator is '*', fitness score is 0.7.

Definition 3 (Individual and Population). Individual is a triple: I= (C, Op, S), where C is chromosome set. Op stands for Individual genetic operator set, such as:

$$Op = Op_i \cup (Op_{c1} \cup Op_{c2} \cup \cdots \cup Op_{cn}, n = length(I(C)))$$

Op_i is an operator for multi-chromosomes, such as chromosome recombination operator, gene random recombination operator; Op_{ci} (i=1... length (I(C))) is each chromosome genetic operator. S is Individual fitness score. Assume Population P= (I), I is an Individual set.

In this paper, the number of chromosome in Individual is 1, which means each Individual has only one chromosome.

2.2 Encoding Method

Encoding is the primary problem in genetic computing. The essential difference among GA, GP, and GEP is in coding. Both genotype and phenotype in traditional genetic code is Tree, and genetic operators (mutation, recombination etc.) manipulate the tree directly. Therefore, there are a lot of invalidation structures in the genetic process. Candida Ferreira proposed ET (Expression Tree) using a different encoding method [4]. The encoding method of GEP is to encode an Individual into a fixation length String. The key points encoding rule are: (a) Translate the expression into a expression tree according the semantic meaning, (b) Go through all the nodes in ET from top to bottom, from left to right, the result is the available parts of gene code.

To ensure the validity of expression, GEP must satisfy following constraints:(a) Let F be a predefined Function set and T be the Terminal set. Gene is divided into head and tail, and the head can include element in F U T, the tail can only include element in T.(b) Let h be the length of the head; t be the length of the tail; n =max {K: K is the number of parameters of f , f in F} t, h, n must satisfy the following equation:

The translating process is as follows:

(a). Scan each element of gene in order. (b).If the current symbol belongs to T, then let it be a leaf-node in ET. (c).If the current symbol belongs to F, then let it be a non-leaf node in ET, the number of its sub-trees equals the number of the function parameters. Let the element which is the directly succeeding of current symbol be the first root node of the sub-trees, the secondary element be the root node of secondary sub-trees, and the rest may be deduced by analogy. If it meets the end of the gene, then let the first element in T as sub-tree root-node.

3 EAOGE Algorithms

EAOGE algorithms simulate the natural biological evolutionary. According to the rule of "natural selection, the survival of the fittest", they implement selection, recombination, and mutation on the Population P which consists of several Individuals. Thus, the Population can evolve generation after generation. The best Individual can be found during the evolution; thereby the problems are solved finally.

The detailed implementations are as follows:

Algorithm 1
Inputs: Configuration (configuration of algorithm parameters such as population number, chromosome length, value of M and rate of IS, RIS etc.),
        Dataset (a training data set);
Output: Best fitness Individual $I = (C, Op, S)$;
1   Generate initial population P (I);
2   Evaluation (P (I)); //Calculate each individual's fitness score.
3   **While** (i < Max_Genaration) **Do**
4   tmpPopulation P'← {Ø}; P'← P'+ {Best Individual of P (I)};
5   For x = 1 To | Op | Do P'← P'+ Operator^x(P (I)); //Execute the x-th operator
6   Evaluation (P' (I)); Sort P' (I) by Individual' Score;
7   P (I) ←P' (I) ; i= i+1;
8   **If** |Best Individual of P (I)-M|< Precision **Then Break; End While;**
9   **Return** Best Individual of P (I);

3.1 Fitness Algorithm

The fitness algorithm in EAOGE does the mapping from genotype to phenotype.

Algorithm 2 fitness algorithm
Input: Individual $I(C, Op)$;
Output: individual fitness I (S);
1 For Each Record r In Training-Dataset **Do**
2 { ParamBuffer ← r; Buffer ← ; rc ← 0;
3   **For Each** Gene G **In** $I.C$ **Do** { rc ←I. C. L (rc, Ovr_Exec (G. E, 1)); }
4   Result ← Result + (r. t − rc)^2;}
5 **Return** |M − Min(sqrt(Result), M)|;

It is easy to see that the range of final fitness is 0~M, the fitness is higher, the inosculation to training data is better. Function Ovr_Exec completes computing the fitness of each gene. The algorithm is recursive, the details is as following:

Algorithm 3 Gene fitness algorithm (Ovr_Exec)
Inputs: genotype Express; current process position;
Output: gene fitness
1 If (Position>**Length**(Express)) Result ← ParamBuffer[1]; **End If**
2 Else If (Express[Position]∈F)
3   { Case Express[Position] **Of**
4   '+': Result ←Ovr_Exec (Position + 1) + Ovr_Exec (Position + 2);
5   '-': Result ←Ovr_Exec (Position + 1) − Ovr_Exec (Position + 2);
6   '*': Result ←Ovr_Exec (Position + 1) * Ovr_Exec (Position + 2);
7   '/': Result ←Ovr_Exec (Position + 1) / Ovr_Exec (Position + 2);}
8   Buffer[Position] ← Result;
9   Express[Position] ←GetCite (Buffer, Position); **End If**
10 Else If (Express[Position]∈T)
11   Result ← GetValue(Buffer, ParamBuffer, Express, Position); **End If**

3.2 Probability Selection Formula

The core of the roulette algorithm is that the probability of individuals' join in the propagation is simply decided by their fitness. Thereby, the individuals with higher fitness are kept. However, if one of the individual densities is too high, it is easy to make the algorithm become locally optimized, and easy to loose the individuals with lower fitness but preserve a good evolution trend. Borrowing idea from immune algorithm[11], this paper introduces a probability selection formula based on individual density. The definition of i-th individual is as following:

$$D(I_k) = 1 \Big/ \sum_{i=1}^{N} |f(I_k) - f(I_i)|, k = 1,2,...,N \tag{1}$$

Where N stands for the number of population. we can infer the probability based on individual density:

$$P(I_k) = \frac{\frac{1}{D(I_k)}}{\sum_{i=1}^{N}\frac{1}{D(I_i)}} = \frac{\sum_{i=1}^{N}|f(I_k)-f(I_i)|}{\sum_{i=1}^{N}\sum_{j=1}^{N}|f(I_i)-f(I_j)|}, k=1,2,...,N \qquad (2)$$

By (2), the more individuals similar to individual I_k, the less selected probability the individual I_k will have. Therefore, the individuals which have lower fitness have the evolution chance. Thus the probability selection formula based on individual density ensures the individual diversity theoretically. Section 5 will compare the difference between roulette probability and the ones based on density.

4 Algorithm Analyses

The essence difference between EAOGE algorithm and other genetic algorithm is in encoding method and will be discussed here.

4.1 Expression Space Analyses

Definition 4 (Expression space). Let I be the individual, I=(C, Op, S), E be I 's Expression, then length (E) is called expression space of I, and denoted as D_I; Then the maximal expression space of the individual I, whose chromosome total length is m, is denoted as $MAX_m(D_I)$.

Lemma 1. Let m be the length of the gene. Let $MAX_m(D_I)$ be the maximal expression space. Then individual I, $MAX_m(D_I)$ =m.

Proof: Omitted by the space limitation, for detail please see [12].

Lemma 2. Let m be the length of the chromosome, k be the number of genes in multi-gene GEP algorithm, then maximal expression space of individual I is $m+k-1$, i.e. $MAX_m(D_I)=m+k-1$.

Proof: Omitted by the space limitation, for detail please see [12].

Theorem 1. Let I be a single gene individual. Let m be the length of gene. Assume the number of parameters in operator set is 2. Then in EAOGE algorithm, the maximal expression space of a single gene individual I is as following:

$$MAX_m(D_I) = \frac{2}{\sqrt{5}}\left(\left(\frac{1+\sqrt{5}}{2}\right)^{m+2} - \left(\frac{1-\sqrt{5}}{2}\right)^{m+2}\right) - 1, \qquad (3)$$

Proof: Omitted by the space limitation, for detail please see[12].

Example 2. From Lemma 1, 2 and Theorem 1, when the number of genes is 1, the length of chromosome ranges from 3 to 17, the expression space comparison between EAOGE algorithm and GEP algorithm is as Table 1:

Table 1. Expression Space Examples

Length of Chromosome	EAOGE	GEP
3	9	3
5	25	5
7	67	7
9	177	9
11	465	11
13	1219	13
15	3193	15
17	8361	17

Theorem 2. Assume the number of parameters in operator set is 3, in EAOGE algorithm, the maximal expression space of a single gene individual I is as following:

$$MAX_m(D_I) = \frac{3}{2}\left(x_1^{m+1} + x_2^{m+1} + x_3^{m+1}\right) - \frac{1}{2}, \qquad (4)$$

Where m is the length of gene, and

$$x_1 = \left(\sqrt[3]{19 + 3\cdot\sqrt{33}} + \sqrt[3]{19 - 3\cdot\sqrt{33}} + 1\right)\big/3,$$

$$x_2 = \left(w\cdot\sqrt[3]{19 + 3\cdot\sqrt{33}} + w^2\cdot\sqrt[3]{19 - 3\cdot\sqrt{33}} + 1\right)\big/3,$$

$$x_3 = \left(w^2\cdot\sqrt[3]{19 + 3\cdot\sqrt{33}} + w\cdot\sqrt[3]{19 - 3\cdot\sqrt{33}} + 1\right)\big/3, \text{ and}$$

$$w = -\frac{1}{2} + \frac{\sqrt{3}}{2}\cdot i$$

Proof: Omitted by the space limitation, for detail please see[12].

In the area of expression space, the analysis and examples show that EAOGE algorithm is better than GEP. The expression space of GEP algorithm gets linear growth with the length of the chromosome, in turn, the expression space of EAOGE algorithm gets exponential growth with the length of the chromosome. Combined the following experiments, we can see that this is an important reason why EAOGE algorithm excels the latter.

4.2 Expression Power Analysis

In EAOGE, the code method from expression tree to linear string is not preorder, inter-order, or post-order, or is not ET code method of GEP. Can EAOGE encode any polynomial? The answer is in the following.

Theorem 3. Assume $H(x_1,x_2,\cdots,x_n) = x_1^{p_1} x_2^{p_2} \cdots x_n^{p_n}$, where x_i is a variant, $p_1,\cdots p_n$ is non-0 integer. Then there must exist a genotype E of EAOGE algorithm, such that the expression of E equals to $f(x_1,x_2,\cdots,x_n)$.

Proof: Omitted by the space limitation, for detail please see[12].

Theorem 4. Assume function sequences f_k satisfy:

$$f_1(x_1,x_2,\cdots,x_n) = H_1(x_1,x_2,\cdots,x_n),$$
$$f_m(x_1,x_2,\cdots,x_n) = H_m(x_1,x_2,\cdots,x_n) * (1 + f_{m-1}(x_1,x_2,\cdots,x_n)),$$

Where $H_i(x_1,x_2,\cdots,x_n)$ satisfies the definition in theorem 3. Then there exist a genotype E_m of EAOGE algorithm such that the corresponding expression of E_m is equal to $f_i(x_1,x_2,\cdots,x_n)$, namely each member of the function sequence can be coded by EAOGE algorithm.

Proof: Omitted by the space limitation, for detail please see[12].

Theorem 5 Assume

$$f(x_1,x_2,\cdots,x_n) = \sum_{i=1}^{k} x_1^{p_{i1}} x_2^{p_{i2}} \cdots x_n^{p_{in}} \qquad (5)$$

Where x_i is a variant; k is a positive integer, $p_{i1},\cdots p_{in}$ are non-0 integer. There exists a genotype E of EAOGE algorithm, an expression tree corresponding E such tat E equals right side of formula (5).

Proof: Omitted by the space limitation, for detail please see[12].

Theorem 5 proves that EAOGE has the capability to encode any polynomials like (5). If there are coefficients in the polynomials, these coefficients can be assumed as variants. In this way, the polynomials turn into formula (5). It proves that EAOGE can encode these polynomials.

According the above discussion, EAOGE can encode any forms of polynomials. Through the same way in prove theorem 5, it can prove that EAOGE can encode the polynomials with other operators.

The encoding method provided by Theorem 5 usually makes the length of expression very long. In practice, there are methods to get much shorter expression. The EAOGE encoding Method provided here shows that EAOGE has the capability to encode any forms of polynomials.

5 Experiments and Analysis

We have applied EAOGE algorithm into function-finding research. The purposes of the experiments includes comparison the characters between EAOGE and GEP algorithm and finding good EAOGE parameters. Experiment environment: CPU: PIII733M, Memory: 512M, Hard disk: 40G, Development tool: Delphi 7.0, Database: Microsoft Access 2000.The key parameters used in the experiment are in the Table 2.

Table 2. Algorithm Parameters

Type	EAOGE	Multi-gene GEP
Max Evolutionary Generation	1000	1000
Size of Population	60	60
Operator Set	+-*/	+-*/
Gene Connector	+	+
Mutation Rate	0.044	0.044
Single-Point Recombination	0.4	0.4
Tow-Points Recombination Rate	0.2	0.2
Gene Recombination Rate	0.1	0.1
Gene transition Rate	0.1	0.1
transition Rate	0.1	0.1
Root transition Rate	0.1	0.1
Precision	0.001	0.001

Experiment 1. 2-member function finding.

Take the function finding of the formula below for instance:

$$Z = X^5 + 2*X^2*Y + Y^3 \tag{6}$$

20 real numbers were generated randomly, the data domain was [-2, 2], M=10000(namely, criterion factor), gene length is from 9~23 for EAOGE and GEP respectively, and ran 100 times respectively, the other parameters were shown in table 2. The results are shown as in figure 1, where *eaoge_time* is the time consumption of EAOGE under different genetic length, *gep_time* is the time consumption of GEP, and the unit of Y-axis is second.

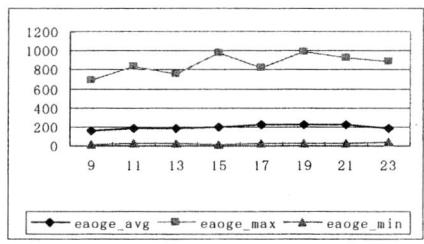 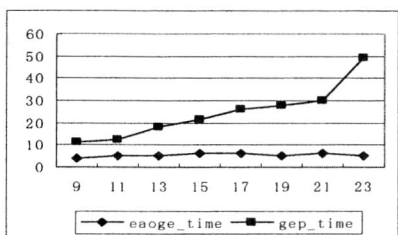

Fig. 1. EAOGE algorithms cooperation under different genetic length and the Comparison of Time Consumption between EAOGE and GEP

Figure 1 shows that (1) under different genetic length, the average evolutionary generation, max evolutionary generation, and min evolutionary generation of EAOGE algorithm does not change a lot. (2) The two algorithm differs greatly on time consumption, the velocity of EAOGE is about 2.8~9.7 times as the one of GEP.

The comparison between average evolutionary generation and success rate of EAOGE and GEP is shown in figure 2, *eaoge_avg* is the average evolutionary generation of EAOGE, *gep_avg* is the average evolutionary generation of GEP.

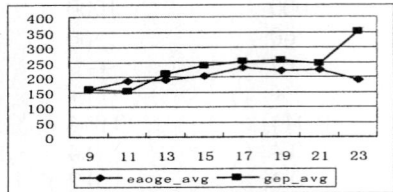
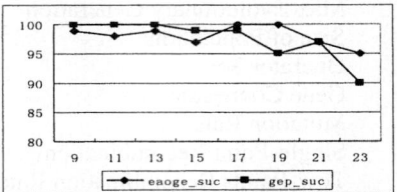

Fig. 2. Averages Evolutionary and Success Rate Comparison between EAOGE and GEP

Figure 2 shows that on success rate of formula (6), the two has little difference, EAOGE is a bit better than GEP as whole. However, on average success generations of different genetic length, EAOGE is obviously better than GEP, the average evolutionary generations save at least 10%.

Experiment 2. Solve the problem of Complex function finding.

Take the formula below for instance:

$$y = f(x_1, x_2, x_3) = x_1^7 + 3*x_1*x_2*x_3 + x_2^2*x_3^4 + x_3^5 \qquad (7)$$

20 real numbers are generated randomly, and the data domain is [-2, 2], M=20000.

To compare the difference in higher-degree polynomial function finding between EAOGE and GEP, the formula (7) was in use of corresponding experiment. The number of gene was changed into 5, the length of single gene is 23, the max evolutionary generation was set to 10000, the other parameters were shown as in table 2, and run it 100 times. The results of the experiment were shown in Table 3, where *OVR_DES* is EAOGE adopted probability selection formula based on density, *OVR-ROU* is EAOGE adopted roulette probability selection formula, *GEP-DES* is GEP adopted probability selection formula which based on density, *GEP-ROU* is GEP adopted roulette probability selection formula and *100-time* is the time consumption to averagely evolve 100 generations.

Table 3. The Comparison of higher-degree polynomial function finding between EAOGE and GEP.

	suc	avg	max	min	Time	suc-time	100-time
OVR-DES	47	4932.78	9901	855	269.31	164.12	3.42
OVR-ROU	44	4011.33	9935	756	273.67	166.39	3.67
GEP-DES	4	3379.50	8331	2582	2183.98	613.14	21.6
GEP-ROU	0				2322.91		23.2

Table 3 shows that:

(1) The success rate of EAOGE is much higher than GEP in higher-degree polynomial function finding. Even if compares with the result of the best GEP, EAOGE still raises 1 order of magnitude at least.

(2) In the process of higher-degree polynomial function finding, the probability selection formulas based on density is good. In EAOGE algorithm, there is a little rise in success rate and number of average evolutionary generation. In GEP algorithm, the success rate is 4%, when the method based on density, whereas there was not even 1 success in 100 run, when the method based on roulette. There force, the probability selection formulas based on density gets obvious advantage in GEP algorithm.

EAOGE possesses comparative applied value, similar to the solutions of complex polynomial function finding problem of formula (7). In the evolutionary computing, whose evolutionary limit is 10000 generations, the success reaches 44% at least. User can continue running it 6 times, the probability of more than once success is $1-(1-0.44)^6=96.9\%$, and the time consumption is $273.67*6=1642.02\approx27.4$ minutes. It is acceptable for users. However, if the success rate is required above 96% in GEP, the algorithm would run more than 80 times $(1-(1-0.04)^{80}=96.1\%)$, and the time consumption is $80*2183.98=174718.4\approx48.5$ hours, is about 106 times to EAOGE. It is obviously too slow.

6 Conclusions

Inspired by the overlapped expression in biological genetics, this study proposes a novel evolutionary algorithm-EAOGE, and describes the genetic expression structures and relevant algorithm of EAOGE. This study systematically analyzes EAOGE, discusses the features of expression space, capability of expression, and compares EAOGE with traditional algorithms.

The detailed experiments show that EAOGE algorithm is 2.8~9.7 times faster than usual GEP method, and in higher-degree polynomial function finding, the success rate of EAOGE is 10 times than usual GEP, discusses the effect of variant criteria factor to algorithm. The experiments results show that the probability selection function based on density works well in higher-degree polynomial function finding.

References

1. M. J. Keith and M. C. Martin, Genetic Programming in C++: Implementation Issues. In K. E. Kinnear, ed., Advances in Genetic Programming, MIT Press, 1994.
2. U.-M. O'Reilly and F. Oppacher, A comparative analysis of genetic programming. In P. J. Angeline and K. E. Kinnear, eds., Advances in Genetic Programming 2, MIT Press, 1996.
3. C. Ferreira. Gene Expression Programming: A New Adaptive Algorithm for Solving Problems. Complex Systems, 2001, 13(2): 87~129
4. C. Ferreira. Gene Expression Programming: Mathematical Modeling by an Artificial Intelligence [OL]. http://www.gene-expression-programming.com/gep/GepBook/Introduction.htm, 2002

5. Thomas H. Cormen, Charles E. Leiserson, Ronald L. Rivest, Clifford Stein. Introduction to Algorithms. Beijing: Higher Education Press, 2002. 184~189
6. Ferreira, C., Gene Expression Programming in Problem Solving [OL]. http://www.gene-expression-programming.com/gep/webpapers/Ferreira-WSC2001/Introduction.htm, 2001
7. Ferreira, C., Mutation, Transposition, and Recombination: An Analysis of the Evolutionary Dynamics. 4th International Workshop on Frontiers in Evolutionary Algorithms, Research Triangle Park, North Carolina, USA, 2002. 614~61
8. Ferreira, C., Discovery of the Boolean Functions to the Best Density-Classification Rules Using Gene Expression Programming. Proceedings of the 4th European Conference on Genetic Programming, EuroGP 2002, volume 2278 of LNCS (Lecture Notes in Computer Science): Berlin: Springer-Verlag , 2002. 51~60
9. Zuo Jie, Tang Changjie, Li Chuan, Chen Anlong, Yuan Chang'an, "Time Series Prediction based on Gene Expression Programming" WAIM04 (International Conference for Web Information Age 2004). LNCS Berlin: Springer-Verlag, July16-17, 2004.
10. C. J. Avers. Genetics Second edition. Willard Grant press, 1991.
11. Gang Lu, De-jian Tan. Improvement on regulating definition of antibody density of immune algorithm[C]. In: Proceedings of the 9th international conference on neural information processing ICONIP'02), 5: 2669~2672
12. http://211.83.120.2/~tangchangjie/buf/download/pj/OverlappeGEP.pdf   The extended version of this paper with appendix

Evolving Case-Based Reasoning with Genetic Algorithm in Wholesaler's Returning Book Forecasting

Pei-Chann Chang, Yen-Wen Wang, Ching-Jung Ting,
Chien-Yuan Lai, and Chen-Hao Liu

Department of Industrial Engineering and Management,
Yuan-Ze University, Nei-Li, Tao Yuan, Taiwan, R.O.C., 32026
iepchang@saturn.yzu.edu.tw

Abstract. In this paper, a hybrid system is developed by evolving Case-Based Reasoning (CBR) with Genetic Algorithm (GA) for reverse sales forecasting of returning books. CBR systems have been successfully applied in several domains of artificial intelligence. However, in conventional CBR method each factor has the same weight which means each one has the same influence on the output data that does not reflect the practical situation. In order to enhance the efficiency and capability of forecasting in CBR systems, we applied the GAs method to adjust the weights of factors in CBR systems, GA/CBR for short. The case base of this research is acquired from a book wholesaler in Taiwan, and it is applied by GA/CBR to forecast returning books. The result of the prediction of GA/CBR was compared with other traditional methods.

1 Introduction

Wholesales in Taiwan are under the extremely competitive environment, in order to face the complex market competitions; they are trying their best to make the ultimate policy. The completeness of the information available to the decision maker is the key influencing the quality of the decisions. A book wholesaler could have better controls if sales forecast is conducted for a new book, and simultaneously another forecast for book returning is evaluated after the release. In business forecasting, managers often apply the outcomes of past similar cases to predict the result of the current one.

Traditionally, the methods to be applied in sales forecasting include naive prediction, statistical methods, or artificial intelligent methods. Among these methods, artificial intelligent (AI) methods are mostly used in academic studies because of the ability to provide rapid solutions with high accuracy and to deal with diversified cases. Among AI methods, Case based reasoning (CBR) has been paid attention gradually. The earliest contributions to the area of CBR were from Schank and his colleagues at Yale University [19, 20]. During 1977-1993, CBR research was highly considered as a conceivable high-level model for cognitive processing. [1] indicated that CBR systems have been successfully used in several domains such as diagnosis, prediction, control, and planning. Based on the survey conducted by [23, 24], there were more than 130 enterprises using CBR systems to solve many kinds of problems in companies at the end of 1997.

For the book industry in Taiwan, it is very difficult to predict sales and returned volumes because the products have various classifications and different lengths of life-cycles, and the environment in this industry is very unique. Average, there are about 3412.6 new books being published every month in Taiwan, and the speed for new released books is really high. The returning rate of books is more than 30% in this industry according to the actual data collected from the wholesaler and from past studies (Council for Culture Affairs [9]). The main reason of high book returning rate is caused by the insufficient information of book sales status in the book supply chain which brings up bullwhip effect and form up the unbalanced situation between supply and demand. Blind returning activities are happening so often because retailing bookstores are often space limited, without efficient computerized managing system, and moreover they do not have to bear any forward and reverse logistics cost. High book returning rate is a very heavy burden for all companies in this industry. Hence, we propose a returning forecasting system for slow-selling books for wholesaler to advise its retailers on returning book decision making to avoid blind returning movements. The system is a hybrid CBR method integrating a conventional CBR with adjusted factor weights by Genetic Algorithms (GAs) method to conduct a high accurate and efficient book returning forecast to reduce high book returning rate to increase profits.

The remainder of this paper is organized as follows: Section 2 describes relevant literature review. Section 3 presents the hybrid method that integrates CBR with GAs based. Section 4 shows problem description. Section 5 depicts experimental design and results. In the final section, the conclusion is presented.

2 Literature Review

In the book industry, returning books forecast is equally important to sales forecast. Under the environment of limited space, low computerized level, frequent release of new books and no forward/reverse logistics cost for retailers, books are returned to wholesales so often without proper evaluations. Retailers might return selling books and place the order again later. This could affect the profit of wholesales, competitive ability of retailers, and also may lead the publishers to re-print a book without proper market demands. Therefore, it should be very important for Taiwan book industry to value the issue of return book forecast, and provide a proper and accurate list of possible slow-selling books to the retailers for correct book returning activities, and also for publishers to evaluate and may introduce promotion strategy for the slow-selling books.

In the early years, studies regarding forecasting mainly relied on statistical techniques such as exponential smoothing, regression model, autoregressive and moving average (ARMA), etc. ([3] [7] [10] [11] and [18]). As time goes by, the internal and external environments for enterprises are becoming more and more complex. Traditional statistical prediction methods are no longer effective enough to deal with the problems. Therefore, Artificial Intelligence algorithms were applied to face the changes as in [21] and [25]. The algorithms such as Artificial Neural Network

(ANNs), Fuzzy method, CBR, Genetic Algorithm (GA) and data envelopment analysis, etc., have been widely applied to many fields such as bankruptcy prediction ([8] and [12]), Stock market prediction ([2], [13], [16] and [22]) and all kinds of sales prediction ([4], [5] and [6]). There were so many researchers that have been comparing different prediction methods ([14] and [15, 17]).

From the literatures reviewed, the study focusing on returning books forecast is rarely discussed. Therefore, this study would like to focus on the book markets and develop an accurate and practical returning books forecasting model.

3 Methodology

GAs and CBR were used in this research to build up an alarm list of slow-selling books and assisting system for returned book handling. The advantages of conveying implicit knowledge, comparing characteristics provided by CBR, and the function of random search by GAs providing different weights of factors could increase the accuracy of forecast. Four models were established in this research: Model A – Hybrid System of GAs and CBR, Model B – Conventional back propagation neural network(BPN), Model C - Conventional CBR and Model D - Multiple-regression analysis. These four models were selected into this research for analysis and comparison.

3.1 Genetic Algorithms

CBR emphasizes on how to describe and retrieve cases, and one of the crucial points is the combination of the weight and each characteristic factor. In this section, we will describe the process of using GAs to find the optimal weight for each factor in CBR). The steps of finding the best combination are described as below:

Step 1. Encoding
The most common encoding method for gene is binary number used as the original calculating system by computer. It is very convenient to operate the encoding, crossover and mutation steps of GAs. Each factor influencing book returning is given a weight with the combination of eight binary numbers.

Step 2. Generate the Initial Population
Initial weights are randomly generated between 0 and 1; these initial solutions form the first population. The weights in the chromosomes will be evaluated by GAs operator later.

Step 3. Compute the objective function
The purpose of finding the objective function is to keep good chromosomes. The objective function of each chromosome will be compared to the best fitness function currently, and if the new chromosome is better the current fitness function, then the new one will be kept to produce next generation. The objective function of this research is to find out the most accuracy for slow-selling books forecast. Description of objected function listed and accuracy as Table 1 and Table 2 below.

Table 1. Description of Notations

Notation	description
M(T)	Objective function of forecasting slow-selling books for set of T training cases
O_i	Comparison of predicted result to actual result for case i. If the same $O_i = 1$; different $O_i = 0$
P_i	Predicted result of case i in training cases
A_i	Actual result of case i in training cases
R	Set of reference cases, $R = \{r_1, r_2, \cdots, r_n\}$.
T	Set of training cases, $T = \{t_1, t_2, \cdots, t_k\}$.
$Y(r_j)$	The result of case j of reference cases that is the most similar to case i of training cases.
S_{ij}	Similarity degree between case i of training cases and case j of reference cases
D	Sum of distances between each weighted factors of training cases and reference cases.
f_{jh}	Value of factor h of case j in reference cases.
f_{ih}	Value of factor h of case i in training cases.
w_h	Weight of factor h in reference cases.

Table 2. Decision Variables and Objective Function for Book Returning Problems

Training cases	P_i	A_i	O_i
$Book_1$	slow-selling	selling	0
$Book_2$	slow-selling	slow-selling	1
⋮	⋮	⋮	⋮
$Book_y$	slow-selling	slow-selling	1
Total $M(T)$	$\sum_{i=1}^{k} O_i$		

1. Objective function:

$$\text{Max } M(T) = \sum_{i=1}^{k} O_i \quad (1)$$

$$\text{s.t. } O_i = 1, \text{ if } P_i = A_i$$

$$O_i = 0, \text{ if } P_i \neq A_i$$

2. Calculation of P_i
Let Set of reference cases $R = \{r_1, r_2, \cdots, r_n\}$, j=1,2,...,n
Set of training cases $T = \{t_1, t_2, \cdots, t_k\}$, i=1,2,...,k

$$P_i = Y(r_j) \qquad (2)$$

if $S_{ij} = \underset{j}{Min}[D(r_j, t_i)]$ and

$D(r_j, t_i) = \sqrt{\sum_{h=1}^{m} w_h (f_{jh} - f_{ih})^2}$, h=1,2,...,m ,where m is the total number of factors

Step 4. Compute the fitness function
The original concept of fitness is "the larger the better", because solutions with larger fitness tend to propagate to the next generation. The objective function for the problem of slow-selling books forecast described in this research is to find the accuracy value which is also "the larger the better." Therefore the objective function is fitness function for a set of training cases.

$$fit(T) = M(T) = \sum_{i=1}^{k} O_i \qquad (3)$$

Step 5. Reproduction / Selection
The roulette wheel selection method is applied in this research and the value of the fitness function represents the area proportion of each string on the roulette wheel, also represents the probability of being selected. Therefore, a chromosome with larger fitness function value means it has greater probability of being selected for crossover. The probability $p(x)$ of each chromosome x will be chosen to re-produce as defined below:

$$p(x) = \frac{fit(x)}{\sum fit(x)} \qquad (4)$$

Step 6. Crossover
After the parameter design, two-point crossover method is applied in the research.

Step 7. Mutation
After the parameter design, one-point mutation method is applied in the research.

Step 8. Elite Strategy
Elite strategy is applied in this research in order to have greater probability for good chromosomes to propagate excellent next generation. 30% of parent chromosomes and 70% offspring chromosomes are used in this research.

Step 9. Replacement
The new population generated by the previous steps updates the old population.

Step 10. Stopping criteria
If the number of generations equals to the maximum generation number then stop, otherwise go to step 3.

3.2 A Hybrid System Combining GAs and CBR

The operation process for the integration is listed as below:

Step 1. Inputs of new case
New case needed to be solved is the input in the CBR system in order to find out the solutions of related problem from the past case-base.

Step 2. Factor analysis of new case
Each new case is composed of many related characteristics, and the factor representing each case would be determined in this state. It is very important to select the related factors since the completeness of a case could influence the computing outcome. Five basic factors including grade of author, grade of publisher, hot or slow season of the publishing date, sales volume for first three months, and returning rate.

Step 3. Calculated Weight of Factors
Using GAs approach to find the optimal weight for each factor.

Step 4. Find out the most matching case from reference cases for the new case using similarity rule.
This stage would find out the most matching case from reference cases using similarity rule in order to predict the possible slow-selling book for the new case.

$$S_{ij} = \min_{j}\left[D(r_j, t_i)\right] \tag{5}$$

$$D(r_j, t_i) = \sqrt{\sum_{h=1}^{m} W_h (f_{jh} - f_{ih})^2} \tag{6}$$

Step 5. Case Adaptation
After the steps above, the most matching case from reference cases was selected and it would have the most similarity to the new case. K-Nearest Neighbors was added to gain more matching cases from reference cases. k numbers of best matching cases from reference cases were produced by K-Nearest Neighbors. We set k = 5 in this research, and determine the new case result to be the same as most results of 5 best matching case from reference cases. For example, the new case would be slow-selling book if the 5 most matching case from reference cases are mostly slow-selling books.

Step 6. Verifying the results
The forecasted values in this research are either 0 or 1 (True/False Question), and mean error method is applied as the measurement benchmark to verify the forecasted results of training cases and testing cases.

$$\text{Mean error rate} = \frac{1}{n}\sum_{i=1}^{n}\frac{e_i}{y_i} \tag{7}$$

Where,

e_i is the forecast error for experiment i
y_i is the total number of forecasted cases in experiment i
n is the total number of experiments

Mean Error values are the forecasting benchmarks to evaluate the accuracy of these four proposed models in this research.

4 Experiment Results and Analysis

In this research, the data were collected from a book wholesaler company in Taiwan. This company is one of the leading book wholesalers in Taiwan, and its distribution channels are widely spread out all around Taiwan. Books to be distributed by this company are covering almost all categories in the market. Therefore, data collected in this research are quite representative for this industry.

Data collected for this research started from May 01, 2002 to April 30, 2003, and total of 904 cases including selling books and slow-selling books. 904 cases were randomly divided into reference cases, training cases, test cases and reserved cases listed as Table 3 below. Reference cases and test cases were used in the GA/CBR returning books forecast system described in this research to find out the best weight for each factor. Test cases were then used to verify the accuracy of this forecast system. Reserved cases would be added into test cases later in order to see if the accuracy of this system would be affected by the numbers of test cases.

Data collecting time for each case would be nine months including actual sales volume for the first three months to be used as a factor in the forecast system, and the actual total sales volume for the six months coming afterward would be used as the base to define a book as a slow-selling book when total sales volume is less then 5 books. Therefore, total collecting time for actual sales volumes for these 904 cases started from May 01, 2002 until Jan. 31, 2004.

Table 3. Groups for collected cases

Group	Reference Cases	Training Cases	Test Cases	Reserved Cases
Volume	404	200	100	200
Selling vs. Slow-selling Books	259:145	102:98	56:44	96:104

Major software used in this research including VISUAL BASIC 6.0, Microsoft Access 2002 (Model A, C), Minitab 13, Neural Works Professional II V5.20 (Model B) and Microsoft Excel 2002 (Model D).

Try and error method is used to find out the best epoch size, and the system becoming stabilized when epoch size exceeds 150,000 times with mean error value of 0.08. We set the epoch size as 180,000 in order to make sure each experiment could reach convergence.

Forecast results for each model under the combination of 404 reference cases, 200 training cases and 100 testing cases are shown as Table 4. Besides, reserved cases are added into reference cases for calculation gradually, and the forecast results are being compared to training cases and testing cases for each model shown as Table 5 and 6.

Table 4. Analysis of forecast errors for each model under 404/200/100 combination

Mo	Reference	Training cases			Testing case		
		Error numbers	Total number	Mean error rate	Error numbers	Total number	Mean Error rate
Model A	Selling	2	102	*0.020**	1	56	*0.018**
	Slow-selling	12	98	*0.122**	6	44	0.136
Model B	Selling	3	102	0.029	4	56	0.071
	Slow-selling	13	98	0.133	4	44	*0.091**
Model C	Selling	8	102	0.078	5	56	0.089
	Slow-selling	18	98	0.184	7	44	0.159
Model D	Selling	16	102	0.157	8	56	0.143
	Slow-selling	14	98	0.143	5	44	0.114

Table 5. Mean error value of training cases under different reference cases numbers for Model A, B, C and D

Mo \ Reference	204	304	404	504	604
Model A	0.1*	0.085*	0.07*	0.022*	0.022*
Model B	0.113	0.085*	0.08	0.067	0.06
Model C	0.155	0.14	0.13	0.065	0.06
Model D	0.15	0.15	0.15	0.15	0.15

*The least mean error value under different reference cases numbers

Table 6. Mean error value of testing cases under different reference cases numbers for Model A, B, C and D

Mo \ Reference	204	304	404	504	604
Model A	0.07*	0.073*	0.07*	0.043*	0.04*
Model B	0.097	0.083	0.077	0.050	0.046
Model C	0.14	0.11	0.12	0.11	0.1
Model D	0.13	0.13	0.13	0.13	0.13

*The least mean error value under different reference cases numbers

Summary and comparison of forecast results:

1. The result of experiment indicates Model A (GA/CBR) has better forecasting ability on selling books than other models, but slightly higher forecast error rates than Model B on slow-selling books. Practically, higher forecast accuracy of selling books could help wholesalers to reduce loss of opportunity costs by misjudge the selling books into slow-selling books.
2. The order of best to worst forecasting ability is Model A, Model B, Model C and Model D. Model A has better performance and higher forecast accuracy then other models under each training cases and each testing cases.
3. Factor weights are both being adjusted under Model A and Model B. Weights being adjusted by Fitness Function under GA in Model A and by bias under Model B. Model A has better forecasting performance under training cases and testing cases than Model B because GA calculates factor weights by global search.
4. Model A with adjusted factor weights under GA presents better forecasting ability than Model C with same factor weights under conventional CBR indicating adjusted factor weights could have better forecasting accuracy and represent the real world.

5 Conclusion

This research discusses how to integrate the GAs and CBR approaches to construct a hybrid system of returning books forecasting. It can help book wholesalers determine the advising list of returning books for the retailers and also the warning list of slow-selling books for publishers. There are so many new books being released each year in Taiwan, and create so many book returning problems. The advising list of returning books could help the space-limited book retailers to make best returning decision and also let the publishers have time to deal with the slow-selling books to make a win-win solution for all parties in the supply chain.

References

1. Aamodt, A. and Plaza, E.: Case-based reasoning: foundational issues, methodological variations, and system approaches. Artificial Intelligence Communication, 7(1) (1994) 39-59.
2. Baba, N. and Kozaki, M.: An Intelligent forecasting system of stock price using neural networks. Proceedings of the International Joint Conference on Neural Networks, 1 (1992) 371-377.
3. Chambers, J.C., Mullick, S.K. and Smith, D.D.: How to choose the right forecasting technique. Harvard Business Review, 49 (1971) 45-79.
4. Chang, P.C. and Lai, C.Y.: A Hybrid System Combining Self-Organizing Maps with Case-Based Reasoning in Wholesaler's New-release Book Forecasting. Expert Systems with Applications, 29(1) (2005)183-192.
5. Chang, P.C. and Lai, K.R.: Combining SOM and Fuzzy Rule Base for Sale Forecasting in Printed Circuit Board Industry. J. Wang, X. Liao, and Z. Yi (Eds.): ISNN, LNCS 3498 (2005) 947-954.

6. Chang, P.C., Wang, Y.W. and Tsai, C.Y.: Evolving Neural Network for Printed Circuit Board Sales. Expert Systems with Applications, 29(1) (2005) 83-92.
7. Chase, C.W.: Ways to improve sales forecasts. Journal of Business Forecasting. 12(3) (1993) 15-17.
8. Cielen, A., Peeters, L. and Vanhoof, K.: Bankruptcy prediction using a data envelopment analysis. European Journal of Operational Research, 154 (2004) 526-532.
9. Council for Culture Affairs: The research for Book published market in R.O.C., Council for Culture Affairs of the Executive Yuan of the Republic of China, Taiwan (2000).
10. Fliedner, E.B. and Lawrence, B.: Forecasting system parent group formation: An empirical application of cluster analysis. Journal of Operations Management. 12 (1995) 119-130.
11. Florance, M.M. and Sawicz, M.S.: Positioning sales forecasting for better results. Journal of Business Forecasting. 12(4) (1993) 27-28.
12. Jo, H. and Han, I.: Integration of Case-based forecasting, Neural network, and Discriminant analysis for bankruptcy prediction. Expert System with Application. 11(4) (1996) 415-422.
13. Krolzig, H.M and J. Toro: Multiperiod forecasting in stock markets: a paradox solved. Decision Support Systems, 37 (2004) 531-542.
14. Kuo, R.J. and Xue, K.C.: A Decision Support System for sales forecasting through fuzzy neural networks with asymmetric fuzzy weights., Decision Support Systems, 24 (1998) 105-126.
15. Kuo, R.J., Wu, P. and Wang, C.P.: An intelligent sales forecasting system through integration of artificial neural networks and fuzzy neural networks with fuzzy weight elimination. Neural Networks, 15 (2002) 909-925.
16. Leigh, W., Purvis, R. and Ragusa, J.M.: Forecasting the NYSE composite index with technical analysis, Pattern Recognizer, Neural Network, and Genetic Algorithm: A case study in romantic decision support. Decision Support Systems, 32(2002) 361-377.
17. Mair, C., Kadoda, G., Lefley, M., Phalp, K., Schofield, C., Shepperd, M. and Webster, S.: An investigation of machine learning based prediction systems. The Journal of Systems and Software, 53 (2000) 23-29.
18. Rice, G. and Mahmoud, E.: Political Risk\Forecasting by Canadian. International Journal of Business Forecasting, 6 (1990) 89-120.
19. Schank, R. and Abelson, R. (eds.): Scripts, Plans, Goals and Understanding, Lawrence Erlbaum Associates, Hillsdale, NJ (1977).
20. Schank, R.: Dynamic Memory: A Theory of Reminding and Learning in Computers and People. Cambridge University Press, New York (1982).
21. Tan, K.C., Lim, M.H., Yao, X., and Wang, L.P. (Eds.): Recent Advances in Simulated Evolution and Learning. World Scientific, Singapore (2004).
22. Wang, X., Phua, P. K. H. and Lin, W.: Stock market prediction using neural networks: does trading volume help in short-term prediction?. Proceedings of the International Joint Conference. 4 (2003) 2438-2442.
23. Watson, I.: Applying Case-Based Reasoning: Techniques for Enterprise Systems. Morgan Kaufmann Publisher Inc., San Francisco (1997).
24. Watson, I. and Marir, F.: Case-based reasoning: A review. Knowledge Engineering Review. 9(4) (1994).
25. Yao, X.:Evolutionary Computation: Theory and Applications. World Scientific, Singapore (1999).

A Novel Immune Quantum-Inspired Genetic Algorithm

Ying Li, Yanning Zhang, Yinglei Cheng, Xiaoyue Jiang, and Rongchun Zhao

School of Computer, Northwest Polytechnical University, Xi'an, 710072, China
lybyp@163.com

Abstract. A new algorithm, the immune quantum-inspired genetic algorithm (IQGA), is proposed by introducing immune concepts and methods into quantum-inspired genetic algorithm (QGA). In application to the knapsack problem, which is a well-known combinatorial optimization problem , the proposed algorithm performs better than the conventional GA (CGA), the immune GA (IGA) and QGA.

1 Introduction

Recently, a novel genetic algorithm called quantum-inspired genetic algorithm (QGA) was presented [1]-[3]. QGA is based on the concept and principles of quantum computing [4] such as qubits and superposition of states. Compared to the conventional GAs, QGA has many advantages such as automatic balance ability between global search and local search, etc. However, the process that QGA evolves the qubit chromosomes is probabilistic, which not only gives the individuals the evolutionary chance but also causes certain degeneracy. In addition, QGA neglects the assistant function of the characteristics or knowledge in a pending problem. Therefore, this Letter introduces immune concepts proposed in [5] into QGA, and presents a new genetic algorithm called the immune QGA (IQGA).

2 The Immune QGA

QGA uses a new representation that is based on the concept of qubits. One qubit is define with a pair of complex numbers, (α, β), which is characterized by

$$|\Psi\rangle = \alpha|0\rangle + \beta|1\rangle \tag{1}$$

where $|\alpha|^2 + |\beta|^2 = 1$. If there is a system of m-qubits, the system can contain information of 2^m states. The basic structure of QGA is described in the following.

```
procedure QGA
begin
    t ← 0
    initialize Q(t)
    make P(t) by observing Q(t) states
    evaluate P(t)
    store the best solution among P(t)
```

```
while (not termination-condition) do
begin
    t ← t+1
    make P(t) by observing Q(t-1) states
    evaluate P(t)
    update Q(t) using quantum gates U(t)
    store the best solution among P(t)
end
end
```

where $Q(t)$ is a population of qubit chromosomes at generation t, and $P(t)$ is a set of binary solutions at generation t. One binary solution is formed by selecting each bit using the probability of qubit. A set of qubit chromosomes $Q(t)$ is updated by applying some appropriate quantum gates $U(t)$, which is formed by using the binary solutions $P(t)$ and the best stored solution.

From the basic structure of QGA, we can easily find that QGA evolves the qubit chromosomes by applying some quantum gates, and makes the binary solutions by observing the states of qubit chromosomes. Because it is a probabilistic operation process which makes individuals change randomly and blindly, it not only give the individuals the evolutionary chance but also cause certain degeneracy. On the other hand, there are many basic and obvious characteristics or knowledge in a pending problem. However QGA neglects the assistant function of the characteristics or knowledge. The loss due to the negligence is sometimes considerable in dealing with some complex problems.

An immune operator is composed with two operations, selecting vaccines, i.e., a vaccination and an immune selection, of which the former is used for raising fitness and the latter is for preventing the deterioration. They are explained as follows:

1) *The Vaccination*: Given an individual x, a vaccination means modifying the genes on some bits in accordance with priori knowledge so as to gain higher fitness with greater probability. Suppose the size of the population is n, select $n_\alpha = n\alpha$ individuals to be subject to vaccination, where α denotes the fraction of individuals.

2) *The Immune Selection*: This operation is accomplished by the following two steps. The first one is the immune test, i.e. testing the antibodies. If the fitness is smaller than that of the parent, the parent will participate in the next competition instead of the individual; the second one is the annealing selection [6].

3 Experiment Results

The knapsack problem, a kind of combinatorial optimization problem, is used to investigate the performance of IQGA. The knapsack problem can be described as selecting from various items those items which are most profitable, given that the knapsack has limited capacity. The 0-1 knapsack problem is used here.

In view of general knowledge of humans, when a person is going to select the items from various items given that the knapsack has limited capacity, he always chooses those items with high values of profit to weight ratios. If the knapsack is overfilled, the selection procedure always chooses the item with low value of profit to weight ratio for deletion. This characteristic is not only one of the properties of the knapsack problem, but also can be used as the information or knowledge for dealing with the problem. So it may act as an approach to abstracting vaccines here.

For the purpose of the comparison, we test the conventional GA (CGA), the immune GA (IGA), QGA, and IQGA on the knapsack problems with 100, 250, and 500 items, respectively. The population size considered for CGA and IGA is equal to 100, and the probabilities of crossover and mutation are fixed as 0.65 and 0.05. The population size of QGA and IQGA is equal to 10, and a qubit chromosome is updated by using the rotation gate $U(t)$ [3] [4]. The i-th qubit value (α_i, β_i) is updated as

$$\begin{bmatrix} \alpha_i' \\ \beta_i' \end{bmatrix} = \begin{bmatrix} \cos(\theta_i) & -\sin(\theta_i) \\ \sin(\theta_j) & \cos(\theta_i) \end{bmatrix} \begin{bmatrix} \alpha_i \\ \beta_i \end{bmatrix} \quad (2)$$

where θ_i is given as $s(\alpha_i \beta_i)\Delta\theta_i$. The parameters used are shown in Table 1, where $f(\cdot)$ is the profit, $s(\alpha_i \beta_i)$ is the sign of θ_i, and b_i and x_i are the i-th bits of the best solution **b** and the binary solution **x**, respectively.

Table 1. Lookup table of θ_i

x_i	b_i	$f(\mathbf{x}) \geq f(\mathbf{b})$	$\Delta\theta_i$	\multicolumn{4}{c}{$s(\alpha_i \beta_i)$}
				$\alpha_i \beta_i > 0$	$\alpha_i \beta_i = 0$	$\alpha_i = 0$	$\beta_i = 0$
0	0	false	0	0	0	0	0
0	0	true	0	0	0	0	0
0	1	false	0	0	0	0	0
0	1	true	0.05 π	-1	+1	±1	0
1	0	false	0.01 π	-1	+1	±1	0
1	0	true	0.025 π	+1	-1	0	±1
1	1	false	0.005 π	+1	-1	0	±1
1	1	true	0.025 π	+1	-1	0	±1

Table 2 shows the experimental results of the knapsack problems found by CGA, IGA, QGA, and IQGA within 1000 generations over 25 runs for 100, 250, and 500 items. The progress of the mean of best profits and the mean of average profits of population is shown in Figure 1. The results show that IQGA performs well in spite of small size of population, which yields superior results as compared to CGA, QGA and IGA.

Table 2. Experiment results of the knapsack problem

No. of items	Profits	Algorithms			
		CGAs	IGAs	QGAs	IQGAs
100	best	583.5	617.8	609.1	617.9
	mean	507.8	601.8	579.2	614.0
	worst	385.4	533.1	508.0	585.2
250	best	1378.9	1503.0	1423.2	1519.5
	mean	1248.6	1449.0	1363.0	1511.4
	worst	1059.0	1268.6	1262.5	1471.3
500	best	2723.3	2973.3	2788.2	3053.4
	mean	2536.0	2861.7	2703.7	3036.5
	worst	2290.4	2564.8	2555.4	2931.7

4 Conclusions

IQGA proposed in this paper leads immune concepts and methods into QGA, whose aim is theoretically to utilize the locally characteristic information for seeking the ways and means of finding the optimal solution when dealing with the difficult problems. The experimental results of the knapsack problem demonstrate the effectiveness and the applicability of IQGA.

Acknowledgment

This works was supported by the Foundation of the National Key Lab for Radar Signal Processing, Xidian University, China, and the National Natural Science Foundation of China under Grant No. 60472072.

References

1. Narayanan and Moore, M.: Quantum-inspired Genetic Algorithm. Proceedings of IEEE International Conference on Evolutionary Computation. (1999) 61-66
2. Han, H., Kim, J. H.: Genetic Quantum Algorithm and Its Application to Combinatorial Optimization Problem. Proceedings of the 2000 IEEE Congress on Evolutionary Computation, (2000) 1354-1360
3. Han, H., Park, K. H., Lee, C. H., Kim, J. H.: Parallel Quantum-inspired Genetic Algorithm for Combinatorial Optimization Problem. Proceedings of the 2001 IEEE Congress on Evolutionary Computation, (2001)1442-1429
4. Hey.: Quantum Computing: An Introduction. Computing & Control Engineering Journal. (1999)105-112
5. Jiao, L.-C., Wang, L.: A Novel Genetic Algorithm Based on Immunity. IEEE Trans. System, Man and Cybernetic. Vol. 30 (2000)552-561
6. Zhang, S., Xu, Z. B., Liang, Y.: The Whole Annealing Genetic Algorithms and Their Sufficient and Necessary Conditions of Convergence. Science in China (Series E), Vol. 27 (1997)154-164.

A Hierarchical Approach for Incremental Floorplan Based on Genetic Algorithms

Yongpan Liu, Huazhong Yang, Rong Luo, and Hui Wang

Department of Electronics Engineering, Tsinghua University, [1]
Beijing, 100084, P.R.China
ypliu99@mails.tsinghua.edu.cn

Abstract. With more and more interactions between high-level and physical-level design, incremental floorplan is becoming a must to deal with such complexity. In this paper, we propose a hierarchical approach for incremental floorplan based on genetic algorithms. It combines the power of genetic optimization and partition algorithms to provide smooth controllable quality/runtime trade-offs. Experiments show that our hierarchy approach can provide magnitudes of speedup compared to traditional flatten floorplan using genetic algorithms without much area overhead. Furthermore, incremental change is also supported in such a hierarchical floorplanner, which makes it very promising to be used in the high-level analysis and synthesis environment.

1 Introduction

With the continuous shrinking of feature size, deep submicron effects cause more and more interactions between high-level and physical-level design. To cope with the complexity of the merging of those design phases, incremental algorithms [1][2] are a must. Furthermore, floorplan is an important stage in the physical design cycle, which can provide necessary information to estimate quality metrics, such as area, timing, interconnect length and congestion. Those physical metrics are important parameters for high-level SoC (Systems-on-a-Chip) synthesis. Thus research on the incremental floorplan algorithm is relevant.

Placement and floorplan of blocks on a 2D surface is a NP complete or NP hard problem, thus many heuristic algorithms are proposed to solve it, e.g. simulated annealing [8][9] and genetic algorithms. Genetic algorithms are proved to be an effective way to solve the floorplan problem and several research papers based on genetic algorithms have been presented recently. In [3], given an initial hard block floorplan, the authors presented how to adjust each soft block's ratio with genetic algorithms, but the quality is also greatly dependent on the previous hard block floorplan. Wang etc [4] proposed a genetic algorithm to simultaneously adjust each soft block's ratio and hard blocks' position, however the incremental approach is not considered and their algorithm does not also have the scalable ability to deal with large design cases.

---

[1] The author would like to thank the grants from the 863 Programs (Grant No. 2004AA1Z1050 and 2005AA1Z1230), and the National Science Foundation of China (Grant No. 60025101 and 90207001).

Partition-based placement (e.g. employed in [5][6]) shows good scalability but can not handle the sizing problem well. Most recently, [7] presented a genetic algorithm to implement the incremental floorplan, however no hierarchical support is considered in their approach, which makes their solution not suitable for large design cases and fast estimation in high-level SoC synthesis.

In this paper, we study the floorplan problem based on genetic algorithms for future IP-based SoC design. Our contributions include: 1) We develop a floorplan algorithm to combine the power of genetic optimization and partition-based algorithms. Our floorplan program can deal with larger design cases (e.g. more than 100 blocks) with a smooth controllable quality/runtime tradeoff, which is not seen in the previous floorplan work based on genetic algorithms. This characteristic is becoming more and more important, because hundreds of IP blocks and hard macros will be integrated into the future SOC designs. 2) We integrate an incremental optimization algorithm into our hierarchical floorplanner. Since more ECO and debugging changes will occur with the increasing complexity of VLSI, handling such changes becomes very important for physical design tools. Incremental optimization will often find an acceptable solution with a magnitude of speedup compared to traditional approaches.

The rest of this paper will be arranged as below: section 2 illustrates partition algorithms, hierarchical genetic algorithms and incremental optimization flow, respectively; then the section 3 and 4 will present the results and conclusions.

2 Hierarchical Floorplan Based on Genetic Algorithms

The basic flow of our hierarchical floorplan based on genetic algorithms is showed in Fig. 1. After the initial floorplan solution is gotten, we may want to make some small changes to it. In traditional floorplan approaches, the floorplanner has to be run again even if only some slight changes are made on the blocks resulting from debugging or ECOs. In fact, using an incremental method will often generate a comparable solution with a much faster speed. Fig. 2 shows the incremental process of resizing two blocks in the previous floorplan solution.

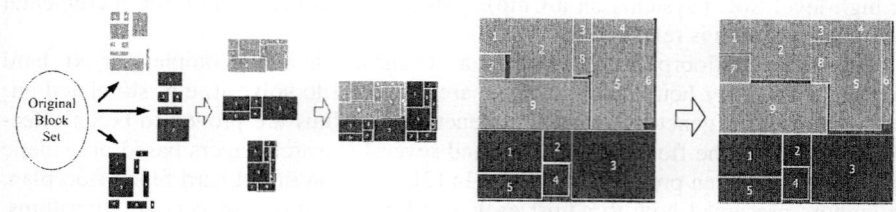

Fig. 1. an example of hierarchical floorplan   **Fig. 2.** resize two blocks incrementally

As we can see, the two green blocks are resized. In our incremental algorithm, we define three kinds of operations to the initial floorplan solution: *add_block, delete_block* and *resize_block*. And their meanings are straightforward.

In the next sections, we will show detail descriptions of the partition algorithms, hierarchical genetic algorithms and the incremental optimization flow respectively.

2.1 Partition Algorithms

In this section, we will present a heuristic partition method to divide the block set B into n subsets B_i $(i = 1...,n)$, in which each subset has a similar number of blocks. Before illustrating the algorithm, we will first define several terminologies:

Given a set B of rectangular blocks and a matrix of inter-rectangle priorities $P = [p_{mn}]_{|B| \times |B|}$ if a link exists from B_m to B_n, we define *a corresponding edge-weighted DAG (directed acyclic graph)* $G(B,E)$, $E = \{(B_m, B_n) | \text{if } m \leq n, \text{then } (B_m, B_n) \in E\}$. An edge $(B_m, B_n) \in E$ has a weight $w_{mn} = p_{mn} + p_{nm}$. Given a graph $G(B,E)$, it can be reduced to a super graph $G'(B', E')$ by recursive clustering. To evaluate the reduction efficiency, we define *a factor* $\alpha = |V'|/|V|$, which is also called the degeneration degree of graph G'. The whole partition procedure is then described as below:

I. Depth-first search is deployed on $DAG\ G(B, E)$.
II. The resulted depth-first trees $G_k(B_k, E_k)$ with more than $\sqrt{|B|}$ blocks are then partitioned into two equal size sub trees recursively until no sub trees exceed $\sqrt{|B|}$. (If the degree of G_k is odd, a special block with zero width and height is added.)
III. After that, block sets with more than M_s blocks are selected as seeds, where M_s is an experimental value to guarantee that the seed number is close to $\sqrt{|B|}$.
IV. For every no-seed block subset, it joins into the seed set with the least blocks.

2.2 Hierarchical Genetic Algorithms

As we know, the encoding method, genetic operators and decoding method are fundamental factors to implement genetic algorithms and we will only discuss encoding method and genetic operators below for limited spaces. The decoding method could be referred to [7], so it isn't discussed in this paper.

1) *Encoding Method:* In order to reduce the complexity of 2D floorplan problem, we use an abstract representation $r = \{S, w\}$ to present the intermediate floorplan result, where w indicates chip width and $S = \{(o_1, d_1), (o_2, d_2), \cdots (o_n, d_n)\}$ is a sequence, in which (o_i, d_i) indicates the place order and the direction of block B_i respectively. Furthermore, we extend the concept of block to enable it represent a single block as well as a block set. Thus our floorplanner can do floorplan hierarchically.

2) *Cross-over Operator:* A two-cut cross-over operator is adopted. Suppose the length of sequence X and Y is n, two number i and j ranging between 0 and n are then randomly generated, with $i < j$, and two new sequences S', S'' are generated by switching two pieces of sequence X and Y. After that, a mapping rule [7] is used on those new generated sequences S', S'' to guarantee the legalization of those sequences.

3) *Mutation Operator:* Two kinds of mutation operators are defined in our floorplanner, called as mutation operator 1 and mutation operator 2, respectively. The first one is the simplest one. We just randomly select several blocks (e.g. two blocks) and change their direction. In mutation operator 2, several pairs of blocks will be randomly picked out and both block's place order and direction will be changed.

4) *Work Flow*: The work flow of our hierarchical genetic algorithm is described as below: The block set B is automatically divided into n subsets B_i $(i=1...,n)$, according to the partition algorithms. For each B_i, we use the encoding method of genetic algorithms to obtain an abstract representation r_i. The heuristic decoder is then called to acquire the width and height of each subset. After that, we can consider each subset as a large block, and hierarchically use the floorplanner to find the final solution.

Suppose that the block set B is divided into L equal-sized subsets with a two-level hierarchical partition, the computation complexity of each subset is $O(M \cdot (|B|/L)^2)$. Thus, the computation cost to obtain the whole floorplan solution is $O(M \cdot |B|^2 /L + M \cdot L^2)$. Though adopting the hierarchical algorithm will greatly reduce the complexity of the problem, it makes us lose the opportunity to find the global optimal solution. However, in most cases, floorplan solutions close to the optimal solution are also acceptable. What's more, the floorplanner also provides controllable quality/runtime tradeoffs by adjusting the partition standard. It is straightforward to prove that the most effective α equals to $\sqrt{|B|}$ for a two-level hierarchy. As the factor α decreases, the floorplanner will operate slower with a better quality.

2.3 Incremental Changes

The basic idea behind our incremental floorplanner is that we try to change the initial floorplan as little as possible to acquire a significant speedup. For flatten incremental floorplan, we can use the algorithm defined in [7]. Suppose that $|B|$ is the number of reshuffled blocks, it is easy to prove that the worst-case computation complexity of the incremental approach will be $O(M \cdot N^2)$, where $N = \lfloor |B|/2 \rfloor + 2$.

Furthermore, the efficiency for the hierarchical approach could be improved. On the assumption that one new block would be added in one subset, what we need to do is to reshuffle part of the sequence corresponding to the subset, and accordingly adjust the sequence in the higher level. Suppose the block set B is divided into L equal-sized subsets with a two-level hierarchical partition, the computation cost for one incremental change is $O(M \cdot K^2 + M \cdot H^2) \approx O(M \cdot (|B|/L)^2 /4 + M \cdot L^2 /4)$, where $K = \lfloor |B|/2L \rfloor + 2$, $H = \lfloor L/2 \rfloor + 2$. In case $L = \sqrt{B}$, we can derive that the complexity of the incremental changes in the hierarchical floorplanner is $O(M \cdot |B|/2)$.

3 Experiment Results

We have implemented the two-level hierarchy floorplan algorithm in a C++/STL style program on a 1.0GHz PC/Intel system running Linux. Because of lacking benchmarks for large cases, we generate the benchmark randomly with the block number ranging from 49 to 225. We believe that our way makes sense for IP-based SoC synthesis. According to the area usage, the initial pool size is set to be 50, while the generation number of genetic algorithms is set to be 50. And the probability to do cross-over and mutation operation is set to be 0.5 and 0.03, respectively. Fig. 3 shows the curves of the relationship between run time and block number in our hierarchical and flatten floorplanner. As we can see, the run time of flatten approach increases very quickly as the number of block on the chip increases. However, the hierarchical algorithm effectively reduces the run time and also keeps an acceptable area usage. In our experiments, it approaches a linear relationship with the block number on the chip, in case that the block number is up to 225.

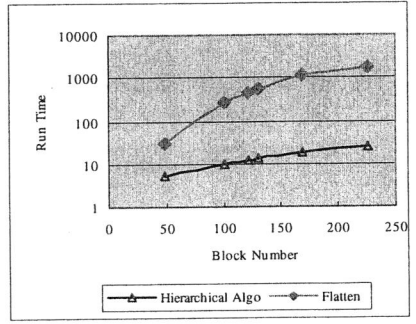 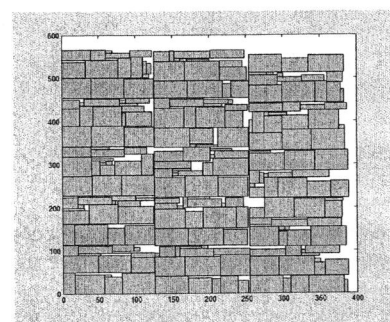

Fig. 3. Run time and block number curve **Fig. 4.** Floorplan result of m225

Fig. 4 gives out the floorplan result of m225. It can be seen that our hierarchical floorplanner partition the whole block set into fifteen subsets and then they are organized in a hierarchical way, it acquires a good tradeoff between quality and running time. Furthermore, the hierarchical approach can use the modularity of block set to obtain extra speedup. For example, in multiprocessor Network Processor, we know that there are many block subsets on the chip, each of which contains the same blocks as others. In a hierarchical approach, we can only find out the floorplan for one of them. It will save lots of time if the number of such block subsets is quite large.

In Table 1, running time of incremental algorithm for two different approaches is showed. As we have analyzed before, the incremental optimization in the hierarchical floorplanner is quite efficient. We only need to modify the corresponding block subset and its high level position. It provides several magnitudes of speedup than simply running the flatten floorplanner again. This characteristic makes our floorplanner quite promising for the estimation tools used in the high-level SOC synthesis, where an iterative process is often needed.

Table 1. Run time of Incremental Optimization Based on Hierarchical Genetic Algorithms

Bench Name	Hier/Incre Run time/Usage	Hier/One-shot Run time/Usage	Flat/One-shot Run time/Usage
m49	1.2/87.1%	5/88.2%	32/89.5%
m100	1.9/88.1%	10/89.4%	258/90.1%
m121	2.0/87.4%	12/88.7%	445/87.2%
m130	2.1/87.1%	13/87.9%	546/88.1%
m169	2.4/85.8%	18/86.7%	1176/86.2%
m225	2.9/88.1%	26/89.3%	1656/89.2%

4 Conclusion and Extension

We showed that our hierarchical floorplan method can produce a reasonably good solution very quickly. By combining the power of genetic optimization and partition algorithms, it provides smooth controllable quality/runtime tradeoffs for large design cases. Furthermore, incremental algorithm is also supported in such a hierarchical floorplanner, which makes it extremely fast and suitable for the quick estimation in high-level SoC synthesis. A possible extension to this work is to extend the current floorplanner to optimize soft blocks as well as hard blocks.

References

1. Coundert,O.,Cong,J.,Malik,S.: Incremental CAD. IEEE/ACM ICCAD, Digest of Technical Papers (2000) 236-243
2. Creshaw,J. Sarrafzadeh,M.,Banerjee,P.: An Incremental Floorplanner. Proceeding of IEEE, Great Lakes Symposium on VLSI (1999) 248-251
3. Rebaudengo,M.,etc.: GALLO: A Genetic Algorithm for Floorplan Area Optimization. IEEE Trans. On CAD Vol.15. (1996)
4. Wang, X., etc.: VLSI Floorplanning Method Based on Genetic Algorithms. Chinese Journal of Semiconductors, Vol.23. (2002)
5. Caldwell,A.,Kahng,A.,Markov,I.: Can Recursive Bisection Alone Produce Routable Placements. Proceedings of DAC. (2000) 477-482
6. Alpert,C.,Huang,J.,Kahng,A.: Multilevel Circuit Partitioning, Proceedings of DAC (1997) 530-533
7. Liu,Y.,Yang,H.,etc.: An incremental floorplanner based on genetic algorithm. Proceedings of 5th International Conference on ASIC, Vol.1. (2003) 331-334
8. Ho,S.Y., Ho,S.J.,etc.: An orthogonal simulated annealing algorithm for large floorplanning problems. IEEE Transactions on VLSI. Vol 12. (2004) 874-876
9. Ranjan,A., Bazargan,K.etc.: Fast floorplanning for effective prediction and construction. IEEE Transactions on VLSI, Vol 9. (2001) 341-350

A Task Duplication Based Scheduling Algorithm on GA in Grid Computing Systems

Jianning Lin and Huizhong Wu

Nanjing University of Science and Technology, post code:210094, Nanjing, China
oliver_ljn@hotmail.com

Abstract. Grid computing is a new computing-framework to meet the growing computational demands. Computational grids provide mechanisms for sharing and accessing large and heterogeneous collections of remote resources. However, task Scheduling is one of the key elements in the grid computing environment, and an efficient algorithm can help reduce the communication time between tasks. So far, the task scheduling algorithms in the grid computing environment have not been based on task duplication. However, the scheduling algorithms based on task duplication will generate too many task replications, which will enlarge the system loads and even add the makespan. As optimal scheduling of tasks is a strong NP-hard problem, this paper presents a scheduling algorithm based on genetic algorithm and task duplication, whose primary aim is to get the shortest makespan, and secondary aim to utilize less number of resources and duplicate less number of tasks. The chromosome coding method and the operator of genetic algorithm are discussed in detail. The relationship between subtasks can be obtained through the DAG. And the subtasks are ranked according to their depth-value, which can avoid the emergence of deadlock. The algorithm was compared with other scheduling algorithm based on GAs in terms of makespan, resource number and task replication number. The experimental results show the effectiveness of the proposed algorithm to the scheduling problem.

1 Introduction

A Grid is a distributed collection of computer and storage resources maintained to serve the needs of some community or virtual organization (VO) [1][2]. These virtual organizations can share their resources collectively as a larger grid. In the grid-computing environment, a large scale-computing program can often be divided into several tasks. In most cases, the amount of tasks is more than that of the computational resource. In order to reduce the makespan of the whole program as possible, scheduling applications among the resource is a very complicate problem. In general, it is a NP-hard problem in a distributed system.

Related earlier work has been done in task scheduling policy. Vincenzo has introduced a scheduling algorithm based on genetic algorithm, which can improve the efficiency and throughput [3][4]. Asim YarKhan addressed the application of simulated annealing algorithm in the resource scheduling of the grid [5]. Xu has also put the ant algorithm into the resource scheduling policy[6]. But they didn't take the relationship among tasks into account. But they all didn't consider the duplication of tasks. Although these algorithms can optimize the execution time of the whole programs, the communication delay between two different computing nodes, seriously affects the efficiency of computation. It is obvious that the communication delay is one of the most important factors that influence the length of schedules. And task duplication is shown to be useful for shortening it. Task duplication means scheduling some copies of a task on more than one computing nodes to eliminate communication delays between processors. So far, several scheduling algorithms using task duplication have already been proposed. Tatsuhiro Tsuchiya first proposed a GA based on task duplication [7]; Samantha Ranaweera proposed another scheduling algorithm TSA based on task duplication in 1998; and two years later, he improved the TSA [8] and proposed the algorithm OSA [9]. However, the previous algorithms were applied in the homogeneous system and didn't consider eliminating the redundancy tasks. In order to overcome the deficiencies, in this paper we propose an alternative approach to find a good schedule based on task duplication and to eliminate the redundancy duplication tasks.

2 System Model

In this paper, a heterogeneous system consists of a set of n identical computing resource $R\{R_1, R_2...R_n\}$, which is completely connected via a network. Each resource executes only one task at one time without interrupting and task preemption is not allowed. A parallel program is modeled as a weighted DAG, $G = \{V, E, C, T\}$ where each node $v \in V$ represents a task whose computation cost is $C(v, r)$ and each edge $(u, v) \in E$ represents the precedence relation that task u should be completed before task v can be started. In addition, at the end of its execution, u sends data to v and the communication cost is $T(u, v)$. The communication cost is zero if u and v are scheduled to the same processor. If there is a path from u to v, then u is called a predecessor of v, while v is called a successor of u. A node without predecessors is called entry node and a node without successors is called exit node.

The height of a node v is denoted by $height(v)$. If the node has no predecessors, the height is zero. If the task has predecessors, the height is the maximum of their heights plus one. A schedule of G, denoted by $S(G)$ is a mapping of tasks onto processors and assigning a start time to each task. For a task $v \in V$, it is scheduled onto processor $r(v) \in R$ and assigned a start time $ST(v, r)$. Therefore, the finishing time of v, denoted by $FT(v, p)$ can be represented as $FT(v, r) = ST(v, r) + C(v, r)$. A node can be mapped onto several processors. In such a case, task duplication is used. The length or makespan of a schedule S is the maximal finishing time of all tasks, that is $makespan(S) = \max\{FT(v, r) | v \in V, p \in P\}$ .Given a weighted DAG $G = \{V, E, C, T\}$, the aim of resource scheduling is to find a schedule with smallest makespan, that is $Min\{makespan(S) \ \forall S\}$. Figure-1 shows a simple DAG, and table-1 shows the computing time of the tasks of DAG in different computing resource.

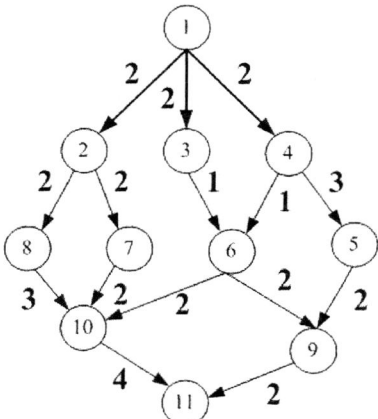

Fig. 1. a simple DAG

Table 1. the computing time in different resource

Resource id→ task id↓	1	2	3	4
1	4	4	4	4
2	5	5	5	5
3	4	6	4	7
4	3	3	3	3
5	3	5	3	4
6	3	7	2	2
7	5	8	5	5
8	2	4	5	3
9	5	6	7	5
10	3	7	5	2
11	5	6	7	8

3 The Proposed Algorithm

Genetic algorithms[10] (GAs) emulate the evolutionary process in nature to solve optimization problems. Unlike other traditional search techniques, GAs uses multiple search nodes simultaneously. Each of the search nodes corresponds to one of the current solutions and is represented by a sequence of symbols. Such a sequence is called a chromosome. Each chromosome has an associated value called a fitness value, which is evaluated by the objective function.

3.1 Chromosomes

One of the most fundamental and important tasks in the design of GAs is devising the encoding mechanism for representing search nodes as chromosomes. Since we consider a scheduling problem, each search node corresponds to a schedule. Therefore, it is desirable that any chromosome can determine a schedule uniquely. For this purpose, we design a chromosome using a planar matrix. Each column in a chromosome is associated with a task and retains information on all tasks assigned to that resource. Each gene of the column corresponds to one of these tasks that run on that resource, which is shown in figure-2.

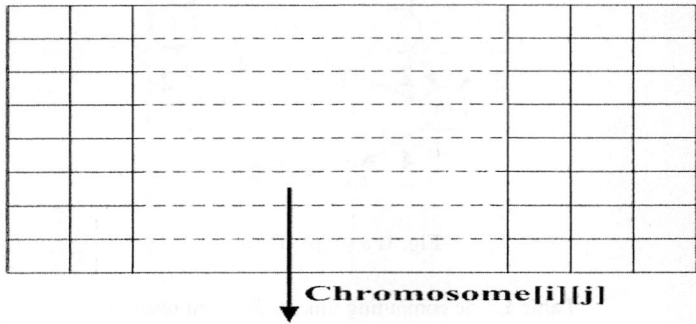

Fig. 2. Chromosome encoding style

The schedule represented by a chromosome must consider the imposed constraints, that is, precedence constraints, communication delays and execution order specified by the chromosome.

Condition 1: For all $n_i, n_j \in V$, if $e_{i,j} \in E$ and $n_i, n_j \in RT(R_k)$, then n_i must execute before n_j.

In order to construct the schedule that satisfies the condition 1, we give the following algorithm I that is used to generate the schedule:

1. Initially, the tasks are classified by the resource that they are assigned;
2. The tasks in the same resource are arranged according to their values of height from the lower to the higher.

The height of a task is defined as

$$height(n_i) = \begin{cases} 0 & \text{parent}(n_i) = \phi \\ 1 + \max\{height(parent(n_i))\} & \text{other tasks} \end{cases} \quad (1)$$

parent (n_i) returns the parent nodes of task n_i.

Claim 1. For the tasks that are assigned to the same resource, if their sequence of execution is according to their height, it will not occur the deadlock.

Proof. Let us be given resources R_i, R_j and task $n_1 - n_4$. It is no matter to suppose that $height(n_1) < height(n_3)$ and $height(n_2) < height(n_4)$. We use the method of reduction to absurdity. Suppose that the sequence of execution of the four tasks is complied with the order according to their height from the lower to higher and a deadlock occurs. So it must be n_1、n_4 are assigned to the same resource R_i and n_4 executes before n_1. And in the same reason n_2、n_3 are assigned to the same resource R_j and n_1 executes before n_2. So we can educe that $height(n_4) < height(n_1)$ and $height(n_3) < height(n_2)$, so $height(n_4) < height(n_2)$. It is obvious that the conclusion is contradicted with our hypotheses. So if their sequence of execution is according to their height, the deadlock will not occur.

3.2 Initialization

In this step, an initial population of chromosomes is generated. First, for every task, the resource value is generated within $[1...n]$; second, for each task, it must be assigned to at least one resource. Consequently, a chromosome is obtained. The initial population of chromosomes is generated by repeating the process as many times as the given population size.

3.3 Fitness and Selection

In this paper, we define the fitness values as the $F = 1/f$, f represents the completion time of the exit task node. So to get the f, we must compute the completion time $f(n_i/R_j)$, which represents the completion time of task n_i runs on the resource R_j. The formula is following:

$$f(n_i / R_j) = s(n_i / R_j) + C(i, j) \qquad (2)$$

And $s(n_i/R_j)$ represents the earliest start time of task n_i in the resource R_j, which is computed as following formula: in (3) $L = \{l \mid chromosome[n_k][l] = 1\}$.

$$S(n_i / R_j) = \max(spare(R_j / n_i),\\ \max_{n_k \in pred(n_i)} (\min_{l \in L} (f(n_k / R_l)_{l=j}, f(n_k / R_l) + C_{i,k})_{l \neq j})) \qquad (3)$$

According to formula (2) and (3) we can compute completion time of the exit node on the resources.

Once fitness values have been evaluated for all chromosomes, we can select good chromosomes through rotating roulette wheel. The chromosomes with higher fitness values have more chance to be selected. Consequently, the same number of chromosomes as the population size is selected.

3.4 Crossover and Mutation

For this algorithm, Crossover is performed by executing the following process for every processor. The crossover operator swaps the columns of two chromosomes, which occurs with the crossover probability. Crossover is performed as follows: first, choose two chromosomes according to the selection method; second, generate two random integers between 1 and the amount of resource as crossover points for each chromosome; third, swap the two columns of the crossover points. As a consequence, two new chromosomes replace the two parents.

Mutation is a basic operator, which occurs with the mutation probability, ensuring that the probability of finding the optimal solution is never zero. The mutation operator is applied to each task in all chromosomes with the mutation probability. We consider three types of mutation: transformation, duplication and deletion. In the following we explain this operator. Let $task(i,r)$ be the ith task on the list for resource and assume that the mutation operator is applied to $task(i,r)$. Deletion operator will remove the task i from the resource r. However, Deletion is executable if and only if there is another resource where the task is assigned. Duplication operator will generate the other resource that task i doesn't run on and duplicate the task i onto it. Transformation operator will generate the other resource that task i doesn't run on and move the task i onto it. Moreover, our mutation operator needs further adjustment. When duplication or transformation operator executes, the resources that the parent of the task i runs on are considered in preference, which will not add the communication delay.

After the crossover or mutation operator, the new schedule represented by the chromosomes that have been altered should be re-scheduled according to the algorithm Ⅰ, which will ensure the deadlock not to occur. Then the new fitness will be computed. If the fitness of the new chromosome is more than that of the old, the old chromosome will be replaced by the new one according to the exchange rate.

4 Redundant Task Elimination

The algorithm terminates when it meets the convergent criterion. Typically, the criterion can be that the best solution in the population obtained does not change after a specific number of generations. The chromosome that meets the convergent criterion represents the tasks schedule scheme in the resources. In this scheme each tasks maybe be replicated at least one time. But not every task replication is needed. It is obvious that the task replication in the grid will consume much resource, such as network bandwidth. And the resource in the grid is costly, so how to eliminate these redundant tasks is a key point.

4.1 Definition of Redundant Task

Definition 1. Redundant task: As for the task n_i that runs in the resource R_j, if n_i was eliminated from the resource and the new fitness of the new chromosome is not more than the old one, then we would define the task n_i as the redundant task for the resource R_j.

4.2 Deletion Algorithm

The algorithm of eliminating the redundant tasks in the scheme is presented here: The input parameters are the old $chromosome[\,][\,]$ and the old fitness.

Algorithm Step:
1. for(i=0;i<nodenumber;i++){
2.   for (j=0;j<resourcenumber;j++) {
3.   if($chromosome[i][j] = 1$){
4.   flag=JudgeCopy(); //judge whether the task has other replications;
5.   if(flag){
6. $chromosome[i][j] = 0$
7.   fitness=computefitness(); //calculate the new fitness
8.   if (oldfitness>=fitness)
9.   oldfitness=fitness;
10.   else
11. $chromosome[i][j] = 1$ //resume the old chromosome
    }}}}

Claim 2. The new fitness calculated according to the new chromosome obtained after the elimination of the redundant tasks is not more than the old one; and the new chromosome must comply with the condition 1.

Proof. According to the algorithm I, after the elimination of a certain replication if the new fitness is smaller than the old one, then the replication will be recovery(line 11); otherwise restore the new fitness and the new chromosome(line 9). So the fitness will not come to be smaller. Moreover, before eliminating the replication of a certain task, it is first to check whether the task has other replication (line 4). If true, the elimination operation will continue; otherwise it will break. So every task in the chromosome must run at least one resource.

5 MGaTds Algorithm Steps

I. Generate the initial population $chromosome[\,popid\,][\,][\,]$, and calculate the fitness of every chromosome in the population;
II. Select two good chromosomes through rotating roulette wheel and make the crossover operator
III. Select one chromosome randomly to make the mutation operator;
IV. When the iterative number is smaller than a certain one return the step one;
V. Optimize the best chromosome by which the smallest completion time is calculated through eliminating the redundant tasks;
VI. The schedule scheme is obtained according to the chromosome whose fitness is largest, and output the completion time and the scheme of task schedule.

6 Experiments

In order to evaluate the performance of the proposed MGaTDS, we coded the algorithm in java language and performed simulation studies. To show the effectiveness, we compared it with a non-genetic algorithm called TDS [8], and GaTDS [7]. The task graph is shown as figure-1. Each node in the DAG represents a task. We also assume the number of computing resource is four and the cost time of each task in different computing resource is shown in table-1. The number beside every arrow represents the communication delay. The population size is 500. The crossover rate is 0.8 and the mute rate is 0.05. The max iterative number is 10000. We make the comparison in three aspect: the minimum makespan□the number of used resources□the number of duplication tasks. The schedules generated by three algorithms are shown as figure-3□figure-4□figure-5. It is obvious that the proposed MGaTDS generates the same makespan with the other two algorithms. However, it occupies less resource and duplicates fewer tasks. We also generate the tree type DAG randomly to represent the task graph, the number of whose nodes are 20□30 and 40. The recourses are 8□10 and 12 correspondingly. The time cost of each task in different resource is generated randomly. We compare the GaTDS and the proposed MGaTDS in the same three aspects. The result is shown in table-2. From table-3, it is clear that the makespan generated by two algorithms are almost equal, but the number of used resources and duplication tasks generated by MGaTds is less than that generated by GaTds, which is more accord with the grid environment.

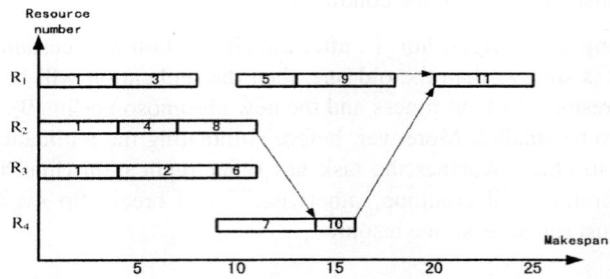

Fig. 3. MGaTDS schedule

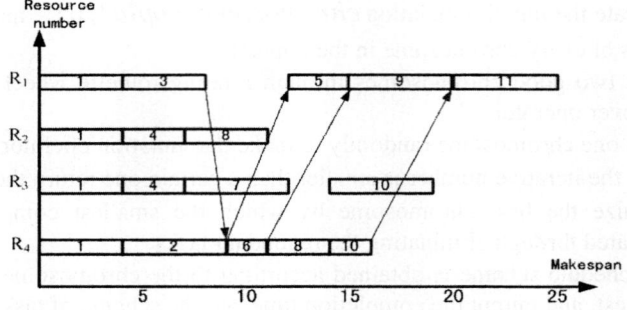

Fig. 4. GaTds schedule

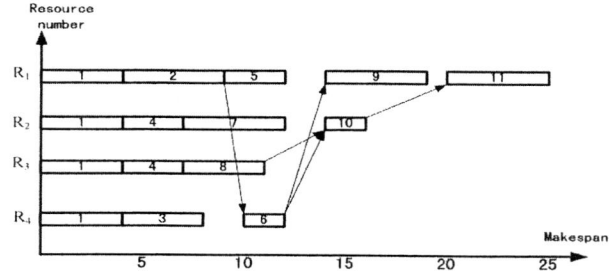

Fig. 5. TDS schedule

Table 2. Two algorithm comparison

	makespan		Resource number		Duplication number	
	CGaTDS	MGaTDS	CGaTDS	MGaTDS	CGaTDS	MGaTDS
T20, R8	66	66	8	6	38	26
T30, R10	151	155	10	9	67	32
T40, R12	229	225	12	10	94	51

7 Conclusion

In this paper, we have proposed a modified genetics-based approach to multi-resources scheduling using task duplication. A novel chromosome encoding scheme is used in our algorithm. In order to show the effectiveness of the proposed GA, we conducted a comparison with the other two algorithms using a number of DAG. As a result, it is found that the resource and duplication tasks number used in the proposed algorithm were less than those in the other algorithms, and the makesapn was also not more than the two others.

References

1. I.Foster and C.Kesselman, editors. The Grid: Blueprint for a New Computing Infrasturcture. Morgan Kauffmann,1999.
2. I. Foster, C. Kesselman, and S. Tuecke. The anatomy of the grid: Enabling scalable virtual organizations. International Journal of High Performance Computing Applications, 15(3):200–222, 2001. http://www.globus.org/research/papers/anatomy.pdf.
3. Vincenzo Di Martino. Scheduling in a grid computing environment using genetic algorithms. Marco Mililotti 16th International Parallel and Distributed Processing Symposium (IPDPS2002). Florida, USA, April 15~19, 2002
4. Vincenzo Di Martino, M. Mililotti. Sub Optimal scheduling in a grid using genetic Algorithms. Parallel computing , 2004, Vol.30: .553~565

5. Ajith Abraham, Rajkumar Buyya. Nature's Heuristics for scheduling Jobs on Computational grids. The 8th International Conference on Advanced Computing and Communications (ADCOM 2000). Cochin, India 2000, Dec 14~16
6. ZhihongXU, Xiangdan HOU, Jizhou SUN. Ant Algorithm-Based Task Scheduling in grid computing. CCECE 2003 - Canadian Conference on Electrical and Computer Engineering. Montreal, Canada, 2003
7. Tsuchiya T.; Kikuno T.; Osada T. genetics-based multiprocessor scheduling using task duplication. Microprocessors and Microsystems. p. 197-207, Vol.22,No.3-4,1998.
8. Samantha Ranaweera; Dharma P. Agrawal. A task duplication based scheduling algorithm for heterogeneous systems. The 14th International Parallel and Distributed Processing Symposium (IPDPS2000), Cancun, Mexico, 1-5 May, 2000. p.445-450
9. Chan-Ik Park; Tae-Young Choe An optimal scheduling algorithm based on task duplication The 8th International Conference on Parallel and Distributed Systems(ICPADS2001), KyongJu City, Korea, June 26-29, 2001. p.9-14
10. D.E. Goldberg, et al. Genetic Algorithm in Search, Optimization, and Machine Learning, Addison-Wesley, Reading, MA, 1989.

Analysis of a Genetic Model with Finite Populations*

Alberto Bertoni[1], Paola Campadelli[1], and Roberto Posenato[2]

[1] Dipartimento di Scienze dell'Informazione,
Università degli Studi di Milano,
via Comelico, 39 - 20135 Milano Italy
{bertoni, campadelli}@dsi.unimi.it
[2] Dipartimento di Informatica,
Università degli Studi di Verona,
strada le Grazie, 15 - 37134 Verona Italy
roberto.posenato@univr.it

Abstract. Simple genetic algorithms on populations of l-binary words usually become iterative systems on 2^l dimensional spaces when populations have size infinite. However, in a particular model (BCCG model) previously introduced, it has been shown that the iterative system works in a l-dimensional space.

In this paper we propose a simplification of the BCCG model and we analyze it in the case of large but finite-size populations. In particular:
1. We exhibit a Markov chain with states in $\mathbb{R}^l$ that approximates the system behavior.
2. We estimate the steady state distribution of the Markov chain.

1 Introduction

Genetic algorithms are probabilistic search algorithms inspired by mechanisms of natural selection. They have received considerable attention because of their applications to several fields such as optimization, adaptive control, and others [1,2,3,4,5,6]. By means of stochastic rules, genetic algorithms simulate natural reproductive processes over a population of individuals or genotypes in an arbitrary environment. In the so-called *simple genetic algorithms*, the individuals are represented by binary words of fixed length.

The behavior of simple genetic algorithms is described by homogeneous Markov chains [7,8,9] whose states encode populations that are multi-sets of binary words. General theoretical results are available in the thermodynamic limit (for *infinite populations*) when the systems become deterministic iterative systems [10]. Unfortunately, simulation of the deterministic system is computationally difficult since the states of the system are represented by vectors in $\mathbb{R}^{2^l}$, where l is the length of the words that represent the individuals.

---
* Partially supported by the PRIN Project "Formal languages and automata: methods, models and applications", MIUR.

In [11] it has been introduced a genetic model, the BCCG model, that preserves most of the properties of the classical genetic systems but, for infinite populations, it has the states in $\mathbb{R}^l$ instead of $\mathbb{R}^{2^l}$. With this condition, the system behavior can be simulated and a general algorithm for finding approximate solutions for a large class of hard combinatorial optimization problems can be derived [11].

In this paper we propose a simplification of the BCCG model obtaining a stochastic system with states in $\mathbb{R}^l$ even when the population size is finite (*finite populations*).

The system behavior is described by an ergodic Markov chain; we show that, under suitable conditions, a random walk of the Markov chain is close to a precise stable state for most of the time.

The paper is organized as follows. In Section 2 we recall the BCCG model and its behavior in case of infinite population. In Section 3 we derive an asymptotic formula which, in the BCCG model, gives the probability of having 1 in a given position of a word in the next generation. In Section 4 we present a simplified model, suggested by the formula obtained in Sect. 3, and we describe the system behavior through a Markov chain. The long-term behavior of the chain is analyzed by using a variant of the Vose's technique. In particular, a weighted digraph is built on the steady state iterative system for infinite populations and it is shown that if this digraph admits a unique rooted spanning tree with minimum cost, the system stays close to a unique state most of the time.

2 Preliminary Definitions and Results

In this section we briefly recall some definitions and some results about the genetic model of Bertoni et al. (BCCG model) [11], which will be used in the following sections.

A population P is a multi-set of n elements of Ω, where n is a positive integer and $\Omega = \{0,1\}^l = \{\omega_1, \ldots, \omega_{2^l}\}$ is the class of binary strings of length l that we assume ordered in the usual lexicographical way. The population P can be represented by the *frequency* vector $\mathbf{F} = [F_{\omega_1}, \ldots, F_{\omega_{2^l}}]$, where $F_{\omega_k} = \frac{n_k}{n}$ and n_k is the number of occurrences of the word ω_k in P. Let Λ_n denote the set of the frequency vectors that represent all the populations of n elements. Note that Λ_n is a finite subset of the *simplex*

$$\Lambda = \left\{ [p_1, \ldots, p_{2^l}] \mid p_i \geq 0 \land \sum_{i=1}^{2^l} p_i = 1 \right\}$$

and $\bigcup_{n=1}^{\infty} \Lambda_n$ is a dense subset of Λ.

Given a function $X : \Omega \to \mathbb{R}$ and a stochastic vector $\mathbf{\Pi} \in \Lambda$, we denote the *expectation* of X by

$$E_{\mathbf{\Pi}}(X) = \sum_{i=1}^{2^l} X(\omega_i) \Pi_i.$$

Let $f : \Omega \to \mathbb{N}^+$ be a *fitness function* and $x_k : \Omega \to \{0, 1\}$ be the function $x_k(\omega) = k$-th bit of ω.

It is possible to represent the fitness function $f : \Omega \to \mathbb{N}^+$ by a multivariate polynomial of degree one at most in each variable, defined in $[0, 1]^l$ and coincident with f on Ω:

$$f(x_1, \ldots, x_l) = \sum_{y_1, \ldots, y_l \in \{0,1\}} \alpha_{y_1 \ldots y_l} x_1^{y_1} x_2^{y_2} \cdots x_l^{y_l} \qquad [x_1, \ldots, x_l] \in [0, 1]^l$$

With abuse of notation, f will denote both the fitness function and the associated polynomial. Since the variables in f have degree one at most, global maxima of f are elements of Ω. Moreover, for every $1 \leq k \leq l$, f can be also represented as a linear combination of multivariate polynomials:

$$f(x_1, \ldots, x_l) = x_k b_k(x_1, \ldots, x_{k-1}, x_{k+1} \ldots, x_l) + a_k(x_1, \ldots, x_{k-1}, x_{k+1}, \ldots, x_l)$$

where polynomials $b_k(\mathbf{x})$ and $a_k(\mathbf{x})$ do not depend on x_k.

In BCCG model, given a population P at time t, represented by the frequency vector $\mathbf{F}$, the population at time $t + 1$, represented by the frequency vector $\mathbf{F}'$, is obtained by the execution of the following stochastic algorithm:

1. calculate the ratio

$$\phi_{k\mathbf{F}} = \frac{E_\mathbf{F}(x_k \cdot f)}{E_\mathbf{F}(f)} \qquad 1 \leq k \leq l$$

2. generate the new candidate members $\{\omega_{s_1}, \ldots, \omega_{s_i}, \ldots, \omega_{s_n}\}$ with probability $\phi_{k\mathbf{F}}$ to obtain 1 at the k-th position of a word, independently from i and k, for $1 \leq i \leq n$ and $1 \leq k \leq l$. This is the *recombination* step.
3. flip the k-th bit of word ω_{s_i} with probability $0 < \eta \leq \frac{1}{2}$ for all $1 \leq k \leq l$ and $1 \leq i \leq n$. This step is called *mutation* and η the *mutation* ratio.

Given a frequency vector $\mathbf{F}$, by applying recombination and mutation the probability of generating words with 1 at the k-th position is

$$g_{k\mathbf{F}} = \phi_{k\mathbf{F}}(1 - \eta) + \eta(1 - \phi_{k\mathbf{F}}) = \frac{E_\mathbf{F}((1 - 2\eta)(x_k \cdot f) + \eta f)}{E_\mathbf{F}(f)} \qquad 1 \leq k \leq l \quad (1)$$

So the population at next generation is obtained by selecting n words with probability distribution

$$\mathcal{G}(\mathbf{F}) = [\mathcal{G}(\mathbf{F})_{\omega_1}, \ldots, \mathcal{G}(\mathbf{F})_{\omega_{2^l}}],$$

where the probability $\mathcal{G}(\mathbf{F})_{\omega_j}$ of obtaining the word ω_j is

$$\mathcal{G}(\mathbf{F})_{\omega_j} = \prod_{k=1}^{l} \left(x_k(\omega_j) g_{k\mathbf{F}} + (1 - x_k(\omega_j))(1 - g_{k\mathbf{F}}) \right). \qquad (2)$$

The analysis of the BCCG model is done by the application of the Vose's technique [10], that describes a genetic system by means of a homogeneous Markov chain. Identifying the populations with the corresponding frequency vectors, the states of the Markov chain are the elements of Λ_n. The probability $Q_{\mathbf{FF'}}$ that the system evolves from a population $\mathbf{F}$ to a population $\mathbf{F'}$ is given by

$$Q_{\mathbf{FF'}} = n! \prod_{j=1}^{2^l} \frac{(\mathcal{G}(\mathbf{F})_{\omega_j})^{nF'_{\omega_j}}}{(nF'_{\omega_j})!}.$$

An important consequence of the mutation step is that if $\eta > 0$, then the Markov chain is ergodic, admitting therefore a stationary distribution. For large n, by Stirling formula, the following asymptotic expression holds

$$Q_{\mathbf{FF'}} = e^{-nK(\mathbf{F'};\mathcal{G}(\mathbf{F}))+O(\log n)}$$

where K is the Kullback-Leibler divergence defined by

$$K(\mathbf{F};\mathbf{F'}) = \sum_{i=1}^{2^l} F_{\omega_i} \log \frac{F_{\omega_i}}{F'_{\omega_i}}. \tag{3}$$

For $n \to \infty$, the state space of the Markov chain becomes dense in Λ and the function $\mathcal{G}$ can be extended to Λ. Moreover, when the population size is infinite, it holds

$$Q_{\mathbf{FF'}} = \delta(\mathbf{F'} - \mathcal{G}(\mathbf{F}))$$

where δ is the impulsive function. Therefore, the system becomes deterministic and its dynamics is given by

$$\mathbf{F}(t+1) = \mathcal{G}(\mathbf{F}(t)). \tag{4}$$

This system has states in $[0,1]^{2^l}$. The main result in [11] is that the behavior of the BCCG model, in the case of infinite populations, can be analyzed by means of a iterative deterministic system with states in $[0,1]^l$ instead of $[0,1]^{2^l}$. More precisely, it is proven that, for large n, with high probability it holds that

$$g_{k\mathbf{F'}} \approx g_{k\mathcal{G}(\mathbf{F})} = \frac{g_{k\mathbf{F}}(b_k(\mathbf{g_F}) + a_k(\mathbf{g_F}))}{f(\mathbf{g_F})}(1 - 2\eta) + \eta, \qquad 1 \leq k \leq l \tag{5}$$

where $\mathbf{g_F} = [g_{1\mathbf{F}}, \ldots, g_{l\mathbf{F}}]$. As a consequence of (4) and (5), for infinite populations, the stochastic genetic system becomes an iterative deterministic one whose states are vectors $\mathbf{g} = [g_1, \ldots, g_l] \in [0,1]^l$ and whose dynamics is described by the equation

$$\begin{aligned} g_k(t+1) &= g_k(t) \frac{b_k(\mathbf{g}(t)) + a_k(\mathbf{g}(t))}{g_k(t)b_k(\mathbf{g}(t)) + a_k(\mathbf{g}(t))}(1 - 2\eta) + \eta \qquad 1 \leq k \leq l \\ &= \tau_k(\mathbf{g}(t)) \end{aligned} \tag{6}$$

We observe that the transformation $\tau(\mathbf{g}(t))$ is continuously differentiable and, for every initial condition $\hat{\mathbf{g}}$, the sequence $\tau^i(\hat{\mathbf{g}})$ converges [11], i.e. the iterative system (6) is *focused*.

In the following section we consider the case of finite populations with $n \gg 0$. In particular, we derive an asymptotic formula for the probability of finding 1 at the k-th position in a word of the generation next to a given population $\mathbf{F}$.

3 Finite Populations Analysis

Let us to start from the Vose's analysis of a genetic system when the population size is finite (*finite populations*) and the system states are in $[0,1]^{2^l}$.

Fixed $n < \infty$, let $\mathbf{F}$ be a population in Λ_n and $\mathbf{F}'$ the random vector representing the generation next to $\mathbf{F}$. Let us assume that $\mathcal{G}(\mathbf{F})_{\omega_j} > 0$ and let us denote by $\boldsymbol{\zeta}$ the random vector with components

$$\zeta_{\omega_j} = \frac{F'_{\omega_j} - \mathcal{G}(\mathbf{F})_{\omega_j}}{\sqrt{\frac{\mathcal{G}(\mathbf{F})_{\omega_j}}{n}}} \qquad 1 \le j \le 2^l.$$

The vector $\boldsymbol{\zeta}$ represents a kind of normalization of the difference vector between $\mathbf{F}'$ and the population $\mathcal{G}(\mathbf{F})$, that would be generated if we assumed the infinite populations model. In [10] it is shown that $\boldsymbol{\zeta}$ can be approximated by a multivariate normal distribution:

Theorem 1. *Let $\boldsymbol{\xi}$ be a random vector of dimension $2^l - 1$ with multi-normal distribution $\mathcal{N}(\mathbf{0}, \mathbf{I})$ and let $\mathbf{C}$ be an $2^l \times 2^l - 1$ matrix having orthonormal columns perpendicular to the vector $\sqrt{\mathcal{G}(\mathbf{F})} = \left[\sqrt{\mathcal{G}(\mathbf{F})_{\omega_1}}, \sqrt{\mathcal{G}(\mathbf{F})_{\omega_2}}, \ldots, \sqrt{\mathcal{G}(\mathbf{F})_{\omega_{2^l}}}\right]$. Then $\boldsymbol{\zeta}$ converges in distribution to $\mathbf{C}\boldsymbol{\xi}^T$ as $n \to \infty$.*

In the case of BCCG model, from equation (2), we can rewrite $\mathcal{G}(\mathbf{F})_\omega$ as

$$\mathcal{G}(\mathbf{F})_{x_1 x_2 \ldots x_l} = \tilde{g}_1(x_1) \cdot \tilde{g}_2(x_2) \cdot \ldots \cdot \tilde{g}_l(x_l)$$

where $\tilde{g}_k(1) = g_{k\mathbf{F}}$ and $\tilde{g}_k(0) = 1 - g_{k\mathbf{F}}$. With this notation, it can be easily verified that:

$$\left[\sqrt{\mathcal{G}(\mathbf{F})_{\omega_1}}, \ldots, \sqrt{\mathcal{G}(\mathbf{F})_{\omega_{2^l}}}\right]$$
$$= \left[\sqrt{\tilde{g}_1(0)}, \sqrt{\tilde{g}_1(1)}\right] \otimes \left[\sqrt{\tilde{g}_2(0)}, \sqrt{\tilde{g}_2(1)}\right] \otimes \cdots \otimes \left[\sqrt{\tilde{g}_l(0)}, \sqrt{\tilde{g}_l(1)}\right],$$

where $\otimes$ is the Kronecker product of matrices.

Consider now the $2^l \times 2^l$ matrix $\tilde{\mathbf{C}}$ defined as

$$\tilde{\mathbf{C}} = \bigotimes_{k=1}^{l} \begin{bmatrix} \sqrt{\tilde{g}_k(0)} & \sqrt{\tilde{g}_k(1)} \\ \sqrt{\tilde{g}_k(1)} & -\sqrt{\tilde{g}_k(0)} \end{bmatrix}.$$

$\tilde{\mathbf{C}}$ is unitary since every matrix $\begin{bmatrix} \sqrt{\tilde{g}_k(0)} & \sqrt{\tilde{g}_k(1)} \\ \sqrt{\tilde{g}_k(1)} & -\sqrt{\tilde{g}_k(0)} \end{bmatrix}$ is unitary and Kronecker product preserves the unitary property; moreover, it can be easily verified that the first column of $\tilde{\mathbf{C}}$ is $[\sqrt{\mathcal{G}(\mathbf{F})}]^T$.

As a consequence of Theorem 1, we have the following corollary:

Corollary 1. *Let $\boldsymbol{\xi}$ be a random vector of dimension $2^l - 1$ with multi-normal distribution $\mathcal{N}(\mathbf{0}, \mathbf{I})$ and let $\tilde{\boldsymbol{\xi}} = [0|\boldsymbol{\xi}]$. The random vector $\boldsymbol{\zeta}$ with components*

$$\zeta_{\omega_j} = \frac{F'_{\omega_j} - \mathcal{G}(\mathbf{F})_{\omega_j}}{\sqrt{\frac{\mathcal{G}(\mathbf{F})_{\omega_j}}{n}}} \qquad 1 \leq j \leq 2^l$$

converges in distribution to $\tilde{\mathbf{C}}\tilde{\boldsymbol{\xi}}^T$ as $n \to \infty$.

Let us now define the random variables

$$\rho_{k\mathbf{F}} = \sum_{j=1}^{2^l} x_k(\omega_j) F'_{\omega_j} \qquad 1 \leq k \leq l$$

i.e., the probability to find 1 at the k-th position in a word of the generation next to $\mathbf{F}$. The following theorem can be considered a specialization of Theorem 1 in the case of the BCCG model.

Theorem 2. *For each $k, 1 \leq k \leq l$, the random variable*

$$\frac{\rho_{k\mathbf{F}} - g_{k\mathbf{F}}}{\sqrt{\frac{g_{k\mathbf{F}}(1 - g_{k\mathbf{F}})}{n}}}$$

converges in distribution to $\mathcal{N}(0, 1)$.

Proof. From the above definitions of the random vector $\boldsymbol{\zeta}$ and from the definition of the random variables $\rho_{k\mathbf{F}}$, it holds that

$$\sum_{j=1}^{2^l} x_k(\omega_j) \sqrt{\mathcal{G}(\mathbf{F})_{\omega_j}} \zeta_{\omega_j} = \sqrt{n}(\rho_{k\mathbf{F}} - \sum_{j=1}^{2^l} x_k(\omega_j)\mathcal{G}(\mathbf{F})_{\omega_j}) \qquad 1 \leq k \leq l.$$

Rewriting this expression in vectorial notation, we obtain

$$\mathbf{x}_k D \boldsymbol{\zeta}^T = \sqrt{n}(\rho_{k\mathbf{F}} - \mathbf{x}_k \mathcal{G}(\mathbf{F})^T) \qquad 1 \leq k \leq l.$$

where
- $\mathbf{x}_k = [x_k(\omega_1), x_k(\omega_2), \ldots, x_k(\omega_{2^l})] = \bigotimes_{i=1}^{k-1}[1,1] \otimes [0,1] \otimes \bigotimes_{i=k+1}^{l}[1,1]$.
- $D = \bigotimes_{k=1}^{l} \begin{bmatrix} \sqrt{\tilde{g}_k(0)} & 0 \\ 0 & \sqrt{\tilde{g}_k(1)} \end{bmatrix}$.

Recall that $\tilde{g}_k(1) = g_{k\mathbf{F}}$ and $\tilde{g}_k(0) = 1 - g_{k\mathbf{F}}$.
- $\mathcal{G}(\mathbf{F}) = [\mathcal{G}(\mathbf{F})_{\omega_1}, \mathcal{G}(\mathbf{F})_{\omega_2}, \ldots, \mathcal{G}(\mathbf{F})_{\omega_{2^l}}] = \bigotimes_{i=1}^{l}[\tilde{g}_i(0), \tilde{g}_i(1)]$.

Now, it holds that

$$\mathbf{x}_k \mathcal{G}(\mathbf{F})^T = \left(\bigotimes_{i=1}^{k-1}[1,1] \otimes [0,1] \otimes \bigotimes_{i=k+1}^{l} [1,1] \right) \cdot \bigotimes_{i=1}^{l} \begin{bmatrix} \tilde{g}_i(0) \\ \tilde{g}_i(1) \end{bmatrix}$$

$$= \left(\bigotimes_{i=1}^{k-1}[\tilde{g}_i(0) + \tilde{g}_i(1)] \right) \otimes [\tilde{g}_k(1)] \otimes \left(\bigotimes_{i=k+1}^{l} [\tilde{g}_i(0) + \tilde{g}_i(1)] \right)$$

$$= \left(\prod_{i=1}^{k-1} \underbrace{(\tilde{g}_i(0) + \tilde{g}_i(1))}_{1} \right) \cdot \tilde{g}_k(1) \cdot \left(\prod_{i=k+1}^{l} \underbrace{(\tilde{g}_i(0) + \tilde{g}_i(1))}_{1} \right)$$

$$= g_{k\mathbf{F}}$$

From Corollary 1, ζ^T converges in distribution to $\tilde{\mathbf{C}}\tilde{\xi}^T$; moreover

$$\mathbf{x}_k D \tilde{\mathbf{C}} \tilde{\xi}^T = \mathbf{x}_k \cdot \bigotimes_{k=1}^{l} \begin{bmatrix} \sqrt{\tilde{g}_k(0)} & 0 \\ 0 & \sqrt{\tilde{g}_k(1)} \end{bmatrix} \cdot \bigotimes_{k=1}^{l} \begin{bmatrix} \sqrt{\tilde{g}_k(0)} & \sqrt{\tilde{g}_k(1)} \\ \sqrt{\tilde{g}_k(1)} & -\sqrt{\tilde{g}_k(0)} \end{bmatrix} \cdot \xi^T$$

$$= \mathbf{x}_k \cdot \bigotimes_{k=1}^{l} \begin{bmatrix} \tilde{g}_k(0) & \sqrt{\tilde{g}_k(0)\tilde{g}_k(1)} \\ \tilde{g}_k(1) & -\sqrt{\tilde{g}_k(0)\tilde{g}_k(1)} \end{bmatrix} \cdot \xi^T$$

$$= \underbrace{([1,0] \otimes \cdots \otimes [1,0])}_{k-1 \text{ terms}} \otimes [\tilde{g}_k(1), -\sqrt{\tilde{g}_k(0)\tilde{g}_k(1)}] \otimes \underbrace{([1,0] \otimes \cdots \otimes [1,0])}_{l-k \text{ terms}} \cdot \xi^T$$

$$= [\tilde{g}_k(1), 0, \ldots, 0, -\sqrt{\tilde{g}_k(0)\tilde{g}_k(1)}, 0, \ldots, 0] \cdot \begin{bmatrix} 0 \\ \xi_1 \\ \vdots \\ \xi_{2^l-1} \end{bmatrix}$$

$$= -\sqrt{\tilde{g}_k(0)\tilde{g}_k(1)} \cdot \xi_{2^l-k}$$

$$= \sqrt{g_{k\mathbf{F}}(1 - g_{k\mathbf{F}})} \cdot \xi_k$$

where $\xi_k = -\xi_{2^l-k}, 1 \leq k \leq l$, are independent normal distributed random variables.

Summarizing,

$$\sqrt{n}(\rho_{k\mathbf{F}} - g_{k\mathbf{F}}) \approx \sqrt{g_{k\mathbf{F}}(1 - g_{k\mathbf{F}})} \cdot \xi_k \qquad 1 \leq k \leq l$$

We can conclude that, for all $k, 1 \leq k \leq l$, $\sqrt{n}(\rho_{k\mathbf{F}} - g_{k\mathbf{F}})$ converges in distribution to $\sqrt{g_{k\mathbf{F}}(1 - g_{k\mathbf{F}})} \cdot \xi_k$ and the thesis follows. □

4 Approximate Model and Its Asymptotic Behavior

In this section we present and analyze a model, suggested by Theorem 2, which is a rough approximation of BCCG model.

Let n the size of population and let $\mathbf{g}(t) \in [0,1]^l$ the state at time t; the state $\mathbf{g}(t+1)$ is obtained by the following steps:

1. For every $1 \leq k \leq l$, compute $\tau_k(\mathbf{g}(t))$ according to (6) as in BCCG model when the population size is infinite.
2. For every $1 \leq k \leq l$, add a random variable $\frac{1}{\sqrt{n}}\psi_k$ to $\tau_k(\mathbf{g}(t))$, where ψ_k is chosen according to the normal distribution $\mathcal{N}(0, \tau_k(\mathbf{g}(t))(1 - \tau_k(\mathbf{g}(t))))$ as suggested by Theorem 2.

More formally, the model behavior is described by the following Markov chain

$$g_k(t+1) = Q_n\left(\tau_k(\mathbf{g}(t)) + \frac{\psi_k}{\sqrt{n}}\right) \quad 1 \leq k \leq l \tag{7}$$

where Q_n is a scalar quantization function defined as:

$$Q_n(x) = \arg\min_{t \in \{\frac{1}{n}, \frac{2}{n}, \ldots, \frac{n-1}{n}\}} |t - x|$$

and ψ_k is a random variable having normal distribution $\mathcal{N}(0, \tau_k(\mathbf{g}(t))(1 - \tau_k(\mathbf{g}(t))))$.

Observe that for infinite population, the system (7) becomes the iterative system (6).

The Markov chain associated to (7) has states in $\{\frac{1}{n}, \frac{2}{n}, \ldots, \frac{n-1}{n}\}^l$ and it is represented by the stochastic matrix $M_{\mathbf{q},\mathbf{p}}^{(n)}$ which, for large n, can be approximated by

$$M_{\mathbf{q},\mathbf{p}}^{(n)} \approx c_\mathbf{q} e^{-\frac{n}{2}\mathcal{K}(\mathbf{q},\mathbf{p})}$$

where $\mathcal{K}(\mathbf{q}, \mathbf{p})$ is a pseudo-distance function defined in $(0, 1)^l$ by

$$\mathcal{K}(\mathbf{q}, \mathbf{p}) = \sum_{k=1}^{l} \frac{1}{q_k(1 - q_k)}(p_k - q_k)^2 \tag{8}$$

and the normalization constant c_q is

$$c_\mathbf{q} = \left(\frac{n}{2\pi}\right)^{\frac{l}{2}} \left(\prod_{k=1}^{l} q_k(1 - q_k)\right)^{-\frac{1}{2}}.$$

In order to derive the long-term behavior of (7), we can apply the technique presented in [5, Chapter 14] since the iterative system (6) is focused. The intuition is that the chain behavior is characterized by periods of relative stability, close to a stable fixed point of the deterministic iterative system, interrupted by fast transitions to another fixed point. This suggests that stable fixed points can be regarded as "states" and the sudden changes as "transitions" between states.

Let $S = \{\mathbf{S}_1, \mathbf{S}_2, \ldots, \mathbf{S}_M\}$ be the set of stable fixed points of the iterative system (6).

Given $\mathbf{p}, \mathbf{q} \in (0, 1)^l$, a *path* between $\mathbf{q}$ and $\mathbf{p}$ is a sequence $\rho = \mathbf{x}_0, \mathbf{x}_1, \ldots, \mathbf{x}_m$ of point in $(0, 1)^l$ such that $\mathbf{x}_0 = \mathbf{q}$ and $\mathbf{x}_m = \mathbf{p}$. The integer m is the length of ρ. The *cost* of ρ, denoted by $|\rho|$, is defined as

$$|\rho| = \sum_{i=0}^{m-1} \mathcal{K}(\mathbf{x}_{i+1}; \boldsymbol{\tau}(\mathbf{x}_i)).$$

The *fixed points graph* $\mathcal{T}$ associated with the iterative system (6) is a weighted digraph with vertices $\mathbf{S}_1, \mathbf{S}_2, \ldots, \mathbf{S}_M$ and edge weights

$$w(\mathbf{S}_i, \mathbf{S}_j) = \inf\{|\rho| \mid \rho \text{ is a path from } \mathbf{S}_i \text{ to } \mathbf{S}_j\}.$$

A *tributary tree* T of $\mathcal{T}$ is a weighted rooted spanning tree such that all edges point towards the root. The *cost* of a tributary tree is the sum of the weights of its edges.

Let us now come back to the Markov chain (7); we recall that for positive mutation ratio $\eta > 0$, the chain is ergodic admitting therefore a steady state distribution Π_n. Following the argument developed in [5, Theorem 14.14], we can conclude:

Theorem 3. *If the fixed point graph $\mathcal{T}$ admits a unique tributary tree with minimum cost and $\mathbf{S}_j$ is its root, then, for all $\varepsilon > 0$,*

$$\Pi_n(\mathbf{x} \mid ||\mathbf{x} - \mathbf{S}_j|| \leq \varepsilon) = 1 - o(1)$$

as $n \to \infty$.

5 Conclusion

In this paper we propose a genetic model that simplifies the BCCG model introduced in [11].

In case of infinite populations, both models are described by the same iterative system with states in $\mathbb{R}^l$ instead of $\mathbb{R}^{2^l}$; this system, experimented in [11] as an heuristic for solving combinatorial optimization problems, has shown good performance as a local optimizer.

In case of finite populations, the new model has still its states in $\mathbb{R}^l$; this makes possible numerical simulations for reasonable values of l; moreover, an advantage of stochastic dynamics is to allow escaping from local maxima of the fitness function.

We analyze the long-term behavior of the new model for large but finite population, according to a technique proposed by Vose [5]. Under suitable conditions this technique allows to find the stable state close to which a random trajectory spends most of its time.

Two main problems are still open and under investigation:

- One of most hard task of Vose's method is its algorithmic implementation. The method consists of two steps: building the fixed point graph and finding the minimum cost tributary tree. The second step can be solved by efficient algorithms working in polynomial-time, while it is an open problem to find an efficient method for constructing the fixed point graph.
- Our genetic model determines, with high probability, a stable state that represents a maximum of the fitness function, not necessarily a global one. It is an open problem to establish conditions which guarantee the convergence to a global maximum with high probability.

References

1. Goldberg, D.E.: Genetic Algorithms in Search. Addison-Wesley Publishing Company (1989)
2. Holland, J.H.: Induction, Processes of Inference, Learning and Discovery. MIT Press, Cambridge, Massachusetts (1989)
3. Holland, J.H.: Adaptation in Natural and Artificial Systems. MIT Press, Cambridge, Massachusetts (1992)
4. Koza, J.R.: Genetic Programming. MIT Press, Cambridge, Massachusetts (1992)
5. Vose, M.D.: The Simple Genetic Algorithms. MIT Press (1999)
6. Tan, K.C., Lim, M.H., Yao, X., Wang, L., eds.: Recent Advances in Simulated Evolution and Learning. Volume 2 of Advances in Natural Computation. World Scientific, Singapore (2004)
7. Eiben, A.E., Aarts, E.H.L., van Hee, K.M.: Global convergence of genetic algorithms: A markov chain analysis. In: Proceedings of the 1st Workshop Parallel Problem Solving from Nature PPSN. (1990) 4–12
8. Goldberg, D.E., Segrest, P.: Finite markov chain analysis of genetic algorithms. In: Proceedings of the Second International Conference on Genetic Algorithms on Genetic algorithms and their application, Lawrence Erlbaum Associates, Inc. (1987) 1–8
9. Nix, A.E., Vose, M.D.: Modeling genetic algorithms with markov chains. Ann. Math. Artif. Intell. **5** (1992) 77–88
10. Vose, M.D.: Modeling simple genetic algorithms. Evolutionary Computation **3** (1995) 453–472
11. Bertoni, A., Campadelli, P., Carpentieri, M., Grossi, G.: A Genetic Model: Analysis and Application to MAXSAT. Evolutionary Computation **8** (2000) 291–309

Missing Values Imputation for a Clustering Genetic Algorithm

Eduardo R. Hruschka[1], Estevam R. Hruschka Jr.[2], and Nelson F.F. Ebecken[3]

[1] Catholic University of Santos (UniSantos), R. Carvalho de Mendonça, 144,
11.070-906, Santos, SP, Brazil
[2] Federal University of São Carlos, CP 676, 13.565-905, São Carlos, SP, Brazil
[3] COPPE / Federal University of Rio de Janeiro, Bloco B, Sala 100,
CP 68.506, 21.945-970, Rio de Janeiro, RJ, Brazil
erh@unisantos.br, estevam@dc.ufscar.br, nelson@ntt.ufrj.br

Abstract. The *substitution* of missing values, also called *imputation*, is an important data preparation task for data mining applications. This paper describes a nearest-neighbor method to impute missing values, showing that it can be useful for a clustering genetic algorithm. The proposed nearest-neighbor method is assessed by means of simulations performed in two datasets that are benchmarks for data mining methods: Wisconsin Breast Cancer and Congressional Voting Records. The efficacy of the proposed approach is evaluated both in prediction and clustering scenarios. Empirical results show that the employed imputation method is a suitable data preparation tool.

1 Introduction

Knowledge discovery in databases (KDD) is the non-trivial process of identifying valid, novel, potentially useful, and ultimately understandable patterns in data [1]. Although the terms KDD and Data Mining (DM) are sometimes employed interchangeably, DM is usually considered as a step in the KDD process that centers on the automated discovery of patterns in data. In this context, data preparation is a step in the KDD process that involves the selection, preprocessing, and transformation of data to be mined. When data preparation is performed in a suitable way, higher quality data are produced, and the outcomes of the KDD process can be improved. In spite of its importance, the data preparation step became an effervescent research area only in the last few years. An important problem to be tackled in this step concerns about missing values. The absence of values is common in real-world datasets and it can occur for a number of reasons like, for instance [2]: malfunctioning measurement equipment, changes in experimental design during data collection, collation of several similar but not identical datasets, refusing of some respondents to answer certain questions in surveys. Missing values resulting from such situations may generate bias in the data, affecting the quality of the KDD process.

Many approaches have been proposed to deal with the missing values problem - e.g. see [3,4,5]. A simple solution involves ignoring instances and/or attributes containing missing values, but the waste of data may be considerable and incomplete datasets may lead to biased statistical analyses. Another alternative is to substitute the missing values by a constant. However, it assumes that all missing values represent the same value, leading to considerable distortions. The substitution by the mean/mode value is common and sometimes can even lead to reasonable results. However, this approach does not take into account the between-attribute relationships, which are usually explored by data mining methods. Therefore, a more interesting approach involves trying to fill missing values by preserving such relationships.

The task of fulfilling missing values is often referred to as either *missing values substitution* or *missing values imputation*. Imputation methods can be helpful for a variety of data mining tasks, such as classification, extraction of association rules and clustering. In this work, we focus on clustering tasks, in which one seeks to identify a finite set of categories (clusters) to describe the data. More specifically, we describe and evaluate a Nearest-Neighbor Method (NNM) to substitute missing values in datasets to be partitioned by the Clustering Genetic Algorithm (CGA) [6], which can find (according to a numeric criterion) the optimal number of clusters. Similar NNMs for imputation have been proposed in the literature – e.g. see [7,8] for classification problems and [9,10] for clustering tasks. NNMs usually do not generate a model to describe the data and, when used for imputation, they basically search for the best instance(s) of the dataset to be used for substituting missing values. This characteristic may produce a high computational cost. On the other hand, as the *learning process* is specific to each *query*, it may be more accurate. Under this perspective, we believe that a NNM can be a suitable data preparation tool for the CGA.

The remainder of this paper is organized as follows. The next section presents our proposed method to substitute missing values. Section 3 reviews the Clustering Genetic Algorithm (CGA) [6]. The employed NNM is evaluated in two datasets that are benchmarks for data mining methods, and the obtained results are described in Section 4. Finally, Section 5 concludes our work.

2   Nearest-Neighbor Method (NNM)

The Nearest-Neighbor Method (NNM) substitutes missing values by the corresponding attribute value of the most similar complete instance, i.e. it is a K-nearest-neighbor method [11] for K=1. Let us consider that each instance is described by ρ attributes. Thus, each instance can be represented by a vector $\mathbf{y}=[y_1,y_2,...,y_\rho]$. The distance between two vectors (instances) $\mathbf{u}$ and $\mathbf{y}$ will be here called $d(\mathbf{u},\mathbf{y})$. Also, let us suppose that the *i-th* attribute value ($1 \leq i \leq \rho$) of vector $\mathbf{u}$ is missing. The NNM calculates distances $d(\mathbf{u},\mathbf{y})$, for all $\mathbf{y} \neq \mathbf{u}$, $\mathbf{y}$ representing a complete instance, and use these distances to compute the value to be imputed in u_i. The Euclidean metric – expression (1) – is used to compute distances between continuous/ordinal instances, whereas the simple matching approach – expression (2) – is employed to compute distances between instances formed by nominal/binary attributes.

$$d(\mathbf{u},\mathbf{y})_E = \sqrt{(u_1 - y_1)^2 + ... + (u_{i-1} - y_{i-1})^2 + (u_{i+1} - y_{i+1})^2 + ... + (u_\rho - y_\rho)^2}. \quad (1)$$

$$d(\mathbf{u},\mathbf{y})_{SM} = \sum_{j=1, j \neq i}^{j=\rho} s_j \; ; \; s_j=0 \text{ if } u_j=y_j; \; s_j=1 \text{ otherwise}. \quad (2)$$

In the above expressions, the i-*th* attribute is not considered, because it is missing in **u**. After computing the distances d(**u**,**y**) for all **y**≠**u**, **y** representing a complete instance, the more similar instance (the neighbor of **u**) is employed to complete u_i. The nearest neighbor of **u** is here called **s**. This way, d(**u**,**s**)=min d(**u**,**y**) for all **y**≠**u**, and u_i is substituted by s_i. For a set of instances whose distances d(**u**,**y**) are equal, the substituted value comes from the first instance of this set. Although expressions (1) and (2) just consider one missing value (in the *i-th* attribute), they can be easily generalized for instances with more missing values.

The imputation by the K-Nearest Neighbor (KNN) method is simple, but it has provided encouraging results [7,8,9,10]. In clustering problems, this approach is particularly interesting, because the imputation is based on distances between instances, as well as the clustering process is. In other words, the inductive biases of clustering and imputation methods are equal.

3 Review of the Clustering Genetic Algorithm (CGA)

Clustering is a task in which one seeks to identify a finite set of categories (clusters) to describe a given dataset, both maximizing homogeneity within each cluster and heterogeneity among different clusters [12]. In other words, instances that belong to the same cluster should be more similar to each other than instances that belong to different clusters. Thus, it is necessary to devise means of evaluating the similarities between instances. This problem is usually tackled indirectly, i.e. distance measures are used to quantify the dissimilarity between instances. Several dissimilarity measures can be employed for clustering tasks, such as the Euclidean distance – expression (1) – or the simple matching approach – expression (2). In both cases, the CGA uses all the available information (attribute values) to calculate such dissimilarities.

The CGA assumes that clustering involves the partitioning of a set **X** of instances into a collection of mutually disjoint subsets C_i of **X**. Formally, let us consider a set of N instances **X**={$x_1,x_2,...,x_N$} to be clustered, where each $x_i \in \Re^p$ is an attribute vector consisting of p measurements. The instances must be clustered into non-overlapping groups **C**={$C_1,C_2,...,C_k$} where k is the number of clusters, such that:

$$C_1 \cup C_2 \cup ... \cup C_k = X, \quad C_i \neq \emptyset, \quad \text{and} \quad C_i \cap C_j = \emptyset \text{ for } i \neq j. \tag{3}$$

The problem of finding an optimal solution to the partition of N data into k clusters is NP-complete [13] and, provided that the number of distinct partitions of N instances into k clusters increases approximately as $k^N/k!$, attempting to find a globally optimum solution is usually not computationally feasible [12]. This difficulty has stimulated the search for efficient approximate algorithms. Evolutionary algorithms [14,15] are widely believed to be effective on NP-complete global optimization problems and they can provide good sub-optimal solutions in reasonable time [13]. Under this perspective, a genetic algorithm specially designed for clustering problems was introduced in [6] and it is here reviewed. Figure 1 provides an overview of the CGA, whose main features are described in the sequel.

> 1) Initialize a population of genotypes;
> 2) Evaluate each genotype in the population;
> 3) Apply a linear normalization;
> 4) Select genotypes by proportional selection;
> 5) Apply crossover and mutation;
> 6) Replace the old genotypes by the ones formed in step 5);
> 7) If the convergence criterion is attained, stop; if not, go to step 2).

Fig. 1. Clustering Genetic Algorithm (CGA)

3.1 Encoding Scheme

The CGA [6] is based on a simple encoding scheme. Let us consider a dataset formed by N instances. Then, a genotype is an integer vector of $(N+1)$ positions. Each position corresponds to an instance, i.e., the i-th position (gene) represents the i-th instance, whereas the last gene represents the number of clusters (k). Thus, each gene has a value over the alphabet $\{1,2,3,...,k\}$. For example, in a dataset composed of 20 instances, a possible genotype is: 223451234533214545525. In this case, 5 instances $\{1,2,7,13,20\}$ form the cluster whose label is 2. The cluster whose label is 1 has 2 instances $\{6,14\}$, and so on. Finally, the last gene represents the number of clusters.

Standard genetic operators may not be suitable for clustering problems for several reasons [6,16]. First, the encoding scheme presented above is naturally redundant. In fact, there are $k!$ different genotypes that represent the same solution. Thus, the size of the search space is much larger than the original space of solutions. This augmented space may reduce the efficiency of the genetic algorithm. In addition, the redundant encoding also causes the undesirable effect of casting context-dependent information out of context under the standard crossover, i.e., equal parents may originate different offspring. Mainly for these reasons, the development of genetic operators specially designed for clustering problems has been investigated [6,16]. In this context, the CGA operators are of particular interest since they operate on constant length genotypes.

3.2 Crossover and Mutation Operators

The crossover operator combines partitions codified in different genotypes. It works in the following way. First, two genotypes (**A** and **B**) are selected. Then, assuming that **A** represents k_1 clusters, the CGA randomly chooses $c \in \{1,2,...,k_1\}$ clusters to copy into **B**. The unchanged clusters of **B** are maintained and the changed ones have their instances allocated to the corresponding nearest clusters (according to their centroids). In this way, an offspring **C** is obtained. The same procedure is employed to get an offspring **D**, but now considering that the changed clusters of **B** are copied into **A**. Thus, the crossover operator produces offspring usually formed by a number of clusters that are neither smaller nor larger than the number of clusters of their parents.

Two operators for mutation are used in the CGA. The first operator works only on genotypes that encode more than 2 clusters. It eliminates a randomly chosen cluster, placing its instances to the nearest remaining clusters (according to their centroids). The second operator divides a randomly selected cluster into 2 new ones. The first cluster is formed by the instances closer to the original centroid, whereas the other cluster is formed by those instances closer to the farthest instance from the centroid.

3.3 Objective Function

The objective function is based on the silhouette [17]. To explain it, let us consider an instance i belonging to cluster **A**. The average dissimilarity of i to all other instances of **A** is denoted by $a(i)$, whereas the average dissimilarity of i to all instances of a different cluster **C** will be called $d(i,\mathbf{C})$. After computing $d(i,\mathbf{C})$ for all clusters $\mathbf{C} \neq \mathbf{A}$, the smallest one is selected, i.e. $b(i) = \min d(i,\mathbf{C})$, $\mathbf{C} \neq \mathbf{A}$. This value represents the dissimilarity of i to its neighboring cluster, and the silhouette $s(i)$ is given by:

$$s(i) = \frac{b(i) - a(i)}{\max\{a(i), b(i)\}} \quad (4)$$

It is easy to verify that $-1 \leq s(i) \leq 1$. Thus, the higher $s(i)$ the better the assignment of instance i to a given cluster. In addition, if $s(i)$ is equal to zero, then it is not clear whether the instance should have been assigned to its current cluster or to a neighboring one [18]. Finally, if cluster **A** is a singleton, then $s(i)$ is not defined and the most neutral choice is to set $s(i) = 0$ [17]. The objective function is the average of $s(i)$ over $i = 1, 2, ..., N$ and the best clustering is achieved when its value is maximized.

3.4 Selection, Settings and Initial Population

The genotypes corresponding to each generation are selected according to the roulette wheel strategy [19], which does not admit negative objective function values. For this reason, a constant equal to one is summed up to the objective function before the selection procedure takes place. In addition, the best (highest fitness) genotype is always copied into the succeeding generation.

The CGA does not employ crossover and mutation probabilities; that is, the designed operators are necessarily applied to some selected genotypes after the roulette wheel selection procedure is performed. Particularly, 50% of the selected genotypes are crossed-over, 25% are mutated by Operator 1 and 25% are mutated by Operator 2.

In this work, we have employed the methodology developed in [17] to set up the initial population. The process is based on the selection of representative instances. The first selected instance is the most centrally located in the set of instances. Subsequently, other instances are selected. Basically, the chance of selecting an instance increases when it is far from the previously selected ones and when there are many instances next to it. After selecting the representative instances, the initial population is formed considering that the non-selected instances must be clustered according to their proximity to the representative ones. Considering k representative instances, the first genotype represents 2 clusters, the second genotype represents 3 clusters,..., and the last one represents k clusters. Thus, we have employed initial populations formed by $(k-1)$ genotypes, each one representing a different data partition.

4 Simulation Results

Imputation methods can be evaluated as *prediction tools*. To do so, known values can be *artificially* excluded from a dataset (missing values simulation), with the goal of predicting them by a particular imputation method. Thus, the *predicted* value can be compared with the real, known value *artificially eliminated* from the dataset. Considering this scenario, the more similar the imputed value is in relation to the real one, the better the imputation method is. In this work, we compare the prediction results obtained by the NNM with those achieved by the mean/mode imputation. Although the prediction results provide an efficient way to compare different imputation methods, requiring few computations after imputation, they do not provide any guarantee that the imputed values will be suitable for the ultimate data mining task – e.g. the clustering process. In summary, the *prediction* results are not the only important issue to be analyzed. Data mining methods usually explore relationships between attributes and, thus, it is critical to preserve them, as far as possible, when replacing missing values [3]. This aspect has motivated us to propose the NNM as an imputation tool for the CGA. Indeed, since both methods (NNM and CGA) are based on distance measures, which can somehow reflect the between-attribute relationships, the patterns inserted by the NNM tend to be consistent with the clustering process performed by the CGA. To assess this aspect, we compare the partitions obtained in the original datasets with those obtained in the imputed datasets. The next section describes the procedure employed to generate datasets formed by imputed values.

4.1 Missing Values Simulation and Imputation

Our simulations consider that there is just one missing value at a time. Let us consider a dataset formed by N instances $\mathbf{x}^i = [x_1^i, x_2^i, ..., x_\rho^i]$. First, we simulate that x_1^1 is missing and it is consequently substituted. Second, x_2^1 is missing and it is consequently substituted. This process is repeated until x_ρ^1 is substituted. After that, we simulate that x_1^2 is missing and it is consequently substituted. In summary, this procedure is repeated for all x_j^i (i=1,...,N; j=1,...,ρ). This way, simulations can be easily reproduced, i.e. they are not influenced by the choice of random samples. After the imputation process, we obtain a substituted dataset, which is formed only by imputed values (same number of instances and attributes of the original dataset). Thus, it is possible to compare the *imputed* values with the *original* ones, as well as the partitions obtained in the original dataset can be compared with those achieved in the imputed datasets.

4.2 Employed Datasets

The assessment of clustering results usually requires datasets for which the clusters are *a priori* known. In this sense, clustering algorithms can be evaluated by means of classification datasets. To do so, the clustering algorithm is applied in the classification dataset (without the class labels) in order to verify whether it finds the correct clusters (according to the known classes) or not. Our simulations were performed in two classification datasets that are benchmarks for data mining methods: Wisconsin Breast Cancer and Congressional Voting Records. These datasets are available at the UCI Machine Learning Repository [20]. These datasets were chosen because they are formed by ordinal and binary attributes, showing the applicability of our method, which can also be employed for continuous and nominal attributes, e.g. using expressions (1) and (2) to compute distances respectively. In this sense, we extend our previous work [21], in which only ordinal attributes were considered.

In the Wisconsin Breast Cancer dataset, each instance has 9 ordinal attributes $(A_1,\ldots, A_9)$ and an associated class (benign or malignant). The attribute values belong to the set $\{1,2,\ldots,9\}$. There are 699 instances, of which 16 have missing values. We removed those instances (to allow evaluating the prediction results) and used the remaining ones to simulate imputations. The Congressional Voting Records dataset includes votes for each of the U.S. House of Representatives Congressmen on 16 key votes (attributes $A_1,\ldots,A_{16}$). There are 435 instances, of which 203 have missing values. These instances were removed (to make the prediction evaluation possible) and the proposed method was employed in the remaining ones.

4.3 Evaluating the NNM as a Prediction Tool

In this section, we compare the imputed values with the original ones (*artificially excluded* from the dataset). This is performed by reporting the average prediction error for each attribute. For the ordinal attributes of the Wisconsin dataset, we calculate the average absolute differences between substituted and original values for each attribute – considering all substitutions. In this case, the NNM imputations are compared with those achieved by the mean value, and the obtained results (average prediction error) are depicted in Figure 2. For the binary attributes of the Congress dataset, the NNM average error rate is compared with the results obtained by the mode imputation (Figure 3). The NNM provided better results than the substitution by the mean in all attributes of Wisconsin, whereas in Congressional the NNM provided better results in 14 out of 16 attributes. The mean/mode imputation was also performed according to the methodology described in Section 4.1.

4.4 Evaluating the Influence of NNM Imputation in a Clustering Task

In this section, we report results that allow estimating the suitability of the NNM in the context of the partitions found by the CGA. As previously mentioned, imputed values should preserve the between-attribute relationships observed in the clean (original) dataset. In a clustering process, it means that the correct clusters should be preserved, i.e. it is expected that the imputed values do not change the *classification* of each particular instance. To evaluate this aspect, it is assumed that the correct clusters are given by the classes. Thus, it is possible to verify to what extent the CGA is capable of finding the correct clusters, which are given by the instances of each class. In this sense, we compare the A*verage Correct Classification Rates (ACCRs)* obtained by CGA in the original dataset with those obtained in the substituted datasets.

The CGA was applied in the original dataset and in the dataset formed only by substituted values, using populations formed by 20 genotypes that, in turn, implies in using 21 clusters at most (see Section 3.4 for details). We simulated the clustering process 11 times (this number is convenient to perform the Wilcoxon/Mann-Whitney test [22]) for each dataset and the maximum number of generations was set to 100. In all simulations, the CGA has found the correct number of clusters. Table 1 shows the obtained results in terms of the Average Correct Classification Rates (ACCRs).

Table 1. ACCRs (%): average (μ); standard deviation (σ)

Dataset	CGA (Original)	CGA (Imputed by NNM)
Wisconsin Breast Cancer	μ=95.45; σ=0.30	μ=95.27; σ=0.30
Congressional Voting	μ=86.41; σ=0.22	μ=88.36; σ=0.00

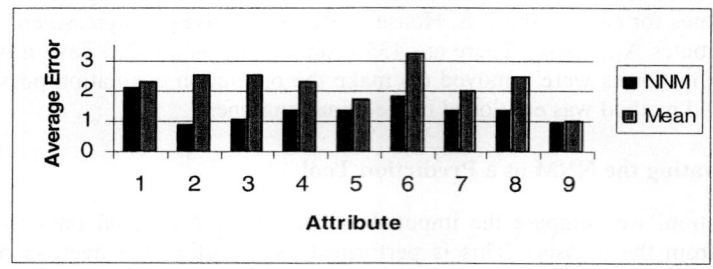

Fig. 2. Average prediction error - Wisconsin Breast Cancer

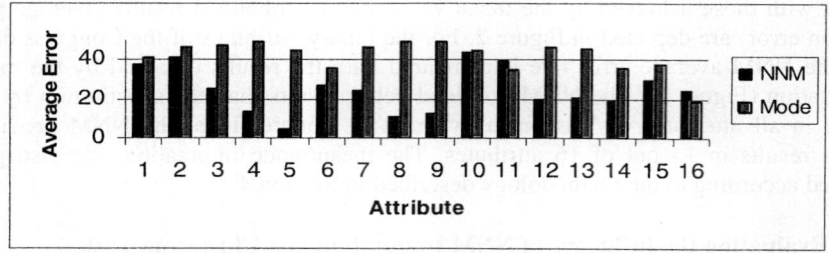

Fig. 3. Average prediction error (%) - Congressional Voting Records

The CGA has provided similar ACCRs in both datasets (original and imputed by NNM). This aspect was statistically evaluated by means of the Wilcoxon/Mann-Whitney test [22]. In the Wisconsin Breast Cancer, it was performed supposing that the ACCR values in the original dataset are equal to those obtained in the substituted dataset, and we concluded that the results are statistically significant at the 5% significance level. In the Congressional Voting Records, there is sample evidence (α=5%) suggesting that the results in the imputed dataset are slightly better than in the original dataset. These results suggest that the proposed method is a suitable estimator for missing values, preserving (Wisconsin) or slightly improving (Congress) the relationships between attributes in the clustering process. Finally, due to the methodology employed in our simulations (Section 4.1), most of the values imputed by the mean/mode are equal across all instances. In this sense, instances in the substituted dataset form only one cluster. In this case, it does not make sense to evaluate the clustering results achieved by the mean/mode imputation. However, the methodology described in Section 4.1 is particularly interesting to evaluate clustering results in the datasets imputed by NNM, because these datasets do not contain any original values and, thus, the corresponding CGA´s results are not *positively* biased by them.

5 Conclusions

Missing values are a critical problem in data mining applications. In this work, we presented a Nearest-Neighbor Method (NNM) to substitute missing values and showed that it can be useful for a Clustering Genetic Algorithm (CGA). In the NNM, each instance containing missing values is compared with the complete instances, using a distance metric, and the most similar complete instance is used to assign the missing value for a particular attribute.

The proposed method was assessed by means of simulations performed in two datasets that are benchmarks for data mining: Wisconsin Breast Cancer and Congressional Voting Records. Our simulations were designed to evaluate the NNM both in prediction and in clustering tasks. In the prediction task, we compared the results obtained by the NNM with those achieved by the mean/mode imputation. In the clustering task, we compared the partitions obtained in original datasets with those achieved in imputed datasets. The prediction results showed that the NNM provided better results than the mean/mode imputation. Although the prediction results are relevant, they are not the only important issue to be analyzed. In fact, imputation methods must generate values that least distort the original characteristics of the original sample, preserving the between-attribute relationships. In our work, we evaluated this aspect in the CGA context, performing clustering simulations and comparing the results obtained in the original datasets with the substituted ones. These results indicated that the proposed method is a suitable estimator for missing values.

Considering our future work, there are many aspects that can be further investigated. One important issue involves evaluating the best number of neighbors (K) in the K-nearest-neighbor method. Finally, we are also going to assess the efficacy of the proposed method in real-world datasets, comparing the NNM results with those obtained by other imputation methods.

Acknowledgements. The authors acknowledge CNPq, FAPESP and FAPERJ for the financial support.

References

1. Fayyad, U. M., Shapiro, G. P., Smyth, P. From Data Mining to Knowledge Discovery: An Overview. In: Advances in Knowledge Discovery and Data Mining, Fayyad, U.M., Piatetsky-Shapiro, G., Smyth, P., Uthurusamy, R., Editors, MIT Press, pp. 1-37, 1996.
2. Witten, I. H., Frank, E., Data Mining – Practical Machine Learning Tools and Techniques with Java Implementations, Morgan Kaufmann Publishers, USA, 2000.

3. Pyle, D., Data Preparation for Data Mining, Academic Press, 1999.
4. Little, R., Rubin, D. B., Statistical Analysis with Missing Data, John Wiley & Sons, New York, 1987.
5. Rubin, D. B., Multiple Imputation for non Responses in Surveys, New York, John Wiley & Sons, 1987.
6. Hruschka, E. R., Ebecken, N.F.F. A genetic algorithm for cluster analysis, Intelligent Data Analysis (IDA), Netherlands, v.7, n.1, 2003.
7. Batista, G. E. A. P. & Monard, M. C., An Analysis of Four Missing Data Treatment Methods for Supervised Learning, Applied Artificial Intelligence, v.17, n.5-6, 519-534, 2003.
8. Hruschka, E. R., Hruschka Júnior, E.R., Ebecken, N.F.F, Towards Efficient Imputation by Nearest-Neighbors: A Clustering Based Approach, Proc. of the 17th Australian Joint Conference on Artificial Intelligence, LNAI 3339, pp. 513-525, Springer, 2004.
9. Hruschka, E. R., Hruschka Junior, E. R., Ebecken, N. F. F. Evaluating a Nearest-Neighbor Method to Substitute Continuous Missing Values In: The 16th Australian Joint Conference on Artificial Intelligence, LNAI 2903, pp. 723-734, Springer-Verlag, 2003.
10. Troyanskaya, O., Cantor, M., Sherlock, G., Brown, P., Hastie, T., Tibshirani, R., Botstein, D., Altman, R.B., Missing value estimation methods for DNA microarrays, Bioinformatics, 17(6), 520-525, 2001.
11. Mitchell, T. M., Machine Learning, McGraw-Hill, 1997.
12. Arabie, P., Hubert, L. J., An Overview of Combinatorial Data Analysis (Chapter 1). Clustering and Classification, ed. P. Arabie, L.J. Hubert, G. DeSoete, World Scientific, 1999.
13. Park, Y., Song, M., A Genetic Algorithm for Clustering Problems, Proceedings of the Genetic Programming Conference, University of Wisconsin, July, 1998.
14. Yao, X., Evolutionary Computation: Theory and Applications, World Scientific, Singapore, 1999.
15. Tan, K. C., Lim, M. H., Yao, X., Wang, L., Recent Advances in Simulated Evolution and Learning, World Scientific, Singapore, 2004.
16. Falkenauer, E., Genetic Algorithms and Grouping Problems, John Wiley & Sons, 1998.
17. Kaufman, L., Rousseeuw, P. J., Finding Groups in Data – An Introduction to Cluster Analysis, Wiley Series in Probability and Mathematical Statistics, 1990.
18. Everitt, B.S., Landau, S., Leese, M., Cluster Analysis, Arnold Publishers, London, 2001.
19. Goldberg, D.E., Genetic Algorithms in Search, Optimization and Machine Learning, Addison Wesley Longmann, 1989.
20. Merz, C.J., Murphy, P.M., UCI Repository of Machine Learning Databases, http://www.ics.uci.edu, University of California, Irvine, CA.
21. Hruschka, E.R, Hruschka Júnior, E.R., Ebecken, N.F.F., A Nearest-Neighbor Method as a Data Preparation Tool for a Clustering Genetic Algorithm, Proceedings of the 18th Brazilian Symposium on Databases, pp. 319-327, Manaus, Brazil, 2003.
22. Triola, M. F., Elementary Statistics, 7th Edition, Addison Wesley Longman Inc., 1999.

A New Organizational Nonlinear Genetic Algorithm for Numerical Optimization

Zhihua Cui and Jianchao Zeng

Division of system simulation and computer application,
Taiyuan University of Science and Technology,
Shanxi, P.R. China, 030024,
cui_zhi_hua_7645@sohu.com

Abstract. Based on the concept of organization in economics, a novel genetic algorithm, organizational nonlinear genetic algorithm (ONGA), is proposed to solve global numerical optimization problems with continuous variables. In ONGA, genetic operators do not act on individuals directly, but on organizations, and four genetic operators,organization establish, organization classify, multi-parent crossover, and multi-parent mutation operators, are designed for organizations. Simulation results indicate that ONGA performs much better than the real-coded genetic algorithm both in the quality of solution and in the computational complexity.

1 Introduction

Multi-parent recombination is an attention-getting research area of GA in recent years,and several multi-parent recombinations have been proposed such as the real-coded center of mass crossover(CMX), multi-parent feature-wise crossover operator(MFX), seed crossover operator(SX), simplex crossover (SPX) and a fitness-weighted crossover(FWX)[1][2].

As an economics concept, organization can decrease the exchanging cost between goods and services. Based on this character, Wilcon J.R. used organization to training classifier system in 1995 firstly and the organization was defined a group or rules. Jing L. ec[3]t gave a new classification method based on organization though the organization defined as a group of training data, and in 2004, Jing L. etc[4] proposed a new organizational evolutionary algorithm while organization is a group of individual.

Enlightened by them, this paper integrates organization with GA to form a new algorithm, organizational nonlinear genetic algorithm (ONGA), for solving the global numerical optimization problem. In ONGA, organization not only provides the group of individuals, but evaluated by multi-parent operations. However the performance of multi-parent recombination is independent with the parent number.

2 Organizational Nonlinear Genetic Algorithm for Global Numerical Optimization

2.1 Organization Establish and Classify Operators

The following global optimization problem is considered:

$$maximize f(x)$$

$$subject to L \leq x \leq U$$

where $x = (x_1, x_2, ..., x_N)$ is a variable vector in R^N, $f(x)$ is the objective function, and $L = (L_1, L_2, ..., L_N)$ and $U = (U_1, U_2, ..., U_N)$ define the feasible solution space. We denote the domain of x_i by $[L_i, U_i]$, and the feasible solution space by $[L, U]$.

(1)Organization Establish Operator

To dynamically create the different organization, gene-pool is needed. Let us assume $X(t) = (X_1, X_2, ..., X_N)$ is the population at time t, where X_k represents the k-th chromosome, and N is the number of chromosomes. $f(X(t))=(f(X_1), f(X_2), ..., f(X_N))$ is the fitness vector of the population at time t, where $f(X_k)$ represents the fitness value of k-th chromosome. Parent populations are selected using roulette wheel approach denoted by $P(t) = (P_1, P_2, ..., P_{2N})$. To balance the diversity and computational efficiency, the parent number within each organization is stochastic established, though it is limited by $2 \leq parent\_number_j \leq \frac{N}{2}$, where $parent\_number_j$ means the number of parent individuals within organization j. Thus the organization group is established. Suppose parent population is divided into M parts. It means $Organization_1, Organization_2, ...,$ and $Organization_M$, where $Organization_i = (P_{Number(i)+1}, P_{Number(i)+2}, ..., P_{Number(i+1)})$, in which $Number(i)$ represents the parent number within organization i.

(2)Organization Classify Operator

Organization fitness is a value determining how well or bad of a organization. Thus, it can be defined with

$$Organization_i - fitness = \max\{fX_j\} \qquad (1)$$

where $j = Number(i) + 1, Number(i) + 2, ..., Number(i + 1)$. Then the M organizations are divided into two parts: good or bad. Organization i is called a good organization if and only if:

$$Organization_i - fitness \geq \frac{\sum_{j=1}^{M} Organization_j - fitness}{M} \qquad (2)$$

while others are called bad organizations. Similarly, we can divide the parent chromosome k of organization i into two parts: good or bad. Parent chromosome j is called a good chromosome of organization i if and only if:

$$f(X_k) \geq \frac{\sum_{j=Number(i)+1}^{Number(i+1)} f(X_j)}{Number(i+1) - Number(i)} \qquad (3)$$

while others are called bad chromosome of organization i.

2.2 Multi-parent Nonlinear Crossover Operator

In this paper, multi-parent nonlinear crossover operator defines a multiple probability distribution. First of all, we need to define two definitions. Suppose $Organization_i = (P_{Number(i)+1}, P_{Number(i)+2}, ..., P_{Number(i+1)})$, where $P_j = (P_{j1}, P_{j2}, ..., P_{jN})$, and $j = Number(i) + 1, Number(i) + 2, ..., Number(i+1)$. Suppose the good interval of kth variable in organization i is $[GL_k, GU_k]$, and better interval of kth variable in organization i is $[BL_k, BU_k]$, where

$$GL_k = min\{P_{jk} | j = Number(i) + 1, Number(i) + 2, ..., Number(i+1)\} \quad (4)$$

$$GU_k = max\{P_{jk} | j = Number(i) + 1, Number(i) + 2, ..., Number(i+1)\} \quad (5)$$

$$BL_k = min\{P_{jk} | P_j \in Organization_i, and P_j is a good chromosome\} \quad (6)$$

$$BU_k = max\{P_{jk} | P_j \in Organization_i, and P_j is a good chromosome\} \quad (7)$$

Now, we can give a probability distribution f as follows:

$$Probability(x \in [BL_k, BU_k]) = \frac{1}{BU_k - BL_k}, if(random() < p_b) \quad (8)$$

$$Probability(x \in [GL_k, GU_k]) = \frac{1}{GU_k - GL_k}, if(p_b \leq random() < p_g) \quad (9)$$

$$Probability(x \in [L_k, U_k]) = \frac{1}{U_k - L_k}, if(p_g \leq random() < 1) \quad (10)$$

It means the multi-parent nonlinear crossover operator has the capability not only to exploitation, but also exploration. Thus the operator can decrease the evendence of premature convergence. Because of the multi-parent crossover operator is a nonlinear function, we call it multi-parent nonlinear crossover operator.

2.3 Multi-parent Nonlinear Mutation Operator

The multi-parent nonlinear mutation operator uses the same information to enhance the operator's exploitation and exploration, and the good interval and bad interval is the same as above, Now, we can give a probability distribution f as follows:

$$Probability(x \in [BL_k, BU_k]) = \frac{1}{BU_k - BL_k}, if(random() < p_b) \quad (11)$$

$$Probability(x \in [GL_k, GU_k]) = \frac{1}{GU_k - GL_k}, if(p_b \leq random() < p_g) \quad (12)$$

$$Probability(x \in [L_k, U_k]) = \frac{1}{U_k - L_k}, if(p_g \leq random() < 1) \quad (13)$$

It means the multi-parent nonlinear mutation operator has the capability not only to exploration, but also exploitation.

3 Computational Results and Comparisons

We have decided to perform experiments on numerical function optimization problems. We have chosen the DeJong function $F3$, and the Spherical functions as test suite, and to compare the performance of ONGA with the performance of real-coded genetic algorithm (RGA). Because of the limitation, here we only give the figure.

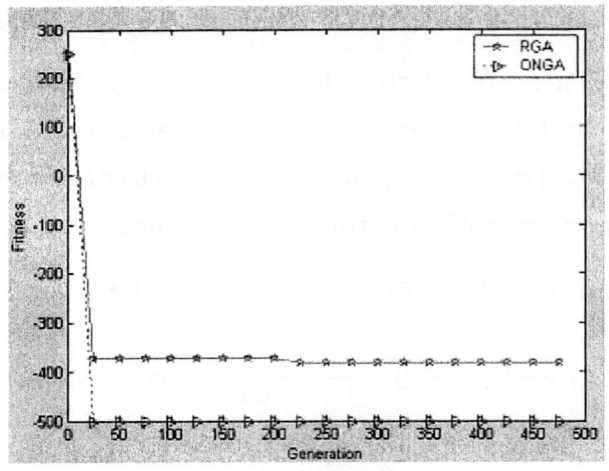

Fig. 1. Comparison of DeJongF3

Acknowledgement

This work was supported by Shanxi Yong Science Funds under Grant 20041017.

References

1. Tsutsui,S., Yamamura,M., Higuchi,T.: Multi-parent Recombination with Simplex Crossover in Real-coded Genetic Algorithms, Proceedings of the GECCO99, 657-664, 1999.
2. Gong D.X.,Ruan X.G.: A New Multi-parent Recombination Genetic Algorithm. Proceedings of the 5th World Congress on Intelligent Control and Automation,2099-2103, 2004.
3. Jing L., Wei C.Z., Fang L., Cheng J.L, Classification Based on Organizational Co-evolutionary Algorithm, Chinese Journal of Computers, 2003, 26(4):446-453. (in Chinese)
4. Jing L., Wei C.Z., Fang L., Cheng J.L,An Organizational Evolutionary Algorithm for Constrained and Unconstrained Optimization Problems,Chinese Journal of Computers, 2004, 27(2):157-167.(in Chinese)

Hybrid Genetic Algorithm for the Flexible Job-Shop Problem Under Maintenance Constraints

Nozha Zribi and Pierre Borne

École Centrale de Lille,
Cité scientifique – BP 48,
59651 Villeneuve d'Ascq Cedex–France
{nozha.zribi, pierre.borne}@ec-lille.fr

Abstract. Most scheduling literature assumes that machines are available at all times. In this paper, we study the flexible Job-shop scheduling problem where the machine maintenance has to be performed within certain intervals and hence the machine becomes unavailable during the maintenance periods. We propose an assignment technique based successively on the use of different priority rules and a local search procedure. An adequate criteria is developed to evaluate the quality of the assignment. The sequencing problem is solved by a hybrid genetic algorithm which takes into account the constraint of availability periods.

1 Introduction

Most of the literature on scheduling assumes that the machines are available at all times. However, in many realistic situations, for typical industrial settings, breakdowns and scheduled maintenance have rather quietly common occurrences. This consideration adds complexity to any scheduling problem.

In this paper, we consider the flexible job-shop scheduling with availability constraints and related machines. We consider the deterministic model where the unavailability periods corresponding to maintenance tasks are known in advance. We also assume that preemption of operations is not allowed. More precisely, an operation O_{ij} of job J_i on machine M_k starts only if its execution can be finished before M_k becomes unavailable. The problem considered is a generalization of the classical job-shop problem and the multi-purpose machine problem studied in [4], where machines are available all time.

As compared to the literature dedicated to classical scheduling problems, studies dealing with limited machine scheduling problems are rather rare. Availability constraints have been firstly introduced in single machine [1], [15] and parallel machines [12], [13]. Lee extensively investigated flow-shop scheduling problems with two machines [6], [8], [9]. In particular, the author defined the resumable, non-resumable and semi-resumable models. An operation is called resumable if it can be interrupted by an unavailability period and completed without penalty as soon as the machine becomes available again. If the part of the operation that has been processed before the unavailability period must be partially (respectively fully) re-executed, then the operation is called semi-resumable (respectively non-resumable). Recently, flow-shop scheduling problems with two machines and resumable jobs have been treated in [3] and [5]. Job-shop problem under unavailability constraints has also been considered recently [17], [2] where authors proposed a branch and bound algorithm for the job-shop problem with heads and tails and unavailability periods. However to our knowledge flexible job shop under availability constraints has not been considered yet. The problem is strongly NP-hard since problem without unavailability periods is already strongly NP-hard [4].Therefore we propose in this paper an approximation method to solve this problem.

The remainder of this paper is organized as follows. After a description of the considered problem in the following section, we propose a heuristic to solve the assignment problem. A hybrid genetic algorithm (HGA) is then used for the sequencing problem.

2 Problem Formulation

The flexible job-shop with availability constraints and related machines can also be called MPM job-shop (job shop with Multi Purpose Machines).

It may be formulated as follows. There are n jobs $J_1, ..., J_n$ to be processed on a set of m machines $R = (M_1, ..., M_m)$. Each machine M_r can process at most one job at a time. Each job J_i consists of a sequence of n_i operations, that must be accomplished according to its manufacturing process. Each operation O_{ij} ($i = 1, ..., n; j = 1, ..., n_i$) can be performed by any machine r in a given set $\mu_{ij} \subset R$ for p_{ij} time units. The operation is non-preemptive, i.e. it must be accomplished without interruption. Moreover, we assume that machine M_r is unavailable during giving periods corresponding to preventive maintenance. The starting times and durations of these tasks are known and fixed in advance. We note K_r the number of maintenance tasks on machine M_r. A_{rl} and D_{rl} represents respectively the starting and the finishing time of the lth maintenance task on machine M_r.

The objective is to construct a schedule with a minimum makespan.

According to the terminology concerning the machine availability introduced in [16], the studied problem can be denoted by $J(MPM), NCwin \mid Cmax$, where NCwin means that non-availability periods are arbitrarily distributed on machines.

The scheduling problem in $J(MPM)NCwin \mid C_{max}$ can be decomposed in two subproblems:

- a routing subproblem that consists in assigning operations to machines;
- an operation scheduling subproblem associated with each machine to minimize the makespan. This is a Job-Shop scheduling Problem with Availability Constraints $J, NCwin \mid Cmax$.

3 The Routing Problem

In classical scheduling problem where machines are available all time we generally adopt for the assignment problem the following priority rule: assigning an operation to the minimum loaded machine. In fact assigning the operation to the minimum loaded machine in classical scheduling is aiming for the operation to be finished as early as possible. Hence assigning operations in this way enable to pre-optimize the makespan. In our problem, however, these two goals are not equivalent and this technique is unsuitable.

3.1 Heuristic for the Assignment Problem

Because of maintenance tasks, the planning horizon is decomposed on subintervals. So our objective, while assigning operations, is to occupy the different time intervals.

Since we deal with a problem presenting precedence constraints, we sort operations in FIFO order using their earliest starting time (definition 1).

Definition 1. *To each operation $O_{i,j}$, we associate an earliest starting time $r_{i,j}$ calculated by the following formula:*

$$\begin{cases} r_{1,j} = r_j \ \forall \ 1 \leq j \leq N \ , r_{i+1,j} = r_{i,j} + p_{i,j} \\ \quad \forall \ 1 \leq i \leq n_j - 1, \ \forall \ 1 \leq j \leq N. \end{cases} \quad (1)$$

On each machine M_r, K_r maintenance tasks are fixed. This decomposes the planning horizon of machine M_r on $K_r + 1$ subintervals $I_{r1}, I_{r2}; ...; I_{rK_r+1}$.

The starting and the finishing time of a subinterval I_{rl} are respectively $D_{r(l-1)}$ and A_{rl}. the last subintervals I_{rK_r+1} are in the shape $[D_{r(l-1)}, +\infty)$. the heuristic starts by assigning operations that could be scheduled in intervals I_{rl} $r = 1...m, l = 1...K_r$

So in Step 2, these intervals are sorted in non decreasing order of their finishing time. For each interval I_{rl}, we try to find the set of operations, noted ε_{rl} in the program, such that $C_{FIFO} \leq A_{rl}$, C_{FIFO} is the makespan where operations are scheduled in FIFO order. Priority is given of course to operations O_{ij} such that $card(\mu_{ij}) = 1$.

Step 3 deals with the remaining operations that means operations that will be scheduled in I_{rK_r+1} $r = 1...m$, the priority rule FAM (First Available Machine)is applied. Let us define S_{ij} the machine that will be assigned to operation O_{ij} by the heuristic of Fig.1.

In order to ensure a high level of the solution quality, we have chosen to improve the assignment given by the assignment heuristic. To this end, a local improvement search has been studied. Such search is based on a Tabu algorithm , an adapted routing move technique and an adapted criteria for the studied problem. In next section, we give a description of the Tabu algorithm.

---
step 1
Sort operations in non-decreasing order of their
earliest starting time.
Sort all available interval of all machines in non-decreasing
order of their finishing time.
step 2
for each interval I_{rl}, $r = 1...m$, $l = 1...K_r$
define the set $E_{1,rl}$ of operations O_{ij} such that:
$\mu_{ij} = \{r\}$ and $r_{ij} + p_{ij} \leq A_{rl}$,
the set $E_{2,rl}$ of operations O_{ij} such that:
$r \in \mu_{ij}$, $card(\mu_{ij}) > 1$ and $r_{ij} + p_{ij} \leq A_{rl}$,
For each operation O_{ij} in $E_{1,rl}$
$\quad S_{ij} = r$
if ($C_{FIFO} = max(C_{FIFO}, r_{ij}) + p_{ij} \leq A_{rl}$)
$\quad C_{FIFO} = max(C_{FIFO}, r_{ij}) + p_{ij}$
$\quad \varepsilon_{rl} = \varepsilon_{rl} \cup O_{ij}$
For each operation O_{ij} in $E_{2,rl}$
Sort operations in $\varepsilon_{rl} \cup O_{ij}$ in non-decreasing order of their
earliest starting time and compute C_{FIFO}.
if ($C_{FIFO} \leq A_{rl}$)
$\quad S_{ij} = r$
$\quad \varepsilon_{rl} = \varepsilon_{rl} \cup O_{ij}$
step 3
For the remaining operations Use the rule FAM (First Available
Machine) for the assignment

Fig. 1. Heuristic for the assignment problem

3.2 A Tabu Search Algorithm for the Assignment Problem

For a classical routing problem where machines are available all time, we choose in general to minimize the workload of the most loaded machine since it is a lower bound for the makespan.

We define for each assignment S a lower bound noted $LB(S)$ for the makespan corresponding to S. This lower bound is based on the one machine relaxation and taking into account the unavailability periods.

The objective of the tabu search algorithm presented here is to minimize $Cr_1 = LB(S)$ and hence to preoptimize the makespan.

Giving an assignment S, to each machine M_k, we associate a single-machine problem π_k with ready times (definition 1), tails (definition 2) and unavailability periods.

A lower bound for π_k is the makespan of a preemptive schedule with unavailability periods based on the Jackson Preemptive Schedule (JPS) defined in Fig.2.

Definition 2. *After the finishing of operation O_{ij}, a time of q_{ij} has to go before job J_i is finished completely. q_{ij} is called the tail of operation O_{ij}*

step1
For each unavailability period we associate
a virtual operation where the ready time is equal to A_{rl}
and the tail is equal to G, G is a big constant :
$(G > qij, \forall O_{ij} \in B_r$)
We add this operation to B_r,
B_r is the set of operations executed by machine M_r.
step2
At time Zero, or the time when operation has just completed
processing, schedule among the available operations in B_r the
operation with the largest tail, If there is no operation
available, leave the machine idle until the first available operation
step3
When a new operation just become available,
compare the tail of this operation with the operation under
processing.
If it is greater, preempt the operation under
processing by this new operation.
Otherwise, add this operation to the list of available operations.
step4
Computation of the makespan:
- Set the tail of the virtual operation associated
to the unavailability period to 0.
- The makespan is equal to $Max_{O_{ij} \in B_r}(C_{ij} + q_{ij})$,
C_{ij} is the completion time of O_{ij} in the preemptive schedule

Fig. 2. Preemptive Schedule

The procedure of preemptive schedule allows constructing the optimal schedule when preempt-resume applies and hence to obtain a lower bound for π_k due to the two following reasons:

1. the unavailability period is treated as an operation, so the problem here is equivalent to the preempt-resume case where JPS give the optimal solution.
2. The unavailability period will start right on its ready time and will never be preempted since it has the largest tail among the available operations. Preemptive schedule is calculated for each machine and $LB(S)$ is the maximal makespan of these schedules.

Description of the Tabu Search (TS) Algorithm. TS was introduced by Glover as a general iterative metaheuristic for solving combinatorial optimization problems [7].
The TS algorithm is as follows.

- The initial solution is obtained by applying the assignment heuristic described above.

- The solution is described as a list of operations with their corresponding machines.
- A routing move is defined by the relocation of a critical operation (operation that belongs to the machine with) to a feasible machine position. For a given solution, we consider every possible relocation of every reroutable critical operation.
  The routing move is based on the following steps:
  1. Find the critical machine M_{k_c}.
  2. Find an operation O_{ij} that it can be assigned to another machine $M_{k_0} \in \mu_{ij}$ without increasing the criterion value.
  3. Reassign O_{ij} to M_{k_0} if possible.
- The Tabu list consists of pairs $(op; m_o)$, where op denotes the operation that is moved from machine m_o to a different machine.
- The choice of the move is based on the value of Cr_1 which is the maximum makespan value of the preemptive schedules.

4 Hybrid Genetic Algorithm for the Job-Shop Problem with Availability Constraints

After the assignment step, the $J(MPM)NCwin \mid C_{max}$ problem is reduced to a job-shop problem with availability constraints (JSPAC).

- to each operation O_{ij}, we define $M_{a(i,j)}$ as the machine on which O_{ij} will be executed (M_k is the machine assigned to O_{ij} in the first part of the algorithm).
- to each machine M_k, we associate the set B_k of operations to be executed on the machine.

The problem is then to assign the starting time t_{ij} and the completion time tf_{ij} to each operation O_{ij} ($tf_{ij} = t_{ij} + p_{ij}$). The considered objective is to minimize the makespan ($C_{max} = max_{i,j} tf_{ij}$).

4.1 Genetic Local Search

We propose a Hybrid Genetic algorithm (HGA) to optimize the makespan in a JSPAC.

Coding: Tasks Sequencing List(T.S.L). We choose to use a simple linear encoding. This encoding has been used for JSP problem [10]. It consists in representing the schedule in a list of NT operations ($\sum_{1 \leq i \leq n} n_i$). Each chromosome will represent the tasks sequencing in the form of a $\overline{NT}$-cell list (Fig.3). Each cell represents a task T_z ($1 \leq z \leq NT$) coded in the following way: (i, j, k).

The computation of the starting times and the completion times (t_{ij}, tf_{ij}) is obtained by applying a Non-delay schedule generation procedure described bellow according to the order z of each task in the list (Fig.4).

T_1	T_2	...	T_z		T_{NT}
(1,2,3)	(2,2,3)		(i,j,k)		(3,2,4)

Fig. 3. Coding

Initialization of the availability date of machine M_k ($DM[k]$) and the availability date of job j_i ($DJ[i]$)
Initialization:
  $DM[k] = 0$ for $k = 1...m$
  $DJ[i] = 0$ for $i = 1...n$
For $z = 1...NT$
$h_{ij} = max(DM[k], DJ[i])$
Compute $A_{k,h_{ij}}$ et $D_{k,h_{ij}}$ the starting and the finishing time of the unavailable period corresponding to h_{ij}
($h_{ij} < D_{k,h_{ij}}$ i.e) Check if T_z can be scheduled before the unavailable period
if($h_{ij} + p_{ij} \leq A_{k,h_{ij}}$)
  $t_{ij} = h_{ij}$
  $tf_{ij} = t_{ij} + p_{ij}$
T_z is scheduled after the unavailable period
Else
  $t_{ij} = max(D_{k,h_{ij}}, h_{ij})$
  $tf_{ij} = t_{ij} + p_{ij}$
Update the availability date of machine M_k and the availability date of job J_i
  $DJ[i] = tf_{ij}$
  $DM[a(i,j)] = tf_{ij}$

Fig. 4. Pseudo-code of Schedule Generation Procedure

Such procedure is based on the sequencing of the tasks (i, j) on the machine M_k according to the availability of machine M_k and the precedence constraints. In fact, for each machine M_k and each job J_i we associate an availability date $DM[k]$ and $DJ[i]$ corresponding respectively to the end of the operation scheduled on machine M_k just before the operation O_{ij} and the end of the operation preceding O_{ij} in the job.

O_{ij} can be scheduled at earliest at date $h_{ij} = max(DM[k], DJ[i])$. But because of the availability constraints we have to check if the operation can be scheduled before or after the corresponding unavailable period (the first unavailable period such that h_{ij} is less than its finishing time).

Operators: In our case, we have to respect the precedence constraints between the operations of each job. Therefore, we can avoid a correction process which will be very expensive in term of computation time. Hence, we propose to use operators developed by Lee and Yamakawa to respect precedence constraints for sequencing problems [9].

Local Search Procedure: It is well known that GA can be enhanced by incorporating local search methods. In fact, an offspring obtained by a recombination operator, such as crossover, is not included in the next generation directly but is used as a "seed" for the subsequent local search. We employ the exchange local search, based on the disjunctive graph model of Roy and Sussmann and the neighborhood of Nowicki and Smutnicki [11]. The local search procedure begins by identifying the critical path. However, because the unavailability periods do not appear in the graph, the classical longest path calculation is not enough precise. In fact the earliest starting time and the latest starting time are calculated using the procedures of Fig.5, Fig.6.

Calculate for each operation O_{ij}
$est_{ij} = max_{O_{i'j'}\ precede\ O_{ij}} est_{i'j'} + p_{i'j'}$
if $A_{k,l} \leq est_{ij} < D_{k,l}$ and then return $D_{k,l}$
else if $est_{ij} < A_{k,l}$ and $est_{ij} + p_{ij} > A_{k,l}$
then return $D_{k,l}$
else return est_{ij}

Fig. 5. Earliest starting time

Calculate for each operation O_{ij}
$lst_{ij} = min_{O_{ij}\ precede\ O_{i'j'}} lst_{i'j'} - p_{ij}$
if (O_{ij} is scheduled just before the unavailable period of machine $a(i,j)$)
Then return $min(lst_{ij}, A_{k,l} - p_{ij})$
Else return lst_{ij}

Fig. 6. Latest starting time

It is possible to decompose the critical path into a number of blocks where a block is a maximal sequence of adjacent critical operations that require the same machine. The approach of Nowicki and Smutnicki can be described as follow:

Given b blocks, if $1 < l < b$, then swap only the last two and first two block operations. Otherwise, if $l = 1$ ($l = b$) swap only the last (first) two block operations. In the case when the first and/or last block contains only two operations, these operations are swapped. If a block contains only one operation, then no swap is made.

5 Experiments Result

Ten classic flexible job-shop instances have been used for computational experiments (LA01, LA02, LA03, LA04, LA05, LA06, ABZ07, LA08, LA09, LA10W).

For these instances, we note C^* the best makespan obtained in the literature without unavailability periods. Unavailability periods are generated as follows:

- the number of unavailability periods on each machine is denoted by z and equals to $n/5$.
- The starting times and the ending times of the lth unavailability period on machine M_{rl} are uniformly generated in $[0; C^* + 3 \times p_{max}(z-1)/2]$ and $[A_{rl} + p_{max}/2, A_{rl} + 3 \times pmax/2]$ respectively. p_{max} represents the maximum processing time of all operations.

This method of generating unavailable periods is used in [17] to generate instances for job-shop problem with availability constraints.

One set of unavailability periods has been generated for each instance, leading to the new instances denoted by (LA01W, LA02W, LA03W, LA04W, LA05W, LA06W, LA07W, LA08W , LA09W and LA10W).

In table I, we report the values of the preemptive lower bound obtained by the assignment procedure ($LB(S_{init})$) and the tabu search ($LB(S_{tabu})$). We report also the value of the makespan obtained by the HGA using the assignment given by the tabu search as well as the relative deviation of C_{max} from LB_{S_tabu}.

We notice from these preliminary simulations that the algorithm of tabu search improve the value of the lower bound and then the value of makespan. And hence we deduce the adaptability of this method and the criteria chosen for the routing problem. The HGA is also efficient ($RD \sim 13.14\%$)for the examples treated. However, we have to test it on larger instances in future work.

Table 1. Simulation results of the HGA

	size	LB_{S_init}	LB_{tabu}	C_{max}	RD
la01W	10x5	933	821	875	6.57%
La02W	10x5	830	780	853	9.35%
La03W	10x5	653	620	769	24%
La04W	10x5	682	660	703	6.51%
La05W	10x5	653	620	781	25.05%
La06W	15x5	977	941	1002	6%
La07W	15x5	919	845	1132	20.5%
La08W	15x5	948	922	1141	33%
La09W	15x5	989	969	1052	8.56%
La10W	15x5	1144	953	1123	17.7%

6 Conclusion

In this paper, we have proposed an algorithm based on a heuristic and the application of a hybrid genetic algorithm to deal with the MPM jobshop with limited machine availability. Preliminary simulations show the quality and the adequation of the proposed method. As future perspective we propose to focus on scheduling jointly and simultaneously jobs and maintenance tasks and propose a multi objective method based on evolutionary algorithm to deal with this problem. Besides the valuation of the results on larger instances.

References

1. Adiri I., Bruno J., Frostig E., and Rinnooy Kan A. H. G. : Single machine flow-time with a single breakdown. Acta Informatica, 26, 679-696.
2. Aggoune, R.: Ordonnancement d'Ateliers sous Contraintes de Disponibilit des Machines(2002) Ph.D. Thesis, Universit de Metz, France.
3. Blazewicz J., Breit J., Formanowicz P., Kubiak W., Schmidt G.: Heuristic algorithms for the two-machine flowshop problem with limited machine availability. Omega Journal (2001), 29, 599-608.
4. Jurisch B.: Scheduling Jobs in Shops with Multi Purpose Machines (1992) Ph.D Thesis, Universitt Osnabrck.
5. Kubiak W., Blazewicz J., Formanowicz P., Breit J., Schmidt G.: Two-machine flow shops with lim-ited machine availability. European Journal of Opera-tional Research (2002) 136: 528-540.
6. Lee C.Y.: Machine scheduling with an availability constraint. Journal of Global Optimization(1996) 9: 395-416.
7. Glover F., Laguna M.: Tabu search, Kluwer Publish- ers, Boston 1997.
8. Lee C.Y.: Minimizing the mazkespan in two-machine flows-hop scheduling with availability constraint. Operations research letters (1997), 20: 129-139, .
9. Lee C.Y.: Two-machine flowshop scheduling with availability constraints. European Journal of Opera-tional Research (1999), 114: 420-429.
10. Lee KM., Yamakawa T.: A Genetic algorithm for general machine scheduling problems. Int.Conf. on Conventional and knowledge-Based Electronics Systems, Vol 2 pp60-66 Australia, 1998.
11. Nowicki E., Smutnicki C.: A Fast Taboo Search Algorithm for the Job-Shop Problem, Management Science (1996), Vol. 42, No. 6, pp. 797-813.
12. Schmidt G.: Scheduling on semi identical processors. Z. Oper.Res.1984, A28, 153-162, .
13. Schmidt G.: Scheduling independent tasks with deadlines on semi-identical processors. Journal of Operational research society, 39, 271-277, 1988.
14. [29] Roy B., Sussmann B.: Les probl'emes dordonnancement avec contraintes disjonctives (in French). Technical Report 9 bis, SEMA, Paris (France), December 1964.
15. Leon V. J., Wu S. D.: On scheduling with ready-times, due-dates and vacations. Naval Research Logistics, 39:5365, 1992.
16. Schmidt G.: Scheduling with limited machine availability. European Journal of Operational Research(2000), 121, 1-15.
17. Mauguiere Ph., Billaut J-C., Bouquard J-L.: New single machine and job-shop scheduling problems with availability constraints. Journal of Scheduling, 2004.
18. Zribi N., Kacem I., EL Kamel A.: Hierarchical Optimization for the Flexible Job-shops Scheduling Problem. INCOM'04, Brazil 5-7 April 2004.

A Genetic Algorithm with Elite Crossover and Dynastic Change Strategies

Yuanpai Zhou and Ray P.S. Han*

Department of Mechanics & Engineering Science,
Fudan University, 200433, Shanghai, China
ray-han@uiowa.edu

Abstract. This paper proposes an elite crossover strategy together with a dynastic change strategy for genetic algorithms. These strategies are applied to the elites, with a different crossover operation applied to the general population. This multi-crossover operation approach is different from the traditional genetic algorithms where the same crossover strategy is used on both elites and general population. The advantage of adopting a multi-crossover operation approach is faster convergence. Additionally, by adopting a dynastic change strategy in the elite crossover operation, the problem of premature convergence does not need to be actively corrected. The inspiration for the dynastic change strategy comes from ancient Chinese history where royal members of a dynasty undertake intermarriages with other royal members in order to enhance their ascendancy. The central thesis of our elite crossover strategy is that a dynasty can never be sustained forever in a society that changes continuously with its environment. A set of 8 benchmark functions is selected to investigate the effectiveness and efficiency of the proposed genetic algorithm.

1 Introduction

Due to their robustness, genetic algorithms (GAs) have become increasingly popular for optimizing real world applications. Another reason for their wide acceptance and popularity is by mimicking the process of biological evolution in the improving search, GAs generally avoid local optima. This is a huge advantage over gradient-based optimization formulations which require objective function derivatives and thus, are prone to convergence to local optima. GAs are based on the mechanics of natural selection and natural genetics rather than a simulated reasoning process and they belong to the category of non-deterministic optimizing algorithms [1], [2]. Good heuristic optima are evolved by operations combining members of an improving population of individual solutions. GAs, on the other hand, may converge too quickly in the early stages or too slowly in the later stages of the iterations [3], [4], [5] leading to a local optimum, the well-known premature convergence problem [6]. Furthermore, because of their statistical approach GAs do not guarantee their solutions are feasible. This leads to another concern, especially among members of the mathematical community, the lack of an established theory explaining why the method works and why it sometimes does not.

---

* Also, Professor of Mechanical Engineering at The Univ. of Iowa, USA.

In the traditional GA, the same crossover strategy is employed on elites as well as the general population, and this can lead to a slow down of the convergence speed. To avoid the problem and perhaps, even enhance the convergence speed, this paper proposes for the elites an elite crossover operation coupled with a dynasty-based crossover strategy while the general population is treated with an ordinary crossover strategy. The method is inspired by dynastic development and change similar to that found in ancient China where royal members of a dynasty undertake intermarriage with other royal members in order to enhance their ascendancy. The central thesis of our dynastic change strategy is that a dynasty can never be sustained forever in a society that changes continuously with its environment.

Another well-known problem in GAs is premature convergence. Up to now, no effective methods have been proposed to overcome this difficulty. While the dynastic change strategy does not actively avoid the premature convergence problem, it reduces its occurrence by renewing the population and saving the best individuals in the former generation when the problem appears.

In the next section a flowchart description of the proposed GA implementation is provided, followed by a section on numerical experimentation to demonstrate and validate the effectiveness of the method and finally, some concluding remarks.

2 Flowchart for the Proposed Elitist and Dynastic-Based GA Implementation

Some of the more salient features of the proposed algorithm are briefly described here. A floating-point representation is adopted in the work. To retain the best members during regeneration, an elite-based operation is used. Furthermore, a dynastic-change strategy is employed to enhance convergence. In addition, offspring of the general population are created by a probabilistic crossover operation. In the fitness selection, several strategies are available: a roulette-wheel method [7], [8], a tournament-based technique or a ranking-based procedure. A tournament-based method is adopted in this paper since it generally converges faster than the other 2 techniques. The flowchart of the proposed GA with elite crossover and dynastic change strategies is outlined in Table 1.

A more detailed explanations of the flowchart is summarized below.

Step 1 is concerned with initialization and evaluation. The maximum number of generations together with other GA parameters are initialized. Furthermore, the initial population which can be chosen randomly or heuristically is fixed. If the size is too small, the population loses diversity and if it is too large, it loses efficiency. Goldberg [8] discusses some ideas on the initial population size selections. In the initial fitness evaluation phase, the values of parameters for each member are randomly extracted.

Step 2 is concerned with elites. The fittest individuals from the population (and offspring) are selected to form the elites. Just as with the initial population, coming up with an appropriate size of the elite pool is equally challenging, if not more. The number of elite members should be set small relative to the population; the term loses its meaning otherwise. Based our numerical experimentations, the elite members were set at 3% of the population.

Table 1. GA Flowchart with Elite Crossover and Dynastic Change Strategies

Step 1: Initialization. Choose generation limit n_{max}, initial population size p, initial starting solutions $\vec{x}^{(1)}, \cdots, \vec{x}^{(n)}$, set generation index $n \leftarrow 0$.

Step 2: Elite Population. Set elite size p_e and choose elites from initial population to form the elite mating pool p_e.

Step 3: Elite Reproduction. Execute nonoverlapping elite crossover among the p_e elites in generation n to complete generation $n+1$ elite population.

Step 4: General Population. Form general population mating pool $k_g p_g$ where $k_g < 1$ and $p_g = p - p_e$, choose $k_g p_g / 2$ nonoverlapping population pairs from generation n and execute population crossover on each pair to complete generation $n+1$ population.

Step 5: Next Elite Generation. Generate elite population of generation $n+1$ from current elites and all their offspring.

Step 6: Next GP Generation. Generate general population of generation $n+1$ from current generation and their offspring using a tournament procedure.

Step 7: Dynastic Change. Increment $n \leftarrow n+1$ and return to Step 3. If premature termination occurs, activate dynastic change strategy and return to Step 2.

Step 8: Stop Condition. The stop condition consists of either the predefined generation limit n_{max} or values remained substantially unchanged after 5 continuous generations.

Step 3 is concerned with elite reproduction. Every elite individual mates with all other elites via an elite non-overlapping pairwise crossover. The p_e individuals in elite mating pool produce $p_e(p_e - 1)$ offspring by the elite crossover.

Step 4 is concerned with the general population reproduction. A mating pool of the general population is formed and their offspring are procreated using the general population crossover with a preset probability. The probability of the population crossover was chosen to lie between $0.8 \sim 1.0 (k_g)$. The $k_g p_g$ parents in the mating pool produce $k_g p_g$ individuals as offspring.

Step 5 selects the fittest individuals from population and offspring to form the next generation elite specie.

Step 6 selects individuals from population and offspring to form the next generation population. The tournament procedure is used in the selection process.

Step 7 is concerned with the premature convergence problem. Steps 3-6 are executed until a premature termination is encountered. If that happens, the dynastic change strategy that includes saving the best individuals is activated. The dynastic change strategy we have implemented is inspired by the practice found in ancient Chinese history. Steps 2-6 are then executed.

Step 8 involves the stop condition. The stop condition consists of either a preset generation limit or converged values are substantially unchanged after 5 continuous generations.

In the next section, the results obtained applying our algorithm to eight real-valued function optimization problems are reported and compared with several genetic algorithms, including the genetic algorithm only with elite crossover strategy, the genetic algorithm only with dynastic changes, and the genetic algorithm without both strategies.

3 Numerical Experimentations and Discussion of Results

In order to study the performance of the proposed strategy, extensive numerical experimentations have been performed with real-valued set of benchmark functions. They include low-dimensional, high-dimensional, unimodal and multimodal functions and are reproduced here as:

1. $\min f_1(\vec{x}) = \sum_{i=1}^{n} x_i^2$, $x_i \in [-50, 50]$, $n = 3$

2. $\min f_2(\vec{x}) = 100(x_1^2 - x_2)^2 + (1 - x_1)^2$, $x_i \in [-50, 50]$

3. $\min f_3(\vec{x}) = 3600 - \left(\dfrac{a}{b + (x_1^2 + x_2^2)}\right)^2 - (x_1^2 + x_2^2)^2$, $x_i \in [-5.12, 5.12]$, $a = 3.0$, $b = 0.05$

4. $\min f_4(\vec{x}) = x_1^2 + 2x_2^2 - 0.3\cos(3\pi x_1) - 0.4\cos(4\pi x_2) + 0.7$, $x_1, x_2 \in [-50, 50]$

5. $\min f_5(\vec{x}) = 0.5 + \dfrac{\sin^2\sqrt{x_1^2 + x_2^2} - 0.5}{\left[1 + 0.001(x_1^2 + x_2^2)\right]^2}$, $x_i \in [-100, 100]$

6. $\min f_6(\vec{x}) = \sum_{i=1}^{n} x_i^2$, $n = 20$, $x_i \in [-20, 20]$

7. $\min f_7(\vec{x}) = \sum_{i=1}^{n} (x_i + 0.5)^2$, $x_i \in [-20, 20]$, $n = 20$

8. $\min f_8(\vec{x}) = -20\exp\left[-0.2\sqrt{(1/n)\sum_{i=1}^{n} x_i^2}\right] - \exp\left[(1/n)\sum_{i=1}^{n} \cos(2\pi x_i)\right] + 20 + e$,

   $x_i \in [-5.12, 5.12]$, $n = 20$

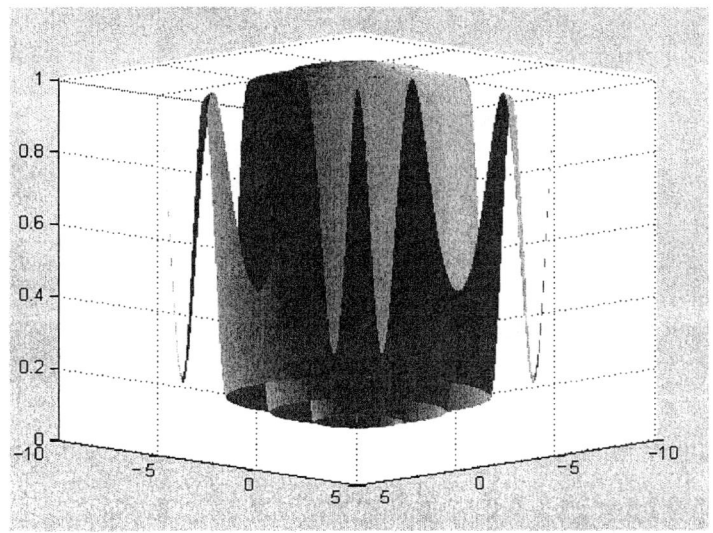

Fig. 1. The diagram of function f_5

As their equations clearly show f_1, f_6 and f_7 are quadratic in nature and hence, are strongly convex with a single optimum and without any local optima [9]. So, the conventional wisdom is that they should be relatively easy to minimize. The f_2 is the generalized Rosenbrock function. Searching for the optimum of this function is challenging because of its narrow curved valley containing the minimum at $(1,1)$ [10]. Function f_3 has 4 local extrema at $(\pm 5.12, \pm 5.12)$ with a function value of 851.22, and a global extremum at $(0,0)$ with a function value of 0 [11]. Function f_4 is taken from Bohachevsky et al. [12] and f_5 is the Schaffer function [13] which has infinite local extrema. A sketch of f_5 with x_1 and x_2 constrained in $(-5,5)$ is depicted in Fig. 1. Additionally, its local extremum of 0.009717 is located in the vicinity of the global

Table 2. Optimization of f_1

	Function f_1			
Method	Mean Gen	Min Func	Appr Time	Mean Best
N-GA	11.16	0.00000006	56	0.05497306
E-GA	9.25	0.00000018	30	0.41757762
D-GA	85.14	0.00000006	99	0.00001052
ED-GA	113.52	0.00000000	100	0.00000003

extremum and thus, most ordinary algorithms will find only the local extremum. Function f_8 is a variation taken from Ackley [14]. Its global minimum is located at the origin with a function value of zero. Simulations were performed using an initial population of 200 and 8 competitions.

Table 3. Optimization of f_2

Function f_2				
Method	Mean Gen	Min Func	Appr Time	Mean Best
N-GA	8.73	0.00000001	21	0.47925830
E-GA	7.39	0.00000000	15	0.81717509
D-GA	82.43	0.00000001	86	0.00040771
ED-GA	82.85	0.00000000	97	0.00058799

Table 4. Optimization of f_3

Function f_3				
Method	Mean Gen	Min Func	Appr Time	Mean Best
N-GA	6.38	0.00045776	1	424.77276611
E-GA	5.56	0.00000000	3	486.30636597
D-GA	83.89	0.00000000	36	0.16390826
ED-GA	78.71	0.00000000	91	10.64427471

Optimization simulations were performed using an initial population of 200 and 8 competitions and results are summarized in Tables 2-9. In these tables, the following notations are employed: *Mean Gen* (mean generation), *Min Func* (minimum function value), *Appr Time* (appearance time of the absolute value < 0.001) and *Mean Best* (mean best objective function value) after the stop condition is attained in over 100 trials. Furthermore, the following nomenclature was used: N-GA (GA without elite crossover and dynastic change strategies), E-GA (GA with elite crossover strategy only), D-GA (GA with dynastic change strategy only) and ED-GA (GA with elite crossover and dynastic change strategies).

Clearly, the results of Tables 2-9 indicate that the performance of GA with both elite and dynastic change strategies is superior to GA without any strategies or with just only one; either the elite or dynastic change strategy. This is especially true in terms of the appearance time. ED-GA has the greatest appearance times compared to all other methods. In terms of mean best fitness, ED-GA is generally better but there are 2 exceptions: from Tables 3 and 8, D-GA produces better mean best fitness values than ED-GA, but ED-GA has better appearance times. Also, comparing between E-GA and N-GA, it can be seen that the former speeds-up the convergence rate compared to the latter. Finally, it appears from our numerical experimentations that the performance of the proposed ED-GA for these functions f_1, f_4, f_6, f_7 and f_8 is better than the lognormal perturbation method introduced in Saravanan et al. [15].

Table 5. Optimization of f_4

	Function f_4			
Method	Mean Gen	Min Func	Appr Time	Mean Best
N-GA	8.45	0.00000001	90	0.02272174
E-GA	6.83	0.00000000	80	0.08100411
D-GA	50.30	0.00000000	100	0.00000249
ED-GA	52.17	0.00000000	100	0.00000001

Table 6. Optimization of f_5

	Function f_5			
Method	Mean Gen	Min Func	Appr Time	Mean Best
N-GA	10.36	0.00000059	1	0.00509341
E-GA	8.64	0.00010571	1	0.00504897
D-GA	48.58	0.00000001	75	0.00365367
ED-GA	65.14	0.00000000	58	0.00281766

Table 7. Optimization of f_6

	Function f_6			
Method	Mean Gen	Min Func	Appr Time	Mean Best
N-GA	15.34	8.39930916	0	22.00690460
E-GA	12.17	17.67862511	0	28.53572273
D-GA	562.46	0.00020634	8	0.00281838
ED-GA	839.79	0.00000237	98	0.00003204

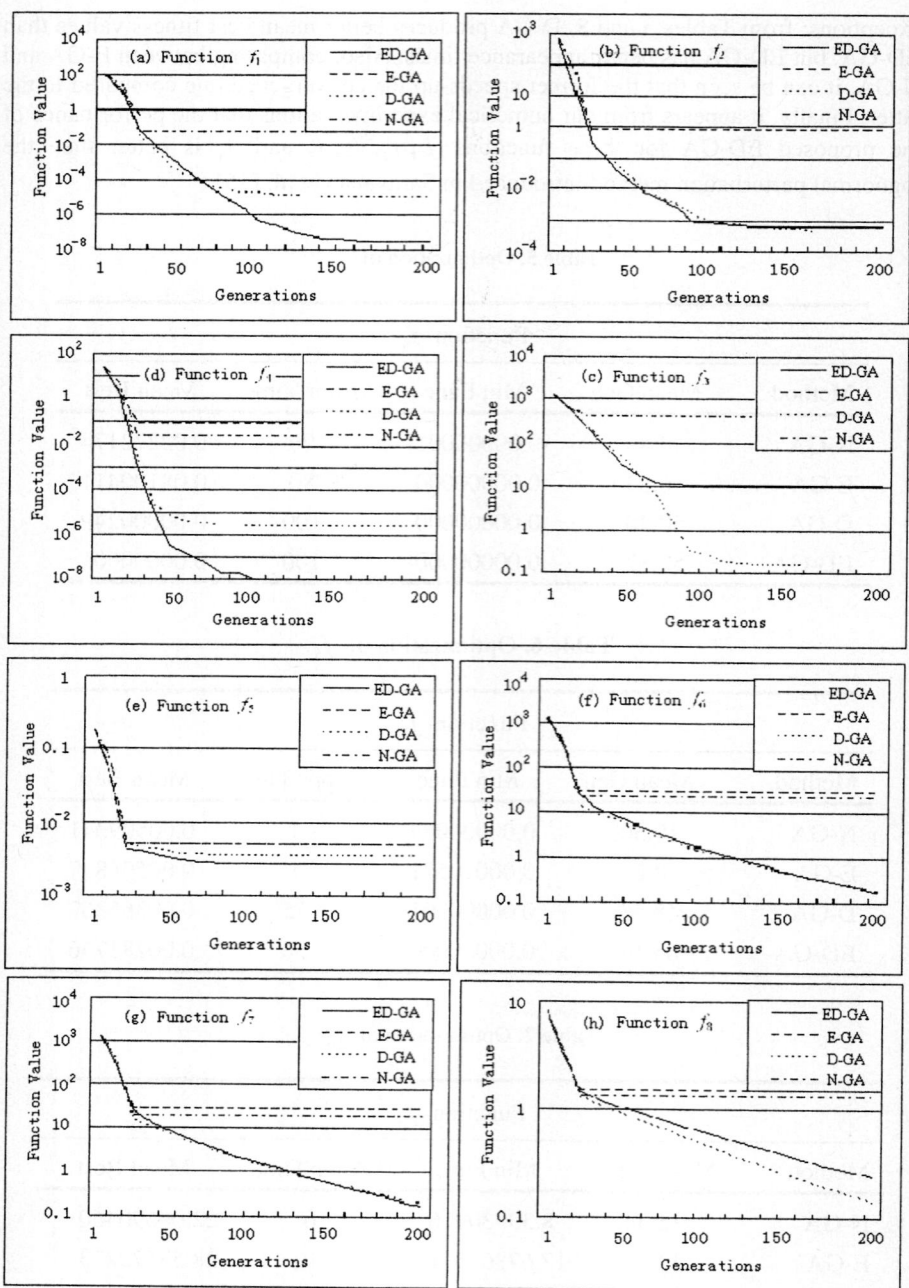

Fig. 2. Optimization of the best scores for functions $f_1 - f_8$

Table 8. Optimization of f_7

	Function f_7			
Method	Mean Gen	Min Func	Appr Time	Mean Best
N-GA	15.45	12.45736885	0	19.12287903
E-GA	12.59	15.91287708	0	27.89656067
D-GA	559.70	0.00072110	5	0.00436221
ED-GA	848.51	0.00000194	98	0.00004552

Table 9. Optimization of f_8

	Function f_8			
Method	Mean Gen	Min Func	Appr Time	Mean Best
N-GA	13.27	1.91737759	0	1.32728183
E-GA	10.80	2.22059083	0	1.48957455
D-GA	527.76	0.00495088	0	0.03247735
ED-GA	773.91	0.00031640	29	0.08787882

Next, the optimization of the best scores in the population averaged over 100 trials in terms of the number of generations for the 8 benchmark functions is collectively graphed in Fig. 2.

4 Conclusion

An elite crossover strategy together with a dynastic change strategy for genetic algorithms is developed in this paper. Elite crossover strategy improves the convergent speed of the optimization procedure whereas the dynastic change strategy assists in the search for global optima and generally, avoids the problem of premature convergence. Eight benchmark functions are employed to demonstrate and validate the effectiveness of the approach. From the results of the numerical experimentation, it appears that the proposed method is effective.

Acknowledgement

The authors would like to acknowledge funding support from National Science Foundation (No. 5047-5048) and also, Professor Li Shouju of Dalian University of Technology for the initial discussion on the research.

References

1. Holland, J.H.: Adapation in Neural and Artificial Systems. Univ. of Michigan Press, Ann Arbor, MI (1975)
2. De Jong, K.A.: An Analysis of the Behavior of Class of Genetic Adaptive Systems. Ph.D. Dissertation, Univ. of Michigan (1975)
3. Baker, J.E.: Reducing Bias and Inefficiency in the Selection Algorithm. Proc. 2nd Ann. Conf. Genetic Algorithms. M.I.T., Cambridge, MA. (1985)
4. Goldberg, D.E., Richardson, J.: Genetic Algorithms with Sharing for Multimodal Function Optimization. Proc. 2nd Int. Conf. Genetic Algorithms, Hillsdale, NJ (1987)
5. Tanese, R.: Distributed Genetic Algorithms. Proc. 3rd Int. Conf. Genetic Algorithms. Morgan Kaufman, Los Altos, CA (1989)
6. Lis, J.: Genetic Algorithm with the Dynamic Probability of Mutation in the Classification Problem. Pattern Recognition Letters. 16 (1995) 1311-1320
7. Michalewiczs, Z.: Genetic Algorithms + Data Structures = Evolution Programs. 3rd ed. Springer-Verlag, Berlin Heidelberg New York (1996)
8. Goldberg, D.E.: Genetic Algorithms in Search, Optimization, and Machine Learning. Addison-Wesley (1989)
9. Fogel, D.B., Fogel, G.B., Ohkura, K.: Multiple-vector Self-adaptation in Evolutionary Algorithms. BioSystems. 61 (2001) 155-162
10. Salomon, R.: Re-evaluating Genetic Algorithm Performance Under Coordinate Rotation of Benchmark Functions: A Survey of Some Theoretical and Practical Aspects of Genetic Algorithms. BioSystems. 39 (1996) 263-278
11. Li Mingqiang, Kou Jisong, Lin Dan, Li Quanshu: Fundamentals and Applications of Genetic Algorithms. Beijing: Science Press, China (2002)
12. Bohachevsky, I.O., Johnson, M.E., Stein, M.L.: Generalized Simulated Annealing for Function Optimization. Technometrics. 28, (1986) 209-218
13. Fogel, D.B.: Evolutionary computation: Toward a New Philosophy of Machine Intelligence. New York: IEEE Press, 2000, 152
14. Ackley, D.H.: A Connectionist Machine for Genetic Hill Climbing. Kluwer, Boston, MA (1987)
15. Saravanan N., Fogel, D.B., Nelson, K.M.: A Comparison of Methods for Self-Adaptation in Evolutionary Algorithms. BioSystems. 36 (1995) 157-166

A Game-Theoretic Approach for Designing Mixed Mutation Strategies

Jun He[1,2] and Xin Yao[1]

[1] School of Computer Science, The University of Birmingham,
Edgbaston, Birmingham B15 2TT, U.K.
j.he@cs.bham.ac.uk
[2] Department of Computer Science, Beijing Jiaotong University, Beijing, China

Abstract. Different mutation operators have been proposed in evolutionary programming. However, each operator may be efficient in solving a subset of problems, but will fail in another one. Through a mixture of various mutation operators, it is possible to integrate their advantages together. This paper presents a game-theoretic approach for designing evolutionary programming with a mixed mutation strategy. The approach is applied to design a mixed strategy using Gaussian and Cauchy mutations. The experimental results show the mixed strategy can obtain the same performance as, or even better than the best of pure strategies.

1 Introduction

Several mutation operators have been proposed in evolutionary programming (EP), e.g., Gaussian, Cauchy and Lévy mutations [1,2,3]. According to no free lunch theorem [4], none of mutation operators is efficient in solving all optimization problems, but only in a subset of problems. Experiments show that Gaussian mutation has a good performance for some unimodal functions and multimodal functions with only a few local optimal points; Cauchy mutation works well on multimodal functions with many local optimal points [2].

An improvement to conventional EP is to apply several mutation operators in one algorithm and integrate their advantages together. This idea is not completely new to the community of evolutionary programming. An early implementation is a linear combination of Gaussian and Cauchy distributions [5]. This combination can be viewed a new mutation operator, whose probability distribution is a convolution of Gaussian and Cauchy's probability distributions. IFEP [2] adopts another technique: each individual implements Cauchy and Gaussian mutations simultaneously and generates two individuals; the better one will be chosen in the next generation. In [3], the idea of IFEP is developed further into mixing Lévy distribution with various scaling parameters.

Different from the above work, this paper presents an alternative approach to design a mixed mutation strategy. Inspired from game theory, individuals in EP are regarded as players in a game. Each individual will choose a mutation strategy from its strategy set based on a selection probability, and then generate an offspring by this strategy.

The central topic of game theory is the interactions and strategies among a group of players [6,7]. Game theory already has a few applications in evolutionary algorithms, mainly in analyzing cooperative co-evolution algorithms [8,9,10]. This paper concentrates on designing co-evolutionary algorithms, rather than analyzing them.

The rest of this paper is organized as follows: Section 2 introduces EP using mixed strategies; Section 3 illustrates a game-theoretic approach to design mixed strategies; Section 4 describes a case study of mixing Cauchy and Gaussian mutations; Section 5 reports experimental results; Section 6 gives conclusions.

2 Evolutionary Programming and Mixed Mutation Strategies

In this paper EP is used to find a minimum $x_{\min}$ of a continuous function $f(x)$, that is,
$$f(x_{\min}) \leq f(x), \quad x \in D, \tag{1}$$
where D is a hypercube in R^n, n is the dimension. Conventional EP using a single mutation operator can be described as follows [2]:

1. **Initialization**: Generate an initial population consisting of μ individuals at random. Each individual is represented a set of real vectors (x_i, σ_i),
$$x_i = (x_i(1), x_i(2), \cdots, x_i(n)), \quad i = 1, \cdots, \mu$$
$$\sigma_i = (\sigma_i(1), \sigma_i(2), \cdots, \sigma_i(n)), \quad i = 1, \cdots, \mu.$$

2. **Mutation**: For each parent $(x_i^{(t)}, \sigma_i^{(t)})$ (where t represents generation), create an offspring (x_i', σ_i') as follows:
$$\begin{aligned}\sigma_i'(j) &= \sigma_i^{(t)}(j) \exp\{\tau N(0,1) + \tau' N_j(0,1)\}, \quad j = 1, \cdots, n,\\ x_i'(j) &= x_i^{(t)}(j) + \sigma_i^{(t+1)}(j) X_j, \quad j = 1, \cdots, n,\end{aligned} \tag{2}$$

where $N(0,1)$ stands for a Gaussian random variable generated for a given i, $N_j(0,1)$ a Gaussian random variable generated for each j, and X_j is a random variable generated for each j. Controlling parameters τ and τ' are chosen as the same as in [2].

3. **Fitness Evaluation**: For μ parents and their μ offspring, calculate their fitness value $f_1, f_2, \cdots, f_{2\mu}$.

4. **Selection**: Define and initialize a winning function for every individual in parent and offspring population as $w_i = 0$, $i = 1, 2, \cdots, 2\mu$. For each individual i, select one fitness function, say f_j and compare the two fitness functions. If f_i is less than f_j, then let $w_i = w_i + 1$. Perform this procedure q times for each inidivual.

5. Select μ individuals that have the largest winning values to be parents for the next generation.

6. Repeat step 2-6, until the stopping criteria are satisfied.

To avoid the step size σ falling too low to zero, a lower bound $\sigma_{\min}$ should be put on σ [11,12]. So a revised scheme of updating σ is given by:

$$\sigma'_i(j) = (\sigma_{\min} + \sigma_i^{(t)}(j)) \exp\{\tau N(0,1) + \tau' X_j\}. \tag{3}$$

where $\sigma_{\min} > 0$ is the minimum value of step size σ.

A mutation operator is called mutation strategy s if the random variable X_j in Eq. (2) satisfies the probability distribution function F_s. A set of mutation strategies consists of Cauchy, Gaussian, Lévy and other probability distributions. The mixed strategy is described as follows: at each generation, an individual chooses one mutation strategy s from its strategy set based on a selection probability $p(s)$. This probability distribution is called a mixed strategy distribution in the game theory.

The key question is to find out a good, if possible an optimal, mixed probability $p(s)$ for every individual. This mixed distribution may be changed over generations.

3 Game-Theoretic Design and Theoretical Analysis

According to [7], each game is specified by a set of rules.

First the players and their strategies are specified. In a game consisting of ν players, players can be denoted by $I = \{1, 2, \cdots, \nu\}$. Each player i has a mutation strategy set available to play in the game, which is denoted by S (assume all players use the same strategy set). A strategy is labeled by a positive integer. A single mutation strategy is called a pure strategy in the terms of game theory. A vector of strategies, $s = (s_1, s_2, \cdots, s_\nu)$ where s_i is a strategy used by player i, is called a strategy profile.

In this paper, only two-player game is considered, in this case, $\nu = 2$. In EP, a population usually consists of more than 2 individuals, so individuals had to be divided into pairs in order to play a two-players game.

Then a payoff is assigned to each strategy. Given a strategy profile s, a real-valued number $\pi_i(s)$ is assigned to each player i, which is called the associated payoff to individual i. The combined payoff function π of the game assigns to each strategy profile s, which is denoted by a vector $\pi(s) = (\pi_1(s), \cdots, \pi_\nu(s))$ of payoffs.

Thirdly, it is needed to define an output for each strategy. Assume at the t-th generation, two players 1 and 2 use strategy s_1 and s_2 respectively to play a game. Then an outcome is generated, which is denoted by $o_1(s_1, s_2)$ and $o_2(s_1, s_2)$. The payoffs $\pi_1(s_1, s_2)$ and $\pi_2(s_1, s_2)$ are dependent on the outcomes $o_1(s_1, s_2)$ and $o_2(s_1, s_2)$. In this paper, only symmetric game is considered, so $\pi_1(s_1, s_2) = \pi_2(s_2, s_1)$.

At the end, the game will be played in the following order. Individuals in EP are selected two-by-two from the population, play the two-player game in the pair of $(1,2),(3,4),\cdots,(\mu-1,\mu)$ (where μ is assumed as an even). They play the game simultaneously. The game is iterated, until some stopping criterion is satisfied.

A mixed strategy for an individual i is defined by a probability distribution $p_i(s)$ over its strategy set. It is used to determine the probability of each strategy being applied in the next iteration. It is dependent on the payoffs of strategies. Denote $\boldsymbol{p} = (p_1, \cdots, p_\nu)$.

In theory mixed strategies have some potential advantages over pure strategies. This can be seen from the following simple facts.

Firstly, the global performance of some mixed strategy may reach the same performance as the best pure strategy.

Proposition 1. *For a pure strategy s, let $E[f^{(t)} \mid s]$ be the mean best fitness outputted at the generation t; for a mixed strategy $\boldsymbol{p}^{(0)}, \cdots, \boldsymbol{p}^{(t-1)}$, let $E[f^{(t)} \mid (\boldsymbol{p}^{(0)}, \cdots, \boldsymbol{p}^{(t-1)})]$ be the mean best fitness outputted at the generation t. Then there exists some mixed strategy $\boldsymbol{p}^{(0)}, \cdots, \boldsymbol{p}^{(t-1)}$, such that,*

$$\min_{s \in S} E[f^{(t)} \mid s] \geq E[f^{(t)} \mid \boldsymbol{p}^{(0)}, \cdots, \boldsymbol{p}^{(t-1)}]. \tag{4}$$

Proof. The proof is trivial. Assume s_* is the best pure strategy, then choose the mixed strategy as follows: all individuals take the best pure strategy s_* at any generation, i.e., $p_i^{(t)}(s_*) = 1$ for all generation t.

The second fact reveals another advantage of mixed strategies: mixed strategies can solve more problems than a pure strategy.

Proposition 2. *Denote $\mathcal{F}(s_1)$ to be the problem set which can be solved efficiently by strategy s_1, $\mathcal{F}(s_2)$ to be the problem set solved efficiently by strategy s_2, and $\mathcal{F}(s_1, s_2)$ the problem set solved efficiently by a mixed strategy consisting of s_1 and s_2, then*

$$\mathcal{F}(s_1) \cup \mathcal{F}(s_2) \subset \mathcal{F}(s_1, s_2). \tag{5}$$

Proof. The proof is straightforward. For any problem in $\mathcal{F}(s_1)$, chose the mixed strategy as: $p(s_1) = 1, p(s_2) = 0$. For any problem in $\mathcal{F}(s_1)$, choose the mixed strategy as: $p(s_1) = 0, p(s_2) = 1$.

4 Case Study: A Mixed Strategy Using Gaussian and Cauchy Mutations

Two mutation operators are used in the mixed strategy:

- **Gaussian Mutation:**

$$x_i^{(t+1)}(j) = x_i^{(t)}(j) + \sigma_i^{(t+1)}(j) N_j(0, 1), \tag{6}$$

where $N_j(0, 1)$ is Gaussian random variable for each component j.
- **Cauchy Mutation:**

$$x_i^{(t+1)}(j) = x_i^{(t)}(j) + \sigma_i^{(t+1)}(j) C_j(0, 1), \tag{7}$$

where $C_j(0, 1)$ is a Cauchy random variable for each j.

The output of an individual is defined by the distance how far an individual moves during a successful mutation. Let $x_i^{(t)}$ be the parent individual, $x_i^{(t+1)}$ be its offspring through a mutation strategy, then the output is

$$o(x_i^{(t+1)}) = \begin{cases} \max_{1 \leq j \leq n}\{|\, x_i^{(t+1)}(j) - x_i^{(t)}(j)\,|\}, & \text{if } f(x_i^{(t+1)}) < f(x_i^{(t)}), \\ 0, & \text{otherwise,} \end{cases}$$

The output of strategy s_1 is defined by:

$$o^{(t+1)}(s_1) = \max_i \{o(x_i^{(t+1)}); x_i^{(t+1)} \text{ is generated by applying strategy } s_1\}. \quad (8)$$

If considering the impact of history strategies, the output (8) is amended as follows:

$$\bar{o}^{(t+1)}(s_1) = \begin{cases} o^{(t+1)}(s_1), & \text{if } o^{(t+1)}(s_1) \geq \alpha \cdot o^{(t)}(s_1), \\ \alpha \cdot o^{(t)}(s_1), & \text{otherwise,} \end{cases} \quad (9)$$

where $\alpha \in [0,1]$ is a controlling parameter of how much the previous output will kept in memory. $\alpha = 0$ means none from historical data; $\alpha = 1.0$ means the output is fully determined by the maximum output in history.

Based on the output (9), the payoff of players are defined by

$$\pi_1(s_1, s_2) = \frac{o(s_1)}{o(s_2)}, \quad \pi_2(s_1, s_2) = \frac{o(s_2)}{o(s_1)}. \quad (10)$$

However there is a danger in Eq. (10): $o(s_2)$ or $o(s_1)$ could be zero. So it is necessary to add a controlling parameter β to avoid this extreme case.

$$\pi_1(s_1, s_2) = \begin{cases} \beta, & \text{if } o(s_1)/o(s_2) \leq \beta, \\ 1/\beta, & \text{if } o(s_1)/o(s_2) \geq 1/\beta, \\ o(s_1)/o(s_2), & \text{otherwise,} \end{cases} \quad (11)$$

where $\beta \in [0,1]$, where $\beta = 0$ allows payoff to be infinity large, and $\beta = 1$ means that payoffs of strategies s_1 and s_2 both are equal to 1.

Now assume the strategy profile is $\mathbf{s} = (s_1, s_2)$, the mixed probability distribution $p(s)$ can be calculated by the proportion of its payoff among the total payoffs, e.g.,:

$$p_1(s_1) = \frac{\pi_1(s_1, s_2)}{\pi_1(s_1, s_2) + \pi_1(s_1, s_2)}. \quad (12)$$

5 Experimental Results and Analysis

The above EP is evaluated on 7 test functions, which was used to test IFEP in [2]. The description of these functions is given in Table 1. Among them, function f_1 and f_2 are unimodal functions, f_3 and f_4 multimodal functions with many local minima, $f_5 - f_7$ multimodal functions with only a few local minima.

The parameter setup in the mixed EP are taken as the same values as those in [2]. Population size $\mu = 100$, tournament size $q = 10$, and initial standard

Table 1. Seven test functions, where the coefficients of $f5 - f7$ are given in [2]

test functions	domain	f_{min}
$f_1 = \sum_{i=1}^{30} x_i^2$	$[-100, 100]^{30}$	0
$f_2 = \sum_{i=1}^{30} \mid x_i \mid + \prod_{i=1}^{30} \mid x_i \mid$	$[-100, 100]^{30}$	0
$f_3 = -20 \exp\left(-0.2\sqrt{\frac{1}{30}\sum_{i=1}^{30} x_i^2}\right)$ $- \exp\left(\frac{1}{30}\sum_{i=1}^{30} \cos(2\pi x_i)\right) + 20 + e$	$[-32, 32]^{30}$	0
$f_4 = \frac{1}{4000}\sum_{i=1}^{30} x_i^2 - \prod_{i=1}^{30} \cos(x_i/\sqrt{i}) + 1$	$[-600, 600]^{30}$	0
$f_5 = -\sum_{i=1}^{5}\left(\sum_{j=1}^{4}(x_j - a_{ij})^2 + c_i\right)^{-1}$	$[0, 10]^4$	-10.15
$f_6 = -\sum_{i=1}^{7}\left(\sum_{j=1}^{4}(x_j - a_{ij})^2 + c_i\right)^{-1}$	$[0, 10]^4$	-10.34
$f_7 = -\sum_{i=1}^{10}\left(\sum_{j=1}^{4}(x_j - a_{ij})^2 + c_i\right)^{-1}$	$[0, 10]^4$	-10.54

Table 2. Comparison of mean best fitness between MEP and IFEP, FEP, CEP

function	evaluation	MEP mean best	IFEP [2] mean best	FEP [2] mean best	CEP [2] mean best
f_1	150,000	9.151e-06	4.16e-5	5.72e-4	1.91e-4
f_2	200,000	1.269e-03	2.44e-2	7.60e-2	2.29e-2
f_3	150,000	6.590e-04	4.83e-3	1.76e-2	8.79
f_4	200,000	1.706e-02	4.54e-2	2.49e-2	8.13e-2
f_5	10,000	-8.774e+00	-6.46	-5.50	-6.43
f_6	10,000	-9.735e+00	-7.10	5.73	7.62
f_7	10,000	-9.841e+00	-7.80	6.41	8.86

deviation is take as $\sigma = 3.0$. The stopping criteria is to stop running at 1500 generations for functions f_1 and f_3, 2000 generations for f_2 and f_4, 100 generations for $f_5 - f_7$. The lower-bound used in this paper is $\sigma_{min} = 10^{-5}$ for all functions except f_4. Since f_4 has a larger definition domain than others, σ_{min} is taken a bigger value 10^{-4}. Parameters α in Eq.(9) and β in Eq.(11) is chosen to be 0.9 and 0.05 respectively. At the initial step, the mixed strategy distribution is taken as $(0.5, 0.5)$. Results for $f_1 - f_4$ are averaged over 50 independent runs, for $f_5 - f_7$ over 1000 independent runs.

In the following, CEP is EP using Gaussian mutation; FEP using Cauchy mutation; IFEP using Gaussian and Cauchy mutations simultaneously; MEP is the mixed mutation given in this paper.

The first experiment aims to compare MEP with IFEP, FEP and CEP. Table 2 gives results generated by MEP against existing results of IFEP, FEP and CEP from [2]. It is observed that MEP is obviously much better than IFEP, CEP and FEP over all test functions. However, to be honest, this improvement is partly due to the well-chosen low bound σ_{min}.

The second experiment intends to compare mixed mutation with Gaussian and Cauchy mutations when they take the same lower bounds. There are three types of results:

1. In Figures 1, 2, 4 and 6, the mixed strategy can reach the same fitness level as the best pure strategy does.
2. In Figure 2, the mixed strategy has a better performance.
3. In Figure 5, the mixed strategy is a little worse than the best pure strategy (Gaussian), however, the difference is very small.

The third experiment describes the dynamics of the mixed strategy. There are two types of dynamics:

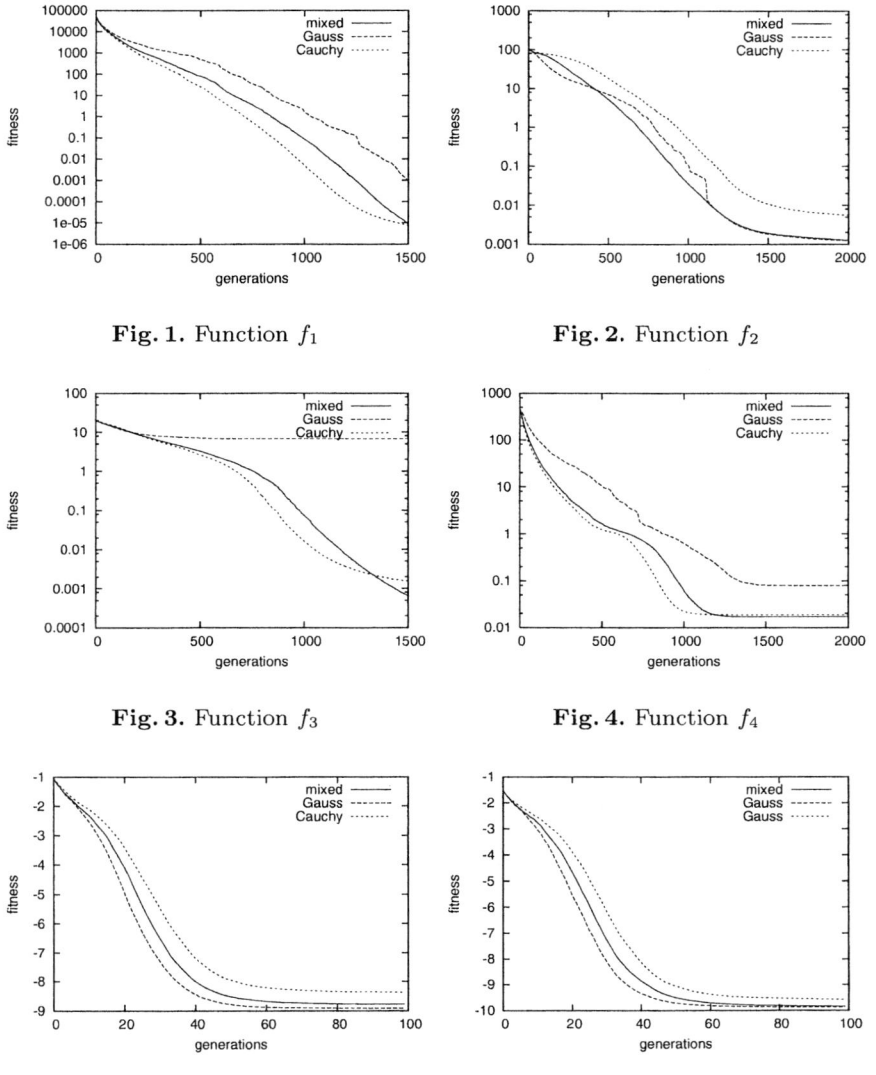

Fig. 1. Function f_1

Fig. 2. Function f_2

Fig. 3. Function f_3

Fig. 4. Function f_4

Fig. 5. Function f_5

Fig. 6. Function f_6

1. In Figures 7-10, Cauchy mutation takes a higher percentage as a global search at the early search phase; and then Gaussian mutation holds a dominant position as a local search.
2. Figures 11 and 12 demonstrate another dynamics of the mixed strategy. The number of individuals using Gaussian mutation is almost the same as that of using Cauchy mutation.

The last experiment studies the impact of parameters α and β on the performance. The parameter α is regraded as a memory of history. From Table 3, it

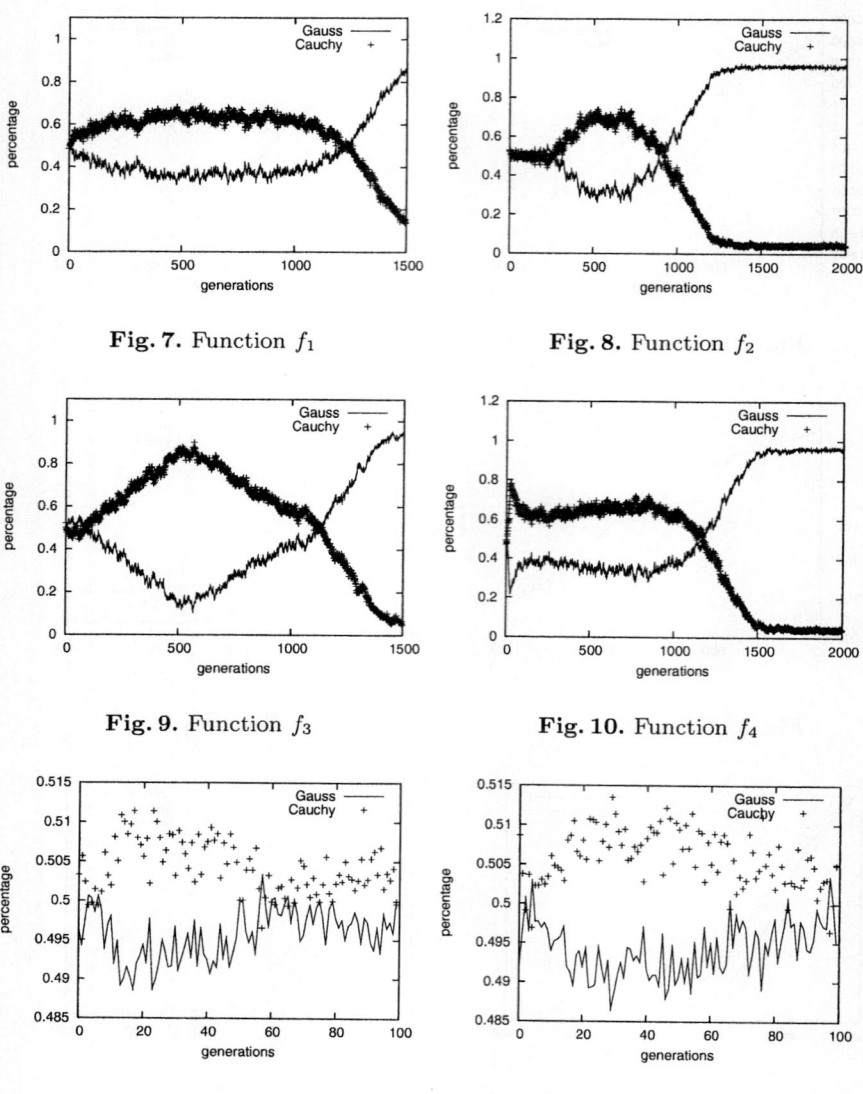

Fig. 7. Function f_1

Fig. 8. Function f_2

Fig. 9. Function f_3

Fig. 10. Function f_4

Fig. 11. Function f_5

Fig. 12. Function f_6

Table 3. Impact of parameter α

	function evaluation	$\alpha = 0.0$ mean best	$\alpha = 0.5$ mean best	$\alpha = 0.9$ mean best	$\alpha = 1.0$ mean best
f_1	150,000	3.342e-05	8.461e-06	9.151e-06	1.974e-05
f_2	200,000	1.224e-03	1.249e-03	1.269e-03	1.760e-03
f_3	150,000	5.720e-04	5.757e-04	6.590e-04	1.464e-03
f_4	200,000	2.967e-02	2.761e-02	1.706e-02	2.123e-02
f_5	10,000	-8.478e+00	-8.627e+00	-8.774e+00	-8.685e+00
f_6	10,000	-9.539e+00	-9.607e+00	-9.735e+00	-9.706e+00
f_7	10,000	-9.814e+00	-9.801e+00	-9.841e+00	-9.658e+00

Table 4. Impact of parameter β

	function evaluation	$\beta = 0.0$ mean best	$\beta = 0.05$ mean best	$\beta = 0.5$ mean best	$\beta = 1.0$ mean best
f_1	150,000	2.696e-05	9.151e-06	9.945e-06	3.864e-05
f_2	200,000	1.207e-03	1.269e-03	1.521e-03	3.692e-03
f_3	150,000	2.238e-01	6.590e-04	1.169e-03	1.239e-03
f_4	200,000	1.884e-02	1.706e-02	1.918e-02	2.147e-02
f_5	10,000	-8.692e+00	-8.774e+00	-8.708e+00	-8.689e+00
f_6	10,000	-9.625e+00	-9.735e+00	-9.610e+00	-9.622e+00
f_7	10,000	-9.776e+00	-9.841e+00	-9.818e+00	-9.786e+00

is seen that for four different values, MEP has produced a similar performance. Parameter β is a threshold to control the scale of each strategy's payoff. Table 4 displays a good performance if $\beta = 0.05, 0.5, 1.0$. However, $\beta = 0.0$ is a bad choice for function f_3.

6 Conclusions

This paper presents a game-theoretic approach to design EP using mixed strategies. The conventional EP usually apply a single mutation strategy. However according to no free lunch theorem, none of a single mutation operators cannot solve all problems efficiently no matter how powerful it is. So it is expected that a mixture of different mutation strategies will solve more problems efficiently than a single mutation strategy does. This paper has confirmed this point.

In theory it s easy to see that some mixed strategies could perform at least as good as or eve better than the best pure strategy, and may solve more problems efficiently than one pure strategy. Through a case study, the theoretic prediction has been validated. The experimental results given in this paper have demonstrated that the mixed mutation has obtained the same or nearly same performance as the best of Cauchy and Gaussian mutations over all test functions, and even better in some cases. If only a single mutation strategy is applied, neither Gaussian nor Cauchy mutation can solve all 7 test functions efficiently.

Further research works include: at present, the evaluation of mixed mutation strategies is only implemented on a few benchmark functions, it is necessary to verify it on more problems; the game designed in this paper is a simple two-player game, it is necessary to study more complex game; if more mutation operators were added into the mixed strategy, it would lead to a more powerful mixed strategy.

Acknowledgements. This work is partially supported by Engineering and Physical Research Council under Grant (GR/T10671/01) and National Natural Science Foundation under Grant (60443003).

References

1. D. Fogel. *Evolution Computation: Toward a New Philosophy of Machine Intelligence.* IEEE Press, Piscataway, NJ, 1995.
2. X. Yao, Y. Liu, and G. Lin. Evolutionary programming made faster. *IEEE Trans. Evolutionary Computation,* 3(2):82–102, 1999.
3. C.-Y. Lee and X. Yao. Evolutionary programming using mutations based on the Lévy probability distribution. *IEEE Trans. on Evolutionary Computation,* 8(2):1–13, 2004.
4. D. H. Wolpert and W. G. Macready. No free lunch theorem for optimization. *IEEE Trans. on Evolutionary Computation,* 1(1):67–82, 1997.
5. K. Chellapilla. Combining mutation operators in evolutionary programming. *IEEE Trans. on Evolutionary Computation,* 2(3):91–96, 1998.
6. J. W. Weibull. *Evolutionary Game Theory.* MIT press, Cambridge, MA, 1995.
7. P. K. Dutta. *Strategies and Games.* The MIT Press, Cambridge, MA, 1999.
8. S. G. Ficici, O. Melnik, and J. B. Pollack. A game-theoretic investigation of selection methods used in evolutionary algorithms. In *Proc. of 2000 Congress on Evolutionary Computation,* pages 880 – 887. IEEE Press, 2000.
9. R. P. Wiegand, W. C. Liles, and K. A. De Jong. Analyzing coperative coevolution with evolutionary game theory. In *Proc. of 2002 Congress on Evolutionary Computation,* pages 1600–1605. IEEE Press, 2002.
10. S. G. Ficici and J. B. Pollack. A game-theoretic memory mechanism for coevolution. In *Proc. of 2003 Genetic and Evolutionary Computation Conference,* pages 286–297. Springer, 2003.
11. K.-H. Liang, X. Yao, and C. S. Newton. Adapting self-adaptive parameters in evolutionary algorithms. *Applied Intellegence,* 15(3):171–180, 2001.
12. D. Fogel, G. Fogel, and K. Ohkura. Multiple-vector self-adaptation in evolutionary algorithms. *BioSystems,* 61:155–162, 2001.

FIR Frequency Sampling Filters Design Based on Adaptive Particle Swarm Optimization Algorithm*

Wanping Huang, Lifang Zhou, Jixin Qian, and Longhua Ma

Institute of Systems Engineering, Control Science and Engineering Department,
Zhejiang University, Hangzhou, 310027
wphuang@iipc.zju.edu.cn

Abstract. Based on the study of Particle Swarm Optimization (PSO) on the mechanism of information communion, a new adaptive method of PSO is presented in this paper. This new adaptive method is to avoid the particles getting into local best solution during the optimization. By applying Adaptive Particle Swarm Optimization (APSO) to optimize transition sample values in FIR filter, the maximum stop band attenuation is obtained. The simulations of designing low-pass FIR have been done and the simulation results show that APSO is better than PSO not only in the optimum ability but also in the convergence speed.

Keywords: particle swarm optimization; adaptive capacity; FIR filter; frequency sampling filter; evolutionary computation.

1 Introduction

As a digital filter design method, the frequency sampling (FS) technique has attracted a great deal of attention [1,2,3]. The FS technique has the advantages that more effective narrow band filters can be found easily, and those filters can be designed with an arbitrary response. However, how to find the values of the transition band frequency sample values that produce a filter with the maximum stop band attenuation is the key task in the FS. Using Tables method to design filter will result in a suboptimal solution [4]. Recently, many evolutionary computation techniques, such as genetic algorithm (GA) and immune algorithm (IA), particle swarm optimization algorithm (PSO), were introduced to solve this problem. They are superior to Tables method.

Particle swarm optimization (PSO) is an evolutionary computation technique developed by Kennedy and Eberhart in 1995 [7,8]. PSO is attractive because there are very few parameters to adjust, and it has been used widely. PSO is similar to GA, in that the system is initialized with a population of random solution, firstly evaluated itself using a fitness function, do some random search according to fitness value [9]. However, it is unlike GA because PSO system updates itself without any genetic operator such as crossover and mutation. In PSO, each potential solution is assigned a andomized velocity, and the potential solutions, named as particles with an important characteristic

---

* This work is supported by the National Natural Science Foundation of China under the Grant No.60474064.

of memory, are then "flown" through the problem space [10]. On the other hand, there're some differences between PSO and GA, IA on the mechanism of information communion. Chromosomes in GA and IA share the information with each other so that the population moves towards to the best location smoothly [11]. But only the particle, which can find the potential solution in the population, can pass on the information to the others. So the whole process of searching and update is to follow the current best solution. In that case, all particles can congregate to the best solution more quickly. The advantage of using PSO to optimize the transition band frequency sample values has been discussed in paper [12].

However, PSO is easy to get into the local best solution in optimization, so that the ability of searching is weaken greatly. To beyond its limitation, PSO is appeal to improve its mechanism of information communion. In this paper, PSO's optimization mechanism is analyzed, and a new mechanism with adaptive ability is proposed. This adaptive PSO (APSO) can avoid getting into local best solution efficiently and improve its searching ability. And, APSO is applied to FIR filter design. Finally, experimental results are presented and compare with PSO, which demonstrate the validity, effectiveness and superiority of APSO.

2 Frequency Sampling Filter

The Discrete Fourier transform (DFT) is an important tool in signal processing applications. Given a sequence h(n) of length N, the DFT evaluate its Z transform X(z) at N equally spaced angles on the unit circle in the Z-plane. In the traditional frequency sampling approach to FIR filter design, the desired frequency response is sampled at N equally spaced frequencies, where N is the filter length. Since the frequency samples are simply the DFT coefficients of the filter impulse response, an N-points inverse DFT (IDFT) is used to computer the filter coefficients.

FS method has attracted a considerable amount of attention as a filter design method. When used to design standard frequency-selective filters, a few variable samples in the transition band are optimized to maximize the filter performance according to its desired use.

Considering a desired frequency response $H_d(e^{jw})$ and its unit sampling response $h_d(n)$, N-points of frequency sampling values $H(k)$ is achieved by $H_d(e^{jw})$ sampled at N equally on the unit circle. Moreover, a sequence $h(n)$ of length N can be obtained through IDFT. For example, $H(z)$ is represented as a system transfer function.

$$H(z) = \sum_{n=0}^{N-1} h(n)z^{-n} = \frac{1-z^{-N}}{N} \sum_{k=0}^{N-1} \frac{H(k)}{1-z^{-1}e^{j2\pi k/N}} \quad (1)$$

As a linear phase filter, $H(k)$ can be expressed just like equation (2).

$$H(k) = H_r(2\pi k/N)e^{j\Phi(k)} \quad (2)$$

where

$$H_r(2\pi k/N) = \begin{cases} H_r(0), & k=0 \\ H_r[2\pi(N-k)/N], & k=1,\cdots,N-1 \end{cases} \quad (3)$$

Also it has symmetrical impulse response.

$$\phi(k) = \begin{cases} -\left(\dfrac{N-1}{2}\right)\left(\dfrac{2\pi k}{N}\right), & k=0,\cdots\left[\dfrac{N-1}{2}\right] \\ \left(\dfrac{N-1}{2}\right)\dfrac{2\pi}{N}(N-k), & k=\left[\dfrac{N-1}{2}\right]+1,\cdots,N-1 \end{cases} \quad (4)$$

where [.] means integral operation.

The interpolated frequency response has considerable ripple in regions where there are sudden transitions in the desired response, e.g. near the band edges of band selective filters. In order to in prove the filter characteristics, a transition band has been introduced in the desired frequency response. A number of samples in the transition band are varied in amplitude so as to minimize the maximum deviation from the desired response over some frequency rang of interest. Since PSO is an effective algorithm to find the global best solution, it's a good idea to use PSO to design the transition band frequency samples based on frequency sampling technique.

3   Particle Swarm Optimization

PSO simulate social behavior, in which a population of individuals exists. These individuals (also called "particles") are "evolved" by cooperation and competition among the individuals themselves through generations. In PSO, each potential solution is assigned a randomized velocity, are "flown" through the problem space. Each particle adjust its flying according to its own flying experience and its companions' flying experience. The ith particle is represented as $X_i = (x_{i1}, x_{i2}, \ldots, x_{iD})$. Each particle is treated as a point in a D-dimensional space. The best previous position (the best fitness value is called *pBest*) of any particle is recorded and represented as $P_i = (p_{i1}, p_{i2},\ldots, p_{iD})$. Anther "best" value (called *gBest*) is recorded by all the particles in the population. This location is represented as $P_g=(p_{g1}, p_{g2},\ldots, p_{gD})$. At each time step, the rate of the position changing velocity (accelerating) for particle i is represented as $V_i = (v_{i1}, v_{i2},\ldots, v_{iD})$. Each particle moves toward its *pBest* and *gBest* locations. The performance of each particle is measured according to a fitness function, which is related to the problem to be solved.

The process for implementing the global PSO is as figure 1.
The particles are manipulated according to the following equation:

$$v_{id} = w*v_{id} + c_1*rand(\ )*(p_{id}-x_{id}) + c_2*Rand(\ )+(p_{gd}-x_{id}) \quad (5)$$

$$x_{id} = x_{id} + v_{id} \quad (6)$$

where C_1 and C_2 in equation (5) are two positive constants, which represent the weighting of the stochastic acceleration terms that pull each particle toward *pBest* and *gBest* positions. In most applications, C_1 and C_2 each equals to 2.0. *rand( )* and *Rand( )* are two random functions in the range [0, 1]. The use of the inertia weight *w* provides a balance between global and local exploration, and results in less iteration to find an optimal solution.

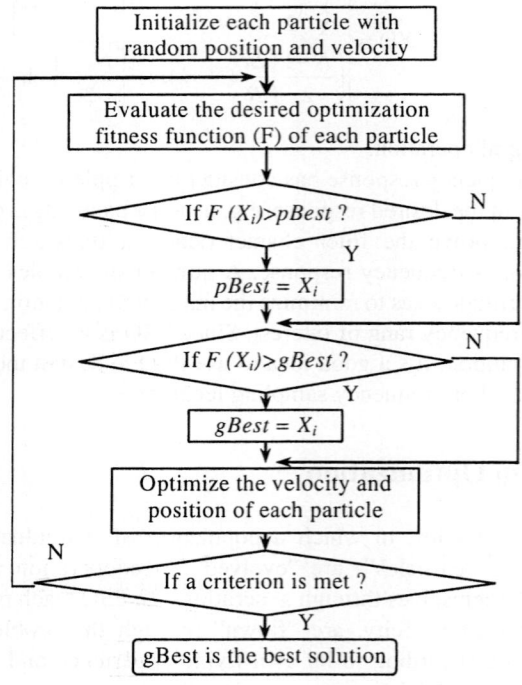

Fig. 1. Flow chart of PSO

4 Adaptive Particle Swarm Optimization

Generally, convergence means that optimization process reaches a steady state. In allusion to PSO, convergence in algorithm relates to both the individual and the whole population. When all particles achieve convergence, the population will never change again and reach a steady state. Accordingly, *gBest* also doesn't change. Convergence in PSO can be described as follow:

Considering in *t* generation, *gBest(t)* is the best location, *gBest** is a fixed position in problem space, when $\lim_{t \to \infty} gBest(t) = gBesst^*$, PSO achieves convergence.

This definition shows that PSO is convergent if *gBest* doesn't change. And PSO achieves the global best convergence if *gBest* is the global best solution. Otherwise, PSO gets into local best solution.

On the other hand, the best search in particle swarm depends on their memory ability and the mechanism of information communion. *pBest* and *gBest* embody their memory ability: *pBest* preserves the best solution which the particle found by itself in history, and *gBest* preserves the best solution which the whole population found. The mechanism of information communion shows that each particle's flying position at next moment is extremely influenced by *gBest*. Particle's flying direction and distance at one step is described as figure 2.

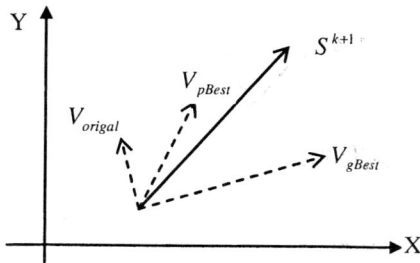

Fig. 2. Particle's flying sketch map

In figure 2, $V_{oringal}$ represents particle's velocity at last step; V_{pBest} represents velocity component based on *pBest*; V_{gBest} represents velocity component based on *gBest*; S^k represents particle's current position; S^{k+1} represents particle's position at last flight.

In PSO, only *gBest* could pass information to other particles, so that information flows unilaterally. Usually all particles are convergent to the best solution faster. However, when the current best solution is a local best solution and all particles are convergent to this solution, it's difficult for them to deviate from the local best solution. Although the increment of particle number is able to extend the searching range, it takes more time to search and can't solve this problem radically.

In order to improve the particle's global searching ability and avoid getting into local solution, this paper ameliorates the searching mechanism as following:

(a) The best reservation is introduced to mechanism, so that the algorithm ensures to achieve the global convergence.

(b) The mean of all particles' current best value $\overline{pBest}$ is introduced. $\overline{pBest}$ is considered to be the criterion whether particle should update or not. When particle's current fitness is better than $\overline{pBest}$, its velocity and position had to update by formula (5)(6). Otherwise, this particle should be deracinated, new location and velocity come into being again, its current *pBest* should be reserved, then new search will begin. It seems to be survival rule in nature. The particle will rebirth after catastrophe. It makes the population to break away from stagnancy.

(c) Particle's max velocity decides the max distance which the particle can move at one step. As result, the limit of max velocity can prevent particles from running out searching space. The particle's searching ability may be restricted when the particle runs over and is limited some fixed value. Therefore, the particle initializes itself randomly at some range when it runs over the max velocity, and the restriction to particle's velocity can reduce.

The algorithm can be written as follow:

```
For each particle
    Initialize particle
END
Do
    For each particle
    Calculate fitness value
    If the fitness value is better than the best fitness value
(pBest) in history
    Set current value as the new pBest
END
    Choose the particle with the best fitness value of all the
particles as the gBest
For each particle
    If the fitness value is better than pBest
        Calculate particle velocity according to equation (5)
        Update particle position according to equation (6)
    Else
            Particle catastrophe
    END
    If particle velocity is more than the max velocity
            Set particle velocity equals to a random value within
range
    End
End
While maximum iterations or minimum error criteria is not
attained
```

5 Experimental Work

Example: Consider the design of a low-pass filter with the specifications: pass band edge $w_p=0.2\pi$, stop band edge $w_s=0.3\pi$, max pass band ripple $R_p=0.4\ dB$, min stop band attenuation $A_s=60\ dB$. Use FS to design a FIR filter.

Suppose sample number N equals to 60, and there are 2 samples in the transition band w ($0.2\pi < w < 0.3\pi$). Since frequency interval $\Delta w=2\pi/60$, samples in the transition band are placed respectively where k=8, 9 and k=53, 54. The transition band values are represented as T_1 and T_2 ($0 < T_1 < 1$, $0 < T_2 < 1$).

Sampling magnitude response can be expressed by function (5) as follow.

$$H_r(k) = [1,1,1,1,1,1,1,1,T_1,T_2,0,\cdots,0,T_2,T_1,1,1,1,1,1,1,1] \qquad (7)$$

where there are 43 zeros in the stop band.

Sampling phase response also can be denoted by function (6) as below:

$$\phi(k) = \begin{cases} -24.5(2\pi/60)k, & 0 \le k \le 20 \\ (50/60)\pi(60-k), & 30 \le k \le 59 \end{cases} \quad (8)$$

Combine (7) and (8) with (2), H(k) is achieved feasibly. Consequently, transferring H(k) into corresponding impulse response *h(n)* of 60 points FIR filter using IDFT, minimum stop band attenuation A_s can be calculated.

On another hand, we chose the population size S=10 and the *j*th particle is represented as $X_j = (T_{j1}, T_{j2})$. (*j*=1,2,...,10). Initialize their location and velocity in order to ensure that the search space is sampled widely and evenly as equation (9) and (10).

$$v_{id} = uniformly\_rand(1,10) \quad (9)$$

$$x_{id} = 0 \quad (10)$$

The particles update by cooperation and competition among the population through generations. The information is passed on by the particle, which finds the potential solution of maximum stop band attenuation. Magnitude response of low pass FIR filter based on PSO and APSO, Table, GA,IA was lied out in figure 3.

Table 1 shows the 10 experimental results of the maximum stop band attenuation (A_s) with PSO and APSO, respectively. In these experiments, the particle's number is chosen 10. When items number was 100, the particles in PSO presented to local best solution, and the arisen probability was 30%. Also, when items number was 200, the PSO presented to local best solution, and the probability was 20%. However, no matter the items number was 100 or 200, the particles in APSO can always find the global best solution, and the successful probability was 100%. Thus it can be seen that APSO's convergence and global search ability are superior to PSO on this problem. On the other hand, the experimental results also demonstrate the impact of items in the APSO on stop band attenuation. The more items we choose the better effect the experiment attained, while the convergence rate reduced substantially.

Figure 4 shows the variation tendency of best solution (stop band attention) in the case of 10 particles and 100 items based on PSO and APSO. Line 1 and line 2 is two experimental tracks in PSO. Line 2 shows the particles in PSO is convergent to global solution. When PSO got into local best solution, the best solution track seems to be Line 1. Here, Line 3 performed in APSO, and outperformed the others.

The successful application of the APSO to this problem leads to consider how it deviated from local best solution. Figure 5 shows the variation tendency of $\overline{pBest}$ (the mean of all particles' current best value). The information in PSO flows unilaterally due to the mechanism of information communion. As the current best solution was a local best solution and all particles were convergent to this solution, it's hard for the population to escape from the local best solution. The information in APSO flows bilaterally. $\overline{pBest}$ was considered to be the criterion whether each particle should update or not. The particles will rebirth after catastrophe. In this case, it makes the population to break away from stagnancy.

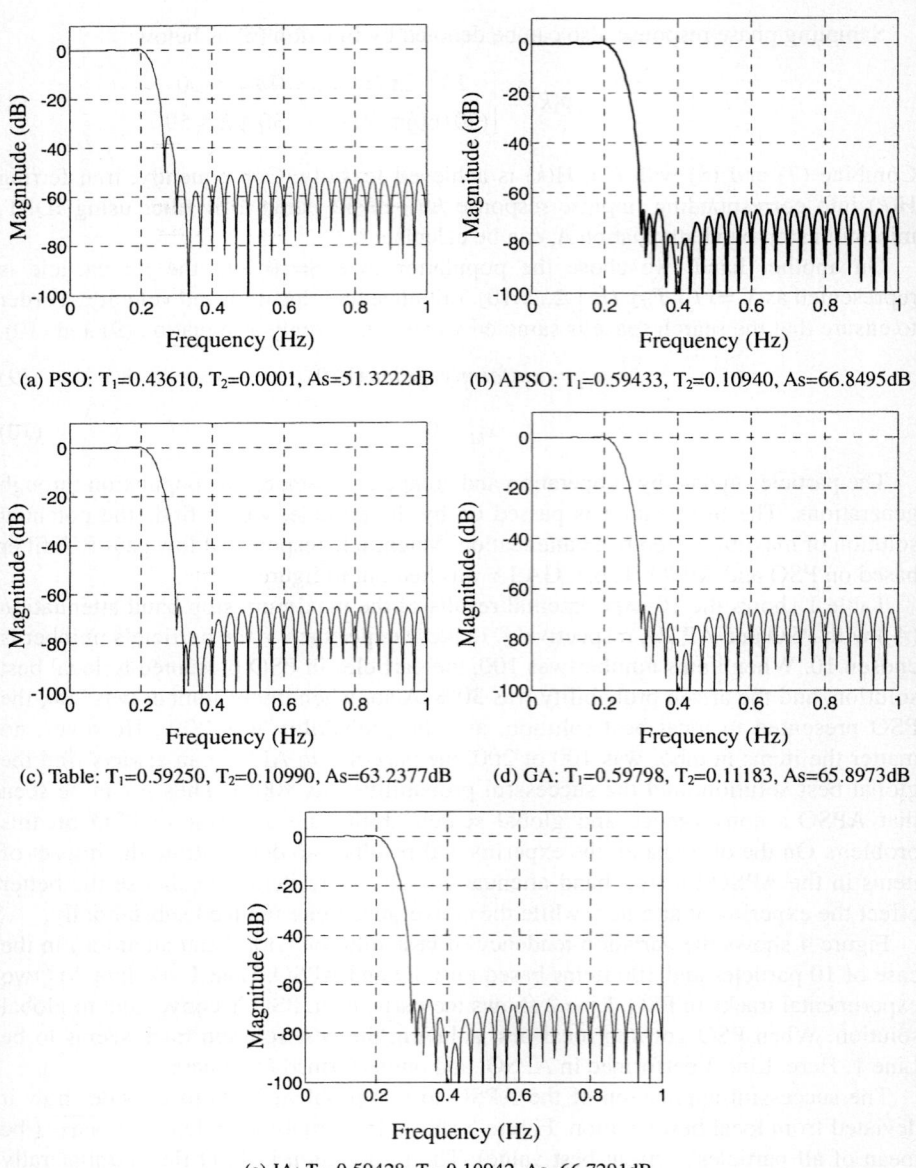

Fig. 3. Comparison between PSO, APSO, Table, GA and IA on magnitude response of low pass FIR filter. (a)PSO: The algorithm is convergent to the local best solution. (b) APSO: The algorithm is convergent to the global best solution, and outperforms other evolutionary computation algorithms.

Table 1. Comparison between PSO and APSO

Items	Algorithm	A_s(dB)				
100	PSO	66.7248	51.3325	51.3325	66.7871	66.7841
	APSO	66.8366	66.8312	66.7748	65.7757	66.817
200	PSO	66.8174	66.8301	51.3325	66.8419	66.8368
	APSO	66.8495	66.8476	66.8476	66.8477	66.8495

Items	Algorithm	A_s(dB)				
100	PSO	66.607	51.3325	64.6607	65.7558	66.651
	APSO	66.7503	66.8366	66.8366	66.837	66.817
200	PSO	66.8428	51.3325	66.8487	66.8419	66.8447
	APSO	66.8495	66.8476	66.8495	66.8393	66.8477

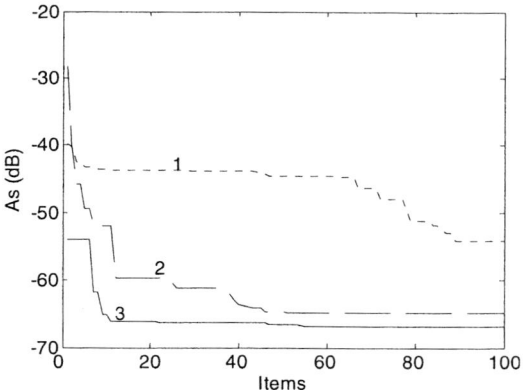

Fig. 4. The variation tendency of best solution in PSO and APSO.

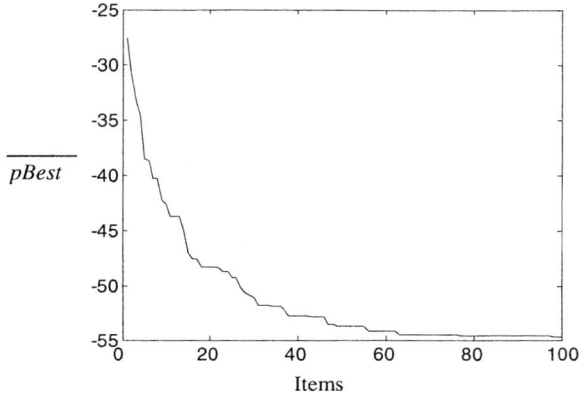

Fig. 5. Variation tendency of $\overline{pBest}$ in APSO (S=10, Items=100)

6 Conclusion

The new improved algorithm APSO proposed in this paper solves the limitation of PSO which the particles easily get into the local best solution. The simulation results show FIR frequency sampling filter design applied APSO is superior to PSO. The feasibility and advantage of APSO is obviously represented.

References

1. P. A. Lynn, "Frequency sampling filters with integer multiplies," *Introduction to Digital Filtering*, R. E. Bogner and A.G Constantinides, Eds. London, U.K. Academic, 1975.
2. E. C. Ifeachor and S.P. Harris, " A new approach to frequency sampling filter design," in *Proc. IEE/IEEE Workshop Natural Algorithms Signal Process*, 1993
3. L. R. Rabiner, B. gold, C. A. McGonegal, "An Approach to the Approximation Problem for Nonrecursive Digital filter", *IEEE Transactions on Audio and Electro-acoustics* Vol. AU-18, No. 2, June, 1970.
4. P.A. stubbenerud and C.T. Leondes, "A frequency sampling filter design method which accounts for finite word length effects," *IEEE Trans. Signal Processing*, vol. 42, pp. 189-193,Jan. 1994.
5. Stephen P. Harris, and Emmanuel C. Ifeachor, "Automatic design of frequency sampling filters by hybrid Genetic Algorithm Techniques", *IEEE Transaction on signal processing*, VOL. 46, NO. 12, December 1998
6. Eberhart, R.C., and Shi, Y. (1998). Comparison between genetic algorithms and particle swarm optimization. In V.W. Porto, N. Saravanan, D. Waagen, and A.E. Eiben, Eds. *Evolutionary Programming VII*: Proc. 7th Ann. Conf. on Evolutionary Computation 2000,San Diego, CA. Berlin: Springer-Verlag.
7. Eberhart, R.C., and Shi, Y. (2001)(b). Particle swarm optimization: developments, applications and resources. Proc. Congress on Evolutionary Computation 2001, Seoul, Korea. Piscataway, NJ: IEEE Service Center.
8. Kennedy, J., Eberhart, R.C., (1999). The particle swarm: social adaptation in information processing systems. In Corne, D., Dorigo, M., and Glover, F., Eds. New ideas in Optimization. London: McGraw-Hill.
9. Eberhart, R.C., and Shi, Y. (2001)(a). Tracking and optimizing dynamic systems with particle swarms. *Proc. Congress on Evolutionary Computation 2001*, Seoul, Korea. Piscataway, NJ: IEEE Service Center.
10. Eberhart, R.C., and Shi, Y. (2000). Comparing inertia weights and constriction factors in particle swarm optimization. *Proc. Congress on Evolutionary Computation* 2000, San Diego, CA, pp 84-88.
11. D.E. Goldberg, Genetic Algorithms in Search, Optimization and Machine Learning. Reading, MA: Addison-Wesley, 1998.
12. Wanpin Huang, Lifang Zhou, Jixin Qian, "FIR Filter Design: Frequency Sampling by Particle Swarm Optimization Algorithm," in *Proc.* The Third International Conference on Machine Learning and Cybernetics, Shanghai, 2004.

A Hybrid Macroevolutionary Algorithm*

Jihui Zhang[1] and Junqin Xu[2]

[1] School of Automation, Qingdao University, Qingdao 266071, China
[2] Department of Mathematics, Qingdao University, Qingdao 266071, China

Abstract. Macroevolutionary algorithm (MA) is a new approach to optimization problems based on extinction patterns in macroevolution. It is different from the traditional population-level evolutionary algorithms such as genetic algorithms. In MAs, evolves at the level of higher taxa is used as the underlying metaphor. It is inspired by the latest models about evolution at large scale-macroevolution, while the traditional evolutionary algorithms are inspired in natural selection of darwinian theory. The MA model exploits the presence of links between "species" that represent candidate solutions to the optimization problem. In this paper, a hybrid MA which combines simulated annealing is proposed to solve complicated multi-modal optimization problems. Numerical simulation results show the power of this hybrid algorithm.

1 Introduction

It is well-known that many practical problems can be modelled as optimization problems. In order to solve various optimization problems, different approaches such as *Newton method, hill-climbing* and *steepest descent*, have been developed in various literature. These classical optimization methods can only be used efficiently to certain kinds of objective functions (e.g. smooth, convex, etc.). But many practical problems are non-convex and have many local optima, thus how to efficiently discover the global optimum of a multi-modal function is still an open problem. Therefore, it is important to develop efficient search methods for general function optimization, especially for large-scale optimization problems with multi-modal objective function. Generally speaking, the methods of global optimization can be classified roughly into two classes: *deterministic* and *random*. If the objective function satisfies some conditions (such as *continuity, existence of Hessian matrix, convexity,* etc.), the global optimum can be discovered by the deterministic method. Unfortunately, it is a strict requirement for the objective functions arising from practical problems to satisfy these conditions, and for this reason, many optimization problems cannot be solved by the classical optimization methods. In contrast, random search generally do not need to satisfy the above conditions, so they have a broader application than deterministic method. Because of these virtues, random search method has prevailed

---
* Supported by SRF for ROCS, SEM; Qingdao NSF (03-2-jz-19); Shandong NSF (Y2002G01); Research Fund of Qingdao Univ. (200204); Research fund of School of Automation (0305).

in engineering practice. Evolutionary computation (EC) methods have been successfully used to solve many diverse problems in search and optimization. This success is in part due to the unbiased nature of their operations, which can still perform well in situations with little or no domain knowledge [1]. Instead of the Darwinian, short-term evolutionary metaphor, however, a different time scale can be considered, namely the macroevolutionary one, where extinctions and diversification of species through internal interactions are at work. Large extinctions can generate coherent population responses that are very different from the slow Darwinian dynamics of a classical GA. Besides, the population of candidate solutions/species might be understood in terms of an ecological system with connections among different species, instead of just a number of independent entities with a given assigned fitness value. In [2], a macroevolutionary algorithm (MA) is proposed, and simulation results show that it is a good alternative to standard GAs.

In this paper, an improved version of MA is proposed for optimization problems with multi-modal objective function. This paper mainly considers the following multi-modal function optimization problem:

$$\begin{aligned}&\text{minimize } f(X)\\&X = (x_1, x_2, \cdots, x_n)^\top \in \Omega \subset \Re^n\\&\ell_i \leq x_i \leq u_i, \ i = 1, 2, \cdots, n\end{aligned} \quad (1)$$

As an evolutionary algorithm, MAs have some of their own shortcomings, too. For example, premature convergence is one common problem in almost all the evolutionary algorithms. Another problem much cared is the convergence speed of the stochastic search methods. Many solution methods are presented to improve the performance of this kind of algorithms. The key problem is to keep a proper balance between "exploration" and "exploitation". "Exploration" is concerned with the ability to search new region and find good solutions, while "exploitation" is concerned with the convergence speed. In fact, much effort is needed to implement this kind of difficult balance in practice.

2 Macroevolutionary Algorithm

Macroevolutionary algorithm (MA) is first proposed by Jesús and Ricard [2]. The biological model of macroevolution (MM) is a network ecosystem where the dynamics are based only on the relation between species. The links between units/species are essential to determine the new state (alive or extinct) of each species at each generation. The state of species i at generation t is defined as

$$S_i(t) = \begin{cases} 1, \text{ if state is "alive"} \\ 0, \text{ if state is "extinct"}. \end{cases} \quad (2)$$

In this model, time is discretized in "generations" and that each generation constitutes a set of P species where P is constant. The relationship between species is represented by a connectivity matrix W, where each entry $w_{i,j}(t)(i, j \in$

$\{1, 2, \cdots, P\}$) of the matrix W measures the influence of species j on species i at t with a continuous value within the interval $[-1, 1]$ (in ecology, this influence is interpreted as the trophic relation between species). At the end of each generation, all extinct species are replaced by the existing species. Briefly, each generation in the biological model consists of a set of steps (the rules) that will be translated to the MA model.

1) *Random variation*: For each species i, a connection $w_{i,j}(t)$ is chosen randomly, and a new random value between -1 and 1 is assigned.
2) *Extinction*: The relation of each species to the rest of the population determines its survival coefficient h defined as

$$h_i(t) = \sum_{j=1}^{P} w_{i,j}(t) \qquad (3)$$

where t is the generation number. The species state in the next generation is updated synchronously as

$$S_i(t+1) = \begin{cases} 1, \text{ (alive) if } h_i(t) \geq 0 \\ 0, \text{ (extinct) otherwise.} \end{cases} \qquad (4)$$

This step allows for the selection and extinction of species.

3) *Diversification*: Vacant sites freed by extinct species are colonized with surviving species. Specifically, a colonizer c will be randomly chosen from the set of survivors. For all vacant sites (i.e., those such that $s_k(t) = 0$) the new connections will be updated as

$$\begin{aligned} w_{k,j} &= w_{c,j} + \eta_{k,j}, \\ w_{j,k} &= w_{j,c} + \eta_{j,k}. \end{aligned} \qquad (5)$$

where is a small random variation and $s_k(t+1) = 1$.

The main idea of MA is that the system will choose, through network interactions, which are the individuals to be eliminated so as to guarantee exploration by new individuals and exploitation of better solutions by further generations. To this purpose, it is essential to correctly establish a relationship between individuals. This is described by the following criteria.

c1) Each individual gathers information about the rest of the population through the strength and sign of its couplings $w_{i,j}$. Individuals with higher inputs h_i will be favored. Additionally, they must be able to out-compete other less-fit solutions.

c2) Some information concerning how close two solutions are in Ω is required (although this particular aspect is not strictly necessary). Close neighbors will typically share similar f-values and will cooperate. In this context, the connection $w_{i,j}$ is defined as

$$w_{i,j} = \frac{f(X_i) - f(X_j)}{\| X_i - X_j \|} \qquad (6)$$

where $X_i = (x_i^1, x_i^2, \cdots, x_i^n)$ is the ith individual.

The main ingredients of MA include:

1) *Selection operator*: It allows calculating the surviving individuals through their relations, i.e., as a sum of penalties and benefits. The state of a given individual S_i will be given by

$$S_i(t+1) = \begin{cases} 1, \text{ if } \sum_{j=1}^{P} w_{i,j}(t) \leq 0 \\ 0, \text{ otherwise} \end{cases} \qquad (7)$$

where t is generation number and $w_{i,j} = w(X_i, X_j)$ is calculated according to (6).

2) *Colonization operator*: It allows filling vacant sites that are freed by extinct individuals (that is, those such that $S_i = 0$). This operator is applied to each extinct individual in two ways. With a probability τ a totally new solution $X' \in \Omega$ will be generated. Otherwise exploitation of surviving solutions takes place through colonization. For a given extinct solution X_i, one of the surviving solutions, say X_b. Now the extinct solution will be "attracted" toward X_b. A possible (but not unique) choice for this colonization of extinct solutions can be expressed as

$$X_i(t+1) = \begin{cases} X_b(t) + \rho\lambda(X_b(t) - X_i(t)), \text{ if } \xi > \tau \\ X_i', \qquad\qquad\qquad\qquad\qquad \text{ if } \xi \leq \tau \end{cases} \qquad (8)$$

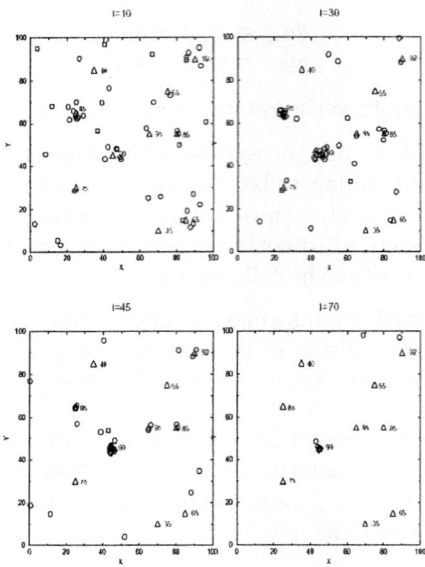

Fig. 1. MA Performance[2]

where $\xi \in [0,1]$ is a random number, $\lambda \in [-1,1]$ (both with uniform distribution) and ρ and τ are given constants of the algorithm. It can be seen that ρ describes a maximum radius around surviving solutions and τ acts as a "temperature". Parameter τ can be set as that in simulated annealing. For example, τ can take the following forms

$$\tau(t,G) = 1 - \frac{t}{G} \qquad (9)$$

$$\tau(t) \propto \exp(-\Gamma t). \qquad (10)$$

Comparison [2] between the performance of MA's and that of genetic algorithm with tournament selection shows that MA is a good alternative to standard GA's, showing a fast monotonous search over the solution space even for very small population sizes. A mean field theoretical analysis also shows that symmetry-breaking (i.e., the choice among one of the two equal peaks) typically occurs because small fluctuations and the presence of random solutions eventually shifts the system toward one of the two peaks (see Fig. 1).

3 The Hybrid Macroevolutionary Algorithm

3.1 Generation of the Initial Population

The main idea can be stated as following: The initial population is selected using uniform design technique [5] such that the individuals are evenly distributed on the whole search space. Experimental design method [3,4] is a sophisticated branch of statistics. *uniform design* is one important experimental design technique and it has been used in many real application. It was proposed by K.T. Fang and Y. Wang [7,8,9,10] in 1981 and it also was developed further by other researchers in recent years [5]. The main objective of uniform design is to sample a small set of points from a given set of points such that the sampled points are uniformly scattered.

Suppose there are n factors and q levels per factor. When n and q are given, the uniform design selects q combinations out of q^n possible combinations, such that these q combinations are scattered uniformly over the space of all possible combinations. The selected q combinations are expressed in terms of a *uniform array* $U(n,q) = (U_{i,j})_{q \times n}$, where $U_{i,j}$ is the level of the jth factor in the ith combination. Then these q points in the unit hypercube are mapped to the space with n factors and q levels. If q is a prime and $q > n$, it was proved that $U_{i,j}$ is given by

$$U_{i,j} = (i\sigma^{j-1} \mod q) + 1, \qquad (11)$$

where σ is a parameter which is different for different experiment [9,5].

3.2 Selection and Extinction Process

The equation (4) is changed to

$$S_i(t+1) = \begin{cases} 1, \text{(alive) if } h_i(t) \geq 0 \\ 1, \text{(alive) if } h_i(t) \geq 0 \ \& \ \eta' > \tau' \\ 0, \text{(extinct) otherwise.} \end{cases} \quad (12)$$

Where, the meaning of η' and τ' is the same with that in equation (17).

After selection process, $N - \ell$ new species are generated, so the remaining $N - \ell$ species will be generated by the following colonization process (here N is the population size, while ℓ is the extinct specie number).

Colonization Process. This process allows filling vacant sites that are freed by extinct individuals. The remaining $N - \ell$ individuals will be generated by two ways: with a probability $\tau \in (0, 1)$, a totally new solution is generated. Otherwise, it is generated based on the current search knowledge. It can be expressed by the following formulae:

$$x_i^j(t+1) = \begin{cases} x_b^j(t) + \eta \cdot \Delta x_i^j(t) + \alpha \cdot sx_i^j(t) \text{ if } \xi > \tau \\ x_{new}^j \quad \text{otherwise} \end{cases} \quad (13)$$

for $j = 1, 2, \cdots, n$. $x_i^j(t)$ is the jth entry of X_i at generation t. t is the current generation number. ξ is a random variable distributed uniformly on $[0, 1]$. $X_b(t)$ is the best individuals in generation t. $sx_i^j(t)$ and $\Delta X_i^j(t)$ have the following forms:

$$\Delta x_i^j(t) = (x_b^j(t) - x_i^j(t)) \cdot |\mathcal{N}(0,1)| \quad (14)$$

$$sx_i^j(t+1) = \eta \cdot acc^i(t) \cdot \Delta x_i^j(t) + \alpha \cdot sx_i^j(t) \quad (15)$$

where $x_i^j(k)$ is the jth variable of an ith individual at the tth generation. η and α are *learning rate* and *momentum rate* respectively. $\mathcal{N}(0, 1)$ is standard Gaussian random variable. $\Delta x_i^j(t)$ is the amount of change in an individual, which is proportional to the temporal error, and it drives the individual to evolve close to the best individual at the next generation. It can be viewed as a tendency of the other individuals to take after or emulate the best individual in the current generation. $sx_i^j(t)$ is the evolution tendency or momentum of previous evolution. It accumulates evolution information and tends to accelerate convergence when the evolution trajectory is moving in a consistent direction. $acc^i(t)$ is defined as follows:

$$acc^i(t) = \begin{cases} 1, \text{ if the current update has improved cost,} \\ 0, \text{ otherwise.} \end{cases} \quad (16)$$

τ in equation (13) is defined as follows

$$\tau(t, G) = 1 - \frac{t}{G} \quad (17)$$

where G is the recycling generations. New individuals X_{new} in equation (13) is generated using uniform design technique. The implementation details are similar to that in section 3.1, but each time the sampling subspace is different such that different sampling points will be trailed.

Local Search. After above steps, a simulated annealing liked local search method[6] is used to improve the quality of candidate solutions. In order to save searching time, only a limited number of local search are executed in each cycle. Therefore computation time is acceptable for large scale instances.

Termination Condition. In this paper, a fixed generation number is used as the termination condition of the procedure.

4 Experimental Results

The following benchmark functions are used to test the performance of HMA. (1) The *Sphere function*; (2) The *Griewangk function*; (3) The *Rosenbrock* and *Colville* functions; (4) *Shekel's Foxholes Function*; (5) *Six Hump Camel Back Function*; (6) *Brain Function*; (7) *Goldstein-Price Function* $f_{GP}(X)$; (8) *Shekel's Family Functions*; (9) *Hartman's Family Functions*; (10) *Rastrigin Function* $f_R(X)$. The characters and global searching difficulty of these functions can be found in related references.

4.1 Experimental Results

During the simulation process, the following parameters are used: population size $N = 100$; generation $G = 100, 300, 500, 1000$ etc. $factor$ =dimension; $s = 8, 16, 32$, etc; $\eta = 1.0$. $\alpha = 1.0$. For each test function, simulation is repeated for 30 times. The best solution in each simulation is recorded. And their average performance and deviation in the 30 simulations are computed and used to compare the different performance between MA and HMA. During all the simulations, HMA has better performance than MA in terms of both search speed and solution quality. Here only the performance of some test problems are shown.

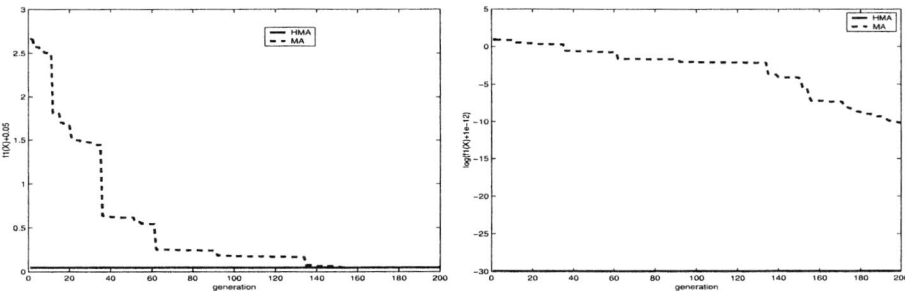

Fig. 2. Performance comparison for test function $f_1(X)$

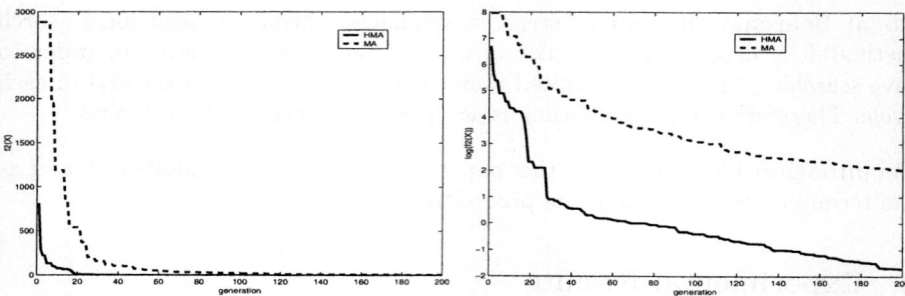

Fig. 3. Performance comparison for test function $f_{G2}(X)$

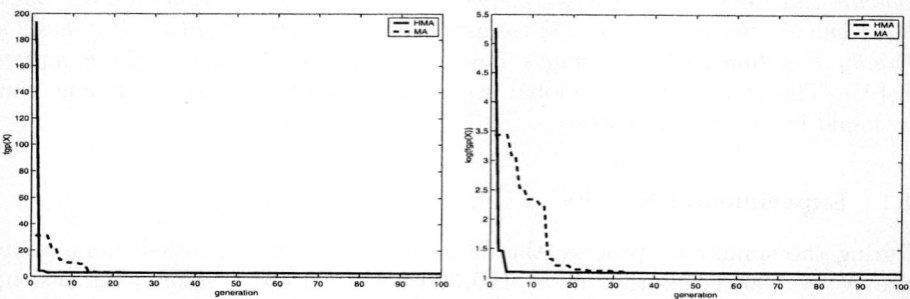

Fig. 4. Performance comparison for test function $f_{G10}(X)$

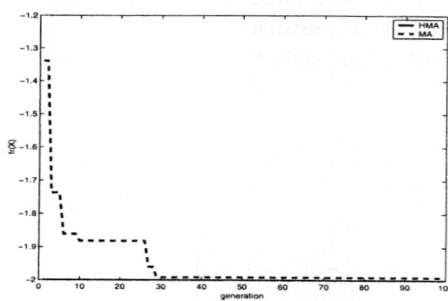

Fig. 5. Performance comparison for test function $f_r(X)$

5   Conclusions

Macroevolutionary algorithm (MA) is a new approach to optimization problems based on extinction patterns in macroevolution. It is different from the traditional population-level evolutionary algorithms. In this paper, a new version

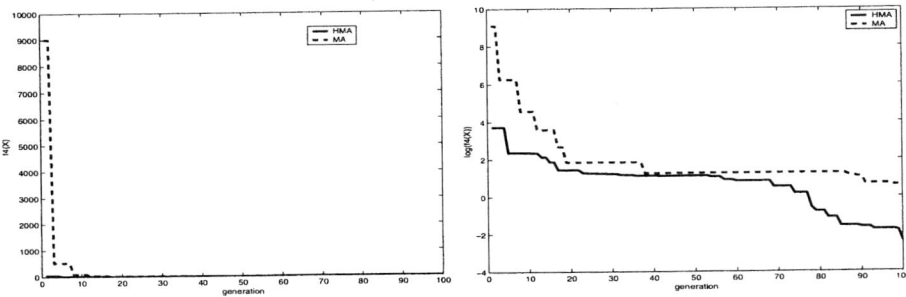

Fig. 6. Performance comparison for test function $f_{co}(X)$

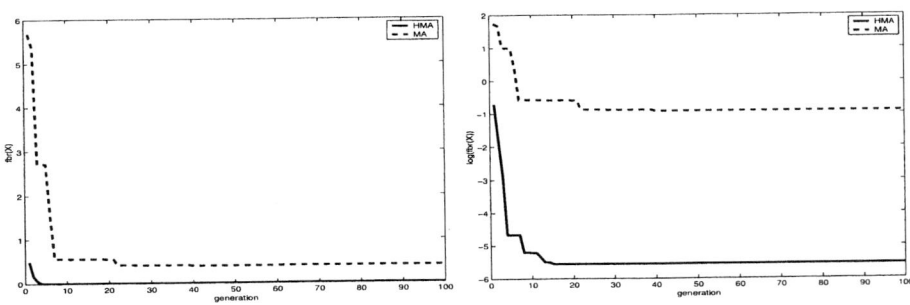

Fig. 7. Performance comparison for test function $f_{BR}(X)$

of MA is proposed to solve complicated multi-modal optimization problems. Numerical simulation results show the power of this new algorithm. Solving constrained and multiobjective optimization problems using MA should be our further research topics.

References

1. R.G. Reynolds and S. Zhu. Knowledge-based function optimization using fuzzy cultural algorithms with evolutionary programming. IEEE Trans. System, Man, and Cybernetics, 31(1), 1–18, 2001.
2. J. Marín and R.V. Solé. Macroevolutionary algorithms: a new optimization method on fitness landscapes, IEEE Trans. on Evolutionary Computation, 3(4), 1999, 272–286.
3. D.C. Montgomery. Design and Analysis of Experiments, 3rd Edition. New York: wiley, 1991.
4. C.R. Hicks. Fundamental Concepts in the Design of Experiments, 4th Edition. New York: Sauders, 1993.
5. P. Winker and K.T. Fang. Application of threshold accepting to the evaluation of the discrepancy of a set of points, SIAM J. Numer. Anal. 34, 2038–2042, 1998.

6. J. Zhang and X. Xu. An efficient evolutionary algorithm, Computers & Operations Research 26, 1999, 645-663
7. Y. Wang and K.T. Fang. A note on uniform distribution and experimental design, KEXUE TONGBAO, 26(6), 485–489, 1981 (in Chinese).
8. K.T. Fang and J.K. Li. Some New Uniform Designs, Hong Kong Baptist Univ., Hong Kong, Tech. Rep. Math-042, 1994.
9. K.T. Fang and Y. Wang. Number-Theoretic Methods in Statistics, London, U.K.: Chapman & Hall, 1994.
10. K.T. Fang. *Uniform Design and Design Tables.* Beijing, China: Science, 1994 (in Chinese).

Evolutionary Granular Computing Model and Applications

Jiang Zhang and Xuewei Li

School of economics and management,
Beijing Jiaotong University, Mailbox 482, Beijing 100044
jakezj@163.com
http://www.swarmagents.com

Abstract. The evolutionary granular computing model (EGCM) combining evolutionary computing and granular computing techniques is introduced in this paper. The model presents a new approach to simulate the cognition of human beings that can be viewed as the evolutionary process through the automatic learning from data sets. The information granule, which is the building block of cognition in EGCM, can be synthesized and created by the basic operators. It also can form the granules network by linking each other among granules. With learning from database, the system can evolve under the pressure of selection. The EGCM creates a dynamic model that can adapt to the environment.

1 Introduction

An information granule is a concept that can be represented by classical set, fuzzy set or random set to reflect the granularity and hierarchy of information [1]. It advocates the higher level "computing with words" rather than computing with numbers. Evolutionary computing[2] is a powerful technique that simulates the evolutionary process in nature by computer programs. Stochastic operators that recombine and reconstruct the building blocks can build adaptive systems. Any trivial change of the building block can be accumulated to lead the evolution of the system. The evolutionary granular computing system (EGCS) mentioned in this paper dedicates to using evolutionary computing technology to recombine and reconstruct adaptive granules from basic information granules. These information granules can form conceptions and knowledge at high level by the self-organizing process. And also, the EGCS is a dynamic model that can evolve through the competition and cooperation among the information granules.

2 Evolutionary Granular Computing Model

2.1 Modeled Cognition Environment

To convenient the discussion, it is assumed that the environment machine confronting is a relational database: D. There exist n records in D and every record is depicted by m attributes. Using $u_1, u_2, ., u_n$ to denote the records and $A_1, A_2, ..., A_m$ are their attributes. The element $a_j(u_i)$ on the row i and the column j represents the record u_i's value on attribute A_j.

2.2 Granule and Relevant Conceptions

According to the literature [3] we can define the formulas on database D. Any formula ϕ is a prediction such as $a_j(u_i) = v$ or $(a_1(u) = v_1) \wedge (a_2(u) = v_2)$, etc. ϕ's meaning denoted as $m(\phi)$ is a set of records satisfing ϕ. Hence, we can define the granule as a combination of formula and set.

Definition 1. *The tuple $\Phi = <\phi, m(\phi)>$ is called a granule. Here Φ is a formula on database D and $m(\phi)$ is its meaning.*

In [3], a granule is the set $m(\phi)$, but in this paper the granule definition is adopted as a tuple because the formula part of a granule should be emphasized.

Formulas can construct new formulas by the operators. Similarly, granules can compose a new granule by using $\wedge$ and $\vee$ operators.

Definition 2. *Suppose there are two granules $\Phi = <\phi, m(\phi)>$ and $\Psi = <\psi, m(\psi)>$. A new granule can be defined as:*

$$\Gamma = \Phi \wedge \Psi = <\phi \wedge \psi, m(\phi) \cap m(\psi)> \qquad (1)$$

Also, we can define "∨" operator of two granules once we adopt the operator " ∧ " and " ∩ " to " ∨ " and " ∪ " respectively. More specific concepts can be obtained by the "∧" operator, more general concepts can be obtained by "∨" operator. These two operators cannot only be used to build very complex granules but also can be simplified by using the logical computing methods.

Definition 3. *Given two granules, they are compatible if and only if their formula parts are compatible.*

So, given a collection of granules denoted as E, and an input granule g, some of elements in E are compatible with g. We call these granules as active granules to g denoted as AE.

One granule can connect other granules. Assume there are two granules: Φ, Ψ, when Φ is activated Ψ is always activated also, that means they are associated, it is denoted as $\Phi \rightarrow \Psi$.

Definition 4. *The directed graph $<V, E>$ is a granule network, if any vertex $v \in V$ is an element in E. Any directed edge $<v_1, v_2>$ represents the connection between granules: $v_1 \rightarrow v_2$.*

When the system is running the connections can be strengthened or weakened if they are activated or not. New connections between any pair of granules can be created randomly.

2.3 Evolutionary Cognitive System

The system that performs the cognitive task is called cognitive system of evolutionary granular computing model. The system contains a collection of granules: E, a granule network N. When it is running another collection of active granules: AE can be obtained. There are two running phases: learning phase and problem solving phase.

In learning phase, the system can read a record from the database at every cycle. Some granules and their connections can be activated. If the input data contains the new granules then they will be added into the E. The system can create some new granules by "∧", "∨" operators randomly with a certain possibility (P_{create}). Also the connections of two granules can be added in the granules network.

The selection mechanism is necessary to evolve the system. Every granule and the link of granules network have a fitness degree when they are running. The fitness degree is the function of right or wrong times, the length of granule and likeness of the input granule and the current granule, etc. In a word, the system can evolve at the equilibrant point of selection pressure and creativity.

As a summary, we can write these steps of the learning in one run.

1. Read the new record as $InputRecord$ from the database;
2. Loop for all elements in E, activate the granules those are compatible with $InputRecord$;
2.1 Loop for all active granules in AE, strengthen or weaken the connections between granules.
2.2 Create new connections in granule network among granules randomly.
3 Separate the formulas group $InputRecord$, add new granules into E.
4 Create new granules with possibility P_{create} to add into E.
5 If the total amount of granules in the E exceeds the threshold $MaxElementNum$, then delete several granules with the smaller fitness degree.

At last, the granules set and granules network can be viewed as the output of the system, because they reflect the cognition and learning results of it. After learning, the system can solve problems. When incomplete records input, the system can reason out the values of the unknown attributes. For example, suppose the information table has m attributes, when a record whose j-th attribute is unknown, the system can reason out the value by activating some granules and their connections with the attribute a_j. The given value of the unknown attribute is the output of solution.

3 Application

To illustrate how to apply EGCM, a specific example of application is selected as the background. In [4], the author presented a real problem of optician's decision. The decision attribute is the type of contact lenses (denoted as e) that can be divided into three classes: hard(1), soft(2), no(3). And some conditional attributes are: age (a), values are young(1), pre-presbyopic(2) and presbyopic(3),

Table 1. Granule connections and their fitness

Connection	fitness
$d = 1 \rightarrow e = 3$	47
$b = 1 \land c = 2 \land d = 2 \rightarrow e = 1$	28
$d = 1 \land a = 2 \rightarrow e = 3$	23
...	...

spectacle(b) values are myope(1) and hypermetrope(2), astigmatic(c) values are no(1) and yes(2), tear product rate (d) values are reduced(1) and normal(2)). The problem is to judge the class of decision attribute according to the conditional attributes. At first, the system can learn from an information table (See reference [4] on page 1 17).

The cognitive system obtains the granules and granules network automatically. These network connections (Table 1) are decision rules those can be used to solve problems. In problem solving phase, the system can not only search the existing decision rules but also can generate the values of empty attitudes. For example if we input a record ($a=1,b=1,c=2,d=2$) and the value of e is empty, then EGCM can output $e=1$ by activating some granules simultaneously to reason out the result which is the emergent computing result. EGCM has other applications such as clustering, classification, etc. Because of the limitation of the paper size, detail introduction is omitted

4 Conclusions

The evolutionary granular computing model can evolve to adapt to the database environment. The information granule is the basic building block to build the concepts and knowledge on higher level. The granule network, which is formed through the self-learning process by scanning the database, can emerge. And this model can be applied to problem solving, decision rules discovery, clustering, etc.

References

1. Bargiela, A.: Granular computing : an introduction(M), Boston: Kluwer Academic Publishers, (2003)
2. Eiben, Agoston E.: Introduction to evolutionary computing. Berlin: Springer-Verlag, (2003)
3. Yao, Y.Y., Granular computing: basic issues and possible solutions, Proceedings of the 5th Joint Conference on Information Sciences, Volume I, Atlantic City, New Jersey, USA, February 27 - March 3, 2000, P.P. Wang (Ed.), Association for Intelligent Machinery, 186–189.
4. Z.Pawlak: Rough Sets, Theoretical Aspects of Reasoning about Data(M), Nowowjska 15/19, Warsaw, Poland, (1990).

Application of Genetic Programming for Fine Tuning PID Controller Parameters Designed Through Ziegler-Nichols Technique

Gustavo Maia de Almeida[1], Valceres Vieira Rocha e Silva[1], Erivelton Geraldo Nepomuceno[1], and Ryuichi Yokoyama[2]

[1] Laboratório de Sistemas e Sinais, Departamento de Engenharia Elétrica, Universidade Federal de São João del-Rei, Pça. Frei Orlando, 170 36307-352 - São João del-Rei, MG, Brazil
[2] Tokyo Metropolitan University, Electrical Engineering, 1-2 Minami-Osawa Hachioji - Tokyo 193.0397 Japan

Abstract. PID optimal parameters selection have been extensively studied, in order to improve some strict performance requirements for complex systems. Ziegler-Nichols methods give estimated values for these parameters based on the system's transient response. Therefore, a fine tuning of these parameters is required to improve the system's behavior. In this work, genetic programming is used to optimize the three parameters K_p, T_i and T_d, after been tuned by Ziegler-Nichols method, to control a high-order process, a large time delay plant and a highly non-minimum phase process. The results were compared to some other tuning methods, and showed to be promising.

1 Introduction

Most industrial processes are controlled by proportional-integral-derivative (PID) controllers [2] and [13]. The popularity of PID controllers is due to their simplicity both from the design and parameter tuning points of view. To implement such a controller, three parameters, namely the proportional gain K_p, the integral time T_i, and the derivative time T_d must be determined in order to make the system operation more efficient. Ziegler and Nichols (1942) proposed a method to determine the values of K_p, T_i and T_d, based on the transient response characteristics of a process to be controlled. When the PID controller parameters are tuned by ZN, the closed loop system's response can present an overshoot up to 25%. Therefore, a fine adjustment is needed to improve the transient response. This fine adjustment can be made by various ways [3], but usually it is done by trial-and-error, what demands experience and certain time.

The approach presented here aims to minimize this problem, by applying GP to optimize the solutions obtained for the PID controllers through ZN method, in order to enhance system's performance and stability.

Since GP has shown to be a valuable and robust technique in assisting the engineers to solve complex engineering problems [1], [6], [7] and [8], we propose the use of this tool for a control tuning purpose, applying a GP algorithm to fine tuning the PID parameters, previously adjusted through the ZN tuning method.

This paper is organized as follows: Section 2 describes ZN tuning. Section 3 gives an overview of GP. Section 4 explains the methodology used. Section 5 presents the results obtained and finally, in Section 6, the conclusions reached on the use of PG applied with ZN are presented.

2   Tuning with Ziegler Nichols Method

The Ziegler-Nichols methods to determine the values of the proportional gain K_p, the integral time T_i and the derivative time T_d, are based on the characteristics of the transient response of a process to be controlled, and is implemented by taking account the experiments with the process. For both methods proposed, the aim is to achieve an overshoot below 25%, for a step input response. For the purpose of this work, the critical period method was used, once this method is suitable to solve the problem of tunning the PID parameters for the plant in question.

The critical period method consists of determining the point where the Nyquist plot of the open-loop system intersects the negative real axis. This point obtained by connecting a purely proportional controller to the system, and by increasing the controller gain until the closed-loop system reaches the stability limit, at which oscillations occur. The oscillation period is denoted by T_c and the corresponding critical gain by K_c. The ZN choice for the three PID parameters according to Table 1, T_c and K_c parameters were applied in the Equation 1.

$$PID = K_p(1 + \frac{1}{T_i s} + T_d s), \qquad (1)$$

However, this needs fine adjustments so that its transient response can present satisfactory characteristics, since the ZN tuning, often gives a high overshoot what is not desirable.

Table 1. PID controller parameters tuning by ZN method

Type of Controller	K_p	T_i	T_d
P	$0.5K_c$		
PI	$0.45K_c$	$\frac{T_c}{1.2}$	
PID	$\frac{K_c}{1.7}$	$\frac{T_c}{2}$	$\frac{T_c}{8}$

3   Genetic Programming

The GP is part of the evolutionary computation [10] and [12] that uses the concepts of the natural selection of Darwin and the genetics of Mendel in the computation environment. In such algorithms, the fittest among a group of artificial creatures can survive and constitute a new generation. In every new generation, a new offspring is created using features of the fittest individuals of the current population.

Even a simple GP can give satisfactory results in a large variety of engineering optimization problems [6], [5], [8]. GP main operators are: reproduction, crossover and mutation. Given an optimization problem, GP run iteratively using the three operators in a random way but based on the fitness function to perform evaluation.

Fitness is a numeric value assigned to each member of a population to provide a measure of the appropriateness of a solution to the problem in question. Fitness functions are generally based upon the error between the actual and predicted solutions. However, error based measures decrease for better solutions.

The overall operation of a GP can be better explained through the flowchart shown in Figure 1, where i refers to an individual in the population of size M.

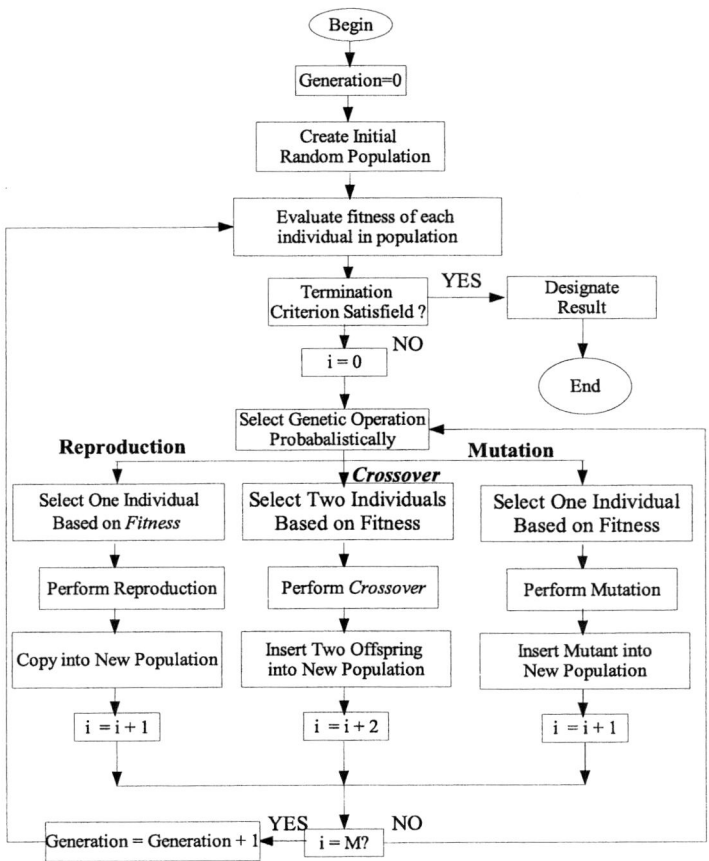

Fig. 1. Flowchart of a generic GP algorithm

The "Generation" gives the number of the current generation. The flowchart can be divided in three parts:

1. creation of an initial population of random functions and terminals;
2. iteratively perform of the following sub-steps until the termination criterion has been achieved:
   a) simulation of the algorithm for each individual in the population and assign a fitness value according to how well it behaves;
   b) creation of a new population of computer programs by,
      (i) copying existing computer programs into the new population;
      (ii) creating new computer programs by genetically recombining randomly chosen parts of two existing programs;
      (iii) creating a new computer program introducing random changes. This operation is applied to the chosen computer program(s) with a probability based on their fitness in the population structure;
3. the best computer program that appeared in any generation, is designated as the result of genetic programming simulation. This result may be a solution (or an approximate solution) to the problem.

4 Genetic Programming and Ziegler-Nichols for PID Controller Design

The GP was applied to fine adjust the three parameters of a PID controller, tuned through ZN, for the closed-loop system shown in Figure 2, where "Plant" is a system to be controlled and "Controller", is a PID strategy controller, described by the transfer function in Equation (1).

Firstly, ZN is applied for determining the three parameters of the controllers. After, the values K_p, T_i and T_d determined by ZN will constitute the set of terminals, having its values varying from 0 to 10 times the values previously determined. In this way, one of the biggest problem of evolutionary computation, of determining the search interval is decided. Whereas, if ZN was not used as initial condition to generate the initial population for the PG, the simulation could have been much higher.

Thus GP algorithm starts by creating a population of 500 individuals that will be evolved for 30 generations, randomly combining elements from the problem specific function sets and terminal sets. Each individual program (controllers) of the initial population is then assessed for its fitness. This is usually

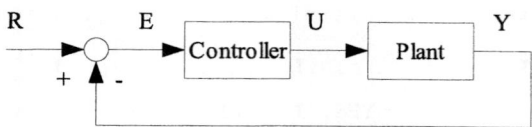

Fig. 2. Closed-loop system

accomplished by simulating each one of them in a set of predefined input data called fitness cases, and by assigning a numerical fitness value for each individual according to some numerical combination.

Genetic operations, including reproduction, crossover, and mutation, are then performed based on each individual fitness value. Individuals are randomly selected to undergo the genetic operations. The selection function is biased towards the highly fit programs and the objectives and constraints to be optimized for these functions are:

- steady-state error (e_{ss}) less than 1%;
- overshoot (M_p) not exceeding 5%;
- the smallest settling time t_s.

The transfer functions used to evaluate the performance of GP are a high-order process $G_1(s)$, a process with a larger time delay $G_2(s)$, and a highly non-minimum-phase process $G_3(s)$. These systems are shown respectively by Equations (2)-(4). GP applied together with ZN tuning was compared to some other tuning methods based on the step responses: the Magnitude Optimum Multiple Integrations (MOMI)[11], the Ziegler Nichols (ZN) [14], Chien-Hrones-Reswick (CHR) [4] and Refined Ziegler Nichols (RZN) [3].

$$G_1(s) = \frac{1}{(1+s)^8} \quad (2)$$

$$G_2(s) = \frac{e^{-5s}}{(1+s)^2} \quad (3)$$

$$G_3(s) = \frac{(1-10s)}{(1+s)^3} \quad (4)$$

The parameters K_p, T_i and T_d used for tuning the controller PID through MOMI, ZN, CHR, RZN have been shown in Vrancic et al., (1998).

5 Results

5.1 Case 1 - High-Order Process

The PID parameters determined by the five different tuning methods, the constraints and objective values are given in Table 2.

The closed-loop step responses obtained for the four PID tuning methods for the system G_1 are shown in Fig. 3. The settling time for the GP tuning method is shorter than the achieved for the three other schemes, and the overshoot is smaller either. In this case, for the ZN tuning method, the system is unstable.

5.2 Case 2 - Large Time Delay Plant

The PID parameters determined by the five different tuning methods, the constraints and objectives values are given in Table 3.

Table 2. PID parameters, constraints and objective values obtained simulating $G_1(s)$

Parameters and variables	GP	MOMI	ZN	RZN	CHR
K_p	0.68	0.75	2.34	0.35	1.48
T_i	4.63	4.80	10.77	4.53	9.06
T_d	1.47	1.37	1.72	1.14	2.02
β	-	-	-	0.88	-
$e_{ss}(\%)$	0.00	0.00	-	0.00	0.00
$M_p(\%)$	4.40	8.17	-	0.00	48.54
$t_s(s)$	10.02	16.74	-	30.04	23.22

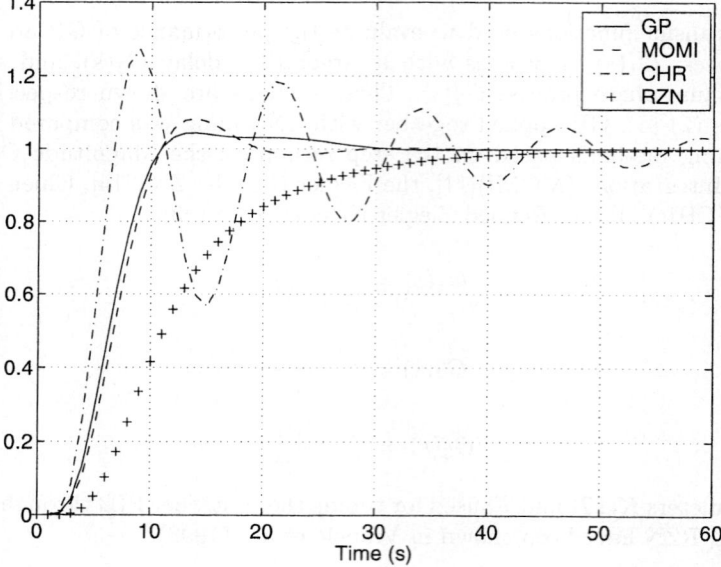

Fig. 3. Step responses of the closed-loop system for $G_1(s)$

Table 3. PID parameters, constraints and objective values obtained simulating $G_2(s)$

Parameters and variables	GP	MOMI	ZN	RZN	CHR
K_p	0.49	0.52	0.77	0.15	0.49
T_i	3.56	3.58	13.20	2.02	3.67
T_d	0.99	1.05	2.11	0.38	2.48
β	-	-	-	2.10	-
$e_{ss}(\%)$	0.00	0.00	0.004	0.00	0.00
$M_p(\%)$	3.41	6.60	7.60	0.00	4.35
$T_s(s)$	9.90	15.21	59.11	23.85	16.31

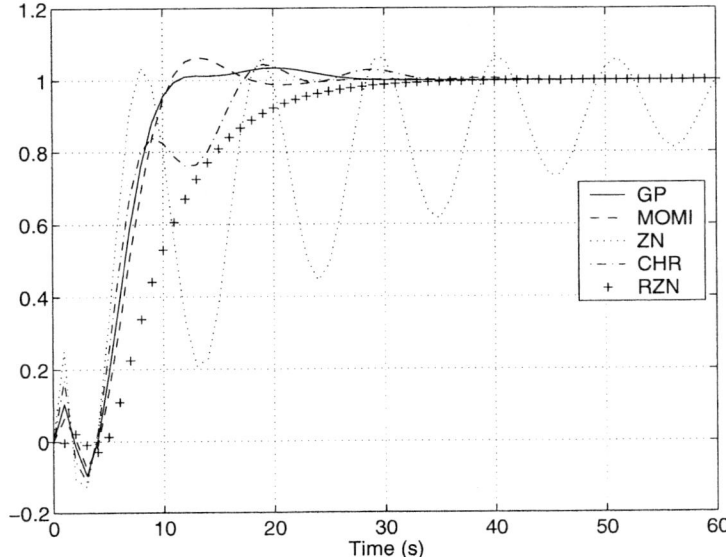

Fig. 4. Step responses of the closed-loop system for $G_2(s)$

The closed-loop step responses obtained for the five PID tuning methods for the system G_2 are shown in Fig. 4. The responses for the GP controller and the MOMI controller are almost indistinguishable, but superior than for the ZN, RZN, and CHR regulators. The system responses for the GP and MOMI controllers exhibits almost no overshoot.

5.3 Case 3 - A Highly Non-minimum-phase Process

The PID parameters determined by the five different tuning methods, the constraints and objective values are given in Table 4.

The closed-loop step responses obtained for the five PID tuning methods for the system G_3 are shown in Fig. 5. It can be observed that the response for the

Table 4. PID parameters, constraints and objective values obtained simulating $G_3(s)$

Parameters and variables	GP	MOMI	ZN	RZN	CHR
K_p	0.14	0.13	0.26	0.15	0.20
T_i	2.31	2.62	9.36	1.91	1.36
T_d	0.006	0.71	2.34	0.37	2.20
β	-	-	-	1.98	-
$e_{ss}(\%)$	0.00	0.00	-	0.01	-
$M_p(\%)$	2.32	0.00	-	118.34	-
$T_s(s)$	24.65	38.14	-	43.73	-

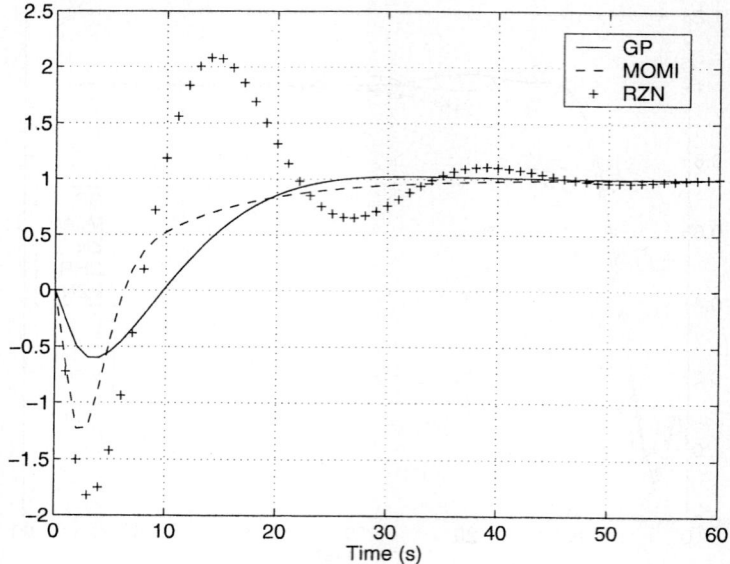

Fig. 5. Step responses of the closed-loop system for $G_3(s)$

MOMI controller has the smallest overshoot but for the GP controller the rise time and settling time are smaller than for the others. The system is unstable for the ZN and CHR tuning methods.

6 Discussion and Conclusion

The individuals (controllers) of the first generation had very poor fitness, which presented a high overshoot, a high settling time and a small steady-state error. As the simulation carried out, and the genetic operations being performed, the parameters started to have fitness values converged around the ideal, what can be seen in Fig. 6, where the best individuals of the first generations do not present a good result, but with elapsing of the generations, could be noticed, they approach to an optimal response. During the simulation, good individuals were preserved, but many of them were lost. The GP algorithm undertook some modifications such that, less good individuals could be rejected. Then, the GP algorithm started to give better individuals in elapsing of the generations until the best individual, with good characteristics is achieved, and for which, fitness is in accordance with the presented in Section 4.

This work presented a novel optimal-tuning technique for the classical PID controllers based on the GP applied to ZN fine tuning. The design, implementation and testing of this approach were discussed and compared with traditional tuning methods. An overview of genetic programming has been offered. Three cases were studied: a high-order process, a process with a larger time delay, and a highly non-minimum-phase process.

GP applied to ZN fine tuning platform revealed to be a simple and efficient tool to controller parameters tuning, showing a great purpose to minimize the settling time of the system with a minimum overshoot, and also with null steady state error. This performance was shown through the simulation of three examples, for five different PID tuning methods. The approach presented here performed better than ZN, RZN, CHR, and MOMI. Comparing the systems responses to a unity step input, the GP method generally gives very small overshoot, little oscillations, and better or comparable settling time, even for the large plant, what suggests to be viable the application of GP to controller parameters tuning.

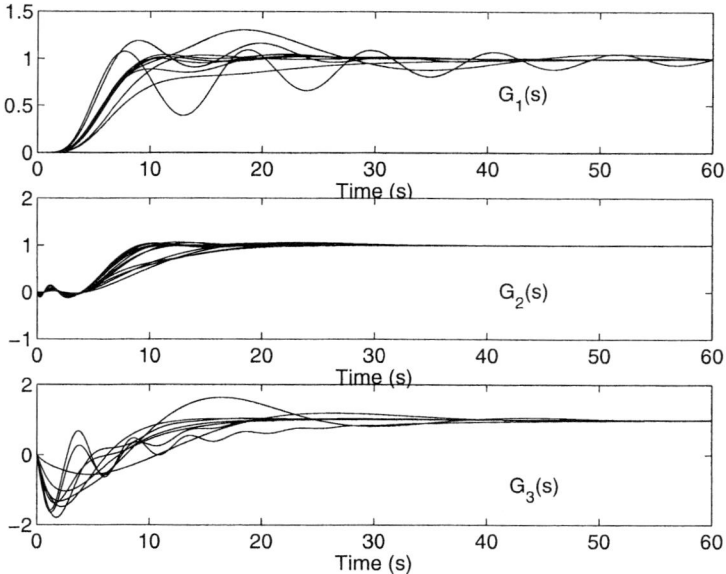

Fig. 6. The best individual of each generation

GP combined with ZN method demonstrated to have an important characteristic of starting the parameters optimization search in a pre-defined interval. Therefore, minimizing the evolutionary computation problem of determining the accurate search interval, which choice has actually been made by trial and error, increasing the computational time of these algorithms simulations.

It is important to stand out also that in systems where ZN is not applied, only GP can be used. However, the search interval must be defined by attempt and error, what will demand higher computation time to reach satisfactory results. But GP can still be applied to any type of system.

References

1. Almeida, G. M., Silva, V. V. R., Nepomuceno, E. G.: Programação Genética em Matlab, Uma aplicação na aproximação de funções matemáticas. Anais do Congresso Brasileiro de Automática. (2004) (in portuguese)
2. Astrom, K. J., Hagglund, T.: PID Controllers: Theory, Design, and Tuning. Instruments Society of America. **2 edn** (1995)
3. Astrom, K. J., Hagglund, T., Hang, C. C., Ho, W. K.: Automatic tuning and adaptation for PID controller - a survey. Control Engineering Practice **4** (1993) 699–714
4. Chien, Hrones, Reswick: On the automatic tuning of generalized passive systems. Transactions ASME **74** (1952) 175–185
5. Grosman, B., Hagglund, Lewin, D. R.: Automated nonlinear model predictive control using genetic programming. Computers and Chemical Engineering **26** (2002) 631–640
6. Hinchliffe, M. P., Willis, M. J.: Dynamic systems modelling using genetic programming. Computers and Chemical Engineering **27** (2003) 1841–1854
7. Koza, J. R.: Genetic Programming: On the Programming of Computers by Natural Selection. MIT Press, Cambridge, MA (1992)
8. Koza,J. R., Bennett III, F.H., Andre, D., Keane, M. A.: A Synthesis of topology and sizing of analog electrical circuits by means of genetic programming. Computer Methods in Applied Mechanics and Engineering **186** (2000) 459–482
9. Luyben, W. L.: Process modelling simulation and control for chemical engineers . Mc Graw Hill **2 edn** (1990)
10. Tan, K.C., Lim, M.H., Yao, X., Wang L.P. (Eds.): Recent Advances in Simulated Evolution And Learning. World Scientific, Singapore (2004)
11. Vrancic, D., Peng, Y., Strmenik, S.: A new PID controller tuning method based on multiple integrations. Control Engineering Practice **7** (1998) 623–633
12. Yao, X.: Evolutionary Computation: Theory and Applications. World Scientific, Singapore (1999)
13. Yu, C. C.: Auto-tuning of PID Controllers. Berlin: Springer **7 edn** (1999)
14. Ziegler, J. G., Nichols, N. B.: Optimum settings for automatic controllers. Transactions ASME **62** (1942) 759–768

Applying Genetic Programming to Evolve Learned Rules for Network Anomaly Detection

Chuanhuan Yin, Shengfeng Tian, Houkuan Huang, and Jun He

School of Computer and Information Technology,
Beijing Jiaotong University, Beijing, 100044, China
{chhyin, sftian, hkhuang}@center.njtu.edu.cn,
j.he@cs.bham.ac.uk

Abstract. The DARPA/MIT Lincoln Laboratory off-line intrusion detection evaluation data set is the most widely used public benchmark for testing intrusion detection systems. But the presence of simulation artifacts attributes would cause many attacks in this dataset to be easily detected. In order to eliminate their influence on intrusion detection, we simply omit these attributes in the processes of both training and testing. We also present a GP-based rule learning approach for detecting attacks on network. GP is used to evolve new rules from the initial learned rules through genetic operations. Our results show that GP-based rule learning approach outperforms the original rule learning algorithm, detecting 84 of 148 attacks at 100 false alarms despite the absence of several simulation artifacts attributes.

1 Introduction

Intrusion detection is an important facet of computer security. It has been extensively investigated since the report written by Anderson [1]. An intrusion detection system (IDS) can detect hostile attacks by monitoring network traffic, computer system sources, audit records, or the access of the file system. There are two models in intrusion detection context, one of which is misuse detection while the other is anomaly detection. The former technique aims to develop models of known attacks, which can be detected through these models. The latter intends to model normal behaviors of systems or users, and any deviation from the normal behaviors is regarded as an intrusion. Due to their nature, misuse detection has low false alarms but its major limitation is that it can't detect novel or unknown attacks until the signatures of attacks are appended to the intrusion detection system, on the contrary, anomaly detection has the advantage of detecting novel or unknown attacks which can't be detected by misuse detection but it has the potential to generate too many false alarms.

With the widespread use of the Internet, intrusion detection systems have become focused on attacks to the network itself. Network intrusion detection system has been developed to detect these network attacks, which can't be detected by host intrusion detection system, by means of examining network traffic. There are a number of network intrusion detection systems using misuse detection or anomaly detection.

Because the models of normal traffic are hard to be obtained, network intrusion detection systems like SNORT [2] typically use misuse detection, matching characteristics of network traffic to the characteristics of known attacks in their database. This method detects known attacks in a very low false alarms rate while omits novel or unknown attacks against intrusion detection systems' database. An alternative approach is anomaly detection, which models normal traffic and regards any deviation from this model as suspicious. But due to its high false alarms rate, anomaly detection hasn't been applied in most commercial intrusion detection systems, leading to the research on network anomaly detection.

This paper focuses on rule learning for network anomaly detection system. We evolve rules learned from the training traffic by using Genetic Programming (GP) [3], and then we use the evolved rules to differentiate attacks traffic from normal traffic.

We present an algorithm called LERAD-GP (LEarning Rules for Anomaly Detection based Genetic Programming) to generate and evolve rules for detecting attacks. LERAD-GP is a variation of LERAD, which has been presented by Mahoney et al. to find the relation of the attributes in network connections [4]. In the process of experimenting, we found that LERAD-GP outperforms LERAD in detecting attacks from modified data set, in which the simulation artifacts had been removed. The presence of simulation artifacts would lead to overoptimistic evaluation of network anomaly detection systems [5]. At the same time, we introduce a simple method to remove simulated artifacts, and validate the effectivity of this remove approach.

The rest of the paper is organized as follows. Section 2 describes an overview of related work in network anomaly detection and Genetic Programming. Section 3 describes the GP algorithm. Section 4 discusses how to use GP to evolve learned rules. Section 5 presents the evaluation of the evolved rules using test dataset and discusses the experimental results. Section 6 concludes the paper.

2 Related Work

Network anomaly detectors look for unusual network traffic by taking some attributes of traffic into account. Some information in network packets such as IP addresses and port numbers can be used for modeling network normal traffic. ADAM (Audit Data and Mining) monitors port numbers, IP addresses and subnets, and TCP state to build normal traffic models which can be used to detect suspicious connections [6]. Like ADAM, SPADE (Statistical Packet Anomaly Detection Engine) monitors addresses and ports to achieve detection [7]. Nevertheless, these few attributes of traffic are far from enough to model network traffic. There are more network attributes should be used to distinguish between hostile and benign traffic.

To use more features of traffic, Mahoney presented several methods in his paper [8]. They are PHAD, ALAD, LERAD, and NETAD [4, 9, and 10]. PHAD (Packet Header Anomaly Detector) [9] is a system that learns the normal range of values for 33 fields of the Ethernet, IP, TCP, UDP, and ICMP protocols. It is implemented by using simple nonstationary models that estimate probabilities based on the time since the last event rather than the average rate of events which is often applied to estimate probabilities. Different from PHAD, ALAD (Application Layer Anomaly Detection) [9] assigns a score to an incoming server TCP connection. It is configured to detect network attacks against the fixed victim, and it distinguishes server ports (0-1023) from client ports (1024-65535). After a testing of a number of attributes and their combinations, Mahoney et al. select five because of their best performance. They are P(source IP address | destination IP address), P(source IP address | destination IP address, destination TCP port), P(destination IP address, destination TCP port), P(TCP flags | destination TCP port), and P(keyword | destination TCP port). During the training stage, these probabilities are estimated and then used to obtain the anomaly score of connections in detecting. As with PHAD, the anomaly score is relevant to the time since the last event. LERAD (LEarning Rules for Anomaly Detection) [4] is a system that learns rules for finding rare events in nominal time-series data with long range dependencies. It constitutes an improvement of the two previous methods by using a rule learning algorithm. LERAD is able to learn important relationships between attributes of benign traffic, and use them to detect hostile traffic. NETAD (NEtwork Traffic Anomaly Detector) [10] models the most common protocols (IP, TCP, Telnet, FTP, SMTP, and HTTP) at the packet level to flag events that have not been observed for a long time. It is based on the consideration of fist 48 bytes of the packet, each of which is treated as an attribute with 256 possible values. The last algorithm can detect anomaly values ever seen in training phase while the others regard values seen in training phase as normal.

One of the major contributions of Mahoney et al. is that they presented a time-based model appropriate for bursty traffic with long range dependencies [8]. There had long been assumed that network traffic could be modeled by a Poisson process, in which events are independent of each other. Therefore, some anomaly detectors like ADAM and SPADE regard the average rate of events x in training as the probability of x. However, this may be inappropriate in this context. Paxson et al. showed that many network processes are self-similar or fractal [11]. In order to depict the features of network traffic, Mahoney et al. proposed a time-based model. Furthermore, Mahoney et al. presented a continuous model to monitor previously seen values of attributes. Using these two models, Mahoney et al. showed that LERAD and NETAD performed quite well on the dataset of DARPA 1999 [12]. They used the inside sniffer traffic from week 3 of the DARPA 1999 valuation dataset for training dataset, and regarded week 4 and 5 as testing dataset. Table 1 shows their results at 100 false alarms.

Table 1. The numbers of detected attacks of LERAD and NETAD at 100 false alarms

Approach	Detections
LERAD	117/177
NETAD	132/177

Mahoney et al. found the presence of simulation artifacts by integrating real network traffic into DARPA 1999 dataset. They deem that the simulation artifacts would lead to overoptimistic evaluation of network anomaly detection systems. In order to eliminate the impact of simulation artifacts of original network traffic dataset, Mahoney et al. collected a real inside traffic dataset which they denoted as FIT dataset. After preprocessing FIT, they mixed the DARPA 99 dataset with FIT dataset.

After that, they modified their detection algorithms to detect attacks of mixed dataset. Table 2 shows their detection results of Probe, DoS (denial of service), and R2L (remote to local) attacks on mixed dataset.

Table 2. Probe, DoS, and R2L attacks detected at 100 false alarms on mixed dataset

Approach	Detections
PHAD	24/148
ALAD	13/148
LERAD	30/148
NETAD	42/148

From their depiction, the performance of their methods on mixed dataset is far worse than that on DARPA 1999 dataset. But the appropriate explanation hadn't been presented. After analyzing their works on detection, we deem that there are several reasons for the worse performance of these four methods on merged dataset.

1. FIT was not free of attacks. Mahoney et al. examined the traffic manually and tested it using SNORT [3], and they found that at least four attacks existed in the FIT dataset. Moreover, it is sure that there are more attacks not found by them. Therefore, their training was based on a dataset contained a few unknown or known attacks. The noisy attacks would influence the training phase, resulting in a deviation from normal model which would be obtained from attack free training dataset. The deviated model led to a decrease in the attacks detection rates at the same false alarms rate.

2. The number of packets in mixed dataset was about double of that in DARPA 1999 dataset. Both traffics will generate false alarms, resulting in a higher error rate than either traffic source by itself. However, the evaluation criterion is the same as that of original traffic, resulting in the lower detection rates.

3. Mahoney et al. claimed that NETAD can model previously seen values, and that this detector can be used for training dataset which contains some attacks. However, from the above results we know that the model of NETAD isn't appropriate for this environment. All of the four detectors performed poorly if the training dataset contains some attacks.

GP has been used to solve many problems since it was developed by Koza [3]. It is also widely used in intrusion detection. Crosbie et al. employed a combination of GP and agent technique to detect anomalous behaviors in a system [13]. They use GP to evolve autonomous agents for detecting potentially intrusive behaviors. But communication among these autonomous agents is still an issue. Su et al. used GP to generate the normal activity profile by modeling system call sequences [14]. If the tested sequences deviate from the normal profile, their system denotes the process as intrusion. Lu et al. proposed a rule evolution approach based on GP to evolve initial rules which were selected based on background knowledge from known attacks [15]. After that, they used initial and evolved rules to detect known or novel attacks on a network. The results showed that the rules evolved based on knowledge of known attacks could detect some novel attacks. But the initial rules they used must be manually specified by domain experts.

3 Overview of GP

3.1 GP

GP is a further extension of Genetic Algorithm (GA) [16, 17]. In contrast to GA, GP typically operates on a population of parse trees which usually represent computer programs. A parse tree is composed of internal nodes and leaf nodes. The internal nodes are called primitive functions while the leaf nodes are called terminals. The terminals can be regarded as the inputs to the program being induced. There are independent variables and the set of constants in the terminals. The primitive functions can form more complex function calls by combining the terminals or simpler function calls. Solving a problem is a search through all the possible combinations of symbolic expressions defined by the programmer.

3.2 GP Operators

GP can be used to evolve rules which are of the form "if antecedents then consequent". In rule evolving, three genetic operators which are called crossover, mutation, and dropping condition can be used [18].

Crossover is a sexual operation that produces two children from two parents. A part of one parent is selected and replaced by another part of the other parent. Mutation is an asexual operation. A part in the parental rule is selected and replaced by a randomly generated part.

Dropping condition can be used to evolve new rules. It selects randomly one condition, and then turns it into "any", resulting in a generalized rule. This operator is a new genetic operator, which is proposed to evolve new rules [18]. For example, the rule

if condition 1 and condition 2 then consequence.
can be changed to
if condition 1 and any then consequence.

3.3 Fitness Function

A fitness function is needed to evaluate evolved rules. In this context, we use the fitness function based on the support-confidence framework and the number of antecedents. Support measures the coverage of a rule while confidence factor (cf) represents the rule accuracy. If a rule has the format of *"if A then B"*, its confidence factor and support are defined as follows:

$$cf = |A \text{ and } B| / |A|; \; support = |A \text{ and } B|/N, \qquad (1)$$

where $|A|$ is the number of records that only satisfy antecedent A, $|B|$ is the number of records that satisfy consequent B, $|A \text{ and } B|$ is the number of records that satisfy both antecedent A and consequent B, and N is the size of training dataset.

As described in [18], some rules may have high accuracy but the rules may be formed by chance and based on a few training examples. This kind of rules does not have enough support. To avoid the waste of evolving those rules of low support, fitness function is defined as:

$$fitness = \begin{cases} support & \text{if } support < min\_support \\ w_1 \times support + w_2 \times cf & \text{otherwise} \end{cases}, \qquad (2)$$

where *min_support* is a minimum threshold of *support*, the weights w_1 and w_2 are user-defined to control the balance between the confidence and the support in searching.

Finally, we use the modified fitness as follows:

$$modified\_fitness = fitness/r, \qquad (3)$$

where r is the number of antecedents in the rule. The idea behind the division by r is that the more antecedents in a rule, the easier the rule will be removed in the validation stage of the algorithm described in next section.

4 Using GP to Generate New Rules

We use a rule learning method which is similar with LERAD to generate the initial rule set. LERAD learns conditional rules over nominal attributes. After evolving rules we obtain a rule set, which can be used to evaluate connections from test dataset and then to detect malicious connections.

The antecedent of a rule is a conjunction of equalities, and the consequent is a set of allowed values, e.g. *if port = 80* and *word3 = HTTP/1.0 then word1 =GET or POST*. Allowed values means that it is observed in at least one training instance satisfying the antecedent. During testing, if an instance satisfies the antecedent but the consequent isn't one of the allowed values, then an anomaly score of *ts/n* is calculated, where t is the time since the last anomaly by this rule, s is the number of training instances satisfying the antecedent, and n is the number of allowed values. In fact, the reciprocal of the anomaly function is the product of two probabilities, *1/t* and *n/s*. Therefore, this anomaly score can be used to identify rare events: those which have not occurred for a long time (large t) and where the average rate of "anomalies" in training is low (small *n/s*). For all violated rules, a total anomaly score is summed. If the summed score exceeds a threshold, an alarm is generated.

The LERAD based GP algorithm is proposed as follows:

1. Rule generation. Randomly select M pairs of training instances from a subset S which is also randomly sampled from the training dataset. Then use these M pairs of instances to generate initial rule set R, in which each rule satisfies both instances with *s/n* = 2/1. Each pair of instances generate up to L rules.

2. Rule evolving. Evolve rules from R using crossover and dropping condition operators. The mutation operator isn't used because the mutated rules may become illegal, e.g. *if port = 80 then word1 = GET*, may mutated to: *if port = HTTP/1.0 then word1 = GET*.

3. Testing coverage. Discard rules from R to find a minimal subset of rules, which cover all instance values in S, favoring rules with higher *modified-fitness* over S.

4. Training. Make sure each of the consequent values of each rule in R is observed at least once when the antecedent is satisfied. If the predefined termination criterion is satisfied, then turn to step 5, otherwise to step 2.

5. Validation. In the whole training dataset, if an instance satisfies the antecedent of a rule but the consequent isn't one of its allowed values, then remove this rule. The reason for rule removing is because the invalidation of this rule has been verified via the unsatisfied instance.

6. Testing. For each instance in testing, assign an anomaly score of $\sum ts/n$ for the violations. The higher score means more suspicious of attacks.

5 Experiments and Results

We test our method using the 1999 DARPA/Lincoln Laboratory intrusion detection evaluation data set, a widely used benchmark using synthetic network traffic [12]. Only the inbound client traffic is used for our experiments because the targets of most R2L attacks, as well as probes and DoS attacks are various servers, leading to the abnormality in the inbound traffic. Our method was trained on week 3 and extra week 3, which contains no attacks, and tested on weeks 4 and 5.

Firstly we reassemble TCP connections from traffic packets. LERAD used 23 attributes of reassembled TCP connection to generate rules and detect suspicious connections. But according to the analysis of Mahoney et al. [5], there are some suspected artifacts attributes in the DARPA 1999 dataset, including client source IP address, TTL, TCP window size, and TCP options. For the purpose of removing artifacts attributes, we omit the above four attributes from reassembled TCP connections, resulting in 16 attributes being remained. The remained 16 attributes are date, time, last two bytes of the destination IP address, source port, destination port, log base 2 of the duration time, log base 2 of the length, and first 8 words of the payload. Because simulation artifacts would help intrusion detectors to detect attacks, some attacks become hardly detected after removing of artifacts attributes. So the detection rate of anomaly detector will be inevitable decreased if we want to keep the same false alarms as before. Nevertheless, the influence of artifacts attributes can be eliminated using this simple removal approach.

We set the sample size $|S| = 200$ and draw $M = 1000$ sample pairs, generating up to $L = 4$ for each rule. As to GP, The rates of crossover and dropping condition operations are 0.6, 0.001 respectively for each rule.

In our experiments, attack is counted as detected if it is "in-spec" (the attack are supposed to be detected) and the detector correctly identifies the IP address of the victim or attacker and the time of any portion of the attack interval within 60 seconds. Out of spec detections are ignored. Duplicate detections of the same attack are counted only once, but every false alarm is counted. Our anomaly detector is designed to detect 148 in-spec attacks, including probe, DoS, and R2L because there is evidence for these attacks in the inside sniffer traffic according to the truth labels.

We also test NETAD and LERAD in the dataset in which four suspected artifacts attributes are omitted. Moreover, for the sake of comparison, we excerpt the results of [7], in which NETAD and LERAD tested on the mixed dataset. Just the same as Mahoney et al., We refer to them as NETAD-C and LERAD-C respectively. Therefore, we compare the performance of LERAD-GP with that of the other two algorithms, which are tested in both modified DARPA 1999 and the mixed dataset in [4]. The results are as follows.

Table 3. Probes, DoS, and R2L attacks detected by LERAD, NETAD, and LERAD-GP at 100 false alarms

Category	Total	LERAD-C	NETAD-C	LERAD-GP	LERAD	NETAD
Probe	34	7(21%)	12(35%)	23(68%)	21(62%)	8(23%)
DoS	60	5(8%)	11(18%)	34(57%)	26(43%)	15(25%)
R2L	54	18(33%)	18(33%)	27(50%)	19(35%)	11(20%)
Total	**148**	**30(17%)**	**41(28%)**	**84(57%)**	**66(45%)**	**34(23%)**

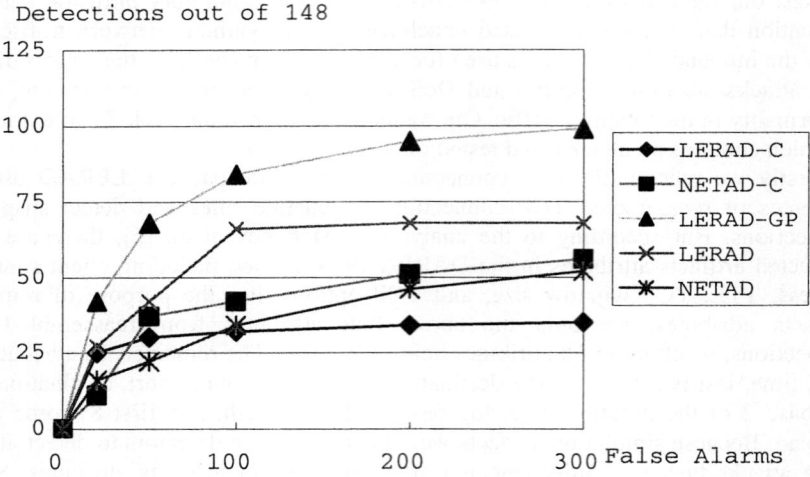

Fig. 1. Probe, DoS, and R2L attacks detected by LERAD, NETAD, and LERAD-GP as 0 to 300 false alarms (*0 to 30 per day*)

6 Conclusion

In this paper, we have presented and evaluated a GP-based rule learning approach for detecting attacks on network. We also introduced a simple removal approach to simulated artifacts attributes, which are regarded as the reason for overoptimistic evaluation of network anomaly detectors. The effectivity of this simple removal has been validated through the experiments conducted in this paper. We can see that LERAD-GP outperforms the original LERAD algorithm. The results show that GP can optimize rules by crossover and dropping condition operations for anomaly detecting.

However, there are some limitations in LERAD-GP. One is that the algorithm needs two passes during training, resulting in the inefficiency of detector. Another is that it requires training dataset which is attack-free whereas explicit training and testing data would not be available in a real setting. How to model network traffic on the training dataset which is mixed with attacks is still an open issue.

Acknowledgements

This paper is supported by the National Natural Science Foundation of China (No. 60442002, No. 60443003) and the Science and Technology Foundation of Beijing Jiaotong University (No. 2004SM010).

References

1. Anderson, J.P.: Computer Security Threat Monitoring and Surveillance. Technical Report, Fort Washington, PA (1980)
2. Roesch, M.: Snort: Lightweight intrusion detection for networks. In: Proc. of USENIX Large Installation System Administration Conference (1999)
3. Koza, J.R.: Genetic Programming. MIT Press (1992)
4. Mahoney, M.V., Chan, P.K.: Learning Rules for Anomaly Detection of Hostile Network Traffic. In: Proc. of International Conference on Data Mining (2003)
5. Mahoney, M.V., Chan, P.K.: An Analysis of the 1999 DARPA/Lincoln Laboratory Evaluation Data for Network Anomaly Detection. In: Proc. of International Symposium on Recent Advances in Intrusion Detection (2003) 220-237
6. Barbara, D., Couto, J., Jajodia, S., Popyack, L., Wu, N.: ADAM: Detecting Intrusions by Data Mining. In: Proc. of IEEE Workshop on Information Assurance and Security (2001) 11-16
7. Hoagland, J.: SPADE, http://www.silicondefense.com/software/spice/ (2000)
8. Mahoney, M.V.: A Machine Learning Approach to Detecting Attacks by Identify-ing Anomalies in Network Traffic. Ph.D. dissertation, Florida Institute of Technology (2003)
9. Mahoney, M.V., Chan, P.K.: Learning Non-stationary Models of Normal Network Traffic for Detecting Novel Attacks. In: Proc. of ACM Special Interest Group on Knowledge Discovery in Data and Data Mining (2002) 376-385
10. Mahoney, M.V.: Network Traffic Anomaly Detection Based on Packet Bytes. In: Proc. of ACM Symposium on Applied Computing (2003)
11. Paxson, V., Floyd, S.: Wide area traffic: the failure of Poisson modeling. IEEE/ACM Transactions on Networking 3 (1995) 226 – 244
12. Lippmann, R., Haines, J.W., Fried, D.J., Korba, J., Das, K.: The 1999 DARPA Off-Line Intrusion Detection Evaluation. Computer Networks 34 (2000) 579-595
13. Crosbie, M., Spafford, G.: Applying Genetic Programming to Intrusion Detection. In: Proc. of AAAI Fall Symposium on Genetic Programming (1995)
14. Su, P.R., Li, D.Q., Feng, D.G.: A Host-Based Anomaly Intrusion Detection Model Based on Genetic Programming. Chinese Journal of Software 14 (2003) 1120-1126
15. Lu, W., Traore, I.: Detecting New Forms of Network Intrusion Using Genetic Programming. Computational Intelligence 20 (2004)
16. Yao, X.: Evolutionary Computation: Theory and Applications. World Scientific, Singapore (1999)
17. Tan, K.C., Lim, M.H., Yao, X., Wang L.P. (Eds.): Recent Advances in Simulated Evolution and Learning. World Scientific, Singapore (2004)
18. Wong, M.L., Leung, K.S.: Data Mining Using Grammar based Genetic Program-ming and Applications. Kluwer Academic Publishers (2000)

A Pattern Combination Based Approach to Two-Dimensional Cutting Stock Problem

Jinming Wan, Yadong Wu, and Hongwei Dai

Shanghai Jiao Tong University, Shanghai, China
{wjm, ydwu, dhwsjtu}@sjtu.edu.cn

Abstract. A new approach for dealing with a huge number of cutting pattern combinations encountered in two-dimensional Cutting Stock Problem (CSP) is described. Firstly, cutting patterns are produced according to a novel cutting method LF(Lease Fit) algorithm which can effectively cuts a sequence of small rectangular pieces from a big stock, heuristically maximizing the stock's utilization ratio. Then Genetic Algorithm (GA) is applied to search for a near optimal solution which consists of many patterns namely a pattern combination. To evaluate the combination's fitness, LP (Linear Programming) algorithm is used in polynomial time without bringing about much error. The performance and efficiency are justified by numerical experiments.

1 Introduction

The two-dimensional non-guillotine cutting stock problem arises in many industry applications such as textile, leather, paper, wood and cloth, etc. It is considered as cutting a number of small rectangular pieces from many pieces of large rectangle stocks of the same width and length. The objective is to minimize the overall cost, such as total number of the stocks to be cut from.

Variant CSP are all NP-Complete problems. Many researchers have formulated them as a kind of Integer Programming problems [1,2]. As for the two-dimensional Cutting Stock Problem, methods mentioned in literatures [3,4] mainly focus on how to cut an infinite long stock to smaller rectangles. Thus the resulted cutting pattern is usually very complex for large scale problem and leads to poor production efficiency. When we consider applying a few cutting patterns to many finite long stocks, from optimization point, it wastes no less than cutting small pieces from an infinite long stock, because the latter mechanism can pack them more tightly. But the former case is usually encountered in real industry application for efficiency consideration. The essential factor that brings complexity to the search process is the huge number of patterns and how to combine them to form a good solution. In [5], how to generate all feasible patterns is described in detail.

The paper is organized as follows. A formal definition of two-dimensional non-guillotine cutting problem is given in the next section. This is followed by a detailed description of all algorithm elements including LF algorithm, pattern combination and GA procedure. Then experimental results show the performance and efficiency of the algorithm. Finally, concluding remarks are summarized.

2 Problem Formulation

There are infinite many rectangular stocks S with the same width W and length L, p kinds of small pieces $R = \{(n_1, w_1, l_1), (n_2, w_2, l_2), ..., (n_p, w_p, l_p)\}$ with each kind's number specified by $n_i (1 \le i \le p)$ and width specified by $w_i (w_i \le W)$ and length specified by $l_i (l_i \le L)$. A cutting pattern P defines how to cut a stock to some small pieces and thus can result in a sequence $(t_1, t_2, ..., t_p)$, where t_i denotes the number of i th kind small pieces generated. The final result would be a cutting pattern combination $C = \{(m_1, P_1), ..., (m_q, P_q)\}$, where $m_i (1 \le i \le q)$ denotes the i th pattern need be applied m_i times. The solution minimizes the cost $\sum_{i=1}^{q} m_i$ that is actually the total number of stocks to be cut from.

3 Approach

3.1 LF Algorithm

For convenience of representing a cutting pattern, a sequence of small piece's kind sequence $[k_1, k_2, ..., k_n](1 \le k_i \le p, 1 \le i \le n)$ is usually adopted. k_i denotes the i th piece generated by this pattern is of k_i th kind. For different pattern, n is randomly set. Each kind is selected according to the probability $n_i / \sum_{j=1}^{p} n_j$. The bigger length of width and length is assigned for each kind as its priority and then the sequence is sorted in priority non-increasing order. It is to accommodate bigger pieces first and then fill smaller ones to small fragments in such cutting order.

All empty rectangles in the stock should be recorded in the cutting process, which are largest possible empty rectangular areas in the stock and may be overlapped. For each piece in the sequence to be cut, the smallest one from those big enough empty

Table 1. Empty areas list

Step	Piece to be cut	Big enough empty areas	Selected area to be cut	Left empty areas
1	(15*5)	(20*15)	(20*15)	(20*10) (5*15)
2	(10*5)	(20*10) (5*15)	(5*15)	(15*10) (20*5)
3	(10*5)	(15*10) (20*5)	(15*10)	(20*5) (5*10)
4	(8*7)	No	No	(20*5) (5*10)
5	(7*4)	(20*5) (5*10)	(5*10)	(1*10) (6*5) (10*5)
6	(7*4)	(10*5)	(10*5)	

rectangles is choose. If needed, small piece can be rotated 90 degree to fit to the empty area. The philosophy is to make good use of space and reserve other empty rectangles as large as possible.

Suppose we have 4 small pieces {(10*5), (8*7), (4*7), (15*5)} and a stock of size (20*15). We randomly generate a index sequence [1,4,3,2,3,1] and the sorted result is [4,1,1,2,3,3].The cutting process is showed in Table.1 and Fig.1 and the final feasible cutting pattern is [4,1,1,3,3].

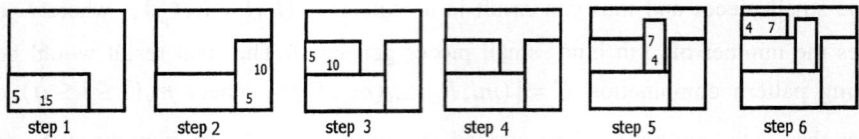

Fig. 1. Cutting process

3.2 Genetic Algorithm

3.2.1 Representation of Gene, Adding New Chromosome and Mutation

The chromosome is constructed as a combination of cutting patterns. After q feasible cutting patterns are available, they form a pattern combination. The real solution may only make use of several of them or even don't exist which is determined by LP algorithm.

Crossover and adding new chromosome to the population which consists of a number of chromosomes is used to realize randomly searching for a near optimal solution. We first specify a fixed operational rate Pr and get a random number between 0 and 1. If it is less than Pr, randomly select two chromosomes and randomly exchange patterns between them, which results in two new chromosomes. Otherwise, simply produce a new chromosome and add it to the population. In our experiment Pr =0.66.

3.2.2 Fitness Evaluation, Selection and Termination

The fitness of a chromosome is defined as the number of stocks needed to cut from. It is easy to formulate it as an Integer Programming (IP) problem. As the pattern number is small, applying LP first in polynomial time and then rounding-up its solution will only bring just a little error. Those infeasible chromosomes should be removed. The following is LP formulation, where t_i^j is the number of i th kind small pieces generated by j th pattern:

$$Min \sum_{j=1}^{q} m_j$$
$$s.t. \sum_{j=1}^{q} (m_j * t_j^i) \leq n_i \ (1 \leq i \leq p)$$

Then rounding-up each $m_j = \lceil m_j \rceil$

To control the population size to be less than m, an individual with higher fitness has a higher chance to be deleted. The possibility is $\min(\max((M-m), 0)*f_i/\sum_{j=1}^{M}f_j, 1)$, where M is the number of all chromosomes at that time and f_i is i th chromosome's fitness. When the fitness decreases less than dif in continuous ite iterations, the algorithm will terminate.

3 Experiments

Bigger parameters for the continuous iteration number ite, fitness difference dif, pattern number q in a combination and population size m may lead to better final solution, because more tests will be tried. In the first 100 tests, all piece' shape and their required numbers are randomly generated by even distribution. Each piece's length and width range from 3 to 17 and its requested number ranges from 5 to 25. The stock's length and width are set between 15 and 30. All tests only involve less than 200 pieces and pattern number for each combination is allowed from 4 to 8 and population size is set to be 40. As Table.2 shows, the majority cases only achieve utility ($u = \sum_{i=1}^{p}(n_i*w_i*l_i)/\min(f_j)$) between 70% and 80%. Increasing q and ite did not improve results much.

Then the algorithm is tested with 10 large scale problems which consist of more than 4000 pieces whose size is a little narrow comparatively. One typical evolution curve is depicted Fig 2. Because they all get final utilities more than 80%, it can be deduced that to get higher utility depends on the problem's constraints more than the algorithm.

Table 2. Test results

Uitility	60%- 70%	70%-80%	80%-90%	90%-100%
Number of tests	14	57	19	2

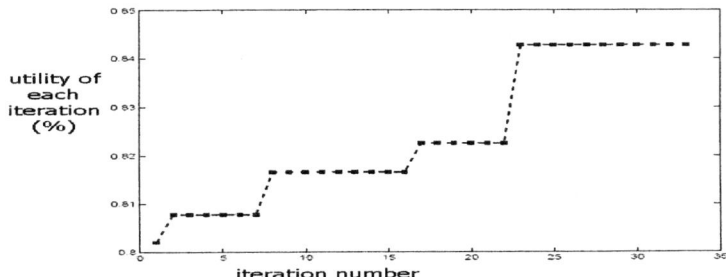

Fig. 2. Utility against iteration curve

4 Conclusions

The proposed approach is based on a heuristic LF conversion method. GA is employed to search for a good combination of patterns and LP is used to evaluate fitness without bringing much error. As the tests of different sizes show, to get a high utility depends heavily on the shapes of stock and pieces in different problem setting. To improve the performance, cutting scheme need to be further studied that incorporate more shape knowledge.

References

1. J.M. Valerio de Carvalho.: LP models for bin packing and cutting stock problems. Journal of Operations Research. 141 (2002) 253-273.
2. P.C.Gilmore., R.E. Gomory.: A linear programming approach to the cutting-stock problem. Journal of Operatiosns Research. 9(1961)849-859.
3. Leo H.W. Yeung and Wallace K.S. Tang.: A hybrid genetic approach for garment cutting in clothing industry, IEEE Transactions on Industrial Electronics. vol. 50, no.3,June 2003, pp. 449-455.
4. T.W. Leung,C.H. Yung, Marvin D.Troutt.: Application of genetic search and simulate annealing to the two-dimensional non-guillotine cutting stock problem", Computers and Industrial Engineering, 40(2001)201-214.
5. Saad M.A. Suliman.: Pattern generating procedure for the cutting stock problem, Journal of Operations Research. 74(2001)293-301.

Fractal and Dynamical Language Methods to Construct Phylogenetic Tree Based on Protein Sequences from Complete Genomes

Zu-Guo Yu[1,2], Vo Anh[1], and Li-Quan Zhou[2]

[1] Program in Statistics and Operations Research, Queensland University of Technology, GPO Box 2434, Brisbane, Queensland 4001, Australia
z.yu@qut.edu.au, v.anh@qut.edu.au
[2] School of Mathematics and Computing Science, Xiangtan University, Hunan 411105, China
zhoulq@xtu.edu.cn

Abstract. The complete genomes of living organisms have provided much information on their phylogenetic relationships. In the past few years, we proposed three alternative methods to model the noise background in the composition vector of protein sequences from a complete genome. The first method is based on the frequencies of the 20 kinds of amino acids appearing in the genome and the multiplicative model. The second method is based on the iterated function system model in fractal geometry. The last method is based on the relationship between a word and its two sub-words in the theory of symbolic dynamics. Here we introduce these methods. The complete genomes of prokaryotes and eukaryotes are selected to test these algorithms. Our distance-based phylogenetic tree of prokaryotes and eukaryotes agrees with the biologists' "tree of life" based on the 16S-like rRNA genes in a majority of basic branches and most lower taxa.

1 Introduction

In our understanding of the classification of the living world as a whole, the most important advance was made by Chatton [5], whose classification is that there are two major groups of organisms, the prokaryotes (bacteria) and the eukaryotes (organisms with nucleated cells). Then the universal tree of life based on the 16S-like rRNA genes given by Woese and colleagues [29,31] led to the proposal of three primary domains (Eukarya, Bacteria, and Archaea). Although the archaebacterial domain is accepted by biologists, its phylogenetic status is still a matter of controversy [13,18]. Analyses of some genes, particularly those encoding metabolic enzymes, give different phylogenies of the same organisms or even fail to support the three-domain classification of living organisms [3,7,13].

It is generally accepted that genome sequences are excellent tools for studying evolution [9]. In building the tree of life, analysis of whole genomes has begun to supplement, and in some cases to improve upon, studies previously done with one or few genes [9]. The availability of complete genomes allows the reconstruction of organismal phylogeny, taking into account the genome content, for example, based on the rearrangement of gene order [23], the presence or absence of protein-coding gene families [12], gene content and overall similarity [26], and occurrence of folds and orthologs [16]. All these approaches depend on alignment of homologous sequences, and it is apparent that much information (such as gene rearrangement and insertions/deletions) in these data sets is lost after sequence alignment, in addition to the intrinsic problems of alignment algorithms [15,24,25]. There have been a number of recent attempts to develop methodologies that do not require sequence alignment for deriving species phylogeny based on overall similarities of the complete genomes (e.g., [15,20,24,25,32-37]).

By overcoming the problem of noise and bias in the protein sequences through the use of appropriate models, whole-genome trees have now largely converged to the rRNA-sequence tree [4]. Qi et al. [20] have developed a simple correlation analysis of complete genome sequences based on compositional vectors without the need of sequence alignment. The compositional vectors calculated from the frequency of amino acid strings are converted to distance values for all taxa, and the phylogenetic relationships are inferred from the distance matrix using conventional tree-building methods. An analysis based on this method using 109 organisms (prokaryotes and eukaryotes) yields a tree separating the three domains of life, Archaea, Eubacteria and Eukarya, with the relationships among the taxa correlating with those based on traditional analyses [20]. A correlation analysis based on a different transformation of compositional vectors was also reported by Stuart et al.[24] who demonstrated the applicability of the method in revealing phylogeny using vertebrate mitochondrial genomes.

In the approach proposed by Qi et al. [20], a key step is to subtract the noise background in the composition vectors of the protein sequences from complete genomes through a Markov model. In the past few years, we proposed three alternative methods to model the noise background in the composition vector of protein sequences from a complete genome. The first method is based on the frequencies of the 20 kinds of amino acids appearing in the genome and the multiplicative model [34]. The second method is based on the iterated function system (IFS) model in fractal geometry [1,32,36]. The last method is based the relationship between a word and its two subwords in the theory of symbolic dynamics [37]. We introduce these methods in the present paper. The results are as good as those previously reported in Qi et al. [20].

2 Methods

A protein sequence is formed by twenty different kinds of amino acids, namely, Alanine (A), Arginine (R), Asparagine (N), Aspartic acid (D), Cysteine (C), Glutamic acid (E), Glutamine (Q), Glycine (G), Histidine (H), Isoleucine (I), Leucine (L), Lysine (K), Methionine (M), Phenylalanine (F), Proline (P), Serine (S), Threonine (T), Tryptophan (W), Tyrosine (Y) and Valine (V) [2, p.109]. Each coding sequence in the complete genome of an organism is translated into a protein sequence using the genetic code [2, p.122].

The phylogenetic signal in the protein sequences is often obscured by noise and bias [4]. There is always some randomness in the composition of protein sequences, revealed by their statistical properties at single amino acid or oligopeptide level (see [28] for a recent discussion on this point). In order to highlight the selective diversification of sequence composition, we subtract the random background (noise and bias) from the simple counting results.

2.1 Methods 1: Measure Representation of Protein Sequences and IFS Simulation

Yu et al. [34] proposed the measure representation of protein sequences. We link all translated protein sequences from a complete genome to form a long protein sequence according to the order of the coding sequences in the complete genome. In this way, we obtain a linked protein sequence for each organism. In this method we only consider these kinds of linked protein sequences and view them as symbolic sequences.

We call any string made of K letters from the alphabet {A, C, D, E, F, G, H, I, K, L, M, N, P, Q, R, S, T, V, W, Y} which corresponds to twenty kinds of amino acids a K-string. For a given K there are in total 20^K different K-strings for protein sequences. In order to count the number of each kind of K-strings in a given protein sequence, 20^K counters are needed. We divide the interval $[0,1[$ into 20^K disjoint subintervals, and use each subinterval to represent a counter.

Letting $s = s_1 s_2 \ldots s_K$, $s_i \in $ {A, C, D, E, F, G, H, I, K, L, M, N, P, Q, R, S, T, V, W, Y}, $i=1,2,\ldots,K$ be a substring with length K, we define $x_l(s) = \sum_{i=1}^{K} \frac{x_i}{20^i}$, where x_i is one of the integer values from 0 to 19 corresponding to $s_i = $ A, C, D, E, F, G, H, I, K, L, M, N, P, Q, R, S, T, V, W, Y respectively, and $x_r(s) = x_l(s) + \frac{1}{20^K}$. We then use the subinterval $[x_l(s), x_r(s)[$ to represent substring s. Let $N_K(s)$ be the number of times that substring s with length K appears in the linked protein sequence ($N_K(s)$ may be zero).

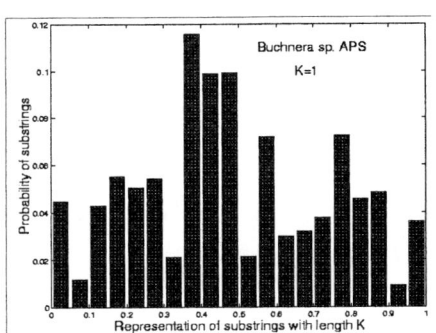 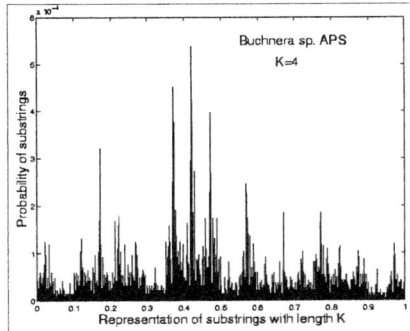

Fig. 1. Histograms of substrings with lengths $K=1$ and 4 in the linked protein sequence from the complete genome of *Buchnera* sp. APS

If the total number of K-strings appearing in the linked protein sequence is denoted as $N_K(total)$, we define $F_K(s) = N_K(s)/(N_K(total))$ to be the frequency of substring s. It follows that $\sum_{\{s\}} F_K(s) = 1$. Now we can define a measure μ_K on $[0,1[$ by $d\mu_K(x) = Y_K(x)dx$, where
$$Y_K(x) = 20^K F_K(s), \quad \text{when} \quad x \in [x_l(s), x_r(s)[.$$

We call μ_K the *measure representation* of the organism corresponding to the given K. As an example, the histogram of substrings in the linked protein sequence of *Buchnera* sp. APS for $K=1$ and 4 are given in Fig. 1.

We can order all the $F(s)$ according to the increasing order of $x_l(s)$. According to the IFS model described in Yu and Anh [32], we can get the IFS simulation of all $F(s)$. As an example, a fragment of the histogram of substrings in the linked protein sequence of *Buchnera* sp. APS for K=5 and its IFS simulation are given in Fig. 2.

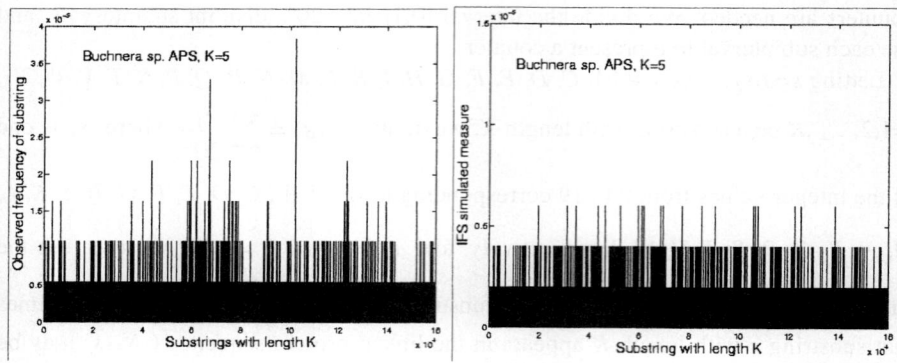

Fig. 2. A segment of measure representation of the linked protein sequence for *Buchnera* sp. APS in the left figure and the IFS simulation for the same set of K-strings in the right figure

We denote this IFS simulation as $F^{pf}(s)$. In this method, we view $F^{pf}(s)$ of the 20^K kinds of K-strings as the noise background. Then we subtract the noise background through defining

$$X(s_1 s_2 ... s_K) = \begin{cases} F(s_1 s_2 ... s_K)/F^{pf}(s_1 s_2 ... s_K) - 1, & \text{if} \quad F^{pf}(s_1 s_2 ... s_K) \neq 0 \\ 0, & \text{if} \quad F^{pf}(s_1 s_2 ... s_K) = 0. \end{cases}$$

2.2 Method 2: Multiplicative Model

In this method, we still consider the linked protein sequences from complete genomes. If s' is one of the 20 letters, we denote by $P(s')$ the frequency of letter s'

in the linked protein sequence. Then for any K-substring $s = s_1s_2...s_K$, where $s_i \in \{A,C,D,E,F, G,H,I,K,L,M, N,P,Q,R,S,T,V,W,Y\}, i = 1,2,...,K$, we define

$$F'(s) = P(s_1)P(s_2)...P(s_K).$$

In this method, we view $F'(s)$ of the 20^K kinds of K-strings as the noise background. Then we subtract the noise background through defining

$$X(s) = F(s) - F'(s).$$

2.3 Method 3: Dynamical Language Model

Let $N = 20^K$. We use a window of length K and slide it through each protein sequence in a genome by shifting one position at a time to determine the frequencies of each of the N kinds of strings. A protein sequence is excluded if its length is shorter than K. The observed frequency $p(s_1s_2...s_K)$ of a K-string $s_1s_2...s_K$ is defined as $p(s_1s_2...s_K) = n(s_1s_2...s_K)/(L - K + 1)$, where $n(s_1s_2...s_K)$ is the number of times that $s_1s_2...s_K$ appears in this sequence. Denoting by m the number of protein sequences from each complete genome, the observed frequency of a K-string $s_1s_2...s_K$ is defined as $(\sum_{j=1}^{m} n_j(s_1s_2...s_K))/(\sum_{j=1}^{m}(L_j - K + 1))$; here $n_j(s_1s_2...s_K)$ means the number of times that $s_1s_2...s_K$ appears in the jth protein sequence and L_j the length of the jth protein sequence in this complete genome.

In this method, we consider an idea from the theory of dynamical language that a K-string $s_1s_2...s_K$ is possibly constructed by adding a letter s_K to the end of the $(K-1)$-string $s_1s_2...s_{K-1}$ or a letter s_1 to the beginning of the $(K-1)$-string $s_2s_3...s_K$. Suppose that we have performed direct counting for all strings of length $(K-1)$ and the 20 kinds of letters, the expected frequency of appearance of K-strings is predicted by

$$q(s_1s_2..s_K) = \frac{p(s_1s_2..s_{K-1})p(s_K) + p(s_1)p(s_2s_3..s_K)}{2}$$

where q denotes the predicted frequency, and $p(s_1)$ and $p(s_K)$ are frequencies of amino acids s_1 and s_K appearing in this genome. [In the previous papers of our group [6,20], we use Markov model to characterize the predictor, in which we need to know the information of the $(K-1)$-strings and $(K-2)$-strings.]. In this method we view $q(s_1s_2...s_K)$ of the 20^K kinds of K-strings as the noise background.

We then subtract the noise background before performing a cross-correlation analysis (similar to removing a time-varying mean in time series before computing the cross-correlation of two time series) through defining

$$X(s_1 s_2 ... s_K) = \begin{cases} p(s_1 s_2 ... s_K)/q(s_1 s_2 ... s_K) - 1, & \text{if } q(s_1 s_2 ... s_K) \neq 0 \\ 0, & \text{if } q(s_1 s_2 ... s_K) = 0. \end{cases}$$

2.4 The Correlation Distance

The transformation $X(s) = F(s)/F^{pf}(s) - 1$, $X(s) = F(s) - F'(s)$ or $X(s) = p(s)/q(s) - 1$ has the desired effect of subtraction of random background (noise and bias) from F or p and rendering it a stationary time series suitable for subsequent cross-correlation analysis.

For all possible K-strings $s_1 s_2 ... s_K$, we use $X(s_1 s_2 ... s_K)$ as components to form a composition vector for a genome. To further simplify the notation, we use X_i for the i-th component corresponding to the string type i, $i = 1,..., N$ (the N strings are arranged in a fixed order as the alphabetical order). Hence we construct a composition vector $X = (X_1, X_2,..., X_N)$ for genome X, and likewise $Y = (Y_1, Y_2,..., Y_N)$ for genome Y.

If we view the N components in vectors X and Y as samples of two random variables respectively, the sample correlation $C(X,Y)$ between any two genomes X and Y is defined as
$$C(X,Y) = \frac{\sum_{i=1}^{N}(X_i - X_{ave}) \times (Y_i - Y_{ave})}{[\sum_{i=1}^{N}(X_i - X_{ave})^2 \times \sum_{i=1}^{N}(Y_i - Y_{ave})^2]^{\frac{1}{2}}},$$
where X_{ave} and Y_{ave} are the mean value of vectors X and Y respectively. The distance $D(X,Y)$ between the two genomes is then defined by $D(X,Y) = (1 - C(X,Y))/2$. A distance matrix for all the genomes under study is then generated for construction of phylogenetic trees.

2.5 Genome Data Sets and Tree Construction

We retrieve the complete genomes from NCBI database (ftp://ncbi.nlm.nih.gov/genbank/genomes/). To test Method 1 and Method 2, we selected 51 bacteria genomes and 3 eukaryotes genomes (data set 1). To test Method 3, we selected a data set used in Qi et al. [20] including 109 organisms (data set 2) for prokaryote phylogenetic analysis.

Qi et al.[19] pointed out that the Fitch-Margoliash method [11] is not feasible when the number of species is as large as 100 or more and an algorithm such as maximum likelihood is not based on the distance matrix alone. So we construct all trees using the neighbour-joining (NJ) method [22] in the PHYLIP package [10].

For the speed problem, we used a PC (Intel Pentium4 CPU 2.80GHz, 512MB of RAM) to calculate the distance matrices on data set 2 for different values of K using method 3 and the one proposed by Qi et al. [20]. The times to run the programs are listed in Table 1. From Table 1, we see that the present method is computational faster than the one proposed by Qi et al. [20] for $K=3$, 4 and 5. And for the case $K=6$, we cannot perform neither the method 3 nor the one in Qi et al. [20] on our PC since this is beyond its computing capacity.

Table 1. The speed comparison of the present method and the one in Qi et al. [20]. In this table "hr" means hour, "min" means minute and "sec" means second.

Value of K	Method of Qi et al. [20]	Method 3
$K=3$	1 hr and 10 mins and 2 secs	1 hr 4 mins and 5 secs
$K=4$	1 hr and 54 mins and 30 secs	1 hr and 40 mins and 33 secs
$K=5$	12 hrs and 1 mins and 25 secs	10 hrs and 25 mins and 33 secs

3 Results and Discussion

Although the existence of the archeabacterial urkingdom has been accepted by many biologists, the classification of bacteria is still a matter of controversy [14]. The evolutionary relationship of the three primary kingdoms, namely archeabacteria, eubacteria and eukaryote, is another crucial problem that remains unresolved [14].

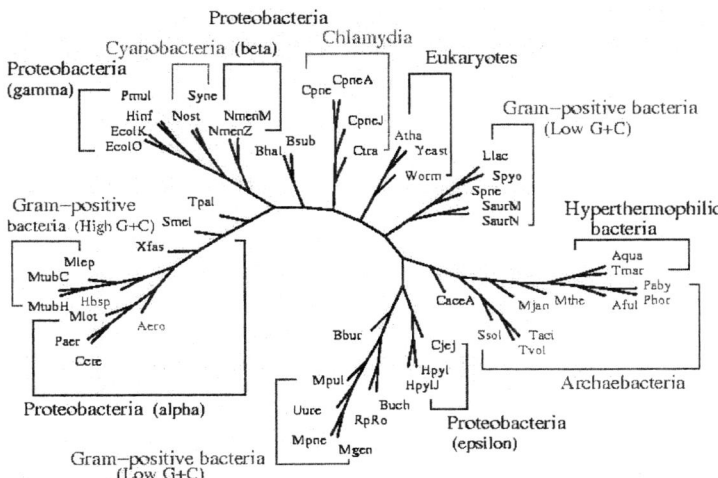

Fig. 3. The neighbor-joining phylogenetic tree of 54 organisms using Method 1 with $K=5$

It has been pointed out [20] that the subtraction of random background is an essential step. Our results show that removing the noise background is also an essential step in our correlation method. In Yu et al. [36], we proposed to use the recurrent IFS model [27] to simulate the measure representation of complete genome and define the phylogenetic distance based on the parameters from the recurrent IFS model. The method of Yu et al. [36] does not include the step of removing multifractal structure, but yielded a tree in which archaebacteria, eubacteria and eukaryotes intermingle with one another.

In the three methods presented here, K must be larger than 3. We can only calculate the distance matrices and construct the trees for K from 3 to 6 because of the limitation on the computing capability of our PCs and supercomputers. We find that the topology of the trees converges with K increasing from 3 to 6 and it becomes stable for $K \geq 5$. We show the phylogenetic tree using $X(s)$ sequences through Method 1 with K=5 in Fig. 3 and through Method 2 with K=5 in Fig. 4. For Method 3, we present the result based on K= 6 in Fig. 5.

The correlation distance based on Method 1 and Method 2 after removing the noise background (via IFS simulation or multiplicative model) from the original information gives a satisfactory phylogenetic tree. Fig. 3 shows that all Archaebacteria except *Halobacterium* sp. NRC-1 (Hbsp) and *Aeropyrum pernix* (Aero) stay in a separate branch with the Eubacteria and Eukaryotes. The three Eukaryotes also group in one branch and almost all other bacteria in different traditional categories stay in the right branch. At a general global level of complete genomes, our result supports the genetic annealing model for the universal ancestor [30]. The two hyperthermophilic bacteria: *Aquifex aeolicus* (Aqua) VF5 and *Thermotoga maritima* MSB8 (Tmar) gather together and stay in the Archaebacteria branch in the tree. We notice that these two bacteria, like most Archaebacteria, are hyperthermophilic. In the phylogenetic analyses based on a few genes, the tendency of the two hyperthermophilic bacteria, *Aquae* and *Thema*, to get into Archaea, has intensified the debate on whether there has been wide-spread lateral or horizontal gene transfers among species [8,17,21]. Eisen and Fraser [9] claimed that analyses of complete genomes suggest that lateral gene transfer has been rare over the course of evolution and it has not distorted the structure of the tree. Fig. 4 based on Method 2 is similar to Fig. 3 based on Method 1. Our results using Method 1 and Method 2 based on the complete genome (Figs. 3 and 4) do not seem to support the views of Eisen and Fraser. Hence more works are required for this problem.

Fig. 5 shows the K=6 tree based on the NJ analysis for the selected 109 organisms using Method 3. The selected Archaea group together as a domain (except *Pyrobaculum aerophilum*). The six eukaryotes also cluster together as a domain. And all Eubacteria fall into another domain. So the division of life into three main domains Eubacteria, Archaebacteria and Eukarya is a clean and prominent feature. At the inter specific level, it is clear that Archaea is divided into two groups of Euryarchaeota and Crenarchaeota. Different prokaryotes in the same group (Firmicutes, Actinobacteria, Cyanobacteria, Chlamydia, Hyperthermophilic bacteria) all cluster together. Proteobacteria (except epsilon division) cluster together. In Proteobacteria, prokaryotes from alpha and epsilon divisions group with those from the same division. It is clear that the branch of Firmicutes is divided into sub-branches Bacillales, Lactobacillales, Clostridia and Mollicutes. Our phylogenetic tree of organisms supports the 16S-like rRNA tree of life in its broad division into three domains and the grouping of the various prokaryotes. So after subtracting the noise and bias from the protein sequences as described in our method, the whole-genome tree converges to the rRNA-sequence tree as asserted in Charlebois et al. [4]. In our tree (Fig. 5) the two hyperthermophlic bacteria group together and stay in the domain of eubacteria. This result is the same as in Qi et al. [20] and also supports the point of view in Eisen and Fraser

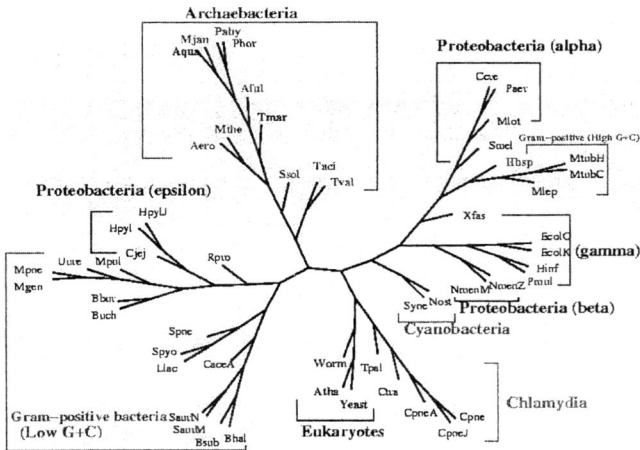

Fig. 4. The neighbor-joining phylogenetic tree of 54 organisms using Method 2 with $K=5$

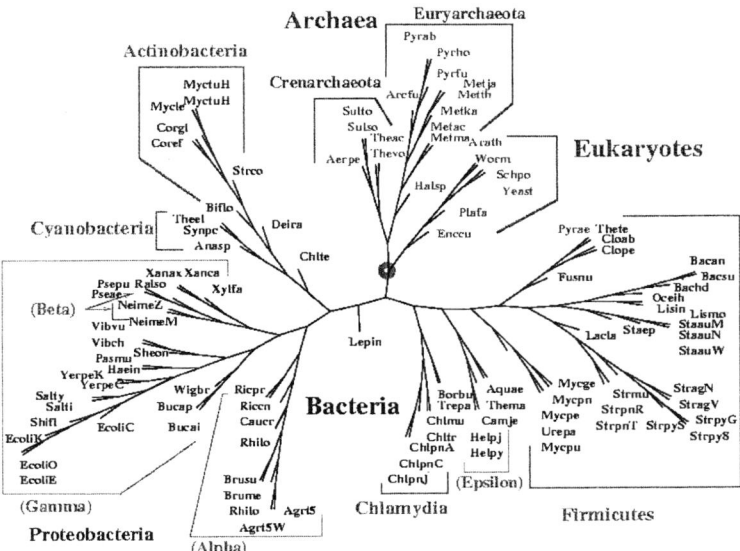

Fig. 5. Phylogeny of 109 organisms (prokaryotes and eukaryotes) based on Method 2 in the case $K=6$

[9]. We gave more comparison between Method 3 and the Markov model proposed by Qi et al. [20] in our recent work [37]. From the biological point of view, Method 3 is better than Methods 1 and 2.

Our approach circumvents the ambiguity in the selection of genes from complete genomes for phylogenetic reconstruction, and is also faster than the traditional approaches of phylogenetic analyses, particularly when dealing with a large number of genomes. Moreover, since multiple sequence alignment is not used, the intrinsic problems associated with this complex procedure can be avoided.

References

1. Anh V. V., Lau K. S. and Yu Z. G., Recognition of an organism from fragments of its complete genome, *Phys. Rev. E*, 66 (2002) 031910
2. Brown T. A., Genetics (3rd Edition), CHAPMAN & Hall, London (1998).
3. Brown, J.R., Doolittle,W.F., Archaea and the prokaryote-to-eukaryote transition, *Microbiol. Mol. Biol. Rev.* 61 (1997) 456-502.
4. Charlebois R.L., R.G. Beiko and M. A. Ragan, Branching out. *Nature*, 421 (2003) 217-217.
5. Chatton, E., *Titres et travaux scientifiques* (Sette, Sottano, Italy) (1937).
6. Chu K.H., J. Qi, Z.G. Yu and V.V. Anh, Origin and Phylogeny of Chloroplasts revealed by a simple correlation analysis of complete genome. *Mol. Biol. Evol.*, 21 (2004) 200-206.
7. Doolittle, R.F., Microbial genomes opened up. *Nature*, 392 (1998) 339-342.
8. Doolittle, R.F., Phylogenetic classification and the universal tree. *Science*, 284 (1999) 2124-2128.
9. Eisen, J.A. and C.M. Fraser, Phylogenomics: intersection of evolution and genomics. *Science*, 300 (2003) 1706-1707.
10. Felsenstein,J. PHYLIP (phylogeny Inference package) version 3.5c. Distributed by the author at http://evolution.genetics.washington.edu/phylip.html, (1993).
11. Fitch, W. M., and E. Margoliash, Construction of phylogenetic trees. *Science* 155 (1967) 279-284.
12. Fitz-Gibbon, S. T., and C. H. House, Whole genome-based phylogenetic analysis of free-living microorganisms. *Nucleic Acids Res.*, 27 (1999) 4218-4222.
13. Gupta, R.S., Protein phylogenies and signature sequences: A reappraisal of evolutionary relationships among Archaebacteria, Eubacteria, and Eukaryotes. *Microbiol. Mol. Biol. Rev.*, 62 (1998) 1435- 1491.
14. Iwabe, N. *et al.*, Evolutionary relationship of archaebacteria, eubacteria and eukaryotes inferred from phylogenetic trees of duplicated genes, *Proc. Natl. Acad. Sci. USA*, 86 (1989) 9355-9359.
15. Li, M., J. H. Badger, X. Chen, S. Kwong, P. Kearney, and H. Zhang, An information-based sequence distance and its application to whole mitochondrial genome phylogeny. *Bioinformatics*, 17 (2001) 149-154.
16. Lin, J., and M. Gerstein, Whole-genome trees based on the occurrence of folds and orthologs, implications for comparing genomes at different levels. *Genome Res.*, 10 (2000) 808-818.
17. Martin, W., and R. G. Herrmann, Gene transfer from organelles to the nucleus: How much, what happens, and why? *Plant Physiol.*, 118 (1998) 9-17.
18. Mayr, E., Two empires or three, *Proc. Natl. Acad. Sci. U.S.A.*, 95 (1998) 9720-9723.

19. Qi, J., H. Luo, and B. Hao, CVTree: a phylogenetic tree reconstruction tool based on whole genomes. *Nucleic Acids Research*, 32 (2004a) W45-W47.
20. Qi, J., B. Wang, and B. Hao, Whole proteome prokaryote phylogeny without sequence alignment: a K-string composition approach. *J. Mol. Evol.*, 58 (2004b) 1-11.
21. Ragan M.A., Detection of lateral gene transfer among microbial genomes. *Curr. Opin. Gen. Dev.*, 11 (2001) 620-626.
22. Saitou, N., and M. Nei, The neighbor-joining method: a new method for reconstructing phylogenetic trees. *Mol. Biol. Evol.*, 4 (1987) 406-425.
23. Sankoff, D., G. Leaduc, N. Antoine, B. Paquin, B. F. Lang, and R. Cedergren, Gene order comparisons for phylogenetic inference: Evolution of the mitochondrial genome. *Proc. Natl. Acad. Sci. U.S.A.*, 89 (1992) 6575-6579.
24. Stuart, G. W., K. Moffet, and S. Baker, Integrated gene species phylogenies from unaligned whole genome protein sequences. *Bioinformatics*, 18 (2002a) 100-108.
25. Stuart, G.W., K.Moffet, and J.J. Leader, A comprehensive vertebrate phylogeny using vector representations of protein sequences from whole genomes. *Mol. Biol. Evol.*, 19 (2002b) 554-562.
26. Tekaia, F., A. Lazcano, and B. Dujon, The genomic tree as revealed from whole proteome comparisons. *Genome Res.*, 9 (1999) 550-557.
27. Vrscay, E.R., in *Fractal Geometry and analysis*, Eds, Belair, J., (NATO ASI series, Kluwer Academic Publishers) (1991).
28. Weiss, O., M. A. Jimenez, and H. Herzel, Information content of protein sequences. *J. Theor. Biol.*, 206 (2000) 379-386.
29. Woese, C.R., Bacterial evolution, *Microbiol. Rev.*, 51 (1987) 221-271.
30. Woese C.R., The universal ansestor, *Proc. Natl. Acad. Sci. USA*, 95 (1998) 6854-6859.
31. Woese, C.R., Kandler, O. & Wheelis, M.L., Towards a natural system of organisms: Proposal for the domains Archaea, Bacteria, and Eucarya, *Proc. Natl. Acad. Sci. USA*, 87 (1990) 4576-4579.
32. Yu, Z.G., V.Anh, Phylogenetic tree of prokaryotes based on complete genomes using fractal and correlation analyses, in *Proceedings of the Second Asia-Pacific Bioinformatics Conference, Dunedin*, New Zealand. (The Australian Computer Society Inc.) (2004).
33. Yu, Z.G., and P. Jiang, Distance, correlation and mutual information among portraits of organisms based on complete genomes. *Phys. Lett. A*, 286 (2001) 34-46.
34. Yu, Z.G., V. Anh and K. S. Lau, Multifractal and correlation analysis of protein sequences from complete genome. *Phys. Rev. E.*, 68 (2003a) 021913.
35. Yu, Z.G., V. Anh and K. S. Lau, Chaos game representation, and multifractal and correlation analysis of protein sequences from complete genome based on detailed HP model. *J. Theor. Biol.* 226 (2004) 341-348
36. Yu, Z.G., V. Anh, K.S. Lau and K. H. Chu, The genomic tree of living organisms based on a fractal model. *Phys. Lett. A*, 317 (2003b) 293-302.
37. Yu,Z.G., L.Q. Zhou, V. V. Anh, K.H. Chu, S.C. Long and J.Q. Deng, Phylogeny of prokaryotes and chloroplasts revealed by a simple composition approach on all protein sequences from whole genome without sequence alignment, *J. Mol. Evol.* 60 (2005) 538-545.

Evolutionary Hardware Architecture for Division in Elliptic Curve Cryptosystems over $GF(2^n)$

Jun-Cheol Jeon, Kee-Won Kim, and Kee-Young Yoo[*]

Department of Computer Engineeing, Kyungpook National University,
Daegu, 702-701 Korea
{jcjeon33, nirvana}@infosec.knu.ac.kr
yook@knu.ac.kr

Abstract. Cellular automata (CA) have been accepted as a good evolutionary computational model for the simulation of complex physical systems. They have been used for various applications, such as parallel processing computations and number theory. In the meanwhile, elliptic curve cryptosystems (ECC) are in the spotlight owing to their significantly smaller parameters. The most costly arithmetic operation in ECC is division, which is performed by multiplying the inverse of a multiplicand. Thus, this paper presents an evolutionary hardware architecture for division based on CA over $GF(2^n)$ in ECC. The proposed architecture has the advantage of high regularity, expandability, and a reduced latency based on periodic boundary CA. The proposed architecture can be used for the hardware design of crypto-coprocessors.

1 Introduction

In cryptography, to achieve a high level of security, many public-key algorithms that rely on computations in $GF(2^n)$ require large field size, some as large as $GF(2^{2000})$. Hence, there is a need to develop an efficient algorithm for the multiplication in $GF(2^n)$. However, significantly smaller parameters can be used in ECC than in other competitive systems such RSA and ElGamal, but with equivalent levels of security. Benefits of having smaller key sizes include faster computations, and reductions in processing power, storage space, and bandwidth. This makes ECC ideal for constrained environments such as pagers, PDAs, cellular phones, and smart cards [6].

ECC was proposed as an alternative to the established public-key cryptosystems such as RSA and ElGamal, and has recently received a great deal of attention in industry and academia [1,2]. The main reason for the attractiveness of ECC is that there is no sub-exponential algorithm known to solve the discrete logarithm problem on a properly chosen elliptical curve.

The main operation of ECC is an inverse/division operation, which can be regarded as a special case of exponentiation [3]. However, since a division operation is quite time consuming, efficient algorithms are required for practical applications, especially for a public key cryptosystem where operands can be as large as 512bits or even lar-

---

[*] Corresponding author.

ger. Fast computation of a division operation can generally be classified into two approaches: a faster architecture design or a novel algorithm development. This current study focused on the former approach.

Finite field GF(2^n) arithmetic operations have recently been applied in a variety of fields, including cryptography and error-correcting codes [4]. A number of modern public key cryptography systems and schemes, for example, Diffie-Hellman key predistribution, the Elgamal cryptosystem, and ECC, require the operations of division and inversion [5]. Wang [15] proposed parallel-in parallel-out division architecture with a latency of ($2n^2$-1.5n) and a critical path of (T_{2AND}+ $3T_{2XOR}$). Kim's serial-in serial-out architecture [16] has a latency of ($2n^2$-2n) and a critical path of ($2T_{2AND}$+$3T_{2XOR}$+T_{MUX}). However, a fast arithmetic architecture is still needed to design dedicated high-speed circuits.

Cellular automata have been used in evolutionary computation for over a decade. They have been used for various applications, such as parallel processing and number theory. CA architecture has been used to design of arithmetic computation as well such that Zhang [8] proposed an architecture with programmable cellular automata, Choudhury [9] designed an LSB multiplier based on a CA, and Jeon [17] proposed a simple and efficient architecture based on periodic boundary CA.

This paper proposes an evolutionary architecture for division based on CA. We focused on the architecture in ECC, which uses restricted irreducible polynomials, especially, trinomials. The structure has a time complexity of ($2n$-1)(n-1)(T_{AND}+T_{XOR}+T_{MUX}) and a hardware complexity of (nAND+(n+1)XOR+($3n$-1)MUX+$4n$REGISTER). In addition, our architecture can easily be expanded for other public key cryptosystem with additional (n-1) XOR gates. Our architecture is focused on both area and time complexity.

The remainder of this paper is organized as follows. The conceptional background, including finite fields, ECC, and CA, is described in section 2. Section 3 presents the proposed division architecture based on CA, and we present our discussion, together with the performance comparison between the proposed architecture and the previous works, in section 4. Finally, section 5 presents our conclusion.

2 Preliminaries

In this section, we discuss the mathematical background in the finite field and ECC, and the characteristics and properties of cellular automata.

2.1 Finite Fields

A finite field or Galois Field (GF), which is a set of finite elements, can be defined by commutative law, associative law, and distributive law and facilitates addition, subtraction, multiplication, and division. A number of architectures have already been developed to construct low complexity bit-serial and bit-parallel multiplications using various irreducible polynomials to reduce the complexity of modular multiplication. Since a polynomial basis operation does not require a basis conversion, it can be readily matched to any input or output system. Additionally, due to its regularity and simplicity, the ability to design and expand it into high-order finite fields with polynomial basis is easier to realize than with other basis operations [10].

A finite field can be viewed as a vector space of dimension n over $GF(2^n)$. That is, there exists a set of n elements $\{1, \alpha, \ldots, \alpha^{n-2}, \alpha^{n-1}\}$ in $GF(2^n)$ such that each $A \in GF(2^n)$ can be written uniquely in the form $A = \sum A_i \alpha^i$, where $A_i \in \{0,1\}$. This section provides one of the most common bases of $GF(2^n)$ over $GF(2)$, polynomial bases [10,13]. Let $f(x) = x^n + \sum_{i=0}^{n-1} f_i x^i$, where $f_i \in \{0,1\}$, for $i = 0, 1, \ldots, n-1$, be an irreducible polynomial of degree n over $GF(2)$. For each irreducible polynomial, there exists a polynomial basis representation. In such a representation, each element of $GF(2^n)$ corresponds to a binary polynomial less than n. That is, for $A \in GF(2^n)$ there exist n numbers $A_i \in \{0,1\}$ such that $A = A_{n-1}\alpha^{n-1} + \ldots + A_1\alpha + A_0$.

The field element $A \in GF(2^n)$ is usually denoted by a bit string $(A_{n-1} \ldots A_1 A_0)$ of length n. The following operations are defined on the elements of $GF(2^n)$ when using a polynomial representation with irreducible polynomial $f(x)$. Assume that $A = (A_{n-1} \ldots A_1 A_0)$ and $B = (B_{n-1} \ldots B_1 B_0)$.

1) Addition: $A + B = C = (C_{n-1} \ldots C_1 C_0)$, where $C_i = (A_i + B_i) \mod 2$. That is, addition corresponds to bitwise exclusive-or.

2) Multiplication: $A \cdot B = C = (C_{n-1} \ldots C_1 C_0)$, where $C(x) = \sum_{i=0}^{n-1} C_i x^i$ is the remainder of the division of the polynomial $(\sum_{i=0}^{n-1} A_i x^i)(\sum_{i=0}^{n-1} B_i x^i)$ by $f(x)$.

In many applications, such as cryptography and digital communication applications, the polynomial basis is still the most widely employed basis [14-16]. In the following, we confine our attention to computations that use the polynomial basis.

2.2 Elliptic Curve Cryptosystem

In ECC, computing kP is the most important arithmetic operation, where k is an integer and P is a point on the elliptic curve. This operation can be computed by the addition of two points k times. ECC can be done with at least two types of arithmetic, each of which gives different definitions of multiplication [11]. The types of arithmetic are Z_p arithmetic (modular arithmetic with a large prime p as the modulus) and $GF(2^n)$ arithmetic, which can be done with shifts and exclusive-ors. This can be thought of as modular arithmetic of polynomials with coefficients mod 2.

We focused on $GF(2^n)$ arithmetic operation. Let $GF(2^n)$ be a finite field of definition. Then the set of all solution to the equation $E: y^2 + xy = x^3 + a_2 x^2 + a_6$, where a_2, $a_6 \in GF(2^n)$, $a_6 \neq 0$, together with special point called the point at infinity O is a non-supersingular curve over $GF(2^n)$. Let $P_1 = (x_1, y_1)$ and $P_2 = (x_2, y_2)$ be points in $E(GF(2^n))$ given in affine coordinates [12]. Assume that $P_1, P_2 \neq O$, and $P_1 \neq -P_2$. The sum $P_3 = (x_3, y_3) = P_1 + P_2$ is computed as follows; if $P_1 \neq P_2$ then $\lambda = (y_1 + y_2)/(x_1 + x_2)$, $x_3 = \lambda^2 + \lambda + x_1 + x_2 + a_2$, $y_3 = (x_1 + x_3)\lambda + x_3 + y_1$, and if $P_1 = P_2$ (called point doubling), then $\lambda = y_1 / x_1 + x_1$, $x_3 = \lambda^2 + \lambda + a_2$, $y_3 = (x_1 + x_3)\lambda + x_3 + y_1$.

In either case, the computation requires one division, one squaring, and one multiplication. The squaring can be substituted by multiplication. From the point addition formulae, it should be noted that no computation except for addition is performed at the same time due to the data dependency. Therefore, sharing hardware between division and multiplication is more desirable than separated implementation of division and multiplication [3,13]

Additive inverse and multiplicative inverses in GF(2^n) can be calculated efficiently using the extended Euclidean algorithm. Division and subtraction are defined in terms of additive and multiplicative inverses: *A-B* is *A+(-B)* in GF(2^n) and *A/B* is $A \cdot (B^{-1})$ in GF(2^n). Here the characteristic 2 finite fields GF(2^n) used should have $n \in \{113, 131, 163, 193, 233, 239, 283, 409, 571\}$ [3]. Addition and multiplication in GF(2^n) should be performed using one of the irreducible binary polynomials of degree *n* in Table1. This restriction is designed to facilitate interoperability while enabling implementers to deploy efficient implementations capable of meeting common security requirements [12].

Table 1. Reduction trinomial representation of GF(2^n)

Field	Reduction Trinomial(s)
GF(2^{113})	$f(x) = x^{113} + x^9 + 1$
GF(2^{193})	$f(x) = x^{193} + x^{15} + 1$
GF(2^{233})	$f(x) = x^{233} + x^{74} + 1$
GF(2^{239})	$f(x) = x^{239} + x^{36} + 1$ or $x^{239} + x^{158} + 1$
GF(2^{409})	$f(x) = x^{409} + x^{87} + 1$

The rule used to pick acceptable reduction polynomials is, if a degree *n* binary irreducible trinomial, $f(x) = x^n + x^k + 1$, for $n > k \geq 1$ exists, use the irreducible trinomial with as small a *k* as possible. These polynomials enable efficient calculation of field operations. The second reduction polynomial at *n*=239 is an anomaly chosen since it has been widely deployed. Our scheme focuses on reduction trinomials as the reduction polynomials.

2.3 Cellular Automata

A CA is a collection of simple cells arranged in a regular fashion. CAs can be characterized based on four properties: cellular geometry, neighborhood specification, the number of states per cell, and the rules to compute to a successor state. The next state of a CA depends on the current state and rules [7]. A CA can also be classified as linear or non-linear. If the neighborhood is only dependent on an XOR operation, the CA is linear, whereas if it is dependent on another operation, the CA is non-linear. If the neighborhood is only dependent on an EXOR or EXNOR operation, then the CA can also be referred to as an additive CA.

Among additive CAs, a CA whose dependency on neighbors is shown only in terms of XOR is called a non-complemented CA, and the corresponding rule is called the non-complemented rule. If the dependency on neighbors is shown only in terms of XNOR, the CA is called a complemented CA, and the corresponding rule is called the complemented rule. A hybrid CA can be subject to either the complemented or non-complemented rule. Additionally, there are 1-dimensional, 2-dimensional, and 3-dimensional CAs according to the structure of arrangement of cells.

Furthermore, if the same rule applies to all the cells in a CA, the CA is called a uniform or regular CA, whereas if different rules apply to different cells, it is called a hybrid CA. In addition, in the structure of CAs, the boundary conditions should be taken into consideration since there exists no left neighbor of the leftmost cell and right neighbor of the rightmost cell among the cells composing the CA. According to the conditions, they are divided into three types: Null Boundary CA (NBCA), Periodic Boundary CA (PBCA), and Intermediate Boundary CA (IBCA). We only consider PBCA, which is mainly used in this area because of their efficient cyclic properties.

We employ the characteristic of PBCA which is that the left neighbor of the leftmost cell becomes the rightmost cell and are adjacent to each other. The evolution of the ith cell can be represented as a function of the present states of the $(i-1)$th, ith, and $(i+1)$th cells for a 3-neighborhood CA: $Q_i(t+1) = f(Q_{i-1}(t), Q_i(t), Q_{i+1}(t))$, where '$f$' represents the evolutionary rule as a CA rule and $Q(t+1)$ denotes the next state for cell $Q(t)$. If the next state is determined by 1 bit shifting to the left, it can be expressed as $Q_i(t+1) = Q_{i-1}(t)$, $(0 \leq i \leq n-1)$. This means that the next state of ith cell is evolved by the right neighbor of the current ith cell. The proposed architecture carries out shift operations and modular reduction using an introduced property.

3   Evolutionary Architecture for Division Based on PBCA

This section presents an A/B architecture based on cellular automata. Finite field division in $GF(2^n)$ can be performed using multiplication and inverse; that is, $A/B = AB^{-1}$, where the A and B are the elements of $GF(2^n)$. Here, the multiplicative inverse of the field element B can be obtained by recursive squaring and multiplication, since the field element B can be expressed as

$$B^{-1} = B^{2^n - 2} = (B(B(B \cdots B(B(B)^2)^2 \cdots)^2)^2)^2 \tag{1}$$

Division also can be easily induced by equation (1).

$$C = AB^{-1} = A(B(B(B \cdots B(B(B)^2)^2 \cdots)^2)^2)^2$$

The above equation can be generalized as follows.

$$C_0 = B$$

$$C_i = B(C_{i-1})^2 = B^{2^{i+1}}, (1 \leq i \leq n-2) \tag{2}$$

$$C_{n-1} = A(C_{n-2})^2 = AB^{2^{n-2}} = AB^{-1} \tag{3}$$

Assume that $A \cdot B = D = (D_{n-1} \ldots D_1 D_0)$; the next equation (4) is held for a certain k in a reduction trinomial.

$$D_{n-2} \cdot x^{n-1} + D_{n-3} \cdot x^{n-2} + \ldots + (D_{n-1} \oplus D_{k-1})x^k + \ldots + D_1 \cdot x^2 + D_0 \cdot x^1 + D_{n-1} \tag{4}$$

Equation (4) can be illustrated by PBCA as shown in Fig. 1.

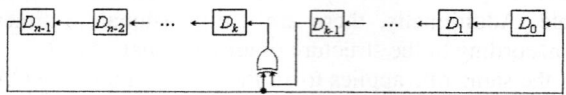

Fig. 1. periodic boundary cellular automata structure using equation (4)

As in Fig.1, shift operations and modular reduction are performed by a given evolutionary rule and reduction trinomial. The evolution shown in Fig.1 should be performed twice in order to accomplish C_i for n-2 times. To satisfy equation (3), A should be multiplied from the squaring of C_{n-2}. The result is $C = A \cdot B^{-1}$ and when $A = 1$, the algorithm realizes the inverse operation B^{-1}.

Fig.2 shows the evolutionary architecture for division. Each initial value is such that cellular automata have all zeros ($C_i^r = 0$, $0 \leq i \leq n$-1), B register has B_i values ($B_i^r = B_{n-1} \ldots B_2 B_1 B_0$), Shift register has B_i values and zeros ($S\_R = B_{n-1} 0 \ldots 0 B_2 0 B_1 0 B_0$), and zero register has 1 bit zero value.

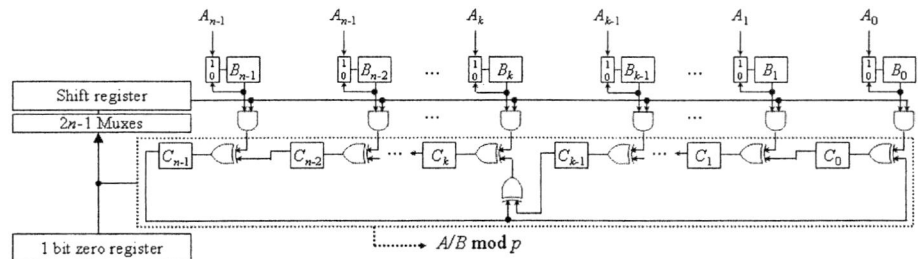

Fig. 2. proposed evolutionary architecture for division using irreducible trinomial

For initial $2n$-1 clock cycles, the values in a shift register are sequentially broadcast to the connected line for multiplying the values in B_i^r, and C_i^r is evolved based on PBCA. After the evolution of C_i^r shown in the dotted box, the values are transferred to the shift register together with 1 bit zero value which will be placed among the computed values one after the other, just as the initialized form in shift register. $(C_{n-2})^2$ is computed according to the process described n-2 times.

After whole previous evolutions, a system chooses A values in the B register for the final resultant values. It is possible to perform A/B division in $(2n-1)(n-1)$ clock cycles using n AND gates, $n+1$ XOR gates, $2n$-1 Muxes, and $4n$ bits registers, plus extra equipment such as control signals for transferring results in cellular automata to the shift register, and for changing the values in the B register right after deriving the values of B^{-1}.

Moreover, our architecture can be easily expanded for other public key cryptosystems using general irreducible polynomials. In the dotted box in Fig.2, by using additional n-1 XOR gates, the proposed architecture can perform a general division operation. Although the architecture is used for a general divider, it has the same latency as Fig.2 because of the parallel property.

4 Comparison and Analysis

A comparison of the proposed evolutionary architecture with existing structures was performed focusing on the time and hardware complexity. As such, Wang's [15] and Kim's [16] division architectures were chosen.

Wang proposed a parallel-in parallel-out A/B architecture, which has a latency of $2n^2$-1.5n and a critical path of (T_{AND}+ $3T_{XOR}$) over GF(2^n). Kim proposed a serial-in serial-out A/B architecture, which has a latency of $2n^2$-2n and critical path of (T_{AND}+ $3T_{XOR}$) over GF(2^n).

Table 2. Performance comparison of A/B Circuits

Item	Wang et al. [15]	Kim et al. [16]	Fig. 3	
Irreducible polynomial	general	general	trinomial	General
Critical path	T_{2AND}+ $3T_{2XOR}$	$2T_{2AND}$+ $3T_{2XOR}$ + T_{MUX}	T_{2AND}+ T_{2XOR}+T_{MUX}	T_{2AND}+ T_{2XOR}+T_{MUX}
Latency	$2n^2$-1.5n	$2n^2$-2n	$2n^2$-3n+1	$2n^2$-3n+1
Hardware Complexity -Registers(R) -Latch(L) -Inverter(I)	$3n^3$ -$3n^2$ AND $3n^3$ -$3n^2$ XOR $8.5n^3$ -$8.5n^2$ (L)	$4n^2$-7n+3 AND $3n^2$-5n+2 XOR $14n^2$-22n+8 (L) n^2-2n+1 Mux $3n^2$-6n+2 (I)	n AND n+1 XOR $4n$+1 (R) $3n$-1 Mux	n AND $2n$ XOR $4n$+1 (R) $3n$-1 Mux
I/O format	Parallel-in parallel-out	Serial-in serial-out	Serial-in parallel-out	

Generally, parallel fashion architectures need much more hardware equipments than serial fashion architectures, and latency is reversed. However, the proposed architecture has better complexity than serial or parallel fashion architectures in the fields of the both sides, area and time. Our architecture only focuses on ECC, which is restricted by using irreducible trinomials. However, our architecture can be easily expanded for other public cryptosystems with additional n-1 XOR gates, while existing systolic architectures including Wang's and Kim's, hardly reduce the complexity although they apply irreducible trinomials for ECC. We have shown that our architecture does not influence in latency after it has been expanded for a general divider.

5 Conclusion

This paper has presented an evolutionary architecture to compute A/B modulo irreducible trinomials, which are restricted in Certicom Standard for ECC. We have proposed a simple evolutionary hardware architecture that is the most costly arithmetic operation schemes in ECC over GF(2^n), such as inverse and division. The proposed architecture includes the characteristics of both an evolutionary PBCA and irreducible trinomials, and has minimized both time complexity and hardware complexity. Moreover, we have shown that our architecture can be easily expanded for general division architectures with no additional latency. Therefore, we have shown that our architecture has outstanding advantages in both hardware complexity and time complexity compared to typical structures. Our evolutionary architecture has a regular structure and modularity. Accordingly, it can be used as a basic architecture not only for ECC, but also for other public key cryptosystems.

Acknowledgement

The authors would like to thank the anonymous referees for their valuable suggestions on how to improve the quality of the manuscript. This research was supported by the MIC (Ministry of Information and Communication), Korea, under the ITRC (Information Technology Research Center) support program supervised by the IITA (Institute of Information Technology Assessment).

References

1. N.Koblitz, Elliptic curve cryptosystems, Mathematics of Computation, Vol. 48. (1987) 203-209
2. V.Miller, Use of Elliptic Curves in Cryptography, Advances in Cryptology-CRYPTO'85, Springer-Verlog Lecture Notes in Computer Science, Vol. 218. (1986)
3. A.J.Menezes, Elliptic Curve Public Key Cryptosystems, Boston, MA: Kluwer Academic Publishers (1993)
4. T. R. N. Rao and E. Fujiwara, Error-Control Coding for Computer Systems, Englewood Cliffs, NJ: Prentice-Hall (1989)
5. W. Drescher, K. Bachmann, and G. Fettweis, "VLSI Architecture for Non Sequential Inversion over $GF(2^m)$ using the Euclidean Algorithm," The International Conference on Signal Processing Applications and Technology, Vol.2. (1997) 1815-1819
6. I. Lopez and R.Dahab, An overview of Elliptic Curve Cryptography, University of Campinas Press, Brazil (2000)
7. J. Von Neumann, The theory of self-reproducing automata, University of Illinois Press, Urbana and London (1966)
8. C. N. Zhang, M. Y. Deng, and R. Mason, "A VLSI Programmable Cellular Automata Array for Multiplication in $GF(2^n)$," PDPTA '99 International Conference (1999)
9. P. Pal. Choudhury and R. Barua, "Cellular Automata Based VLSI Architecture for Computing Multiplication and Inverses in $GF(2^m)$," IEEE 7th International Conference on VLSI Design (1994) 279-282
10. A. J. Menezs, Applications of Finite Fields, Boston, MA: Kluwer Academic Publishers (1993)
11. C. Kaufman, R. Perlman, and M. Speciner, Network Security private communication in a public world, New Jersey: Prentice Hall (2002)
12. SEC 1: Elliptic Curve Cryptography version 1.0, Certicom Reserch (2000)
13. IEEE P1363, Standard Specifications for Public Key Cryptography (2000)
14. S. W. Wei, "VLSI architecture of divider for finite field $GF(2^m)$", IEEE International Symposium on Circuit and Systems, Vol.2. (1998) 482-485
15. C. L. Wang and J. H. Guo, "New Systolic Arrays for C+ AB^2, inversion, and division in $GF(2^m)$", IEEE Trans. on Computer, Vol.49, No.10. (2000) 1120-1125
16. N. Y. Kim and K. Y. Yoo, "Systolic architecture for inversion/division using AB^2 circuits in $GF(2^m)$", Integration, the VLSI journal, Vol.35. (2003) 11-24
17. Jun-Cheol Jeon and Kee-Young Yoo, "An Evolutionary Approach to the Design of Cellular Automata Architecture for Multiplication in Elliptic Curve Cryptography over Finite Fields," Lecture Notes in Artificial Intelligence PRICAI 2004: Trends in Artificial Intelligence (LNAI 3157), Springer-Verlag, Vol.3157. (2004) 241-250

An Evolvable Hardware System Under Varying Illumination Environment

In Ja Jeon and Phill Kyu Rhee

School of Computer Science & Engineering, Inha University,
253 Yonghyun-Dong, Nam-Gu, Incheon, Korea
juninja@im.inha.ac.kr, pkrhee@inha.ac.kr

Abstract. This paper proposes an evolvable hardware system with capability of evolution under varying illumination environment, which is implemented on reconfigurable field programmable gate array platform with ARM core and genetic algorithm processor. The proposed evolvable hardware system for image processing consists of the reconfigurable hardware module and the evolvable software module, which are implemented using SoC platform board with the Xilinx Virtex2 FPGA, the ARM core and the GAP. The experiment result shows that images affected by environment changes are enhanced for various illumination image environments.

1 Introduction

The concept of a reconfigurable hardware and evolvable hardware has been studied actively [1, 3, 5, 6]. The evolvable hardware architecture is a functional evolvable module, which can be implemented by reconfigurable field programmable gate arrays (FPGAs) [8]. In this paper presents evolvable hardware system that is effective for implementing adaptive image processing. The reconfigurable hardware module process the median, histogram equalization, contrast stretching and illumination compensation algorithm, which are implemented on Xilinx Virtex2 FPGA. The evolvable software module consists of genetic algorithm and feature space search block, which are implemented by genetic algorithm processor (GAP) and ARM core, respectively [2]. Section 2 describes the evolvable hardware system for adaptive image processing applications. The experimental results are given in Section 3. In Section 4, the conclusions are given.

2 The Situation-Awareness Using the Neural Network

The evolvable neural network analyzes and decides the category of a given illumination environment. The changes of illumination environment can be decided by either analyzing the input images or monitoring the system performance. The evolvable neural network is trained by supervised learning. We define nine categories of illumination environments in the proposed illumination model by distinguishing the brightness level and the coarse lighting direction. The weighted node is threshold. We have tested three methods for illumination discrimination: the simple rule based discrimination (SR), the back propagation neural network based discrimination (BP), and the evolvable neural network based discrimination (E-NN). The training of evolutionary neural network is done 100 original face images accumulated in IT lab, and 800 virtually generated mosaic face images using the image synthesis method described above. The modeling face image reflecting a brightness variation can be done by the additive, the multiplicative, and the hybrid functions. Directional illumination variations are modeled by the sine and the cosine weight function.

3 Evolvable Hardware System for Image Processing

The proposed evolvable hardware system consists of the reconfigurable hardware module for the image preprocessing algorithms and the evolvable software module for feature space of Gabor representation and fitness evaluation, as shown in Fig. 1.

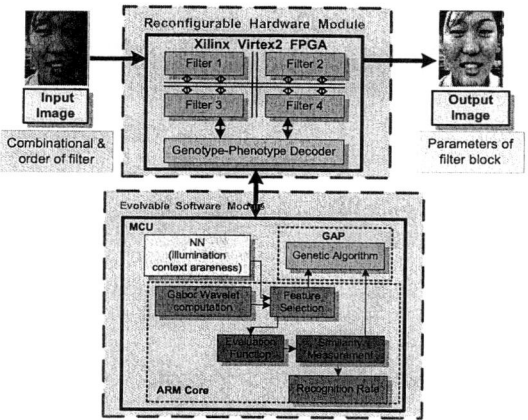

Fig. 1. The block diagram of evolvable hardware system.

3.1 Reconfigurable Hardware Module

The reconfigurable hardware module processes the image preprocessing algorithms, which are the median, the histogram equalization, the contrast stretching and the illumination compensation algorithm for object recognition [7]. This module consists of the genotype-phenotype decoder and 4 types of image filters, and it is implemented on Xilinx Virtex2 FPGA. The optimal image filter function can be searched and selected using genetic algorithm running on the genetic algorithm processor (GAP) and the genotype-phenotype decoding [2]. The input of reconfigurable hardware module is illumination image, which is suitable image to achieve processing. Therefore, the image filter function can be selected using the GAP about used order or used existence, and nonexistence of image that is most suitable to recognize. Used algorithm's order and existence and nonexistence are selected using the GA method. Composite processed image after image preprocessing is accomplished. The image filters are operated in parallel using multiple memory blocks in order to decrease processing time in hardware. The four types of image preprocessing filters are processed in parallel and synchronously. When this parallel processing method is applied to filters in hardware, the processing speed is increased more than about three times. The gene of GAP includes the sequent order and parameter values of filters. Each filter sets their parameter values and images are filtered in the order. The filtered images are sent to the fitness evaluating part. Selected filter gets the parameter values and image.

3.2 Evolvable Software Module

The role of evolvable software module controls a Gabor feature vector of a face for achieving optimal performance of recognition system in varying environment. The evolvable software module consists of a genetic algorithm block and a feature space search block for feature space of Gabor representation and fitness evaluation, which are implemented by software and processed by GAP and ARM processor [6]. GA block has two times repeatable functional block. The first module of GA block sends the information of the use existence, nonexistence, order, parameter value and window size of median filter to image preprocessing algorithm. The second module of GAP generates the possible combination of fiducial points, Gabor feature vectors and the optimality of the chromosome, which is defined by classification accuracy and generalization capability. The total Gabor feature vector for all fiducial points, V is evolved from a larger vector set defined as follows:

$$V = (F^{(e)}(\vec{x_1}) F^{(e)}(\vec{x_2}),,,, F^{(e)}(\vec{x_n})) \tag{1}$$

As it searches the geno-space, the GA makes its choices via genetic operators as a function of probability distribution driven by fitness function. The evolvable hardware system needs a salient fitness function to evaluate current population and choose offspring for the next generation. The system performance denotes the correctness that the evolvable adaptation has achieved so far, and the class scattering indicates the expected fitness on future generations.

4 Experimental Results

The proposed evolvable hardware system using FPGA platform with ARM processor has been tested to adapt the system for the image processing under uneven illumination.

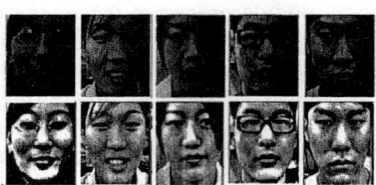

Fig. 2. Preprocessed image with uneven illumination by the proposed evolvable hardware system

IT Lab., FERET, and Yale databases are used for the performance evaluation of the proposed system. A-NN algorithm [8] is employed for face identification. For experiments, the number of initial population is set to 32 and each chromosome is evolved with crossover of 0.8 and mutation of 0.03. Fig. 2 shows the enhanced result for various illumination conditions. The sine shaped illumination is synthesized with the half region of input facial image.

Table 1 shows the experiment result in which we used 4 types of image preprocessing algorithms to compare the performance. As see in Table 1, we know that similarity rate is improved when used preprocessing algorithm used preprocessing algorithm variously according to the input image. Object recognition is performed in the action mode which consists of four phase: the situation-aware phase, the preprocessing phase, the Gabor feature space phase, and the class decision phase. The input image is preprocessed by the restructured filter bank using the filter chromosome corresponding to the detected environmental category. The preprocessed image is transformed into the Gabor feature vector. Finally, the class is decided by the class decision phase. A-nn algorithm is employed for the recognition. Experiment for the face recognition is performed using the data set accumulated by our lab and Yale dataset.

Table 1. Comparison of the performance between the image processing evolvable hardware image and traditional image processing method

	Histogram Equalization filter only	Median filter only	Illumination compensation filter only	Homommorphic filter only	Proposed method
IT Lab.	87.8%	90.8%	86.3%	89.6%	92.3%
FERET	91.3%	89.5%	88.5%	90.4%	92.5%
Yale	84.5%	90.4%	77.2%	87.5%	91.1%

Table 2. IT Lab and Yale dataset

Data	Number of image		Number of person		Success		Reject		Successful rate(%)	
	IT lab.	Yale	IT lab.	Yale	IT lab.	Yale	IT lab.	Yale	IT lab.	Yale
Histogram	4500	45	100	15	4385	39	29	3	97.44	86.66
Illumination compensation	4500	45	100	15	4170	36	39	4	92.66	80.00
Simple rule	4500	45	100	15	4395	43	28	0	97.66	95.56
BP	4500	45	100	15	4319	41	42	1	95.98	91.11
ENN	4500	45	100	15	4409	43	2	0	97.98	95.56

Table 2 shows a recognition rate of proposed method. It was successful rate in 97.98 % for IT Lab DB and 95.56 % for Yale dataset. The experimental result of proposed method shows the average recognition rate of 97% and an image filtering recognition rate of 93.06%. From Tables, it becomes apparent that selected image filter bank by genetic algorithm method shows good recognition performance while general illuminant filter single filter do. Evolvable neural network improved performance over the two during testing. This can interpret use existence and nonexistence and parameter of each image filter using genetic algorithm, because general filtering may appear result that flow image filter unconditionally, and drops preferably quality of original above zero because suitable parameter control is impossible.

5 Conclusions

Most existing technologies are not sufficiently reliable under changing illumination and various noises. The proposed evolvable hardware system performs well especially in changing illumination and noisy environments, since it can adapt itself to external environment. In this paper, we proposed an evolvable hardware system, which is implemented on Xilinx FPGA, ARM processor and GAP, for adaptive image processing applied to the face recognition in object recognition. The face recognition performs by Gabor wavelet, which is intrinsically robust to uneven environments. The face recognition is optimized using evolvable approach. The proposed system for face recognition adapts itself to varying illumination and noisy environments, and shows much robustness especially for changing environments of illumination and noisy.

References

1. T. Higuchi, M. Iwata and W. Liu: Evolvable Systems: From Biology to Hardware, Tsukuba, Springer, (1996)
2. D.E. Goldberg: Genetic Algorithms in Search, Optimization, and Machine Learning, Addison Wesley, (1989)
3. A. Stoica, et. al.: Reconfigurable VLSI Architectures for Evolvable Hardware: From Experimental Field Programming Transistor Arrays to Evolution-Oriented Chip, IEEE Trans. on VLSI Systems, Vol. 9, No. 1 (2001)
4. Bossmaier, T.R.J: Efficient image representation by Gabor functions - an information theory approach, in J.J. Kulikowsji, C.M. Dicknson, and I.J. Murray(Eds.), Pergamon Press, Oxford, U.K. 698-704.
5. A. Marshall, T. Stansfield, I. Kostarnov, et. al.: A Reconfigurable Arithmetic Array for Multimedia Applications, ACM/SIGDA International Symposium on FPGAs (1999) 135-143
6. K. K. Bondalapati: Modeling and Mapping for Dynamically Reconfigurable Hybrid Architectures, PhD thesis, University of Southern California (2001)
7. D. Goldberg: Genetic Algorithm in Search, Optimization, and Machine Learning, Addison-Wesley, (1989)
8. J. Faugman: Uncertainty relation for resolution in space, spatial frequency, and orientation optimization by two-dimensional cortical filters, Jounal Opt. Soc. Amer. Vol 2, No 7 (1985) 675-676
9. L. Wiskott, J.-M. Fellous, N. Kuiger and C. von der Malsburg: Face Recognition by Elastic Bunch Graph Matching, IEEE Transactions on Pattern Analysis and Machine Intelligence, vol. 19 (1997) 775-779

An Evolvable Hardware Chip for Image Enhancement in Surface Roughness Estimation

M. Rajaram Narayanan[1], S. Gowri[2], and S. Ravi[3]

[1] Research Scholar, Dept of Manufacturing Engg., Anna University, India
[2] Professor & Head, Dept of Manufacturing Engg., Anna University, India
[3] Member IEEE and Professor, Electronics and Communication,
Dr. M.G.R. Engg., College, India
rajaram_1967@yahoo.com, ravi_mls@yahoo.com

Abstract. Surface roughness is one of the essential quality control processes that the carried out to ensure that manufactured parts conform to specified standards and influences the functional characteristics of the work-piece such as fatigue, fracture resistance and surface friction. The most widely used surface finish parameter in industry is the average surface roughness (R_a) and is conventionally measured by using a stylus type instrument, which has a disadvantage that it requires direct physical contact and may not represent the real characteristics of the surface. Alternately, surface roughness monitoring techniques using non – contact methods based on computer vision technology [1] are becoming popular. In this paper, an evolvable hardware (EHW) configuration using Xilinx Virtex xvc1000 architecture to perform adaptive image processing i.e. noise removal and improve the accuracy of measurement of surface roughness is presented.

1 Introduction

Evolvable systems (EHW) are hardware units that are built on software reconfigurable logic devices such as FPGA and PLD and whose architecture can be reconfigured using genetic learning. To design conventional hardware, it is necessary to prepare all the specification of the hardware functions in advance. In contrast to this, EHW continues to reconfigure itself without such specifications to achieve a better performance. The basic idea of EHW is to regard architecture bits of a reconfigurable device as a chromosome for GA, which searches for an optimal hardware structure.

In the field of digital image processing particularly, a broad and disparate range of applications using evolutionary computation may be found in the literature, including the use of genetic algorithms in the segmentation of medical resonance imaging scans [3], a genetic program that performs edge detection on one-dimensional signals [4], the evolution of genetic programs to detect edges in petrographic images [5], and the evolution of spatial masks to detect edges within gray scale images.

This paper, presents evolvable hardware architecture, dedicated for implementing high performance image noise filtering on a custom Xilinx Virtex FPGA xcv1000, together with a flexible local interconnect hierarchy. After processing the initially grabbed images using the EHW system, the improved quality images of surfaces are used for evaluation of surface finish. Section 2 of this paper describes the classification of an EHW system. Section 3 describes the details of reconfigurable chip. The chip evolution is described in section 4. The experimental results are presented in section 5.

2 Evolvable Hardware System

The EHW architecture can be classified into functional and gate level [2] and is shown in figure1 and 2. In gate-level EHW, the architecture bits of PLDs are treated as GA chromosome. The architecture bits can be downloaded on PLDs. Such downloading can be engaged in either during or after the learning process.

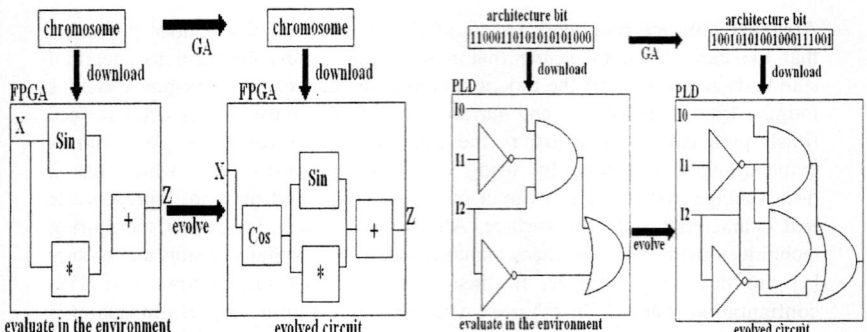

Fig. 1. Functional level evolution   **Fig. 2.** Gate level evolution

3 Reconfigurable Architecture

The virtual reconfiguration chip (VRC) of the EHW unit is shown in figure 3. In the present work, each PE except the first stage is assumed to receive inputs from any of the previous two stages. A total of 25 PE's used in the VRC. The genetic unit is programmed to give the best chromosome and using this, the initial configuration of the VRC is chosen. Each PE can handle 16 different function as listed in Table 1.

Table 1. Function codes

Code	Function	Code	Function
F0: 0000	X >> 1	F8 : 1000	(X+Y+1) >> 1
F1: 0001	X >> 2	F9 :1001	X & 0x0F
F2: 0010	~ X	F10: 1010	X & 0xF0
F3: 0011	X & Y	F11: 1011	X	0x0F
F4: 0100	X	Y	F12: 1100	X	0x F0
F5: 0101	X ^ Y	F13: 1101	(X&0x0F)	(Y&0xF0)
F6: 0110	X + Y	F14: 1110	(X&0x0F) ^ (Y&0xF0)
F7: 0111	(X+Y) >> 1	F15: 1111	(X&0x0F) & (Y&0xF0)

The logical configuration of the circuit is defined by a set of 25 inter triplets, one for each of the 25 PEs in the reconfigurable architecture. The first two integers of each triplet represent the source of inputs to the PE (cfg1 & cfg2) and the third integer of the triplet (cfg3) indexes the function (refer Table 1) to be applied by the PE.

4 Evolution of Chip

The proposed EHW system is shown in figure 4. The configuration word contains details about the interconnection between the PE's of the VRC and the functional operations performed within each PE. For each PE, the multiplexer inputs are chosen from the outputs of the previous two columns. Both cfg1 and cfg2 are constrained such that they should not exceed the number of the multiplexer inputs. The cfg3 input is the binary representation of the number of functions in store.

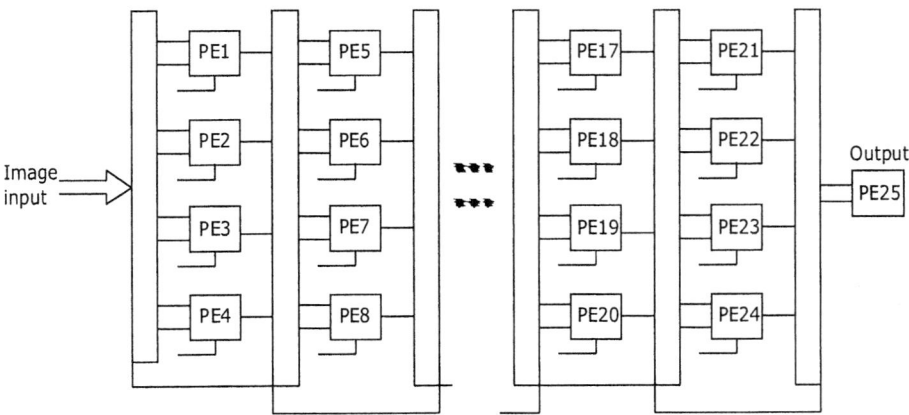

Fig. 3. Reconfigurable architecture

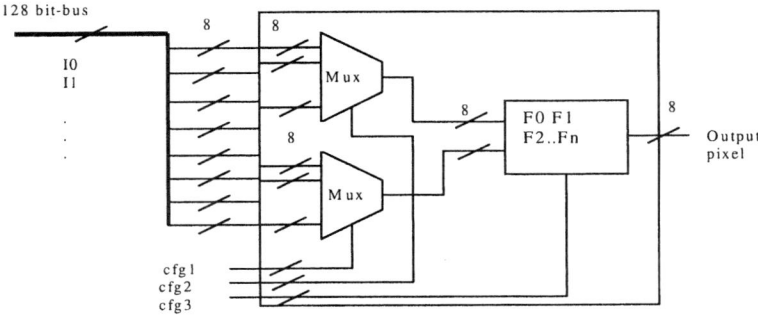

Fig. 4. Architecture of a single PE [output = F {mux(cfg1), mux(cfg2), cfg3}]

5 Experimental Results

The surface images of the specimens grabbed using the CCD camera are given to the EHW Chip and the configuration word is selected to eliminate the effects of improper illumination and noise. Preprocessing is performed to enhance the quality of images. Given an input images. 'I' with a resolution m x n , the chip extracts the edges and replaces the original low quality image with an output image 'O'. For experiments the number of initial population is set to 16 each chromosome is evolved with crossover 0.9 and mutation 0.01. Figure 5 shows the images corrupted by noise and figure 6 shown the preprocessed images using the EHW system. The two images in figure5 are the raw images obtained using vision system. The quality of the images is enhanced by 60.5% with the evolvable hardware chip unit.

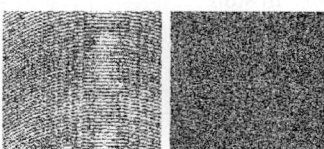
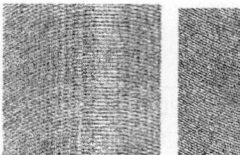

Fig. 5. Images with noise **Fig. 6.** Images without noise

The surface roughness values obtained using the styles approach along with the parameters feed, depth of cut (doc) and spindle speed are listed and the surface finish values obtained by using the evolvable hardware system on the milled surface is compared with other approaches and given in Table 2.

Table 2

S.No	feed (mm/rev)	doc (mm)	Speed (m/min)	R_a (Stylus) (µm)	R_a Reg. Analysis (µm)	R_a EHW (µm)
1	150	.5	123	3.05	3.23	3.17
2	150	.8	123	3.19	2.61	3.08
3	150	.5	153	5.35	6.05	5.48
4	200	.5	123	5.62	6.13	5.44
5	200	.8	123	3.75	3.38	3.68
6	200	.5	153	2.94	1.95	2.96

6 Conclusion

This paper has presented a genetic algorithm based EHW chip to inspect the surface roughness of components generated using milling process by preprocessing the images to remove the noise. The correlation obtained using regression approach after improving the quality of the surfaces using EHW system was better than that without enhancing the images. The experimental results clearly indicate that the proposed technique can be used to evaluate the roughness of the machined surfaces. Future direction of study is to be focused on using an artificial neural network (ANN) to predict the surface roughness using spindle speed, feed rate and depth of cut.

References

1. Vandenberg et al: "Digital image processing techniques, fractal dimensionality and scale-space applied to surface roughness", Wear, 159, (1992) 17-30
2. P. Layzell. A New research Tool for Intrinsic Hardware Evolution. Proc. 2nd Int. Conf. On Evolvable Systems (ICES'98), 47-56, Springer-Verlag, 1998.
3. R. Poli: Genetic Programming for Image Analysis. Genetic Programming: Proceedings of the first Annual Conference (1996) 363-368.
4. C. Harris and B. Buxton: Evolving Edge Detectors. Research Note RN/96/3(1996). University College London,
5. B. Ross, F. Feutan and D. Yashkir: Edge Detection of Petrigraphic Images using Genetic Programming
6. Brock Computer Science Technical Reports, Brock University, Ontario, Canada CS-00-01 (2000).

Evolutionary Agents for n-Queen Problems

Weicai Zhong, Jing Liu, and Licheng Jiao

Institute of Intelligent Information Processing, Xidian University, Xi'an 710071, China
neouma@163.com

Abstract. A novel algorithm, Multi-Agent Evolutionary Algorithm for n-Queen Problem (MAEAqueen), is proposed. In MAEAqueen, all agents live in a latticelike environment, with each agent fixed on a lattice-point. In order to increase energies, they compete with their neighbors, and they can also use knowledge. Theoretical analyses show that MAEAqueen has a linear space complexity. In the experiments, a comparison is made between MAEAqueen and the existing method based on agents. The results show that MAEAqueen outperforms the other method. Furthermore, to study the time complexity of MAEAqueen, the $10^4 \sim 10^7$-queen problems are used. The results show that MAEAqueen has a linear time complexity. Even for 10^7-queen problems, it can find the exact solutions only by 150 seconds.

1 Introduction

Traditional approaches to the n-queen problems are based on backtracking. Backtracking search techniques can systematically generate all possible solutions, but backtracking searching is exponential in time and is not able to solve a large-scale n-queen problem. Therefore, lots of new searching methods are proposed [1, 2], with a good performance obtained. Agent-based computation has been studied for several years in the field of distributed artificial intelligence and has been widely used in other braches of computer science [3, 5]. With the intrinsic properties of the n-queen problems in mind, we integrate the multi-agent systems and evolutionary algorithms (EAs) to form a new algorithm, Multi-Agent Evolutionary Algorithm for n-Queen Problems (MAEAqueen). MAEAqueen has a fast convergence rate. The convergence rate is slow has always been one of the key factors limiting the practical application of EAs, especially for large-scale problems. Homaifer et al. has solved the 200-queen problems by genetic algorithms [4], and [2] has solved the 7000-queen problem by an energy-based multi-agent model. But MAEAqueen can solve the 10^7-queen problems by only 150 seconds. This demonstrates that the methods integrating EAs and multiagent systems have a high potential in solving NP-complete problems.

2 The Evolutionary Agent for n-Queen Problems

According to [3], an agent is a physical or virtual entity that essentially has the following properties: (a) it is able to live and act in the environment; (b) it is able to sense its local environment; (c) it is driven by certain purposes and (d) it has some reactive behaviors. Therefore, the meaning of an agent is comprehensive, and what an agent represents is different for different problems. In general, three elements should be defined when agents are used to solve problems. They are the environment where all agents live, the purpose of each agent and the behaviors that agents can take.

2.1 The Evolutionary Agent for the *n*-Queen Problems

For the *n*-queen problems, the collisions on rows and columns can simply be avoided by a permutation of 1,2,...,*n*, thus the search space S can be expressed as

$$S = \{P_1, P_2, ..., P_{n!}\}$$
$$P_i = (queen_{i,1}, queen_{i,2}, ..., queen_{i,n}), \ 1 \leq i \leq n! \quad (1)$$
$$queen_{i,j} \in \{1, 2, ..., n\}, \ 1 \leq j \leq n$$
$$\forall 1 \leq k, l \leq n, \ (k \neq l) \Rightarrow (queen_{i,k} \neq queen_{i,l})$$

For $\forall (queen_1, queen_2, ..., queen_n) \in S$, $queen_i$ denotes the queen placed on the *i*th row and the $queen_i$th column. Thus, the collisions on rows and columns are avoided naturally, and then what needed to do is to find the permutations satisfying the constraints on the diagonal lines in S. An $n \times n$ grid has $(2n-1)$ positive diagonal lines and $(2n-1)$ negative diagonal lines, and they have the following characteristics: the difference between the row index and the column index is constant on any positive diagonal lines, and the sum of both indexes is constant on any negative diagonal lines. Therefore, the solutions of the *n*-queen problems must satisfy (2):

$$(queen_1, queen_2, ..., queen_n) \in S$$
$$\forall 1 \leq i, j \leq n, \ (i \neq j) \Rightarrow (i - queen_i \neq j - queen_j) \text{ and } (i + queen_i \neq j + queen_j) \quad (2)$$

The number of queens on the positive and negative diagonal lines that $queen_i$ is placed are labeled as $|queen_i^{pos}|$ and $|queen_i^{neg}|$, respectively. The number of queens on the *j*th positive and negative diagonal lines are labeled as $|posLine_j|$ and $|negLine_j|$, respectively. Where $1 \leq i \leq n$, $1 \leq j \leq (2n-1)$, and $|\cdot|$ denotes the number of elements in the set. An agent for the *n*-queen problems is defined as follows:

Definition 1: An agent, $a = (queen_1, queen_2, ..., queen_n) \in S$, is an element in the search space S. Its energy is equal to

$$Energy(a) = -\sum_{i=1}^{2n-1} Collisions(|posLine_i|) - \sum_{i=1}^{2n-1} Collisions(|negLine_i|) \quad (3)$$

where $Collisions(x) = \begin{cases} x & x \geq 2 \\ 0 & x < 2 \end{cases}$. The purpose of an agent is to increase its energy as much as possible.

All agents live in a latticelike environment, L, which is called an agent lattice. The size of L is $L_{size} \times L_{size}$, where L_{size} is an integer (see Fig.1). In Fig.1, each circle represents an agent, and the data in a circle represents its position in the lattice. The agent located at the ith row and the jth column is labeled as $L_{i,j}$, $i, j=1,2,\ldots,L_{size}$. Each agent is fixed on a lattice-point and it can only interact with its neighbors.

Definition 2: The neighbors of $L_{i,j}$ is $Nb_{i,j}=\{L_{i_1,j},L_{i,j_1},L_{i_2,j},L_{i,j_2}\}$, where $i_1=\begin{cases}i-1 & i\neq 1\\ L_{size} & i=1\end{cases}$,

$j_1=\begin{cases}j-1 & j\neq 1\\ L_{size} & j=1\end{cases}$, $i_2=\begin{cases}i+1 & i\neq L_{size}\\ 1 & i=L_{size}\end{cases}$, $j_2=\begin{cases}j+1 & j\neq L_{size}\\ 1 & j=L_{size}\end{cases}$.

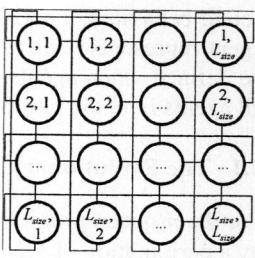

Fig. 1. The agent lattice

2.2 The Behaviors of the Evolutionary Agent

For the n-queen problems, the purpose of an algorithm is to find solutions by a computational cost as low as possible. Therefore, the computational cost can be considered as the resources of the environment in which all agents live. Because the resources are limited and the behaviors of the agents are driven by their purposes, an agent will compete with others to gain more resources.

Competition behavior: The energy of an agent is compared with those of its neighbors. If its energy is greater than that of any agent in its neighbors, then it can survive; otherwise it must die, and its lattice-point is taken up by the child of the agent whose energy is maximum in its neighbors. The details are described as follows:

Let $L_{i,j}=(queen_{i,j,1}, queen_{i,j,2}, \ldots, queen_{i,j,n})$, $a_{max}=(queen_{a1}, queen_{a2}, \ldots, queen_{an}) \in Nb_{i,j}$ and $\forall a \in Nb_{i,j}$, $Energy(a) \leq Energy(a_{max})$. If $Energy(L_{i,j}) \leq Energy(a_{max})$, then a_{max} generates a child agent, $c=(queen_{c1}, queen_{c2}, \ldots, queen_{cn})$ by following two steps to replace $L_{i,j}$:

$$\begin{aligned}&\text{(a)}\ queen_{ck} \leftarrow queen_{ak}, \text{ for } 1\leq k \leq n\\ &\text{(b)}\ queen_{ck} \leftrightarrow queen_{cl}, \text{ for } U_k(0,1) < p_c, 1 \leq k \leq n\end{aligned} \quad (4)$$

where l is a random integer in $1\sim n$ and is not equal to k, $U_k(0,1)$ is a uniform random number between 0 and 1 for each k, and $p_c \in (0, 0.1)$ is a predefined parameter. In fact, due to the small value of p_c, c is generated by exchanging a small part of a. The purpose of the competition behavior is to eliminate the agents with low energy, and give more chances to the potential agents.

Self-learning behavior: An agent increases its energy by using its knowledge. Suppose that the behavior is applied to $L_{i,j}=(queen_{i,j,1}, queen_{i,j,2}, \ldots, queen_{i,j,n})$, and then the details is described in Algorithm 1. $Swap(x, y)$ performs a swap of x and y.

Algorithm 1 The self-learning behavior

Step 1: $Repeat \leftarrow False$, $k \leftarrow 1$, $Iteration \leftarrow 1$;
Step 2: If $\left(|queen_{i,j,k}^{pos}|=1\right)$ and $\left(|queen_{i,j,k}^{neg}|=1\right)$, then go to Step 9;
Step 3: Select a random integer l in $1\sim n$ such that $k \neq l$;
Step 4: $Collision_{old} \leftarrow |queen_{i,j,k}^{pos}|+|queen_{i,j,k}^{neg}|+|queen_{i,j,l}^{pos}|+|queen_{i,j,l}^{neg}|$;
Step 5: $Swap(queen_{i,j,k}, queen_{i,j,l})$;

Step 6: $Collision_{new} \leftarrow |queen_{i,j,k}^{pos}|+|queen_{i,j,k}^{neg}|+|queen_{i,j,l}^{pos}|+|queen_{i,j,l}^{neg}|$;
Step 7: If $Collision_{old} > Collision_{new}$, then $Repeat \leftarrow True$; otherwise, $Swap(queen_{i,j,k}, queen_{i,j,l})$;
Step 8: If $Iteration < n-1$, then $Iteration \leftarrow Iteration+1$, go to Step 2; otherwise $Iteration \leftarrow 1$;
Step 9: $k \leftarrow k+1$; If $k \leq n$, then go to Step 2;
Step 10: If $Repeat = True$, go to Step 1; otherwise calculate the energy of $L_{i,j}$ and stop.

The purpose of Algorithm 1 is to find a swap for each queen which has collisions in $L_{i,j}$ such that the energy of $L_{i,j}$ is increased after the swap is performed. For a queen which has collisions, the algorithm iteratively performs the swap until the queen has not collisions or the predefined iterative count, $Iteration=(n-1)$, is achieved. Then, the algorithm goes to deal with the queen in the next row. $Iteration$ can prevent the algorithm from repeating infinitely. Because each queen only involves two diagonal lines, Step 4 and Step 6 only deal with the four diagonal lines in which $queen_{i,j,k}$ and $queen_{i,j,l}$ locate. To explain Algorithm 1 explicitly, Fig.2 gives the performing process of Algorithm 1 for the agent, $a=(1,2,8,4,5,7,3,6)$.

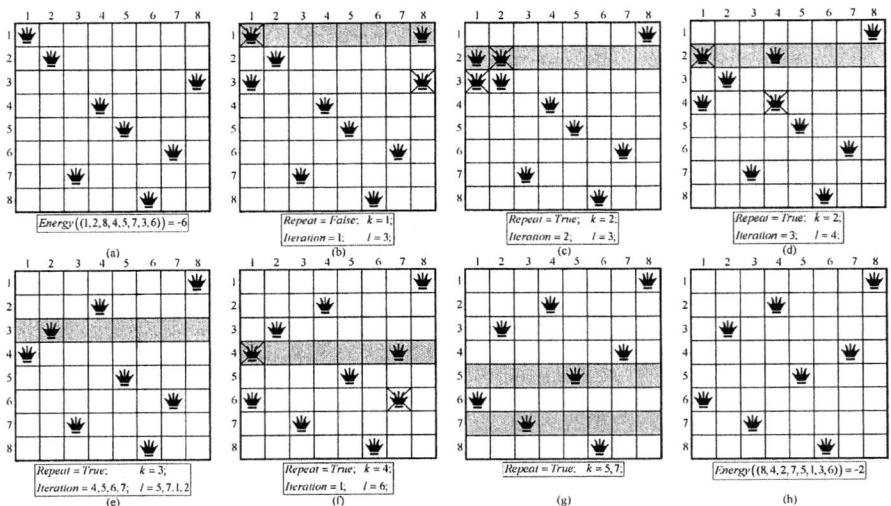

Fig. 2. The performing process of ALAORITHN 1 for the agent, $a = (1,2,8,4,5,7,3,6)$

For more clarity, Fig.2 is explained further. Because the queen in the first row has collisions, the algorithm first searches a swap for it, see Fig.2(b). Suppose that the selected l is 3, then after the swap, we have $Collision_{old}=7 > Collision_{new}=6$. So the swap is successful, $Repeat$ is set to $True$, and $Iteration$ increases 1. Here the queen in the first row has no collisions, so the algorithm deals with the queen in the second row, see Fig.2(c). Suppose that 3 is chosen for l. Although the swap is successful, the queen still has collisions, see Fig.2(d). Suppose that 4 is chosen for l, then the swap is successful and the algorithm deals with the queen in the third row, see Fig.2(e). Suppose that 5,7,1,2 are chosen for l in turn, but all swaps are failed. At the moment, *Iteration* is equal to 7, so *Iteration* is set to 1 and the algorithm deals with the queen in the fourth row, see Fig.2(f). Suppose that 6 is chosen for l, then the swap is successful. Presently, because the queen has not collisions, the algorithm deals with the queens in following rows, see Fig.2(g). Since the queens in the sixth and eighth row have not collisions, the algorithm deals with the queens in the fifth and seventh rows. But all swaps are failed. Because *Repeat* is *True*, the algorithm restarts from Step 1. During this time, the collisions of the queens in the fifth and seventh row cannot be eliminated yet. So *Repeat* is equal to *False* and the algorithm is stopped. The final state of a is shown in Fig.2(h) and its energy increases from –6 to –2.

3 The Implementation of MAEAqueen and Its Space Complexity

To solve the n-queen problems, all agents must orderly adopt the two behaviors aforementioned. Here the behaviors are controlled by means of evolution. The details are described in Algorithm 2.

Algorithm 2 Multi-Agent Evolutionary Algorithm for n-Queen Problem

L^t is the agent lattice in the tth generation. a^t_{Best} is the best agent among $L^0, L^1, \ldots,$ L^t, a^t_{tBest} the best agent in L^t. $Gens_{Max}$ is the maximum number of generations.

Step 1: Initialize the agent lattice L^0, update a^0_{Best}, and $t \leftarrow 0$;

Step 2: Perform the competition behavior on each agent in L^t: If $L^t_{i,j}$, $i,j=1,2,\ldots,L_{size}$ wins, then $L^t_{i,j}$ go into L^{t+1}; otherwise the child agent of the best agent among the neighbors of $L^t_{i,j}$ generated by (4) go into L^{t+1};

Step 3: Update $a^{t+1}_{(t+1)Best}$, and perform the self-learning behavior on $a^{t+1}_{(t+1)Best}$ according to Algorithm 1;

Step 4: If $Energy(a^{t+1}_{(t+1)Best}) \geq Energy(a^t_{Best})$, then $a^{t+1}_{Best} \leftarrow a^{t+1}_{(t+1)Best}$; otherwise $a^{t+1}_{(t+1)Best} \leftarrow a^t_{Best}$, $a^{t+1}_{Best} \leftarrow a^t_{Best}$;

Step 5: If $\left(Energy(a^{t+1}_{Best}) = 0\right)$ or ($t=Gens_{Max}$), then output a^{t+1}_{Best}, and stop; otherwise $t \leftarrow t+1$, go to Step2.

When a large-scale problem is dealt with, the memory required by an algorithm must be taken into account. For example, although the method proposed in [2] obtained a good performance, it needs to store a $n \times n$ lattice to record the number of collisions in each grid and its space complexity is $O(n^2)$. Even if each grid is recorded by an integer with 4 bytes, 38,147M memories still needed for a 10^5-queen problem.

Theorem 1: The space complexity of multi-agent evolutionary algorithm for n-queen problem is $O(n)$.

Proof: The main contribution to the space complexity is from the storage for the agent lattices in current generation and the next generation and the best agent. Therefore, the number of agents required be recorded is

$$Num_a = 2 \times L_{size} \times L_{size} + 1 \tag{5}$$

For each agent, a permutation with n integers and the value of energy require to be recorded, and so the number of space units required is

$$Units_a = n+1 \tag{6}$$

Therefore, the number of space units in total is

$$Num_{Units} = Num_a \times Units_a = (2L_{size}^2 + 1)n + (2L_{size}^2 + 1) \tag{7}$$

That is to say, the space complexity of MAEAqueen for n-queen problem is $O(n)$. □

If an integer requires 4 bytes and L_{size} is equal to 3, MAEAqueen requires 725M for 10^7-queen problems. So it can be used to solve the large-scale problems.

4 Experiments

All experiments are made on a 2.4-GHz Pentium IV with 1G RAM PC. The termination criterion of MAEAqueen is to find a solution satisfying the constraints.

4.1 The Effect of p_c on the Performance of MAEAqueen

The problems with 50, 100 and 500 queens are used, and p_c is increased from 0.01 to 0.5 in steps of 0.01. At each sampled value of p_c, 50 trials are carried for each problem, and the average running time is shown in Fig.3. As can be seen, the running time for the three problems increases with p_c. When p_c is in [0, 0.1], the running time is smaller than 0.05s, so we restrain p_c in [0, 0.1] in Section 2.2. To be consistent, p_c is set to 0.05 in all followed experiments.

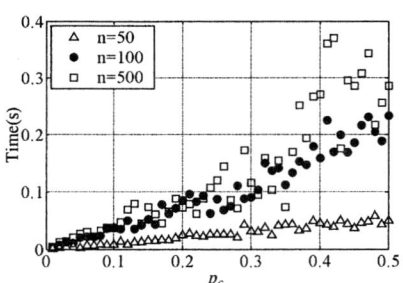

Fig. 3. The running time of MAEAqueen

Table 1. The average running time of MAEAqueen and [2] (s)

n	1000	2000	3000	4000	5000
MAEAqueen	9.4×10⁻⁴	1.6×10⁻³	2.2×10⁻³	3.4×10⁻³	3.7×10⁻³
[2]	1.5	10.9	21.8	40.7	118.4
n	6000	7000	8000	9000	10,000
MAEAqueen	4.7×10⁻³	5.9×10⁻³	5.3×10⁻³	7.5×10⁻³	9.1×10⁻³
[2]	284.5	400.7	—	—	—

Reference [2] designed the ERA model that can solve 7000-queen problems. So a comparison is made between MAEAqueen and [2], and the results are shown in Table 1. The results of [2] are obtained by running its software[1]. The software restrains n in 4~7000. As can be seen, the performance of MAEAqueen is much better than that of [2], and it only uses 9 milliseconds to solve 10^4-queen problem.

4.2 The performance of MAEAqueen on 5×10^4~10^7-Queen Problems

n is increased from 5×10^4 to 10^7 in steps of 50,000. At each sampled value of n, 50 trials are carried out, and the average running time is shown in Fig.4. As can be seen, the running time of MAEAqueen can be approximated by the function, $(5.04 \times 10^{-6} \times n^{1.07})$. That is to say, MAEAqueen has a linear time complexity and can solve problems with large scale.

For more clarity, the average running time and the standard deviation of MAEAqueen are shown in Table 2 for

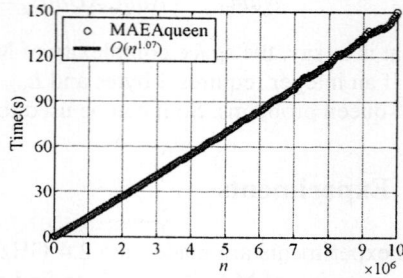

Fig. 4. The running time of MAEAqueen

the problems with 1×10^6, 2×10^6, ..., 1×10^7 queens. MAEAqueen only uses 13 seconds to solve the problem with 1×10^6 queens, and 150 seconds to solve the problem with 1×10^7 queens. Moreover, all standard deviations are very small, and the maximum one is only 1.15. All results show that MAEAqueen not only has a fast convergence rate, but also has a stable performance.

Table 2. The average running time and the standard deviation of MAEAqueen

n	1×10^6	2×10^6	3×10^6	4×10^6	5×10^6
Time(s)	12.88	26.75	40.83	55.06	69.75
St. Dev.	0.04	0.08	0.11	0.21	0.22
n	6×10^6	7×10^6	8×10^6	9×10^6	1×10^7
Time(s)	84.06	98.76	114.69	131.85	149.81
St. Dev.	0.32	0.30	0.45	1.10	1.15

5 Conclusions

In this paper, multi-agent systems and EAs are combined to form a new algorithm to solve n-queen problems. In the experiments, the 10^4~10^7-queen problems are used to test the performance of MAEAqueen. The results show that the time complexity of MAEAqueen is $O(n^{1.07})$ and MAEAqueen is competent for dealing with the large

---

[1] http://hjworm.edu.chinaren.com/myresearch.htm

scale problems. Moreover, all experimental results are obtained in the same parameter value, and the standard deviations are very small. It illustrates that MAEAqueen has a fast convergence rate, a stable performance, and is easy to use.

References

1. Sosič, R., Gu, J.: Efficient Local Search with Conflict Minimization: a Case Study of the n-queen Problem. IEEE Trans. on Knowledge and Data Engineering 6(5) (1994) 661-668
2. Liu, J., Han, J., Tang, Y. Y.: Multi-agent Oriented Constraint Satisfaction. Artificial Intelligence 136(1) (2002) 101-144
3. Liu, J.: Autonomous Agents and Multi-agent Systems: Explorations in Learning, Self-organization, and Adaptive Computation. Singapore: World Scientific (2001)
4. Homaifar, A., Turner, J., Ali, S.: The N-queens Problem and Genetic Algorithms. Proceedings of IEEE SOUTHEASTCON, Birmingham, USA, (1992) 262-267
5. Zhong, W., Liu, J., Xue, M., Jiao, L.: A Multiagent Genetic Algorithm for Global Numerical Optimization. IEEE Trans. Syst., Man, and Cybern. B 34(2) (2004) 1128-1141

Fictitious Play and Price-Deviation-Adjust Learning in Electricity Market

Xiaoyang Zhou[1], Li Feng[1], Xiuming Dong[1], and Jincheng Shang[2]

[1] Huazhong University of Science and Technology, Wuhan 430074, P.R. China
z_z7613@yahoo.com.cn
[2] Henan Electric Power Company, Zhengzhou 450052, P.R. China

Abstract. Investigate how the level of rationality of power suppliers impacts on equilibrium. First fictitious play was established to electricity market. Then a leaning model Price-deviation-adjust (PD-adjust) was proposed, which inherits main characters of the fictitious play but in a lower rationality because of poor information. An interesting phenomenon is observed in numerical simulations: the errors coming from lower rationality of the agents can be reinforced and often bring the agents extra profits rather than loss, and eventually drive the market to enter an unstable state from the stable equilibrium one. The conclusion is a set of game models identified by a rationality variable should be introduced to understand the electricity market better.

1 Introduction

Electric power industries around the world are undergoing restructuring. Price spikes have been observed in almost every electricity market but explicit analysis of these phenomena is rare[1]. The price spikes give profits to suppliers much in excess of their marginal costs even when sufficient supply is available, and introduce price volatility which can cause serious economic damage. The oligopoly equilibrium approach helps to analyze and detect such situations. The game-theoretic concepts have been prominently applied to electricity markets such as the supply function and the Cournot equilibrium model[2].

However, standard game theory is based on the assumption of perfect rationality and has focused mainly on equilibrium concepts. Agents in perfect rationality have commonly known identical beliefs in equilibrium and by definition it is a self-enforcing state. Once equilibrium is reached no agent has incentives to leave the strategy (or mixed strategy). However, equilibrium concepts do not explain how rational agents get to have identical beliefs or, in other words, how this self-enforcing state arises.

It is helpful to re-understand the electricity market from game learning[3] and behavior game[4] viewpoint. Ideally, we would like a model of bounded rationality which allows "decision makers may simplify, misunderstand, lack ability, miscalculate, forget, and make evaluations of alternatives that depend on seemingly irrelevant details about how a problem is framed"[5]. This kind of game models pay more attention to explain how people learn, adapt or evolve toward equilibrium. Therefore different learning models have different convergence (hence different equilibrium) and stability properties and often these properties depend on the properties of specific games.

In this paper, we establish a fictitious play model to electricity market (that is a well-known learning model but little literature in electricity market has discussed it), and then suggest a price deviation adjust (PD adjust) learning which provides a power supplier who has poor information about his opponents with a tool to detect extra profit in equilibrium case. Our main interest is to observe what the assumption (the agents are in lower level of rationality) will bring to the market. We believe a multi-game learning model (i.e. a set of game learning models identified by rationality level of the agents) should be introduced to get better insight into the electricity market but in fact we know little about this issue.

A good example of this can be provided by the PD-adjust learning. This learning model is at a lower level of rationality due to poor information. However, our numerical simulations show a little surprising result: the agents often benefit from, rather than lose by, the errors coming from the lower rationality, and the errors can be continuously reinforced in bidding process eventually drive the market to enter an unstable state from the stable equilibrium one. The interesting phenomenon hints to us that the level of rationality of agents is a noteworthy variable. The variable will bring a multi-game model to the electricity market in different way, which will be helpful to understand the market better.

2 Learning and Evolution

2.1 Information Feedback Construction of Market Power

We consider an electricity market in which there are K power suppliers and a power exchange (PX). Suppose that supplier i has the cost function $C(q_i) = a_i q_i^2 + b_i q_i + c_i$, where q_i is his output such that $0 \leq q_i \leq \overline{q}_i$ and $\overline{q}_i$ his maximum capacity ($i = 1,2,\cdots,K$). At stage t, all suppliers present the supply functions

$$q_i = q_i(\lambda), \; i = 1,\cdots,K \tag{1}$$

to the electricity pool, then the PX determines a market clearing price(MCP) λ_{MCP} by solving supply-demand balance equation

$$\sum_{i=1}^{K} q_i(\lambda) = Q - r\lambda \tag{2}$$

where Q is the load at stage t and r the elasticity coefficient of the market.

The supply function (SF) $q_i = q_i(\lambda)$ represents supplier i's willingness to provide output q_i at price λ. Bidding function is its inverse function denoted by $\lambda = \lambda_i(q_i)$. Let S_i represent bidding strategy set of supplier i. The supplier selects a strategy $s_i^t \in S_i$ and establishes the bidding function by

$$\lambda = \lambda_i(q_i, s_i^t) = s_i^t \cdot C_i'(q_i) = s_i^t \cdot (2a_i q_i + b_i), \; 0 \leq q_i \leq \overline{q}_i \tag{3}$$

where $C_i'(q_i)$ is his marginal cost function.

From the viewpoint of supplier i, the supply-demand balance equation (3) has an equivalent expression

$$q_i + q_{-i}(\lambda) + r\lambda = Q \quad (4)$$

where $q_{-i}(\lambda) = \sum_{j \neq i} q_j(\lambda)$ is the aggregated supply of the supplier's opponents at price λ. Denote the inverse function of $q_{-i} = q_{-i}(\lambda) + r\lambda$ by

$$\lambda = \lambda_{-i}(q_{-i}, r), \quad \forall \ q_{-i} \in [0, \overline{q}_{-i}] \quad (5)$$

where $\overline{q}_{-i} = \sum_{j \neq i} \overline{q}_j$ is maximum supply of the supplier's opponents. Thus Equation (4) becomes

$$\lambda = \lambda_{-i}(Q - q_i, r), \quad 0 \leq q_i \leq \overline{q}_i \quad (6)$$

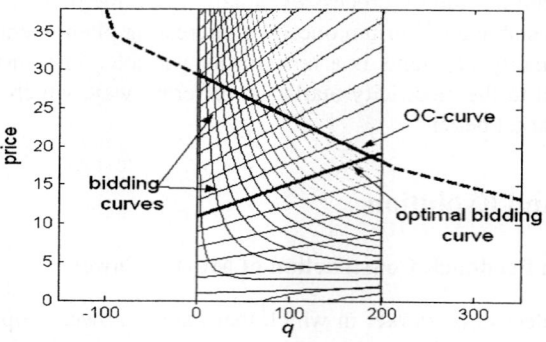

Fig. 1. OC-curve and bidding curve of supplier i

For the purpose of simplification, we call function $\lambda = \lambda_{-i}(Q - q_i, r)$ the opponent constrain curve (OC-curve) of supplier i. Fig. 1 shows OC-curve which is a monotonically descending function on the supplier's output interval $[0, \overline{q}_i]$. Two remarks are (1) the slope of the curve is completely determined by the bidding strategies of the supplier's opponents and the market elasticity, i.e. supplier i can't directly determine this curve, and (2) when supplier i chooses an output $\tilde{q}_i$ then the MCP will be just equal to $\tilde{\lambda} = \lambda_{-i}(Q - \tilde{q}_i, r)$, therefore a steep OC-curve may provide the supplier with a stronger motivation to release his market power for driving market price up.

Moreover, OC-curve reveals a market-power-information-feedback-loop. An agent in the oligopolistic competition can realize the market price is the result of the interaction of himself and his opponents: his OC-curve is determined by his opponents but at the same time his bidding affects the opponents' OC-curves too. For example, a possible interaction (positive feedback) can be illustrated as follows bids higher(agent) → steeper OC-curve (opponents) → bid higher(opponents) → steeper OC-curve(agent) → bid higher (agent) →...

Obviously, the OC curves provide the suppliers a bridge to exchange their information without direct collusion.

2.2 Fictitious Play

Fictitious play is a belief-based learning model which assumes that an agent has available information of his opponents' strategy before current period. The OC-curve construction is great helpful to build the learning in the electricity market

Agent i has an exogenous initial weight function $\kappa_0^j : S^j \rightarrow R^+$. This weight is updated by adding 1 to the weight of his j-th opponent's strategy each time it is played, so that:

$$\kappa_t^j(s^j) = \kappa_{t-1}^j(s^j) + \begin{cases} 1 & \text{if } s^j = s_{t-1}^j \\ 0 & \text{if } s^j \neq s_{t-1}^j \end{cases}, \forall s^j \in S^j \text{ for } j \neq i \quad (7)$$

The probability that agent i endows agent j's strategy s^j with at period t is given by

$$\gamma_t^j(s^j) = \frac{\kappa_t^j(s^j)}{\sum_{\tilde{s}^j \in S^j} \kappa_t^j(\tilde{s}^j)}, \forall s^j \in S^j \quad \forall j \neq i \quad (8)$$

In order to establish the fictitious play learning, which is the best response to the expected value of the agent's profit, the agent can firstly generate a pure strategy s^j of agent j at random, based on the belief $\{\gamma_t^j, j \neq i\}$. Thus he gets a pure strategy profile of his opponents $s^{-i} = (s^1, \cdots, s^{i-1}, s^{i+1}, \cdots, s^K)$ that determines an OC-curve $\lambda_{-i}(Q - q_i, r)$, $0 \leq q_i \leq \bar{q}_i$. N OC-curves are simulated in this way, denoted $\{\lambda_{-i,l}(Q - q_i, r), l = 1, \cdots N\}$, then an expected value of OC-curves based on the belief $\gamma_t^{-i} = \gamma_t^1 \times \cdots \times \gamma_t^{i-1} \times \gamma_t^{i+1} \times \cdots \times \gamma_t^K$ can be estimated by

$$E_{\gamma_t^{-i}}(\lambda_{-i}(Q - q_i, r)) \approx (1/N) \cdot \sum_{i=1}^{N} \lambda_{-i,l}(Q - q_i, r), 0 \leq q_i \leq \bar{q}_i \quad (9)$$

where $E_{\gamma_t^{-i}}$ is an expectation operator on the distribution γ_t^{-i}. Now an optimal output is determined by

$$\hat{q}_i = \arg \max_{q_i \in [0, \bar{q}_i]} \left\{ \left((1/N) \cdot \sum_{i=1}^{N} \lambda_{-i,l}(Q - q_i, r)\right) q_i - C_i(q_i) \right\} \quad (10)$$

i.e. the output $\hat{q}_i$ maximizes the agent's expected profit. Then the best strategy response of the agent can be obtained by directly solving the following equation

$$s \cdot (2a_i \hat{q}_i + b_i) = (1/N) \cdot \sum_{i=1}^{N} \lambda_{-i,l}(Q - \hat{q}_i, r) \quad (11)$$

according to the bidding scheme of the agent mentioned as above (see Equation (3),(6) or Fig.1)). Then the best strategy is

$$\hat{s}^i = (1/N) \cdot \sum_{i=1}^{N} \lambda_{-i,l}(Q - \hat{q}_i, r)/(2a_i\hat{q}_i + b_i) \tag{12}$$

We can also define a marginal empirical distribution of agent i as

$$d_t^i(s^i) = (\kappa_t^j(s^i) - \kappa_0^j(s^i))/t \tag{13}$$

Its limit (if existing) is usually regarded as mixed strategy equilibrium of the agent ($t \to \infty$).

2.3 Price Deviation Adjust Learning

OC-curve provides a supplier with detailed information about his opponents' strategy. However, in the real world only the information about MCP and agent's own output is usually available to the agent. In other words, an agent may have to estimate roughly the aggregated supply of his opponents by a linear function $q_{-i} = q_{-i}(\lambda) = \beta_{-i}\lambda + \alpha_{-i}$. Then his OC- curve becomes

$$\lambda = s_{-i} \cdot (Q - \alpha_{-i} - q_i) \ , 0 \leq q_i \leq \overline{q}_i \ , \overline{s}_{-i} = 1/(\beta_{-i} + r) \tag{14}$$

Notice our focus is to observe influence of the rationality level of agents, so in here we should realize Equation (14) shows a lower level of rationality. But even so, the supplier still faces the difficulty in dealing with the randomness of the slope and intercept parameter (s_{-i}, α_{-i}) in this equation, which comes from the random behavior of his opponents (mixed strategies). An approximation

$$\lambda = \overline{s}_{-i} \cdot (Q - \overline{\alpha}_{-i} - q_i) + \varepsilon \ , 0 \leq q_i \leq \overline{q}_i \tag{15}$$

may be used to reduce the difficulty but it shows much lower level of rationality than equation (14). In Equation (15) the randomness is simply expressed by the noise term ε ($E(\varepsilon) = 0$), and $\overline{s}_{-i}, \overline{\alpha}_{-i}$ are respectively the expected values of s_{-i}, α_{-i}. It is easy to know the equation has an equivalent expression

$$\lambda = E\lambda^R - \overline{s}_{-i} \cdot (q_i - Eq_i^R) + \varepsilon \ , 0 \leq q_i \leq \overline{q}_i \tag{16}$$

where (λ^R, q_i^R) is real market price and the supplier's output. The expectations included in Equation (16) can be estimated by history samples available to the supplier. Obviously, we can build a learning model similar to the fictitious play described in section 2.2 if the slope parameter $\overline{s}_{-i}$ is known. Instead of Equation (9), the average of OC-curve now is

$$\lambda = E\lambda^R - \overline{s}_{-i} \cdot (q_i - Eq_i^R) \tag{17}$$

and the optimal output (see equation (10)) is determined by

$$\hat{q}_i(\overline{s}_{-i}) = \arg\max_{q_i \in [0, \overline{q}_i]} (E\lambda^R - \overline{s}_{-i}(q_i - Eq_i^R))q_i - C_i(q_i) \tag{18}$$

At the same time the price corresponding the optimal output $\hat{q}_i(\overline{s}_{-i})$

$$\lambda(\overline{s}_{-i}) = E\lambda^R - \overline{s}_{-i} \cdot (\hat{q}_i(\overline{s}_{-i}) - Eq_i^R) \tag{19}$$

in fact is regarded by the supplier as an optimal expected price. Hence his optimal bidding strategy will be

$$s_i^{opt} = \lambda(\overline{s}_{-i})/(2a_i\hat{q}_i + b_i) \tag{20}$$

which is determined by solving the equation $s_i \cdot (2a_i\hat{q}_i(\overline{s}_{-i}) + b_i) = \lambda(\overline{s}_{-i})$ (see Equation (11)).

However, the slope parameter $\overline{s}_{-i}$ is actually unknown so need to be learned by the agent. We suggest a learning model, call it *price deviation adjust* (PD adjust) for statement simplification. Suppose the market has reached equilibrium after a long adjustment. In this case, a supplier may think he has a proper market share. But the profit motive encourages him to detect higher profit. In his mind

$$\lambda^R = E\lambda^R - \overline{s}_{-i} \cdot (\hat{q}_i(\overline{s}_{-i}) - Eq_i^R) + \varepsilon^R = \hat{\lambda}(s_{-i}) + \varepsilon^R \tag{21}$$

is the real market price λ^R corresponding to the optimal output $\hat{q}_i(\overline{s}_{-i})$ (see Equation(15) or (16), which in fact is an evaluation of the market clearing condition in the supplier mind). According to Equation (21), the true slope parameter $\overline{s}_{-i}$ should satisfy

$$E(\lambda^R) - \hat{\lambda}(\overline{s}_{-i}) = E(\varepsilon^R) = 0 \tag{22}$$

which means $\overline{s}_{-i} \cdot (\hat{q}_i(\overline{s}_{-i}) - Eq_i^R) = 0$. $\overline{s}_{-i} = 0$ implies the supplier abandons his own market power hence a reasonable selection is

$$s_{-i}^* = (E\lambda^R - 2a_i Eq_i^R - b_i)/Eq_i^R \tag{23}$$

i.e. s_{-i}^* is the root of equation $\hat{q}_i(\overline{s}_{-i}) = Eq_i^R$. We omit some details for but indicate the condition $s_{-i}^* \geq 0$ is necessary. That will be true if the average of the market price is higher than the average of the supplier's marginal cost, that is usually right in oligopolistic competition case, otherwise s_{-i}^* has to be taken as 0.

Notice that the assumption $E(\varepsilon^R) = 0$ indicates a lower rationality of the supplier brought by poor information. In fact the price is $\lambda^R = \lambda_{-i}(Q - q_i^R, r)$ according to Equation (6) hence real error in Equation (22) should be

$$\varepsilon^R = \lambda_{-i}(Q - q_i^R, r) - \left(E\lambda^R - \overline{s}_{-i} \cdot (\hat{q}_i(\overline{s}_{-i}) - Eq_i^R)\right) \tag{24}$$

Obviously, it is difficult to conclude $E(\varepsilon^R) = 0$. However, Equation (22) is still helpful for the supplier to capture some useful information about his opponents, otherwise he can do nothing except maintaining the equilibrium.

We now outline the PD-adjust learning model: Suppose the market has reached equilibrium and profit ue_i (corresponding to the equilibrium) is acceptable for supplier i. In this case, PD-adjust suggests the supplier detect higher profits by evaluating his opponents' behavior, rather than maintain the equilibrium. The strategy (20) suggested by PD-adjust is based on his lower rational belief (17) and the (possibly poor) estimation (22) for unknown slope parameter. The strategy will be reinforced if it brings the supplier extra profit, otherwise the supplier will choose to maintain the equilibrium.

Table 1. Cost parameter and supply quantity of six firms

Suppliers	a	b	c	The lowest supply (MW)	The highest supply (MW)
1	0.0037	200	0	0	200
2	0.0083	325	0	0	200
3	0.0175	175	0	0	200
4	0.0250	300	0	0	200
5	0.0250	300	0	0	200
6	0.0625	100	0	0	200

2.4 Evolutionary Analysis

In numerical simulations, we use the cost data in IEEE30 (six suppliers), as shown in Table 1. The load interval is considered as [200,1200](MW) and market elasticity coefficient $r = 0$ in all simulations.

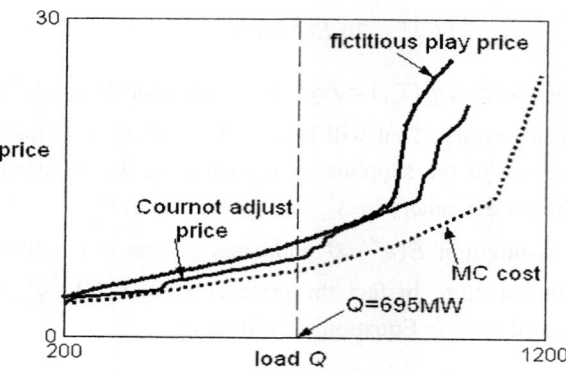

Fig. 2. Fictitious play price, Cournot-adjust price and marginal cost price

The first experiment is about the fictitious play in complete information case. Fig. 2 shows the results, in which the marginal cost price (MC Price, the price when all suppliers bid with their marginal costs) curve is at the bottom. The Cournot-adjust price curve is beyond it. Cournot-adjust is another well-known learning model in game learning theory, which suggests each agent choose a best response to behavior of his opponents the previous period rather than an average of all the past as done in fictitious play. Therefore, it is not strange that the equilibrium price corresponding to fictitious play should be higher than that of the Cournot-adjust as shown in Fig. 2.

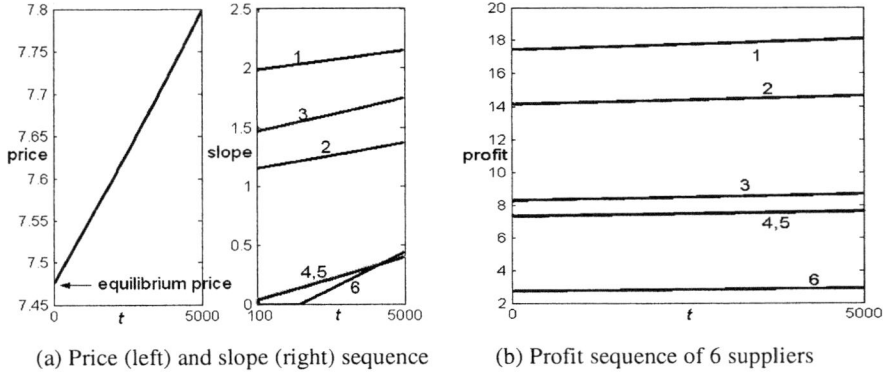

(a) Price (left) and slope (right) sequence   (b) Profit sequence of 6 suppliers

Fig. 3. PD-adjust (Initial state is the Cournot-adjust equilibrium, Number 1~6 indicate the suppliers' index)

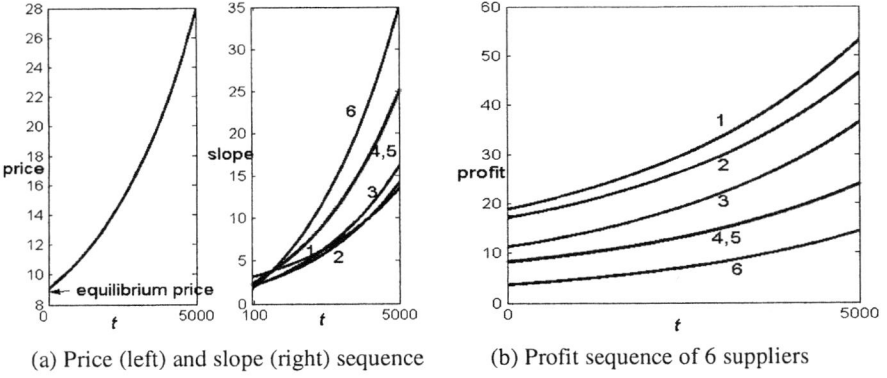

(a) Price (left) and slope (right) sequence   (b) Profit sequence of 6 suppliers

Fig. 4. PD-adjust (Initial state is the Fictitious Play equilibrium, Number 1~6 indicate the suppliers' index)

The second class of experiments is about the PD-adjust learning. We design the experiments in the following way: Load is fixed to $Q = 695$MW such that both Cournot-adjust and fictitious play learning can reach equilibriums. Then the suppliers are assumed to play PD-adjust with the initial equilibrium strategies.

Fig. 3 and Fig. 4 show respectively the price evolutionary processes from the Cournot-adjust and Fictitious Play equilibrium. 5,000 iterations are carried out. We observe an increasing price sequence in both cases (see the left sub-plot in Fig.3 and 4 (a)) and a positive feedback process mentioned in section 2.1: the suppliers capture the increasing price signal by estimating their slope parameters of OC curves. The increasing slope parameters (see the right sub-plot of Fig. 3 and 4 (a)) then encourage the suppliers to try higher bidding, which will result in the price increase further. In this process, the output of each supplier has no change from his equilibrium. We also observe in this process all agents obtain persistently increasing profits, which are higher than their equilibrium ones (see Fig.3~4 (b)), hence all of them will prefer playing PD-adjust to maintaining the old equilibrium.

Remark: In this paper we focus our study on what will appear if considering the level of rationality of agents as a variable. In fact the study is initial and in theory. For example in the real world, it is impossible that the price can increase persistently to reach such high level as in our numerical simulations. PX may restrict it by so-called price-cap strategy. However, how prevent the electricity market from crisis, which means restrict the price into a *reasonable range*, is a very important and challenge topic. We hope our discovery is helpful to the topic.

3 Conclusion and Discussion

In fictitious play game, agents behave as if they thought they were facing a stationary but unknown distribution of opponents' strategies. Then the beliefs will be formed and updated by observing the history or past behavior of opponents. By choosing a best response with those given beliefs, the agents interact strategically until they are mutually consistent (equilibrium). In poor information case, some learning models at lower level of rationality are developed such as reinforce learning[6-8]. Different from them, the PD-adjust inherits main characters of the fictitious play except replacing the exact belief with a rougher one in which an unknown slope parameter needs to be estimated from the price information. Obviously, the learning is at lower level of rationality due to poor information so no agent is willing to play it before he feels his output or profit has reached a satisfactory share. However, after the market reaches equilibrium, PD-adjust is helpful for agents to drive price up for detecting extra profits. In this process, the deviations coming from the lower rationality can be gradually reinforced through the information feedback loop of market power. For example, an agent may believe his opponents bid higher based on his belief function. But in fact that is a wrong inference because the market is in equilibrium at this time. This error comes from the level of rationality of the agent, e.g. a rough OC-curve (16) and assumption (22) on the distorted noise. Obviously, it is unrealistic to expect the rough belief can bring a good estimation of the opponent's behavior, so the action of agent based on the belief is in lower rationality. However, the reinforcement "errors" often bring extra profits to the agents rather than loss and eventually drive the market to enter an unstable state from the stable equilibrium one. That is a very interesting phenomenon.

It is not a surprise that the agents often benefit from their rationality error. If we take the level of rationality as a variable and regard the "error" coming from lower rationality as a disturbance to the perfect rationality, then equilibrium in fact will depend on rationality of the agents and the perfect rationality is only a special case. So the standard game theory only provides the electricity market with a "local description". We need a "global description": a multi-game-model including a rationality variable is more reasonable and helpful to understand the market better. For example, the perfect-rationality tells the suppliers to maintain the equilibrium, as is advised by Nash equilibrium in standard game theory. However, the multi-model suggests them to try extra profits. Similarly, a single game model provides PX with the equilibrium and regards equilibrium as the prediction of the market. In reverse, the multi-model advises PX to focus on reducing the behavior diversity of the suppliers in order to prevent the market from crisis.

Acknowledgments

This work is supported by the National Natural Science Foundation of China under Grant Nos. 70271069.

References

1. Xiaohong, G., Yuchi, H., David, L.P.: Gaming and Price Spikes in Electric Power Markets. IEEE Transactions on Power Systems, 16 (2001) 402–408
2. Aleksandr, R., Tabors, C.: Supply Function Equilibrium: Theory and Applications. 36th Annual Hawaii International Conference on System Sciences (HICSS'03) Track 2, Big Island, Hawaii, (2003)
3. Drew, F., David, K.L.: The Theory of Learning in Games .The MIT Press (1998)
4. Camerer, C.F.: Behavioral Game Theory: Experiments in Strategic Interaction. Princeton, N.J. Princeton University Press (2003)
5. Martin, D.: Review of Ariel Rubinstein's Modeling Bounded Rationality. Economics & Philosophy, 17 (2001) 134–140
6. Ido, E., Alvin E.R.: Predicting How People Play Games: Reinforcement Learning Experimental Games with Unique, Mixed Strategy Equilibria. The American Economic Review, 88 (1998) 847–880
7. Sarin, R, Vahid, F.: Predicting How People Play Games: A Simple Dynamic Model of Choice. Games and Economic Behavior, 34 (2001) 104–122
8. Sarin, R., Vahid, F.: Payoff Assessments without Probabilities: A Simple Dynamic Model of Choice. Games and Economic Behavior, 28 (1999) 294–309

Automatic Discovery of Subgoals for Sequential Decision Problems Using Potential Fields

Huanwen Chen*, Changming Yin, and Lijuan Xie

Changsha University of Science and Technology,
Changsha 410076, Hunan, China
hwchen@csust.edu.cn

Abstract. This paper presents a new method by which a sequential decision agent can automatically discover subgoals online. The agent discovers subgoals using potential field. The method uses a reward function to generate a potential field, and then abstracts some features from the potential field as candidates of subgoals. Based on the candidates, the agent can determine its behaviors online through some heuristics in unknown environment. The best-known and most often-cited problem with the potential field method is local minima. But our method does not have this limitation because the local minima are used to form subgoals. The disadvantage of the local minima in the previous approaches of potential field turns out to be an advantage in our method. We illustrate the method using a simple gridworld task.

1 Introduction

In sequential decision problems, as studied in the dynamic programming and reinforcement learning literatures, the "task" or "problem" is represented by a reward function. Given the reward function and a model of the domain, an optimal policy is determined. The ability to decompose such a complex problem into a set of simple problems is necessary for solving large scale sequential decision problems. One way to do this is to discover useful subgoals automatically.

Methods for automatically introducing subgoals have been studied in the context of adaptive production systems, where subgoals created are based on examinations of problem-solving protocols (e.g., [1,2,3]). Recently, several researchers have proposed reinforcement learning approaches which introduce subgoals. In Digney's system [4,5], states that are visited frequently or states where their reward gradients are high are chosen as subgoals. Drummond [6] proposed a system where a reinforcement learning agent detected walls and doorways through the use of vision processing techniques applied to the learned value function. McGovern and Barto [7] introduced a method for automatically creating subgoal options online by searching for bottlenecks in observation space. The method formulated the problem as a multiple-instance learning problem and used the concept of diverse density to solve it.

---

* This research was funded by NSFC60075019.

Potential field principle is particularly attractive because of its elegance and simplicity. Previous researches of potential field are mainly focused on obstacle avoidance applications for mobile robots and manipulators [8]. In these approaches obstacles exert repulsive forces onto the robot, while the target applies an attractive force to the robot. The sum of all forces determines the subsequent direction and speed of travel. The best-known and most often-cited problem with these approaches is local minima or trap situations[9]. Therefore, many researchers have abandoned potential field methods because of such a drawback.

In attempt to overcome the specific cost of local minima in the previous approaches of potential field, this paper focuses on building of a reward function to generate potential field. A set of features as possible candidates are abstracted from the potential field. The agent guided by these candidates can further determines its behaviors online. Through an intuitive gridworld task, such a method was demonstrated to be useful to automatically discover subgoals.

2 Representation of the Sequential Decision Problems

This section describes the framework of sequential decision problems from a reinforcement learning perspective. The decision-maker is called the agent. The things it interacts with, comprising everything outside the agent, is called the environment. On each step of interaction the agent receives input, o, some indication of the current state, s, of the environment, and the value of this state transition is perceived by the agent through a scalar reinforcement signal, r. The agent's goal, roughly speaking, is to choose actions that tend to increase the long-run sum of values of the reinforcement signal. The model of the sequential decision process is illustrated in Fig. 1.

The model consists of a discrete set of environment states, S; a discrete set of agent actions, A; a set of scalar reinforcement signals, R.

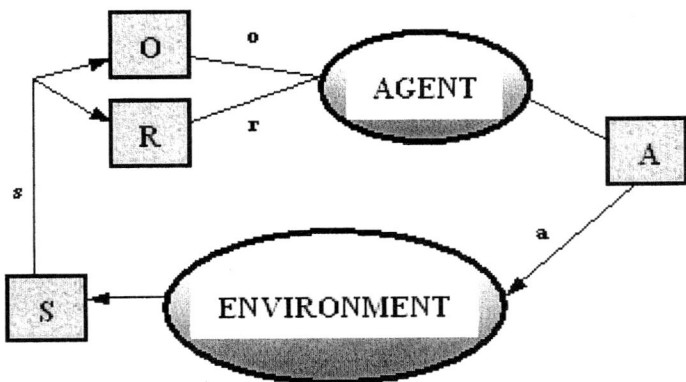

Fig. 1. The sequential decision process model

In many real-world environments, it will not be possible for the agent to have perfect and complete perception of the state of the whole environment. Therefore the model also includes a discrete set of agent observations, O, consists of a set of states that the agent perceives from the environment. Before the agent interacts with the environment to achieve a goal, the designer must determine how to represent S or O, A and R. Given the reward function R and the domain-dependent variables S or O and A, the problem or task of the sequential decision is determined.

3 Potential Field Method

This section describes the principles and processes of our approach in detail.

3.1 Generation of the Potential Field Based on the Reward Function

There are many choices of the potential function. If we imagine that each state in the sequential decision problem carries an electric change, we can write down an expression of the potential field with a reward function, it is

$$F_{ij} = -r_i e^{-\frac{d(s_j - s_i)^2}{2\sigma^2}} \qquad (1)$$

where, the state space $S = \{s_1, s_2, ..., s_N\}$, the states in the space interact with each other. F_{ij} is the potential of the state s_i over the state s_j. r_i is a numerical reward which agent receives at state s_i, describing the strength of the potential field. $d(s_j - s_i)$ is the Euclidean distance between the state s_i and s_j. σ is a constant named as radiate factor. When $d(s_j - s_i) \geq 3\sigma$, $F_{ij} \approx 0$. Usually the σ is a real number and $\sigma \in (0, 1]$, so the $d(s_j - s_i)$ needs to be normalized as $(0, 1]$ in practice. The potential in state s_j can be obtained by summing up all of the potentials of the states over the state s_j,

$$F_j = \sum_{i=1}^{N} F_{ij}. \qquad (2)$$

State space is constructed by n state variables, this forms a n-dimension state space. The potential field generated by Eq.(2) is also n-dimension. Fig. 2 shows a simple two-room gridworld environment. The reward function is: $+1$ for goal state, -1 for obstacle, and 0 for other states.

$$r_i = \begin{cases} +1, & \text{goal} \\ -1, & \text{obstacle} \\ 0, & \text{others} \end{cases} \qquad (3)$$

The potential field generated by the reward function of the simple two-room gridworld using Eq.(1), (2) and (3) is shown in Fig. 3.

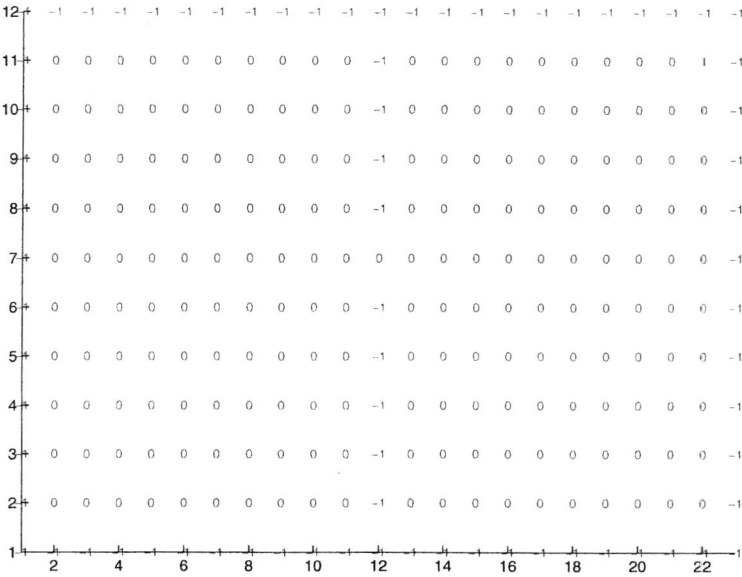

Fig. 2. The reward function of a simple two-room gridworld

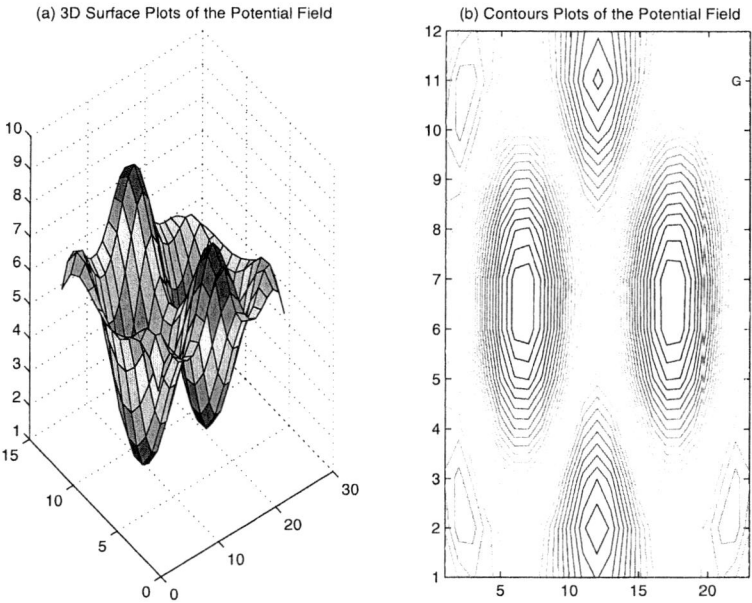

Fig. 3. The potential field generated by reward function

3.2 Forming Candidates of Subgoals

To form useful candidates of subgoals, the agent searches for features in the potential field. Candidates of subgoals (CS) can be defined as a set of saddle states and locally minimum states. In other words, if a state $s_i \in CS$, there is at least one direction along which the potential achieves its local minimum at s_i. The above definition of CS makes it clear how the CS captures the features of the potential field. Using this definition CS is motivated by studying room-to-room navigation tasks where the agent should quickly discover the utility of doorways as subgoals[7]. The doorways are usually saddle states in the potential field. The second motivation of using the definition CS is that the similar definition (Minimum Potential Valleys, MPV) is successfully applied to path planning [10]. Since the task of the sequential decision is to choose actions that tend to increase the long-run sum or decrease long-run cost of values of the reinforcement signal, it is rational that the local minimum states of the potential field are used as candidates of subgoals. As shown in Fig. 4, the minimum points in the potential field are the local maximum points of the reward function. This treatment is to keep consistent with normal concept in the potential field literature.

In Fig. 4, $*$ indicates the saddle point, $\triangledown$ indicates the minimum point, and $\triangle$ indicates the maximum point. The candidates of subgoals include the saddle points and minimum points. We will find useful subgoals from the candidates of subgoals automatically in the next section.

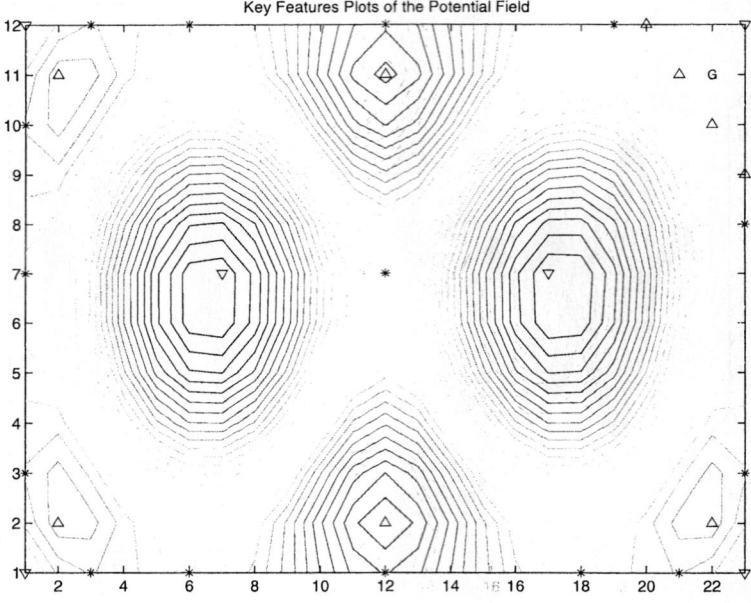

Fig. 4. Candidates of the subgoals

3.3 Autonomous Subgoal Discovery and Control Strategy

1. Dynamic subgoal discovery
   This paper uses a heuristics to choose a subgoal state from the candidates of subgoals as follows.

   Heuristics 1. *Let the goal state S_g, a state $S_n \in CS$, and the current state of the agent S_c be given. We say S_n is the subgoal of S_c if $d(S_n, S_c) < d(S_c, S_g)$, $d(S_n, S_g) < d(S_c, S_g)$, and $d(S_n, S_c) = min(d(S_c, CS))$. Where $d(s_j - s_i)$ is the Euclidean distance between the state s_i and s_j; $d(S_c, CS)$ is a set of the Euclidean distance between S_c to every state in CS.*

2. Control strategy generation
   After the subgoal of current state is determined, a lot of methods may be applied to decide which action will be performed at the next step. This paper uses a very simple method to do this: Choose one action which can make the agent close to the subgoal until the agent arriving at the subgoal. If the agent can not get to the subgoal during some limit steps, we will remove the subgoal from the CS and use Heuristics 1 to choose a new subgoal again.

The experimental results for the different start states in the two-room gridworld environment are illustrated in Fig. 5. In the experiments, the agent can reach the goal, but the paths are not the optimal solutions as in most of reinforcement learning methods. One of the main advantages in our method is more simple and less time consumed than other methods do.

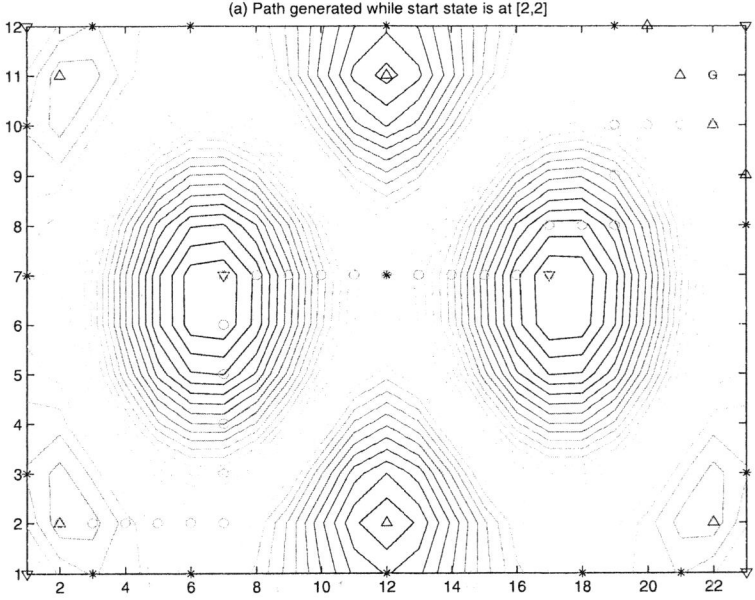

(a) Path generated while start state is at [2,2]

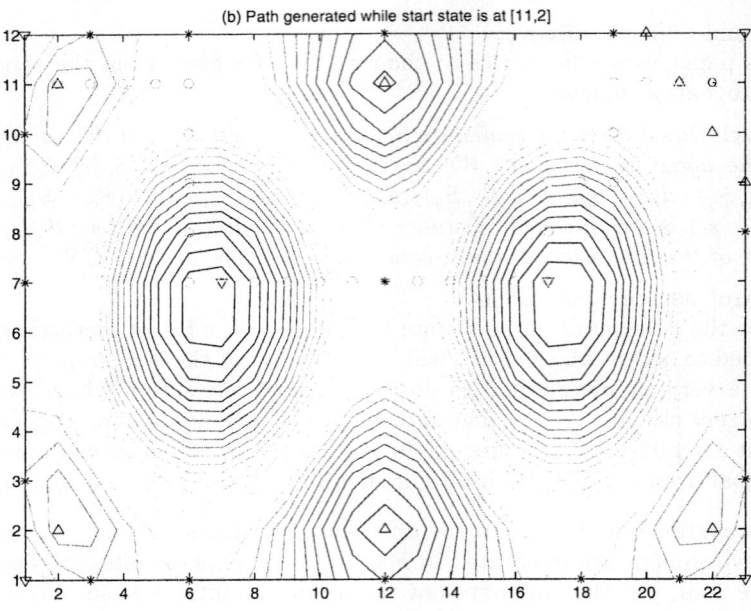

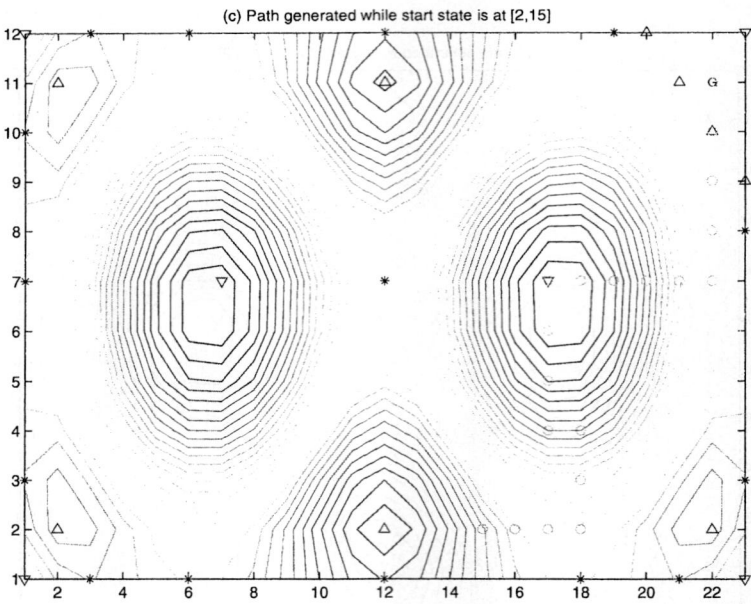

Fig. 5. Path generated for the different start states

4 Conclusions

In this paper, the application of the potential field method in a sequential decision problem environment is presented. The method proposed is tested in a simple two-room gridworld environment. The test results show that the method can discover subgoals dynamically and automatically. In the future work, we will test the method proposed in this paper in real environment. To find subgoal from the candidates of subgoals, more effective methods are still needed in the practical applications.

References

1. Amarel, S. : On representations of problems of reasoning about actions. In D. Michie (Ed.), Machine Intelligence **3** (1968) 131–171
2. Anzai, Y., and Simon, H. A. : The theory of learning by doing. Psychological Review **86** (1979) 124–140
3. Iba, G. A. : A heuristic approach to the discovery of macro-operators. Machine Learning **3** (1989) 285–317
4. Digney, B. : Emergent hierarchical control structures: Learning reactive hierarchical relationships in reinforcement environments. From Animals to Animats **4** (1996)
5. Digney, B. : Learning hierarchical control structure for multiple tasks and changing environments. From Animals to Animats **5** (1998)
6. Drummond, C. : Composing functions to speed up reinforcement learning in a changing world. European Conference on Machine Learning (1998) 370–381
7. McGovern, A. and Barto, A.G. : Automatic discovery of subgoals in reinforcement learning using diverse density. Proceedings of the 18th International Conference on Machine Learning (2001) 361–368
8. Arkin, R. C. : Intelligent Robots and Autonomous Agents. The MIT Press, Cambridge, Massachusetts. (1998)
9. Koren, Y., and Borenstein, J. : Potential field methods and their inherent limitations for mobile robot navigation. Proceedings of the IEEE Conference on Robotics and Automation (1991) 1398–1404
10. Hwang, Y. K. and Ahuja, N. : A potential field approach to path planning. IEEE Transaction on Robots and Automation **8** (1992) 23–32

Improving Multiobjective Evolutionary Algorithm by Adaptive Fitness and Space Division*

Yuping Wang[1] and Chuangyin Dang[2]

[1] School of Computer, Xidian University, Xi'an, 710071, China
ywang@xidian.edu.cn
[2] Department of Manufacturing Engineering and Engineering Management,
City University of Hong Kong, Kowloon Tong, Hong Kong
mecdang@cityu.edu.hk

Abstract. In this paper, a novel evolutionary algorithm based on adaptive multiple fitness functions and adaptive objective space division for multiobjective optimization is proposed. It can overcome the shortcoming of those using the weighted sum of objectives as the fitness functions, and find uniformly distributed solutions over the entire Pareto front for non-convex and complex multiobjective programming. First, we divide the objective space into multiple regions with about the same size by uniform design adaptively, then adaptively define multiple fitness functions to search these regions, respectively. As a result, the Pareto solutions found on each region are adaptively changed and eventually are uniformly distributed over the entire Pareto front. We execute the proposed algorithm to solve five standard test functions and compare performance with that of four widely used algorithms. The results show that the proposed algorithm can generate widely spread and uniformly distributed solutions over the entire Pareto front, and perform better than the compared algorithms.

1 Introduction

Many real-world problems involve simultaneous optimization of several incommensurable and often competing objectives, that is,

$$\min_{x \in \Omega} \{f_1(X), f_2(X), ..., f_s(X)\}, \qquad (1)$$

where $X = (x_1, x_2, ..., x_n) \in R^n$ and Ω is the feasible solution space. After the first pioneering studies on evolutionary multiobjective optimization appeared in the middle of 1980's, a couple of EAs were proposed in the last two decades (e.g., [2]~[9]). These approaches and their variants have been successfully applied to various multiobjective optimization problems. Among them the weighted-sum

---

* This work was supported by the National Natural Science Foundation of China (60374063) and SRG: 7001639 of City University of Hong Kong.

method is one of the simplest and most effective methods, however, it is difficult to find a set of uniformly scattered solutions on the Pareto front ([9]).

In this paper, we develop a novel multiobjective evolutionary algorithm, which can find a set of solutions scattered uniformly on the entire Pareto solution front. In the algorithm, the objective space is divided into multiple regions and on each region a fitness function is defined to search for the Pareto solutions in it. If some region contains fewer Pareto solutions, we will further divide it into several sub-regions and define one additional fitness function on each sub-region. In addition, we carry out the search in each sub-region independently so that more potential solutions can be generated in this region. This process is repeated adaptively. As a result, the number of Pareto solutions in this region will be increased gradually, and finally a set of well distributed solutions on the entire Pareto solution front will be obtained. At last, we demonstrate the effectiveness of the proposed algorithm by numerical experiments.

2 Uniform Design and Evolutionary Operators

2.1 Uniform Design

In this subsection we briefly introduce main idea of uniform design. The main objective of a uniform design is to sample a small set of points from a given closed and bounded set $G \subset R^M$ such that the sampled points are uniformly scattered on G. In this paper, we only consider two specific cases of G, that is, $G = [l, u]$ and $G = U(s)$, where

$$[l, u] = \{(\theta_1, \theta_2, ..., \theta_M) \mid l_i \leq \theta_i \leq u_i, \ i = 1 \sim M\}$$

and

$$U(s) = \{(f_1, \cdots, f_s) \mid f_1^2 + \cdots + f_s^2 = 1\}.$$

For details of the methods to generate uniformly distributed points in these two sets, please refer to [10].

2.2 Crossover and Mutation

In this subsection we use the uniform design method to construct a crossover operator. The main idea is as follows: Select parents for undergoing crossover according to the crossover probability p_c, and randomly match every two parents as a pair. For each pair of parents $Y = (y_1, \cdots, y_n)$ and $X = (x_1, \cdots, x_n)$, we define two vectors

$$l = (l_1, \cdots, l_n) \text{ and } u = (u_1, \cdots, u_n), \tag{2}$$

where $l_i = \min\{x_i, y_i\}$ and $u_i = \max\{x_i, y_i\}$ for $i = 1 \sim n$. These two vectors define a hyper-rectangle

$$[l, u] = \{(z_1, \cdots, z_n) \mid l_i \leq z_i \leq u_i, \ i = 1 \sim n\}. \tag{3}$$

Choose a proper integer q_1. The uniform design on $[l, u]$ is then used to generate $q = q_1$ points uniformly distributed on $[l, u]$, and these q_1 points can be regarded as the offspring of two parents X and Y.

Select individuals from the offspring of crossover according to the mutation probability p_m. For each selected offspring, say $X = (x_1, x_2, \cdots, x_n)$, randomly change it into another individual $X = X + \Delta X$, where each component of ΔX obeys Gaussian distribution with mean 0 and deviation σ and all components are independent.

2.3 Selection

Suppose that we have totally q_3 direction vectors including all additional direction vectors and denote them by $\{V_1, V_2, \cdots, V_{q_3}\}$. These direction vectors have divided the objective space into q_3 regions or sub-regions denoted by $R(V_1), \cdots, R(V_{q_3})$, and each direction vector defined one region or sub-region and one fitness function was defined on this region or sub-region by the weighted sum of the objective functions. The selection is carried out on each region or sub-region independently by selecting the same number of individuals.

3 A Novel Multiobjective Evolutionary Algorithm

In this section, we will develop a new multiobjective evolutionary algorithm. The main idea is as follows.

We first generate multiple direction vectors by the uniform design method on the unit sphere $U(s)$ of the objective space in subsection 2.1, and then employ them to divide the objective space into multiple regions of the approximately same size. On each region, one fitness function is defined. In order to generate a set of uniformly distributed and widespread solutions on the entire Pareto front, we try to generate about the same number of Pareto solutions in each region. If a region contains fewer solutions, we further divide this region into several sub-regions and on each sub-region we define one additional fitness function. Thus more fitness functions are used to search for the potential solutions in this region. As a result, more and more candidate solutions can be generated in this region during evolution, and finally, a set of uniformly distributed and wide spread Pareto solutions can be obtained.

3.1 Divide Objective Space and Define Multiple Fitness Functions

In order to divide the objective space into multiple regions of about the same size, a set of uniformly distributed points (can be seen as direction vectors) on the unit sphere $U(s)$ in the objective space is first generated by the uniform design in subsection 2.1. Then the objective space is divided into multiple regions of about the same size by applying the direction vectors as follows.

Algorithm 3.1

1. Generate q_0 points uniformly scattered on the surface of the unit sphere $U(s)$ in the objective space by the uniform design in subsection 2.1. Each of these points is a direction vector originating from the origin. The direction vectors constitute a set denoted by $D(s, q_0)$.
2. The objective space is divided into q_0 regions by applying the q_0 direction vectors. Each direction vector $V_k \in D(s, q_0)$ defines a region, denoted by $R(V_k)$, in the following way:

$$R(V_k) = \{Y \in R^s |\ \text{ang}(Y, V_k) = \min\{\text{ang}(Y, V_i)|V_i \in D(s, q_0)\}\},$$

where $\text{ang}(Y, V_k)$ represents the angle between vectors Y and V_k.
3. The current Pareto front, denoted by FT, is divided into q_0 Pareto subfronts similarly. Each direction vector $V_k \in D(s, q_0)$ defines a Pareto subfront, denoted by $FT(V_k)$, in the following way:

$$FT(V_k) = \{F(X_j)|\ F(X_j) \in FT,$$

$$\text{ang}(F(X_j), V_k) = \min\{\text{ang}(F(X_j), V_i)|V_i \in D(s, q_0)\}\},$$

where $F(X_j) = (f_1(X_j), \cdots, f_s(X_j))$ is the objective function vector at X_j. Obviously, $FT(V_k)$ is contained in $R(V_k)$.
4. Form multiple fitness functions. Each direction vector $V_k = (V_{k1}, V_{k1}, \cdots, V_{ks}) \in D(s, q_0)$ defines a fitness function on $R(V_k)$ by

$$f(X, V_k) = V_{k1}f_1(X) + V_{k1}f_2(X) + \cdots + V_{ks}f_s(X),\ k = 1 \sim q_0.$$

For any region $R(V_k)$ containing fewer Pareto solutions, we further divide it into several sub-regions and define one additional fitness function for each sub-region. Thus several additional fitness functions are defined for each such region. In the selection process, for each sub-region of region $R(V_k)$, we use the corresponding additional fitness function to select some individuals. Therefore, more individuals with a good diversity on $R(V_k)$ will be selected for the next generation population. As a result, a set of uniformly distributed solutions will be finally found.

3.2 Proposed Algorithm

Algorithm 3.2

1. Choose the proper parameters q_0, q_1, population size N_{pop}, crossover probability p_c and mutation probability p_m. Generate an initial population and a set of initial multiple weight vectors $D(s, q_0) = \{V_k | k = 1 \sim q_0\}$.
2. Divide the objective space into q_0 regions $R(V_1), \cdots, R(V_{q_0})$. Construct one Pareto subfront $FT(V_k)$ and define one fitness function $FT(X, V_k)$ on each region $R(V_k)$ by Algorithm 3.1.
3. Execute crossover and mutation.

4. Revise the current Pareto subfronts $FT(V_1), \cdots, FT(V_{q_0})$. Compute the mean number of solutions in all q_0 Pareto subfronts and denote it by $\bar{S}$.
5. For each region $R(V_j)$ containing Pareto subfront $FT(V_j)$ with fewer than $\bar{S}$ Pareto solutions, further divide it into q_1 sub-regions and define q_1 additional fitness functions.
6. Select points to form the next generation population.
7. If stopping criterion is not met, go to step 3; otherwise, stop.

4 Computer Simulations

In simulations, We take the parameter values as follows: $N_{pop} = 100$, $p_c = 0.2$, $p_m = 0.02$, $q_0 = 11$, $q_1 = 5$, maximum number of generations is 200. We run the proposed algorithm (called Nmea hereinafter) 30 times on five widely used test functions: $ZDT1 \sim ZDT4$ and $ZDT6$ ([11], [12]), and compared its performance with the existing four ones, namely: Spea ([5]), Nsga ([4]), Spea-II ([8]) and Nsga-II ([7]). For details of these functions, please refer to [12]. In order to compare the performance of these algorithms, we used C measure ([5]) and U measure ([1]) as the quantitative measures of the solution quality. The former is used for the comparison of the quality of the solutions found by two algorithms, and the later is for measuring the uniformity of the solutions found by each algorithm. For details, please refer to [5] and [1]. The results are summarized in Tables 1 and 2.

For $ZDT1$, $ZDT2$ and $ZDT4$, it can be seen from Table 1 that all solutions obtained by Spea and Nsga are dominated by those obtained by Nmea, but none of solutions from Nmea is dominated by those from any of Spea and Nsga. For $ZDT3$ and $ZDT6$, much more solutions obtained by Spea and Nsga are dominated by those obtained by Nmea, while only fewer solutions from Nmea is dominated by those from any of Spea and Nsga. For example, 71% solutions obtained by Spea and 81% solutions obtained by Nsga are dominated by those obtained by Nmea, but 23% and 20% solutions obtained by Nmea are dominated

Table 1. Comparison of C metric between Nmea and each of Spea, Nsga, Spea-II and Nsga-II in a typical run, where Nm, Sp, Ns, Sp-II and Ns-II represent Nmea, Spea, Nsga, Spea-II and Nsga-II, respectively

	C(Nm,Sp)	C(Sp,Nm)	C(Nm,Ns)	C(Ns,Nm)
$ZDT1$	1	0	1	0
$ZDT2$	1	0	1	0
$ZDT3$	0.71	0.23	0.81	0.20
$ZDT4$	1	0	1	0
$ZDT6$	0.75	0.03	0.79	0.12
	C(Nm,Sp-II)	C(Sp-II,Nm)	C(Nm,Ns-II)	C(Ns,Nm-II)
$ZDT6$	0.11	0	0.17	0

Table 2. Comparison of U measure among Spea, Nsga, Spea-II, Nsga-II, and Msea on $ZDT6$ in five independent runs

	1	2	3	4	5
Spea	0.1156	0.1185	0.13376	0.1268	0.1235
Nsga	0.1012	0.2293	0.2512	0.1147	0.1039
Spea-II	0.1003	0.1328	0.1218	0.1146	0.1129
Nsga-II	0.0974	0.0991	0.0965	0.0964	0.0968
Nmea	0.0667	0.0789	0.0798	0.0693	0.0678

by those obtained by Spea and Nsga, respectively. It can be seen from Table 2 that the values of U measure from Spea-II are smaller than those from Spea, the values from Nsga-II are smaller than those from Nsga, and the values from Nmea are the smallest. This indicates the distribution of solutions from Nmea is the most uniform, then those from Spea-II and Nsga-II, and the last those from Spea and Nsga.

5 Conclusion

In this paper, we develop a novel multiobjective evolutionary algorithm, which uses the space division and defines multiple fitness functions to search in the divided spaces. As a result, the proposed algorithm can find a set of solutions scattered uniformly on the entire Pareto solution front. The simulation also indicates the effectiveness of the proposed algorithm.

References

1. Y.W. Leung and Y.P. Wang: U-Measure: A quality measure for multiobjective programming. IEEE Trans. Systems, Man, and Cybernetics-Part A: Systems and Humans, 33(2003) 337-343
2. H. Ishibuchi, T. Yoshida and T. Murata: Balance between genetic search and local search in memetic algorithms for multiobjective permutation flowshop scheduling. IEEE Trans. Evolutionary Computation, 7(2003) 204-223
3. C.M. Fonseca and P.J. Fleming: Genetic algorithms for multiobjective optimization: Formulation, discussion and generalization. In: S. Forrest (Ed.). Proc. 5th Inter. Conf. Genetic Algorithms, Morgan Kaufman, San Mateo, California (1993) 416-423
4. N. Srinivas and K. Deb: Multiobjective optimization using nondominated sorting in genetic algorithms. Evolutionary Computation, 2(1994) 221-248
5. E. Zitzler, K. Deb, and L. Thiele: Multiobjective evolutionary algorithms: A comparative case study and the strenth Pareto approach. IEEE Trans. on Evolutionary Computation, 3(1999) 257-271
6. Y.W. Leung and Y.P. Wang: Multiobjective programming using uniform design and genetic algorithm. IEEE Trans. Systems, Man, and Cybernetics-Part C: Applications and Reviews, 30(2000) 293-304

7. K. Deb, A. Pratap, S. Agrawal, and T. Meyarivan: A fast and elitist multiobjective genetic algorithm: NSGA-II. IEEE Trans. Evolutionary Computation, 6(2002) 182-197
8. E. Zitzler: SPEA-II: Improving the strength Pareto evolutionary algorithm. Swiss Federal Institute of Technology, Lausanne, Switzerland. Tech. Rep. TIK-Rep. 103(2001)
9. E. Zitzler: Evolutionary algorithms for multiobjective optimization: Methods and applications. Ph.D. Thesis, Swiss Federal Institute of Technology Zurich (1999)
10. K.T. Fang and Y. Wang: Number-Theoretic Method in Statistics, Chapman and Hall, London (1994)
11. E. Zitzler, K. Deb, and L. Thiele: Comparison of multiobjective evolutionary algorithms: Empirical results. Evolutionary Computation, 8(2000) 1-24
12. K. Deb: Multiobjective genetic algorithms: Problem difficulties and construction of test problems. Evolutionary Computation, 7(1999) 205-230

IFMOA: Immune Forgetting Multiobjective Optimization Algorithm

Bin Lu[1], Licheng Jiao[1], Haifeng Du[2], and Maoguo Gong[1]

[1] Institute of Intelligent Information Processing, P.O. Box 224, Xidian University,
Xi'an, 710071, P.R. China
blu@mail.xidian.edu.cn
[2] School of Mechanical Engineering, Xi'an Jiaotong University,
710049 Xi'an, P.R. China

Abstract. Based on the Antibody Clonal Selection Theory and the dynamic process of immune response, a novel Immune Forgetting Multiobjective Optimization Algorithm (IFMOA) is proposed. IFMOA incorporates a Pareto-strength based antigen-antibody affinity assignment strategy, a clonal selection operation, and a technique simulating the progress of immune tolerance. The comparison of IFMOA with other two representative methods, Multi-objective Genetic Algorithm (MOGA) and Improved Strength Pareto Evolutionary Algorithm (SPEA2), on different test problems suggests that IFMOA extends the searching scope as well as increasing the diversity of the populations, resulting in more uniformly distributing global Pareto optimal solutions and more integrated Pareto fronts over the tradeoff surface.

1 Introduction

Artificial Immune System (AIS) is a new hotspot following the neural network, fuzzy logic and evolutionary computation [1]. Its research production refers to many fields like control, data processing, optimization learning and trouble diagnosing. The Antibody Clonal Selection Theory is put forward by Burnet in 1958 [2], giving a reasonable explanation for its three important features (autoimmunity forbidden, elaborate specific reorganization and immune memory). The main idea lies in that the antibodies are the native production, existing on the cell surface in the form of peptides, and the antigens can selectively react to the antibodies. So the clonal selection is a dynamic self-adaptive process of the immune system, and some biologic characters such as learning, memory and regulation can be used in Artificial Immune System.

In this paper, based on the Antibody Clonal Selection Theory and the dynamic process of immune response, Immune Forgetting Multiobjective Optimization Algorithm (IFMOA) is put forwards. The new method tires to preserve more nondominated solutions by incorporating previous multiobjective evolutionary techniques and immune-strategy inspired operations. The experimental results demonstrated that the capabilities of IFMOA to generate well-distributed Pareto optimal solutions and more integrated Pareto fronts of the test problems. The further comparison with two classical algorithms: MOGA [3] and SPEA2 [4], confirm its potential to solve multiobjective optimization problems.

2 Algorithm

In this paper, the main operations of IFMOA are included in the following sections. Here, the antigen means the problem and its constraints, while the antibody is the candidate of the problem. The antibody-antigen affinity and the antibody-antibody affinity indicate the match between solution and the problem, and the total combines power between the antibodies respectively [5]. Without loose of generality, $a = a_1 a_2 \cdots a_l$ is defined as the antibody and $\mathbf{A} = \{\mathbf{a}_1, \mathbf{a}_2, \cdots, \mathbf{a}_n\}$ is the antibody population; f is a positive real-value function defined as antibody-antigen avidity function. Furthermore, an external set called antibody archive $\overline{P}$ saves the nondominated solutions of each generation, which has the same structure as antibody population A.

2.1 Computation of Avidity

In IFMOA each individual is assigned an antibody-antigen affinity $F(i)$. The first part of $F(i)$ is the raw antibody-antigen affinity $R(i)$, which is determined based on the concept of Pareto strength [4]. $R(i) = 0$ indicates that the individual p_i is not dominated by any other individuals, corresponding to a nondominated solution. The second part of $F(i)$ is antibody-antibody affinity $D(p_i)$, which is additionally incorporated to guide a more precise search process. $D(p_i) = \dfrac{1}{(d(p_i)+1)}$, Where $d(p_i)$ is the sum of two smallest Euclidian distances between p_i and other individuals. The smaller $D(p_i)$ is, the lower is the comparability between p_i and other antibodies, accordingly, it is beneficial to the diversity of the population. Thus the overall antibody-antigen should be minimized.

2.2 Clonal Selection

Concretely, the Clonal Selection Operator (CSO) is to implement three steps including clone, clonal mutation and clonal selection on the antibody population [6], and a new antibody population will be attained after CSO. The evolvement process can be denoted as follows:

$$\mathbf{A}(k) \xrightarrow{Clone} \mathbf{Y}(k) \xrightarrow{Clonal\ Mutation} \mathbf{Y}'(k) \xrightarrow{Clonal\ Selection} \mathbf{A}(k+1) \qquad (1)$$

Clone $T_c^C(*)$: The clonal operator $T_c^C(*)$ is defined as:

$$\mathbf{Y}(k) = T_c^C(\mathbf{A}(k)) = \left[T_c^C(\mathbf{a}_1(k)), T_c^C(\mathbf{a}_2(k)), \cdots, T_c^C(\mathbf{a}_n(k))\right]^T \qquad (2)$$

Where $T_c^C(\mathbf{a}_i(k)) = I_i \times \mathbf{a}_i(k)$, $i = 1, 2 \cdots n$, and I_i is n_c dimension row vector. Here, n_c is a given integer called clonal scale and n_c copies of each antibody will be produced by cloning. After the clonal operator, the antibody population is like this:

$$\mathbf{Y}(k) = \{\mathbf{y}_1(k), \mathbf{y}_2(k), \cdots, \mathbf{y}_n(k)\} \qquad (3)$$

$$\mathbf{y}_i(k) = \{\mathbf{y}_{ij}(k)\} = \{\mathbf{a}_i(k), \mathbf{y}_{i1}(k), \mathbf{y}_{i2}(k), \cdots, \mathbf{y}_{in_c}(k)\}, \text{ and } \mathbf{y}_{ij}(k) = \mathbf{a}_i(k), j = 1, 2, \cdots, n_c \quad (4)$$

Cloanal Mutation $T_m^C(*)$: unlike the general mutation operator in GA, the clonal mutation is not applied to the $\mathbf{a}_i \in \mathbf{y}_i$ in order to save the information of original population, namely,

$$P\left(T_m^C\left(\mathbf{y}_i = \mathbf{y}_i^{'}\right)\right) = \begin{cases} P_m \succ 0 & \mathbf{y}_i \in \mathbf{y}_{ij} \\ 0 & \mathbf{y}_i \in \mathbf{a}_i \end{cases} \quad i = 1, 2, \cdots n, \ j = 1, 2, \cdots, n_c \quad (5)$$

P_m is the mutation probability, after clonal mutation, the antibody population is :

$$\mathbf{Y}'(k) = \{\mathbf{y}_1^{'}(k), \mathbf{y}_2^{'}(k), \cdots, \mathbf{y}_n^{'}(k)\} = \{\mathbf{a}_i(k), \mathbf{y}_{i1}^{'}(k), \mathbf{y}_{i2}^{'}(k), \cdots, \mathbf{y}_{in_c}^{'}(k)\} \quad (6)$$

Clonal Selection $T_s^C(*)$: $\forall\ i = 1, 2 \cdots n$, if

$$b = \{\mathbf{y}_{im}^{'} \mid \min f(\mathbf{y}_{ij}^{'}), \ j = 1, 2, \cdots n_c, \ m \in j\} \text{ and } f(\mathbf{a}_i) < f(b) \text{ , } \mathbf{a}_i \in \mathbf{y}_n^{'} \quad (7)$$

Then b will replace $\mathbf{a}_i$ in the antibody population. So the antibody population is updated, and the information exchanging among the antibody population is realized.

2.3 Updating Antibody Archive and Clonal Forgetting Unit

In the iterative of IFMOA, the antibody archive saves the nondominated solutions of current antibody population, which it is preserved and updated unremittingly. The update of the antibody archive space is as follows:

Operation 1: Antibody Archive Update in IFMOA

Step1: Copy all nondominated individuals in antibody population $A(k)$ to the antibody archive $\overline{P}(k+1)$, $\overline{P}(k+1) = \{a_i(k) | i \in A(k) \wedge F(i) \prec 1\}$ and $\left|\overline{P}(k+1)\right|$ repre sents its size. If $\left|\overline{P}(k+1)\right| = N_f$, go to Step3; or else, go to Step2.

Step2: If $\left|\overline{P}(k+1)\right| \prec N_f$, copy $\left(N_f - \left|\overline{P}(k+1)\right|\right)$ dominated individuals having the best affinity to $\overline{P}(k+1)$; or else, compress $\overline{P}(k+1)$ until $\left|\overline{P}(k+1)\right|$ is equal to N_f .

Step3: Apply Clonal Selection Operation(CSO) to $\overline{P}(k+1)$.

Fig. 1. Antibody archive update

We assume that $|i|$ is the actual number of the individuals found to be deleted each time, and $|\overline{P}(t+1)| - N_f$ is the number of the individuals should be deleted. The clustering technique in SPEA2 only deletes one suited individual once, so $|\overline{P}(t+1)| - N_f$ repetition is needed. Then the computation complexity of SPEA2 is larger and the efficiency is weakened accordingly. Based on the clustering principle in SPEA2, we proposed an improved operation of updating the antibody archive. In detail, if $|i| \leq |\overline{P}(t+1)| - N_f$ and more than one suited individual could be found, we delete all of them once instead, without comparing one individual with the others repeatedly, which will reduce the computation complexity and the whole number of repetition during the clustering operation is far smaller than $|\overline{P}(t+1)| - N_f$.

2.4 Updating Clonal Forgetting Unit

In immunology, immune tolerance means the non-response expressed by immune active cell when they are exposed to antigens. It is an important and necessary part of immune regulation. Both clonal deletion and clonal anergy are considered to be certain mechanisms of immune tolerance, on which the models of immune adjusting and control could be built [7]. In our paper, the phenomenon of immune tolerance is nameed as "forgetting" and we construct a clonal forgetting unit, whose members are charactered by not participating in clonal proliferation. However, the clonal forgetting

---

Operation 2: Activate Clonal Forgetting Unit in IFMOA

Step1: Sort the antibody population $A(k)$ based on the Affinity, named by

$$A'(k) = \{a'_1(k), a'_2(k), \cdots, a'_n(k)\}, \text{ where } F(a'_i(k)) \leq F(a'_{i+1}(k)), i = 1, 2, \cdots, n-1;$$

Step2: Randomly select r individuals in the $A'(k)$ to constitute the clonal forgetting unit, Now $A'(k) = \{a'_1(k), a'_2(k), \cdots, a'_j(k), a'_{j+1}(k), a'_{j+2}(k), \cdots, a'_{j+r}(k)\}$, $j + r = n$,

Step3: Replace the whole clonal forgetting unit with individuals $b_i(k)$, $i = 1, 2, \cdots r$ from the antibody archive $\overline{P}(k)$ to activate the clonal forgetting unit, and the final antibody population is $A''(k) = \{a'_1(k), a'_2(k), \cdots, a'_j(k), b_1(k), b_2(k), \cdots, b_r(k)\}$

Fig. 2. Activate clonal forgetting unit

unit could be activated by some external stimulation, which is denoted as the process of activation of clonal forgetting unit.

In the above steps, $r = round(T\% * n)$, where the function $round(*)$ returns the nearest integer of x. The value of clonal forgetting ratio $T\%$ is related to antibody population size and antibody-antigen affinity, it can be self-adaptive or fixed.

2.5 Immune Forgetting Multiobjective Optimization Algorithm

The Clonal Selection Operator (CSO) described above emphasizes mainly on the proliferation and the single compression of individuals, not mentions antibody's death. However, the course of clonal proliferation is accordant with the course of clonal death. Therefore, the multiobjective algorithm inspired by clonal selection and clonal forgetting is called Immune Forgetting Multiobjective Optimization Algorithm, and the overall flow of IFMOA is described as follows:

Algorithm: The Immune Forgetting Multiobjective Optimization Algorithm

Step1: Generate the initial antibody population $A(0) = \{a_1(0), a_2(0), \cdots a_n(0)\}$ and create an empty matrix (antibody archive) $\overline{P}(0)$. $k = 0$

Step2: Assigning antibody-antigen affinity to the individuals in the antibody population $A(k)$ and archive $\overline{P}(k)$.

Step3: If the termination criterion is not satisfied, carry on the following operations, otherwise, stop.

  Step 3.1: Apply Clonal Selection Operator to antibody population $A(k)$.

  Step 3.2: Update the antibody archive $\overline{P}(k)$ and get $\overline{P}(k+1)$.

  Step 3.3: Perform activation of the clonal forgetting unit and get $A(k+1)$.

  Step 3.4: $k = k+1$, go to Step 2.

Fig. 3. Immune Forgetting Multiobjective Optimization Algorithm

3 Experiments and Discussion

In order to validate our new algorithm, we compare IFMOA with another two representative algorithms, MOGA and SPEA2. For all algorithms, we apply binary coding, the terminal generation $G_{max} = 150$, the population size N is 100, which is referred to Reference [4]. In IFMOA, antibody archive size $N_f = 100$, clonal scale $n_c = 3$, mutation probability $P_m = 1/l$; In MOGA, the number of elite solutions is 10, crossover probability $P_c = 0.9$, mutation probability $P_m = 0.06$. In SPEA2, archive size $N_e = 100$, crossover probability $P_c = 0.9$, mutation probability $P_m = 0.06$.

3.1 Metrics of Performance Assessment

The goal of multiobjective optimization is to find a Pareto-optimal set or approximate it. Therefore, quantitative performance assessments of MOEAs should better take three objectives including the distance to the Pareto front, distribution of solutions, and the scope extended by solutions into account.

First of all, let's refer to the metric "Coverage of Two Sets" proposed in Reference [8]. This metric is described as: Let $A', A'' \subseteq X$ be two sets of decision vectors, the function ς maps the ordered pair (A', A'') to the interval [0, 1]:

$$\varsigma(A', A'') \Box \frac{|\{a'' \in A''; \exists a' \in A' : a' \geq a''\}|}{|A''|} \tag{8}$$

Where "$\geq$" means Pareto dominate or equal. The value $\varsigma(A', A'') = 1$ means that all points in A'' are dominated by or equal to points in A', while $\varsigma(A', A'') = 0$ indicates the opposite. Note that both $\varsigma(A', A'')$ and $\varsigma(A', A'')$ have to be considered because $\varsigma(A', A'')$ is not necessarily equal to $1 - \varsigma(A'', A')$.

Another metric called "Spacing" proposed by Schott [9] as a way of measuring the range variance of neighboring vectors in the tradeoff front has also been cited many times in different papers [10].

Let $A' \subseteq X$ be a set of decision vectors. The function S

$$S \Box \sqrt{\frac{1}{|A'|-1}\sum_{i=1}^{|A'|}(\bar{d}-d_i)^2} \tag{9}$$

Where

$$d_i = \min_j \left\{ \sum_{k=1}^{p} |f_k(\mathbf{x}_i) - f_k(\mathbf{x}_j)| \right\} \quad \mathbf{x}_i, \mathbf{x}_j \in A' \quad i, j = 1, \cdots |A'| \tag{10}$$

$\bar{d}$ is the mean of all d_i, and p is the number of objective functions.

Since both of the two metric have deficiency, we can not objectively evaluate the performance between different algorithms based on only one metric; both of them are adopted in the performance assessment so that they can complement each other.

3.2 Test Problems

In the following, 6 benchmark multiobjective problems are selected to compare IFMOA with MOGA and SPEA2 based on the parameters set above. All of these test problems are described in Table 1 [11]:

Table 1. Multiobjective optimization problem (Mop)

Mop 1 $\min F = (f_1(x,y), f_2(x,y))$ $f_1(x,y) = 1 - \exp(-(x-1)^2 - (y+1)^2)$, $f_2(x,y) = 1 - \exp(-(x+1)^2 - (y-1)^2)$	Mop 2 $\min F = (f_1(x,y), f_2(x,y))$, $f_1(x,y) = \dfrac{1}{x^2 + y^2 + 1}$, $f_2(x,y) = x^2 + 3y^2 + 1$ S.T. $-3 \le x, y \le 3$
Mop 3 $\min F = (f_1(x,y), f_2(x,y))$, $f_1(x,y) = x + y + 1$, $f_2(x,y) = x^2 + 2y - 1$ S.T. $-3 \le x, y \le 3$	Mop 4 $\min F = (f_1(x,y), f_2(x,y))$ $f_1(x,y) = x$, $f_2(x,y) = (1+10y) \left[1 - \left(\dfrac{x}{1+10y}\right)^a - \dfrac{x}{1+10y}\sin(2\pi q x) \right]$ S.T. $\begin{cases} 0 \le x, y \le 1 \\ q = 4; a = 2 \end{cases}$
Mop 5 $\min F = (f_1(x,y), f_2(x,y), f_3(x,y))$ $f_1(x,y) = x^2 + (y-1)^2$, $f_2(x,y) = x^2 + (y+1)^2 + 1$, $f_3(x,y) = (x-1)^2 + y^2 + 2$ S.T. $-2 \le x, y \le 2$	Mop 6 $\min F = (f_1(x,y), f_2(x,y), f_3(x,y))$ $f_1(x,y) = \dfrac{(x-2)^2}{2} + \dfrac{(y+1)^2}{13} + 3$, $f_2(x,y) = \dfrac{(x+y-3)^2}{36} + \dfrac{(-x+y+2)^2}{8} - 17$, $f_3(x,y) = \dfrac{(x+2y-1)^2}{175} + \dfrac{(2y-x)^2}{17} - 13$ S.T. $-4 \le x, y \le 4$

3.3 Simulations Results

It is observed in the experiments that the performance of IFMOA to solve the same problem varies with the clonal forgetting proportion $T\%$. In order to verify the phenomena, $T\%$ is assigned 10 different values, in detail, 0.05, 0.06, 0.07, 0.08, 0.09, 0.1, 0.2, 0.3, 0.4 and 0.5. For most test problems, we get the best evaluation values when $T\%$ is set round 0.08. On this condition, the value of S, $\varsigma(X^M, X^I)$ and $\varsigma(X^S, X^I)$ are minimums while the value of $\varsigma(X^I, X^M)$ and $\varsigma(X^I, X^S)$ are maximums. However, when $T\%$ deviates 0.08 too much, the performance of IFMOA degenerates obviously.

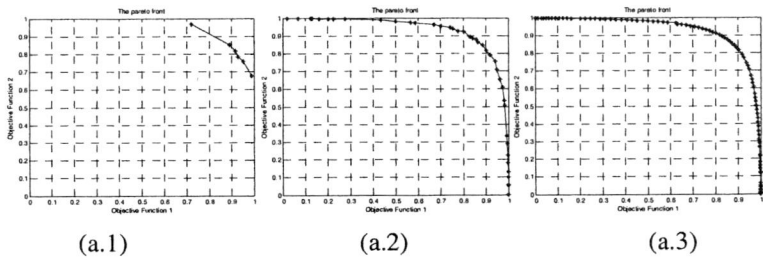

(a.1)   (a.2)   (a.3)

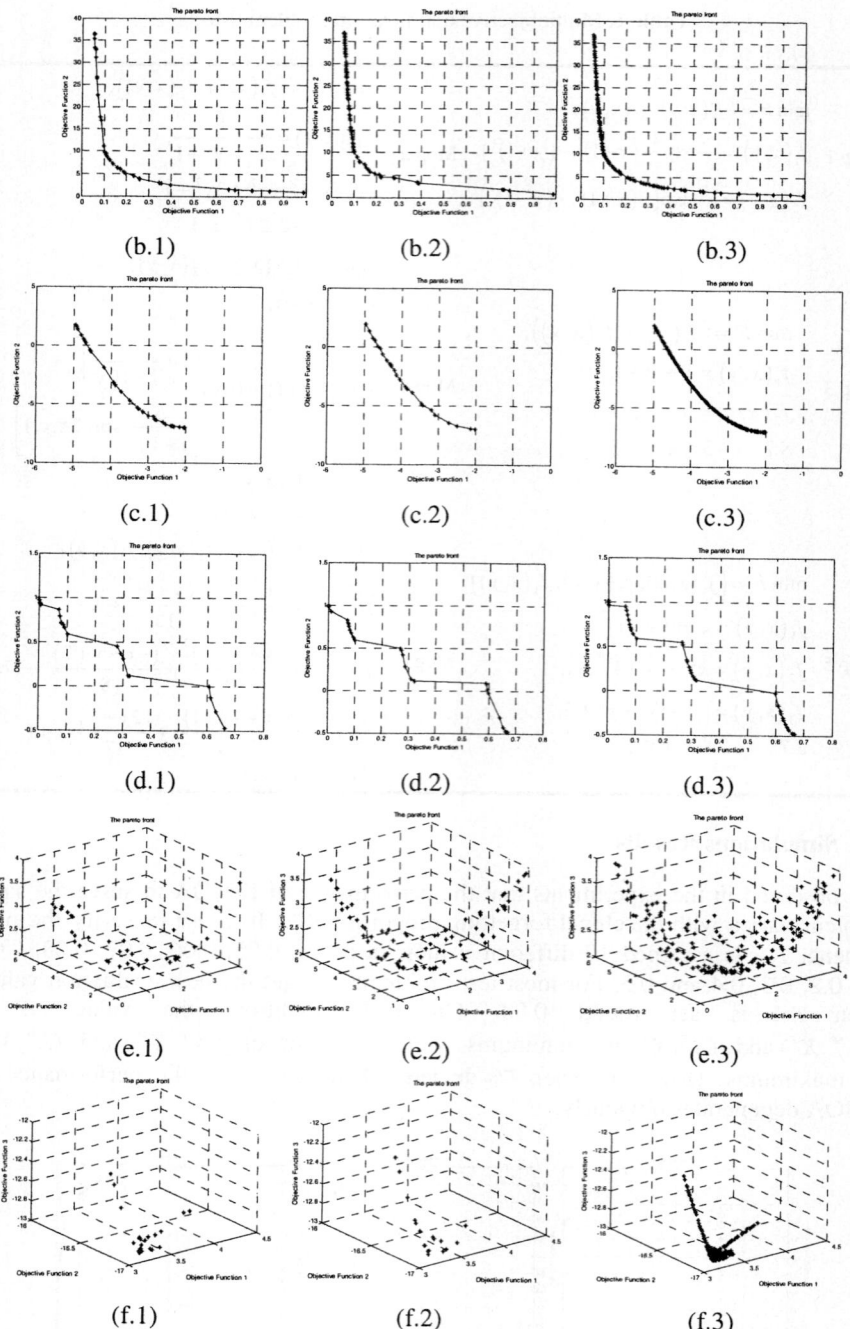

Fig. 4. The performance comparison of MOGA, SPEA2, and IFMOA on Mop1 to Mop6

With $T\% = 0.08$ and the other parameters set above, 30 runs with randomly generated population are carried on for each test problem and each algorithm. The Pareto fronts and statistical results of the two metrics are presented in Fig 6, Table 2 and Table 3 to make direct comparisons of IFMOA with MOGA and SPEA2.

Comparing the actual solutions obtained by three algorithms, it is easy to find that IFMOA could converge to the ideal Pareto front but fewer nondominated solutions are found when using MOGA and SPEA2. For these problems, the proportion of IFMOA converging to the ideal Pareto front is far higher than the other two algorithms. The effectiveness of IFMOA to guide the search of boundary solution, e.g. Mop1 and Mop5, also reveals the stronger search ability of IFMOA

Table 2. The performance comparison by Coverage of two sets

	$\varsigma(A',A'')$	$\varsigma(X^M,X^S)$	$\varsigma(X^S,X^M)$	$\varsigma(X^M,X^I)$	$\varsigma(X^I,X^M)$	$\varsigma(X^S,X^I)$	$\varsigma(X^I,X^S)$
Mop 1	0.034211	0.472222	0.007906	0.911111	0.077991	0.891228
Mop 2	0.070743	0.405714	0.038333	0.498095	0.189074	0.321343
Mop 3	0.258889	0.102299	0.068323	0.790805	0.033333	0.820000
Mop 4	0.356863	0.080000	0.116667	0.348000	0.046667	0.594118
Mop 5	0.032993	0.082051	0.021481	0.128205	0.050370	0.109524
Mop 6	0.158730	0.079487	0.014991	0.339744	0.007937	0.574603

Table 3. The performance comparison by Spacing

S	MOGA	SPEA2	IFMOA
Mop 1	0.109008	0.016340	0.007752
Mop 2	0.695562	0.169204	0.111575
Mop3	0.239585	0.243787	0.037497
Mop 4	0.141775	0.231693	0.028540
Mop 5	0.294516	0.185243	0.124811
Mop 6	0.155836	0.119814	0.011588

From Table 2, we can observe that the solution sets obtained by IFMOA dominated the ones get from SPEA2 and MOGA. The average statistical results of S metric in Table 3 also indicates the more reasonable distribution obtained by IFMOA. Even for the discrete Pareto front, e.g. Mop4 or the tri-objective problems, e.g. Mop6, IFMOA are capable of converging to ideal Pareto front, while the other two algorithms shows the lack of effective search to different extent.

4 Conclusion

In this paper, we proposed a novel algorithm Immune Forgetting Multiobjective Optimization Algorithm (IFMOA). It simulates the dynamic process of immune response on the basis of the Antibody Clonal Selection Theory and the character of immune tolerance. When compared with MOGA and SPEA2, IFMOA is more effective for multiobjective optimization problems in the two popular metrics, Coverage of Two Sets and Spacing.

Although IFMOA can solve some benchmark multiobjective problems preferably, it adopts binary coding, so it can not solve high-dimensional problems with low computational complexity. How to design a suitable antibody encoding mode and more effective antibody-antigen function for high-dimensional or constrained multiobjective problems demands our research in future.

References

1. Dasgupta, D., Forrest, S.: Artificial immune systems in industrial applications[A]. IPMM '99. Proceedings of the Second International Conference on Intelligent Processing and Manufacturing of Materials[C]. IEEE press (1999) 257-267
2. Abbas, A. K., Lichtman, A. H., Pober, J. S.: Cellular and Molecular Immunology. 3rd ed.. W. B. Saunders Company, New York (1998)
3. Murata, T., Ishibuchi, H., Tanaka H.: Multi-Objective Genetic Algorithm and Its Application to Flowshop Scheduling. Computers and Industrial Engineering Journal (1996) 30(4):957-968
4. Zitzler, E., Laumanns, M. and Thiele, L.: SPEA2: Improving the Strength Pareto Evolutionary Algorithm. Technical Report 103, Computer Engineering and Networks Laboratory (TIK), Swiss Federal Institute of Technology (ETH) Zurich, Gloriastrasse 35, CH-8092Zurich, Switzerland (2001)
5. Li cheng, J., Wang, L.: A novel genetic algorithm based on immunity. IEEE Transactions on Systems, Man and Cybernetics, Part A (2000) Vol.30, No.5: 552-561
6. Li cheng, J., Hai feng, D.: Development and Prospect of the Artificial Immune System. Acta Electronica Sinica. 31 (2003) 73-80
7. Akdis, CA, Blaser K., Akdis, M. Genes of tolerance. Allergy (European Journal of Allergy and Clinical Immunology) (2004) 59(9): 897-913
8. Eckart, Z.: Evolutionary Algorithms for Multiobjective Optimization: Methods and Applications. A dissertation submitted to the Swiss Federal Institute of Technology Zurich for the degree of Doctor of Technical Sciences. Diss. Eth No. 13398 (1999)
9. Schott, J. R.: Fault Tolerant Design Using Single and Multictiteria Gentetic Algorithm Optimization. Master's thesis, Massachusetts Institute of Technology, Cambridge, Massachusetts (1995)
10. Van Veldhuizen, D. A., Lamont, G. B.: On measuring multiobjective evolutionary algorithm performance. In proceeding of the Congress on Evolutionary Computation (CEC2000), A. Zalzala and R. Eberhart, Eds. Piscataway, NJ: IEEE Press (2000) vol. 1, pp. 204-211
11. Van Veldhuizen, D. A.: Multiobjective Evolutionary Algorithms: Classification, Analyses, and New Innovations. Air Force Institute of Technology (1999) AFIT/DS/ENG/99-01

Genetic Algorithm for Multi-objective Optimization Using GDEA

Yeboon Yun[1], Min Yoon[2], and Hirotaka Nakayama[3]

[1] Kagawa University, Kagawa 761-0396, Japan
yun@eng.kagawa-u.ac.jp
[2] Yonsei University, Seoul 120-749, Republic of Korea
myoon@base.yonsei.ac.kr
[3] Konan University, Kobe 658-8501, Japan
nakayama@konan-u.ac.jp

Abstract. Recently, many genetic algorithms (GAs) have been developed as an approximate method to generate Pareto frontier (the set of Pareto optimal solutions) to multi-objective optimization problem. In multi-objective GAs, there are two important problems : how to assign a fitness for each individual, and how to make the diversified individuals. In order to overcome those problems, this paper suggests a new multi-objective GA using generalized data envelopment analysis (GDEA). Through numerical examples, the paper shows that the proposed method using GDEA can generate well-distributed as well as well-approximated Pareto frontiers with less number of function evaluations.

1 Introduction

Most decision making problems involve multiple and conflicting objectives, and are formulated as multi-objective optimization problems. There does not necessarily exist a solution that optimizes simultaneously all objectives, because the presence of conflicting objectives. Thus, the concept well known as Pareto optimal solution has been used. Usually, there are a lot of Pareto optimal solutions which are considered as candidates of a final solution to the decision making problem. It is an issue how a decision maker chooses her/his most preferable solution from the set of Pareto optimal solutions in the objective function space (i.e., Pareto frontier). In cases with two or three objective functions, if it does not take so much time to evaluate the value of each objective function, Pareto frontier can be depicted relatively easily. Seeing Pareto frontiers, we can grasp the trade-off relation among objectives totally. Therefore, it would be the best way to depict Pareto frontiers in cases with two or three objectives. In recent years, the research applying genetic algorithms (GAs) to generate Pareto frontiers has been extensively developed, and also has been observed to be useful for visualizing Pareto frontiers In this research, the important subjects are how fast individuals converge to Pareto frontier and how well-distributed they are on the whole Pareto frontier. To this end, many contrivances have been reported for gene operators and fitness function [1,2,3,4,5,6,7,8]. Most conventional algorithms are adopting Pareto optimality-based ranking method which is the way by the number of dominant individuals, although the rank does not reflect the "distance" itself between each individual and Pareto frontier. Therefore, we have suggested several multi-objective GAs using generalized data envelopment analysis (GDEA) to generate Pareto frontier, in short, GDEA methods [10], [12]. The characteristic of GDEA methods is in measuring the degree how far each individual is from Pareto frontier by solving some linear programming problem [11]. As a result, we have observed through several applications that GDEA methods can provide much closer Pareto frontier to the real one with less number of generations. In this paper, we propose a new method of crossover using GDEA in order to generate well-distributed Pareto frontier. In addition, we show that the proposed method can provide much well-distributed Pareto frontier through the comparison with the results by several methods.

2 Multi-objective Genetic Algorithm Using GDEA

Multi-objective optimization problems are formulated as follows:

$$\underset{x}{\text{minimize}} \quad f(x) = (f_1(x), \ldots, f_m(x))^T \qquad \text{(MOP)}$$

$$\text{subject to} \quad x \in X = \{\, x \in \mathbb{R}^n \mid g_j(x) \leqq 0, \ j = 1, \ldots, l \,\},$$

where $x = (x_1, \ldots, x_n)^T$ is a vector of design variable and X is the set of all feasible solutions.

Generally, unlike traditional optimization problems with a single objective function, there does not always exist an optimal solution that minimizes all objective functions $f_i(x)$, $i = 1, \ldots, m$, simultaneously does not necessarily exist in the problem (MOP). Based on Pareto domination relation, Pareto optimal solution is introduced, and there may be many Pareto optimal solutions. Pareto frontier is the set of them in the objective function space. (See Fig. 1.)

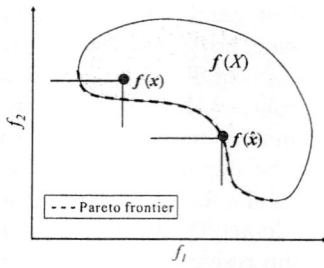

Fig. 1. Pareto frontier in the objective function space

Definition 1 (Pareto optimal solution). *A point $\hat{x} \in X$ is said to be Pareto optimal if there exists no $x \in X$ such that $f_i(x) \leq f_i(\hat{x})$, $\forall\ i = 1, \ldots, m$ and $f(x) \neq f(\hat{x})$.*

For assessing a fitness for each individual x^o, $o = 1, \ldots, p$ (p : the number of population), we suggested GDEA method of fitness evaluation given by an optimal value to the following linear programming problem [10]:

$$\underset{\Delta, \nu_i}{\text{maximize}}\ \Delta \qquad\qquad\text{(GDEA)}$$

$$\text{subject to}\quad \Delta \leq \tilde{d}_j - \alpha \sum_{i=1}^{m} \nu_i(f_i(x^o) - f_i(x^j)),\ j = 1, \ldots, p,$$

$$\sum_{i=1}^{m} \nu_i = 1,$$

$$\nu_i \geq \varepsilon,\ i = 1, \ldots, m,$$

where ε is a sufficiently small number, and $\tilde{d}_j$, $j = 1, \ldots, p$, is the value of multiplying $\underset{i=1,\ldots,m}{\max} \left(-f_i(x^o) + f_i(x^j)\right)$ by its corresponding weight, for example,

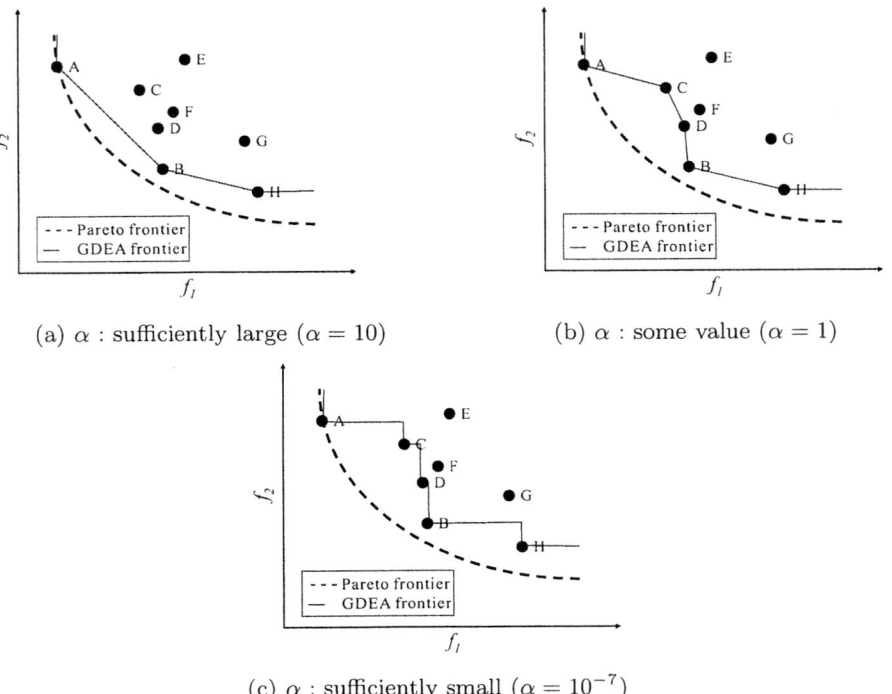

Fig. 2. GDEA frontiers by varying the parameter α

$\tilde{d}_j = 2\nu_1$ if $-\boldsymbol{f}(\boldsymbol{x}^o) + \boldsymbol{f}(\boldsymbol{x}^j) = (2, -1)$. α is a value of monotonically decreasing with respect to the number of generation. The parameter α decides so-called GDEA frontier as shown in Fig. 2, and the optimal value Δ^* means the degree how far an individual $\boldsymbol{x}^o$ is from GDEA frontier in the objective space. By adjusting the parameter α, we have observed that GDEA method can generate well-approximated Pareto optimal solutions with small number of generations.

Furthermore, in the paper, we consider the dual problem (GDEA$_D$) to the primal problem (GDEA) as follows:

$$\underset{\omega, \lambda_j, s_i}{\text{minimize}} \quad \omega - \varepsilon \sum_{i=1}^{m} s_i \qquad \text{(GDEA}_D\text{)}$$

$$\text{subject to} \quad \sum_{j=1}^{p} \left\{ \alpha \left(-f_i(\boldsymbol{x}^o) + f_i(\boldsymbol{x}^j) \right) + d_{ij} \right\} \lambda_j - \omega + s_i = 0, \quad i = 1, \ldots, m,$$

$$\sum_{j=1}^{p} \lambda_j = 1, \ \lambda_j \geqq 0, \ j = 1, \ldots, p,$$

$$s_i \geqq 0, \ i = 1, \ldots, m,$$

where d_{ij} is a component of a matrix $\left[-\boldsymbol{f}(\boldsymbol{x}^o) + \boldsymbol{f}(\boldsymbol{x}^1), \cdots, -\boldsymbol{f}(\boldsymbol{x}^o) + \boldsymbol{f}(\boldsymbol{x}^p) \right]^T$ replaced by 0, except for the maximal component in each column.

Let ω^*, $(\lambda_1^*, \ldots, \lambda_p^*)$ and $(s_1^*, \ldots, s_m^*)$ be the optimal solution to the problem (GDEA$_D$) for an individual $\boldsymbol{x}^o$. Then, as well known from the duality theory of linear programming problem, ω^* has the same meaning with Δ^* in the primal problem (GDEA). $(s_1^*, \ldots, s_m^*)$ represents the slackness which can distinguish easily individuals to be weak Pareto optimal. $(\lambda_1^*, \ldots, \lambda_p^*)$ represents a domination relation between an individual $\boldsymbol{x}^o$ and another individuals. That is, if λ_j^* is positive for some $j \neq o$, $\boldsymbol{x}^o$ is dominated by $\boldsymbol{x}^j$ which may be regarded as a reference individual. Making efficient use of the reference individual, we suggest that the new offspring is generated by the parents with same reference individuals in order to keep the diversity of individuals. As is shown in Fig. 3,

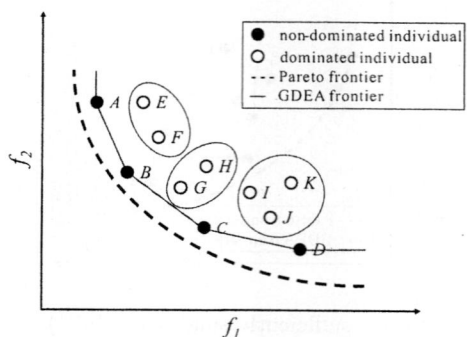

Fig. 3. Crossover by the proposed method

for instance, the reference individuals of E and F are A and B, and the children are generated by the parents E and F. This means that E and F are evolved toward GDEA frontier of between A and B. By divide the population into several sub-populations, Pareto frontier is generated piecewise. Consequently, the proposed method can not only generate well-distributed Pareto frontier, but also converge much faster and more effectively to the real Pareto frontier than the conventional algorithms.

3 Numerical Examples

In this section, we illustrate the effectiveness of the proposed method through the following examples [9]:

$$\underset{x}{\text{minimize}} \qquad f_1(x) = x_1 \qquad \text{(ZDT4)}$$

$$\underset{x}{\text{minimize}} \qquad f_2(x) = g(x) \times \left(1 - \sqrt{\frac{f_1(x)}{g(x)}}\right)$$

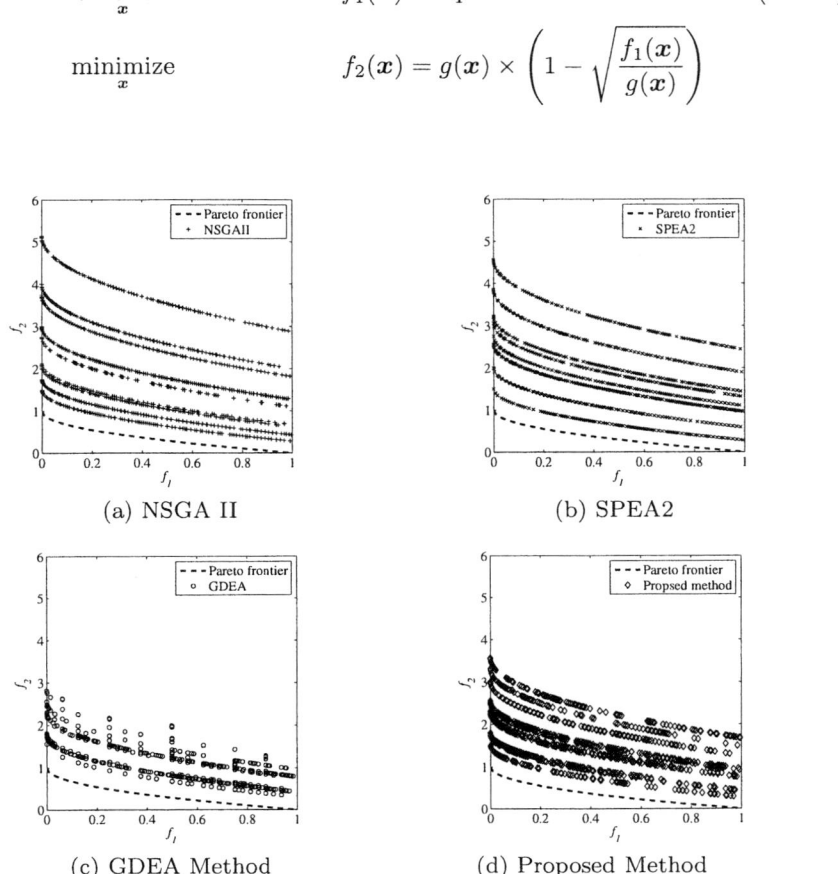

Fig. 4. Results for ZDT4

subject to $g(\boldsymbol{x}) = 1 + 10(N-1) + \sum_{i=2}^{N} \left(x_i^2 - 10\cos(4\pi x_i)\right),$

$x_1 \in [0,1], \ x_i \in [-5,5], \ i = 1, 2, \ldots, N.$

$\underset{\boldsymbol{x}}{\text{minimize}} \quad f_1(\boldsymbol{x}) = 1 - \exp(-4x_1)\sin^6(6\pi x_1)$ (ZDT6)

$\underset{\boldsymbol{x}}{\text{minimize}} \quad f_2(\boldsymbol{x}) = g(\boldsymbol{x}) \times \left(1 - \left(\frac{f_1(\boldsymbol{x})}{g(\boldsymbol{x})}\right)^2\right)$

subject to $g(\boldsymbol{x}) = 1 + 9 \left(\frac{\sum_{i=2}^{N} x_i}{N-1}\right)^{0.25},$

$x_i \in [0,1], \ i = 1, \ldots, N.$

In the above problems, $N = 10$, and both the true Pareto frontiers are formed with $g(\boldsymbol{x}) = 1$. Under the following parameters, we simulate 10 times with random initial population, and show the results in Fig. 4 and Fig. 5.

generation : 100 (ZDT4), 120 (ZDT6),   population size : 100
crossover rate : 1.0,   mutation rate : 0.05

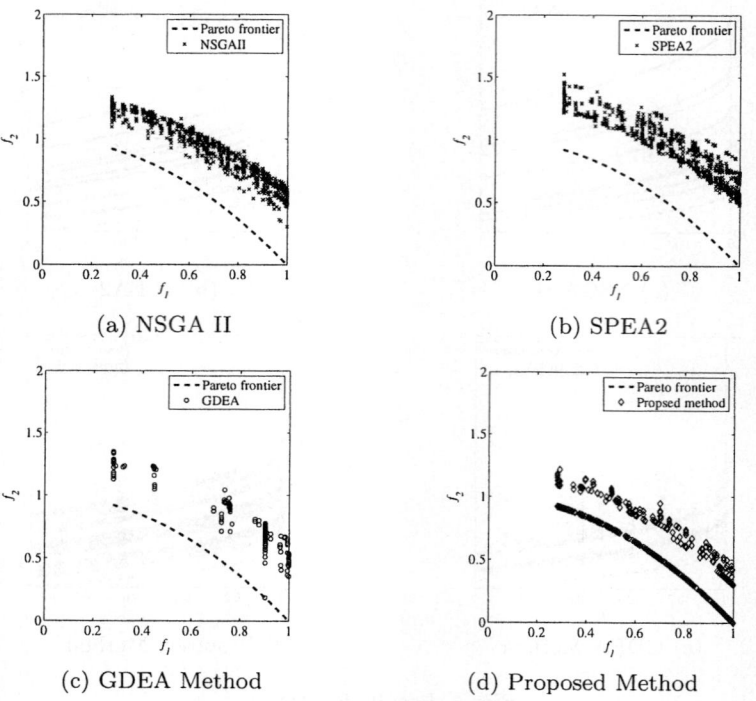

Fig. 5. Results for ZDT6

The problem (ZDT4) is used the test for the ability to deal with multimodality, because of containing many local Pareto frontiers. The problem (ZDT6) has the feature that the Pareto optimal solutions are non-uniformly distributed on the true Pareto frontier. As is seen from the computational results of the figures, the proposed method gives the results that the obtained solutions are more widely distributed and closer to the real Pareto frontiers, comparing the results by two conventional NSGAII and SPEA2.

4 Concluding Remarks

In many practical engineering problems, we have black-box objective functions whose forms are not explicitly known in terms of design variables. The values of objective functions for each design variable can be given by sampled real/computational experiments, for example, structural analysis, fluid mechanical analysis, thermodynamic analysis, and so on. Usually, these analyses are considerably expensive, and take too much computation time. Also, we do not know when to stop the computation in advance, and the computation is terminated relatively early by the given computation time and cost limitation. Under this circumstance, it is an important issue to generate well-approximated solution with less function evaluations (= the size of population × the number of generations) as possible. From this point of view and the experimental results, it can be concluded that the proposed method using GDEA has the desirable performance.

References

1. M. Arakawa, H. Nakayama, I. Hagiwara, H. Yamakawa, Multiobjective Optimization Using Adaptive Range Genetic Algorithms with Data Envelopment Analysis, *A Collection of Technical Papers on 7th Symposium on Multidisciplinary Analysis and Optimization (TP98-4970), AIAA*, Vol.3, pp.2074–2082, 1998
2. C.A. Coello Coello, D.A. Van Veldhuizen, G.B. Lamont, Evolutionary Algorithms for Solving Multi-Objective Problems, *Kluwer Academic Publishers*, 2002
3. K. Deb, Multi-Objective Optimization using Evolutionary Algorithms, *John & Wiley Sons, Ltd.*, 2001
4. K. Deb, S. Agarwal, A. Pratap, T. Meyarivan, A Fast Elitist Non-dominated Sorting Genetic Algorithm for Multi-objective Optimisation: NSGA-II, *Proceedings of 6th International Conference on Parallel Problem Solving from Nature*, pp.849–858, 2000
5. C.M. Fonseca, P.J. Fleming, Genetic Algorithms for Multi-objective Optimization: Formulation, Discussion and Generalization", *Proceedings of the Fifth International Conference on Genetic Algorithms*, pp.416–426, 1993
6. D.E. Goldberg, Genetic Algorithms in Search, Optimization and Machine Learning, Massachusetts : Addison-Wesley, Inc., 1989
7. J.D. Schaffer, Multiple Objective Optimization with Vector Evaluated Genetic Algorithms", *Proceedings of the First International Conference on Genetic Algorithms*, pp. 93–100, 1985

8. N. Srinivas, K. Deb, Multi-Objective Function Optimization using Non-Dominated Sorting Genetic Algorithms, Evolutionary Computation, Vol.3, pp.221–248, 1995
9. E. Zitzler, K. Deb, L. Thiele, Comparison of Multiobjective Evolutionary Algorithms: Empirical Result, Evolutionary Computation, Vol.8, No.2, pp. 173–195, 2000
10. Y.B. Yun, H. Nakayama, T. Tanino, M. Arakawa, Generation of efficient frontiers in multi-objective optimization problems by generalized data envelopment analysis, European Journal of Operational Research, Vol.129, No.3, pp.586–595, 2001
11. Y.B. Yun, H. Nakayama, T. Tanino, A generalized model for data envelopment analysis, European Journal of Operational Research, Vol.157, No.1, pp.87–105, 2004
12. Y.B. Yun, H. Nakayama, M. Arakawa, Multiple criteria decision making with generalized DEA and an aspiration level method, European Journal of Operational Research, Vol.158, No.1, pp.697–706, 2004

A Quantum-Inspired Genetic Algorithm for Scheduling Problems

Ling Wang, Hao Wu, and Da-zhong Zheng

Department of Automation, Tsinghua University, Beijing 100084, China
wangling@mail.tsinghua.edu.cn

Abstract. This paper is the first to propose a quantum-inspired genetic algorithm (QGA) for permutation flow shop scheduling problem to minimize the maximum completion time (makespan). In the QGA, Q-bit based representation is employed for exploration in discrete 0-1 hyperspace by using updating operator of quantum gate as well as genetic operators of Q-bit. Meanwhile, the Q-bit representation is converted to random key representation, which is then transferred to job permutation for objective evaluation. Simulation results and comparisons based on benchmarks demonstrate the effectiveness of the QGA, whose searching quality is much better than that of the famous NEH heuristic.

1 Introduction

Quantum computing is a research area that includes concepts like quantum mechanical computers and quantum algorithms. So far, many efforts on quantum computer have progressed actively due to its superiority to classical computer on various specialized problems. There are well-known quantum algorithms such as Grover's database search algorithm [1] and Shor's quantum factoring algorithm [2]. During the past two decades, evolutionary algorithms have gained much attention and wide applications, which are essentially stochastic search methods based on the principles of natural biological evolution [3]. Since later 1990s, research on merging evolutionary computing and quantum computing has been started and gained attention both in physics, mathematics and computer science fields. One of the important topics concentrates on quantum-inspired evolutionary computing characterized by certain principles of quantum mechanisms for a classic computer [4,5].

Recently, some quantum-inspired genetic algorithms (QGAs) have been proposed for some combinatorial optimization problems, such as traveling salesman problem [4] and knapsack problem [5-6]. However, to the best of our knowledge, there is no published research work on QGA for scheduling problems. So, this paper proposes a QGA for flow shop scheduling problems. In the QGA, Q-bit based representation is employed for exploration in discrete 0-1 hyperspace by using updating operator of quantum gate as well as genetic operators of Q-bit. Meanwhile, the Q-bit representation is converted to random key representation, which is then transferred to job permutation for objective evaluation. Simulation results and comparisons based on benchmarks demonstrate the effectiveness of the QGA, whose searching quality is much better than that of the famous NEH heuristic.

2 Flow Shop Scheduling

Flow shop scheduling is a typical combinatorial optimization problem that has been proved to be strongly NP-complete [7]. Due to its strong engineering background, flow shop scheduling problem has gained much attention and wide research in both Computer Science and Operation Research fields.

The permutation flow shop scheduling with J jobs and M machines is commonly defined as follows. Each of J jobs is to be sequentially processed on machine 1, ..., M. The processing time $p_{i,j}$ of job i on machine j is given (usually the setup time is included). At any time, each machine can process at most one job and each job can be processed on at most one machine. The sequence in which the jobs are to be processed is the same for each machine. The objective is to find a permutation of jobs to minimize the maximum completion time, i.e. makespan C_{max} [7-13]. Due to its significance in both theory and applications, it is always an important and valuable study to develop effective scheduling approaches.

Denote $c_{i,j}$ as the complete time of job i on machine j, and let $\pi = (\sigma_1, \sigma_2, ..., \sigma_J)$ be any a processing sequence of all jobs. Then the mathematical formulation of the permutation flow shop problem to minimize makespan can be described as follows:

$$\begin{cases} c_{\sigma_1,1} = p_{\sigma_1,1}, \\ c_{\sigma_j,1} = c_{\sigma_{j-1},1} + p_{\sigma_1,1}, & j = 2,...,J \\ c_{\sigma_1,i} = c_{\sigma_1,i-1} + p_{\sigma_1,i}, & i = 2,...,M \\ c_{\sigma_j,i} = \max\{c_{\sigma_{j-1},i}, c_{\sigma_j,i-1}\} + p_{\sigma_j,i}, & i = 2,...,M; j = 2,...,J \\ C_{max} = c_{\sigma_J,M} \end{cases} \quad (1)$$

The optimal solution π^* should satisfies the following criterion:

$$\pi^* = \arg\{C_{max}(\pi) \to \min\} \quad (2)$$

So far, many approaches have been proposed for flow shop scheduling. However, exact techniques are applicable only to small-sized problems in practice, and the qualities of constrictive heuristics [8] are often not satisfactory. So, intelligent methods have gained wide research, such as simulated annealing [9], genetic algorithm [10], evolutionary programming [11], tabu search [12] and hybrid heuristics [13], etc. Recently, Han and Kim [5-6] proposed a quantum-inspired genetic algorithm (QGA) for knapsack problem and achieved good results. However, solution of flow shop scheduling should be a permutation of all jobs, while in knapsack problem solution is a 0-1 matrix. That is to say, the QGA cannot directly apply to scheduling problems. Thus, in this paper, we propose a QGA for flow shop scheduling problems.

3 Quantum-Inspired GA for Flow Shop Scheduling

3.1 Representation

In QGA for a minimization problem, a Q-bit chromosome representation is adopted based on the concept and principles of quantum computing [5-6]. The characteristic of the representation is that any linear superposition of solutions can be represented. The smallest unit of information stored in two-state quantum computer is called a Q-bit, which may be in the "1" state, or in the "0" state, or in any superposition of the two. The state of a Q-bit can be represented as follows:

$$|\Psi\rangle = \alpha|0\rangle + \beta|1\rangle \quad (3)$$

where α and β are complex numbers that specify the probability amplitudes of the corresponding states.

Thus, $|\alpha|^2$ and $|\beta|^2$ denote the probabilities that the Q-bit will be found in the "0" state and "1" state respectively. Normalization of the state to the unity guarantees $|\alpha|^2 + |\beta|^2 = 1$.

A Q-bit individual as a string of m Q-bits is defined as follows:

$$\begin{bmatrix} \alpha_1 | \alpha_2 | \cdots | \alpha_m \\ \beta_1 | \beta_2 | \cdots | \beta_m \end{bmatrix} \quad (4)$$

where $|\alpha_i|^2 + |\beta_i|^2 = 1$, $i = 1,2,...,m$.

For example, for a three-Q-bit with three pairs of amplitudes $\begin{bmatrix} 1/\sqrt{2} | 1/\sqrt{2} | 1/2 \\ 1/\sqrt{2} | -1/\sqrt{2} | \sqrt{3}/2 \end{bmatrix}$, the states can be represented as $\frac{1}{4}|000\rangle + \frac{\sqrt{3}}{4}|001\rangle - \frac{1}{4}|010\rangle - \frac{\sqrt{3}}{4}|011\rangle + \frac{1}{4}|100\rangle + \frac{\sqrt{3}}{4}|101\rangle - \frac{1}{4}|110\rangle - \frac{\sqrt{3}}{4}|111\rangle$. This means that the probabilities to represent the states $|000\rangle$, $|001\rangle$, $|010\rangle$, $|011\rangle$, $|100\rangle$, $|101\rangle$, $|110\rangle$ and $|111\rangle$ are 1/16, 3/16, 1/16, 3/16, 1/16, 3/16, 1/16 and 3/16, respectively.

By consequence, the above three-Q-bit system contains the information of eight states. Evolutionary computing with Q-bit representation has a better characteristic of population diversity than other representation, since it can represent linear superposition of state's probabilities.

3.2 Genetic Operators

As for the genetic operators in QGA, following selection, crossover and mutation operators are used in this paper.

Rank-based selection: all individuals of the population are firstly ordered from the best to the worst, then the top $N/5$ individuals are copied and the bottom $N/5$ individuals are discarded to maintain the size of population, N. In such a way, good individuals also have more chance to be reserved or to perform evolution.

One point crossover: one position is randomly determined (e.g. position i), and then the Q-bits of the parents before position i are reserved while the Q-bits after position i are exchanged.

Mutation: one position is randomly determined (e.g. position i), and then the corresponding α_i and β_i are exchanged.

To avoid premature convergence, a *catastrophe operation* is used in QGA. In this paper, if the best solution does not change in certain consecutive generations, we regard it is trapped in local optima, then the best solution is reserved and the others will be replaced by solutions randomly generated.

3.3 Rotation Operator

A rotation gate $U(\theta)$ is employed in QGA to update a Q-bit individual as a variation operator. (α_i, β_i) of the i-th Q-bit is updated as follows:

$$\begin{bmatrix}\alpha_i'\\ \beta_i'\end{bmatrix} = U(\theta_i)\begin{bmatrix}\alpha_i\\ \beta_i\end{bmatrix} = \begin{bmatrix}\cos(\theta_i) & -\sin(\theta_i)\\ \sin(\theta_i) & \cos(\theta_i)\end{bmatrix}\cdot\begin{bmatrix}\alpha_i\\ \beta_i\end{bmatrix} \quad (5)$$

where θ_i is rotation angle. $\theta_i = s(\alpha_i, \beta_i)\Delta\theta_i$, $s(\alpha_i, \beta_i)$ is the sign of θ_i that determines the direction, $\Delta\theta_i$ is the magnitude of rotation angle whose lookup table is shown in Table 1. In the Table, b_i and r_i are the i-th bits of the best solution b and the binary solution r respectively.

Table 1. Look up table of rotation angle

r_i	b_i	$f(r)<f(b)$	$\Delta\theta_i$	$s(\alpha_i,\beta_i)$			
				$\alpha_i\beta_i>0$	$\alpha_i\beta_i<0$	$\alpha_i=0$	$\beta_i=0$
0	0	false	0	0	0	0	0
0	0	true	0	0	0	0	0
0	1	false	0	0	0	0	0
0	1	true	0.05π	-1	+1	±1	0
1	0	false	0.01π	-1	+1	±1	0
1	0	true	0.025π	+1	-1	0	±1
1	1	false	0.005π	+1	-1	0	±1
1	1	true	0.025π	+1	-1	0	±1

3.4 Evaluation

In flow shop scheduling, the problem solution is a permutation of all jobs. So, it should convert Q-bit representation to permutation for evaluation. When evaluate the solution, a binary string ***r*** with length m is firstly constructed according to the probability amplitudes of individual p with Q-bit representation. In particular, for $i = 1,2,...,m$, firstly generate a random number η between [0, 1], if α_i of individual p satisfies $|\alpha_i|^2 > \eta$, then set r_i as 1, otherwise set it as 0.

Then the binary representation is viewed as random key representation [14]. Finally, job permutation is constructed based on random key.

For example, consider a 3-job, 3-machine problem, let 3 Q-bits be used to represent a job. Suppose a binary representation is [0 1 1| 1 0 1| 1 0 1] that is converted from Q-bit representation, then the random key representation is [3 5 5]. If two random key values are different, we let smaller random key denote the job with smaller number; otherwise, we let the one first appears denote the job with smaller number. So, the above random key representation is corresponding to job permutation [1 2 3]. Obviously, if enough Q-bits are used to represent a job, any job permutation would be constructed with the above strategy from binary representation based space.

3.5 Procedure of QGA

The procedure of quantum-inspired genetic algorithm for flow shop scheduling is described as follows:

Step 1: randomly generate an initial population $P_Q(t) = \{p_1^t, \cdots, p_N^t\}$, where p_j^t denotes the j-th individual in the t-th generation with the Q-bit representation

$$p_j^t = \begin{bmatrix} \alpha_1^t & \alpha_2^t & \cdots & \alpha_m^t \\ \beta_1^t & \beta_2^t & \cdots & \beta_m^t \end{bmatrix}.$$

Step 2: evaluate each solution of $P_Q(t)$ with the method described in Section 3.4, and then record the best one denoted by ***b***.

Step 3: if stopping condition is satisfied, then output the best result; otherwise go on following steps.

Step 4: perform selection and quantum crossover, mutation for $P_Q(t)$ to generate $P'_Q(t)$.

Step 5: if catastrophe condition is satisfied, perform catastrophe for $P'_Q(t)$ to generate $P_Q(t+1)$ and go to Step 7; otherwise go to Step 6.

Step 6: applying rotation gate $U(\theta)$ to update $P'_Q(t)$ to generate $P_Q(t+1)$.

Step 7: evaluate every individual of $P_Q(t+1)$, and update the best solution ***b*** if possible. Then let $t = t+1$ and go back to step 3.

4 Simulations and Comparisons

In this paper, 8 problems named car1 through car8 by Carlier [15] are selected as benchmarks for simulation test. We set population size as 40, maximum generation (stopping condition of QGA) as $J \times M$, the length of each chromosome as $10 \times J$ (i.e., every 10 Q-bits correspond to a job), crossover probability as 1, mutation probability as 0.05, catastrophe happens in QGA if the best solution does not change in consecutive $J \times M / 10$ generations.

We run the QGA 20 times for every problem, and the statistical results are summarized in Table 2, where BRE, ARE and WRE denote the best, average and worst relative errors with C^* (optimal makespan or lower bound) respectively.

Table 2. The statistical results of testing algorithms

Problem	J, M	C^*	NEH RE	QGA BRE	QGA ARE
Car1	11,5	7038	0	0	0
Car2	13,4	7166	2.93	0	1.90
Car3	12,5	7312	1.19	1.19	1.65
Car4	14,4	8003	0	0	0.06
Car5	10,6	7720	1.49	0	0.11
Car6	8,9	8505	3.15	0	0.19
Car7	7,7	6590	0	0	0
Car8	8,8	8366	2.37	0	0.03

From the simulation results, it can be seen that the results obtained by QGA are much better than that of NEH heuristic except problem Car3. Secondly, the BRE values resulted by QGA are all 0 except Car3, which means QGA is able to obtain good solutions in global sense. Thirdly, the BRE and ARE values resulted by QGA are very close, which means QGA has good robustness and consistence on initial conditions. So, QGA is a novel and viable approach for flow shop scheduling.

5 Conclusion

To the best of our knowledge, this paper is the first to propose a genetic algorithm inspired by quantum computing for flow shop scheduling. Simulation results and comparisons based on benchmarks demonstrate the effectiveness of the QGA. The future work is to develop more effective hybrid QGA for flow shop scheduling, and study QGA for job shop scheduling problems as well.

Acknowledgements

This research is partially supported by National Science Foundation of China (60204008, 60374060) and 973 Program (2002CB312200).

References

1. Grover, L.K.: A fast quantum mechanical algorithm for database search. In: Proceedings of the 28th Annual ACM Symposium on the Theory of Computing, Pennsylvania, (1996) 212-221
2. Shor, P.W.: Algorithms for quantum computation: discrete logarithms and factoring. In: Proceedings of the 35th Annual Symposium on the Foundation of Computer Sciences. Los Alamitos, (1994) 20-22
3. Wang, L.: Intelligent Optimization with Applications. Tsinghua University & Springer Press, Beijing, (2001)
4. Narayanan, A., Moore, M.: Quantum inspired genetic algorithm. In: IEEE International Conference on Evolutionary Computation, Piscataway, (1996) 61-66
5. Han, K.H., Kim, J.H.: Quantum-inspired evolutionary algorithm for a class of combinatorial optimization. IEEE Trans. Evolutionary Computation, **6** (2002) 580-593
6. Han, K.H., Kim, J.H.: A Quantum-inspired evolutionary algorithms with a new termination criterion, He gate, and two-phase scheme. IEEE Trans. Evol. Comput., **8** (2004) 156-169
7. Garey, M.R., Johnson, D.S.: Computers and Intractability: a Guide to the Theory of NP-Completeness. Freeman, San Francisco, (1979)
8. Nawaz, M., Enscore, E.Jr., Ham, I.: A heuristic algorithm for the m-machine, n-job flow-shop sequencing problem. Omega, **11** (1983) 91-95
9. Ogbu, F.A., Smith, D.K.: Simulated annealing for the permutation flowshop problem. Omega, **19** (1990) 64-67
10. Wang, L., Zhang, L., Zheng, D.Z.: A class of order-based genetic algorithm for flow shop scheduling. Int. J. Advanced Manufacture Technology, **22** (2003) 828-835
11. Wang, L., Zheng, D.Z.: A modified evolutionary programming for flow shop scheduling. Int. J. Advanced Manufacturing Technology, **22** (2003) 522-527
12. Nowicki, E., Smutnicki, C.: A fast tabu search algorithm for the permutation flow-shop problem. European J. Operational Research, **91** (1996) 160-175
13. Wang, L., Zheng, D.Z.: An effective hybrid heuristic for flow shop scheduling. Int. J. Advanced Manufacture Technology, **21** (2003) 38-44
14. Bean, J.C.: Genetic algorithms and random keys for sequencing and optimization. ORSA Journal on Computing, **6** (1994) 154-160
15. Carlier, J.: Ordonnancements a contraintes disjonctives. R.A.I.R.O. Recherche operationelle/ Operations Research, **12** (1978) 333-351

Consensus Control for Networks of Dynamic Agents via Active Switching Topology

Guangming Xie and Long Wang

Center for Systems & Control,
LTCS and Department of Mechanics and Engineering Science,
Peking University, Beijing, 100871, China
xiegming@mech.pku.edu.cn

Abstract. This paper investigates the average-consensus problem for networks of dynamic agents. A consensus protocol based on active switching topology for solving the average-consensus problem of the network is proposed. Within such a topology, a finite set of candidate unconnected graphs is used and we change the topology actively according to the state of the network. The advantage of such mechanism is that it decreases the communication complexity/cost dramatically. The simulation results are presented that are consistent with our theoretical results.

1 Introduction

In recent years, decentralized control of communicating-agent systems has emerged as a challenging new research area. It has attracted multi-disciplinary researchers in a widely range including physics, biophysics, neurobiology, systems biology, apply mathematics, mechanics, computer science and control theory. The applications of multi-agent systems are diverse, ranging from cooperative control of unmanned air vehicles, formation control of mobile robots, control of communication networks, design of sensor-network, to flocking of social insects, swarm-based computing, etc. A common characteristics of the relevant analytical techniques is that they are deeply connected with decentralized, or networked control theory.

Agreement and consensus protocol design is one of the important problems encountered in decentralized control of communicating-agent systems. It has been paid attention for a long time by computer scientists, particularly in the field of automata theory and distributed computation [1]. Agreement upon certain quantities of interest is required in many applications such as multivehicle systems, multirobot systems, groups of agents and so on.

In the past decade, quite a tremendous amount of interesting results have been addressed for agreement and consensus problems in different formulations due to different type of agent dynamics and different type of tasks of interest. In [2], the problem of cooperation among a collection of vehicles performing a shared task using intervehicle communication to coordinate their actions was considered. The agents in the group were with linear dynamics. Tools from algebraic graph theory were used to prove the formation stability. In [3], a dynamic graph structure was provided as a convenient framework for modelling distributed dynamic systems where the topology of the interaction among its elements evolves in time. Some promising directions were highlighted as well.

Followed the pioneering work in [4], there are many researchers have worked in analysis of swarms [5-9], [13-24]. In [5], the stability analysis for swarms with continuous-time model in n-dimensional space was addressed. Following this direction, stability analysis of social foraging swarms that move in an n-dimensional space according to an attractant/repellent or a nutrient profile was addressed in [6]. The corresponding results in the case of noisy environment was given in [7].

Different from the above disciplinary, in [8] and [9], a model of coordinated dynamical swarms with physical size and asynchronous communication was introduced and analysis of stability properties of such swarms were presented with a fixed communication topology. A potential application of these theoretical results is in the field of the leader-follower formation control of multi-robot systems [10-12].

In [13], a simple discrete-time model of finite autonomous agents all moving in the plane with same speed but with different heading was proposed. Moreover, the concept of Neighbors of agents was introduced. Some simulation results to demonstrate the nearest neighbor rule were obtained. Based on this model, theoretical explanations were first given in [14] for the simulation results in [13]. Some sufficient conditions for coordination of the system of agents in the point of view of statistical mechanics. Another qualitative analysis for this model under certain simplifying assumption was given in [15].

In [16], a systematical framework of consensus problem in networks of dynamic agents with fixed/switching topology and communication time-delays was addressed. Under the assumption that the dynamic of the agent is a simple scalar continuous-time integrator $\dot{x} = u$, three consensus problems were discussed. They are directed networks with fixed topology, directed networks with switching topology and undirected networks with communication time-delays and fixed topology. Moreover, a disagreement function was introduced for disagreement dynamics of a directed network with switching topology. The undirected networks case was discussed by the same authors in [17]. Some other interesting results can be seen in [18-24] and the references therein.

Meanwhile, there are many researchers in physics, biophysics who consider a closely related to consensus problems on graphs, named as synchronization of coupled oscillators where a consensus is reached regarding the frequency of oscillation of all agents [25-34].

In this paper, we follow the work in [16-17] and consider consensus problem for a more general class of networks. A novel consensus control protocol is proposed which is base on active switching topology. An important aspect of performing coordinated tasks in a distributed fashion in multiagent systems is to keep communication and interagent sensing costs limited. The main advantage of the control protocol with active switching topology is that it decreases the communication complexity/cost dramatically, since it does not ask the graph is connected.

An outline of this paper is as follows. In Section 2, we recall the consensus problems on graphs. In Section 3, the control protocol is given. The convergence analysis and performance discussion are presented in Section 4. The simulation results are presented in Section 5. Finally, we conclude the paper in Section 6.

2 Consensus Problems on Graph

In this section, we introduce networks of dynamic agents and consensus problems.

2.1 Algebraic Graph Theory

Let $\mathcal{G} = (\mathcal{V}, \mathcal{E}, \mathcal{A})$ be a undirected graph with the set of vertices $\mathcal{V} = \{v_1, v_2, \cdots, v_M\}$, the set of edges $\mathcal{E} \subseteq \mathcal{V} \times \mathcal{V}$, and a weighted adjacency matrix $\mathcal{A} = [a_{ij}]$ with nonnegative adjacency elements a_{ij}. The node indexes of $\mathcal{G}$ belong to a finite index set $\mathcal{I} = \{1, 2, \cdots, M\}$. An edge of $\mathcal{G}$ is denoted by $e_{ij} = (v_i, v_j)$. The adjacency elements associated with the edges are positive, i.e., $e_{ij} \in \mathcal{E} \iff a_{ij} > 0$. Moreover, we assume $a_{ii} = 0$ for all $i \in \mathcal{I}$. Since the graph considered is undirected, it means once e_{ij} is an edge of $\mathcal{G}$, e_{ji} is an edge of $\mathcal{G}$ as well. As a result, the adjacency matrix $\mathcal{A}$ is a symmetric nonnegative matrix.

The set of *neighbors* of node v_i is denoted by $N_i = \{v_j \in \mathcal{V} : (v_i, v_j) \in \mathcal{E}\}$. A *cluster* is any subset $J \subseteq \mathcal{V}$ of the nodes of the graph. The set of neighbors of a cluster N_J is defined by

$$N_J = \bigcup_{v_i \in J} N_i. \tag{1}$$

The *degree* of node v_i is the number of its neighbors $|N_i|$ and is denoted by $\deg(v_i)$. The *degree matrix* is an $M \times M$ matrix define as $\Delta = [\Delta_{ij}]$ where

$$\Delta_{ij} = \begin{cases} \deg(v_i), & i = j; \\ 0, & i \neq j. \end{cases}$$

The *Laplacian* of graph $\mathcal{G}$ is defined by

$$L = \Delta - A \tag{2}$$

An important fact of L is that all the row sums of L are zero and thus $\mathbf{1}_M = [1, 1, \cdots, 1]^T \in \mathbb{R}^M$ is an eigenvector of L associated with the eigenvalue $\lambda = 0$.

A *path* between each distinct vertices v_i and v_j is meant a sequence of distinct edges of $\mathcal{G}$ of the form $(v_i, v_{k_1}), (v_{k_1}, v_{k_2}), \cdots, (v_{k_l}, v_j)$. A graph is called *connected* if there exist a path between any two distinct vertices of the graph.

Lemma 1. *[35] The graph $\mathcal{G}$ is connected if and only if $rank(L) = M - 1$. Moveover, for a connected graph, there is only one zero eigenvalue of L, all the other ones are positive and real.*

2.2 Consensus Problem on Network

Given a graph $\mathcal{G}$, let $x_i \in \mathbb{R}$ denote the state or value of node v_i. We refer to $\mathcal{G}_x = (\mathcal{G}, x)$ with $x = (x_{1,2}, \cdots, x_M)^T$ as a *network* with value $x \in \mathbb{R}^M$ and topology G. Suppose each node of a graph is a dynamic agent with dynamics

$$\dot{x}_i = u_i \tag{3}$$

where x_i is aforementioned state of node v_i and u_i is the control input that will be used for consensus problem.

Let $\chi : \mathbb{R}^M \to \mathbb{R}$ be a function of M variables $x_1, x_2, \cdots, x_M$ and $x_0 = x(0)$, denote the initial state of the system. The χ-*consensus problem* in a dynamic graph is distributed way to calcualted $\chi(x_0)$ by applying inputs u_i that only depend on the states of node v_i and its neighbors. We say a state feedback

$$u_i = k_i(x_{j1}, x_{j2}, \cdots, x_{jl_i}) \tag{4}$$

is a *protocol* with topology $\mathcal{G}$ if the cluster $J_i = \{v_{j1}, v_{j2}, \cdots, v_{jl_i},\}$ of nodes with indexes $j1, j2, \cdots, jl_i \in \mathcal{I}$ satisfies the property $J_i \subseteq \{v_i\} \bigcup N_i$. In addition, if $|J_i| < M$ for all $i \in \mathcal{I}$, (4) is called a *distributed protocol*.In a dynamic network with switching topology, the graph $\mathcal{G}$ is a discrete-state of the system that changes in time.

We say protocol (4) asymptotically solves the χ-consensus problem if and only if there exists an asymptotically stable equilibrium x^* of the network satisfying $x_i^* = \chi(x_0)$ for all $i \in \mathcal{I}$, and meanwhile, the speed of each agent satisfying $\lim_{t\to\infty} v_i = 0, i \in \mathcal{I}$. Whenever the nodes of a network are all in consensus, the common value of all nodes is called the *group decision value*.

In this paper, we are interested in distributed solutions of the special case with $\chi(x) = \text{Ave}(x) = 1/M(\sum_{i=1}^M x_i)$ which is called *average-consensus*. This is a very representative case with broad applications in distributed decision-making for multi-agent system.

3 Control Protocol and Network Dynamics

In this section, we present the control protocol that solve the aforementioned average-consensus problem. We will use a linear protocol with switching topology and no communication time-delays:

$$u_i = \sum_{j \in N_i} a_{ij}(x_j - x_i) \tag{5}$$

where the set of neighbors N_i of node v_i is variable in networks with switching topology.

By using the above protocol (5), the agent dynamic is given as follows:

$$\dot{x}_i = \sum_{j \in N_i} a_{ij}(x_j - x_i) \tag{6}$$

Then, the network dynamic is summarized as follows:

$$\dot{x}(t) = -L_{\mathcal{G}(t)}x(t) \tag{7}$$

where $L_{\mathcal{G}(t)}$ the aforementioned Laplacian associate with the graph $\mathcal{G}(t)$ at time instant t.

The dynamics of the network is typically *hybrid* with the continuous state $x \in \mathbb{R}^M$ and the discrete state $\mathcal{G}$. As a result, the network is a typically switched system.

In what follows, we introduce the active switching topology in details.

We first develop some results for algebraic graph theory. Given a graph $\mathcal{G} = (\mathcal{V}, \mathcal{E}, \mathcal{A})$, a *partition* of $\mathcal{E}$, is a set of finite subsets of $\mathcal{E}$, $\{\mathcal{E}_1, \cdots, \mathcal{E}_N\}$ which satisfies that

$$i) \quad \bigcup_{i=1,\cdots,N} \mathcal{E}_i = \mathcal{E};$$

$$ii) \quad \mathcal{E}_i \cap \mathcal{E}_j = \varnothing, \ \forall i \neq j.$$

Based on the partition of $\mathcal{E}$, an induced *partition* of the graph $\mathcal{G}$ is obtained as

$$\{\mathcal{G}_i : \mathcal{G}_i = (\mathcal{V}, \mathcal{E}_i, \mathcal{A}_i), \ i = 1, \cdots, N.\}$$

It is easy to see that

$$\sum_{i=1,\cdots,N} \mathcal{A}_i = \mathcal{A}. \tag{8}$$

It follows that

$$\sum_{i=1,\cdots,N} L_i = L. \tag{9}$$

where L_i is the Laplacian of $\mathcal{G}_i$, $i = 1, \cdots, N$.

Then, the active switching topology is to design a state-dependent switching signal

$$\mathcal{G}(t) = \mathcal{G}(x(t)) \tag{10}$$

such that it can solve the average-consensus problem for the network (7).

4 Network with Active Switching Topology

In this section, we investigate the convergence of the control protocol with active switching topology.

Since $\mathbf{1}_M$ is the common eigenvector of the matrices $L_1, \cdots, L_N$, it allows the decomposition of x in the form

$$x(t) = \text{Ave}(x_0)\mathbf{1}_M + \delta(t).$$

Therefore, the induced disagreement switched system takes the form

$$\dot{\delta}(t) = -L_{\mathcal{G}(t)}\delta(t). \tag{11}$$

Lemma 2. *Given a connected graph* $\mathcal{G} = (\mathcal{V}, \mathcal{E}, \mathcal{A})$, *assume* $\{\mathcal{G}_1, \cdots, \mathcal{G}_N\}$ *is a partition of* $\mathcal{G}$, *then the disagreement system (11) is globally asymptotically stable under the following active switching topology.*

$$\mathcal{G}(t) = \arg \min_{i=1,\cdots,N} -\delta^T(t) L_i \delta(t) \tag{12}$$

Furthermore, the following smooth positive definite and proper function

$$V(\delta) = \frac{1}{2}\delta^T \delta \tag{13}$$

is a valid Lyapunov function for the disagreement dynamics given by (11).

Proof. Since the graph $\mathcal{G}$ is connected, by Lemma 1, we have

$$-\delta^T(t) L \delta(t) = -\delta^T(t) (\sum_{i=1,\cdots,N} L_i) \delta(t) < 0$$

It follows that

$$\min_{i=1,\cdots,N} -\delta^T(t) L_i \delta(t) < 0.$$

Consider the derivative of V, we have

$$\dot{V}(\delta(t)) = -\delta^T(t) L_{\mathcal{G}(t)} \delta(t) = \min_{i=1,\cdots,N} -\delta^T(t) L_i \delta(t) < 0.$$

This shows that V is a Lyapunov function which guarantee the asymptotically stability of (11).

This completes the proof. □

Based on Lemma 2, we establish the following theorem for convergence of the consensus protocol via active switching topology.

Theorem 1. *Given a connected graph* $\mathcal{G} = (\mathcal{V}, \mathcal{E}, \mathcal{A})$, *assume* $\{\mathcal{G}_1, \cdots, \mathcal{G}_N\}$ *is a partition of* $\mathcal{G}$, *then the network (7) is globally asymptotically convergent under the following active switching topology.*

$$\mathcal{G}(t) = \arg \min_{i=1,\cdots,N} -x^T(t) L_i x(t) \tag{14}$$

Furthermore,

$$\lim_{t \to \infty} x(t) = Ave(x_0). \tag{15}$$

Proof. Noticing for any i,

$$-x^T(t) L_i x(t) \equiv -\delta^T(t) L_i \delta(t).$$

It follows that the switching signal generated by (12) is the same as the one generated by (14). By Lemma 2, we have

$$\lim_{t \to \infty} \delta(t) = 0.$$

Since $x = Ave(x_0) + \delta$, thus, we get (15).

This completes the proof. □

5 Simulations

In this section, we present a numerical example to verify the theoretic result in the previous section. Consider a connected graph $\mathcal{G}$ with 10 nodes shown in Fig.1 and the adjacency matrices are limited to $0, 1$ matrices. A partition of $\mathcal{G}$ is given as $\{\mathcal{G}_1, \mathcal{G}_2, \mathcal{G}_3\}$ in Fig.2. Then we adopt the control protocol via active switching topology given by (14) to solve the average-consensus problem. Fig. 3 and Fig. 4

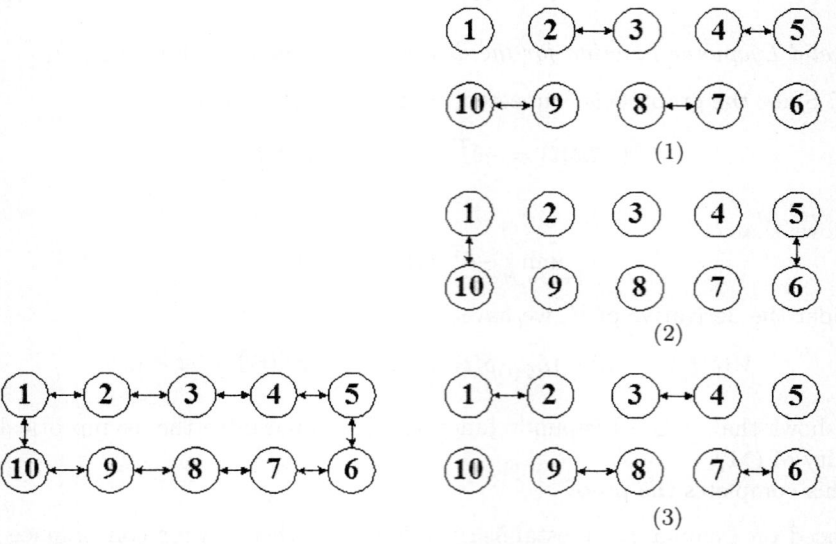

Fig. 1. Undirected connected graph $\mathcal{G}$

Fig. 2. A partition of graph $\mathcal{G}$: (1) $\mathcal{G}_1$, (2) $\mathcal{G}_2$, (3) $\mathcal{G}_3$

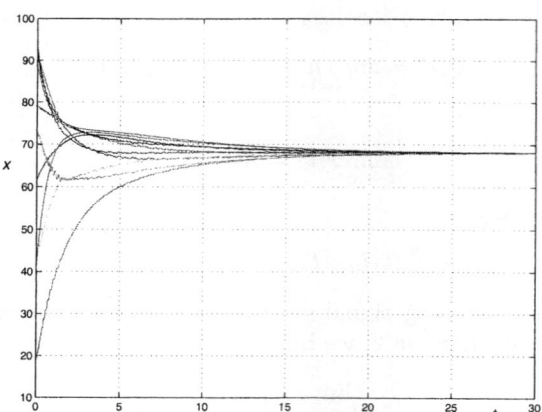

Fig. 3. State trajectories of the network

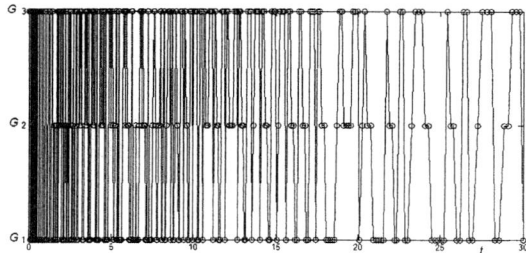

Fig. 4. The active switching signal for the network

show the simulation results for the consensus protocol (5) for a network with graphs $\{\mathcal{G}_1, \mathcal{G}_2, \mathcal{G}_3\}$ with random set of initial conditions.

6 Conclusion

In this paper, convergence analysis of a consensus protocol for networks of dynamic agents with active switching topology was presented. The future work includes extending the obtained results to more general class of networks of agents with more general dynamics.

Acknowledgements

This work was supported by National Natural Science Foundation of China (No. 10372002, No. 60404001 and No. 60274001) and National Key Basic Research and Development Program (2002CB312200).

References

1. Lynch, N.A.: Distributed Algorithms. San Mateo, CA: Morgan Kaufmann, (1997)
2. Fax, A. Murray, R.M.: Information flow and cooperative cotnrol of vehicle formations. IEEE Trans. Automat. Contr. **49** (2004) 1465–1476
3. Mesbahi, M.: On a dynamic extension of the theory of graphs. Proceedings of the American Control Conference. (2002) 1234–1239
4. Reynolds, C.W.: Flocks, herds, and schools: a distributed behavioral model. Computer Graphics(ACM SIGGRAPH'87). **21** (1987) 25–34
5. Gazi, V., Passino, K.M.: Stability Analysis of Swarms. IEEE Trans. Automat. Contr. **48** (2003) 692–697
6. Gazi, V., Passino, K.M.: Stability Analysis of Social Foraging Swarms. IEEE Trans. System, Man and Cybernetics-B. **34** (2004) 539–557
7. Liu, Y., Passino, K.M.: Stable Social Foraging Swarms in a Noisy Environment. IEEE Trans. Automat. Contr. **49** (2004) 30–44
8. Liu, Y., Passino, K.M., Polycarpou, M.M.: Stability Analysis of M-Dimensional Asynchronous Swarms With a fixed Communication Topology. IEEE Trans. Automat. Contr. **48** (2003) 76–95

9. Liu, Y., Passino, K.M., Polycarpou, M.M.: Stability Analysis of One-Dimensional Asynchronous Swarms. IEEE Trans. Automat.Contr. **48** (2003) 1848–1854
10. Mesbahi, M., Hadegh, F.: formation flying of multiple spacecraft via graphs, matrix ineuqalities and switching. AIAA J. guid., Control, Dyna. **24** (2000) 369–377
11. Desai, J.P., Ostrowski, J.P., Kumar, V.: Modeling and control of formations of nonholonomic mobile robots. IEEE Trans. Robot. Automat. **17** (2001) 905–908
12. Lawton, J.R.T., Beard, R.W., Yong, B.J.: Adecentralized apprach to formation maneuvers. IEEE Trans. Robot. Automat. **19** (2003) 933–941
13. Vicsek, T., Czirok, A., Jacob, EB., Cohen, I., Schochet, O.: Novel type of phase transitions in a system of self-driven particles. Phys. Rev. Lett. **75** (1995) 1226–1229
14. Jadbabaie, A., Lin, J., Morse, A.S.: Coordination of groups of mobile autonomous agents using nearest neighbor rules. IEEE Trans. Automat. Contr. **48** (2003) 988–1001
15. Savkin, A.V.: Coordinate collective motion of groups of autonomous mobile robots: analysis of vicsek's model. IEEE Trans. Automat. Contr. **49** (2004) 981–983
16. Saber, R.O., Murray, R.M.: Consensus Problems in Networks of Agents with Switching Topology and Time-delays. IEEE Trans. Automat. Contr. **49** (2004) 1520–1533
17. Saber, R.O., Murray, R.M.: Consensus Protocols for networks of dynamic agents. Proc. Amer. Control Conf. (2003) 951–956
18. Tanner, H.G., Jadbabaie, A., Pappas, G.J.: Stable Flocking of Mobile Agents, Part I: Fixed Topology. Proceedings of the IEEE Conference on Decision and Control. **2** (2003) 2010–2015
19. Tanner, H.G., Jadbabaie, A., Pappas, G.J.: Stable Flocking of Mobile Agents, Part II: Dynamic Topology. Proceedings of the IEEE Conference on Decision and Control. **2** (2003) 2016–2021
20. Shi, H., Wang, L., Chu, T.: Swarming behavior of multi-agent systems. Proc. of the 23rd Chinese Control Conference. (2004) 1027–1031
21. Shi, H., Wang, L., Chu, T., Zhang, W.: Coordination of a group of mobile autonomous agents. International Conference on Advances in intelligent Systems—Theory and Applications. (to appear)
22. Wang, L., Shi, H., Chu, T., Chen, T., Zhang, L.: Aggregation of forging swarms, Lecture Notes in Artificial Intelligence. **3339** (2004) 766–777
23. Liu, B., Chu, T., Wang, L., Wang, Z.: Swarm Dynamics of A Group of Mobile Autonomous Agents. Chin. Phys. Lett. **22** (2005) 254–257
24. Liu, B., Chu, T., Wang, L.: Collective Motion in A Group of Mobile Autonomous Agents. IEEE International Conference on Advance in Intelligent Systems-Theory and Applications. (to appear)
25. Strogatz, S.H.: Exploring complex networks. Nature. **410** (2001) 268–276
26. Graver, J., Servatius, H., Servatius, B.: Chemical Oscillators, Waves, and Turbulance. Berlin, Germany: Springer-Verlag (1984)
27. Acebron, J.A., Spigler, R.: Adaptive frequency model for phase-frequency synchronization in large populations of globally coupled nonlinear oscillators. Physical Review Letters. **81** (1998) 2229-2232
28. Toner, J., Tu, Y.H.: Flocks, herds, and schools: A quantitative theory of flocking. Physical Review E. **58** (1998) 4828–4858
29. Levine, H., Rappel, W.J., Cohen, I.: Self-organization in systems of self-propelled particles. Physical Review E. **63** (2001) 017101-1–017101-4

30. Rosenblum, M.G., Pikovsky, A.S.: Controlling Synchronization in an Ensemble of Globally Coupled Oscillators. Physical Review Letters. **92** (2004) 114102-1–114102-4
31. Kiss, I.Z., Hudson, J.L., Escalona, J., Parmananda, P.: Noise-aided synchronization of coupled chaotic electrochemical oscillators. Physical Review E. **70** (2004) 026210-1–026210-8
32. Scire, A., Colet, P., Miguel, M.S.: Phase synchronization and polarization ordering of globally coupled oscillators. Physical Review E. **70** (2004) 035201-1–035201-4
33. Woafo, P., Kadji, H.G.E.: Synchronized states in a ring of mutually coupled self-sustained electrical oscillators. Physical Review E. **69** (2004) 046206-1–046206-9
34. Rosenblum, M.G., Pikovsky, A.S.: Controlling Synchronization in an Ensemble of Globally Coupled Oscillators. Physical Review Letters. **92** (2004) 114102-1–114102-4
35. Biggs, N.: Algebraic Graph Theory. Cambridge, U.K.: Cambridge Univ. Press (1974)

Quantum Search in Structured Database*

Yuguo He[1,2] and Jigui Sun[1,3]

[1] College of Computer Science and Technology, Jilin University,
130012 Changchun, China
[2] Department of Computer Science and Engineering, Beijing Institute of Technology,
100081 Beijing, China
yuguo@bit.edu.cn
[3] Key Laboratory of Computation and Knowledge Engineering of Ministry of Education,
Jilin University, 130012 Changchun, China
jgsun@jlu.edu.cn

Abstract. This paper is mainly about methodology in designing quantum algorithm. Based on study of Grover's algorithm, we argue that it is a short cut to design and interpret quantum algorithms from the viewpoint of Householder transformation directly. We give an example for this claim, which extends Grover's quantum search algorithm to some structured database. In this example, we show how to exploit some special structure information of problem, which restricts the search in some subspace. Based on an instantiation of this framework, we show that it does can utilize the information to the full extent. This paper gives the details that produce the algorithm framework. The idea, which is simple and intelligible, is universal to some extent, and therefore can be applied to other similar situations.

1 Introduction

Computation occurs everywhere, because a series of change can be regarded as computing. And movement and change is universal and eternal. In the viewpoint of Pilip Ball and some other physicists, the universe is just a computer. Seth Llod has estimated the number of computation that our universe had done since the big bang [9].

In a traditional computer, input states and output states are orthogonal. But in a quantum computer, states can be superposition states. Any unitary transformation is a valid quantum transformation, and vice versa. Indeed, it is a more or less strong restriction for algorithm design. In the end of computation, after some measurement, the quantum computer can give an answer.

In the 1990's, several milestones, such as Grover's quantum search algorithm and Shor's number factoring algorithm, were known to related societies and spur a flurry of activity. However little leap in quantum algorithm design can be seen after that period, though there are some improvements and achievements in many fields. Analyzing, assimilating, summarizing of previous works and accumulating experience are therefore becoming more important nowadays.

---

* Supported by the National Natural Science Foundation of China under Grant No. 60273080, 60473003, and Natural Science foundation of Jilin Province grant number 20030107.

The topic, quantum search that we will discuss in this paper, plays an important role in quantum computation. Many experiments were done to verify these search algorithms. It is perhaps due to the crucial role of search in many fields, especially computer science. And there are some impressive achievements, the representative works among which were done by Grover and Ted Hogg. And Grover's search algorithm has influenced quantum computation deeply and widely. Grover not only brought forward the well-known unstructured algorithm [3], but also made many improvements to his algorithm later, e.g. [4][5]. And he also wrote an unusual paper that recalled the details of procedure when he designed his algorithm [6].

Some people argued that Grover's unstructured algorithm is not practical [11]. They argue that to be useful, a search algorithm has to use structure information. In fact, some search algorithms are designed for problems that have structure. For example, one early work of Ted Hogg [7] has used one kind of general structure information. That is, part of solution should not violate any constrain on solution. In this paper, we will also show how we can exploit certain explicit structure to full extent in quantum search. And we can use the same thoughts to reconstruct Grover's algorithm in another simpler viewpoint.

This paper is written for the readers who have limited physics background. Because of limited space, no background knowledge is introduced here. However, readers can find the necessary concepts and notations in many papers, such as [2].

The rest of this paper is organized as follows. Section 2 introduces Grover's seminal search algorithm. Section 3 gives a new search algorithm frame with some discussions. We argue that Householder transformation is a useful tool for designing quantum algorithms. Section 4 concludes.

2 Grover's Quantum Search Algorithm [3]

Before introducing quantum search algorithm, we need recall the classical counterparts. There are many classical search algorithms, such as hill-climbing, depth-first search, A* search, local search, simulated annealing, etc. Then what is the nature of search problem? If there is no turnoff, even a blind man can get out labyrinth easily and no search technique is needed. Therefore, the nature of search problem is that we have to choose. Search is a process that finds the proper one when we face to many choices (possibilities). Searching is choosing. It is not only sound for Turing machine, but also fit for quantum Turing machine. "Selectivity" in quantum search algorithms is to enhance or weaken amplitudes of basis states selectively.

A searching technique gives people certain principle and strategy when they face to choices. If a problem doesn't offer any structure information, or there is no constraint on problem space, then there exists no effective search skill. It is just like the case when we face to a crossing. If no information can give some hint about the next step, we have to choose one path randomly. In other words, we choose every possible path with identical probability, the sum of which is 1. In this case, even if we comply with some strategy, the possibility of success is the same as the case we select randomly, in average cases.

What Grover set out to solve is just this kind of problem. That is, find one element x satisfying some condition from a given set. And no structure information is available.

Here is the abstracted problem it solves: Let a system have $N = 2^n$ states that are labeled $S_1, S_2, ...S_N$. These 2^n states are represented as n bit strings [3]. $C(S_t)=1$ if S_t is a solution, and $C(S_t)=0$ if S_t is not a solution. The problem is to identify one solution. Here the number of solutions, M, is assumed known.

Below is the description of Grover's algorithm:

(i) Initialization: $\left(\frac{1}{\sqrt{N}}, \frac{1}{\sqrt{N}}, \cdots, \frac{1}{\sqrt{N}}\right)^T$, i.e. there is the same amplitude to be in each of N states. This state can be obtained in $O(\log N)$ steps [3].

(ii) Perform Grover iteration G ($G=DU_f=WRWU_f$): Repeat (a) (b) $O(\sqrt{N/M})$ times (exact estimation of the number of repetition is important [1]):

(a) Marking the solution set using selective rotation transformation U_f:
Let S be one basis state:
In case $C(S)=1$, rotate the phase by π radians;
In case $C(S)=0$, leave the system unaltered.

(b) Apply the diffusion transform D which is defined by the matrix D as follows:

$$D_{ij} = \frac{2}{N} \text{ if } i \neq j \,\&\, D_{ii} = -1 + \frac{2}{N}.$$

D can also represented as: WRW, where W is the Walsh-Hadamard transform matrix, and R, the conditional phase shift matrix, is defined as follows:

$R_{ij}=0$ if $i \neq j$; $R_{ii}=1$ if $i=0$; $R_{ii}=-1$ if $i \neq 0$. This matrix rotate the phases of all basis states by π radians except that of the state $|00...0\rangle$.

(iii) Read (measure) the result.
Assume the output is Sv. If $C(Sv)=1$, then stop, else restart the algorithm.

In this algorithm, step (i) is often adopted in other algorithms. It can be done by perform W on $|00...0\rangle$. Step (ii) (a) marks the solution set with the help of an auxiliary qubit or oracle qubit b. Here, $U_f : |x,b\rangle \rightarrow |x, b \oplus C(x)\rangle$, where $|b\rangle = \frac{1}{\sqrt{2}}(|0\rangle - |1\rangle)$. It can be regarded as a derivation of Deutsch's first algorithm. Step (ii) (b) is the key point of Grover's algorithm, which is also the focus of our study. From section 3.2, the reader can find a similar algorithm and know how to reconstruct the algorithm in a simple way. Measurement in step (iii) is a step needed by all quantum algorithms. We make a slight change to it: when we haven't obtained a solution, the algorithm will be restarted.

From Grover's algorithm, we can see that, the core feature of quantum search algorithms is to converge amplitudes to solutions by reducing or removing the amplitudes of other basis states. And interference plays a key role in this process, which has no counterpart in classical search algorithms.

Notice of difference between quantum search algorithms and classical counterparts will help us to grasp the gist. An analogy can be used to illustrate the difference.

Using searching algorithms to solve problem is just like finding the target points in a huge drawing. The traditional method acts as a man who has myopia. To see the points clearly, he has to close with the picture. As a consequence, every time he can only see one (or several) point. Therefore, to see the target points, he has to depend on structure information to select the positions of observation. On the contrary, a quantum algorithm acts just as a man who looks out over the picture. He can see the whole drawing because he stands far away from the picture. But what he can see is a blurred picture. Now assume there is a pixy near the drawing, and the man can let the pixy do something for him by some orders written in quantum mechanics language. To see the targets clearly, he has to let the pixy know how to mark the goals with distinct "color" and thicken it, while in the same time lighten the colors of other points. Thus the target points become more and more clear. Here the thickness of "color" is an analogy of the norm of amplitude.

3 An Improvement: Searching in a Specific Subspace

If we know or can infer something about solutions, such as the region solutions falls into, or any solution can be divided by some integer, etc., we can use this kind of information to speed search. The point is that the problem space can be reduced by the information. And the search can be narrowed to a specific subspace.

For example, $\begin{cases} x^2+y^2=16 & (1) \\ x \cdot y + \sqrt[3]{x^2+2x-3y^3} > 5 & (2) \end{cases}$ (x and y are all nonnegative integers)

From (1), we can see that: $0 \le x \le 4$ and $0 \le y \le 4$.

Another example comes from some problem that requires finding positive integer solutions of indeterminate equations. We can also infer something about the solutions easily.

Below, we will show how to design a quantum search algorithm that uses such kind of information, from the viewpoint of Householder transformation.

3.1 Householder Transformation

Let $w=(w_1, w_2, \cdots w_n)^T \in R^n$, $\|w\|^2=1$. The Householder transformation determined by vector w is matrix $H=I-2ww^T$ where I is the identity matrix.

We have: if $Hx=y$, then $w = \dfrac{y-x}{\|y-x\|_2}$ (Proof is omitted here).

Thus, if $-Hx=y$, we have: $w = \dfrac{y-(-x)}{\|y-(-x)\|_2}$ (formula *)

Householder transformation can be used to realize any specific unitary transformation when the difference of two vectors is ascertained.

In next section, we will give an algorithm, which can combine the thoughts of Michel Boyer et al. [1] easily in the case we don't know the number of solutions.

3.2 The Algorithm

Assume the problem space has such a structure that we can infer a subspace of size K, which holds all the p solutions. Below is the brief description of the algorithm.

(1) Initialization: assign amplitudes evenly to the subspace that holds all solutions.
   Assume w is the initial state.
(2) Iterate following $O\left(\sqrt{\frac{K}{p}}\right)$ times:
   (a) Marking the solution set using selective rotation transformation U_f:
       Let S be any basis state:
       In case $C(S)=1$, rotate the phase by π radians;
       In case $C(S)=0$, leave the phase unaltered.
   (b) Apply the transformation H, which is defined as follows:
       $H=2ww^T-I$ (H can be further decomposed)
(3) Read the result.
   Assume the output is Sv. If $C(Sv)=1$, then stop. Otherwise, restart the algorithm.

3.3 The Thoughts That Generate the Algorithm

Just as mentioned before, quantum algorithm acts as a man who looks far away from the picture. He can see the whole drawing without difficulty. However what he see is not clear. Can we let him go somewhat closer to the drawing? He perhaps cannot see the whole picture in this way. But if he knows in advance, by being told or probing, that there is no solution in some regions of the drawing, then he can possibly assure no solution will be out of sight when he goes closer to picture. The nature of our algorithm is some techniques that avoid considering regions that have no solutions.

Here are the details of the thoughts that produce our algorithm:

(1) A basic problem in quantum algorithm design is how to exploit "phase" of amplitude. It is clear that the phases of all targets (solutions) need not be different. How about other basis states? For these states, if there is some structure information that includes some distance metric, assigning different phase to them will probably speed search. However, in our problem, the structure information can only tell us a state is or is not a target. In other words, we lack some distance metric to tell us how "far" a state is from a target state. Therefore, it's better to assign the same phase to all these basis states that are not targets. Hence, two kinds of phases are enough for our purpose. And the simplest choice is to assign either "0" or "π" radians to these phases.
(2) Because the constraints are ascertained before search, the subspace that needs to be searched has an explicit structure that can be exploited.

When we have to choose a branch at a road junction, we will choose a promising one that leads us to our goal. But if no information is available for us to make the decision, we will give every branch, which probably leads to a goal, an equal chance (equal amplitude), and in the same time avoid exploring the wrong ways which are known invalid. Thus, the first step of the algorithm is to assign amplitudes to the subspace evenly, as shown in Fig. 1(a).

Fig. 1. (a). Initial state

(3) Clearly, if the amplitudes of solutions are to be increased, we must mark the solutions first. Otherwise the algorithm doesn't know how to enhance the amplitudes of solutions selectively. The simplest way is using transformation U_f to overturn the phases of solutions, as shown in Fig. 1(b). It is similar to Deutsch's first quantum algorithm and the same as Grover's. The method of Tad Hogg [8] doesn't fit to our problem. Why? We leave it to readers.

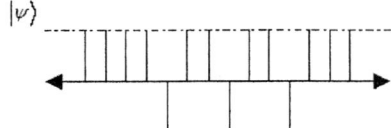

Fig. 1. (b). Marking solutions

(4) The initial amplitudes assigned to solutions are too small. So we need increase the amplitudes of solutions gradually, which possibly needs iterations. Inspired by Grover's work, we turn the state $|\psi\rangle$ to $|\psi'\rangle$, as shown in Fig. 1(c):

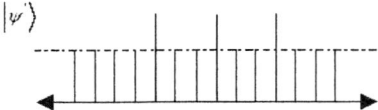

Fig. 1. (c). Increase of amplitudes of solutions

We leave this question to readers: can we do not invert the phases of solutions, whereas still expect the increase of their amplitudes with some transformation?

(5) From Fig. 1(b) to Fig. 1(c), we can see the phase of the former state is inverted again. And the amplitudes of solutions are expected to increased, which means we cannot simply apply U_f again this time. Therefore, we can assume a component, $-I$, in the transformation, and the remainder is X that is to be specified. Thus the transformation has the form: $X-I$. As well known, Householder transformation is a special case of it, and *Householder transformation can be used to realize any specific rotation (unitary) transformation, where w reflects the difference caused by the rotation.* So we can let $X=2ww^T$. In fact, from (formula *) we know the following is preferred:

$|\phi\rangle = |\psi'\rangle - (-|\psi\rangle) = \sum_{x=0}^{N-1} a_x |x\rangle$ be such a special vector that its components are zero eve-

rywhere except this kind of component a_x when $|x\rangle$ is *possibly* a solution. The principle for assigning this kind of component is: since we don't know beforehand whether $|x\rangle$ is a solution or not, we have to set identical quantity to such components. It is reasonable and also implies optimality since any biased guess won't benefit average-case time complexity. In fact, the thought can extend to other cases whenever we can ascertain the difference reflected by w, using the same principle.

Now, let's look at Grover's original algorithm again. It is easy to see that Grover's algorithm can also be designed in this way. But here $w=W|00\cdots0\rangle$. W is Walsh-Hadamard transform.[1] It is readily apprehensible because when we have no idea about where the solutions are, we have to assign equal amplitude everywhere.

We can use this thought to analyze Grover's algorithm.

$(2ww^T - I)|\psi\rangle = 2ww^T|\psi\rangle - |\psi\rangle$. And when $w = W|00\cdots0\rangle = \left(\overbrace{\frac{1}{\sqrt{N}}, \frac{1}{\sqrt{N}}, \cdots, \frac{1}{\sqrt{N}}}^{N}\right)^T$,

$ww^T|\psi\rangle = \frac{1}{N}\sum_{i=1}^{N}|\psi\rangle_i \sum_{x=0}^{N-1}|x\rangle$ where $|\psi\rangle_i$ is the ith component in $|\psi\rangle$. Firstly, amplitudes of solutions increase when $w^T|\psi\rangle$ is positive. When $w^T|\psi\rangle = 0$, the amplitudes stop enlarging and $\sum_{i=1}^{N}|\psi\rangle_i = 0$. Assume in this case the amplitudes of M solutions is Mk and the amplitudes of $(N-M)$ non-solutions is $(N-M)l$, we have $(N-M)l = Mk$ and $(N-M)l^2 + Mk^2 = 1$. Thus, $k = \sqrt{\frac{N-M}{NM}}$. Therefore, $Mk^2 = \frac{N-M}{N}$. It means that there exists an integer r, which satisfies that the amplitudes of solutions reach the maximum when the algorithm iterates r times, the time making $w^T|\psi\rangle \leq 0$. And a solution can be observed with a probability of at least $\frac{N-M}{N}$. Clearly, when $M \ll N$, we can find a solution with a high probability if we iterate the algorithm r times.

The last thing we should mention here is that our algorithm is adoptable only when the initial state is easy to prepare.

3.4 Instantiation of the Algorithm Frame

The algorithm that we've proposed is a general framework. Now we will give an example about how to fill the framework with additional information "any solution can be divided by t".

The algorithm: (Let $\lfloor x \rfloor$ be the floor of x: $max\{n|n \leq x,$ integer $n\}$)

(i) Initialization:

$$\frac{1}{\sqrt{\lfloor \frac{N}{t} \rfloor + 1}}(1,\overbrace{0,0,\cdots 0}^{t},1,\overbrace{0,0,\cdots 0}^{t},1,0,\cdots)^T$$

(ii) Iterate (a) and (b): (It is important to make sure the number of iterations, which will be discussed in complexity analysis)

---

[1] In fact, in [10] Grover iteration is just rewritten as $(2|\psi\rangle\langle\psi| - I)O$, where $|\psi\rangle = W|0\rangle$, and O: $|x\rangle|q\rangle \xrightarrow{O} |x\rangle|q \oplus f(x)\rangle$. These authors also derived Grover's algorithm by guessing the Hamiltonian that solves unstructured search problem and simulating the action of the Hamiltonian using a quantum circuit.

(a) Marking the solution set using selective rotation transformation U_f:
   Let S be one basis state:
      In case $C(S)=1$, rotate the phase by π radians;
      In case $C(S)=0$, leave the phase unaltered.
(b) Apply the transformation H which is defined as follows:

$$H = 2ww^T - I, \text{ where } w = \frac{1}{\sqrt{\left\lceil \frac{N}{t} \right\rceil + 1}} \overbrace{(1,0,0,\cdots 0,1,0,0,\cdots 0,1,0,\cdots)^T}$$

(iii) Read the result.
Assume the output is Sv. If $C(Sv)=1$, then stop. Otherwise, restart the algorithm.

3.5 Complexity Analysis of the Algorithm in Sec. 3.4

Now assume there is M solutions in N basis states. We can project them onto a plane spanned by two orthogonal vectors $|k\rangle = \frac{1}{\sqrt{M}} \sum_{x \in X_1} |x\rangle$ and $|u\rangle = \frac{1}{\sqrt{\left\lceil \frac{N}{t} \right\rceil + 1 - M}} \sum_{x, x \in X_0} |x\rangle$,

as shown in Fig. 2. Here, $X_1 = \{x | C(|x\rangle) = 1\}$ and $X_0 = \{x | C(|x\rangle) = 0\}$.

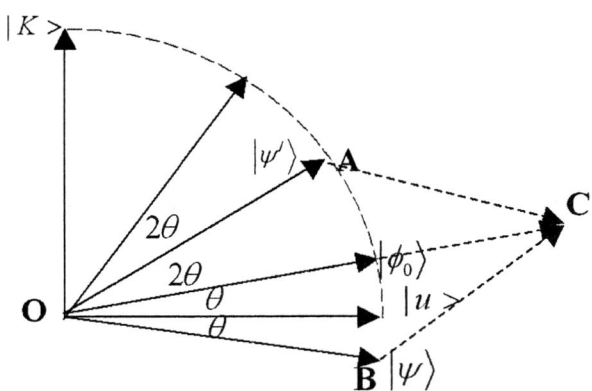

Fig. 2. Geometric interpretation of the iterative procedure

Initial state:
$$|\phi_0\rangle = \frac{1}{\sqrt{\left\lceil \frac{N}{t} \right\rceil + 1}} \sum_{x, x \in [0, N-1]} |x\rangle = \frac{\sqrt{M}}{\sqrt{\left\lceil \frac{N}{t} \right\rceil + 1}} |k\rangle + \frac{\sqrt{\left\lceil \frac{N}{t} \right\rceil + 1 - M}}{\sqrt{\left\lceil \frac{N}{t} \right\rceil + 1}} |u\rangle.$$

It is easy to see that U_f reflects acted vector about $|u\rangle$, for it shifts the phase of $|k\rangle$. Because $|\psi'\rangle = HU_f|\phi_0\rangle = H|\psi\rangle = (2ww^T - I)|\psi\rangle$, from [formula *] we have $|\phi_0\rangle = w = \frac{|\psi\rangle + |\psi'\rangle}{\||\psi\rangle + |\psi'\rangle\|_2}$. Since $|\psi\rangle$ 与 $|\psi'\rangle$ are unitary vector. Therefore, quadrangle OACB is a rhombus and OC is its axis. As a consequence, transformation H reflects acted vector about $|\phi_0>$. Hence, transformation HU_f rotates acted vector 2θ radians. Here $\theta = \sin^{-1}\sqrt{\frac{M}{\left[\frac{N}{t}\right]+1}}$.

Assume the algorithm should iterate i times to reach the maximum of the amplitudes of solutions, we have: $\frac{\pi}{2} > (2i+1)\theta > (2i+1)\sin\theta \geq (2i+1)\sqrt{\frac{tM}{N+t}}$. Therefore, $i < \frac{\pi}{4}\sqrt{\frac{N+t}{tM}}$.

Although it also takes some price in initializing, the price is relative small in this case. It is easy to see that this algorithm is about $\sqrt{t}$ times fast than Grover's. In addition, when $tM<<N$, $\theta \approx \sin\theta$. In this case, from $\sqrt{\frac{M}{\left[\frac{N}{t}\right]+1}} / \sqrt{\frac{M}{N}} \approx \sqrt{t}$ we can also see that the algorithm has exploited related information, that is " the solution can be divided by t", to the full extent, which is supported by a proposition.

Proposition: when problem space can be reduced t times and no other information is exploited, any quantum algorithm can at most be $\sqrt{t}$ times faster than Grover's in the sense of number of queries.

Proof: It is easy to prove. ∎

4 Conclusions

This paper emphasize particularly on some simple thoughts and methods that generate a quantum algorithm. As have been pointed out by Michael A. Nielson and Isaac L.Chuang, quantum phenomenon is often out of reach of our intuition and common sense because our intuition root in classical physics world[10]. Hence, it is not easy to design quantum algorithms that cleverly use quantum dynamics effects, such as interference and entanglement. More works on the principles, skills and methods of algorithm design are therefore needed for the people who are interested in the algorithm aspect but have no idea of it.

In section 3 we've discussed how to exploit a kind of structure information to full extent. In fact, Grover has also discussed possibilities of integrating some structure information into his original algorithm [4]. He has obtained a series of algorithms from another viewpoint. The related work, though similar, is different, and cannot deduce our algorithm.

As well known, Grover's original algorithm is optimal. However, "The arguments used to prove this are very subtle and mathematical. What is lacking is a simple and convincing two line argument that shows why one would expect this to be the case" [4]. Our paper shows that it is natural to expect the optimality of Grover's algorithm. And we claim that, for some kinds of problems, Householder transformation can be a useful tool in algorithm design. And sometimes we can design an algorithm directly from the connotation of it.

References

1. Boyer, M., Brassard, G., Hoyer, P., Tapp, A.: Tight Bounds on Quantum Searching. In Proceedings of the Workshop on Physics of Computation:PhysComp'96. IEEE Computer Society Press, (1996)
2. Ekert, A., Hayden, P., Inamori, H.: Basic Concepts in Quantum Computation. quant-ph/0010077
3. Grover, L.: A Fast Quantum Mechanical Algorithm for Database Search. In Proceedings of the 28th Annual ACM Symposium on the Theory of Computing. Philadelphia (1996) 212-219
4. Grover, L.: Quantum search on structured problems. In the Proceedings of the 1st NASA International Conference on Quantum Computation and Quantum Communications, Berlin (1998)
5. Grover, L.: Tradeoffs in the Quantum Search Algorithm. Manuscript quant-ph/0201152 (2002)
6. Grover, L.: From Schrödinger's Equation to the Quantum Search Algorithm. American Journal of Physics, 7 (2001) 769-777
7. Hogg, T.: Quantum Computing and Phase Transitions in Combinatorial Search. Journal of Artificial Intelligence Research, 4 (1996) 91-128
8. Hogg, T.: Highly Structured Searches with Quantum Computers. Physical Review Letters, (1998) 2473-2476
9. Lloyd, S.: Computational capacity of the Universe. Physical Review Letters, 88 (2002) 237901
10. Nielsen, M., Chuang, I.: Quantum Computation and Quantum Information. Originally published by Cambridge University Press in 2000. Reprinted by Higher Education Press (2003)
11. Viamontes, G., Markov, I., Hayes, J.: Is Quantum Search Practical? quant-ph/0405001

A Fuzzy Trust Model for Multi-agent System*

Guangzhu Chen[1,2], Zhishu Li[1], Zhihong Cheng[2],
Zijiang Zhao[2], and Haifeng Yan[2]

[1] School of Computer, Sichuan University, Chengdu, 610065, P.R. China
[2] College of Mechanical & Electrical Engineering,
China University of Mining and Technology, Xuzhou, 221008, P.R. China
Cgzhu@126.com

Abstract. In the dynamic and uncertain network environment, the trust is an important mechanism for security and reliability of multi-agent system. This paper proposes a trust model for multi-agent system using fuzzy sets (TMMASFS). The distinguishing feature of TMMASFS is that there is the self-recommendation trust besides the direct trust and the recommendation trust. The self-recommendation trust is useful very much when the manager agent has neither the direct experience nor the recommendation experience about the contractor agents. Then the trust dynamic modification theorem is introduced, which can not only valuate the trust but also monitor the executed process of the task. At last, the trust valuation algorithm is presented, and the result of the experiment shows TMMASFS is efficient and adapted to the dynamic and uncertain network environment.

1 Introduction

In a multi-agent system, the trust is an important mechanism. Some trust models [1,2,3,4,5] have been presented, but they have common shortcomings: (1) only include the direct trust and the recommendation trust, which brings a problem that when the manager agent has no transcendental experience about the contractor agents, the manager agent can't valuate the trust of the contractor agents;(2) some trust valuation methods don't take the uncertain environment into account;(3) can't monitor the executed process of the task.

This paper proposes a trust model for multi-agent system using fuzzy sets (TMMASFS). In order to overcome the shortcoming of the presented models in [1,2,3,4,5], There are three kinds of trusts in TMMASFS: the direct trust, the recommendation trust and the self-recommendation trust. The membership function of trust is not given subjectively, but it is evaluated using the trust dynamic modification theorem, which can also monitor the executed process of the task. At last, the trust valuation algorithm and the experiments are introduced.

---

* This work has been supported by the Science and Technology Foundation of China University of Mining and Technology under Grant No.E200412.

2 A Trust Model for Multi-agent System Using Fuzzy Sets

This model is graphically shown in the Fig.1.

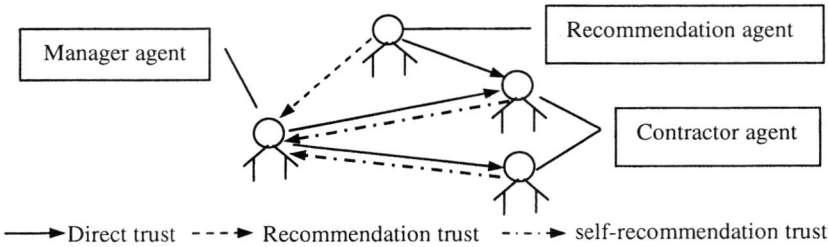

Fig. 1. This shows a figure consisting of different types of trust entities and trusts.

TMMASFS may be described as 4-tuple:

$$M =< Ag, TA, D, TR >. \quad (1)$$

Where $Ag = \{Ag_1, \cdots, Ag_m\}$ is a set of trust entities (the manager agent, the contractor agent and the recommendation agents). Let $X = \{x_1, \cdots, x_n\}$ be the set of issues in a task, and $E = \{e_1, \cdots, e_n\}$ be the domain of expectation values taken by X, thus, a task is a set of issue-value assignments noted as $TA = \{x_1 = e_1, \cdots, x_n = e_n\}$. $D = \{d_1, \cdots, d_n\}$ is a fuzzy set of executed degrees of subtasks, therefore, it may be described as

$$\mu_D : X \rightarrow [0,1]. \quad (2)$$

The membership function μ_D is triangle. Suppose e is the expected value of an issue x, d_1 and d_2 are two maximal difference between the actual value(r) of an issue x and e(d_1, $d_2 \geq 0$, and $d_1 < d_2$). If $|r-e| \leq d_1$, it denotes the subtask is performed well; if $d_1 < |r-e| \leq d_2$, it denotes the subtask is performed averagely; if $|r-e| > d_2$, it denotes the subtask is performed badly.

TR is the total trust of the contractor agent, it may be described as 3-tuple:

$$TR =< TR_d, TR_r, TR_s >. \quad (3)$$

Where TR_d, TR_r and TR_s are fuzzy sets of the direct trust, the recommendation trust and the self-recommendation trust of the contractor agents respectively. Their membership functions (namely, trust degrees) may be described as

$$\mu_{TV_x} : D \rightarrow [0,1]. \quad (4)$$

TV_x is one of TR_d, TR_r and TR_s. Ramchurn[1] regarded μ_{TV_x} as a trigonometric function, we think it is subjective, we will discuss μ_{TV_x} in the section 3.

Suppose ω_d, ω_r and ω_s are the weights of the direct trust, the recommendation trust and the self-recommendation trust respectively, they satisfy $\omega_d + \omega_r + \omega_s = 1$. If $\omega_s = 0$, TMMASFS become the model presented in the literature [1,2,3,4,5]. It is obvious that TMMASFS is a universal model, while the other models are the special cases of TMMASFS. The total trust degree (noted as μ_{TV}) can be denotes as

$$\mu_{TV} = \omega_d \cdot \mu_{TV_d} + \omega_r \cdot \mu_{TV_r} + \omega_s \cdot \mu_{TV_s}. \tag{5}$$

3 Trust Dynamic Modification

Definition 1. $\forall t_i$ (t_i is i'th subtask), suppose that e_i and r_i are the expectation value and actual value of t_i respectively, if $e_i \neq r_i$, the trust degree after executing t_i (noted as $\mu_{TV_x}(i)$) will be modified by a quantity noted as $\varepsilon_i = 1 - \dfrac{|r_i - e_i|}{r_i + e_i}$. It is obviously $0 \leq \varepsilon_i \leq 1$.

Definition 2(Trust modification principle). If $|r_i - e_i| \leq d_1$, μ_{TV_x} will increase, and the smaller $|r_i - e_i|$ is, the more μ_{TV_x} increases; if $d_1 < |r_i - e_i| \leq d_2$, μ_{TV_x} will be unchanged; if $|r_i - e_i| > d_2$, μ_{TV_x} will decrease, and the smaller $|r_i - e_i|$ is, the less μ_{TV_x} decreases.

Theorem 1 (Trust dynamic modification). $\forall t_i$,

$$\mu_{TV_x}(i) = \begin{cases} \mu_{TV_x}(i-1) + \varepsilon_i \cdot (1 - \mu_{TV_x}(i-1)) & |r_i - e_i| \leq d_1 \\ \mu_{TV_x}(i-1) & d_1 < |r_i - e_i| \leq d_2 \\ \mu_{TV_x}(i-1) - \mu_{TV_x}(i-1) \cdot (\dfrac{1}{1+\varepsilon_i}) & |r_i - e_i| > d_2 \end{cases} \tag{6}$$

Satisfies definition 2(Trust modification principle).

Prove. When $|r_i - e_i| \leq d_1$, if $|r_i - e_i|$ is smaller, $\varepsilon_i = 1 - \dfrac{|r_i - e_i|}{r_i + e_i}$ will be bigger, and $\varepsilon_i \cdot (1 - \mu_{TV_x}(i-1))$ will also be bigger, it makes $\mu_{TV_x}(i)$ increase more;

When $d_1 < |r_i - e_i| \le d_2$, $\mu_{TV_x}(i) = \mu_{TV_x}(i-1)$, namely μ_{TV_x} is unchanged;

When $|r_i - e_i| > d_2$, if $|r_i - e_i|$ is smaller, $\varepsilon_i = 1 - \dfrac{|r_i - e_i|}{r_i + e_i}$ will be bigger, and $\mu_{TV_x}(i-1) \cdot (\dfrac{1}{1+\varepsilon_i})$ will be smaller, it makes $\mu_{TV_x}(i)$ decrease less.

Therefore, Equation (6) satisfies definition 2(Trust modification principle).

4 Trust Valuation Algorithm

The algorithm consists of three steps: Initializing (Initialize());choosing the optimal contractor agent (Choose_Agent ()) and modifying the trust degree dynamically (Modify_trust()).

Step 1. Initialize ()   //choose the optimal contractor agent primarily.
        { Input $\mu_{TV_d}, \mu_{TV_r}, \mu_{TV_s}$ of the contractor agents;
        Computer μ_{TV} ; }

Step 2. Choose_Agent ()   //choose the optimal contractor agent.
        { Compare and Choose the optimal contractor agent;
        Start doing the i'th subtask; }
Step 3. Modify_Trust ()   //modifying the trust degree.
        { Modify $\mu_{TV_d}, \mu_{TV_r}, \mu_{TV_s}$;
        Restart compute μ_{TV} ;
        Go to Step 2; }

5 Experiments

Suppose that there are three agents: Ag_1, Ag_2 and Ag_3. Ag_1 is the manager agent, Ag_2 and Ag_3 are the contractor agents. The amount of subtasks is 10. At beginning, TV_d, TV_r, TV_s of each contractor agent are given randomly. $\omega_d = 0.5$, $\omega_r = 0.3$, $\omega_s = 0.2$. The trust modifications of contractor agents are illustrated in the Fig.2.

6 Conclusions

It is important of the trust mechanism to safeguard the runs of multi-agent system in the dynamic and uncertain network environment. TMMASFS overcomes the shortcomings of the presented trust models, and is adapted to the uncertain network environment more effectively. There are many difficulties in studying the self-recommendation trust, but we think that we have made a start in this direction.

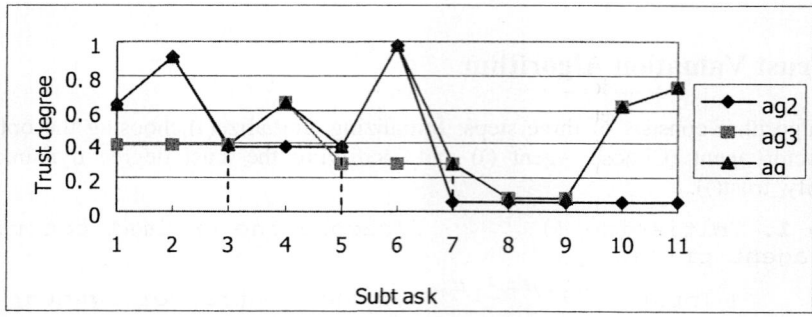

Fig. 1. Curve ag2 is the total trust degree of Ag_2, curve ag3 is the total trust degree of Ag_3, and curve ag is the total trust degree of the optimal contractor agent. It is observed that the trust degree changes continuously and the optimal contract agent alternates in the executed process of subtasks (for example the 3'th, the 5'th and the 7'th subtask in the figure).

References

1. Ramchurn, S. D., Sierra, C., Godo, L.:A Computational Trust Model for Multi-Agent Interactions based on Confidence and Reputation. In Proceedings of 6th International Workshop of Deception, Fraud and Trust in Agent Societies, Melbourne, Australia (2003) 69-75
2. Anthony G.Bower.et al.: Learning about a Population of Agents and the Evolution of Trust and Cooperation. International Journal of Industrial Organization (1996) 165-190
3. Xu F,Lü J,Zheng W,Cao C.:Design of a Trust Valuation Model in Software Service Coordination. Journal of Software (2003) 1043-1051
4. Chen Gang,Lü Ruiqian.:The Relation Web Model-An Organizational Approach to Agent Cooperation based on Social Mechanism. Journal of Computer Research and Development (2003) 107-114
5. B. Yu and M.P. Singh.:A Social Mechanism of Reputation Management in Electr- onic Communities. In Cooperative Information Agents (2000) 154–165

Adaptive Particle Swarm Optimization for Reactive Power and Voltage Control in Power Systems

Wen Zhang and Yutian Liu*

School of Electrical Engineering, Shangdong University,
73 Jingshi Avenue, Jinan 250061, P.R. China
zhangwen@sdu.edu.cn

Abstract. The particle swarm optimization (PSO) algorithm, a new evolutionary computation method, has been proved to be powerful but needs parameters predefined for a given problem. In this paper, a new adaptive particle swarm optimization (APSO) algorithm is proposed and applied to reactive power and voltage control in power systems. The proposed APSO method can adjust parameters automatically in optimization process. The simulation results show that the APSO algorithm is more efficient in searching global optimization solution compared with the PSO algorithm.

1 Introduction

The particle swarm optimization (PSO) [1] has been proposed recently and proved to be a powerful competitor in the field of optimization. It has been recently applied to several power system problems and has been shown to perform well [2]. However, the parameters of PSO should be selected carefully for efficient performance in applications. In order to find a "good" set of parameters, the algorithm has to be run several times with different parameter sets. The use of rigid parameters that do not change their values may not be optimal, since different values of parameters may work better/worse at different stages of the evolutionary process. Some attempts have been made to define an adaptive PSO [3] [4].

This paper presents a new adaptive particle swarm optimization (APSO) algorithm which can adjust all three parameters automatically in the optimization process. The effectiveness of the proposed algorithm has been showed by the simulation results of a practical power system.

2 Adaptive Particle Swarm Optimization

For a given particle P_i, its position and velocity in a D-dimensional space are represented as $x_i(t) = (x_{i,1}(t), x_{i,2}(t), \ldots x_{i,D}(t))$ and $v_i(t) = (v_{i,1}(t), v_{i,2}(t), \ldots v_{i,D}(t))$ respectively. The best previous position found so far by particle P_i is recorded as $P_i = (P_{i,1}, P_{i,2}, \ldots P_{i,D})$. The best previous position among the neighborhood is represented as $g_i = (g_{i,1}, g_{i,2}, \ldots g_{i,D})$. Mathematically, the particles are manipulated according to the following equations [5]

---

* Senior Member, IEEE

$$\begin{cases} v_{i,d}(t+1) = \chi(v_{i,d}(t) + rand(0,\varphi/2)(p_{i,d}(t) - x_{i,d}(t)) \\ \qquad\qquad + rand(0,\varphi/2)(g_{i,d}(t) - x_{i,d}(t))) \\ x_{i,d}(t+1) = x_{i,d}(t) + v_{i,d}(t+1) \end{cases} \quad 1)$$

$$\begin{cases} \varphi > 4 \\ \chi = 2/(\varphi - 2 + \sqrt{\varphi^2 - 4\varphi}) \end{cases} \quad (2)$$

Where χ is called constriction coefficient, rand$(0,\varphi/2)$ stands for a random number in$[0,\varphi/2]$.

2.1 Adaptive Strategy of Swarm Size N

Swarm size or the number of particles in the swarm affects the performance of PSO significantly. Too few particles will cause the algorithm to become stuck in a local minimum, while too many particles will slow down the algorithm. Therefore a balance between variety and speed must be sought.

If a particle has an enough improvement but still is the worst particle in its neighborhood, remove the particle from the swarm to reduce redundant.

$$\text{Remove } P_i, \text{ if } P_i = P_{worst,i} \text{ and } \delta(P_i) > \Delta. \quad (3)$$

where $\delta(P_i)$ is the improvement of P_i by comparing its position when it has been generated and the best position it has found after that.

On the contrary, if a particle hasn't any enough improvement but still is the best particle in its neighbors, generate a new particle to improve diversity.

$$\text{Add a particle, if } P_i = P_{best,i} \text{ and } \delta(P_i) < \Delta. \quad (4)$$

2.2 Adaptive Strategy of Coefficient φ_i

The value of φ_i determines how much the particle attracted by the best points found previously by itself and its neighborhood.

If a particle has improved itself enough, it can try to decrease its velocity and thus decrease the exploring regions in the search space. This can be implemented by increasing φ_i in a proper range $[\varphi_{min}, \varphi_{max}]$.

$$\varphi_i = \varphi_{i+}(\varphi_{max} - \varphi_i)m_i \text{ if } m_i = \delta(P_i) - \Delta > 0. \quad (5)$$

where $\Delta = 1 - f_{best}/f_{worst}$ is the improvement threshold of a particle.

On the contrary, if a particle hasn't made enough improvement, it would be better to slow down the rate of convergence and explore a wider part of the search space.

2.3 Adaptive Strategy of Neighborhood Size h_i

The smaller value of h_i, the more slowly the best positions are communicated between particles as particles only exchange information with neighboring particles. As h_i increases, the algorithm converges faster but might be trapped into local optimum.

If a particle is the local best and has improved enough, the particle doesn't need to inquire so many neighbors for more information and its neighborhood size is reduced.

$$\delta(h_i) = \delta(h_i) + (\delta(h_i)-1)/(N-1), \text{ if } P_i = P_{best,i} \text{ and } \delta(P_i) > \Delta. \tag{6}$$

This will be effective when the accumulating absolute value is greater than or equal to 1. That is

$$h_i = h_i - 1 \text{ and } \delta(h_i) = 0, \text{ if } |\delta(h_i)| \geq 1. \tag{7}$$

On the contrary, if a particle is the local best but hasn't improved enough, the particle needs more information and its neighborhood size is increased.

3 Simulation Results of Optimal Reactive Power and Voltage Control Based on APSO

Usually, the optimal reactive power and voltage control in power systems can be represented as a mixed integer nonlinear programming problem.

$$\text{Min } P_{loss}(x_1, x_2)$$

$$\text{s.t. } h(x_1, x_2) = 0 \tag{8}$$

$$x_{1min} \leq x_1 \leq x_{1max}$$
$$x_{2min} \leq x_2 \leq x_{2max}$$

where $P_{loss}(x_1,x_2)$ denotes the real power loss in a power system; x_1 is the control variable vector including generator voltages (V_G, continuous), transformer taps (K_T, integer) and shunt capacitors(Q_C, integer); x_2 is the dependent variable vector including load-bus voltages(V_L) and reactive power generations(Q_G); $h(x_1,x_2)=0$ is the power flow equation.

The fitness function considering the constrains on V_L and Q_G used in this paper is

$$\min f = P_{loss} + \lambda_V \sum_\alpha \Delta V_L^2 + \lambda_Q \sum_\beta \Delta Q_G^2 . \tag{9}$$

where λ_V and λ_Q are penalty factors; $\triangle V_L$ and $\triangle Q_G$ are the violations of load-bus voltages and generator reactive powers; α and β are sets of buses whose voltage and reactive power generation violate their constraints, respectively.

Both the APSO and the PSO are applied to reactive power optimization of a practical 125-bus power system. The system control variables are the same with that of reference [6]. The parameters adopted in PSO are $N=20$, $\varphi_i=4.1$ and $h_i=3$. The initial values of the APSO parameters are equal to that of PSO. The stop criterion for the PSO is 20,000 fitness value evaluations (20 particles iterate 1000 times). The PSO has been run 100 times with random initial values and the mean computation time T for a trial is evaluated. For comparison, every trial of the APSO was permitted to run for time T. There may be fewer fitness evaluations than 20,000 because of the adaptive process, but the results are better than that of the PSO for the same reason.

Some average results of 100 trails are listed in Table 1. It can be seen that APSO algorithm outperforms PSO. The active power losses before and after the APSO optimization are 0.3584 and 0.3584 respectively. It is clear that the power loss is greatly reduced (14.17% reduction) and the voltage profile qualification has been improved from 84.8% to 100%. It is evident that the APSO approach outperforms the PSO algorithm.

Table 1. Average results of the practical power system

Item	P_{loss}(p.u.)	$P_{reduced}$(%)	$V_{qualified}$(%)
Original	0.3584	--	84.8
APSO	0.3584	14.17	100
PSO	0.3080	14.06	100

4 Conclusion

This paper presents an APSO algorithm and its application to reactive power optimization in power systems. In the APSO, all three parameters, swarm size N, coefficient φ_i and neighborhood size h_i of each particle, are adapted based on the fitness values of particles during optimization process. Optimization results of a practical power system show that the APSO can adjust parameters automatically in searching process and yield better solution comparing with PSO.

References

1. Kennedy, J., Eberhart, R.C.: Particle swarm optimization. Proceedings of International Conference on Neural Networks, Australia, (1995) 1942-1948
2. Abido, M. A.: Optimal power flow using particle swarm optimization. International Journal of Electric Power and Energy Systems 24(7) (2002) 563-571
3. Clerc, M., The Swarm and the Queen: Towards a Deterministic and Adaptive Particle Swarm Optimization. Congress on Evolutionary Computation, CEC 1999, Washington DC, USA, (1999) 1951-1957
4. Shi, Y., Eberhart, R.C.: Fuzzy adaptive particle swarm optimization. Proceedings of International Congress on Evolutionary Computation, Korea, (2001) 101-106
5. Clerc, M., Kennedy, J.: The particle swarm - explosion, stability, and convergence in a multidimensional complex space. IEEE Trans on Evolutionary Computation, 6(1), (2002) 58-73
6. Liu, Y., Ma, L., Zhang J.: Reactive power optimization by GA/SA/TS combined algorithms. Int. J. of Electric Power & Energy Systems, 24(9), (2002) 765-769

A Dynamic Task Scheduling Approach Based on Wasp Algorithm in Grid Environment*

Hui-Xian Li[1,2] and Chun-Tian Cheng[2,**]

[1] School of Electronic and Information Engineering, Dalian University of Technology,
116024 Dalian, China
hxli@Student.dlut.edu.cn
[2] Institute of Hydroinformatics, Dalian University of Technology, 116024 Dalian, China
ctcheng@dlut.edu.cn

Abstract. Task scheduling is one of the bottlenecks in realizing grid computing. We introduce swarm intelligence into task scheduling in a grid environment, and propose a new dynamic task-scheduling algorithm. This algorithm schedules effectively a group of independent tasks based on the interaction model between a wasp colony and its environment. We also present an effective method, using the self-organized dominance hierarchy of wasp colony to solve the dominance struggle problem that occurs in the proposed algorithm. Our evaluation results show that the proposed algorithm is more efficient and more adaptive to the dynamic grid environment than other task-scheduling algorithms.

1 Introduction

Grid computing aims to implement large-scale resource sharing and interactive collaboration [1]. Allocating tasks to different resources reasonably and optimally, that is, task scheduling, is an NP-complete problem, and aims to minimize the overall execution time (or *makespan*) of all tasks. Task scheduling is one of the bottlenecks of grid computing and is mainly based on a meta-task model [2]. However, most algorithms based on a meta-task model belong to a centralized scheme [3]; because they lack good adaptability, they are not adaptive to the complex grid environment.

In the last ten years, swarm intelligence has received increasing attention in the research community. The collective behavior that emerges from a swarm of social insects is referred to as swarm intelligence [4]. Social insect colonies solve complex problems collectively by the distributed and intelligent methods. These problems are beyond the capabilities of each individual insect, and the cooperation among them is largely self-organized without any supervision. Through studying social insect colonies behaviors, scholars have proposed some algorithms or theories for combinational optimal problems, such as the wasp algorithm [5] and the ant algorithm [6]; these approaches have already been applied to many fields [7]. Task scheduling in the grid

---

* This research was supported in part by the Chinese National Natural Science foundation no. 50479055.
** Corresponding author.

is also a combinational optimal problem. Motivated by these concerns, we proposed a new dynamic task-scheduling algorithm based on the wasp algorithm. We proved through experiment that the proposed algorithm is more adaptive to the grid environment than other task-scheduling algorithms.

2 The Proposed Algorithm

2.1 Problem Definition

Let $C=\{c_1, c_2, ...,c_n\}$ denote a set of n heterogeneous computing resources, $D=\{d_1, d_2, ...,d_r\}$ denote a set of r data sources, and $T=\{t_1, t_2, ...,t_m\}$ denote a set of m tasks. Tasks are submitted to the grid system randomly. Without loss of generality, suppose that the input of each task is a group of data units stored in some data source, and each task needs one computing resource. In each computing resource, there is a waiting list labeled as L, which is used to describe its workload size.

There exist two length thresholds for each waiting list: idle threshold L_{in} and busy threshold L_{stop}. Let $Tran(t_i, c_j, d_k)$ denote the data transfer time from d_k to c_j of a task t_i. Let $Exe(t_i, c_j)$ denote the estimated execution time of a task t_i on c_j. Let $Comp(t_i, c_j)$ denote the completion time of a task t_i on c_j; this is the sum of the estimated execution time and the data transfer time of the task t_i on c_j. Let $WT(t_i)$ denote the time interval from the submission to the execution for a task t_i. Let $Length(c_j, L)$ denote the length of the waiting list L of c_j; this is the sum of completion times of all tasks in the waiting list L.

2.2 The Design of the Proposed Algorithm

Grid task scheduling is very similar to task allocation of a wasp colony. In our algorithm, each computing resource c_j has an associated agent wasp w_j, which is in charge of leaving its computing resource and returning with tasks. Tasks submitted by users first enter into the task list in the scheduling center of the grid. The scheduling center is responsible for receiving tasks and is not involved in task scheduling. Each wasp w_j has a set of response thresholds $\Theta_j=\{\theta_{j,1}, \theta_{j,2}, ..., \theta_{j,m}\}$ to m tasks. When the stimulus emitted by t_i reaches $\theta_{j,i}$, w_j will transfer the task t_i to the corresponding resource c_j. $\theta_{j,i}$ is defined as follows:

$$\theta_{j,i} = \eta + u \cdot Exe(t_i,c_j) + l \cdot Tran(t_i,c_j,d_k). \tag{1}$$

where η, u and l are constants. A task t_j that has not been allocated computing resources emits a stimulus S_j to all agent wasps, defined as follows:

$$S_j = S_0 + h \cdot WT(t_j). \tag{2}$$

where h is a constant and S_0 is the initial stimulus of the task t_j. A high priority task is assigned a high initial stimulus so that some wasp will transfer it preferentially.

The agent wasp w_j transfers a task t_i emitting a stimulus S_i with probability

$$P(\theta_{j,i},S_i) = S_i^2 / (S_i^2 + \theta_{j,i}^2). \tag{3}$$

In the way, agent wasps will tend to transfer tasks whose response thresholds are lower. But if a task emits a high enough stimulus, agent wasps will also tend to transfer it. The algorithm for each agent wasp w_i can be described as follows:

```
1  CurLen = Length(c_j, L);
2  while (CurLen ≤ L_in) do
   2.1 for i = 1 to m do   /*for m tasks*/
       2.1.1 Query the S_i emitted by the task t_i;
       2.1.2 Compute the probability P(θ_{j,i}, S_i)
       end for i
   2.2 while (CurLen ≤ L_stop) do
       2.2.1 Add t_i to L of c_j in the order of P(θ_{j,i}, S_i);
       2.2.2 CurLen = Length(c_j, L);
       end while
   end while
```

2.3 Dominance Struggle

Formula (3) does not address the real problem of many wasps often trying to transfer the same task. According to the self-organized dominance hierarchy of a wasp colony, we proposed an effective method to solve the contest problem in our algorithm, more effective than the method of Cicirello et al. [7]. Suppose agent wasps, $w_1, w_1, \ldots, w_q$, contend for a task t_i. In our method, each agent wasp $w_j (1 \le j \le q)$ is given a force F_j

$$F_j = Length(c_j, L) + Comp(t_i, c_j) \quad 1 \le j \le q. \quad (4)$$

They may with their forces interact with each other. The wasp with the least force will win and transfer the task. In fact, the force of an agent wasp is the length of the new waiting list into which t_i is added. So the corresponding computing resource is optimal to process the task. In addition, if there are several agent wasps with the same least force, the scheduling center will select one among them randomly.

3 Simulation and Discussion

In this section, we will evaluate the proposed algorithm (hereafter called the wasp-based algorithm) and use a simulation environment based on discrete event simulation. We simulate six computing resources and ten data sources and implement our scheduling algorithm, the min-min heuristic algorithm, and the sufferage heuristic algorithm. Ding et al. illustrated the good performance of the last two algorithms [2].

Table 1. Comparison of the *makespan*(s). Three groups of tasks are chosen in our experiment. The amounts of three groups are 500, 1000 and 2000, respectively.

	500	1000	2000
Wasp-based	1500	3100	7650
Sufferage	1750	3600	8950
Min-min	1830	3750	9500

From Table 1, it is obvious that the *makespan* of the wasp-based algorithm is less than the other two for each number of tasks. Our experiment concludes that the wasp-based algorithm performs better than the other two algorithms and shows a fine adaptability to the complex grid environment.

4 Conclusions

In this paper, we apply swarm intelligence to solve task scheduling in the grid environment, and design a dynamic task-scheduling algorithm based on a wasp algorithm. In our algorithm, task scheduling is implemented by adding tasks to the waiting list of each computing resource instead of allocating the required resources to a group of tasks once. Results show that the proposed algorithm is higher in efficient than the sufferage and the min-min algorithms, and more adaptive to the complex grid environment.

References

1. Foster I., Kesselman C.: The GRID Blueprint for a New Computing Infrastructure. Morgan Kaufmann Publishers, San Francisco (1998)
2. Ding Q., Chen G.-L.: A Benefit Function Mapping Heuristic for a Class of Meta-tasks in Grid Environments. In: Proc. of First IEEE/ACM International Symposium on Cluster Computing and the Grid, IEEE Computer Society, Brisbane, Australia (2001) 654–659
3. Hamscher, V., Schwiegelshohn, U., Streit, A., Yahyapour, R.: Evaluation of Job-Scheduling Strategies for Grid Computing. In Buyya, R., Baker, M. (eds.): Proc of 7th Int'l Conf on High Performance Computing. Lecture Notes in Computer Science, Vol. 1971. Springer-Verlag, Berlin Heidelberg New York (2000) 191–202
4. Bonabeau, E., Dorigo, M., Theraulaz, G.: Swarm Intelligence: From Natural to Artificial System. Oxford University Press, Oxford (1999)
5. Theraulaz, G., Goss, S., Gervet, J., Deneubourg, J.-L.: Task Differentiation in Polistes Wasp Colonies: A Model for Self-organizing Groups of Robots. In Meyer, J.A., Wilson, S.W. (eds.): Proc. of the First International Conference on Simulation of Adaptive Behavior on From Animals to Animats, MIT Press, Paris, France, (1991) 346–355
6. Dorigo, M., Maniezzo, V., Colorni, A.: The Ant System: Optimization by a Colony of Cooperation Agents. IEEE Tran. on Systems, Man, and Cybernetics-Party B, 26(1) (1996) 1–13
7. Cicirello, V.A., Smith, S.F.: Improved Routing Wasps for Distributed Factory Control. In: Proc. of IJCAI-01 Workshop on AI and Manufacturing: New AI Paradigms and Manufacturing, Seattle, WA (2001) 26–32

A Novel Ant Colony Based QoS-Aware Routing Algorithm for MANETs

Lianggui Liu and Guangzeng Feng

Department of Communications Engineering, Nanjing University of Posts & Telecommunications, Nanjing 210003, China
liangguiliu@126.com, gzfeng@njupt.edu.cn

Abstract. Ant based routing protocols for MANETs have been widely explored, but most of them are essentially single-path routing methods which tend to have heavy burden on the hosts along the shortest path from source to destination. The robustness of these protocols is comparatively not good which is further weakened by the positive feedback mechanism of ant. Link-disjoint multi-path routing is more robust and can support QoS better than single-path routing in MANETs. In this paper we combine swarm intelligence and link-disjoint multi-path routing to solve the problem mentioned above. A novel approach named Ant colony based Multi-path QoS-aware Routing (AMQR) is proposed. AMQR establishes and utilizes multiple routes of link-disjoint paths to send data packets concurrently and adopts pheromone to disperse communication traffic, thus it can adapt to the dynamic changes of the network and support QoS better. The simulation results show that the proposed approach outperforms other pertinent algorithms.

1 Introduction

Mobile ad hoc networks (MANETs) [1] are wireless, self-organizing systems formed by co-operating nodes within communication range of each other that form temporary networks. Their topology is dynamic, decentralized, ever changing and the nodes may move around arbitrarily. Routing algorithms in ad hoc networks need to match the special network characteristics such as mobility, limited energy and bandwidth, higher bit error rate. Routing algorithms for ad hoc networks can be categorized into table-driven and on–demand. Most of them may introduce much uncontrolled overheads to solve the routing problem. The large routing overheads affect the scalability of the networks and the network performance since it use a significant part of the wireless bandwidth and the node's energy. The routing algorithms based on ant can self-configure and self-adapt to the dynamic changes of the network. Some protocols based on ant have been performed in wired telecommunication network routing optimization [2~5]. But because of the own special character of ad hoc networks, the ant-based routing for static, wired network can not be directly applied to ad hoc networks. Using periodic broadcast ants to discover routes in ad hoc networks could incur a large traffic which will lead large delay and the adaptability to topology changes would be unacceptably slow. So in order to use ant based routing protocol, some new mechanisms must be performed in ad hoc networks [6~12]. As far as the present ant-based routing in ad hoc networks are concerned, the drawbacks exist as follows. To the best of our knowledge, although protocols in [6] [8] [9] [12] adopt backup routes to send data packets when route failure happens, they are essentially single-path routing methods as well as other conventional protocols such as DSR [13]. The robustness of ant based protocols is comparatively not good, which is further weakened by the positive feedback mechanism of ant. So these protocols among which ADRA [12] is tend to have heavy burden on the hosts along the shortest path from a source to a destination. As a result, heavily loaded hosts may deplete power energy quickly, routing load brought by rebroadcasting route request packets will be aggravated when route failure happens, and congestion will be a most serious problem for these hosts and most of these algorithms can not deal with the problems effectively, thus the performance of network will be greatly aggravated.

In this paper, a novel ant colony based multi-path routing protocol named AMQR is proposed which combines swarm intelligence and link-disjoint multi-path routing to solve the problem mentioned above. The new method establishes and utilizes multiple routes of link-disjoint paths to send data packets concurrently and adopts pheromone to disperse communication traffic. We validate its performance with extensive simulation.

The rest of this paper is organized as follows. The novel routing protocol AMQR is proposed in Section 2. Section 3 gives the simulation results. Finally, we draw conclusions in Section 4.

2 AMQR Description

2.1 Pertinent Definitions

Definition 1. A graph, $G = (V, E)$ is used to describe an ad hoc network with a finite non-empty node set V and a link set E the member of which has two endpoints that can communicate with each other directly. When ants locate at node i, it will select the next hop j with the transition probability calculated by the formula (1):

$$P(i, j) = \begin{cases} \dfrac{\mathcal{P}_{ij}}{\sum_{u \in N(i)} \mathcal{P}_{iu}} & \text{if } u \in N(i) \\ 0 & \text{otherwise} \end{cases} \quad (1)$$

In formula (1), N(i) is the neighbor node set of i. $\mathcal{P}_{ij}$ is the amount of pheromone on the link e(i,j). During the route discovery and maitenance periods, $\mathcal{P}_{ij}$ is updated using formula:

$$\mathcal{P}_{ij} \leftarrow (1-\alpha) \cdot \mathcal{P}_{ij} + \Delta \mathcal{P}_{ij} \quad (2)$$

where $0 < \alpha < 1$ is a pheromone decay parameter, $\Delta \mathcal{P}_{ij}$ is the increment of $\mathcal{P}_{ij}$ caused by the received ant which is caculated by formula:

$$\Delta \mathcal{P}_{ij} = q^{-m} h^{-n} \tag{3}$$

In (3), q is the time delay of ant, h is the hop count the ant passed by from its source to the current node. m and n are parameters which determine the relative importance of time delay versus hop count.

Definition 2. During the route discovery period, the use of forward ants and backward ants are required. They are called mobile agents. A forward ant establishes the pheromone track to the source node. In contrast, a backward ant establishes the pheromone track to the destination node.

Frame format: Here two types of control packets in AMQR are listed, the Forward ant (F) and the Backward ant (B). The following are the formats of these packets.

(i). F packet is shown in Fig. 1a, which includes the following items: SID — source node ID, DID — destination node ID, SeqN — the unique sequence number, HopC — hop counter field which calculates the hop the ant passed by from its source, and the dynamically increasing list which consists of the passed node's ID (PasN) and the corresponding arriving time (ArrT).

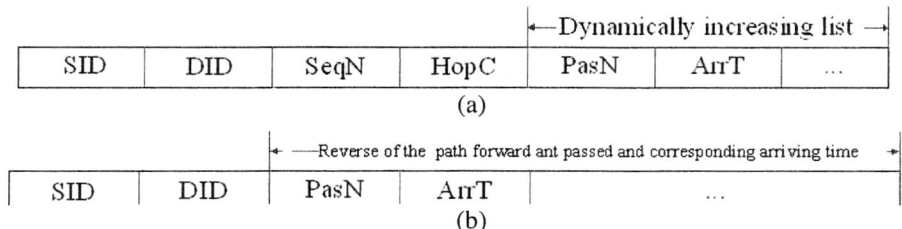

Fig. 1. Frame formats (a) Forward ant (F) (b) Backward ant (B)

(ii). B packet is shown in Fig. 1b. Here DID represents the ID of the intermediate node or the destination node which creates the backward ants. The other items have the same meaning as in F packet.

2.2 Description of AMQR

AMQR is an on-demand routing protocol and it consists of three phases: route discovery phase, route maintenance phase and route failure handling phase.

Phase 1: route discovery

To find the route to the destination node d, the source node s firstly broadcasts HELLO packets to get information of its neighbor nodes, then s broadcasts forward ant F.

(i). If node j which receives F for the first time has met with congestion, it discards the F; otherwise, it checks the F's destination ID. If the F's destination ID is not the same as node j's, node j will add its ID and arriving time to the list of this F. Then node j creates a record in its routing table. A record in the routing table is triple and consists of destination ID, next hop and pheromone value $\mathcal{P}$. Node j interprets the source ID of F as the destination ID, the ID of the previous node as the next hop, and computes the pheromone value depending on the number of hops and the time delay that F needed to reach node j. After that, node j updates the hop counter field HopC by $HopC \leftarrow HopC+1$ and records HopC as $Hops_{old}$ which represents the currently received F's number of hops. In the end, node j relays F to its neighbors. Duplicate F can be identified through the unique sequence number and discarded.

(ii). If it is not the first time for an intermediate node to receive F came from the same source with the same sequence number, and if the received F's HopC (set $Hops_{new} = HopC$) accords with $Hops_{new} \leq Hops_{old} + \Delta hops$ where $\Delta hops$ is the acceptable number of the extra hops, the node will record the corresponding path in its route buffer. Meanwhile, every intermediate node records SID (source node ID) and the maximum sequence number which is the newest one of the ever received forward ants came from the same source node. If the sequence number of the presently received F coming from the same source node is smaller than or equivalent to the corresponding maximum sequence number and the F's node list includes the present node, then the F will be killed. When F arriving at the intermediate node, because its priority is the same as the data packets', just like a data packet does, it abides by the FIFO rule and suffers time delay and congestion, both of which will be represented by the recorded data and will be the gist according as which the route is confirmed and optimized. When F arrives at the destination node, the destination node will postpone for a short period of time in order to get the information from the other routes. After that, the destination node extracts the information of the received F and destroys it. Then it encapsulates the routing path information and gives this to the backward ant B which is then sent back to the source node through the shortest route. The intermediate nodes also create backward ants and send them back to the source node. When B is sent to the source node by source routing according to its list, it updates intermediate node's pheromone using formula (2). Intermediate node that receives B does the same work as when it receiving F. The source node can construct its own network topology graph after the routing information coming from these different nodes is superposed. While B is sent to the source, the destination will send some messages to the up hop nodes on the routing paths which are not the shortest to get response. Finally, route table of each node is created and in the next hop field of the table which corresponds to every destination node is placed by the pheromone.

Example: route discovery

In Fig. 2a, the solid arrowhead line represents the first received F and the broken arrowhead line represents the repeated F. Table near the node which is the route buffer contains the redundant paths. To find the route to destination node d, source node s broadcasts forward ant F. Then the intermediate node will process according to Phase 1(i)(ii). For example, here we let $\Delta hops = 1$. Node 4 receives F from node 2 for the first time. Having finished its work it then broadcasts F to the neighbor nodes. After a while, if it will again receive the same F coming from the same source node s and having the same sequence number, it judges whether this path is efficient or not according to formula $Hops_{new} \leq Hops_{old} + \Delta hops$ and then record this path in its route buffer if the path is efficient. In Fig. 2b, destination node d encapsulates the routing path information and gives this to the backward ant B which is then sent back to source node s through the shortest path s-2-3-d. The other intermediate node also feedback their recorded paths to the source node through the shortest one of the recorded paths in the route buffer. Here the polygonal line represents the path which backward ants will pass, and the data on the polygonal line represents the path information recorded by the corresponding backward ants. In Fig. 2c, the source node constructs its own network topology graph after the routing information coming from these different nodes is superposed.

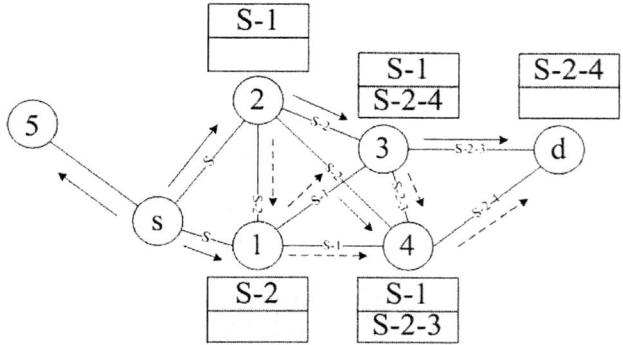

(a) Forward ants and recorded paths

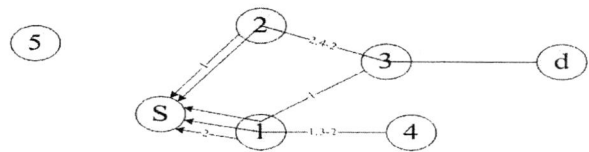

(b) Backward ants

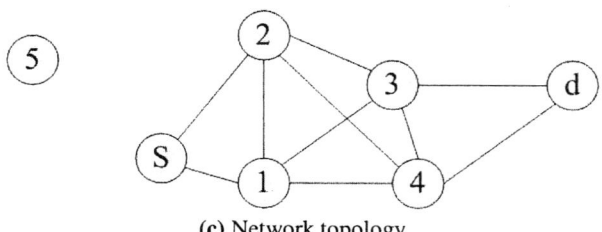

(c) Network topology

Fig. 2. Route discovery

Phase 2: route maintenance

In the condition of polynomial complexity, the method presented in [14] is used to find n paths which are link disjoint from the shortest path got in Phase 1.

(i). Build two disjoint paths from one flow network.

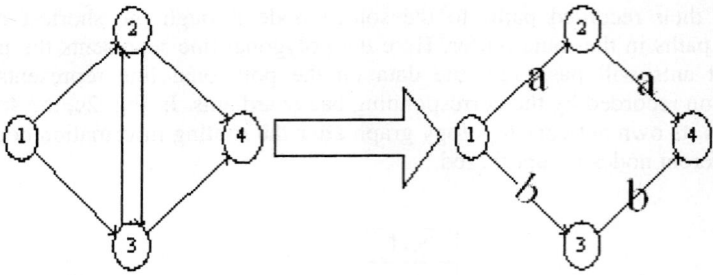

Fig. 3. Build two disjoint paths from one flow network

From Fig. 3, It can be seen that when a flow like 1->2->3->4 exists and if one augmented path like 1->3->2->4 can be found, two link disjoint paths such as 1->3->4 and 1->2->4 represented by a and b respectively can be built.

(ii). Path construction

Step 1: Regard the present network state graph as the flow network, and set the weight of every edge 1.

Step 2: Regard the shortest path from the source node to the destination node as one augmented path.

Step 3: Add this augmented path to the former flow network, then construct a new flow network.

Step 4: Repeat Step 2 and Step 3 for n times or until no new augmented path can be obtained (here we assume that Step 2 and Step 3 have been repeated for n' times), then a network flow can be obtained. After that, we construct n disjoint paths from this network flow (if we can not repeat for n times, then only n' paths can be obtained). Let m=n, and only when we can not repeat for n times, m= n'.

Step 5: Look for the conceivable paths according to the obtained network flow along the source node. Assume that the presently visited node is i , then i is the source node.

Step 6: Select one edge or link which is originated from i arbitrarily and let it be (i,j) . Then delete this one and let i=j.

Step 7: Repeat Step 6 until i is the destination node.

Step 8: Repeat Step6 ~ Step7 for m times and m paths can then be constructed.

Routing information is stored in source node s, according to which s calculates their hops respectively in order to update the corresponding $\mathcal{P}_{ij}$. Then, s selects one of the existing paths randomly to send data packets according to a random number. Data packet updates the pheromone value using formula (2) when it is sent along the route. On receiving the data packet successfully, destination node d returns ack ants periodicly, then the ack ants update the pheromone value according to formula (2) just as the data packets do.

(iii). Deal with the congestion problem

When congestion emerges in network, packets will be lost, time delay will be extended and precious bandwidth will be wasted. Since AMQR can balance the traffic through different paths, probability of congestion happening will be bound to be lowered. Further more, the node in network monitor the state of the network. Once the time delay of the returning ack ants from a destination node is larger than one limit which has been set in the beginning, the source node sets the pertinent $\mathcal{P}_{ij}$ to zero and updates the pheromone value of other feasible paths immediately. When an intermediate node finds that the load is beyond its own limit, it will send back backward ant to the source node to inform it of changing route.

Phase 3: route failure handling

The third and last phase of AMQR handles routing failures, which are caused especially by node mobility and thus very common in mobile ad hoc networks. AMQR recognizes a route failure through a missing acknowledgement. If a node i gets a route_error message for a certain link such as (i,j) , it first deactivates this link by setting the corresponding pheromone value to 0, then it informs the source node of selecting other valid paths to go on sending packets. Only when all paths fail, source node will rebroadcast the route request.

3 Simulation and Performance Analysis

The performance of AMQR was compared with ADRA [12] and DSR [13] for the same network and load characteristics, because by comparison ADRA outperforms other existing ant-based algorithms and DSR is a standard non-ant algorithms. Both of these two protocols build and relay on single route for each data session essentially. 50 nodes using the Random Waypoint Model moves within a of $2000m \times 1500m$ area with the minimum and maximum speeds set to $0 \sim 15 m/s$ respectively. The channel capacity is 2 Mbps. The direct communication distance is 250m. MAC layer uses the mechanism of IEEE802.11 DCF. 40 CBR flows each send 3 data packets per second were used. The size of data payload is 512 bytes per packet.

Three key performance metrics are evaluated: Packet successful delivery ratio, average end-to-end delay and routing load. The simulation results are shown in Fig. 4~6.

From Fig. 4, we see that packet successful delivery ratio of AMQR improves as the pause time increases. In the case with low pause time, which means frequent moves and consequently frequent topology changes, because AMQR establishes and utilizes multiple routes of link disjoint paths and adopts pheromone to disperse communication traffic, traffic in network can be well balanced, AMQR shows better than ADRA and DSR.

Fig. 5 depicts the the delay characteristics of three protocols. Delay consists of queueing delay, transmission delay, propagation delay, processing delay and retransmission delay. AMQR can adjust routing tactic according to congestion, that is, when one of the multiple paths meets slight congestion, the source node can pick another available path to go on sending data packets instantly not having rebroadcasted F to discover route. Thus it can reduce queuing buffer delay and retransmission delay.

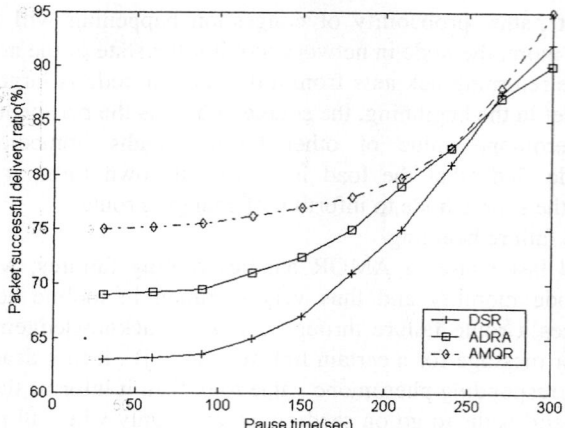

Fig. 4. Packet successful delivery ratio

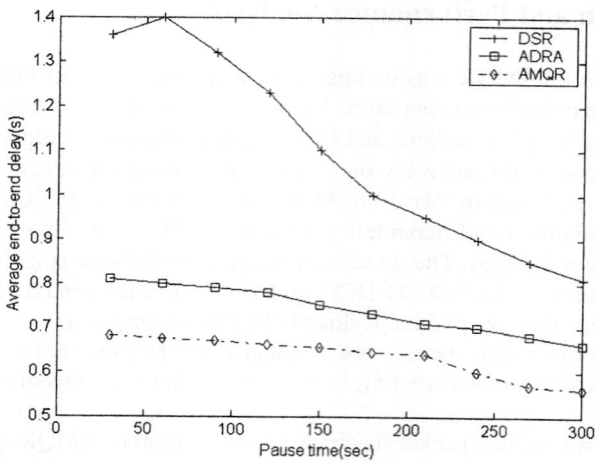

Fig. 5. Average end-to-end delay

Fig. 6 shows the routing overhead. For AMQR control packets only include forward ants, backward ants, ack ants which are sent back to the source periodicly and route_error packet. When pause time is short, because of the overfull route error information caused by the buffer mechanism mainly, DSR must use more control packets to reconstruct route path. ADRA adopt not buffer mechanism but enforce ants and anti-ants to improve routing. When topology changes severely, because of frequently routing discovering ADRA brings only more overhead and can not get better effect. AMQR adopts multi-path to obtain the routing robustness, monitors the state of links without lost of time, then dynamically adjusts routing tactic, so the number of route request packets, route reply packet, ack packets and route-error packets can be reduced.

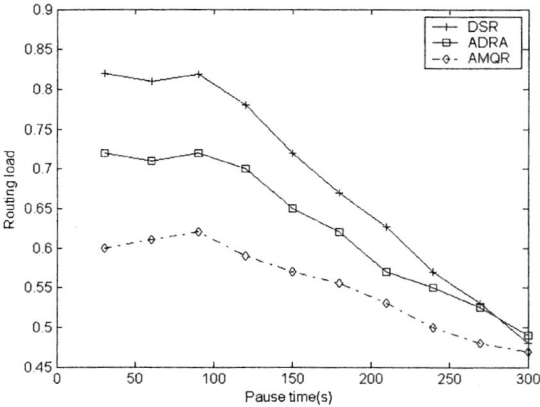

Fig. 6. Routing load

4 Conclusion

We presented AMQR for ad hoc networks to solve the routing problem effectively. In conclusion, it has the following features:

a) It is an on-demand routing protocol.
b) It establishes and utilizes multiple paths for data session, thus routing robustness which is very necessary in computer networks especially mobile ad hoc networks can be obtained.
c) It adopts probability routing tactics using pheromone to disperse communication traffic.

Therefore, this protocol is assure to provide QoS (quality of service) guarantee and improve the performance of the network. Simulation results indicate that AMQR is a very attractive approach for ad hoc network that need to provide QoS guarantee.

References

1. MACKER, J.P., and SCOTT CORSON, M. : Mobile ad-hoc networking and the IETF in Mob. Comput. Commun. Rev. vol.2. ACM Press, New York, NY (1998) 9–15
2. G DiCaro,M Dorigo.: AntNet: Distributed stigmergetic control for communications networks. Journal of Artificial Intelligence Research (JAIR) (1998) 317–365
3. Lianyuan Li ,Zemin Liu ,Zheng Zhou.: A new dynamic distributed routing algorithm on telecommunication networks. Proceedings of the International Conference on Communication Technology. January 2000, Beijing China, 849–852
4. DiCaro G,DORIGO M.: AntNet: a mobile agents approach to adaptive routing. Belgium: Tech Rep IRIDIA, Université Libre de Bruxelles,Belgium,1997
5. Di Caro ,GDorigo M.: Mobile agents for adaptive routing. Proceedings of the Thirty-First Hawaii International Conference on System Sciences, Jan 1998, Kohala Coast, HI USA, Vol. 7, 74–83

6. Daniel Camara and Antonio Alfredo F.Loureiro.: A GPS/Ant-Like Routing Algorithm for Ad Hoc Networks. Proceedings of the IEEE Wireless Communications and Networking Conference(WCNC'00), September 2000, Chicago.IL
7. D. Camara and A. A. F. Loureiro.: A Novel Routing Algorithm for Ad Hoc Networks. 33rd Hawaii International Conference on System Sciences, January 2000, Vol. 8
8. S. Marwaha, C.K.Tham, and D. Srinavasan.: Mobile Agents based Routing Protocol for Mobile Ad hoc Networks. in IEEE Global Telecommunications Conference (GLOBECOM'02), November 2002, Taiwan, Taipei, 17–21
9. S. Marwaha, C. K. Tham, and D. Srinavasan.: A Novel Routing Protocol using Mobile Agents and Reactive Route Discovery for Ad-hoc Wireless Networks. Towards Network Superiority, Proceedings of IEEE International Conference on Networks 2002 (ICON 2002), August 2002
10. Mesut Gunes,Udo Sorges,and Imed Bouazizi. : ARA-The Ant-Colony Based Routing Algorithm for MANETs. In International Conference on Parallel Processing Workshops (ICCPW'02), August 2002, Vancouver, B. C., Canada, 79–85
11. M. Heissenbttel and T. Braun.: Ants-Based Routing in Large Scale Mobile Ad-Hoc Networks. Technical report, University of Bern, Kommunikation in verteilten System (KiVS03), March 2003, 181–190
12. Xiangquan Zheng, Wei Guo, Renting Liu.: An Ant-Based Distributed Routing Algorithm for Ad-hoc Networks. International Conference on Communications, Circuits and Systems, 2004 (ICCCAS 2004), June 2004, Vol.1, 412–417
13. Broch J, Johnson DB, Maltz DA. : The dynamic source routing protocol for mobile ad hoc networks. Internet-Draft, draft-ietf-manet-dsr-09.txt, April 2003
14. Thomas H Cormen, Charles E Leiserson Ronald L Rivest, Clifford Stein.: Introduction To Algorithms. second edition. MIT Press, Cambridge, MA (2001)

A Differential Evolutionary Particle Swarm Optimization with Controller

Jianchao Zeng, Zhihua Cui, and Lifang Wang

Division of system simulation and computer application,
Taiyuan University of Science and Technology, Shanxi, P.R. China, 030024
zengjianchao@263.net

Abstract. To improve the computational efficiency,a new uniform model of particle swarm optimization (PSO) and corresponding algorithm, differential evolutionary PSO (DEPSO), are described, and the convergence is analyzed with transfer function. To enhance the diversity of swarm, PID controller is used to control dynamic evolutionary behavior of DEPSO. Simulation results have proved the algorithm's efficiency.

1 Introduction

Since the particle swarm optimization[1][2] was proposed, many modified algorithms have been introduced such as the PSO with inertia weight[3](in briefly, standart PSO), the PSO with constriction factors[4],etc.. Many theoretical analysis have been done through discrete time linear system theory[5], algebra method[6], analytic method or state space mode[7].

Frans van den Bergh[8] has proved the original PSO can not be guaranteed to converge on a global optima or local optima. In other words, the original PSO can result premature convergence. To solve the problem, the key point is enlarging the probability of global convergence through increasing the diversity of the swarm in evolutionary process.

To improve the diversity of PSO, a new uniform model of PSO is proposed, and the corresponding algorithm structure is modified with different controllers.As a example, PID-controller is used to test the new model's efficiency.

2 Differential Evolutionary PSO (DEPSO)

Consider the following differential equations:

$$\frac{dv_i(t)}{dt} = \chi[(w - \frac{1}{\chi})v_i(t) + c_1 r_1(p_i - x_i(t)) + c_2 r_2(p_g - x_i(t))] \quad (1)$$

$$\frac{dx_i(t)}{dt} = v_i(t+1)$$

if the Euler numerical integration method is used to differential equations (1) and integral step is one, we have:

(1) the original PSO can be obtained when $w = 1 and \chi = 1$;
(2) the standard PSO(the PSO with inertia weight) can be obtained when $w \neq 1 and \chi = 1$;
(3) the PSO with constriction factors can be obtained when $w = 1 and \chi = \frac{2}{|2-\varphi-\sqrt{\varphi^2-4\varphi}|}(\varphi = c_1 r_1 + c_2 r_2)$;
(4) the stochastic PSO[9] can be obtained when $w = 0 and \chi = 1$.

It means that equation (1) can be considered as a uniform model of PSO and represents different PSO's evolutionary equation while parameter w and χ have different values. Hence, equation (1) can be considered the unified model of different PSO. For the convenience, define: $\varphi_0 = \chi(w - \frac{1}{\chi})$, $\varphi_1 = \chi c_1 r_1$, $\varphi_2 = \chi c_2 r_2$,

Substituting the definition into (1) results in

$$\frac{dv_i(t)}{dt} = \varphi_0 v_i(t) + \varphi_1(p_i - x_i(t)) + \varphi_2(p_g - x_i(t)) \quad (2)$$

$$\frac{dx_i(t)}{dt} = v_i(t+1)$$

The PSO algorithm described by differential evolutionary equations (2) is called differential evolutionary PSO (DEPSO).

The analysis of the evolutionary behavior of DEPSO is made by transfer function as follows. The first order difference approximation of $v_i(t+1)$ is $v_i(t+1) = v_i(t) + \frac{dv_i(t)}{dt}$, then equation 2 will be

$$\frac{dv_i(t)}{dt} = \varphi_0 v_i(t) + \varphi_1(p_i - x_i(t)) + \varphi_2(p_g - x_i(t)) \quad (3)$$

$$\frac{dx_i(t)}{dt} = (\varphi_0 + 1) v_i(t) + \varphi_1(p_i - x_i(t)) + \varphi_2(p_g - x_i(t))$$

Laplace transformation is made on equation (3), and suppose initial values of $v_i(t)$ and $x_i(t)$ are zero, we have

$$sV_i(s) = \varphi_0 V_i(s) + \varphi_1(P_i(s) - X_i(s)) + \varphi_2(P_g(s) - X_i(s)) \quad (4)$$

$$sX_i(s) = (\varphi_0 + 1)V_i(s) + \varphi_1(P_i(s) - X_i(s)) + \varphi_2(P_g(s) - X_i(s)) \quad (5)$$

From equation(4), it is known that

$$V_i(s) = \frac{\varphi_1}{s - \varphi_0}(P_i(s) - X_i(s)) + \frac{\varphi_2}{s - \varphi_0}(P_g(s) - X_i(s)) \quad (6)$$

Substituting (6) into (5) yields

$$X_i(s) = \frac{\varphi_1(s+1)}{s(s - \varphi_0)}(P_i(s) - X_i(s)) + \frac{\varphi_2(s+1)}{s(s - \varphi_0)}(P_g(s) - X_i(s)) \quad (7)$$

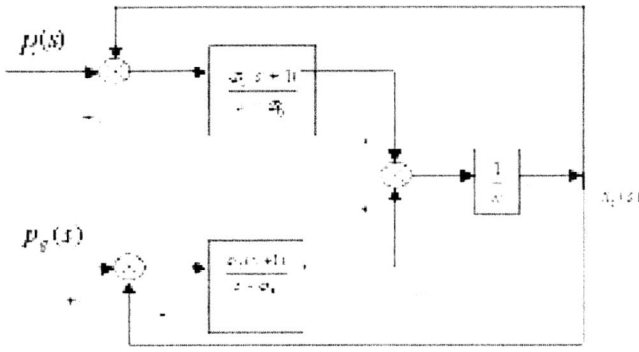

Fig. 1. The System Diagram of DEPSO

Suppose $P_i(s)$ and $P_g(s)$ are two input variables, $X_i(s)$ is output variable, then the system structure reflecting by equation (7) can be shown as in Fig.1. The open-loop transfer function from $P_i(s)$ to $X_i(s)$ is

$$G_{K_1}(s) = \frac{\varphi_1(s+1)}{s(s-\varphi_0)} \tag{8}$$

And the eigenequation is $1 + G_{K_1}(z) = 0$, thus results in

$$s^2 + (\varphi_1 - \varphi_0)s + \varphi_1 = 0 \tag{9}$$

the two eigenvalues are

$$\lambda_{1,2} = \frac{\varphi_0 - \varphi_1 \pm \sqrt{(\varphi_1 - \varphi_0)^2 - 4\varphi_1}}{2} \tag{10}$$

DEPSO will converge when λ_1 and λ_2 have negative real parts. If $(\varphi_1 - \varphi_0)^2 - 4\varphi_1 > 0$, $(\varphi_1 - \varphi_0)^2 - 4\varphi_1 < \varphi_1 - \varphi_0$. So, the convergence of DEPSO with $P_i(s)$ as input can be guaranteed if

$$\varphi_1 - \varphi_0 > 0 \tag{11}$$

By the same way, the convergence of DEPSO with $P_g(s)$ and $X_i(s)$ as input and output respectively can be guaranteed if $\varphi_2 - \varphi_0 > 0$. Therefore, the convergence condition of DEPSO is

$$\varphi_0 < \min\{\varphi_1, \varphi_2\} \tag{12}$$

From Fig.1, it is obviously that

$$X_i(s) = \frac{\varphi_1(s+1)P_i(s) + \varphi_2(s+1)P_g(s)}{s(s-\varphi_0) + \varphi_1(s+1) + \varphi_2(s+1)} \tag{13}$$

From (12), we have

$$lim_{t\to\infty} X_i(t) = lim_{s\to 0} \frac{\varphi_1(s+1)P_i(s) + \varphi_2(s+1)P_g(s)}{s(s-\varphi_0) + \varphi_1(s+1) + \varphi_2(s+1)} \tag{14}$$

it means

$$-(\varphi_1+\varphi_2)lim_{t\to\infty}x_i(t)+\varphi_1 P_i+\varphi_2 P_g=0$$

because φ_1 and φ_1 are stochastic variables, it is obviously that the above equation is satisfied only if

$$lim_{t\to\infty}X_i(t)=P_i=P_g \tag{15}$$

3 Introduction of PID-DEPSO

To improve the dynamic evolutionary behaviour of DEPSO, the evolutionary function of DEPSO is considered as a control plant and PID controller is introduced. The parameter of PID controller can be dynamically adjusted in the evolutionary process, and the new algorithm is called PID-DEPSO.

The system structure is showed in Fig.2 From Fig.2, we have

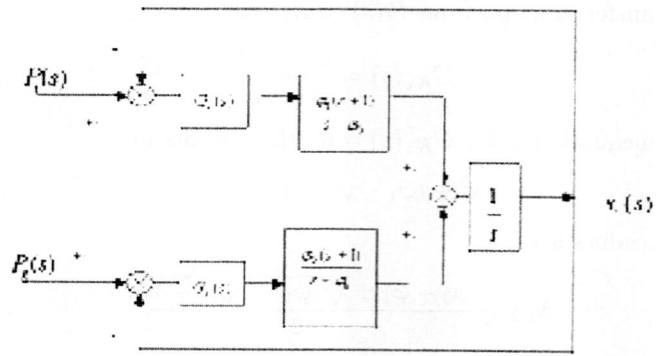

Fig. 2. The System Diagram of PID-DEPSO

$$G_c(s)=K_p(1+\frac{1}{T_1s}+T_Ds)=K'_p\frac{T_DT_1s^2+T_1s+1}{s} \tag{16}$$

where $K'_p=\frac{K_p}{T_1}$.

The open-loop transfer function taking $P_i(s)$ as input is :

$$G_{Kc_1}(s)=G_c(s)\frac{\varphi_1(s+1)}{s(s-\varphi_0)}=\frac{\varphi_1 K'_p(s+1)(T_DT_1s^2+T_1s+1)}{s^2(s-\varphi_0)} \tag{17}$$

its eigenequation is $1+G_{Kc_1}(s)=0$, then

$$(K'_p\varphi_1 T_D T_1)s^2=(K'_p\varphi_1 T_1+K'_p\varphi_1 T_D T_1-\varphi_0)s^2 \tag{18}$$

$$+K'_p\varphi_1(1+T_1)s+K'_p\varphi_1=0$$

According to Routh's stability criteria, the stability condition of the system with $P_i(s)$ and $X_i(s)$ as input and output respectively are

$$K'_p T_D (T_1 + 1) > \frac{\varphi_0}{\varphi_2} \qquad (19)$$

As a result, the stability of PID-DEPSO is stability if

$$K'_p T_D (T_1 + 1) > \max\{\frac{\varphi_0}{\varphi_1}, \frac{\varphi_0}{\varphi_2}\} \qquad (20)$$

Similarly, if (20) is satisfied, $lim_{t \to \infty} x_i(t) = lim_{s \to 0} s X_i(s)$. From Fig.2, we have

$$X_i(s) = \frac{K'_p (s+1)(T_D T_1 s^2 + T_1 s + 1)(\varphi_1 P_i(s) + \varphi_2 P_g(s))}{s^2(s - \varphi_0) + K'_p(s+1)(T_D T_1 s^2 + T_1 s + 1)(\varphi_1 + \varphi_2)} \qquad (21)$$

Thus

$$lim_{t \to \infty} X_i(t) = \frac{\varphi_1 P_i + \varphi_2 P_g}{\varphi_1 + \varphi_2} \qquad (22)$$

The evolutionary equation of PID-DEPSO is deduced as follow:

$$X_i(s) = G_{Kc_1}(s)(P_i(s) - X_i(s)) + G_{kc_2}(P_g(s) - X_i(s)) \qquad (23)$$

$$= \frac{(s+1)(T_D T_1 s^2 + T_1 s + 1)}{s^2(s - \varphi_0)}$$

$$\times [K'_p \varphi_1 (P_i(s) - X_i(s)) + K'_p \varphi_2 (P_g(s) - X_i(s))]$$

it means:

$$\frac{s^2(s - \varphi_0)}{(s+1)(T_D T_1 s^2 + T_1 s + 1)} X_i(s) \qquad (24)$$

$$= [K'_p \varphi_1 (P_i(s) - X_i(s)) + K'_p \varphi_2 (P_g(s) - X_i(s))]$$

Suppose

$$\frac{dx_i(t)}{dt} = v_i(t+1) = v_i(t) + \frac{dv_i(t)}{dt}$$

then $V_i(s) = \frac{s}{s+1} X_i(s)$, substituting it into (24), we have

$$\frac{s(s - \varphi_0)}{(T_D T_1 s^2 + T_1 s + 1)} V_i(s) \qquad (25)$$

$$= [K'_p \varphi_1 (P_i(s) - X_i(s)) + K'_p \varphi_2 (P_g(s) - X_i(s))]$$

Let
$$\frac{dv_i(t)}{dt} = \varphi_0 v_i(t) + a_i(t) \qquad (26)$$

then $A_i(s) = (s - \varphi_0)V_i(s)$, substituting it into (26), we have

$$\frac{sA_i(s)}{(s+1)(T_D T_1 s^2 + T_1 s + 1)} \qquad (27)$$

$$= [K'_p \varphi_1 (P_i(s) - X_i(s)) + K'_p \varphi_2 (P_g(s) - X_i(s))]$$

Let $\alpha = 1 + K'_p T_D T_1 (\varphi_1 + \varphi_2)$, $\beta = K'_p T_1 (\varphi_1 + \varphi_2)(\varphi_0 T_D + T_D + 1)$, and the Laplace inverse transformation of $sP_i(s), s^2 P_i(s), sP_g(s)$ is zero, then

$$\frac{da_i(t)}{dt} = -\frac{\varphi_0 \beta}{\alpha} V_i(t) - \frac{\beta}{\alpha} a_i(t) \qquad (28)$$

$$+ K'_p \frac{\varphi_1}{\alpha}(P_i - X_i(t)) + K'_p \frac{\varphi_2}{\alpha}(P_g - X_i(t))$$

Let $\frac{\beta}{\alpha} = \gamma$, $\frac{\varphi_1}{\alpha} = \varphi'_1$, $\frac{\varphi_2}{\alpha} = \varphi'_2$, then the evolutionary equations of PID-DEPSO are

$$\frac{da_i(t)}{dt} = -\varphi_0 \gamma v_i(t) - \gamma a_i(t) + varphi_1 (p_i - x_i(t)) + \varphi_2 (p_g - x_i(t)) \qquad (29)$$

$$\frac{dv_i(t)}{dt} = \varphi_0 v_i(t) + a_i(t)$$

$$\frac{dx_i(t)}{dt} = v_i(t+1) = v_i(t) + \frac{dv_i(t)}{dt} = (\varphi_0 + 1)v_i(t) + a_i(t)$$

4 The Analysis of PID-DEPSO

The original PSO describes the particles' evolutionary process only by the velocity and the position. From equation (29), it is obviously that PID-DEPSO is a modified algorithm by adding accelerator $a_i(t)$. Further more, it is satisfied with the flying behavior of the bird flocking that introducing the accelerator by analyzing the background of original PSO. When a bird flies away from the flocking to a habitat, the other birds around it will adjust their direction and velocity according to their own current position respectively. The altering rate of a bird's flying velocity (i.e. acceleration) is decided by its distance to the special bird. Therefore, the velocity of a bird is decided by both its current velocity and the acceleration. Equation (29) is just the description of this phenomenon, so the evolutionary equation of PID-DEPSO is reasonable in biological mechanism.

We know that original PSO is a typical two-order stochastic system and PID-DEPSO is a three-order stochastic system. From system theory we know that three order stochastic system is more complex than two-order in dynamic behavior. Further more, because $\gamma, \varphi_1, \varphi_2$ are all stochastic variables, the system of PID-DEPSO processes better global exploration ability when the convergence condition satisfied. Therefore, the probability of global convergence is enhanced.

In the view of system control theory, the introduction of PID controller can make system jump out of the local optima and avoid the "premature" in evolutionary process. P-type controller can change only the parameter φ_1 and φ_2 of DEPSO. According to equation (12), the evolutionary process changes from stable state to unstable state, which enlarges the exploration area with small K_p, and the convergence velocity accelerates with large K_p. Introduction of integral action increases the order of system and decrease the convergence velocity. At the same time, it makes the state convergence accurately to the historical best location. Therefore, the PID controller can balance profitably between exploration and exploitation according to different parameters in the evolutionary process.

When three parameters $K_p K_D$ and K_1 are satisfied with equation (20), PID-DEPSO converges to global optima. In the first stage of PID-DEPSO, the algorithm increases the global search capability and enhances the local search capability in the last stage. Thus, K_p and K_D are small and K_1 is large in the early stages, with the evolutionary process, K_p and K_D increase and K_1 decrease. The global optima and convergence speed can be adjusted by changing the three parameters of PID-DEPSO for the special problems.

5 Simulation Results

Two benchmark functions are used to test the above mentioned algorithms.
Spherical Function:

$$f_1(X) = \sum_{j=1}^{n} x_j^2, |x_j| \le 100$$

its optima is $f_1(0, 0, ..., 0) = 0.0$.
Schwefel Function:

$$f_2(X) = 418.9829n + \sum_{j=1}^{n} x_j sin(\sqrt{|x_j|}), |x_j| \le 500$$

its optima is $f_2(-420.9687, -420.9687, ..., -420.9687) = 0.0$.

The above two test functions are optimized using both PSO and PID-DEPSO. Each algorithm runs 50 times and the max generation is 5000. To ensure the algorithm search finely, the maximal acceleration A_{max} is defined to restrict the accelerator $a_i(t+1)$. The velocity $V_i(t+1)$ cannot be guaranteed non-negative because of the item $a_i(t+1)$. So we define the following equations to adjust accelerator and velocity.

$$a_i(t+1) = A_{max}, if(a_i(t+1) > A_{max})$$

$$a_i(t+1) = -A_{max}, if(a_i(t+1) < -A_{max})$$

$$a_i(t+1) = a_i(t+1), otherwise$$

where V_{max} is the maximal velocity. In the simulations, we take the parameters as the following: $\chi = 2, w = 1, \varphi_0 = 1, \varphi_1 = 2c_1r_1, \varphi_2 = 2c_2r_2, c_1 = c_2 = 0.9, \alpha = 1 + K'_p T_D T_1(\varphi_1 + \varphi_2)$, where α is decreased linearly from 2 to 1. $\beta = K'_p T_1(\varphi_1+\varphi_2)(\varphi_0 T_D)+T_D+1$, where β is increased linearly from 3 to 4. Obviously, there are many sets of K_p, T_1, T_D to satisfy equation (20). The test results are showed in Tab.1. Notes: ACG represents average convergence generations and

Table 1. The Comparison Results of Two Functions

Function	Algorithm	ACG	ACR
F1	PSO	133.66	100
F1	PID-PSO	47.44	100
F2	PSO	1613.0	4
F2	PID-PSO	451.6	100

ACR represents average convergence ratio.

The two functions' dynamical performances are showed in Fig.3 and Fig.4 respectively. It is showed that PID-PSO converges faster and owns a good performance on global optima.

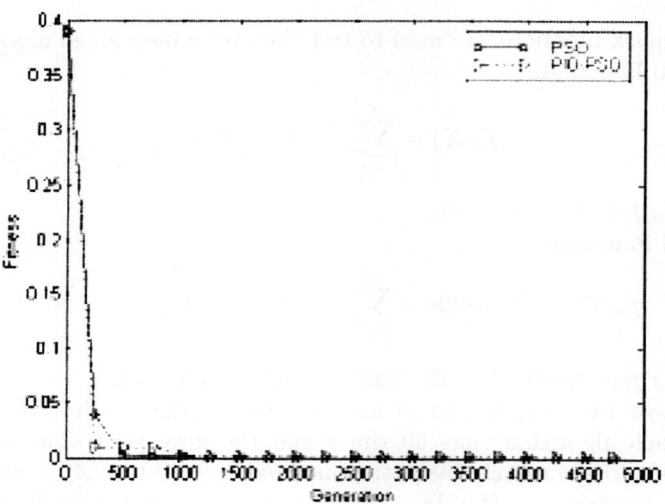

Fig. 3. The Comparison of $f_1(X)$

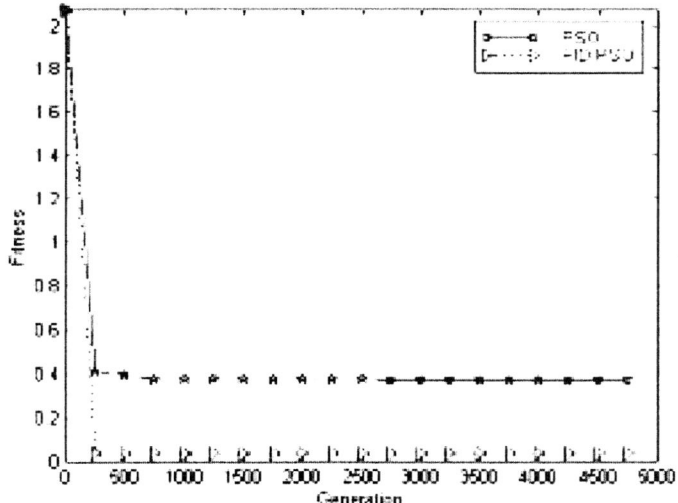

Fig. 4. The Comparison of $f_2(X)$

Table 2. The Comparison of PSO and GPSO

Function	Algorithm	F_{per}	F_{eval}
Spherical	PSO	100	206.22
Spherical	GPSO	100	150.9
Rosenbrock	PSO	100	214.66
Rosenbrock	GPSO	100	176.02
$Goldstein_price$	PSO	98	184.04
$Goldstein_price$	GPSO	100	155.36
Schaffer	PSO	30	67.07
Schaffer	GPSO	96	54.27

References

1. Kennedy, J., Eberhart, R.C.: Particle Swarm Optimization. IEEE International Conference on Neural Networks. (1995) 1942–1948
2. Eberhart, R.C., Kennedy, J.: A New Optimizer Using Particle Swarm Theory. Proceedings of the 6th International Symposium on Micro Machine and Human Science.(1995) 39-43
3. Shi,Y., Eberhart,R.C.: A Modified Particle Swarm Optimizer. IEEE International Conference of Evolutionary Computation. (1998)
4. Clerc,M.:The Swarm And The Queen: Toward A Determined and Adaptive Particle Swarm Optimization. Proceedings of the Congress on Evolutionary Computation, (1999) 1951-1957
5. Tan Ying, Zeng Jianchao, Gao Huimin:Particle Swarm Optimization Analysis Based on Discrete Time Linear System Theory, Proceedings of 5th World Congress on Intelligent Control and Automation,(2004) 2210-2213 (in Chinese)

6. Ozcan, E.,Mohan,C.K.: Analysis of A Simple Particle Swarm Optimization System. Intelligent Engineering Systems Through Artificial Neural Network, (1998) 253-258
7. Clerc,M.,Kennedy,J.: The Particle Swarm-Explosion, Stability, and Convergence in a Multidimensional Complex Space. IEEE Trans. On Evolutionary Computation, (2002) 6(1):58-73
8. Van den Bergh,F.: An Analysis of Particle Swarm Optimizers. Ph.D thesis, University of Pretoria. 2001
9. Cui Zhihua,Zeng Jianchao: A Guaranteed Global Convergence PSO Algorithm. Lecture Notes in Artificial Intelligence,2004 Vol.3066:762-767.

A Mountain Clustering Based on Improved PSO Algorithm*

Hong-yuan Shen[1,2], Xiao-qi Peng[1,3], Jun-nian Wang[2,3], and Zhi-kun Hu[3]

[1] Institute of Energy and Power Engineering,
Central South University, Changsha, 410083, China
[2] Institute of Information and Electrical Engineering,
Hunan University of Science and technology, Xiangtan, 411201, China
[3] Institute of Information Science and Engineering,
Central South University, Changsha, 410083, China

Abstract. In order to find most centre of the density of the sample set this paper combines MCA and PSO, and presents a mountain clustering based on improved PSO (MCBIPSO) algorithm. A mountain clustering method constructs a mountain function according to the density of the sample, but it is not easy to find all peaks of the mountain function. The improved PSO algorithm is used to find all peaks of the mountain function. The simulation results show that the MCBIPSO algorithm is successful in deciding the density clustering centers of data samples.

1 Introduction

The clustering analysis is a process to categorize the sample set of similar characteristics. The clustering analysis is not only an important means of obtaining knowledge from a great deal of samples, but also a general technique used in the data mining [1,2]. According to the different clustering rules, there are variety of clustering algorithms, such as clustering algorithms based on the model, the layer, the flat surface partition, the density, the mesh and sub-space and so on [3]. But there are two problems in most clustering algorithms: The first is that some parameters have to be given in advance, but under the condition of no prior knowledge, it's very hard to determine these parameters. The second is hard to assure the time and space efficiency of clustering analysis to a big sample set or a high dimensions sample set. Therefore, this paper puts forward a mountain clustering method based on improved PSO (MCBIPSO) algorithm, which makes improvements in the particle swarm optimization algorithm and is combined to the mountain clustering. The simulation result shows that the mechanism of the MCBIPSO is clear, and it can efficiently search for the most density clustering centers of the sample data.

---

* This research was supported by National Nature Science Foundation of China (50374079).

2 The Mountain Clustering Algorithm (MCA)

The Mountain Clustering Algorithm, presented by Yager and Filev [4,5], is an simple and effective method to estimate the density clustering center, which is not only able to find the density clustering centre of the sample data, but also provide the beginning clustering centers for other clustering methods. The principle of the MCA is to construct a mountain function according to the density of sample distribution, that is, the height of the mountain function has a direct proportion of the distribution density, and the peaks of the mountain are the sample clustering centers.

In the MCA, the denser the density of the mesh is, the higher the accuracy of the calculation result is. The calculation load increases in the index number way along with the growth of the sample space dimensions, then "the dimensions disaster" appears. A better solution is the subtraction clustering method putted forward by Chiu [6]. The subtraction clustering method is to regard every sample point as calculation point, thus the computation load can be reduced.

In order to increase the efficiency of calculating, the mountain clustering method or the subtraction clustering method should be simplified. One solution is to look for a kind of mountain function optimization algorithm getting every peak value at one time. This algorithm is known as the multi-modal function optimization algorithm. Another is to make use of heuristic optimization algorithms to get every peak value instead of visiting all the samples of the data set, and decrease the calculation workload.

3 The Particle Swarm Optimization Algorithm

There are variety of heuristic optimization algorithms, among which some are very successful, for instance, the genetic algorithm [7,8] and the particle swarm optimization algorithm [9,10]. Among multi-modal function optimization algorithms, the artificial immune algorithm [11□12] is a good one. The particle swarm optimization algorithms are got more and more attention according its explicit mechanism and simple calculation.

The particle swarm optimization algorithm hypothesizes that there are m particles in the D dimensions space, whose position is $x_i=(x_{i1}, x_{i2} \ldots x_{iD})$, and have a fitness function fit_i, related with optimization target function. The optimization target function can also be a fitness function. Every particle moves gradually in a certain speed $v_i=(v_{i1}, v_{i2} \ldots v_{iD})$ in the D dimensions space. During the moving $x_{pi}=(x_{p1}, x_{p2} \ldots x_{pD})$ records the best position of the fitness function of the particle i, x_g records the best position of the fitness function of the whole particle swarm. For the particle i of iterative j generation, its position is calculated as follows

$$v_i(j+1) = \omega \cdot v_i(j) + rand() \cdot c_1 \cdot (x_{p_i} - x_i(j)) + rand() \cdot c_2 (x_g - x_i(j)) \tag{1}$$

$$x_i(j+1) = x_i(j) + v_i(j+1), \tag{2}$$

where ω is a inertial effect coefficient, rand( ) is a random function whose value is between 0 and 1, C_1 is a weight coefficient of the particle individual, C_2 is a weight coefficient of the particle community, and the maximum speed of the particle is limited by v_{max}. The speed of the particle consists of three parts: the first item comes from particle itself inertial, the second comes from the experience of the particle itself during moving, and the third comes from the experience of the particle community during moving. Because of the existence of the individual and the community experience, the particle swarm optimization algorithm is a kind of heuristic optimization algorithms. Compared with other algorithms, such as the genetic algorithms, the simulated annealing algorithms etc, its calculation is easier and faster.

4 The Improved Particles Swarm Optimization Algorithm

Analyzing every item of Equation (1), it can be discovered that ,the item containing C_2 embodies the property of the community and makes the community moving to the optimization direction, the item containing C_1 embodies the property of the individual. In order to carry out a multi-modal function optimization, the item multiplied by C_2 should be reduced and the item multiplied by C_1.should be enlarged. Under the ideal condition, the cognition of each individual particle represents the optimization peak value of the multi-modal function optimization therefore the particles swarm optimization algorithm can be used in the multi-modal function optimization.

In the multi-modal function optimization, for making each peak of the mountain function be the "only route" of some particles, this paper makes three aspects improvements to the particles swarm optimization algorithm. The first is making $C_2=0$ to get most local optimization values, not the global optimization value. The second is taking variable step to make each peak of the mountain function be passed by the particle. At the beginning of the calculation, the step should be long enough to enlarge the diversity of the particles. During the calculating process, the step should be reduced gradually, and the particles converge at different local optimization point in the end of the calculation. The third is throwing away the random function rand(), making every particle convergence likely at a certain local optimization point.

Suppose the number of the particles is n, and the generation of the iterative is j, then the improved calculation formula of the particle position is as follows

$$v_i(j+1) = \omega \cdot v_i(j) + c_1 \cdot ((2n-j)/n) \cdot (x_{p_i} - x_i(j)) \quad (3)$$

$$x_i(j+1) = x_i(j) + v_i(j+1) \quad (4)$$

5 The MCBIPSO Algorithm

The MCBIPSO algorithm combines the particle swarm optimization algorithm with the Mountain Clustering Method. Its calculation step is as follows:

Step 1. Initializing
Step 2. Constructing the mountain function

Regard every sample value as a center of the Gauss function, and the mountain function is given by the summation of the Gauss function.
Step 3. Getting new position of the particles based on Equation (3) and (4).
Step 4. Evaluating the fitness
Step 5 Deciding the current optimization value of particles
To each particle, keep its history optimization value if it is more excellent than the current fitness. Otherwise, it is replaced by the current fitness.
Step 6 Judging end condition

Judge whether the end condition is sufficient: if not then return to step (3), otherwise, end the process of searching for optimization values and give the current optimization fitness value and the position of the particle.

When the process is over, the position of every particle will be converged at local optimization value of the mountain function. These local optimization points are also the clustering centers.

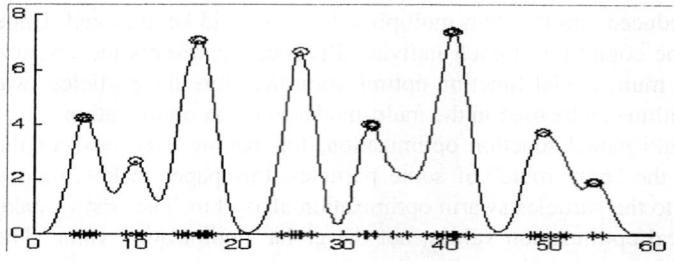

Fig. 1. A example of mountain clustering based on improved PSO algorithm

An example of a dimension sample data set is supplied. The mountain function and MCBIPSO algorithm simulation result are showed in figure 1. The stars mark the position of the sample data on the x coordinate and the circle stands for the clustering center found by MCBIPSO on the mountain function. Suppose the number of the particles is 30 and the number of the iteration is 100. In running 10 times, all of the clustering centers can be found every time.

6 Conclusions

1) A clustering method based on improved PSO algorithm can find the clustering centers of the sample data fast and accurately.
2) the improved particles swarm algorithm can find most of local optimization of the mountains function, and is simple and valid.
3) the simulation process shows that the particles swarm optimization algorithm is sensitive to the change of ω, C_1 and C_2.

References

1. David Hand, Heikki Mannila, Padhraic Smyth: Principles of Data Mining, The MIT Press, 2001.
2. Jain A K, Dubes R C: Algorithms for Clustering Data. Englewood Cliffs, NJ: Prentice Hall, 1988.
3. Xing xiaoshuai, Jiao Licheng: Clustering Method in the Field of Data Mining, Journal of Circuits and Systems, 8(1), 2003.
4. R. R. Yager, D.P. Filve: Generation of fuzzy rules by mountain clustering. Journal of Intelligent and Fuzzy Systems,2:209-219,1994.
5. Ronald R Yager, Dimitar P. Filve: Essential of fuzzy modeling and control. John Wiley &Sons,Inc,1994.
6. S. L. Chiu: Fuzzy model identification based on cluster estimation. Journal of Intelligent and Fuzzy System, 2(3), 1994.
7. Vose M. D: The simple genetic algorithms: foundations and theory. The MIT Press,1999.
8. Li Mingqiang, Kou Jishong, Ling Dan et al: principle and application of the genetic algorithms, Beijing: Science press, 2002.
9. Kennedy J, Eberhart R. Particle swarm optimization. Proc IEEE, Int Conf on Neural Networks. Perth, 1995. 1942-1948.
10. Eberhart R, Kennedy J. A new optimizer using particle swarm theory, Proc 6th Int Symposium on Micro Machine and Human Science. Nagoya, 1995, 39-43.
11. Dasgupta D: Artificial Immune Systems and Their Applications. Berlin: Springer-Verlag. 1999.
12. Ge Hong, Mao Zongyuan: Research on of Parameters Immune Algorithm. Journal of South China University of Technology (Natural Science Edition), Vol. 30 No. 12. December 2002.

Multi-agent Pursuit-Evasion Algorithm Based on Contract Net Interaction Protocol

Ying-Chun Chen, Huan Qi, and Shan-Shan Wang

Dept. of Control Science & Engineering, Huazhong University of Science & Technology,
Wuhan 430074, Hubei Province, China
chyc@21cn.com, qihuan@hust.edu.cn, hustsunny2003@163.com

Abstract. The motivation is the deployment of large numbers of inexpensive robots in hostile environments to pursue evasive targets. Based on the interaction protocols of contract net and subscribe-publish, a distributive pursuit-evasion algorithm is proposed for multi-agents to pursue multiple evasive agents. The pursuit agents engaged in teams adopt a tail-chase strategy while the rest pursuit agents use a hug-a-tree policy. The evading agents move towards directions with fewer pursuit agents in their neighborhood. All agents communicate according to the subscribe-publish protocol and the pursuit agents coordinate their acts through the contract net protocol. The result of simulation under JADE platform shows that the pursuit agents can dynamically form several teams to catch respective evaders efficiently without centralized leadership or hierarchical coordination. Distributive in nature, it allows a large-scale agent fleet to perform complex tasks in a coordinated way.

1 Introduction

Search is widely used in mapping mine fields, exploring extraterrestrial and undersea areas, exploring volcanoes, locating chemical, biological weapons and explosive devices and so on [1]. The principles of search theory have been applied successfully in numerous important operations, such as the 1966 search for a lost H-bomb in the Mediterranean, the 1968 search for the lost nuclear submarine Scorpion near the Azores, and the 1974 underwater search for unexploded ordnance in the Suez Canal [2].

Search theory is still a field of active research despite considerable advance has been made since its inception more than 50 years ago. Many problems remain to be solved, particularly in cases involving multiple targets. Systematic methods are needed for building maps from inconsistent and sometimes even conflicting sensor sources. More work is also needed for moving targets. Two-sided pursuit-evasion problems are of great importance in military applications. It is desirable in many instances to formulate these problems as differential games to obtain the essential characteristics of the solutions that arise from the differential motions of the searcher and evader. Difficult to solve, the only pursuit-evasion differential games that have been solved are those that the conditional detection functions and motion constraints have been made unrealistically simple [2]. These problems remain intractable, although some progress has been made.

The motivation is the deployment of large numbers of inexpensive robots in hostile environments to catch evasive targets. Designing a mobile robot team to search a sensate region for evasive targets is very challenging because human intervention is not always possible in these environments and participants are prone to failure [3]. Decentralized coordination schemes are the most promising avenues of research [1][3][4]. The limitations of crude but inexpensive sensors can be overcome by using distributed pursuit-evasion algorithms that utilize shared data from a large number of agents. The paper is concerned with solving the coordination problem using a decentralized coordination strategy based on interaction protocols of contract net and subscribe-publish. The coordination strategy allows a team of communicating agents to coordinate their search activities through a division of labor based on commitments and conventions, similar to that of human societies.

2 Mission Description

The mission is to catch several evasive agents $E = \{E_1, E_2, ..., E_n\}$ by a team of pursuit agents $P = \{P_1, P_2, ..., P_m\}$ in a bounded 2D region $\Omega = \{(x, y) | x, y \in R, 0 \leq x, y < M\}$, where M is a given real number. It is assumed that this region is known beforehand or can be known using map-learning techniques [3][4][5][6]. Time belongs to the set of integer $T = \{1, 2, ...\}$. Evader type $K(E_j) = \{1, 2, 3, ...\}$ is defined as the minimum number of pursuers required for the capture of the evader. $V(E_j) \in R^+$ is defined as the bonus that team members can share if they catch the evader. Target E_i is caught at time $t \in T$ if there exist at least $K(E_j)$ pursuers P_j satisfying

$$d(E_i, P_j)(t) \leq r. \tag{1}$$

Where $d(E_i, P_j)(t)$ is the distance between evader E_i and pursuer P_j at time t, and r is the detection radius of the pursuers. It is easy to see that a single pursuer cannot catch evasive agents with type $K(E_j) > 1$. At least $K(E_j)$ pursuers are required to form a team for the capture of the evader E_j.

3 Interaction Protocol

3.1 Contract Net Interaction Protocol

According to the Foundation for Intelligent Physical Agents (FIPA) contract net interaction protocol [7], the initiator agent takes the role of a manager who wishes to catch an evader with one or more participants. The initiator calls for proposals for catching a given evader; the participants may respond with a proposal, refuse or reply with a not-understand message before a deadline set by the initiator. Negotiations then continue with the participants that proposed.

Each participant's proposal includes its distance to the evader. Once the deadline arrives, the initiator evaluates the received proposals and selects the nearest agents to pursue the evader. The selected agents will receive an accept-proposal act and the rest reject-proposal acts.

The proposals are binding on each participant. Once the initiator accepts the proposal, the participant acquires a commitment to perform the task. Once the participant has completed the task, it sends an inform-done message to the initiator. However, if the participant fails to complete the task, a failure message is sent. Before the action has been performed and the last message has been received, the initiator can even decide to cancel the task by sending cancel messages if the initiator is no longer interested in continuing the task and that it can be terminated in a manner acceptable to both the initiator and the participants. The architecture of the contract net interaction protocol is shown in Fig. 1.

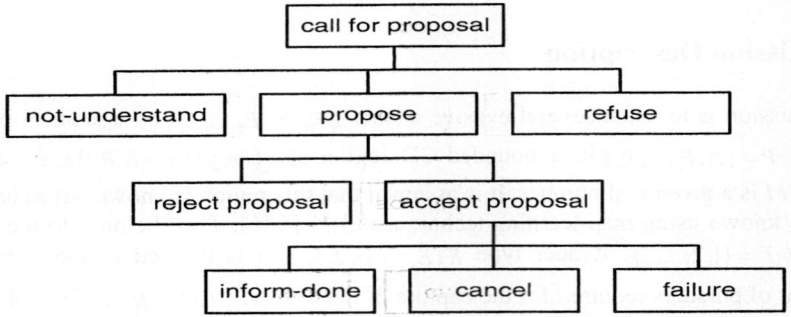

Fig. 1. FIPA Contract Net Interaction Protocol

3.2 Subscribe-Publish Protocol

The subscribe-publish protocol [8] allows the subscription initiator to send a subscription message indicating its desired subscription to the participant via the subscription manager. The participant processes the subscription message and responds to the initiator via the manager by either accepting or rejecting the subscription. Once the participant agrees to a subscription, it communicates all content matching the subscription condition using an inform-result. The participant continues to send inform-results until either the initiator cancels or the participant experiences a failure. The architecture of the protocol is shown in Fig. 2.

There are three roles in the protocol: the initiator, responder and manager. The initiator sends the subscription message and receives notifications each time the subscription condition becomes true. The responder replies by sending a not-understood message, a *refuse* message or an *agree* message. Each time the subscription condition becomes true, the responder sends a notification message to the initiator via the manager. The initiator behavior terminates if no response has been received before the subscription timeout expires, or all responders reply with a *refuse* or *not-understood* message. Otherwise, the behavior will run forever. The subscription manager is responsible for the registry and cancellation of subscriptions.

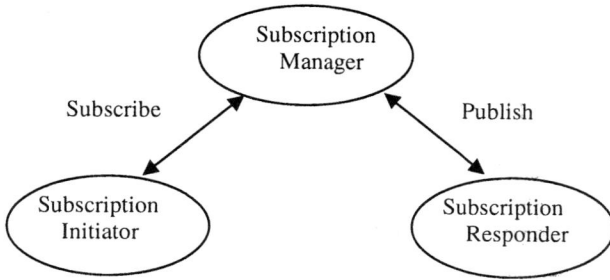

Fig. 2. Architecture of Subscribe-publish Protocol

4 Pursuit-Evasion Algorithm

Since each pursuer can pursue several evaders and one evader requires several pursuers to catch, it is necessary to assign tasks among pursuers. Based on interaction protocols of contract net and subscribe-publish, a greedy algorithm is applied for task assignment.

4.1 Pursuit Strategy

The nearest pursuer of evader E_j is chosen as the initiator. It sends call-for-proposal messages to the rest pursuers with a deadline for reply message. When the deadline arrives, it picks up the participants' proposals and evaluates their distances to the evader. The initiator chooses $K(E_j)$ nearest participants and sends accept-proposals to the selected agents, forming a team to pursue evader E_j.

The team members subscribe position information from the evader. Whenever a notification message of position updates is arrived from the evader, each member decides by itself what to do next: it will inform the initiator that the task is done if the evader is within its detection radius; otherwise, a tail-chase method is applied to pursue the evader. If the initiator receives this information from all its team members, it will dissolve the team after giving each member a bonus. If any member counters a failure, the initiator will call for new proposals from free pursuers and choose another pursuer to join the team.

4.2 Evasion Strategy

The neighborhood of an evader is divided into 8 equal sectors with a central angle $45°$. The evader counts the number of pursuit agents in each sector within a given radius, and moves towards the sector with less or no pursuit agents.

4.3 Strategy of Free Pursuers

If a pursuit agent is not accepted for any pursuit teams, it is called a free pursuer. It adopts a hug-a-tree strategy to save energy, i.e., they stay where they are if no accept-proposal message is received. For comparison, they can also move randomly.

4.4 Pursuit-Evasion Procedure

Since each pursuer can pursue several evaders and an evader requires several pursuers to catch, it is necessary to assign tasks among pursuers. A greedy algorithm based on contract net interaction protocol is applied for task assignment. The pursuit-evasion procedure based on the greedy algorithm is described as follows.

Step 1: Generate pursuit agents with random positions and register them in JADE (Java Agent Development Environment) platform along with their position information; generate evasive agents and register them along with their position, value and type information.

Step 2: Find out the evasive agent E_j with the highest value from set E; find out its nearest pursuit agent P_j from set P.

Step 3: Agent E_j subscribes position information from all pursuit agents. Whenever an updated notification message about position information is received, it acts according to its evasion strategy.

Step 4: The nearest pursuit agent P_j of evader E_j takes the role of a manager and sends call-for- proposal message to the rest pursuit agents with a deadline for reply. It manages the pursuit team according to the above mentioned pursuit strategy. It chooses $K(E_j)$ pursuit agents with the nearest distances to evader E_j, sends an accept-message to each of them. Remove these selected pursuit agents and P_j from set P.

Step 5: Agent P_j subscribes position information from its team members and E_j.

Step 6: Remove E_j from set E. If set E is not empty, go back to step 2.

Step 7: If the position of E_j is updated, agent P_j informs its team members. Thus it is not necessarily for evasive agents to broadcast their position information, significantly reducing network flow. If done-notification messages have been received from all its members, agent P_j will dissolve the team after giving each member a bonus.

Step 8: If all evaders are caught, game is over. Otherwise, go back to Step 7.

5 Simulation Results

JADE is a middleware that enables faster time-to-market for developing multi-agent distributed applications [8]. JADE is used as the simulation platform for the pursuit-evasion problem.

The site is a square of 100m×100m, free of obstacles. The speeds of pursuit and evasion agents are all 1 m/s. Evaders are not allowed to move out of the site. Communications between agents are assumed reliable and on time. Each participant can locate itself, without error. Each pursuer can recognize the types of the evaders, with a 360° field of vision. There are 5 evaders with type 1,2,3,4,5 respectively. Their values are the squares of their types. The number of pursuers is 40, but only 15 pursuers are assigned tasks. Since the pursuers that are not selected adopt a hug-a-tree strategy, they have little influence on the simulation result. So they are not shown in the simulation figures.

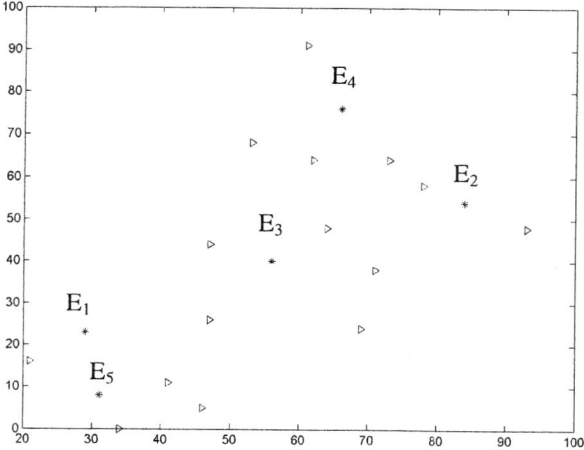

Fig. 3. The State after Task Assignment

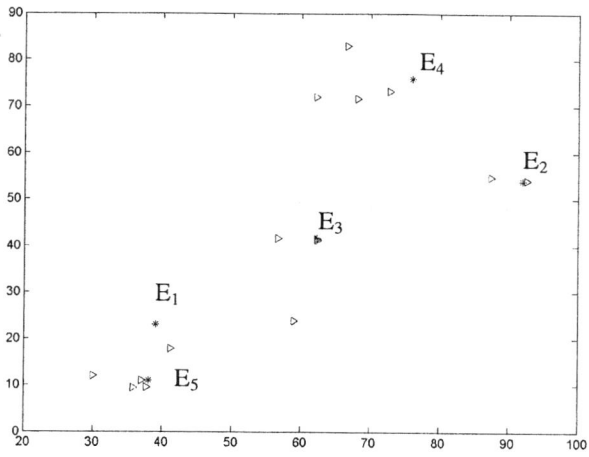

Fig. 4. The State after 5s

If the free pursuit agents adopt a hug-a-tree policy, the average capture time for 1, 2, 3, 4 and 5 evaders in 100 runs are 7s, 11s, 20s, 38s and 71s, respectively; if they move randomly, the average capture time for 1, 2, 3, 4 and 5 evaders are 7s, 11s, 21s, 36s and 67s, respectively. The random movements of the free agents do little help to the result. Therefore, it is better for them to keep immobile. If $j+1$ pursuit agents are chosen to catch evasive agents E_j, the average capture time of 1, 2, 3, 4 and 5 evaders are 11s, 28s, 47s, 68s and 86s, respectively.

The states after task assignment, after 5s, 10s and 40s are shown in Fig. 3, 4, 5 and 6 respectively. In the figures, asterisks represent evasive agents $E_j, j = 1, 2, 3, 4, 5$

while triangles stand for pursuit agents, where j is the minimum number of pursuit agents required for the capture of the evasive agent E_j. For example, at least 4 pursuit agents are needed for the capture of evader E_4.

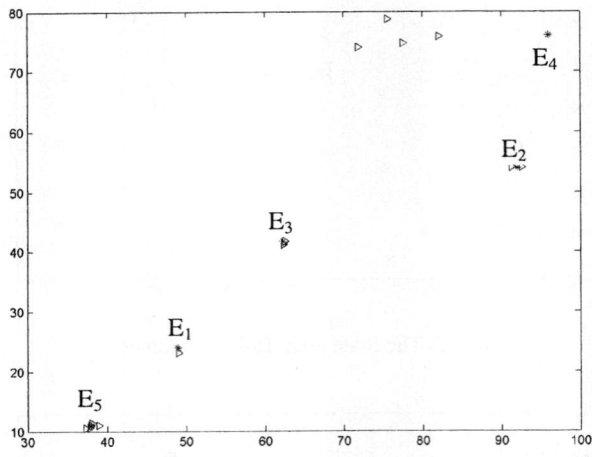

Fig. 5. The State after 10s

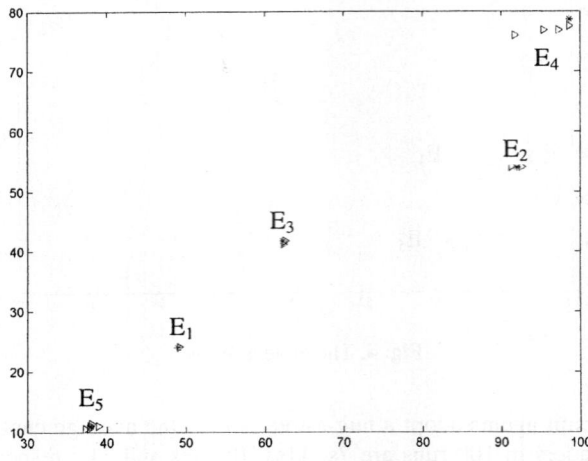

Fig. 6. The State after 40s

6 Conclusions

The motivation of the paper is the deployment of large numbers of inexpensive robots in hostile environments to pursue evasive targets. Based on the interaction protocols of contract net and subscribe-publish, a distributive greedy pursuit-evasion algorithm is proposed for multiple pursuit agents to pursue multiple evasive agents. The pursuit agents engaged in teams adopt a tail-chase strategy while the rest pursuit agents use a hug-a-tree policy. The evading agents move towards the direction with fewer pursuit agents. The simulation result shows that the pursuit agents can dynamically form several teams to catch evaders efficiently. Distributive in nature, it allows large-scale agent fleet to perform complicated tasks.

For convenience, some assumptions and simplifications have been made. The world is free of obstacles, ambient noise and location error. Communications between agents are assumed perfect. Both pursuit agents and evasive agents are not intelligent enough to forecast the moves of each other. If the pursuers look ahead what moves the evaders can take, the performance is likely to be improved. They are left as recommendations for further work.

References

1. Steven Y. Goldsmith, Rush Robinett,□.: Collective Search by Mobile Robots using Alpha-Beta Coordination. (1998) Internet: http://www.aisl.sandia.gov/papers
2. David V. Chudnovsky, Gregory V. Chudnovsky: Search Theory: Some Recent Developments. Marcel Dekker, New York (1989)
3. Jeff Ko, Amit Mahajan, Raja Sengupta: A Network-Centric UAV Organization for Search and Pursuit Operations. In: Aerospace Conference Proceedings, Vol. 6. IEEE, New York (2002) 2697-2713
4. Jiming Liu, Xiaolong Jin, Shiwu Zhang, Jianbing Wu: Multi-Agent Systems: Models and Experimentation. Tsinghua University Press, Beijing (2003)
5. Hespanha J, Prandini M, Sastry S.: Probabilistic Pursuit-evasion Games: a One-step Nash Approach. In: Proceedings of the 39th IEEE Conference on Decision and Control, Vol. 3. IEEE, New York (2000) 2272-2277
6. Rene Vidal, Omid Shakernia, H. Jin Kim, David Hyunchul Shim, Shankar Sastry: Probabilistic Pursuit-evasion Games: Theory, Implementation, and Experimental Evaluation. IEEE Transactions on Robotics and Automation, Vol. 18, No. 5, (2002) 662-669
7. Internet: http://www.fipa.org/specs/fipa00029/SC00029H.html
8. Fabio Bellifemine, Giovanni Caire, Tiziana Trucco, Giovanni Rimassa: JADE Programmer's Guide. (2004) Internet: http://jade.cselt.it

Image Compression Method Using Improved PSO Vector Quantization

Qian Chen[1], Jiangang Yang[2], and Jin Gou[2]

[1] Ningbo Institute of Technology, Zhejiang University,
315100 Ningbo, China
march@zj165.com
[2] Ningbo Institute of Technology, Zhejiang University,
315100 Ningbo, China
{yangjg, goujin}@zju.edu.cn

Abstract. VQ coding is a powerful technique in digital image compression. Conversional methods such as classic LBG algorithm always generate local optimal codebook. In this paper, we introduce Particle Swarm Optimization (PSO) cluster method to build high quality codebook for image compression. We also set the result of LBG algorithm to initialize global best particle by which it can speed the convergence of PSO. Both image encoding and decoding process are simulated in our experiments. Results show that the algorithm is reliable and the reconstructed images get higher quality to images reconstructed by other methods.

1 Introduction

Image compression is essential for applications as video conferencing, TV transmission, transmission of printed graphics images and image data store systems. The fundamental goal of image compression is to reduce the bit rate for transmission or data storage with an acceptable fidelity or image quality. In recent years, a lot of compression methods have been developed, such as differential pulse code modulation, transform coding, hybrid coding.

Vector Quantization algorithms have been performed by many researchers for image compression recently [1, 2, 3, 4, 5, 6]. In VQ systems, a vector quantizer can be defined as a mapping Q of K-dimensional Euclidean space R^K into a finite subset Y of R^K as

$$Q : R^K \rightarrow Y \tag{1}$$

Where $Y=(Y_1, Y_2, Y_3 ... Y_M)$ is called a codebook and Y_i is the codeword. When VQ method used in image compression, the vector quantizer generates a codebook for input image vectors. Then, encoder computes the distortion $d(x,y_i)$ between the input vector x and codeword y_i, $i=1,2,3...M$. Encoder also finds the index of the codeword vector with *nearest neighbor rule*, and the index i is transmitted to the decoder if codeword y_i yields the least distortion. On the other hand, the decoder uses the index to generate reproduction vector. Fig.1. shows us the overall process of a simple VQ used in image compression.

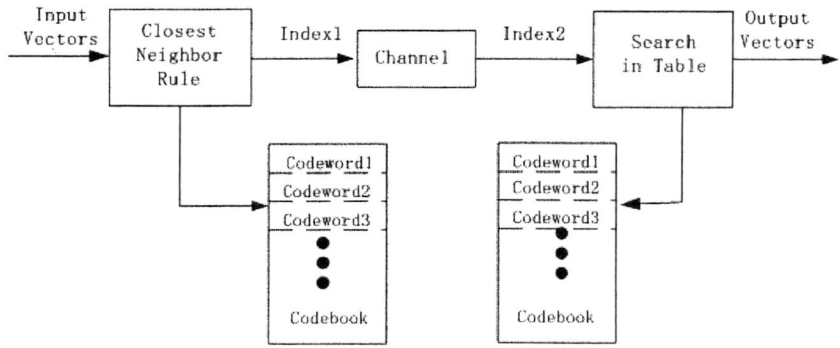

Fig. 1. This shows the detail process of vector quantization when used in image compression

The essential problem to image vector quantization coding is to search a perfect codebook from the training image samples. Previous methods use cluster algorithms such as the classic LBG algorithm to generate codebook. However, these algorithms always get a local optimal result and the reconstructed images are not ideal. In this paper, an improved PSO cluster algorithm will be introduced into designing high quality codebook. PSO is a new evolutionary computational model. In such a model, particles fly in the vector space with a velocity that is dynamically adjusted according to its own flying experience and its neighbors' experience. So it can find good solution effectively. We use the result of LBG algorithm to initialize the particles of PSO algorithm. Thus, the improved PSO cluster method can enhance its performance.

2 The Basic of PSO

Particle Swarm Optimization (PSO) is a new branch of evolutionary computation technique originally presented by Kenney and Eberhart [7] in 1995. It is inspired by the social behavior of birds flocking or fish schooling. In a multi-dimensional space, each particle (individual) represents a potential solution to a problem. There also exists a fitness evaluation function that assigns a fitness value to a particle's position. Two positions are recoded by every particle. One is named global best (*gbest*) position, which has the highest fitness value in the whole population. The other is called personal best (*pbest*) position, which has the highest fitness value of itself at present. A population of particles is flying in the search space and every particle changes his position according to global best position and personal best position with formula (2) and (3)

$$v_{ik}^{n+1} = v_{ik}^n + c_1 rand_1^n (pbest_{ik}^n - x_{ik}^n) + c_2 rand_2^n (gbest_k^n - x_{ik}^n) \qquad (2)$$

$$x_{ik}^{n+1} = x_{ik}^n + v_{ik}^{n+1} \qquad (3)$$

Here, k is the number of dimensions and i represents a particle of the population. x means the position of particle in search space, v is the velocity vector for the particle to change its position. *Pbest* and *gbest* are the personal best position and global best position memorized by this particle. Parameter c_1 and c_2 are the cognitive and social learning rates respectively. $Rand_1$ and $rand_2$ are two random numbers that belongs to *[0,1]*. Fig.2. depicts a particle how to change his position according equation (2) and (3) in a two-dimension space.

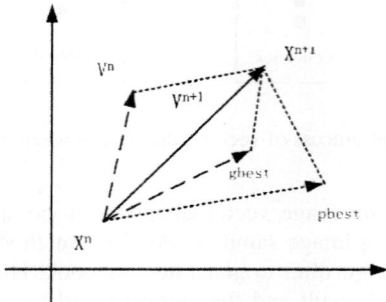

Fig. 2. This shows a particle changes its position from x^n to x^{n+1} in a two-dimension space

Previous studies show us such a behavior of particle population takes more chance into better solution areas quickly, so it can find the high quality solution much faster than other evolutionary algorithms such as GA.

3 Improved PSO Cluster Used in VQ

In this section, we will introduce how to build high quality VQ codebook by improved PSO cluster method. PSO cluster method has much powerful capability to find the codeword vectors of codebook in multi-dimensions space [8,9].

3.1 The Fitness Function and Encoding

Given a $N \times N$ digital image, we can divided the image into a number of $n \times n$ blocks. Thus, Every block is K-dimension vector where $K=n \times n$. The image can be represented as $(N/n) \times (N/n)$ vectors. We measure the distortion of input vector x_i and reconstructed vector y_i with Mean Square Error (MSE) as

$$d(x, y) = \sum_{i=1}^{K}(x_i - y_i)^2 \qquad (4)$$

Then the overall distortion between input image and reconstructed image can be expressed as

$$D = \frac{1}{M}\sum_{j=1}^{M}\sum_{i=1}^{N \times N} \forall x_i \in C_{ij} \, d(x_i, y_j) \qquad (5)$$

Moreover, The fitness function can be expressed as

$$f_{fitness} = 1/D \qquad (6)$$

The key point to generate a high quality is to find the perfect codewords $Y=(Y_1,Y_2,Y_3 ...Y_M)$ which minimizes the fitness function for all training vectors. So, In our PSO method, every particle is constructed by string sequence of real value. For a M-length codebook, a particle is constituted of M codewords and the length of a particle is $M \times K$, where K is the dimension of search space. Thus, every particle represents a construction of codebook. The task of PSO is to find the perfect particle position in search space, where particle gets a very high fitness value. Fig.3. is an example of encoded string for a particle in the PSO population. Given the search space is three-dimension and the length of codebook is 8, the string of this particle is encoded as follows:

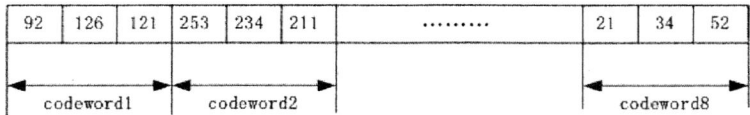

Fig. 3. This figure shows the encoded string of a particle for an eight-length in a three-dimension

3.2 Detail Algorithm

The traditional LBG algorithm seems converges faster but usually stops at local minimum point. PSO searchs the global best solution but slower than LBG. So in this section, we improved PSO method by set the result of LBG algorithm to initial global best particle. Followings are the detail Algorithm:

Step 1. Run the LBG algorithm once.
Step 2. Assign the result of LBG algorithm to one particle and initialize positions of rest particles and associated velocity of all particles randomly.
Step 3. To each particle, cluster the training vectors to particle. Then, calculate the fitness value for the particle according to function (5) and (6).
Step 4. To each particle, compare fitness evaluation with this particle's personal best value. If better, update *pbest* and take record current position as the particle's personal best position.
Step 5. Find the highest fitness value of the whole particles. If the value is better than *gbest*, replace *gbest* with this fitness value, and take record the global best position.
Step 6. Change velocities and positions with equation (3) and (4) for every particle.
Step 7. Repeat *Step3* to *Step7* until end condition is satisfied or predefined iterations are reached.

4 Experiment

Our experiment is implemented on 8 gray images of 256×256×8 resolution. We divide the images to 4×4 blocks, Then, 4096×8 16-dimension vectors are contained for training and test. 4 image block vectors are used for training and 2 images outside are used to test. Codebooks are generated on training set by LBG and PSO cluster methods respectively. Different codebook sizes are used in test phase. We measure the performance of our methods with average Signal-To-Noise Ration (SNR), which is defined as follows

$$SNR = 10\log \frac{\frac{1}{N^2}\sum_{i=1}^{N}\sum_{j=1}^{N}x_{ij}^2}{\frac{1}{N^2}\sum_{i=1}^{N}\sum_{j=1}^{N}(x_{ij}-y_{ij})^2} \qquad (7)$$

where x_{ij} and y_{ij} are the pixel gray levels of the original and reconstructed images of $N \times N$ pixels. The average rate can be calculated using

$$rate = \log_2 C/N^2 \qquad bit/pixel \qquad (8)$$

Table 1 presents us the result of designing two vector quantizers for training set under different rate. It is obvious that LBG cluster has larger design SNR variation of 5 db for LBG VQ codebook and random initial codebooks.

Fig.4. and Fig.5. are the result of two test image with the two well trained vector quantizers. (a) are the two original image and the correspondence reconstructed images using LBG VQ and PSO VQ are shown in (b) and (c). It is also very clear that the reconstructed image in (c) has higher quality than the images in (b).

Table 1. Average SNR(db) for images with different rate using LBG and PSO clustering methods

Bit/pixel	0.3125	0.375	0.4375	0.5
SNR(LBG)	6.81	7.23	8.34	10.20
SNR(PSO)	11.71	13.55	14.59	15.84

(a)　　　　　　　　　(b)　　　　　　　　　(c)

Fig. 4. (a) Original image (b) Reconstructed image using LBG VQ with 0.375 bit/pixel(c) Reconstructed image using PSO VQ with 0.375 bit/pixel

(a)　　　　　　　　(b)　　　　　　　　(c)

Fig. 5. (a) Original image (b) Reconstructed image using LBG VQ with 0.4375 bit/pixel(c) Reconstructed image using PSO VQ with 0.4375 bit/pixel

5 Conclusion

In this paper, we use PSO method initialized by LBG method to generate VQ codebook for image compression. The result of experiments proves it is a very effective and the reconstructive images have higher quality than traditional LBG method. Moreover, this method can also be used in other applications such as image storage, speaker recognition etc.

References

1. Nasrabadi, N.M., King, R.A.: Image Coding Using Vector Quantization: a review. Communications, IEEE Transactions On. (1988) 957-971
2. Feng, J., Kwork-Tunk, L.: Dynamic Codebook Adaptive Vector Quantization for Image Coding. Consumer Electronics, IEEE Transactions on. (1999) 327-332
3. Torres, L., Casas, J.R.., Arias, E.: Stochastic Vector Quantization of Images. Signal Processing. (1997) 291-301
4. Shigang, W., Hexin, C.: Multistage vector quantization based on simulated annealing for image coding. Intelligent Processing Systems, 1997 ICIPS '97. 1997 IEEE International Conference on. (1997) 1014-1017
5. Wu, Y.-G.: GA-based DCT quantisation table design procedure for medical images. IEE Proceedings- Vision, Image and Signal Processing, 151 (2004) 353-359
6. Tan, Y.P., Yap, K.H., Wang, L.P. (Eds.): Intelligent Multimedia Processing with Soft Computing. Springer, Berlin Heidelberg New York (2004)
7. Kennedy, J., Everhart, R.: Particle Swarm Optimization. Proc. Of IEEE international Conference on Neural Networks (ICNN).(1995) 1942-1948
8. Merwe, D.W.: Engelbrecht A P. Data Clustering Using Particle Swarm Optimization. Evolutionary Computation, 2003. CEC '03. The 2003 Congress on. (2003) 215 - 220
9. Ching-Yi, C., Fun, Y.: Particle Swarm Optimization Algorithm and Its Application to Clustering Analysis. Networking, Sensing and Control, 2004 IEEE International Conference on . (2004) 789 - 794

Swarm Intelligence Clustering Algorithm Based on Attractor*

Qingyong Li[1,2], Zhiping Shi[1,2], Jun Shi[1,2], and Zhongzhi Shi[1]

[1] Key Laboratory of Intelligent Information Processing,
Institute of Computing Technology, Chinese Academy of Sciences,
100080, Beijing, China
{liqy, shizp, shij, shizz}@ics.ict.ac.cn
[2] Graduate School of the Chinese Academy of Sciences, 100039, Beijing, China

Abstract. Ant colonies behavior and their self-organizing capabilities have been popularly studied, and various swarm intelligence models and clustering algorithms also have been proposed. Unfortunately, the cluster number is often too high and convergence is also slow. We put forward a novel structure-attractor, which actively attracts and guides the ant's behavior, and implement an efficient strategy to adaptively control the clustering behavior. Our experiments show that swarm intelligence clustering algorithm based on attractor (**SICABA** for short) greatly improves the convergence speed and clustering quality compared with LF and also has many notable virtues such as flexibility, decentralization compared with conventional algorithms.

1 Introduction

Swarm Intelligence emerged out of social insect collective behavior shows many interesting properties such as flexibility, robustness, decentralization and self-organization. Implementations of optimization and control algorithms based on swarm intelligence such as Ant Colony Optimization and Ant Colony Routing have been well known [1,2,3]. Clustering models and algorithms based on swarm intelligence, inspired by co-operative brood sorting of ants or other behaviors, are also put forward, though they are still in a preliminary, proof-of-concept stage [4,5].

The swarm intelligence clustering models and algorithms have advantages in many aspects, such as no need of priori information, self-organization. However, the number of result cluster is often too high and the convergence is slow because of the ant's inefficient behaviors: randomly picking up items and dropping down items. Are there any methods to make ant perform efficiently?

After some careful research, we believe that the algorithms inefficient performance is mainly because of the ant's inefficient moving. Especially in the first stage, items are distributed sparsely, the probability for an ant to move to a

---

* This paper is supported by National Natural Science Foundation of China No. 60435010 and National Basic Research Priorities Programme No. 2003CB317004.

place to pick up items or to drop down items is often small, so most of the ant's movings are inefficient. At the same time, the number of items loaded by an ant is an important factor for cluster number and accuracy.

In this paper, we put forward a new algorithm, named swarm intelligence clustering algorithm based on attractor (SICABA for short). SICABA attacks the problem in following two aspects:

Firstly, a novel, efficient structure, called attractor, is constructed. Simply, it is an item set converging the homogeneous items. Moreover, it contains not only local environment information, such as inner distance, but also global information, such as outer distance between attractors in the system. So it can actively attracts the ant to pick up dissimilar items or drop down similar items.

Secondly, an ant can pick up the farthest item or all items from an attractor controlled by a simple rule. Furthermore, a parameter is applied to form a strategy: first stage an ant is prior to pick up all items coarsely but fast from a cluster; last stage the ant is mostly to pick up the farthest item to precisely partition. So it can distinctly improve the convergence speed and accuracy.

The paper is organized as follow: the following section introduces the related work; the next section describes the details of SICABA; the experiments are showed in the section 4; at last we make our conclusion.

2 Related Work

Deneubourg et al [4] proposed an agent-based model to explain how ants manage to cluster the corpses of their dead nestmates. Artificial ants (or agents) are moving randomly on a square grid of cells on which some items are scattered. Each cell can only contain a single item. Whenever an unloaded ant encounters an item, this item is picked up with a probability which depends on an estimation of the density of items of the same type in the neighborhood. When a loaded ant encounters a free cell on the grid, the probability that this item is dropped also depends on an estimation of the local density of items of the same type.

Lumer and Faieta [5] (LF for short)extended the model of Deneubourg et al., using a dissimilarity-based evaluation of the local density, in order to make it suitable for data clustering. Unfortunately, the resulting number of clusters is often too high and convergence is slow. Therefore, a number of modifications were proposed, by Lumer and Faieta themselves as well as by others [6,7].

3 Swarm Intelligence Clustering Algorithm Based on Attractor

3.1 Basic Concept

Definition 1. *Attractor is a data set which has similar items as a whole.*

The attractor can attract the ants to pick up the furthest item or all items from them according to a pick-attractive rate, and drop down an item or an item collect in it according to a drop-attractive rate. Furthermore, the attractor has it own status: active and inactive, if the attractor has not any item the attractor is considered as inactive, and it can't attract ant to pick up items or drop down items any longer; otherwise, it is considered as active and can attract any ant.

Definition 2. *Inner distance is the average distance between the items and the attractor's centroid for an attractor, represented by $D_i \in [0, 1]$.*

Definition 3. *Outer distance is the average distance with the other attractors in the system for an attractor, represented by $D_o \in [0, 1]$.*

Attractor's pick-attractive rate and drop-attractive rate are two very important features to control an ant to load items or unload items, differentiating the ant's randomly choosing method in [4,5]. Pick-attractive rate (PAR) for an attractor is a numeric feature to indicate the attractor's affinity attracting the ant to pick up items, in other word, it indicates the probability for an ant to pick up an item or all the items from the attractor. If the PAR is greater, the probability for an ant to pick up items is also greater. The PAR value depends on the attractor's item number marked as C, if the number C is less than a threshold θ, the attractor is a small attractor whose PAR is determined by its inner distance, outer distance and item number. If the inner distance, the outer distance and item number are less the PAR is greater; otherwise, if C is greater than θ the attractor is considered as big one and its PAR is effected by the maximal distance in the attractor and outer distance. The PAR is given by

$$PAR = \begin{cases} f_1(D_i) \times \alpha_1 + f_1(D_o) \times \alpha_2 + T(C, \theta) \times \alpha_3 + \delta & \text{if } C < \theta \\ D_m \times \beta_1 + f_1(D_o) \times \beta_2 & \text{if } C \geq \theta \end{cases} \quad (1)$$

where the function f_1 and T are both descending functions, and we experimented with $T(C, \theta) = \theta/(C + \theta)$ and $f_1(x) = 1 - x$, $0 \leq \alpha_1, \alpha_2, \alpha_3 \leq 1$ and $\alpha_1 + \alpha_2 + \alpha_3 = 1$. δ is a constant parameter to control the choosing strategy: if $\delta > 1$, the attractor which has few items will have the absolute priority to be chosen comparing with the attractor which has many items and PAR smaller than 1. D_m is the maximal distance in the attractor. $0 \leq \beta_1, \beta_2 \leq 1$ and $\beta_1 + \beta_2 = 1$.

Drop-attractive rate (DAR) for an attractor is a contrast feature to indicate the attractor's affinity attracting the ant to drop down items. In the same way, The DAR value firstly depends on C, if the number C is less than the threshold θ the attractor is small one and the DAR is always small; if $C \geq \theta$ the attractor is a big one and its DAR is determined by the distance between the items loaded by an ant and the attractor's items, and the outer distance also has slight influence. The DAR is given by

$$DAR = \begin{cases} C/T & \text{if } C < \theta \\ (1 - D) \times \beta_1 + D_o \times \beta_2 & \text{if } C \geq \theta \end{cases} \quad (2)$$

where T is the total number of items in the system, D is the distance between the loaded items by an ant and the attractor's items, $0 \leq \beta_1, \beta_2 \leq 1$ and $\beta_1 + \beta_2 = 1$ β_1 is always greater than β_2.

3.2 Probability Conversion Function

Probability conversion function converts the attractor's quality and quantity characters into a pick up probability for an unloaded ant or drop down probability for an loaded ant. There are usually two related functions. One is for picking-up probability; another is for dropping probability. Bonabeau et al [8] put forward a model of division of labour in social insects. In this model, a certain stimulus and a response threshold value are associated with each task an ant can perform. The response threshold value is fixed, but the stimulus can change and represent the need for someone to perform the task. The probability that an ant starts performing a task with stimulus S and response threshold value μ is given by

$$T_n(S;\mu) = \frac{S^n}{S^n + \mu^n} \tag{3}$$

where n is a positive constant value.

We utilize the model to the problem at hand simplifying the formula with $n = 1$. μ is associated with the items collection for the problem, and the S is determined by the attractor and ant.

Picking up stimulus. An unloaded ant can perform the task: picking up an item or picking up all items. When the item number of the target attractor C is less than θ the ant picks up all the items. Obviously, the unloaded ant should pick up an entire attractor if the attractor is small, homogeneous and not isolated. It implies that such attractor's inner distance and outer distance are small relatively. So the $S_{\text{pick-all}}$ is given by

$$S_{\text{pick-all}} = f_1(D_i) \times \alpha_1 + f_1(D_o) \times \alpha_2 \tag{4}$$

where $D_i, D_o \in [0,1]$ represent inner distance and outer distance, $0 \leq \alpha_1, \alpha_2 \leq 1$ and $\alpha_1 + \alpha_2 = 1$.

While the item number C is greater than θ the attractor is considered as a big one, so only the most dissimilar item should be picked up. The stimulus $S_{\text{pick-one}}$ for picking up one item is mainly influenced by the furthest distance and slightly by the outer distance. $S_{\text{pick-one}}$ is given by

$$S_{\text{pick-one}} = D_m \times \beta_1 + f_1(D_o) \times \beta_2 \tag{5}$$

where D_m is the maximal distance in the attractor, and $0 \leq \beta_1, \beta_2 \leq 1$ and $\beta_1 + \beta_2 = 1$.

Drop down stimulus. The stimulus for a loaded ant to drop its items L in an attractor is mainly based on the local distance D between the loaded items and the attractor's items. If the ant loads an item collect, the center of the loaded items is used to measure the similarity. Furthermore, we also consider the global factor - outer distance because the outer distance indicates the dependence among the attractors in the system. Stimulus for dropping down S_{drop} is given by

$$S_{\text{drop}} = (1 - D_m) \times \beta_1 + D_o \times \beta_2 \tag{6}$$

where $0 \leq \beta_1, \beta_2 \leq 1$ and $\beta_1 + \beta_2 = 1$, β_1 is always greater than β_2

3.3 Algorithm Description

Based on the above description we have the following algorithm.

Algorithm. (SICABA: Swarm Intelligence Clustering Algorithm Based on Attractor)

```
1. Initialize theta,delta  and other parameters;
2. Run k-means algorithm assigned with ATTRACTORNUMBER clusters to
   form the original ATTRACTORNUMBER attractors;
3. Giving ants initial attractors, initial states of ants are
   unloaded;
4. WHILE(cycle_counter<MAXCYCLENUMBER and NotConvergent){
5. FOR(number of  ants  ) {
6. IF the ant is unloaded, THEN {
      Calculate Pp ;
      Compare  Pp  with a random probability Pr ,
      IF  Pp < Pr   THEN {
        Not pick up anything;
        According to PAR values, the unloaded ant moves to
        the greatest attractor; }
      ELSE {
        Pick up the most farther items or all items;
        Update the attractor's state according to the
        picking task;
        According to DAR values, the loaded ant moves to
        the greatest attractor; }}
   ELSE { //the ant is loaded
      Calculate Pd ;
      Compare  Pd  with a random probability  Pr,
      IF  Pd < Pr THEN {
        Not drop down;
        According to DAR values, the loaded ant moves to
        the greatest attractor; }
      ELSE {
        Drop down the load;
        Update the attractor's state according to the
        dropping task;
        According to PAR values, the loaded ant moves to
        the greatest attractor; }}}}
```

4 Experimental Results

In this section, we'll demonstrate the experimental results about the performance of SICABA and the influence of the parameter δ for clustering performance.

The dataset IRIS chosen from UCI machine learning repository (http://www.ics.uci.edu/ mlearn/MLRepository.html) are used in this paper.

IRIS database has 150 records with 4 attributes and 3 classes. All experiments are performed on a 800-MHz Pentium machine which 512 megabytes main memory, running on Windows 2000 professional. Programs are written in Windows/Visual C++ 6.0.

4.1 Clustering Convergence Performance

In this experiment we compare SICABA with LF about the clustering convergent performance. As we know, the cluster number and convergence performance are two very important factors for swarm intelligence clustering algorithms. We here measure the clustering result number when run N cycles. The result is shown in the Fig.1.

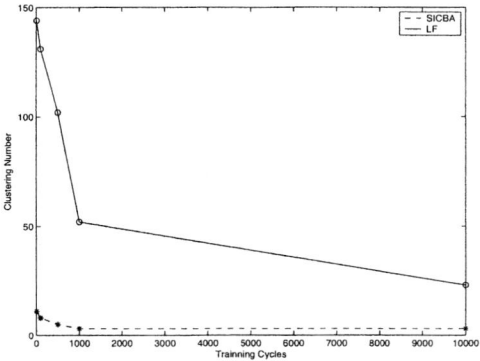

Fig. 1. Clustering number with training cycle

Fig.1 shows that convergence speed of SICABA is greatly faster than LF, especially in the first stage, SICABA quickly partitions dataset into a few clusters, how-ever, the LF is very slow to be convergent. The last cluster number of SICABA is also better than LF. Fig.1 shows that the last number of SICABA is 4 a little greater than the real number 3, but LF is much greater than 3. Because SICABA initialize $ATTRACTORNUMBER$ (here we experimented with 20) attractors with K-means, moreover, it picks up all items in the small attractor at first stage and picks up the farthest items in the big attractor at last stage, so SICABA can converge greatly faster than LF, furthermore, it also can get much better clustering result.

4.2 Clustering Accuracy Performance

After demonstrating the good convergence performance we experiment the accuracy performance in this section. We analysis the clustered results compared with LF and k-means. Noted that all the clustered results are best results among 10

Table 1. Comparison with LF and K-means about clustering accuracy performance

Original	SICABA	LF	k-means
Iris-setosa (50)	Class2(50)	Class4(41) Class1(9)	Class0(50)
Iris-versicolor(50)	Class1(32) Class3(18)	Class2(30) Class0(20)	Class1(48) Class2(2)
Iris-virginica(50)	Class3(26) Class0(24)	Class3(24) Class0(19) Class1(7)	Class2(36) Class1(14)
Totle(3)	Total(4)	Total(5)	Total(3)

times repeats. The details of the clustered results for these clustering algorithms are shown in Table1. SICABA is notablely better than LF: The LF partitions the dataset into five clusters and two clusters (class0 and class1) mixing the elements from different original classes, for example, class1 is composed of 7 elements from Iris-virginica and 9 elements from Iris-setosa. But there is just one mixed cluster for SICABA. However, SICABA has approximate accuracy performance compared with k-means except one more total cluster number. Surprisingly, they both precisely cluster the Iris-setosa into a complete cluster and the number of mixed clusters in SICABA is also smaller than k-means. Because SICABA picks up all items coarsely but fast from cluster in the first stage and picks up the furthest item to precisely fine-tune in the last stage, it can converge to fewer clusters and get better accuracy than LF, even get more homogeneous cluster than k-means though with more clusters.

4.3 Influence of Parameter δ for the Clustering Performance

The parameter δ in formula (1) is a most important factor to affect the clustering performance, because it directly determines the picking up strategy. In this experiment the clustering performance is measured by clustering result number through 1000 times training. The influence shows in Fig.2.

Fig. 2 shows that if value of δ is greater the clustering performance is better. From formula 1, we can easily get that directly effect the PAR value, that is to say, δ affects the probability for the small attractors to be chosen to pick up items. If δ is greater, the small attractor is more prior to be chosen than the big one, so SICABA is quicker to converge. As to the last stage, most of the active attractors are all big one, and doesn't effect any longer. The probability of picking up item is mainly determined by the attractor's furthest item, so SICABA can precisely adjust the cluster and get better accuracy performance. Because the PAR values in the case of $C > \theta$ is always smaller than 1, obviously, δ greater than 1 is none meaning. In conclusion, when δ equals 1 SICABA can get the best performance and implement the efficient strategy: small attractors prior.

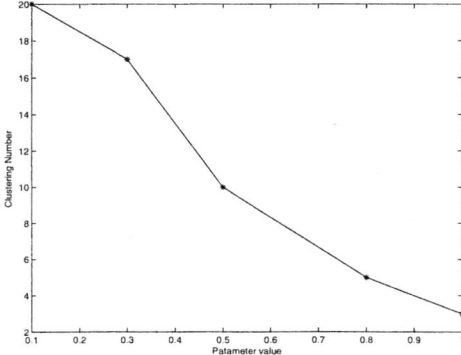

Fig. 2. Influence of parameter δ

5 Conclusion

This paper puts forward a novel structure in swarm intelligence clustering algorithm, named attractor, which contains not only the local information but also the global information, so it can actively attract the ant to pick up items or drop down items and avoid the ant aimless moving. Furthermore, we also implement an efficient strategy: *small attractors prior*, based on the attractor. The strategy makes SICABA picks up all items coarsely but fast from cluster in the first stage and picks up the furthest item to precisely fine-tune. The experiments prove that it can greatly improve the algorithm convergence speed and clustering quality compared with LF algorithm and k-means. Although SICABA has no advantages over classic k-means algorithms on the aspect of space and time complexity, as a self-organization clustering algorithm, it has great advantages in robustness, visualization, flexibility and decentralization.

References

1. Becker R., Holland O.E. and Deneubourg J.L: 'From local actions to global tasks: Stigmergy and collective robotics'. in Brooks R. and Maes P. Artificial Life IV, MIT Press, 1994.
2. E.Bonabeau, M.Dorigo, G.Theraulaz: Inspiration for optimization from social insect behaviour. Nature. 406 (2000) 39-42.
3. Gianni Di Caro and Marco Dorigo: AntNet: Distributed Stigmergetic Control for Communications Networks. Journal of Artificial Intelligence Research 9 (1998) 317-355.
4. Deneubourg J.L., Goss S., Frank N., Sendova-hanks, A.,Detrain C.,Chrerien L.: The dynamics of collective sorting: robot-like ants and ant-like robots, in: Meyer J., Wilson S.W. (Eds.), Proceedings of the First International Conference on Simulation of Adaptive Behavior: From Animals to Animats, MIT Press/Bradford Books, Cambridge, MA. (1991) 356-363.

5. E.Lumer, B.Faieta: Diversity and adaptation in populations of clustering ants . in J.-A.Meyer, S.W. Wilson(Eds.), Proceedings of the Third International Conference on Simulation of Adaptive Behavior: From Animals to Animats, Vol.3, MIT Press/ Brad-ford Books, Cambridge, MA. (1994) 501-508.
6. J. Handl, B. Meyer: Improved Ant-Based Clustering and Sorting in a Document Retrieval Interface. Proc. of the 7th Int. Conf. on Parallel Problem Solving from Nature. (2002) 913-923.
7. V. Ramos, F. Muge, P. Pina: Self-Organized Data and Image Retrieval as a Consequence of Inter-Dynamic Synergistic Relationships in Artificial Ant Colonies. Soft Computing Systems: Design, Management and Applications. 87 (2002) 500-509.
8. Bonabeau,E, Dorigo,M, Theraulaz,G: Swarm Intelligence: From Natural to Artificial Systems ,Oxford Univ. Press, NewYork,1999

An Agent-Based Soft Computing Society with Application in the Management of Establishment of Hydraulic Fracture in Oil Field

Fu hua Shang[1], Xiao feng Li[2], and Jian Xu[3]

[1] The department of computing Harbin Institute of Technology
sfh@mtlab.hit.edu.cn
[2] School of the application of computing DaQing Petroleum Institute
xfli@pislab.com
[3] School of the application of computing DaQing Petroleum Institute
xujian@pislab.com

Abstract. Establishment of Hydraulic Fracture in Oil field is a complicated system. The process of establishment of project involves many departments, which frequently interact each other. In general, The Orient-Object technology is not suitable to construct this system, which has these characters. The technology of Agent is a new method that analyses and designs the complicated system, which is suitable to develop the intricate and dynamic system and is able to simulate the society. This paper presents a soft computing society model by the methodology of Gaia, based on the characters of establishment of Hydraulic Fracture.

1 Introduction

The measure of the Hydraulic Fracture is indispensable in order to effectively exploit the reservoir. Because of the complexity and uncertainty of the geological deposition, the measure of Hydraulic Fracture is complicated. On the other hand, the process of establishment of project involves many departments that are frequently interacting each other, thus put forward the pressing requirements: how to effectively cooperate with each department and complete the establishment of Hydraulic Fracture in the sound time and how to construct the system? Traditionally the modeling method of information system has been applied widely in the process of information development of corporation such as the orient-requirement methodology [6], the orient-data methodology and the orient-object methodology. But these methods have some flaws: firstly these methods are suitable to construct the system that has the constant framework and every details of interaction have been set down. That is we must know the details of interaction and interaction pattern can't be changed. Secondly the extensibility of the system is poor. The function of the system can't be easily added. When the framework of the system is changed we must do a lot work that is almost equivalent to redevelop the system.

With the development of the view point of management, the corporation often alters the process of manipulation and workflow. Traditional method can not adapt to this transition. Existent information system of corporation is a distributed system, which is a loosely coupled network of entities that work together to make decisions or solving problem. In this system data knowledge and control is averagely distributed at each node and no node can control all others. As no node has enough resources to solving the whole problem, each node need to exchange data knowledge and the state of entity and cooperate with each other to solving problems [13] Traditional modeling technology can not develop the system which has these above properties.

Orient-Agent methodology can be useful [9].

It is open environment that is at least highly dynamic uncertainty and complex [9]. In this environment the only method to solve problem is by autonomous Agent.

Agent is a natural metaphor. Agent society naturally simulates the entities of much environment including competitive conditions of many organizations and business, a Agent can cooperate with the others to solve problem or compete with the others to get resources.

Data control expertise and resources are distributed [9]. Under some conditions distribution data control expertise and resources mean that the centralized method is quite difficult to solve these problem. For example the distributed data base system that is made up of many distributed data bases which is located at different nodes is not adopted to the centralized method to solve problems. In general, we transform this system into Multi-Agent systems, in which each data base is half autonomous Agent. This paper analyzes and designs the information system of establishment of hydraulic fracture, at last presents a Agent soft computing society model by orient-Agent methodology. This system that has some characters such as extensibility robustness flexibility maintainability fulfils the requirements of corporation.

2 The Agent-Oriented Methodology

Existing software development technique (for example, object-oriented analysis and design) are inadequate for multi-Agent system analysis and design [6]. There is a fundamental mismatch between the concepts used by object-oriented developers and the agent-oriented perspective. In particular, extant approaches fail to adequately capture an agent's flexible, autonomous problem-solving behavior, the richness of an agent's interactions, and the complexity of an agent system's organizational structure. For these reason, this section outlines a methodology that has been specifically tailored to the analysis and design of agent-based complicated system. The main models used in this methodology are summarized in Figure 1, which are mainly based on the Gaia methodology [6].

The analysis phase aims to identify what the actual organization of the multiple agents should look like. It does this by decomposing the system into abstract "loci of control"; i.e., the role to be played in the organization, and the way in which they interact accordingly to specific protocols. This defines the role model and interaction model, respectively.

The role model identified the key role in the system. Here a role can be viewed as an abstract description of an entity's expected function. A role is defined by four attributes: responsibility, permission, activities, and protocols.

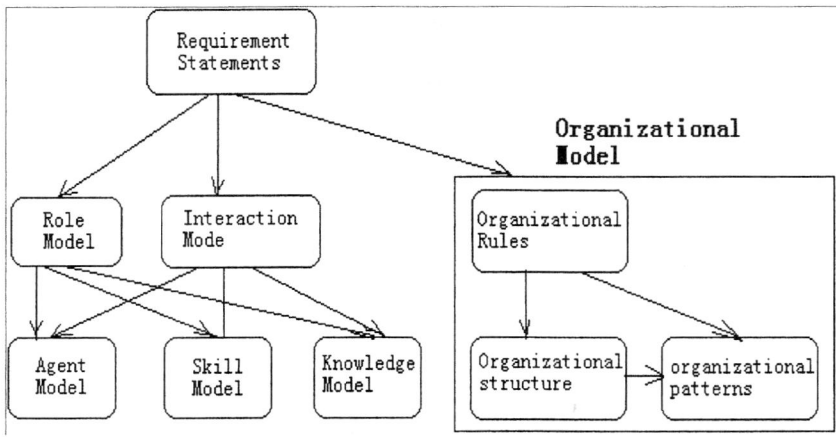

Fig. 1. Relationship between Models

Responsibilities determine functionality and, as such, are perhaps the key attribute associated with a role. Responsibility is divided into two types: liveness properties and safety properties. Liveness properties intuitively state that "something good happens". They describe those states of affairs that an agent must bring about, given certain environmental conditions. Following the Gaia notation, liveness properties are specified via a liveness expression, which defines the "life-cycle" of the role and is a regular expression. Safety properties are invariant. Intuitively, a safety property states that " nothing bad happens"(i.e., that an acceptable state of affairs is maintained across all states of execution). Safety requirement are specified by means of a list of predicated. These predicates are typically expressed over the variables listed in a role's permission attribute.

In order to realize responsibilities, a role has a set of permissions. Permissions are the "rights" associated with a role. The permissions of a role thus identify the resources that are available to that role in order to realize its responsibilities.

Finally, a role is identified with a number of protocols, which define the way that it can interact with other roles. A role model is comprised of a set of role schemata, one for each role in the system. A role schema draws together the various attributes discussed above into a single place (see Figure 2).

In summary, the analysis phase is tasked with collecting all the specification from which the design of the computational organization can start (refer to Figure 1). The output of the analysis phase should be a triple < PR, PP, OL>, where PR are the preliminary roles of the system, PP are the preliminary protocols (which have already been discovered to be necessary for the preliminary roles), and OL are the organizational rules.

The design phase starts from the models defined during the analysis phase and aims to define the actual agent system in such a way that it can easily be implemented. To this end, the design phase has to decide which classes of agents (and how many) have to play the roles identified during the analysis phase, which services agents must provide to fulfill their role, and what is the actual topology of the interaction that flows from the interaction and agent models.

Role Schema	name of role
Description	short English description of the role
Protocols and Activities	protocols and activities in which the role plays a part
Permissions	"rights" associated with the role
Responsibilities	
Liveness	liveness responsibility
Safety	safety responsibility

Fig. 2. Template for Role Schema

The purpose of the agent model is to document the various agent types that will be used in the system under development, and the agent instances that will realize these agent types at run-time.

An agent type is best thought of as a set of agent roles. There may, in fact, be a one-to-one correspondence between roles (as identified in role model) and agent types. However this need not be the case. A designer can choose to package a number of closely related roles in the same agent type for the purpose of convenience.

The agent model is defined using a simple agent type tree, in which leaf nodes correspond to roles, and other nodes correspond to agent types. If an agent type m1 has children m2 and m3, then this means that m1 is composed of the roles that make up m2 and m3.

The aim of the skill model is to identify the main skills with each agent role. Skills mainly consist of the basic services required to be able to perform a role. A service is defined as a function of the agent. For each agent service that may be performed by an agent, it is necessary to document its properties. Specifically, one must identify the inputs, outputs, pre-conditions, and post-conditions of each service.

The design phase builds on the output of the analysis phase and produces a complete specification of the multi-agent system. The design stage can now be summarized as the following:

- .Create an agent model: (1) aggregate roles into agent types, and refine to form an agent type hierarchy; (2) document the instance of each agent type using instance annotations.
- .Develop a skill model, by examining activities, protocols, and safety and liveness properties of roles.
- .Develop a knowledge model from interaction model and agent model. Identify organizational structures and organizational patterns that respect the organizational rules.

3 Agent-Based Soft Computing Society Model for Establishment of Hydraulic Fracture

In order to identify which components should be contained in a establishment system of hydraulic fracture, without loss of generality, we are based on real process of the corporation to extract the components. In this system, firstly a geological requisition in which gives the fundamental data of a well is sent to the collaborating department of hydraulic fracture, then collaborating department transfer the geological requisition to the department of establishment. The department of establishment corresponds with six groups: the discussing group of planning, the decision making group, The measure group of conventional fracture, the measure group of CO_2 fracture, the measure group of multi-fracture, the measure group of limited flow fracture. Every fracturing group is corresponding with a group of expertise: such as the analysis of geological stress, the production forecast, the evaluation of economy, the design of tubing. In addition, a share database is needed. Flow chart sees Fig.3.

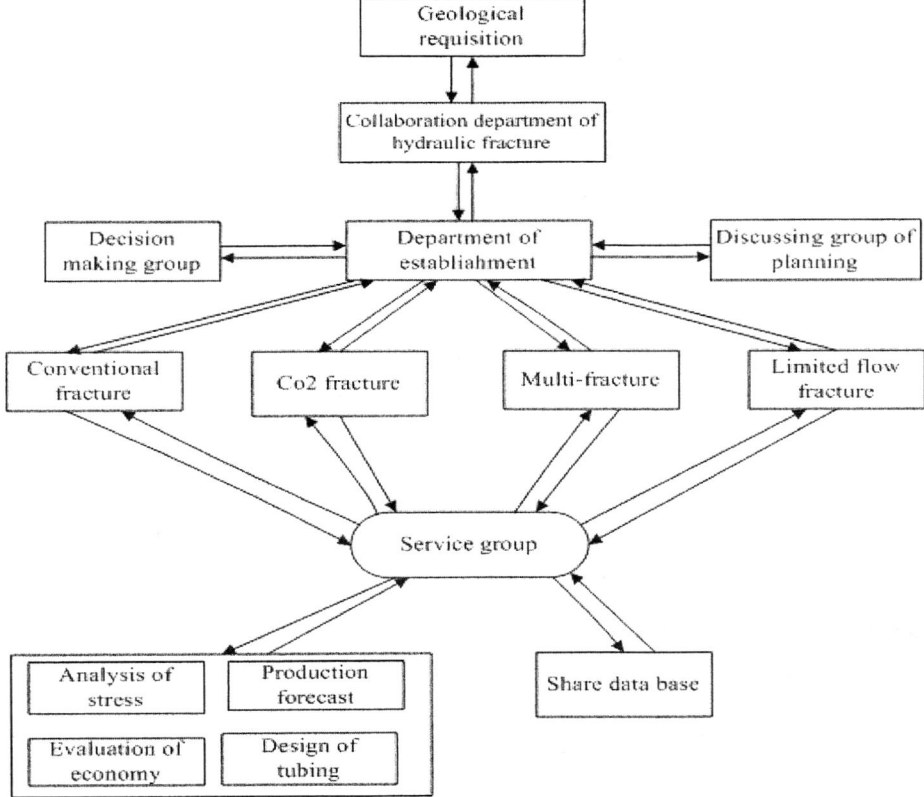

Fig. 3. Flow Char of System

3.1 Analysis of Agent-Based Soft Computing Society

Based on the above description and the methodology proposed in the previous section, it is comparatively straightforward to identify the roles in the system. A role of the collaborating department of fracture is an interface to the user. The department of establishment acts as planning and collaboration. The discussing group of planning falls into two roles: one keeping track of the profiles and one checking the profiles. The decision making group aggregates the final results.

The measure group of conventional fracture, the measure group of CO_2 fracture, the measure group of multi-fracture, and the measure group of limited flow fracture act as the roles that cooperate with the expertise to complete the analysis of planning. The analysis of geological stress, the production forecast, the evaluation of economy, and the design of tubing act as expertise roles.

With the respective role definitions in place, the next stage is to define the associated interaction models for these roles. Here we focus on the interactions associated with the department of establishment.

This role interacts with the collaborating department to obtain the task and transfers the task to the discussing group. In there, the mode of fracture is determined and the result is returned to the department of establishment, perhaps multi-modes are adopted. Following, the department of establishment sends the details of task to the concrete measure group and receives the results of the computing. Finally, the decision making group aggregate the final results.

3.2 Design of the Society

Having completed the analysis of the society, the design phase follows. The first model to be generated is the agent model (Fig.4). This shows, for most cases, a one to one correspondence between roles and agent types.

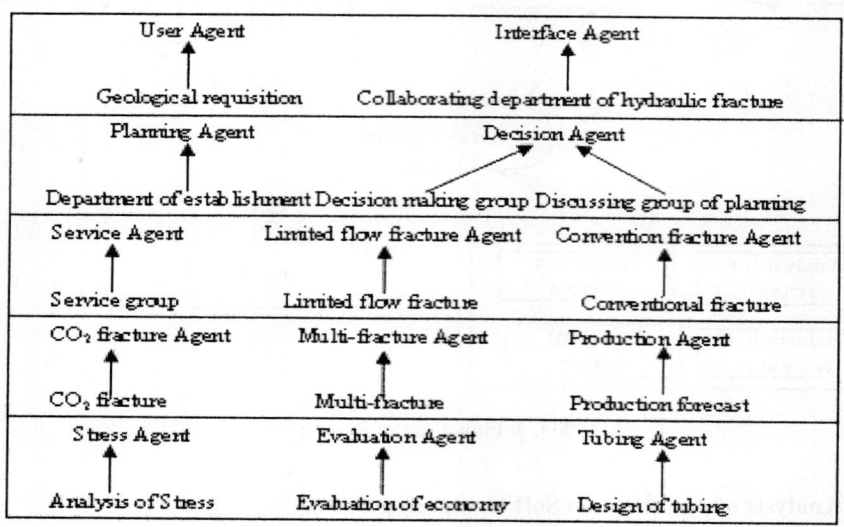

Fig. 4. The Agent Model of the Society

3.3 Architecture of the Society

From the above analysis and design phases, it is clear that there are eleven types of agents in the soft computing society –user agent, interface agent, planning agent, decision making agent, convention fracture agent, CO_2 fracture agent, multi-fracture agent, limited flow fracture agent, share data base agent, service Agent, service provider agents are made up of the analysis of geological stress agent, the production forecast agent, the evaluation of economy agent, and the design of tubing agent. To this end, the architecture of the agent-based soft computing society is shown in Figure 5.

- **Interface Agent** This agent interacts with the user (or user agent). It asks user to provide his personal information and requirements, and provides the user with a final decision or advice that best meets the user's requirement.
- **Planning Agent** The planning agent is in charge of the activation and synchronization of different agents. It elaborates a work plan and is in charge of ensuring that such a work plan is fulfilled. It receives the assignment from the interface agent.
- **Decision Making Agent** It is in charge of keeping track of the profiles, checking the profiles and aggregating the results of computing.
- **Service Agent** The service agent is a matchmaker of expertise-one kind of middle agent, besides in charge of accessing the share database.
- **Service Provider Agents** Service Provider Agents are made up of much expertise. It can send back the processed results to the service agent.
- **Share Data Base Agent** share data base agent consists of all kinds of data.

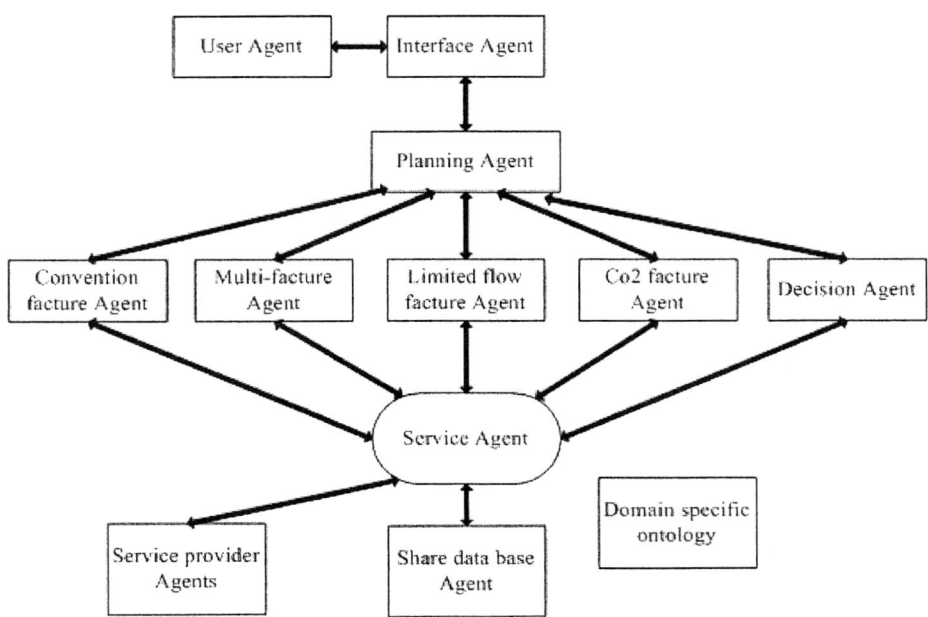

Fig. 5. Architecture of Agent-based Soft Computing Society

4 The Prototype of System

The most important implementation criterion of such a system is platform independent. With this in mind, the AgentBuilder (Java Agent Template, http://www.reticular.com,

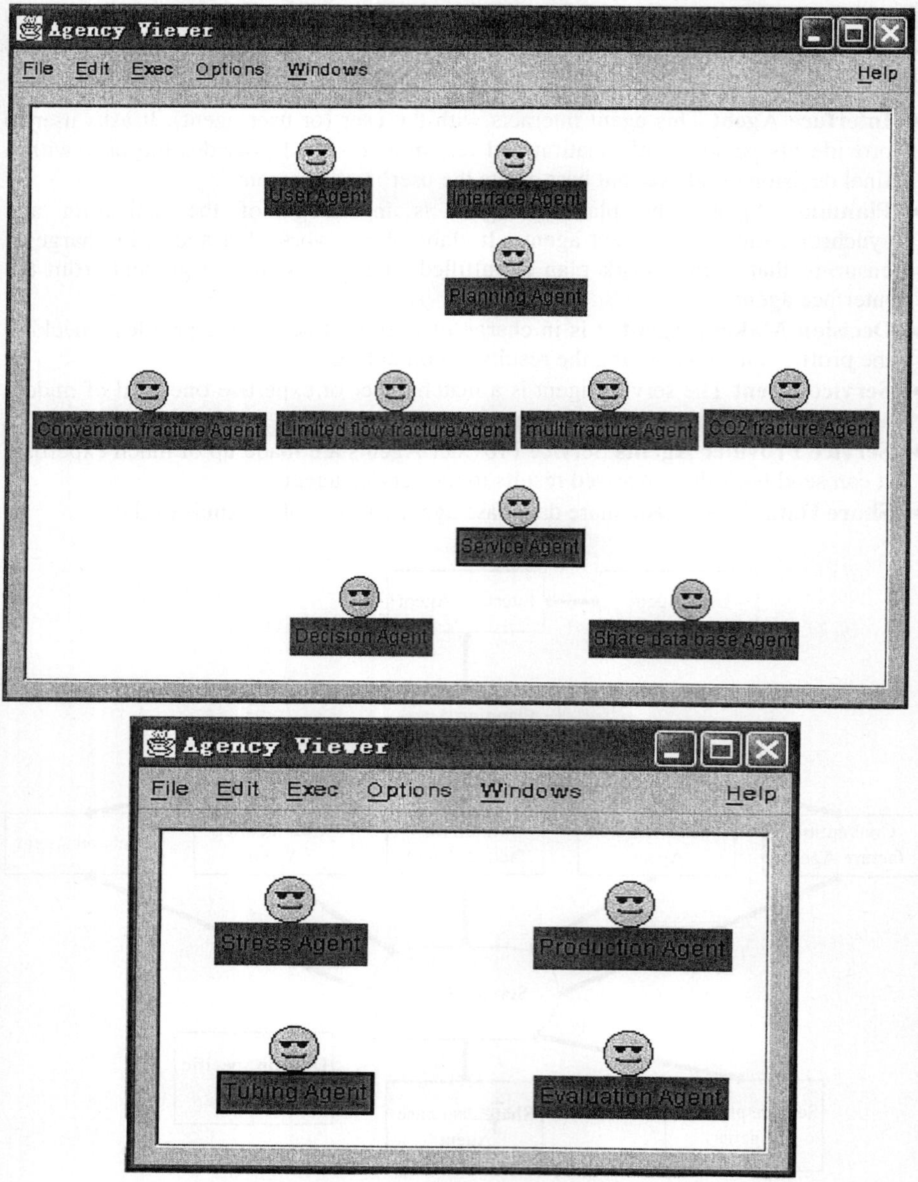

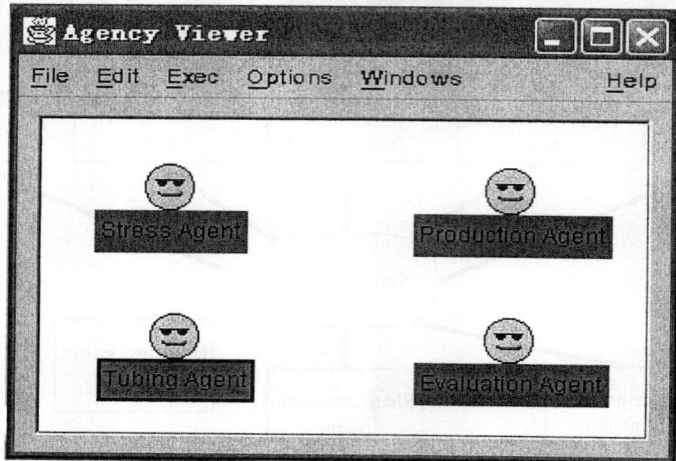

Fig. 6. Agencies of the system

http://www.agentbuild.com) was chosen to support the implementation. AgentBuilder provides a set of Java templates and a ubiquitous Java agent infrastructure that makes it easy to build systems in a common way. AgentBuilder especially facilitates construction of agents that send and receive messages using the emerging standard agent communication language KOML(Knowledge Query and Manipulation Language). All agents implemented have the ability to exchange KOML messages. This greatly increases the interoperability of the system.

Following the analysis and design phases of the proposed methodology, we worked out that the prototype consists of the following agents: one interface agent, one planning agent, four measure agents, one decision making agent, one service agent, one share data base agent, service provider agents. The system sees Fig.6.

5 Summary

This prototype system presents a agent soft computing society model by the orient-agent methodology. This model can dynamically collaborate with each department to work together. In intranet and virtual office, it transparently completes the process of establishment of hydraulic fracture, achieves the prospective purpose and satisfies the requirement of the corporation.

References

1. Ke Zhang, JiNan Sun: The Application of Agent Technology in Mining Management and Decision making System. Journal of computer and modernization. 2002 No.10
2. Gang Li, Linyan Sun: Study on the Architecture of Flexible Enterprise Resource Planning System Based on Multi-agent Computer Engineering. 2002 Vol.28 No. 9
3. Sanyuan Zhou: A Agent Oriented Method for Designing Enterprise Information System Model Journal of missile and spaceflight delivery technology. 2003 No.2
4. Liang Guo: Agent-Oriented Software Engineer Journal of chongqing University. 2002 Vol. 25 No.10
5. Nicholas R. Jennings: On agent-based software engineering Artificial Intelligence 117 (2000) 277–296
6. M. Wooldrige, N. Jennings, D. kinny: The Gaia Methodology for Agent-Oriented Analysis and Design. *Journal of Autonomous Agents and Multi-Agent Systems*, 3, 12, 2000
7. ZiLi Zhang and Chengi Zhang: An Agent-Based Soft Computing Society with Application in Financial Investment Planning. *Studies in Fuzziness and Soft Computing: Applied Decision Support with Soft Computing*, pp. 99-126.
8. Nicholas R. Jennings: On agent-based software engineering. *Artificial Intelligence* 117 (2000) 277–296
9. Jennings, N. R. and Wooldridge, M. J. (1998): *Applications of Intelligent Agents*, in Jennings, N. R. and Wooldridge, M. J., Eds: *Agent Technology: Foundations, Applications and Markets*, pages pp. 3-28

10. K. Decker, K. Sycara, and M. Williamson: Middle Agents for the internet, Proceedings of 15th international Joint Conference on Artificial Intelligence. Nogoya, Japan, 1997, 578-583.
11. Zhang Y, Shi ML, Zhang SH: An agent-based framework for cross-domain cooperation of virtual enterprise. Journal of Software, 2003,14 (Suppl.): 61~73
12. L. C. Jain and R. K. Jain (Eds.): Hybrid Intelligent Engineering Systems. World Scientific, Singapore, 1997
13. Moulin, B., Chaib-Draa, B.,: "An Overview of Distributed Artificial Intelligence", in Foundations of Distributed Artificial Intelligence. O'Hare, G.M.P. & Jennings, N.R. (eds.), Sixth-Generation Computer Technology Series, 1996

Two Sub-swarms Particle Swarm Optimization Algorithm

Guochu Chen and Jinshou Yu

Research Institute of Automation, East China University of Science and Technology,
Shanghai, 200237, China
chgcsh@sohu.com

Abstract. This paper proposes a two sub-warms particle swarm optimization algorithm (TSPSO) and its iteration equations. The new algorithm assumes that particles are divided into two sub-swarms. The two sub-swarms have different move directions. One sub-swarm moves toward the global best position. Another moves in the opposite direction. Not only its own move experience and the best individual's position of its own sub-swarm, but also the global best position of the whole swarm can affect each particle's move in every iteration. If the fitness of the global best position can't be improved for fifteen successive steps, the particles of the two sub-swarms are exchanged. At the same time, the worst individual of one sub-swarm is replaced with the best individual of another. Then, both TSPSO and PSO are used to resolve ten well-known and widely used test functions' optimization problems. Results show that TSPSO has greater optimization efficiency, better optimization performance and more advantages in many aspects than PSO.

1 Introduction

Particle swarm optimization algorithm (PSO) is an evolutionary computation technique inspired by social behavior observable in nature, such as flocks of birds and schools of fish, proposed by Eberhart and Kennedy in 1995 [1,2]. It is a simple algorithm and can be developed over a very simple theoretical framework and can be implemented with a few lines of computer code, requiring only primitive mathematical operators. Besides, it is computationally inexpensive in terms of both memory requirements and speed [3-5]. It was originally developed for optimization in a continuous space and it has been recently adapted to optimization in binary spaces, presenting good performance also when applied to discontinuous objective functions and used in the optimization of many nonlinear functions and in neural networks training [4-8].

As an evolutionary computation algorithm, PSO is an attractive choice for nonlinear programming because of the characteristics mentioned above. Even so, it is not without problems. PSO suffers from premature convergence, tending to get stuck in local optima [3,4,7]. We have also found that it suffers from an ineffective exploration strategy, especially around local optima, and thus does not find best solutions as quickly as it could. Moreover, adjusting the tunable parameters of PSO to obtain good performance can be a difficult task [3,7]. This paper proposes a two sub-warms particle swarm optimization algorithm (TSPSO), analyses outline of TSPSO and then uses TSPSO to resolve ten well-known test functions' optimization problems.

2 Two Sub-warms Particle Swarm Optimization Algorithm

2.1 PSO Algorithm

Suppose that the search space is D-dimensional and a particle swarm consists of m particles, then the i-th particle of the swarm can be represented by a D-dimensional vector, $X_i = (x_{i1}, x_{i2}, x_{i3}, \cdots, x_{iD})$, $i = 1, 2, \cdots, m$. The velocity of this particle can be represented by another D-dimensional vector, $V_i = (v_{i1}, v_{i2}, v_{i3}, \cdots, v_{iD})$. The fitness of every particle can be evaluated according to the objective function of optimization problem. The best previously visited position of the i-th particle is noted as its individual best position, $P_i = (p_{i1}, p_{i2}, p_{i3}, \cdots, p_{iD})$. Define g as the index of the best particle of the whole swarm, the position of the best individual of the whole swarm is noted as the global best position P_g, and the fitness of the global best position is noted as the global best fitness F_g. Then the velocity of particle and its new position will be assigned according to the following two equations [1,2,7]:

$$v_{id} = \chi \cdot (\omega v_{id} + c_1 r_1 (p_{id} - x_{id}) + c_2 r_2 (p_{gd} - x_{id})) \tag{1}$$

$$x_{id} = x_{id} + v_{id} \tag{2}$$

where χ is a constriction factor; ω is called inertia weight; c_1 and c_2 are two positive constants called acceleration coefficients; r_1 and r_2 are two random numbers uniformly from the interval [0, 1].

2.2 Outline of TSPSO

Although PSO finds the optimal value quickly and has attractive optimization performance to many optimization problems, PSO have two limitations. First, to avoid being trapped in local optima, the search space usually is very large so that PSO wastes a considerable amount of computational effort by visiting states of poor fitness values. Second, each particle in PSO often continues to move roughly in the same direction (towards the global best position) until there is a change in the global best position. This leads to the convergence of all particles towards local optima whose fitness may be low.

TSPSO is an extension of PSO based on the idea that changing direction can lead to a better solution while PSO searches for the global optima. TSPSO assumes that the particles are divided into two sub-swarms. The move directions of the two sub-swarms are different. One sub-swarm moves toward the global best position. Another moves in the opposite direction. Not only its own search experience and the best individual's position of its own sub-swarm, but also the global best position of the whole swarm can affect each particle's search in every iteration. If the fitness of the global best position can't be improved for fifteen successive steps, the particles of the two sub-swarms are exchanged. To extend the superiority of the best individual of each sub-swarm, the worst individual of one sub-swarm is replaced with the best individual of another at the same time. Once the fitness of the global best particle cannot be improved for some successive iteration steps, TSPSO can improve the exploration strategy of the whole swarm to get better solution by changing the move direction and renewing move information of particles. So, the particles in TSPSO may often change move direction and can continue to move even if they are trapped in local optima temporarily. The probability of being trapped in the local optima can be decreased and the probability of finding the global optimum can be increased enormously.

2.3 Algorithm Equations of TSPSO

TSPSO have not only the best individual of its own sub-swarm but also the global best position of the whole swarm. So in TSPSO, each particle not only moves toward the global best position of the whole swarm but also can get information from its own search experience and the best individual's experience of its own sub-swarm. Then the velocity of particle and its new position in TSPSO will be assigned according to the following two new equations:

$$v_{id} = \chi \cdot (\omega v_{id} + c_1 \cdot r_1 \cdot (p_{id} - x_{id}) + \mu_1 \cdot c_2 \cdot r_2 \cdot (p_{gd} - x_{id}) + \mu_2 \cdot c_3 \cdot r_3 \cdot (p_{pd} - x_{id})) \quad (3)$$

$$x_{id} = x_{id} + k \cdot v_{id} \quad (4)$$

where, as PSO, χ is a constriction factor; ω is called inertia weight; c_1, c_2 and c_3 are three positive constants called acceleration coefficients; r_1, r_2 and r_3 are three random numbers uniformly from the interval [0, 1].

p_{id} is the individual best position in the d-th dimension of the i-th particle; P_p is the best position of a sub-swarm. P_g is the global best position of the whole swarm.

μ_1 and μ_1 are called influence factors. μ_1 reflects the influence that the experience of the best position of sub-swarm imposes on the i-th particle. μ_2 reflects the influence that the experience of the global best position of the whole swarm imposes on the i-th particle. As a rule, μ_1 and μ_1 are positive decimal fraction. Default values of μ_1 and μ_1 could be $\mu_1 = \mu_2 = 0.5$.

k is a sign of movement direction. There are two possible values, -1 and 1, for k. If the particle moves toward the global best position, the value of k is 1. Otherwise, the value of k is -1 if the particle moves in the opposite direction.

2.4 TSPSO Algorithm

TSPSO algorithm can be summarized in the following steps:

1. Initialize the parameters of TSPSO.
2. Initialize the state of each particle. Store the individual best position of each particle. Evaluate and store individual best fitness of each particle. Evaluate and store the best position and the best fitness of each sub-swarm. Evaluate and store the global best position and global best fitness of whole swarm.

3. Update the velocity of particle according to equation (3). Update the position of particle according to equation (4). If necessary, deal with particle.
4. If necessary, update and store the individual best position and individual best fitness of each particle, update and store the best position and the best fitness of each sub-swarm, update and store the global best position and global best fitness of whole swarm.
5. If the global fitness is not improved for fifteen successive iteration steps, go to step 6. Otherwise, go to step 7.
6. The particles of the two sub-swarms are exchanged. And the worst individual of one sub-swarm is replaced with the best individual of another.
7. If the stopping condition is not satisfied, go to step 3. Otherwise, stop iterating and obtain the result from the global best position and the global best fitness of the whole swarm.

3 Experiments

3.1 Test Functions

In order to compare the performance of TSPSO with that of PSO, both TSPSO and PSO are employed to resolve ten well-known and widely used test functions' optimization problems. The ten test functions are described as follows:

The first test function is called Function 1:

$$\max f(x_1, x_2) = 21.5 + x_1 \cdot \sin(4 \cdot \pi \cdot x_1) + x_2 \cdot \sin(20 \cdot \pi \cdot x_2), \quad -3.0 \le x_1 \le 12.1, \quad 4.1 \le x_2 \le 5.8. \quad (5)$$

Function 1 is a very difficult optimization function and has a global optimum (maximum) situated at $x=(11.6255, 5.725)$ with function value $f(x)=38.8503$.

The second test function is called Function 2:

$$\max f(x_1, x_2) = \frac{\sin(\sqrt{(x_1-50)^2 + (x_2-50)^2} + e)}{\sqrt{(x_1-50)^2 + (x_2-50)^2} + e} + 1, \quad -100 \le x_1, x_2 \le 100. \quad (6)$$

Function 2 is also a very difficult optimization function and have many local optima (maxima) but only one global optimum (maximum) situated at $x=(50, 50)$ with function value $f(x)=1.1511$.

The third test function is Schaffer F6 function:

$$\max f(x_1, x_2) = 0.5 - \frac{\left(\sin \sqrt{x_1^2 + x_2^2}\right)^2 - 0.5}{\left(1 + 0.001 \cdot (x_1^2 + x_2^2)\right)^2}, \quad -10 \le x_1, x_2 \le 10. \quad (7)$$

Schaffer F6 function is a difficult optimization function and have a lot of local optima (maxima) but only one global optimum (maximum) situated at $x=(0, 0)$ with function value $f(x)=1$.

The fourth test function is Shubert function:

$$\min f(x_1,x_2) = \left\{\sum_{i=1}^{5} i \cdot \cos[(i+1)\cdot x_1 + i]\right\} \cdot \left\{\sum_{i=1}^{5} i \cdot \cos[(i+1)\cdot x_2 + i]\right\} +$$
$$0.5 \cdot \left[(x_1 + 1.42513)^2 + (x_2 + 0.80032)^2\right]. \quad -10 \le x_1, x_2 \le 10. \quad (8)$$

There are about 760 local optima (minima) for Shubert function and one global optimum (minimum) situated at $x=(-1.42513, -0.80032)$ with function value $f(x)=-186.7309$. Shubert function is a difficult optimization function.

The fifth test function is Griewangk function (here, n=2):

$$\min f(x) = \sum_{i=1}^{n} \frac{x_i^2}{4000} - \prod_{i=1}^{n} \cos(\frac{x_i}{\sqrt{i}}) + 1 \quad -600 \le x_i \le 600. \quad (9)$$

Griewangk function is also a difficult optimization function and has one global optimum (minimum) situated at $x=(0, 0)$ with function value $f(x)=0$.

The sixth test function is Levy F5 function:

$$\min f(x_1,x_2) = \left\{\sum_{i=1}^{5} i \cdot \cos[(i-1)\cdot x_1 + i]\right\} \cdot \left\{\sum_{i=1}^{5} i \cdot \cos[(i+1)\cdot x_2 + i]\right\} +$$
$$\left[(x_1 + 1.42513)^2 + (x_2 + 0.80032)^2\right] \quad -10 \le x_1, x_2 \le 10 \quad (10)$$

There are about 760 local optima (minima) for Levy F5 function and one global optimum (minima) situated at $x=(-1.3068, 1.4248)$ with function value $f(x)=-176.1376$.

The seventh test function is Schaffer F7 function:

$$\max f(x_1,x_2) = (x_1^2 + x_2^2)^{0.25} \cdot (\sin^2(50\cdot(x_1^2 + x_2^2)^{0.1}) + 1.0), \quad -10 \le x_1, x_2 \le 10. \quad (11)$$

Schaffer F7 function have many local optima (maxima) but only one global optimum (maximum) with function value $f(x)=7.1580$.

The eighth test function is Rosenbrock function:

$$\min f(x_1,x_2) = 100\cdot(x_1^2 - x_2)^2 + (1 - x_1)^2, \quad -2.048 \le x_1, x_2 \le 2.048. \quad (12)$$

Rosenbrock function has one global optimum (minimum) situated at $x=(1, 1)$ with function value $f(x)=0$.

The ninth test function is De Jong function (here, $n=2$):

$$\min f(x) = \sum_{i=1}^{n} x_i^2, \quad -10 \le x_i \le 10, \quad (13)$$

De Jong function has one global optimum (minimum) situated at $x=(0, 0)$ with function value $f(x)=0$.

The tenth test function is Camel function:

$$\min f(x_1,x_2) = (4 - 2.1\cdot x_1^2 + \frac{x_1^4}{3})\cdot x_1^2 + x_1 \cdot x_2 + (-4 + 4\cdot x_2^2)\cdot x_2^2, \quad -100 \le x_1, x_2 \le 100. \quad (14)$$

There are four local optima (minima) for Camel function and two global optima (minima) situated at $x=(-0.0898, 0.7126)$ or $(0.0898, -0.7126)$ with function value $f(x)= -1.031628$.

3.2 Experiments

The success rate (the probability of algorithm's finding the global optimal solution) is very important for any optimization algorithm. If the success rate is higher, the algorithm can find the global optimal solution easier. So, the first experiment is to compare the success rate of TSPSO with that of PSO. In this experiment, both TSPSO and PSO run for 4000 iteration steps for every test to ensure that the two algorithms can find optimal solution for the last five test functions. In the two algorithms, c_1, c_2 and c_3 are set to 2.0. ω is gradually decreased from 1.8 to 0.02. μ_1 and μ_2 are set to 0.5. χ is set to 0.75. The population of each sub-swarm of TSPSO is set to 30. To compare fairly, the population of PSO is set to 60. Because TSPSO and PSO both are stochastic optimization algorithms, the optimization result of every test may be different. It is hard to compare fairly the two algorithms' optimization performance with result of one or two times test. So, both TSPSO and PSO are testing for 500 times respectively for the ten test functions. Then, the test results are statistical accounted. The results are averaged and summarized in Table 1.

The convergence time (the time that algorithm spends to find the global optimal solution) is also important for any optimization algorithm. If the convergence time is shorter, the algorithm converges at the global optimal solution faster. So, the second experiment is to compare the convergence time of TSPSO with that of PSO. The algorithm parameters of this experiment are the same as that of the first experiment. Furthermore, in this experiment, the error limit is set to 10^{-5}. That is, if the absolute value of the error between the optimal solution of test function and the global best fitness of the m-th iteration is less than 10^{-5}, then the success iteration of this test is m. As the first experiment, both TSPSO and PSO take 500 times trial runs respectively for last five test functions, because the last five test functions are comparative easy optimization functions. Then, the test results are also statistical accounted. The results are averaged and summarized in Table 2.

3.3 Discussion About N, the Successive Iteration Steps of the Global Optimal Fitness' not Being Improved

In TSPSO, if the value of N is too small, the flight of some potential particles may be impaired so that the success rate during the search will be decreased, although TSPSO keeps the best particle while exchanging particles. On the contrary, if N is too large, excessively computing is wasted on the search of poor fitness so that the superiority of TSPSO cannot be embodied. To choose appropriate value of N, this paper designs three groups of tests as following: the first test is to test the relationships between N and success rates with different test functions, the second test is to test the relationships between N and success rates with different sizes of sub-swarms, and the last test is to test the relationships between N and success rates with different largest permission iteration steps. During the three tests, ω is gradually decreased from 1.8 to 0.02. c_1, c_2 and c_3 are set to 2.0. χ is set to 0.5. μ_1 and μ_2 are set to 0.5. the values of N are respectively 0, 1, 5, 10, 15, 20, 30, 40, 50, 60, 80 and 100. In the first test, the largest permission iteration steps is set to 2000, the sizes of sub-swarms are 30 for the first five test functions above, to test the relationship between the success rates and the value of N with different test functions. In the second test, the largest permission iteration steps is set to 2000, the sizes of sub-swarms are respectively 10, 20, 30 and 50 for the test function F1, to test the relationship between the success rates and the value of N with different sub-swarm sizes of the test function F1. In the third test, the size of sub-swarms are set to 30, the largest permission iteration steps are set to 1000, 2000 and 4000 respectively for the function F1, to test the relationship between the success rates and the value of N with different largest permission iteration steps. Because TSPSO is a stochastic optimization algorithm, the three tests are testing for 500 times respectively for every case. Then, the test results are statistical accounted. The statistics results of the tests are showed respectively in Fig. 1, Fig. 2 and Fig. 3.

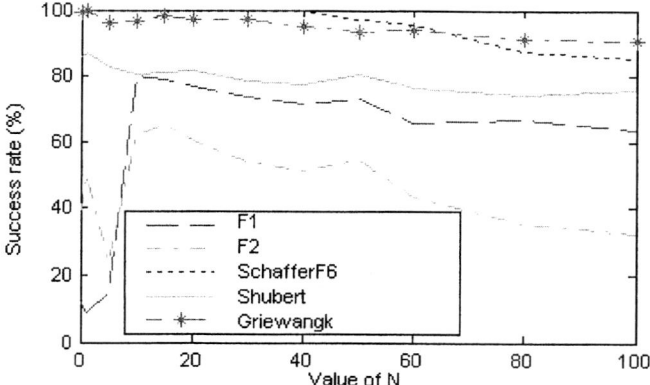

Fig. 1. Relationships between N and success rates with different test functions

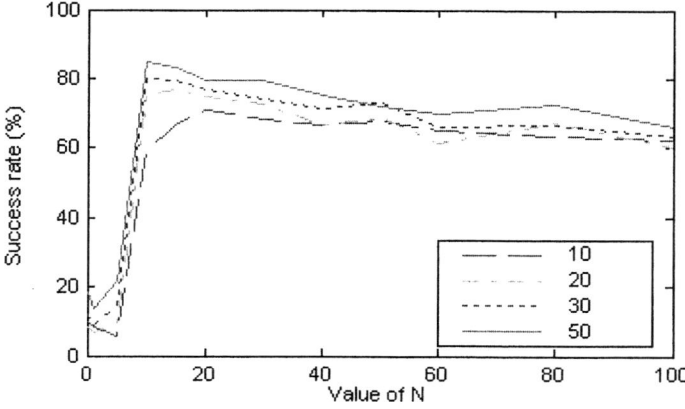

Fig. 2. Relationships between N and success rates with different sizes of sub-swarms

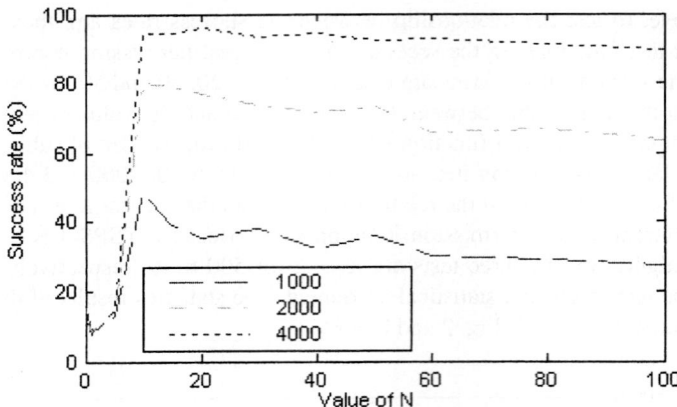

Fig. 3. Relationships between N and success rates with different largest iteration steps

In Fig. 1, for the functions F1 and F2, when N is small, the success rate is quite low, with the increasing of N, the success rate becomes gradually higher and achieves the highest value with $N=15$, then with the increasing of N, the success rate decreases gradually. For the test function Schaffer F6, the success rate has been 100 percent before N reaches 20, then with the increasing of N, it decreases slowly. For the test function Shubert and Griewangk, the success rates both achieve the highest value with $N=1$, then they decrease slowly too. On the whole, the value of N ranging from 10 to 20 is relatively proper.

In Fig. 2, with the increasing of particles' size, both of the search computing and the success rate increase, but the relationship between the success rates of different sub-swarms' sizes and the value of N is similar, the sub-swarms' sizes have little impact on the choice of N.

In Fig. 3, with the increasing of the largest permission iteration steps, the search computing and the success rate also increase, but the relationship between the success rates of the different largest permission iteration steps and the value of N is similar and the different largest permission numbers of iterative steps have also little impact on the choice of N.

So, this paper assumes that the value of N is set to 15 in the two experiments.

4 Results and Discussions

Table 1 shows the success rate and mean number of fitness of the global best position found for the ten test functions with the two algorithms, TSPSO and PSO respectively after 500 trial runs.

By comparing the results of the two algorithms, it is clear to see that the success rate of TSPSO is higher than that of PSO for the first five difficult optimization functions and the mean number of fitness of the global best position of TSPSO is also better than that of PSO for the first five difficult optimization functions. For the last five comparable easy optimization functions, the optimization performance of TSPSO and the optimization performance of PSO are comparable and both of them are attractive. So, it is clear that TSPSO has greater optimization efficiency and better optimization performance than PSO.

Table 1. Success rate and mean fitness of functions found for the ten test functions with TSPSO and PSO

Test Functions	TSPSO		PSO	
	Succ. Rate, %	Mean Fitness	Succ. Rate, %	Mean Fitness
Function 1	93.2	38.843	1	38.666
Function 2	89.2	1.1493	18.4	1.1332
Schaffer F6	100	1	56	0.99803
Shubert	96	-186.58	59.4	-186.44
Griewangk	99.2	5.8216e-05	68.6	0.00208
Levy F5	100	-176.1376	100	-176.1376
Schaffer F7	100	7.1580	100	7.1580
Rosenbrock	100	0	100	0
De Jong	100	0	100	0
Camel	100	-1.0316	100	-1.0316

Table 2 shows the mean number of success iteration, the maximal number of success iteration and the minimal number of success iteration for the last five test functions with the two algorithms, TSPSO and PSO respectively after 500 trial runs. Table 2 also shows the time needed of one iteration for the last five test functions with TSPSO and PSO respectively.

According to Table 2, the time needed of one iteration of TSPSO is longer than that of PSO (the time needed of one iteration of TSPSO is about 1.5 times that of PSO), but the mean number of the success iteration of TSPSO is much less than that of PSO (the mean number of the success iteration of TSPSO is about 0.3 times that of PSO). Besides, the maximal number of success iterations and minimal number of success iterations of TSPSO are also less than that of PSO. So it is clear that TSPSO can find the global optimal solution more quickly than PSO.

Table 2. Mean number of success iterations, maximal number of success iterations, minimal number of success iterations and the time needed of one iteration for the last five test functions with TSPSO and PSO

Test Functions	TSPSO				PSO			
	Mean Iter.	Max. Iter.	Min. Iter.	Time Nee./ms	Mean Iter.	Max. Iter.	Min. Iter.	Time Nee./ms
Levy F5	1061	1765	45	0.89475	3231	3305	3210	0.574
Schaffer F7	54	404	1	0.8865	2995	3245	1	0.6055
Rosenbrock	1550	1689	37	0.621	3256	3349	3214	0.375
De Jong	669	1497	30	0.63275	3212	3221	3189	0.40625
Camel	1196	1849	72	0.67575	3225	3237	3206	0.40625

5 Conclusions

This paper proposed TSPSO, which is based on the idea that changing move direction can lead to a better solution while searching for the global optimal solution with PSO. TSPSO assumes that the particles are divided into two sub-swarms, and each sub-swarm has a different move direction so that the particle in TSPSO can escape from local optima easily by changing move direction. The simulation results for ten well-known test functions show that TSPSO has greater optimization efficiency, better optimization performance and more advantages in many aspects than PSO. However, only ten optimization functions had been tested. To fully claim the benefits of TSPSO, more researches need to be done.

References

1. Kennedy J, Eberhart R C: Particle Swarm Optimization. Proc. IEEE Int. Conf. on Neural Networks. Perth, WA, Australia (1995) 1942-1948
2. Eberhart R C, Kennedy J: A New Optimizer Using Particle Swarm Theory. Proc. the Sixth Int. Symposium on Micro Machine and Human Science. Nagoya, Japan (1995) 39-43
3. Shi, Y, Eberhart, R C: Parameter Selection in Particle Swarm Optimization. Evolutionary Programming VII: Proceedings of The Seventh Annual Conference on Evolutionary Programming. New York (1998) 591–600
4. Eberhart R C, Shi Y: Particle Swarm Optimization: Developments, Applications and Resources. Proc. 2001 Congress on Evolutionary Computation. Seoul, South Korea (2001) 81-86.
5. James Kennedy, Russell C. Eberhart: Swarm Intelligence. Morgan Kaufmann Publishers, San Francisco, California, USA (2001)
6. Frans Van Den Bergh, Engelbrecht A P: Training Product Unit Networks Using Cooperative Particle Swarm Optimizers. Proc. of The Third Genetic and Evolutionary Computation Conference. San Francisco, USA (2001)
7. K. E. Parsopoulos, M. N. Vrahatis: Recent Approaches to Global Optimization Problems Through Particle Swarm Optimization. Natural Computing 1 (2002) 235–306
8. W Z Lu, H Y Fan, S M Lo: Application of Evolutionary Neural Network Method in Predicting Pollutant Levels in Downtown Area of Hong Kong. Neurocomputing 51 (2003) 387 – 400

A Mobile Agent-Based P2P Autonomous Security Hole Discovery System

Ji Zheng[1], Xin Wang[2], Xiangyang Xue[3], and C.K. Toh[4]

[1] Software School, Fudan University, Shanghai, 200433, China
032053001@fudan.edu.cn
[2] Shanghai Key Laboratory of Intelligent Information Processing,
Fudan University, Shanghai, 200433, China
xinw@fudan.edu.cn
[3] Department of Computer Science and Engineering,
Fudan University, Shanghai, 200433, China
xyxue@fudan.edu.cn
[4] Dept. of Electronic Engineering, Queen Mary University of London
c.k.toh@elec.qmul.ac.uk

Abstract. A general or agent-based security system is usually constructed hierarchically and has a central manager acting as head of the whole system. However, the manager becomes a bottleneck for being connected by each client. It can even overload when too many clients request service simultaneously. The whole system may collapse when the central manager is attacked. And these systems are passive to detect and deal with the secure problem. Hereby we present a mobile agent-based P2P Autonomous Security Hole Discovery system (PASHD). It can detect infection and network intrusion based on knowledge of the local host. Viruses will be removed and connection will be refused after identification. In case of a suspicious activity, PASHD initiates a voting approach to make a collective decision and take further action. This system acts self-learning when encountering intrusion or infection with new patterns. And it has the capability of autonomous discovery the security hole of hosts in network. The integration of peer-to-peer behavior with mobile agents reduces latency and load; however, flexibility, effectivity, security and cooperation of the system are enhanced.

1 Introduction

The amount of information is growing incredibly nowadays, including almost everything: various data, files and documents, etc. In 1997 the web search engine-World Wide Web Worm had an index of 110,000 web pages [1] while www.google.com now claims to index more than a billion web sites and to support more than 220 file types [2]. At the same time, relevant security incidents such as unauthorized access, system intrusion and virus infection, occur more frequently. It becomes difficult to detect viruses and remove them since they turn more sophisticated and follow novel infecting patterns. Other unforeseen ways will certainly be employed in future security critical incidents. Moreover, the impact of a nefarious activity is extensive for it spreads quickly through a network and does severe harm to companies, organizations or even whole countries. For example, within 14 hours after the debut of its first copy, Code-red virus infected more than 359000 machines, at a rate of 2000 machines per minute at its peak [3]. In January 2003, the SQL Slammer worm spread out and within 10 minutes infected more than 90% of computers that were vulnerable [4].

How can we protect information from theft, destruction or misuse? There are some traditional methods to protect our information. Firewalls prevent unauthorized connection, and antivirus software detects corruptive files. Although some ways are explored to advance these technologies [5] [10], they are not perfect since they are only suitable for some situations. The former cannot distinguish appropriate activities from illegal ones. The latter only discovers the infected files and fixes them, but is incapable of preventing intrusion. An Intrusion Detection System (IDS) alerts the system administrator for potential attack within network environment so that the administrator takes appropriate action to avoid damage or loss. So it is regarded as a better paradigm in enterprise network. Intrusion detection technology is broadly studied for its advantages, and has developed quickly since proposed by James Anderson in 1980. Denning published an intrusion detection model seven years later. Subsequently, on this base some prototype systems were generated in the lab. With the development of distributed technology, IDS based on distributed technology was studied. The Information-technology Promotion Agency in Japan, Purdue University and Iowa State University had built their IDS based on agents or mobile agents [8] [9] [12]. They all have a manager at top level, which analyzes the information collected by agents at lower level residing on various hosts and takes relevant action. Geetha Ramachandran and Delbert Hart built a peer-to-peer (P2P) IDS based mobile agents [11]. They proposed a concept of "virtual neighbors" consisting of neighbor nodes. Mobile agents are periodically dispatched to neighbors for checking. In this paper we propose a mobile agent-based P2P Autonomous Security Hole Discovery system (PASHD). In PASHD mobile agents are only transferred in network when a suspicious activity is found. Otherwise, the host takes action according to its judgment based on the local knowledge library. And it has the capability of autonomous discovering secure problems in the network.

The remaining sections of this paper are organized as follows. Section 2 introduces the related work. Section 3 describes the architecture of PASHD and its work approaches. Section 4 gives the result of simulation on comparison between PASHD and traditional IDS. In Section 5 conclusions are drawn about PASHD.

2 Related Work

Autonomous Agents for Intrusion Detection (AAFID) [9] follows a hierarchy with root agents coordinating information, leaf agents collecting data and transceivers sending them back to root agents. These agents are lightweight components and are reconfigurable. The lowest leaf agents collect event information and report it to resident transceivers, which extract and reduce the data and then transmit it to the monitor above it. A monitor can manage and control many transceivers residing on various hosts.

The Information-technology Promotion Agency in Japan has developed a multi-hosts-IDS named after the Intrusion Detection Agent system (IDA) [8]. IDA watches suspicious events referred to as Marks Left by Suspected Intruder (MLSI). Agents roam among hosts involved in an intrusion incident in the network. If a sensor that resides inside the host searching for MLSIs finds a MLSI, the sensor gathers related information and reports to the top manager, which integrates and analyzes the information to decide whether or not a malicious act has occurred.

The first generation IDS based on agents has only two types of components. One collects data from the original host through monitoring packets in the network, and sends it to the other to simply analyze. They are static and are not scalable. AAFID and IDA are improved, which follow a hierarchical structure. Collected data are classified and reduced, then the relevant information is sent up to the top level component to analyze. The top manager decides whether the network is healthy or not.

Multi-Agent Intrusion Detection System (MAIDS) [12] is a prototype of IDS with lightweight mobile agents. Agents roam among monitored systems, obtain information from data cleaning agents, classify and extract information, and then transfer it up to a user interface and database via mediators. It emphasizes on cooperation of self-learning algorithm, data warehouse and mobile agents. The network load is reduced due to lightweight agents.

MA-IDS [7] is a distributed IDS with four components: Manager, Assistant MA, Response MA, and Monitor MA. If a certain monitored host detects an intrusion, the Monitor directly reports to the Manager on the local host. Otherwise, the Manager dispatches the Assistant MA to other monitored hosts to gather information when receiving request of the Monitor. The Manager analyzes gathered information to make the distributed intrusion identification. A Response MA is dispatched to each monitored host to take an intelligent action if a distributed intrusion is found.

Compared with AAFID and IDA, MAIDS and MA-IDS are enhanced to a certain extent. They are built in the architecture, which has monitors at low level to collect data and send it back to the central manager. Then the manager analyzes the suspicious activity and makes a decision on what action to respond, so it is vulnerability of the whole system. Although it's hard to directly attack the manager, the system is in a dangerous situation if hackers find and attempt to enter it. The unparalleled features of mobile agents such as autonomous, intelligent and continuous running are not taken full advantage of. Geetha Ramachandran and Delbert Hart try to build a peer-to-peer IDS based on mobile agents (IDSA), which uses "virtual neighbors" to find viruses and to prevent illegal intrusion [11]. "Virtual neighbors" are neighbor nodes as a unit to take collective actions on suspicious activities. When inconsistent or anomalous behaviors are observed, the observer-neighbor initiates a voting approach to take action against the compromised site. However, a node must keep some critical data and system configuration information of neighbors, and periodically dispatch agents to them. Periodic detection and frequent communication may result in network overload and have impact on the overall performance. The most important is that all these works only passively discover the fault of network. So we present PASHD without periodically dispatching agents between "Virtual neighbors", which only sends agents to the network when finding suspicious activities. It responses rapidly and autonomously processes security hole.

3 Architecture

PASHD chiefly consists of seven types of mobile agents, including Monitor, Executor, Controller, Coordinator, Voting-Agent, Result-Agent and Response-Agent. These components are classified into two groups: static and mobile agents. Monitor, Executor, Controller and Coordinator belong to the former. The latter includes Voting-Agent, Result-Agent and Response-Agent. Monitors reside on target hosts to watch all local activities. When a corruptive event happened and was found by a Monitor, it gathers relevant information and reports up to a Controller that analyzes the data to make a decision on what to do. If the Controller identifies the event as infection or intrusion, it will have an Executor clear the viruses or prevent the network from intrusion. Else, it extracts some key data and forwards it to a Coordinator. Then the Coordinator randomly selects some hosts from its host list to make an itinerary, and initiates a voting approach, which is applied to all hosts in the itinerary in order to monitor the suspicious incident and then make a distributed decision as a unit on whether it is illegal or not. If it is considered as vicious, the Coordinator dispatches Result-Agents to all other hosts in the group to raise the alarm level and to prepare for virus infection and network intrusion. It works as follows in Fig. 1.

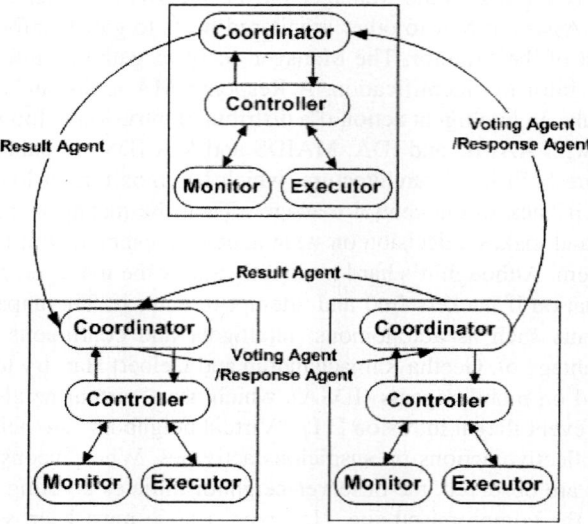

Fig. 1. Approach of voting and response

A node pretends to attack others and sends vicious agents to the network. So the whole system is running to acquire the attack characters, and then update all knowledge libraries. In this way, PASHD can autonomously detect the security hole of hosts.

3.1 Monitor

In PASHD there are various monitors watching all critical activities such as file operation, privilege access and network connection. Each type of monitor is in charge of a specific task. For instance:

1. To monitor critical system files and execute files. It informs its supervisor Controller if it finds suspicious incidents.
2. To look for signatures of viruses in files.
3. To collate the sizes of files with stored ones, if there is a change of a certain file, the system will pay special attention to it.
4. To find unauthorized connections

As a whole, the monitor is a primary unit of PASHD to find problems.

3.2 Executor

The Executor is also a primary agent in PASHD, which is responsible for executing tasks coming from the Controller above it. These tasks include erasing viruses, fixing files, refusing privilege operation or connection request, and disconnecting network. There are various kinds of Executors, and each does a kind of task. There are 3 primary types of Executors as follows:

1. to clear viruses
2. to restore files
3. to prevent network connection

3.3 Controller

The Controller is a medium component between Executor, Monitor and Coordinator. It integrates and analyzes the data reported by Monitors to make a decision on the security incident. If there is an infection or intrusion, it will dispatch a command to the Executor to separate corrupt files, remove viruses or refuse network connections. Otherwise the Controller will inform the Coordinator to make sure that the incident is malicious and the alarm level of PASHD will rise. Then the Coordinator will launch a voting approach to reach a decision. Instead of storing information on neighbor hosts as in IDSA, each host has a local knowledge library which stores important configuration information of the local host, sizes of files, patterns of network attack, signatures of viruses, etc. The Coordinator updates the library when gaining new security knowledge by a voting approach, which is called self-learning. Furthermore, each activity of security is assigned a certain weight. The Controller changes the weight of a suspicious activity dynamically according to frequency of occurrence over a certain time range, which is specified by the agent who notified this host. The weight rises with the increasing frequency of an activity, otherwise it drops. However, the weight changes without geometric proportion, which rises more and more quickly with the increasing frequency of the incident. For example, the weight collection may be $\{\ldots 1/16, 1/15, 1/14, 1/12, 1/10, 1/8, 1/4, 1/2, 1\}$. The weight is added up to $1/10$ when a certain frequency is arrived. The next weight is $1/8$, then $1/4$, $1/2$, and the last is 1, which is the threshold here. Otherwise, the weight is degressive in the reverse direction. When it exceeds the threshold, PASHD identifies it as an infection or intrusion. Of course, it is not easy to distinguish normal activities from malicious ones. The administrator can correct it if something wrong happened.

3.4 Coordinator

As the name implies, the Coordinator coordinates PASHDs in the group. It initiates voting to arrive at a decision when informed by the Monitor that there is a suspicious incident. First a Coordinator makes an itinerary by randomly selecting hosts from its host list. The itinerary includes the number of destination hosts, IP addresses of hosts and source address of the incident. The information consists of the time, the type and the characteristic of .the incident. Then the agent is dispatched to hosts one by one according to the itinerary. A Result-Agent with a voting paper is sent back to the original Coordinator, which adds up all voting papers with YES-vote. If 2/3 is exceeded, the incident is regarded as dangerous. The Coordinator is in charge of informing all hosts in the group by Response-Agents to take action, and new knowledge is stored in the library via the Controller. When a Coordinator dispatches Response-Agents to other hosts, there are two patterns to choose: master-slave and sequential. The former is a pattern where a master can delegate a task split between two computers to a slave. While the slave is away doing its task, the master can continue with its task until the result of its task is sent back. The latter is a pattern where the itinerary is separated from agents. The same itinerary can be plugged into different agents while the code of agent needs no modifying [6]. Moreover, the Response-Agent takes a task specified by one of three execution strategies: immediately, when idle or per x minutes (x is set by system administrator). Of course, the PASHD can refuse to comply with the strategy carried by a Response-Agent. Whether or not to execute is determined by the system configuration.

3.5 Voting-Agent

The main goal of Voting-Agent is to inform some hosts in the group to make a collective decision on a suspicious incident. There are five chief parts in a Voting-agent: voting sequence no, source address, the itinerary, characteristics of the incident, vote ('Yes' or 'No'), times of report and time to life (TTL). The Voting-agent will be dissolved when it finishes its task or when TTL is reached.

3.6 Result-Agent

A Result-Agent with a voting paper is going to be sent back to the original host where a suspicious incident is found after a certain time. It is encrypted for security reason. The Coordinator adds up all voting papers to make a final decision whether it is malicious activity or not.

Seq No	Src	Itinerary	Characteristics	Times	Vote	TTL

Fig. 2. Format of Voting sheet carried by Voting-Agent

3.7 Response-Agent

After identification of infection or intrusion, Response-Agents are dispatched to all hosts in the group. Each PASHD host receiving this agent will take appropriate action to prevent viruses' infection or network intrusion.

4 Simulation and Analysis

The main principle for computer security is preventing any infection or intrusion. The next is preventing infection spreading, and the last is identifying the area that has been already infected. So it is a key factor for the antivirus software and IDS to detect infection or intrusion and take action as early as possible. Low latency will improve the performance of IDS. A reduction of communication in the network will do, too. We did a simulation in Java to study the latency and communication of traditional IDS, MAIDS, IDSA and PASHD. The network topology is randomly generated, and the host where a security incident occurs and the host owning the manager in traditional IDS and MAIDS are also randomly selected from all hosts. Let's consider the scenario: a certain host is infected and detected, it is reported to the central manager first in traditional IDS and MAIDS, and then the Manager informs all hosts to take action. In IDSA and PASHD this host directly notifies all other hosts. We define the range from the time that incident occurs, till the time when all hosts took action as the total latency of the whole system. All communications including reporting and giving notices are defined as the total load of the whole system. The average latency is the value that the total latency divides the number of nodes involved in the voting approach, and the average load is the value that the total load divides the number of nodes involved in the voting.

It is assumed that those hosts in close range to each other will be arranged together in the itinerary and that periodically dispatching mobile agents to neighbors only happens once in IDSA. Fig. 3 and Fig. 4 show the total latency and total load of the whole system. Fig. 5 and Fig. 6 show the average latency and load.

Conclusions are drawn as follows from Figures 3 and Figure 4:

1. The total latency and total load of IDS, MAIDS, IDSA and PASHD are increased with the rising number of hosts
2. Compared with IDS, the total latency of MAIDS, IDSA and PASHD increases gradually with rising number of network nodes. When there are 5 nodes in the network, the total latency of them are almost the same. However, when there are 10, 15, and 20 nodes, the total latency of IDS based on agent is 65%, 60%, 45% of that of IDS respectively. It is obvious that IDS based on mobile agents would be more effective.
3. The total latency of PASHD is lower than that of IDS, MAIDS and IDSA. So it can take action earlier than others when encountering infection or intrusion.
4. The total load of PASHD is the lowest of all. Although we assume that periodically dispatching agents to neighbors only happens once, the total load of IDSA is higher approximately 50% than that of others. It will have a bad influence on its performance.

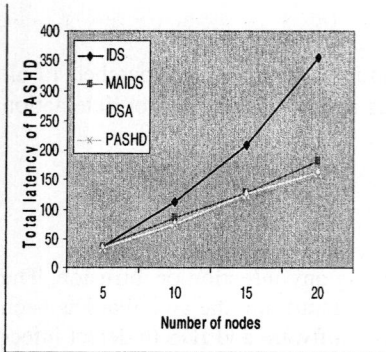 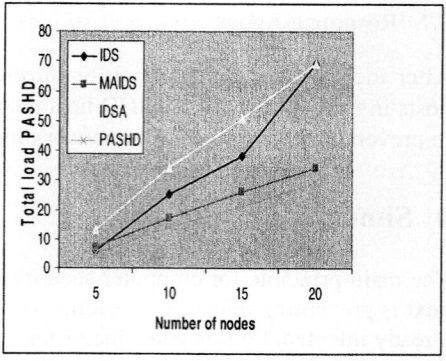

Fig. 3. Total latency of IDS, MAIDS, IDSA and PASHD

Fig. 4. Total load of IDS, MAIDS, IDSA and PASHD

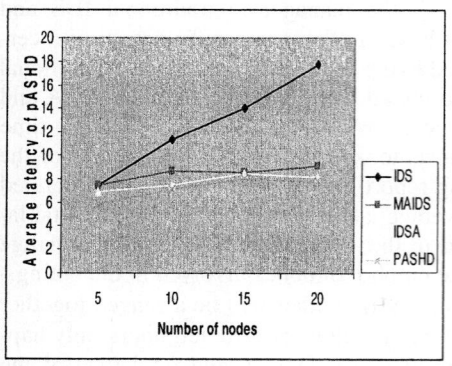 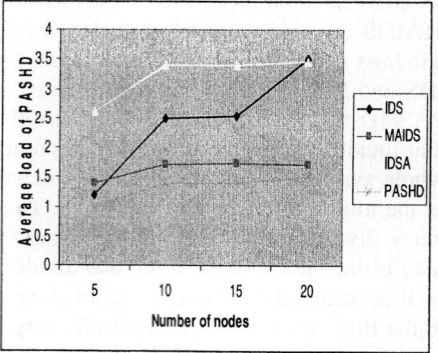

Fig. 5. The average latency of IDS, MAIDS, IDSA and PASHD

Fig. 6. The average load of IDS, MAIDS, IDSA and PASHD

Like above, again Figures 5 and Figure 6 are almost the same. So as far as the average latency and load are concerned, we arrive at similar conclusions.

1. The average latency and load of IDS, MAIDS, IDSA and PASHD are increased with the rising number of hosts
2. Compared with IDS, the average latencies of MAIDS, IDSA and PASHD rises gradually with the rising number of network nodes. The average latencies of MAIDS, IDSA and PASHD are approximately 65%, 60% and 45% of that of IDS when the number of nodes in the network is 10, 15, and 20 respectively. Again it is obvious that IDS based on mobile agents is more suitable for large-scale network than traditional IDS.
3. The average latency of PASHD is lower than that of others. It is more effective for taking action earlier than others when encountering infection or intrusion.
4. The average latency of IDSA is close to that of PASHD and that of MAIDS. However, the load of PASHD is 50% lower than that of IDSA.

In a word, PASHD does well in latency and overhead. Its average latency and load rise gradually with the number of nodes rising, so it is suitable for the large-scale network. The performance of MAIDS seems to be similar to that of PASHD. However, the architectures of them are essentially different. By using distributive detection approach for monitoring critical information, it is harder for someone to compromise the data and thereby affect the whole system. In PASHD all hosts are peer-to-peer and without the central host, so it is not easy to collapse when attacked.

5 Conclusion

Integrating peer-to-peer behavior with mobile agents, the flexibility, extensibility, security and cooperation ability of PASHD are enhanced. It uses a knowledge library including critical information about the system and signatures of viruses on the local host. It only launches voting approaches to reach a cooperative decision when a suspicious event occurs. Otherwise, PASHD makes decisions about infection or intrusion depending on its local knowledge library instead of being periodically checked by its neighbors. Thus the latency and load of the network is reduced and fault-tolerance is increased. When compared with IDSA, overhead is successfully dropped with low latency at the same time in PASHD. The library of PASHD can be updated by itself through voting. A Response-Agent roaming in network according to its itinerary skips a host, which is inactive and cannot be reached. The host will be recorded by sending back an agent to the original host, which initiates a Response-Agent with that same task again when it reboots.

For the asynchronous nature and continuity of mobile agents, the network needn't be active when mobile agents are sent out for work. An agent can wait until the network turns active before it returns. PASHD based on mobile agents works well in high latency links (i.e. slow networks). Agents are transferred on ATP, which is modeled on top of the HTTP protocol, so PASHD can scale to wide area networks, too.

Otherwise, PASHD can send testing agent to other hosts to detect the fault of the whole system. So it owns the ability to autonomously discover the security hole of network and remedy it.

There is much further work to improve the performance of PASHD. More Monitors, Executors need to be developed to detect intrusion with unexpected patterns and viruses with unknown signatures.

This work was supported in part by 863-2002AA103011-5, Shanghai Municipal R&D Foundation under contracts 035107008, MoE R&D Foundation and Shanghai Key Laboratory of Intelligent Information Processing (IIPL).

References

1. Brin S., Page L., "The anatomy of a large-scale hypertextual web search engine", In Proceedings of the 7 International World Wide Web Conference, Brisbane, Australia, 1997, vol.3, ACM Press.
2. www.google.com/why_use.html
3. David Moore, Colleen Shannon. The spread of the code-red worm (CRv2), July 2001

4. D. Moore, V. Paxson, S. Savage, C. Shannon, S.Staniford, and N. Weaver. Inside the Slammer Worm. IEEE Security and Privacy, 1(4):33-39, July 2003.
5. Mihai Christodorescu and Somesh Jha. Static analysis of executables to detect malicious patterns. In Proc. of the 12th USENIX Security Symp., Washington, DC, August 2003.
6. http://www.trl.ibm.com/aglets/documentation_e.htm
7. C. Li, Q. Song, C. Zhang, "MA-IDS Architecture for Distributed Intrusion Detection using Mobile Agents", Proc. of the 2nd International Conference on Information Technology for Application (ICITA 2004), 2004, 451-455.
8. http://www.ipa.go.jp/STC/IDA/paper/ida-client-install-e.pdf
9. Balasubramaniyan,j.,Carcia-Fernandez,J.O.,Isacoff,D.,Spafford,E.H., and Zamboni, D. An Architecture for Intrusion Detection using Autonomous Agents, Department of Computer Science, Purdue University: Coast TR, 98-05, 1998
10. 10.B. Hickman, D. Newman, S. Tadjudin, and T. P. Martin. Benchmarking Methodology for Firewall Performance. Internet Engineering Task Force, RFC 3511, April 2003.
11. Geetha Ramachandran, Delbert Hart. A P2P Intrusion Detection System based on Mobile agents. Proceedings of the 42nd annual Southeast regional conference citation 2004, Huntsville, Alabama April 02 - 03, 2004.
12. Helmer, G., Wong, J., Honavar, V., Miller , L. and Wang, Y.. Lightweight Agents for Intrusion Detection. Journal of Systems and Software. Elsevier. PP.109-122, 2003.

A Modified Clustering Algorithm Based on Swarm Intelligence[1]

Lei Zhang[1], Qixin Cao[1], and Jay Lee[2]

[1] State Key Laboratory of Vibration, Shock & Noise,
Shanghai Jiao Tong Univ., 200030, Shanghai, China
{Lei Zhang, zhanglei75}@sina.com,
{Qixin Cao, qxcao}@sjtu.edu.cn
[2] NSF I/UCR Center for Intelligent Maintenance Systems,
Univ. of Cincinnati, OH 45221, USA
{Jay Lee, jay, lee}@uc.edu

Abstract. A modified clustering algorithm based on swarm intelligence (MSIC) is proposed in this paper. To improve the running efficiency of the SIC algorithm, the random projection of the patterns into the plane is modified. The patterns are firstly analyzed by principal component analysis (PCA) and the first two principal components (PCs) are retained. The patterns are projected into the plane according to their corresponding PCs, which are processed as the projection coordinates. This modification ensures that the pattern will be similar to the ones in its local surroundings and the rough clustering has been formed at the beginning time of the algorithm. Moreover, to reduce the influence of the parameters on the algorithm, a simple way to calculate the swarm similarity of the pattern is presented. The adjusting formula of the similarity threshold is also proposed. Finally, the modified algorithm is compared with the original one and the results prove the efficiency has been improved significantly.

1 Introduction

Swarm Intelligence is one kind of intelligent behavior shown by the cooperation of collective insects, such as ants and bees. Swarm Intelligence Clustering (SIC) is a clustering algorithm imitating the behavior of ants. Researchers have found that some ants can pick up the dead bodies randomly distributed in the nests and group them with different sizes. The large group of bodies attracts the ant workers to deposit more dead bodies and becomes larger and larger. The essence of this phenomenon is a positive feedback [1]. Deneubourg etc [2] gave the basic model to explain it, which was called BM model. Lumer and Faieta [3] extended the model and applied it in data analysis. In their analysis, the data object with n attributes can be looked as a point in n dimensional space. The point in the R^n space is projected into a low dimensional space (often a two dimensional plane). The similarity of the data object with other

---

[1] Supported by the National Natural Science Foundations of China under grant No. 50128504 and No.60443007.

ones in local surroundings is calculated to decide whether the object should be picked up or dropped. Wu[4] studied the SIC algorithm systematically. He defined some important concepts such as swarm similarity, similarity coefficient and probability conversion function. He also suggested a more simple probability conversion function to reduce the dependence of the algorithm on the parameters.

Compared with other clustering algorithms, such as k-means clustering, the SIC algorithm can find the number of clustering centers self-organizationally. The visualization and robustness of the algorithm are also very distinct. The parallel property built in the algorithm makes it very suitable to the clustering of big data sets. But the SIC algorithm also has some disadvantages. For example, its running efficiency is not high and there are no theories to guide the selections of the parameters [5]. To solve these problems, a modified SCI algorithm is proposed in this paper. First, Principal Component Analysis (PCA) is suggested to reduce the randomicity when the patterns are projected into the plane. Namely, the patterns are processed by PCA, then the first two principal components (PCs) are retained and processed as the pattern's projection coordinates. This pro-processing ensures that the patterns close in the R^n space are also close in the projection plane. So the pattern is of high similarity with others in its local surroundings at the beginning of the algorithm. Moreover, the similarity of the pattern is calculated by a more simple way, which reduces the influence of the parameters on the algorithm.

The paper is organized as follows. The SIC algorithm is introduced in section 2. Then the modified SIC algorithm is proposed in section 3. The simulation and the comparison of SIC and MSIC algorithm are shown in section 4. Finally the conclusion is given in section 5.

2   The Swarm Intelligence Clustering Algorithm (SIC)

Some important concepts in the SIC algorithm are firstly introduced as follows [4,5].

> Local surroundings: it is a neighboring region of one pattern, which is often a circle region. The center of the circle is the point of the pattern's coordinates and the radius is r.
> Swarm similarity: the integrated similarity of the pattern with other patterns in its local surroundings. The similarity is usually measured by the distance between the patterns.
> Probability conversion function: it is a function that converts the swarm similarity into the probability of picking up or dropping the pattern by the ant.

In the SIC algorithm, the patterns which are going to be clustered are projected into a two-dimensional plane randomly. Then the ant calculates the swarm similarity of the pattern with others in its local surroundings. And the swarm similarity will be turned into the probability to pick up or drop the pattern through the probability conversion function. The patterns can be clustered after many cycles via the actions of the ant swarm.

The swarm similarity is calculated by the following formula,

$$f(O_i) = \sum_{O_j \in Neigh(r)} [1 - \frac{d(O_i, O_j)}{\alpha}] \quad (1)$$

Where, $Neigh(r)$ represents the local surroundings of the pattern O_i, which is a circle region with the radius r. $d(O_i, O_j)$ is the distance between the pattern O_i and O_j, and usually Euclidean distance is preferred. α is the swarm similarity coefficient, which has an important influence on the number of the clustering centers and the speed of the algorithm.

The probability conversion function converts the swarm similarity into the probability of picking up or dropping the patterns by the ant. In the reference [4], a more simple probability conversion function than that in BM was applied, which is shown in the formula (2) and (3).

$$P_p = \begin{cases} 1 - \varepsilon & f(O_i) \leq 0 \\ 1 - k \times f(O_i) & 0 < f(O_i) \leq 1/k \\ 0 + \varepsilon & f(O_i) \geq 1/k \end{cases} \quad (2)$$

$$P_d = 1 - P_p \quad (3)$$

Where, P_p, P_d are the probabilities of picking up and dropping the pattern respectively. ε is a little real number. P_p, P_d are compared with the threshold P_r to decide whether the patter should be picked up or dropped. Only the parameter k is needed to choose properly after the simplicity rather than k_1 and k_2 in the BM algorithm[2]. So the parameters are simplified. But there is still no theoretical guidance to determine the value of k in the practical application.

The process of SIC algorithm can be referred the document [5] and [6]. The terminating condition of the algorithm has two cases: one is up to the maximum cycle times, the other is no pattern is moved again. The former one is usually applied because the latter is complex in computation.

3 The Modified Swarm Intelligence Clustering Algorithm (MSIC)

To improve the efficiency and simplify the parameters of the SIC algorithm, a modified algorithm is proposed as follows.

3.1 Modifying the Random Projection of the Patterns Based on PCA

At the beginning time of SIC algorithm, the patterns are projected into the plane randomly and one pattern is corresponded with a pair of coordinates. Because the coordinates is randomly selected, the similarity of the pattern with the ones in its local surroundings is very low. This will induce that the pattern is easily picked up but not easily dropped by the ant. Therefore, it will take a long time from the beginning to the time when the pattern is similar to the ones near it.

How to keep the patterns close after the projection if they are close in the R^n space? We suggest that the patterns should be pre-processed by principal component analysis (PCA). Then the first two principal components (PCs) are retained and processed. According to the principles of PCA [7], the first two PCs can remain the most information of original patterns. If the patterns are projected corresponding with the coordinates composed by the processed two PCs, it will be ensured that the patterns near in the R^n space will be near in the projection plane. As a result, the rough clustering of the patterns has been formed at the beginning time of the modified algorithm. This result is the similar as that of the SIC algorithm after many cycles, so the running time is reduced significantly.

How to process the PCs will be introduced detailed in sections 4.

3.2 Modifying the Formula of Swarm Similarity

The similarity of the pattern is computed as the formula (1) in the SIC algorithm, where the similarity coefficient will influence on the number of the clustering centers as well as the speed of the algorithm. If α is too large, the patterns which are not similar will be clustered together. If α is too small, the patterns which are similar will be clustered into different groups. In the reference [4], Wu suggested that α should be changed with the cycles increasing. But there is no theory to guide how to change it. The change of α is various at different applications, so it is difficult to determine it properly. In addition, the probability conversion function is calculated as the formula (2) and (3), where the parameter k has an important influence on the probability. But how to select k is also a problem.

To avoid the influence of α and k on the clustering results, a more simple similarity computing method is presented. From the formula (1), it can be seen that the essence to measuring the similarity is the distance between the patterns. Therefore, the similarity is represented directly by the distance between the patterns in this paper. The similarity of the pattern O_i with others is.

$$f(O_i) = \frac{1}{n} \sum_{O_j \in Neigh(r)} d(O_i, O_j) \qquad (4)$$

Where, n is the number of the patterns in the local surroundings of the pattern O_i. The means of other signs are the same as those in formula (1). The larger $f(O_i)$ is, the smaller the pattern O_i 's similarity is.

Dissimilar to the SIC algorithm, the MSIC algorithm doesn't apply the probability conversion function. The threshold of the similarity F is set, and $f(O_i)$ is compared with F to determine whether the pattern is picked up or dropped. This simple way is easily computed and avoiding the influence of k on the algorithm. Because the distances of the patterns are large at the beginning time of the clustering, F should be set a large value. With the increasing of the cycles, $f(O_i)$ will be decreased, so F should be reduced correspondingly. The adjusting formula of F in the MSIC algorithm is

$$F(t) = \begin{cases} F(t) & \text{if } \mod(t,500) \neq 0 \\ kF(t) & \text{otherwise} \end{cases} \qquad (5)$$

Where, k is a real number smaller than 1. t is the number of cycles The formula (5) means $F(t)$ will be reduced per 500 cycles. "500 cycles" is a relative concept, which influences the reducing speed of $F(t)$ as well as k. These two parameters can be adjusted according to the changing speed of the similarity.

3.3 The Process of MSIC Algorithm

The detailed process of the MSIC algorithm is as follows.
    Algorithm: the MSIC algorithm
    Inputs: The patterns waiting to be clustered
    Outputs: The clustered patterns or the centers of the clustered groups
    Process: 1: The initialization of all parameters: cycle_number (the maximum cycle times); ant_number (the number of the ants), the radius r; the initial threshold of the similarity $F(1)$; the adjusting parameter of the similarity threshold k.
          2: The patterns are processed by PCA, and the first two PCs are retained. Then the PCs are processed as the coordinates and the patterns are projected into the plane according to its processed PCs.
          3: Set the initial patterns and set the coordinates of the patterns to the ants. The initial load states of the ants are without any load.
          4: for i=1:cycle_number
             4.1 for j=1:ant_number
                  4.1.1 take the coordinates of the ant as the center, r as the radius, calculate the similarity f of the ant's pattern in its local surroundings by the formula (4)
                  4.1.2 if load_ant(j)=0, compare f with the threshold $F(i)$. If $f \leq F(i)$☐the ant picks up the pattern and the ant's load is set to 1, namely load_ant(j)=1. Otherwise, the ant doesn't pick up the pattern and new pattern and corresponding coordinates are set to the ant.
                  4.1.3 If load_ant(j)=1, compare f with the threshold $F(i)$. If $f>F(i)$, the ant drops the pattern and the current coordinates of the ant are set to the pattern. load_ant(j)=0. Then a new pattern and its coordinates are set to the ant randomly. Otherwise, the ant doesn't drop the pattern and new coordinates are set to the ant again.
            End j (up to the maximum number of the ants)
            4.2 Calculate the threshold F(i) by the formula (5)
          End i (up to the maximum number of the cycles)
          5: Calculate the clustering center of all groups and output the clustered

4 The Comparison of MSIC and SIC Algorithms

To compare the performance of SIC and MSIC algorithms, the data in the reference [4] is analyzed by the MSIC algorithm. The experiment data is from the machine learning database of the website http://www.ics.uci.edu/~mlearn/MLRepository.html. It is the data of the iris. The number of the items in the data set is 150 and each item has 4 attributes. The number of classes is 3.

The parameters in two algorithms are listed in the table 1. It can be seen that the MSIC algorithm avoids the influence of the parameters α and k, which may be selected improperly.

Table 1. The comparison of two algorithms

Parameters	SIC algorithm	MSIC algorithm
The maximum cycle times	60000	10000
The number of ants:	6	6
The size of the projection plane	480×450	80×80
The radius	$r=20$	$r=5$
The similarity coefficient	$\alpha =0.4-0.3$	\
Others	$k=0.1$ (in the formula 2)	$k=0.95$ (in the formula 5)
Others	P_r (not mentioned)	$F(1)=1.8$

In the MSIC algorithm, the patterns are firstly analyzed by PCA and the first two PCs are retained. The two PCs remain about 97.76 percent of the information of original data. Then the PCs are processed as follows:

(1) Enlarging: Because the PCs are very small, they are multiplied by 10 to be distinguished easily.
(2) Rounding
(3) Shifting: Finding the minimums of the fist PC and the second PC respectively. Subtracting the minimums from the pair of PCs and the last processed values are obtained.

The two PCs after the processing are taken as the projection coordinates of the pattern (The first PC as x-coordinate and the second PC as y-coordinate). The aim of these processing is making the coordinates of the patterns distributed in the first quadrant and identified easily.

The projections of the patterns at the beginning of the algorithms are shown in the Fig. 1. We apply three signs to identify different classes. It can be seen from (a) in Fig.1, the patterns are randomly distributed in the projection plane in the SIC algorithm. While in (b) of Fig. 1, some patterns have been divided from others after they are projected according to their processed PCs. Especially the patterns of the class one (signed as *) are distinct from other two classes. The projection way in the MSIC algorithm ensures that the rough clustering has been formed at the beginning of the algorithm, which is similar as the result of the SIC algorithm after several hundreds or thousands of cycles.

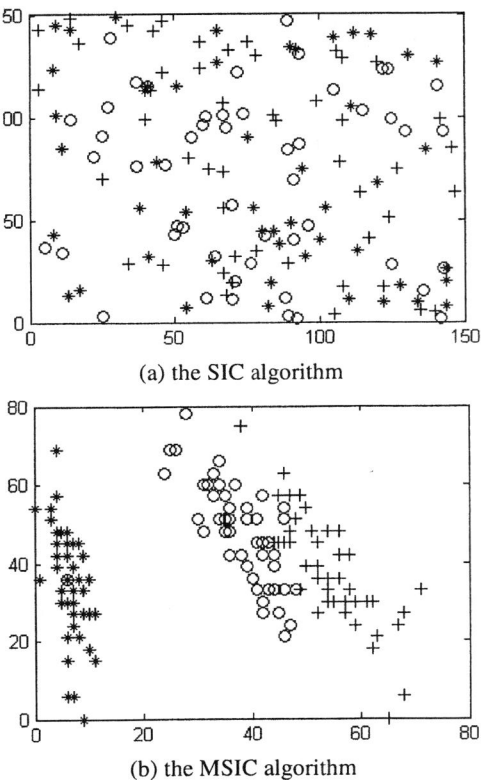

Fig. 1. The projection of the patterns in two algorithms

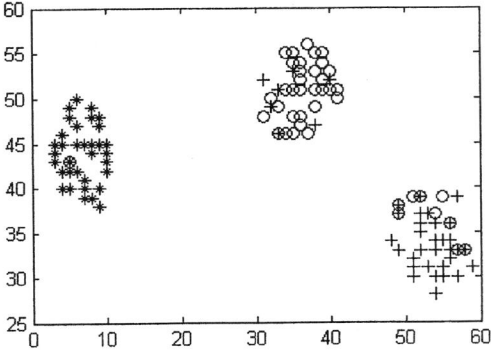

Fig. 2. The clustering result of the MSIC algorithm

In this sample, the MSIC algorithm will cluster the patterns into three classes after about 8000-10000 cycles while the SIC algorithm needs 60000 cycles. If the parameters in the two algorithms, such as the number of the ants, are the same, the running efficiency of the algorithm is dependent mainly on the number of cycles. So the running time of the MSIC algorithm is reduced. The clustering results of the MSIC algorithm are shown in the Fig 2. The average accuracy is 90.3 percent which has no big difference with 90 percent of the SIC algorithm in the reference [4].

5 Conclusions

This paper focuses on a modified clustering algorithm based on swarm intelligence (MSIC). To improve the efficiency of the SIC algorithm, PCA is suggested to reduce the randomicity when the patterns are projected into the plane. The first two PCs of the pattern are processed as the corresponding projection coordinates. This projection way ensures the running time of the algorithm can be reduced because the rough clustering has been formed. Moreover, a simple way to calculate the similarity based on the distance between the patterns is presented and the adjusting formula of the similarity threshold is given. The comparison results of the MSIC algorithm and the SIC algorithm prove the running efficiency of the MSIC algorithm is improved. In the MSIC algorithm, how to measure the swarm similarity more properly and how to adjust the similarity threshold need to be further studied.

References

1. Marco D., Eric B., Guy T. Ant Algorithms and Stigmercy. Future Generation Computer System, 16(2000)851-871
2. Deneubourg J. L., Goss S., Frank N., etc. The Dynamics of Collective Sorting: Robot-like Ants and Ant-like Robots. In: Proceedings of the 1st International Conference on Simulation of Adaptive Behavior: From Animals to Animats. MIT Press/Bradford Books, Cambridge, MA, (1991)356-363
3. Lumer E., Faieta B. Diversity and Adaptation in Populations of Clustering Ants. In: Processing of the 3rd International Conference on Simulation of Adaptive Behavior: From Animals to Animats. MIT Press/Bradford Books, Cambridge, MA, (1994)501-508
4. Bin W. Research on Swarm Intelligence and Its Application in Knowledge Discovery. Ph.D. Thesis, Institute of Computing Technology, Chinese Academy of Science, Beijing. (2002) 40-47
5. Bin W., Yi Z., Wei-peng F., etc. A Customer Behavior Analysis Algorithm Based on Swarm Intelligence. Chinese Journal of Computers, Vol.26 No.8 (2003)913□918
6. Bin W., Zhong-zhi S. A Clustering Algorithm Based on Swarm Intelligence. International Conference on Info-tech and Info-net (ICII 2001), Beijing, 29 Oct.-1 Nov. Vol.3 (2001)58-66
7. Partridge M., Rafael A.C. Fast Dimensionality Reduction and Simple PCA. Intelligent Data Analysis. 2(1998)203-210

Parameter Selection of Quantum-Behaved Particle Swarm Optimization

Jun Sun, Wenbo Xu, and Jing Liu

School of Information Technology, Southern Yangtze University,
No. 1800, Lihudadao Road, Wuxi, Jiangsu 214036, China
sunjun_wx@hotmail.com

Abstract. Particle Swarm Optimization (PSO) is a population-based evolutionary search technique, which has comparable performance with Genetic algorithm. The existing PSOs, however, are not global-convergence-guaranteed algorithms, because the evolution equation of PSO, make the particle only search in a finite sampling space. In [10,11], a Quantum-behaved Particle Swarm Optimization algorithm is proposed that outperforms traditional PSOs in search ability as well as having less parameter. This paper focuses on discussing how to select parameter when QPSO is practically applied. After the QPSO algorithm is described, the experiment results of stochastic simulation are given to show how the selection of the parameter value influences the convergence of the particle in QPSO. Finally, two parameter control methods are presented and experiment results on the benchmark functions testify their efficiency.

1 Introduction

Particle Swarm Optimization (PSO), originally proposed by J. Kennedy and R. Eberhart [5], has become a most fascinating branch of evolutionary computation. The underlying motivation for the development of PSO algorithm was social behavior of animals such as bird flocking, fish schooling, and swarm theory. Like genetic algorithm (GA), PSO is a population-based random search technique but that outperforms GA in many practical applications, particularly in nonlinear optimization problems. In the Standard PSO model, each individual is treated as a volume-less particle in the D-dimensional space, with the position and velocity of ith particle represented as $X_i = (X_{i1}, X_{i2}, \cdots, X_{iD})$ and $V_i = (V_{i1}, V_{i2}, \cdots, V_{iD})$. The particles move according to the following equation:

$$V_{id} = w * V_{id} + c_1 * rand(\cdot) * (P_{id} - X_{id}) + c_2 * Rand(\cdot) * (P_g - X_{id}) \tag{1a}$$

$$X_{id} = X_{id} + V_{id} \tag{1b}$$

where c_1 and c_2 are positive constant and rand() and Rand() are two random functions in the range of [0,1]. Parameter w is the inertia weight introduced to accelerate the convergence speed of the PSO. Vector $P_i = (P_{i1}, P_{i2}, \cdots, P_{iD})$ is the best previous position (the position giving the best fitness value) of particle i called **pbest**, and vector $P_g = (P_{g1}, P_{g2}, \cdots, P_{gD})$ is the position of the best particle among all the particles in the population and called **gbest**.

Since the origin of PSO, many researchers have been devoted to improving its performance, and therefore, many revised versions of PSO have been proposed, among which the most important are those proposed in ([8], [4], [1], [9], [6], [7], [2]). These various improved versions, generally speaking, can enhance the convergence performance and the search ability of PSO considerably. However, the evolution equation (1) that these PSO algorithms are based on cannot guarantee the algorithm to find out the global optimum with probability 1, that is, SPSO is not a global optimization algorithm, as F. van den Bergh has demonstrated [3]. In the previous work presented in [10] and [11], we proposed a global convergence-guaranteed search technique, Quantum-behaved Particle Swarm Optimization algorithm, whose performance is superior to the Standard PDO (SPSO) and PSO with contractor.

The purpose of this paper is to discuss how to select the parameter of ensure that the QPSO has a good performance. The rest part of the paper is organized as follows. In Section 2, the ideology of QPSO is formulated in detail. In Section 3, some experiment result of stochastic simulation is presented to show how to select the parameter to guarantee the convergence of the individual particle. Two methods of parameter control are proposed, one of which is adaptive control approach. The experiment results of the two methods on benchmark functions are given in Section 4. And the paper is concluded in Section 5.

2 Quantum-Behaved Particle Swarm Optimization

In Quantum-behaved Particle Swarm Optimization (QPSO), the particle moves according to the following equation:

$$mbest = \frac{1}{M}\sum_{i=1}^{M} P_i = \left(\frac{1}{M}\sum_{i=1}^{M} P_{i1}, \frac{1}{M}\sum_{i=1}^{M} P_{i2}, \cdots, \frac{1}{M}\sum_{i=1}^{M} P_{id}\right) \qquad (2a)$$

$$p_{id} = \varphi * P_{id} + (1-\varphi) * P_{gd}, \quad \varphi = rand() \qquad (2b)$$

$$X_{id} = p_{id} \pm \alpha * |mbest_d - X_{id}| * \ln(1/u), \quad u = Rand() \qquad (2c)$$

where *mbest* is the mean best position among the particles. p_{id}, a stochastic point between P_{id} and P_{gd}, is the local attractor on the *d*th dimension of the *i*th particle, φ is a random umber distributed uniformly on [0,1], u is another uniformly-distributed random number on [0,1] and α is a parameter of QPSO that is called Contraction-Expansion Coefficient. The Quantum-behaved Particle Swarm Optimization (QPSO) Algorithm in [11] is described as follows.

(1) Initialize an array of particles with random position and velocities inside the problem space.
(2) Determine the mean best position among the particles by

$$mbest = \frac{1}{M}\sum_{i=1}^{M} P_i = \left(\frac{1}{M}\sum_{i=1}^{M} P_{i1}, \frac{1}{M}\sum_{i=1}^{M} P_{i2}, \cdots, \frac{1}{M}\sum_{i=1}^{M} P_{id}\right)$$

(3) Evaluate the desired objective function (for example minimization) for each particle and compare with the particle's previous best values: If the current value is less than the previous best value, then set the best value to the current value. That is, if $f(X_i) < f(P_i)$, then $X_i = P_i$.

(4) Determine the current global position minimum among the particle's best positions. That is: $g = \arg\min_{1 \le i \le M}(f(P_i))$ (M is the population size).

(5) Compare the current global position to the previous global: if the current global position is less than the previous global position; then set the global position to the current global.

(6) For each dimension of the particle, get a stochastic point between P_{id} and P_{gd}:

$$p_{id} = \varphi * P_{id} + (1-\varphi) * P_{gd}, \quad \varphi = rand()$$

(7) Attain the new position by stochastic equation:

$$X_{id} = p_{id} \pm \alpha * |mbest_d - X_{id}| * \ln(1/u), \quad u = Rand()$$

(8) Repeat steps (2)-(7) until a stop criterion is satisfied OR a pre-specified number of iterations are completed.

The stochastic evolution equation comes from a quantum δ potential well model proposed in [10]. By establishing a δ potential well on point p_{id} for each dimension to prevent the particle from explosion, we can get the particle's probability distribution in space

$$D(X_{id} - p_{id}) = \frac{1}{L} e^{-2|X_{id} - p_{id}|/L} \tag{3}$$

where L, which is relevant to mass of the particle and the intensity of the potential, is characteristic length of the distribution function. In practice, L is the most important variable in this model and determines the probable search scope of the individual particle.

Through Monte Carlo Anti-transformation, we can get following stochastic equation

$$X_{id} = p_{id} \pm \frac{L}{2} \ln(1/u), \quad u = Rand() \tag{4}$$

where u is random number uniformly distributed on $(0,1)$.

There two approaches of evaluating the variable L. In [10], L is evaluated by the gap between the particle's current position and point p_{id}. That is

$$L = 2 * \alpha * |p_{id} - X_{id}| \tag{5}$$

and thus equation (5) can be written as

$$X_{id} = p_{id} \pm \alpha * |p_{id} - X_{id}| * \ln(1/u) \tag{6}$$

where α is the only parameter of the algorithm. The PSO with evolution equation (6) is called Quantum Delta-Potential-Well-based Particle Swarm Optimization (QDPSO).

In [11], a global point, Mean Best Position of the population is introduced in PSO system. The global point denoted as *mbest* is defined by (2a). The L is evaluated by

$$L = 2 * \alpha * |mbest_{id} - X_{id}| \qquad (7)$$

and therefore the equation (6) become equation (2c). Here we rewrite it as

$$X_{id} = p_{id} \pm \alpha * |mbest_{id} - X_{id}| * \ln(1/u) \qquad (8)$$

where α is the same as that in equation (5), (6) and is called Contraction-Expansion Coefficient, which can be used to control the convergence of the PSO algorithm. The PSO with equation (8) is named Quantum-behaved Particle Swarm Optimization (QPSO). The experiment results testify that QPSO has better performance than QDPSO [11].

3 Parameter Selection and Convergence Behavior of the Particle in QPSO

In QPSO, Contraction-Expansion Coefficient is a vital parameter to the convergence of the individual particle in QPSO, and therefore exerts significant influence on convergence of the algorithm. Mathematically, there are many forms of convergence of stochastic process, and different forms of convergence have different conditions that the parameter must satisfy. In this paper, we do not mean to analyze theoretically the convergence process of the individual particle in QPSO, but implement stochastic simulation to discover the knowledge about convergence of the particle.

For simplicity, we consider the evolution equation (6) of QDPSO in one-dimensional space. The p_{id} is denoted as point *p*. In practice, when $t \to \infty$, the point *p* of the individual particle and the Mean Best Position point *mbest* will converge to the same point, and consequently, the particle in QDPSO and that in QPSO have the same convergence condition for parameter α, except that they have different convergence rate.

In our stochastic simulation, the point *p* is fixed at *x*=0, and the initial position of the particle is set to be 1000, that is *x*(0)=1000 when t=0. In the simulation processes, the value of Contraction-Expansion Coefficient are set to be 0.7, 1.0, 1.5, 1.7, 1.8 and 2.0 respectively, and the number of times the stochastic simulation executes are 1000, 1500, 5000, 1500, 50,000, and 7000 respectively. When the stochastic simulation is executing, the logarithmic value of the distance between current position *x*(t) and the point *p* is recorded. The results of simulation experiment are shown in from Figure 1 to Figure 6.

From the results of stochastic simulation, we can conclude that when $\alpha \leq 1.7$, the particle will converge to the point p, and when $\alpha \geq 1.8$, it will diverge. Therefore there must be such a threshold value $\alpha_0 \in [1.7, 1.8]$ that the particle converges if $\alpha \leq \alpha_0$, and diverges otherwise. To get more precise value of α_0, we need to do simulation experiment with α set to be the value between 1.7 and 1.8 by more times. However, for practical application of QPSO, the knowledge about parameter α we acquired so far is adequate.

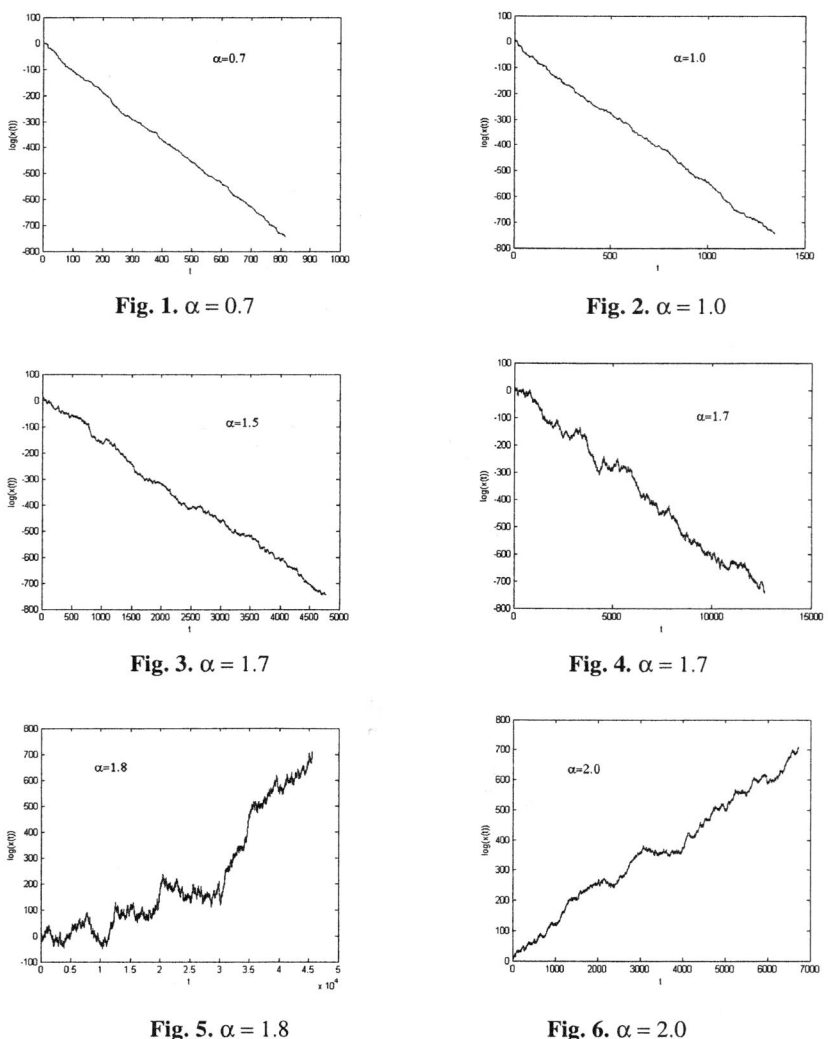

Fig. 1. α = 0.7

Fig. 2. α = 1.0

Fig. 3. α = 1.7

Fig. 4. α = 1.7

Fig. 5. α = 1.8

Fig. 6. α = 2.0

4 Parameter Control and Experiment Results

When Quantum-behaved Particle Swarm Optimization algorithm is applied to practical problems, there are several control methods for parameter α. A simple one is that α is set to be a fixed value when the algorithm is running. But this approach is lack of robustness. Another efficient method is linear-decreasing method that decreasing the value of α linearly as the algorithm is running. That is, the value of α is determined by

$$\alpha = (\alpha_1 - \alpha_2) \times \frac{(MAXITER - t)}{MAXITER} + \alpha_2 \tag{9}$$

where α_1 and α_2 are the initial and final values of the parameter α, respectively, t is the current iteration number and *MAXITER* is the maximum number of allowable iterations. Through empirical study, we observed that QPSO has relatively better performance by varying the value of α from 1.0 at the beginning of the search to 0.5 at the end of the search for most problems.

The better parameter control method is to use adaptive mechanism. Next, an adaptive parameter control method will be discussed, but firstly, we introduce the following error function

$$\Delta F = (F_i - F_{gbest})/MIN(ABS(F_i), ABS(F_{gbest})) \quad (10)$$

where F_i is the fitness of the *i*th particle, F_{gbest} is the fitness of *gbest*, ABS(x) gests the absolute value of *x*, and $MIN(x_1,x_2)$ gets the minimum value between x_1 and x_2. This error function is used to identify how the particle is close to the global best position, *gbest*. The small the value of the error function for a certain particle, the closer to the *gbest* the particle is, and therefore the narrower the search scope (possible value of *L*) of the particle is. To endow the QPSO with self-adaptation, the particles far away from the *gbest* should have smaller value of α, whereas those close to the *gbest* might be given large value of α as well. It is because that the latter properly has little chance to search other position far away from its local attractor p_{id} and should have larger α; otherwise its evolution will stagnate and not be able to discover new better position. On the contrary, the purpose of giving small value of α the particles far away from the gbest is to guarantee the collectiveness of the swarm. The critical technique of this adaptive approach is working out a self-adaptation function that computes the value of α in accord with the value of the error function (error value) for a certain particle.

Here we propose a self-adaptation function with each subsection zone of error value has the same value of α. It is formulated as follows.

Let $z = \log(\Delta F)$, then the function is

$$\alpha(z) = \begin{cases} 0.6 & z > 0 \\ 0.7 & -2 < z \leq 0 \\ 0.6 + 0.1 \times k & -k-1 < z \leq -k \quad (k = 2,3,4) \\ 1.0 + 0.2 \times (k-4) & -k-1 < z \leq k \quad (k = 5,6,7) \\ 1.8 & z \leq -8 \end{cases} \quad (11)$$

The QPSO employing the above adaptive function is called Adaptive Quantum-behaved Particle Swarm Optimization (AQPSO).

To test the performance of QPSO with the two methods of parameter control, five benchmark functions, listed in Table 1, are used here for comparison with SPSO in [10] and QPSO in [9]. These functions are all minimization problems with minimum value zero.

In all experiments, the initial range of the population listed in Table 2 is asymmetry and Table 2 lists V_{max} and X_{ma} values for all the functions, respectively, as used in [9, 10]. The fitness value is set as function value and the neighborhood of a particle is the whole population. We had 50 trial runs for every instance and recorded mean best fitness. In order to investigate the scalability of the algorithm, different population sizes are used for each function with different dimensions. The population sizes are 20, 40 and 80. Generation is set as 1000, 1500 and 2000 generations corresponding to the dimensions 10, 20 and 30 for first four functions, respectively, and the dimension of the last function is 2.

Table 1. Benchmark Functions

Function	Formula
Sphere function f_1	$f(x)_1 = \sum_{i=1}^{n} x_i^2$
Rosenbrock function f_2	$f(x)_2 = \sum_{i=1}^{n}(100(x_{i+1} - x_i^2)^2 + (x_i - 1)^2)$
Rastrigrin function f_3	$f(x)_3 = \sum_{i=1}^{n}(x_i^2 - 10\cos(2\pi x_i) + 10)$
Griewank function f_4	$f(x)_4 = \frac{1}{4000}\sum_{i=1}^{n}(x_i - 100)^2 - \prod_{i=1}^{n}\cos(\frac{(x_i - 100)}{\sqrt{i}}) + 1$
Shaffer's function f_5	$f(x)_7 = 0.5 + \frac{(\sin\sqrt{x^2 + y^2})^2 - 0.5}{(1.0 + 0.001(x^2 + y^2))^2}$

Table 2

Function	Initialization Range	X_{max}	V_{max}
f_1	(50, 100)	100	100
f_2	(15, 30)	100	100
f_3	(2.56, 5.12)	10	10
f_4	(300, 600)	600	600
f_5	(30, 100)	100	100

Table 3. Sphere Function

M	Dim.	Gmax	SPSO Mean Best	SPSO St. Dev.	QPSO Mean Best	QPSO St. Dev.	AQPSO Mean Best	AQPSO St. Dev.
20	10	1000	3.16E-20	6.23E-20	2.29E-41	1.49E-40	1.62E-70	2.28E-70
20	20	1500	5.29E-11	1.56E-10	1.68E-20	7.99E-20	2.52E-50	6.04E-50
20	30	2000	2.45E-06	7.72E-06	1.34E-13	3.32E-13	6.26E-40	1.63E-39
40	10	1000	3.12E-23	8.01E-23	8.26E-72	5.83E-71	3.2E-120	5.1E-120
40	20	1500	4.16E-14	9.73E-14	1.53E-41	7.48E-41	1.12E-95	4.12E-95
40	30	2000	2.26E-10	5.10E-10	1.87E-28	6.73E-28	5.35E-71	1.65E-71
80	10	1000	6.15E-28	2.63E-27	3.1E-100	2.10E-99	4.3E-149	7.1E-149
80	20	1500	2.68E-17	5.24E-17	1.56E-67	9.24E-67	1.6E-128	8.2E-128
80	30	2000	2.47E-12	7.16E-12	1.10E-48	2.67E-48	2.4E-105	3.1E-105

We make two groups of experiments to test the QPSO algorithm. In the first set of experiment, the QPSO is tested, and the coefficient α decreases from 1.0 to 0.5 linearly when the algorithm is running as in [11]. The second set is done to test the performance of AQPSO, in which the position of each particle is free from the constraint of X_{max}. The best fitness values for 50 runs of each function in Table 3 to Table 7.

Table 4. Rosenbrock Function

M	Dim.	Gmax	SPSO		QPSO		AQPSO	
			Mean Best	St. Dev.	Mean Best	St. Dev.	Mean Best	St. Dev.
20	10	1000	94.1276	194.3648	59.4764	153.0842	46.6669	66.9602
	20	1500	204.337	293.4544	110.664	149.5483	100.253	173.209
	30	2000	313.734	547.2635	147.609	210.3262	70.6362	81.0009
40	10	1000	71.0239	174.1108	10.4238	14.4799	13.9107	15.9653
	20	1500	179.291	377.4305	46.5957	39.5360	29.0769	22.1808
	30	2000	289.593	478.6273	59.0291	63.4940	45.5361	58.4595
80	10	1000	37.3747	57.4734	8.63638	16.6746	19.6623	23.9647
	20	1500	83.6931	137.2637	35.8947	36.4702	20.2816	22.7247
	30	2000	202.672	289.9728	51.5479	40.8490	16.0450	18.8032

Table 5. Rastrigrin Function

M	Dim.	Gmax	SPSO		QPSO		AQPSO	
			Mean Best	St. Dev.	Mean Best	St. Dev.	Mean Best	St. Dev.
20	10	1000	5.5382	3.0477	5.2543	2.8952	7.9675	9.4235
	20	1500	23.1544	10.4739	16.2673	5.9771	26.0826	14.9771
	30	2000	47.4168	17.1595	31.4576	7.6882	41.8044	15.8808
40	10	1000	3.5778	2.1384	3.5685	2.0678	7.5200	8.5370
	20	1500	16.4337	5.4811	11.1351	3.6046	17.0793	8.8016
	30	2000	37.2796	14.2838	22.9594	7.2455	28.4931	14.3873
80	10	1000	2.5646	1.5728	2.1245	1.1772	5.1044	6.3375
	20	1500	13.3826	8.5137	10.2759	6.6244	17.2010	11.2018
	30	2000	28.6293	10.3431	16.7768	4.4858	26.5024	12.9643

The results in Table 3 show that the adaptive method can enhance the local search ability of the QPSO tremendously. The results in Table 4 show that with adaptive parameter control method, the AQPSO outperform the other PSO algorithm in global search ability. The numerical results show that the AQPSO works better than other PSO algorithm except on Rastrigrin function. It is because that the APSO has ability to evolve persistently, and when the search iteration terminated, the algorithm can search the solution space fatherly without converging.

Table 6. Griewank Function

M	Dim.	Gmax	SPSO		QPSO		AQPSO	
			Mean Best	St. Dev.	Mean Best	St. Dev.	Mean Best	St. Dev.
20	10	1000	0.09217	0.08330	0.08331	0.06805	0.08645	0.06454
	20	1500	0.03002	0.03255	0.02033	0.02257	0.02412	0.02325
	30	2000	0.01811	0.02477	0.01119	0.01462	0.01401	0.01716
40	10	1000	0.08496	0.07260	0.06912	0.05093	0.07702	0.05619
	20	1500	0.02719	0.02517	0.01666	0.01755	0.01478	0.01750
	30	2000	0.01267	0.01479	0.01161	0.01246	0.01033	0.01218
80	10	1000	0.07484	0.07107	0.03508	0.02086	0.05364	0.02376
	20	1500	0.02854	0.02680	0.01460	0.01279	0.01302	0.01474
	30	2000	0.01258	0.01396	0.01136	0.01139	0.00668	0.07163

Table 7. Shaffer's Function

M	Dim.	Gmax	SPSO		QPSO		AQPSO	
			Mean Best	St. Dev.	Mean Best	St. Dev.	Mean Best	St. Dev.
20	2	2000	2.78E-04	0.001284	0.001361	0.003405	0.001958	0.003919
40	2	2000	4.74E-05	3.59E-05	3.89E-04	0.001923	0.001166	0.003189
80	2	2000	2.57E-10	3.13E-10	1.72E-09	3.30E-09	1.52E-05	1.04E-04

5 Conclusions

We have described in this paper the Quantum-behaved Particle Swarm Optimization and the relationship between parameter α and convergence of the individual particle. We also have presented two parameter control methods, one of which is adaptive, for QPSO algorithm. The AQPSO outperforms QPSO with linear-decreasing method both in global search ability and local search ability, because the adaptive method is more approximate to the learning process of social organism with high-level swarm intelligence and can make the population evolve persistently. In our future work, we will be devoted to find out a more efficient self-adaptation function to evaluate the coefficient α, and therefore to improve the performance of QPSO fatherly.

References

1. P. J. Angeline: Evolutionary Optimization Versus Particle Swarm Optimization: Philosophy and performance Differences. Evolutionary Programming VII (1998), Lecture Notes in Computer Science 1447, pp. 601-610, Springer.
2. F. Van den Bergh, A. P. Engelbrecht: A New Locally Convergent Particle Swarm Optimizer. 2002 IEEE International Conference on systems, Man and Cybernetics, 2002.
3. F. Van den Bergh, An Analysis of Particle Swarm Optimizers. PhD Thesis. University of Pretoria, Nov 2001.
4. M. Clerc: The Swarm and Queen: Towards a Deterministic and Adaptive Particle Swarm Optimization. Proc. CEC 1999, pp. 1951-1957.
5. J. Kennedy, R. C. Eberhart: Particle Swarm Optimization. Proc. IEEE Int'l Conference on Neural Networks, IV. Piscataway, NJ: IEEE Service Center, 1995, pp. 1942-1948.
6. J. Kennedy: Small Swrlds and Mega-minds: Effects of Neighborhood Topology on Particle Swarm Performance. Proc. Congress on Evolutionary Computation 1999, pp. 1931-1938.
7. Jacques Riget and Jakob S. Besterstr, A Diversity-guided Particle Swarm Optimizer-the ARPSO.
8. Y. Shi, R. C. Eberhart: A Modified Particle Swarm. Proc. 1998 IEEE International Conference on Evolutionary Computation, pp. 1945-1950.
9. P. N. Suganthan: Particle Swarm Optimizer with Neighborhood Operator. Proc. 1999 Congress on Evolutionary Computation, pp. 1958-1962.
10. J. Sun et al: Particle Swarm Optimization with Particles Having Quantum Behavior. Proc. 2004 Congress on Evolutionary Computation, pp. 325-331.
11. J. Sun et al: A Global Search Strategy of Quantum-behaved Particle Swarm Optimization. Proc. 2004 IEEE Conference on Cybernetics and Intelligent Systems.
12. Y. Shi and R. Eberhart: Empirical study of particle swarm optimization. Proc. of Congress on Evolutionary Computation, 1999, 1945-1950.

An Emotional Particle Swarm Optimization Algorithm

Yang Ge and Zhang Rubo

College of Computer Science and Technology, Harbin Engineering University,
150001,Nantong Street 145-11,Harbin, Heilongjiang Province
yangge@hrbeu.edu.cn, zrbzrb@hrbeu.edu.cn

Abstract. This paper presents a modification of the particle swarm optimization algorithm (PSO) intended to introduce some psychology factor of emotion into the algorithm. In the new algorithm, which is based on a simple perception and emotion psychology model, each particle has its own feeling and reaction to the current position, and it also has specified emotional factor towards the sense it got from both its own history and other particle. The sense factor is calculated by famous Weber-Fechner Law. All these psychology factors will influence the next action of the particle. The resulting algorithm, known as Emotional PSO (EPSO), is shown to perform significantly better than the original PSO algorithm on different benchmark optimization problems. Avoiding premature convergence allows EPSO to continue search for global optima in difficult multimodal optimization problems, reaching better solutions than PSO with a much more fast convergence speed.

1 Introduction

The Particle Swarm Optimization algorithm (PSO), originally introduced in terms of social and cognitive behavior by Kennedy and Eberhart in 1995 [1], [2], has proven to be a powerful competitor to other evolutionary algorithms such as genetic algorithms [3].

In fact, the PSO algorithm simulates social behavior among individuals (particles) "flying" through a multidimensional search space, each particle representing a single intersection of all search dimensions. The particles evaluate their positions relative to a goal (fitness) at every iteration, and companion particles share memories of their "best" positions, then use those memories to adjust their own velocities and positions as shown in equations (1a) and (1b) below. The PSO formulae define each particle as a potential solution to a problem in a D-dimensional space, with the *ith* particle represented as $X_i = (x_{i1}, x_{i2}, x_{i3}, \ldots .. x_{iD})$. Each particle also remembers its previous best position, designated as as *pbest*, $P_i = (p_{i1}, p_{i2}, p_{i3}, \ldots .. p_{iD})$ and its velocity $V_i = (v_{i1}, v_{i2}, v_{i3}, \ldots ..v_{iD})$ [7]. In each generation, the velocity of each particle is updated, being pulled in the direction of its own previous best position (p_i) and the best of all positions (p_g) reached by all particles until the preceding generation. The original PSO formulae developed by Kennedy and Eberhart were modified by Shi and Eberhart [4] with the introduction of an inertia parameter, ω, that was shown empirically to improve the overall performance of PSO.

$$V_{id} = \omega \times V_{id} + c_1 \times rand_1() \times (p_{id} - X_{id}) + c_2 \times rand_2() \times (p_{gd} - X_{id}) \quad (1a)$$

$$X_{id}^{t+1} = X_{id}^t + v_{id}^t \quad (1b)$$

In [3], Angeline compared the philosophy and performance differences between the evolutionary programming algorithm and PSO algorithm by conducting experiments on four non-linear functions well studied in the evolutionary optimization literature. Through adapting the strategy parameters to adjust the mutation step size, the evolutionary programming algorithm employed ideally has the ability to fine tune the search area around the optima. Many further research focus on control the diversity of the particles and slow the spread speed of the share information. Researchers developed new modifications of PSO by estimate the diversity of the swarm, such as PSO with self-organized criticality showed in [8], diversity-guided PSO in [9], and spatial particle extension [10], and when it is less than a lower limit, the swarm was dispersed. There are also some improvements made by constrain the spread speed of share information, as subpopulation model in [11].

Research in psychophysics indicate the principle of sensation to stimulus outward, that is the intensity of a sensation varies by a series of equal arithmetic increments as the strength of the stimulus is increased geometrically. In this paper, in an effort to extend PSO models beyond real biology and physics and push the limits of swarm intelligence into the exploration of swarms as they could be, we study the PSO with psychology, through the use of psychology model to control the particles in a PSO.

Section 2 describes how to use psychological theory in PSO to understand the swarm intelligence from a system complexity view of point. The settings and variations of the experiments are discussed in Section3. We compared the new algorithm with standard PSO in Section 4. In Section 5, a brief restatement of our findings and future direction is reported and discussed.

2 Emotional PSO

2.1 Psychology Models

Psychophysics shows that perceptions and consciousness are produced when external object act on nerve system which is thus caused to be busy. And recognition and interpretation of sensory stimuli based chiefly on memory. But not all the stimulation would cause perception. In one of his classic experiments, Weber, the first psychologist who quantitatively studies the human response to a physical stimulus, found that the response was proportional to a relative increase in the weight. That is to say, if the weight is 1 kg, an increase of a few grams will not be noticed. Rather, when the mass in increased by a certain factor, an increase in weight is perceived. If the mass is doubled, the threshold is also doubled. This kind of relationship can be described by a differential equation as,

$$dp = k \frac{dS}{S} \quad (2)$$

where dp is the differential change in perception, dS is the differential increase in the stimulus and S is the stimulus at the instant. A constant factor k is to be determined experimentally.

Integrating the above equation

$$p = k \ln S + C \qquad (3)$$

with C is the constant of integration, ln is the natural logarithm.

To determine C, put $p = 0$, i.e. no perception; then

$$C = -k \ln S_0 \qquad (4)$$

where S_0 is that threshold of stimulus below which it is not perceived at all, and can be called Absolute Stimulus Threshold (AST).

Therefore, our equation becomes

$$p = -k \ln \frac{S}{S_0} \qquad (5)$$

The relationship between stimulus and perception is logarithmic. This logarithmic relationship means that if the perception is altered in an arithmetic progression (i.e. add constant amounts) the corresponding stimulus varies as a geometric progression (i.e. multiply by a fixed factor). That is famous Weber-Fechner Law.

On the other hand, in psychology, emotion is considered a response to stimuli that involves characteristic physiological changes—such as increase in pulse rate, rise in body temperature, and so on. In the 1960s, the Schachter-Singer theory pointed out that the cognitive processes, not just physiological reactions, played a significant role in determining emotions. Robert Plutchik developed (1980) a theory showing eight primary human emotions: joy, acceptance, fear, submission, sadness, disgust, anger, and anticipation, and argued that all human emotions can be derived from these. But since emotions are abstract and subjective, however, they remain difficult to quantify. The *Cannon-Bard Approach* proposes that the lower brain initially receives emotion-producing information and then relays it simultaneously to the higher cortex for interpretation and to the nervous system to trigger physiological responses.

2.2 Emotional PSO

Assume the particles have psychology; thus we can introduce the models mentioned before to improve PSO's performance. The particle can sense the stimulus from the difference between it current location and the best location it ever arrived, and it can also feel the difference from other particles. When the stimulus can cause noticeable perception, which is much more bigger than threshold, the particle will respond to the stimulus strongly. On the other hand, the stimuli will be compared with the history it ever experienced. As we have discussed in psychology model, if the history value is also very high, the respondence will not be very notable. Along with experience, the emotion state of particles will change. To be simplified, we define only two emotions particles could have, joy and sadness, and correspond to two reaction to perception respectively. If the particle is joyful, it will exploit both history experience and global experience, and it will be more vibrant at its current position. If it is sad, it will emphasis more on its own history, and it also will shrink from its normal position. Just as human, it's emotion change by inner factors.

So the perception of particles can be described by following:

$$r_g = -k \ln \frac{S(f(P_{gd}) - f(X_i))}{S_0} \quad (6a)$$

$$r_h = -k \ln \frac{S(f(P_{id}) - f(X_i))}{S_0} \quad (6b)$$

Here r_g is the perception from global, and r_h is the sense of the history, S means stimulus function. And the emotional effect can be described by following:

$$V_{id} = \omega \times V_{id} + c_1 \times r_g \times rand_1() \times (p_{id} - X_{id}) + c_2 \times r_k \times rand_2() \times (p_{gd} - X_{id}) \quad (7a)$$

$$V_{id} = \omega \times V_{id} + c_1 \times rand_1() \times (p_{id} - X_{id}) + c_2 \times \frac{r_k}{r_g} r_k \times rand_2() \times (p_{gd} - X_{id}) \quad (7b)$$

(7a) means particle is joyful and (7b) means particle is sad. The choice is made by following:

$$\textbf{IF } (rand() < e_s) \textbf{ THEN } (7a) \textbf{ ELSE } (7b) \quad (8)$$

Here e_s is emotion factor.

Then the news algorithm can be demonstrated by following:

Step (a): Initialize a population (array) which including m particles, For the ith particle, it has random location Xi in the problem space and for the dth dimension of velocity V_i, $V_{id} = Rand2() * V_{max,d}$, where $Rand2()$ is in the range [-1, 1];
Step (b): Evaluate the desired optimization fitness function for each particle;
Step (c): .Compare the evaluated fitness value of each particle with its p_{id}, which means the best position of its history. If current value is better than p_{id}, then set the current location as the p_{id} location. Furthermore, if current value is better than p_{gd}, which is the best position of global, then reset p_{gd} to the current index in particle array;
Step (d): Change the velocity and location of the particle according to the equations (7a) and (7b) which is decided by equations (8);
Step (e): Loop to step (2) until a stop criterion is met, usually a sufficiently good fitness value or a predefined maximum number of generations G_{max}.

3 Experimental Setting

In order to be able to evaluate the emotional PSO, we compared it with GA algorithm, standard PSO and a number of other update rules, and four non-linear functions in [3] are used in our tests. But f1, the function Sphere is not showed here because in tests, the function quickly get value of zero, with no comparative meaning.

The first function is the Rosenbrock function described by equation (9):

$$f_2(x) = \sum_{i=1}^{n}(100(x_{i+1} - x_i^2)^2 + (x_i - 1)^2) \tag{9}$$

The third function is the generalized Rastrigrin function described by equation (10):

$$f_3(x) = \sum_{i=1}^{n}(x_i^2 - 10\cos(2\pi x_i) + 10) \tag{10}$$

The last function is the generalized Griewank function described by equation (11)

$$f_4(x) = \frac{1}{4000}\sum_{i=1}^{n}x_i^2 - \prod_{i=1}^{n}\cos(\frac{x_i}{\sqrt{i}}) + 1 \tag{11}$$

Following the suggestion in [12] and for the purpose of comparison, the asymmetric initialization method used is [3] is adopted here for population initialization. Table 1 lists the initialization ranges of the four functions.

Table 1. Asymmetric initialization ranges

Fucntion	Asymmetric Initialization Range
f_2	(15,30)
f_3	(2.56,5.12)
f_4	(300,600)

For each function, three different dimension sizes are tested. They are dimension sizes:10, 20 and 30. The maximum number of generations is set as 1000, 1500, 2000 corrsponding to the dimensions 10, 20, and 30, respectively. In the experiment different population sizes are used for each function with different dimensions. They are population sizes of 20, 40, 80 and 160. a linearly deceasing inertia weight is used which starts at 0.9 and ends at 0.4, with c_1=1.0,c_2=0.001, which was determined by a series of experiment. V_{max} and X_{max} are set to be equal and their values for each function are listed in table 2.

Table 2. Vmax and Xmax calues for each function

Function	$V_{max} = X_{max}$
f_2	100
f_3	10
f_4	600

As to Emotional PSO, the values for S_0 is 1, k is -1/2.

4 Experimental Results and Discussion

Tables 3 to 5 list the mean fitness values of the best particle found for the 10 runs for the other three functions, respectively. In the function f_2 and f_3, which are showed in Table 3 and Table 4, we can see the EPSO shows significant better performance than standard PSO. The EPSO shows to be less susceptible to premature convergence, and less likely to be stuck in local optima. In function f_4, the EPSO shows not so good as it shows in the fucntion f_2 and f_3, but it also shows along with the increase of population size and dimensions, the performance of EPSO improved fast, which means it is more suitable to large optimization problems.

Table 3. Mean fitness values for the Rosenbrock fucntion

Popu. Size(m)	Dimension	Generation	Mean Best Fitness EPSO	PSO
20	10	1000	22.7642	39.1026
	20	1500	14.4449	24.9219
	30	2000	49.2848	98.0279
40	10	1000	13.3361	10.1767
	20	1500	44.7021	70.9678
	30	2000	56.2189	136.9933
80	10	1000	8.2491	7.3112
	20	1500	38.0797	35.4722
	30	2000	33.2934	47.6875
160	10	1000	5.7420	12.9636
	20	1500	28.6470	41.2685
	30	2000	26.8016	66.0944

Table 4. Mean fitness values for the generalized Rastrigrin fucntion

Popu. Size(m)	Dimension	Generation	Mean Best Fitness EPSO	PSO
20	10	1000	0.3979	5.5087
	20	1500	3.2296	22.1879
	30	2000	15.0611	51.10412
40	10	1000	0.0994	3.6816
	20	1500	1.5113	19.2325
	30	2000	7.6086	35.7287
80	10	1000	0.0000	1.7070
	20	1500	1.3593	13.3324
	30	2000	4.3004	31.6400
160	10	1000	0.0000	1.3929
	20	1500	0.2985	10.3555
	30	2000	3.2947	26.5671

Figure 1 to 3 showed the results of the experiments. We can see it clearly that the improved algorithm perfermance much more better than standard PSO both in Rosenbrock funtion and generalized Rastrigrin function, and performance little better than standard PSO in generalized Griewank function. But all the three experimental functions show that for larger population size and bigger dimension and more generation , the EPSO will perform better. Also from the three figures we can that EPSO's curve decend steepper than PSO's, which means a faster convergence speed.

Table 5. Mean fitness values for the generalized Griewank fucntion

Popu. Size(m)	Dimension	Generation	Mean Best Fitness EPSO	PSO
20	10	1000	2.1142	0.0698
	20	1500	0.1521	0.0322
	30	2000	0.1786	0.0169
40	10	1000	0.4633	0.1006
	20	1500	0.0258	0.0361
	30	2000	0.0152	0.0120
80	10	1000	0.3286	0.0787
	20	1500	0.0285	0.0221
	30	2000	0.0064	0.0175
160	10	1000	0.3364	0.0487
	20	1500	0.0358	0.0398
	30	2000	0.0083	0.0091

Clearly that EPSO's curve decend steepper than the standard PSO's, which shows the new algorithm has a faster convergence speed.

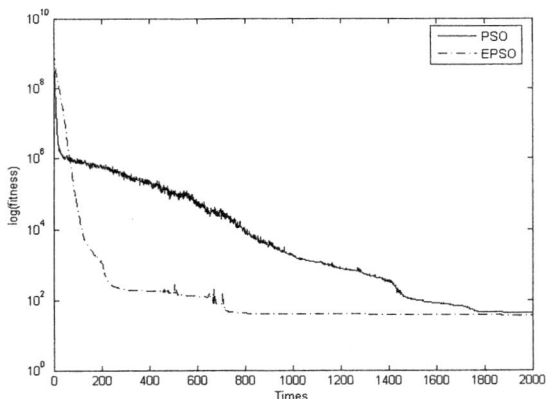

Fig. 1. Mean relative performance for Rosenbrock function

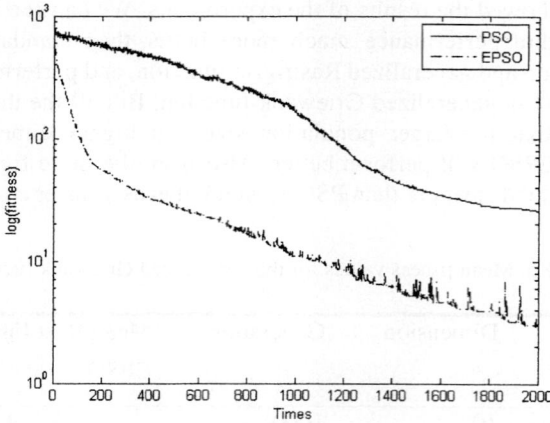

Fig. 2. Mean relative performance for generalized Rastrigrin function

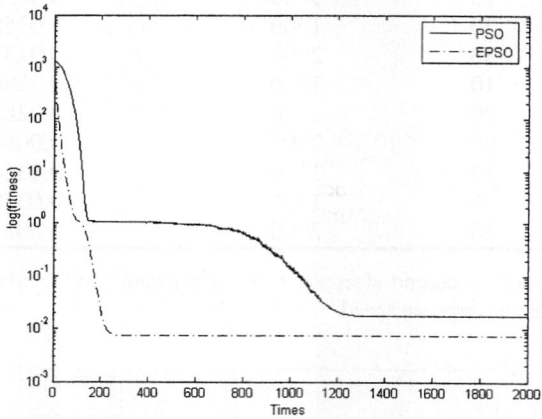

Fig. 3. Mean relative performance for generalized Griewank fucntion

5 Conclusion

This paper has proposed a new variation of the particle swarm optimization algorithm called EPSO, introducing a so called psychology model into the update rules of the particle. Each particle caculates the perception of its history position and the global postion. Then a emotional factor is caculated to guide the next action of the particle with the considerate of the percetion. That means the particles choose to emphasize the history or the global experience according to its own emotion and with the percetion function. The new algorithm outperfoms PSO on four test functions, being less susceptible to premature convergence, and less likely to be stuck in local optima. EPSO algorithm outperforms the PSO even in its faster convergence speed.

The psychology model is the base that intruct the living beings to react reasonable to out stimulus. The introduce of the model makes particle swarm have the ability of self-adapting during the progress of exploring and exploiting. In current work, a promising variation of the algorithm, with the simultaneous influence of psychology model is being explored. Future work includes further experimentation with parameters of EPSO, testing the new algorithm on other benchmark problems, and evaluating its performance relative to a more complex emotion model.

References

1. Kennedy, J., Eberhart, R.C.: Particle Swarm Optimization. Proc. IEEE Int. Conf. on Neural Networks. (1995) 1942–1948
2. Eberharyt, R.C., Kennedy, J.: A New Optimizer Using Particle Swarm Theory. Proc. 6th international Symposium on Micro Machine and Human Science(Nagoya, Japan), IEEE Service Center, Piscataway, NJ. (1995) 39-43
3. Angeline, P.J.: Evolutionary Optimization Versus Particle Swarm Optimization: Philosophy and Performance Difference. 1998 Annual Conference on Evolutionary Programming, San Diego. (1998) 601-610
4. Shi, Y. Eberhart, R.C.: Parmeter Selection in Particle Swarm Optimization. Proc. 7th Annual Conf. on Evolutionary Programming. San Diego. (1998) 591-600
5. Shi, Y. Eberhart, R.C.: Empirical study of Particle Swarm Optimization. Proc. Congress on Evolutionary Computation. (1999) 1945-1950
6. Cristian T.I.: The Particle Swarm Optimization Algorithm: Convergence Analysis and Parameter Selection. Information Processing Letters, 2003, Vol. 85 (2003) 317-325
7. Carlisle, A., Dozier, G.: Adapting Particle Swarm Optimization to Dynamic Environments. Proc. International Conf. on Artificial Intelligence, Las Vegas, Nevada. (2000) 429-434
8. Morten, L., Krink, T.: Extending Particle Swarm Optimizers with Self-Organized Criticality. Proc. 4th Congress on Evolutionary Computation (CEC) (2002)
9. Riget, J., Vestertrøm, J.S.: A Diversity-Guided Partilce Swarm Optimizer – the arPSO. EVALife Technical Report. Denmark. Vol. 2. (2002)
10. Morten, L., Rasmussen, T.K.: Hybrid Particle Swarm Optimiser with Breeding and Subpopulations. EVALife Project Group, Dept. of Computer Science. (2001)
11. Kennedy, J., Mendes, R.: Population Structure and Particle Swarm Performance. Proc. Conf. Evolutionary Computation. Vol. 2, (2002) 1671-1676
12. Fogel, D., Beyer, H.: A note on the empirical Evaluation of intermediate recombination. Evolutionary Computation, Vol. 3, no. 4. (1995) 491-495
13. Holland, J.H.: Adaptation in Natural and Artificial Systems. University of Michigan Press, Ann Arbor, MI, (1975)
14. Kennedy, J.: The Particle Swarm: Social Adaptation of Knowledge. Proc. IEEE Int. Conf. on Evolutionary Computation. (1997) 303-308
15. Eberhart, R., Shi, Y.: Particle Swarm Optimization: Developments, Applications and resources. Proc. IEEE Int. Conf. on Evolutionary Computation. (2001). 81-86

Multi-model Function Optimization by a New Hybrid Nonlinear Simplex Search and Particle Swarm Algorithm

Fang Wang[1], Yuhui Qiu[1], and Naiqin Feng[1,2]

[1] Faculty of Computer & Information Science,
Southwest-China Normal University, Chongqing, 400715, China
{teresa78, yhqiu}@swnu.edu.cn
[2] Faculty of Computer & Information Science,
Henan Normal University, Xinxiang, 453002, China
fengnq@henannu.edu.cn

Abstract. A new hybrid Particle Swarm Optimization (PSO) algorithm is proposed based on the Nonlinear Simplex Search (NSS) method. At late stage of PSO, when the most promising regions of solutions are fixed, the algorithm isolates particles that are very close to the extrema, and applies the NSS method to them to enhance local exploitation searching. Explicit experimental results on famous benchmark functions indicate that this approach is reliable and efficient, especially on multi-model function optimizations. It yields better solution qualities and success rates compared to other published methods.

1 Introduction

The particle swarm algorithm, which is mostly used for continuous function optimizing, was originally proposed by Eberhart and Kennedy in 1995 [1]. It exhibits good performance in solving hard optimization problems and engineering applications, and compares favorably to other optimization algorithms.

Numerous variations of the basic PSO algorithm have been projected to improve its overall performance since its introduction [2]. Hybrid PSO algorithms with determinate methods, such as the nonlinear simplex search method [3], are proved to have many advantages over other techniques, such as genetic algorithms and tabu search, because these hybrid methods can perform exploration search with PSO and exploitation search with determinate methods [4,5]. Generating initial swarm by the NSS might improve, but is not satisfying for multi-modal function optimizing tasks [5]. Developing the NSS as an operator to the swarm during the optimization may increase the computational complex considerably.

2 The Particle Swarm Algorithm

In the original PSO formulae, particle i is denoted as $X_i = (x_{i1}, x_{i2}, \cdots, x_{iD})$, which represents a potential solution to a problem in D-dimensional space. Each particle maintains a memory of its previous best position, $P_i = (p_{i1}, p_{i2}, \cdots, p_{iD})$, and a velocity along each dimension, represented as $V_i = (v_{i1}, v_{i2}, \cdots, v_{iD})$. At each iteration, the P vector of the particle with the best fitness in the local neighborhood, designated g, and the P vector of the current particle are combined to adjust the velocity along each dimension, and that velocity is then used to compute a new position for the particle.

The computational model of the swarm are [6]:

$$v_{id} = w * v_{id} + c1 * rand() * (p_{id} - x_{id}) + c2 * Rand() * (p_{gd} - x_{id}) \quad (1)$$

$$x_{id} = x_{id} + v_{id} \quad (2)$$

Constants $c1$ and $c2$ determine the relative influence of the social and cognition components, which often both are set to the same value to give each component equal weight. A constant, V_{max}, was used to limit the velocities of the particles. The parameter w, which was introduced as an inertia factor, can dynamically adjust the velocity over time, gradually focusing the PSO into a local search.

Maurice Clerc has derived a constriction coefficient K, a modification of the PSO [7] that runs without V_{max}, reducing some undesirable explosive feedback effects. Carlisle and Doziert investigated the influence of different parameters in PSO, selected a set of reasonable parameters, and proposed the canonical PSO [8].

3 The Proposed Algorithm and Experimental Design

We propose a hybrid PSO algorithm, which isolates a particle and apply the NSS to it when it reaches quite close to the extrema (within the diversion radius). If the particle lands within a specified precision of a goal solution (*ErrorGoal*) during the NSS running, a PSO process is considered to be successful, otherwise it may be laid back to the swarm and start the next PSO iteration.

The diversion radius is computed as:

$$DRadius = ErrorGoal + \delta \quad (3)$$

$$\delta = \begin{cases} 100 * ErrorGoal, & \text{if } ErrorGoal \leq 10^{-4} \\ 0.01 * ErrorGoal, & \text{otherwise} \end{cases} \quad (4)$$

In a NSS process, an initial simplex is consists of the isolated particle i and other D vertices randomly generated with the mean of X_i and standard deviation of $DRadius$. We tested the proposed algorithm and compared it to other methods on more than 20 benchmark functions taken from [4] and [5], but only listed some typical results in section 4.

To eliminate the influence of different initial swarms, we implement 200 experiments for each test and the maximum number of PSO iterations is set to be 500, swarm size is 60 for 30-dimension functions and 30 for others. Parameters used in the NSS are: $\alpha = 1.0, \gamma = 2.0, \beta^+ = \beta^- = 0.5$.

Table 1. Rate of success and mean function evaluations for each test function

Test Function	Rate of success			Mean function evaluations		
	NSSPSO	NS-PSO	CPSO	NSSPSO	NS-PSO	CPSO
Rastrigin$_2$	1	0.84	1	2970.6	5573.3	3181.8
LevyNo3$_2$	1	0.83	1	2595.7	4827	2853.3
Schaffer$_2$	0.7	0.57	0.645	8662.6	9906.8	9119.7
Rosenbrock$_2$	0.99	0.845	0.97	7589.6	9421.8	8450.3
Grienwank$_2$	0.8	0.685	0.735	8383.9	9397.6	8985.9
Sphere$_{10}$	1	1	1	9677.9	5723.4	6306.8
Rosenbrock$_{10}$	0.83	0.945	0.84	5365.1	3552	5461.6
Rastrigin$_{10}$	0.963	0.83	0.96	5390.7	5929.5	5094.3
Griewank$_{10}$	0.845	0.8	0.845	8997.5	7084.1	7332.3
Sphere$_{30}$	1	1	1	11716	13789	15448
Rosenbrock$_{30}$	0.825	0.94	0.795	14945	10697	16576
Rastrigin$_{30}$	0.995	1	1	8987.1	3475.5	8511.3
Grienwank$_{30}$	0.99	1	0.995	11019	8999.1	10801

Table 2. Average optima and total CPU time for each test function

Test Function	Average optima			Total CPU time		
	NSSPSO	NS-PSO	CPSO	NSSPSO	NS-PSO	CPSO
Rastrigin$_2$	4.7472e−9	0.42783	4.9856e−9	14.875	27.156	14.906
LevyNo3$_2$	−176.54	−163.17	−176.54	13.063	22.688	12.813
Schaffer$_2$	−0.99716	−0.99334	−0.99664	30.609	35.484	31.047
Rosenbrock$_2$	7.82995e−9	0.76162	0.002373	31.031	36.422	31.781
Grienwank$_2$	1.0012	1.003	1.0016	42.469	49.141	44.813
Sphere$_{10}$	8.9723e−9	8.2146e−9	8.2073e−9	40.453	23.125	24.656
Rosenbrock$_{10}$	298.01	461.95	20.688	22.172	15.266	22.547
Rastrigin$_{10}$	9.6195	10.14	9.7158	29.359	32.625	27.641
Griewank$_{10}$	9.0979	9.1038	9.1003	102.311	42.25	43.156
Sphere$_{30}$	9.2039e−5	9.3474e−5	9.2407e−5	341.98	67.594	68.609
Rosenbrock$_{30}$	2009.3	100.63	2856.7	79.952	56.281	80.047
Rastrigin$_{30}$	97.418	95.818	97.752	64.094	27.574	60.75
Grienwank$_{30}$	29.098	29.094	29.094	83.063	71.609	81.547

4 Experimental Results

The rate of success, mean function evaluations, average optima and total CPU time for each test are listed in Table 1 and Table 2. The subscript of each test function denotes its dimension. The proposed algorithm is denoted as NSSPSO, NS-PSO is another NSS hybrid PSO proposed by Parsopoulos and Vrahatis [5], and CPSO is the canonical PSO by Carlisle [8]. From the tables we can see that the overall performance of NSSPSO algorithm is competitive to other algorithms in terms of success rate, solution quality and convergence speed as well, especially on multi-model functions. As to high dimension function optimizing, NSSPSO operates appreciably inferior to NS-PSO due to its computational expense, but is still equal to the CPSO algorithm.

5 Conclusions and Future Work

In this paper, we propose a new hybrid particle swarm algorithm and implement wide variety of experiments to test it. The results compared to other published methods demonstrate that this method is very effective and efficient, especially for continuous multi-model function optimization tasks.

Future work may focus on accelerating the convergence for high dimension problems, extending the approach to constrained multi-objective optimization, and developing parallel algorithm of this hybrid technique.

References

1. Kennedy, J., Eberhart, R. C.: Particle swarm optimization. Proceedings of IEEE International Conference on Neural Networks, Piscataway, NJ (1995) 1942–1948
2. Parsopoulos, K. E., Vrahatis, M. N.: Recent approaches to global optimization problems through particle swarm optimization, Natural Computing, vol. 1 (2002) 235–306
3. Nelder, J., Mead, R.: A simplex method for function minimization. Computer Journal, vol. 7 (1965) 308–313
4. Shu-Kai S. Fan, Yun-Chia Liang, Erwie Zahara: Hybrid Simplex Search and Particle Swarm Optimization for the Global Optimization of Multimodal Functions, Engineering Optimization, vol. 36, no. 4 (2004) 401–418
5. Parsopoulos, K. E., Vrahatis, M. N.: Initializing the particle swarm optimizer using the nonlinear simplex method. Advances in Intelligent Systems, Fuzzy Systems, Evolutionary Computation, WSEAS Press (2002) 216–221
6. Shi, Y. H., Eberhart, R. C.: A modified particle swarm optimizer. Proceedings of the IEEE Congress on Evolutionary Computation (CEC 1998), Piscataway, NJ (1998) 69–73
7. Clerc, M.: The swarm and the queen: towards a deterministic and adaptive particle swarm optimization. Proceedings of the IEEE Congress on Evolutionary Computation (1999) 1951–1957
8. Carlisle, A., Dozier, G.: An off-the-shelf PSO. Proceedings of the Workshop on Particle Swarm Optimization, Indianapolis (2001)

Adaptive XCSM for Perceptual Aliasing Problems

Shumei Liu and Tomoharu Nagao

Faculty of Environment and Information Sciences,
Yokohama National University,
79-7, Tokiwadai, Hodogaya-ku, Yokohama 240-8501, Japan

Abstract. Recently, works about Non-Markov environment has attracted increasing attention in autonomous agent control. Based on XCS, XCSM introduced a constant length of bit-register memory into general classifier system structure to record agent's experience. Then combining the current perception with its past experience, the agent gets suitable action successfully. But when the memory becomes longer, its performance will decrease urgently with the expansion of search space. In this paper, an adaptive XCSM (AXCSM) method has been proposed by adapting variable length of memory. The proposal composes of a hierarchical structure. In the first hierarchy, we learn a suitable memory length for this position using general XCS. Then action of the agent is acquired in the second hierarchy using XCSM. The proposal converges to optimal policy as that of XCSM, within shortened search space.

1 Introduction

Due to the limitation of agent's sensor, it maybe result an agent failing to obtain enough information to distinguish between two different situations, which appear identical to the agent, but require two different actions to behave. Such an environment is said to be Non-Markov and the agent is suffering from a perceptual aliasing problem, which disturbs the agent's learning capability seriously [1]. To overcome this problem, generally, we endeavor to expand agent's sensation to convert the Non-Markov environment into a Markov one.

In [2], an improved classifier system [3], XCS, has been introduced, based on the accuracy of the classifier's payoff prediction instead of the prediction itself. It has been shown to reach optimal performance in Markov problem, but failure in Non-Markov problem.

Based on [4], XCSM [5] has been proposed by adding bit-register memory to XCS. For the fixed-length memory, assigned in advance by experience, there are two flaws. One is how to define the fixed length. Generally, we set it by counting the aliasing positions in a given environment. For a simple map, it is easy. But for a harder one, it is not always so exactly to count. The second problem is that, assume that we have gotten a suitable memory length for the maximum aliasing positions, but for any other positions, it is not necessary to use so much long memory. This results in the space wasteful also.

Therefore, we proposes an adaptive XCSM (AXCSM), in which only the maximum memory length is set beforehand, the appropriate length for each rule varies from 0 to the maximum. AXCSM can be seen as a hierarchical structure. The first hierarchy is to learn a suitable memory length for any given position, using general XCS. In the second hierarchy, action is obtained by XCSM. Experiment is pursued to verify the validity of AXCSM.

The remainder of the report is organized as follows. Section 2 presents the perceptual aliasing problem and related works. Section 3 describes the adaptive memory implementation. Experiments are presented and analyzed in Section 4. In section 5, the future work has been prospected.

2 Perceptual Aliasing Problem and Related Work

2.1 Perceptual Aliasing Problem

A typical perceptual aliasing problem is shown in Fig. 1(a), where '■' is wall, 'G' is goal, and ' ' is free. In this report, we indicate that the agent perceives environment by means of Boolean sensors that report the contents of its eight squares adjacent to itself. And the agent moves into 8 free adjacent directions. The learning goal is to find a shortest path to goal state from random start. From

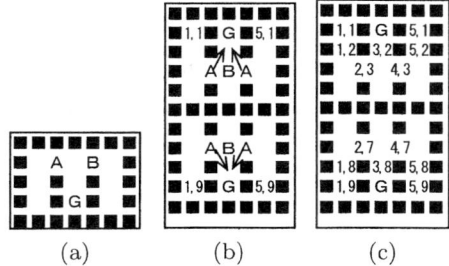

Fig. 1. (a) Environment Woods101; (b) Environment Woods102 marked with two aliasing states and start coordinate; (c) Environment Woods102 marked with coordinates

Fig. 1(a), we can see that the agent has an identical sensation for two distinct locations A and B. To reach goal state 'G', for A, the optimal action is "go-SE"; for B, it is "go-SW". The agent couldn't distinguish the two locations, simply basing on its sensation of the current position in environment.

So, learning for a perceptual aliasing problem is necessary and urgent.

2.2 XCS and XCSM

Classifier in XCS [2] [6] consists of {*condition, action, parameters*}, defined as *strXCS*. Here the *condition*, consisting of {0, 1, #} ("don't care" symbol), specifies agent's sensation; *action* is an integer, towards 8 directions movement; and *parameters* are used to judge the accuracy of a classifier.

When agent perceives its present position, it searches all the classifiers whose condition match to this sensation, gets an optimal action from these matching classifiers, and then performs it to environment. Eventually, a scalar reward is returned to update parameters of these classifiers.

In XCSM, which has been proposed in [5] to Non-Markov environment, a register has been added to agent to record its experience. And the classifier consists of {*strXCS, inCondition, inAction*}, defined as *strXCSM*. The memory space, *inCondition* and *inAction*, consists of symbols {0/1/#}. For the *inCondition*, the symbols retain the same meaning as *condition* in XCS, but they match with content of register. For *inAction*, '0' and '1' set the corresponding bit of the register to '0' and '1', respectively, '#' leaves the corresponding bit unmodified.

However, when *inCondition* and *inAction* are composed of m bit, the search space of *inAction* will possible be a maximum of 3^m. With the m becomes larger, the search space of memory will increase urgently.

Therefore, adaptive XCSM (AXCSM) is proposed in this report. Here, we try to get a smaller classifier set, and a shorter memory for each single classifier.

3 AXCSM

3.1 Framework of AXCSM

The classifier in AXCSM is expanded to {*strXCSM, inLength, inParameters*}. *inLength* is an integer value to define the memory length, and *inParameters*, the same as *parameters* in XCSM, is used to evaluate accuracy of *inLength*. Besides these, the length of *inCondition* and *inAction* are not fixed, but varying with *inLength* from 0 to the assigned maximum in advance.

The framework of AXCSM is outlined as below. Continue this loop until termination criteria is met.

1. get suitable inLength of memory by general XCS
   (a) *set start position and Register randomly*
   (b) *Generate inMatchSet, composed of all classifiers from PopulationSet whose condition and inCondition matched with agent's perception and register respectively, regardless the inLength*
   (c) *select memory length. From inMatchSet, calculate average(fitness) for each inLength, and set this maximum one as suitable memory length*
2. get optimal action for this position by XCSM
   (a) *get MatchSet, composed of all classifiers from inMatchSet, whose* inLength *equals to selected memory length*
   (b) *get Action and inAction; generate ActionSet*
   (c) *execute Action and inAction; update agent's perception and Register*
   (d) *get Reward*
   (e) *update parameters in ActionSet by reward; update inParameters in inMatchSet by discounted reward; run GA to search new classifier*

3.2 Reward-Discounted Policy

As mentioned in Sect. 3.1, *inParameters* in *inMatchSet* will be updated with discounted reward, according to (1). The *r* decreases with the *inLength* linearly.

$$r = reward * f(inLength) = reward * \left(\frac{(disRate - 1) * inLength}{maxLength} + 1 \right) \quad (1)$$

Here, *reward* is real value received from environment; *maxLength* is the maximum memory length; *disRate* is discounted rate for *maxLength*(we set it 0.5).

3.3 Delete Unusually Accessed and Low Fitness Classifier

Analyzing the PopulationSet in XCSM, we knew that there exists some rules, which are generated at the beginning of the learning process, and are seldom accessed. Then we delete those ones, satisfied with (2).

$$\frac{exp}{t - gTime} * \frac{inExp}{t\text{-}ingTime} < p1 * p2 \quad (2)$$

Here, for each classifier, *t* is the present timer value; *exp* is accessed times, *gTime* is last accessed time in XCSM; *inExp* is accessed times, *ingTime* is last accessed time in general XCS; *p1* and *p2* are discounted coefficient, set 0.01 here.

Meanwhile, there are also some rules, with low fitness, and contributes less to learning procedure. Then delete them satisfying with (3). α is set as 0.05.

$$fitness < \alpha * \frac{\sum_{CS}(fitness * num)}{\sum_{CS}(num)} \quad (3)$$

4 Experiment and Result

4.1 Experiment Design

In this report, we consider the maze of Woods102, shown in Fig. 1(b). The agent perceives eight squares adjacent to itself as WALL ('■'), Free (Empty) or Goal ('G'). The action is 8 directions movement. The learning goal is to get shortest route to Goal position.

See the maze in Fig. 1(b), to recognise the two aliasing states, marked with 'A' and 'B', we set the agent starting from four corner positions, (1,1) (1,9) (5,1) and (5,9), as in Fig. 1(c).

During the learning procedure, action selection is changed alternatively between explore and exploit strategy. And explore action part is turned off in the final 2000 problems. Other parameters are set the same as those of [5].

4.2 Experiment on Woods102

We set AXCSM with 8 bit of maximum memory here, the max population is 6000, and 20000 problems has been pursued. Results for AXCSM have been shown in Fig. 2, compared with that of XCSM.

The first result is about average steps to goal position, which is not shown here. It converged to the same optimum as that of XCSM finally.

Figure 2(a) shows the population size fluctuating with the learning procedure, averaged for every 100 problems. The population size in AXCSM is less than that of XCSM. Research space decreases within this compacted Population Set.

Figure 2(b) shows the memory length of all rules in the final Population Set after 20000 problems. The horizontal axis is the rule's serial number, and the vertical axis is memory length for each rule. We have mentioned in Sect. 3.2 that we return a discounted reward to rule according to its different memory length. Supposing that the agent receives an identical reward from environment, the rules with shorter memory length will be more valuable and will survive with high opportunity. Adversely, the rules with longer memory length will be eliminated more easily.

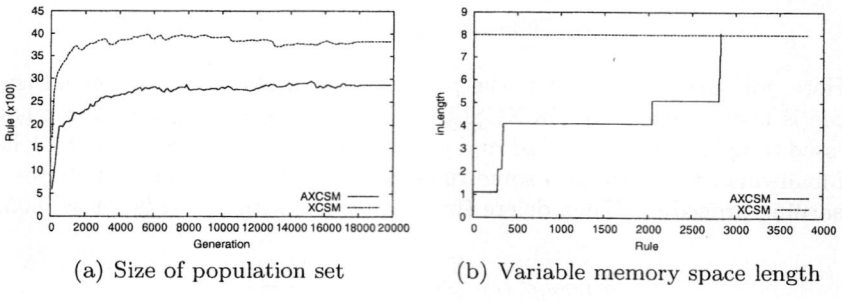

(a) Size of population set   (b) Variable memory space length

Fig. 2. Performance of AXCSM compared with XCMS

From Fig. 2(b), we can firstly see that the curve of XCSM ended at about 3824 in horizontal axis. This means that there are 3824 rules in final population, while in AXCSM, it is about 2829. The proposal has less rules than that of XCSM. It is in coherent with the result of Fig. 2(a). Secondly, in XCSM all the rules are with the same memory length, 8 bit. While in AXCSM, the rules construct hierarchical distribution, with memory length ranging from 0 bit to 8 bit, and average to 3.95 bit. Thus the whole memory space becomes more contractible.

Finally, we observe the agent's trail track with the optimal policy obtained by AXCSM in Table 1, to validate that the memory length works as we designed. The "inLen" item means that when agent reaches to this position, it needs this number of memory bit to remember its past experience. The "Register" item is Register content for each position.

We can summary that, on the route to Goal position, the memory length has been changed, and the Register content varies with it also.

Table 1. Register Content on Woods102

pos	inLen	Register	pos	inLen	Register	pos	inLen	Register	pos	inLen	Register
(1,1)	1	0	(5,1)	1	0	(1,9)	1	0	(5,9)	1	0
(1,2)	1	0	(5,2)	4	0000	(1,8)	4	0000	(5,8)	4	0100
(2,3)	**5**	**1000,0**	**(4,3)**	**5**	**0101,0**	**(2,7)**	**5**	**0000,0**	**(4,7)**	**5**	**0110,0**
(3,2)	1	0	(3,2)	1	0	(3,8)	1	0	(3,8)	1	0

5 Summary and Future

This work proposes an adaptive XCSM (AXCSM) to harder Non-Markov environment. The classifier in XCSM owns a fixed length of memory to record its past experience. But with the fixed length becomes longer, the search space will expand also. Upon that, we involved a variable memory length to XCSM (AXCSM), ranging from 0 bit to the maximum length, which is defined beforehand. By experiment, we summarized that the proposal obtained smaller population, and the memory length for each rule also decreased.

Based on the analysis above, we confirmed that the AXCSM performed better than XCSM determinately, especially for complicated maze. But we haven't applied it on a real-value environment till now, and could not foresee how it will behave. On the other hand, how to get a suitable maximum memory length autonomously is also another concern for future research.

References

1. Crook, P.A., Hayes, G.: Learning in a state of confusion:perceptual aliasing in grid word navigation. In: Proceedings of Towards Intelligent Mobil Robots(TIMR 2003)4th British Conference on(Mobile) Robotics. (2003)
2. Wilson, S.: Classifier fitness based on accuracy. Evolutionary Computation **3** (1995) 149–175
3. Boer, B.D.: Classifier Systems: A useful approach to Machine Learning? Master's Thesis Leiden University, Holland (1994)
4. Cliff, D., Ross, S.: Adding temporary memory to ZCS. Adaptive Behavior **3** (1995) 101–150
5. Lanzi, P., Wilson, S.: Toward optimal classifier system performance in non-markov envionments. Evolutionary Computation **8** (2000) 393–418
6. Butz, M., Wilson, S.W.: An algorithmic descriptions of XCS. In: Advcnaes in Learning Classifier Systems, Third International Workshop,Lecture Notes in Artificial Intelligence, Berlin:Springer-Verlag (2000)

Discrete Particle Swarm Optimization (DPSO) Algorithm for Permutation Flowshop Scheduling to Minimize Makespan

K. Rameshkumar[1], R.K. Suresh[1], and K.M. Mohanasundaram[2]

[1] Department of Production Engineering,
Amrita School of Engineering, Amrita Vishwa Vidyapeetham,
Ettimadai, Coimbatore 641105, India
k_rameshkumar@ettimadai.amrita.edu
[2] Department of Mechanical Engineering,
PSG College of Technology, Coimbatore, India

Abstract. In this paper a discrete particle swarm optimization (DPSO) algorithm is proposed to solve permutation flowshop scheduling problems with the objective of minimizing the makespan. A discussion on implementation details of DPSO algorithm is presented. The proposed algorithm has been applied to a set of benchmark problems and performance of the algorithm is evaluated by comparing the obtained results with the results published in the literature. Further, it is found that the proposed improvement heuristic algorithm performs better when local search is performed. The results are presented.

1 Introduction

Flowshop scheduling is one of the best-known production scheduling problem which has been proved to be strongly NP Complete [1]. It involves determination of the order of processing jobs on machines, arranged in series, to optimize the desired measure of performance such as makespan, total flowtime, etc. Makespan is the completion time of the last job. Minimization of the makespan time ensures increased utilization of the machines and thus leads to a high throughput [2,3]. The order of processing of jobs affects the performance measures.

Flowshop scheduling problem is a widely researched problem. Exact and constructive heuristic algorithms for solving static permutation flowshop scheduling problems (PFSPs) have been proposed by various researchers [4] over the years with the objective of minimizing makespan. The exact techniques are computationally effective for small size problems. But, for large size problems, such methods are computationally expensive and heuristics are resorted to. Heuristics for the flowshop scheduling problems can be a constructive heuristics or improvement heuristics. Johnson [5], Gupta [6], Palmer [7], Dannenbring [8], Koulamas [9] and Nawaz *et al.* [10] have proposed constructive heuristics. Among these, the NEH heuristics developed by Nawaz *et al.* performs better [11].

Unlike constructive heuristics, improvement heuristics take a solution and try to improve it. Dannenbring [8], Ho and Chang [12], Suliman [13] have proposed

DPSO Algorithm for Permutation Flowshop Scheduling to Minimize Makespan 573

improvement heuristics. General purpose metaheuristics such as genetic algorithm [14-19], simulated annealing [20,21] and tabu search [11,23,24] have also been applied successfully for PFSPs.

In this paper, a discrete particle swarm optimization algorithm has been proposed for solving a set of benchmark FSPs published in the literature [25,15]. The performance measure under study is the makespan value. The proposed approach is based on the PSO heuristic proposed in [26]. Performance of the proposed approach is evaluated by comparing the obtained results with the results published in the literature [18,19].

2 Notations and Conventions

n	Number of jobs to be scheduled
m	Number of machines in the flowshop
t_{ij}	Processing time of operation j of job i
C_i	Completion time of job i
C_{max}	Makespan
C^*	Optimal makespan value or lower bound value reported in the literature.
N	Swarm size
t	Iteration counter
t_{max}	Maximum number of Iterations
P_k^t	Sequence of the kth particle during t^{th} iteration i.e, $P_{current}$
$Z(P_k^t)$	Makespan value of kth particle during t^{th} iteration
$P_{k(best)}$	Particle best, i.e., the sequence with least makespan value, found by the particle up to 't' iterations, i.e, P_{best}
$Z(P_{k(best)}^t)$	Makespan value of the P_{best} sequence of the kth particle
G	Global best sequence (G_{best}) = Min $\{ Z(P_{k(best)}^t); k = 1, N \}$
L	Length of the velocity list
v_k^t	Velocity of kth particle during t^{th} iteration
c_1, c_2, c_3	Learning coefficients

3 Formulation of the Static Permutation Flowshop Scheduling Problem

The permutation flowshop scheduling problem under study consists of scheduling 'n' jobs, with known processing times t_{ij}, on 'm' machines with the sequence of processing as identical and unidirectional. A schedule of this type is called a permutation schedule. The objective is to find the job sequence that minimizes the makespan. The makespan of the flowshop problem is defined by the time span necessary to complete processing of all jobs. The makespan is given by equation 1.

$$C_{max} = \max\{C_i, i=1,2,\cdots,n\} \qquad (1)$$

It is assumed that machine can process only one job at a time and no pre-emption is allowed.

4 Proposed Discrete Particle Swarm Optimization (DPSO) Algorithm

Particle swarm optimization (PSO) is a recently developed population based optimization method inspired by the social behavior of organisms such as bird flocking and fish schooling. PSO was first applied to optimize various continuous nonlinear functions by Kennedy and Eberhart [27, 28]. Later, PSO has been successfully applied to a wide variety of problems such as power and voltage control [29], neural network training [30], mass-spring system [31], task assignment [32], supplier selection and ordering problem [33], optimal operational path finding for automated drilling operations [34], traveling salesman problems [26], etc. Application of DPSO algorithm for solving scheduling problem is not reported in the literature.

4.1 DPSO Algorithm for FSPs

The PSO starts with a population of randomly generated initial solutions and searches iteratively in the problem space for optimal solution. The potential solutions are called particles which fly through the problem space by following their best particles. PSO starts the search process with a group of randomly generated sequences called particles. After this, P_{best} and G_{best} sequences are identified. Now, the iterative search process starts with computing velocity of each particle v_k using equation 2.

$$v_k^{t+1} = c_1 \times v_k^t + c_2 (P_{Best} - P_{Current}) + c_3 (G_{Best} - P_{Current}) \qquad (2)$$

New position of a particle at time (t+1) is determined by its current velocity v_k^t, and $P_{k(best)}$ and G_{best} sequences. c_1, c_2 and c_3 are learning co-efficients. Particle position i.e, sequence is updated after every iteration using equation 3.

New position = Current position + Particle velocity.

$$P_k^{t+1} = P_k^t + v_k^{t+1} \qquad (3)$$

The velocity index of a particle k at time t is computed using equation 4.

$$v_k = ((i_q, j_q)); q = 1, L \qquad (4)$$

Where i, j represents job positions, and L represents the length of the list or the maximum number of possible transpositions which is randomly generated between 1 and n.

Here v_k refers to exchange of job positions (i_1, j_1), then positions (i_2, j_2), etc. After generating the velocity index v_k, particle velocity v_k^t is computed using the equation 2. Various operations performed for computing particle velocity and updating particle positions are explained below:

Subtraction (position – position) operator: Let x_1 and x_2 be two positions representing two different sequences. The difference $x_2 - x_1$ is a velocity v. In the equation 2, for example subtracting two positions i.e. ($P_{best} - P_{current}$) results in a velocity which is a set of transpositions.

Addition (position + velocity) operator: Let x be the position and v be the velocity. New position x_1 is found by applying the first transposition of v to p, i.e, $x_1 = x + v$ then the second one to the result etc.

Addition (velocity + velocity) operator: Let v_1 and v_2 be two velocities. In order to compute $v_1 + v_2$, we consider the list of transpositions which contains first the 'ones' of v_1, followed by the 'ones' of v_2.

Multiplication (Coefficient × velocity) operator: Let c be the learning coefficient and v be the velocity. $c \times v$ results in a new velocity.

A numerical illustration of the above operations used in the proposed DPSO algorithm is presented in the section 4.3. Pseudocode of the DPSO algorithm for the flowshop scheduling problem is presented in Fig. 1.

4.2 Pseudocode of the DPSO Algorithm

$t = 0$
For (k = 1, N)
        Generate P_k^t
        Evaluate $Z(P_k^t)$
        $P_{k(best)} = P_k^t$
        G_{best} = best particle found in P_k^t
do {
        For (k = 1, N)
        $v_k^{t+1} = c_1 \times v_k^t + c_2 (P_{best} - P_{current}) + c_3 (G_{best} - P_{current})$
        $P_k^{t+1} = P_k^t + v_k^{t+1}$
        If (P_k^{t+1} is better than P_k^t)
        $P_{k(best)} = P_k^{t+1}$
        If (P_k^{t+1} is better than G_{best})
        $G_{best} = P_k^{t+1}$
        $t = t + 1$;
} (while $t < t_{max}$)
Output G_{best}

Fig. 1. Pseudocode of the DPSO algorithm for FSP

4.3 Numerical Illustration of DPSO Algorithm

Let us assume the following data during t^{th} iteration.

P_k^t = {2,3,1,4} ($P_{Current}$ Sequence);

$P_{k(best)}^t$ = {2,3,1,4} (P_{Best} Sequence), and

G^t = {3,4,2,1} (G_{Best} Sequence)

Computation procedure for calculating particle velocity and particle movement is explained as follows:

4.3.1 Generating Velocity Index

Velocity index v_k for the particle k is computed as follows:

Let length of the velocity list L_k be equal to 2 with the randomly generated list {(2,4), (4,1)}. Similarly, velocity index is computed for other particles.

4.3.2 Calculation of Particle Velocity

For each particle in the population, velocity for moving the particle from one position to the other position is calculated using equation 2. The coefficient times the velocity operator is used to find out the number of velocity components to be applied over the position. For example, if the coefficient value is 0.5, then 50 percent of the velocity components are randomly selected from the velocity list and applied over the position.

$$v_k^{t+1} = 0.5 \times [(2,4),(4,1)] + 0.5 \times [(2,3,1,4) - (2,3,1,4)] + 0.5[(3,4,2,1) - (2,3,1,4)]$$

$$= [(2,4)] + 0.5 \times [0] + 0.5[(1,2),(2,4),(3,4)] = [(2,4),(1,2),(2,4)]$$

4.3.3 Particle Movement

Moving the particles from their current position to the new position is done using equation (3).

i.e. $P_k^{t+1} = P_k^t + v_k^{t+1} = \{2,3,1,4\} + [(2,4),(2,3),(2,4)]$

$= \{2,4,1,3\} + [(2,3),(2,4)] = \{2,1,4,3\} + [(2,4)] = \{2,3,4,1\}$

$P_k^{t+1} = \{2,3,4,1\}$

Similarly for all the particles P_k^{t+1} is computed and $P_{k(best)}^t$ (P_{best}) and G (G_{best}) are updated.

5 Experimental Investigation

The DPSOA has been tested on 14 benchmark problems given by Carlier [25] and Reeves [15]. These test problems have number of jobs (n) varying from 7 to 20, and the number of machines (m) from 4 to 15. By trial and error, optimum swarm size is found to be 10. In all our computational effort, the total number of sequences evaluated by the algorithm is limited to $50n^2$.

The problem of solving FSPs using DPSO has been done in two phases. In the first phase of our study, DPSO algorithm is applied for solving a set of Carlier FSPs [25]. It is found that the DPSO algorithm obtained the best results (C^*) for six out of the eight benchmark problems. The results presented in Table 1 indicate that DPSO algorithm performs better when problem size is comparatively small. Further, in order to improve the performance of DPSO algorithm, a local search is applied at the end of every iteration. During local search every job except the last one is interchanged with its successor. There will be (n-1) number of interchanges. It is to be noted that an interchange which does not improve the makespan value is ignored. The result obtained by the DPSO algorithm with local search is presented in column number 6 of Table 1. When DPSO algorithm assisted by local search it is able to find the best solutions for all the eight Carlier problems.

Table 1. Carlier benchmark results (makespan)

Problem	Problem Size		C^*	DPSO	DPSO + Local search
	n	m			
Car1	11	5	7038	7038	7038
Car2	13	4	7166	7166	7166
Car3	12	5	7312	7392	7312
Car4	14	4	8003	8003	8003
Car5	10	6	7720	7768	7720
Car6	8	9	8505	8505	8505
Car7	7	7	6590	6590	6590
Car8	8	8	8366	8366	8366

In the second phase our study both the DPSO algorithm and the hybrid approach, i.e, DPSO assisted by local search, are applied to solve large size problems. Results are presented in Table 2. It is found that the DPSO algorithm assisted by local search perform better even with the large size problems.

Table 2. Reeves benchmark results (makespan)

Problem	Problem Size		C^*	DPSO	DPSO + Local search
	n	m			
Rec01	20	5	1247	1264	1249
Rec03	20	5	1109	1115	1111
Rec05	20	5	1242	1254	1245
Rec07	20	10	566	1624	1584
Rec09	20	10	1537	1621	1574
Rec11	20	10	1431	1590	1446

In order to evaluate the performance of DPSO algorithms proposed in this paper, a comparative study is performed with the results obtained by the popular constructive heuristics such as NEH, CDS, RA, GUPTA and PALMER [18] and the results are presented in Tables 3 and 4.

Table 3. Carlier benchmark results (makespan)

Problem	Problem Size		Constructive Heuristics (Makespan value)					DPSO	
	n	m	Palmer	Gupta	CDS	RA	NEH	no local search	with local search
Car1	11	5	7472	7348	7202	7817	7038	7038	7038
Car2	13	4	7940	7534	7410	7509	7940	7166	7166
Car3	12	5	7725	7399	7399	7399	7503	7312	7312
Car4	14	4	8423	8423	8423	8357	8003	8003	8003
Car5	10	6	8520	8773	8627	8940	8190	7720	7720
Car6	8	9	9487	9441	9553	9514	9159	8505	8505
Car7	7	7	7639	7639	6819	6923	7668	6590	6590
Car8	8	8	9023	9224	8903	9062	9032	8366	8366

Table 4. Reeves benchmark results (makespan)

Problem	Problem Size		Constructive Heuristics (Makespan value)					DPSO	
	n	m	Palmer	Gupta	CDS	RA	NEH	no local search	with local search
Rec01	20	5	1391	1434	1399	1399	1334	1264	1249
Rec03	20	5	1223	1380	1273	1159	1136	1115	1111
Rec05	20	5	1290	1429	1338	1434	1294	1254	1245
Rec07	20	10	1715	1678	1697	1722	1637	1624	1584
Rec09	20	10	1915	1792	1639	1714	1692	1621	1574
Rec11	20	10	1685	1765	1597	1636	1635	1590	1446

The relative percentage increase in makespan yielded by the proposed DPSO algorithms, genetic algorithm [18] and a hybrid genetic algorithm [19] for these benchmark problems, are presented in Tables 5 and 6.

Table 5. Relative percentage increase in makespan (Carlier Problems)

Problem	Problem Size		Relative percentage increase in makespan			
	n	m	DPSO		Hybrid GA (Wang)	GA (Ponnambalam)
			no local search	with local search		
Car1	11	5	0.00	0.00	0.00	0.00
Car2	13	4	0.00	0.00	0.00	0.00
Car3	12	5	1.09	0.00	0.00	2.42
Car4	14	4	0.00	0.00	0.00	0.00
Car5	10	6	0.62	0.00	0.00	0.36
Car6	8	9	0.00	0.00	0.76	0.00
Car7	7	7	0.00	0.00	0.00	0.00
Car8	8	8	0.00	0.00	0.00	0.00

Table 6. Relative percentage increase in makespan (Reeves Problems)

Problem	Problem Size		Relative percentage increase in makespan			
	n	m	DPSO no local search	DPSO with local search	Hybrid GA (Wang)	GA (Ponnambalam)
Rec01	20	5	1.36	0.16	0.14	8.26
Rec03	20	5	0.54	0.18	0.09	7.21
Rec05	20	5	0.97	0.24	0.29	5.23
Rec07	20	10	3.70	1.15	0.69	8.56
Rec09	20	10	5.47	2.41	0.64	5.14
Rec11	20	10	11.11	1.05	1.1	8.32

Since the data available in [19] is the relative percentage increase in makespan, the same has been computed and presented in Tables 4 and 5. The relative percentage increase in makespan is computed as follows:

$$\frac{(Makespan\ obtained\ by\ the\ heuristic - optimal\ makespan\ value)}{optimal\ makespan\ value} \times 100 \quad (5)$$

The results presented in Tables 1 and 2 indicate that the performance of DPSO algorithm is better when local search is employed. It is clear from the results presented in Tables 3 and 4 that DPSO algorithms outperform constructive heuristics. From the Table 5, performance of the DPSO algorithm is found to be better than the genetic algorithms [18] and the hybrid GA [19] for the small size PFSPs [25]. The results of large size PFSPs [15] are presented in Table 6. It indicates that the results of the Hybrid GA are better than the DPSO algorithms proposed in our paper. Better performance of the hybrid GA is due to high computational effort applied in [19]. The computational complexity of the DPSO algorithm is $50(n^2)$ where as for the hybrid GA it is approximately $800\ (n^2)$.

6 Conclusions

In this paper a discrete particle swarm optimization (DPSO) algorithm is proposed to solve permutation flowshop scheduling problems. Drawbacks of DPSO in solving FSP have been identified. Local search procedure has been found to help the DPSO algorithm to escape from the local optima. The obtained results are compared with the results published in the literature. DPSO algorithms proposed in this paper found to perform better in terms of quality of the solutions and computational complexity.

Acknowledgment

The authors are thankful to the three anonymous reviewers for their comments to improve the earlier version of this paper.

References

1. Garey, M.R., Johnson, D. S.:Computers and Intractability: a guide to theory of NP – Completeness, Freeman, SanFrancisco (1979).
2. Pinedo, M.:Scheduling: Theory, Algorithms and systems, Second ed. Prentice-Hall, Englewood Cliffs, NJ (2002).
3. Chandraseakaran Rajendran, Sudipta Lahiri, Narendran, T.T.:Evaluation of heuristics for scheduling in a flowshop : a case study, Production Planning and control, 4 (2), (1993), 153-158.
4. Dimopoulos, C., Ali. M. S. Zalza.:Recent developments in evolutionary computation for manufacturing optimization: problems, solutions, and Computations, IEEE Transactions on Evolutionary Computation, 4(2), (2000), 93-113.
5. Johnson, S.:Optimal two and three stage production schedules with setup times included, Naval Research Logistics Quarterly, 1, (1954), 61.
6. Gupta, J.N.:A functional heuristic algorithm for flowshop scheduling problem, Operational Research Quarterly, 22(1), (1971), 39-47.
7. Palmer, D.:Sequencing jobs through a multi stage process in the minimum total time- a quick method of obtaining near optimum, Operational Research Quarterly, 16(1), (1965), 101-107.
8. Dannenbring, D. G.:An evaluation of flowshop sequencing heuristic, Management science 23(11), (1977) 1174-1182.
9. Koulamas, C.:A new constructive heuristic for flow-shop scheduling problem, European Journal of Operational Research 105, (1998) 66-71.
10. Nawaz, M., Enscore Jr, E., Ham, I.: A heuristics algorithm for the m-machine, n-job flowshop sequencing problem, Omega, 11(1), (1983) 91-95.
11. Taillard, E.:Some efficient heuristic methods for flowshop sequencing problem, European journal of Operational research 47, (1990), 67-74.
12. Ho, J.C., Chang, Y. L.:A new heuristic for n-job , m-machine flow-shop problem, European Journal of Operational Research, 52, (1991), 194-202.
13. Suliman, S.:A two-phase heuristic approach to the permutation flow-shop scheduling problem, International Journal of Production Economics, 64, (2000), 143-152.
14. Chen, C.L., Vempati, V.S., Aljaber, N.:An application of genetic algorithms for flowshop problems, European Journal of Operational Research, 80, (1995), 389-396.
15. Reeves, C. R.: A Genetic Algorithm for Flowshop Sequencing, Computers and Operations Research, 22(1), (1995) 5-13.
16. Murata, T., Ishibuchi, H., Tanaka, H.:Genetic algorithms for flowshop scheduling problems, Computers and industrial Engineering, 30(4), (1996), 1061-1071.
17. Reeves, C., Yamada, T.:Genetic algorithms, path relinking, and the flowshop sequencing problem, Evolutionary Computation, 6(1), (1998),45-60.
18. Ponnambalam, S. G., Aravindan, P., Chandrasekaran , S.:Constructive and improvement flow shop scheduling heuristics: an extensive evaluation, Production Planning & Control, Vol. 12, No. 4, (2001) 335- 344.
19. Wang, L., Zheng, D. Z. :An Effective Hybrid heuristic for flowshop scheduling, International Journal of Advanced manufacturing technology, 21, (2003), 38-44.
20. Osman, I., Potts, C.:Simulated annealing for permutation flow-shop scheduling, OMEGA, The international Journal of Management Science, 17(6), (1989), 551-557.
21. Ogbu, F., Smith, D.:Simulated Annealing for the permutation flow-shop problem, OMEGA, The international Journal of Management Science, 19(1), (1990), 64-67.

22. Ishibuchi, H., Misaki, S., Tanaka, H.:Modified simulated annealing algorithms for the flowshop sequencing problem, European Journal of Operational Research, 81, (1995), 388-398.
23. Nowicki, E., Smutnicki, C.:A fast Tabu Search algorithm for the permutation flow-shop problem, European Journal of Operational Research, 91, (1996), 160-175.
24. Moccellin, J.A.V., Dos Santos, M.O.:A new heuristic method for the permutation flowshop scheduling problem, Journal of the Operational Research Siciety, 105, (2000), 883-886.
25. Carlier, J.:Ordonnancements a contraintes disjonctives, Rairo Recherehe operationelle / Operations Research, 12, (1978) 333-351.
26. Clerc, M.:Discrete particle swarm optimization, illustrated by the Traveling Salesman Problem, New Optimization Techniques in Engineering. Heidelberg, Germany: Springer, (2004) 219-239.
27. Kennedy, J., Eberhart, R.C.:Particle swarm optimization, Proceedings of IEEE International Conference on Neural Networks, Piscataway, NJ, USA, (1995), 1942-1948.
28. Eberhart, R. C., Kennedy, J.:A new optimizer using particle swarm theory, Proceedings of the Sixth International symposium on Micro machine and Human Science, Nagoya, Japan, IEEE Service center, Piscataway, NJ, (1995) 39-43.
29. Abido, M.A.:Optimal power flow using particle swarm optimization, Electrical Power and Energy Systems 24, (2002) 563-571
30. Van den Bergh, F., Engelbecht, A.P.: Cooperative learning in neural networks using particle swarm optimizers, South African Computer Journal 26 (2000) 84-90.
31. Brandstatter, B. , Baumgartner, U. :Particle swarm optimization: mass-spring system analogon, IEEE Transactions on Magnetics 38 (2002) 997- 1000.
32. Salman, A., Ahmad, I., Al-Madani, S.:Particle swarm optimization for task assignment problem", Microprocessors and Microsystems, 26, 2003.
33. Yeh, L. W.:Optimal Procurement Policies for Multi-product Multi-supplier with Capacity Constraint and Price Discount, Master thesis, Department of Industrial Engineering and Management, Yuan Ze University, Taiwan, R.O.C., (2003).
34. Onwubolu, G.C., Clerc, M.: Optimal operational path for automated drilling operations by a new heuristic approach using particle swarm optimization, International Journal of Production Research, 42(3), (2004), 473-491.

Unified Particle Swarm Optimization for Solving Constrained Engineering Optimization Problems

K.E. Parsopoulos[1] and M.N. Vrahatis[2]

[1] Computational Intelligence Laboratory (CI Lab), Department of Mathematics,
University of Patras, GR–26110 Patras, Greece
{kostasp, vrahatis}@math.upatras.gr
[2] University of Patras Artificial Intelligence Research Center (UPAIRC),
University of Patras, GR–26110 Patras, Greece

Abstract. We investigate the performance of the recently proposed Unified Particle Swarm Optimization method on constrained engineering optimization problems. For this purpose, a penalty function approach is employed and the algorithm is modified to preserve feasibility of the encountered solutions. The algorithm is illustrated on four well–known engineering problems with promising results. Comparisons with the standard local and global variant of Particle Swarm Optimization are reported and discussed.

1 Introduction

Many engineering applications, such as structural optimization, engineering design, VLSI design, economics, allocation and location problems [1], involve difficult optimization problems that must be solved efficiently and effectively. Due to the nature of these applications, the solutions usually need to be constrained in specific parts of the search space that are delimited by linear and/or nonlinear constraints.

Different deterministic as well as stochastic algorithms have been developed for tackling such problems. Deterministic approaches such as Feasible Direction and Generalized Gradient Descent make strong assumptions on the continuity and differentiability of the objective function [1,2]. Therefore their applicability is limited since these characteristics are rarely met in problems that arise in real–life applications. On the other hand, stochastic optimization algorithms such as Genetic Algorithms, Evolution Strategies, Evolutionary Programming and Particle Swarm Optimization (PSO) do not make such assumptions and they have been successfully applied for tackling constrained optimization problems during the past few years [3,4,5,6,7].

Most of the aforementioned optimization algorithms have been primarily designed to address unconstrained optimization problems. Thus, constraint–handling techniques are usually incorporated in the algorithm in order to direct the search towards the desired (feasible) regions of the search space. The most common constraint–handling technique is the use of penalty functions [3,8,9,7]. In these approaches, the problem is solved as an unconstrained one, where the objective function is designed such that non–feasible solutions are characterized by high function values (in minimization cases). The popularity of penalty–based approaches for constraint–handling is based mostly on their simplicity and direct applicability that does not involve neither modifications of the employed algorithm nor development of specialized operators to tackle constraints.

Unified Particle Swarm Optimization (UPSO) is a recently proposed PSO scheme that harnesses the local and global variant of PSO, combining their exploration and exploitation abilities without imposing additional requirements in terms of function evaluations [10]. Preliminary studies have shown that UPSO can tackle efficiently different optimization problems [10,11].

We investigate the performance of UPSO on four well–known constrained engineering optimization problems. A penalty function approach is adopted and the obtained results are compared to that of the standard PSO algorithm, providing useful conclusions regarding the efficiency of the unified scheme. The rest of the paper is organized as follows. The employed penalty function is described in Section 2, while Section 3 is devoted to the description of UPSO. The considered test problems as well as the obtained results are reported and discussed in Section 4. The paper closes with conclusions in Section 5.

2 The Penalty Function Approach

The constrained optimization problem can be formulated, in general, as:

$$\min_{X \in S \subset \mathbb{R}^n} f(X), \tag{1}$$

$$\text{subject to } g_i(X) \leqslant 0, \quad i = 1, \ldots, m, \tag{2}$$

where m is the number of constraints. Different inequality and equality constraints can be easily transformed into the form of Eq. (2). The corresponding penalty function can be defined as [3]:

$$F(X) = f(X) + H(X), \tag{3}$$

where $H(X)$ is a *penalty factor* that is strictly positive for all non–feasible solutions. Penalty functions with static, dynamic, annealing and adaptive penalties have been proposed and successfully applied in different applications [3,7].

In the current study, we employed a penalty function that includes information about both the number of the violated constraints as well as the degree of violation. Thus, the penalty factor is defined as [8]:

$$H(X) = w_1 \operatorname{NVC}_X + w_2 \operatorname{SVC}_X, \tag{4}$$

where NVC_X is the number of constraints that are violated by X; SVC_X is the sum of all violated constraints, i.e.,

$$\operatorname{SVC}_X = \sum_{i=1}^{m} \max\{0, g_i(X)\},$$

and w_1, w_2, are static weights. The selection of this form of penalties was based on the promising results obtained by using such penalty functions with evolutionary algorithms [8].

In general, the penalty function influences heavily the performance of an algorithm in solving constrained optimization problems. Sophisticated and problem–based penalty functions can increase the algorithm's performance significantly. To avoid the possibly large influence of the employed penalty function on the performance of the algorithms, we used static weights w_1 and w_2, although self–adaptive approaches that modify the weights dynamically through co–evolution schemes, as well as more complicated penalty functions, have been successfully applied in relative works [8,6].

3 Unified Particle Swarm Optimization

PSO is a stochastic, population–based algorithm for solving optimization problems. It was introduced in 1995 by Eberhart and Kennedy for numerical optimization tasks and its dynamic is based on principles that govern socially organized groups of individuals [12].

In PSO's context, the population is called a *swarm* and its individuals (search points) are called *particles*. Each particle has three main characteristics: an adaptable velocity with which it moves in the search space, a memory where it stores the best position it has ever visited in the search space (i.e., the position with the lowest function value), and the social sharing of information, i.e., the knowledge of the best position ever visited by all particles in its neighborhood. The neighborhoods are usually determined based on the indices of the particles, giving rise to the two main variants of PSO, namely the *global* and the *local* variant. In the former, the whole swarm is considered as the neighborhood of each particle, while in the latter strictly smaller neighborhoods are used.

Assume an n–dimensional function, $f : S \subset \mathbb{R}^n \to \mathbb{R}$, and a swarm, $\mathbb{S} = \{X_1, X_2, \ldots, X_N\}$, of N particles. The i-th particle, $X_i \in S$, its velocity, V_i, as well as its best position, $P_i \in S$, are n–dimensional vectors. A neighborhood of radius m of X_i consists of the particles $X_{i-m}, \ldots, X_i, \ldots, X_{i+m}$. Assume b_i to be the index of the particle that attained the best previous position among all the particles in the neighborhood of X_i, and t to be the iteration counter. Then, according to the *constriction coefficient* version of PSO, the swarm is updated using the equations [13],

$$V_i(t+1) = \chi \Big[V_i(t) + c_1 r_1 \big(P_i(t) - X_i(t) \big) + c_2 r_2 \big(P_{b_i}(t) - X_i(t) \big) \Big], \quad (5)$$

$$X_i(t+1) = X_i(t) + V_i(t+1), \quad (6)$$

where $i = 1, 2, \ldots, N$; χ is the constriction coefficient; c_1 and c_2 are positive constants, referred to as *cognitive* and *social* parameters, respectively; and r_1, r_2 are random vectors with components uniformly distributed in $[0, 1]$. Default values for χ, c_1 and c_2 are determined in the theoretical analysis of Clerc and Kennedy [13].

The performance of a population–based algorithm is heavily dependent on the trade–off between its *exploration* and *exploitation* abilities, i.e., its ability to explore wide areas of the search space and its ability to converge rapidly towards the most promising solutions, respectively. The global variant of PSO promotes exploitation since all particles are attracted by the same best position, thereby converging faster towards the same point. On the other hand, the local variant has better exploration properties since the information regarding the best position of each neighborhood is communicated to the rest of the swarm through neighboring particles. Therefore, the attraction to specific points is weaker, thus, preventing the swarm from getting trapped in local minima. Obviously, the proper selection of neighborhood size affects the trade–off between exploration and exploitation. However, the selection of neighborhood size is heavily based on the experience of the user [10].

The *Unified Particle Swarm Optimization* (UPSO) scheme was recently proposed as an alternative that combines the exploration and exploitation properties of both the local and global PSO variant [10]. Let $\mathcal{G}_i(t+1)$ and $\mathcal{L}_i(t+1)$ denote the velocity update of the particle X_i for the global and local PSO variant, respectively [10],

$$\mathcal{G}_i(t+1) = \chi \left[V_i(t) + c_1 r_1 \big(P_i(t) - X_i(t)\big) + c_2 r_2 \big(P_b(t) - X_i(t)\big) \right], \quad (7)$$

$$\mathcal{L}_i(t+1) = \chi \left[V_i(t) + c_1 r'_1 \big(P_i(t) - X_i(t)\big) + c_2 r'_2 \big(P_{b_i}(t) - X_i(t)\big) \right], \quad (8)$$

where t denotes the iteration number; b is the index of the best particle of the whole swarm (global variant); and b_i is the index of the best particle in the neighborhood of X_i (local variant). The main UPSO scheme is defined by [10]:

$$\mathcal{U}_i(t+1) = (1-u)\,\mathcal{L}_i(t+1) + u\,\mathcal{G}_i(t+1), \quad (9)$$

$$X_i(t+1) = X_i(t) + \mathcal{U}_i(t+1), \quad (10)$$

where $u \in [0,1]$ is a parameter called the *unification factor*, which balances the influence of the global and local search directions in the unified scheme. The standard global PSO variant is obtained by setting $u = 1$ in Eq. (9), while $u = 0$ corresponds to the standard local PSO variant. All values $u \in (0,1)$, correspond to composite variants of PSO that combine the exploration and exploitation characteristics of the global and local variant.

Besides the aforementioned scheme, a stochastic parameter that imitates mutation in evolutionary algorithms can also be incorporated in Eq. (9) to enhance the exploration capabilities of UPSO [10]. Thus, depending on which variant UPSO is mostly based, Eq. (9) can be written as [10],

$$\mathcal{U}_i(t+1) = (1-u)\,\mathcal{L}_i(t+1) + r_3\,u\,\mathcal{G}_i(t+1), \quad (11)$$

which is mostly based on the local variant, or

$$\mathcal{U}_i(t+1) = r_3\,(1-u)\,\mathcal{L}_i(t+1) + u\,\mathcal{G}_i(t+1), \quad (12)$$

which is mostly based on the global variant, where $r_3 \sim \mathcal{N}(\mu, \sigma^2 I)$ is a normally distributed parameter, and I is the identity matrix. Although r_3 imitates mutation, the obtained scheme is consistent with the PSO dynamics.

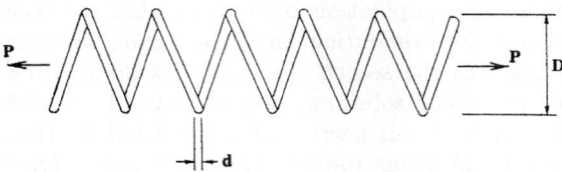

Fig. 1. The tension/compression spring problem

4 Results and Discussion

In the experiments we used four well–known constrained engineering optimization problems:

Problem 1: *Design of a tension/compression spring* [14]. This problem consists of the minimization of the weight of the tension/compression spring illustrated in Fig. 1, subject to constraints on the minimum deflection, shear stress, surge frequency, diameter and design variables. The design variables are the wire diameter, d, the mean coil diameter, D, and the number of active coils, N. The problem is formulated as:

$$\min_X \; f(X) = (N+2)Dd^2,$$

subject to:

$$g_1(X): \; 1 - \frac{D^3 N}{71785 d^4} \leqslant 0,$$

$$g_2(X): \; \frac{4D^2 - dD}{12566(Dd^3 - d^4)} + \frac{1}{5108 d^2} - 1 \leqslant 0,$$

$$g_3(X): \; 1 - \frac{140.45 d}{D^2 N} \leqslant 0,$$

$$g_4(X): \; \frac{D+d}{1.5} - 1 \leqslant 0,$$

where $X = (d, D, N)^\top$. The desired ranges of the design variables are:

$$0.05 \leqslant d \leqslant 2.0, \quad 0.25 \leqslant D \leqslant 1.3, \quad 2.0 \leqslant N \leqslant 15.0.$$

Problem 2: *Design of a welded beam* [15]. This problem consists of the minimization of the cost of a welded beam illustrated in Fig. 2, subject to constraints on the shear stress, τ, bending stress in the beam, σ, buckling load on the bar, P_c, end deflection of the beam, δ, and side constraints. There are four design variables, h, l, t and b that will be denoted as x_1, x_2, x_3 and x_4, respectively. The problem is formulated as:

$$\min_X \; f(X) = 1.10471 x_1^2 x_2 + 0.04811 x_3 x_4 (14.0 + x_2),$$

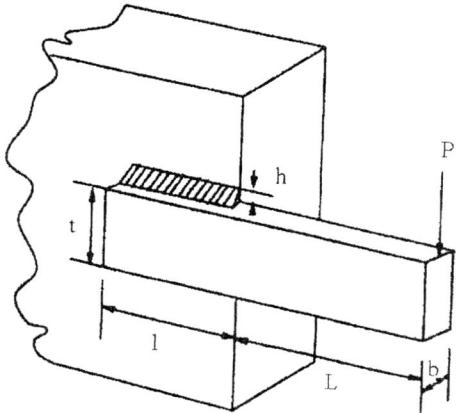

Fig. 2. The welded beam problem

subject to:

$$g_1(X): \quad \tau(X) - \tau_{\max} \leqslant 0,$$
$$g_2(X): \quad \sigma(X) - \sigma_{\max} \leqslant 0,$$
$$g_3(X): \quad x_1 - x_4 \leqslant 0,$$
$$g_4(X): \quad 0.10471x_1^2 + 0.04811x_3x_4(14.0 + x_2) - 5.0 \leqslant 0,$$
$$g_5(X): \quad 0.125 - x_1 \leqslant 0,$$
$$g_6(X): \quad \delta(X) - \delta_{\max} \leqslant 0,$$
$$g_7(X): \quad P - P_c(X) \leqslant 0,$$

where,

$$\tau(X) = \sqrt{(\tau')^2 + 2\tau'\tau''\frac{x_2}{2R} + (\tau'')^2},$$

$$\tau' = \frac{P}{\sqrt{2}x_1x_2}, \quad \tau'' = \frac{MR}{J}, \quad M = P\left(L + \frac{x_2}{2}\right),$$

$$R = \sqrt{\frac{x_2^2}{4} + \left(\frac{x_1+x_3}{2}\right)^2}, \quad J = 2\left\{\sqrt{2}x_1x_2\left[\frac{x_2^2}{12} + \left(\frac{x_1+x_3}{2}\right)^2\right]\right\},$$

$$\sigma(X) = \frac{6PL}{x_4x_3^2}, \quad \delta(X) = \frac{4PL^3}{Ex_3^3x_4}, \quad P_c = \frac{4.013E\sqrt{\frac{x_3^2x_4^6}{36}}}{L^2}\left(1 - \frac{x_3}{2L}\sqrt{\frac{E}{4G}}\right),$$

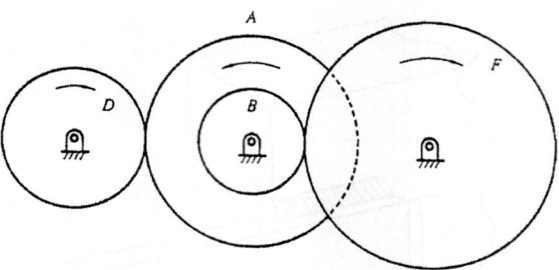

Fig. 3. The gear train problem

$$P = 6000 \text{ lb}, \quad L = 14 \text{ in}, \quad E = 30 \times 10^6 \text{ psi}, \quad G = 12 \times 10^6 \text{ psi},$$

$$\tau_{\max} = 13600 \text{ psi}, \quad \sigma_{\max} = 30000 \text{ psi}, \quad \delta_{\max} = 0.25 \text{ in},$$

and $X = (x_1, x_2, x_3, x_4)^\top$. The desired ranges of the design variables are:

$$0.1 \leqslant x_1, x_4 \leqslant 2.0, \quad 0.1 \leqslant x_2, x_3 \leqslant 10.0.$$

Problem 3: *Design of a gear train* [16]. This problem consists of the minimization of the cost of the gear ratio of the gear train illustrated in Fig. 3. The gear ratio is defined as:

$$\text{gear ratio} = \frac{n_B n_D}{n_F n_A},$$

where n_j denotes the number of teeth of the gearwheel j, with $j = A, B, D, F$. The design variables, n_A, n_B, n_D and n_F will be denoted as x_1, x_2, x_3 and x_4, respectively, and they are all integers in the range $[12, 60]$. The problem is formulated as:

$$\min_X f(X) = \left(\frac{1}{6.931} - \frac{x_3 x_2}{x_1 x_4} \right)^2,$$

subject to:

$$12 \leqslant x_i \leqslant 60, \quad i = 1, \ldots, 4.$$

Problem 4: *Design of a pressure vessel* [16]. This problem consist of the minimization of the cost of the pressure vessel illustrated in Fig. 4. The design variables are the shell's thickness, T_s, the thickness of the head, T_h, the inner radius, R, and the length, L, of the cylindrical section of the vessel, and they will be denoted as x_1, x_2, x_3 and x_4, respectively. The variables T_s and T_h are integer multiples of 0.0625, which represent the available thicknesses of rolled steel plates. The problem is formulated as:

$$\min_X f(X) = 0.6224 x_1 x_3 x_4 + 1.7781 x_2 x_3^2 + 3.1661 x_1^2 x_4 + 19.84 x_1^2 x_3,$$

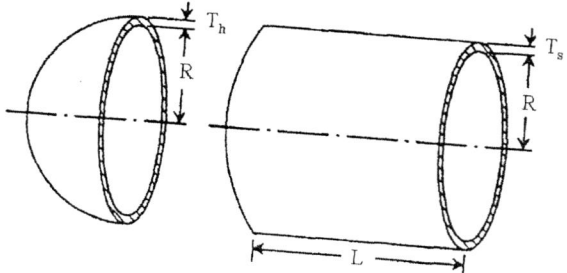

Fig. 4. The pressure vessel problem

subject to:

$$g_1(X): \quad -x_1 + 0.0193x_3 \leqslant 0,$$

$$g_2(X): \quad -x_2 + 0.00954x_3 \leqslant 0,$$

$$g_3(X): \quad -\pi x_3^2 x_4 - \tfrac{4}{3}\pi x_3^3 + 1296000 \leqslant 0,$$

$$g_4(X): \quad x_4 - 240 \leqslant 0,$$

where $X = (x_1, x_2, x_3, x_4)^\top$. The desired ranges of the design variables are:

$$1 \leqslant x_1, x_2 \leqslant 99, \quad 10.0 \leqslant x_3, x_4 \leqslant 200.0.$$

In all cases, the constriction coefficient PSO version was used with $\chi = 0.729$, $c_1 = c_2 = 2.05$. The neighborhood radius for the determination of the velocities in the local PSO variant was always equal to 1 (smallest possible neighborhood) in order to take full advantage of its exploration capabilities. For each test problem we applied the standard UPSO algorithm with $u = 0.2$ and 0.5, as well as UPSO with mutation (denoted as UPSOm) with $u = 0.1$, $\mu = (0,\ldots,0)^\top$ and $\sigma = 0.01$. These choices were based on prior good performance on static optimization problems [10]. Also, the standard global and local PSO versions (derived for $u = 1$ and $u = 0$, respectively), were applied. In all problems, the swarm size was equal to 20, and the algorithm was allowed to perform 5000 iterations per experiment. We conducted 100 independent experiments per algorithm per problem, recording at each experiment the best solution detected by the swarm.

In order to preserve feasibility of the solutions, the update of the best positions of the particles was performed according to the scheme adopted by Hu *et al.* in [4]. More specifically, the best position of a particle was updated only if the new candidate best position was feasible, otherwise, it remained unchanged. Regarding the weights w_1 and w_2 of the penalty function in Eq. (4), the values $w_1 = w_2 = 100$ were used.

Table 1. The obtained results

Pr.		Standard UPSO				UPSOm
		$u=0$	$u=0.2$	$u=0.5$	$u=1$	
1	Mean	2.32563×10^{-2}	1.19291×10^{-1}	4.67351×10^{-2}	4.19581×10^{-2}	2.29478×10^{-2}
	StD	7.48230×10^{-3}	5.42710×10^{-1}	2.14505×10^{-1}	2.84724×10^{-2}	7.20571×10^{-3}
	Min	1.28404×10^{-2}	1.31269×10^{-2}	1.28158×10^{-2}	1.30803×10^{-2}	1.31200×10^{-2}
	Max	4.87550×10^{-2}	4.12260×10^{0}	1.57998×10^{0}	1.98921×10^{-1}	5.03651×10^{-2}
2	Mean	2.58869×10^{0}	2.29718×10^{0}	1.96820×10^{0}	4.27985×10^{0}	2.83721×10^{0}
	StD	5.01437×10^{-1}	4.10969×10^{-1}	1.55415×10^{-1}	1.36945×10^{0}	6.82980×10^{-1}
	Min	1.83008×10^{0}	1.82440×10^{0}	1.76558×10^{0}	1.91853×10^{0}	1.92199×10^{0}
	Max	4.13207×10^{0}	4.17382×10^{0}	2.84406×10^{0}	8.91270×10^{0}	4.88360×10^{0}
3	Mean	3.92135×10^{-8}	7.55581×10^{-8}	2.83820×10^{-7}	1.64225×10^{-6}	3.80562×10^{-8}
	StD	7.71670×10^{-8}	1.83057×10^{-7}	6.87035×10^{-7}	8.25521×10^{-6}	1.09631×10^{-7}
	Min	2.70085×10^{-12}	2.70085×10^{-12}	2.30781×10^{-11}	8.88761×10^{-10}	2.70085×10^{-12}
	Max	6.41703×10^{-7}	8.94899×10^{-7}	5.69940×10^{-6}	8.19750×10^{-5}	8.94899×10^{-7}
4	Mean	9.19585×10^{3}	8.66971×10^{3}	8.01637×10^{3}	1.35035×10^{5}	9.03255×10^{3}
	StD	9.60268×10^{2}	6.24907×10^{2}	7.45869×10^{2}	1.51116×10^{5}	9.95573×10^{2}
	Min	7.56796×10^{3}	6.77080×10^{3}	6.15470×10^{3}	7.52706×10^{3}	6.54427×10^{3}
	Max	1.26720×10^{4}	1.01895×10^{4}	9.38777×10^{3}	5.59300×10^{5}	1.16382×10^{4}

All results are reported in Table 1. More specifically, the mean, standard deviation, minimum and maximum value of the function values of the best solutions obtained in 100 experiments for each algorithm and problem are reported. In Problem 1, UPSOm (UPSO with mutation) had the overall best performance with respect to the mean objective function value of the best solutions as well as the standard deviation, although, the lowest minimum function value was obtained for the standard UPSO scheme with $u = 0.5$. In Problem 2, UPSO with $u = 0.5$ had the smallest mean, standard deviation and minimum of the objective function value of the best solutions, which is also true for Problem 4 with the exception of the standard deviation. In Problem 3, UPSOm had again the best mean, although the local PSO variant (UPSO with $u = 0$) was more robust, exhibiting the smallest standard deviation, while they had the same minimum value. In all cases except Problem 1, the global PSO variant had the worst mean and maximum value.

Summarizing the results, UPSO with $u = 0.5$ and UPSOm proved to be the most promising schemes, conforming with results obtained for different unconstrained optimization problems [10, 11]. The global PSO variant had the worst overall performance, while the local variant was competitive, however only in Problem 3 it outperformed UPSO with respect to the standard deviation and the minimum objective function value.

5 Conclusions

We investigated the performance of the recently proposed Unified Particle Swarm Optimization method on four well–known constrained engineering optimization problems, using a penalty function approach and a feasibility preserving modification of the algorithm. The results were very promising, with UPSO outperforming the standard PSO algorithm, conforming with previous results for different unconstrained optimization problems.

Further work will consider the investigation of the effect of the penalty function on the algorithm's performance as well as different feasibility preserving mechanisms.

Acknowledgment

This work was partially supported by the PENED 2001 Project awarded by the Greek Secretariat of Research and Technology.

References

1. Floudas, C.A., Pardalos, P.M.: A collection of test problems for constrained global optimization algorithms. In: LNCS. Vol. 455. Springer-Verlag (1987)
2. Himmelblau, D.M.: Applied Nonlinear Programming. McGraw–Hill (1972)
3. Coello Coello, C.A.: A survey of constraint handling techniques used with evolutionary algorithms. Techn. Rep. Lania–RI–99–04, LANIA (1999)
4. Hu, X., Eberhart, R.C., Shi, Y.: Engineering optimization with particle swarm. In: Proc. 2003 IEEE Swarm Intelligence Symposium. (2003) 53–57
5. Joines, J.A., Houck, C.R.: On the use of non–stationary penalty functions to solve nonlinear constrained optimization problems with ga's. In: Proc. IEEE Int. Conf. Evol. Comp. (1994) 579–585
6. Parsopoulos, K.E., Vrahatis, M.N.: Particle swarm optimization method for constrained optimization problems. In Sincak et al., eds.: Intelligent Technologies–Theory and Application: New Trends in Intelligent Technologies. Volume 76 of Frontiers in Artificial Intelligence and Applications. IOS Press (2002) 214–220
7. Yeniay, Ö.: Penalty function methods for constrained optimization with genetic algorithms. Mathematical and Computational Applications **10** (2005) 45–56
8. Coello Coello, C.A.: Self–adaptive penalties for ga–based optimization. In: Proc. 1999 IEEE CEC. Volume 1., Washington, D.C., USA (1999) 573–580
9. Coello Coello, C.A.: Use of a self–adaptive penalty approach for engineering optimization problems. Computers in Industry **41** (2000) 113–127
10. Parsopoulos, K.E., Vrahatis, M.N.: UPSO: A unified particle swarm optimization scheme. In: Lecture Series on Computer and Computational Sciences, Vol. 1, Proc. Int. Conf. Computational Methods in Sciences and Engineering (ICCMSE 2004), VSP International Science Publishers, Zeist, The Netherlands (2004) 868–873
11. Parsopoulos, K.E., Vrahatis, M.N.: Unified particle swarm optimization in dynamic environments. LNCS **3449** (2005) 590–599
12. Eberhart, R.C., Kennedy, J.: A new optimizer using particle swarm theory. In: Proceedings Sixth Symposium on Micro Machine and Human Science, Piscataway, NJ, IEEE Service Center (1995) 39–43
13. Clerc, M., Kennedy, J.: The particle swarm–explosion, stability, and convergence in a multidimensional complex space. IEEE Trans. Evol. Comput. **6** (2002) 58–73
14. Arora, J.S.: Introduction to Optimum Design. McGraw–Hill, New York (1989)
15. Rao, S.S.: Engineering Optimization–Theory and Practice. Wiley (1996)
16. Sandgen, E.: Nonlinear integer and discrete programming in mechanical design optimization. Journal of Mechanical Design (ASME) **112** (1990) 223–229

A Modified Particle Swarm Optimizer for Tracking Dynamic Systems

Xuanping Zhang, Yuping Du, Zheng Qin, Guoqiang Qin, and Jiang Lu

Department of Computer Science, Xi'an Jiaotong University, Xi'an, P.R.C
{zxp, ypdu, zhqin, gqqin, jlu}@mail.xjtu.edu.cn

Abstract. The paper proposes a modified particle swarm optimizer for tracking dynamic systems. In the new algorithm, the changed local optimum and global optimum are introduced to guide the movement of each particle and avoid making direction and velocity decisions on the basis of the outdated information. An environment influence factor is put forward based on the two optimums above, which dynamically decide the change of the inertia weight. The combinations of the different local optimum update strategy and local inertia weight update strategy are tested on the parabolic benchmark function. The results on the benchmark function with various severities suggest that modified particle swarm optimizer performs better in convergence speed and aggregation accuracy.

1 Introduction

The Particle Swarm Optimization (PSO) algorithm, regarded as a member of swarm intelligent stochastic optimizer, has been found to be robust and fast in solving nonlinear, non-differentiable, multi-modal problems. As the implementation of the PSO is very simple and a few parameters need to be adjusted, lots of modified PSO have been developed and applied in a great deal of science and engineering fields. The PSO exhibits good performance in finding solutions to static optimization problems. A lot of work and researches are progressed in this field [1,2]. But the real-world problems change over time. As the fitness function is defined as a dualistic function $F(X, G)$ in the dynamic system, the change of the goal will certainly lead to the change of the fitness function. In order to track the dynamic system, the PSO must have a method to detect the environment changes automatically and after the detection of the environment changes, and there must be a strategy to effectively respond to a variety of changes. Various adaptations to PSO have been suggested [3-6].

In this paper, a new modified PSO is introduced. After every movement of the goal, the algorithm updates its own local optimum (called as pBest) and global optimum (called as gBest) according to the current location of the goal. And a new detection method is introduced based on the two updated optimums. At the same time, the inertia weight is respectively dependent on the influence of the moving goal on each particle. The experiments show that the modified PSO with the new detection method and changed inertia weight improves the accuracy of the search result and converges fast in tracking dynamic systems.

L. Wang, K. Chen, and Y.S. Ong (Eds.): ICNC 2005, LNCS 3612, pp. 592–601, 2005.
© Springer-Verlag Berlin Heidelberg 2005

The remaining of the paper is organized as follows. In section 2, an overview over existing approaches to use PSO for dynamic systems is given. A modified PSO is then discussed in section 3. The new detection method and the change mechanism of the inertia weight are introduced, and then the algorithm is given. In section 4, the experiments in different cases are described. The performance analyses of the results are exhibited as well. Finally, the conclusions and future work are presented.

2 Related Work

The experiment results indicate that the basic PSO has the ability to cope with noisy environments effectively and in a stable manner [7]. In fact, in many cases, the presence of noise seems to help PSO to avoid local optimum of the objective function and locate the global one. Anthony Carlisle and Gerry Dozier [8] also discovered that when the changes of the optimized goal are small, the PSO has certain ability to self-correct. But the performance of the basic PSO is bad when there are big dynamic changes. There are two main problems to be solved for PSO to track dynamic systems. One is the environment detection method. And the other is the response method to the changed goal.

Two methods commonly used to detect environment changes are changed-gbest-value method and fixed-gbest-value method [10]. Both of these two methods can successfully detect the various dynamic changes. The former is faster but needs extra time to re-evaluate the fitness value, while the latter is slow but can be applied in any situation.

For response techniques to the change of the goal, two main methods exist: re-randomizing a certain number of particles and replacing the history memory of the particle swarm. Hu and Eberhart [10] randomized a certain scale of particles to response the movement of the goal, making them break away from the moving direction to the previous goal. But the randomization implies loss of information gathered during the search so far. At the same time, Carlisle and Dozier studied several variants of a PSO algorithm for dynamic environments[8,9]. One approach was to let the particles periodically replace their previous best position by the current position. The previous best position is reevaluated after the goal moves, and is exchanged by the current position when the current position is better.

3 Model of the Modified PSO

In the algorithm modified by Carlisle[8], the update strategy of pBest just considers the influence of the previous personal best position, but the previous particle position does have an influence on the algorithm. Because the memories of particles are incompletely reset and there is still part of the history memories existing in each particle, the algorithm does not take full use of the memorial information of the particles, and this decreases the particles' ability to search for optimum. We must consider this again to settle the problem perfectly.

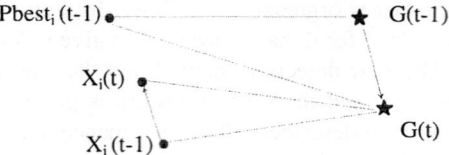

Fig. 1. Influence of goal's movement on Pbest

Suppose the movement process of the goal and the particles is displayed as Figure 1. The goal moves from the position G(t-1) to G(t) and a particle i moves from the position X_i(t-1) to X_i(t). At time t-1, personal best position of particle i is Pbest$_i$(t-1). We assume that it is a process to search for minimum, that is, F(Pbest$_i$(t-1), G(t-1))≤ F(X_i(t-1), G(t-1)). According to the algorithm developed by Carsile and Dozie, When the goal moves, the fitness value of Pbest$_i$(t-1) to the new goal is reevaluated, marked as F(Pbest$_i$(t-1),G(t)). The fitness value of the current particle position X_i(t) is evaluated marked as F(X_i(t),G(t)) as while. Comparing the two values above, if F(Pbest$_i$(t-1),G(t))>F(X_i(t),G(t)), then Pbest$_i$(t) is set as X_i(t). However, if F(X_i(t-1),G(t)) is less than F(X_i(t),G(t)) , it is more reasonable to set Pbest$_i$(t) by X_i(t-1) instead of X_i(t), although F(X_i(t-1),G(t-1)) is greater than F(Pbest$_i$(t-1),G(t)).

Generally considering the influence of Pbest$_i$(t-1) and X_i(t-1) on the algorithm to settle the problem, the F(Pbest$_i$ (t-1),G(t)) and F(X_i(t-1),G(t)) are compared after the goal moves and the better of them is chosen as Pbest′$_i$(t-1). At the same time, the best of the Pbest′$_i$(t-1) is selected as Gbest′(t-1). And then Pbest′$_i$(t-1) is compared with the current positon X_i(t) and the better of them is Pbest$_i$(t). If the Pbest′$_i$(t-1) is different from Pbest$_i$(t-1) or Gbest′(t-1) is different from Gbest(t-1), the movement of the goal will change the direction of the particles. Otherwise, it doesn't take any impact on the swarm.

It is simple to testified that Pbest$_i$(t) is the best position of Pbest$_i$(t-1), X_i(t-1) and X_i(t), and Gbest(t) must be the best among the particles' memory. Based on the model of the modified PSO, a new detection method and changed inertia weight are proposed.

3.1 Improved Environment Detection Method

The movement of the particle is closely related with local optimum and global optimum on the basis of the velocity update function:

$$V_k = w \times V_{k-1} + c1 \times rand()(pBest - p\Pr esent) + c2 \times rand()(gBest - p\Pr esent) \tag{1}$$

Because the movement of the goal may change the fitness values of pBest and gBest, the values of F(Pbest$_i$(t-1),G(t)), F(X_i(t-1),G(t)) and F(Gbest(t-1),G(t)) should be recalculated after the goal moves, and the better of Pbest$_i$(t-1) and X_i(t-1) is chosen as Pbest′$_i$(t-1). The local influence factor η_{Pi} can be defined as follow:

$$\eta_{Pi} = \begin{cases} \dfrac{F(Pbest'_i(t-1), G(t)) - F(Pbest_i(t-1), G(t-1))}{F(Pbest'_i(t-1), G(t)) - F(Pbest_i(t-1), G(t))} \\ \qquad if \quad F(Pbest'_i(t-1), G(t)) \neq F(Pbest_i(t-1), G(t)) \\ 0 \qquad Otherwise \end{cases} \quad (2)$$

$|\eta_{Pi}|$ reflects the influence of the goal's movement on the particle i. Smaller the $|\eta_{Pi}|$ is, smaller the influence is. Bigger the $|\eta_{Pi}|$ is, bigger the influence is. If $\eta_{Pi} = 0$, it means that the goal's movement does not change the local optimum or the goal is still.

The Gbest'(t-1) is the best of the all Pbest'$_i$(t-1). Similarly to the definition of the local influence factor η_{Pi}, we define the global influence factor η_G as:

$$\eta_G = \begin{cases} \dfrac{F(Gbest'_i(t-1), G(t)) - F(Gbest_i(t-1), G(t-1))}{F(Gbest'_i(t-1), G(t)) - F(Gbest_i(t-1), G(t))} \\ \qquad if \quad F(Gbest'_i(t-1), G(t)) \neq F(Gbest_i(t-1), G(t)) \\ 0 \qquad Otherwise \end{cases} \quad (3)$$

According to the influence of η_{Pi} and η_G on the particles, a parameter η_i, named environment influence factor, is introduced. η_i is defined as follows:

$$\eta_i = \lambda * \eta_{Pi} + (1 - \lambda) * \eta_G \quad (4)$$

Where $0 < \lambda < 1$. λ is the influence weight of Pbest and Gbest. Bigger the λ is, bigger the influence of local optimum is and smaller the influence of global optimum is.

$|\eta_i|$ reflects the goal's movement on local optimum and global optimum. Smaller the $|\eta_i|$ is, smaller the influence is. Bigger the $|\eta_i|$ is, bigger the influence is. If $|\eta_i|$ equates to zero, the goal is considred to be still or the goal's movement does not bring any changes to both local and global optimum, and has no influence on the next iteration.

3.2 The Weight and the Particle's Velocity Update Mechanism

The inertia weight in the dynamic system is defined as $w = 0.5 + r(t)/2.0$ in the papers [10, 11]. $r(t)$ is a random number in (0,1), while the average of w is 0.75. For the dynamic random inertia weight, as the last part of the formula $r(t)/2.0$ is random, it can not reflect the influence of the goal's movement. In order to improve this problem, a new changed method to update w on the basis of changed situation is proposed. The idea is described as follows.

When $\eta_i > 0$, the goal moves far away from the particle, and w_i should be increased to make the particle have a higher velocity to track the goal. When $\eta_i < 0$, the goal moves close to the particle, w_i should be decreased to make the particle can find the optimum in a precise way. When $\eta_i = 0$, w_i changes as the method mentioned in the paper[12].

Based on the analysis above, when $\eta_i \neq 0$, w_i should increase as η_i increases, and shoud decrease as η_i decreases. According to the dynmic random inertia weight formula, when w variety is near 0.5, the performance of the algorithm is good. So, let:

$$w_i = (\eta_i + 1)/2 \qquad (5)$$

Here, w_i is limited to [0.1, 1]. Let w_i=0.1 if w_i<0.1, and let w_i=1 if w_i>1.

On the basis of formula (1), different particles have different w_i in different iterations because influence of the goal's movement is different on each particle. After w_i is calculated, the velocity $Vi(t)$ and position $X_i(t)$ of the next iteration can be obtained, and then fitness value $F(X_i(t),G(t))$ is evaluated. The swarm follows the current goal's position during the iterations, and is influenced by it. As a result, it can track the moving goal.

3.3 Modified PSO Algorithm

As the movement of the goal lead to the changes of the environment, the modified PSO algorithm detects the changes and updates the value of pbest and gbest. Then the w is changed based on the influence of the moving goal. The updated w, gbest and pbest are used to guide the particles to track the goal, and result in the new local optimum and global optimum.

The modified algorithm is described as follows:

```
Algorithm PSO {
  Initialize();
  do {
    Update the fitness function;
    for (i=1; i<N; i++){
      Reevaluate the fitness value of Pbest_i(t-1)
        and  X_i(t-1);
      if Pbest_i(t-1) is better than X_i(t-1)
        Choose Pbest_i(t-1) as Pbest'_i(t-1);
      else
        Choose X_i (t-1) as Pbest'_i (t-1);
      Choose the best of Pbest'_i(t-1) as Gbest'(t-1);
    }
    for (i=1; i<N; i++){
      Calculate wi;
      Update Velocity of particle i at time t;
      Limit Velocity Vi (t);
      Update the Position of particle i at time t;
      Evaluate the fitness value of X_i;
      if X_i(t) is better than Pbest'_i(t-1)
        choose X_i(t) as Pbest_i(t);
      else
        choose Pbest'_i(t-1) as Pbest_i(t);
      Choose the best of Pbest_i(t) as Gbest(t);
    }
  } WHILE the convergence criteria is not attained
} /* END PSO */
```

The modified PSO can automatically detect the movement of the goal, and the state of the new particle is updated according to the influence of the movement on the current situation, in order to get the newest guiding information to track the goal.

4 Experiments and Evaluation

As the parabolic function is easy to control the dynamic change, it is chosen as the test function described as formula (6). There is a dynamic parameter offset in the function that changes in various ways.

$$F(\vec{x}) = \sum_{i=1}^{n} (x_i - \text{offset})^2 \quad \forall x_i \in [-50, 50] \tag{6}$$

In the experiments, the number of particles is set as 30 and the dimension of each particle is 10. The algorithm is tested in two cases.

Case 1: First, PSO finds the optimum and records the number of iterations needed to reach the required accuracy. In this experiment, accuracy e=0.0001. Then the function changes dynamically and PSO continues to find the new optima and records the number of iterations needed to re-reach the accuracy. For each experiment, PSO is repeated for 100 runs.

Case 2: The offset changes continuously. When the change of the goal is less than 1, the goal moves once and the swarm iterates once. When the change of the goal is equal to 10, the goal moves once, the swarm iterates 100 times. For each experiment, PSO is repeated for 20 runs.

4.1 The Influence of Different λ on PSO

The influence of different λ on PSO is tested in case 1. The result is showed as table 1. The row 'first time' is the average number of iterations that PSO used to find the optimum. The row 'second time' is the average iterations PSO used after the dynamic changes. We can see from table 1, the influence of λ is little. According to the result, we set $\lambda=0.4$ in all following experiments.

Table 1. The influence of λ on the PSO performance

offset		$\lambda=0$	$\lambda=0.2$	$\lambda=0.4$	$\lambda=0.5$	$\lambda=0.8$	$\lambda=1$
1	First time	152.05	152.14	147.14	158.29	153	156.48
	Second time	82.35	79.19	80.95	82.95	84.71	82.34
10	First time	156.42	152.84	150.51	154.5	157.65	155.49
	Second time	135.48	135.78	135.41	144.3	131.18	140.67

4.2 Performance Comparison

The performance of PSO is tested in case 2. In order to compare the influence of different pbest update strategy on PSO, the algorithm adopts the same w update strategy and different pbest update strategy. In the experiment, the offset verifies from 0.001 to 10. The results show that the evolution curves have the same characteristic. In figure 2, the Linearly Decreasing Weight is applied in the experiment and the movement of the goal is 0.01. In figure 3, the Random Weight is applied in the experiment and the movement of the goal is 10. The conclusion can be drawn that for the linearly decreasing weight, the performance of the two pbest update strategies is equivalent, and for the random weight, the modified pbest update strategy exhibits better performance in accuracy.

In order to test the influence of the weight update strategy on PSO, the algorithm adopts the same pbest update strategy and different weight update strategy. Figure 4 shows the comparison of different weight update strategy with the modified pbest strategy when the movement of the goal is 0.01.

Figure 4 shows that although the linearly decreasing weight strategy exhibits good performance in accuracy, the algorithm searches is in a big space so that the convergence speed is low as the weight is large in the early time. On the contrast, the accuracy of the modified dynamic weight strategy is as good as that of the linearly decreasing weight strategy and the convergence speed is fast. Conclusion can be drawn that PSO with the modified dynamic weight strategy outperforms the PSO with dynamic random weight under the same circumstance.

Figure 5 and table 2 shows the comparison of the modified PSO and the PSO developed by Hu and Eberhart.

For the reason that the modified PSO applies the dynamic changing weight of the static PSO when the goal is detected unchanged, the modified PSO outperforms the PSO developed by Hu and Eberhart. When the goal has a change, the latter

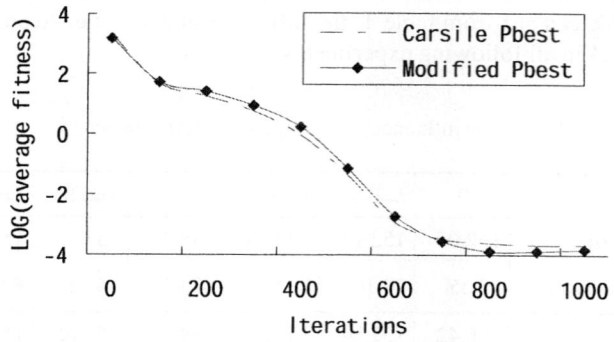

Fig. 2. Comparison of two pbest update strategies for LDC

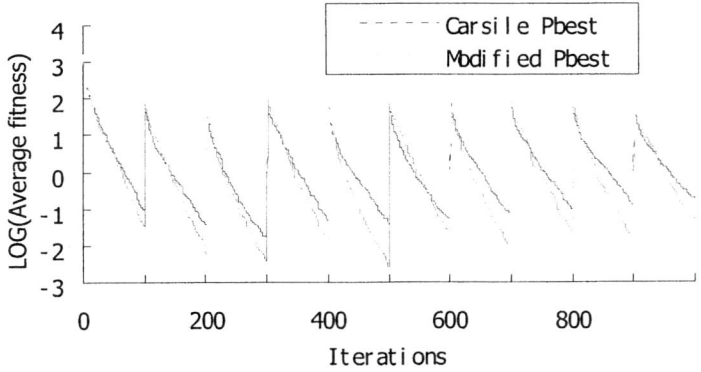

Fig. 3. Comparison of two pbest update strategies for Random w

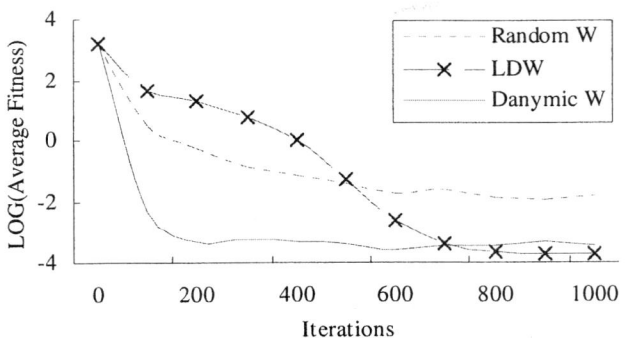

Fig. 4. Comparison of weight update strategies

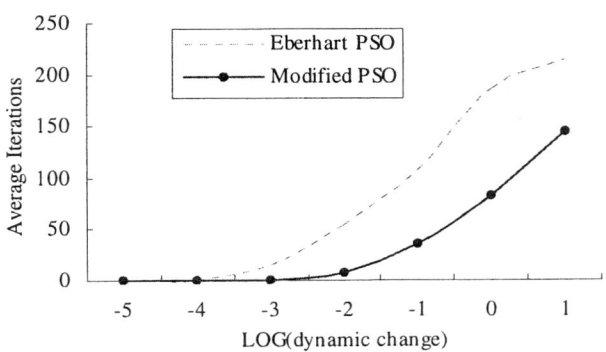

Fig. 5. Comparison of two PSO

Table 2. Mean iterations needed to follow the optimum

Dynamic change	My PSO		Eberhart PSO	
	First time	Second time	First time	Second time
0.00001	154.14	0	222.79*	0.06*
0.0001	159.85	0	221.68*	0.77*
0.001	150.28	0.56	221.48*	14.86*
0.01	152.06	6.72	220.55*	54.86*
0.1	154.81	35.56	223.35*	108*
1	158.29	82.95	220.2*	186.74*
10	154.5	144.3	220.46*	213.97*

Remark: The data come from reference [11]

randomizes a certain number of particles and make them break away from the trend to move toward the previous goal and search in the whole space again. But this method does not enable to make the particles move towards the new goal or randomize around the area of the new goal, so that it is a random process during iterations.

When offset is a little more severe, in contrast with the algorithm of Hu and Eberhart, the modified PSO can find the moved goal more quickly. When the offset is less than 0.001, the PSO does not need any iteration to find the goal again. In figure 5, the curve shows that whatever the offset is, the superiority of the modified PSO is evident.

5 Conclusions and Further Research

In this paper, a new modified PSO for dynamic function optimization has been proposed. The new environment detection method is put forward based on a parameter that can reflect the influence of the moving goal on each particle. The weight is updated depending on the parameter mentioned above. As a result, the methods in the static PSO are available in the modified PSO since the parameter can judge the fact whether the goal is moving or not. The modified pbest update strategy effectively and completely uses the particles' position information, with which the algorithm can find a more accurate solution than Carlisle's algorithm. At the same time, modified dynamic weight increases the convergence speed and aggregation accuracy. The test results on the parabolic benchmark function with various severities under the same circumstance show that the modified PSO can successfully track the dynamic systems in a more effective way than the PSO developed by Hu and Eberhart.

Here only a parabolic function test case is presented. For more complex problems, further investigation is needed to test the performance of PSO. More researches on the influence of λ on the PSO should be done in the future.

References

1. Eberhart RC, Shi YH. Particle Swarm Optimization: Development, Applications and Resources. Proceedings of Congress on Evolutionary Computation[C]. Seoul, Korea, 2001. pp. 81-86.
2. Kennedy J, Eberhart RC, Shi Y. Swarm Intelligence[M]. San Francisco CA: Morgan Kaufmann Publishers. 2001.
3. Blackwell,T.: Swarms in Dynamic Environments. In et al., E.C.P., ed.: Genetic and Evolutionary Computation—GECCO 2003. Proceedings, Part I, Springer. Lecture Notes in Computer Science Vol. 2723 (2003) pp. 1–12
4. Susana C. Esquivel, Carlos A. Coello Coello. Particle Swarm Optimization in Nonstationary Environments, Lecture Notes in Computer Science, Volume 3315/2004. pp. 757-766
5. Tim Blackwell and Jürgen Branke, Multi-swarm Optimization in Dynamic Environments, Lecture Notes in Computer Science, Volume 3005/2004. pp. 489 - 500
6. Stefan Janson, Martin Middendorf. A Hierarchical Particle Swarm Optimizer for Dynamic Optimization Problems Lecture Notes in Computer Science Volume 3005/2004. pp.513-524
7. Parsopoulos K. E.and Vrahatis. M. N. Particle Swarm Optimizer in noisy and continuously changing environments[A]. Hamza M H. Proceeding of the IASTED International Conference on Artificial Intelligence and Soft Computing[C]. Cancun, Mexico: ISATED/ACTA Press, 2001, pp.289-294.
8. Carlisle. A and Dozier. G, Adapting PSO to dynamic environment, Proceedings of international conference on artificial Intelligence. Las Vegas, Nevada, USA, 2000. pp.429-434,
9. Carlisle A, Dozier G. Tracking Changing Extrema with Particle Swarm Optimization. Auburn University Technical Report CSSE01-08 [R]. 2001.
10. Xiaohui Hu and Eberhart, R. C. Adaptive Particle swarm optimization: Detection and Response to Dynamic Systems, 2002. pp. 1666-1670.
11. Eberhart, R. C. and Shi, Y. Tracking and Optimizing Dynamic Systems with Particle Swarms. Proceedings Congress On Evolutionary Computation 2001, Piscataway, NJ: IEEE Press, 2001,pp.94-97.
12. Zhang Xuanping, Du Yuping, Qin Guoqiang, Qin Zheng. An Adaptive Particle Swarm Optimization with Dynamically Changing Weight (in Chinese). Journal of Xi'an Jiaotong University. Agust, 2005.

Particle Swarm Optimization for Bipartite Subgraph Problem: A Case Study*

Dan Zhang[1], Zeng-Zhi Li[1], Hong Song[2], and Tao Zhan[3]

[1] School of Electronics & Information Engineering, Xi'an Jiaotong University,
Xi'an Shaanxi 710049, China
danzhang@mailst.xjtu.edu.cn
[2] School of Mechanical Engineering, Xi'an Shiyou University,
Xi'an Shaanxi 710065, China
[3] Dept. of Computer Science & Engineering, Northwest Polytechnical University,
Xi'an Shaanxi 710072, China

Abstract. The goal of bipartite subgraph problem is to partition the vertex set of an undirected graph into two parts in order to maximize the cardinality of the set of edges cut by the partition. This paper proposes a modified particle swarm optimization (PSO), called MPPSO (Mutated Personalized PSO), for this NP-hard problem. The proposed MPPSO algorithm contains a key improvement by introducing a personality factor from a psychological standpoint and a mutation operator for global best. Additionally the symmetry issue of solution space of bipartite subgraph problem is coped well with too. A large number of instances have been simulated to verify the proposed algorithm. The results show that the personality factor and mutation operator are efficient and the quality of our algorithm is superior to those of the existing algorithms.

1 Introduction

One of the best known combinatorial optimization graph problem is the bipartite subgraph problem, which is to find a partition of undirected graph into two disjoint vertex set such that the cut size is maximized. It has been studied in several real world applications such as the VLSI design and the statistical physics [1] [2].

Particle Swarm Optimization (PSO) is a population-based stochastic optimization technique developed by Eberhart and Kennedy in 1995 [3] [4], inspired by social behavior of bird flocking and fish schooling. In PSO, each particle represents a potential solution within the search space and a position, a velocity and a record of its past behavior characterize it. At each flight cycle the objective function is evaluated for each particle with respect to its current position. The obtained value measures the quality of the particle. Many optimization problems involve in discrete or binary variables. The updating equation of PSO and procedures are oriented from and designed for continuous spaces. Some changes have

---

* Supported by the Nation Science Foundation of China (No.60173059).

to be made to adapt to the discrete spaces. The coding changes may be simple, but it is hard to define the meanings of velocities and determine the changes of trajectories. Few researches has been made in this direction [5] [6] [7] [8].

In this paper, we represent the bipartite subgraph potential solutions as particles and let them fly to get optimal solutions. The proposed PSO, called MPPSO, contains a key improvement by introducing a "personality" factor from a psychological standpoint and a mutation operator for global best. In addition, the special symmetry issue of bipartite subgraph problem is coped well with to speed up the convergence of MPPSO. A large number of randomly generated examples are simulated to verify the proposed algorithm. The efficacy of our algorithm is compared with those of previous algorithms.

The remainder of this paper is organized as follows. In section 2 bipartite subgraph problem is described. The basic PSO algorithm is outlined in section 3. MPPSO for bipartite subgraph problem is presented in section 4. Experiments results are provided in section 5. Finally, the conclusions are given in Section 6.

2 Bipartite Subgraph Problem

Definition 1. *Let $G = (Vert, E)$ be an undirected graph, where $Vert$ is the set of vertices and E is the set of edges. The edge from vertex $vert_i$ to vertex $vert_j$ is represented by $e_{ij} \in E$. $e_{ij} = e_{ji}$ indicates whether there is an edge which endpoints are vertex $vert_i$ and $vert_j$ (1 indicates existence, and 0 indicates inexistence). The goal of the bipartite subgraph problem of $G = (Vert, E)$ is to find a partition of $Vert$ into two disjoint vertex sets S_0 and S_1 such that the cut size is maximized. The cut size is the sum of edges in E which have one endpoint in S_0 and another one in S_1.*

The bipartite subgraph problem is a well-known NP-hard problem [9]. In 1983, a sequential heuristic algorithm for this problem was proposed by Hsu [1]. In 1992, Lee et al. proposed a binary neural network using the maximum neuron model [10].

3 Basic Particle Swarm Optimization

Like Genetic Algorithm (GA), PSO is initialized with a population of random solutions. Its development was based on observations of the social behavior of animals such as bird flocking, fish schooling and swarm theory. Each individual in PSO is assigned with a randomized velocity according to its own and its companions' flying experiences, and the individuals, called particles, are then fly through hyperspace. Compared to GA, PSO has some attractive characteristics. It has memory, so knowledge of good solutions is retained by all particles; whereas in GA, previous knowledge of the problem is destroyed once the population changes. It has constructive cooperation between particles, particles in the swarm share information between them.

$$v_{id} = wv_{id} + c_1 rand()(p_{id} - x_{id}) + c_2 Rand()(p_{nd} - x_{id}) \qquad (1)$$

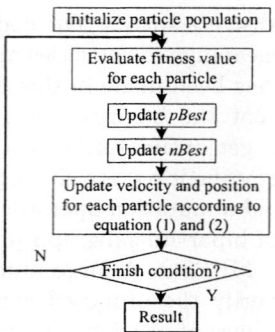

Fig. 1. General flowchart of particle swarm optimization

$$x_{id} = x_{id} + v_{id} \qquad (2)$$

The particle swarm works by adjusting trajectories through manipulation of each coordinate and velocity of a particle per iteration. PSO is initialized with a group of random particles (solutions) and then searches for optima by updating each generation. The core of PSO is the updating equations of the particle, which can be represented as follows. A particle (potential solution) $X_i = (x_{i1}, x_{i2}, \ldots, x_{iD})$ is looked as a point without quality and volume in D-dimension search space. The velocity of X_i is presented as $V_i = (v_{i1}, v_{i2}, \cdot, v_{iD})$. Equation (1) calculates the dth-dimension of a new velocity for each particle based on its previous velocity (v_{id}), the particle's position at which the best fitness so far has been achieved $(pBest)$, and the neighbor's best position $(nBest)$ at which the best fitness in a neighborhood so far has been achieved (if all the population is taken as its neighbors, $nBest$ is called $gBest$). Equation (2) updates each particle's position in the solution hyperspace. $Rand()$ and $rand()$ are two random numbers independently generated. c_1 and c_2 are two learning factors, which control the influence of $pBest$ and $nBest$ on the search process. From a psychological standpoint, the cognitive term (c_1) represents the tendency of individuals to duplicate past behavior that has been proven successful, whereas the social term (c_2) represents the tendency to follow the successes of others. The function of inertia weight w is to balance global exploration and local exploitation. The general flowchart of PSO is shown in fig. 1.

4 MPPSO for Bipartite Subgraph Problem

For the bipartite subgraph problem, we represent a potential sub-graph partition as a position in n-dimension binary space. A particle may be seen to move to nearer and farther corners of the hypercube by flipping various numbers of bits; thus velocity of the particle should reflect the probability the bit changing on a dimension per iteration. In this paper, therefore, each v_{id} ($v_{id} \in (-V_{max}, +V_{max})$) reflects the probability of bit x_{id} taking value 1. As equation (3) shows, the probability that a bit will be a one = $S(v_{id})$, and the probability that it will be a zero $= 1 - S(v_{id})$. In other words, the greater v_{id}, the higher probability x_{id} will be 1; the smaller v_{id}, the higher probability x_{id} will be 0. The value of $(p_{id} - x_{id})$ can be reasonably calculated as -1, 0, +1, and used to weight the change in probability v_{id} at the next step. The equation (1) remains unchanged except that p_{id} and v_{id} is binary integers in $\{0, 1\}$. Furthermore, if it is a zero already, then the probability that it will change $= S(v_{id})$, and if it is a one then probability it will change $= 1 - S(v_{id})$. Hence the probability of bit changing is given by equation (5), which is the absolute rate of change for that bit given a value of v_{id} [5].

$$S(v_{id}) = \frac{1}{1 + e^{-\alpha v_{id}}} \tag{3}$$

$$x_{id} = \begin{cases} 1, & \text{if } rand() < S(v_{id}), \\ 0, & \text{elsewise.} \end{cases} \tag{4}$$

$$p(\Delta) = S(v_{id})(1 - S(v_{id})) \tag{5}$$

The new coordinate x_{id} is calculated according to equation (4), where function $S(v_{id})$ is a sigmoid limiting transformation and $rand()$ is a quasi-random number selected from a uniform distribution in [0.0, 1.0]; thus $S(v_{id})$ determine the next value of x_{id}. Another parameter V_{max} is to limit the absolute value of v_{id}; thus the function of V_{max} is to set a limit to further exploration after the population has converged. From the equation (3), (4) and (5), smaller V_{max} implies higher probability of bit changing. To solve bipartite subgraph problem efficiently, we proposed mutated personalized PSO (MPPSO). The following subsections describe three key techniques of MPPSO - personality factors, mutation operator and symmetry issue - in detail.

4.1 Personalized Particle Swarm Optimization

According to equation (1), the inertia weight w and two learning factor c_1 and c_2 are key parameters. From a psychological standpoint, the cognitive term c_1 represents the tendency of individuals to duplicate past behaviors that have proven successful, whereas the social term c_2 represents the tendency to follow the successes of others. Both c_1 and c_2 are sometimes set to 2.0 obviously for it will make the search cover all surrounding regions which is centered at the $pBest$ and $nBest$. 1.49445 is also used according to the work by Clerc [11] which indicates that a constriction factor may be necessary to insure convergence of PSO [12]. In most cases, the learning factors are identical. That puts the same weights on social searching and cognitive searching. Kennedy studied two extreme cases: social-only model and cognitive-only model, and found out that both parts are essential to the success of PSO searching [13]. No definitive conclusions about asymmetric learning factors have been reported.

However, all previous studies on learning factors only think the particle swarm as a whole, but not consider the speciality of every particle. In this paper, we propose a property of single particle - "personality", which represents a kind of psycology inclination of each particle. The extrovert has higher social learning ability and is easy to be influenced by others. The introvert has lower social learning ability and incline to learning from the experience of itself. The social learning factor c_1 and cognitive learning factor c_2 are not equal for each particle, but the whole swarm has equal social and personal learning ability. It is hard to say whether the extrovert is superior to introvert or vice versa for single individual. But from the whole standpoint, this property increases the exploration and exploitation abilities of particle swarm and makes particles search larger region.

According to the *Gaussian* distribution of personalities from the standpoint of social psycology, we assume the particles conforming to *Gaussian* distribution. Therefore, the personality property p_i of particle X_i is calculated according to equation (6) and (7) in the initialization stage. k_1 and k_2 are two factors to control the particle personality distribution. Their values are inversely proportional to personality percentage in population. In other words, these two factors control how "bias" the particles could be from balance personality as a whole swarm. The greater these two factors, the more ordinary and centralized individuals are. In the extreme case of $k_1=k_2=0$, p_i is set to 0 or 1 randomly; thus c_1, c_2 will be 0, 1 or 1, 0 for a particle, which means that one half-part of population is social-only and another half-part is cognitive-only. While in another extreme case of $k_1 = k_2 = +\infty$, $p_i \equiv 0.5$, then c_1 and c_2 will be invariable values (1.49445 in this paper) without personalities.

$$p_i = \begin{cases} 0.5 - \frac{1}{1+e^{-k_1 r}}, & r < 0; \\ 1.5 - \frac{1}{1+e^{-k_2 r}}, & r > 0. \end{cases} \quad (6)$$

r: uniform random number on $(-rand\_max, 0) \cup (0, +rand\_max)$;
k_1: introvertive proportional factor, $k_1 > 0$;
k_2: extrovertive proportional factor, $k_2 > 0$.

$$\begin{cases} c_{i1} = p_i \times sum\_c \\ c_{i2} = (1 - p_i) \times sum\_c \end{cases} \quad (7)$$

sum_c: the sum of c_1 and c_2, equals 2.9889 according to [11].

4.2 Mutated Particle Swarm Optimization

Another improvement is mutation operator for global best. One drawback of PSO is local-optimal, because all particles tend to congregation towards global best. However, global best is hard to learn from social and personal experiences. Thus, we adopt mutation operator to global best, which is from Genetic Algorithm. m coordinates of n-dimension $gBest$ are selected randomly and mutated (reverses 0 to 1 or vice versa) according to mutation probability P_m. If the fitness after mutation is better than the one before, mutation takes effect. Otherwise, the old value is retained. m is linearly decreasing with iteration and defined as follows.

$$m = n \times (iter/iter_{max})$$
$iter$: The current iteration;
$iter_{max}$: The maximum iteration.

4.3 Symmetry Issue of Solution Space

Another important issue of bipartite subgraph problem is the symmetry of solution space, which means in n-dimension binary space, a position and its symmetrical position represent the same sub-graph partition (e.g. 01010 equals 10101 in 5-dimension space). Thus, when we calculate the v_{id} and x_{id} according to the equation (1) and (4), particle move on the edges of hypercube to close to the corner (position) $pBest$ and corner $gBest$. For the bipartite subgraph problem, sub-graphs partition $\{S_0, S_1\}$ has no order, thus two solutions exist as a pair in solution space.

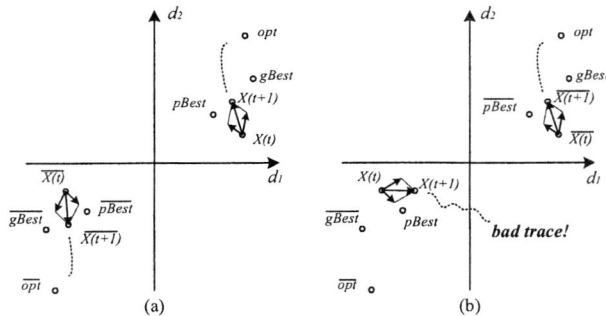

Fig. 2. Illustration for symmetry issue of particle solution space

We illustrate this issue by a simple example in fig. 2. $\overline{pBest}$ and $\overline{gBest}$ represent the symmetrical corners of $pBest$ and $gBest$ in hypercube. To simplify analysis, the calculation can be seen as vector addition approximately in continuous space; thus the main part of velocity V is computed stochastically by vector-adding up $(pBest-X)$ and $(gBest-X)$. As fig. 2(a) shows (in 2-dimension case), $pBest$, $gBest$, X and opt reside in first phase, while $\overline{pBest}$, $\overline{gBest}$, $\overline{X}$ and $\overline{opt}$ reside in third phase; then particle X will fly towards opt in terms of $pBest$ and $gBest$ ($\overline{X}$ will fly towards $\overline{opt}$ according to $\overline{pBest}$ and $\overline{gBest}$). But in the case of fig. 2(b), where X and $pBest$ reside in third phase while $gBest$ and opt resides in first phase, the trajectory of X will oscillate and converge very slowly to opt or $\overline{opt}$ according to $pBest$ and $gBest$ (same to $\overline{X}$ according to $\overline{pBest}$ and $\overline{gBest}$). We call this phenomena *bad trace*. However, if X adjusts trajectory according to $pBest$ and $gBest$ reside in third phase, it will converge to $\overline{opt}$ rapidly. This situation is shown in first phase of fig. 2(b), where $\overline{X}$ flies towards opt according to $\overline{pBest}$ and $gBest$. Therefore, the new position with highest fitness is selected as the final new position and velocity of a particle per iteration. The following experiments also show that this strategy guarantees the convergence.

4.4 Steps of MPPSO

Step 1. The solutions are presented as particles, which are binary encoding schemes (n-dimension binary vector). For an undirected graph $G = (Vert, E)$, a potential solution is $X = (x_1, \ldots, x_n)$, $n = |Vert|, x_i \in \{0, 1\}$. A vertex is represented as x_i with value 0 or 1, which denotes x_i belong to sub-graph S_0 or S_1.

Step 2. The initial particles population is generated randomly. The population size is N. The population P is a set containing N particles. $P = X_1, \ldots, X_N$. The personal and social cognitive learning factors are generated for each particle according to equation (6) and (7).

Step 3. The edges of G is a $n \times n(n = |Vert|)$ triangle matrix W. $e_{ij} = 1$ denotes whether the edge exists whose endpoints are vertices $vert_i$ and $vert_j$, otherwise $e_{ij} = 0$. The fitness value $f(X)$ is computed according to equation (8), which denotes the cut number in the case of partition X.

$$f(X) = \frac{\sum_{i=1}^{n} \sum_{j=1}^{i-1} \left(e_{ij} \times (x_i \ XOR \ x_j)\right)}{\sum_{i=1}^{n} \sum_{j=1}^{i-1} e_{ij}}; 1 \leq i, j \leq n; x_i, x_j \in X \quad (8)$$

XOR: exclusive or operator.

Step 4. If the current fitness value of a particle is better than $pBest$, it is updated by current position.

Step 5. If the current global best fitness value of the whole swarm is better than $gBest$, it is updated by current global best position.

Step 6. The velocity and position of each particle are updated according to equation (1) and (4), and the symmetry issue should be considered in calculation.

Step 7. Perform mutation operation for $gBest$.

Step 8. Check the finish condition (maximum iteration I_{max}). If the process is finish, $gBest$ is decoded and result is gained. Otherwise return to step3.

5 Experimental Results and Analysis

In order to evaluate the efficiency of the proposed algorithm, we have implemented it in C++ on AMD Athlon XP1700+ 512M. As graph instances, each edge is randomly generated at the 5% 15% and 20% probability for random graphs. A total of 100 trials are performed in each case. The parameters used in our experiments are as follows: population size = 20, maximum iteration = 500, inertia weight $w = [0.5 + (\text{Rnd}/2.0)]$, learning factors $c_1 = c_2 = 1.49445$ (only for PSO and MPSO algorithm), max velocity $V_{max} = 50$, sigmoid function $\alpha = 1$, $sum\_c = 2.9889$. After a number of simulations, we select key personality factors as $k_1 = 2$, $k_2 = 1$.

Table 1 shows the comparison among PSO, PPSO (Personalized PSO), MPSO (Mutated PSO) and MPPSO (Mutated Personalized PSO). Column 1 shows the number of vertices. The results of PSO, PPSO, MPSO and MPPSO are shown in column 2 to 13. Table 1 shows that both personality factors and mutation operator contribute to the improvement of the solution quality.

Table 2 shows the results of PSO compared with those of the algorithms of Hsu's Greedy Search (GS) [1], Lee's Max Neural Network (MNN) [10] and

Table 1. The results of PSO, PPSO, MPSO and MPPSO (MPP)

Node	5% PSO	5% PPSO	5% MPSO	5% MPP	15% PSO	15% PPSO	15% MPSO	15% MPP	20% PSO	20% PPSO	20% MPSO	20% MPP
10	2	2	2	2	6	7	5	7	8	8	8	8
20	9	9	9	9	23	24	25	24	30	30	31	31
30	22	21	21	21	52	52	52	53	66	65	66	66
40	36	36	35	36	89	88	89	89	112	113	112	113
50	53	54	53	53	134	133	136	134	172	173	171	173
60	75	76	76	77	188	190	191	191	241	240	240	242
70	100	103	101	101	253	254	256	254	323	323	323	324
80	130	130	132	130	324	323	327	329	412	414	418	420
90	160	160	160	164	400	402	405	405	516	516	523	521
100	193	192	195	196	490	494	498	497	631	635	638	638

Table 2. The results of GS, MNN, GA and MPPSO

Node	5% GS	5% MNN	5% GA	5% MPPSO	15% GS	15% MNN	15% GA	15% MPPSO	20% GS	20% MNN	20% GA	20% MPPSO
10	2	2	2	2	6	6	7	7	6	6	9	8
20	8	8	9	9	24	25	24	24	26	28	30	31
30	19	20	21	21	49	50	51	53	52	56	65	66
40	36	36	35	36	90	90	88	89	96	99	111	113
50	50	53	52	53	128	135	131	134	143	149	169	173
60	78	80	75	77	191	195	187	191	210	218	240	242
70	102	107	98	101	246	254	250	254	282	282	318	324
80	125	132	128	130	311	330	320	329	363	367	411	420
90	158	162	157	164	390	405	400	405	445	459	513	521
100	185	195	189	196	478	494	487	497	553	564	628	638

Table 3. The results of PSO with symmetry and without symmetry

iteration	un-symmetry PSO	symmetry PSO
5	403	413
20	412	435
50	419	462
100	424	480
500	442	490

Genetic Algorithm (GA). From table 2, the results of MPPSO are superior to others.

Table 3 shows the comparison between PSO with symmetry and PSO without symmetry in the case that node size is 100 and edge-density is 15%. It shows that the PSO without symmetry converges very slowly. The symmetry issue is very important for bipartite subgraph problem.

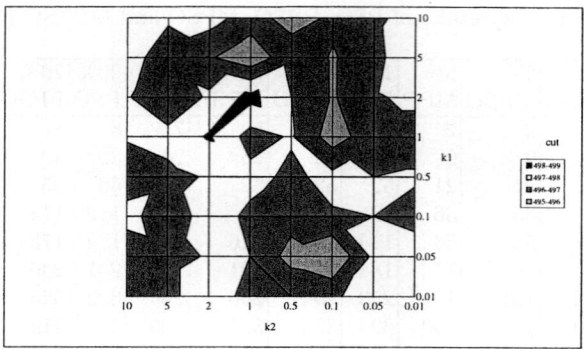

Fig. 3. The influence by the personality factors k_1 and k_2

Fig. 3 shows the influence by the personality factors k_1 and k_2. We measure the results of k_1 and $k_2 = 0.01, 0.05, 0.1, 0.5, 1, 2, 5$ and 10 respectively in the case that node size is 100, edge-density is 15% and total 100 trials are executed. The results shows that the optimal result appears where $k_1 = 2$ and $k_2 = 1$.

6 Conclusions and Future Works

A modified PSO algorithm MPPSO was proposed, which introduced an important "personality" factor and a mutation operator into basic PSO. For bipartite subgraph problem, the particles representing a sub-graphs partition solutions move on the corners of hypercube to close the optimal solution. Meanwhile, the symmetry of solution space is also considered such that convergence of MPPSO is guaranteed. MPPSO has the advantages of few parameters and simplicity. In comparison with greedy search, genetic algorithm and neural networks, the results of MPPSO are better than others, and the efficiency of personality factors and mutation operator are illustrated too. This personality factor should be able to be extended to solve other continuous and discrete optimization problems. It is necessary for us to study more.

References

1. Hsu, C.P.: Minimum-via topological routing. IEEE Trans. on Computer-Aided Design **2** (1983) 235–246
2. Barahona, F., et al.: An application of combinatorial optimization to statistical physics and circuit layout design. Operation Research **36** (1988) 493–513
3. Eberhart, R., Kennedy, J.: A new optimizer using particle swarm theory. In: Int. Sym. Micro Machine and Human Science, Nagoya, Japan (1995) 39–43
4. Kennedy, J., Eberhart, R.: Particle swarm optimization. In: IEEE Int. Conf. Neural Networks, Perth, Australia (1995) 1942–1948
5. Kennedy, J., Eberhart, R.: A discrete binary version of the particle swarm algorithm. In: The World Multiconference on Systemics, Cybernetics and Informatics, Piscataway, NJ (1997) 4104–4109

6. Mohan, C.K., Al-kazemi, B.: Discrete particle swarm optimization. In: The Workshop on Particle Swarm Optimization, Indianapolis, IN (2001)
7. Hu, X., Eberhart, R.C., Shi, Y.: Swarm intelligence for permutation optimization: a case study on n-queens problem. In: IEEE Swarm Intelligence Symposium 2003 (SIS2003), Indianapolis, Indiana, USA (2003) 37–44
8. Cagnina, L., Esquivel, S., Gallard, R.: Swarmparticle swarm optimization for sequencing problems: a case study. In: IEEE Congress on Evolutionary Computation 2004 (CEC2004). Volume 1., Indianapolis, Indiana, USA (2004) 536–541
9. Garey, M.R., Johnson, D.S. In: Computers and intractability. Freeman, San Francisco (1979)
10. Lee, K.C., Funabiki, N., Takefuji, Y.: A parallel improvement algorithm for the bipartite subgraph problem. IEEE Trans. on Neural Networks **3** (1992) 139–145
11. Eberhart, R.C., Shi, Y.: Particle swarm optimization: Developments, applications and resources. In: IEEE Congress on Evolutionary Computation. (2001) 81–86
12. Clerc, M.: The swarm and the queen: towards a deterministic and adaptive particle swarm optimization. In: IEEE Congress on Evolutionary Computation. (1999) 1951–1957
13. Kennedy, J.: Minds and cultures: particle swarm implications. In: AAAI Fall Symposium on Socially Intelligent Agents. (1997) 67–72

On the Role of Risk Preference in Survivability

Shu-Heng Chen[1] and Ya-Chi Huang[2]

[1] AI-ECON Research Center, Department of Economics,
National Chengchi University, Taipei, Taiwan
chchen@nccu.edu.tw
[2] AI-ECON Research Center, Department of Economics,
National Chengchi University, Taipei, Taiwan
yachi@aiecon.org

Abstract. Using an agent-based multi-asset artificial stock market, we simulate the survival dynamics of investors with different risk preferences. It is found that the survivability of investors is closely related to their risk preferences. Among the eight types of investors considered in this paper, only the CRRA investors with RRA coefficients close to one can survive in the long run. Other types of agents are eventually driven out of the market, including the famous CARA agents and agents who base their decision on the capital asset pricing model.

1 Introduction

The paper is concerned with a part of the debate on the *market selection hypothesis*. The debate, if we trace its origin, started with the establishment of what become known as the *Kelly criterion* ([8]), which basically says that a rational long-run investor *should* maximize the expected growth rate of his wealth share and, therefore, should behave as if he were endowed with a logarithmic utility function. Alternatively speaking, the Kelly criterion suggests that there is an optimal preference (rational preference) which a competitive market will select and that is logarithmic utility. The debate on the Kelly criterion has a long history, so not surprisingly, there is a long list of both pros and cons standing alongside the developments in the literature.[1]

The Kelly criterion may further imply that an agent who maximizes his expected utility under the *correct* belief may be driven out by an agent who maximizes his expected utility under an *incorrect* belief, simply because the former does not maximize a logarithmic utility function, whereas the latter does. [1] were the first to show this implication of the Kelly criterion in a standard asset pricing model. As a result, the market selection hypothesis fails because agents with accurate beliefs are not selected. A consequence of this failure is that asset prices may not eventually reflect the beliefs of agents who make accurate predictions, and hence may persistently deviate from the *rational expectations equilibrium* and violate the *efficient market hypothesis*.

---
[1] See [11] for a quite extensive review.

However, a series of recent studies indicates that the early analysis of [1] is not complete. [10] shows that, if the saving behavior is endogenously determined, then the market selection hypothesis is rescued, and in the long run, only those optimizing investors with *correct beliefs* survive. The surviving agents do not have to be log-utility maximizers, and they can have diverse risk preferences. [10]'s analysis is further confirmed by [2] in a connection of the market selection hypothesis to the *first theorem of welfare economics*. [2] show that in a dynamic and complete market *Pareto optimality* is the key to understanding selection either for or against traders with correct beliefs: in any optimal allocation the survival or disappearance of a trader is determined entirely by beliefs, and not by risk preferences.

Despite the rigorousness of these theoretical studies, there exists a fundamental limitation, which may make it difficult to grasp their empirical counterparts, namely, they are *non-constructive*.[2] Take [10] as an example. First, the analysis crucially depends on the appearance of agents who *eventually make accurate predictions* or *eventually make accurate next period predictions*. Nevertheless, the process that shows the emergence of these sages is unknown. It is, therefore, not clear how these agents emerge, or whether they will ever emerge.[3] Second, maximizing expected utility is equivalent to assuming that agents are able to solve any infinite-time stochastic dynamic optimization problem implied by their utility function. However, current dynamic optimization techniques, regardless of whether they include stochastic optimal control or stochastic dynamic programming, can only help us solve a very limited subset of the whole problem space. As for the rest of them, it is necessary to rely on numerical approximations, and their effectiveness to a large extent is also unknown.

Given these practical limitations, we are motivated to re-examine the issue from a more realistic perspective or, technically speaking, a computational perspective. By remaining in the general equilibrium analysis framework, we replace the rational agents with bounded-rational agents. More precisely, these agents are constructed in terms of what is known as *autonomous agents* in agent-based computational economics ([12]). Basically, these agents are able to learn to optimize and to forecast in an autonomous manner. So, they are not necessarily utility-maximizers. Instead, they use adaptive computing techniques to approximate the optimal solution. In this sense, they are Herbert Simon's *satisfying* agents. Similarly, they base their decisions upon beliefs which may not be and may never be correct, but are reviewed and revised continuously ([9]).

By introducing autonomous agents, we are getting closer to the world of flesh and blood, and enhancing the study of the empirical relevance of risk preference to survival dynamics.

---

[2] This kind of issue is generally shared in many general equilibrium analyses.

[3] Back to the real world, we have not been convinced that these agents have ever appeared in human history.

2 A Simple Multi-asset Model

The simulations presented in this paper are based on an agent-based version of the multi-asset market as per the studies of [1] and [10]. The market is complete in the sense that the number of states is equal to the number of assets, say M. At each date t, the outstanding volume of each asset is exogenously fixed at one unit. There are I investors in the market, with each being indexed by i. At time t asset m will pay dividends w_m if the corresponding state m occurs, and 0 otherwise. The behavior of these states follows a finite-state stochastic process, which does not have to be stationary. The dividends w_m will be distributed among the I investors proportionately according to their owned shares of the respective asset. The dividends can only be either re-invested or consumed. Hoarding is prohibited. If agent i chooses to consume c, her satisfaction is measured by her utility function $u(c)$. This simple multi-asset market clearly defines an optimization problem for each individual as follows:

$$\max_{\{\{\delta^i_{t+r}\}_{r=0}^{\infty}, \{\alpha^i_{t+r}\}_{r=0}^{\infty}\}} E\{\sum_{r=0}^{\infty}(\beta^i)^r u^i(c^i_{t+r}) \mid B^i_{t-1}\} \quad (1)$$

subject to

$$c^i_{t+r} + \sum_{m=1}^{M} \alpha^{i,*}_{m,t+r} \cdot \delta^{i,*}_{t+r} \cdot W^i_{t+r-1} \leq W^i_{t+r-1} \quad \forall r \geq 0, \quad (2)$$

$$\sum_{m=1}^{M} \alpha^i_{m,t+r} = 1, \quad \alpha^i_{m,t+r} \geq 0 \quad \forall r \geq 0. \quad (3)$$

In equation (1), u^i is agent i's temporal utility function, and β^i, also called the discount factor, reveals agent i's time preference. The expectation $E(\ )$ is taken with respect to the most recent belief B^i_t, which is a probabilistic model used to represent agent i's subjective belief regarding the stochastic nature of the state. The maximization problem asks for two sequences of decisions, one related to saving, and the other to the portfolios, denoted by

$$\{\{\delta^i_{t+r}\}_{r=0}^{\infty}, \{\alpha^i_{t+r}\}_{r=0}^{\infty}\},$$

where δ^i_t is the saving rate at time t, and

$$\alpha^i_t = (\alpha^i_{1,t}, \alpha^i_{2,t}, ..., \alpha^i_{M,t})$$

is the portfolio comprising the M assets.

Equations (2) and (3) are the budget constraints. W^i_t is the wealth of agent i at time t, which is earned from the dividends paid at time t. Notice that these budget constraints do not allow agents to consume or invest by borrowing.

The equilibrium price $\rho_{m,t}$ is determined by equating the demand for asset m to the supply of asset m, i.e.

$$\sum_{i=1}^{I} \frac{\alpha^{i,*}_{m,t} \cdot \delta^{i,*}_t \cdot W^i_{t-1}}{\rho_{m,t}} = 1, \quad m = 1, 2, ..., M. \quad (4)$$

By rearranging Equation (4), we obtain the market equilibrium price of asset m:

$$\rho_{m,t} = \sum_{i=1}^{I} \alpha_{m,t}^{i,*} \cdot \delta_t^{i,*} \cdot W_{t-1}^i. \tag{5}$$

3 The Agent-Based Multi-asset Artificial Stock Market

An agent-based version of the Blume-Easley-Sandroni standard multi-asset model is developed in [4]. There they ([4]) propose a sliding-window adaptation scheme to approximate the original infinite-time horizon optimization problem (Equations (1) – (3)) by a finite-time horizon optimization problem. The stochastic optimization problem (1) has two mainstays: first, finding an appropriate belief, and second, under that belief, searching for the best decisions regarding saving and portfolios. To distinguish the two, [3] calls the former *"learning how to forecast,"* and the latter *learning how to optimize*. Genetic algorithms are then applied to evolve both beliefs and investment strategies.[4]

To simulate this agent-based multi-asset artificial stock market, a software called *AIE-ASM Version 5.0* is written using *Delphi, Version 7.0*. In each single run, we generate a series of artificial data.

4 Experimental Design

Since the main focus of this paper is to examine the relevance of risk preference to survivability, we shall assume that the autonomous agents are identical in all aspects except in terms of their preferences over risk. With this assumption, we run two series of experiments. These two experiments differ in their constituent agent types. In Experiment 1, the market is composed of eight types of agents, and they are distributed evenly among 40 market participants, i.e. five agents for each type. These eight types of agents are agents with the seven utility functions specified in Table 1 plus the CAPM (capital asset pricing model) believers.

The type-one agent has the logarithmic utility function. We are very much interested in knowing whether this type of agent has any advantage over others in the long-run wealth share. As to types two to six, they are also frequently used in economic analysis.[5] Among them, type four has the well-known *CARA* (constant absolute risk aversion) utility function. In addition to these six familiar types of utility functions, we also consider any arbitrary utility function. By using Taylor's expansion, an arbitrary analytical utility function can be approximated by a finite-order polynomial function. Here, we consider the approximation only up to the sixth order.

Notice that types 3 to 7 refer to a class of parametric utility functions. Parameters of these types of utility functions, namely, $\alpha_1, ..., \alpha_4$, $\beta_1, ..., \beta_3$, and $a_0, a_1, ..., a_6$, can in principle be randomly or manually generated as long as they

---

[4] Details can be found in [4].
[5] See, for example, [6], pp. 27-33.

Table 1. Types of the Utility Function $u(c)$: Experiment 1

	Utility Type	Relative Risk Aversion (RRA)
Type 1	$u(c) = \log(c)$	1
Type 2	$u(c) = \sqrt{c}$	0.5
Type 3	$u(c) = \alpha_1 + \beta_1 c$	0
Type 4	$u(c) = \frac{\alpha_2}{\beta_2} \exp\{\beta_2 c\}$	$-\beta_2 c$
Type 5	$u(c) = \frac{1}{(\gamma_3+1)\beta_3}(\alpha_3 + \beta_3 c)^{\gamma_3+1}$	$-\frac{\beta_3 \gamma_3}{\frac{\alpha_3}{c}+\beta_3}$
Type 6	$u(c) = c - \frac{\alpha_4}{2}c^2$	$\frac{\alpha_4}{\frac{1}{c}-\alpha_4}$
Type 7	$u(c) = a_0 + \sum_{i=1}^{6} a_i c^i$	$-\frac{2a_2 c + 6a_3 c^2 + 12a_4 c^3 + 20a_5 c^4 + 30a_6 c^5}{a_1 + 2a_2 c + 3a_3 c^2 + 4a_4 c^3 + 5a_5 c^4 + 6a_6 c^5}$

satisfy the regular first- and second-order conditions: $u' > 0$ and $u'' < 0$. Since each type of utility function is assigned to five agents, parameter values are generated for each agent for each type separately. So, type 3 agents may have different values of (α_1, β_1), type 4 agents have different values of (α_2, β_2), and so on and so forth.

In Experiment 2, all agents are restricted to the family of the CRRA (constant relative risk aversion) utility functions,

$$u(c) = \begin{cases} c^\rho/\rho, & if \quad -\infty < \rho < \infty, \\ \ln^c, & if \quad \rho = 0. \end{cases} \qquad (6)$$

They, however, differ in terms of their RRA coefficients, i.e. $1 - \rho$. The smaller the ρ, the larger the risk aversion coefficient. Eleven different ρs, starting from 0, 0.1., 0.2.,..., to 0.9, and 1.0, are distributed evenly to all 55 agents, with five agents for each ρ.

5 Simulation Results

5.1 Wealth Share Dynamics

Figure 1 shows the wealth-share dynamics of the eight types of investors in Experiment 1. Notice that each line is based on the average of 100 simulations. The results clearly indicate the strong dominance of the type-one investors, i.e. the agents who have a log utility function. While in some cases type-two investors are still hanging in there for the first 100 periods, their shares eventually decline toward zero. Maybe the most striking result is the extinction of the CARA type of agents (type-4 agents). It is striking because the CARA utility function has been used so extensively in the finance literature that one can hardly cast any doubt on its appropriateness.[6] Equally surprising is the finding that CAPM believers also fail to survive. This result is consistent with an earlier finding by [11], who shows that a sufficient condition to drive CAPM traders to extinction is that an investor endowed with a logarithmic utility function enters the market.

---
[6] For example, it was used to develop the standard asset pricing model ([5]), and was also used in agent-based artificial stock market simulations ([7]).

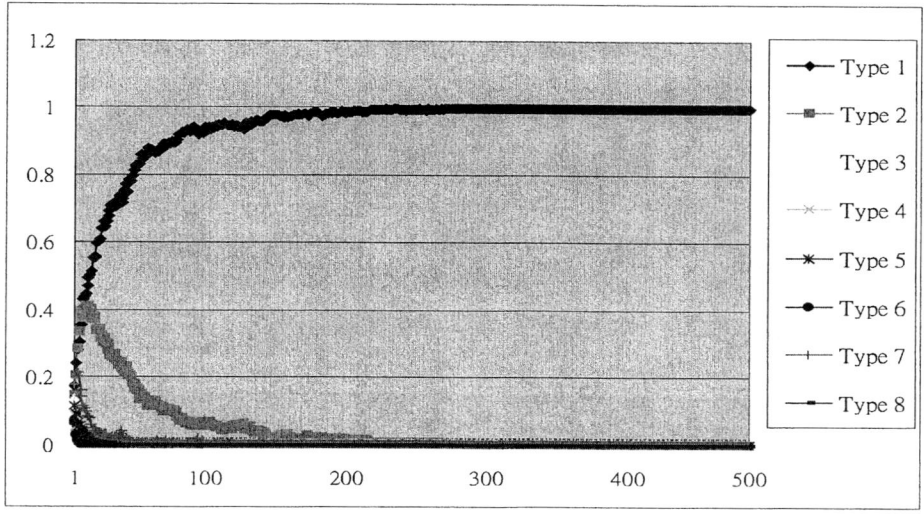

Fig. 1. Time Series Plot of the Wealth Share of Eight Types of Investors: Experiment 1

Since the type-one investors have a constant relative risk aversion coefficient that is one, our experimental results also lend support to Blume and Easley's main argument: *the market selects those investors whose coefficient of relative risk aversion is nearly one.*[7] To further examine this claim, the wealth share dynamics of Experiment 2 is depicted in Figure 2.

As can be seen from Figure 2, the wealth share seems to be positively correlated with the RRA coefficient. Agents with very low values for their the RRA coefficients are driven out of the market at different speeds. The lower the RRA, the faster the evaporation. Towards the end of this 100-period simulation, all agents with RRA values of less than 0.6 are driven out of the market. However, when the RRA coefficient increases to 0.9, the respective agents perform equally well, and sometimes even better, in terms of their wealth shares, as compared with the log-utility agents.

5.2 Saving Rates

Since we assume that the autonomous agents are identical in all aspects except in terms of their preferences over risk, there are only two decision variables left for us to trace the reason why *the market selects those investors whose coefficient of relative risk aversion is nearly one,* namely *saving* and *portfolio*.

Figure 3 is the box-whisker plots of the saving rates. Each plot shows the lifetime distribution of the saving rate δ_t associated with a specific RRA coefficient.

---

[7] See [1], Theorem 5.4, pp. 23-24. The words in italics shown in the main text are not quoted exactly from that theorem, which was originally made by controlling saving rates. Since saving rates are treated endogenously in our paper, our finding suggests that the theorem can still hold true even if the assumption of saving rates is relaxed.

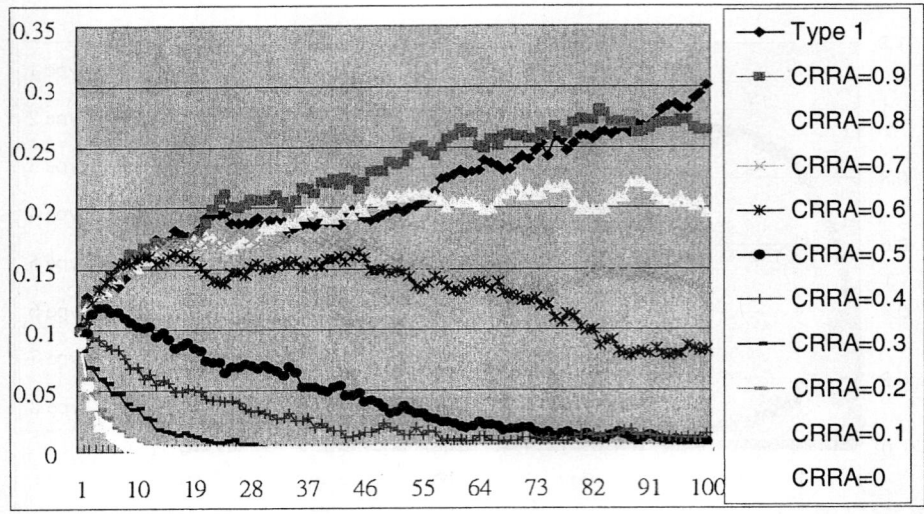

Fig. 2. Time Series Plot of the Wealth Shares of Eleven Types of Investors: Experiment 2

To generate each plot, we first take an average of the saving rate of the five agents for the same RRA coefficient. This is done period by period. A single history of δ_t ($t = 1, 2, ..., 100$) is then derived by further taking an average over the entire 100 simulation runs. So, in the end, we have a single time history of δ_t for each RRA coefficient. The eleven boxes are drawn accordingly.

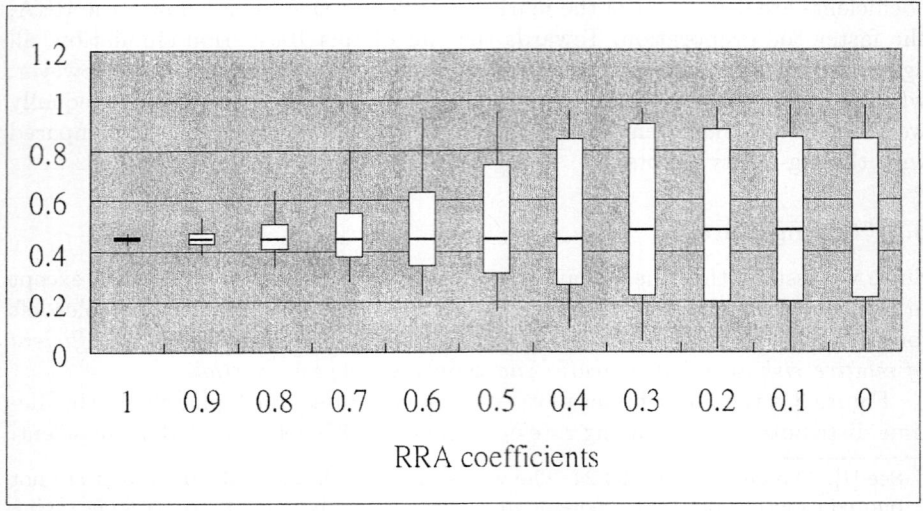

Fig. 3. Distribution of Saving Rates

The line appearing in the middle of the box indicates the median of the 100 observed saving rates for a specific RRA coefficient. While higher saving rates, as what Blume and Easley suggested, will place agents in an advantageous position to survive, we find that the saving rate of the log-utility agents (the case where the RRA coefficient is one) are not significantly higher than other types of agents. This is evidenced by the very close medians observed from the eleven types of agents. Thus, even though the level of saving rate may contribute to survival to a certain degree, our medians simply vary too little to give us a chance to test it.

However, that does not mean all agents have the saving behavior. This is revealed by comparing the boxes and whiskers. Compared to other types of agents, log-utility agents obviously have a very narrow box with a very short whisker, which indicates an unique feature of log-utility agents' saving behavior, namely, *a very stable saving behavior*.

From what we have seen in Figure 3, agents with lower RRA coefficient compared with the log-utility agents suffer from more unstable saving behavior, especially the lower *down-side* saving rates, which may contribute to the faster decline in their wealth share. This provides an significant evidence to explain why *the lower the RRA, the faster the evaporation*.

5.3 Portfolio Performance

In addition to the saving rate, portfolio performance may be another contributing factor to survivability. However, this possibility has already been excluded in [4], and is excluded here again. Table 2 gives the three basic performance measures: the mean return, the risk (variance), and the Sharpe ratio.[8] These statistics are averaged over the five agents of the identical type and are further averaged over the entire 100 simulation runs.

Table 2. Performance Measurements

RRA	1.0	0.9	0.8	0.7	0.6	0.5	0.4	0.3	0.2	0.1	0.0
Mean	2.037	2.083	2.126	2.192	2.276	2.340	2.411	2.428	2.412	2.400	2.374
Variance	7.627	8.424	9.392	11.10	13.31	15.48	18.39	20.36	25.11	27.36	30.61
Sharpe Ratio	0.738	0.718	0.694	0.658	0.624	0.595	0.562	0.538	0.481	0.459	0.429

As we have seen in [4], the surviving agents do not have the highest rates of return. Nonetheless, the column "variance of return" indicates that these agents are under different exposures to risk. Agents with higher relative risk aversion coefficients choose to behave more prudently. Motivated by this finding, we go further to examine the *risk-adjusted return*, also known as the *Sharpe ratio*, and we find that, despite their low mean rate of return, the precautionary behavior of highly risk-averse agents actually helps them to earn a higher

---

[8] For the definition or calculation of these statistics, please see [4], Equations (21) and (22), for details.

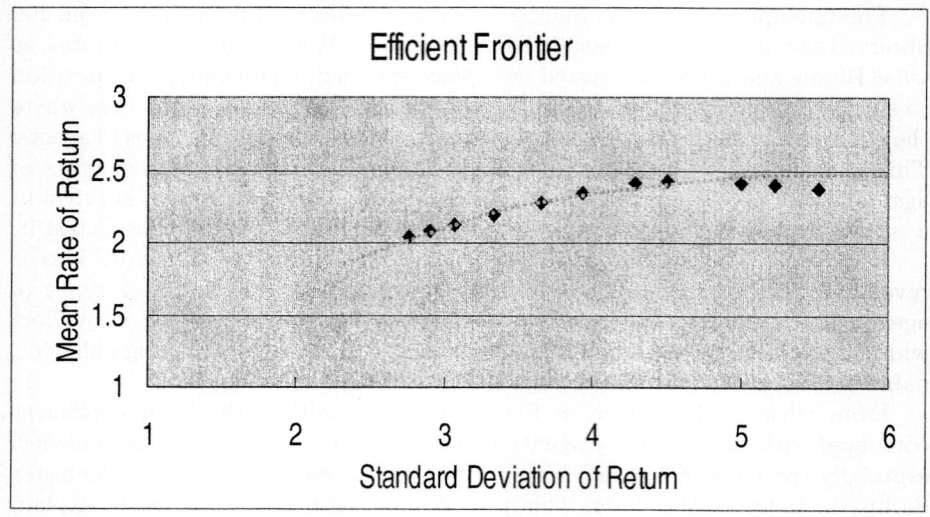

Fig. 4. Efficient Frontier

Sharpe ratio. However, there is no simple intuition to tell us why the agents with higher Sharpe ratios would survive. At least, one may suppose that every investor whose performance is situated at the *efficient frontier* has an equal chance to survive.[9] Therefore, we see no particular reason to attribute the survivability of agents with the RRA coefficient nearly one to their portfolio performance.

6 Concluding Remarks

The irrelevance of risk preference to the survivability of agents is dismissed in this paper. Our first experiment indicates that the only agents who survive in the long run (up to a 500-period simulation) are the log-utility agents. The rest are all driven out, including the CARA agents and the CAPM believers. In the second experiment, we further test for the significance of the RRA coefficient by assuming that all agents are CRRA types, and it is found that the agents' wealth share is affected by how close their RRA coefficients are to 1.

---

[9] To see this, the risk-return plot is drawn in Figure 4. The continuous frontier line is constructed by smoothly connecting the eight points on the frontier. The eight points on the frontier correspond to agents with RRA values of 1, 0.9, 0.8, 0.7, 0.6, 0.5, 0.4, 0.3. From this point of view, their portfolio performance offer them equal survivability. Furthermore, while the other three types of agents do not lie exactly on the frontier, they are not far away from it.

References

1. Blume, L., Easley, D.: Evolution and Market Behavior. Journal of Economic Theory. **58** (1992) 9–40
2. Blume, L., Easley, D.: If You're So Smart, Why Aren't You Rich? Belief Selection in Complete and Incomplete Markets. Working paper. (2001)
3. Bullard, J., Duffy, J.: Using Genetic Algorithms to Model the Evolution of Heterogeneous Beliefs. Computational Economics. **13(1)** (1999) 41–60
4. Chen, S.-H., Huang, Y.-C.: Risk Preference, Forecasting Accuracy and Survival Dynamics: Simulations Based on a Multi-Asset Agent-Based Artificial Stock Market. Working Paper Series 2004-1, AI-ECON Research Center, National Chengchi University.
5. Grossman, S. J., Stiglitz, J.: On the Impossibility of Informationally Efficient Markets. American Economic Review. **70** (1980) 393–408
6. Huang, C. F., Litzenberger, R. H.: Foundations for Financial Economics. Prentice Hall, Inc., Englewood Cliffs, New Jersy (1988)
7. Izumi, K., Nakamura, S., Ueda, K.: Development of an Artificial Market Model Based on a Field Study. Information Sciences, forthcoming. (2004)
8. Kelly, J. L.: A New Interpretation of Information Rate. Bell System Technical Journal **35** (1956) 917–926
9. Lucas, R.: Adaptive Behaviour and Economic Theory. In: Hogarth, R., Reder, M. (eds.): Rational Choice: The Contrast between Economics and Psychology. University of Chicago Press (1986) 217–242
10. Sandroni, A.: Do Markets Favor Agents Able to Make Accurate Predictions? Econometrica. **68(6)** (2000) 1303–1341
11. Sciubba, E.: The Evolution of Portfolio Rules and the Capital Asset Pricing Model. DAE Working Paper No. 9909, University of Cambridge. (1999)
12. Tesfatsion, L.: Introduction to the Special Issue on Agent-Based Computational Economics. Journal of Economic Dynamics and Control. **25** (2001) 281–293

An Agent-Based Holonic Architecture for Reconfigurable Manufacturing Systems

Fang Wang, Zeng-Guang Hou, De Xu, and Min Tan

Laboratory of Complex Systems and Intelligence Science, Institute of Automation,
Chinese Academy of Science, P.O. Box 2728, Beijing 100080, China
{fang.wang, zengguang.hou, de.xu, min.tan}@mail.ia.ac.cn

Abstract. Holonic architectures are more suitable for reconfigurable manufacturing systems compared with hierarchical and heterarchical architectures. A holonic architecture is proposed for reconfigurable manufacturing systems based on the well-known reference architecture PROSA. Considering the special status of the configuration in reconfigurable manufacturing systems, configuration holon is introduced besides the basic holons in PROSA. The basic structure of this holonic architecture, the details of basic holons and cooperation of holons are described in detail. Finally an agent-based holon model is introduced for the realization of the proposed holonic architecture.

1 Introduction

Aggressive competition on a global scale and rapid changes in process technology requires that manufacturing systems must be rapidly designed, able to adjust functionality and capacity quickly to the new demand, and able to integrate new technology easily. It brings the birth of reconfigurable manufacturing system (RMS).

Proper system architecture is the foundation of design and realization of manufacturing system. Holonic architectures integrate the merits of hierarchical architectures and heterarchical architectures and become the focus in the research of RMS [1,2]. Holonic technique is motivated by solving problems encountered and enhancing performances of the system, and oriented its research towards the real-time end of the manufacturing process. However multi-agent technique does well in information processing, but lacks of access to control of physical entities. It is natural to combine these two techniques to complement each other as reported in [2,3,4].

In this paper a holonic architecture for RMS is proposed whose holons are designed based on agent. The rest of this paper is organized as follows. In section 2 three control architectures are compared with each other, and a conclusion is drawn that holonic architecture suits RMS better. Section 3 depicts the proposed holonic architecture for RMS. The agent-based holon framework is described in section 4. Section 5 is the conclusion.

2 Manufacturing System Architectures Comparison

The traditional control architecture for the design of computer integrated manufacturing systems is the hierarchical architecture. Hierarchical architecture is motivated by the tree structure of complex systems. In hierarchical architecture system modules, their functionalities and hierarchic ranks are strictly defined. Commands flow top-down, and feedback information flows bottom-up. All hierarchical architectures keep a fixed structure while the system is running on the assumption that behaviors of the components are deterministic. Therefore the relevant system is very rigid, sensitive to disturbances, expensive to develop and difficult to maintain [5].

Heterarchical architecture is an approach to alleviate the problems of hierarchical architecture [5]. They have a flat structure and are composed of independent intelligent entities, which represent resources and/or tasks. Unlike the master-slave relationship in hierarchical architecture, information and commands are exchanged between entities by the use of a negotiation protocol, which makes it robust to disturbance. But it only functions under condition that resources are abundant and system is homogeneous and not too complex.

Holon is possessed of two significant features: autonomy and cooperation. Autonomy provides the system with abilities to response to disturbances and to reconfigure itself to face new requirements. Holarchy that defines the basic rules for cooperation of the holons can be regarded as a kind of flexible or loose hierarchy. Hence holonic architecture avoids the uncontrollability of heterarchical architecture, as hierarchy is an essential tool to master complexity. So holonic architecture combines the advantages of both hierarchical and heterarchical architecture while avoiding their drawbacks [5]. Considering the characteristics of RMS the architecture for it should be reconfigurable, adaptable to environment variance, of course steady and reliable. With connatural shortcomings, neither hierarchical nor heterarchical architecture is suitable for RMS. Holonic architectures are stable, robust and scalable. Hence it is a reasonable and practical choice for RMS structuring, which becomes a general consensus [2,3,4].

3 Proposed Holonic Architecture for RMS

3.1 Basic Structure of the Holonic Architecture

RMS is capable of changing its configuration to adapt for external or internal disturbances, which distinguishes RMS from other manufacturing systems. So in RMS the configuration not only fills the role of describing the temporary state of the system, but also acts as the object of management, control, reconfiguration optimizing and reconfiguration adjusting. The configuration of RMS may include the following elements [6]:

- Completes set of constituent components and their attributes;
- System internal and external relationships;
- Concepts, rules, principles, methodologies and technologies including human skills and knowledge;
- Methodologies and technologies including human skills and knowledge.

PROSA is a reference architecture for holonic manufacturing systems, which comprises three types of basic holon: order holon, product holon and resource holon, each of which is responsible for one aspect of manufacturing control of logistics, technological planning and resource capabilities [7]. Each type of the holons holds some data and functions.

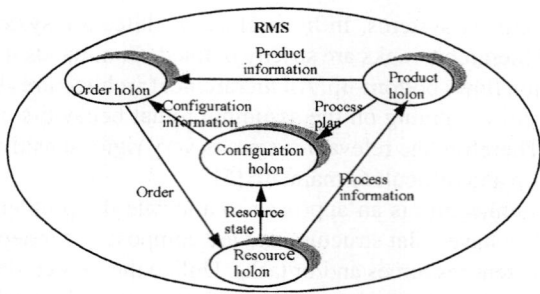

Fig. 1. Illustration of the proposed holonic architecture for RMS

The holonic architecture for RMS proposed in this paper is derived from PROSA. Since configuration plays an important role in RMS as mentioned above, a new type of holon named configuration holon is inducted besides basic types of holon in PROSA. The basic structure of this holonic architecture for RMS is shown in Fig. 1. The detailed explanation will be given in the following.

3.2 Details of Basic Holons

Configuration Holon. A configuration holon possesses the information of current system configuration and capabilities of configuration management with the detail as follows:
- Data: List of resource, Relationship of resources
- Functions: Configuration design, Reconfiguration cost evaluating, Configuration adjusting.

The function of configuration design can deduce a new configuration according to current configuration and process plan supplied by a product holon. To a configuration candidate the index of reconfiguration cost is defined as the spending of time, money, personal efforts or the integration of them all to convert the system from the old configuration to the new one. It indicates that the reconfiguration plan is acceptable or not, and is calculated by the function of reconfiguration cost evaluating. During production equipment failure is inevitable. When configuration holon receives failure information from resource holons, the function of configuration adjusting will adjust system configuration partly by triggering redundancy equipment or equipment with similar function.

Resource Holon. A resource holon combines the information of a physical device and ability to control this device, the detail of which is listed as follows:
- Date: Capabilities, Running tasks, Sub-resources, Activity log
- Functions: Starting processing, Control processing, Control sub-resources, Plan/perform maintenance, Self/sub-resources examining

The detail of the resource holon in the proposed architecture is similar to that in PROSA except that a function of self/ sub-resources examining is added to catch and report failures of its own or sub-resources.

Product Holon. The Product holon contains the product model of the type, up-to-date information on the product life cycle, the knowledge about product design and process plan, which is shown as follows:

- Data: Product model, Process plan, Quality requirements, State of product
- Functions: Modular (re-)design, Process (re-)planning, Quality verification

It is noted that modular design method should be adopted during the product design in RMS.

Order Holon. Order holon is in charge of production scheduling and control. It schedules the task progress after synthesizing the knowledge of process from product holon and configuration from configuration holon, triggers process execution properly and opportunely according to the up-to-date products state and task log, monitors the whole progress to find system deadlock and handle it in time. The detail is as follows:

- Data: Task progress, Task log
- Functions: Scheduling, Progress monitoring, Deadlock handling

3.3 Cooperation of Basic Holons

Holons are autonomous, which means each holon can create and control the execution of its own plans and/or strategies. However the autonomy of the holon is not absolute, and may be broken by the cooperation among holons. It is the characteristic cooperation of holons that generate mutually acceptable scheme and perform it in order to accomplish global goal. In this subsection the cooperation among holons as shown in Fig. 1 are stated in detail.

After the RMS receiving an order form of new product, the product holon of this new type will generate. The product holon sends process plan generated by the modular design function within it to the configuration holon. Maybe more than one configuration candidate is produced by the function of configuration design in the configuration holon. Then the evaluation function of reconfiguration cost calculates the index of every configuration candidate. The configuration holon selects the most efficient one, generates a new configuration holon and informs the product holon of a success signal. The product holon writes the process plan into its data area. If configuration holon fails to educe a reconfiguration plan, a failure signal sends to the product holon. The product holon redesigns this product to generate another process plan and send it to configuration holon again. If all efforts of the product holon have no fruit, that is the RMS can't change its configuration to achieve the new mission within acceptable cost, the system refuses the order form. A staff holon like in PROSA might be imported to assist above reconfiguration negotiation process.

When current mission finishes, current order holon and product holon will be dismissed. After the RMS changes from the old configuration to the new one, the old configuration holon vanishes and an order holon is initialized. Then the new configuration holon and product holon sends configuration information and process plan respectively to the order holon. According them the function of scheduling in order holon frames the task progress. Product holon informs order holon of the real-time state of physical product. Order holon order the related resource holons to start after synthesizing the product state and task progress.

If the resource holon receiving the start order is free, it executes the process immediately, otherwise it puts the order into the running task queue. At the end of process execution resource holon sends the process information such as machining errors to the product holon, which helps the product holon master the product state in time. At the same time resource holons examine the physical devices of itself and sub-resource holons and report resource state to configuration holon.

4 Agent-Based Holon Framework

After structure design of the holonic architecture, the realization of holons and furthermore the whole system based on above blueprint is an important and quite difficult task. Here a means combining both the IEC 61499 function block model and multi-agent technology is adopted, which is mentioned in the paper [3]. This holon framework encapsulates one or more function block oriented devices into a wrapper containing a higher-level software component. The holons of this framework and their relationship are illustrated in Fig. 2.

The polygons in Fig. 2 are function blocks that act in accord with IEC 61499 standard, which builds on the function block part of the IEC 61131-3 standard for languages in PLCs, significantly extends the function block language in the direction needed for holonic control [3].

In such a holon shown in Fig. 2, three types of communications should be considered:

- Intra-holon communication among the function block parts and the software agent;
- Inter-holon communication among the agent-based parts of holons (FIPA standards are used);
- Direct communication among function block parts of the neighboring holons (IEC 61499 standard is used).

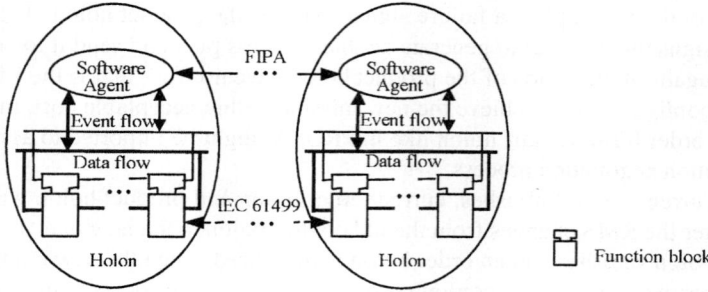

Fig. 2. Holons with wrapper model

5 Conclusions

Via comparison of hierarchical, heterarchical and holonic architecture, a conclusion can be drawn that holonic architectures are much more suitable for RMS. In this paper a holonic architecture for RMS is presented based on PROSA the well studied holonic reference architecture. As configuration of RMS is the carrier of reconfiguration and the pivot of management and control, a new type of holon called configuration holon is introduced in the proposed holonic architecture besides resource holon, product holon and order holon in PROSA. The basic structure of the proposed architecture, details of each basic holon and cooperation of holons are amply described. Then an agent-based holon framework is introduced for further realization. Future work will focus on designing of functions of holons and negotiation rules among holons on the ground of the agent-based holon model.

Acknowledgements

This research has been supported in part by the National Basic Research Program (973) of China (Grant No. 2002CB312200), the National Natural Science Foundation of China (Grant Nos. 60205004, 50475179 and 60334020), the Hi-Tech R&D Program (863) of China (Grant No. 2005AA420040), and the Science and Technology New Star Program of Beijing (Grant No. H02082 0780130).

References

1. Sugi, M., Maeda, Y., Aiyama, Y., et al.: A holonic architecture for easy reconfiguration of robotic assembly systems. IEEE Transactions on Robotics and Automation, **19** (3) (2003) 457-464
2. Huang, X.M., Wang, Y.C., Tan, D.L., et al.: Theoretical analyze and implementation method of reconfigurable assembly line based on Agent and Holon. Proceedings of the 5th World Congress on Intelligent Control and Automation, Hangzhou, China, (2004)
3. Marík, V., Fletcher, M., Pechoucek, M.: Holons & agents: recent developments and mutual impacts. Lecture Notes in Computer Science, **2322** (2002) 233-267
4. Zudor, E.I., Monostori, L.: An agent-based approach for production control incorporating environmental and life-cycle issues together with sensitivity analysis. Lecture Notes in Computer Science, **2358** (2002) 157-167
5. Brussel, H.V., Bongaerts, L., Wyns, J., et al.: A conceptual framework for holonic manufacturing: Identification of manufacturing holons. Journal of Manufacturing Systems, **18** (1) (1999) 35-52
6. Brehmer, N., Wang, C.E.: Reconfigurable manufacturing systems and environment consciousness. Proceedings of First International Symposium on Environmentally Conscious Design and Inverse Manufacturing, (1999) 463-468
7. Brussel, H.V., Wyns, J., Valckenaers, P., et al.: Reference architecture for holonic manufacturing systems: PROSA. Computers in Industry, **37** (3) (1998) 255-274

Mobile Robot Navigation Using Particle Swarm Optimization and Adaptive NN

Yangmin Li and Xin Chen

Department of Electromechanical Engineering, Faculty of Science and Technology,
University of Macau, Av. Padre Tomás Pereira S.J., Taipa, Macao SAR, P.R. China
{ymli, ya27407}@umac.mo

Abstract. This paper presents a novel design for mobile robot using particle swarm optimization (PSO) and adaptive NN control. The adaptive NN control strategy guarantees that robot with nonholonomic constraints can follow smooth trajectories. Based on this property, a PSO algorithm for path planning is proposed. The path planning generates smooth path with low computational cost to avoid obstacles, so that robot can use smooth control strategy to track the trajectory.

1 Introduction

Mobile robot navigation are usually classified into two ways: The first one is real-time reactive way, called artificial potential method, which is difficult to estimate whether the trajectory is optimal or not; The second way is motion planning, namely path planning. Analytical path planning describes paths in the form of high order polynomial [1], then one can estimate the feasibility of path ahead of robot moving. But computation referred is complex and difficult to be realized. Genetic algorithm(GA) has low computational cost for path planning, but the path is a nonsmooth one which can hardly be followed by a mobile robot using smooth control strategy. In this paper, a new path planning method using particle swarm optimization(PSO) is presented [2], which can produce smooth trajectory to make robot via adaptive NN controller [3] track the trajectory to arrive at destination without touching obstacles on the way.

2 NN Control Strategy

2.1 Mobile Robot

A mobile robot is two-wheel driven mini car-like robot with nonholonomic constraints. The position of robot is $p = [\,x\ \ y\,]^T$. Defining $T = \begin{bmatrix} \cos\theta & \sin\theta \\ -\sin\theta & \cos\theta \end{bmatrix}$ and $M_0 = \begin{bmatrix} m & 0 \\ 0 & \frac{I}{d} \end{bmatrix}$, we have the dynamic model: $M_0 T \ddot{p} + M_0 \dot{T} \dot{p} = S^T B \tau - \bar{\tau}_d$, where $\bar{\tau}_d$ represents bounded disturbance and unmodeled dynamics.

2.2 Control Law for Individual Robot

Let p^d denote the reference point. Then the position error is $e = p - p^d$. A filtered error is $z = \dot{e} + \Lambda e$. Define $\dot{p}^r = \dot{p}^d - \Lambda e$, $z = \dot{p} - \dot{p}^r$, $\tilde{z} = Tz$.

A NN function $\hat{f}(X) = \hat{W}^T \sigma(\hat{V}^T X)$ is chosen to estimate $\bar{M}\ddot{p}^r + \bar{V}\dot{p}^r$ on line, where $\hat{W}$ and $\hat{V}$ are estimates of NN weights. An input-output feedback linearization control technology with adaptive BP algorithm is [4]

$$\tau = (S^T B)^{-1}(\hat{W}^T \sigma(\hat{V}^T X) - K\tilde{z} + \gamma), \tag{1}$$

$$\begin{aligned}\dot{\hat{W}} &= F\hat{\sigma}'\hat{V}^T X \tilde{z}^T - F\hat{\sigma}\tilde{z}^T - \kappa F\|\tilde{z}\|\hat{W} \\ \dot{\hat{V}} &= -UX(\hat{\sigma}'^T \hat{W}\tilde{z})^T - \kappa U\|\tilde{z}\|\hat{V}\end{aligned}, \tag{2}$$

where $K = diag\{k_1, k_2\}$, $k_1, k_2 > 0$. F and U are positive definite matrices governing the speed of learning, γ is a robust control term to suppress $\bar{\tau}_d$ and approximation error, $\gamma = \begin{cases} -K_Y(\|\hat{Y}\|_F + Y_M)\tilde{z} - J\frac{\tilde{z}}{\|\tilde{z}\|}, & \|\tilde{z}\| \neq 0 \\ -K_Y(\|\hat{Y}\|_F + Y_M)\tilde{z}, & \|\tilde{z}\| = 0 \end{cases}$, where J and K_Y are positive scalars. It has been proved that the control strategy ensures the robot track the reference point on any smooth path [4].

3 Path Planning Using PSO

3.1 Description of Desired Trajectory

Let $P^d = [p_1^d, p_2^d]^T$ represent the position on the desired trajectory. To avoid obstacles, a five order polynomial for path planning is chosen

$$p_2^d = a_5(p_1^d)^5 + a_4(p_1^d)^4 + a_3(p_1^d)^3 + a_2(p_1^d)^2 + a_1(p_1^d) + a_0. \tag{3}$$

According to boundary conditions, in a_0 to a_5, two of six parameters are free parameters. Other four parameters can be expressed as functions of these two.

3.2 Algorithm of PSO

(1) General algorithm of PSO

Let N denote the size of the swarm, D denote the dimension of the solution space. For particle i, its current position is denoted as $X_i = [x_{i1} \ x_{i2} \ \cdots \ x_{iD}]^T$, and its current velocity is denoted as v_i. $r_1 \sim U(0,1)$ and $r_2 \sim U(0,1)$ represent the two random numbers in the range $(0,1)$. The adjustment of velocity is [5]:

$$v_{ij}(t+1) = Kv_{ij}(t) + c_1 r_{1i}(t)[Y_{ij}(t) - x_{ij}(t)] + c_2 r_{2i}(t)[Y_{ij}^g(t) - x_{ij}(t)], \tag{4}$$

where $j = 1, 2, \cdots, D$, c_1 and c_2 are positive scalars. K is the constriction factor defined as $K = 2/|2 - \phi - \sqrt{\phi^2 - 4\phi}|$, where $\phi = c_1 + c_2$, $\phi > 4$.

The new position of particle i and its best position record are calculated by

$$X_i(t+1) = X_i(t) + v_i(t+1). \tag{5}$$

$$Y_i(t+1) = \begin{cases} Y_i(t), & f(X_i(t+1)) \geq f(Y_i(t)) \\ X_i(t+1), & f(X_i(t+1)) < f(Y_i(t)) \end{cases}. \quad (6)$$

The global best position found by particle i's neighborhoods is modified by

$$Y_i^g(t+1) = arg \min_{k \in \Pi_i} f(Y_k(t+1)), \quad (7)$$

where Π_i represents the neighborhoods of particle i.

(2) Interaction topology in the swarm
A ring interaction graph is used to describe relationship of interaction.

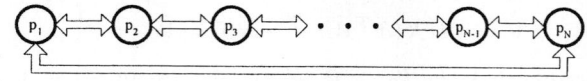

Fig. 1. The ring interaction topology

(3) Fitness evaluation
The fitness function includes two parts:

1) If the x-axis of the reference frame is along the beeline connecting the begin and end of the trajectory, the fitness function is $F_{path} = \int_0^{p_1^{d(t_f)}} (p_2^d)^2 dp_1^d$, where $p_1^{d(t_f)}$ is the coordinate in x-direction of the destination.

2) Given obstacle i, let $P_i^c = [p_{i1}^c, p_{i2}^c]^T$ denote the cross point on which a beeline through obstacle position intersects with the trajectory perpendicularly. Therefore an evaluation function for the cross point is defined as $F_{crosspoint} = \left(1 - \frac{p_{i2}^o - p_{i2}^c}{p_{i1}^o - p_{i1}^c} \cdot \frac{dp_2^d}{dp_1^d}\Big|_{P^d = P_i^c}\right)^2$. And an evaluation function for obstacle avoidance is $F_{obstacle} = \begin{cases} \mu(\frac{1}{\|\rho_i^o\|} - \frac{1}{\rho_{eff}}), & \|\rho_i\| \leq \rho^{eff} \\ 0, & \|\rho_i\| > \rho^{eff} \end{cases}$, where $\rho_i = P_i^o - P_i^c$, ρ^{eff} denotes the maximal effective range of obstacle i.

Consequently the fitness function for path planning is of the form

$$F = L_1 \cdot F_{path} + L_2 \cdot F_{crosspoint} + L_3 \cdot F_{obstacle}, \quad (8)$$

where L_1, L_2, and L_3 represent positive weights.

If we assume there are M obstacles and adopt five order polynomial, the dimension of the particle is $D = M + 2$, or $X = [\, a_5 \quad a_3 \quad p_{11}^c \quad p_{21}^c \quad p_{31}^c \,]^T$.

4 Simulations

The boundary conditions for polynomial are chosen as $P^d(0) = 0$, $P^d(t_f) = 4$, $\frac{dp_2^d}{dp_1^d}\big|_{t=0} = 0$, $\frac{dp_2^d}{dp_1^d}\big|_{t=t_f} = 0$. There are three obstacles at $(1, 0.25)$, $(2, 0.5)$ and $(3, -0.3)$. Hence $X_i = [\, a_{i5} \quad a_{i3} \quad p_{i11}^c \quad p_{i21}^c \quad p_{i31}^c \,]^T$, $i = 1, 2, \cdots, N$. Other parameters include: $N = 20$, $K = 0.729$, $c_1 = c_2 = 2.05$, $L_1 = L_2 = L_3 = 1$. Fig. 2 shows the simulation results. There are two robots forming a leader-

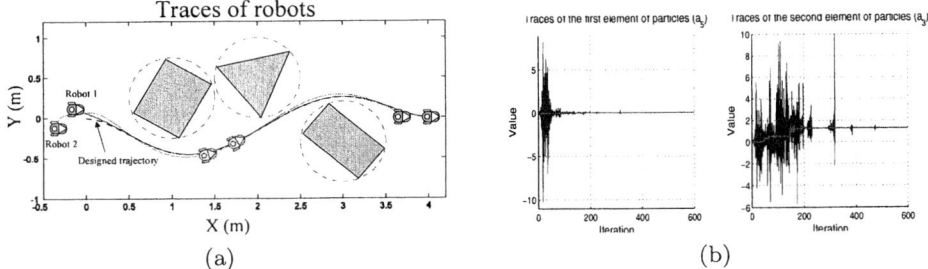

Fig. 2. Simulation results

follower pair to pass through field with obstacles. Fig. 2 (b) displays the evolution process of two elements, a_5 and a_3, during the first 600 iterations. After 1200 iterations, all particles aggregate to a single position where $a_3 = 1.2917$ and $a_5 = 0.0380$, so that the desired trajectory is $p_2^d = 0.0380(p_1^d)^5 - 0.3892(p_1^d)^4 + 1.2917(p_1^d)^3 - 1.3687(p_1^d)^2$. Once the path is generated, a moving point on the trajectory is designed. And robot 1 is required to follow this moving point using the control strategy shown in (1) and (2).

5 Conclusions

A kind of practical technique for mobile robot navigation is proposed in this paper. The analysis and simulation demonstrate the feasibility of mobile robot navigation using PSO and ANN. Because of its low computational cost, it is easily realized in practical applications in case of real-time path planning required.

Acknowledgements

This work was supported by the Research Committee of University of Macau under grant RG082/04-05S/LYM/FST.

References

1. Dyllong, E., Visioli, A.: Planning and Real-time Modifications of a Trajectory Using Spline Techniques. Robotica, **21** (2003) 475 - 482
2. Kennedy, J., Eberhart, R. C.: Particle Swarm Optimization. Proc. of IEEE Int. Conf. on Neural Network, Perth, Australia (1995) 1942-1948
3. Lewis, F. L., Yesildirek, A., Liu, K.: Multilayer Neural-Net Robot Controller with Guaranteed Tracking Performance. IEEE Trans. on Neural Networks, **7** (1996) 388-399
4. Li, Y., Chen, X.: Control and Stability Analysis on Multiple Robots. The 2nd Int. Conf. on Autonomous Robots and Agents. New Zealand (2004) 158-163
5. Clerc, M., Kennedy, J.: The Particle Swarm: Explosion, Stability, and Convergence in a Multi-dimentional Complex Space. IEEE Trans. on Evolutionary Computation. **6** (2002) 58-73

Collision-Free Path Planning for Mobile Robots Using Chaotic Particle Swarm Optimization

Qiang Zhao and Shaoze Yan

Department of Precision Instruments and Mechanology, Tsinghua University,
Beijing 100084, P.R. China
{zhao-q, yansz}@mail.tsinghua.edu.cn

Abstract. Path planning for mobile robots is an important topic in modern robotics studies. This paper proposes a new approach to collision-free path planning problem for mobile robots using the particle swarm optimization combined with chaos iterations. The particle swarm optimization algorithm is run to get the global best particle as the candidate solution, and then local chaotic search iterations are employed to improve the solution precision. The effectiveness of the approach is demonstrated by three simulation examples.

1 Introduction

Mobile robots are expected to have more wide applications in the future. Planning a collision-free path is one of the fundamental requirements for a mobile robot to execute its tasks. There are many approaches suggested by researchers to solve this problem [1]. Recently, it is widespread to use genetic and evolutionary algorithms. A chaotic genetic algorithm was used to find the shortest path for a mobile robot to move in a static environment [2]. A particle swarm optimization (PSO) algorithm with mutation operator was employed in the path planning to meet the real-time requests of the mobile robot navigation [3].

The PSO algorithm, as a new evolution technology, has many advantages, such as simple algorithm and quick convergence, but in the last stage of iterations of the algorithm when all particles approach the best solution, the convergence may become slow and the solution precision may not be absolutely satisfactory. The chaotic search algorithm was developed for nonlinear constrained optimization problems [4]. This paper introduces the chaos with its ergodicity into the PSO algorithm for the path planning of mobile robots so as to intensify the local search ability and improve the solution precision.

2 Chaotic Particle Swarm Optimization

The particle swarm optimization algorithm, proposed by Kennedy and Eberhart [5], has proved to be a very effective approach in solving multi-dimensional optimization problems. The PSO algorithm first randomly initializes a swarm of particles. Each particle is represented as $X_i = (x_{i,1}, x_{i,2}, ..., x_{i,n})$, $i = 1, 2, ..., N$, where N is the swarm size, and n is the total dimension number of each particle. Each particle adjusts its trajectory toward its own previous best position *pbest* and the previous best position *gbest* attained by the whole swarm. In each iteration k, the i th particle with respect to the j th dimension is updated by

$$v_{ij}^{(k+1)} = v_{ij}^{(k)} + c_1 r_1 (pbest_{ij}^{(k)} - x_{ij}^{(k)}) + c_2 r_2 (gbest_j^{(k)} - x_{ij}^{(k)}), \qquad (1)$$

$$x_{ij}^{(k+1)} = x_{ij}^{(k)} + v_{ij}^{(k+1)}. \qquad (2)$$

where $x_{i,j}^{(k)}$ and $v_{i,j}^{(k)}$ are the current position and velocity, respectively. c_1 and c_2 are acceleration constants, r_1 and r_2 are random numbers within the interval of [0,1].

Chaos is one of the important achievements in nonlinear system search. The chaotic model adopts a logistic mapping [6]: $z^{(k+1)} = \mu z^{(k)}(1-z^{(k)})$, where μ is the control parameter. When $\mu = 4$, the system enters into a chaos state.

In our chaotic particle swarm optimization (CPSO) approach, the PSO algorithm is first run to find the global best position as a candidate solution, and then the chaotic space (0, 1) is mapped into the neighborhood of this candidate solution. Thus the better solution can be searched by means of the ergodicity of the chaos.

3 Path-Planning Using the CPSO Algorithm

The mobile robot path-planning problem is typically stated as follows: given a robot, start location S, target location T and two-dimensional map of workplace including static obstacles, plan the shortest collision-free path between the two locations.

The particle representation can be taken as the same way as chromosome encoding in literature [2]. Divide line ST into $n+1$ equal segments with n points, and further draw n vertical lines, $L_1, L_2, \cdots, L_n$, through these points, respectively. Take one random point on each vertical line according to priority and construct a path: $X = \{P_1, P_2, \cdots, P_i, \cdots, P_n\}$, $P_i \in L_i$. Described by two-dimensional coordinates for each point, the above path can be extended to $X = \{x_1, y_1, \cdots, x_i, y_i, \cdots, x_n, y_n\}$. In order to decrease the dimension number in X, a coordinate transformation is used to locate the X-axis to coincide with line ST. The new coordinates of P_i can be described:

$$\begin{bmatrix} x_i' \\ y_i' \end{bmatrix} = \begin{bmatrix} -x_s \cos\theta - y_s \sin\theta \\ x_s \sin\theta - y_s \cos\theta \end{bmatrix} + \begin{bmatrix} \cos\theta & \sin\theta \\ -\sin\theta & \cos\theta \end{bmatrix} \begin{bmatrix} x_i \\ y_i \end{bmatrix}, \qquad (3)$$

where x_s and y_s are the coordinates of point S, θ is the anti-clockwise rotation angle from the X-axis to line ST.

The new located coordinate frame is shown as S-$X'Y'$ in Fig. 1. The particle representation can be simplified into $X = \{y_1', y_2', \cdots, y_i', \cdots, y_n'\}$. Additionally, the particle must satisfy the collision-free constraint conditions as follows: Each node in the path must not be within the areas taken by all the obstacles, and any one of the line series $\{SP_1, P_1P_2, \ldots, P_{n-1}P_n, P_nT\}$ must not intersect with any obstacle.

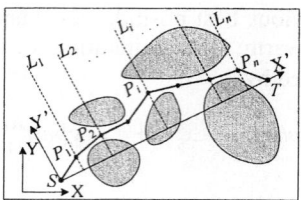

Fig. 1. Representation of a collision-free path

Considering that the shortest path is as the optimization criterion for our problem, the objective function, also as the fitness function in the PSO, is taken as

$$f(X) = \frac{d}{\sqrt{\frac{d^2}{n+1} + \sum_{i=0}^{n}(y'_{i+1} - y'_i)^2}}, \qquad (4)$$

where d is the distance between point S and T, $d = |ST|$. $y'_0 = y'_{n+1} = 0$.

The path planning procedure of the CPSO approach can be described as follows:

Step 1. Initialization: Generate randomly N particles $X_i^{(0)}$, and with velocities, $V_i^{(0)}$.
Step 2. Evaluate the fitness of each particle according to Eq. (4), and determine the individual and global best positions: $pbest_i$ and $gbest$.
Step 3. Velocity and position updating: update $v_{ij}^{(k)}$ and $x_{i,j}^{(k)}$ using Eq. (1) and (2).
Step 4. Collision-free constraint conditions checking: if the path satisfies the conditions, continue, else reset $v_{ij}^{(k)}$ and $x_{ij}^{(k)}$ to their previous values and goto step 3.
Step 5. Loop to step 2 and repeat until a given maximum iteration number is attained.
Step 6. Local chaotic search: select $gbest$ as the initial condition, the chaotic iteration is as $x_i^{(k+1)} = a_i + \mu(b_i - a_i)z^{(k)}(1-z^{(k)})$, where $z^{(0)} = (gbest_i + \Delta r_i - a_i)/(b_i - a_i)$, Δr_i is a small random variant, a_i and b_i is the lower and upper boundary of a neighborhood of $gbest_i$.
Step 7. Check the new path whether to satisfy the collision-free constraint conditions, evaluate the path using Eq. (4) and if it is the better one, update the optimum.
Step 8. Loop to step 6 and repeat until a given maximum iteration number is attained.

4 Numerical Simulations

Some simulations are carried out to illustrate the proposed algorithm using Matlab. The two-dimensional map of workplace is a rectangle area with size of 100×100, and the mobile robot is simplified as a circle with a diameter of 3. Three cases with different distribution density of obstacles are considered. Related parameters are set as: $N = 50$, $n = 19$, $c_1 = c_2 = 2$. The optimized paths and corresponding fitness functions are shown in Table 1 and Fig. 2, respectively. It can be seen that, compared with the PSO, the CPSO approach can get a shorter path with higher solution precision.

Table 1. Fitness functions for 3 cases under the PSO and CPSO algorithms

Method	Fitness function $f(X)$		
	Case a	Case b	Case c
PSO	0.8672	0.9375	0.9517
CPSO	0.9712	0.9659	0.9726

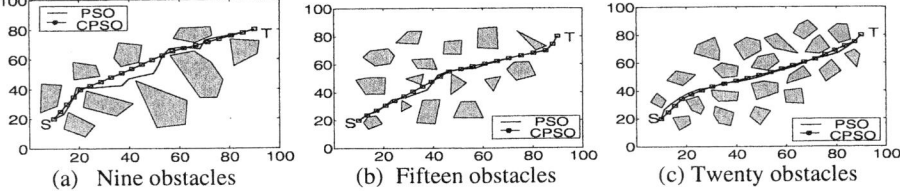

(a) Nine obstacles (b) Fifteen obstacles (c) Twenty obstacles

Fig. 2. Simulation results of the PSO and CPSO algorithms

5 Conclusions

A chaotic particle swarm optimization approach is developed for mobile robots to obtain the shortest collision-free path in two-dimensional environment. This approach introduces chaos with its ergodicity property into the particle swarm optimization so as to intensify the local search ability and improve the solution precision. Simulation results show the feasibility and effectiveness of the proposed approach.

References

1. Latombe, J. C.: Robot Motion Planning. Kluwer, Norwell, MA (1991)
2. Zhou, P. C., Hong, B. R., Yang, J. H.: Chaos Genetic Algorithm Based Path Planning Method for Mobile Robot. Journal of Harbin Institute of Technology. 7 (2004) 880–883
3. Qin, Y. Q., Sun, D. B., Li. N., CEN. Y. G.: Path Planning for Mobile Robot Using the Particle Swarm Optimization with Mutation Operator. Proceedings of the Third International Conference on Machine Learning and Cybernetics, Shanghai. (2004) 2473-2478
4. Jiang, C. W., Bompard, E.: A Hybrid Method of Chaotic Particle Swarm Optimization and Linear Interior for Reactive Power Optimization. Mathematics and Computers in Simulation. 68 (2005) 57–65
5. Kennedy, J. E., Eberhart, R.: Particle Swarm Optimization. In: Proceedings of the IEEE International Conference on Neural Networks, Vol. 4. Perth. Australia. (1995) 1942-1948
6. Wu, X. X., Chen, Z.: Introduction of Chaos Theory. Shanghai Science and Technology Bibliographic Publishing House, Shanghai (1996)

Analysis of Toy Model for Protein Folding Based on Particle Swarm Optimization Algorithm*

Juan Liu[1], Longhui Wang[1], Lianlian He[2], and Feng Shi[2]

[1] School of Computer, Wuhan University, Wuhan, 430079, China
liujuan@whu.edu.cn
[2] School of Mathematics, Wuhan University, Wuhan, 430072, China

Abstract. One of the main problems of computational approaches to protein structure prediction is the computational complexity. Many researches use simplified models to represent protein structure. Toy model is one of the simplification models. Finding the ground state is critical to the toy model of protein. This paper applies Particle Swarm Optimization (PSO) Algorithm to search the ground state of toy model for protein folding, and performs experiments both on artificial data and real protein data to evaluate the PSO-based method. The results show that on one hand, the PSO method is feasible and effective to search for ground state of toy model; on the other hand, toy model just can simulate real protein to some extent, and need further improvements.

1 Introduction

The structure of protein determines its function in molecular. Experimental methods of determining protein structure include X-ray crystallography and NMR-spectroscopy. However some proteins are hard to crystallize, and NMR-spectroscopy method only works on small proteins. Moreover, these two methods are expensive and time-consuming [1]. So predicting protein structure by computational method is very necessary, and it has become one of the most important research topics in modern molecular biology. However, it is very complex to determine the native three-dimensional structure of a protein when only given the sequence of amino acid residues that compose the protein chain [2].

Due to the complexity of the protein-folding problem, scientists have proposed a variety of models such as hydrophobic-polar (HP) model to simplify the problem by abstracting only the "essential physical properties" of real proteins. Generally speaking, there are three representative simplified HP models for protein folding: lattice model [3], triangle lattice model [4], and toy model[5]. In lattice model, the three dimensional space is represented by a lattice, and the 20 amino acids are grouping into two classes: hydrophobic (or non-polar) residues and hydrophilic (or polar) residues, where P represents polar residues, and H represents hydrophobic residues. Residues that are adjacent in the primary sequence must be placed at adjacent points in the lattice. A conformation of a

---

* This work was supported by the National Natural Science Foundation of China under grant no. 60301009.

protein is a self-avoiding walk along the lattice. The protein folding problem is to find a conformation of the protein sequence on the lattice such that the overall energy is minimized, for some reasonable definition of energy [6]. Dill et.al. surveyed some works on this model in [7].

Richa Agarwada et.al. tested the HP model on a triangle lattice [4]. They examined the choice of a lattice by considering its algorithmic and geometric implications and argued that triangular lattice is a more reasonable choice. Though the structures derived from triangle lattice model are probably still far from biological reality, it's much better than basic lattice model [4].

Stillinger et al. had done further improvements and presented the toy model [5]. In this model, amino acid residues are still classified into two kinds: hydrophobic and hydrophilic, but what differences from previous lattice models are that there is only one bond between two consecutive residues, and the angle between the two bonds can change freely. So it is more like the real protein structure than the previous two lattice models [5]. One major advantage of the toy model is that it becomes feasible to determine a complete database of ground state structures for all "polypeptides" up to some modest (but non-trivial) degree of polymerization.

How to find the ground state of toy model of protein? People have tried many methods such as Neural Network [5,8] and Simulated Annealing Algorithm [9]. In this paper, we will try to use PSO algorithm to search the ground state and analyze the experiment results.

PSO is a recently proposed algorithm by J.Kennedy and R. C. Eberhart in 1995 [10], motivated by social behavior of organisms such as bird flocking and fish schooling [11]. In a PSO system, **particles**(individuals) **fly** around in a multidimensional search space. During flight, each particle adjusts its **position**(state) according to its own experience, the experience of a neighboring particle, making use of the best position encountered by itself and its neighbor. Thus, as in modern GAs and memetic algorithms, a PSO system combines local search methods with global search methods, attempting to balance exploration and exploitation [10,12]. In the past several years, PSO has been successfully applied in many research and application areas.

In this paper, we will discuss the application of PSO on toy model for protein folding. The rest part of the paper is organized as following: In section 2, we give a brief description of toy model for protein folding. In section 3, we introduce the basic ideas of PSO. Section 4 includes the experiments and the results. The final section is the conclusion part of this paper.

2 Description of Toy Model

In 1993, Stillinger et al. presented the toy model for protein sequence [5]. This model incorporates only two "amino acids", to be denoted by **A** and **B**, in place of the real 20 amino acids. **A** and **B** are linked together by rigid unit-length bonds to form linear un-oriented polymers that reside in two dimensions. As figure 1 illustrates, the configuration of any n-mer is specified by the $n-2$

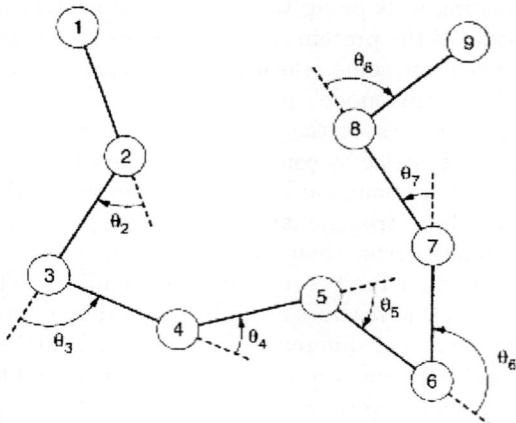

Fig. 1. A schematic diagram of a generic 9-mer, with serially numbered residues, and backbone bend angles

angles of bend $\theta_2 \ldots \theta_{n-1}$ at each of the non-terminal residues. We adhere to the conventions that: $-\pi < \theta_i < \pi$, $\theta_i = 0$ corresponds to linearity of successive bonds, and positive angles indicate counterclockwise rotations.

In the following, we do not consider intermolecular interactions. We suppose that two kinds of interactions compose the intra-molecular potential energy for each molecule: backbone bend potentials (V_1) and non-bonded interactions (V_2). The former is independent of the **A**, **B** sequence, whereas the later varies with the sequence and receives contribution from each pair of residues that are not directly attached by a backbone bond. Residues along the backbone can be conveniently encoded by a set of binary variables $\xi_1 \ldots \xi_n$, where $\xi_i = 1$ means that the ith residue is **A**; and $\xi_i = $ -1 means that it is **B**. Thus for any n-mer, the intra-molecular potential-energy function Φ can be expressed as formula (1):

$$\Phi = \sum_{i=2}^{n-1} V_1(\theta_i) + \sum_{i=1}^{n-2} \sum_{j=i+2}^{2} V_2(r_{ij}, \xi_i, \xi_j) \qquad (1)$$

Where, the distances r_{ij} can be written as functions of the intervening angles (backbone bonds have unit length):

$$r_{ij} = \left\{ \left[1 + \sum_{k=i+1}^{j-1} \cos\left[\sum_{l=i+1}^{k} \theta_l\right] \right]^2 + \left[\sum_{k=i+1}^{j-1} \sin\left[\sum_{l=i+1}^{k} \theta_l\right] \right]^2 \right\}^{1/2} \qquad (2)$$

Toy model assigns a simple trigonometric form to V_1:

$$V_1(\theta_i) = \frac{1}{4}(1 - \cos\theta_i) \qquad (3)$$

And the non-bonded interactions V_2 have a species dependent Lennard-Jones 12, 6 form:
$$V_2(r_{ij}, \xi_i, \xi_j) = 4[r_{ij}^{-12} - C(\xi_i, \xi_j)r_{ij}^{-6}] \quad (4)$$
Where,
$$C(\xi_i, \xi_j) = \frac{1}{8}(1 + \xi_i + \xi_j + 5\xi_i\xi_j) \quad (5)$$

On account of Equation (4), successive bonds would tend towards linearity ($\theta_i = 0$), if nothing else mattered.

Toy model is also based on the famous judgement presented by Anfinsen in 1960s: The native structure of protein is the structure with the lowest free energy [13]. This conclusion is the thermodynamics base of using energy minimization method to predict protein structure. For a protein sequence with n residues, we need to search out a group of suitable θ_i ($i = 2, \ldots, n-1$), $\theta_i \in (-\pi, \pi)$, to make the energy function (1) achieve the minimal value in the solution space.

3 Particle Swarm Optimization

PSO algorithm is similar to other genetic algorithms (GA). What makes it different with GAs is that, PSO does not use evolutionary operators to evolve the population, instead, it takes each individual as a particle without weight and volume in the n-dimensional search space, the particle flies at certain speed in the search space. The flying speed of the particle adjusts dynamically according to its flying experience and population's flying experience [14].

3.1 Basic Particle Swarm Optimization Method

Considering the minimal problem, given a particle i, let $X_i = (x_{i1}, x_{i2}, \cdots, x_{in})$ be its current position, $V_i = (v_{i1}, v_{i2}, \cdots, v_{in})$ be its current flying speed, $P_i = (p_{i1}, p_{i2}, \cdots, p_{in})$ be the best position it has experienced. Suppose $f(X)$ is the objective function, obviously, P_i would minimize $f(X)$. P_i is called as the best individual place. Suppose that the particle number in the swarm is s, the best position P_g that all particles in the swarm have experienced is called the global optimal position, so we have $P_g \in \{P_1, P_2, \cdots, P_s\}$, and $f(P_g) = \min\limits_{i \in \{1,2,\cdots,s\}} \{f(P_i)\}$.

With the definition presented as above, basic PSO function can be described as following:
$$v_{ij}(t+1) = v_{ij}(t) + c_1 r_{1j}(t)(p_{ij}(t) - x_{ij}(t))$$
$$+ c_2 r_{2j}(t)(p_{gj}(t) - x_{ij}(t)) \quad (6)$$
$$x_{ij}(t+1) = x_{ij}(t) + v_{ij}(t+1) \quad (7)$$

Where, j indicates the jth dimension of particle, i indicates the ith particle, t indicates the tth generation, c_1, c_2, varying from 0 to 2, are the acceleration speed constants, they determine the relative influence of the social and cognitive components, and are usually both set the same to give each component equal weight as the cognitive and social learning rate. $r_1 \sim U(0,1), r_2 \sim U(0,1)$ are two independent random function [15].

3.2 Canonical Particle Swarm Optimization Method

Due that basic PSO usually failed in some applications, Carlisle and Doziert presented the following typical PSO Algorithm model (Canonical PSO) [16].

$$v_{ij} = \begin{cases} K(v_{ij} + c_1 r_1 (P_{ij} - x_{ij}) + c_2 r_2 (P_{gj} - x_{ij})), & X_{\min} < x_{ij} < X_{\max} \\ 0 & otherwise \end{cases}$$

$$x_{ij} = \begin{cases} x_{ij} + v_{ij}, & X_{\min} < x_{ij} < X_{\max} \\ X_{\max}, & (x_{id} + v_{ij}) > X_{\max} \\ X_{\min}, & X_{\min} < (x_{ij} + v_{ij}) \end{cases} \quad (8)$$

Where K is the constriction factor,

$$K = \frac{2}{|2 - C - \sqrt{c_2 - 4C}|} \quad (9)$$

In the following experiments, we use this kind of PSO to analyze toy model. We use the classic parameter set [16], in which, $c_1 = 2.8$, $c_2 = 1.3$, $C = c_1 + c_2$, population size $N = 30$. In each generation, we produce new candidate solutions, and calculate the energy function, if the result of the function becomes smaller, we reserve the solution, otherwise we reject the solution. The iteration procedure repeats until the terminal conditions are satisfied. In this article, the procedure will stop when it reaches the maximal iteration steps.

4 Experiments and Results

In this section, we do several experiments to analyze the toy model for protein folding. Canonical PSO described in secion 3.2 is used to search the ground state of the toy model that minimizes Equation(1).

4.1 Experiments on Artificial Sequences

We use some artificial sequence to do two kinds of experiments. First, we use the same sequences as [5] to see whether our method can get the ground state. For these short sequences, the maximal iteration step $L = 30$. From the results illustrated in table 1, we can see that our method can also reach the ground state presented by Stillinger [5].

To explore whether our method can get the correct protein secondary structure elements, we then use two testing sequences "AABABB" and "AAABAA" just like [5] for experiments. The secondary structures on the 2D toy model is shown in figure 2. Figure 3 shows the computational results. Because these two sequences are short, our program got the results in a very short time.

From figure 3 we can see that our method is effective to simulate protein folding as it can correctly give out the secondary structure motif: α-helix and β-sheet.

Table 1. Ground state properties of toy-model polypeptides

Molecular	Φ	Molecular	Φ
AAA	-0.658 21	AAAAA	-2.848 28
AAB	0.032 23	AAAAB	-1.589 44
ABA	-0.658 21	AAABA	-2.444 93
ABB	0.032 23	AAABB	-0.546 88
BAB	-.0.030 27	AABAA	-2.531 70
BBB	-0.030 27	AABAB	-1.347 74
		AABBA	-0.926 62
AAAA	-1.676 33	AABBB	0.040 17
AAAB	-0.585 27	ABAAB	-1.376 47
AABA	-1.450 98	ABABA	-2.220 20
AABB	0.067 20	ABABB	-0.616 80
ABAB	-0.649 38	ABBAB	-0.005 65
ABBA	-0.036 17	ABBBA	-0.398 04
ABBB	0.004 70	ABBBB	-0.065 96
BAAB	0.061 72	BAAAB	-0.521 08
BABB	-0.000 78	BAABB	0.096 21
BBBB	-0.139 74	BABAB	-0.648 03
		BABBB	-0.182 66
		BBABB	-0.240 20
		BBBBB	-0.452 66

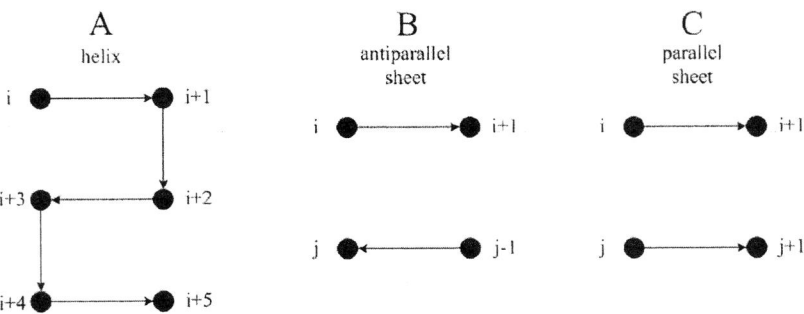

Fig. 2. Secondary structures on the 2D toy model. A: helix, at least two sequential noncovalent contacts between residues [(i, i+3), (i+2,i+5)...(i+2n, i+2n+3)]. B: Antiparallel sheet [(i, j), (i+1, j-1)...(i+n, j+n)]. C: Parallel sheet [(i, j), (i+1, j+1)...(i+n, j+n)]

4.2 Experiments on Real Protein Sequences

Then we test our method on real protein sequences. When sequence becomes long, the determination of the objective function value is extremely time-consuming. So only two real proteins with short sequences are discussed in our paper, i.e., 1agt and 1aho. All information of these two proteins can be downloaded from PDB (http://www.rcsb.org/pdb/).

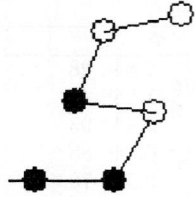 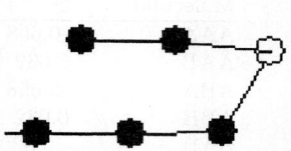

(a) The lowest-energy conformer of sequence AABABB may be classified as "helical". Φ=-1.335366, x=[-1.045231 -1.951874 1.738942 0.147911]

(b) The lowest-energy conformer for sequence AAABAA is a "β-sheet" motif. (Φ=-3.697501, x= [0.020746 1.040153 1.958890 0.133675]

Fig. 3. Testing sequence results. In fig.3 and the following pictures, the circle indicates hydrophilic residue, and the black dot indicates hydrophobic residue

In the experiments, we use K-D method to distinguish hydrophobic and hydrophilic residues of 20 amino acids in real proteins. Briefly speaking, amino acids I, V, L, P, C, M, A, G are hydrophobic and D, E, F, H, K, N, Q, R, S, T, W, Y are polar [17].

Experiment on 1AGT. First, we experimented on 1agt. The information about its sequence and secondary structure from PDB are as follows:

1 GVPINVSCTG SPQCIKPCKD QGMRFGKCMN RKCHCTPK
    EE   B SS STTHHHHHHH HTBSEEEEET TEEEEEE

The first line is amino acid sequence, and the second line is its secondary structure. It contains 38 residues, one helical segment and two β-sheet segments.

With the maximal iterate steps $L = 5,000$, we got ground state shown in figure 4, from which we can see that the final toy model can simulate the real protein to some extent.

Experiment on 1AHO. And then, we discussed on protein 1aho; its protein sequence and secondary structure information are as follows:

1 VKDGYIVDDV NCTYFCGRNA YCNEECTKLK GESGYCQWAS PYGNACYCYK
   B EEEE TT S B   S HH HHHHHHHHTT   SEEEEETTB TTBSEEEEES

51 LPDHVRTKGP GRCH
    B TTS B   S S

It contains 64 residues. Residue 19 to 28 is a helix segment in native conformation. With $L = 10,000$, we got the result shown in figure 5, which also approaches to the real protein structure.

To evaluate the performance of our method, we also compared it with Simulated Annealing (SA) Algorithm implemented in [9] on 1agt and 1aho sequences.

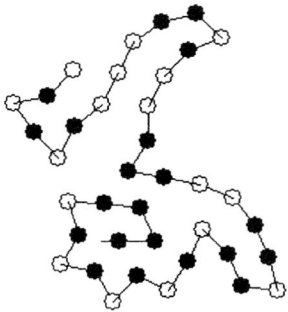

Fig. 4. Φ = -19.616866, x = [1.968670 1.039088 0.068094 1.922932 -0.834257 1.907747 -0.833636 1.912368 -1.340518 1.479550 0.137488 -1.933330 -0.375798 1.044901 1.953578 0.125628 0.280929 0.528956 0.144413 0.067585 -1.937305 0.497480 -0.420421 -0.306854 -0.404344 1.946600 1.041268 0.396669 0.504622 -0.058998 -0.411684 0.426404 -1.939082 -0.130507 -1.945389 0.570014]

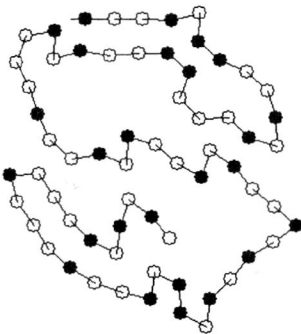

Fig. 5. Φ = -15.181101, x = [-0.010702 -0.060948 0.362086 -1.926352 0.904857 0.301411 -0.299284 -0.573455 -0.201756 -1.900080 -0.531997 0.810784 -0.829126 - 1.096663 1.186948 0.746497 0.050294 -0.262349 0.501073 -1.922822 1.787451 1.047013 0.815521 -0.145761 0.093422 0.404816 0.928052 -0.562520 1.924269 -1.820003 -0.455601 0.188326 1.842072 -1.918896 -0.259529 0.200091 -0.056049 -1.756343 -0.071092 0.340538 -0.165433 0.691833 -1.951029 -1.040509 1.052306 1.944196 -1.725629 -0.051463 - 0.258637 -0.097700 -0.364711 0.076348 -0.312131 -1.820869 -0.995589 -0.052073 0.215089 0.307311 1.937550 -0.175043 -1.938866 -0.222515]

Both methods were used to search the minimal energy state of toy model for protein folding, and the comparison results are listed in table 2 and table 3.

From table 2 and table 3, we can see that PSO is much faster than SA and it can search better results. This may due that PSO has less parameters than SA, furthermore, since SA often lead to huge computational task, thus it usually can not get the global minimal in reasonable time.

Table 2. Comparison PSO with SA: ground state

	PSO	SA
1AGT	-19.6168 66	-17.3628 15
1AHO	-15.1911 01	-14.9612 73

Table 3. Comparison PSO with SA: searching time

	PSO	SA
1AGT	8,376 s	12, 065 s
1AHO	10,149 s	15, 832 s

From the results shown in figure 4 and figure 5, we can also see that, although the toy model can simulate the real protein to some extent, the results are still some different from the real proteins. That is to say, toy model needs further improvements.

5 Conclusions

Toy model is a great improvement of simplification models of protein folding. Because comparing with lattice model, the angle of its bond can turn freely and thus it is more like real protein structure. In this paper, we applied PSO on toy model for protein folding and got good results. Our experiment results show that PSO has strong ability to search extremum in consecutive space. At present, Our method only considered two kinds of residues and only two kinds of interaction energy. Maybe we can improve the model by considering more interaction energy and more properties of amino acid residues, not just only the polar and non-polar characters. However, we should note that not all properties are mattered with the structure of protein, for unnecessary conditions will make the question too complicated. We will address this direction in the future.

References

1. Park, B.H. and Levitt, M.: The Complexity and Accuracy of Discrete State Models of Protein Structure, J.Mol.Biol. **249** (1995) 493-507
2. Kolinski, A. and Skolnick, J.: (2004) Reduced Models of Protein and Their applications, Polymer **45** (2004) 511-524
3. Dill, K. A.: (1985), Theory for the folding and stability of globular proteins, Biochemistry **24** (1985) 1501-1512
4. Afarwala, R., Batzoglou, S., et al.: Local Rules for Protein Folding on a Triangular Lattice and Generalized Hydrophobicity in the HP Model, Proceedings of the first annual international conference on Computational molecular biology (1997) 1-2
5. Stillinger, F. H., Gordon, T. H., and Hirshfeld, C. L.: Toy Model for Protein Folding, Physical Review E **48** (1993) 1469-1477
6. Morrissey, M.P., Ahmed, Z. and Shakhnovich, E. I.: The Role of Cotranslation in Protein Folding: a Lattice Model Study, Polymer **45** (2004) 557-571
7. Dill, K. A., Bromberg, S., and Yue, K., et al.:(1995) A perspective from simple exact models, Prot. Sci. **4** (1995) 561-602
8. Caspi, S. and Jacob, E.B.: Conformation Changes and Folding of Protein Mediated by Davydov's Soliton, Physics Letters A **272**, (2000) 124-129

9. Wang, L, Zhou, H., et al.: Perspective Roles of Short- and Long-Range Interactions in Protein Folding, Wuhan University Journal of Natural Sciences **9** (2004) 182-187
10. Kennedy, J. and Eberhart, R.C.: Particle Swarm Optimization, In Proceedings of the IEEE Int. Conf. Neural Networks (1995) 1942-1948
11. Shi, Y. and Eberhart, R.C.: A Modified Particle Swarm Optimizer. In: Proceedings of the IEEE International Conference on Evolutionary Computation. (1998) 69-73
12. Eberhart, R.C., Kennedy, J.: Swarm Intelligence, Morgan Kaufmanns (2001)
13. Anfisen, C.B.: Developmental Biology Supplement 2, Academic Press Inc., USA (1968)
14. Parsopoulos, K.E., Vrahatis, M.N.: Particle Swarm Optimization method in Multiobjective Problems, In: Proceedings ACM Symposium on Applied Computing (2002) 603-607
15. Shi, Y., Eberhart, R.C.: Empirical Study of Particle Swarm Optimization, In: Proceedings of the 1999 Congress on Evolutionary Computation, (1999) 1945-1950
16. Carlisle, A., Dozier, G.: An Off-the-Shelf PSO, In :Proceedings of the Workshop on Particle Swarm Optimization (2001) 1-6
17. Thorton, J., Taylor, W. R.: Structure Prediction, In:Findlay J.B.C, Geisow M.J. (eds.): Protein Aequencing, Oxford: IRL Press (1989) 147-190

Selective Two-Channel Linear Descriptors for Studying Dynamic Interaction of Brain Regions

Xiao-mei Pei, Jin Xu, Chong-xun Zheng, and Guang-yu Bin

Institute of Biomedical Engineering of Xi'an Jiaotong University,
710049, Xi'an, China
{pei@zy165.com}
{xujin, cxzheng}@mail.xjtu.edu.cn

Abstract. This paper demonstrates an effective approach to studying functional coupling of different brain regions in event-related paradigm. The selective two-channel complexity (TCC) and field power ($TCFP$) were investigated between contralateral sensorimotor and mid-central region (close to Cz), and between ipsilateral sensorimotor and mid-central region during left or right hand motor imagery. It is demonstrated that TCC and $TCFP$ can provide information regarding the dynamic interaction of spatially separated brain regions. In the upper alpha band (10-12Hz), TCC and $TCFP$ with mu rhythm of the mid-central region and contralateral sensorimotor hand area show a pronounced increase and decrease respectively at imagination onset, which indicates that there are independent, parallel functional processes over contralateral sensorimotor area and mid-central region with the respective regions becoming active. The preliminary results show that TCC and $TCFP$ could characterize the information exchange between different brain regions and also that the two parameters display good separability for left and right hand motor imagery tasks, so that they could be considered for the classification of two classes of EEG patterns in BCI (Brain Computer Interface).

1 Introduction

Studies at Graz University of technology have shown that unilateral hand motor imagery results in desynchronization of alpha and beta rhythmic activities over contralateral hand area which is called event-related desynchronization (ERD) and simultaneously results in synchronization of rhythmic activities over ipsilateral area which is called event-related synchronization (ERS) [1]. For the antagonistic ERD/ERS pattern, the hypothesis has been proposed about 'focal ERD/surround ERS' reflecting a thalamo-cortical mechanism to enhance focal cortical activation by simultaneous inhibition of other cortical areas [2, 3]. So, whatever the brain state of the mid-central region is, it would be reasonable to expect some different functional interaction between the contralateral, ipsilateral hand area and mid-central region respectively. Synchrony (high coherence) between scalp signals has been taken as evidence for functional coupling of the underlying cortical areas [4]. ERCoh (event-

functional coupling of the underlying cortical areas [4]. ERCoh (event-related coherence) has been suggested to provide a means of studying the functional coupling between different brain regions, which calculates the ratio of cross-spectrum and auto-spectrum [5]. Within this method, spectral leakage effects, although reduced with Hanning window processing, could not be eliminated completely in calculating spectrum with DFT, which has more or less effects on the analysis results. This paper introduces a simple approach for characterizing dynamic functional interaction between brain regions in relation to event-related EEG by TCC and $TCFP$. The preliminary results show that TCC and $TCFP$ could characterize the information exchange between different brain regions and also have good separability for left and right hand motor imagery so that they could be considered for the classification of two classes of EEG patterns in BCI application.

2 The Experimental Data

The event-related EEG changes were investigated in a feedback-guided motor imagery experiment [3, 6, 7]. The subject performed the following task repeatedly in a series of sessions. During the first 3 sec reference period of each trial, the subject was asked to keep relaxed with eyes open, followed by an arrow pointing either to the right or left (cue stimulus) indicating the imagery task of either a movement with right or left hand till t=4.25s. The feedback bar, presented during the following about 4-s period, was moving horizontally toward the right or left boundary of the screen dependent on the on-line classification of the EEG signals, which directs the subject performing hand motor imagery [3, 6, 7].

Three bipolar EEG channels were measured over the anterior and posterior of C3, Cz, C4 with inter-electrode intervals of 2.5cm. EEG was sampled with 128Hz and filtered between 0.5 and 30Hz. EEG dataset were provided by Graz University of technology available at the BCI2003 competition website. The MATLAB data files, x_train.mat, y_train.mat are train datasets and the files x_test.mat, y_test.mat are test datasets, which both include 140 trials and the class labels respectively. The details could be found in relevant website and references [3, 6, 7].

3 Methods

Wackermann proposed $\Sigma - \phi - \Omega$ system for describing the comprehensive global brain macro-state [8, 9]. The three linear descriptors Σ, ϕ, Ω were used to describe the three most salient features of the state space trajectories directly constructed by simultaneous EEG measurements from K electrodes. Σ is a measure of global field strength [μV]; Ω is a measure of spatial complexity, reflected by different extensions along the principal axes of the data cloud; φ is a measure of global frequency of field changes [Hz] [8, 9]. In this paper, to describe the interactions between EEG signals of different channels, only Σ, Ω are discussed. Considering N EEG samples in the observed time window at K electrode sites to form voltage vectors $\{u_1, \cdots u_N\}$, where each u_i $(i = 1, \cdots N)$ corresponds to the state vector representing the spatial distribution of EEG voltage over the scalp at the ith sample point. Σ, Ω can be calculated as follows [8, 9]:

$$m_0 = \frac{1}{N} \sum_i \|u_i\|^2 \qquad (1a)$$

$$\Sigma = \sqrt{m_0 / K} \qquad (1b)$$

The covariance matrix is constructed as:

$$C = \frac{1}{N} \sum_i u_i u_i^T \qquad (2)$$

The eigenvalues $\lambda_1 \cdots \lambda_K$ of matrix C is calculated, then Ω complexity can be obtained:

$$\log \Omega = -\sum_k \lambda_k' \log \lambda_k' \qquad (3)$$

where λ_k' is the normalized eigenvalue. The details can be found in references [8, 9].

Considering the antagonistic ERD/ERS pattern over the contralateral and ipsilateral sensorimotor area during hand motor imagery, the spatial complexity Ω and field power Σ calculated by EEG between the selective two channels C3 and Cz, between C4 and Cz are studied. Therefore the number of electrodes K in equation (1b) is 2 and the multichannel linear descriptors are reduced to two-channel complexity and filed power, which are defined TCC and $TCFP$ respectively. Ω complexity quantifies the amount of spatial synchrony [9]. Large value of Ω indicates little linear spatial correlation between the different electrodes and the low value corresponds to the minimal complexity or high synchronization [8, 9]. It's reasonable to describe the correlation between two brain regions by TCC. $TCFP$ reflect the field strength between two-channel EEG signals, which also describe the simultaneous power information of the two corresponding brain regions.

Before calculating the linear descriptors, EEG data are to be centered to zero mean value and transformed to the average reference. There is little influence from reference derivation and no need to transform data to average reference because EEG was recorded by bipolar derivation acting as a spatial high-pass filter to allow local cortical activity to be measured [10, 11]. In addition, ERD/ERS results in the large difference in the EEG amplitude over the contralateral and ipsilateral areas. To reduce the effect of EEG amplitude on Ω, the data were normalized by the EEG maximum of each channel before calculating TCC [12].

TCC and $TCFP$ reflect brain macro-state averaged within the observed time segment. However, the event-related EEG is typical of non-stationary signal. Linear descriptors observed in long time window would result in information with a poor time resolution. By studies reported by Andrew [5], a 1 sec segment is short enough to approximate a stationary signal, so the time segment was chosen 1 sec here.

To obtain the time course of Ω and Σ, a 1-second segment is extracted from the trial to calculate Σ, Ω. By shifting the segment in steps of 7.8125 milliseconds from the start to the end of the trial, and calculating averaged Σ, Ω across all the trials for each segment, time sequences of Ω and Σ are obtained. In event-related paradigm, the experimental situation is controlled under the same stimulation, in which each trial is repeated a number of times. So parameters Σ and Ω calculated from the ensemble of trials recorded for each repetition of the event can yield information which reveals short time changes in parameters due to the specific event i.e. left or right hand motor imagery involved [5].

4 Results

The analysis results for train dataset were given. Figure 1 summarizes the results of TCC and $TCFP$ obtained from event-related EEG data within 10-12Hz during left or right hand motor imagery. The upper alpha band within 10-12Hz was chosen based on priori knowledge from previous analysis of the data, which indicated that this band contained rhythms that were the most reactive to planning and execution of hand movement [5]. The three rows (Fig1 (a, b), Fig1 (c, d), Fig1 (e, f)) refer respectively to TCC time courses including $Cc3z, Cc4z$ computed by EEG signals between C3 and Cz and between C4 and Cz, $TCFP$ time courses including $Pc3z, Pc4z$, and ERD/ERS time courses quantified by the classical power method. The two columns (Fig1 (a, c, e), Fig1 (b, d, f)) correspond to left and right hand imagery tasks respectively. From figure 1 (e, f), a large decrease in power corresponding to ERD phenomenon occurs not only over the contralateral hand area but also over mid-central region close to Cz accompanied simultaneously with ERS over ipsilateral hand area at imagination onset of hand movement. Accordingly, a pronounced increase with spatial complexity $Cc3z$ for right ($Cc4z$ for left) of contralateral and mid-central region occurs at imagination onset. In contrast, in associated with ERD over mid-central region and simultaneous ERS over ipsilateral hand area, a pronounced decrease with the corresponding spatial complexity occurs. Besides, $Pc3z, Pc4z$ time courses show the opposite changes to $Cc3z, Cc4z$ time courses.

From the Figure 1, it is clearly seen that the two parameters i.e. the two channel spatial complexity TCC and the two channel field power $TCFP$ show the different behaviors during the left or right hand motor imagery so that the dynamic interaction of two different brain regions is characterized from the two aspects. In addition, for the left and right hand imagery tasks, the time course changes of $Cc3z, Cc4z, Pc3z, Pc4z$ show the good separability.

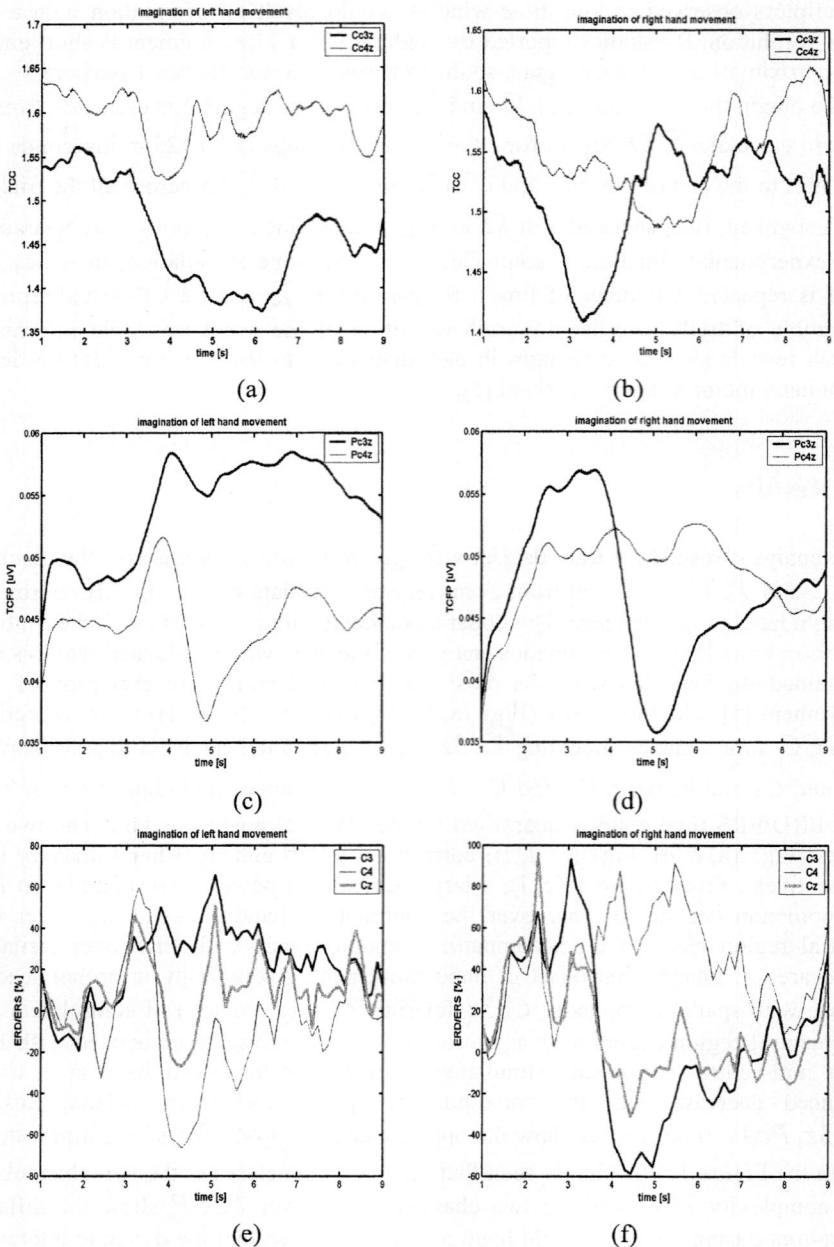

Fig. 1. Spatial complexity $Cc3z, Cc4z$ time course in (a), (b); and the local field power $Pc3z, Pc4z$ time course in (c), (d); ERD/ERS time course quantified by classical band power method in (e), (f); The left panels correspond to left hand motor imagery and the right panels correspond to right hand motor imagery.

To testify the validity of TCC and $TCFP$ for characterizing the different interaction information between the contralateral, ipsilateral brain regions and mid-central region respectively, the features $Cc3z, Cc4z, Pc3z, Pc4z$ within 10-12Hz are extracted to discriminate left and right hand motor imagery for the test dataset and the satisfactory classification results could be used to show the validity of the selected parameters. By a Fisher discriminant linear classifier, the classification accuracy time course could be obtained in Fig 2 (a). Another effective index for measuring the separability of two classes of EEG patterns is Mutual Information (MI) [13]. MI is proposed for quantifying the information transferred by a BCI system which could reflect the effective information contained in brain consciousness [6, 13]. Fig 2 (b) gives the time course of MI. The maximum classification accuracy with 87.14% was obtained at about t=5s. Also at this time point, the maximum mutual information was obtained with 0.52 bit. Both classification accuracy and MI time course show that two parameters i.e. the spatial complexity and the field power between the two-channel EEG TCC and $TCFP$ could well characterize the effective separate features for left and right hand motor imagery tasks.

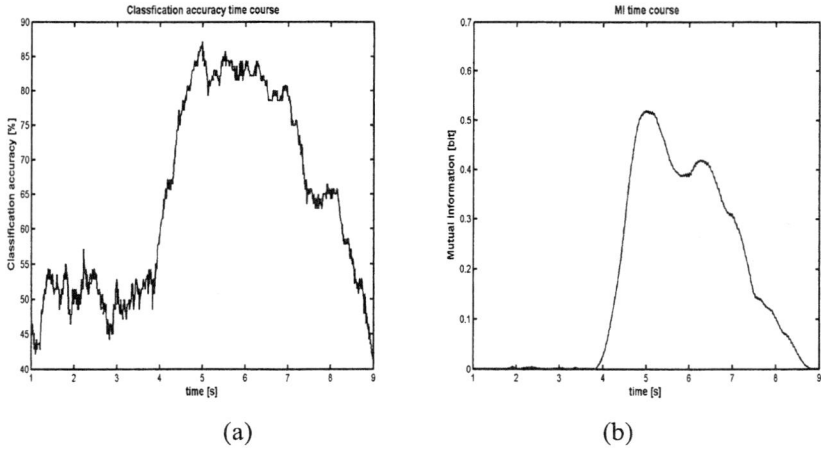

Fig. 2. Classification accuracy time course in (a) and MI time course in (b)

5 Discussions

Ω complexity reflects the degree of synchronization between functional processes spatially distributed over different brain regions. TCC increase of the contralateral sensorimotor area and mid-central region during unilateral hand motor imagery suggests there are stronger independent, parallel, functional processes active between these two regions, which is just in accordance with the fact that ERD appears over the two regions. This result is also similarly consistent with the findings of Andrew et al.

[5]. The dynamic complexity analysis of the single channel event-related EEG also suggests that ERD/ERS correspond to the increase and decrease of EEG complexity [14]. During unilateral hand motor imagery, the mu rhythms were desynchronized when each of the underlying areas becomes active and then the degree of synchrony between the rhythms is decreased [5]. The desynchronized functional processes underlying the two brain areas result in the amplitude attenuation of EEG signals over the corresponding regions, which are reflected by the field power $TCFP$ decrease between the contralateral and mid-central region. In contrast, ERS with amplitude enhancement appears over the ipsilateral area so that the field power $TCFP$ between the ipsilateral and mid-central region shows a pronounced increase.

In recent application to brain global state by linear descriptors Σ, Ω, at least 19 channels are used to study global brain functional states for different studying purposes such as sleep and wakefulness, sensory and motor processes, etc [8, 15, 16, 17]. However, the results presented in this paper show that the two-channel linear descriptors TCC and $TCFP$ are also sensitive to local brain macro-state change and could be considered as a tool for studying dynamic interaction of two brain regions. In fact, TCC and $TCFP$ could be regarded as the simplest case of multichannel Ω and Σ. The method by TCC and $TCFP$ describing functional coupling of brain regions avoids difficulties such as spectral leakage effects resulting from DFT of the windowed data and the spectral resolution consideration within ERCoh method. Thus, the parameters TCC and $TCFP$ together provide more accurate and comprehensive information about functional coupling between different brain regions.

Finally, TCC and $TCFP$ reflect the more information including EEG features over left and right hemispheres and mid-central region, the satisfactory classification accuracy and MI are obtained. So, TCC and $TCFP$ could be considered for the classification of left and right hand motor imagery tasks in BCI application.

Acknowlegements

This work is funded by National Nature Science foundation of China (#30370395 and #30400101). And the authors would like to thank Graz University of technology for providing the data.

References

1. Pfurtscheller G., Lopes da Silva, F.H. Event-related EEG/MEG synchronization and desynchronization: basic principles. Clincal Neurophsiol, (1999); 110: 1842-1857.
2. Suffczynski P., Pijn P.J.M., Pfurtscheller G., Lopes da Silva, F.H. (Eds.), Event-related dynamics of alpha band rhythms: a neuronal network model of focal ERD/surround ERS. Handbook of Electronceph Clin Neurophysiol, (1999); vol. 6, Elsevier, Amsterdam, pp.67-85.
3. Neuper C, Pfurtscheller G. Event-related dynamics of cortical rhythms: frequency-specific features and functional correlates. Int. J. Psychophysiol, (2001); 43: 41-58.

4. Thatcher R.W., Krause P.J., Hrybyk M. Cortico-cortical associations and EEG coherence: A two compartmental model. Electroenceph. Clin. Neurophysiol, (1986); 64, 58-75.
5. Andrew C., Pfurtscheller G. Event-related coherence as a tool for studying dynamic interaction of brain regions. Electroenceph Clin Neurophysiol, (1996); 98, 144-148.
6. Schlögl A., Lugger K., Pfurtscheller G. Using Adaptive Autoregressive Parameters for a Brain-Computer-Interface Experiment, Proceedings of the 19th Annual International Conference if the IEEE Engineering in Medicine and Biology Society, (1997); 19, 1533-1535.
7. Neuper C., Schlogl A., Pfurtscheller G. Enhancement of left-right sensorimotor EEG differences during feedback-regulated motor imagery. J. Clin. Neurophysiol, (1999); 16, 373-382.
8. Wackermann J. Beyond mapping: estimating complexity of multichannel EEG recordings. Acta Neurobiol, Exp. (1996); 56, 197-208.
9. Wackermann J. Towards a quantitative characterization of functional states of the brain: from the non-linear methodology to the global linear description. Int. J. Psychophysiol, (1999); 34, 65-80.
10. Pfurtscheller G., Neuper Ch., Flotzinger D., Pregenzer M. EEG-based discrimination between imagination of right and left hand movement. Electroenceph Clin Neurophysiol, (1997); 103, 642-651.
11. Nunez P.L., Srinivasan R., Westdorp A.F., Wijesinghe R.S., Tuchker D.M., Silberstein R.B., Cadusch P.J. EEG coherency I: statistics, reference electrode, volume conduction, Laplacians, cortical imaging, and interpretation at multiple scales. Electroenceph Clin Neruophysiol, (1997); 103, 499-515.
12. Xiao-mei Pei, Chong-xun Zheng, Ai-hua Zhang, Fu-jian Duan, Guang-yu Bin. Discussion on "Towards a quantitative characterization of functional states of the brain: from the nonlinear methodology to the global linear description" by J. Wackermann". Int. J. Psychophysiol, (2005); 56, 201-207.
13. Schlögl A., Neuper C., Pfurtscheller G. Estimating the mutual information of an EEGbased brain-computer interface. Biomedizinische Technik, (2002); 47, 3-8.
14. Pei Xiaomei, Zheng Chongxun, He Weixing. Dynamic complexity analysis of event-related EEG. 2nd international BCI workshop and Training Course. Biomedizinische Technik, (2004); 49, 87-88.
15. Szelenberger W., Wackermann J., Skalski M., Niemcewicz S., Drojewski J. Analysis of complexity of EEG during sleep, Acta Neurobiol. (1996); Exp. 56, 165-169.
16. Kondakor I.., Brandeis D., Wackermann J., Kochi K., Koenig T., Frei E., Pascual-Marqm, R., Yagyu, T., Lehmann. D. Multichannel EEG fields during and without visual input: frequency domain model source locations and dimensional complexities. Neurosci. Lett, (1997); 226, 49-52.
17. Saito N., Kuginuki T, Yagyu T, Kinoshita T, Koenig T, Pascual-Marqui R, Kochi K, Wackermann J, and Lehmann D. Global, regional, and local measures of complexity of multichannel electroencephalography in acute, neuroleptic-naive, first-break schizophrenics. Biol Psychiatry, (1998); 43, 794-802.

A Computational Pixelization Model Based on Selective Attention for Artificial Visual Prosthesis

Ruonan Li[1], Xudong Zhang[2], and Guangshu Hu[3]

[1,2] Department of Electronic Engineering, Tsinghua University, Beijing, China
[3] Department of Biomedical Engineering, Tsinghua University, Beijing, China
liruonan00@mails.tsinghua.edu.cn
{zhangxd, hgs-dea}@tsinghua.edu.cn

Abstract. Inspired by the ongoing research on artificial visual prosthesis, a novel pixelization visual model based on the selection of local attention-drawing features is proposed, and a subjective scoring experiment as a cognitive assessment is designed to evaluate the performance of the model. The results of the experiment reveal that the model can accentuate the areas with prominent features in the original image, so as to give observers a subjective perception of rich visual information. Thus, the model will provide a new approach for future research.

1 Introduction

It is gradually coming true to partially restore vision capability to the visually-impaired or blind person due to the effort of international research groups working on the 'visual prosthesis' (also called 'artificial vision') project[1-3]. The approach is to try to implant an array of electrodes into human's optic neural pathway like visual cortex or retina. The visual signal captured by camera is converted by the visual prosthetic system to electronic pulses. When the pulses are received by the electrodes, the blind person is expected to feel points of lights called 'phosphenes' and all the phosphenes are expected to form a virtual 'image' finally perceived by the blind one[1,2]. Thus, the visual information is said to be conveyed to the blind through a 'pixelized vision' method because each phosphene is regarded as a 'pixel' in the virtual image [4,5].

A conventional image usually contains more than thousands of pixels, but unfortunately, prototype experiments have not been able to confirm the safety, long-term efficiency and biological compatibility to implant so many electrodes into human bodies, and the number of implantable electrodes must be constrained because of surgical techniques and electronic devices[6-10]. Meanwhile, early research predicted that about hundreds of phosphenes would be sufficient to convey quite a little visual information[4]. Therefore, a key component of visual prosthetic system is to reduce the resolution of the original image to several hundred, called a 'pixelization' procedure. Apparently, the limited phosphenes must be utilized effectively to present the important and prominent information preferentially. In fact, it has been pointed out that a good computational vision model for pixelization is significant for obtaining and presenting those important and prominent visual information[11].

Moreover, not only the implantable electrodes are limited, but the implantation is constrained to carry out due to technical and social reasons. It is therefore necessary to use simulations with normally sighted subjects called 'simulated visual prosthesis' to investigate whether the pixelization model can best keep the most prominent visual information. Assuming the normally sighted will receive the same perception as real blind recipients, simulated cognitive experiment has been widely performed by early researchers[4,5] and recent groups[12-15]. In simulated cognitive experiments, low-resolution pixelization results are observed by subjects with naked eyes, who are required to response to or to give assessment on these results. In fact, the purpose of these cognitive assessments is to search for psychophysical evidences and effective vision models in advance before the complex relationship between the perception of the blind and what the normally-sighted see is totally found out.

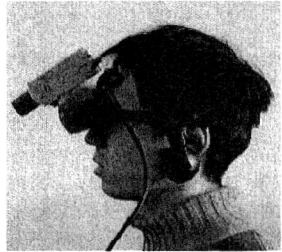

Fig. 1. A prospective artificial visual prosthetic system

A novel computational pixelization model is proposed in this paper. The proposed method will give a multi-resolution pixelization result similar to the algorithm by Gilmont et al.[16], while the high resolution will not be simply allocated to the central area but will be selectively given to the 'prominent areas' based on the analysis of the scene. Instead of simple segmentation algorithms, the proposed pixelization model will conform to the verified principles on vision information processing and selective attention mechanism. Simulated cognitive assessment experiments are designed and performed to evaluate the proposed model, and the results are promising thus can be used for reference for future research.

2 The Model

2.1 General Framework

Former research reveals that some local structural feature in the original image is interesting to human vision system. Without high-level visual processing such as segmentation, classification and recognition, human vision will pay more attention to these local areas[17], which are thus 'prominent' areas considered to be rich in visual information. On one hand all types of these prominent features are attractive to vision system; on the other hand there exists 'lateral inhibition' effect among visual perception units and 'reception field' model by Hartline and Rodieck can depict the interaction between the prominent features from different local areas[18]. Based on the basic principles above, the computational pixelization model can be illustrated as Figure 2.

As shown in Figure 2, the processing procedure of the model includes three main steps: 1) Some local operators are applied to the original image to extract the local prominent feature maps; 2) A 'competition' step is designed to simulate the enhancement and inhibition effect of the reception field, then an 'integration' step is used to integrate the maps into a final attention map; 3) Pixelization is performed under the supervising of the final attention map, in which prominent areas are given high resolution and vice versa. Generally speaking, the model aims to give fine presentation to those areas that are attractive to human vision, so that the scene details rich of visual information would be conveyed to the recipient foremost.

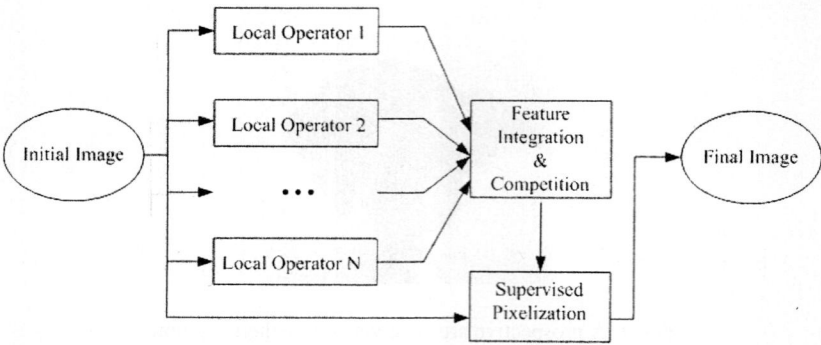

Fig. 2. The framework of the pixelization model based on selective prominent features

2.2 Local Operators

Various local image features, including symmetry, wavelet coefficient, edge density, entropy, DCT coefficient and contrast, have been inspected[17] and it is found through eye-tracking experiments that areas with strong contrast, strong symmetry as well as dense edges are more attractive to human vision. Other research also reported that the areas with a different orientation from surrounding are attention-drawing[19]. Therefore, the above four prominent features are brought into our model which may be expanded after more attention-drawing feature are found out.

For contrast feature, we bring Michaelson Contrast[20] to identify the areas with strong contrast against the whole background. Michaelson Contrast at location (x, y) is calculated as

$$C(x, y) = \frac{|L_m - L_M|}{L_m + L_M} \qquad (1)$$

in which L_m is the mean luminance within a 7*7 surrounding of the center location (x, y) and L_M is the overall mean luminance of the image.

For edge density feature, we use the popular Canny edge detector to obtain the edge map. Given the image I convolved with Gaussian filter G, the normal vector map **n** is

$$\mathbf{n} = \frac{\nabla(G \otimes I)}{\|\nabla(G \otimes I)\|} \quad (2)$$

Then the edge location (x, y) satisfies

$$\frac{\partial^2}{\partial \mathbf{n}^2} G \otimes I = 0 \quad (3)$$

Numbers of edges per unit area around (x, y) gives the edge density measure.

For orientation difference feature, the center-surrounding orientation difference at (x, y) is determined first by convoluting the image with four Gabor masks as

$$Ga(x, y) = \frac{1}{2\pi\sigma^2} \exp\left\{-\frac{x^2+y^2}{2\sigma^2}\right\} \cos(2\pi f(x\cos\theta + y\sin\theta)) \quad (4)$$

with angle θ equal to $0°$, $45°$, $90°$, and $135°$ respectively. Then the area whose response is significantly dissimilar to surrounding is regarded as having a high orientation difference.

For symmetry feature, we define the symmetric magnitude at (x, y) as

$$S(x, y) = \sum_u \sum_v \|\mathbf{p}(x+u, y+v)\| \cdot \|\mathbf{p}(x-u, y-v)\| \cdot S_{x,y}(u, v) \quad (5)$$

in which

$$S_{x,y}(u,v) = 1 - \left|\left\langle \frac{\mathbf{p}_n(x+u, y+v) + \mathbf{p}_n(x-u, y-v)}{\|\mathbf{p}_n(x+u, y+v) + \mathbf{p}_n(x-u, y-v)\|}, \frac{\mathbf{q}(u,v)}{\|\mathbf{q}(u,v)\|} \right\rangle\right| \quad (6)$$

where $\mathbf{p}_n(x,y)$ denotes the normalized luminance gradient at (x,y) and $\mathbf{q}(u,v)$ denotes the vector connecting $(x+u, y+v)$ to $(x-u, y-v)$.

2.3 Feature Competition and Integration

The prominent feature map produced by each local detector is a response map which quantitatively indicates the strength of the attention-drawing stimulus. Early research by Hartline and Rodieck[18], together with latest psychophysical theories[20-24], concludes that visual response to the attention-drawing stimulus has following properties: the response to a large range of stimulus is not significant; a strong stimulus surrounded by the weak is further enhanced; the weak stimulus next to the strong is further inhibited. Thereby a linear combination of two Gaussian masks

$$R(x, y) = c_1 \exp(-\frac{x^2+y^2}{2\sigma_1^2}) - c_2 \exp(-\frac{x^2+y^2}{2\sigma_2^2}) \quad (7)$$

is introduced to simulate the above 'competition' effect. A special adjusting of the parameter $c_1, \sigma_1, c_2, \sigma_2$ will generate a mask with its 2-D section as depicted in Figure 3. Convoluting the mask with the feature map will just simulate the competition effect.

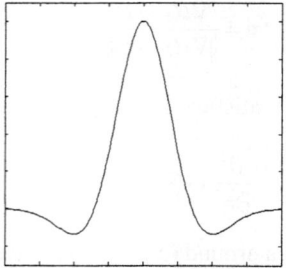

Fig. 3. The 2-D section of the feature competition mask

The maps after the competition processing, each of which quantitatively represents a particular local attention-drawing feature, must be integrated to a unitary map. Since no many computational psychophysical evidences on the combination effect have been found out, we take a weighted addition as a simulation

$$F(x, y) = \sum_{n=1}^{N} w_n F_n(x, y) \qquad (8)$$

in which $F_n(x, y)$ denotes the map from the competition processing. Appropriate weights w_n should be achieved through subjective cognitive experiment to be discussed later.

2.4 Pixelization

Finally the original image is to be pixelized. The reduction of the resolution should be supervised by the unitary feature map from integration: the areas with a large value in the map will be allocated with finer resolution. Figure 4 illustrates a multi-resolution pixelization pattern in which the small block regions have a large value at corresponding areas in the feature map. The amount of total blocks would be artificially controlled nearest to four hundred in order to agree with early research conclusion[4].

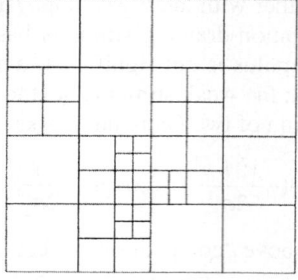

Fig. 4. A multi-resolution pixelization configuration

3 Subjective Cognitive Experiment

To evaluate the performance and effectiveness of the proposed model for visual prosthesis, subjective assessment experiment is designed as others adopted[12-15]. The normally-sighted subjects are required to observe the pixelization results with naked eyes, and then to score each result according to whether it has best presented the prominent and important visual information.

3.1 Single Feature Assessment

The purpose of single feature experiment is to investigate the four local features separately to provide evidence for the appropriate weights factor in (8). To distinguish the possible difference between scene types, the test images are classified into four groups-faces, typical objects, indoor scenes, outdoor scenes- according to their contents. These test images are specially prepared without any from standard image database to prevent any prior knowledge about the images. For each image in each group, the four local feature maps are obtained respectively, and four separate pixelization results are produced without feature integration step.

Ten volunteer college students as subjects participated the experiments. They were requested to observe the results and to give a one point to five points score to each of them. Though having been notified the basic background of the research, none of the subjects knew any about the model. The test results are displayed in a head-mounted interface as in Figure 1, and the scores are afterward adjusted to distribute uniformly among one to five. Statistics of the scoring results is shown in Table 1.

An analysis of variance as a tool of mathematical statistics was performed to answer whether the four prominent features behave distinctly, and the p-values calculated from Table 1 for each scene group is shown in Table 2. The small p-values prove that extracting the attention-drawing features respectively is reasonable and necessary.

Table 1. Statistics of single feature experiments (mean ± standard deviation)

Feature Group	Contrast	Edge Density	Orientation Difference	Symmetry
Human Faces	2.77±0.42	3.02±0.51	2.12±0.22	2.51±0.24
Typical Objects	3.30±0.43	2.95±0.55	2.20±0.27	2.70±0.10
Indoor Scenes	2.95±0.21	2.56±0.25	2.12±0.15	0.41±0.17
Outdoor Scenes	3.17±0.21	2.40±0.12	2.52±0.18	2.57±0.14

Table 2. Results of the analysis of variance

Group	Human Faces	Typical Objects	Indoor Scenes	Outdoor Scenes
p-value	3.8×10^{-3}	3.3×10^{-4}	4.2×10^{-4}	1.3×10^{-4}

3.2 Assessment of the Complete Model

Now we can calculate the weights in (8) for each scene group as

$$w_k = S_k \bigg/ \sum_{l=1}^{4} S_l \qquad (9)$$

in which w_k denotes the weight for the k feature and S_k is the mean score for that feature obtained in single feature experiment. Given the weights, each original image is processed according to the complete pixelization model and the final pixelization results are produced. For comparison, other two kinds of pixelization results from feature averaging (all weights are 1/4) and conventional image segmentation are produced. The subjects then scored the three kinds of pixelization results for each test image, allocating a zero point, a one point and a two point among the three. The score ratio for each group is shown in Figure 5. It is easy to see that the results from supervised pixelization achieve the most score, indicating that the weighted map rather than feature averaging is more effective.

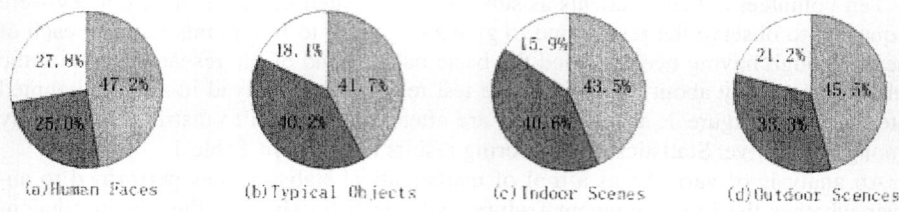

Fig. 5. Score ratio of the three pixelization schemes: White-conventional segmentation; Black-feature averaging; Gray-the complete model

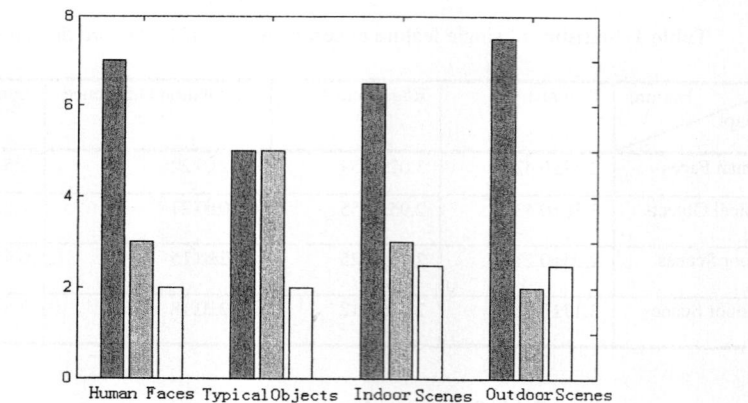

Fig. 6. Score counts for the proposed model. Black-2 points, Gray-1 point, White-0 point

We inspect the mean counts of two points, one point and zero point achieved by the supervised pixelization results, which are shown in Figure 6. The mean count of two points significantly exceeds that of one or zero point, which again supports the effectiveness and reasonableness of the model.

In general, the subjective cognitive experiments that are elaborately designed and performed provide satisfactory evidences to support the vision model proposed above.

4 Conclusion

Based on the ongoing research about vision prosthesis, a computational pixelization vision model is proposed in this paper. The attention-based model, which utilizes psychophysical principles of vision information processing, aims to selectively present the attention-drawing prominent areas with higher resolution under the strict phosphene (pixel) limitation. Subjective scoring experiments as a cognitive assessment of the model are carried out, and the results support that the model can first and foremost extract and present the prominent feature that human vision is interested in, so the model will potentially provide a new approach for future research on visual prosthesis.

It must be mentioned that modeling of pixelized vision for visual prosthesis is newly-risen. It is believed that the development of computational vision and related theory will benefit the research progress, and more other achievements will appear in the near future.

Acknowledgment

The authors want to thank Lin FU, Tao QIN and the volunteers for their contribution to this paper. This research is supported by the Fundamental Research Foundation of Tsinghua University under Grant No. JC2003063.

References

1. Dagnelie G., Massof R.W.: Toward an Artificial eye, IEEE Spectrum (1996) vol.33 21–29
2. Liu W., Sivaprakasam M., et al: Electronic Visual Prosthesis, Artificial Organs (2003) vol.27 (11) 986–995
3. Mehenti N.Z., Fishman H.A., Bent S.F.: Pushing the limits of artificial vision, IEEE Potentials (2004) vol.23 (1) 21-23
4. Cha K., Horch K.W., Normann R.A.: Mobility performance with a pixelized vision system, Vision Research (1992) vol.32 1367–72
5. Normann R.A., Maynard E.M., et al: A neural interface for a cortical vision prosthesis, Vision Research (1999) vol.39 (15) 2577-2587
6. Dobelle W.H.: Artificial vision for the blind by connecting a television camera to the visual cortex, ASAIO Journal (2000) vol.46 3–9
7. Veraart C., Wanet-Defalque M-C, et al: Pattern Recognition with the Optic Nerve Visual Prosthesis, Artificial Organs (2003) vol.27 (11) 996-1004

8. Suaning G.J., Hallum L.E., et al: Phosphene Vision: Development of a portable visual prosthesis system for the blind, Proceedings of the 25th Annual International Conference of the IEEE/EMBS (2003) 3 2047-2050
9. Humayun M.S., Weiland J.D., et al: Visual perception in a blind subject with a chronic microelectronic retinal prosthesis, Vision Research (2003) vol.43 (24) 2573-2581
10. Rizzo J., Wyatt J., et al: Methods and Perceptual Thresholds for Short-Term Electrical Stimulation of Human Retina with Microelectrode Arrays, Investigative Ophthalmology and Visual Science (2003) vol. 44 (12) 5355-5361
11. Boyle J.R., Maeder A.J., Boles W.W.: Challenges in digital imaging for artificial human vision, Proceedings of SPIE (2001) vol. 4299 533-543
12. Hayes J.S., Yin V.T., et al: Visually Guided Performance of Simple Tasks Using Simulated Prosthetic Vision, Artificial Organs (2003) vol. 27 (11) 1016-1028
13. Thompson R., Barnett G., et al: Facial recognition using simulated prosthetic pixelized vision, Investigative Ophthalmology & Vision Science (2003) vol.44 (11) 5035-5042
14. Dowling J., Maeder A.J., Boles W.W.: Mobility enhancement and assessment for a visual prosthesis, Proceedings of SPIE (2004) vol.5369 780-791
15. Sommerhalder J., Rappaz B., Haller R.d., Fonrnos A.P., Safran A.B., et al: Simulation of artificial vision: II. Eccentric reading of full-page text and the learning of this task, Vision Research (2004) vol.44 1693-1706
16. Gilmont T., Verians X., Legat J. D., Veraart C.: Resolution reduction by growth of zones for visual prosthesis, Proceedings of International Conference on Image Processing (1996) vol.1 299 – 302
17. Privitera C.M., Stark L.W.: Algorithms for defining visual region-of-interest: comparison with eye fixations, IEEE Transactions on Pattern Analysis and Machine Intelligence (2000) vol.22 (9) 970–981
18. Bai J.: Simulation and modeling of biological systems, Tsinghua University Press (1994)
19. Itti L., Koch C.: A saliency-based search mechanism for overt and covert shifts of visual attention, Vision Research (2000) vol.40 1489–1506
20. Mannan S.K., Ruddock K.H., Wooding D.S.: The relationship between the Locations of Spatial Features and Those of Fixations Made during Visual Examination of Briefly Presented Images, Spatial Vision (1996) vol.10 (3) 165-188
21. Gilbert C.D., Wiesel T.N.: Columnar specificity of intrinsic horizontal and corticocortical connections in cat visual cortex, Journal of Neuroscience (1992) vol.9 2432–2442
22. Levitt J.B., Lund J.S.: Contrast dependence of contextual effects in primate visual cortex, Nature (1997) vol.387 73–76
23. Sillito A.M., Grieve K.L., Jones H.E., Cudeiro J., Davis J.: Visual cortical mechanisms detecting focal orientation discontinuities, Nature (1995) vol.378 492–496
24. Zenger B., Sagi D.: Isolating excitatory and inhibitory nonlinear spatial interactions involved in contrast detection, Vision Research (1996) vol.36 2497–2513

Mosaicing the Retinal Fundus Images: A Robust Registration Technique Based Approach

Xinge You[2,3], Bin Fang[1,3], and Yuan Yan Tang[2,3]

[1] Center for Intelligent Computation of Information , Chongqing University, China
[2] Faculty of Mathematics and Computer Science, Hubei University, 430062, China
[3] Department of Computer Science, Hong Kong Baptist University

Abstract. Mosaicing fundus retinal images is fundamental to reveal helpful information of the eyes in order to track the progress of possible diseases. We propose the use of a simple rigid model to globally match vascular trees via a multi-resolution scheme. An elastic matching algorithm is employed to achieve accurate local alignment. We build mosaic maps by merging gray intensities of pixels from different fundus images at the same transformed locations with arithmetic average operation. Experiment results show that successful matching can be achieved with improved accuracy and the mosaic maps seem perfect in terms of visual inspection.

1 Introduction

Mosaiced fundus retinal image is helpful to provide valuable information for doctors to evaluate the progress of eye-related diseases and to decide on the appropriate treatments to be taken [1]. Mosaicing a number of images is usually based on the correct registration between different pairs of images. Since vascular tree is more reliable to be extracted and more representative of the eye surface, it is expected to use tree structure of blood vessels as object features for retinal fundus registration [2,3].

In this paper, we bring forward the idea of employing a 'global-to-local' matching strategy. First, extracted vascular trees are globally aligned using rigid model of translation and rotation. The adoption of comparative simple model enables us to compute the optimal transformation effectively and efficiently by multi-resolution matching technique. Then, we adopt a structure-deformed elastic matching algorithm to improve local alignment accuracy. The construction of the mosaic map starts with a reference sample which can be conveniently identified by human operator from a number of retinal images.

2 Registration Using Vascular Trees

The registration between retinal fundus images is based on the identified features of vascular tree. To extract blood vessels from background, we employ the technique described in [4] which has been demonstrated to be robust in extracting vascular trees.

2.1 Global Multi-resolution Matching

Although a quadratic surface model is more suitable to describe human eye surface, it is difficult to calculate relative model parameters where local optima traps often exist. It is shown that a weak affine model may be sufficient without losing too much accuracy. This motivates us to adopt the simplified rigid model of translation and rotation for globally matching two vascular trees of retinal fundus images. The model can be mathematically expressed as follows:

$$\begin{bmatrix} x' \\ y' \end{bmatrix} = \begin{bmatrix} \cos\theta & -\sin\theta \\ \sin\theta & \cos\theta \end{bmatrix} \begin{bmatrix} x \\ y \end{bmatrix} + \begin{bmatrix} \Delta x \\ \Delta y \end{bmatrix} \quad (1)$$

One of the two vascular features to be registered is called the *Template* and the other the *Input*. Thinning is performed for both the *Template* and the *Input* so that the resulting patterns consist of lines with one pixel width only. A sequential distance transformation (DT) is applied to create a distance map for the *Template* by propagation local distances [5]. The *Input* at different positions with respect to the corresponding transformations is superimposed on the *Template* distance map. A centreline mapping error (CME) to evaluate matching accuracy is defined as the average of feature points distance of the *Input* as follows:

$$CME = \frac{1}{N} \sum_{p(i,j) \in Input} DM_{Template}(p(i,j))^2 \quad (2)$$

N is the total number of feature points in the *Input*, $p(i,j)$ are the transformed positions of the original feature points in the *Input* and DM is the distance map created for the *Template* vascular features. It is obvious that a perfect match between the *Template* and *Input* images will result in a minimum value of CME.

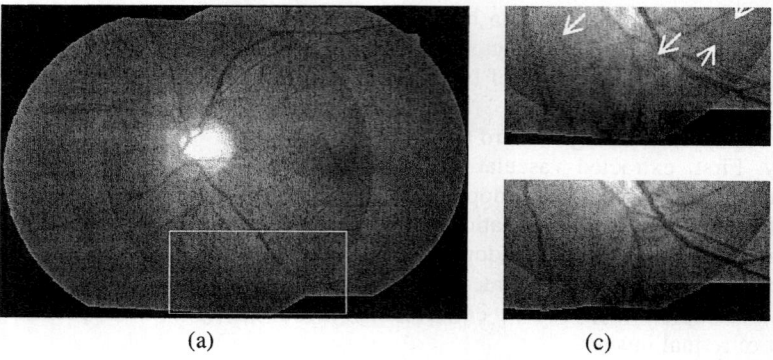

Fig. 1. A mosaic of two retinal fundus images formed by the computed rigid global transformation is shown in (a). The misaligned vessels ('ghost vessel') enclosed in the outlined frame in (a) have been clearly illustrated in (b) indicated by white arrows. (c) By applying the local elastic matching algorithm, near perfect alignment has been produced.

A search for the optimal transformation is to find the global minimum of the CME and can be done in different levels of resolution to avoid local optima traps. The idea behind multi-resolution matching is to search for the local optimal transformation at a coarse resolution with a large number of initial positions. Only a few promising local optimal positions with acceptable CME are selected as seeds before proceeding to the next level of finer resolution. The assumption is that at least one of them is a good approximation to the global optimal matching.

The final optimal match is determined by the transformation which has the smallest centreline mapping error at level 0 (the finest resolution). Once the relative parameters for the global transformation model have been computed, the registration between two retinal images is ready. One example is illustrated in Figure 1(a).

2.2 Local Elastic Matching

While the multi-resolution matching strategy is able to efficiently align retinal images globally, the local alignment errors inevitably exist because of the inherent imprecise characteristics of the simplified model. The phenomenon of 'ghost vessels' that is more obvious around boundaries of overlapped region is clearly perceptible (see Figure 1(b)). In order to rectify the pitfall of the rigid model, we adopt a local elastic matching algorithm to further improve matching accuracy by eliminating the existence of 'ghost vessels' (Figure1(c)). For process details, refer to [6].

3 Mosaicing Retinal Fundus Images

Once having identified correspondence of each feature point by local elastic matching method, we are able to calculate the transformed positions for registered fundus images. Assuming mid-point and two end points of each *Template* element as feature points, the elastic local move vector for each feature point can be computed directly by referring to location in the *Template* and the matched location in the *Input*. In addition, the local elastic transformed positions for all pixels other than the feature points of the *Template* can be defined as follows.

$$\Delta M = \sum_{j=1}^{N} w_j \mathbf{P}_j \tag{3}$$

N is the size parameter of the Gaussian window which establishes neighborhoods of correlation, w_j are the correlation weights in the Gaussian correlation window where $w_j = \exp(-(j-1)^2/(2 \times N^2))$ and $j = 1,2,\ldots,N$. $\mathbf{P}_j$ is the local move vector of feature point j in the Gaussian window sorted in the order of increasing distance from that pixel. $\mathbf{P}_j = \mathbf{T}_j - \mathbf{I}_{i(j)}$, where $\mathbf{T}_j$ is the move vector of feature point j of the *Template* and $\mathbf{I}_{i(j)}$ is the position vector of the feature point of *Input* which is matched to j.

Since we have applied the global-to-local strategy to achieve accurate alignment between pair of vascular tree features, the final transformed vectors for pixels in the input fundus image which is used to be registered to the reference fundus image are conveniently to be calculated by adding the elastic local move vector and the global model-transformed vector. Let the registered image I_q be matched to the reference image I_p. If the transformed position of a certain pixel P_q in I_q is overlapped with a pixel P_p in the retinal region of I_p, the gray density of pixel of the mosaic map which has the same position as P_p is to be calculated by merging the gray densities of P_q and P_p. The merging strategy adopted in the experiment is the arithmetic average operation of the gray intensities. For those pixels of I_q whose transformed positions are not located inside the retinal region of image I_p, they augment the mosaic map with their original gray intensities to the transformed positions in the mosaic map.

4 Experiment Results

The image database that we use to evaluate the performance of the proposed registration algorithm consists of 115 gray level fundus images of both left and right eyes from eleven patients. The image size is 512×512×8 bits. We randomly pair retinal fundus images captured at different times from the same eye of the same person resulting 268 pairs.

The depth for the fast multi-resolution matching method is set to 3, we have 7×7 translation positions and 5 equidistant rotation angles. The step-length for the translation parameters X or Y in vertical or horizontal coordinate directions is one pixel shift. The step-length for the rotation angle is $\Delta\theta = 180 / (\sqrt{2} \times \pi \times width)$ degrees. Figure 2 shows examples of successful registration.

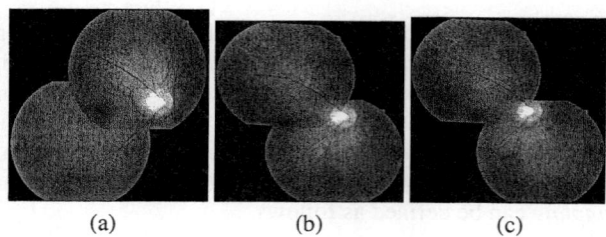

Fig. 2. Successful registration of retinal fundus images with varying overlaps: (a) 17.83% (b) 11.82% (c) 5.30 %

5 Conclusion

In this paper, a mosaicing method for fundus retinal images based on robust registration techniques is proposed. In order to construct precise masaic map, we apply a 'global-to-local' matching strategy to accurately align pairs of vascular trees with improved registration accuracy. We build mosaic maps by merging gray intensities of pixels from different fundus images at the same transformed locations referring to the reference with arithmetic average operation. Experiment results demonstrate nearly perfect mosaic maps in terms of visual inspection.

References

1. D. E. Singer, D. M. Nathan, H. A. Fogel, A. P. Schachar , "Screening for diabetic retinopathy," *Ann. Intern. Med.*, no. 116, pp. 660-671, 1992
2. A. Pinz, S. Bernogger, P. Datlinger and A. Kruger, "Mapping the Human Retina," *IEEE Trans. Med. Imag.*, vol. 17, no. 4, pp. 606-619, Aug. 1998
3. G. K. Matsopoulos, N. A. Mouravliansky, K. K. Delibasis, and K. S. Nikita, "Automatic retinal image registration scheme using global optimization techniques," *IEEE Trans. Info. Tech. Biomed.*, vol. 3, no. 1, pp. 47 –60, Mar. 1999
4. B. Fang, W. Hsu, M. L. Lee, "Reconstruction of vascular structures in retinal images," in *Proceedings. ICIP'2003*, Barcelona, Spain, September 2003
5. G. Borgefors, "Hierarchical Chamfer Matching: a parametric edge matching algorithm," *IEEE trans. Pattern Analysis Machine Intelligence*, vol. 10, no. 6, pp. 849-865, 1988
6. C. H. Leung and C. Y. Suen, "Matching of Complex Patterns by Energy Minimization," *IEEE Transactions on Systems, Man and Cybernetics*, Part B, vol. 28, no. 5, pp. 712-720, 1998

Typing Aberrance in Signal Transduction[*]

M. Zhang[1,**], G.Q. Li[2], Y.X. Fu[1], Z.Z. Zhang[3], and L. He[3]

[1] BASICS, Department of Computer Science and Engineering,
Shanghai Jiao Tong University, Shanghai 200030, China
{zhangmin, yxfu}@sjtu.edu.cn

[2] Japan Advanced Institute of Science and Technology,
Asahidai, Nomi, Ishikawa 923-1292, Japan
guoqiang@jaist.ac.jp

[3] BDCC, College of Life Science and Biotechnology,
Shanghai Jiao Tong University, Shanghai 200030, China
{zhangzz, helin}@sjtu.edu.cn

Abstract. We have developed a calculus, called *Ipi*, for describing the aberrance in biological models. Our approach extends the traditional pi calculus to handle aberrant process in the signal transduction. In this paper we propose a typing system that replaces the tag system of Ipi calculus. It is shown that the typing system is equal to the tag system in terms of the expressive power.

1 Introduction

There are several pieces of related work about modelling various biological systems based on pi calculus [1,6], some of which are about modelling signal transduction (ST) [4,5,2,3]. In these works however the biological systems are considered under normal conditions, assuming that there are no exceptions when they evolve.

In fact, part of the purpose of this research is to investigate the ways in which the biological systems can be subverted. There is an important reason for modelling these systems in all their complexity: many drugs and natural defenses work by subverting natural pathways. We need to model the aberrant biological systems to understand them. For this purpose, we have introduced Ipi calculus [8], extended from pi calculus, to describe more complex biochemical systems like aberrant ST. The calculus is obtained by adding two aberrant actions into pi calculus and a tag system to check existing aberrance.

We used the tag system to check the existence of aberrance in [8] by sets computation, such as union, disjoint, etc. It is quite intuitive but difficult to implement. Biological systems however are most complicated systems, so without an automatic tool we can hardly go any further. In this paper we introduce a

---

[*] The work is supported by The National Distinguished Young Scientist Fund of NNSFC (60225012), BDCC (03DZ14025), The National Nature Science Foundation of China (60473006), and The BoShiDian Research Fund (20010248033).
[**] The author is also supported by PPS, Paris 7 University, France.

typing system that is simple enough to be enforced statically and that is easily implemented into an automatic tool design (It had been implemented by Simon Gay). We will establish some properties of the typing system and show that it is equivalent to the tag system of [8].

2 The Pure Ipi Calculus

In this section we present the pure version of Ipi calculus that serves as the preliminary setting for our formal work. The pure Ipi calculus is Ipi calculus without the tag system.

2.1 Syntax

Processes evolve by performing actions. In process algebra actions capabilities are introduced by prefix capabilities. In Ipi calculus, we introduce two capabilities in addition to the prefix defined by pi calculus.

We assume that an infinite countable set $\mathcal{N}$ of names and an infinite countable set $\mathcal{V}$ of variables. Let $a, b, \cdots$ range over the names and $x, y, \cdots$ range over the variables. We also define two symbols § and ♯ to represent the aberrance capability. Here § represents the killer capability and ♯ the propagation capability. When a process has the killer capability, it terminates immediately. And when a process has the propagation capability, it will duplicate itself infinitely.

Definition 1 (Prefix). *The prefix of Ipi calculus are defined as follows:*

$$\pi ::= \overline{a}(b) \mid a(x) \mid \overline{a} \mid a \qquad \pi_i ::= \pi \mid \S(\pi_i) \mid \sharp(\pi_i)$$

The capability of π is the same as in pi calculus. $\S(\pi_i)$ and $\sharp(\pi_i)$ are the substitution capabilities. They are respectively the capabilities § and ♯ if the subject of π is in an aberrant state.

Definition 2 (Process). *The Ipi processes are defined as follows:*

$$P ::= 0 \mid \pi_i.P \mid \pi_i.P + \pi'_i.P' \mid P|P' \mid (\nu a)P \mid P; P'$$

Intuitively the constructs of Ipi processes have the following meaning: 0 is the inert process. The prefix process $\pi_i.P$ has a single capability imposed by π_i, that is, the process P cannot proceed until that capability has been exercised. The capabilities of the sum $\pi_i.P + \pi'_i.P'$ are those of $\pi_i.P$ plus those of $\pi'_i.P'$. When a sum exercises one of its capabilities, the other is rendered void. In the composition process $P|P'$, the components P and P' can proceed independently and can interact via shared channel. In the restriction process $(\nu a)P$, the scope of the name a is restricted to P. The sequential process $P; P'$ can run the process P' after the process P.

We write $fn(P)$ for the set of names free in process P, and $fv(P)$ for the set of variables free in P. An expression is closed if it has no free variables. Notice that a closed expression may have free names.

2.2 Semantics

The structural congruence $\equiv$ is the least equivalent relation on closed processes that satisfies the following equalities:

$$P \mid Q \equiv Q \mid P$$
$$(P \mid Q) \mid R \equiv P \mid (Q \mid R)$$
$$P + Q \equiv Q + P$$
$$(P + Q) + R \equiv P + (Q + R)$$
$$(\nu a)0 \equiv 0$$
$$(\nu a)(\nu b)P \equiv (\nu b)(\nu a)P$$
$$((\nu a)P) \mid Q \equiv (\nu a)(P \mid Q) \text{ if } a \notin fn(Q)$$

The reaction relation, introduced initially by Milner [1], is a concise account of computation in the pi calculus. In addition to the well-known interaction rule(Com-N), our reaction relation also includes two new rules about reactions with aberrance(Pre-§ and Pre-♯).

$$\dfrac{}{\S(\pi_i).P \longrightarrow 0} \text{ Pre-§ ;} \qquad \dfrac{}{\sharp(\pi_i).P \longrightarrow \pi_i.P; \sharp(\pi_i).P} \text{ Pre-♯ ;}$$

$$\dfrac{}{\overline{a}(b).Q \mid a(x).P \longrightarrow Q \mid P\{b/x\}} \text{ Com-N;}$$

$$\dfrac{P \longrightarrow P'}{P + Q \longrightarrow P'} \text{ Sum;} \qquad \dfrac{P \longrightarrow P'}{P \mid Q \longrightarrow P' \mid Q} \text{ Com;}$$

$$\dfrac{P \longrightarrow P'}{(\nu a)P \longrightarrow (\nu a)P'} \text{ Res;} \qquad \dfrac{Q \equiv P \quad P \longrightarrow P' \quad P' \equiv Q'}{Q \longrightarrow Q'} \text{ Stc.}$$

The first two rules deal with reactions with aberrance: the former says that the resulting process is terminated; the latter declares that the resulting process duplicates itself infinitely. The third reaction rule deals with the interaction in which one sends a message with a channel while the other receives a message with the same channel so that they have an interactive action. Each of the reduction rules are closed in the summation, composition, restriction and structural congruence.

3 An Example in ST Pathway with the Aberrance

In order to illustrate the use of our calculus, we consider an example in ST pathway with aberrance. We focus our attention on the well-studied RTK-MAPK pathway. Here we choose a small yet important part, *Ras* Activation, for explanation.

Fig.1 gives an example of Ras Activation of the ST pathway, RTK-MAPK. At the normal state, the protein-to-protein interactions bring the SOS protein close to the membrane, where Ras can be activated. SOS activates Ras by exchanging Ras's GDP with GTP. Active Ras interacts with the first kinase in the MAPK cascade, Raf. GAP inactivates it by the reverse reaction.

Within the framework of Ipi calculus, we set some principles for the correspondence. Firstly, we choose the functional signaling *domain* as our primitive *process*. This captures the functional and structural independence of domains in signaling molecules. Secondly, we model the component *residues* of domains as communication *channels* that construct a process. Finally, molecular interaction and modification is modelled as communication and the subsequent change of channel names. Aviv Regev and his colleagues have given the representation of normal RTK-MAPK using the pi calculus [4].

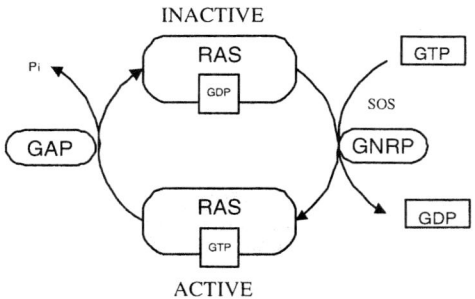

Fig. 1. Ras Activation

A protein molecule is composed of several domains, each of which is modelled as a process as well. In (1) through (4) the detailed Ipi calculus programs for the proteins Ras, SOS, Raf and GAP are given:

$$RAS ::= INASWI\_I \mid INASWI\_II \qquad (1)$$
$$SOS ::= S\_SH3\_BS \mid S\_GNEF \qquad (2)$$
$$RAF ::= R\_Nt \mid R\_ACT\_BS \mid R\_M\_BS$$
$$\mid INA\_R\_Ct \mid R\_ATP\_BS \qquad (3)$$
$$GAP ::= sg(c\_ras).\overline{c\_ras}(gdp).GAP \qquad (4)$$

The molecules (or domains) interact with each other based on their structural and chemical complementarity. Interaction is accomplished by the motifs and residues that constitute a domain. These are viewed as channels or communication ports of the molecule:

$$INASWI\_I ::= \overline{bbone}.ACTSWI\_I \qquad (5)$$
$$INASWI\_II ::= \overline{sg}(rs\_1).rs\_1(x).bbone.ACTSWI\_II \qquad (6)$$
$$S\_GNEF ::= bbone.S\_GNEF + sg(c\_ras).\overline{c\_ras}(gtp).S\_GNEF \qquad (7)$$

The following interactions are possible:

$$INASWI\_I \mid S\_GNEF \longrightarrow ACTSWI\_I \mid S\_GNEF \qquad (8)$$
$$INASWI\_II \mid S\_GNEF \longrightarrow bbone.ACTSWI\_II \mid S\_GNEF \qquad (9)$$

The interaction (8) shows that the domain $INASWI\_I$ of Ras is activated by the domain of S_GNEF of SOS. The interaction (9) shows that the domain $INASWI\_II$ of Ras is activated by the domain S_GNEF of SOS.

The detailed Ipi programs for activated domains, $ACTSWI\_I$, $ACTSWI\_II$ of the protein Ras and the domain R_Nt of Raf are defined in (10) through (12):

$$ACTSWI\_I ::= \overline{s}(rs\_2).\overline{rs\_2}.ACTSWI\_I + \overline{bbone}.INASWI\_I \quad (10)$$

$$ACTSWI\_II ::= \overline{sg}(r\_swi\_1).\overline{r\_swi\_1}(x).\overline{bbone}.ACTSWI\_II \quad (11)$$

$$R\_Nt ::= s(c\_ras).\overline{c\_ras}.ACTR\_Nt \quad (12)$$

The processes so defined have the following interactions:

$$ACTSWI\_I \mid R\_Nt \longrightarrow^* ACTSWI\_I \mid ACTR\_Nt \quad (13)$$

$$ACTSWI\_II \mid GAP \longrightarrow^* \overline{bbone}.ASWI\_II \mid GAP \quad (14)$$

$$\overline{bbone}.ACTSWI\_II \mid ACTSWI\_I \longrightarrow INASWI\_II \mid INASWI\_I \quad (15)$$

The interaction (13) shows that the active domain $ACTSWI\_I$ of Ras interacts with the domain R_Nt of Raf. (14) shows that GAP inactivates the domain $ACTSWI\_II$ of Ras. (15) says that the domains of Ras interact with each other and that Ras rollbacks to the initial inactivated state.

When Ras mutates aberrantly, it does not have any effect on the Ras's binding with GTP but will reduce the activity of the GAP hydrolase of Ras and lower its hydrolysis of GAP greatly; in the meantime Ras will be kept in an active state; they keep activating the molecule, inducing the continual effect of signal transduction, which result in cell proliferation and tumor malignancy.

(16) defines the Ipi representation of GAP in the aberrant state. (17) shows that GAP loses its function and does nothing, meaning that it can not inactivate the domain $ACTSWI\_II$ of Ras.

$$GAP ::= \S(sg(c\_ras)).\overline{c\_ras}(gdp).GAP \quad (16)$$

$$GAP \longrightarrow 0 \quad (17)$$

But then the interaction (15) will not occur whereas the interaction (13) will occur infinitely. Now observe that

$$\sharp ACTSWI\_I \longrightarrow ACTSWI\_I; \sharp ACTSWI\_I$$

It reaches an abnormal state with exceptions. Pi calculus could not easily describe this aberrant case. Ipi calculus, on the contrary, can describe it quite precisely.

4 The Tag System

The occurrence of aberrance is affected by temperature, environment, and concentration, etc. We will express the aberrance using two functions. We assume an infinite countable set $\mathcal{A}$ of values. Let σ, ρ be functions from $\mathcal{N}$ to $\mathcal{A}$. One can think of σ as an interference function and that $\sigma(a)$ as the interference degree of a. The function ρ is a critical function and that $\rho(a)$ is the critical value of the interference degree of a. The interference coefficient can be defined below:

Definition 3 (Interference Coefficient). *For $a \in \mathcal{N}$, let i_a be $|\rho(a) - \sigma(a)|$. We say that i_a is the interference coefficient of a.*

Therefore, when the aberrance occurs, it will be marked into the interference coefficient. We call such a system the tag system of Ipi calculus. Intuitively, when i_a is equal to zero, we take that a is in an aberrant state; when i_a is not zero, we think that a is still in a normal state. For convenience of representation, when i_a is equal to zero, we write 0 as the tag of a. Otherwise we write i_a as the tag of a.

For every prefix, we write a pair $\langle i_{\pi_i}, \pi_i \rangle$ instead of π_i, where i_{π_i} is the tag of π_i. When $\pi_i = \pi$, i_{π_i} is the tag of the subject of π; when $\pi_i = \S(\pi_i')$ or $\pi_i = \sharp(\pi_i')$, $i_{\pi_i} = 0$.

For a process, the expression of a process is also a pair $\langle I_P, P \rangle$ where I_P is the tag of the process P. The syntax of the tags is defined inductively by the following rules, where the symbol $\uplus$ means disjoint union: $\overset{\infty}{\underset{n=1}{\uplus}} I_P \triangleq I_P \uplus I_P \uplus \cdots$:

$$\frac{}{I_0 = \emptyset} \text{ 0-t} \qquad \frac{\langle I_P, P \rangle = \langle i_\pi, \pi \rangle.\langle I_Q, Q \rangle}{I_P = \{i_\pi\} \uplus I_Q} \text{ N-t}$$

$$\frac{\langle I_P, P \rangle = \langle 0, \S(\pi_i) \rangle.\langle I_Q, Q \rangle}{I_P = \{0\}} \text{ §-t} \qquad \frac{\langle I_P, P \rangle = \langle 0, \sharp(\pi_i) \rangle.\langle I_Q, Q \rangle}{I_P = \overset{\infty}{\underset{n=1}{\uplus}}(\{0\} \uplus \{i_{\pi_i}\} \uplus I_Q)} \text{ }\sharp\text{-t}$$

$$\frac{\langle I_P, P \rangle = \langle i_{\pi_i}, \pi_i \rangle.\langle I_Q, Q \rangle + \langle i_{\pi_i'}, \pi_i' \rangle.\langle I_R, R \rangle}{I_P = f(\langle \{i_{\pi_i}\} \uplus I_Q, \{i_{\pi_i'}\} \uplus I_R \rangle)} \text{ Sum-t}$$

$$\frac{\langle I_P, P \rangle = \langle I_Q, Q \rangle | \langle I_R, R \rangle}{I_P = I_Q \cup I_R} \text{ Com-t} \qquad \frac{\langle I_P, P \rangle = (\nu x)\langle I_Q, Q \rangle}{I_P = I_Q} \text{ Res-t}$$

$$\frac{\langle I_P, P \rangle = \langle I_Q, Q \rangle; \langle I_R, R \rangle}{I_P = I_Q \uplus I_R} \text{ Seq-t}$$

In the above definition, $\langle I_P, I_Q \rangle$ is a pair, f is the projection, and $f(\langle I_P, I_Q \rangle)$ represents the tag of the process which has the operator "sum". I_P and I_Q are nondeterministically chosen as the process P or Q is chosen to act.

Let I_P, I_Q be the tags of the processes P and Q. We define

$$I_P = I_Q \Leftrightarrow \langle I_P, P \rangle \equiv \langle I_Q, Q \rangle$$

So we have defined an equivalence on the tags in terms of the structural equivalence.

For the reaction relations, all the rules react with their tags reacting simultaneously. We define them as follows:

$$\frac{}{\{0\} \setminus \{0\} = \emptyset} \text{pre-§};$$

$$\frac{\biguplus_{n=1}^{\infty}(\{0\} \uplus \{i_{\pi_i}\} \uplus I_P) \setminus \{0\} = \{i_{\pi_i}\} \uplus I_P \uplus \biguplus_{n=1}^{\infty}(\{0\} \uplus \{i_{\pi_i}\} \uplus I_P)}{}\text{pre-}\sharp;$$

$$\frac{}{(\{i_x\} \uplus I_Q) \cup (\{i_x\} \uplus I_P) \setminus \{i_x\} = I_Q \cup I_P}\text{com-N};$$

$$\frac{I_P \setminus \{i_y\} = I_{P'}}{f_P(\langle I_P, I_Q \rangle) \setminus \{i_y\} = I_{P'}}; \quad \frac{I_P \setminus \{i_y\} = I_{P'}}{I_P \cup I_Q \setminus \{i_y\} = I_{P'} \cup I_Q};$$

$$\frac{I_Q = I_P \quad I_P \setminus \{i_x\} = I_{P'} \quad I_{P'} = I_{Q'}}{I_Q \setminus \{i_x\} = I_{Q'}}.$$

The section is a brief introduction to the tag system. To know more, see [8].

5 The Typing System

As we have mentioned, for a biochemical network with aberrance, we hope to know whether the proteins are aberrant or not in the network. So in Ipi calculus, we need to control the information flow when modelling an aberrant biochemical network. This section describes rules for controlling information flow in Ipi calculus. There are several ways of formalizing those ideas, just like the tag system introduced in [8]. Here we embody them in a typing system for Ipi calculus. Typing system was firstly introduced by Martin Abadi in studying security protocols [7].

5.1 The Typing System

In order to represent the aberrance of ST we classify signals into three classes:

- A *Normal* signal is one that takes part in the normal processes.
- An *Aberrant* signal is one that takes part in the aberrant processes.
- An *Unknown* signal could be any signal.

To simplify we define a reflexive order relation $<:$ among these three classes:

Normal $<:$ *Unknown*;
Aberrant $<:$ *Unknown*.

For convenience of representation, we denote M as a name or a variable. M is called *term*. Corresponding to these three classes the typed system has three kinds of assertions:

- "$\vdash \Gamma$ well formed" means that the environment Γ is well-formed.
- "$\Gamma \vdash M : T$" means that the term M is of the class T in Γ.
- "$E \vdash P : ok$" means that the process P type checks in E.

Typing rules are given under an environment. An environment is a list of distinct names with associated classifications.

Definition 4 (Typed Environment). *Typed environments are given by the following rules:*

$$\frac{}{\vdash \emptyset \; well \; formed} Environment \; Empty$$

$$\frac{\vdash \Gamma \; well \; formed, M \notin \Gamma}{\vdash \Gamma, M:T \; well \; formed} Environment \; Term$$

Having defined the environments, one can define rules for terms and processes.

Definition 5 (Terms). *The rules for terms of typing system are as follows:*

$$\frac{\Gamma \vdash M:T \quad T <: R}{\Gamma \vdash M:R} Level \; Subsumption$$

$$\frac{\vdash \Gamma \; well \; formed \quad M:T \; in \; \Gamma}{\Gamma \vdash M:T} Level \; Term$$

Intuitively the rule Level Subsumption says that a term of level *Normal* or *Aberrant* has level *Unknown* as well.

Definition 6 (Processes). *The rules for typing processes are as follows:*

$$\frac{\Gamma \vdash a: Normal \quad \Gamma \vdash b: Normal \quad \Gamma \vdash P:Ok}{\Gamma \vdash \overline{a}(b).P:Ok} T\text{-}out$$

$$\frac{\Gamma \vdash a: Normal \quad \Gamma \vdash x: Normal \quad \Gamma \vdash P:Ok}{\Gamma \vdash a(x).P:Ok} T\text{-}in$$

$$\frac{\Gamma \vdash a: Normal \quad \Gamma \vdash P:Ok}{\Gamma \vdash \overline{a}.P:Ok} T\text{-}sout \quad \frac{\Gamma \vdash a: Normal \quad \Gamma \vdash P:Ok}{\Gamma \vdash a.P:Ok} T\text{-}sin$$

$$\frac{\Gamma \vdash a: Aberrant \quad \Gamma \vdash b: Unknown \quad \Gamma \vdash P:Ok}{\Gamma \vdash \S(\overline{a}(b)).P:Ok} T\text{-}kout$$

$$\frac{\Gamma \vdash a: Aberrant \quad \Gamma \vdash x: Unknown \quad \Gamma \vdash P:Ok}{\Gamma \vdash \S(a(x)).P:Ok} T\text{-}kin$$

$$\frac{\Gamma \vdash a: Aberrant \quad \Gamma \vdash P:Ok}{\Gamma \vdash \S(\overline{a}).P:Ok} T\text{-}ksout \quad \frac{\Gamma \vdash a: Aberrant \quad \Gamma \vdash P:Ok}{\Gamma \vdash \S(a).P:Ok} T\text{-}ksin$$

$$\frac{\Gamma \vdash a: Aberrant \quad \Gamma \vdash b: Unknown \quad \Gamma \vdash P:Ok}{\Gamma \vdash \sharp(\overline{a}(b)).P:Ok} T\text{-}pout$$

$$\frac{\Gamma \vdash a: Aberrant \quad \Gamma \vdash x: Unknown \quad \Gamma \vdash P:Ok}{\Gamma \vdash \sharp(a(x)).P:Ok} T\text{-}pin$$

$$\frac{\Gamma \vdash a: Aberrant \quad \Gamma \vdash P:Ok}{\Gamma \vdash \sharp(\overline{a}).P:Ok} T\text{-}psout \quad \frac{\Gamma \vdash a: Aberrant \quad \Gamma \vdash P:Ok}{\Gamma \vdash \sharp(a).P:Ok} T\text{-}psin$$

$$\frac{\vdash \Gamma \; well \; formed}{\Gamma \vdash 0:Ok} T\text{-}nil \quad \frac{\Gamma, a: Normal \vdash P:Ok}{\Gamma \vdash (\nu a)P:Ok} T\text{-}res$$

$$\frac{\Gamma \vdash P : Ok \quad \Gamma \vdash Q : Ok}{\Gamma \vdash P \mid Q : Ok} \textit{T-com} \quad \frac{\Gamma \vdash P : Ok \quad \Gamma \vdash Q : Ok}{\Gamma \vdash P + Q : Ok} \textit{T-sum}$$

$$\frac{\Gamma \vdash P : Ok \quad \Gamma \vdash Q : Ok}{\Gamma \vdash P; Q : Ok} \textit{T-seq}$$

5.2 Properties of Typing

Having defined the typing system for Ipi calculus, we can show that the checking capability of the typing system is equal to the tag system of [8]. We firstly establish some properties of typing system before proving the main result. The first three are fundamental properties satisfying a typing system. The last one is a precondition for the theorem. The proofs of properties are obvious so we omit them here.

Proposition 1. *Assume that $\vdash \Gamma$ well formed and that the terms in $dom(\Gamma)$ are all normal. Then the following properties hold:*

- If M is a term and $M \in dom(\Gamma)$, then $\Gamma \vdash M : Normal$.
- if P is a process with $f_n(P) \cup f_v(P) \subseteq dom(\Gamma)$, then $\Gamma \vdash P : ok$.

Proposition 2 (Strengthening). *Assume that the term M is not free in the process P and that $N \neq M$. The following properties hold:*

- If $\Gamma, M : T \vdash N : S$, then also $\Gamma \vdash N : S$.
- If $\Gamma, M : T \vdash P : Ok$, then also $\Gamma \vdash P : Ok$.

Proposition 2 enables us to condense an environment, moving out the declaration of a term that is not used.

Proposition 3 (Weakening). *Let M is not defined on the environment Γ,*

- If $\Gamma \vdash N : S$, then $\Gamma, M : T \vdash N : S$.
- If $\Gamma \vdash P : Ok$, then $\Gamma, M : T \vdash P : Ok$.

Proposition 3 declares that anything that can be proved in a given environment can also be proved with more assumptions.

Proposition 4 (Signal checking). *Let i_M be the interference coefficient of the term M. Then*

- $i_M = 0$ if and only if $M : Aberrent$;
- $i_M \neq 0$ if and only if $M : Normal$.

Now, we bring out the key theorem of this paper, presented as follows. It can be concluded that the typing system is equal to the tag system in terms of the expressive power.

Theorem 1 (Full Abstraction). *Let I_P be the tag of P. Then $0 \in I_P$ iff 'If $\Gamma \vdash P : ok$, then there is a term M in P such that $\Gamma \vdash M : Aberrant$'.*

It can be proved by induction on the derivation of I_P and the P.

With this brief typing system, we can verify the aberrant ST pathways without complex tags, and implement into an automatic tool to run it correctly.

6 Future Prospects

This work brings out the static checking for Ipi calculus, opening up new possibilities in the study of biochemical systems with exceptions. Our next work is to investigate properties of Ipi calculus, finding out the relations between these properties and the properties of biochemical systems.

We can also modify the typing system to suit for regulating various biochemical systems, including transcriptional circuits, metabolic pathways etc. Also, while we get further knowledge of biochemistry, we will refine our typing system in a more precise way to type check errors when we design automatic tools.

References

1. Milner, R., Parrow, J., Walker, D.: A Calculus of Mobile Processes, parts I and II. In: Information and Computation. (1992)1-77
2. Priami, C., Regev, A., Silverman, W., and Shapiro,E.: Application of a stochastic name passing calculus to representation and simulation of molecular processes. In: Information Processing Letters. **80**(2001)25-31
3. Regev, A.: Representation and simulation of molecular pathways in the stochastic pi calculus. In: Proceedings of the 2nd workshop on Computation of Biochemical Pathways and Genetic Networks. (2001)
4. Regev, A., Silverman, W., and Shapiro, E.: Representing biomolecular processes with computer process algebra: pi calculus programs of signal transduction pathways. In: http://www.wisdom.weizmann.ac.il/ aviv/papers.htm (2000)
5. Regev, A., Silverman, W., and Shapiro, E.: Representation and simulation of biochemical processes using the pi calculus process algebra. In: Proceedings of the Pacific Symposium of Biocomputing. **6**(2001)459-470
6. Sangiorgi, D., and Walker, D.: The pi calculus: a Theory of Mobile Process. In: Cambridge University Press. (2001)
7. Abadi, M.: Secrecy by Typing in Security Protocols. In Proceedings of Theoretical Aspects of Computer Software, Third International Symposioum. **1281**(1997) 611-638
8. Zhang, M., Li, G., and Fu, Y, et al.: Representation of the Signal Transduction with Aberrance Using Ipi Calculus. In : Computational and Information Science: First International Symposium, **3314**(2004)477-484

Local Search for the Maximum Parsimony Problem

Adrien Goëffon, Jean-Michel Richer, and Jin-Kao Hao*

LERIA - University of Angers 2 Boulevard Lavoisier,
49045 Angers Cedex 01, France
{goeffon, richer, hao}@info.univ-angers.fr

Abstract. Four local search algorithms are investigated for the phylogenetic tree reconstruction problem under the Maximum Parsimony criterion. A new subtree swapping neighborhood is introduced and studied in combination with an effective array-based tree representation. Computational results are shown on a set of randomly generated benchmark instances as well as on 8 real problems (sequences of phytopathogen γ-proteobacteria) and compared with two references from the literature.

1 Introduction

Phylogeny concerns the reconstruction of the evolutionary history of a set of species identified by their nucleic acid (DNA) or amino acid (AA) sequences, also called taxa. The evolutionary relationships between species are represented by a tree, called a phylogenetic tree, whose branches reflect historical relationships. The applications of phylogeny range from classification and taxonomy to molecular epidemiology [5].

The problem of phylogeny reconstruction can be addressed using several methods. The *distance-based approach* computes a distance matrix from the taxa and tries to find a tree that approximates this matrix. Agglomerative clustering algorithms such as NJ (Neighbor-Joining) [11] and BIONJ [8] are well-known examples. The *character-based approach* searches through tree topologies to find the best tree according to an optimality criterion. The widely used Maximum Parsimony criterion [3] is such an example which states that the tree requiring the fewest number of changes (mutations) should be preferred. This *Maximum Parsimony Problem (MPP)* is known to be NP-Hard [7]. Therefore, several heuristics have been developed, including branch-swapping used in PHYLIP [4] and PAUP [12], simulated annealing [2] and other metaheuristics [1]. *Maximum Likelihood* is yet another approach for the inference of phylogeny using probabilistic estimation.

In this paper, we are interested in studying Local Search algorithms for the MPP and studying two important elements: the neighborhood relation and the internal tree representation. We evaluate a new neighborhood called Subtree Swapping Neighborhood (SSN) as well as an array-based tree representation.

---
* Corresponding author.

2 The Maximum Parsimony Problem

Definition 1 (Phylogenetic tree). *A phylogenetic tree is a directed graph showing the relationships between a group of contemporary taxa (labels of the leaves) and their hypothetical common ancestors (internal nodes labeled by consensus sequences). If a rooted tree is used, the root is the common ancestor of all the contemporary taxa.*

Definition 2 (Consensus sequences). *Given two sequences S_1 and S_2 of length k: $S_1 = <x_1^1, x_2^1, \cdots, x_k^1>$, $S_2 = <x_1^2, x_2^2, \cdots, x_k^2>$ with x_i^j taken from some alphabet $\sum$, the consensus sequence S_c (parent node in a phylogenetic tree) is obtained from S_1 and S_2 by:*

$$\forall i, 1 \leq i \leq k, x_i^c = \begin{cases} x_i^1 \cup x_i^2, \text{if } x_i^1 \cap x_i^2 = \emptyset \\ x_i^1 \cap x_i^2, \text{if } x_i^1 \cap x_i^2 \neq \emptyset \end{cases}$$

The cost of the consensus sequence S_c is defined by:

$$f(S_c) = \sum_{i=1}^{k} c_i \quad \text{where} \quad c_i = \begin{cases} 1, \text{if } x_i^1 \cap x_i^2 = \emptyset \\ 0, \text{otherwise} \end{cases}$$

Definition 3 (Parsimony score of a phylogenetic tree). *Given a phylogenetic tree t and V a set of nodes whose leaves are labeled with the sequences of an initial set S, the parsimony score of t is given by:*

$$f(t) = \sum_{v \in V \setminus S} f(S_c^v)$$

where S_c^v are the consensus sequences associated to the internal nodes of t.

The goal of the Maximum Parsimony Problem is then to find a tree $t^* \in \mathcal{T}$ with the lowest parsimony score $f(t^*)$, $\mathcal{T}$ being the set of all the possible phylogenetic trees for a given set of taxa S.

3 Local Search for the Maximum Parsimony Problem

Given the NP-hardness of the MPP, local search (LS) heuristics have been massively used to find approximate phylogenetic trees. In this Section, we study four LS algorithms using a new neighborhood. First, the basic and common elements of these LS algorithms are introduced.

3.1 Tree Representation and Evaluation

One important issue of LS algorithms for the MPP concerns the way the trees are represented and evaluated. Here, we use an array-based representation (Fig. 1). Each node is identified by a number (N), associated with its left (L) and right (R) son, the parent (P) and the cost (C) of the node. This representation is particularly suitable for applying changes in the SSN neighborhood and convenient for computing the cost of each neighboring tree.

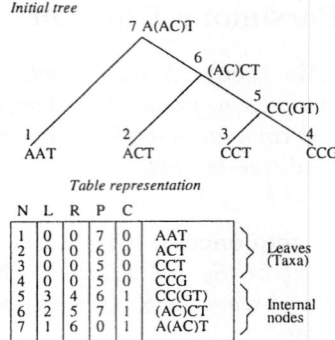

Fig. 1. Tree representation

3.2 Neighborhood

Neighborhood is a critical element of local search algorithms. The literature offers three major neighborhoods for trees: NNI (*Nearest neighborhood interchanges*) [14], SPR (*Subtree pruning and Regrafting*) and TBR (*Tree Bisection Reconnection*) [13]. NNI is a restricted neighborhood which consists in swapping two adjacent branches. SPR removes a subtree and reinserts it in other branches of the tree. TBR breaks the initial tree into two subtrees which can be reconnected to any branches of one another. It is easy to see that NNI $\subseteq$ SPR $\subseteq$ TBR.

In this study, we introduce a new neighborhood, that we call SSN (for *Subtree Swapping Neighborhood*). SSN consists in swapping two subtrees of a tree. Let $SSN_{X,Y}(t)$ be the tree obtained by exchanging the subtrees with roots X and Y of tree t such that Y (resp. X) must not be contained in the subtree rooted from X (resp. from Y). Then the SSN neighborhood $\mathcal{N}$ can be formally defined as follows $\mathcal{N} : \mathcal{T} \to 2^{\mathcal{T}}$ is such that for each $t = <N, V> \in \mathcal{T}$, a tree $t' \in \mathcal{T}$ is a neighbor of t, i.e. $t' \in \mathcal{N}(t)$, if and only if $\exists (X, Y) \in V \times V$, $SSN_{X,Y}(t) = t'$ where V is the set of nodes. As shown later, SSN, combined with our internal tree representation, contributes greatly to the efficiency of our LS algorithms.

3.3 Implemented Local Search Algorithms

Pure Descent (PD). The Pure Descent (PD) algorithm accepts only better neighboring solutions. A neighboring tree t' is accepted to replace the current tree t only if $f(t') < f(t)$ (t' is more parsimonious than t). This algorithm needs no parameter and stops automatically when a local optimum (minimum) is encountered. The pure descent is very fast and may serve as a baseline reference for evaluating other algorithms.

Random Walk Descent (RWD). This algorithm combines the pure descent with the random walk strategy to accept from time to time a random neighbor (which is not necessarily better). At each iteration, with probability $p \in [0, 1]$, a neighbor is taken randomly from the neighborhood to replace the current solution regardless of its cost; with probability $1-p$, a pure descent iteration is carried out. Here, $p = \frac{1}{\alpha.|S|^2}$, α taking values from 1 to 10 and $|S|$ being the number of species of the problem instance.

Iterative Local Search (ILS). ILS uses the pure descent to reach a first local optimum and then perturbs this local optimum by carrying out a limited number of random walks. This leads to a new solution which is then used by the pure descent to seek another local optimum. The two-steps process *Descent-Perturbation* is repeated until a predefined stop condition is met.

Simulated Annealing (SA). At each iteration, a neighbor t' is taken randomly from $\mathcal{N}(t)$ of the current tree t. t' is accepted to replace t if t' is better than t. Otherwise, t' is accepted with a probability $e^{-\frac{f(t')-f(t)}{\tau}}$ where f is the evaluation (cost) function given in Section 2 and τ is the temperature parameter which is decreased by a simple linear function. The algorithm stops when the current solution is not replaced for a fixed number of iterations.

4 Experimental Results

In this section, we compare the four LS algorithms presented above and assess their performances with respect to two references: DNAPARS of PHYLIP package [4] and LVB (both fast and slow versions) [2]. Implemented in C++, PD, RWD, ILS and SA are compiled using the -O2 optimization option of the gcc/g++ compiler and run on Sun Fire V880 with 8 GBytes of RAM.

4.1 Benchmarks

Our benchmarks include problems having 100 to 180 sequences of a length of 100 nucleotides and were generated with *Dnatree* [10] and the Kimura two-parameter model [9] with a transition/transversion ratio fixed to 2, and an evolution rate of 0.05. We used also 8 real instances from plant pathology, composed of 69 to 95 sequences of phytopathogen γ-proteobacteria (denoted by phyto here) with 409 to 645 sites and report only here the results on one real instance since we observed very similar behavior on these instances. To run the programs, an initial tree is generated either with a random construction (Rand) or with a distance-based method (Dist). Each algorithm is run 20 to 50 times.

4.2 Comparison of PD, RWD, ILS and SA

Table 1 shows the comparative results of (PD, RWD, ILS and SA) on five classes of random instances and the phytopathogen instance, with the following information: the best cost found (f_b), the average cost (f_m), the standard deviation of the cost (σ) and the average computing time (time).

Table 1. Comparison of PD, ILS, RWD, SA, DNAPARS and LVB

Algorithm	f_b	f_m	σ	time	Algorithm	f_b	f_m	σ	time
100.100					**160.100**				
PD	419	420,9	1,5	3m30	PD	655	658,9	2,6	13m
RWD	419	420,1	1,4	30m	RWD	655	656,6	1,9	1h20
ILS	419	419,0	0	20m	ILS	655	655,5	0,7	1h
SA	419	419,0	0	30m	SA	654	654,0	0	1h10
DNAPARS	419	419	–	4m	DNAPARS	654	654	–	65h
LVB Slow	420	420	–	>2h	LVB Slow	655	655	–	>3h
LVB Fast	421	421	–	>2h	LVB Fast	655	655	–	>3h
120.100					**180.100**				
PD	495	495,8	1,4	6m	PD	753	755,4	1,8	15m
RWD	495	495	0	40m	RWD	752	754,0	1,3	1h40
ILS	495	495,3	0,6	30m	ILS	752	753,0	1,4	1h20
SA	495	495,0	0	40m	SA	751	751,0	0	1h40
DNAPARS	495	495	–	40h	DNAPARS	751	751	–	1h20
LVB Fast	496	496	–	>1h	LVB Slow	752	752	–	>3h
LVB Slow	496	496	–	>1h	LVB Fast	752	752	–	>3h
140.100					**phyto**				
PD	683	684,6	1,2	8m	PD	731	734,8	2,6	6m
RWD	682	683,6	1,0	1h	RWD	730	731,0	1,1	40m
ILS	683	684,2	1,1	40m	ILS	731	732,8	1,5	30m
SA	682	682,0	0	50m	SA	729	729,8	0,7	40m
DNAPARS	682	682	–	51h	DNAPARS	731	731	–	14h
LVB Slow	683	683	–	>5h	LVB Slow	764	764	–	>4h
LVB Fast	685	683	–	>4h	LVB Fast	740	740	–	>4h

From Table 1, one observes that PD is able to find good solutions with very short computation times compared with other algorithms. RWD finds a little better solutions, but needs more computation time. We suspect that executing RWD more times may lead to even better solutions. ILS, even with a long computation time, is not competitive. This is somewhat unexpected given that it uses a perturbation techniques to re-start PD. One possible explanation would be that the simple re-start technique used by PD (recall that PD was run 5 times) is more appropriate than re-starting PD with a solution near a local optimum. Finally, SA is the most powerful algorithm, able to find the most parsimonious trees with reasonable computation times.

4.3 Comparisons of LS Algorithms with LVB and DNAPARS

From Table 1, one observes first that in terms of solution quality, SA and DNA-PARS find the same results for random instances, and SA finds better solutions for the real instance. However, SA is much faster than DNAPARS to find solutions of the same quality. This is particularly true when the problem instance is of larger size. Indeed for still larger instances (with more than 200 sequences, not reported here), DNAPARS did not finish after 2 days of computation while SA needs 1 to 2 hours to obtain near-optimal solutions. For the phytopathogen instance, our SA algorithm obtains better result than DNAPARS (with a cost of 729 against 731). If we consider the results of LVB, one observes easily that both the fast and slow versions of LVB are often dominated by our algorithms, both in terms of solution quality and computation time.

5 Conclusion

An empirical study of four local search algorithms is carried out for the phylogenetic tree reconstruction with the Maximum Parsimony criterion. These algorithms are tested on both random instances and real problems. They are also compared with two references from the literature, showing competitive results. This study confirms that local search remains a very promising approach for the Maximum Parsimony Problem. This study has allowed us to assess the proposed SSN neighborhood and the array-based tree representation. Based on the results, we are investigating an improved local search algorithm using an evolutionary SSN neighborhood combined with a noisy evaluation function. Experimental validations are on the way by using very large instances (up to 500 taxa and 2 000 sites, including the *Zilla* data set).

Acknowledgment. This work is partially supported by the French Ouest Genopole®. We thank the Plant Pathology Lab. from the INRA of Angers for providing us with the phytopathogen sequences.

References

1. A.A. Andreatta and C.C. Ribeiro.Heuristics for the phylogeny problem. *Journal of Heuristics* 8:429-447, 2002.
2. D. Barker. LVB: parsimony and simulated annealing in the search for phylogenetic trees. *Bioinformatics* 20:274-275, 2003.
3. J.H. Camin and R.R. Sokal. A method for deucing branching sequences in phylogeny. *Evolution* 19:311-326, 1965.
4. J. Felsenstein. *Phylogenetic Inference Package (PHYLIP)*, 1993.
5. J. Felsenstein. Inferring Phylogenies. *Sinauer*, 2003.
6. W. Fitch. Towards defining course of evolution: minimum change for a specified tree topology. *Systematic Zoology* 20:406-416, 1971.
7. L.R. Foulds and R.L. Graham. The Steiner problem in phylogeny is NP-complete. *Advances in Applied Mathematics* 3:43-49, 1982.
8. O. Gascuel. BIONJ: An improved version of the NJ algorithm based on a simple model of sequence data. *Molecular Biology and Evolution* 14:685-695, 1997.
9. M. Kimura. A simple model for estimating evolutionary rates of base of base substitutions through comparative studies of nucleotide sequence. *Journal of Molecular Evolution* 16:111-120, 1980.
10. M.K. Kuhner and J. Felsenstein. A simulation comparison of phylogeny algorithms under equal and unequal evolutionary rates. *Molecular Biology and Evolution*, 11:459-468, 1994 (Erratum 12:525, 1995).
11. N. Saitou and M. Nei. Neighbor-joining method : A new method for reconstructing phylogenetic trees. *Molecular Biology and Evolution* 4:406-425, 1987.
12. D.L. Swofford. *PAUP: Phylogenetic analysis using parsimony.* Sinauer Associates, 1998.
13. D.L. Swofford and G.J. Olsen. in D.M. Hillis and C. Moritz (Ed.) Phylogeny Reconstruction. *Molecular Systematics*, chapter 11:411-501, 1990.
14. M.S. Waterman and T.F. Smith. On the similarity of dendograms. *Journal of Theoretical Biology* 73:789-800, 1978.

Optimization of Centralized Power Control by Genetic Algorithm in a DS-CDMA Cellular System

J. Zhou[1], H. Kikuchi[2], S. Sasaki[2], and H. Luo[1]

[1] Dept. of Information and Communications,
Nanjing University of Information Science and Technology, P.R. China
zhoujie45@hotmail.com
[2] Dept. of Electrical and Electronic Engineering, Niigata University, Japan

Abstract. Here, we propose an approach to solve the power control issue in a DS-CDMA cellular system using genetic algorithms (GAs). The optimal centralized power control (CPC) vector is characterized and its optimal solution for CPC is presented using GAs in a DS-CDMA cellular system. Emphasis is put on the balance of services and convergence rate by using GAs.

1 Introduction

Transmitter power control is an effective way to increase the system capacity and transmission quality in cellular wireless systems. Significant works are on power control strategy, such as Refs.[1],[2] and [3] which have focused on centralized power control(CPC) and distributed power control strategy (DPC). Ref.[1] investigated just a simplified case because of difficulties in computation and search for an optimal solution. Refs.[2]-[4] have focused on maximizing the minimum SIR using a complicated method to obtain a local optimum in the solution space using DPC for simplicity. In this paper, we first propose an approach to solve the power control issue in a DS-CDMA cellular system using genetic algorithms (GAs)[4] to obtain a global optimal solution.

2 CPC Problem

We assume N users and M base stations. All users use the common radio channel in a DS-CDMA cellular system. Let p_i denote the transmitter power of user i so that $\mathbf{P}=[p_1, p_2, ...p_N]$ denotes the transmitter power vector of the DS-CDMA cellular system. The corresponding received signal power of user i at base station k is $p_i L(i,k)$ where $L(i,k)$ denotes the gain for user i to base station k. The interference seen by user i at base station k is $\sum_{j=1, j \neq i}^{N} p_j L(j,k)$. Then, the signal to interference ratio (SIR) of mobile user i at its base station k is then written by

$$SIR_i = \frac{p_i L(i,k)}{\alpha \sum_{j=1,j \neq i}^{N} p_j L(j,k)} = \frac{p_i}{\alpha \sum_{j=1,j \neq i}^{N} p_j G_{j,k}} \quad for \quad 1 \leq i \leq N \quad (1)$$

where, α is defined as the voice activity factor. In order to achieve the balance of services, the optimization problem of the same SIR for all users in the system is expressed as[3][4]

$$SIR_{opt}^- = \min_{1 \leq i \leq N} SIR_i \quad and \quad SIR_{opt}^+ = \max_{1 \leq i \leq N} SIR_i \qquad (2)$$

Due to the theorems and lemmas of R.Vijayan and J.Zender[1], let us define G as an $N \times N$ matrix that has $G_{j,k}$ as its elements. The matrix G has a few important properties that are described as follows.

A. G is an irreducible nonnegative matrix
B. There exists a unique SIR^* given by

$$SIR^* = \max_{\mathbf{P} \in \Re} SIR_{opt}^- = \min_{\mathbf{P} \in \Re} SIR_{opt}^+, \quad \Re = \{\mathbf{P} : 0 \leq p_i \leq p_{max}, i = 1, 2, ...N\} \quad (3)$$

3 Performance Evaluation

The objective function will essentially determine the survival of each chromosome by providing a measure of its relative fitness. By assigning the power to each user in order to satisfy the same SIR for all users, a comprehensive objective function that involves all of the considerations is described as

$$\min \eta(t) = \min |SIR_{opt}^+(t) - SIR_{opt}^-(t)| \qquad (4)$$

In order to greatly speed up the convergence rate and computation, evolution is then proceeded via the partially matched crossover (PMX)[7] operator. In order to achieve PMX easily, each individual is represented by a real number vector, that means the decimal encode. We also created two First-In First-Out (FIFO) stacks with stack depth, N, to store the genes. The crossover is performed by the combination of two parents, $p_i(t)$ in t-th generation with SIR_{opt}^+ and $p_j(t)$ in t-th generation with SIR_{opt}^-. It is expressed as follows

$$p_i(t+1) = p_i(t) - \lambda p_j(t) \quad and \quad p_j(t+1) = p_j(t) + \lambda p_i(t) \qquad (5)$$

where the two types of nonlinear decreasing functions for the crossover factor in which λ is introduced in the crossover operation as

$$Case\ 1: \quad \lambda = \frac{1}{\beta + \mu t} \quad and \quad Case\ 2: \quad \lambda = \tau^{-\gamma t} \qquad (6)$$

where β, μ, τ, and γ are control parameters. In each iteration step, the search can also be terminated, when there are no significant changes in the difference between $SIR_{opt}^+(t)$ and $SIR_{opt}^-(t)$ as the following stopping conditions by the termination constant δ as $min|\eta(t)| \leq \delta$.

4 Simulation Results

We consider the system as a general multi-cell DS-CDMA cellular system on a rectangular grid shown in Fig.1. that shows the positions of base stations and an example of randomly distributed users in the system. During investigation, each user is assigned to its nearest base station.

We observed that GAs with FIFO stacks has a better convergence property to produce the unique optimal solution. In the investigation of a DS-CDMA cellular system, unless the FIFO stacks are adopted, it takes a very long processing delay time. For real-time applications, this strategy will be useless for solving the CPC problem. The FIFO stacks genetic algorithm can be a better and enough

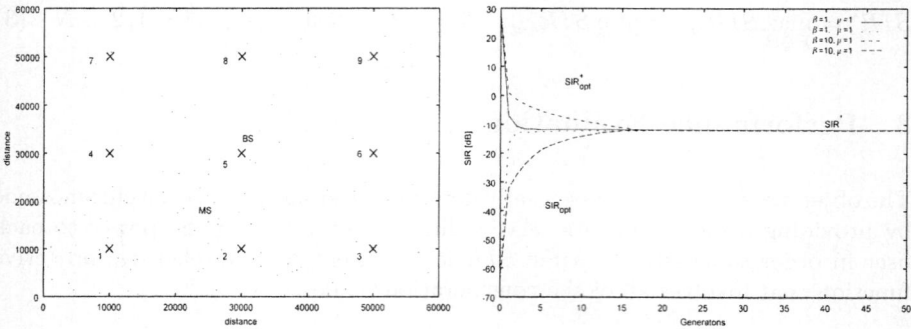

Fig. 1. Simulation environment for the number of active users N, and SIR_{opt}^+, SIR_{opt}^- versus the generation using by Case 1 $(1)\beta = 10$, $\mu = 1$ $(2)\beta = 1$, $\mu = 1$ ($\delta = 0.1dB$, $\alpha = 0.375$, $p_c = 1$, $p_m = 0.01$, $N = 270$)

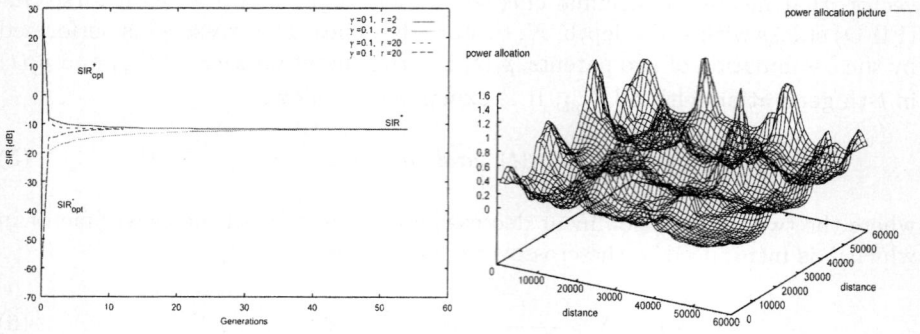

Fig. 2. SIR_{opt}^+, SIR_{opt}^- versus the generation by Case 2 $(1)\gamma = 0.1$, $\tau = 2$ $(2)\gamma = 0.1$, $\tau = 20$, and the allocation of transmitted power for Fig.1 in the entire coverage area ($\delta = 0.1dB$, $\alpha = 0.375$, $p_c = 1$, $p_m = 0.01$, $N = 270$)

approach to realistic large-scale problems. Figure 1 shows the convergence rate of user SIR being maximum value of SIR and with minimum value of SIR by Case 1. We see that SIR^* reaches the target optimal value after about 20 generations as $\beta = 10$ and $\mu = 1$. When $\beta = 1$ and $\mu = 1$, it shows better results, because the SIR reaches the target optimal value after near 7 generations.

As a result, the final unique optimal solution, that is the best SIR^*, takes the value of -11.812542 dB whatever the nonlinear decreasing functions are used in GAs. In Ref.[1], Bit-Error-Rate is given as $BER \leq 10^{-3}$ to get better transmission quality. To achieve this, the bit-energy to noise density ratio, E_b/N_0 must be larger than 7dB in the DS-CDMA system where $SIR = (E_b/N_0)/PG$, and processing gain, $PG = W_{ss}/R_b$ in which W_{ss} is the spreading bandwidth and R_b is the information bit rate. When IS-95 protocol ($W_{ss} = 1.25MHz$, and $R_b = 9.6kbps$) is used in the system, $SIR \geq -14dB$.

In order to achieve this purpose, the power allocation plot by CPC has been obtained as shown in Fig.2 for the system structure of Fig.1. One can see that a larger amount of power will be allocated to users located at the boundaries among the cells. The largest power demanded by users is located at the coordinates approximately (0, 40000) and the smallest power is located at approximate (10000, 30000) around the 4th BS.

5 Conclusions

To speed up the convergence rate and to filter out the illegal solutions, we introduced nonlinear decreasing functions and FIFO stacks. Then we have effectively simulated the centralized power control in a DS-CDMA cellular system and obtained better results. The main benefit of these simulation results is that they provide an estimate of CPC and it can be developed as some basics for the design of DPC in the system.

References

1. S.A.Grandhi and J.Zender: Centralized Power Control in Cellular Radio System, IEEE Trans. on Veh. Technol., Vol.42, No.4, pp.466-469, Nov. 1993
2. T.P.Wang, S.Y.Hwang and C.C.Tseng: Registration Area Planning for PCS Networks Using Genetic Algorithms, IEEE Trans. on Veh. Technol., Vol.47, No.3, pp.987-995, Aug. 1998
3. C.Y.Ngo and V.O.K.Li: Fixed Channel Assignment in Cellular Radio Networks Using a Modified Genetic Algorithm, IEEE Trans. on Veh. Technol., Vol.47, No.1, pp.164-172, Feb. 1998
4. M.Gen and R.W.Cheng: Genetic Algorithms and Engineering Design, A Wiley-Interscience Publication, JOHN WILEY AND SONS, INC. 1997

Cascade AdaBoost Classifiers with Stage Features Optimization for Cellular Phone Embedded Face Detection System

Xusheng Tang, Zongying Ou, Tieming Su, and Pengfei Zhao

Key Laboratory for Precision and Non-traditional Machining Technology
of Ministry of Education, Dalian University of Technology, Dalian 116024, P.R. China
tribology88@yahoo.com, {ouzyg, tiemings}@dlut.edu.cn

Abstract. In this paper, we propose a novel feature optimization method to build a cascade Adaboost face detector for real-time applications on cellular phone, such as teleconferencing, user interfaces, and security access control. AdaBoost algorithm selects a set of features and combines them into a final strong classifier. However, conventional AdaBoost is a sequential forward search procedure using the greedy selection strategy, redundancy cannot be avoided. On the other hand, design of embedded systems must find a good trade-off between performances and code size due to the limited amount of resource available in a mobile phone. To address this issue, we proposed a novel Genetic Algorithm post optimization procedure for a given boosted classifier, which leads to shorter final classifiers and a speedup of classification. This GA-optimization algorithm is very suitable for building application of embed and resource-limit device. Experimental results show that our cellular phone embedded face detection system based on this technique can accurately and fast locate face with less computational and memory cost. It runs at 275ms per image of size 384×286 pixels with high detection rates on a SANYO cellular phone with ARM926EJ-S processor that lacks floating-point hardware.

1 Introduction

Many commercial applications embedded in cellular phone demand a fast face detector, such as teleconferencing, user interfaces, and security access control. Several face detection techniques have been developed in recent years [1], [2], [3], [4]. However, due to the limitation of hardware of the mobile phone (only a few KB memory and a processor with low frequency), fast face detection embedded on mobile phone is a challenging task. It must find a good trade-off between the high detection rates, runtime and code size.

Recently, Viola [2] introduced an boosted cascade of simple classifiers using Haar-like features capable of detecting faces in real-time with both high detection rate and very low false positive rates, which is considered to be one of the fastest systems. Viola implemented this face detector on the Compaq iPaq handheld and has achieved detection at two frames per second (this device has a 200MIPS Strong Arm processor) [2]. The central part of their method is a feature selection algorithm based on

AdaBoost [5]. Much of the recent work on face detection following Viola-Jones has explored alternative-boosting algorithms such as Float-Boost [6], GentleBoost [7], and Asymmetric AdaBoost [8]. However, AdaBoost is a sequential forward search procedure using the greedy selection strategy. Because of its greedy character, neither the found weak classifiers nor their coefficients are optimal. In this paper we proposed a post optimization procedure for each completed stage classifier based on Genetic Algorithm, which removes the redundancy feature and leads to shorter final classifiers and a speedup of classification. This is very important to the mobile phone because its memory is only a few KB. A face location system on mobile phone using our proposed framework is built and tested on test database. The experimental results demonstrate that our face location system can be implemented on a wide range of small resource-limit devices, including handholds and mobile phones.

The remainder of the paper is organized as follows. In section 2 the Adaboost learning procedure proposed in [2] is introduced. The stage Optimization procedure based on Genetic Algorithms is presented in section 3. Section 4 provides the experimental results and conclusion is drawn in section 5

2 Cascade of AdaBoost Classifiers

There are three elements in the Viola-Jones framework: the cascade architecture, a rich over-complete set of Haar-like feature, and an algorithm based on AdaBoost for constructing ensembles of simple features in each classifier node.

A cascade of face classifiers is degenerated decision tree where at each stage a classifier is trained to detect almost all frontal faces while rejecting a certain fraction of non-face patterns. Those image-windows that are not rejected by the initial classifier are processed by a sequence of classifiers, each slightly more complex than the last. If any classifier rejects the image-windows, no further processing is performed, see the Fig.1. The cascade architecture can dramatically increases the speed of the detector by focusing attention on promising regions of the images.

Each stage classifier was trained using the Adaboost algorithm [5]. AdaBoost constructs the strong classifier as a combination of weak classifiers with proper coefficients. This is an iterative supervised learning process. Given a training set $\{x_i, y_i\}$, the weak classifier h_j is to find a threshold θ_j which best separates the value of the Haar-like feature f_j of the positively labeled samples from the negatively labeled samples. Thus, the weak classifier can be defined as follow:

$$h_j(x) = \begin{cases} 1 & p_j f_j < p_j \theta_j \\ 0 & otherwise \end{cases} \quad . \tag{1}$$

where p_j is 1 if the positive samples are classified below the threshold or −1 is the positive samples are classified above the threshold. After T rounds of Adaboost training, T numbers of weak classifiers h_j and ensemble weights α_j are yielded by learning. Then a final strong classifier H (x) is defined as follow:

$$H(x) = \begin{cases} 1 & \sum_{j}^{T} \alpha_j h_j(x) \geq \theta \\ 0 & otherwise \end{cases}. \quad (2)$$

The threshold θ is adjusted to meet the detection rate goal.

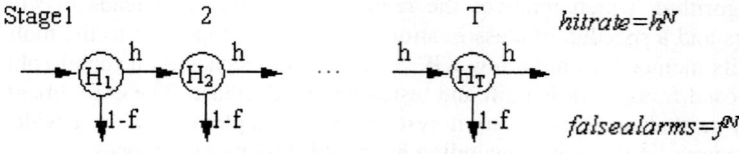

Fig. 1. Cascade of classifiers with N stages. At each stage a classifier is trained to achieve a hit rate of h and a false alarm rate of f

3 Genetic Algorithms for Stage Optimization

According to the model of the boosting classifier (Equ.2), the stage classifier could be regarded as the weight combination of weak classifier $\{h_1, h_2, \cdots, h_T\}$. Each weak classifier h_i will be determined after the boosting training. When it is fixed, the weak classifier maps the sample x_i from the original feature space F to a point

$$x_i^* = h(x_i) = \{h_1(x_i), h_2(x_i), \cdots, h_T(x_i)\}. \quad (3)$$

in a new space F^* with new dimensionality T.

As AdaBoost is a sequential forward search procedure using the greedy selection strategy, neither the found weak classifiers nor their coefficients are optimal. At the same time, classifiers with more features require more time to evaluate and more memory to occupy. However, the more features used the higher detection accuracy may be achieved. So performance at each stage classifier involves a tradeoff between accuracy, speed and hardware resources. This problem is more importance in embedded system. To address this issue, we use the Genetic algorithms to remove the redundancy and optimize the parameter. The procedure is summarized in Algorithm.1.

- Given example images $(x_1, y_1), \cdots, (x_n, y_n)$ where $y_i = 0, 1$ for negative and positive examples respectively.
- Initialize weights $\omega_{1,i} = 1/2m, 1/2l$, for $y_i = 0, 1$ respectively, where m and l are the number of negatives and positives respectively.
- For $t = 1, \ldots, T$

  1. Normalize the weights, $\omega_{t,i} \leftarrow \dfrac{\omega_{t,i}}{\sum_{j=1}^{n} \omega_{t,i}}$ so that ω_t is a probability distribution.

2. For each feature, j, train a classifier h_j which is restricted to using a single Haar-like feature. The error is evaluated with respect to ω_t, $\varepsilon_j = \sum_i \omega_i |h_j(x_i) - y_i|$.

3. Choose the classifier, h_t, with the lowest error ε_t.

4. Update the weights: $\omega_{t+1,i} = \omega_{t,i} \beta_t^{1-e_i}$ where $e_i = 0$ if example x_i is classified correctly, $e_i = 1$ otherwise, and $\beta_t = \dfrac{\varepsilon_t}{1-\varepsilon_t}$.

- The final stage classifier is: $h(x) = \begin{cases} 1 & \sum_{t=1}^{T} \alpha_t h_t(x) \geq \theta \\ 0 & \text{otherwise} \end{cases}$ where $\alpha_t = \log \dfrac{1}{\beta_t}$.

- Genetic Algorithms Stage Classifier Post-Optimization (See Algorithm 2)

Algorithm. 1. Post-optimization procedure of a given boosted stage classifier based on Genetic algorithms

3.1 Evolutionary Search

Genetic algorithms [9] are nondeterministic methods that employ crossover and mutation operators for deriving offspring. The power of GA lies in its ability to exploit, in a highly efficient manner, information about a large number of individuals.

3.1.1 Individual Representation

In order to apply genetic search a mapping must be established between concept descriptions and individual in the search population. The representation scheme that we use can be described as follows. Assume that the stage classifier contains T weak classifiers (h_i) with T weight values α_i a stage threshold value (b). This information is encoded a string just like Fig.2.

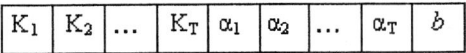

Fig. 2. The representational structure of individual

$K_1 \sim K_T$ denotes the weak classifiers, $K_i = 0$ means the weak classifier is removed and $K_i = 1$ means the weak classifier is present. $\alpha_1 \sim \alpha_T$ denotes the weight values, which range in [0, 10]. The b denotes the stage threshold value, which range in [-6,1].

3.1.2 Fitness Function

The fitness function is composed of two functions that satisfy the two characteristics of fewer weak classifier and lower error rate.

The first fitness component concerns the efficiency of stage classifier and mode size. In terms of these, it is preferable that fewer weak classifiers give a correct prediction for a given object rather more weak classifiers. The following component is designed to encourage this behavior.

$$F_1 = 1 - l/T \ . \tag{4}$$

Where l is the number of weak classifier is selected, that is $l = \sum_{i=1}^{T} K_i$, T is the total number of weak classifiers.

The next fitness component concerns accuracy measures-high hit rate (h) and low false alarm rate (f). We defined as follow:

$$F_2 = \begin{cases} 1 - n^-/N^- & if \quad m^+/M^+ \geq h \\ 0 & if \quad m^+/M^+ < h \end{cases} \ . \tag{5}$$

where: m^+ is the number of labeled positive samples correctly predicted,
 M^+ is the total number of labeled positives samples in the training set,
 n^- is the number of labeled negative samples wrongly predicted,
 N^- is the total number of labeled negative samples in the training set,
 h is the hit rate of the original stage classifier in the training set.

Given samples $(x_1, y1)\ldots(x_n, y_n)$ where $y_i=0,1$ for negative and positive samples respectively and a set of weak classifiers $\{h_1, h_2, \cdots, h_T\}$. According to the chromosome representation in the Section 3.1.1, the prediction function is defined as follow:

$$H^{'}(x_i) = \begin{cases} 1 & \sum_{i=1}^{T} K_i \alpha_i h_i(x_i) + b \geq 0 \\ 0 & otherwise \end{cases} \ . \tag{6}$$

Thus the total fitness function for the genetic algorithm can be represented as the weighted function of the two components (F_1, F_2) defined above. Then the total fitness function is defined as follow:

$$F = w_1 F_1 + w_2 F_2 \ . \tag{7}$$

where w_1 and w_2 are fitness weights that can be adjusted to balance the efficiency, mode size and accuracy of the classifier.

3.1.3 Genetic Operators

As the representational structure of individual is composed of three parts, the crossover and the mutation operators must be work on each part respectively. This ensures that the representational structure of individuals is preserved through crossover and mutation. In this paper, we adopt the point crossover and mutation. The process of crossover and mutation is shown in Fig.3 and Fig.4. (P, X and β are the random value of mutation)

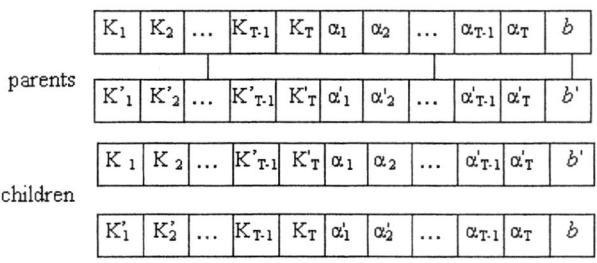

Fig. 3. The illumination of the crossover

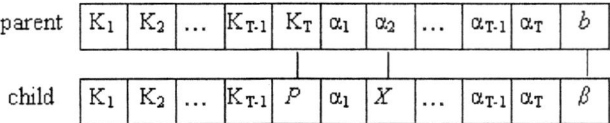

Fig. 4. The illumination of the mutation

3.1.4 Search

Search is performed as per standard genetic search. An initial population of individuals is generated. These individuals are then evaluated according to Equ.7. And the fitter individuals are chosen to undergo reproduction, crossover, and mutation operations in order to produce a population of children for the next generation. This procedure is continued until either convergence is achieved, or a sufficiently fit individual has been discovered. The evolutionary search algorithm is shown in Algorithm. 2. Further information on genetic algorithms can be found in [9].

- Choose initial population
- Evaluate each individual's fitness function
- Repeat
  1. Select individuals to reproduce
  2. Mate pairs at random
  3. Apply crossover operator
  4. Apply mutation operator
  5. Evaluate each individual's fitness function
- Until terminating condition

Algorithm. 2. Genetic Algorithms Stage Classifier Post-Optimization

3.2 Cascade Face Classifiers Learning Framework

Training a classifier for the face detection task is challenging because of the difficulty in characterizing prototypical "nonface" images. It is easy to get a representative sample of images which contain faces, but much harder to get a representative sample of those which do not. We adapted "bootstrap" method [10] to reduce the size of the training set needed. The negative images are collected during training, in the following manner, instead of collecting the images before training is started.

1. Create an initial set of nonface images by collecting m numbers of random images. Create an initial set of face images by selecting l numbers of representative face images. Given the stage number N, the total false alarm rate of total stage f.
2. Train a stage face classifier using these $m+l$ numbers of samples by Algorithm.1.
3. Add this stage face classifier to ensemble a cascade face classifier system. Run the system on an image of scenery that contains no faces and filter out m numbers of negative images that the system incorrectly identifies as face. Stage number=stage number+1;
4. If (stage number <N and m/the numbers of detected image>f) Go to step 2. Else Exit.

4 Experiment

In this section, a face detection system on the cellular phone using our proposed algorithm is implemented. The performance of our algorithm and standard AdaBoost algorithm is also compared. The performance evaluation concentrates on the speed, complexity of the learned cascaded classifiers and the memory occupy under the cellular phone environment.

4.1 Training Dataset

We collected 10000 face images and 20,000 non-faces images from various sources, such as AR, FERET, and from WEB, covering the out-of-plane rotation in the range of [-20°, +20°] of out-of-plane rotations. The dataset contains face images of variable quality, different facial expressions and taken under wide range of lightning conditions. The 10000 face images are cropped and rescaled to the size of 20×20. 5000 face images and 10000 non-face images are used in training and other images are used in GA post optimization.

4.2 Training Process

The training is implement on PC with CPU of AMD AlthonXP2500+. Two face detection systems were trained: One is standard AdaBoost and one with our novel post-optimization procedure for each completed stage classifier.

Parameters used for evolution were: 80% of all individuals undergo crossover ($p_c = 0.8$), 10% of all individuals were mutated ($p_m = 0.1$) and the population was initialized randomly. The GA terminated if the population was converged to a good solution so that no better individual was found within the next 5000 generations. If convergence did not occur within 10000 generations, the GA was stopped as well.

4.3 Experiment Results

Our face detection system is implemented using C language with ARM compiler. The system is tested on a mobile phone that integrates with a CCD camera; 2MB of RAM and ARM926EJ-S processor that lacks floating-point hardware.

We tested our system on the BIO face test set [11]. This set consists of 1520 images with 1521-labeled frontal faces with a large variety of illumination and face size, and very complex background. This database is believed to be more difficult than some commonly used head-and-shoulder face database without complex background.

The ROC curve over the Bio-FaceDabase test is shown in Figure 5. The mode and the average detection time of two face detection systems are listed in Table 1.The numbers of weak classifiers trained by standard Adaboost and our novel GA-post-optimization procedure for each completed stage classifier are summarized in Table 2.

Table 1. Model size and detection time of two face detector on the cellular phone

Face Detector	Model size	Average detection time
With GA-post-optimization	80KB	275ms
Without GA-post-optimization	110KB	395ms

Table 2. the nuber of weak classifiers by with and without GA-post-optimization

Stage No.	Number of weak classifiers		Stage No.	Number of weak classifiers	
	AdaBoost	GA-post-optimization		AdaBoost	GA-post-optimization
1	13	10	8	82	60
2	17	11	9	113	86
3	22	15	10	128	94
4	29	20	11	157	107
5	39	29	12	160	122
6	48	34	13	138	97
7	58	41	Total	1004	726

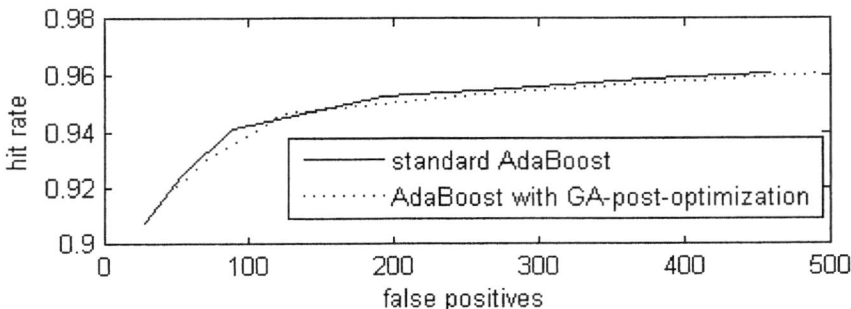

Fig. 5. ROC cures for the face detector based on AdaBoost with and without GA-post-optimization on the Bio test set. The tests were run on a SANYO cellular phone with ARM926EJ-S processor that lacks floating-point hardware.

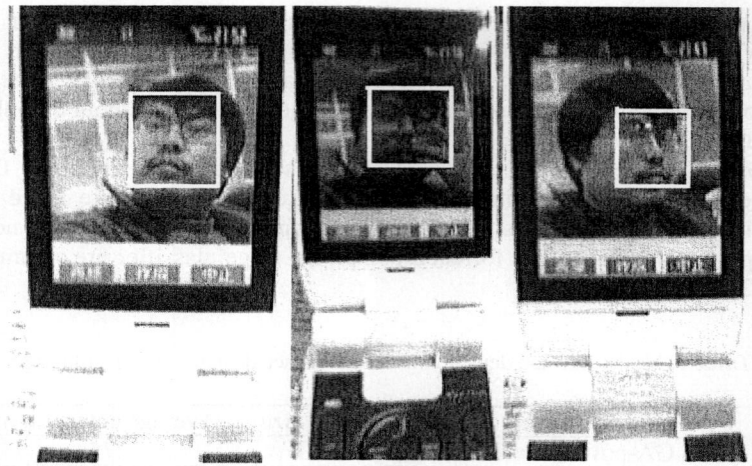

Fig. 6. Sample experiment results of our mobile phone embedded face detection system on real-time detection

From the experiment results shown in Table 1 and Table 2, we can see that the numbers of weak classifier of each stage classifiers are reduced due to the Genetic Algorithms optimization. The model size of face detector with GA-optimization is also about 30% smaller. This is very important, as the memory resource of the mobile phone is only a few KB. Due to the features reduction, the average detection time of face detector with GA-optimization is about 30% faster. And the performance of detection is only slightly dropped, which can be seeing from Fig.5.

Some real-time detection results using our mobile phone embedded face detection system are shown in Fig.6. As can be seen in Fig.6, our system is able to detect face in variable lighting conditions and movements such as rotation, scaling, up and down, profile, and occlusion.

5 Conclusion

In this paper, we present a novel stage post-optimization procedure for boosted classifiers by applying the genetic algorithms. This method effectively improves the learning results. The classifier trained by the novel method was about 22% faster and consists of only 70% of the weak classifiers needed for a classifier trained by standard AdaBoost while the detection rate only slightly decrease. The reduction of the model size can be very important in mobile phone context where the weak classifiers are expensive to compute and implement. Experimental results show that our object detection framework is very suitable for the resource-limit devices, including mobile phones, smart cards or other special purpose due to the reduction of the number of weak classifiers. Our GA-post-optimization algorithms can also be applied with other boosting algorithms like e.g. FloatBoost [5] or GentleBoost [7].

References

1. Rowly, H., Baluja, S., and Kanade, T.: Neural network-based face detection. PAMI, Vol. 20 (1998) 23-38
2. Viola, P., Jones, M.: Rapid object detection using a boosted cascade of simple features. IEEE CVPR, (2001) 511~518
3. Romdhani, S., Torr, P., Schoelkopf, B., and Blake, A.: Computationally efficient face detection. In Proc. Intl. Conf. Computer Vision, (2001) 695–700
4. Henry, S., Takeo, K.: A statistical model for 3d object detection applied to faces and cars. In IEEE Conference on Computer Vision and Pattern Recognition. (2000)
5. Freund, Y., Schapire, R.: A diction-theoretic generalization of on-line learning and an application to boosting. Journal of Computer and System Sciences, Vol. 55 (1997) 119-
6. Li,S.Z., Zhang, Z.Q., Harry, S., and Zhang, H.J.: FloatBoost learning for classification. In Proc.CVPR, (2001) 511-518
7. Lienhart, R., Kuranov, A., and Pisarevsky, V.: Empirical analysis of detection cascades of boosted classifiers for rapid object detection. Technical report, MRL, Intel Labs, (2002)
8. Viola, P., Jones, M.: Fast and robust classification using asymmetric AdaBoost and a detector cascade. In NIPS 14, (2002)
9. Goldberg, D.E.: Genetic algorithms in search, optimization, and machine learning, Addison-Wesley, Reading, A (1989)
10. Sung, K.K.: Learning and Example Selection for Object and Pattern Detection. PhD thesis, MIT AI Lab, January (1996)
11. http://www.bioid.com/downloads/facedb/facedatabase.html

Proper Output Feedback H$_\infty$ Control for Descriptor Systems: A Convex Optimization Approach

Lei Guo[1], Keyou Zhao[2], and Chunbo Feng[1]

[1] Research Institute of Automation,
Southeast University, Nanjing 210096, China
[2] School of Automation Engineering,
Qingdao University, Qingdao, 266071, China

Abstract. In this paper, the H$_\infty$ control problem is considered for linear descriptor systems by using convex optimization approaches. By giving sufficient and necessary conditions for the output feedback H$_\infty$ control problem, feasible LMI-based design approaches are presented for both generalized and proper H$_\infty$ controller. All proper H$_\infty$ controllers are constructed via solutions of LMIs based on convex algorithms. These results generalize the standard H$_\infty$ control theory for normal systems to that for descriptor ones.

1 Introduction

In the last decade, the control problems for descriptor systems (or generalized systems, singular systems) have drawn the considerable attention of many researchers due to their extensive applications in chemical processes, large scale systems, singular perturbation theory, electrical networks, economic systems, macroeconomic systems, and other areas. Recently, many LMI-based analysis and synthesis approaches have extensively been presented for H_∞ control problems (see *e.g.* [1]~[6]). However, the existing results only considered the generalized output feedback controller design problems, which required re-computations of perturbed synthesis LMIs and inversion of the possible ill-conditioned results. In this paper, 3-LMIs based sufficient and necessary conditions are presented for both generalized and proper H_∞ controller design.

2 Main Results

Consider the unforced descriptor system Σ_D^f described by $\begin{cases} E\dot{x} = Ax + Bw \\ z = Cx + Dw \end{cases}$, Σ_D^f is called to be *admissible* if Σ_D^f is regular and has neither impulsive modes nor unstable finite modes. It can be shown that Σ_D^f is admissible and satisfies

$$\|G(s)\| := \left\|C(sE - A)^{-1}B + D\right\|_\infty < \gamma$$

if and only if there exists X satisfying (see [6])

$$E^T X = X^T E \geq 0, \quad \begin{bmatrix} X^T A + A^T X & X^T B & C^T \\ B^T X & -\gamma^2 I & D^T \\ C & D & -I \end{bmatrix} < 0. \quad (1)$$

The generalized descriptor plant Σ_D can be described by

$$\Sigma_D : \begin{cases} E\dot{x} = Ax + B_1 w + B_2 u \\ z = C_1 x + D_{11} w + D_{12} u \\ y = C_2 x + D_{21} w \end{cases}, \quad (2)$$

where $x \in R^n$, $w \in R^{m_1}$, $u \in R^{m_2}$, $y \in R^{p_2}$ and $z \in R^{p_1}$ are the state, the exogenous input, the control input, the measurement output and the controlled output, respectively. Consider the controller Σ_c with order n_c described as $\begin{cases} E_c \dot{x}_c = A_c x_c + B_c y \\ u = C_c x_c + D_c y \end{cases}$, where x_c is the state of the controller. We call Σ_c as a *generalized* controller if $rank E_c < n_c$, and a *proper* one if $E = I$. Σ_c is named as an H_∞ *controller* if Σ_{cl} is admissible and satisfies

$$\|C_{cl}(sE_{cl} - A_{cl})^{-1} B_{cl} + D_{cl}\|_\infty < \gamma.$$

Correspondingly the closed-loop system Σ_{cl} is given by $\begin{cases} E_{cl} \dot{x} = A_{cl} x + B_{cl} w \\ z = C_{cl} x + D_{cl} w \end{cases}$, where

$$\begin{bmatrix} A_{cl} & B_{cl} \\ C_{cl} & D_{cl} \end{bmatrix} := \begin{bmatrix} \hat{A} & \hat{B}_1 \\ \hat{C}_1 & \hat{D}_{11} \end{bmatrix} + \begin{bmatrix} \hat{B}_2 \\ \hat{D}_{12} \end{bmatrix} G \begin{bmatrix} \hat{C}_2 & \hat{D}_{21} \end{bmatrix}, \quad E_{cl} := \begin{bmatrix} E & 0 \\ 0 & E_c \end{bmatrix},$$

and

$$\begin{bmatrix} \hat{A} & \hat{B}_1 & \hat{B}_2 \\ \hat{C}_1 & \hat{D}_{11} & \hat{D}_{12} \\ \hat{C}_2 & \hat{D}_{21} & G^T \end{bmatrix} := \begin{bmatrix} A & 0 & B_1 & B_2 & 0 \\ 0 & 0 & 0 & 0 & I_{n_c} \\ C_1 & 0 & D_{11} & D_{12} & 0 \\ C_2 & 0 & D_{21} & D_c^T & B_c^T \\ 0 & I_{n_c} & 0 & C_c^T & A_c^T \end{bmatrix}. \quad (3)$$

In the following, we will give 3-LMI based results for output feedback H_∞ control of descriptor system. Applying Lemma 1 to the closed-loop system Σ_{cl}, the first equation of (1) can be rewritten as

$$\begin{bmatrix} E & 0 \\ 0 & E_c \end{bmatrix}^T \begin{bmatrix} X_{11} & X_{12} \\ X_{21} & X_{22} \end{bmatrix} = \begin{bmatrix} X_{11} & X_{12} \\ X_{21} & X_{22} \end{bmatrix}^T \begin{bmatrix} E & 0 \\ 0 & E_c \end{bmatrix} \geq 0, \quad (4)$$

where $\begin{bmatrix} X_{11} & X_{12} \\ X_{21} & X_{22} \end{bmatrix} := X$ compatible with A_{cl}. Correspondingly we denote $Y := X^{-T} = \begin{bmatrix} Y_{11} & Y_{12} \\ Y_{21} & Y_{22} \end{bmatrix}$, where

$$\begin{cases} Y_{11} := (X_{11}^T - X_{21}^T X_{11}^{-T} X_{12}^T)^{-1}, Y_{12} := -Y_{11} X_{21}^T X_{22}^{-T}, \\ Y_{21} := -X_{22}^{-T} X_{12}^T Y_{11}, Y_{22} := X_{22}^{-T} + X_{22}^{-T} X_{12}^T Y_{11} X_{21}^T X_{22}^{-T}. \end{cases} \quad (5)$$

(5) implies
$$R^T - S^{-1} = X_{21}^T X_{22}^{-T} X_{12}^T, \tag{6}$$
and (4) results to $E^T X_{11} = X_{11}^T E \geq 0$ and
$$\begin{cases} E^T X_{12} = X_{21}^T E_c, \\ E_c^T X_{22} = X_{22}^T E_c \geq 0. \end{cases} \tag{7}$$

On the other hand, similarly to the derivation for the conventional systems (see [2]), the second equation of (1) yields
$$\hat{U} G \hat{V} + (\hat{U} G \hat{V})^T + \hat{\Omega} < 0, \tag{8}$$
where
$$\hat{U} := \begin{bmatrix} X^T \hat{B}_2 \\ 0 \\ \hat{D}_{12} \end{bmatrix}, \ \hat{V}^T := \begin{bmatrix} \hat{C}_2^T \\ \hat{D}_{21}^T \\ 0 \end{bmatrix}, \ \hat{\Omega} := \begin{bmatrix} \hat{A}^T X + X^T \hat{A} & X^T \hat{B}_1 & \hat{C}_1^T \\ \hat{B}_1^T X & -\gamma^2 I & \hat{D}_{11}^T \\ \hat{C}_1 & \hat{D}_{11} & -I \end{bmatrix}.$$

Denote $R := X_{11}$ and $S := Y_{11}$. It can be verified that (8) holds if and only if
$$\begin{bmatrix} C_2^T \\ D_{21}^T \\ 0 \end{bmatrix}^\perp \begin{bmatrix} A^T R + R^T A & R^T B_1 & C_1^T \\ B_1^T R & -\gamma^2 I & D_{11}^T \\ C_1 & D_{11} & -I \end{bmatrix} \begin{bmatrix} C_2^T \\ D_{21}^T \\ 0 \end{bmatrix}^{\perp T} < 0, \tag{9}$$
and
$$\begin{bmatrix} B_2 \\ 0 \\ D_{12} \end{bmatrix}^\perp \begin{bmatrix} SA^T + AS^T & B_1 & SC_1^T \\ B_1^T & -\gamma^2 I & D_{11}^T \\ C_1 S^T & D_{11} & -I \end{bmatrix} \begin{bmatrix} B_2 \\ 0 \\ D_{12} \end{bmatrix}^{\perp T} < 0. \tag{10}$$

Theorem 1. *For the system Σ_D described by (2), there exists a generalized H_∞ controller Σ_c if and only if there exist nonsingular matrices S, R satisfying (9), (10), and*
$$(R^T - S^{-1})E \geq 0, E^T R = R^T E \geq 0, SE^T = ES^T \geq 0. \tag{11}$$

In this case, for any X_{12}, X_{21}, X_{22} and E_c satisfying the constraint (6) and (7), then the controllers with order $\text{rank} X_{22}$ can be solved via (8). Especially, X_{12}, X_{21}, X_{22} and E_c can be selected to be
$$X_{12} := X_{22} := X_{21} := R - S^{-T}, \ E_c := E, \tag{12}$$
which satisfy (6) and (7) naturally.

Proof is omitted for brevity.

Without loss of generality, in the following we assume $E := \begin{bmatrix} I & 0 \\ 0 & 0 \end{bmatrix}$ to find feasible approaches compatible with Matlab. The following result can be obtained by using Theorem 1.

Theorem 2. *For the system Σ_D described by (2) with $E := \begin{bmatrix} I & 0 \\ 0 & 0 \end{bmatrix}$, there exists a generalized H_∞ controller Σ_c if and only if there exist nonsingular matrices S, R, described by*

$$S = \begin{bmatrix} S_1 & S_{12} \\ 0 & S_2 \end{bmatrix}, R = \begin{bmatrix} R_1 & 0 \\ R_{21} & R_2 \end{bmatrix}, \tag{13}$$

satisfying $\begin{bmatrix} R_1 & I \\ I & S_1 \end{bmatrix} > 0$, (9) and (10). In this case, for any X_{12}, X_{21}, X_{22} and E_c satisfying the constraint (6) and (7), then the controllers with order $\text{rank} X_{22}$ can be solved via (8). Especially, X_{12}, X_{21}, X_{22} and E_c can also be constructed by (12) and consequently obtain the controllers via (8).

Based on this result, the LMI-toolbox in Matlab can be applicable directly and the feasible design steps can be given as follows: (i) solve the LMIs (9), (10) to obtain a pair of R and S with the description of (13); (ii) construct X using (12) and then solve LMI (8) for the parameters A_c, B_c, C_c and D_c of Σ_c.

In the above two results, only generalized controllers were studied, which generally are difficult to realize. The following result gives a necessary and sufficient condition for the proper H_∞ control problem for Σ_D.

Theorem 3. *For the system Σ_D with $E := \begin{bmatrix} I & 0 \\ 0 & 0 \end{bmatrix}$, there exists a proper H_∞ controller Σ_c if and only if there exist nonsingular matrices S, R described as (13) which satisfy (9), (10), $\begin{bmatrix} R_1 & I \\ I & S_1 \end{bmatrix} > 0$ and $S_2 R_2^T = I$. In this case, for any X_{11}, X_{12}, X_{21}, X_{22} constructed by*

$$X_{11} := R, X_{21} = \begin{bmatrix} X_{121}^T & 0 \end{bmatrix}, X_{12}^T = \begin{bmatrix} X_{121}^T & X_{122}^T \end{bmatrix}, X_{22} > 0, \tag{14}$$

which satisfy

$$\begin{cases} X_{121} X_{22}^{-1} X_{121}^T = R_1^T - S_1^{-1} \\ X_{121} X_{22}^{-1} X_{122}^T = R_{21}^T + S_1^{-1} S_{12} S_2^{-1} \end{cases}, \tag{15}$$

the controllers with $n_c = \text{rank} X_{22}$ can be solved via (8). Especially, we can choose

$$X_{121} := X_{22} := R_1^T - S_1^{-1}, X_{122} := R_{21} + S_2^{-T} S_{12}^T S_1^{-T},$$

which satisfy (15) naturally.

Proof: $(ii) \Longrightarrow (i)$: If there exist matrices S, R described by (13) satisfying (9), (10) and (11), then we have

$$R^T - S^{-1} := \begin{bmatrix} R_1^T - S_1^{-1} & R_{21}^T + S_1^{-1} S_{12} S_2^{-1} \\ 0 & 0 \end{bmatrix}. \tag{16}$$

Partitioning $X_{12} := \begin{bmatrix} X_{121} \\ X_{122} \end{bmatrix}$ compatible with E. Based on the second equation of (7), we can choose X_{22} as any positive definite matrix, such as I, without loss of generality. From the second equation of (7) we select $X_{21}^T = \begin{bmatrix} X_{121} \\ 0 \end{bmatrix}$, and from the first one, select X_{121} and X_{122} by (15). And $R_1^T - S_1^{-1} > 0$ guarantees the existence of a nonsingular X_{121}. Then we can construct X as (14) and (15) to satisfy (8).

$(i) \Longrightarrow (ii)$: If (i) holds, there then exists a partitioned matrix X satisfying (4) and (1) for the closed loop system. From (4), or equivalently, (7), we can also get (11), where S and R constructed by (13) satisfy $\begin{bmatrix} R_1 & I \\ I & S_1 \end{bmatrix} > 0$. Partitioning $X_{12} := \begin{bmatrix} X_{121} \\ X_{122} \end{bmatrix}$ compatible with E, from the second equation of (7) we have $X_{21}^T = \begin{bmatrix} X_{121} \\ 0 \end{bmatrix}$, which implies $R_2^T - S_2^{-1} = 0$ by means of the first one of (7). Similarly to necessity of Theorem 1, (9) and (10) result from the first equation of (1). Q.E.D

Based on Theorem 3, we can give an LMI-based iterative procedure to design proper H_∞ controllers for descriptor systems.

3 Conclusions

This paper presents LMI-based approaches to the output feedback H_∞ control problem for descriptor systems. Feasible LMI-based procedures are given to design both of the generalized and proper output feedback H_∞ controllers. The results can be generalized to some other dissipative control problems with quadratic performance for descriptor systems.

Acknowledgement. This work is jointly supported by *National Science Foundation of China under Grant 60474050 and 60174040.*

References

1. Guo, L., Lam, L.: Robust H_∞ performance problem for linear systems with nonlinear uncertainties in all system matrices. Int. J. Systems Sci., **33** (2002) 885-900
2. Guo, L., Malabre, M.: Robust H_∞ control for descriptor systems with non-linear uncertainties. Int. J. Control, **76** (2003) 1254-1262
3. Lin, C., Wang, J., Yang, G. H., Lam, J.: Robust stabilization via state feedback for descriptor systems with uncertainties in the derivative matrix. Int. J. Control, **73** (2000) 407-415
4. Masubuchi, I., Kamitane, Y., Ohara, A., Suda, N.: H_∞ control for descriptor systems: A matrix inequalities approach. Automatica, **33** (1997) 669-673
5. Rehm, A., Allgower, F.: Descriptor and non-descriptor controllers in H_∞ control of descriptor systems. In Proc. 3th IFAC Symposium on Robust Control Design, Prague, (2000) pages 63-69
6. Takaba, K.: Robust H^2 control of descriptor system with time-varying unceratinty. Int. J. Control, **71** (1998) 559-579

Planning Optimal Trajectories for Mobile Robots Using an Evolutionary Method with Fuzzy Components

Serkan Aydin and Hakan Temeltas

Istanbul Technical University,
Electric-Electronic Faculty, Electric Engineering Department,
34390, Maslak, Istanbul, Turkey,
{aydinsk, temeltas}@elk.itu.edu.tr

Abstract. This study describes a generation of globally time optimal trajectories for a mobile robot in predefined environment. The primary task in the study is to apply Differential Evolution (DE) method for definition of globally time-optimal trajectories under environmental and dynamical constraints. The planned trajectories are composed of line segments and curve segments. The structures of the curve segments are determined by using only two parameters such as a turn angle θ and a translation velocity on the curve v_{t_start}. All possible curve segments in parameters range $\theta \in (0, \pi]°$, v_{t_start} [0,40] inch and $a_{t\_turn} \in [-a_{t\_max}, a_{t\_max}]$ inch/sec^2 form a curve segments set. Then DE, is used to find time optimal trajectory from this set. Experimental results are given and the results are shown successfully.

1 Introduction

Motion planning is an important task in the robot navigation that defines a path between initial and final configuration of a mobile robot. The motion planning studies can be separated into two groups such as explicit and implicit motion planning [1,2,3,4]. If the aim of robot motion is only reaching the desired configuration or final point, explicit methods are sufficient. However the implicit planning techniques are widely used when optimization criteria on the path are desired or to make sure the certain properties of the trajectory (i.e. optimal-time or distance). In this approach, obstacle information from the environment and the constraints of the mobile robot are used and consequently global-optimal solutions can be obtained. But it has two disadvantages: 1) random supplied initial values starting to numerical solutions. In some cases the correct results cannot be obtained. 2) Still, there is a necessity for using a controller. Aim of this study is to obtain global-time optimal trajectory planning for mobile robots using a derivative free optimization method such as DE approach. The most important disadvantage of the evolutionary methods is long optimization time. To partially overcome this problem a Fuzzy Inference System (FIS) model is used to form the curve segments instead of serial expansion of the robot's equations. In the next section, line and curve segments are derived from MR's equations. In section 3,

Modified DE is introduced and objective function and nonlinear constraints are formed. Global optimality of the obtained results is investigated in section 4. After that, applications and experimental results are given and the paper is concluded at the last section 6.

2 Trajectory Components

In this study, the planned trajectories are composed of *line segments* (steering deceleration/deceleration (acc/dec) $a_S=0$, velocity $v_S=0$ and translation acc/dec $a_t=a_{t\_max}$) and *curve segments* (translation acceleration/deceleration and $a_t=a_{t\_turn}$ =constant, $v_{t0}=v_{t\_start}$ =constant and steering acc/dec $a_s=a_{s\_max}$). The state vector of the Nomad 200 is $\mathbf{x}=(x, y, \theta)^T$ where x and y represent coordinates for center of the MR while θ represents orientation of the MR. MR's equations are given by :

$$\dot{x}=v_t\cos(\theta)=v_x \;,\; \dot{y}=v_t\sin(\theta)=v_y \;,\; \dot{\theta}=v_s, \; \dot{v}_t=a_t, \; \dot{v}_s=a_s. \qquad (1)$$

These parameters, however have boundaries to used in the optimization procedure. Numericaly, the maximum value of velocities and accelerations of the mobile robot system are $v_{t\_max}=40"/s$, $v_{s\_max}=0.785$ rad/s, $a_{t\_max}=30"/s^2$ and $a_{s\_max}=0.875$ rad/s^2. If $a_t=a_{t\_max}$, $a_s=a_{s\_max}$ and then Eq. 1 can be solved [7].

Line Segments. In the solved Eqs, if $a_s=0$ and $v_s=0$ are taken Eq. 2 is obtained:

$$x=x_0+\int_0^t\{(v_{t0}+a_tt)\cos(\theta_0)\}_{a_t=a_{t\_max}}dt=\left\{x_0+\left(v_{t0}t+a_t\frac{t^2}{2}\right)\cos(\theta_0)\right\}_{a_t=a_{t\_max}}$$

$$y=y_0+\int_0^t\{(v_{t0}+a_tt)\sin(\theta_0)\}_{a_t=a_{t\_max}}dt=\left\{y_0+\left(v_{t0}t+a_t\frac{t^2}{2}\right)\sin(\theta_0)\right\}_{a_t=a_{t\_max}} \qquad (2)$$

Curve Segments. Again from the definition of the curve segments, v_t and a_t are taken as constant values, v_{t_start} and a_{t_turn} respectively, Eq. 3 is obtained:

$$x=x_0+\int_0^t\left\{(v_{t0}+a_tt)\cos\left(\theta_0+v_{s0}t+\frac{a_st^2}{2}\right)\right\}_{\substack{a_s=a_{s\_max}\\a_t=a_{t\_turn}\\v_{t0}=v_{t\_start}}}dt \;;$$

$$y=y_0+\int_0^t\left\{(v_{t0}+a_tt)\sin\left(\theta_0+v_{s0}t+\frac{a_st^2}{2}\right)\right\}_{\substack{a_s=a_{s\_max}\\a_t=a_{t\_turn}\\v_{t0}=v_{t\_start}}}dt \qquad (3).$$

Eq. 3 can only be solved with using Mclauren series expansion. At the curve segments the turning angle is known, that's why switching times of a_s and a_t. If θ_0, v_{s0} and a_{smax} are known in Eq. 3 then x and y can be obtained according to the switching times of a_s [7]. It's meant that, the structures of the curves are determined by only two parameters (θ: turn angle and v_{t0}: translation velocity in the curve segment). A curves set is formed by all possible curves in parameters range $\theta \in (0,\pi]°$ and vt0 [0, v_{t_max}] inch. It is clear that, if the ($\theta, v_{t\_start}, a_{t\_turn}$) triple is known, the curve segment is known and there is no need to design a controller to track this curve segment.

3 DE Optimization in Trajectory Planning

DE [5] operates on candidate solutions of *population* P_G in G^{th} *generation* and these are *individuals* of the population. The representation of NP vectors of the Gth generation of the population may be written as $P_G = (V_{1,G},......,V_{NP,G})$ $G=0,...,G_{max}$,

$$V_i=(\theta_1, \theta_2,...\theta_{D-1}, v_{t\_start1}, v_{t\_start\ 2},...v_{t\_start\ D}, x_1, y_1, k_2,...k_D, a_{t\_turn1}, a_{t\_turn2},...a_{t\_turnD}) \quad (4)$$

where i=1,...,NP, D is the number of the curve segments in the trajectory (so that, there are D+1 line segments in the trajectory), θ_i is the turn angle of the orientation which is realized by the ith curve segment, $v_{t\_start\ i}$ is the starting translation velocity to the ith curve segment, a_{t_turni} is the acc/dec value in the ith curve segment, (x_1,y_1) is the first curve segments center position (in T region) and k_i is the ith line segment length (Fig. 1a). There are 4D parameters in a parameter vector V_i.

3.2 Optimization Function and Equations of Constraints

Before giving the objective function, some symbols will be declared in Fig. 1b. In Fig. 1b: θ_i : turn angle and v_{ti} is the constant translation velocity of ith curve segment which are given above. α_i : distance from the initial point of the ith curve segment and the intersection point of the ith and $(i+1)^{th}$ line segments and if the ith curve segment's initial point is taken as (0,0) and final point is taken as (x_i, y_i) (calculated from Eq. 3), α_i can be calculated from the equation

$$\alpha_i = \sqrt{\frac{(x_i^2 + y_i^2)}{4}\left(1 + \frac{1}{(\tan(\pi - |\theta_i|))^2}\right)} \quad (5)$$

d_i : necessary distance to increase/decrease v_{ti} to v_{ti+1}, if $v_{ti} \neq v_{ti+1}$. c_i : difference distance between i^{th} line segment length, L_i and d_i. It is clear that c_i must be equal or greater than 0 for a feasible trajectory. These, $c_i(V) = L_i - d_i \geq 0$ $i = 1,...D+1$ are the first D+1 constraints of the problem. In these constraints, d_i can be calculated by:

$$d_i = \begin{cases} v_{t\_starti-1}t_{di} + t_{di}\dfrac{1}{2a_{t\_max}}(v_{t\_starti-1} - v_{t\_starti})^2 & \text{if} \quad v_{t\_starti-1} < v_{t\_starti} \\ v_{ti\_start-1}t_{di}) - t_{di}\dfrac{1}{2a_{t\_max}}(v_{t\_starti-1} - v_{t\_starti})^2 & \text{if} \quad v_{t\_starti-1} \geq v_{t\_starti} \end{cases}$$

$$t_{di} = \begin{cases} \dfrac{v_{t\_starti}}{a_{t\_max}} & \text{for} \quad i=1 \quad i = D+1 \\ \dfrac{(v_{t\_starti} - v_{t\_starti-1})}{a_{t\_max}} & \text{if} \quad v_{t\_starti-1} < v_{t\_start\,i} \\ \dfrac{(v_{t\_starti-1} - v_{t\_starti})}{a_{t\_max}} & \text{if} \quad v_{t\_start\,i-1} \geq v_{t\_start\,i} \end{cases} \quad i=[2,D] \quad (6)$$

The other 2D+1 constraints are:

$$c_k(V) = -(L_i \cap (O_1 \cup .... \cup O_n)), \quad c_k(V) = -(Y_i \cap (O_1 \cup .... \cup O_n)),$$
$$k = D+2, ... 2(D+1) \quad i=1,...D+1 \qquad k = 2(D+1)+1,...,3(D+1)-1 \quad i=1,...D$$

Where L_i: i^{th} line segment length, O_i: i^{th} polygonal obstacle, Y_i: i^{th} curve segment and n: the number of obstacles. In these Eqns, there are 3D+2 constraints.

The objective function f(V) is:

$$f(V) = \sum_{i=1}^{D+1} \begin{cases} t_{ci} + t_{di} + t_{vti}/2 & \text{for} \quad i = 1 \\ t_{vti-1}/2 + t_{di} + t_{ci} + t_{vti}/2 & \text{for} \quad i \in [2, D] \\ t_{vti-1}/2 + t_{ci} + t_{di} & \text{for} \quad i = D+1 \end{cases} \quad (7)$$

where t_{ci}, t_{vti} and t_{di} necessary times for c_i distance on i^{th} line segment, for i^{th} curve segment and d_i distance on i^{th} line segment respectively. t_{vti} can be written as:

$$t_{vti} = \begin{cases} \dfrac{\theta_i - (a_{s\_max} t_{as\_max}^2)}{v_{s\,max}} + 2t_{as\_max} & \text{for} \quad \theta_i > (a_{s\_max} t_{as\_max}^2) \\ 2\sqrt{\dfrac{\theta_i}{a_{s\_max}}} & \text{otherwise} \end{cases} \quad (8)$$

where $t_{as\_max} = t_{ds\_max} = \dfrac{v_{s\_max}}{a_{s\_max}}$ (t_{as_max}, is the necessary time from 0 to v_{s_max}

and t_{ds_max}, is necessary time from v_{s_max} to 0). θ_i i^{th} turn angle (Fig. 1). t_{ci} in Eq. 7 is:

$$t_{ci} = \begin{cases} t_{cia} + t_{cik} + t_{cid} & \text{for} \quad v_{tci} = v_{t\_max} \\ t_{cia} + t_{cid} & \text{for} \quad v_{tci} < v_{t\_max} \end{cases} \quad (9)$$

Planning Optimal Trajectories for Mobile Robots   707

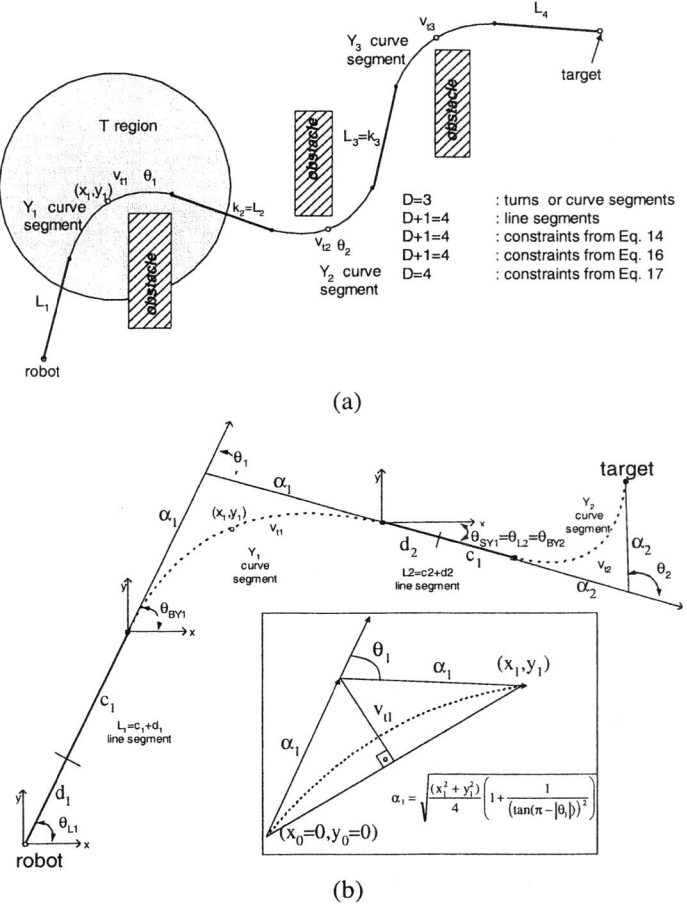

Fig. 1. a) A 3 curve segmented trajectory b) L_1, L_2 line segment lengths; α_1 α_2 necessary distance to achieve the turn in $v_{t\_start\ 1}$ $v_{t\_start\ 2}$ respectively; d_1 is distance to velocity change 0 to v_{t1}; d_2 is distance to velocity change v_{t1} to v_{t2}; $L_1=c_1+d_1$, $L_2=c_2+d_2$

where, v_{tci}: max reachable translation velocity on i^{th} line segment, t_{cia}: necessary time to reach from v_{ti-1} to v_{tci}, t_{cid}: from v_{tci} to v_{ti} and t_{cik}: if v_{tci} is equal to v_{t_max}, then the time to travel at v_{t_max} velocity. It is clear that, v_{tci}, t_{cia}, t_{cik} and t_{cid} values must be calculated for Eq. 9. By using:

$$K1_i = \sqrt{\frac{v_{t\_starti}^2}{2} + (c_i + d_i)a_{t\_max}} \quad , \quad K2_i = \sqrt{\frac{v_{t\_starti-1}^2}{2} + \frac{v_{t\_starti}^2}{2} + (c_i + d_i)a_{t\_max}} \quad \text{and}$$

$$K3_i = \sqrt{\frac{v_{t\_starti-1}^2}{2} + (c_i + d_i)a_{t\_max}} \quad , \quad v_{tci} \text{ can be found from:}$$

$$v_{tci} = \begin{cases} K1_i & if \quad K1_i \leq v_{t\_max} \wedge i=1 \\ K2_i & if \quad K2_i \leq v_{t\_max} \wedge i \in [2,D] \\ K3_i & if \quad K3_i \leq v_{t\_max} \wedge i = D+1 \\ v_{t\_max} & otherwise \end{cases} \quad (10)$$

t_{cia}, t_{cid} and t_{cik} can be represented by:

$$t_{cia} = \begin{cases} \dfrac{v_{tci} - v_{t\_starti}}{a_{t\_max}} & for \quad i \in [1,D] \\ \dfrac{v_{tci} - v_{t\_starti-1}}{a_{t\_max}} & for \quad i = D+1 \end{cases} ; \quad t_{cid} = \begin{cases} \dfrac{v_{tci} - v_{t\_starti}}{a_{t\_max}} & for \quad i \in [1,D] \\ \dfrac{v_{tci} - v_{t\_starti-1}}{a_{t\_max}} & for \quad i = D+1 \end{cases} \quad (11)$$

$$t_{cik} = \begin{cases} \left[c_i - \left(v_{t\_starti} t_{cia} + \dfrac{1}{2} a_{t\_max} t_{cia}^2 + v_{t\_starti} t_{cid} - \dfrac{1}{2} a_{t\_max} t_{cid}^2 \right) \right] / v_{tci} & for \quad i \in [1,D] \\ \left[c_i - \left(v_{t\_starti-1} t_{cia} + \dfrac{1}{2} a_{t\_max} t_{cia}^2 + v_{t\_starti-1} t_{cid} - \dfrac{1}{2} a_{t\_max} t_{cid}^2 \right) \right] / v_{tci} & for \quad i = D+1 \end{cases} \quad (12)$$

The trajectory length is found by

$$g(V) = \sum_{i=1}^{D+1} \begin{cases} d_i + c_i + \ell\_curve_i / 2 & for \quad i = 1 \\ \ell\_curve_{i-1}/2 + d_i + c_i + \ell\_curve_i / 2 & for \quad i \in [2, D] \\ \ell\_curve_{i-1}/2 + c_i + d_i & for \quad i = D+1 \end{cases} \quad (13)$$

Where,

$$\ell\_curve_i = \begin{cases} \begin{rcases} (v_{t\_starti} t_{ai}) + (v_{t\_max}(t_{\theta i} - t_{ai})) & if \quad a_{t\_turni} \geq 0 \\ v_{t\_starti} t_{ai} & if \quad a_{t\_turni} < 0 \end{rcases} & if \quad t_{\theta i} \geq (t_{ai} + t_{di}) \\ \begin{rcases} \left(2v_{t\_starti} + a_{t\_turni} \dfrac{t_{\theta i}}{2} \right) \dfrac{t_{\theta i}}{2} & if \quad a_{t\_turni} \geq 0 \\ \left(2v_{t\_starti} - a_{t\_turni} \dfrac{t_{\theta i}}{2} \right) \dfrac{t_{\theta i}}{2} & if \quad a_{t\_turni} < 0 \end{rcases} & if \quad t_{\theta i} < (t_{ai} + t_{di}) \end{cases}$$

here $t_{di} = t_{ai} = \begin{cases} \dfrac{v_{t\_max} - v_{t\_starti}}{a_{t\_turni}} & a_{t\_turni} \geq 0 \\ \dfrac{v_{t\_starti} - 0}{a_{t\_turni}} & a_{t\_turni} < 0 \end{cases} \quad i \in [1,D]$ and $t_{\theta i} = t_{vti}$.

3.3 Building FIS for α

At the calculation of α (Eq. 5), Eq. 3 must be evaluated. Alternatively, to decrease the calculation time of the objective function, fuzzy inference system (FIS), which is trained, by adaptive fuzzy inference system (ANFIS) [6] is used. There are three inputs, turning angle ($\theta \in [1°\text{-}150°]$), velocity ($v_{t\_starti} \in [1\text{-}40]$ inch) and acc/dec ($a_{t\_turni} \in [-a_{t\_max}, a_{t\_max}]$ inch/sec^2) one output, α_i. ANFIS is trained with 1064 pairs and tested with 23779 pairs. Different membership functions are trained and Triangle 2:2:2 (3 input and each has 2 triangle Mfs) is taken. The error values relative percent max error, E_M, mean error, E_O, and bigger than %5, E_5 are evaluated by using:

$$E_O(\%) = 1/n \sum_{i=1}^{n} 100|\varepsilon_i| \; ; E_M = \max(|100E|) \% \, , \, E_5 = \{\varepsilon_i | \; |100\varepsilon_i| > 5; i \in [1,n]\}$$

where, $E = \{\varepsilon_i | \; \varepsilon_i = (\alpha_{di} - \alpha_{ri})/\alpha_{ri} \; i \in [1,n]\}$ is defined as the relative error set, α_{di}: desired α_i value, α_{ri}: FIS output value and ε_i: relative error value. In the training and test phase error values are E_M=14.43 %, E_M=14.43 %, E_O =1.52 %, E_O =1.49 %, and E_5 = 18, E_5 = 295 respectively. 23779 curve segments calculation times with using Eq. 5 and FIS model are 40.0929 sec and 6.209 respectively.

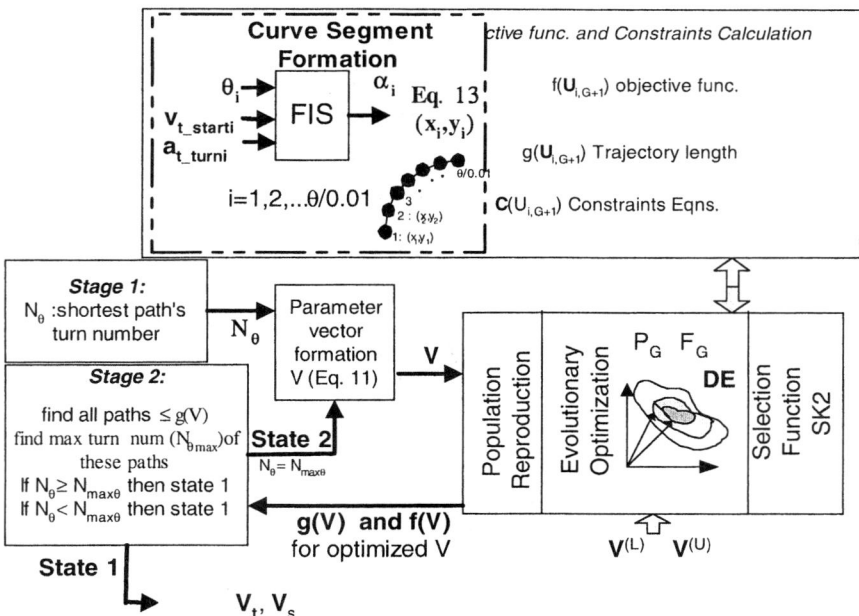

Fig. 2. Overall structure of the global optimization process

4 Global Optimization Process

The possible largest range ($-\pi, \pi$] for θ_i, [0,v_{t_max}] for v_{t_starti} and [$-a_{t\_max}, a_{t\_max}$] inch/sec^2 for a_{t_turni} are taken as elements of the parameter vector $V^{(L)}$ and $V^{(U)}$. Other elements of the parameter vector are taken the environments big edge length. Obtaining global optimal results are done in two stages. These are:

Stage 1: N_θ is taken equal to the turn number of the shortest path. Then optimization process is implemented.

Stage 2: Proof of the global optimality: Maximum number of turns ($N_{max\theta}$) is searched in the paths, that are shorter or equal to the g(V) optimized in stage 1.

State 1: If $N_\theta \geq N_{max\theta}$: The trajectory found in stage 1 is the global optimal trajectory.

State 2: If $N_\theta < N_{max\theta}$: The optimization process is repeated according to the $Nmax_\theta$. The stage 2 is repeated until state 1 condition is obtained.

After the implementation of these 2 stages, obtained result is global time optimum. The overall view of the trajectory generation is shown in Fig. 2. g to the Stage 2. The optimization process continues until the state 1 condition will be obtained. After the overall optimization process, control variables V_s and V_t can be produced easily, so that the MR can move on the global time optimal trajectory without feedback control.

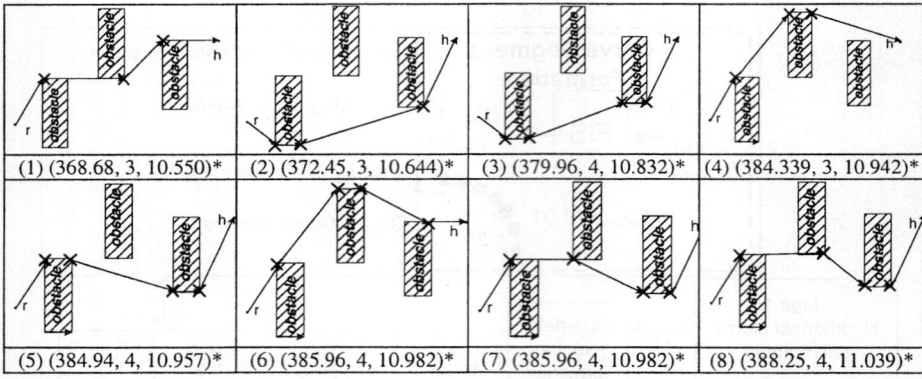

Fig. 3. The first 8 path. 1 is the shortest path. ✗ : turn points. r :robot position, h: target position. *: (Path lenght H (inch), Turn Number N_θ, Tracking time T_H sec.)

5 Application and Experimental Results

In this section, the global time optimal trajectory is found for two different environments shown in Fig. 3 and Fig. 5. In Fig 3, T_H (suppose that the path has not any turns, i.e. straight line) is calculated by the equation :

$$T_H = \begin{cases} \dfrac{\left(H - a_{t\_max}\left(\dfrac{v_{t\_max}}{a_{t\_max}}\right)^2\right)}{v_{t\_max}} + 2\left(\dfrac{v_{t\_max}}{a_{t\_max}}\right) & \text{if } H > a_{t\_max}\left(\dfrac{v_{t\_max}}{a_{t\_max}}\right)^2 \\ \sqrt{\dfrac{H}{a_{t\_max}}} & \text{if } H > a_{t\_max}\left(\dfrac{v_{t\_max}}{a_{t\_max}}\right)^2 \end{cases}$$

and shortest tracking time, $T_{g(V)}$ for g(V) length path (i.e. g(V) length straight line) can be calculated similar to the above equations replacing H with g(V). Here, H is the total path length (i.e. sum of the line segments lengths of the path,). The shortest path, 1 has $N_\theta=3$. That's why, N_θ is taken equal to 3 in Stage 1 and time optimal trajectory is found (in Fig 4a). Table 1 gives the f(V), g(V), $T_{g(V)}$ (the shortest tracking time for a straight line of g(V) inch length) and $H_{f(V)}$ (the maximum path length (straight line length) to track in f(V) sec.) values of this trajectory's ($N_\theta=3$ row in the Table 1). After the implementation of Stage 2, it is seen in Fig. 3 that, there are seven paths shorter than $g(V)|_{N\theta=3}$ and the biggest N_θ, $N_{max\theta}$ is found 4 in these 7 paths. The optimization process is done again for $N_\theta=4$ according to State 2 and results are given in Table 1. After that, Stage 2 is repeated and 5 paths shorter than g(V) $|_{N\theta=4}$ is found in Fig. 3 and the biggest N_θ, $N_{max\theta}$ is found 4 again in these 5 paths. Due to, N_θ is equal to $N_{max\theta}$, it is said that, this trajectory is global time optimal trajectory. But the optimization results obtained for $N_\theta=5$ are also given in tables. In the second environment, there are narrow passages. So that optimal acc/dec values on the curve segments are found different from zero (Table 8).

Table 1. The comparison results for the trajectories in Fig. 5

N_θ (rad)	f(V) (sec)	g(V) (inch)	$H_{f(V)}$ (inch) path length	$T_{g(V)}$ (sec)
(-0.100, -1.437, 0.031)	10.986	386.110	386.106	10.986
(-0.107, 0, -1.421, -0.003)	10.975	385.547	385.666	10.972
(-0.095, -0.019, -1.424, 0, 0.014)	10.963	384.802	385.186	10.953

6 Conclusions

A novel approach to the global time optimal trajectory planning for a unicycle MR is introduced. Constraints from environment (obstacles) and physical constraints (i.e. steering and translation accelerations/velocities) are taken into consideration in the method. Then DE, which is an evolutionary optimization method, is used to find the time optimal trajectory from this set. The curves are formed in two ways: a) serial expansion of the robots equations (Mclauren series) and b) fuzzy inference system (FIS) which reduces the optimization time. Approximately the optimization time with FIS decreased to 1/7 of the series expansion method. The planned trajectories are tracked by Nomad 200.

Table 2. The comparison results for the trajectories in Fig. 5.

	II (Optimized path)	I (shortest path)
f(V)(s)	14.2347	22.2648
g(V)(inch)	446.154	416.138

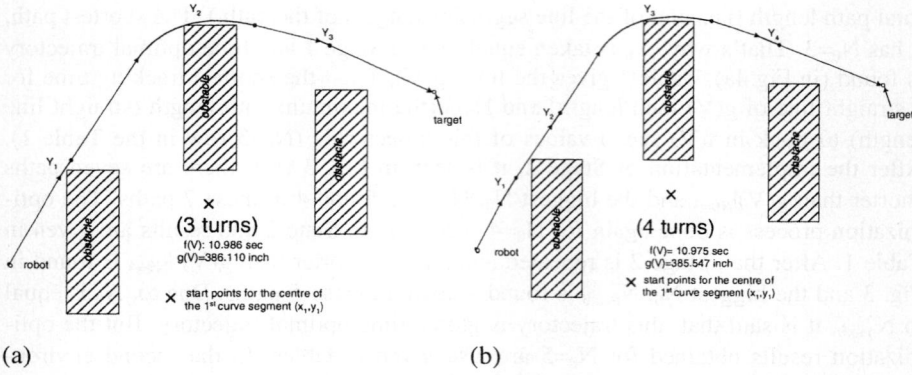

Fig. 4. a) Time optimal trajectory for $N_\theta=3$. b) Time optimal trajectory for $N_\theta=4$

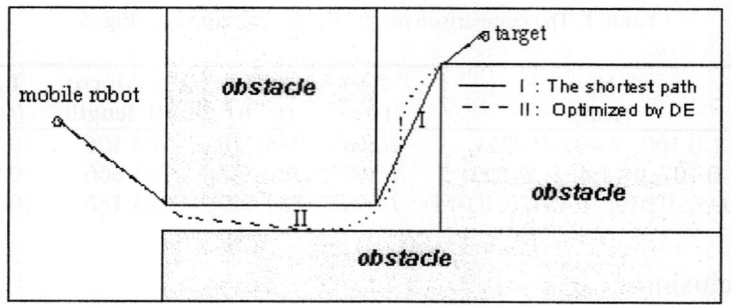

Fig. 5. An environment with a narrow passage.

References

1. Zefran, M..: Continious Methods for Motion Planning. PhD Thesis, University of Pennsylvania, Philadelphia (1996)
2. Weber, H.: A motion planning and execution system for mobile robots driven by stepping motors", Robotics and Autonomous Systems 33 (2000) 207–221
3. Lee, C., Xu Y.: Trajectory fitting with smoothing splines using velocity information. IEEE Proc. Of Int. Conf on Robotics&Automation, San Francisco CA, April (2000)
4. Reuter, J.: Mobile robots trajectories with continiously differentiable curvature: An optimal control approach. IEEE/RSJ Proc. Of Int. Conf on Intelligent Robots and System, Victoria B.C., Canada, October (1998)
5. Storn, R.: System Design by Constraint Adaptation and Differential Evolution. IEEE Transactions on Evolutionary Computation, 3(1): April (1999) 22–34 ISSN 1089-778X
6. Jang, R.J.-S., Sun, C.-T., Mizutani, E.: Neuro-Fuzzy and Soft Computing: A Computational Approach to Learning and Machine Intelligence. Prentice Hall, USA (1997)
7. Aydın, S., Temeltaş, H.: Real-Time Mobile Robot Optimal Motion Planning in Dynamic Environment. Proc. Of 1th Int. Conf. On Information Technology in Mechatronics ITM'01., 1-3 October, Istanbul, TURKEY 2001 161-167

Hexagon-Based Q-Learning for Object Search with Multiple Robots*

Han-Ul Yoon[1] and Kwee-Bo Sim[2]

[1] School of Electrical and Electronics Engineering, Chung-Ang University,
221 Heukseok-Dong, Dongjak-Gu, Seoul 156-756, Korea
huyoon@wm.cau.ac.kr
[2] School of Electrical and Electronics Engineering, Chung-Ang University,
221 Heukseok-Dong, Dongjak-Gu, Seoul 156-756, Korea
kbsim@cau.ac.kr

Abstract. This paper presents the hexagon-based Q-leaning for object search with multiple robots. We set up an experimental environment with five small mobile robots, obstacles, and a target object. The robots were out to search for a target object while navigating in a hallway where some obstacles were placed. In this experiment, we used three control algorithms: a random search, an area-based action making (ABAM) process to determine the next action of the robots, and hexagon-based Q-learning to enhance the area-based action making process.

1 Introduction

Nowadays, robots are performing tasks previously performed by men in dangerous field, such as rescue missions at fire-destroyed building or at gas contaminated sites; information retrieval from deep seas or from space; and weather analysis at extremely cold areas like Antarctica. Sometimes, multiple robots are especially needed to penetrate into hard-to-access areas, such as underground insect nests, to collect more reliable and solid data.

Multiple robot control has received much attention since it can offer a new way of controlling multiple agents more flexibly and robustly. For instance, Parker used the heuristics approach algorithm for multiple robots and applied it to cleaning tasks [1]. Ogasawara employed distributed autonomous robotic systems to control multiple robots that transporting a large object [2]. In this paper, we propose an area-based action making (ABAM) process. This, in turn, becomes incorporated with hexagon-based Q-learning, which helps multiple robots to navigate, to avoid collision, and to search through their own trajectories.

Reinforcement learning through the explorations of its environment enables an agent to actively decide what the following action should be. During the exploration of an uncertain state space with reward, it can learn what to do by

---

* This research was supported by the project of Developing SIC and Applications under the Next Generation Technologies program in 2000: The Ministry of Commerce, Industry, and Energy in Korea.

continuous tracking of its state history and appropriately propagating rewards through the state space [3]. In our research, we focused on Q-learning as a reinforcement learning technique. It is because Q-learning is a simple way to solve Markovian action problems with incomplete information. Also, it can map state-action pairs onto expected returns on the basis of the action-value function Q [4]. In addition to this simplicity, Q-learning can adopt to the real world situation. For example, the state space can be matched with the physical space of the real world. An action can also be regarded as physical robot movement. In this paper, we propose that the hexagon-based Q-learning can enhance the area-based action making process so that the learning process can adapt to real world situations better.

The organization of this paper is as follows. In section 2, the area-based action making process is introduced. In section 3, hexagon-based Q-learning adaptation is presented. In section 4, experimental results from the application of three different searching methods to find the object are presented. In section 5, conclusions are presented.

2 Area-Based Action Making Process

Area-based action making (ABAM) process is a process that determines the next action of a robot. The reason why this process is referred to as ABAM is because a robot recognizes surrounding not by distances, i.e., from itself to obstacle, but by areas around itself. The key idea of the ABAM process is to reduce the uncertainty of its surrounding. It is similar to the behavior-based direction change in regards to controlling the robots [5][6]. Under ABAM process robots recognize the shape of their surrounding and then take an action, i.e., turn and move toward where the widest space will be guaranteed. Consequently, each robot can avoid colliding into obstacles and other robots. Figure 1 depicts the different actions taken by distance-based action making (DBAM) and by ABAM in the same situation, respectively [7].

The advantage of ABAM over DBAM is illustrated in Fig. 2 which presents the result of each action making process by DBAM and ABAM. In both case, the robot is surrounded by 4-obstacles. Under DBAM, the robot perceives that there is no obstacle in the southwest. Thus, it will try to proceed toward that direction,

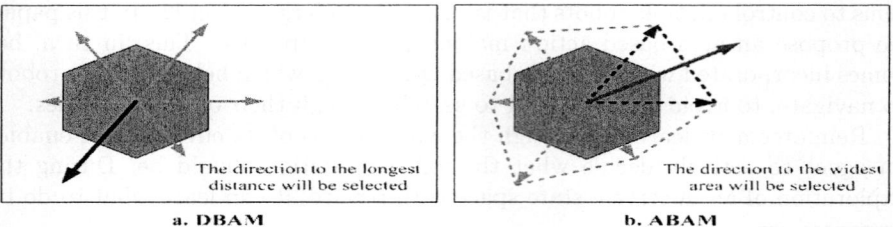

Fig. 1. Different actions taken under DBAM and ABAM

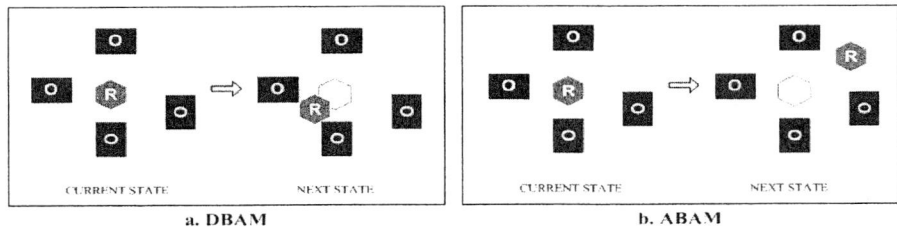

Fig. 2. Illustrative examples of robot maneuvers

which will result in being stuck two obstacles. This scenario is shown in Fig. 2a. Under ABAM, however, the robot will calculate the areas of its surrounding, and then it will recognize that an action toward the northeast will guarantee the widest space. Therefore, the robot will change its direction accordingly. This scenario is presented in the right picture in Fig. 2b.

To explain how the robots can navigate through the hallway and search a target, let's assume that we try to search some data in the huge memory space (i.e. database server) using multiple computers. All of data in this memory are neither stored regularly nor sorted. Also, the memory has some parts of reserved space which contains security data. The best way to solve this problem is to assign the block of memory to each computer so that it searches its own space. Interestingly, assigning a part of memory space to each computer is equivalent to using ABAM for each robot, because a robot becomes greedy to occupy it own searching space. The reserved memory spaces correspond to obstacles in the hallway. The increment of pointer corresponds to making an action to the next state. Therefore, we can improve the object search using multiple robots with ABAM as similarly increase a processing speed by multi-processing (*Amdahl's law*) [8]. Figure 3 shows the similarity.

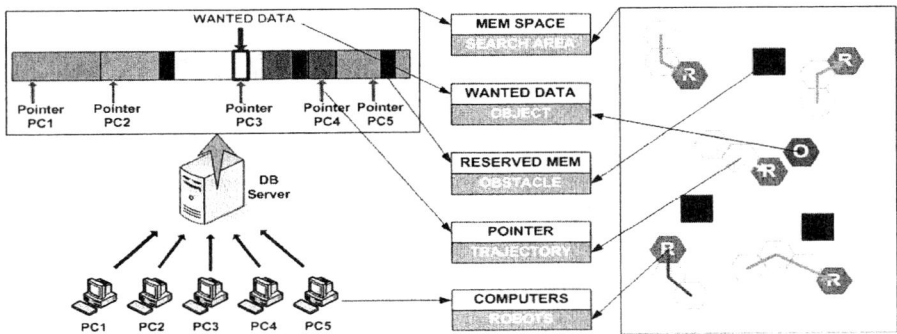

Fig. 3. Similarity between data search using multiple computers and an object search using multiple robots

3 Hexagon-Based Q-Learning

Q-learning is a well-known algorithm for reinforcement learning. It leads an agent to acquire optimal control strategies from delayed rewards, even when it has no prior knowledge of the effects of its actions on the environment [9][10]. Q-learning algorithm is presented in Table 1, where s is a possible state, a is a possible action, r indicates an immediate reward value, and γ is the discount factor.

Table 1. Q-learning algorithm

For each s, a initialize the table entry $\widehat{Q}(s,a)$ zero
Observe the current state s
Do forever
- Select the action a and execute it
- Receive the immediate reward r
- Observe the new state s'
- Update the table entry for $\widehat{Q}(s,a)$
- $s \leftarrow s'$

The formula to update the table entry value is:

$$\widehat{Q}(s,a) \leftarrow r + \gamma \max_{a'} \widehat{Q}(s',a') . \tag{1}$$

Figure 4 explains Q-learning algorithm more clearly more clearly. Each grid square presents the possible states. 'R' stands for a robot or an agent. The values upon the arrows are relevant $\widehat{Q}$ values with the state transition. For example, the value $\widehat{Q}(s_1, a_{right}) = 72$, a_{right} refers to the action that moves R to its right [9]. If the robot takes the action to the right, the value will be updated for this entry where $r=0$, $\gamma=0.9$ are predetermined values. The formula is as follows.

$$\widehat{Q}(s_1, a_{right}) \leftarrow r + \gamma \max_{a_2} \widehat{Q}(s_2, a_2)$$

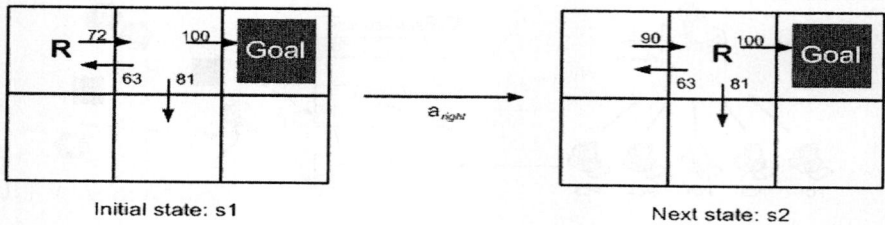

Fig. 4. An illustrative example of Q-learning

$$\leftarrow 0 + 0.9 \max_{a_2}\{63, 81, 100\} \quad (2)$$
$$\leftarrow 90 .$$

The Q-learning for our robot system is adapted to enhance the ABAM process. The adaptation can be performed with a simple and easy modification, namely, hexagon-based Q-learning. Figure 5 illustrates example of hexagon-based Q-learning. In Fig. 5, the only thing that was changed is the shape of state space. We changed the shape of the space from a square to a hexagon, because the hexagon is a polygon which can be expanded infinitely by its combination. According to this adaptation, the robot can take an action in 6-direction and have 6-table entry $\widehat{Q}$ value. In Fig. 5, the robot is in the initial state. Now, if the robot decides that +60 degree guarantee the widest space after calculating of its 6-areas of surrounding, the action of the robot would be $a_{+60°}$. After the action is taken, if $Area6'$ is the widest area, the value of $\widehat{Q}(s_1, a_{+60°})$ will be updated by the formula (1) in the Q-learning algorithm as

$$\widehat{Q}(s_1, a_{+60°}) \leftarrow r + \gamma \max_{a'_\theta} \widehat{Q}(s_2, a'_\theta)$$
$$\leftarrow 0 + \gamma \max_{a'_\theta}\{Area1', Area2', \cdots, Area6'\} \quad (3)$$
$$\leftarrow \gamma Area6' .$$

where 0 is the predetermined immediate reward. After the movement from the initial state to the next state, immediate reward becomes the difference between *the sum of total area before action is taken* and *the sum of total area after action is taken*. Thus, the reward is:

$$r = \sum_{j=1}^{6} Area_j - \sum_{i=1}^{6} Area_i . \quad (4)$$

where $Area_i \in s$ and $Area_j \in s'$ respectively.

The robot would ultimately acquire the environmental information and determine its trajectory by learning this value. In the real world experiment, however,

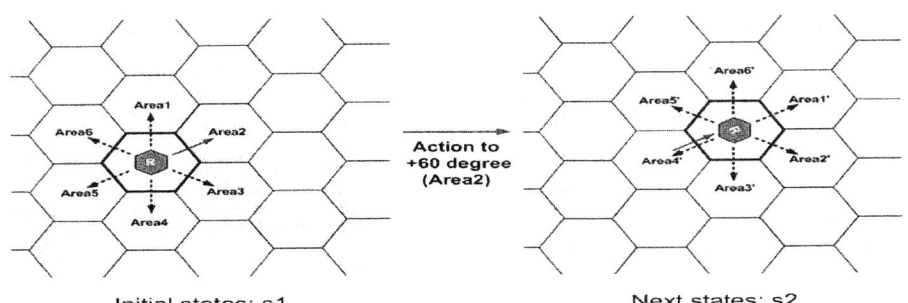

Fig. 5. An illustrative example of Hexagon-Based Q-learning

battery consumption presents a problem. If the robot had to perform infinite iterations to complete task, total system would fail. Therefore, a system must be set up to cancel the former action and move back to the previous state, when the former action causes any critical result. The hexagon-based Q-learning algorithm is presented in Table 2.

Table 2. Hexagon-based Q-learning algorithm

For each s, a initialize the table entry $\widehat{Q}(s, a_\theta)$ zero
Calculate 6-areas at the current state s
Do until the task is completed
- Select the action a_θ to the widest area, and execute it
- Receive the immediate reward r
- Observe the new state s'
    If $\widehat{Q}(s', a'_\theta)$ is greater or equal than $\widehat{Q}(s, a_\theta)$
    - Update the table entry for $\widehat{Q}(s, a_\theta)$
    - $s \leftarrow s'$
    Else, if $\widehat{Q}(s', a'_\theta)$ is far less than $\widehat{Q}(s, a_\theta)$
    - Move back to the previous state
    - $s \leftarrow s$

---

4 Experiments with Three Different Control Methods

We performed experiments by using three different control methods: random search, ABAM, and enhanced ABAM by hexagon-based Q-learning. In section 4.1, we introduce our small mobile robot system. Experimental result with three different control methods will be presented in the following sections.

4.1 Architecture of Small Mobile Robot

Our small mobile robot system consists of four subparts and a main micro-controller part. The subparts were camera vision, sensor, motor, and Bluetooth communication module. Each subpart has its own controller to perform its unique function more efficiently. The main micro-controller part controls the four subparts to avoid process collision and generates actions with the data from its subparts. Figure 6 shows the appearance, anatomy, and functional block diagram of the robot.

The main components of the robot are as follows. For the eye of the robot, Movicam II made by Kyosera is used. It is the CCD camera and its size is $30 \times 16.4 \times 47$ ($width \times length \times height$) mm^3. The robot has the six emitter-detector infrared sensor pairs, which are placed at an angle of 60 degrees with one another to cover 360 degrees, to measure the distance around itself. The emitter is Kodenshi EL-1kl3, high-power GaAs infrared sensor. The detector is ST-1kla, high sensitivity NPN silicon photo-transistor. NMB PG25L-024 stepping motor is used as the driving part. Its characteristics are the following: drive voltage-12V, drive method 2-2 phase and 0.495 step angle. Bluetooth communication module is mounted to make the robot very suitable for wireless communication systems [11].

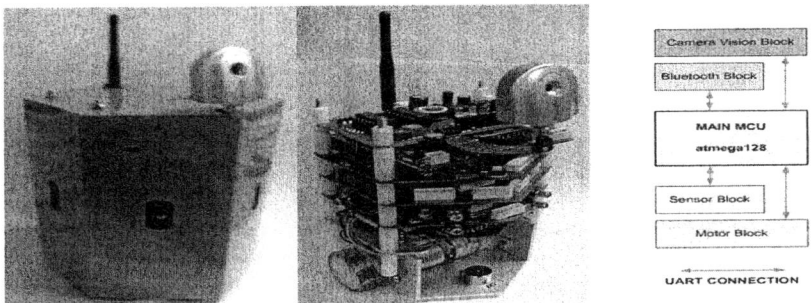

Fig. 6. Small mobile robot employed in the experiments

4.2 Experiments

The task of the robots is: *"Find the hidden target object while tracking through an unknown hallway."* We set up the color of the target object as green and that of 5-robots as orange. The target was a stationary robot with the same shape as other robots. It was a located at a hidden place behind one obstacle. Five robots, whose mission is to find the target, would recognize it by its color and shape. They would decide whether they finished the task by detecting the target after each action was taken.

Random search. We adapted the random search control method to find the hidden target. The main controller generated a random number and decided the next action corresponding to this number. It did not perform well. Therefore, it is clear that random search was not so strong a method to control the robots efficiently. Moreover, it would be very time and power consuming in the real world situation. The result showed that random search was a horrible method to be adapted to a real robot system. In Fig. 7, the white arrow points out the target object, which will be the case in Fig. 8 and Fig. 9 as well. During random search, even though the robots were within a close distance to the target object, some robots failed to detect it.

ABAM. We applied ABAM to the robots. They could sense their environment with 6-infrared sensors and calculate 6 areas. When the calculation was done, each robot tried to move toward the direction where the widest area would be guaranteed. Once the robots started to move, each robot spread out into the environment. Consequently, the ABAM performed better than random search.

Fig. 7. Five-robots are searching the object using random search

Fig. 8. Five-robots are searching the object using ABAM

Fig. 9. Five-robots are searching the object using hexagon-based Q-learning

Figure 8 shows that the two robots located at the right side of the target succeeded to complete the task. These two robots are marked by black arrow in Fig. 8.

Enhanced ABAM by hexagon-based Q-learning. We used the hexagon-based Q-learning to ABAM as a modified control method. This method allowed the robots to reduce the probability of wrong judgment and to compensate wrong judgment with reinforcement learning. Each robot tried to search its own area, which was the case under ABAM. However, it learned the experimental environment, state by state, and canceled the state transition if the action caused critical reduction of $\widehat{Q}$ value. By using the hexagon-based Q-learning adaptation to ABAM, more than two robots completed the task during ten trials. The search with hexagon-based Q-learning is presented in Fig. 9.

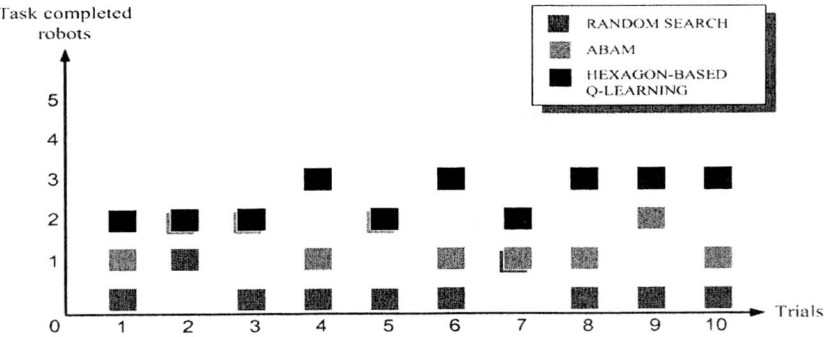

Fig. 10. Experimental result with three different control methods

Results. The results of our experiment are presented in Fig. 10. With random search, one robot found the target at the second trial and sixth trial, although these detections could be considered just a coincidence. Therefore, we can state that the random search has no significant success. With ABAM, the robots performed better than they did with random search. The average performance was above 1 during the all trial. Finally, with the adaptation of hexagon-based Q-learning to ABAM, the results were remarkable. Three robots succeeded to find the target at the fourth, sixth, eighth, ninth, and tenth trials.

5 Conclusions

In this paper, we presented the area-based action making (ABAM) process and hexagon-based Q-learning. Five small mobile robots were used to search for the object hidden in the unknown space. The experimental results from the application of the three different control methods in the same situations were presented.

The area-based action making process and hexagon-based Q-learning can be a new way for robots to search for an object in the unknown space. This algorithm also enables the agents to avoid obstacles during their search.

For the future research, first, we need to clarify the problem of accessing the object. In other words, if multiple robots are to carry out a task such as object transporting or block stacking, they need to recognize the object first and then proceed to approach it. Second, our robot systems desire to be improved so that the main part and the subparts could adhere more strongly. In addition, stronger complex algorithms, such as Bayesian learning or TD(λ) method, need to be adapted. Third, a self-organizing Bluetooth communication network should be built so that robots can communicate with one another robustly even if one or more robots are lost. Finally, the total system needs to be refined to obtain better results.

References

1. Parker, L.: Adaptive Action Selection for Cooperative Agent Teams. Proc. of 2nd Int. Conf. on Simulation of Adaptive Behavior (1992) 442–450
2. Ogasawara, G., Omata, T., Sato, T.: Multiple Movers Using Distributed, Decision-Theoretic Control. Proc. of Japan-USA Symp. on Flexible Automation **1** (1992) 623–630
3. Ballard, D.: An Introduction to Natural Computation. The MIT Press Cambridge (1997)
4. Jang, J., Sun, C., Mizutani, E.: Neuro-Fuzzy and Soft Computing. Prentice-Hall New Jersey (1997)
5. Ashley, W., Balch, T.: Value-Based Observation with Robot Teams (VBORT) using Probabilistic Techniques. Proc. of Int. Conf. on Advanced Robotics (2003)
6. Ashley, W., Balch, T.: Value-Based Observation with Robot Teams (VBORT) for Dynamic Targets. Proc. of Int. Conf. on Intelligent Robots and Systems (2003)
7. Park, J.B., Lee, B.H., Kim, M.S.: Remote Control of a Mobile Robot Using Distance-Based Reflective Force. Proc. of IEEE Int. Conf. on Robotics and Automation **3** (2003) 3415–3420
8. Patterson, D., Hennessy, J.: Computer Organization and Design. 3rd edn. Morgan-Kaufmann Korea (2005)
9. Mitchell, T.: Machine Learning. McGraw-Hill Singapore (1997)
10. Clausen, C., Wechsler, H.: Quad-Q-Learning. IEEE Trans. on Neural Network **11** (2000) 279–294
11. Yoon, H.U., Whang, S.H., Kim, D.W., Sim, K.B.: Strategy of Cooperative Behaviors of Distributed Autonomous Robotic Systems. Proc. of 10th Int. Symp. on Artificial Life and Robotics (2005) 151–154

Adaptive Inverse Control of an Omni-Directional Mobile Robot

Yuming Zhang, Qixin Cao, and Shouhong Miao

Shanghai Jiaotong University, Research Institute of Robotics,
200030 Shanghai, P.R. China
{rieman, qxcao, motsler}@sjtu.edu.cn

Abstract. The omni-directional mobile robot developed by Shanghai Jiaotong University was introduced. The inverse kinematics and dynamics of the robot were modeled for decoupled control simulation. An adaptive inverse control (AIC) scheme incorporating Dynamic neural network (DNN) controller and conventional feedback controller was presented. Finally, linear and circular trajectories following simulation results demonstrate that the AIC can decouple the dynamic control of the robot motion in the plane to direct rotational speed control of independent wheels, and precise trajectory following is achieved.

1 Introduction

Omni-directional mobile robots have good maneuverability that make them widely studied in the dynamic environmental applications, such as the RobCup competition. The Omni-directional mobile robot named JiaoLong developed by Shanghai Jiaotong University is a cross-disciplinary research platform for the full integration of AI and robotics research. It has three Swedish wheels [1], which are arranged 120° apart and locate at the vertices of the frame that has the form of an equilateral triangle. A DC motor installed with shaft optical encoder and a gear train drives each wheel. A DSP (digital signal processor) is used for the motion control.

From the robot testing and competition at the past games, it is realized that a precise trajectory control for the robot is one of the key areas to improve the robot's performance. It appears that most research on the control of omni-directional mobile robot is based on dynamic model and feedback method, such as PID control, self-tuning PID control, fuzzy control, and trajectory linearization control [2-4]. The robot dynamic models are generally assumed that the robot motors' dynamics is identical, and the motors are controlled by ideal servos, and the motor output can perfectly follow the command [2-5]. In fact, the motors and servos' dynamics could hardly be identical, and their constraints can greatly affect the behavior of the robot. Since the omni-directional robot is a complex coupled nonlinear dynamic plant, it is difficult to precisely modeling the plant dynamics in an analytic way.

In this paper, an adaptive inverse control scheme incorporating dynamic neural network and conventional feedback control was developed for the omni-directional mobile robot. When it is difficult to model the robot dynamics precisely in an analytic way, the neural network adaptive inverse controller can adapt its weights to achieve optimal dynamic performance by learning the output of the conventional feedback controller [6-7].

2 Kinematics Modeling

We assume that the robot under study is moving on a horizontal plane. The posture is defined in Fig. 1(a), where $X_W O Y_W$ is the world coordinate system, point O is the reference point; $X_R P Y_R$ is the robot coordinate system, point P is the center of the robot chassis. We define the 3-vector describing the robot posture:

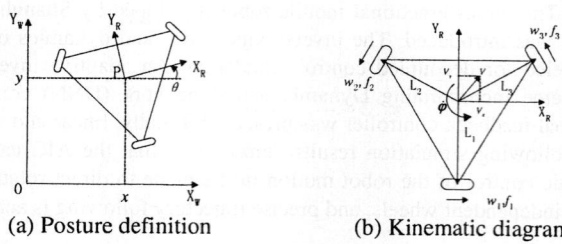

(a) Posture definition   (b) Kinematic diagram

Fig. 1. Kinematic parameters definition of the omni-directional robot

$$\xi = (x \quad y \quad \theta)^T. \tag{1}$$

where x, y are the coordinates related to the reference point P in the world frame, θ is the orientation of the robot frame with respect to the world frame. In our design, the inverse kinematic equations are given by

$$(w_1 \quad w_2 \quad w_3)^T = \frac{1}{r} A R(\theta) (\dot{x} \quad \dot{y} \quad \dot{\theta})^T. \tag{2}$$

where w_i, $i=1,2,3$, is the rotational speed of each wheel of the robot, r is the wheel radius, $A = \begin{bmatrix} 1 & 0 & L_1 \\ -\frac{1}{2} & -\frac{\sqrt{3}}{2} & L_2 \\ -\frac{1}{2} & \frac{\sqrt{3}}{2} & L_3 \end{bmatrix}$, $R(\theta) = \begin{bmatrix} \cos\theta & \sin\theta & 0 \\ -\sin\theta & \cos\theta & 0 \\ 0 & 0 & 1 \end{bmatrix}$, L_i is the distance from the center of the robot chassis to the contact point to the ground of each wheel along a radial path (see Fig. 1(b)). Using equation (2), we can calculate the rotational speed command given to each wheel of the robot from trajectory planner that specifies the vector ξ.

3 Robot Dynamics Modeling for Decoupled Control Simulation

By Newton's Law we have $(m\ddot{x} \quad m\ddot{y} \quad J_R \ddot{\theta})^T = A^T (f_1 \quad f_2 \quad f_3)^T$, so there is

$$(f_1 \quad f_2 \quad f_3)^T = (A^-)^T (m\ddot{x} \quad m\ddot{y} \quad J_R \ddot{\theta})^T. \tag{3}$$

Where m is the robot mass, J_R is the robot moment inertia, f_i is the traction force of each wheel. Assuming the robot can follow the command fast, f_i will be very closely approximate the real traction force given by each motor driving unit.

The dynamics of each wheel driven by a DC motor can be described as

$$J_m \dot{w}_m = -(\frac{C_m C_e}{R_a} + b_m)w_m - \frac{r}{n}f + \frac{C_m}{R_a}u \cdot \qquad (4)$$

Where J_m is the combined moment of inertia of the motor, gear train and wheel referred to the motor shaft, w_m is the rotational speed of the motor shaft, R_a is the armature resistance C_e is the electromotive force (EMF) constant, C_m is the motor torque constant, b_m is the vicious friction efficient of the combination of the motor and gear train, n is the gear ratio, f is one of f_i, u is the applied armature voltage. Similarly, we can copy equation (4) for the other two wheel dynamic models. Using Equation (3) and (4), we can construct the simulation model for the following adaptive inverse control scheme.

4 Adaptive Inverse Control of Nonlinear Plant

The overall adaptive inverse control scheme based on neural network is depicted in Fig. 2, where z^{-1} is unit delay of the discretized time. The neurocontroller is a dynamic neural network with tapped-delay-line (TDL). The input of the plant is the output sum of the neurocontroller and the PID controller: $u=u_N+u_F$. The main idea is to adapt the neurocontroller via learning the output of the PID controller u_F, which is called feedback error method. When the neurocontroller is converged, there will be $u_F \rightarrow 0$, $u_N \rightarrow u$, $y \rightarrow r$, $e \rightarrow 0$, and the PID controller will not act, then the neurocontroller approaches the inverse model of the plant.

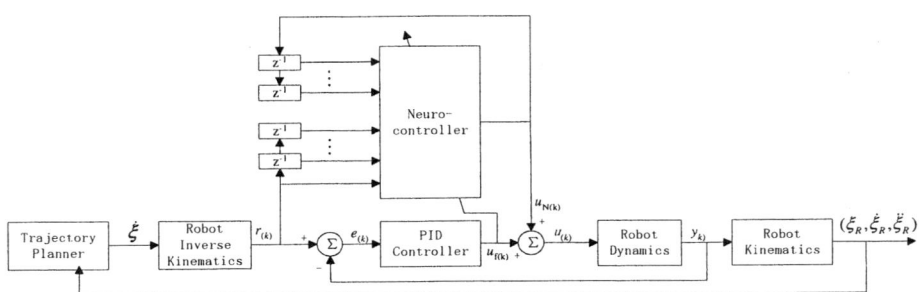

Fig. 2. Adaptive inverse control scheme

5 Simulation

We designed two trajectories in the simulation to follow by the robot: a linear trajectory and a circular trajectory. For linear trajectory, the command is to accelerate the robot from the original position to the desired speed $\dot{x}=1m/s$, $\dot{y}=1m/s$, $\dot{\theta}=0.15rad/s$

with fixed acceleration $\ddot{x} = 1\text{m/s}^2$, $\ddot{y} = 1\text{m/s}^2$, $\ddot{\theta} = 0.1\text{rad/s}^2$. The linear speed error is 1.2mm/s and the rotational speed error is 0.0013 rad/s. For circular trajectory, the robot is commanded to accelerate from initial state to circle around the center of the trajectory with the desired angular rate 0.754 rad/s. The center of the circular trajectory is at [0 0.5], the radius of the circular trajectory is 0.5m. The position error is 0.8mm and the orientation error is 0.0011rad.

6 Conclusion

In this paper, the inverse kinematics and dynamics of an omni-directional mobile robot was analyzed. The adaptive inverse controller was designed for dynamic decoupled control. So unlike those model-based control methods, it is not sensitive to the parameters of the robot dynamic model. The simulation results demonstrate that the adaptive inverse control can decouple the control of the robot motion in the plane to direct rotational speed control of the independent wheels, and the robot can be controlled to follow different trajectory precisely. The next step is to implement and test the control scheme on the real robot that is controlled by a DSP system.

References

1. Campion, G., Bastin, G., Dandrea-Novel, B.: Structural properties and classification of kinematic and dynamic models of wheeled mobile robots. Robotics and Automation, IEEE Transactions on, Vol.12(1), (1996) 47 - 62
2. Yong Liu, Xiaofei Wu, Jim Zhu J., Jae Lew: Omni-directional mobile robot controller design by trajectory linearization. American Control Conference, Proceedings of the 2003, Vol.4, 3423 - 3428
3. Watanabe, K., Shiraishi, Y., Tzagestas, S. G., Tang, J.: Feedback Control of an Omnidirectonal Autonomous Platform for Mobile Service Robots. Journal of Intelligent and Robotic Systems (1998), Vol.22(3), 315-330
4. Keigo Watanabe. : Control of Omni-directional Mobile Robot. 2nd Int. Conf. On Knowledge-Based Intelligent Electronic Systems (1998)
5. Jong-Suk Choi, Byung Kook Kim.: Near Minimum-Time Direct Voltage Control Algorithms for Wheeled Mobile Robots with Current and Voltage Constrain. Robotica (2001), Vol. 19, 29-39
6. H.Gomi, M.Kawato.: Learning control for closed loop system using feedback-error-learning. Proceedings of 29th International Conference On Decision and Control (1990), 3289-3294
7. H.Miyamoto, M.Kawato, T.Setoyama, R.Suzuki. Feedback error learning neural network for Trajectory control of robotic manipulator. Neural Networks (1998), Vol.11, 251-265

A Closed Loop Algorithms Based on Chaos Theory for Global Optimization

Xinglong Zhu[1,2], Hongguang Wang[1], Mingyang Zhao[1], and Jiping Zhou[2]

[1] Robotics Laboratory, Shenyang Institute of Automation, Chinese academy of Sciences,
Shenyang 110016, Liaoning, P.R. China
xinglongzhu@263.net, {hgwang, myzhao}@sia.cn
[2] Mechanical Engineering College of Yangzhou University,
Yangzhou 225009, Jiangsu, P.R. China
jpzhou@yzu.zdu.cn

Abstract. Numerical optimization problems enjoy a significant popularity in chaos theory fields. All major chaotic techniques use such problems for various tests and experiments. However, many of these techniques encounter difficulties in solving some real-world problems which include non-trivial constrains. This paper discusses a closed loop algorithms (CLA) which based on chaos theory. Thus, for many constrained numerical optimization problems it might be beneficial to add a constraint, and make up of closed loop, using feedback theory. Given an initial best function value (BFV), after the first runs computation we subtract variable increment from obtained BFV, and name it as the new value. That the new value subtracts the new BFV in the next runs computation is defined the accessional constraints. Substituting the new BFV in the next runs for the old BFV and go on, until the global solution is searched. Eventually, some difficult test cases illustrate this approach is very available.

1 Introduction

Constrained function optimization id an extremely important tool in almost every facet of engineering, operation research, mathematics, and etc. Let us consider the following constrained numerical optimization problems [1],[2]:

$$\text{minimize} \quad f(x)$$

Subject to (nonlinear and linear) constraints:

$$g_i(x) \geq 0, \quad i=1,\ldots,m; \; h_j(x) = 0, \quad j=1,\ldots,p.$$

In the past ten years, there has been a growing effort to apply chaos theory to solve general constrained optimization problems [3],[4],[5],[6], Chaotic algorithms have been widely applied to unconstrained optimization where their appeal is their ability to solve ill-conditioned problems. Traditional calculus-based or deterministic global search methods typically make strong assumptions regarding the objective function, i.e., continuity, differentiability, satisfaction of the Lipschitz Condition, etc., in order to make the search method justifiable. These conditions also hold for any linear and nonlinear constraints of a constrained optimization problem. It is our expectation that chaotic algorithms can overcome these limitations as well.

This paper is organized into four sections. The following section, Section 2, describes existing methods used to solve constraint optimization problems with the simplex algorithms, the penalty methods and chaotic algorithms. Section 3 introduces the process implementation of the closed loop algorithms for nonlinear constrained problems. Section 4 details the results obtained from applying these techniques to the some difficult test cases. The last section of this paper will state the conclusion developed from the experiments and the work of future research.

2 Previous Constrained Optimization Methods

Form the initial basic feasible solution (BFS), simplex algorithm searched a new BFS, which enabled objective function to decrease dramatically, then substituted the new BFS for the old BFS [7],[8]. By criterion, if objective function was not the best value, then continued iterating, until numbered iteration, simplex algorithm found the global /local solution.

Penalty functions method was a numerical solution which widely applied to the nonlinear programming problems. Its principle was that transformed the constrained optimization problems into the unconstrained extremum problems by selecting a series of non-stationary penalty factors. This method was named Sequential Unconstrained Minimization Technique [9],[10].

Sheela B.V. and Ramamoorthy P. presented an approach that the combined simplex algorithm with penalty functions method in 1975. In each iterative, this method adopted the simplex algorithm to solve extremum problems. The penalty factor of penalty items was given by the last iterative, and computation speed was accelerated. This method was entitled sequential weight increasing factor technique (SWIFT).

The process of the SWIFT implementation is following. Let searching for the minimum to nonlinear constrained problems,

$$J = \min f(x) , x = (x_1, x_2, ..., x_n) . \quad (1)$$

Subject to,

$$g_i(x) \leq 0 , (i=1,2,...,m). \quad (2)$$

$$h_j(x) = 0 , (j=1,2,...,p). \quad (3)$$

$$l_i \leq x_i \leq u_i \quad (i=1,2,...,n). \quad (4)$$

Where $x(x_1, x_2, ..., x_n)$ is the set of independent design variables with their lower and upper bounds as l_i and u_i. $f(x)$ is the objective function to be optimized, $g_i(x)$ and $h_j(x)$ are the constraints inequality and equality.

SWIFT method is going to transform Eq.(1)-(4) into following Eq.(5),

$$P(x, r_w) = \min J + r_w (\sum_{j=1}^{p} h_j^2 + \sum_{i=1}^{m} \max[g_i, 0]) . \quad (5)$$

In Eq.(5), $\max[g_i, 0] = \begin{cases} 0 & \text{if } g_i \leq 0 \\ g_i & \text{if } g_i > 0 \end{cases}$, and let $G'(x) = \sum_{j=1}^{p} h_j^2 + \sum_{i=1}^{m} \max[g_i, 0]$.

The n-dimensional simplex has $(n+1)$ vertexes, assumption using i^{th} vertex $x^{(i)}, (i = 1, 2, \ldots, n)$ to construct the simplex, using matrix $S_{n \times (n+1)}$ to be denoted as follows,

$$S_{n,n+1} = \begin{bmatrix} s_{1,1} & s_{1,2} & \cdots & s_{1,n} & s_{1,n+1} \\ s_{2,1} & s_{2,2} & \cdots & s_{2,n} & s_{2,n+1} \\ \cdots & \cdots & \cdots & \cdots & \cdots \\ s_{n,1} & s_{n,2} & \cdots & s_{n,n} & s_{n,n+1} \end{bmatrix} = \begin{bmatrix} x_1^{(i)} & x_1^{(i)} + d_1 & \cdots & x_1^{(i)} + d_2 & x_1^{(i)} + d_2 \\ x_2^{(i)} & x_2^{(i)} + d_2 & \cdots & x_2^{(i)} + d_1 & x_2^{(i)} + d_2 \\ \cdots & \cdots & \cdots & \cdots & \cdots \\ x_n^{(i)} & x_n^{(i)} + d_2 & \cdots & x_n^{(i)} + d_2 & x_n^{(i)} + d_1 \end{bmatrix},$$

$d_1 = \frac{t}{n\sqrt{2}}(\sqrt{n+1} + n - 1), d_2 = \frac{t}{n\sqrt{2}}(\sqrt{n+1} - 1)$, t is the side length of the simplex.

For selecting of the penalty factor r_w, let the barycenter of simplex is $x^{(G)}$,

$$x^{(G)} = \frac{1}{n+1} \sum_{i=1}^{n+1} x^{(i)}. \tag{6}$$

From the vertex of simplex to the barycenter, the mean distance d equals

$$d = \frac{1}{n+1} \sum_{i=1}^{n+1} \|x^{(i)} - x^{(G)}\|. \tag{7}$$

And then calculating mean value R, the expression R is defined as follows,

$$R = \frac{1}{\frac{1}{n+1} \sqrt{\sum_{j=1}^{n+1} [f(s_j) - f(x^{(i)})]^2}}. \tag{8}$$

Selecting a new penalty factor by the following Eq.(9),

$$r_w = \max(R, d^{-1}). \tag{9}$$

Calculating the function value $P(x, r_w)$ again, after numbered iteration, SWIFT enables the vertex of simple to limit to the barycenter of simplex, and stopping till satisfying the differentiate criterion, as the Eq.(10).

$$\{\frac{1}{n+1} \sum_{i=1}^{n+1} [P(x^{(i)}, r_w) - P(x^{(G)}, r_w)]^2\}^{\frac{1}{2}} < \varepsilon. \tag{10}$$

In Eq.(10), ε is iteration control accuracy.

Although SWIFT approach has an effective convergence property, and penalty function may be exact non-continuous and non-differentiable, the searching results have a bearing up on the initial iterative value. SWIFT approach is prone to fall into the local optimization solution in searching multi-peak function. In order to solve this problem, chaotic algorithms, which was a new method for optimization problems, had been adopted.

Chaos methods can find global optimization solution or approximate optimization solution, due to adopting an adaptive global probability searching algorithm. Chaos is a kind of universal nonlinear phenomenon. It seems out-of-order that actually exist regularity. A chaotic variable has three traits. They are randomicity, ergodicity and regularity in chaotic motion [11].

A hybrid algorithm, which combined the chaos optimization methods and SWIFT approach, was as in [12]. SWIFT approach that combines the simplex algorithms and the penalty function method transforms the constrained optimization problems into the unconstrained optimization problems. It can search the global/local minimum by the simplex algorithms for the constrained nonlinear optimization problems.

3 Closed Loop Algorithms

The mathematical expression of the logistic mapping of chaos optimization method is given in Eq. (11).

$$x'_i = \mu x'_i(1 - x'_i), i=1,..,n, \mu = 4, x'_i \in [0,1]. \tag{11}$$

Where μ is the growth rate or fecundity, x'_i is initial value, it generated by random function as follows, $x'_i = \text{rand}()\%100/100$.

Since there are n independent design variables for the objective function, supplying x'_i of Eq.(1) with n starting values, which avoid choosing such fixed points as $0, 0.25, 0.75, 1, (2 \pm \sqrt{3})/4$.

The elements on n chaotic orbits are computed as following mapping,

$$x_i = l_i + (u_i - l_i)x'_i, (i = 1,2,...,n). \tag{12}$$

Using Eq.(12), we can change chaotic number on the interval [0,1] into function independent variables on the interval $[l_i, u_i]$.

Substitution $x = (x_1, x_2, ... x_i, ... x_n), (i = 1,2,..,n)$ to Eq.(5), and then called for the SWIFT algorithms to search for feasible solution. In simulation experiment processing, we find that chaos method is easy to appear the pre-maturity phenomenon [4], Except for with many strong points. In order to surmount the pre-maturity phenomenon, we propose a closed loop algorithms (CLA) for global optimization solution to constrained nonlinear problems.

The idea of CLA is that we subtract variable increment Δ_k on the BFV had searched after the first runs computation. That is, in the first runs computation, we obtained a BFV, named it as J_1. Let

$$J_1^{(new)} = J_1 - \Delta_1. \tag{13}$$

Then adding the constraints imposed which the expression is as follows,

$$g_0^{(1)} = J_2 - J_1^{(new)} = J_2 - J_1 + \Delta_1. \tag{14}$$

In Eq.(14), J_2 is the best function value in the second runs computation, Δ_1 is a alterable positive number.

If $g_0^{(1)} \leq 0$, then $J_2 \leq J_1 - \Delta_1 < J_1$.

In a similar way, let

$$J_k^{(new)} = J_k - \Delta_k . \tag{15}$$

Added the constraints imposed which the expression is as follows,

$$g_0^{(k)} = J_{k+1} - J_k^{(new)} = J_{k+1} - J_k + \Delta_k . \tag{16}$$

If $g_0^{(k)} \leq 0$, then $J_{k+1} \leq J_k - \Delta_k < J_k$. (k=1,2,...,count)

Therefore, $J_1 > J_2 > ... > J_k > J_{k+1} > ... > J_{count}$, where count is recurrence number.

We name Δ_k as self-heuristic factor. Due to Δ_k function, CLA method in the searching process can jump out local optimization solution, and find out the global optimization.

Definition as,

$$\max[g_0, 0] = \begin{cases} 0 & \text{if } g_0^{(k)} \leq 0 \\ g_0^{(k)} & \text{if } g_0^{(k)} > 0 \end{cases} . \tag{17}$$

Substitution Eq.(17) to Eq.(5), new penalty function is defined as follows.

$$\begin{aligned} P(x, r_w) &= \min J + r_w (G'(x) + \max[g_0, 0]) \\ &= \min J + r_w (\sum_{j=1}^{p} h_j^2 + \sum_{i=1}^{m} \max[g_i, 0] + \max[g_0, 0]) \\ &= \min J + r_w (\sum_{j=1}^{p} h_j^2 + \sum_{i=0}^{m} \max[g_i, 0]) = \min J + r_w G(x) \end{aligned} \tag{18}$$

Definition as $G(x) = r_w (G'(x) + \max[g_0, 0])$.

The configuration diagram of the CLA is denoted as follows, sees Fig.1.

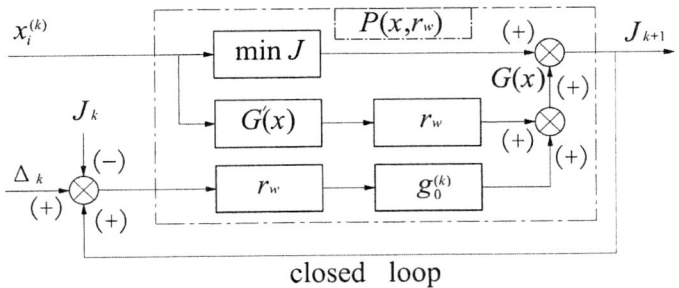

Fig. 1. The configuration diagram of the CLA

The CLA program is described as follows.
```
Initialization();
int    count;    // deposit recurrence number
int    counter;  // deposit searching number
double best[n+2]=1e10;//definition array
best[0];//  deposit the best function value J
best[i]=x[i];//deposit  optimization vari-
ables(i=1,2,…,n)
best[n+1]; //deposit G(x) value
int    max=1000;// deposit self-heuristic factor
CLA();
```
Δ_k =max;
```
while(count!=0){
num=counter;
while(num!=0){
c[0]=rand()%100/100.0;
if(c[0]==0||c[0]==0.25||c[0]==0.5||c[0]==0.75||c[0]==
```
$(2\pm\sqrt{3})/4$)
```
{c[0]=c[0]+0.1;}
if(c[0]==1){c[0]=c[0]-0.1;}
for(j=1;j<=n;j++){
c[j]=c[0]+rand()%1000/10000.0;
if(c[j]==0||c[j]==0.25||c[j]==0.5||c[j]==0.75||
```
$c[0]==(2\pm\sqrt{3})/4$){c[j]=c[j]+0.1;}
```
if(c[j]==1){c[j]=c[j]-0.1;}
x[j]=4*c[j]*(1-c[j]);
x[j]=l[j]-(l[j]-u[j])*x[j];}
SWIFT();//call for penalty function
if(J<=best[0]&&G(x)<=ε){
best[0]=J;
best[n+1]=G(x);
for(j=1;j<=n;j++){best[j]=x[j];}
```

```
num=1;}
num--;}
count--;
```
Δ_k =max/2.0;
if (Δ_k) < ε) { Δ_k =max;}}.

4 Test Cases

Eight typical optimization problems are used to test our algorithms.

Example 1: Design of a pressure vessel as presented by Sandgren[13]. The design variables are the dimensions required for the specifications of the vessel, as follows. $(x, y) = (x_1, x_2, y_1, y_2)$, x is real variables, and y is integer variables.

The objective function is the combined costs of material, forming and welding of the pressure vessel. The constraints are set in accordance with the respective ASME codes the mixed-integer optimization problem is expressed as,

$$\min f(x, y) = 0.6224(0.0625 y_1) x_1 x_2 + 1.7781(0.0625 y_2) x_1^2$$
$$+ 3.1661(0.0625 y_1)^2 x_2 + 19.84(0.0625 y_1)^2 x_1,$$

Subject to,
$g_1(x, y) = 0.0193 x_1 - 0.0625 y_1 \leq 0$,
$g_2(x, y) = 0.00954 x_1 - 0.0625 y_2 \leq 0$,
$g_3(x, y) = 750 \times 1728 - \pi x_1^2 x_2 - 4/3 \pi x_1^3 \leq 0$,
$g_4(x, y) = x_2 - 240 \leq 0$,
and bounds, $20 \leq x_1 \leq 80, 0 \leq x_2 \leq 240, 0 \leq y_i \leq 20$, ($i$=1,2).

The best solution is, as in [14], $(x, y) = (37.699, 239.999, 0.72759, 0.35965)$, with min $f(x) = 5804.3876$, but optimization variables $y_1 = 0.72759/0.0625$ and $y_2 = 0.35965/0.0625$ is not integer. The optimal solutions obtained by CLA in

Table 1. Comparsion of the best solution for 1st example with real variables

Design variables	Kannan[16]	Carlos[15]	CLA
y_1	18	13	12
y_2	10	7	6
x_1	58.291	40.3239	38.8601
x_2	43.690	200.0000	221.3654
g_1	-0.000016	-0.034324	0.0000
g_2	-0.068904	-0.052847	-0.0042
g_3	-21.220	-27.1059	-3.38-007
g_4	-196.310	-40.0000	-18.6345
$f(x)$	7198.0428	6288.7445	5850.3831

Table 1. From the Table 1, we can find the optimization results are better than of [15],[16].

Example 2: A limited set of experiments reported by Michalewicz indicated that the method can provide good results if violation levels and penalty coefficients are tuned to the problem. Minimize a function of 5 variables, as in [1],

$\min f(x) = 5.3578547 x_3^2 + 0.8356891 x_1 x_5 + 37.293239 x_1 - 40792.141$,

Subject to three double inequalities,

$0 \le g_1(x) \le 92, 90 \le g_2(x) \le 110, 20 \le g_3(x) \le 25$,

$g_1(x) = 85.334407 + 0.0056858 x_2 x_5 + 0.00026 x_1 x_4 - 0.0022053 x_3 x_5$,

$g_2(x) = 80.51294 + 0.0071317 x_2 x_5 + 0.0029955 x_1 x_2 + 0.0021813 x_3^2$,

$g_3(x) = 9.300961 + 0.0047026 x_2 x_3 + 0.0012547 x_1 x_3 + 0.0019085 x_3 x_4$,

and bounds, $78 \le x_1 \le 102, 33 \le x_2 \le 45$, and $27 \le x_i \le 45$ for $i=3,4,5$. The best solution obtained was, as in [9],

$x = (78.0495, 33.0070, 27.0810, 45.0000, 44.9400)$, with $\min f(x) = -31020.859$, whereas the optimum solution was, as in [17],

$x = (78.0000, 33.0000, 29.9950, 45.0000, 36.7760)$, with $\min f(x) = -30665.5$.

So far, the best solution by CLA is,

$x = (78.000947, 33.000006, 27.071141, 45.000000, 44.960241)$,

with $\min f(x) = -31025.44$, and sees Table 2. From the Table 2, we can find the optimization results are better than of [15],[16].

Example 3: This problem is, as in [18],

$\min f(x) = x_1 + x_2 + x_3$.

Subject to the linear and nonlinear constraints,

$g_1(x) = 0.0025(x_4 + x_6) - 1 \le 0$,

$g_2(x) = 0.0025(x_5 + x_7 - x_4) - 1 \le 0$,

$g_3(x) = 0.01(x_8 - x_5) - 1 \le 0$,

Table 2. Comparsion of the best solution for 2nd example with real variables

Design variables	Carlos[15]	Homaifar[17]	CLA
x_1	78.0495	78.0000	78.000947
x_2	33.0070	33.0000	33.000006
x_3	27.0810	29.9950	27.071141
x_4	45.0000	45.0000	45.000000
x_5	44.9400	36.7760	44.969241
g_1	91.9976	90.7146	91.999998
g_2	100.4078	98.8409	100.40535
g_3	20.0019	19.9999	20.000089
$f(x)$	-31020.86	-30665.5	-31025.44

$g_4(x) = 833.33252x_4 + 100x_1 - 83333.333 - x_1x_6 \leq 0$,
$g_5(x) = 1250x_5 + x_2x_4 - 1250x_4 - x_2x_7 \leq 0$,
$g_6(x) = 1250000 + x_3x_5 - 2500x_5 - x_3x_8 \leq 0$,
and bounds: $100 \leq x_1 \leq 10000$, $1000 \leq x_i \leq 10000$, (i=2,3), and $10 \leq x_j \leq 1000$, (j=4,5,6,7,8).

The best known solution is 7049.24. According to this point was not completely feasible. Again the sum of the violated constraints was 0.234×10^{-7}. The optimal solutions obtained by CLA in Table 3.

Table 3. Comparsion of the best solution for 3rd example with real variables

Design variables	Zbigniew[1]	CLA
x_1	579.3167	573.1781548957
x_2	1359.9430	1357.5456017193
x_3	5110.0710	5118.5602905953
x_4	182.0174	181.5035089338
x_5	295.5985	295.2575886174
x_6	217.9799	218.4962215241
x_7	286.4162	286.2459203163
x_8	395.5979	395.2575886172
g_1	-6.75e-6	-6.74e-7
g_2	-0.7160	0.00000
g_3	-3.9559	-2.60e-12
g_4	-3.22e-7	-1.69e-8
g_5	-1.08e-7	-7.24e-10
g_6	-1.40e-7	-2.97e-10
$f(x)$	7049.3309	7049.2840

Example 4: This problem is, as in [19],
 min $f(x) = (x_1 - 10)^3 + (x_2 - 20)^3$.
Subject to the linear and nonlinear constraints,
$g_1(x) = 100 - (x_1 - 5)^2 - (x_2 - 5)^2 \leq 0$,
$g_2(x) = (x_1 - 6)^2 + (x_2 - 5)^2 - 82.81 \leq 0$,
and bounds: $13 \leq x_1 \leq 100$, $0 \leq x_2 \leq 100$.

The best known solution is -6961.81381. The optimal solutions obtained by CLA in Table 4.

Example 5: This problem is, as in [19],
 min $f(x) = e^{x_1 x_2 x_3 x_4 x_5}$.
Subject to the linear and nonlinear constraints,
$h_1(x) = x_1^2 + x_2^2 + x_3^2 + x_4^2 + x_5^2 = 0$,

Table 4. Comparsion of the best solution for 4th example with real variables

Design variables	Jong[19]	CLA
x_1	14. 095	14.095
x_2	0.84296	0.842960789
g_1	6.52256e-9	3.33955e-13
g_2	-6.52258e-9	-3.41061e-13
$f(x)$	-6961.8138747	-6961.81387561

Table 5. Comparsion of the best solution for 5th example with real variables

Design variables	Jong[19]	CLA
x_1	-1.717143	-1.7171435996750
x_2	1.595709	1.5957097333077
x_3	1.827247	1.8272457685642
x_4	-0.7636413	0.76364314821295
x_5	-0.763645	0.76364316938380
h_1	6.1522969119e-7	5.41572642731e-7
h_2	1.8043050031e-7	-5.11854597373e-7
h_3	-2.2665673693e-7	7.04107598892e-8
$f(x)$	0.0539498310941	0.05394980622265

$h_2(x) = x_2 x_3 - 5 x_4 x_5 = 0$,
$h_3(x) = x_1^3 + x_2^3 + 1 = 0$,
and bounds: $-2.3 \leq x_i \leq 2.3$, ($i=1,2$), $-3.2 \leq x_j \leq 3.2$, ($j=3,4,5$).

The best known solution is 0.0539498473. The solutions obtained by CLA in Table 5.

Example 6: This problem is, as in [20],

min $f(x) = 6.5 x_1 - 0.5 x_1^2 - x_2 - 2 x_3 - 3 x_4 - 2 x_5 - x_6$.

Subject to the linear and nonlinear constraints,

$g_1(x) = x_1 + 2 x_2 + 8 x_3 + x_4 + 3 x_5 + 5 x_6 - 16 \leq 0$,
$g_2(x) = -8 x_1 - 4 x_2 - 2 x_3 + 2 x_4 + 4 x_5 - x_6 + 1 \leq 0$,
$g_3(x) = 2 x_1 + 0.5 x_2 + 0.2 x_3 - 3 x_4 - x_5 - x_6 - 24 \leq 0$,
$g_4(x) = 0.2 x_1 + 2 x_2 + 0.1 x_3 - 4 x_4 + 2 x_5 + 2 x_6 - 12 \leq 0$,
$g_5(x) = -0.1 x_1 - 0.5 x_2 + 2 x_3 + 5 x_4 - 5 x_5 + 3 x_6 - 3 \leq 0$,
and bounds: $x_i \geq 0$, (,$i=1,2,3$), $0 \leq x_j \leq 1$, ($j=1,2$),and $1 \leq x_6 \leq 2$.

The best known solution is -11. The optimal solutions obtained by CLA in Table 6.

Table 6. Comparsion of the best solution for 6th example with real variables

Design variables	Zbigniew[20]	CLA
x_1	0.0000000	0.0000000
x_2	5.9760890	6.0065110
x_3	0.0059780	0.0001520
x_4	0.9999990	0.9999980
x_5	1.0000000	0.9928240
x_6	0.0000000	0.0000000
g_1	1.0000e-6	-0.0072920
g_2	-16.916314	-17.055056
g_3	-25.0107569	-24.9895321
g_4	-2.04722020	-2.0013068
g_5	-5.97609350	-5.9670815
$f(x)$	-10.988042	-10.992457

Example 7: This problem is, as in [1],

$$\min f(x) = x_1^2 + x_2^2 + x_1 x_2 - 14x_1 - 16x_2 + (x_3 - 10)^2 + 4(x_4 - 5)^2 + (x_5 - 3)^2$$
$$+ 2(x_6 - 1)^2 + 5x_7^2 + 7(x_8 - 11)^2 + 2(x_9 - 10)^2 + (x_{10} - 7)^2 + 45.$$

Subject to the linear and nonlinear constraints,

$g_1(x) = 4x_1 + 5x_2 - 3x_7 + 9x_8 - 105 \leq 0$,
$g_2(x) = 10x_1 - 8x_2 - 17x_7 + 2x_8 \leq 0$,
$g_3(x) = -8x_1 + 2x_2 + 5x_9 - 2x_{10} - 12 \leq 0$,
$g_4(x) = -3x_1 + 6x_2 + 12(x_9 - 8)^2 - 7x_{10} \leq 0$,
$g_5(x) = 3(x_1 - 2)^2 + 4(x_2 - 3)^2 + 2x_3^2 - 7x_4 - 120 \leq 0$,
$g_6(x) = x_1^2 + 2(x_2 - 2)^2 - 2x_1 x_2 + 14x_5 - 6x_6 \leq 0$,
$g_7(x) = 5x_1^2 + 8x_2 + (x_3 - 6)^2 - 2x_4 - 40 \leq 0$,
$g_8(x) = 0.5(x_1 - 8)^2 + 2(x_2 - 4)^2 + 3x_5^2 - x_6 - 30 \leq 0$,

and bounds: $-10 \leq x_i \leq 10$, (i=1,...,10).

The best known solution is 24.3062091. The optimal solutions obtained by CLA in Table 7.

Example 8: This problem is, as in [21],

$$\max f(x) = |\frac{\sum_{i=1}^{n} \cos^4(x_i) - 2\prod_{i=1}^{n} \cos^2(x_i)}{\sqrt{\sum_{i=1}^{n} i x_i^2}}|.$$

Table 7. Comparsion of the best solution for 7th example with real variables

Design variables	Zbigniew[1]	CLA
x_1	2.171996	2.1719961347540
x_2	2.363683	2.3636837460409
x_3	8.773926	8.7739258668515
x_4	5.095984	5.0959845191403
x_5	0.9906548	0.99065499761948
x_6	1.430574	1.4305739055145
x_7	1.321644	1.3216436144857
x_8	9.828726	9.8287263202019
x_9	8.280092	8.2800923143635
x_{10}	8.375927	8.3759262624081
g_1	9.999999e-7	9.307580498330e-6
g_2	0.000000	2.573359697777e-6
g_3	3.999999e-6	7.461051101387e-6
g_4	-50.0239606	-50.023949310087
g_5	1.207695e-5	1.113507011041e-7
g_6	4.304579e-7	1.556877339936e-6
g_7	-5.42644e-6	1.691766030376e-6
g_8	-6.14850124	-6.1485056399865
$f(x)$	24.30620316	24.306180627377

Subject to the linear and nonlinear constraints,

$g_1(x) = \prod_{i=1}^{n} x_i \geq 0.75$,

$g_2(x) = \sum_{i=1}^{n} x_i \leq 7.5n$,

and bounds: $0 \leq x_i \leq 1$, ($i=1,\ldots,20$).

The known best value found (namely 0.803553) was better than the best values of any method discussed earlier. The optimal solutions obtained by CLA is

x=(3.1623727281345, 3.1280419375461, 3.0946389687528, 3.0614422804305, 3.0283524299799, 2.9936728284571, 2.9585306527356, 2.9217381410116, 0.49557615940763, 0.48959098750755, 0.48215047020186, 0.47736554194251, 0.47231988466596, 0.46541746361325, 0.46126836591559, 0.45633003676137, 0.45258207080319, 0.44773893307735, 0.44346139458823, 0.43978895941492), and $f(x)$=0.80361847330915.

$g_1(x) = \prod_{i=1}^{n} x_i = 0.75000000010132 \geq 0.75$,

$g_2(x) = \sum_{i=1}^{n} x_i = 29.932380234948 \leq 7.5n$.

According to the computation results, we can find the optimal objective function value is smaller than that obtained, as in [21].

5 Conclusion

We proposed a closed loop algorithms with SWIFT can search for global solution. The simulation results on the eight difficult test functions show the proposed CLA is effective for nonlinear optimization problems. In further work, the investigation problem is how to select the optimal increment and to accelerate the convergence of the proposed CLA.

Acknowledgment

This work was supported in part by the Hi-Tech Research and Development Program, Ministry of Science and Technology, P. R. China under Grant 2002AA420110.

References

1. Michalewicz Z., Schoenauer M.: Evolutionary algorithms for constrained parameter optimization problems. Evolutionary Computation, 1996, 4(1):1-32
2. Lin Y.Ch., Wang F.Sh.: Hybrid differential evolution with multiplier updating method for nonlinear constrained optimization problems. In: Proceedings of the Congress on Evolutionary Computation, Piscataway, U.S.A., Vol.1 (2002) 872-877
3. Chen L.N, Aihara K.: Global searching ability of chaotic neural networks. IEEE Transactions on Circuits and Systems-I: Fundamental Theory and Applications, 1999, 46(8):974-993
4. Wang L.P., Smith K.: On chaotic simulated annealing. IEEE Transactions on Neural Networks, 1998, 9(4):716-718
5. Chen Zh.F, Shi H.Y, An Y.J, Sun Ch.Zh.: Globally convergent approach based on chaotic theory for underwater robot motor optimization. In: Proceedings of the IEEE International Conference on Robotics, Intelligent Systems and Signal processing, Changsha, China, Vol.2 (2003)996-1001
6. Liu Sh.S, Hou Zh,J.: Weighted gradient direction based on chaos optimization algorithm for nonlinear programming problem. In: Proceedings of the 4th World Congress on Intelligent Control and Automation, Shanghai, China, Vol.3 (2002)1779-1783
7. Teixeira F.H., Loureiro Legey L. F.: Generation expansion planning: an iterative genetic algorithm approach. IEEE Transactions on Power Systems, 2002, 17(3):901-906
8. Jean M. R., Stephane P.F.: Hybrid methods using genetic algorithms for global optimization. IEEE Transactions on System, Man, and Cybernetics-Part B: Cybernetics, 1996, 26(2):243-258
9. Fogel D.B.: An introduction to simulated evolutionary optimization. IEEE Transaction on Neural Networks, 1994, 5(1):3-14
10. Zhu X.L., Zhou J.P., Zhou J.H.: Optimization design of hydraulic servo actuators with 3-D.O.F. and motion decoupling. In: Proceedings of the Europe-Asia Symposium on Advanced Engineering Design and Manufacture, Xi'an, China, Vol.1 (2004)479-488
11. Leahy R., Jeffs B.,Wu Z. : A nonlinear simplex algorithm for minimum order solutions. In: International Conference on Acoustics, Speech, and Signal Processing, New York, U.S.A., Vol.2 (1988)745-748

12. Yang J., Yamaguchi, Y., Boerner, W.M.: Numerical methods for solving the optimal problem of contrast enhancement. IEEE Transactions on Geoscience and Remote Sensing, 2000, 38(2):965-971
13. Sandgren E.: Nonlinear integer and discrete programming in mechanical design. ASME Journal of Mechanical Design, 1990, 112(2):223-229
14. Zeng S.Y., Ding L.X., Kang L.S.: An evolutionary algorithm of contracting search space based on partial ordering relation for constrained optimization problems. In: Proceedings of the Fifth International Conference on Algorithms and Architectures for Parallel Processing, Beijing, China, Vol.1 (2002)76-81
15. Carlos A.,Coello C.: Self-adaptive penalties for GA-based optimization. In: Proceedings of the Congress on Evolutionary Computation, Washington, DC, U.S.A., Vol.1 (1999)573-580
16. Kannan B.K., Kramer S.N.: An argumented Lagrange multiplier based method for mixed integer discrete continuous optimization and its application to engineering design optimization. Journal of mechanical Design, 1994, 116(3):318-320
17. Homaifar A., Lai S.H.Y., Qi X.: Constrained optimization via genetic algorithms. Simulation, 1994, 62(4):242-254
18. Jeffrey A.J.,Christopher R.H.: On the use of non-stationary penalty functions to solve nonlinear constrained optimization problems with GAs. In: IEEE International Conference on Evolutionary Computation, Orlando, U.S.A., Vol.1 (1994)579-584
19. Kim J.H., Hyun M.: Evolutionary programming techniques for constrained optimization problems. IEEE Transactions on Evolutionary Computation, 1997, 1(2):129-140
20. Michalewicz Z., Thomas D.L.: Evolutionary operations for continuous convex parameter spaces. In: Proceedings of the 3rd Annual Conference on Evolutionary Programming, San Diego, U.S.A., Vol.1 (1994)84-97
21. Schoenauer M., Michalewicz Z.: Evolutionary computation at the edge of feasibility. In: Proceedings of the 4th Parallel Problem Solving from Nature, Berlin, Germany, Vol.1 (1996)245-254

Harmony Search for Generalized Orienteering Problem: Best Touring in China

Zong Woo Geem[1], Chung-Li Tseng[2], and Yongjin Park[3]

[1] Johns Hopkins University, Environmental Planning and Management Program,
729 Fallsgrove Drive #6133, Rockville, Maryland 20850, USA
geem@jhu.edu
[2] University of Missouri,
Department of Engineering Management,
215 Engineering Management, Rolla,
Missouri 65409, USA
chungli@umr.edu
[3] Keimyung University,
Department of Transportation Engineering,
1000 Sindang, Dalseo, Daegu, 704-701, South Korea
ypark@kmu.ac.kr

Abstract. In order to overcome the drawbacks of mathematical optimization techniques, soft computing algorithms have been vigorously introduced during the past decade. However, there are still some possibilities of devising new algorithms based on analogies with natural phenomena. A nature-inspired algorithm, mimicking the improvisation process of music players, has been recently developed and named Harmony Search (HS). The algorithm has been successfully applied to various engineering optimization problems. In this paper, the HS was applied to a TSP-like NP-hard Generalized Orienteering Problem (GOP) which is to find the utmost route under the total distance limit while satisfying multiple goals. Example area of the GOP is eastern part of China. The results of HS showed that the algorithm could find good solutions when compared to those of artificial neural network.

1 Introduction

Over the several decades, optimization techniques such as linear programming (LP), non-linear programming (NLP), and dynamic programming (DP) have gathered attention among engineers. However, the mathematical techniques can excellently perform mostly in simple and ideal models.

In order to overcome the shortcomings of mathematical techniques, nature-inspired soft computing algorithms have been introduced. Many evolutionary or meta-heuristic algorithms have been developed that combine rules and randomness mimicking natural phenomenon [1-8].

The purpose of this paper is to introduce a recently-developed nature-inspired algorithm, Harmony Search, and to apply the algorithm to a TSP-like NP-hard Generalized Orienteering Problem (GOP), proposed by Wang et al. [9].

2 Harmony Search Algorithm

Harmony Search (HS) algorithm was recently developed in an analogy with music improvisation process where music players improvise the pitches of their instruments to obtain better harmony [10].

The HS algorithm has been successfully applied to various benchmarking and real-world problems including traveling salesperson problem [10], parameter optimization of river flood model [11], design of pipeline network [12], and design of truss structures [13]. Consequently, the HS algorithm provides a possibility of success in a TSP-like NP-hard problem.

As existing soft computing algorithms are found in the paradigm of natural processes, a new algorithm can be conceptualized from a musical performance process (for example, a jazz trio) involving searching for a better harmony. Musical performance seeks a best state (fantastic harmony) determined by aesthetic estimation, as the optimization process seeks a best state (global optimum: minimum cost; minimum error; maximum benefit; or maximum efficiency) determined by objective function evaluation. Aesthetic estimation is done by the set of the pitches sounded by joined instruments, as objective function evaluation is done by the set of the values produced by composed variables; the aesthetic sounds can be improved practice after practice, as the objective function values can be improved iteration by iteration.

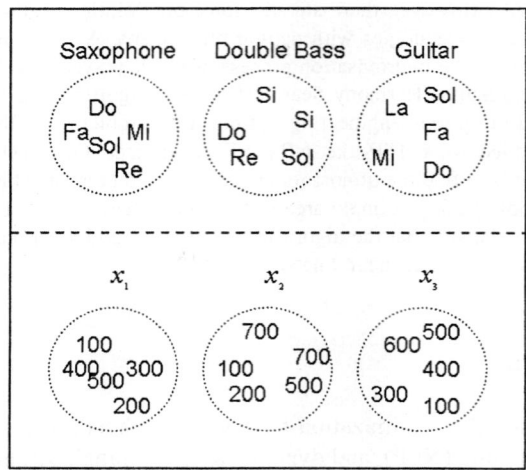

Fig. 1. Structure of Harmony Memory

Figure 1 shows the structure of the Harmony Memory (HM) that is the core part of the HS algorithm. Consider a jazz trio composed of saxophone, double bass, and guitar. There exist certain amount of preferable pitches in each musician's memory: saxophonist, {Do, Fa, Mi, Sol, Re}; double bassist, {Si, Do, Si, Re, Sol}; and guitarist, {La, Sol, Fa, Mi, Do}. If saxophonist randomly plays Sol out of its memory {Do, Fa, Mi, Sol, Re}, double bassist Si out of {Si, Do, Si, Re, Sol}, and guitarist Do out of

{La, Sol, Fa, Mi, Do}, the new harmony (Sol, Si, Do) becomes another harmony (musically C-7 chord). And if this new harmony is better than existing worst harmony in the HM, the new harmony is included in the HM and the worst harmony is excluded from the HM. This procedure is repeated until fantastic harmony is found.

In real optimization, each musician can be replaced with each decision variable, and its preferred sound pitches can be replaced with each variable's preferred values. Let us set that each decision variable represents pipe diameter between two nodes and the music pitches {Do, Re, Mi, Fa, Sol, La, Si} correspond to pipe diameters {100mm, 200mm, 300mm, 400mm, 500mm, 600mm, 700mm}, respectively. And if first variable chooses 500mm out of {100mm, 400mm, 300mm, 500mm, 200mm}, second one {700mm} out of {700mm, 100mm, 700mm, 200mm, 500mm}, and third one {100mm} out of {600mm, 500mm, 400mm, 300mm, 100mm}, those values (500mm, 700mm, 100mm) make another solution vector. And if this new vector is better than existing worst vector in the HM, the new vector is included in the HM and the worst vector is excluded from the HM. This procedure is repeated until certain stopping criterion is satisfied.

According to the above algorithm concept, the steps of HS for the generalized orienteering problem are as follows:

Step 1. Initialize the Parameters for Problem and Algorithm.

Step 2. Initialize the Harmony Memory (HM).

Step 3. Improvise a New Harmony.

Step 4. Update the Harmony Memory.

Step 5. Check the stopping criterion.

2.1 Initialize Parameters

In Step 1, the optimization problem is specified as follows:

$$\text{Minimize } f(\mathbf{x}). \tag{1}$$

$$\text{Subject to } x_i \in \mathbf{X}_i, i = 1, 2, ..., N. \tag{2}$$

where $f(\mathbf{x})$ is an objective function; $\mathbf{x}$ is the set of each decision variable x_i; $\mathbf{X}_i$ is the set of possible range of values for each decision variable, that is, $\mathbf{X}_i = \{x_i(1), x_i(2), ..., x_i(K)\}$ for discrete decision variables $(x_i(1) < x_i(2) < ... < x_i(K))$; N is the number of decision variables (number of music instruments); and K is the number of possible values for the discrete variables (pitch range of each instrument).

For the GOP, the objective function becomes the total score of individual goals, as shown in Equation 7; and each decision variable represents each city, having the value of next city number to move.

The HS algorithm parameters are also specified in this step: Harmony Memory Size (HMS) (= number of solution vectors), Harmony Memory Considering Rate (HMCR), Pitch Adjusting Rate (PAR), and Stopping Criteria (= number of improvisation). Here, HMCR and PAR are the parameters of HS algorithm explained in Step 3.

2.2 Initialize Harmony Memory

In Step 2, the Harmony Memory (HM) matrix, as shown in Equation 3, is filled with as many randomly generated solution vectors as the size of the HM (HMS).

$$\begin{bmatrix} x_1^1 & x_2^1 & \cdots & x_{N-1}^1 & x_N^1 \\ x_1^2 & x_2^2 & \cdots & x_{N-1}^2 & x_N^2 \\ \vdots & \cdots & \cdots & \cdots & \cdots \\ x_1^{HMS-1} & x_2^{HMS-1} & \cdots & x_{N-1}^{HMS-1} & x_N^{HMS-1} \\ x_1^{HMS} & x_2^{HMS} & \cdots & x_{N-1}^{HMS} & x_N^{HMS} \end{bmatrix} \Rightarrow \begin{matrix} f(x^1) \\ f(x^2) \\ \vdots \\ f(x^{HMS-1}) \\ f(x^{HMS}) \end{matrix} \qquad (3)$$

2.3 Improvise New Harmony

A new harmony vector, $x' = (x_1', x_2', \ldots, x_N')$ is generated by following three rules: HM consideration; Pitch adjustment; or totally random generation. For instance, the value of the first decision variable (x_1') for the new vector can be chosen from values stored in HM ($x_1^1 \sim x_1^{HMS}$). Value of other variables (x_i') can be chosen in the same style. There is also a possibility that totally random value can be chosen. HMCR parameter, which varies between 0 and 1, sets the rate whether a value stored in HM is chosen or a random value is chosen, as follows:

$$x_i' \leftarrow \begin{cases} x_i' \in \{x_i^1, x_i^2, \ldots, x_i^{HMS}\} & \text{w.p.} \quad HMCR \\ x_i' \in X_i & \text{w.p.} \quad (1-HMCR) \end{cases} \qquad (4)$$

The HMCR is the rate of choosing one value from historical values stored in HM while (1-HMCR) is the rate of randomly choosing one value from the possible value range.

After choosing the new harmony vector $x' = (x_1', x_2', \ldots, x_N')$, pitch-adjusting decision is examined for each component of the new vector. This procedure uses the PAR parameter to set the rate of pitch adjustment as follows:

$$x_i' \leftarrow \begin{cases} \text{Adjusting Pitch} & \text{w.p.} \quad PAR \\ \text{Doing Nothing} & \text{w.p.} \quad (1-PAR) \end{cases} \qquad (5)$$

In the pitch adjusting process, a value moves to its neighboring value with probability of PAR, or just stays in its original value with probability (1-PAR). If the pitch adjustment for x_i' is determined, its position in the value range X_i is identified in the form of $x_i(k)$ (the kth element in X_i), and the pitch-adjusted value for $x_i(k)$ becomes

$$x_i' \leftarrow x_i(k+m). \qquad (6)$$

where $m \in \{\ldots, -2, -1, 1, 2, \ldots\}$ is a neighboring index used for discrete-type decision variables.

The HMCR and PAR parameters in Harmony Search help the algorithm find globally and locally improved solution, respectively.

2.4 Update Harmony Memory

If the new harmony vector, $x' = (x'_1, x'_2, ..., x'_N)$ is better than the worst harmony in the HM, judged in terms of the objective function value, the new harmony is included in the HM and the existing worst harmony is excluded from the HM.

2.5 Check Stopping Criterion

If the stopping criterion (maximum number of improvisations) is satisfied, computation is terminated. Otherwise, Steps 3 and 4 are repeated.

3 Generalized Orienteering Problem

In this study, HS is applied to generalized orienteering problem (GOP). The objective of GOP is to find the optimal tour under the constraint of total distance limit while satisfying multiple goals.

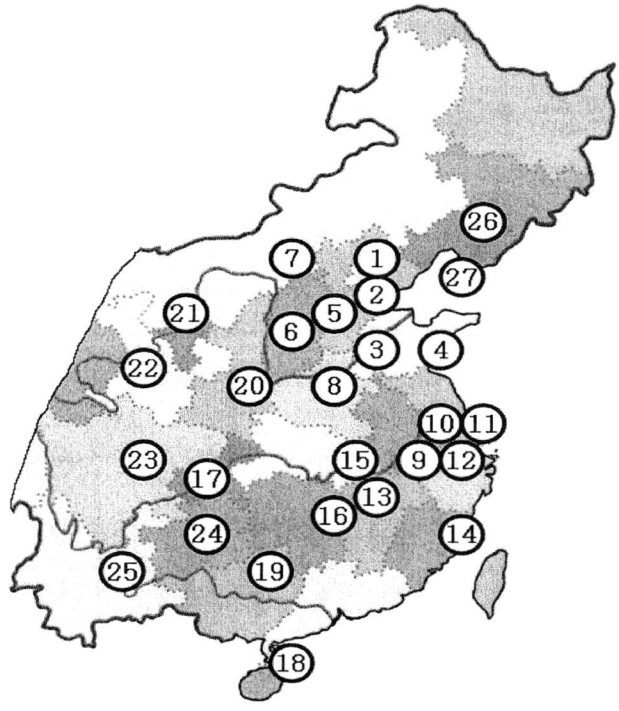

Fig. 2. Map of 27 cities in eastern part of China

If a traveler visits eastern part of China, as shown in Figure 2, and he/she wants to travel as many cities as possible with the purpose of best fulfilling multiple factors such as 1) natural beauty, 2) historical interest, 3) cultural event, and 4) business opportunities under the limited total moving distance, his/her travel can become generalized orienteering problem where each city has certain quantified scores for all factors and the estimation of a tour is performed based on the summation of those scores in the tour.

The GOP is a generalization of the orienteering problem (OP) and the main difference between the two is that each city in GOP has multiple scores while each city in OP has only one score [14-16].

Table 1. Physical location and score vector for each city

No.	Name	Longitude	Latitude	S_1	S_2	S_3	S_4
1	Beijing	116.40	39.91	8	10	10	7
2	Tianjin	117.18	39.16	6	5	8	8
3	Jinan	117.00	36.67	7	7	5	6
4	Qingdao	120.33	36.06	7	4	5	7
5	Shijiazhuang	114.50	38.05	5	4	5	5
6	Taiyuan	112.58	37.87	5	6	5	5
7	Huhehaote	111.70	40.87	6	6	5	5
8	Zhengzhou	113.60	34.75	5	6	5	5
9	Huangshan	118.29	29.73	9	3	2	2
10	Nanjing	118.75	32.04	7	8	8	6
11	Shanghai	121.45	31.22	5	4	9	9
12	Hangzhou	120.15	30.25	9	8	7	6
13	Nanchang	115.88	28.35	7	6	5	5
14	Fuzhou	119.30	26.10	6	5	5	7
15	Wuhan	114.30	30.55	6	6	8	6
16	Changsha	113.00	28.20	6	6	6	5
17	Guangzhou	113.15	23.15	6	6	5	10
18	Haikou	110.35	20.02	7	3	4	8
19	Guilin	110.29	25.28	10	4	4	4
20	Xi'an	108.92	34.28	5	9	8	6
21	Yinchuan	106.27	38.48	5	7	5	5
22	Lanzhou	103.80	36.03	7	6	5	6
23	Chengdo	104.07	30.66	6	7	6	5
24	Guiyang	106.00	26.59	8	5	4	5
25	Kunming	102.80	25.05	9	7	7	6
26	Shenyang	123.40	41.80	5	8	5	6
27	Dalian	121.60	38.92	7	5	6	7

Let V be the set of N points and E the set of edges between points in V. G = {V, E} is a complete graph. Each edge in E has a symmetric, non-negative cost d(i, j) which becomes the distance or travel time between point i and j. Assume the starting point is point 1 and the end point is point N. Each point i in V has a non-negative score vector $S(i) = (S_1(i), S_2(i), ..., S_m(i))^T$, where m is the number of individual goals, and $S_g(i)$ is the score of point i with respect to goal g.

A differentiable objective function that defines total score of a path P, which starts at point 1 and ends at point N can be formulated as follows:

$$Z = \sum_{g=1}^{m} W_g \left[\left\{ \sum_{i \in P} [S_g(i)]^k \right\}^{1/k} \right]. \quad (7)$$

where W_g is the weight of goal g, and the exponent k is set to 5 in this problem.

Table 1 presents city data such as city number, longitude, latitude, and score vector. S_1, S_2, S_3, and S_4 are the scores approximately scaled from 1 to 10 in the aspects of natural beauty, historical interest, cultural event, and business opportunities, proposed by Wang et al. [9].

4 Computation and Results

For applying HS to GOP, the values of algorithm parameters such as number of music instruments (= number of decision variables), number of improvisations (= number of function evaluations), HMCR, PAR, and HMS are specified.

In GOP, number of music instruments (= 27) is substituted with the number of decision variables that represent every city, and the value of each decision variable represents its next assigned city; Number of improvisations (= 50,000) stands for the number of maximum iterations or objective function evaluations.

HMCR is the rate of choosing any one value from the HM, and thus (1 - HMCR) is the rate of choosing any value from all the possible range of each decision variable. For the computation, various HMCR's are used.

PAR is originally the rate of moving to a neighboring value from one value in HM, but this parameter is modified for GOP. In this computation, PAR becomes the rate of moving to the nearest city from one city. There are total three PAR's (PAR1 = 0.35, PAR2 = 0.105, and PAR3 = 0.045) that are the rates of moving to nearest, second nearest, and third nearest cities, respectively.

HMS is the number of harmony vectors simultaneously stored in HM. For this computation, various HMS's are used.

In this computation, a tour starts from city 1, and next city is assigned based on the following three rules:

Rule 1. Choose any city stored in HM as a next city with probability HMCR × (1-PAR), where PAR = PAR1 + PAR2 + PAR3.

Rule 2. Choose the nearest city as a next city with probability HMCR × PAR1; Or choose the second nearest city with probability HMCR × PAR2; Or choose the third nearest city with probability HMCR × PAR3.

Rule 3. Choose next city randomly with probability (1-HMCR).

Whenever the HS visits new city, the scores of four goals in the city are added using Equation 7 and the distance up to the city is also added using trigonometric formulas on spherical surface (average earth radius, r = 6,371 km) using Equation 8.

$$d(x, y) = r \cdot \arcsin\left(\sin(c_1)\sin\left(\frac{\pi(90-b_1)}{180}\right) \Big/ \sin(e)\right) \qquad (8)$$

where

$$e = \arctan(d_1) + \arctan(d_2)$$

$$d_1 = \cos\frac{c_2}{2} \Big/ \cos\frac{c_3}{2} \tan\frac{c_1}{2}, \quad d_2 = \sin\frac{c_2}{2} \Big/ \sin\frac{c_3}{2} \tan\frac{c_1}{2}$$

$$c_1 = (a_1 - a_2)\frac{\pi}{180}, \quad c_2 = (b_2 - b_1)\frac{\pi}{180}, \quad c_3 = \pi - (b_1 + b_2)\frac{\pi}{180}.$$

where $d(\cdot)$ is a function calculating the distance (in kilometer) between two cities (x and y); a_1 is longitude of city x; b_1 is latitude of city x; a_2 is longitude of city y; and b_2 is latitude of city y.

If the total distance of a tour is over the distance limit (5,000 km in the problem), penalty (the absolute difference between computed distance and limit distance) is also taxed to the original summarized score.

There are five different weight vectors including W_0 = (0.25, 0.25, 0.25, 0.25), W_1 = (1, 0, 0, 0), W_2 = (0, 1, 0, 0), W_3 = (0, 0, 1, 0), and W_4 = (0, 0, 0, 1). The first weight gives equal weight to each of the four goals. The four other weight vectors stress one goal and ignore the other three. And, each weight case runs 45 times with different HMS's and HMCR's.

Table 2. Comparison of GOP results from HS and ANN

Weight	Method	Score	Distance	Tour
W_0	HS	12.38	4993.4	1-2-3-10-11-12-9-13-17-19-16-20-6-5-1
	ANN	12.38	4993.4	1-2-3-10-11-12-9-13-17-19-16-20-6-5-1
W_1	HS	13.08	4985.4	1-2-3-15-24-19-13-9-12-10-4-27-1
	ANN	13.05	4987.7	1-2-3-4-10-11-12-9-13-16-19-24-20-6-5-1
W_2	HS	12.56	4910.6	1-26-27-4-10-12-9-13-16-15-20-8-3-2-1
	ANN	12.51	4875.1	1-2-26-27-3-10-11-12-9-13-15-20-6-5-1
W_3	HS	12.78	4987.5	1-2-3-5-6-20-8-15-16-13-9-12-11-10-4-27-1
	ANN	12.78	4987.5	1-2-3-5-6-20-8-15-16-13-9-12-11-10-4-27-1
W_4	HS	12.40	4845.2	1-2-27-4-10-11-12-14-17-16-15-3-1
	ANN	12.36	4989.8	1-2-3-10-9-13-16-17-14-12-11-4-27-1

Table 2 represents the best tours in five different weight vector cases and compares them with the tours obtained using artificial neural network (ANN) approach [9]. Compared to the results of ANN, HS could find better score solutions in cases of W_1, W_2, and W_4 while find same score solutions in cases of W_0 and W_3: With the weight vector W_0, HS found 12.38 as the best score with the score range between 11.95 ~ 12.38; with the weight vector W_1, HS found 13.08 as the best score with the score range between 12.58 ~ 13.08; with the weight vector W_2, HS found 12.56 as the best score with the score range between 12.34 ~ 12.56; with the weight vector W_3, HS found 12.78 as the best score with the score range between 12.50 ~ 12.78; with the weight vector W_4, HS found 12.40 as the best score with the score range between 12.14 ~ 12.40.

5 Conclusions

In this study, a recently-developed nature-inspired algorithm, HS, has been introduced and applied to an NP-hard GOP whose objective is to find the best tour in eastern part of China. The algorithm, HS, mimics three major behaviors of music players: 1) memory consideration; 2) pitch adjustment; and 3) random choice. These behaviors can be successfully translated in GOP: 'memory consideration' becomes that HS chooses any one city from the cities stored in HM; 'pitch adjustment' is that HS chooses the nearest city as next city; and 'random choice' is that HS chooses any one city from all the possible cities.

After applied to GOP, HS could find equal or better solutions when compared with those of ANN. In order for HS to obtain better results in GOP in the future, some additional operators especially for GOP might be implemented along with existing memory consideration and pitch adjustment operators. Also, it is expected that HS, as a nature-inspired algorithm, can be applied to other optimization problems in various fields.

References

1. Fogel, L. J., Owens, A. J. and Walsh. M. J.: Artificial Intelligence Though Simulated Evolution. John Wiley, Chichester, UK (1966)
2. De Jong, K.: Analysis of the Behavior of a Class of Genetic Adaptive Systems. Ph.D. Thesis, University of Michigan, Ann Arbor, MI, USA (1975)
3. Koza, J. R.: Genetic Programming: A Paradigm for Genetically Breeding Populations of Computer Programs to Solve Problems. Report No. STA-CS-90-1314, Stanford University, Stanford, CA, USA (1990)
4. Holland, J. H.: Adaptation in Natural and Artificial Systems. University of Michigan Press, Ann Arbor, MI, USA, (1975)
5. Goldberg, D. E.: Genetic Algorithms in Search Optimization and Machine Learning. Addison Wesley, MA, USA (1989)

6. Glover, F.: Heuristic for Integer Programming using Surrogate Constraints. Decision Sciences. 8(1) (1977) 156-166
7. Dorigo, M., Maniezzo, V., and Colorni, A.: The Ant System: Optimization by a Colony of Cooperating Agents. IEEE Transactions on Systems, Man, and Cybernetics-Part B. 26(1) (1996) 29-41
8. Kirkpatrick, S., Gelatt, C., and Vecchi, M.: Optimization by Simulated Annealing. Science. 220(4598) (1983) 671-680
9. Wang, Q., Sun, C., and Golden, B. L.: Using Artificial Neural Networks to Solve Generalized Orienteering Problems. Proceedings of Artificial Neural Networks in Engineering Conference (ANNIE '96). (1996)
10. Geem, Z. W., Kim, J. H., and Loganathan, G. V.: A New Heuristic Optimization Algorithm: Harmony Search. Simulation. 76(2) (2001) 60-68
11. Kim, J. H., Geem, Z. W., and Kim, E. S.: Parameter Estimation of the Nonlinear Muskingum Model using Harmony Search. Journal of the American Water Resources Association. 37(5) (2001) 1131-1138
12. Geem, Z. W., Kim, J. H., and Loganathan. G. V.: Harmony Search Optimization: Application to Pipe Network Design. International Journal of Modelling and Simulation. 22(2) (2002) 125-133
13. Kang, S. L., and Geem, Z. W.: A New Structural Optimization Method Based on the Harmony Search Algorithm. Computers and Structures. 82(9-10) (2004) 781-798
14. Chao, I. -M., Golden, B. L., and Wasil, E. A.: The Team Orienteering Problem. European Journal of Operational Research. 88 (1996) 464-474
15. Chao, I. -M., Golden, B. L., and Wasil, E. A.: A Fast and Effective Heuristic for the Orienteering Problem. European Journal of Operational Research. 88 (1996) 475-489
16. Tasgetiren, M. F., and Smith, A. E.: A Genetic Algorithm for the Orienteering Problem. Proceedings of Congress on Evolutionary Computation 2000 (CEC 2000). (2000), 1190-1195.

Harmony Search in Water Pump Switching Problem

Zong Woo Geem

Johns Hopkins University, Environmental Planning and Management Program,
729 Fallsgrove Drive #6133, Rockville, Maryland 20850, USA
geem@jhu.edu

Abstract. The purpose of this paper is to introduce a recently-developed nature-inspired algorithm, harmony search (HS), and to apply the algorithm to water pump switching problem. The HS algorithm is conceptualized using the musical improvisation process of searching for a better state of harmony. This paper describes a HS algorithm-based approach for the optimal switching problem in serial water pumping system. A standard example from the literature is presented to demonstrate the effectiveness of the proposed method, and the results are compared to genetic algorithm and branch & bound method. Computational results indicate that the HS approach becomes a good optimization model for solving water pump switching problem.

1 Introduction

The water system optimization is a challenging activity that has received considerable attention over the decades. Engineers are able to produce better designs while saving time and money through optimization. Traditionally, various mathematical models such as linear programming, nonlinear programming, and dynamic programming have been applied to optimize water systems. In these algorithms, however, an increase in terms of the number of variables would exponentially increase the number of function evaluations and require huge memory space in computer. These characteristics are limiting their application to a variety of water system optimization problems.

The computational drawbacks of mathematical algorithms have forced engineers to rely on evolutionary or meta-heuristic algorithms such as genetic algorithm, simulated annealing and tabu search to solve various water system optimization problems. The common factor in these soft computing algorithms is that they combine rules and randomness to imitate natural phenomena.

In the past two decades, these soft computing algorithms have been broadly applied to solve various water system optimization problems [1-7]. These algorithms have successfully overcome several deficiencies of conventional mathematical optimization algorithms. However, a new nature-inspired algorithm based on analogies with natural phenomena still remains to be explored.

Recently, Geem et al. [8] developed a harmony search (HS) algorithm that was conceptualized using the musical improvisation process of searching for a perfect state of harmony. The harmony in music is analogous to the solution vector, and the behavior of musician's improvisation is analogous to local and global search schemes in optimization techniques. These behaviors were successfully translated in various optimization applications [8-11].

The purpose of this paper is to introduce the nature-inspired HS algorithm applied to least-energy water pump switching problem. A standard example from the literature is presented to demonstrate the effectiveness of the proposed approach compared to other optimization algorithms.

2 Water Pump Switching Problem

Water pump switching problem is to supply water in a system while minimizing energy cost and satisfying adequate pressure requirement in the system. The pumping system consists of n pipes and n pumping stations with m pumps in series within each station, as illustrated in Figure 1. Although Goldberg and Kuo [1] first tackled the problem using basic genetic algorithm, there has not been any better research so far using advanced genetic algorithm techniques.

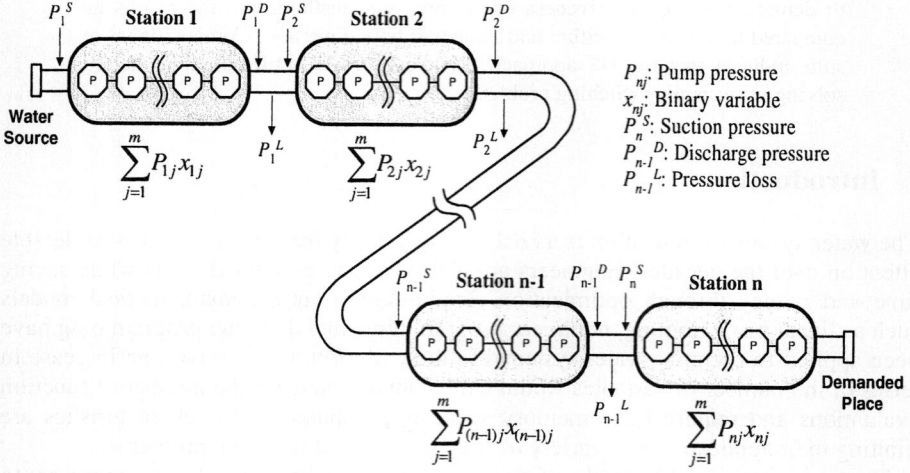

Fig. 1. Schematic of Water Pump Switching Problem

Water can be delivered from water source into demanding place by the pressure which is added by each pump and consumed along each pipeline due to the friction between water and pipe. Suppose that a pump j in station i can add pressure P_{ij} using energy E_{ij} if the pump is turned on. The energy E_{ij} (horsepower) can be calculated using a function of specific weight γ (= 62.4 lb/ft^3), flow rate Q_0 (= 19 cfs in this study), pressure rise P_{ij} (in psi) across pump, and motor-pump efficiency η_{ij}.

$$E_{ij} = \frac{\gamma Q_0 P_{ij}}{238.3 \, \eta_{ij}} \tag{1}$$

By assigning a binary variable $x_{ij} \in \{0,1\}$ to each pump at each station to denote the on/off scheduling of the pump, the objective function of the problem is to minimize the total electrical energy (horsepower) as follows:

$$\text{Minimize} \quad f(\mathbf{x}) = \sum_{i=1}^{n}\sum_{j=1}^{m} E_{ij} x_{ij} \qquad (2)$$

The objective function for water pump switching problem, as in Equation 2, subjects to the following constraints:

Discharge Pressure Constraint: A discharge pressure P_i^D in pumping station i should be equal to the summation of suction pressure P_i^S and all operating pump pressures $\sum_{j=1}^{m} P_{ij} x_{ij}$.

$$P_i^D = P_i^S + \sum_{j=1}^{m} P_{ij} x_{ij}, \quad i = 1,\ldots,n \qquad (3)$$

Discharge Pressure Bound Constraint: Discharge pressure in any station should be placed less than upper-limit discharge pressure $_U P_i^D$.

$$P_i^D \leq {_U P_i^D}, \quad i = 1,\ldots,n \qquad (4)$$

Suction Pressure Constraint: A suction pressure in pumping station $i+1$ should be calculated by subtracting pressure loss P_i^L, which is occurred along the pipeline i, from discharge pressure in pumping station i.

$$P_{i+1}^S = P_i^D - P_i^L, \quad i = 1,\ldots,n-1 \qquad (5)$$

Suction Pressure Bound Constraint: Any suction pressure should be placed between lower suction pressure $_L P_i^S$ and upper suction pressure $_U P_i^S$.

$$_L P_i^S \leq P_i^S \leq {_U P_i^S}, \quad i = 1,\ldots,n \qquad (6)$$

Initial Suction Pressure Constraint: Initial suction pressure is assumed to be zero.

$$P_1^S = 0 \qquad (7)$$

Binary Decision Variable Constraint: The binary value (0 or 1) is assigned to decision variable x_{ij}.

$$x_{ij} \in \{0,1\}, \quad i = 1,\ldots,n \quad j = 1,\ldots,m \qquad (8)$$

3 Harmony Search Algorithm

The recently-developed HS algorithm is based on music performing process that occurs when musicians search for the better state of harmony, such as during jazz improvisation. Jazz improvisation seeks to find musically pleasing harmony (a perfect state) determined by an aesthetic standard, just as the optimization process seeks to find a global solution (a perfect state) determined by an objective function. The pitch of each musical instrument determines the aesthetic quality, just as the objective function value is determined by the set of values assigned to each design variable.

The procedure of the HS algorithm consists of Steps 1 through 5, as follows:

Step 1. Initialize optimization problem and HS algorithm parameters.
Step 2. Initialize harmony memory (HM).
Step 3. Improvise a new harmony from HM.
Step 4. Update HM.
Step 5. Check the stopping criterion.

Step 1: First, the optimization problem is specified as follows:

$$\text{Minimize } f(x) \text{ s.t. } x_i \in \mathbf{X}_i, i = 1, 2, ..., N \tag{9}$$

where $f(x)$ is an objective function (Equation 2 in this study); x is the set of each decision variable x_i; $\mathbf{X}_i$ is the set of possible range of values for each decision variable (0 or 1 in this study); N is the number of musical instruments (number of decision variables); and K is the pitch range of each instrument (number of possible values for the discrete variables).

The HS algorithm parameters that are required to solve the optimization problem of Equation 9 are also specified in this step: harmony memory considering rate (HMCR), pitch adjusting rate (PAR), harmony memory size (HMS, that is, number of solution vectors), and termination criterion (number of improvisations, that is, number of function evaluations). Here, HMCR and PAR are parameters that are used to improve solution vectors. Both are defined in Step 3.

Step 2: Harmony memory (HM), which is a matrix shown in Equation 10, is filled with as many randomly generated solution vectors as the HMS.

$$\text{HM} = \begin{bmatrix} x_1^1 & x_2^1 & \cdots & x_{N-1}^1 & x_N^1 \\ x_1^2 & x_2^2 & \cdots & x_{N-1}^2 & x_N^2 \\ \vdots & \cdots & \cdots & \cdots & \cdots \\ x_1^{HMS-1} & x_2^{HMS-1} & \cdots & x_{N-1}^{HMS-1} & x_N^{HMS-1} \\ x_1^{HMS} & x_2^{HMS} & \cdots & x_{N-1}^{HMS} & x_N^{HMS} \end{bmatrix} \begin{matrix} \Rightarrow f(x^1) \\ \Rightarrow f(x^2) \\ \Rightarrow \vdots \\ \Rightarrow f(x^{HMS-1}) \\ \Rightarrow f(x^{HMS}) \end{matrix} \tag{10}$$

Step 3: A new harmony vector, $x' = (x_1', x_2', ..., x_N')$ is generated based on three rules: memory considerations, pitch adjustments, and randomization.

For instance, the value of the first decision variable (x'_1) can be chosen from any value in the specified HM range ($x^1_1 \sim x^{HMS}_1$). However, there is also a possibility that totally random value can be chosen for the decision variable x'_1:

$$x'_i \leftarrow \begin{cases} x'_i \in \{x^1_i, x^2_i, ..., x^{HMS}_i\} & w.p. \quad HMCR \\ x'_i \in X_i & w.p. \quad (1-HMCR) \end{cases} \quad (11)$$

where HMCR, which varies between 0 and 1, is the probability of choosing one value from the historical values stored in the HM, and the complement (1-HMCR) is the probability of random feasible value, not limited to those stored in the HM. Values of the other decision variables ($x'_2, ..., x'_N$) can be chosen in the same manner.

After the memory considering operation, pitch adjusting operation follows. The pitch adjusting operation is performed only for the values which were chosen from the HM. This operation uses the PAR parameter that sets the rate of moving to neighboring values for the originally chosen value from the HM.

For the water pump switching problem in this study, however, the pitch adjusting operation is not performed because candidate values for each decision variable are only 0 or 1.

Step 4: If the new harmony vector $x' = (x'_1, x'_2, ..., x'_N)$ is better than the worst harmony in the HM in terms of the objective function value, the new harmony is included in the HM and the existing worst harmony is excluded from the HM.

Step 5: The computations are terminated when the termination criterion (number of function evaluations in this study) is satisfied. If not, Steps 3 and 4 are repeated.

4 Computation and Results

The HS algorithm is applied to the water pump switching system which consists of 10 pipes ($n = 10$) and 10 pump stations ($n = 10$) with 4 pumps ($m = 4$) in series within each station. Thus, the number of decision variables (pump status variables) is 40 ($= n \times m$). In applying the HS algorithm to the problem, each decision variable x_{ij} ($i = 1, ..., n$, $j = 1, ..., m$) has a binary value (0 or 1), representing pump status: if x_{ij} equals to 1, pump is on; and if x_{ij} equals to 0, pump is off.

Pumping pressure P_{ij} across each pump is tabulated in Table 1, and corresponding energy E_{ij} can be calculated using Equation 1, where motor-pump efficiencies η_i for ten stations are 0.9789, 0.9810, 0.9810, 0.9630, 0.9660, 0.9830, 0.9840, 0.9700, 0.9800, 0.9600, respectively.

The pressure loss P^L_i along the pipeline i, which can be calculated using Darcy-Weisbach and Colebrook-White equations, is tabulated in Table 2. The lower suction pressure bound $_LP^S_i$, upper suction pressure bound $_UP^S_i$, and upper discharge pressure bound $_UP^D_i$ in pumping station i are also shown in Table 2.

Table 1. Pumping Pressure Data

Pump Number (i, j)	Pumping Pressure P_{ij} (psi)	Pump Number (i, j)	Pumping Pressure P_{ij} (psi)
(1, 1)	173.22	(6, 1)	209.82
(1, 2)	173.22	(6, 2)	209.82
(1, 3)	173.22	(6, 3)	209.82
(1, 4)	86.62	(6, 4)	104.91
(2, 1)	191.78	(7, 1)	229.13
(2, 2)	191.78	(7, 2)	229.13
(2, 3)	191.78	(7, 3)	229.13
(2, 4)	95.89	(7, 4)	114.56
(3, 1)	191.78	(8, 1)	169.51
(3, 2)	191.78	(8, 2)	169.51
(3, 3)	191.78	(8, 3)	169.51
(3, 4)	95.89	(8, 4)	84.75
(4, 1)	100.07	(9, 1)	211.32
(4, 2)	100.07	(9, 2)	211.32
(4, 3)	100.07	(9, 3)	211.32
(4, 4)	50.04	(9, 4)	105.66
(5, 1)	110.35	(10, 1)	192.31
(5, 2)	110.35	(10, 2)	192.31
(5, 3)	110.35	(10, 3)	192.31
(5, 4)	55.18	(10, 4)	96.15

Table 2. Pressure Loss and Pressure Limit

n	P_i^L (psi)	$_L P_i^S$ (psi)	$_U P_i^S$ (psi)	$_U P_i^D$ (psi)
1	309.85	0	200	900
2	154.98	25	200	900
3	258.19	25	200	800
4	309.85	25	400	900
5	154.98	25	250	900
6	309.85	25	350	900
7	309.85	25	450	1100
8	284.07	25	550	1100
9	82.675	25	400	1100
10	51.658	25	400	1100

Table 3. Solutions from Different Algorithms

Method	Energy (HP)	Pump Status
GA	11263.19	1100 1001 1001 1101 1001 1100 1100 0000 0000 0000
B&B[a]	11187.00	1100 1000 1110 1000 0000 1100 1101 0000 0000 0000
B&B[b]	11181.37	1011 0001 1110 0000 1010 0110 0110 0000 0000 0000
HS	11169.43	1100 0010 1011 0110 0000 1011 1010 0000 0000 0000

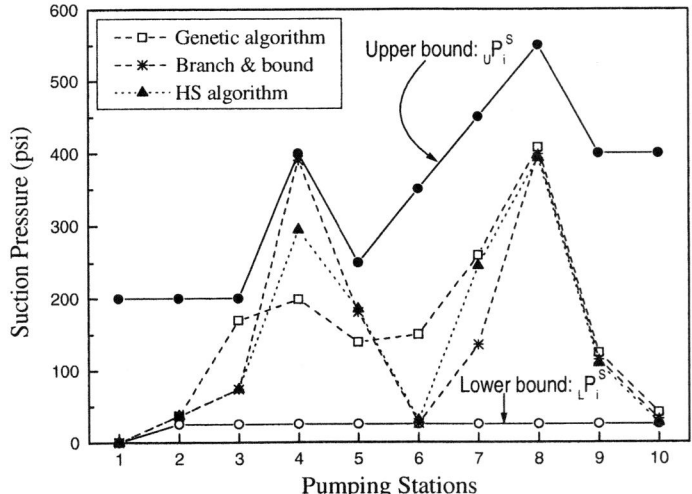

Fig. 2. Suction Pressures of Different Solutions

For the HS algorithm, HMCR of 0.95 is used, and 10 different runs with different HMS (1 ~ 100) are investigated. For all cases, maximum improvisations (function evaluations) of 3,500 are used.

After 3,500 improvisations (it took 19 seconds on 200MHz IBM-compatible PC), the HS algorithm found pumping energy solutions (in horsepower) for 10 runs: 11,210.72 for HMS = 1; 11,169.43 for HMS=2; 11,215.11 for HMS = 3; 11,202.86 for HMS = 5; 11,181.37 for HMS = 10; 11,194.71 for HMS = 15; 11,184.16 for HMS = 20; 11,234.20 for HMS = 30; 11,187.33 for HMS = 50; and 11,724.05 for HMS = 100. Among them, the minimal pumping energy 11,169.43 was obtained with HMS = 2.

The best HS solution (11,169.43) was also compared to earlier solutions reported by Goldberg and Kuo [1], as shown in Table 3. Goldberg and Kuo obtained the best GA solution (11,263.19) and compared the GA solution with branch & bound method solution (B&Ba, 11,187.00) because they believed that branch & bound method could find global optimal solution at that time. However, this study found the better solution (B&Bb, 11,181.37) using different branch & bound method code, taking 28 minutes

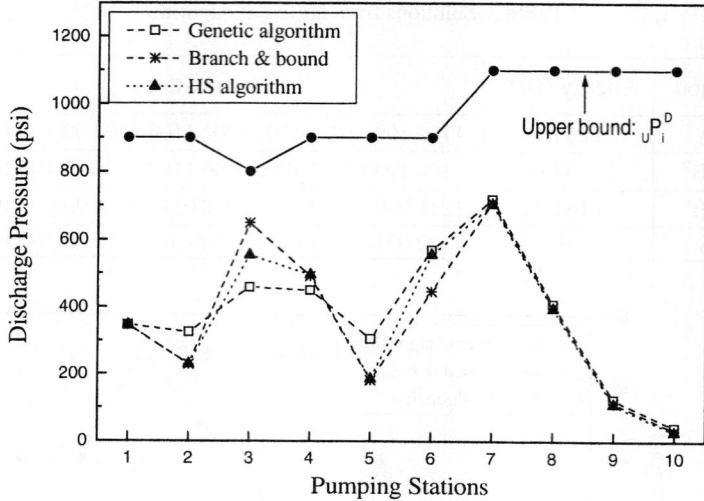

Fig. 3. Discharge Pressures of Different Solutions

on 200MHz PC. And, the HS could find even better solution (11,169.43), taking 19 seconds on the same machine. The lower limit of the solution for the water pump switching problem can be calculated using simplex method. Any feasible solution for the problem cannot be placed below the lower limit (11,149.56) which consists of non-binary infeasible values for decision variables.

Although the difference between GA solution (11263.19) and HS solution (11169.43) looks very small, the distance between GA solution and lower limit is 5.7 times longer than the distance between HS solution and lower limit.

The suction and discharge pressures for GA, B&B[a], and HS solutions in Table 3 are profiled in Figure 2 and Figure 3, respectively. All pressure profiles satisfy the constraints of upper and lower pressure bounds in Table 2.

Expanding the above 10 runs, 200 different runs which used randomly generated HMS (= 2 ~ 30 in integer) and HMCR (= 0.8 ~ 0.98), were carried out in order to demonstrate the HS algorithm's convergence effectiveness to the optimal solution. 200 different runs using GA with randomly generated crossover rate (= 0.5 ~ 1.0) and mutation rate (= 0.001 ~ 0.05) were also compared.

The statistical values (minimum, arithmetic average, and standard deviation of solutions) from both algorithms were obtained and compared. HS produced 11,164.47 (HMS = 19; and HMCR = 0.9710) as minimum solution; 11,215.11 as arithmetic average; and 48.13 as standard deviation, taking 15 seconds per each computation while genetic algorithm found 11,172.74 (crossover rate = 0.9480; and mutation rate = 0.0090) as minimum solution; 11,320.19 as arithmetic average; and 196.61 as standard deviation, taking 20 seconds per each computation.

The distribution of the 200 HS solutions showed a narrower shape than that of the 200 GA solutions. It should be noted that the HS algorithm parameters (HMS and HMCR) do not exert a significant influence on the optimized solutions in terms of standard deviation, and the solutions of HS algorithm are relatively well optimized than those of GA in terms of minimum and arithmetic average of solutions. In addition, HS algorithm found the solutions faster (15 seconds) than GA (20 seconds) in terms of mean time elapsed in both algorithm computations.

5 Conclusions

Recently-developed nature-inspired HS algorithm was applied to the optimal water pump switching problem to demonstrate the effectiveness of the proposed algorithm. The results of HS model were also compared to those of other evolutionary and mathematical algorithms.

The computational results revealed that the proposed HS algorithm was effectively capable of solving the water pump switching problem. The HS results were better than those obtained using GA in terms of minimal energy as well as average energies or computing time. Furthermore, the HS algorithm parameters (HMS and HMCR), which were arbitrarily selected from preferable ranges, did not exert a significant influence on the results with respect to statistical standard deviation.

In conclusion, this study suggests that the new HS-based approach is potentially a powerful search and optimization algorithm for solving the water pump switching problem. It is also expected that HS algorithm, as a nature-inspired algorithm, can be applied to various optimization problems with discrete and/or continuous decision variables.

References

1. Goldberg, D. E., and Kuo, C. H.: Genetic Algorithms in Pipeline Optimization. Journal of Computing in Civil Engineering, ASCE. 1(2) (1987) 128-141
2. Wang, Q. J.: The Genetic Algorithm and Its Application to Calibrating Conceptual Rainfall-Runoff Models. Water Resources Research. 27(9) (1991) 2467-2471
3. Dandy, G. C., Simpson, A. R. and Murphy, L. J.: An Improved Genetic Algorithm for Pipe Network Optimization. Water Resources Research. 32(2) (1996) 449-458
4. Mohan, S.: Parameter Estimation of Nonlinear Muskingum Models using Genetic Algorithm. Journal of Hydraulic Engineering, ASCE. 123(2) (1997) 137-142
5. Sharif, M., and Wardlaw, R.: Multireservoir Systems Optimization using Genetic Algorithms: Case Study. Journal of Computing in Civil Engineering, ASCE. 14(4) (2000) 255-263
6. Maryott, R. A., Dougherty, D. E., and Stollar, R. L.: Optimal Groundwater Management: Application of Simulated Annealing to a Field-Scale Contamination Site. Water Resources Research. 29(4) (1993) 847-860
7. Cunha, M. Da C., and Sousa, J.: Water Distribution Network Design Optimization: Simulated Annealing Approach. Journal of Water Resources Planning and Management, ASCE. 125(4) (1999) 215-221

8. Geem, Z. W., Kim, J. H., and Loganathan, G. V.: A New Heuristic Optimization Algorithm: Harmony Search. Simulation. 76(2) (2001) 60-68
9. Kim, J. H., Geem, Z. W., and Kim, E. S.: Parameter Estimation of the Nonlinear Muskingum Model using Harmony Search. Journal of the American Water Resources Association. 37(5) (2001) 1131-1138
10. Geem, Z. W., Kim, J. H., and Loganathan. G. V.: Harmony Search Optimization: Application to Pipe Network Design. International Journal of Modelling and Simulation. 22(2) (2002) 125-133
11. Kang, S. L., and Geem, Z. W.: A New Structural Optimization Method Based on the Harmony Search Algorithm. Computers and Structures. 82(9-10) (2004) 781-798

A Selfish Non-atomic Routing Algorithm Based on Game Theory[*]

Jun Tao[1,2], Ye Liu[1,2], and Qingliang Wu[1,2]

[1] Key Laboratory of Computer Networks and Information Integration of Ministry of Education, Southeast University, Nanjing 210096
[2] Department of Computer Science and Engineering, Southeast University, Nanjing 210096
{juntao, yliu, qwu}@seu.edu.cn

Abstract. To avoid the low efficiency in Internet routing, end users adopt many routing technologies, such as source routing and active routing. As the result of user's participation, these routing technologies possess selfish character. Firstly, selfish routing game model is put forward in the paper based on the discussion of selfish routing problem. And then, we discuss the existence and uniqueness of Nash Equilibrium Point. Moreover, atomic and non-atomic routing in game model is discussed. Finally, SRAG algorithm is simulated in the specific network environment. The results of simulation show the good routing results of SRAG. The feasibility and effectivity of the algorithm is suggested by the results of experiment.

1 Introduction

Nowadays Internet routing is based on single metric that is related to the delay and distance between source and destination [1]. It is numerous independent and selfish users in the Internet that provide Internet with economics and computer science characters. So Internet routing is becoming a very ordinary problem [2]. After the inhered low efficiency of routing over network layer, the method in which users adopt source routing has been put forward to avoid the inefficient routing. Whereas, the source side independently chooses the routing using source routing. Therefore, the routing behaviors of the data flow are selfish because of the selfish characters in non-cooperative network users [3].

If the routing of the flow is decided by non-cooperative and selfish users to minimize the cost and transfer delay, the routing allocation is expected to be stable. At the stable allocation, there are no users can minimize the transfer cost through change the routing. The selfish non-atomic routing is studied in this paper.

2 The Model of Selfish Routing Game

Long time ago, non-cooperative game theory was applied to study the routing problem in traffic network [4]. Users are regarded as the entity that control very small part

---

[*] Foundation Items: Supported by the National Grand Fundamental Research 973 Program of China under Grant (2003CB314801) and the research fund for the doctoral program of higher education (20040286001).

of network flows, which can be even ignored when compared with the whole network flows, such as the automobiles on the highway [5].

2.1 Mathematic Model

We assume that there is a N users set, $\mathcal{N} = \{1, \cdots, N\}$, which share a set of L parallel links $\mathcal{L} = \{1, \cdots, L\}$ interconnecting a common source node S to a common destination node D (Showed in Fig.1.). The link set and link capability set $\mathcal{L} = \{1, \cdots, L\}$ and $\{c_l\}_{l \in \mathcal{L}}$. Each user ships data (non-atomic) flow by splitting it over the communication links. The data flow set, $\{f_i\}_{i \in \mathcal{N}}$, corresponds to flow rate set, $\{x_i\}_{i \in \mathcal{N}}$.

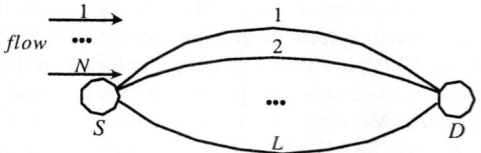

Fig. 1. Network environment with parallel links

We study the system flow configuration vector **f** sent by the source S as follows:

1. End User: the system flow vector is $\mathbf{f} = (\mathbf{f}_1, \cdots, \mathbf{f}_i, \cdots, \mathbf{f}_N)$. The flows of user i on each link constitute the routing vector of flow i: $\mathbf{f}_i = (f_i^1, \cdots, f_i^l, \cdots, f_i^L)$.

Obviously, $f_i^l \geq 0$ [1]. And any value can be assigned to f_i^l, the flow f_i can be arbitrarily split to ship.

2. Link: the system flow vector is $\mathbf{f} = (\mathbf{f}^1, \cdots, \mathbf{f}^l, \cdots, \mathbf{f}^L)$.

Similarly, the flows of each user on link l constitute the routing vector on link l, $\mathbf{f}^l = (f_1^l, \cdots, f_i^l, \cdots, f_N^l)$. Obviously, $f_i^l \leq c_l$.

For convenience of the following discussion and without loss of generality, we assume that the link capacity satisfies $c_1 \geq c_2 \geq \cdots \geq c_L$ and the flow rate satisfies $x_1 \geq x_2 \geq \cdots \geq x_N$.

In non-cooperative game, all users choose the strategies to maximize their profit. We measure the users' profit with their cost function.

The transfer delay is added into cost function. The transfer delay over the link l

---

[1] We think that the flow traffic be function about the traffic of user i on link l, $f_i^l : \mathcal{L} \to R^+$. In this paper, how to split the flow and how to ship the flow with appropriate routing will be studied.

$$d_l \triangleq \begin{cases} 1/(c_l - f^l), & f^l < c_l \\ \infty, & f^l \geq c_l \end{cases}$$

Different kinds of routing cost functions were discussed in the Ref. [6, 7, 8]. Subsequently, we define the cost functions in non-cooperative selfish routing game.

Definition 1 (cost function). In the non-cooperative selfish routing game, the cost function of user i ($i \in \mathcal{N}$) is $J_i(\mathbf{f}) \triangleq J_i(\mathbf{f}_i, \mathbf{f}_{-i}) = \sum_{l \in L} J_i^l(\mathbf{f}^l)$.

$\mathbf{f}_{-i}$ is the flow vector except flow i. The cost function of user i over link l is $J_i^l(\mathbf{f}^l) = f_i^l \cdot d_l$.

The cost of user i is the sum of his cost over each link. So the cost function quantifies the service level received by the flow. The greater $J_i(\mathbf{f})$ is, the lower grade the service received by user i will be [7].

Definition 2 (NEP, Nash Equilibrium Point). $J_i(\mathbf{f}_i, \mathbf{f}_{-i})$ is the cost function of user i. $(\mathbf{f}_1^*, \cdots, \mathbf{f}_i^*, \cdots, \mathbf{f}_N^*)$ is a NEP iff $J_i(\mathbf{f}_i^*, \mathbf{f}_{-i}^*) \leq J_i(\mathbf{f}_i, \mathbf{f}_{-i}^*)$, $\forall \mathbf{f}_i \in F_i$, $0 \leq f_i \leq c_l$. F_i is the set of all users' possible flow configuration.

From Def. 2., we can see NEP is a stable point in N users joined selfish routing game. User i split the flow and ship the flow to the corresponding routing with the cost $J_i(\mathbf{f}_i, \mathbf{f}_{-i})$. After the system reaches NEP, any flow routing vector $\mathbf{f}'$ of users who deviate NEP, the cost of $\mathbf{f}'$ is not less than the cost of $\mathbf{f}^* = (\mathbf{f}_1^*, \cdots, \mathbf{f}_N^*)$. The routing vector $\mathbf{f}_i^*$ in Def. 2. is the dominated strategy of user i. Def. 2. also discusses the seeking NEP method in which user i chooses $\mathbf{f}_i$ to minimize the cost, $\min_{\mathbf{f}_i \in F_i} J_i(\mathbf{f}_i, \mathbf{f}_{-i}^*)$.

In the following, we will discuss the existence and uniqueness of selfish routing game equilibrium.

Proposition 1 (Existence and Uniqueness). N users share L links. If the cost function of user i ($i = 1, \cdots, N$) defined in Def. 1., there is exists a unique NEP in the game.

Proof: Seen in Ref [9].

In the following, how to allocate the flow over each link at the NEP for minimizing the cost will be studied. To extend the following discussion, we introduce several lemmas that can be applied to the discussion and proved by Ref. [6].

Lemma 1. At the NEP, the flow vector, $(f_i^1, f_i^2, \cdots, f_i^L)$, satisfies $f_i^1 \geq f_i^2 \geq \cdots \geq f_i^L$.

Lemma 2. At the NEP, the flow vector, $(f_1^l, f_2^l, \cdots, f_N^l)$, satisfies $f_1^l \geq f_2^l \geq \cdots \geq f_N^l$.

Lemma 3. The residual link capacity satisfies $c_1 - f^1 \geq c_2 - f^2 \geq \cdots \geq c_L - f^L$.

Lemma 4. At the NEP, the residual capacity of link l for user i, $\gamma_i^l = c_l - f_{-i}^l$, satisfies $\gamma_i^1 \geq \gamma_i^2 \geq \cdots \geq \gamma_i^L$.

In addition, if user i does not ship the flow to link l, $f_i^m = f_i^l = 0$ ($\forall m > l$) holds from lemma 1. We denote the link set that user i chooses L_i. So $f_i^l = 0$ ($\forall l \notin L_i$) and $f_i^l > 0$ ($\forall l \in L_i$) hold.

According to the above lemmas, we will study the allocation of user i over link l.

Corollary 1. At the NEP, the flow that user i allocates over link l satisfies:

$$f_i^l = \begin{cases} \left(\gamma_i^l - \left(\sum_{m \in L_i} \gamma_i^m - x_i\right) \cdot \sqrt{\gamma_i^l} \middle/ \sum_{m \in L_i} \sqrt{\gamma_i^m}\right) & , l \in L_i \\ 0 & , l \notin L_i \end{cases}$$

Proof: Seen in Ref [9].

Obviously, the method of allocating the flow over the links is given in Prop. 1. How to compute the chosen link set is the precondition of the above method. Subsequently, we study how to compute the chosen link set by an example of computing the chosen link set of user i, L_i.

Corollary 2. We assume the chosen link set of user i is $L_i = \{1, \cdots, L_i\}$. The relationship between the flow rate and the residual link capacity of user i satisfies

$$\sum_{m=1}^{L_i - 1} \gamma_i^m - \sqrt{\gamma_i^{L_i}} \cdot \sum_{m=1}^{L_i - 1} \sqrt{\gamma_i^m} < x_i \leq \sum_{m=1}^{L_i} \gamma_i^m - \sqrt{\gamma_i^{L_i + 1}} \cdot \sum_{m=1}^{L_i} \sqrt{\gamma_i^m}$$

Proof: Seen in Ref [9].

2.2 Network Link and Network Route

Whether the routing model based on this game environment can be applied to general network topology in the same way?

In general network topology, $E = \{E_1, \cdots, E_M\}$ denotes the node set. The link set among nodes is $L = \{1, \cdots, L\}$. We assume that the route set between source node and destination node should be $R = \{R_1, R_2, \cdots, R_N,\}$, $R_i = \{l_S, l_K, \cdots, l_D\}$ and $R_i \cap R_j = \{l_S, l_D\}$. The route capacity, $C = (c_1, \cdots, c_r, \cdots, c_N)$, is equal to the lowest capacity of links along the route, the capacity of bottleneck link. We can deal with route set R using the same method as dealing with link set. Thus the methods and conclusions in the link model can be applied to general network topology.

2.3 "Atomic" Routing and "Non-atomic" Routing

The flow is atomic for its serial transfer and not being split. Once a packet completes routing, packets subsequent to the former will be transferred according to the chosen route until different route is selected. Similarly, in the connection data transfer (TCP). Consequently, this serial transfer mode has severely impacted the transfer rate and efficiency. Furthermore, the serial transfer mode demands quite high bandwidth of the route. If any route cannot meet its requirement, this application's request will be denied, while the sum of available bandwidth greatly exceeds the request from the application at the same time.

To overcome the defects of atomic flow transfer mode, we assume that the (non-atomic) flow be split when the traditional routing problem is discussed. That is to say, the data flow can be arbitrarily split into task flows with any size over many paths. The transfer mode is non-atomic.

The non-atomic data we discussed is relative to atomic data. Hence, non-atomic selfish routing game differs from active routing in which each packet can carry routing strategy and differs from the routing of traffic vehicle that is a routing decision-maker.

3 Selfish Routing Algorithm Based on Game Theory

3.1 SRAG Algorithm

The objective of designing SRAG algorithm:

1. Based on non-cooperative game theory, the routing is chosen for minimizing the user's cost.
2. Through the running of SRAG algorithm, the routing chosen by each user will reach or converge at NEP.
3. SRAG algorithm is distributed over users and asynchronously chooses routing.

Using the conclusion of corollary 1, we design the SRAG algorithm seen in Ref [9].

3.2 Results of Simulation

Experiment 1. The changes in chosen link set in SRAG algorithm of single flow.

There are one user and six parallel links with capacity $c_{1\sim 6}$ (showed in Tab. 1) in the network environment (showed in Fig. 1).

Table 1. The distribution of link capacity

	c_1	c_2	c_3	c_4	c_5	c_6
Link	10.67	8.31	7.946	5.32	4.135	2.01

The results are showed in Fig. 2 at different flow rates. Obviously, the ladder shape figure accords with design idea of computing the chosen link set.

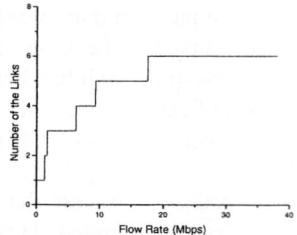
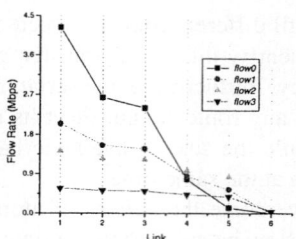

Fig. 2. The changes in chosen link set   Fig. 3. The routing result

Table 2. The distribution of flows

	f_0	f_1	f_2	f_3
Traffic	10.17	6.463	5.687	2.463

Experiment 2. The routing results of SRAG algorithm with different flows.

In experiment 2, the flows satisfy $f_0 > f_1 > f_2 > f_3$. Obviously, $f_i^1 > f_i^2 > \cdots > f_i^6$ ($i=0,\cdots,3$) and $f_0^l > f_1^l > f_2^l > f_3^l$ ($l=1,\cdots,6$) hold in Fig. 3. The experiment 2 is consistent with the lemma 1 and lemma 2 and validates the rationality of SRAG algorithm.

4 Conclusions

The non-cooperative behaviors in selfish routing are further studied with game theory. And then, the existence and uniqueness of NEP in routing game model is proved. Meanwhile, the user's cost is minimized according to SRAG algorithm. The feasibility and effectivity of the algorithm is suggested by results of experiment and simulation.

References

1. Altman, E., Azouzi, R. El., Jimenez, T.: Slotted Aloha as a Stochastic Game with Partial Information. Computer Networks, 2004, 45: 701-713.
2. Feigenbaum, J., Papadimitriou, C., Sami, R.: Incentive-Compatible Interdomain Routing. Working Paper, Yale University, 2002.
3. Roughgarden, T.: Designing Networks for Selfish Users is Hard. In Proc. of the 43rd Annual IEEE Symposium on the Foundations of Computer Science, October 2001, 472-481.
4. Altman, E., Azouzi, R. E., Vyacheslav, A.: Non-Cooperative Routing in Loss Networks. Performance Evaluation, September 2002, 49(1-4): 257-272.
5. Korlis, Y. A., Lazar, A. A., Orda, A.: Avoiding the Braess Paradox in Non-Cooperative Networks. Journal of Applied Probability, 1999, 36(1): 211-222.
6. Orda, A., Rom, R., Shimkin, N.: Competitive Routing in Multi-user Communication Networks. INFOCOM '93, San Francisco, CA, 1993, 3: 964 - 971.

7. Korilis, A., Lazar, A., Orda, A.: Achieving Network Optima Using Stackelberg Routing Strategies. IEEE/ACM Transactions on Networking, 1997, 5(1): 161-173.
8. Korilis, Y. A., Lazar, A., Orda, A.: Capacity Allocation under Noncooperative Routing. IEEE Transactions on Automatic Control, March 1997, 42(3): 309-325.
9. Tao Jun, Research on the Key Technologies of QoS-Allocation based on Non-cooperative Game Theory Model. Dissertation submitted to the Graduate of Southeast University for the degree Doctor of Philosophy in Computer Science and Engineering(CSE), January 2005
10. Luenberger, D. G.: Linear and Nonlinear Programming. MA: Addison Wesley, 2nd Edition, 1984.
11. Chen, BL.. Theory and Algorithm of Optimization. Beijing: Tsinghua University Publishing Company, 2003, 239-246.

Clone Selection Based Multicast Routing Algorithm

Cuiqin Hou, Licheng Jiao, Maoguo Gong, and Bin Lu

Institute of Intelligent Information Processing, P.O. Box 224, Xidian University,
Xi'an, 710071, P.R. China
houcuiqin0304@163.com

Abstract. The problem of multicast routing with delay constraints is of great interest in the communication area in the last few years and has been proved a NP-Complete problem. A novel multicast routing algorithm based on clone selection operator is proposed to solve the problem. Simulations illustrate that compared with other algorithms, the proposed algorithm has a fast convergence speed and powerful search ability. The result shows that the proposed algorithm can find a better solution in the same time or even the shorter time.

1 Introduction

With rapid development of communication network and multimedia, the problem of multicast routing with delay constraints is of great interest in the last few years. The multicast routing with delay constraints problem has been proved a NP-complete problem [1]. Therefore, many heuristic algorithms have been proposed. E.g. KPP Algorithm [2], Bounded Shortest Multicast Algorithm (BSMA) [3], Constrained Dijkstra Heuristic Algorithm (CDKS) [4]. And more and more multicast routing algorithms based on genetic algorithm [5] are proposed to solve this problem.

In this paper, an algorithm based on clone selection operator [6] which solves the multicast routing with delay constraints problem is proposed. The paper will show that the proposed algorithm can perform better than orthogonal genetic algorithms which can search the solution space in a statistically sound manner.

2 The Model of the Multicast Routing with Delay Constraints Problem

A communication network is modeled as a graph $G = (V, E)$, where V denotes a set of nodes and E denotes a set of edges. $\forall (x, y) \in E$, there exists $(d(x, y), c(x, y))$, where $d(x, y)$ and $c(x, y)$ are positive real number. Then $\forall a, b \in V$, the total delays of the path between a and b is $\text{Delay}(a,b) = \sum_{(x,y) \in P(a,b)} d(x, y)$ and the total cost is $\text{Cost}(a,b) = \sum_{(x,y) \in P(a,b)} c(x, y)$. Mathematically, when the given source node is s and $D \subseteq V - \{s\}$ denotes the set of destination nodes, the problem is to find the multicast tree $T = (V_T, E_T)$ ($V_T \in V$ $E_T \in E$) such that $\text{Cost}(T) = \min(\sum_{(x,y) \in E_T} c(x, y))$

and delay$(s,v) \leq \Delta d_i, \forall v \in D$, where Cost(T) is the total cost of the multicast tree, Δd_i is the given delay for the ith destination node and depends on applications.

3 The Multicast Routing Algorithm Based on Clone Selection

3.1 Coding Scheme

Just as genetic algorithm, when designing a clone selection algorithm, the first step is to determine a coding scheme translating problem space to coding space. Coding scheme is a very important element of influencing the performance of a clone selection algorithm.

After comparing in many respects, we adopted binary coding based on edges proposed by Qingfu Zhang. This scheme is capable of representing all possible trees and the length of code is equal. In addition, it is easy to design clone selection operator employing this coding scheme.

3.2 Antibody-Antigen Affinity Function

Antibody-antigen affinity not only reflects the quality of this antibody for the problem, but also has to do with the number of this antibody been cloned. We proposed the antibody-antigen affinity function as follows:

$$\Psi(\mathbf{a}) = 1/\text{cost}(\mathbf{a}) - \sum_{i=0}^{d} \alpha_i * \max(0, (\text{delay}_i(\mathbf{a}) - \text{maxdelay}_i)) \quad (1)$$

where cost($\mathbf{a}$) is the total cost of the tree induced by antibody $\mathbf{a}$, delay$_i(\mathbf{a})$ is the total delay from the source node to the ith destination node, maxdelay$_i$ is the given delay for the ith destination, α_i is a penalty coefficient which can be set.

3.3 The Proposed Algorithm

Based on the clone selection operator, we proposed a new multicast routing algorithm, or clone selection based multicast routing algorithm CSMA.

The steps are as follows:

Table 1. The Steps of the proposed algorithm CSMA

Step1: set $gen = 0$, generate an initial population $\mathbf{A} = [\mathbf{a}_1, \mathbf{a}_2..., \mathbf{a}_n]$ and perform repair operation on every antibody. Then the population is $\mathbf{A}_r = \{R(\mathbf{a}_1), R(\mathbf{a}_2), ...R(\mathbf{a}_n)\} = [\mathbf{a}_{r1}, \mathbf{a}_{r2}, ..., \mathbf{a}_{rm}]$;

Step2: evaluate the affinity of every antibody;

Step3: perform clone selection operator, or clone operation and immune genic operation and clone selection operation, on this population, and then produce the next generational population $\mathbf{A}_c = [\mathbf{a}_{c1}, \mathbf{a}_{c2}, ..., \mathbf{a}_{cn}]$;

Step4: $gen = gen + 1$, if no given termination criterion is satisfied, then go to Step2;else end.

4 Simulation Result

The simulation network is created by the RNTGA algorithm [7] which guarantees the network is connective, the degree of every node is 2 at least and the average degree is invariable.

In our experiments, we randomly generate networks and let the average node degree be 4. We get destination nodes or multicast group, by randomly choosing from nodes in network. The cost and delay of an edge is randomly generated. In our simulation, our proposed algorithm is compared with the algorithms, or OGA_4 and OGA_9, proposed in [5]. We let the number of individual in a population be 60 in OGA_4, 30 in OGA_9 and 20 in our algorithm. We let the clone scale be 5, thus the true search space in three algorithms is approximate equal. And we let the maximum generation be 200 such that the running time is acceptable. And we let the mutation probability equals to $\frac{10}{numside}$, where *numside* is the length of code.

We do the simulation experiments on the networks of 100 200 300 nodes generated by the RNTGA algorithm, with multicast group size equal to 5%, 15%, and 30% of the number of network nodes. Every program is executed for 10 runs under any situation respectively. Then the average cost was evaluated, or $\overline{cost} = \frac{1}{m}\sum_{i=1}^{m} cost$, where *m* is the time of all the delay constraints being satisfied in the 10 times and *cost* is the cost of a multicast tree that satisfied all the delay constraints. In table 2, blank units denote there was no multicast tree satisfying constraints that has been found in the 10 times.

Table 2. Cost values of multicast trees constructed by OGA_4、OGA_9 or CSMR for network nodes equaling 100、200 and 300 with multicast group equaling 5%、15% and 30%

	Number of nodes=100			Number of nodes=200			Number of nodes=300		
	5%	15%	30%	5%	15%	30%	5%	15%	30%
OGA_4	830.2	1386.9	1910.8	1349.1		4234.5	2523.0		
OGA_9	789.7	1256.2	2338.6	1235.1		3807.9	2119.8	4171.5	6847.5
CSMR	671.4	1136.9	2011.6	1208.0	2890.8	3695.0	1875.3	4106.7	6090.0

Table 3. Time for OGA_4、OGA_9 or CSMR to construct multicast trees in all situations respectively

	Number of nodes=100			Number of nodes=200			Number of nodes=300		
	5%	15%	30%	5%	15%	30%	5%	15%	30%
OGA_4	6.21	7.06	8.51	16.97	21.56	24.59	33.03	39.95	52.83
OGA_9	6.66	7.56	9.31	18.35	23.73	27.51	36.99	44.32	56.99
CSMR	5.42	6.91	9.75	14.51	19.96	24.21	27.44	35.27	47.34

From table 2, we can see that cost of the tree constructed by our algorithm is lower than OGA_4 and OGA_9 for different network with different multicast group size. It is more encouraged that our program has a less running time in general from table 3. From these results, we can conclude our algorithm has a faster convergence speed and more powerful search ability. We can also find OGA_9 is better than OGA_4, this is consistent with what the author in [5] has concluded.

5 Conclusion

Multicast routing with delay constraints problem has been proved to be NP-Complete. In this paper, we proposed a multicast routing algorithm based on clone selection. Compared with OGA_4 and OGA_9, CSMR has a fast convergence speed and powerful search ability

References

1. Garey, M., Johoson, D.: Computers and Intractability :A Guide to the Theory of NP-completeness. W.H.Freeman,San Francisco(1979)
2. Kompella, V., Pasquale, J. Polyzos, G.: Multicast Routing for Multimedia Communication. IEEE/ACM Trans on Networking, Vol. 1. (1993) 286–292
3. Parsa, M, Zhu, Q, Garcia-Luna-Aceves, J.J.: An Iterative Algorithm for Delay-constrained Minimum-cost Multicasting. IEEE/ACM Trans On Networking, Vol. 6. (1998) 461–474
4. Salama, H.F., Reeves, D.S., Vinitos, I.: Evaluation of Multicast Routing Algorithms for Real-Time Communication on High Speed Networks. IEEE Journal on Selected Area in Communications, Vol. 15. (1997) 332–345
5. Zhang, Q.F., Leung, Y.W.: An Orthogonal Genetic Algorithm for Multimedia Multicast Routing. IEEE Transations on Evolutionary Computation, Vol.3. (1999) 53–62
6. Du H.F., Jiao L.C., Gong M.G., Liu R.C.: Adaptive Dynamic Clone Selection Algorithms. In: Zdzislaw P., Lotfi Z. (eds): Proceedings of the Fourth International Conference on Rough Sets and Current Trends in Computing (RSCTC'2004). Uppsala, Sweden. (2004) 1-5
7. Wang, Z.Y.: Reach of high Speed network QoS routing technique and simulation environment(Chinese). PHD. Huazhong University of science and technology, Wuhan. (2001)

A Genetic Algorithm-Based Routing Service for Simulation Grid

Wei Wu, Hai Huang, Zhong Zhou, and Zhongshu Liu

School of Computer Science and Engineering,
Beihang University, Beijing 100083, P.R. China
huanghai@vrlab.buaa.edu.cn

Abstract. A genetic algorithm-based routing service for building a multicast distributed tree on Simulation Grid is proposed. Different from existing algorithms, the proposed routing algorithm doesn't demand that all the routers in the whole network have multicast functionality. It can meet federates' QoS requirements and minimize the bandwidth consumption. We formalize the routing as a multi-objective optimization problem, which is NP-hard, and apply GA (Genetic Algorithm) to solve it. Also, we focus on the two important aspects of encoding & decoding and fitness function construction in our GA, and present the procedure of seeking the optimal paths. Experiment results have showed that the proposed approach is feasible.

1 Introduction

Distributed interactive simulation has already been applied in many fields and is becoming the third important approach to know and change the objective world subsequent to theoretical and experimental research. At present, HLA is dominating the modeling & simulation world. However, a lot of limitations have emerged as HLA has been used in more and more fields. Over the past several years, the concept of "Grid" computing, which was proposed by Ian Foster as secure and coordinated resource sharing and problem solving in dynamic, multi-institutional virtual organizations has become a hot topic, and a number of scholars are attempting to introduce Grid into the modeling & simulation world to overcome the defects of HLA. Such an intention brings about the naissance of Simulation Grid. One important objective of Simulation Grid is to provide integrated dynamic management ability for such massive data resources as the terrain, models and texture in the simulation system to eliminate the defect of tight coupling between federates and data resources [1,2].

In Simulation Grid, massive data resources are stored in different organizations connected by wide-area network. At runtime, for a federate, there is a strong need for remote access to large data sets, or models, as well as live data feeds from other immersive spaces. For many applications, the (3D) data models to be rendered can easily be 10's of gigabytes, consisting of a time series of large polygonal meshes, massive volumetric data and texture maps. Although the network infrastructure is improved continuously, the available bandwidth is far from satisfaction because of the increasing demand in bandwidth. Consequently, designing a transport mechanism for virtual environment data capable of meeting the (soft) real-time transmission requirements of these immersive systems is a significant challenge [3].

Multicast is a kind of one-to-many communications, in which one source sends desired data to many destinations, and the data is duplicated and distributed at key routers during transport. Compared with unicast, multicast has great advantage in band saving. In Simulation Grid, multicast is employed to transport virtual environment data based on the following consideration. First of all, in order to construct an immersive environment, the data should bear continuity in both time and space. That is, multiple federates located in the same area usually access the same virtual environment data at the same time. Secondly, different from interactive data, the virtual environment data transported in Simulation Grid is enormous in quantity. The transport is only in one direction from source to destinations. Above characteristics indicate that multicast is a good candidate used to transport virtual environment data in Simulation Grid.

An important aspect of multicast is routing. By now, almost all of the multicast routing algorithms are based on the presupposition that all the routers in the network have multicast ability [6,7,11]. Grid environment is grounded on the existing network substrate and consists of a lot of routers bearing no multicast functionality. Therefore, research on multicast routing for Simulation Grid is a meaningful work.

In this paper, we consider the design of a multi-objective routing service for simulation grid to support real-time data transport using multicast. The rest of the paper is organized as follows. In Section 2, we describe the system-level architecture and the role of multi-objective routing service in simulation grid. Section 3 formulizes the multi-objective routing as a constrained multi-objective programming problem. In Section 4, we apply genetic algorithm to solve the problem and describe the genetic algorithm we use. We then discuss results of experiments. In Section 5, we present concluding remarks and discuss future work.

2 Simulation Grid and Its Routing Service

A federation refers to a distributed simulation consisting of two or more autonomous simulators, or federates. Figure 1 shows the system-level architecture of a typical Grid-based federation federates interface through a remote server that manages federation state and provides all simulation-related services [4,5]. All the system components, such as computing resources, storage resources, federates, etc., are published as services. Grid infrastructure is used as the lower level communication channel, and the proxy acts on behalf of the HLA-compatible legacy federate to translate normal federate-RTI communication into Grid service invocations and vice versa. Besides services shown in Figure 1, there exist some other services, such as, Computing Service accessed by computation-intensive federates, Work Flow Service supporting automatic setup of a feder-

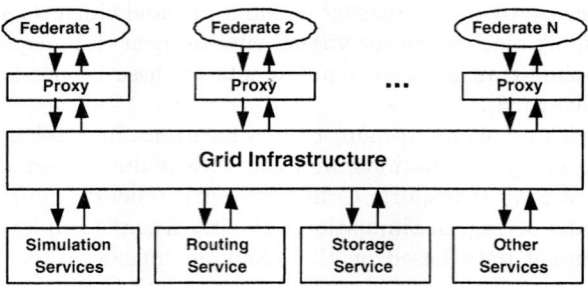

Fig. 1. A Grid-base federation

ation, Monitoring Service used for monitoring federation execution, etc. Grid-based communication may introduce more overhead than existing HLA [5], and yet it is beyond the scope of this paper, which focuses on the Routing Service.

The goal of Routing Service is to find the optimal paths for virtual environment data based on multicast technology. When a number of federates concurrently download virtual environment data from multiple storage nodes, which can collaboratively provide data service for them, the overall process involves several steps. Firstly, federates query Index Service of Grid to locate the Storage Service and Routing Service and get their access methods. Secondly, they access Routing Service to provide their desired bandwidth, delay and jitter, which are needed to build a multi-objective multicast tree. Finally, data transport begins based on the calculated multicast tree.

3 Multi-objective Routing Formulation

In Simulation Grid, two important aspects should be considered when building a multicast distributed tree. Firstly, the bandwidth, end-to-end delay and jitter should meet the requirements of federates. Secondly, the network resources should be used in an optimal way. We choose bandwidth as the network optimization parameter. Therefore, the optimal multicast distributed tree should be the one that can guarantee the desired bandwidth, delay and jitter and at the same time minimize them.

In order to deliver multicast data to all the destinations, multicast distributed tree is used to describe the multicast paths. There exist four types of multicast distributed tree: flooding technique, source tree, core based tree and Steiner tree. In consideration of meeting the real-time requirement of Grid-based simulation applications, which bears strict delay bound and massive data traffic, and of balancing their data traffic in the Grid environment, source tree is adopted as the multicast distributed tree in this paper. Below is the formal description for multi-objective routing, which can be employed to build a source tree.

The underlying communication network is modeled by an undirected graph $N = (V, E, M)$, which is a structure consisting of a finite set of vertices

$V = \{v_1, v_2, ..., v_n\}$ and a finite set of edges $E = \{(v_i, v_j) | v_i, v_j \in V \text{ and } v_i \neq v_j\}$, where each edge is an unordered pair. V corresponds to the set of routers and E to the set of physical links between them. M is a subset of all the V's elements whose corresponding routers bear multicast functionality. The weight on an edge is multicast cost, which usually refers to bandwidth cost and can be defined as:

$$cost(e) : V \times V \longmapsto (0, \infty), \forall e \in E.$$

There is a delay corresponding to each edge:

$$delay(e) : V \times V \longmapsto (0, \infty), \forall e \in E.$$

In addition, for each vertex $v \in V$, a third function is associated, which denotes whether the corresponding router bears multicast functionality:

$$cost(v) = \begin{cases} 0 & \text{if } v \in M \\ \infty & \text{if } v \in V - M \end{cases} \quad (1)$$

Based on above definitions and inspired by the seminal work of [6,7,11], in this paper we model the multi-objective routing problem as follows: given a multicast source $s \in V$ and a multicast destination set $D \in V$, find a *RPT* (Rendezvous Point Tree) T such that

$$\begin{aligned} & Minimize \; f_1(T) = \sum_{e \in E_T} cost(e) + \sum_{v \in V_T} cost(v) \\ & f_2(T) = \sum_{e \in P_T(s,d)} delay(e), \forall d \in D \\ & f_3(T) = |\sum_{e \in P_T(s,d_1)} delay(e) - \sum_{e \in P_T(s,d_2)} delay(e)|, \\ & \quad \forall d_1, d_2 \in D \\ & Subject \; to \; c_1 = \min_{e \in P_T(s,d)} \{cost(e)\} \geq B_{min}, \forall d \in D \\ & c_2 = \min_{e \in P_T(s,d)} delay(e) \leq D_{max}, \forall d \in D \\ & c_3 = |\sum_{e \in P_T(s,d_1)} delay(e) - \sum_{e \in P_T(s,d_2)} delay(e)| \leq J_{max}, \\ & \quad \forall d_1, d_2 \in D \end{aligned} \quad (2)$$

where $s \in V_T$, $D \subseteq V_T$, $T \subseteq N$, and V_T is the set of nodes in T. $P_T(s,d)$ is the unique path from source s to destination d in tree T. B_{min}, D_{max} and J_{max} are the desired bandwidth, acceptable delay and jitter, respectively. f_1, f_2 and f_3 are objective functions that seek to minimize the total connecting cost, delay and jitter between nodes. c_1, c_2 and c_3 are inequality constrained functions that specify the lower bound for desired bandwidth and the upper bound for acceptable delay and jitter.

4 Applying GA to Solve Multi-objective Routing

Most of the constrained minimum spanning tree problems are NP-hard, which cannot be solved in polynomial time. Because of their complexity, Genetic algorithm [8,13,14] are deployed to tackle these questions in the paper. This approach has been successful since GA is computationally simple, not affected by data distributions, and uses parallel search capability to evaluate the entire solution space.

GA is search algorithm that mimics the behavior of natural selection. GA attempts to find the best solution to some problem (e.g., the maximum of a function) by generating a collection ("population") of potential solutions ("chromosomes") to the problem. Through mutation and recombination (crossover) operations, better solutions are hopefully generated out of the current set of potential solutions. This process continues until an acceptably good solution is found. In order to solve model (2), some preparations need to be done.

We extend the arbitrary graph $N = (V, E, M)$ to a complete graph $G = (V, \overline{E}, M)$, in which $E \subseteq \overline{E}$ is obvious. The cost and delay on an edge $e \in \overline{E}$ are defined as:

$$\overline{cost}(e) = \begin{cases} cost(e), \forall e \in E \\ \infty, \forall e \in \overline{E} - E \end{cases} \text{ and } \overline{delay}(e) = \begin{cases} delay(e), \forall e \in E \\ \infty, \forall e \in \overline{E} - E \end{cases}, \quad (3)$$

respectively. Other definition remains unchanged. Therefore, the multi-objective optimization problem illustrated in model (2) can be rewritten as:

$$\begin{array}{rl} Maximize & z_1 = z_1(T) = -\sum_{e \in E_T} \overline{cost}(e) - \sum_{v \in V_T} cost(v) \\ & z_2 = z_2(T) = -\sum_{e \in P_T(s,d)} \overline{delay}(e), \forall d \in D \\ & z_3 = z_3(T) = -|\sum_{e \in P_T(s,d_1)} \overline{delay}(e) - \sum_{e \in P_T(s,d_2)} \overline{delay}(e)|, \\ & \forall d_1, d_2 \in D \\ Subject\ to & g_1 = B_{min} - \min_{e \in P_T(s,d)}\{\overline{cost}(e)\} \leq 0, \forall d \in D \\ & g_2 = \min_{e \in P_T(s,d)} \overline{delay}(e) - D_{max} \leq 0, \forall d \in D \\ & g_3 = |\sum_{e \in P_T(s,d_1)} \overline{delay}(e) - \sum_{e \in P_T(s,d_2)} \overline{delay}(e)| - J_{max} \leq 0, \\ & \forall d_1, d_2 \in D \end{array} \quad (4)$$

Before performing reproduction operators of GA such as crossover, which mimics propagation, and mutation, which mimics random changes occurring in nature, it is needed to decide how to encode and decode chromosomes, generate initial population and construct fitness function. This section we focus on the two important aspects of encoding & decoding and fitness function construction in GA, and give a preliminary experiment to validate the algorithm.

4.1 Prüfer Sequence-Based Encoding and Decoding

Genetic algorithms operate on encoded representations of the solutions, equivalent to those chromosomes of individuals in nature. It is assumed that a potential solution to a problem may be represented as a set of parameters and encoded as a chromosome. In this paper, Prüfer sequence [8,11,12,15] is chosen as the coding technique for tree structure, considering its concision and convenience when a computer processes it based on genetic algorithms.

A spanning tree for a graph N is a subgraph of N that is a tree and contains all the vertices of N. For the k-vertex complete graph $G = (V, \overline{E}, M)$ the number of deferent spanning trees is k^{k-2}, and there exists a bijective from the spanning trees to the Prüfer sequences which consist of $k-2$ numbers. Given a labeled tree, we suppose that the least leaf is labeled i_1, and that its unique neighbor is labeled j_1. Remove i_1 and its edge from the tree, and let i_2 be the least leaf on the new tree, with its unique neighbor j_2. This process is repeated until there are only two vertices left, the Prüfer sequence $(j_1, j_2, \ldots, j_{k-2})$ uniquely determines the tree. However, the chromosomes cannot be obtained simply by recovering a trees form the Prüfer sequences because its corresponding spanning tree $\overline{T}$ has no root and some of the leaves of $\overline{T}$ may not be the multicast destinations. This problem can be easily tackled based on the technique stated in [11].

4.2 Fitness Function Construction

A shown in model (4), it is an optimization problem with multiple objectives. The fitness function construction mainly involves handling its multiple objectives and constraints. Assigning a weigh, which states the preference, to each objective is the usual way to convert multiple objectives into a single objective. Recently a lot of weight approaches have been proposed, such as random-weight approach, adaptive weight approach [8], etc. This paper adopts fixed-weight approach [8] due to its concision and convenience to implement. As a result, the fixed-weight-based single objective function is expressed as

$$Maximize\ z = z(T) = \tfrac{1}{3}\sum_{i=1}^{3} z_i(T), \forall T \in Pop$$
$$Subject\ to\ g_i \leq 0, j = 1, 2, 3$$

where we simply assume that all the three objectives bear the same importance.

Genetic algorithm, like other evolutionary algorithms, is unconstrained optimization procedures. Therefore it is necessary to device ways of incorporating the constraints into the fitness function. Use of penalty function is the most common approach in GAs to handle constraints. The basic principle is to define the fitness value by adding penalties into the objective function. This paper chooses adaptive penalty function described in reference [8], which can adapt penalties according to the population, because of its use in prior studies and better performance, as follows:

$$p(T) = 1 - \frac{1}{3}\sum_{i=1}^{3}\left(\frac{\Delta b_i(T)}{\Delta b_i^{max}}\right)^{\alpha},$$

where

$$\Delta b_i(T) = max\{0, g_i(T)\},$$
$$\Delta b_i^{max} = max\{\varepsilon, \Delta b_i(T) | T \in Pop\}, i = 1, 2, 3,$$

among which ε is a positive infinitesimal. As a result of introducing weights and penalties, the single objective function with no constraints, which is called fitness function, can be expressed as:

$$fitness(T) = z(T)p(T). \tag{5}$$

Observing functions (1), (3), (4) and (5) simultaneously, we can deduce that the value of $fitness(T)$ would be positive infinity if T contained either a router bearing no multicast functionality or an edge $e \in \overline{E} \bigwedge e \notin E$. Therefore, T would eventually be eliminated through selection. That is, the multicast distributed tree corresponding to the optimal solution is made up of the vertices $v \in M$ and the edges $e \in E$. It is exactly our original intention.

4.3 Preliminary Experiment and Results

In order to validate the genetic algorithm-based approach used to tackle our problem, we conducted a simple experiment, in which a variation of the famous Simple Genetic Algorithm or SGA was used. Both our encoding & decoding technique and our fitness function were incorporated into the variation, as follows:

```
Algorithm: ExpeAlgorithm
BEGIN
    t := 0;
    randomly initialize population;
    evaluate population based on fitness function fitness(T);
    while t < pop_size do
    BEGIN
        select solutions for next population based on
            roulette wheel selection approach;
        perform two-point crossover and uniform mutation;
        evaluate population based on fitness function fitness(T);
        t := t + 1;
    END
END
```

ExpeAlgorithm proceeded by first Random initialization. A pseudo random number generator was used to generate the initial population, which did not build in any bias in its selection. For each gene, an integer in the range of 1 to $k-2$ was randomly generated. The initial chromosomes were not required to be legal or generate a feasible tree. They wre expected to be widely varied to enable exploration of a wider solution space without being trapped in local optima. Then selection, crossover and mutation operators were performed repeatedly until the max step *pop_size* was reached. Roulette wheel selection [8], two-point crossover [10] and uniform mutation [9] were used, respectively. Basic parameters of GAs include: population size, probability and type of crossover, and probability and type of mutation, whose values in the experiment were shown as Figure 2(a).

The experiment scenario was based on the network topology shown as Figure 2(b), in which the node labeled 1 was multicast source node, 6, 7, 8 and 9 were destination nodes. The ordered pairs on links represented available bandwidth and delay. For such requirements as 1 unit of bandwidth and 5 units of end-to-end delay, the optimal multicast distributed tree would be denoted as the

Parameter	Value
Population Size	70
Two-Point Crossover	0.65
Uniform Mutation	0.007

(a) Parameters of GA

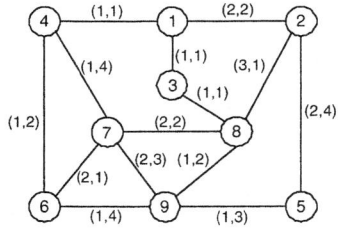

(b) Network Topology

Fig. 2. Parameters of GA and network topology used in the experiment

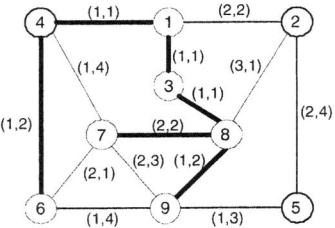

(a) All the nodes have multicast functionality

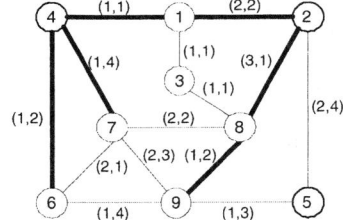

(b) Node 3 has not multicast functionality

Fig. 3. Optimal multicast distributed trees

thick lines in Figure 3(a) if all the nodes in the network had multicast functionality, and would be thick-lined tree in Figure 3(b) if node 3 had not multicast functionality.

In our experiment, ExpeAlgorithm was run one hundred times with a max step 600 in the latter case, in which node 3 had no multicast ability. The probability of getting the optimal tree was 87%, which showed that the proposed multi-objective routing service had strong ability in finding the optimal multicast distributed tree.

5 Conclusions and Future Work

In Grid-based interactive simulation, federates need remotely access massive virtual environment data, which is stored in different organizations connected by wide-area network. Heavy bandwidth burden is imposed upon the underlying network infrastructure. Multicast is chosen as the data transport technology due to its band-saving advantage. The traditional multicast routing algorithms cannot gracefully be applied to Simulation Grid environment since Grid is based on the existing network substrate and consists of a lot of routers bearing no multicast functionality.

In this paper, we have presented a multi-objective routing service for building a multicast distributed tree on the Grid infrastructure, which consists of a lot of routers bearing no multicast functionality. The goal of multi-objective routing service is two-fold. Firstly, we want to take full advantage of the existing network substrate to deliver data based on multicast technology. Secondly, we want to improve the overall network utilization and transport the virtual environment data in a way of meeting federates' requirements. We have formalized the routing as a multi-objective optimization problem, which is NP-hard, and applied genetic algorithm to solve it. Also, we have focused on the two important aspects of encoding & decoding and fitness function construction in our GA, and presented the procedure seeking the optimal solution. Experiment results have showed that the proposed approach is feasible. Besides the modeling & simulation world, the proposed approach can be used in such applications as Grid-based Video Conference, etc.

Clearly, employing multicast technology to transport massive real-time data in Grid environment involves many aspects that cannot be addressed in a single paper. Much work remains to be done.

As our research proceeds, we will further investigate the genetic algorithm used in this paper. The success rates in finding the optimal solution still have much space to improve. Perhaps this can be achieved by design more efficient weight functions for the three objectives and penalty functions for the constraints. Of course, there is a need to estimate the available bandwidth information used by the routing service. The active probing or passive monitoring approach can be employed for such purpose.

We will also take such factor into account that the process of searching optimal multicast tree based on genetic algorithm may be time-consuming. In order to not make federates "wait" too long for the finish of searching, predicting data transport and building multicast tree in advance may be beneficial.

We will strengthen the proposed multi-objective routing service to allow a destination to exit or new destination to join the multicast distributed tree since a federate may exit or new one may join the federation in the simulation process.

Finally, we need to test its overall performance in a Grid environment. Furthermore, such experimentations may also help to determine the appropriate mutation rate in population size, and thus help to improve the overall performance of our GA.

Acknowledgements

Thanks to Dr. PAN Yun in China University of Mining & Technology (Beijing) for her helpful suggestions on GAs. This paper is supported by the National Grand Fundamental Research 973 Program of China (No. 2002CB312105).

References

1. Wu, W., Zhou, Z., Wang, S.F., Zhao, Q.P.: Aegis: a Simulation Grid Oriented to Large-scale Distributed Simulation. The Third International Conference on Grid and Cooperative Computing, Lecture Notes in Computer Science, Vol. 1000 (2004) 413–422
2. Cai, W.T., Turner, S.J., Zhao, H.: A Load Management System for Running HLA-Based Distributed Simulations over the Grid. Proceedings of the 6th IEEE International Workshop on Distributed Simulation and Real-Time Applications (2002) 7–14
3. Shi, S., Wang, L.L., Calvert, K.L., Griffioen, J.N.: A multi-path Routing Service for Immersive Environments. 2004 IEEE International Symposium on Cluster Computing and the Grid (2004) 699–706
4. Fitzgibbons, J.B., Fujimoto, R.M., Fellig, D., Kleban, S.D., Scholand, A.J.: IDSim: An Extensible Framework for Interoperable Distributed Simulation. Proceedings of the IEEE International Conference on Web Services (2004) 532–539
5. Xie, Y., Teo, Y.M., Cai, W.T., Turner, S.J.: Extending HLA's Interoperability and Reusability to the Grid. 19th ACM/IEEE/SCSWorkshop on Principles of Advanced and Distributed Simulation (2005)
6. Pan, Y., Yu, Z.W., Liu, K.J., Dou, W.: A New Multi-Objective Programming Model of QoS-based Multicast Routing Problem. Computer Engineering and Application, No. 19 (2003) 155–157
7. Wang, Z.Y., Shi, B.X.: Solving QoS Multicast Routing Problem Based on Heuristic Genetic Algorithm. Journal of Computers, Vol. 24, No. 1 (2001) 55–61
8. Gen, M., Cheng, R.W.: Genetic Algorithms and Engineering Optimization. Tsinghua University Press (2004)
9. Michalewicz Z.: Genetic Algorithm for Optimal Control Problems. Computer Math. Application, 23 (12) (1992) 83–94
10. Pezeshk, S., ASCE, M., Camp, C.V.: State of the Art on the Use of Genetic Algorithms in Design of Steel Structures. http://www.ce.memphis.edu/pezeshk/PDFs/genetic.pdf
11. Pan, Y., Yu, Z.W., Dou, W.: A Novel Genetic Algorithm for multicast Service Routing Problems. Computer Engineering, Vol. 29, No. 10 (2003) 30–31
12. Wu, B.Y., Chao, K.M.: Spanning Trees and Optimization Problems. Chapman & Hall/CRC PRESS, http://www.csie.ntu.edu.tw/~kmchao/tree04spr/counting.pdf
13. Yao, X.: Evolutionary Computation: Theory and Applications. World Scientific, Singapore (1999)
14. Tan, K.C., Lim, M.H., Yao, X., Wang L.P. (Eds.): Recent Advances in Simulated Evolution And Learning. World Scientific, Singapore (2004)
15. Gen, M., Cheng, R.W.: Genetic Algorithms and Engineering Design. Wiley, New York (1997)

Clustering Problem Using Adaptive Genetic Algorithm[*]

Qingzhan Chen[1,2], Jianghong Han[2], Yungang Lai[1], Wenxiu He[1], and Keji Mao[1]

[1] Zhejiang University,of Technology, 310032 Hangzhou, Zhejiang, China
[2] Heifei University of Technology, 230009 Hefei, Anhui, China
qzchen@zjut.edu.cn

Abstract. Clustering is very important to data analysis and data minig. The K-Means algorithm, one of the partitional clustering approaches, is an iterative clustering technique that has been applied to many practical clustering problems successfully. However, the K-Means algorithm suffers from several drawbacks. In this paper, an adaptive genetic algorithm be present , it solve disadvantages of K-Means by combine parallel genetic algorithm, evolving flow and adaptive. Experimental results show that the adaptive genetic algorithm have advantages over traditional Clustering algorithm.

1 Introduction

There are two ways of data clustering, hierarchical clustering and partitional clustering. The former can find out the relationship from the ungrouped data through separation and combination; the latter can do it through partition. The K-Means algorithm is the most common one in the traditional partitional clustering approaches. But we find that the K-Means algorithm is not a perfect one. The K-Means algorithm cannot cluster and deal with the overlap groups when handles the huge data. The main shorts of the K-Means algorithm are as follows: (1) We must know the number of the cluster before using the K-Means algorithm; (2) K-Means algorithm must depend on the initial cluster pivot; (3) The result of the K-Means algorithm may be the local optimum; (4) K-Means algorithm cannot deal with the overlap data properly.

We take the Genetic-algorithms-based clustering algorithm presented by Maulik and Bandyopadhyay [1] as reference, and we also consult the Adaptive genetic algorithms presented by Srinivas and Patnaik [2]. So in this paper we put forward a clustering approach based on Adaptive Genetic Algorithms.

2 Related Research

2.1 Genetic Algorithms

J. Holland presented the essential theory of Genetic algorithms in 1975. Genetic algorithms is an optimization searching mechanism of emulating the evolvement of nature. At the beginning of Genetic algorithms, many random results are produced.

---

[*] The Project Supported by Zhejiang Provincial Science Foundation of China (601081) and Key Lab of Information Processes of Jiangsu Province(Suzhou University).

Through the competition of these results, good results will be remained and become the objects of partnership and reproduction so as to produce the offspring after regrouped. However the bad results will be eliminated. In the second-generation results, these who have favorable adaptability will be selected to match and reproduce. In this way, like the evolvement of nature, we can approach the best result little by little. Because of the obvious characteristics of Genetic algorithms, it is always used to resolve optimization problem.

2.2 Adaptive Genetic Algorithms

The adaptive concept was derived from Messy Genetic algorithms, which presented by Goldberg [3] in 1989. Through the variable-length of chromosome presented in Messy Genetic algorithms [4], some scholars began to study the Adaptive genetic algorithms.

During the evolvement of nature, the change of a clan, the selection, crossover and mutation of the offspring vary with the environment to adapt it. In order to make the evolving process be up to the evolvement of nature, it is necessary to improve the traditional Genetic algorithm and add adaptive concept. The purposes of the Adaptive genetic algorithms are as follows [4]: (1) Maintain the difference of chromosomes in the clan;(2) Improve the state of premature convergence in Genetic algorithms;(3) Avoid destroying schemata because of crossover.

3 Clustering with Adaptive Genetic Algorithms

If we use traditional Genetic algorithm to get approximate optimal result, it may be the local optimum one, the reason may be that the probability of crossover and mutation are fixed. There are many unknown factor hidden in the evolvement of nature, the change, the selection, crossover and mutation of clans vary with the environment to adapt it. In this paper, we combine the concept of the adaptive with Genetic algorithms to approach the evolvement of nature, and try to change the fixed probability of crossover and mutation to adaptive one, and apply the theory to resolve the misjudging problem of clustering by K-Means algorithms and speed up the evolvement of huge data.

3.1 The Coding of Chromosome and the Initialization of Clans

Partitional clustering can divide the multi-dimensional space data into k groups according to the attribute or character. In this way, if we know the number of cluster then we can code the vector caused by the points of k groups into chromosome. Every chromosome denotes a result of clustering. We define the length of chromosome as follows:

$$l = d \times k \tag{1}$$

Here, l denotes the length of chromosome; d denotes the space dimension or data attribute dimension, and k denotes the number of the cluster. In this paper, we use continuous data as the test data, and adopt real number coding as the chromosome coding. We randomly choose the k points of the groups as the initialization of every chromosome of a clan, to make things convenient for the later calculation.

3.2 Function

In the calculation of adaptive value, we cluster the data by an algorithm just like the K-Means, and then update the previous collocated pivot by the new pivot in the chromosome. Since the K-Means algorithms take the distance between the pivot and every data point in the group as the reference, we can define the adaptive function as follows:

$$F = \sum_{X_j \in C_i} \| x_j - z_i \|, i = 1, \ldots, k, j = 1, \ldots, n \quad (2)$$

In formula (2), X_j denotes the data point of C_i, $i=1\ldots k$; Z_i is the pivot of group C_i.

3.3 Evolving Flow

In this paper, tournament selection scheme is adopted as the selecting mode. It is one of the multi-chosen modes and extremely suitable for the application of parallel Genetic algorithms. Through this way, N_{tour} ($N_{tour} \geq 2$) chromosomes are chosen at random. Then the best one will be the seed for producing next generation by judging the adaptive value.

One-point crossover is adopted as crossover mode mainly because it is a very basic one. The mutation rule of evolutionary method is adopted in mutation mode. In formula (3), v denotes the genetic value of chromosome. δ denotes a random constant which ranges between 0 and 1. The probability of selecting addition or subtraction is equal in the evolutionary method.

$$v \leftarrow v \pm \delta \times v \quad (3)$$

The adaptive probability mode is adopted to judge the probability of crossover and mutation. As we know, the reference information of Genetic algorithms comes from the adaptive value of chromosome. So, the adaptive probability in this paper is also based on the adaptive value of chromosome. The value of adaptive determines the quality of chromosome. At the same time, we can judge whether the adaptive value is involved in the local optimum by the difference between the f_{max} and adaptive value $\bar{f}$ in the evolution of every generation.

So, we take the difference between f_{max} and $\bar{f}$ as the basic rule of the crossover probability (P_c) and the mutation probability (P_m), and the traditional P_c and P_m are changed as (4) and (5):

$$P_c = k_1/(f_{max} - \bar{f}), k_1 \leq 1.0 \quad (4)$$

$$P_m = k_2/(f_{max} - \bar{f}), k_2 \leq 1.0 \quad (5)$$

According to the above two formulas, the values of traditional invariable P_c and P_m have been changed into variables, where, k_1 and k_2 are random variables between 0 and 1.0. We can adjust those two formulas according to the crossover and mutation. The process of crossover is selecting two couples of chromosomes randomly from clusters as Parents to make genetic exchange to produce another two couples of chromosomes, which will be considered as offspring. While mutation is the process of genetic mutating, to expect that the adaptive value can reverse the trend of P_c and P_m, in another word, the higher the adaptive value is, the lower the P_c and P_m are. So we can change formula (4) and (5) to (6) and (7).

$$P_c = k_1(f_{max} - \tilde{f})/(f_{max} - \bar{f}), k_1 \leq 1.0 \tag{6}$$

$$P_m = k_2(f_{max} - f)/(f_{max} - \bar{f}), k_2 \leq 1.0 \tag{7}$$

In formula (6), $\tilde{f}$ denotes the maximum of the adaptive values in any two chromosomes preparing to copulate, in format (7), f means the adaptive value of every chromosome, where, k_1 and k_2 are also random variables between 0 and 1.0. From formula (6) and (7), we can see that P_c and P_m may vary with the crossover parents and chromosomes.

In the P_c, if the D-value between f_{max} and $\bar{f}$ becomes smaller relatively, it means that the whole process of the evolving turns to the case of slow moving. At this time, the value of P_c, which will increase relatively, can make all the chromosomes in the clusters to copulate to generate new generations, to speed up the process of mutation. In the P_m, if the D-value between f_{max} and $\bar{f}$ becomes smaller, it means that the whole process of the evolvement may drop into the station of local optimum. While the $f_{max} = \tilde{f}$ or $f_{max} = f$, the value of P_c or P_m will be zero, means reserving the best chromosome to produce better generation.

In addition, we also should consider the cases of $\tilde{f} < \bar{f}$ and $f < \bar{f}$. In these cases, we must redefine the values of P_c and P_m. We set the $Pc = 1.0$ and $P_m = 0.5$, in order to make the worse chromosomes generate the better chromosomes by copulating and mutating, so that the complete adaptive of P_c and P_m can show as following:

$$P_c = \begin{cases} k_1(f_{max} - \tilde{f})/(f_{max} - \bar{f}), \tilde{f} \geq \bar{f}, k_1 = 1.0 \\ 1.0, otherwise \end{cases} \tag{8}$$

$$P_m = \begin{cases} k_2(f_{max} - f)/(f_{max} - \bar{f}), f \geq \bar{f}, k_2 = 0.5 \\ 0.5, otherwise \end{cases} \tag{9}$$

From the above description, the evolvement parameter are as follows: Selecting mode is Crossover mode, Crossover mode is Single-point crossover, Crossover probability is Adaptive probability, Mutating mode is Evolutionary mutation, and Mutating probability is Adaptive probability.

4 The Result and Analysis of Experimentation

The test data in this paper is practical, which is Glass data provided by the University of California[6]. The experimental result of the four clustering method is shown in

Table 1. The data in Table 1 show the results of Genetic algorithms and Adaptive genetic algorithms are better than that of K-Means and are the same as that of the other method. The max value almost decreases 31% misjudgments.

Table 1. The Experimental Data of Glass Data

Data / Method	Type1 (70)	Type2 (76)	Type3 (17)	Type 5(13)	Type 7(29)	Total Distance	Misjudgment Rate
K-Means	60	65	17	15	26	206.18	26.17%
H-Means[5]	125	26	15	14	29	220.10	52.34%
Pure Genetic algorithms +K-Means	78	51	17	33	26	200.95	28.04%
Adaptive Genetic algorithms+K-Means	71	58	17	33	26	200.65	21.50%

5 Conclusion

We test Glass data by K-Means, H-Means, Genetic Algorithms and adaptive Genetic algorithms respectively during the experimental process. Through the experimental result, we discover that Adaptive genetic algorithms can greatly improve the misjudgments of K-Means and H-Means, and find out the proper representative pivot when solving clustering problem, and is better than Genetic algorithms in evolving speed. It is more effective especially the vast amount of data.

References

1. Maulik U., Bandyopadhyay S.: Genetic algorithm-based clustering technique, Pattern Recognition, Vol. 33, (2000)1455-1465.
2. Srinivas M., Patnaik L. M.: Adaptive probabilities of crossover and mutation in genetic algorithms, IEEE Transactions on Systems, Man, and Cybernetics, Vol. 24, No. 3, (1994)656-667.
3. Goldberg D. E.: Genetic Algorithms in Search, Optimization and Machine Learning, Addison Wesley, Reading(1989).
4. Dumitrescu D., Lazzerini B., Jain L. C.: Dumitrescu A., Evolutionary Computation, CRC Press Boca Raton, (2000) 223-224.
5. Hansen P., Mladenovic N,: J-MEANS: a new local search heuristic for minimum sum of squares clustering, Pattern Recognition, Vol. 34, (2001)405-413.
6. Merz C., Murphy P., Aha D.: UCI repository of Machine Learning databases. Dept. of Information and Computer Science, University of California, Irvine(1997).
7. http://www.ics.uci.edu/~mlearn/MLRepository.html.

FCACO: Fuzzy Classification Rules Mining Algorithm with Ant Colony Optimization

Bilal Alatas and Erhan Akin

Department of Computer Engineering, Faculty of Engineering,
Firat University, 23119, Elazig / Turkey
{balatas, eakin}@firat.edu.tr

Abstract. Ant colony optimization (ACO) is relatively new computational intelligence paradigm and provides an effective mechanism for conducting a global search. This work proposes a novel classification rule mining algorithm integrating ACO for search strategy and fuzzy set for representation of the rule terms to give the system flexibility to cope with continuous values and uncertainties typically found in real-world applications and improve the comprehensibility of the rules. The algorithm uses a strategy that is different from 'divide-and-conquer' and 'separate-and-conquer' approaches used by decision trees and lists respectively; and simulates the ants' searching different food sources by using attribute-instance weighting and an effective pheromone update strategy for mining accurate and comprehensible rules. Obtained results from several real-world data sets are analyzed with respect to both predictive accuracy and simplicity and compared with C4.5Rules algorithm.

1 Introduction

Ant colony optimization (ACO) is recently developed heuristics for finding solutions to difficult search and optimization problems based on simulation of foraging behavior of ant colonies [1]. The application of ACO to classification is a research area still relatively unexplored. In fact, mining of classification rules is a search problem and ACO is very successful in global search and can cope better with attribute interaction than greedy rule induction algorithms. Furthermore, the application of ant algorithms requires minimum understanding of the problem domain. Parpinelli et al first worked on the application of ant algorithms to classification rule mining in [2] and then extended their work on optimizing parameter values and on the complexity of the algorithm and republished in [3]. The overall approach of Ant-Miner is a 'separate-and-conquer' one. It starts with a full training set, creates a 'best' rule that covers a subset of the training data, adds the best rule to its discovered rule list, removes the instances covered by said rule from the training data, and starts again with a reduced training set. This goes on until only a few instances are left in the training data, at which point a default rule is created to cover those remaining instances. This algorithm and its extended version [4-5] generate rule sets from data sets that have only nominal attributes that is why, a discretization process is necessary for the continuous attributes. Also Cordon et al have used an ant algorithm designed for solving the quadratic assignment problem to learn fuzzy control rules [6]; however it is outside the scope of data mining.

The algorithm proposed in this paper, called FCACO (**F**uzzy **C**lassification Rules Mining **A**lgorithm with **A**nt **C**olony **O**ptimization), is the first ACO algorithm for discovering fuzzy classification rules. Continuous attributes are dealt with using fuzzy sets. The fuzzy representation of the rule conditions not only gives the system more flexibility to cope with uncertainties typically found in real-world applications, but also improves the comprehensibility of the rules. The proposed approach performs a different strategy used in Ant-Miner. Instead of 'separate-and-conquer' strategy, this approach uses attribute-instance weighting and an effective pheromone update strategy.

2 The Proposed Method: FCACO

Each fuzzy rule covers a particular region of the attribute space described by the rule antecedent. The rule consequent that maximizes the rule quality is assigned to the rule once the rule antecedent is completed. This is done by assigning the rule consequent to the majority class among the instances covered by the rule.

Assume a training set of K instances $T = \{(x^1, c^1), ..., (x^K, c^K)\}$ where $x^k = \{x^k{}_1, ..., x^k{}_N\}$ is an instance taken from some attribute space $\{X_1, ..., X_n\}$, and $c^k \in \{C_1, ..., C_m\}$ is the class label associated with x^k. Upper indices k is used to denote the k-th training instance, and lower indices n to denote the n-th attribute $x^k{}_n$ of a training instance x^k. Fuzzy rules are of the form R_i: if X_1 is A_{1i} and ... X_N is A_{Ni} then $Y = c_i$ in which X_n denotes the n-th input variable, A_{ni} the fuzzy set associated to X_n and $c_i \in \{C_1, ..., C_M\}$ represents the class label of rule R_i. For a particular instance x_k, the rule activation

$$\mu_{Ri}(x^k) = \mu_{Ri}(\{x^k{}_1, ..., x^k{}_n\}) = \min_{n=1}^{N} \mu_{A_{ni}}(x^k{}_n) \tag{1}$$

describes the degree of matching between the rule and the instance. Each possible classification C_m accumulates the degree of activation of fuzzy rules R_i with a matching consequent $c_i = C_m$. The instance x^k is classified according to the class label

$$C_{max}(x^k) = \mathrm{argmax}_{Cm} \sum_{R_i | c_i = C_m} \mu_{R_i}(x^k) \tag{2}$$

that obtains the majority class.

Ant-Miner and improved Ant-Miner proposed for only data sets that have only nominal attributes are run sequentially several times for mining classification rules, each time being run against a reduced data set. Ordered rule sets, or lists used in Ant-Miner, come with an inherent deterrent to comprehensibility – the meaning of a single rule in the list is dependent on all the previous rules and the further down the list you get the more difficult it is to make sense of the rule. The instances that are correctly classified by the mined rule are removed from the training set. Rules mined in later stages are unaware of the previously removed instances and therefore might be in conflict with rules mined earlier. Unexpected interactions between rules can appear when an instance is covered by several rules of different classes.

Let T rules of a class have been mined and we wish to mine the $T+1$ rule for the same class. The information that the system has about the T rules, are the instances from the training set that were not covered by them, but for the system is not known as the T rules affect on the instances from other classes. Furthermore, when working with fuzzy rules and instances, this problem increases since the instances are covered by a rule in a degree. This can cause unexpected interaction between rules. That is why, in this study 'separate-and-conquer' approach has not been followed; a different method that simulates the ants' finding different food sources by using attribute-instance weighting with different pheromone update strategy has been performed. The main steps of FCACO are shown in Figure 1.

```
Fuzzify continuous attributes
Discovered_Rule_List = [] // empty initially
Initialize all trails with the same amount of pheromone
While (Number of unweighted instances in the Training Set >
       maxInstUnweighted OR yielding a positive fitness)//'AntRun'
    i=0
    Repeat // 'iteration'
        i=i+1
        Ants incrementally construct classification rule
        Assign rule consequents
        Prune just-constructed rules
        Update pheromone of trail followed by the best Ant
    Until (i >= NoOfIterations) OR (Best rule does not change
                          throughout MaxRulesConverge-1 iteration)
    Select the best rule among all constructed rules
    Add rule to Discovered_Rule_List
    Weight the instances covered by mined rule
    Update amount of pheromone for mining of other rules
                //simulation of searching different food sources
End While
output Discovered_Rule_List
```

Fig. 1. Main steps of FCACO

Each run generates a number of AntRuns in succession. An AntRun uses the training set to generate a number of fuzzy if-then rules with a number of ants, NoOfAnts. At the end of an AntRun, the best rule generated is added to the rule set for that run. All instances and attributes in the training set covered by this newly added rule are reweighted, and amount of pheromone in these instances is reduced for mining other rules. The next AntRun then uses the resulting training set with different amount of pheromone. The number of AntRuns is determined dynamically based on the predetermined value of a parameter: maxInstUnweighted, i.e. the maximum number of instances in the training set that may be left unweighted by the rules in the rule set. No more AntRuns will be generated if the remaining number of instances in the unweighted training set is less than or equal to the value of this predefined parameter. The motivation for using this criteria is to avoid overfitting of a rule to just a very small number of instances. In this way, simpler rule sets that are more easily interpreted by a human user are mined. Furthermore in this study, an additional stopping criterion for the number of AntRuns has also been implemented.

Occasionally, towards the end of a run, the best rule generated by an AntRun has a quality value of zero. This happens when the instances remaining in the training set are few and disparate, and the minimum number of instances that must be covered by any rule is generally too great at this point to generate useable rules. Therefore if the best rule of the current AntRun has quality equal to zero, though the `maxInstUnweighted` criteria may not yet be satisfied, no more AntRuns are generated, and the best rule is not added to the final rule set.

For each rule, the system prunes the rule. The basic idea of this rule pruning procedure is that, the lower the predictive power of a condition; the more likely the condition will be removed from the rule. The predictive power of a condition is estimated by its information gain, a very popular heuristic measure of predictive power in data mining. This rule pruning procedure was chosen because the computation has already been done in heuristic function and this is both effective and computationally efficient.

After pruning, each rule is assigned a quality value based on how well it covers instances in the training set. The best rule of each iteration is saved in a temporary storage structure, `BestRulesOfIterations`, and is used to update the amount of pheromone of the terms before the next iteration is initiated. There are two user-defined parameters that control the number of iterations that may be executed by an AntRun: `maxRulesConverge` and `NoOfIterations`. The first parameter sets the value, p, for the maximum number of best rules from successive iterations that are allowed to be the same. If this value is reached then the current AntRun will halt. At this point the best rule from `BestRulesOfIterations` is selected and added to the final rule set for the run. The `NoOfIterations` parameter controls the maximum number of iterations that may be executed if the `maxRulesConverge` value is not reached during that AntRun.

2.1 Problem Dependent Elements

The elements of an ACO algorithm that must be adapted to the particular problem domain are heuristic and fitness functions. Heuristic function will be used for constructing of a rule antecedent and fitness function assesses how well a rule constructed by an ant covers instances in the training data in this study.

2.1.1 Heuristic Function

Each *term*$_{ij}$ that can be added to the current rule antecedent has an associated heuristic value η_{ij}. This value gives an estimate of the quality of this term with respect to its ability to improve the predictive accuracy of the rule being constructed. The term heuristic values are calculated at the beginning of each AntRun as they depend on the weights of the instances in the training set, i.e. after the training set has been weighted they need to be recalculated. Heuristic values are recalculated each time after a term is selected for addition to the current rule antecedent being constructed; when this happens the term selected needs to be ignored in subsequent term selections as do other terms belonging to the same attribute of the chosen term. Since the heuristic function is a normalized one the heuristic values of the remaining terms, i.e. the terms that may still be selected by the current ant, need to be recalculated.

$$\eta_{ij} = \frac{\log_2 k - infoA_{ij}}{\sum_{i=1}^{a} x_i \sum_{j=1}^{b_i} \left(\log_2 k - infoA_{ij}\right)} \quad (3)$$

$$infoA_{ij} = -\sum_{c=1}^{k} \left(\frac{\sum_{n \in I_c} w_{ij} \mu A_{ij}{}^n}{\sum_{n=1}^{N} w_{ij} \mu A_{ij}{}^n} \right) \log_2 \left(\frac{\sum_{n \in I_c} w_{ij} \mu A_{ij}{}^n}{\sum_{n=1}^{N} w_{ij} \mu A_{ij}{}^n} \right) \quad (4)$$

a is the total number of attributes, x_i is set to 1 if the attribute A_i is not yet used by the current ant, otherwise 0. b_i is the number of domain values of the i-th attribute.

w_{ij} is the weight of the attribute computed whenever a rule is inserted to the rule list. The idea is to reduce the weights of the attributes contained by the mined rules to avoid from mining the same rule and to mine the other rules. Initially all the weights are set to 1. When the j-th value of the i-th attribute is included in the rule its weight is reduced as $w_{ij} = w_{ij} - \eta \, w_{ij}$ with $\eta = 0.001$

This heuristic is a local heuristic as it is applied to individual terms and this makes it sensitive to attribute interaction. The amount of pheromone of a term actually acts as another heuristic in an ACO, but of a more global kind. In fact, ACO does not need accurate information in its heuristic value, since the amount of pheromone compensates for small potential errors in the heuristic values [4]. The pheromone values are changed depending on the fitness of the rule as a whole, i.e. taking into account attribute interactions occurring in the rule.

2.1.2 Fitness Function

The fitness function that shows the quality of a rule consists of three parts. The first part considers sensitivity, specificity, and accuracy criteria and can be defined as

$$Q_1 = \frac{Sensitivity \times Specificity + aw \times Accuracy'}{1 + aw} \quad (5)$$

$$Sensitivity = \frac{TP}{TP+FN}, \quad Specificity = \frac{TN}{TN+FP}, \text{ and } Accuracy = \frac{TP+TN}{TP+TN+FP+FN}$$

$Accuracy' = Accuracy$ when $Accuracy > 0.7$ and $Accuracy' = 0$ otherwise. aw is the weight of the accuracy and is set to 0.01. This term of this part of fitness slightly reinforces the fitness of high-accuracy rules.

In case of nominal attribute, sensitivity is the accuracy among positive instances, and specificity is the accuracy among negative instances and TP is true positives, the number of instances covered by the rule that have the same class label as the rule; FP is false positives, the number of instances covered by the rule that have a different class label from the rule; FN is false negatives, the number of instances that are not covered by the rule but have the same class label as the rule, and TN is true negatives, the number of instances that are not covered by the rule and do not have the same class label as the rule. However, in this study fuzzy classification rules are mined, and an instance can be covered by a rule antecedent to a certain degree in the range [0...1], which corresponds to the membership degree of that instance in that rule antecedent. Therefore, the system computes fuzzy values for TP, FP, FN, and TN as

$$TP = \sum_{k|c^k=c_i}^{p} w^k \mu R_i(x^k), \; FP = \sum_{k|c^k \neq c_i}^{p} w^k \mu R_i(x^k), \; FN = \sum_{k|c^k=c_i}^{p} (1 - w^k \mu R_i(x^k)), \; TN = \sum_{k|c^k \neq c_i}^{p} (1 - w^k \mu R_i(x^k)),$$

Here, p is the number of instances in the training data set; w^k is weight of the instance and is computed as the minimum weight of its attributes.

The number of correctly and incorrectly classified instances irrespective of their weight is a consistency criterion and must be included in the fitness function as second part. The rationale is to avoid that rules generated in the later stages sequentially make inaccurate generalizations based on the few remaining instances with high weights, while ignoring previously down-weighted instances. Part of the fitness for rule consistency of unweighted instances is accordingly computed by considering the number of correctly and incorrectly classified instances covered by the rule R_i and can be defined as

$$Q_2 = \begin{cases} 0 & \sum_{k|c_k=c_i} \mu R_i(x^k) < \sum_{k|c_k \neq c_i} \mu R_i(x^k) \\ \dfrac{\sum_{k|c_k=c_i} \mu R_i(x^k) - \sum_{k|c_k \neq c_i} \mu R_i(x^k)}{\sum_{k|c_k=c_i} \mu R_i(x^k)} & \text{otherwise} \end{cases} \quad (6)$$

Another criterion considered for fitness function, third part, is the length of the rule. This part of fitness rewards a concise rule and is computed as

$$Q_3 = 1 - \frac{NumberOfTerms}{20} \quad (7)$$

The final fitness function is weighted sum of these described criteria:

$$Q = \sum_{i=1}^{3} weight_i Q_i \quad (8)$$

$weight_1=1$, $weight_2=1$, and $weight_3=0.0005$ were empirically determined.

2.2 Problem Independent Elements

Problem independent elements of an ACO are transition rule and pheromone update strategy. The balance between exploration and exploitation has been ensured with these elements in this study.

2.2.1 Transition Rule

The probability that the condition is added to the current partial rule that the ants areconstructing is given in Figure 2 [5]. In order to enhance the role of exploration this transition rule is used.

```
if q₁ ≤ φ
    repeat
        ∑ Pᵢⱼ
    until (q₂ ≤ ∑_{j∈Jᵢ} Pᵢⱼ)
        select termᵢⱼ
Else
    Choose termᵢⱼ with max Pᵢⱼ
```

Fig. 2. Transition Rule

Here q_1 and q_2 are random numbers, φ is a parameter in [0, 1] and is set to 0.4 in simulations, j_i is the number of i-th attribute values, and P_{ij} is the probability calculated using

$$P_{ij} = \frac{[\tau_{ij}(t)]^\alpha [\eta_{ij}]^\beta}{\sum_{i=1}^{a} \sum_{j=1}^{b_i} [\tau_{ik}(t)]^\alpha [\eta_{ik}]^\beta}, \forall i \in I \quad (9)$$

Pij is the probability that termij is selected to be added to the current partial rule antecedent; ηij is the heuristic value associated with termij; τij(t) is the amount of pheromone associated with a termij at iteration t; a is the total number of attributes; bi is the number of domain values of the i-th attribute; I are the attributes not yet used by the ant; α and β are two adjustable parameters that control the relative weight of the heuristic and pheromone values respectively. In FCACO, these are kept fixed at 1, thereby giving them equal importance.

2.2.2 Pheromone Update Strategy

Note that in Ant-Miner, the amount of pheromone of terms is updated after the creation of each ant, while in this implementation the amount of pheromone is updated once at the start of each iteration, based on the best ant from the previous iteration. This makes the pheromone updating of terms more discriminatory and therefore provides more direction to the search of ants in successive iterations.

At the start of an AntRun, the amount of pheromone of all terms is initialized and given equal value, the inverse of the total number of terms.

$$\tau_{ij}(z,t) = \frac{1}{\sum_{i=1}^{a} b_i} \qquad z=0, t=0 \tag{10}$$

Here, z represents the z-th rule and t is the t-th iteration in mining of z-th rule. Each time an ant completes the construction of a rule, the amount of pheromone for all terms is updated. The amount of pheromones of terms that occur in the constructed rule R is increased in proportion to the quality, Q, as follows.

$$\tau_{ij}(z,t+1) = \tau_{ij}(z,t) + \tau_{ij}(z,t)Q \qquad \forall i,j \tag{11}$$

The amount of pheromone associated with each $term_{ij}$ that does not occur in the constructed rule has to be decreased, to simulate the phenomenon of pheromone evaporation in real ant colony systems. Dividing the value of each τ_{ij} by the summation of all τ_{ij} performs the reduction of pheromone of an unused term. Only the best ant is used for pheromone updating, ensuring that exploration is more directed. This formula is used for constructing one rule for Discovered_Rule_List. For simulation of searching different food sources, after best rule from BestRulesOfIterations is selected and added to the Discovered_Rule_List, amount of pheromone of the terms included in the best rule is decreased and other best rules are forced to be found. That is why; another amount of pheromone of terms must be kept for mining other rules. Each time a best rule is included in the list, amount of pheromone is initialized using

$$\tau_{ij}(z+1,0) = \begin{cases} \tau_{ij}(z,0) & , A_{ij} \in R \\ \tau_{ij}(z,0) \times \chi^k & , A_{ij} \notin R \end{cases} \tag{12}$$

$$\chi^k = \left(\frac{E(R_t)}{1-E(R_t)}\right)^{\mu_{R_t}(x^k)} \tag{13}$$

The computation of $E(R_t)$ was previously used for boosting in induction of fuzzy rule-based classifiers [7]. Here $E(R_t)$ is the error of the fuzzy rule R_t mined at iteration t. $E(R_t)$ of a fuzzy rule R_t is weighted by the degree of matching $\mu R_t(x^k)$ between the k-th training instance (x^k, c^k) and the rule antecedent as well as its weight w^k and can be defined as

$$E(R_t) = \frac{\sum_{k|c_k \neq c_t} w^k \mu R_t(x^k)}{\sum_k w^k \mu R_t(x^k)} \tag{14}$$

In other words, the goal of simulation of searching different food source is to find rules that perform well over the current distribution of training instances.

3 Simulation Results

Five data sets described in Table 1 available from the UCI ML repository were used. The first column gives the name of the data set, the second the number of attributes (excluding the conclusion attribute), the third the total number of instances in the data set, and the final column gives the number of class labels. Three of the data sets have binary class labels while the other two represent multi-class domains. All of the data sets have continuous attributes. Note that the number of instances includes the missing valued instances. In this study, instances that had any attribute with missing value were removed from the data sets.

User specified membership functions were used for fuzzy classification. In the simulations, ten iterations of the whole ten-fold cross-validation (10-CV) procedure were used for estimating predictive accuracy. Since FCACO is based on a stochastic process and the results produced therefore vary from one 10-CV to the next, the same folds were used for each of the ten 10-CV tests. That is, the data set was not re-shuffled and split into k different subsets before each of the ten 10-CV runs. This was done in order to test the deviation in the performance statistics arising from FCACO, and not due to any changes in the folds used.

In the simulations, user-specified system parameters were set as `NoOfIterations=80`, `NoOfAnts=30`, `maxInstUnweighted=10`, and `maxRulesConverge=10`.

Table 1. The used data sets

Data set	Attributes	Instances	Classes
Breast W	9	699	2
Bupa	6	345	2
Diabetes	8	768	2
Glass	9	214	6
Wine	13	178	3

Table 2. Comparison of accuracy rates

FCACO		C4.5Rules	
Training	Test	Training	Test
98.3	95.26	96.9	94.0
69.91	65.5	71.1	66.3
78.9	75.3	76.0	73.0
80.5	78.9	80.4	78.9
96.9	96.76	94.4	93.3

Table 3. Comparison of simplicity

Data set	Rules		Terms	
	FCACO	C4.5Rules	FCACO	C4.5Rules
Breast W	6.9	8.1	11.8	19.8
Bupa	8.6	14.0	17.1	36.8
Diabetes	10.9	13.1	24.5	29.7
Glass	13.9	14.0	28.0	29.1
Wine	5.4	4.6	12.5	14.5

Table 2 shows the average accuracy rate on training and test data for FCACO and C4.5Rules. In the simulations, all C4.5 parameters had their default values. In this table, the rules obtained by FCACO have higher accuracy on training and test data than the rules obtained by C4.5Rules in four out of five data sets. The differences in accuracy rates are significant in some data sets. C4.5Rules found rules that have higher accuracy than FCACO in one data set, Bupa, and the difference is significant. Too simple rules mined by FCACO that were underfitted to the data seem the reason of this situation.

The results of the simplicity of the mined rule set measured by the number of mined rules and the average total number of terms in all mined rules of both FCACO and C4.5Rules are shown in Table 3. The results obtained by FCACO are much better than the results obtained by C4.5Rules in four out of all data sets. FCACO mined a slight more number of rules in Wine data set, however it mined simpler rules.

4 Conclusions and Future Works

This work proposed a new ACO algorithm, called FCACO, for mining fuzzy classification rules. Furthermore it requires minimum understanding of the problem domain. The strategy used in FCACO is different from 'divide-and-conquer' and 'separate-and-conquer' approaches used by decision trees and lists respectively. It simulates the ants' searching different food sources by a different pheromone updating strategy and attribute-instance weighting. FCACO was compared with C4.5Rules algorithm in five real-world data sets. Overall the results show that, concerning predictive accuracy, FCACO is competitive with C4.5Rules and finds considerably simpler rules. These results are promising since C4.5Rules has been evolving from the research of decades in decision tree and rule induction algorithms.

One research direction is to investigate the sensitivity of FCACO to its system parameters by performing more elaborated experiments by using optimized parameters. Another research direction consists of simultaneously searching for intervals of continuous attributes and mining of classification rules that these intervals conform to avoid from conveying a loss of information. The proposed method has a very convenient structure for parallel or distributed architecture and that is why, it would be interesting to try parallel implementation of this method using different heuristic and fitness functions, pheromone update strategies, and more transition rules.

References

1. Dorigo, M., Maziezzo, V., Colorni, A.: The Ant System: Optimization by a Colony of Cooperating Ants. IEEE Trans. on Systems, Man and Cybernetics B,26(1) (1996) 29-41
2. Parpinelli, R.S., Lopes, H.S., Freitas, A.A.: An Ant Colony Based System for Data Mining: Applications to Medical Data. GECCO Proceedings USA (2001) 791-798
3. Parpinelli, R.S., Lopes, H.S., Freitas. A.A.: An Ant Colony Algorithm for Classification Rule Discovery. In: Abbas, H.A., Sarker, R.A., Newton CS, editors, Data Mining: A Heuristic Approach. Idea Group Publishing, London (2002) 190-208

4. Liu, B., Abbass, H.A., McKay, B.: Classification Rule Discovery with Ant Colony Optimization. IEEE Computational Intelligence Bulletin, 3(1) (2004)
5. Galea, M.: Applying Swarm Intelligence to Rule Induction. MSc Artificial Intelligence, Divison of Informatics University of Edinburgh (2002)
6. Casillas, J., Cordón, O., Herrera, F.: Learning Fuzzy Rules Using Ant Colony Optimization. Proc. ANTS'2000 From Ant Colonies to Artificial Ants: Second International Workshop on Ant Algorithms (2000) 13-21
7. del Jesus, M.J., Hoffman, F., Navacués, L.J., Sánches, L.: Induction of Fuzzy-Rule-Based Classifiers with Evolutionary Boosting Algorithms. IEEE Transactions on Fuzzy Systems, 12:3 (2004) 296-308

Goal-Directed Portfolio Insurance

Jiah-Shing Chen[1] and Benjamin Penyang Liao[2]

[1] National Central University, Jungli, Taiwan 320
jschen@mgt.ncu.edu.tw
[2] Overseas Chinese Institute of Technology, Taichung,
Taiwan 407 & National Central University, Jungli, Taiwan 320
lpy@ocit.edu.tw

Abstract. In an investment process, there is usually a goal implicitly or explicitly designated by an investor. However, traditional constant proportion portfolio insurance (CPPI) strategy considers only the floor constraint but not the goal aspect. In addition, empirical evidences show that a mutual fund manger's risk-attitude changes when the mid-year performance outperforms or under-performs the benchmark. There seems to be two contradictory risk-attitudes according to different studies: low wealth risk aversion and high wealth risk aversion. Although low wealth risk aversion can be explained by the CPPI strategy, high wealth risk aversion can not be explained by CPPI. We argue that these contradictions can be explained from two perspectives: the portfolio insurance perspective and the goal-directed (or goal-seeking) perspective. This paper proposes a goal-directed (GD) strategy to express an investor's goal-directed trading behavior and combines it with the portfolio insurance perspective to form a goal-directed constant proportion portfolio insurance (GDCPPI) strategy. In order to compare these 3 strategies, we build an effectiveness measure using deviation of absolute distance. From our statistical test results, the GDCPPI strategy dominates the other two strategies under this measure. We also apply the genetic algorithm (GA) technique to find a satisfactory set of parameter values for the GDCPPI strategy to improve its performance.

1 Introduction

Portfolio insurance is a way of investment with the constraint that the wealth can never fall below a pre-assigned protecting wealth floor. The optimal trading strategy for a constant floor turns out to be the popular constant proportion portfolio insurance (CPPI) strategy [1,2] and can be expressed as $x_t = c(W_t - F)$, where x_t is the amount invested in the risky asset at time t, W_t is the wealth at time t, c is a constant risk multiplier, and F is the floor. This optimal strategy states that one should invest more in the risky asset when the wealth increases. In practice, a mutual fund manager generally sets up a performance objective in terms of wealth or return at the beginning of a period. Then the fund manager has to do his best to achieve this objective or goal. Now if a fund manager follows the CPPI strategy and the current wealth is very close to the goal, he will invest a large portion in the risky asset and will have a greater chance of failing his almost reached goal. This possibility is not favorable to mutual fund managers. The major reason of this is that CPPI strategy only considers the floor but does not take the goal state into account, while fund managers do have the goal state in mind during the investment process.

Evidences show that an investor will change his risk-attitude under different wealth levels. CPPI strategy demonstrates this phenomenon. In addition, some studies showed fund managers change their risk-attitudes based on their performance compared to the benchmark. However, there are contradictory observations among these studies. Some studies observed that fund managers take risk-seeking behavior when their performance is worse than the benchmark while some other studies observed that fund managers take risk-averse behavior when their performance is worse than the benchmark.

These contradictions in fact can be explained by portfolio insurance perspective and goal-directed perspective, respectively. Goal-directed perspective proposes that an investor in financial markets will consider some investment goals. A goal-directed investor will take risk-seeking behavior when the distance from current wealth to the goal is large and will take risk-averse behavior when the distance from current wealth to the goal is small. Obviously, a CPPI investor's risk-attitude changing direction is opposite to a goal-directed investor's.

We therefore construct a *goal-directed (GD)* strategy $x_t = c(G - W_t)$ under constraint $W_t \leq G$, where G is the goal. We further combine the portfolio insurance constraint and goal-directed constraint as $F \leq W_t \leq G$ to construct a *goal-directed CPPI (GDCPPI)* strategy, $x_t = c[\alpha(W_t - F) + (1 - \alpha)(G - W_t)]$, $0 \leq \alpha \leq 1$. Since the GDCPPI strategy reduces to the CPPI strategy when $\alpha = 1$ and reduces to the GD strategy when $\alpha = 0$, the proposed GDCPPI strategy is a generalization of both CPPI and GD strategies.

To compare feasible strategies under some constraints, we only need to compare their objective function values. However, to compare arbitrary strategies, feasible or not, under some constraints, we need a more sophisticated measure. Since CPPI strategy is the optimal strategy under the floor constraint, we can use a strategy's mean absolute distance (error) to the CPPI strategy as a measure for the floor constraint. We use the mean absolute distance to the GD strategy as a measure for the goal constraint by symmetry. For both the floor and the goal constraints, we construct two measures: the mean absolute distance $\mu_h(x)$ and the standard deviation of absolute distance $\sigma_h(x)$ for a strategy x. Since the forms of $\mu_h(x)$ for strategies CPPI, GD, and GDCPPI are identical, this measure does not show which strategy dominates the others all the time. This paper therefore applies the measure $\sigma_h(x)$ to show that GDCPPI strategy dominates the CPPI and GD strategies all the time in the statistical tests.

We also apply the genetic algorithm (GA) technique to find a better set of strategy parameter values. We execute 30 GA learning runs to show that GA technique does indeed find a better set of strategy parameter values.

The remainder of this paper is organized as follows. Section 2 formulates the models of our goal-directed strategies. Section 3 builds two measures to evaluate an arbitrary strategy. Section 4 performs some experiments to show the measurement effects of these strategies and the GA learning experiments. Section 5 describes our conclusions and directions for future works.

2 Trading Strategies

2.1 CPPI Strategy

The formulation and solution of optimal portfolio insurance problem will be described following Grossman's work [3]. Assume there are two assets: a risk-free asset such as a T-bill and a risky asset such as a stock. Let the stock price dynamic be $\frac{dP_t}{P_t} = \mu dt + \sigma dz_t$, where μ is the mean of returns, σ is the standard deviation of returns, and z_t is a Brownian motion at time t. The portfolio wealth dynamic is then $dW_t = rW_t dt + x_t(\mu dt + \sigma dz_t)$, where r is the risky-free rate of return and x_t is the dollar amount invested in the risky asset. Suppose an investor tries to maximize the growth rate of expected utility of the final wealth under the portfolio insurance constraint. The problem becomes:

$$\xi = \sup_{\mathcal{A}} \lim_{T \to \infty} \frac{1}{\gamma T} \ln E[\gamma U(W_T)] \qquad (1)$$
$$\text{s.t. } W_t \geq K, \forall t \leq T$$

where $\mathcal{A}$ denotes the set of admissible trading strategies, $0 \neq \gamma \leq 1$, and $K > 0$ is the floor. The optimal strategy to the above optimization problem is:

$$x_t^* = \frac{\mu}{\sigma^2(1-\beta)}(W_t - K), \qquad (2)$$

where $\beta = \frac{1}{1+\frac{\mu^2}{2\gamma\xi\sigma^2}} = \frac{2\gamma\xi\sigma^2}{2\gamma\xi+\mu^2}$.

Equation (2) can be simplified as:

$$\zeta_t \equiv x_t = c(W_t - K), W_t \geq K, \qquad (3)$$

where $c = \frac{\mu}{\sigma^2(1-\beta)}$ can be regarded as an investor's risk multiplier, K is the protecting floor. This ζ_t is the popular CPPI strategy.

2.2 Risk Attitudes

Studies showed that there are two different types of risk attitudes. Tournament theory studies the behaviors of fund managers comparing to the benchmark. Some studies observed that under-performers become risk-averse and outperformers become risk-seeking [4,5,6]. Other studies observed that the underperformers will become more risky than the better-performers in mutual fund markets [7]. We name these two risk attitudes as low wealth risk aversion and high wealth risk aversion, respectively and summarize them as follows.

Low Wealth Risk Aversion: An investor will become risk-averse when his current wealth is low and will become risk-seeking when his current wealth is high.

High Wealth Risk Aversion: An investor will become risk-averse when his current wealth is high and will become risk-seeking when his current wealth is low.

Although low wealth risk aversion can be explained by the CPPI strategy, high wealth risk aversion can not be explained by CPPI. We argue that these contradictions can be explained from two perspectives: the portfolio insurance perspective and the goal-directed (or goal-seeking) perspective.

2.3 Goal-Directed Strategy

The CPPI strategy in equation (3)

$$x_t = c(W_t - K), W_t \geq K$$

can be generalized to

$$x_t = c|W_t - K|. \quad (4)$$

Equation (4) can be regarded as a general strategy of the following two special cases defined by different constraints.

Floor-Protected: $x_t = c(W_t - K) \geq 0, W_t \geq K$. This trading strategy is reasonably regarded as the CPPI strategy to protect the floor K such as $K = F$.

Goal-Directed: $x_t = c(K - W_t) \geq 0, W_t \leq K$. Here, since $W_t \leq K$, K should not be regarded as the protecting floor. As we have argued that a fund manger will take a riskier activity when goal distance is large and will take less risky activity when goal distance is small from goal-seeking perspective. Then, the K can be reasonably regarded as the *goal*, i.e., K is replaced by a gaol G. Therefore, we propose a *goal-directed (GD)* strategy as $\eta_t \equiv x_t = c(G - W_t), W_t \leq G$, where G is the goal and c is a constant.

2.4 Goal-Directed CPPI Strategy

CPPI strategy considers the floor but not the goal while GD strategy considers the goal but not the floor. Neither strategy considers both the floor and goal. We therefore further generalize them to derive a goal-directed CPPI strategy as follows.

Equation (4), $x_t = c|W_t - K|$, can be rewritten as

$$x_t = c|W_t - K| = c(\alpha|W_t - K| + (1-\alpha)|W_t - K|), 0 \leq \alpha \leq 1$$
$$x_t = c(\alpha|W_t - K| + (1-\alpha)|W_t - K'|), 0 \leq \alpha \leq 1, \text{if } K = K'$$
$$x_t = c[\alpha(W_t - F) + (1-\alpha)(G - W_t)], 0 \leq \alpha \leq 1, F \leq W_t \leq G,$$

where K and K' are generalized to $F = K \leq K' = G$. Finally,

$$\theta_t \equiv x_t = c[\alpha(W_t - F) + (1-\alpha)(G - W_t)], 0 \leq \alpha \leq 1, F \leq W_t \leq G.$$

We define θ_t as the goal-directed CPPI (GDCPPI) strategy, which combines portfolio insurance perspective and goal-directed perspective and is under constraint $F \leq W_t \leq G$. It is easy to see that GDCPPI strategy is a generalization of both CPPI and GD strategies.

- When $\alpha = 1$, $x_t = c(W_t - F)$ and the GDCPPI strategy reduces to the CPPI strategy.
- When $\alpha = 0$, $x_t = c(G - W_t)$ and the GDCPPI strategy reduces to the GD strategy.

3 Measures for Strategies with Floor and Goal Constraints

To compare feasible strategies under some constraints, we only need to compare their objective function values. However, to compare arbitrary strategies, feasible or not, under some constraints, we need a more sophisticated measure. Since CPPI strategy is the optimal strategy under the floor constraint, we can use a strategy's mean absolute distance (error) to the CPPI strategy as a measure for the floor constraint. We use the mean absolute distance to the GD strategy as a measure for the goal constraint by symmetry. For both the floor and the goal constraints, we construct two measures: the mean absolute distance $\mu_h(x)$ and the standard deviation of absolute distance $\sigma_h(x)$ for a strategy x. A strategy with smaller mean absolute distance then is a better one. Since the forms of $\mu_h(x)$ for strategies CPPI, GD, and GDCPPI are identical, this measure does not show which strategy dominates the others all the time. Therefore, we finally apply the measure $\sigma_h(x)$ to compare arbitrary strategies.

3.1 Mean Absolute Distance

The ζ strategy and the η strategy are taken in this paper as two reference strategies to calculate an arbitrary strategy's mean absolute distances under different constraints. Let strategy s_t be an reference strategy. For any strategy x_t, its absolute distance is $|x_t - s_t|$ at time t.

Under floor constraint $W_t \geq F$, since ζ is the optimal strategy, ζ is taken as the reference strategy. Then the absolute distance for any strategy x_t is $|x_t - \zeta_t|$ at time t. Let $f(x_t) = |x_t - \zeta_t|$ and $F(x) = \{f(x_t)\}$. We build a measure:

$$\mu_f(x) = \mu(F(x)) = \mu(\{f(x_t)\}) = \frac{\sum_{t=1}^{N} |x_t - \zeta_t|}{N}. \tag{5}$$

When $x_t = c(W_t - F)$, i.e., $x_t = \zeta_t$, the absolute distance at each time t is $f(x_t) = |\zeta_t - \zeta_t| = 0$ and $\mu_f(\zeta) = 0$ which attains 100% optimality.

Under goal constraint $W_t \leq G$, η is taken as the reference strategy by symmetry. Then the absolute distance for any strategy x_t is $|x_t - \eta_t|$ at time t. Let $g(x_t) = |x_t - \eta_t|$ and $G(x) = \{g(x_t)\}$. We build a measure:

$$\mu_g(x) = \mu(G(x)) = \mu(\{g(x_t)\}) = \frac{\sum_{t=1}^{N} |x_t - \eta_t|}{N}. \tag{6}$$

When $x_t = c(G - W_t)$, i.e., $x_t = \eta_t$, the absolute distance at each time t is $g(x_t) = |\eta_t - \eta_t| = 0$ and $\mu_g(\eta) = 0$ which attains its minimum.

Since ζ is used as the reference strategy under constraint $W_t \geq F$ and η is used as the reference strategy under constraint $W_t \leq G$, it is natural to use both of them as the reference strategies under constraint $F \leq W_t \leq G$. Since the absolute distance is $f(x_t)$ under constraint $W_t \geq F$ and the absolute distance is $g(x_t)$ under constraint $W_t \leq G$, the average of $f(x_t)$ and $g(x_t)$ is a suitable start to calculate the absolute distance under constraint $F \leq W_t \leq G$.

Let $H(x) = F(x) \cup G(x) = \{f(x_t), g(x_t)\}$. Therefore, by taking ζ and η as the reference strategies, we build a measure:

$$\mu_h(x) = \mu(H(x)) = \mu(\{f(x_t), g(x_t)\}) = \frac{\sum_{t=1}^{N}(|x_t - \zeta_t| + |x_t - \eta_t|)}{2N}. \tag{7}$$

We can therefore compare the three strategies ζ, η, and θ by measure $\mu_h(x)$:

$$\mu_h(\zeta) = \frac{c}{N} \sum_{t=1}^{N} |W_t(\zeta) - \frac{F+G}{2}| \tag{8}$$

$$\mu_h(\eta) = \frac{c}{N} \sum_{t=1}^{N} |W_t(\eta) - \frac{F+G}{2}| \tag{9}$$

$$\mu_h(\theta) = \frac{c}{N} \sum_{t=1}^{N} |W_t(\theta) - \frac{F+G}{2}| \tag{10}$$

We can see that equations (8), (9) and (10) have the same form. These measures in fact are their mean absolute distance of wealth to the average of floor and goal. This seems to imply that the μ_h measure can not distinguish among the 3 strategies. Therefore, it is necessary to find another measure to compare these strategies.

3.2 Distance Volatility

Since $\mu_h(\zeta)$, $\mu_h(\eta)$ and $\mu_h(\theta)$ can not always dominate each others in all circumstances, we will build a new measure from the concept of distance volatility. In general, under the same mean of returns, a strategy with smaller standard deviation of returns is better then the others. Applying this concept, we build a new measure:

$$\sigma_h(x) = \sigma(H(x)) = \sigma(\{f(x_t), g(x_t)\})$$
$$= [\frac{1}{2N}\sum_{t=1}^{N}((f(x_t) - \mu_h(x))^2 + (g(x_t) - \mu_h(x))^2)]^{\frac{1}{2}}. \quad (11)$$

We can see that $\sigma_h(x)$ is the standard deviation of absolute distance and smaller $\sigma_h(x)$ is preferred. Therefore, we can compare strategies ζ, η and θ by measures $\sigma_h(\zeta)$, $\sigma_h(\eta)$ and $\sigma_h(\theta)$, respectively.

4 Experiments

This study performs experiments for strategy comparison and strategy optimization by genetic algorithms.

4.1 Strategy Comparison

This experiment compares the 3 strategies by the σ_h measure.

Generate Price Random Walk Series: In order to get sufficient random walk series, we set up the admissible price-related parameter sets for μ and σ as: $\mu \in \{-23\%, 0\%, 23\%\}$ and $\sigma \in \{20\%, 30\%, 40\%\}$. Then we have 9 price-related parameter combinations. In addition, under each combination instance, we generate 20 price random walk series. Therefore, we have 180 price random walk series.

Strategy Parameter Sets: The strategy parameter sets are set up as follows: $c \in \{1.5, 2.5, 3.5\}$, $\alpha \in \{0.25, 0.5, 0.75\}$, $F/W_0 \in \{0.74, 0.84, 0.94\}$, $G/W_0 \in \{1.06, 1.16, 1.26\}$. F/W_0 is the ratio of floor and initial wealth and G/W_0 is the ratio of goal and initial wealth. Therefore, there are 81 strategy parameter combinations.

Statistical Test: For each strategy parameter combination, we compute $\sigma_h(\zeta)$, $\sigma_h(\eta)$, $\sigma_h(\theta)$ for each of the 180 price random walk series. Then we perform the paired-samples t test for pair $\sigma_h(\zeta)$-$\sigma_h(\theta)$ and pair $\sigma_h(\eta)$-$\sigma_h(\theta)$. The hypotheses and the t test results are as follow.

- For pair $\sigma_h(\zeta)$-$\sigma_h(\theta)$, the null hypothesis is $H_0 : \sigma_h(\zeta) \leq \sigma_h(\theta)$. The testing results show that its mean difference is 6.617855, $t = 130.083$, degree of freedom is 14579, $p = 0.000$. For 95% significance level, the test shows that the result has reached the statistical significance. Therefore, we can reject the hypothesis H_0 and then we can reasonably accept that $\sigma_h(\zeta) \geq \sigma_h(\theta)$.
- For pair $\sigma_h(\eta)$-$\sigma_h(\theta)$, the null hypothesis is $H_0 : \sigma_h(\eta) \leq \sigma_h(\theta)$. The testing results show that its mean difference is 6.960135, $t = 131.062$, degree of freedom is 14579, $p = 0.000$. For 95% significance level, the test shows that the result has reached the statistical significance. Therefore, we can reject the hypothesis H_0 and then we can reasonably accept that $\sigma_h(\eta) \geq \sigma_h(\theta)$.

In sum, the GDCPPI strategy θ dominates the CPPI strategy ζ and the GD strategy η under the σ_h measure.

4.2 Strategy Optimization by Genetic Algorithms

We have shown that θ (GDCPPI strategy) is better than ζ (CPPI strategy) and η (GD strategy) by the σ_h measure under constraint $F \leq W_t \leq G$. However, we still do not know which θ strategy parameter values are the best. For this problem, we apply genetic algorithm (GA) [8] technique to search satisfactory strategy parameter values. GAs apply the concept of natural evolution by selecting and crossing over better chromosomes, and mutating genes in order to build new possibly better solutions. The GA optimization design and testing results are as follow.

Optimization Design: The purpose of applying GA technique in this experiment is to search satisfactory strategy parameter values: $\{c, \alpha, F/W_0, G/W_0\}$. Therefore, each parameter stands for a gene in the chromosome by GA's terminology. The detail designs are as follows.

- Each chromosome consists of 4 genes $\{c, \alpha, F/W_0, G/W_0\}$, with total 21 bits.
- Gene c: 5 bits. If the decimal value of this gene is D, then the decoded value of c is $1 + D/10$, i.e., $c \in [1.1, 4.1]$.
- Gene α: 6 bits. If the decimal value of this gene is D, then the decoded value of α is $D/63$, i.e., $\alpha \in [0.00, 1.00]$.
- Gene F/W_0: 5 bits. If the decimal value of this gene is D, then the decoded value of F/W_0 is $1 - (D+1)/100$, i.e., $F/W_0 \in [0.68, 0.99]$. Therefore, the floor will be in $[0.68, 0.99]$ times the initial wealth.
- Gene G/W_0: 5 bits. If the decimal value of this gene is D, then the decoding value of G/W_0 is $1 + (D+1)/100$, i.e., $G/W_0 \in [1.01, 1.32]$. Therefore, the goal will be in $[1.01, 1.32]$ times the initial wealth.
- Fitness function and GA parameters: The fitness function is to minimize $\sigma_h(\theta)$. The other important GA parameters are as follow: the population size is 80, each run executes 40 generations, crossover is two-point, mutation rate is 0.001 per bit, and selection method is expected value.
- Testing design: We use the independent-samples t test to validate whether the strategy parameter values found by GA are better than arbitrary strategy parameter values. Therefore, there are two sample groups: (i) the $\sigma_h(\theta)$ values computed from the artificial predetermined strategy parameter values: $c \in \{1.5, 2.5, 3.5\}$, $\alpha \in \{0.25, 0.5, 0.75\}$, $F/W_0 \in \{0.74, 0.84, 0.94\}$, $G/W_0 \in \{1.06, 1.16, 1.26\}$, which generate 81 samples, (ii) the $\sigma_h(\theta)$ values computed from GA search by 30 runs, which then generate 30 samples. For independent-samples t test, this sample size is acceptable.

GA Statistical Test: The null hypothesis is $H_0 : \sigma_h(\theta_{comb}) \leq \sigma_h(\theta_{ga})$, where *comb* stands for the predefined parameter combinations, and *ga* stands for the GA search. The results of independent-samples t test are described as follow. The mean of $\sigma_h(\theta_{comb})$ for 81 strategy parameter combinations is 6.7171 and the mean of $\sigma_h(\theta_{ga})$ for 30 GA runs is 0.0832. Since the Levene's equality of variance test shows $p = .000$, it means these two sample groups have different variance. The t-test shows $p = .000$, that is this test has reached statistical significance.

Then, we can reject the null hypothesis. That is, the GA does really find better parameter values by the σ_h measure under constraint $F \leq W_t \leq G$.

5 Conclusions

Traditional portfolio insurance strategy such as CPPI does not consider the goal perspective and may fail an almost reached goal as a result. This paper considers the goal-seeking perspective in order to formulate new goal-related strategies. We first generalize the CPPI strategy into a general form and then derive a new goal-directed (GD) strategy under constraint $W_t \leq G$. Furthermore, this paper builds a goal-directed CPPI (GDCPPI) strategy under constraint $F \leq W_t \leq G$. To compare feasible strategies under some constraints, we only need to compare their objective function values. However, to compare arbitrary strategies, feasible or not, under some constraints, we need a more sophisticated measure. Since CPPI strategy is the optimal strategy under the floor constraint, we can use a strategy's mean absolute distance (error) to the CPPI strategy as a measure for the floor constraint. We use the mean absolute distance to the GD strategy as a measure for the goal constraint by symmetry. For both the floor and the goal constraints, we construct two measures: the mean absolute distance $\mu_h(x)$ and the standard deviation of absolute distance $\sigma_h(x)$ for an arbitrary strategy x. Since the forms of $\mu_h(x)$ for strategies CPPI, GD, and GDCPPI are identical, this measure does not show which strategy dominates the others all the time. This paper therefore constructs the measure $\sigma_h(x)$ to show that GDCPPI strategy dominates the CPPI and GD strategies statistically. This paper also applies the GA technique to optimize the GDCPPI strategy.

Future directions of this research include the followings.

- To derive the optimal GD and GDCPPI strategies in a more rigorous way.
- To generalize the parameters c and α as expressions rather than constants: We have shown that an investor's risk-attitude will be changed under different wealth state. Since c plays as a risk multiplier, making c varying according to some risk factors is a reasonable generalization. In addition, the CPPI strategy and the GD strategy are two opposite strategies which may dominate each other under different situations. Therefore, dynamic α is also a possible generalization.

Finally, goal-directed behavior is an interesting and important topic in practical investment. This kind of investors' behavior is worth exploiting in the future.

References

1. Black, F., Perold, A.F.: Theory of constant proportion portfolio insurance. Journal of Economic Dynamics and Control **16** (1992) 403–426
2. Perold, A.F., Sharpe, W.F.: Dynamic strategies for asset alocation. Financial Analyst Journal **Jan/Feb** (1988) 16–27

3. Grossman, S.J., Zhou, Z.: Optimal investment strategies for controlling drawdowns. Mathematical Finance **3** (1993) 241–276
4. Tayler, J.: Risk-taking behavior in mutual fund tournaments. Journal of Economic Behavior & Organization **50** (2003) 373–383
5. Chevalier, J., Ellison, G.: Risk taking by mutual funds as a response to incentives. Journal of Political Economy **105** (1997) 1167–1200
6. Busse, J.A.: Another look at mutual fund tournaments. Journal of Financial and Quantitative Analysis **36** (2001) 53–73
7. Brown, K., Harlow, W., Starks, L.: Of tournaments and temptations: An analysis of managerial incentives in mutual fund industry. Journal of Finance **51** (1996) 85–110
8. Holland, J.H.: Adaptation in Natural and Artificial Systems: An Introductory Analysis with Applications to Biology, Control, and Artificial Intelligence. The University of Michigan (1975)

A Genetic Algorithm for Solving Portfolio Optimization Problems with Transaction Costs and Minimum Transaction Lots*

Dan Lin[1], Xiaoming Li[1], and Minqiang Li[2]

[1] School of Sciences, Tianjin University, Tianjin 300072, P.R. China
{dlin, xmli }@tju.edu.cn
[2] School of Management, Tianjin University, Tianjin 300072, P.R. China
mqli@tju.edu.cn

Abstract. A mean-variance model is proposed for portfolio rebalancing optimization problems with transaction costs and minimum transaction lots. The portfolio optimization problems are modeled as a non-smooth nonlinear integer programming problem. A genetic algorithm based on real value genetic operators is designed to solve the proposed model. It is illustrated via a numerical example that the genetic algorithm can solve the portfolio rebalancing optimization problems efficiently.

1 Introduction

When taking into account a practical situation such as transaction costs and/or minimum transaction lots, portfolio optimization becomes more complicated. The issue of transaction costs is one of the main sources concerned by portfolio managers, and minimum transaction lots is another practical issue in portfolio selection and rebalancing.

Recently, some study including transaction costs and/or minimum lots into portfolio optimization problems [1], [2], [3]. It was shown that a portfolio optimization problem with minimum lots and without any fixed costs is a NP-complete problem [2], so a few heuristics have been developed and shown to be effective for solving a portfolio selection problem with minimum lots. Among these heuristics are the genetic algorithms (GAs, [4]).

GAs are stochastic, heuristic techniques based on the natural selection principles, and they can deal with the nonlinear optimization problems with non-smooth and even non-continuous objective, and continuous and/or integer variables.

In this paper, we propose a model for portfolio rebalancing optimization problems with transaction costs and minimum lots. A GA based on the traditional real value genetic operators is then designed to solve these models.

---

* Supported by National Sciences Foundation of China (No. 70301005) and the Liu Hui Center of Applied Mathematics of Nankai University and Tianjin University.

2 Models

Denote by S the set of securities to invest a capital $C_0 \leq C \leq C_1$ and let $s = |S|$ be the number of the securities. A portfolio can be represented as $k = (k_1,...,k_s)$, where k_j represents the number of shares of security j. Let r_j be the random rate of return on security $j \in S$. Let n_j^s be the minimum transaction lot when selling security j and n_j^b be the minimum lot when buying security j. Denote $R_j = E(r_j)$ the expected rate of return on security j and $\sigma_{ij} = \text{cov}(r_i, r_j)$ the covariance between r_i and r_j. For security j, denote u_j the maximum amount of capital that can be invested in it. d_j represents the fixed proportion parameter of transaction cost associated with security j and p_j represents the quoted price, and $y_j = (p_j k_j)/C$.

The expected return $R(k)$ and the variance $V(k)$ can be written as

$$R(k) = (\sum_{j \in S} R_j p_j k_j - \sum_{j \in S} d_j p_j |k_j - k_j^0|)/C. \tag{1}$$

$$V(x) = \sum_{i \in S} \sum_{j \in S} \sigma_{ij} y_i y_j. \tag{2}$$

A portfolio rebalancing problem can be stated as follows:

$$\min \ f(k) = -\lambda \cdot R(k) + (1-\lambda) \cdot \omega \cdot V(k) \tag{3}$$

s.t. $C_0 \leq \sum_{j \in S} p_j k_j = C \leq C_1$,

$0 \leq p_j k_j \leq u_j$, for all $j \in S$

$n_j^b | (k_j - k_j^0)$, for all $j \in S$, if $k_j > k_j^0$,

$n_j^s | (k_j^0 - k_j)$, for all $j \in S$, if $k_j^0 > k_j$.

Here parameter λ varying in [0,1] and ω is a scaling parameter.

3 Genetic Algorithms

Representation Structure. Each portfolio in the population is coded as a string of non-negative integer numbers.

Repair Process. For an existing portfolio $k^0 = (k_1^0,...,k_s^0)$, a real vector $x = (x_1,...,x_s)$ can be repaired into a new portfolio by the following formula:

$$d_i = \begin{cases} \left\lceil \dfrac{x_i - k_i^0}{n_i^b} \right\rceil & \text{if } x_i \geq k_i^0 \\ \left\lceil \dfrac{k_i^0 - x_i}{n_i^s} \right\rceil & \text{if } x_i \leq k_i^0 \end{cases} \tag{4}$$

$$m_i = \begin{cases} k_i^0 + d_i \cdot n_i^b & \text{if } x_i \geq k_i^0 \\ k_i^0 - d_i \cdot n_i^b & \text{if } x_i \leq k_i^0 \end{cases} \quad (5)$$

$$m_i' = \begin{cases} k_i^0 + (d_i+1) \cdot n_i^b & \text{if } x_i \geq k_i^0 \\ k_i^0 - (d_i+1) \cdot n_i^b & \text{if } x_i \leq k_i^0 \end{cases} \quad (6)$$

$$k_i = m_i \text{ or } m_i' \text{ randomly}. \quad (7)$$

The GA based on the SBX and PM genetic operators [5] can be written as follows:

Step 0. Input parameters: pop_size, P_c and P_m, the parameters of SBX and PM operators, total evolutionary generations gen.
Step 1. Initialize pop_size individuals to generate the initial population.
Step 2. Update the individuals in the current population by SBX crossover and PM mutation operators. Repair the individuals as described in the repair process.
Step 3. Calculate the fitness values for all individuals.
Step 4. Select the individuals by using the binary tournament selection strategy.
Step 5. Repeat steps 2 to 4 until the given gen generations.

4 Simulation Results

The returns of six stocks from time t-7 to t and price per share are given in Table 1.

Table 1. Stock returns and price

Period	t-7	t-6	t-5	t-4	t-3	t-2	t-1	t	Price
Stock 1	0.04	0.07	0.09	0.13	0.14	0.17	0.21	0.24	12.44
Stock 2	0.14	0.06	0.08	0.15	0.11	0.13	0.10	0.11	18.59
Stock 3	0.13	0.13	0.11	0.15	0.10	0.07	0.14	0.11	45.12
Stock 4	0.12	0.04	0.18	0.13	0.19	0.16	0.14	0.11	26.45
Stock 5	0.18	0.06	0.22	0.15	0.14	0.06	0.08	0.09	19.78
Stock 6	0.15	0.04	0.08	0.06	0.13	0.05	0.10	0.09	35.21

The minimum buying and selling lot is set to be 100 and 1. The total amount of the present capital value of k^0 is 1,004,482.36. $C_0 = 1,000,000$ and $C_1 = 1,00,5000$. $u_i = 0.2 \cdot C_0 = 200,000$ and d_j is set to be 0.01. $P_c = 0.95$ and $P_m = \frac{1}{6}$. The pop_size is set to be 400 and the run ends until 300 generations. The scaling parameter ω is set to be 100 in all the experiments. The results for the average of 100 independent runs are given in Table 2.

Table 2. Results of portfolio rebalancing with different λ

λ	0.0	0.2	0.4
return	1.1284e-1	1.1356e-1	1.1522e-1
risk	4.1912e-4	4.1957e-4	4.2757e-4
fitness	4.1912e-2	1.0854e-2	-2.0434e-2
λ	0.6	0.8	1.0
return	1.1858e-1	1.2000e-1	1.2007e-1
risk	4.6165e-4	4.9867e-4	5.1007e-4
fitness	-5.2681e-2	-8.6028e-2	-1.2007e-1

5 Conclusion

In this paper, we have proposed a new mean-variance model for portfolio optimization with transaction costs and minimum transaction lots, and a GA has been designed to solve the model. Computational results have shown the efficiency of the proposed GA.

References

1. Masini, R., Speranza, M.G.: Heuristic Algorithms for a Portfolio Selection Problem with Minimum Transaction Lots. European Journal of Operational Research. 114(1999) 219-233
2. Kellerer, H., Mansini, R., Speranza, M.G.: On Selecting a Portfolio with Fixed Costs and Minimum Lots. Annals of Operations Research. 99(2000) 287-304
3. Konno, H., Wijayanayake, A.: Portfolio Optimization Problems under Concave Transaction Costs and Minimal Transaction Unit Constraints. Mathematical Programming. 89(2001) 233-250
4. Bäck, T., Fogel, D.B., Michalewicz, Z.: Handbook of Evolutionary Computation. Oxford University Press, Oxford (1997)
5. Deb, K., Agrawal, R.B.: Simulated Binary Crossover for Continuous Search Space. Complex Systems. 9(1995) 115-148

Financial Performance Prediction Using Constraint-Based Evolutionary Classification Tree (CECT) Approach

Chi-I Hsu[1], Yuan Lin Hsu[2], and Pei Lun Hsu[3]

[1] Department of Information Management,
Kai Nan University, Taiwan, R.O.C.
imchsu@mail.knu.edu.tw
[2] Department of Finance,
National Cheng Chi University, Taiwan, R.O.C.
g88357501@nccu.edu.tw
[3] Department of Electricity Engineering,
Chin Yun University, Taiwan, R.O.C.
hsupl@cyu.edu.tw

Abstract. Financial ratios are commonly employed to measure a corporate financial performance. In recent years a considerable amount of research has been directed towards the analysis of the predictive power of financial ratios as influential factors of corporate stock market behavior. In this paper we propose a constraint-based evolutionary classification tree (CECT) approach that combines both the constraint-based reasoning and evolutionary techniques to generate useful patterns from data in a more effective way. The proposed approach is experimented, tested and compared with a regular genetic algorithm (GA) to predict corporate financial performance using data from Taiwan Economy Journal (TEJ). Better prediction effectiveness of CECT approach is obtained than those of regular GA and C5.0.

1 Introduction

Financial ratios are commonly employed to measure a corporate financial performance. In recent years a considerable amount of research has been directed towards the analysis of the predictive power of financial ratios as influential factors of corporate stock market behavior. Some of the financial ratios, such as Current Ratio, Receivables Turnover, and Times Interest Earned, Capital, were used for bankruptcy prediction [16], financial distress prediction [5, 7], and so forth. Revealing valuable knowledge hidden in financial data becomes more critical for decision making.

Rule induction is one of the most common methods of knowledge discovery. Basically an ideal technique for rules induction has to carefully tackle those aspects, such as model comprehensibility and interestingness, attributes selection, learning efficiency and effectiveness, and etc. Genetic algorithms (GAs), one of the often used evolutionary computation technique, has been increasingly aware for its superior flexibility and expressiveness of problem representation as well as its fast searching capability for knowledge discovery [27].

This research applies CECT (constraint-based evolutionary classification tree) approach [3] to construct a classification model for predicting the corporate finance performance using various financial ratios.

Generally, rule induction methods are used to automatically produce rule sets for predicting the expected outcomes as accurately as possible. However the emphasis on revealing novel or interesting knowledge has become a recent research issue in data mining. These attempts may impose additional rule discovery constraints, and thereby produce additional computation overhead. For regular GAs operations, constraint validation is proceeded after a candidate chromosome is produced. That is, several iterations may be required to determine a valid chromosome. One way to improve the computation load problem is to prevent the production of invalid chromosomes before a chromosome is generated; thereby accelerating the efficiency and effectiveness of evolution processes. Potentially, this can be done by embedding a well-designed constraint mechanism into the chromosome-encoding scheme.

In this research we adopt CECT approach that integrates an association rule algorithm and constraint-based reasoning with GAs to discover classification trees. Apriori algorithm, one of the common seen association rule algorithms, is used for attributes selection; therefore those related input attributes can be determined before proceeding the GA's evolution. The constraint-based reasoning is used to push constraints along with data insights into the rule set construction. This research applied tree search and forward checking techniques to reduce the search space from possible gene values that can not meet predefined constraints during the evolution process. This approach allows constraints to be specified as relationships among attributes according to predefined requirements, user preferences, or partial knowledge in the form of a constraint network. In essence, this approach provides a chromosome-filtering mechanism prior to generating and evaluating a chromosome. Thus insignificant or irreverent rules can be precluded in advance via the constraint network.

The CECT approach was employed to predict corporate financial performance using TEJ finance data of year 2001. Other, in order to compare with often used classification tree techniques, C5.0 is applied to the same data sets.

2 The Literature Review

2.1 The Evaluation of Corporate Financial Performance

Tobin's Q is a measure for evaluating a corporate financial performance [4, 11]. The higher value a Tobin's Q is, the better a corporate financial performance is. On the other hand, the lower value a Tobin's Q is, the inferior a corporate financial performance is. This research denotes the dependent variable as "Good" if Tobin's Q > 1; "Bad" if Tobin's Q =< 1. The data used was derived from Taiwan Economic Journal (TEJ) database, a standard source of financial market database. 510 financial data records of the listed companies on Taiwan Stocks Market for the entire period of year 2001 were collected. Each data record includes eight input financial ratios and one output Tobin's Q. Tobin's Q value is converted into either "Good" or "Bad" before executing the learning process.

2.2 Genetic Algorithm for Rule Induction and Constraint Satisfaction

Rule induction methods can be categorized into either tree based or non-tree based methods [1]. Some of the often-mentioned decision tree induction methods include C4.5 [15], CART [2] and GOTA [9] algorithms. Quinlan [15] introduced techniques to transform an induced decision tree into a set of production rules. GAs have been successfully applied to data mining for rule discovery in literatures. There are some techniques using one-rule-per-individual encoding proposed in [8, 13]. For the one-rule-per-individual encoding approach, a chromosome usually can be identical to a linear string of rule conditions, where each condition is often an attribute-value pair, to represent a rule or a rule set. Although the individual encoding is simpler and syntactically shorter, the problem is that the fitness of a single rule is not necessarily the best indicator of the quality of the discovered rule set. Then, the several-rules-per-individual approach [6, 10] has the advantage by considering its rule set as a whole, by taking into account rule interactions.

Problem solving in a constraint satisfaction problem (CSP) that is basically belongs to NP-Complete problems normally lacks suitable methods. A number of different approaches have been developed for solving the CSP problems. Some of them adopted constraint propagation to reduce the solutions space. Others tried "backtrack" to directly search for possible solutions. Some applied the combination of these two techniques including tree-search and consistent algorithms to efficiently find out one or more feasible solutions. Nadel [12] compared the performance of the several algorithms including "generate and test", "simple backtracking", "forward checking", "partial lookahead", "full lookahead", and "really full lookahead." The major differences of these algorithms are the degree of consistency performed at the node during the tree-solving process. Besides the "generate and test" method, others performed hybrid techniques. In other words, whenever a new value is assigned for the variable, the domains of all unassigned ones are filtered and left only with those values that are consistent with the one already being assigned.

Dealing with constraints for search space reduction seems to be an important research issues for many artificial intelligence areas. GAs maintain a set of chromosomes (solutions), called population. The population consists of parents and offspring. When the evolution process proceeds, the best N chromosomes in the current population are selected as parents. Through performing genetic operators, offspring are selected according to the filtering criterion that is usually expressed as fitness functions along with some predefined constraints. The GA evolves over generations until stopping criterions are met. However valid chromosomes are usually produced by trials and errors. That is, a candidate chromosome is produced and tested against the filtering criterions. Therefore a GA may require more computation, especially in dealing with complicated or severe filtering criterions. To resolve this problem, an effective chromosome construction process can be applied to the initialization, crossover, and mutation stages respectively.

3 The Proposed Constraint-Based Evolutionary Classification Tree(CECT) Approach

The proposed CECT approach consists of three modules: the user-interface, the symbol manager, and constraint-based GA (CBGA). According to Fig. 1, the user interface module allows users to execute the following system operations including:

- Loading a constraint program,
- Adding or retracting the constraints,
- Controlling the GA's parameter settings, and
- Monitoring the best solutions.

The constraint program here is a set of any first order logic sentence (atomic, compound or quantified) about a many-sorted universe of discourse that includes integers, real numbers, and arbitrary application-specific sorts.

Three types of data sources: GA parameter settings, human knowledge, and data sets are converted into the constraint programs. Each gene in a GA here is equal to each object of constraint program. The range for each gene can be viewed as a domain constraint for each object. The predefined hard constraints are represented by the first order logic sentences. The human knowledge specifies the user preferences, or partial expert experiences. For example, the user's preference such as "people high

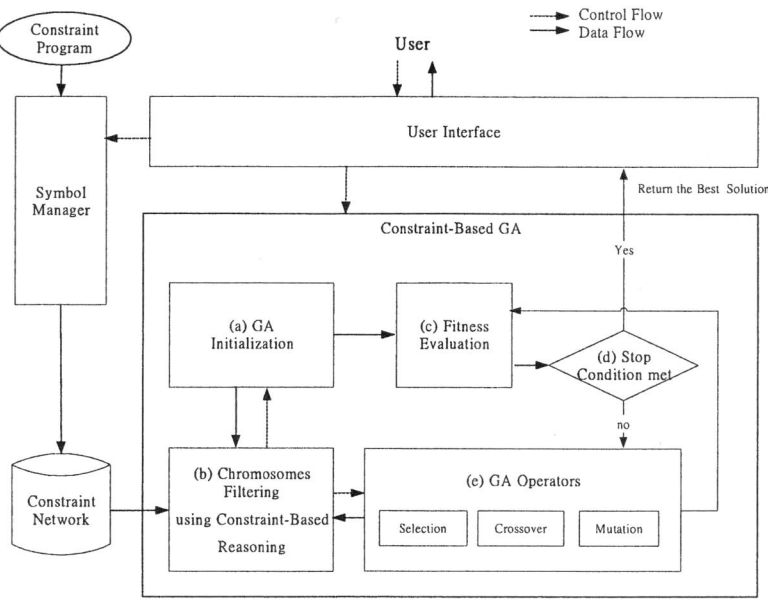

Fig. 1. The Conceptual Diagram of the Proposed CECT System

blood pressure cannot take certain drugs" can be treated as one type of expert knowledge. It can be translated into the user's defined constraints in the form of first order logic sentence. The association rule mining module generates association rules by apriori algorithm. In this research the derived association rules has to satisfy user-defined minimum support and minimum confidence levels. The symbol manager examines the syntax of the first order logic sentences in the constraint program and translates the syntax into a constraint network for further processing.

In the CBGA module, the constraint-based reasoning filters each gene value and processes both the GA initial population and regular populations.

To speed up the reasoning process, both the variable ordering and backtrack-free search methods are adopted in the CBGA to derive contradiction-free chromosomes. Details of the above mentioned processes can be found in [3].

4 The Experiments and Results

Two other approaches: a simple GA (SGA) and apriori algorithm with GA (AGA) were employed to compare our proposed approach that is denoted by ACECT (i. e., apriori algorithm with CECT). Also, C5.0, a commonly used classification tree technique, was applied to the same data sets. Generally association rules extracted by apriori algorithm could be varied depending on the defined support and confidence values. Different association rules extracted may result in different impacts on CECT learning performances. Therefore this research experimented with different sets of minimum support and confidence values to both the credit screening and financial performance prediction problems. The evaluation of those classification trees generated by each of the three approaches as well as C5.0 was based on five-fold cross validation. That is, each training stage used 4/5 of the entire data records; with the rest 1/5 data records used for the testing stage. The GA parameter settings for both the applications are summarized in Table 1.

This research applies CECT approach to construct a classification model for predicting the corporate finance performance using various financial ratios. The notation for the variables (i. e., the seven financial ratios) is specified in Table 2. The dependent variable is a categorical type of data labeled by either "Good" or "Bad" according to the Tobin's Q value.

Table 1. The GA Parameter Settings

Item	Value
Population Size	100
Generations	100/200/300/400/500
Crossover rate	0.6
Mutation rate	0.01
Crossover method	Uniform
Selection method	Roulette wheel
Training time (Credit Screening)	1.4 Minutes*
Training time (Financial Performance Prediction)	1.7 Minutes*

* The hardware platform is Pentium III 800 MHz with 512 MB RAM.

Among the entire data records, 181 records are "Good" while 329 records are "Bad". After several trials with different sets of minimum support values and confidence values, the best ACECT learning performance is obtained. Both the training and testing performance are summarized in Table 3, along with their corresponding representation depicted in Fig. 2 & 3. These results are based on the minimum support value (=7) and confidence value (=100). The derived association rule sets consists of 12 rules for "Good" output category and 14 association rules for "Bad" output category. In order to obtain more details about the learning progress for the three approaches, learning tract behavior were recorded in sessions. Fig. 4 & 5 depict the entire learning progresses monitored over generations and time. The details of the optimal results derived are illustrated in Appendix A. C5.0 learning performance of each testing fold for both data sets are illustrated in Appendix B.

Table 2. The Various Financial Ratios Used in the Model

	Descriptions	Data Type
X1:	Industry type (22 types)	category
X2:	Credit rating (1-10 rating)	category
X3:	Employee size (1-4 level)	category
X4:	Capital scope (1-4 level)	category
X5:	Current ratio	continuous
X6:	Debt ratio	continuous
X7:	Times interest earned	continuous
X8:	Receivables turnover	continuous

5 Discussion

According to the results indicated above ACECT achieves superior learning performance than SGA and AGA in terms of computation efficiency and accuracy. By applying association rule process, the partial knowledge is extracted and transformed as seeding chromosomes. It can be seen that the initial training results for both AGA and ACECT exhibit significantly higher accuracy and efficiency than SGA. As shown in Fig. 4 both AGA and ACECT approach relative convergence within 50 generations, while SGA requires 500 generations to reach the similar result in the training stage. The outcomes can be attributed to the adoption of apriori algorithm by which the GA search space is substantially reduced.

Table 3. The Summarized Learning Performance for SGA, AGA, and ACECT

Gen.	100		200		300		400		500	
	Train	Test	Train	Test	Train	Test	Train	Test	Train	Test
SGA	75.64	71.18	77.5	72.75	78.38	73.53	79.07	73.92	79.61	74.12
AGA	80.34	74.90	81.32	75.49	82.01	74.90	82.50	75.1	82.79	74.90
ACECT	81.13	77.45	82.25	77.25	82.79	77.65	83.28	77.45	83.58	77.65
C5.0	Test: 77.08 (in %)									

For the ACECT approach, the derived partial knowledge is not only encoded as seeding chromosomes, but also converted into the constraint network. As shown in the figures displaying learning progresses, ACECT outperforms AGA less significantly than outperforms SGA. Nevertheless, the improvement of ACECT over AGA positively demonstrates its learning effectiveness for both the applications data. As compared with C5.0, ACECT marginally exhibits superior testing performance than C5.0 for both data sets based on 5-fold cross-validation.

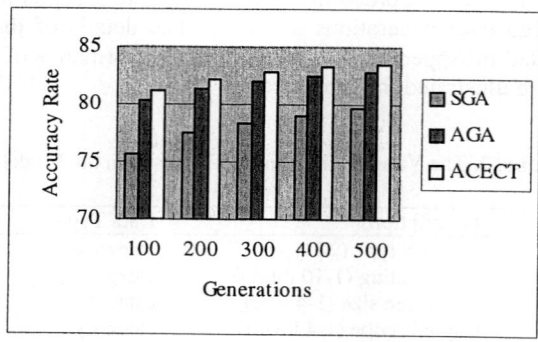

Fig. 2. Training Results with Various Generations (based on 5-fold average)

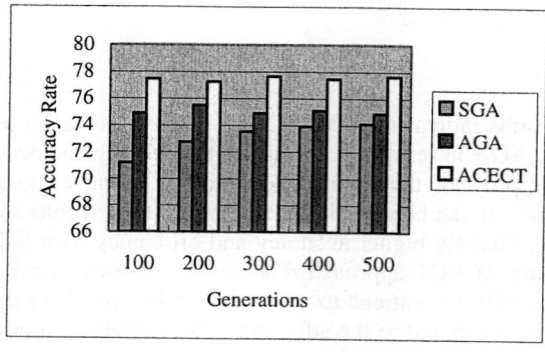

Fig. 3. Testing Results with Various Generations (based on 5-fold average)

6 Conclusions and Future Development

We have introduced CECT approach that hybridizes constraint-based reasoning within a genetic algorithm for classification tree induction. Incorporating the partial knowledge or user-control information into mining process is not straightforward and, typically, requires the design of novel approaches. By employing the rule association algorithm to acquire partial knowledge from data, our proposed approach is able to induce a classification tree by pushing the partial knowledge into chromosome construction. Most importantly, the adoption of constraint-based reasoning mechanism into the GA process can filter invalid chromosomes; therefore feasible solutions can be more efficiently derived.

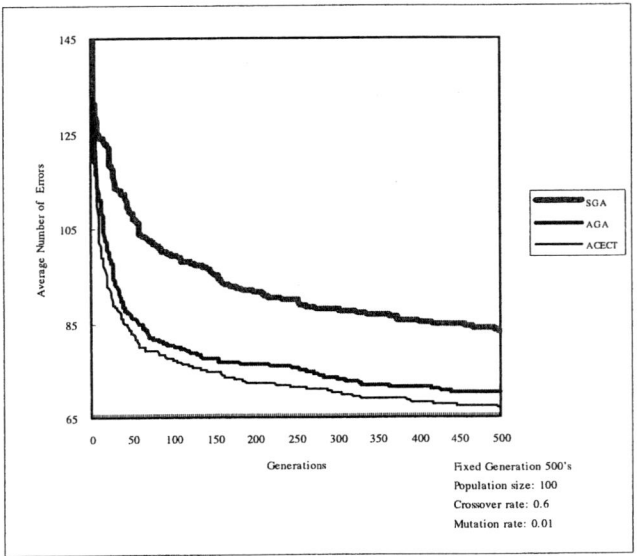

Fig. 4. The Learning Progress over Generations (based on 5-fold average)

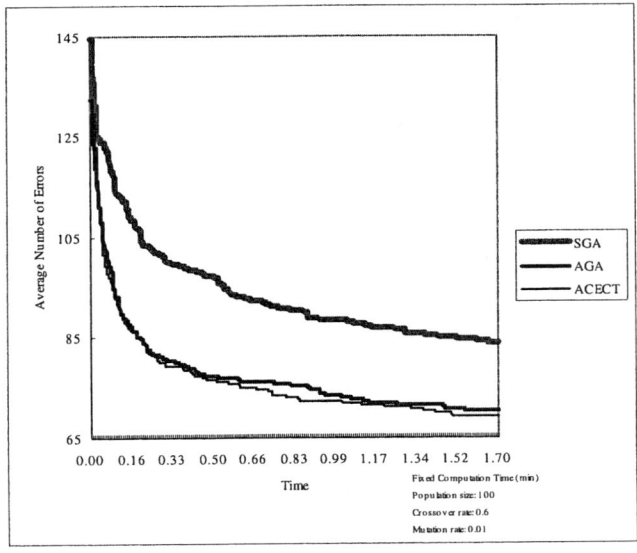

Fig. 5. The Learning Progress over Time (based on 5-fold average)

Comparing with SGA and AGA, ACECT achieves higher predictive accuracy and less computation time required for classification trees inductions using a benchmark data set as well as real financial data set. In addition, the classification trees discovered by ACECT not only obtain higher predictive accuracy and computation efficiency, but also may produce more user transparent or significant knowledge. This approach is not only applicable for binary classification problems, but also applicable for multi-category classification problems, though the experiment examples are binary classification problems. Currently CECT approach is able to reveal tree splitting nodes that may allowed complex rule sets-like discriminating formats such as "Attribute$i$ <= w * Attribute$j$" relationship which can be extended to express more complicated multivariate inequations with either a linear or nonlinear format in the future.

Improving Financial Performance by Exploring the Financial Ratios

Basically prediction models map the inputs values to produce the outcome(s). When the model is complex, it is not possible to easily figure out the appropriate inputs that can best approximate the expected output. Usually this type of research is called parameters design. The classification tree constructed by our proposed CECT approach can be a multivariate-split based classification tree. It would be relatively difficult to find out suitable inputs values in order to match an expected outcome. The mechanism that allows proceeding "what-if" as well as "goal-seeking" analysis can be a useful aid for financial managers in further exploring those financial ratios that are most likely or most unlikely to be adjusted to improve a corporate financial performance. In addition to our proposed CECT approach, this research is currently working on adopting another optimization technique to support the "goal-seeking" function. It is believed that such information provides highly strategic values for the corporate financial management.

References

1. Abdullah, M.K.: CAN: Chain of Nodes Approach to Direct Rule Induction. IEEE Transactions on Systems, Man, and Cybernetics, Part B: Cybernetics, Vol. 29. No. 6. December, (1999) 758-770
2. Breiman, L., Friedman, J.H., Olshen, R.A., Stone, C.J.: Classification and Regression Trees. Los Angeles, CA: Wadsworth. (1984)
3. Chiu, C, Hsu, P.L.: A Constraint-Based Genetic Algorithm Approach for Mining Classification Rules. IEEE Transactions on Systems, Man, and Cybernetics (forthcoming)
4. Ciccolo, J., Fromm, G.: 'Q' and the Theory of Investment. Journal of Finance, Vol. 34. No. 2. (1979) 535-547
5. Coats, P.K., Fant, L.F.: A Neural Network Approach to Forecasting Financial Distress. The Journal of Business Forecasting, winter 1991-'92, (1991) 9-12
6. De Jong, K.A., Spears, W.M., Gordon, D.F.: Using Genetic Algorithms for Concept Learning. Machine Learning, Vol. 13. (1993) 161-188
7. Ganesalingam, S.: Detection of Financial Distress via Multivariate Statistical Analysis. Managerial Finance, Vol. 27. No. 4. (2001) 45-55
8. Greene, D.P., Smith, S.F.: Competition-Based Induction of Decision Models from Examples. Machine Learning, Vol. 13. (1993) 229-257
9. Hartmann, C.R.P., Varshney, P.K., Mehrotra, K.G., Gerberich, C.L.: Application of Information Theory to the Construction of Efficient Decision Trees. IEEE Trans. Inform. Theory, Vol. IT-28. (1982) 565-577

10. Janikow, C.Z.: A Knowledge-Intensive Genetic Algorithm for Supervised Learning. Machine Learning, Vol. 13. (1993) 189-228
11. Lindenberg, E.B., Ross, S.A.: Tobin's q Ratio and Industrial Organization. Journal of Business, Vol. 54. Jan. (1981) 1-32
12. Nadel, B.: Tree Search and Arc Consistency in Constraint-Satisfaction Algorithms. In Search in Artificial Intelligence, New York (1988) 287-342
13. Noda, E., Freitas, A.A., Lopes, H.S.: Discovering Interesting Prediction Rules with a Genetic Algorithm. In Proc. Congress on Evolutionary Computation, Washington D.C., July (1999) 1322-1329
14. Purdom, P.: Search Rearrangement Backtracking and Polynomial Average Time. Artificial Intelligence, Vol. 21. (1983) 117-133
15. Quinlan, J.R.: C4.5: Programs for Machine Learning. Morgan Kaufman Series, in Machine Learning, Kluwer Academic Publishers (1993)
16. Shah, J.R., Murataza, M.B.: A Neural Network Based Clustering Procedure for Bankruptcy Prediction. American Business Review, Jun. (2000) 80-86
17. Tan, K.C., Lim, M.H., Yao, X., Wang, L.P.: Recent Advances in Simulated Evolution and Learning. World Scientific, Singapore (2004)

Appendix A: The Inferred Classification Tree

Node 1. IF $x_3 = 4$ AND $x_8 > 120.838$ THEN Good
Node 2. IF $x_2 = 6$ AND $x_5 <= 526.554$ THEN Bad
Node 3. IF $x_2 = 7$ THEN Bad
Node 4. IF $x_1 = 23$ AND $x_4 = 1$ AND $x_8 <= 20.5695$ THEN Good
Node 5. IF $x_1 = 24$ THEN Good
Node 6. IF $x_1 = 23$ AND $x_3 = 3$ THEN Good
Node 7. IF $x_2 = 9$ AND $x_3 = 2$ AND $x_4 = 1$ AND $x_5 > 295.631$ AND $x_6 <= -1.97058 * x_7$ THEN Bad
Node 8. IF $x_3 = 3$ AND $x_4 = 3$ THEN Bad
Node 9. IF $x_2 = 4$ AND $x_5 <= 1280.3$ AND $x_7 <= 123.463$ AND $x_5 <= 7.85272 * x_7$ THEN Good
Node 10. IF $x_2 = 5$ THEN Bad
Node 11. IF $x_1 = 14$ AND $x_4 = 4$ AND $x_5 > 891.989$ AND $x_8 > 140.889$ AND $x_7 <= -5.07187 * x_5$ THEN Bad
Node 12. IF $x_1 = 14$ AND $x_2 = 7$ AND $x_8 <= 443.831$ THEN Bad
Node 13. IF $x_4 = 1$ AND $x_6 <= 56.013$ THEN Good
Node 14. IF $x_2 = 4$ AND $x_6 <= 16.6635$ THEN Good
Node 15. IF $x_4 = 4$ THEN Bad
Node 16. IF $x_3 = 4$ AND $x_4 = 3$ THEN Good
Node 17. IF $x_2 = 5$ AND $x_4 = 3$ AND $x_6 <= -8.10053 * x_8$ THEN Good
Node 18. IF $x_8 <= 91.2198$ THEN Bad

Appendix B: C5.0 Learning Performance

Decision Tree

Fold	Size	Accuracy Rate
1	32	76.5%
2	39	77.5%
3	30	81.4%
4	30	74.5%
5	27	75.5%
Average		77.1%

A Genetic Algorithm with Chromosome-Repairing Technique for Polygonal Approximation of Digital Curves

Bin Wang and Yan Qiu Chen*

Department of Computer Science and Engineering,
School of Information Science and Engineering,
Fudan University, Shanghai, 200433, P.R. China
chenyq@fudan.edu.cn

Abstract. A genetic algorithm with chromosome-repairing scheme (CRS) is proposed in this paper to solve the polygonal approximation problem. Different from the existing approaches based on genetic algorithms, the proposed algorithm adopts variable-length chromosome encoding for reducing the memory storage and computational time, and develops a special crossover named gene-removing crossover for removing the redundant genes. It is known that Genetic operators may yield infeasible solutions, and it is generally difficult to cope with them. Instead of using the penalty function approach, we propose a chromosome-repairing scheme to iteratively add the valuable candidate gene to the chromosome to deal with the infeasible solution and an evaluating scheme for the candidate genes. The experimental results show that the proposed CRS outperforms the existing approaches based on genetic-algorithms, ant-colony-optimization and tabu-search.

1 Introduction

In image processing, the contours extracted from the regions or objects can be viewed as digital curves. How to represent digital curves is a key issue in image processing and pattern recognition. Polygonal approximation is one of the most effective approaches. The idea of this approach is to approximate a given curve using a polygon with the fewest line segments such that the approximation error is no more than a pre-specified tolerance. Polygonal approximation not only provides compact representation with less memory requirement, but also facilitate feature extraction for further image analysis. Hence, the representation scheme has been widely used in shape analysis, image compression, pattern recognition, CAD and GIS applications.

Many approaches have been proposed for solving the polygonal approximation problem, such as sequential approaches [1], split-and-merge approaches [2], dominant point detection approaches [3] and k-means based approaches [4]. Most of the above approaches are based on local search technique. They are very fast

* Corresponding author.

but lack of global optimality, this is because the results depend on the selection of initial points and the given arbitrary initial solution. However, exhaustive search in the solution space will result in an exponential complexity. Recently, nature-inspired algorithms such as genetic algorithms (GA), ant colony optimization (ACO), tabu search (TS), particle swarm optimization (PSO) and so on, which are inspired by natural phenomena, have been widely used to solve the various optimization problems due to their global search ability. Approaches based on GA [5], TS [6] and ACO [7] have already been proposed for solving the polygonal approximation problem and shown their better performance compared with those based on local search method.

In this paper, we focus our attention on using genetic algorithms to solve the polygonal approximation problem. Many existing GA-based methods have the following disadvantages which limit their performance. Firstly, they adopted traditional binary-string chromosome encoding with fixed length such that each gene corresponds to a curve point. When the curve has a large amount of points, the chromosome's length will be very long. Hence, the computation time and memory requirement are both large. Secondly, they use the traditional crossover convention such as one-cut-point crossover and two-cut-point crossover, but, for the polygonal approximation problem, this kind of crossover does not reflect the fundamental characteristics of the task and may result in poor search performance. Thirdly, They usually adopt the penalty function approach to cope with infeasible solutions, but it is usually difficult to determine an appropriate penalty function. Since, if the strength of the penalty function is too large, more time will be spent on finding the feasible solutions than searching the optimum. However, if the strength of penalty function is too small, more time will be spent on evaluating infeasible solutions. In addition, the eliminated infeasible solution may also contain valuable genes, so, the penalty function approach may result in the losing of valuable genes. In this paper, A genetic algorithm with chromosome-repairing scheme (CRS) is proposed. The contribution and main work of this paper are: (1) An variable-length chromosome encoding scheme is proposed. Under this scheme, each gene corresponds to a vertex of the polygon and the length of the chromosome is equal to the number of vertices of the polygon, So the length of the chromosome is variable and this encoding scheme shorten the length of the chromosome greatly. (2) Since the approximation problem can be transformed into the problem of obtaining a chromosome with the fewest genes which can represents a feasible solution under the above chromosome encoding scheme, we develop a peculiar crossover named gene-removing crossover for removing the redundant genes. (3) A chromosome-repairing scheme of iteratively adding the valuable candidate gene to the chromosome is proposed to deal with the infeasible solution and A function is developed for evaluating the candidate genes. (4) Three benchmark curves are used to evaluate CRS for comparing it with the existing approaches based on GA, ACO and TS. The experimental results show the superiority performance of CRS.

The remainder of this paper is organized as follows: Section 2 gives the definitions of the polygonal approximation problem. Section 3 illustrates the details of CRS. In section 4, we present the experimental results and performance comparisons. Section 5 gives the conclusion.

2 Problem Formulation

The polygonal approximation problem can be formulated as follows:

Definition 1. *A digital closed curve C can be represented by a clockwise ordered sequence of points, that is $C = \{p_1, p_2, \ldots, p_N\}$ and this sequence is circular, namely, p_1 is considered as the succeeding point of p_N, where N is the number of points on the curve.*

Definition 2. *Let $\widehat{p_i p_j} = \{p_i, p_{i+1}, \ldots, p_j\}$ represent the arc starting at point p_i and continuing through point p_j in the clockwise direction along the curve. Let $\overline{p_i p_j}$ denote the line segment connecting points p_i and p_j.*

Definition 3. *The approximation error between $\widehat{p_i p_j}$ and $\overline{p_i p_j}$ is defined as follows:*

$$e(\widehat{p_i p_j}, \overline{p_i p_j}) = \sum_{p_k \in \widehat{p_i p_j}} d^2(p_k, \overline{p_i p_j}), \qquad (1)$$

where $d(p_k, \overline{p_i p_j})$ is the perpendicular distance from point p_k to the line segment $\overline{p_i p_j}$.

Definition 4. *The polygon V approximating the curve $C = \{p_1, p_2, \ldots, p_N\}$ is a set of ordered line segments such that*

(1) $V = \{\overline{p_{t_1} p_{t_2}}, \overline{p_{t_2} p_{t_3}}, \ldots, \overline{p_{t_{M-1}} p_{t_M}}, \overline{p_{t_M} p_{t_{M+1}}}\}$, *where* $t_i \in \{1, 2, \ldots, N\}$, $t_{M+1} = t_1$ *and M is the number of vertices of the polygon V.*
(2) $\forall i \neq j \in \{1, 2, \ldots, M\}$, $(\widehat{p_{t_i} p_{t_{i+1}}} \sim \{p_{t_i}, p_{t_{i+1}}\}) \bigcap (\widehat{p_{t_j} p_{t_{j+1}}} \sim \{p_{t_j}, p_{t_{j+1}}\}) = \phi$.
(3) $\bigcup_{i=1}^{M} \widehat{p_{t_i} p_{t_{i+1}}} = C$.

Definition 5. *The approximation error between the curve $C = \{p_1, p_2, \ldots, p_N\}$ and its approximating polygon $V = \{\overline{p_{t_1} p_{t_2}}, \overline{p_{t_2} p_{t_3}}, \ldots, \overline{p_{t_{M-1}} p_{t_M}}, \overline{p_{t_M} p_{t_{M+1}}}\}$ is defined as follows:*

$$E(V, C) = \sum_{i=1}^{M} e(\widehat{p_{t_i} p_{t_{i+1}}}, \overline{p_{t_i} p_{t_{i+1}}}), \qquad (2)$$

Then the polygonal approximation problem is formulated as follows: Given a digital curve C and the error tolerance ε. Let $SP = \{V \mid E(V, C) \leq \varepsilon\}$ be a subset of polygons which approximate the curve C. Find a polygon $P \in SP$ such that

$$|P| = \min_{V \in SP} |V|, \qquad (3)$$

where $|P|$ denotes the cardinality of P.

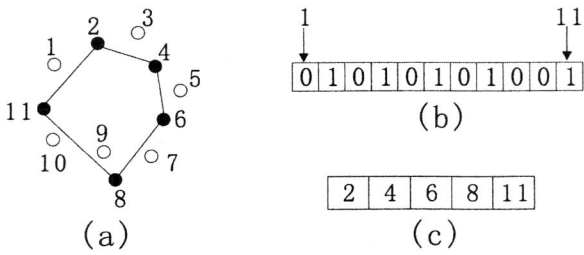

Fig. 1. An example to illustrate the two types of chromosome encoding schemes. (a) A curve with 11 points and its approximating polygon. (b) Binary-string chromosome encoding. (c) Variable-length chromosome encoding.

3 The Proposed Genetic Algorithms

In this section, we illustrate the details of CRS, including chromosome encoding scheme, fitness function, genetic operators and the disposal of the infeasible solution.

3.1 Variable-Length Chromosome Encoding

For reducing the computational cost, we propose a variable-length chromosome encoding scheme. Let $C = \{p_1, p_2, \ldots, p_N\}$ denotes a digital curve, and $V = \{\overline{p_{t_1}p_{t_2}}, \overline{p_{t_2}p_{t_3}}, \ldots, \overline{p_{t_{M-1}}p_{t_M}}, \overline{p_{t_M}p_{t_1}}\}$ represent its approximating polygon. Then, we use the circular integer string $t_1 t_2 \ldots t_M$ to encode the polygon V. Consequently, the gene value is a integer and lying in the range of $[1, N]$. Fig. 2(c) gives an example to illustrate this chromosome encoding scheme compared with the Binary-string encoding scheme. The characters of this encoding scheme are that: (1) Each gene of the chromosome correspond to a vertex of the polygon and the chromosome's length is equal to the number of the vertices of the polygon. Hence, the chromosome's length is variable. (2) There is no need to perform the decoding operator. This is because , from the chromosome, the numbers of all the vertices on the polygon can be directly obtained.

3.2 Fitness Evaluation and Parent Selection

Given a digital curve C. Let α denote a chromosome. Let $|\alpha|$ denote the length of the chromosome α and $e(\alpha)$ denote the approximation error between the curve c and the polygon represented by the chromosome α. The fitness function is defined as

$$f(\alpha) = (|\alpha|, e(\alpha)) \qquad (4)$$

such that for two arbitrary chromosomes, we have

$$\begin{cases} f(\alpha_1) > f(\alpha_2) \text{ if } |\alpha_1| < |\alpha_2| \text{ or } (|\alpha_1| = |\alpha_2| \text{ and } e(\alpha_1) < e(\alpha_2)) \\ f(\alpha_1) < f(\alpha_2) \text{ if } |\alpha_1| > |\alpha_2| \text{ or } (|\alpha_1| = |\alpha_2| \text{ and } e(\alpha_1) > e(\alpha_2)) \\ f(\alpha_1) = f(\alpha_2) \text{ if } |\alpha_1| = |\alpha_2| \text{ and } e(\alpha_1) = e(\alpha_2) \end{cases}$$

On the parent selection, we adopt tournament-selection strategy. The operation process is illustrated as follows: select two individual from the population randomly and compare their fitness value, then choose the one with the larger fitness value as the parent individual.

3.3 Gene-Removing Crossover

Let $C = \{p_1, p_2, \ldots, p_N\}$ be the digital curve. Assume that $U = u_1 u_2 \ldots u_M$ and $V = v_1 v_2 \ldots v_K$ are two selected parent chromosomes. The details of the gene-removing crossover operator are described as follows:

step 1. Select two pairs of adjacent genes $u_i u_{i+1}$ and $v_j v_{j+1}$ randomly from U and V, respectively.

step 2. For each gene u_t of the chromosome U, if $p_{u_t} \in (p_{v_j} \widehat{p_{v_{j+1}}} \sim \{p_{v_j}, p_{v_{j+1}}\})$, then remove it from the U. Through this gene-removing process, we obtain a new chromosome U_C.

step 3. For each gene v_t of the chromosome V, if $p_{v_t} \in (p_{u_i} \widehat{p_{u_{i+1}}} \sim \{p_{u_j}, p_{u_{j+1}}\})$, then remove it from the V. Through this gene-removing process, we obtain another chromosome V_C.

step 4. return U_C and V_C.

Fig. 2 gives an example to depict this operation process. In Fig. 2, 9 and 16 are adjacent genes which are selected from the parent 1. Since $p_{11}, p_{14} \in (\widehat{p_9 p_{16}} \sim \{p_9, p_{16}\})$, we remove the genes 11 and 14 from parent 2, and obtain a new chromosome offspring 2. Similarly, we obtain another chromosome offspring 1.

In general, The crossover is considered as the exchange of the part genes on the two selected parent chromosomes. For the Gene-removing crossover, The two selected parent chromosomes don't exchange their genes. But it can be still considered as a kind of crossover, this is because, the removed genes of one parent chromosome are determined by another parent chromosome's adjacent genes which is selected randomly, in fact, the two parent chromosome exchange their gene information. The advantage of this crossover is that, through it, we can remove a part of redundant genes.

3.4 Single-Point Mutation

Here, we adopt-single point mutation. Let $C = \{p_1, p_2, \ldots, p_N\}$ be the digital curve, $U = u_1 u_2 \ldots u_M$ be a selected parent chromosome. The single point mutation is illustrated as follows: Firstly, select a gene u_i randomly from the chromosome U. Secondly, add 1 to or subtract 1 from u_i randomly, note that if $u_i = N + 1$, then set $u_i = 1$ and if $u_i = 0$, then set $u_i = N$. Finally, if u_i is equal to its neighbor gene value, then remove u_i from U. Fig. 3 gives an example of the Single-point mutation.

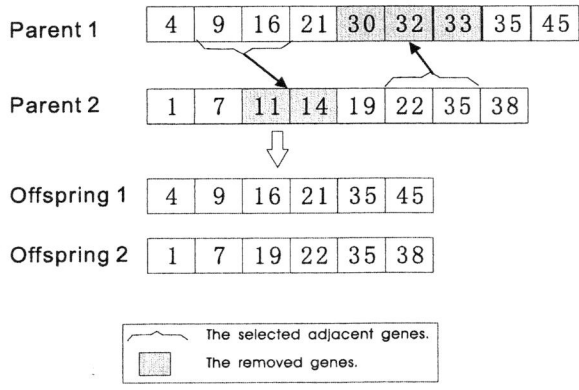

Fig. 2. An example to depict the gene-removing crossover

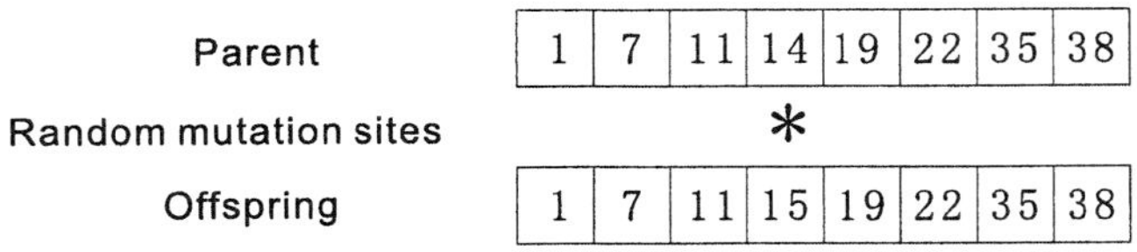

Fig. 3. An example to illustrate the single-point mutation

3.5 Chromosome-Repairing Scheme

The main idea of the chromosome-repairing scheme is that, for a infeasible solution, repair it for transforming it into a feasible solution. For facilitating the illustrating, the chromosome which represents a infeasible solution is called infeasible chromosome. For the polygonal approximation problem, infeasible solutions are those whose approximation error are lager than the pre-specified error tolerance. Adding a curve's point to the polygon may decrease the approximation error and, when all the points on the curve are the vertices of the polygon, the approximation error will be 0. Hence, if we iteratively add vertices to the polygon, the approximation error of the polygon will be eventually smaller than the pre-specified error tolerance. Then a infeasible chromosome can be transformed into a feasible one through iteratively adding gene to it. For adding the valuable genes to the chromosome as possible. we develop a function for evaluating the candidate genes. Let $C = \{p_1, p_2, \ldots, p_N\}$ be the digital curve. Let ε be the pre-specified error tolerance and $U = u_1 u_2 \ldots u_M$ be a infeasible chromosome.

Definition 6. *Let $cand(U) = \{1, 2, \ldots, N\} \sim \{u_1, u_2, \ldots, u_M\}$ be the set of candidate genes of the chromosome U.*

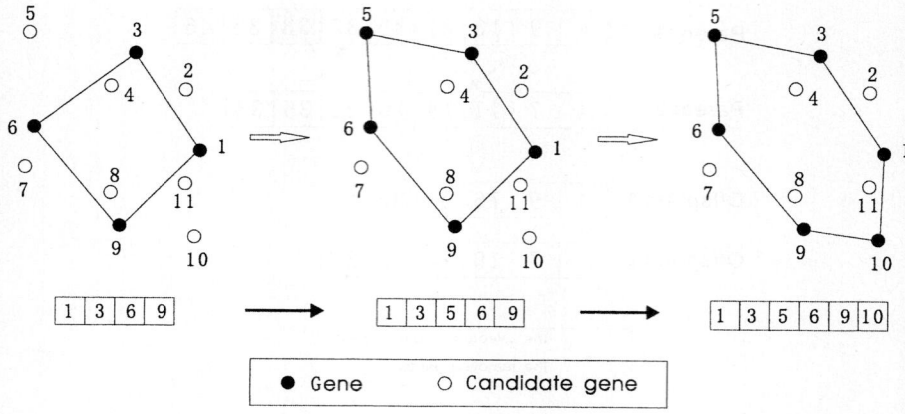

Fig. 4. An example to illustrate the Chromosome-repairing scheme

Definition 7. *Let α be a candidate gene of U and $p_\alpha \in \widehat{p_{u_i} p_{u_{i+1}}}$. The quality of the candidate gene α can be evaluated by function*

$$q(\alpha) = d(p_\alpha, \overline{p_{u_i} p_{u_{i+1}}}) \tag{5}$$

Then the chromosome-repairing scheme is illustrated as follows.

step 1. For all $\alpha \in cand(U)$, calculate function value $q(\alpha)$. Calculate approximation error $E(U, C)$. If $E(U, C) \leq \varepsilon$, then go to step 4.

step 2. Select the candidate gene $\beta \in cand(U)$ such that $q(\beta) = \max_{\alpha \in cand(U)} q(\alpha)$.

step 3. Insert the candidate gene β to the chromosome U and remove it from $cand(U)$. Then go to step 1.

step 4. Return U.

We give an example to illustrate this chromosome-repairing process in Fig. 4. From the above expatiation, we can see, the chromosome-repairing process is an iteration process, in each iteration, the quality of all the candidate genes are evaluated, and the valuable candidate gene is chosen to be added to the infeasible chromosome. Finally, we obtain a feasible chromosome.

3.6 Algorithm Flow

Let p_m, p_c and N_s be the mutation rate, crossover rate and population size, respectively. Let G_n be the pre-specified number of generation. They are all the control parameters of the algorithm. The proposed algorithm (CRS) is illustrated as follows:

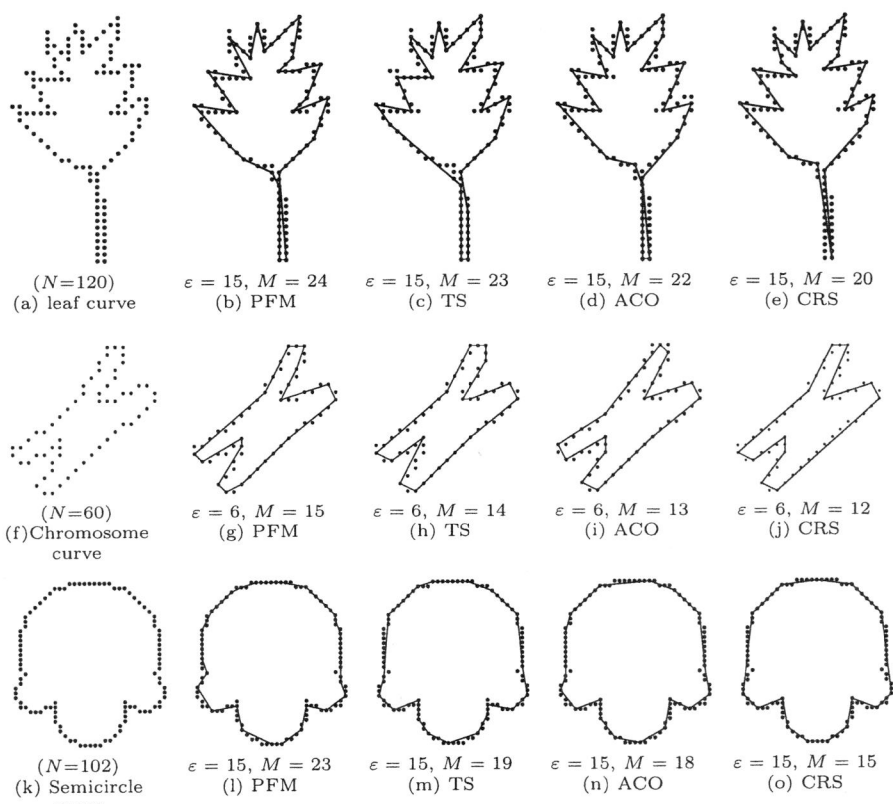

Fig. 5. Three benchmark curves and the comparative results of PFM, TS, ACO and CRS, where N, ε and M denote the number of points on the curve, the error tolerance and the number of vertices of the polygon approximating the curve, respectively.

input. the digital curve $C = \{p_1, p_2, \ldots, p_N\}$, the error tolerance ε.

output. the polygon U which approximates C.

step 1. Generate a initial population W_p having N_s individuals and the generation number g is initially set to 0.

step 2. Calculate the fitness value of each individual in population W_p and repair all the infeasible chromosomes of population W_p using the proposed chromosome-repairing scheme.

step 3. Copy the individual having the largest fitness value of population W_p to the next generation population W_c.

step 4. Generate $N_s - 1$ individuals by performing selection, crossover and mutation in the population W_p, and add them to population W_c.

step 5 Replace population W_p with W_c and update the generation number g=g+1. If $g < G_n$, then go to step 2, otherwise output U.

4 Experimental Results and Performance Comparisons

Global search approaches [5,6,7] based on genetic algorithms with penalty function method, tabu search algorithm, ant colony optimization, here, we call them PFM, TS and ACO, respectively, have been proposed to solve the polygonal approximation problem and shown to be superior to those existing methods based on local search. Therefore, we do nothing but comparing the proposed algorithm (CRS) with PFM, TS and ACO.

Three benchmark curves, leaf curve, chromosome curve and semicircle curve (see Fig. 5 (a),(f),(k)) have been widely used in literature [5,6,7,1,2,3]. So, we also use these benchmark curves to evaluate the performance of CRS. The platform of all experiments is a PC with CPU Pentium III 550 under Windows 2000. We set the control parameters of CRS as follows: $p_m = 0.3$, $p_c = 0.7$, $N_s = 31$ and $G_n = 80$. the parameters of the other compared algorithms are same as the ones presented by the literature [5,6,7]. Since all the compared algorithms are based on stochastic search, the simulation conducts ten independent runs for them. The simulation results, including the average results M, the standard deviation σ and the average time t over ten independent runs are reported in table 1 and Fig. 5 shows the finally obtained approximation polygons with its number of

Table 1. Eperimental results of three benchmarks curves for PFM, TS, ACO and CRS. Where N, M and ε are the number of points on the curve, the average solution and the error tolerance, respectively. σ and t are the standard deviation of solutions and the average computation time (in seconds), respectively

Curves	ε	PFM		TS		ACO		CRS	
		$M(\sigma)$	t	$M(\sigma)$	t	$M(\sigma)$	t	$M(\sigma)$	t
	150	15.6(0.6)	0.81	10.6(0.5)	0.13	11.2(0.5)	0.10	10.0(0.0)	0.08
	100	16.3(0.5)	0.64	13.7(0.6)	0.13	13.0(0.3)	0.10	12.3(0.2)	0.07
Leaf	90	17.3(0.5)	0.76	14.6(0.5)	0.13	13.2(0.4)	0.10	12.5(0.3)	0.07
($N = 120$)	30	20.5(0.6)	0.66	20.1(0.5)	0.13	17.2(0.4)	0.10	16.5(0.3)	0.08
	15	23.8(0.6)	0.77	23.1(0.5)	0.13	22.2(0.5)	0.10	20.0(0.0)	0.08
	30	7.3(0.4)	0.42	6.7(0.4)	0.06	6.0(0.0)	0.05	6.0(0.0)	0.04
	20	9.0(0.6)	0.45	8.0(0.3)	0.06	8.0(0.3)	0.05	7.0(0.0)	0.04
Chromosome	10	10.2(0.4)	0.46	11.0(0.4)	0.05	10.0(0.3)	0.05	10.0(0.0)	0.04
($N = 60$)	8	12.2(0.5)	0.45	12.2(0.5)	0.06	11.0(0.4)	0.05	11.0(0.0)	0.04
	6	15.2(0.6)	0.50	14.4(0.5)	0.06	12.8(0.3)	0.05	12.1(0.1)	0.04
	60	13.2(0.4)	0.58	11.0(0.4)	0.12	10.0(0.0)	0.09	10.0(0.0)	0.07
	30	13.9(0.7)	0.60	13.6(0.5)	0.10	12.6(0.4)	0.09	12.0(0.0)	0.07
Semicirle	25	16.8(0.7)	0.54	14.9(0.6)	0.10	13.4(0.5)	0.09	13.0(0.0)	0.07
($N = 102$)	20	19.2(0.6)	0.59	16.2(0.6)	0.10	16.4(0.5)	0.09	14.0(0.0)	0.07
	15	23.0(0.9)	0.55	18.3(0.7)	0.10	18.0(0.7)	0.09	15.4(0.3)	0.08

vertices (M) under the pre-specified error tolerance (ε) for visual comparison of the approximation. The simulation results show that:

(1) For the same testing curve, under the same pre-specified error tolerance, CRS produces approximating polygon with fewer number of vertices than the other approaches and its standard deviation of the solutions obtained is smaller than the other methods.
(2) CRS achieves significant reduction of computation time compared with PFM, TS and ACO. It is noticeable that CRS achieves more than 87% reduction of computation time compared with PFM.

5 Conclusions

A genetic algorithm with chromosome-repairing scheme has been proposed for polygonal approximation. For improving the performance of GA-based approaches, we have presented variable-length chromosome encoding instead of traditional binary-string encoding, designed a gene-removing crossover instead of traditional crossover and developed a chromosome-repairing scheme instead of the penalty function method. The results demonstrate that the proposed CRS has improved the performance of the GA-based approaches greatly and show that CRS is superior to the existing methods based on GA, ACO and TS.

Acknowledgements

The research work presented in this paper is supported by National Natural Science Foundation of China, project No.60275010; Science and Technology Commission of Shanghai Municipality, project No. 04JC14014; and National Grand Fundamental Research Program of China, project No. 2001CB309401.

References

1. Ray, B.K., Ray, K.S.: Determination of optimal polygon from digital curve using L_1 norm. Pattern Recognition. **26** (1993) 505–509
2. Ray, B.K., Ray, K.S.: A new split-and merge technique for polygonal approximation of chain coded curves. Pattern Recognition letter. **16** (1995) 161–169
3. Teh, H.C., Chin, R.T.: On detection of dominant points on digital curves. IEEE Trans Pattern Anal Mach Intell. **11(8)** (1989) 859–872
4. Phillips, T.Y., Rosenfeld, A.: An ISODATA algorithm for straight line fitting. Pattern Recognition letter. **7** (1988) 291–297
5. Yin, P.Y.: Genetic algorithms for polygonal approximation of digital curves. Int. J. Pattern Recognition Artif. Intell. **13** (1999) 1–22
6. Yin, P.Y.: A tabu search approach to the polygonal approximation of digital curves. Int. J. Pattern Recognition Artif. Intell. **14** (2000) 243–255
7. Yin, P.Y.: Ant colony search algorithms for optimal polygonal approximation of plane curves. Pattern Recognition. **36** (2003) 1783–1997

Fault Feature Selection Based on Modified Binary PSO with Mutation and Its Application in Chemical Process Fault Diagnosis

Ling Wang and Jinshou Yu

Research Institution of Automation, East China University of Science & Technology
200237, Shanghai, China
shwl_1212 @ 163.com

Abstract. In large scale industry systems, especially in chemical process industry, large amounts of variables are monitored. When all variables are collected for fault diagnosis, it results in poor fault classification because there are too many irrelevant variables, which also increase the dimensions of data. A novel optimization algorithm, based on a modified binary Particle Swarm Optimization with mutation (MBPSOM) combined with Support Vector Machine (SVM), is proposed to select the fault feature variables for fault diagnosis. The simulations on Tennessee Eastman process (TEP) show the BMPSOM can effectively escape from local optima to find the global optimal value comparing with initial modified binary PSO (MBPSO). And based on fault feature selection, more satisfied performances of fault diagnosis are achieved.

1 Introduction

With the high automation of chemical process industry, control systems are adopted to keep the steady operation of production process. Once abnormal situation occurs, control systems will be out of work, which makes the process to make off-grade products, even causes casualty. Fault diagnosis, which can provide early warning for process upset and reduce loss, plays an important role in industry process.

But it is hard for fault diagnosis in complex chemical process because there are large amounts of data monitored. When all collected variables are used as the inputs, high-dimensions of data not only reduce the performance of fault diagnosis because of containing too much irrelevant variables, but also spoil the real-time requirement due to increased complexity of computation. So it is essential to execute fault feature selection or fault feature extraction in the developing fault diagnosis system for an industrial system to improve its performance.

There are several approaches to fault feature extraction developed and applied, such as Principal Component Analysis (PCA), which is a well-known method for feature extraction, and has been widely researched in fault diagnosis applications [1], [2], [3].But the data preprocessed by data dimension redundant method may be unsatisfied for fault diagnosis due to the method own characters, for example, PCA does not fit nonlinear, dynamic system, etc. And sometimes, the number of selected components is still large in order to contain enough information for fault diagnosis. And even worse, the extracted data is not exactly fit to fault diagnosis because PCA do not just extract the fault information of system. To make up for this shortage, the approach to directly search the fault feature variables was presented [4]. In this paper, a novel algorithm based on a modified binary PSO with mutation combined with SVM is developed to search the key fault feature variables, and then take them as inputs for fault diagnosis.

The reminder of the paper is organized as follows. Section 2 presents the modified binary PSO with mutation algorithm in detail and introductions of the concerned methods are also given. Section 3 introduces simulations setup. Performances of presented BMPSOM algorithm and fault diagnosis on TEP are given in Section 4. Comparisons with PCA method are also given. Section 5 concludes the results of simulations.

2 Theory

2.1 Particle Swarm Optimization

PSO was inspired by the movement of flocks of birds randomly to look for food in an area, which firstly was presented by Kennedy and Eberhart [5]. No bird knows where food is, except the one that is nearest to food. So it is an effective strategy for other birds to follow the nearest one to find food. Simulating this scenario, PSO was developed and used as a useful computation technique to solve the optimization problem, such as evolving weights and structure for artificial neural networks [6], solving the optimal power flow problem [7], evaluating the parametric regions of chemical process [8], combinatorial optimization problem [9] and so on.

The basic PSO model consists of a swarm of m particles moving about in a D-dimensional real value search space. Each particle, which is a potential global optimum of the function f(x) over a given domain D, is looked as a point in the D-dimensional space and represented as xi = (x_{i1}, x_{i2}... x_{id}). Here subscript i means *ith* particle. Fitness value of all particles is evaluated by the fitness function to be optimized. And according to that value, the particle is updated to move towards the better area by the corresponding operators till the best point is found. In the iterative process, the position of each particle with its best fitness value, that is its local best, is remembered and denoted Pi = (p_{i1}, p_{i2}... p_{id}). At the same time, the globe best, which is the position with the best fitness value of all particles, is also recorded as Pg = (p_{g1}, p_{g2}... p_{gd}). Velocity, the rate of the position change for the *ith* particle is represented as Vi = (v_{i1}, v_{i2}...v_{id}). At each times step, the velocity of all particles is adjusted as a sum of its local best value, globe best value and its present velocity, multiplied by the three constants w, *c1*, *c2* respectively, shown in Eq. (1). The position of each particle is also modified by adding its velocity to the current position, see Eq. (2).

$$V_{id} = V_{id} + c_1 \times rand() \times (p_{id} - x_{id}) + c_2 \times rand() \times (p_{gd} - x_{id}). \quad (1)$$

$$x_{id} = x_{id} + V_{id}. \quad (2)$$

The parameters, c1 and c2, are two positive constant named as learning factors, normally set as c1=c2=2. With the development of the PSO, new modified PSO algorithms were developed, such as PSO combined with GA [10], PSO with mutation operating [11].

2.2 Binary Particle Swarm Optimization

The basic PSO and its modified forms mentioned above all work in the continuous space, which can not be used to optimize the pure combinational problem. Kennedy and Eberhart firstly extended the basic PSO to the discrete space in 1997 [12]. The binary PSO algorithm where the particles take the values of binary vectors of length n and the velocity defined the probability of bit x_{id} to take the value 1 reserved the updating formula of the velocity (see Eq.(1)) while velocity was constrained to the interval [0.0, 1.0] by a limiting transformation function S(v). Then the particle changes its bit value by Eq. (3)

$$p_{ij} = \begin{cases} 1 & \text{if rand()} \leq S(v_{ij}) \\ 0 & \text{otherwise} \end{cases} \quad (3)$$

Based on Kennedy's work, Qi[13] developed a modified binary PSO (MBPSO) and applied to feature selection in MLR and PLS modeling. The modified binary particle swarm optimization algorithm changed the updating formula as Eq. (4-6)

$$\text{If } (0 < v_{id} \leq \alpha) \text{ then } x_{id}(mid) = x_{id}(old). \quad (4)$$

$$\text{If } (\alpha < v_{id} \leq \frac{1}{2}(1+\alpha)) \text{ then } x_{id}(mid) = p_{id}. \quad (5)$$

$$\text{If } (\frac{1}{2}(1+\alpha) < v_{id} \leq 1) \text{ then } x_{id}(mid) = g_{id}. \quad (6)$$

Where α is a random value in the range of (0, 1) named static probability, which plays an important role in balancing the globe and local search. The larger value of the parameter a, the greater the probability for PSO to overleap local optima, while a small value of the parameter a guide effectively particles to follow their two best value to converge more quickly. Although its forms of formulas are different from the basic PSO presented, information sharing mechanism and the updating model of particles are the same. That is to say, particles still share and only share the information of its best and the globe best.

MBPSO can search the best solution more effectively, but it tends to converge to local optimal. To overcome this shortage, 10% particles are forced to be set value randomly without sharing information with the two best particles.

2.3 Support Vector Machines

SVM is a relatively new class of machine learning techniques introduced by Vapnik. It implements the Structural Risk Minimization Principal by seeking to minimize an upper bound of the generalization error instead of minimizing the training error. The training of SVM is equivalent to solving a linearly constrained convex quadratic programming problem, so SVM can escape from the local minima and get the global optimal solution, which is determined only by support vectors and represented sparsely. More details see [14] Because the remarkable characteristics of SVM such as good generalization performance, the absence of local minima and the sparse representation of solution, now SVM is popularly used in the application of fault diagnosis[15-17].

In this paper, the selected feature variables of each particle will be taken as input variables of SVM to class testing sample data, and then the correct classification rates will be provided to fitness function to evaluate each particle's fitness.

2.4 Fitness Function

In order to measure the performance of each particle, a pre- defined fitness function is applied to evaluate the fitness of each particle. In this paper, the fitness function is normally defined as the correct classification rate by using the fault feature variables picked by each particle. As mentioned above, unnecessary variables are useless and increase the computing time, the adjusted fitness function is given here to remove the irrelated variables, denoted as Eq. (7)

$$f(x_{id}) = f(id) - p \times \frac{m_c}{m_{all}}. \qquad (7)$$

$f(x_{id})$ means the fitness function, $f(id)$ represents the correct classification rate of the data samples, mc is the number of variable chosen by the particle while mall is the dimension of data samples, p is a parameter which balances the maximum correct classification rate and the numbers of retained variables. An appropriate value of p will ensure to get the maximum correct classification rate using the least variables, for example, p is set less than $1/mall$.

2.5 Modified Binary PSO with Mutation Algorithm for Fault Feature Selection

MBPSO introduced by Qi is an effective evolution optimization algorithm for feature selection [13] with the excellent characters such as easy to implement, few set parameters, rapid convergence. But it is tendentious to stick in the local optimal solutions for solving complex problems. Looking at the positions of the particles when the swarm had stagnated, the particles are highly similar with their two best values, which cause that no more new solutions can be generated, and the swarm traps in the local optimum. To make up for this deficiency, a novel modified binary PSO with mutation (BMPSOM) algorithm is presented. The introduction of mutation will make the swarm keeping searching new area of solution space which ensures swarm from sticking in local optima.

In the first part of the iteration, just the globe best individual is operated by mutation. In each turn, the lowest fitness particle will be replaced with the current mutated globe best individual to speed up the search with a little additional computation. With the iteration going on, all particles will be mutated with probability p_{mute} to find the best solution more effectively and ensure to escape from local optima. Some discussion about the value of p_{mute} is given by in detail.

The whole steps of the MBPSOM combined with SVM for feature selection are following:

Step 1. set particles number of the swarm and initial particles;
Step 2. get the training data samples and validation data samples according to the retained variables of particles;
Step 3. classify with SVM and calculate the fitness function of each particle according to Eq. (7);
Step 4. update the local optima and the global optima;
Step 5. mutation operation;
Step 6. stop the iterative if the terminal rule is satisfied or goto step2.

3 Experimental Setup

3.1 Tennessee Eastman Process

The Tennessee Eastman is a well-known benchmark chemical process, which was firstly introduced by Downs and Vogel [18]. The TEP provides a realistic industrial process for evaluating process control and monitoring methods. The process consists of five major units: a reactor, condenser, compressor, separator, and stripper. The TEP produces two products from four reactants. The gaseous reactants A, C, D, E and the inert B are fed to the reactor where liquid products G, H and byproduct F are formed. Now, the TEP has been widely used for the process monitoring community as a source of data for comparing various approaches [19].

The TEP simulator, coded in Matlab, was used to generate normal data and faulty data. The faults of this paper to research are those with stable operating conditions before and after the fault occur because of the characteristic of SVM, and will be called as Fault1, Fault2 and Fault3 below.

The first simulation ran 25 hour and sampled per 3 minutes to generate 500 observations under the normal operating conditions. The next three simulations also ran 25 hour and each of them corresponded to three different faults mentioned above. These three simulations started without faults, and the faults were introduced 1 simulation hour into the run. So the total number of observations generated for each run was n=500, but only 480 observations were collected after the introduction of the fault. Each observation contains 52 observation variables. As SVM is fit to limited samples, so just 30 samples as SVM training data and 60 data samples as SVM validation data were chosen randomly from each simulation run. These two dataset were used in the process of fault feature selection.

Another 4 simulations ran to generate test data for fault diagnosis. Like the former 4 simulations, one simulation ran in the normal condition, and the other 3 simulations ran corresponding to Fault1-3. But the simulation time for each run was 48 hours. Each simulation started with no faults, and the faults were introduced 8 simulation hours into the run. The total number of observations generated for each run was n=960.

To make the results comparable, the data used for experiment are given by http://brahms.scs.uiuc.edu.

4 Result and Discussion

4.1 Experiment with Testing Function

Six testing function used in [20] are adopted here to validate MBPSO and MBPSOM.

$$F_1 = 100(x_1^2 - x_2)^2 + (1-x_1)^2 \qquad -2.048 \le x_i \le 2.048. \tag{8}$$

$$F_2 = 4 + 4.5x_1 - 4x_2 + x_1^2 + 2x_2^2 - 2x_1 x_2 + x_1^4 - 2x_1^2 x_2 \qquad -8 \le x_i \le 8. \tag{9}$$

$$F_3 = (x_1^2 + x_2^2)^{0.25}[\sin^2(50(x_1^2 + x_2^2)^{0.1}) + 1.0] \qquad -100 < x_i < 100. \tag{10}$$

$$F_4 = (4 - 2.1x_1^2 + x_1^4/3)x_1^2 + x_1 x_2 + (-4 + 4x_2^2)x_2^2 \qquad -100 < x_i < 100. \tag{11}$$

$$F_5 = 0.5 - \frac{\sin^2 \sqrt{x_1^2 + x_2^2} - 0.5}{(1 + 0.001(x_1^2 + x_2^2))^4} \qquad -100 < x_i < 100. \tag{12}$$

$$F_6 = \sum_{i=1}^{5} \operatorname{integer}(x_i) \qquad -5.12 \le x_i \le 5.12. \tag{13}$$

Where F5 has the global maximum, others have the global minimum. The experiment results are list in the Table1.

4.2 Fault Feature Selection

Because PSO algorithm is affected by the initial of the particles, the MBPSO and the MBPSOM both run 10 times to select fault feature variables and the average value is used to compare each other.

Table 1. Results of compared MBPSPOM with MBPSO

NO.	Global value	MBPSOM		MBPSO	
		Correct rate (%)	worst value	Correct rate (%)	worst value
Fun1	0	100	0	60	1.67×10^{-7}
Fun2	-0.5134	100	-0.5134	90	-0.5121
Fun3	0	100	0	60	0.004
Fun4	-1.316	100	-1.316	100	-1.316
Fun5	1.00	100	1.00	70	0.9980
Fun6	-30	100	-30	100	-30

In the fault1 case, all variables remained steady except the 51th variable induced a change when the fault occurred. So the fault feature variable of fault1 is just variable 51. Both of MBPSO and MBPOSM found the fault feature variable correctly. MBPSO found the global optima after minimum 48th iteration, average 68 times iteration, and stuck in the local optima once. While the MBPSOM searched the fault feature variable in the minimum 5th iteration and average 7 times iteration. The average fitness changes of the global optimal particle are given by Fig.1.

Fault2 involves a step changes in variable 1and variable 44, and the other variables are all bothered. The change of variable 1 or variable 44 is so remarkable that any one of them can be taken as fault feature. MBPSO and MBPOSM chose the variable 44 as fault feature variable, and their minimum, average iterative times are 43, 50, 5, and 6 respectively. The average fitness changes of the whole simulation see Fig.2.

Variable 45 had a noticeable step change when the fault3 was introduced into the process. And affected by it, other 34 variables deviated significantly from their normal operation behavior and went aback to normal values later by the control of closed loop. MBPSO searched the global optima with minimum iteration 58 times, average iteration 70 times, but it stuck in the local optima in 7 simulations. As a comparison, MBPSOM found the fault feature variable correctly all 10 simulations with the minimum 6 times iterations and the average 8 times iteration. The changes of the maximum fitness during the process are presented in Fig.3.

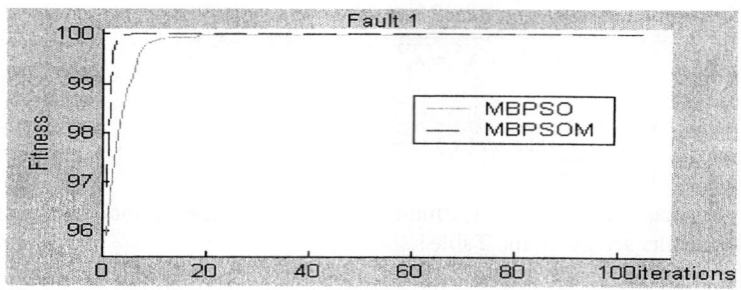

Fig. 1. Fitness changing of MBPSO and MBPSOM in the fault1case

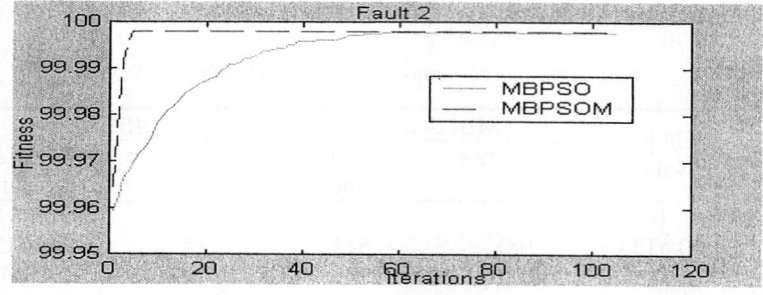

Fig. 2. Fitness changing of MBPSO and MBPSOM in the fault2 case

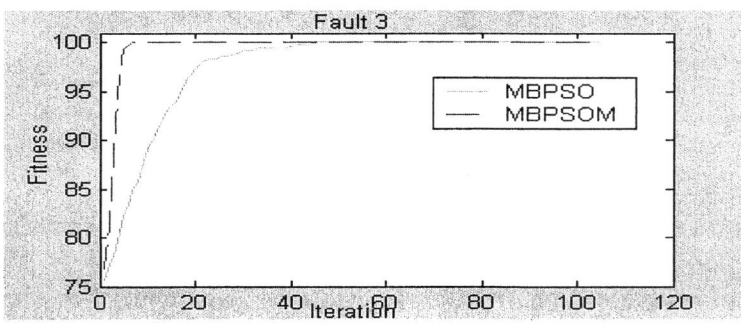

Fig. 3. Fitness changing of MBPSO and MBPSOM in the fault3 case

It is obvious that MBPSO is hard to escape from the local minimum in solving complex problems although it randomly re-initialize particles with 10% probability to prevent overlapping local optima. On the other hand, mutation operator makes MBPSOM effectively escape from the local minimum successfully, and come to convergence more effectively.

4.3 Fault Diagnosis Based on Fault Feature Selection

Table 2 presents the results of fault diagnosis based on fault feature variable selection. To give a comparison, the same data were used for fault diagnosis based on all variables and data extracted by PCA.SVM is applied to classify the fault class. Because the focus of this paper is to develop a more effective algorithm to select fault feature, and fault diagnosis is just to validate its performance, the whole fault diagnosis strategy is not described here.

Table 2. The misclassifications rates of three methods

~	MBPSOM/SVM	All variables	PCA
Fault 1	0.0%	38.7%	31.8%
Fault 2	0.0%	0.0%	0.0%
Fault 3	0.0%	48.2%	40.3%

5 Conclusion

The developed MBPSOM performs better and convergent more quickly because it can effectively escape from the local optima. SVM works better in the applications of fault diagnosis based on fault feature selected than data extracted by PCA. Considering SVM is suitable for the limited data sample application and the fault data lack in the real industrial process, all of these make fault feature selection based on MBPSOM combined with SVM noticeable and attractive in fault diagnosis applications.

References

1. Wang Shengwei, Xiao Fu: Detection and diagnosis of AHU sensor faults using principal component analysis method. Energy Conversion and Management. 45 (2004) 2667-2686
2. Russell, Evan L., Chiang, Leo H. Braatz, Richard D.: Fault detection in industrial processes using canonical variate analysis and dynamic principal component analysis. Chemometrics and Intelligent Laboratory Systems. 51 (2000) 81–93
3. Huang Yunbing, Gertler, Janos,McAvoy, Thomas J.: Sensor and actuator fault isolation by structured partial PCA with nonlinear extensions. Journal of Process Control. 10 (2000) 459–469
4. Chiang, Leo H. Pell, Randy J.: Genetic algorithms combined with discriminant analysis for key variable identification. Journal of Process Control. 14 (2004) 143-155
5. P. Kennedy, R. Eberhart.: Particle Swarm Optimization, In: Proceeding of IEEE International Conference on Neural. 4 (1995) 1942-1948
6. Eberhart, R.C., Shi, Y.: Evolving artificial neural networks, In: Proceeding of the International Conference on Neural Networks and Brain. (1998) 5-13
7. Abido, M.A. Optimal power flow using particle swarm optimization, International Journal of Electrical Power and Energy Systems. 24 (2002) 563-571
8. Ourique, Claudia O, Biscaia Jr.: The use of particle swarm optimization for dynamical analysis in chemical process, Computers and Chemical Engineering. 26 (2002) 1783-1793
9. Kannan, S., Slochanal, S.: Application of particle swarm optimization technique and its variants to generation expansion planning problem. Electric Power Systems Research. 70 (2004) 203-210
10. Stacey, A., Jancic, M., Grundy, I.: Particle swarm optimization with mutation. Evolutionary Computation. 2 (2003) 1425 -1430
11. Juang, C.F.: A Hybrid of Genetic Algorithm and Particle Swarm Optimization for Recurrent Network Design. Systems, Man and Cybernetics (B). IEEE Transactions on. 34 (2004) 997-1006
12. Kennedy.J., Eberhart, R.C.: A discrete binary version of the particle swarm algorithm, Systems, Man, and Cybernetics. 'Computational Cybernetics and Simulation'., 1997 IEEE International Conference on . 5 (1997) 4104-4108
13. Shen Qi, Jiang Jianhui.: Modified particle swarm optimization algorithm for variable selection in MLR and PLS modeling: QSAR studies of antagonism of angiotensin II antagonists. European Journal of Pharmaceutical Sciences. 22 (2004) 145-152
14. V.N. Vapnik.: The Nature of Statistical Learning Theory. Springer, New York. (1995)
15. Ge. Ming, Du, R.: Fault diagnosis using support vector machine with an application in sheet metal stamping operations, Mechanical Systems and Signal Processing. 18 (2004) 143–159
16. Samanta, B., Al-Balushi, K.R.: Artificial neural networks and support vector machines with genetic algorithm for bearing fault detection. Engineering Applications of Artificial Intelligence. 16 (2003) 657 – 665
17. Samanta, B.: Gear fault detection using artificial neural networks and support vector machines with genetic algorithms, Mechanical Systems and Signal Processing. 18 (2004) 625 – 644
18. Downs J. H., Vogel E.F.: A plant-wide industrial process control problem, Comput. Chem. Eng. 17 (1993) 245–255
19. L.H. Chiang, E.L. Russell, R.D. Braatz.: Fault Detection and Diagnosis in Industrial Systems. Springer-Verlag Berlin Heidelberg London (2001)
20. Xihuai. Wang, Junjun L.: Hybrid particles swarm optimization with simulated annealing. In: Proceedings of the 3nd international Conference on Machine Learning and Cybernetic. (2004) 2403-2405

Genetic Algorithms for Thyroid Gland Ultrasound Image Feature Reduction

Ludvík Tesař[1], Daniel Smutek[2], and Jan Jiskra[2]

[1] Institute of Information Theory and Automation,
Czech Academy of Sciences, Prague, Czech Republic
[2] 3rd Department of Medicine, 1st Medical Faculty,
Charles University, Prague, Czech Republic

Abstract. The problem of automatic classification of ultrasound images is addressed. For texture analysis of ultrasound images quantifiable indexes, called features, are used. Classification was performed using Gaussian mixture model based on Bayes classifier. The common problem of texture analysis is a feature selection for classification tasks. In this work we use genetic algorithms for a feature subset selection. Total number of 387 features was used, consisting of spatial and co-occurance statistical texture features (proposed by Muzzolini and Haralick). The classification infers between healthy thyroid gland and thyroid gland with chronic inflammation.

1 Introduction

Ultrasound imaging is a very important cost-effective method for diagnostics of thyroid gland diseases. For most thyroid disorders it surpasses the more expensive magnetic resonance. Image analysis can give more objective way of diagnosing patient than a physician who relies on his experience only.

We use Bayes classifier, where diagnose was verified by other methods. The method we use very successfully (See [1,2]) employs Gaussian Mixture model in feature space. Reduction of number of features can help to reduce number of computations substantially, and to better understand, which pattern feature characterize thyroid gland inflammation in ultrasound image. In this work we are using genetic algorithm for feature selection.

2 Classification Method Description

Texture features are computed from a set of fixed-size rectangular regions referred to as texture samples. The non-overlapping samples are obtained from a manually segmented sonographic B-mode image of thyroid gland. Haralick texture features [4] were computed from the co-occurrence matrix. Muzzolini's spatial features, originally suggested by Muzzolini [5], are based on the original pixel gray levels. For closer feature description refer to [3]. Finally 387 different texture feature values were known for each patient.

The vector Y of features, is modeled using Gaussian mixture model:

$$p(Y) = \sum_{i=1}^{n} \frac{\alpha_i \exp\left[-\frac{1}{2}(Y - Y_i)^{\mathrm{T}} C_i^{-1}(Y - Y_i)\right]}{(2\pi)^{\frac{d}{2}} |C_i|^{\frac{1}{2}}} \quad (1)$$

Where n is order of the mixture, d dimension of vector Y, $|\cdot|$ denotes determinant of matrix, symbol $()^{\mathrm{T}}$ denotes transposition. Important condition is, that $\sum_{i=1}^{n} \alpha_i = 1$.

During learning process, parameters of the model (1) are estimated. Two sets of parameters are calculated, one for healthy and one for inflamed tissue. The diagnosis is obtained by applying features of given patient to probability density functions from equation (1) fitted to healthy and unhealthy patients. The method is more more in detail described in [2]. The result of classification method is used in genetic algorithm to evaluate the fitness of an individual, by selecting only features that are attached to this individual and by doing classification only on such subset of features.

3 Genetic Algorithm Description

In explanation of the genetic algorithm, we will use terms *population*, *generation* and *individual* as follows: Each individual in our population was representing the set of features (its chromosomes). The population is set of individuals. In every generation, chromosomes (features) of individuals in the population are crossed in order to create the next generation. Fitness of individual is evaluated according to the success of its features in classification.

Every individual in our population have given number (in our experiments 5 or 10) of chromosomes. Every chromosome represents one feature. Features are numbered by numbers between 1 and 387, so chromosome is simply one number between 1 and 387. If two parents are to have an offspring, chromosomes of an offspring are randomly selected from its parents. Let $D_1 = [c_{1,1}, c_{1,2}, \ldots, c_{1,n}]$ is an ordered n-tuple representing chromosomes of the first parent and $D_2 = [c_{2,1}, c_{2,2}, \ldots, c_{2,n}]$ of the second parent, then $D_3 = [c_{2,1}, c_{2,2}, \ldots, c_{2,n}]$ defined as $D_3 = [c_{i(1),1}, c_{i(2),2}, \ldots, c_{i(n),n}]$ is genetic information of the offspring, where $i(1), i(2), \ldots, i(n)$ is vector of binary random numbers ($i(k) \in \{1, 2\}$), and n is number of chromosomes in individuals of our population. In every new offspring, mutation was made randomly with mutation rate given in per-individual basis, i.e. if mutation rate was 0.5, it means that there was one mutation per two new offsprings in average.

Algorithm is started by randomly chosen generation $\mathcal{G} = \{D_1, D_2, \ldots, D_h\}$ of h individuals with n chromosomes. Following steps are repeated for given number of generations:

1. **Selection.** Fitness of every individual $D_k \in \mathcal{G}$ is evaluated and only first ℓ are selected (Fitness of the individual is evaluated based on classification method described in Section 2). I.e. worst $h - \ell$ individuals are removed from

population. The new set will be $\mathcal{G} := \{D_1, D_2, \ldots, D_\ell\}$, assuming that D_k was already sorted by fitness. Note that in algorithm, we are using the same letter to represent different thing.
2. **Making offsprings.** h new individuals are created as offsprings of individuals in set $\mathcal{G}$. I.e. two individuals from the set $D_1, D_2 \in \mathcal{G}$ are repeatedly randomly selected as parents and new individual E_k is created (as explained above) as their offspring for $k \in \{1, 2, \ldots, h\}$. Now the set $\mathcal{G}$ is changed to hold the new generation: $\mathcal{G} := \{E_1, E_2, \ldots, E_h\}$.
3. **Mutation.** Every individual $E_k \in \mathcal{G}$ is mutated with given mutation rate.

Chromosomes of individuals from the last generation represent an optimal selection of features.

4 Testing of the Genetic Algorithm

We tested the proposed algorithm using the data with 100 subjects, of which 62 were patients with lymphocytic thyroiditis. The diagnosis was confirmed by fine-needle aspiration biopsy, an increased level of antibodies (anti-thyroperoxidase and anti-thyroglobulin) and by clinical examination. Another 38 subjects were healthy test persons (volunteers) with mean age 28 ± 14 years with no known thyroid disease.

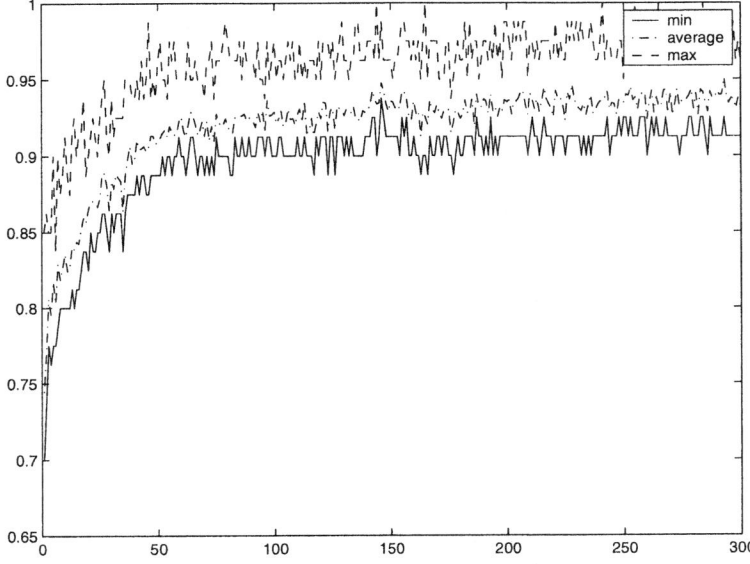

Fig. 1. Results of run with 300 generations. Graphs show minimum, average and maximum of the success rate of individuals from the population

The principal parameters of the sonograph were fixed in the study. Details concerning data acquisition and processing are the same as in [3].

We made several runs with number of generations between 10 and 300 and with number of chromosomes between 5 and 10. Number of mutations was 0.5 to 3 per generation. Population size h was between 40 and 80 and parameter ℓ was selected to be 10 to 20.

Graph in Figure 1 shows minimum, average and maximum of the success rate of individuals from the population in the typical run of algorithm. We can see that genetic algorithm converged after 70 generations already.

5 Conclusions

Compared to our earlier paper [6], results of classification are better, because of much better classifier, which was developed in [2]. We have found the most suitable quantitative indicators of an ultrasound examination of thyroid gland, assuming they include the highest amount of information for texture recognition of chronic inflammation in thyroid tissue. Such indicators enable reproducibility of the examination, facilitate an assessment of changes of the disease in time and make the comparison of different physicians' ultrasound findings possible.

Acknowledgment

Paper was supported by Grant agency of Academy of Sciences of the Czech Republic by project 1ET101050403.

References

1. Tesař, L., Smutek, D.: Bayesian classification of sonograms of thyroid gland based on Gaussian mixtures. In: Proceedings of Norwegian Conference on Image Processing and Pattern Recognition, NOBIM 2004, Stavanger, Norway (2004) 36–40
2. Smutek, D., Šára, R., Jiskra, J., Tesař, L.: Ultrasound of thyroid gland - what is hidden inside and physician does not see. In Cikes, Nada, eds.: Lijecnicki Vjesnik; Abstracts from European Congress on Ultrasound in Medicine and Biology 126 (Suppl. 2), Zagreb, Croatia, Kratis - Zagreb (2004) 57
3. Smutek, D., Šára, R., Sucharda, P., Tjahjadi, T., Švec, M.: Image texture analysis of sonograms in chronic inflammations of thyroid gland. Ultrasound in Medicine and Biology **29** (2003) 1531–1543
4. Haralick, R.M., Shapiro, L.G. In: Computer and Robot Vision. Volume 1. Addison-Wesley Publishing Company, Reading MA (1993) 453–508
5. Muzzolini, R., Yang, Y.H., Pierson, R.: Texture characterization using robust statistics. Pattern Recognition **27** (1994) 119–134
6. Smutek, D., Semecký, J.: Feature selection by genetic algorithms in image texture analysis of thyroid gland ultrasound. In: IFBBE Proceedings: 2nd European Medical and Biological Engineering Conference EMBEC'02. Volume 3., Verlag der Technischen Universität Graz (2002) 878–879

Improving Nearest Neighbor Classification with Simulated Gravitational Collapse

Chen Wang and Yan Qiu Chen*

Department of Computer Science and Engineering,
School of Information Science and Engineering,
Fudan University, Shanghai, 200433, P. R. China
chenyq@fudan.edu.cn

Abstract. The performance of the Nearest Neighbor classifier drops significantly with the increase of the overlapping of the distribution of different classes. To overcome this drawback, we propose to simulate the physical process of gravitational collapse to trim the boundaries of the distribution of each class to reduce overlapping. The proposed simulated gravitational collapse(SGC) algorithm is tested on 7 real-world data sets. Experimental results show that the nearest prototype classifier based on SGC outperforms conventional NN and k-NN classifiers.

1 Introduction

The nearest neighbor(NN) classification method and its improved versions have been shown to perform well for pattern classification in many domains. NN assigns the class label of the nearest reference instance to the query, i.e. any unknown sample is believed to have the same class label as its nearest neighbor.

Cover and Hart[14] have proved that the error for the NN classifier is bounded by twice the Bayes error when the number of samples is infinite. However, in practice, we never have an infinite sample size and the performance of NN classifier is away from the theoretic boundary. Hence, a lot of methods have been proposed to find "good" and representative prototypes from the original training set and the NN rule based on the result prototypes will perform better, even approximate the Bayes classifier.

There are mainly 2 kinds of prototype generators. One is prototype selection. In these methods, prototypes are selected or edited from the original set. One of the original literatures in this kind is the condensed nearest neighbor(CNN)[9]. It produces a reduced set without "interior" instances which maintain the performance of the result classifier. Other selective methods have been proposed successively, such as the reduced nearest neighbor rule(RNN)[10], the selective nearest neighbor rule(SNN)[12]. Besides, Wilson's edited neighbor rule (ENN)[4] is a typical method of another kind of prototype selection, which focus on editing the boundary by eliminating border instances.

---

* Corresponding author.

In Wilson's method, the k-NN algorithm is run once on the training set, and simply discard misclassified instances after the run. One intrinsic problem comes from using the k-NN(K=3, recommended by Wilson) rule to estimate Bayes decision boundary in a finite sample size situation. From a practical point of view, it's not possible to remove only instances lying in wrong decision regions without also removing some "correct" ones[5].

Another kind of prototype generator is prototype replacement, which generates prototypes to take the place of the original ones. Chang's the prototypes for nearest neighbor classifier(PNN) generates representative prototypes by merging similar intances[11]. Hamamoto introduced a bootstrap technique of generating prototypes by locally conbining original training instances[2]. Li's Nearest Feature Line(NFL)[13] generates a line linking each pair of instances as the prototypes. Besides these, learning update strategy is also employed in generating prototypes by a family of learning vector quantization(LVQ) methods, which is first proposed in Kohonen's LVQ1[6].

LVQ1 uses a learning update strategy to make prototypes move away from samples of other classes but come close to samples belonging to the same class. Asymptotic convergence of LVQ1 has only been studied when the number of training instances tends to ∞[7]. For finite sample cases, the use of LVQ1 only supported by empirical evidence rather than convergence from a theoretical point of view.

Prototype selection methods are usually simple and fast. However, prototypes generated by replacement schemes can be more representative than the ones obtained by instance selection. Lam[8] proposed a framework of combining these two kinds of generation methods. For more details of these algorithms, a recent survey about the nearest prototype classifier can be found in[1].

In this paper we propose to use simulated gravitational collapse(SGC) model to construct the nearest prototype classifier. Prototypes are generated by the migration of original instances, which is a natural computing process by simulating gravitational collapse in astronomy and different from selection and simple replacement schemes. The motivation of the SGC algorithm comes from the following observation.

Samples can be divided roughly into 2 types according to their location: interior instances and border instances. Since interior instances hardly contribute to the decision boundary, in the NN case, this kind of instances are often useless. On the contrary, due to their locality, border instances play a critical role in NN classification.

Border instances are important to NN classifier, while they also bring misclassification. Figure 1 illustrates that, with the apparent probability density functions of two classes, the training instances(border instances) falling in a wrong Bayes acceptance region may lead misclassifications under the NN rule, by which NN's intrinsic drawback of over-fitting is demonstrated clearly. Due to possible overlapping among classes, the Voronoi decision region based on the NN rule is still far away from the optimal Bayes decision boundary. By eliminating those "mislabelled" instances, the remaining prototypes will be well clustered

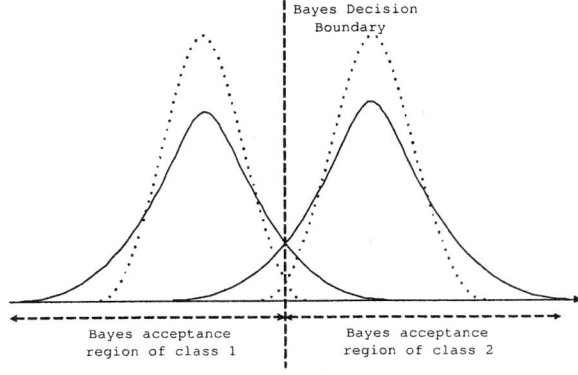

Fig. 1. Bayes decision region and NN's possible misclassification region(overlapping)

and form a compact decision boundary which could approximate the Bayes optimal one for infinite samples[3].

However, infinite instances do not exist in real world problems, so these algorithms always lead suboptimal results without detailed knowledge about actual class distribution. Under such circumstance, we have to make a trade-off between cleaning class boundary thoroughly and leaving some small overlapping among classes. Nonetheless, those existing algorithms and analysis have strongly illustrated that reducing overlapping by changing the class distribution is an effective and efficient way to improve NN classifier. It's believed that, as shown in Figure 1, the overlapping region will be reduced by contracting the original distribution properly(distribution contracting from real curve to dashed curve).

For this purpose, by simulating the gravitational collapse phenomenon in astronomy, we propose a novel scheme to generate prototypes. The genenrated samples distribute more compactly, by moving the original instances to contract distribution and reduce overlapping.

2 Simulated Gravitational Collapse

The notion of gravitational collapse in astronomy describes a contracting cloud that gathers enough density to acquire an inward gravitational force. It is observed that, interstellar space is filled with huge clouds of dust and hydrogen gas as shown in Figure 2, in which the particles are usually moving too fast to allow gravity to pull them together. Occasionally a cloud will be compressed enough by external forces to enable gravity to overcome the speed of the particles. The gravitational attraction of the cloud's center begins to pull upon its outer regions and the cloud begins to collapse. The contracting cloud eventually builds up enough pressure and heat to counter the inward pull and the collapse is halted. Although a detailed description of such a collapse is still missing, in astronomy, gravitational collapse could be described as the inward collapse of

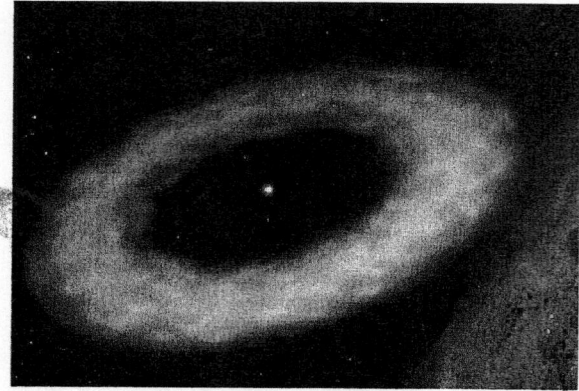

Fig. 2. The beginning of Vega's Solar System, surrounded by a disk of small particles

interstellar matter or stars caused by gravitation, the force of attraction between all objects that tends to pull them together.

We apply a simulated process of gravitational collapse to the samples of each class to effect distribution contraction which reduces overlapping to lower the error probability of the NN classifier. The whole training set is a finite point set of Euclidean N-space. Each class constitutes a subspace of E^N. In each class' subspace, if training instance is considered as particle in cloud of the interstellar space, there are attractions between each instance in the process of gravitational collapse. If this phenomenon is applied in our sample space, for the instances belonging to same class, it seems that they become increasingly compact under attractions in their subspace. For the problem shown in Figure 1, obviously, instances of the same class will be more concentrated after such a process and the class distribution will be contracted. If the collapse halts properly, the process of instances' movement will lead to a tighter class distribution, which eliminates "mislabelled" instances naturally and does good to the NN classifier.

The proposed simulated gravitational collapse is simplified, that is, except universal gravitation between each pair of particles, other forces will be omitted during the collapse. According to Newton's Universal Gravitation Law, attraction(the universal gravitation) exists between any two objects whose mass are m_1, m_2 respectively. When their distance is r, the universal gravitation between two objects is

$$F = G_0 \frac{m_1 m_2}{r^2} \qquad (1)$$

where G_0 is a constant, reflecting the characters about attraction between objects.

To make it applicable to pattern classification, we expand it into E^N. Besides, as shown in Eq.1, $F \propto \frac{1}{r^2}$, which means when $r \to 0$, F will suddenly increase. Under this circumstance, all particles are ignored except the closest one, which is unfair for other instances in pattern classification. So we should smooth the force function, especially when r comes to 0. Moreover, objects' movements caused by the force is a continuous process. We have to simulate it by computer in our algorithm.

Firstly, we simulate the universal gravitation between objects to a "force" between our training instances who have same class label, which is defined as follows.

$$F(x) = \frac{C}{(x+\varepsilon)^2} \qquad (2)$$

where C substitutes $G_0 \cdot m_1 m_2$ as a constant, ε caps the force function curve. In E^N, the direction of force between 2 instances(points in E^N) can be represented by the vector from one point to another. Therefore, the resultant force equals to the vector addition of all forces it suffers.

Under the effects of resultant force, each instance gets an acceleration following the direction of resultant force when time is t. During a very short time Δt, the resultant force of any instance can be seen unique, i.e. the acceleration of instance will not change during Δt. Hence we could consider each Δt as one iterative step in our algorithm. In physics domain, if muzzle velocity doesn't equal to 0, the movement is determined by both muzzle velocity and acceleration. For the sake of simplicity, we could assume that muzzle velocity is 0 at the beginning of each iterative period. Therefore, the displacement of instance coincides with the orientation of resultant forces it suffers.

The simulated gravitational collapse model can be clearly and integrally described in this way: any instance is attracted by all other instances who belong to the same class. We compute all instance's resultant force at first, and then each instance moves a step according to its suffering force. This is called an iterative period. After the migration of all instances, we recompute the force and displacement of each instance, and then start a new iterative period. This process could be terminated when iteration reaches the appointed upper limit.

3 The Simulated Gravitational Collapse Algorithm

The training set of classifier is denoted by $\{A^1, A^2, \cdots, A^m \mid \forall_{k \neq j}, A^k \bigcap A^j = \emptyset\}$, in which A^k is the subset of samples in class ω_k. Nearest prototype classifiers select a subset or generate a new set from each A^k, denoted by A'^k, and then, any unknown sample is classified based on the new training samples by the NN rule.

For each $A_{Nk}^k = \{a_1^k, a_2^k, \cdots, a_{Nk}^k\}$, SGC algorithm generates a new set $A_{Nk}'^k = \{a_1'^k, a_2'^k, \cdots, a_{Nk}'^k\}$ through applying simulated gravitational force on the samples to condense the distribution.

3.1 The Procedure

One iteration of the procedure of the SGC algorithm could be given as follows, for each class ω_k of the whole original training set:

1) For each sample a_i^k, compute the force $\vec{F_{ij}}$ between a_i^k and $a_j^k (1 \leq j \leq N_k$ and $j \neq i)$ using Eq.2, where $a_i^k \in A_{Nk}^k$ and $a_j^k \in A_{Nk}^k$ and obtain the resultant force $\vec{F_i}$ of a_i^k

$$\vec{F_i} = \sum_{j=0}^{Nk} \vec{F_{ij}} \qquad (3)$$

The direction vector v_i of the resultant force for a_i^k is

$$\vec{v_i} = \frac{\vec{F_i}}{\|F_i\|} \qquad (4)$$

2) Let each sample move a small constant distance along this direction

$$a_i^k = a_i^k + S\vec{v_i} \qquad (5)$$

where S is the length of each step

This procedure will repeat until reach the prefixed maximum number of iterations(denoted by N).

The length of step can also be a variable according to its suffering force. Then Eq.5 could be rewrite as follows

$$a_i^k = a_i^k + \frac{\|F_i\|}{\max_i \|F_i\|} S\vec{v_i} \qquad (6)$$

For this case, the length of step $\propto F$ and S is maximum value of step length. In this paper, the length of step is seemed as a constant with value S.

At the end of algorithm, we will gain a new set of generating prototypes, which replaces the original set as the preprocessed training set for the NN classifier. In fact, unlike most other replacement methods for generating new prototypes instead of old ones by merging or update strategy, the migration of the original instances forms "new" prototypes in our model.

3.2 Determination of Parameters

There are 3 parameters should be prefixed in our algorithm. Constant C will be eliminated in step 3, so we can ignore it. ε is a bias used to keep away from the sudden growth when $x \to 0$. At first it must be a positive number. Further more, it should not affect the relationship between F and x^2 except that x is small enough. Therefore, a positive number between 0 and 1 is apt for the value of ε.

The other 2 parameters are S and N, which are dependent on each other. Actually the degree of distribution contraction is determined by the number of iterations and the step length. For finite instances problems, we can eliminate overlaps by a more compact class boundary. On the other hand, for the limitation case, the distribution of one class will converge to their class center, i.e. this class will be represented by its central sample when $N \to \infty$. If so, although the probability density function of each class becomes 0 at their Bayes decision boundary, their representational capacity will seriously degrade for most cases. Besides, if the length of each step is small, it will lead to a large iteration number. If too large, it's illogical for the actual physics model, and at the same time it will bring a frequently surge among some states of class distribution without contraction. Consequently, these 2 parameters should be balanced to control the degree of class distribution's contraction.

3.3 Analysis of The Algorithm

An intrinsic advantage of this algorithm is local contraction rather than total contraction, i.e. it could deal with concave problems as well as convex cases without any special consideration. In fact, simple replacement methods always fails to describe concepts formed by concave decision boundaries[8]. This can be clearly shown in the NFL algorithm. NFL replaces the original points by all the lines between each pair of instances. The concave parts of the decision boundary where sample doesn't exist, are fulfilled by this algorithm. It obviously distorts the distribution, and if other class occupies these concave space originally, the NFL will cause a serious misclassification.

The local contraction of our algorithm can be illustrated as follows. For an appointed instance a, the Euclidean distance from any other two points to a is r_1, r_2 respectively. If $r_1 < r_2$

$$\varepsilon > 0 \to (r_1 + \varepsilon)^2 < (r_2 + \varepsilon)^2 \tag{7}$$

Hence,

$$F_1 = \frac{C}{(r_1 + \varepsilon)^2} > F_2 = \frac{C}{(r_2 + \varepsilon)^2} \tag{8}$$

According to the definition of the value of ε, it can be ignored in most case. We can rewrite Eq.8:

$$F_1 = \frac{C}{r_1^2} > F_2 = \frac{C}{r_2^2} \tag{9}$$

If define $n = \frac{r_2}{r_1}$, we can get $F_2 = \frac{1}{n^2} F_1$. That means when the distance from one point to a is another's n times large, the force it generates is $\frac{1}{n^2}$ of the latter one. When n comes large, the effect of F_2 could be even omitted.

If x is small enough, ε begins to make sense. When r_1, r_2 meet this problem at the same time, although $r_1 < r_2$, actually they are both small enough so that the should be seen "equal" in practice. It can also be demonstrated by the formula

$$F_1 = \frac{C}{\varepsilon^2} > F_2 = \frac{C}{\varepsilon^2} \tag{10}$$

Because r_1, r_2 are small enough, they are left out by the above formula. If r_2 has a normal value, it's obviously that $F_1 \gg F_2$ according to ε's definition.

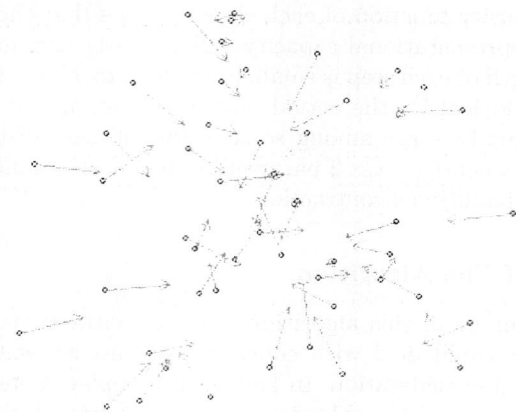

Fig. 3. The movement of a sphere sample set after 2 iterations of SGC algorithm(Arrow and its length stand for direction and distance of the original instance's movement respectively)

From the analysis, we can draw the conclusion that SGC algorithm assign a natural weight for each instance in terms of the distance from them to the fixed one. Briefly speaking, although all instances are computed, only samples near the fixed instance are taken into account, since the force generating by far instances is much smaller than near ones. Therefore, our algorithm will not meet the same problem as other simple replacement methods when dealing with concave distributional cases, due to its locally disposal.

As discussed, the preprocessing will take effects under the NN rule, if the class distribution is contracted aptly. For interior instances, their surrounding instances exist in all directions, according to the locally effect of the force, their suffering forces are often symmetrical. Even though the resultant force doesn't equal to 0, they won't migrate toward one unique direction during iterations and their movement are still bounded in a local region. On the contrary, outliers and border instances face a different situation. Since instances of the same class seldom exist in their outward direction, their migration always toward the majority of instances belonging to same class. Obviously, a more compact class distribution can be generated by the SGC algorithm. This discussion can be demonstrated well in Figure 3.

4 Experimental Results

The simulated gravitational collapse algorithm was tested on 7 real-world data sets. The correct classification rate(CCR) of the test set is defined to be the ratio of the number of correctly classified patterns over the total patterns.

Table 1. CCR Comparison Results on 7 UCI benchmarks

	NN	3-NN	5-NN	NFL	SGC(Iteration 1)	SGC(Iteration 5)
Iris(%)	94.7	94.7	94.7	88.7	**96.0**	**96.0**
Wine	95.5	95.5	97.2	92.7	96.1	**97.8**
Bupa	63.2	65.5	61.4	63.5	60.0	**66.7**
Pima	70.6	73.6	**74.2**	67.1	74.0	71.7
Ionosphere	86.3	84.6	84.9	85.2	**89.2**	87.2
Wdbc	95.1	96.5	97.0	95.3	**97.5**	95.4
Glass	70.1	**72.0**	65.9	66.8	**72.0**	66.4

In this part, we compare NN, k-NN , NFL along with the SGC algorithm on some real-world data sets. All of these algorithms are tested on 7 benchmark data sets from the UCI database[15]. To hold fair, all the instances in each data set are standardized(Normalized) by their means and standard deviations. Leave-one-out estimating strategy is taken in the test.

Parameter ε is assigned 0.1 according to the value of sample. The length of step(S in our algorithm) is an adaptive parameter in this experiment. We record all distance between each instance and its nearest neighbor in each iteration, and then assign the mean value of all nearest distance to S. The number of iterations is assigned 1 and 5 for test respectively.

The result is shown in Table 1. For all of 7 benchmark data sets, the prototypes generated by the SGC algorithm perform better than the original set under the NN rule. For most case, the SGC algorithm achieves the highest classification accuracy, even outperform the k-NN classifier.

5 Conclusion

We have proposed in this paper a novel prototype generating technique for the NN classifier. The performance of the NN classifier using the prototypes generated by the SGC algorithm was evaluated on several data set. The experimental results show that the SGC algorithm outperforms the NN classifier as well as k-NN classifier using the original data sets. The proposed SGC has been inspired by a fundamental process in nature and has shown promising results. This is another indication that we can learn a lot from nature.

Acknowledgement

The research work presented in this paper is supported by National Natural Science Foundation of China, project No.60275010; Science and Technology Commission of Shanghai Municipality, project No. 04JC14014; and National Grand Fundamental Research Program of China, project No. 2001CB309401.

References

1. Bezdek JC, Kuncheva LI, Nearest prototype classifier designs: An experimental study. International Journal of Intelligent Systems 16(12), 1445-1473, 2000.
2. Hamamoto Y, Uchimura S, Tomita S, A bootstrap technique for nearest neighbor classifier design. IEEE Transactions on Pattern Analysis and Machine Intelligence 19(1), 73-79, 1997.
3. P.A.Devijver and J.Kittler, Pattern Recognition. A Statistical Approach. Englewood Cliffs, NJ: Prentice-Hall, 1982.
4. Wilson, Dennis L, Asymptotic Properties of Nearest Neighbor Rules Using Edited Data. IEEE Transactions on Systems, Man, and Cybernetics, 2(3), 403-411, 1972.
5. Francesc J. Ferri, J. V. Albert, Enrique Vidal, Considerations about sample-size sensitivity of a family of edited nearest-neighbor rules. IEEE Transactions on Systems, Man, and Cybernetics, Part B 29(5), 667-672, 1999.
6. T. Kohonen, The Self-Oragnization Map. Proceding of IEEE, 78(9), 1464-1480, 1990.
7. Lavigna A, Nonparametric classification using learning vector quantization. Ph.D. Thesis, University of Maryland, 1990.
8. Wai Lam, Chi-Kin Keung, Danyu Liu, Discovering Useful Concept Prototypes for Classification Based on Filtering and Abstraction. IEEE Transactions on Pattern Analysis and Machine Intelligence, 24(8), 1075-1090 ,2002.
9. P.E.Hart, The Condensed Nearest Neighbor Rule. IEEE Transactions on Information Theory, 14, 515-516, 1968.
10. G.W.Gates, The Reduced Nearest Neighbor Rule. IEEE Transactions on Information Theory, 18, 431-433, 1972.
11. C.L.Chang, Finding Prototypes for Nearest Neighbor Classifiers. IEEE Transactions on Computers, 23(11), 1179-1184, 1974.
12. G.L.Hitter, H.B.Woodruff, S.R.Lowry and T.L.Isenhour, An algorithm for a selective nearest neighbor rule, IEEE Transaction on Information Theory, 21, 665-669,1976.
13. Stan Z. Li and Juwei Lu, Face Recognition Using the Nearest Feature Line Method. IEEE Transactions on Neural Network, 10(2), 439-443, 1999.
14. T.M.Cover, P.E.Hart, Nearest Neighbor Pattern Classification. IEEE Transaction on Information Theory, 13(1), 21-27,1967
15. P.M.Murphy, D.W.Aha, UCI Repository of Machine Learning Database, University of California, Irvine, 1994.

Evolutionary Computation and Rough Set-Based Hybrid Approach to Rule Generation

Lin Shang[1], Qiong Wan[1], Zhi-Hong Zhao[2], and Shi-Fu Chen[1]

[1] National Laboratory for Novel Software Technology,
Nanjing University, Nanjing 210093, P.R. China
{shanglin, chensf}@nju.edu.cn, wanqiong@ai.nju.edu.cn
[2] Software Institute,
Nanjing University, Nanjing 210093, P.R. China
{zhaozh}@software.nju.edu.cn

Abstract. This paper presents the rule generation method based on evolutionary computation and rough set, which integrates the procedure of discretization and reduction using information entropy-based uncertainty measures and evolutionary computation. Based on the definitions of certain rules and approximate certain rules, the paper focuses on the reduction by meanings of evolutionary computation. Experimental results reveal that the proposed method leads to better classification quality and smaller number of decision rules comparing with other methods.

1 Introduction

We are considering the algorithm of generation for "if...then..." decision rules discovered from data. Various rough set-based rule induction methods have been applied to knowledge discovery in databases [1, 2, 3, 4]. The results show that the rough set methods are powerful and that some important knowledge has been extracted. For rule generation, reducts play important roles. Rough set-based knowledge acquisition is primarily achieved by the reduction with the invariability of dependency between the decision attributes and the conditional attributes. Derived from the reduction, the decision rules are generated, where attributes values are for the "if" conditions, and the decision attribute values are for the "then" decisions.

The present methods for reduction are mainly applicable to information systems with discrete values. For the continuous-valued attributes reduction, the common way is to get discrete intervals of values first and then transform the continuous values into the discrete ones. In such discretization, some information will be lost, which may influence the reduction. In this paper, we present a new approach for reduction of continuous-valued attributes, which integrates the procedure of discretization and reduction using information entropy-based uncertainty measures and evolutionary computation. Experimental results show that the approach is effective to generate rules with the high classification quality for continuous-valued attributes, and can achieve higher precisions comparing with the results computed by the RSES [5].

The paper begins with some notations of rough set [6]. We emphasize on the certain rules and approximate certain rules definitions. Then, we present the evolutionary algorithm in detail. The next section describes the experiments and results on UCI repository datasets and comparison results with the RSES system. The last is the conclusion and future works.

2 Basic Notions

Rough set is a powerful tool to deal with imprecise or vague concepts [6]. In this paper, we only introduce some relevant basic notations.

2.1 Decision Rules [7]

Let $S=(U, A)$ be an information system, where U and A are finite, non-empty sets called the universe and the set of attributes, respectively. If in the set A two disjoint classes of attributes, called condition and decision attributes, are distinguished, then the system is called a decision table and is denoted by $S = (U, C \cup D)$, where C and D are sets of condition and decision attributes, respectively. With every subset of attributes, one can associate a formal language of formulas L defined in a standard way and called the decision language.

Definition 1. A decision rule induced from S and expressed in L is an implication $\phi \rightarrow \psi$, read "if ϕ, then ψ", where ϕ and ψ are condition and decision formulas in L, respectively.

2.2 Information View of Rough Set [8]

The definition of reduct of a relatively consistent decision table in the information view is equivalent to its definition in the algebra view. In the paper, information entropy-based uncertainty measures are employed in the evolutionary algorithm for rule generation. Here we give some basic notions about the information view of rough set.

Definition 2. Given an information system $S = (U, C \cup D)$. The entropy of attribute subset $B \subseteq C$ is defined as $H(B) = -\sum_{i=1}^{n} p(X_i) \log(p(X_i))$,

$X_i \in U/IND(B) = \{X_1, X_2, ...X_n\}, (i=1,...,n)$, where $p(X_i) = \dfrac{|X_i|}{|U|}$

Definition 3. Given an information system $S = (U, C \cup D)$, the conditional entropy of D $(U/IND(D) = \{Y_1, Y_2, ..., Y_m\})$ given $B \subseteq C$ $(U/IND(B) = \{X_1, X_2, ..., X_n\})$ is defined as

$$H(D|B) = -\sum_{i=1}^{n} p(X_i) \sum_{j=1}^{m} p(Y_j | X_i) \log(p(Y_j | X_i)),$$

where $p(Y_j | X_i) = |Y_j \cap X_i|/|X_i|, i=1,2,...,n, j=1,2,...,m$.

From two-part version of MDL Principle [9], the best point to get the attributes subset in a decision information system is the one which minimizes the sum $H(B) + H(D|B)$. Some attempts have been made to define the appropriate conditional entropy as the criteria for certain heuristic methods [10,11].

As denoted in Definition 3, the conditional entropy is counted by its crisp inconsistent part, where the noise or the boundary objects are neglected. In this paper, we present the evolutionary algorithm, where the fitness function is based on the sum of new defined $H(B)$ and the $H(D|B)$. In the next section we will give the redefinition of $H(B)$ and $H(D|B)$.

3 Redefinition of Entropy and Conditional Entropy

First the definitions of certain rules and approximate certain rules are presented.

Definition 4. Given a decision table $S = (U, C \cup \{d\})$, where C and $\{d\}$ are sets of condition and decision attributes. Assume that $U / IND(C) \models m$ and the set of decision values is finite. The j-th decision class is a set of objects $Y_j = \{o \in U \mid d(o) = d_j\}$, where d_j is the j-th decision value taken from decision value set $V_d = \{d_1, ..., d_k\}$, here k is the number of decision values. For any $X_i \in U / IND(C) (i = 1, ..., m)$, $X_i \rightarrow d_j$ are decision rules. We say that

(1) $X_i \rightarrow d_j$ are certain rules iff
$X_i \in U / IND(C) \& |X_i| \neq 0 \& \forall k (k \neq j \& 1 \leq k \leq d \& Y_k \cap X_i = \Phi)$

(2) $X_i \rightarrow d_j$ are β - approximate certain rules iff

$$X_i \in U / IND(C) \& |X_i| \neq 0 \& \forall k (k \neq j \& \beta * \sum_{k=1}^{d} |Y_k \cap X_i| \leq |Y_j \cap X_i| k \sum_{k=1}^{d} |Y_k \cap X_i|)$$

$(j = 1, ..., d)$, $0.5 < \beta < 1$

(3) Otherwise, $X_i \rightarrow d_j$ are uncertain rules.

From the definition of certain rules and uncertain rules shown above, the entropy $H'(B)$ and the conditional entropy $H'(D|B)$ for X_i ($X_i \in U / IND(C)$) are defined as follows:

Definition 5.

(1) If $X_i \rightarrow d_j$ are certain rules, then

$H_i'(B) = -p(X_i) \log(p(X_i))$

$H_i'(D|B) = 0$

(2) If $X_i \rightarrow d_j$ are β-approximate certain rules, then

$$H_i'(B) = -\frac{\max_{j=1,...,k}(|X_i \cap Y_j|)}{|U|} * \log \frac{\max_{j=1,...,k}(|X_i \cap Y_j|)}{|U|} - \frac{|X_i| - \max_{j=1,...,k}(|X_i \cap Y_j|)}{|U|} * \log \frac{1}{|U|}$$

$$H_i'(D|B) = -\frac{|X_i| - \max_{j=1,...,k}(|X_i \cap Y_j|)}{|U|} * \log \frac{1}{|X_i| - \max_{j=1,...,k}(|X_i \cap Y_j|)}$$

(3) If $X_i \to d_j$ are uncertain rules, then

$$H_i^{'}(B) = -\frac{|X_i|}{|U|} * \log\frac{1}{|U|}$$

$$H_i^{'}(D|B) = -\frac{|X_i|}{|U|} * \log\frac{1}{|X_i|}$$

Computed by the Definition 5, the entropy $H(B)$ and $H(D|B)$ are the sum of each $H^{'}(B)$ and $H^{'}(D|B)$, which are defined as follows:

$$H(B) = \sum_{i=1}^{m} H_i^{'}(B) \qquad (1)$$

$$H(D|B) = \sum_{i=1}^{m} H_i^{'}(D|B) \qquad (2)$$

The algorithm presented in the paper is based on the $H(B)$ and $H(D|B)$ defined as formula (1) and (2), which are employed as the uncertainty measurements.

4 Evolutionary Computation and Rough Set-Based Algorithm for Rule Generation

In this section, we propose the method for rule generation based on the evolutionary computation and rough set reduction.

By analogy to natural evolution, the solution candidates are called *individuals* and the set of solution candidates is called the *population*. Each individual represents a possible solution, i.e., a decision vector, to the problem at hand. For the continuous-valued attributes, we encode the cuts in the genes of individuals. For $V_a = [l_a, r_a] \subset R$, where $a \in A$ (attributes set) and R is set of real, any cuts c_i^a are belonging to c_a, where $c_a = \{c_0^a, c_1^a, c_2^a, c_3^a, ..., c_k^a, c_{k+1}^a\}$ and $l_a = c_0^a < c_1^a < c_2^a < \cdots < c_{k_a}^a < c_{k_a+1}^a = r_a$. Given $V_a = [l_a, r_a] = \{v_1^a, v_2^a, ..., v_n^a\} = \{a(x): x \in U\}$, here $l_a = v_1^a < v_2^a < ... < v_n^a = r_a$ and n is objects number. The candidate cuts set $P_a = \{[c_0^a, c_1^a), [c_1^a, c_2^a), \cdots, [c_{k_a}^a, c_{k_a+1}^a)\}$, where $c_i^a = \frac{v_{i-1}^a + v_i^a}{2} (i = 1...k_a)$.

Here in the method, we encode individuals in two segments. The genes for the first segment are attributes bits, where amount of bits is equal to attributes number and each bit denotes the selection of the corresponding attribute. The second segment is encoded for cuts genes, where genes k$_{im1}$, k$_{im2}$, ...k$_{imi}$ in the second segment denote the selection of cuts for attribute i. The candidate cuts set for the attributes is P_a described above. Binary codes are employed in the representation of bits, in which value '1' means being-selected and '0' means no selection.

A new individual is created by mutation, which is implemented on the two segments of genes respectively. When changing the bits from one generation to next generation, the random number r (0<r<1) for each bit is generated, which is the criteria for modification. If $r >= \theta_a$, θ_a is the mutation threshold (0< θ_a <1), the bit is to be changed from '0' to '1' or from '1' to '0'. If $r<\theta_a$, the mutation will not be activated. The two segments of genes are interrelated. If the bit in attributes segment is set to '1', then corresponding cuts will be changed by mutation with the probability $P_b (0 < P_b < 1)$, whereas the bit in attribute segment will be set to '0' if the corresponding bits in second segment all go to '0'.

The probability of survival of any individual is determined by its fitness. In the paper, the fitness function we use is:

$$H = \alpha * (1 - \frac{H(B)}{\log(|U|)}) + (1-\alpha) * (1 - \frac{H(D|B)}{\log(|U|)}) \quad (3)$$

where $0 \le \alpha \le 1$ and $H(B)$ and $H(D|B)$ are defined as formula (1) and (2).

The description of basic steps of the proposed algorithm is given as follows, where some parameters are used: m denotes the number of attributes, d denotes decision classes number, n denotes the initial solutions in a population, s denotes number of individuals in the next generation by mutation from one solution, $maxgen$ is maximum of generations, $maxfitness$ is threshold of fitness, $cycle$ is variable of evolutionary generation.

Algorithm. Evolutionary Computation and Rough Set-Based Algorithm For Rule Generation
Input. Decision table $S = (U, C \cup D)$, where U is a finite, non-empty set of objects(universe), C is a set of condition attributes and D is set of decision attributes.
Output. Decision Rules

Step 1 initial($m,d,n,s,maxgen,maxfitness,cycle$) //initialization
Step 2 for i=1 to m do   // generate candidate cuts set
        SortSamples( );
        CUT(i,:)= SelectCuts( );
     end
Step 3 CalculateCutImportance( ) //calculate the importance of cuts
Step 4 InitialChromosome(n)   //generate the initial population
Step 5.MutationChromosome(n,s) //mutation
Step 6 DecodeChromosomeToDecisionTable( )   //Decode for the $n*(1+s)$ individuals
                                              //in the filial generation and the parent
                                              //generation
Step 7 for i=1 to $n(s+1)$ do
        efitness(i)=CalculateFitness(i)   //calculate the fitness by formula (3)
     end;
Step 8 fitness=max(efitness);
Step 9 chromosome=ChooseBestChromosome( )   // $(1+s)$-ES evolutionary strategy
Step 10 cycle=cycle+1;
Step 11 if cycle<maxgen & fitness<maxfitness
            goto step 5
        else
            goto step 12
Step 12 rules=GetRulesFromTheBestChromosome( ) //get the rules form the genes
                                               // for the finial solution
        finalRules=simplify(rules)   // simplify the rules

5 Experiments and Results

We did a series of experiments with two UCI machine learning datasets *Iris* and *Thyroid-disease* to get the decision rules [13]. Table 1 gives the summary of these two data sets.

Table 1. Summary of data sets

Data set	Number of records	Number of conditional attributes	Number of decision classes
Iris	150	4	3
Thyroid-disease	215	5	3

Table 2. Results on *Iris* data set

	$\beta = 0.8$			$\beta = 0.9$			$\beta = 1.0$		
No. of Cuts	reduct	No. of decision rules	Precision (%)	No. of Cuts	reduct	No. of decision rules	Precision (%)	No. of Cuts	reduct	No. of decision rules	Precision (%)
1	3	a3	3	93.33	6	a3,a4	5	96.67	10	a3,a4	7	91.67
2	3	a4	3	96.67	4	a3	3	93.33	8	a3,a4	6	91.67
3	2	a4	3	96.67	6	a3,a4	4	98.33	8	a3,a4	7	96.67
4	6	a3,a4	4	98.33	10	a3,a4	7	96.67	10	a3,a4	6	96.67
5	3	a4	4	95	9	a3,a4	6	96.67	6	a3,a4	6	96.67
average				96				96.33				94.67

Table 3. Results on *Thyroid-disease* data set

	$\beta = 0.8$			$\beta = 0.9$			$\beta = 1.0$		
No. of Cuts	reduct	No. of decision rules	Precision (%)	No. of Cuts	reduct	No. of decision rules	Precision (%)	No. of Cuts	reduct	No. of decision rules	Precision (%)
1	5	a2,a5	4	94.12	9	a2,a5	6	91.76	15	a1,a2,a3,a5	14	90.59
2	5	a2,a4,a5	4	91.76	11	a2,a3,a5	8	92.94	13	a1,a2,a3,a5	12	90.59
3	9	a2,a4,a5	8	96.47	10	a2,a5	6	92.94	14	a2,a3,a5	12	90.59
4	5	a2,a5	5	91.76	9	a2,a5	7	91.76	14	a1,a2,a4,a5	11	92.94
5	5	a2,a5	4	95.29	8	a2,a5	6	90.59	14	a1,a2,a4,a5	9	90.59
average				93.88				91.99				91.06

For the *Iris* data set, we randomly use 90 instances as the training set and others as the testing set, and for the data set *Thyroid-disease*, we randomly select 130 instances as training set. All tests are made five times.

Table 4. Comparison with methods in RSES system

	Methods	*Iris*		*Thyroid-disease*	
		Rules number	Testing precision(%)	Rules number	Testing Precision(%)
R S E S	Local Discretization+Exhaustive Algorithm	8.2	96.33	11.8	92.00
	Local Discritization+LEM2 Algorithm	5.0	93.33	7.2	91.76
	Global Discretization+Exhaustive Algorithm	7.0	91.33	11.2	91.76
	Global Discretization+Genetic Algorithm	6.8	93.33	11.0	91.76
	Global Discretization+LEM2 Algorithm	5.0	91.67	7.0	90.82
	Proposed method	5.0	96.33	5.0	93.88

All Parameters have been tuned experimentally, which are set as $n=4$, $s=5$, $\theta_a = 0.6$~0.7, $\alpha = 0.05$~0.15. Now the results are summarized in Table 2 and Table 3.

Results in Table 2 and Table 3 show the reducts and generated decision rules numbers along with the changed value of β described in section 3. From the definition, β is set for the tolerance of noise and for the boundary uncertainty measurement, which has been tuned experimentally. Setting greater value of β will keep out the appropriate rules, whereas lower value will get more faulty rules. It is noteworthy that how β works in different data sets. It can be seen from table 2 of *Iris* data set that 0.9 is best value of β comparing with three settings ($\beta = 0.8$, $\beta = 0.9$, $\beta = 1.0$), with which the testing precision is highest. From table 3 of *thyroid-disease* data set we can see that $\beta = 0.8$ is the appropriate assignment. Experimental results reveal that assignment of β keeps close relation with the distribution of data sets.

Some experiments are done to compare with other methods. In the paper, we use *Rough Set Exploration System*2.2 [5] to get the average rules numbers and precisions by five times of experiments. Results are presented in Table 4, in which the listed methods in the left column are embedded in system RSES except the last row for our proposed method.

Results shown above reveal that rules generated by the proposed method are fewer than the listed RSES methods, and the precision is higher, which indicates that it is effective to generate decision rules employing our proposed method and to get higher classification quality.

6 Remarks

The work presented in the paper shows that it is possible to generate decision rules with evolutionary computation and rough set-based hybrid approach. Different from other methods, the algorithm integrates procedure of discretization and reduction using information entropy-based uncertainty measures and evolutionary computation. Experimental results show that the proposed method leads to better classification quality and smaller number of decision rules. Unfortunately, it takes time to implement the evolutionary computation and tune the parameters. Once tuned and trained, the method exhibits excellent classification quality. Future work will emphasize on the optimization of fitness function and tuning of parameters.

Acknowledgements. This work is supported by the National Natural Science Foundation of China under Grant No.60273033 and the Natural Science Foundation of Jiangsu Province of China under Grant No.BK2004079.

References

1. Polkowski, L., Skowron, A. (Ed.): Rough Sets and Knowledge discovery 1, 2, Physica Verlag, Heidelberg (1998)
2. Tsumoto, S.: Automated Discovery of Positive and Negative Knowledge in Clinical Databases based on Rough Set Model. IEEE EMB Magazine (2000) 56-62
3. Yao, J. T., Yao, Y. Y.: Induction of Classification Rules by Granular Computing. In: Proceedings of the Third International Conference, RSCTC 2002, Malvern, USA, LNAI 2475 (2002) 331-338
4. Sankar, K. P., Sushmita, M., Pabitra, M.L: Rough-Fuzzy MLP: Modular Evolution, Rule Generation, and Evaluation. IEEE Trans. Knowledge and Data Engineering 15 (2003) 14-25
5. RSES. Rough Set Exploration System ver. 2.1.1 Institute of Mathematics, Warsaw University, Poland (2004) http://logic.mimuw.edu.pl/~rses
6. Pawlak, Z.: Rough Sets. Theoretical Aspects of Reasoning about Data. Dordrecht: Kluwer Acasemic Publisher (1991)
7. Salvatore, G., Zdzislaw, P., Roman, S.: Generalized Decision Algorithms, Rough Inference Rules, and Flow Graphs. In: Proceedings of the Third International Conference, RSCTC 2002, Malvern, USA,LNAI 2475 (2002) 93-104
8. Wang, G.Y.: Algebra View and Information View of Rough Sets Theory, in Data Miming and Knowledge Discovery: Theory, Tools, and Technology III, Belur V. Dasarathy, Editor, Proceedings of SPIE Vol. 4384(2001) 200-207
9. Rissanen, J.: Minimum-Discription-Length Principle. In: S Kotz,N L Johnson (Eds).: Encyclopedia of Statistical Science[C]. New York: Wiley (1985) 523-527
10. GrÄunwald, P., Myung, P.: Advances in Minimum Description Length: Theory and Applications. MIT Press (2004)
11. Ivo, D., Guncher, G.: Uncertainty Measures of Rough Set Prediction. Artificial Intelligence 106 (1998) 109-137
12. HAN, B., WU, T.-J., YANG, M.-H.: Reduct Algorithm Based on Information Entropy and Rough Set Theory. Journal of Circuits and Systems, Vol.7, No.2 (2002) 96-100
13. Blake, C. L., Merz, C. J.: UCI Repository of Machine Learning Databases (1998) http://www.ics.uci.edu/~mlearn/MLRepository.html.

Assessing the Performance of Several Fitness Functions in a Genetic Algorithm for Nonlinear Separation of Sources

F. Rojas[1], C.G. Puntonet[1], J.M. Górriz[2], and O. Valenzuela[3]

[1] Dpt. Arquitectura y Tecnología de Computadores. E.T.S.I.Informática,
University of Granada, 18071, Spain
frojas@atc.ugr.es, http://atc.ugr.es
[2] Dpt. Teoría de la Señal, Telemática y Comunicaciones. University of Granada
[3] Dpt. Matemática Aplicada. University of Granada

Abstract. In this contribution, we propose and analyze three evaluation functions (contrast functions in Independent Component Analysis terminology) for the use in a genetic algorithm (PNL-GABSS, Post-NonLinear Genetic Algorithm for Blind Source Separation) which solves source separation in nonlinear mixtures, assuming the post-nonlinear mixture model. Blind source separation refers to the problem of recovering a set of unknown sources from another set of mixtures directly observable and little more information about the way they were mixed. Assuming statistical independence as the assumption to obtain the original sources we can apply ICA (Independent Component Analysis) as the technique to recover the signals. In order to analyze in practice the performance of the chosen fitness functions in our proposed algorithm, we applied ANOVA (Analysis of Variance) to the results, showing the validity of the three approaches.

1 Blind Source Separation and Independent Component Analysis

The guiding principle for ICA is statistical independence, meaning that the value of any of the components gives no information on the values of the other components. This method differs from other statistical approaches such as principal component analysis (PCA) and factor analysis precisely in the fact that is not a correlation-based transformation, but also reduces higher-order statistical dependencies. The extensive use of ICA as the statistical technique for solving blind source separation (BSS), may have lead in some situations to the erroneous utilization of both concepts as equivalent. In any case, ICA is just the technique which in certain situations can be sufficient to solve a given problem, that of blind source separation. In fact, statistical independence insures separation of sources in linear mixtures, up to the known indeterminacies of scale and permutation.

In linear ICA, which is the most extensively studied case, the transformation F is restricted to being linear. Nonlinear ICA allows F to be nonlinear. If we generalize to the situation in which mixtures are the result of an unknown transformation (linear or not) of the sources, independence alone is not a sufficient condition in order to accomplish blind source separation successfully. Indeed, in [1] it is formally demonstrated how for nonlinear mixtures, an infinity of mutually independent solutions can be found that have nothing to do with the unknown sources. Thus, in order to successfully separate the observed signals into a wave-preserving estimation of the sources, we need additional information about either the sources or the mixing process.

Therefore nonlinear ICA, is rather unconstrained, and normally demands additional information to make the estimations coincide with the estimations. Applying the post-nonlinear constraint, other authors (Taleb and Jutten [2], Rojas et al. [3], [4]) proposed several contrast functions which approximate the mutual information of the estimated components. Assuming the post-nonlimear model, the indeterminacies are the same as for the basic linear instantaneous mixing model: invertible scalings and permutations. The mixture model can be described by the following equation:

$$\mathbf{x(t)} = \mathbf{f}(A \cdot \mathbf{s(t)}). \tag{1}$$

We propose in this contribution the use of a genetic algorithm to solve post-nonlinear blind source separation. We also present three different evaluation functions that asses each candidate solution in distinct versions of the genetic algorithm. Neural network approaches have the drawback of possibly being trapped into near-optimal solutions in situations where the search space presents many local minima. As an alternative, genetic algorithms deal simultaneously with multiple solutions, not a single solution, and also include random elements, which help to avoid getting trapped into sub-optimal solutions.

Starting from the observed mixtures ($\mathbf{x}$), our algorithm will The unmixing stage, which will be performed by the algorithm here proposed is expressed by equation 2:

$$\mathbf{y(t)} = W \cdot \mathbf{g(x(t))}. \tag{2}$$

2 PNL-GABSS: Genetic Algorithm for Post-Nonlinear Blind Source Separation

The proposed algorithm will be based on the estimation of mutual information, value which cancels out when the signals involved are independent. Mutual information between the elements of a multidimensional variable $\mathbf{y}$ is defined as:

$$I(y_1, y_2, ..., y_n) = \sum_{i=1}^{n} H(y_i) - H(y_1, y_2, ..., y_n). \tag{3}$$

In order to exactly compute mutual information, we need also to calculate entropies, which likewise require to know the analytical expression of the probability density function (PDF) which is generally not available in practical applications of speech processing. Thus, we propose several evaluation functions (or contrast function in BSS terminology) that approximate mutual information. A *contrast function*, $\Psi(\cdot)$, is any non-linear function which is invariant to permutation and scaling matrices, and attains its minimum value in correspondence of the mutual independence among the output components.

Independently of the selected fitness or contrast function, the operation of the basic genetic algorithm is invariant, needing the following features to be completely characterized:

1. Encoding Scheme. The genes will represent the coefficients of the odd polynomials which approximate the family of nonlinearities g (see equation 2). The linear matrix will be approximated by a well-known method such as JADE [5].
2. Initialization Procedure. Both polynomial and matrix coefficients which form part of the chromosome are randomly initialized.
3. Fitness Function. The key point in the performance of a GA is the definition of the fitness function. In this case, the fitness function that we want maximize will be precisely the inverse of the approximation of mutual information given in equation 3:

$$Fitness(y) = \frac{1}{I(y)} = \frac{1}{\sum_{i=1}^{p} H(y_i) - H(y_1, y_2, ..., y_p)} \qquad (4)$$

4. Genetic Operators. Typical crossover and mutation operators will be used for the manipulation of the current population in each iteration of the GA. The

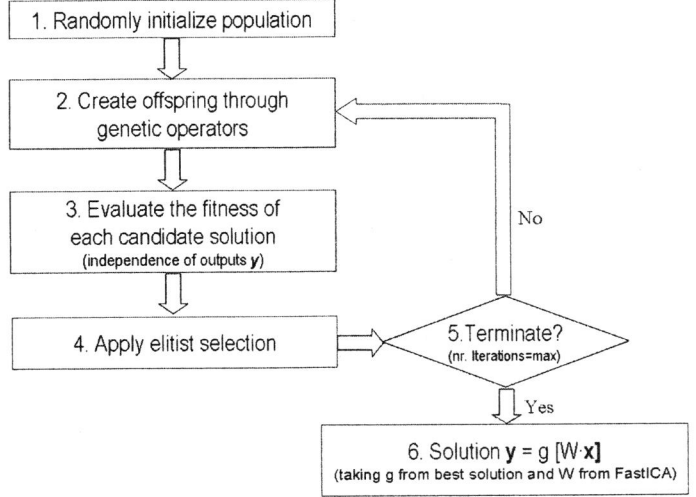

Fig. 1. Flow chart of the genetic algorithm for source separation of post-nonlinear mixtures

crossover operator is "Simple One-point Crossover". The mutation operator ("Non-Uniform Mutation" [6]), is more favorable to exploration in the early stages of the algorithm, while exploitation takes more importance when the solution given by the GA is closer to the optimal.
5. Parameter Set. Population size, number of generations, probability of mutation and crossover and other parameters relative to the genetic algorithm operation were chosen depending on the characteristics of the mixing problem.

The flow chart for the genetic algorithm that solves blind source separation in post-nonlinear mixtures is shown in Figure 1.

3 Proposed Fitness Functions

In order to calculate the degree of independence of a set of variables precisely it is necessary to have the mathematical expression of their probability density functions. Actually, since that information is not typically available, it is usual to utilize approaches of independence measures. In this research work, several functions have been evaluated, most of them based on the calculation of approaches of the mutual information or measures derived from it. One of the great advantages of genetic algorithms is its flexibility in the use of evaluation functions.

3.1 Cross-Cumulants Minimization

It is possible to build a fitness function based on the simultaneous minimization of several cumulants, cross-cumulants 2-2, 3-1 and 1-3 to be precise. We can also add some penalization factors to the fitness functions, promoting solutions whose estimations are closed to zero mean and unit variance (C_1 and C_2, respectively).

$$\Psi_{CrossCumulants}(y_i, y_j) = cum_{22}(y_i, y_j) + \\ + cum_{31}(y_i, y_j) + cum_{13}(y_i, y_j) + \alpha C_1 + \beta C_2 \quad (5)$$

where α and β are weights (real numbers) for the penalization functions.

Unfortunately, this simple approach is only valid for separating two signals. Although it can be extended to three or more computing the fitness function by pairs, the computational cost would exponentially increase with the number of mixtures.

3.2 PDF Direct Approximation Using Histograms

We propose to approximate densities through the discretization of the estimated signals building histograms and then calculate their joint and marginal entropies. In this way, we define a number of bins m that covers the selected estimation space and then we calculate how many points of the signal fall in each of the bins (B_i $i = 1, ..., m$). Finally, we easily approximate marginal entropies using the following formula:

$$H(y) = -\sum_{i=1}^{n} p(y_i) \log_2 p(y_i) \approx -\sum_{j=1}^{m} \frac{Card(B_j(y))}{n} \log_2 \frac{Card(B_j(y))}{n} \quad (6)$$

where $Card(B)$ denotes cardinality of set B, n is the number of points of estimation y, and B_j is the set of points which fall in the jth bin.

The same method can be applied for computing the joint entropies of all the estimated signals:

$$H(y_1, ..., y_p) = \sum_{i=1}^{p} H(y_i | y_{i-1}, ..., y_1) \approx$$

$$\approx -\sum_{i_1=1}^{m} \sum_{i_2=1}^{m} \cdots \sum_{i_n=1}^{m} \frac{\#B_{i_1 i_2 ... i_p}(y)}{n} \log_2 \frac{\#B_{i_1 i_2 ... i_p}(y)}{n}. \quad (7)$$

where p is the number of components which need to be approximated.

Therefore, substituting entropies in equation 3 by approximations of equation 6 and 7, we obtain a fitness function which will reach its minimum value when the estimations are independent.

3.3 Gram-Charlier Expansion for Mutual Information Approximation

A widely applied method for mutual information approximation is the application of the Gram-Charlier expansion, which only needs some moments of y_i as suggested by Amari et al.[7] to express each marginal entropy of y as:

$$H(y_i) \approx \frac{\log(2\pi e)}{2} - \frac{(k_3^i)^2}{2 \cdot 3!} - \frac{(k_4^i)^2}{2 \cdot 4!} + \frac{3}{8} (k_3^i)^2 k_4^i + \frac{1}{16} (k_4^i)^3 \quad (8)$$

where $k_3^i = m_3^i$, and $k_4^i = m_4^i - 3$.

Substituting equation 8 in the calculation of mutual information (equation 3), we obtain a new fitness function:

$$\text{eval}_{IM-GramCharlier}(\mathbf{g})^{-1} = \Psi_{IM-GramCharlier}(\mathbf{y})$$

$$= \sum_{i=1}^{n} \left[\frac{\log(2\pi e)}{2} - \frac{(k_3^i)^2}{2 \cdot 3!} - \frac{(k_4^i)^2}{2 \cdot 4!} + \frac{3}{8} (k_3^i)^2 k_4^i + \frac{1}{16} (k_4^i)^3 \right] -$$

$$- \log |\det(\mathbf{W})| - \sum_{i=1}^{n} E \left[\log \left| \sum_{k=1}^{P} (2k-1) p_{ik} x_i^{2k-2} \right| \right] \quad (9)$$

The approximation of entropy in equation 8 is only valid for uncorrelated random variables, being necessary to preprocess the mixed signals (*prewhitening*) before estimating their mutual information. Whitening or sphering of a mixture of signals consists of filtering the signals so that their covariances are zero (uncorrelatedness), their means are zero, and their variances equal unity.

4 Analysis of Variance of the Results

Once the algorithm has been proposed, we will test its robustness and computational load using a well-known statistical tool as the Analysis of Variance (ANOVA). ANOVA is a statistical method that yields values that can be tested to determine whether a significant relation exists between variables of interest [8].

In our case, we will use ANOVA in order to analyze the estimations in terms of their similarity to the original sources and testing which variables (factors) affect more to the performance of the proposed algorithm. It will be of special interest the influence of the fitness function chosen, so that we can determine which one works better in practice. Table 1 shows the factors defined for the analysis of variance and their corresponding levels (using ANOVA terminology). We will also apply ANOVA in order to test which factors affect more to the computational time of the PNL-GABSS algorithm. Therefore, the response variables will be the crosstalk between the sources and the estimations (measured in decibels) and the time of execution of the algorithm.

Table 1. Chosen factors for the ANOVA

Factor	Levels of the chosen factors			
	Level 1	Level 2	Level 3	Level 4
Fitness Function	$\Psi_{IM-GramCharlier}$	$\Psi_{Histograms}$	$\Psi_{CrossCumulants}$	
Nr. Samples	2000	4000	8000	
Population Size	10	20	30	40
Generations number	10	20	40	80
Crossover probability	0.05	0.2	0.5	
Mutation probability	0.01	0.1	0.3	
Selection probability	0.01	0.1	0.2	

The algorithm is run over a mixture of signals generated after applying the following linear and non-linear transformation to a set of two voice signals of 10.165 samples each one (see mixtures in figure 2):

$$\mathbf{A} = \begin{bmatrix} 0.4891 & -0.1202 \\ -0.4641 & 0.8668 \end{bmatrix}, \quad \mathbf{F} = \begin{bmatrix} \tanh(x) \\ \tanh(x/2) \end{bmatrix} \quad (10)$$

Once the results after applying the PNL-GABSS algorithm were obtained, we performed an ANOVA with the output variable as the average crosstalk between estimations and the sources and another ANOVA for the execution time (CPU

Table 2. Multiple range table for the factor "Fitness Function" in the ANOVA (response variable: crosstalk)

Fitness Func.	Nr. of runs	Avg. Crosstalk	Homogenous Group
$\Psi_{Histograms}$	1296	-11.399 dB	B
$\Psi_{CrossCumulants}$	1296	-10.201 dB	C
$\Psi_{IM-GramCharlier}$	1296	-15.638 dB	A

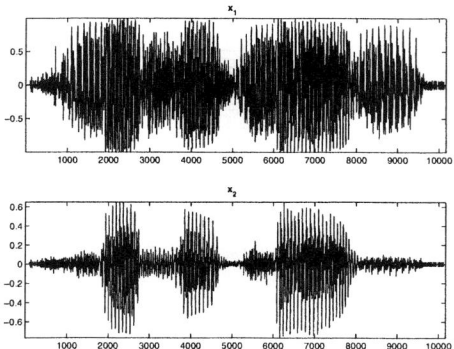

Fig. 2. Post-nonlinear mixtures as the inputs for the PNL-GABSS algorithm

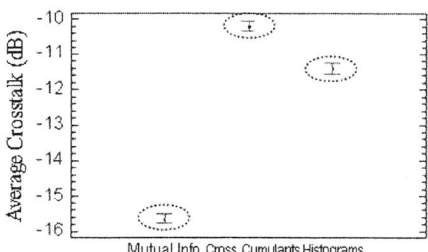

Fig. 3. Homogenous groups for each fitness function for the average crosstalk

time). Table 2 and Figure 3 show the different results obtained depending on the fitness function chosen for the genetic algorithm.

Table 3. Multiple range table for the factor "Number of samples in the signals" in the ANOVA (response variable: crosstalk)

Nr. Generations	Nr. of runs	Avg. Crosstalk	Homogenous Group
8000	1296	-13.472 dB	A
4000	1296	-11.884 dB	B
2000	1296	-11.883 dB	B

Table 4. Multiple range table for the factor "Number of generations" in the ANOVA (response variable: crosstalk)

Nr. Generations	Nr. of runs	Avg. Crosstalk	Homogenous Group
80	972	-12.659 dB	A
40	972	-12.586 dB	A and B
20	972	-12.315 dB	B and C
10	972	-12.091 dB	C

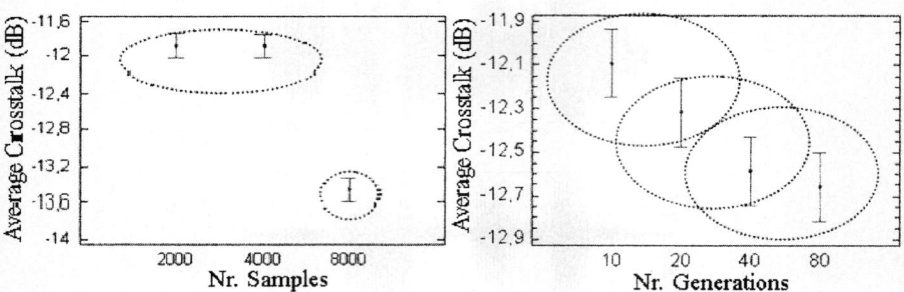

Fig. 4. Homogenous groups for different number of samples at the input of the algorithm (left) and number of generations (right) for the average crosstalk

Table 5. Multiple range table for the factor "Fitness Function" in the ANOVA (response variable: CPUTime)

Fitness Func.	Nr. of runs	Avg. CPU time	Homogenous Group
$\Psi_{Histograms}$	1296	25.23	A
$\Psi_{CrossCumulants}$	1296	21.92	B
$\Psi_{IM-GramCharlier}$	1296	19.88	C

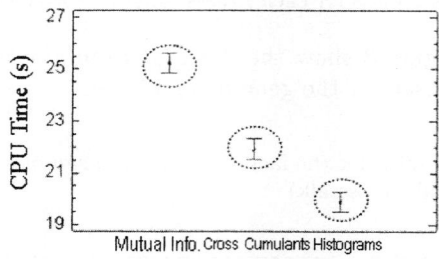

Fig. 5. Homogenous groups for each fitness function for the computation time

The number of samples in the signals refers to the amount of data from the mixture signals which is used by the algorithm PNL-GABSS. A higher number of data must give better results (see Table 3) and Figure 4 (left), although the response time will be also higher.

Table 4 and Figure 4 (right) show how the number of generations in the genetic algorithm affects the crosstalk between the estimations and the sources. As can be expected, as the number of generations is higher, the solution is slightly better. However, the differences in crosstalk are not so noticeable as those obtained depending on the chosen fitness function. Other factors regarding the genetic algorithm design, such as crossover and mutation probability, population size and selection probability do not have either a strong effect on the obtained crosstalk.

From the results, it can be drawn that the fitness function based on the Gram-Charlier expansion for mutual information approximation achieves better results. Also, from the ANOVA is deduced that results also improve if the number of samples increases, as it is normally expected. Other factors, as the crossover or mutation probabilities do not have a strong influence on the crosstalk results (their tables and figures were not included in this paper).

Regarding the ANOVA with the computation time as the response variable, all the factors listed in Table 1 have a strong statistical significance over the algorithm response time (e.g. as population size increases, computation time also increases). Specifically, concerning the effect of the chosen fitness function over the computation time, algorithm using $\Psi_{IM-GramCharlier}$ takes an average time of $25.23s$, while using $\Psi_{CrossCumulants}$ and $\Psi_{Histograms}$ takes an average of $21.92s$ and $19.88s$, respectively. Therefore, fitness function $\Psi_{IM-GramCharlier}$, although is the one which gives the best results in terms of crosstalk, is also the most complex regarding time of computation, as it is shown in Table 5 and Figure 5.

5 Conclusion

This paper discusses the application of three fitness functions in a genetic algorithm proposed for post-nonlinear blind source separation. After showing the theoretical basis of the new approaches, a thorough analysis such as ANOVA was applied in order to assess the capability of the approaches, showing that the function based on the mutual information approximation by means of the Gram-Charlier expansion achieves the best similarity results between the estimations and the sources.

Furthermore, another ANOVA analyzing the most relevant factors affecting computation time shows that mutual information approximation is also the function which takes more time to compute among the three functions proposed.

References

1. Hyvärinen, A., Pajunen, P.: Nonlinear independent component analysis: Existence and uniqueness results. Neural Networks **12** (1999) 429–439
2. Taleb, A., Jutten, C.: Source separation in post-nonlinear mixtures. IEEE Trans. on Signal Processing **47** (1999) 2807–2820
3. Rojas, I., Puntonet, C., Cañas, A., Pino, B., Fernández, J., Rojas, F.: Genetic algorithms for the blind separation of sources, IASTED (2001)
4. Rojas, F., Puntonet, C., Rodríguez, M., Rojas, I., Clemente, R.: Blind source separation in post-nonlinear mixtures using competitive learning, simulated annealing and a genetic algorithm. IEEE Transactions on Systems, Man and Cybernetics, Part C **34** (2004) 407 – 416
5. Cardoso, J.F., Souloumiac, A.: Blind beamforming for non Gaussian signals. IEE Proceedings-F **140** (1993) 362–370
6. Michalewicz, Z.: Genetic Algorithms + Data Structures = Evolution Programs. Tercera edn. Springer-Verlag, New York (1999)
7. Amari, S.I., Cichocki, A., Yang, H.: A new learning algorithm for blind source separation. In: Advances in Neural Information Processing Systems 8. MIT Press (1996) 757–763
8. Mead, R.: The design of experiments. Statistical principles for practical application. Cambridge University Press (1988)

A Robust Soft Decision Mixture Model for Image Segmentation

Pan Lin[1], Feng Zhang[1], ChongXun Zheng[1], Yong Yang[1], and Yimin Hou[2]

[1] Institute of Biomedical Engineering, Xi'an Jiaotong University,
Xi'an 710049, P.R. China
linpan@mailst.xjtu.edu.cn
[2] Department of Automatic Control of Northwestern Polytechnical University,
Xi'an, 710072, P.R. China

Abstract. In this paper, we present a novel soft decision mixture model for image segmentation. This model adopts the soft decision classify into gaussian mixture model to represent the probability distribution of the observed image feature. The model for the underlying true context images is designed to serve as prior contextual constraints on unobserved pixel labels in term of markov random field model. Experiments with synthetic image and real image show that the use of soft decision mixture model definitely improves the quality of the segmentation results for noisy images and results in reduced classification errors in the interior area of the region.

1 Introduction

Image segmentation is one of the major challenges in image processing and computer vision. Recently, finite mixture models [1]-[5] have attracted considerable interest for image segmentation. However, the application of finite mixtures model to image segmentation faces some difficulties. For the classical mixture statistical model each image pixel to be associated with exactly one class. This assumption may be not realistic. The fuzzy-c mean algorithm, which has widely been used in image segmentation. Some methods mixing fuzzy and statistical model have been developed by Gath[6]. Recently, the Markov Random Field (MRF) models [7] were used with images in an important number of works to add spatial smoothness into the process of image segmentation [8]-[9]. This approach provide satisfactory results in many case, but most case the assumption of a single Gaussian distribution typically limits image segmentation accuracy.

In this work, we incorporate a "soft-decision" idea into mixture model segmentation scheme, in contrast to "hard-decision" schemes, which use the current segmentation to estimate parameters at each stage of the mixture model. To overcome the difficulty of classical mixture model method for noisy image segmentation, we consider spatial contextual information by incorporating the prior spatial information based on the Markov Random field. From experiments with both synthetic and real image, the proposed method was quite effective for unsupervised image segmentation.

2 The New Image Segmentation Method

Our goal to image segmentation is based on mixture model. Let $X = \{x_1, x_2, ..., x_N\}$ be a finite set of pixel of an image. The image can model by Gaussian mixture model, the probability distribution function of the image pixel x is:

$$p(x|\theta_i) = \frac{1}{\sqrt{2\pi}\sigma_i} \exp\left\{-\frac{(x-\mu_i)^2}{2\sigma_i^2}\right\} \quad i=1,2,....,N , \quad (1)$$

where $\theta_i = (\mu_i, \sigma_i)$ is the Gaussian mixture distribution parameter.

Given X, fuzzy subsets $\{u_i : X \to [0,1], 1 \le i \le c\}$ constitute a fuzzy c-partition of X. Matrix $U = [u_{ik}]\{1 \le i \le c \text{ and } 1 \le k \le n\}$ where u_{ik} is the degree of membership of pattern x_k in cluster C. The fuzzy partition satisfy the following conditions:

$$\sum_{i=1}^{c} u_{it} = 1 \quad \forall t \quad 0 \le u_{it} \le 1 \quad \forall i,t \quad 0 < \sum_{t=1}^{T} u_{it} < T \quad \forall i \quad (2)$$

Then we can write the soft-mixture density for class i as:

$$p(x|\theta_i) = \sum_{t=1}^{C} u_{it} \frac{1}{\sqrt{2\pi}\sigma_{it}} \exp(-\frac{(x-\mu_{it})^2}{2\sigma_{it}^2}) \quad (3)$$

One common approach to introduce spatial information is to model the label field image X by a Gibbs random field (GRF). Hence its probability density $P(x)$, is given by a Gibbs distribution expressed as

$$P(x) = \frac{1}{Z} \exp\{-\beta \sum_{C} V_{ij}(x)\} \quad (4)$$

Where Z is a normalizing constant and the summation is over all cliques C, β is a positive parameter that controls the granularity of the image region. The clique potentials can be defined as

$$V_{ij}(x_i, x_j) = \begin{cases} 1, & \text{if } x_i = x_j \\ 0, & \text{if } x_i \ne x_j \end{cases} \quad (5)$$

This is known as Potts model with an external field V_{ij}, that weights the relative importance of different class present in the image. The second term which takes into account the spatial neighbors information relative to the image data. Here, we define the neighborhood of pixel i, denote by ∂i, by 3X3 windows with pixel i being the central pixel. According to the Bayes rule, combining Eq(3) and Eq(4), to find the probability function

$$P(x\mid y,\theta) = \frac{P(y\mid x,\theta)P(x)}{P(y\mid \theta)} \quad (6)$$

The segmentation solution is the choice of x which maximizes this posterior distribution, $P(x\mid y,\theta)$, this is the MAP estimate, $\hat{x}$. We use the iterated conditional models (ICM) algorithm proposed by Besag[9] to search for an optimal image labeling.

3 Experimental Results

In this section, we use synthetic images to compare the experiment performance of the new method presented in this paper with that of classical EM and MRF models.

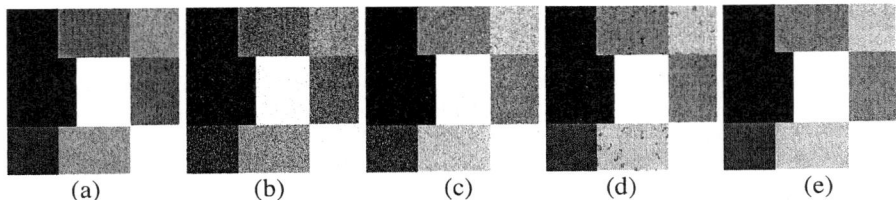

(a) (b) (c) (d) (e)

Fig. 1. Segmentation experiment on a synthesis image with five classes. (a) The original image (b) Noisy synthetic image (add Gaussian noise 0,20) (c) traditional EM (d) traditional MRF segmentation results. (e) Proposed method results.

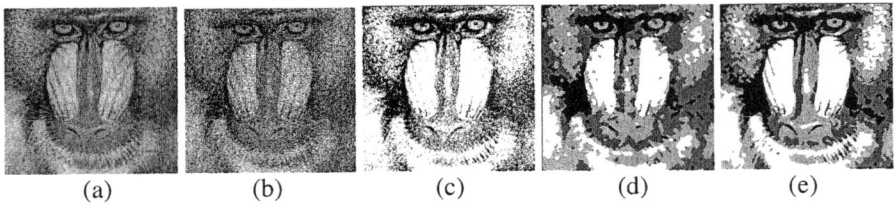

(a) (b) (c) (d) (e)

Fig. 2. Segmentation experiment on a Baboon image with 4 class. (a) The original image (b) Noisy synthetic image (add Gaussian noise 0,20) (c) traditional EM(d)traditional MRF segmentation results.(e)Proposed method results.

The first experiment image is obtained by adding some Gaussian noise to the synthesis image of Fig.1 (a), leading to Fig. (b). Here the Gaussian noise parameters are $(\mu,\sigma) = (0,25)$. The value $\beta = 1.5$ would be suggested in this example.Fig.1 shows 5-class image segmentation. The different segmentation obtained with the different methods is shown in Fig1. (c)-Fig.(e). The result displayed in Fig.1 (e) demonstrates the parameters of each class are properly estimated and the segmented regions are uniform respectively. This is great improvement over the EM and classical MRF model. Second experiment on Baboon image, we consider the 256X256 images of baboon's face presented in fig.2 (a). Fig.2 (b) add Gaussian noise to baboon image, here the Gaussian noise parameters are $(\mu, \sigma) = (0, 25)$. The value $\beta = 2$ would be suggested in this example.

4 Conclusions

In this paper, we present a new statistical model-based image segmentation method. We present some examples on synthetic image and real image to illustrate the versatility of our approach. The experimental results show that this method has a significant improvement over classical MRF-based image segmentation. We conclude from the experiments for the synthesis and real images that our algorithm is robust to resist noise.

References

1. G.McLachlan and D.Peel, Finite mixture models,New York:John Wiley&Sons,2000.
2. H. S. Choi, D. R. Haynor, and Y. Kim, Partial volume tissue classification of multichannel magnetic resonance images—A mixel model, IEEE Trans. Med. Imag., vol. 10, pp. 395–407, 1991.
3. P. Santago and H. D. Gage, Statistical models of partial volume effect, IEEE Trans. Image Processing, vol. 4, pp. 1531–1540, 1995.
4. Roberts, S.J Husmeier, D Rezek, I, Penny, W, Bayesian approaches to Gaussian mixture modeling, Pattern Analysis and Machine Intelligence, IEEE Transactions on, vol.20 (11), pp.1133 – 1142,1998.
5. M.A.T. Figueiredo, A.K. Jain, Unsupervised learning of finite mixture models, IEEE Trans. Pattern Anal. Mach. Intell.vol.24 (3), pp.381–396,2002.
6. Gath, I., Geva, A.B., Fuzzy clustering for the estimation of the parameters of the components of mixtures of normal distributions, Pattern Recognition Letters, vol.9 (3), Elsevier, pp. 77-78,1989.
7. R. Chellapa, and A. Jain Ed., Markov Random Fields, Academic Press, 1993.
8. Geman, S., Geman, D, Stochastic relaxation, Gibbs distributions, and the Bayesian restoration of images. IEEE Trans. on Pattern Analysis and Machine Intelligence, vol.6, pp. 721–741, 1984.
9. J. Besag, Towards Bayesian image analysis, Journal of Applied Statistics, vol.16, pp. 395-407, 1989.

A Comparative Study of Finite Word Length Coefficient Optimization of FIR Digital Filters

Gurvinder S. Baicher, Meinwen Taylor, and Hefin Rowlands

School of Computing & Engineering, University of Wales Newport, Allt-yr-yn Campus,
P.O.Box 180, Newport, NP20 5XR, South Wales, U.K
g.singh-baicher@newport.ac.uk

Abstract. The accuracy of a real-time digital filter frequency response is affected by the finite word length (FWL) constraint of coefficients used in its implementation. In this paper, we consider the FWL problem in regard to the finite impulse response (FIR) digital filters. Some theoretical issues and statistical error bound conditions of the maximum deviation between the exact and the approximate magnitude responses are also considered. We use real-valued genetic algorithms (GA) as an optimisation tool and derive results for the maximum error bounds and error deviation due to FWL effects for a number of design examples. Finally, a comparison is drawn between the simply rounded, the GA optimised, integer programming and the simple hill climber methods.

1 Introduction

FIR digital filters are used extensively in image processing, mobile communications, medical electronics and various other signal processing applications. For low power dissipation and high computational throughput, it is advantageous to truncate the coefficients to a limited length. However, this truncation can cause a shift in the design parameters of the filter that in some cases may become unacceptable. This leads to an optimisation issue that endeavours to select small variations of the approximated coefficient values in order to best serve the design specifications. The linear phase, direct form structure of finite impulse response (FIR) filters has been shown to be robust and therefore, attractive for the realisation of FWL coefficient implementation [1]. The problem of FWL FIR symmetric digital filters involves choosing a set of coefficients so that the new frequency response, as a consequence of truncation of the infinite precision coefficients, approximates as closely as possible to a given specified frequency response in a minimax sense.

Prior algorithms reported in literature for solving this problem have been based upon two methods; the local search method [2] and the integer programming 'branch and bound' method [3, 4]. The local search algorithm involves selecting a feasible set of FWL coefficients (say rounded valued) to give a frequency response and examining the neighbourhood of H, the transfer function of the filter, for a better filter H' i.e. one with lower error function. If such a filter is found then H', replaces H and the algorithm moves to the next step or else it stops. The 'branch and bound' algorithm is involved with systematically pruning a tree of several possible solutions based upon certain lower bounds as the enumeration proceeds. Both of these methods are intrinsically computationally intensive and global optimality is not assured. The problem is further compounded and becomes acute for longer filter lengths.

2 FWL Coefficients and Error Objective Function

The most commonly used method of deriving FWL coefficients for fixed-point arithmetic is the direct quantisation method. In this method, high precision coefficients that are derived using standard filter design techniques are first rounded to yield FWL quantised coefficients. The starting solution of quantised coefficients is thus given by

$$h_{ri} = \text{round}[h_{ei}\, 2^{B-1}] \; . \qquad i=0,1,2,\ldots\ldots,N-1 \qquad (1)$$

Where 'h_{ri}' is the rounded coefficient, 'h_{ei}' is the high precision coefficient, 'B' is the number of bits used to represent the coefficients and 'N' is the filter length.

The main purpose of the optimisation process is to minimise the objective function with the specific aim of obtaining an approximated frequency response of the filter that is as close as possible to the desired response. The objective function is calculated for 500 equally spaced frequency grid points.

The objective function is then evaluated using the following

$$\text{ObjV} = \left\{ \sum_{i_p=0}^{p} |1 - H_{i_p}|^2 + \sum_{i_s=s}^{L} |H_{i_s}|^2 \right\} + 10\,\max\left\{ \max |1 - H_{i_p}|,\, \max |H_{i_s}| \right\}. \qquad (2)$$

Where

H_{ip} = magnitude response of GA optimised filter at frequency ip in the pass band
H_{is} = magnitude response of GA optimised filter at frequency is in the stop band
L = number of frequency grid points (=500)
p = pass band cut-off point
s = stop band cut-off point

A combination of the summation of squared deviations and a weighted maximum deviation as seen in equ.(2) generated good overall frequency responses. These responses did not show the effects of skewing that was observed during initial trials when only the maximum deviation was used to optimise the objective function.

3 GA Optimisation of Band Select FIR Filters

In this section we consider the case of band select filters for which the desired response is specified over the selected pass and stop bands. The desired function $D(\omega)$ consists of a number of disjointed frequency bands $\Omega_k \subset [0,\pi]$, where k=1,...,M such that for each k, $D(\omega)$ is to be approximated to within a specified error bound $\delta(k)$ for all $\omega \in \Omega_k$. If the transfer function of the filter with infinite precision coefficients is $H(\omega)$ and that of the approximate filter using FWL coefficients is $\hat{H}(\omega)$, then the maximum error bound is given by

$$\max \left| |\hat{H}(\omega)| - D(\omega) \right| = Q\sqrt{\frac{2N-1}{3}} + \delta(k) \text{ . for } \omega \in \Omega_k \qquad (3)$$

In order to conduct a comparative study, the 10 filter examples used by Kodek and Steiglitz [4] for coefficient optimisation based on integer programming method are also used here. The 10 filters are divided into 4 sets of filters as shown in Table 1. The optimised coefficients using the integer programming method have been taken from Kodek and Steiglitz [4].

Table 1. Sets of Filter Specifications

Filter	Pass-band	Stop-band	Pass-band
A: range	0 to 0.4	0.5 to 1.0	
Weighting:	1	1	
Desired value:	1	0	
B: range	0 to 0.4	0.5 to 1.0	
Weighting:	1	10	
Desired value:	1	0	
C: range	0 to 0.24	0.4 to 0.68	0.84 to 1.0
Weighting:	1	1	1
Desired value:	1	0	1
D: range	0 to 0.24	0.4 to 0.68	0.84 to 1.0
Weighting:	1	10	1
Desired value:	1	0	1

Table 2 shows results for the maximum error deviation relative to the desired response for all $\omega \in \Omega_k$. The bounded value used in Table 2 is obtained using equ.(3). A comparison with the integer programming (IP) method clearly shows a distinct improvement for the case of GA optimised filters. It is also observed that the bounded value of equ.(3) is consistent with the maximum error deviation obtained using the GA optimised filters. The GA optimised filters have generated slightly lower maximum error deviation values as compared to the value of bounded error for all but two of the ten filters namely, the A25/5 and the C15/5 filters. On the other hand, the IP optimised filters have better performance compared to the bounded value in just two of the ten filters.

An example response for filter B25/7 is shown in Fig.1(a). It is observed that while the rounded response follows the exact response as is to be expected, the GA optimised response follows the requirement of the desired response which is 1 in the pass band for the filter B25/7. Fig. 1(b) shows a comparison of maximum error magnitudes against number of bits B for filter B25.

Table 2. Maximum error deviation relative to the desired response for all $\omega \in \Omega_k$

filter	GA-op	Rounded	IP-op	exact	Bounded value equ.(3)
A15/5	0.1978	0.2309	0.2002	0.1324	0.2296
A25/5	0.1873	0.2309	0.1873	0.0508	0.1771
B15/7	0.2315	0.2813	0.3273	0.2797	0.3040
B25/7	0.0993	0.1251	0.2157	0.1231	0.1547
B35/7	0.0637	0.0869	0.1865	0.0528	0.0903
C15/5	0.1672	0.1873	0.1667	0.0596	0.1568
C25/5	0.1265	0.1873	0.1265	0.0173	0.1436
D15/7	0.1483	0.2143	0.2542	0.2006	0.2249
D25/7	0.0428	0.0651	0.1306	0.0570	0.0886
D35/7	0.0425	0.0558	0.0668	0.0152	0.0526

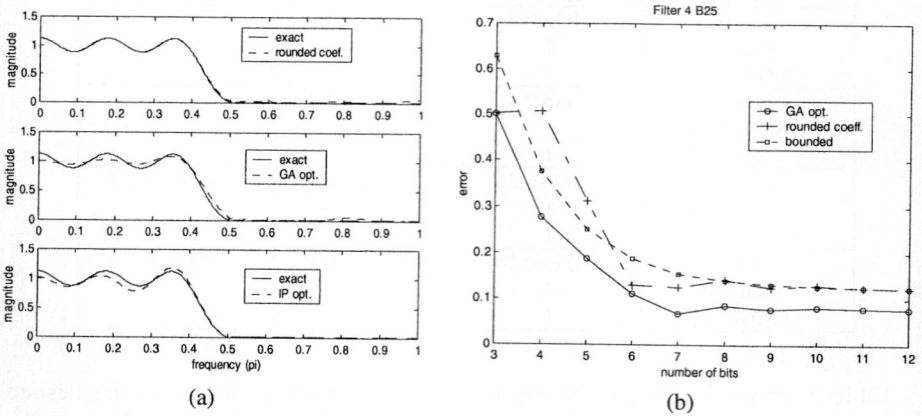

Fig. 1. (a) Magnitude response of simply rounded, GA optimised and IP optimised coefficients for the case of filter B25/7, (b) Comparison of error magnitudes against number of bits B for filter B25

4 Simple Hill Climber Techniques and Exhaustive Search

To test the robustness and accuracy of the GA optimised results, the methods of simple hill climber algorithms such as steepest ascent (SAHC) and nearest ascent (NAHC) were applied to a selection of filters shown in Table 1. Random sampling tests for the search space as used for GA optimisation were also conducted. Furthermore, for a small selection of low order filters, an exhaustive search was conducted over a matching search space. The hill climber algorithms for this search were based on the standard techniques used for binary strings [5] and adapted for the case of integer valued numbers representing the FIR filter coefficients. The starting 'seed' individual of an integer valued coefficient set is generated by randomly perturbing the rounded coefficients by +1, 0 or –1. The flow chart shown in Fig.2 describes the hill climber algorithm used for this application.

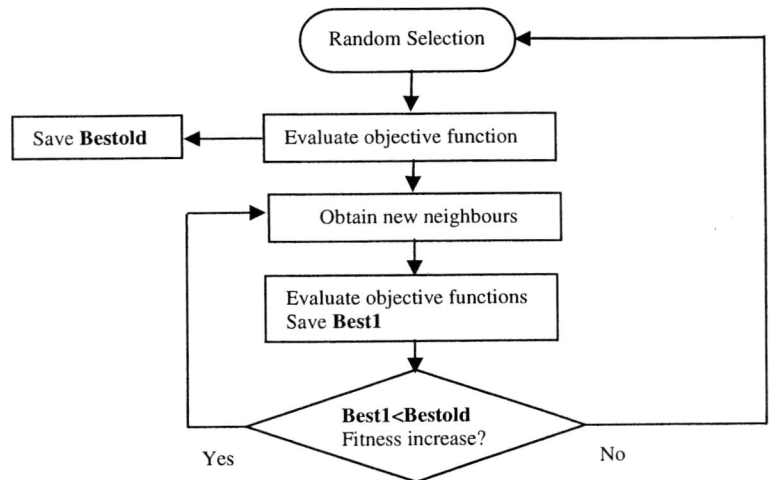

Fig. 2. A flow chart for the simple hill climber algorithm

Table 3. Maximum error deviation relative to the desired response for all $\omega \in \Omega_k$

Filter	Exh. search	Random	SAHC	NAHC	GA
A15/5	0.1978	0.1978	0.1978	0.3536	0.1978
A25/5	None	0.3051	0.1873	0.2517	0.1873
B15/7	0.2208	0.2322	0.1418*	0.1972*	0.2315
B25/7	None	0.1088	0.0678*	0.0740*	0.0993
C15/5	0.1667	0.1875	0.1667	0.2796	0.1672
C25/5	None	0.2468	0.1576	0.2623	0.1265

Exh. = Exhaustive
SAHC=steepest ascent hill climber
NAHC=nearest ascent hill climber
* indicates search space exceeded +1 and/or –1 of rounded coefficient values

The results of SAHC, NAHC, the random sampling and exhaustive search for a selection of the FIR filters are shown in Table 3. The results shown with an asterisk (*) are the ones for which the search space has deviated greater than +1 or -1 of the rounded coefficient values. Note also that the exhaustive search was confined to deviation of +1, 0 or –1 of the rounded coefficients. There is clear evidence that the GA optimisation has generated consistently good results (see Table 2). Although the hill climber of steepest ascent form (SAHC) has also shown remarkably good results for a selected number of filters.

5 Conclusions

In this paper, we explored the GA optimisation of finite word length coefficient FIR digital filters. GA optimisation of a number of band-select filters is considered. For such filters, comparison has been drawn with the optimised results based on integer programming method reported in [4] and also with the simple hill climber techniques. Again GA optimised results indicate consistent improvement for majority of the selected filters.

Optimisation using the simple hill climber technique (especially SAHC) has shown potential by generating some good results; in general these have been inconsistent over the range of example filters that were considered. However, the GA technique has demonstrated a valid, effective and robust optimisation tool for this application. Furthermore, it is efficient as the GA code running on a 600MHz pentium-3 computer with the parameters given in Section 2 above completed the optimisation in approximately 30 seconds for each filter.

References

1. Chan, D.S.K., Rabiner L.R.: Analysis of Quantization Errors in the Direct Form for Finite Impulse Response Digital Filters. IEEE Trans. Audio and Electroacoustics. **21**(4) (1973) 354-366
2. Avenhaus, E.: On the Design of Digital Filters with Coefficients of Limited Word Length. IEEE Trans. Acoustics, Speech, Signal Processing. **20** (1972) 206-212
3. Kodek, D.M.: Design of Optimal Finite Wordlength FIR Digital Filters using Integer Programming Techniques. IEEE Trans. Acoustics, Speech and Signal Processing. **28**(3) (1980) 304-308
4. Kodek, D.M., Steiglitz, K.: Comparison of Optimal and Local Search Methods for Designing Finite Wordlength FIR digital filters. IEEE Trans. Circuits and Systems. **28**(1) (1981) 28-32
5. Mitchell, M.: An Introduction to Genetic Algorithms. Bradford Books, MA Cambridge (1996)

A Novel Genetic Algorithm for Variable Partition of Dual Memory Bank DSPs*

Dan Zhang[1], Zeng-Zhi Li[1], Hai Wang[1], and Tao Zhan[2]

[1] School of Electronics & Information Engineering, Xi'an Jiaotong University,
Xi'an Shaanxi 710049, China
danzhang@mailst.xjtu.edu.cn
[2] Dept. of Computer Science & Engineering, Northwest Polytechnical University,
Xi'an Shaanxi 710072, China

Abstract. DSPs provide high performance and low cost through their use of specialized hardware features. One feature commonly found in DSPs is the dual data memory banks to offer high memory bandwidth. However, it poses problems for C compilers, which are mostly not capable of assigning variables between banks. In this paper, an immune genetic algorithm for variable partition between data banks is presented to maximize the benefit of this feature. In our approach, the reduced interference graph of variable accesses is constructed, the potential variable partitions are represented as antibodies and the vaccines are abstracted; then through some operations including adaptive vaccination, immune selection and so on, the antibodies can converge at optimal variable partitions. Experimental results show that our algorithm is superior to previous works in terms of performance and code size.

1 Introduction

Currently, there is a high demand for digital signal processors (DSPs) with high performance, low code size, low power dissipation and low energy consumption in many areas. Some common hardware features of DSPs, e.g. hardware low-overhead looping, accumulator-based data paths, tightly-encoded instructions that specify the parallel execution of multiple independent operations, multiple pipelined functional units, and an instruction memory plus two data memory banks [1], are designed to exploit compute-intensive program constructs that occur frequently in the signal processing algorithms that are at the core of many embedded applications. However, existing compilers for DSPs are generally unable to exploit these features and generate sufficiently efficient and compact code. Hence, system designers often resort to hand-programming the embedded software in assembly - a very time-consuming and high development cost task.

One important feature of DSP is dual data memory banks. These DSPs, e.g. Motorola DSP 56000, NEC uPD77016, Analog Device ADSP2100, are equipped with one program memory bank plus two data memory banks (X and Y) accessible in parallel for increasing the memory bandwidth. The data ALU of Motorola

---
* Supported by the Nation Science Foundation of China (No.60173059).

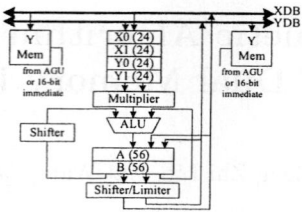

Fig. 1. Data ALU of Motorola 56000

```
sum = 0;                <1> CLR   A         X:(R0)+,X0  Y:(R4)-,Y0
for (i=0; i<N; i++)     <2> REP   #N-1
    sum += A[i] * B[N-1-i]; <3> MAC X0,Y0,A  X:(R0)+,X0  Y:(R4)-,Y0
            (a)         <4> MACR  X0,Y0,A
                                    (b)
```

Fig. 2. (a) C code of FIR filter (b) Motorola DSP56k assembly code

56000, shown in fig. 1, consists of four 24-bit input registers called X0, X1, Y0 and Y1, and two 56-bit accumulators called A and B. Data transfers between the data ALU registers and the X or Y data memory bank occur over XDB, YDB. This feature of memory architecture can be shown to be very effective to many DSP algorithms such as the FIR filter algorithm. Fig. 2(a) shows the filter written in C while fig. 2(b) shows the corresponding code in the assembly language of Motorola DSP56000 [2]. Instructions $<1>$ and $<3>$ demonstrate the effective use of the dual memory banks. By allocating array A to one memory bank and array B to the other, it is possible to access an element from each array in one instruction. If the arrays had both been allocated to the same memory bank, the elements would have to be accessed sequentially with two instructions and thus increase the size of the loop from one instruction to two instructions, reducing performance by a factor of two. For scalar variables, the partition to either X or Y plays an important role for code quality too.

Many existing C compilers, e.g. GCC for M56000 and ADSP-2100, cannot cope well with dual memory banks, but all variables are assigned to just one bank, which implies a great performance and area loss. In this paper a novel immune genetic algorithm (IGA) for the variable partition problem of dual memory bank DSPs is proposed. In our approach, the reduced interference graph of variable accesses is constructed and the maximum-cut two parts are gained by using IGA for maximizing parallelism. we represent potential variable partitions as antibodies and propose a vaccine abstraction technique. Through adaptive evolution process, composed of selection, crossover, mutation, vaccination, immune selection, and so on, the antibodies can converge at optimal variable partitions. The experimental results demonstrate that our approach can improve code quality in terms of performance and code size.

The remainder of this paper is organized as follows. In section 2 related works are discussed. The immune genetic algorithm for variable partition is presented in section 3. Experiments results are provided in section 4. Finally, the conclusions and future works are given in Section 5.

2 Related Works

Variable partition problem for exploiting dual memory banks was studied early by Powell et al. [3]. Their approach assign variables to the X/Y banks by using a greedy strategy: variables are assigned to X and Y in an alternating way according to their access sequence in the program. This simple greedy method may produce poor results for complex programs.

Saghir et al. [4] proposed two algorithms - compaction-based data partitioning and partial data duplication - are both performed in the data allocation pass of the post-optimizer. The partitioning algorithm uses an interference graph to partition a program's variables into two sets, which correspond to the two memory banks. The partial duplication algorithm identifies memory accesses that could be executed in parallel but cannot because their corresponding variables cannot be allocated appropriately. A problem with this approach is that it is for a hypothetical VLIW DSP. Additionally, duplicating partial variables makes parallel execution possible, but increases storage requirements.

Sudarsanam et al. [5] tried to use the dual data memory optimally using simultaneous reference allocation (memory bank + register allocation). They performed both phases of register allocation and memory bank allocation in single phase. Their algorithm is based on graph labelling, whose objective is to find an optimal labelling of a constraint graph representing conditions on the register and memory bank allocation. To solve this NP-hard problem, simulated annealing algorithm is applied to it and has achieved code size reductions between 5 and 10 % compared to machine code without exploitation of dual memory banks. A problem is that compilation time is too long.

3 Immune Algorithm for Variable Partition of Dual Data Memory Banks

The main steps of our variable partition approach are as follows.

1) DDG of variable accesses is constructed according to definition 1;
2) IG is constructed from DDG according to definition 2;
3) IG is reduced into RIG according to definition 3;
4) RIG is divided into two parts with maximum-cut weight by using IGA;
5) These two sub-graphs are mapped into variable assignment of X and Y banks.

3.1 DDG, IG and RIG Construction

Our approach is based on interference graph [4], which reflects the inherent parallelism between variables of program.

Definition 1. *A data dependency graph (DDG) is a directed node-labeled graph $G = (A, E, l)$, where each node $a_i \in A$ represents a memory access in program, and each edge $(a_i, a_j) \in E$ denotes a scheduling precedence between a_i and a_j. A node label $l(a_i)$ denotes the name of the variable accessed by a_i.*

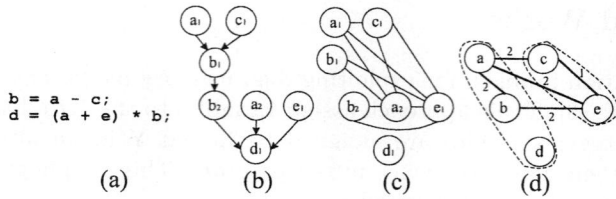

Fig. 3. (a) code sequence; (b) DDG; (c) IG; (d) RIG and optimal variable partition

Definition 2. *For a DDG $G = (A, E, l)$, the interference graph (IG) is an undirected graph $I = (A', E', l')$ with $A' = A$, $l' = l$. There is an edge $(a_i, a_j) \in E'$, if and only if a_i and a_j are not reachable from each other via a path in G.*

Definition 3. *The reduced interference graph (RIG) is an undirected graph $R = (V, E^*, W)$, which constructed from IG as follows. Each node $v_k (v_k \in V)$ represents a node set $A'_k = \{a_{k_1}, \ldots, a_{k_m}\}$, $A'_k \in A'$, $l(a_{k_i}) = v_k$, which means the nodes in A' with the same variable v_k are reduced into a single node v_k. All edges in E' containing nodes in A'_k are redirected to v_k. Finally, all edges (v_k, v_l) between two variables v_k and v_l are reduced to one edge and a weight $w(v_k, v_l)$ denoting the sum of the total edges between A'_k and A'_l in E'. The weight $w(v_k, v_l)$ reflects the gain achieved by assigning v_k and v_l to different memory banks. $|V| = n$, W is a $n \times n$ triangular matrix (R is undirected graph), in which each $w(i, j)$ denotes the sum of potential parallel accesses of v_i and v_j.*

$$W = \{w(i,j) | w(i,j) = sum\ of\ edges\ between\ v_i\ and\ v_j\ in\ E', 1 \leq i, j \leq n\} \quad (1)$$

An example of DDG, IG, RIG and optimal variable partition are shown in fig. 3. The DDG (fig. 3(b)) is constructed according to definition 1. a_1 stands for the first access of variable a, b_1 depends on a_1 and c_1 since b_1 is the l-value and a_1 and c_1 are r-values of assignment expression, b_2 depends on b_1 since b_1 is the last write-access of variable b. The IG (fig. 3(c)) is constructed according to definition 2. a_1 is depended by b_1, b_2, d_1, so a_1 can be accessed in parallel with a_2, c_1, e_1 (one edge represents potential parallel access between two variable accesses). The RIG (fig. 3(d)) is constructed according to definition 3. The accesses of same variable is reduced to a single node, and the edges of them is summed and represented as weight of edge. The edge-weight between a and c is 2 because of edges (a_1, c_1) and (a_2, c_1) in IG. Therefore, the best partition is achieved if the RIG is divided into two sub-graphs X and Y, such that the sum of the edge weights between X and Y is maximal. In this case, the most parallel memory accesses can be gained. This problem is known as a NP-hard problem - maximum cut problem [6], which is solved by using proposed IGA in following.

3.2 Immune Genetic Algorithm

Immune Genetic Algorithm (IGA) [7] is based on Genetic Algorithm (GA). GA [8] presents the solving process of problem as the evolving process of genes, and

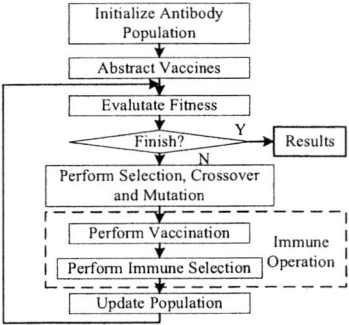

Fig. 4. Flowchart of immune genetic algorithm

gets the fittest individuals (best or satisfying solutions) by selecting, crossing and mutating individuals in population. However, because crossover and mutation genetic operators make individuals change randomly and indirectly during evolution, they not only make the individuals evolve better but also cause certain degeneracy. On the other hand, there are many basic and obvious characteristics or knowledge in the pending problem. However GA lacks the capability of meeting an actual situation. On condition of preserving GA's advantages, IGA utilizes some characteristics and knowledge in the pending problems for restraining the degenerative phenomena during evolution, so as to improve the algorithmic efficiency. The general flowchart of IGA is shown in fig. 4. The individuals in GA are called antibodies in IGA, and the key step - immune operation, which contains vaccination and immune selection, is used to restrain the degeneration of antibodies. The population of antibodies are initialized randomly. The vaccines are abstracted as local maximum spanning tree from RIG. Then through the iterative steps including selection, crossover, mutation, vaccination and immune selection, finally the antibodies can evolve into optimal solutions.

3.3 Representation of Antibody

Definition 4. *For the X and Y banks, the representation of antibody B is defined as a binary string of length n. A gene (bit) denotes whether a variable belong to X or Y banks $(0 \to X, 1 \to Y)$. $B = (b_1, \ldots, b_n), b_i \in \{0, 1\}, n = |V|$*

3.4 Fitness Evaluation

Matrix W is computed according to equation (1) in definition 3. For an antibody $B = (b_1, \ldots, b_n)$, the fitness $f(B)$ is computed according to equation (2), which denotes the parallel gain in the case of variable partition of B.

$$f(B) = \frac{\sum_{i=1}^{n} \sum_{j=1}^{i-1} \left(w(i,j) \times (b_i \text{ XOR } b_j) \right)}{\sum_{i=1}^{n} \sum_{j=1}^{i-1} w(i,j)}; 1 \leq i, j \leq n; b_i, b_j \in B \quad (2)$$

XOR: exclusive or operator.

3.5 Vaccine Abstraction

The vaccine contains some basic features of the problem, while antibodies are potential solutions. In other words, a vaccine can be regarded as an estimation on some genes of the optimal antibody. For RIG maximum cut problem, some gene fragments are generated as vaccines. The algorithm is shown in fig. 5. A vaccine is a local maximum spanning tree (MST). Two nodes connected by a tree edge can be simply assigned to different banks because the tree found by MST does not form a cycle. MST ensures that we can assign nodes connected via an edge with heavy weight, which implies that the bank assignment we get would be local optimal. These vaccines are used to gain better antibodies by vaccination and immune selection operations. An example of abstracting vaccine is illustrated in fig. 6 (vaccine size = 4). Fig. 6(a) shows the RIG. In fig. 6(b), node i is selected randomly firstly, then choose node k with maximum-weight edge (i, k), finally c and d are selected into node set and (i, c) and (i, d) are selected into edge set. So as fig. 6(e) shows, this vaccine, named $vac1$, is abstracted. All nodes in $vac1$ and related edges are removed from RIG. In fig. 6(c), node p is selected firstly randomly, then q, h and l are selected orderly, finally formed $vac2$. Fig. 6(d) shows $vac3$ and $vac4$. As fig. 6(e) shows, after all vaccines are abstracted, their vaccination probabilities P_v are computed. According to the depth of a vaccine tree, nodes are assigned 0 and 1 alternately.

```
while (remainder(V) > 0) { /* finish condition: V does not have remainders */
    create a new vaccine vac;
    select a node randomly, add it to vac;
    num_of_nodes = 1; /* number of nodes of vaccine */
    while (num_of_nodes <= T) { /* T is maximum nodes in a vaccine */
        select a adjacent node v to vac with maximum weight edge e;
        if (weight(e) <= 0) break; /* no other edges, vaccine is done */
        add node v and edge e into vac;
        num_of_nodes++;
    }
    if (num_of_nodes >= 2) { /* a vaccine contains two nodes at least */
        compute average weight of vac;
        assign 0 and 1 alternately according to the depth level of vac;
        add vac into vac_set;
        all edges related with nodes in vac are removed from W;
    }
    nodes whose degree = 0 are removed from V;
}
compute vaccination probability P_v of each vaccine of vac_set according to equation (3);
```

Fig. 5. Algorithm for abstracting vaccine

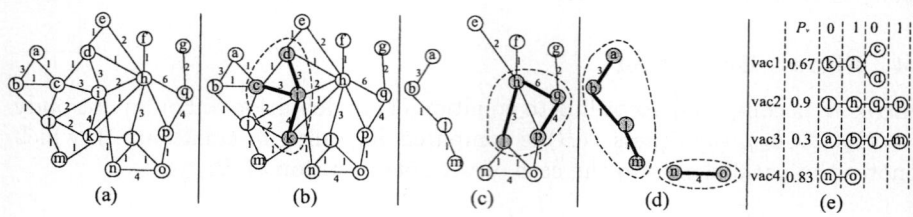

Fig. 6. Example of abstracting vaccine (Vaccine size = 4): (a) RIG (b) first vaccine; (c) second vaccine; (d) third and fourth vaccine; (e) vaccines and their P_v

$$P_{v_{vac}} = P_{v\_min} + \frac{(P_{v\_max} - P_{v\_min})(AW_{vac} - AW_{min})}{AW_{max} - AW_{min}}, vac \in vac\_set \quad (3)$$

P_{v_max} (P_{v_min}) : The maximum (minimum) vaccination probability;
AW_{max} (AW_{min}) : The maximum (minimum) average-weight in vaccine set vac_set;
AW_{vac} : The average-weight of a vaccine vac.

3.6 Selection, Crossover, Mutation and Adaptive Strategy

The parents are selected by tournament selection method. Uniform crossover method is executed. Mutation is performed by exchanging two stochastic gene-bits of an antibody, which means that the assigned banks are exchanged. However, The behavior and performance of IGA are affected significantly by selection of parameters crossover probability P_c and mutation probability P_m. Hence, an adaptive method [9] is adopted to speed up convergence and preserve population-diversity. Shown in equation (4) and (5), P_c and P_m are adaptive to the fitness of individual and generation. Another mutation method is to reverse a stochastic gene of antibody, which means changing the partition of a variable.

$$P_c = \begin{cases} P_{c1} - \frac{(P_{c1}-P_{c2})(f'-f_{avg})}{f_{max}-f_{avg}}, & \text{if } f' \geq f_{avg}, \\ P_{c1}, & \text{if } f' < f_{avg}. \end{cases} \quad (4)$$

$$P_m = \begin{cases} P_{m1} - \frac{(P_{m1}-P_{m2})(f_{max}-f)}{f_{max}-f_{avg}}, & \text{if } f \geq f_{avg}, \\ P_{m1}, & \text{if } f < f_{avg}. \end{cases} \quad (5)$$

f_{max} (f_{avg}) : The maximum (average) fitness of current population;
f' : The higher fitness of two individuals to crossover;
f : The fitness of individual to mutate;

3.7 Vaccination

The vaccines are not solutions, but some local optimal variable partition. Therefore, vaccination is to modify some gene-bits according to a vaccine's scheme, so that antibodies have higher probabilities to get higher fitness. For an antibody, the vaccination operation is performed with each vaccine according to its vaccination probability P_v, which is initialized in the vaccine abstraction phase (see fig. 5). The whole vaccination process is performed according to immunity probability P_i to each antibody. Because of the symmetry of vaccine(e.g. all-0 equals all-1), vaccination is performed as follows: two new antibodies can be generated by replacing the gene-bits of one parent antibody by a vaccine and its opposite-vaccine (reverse 1-bit into 0-bit and vice versa) respectively. The one with higher fitness is chosen as the new antibody after vaccination.

The vaccination probability P_v of a vaccine is adaptive to evolving process. After vaccination, the average difference between new fitness and old fitness of antibodies is used to adjust P_v of this vaccine according to equation (7).

$$P_{v_{new}} = \begin{cases} P_{v_{old}} + (1 - P_{v_{old}}) \times diff, & \text{if } diff \geq 0, \\ P_{v_{old}} \times (1 + diff), & \text{if } diff < 0. \end{cases} \quad (6)$$

$$diff = \frac{\sum_{j=1}^{N_{P_i}}(f(B_j)_{new}-f(B_j)_{old})}{N_{P_i}};$$

N_{P_i} : The number of antibodies for vaccination according to P_i;
$f(B_j)_{old}$ ($f(B_j)_{new}$) : The fitness of antibody B_j before (after) vaccination;

3.8 Immune Selection

Immune selection performed after vaccination is divided into two steps. Firstly immune inspection is used to check whether the fitnesses of new antibodies are higher than their parents. The case that child is lower than parents indicates a degeneracy, so parents are preserved. Otherwise the second step - *annealing selection* [10] is performed, which means that each antibody B_i of population D_k is selected into new parent population A_{k+1} according to probability $P(B_i)$.

$$P(B_i) = \frac{e^{f(B_i)/T_k}}{\sum_{j=1}^{N} e^{f(B_j)/T_k}} \qquad (7)$$

$$T_k = ln(\frac{T_0}{k} + 1)$$

k : The current order number of generation; N : The size of population;
$D_k = (B_1, \ldots, B_N)$: The current children population after vaccination;
$f(B_i)$: The fitness of antibody B_i;
T_k : The annealing temperature sequence, $T_0 = 80$ in this work.

4 Experimental Results and Analysis

We evaluated the quality of our algorithm with DSP kernels from DSPStone C benchmarks [11] on the Motorola DSP56000 [2]. The experimental platform is

Table 1. The results of IGA for variable partition of dual memory bank

kernel	var	acc	opt-gain	time(s)	X bank	Y bank
complex_mul	6	18	69	5.548	ar, br, ci	ai,bi,cr
complex_up	4	22	117	4.697	A,B,C	D
convolution	4	82	1550	5.067	y,x	i,h
dot_product	3	13	32	3.956	Z	A,B
fir	5	161	5950	3.786	x,x0	h,i,y
fir2dim	6	882	193190	7.401	image,output,array2,array3	coeffs,array
biquad_N	6	157	5161	4.947	w, f, coeffs	wi,x,y
bi_one	10	27	163	6.199	y,x,w2,b0,b1	w,w1,b2,a1,a2
lms	7	203	9550	8.523	X,delta,x	H,d,y,error
matrix1	3	3900	3594900	17.605	C	A,B
matrix2	3	3600	2879000	24.876	A,C	B
mat1x3	3	27	153	10.665	h,y	x
n_complex_up	5	480	57088	4.797	A,C	B,D
n_real_up	4	192	9152	3.565	A,C	B,D
real_up	4	10	21	3.104	C,D	A, B

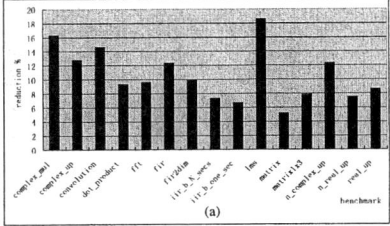 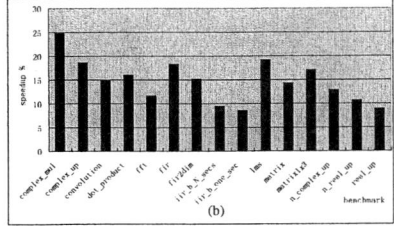

Fig. 7. (a) Code size reduction (%); (b) Performance speedup (%)

Pentium IV 2.0G, 512M. The parameters are following: population size = 20, maximum iteration = 500, $P_{c1} = 0.9$, $P_{c2} = 0.6$, $P_{m1} = 0.1$, $P_{m2} = 0.001$, $P_i = 0.3$, P_r (reversion mutation probability) = 0.05, $Tour$ (tournament size) = 3, T (vaccine size) = 3, $P_{v\_max} = 0.9$, $P_{v\_min} = 0.3$, $T_0 = 80$.

The results of our approach are showed in Table 1. Column 1 is kernel name. Column 2 is the number of variables. Column 3 is the number of accesses. Column 4 is the optimized gain. The computing time is listed in Column 5. The variable partition to X and Y banks are shown in column 6 and 7.

Code quality improvements are gained in terms of performance and code size. Code size is reduced because parallel memory accesses are encoded into a single instruction. The performance is improved for higher data memory bandwidth. Fig. 7(a) shows the percentage of code size reduction, as compared to unoptimized code, which ranges from 5.16% (matrix2) to 18.6% (lms). On average 2.32% improvement is gained in comparison with the results reported in [5]. Fig. 7(b) gives the percentage of speedup of performance, which ranges from 8.52% (biquad_one_sec) to 24.73% (complex_mul).

5 Conclusions and Future Works

An immune genetic algorithm for variable partition of dual data memory banks DSPs is proposed to get the maximum cut of reduced interference graph of variables accesses. The vaccines, which are abstracted according to special variable partition problem, are vaccinated on antibodies in the evolving process, and accelerate convergence. Moreover, the vaccination probabilities of vaccines are adaptive to their effects. Additionally, the adaptive crossover and mutation methods are adopted too. Experimental results show that compared to previous works, the code quality is improved in terms of code size and performance.

References

1. Lee, E.A.: Programmable dsp architectures. IEEE ASSP Magazine (1988, 1989) Part I, 4–19; Part II, 4–14
2. Motorola: Dsp56000/dsp56001 digital signal processor user's manual (1990)

3. D. B. Powell, e.a.: Direct synthesis of optimized dsp assembly code from signal flow block diagrams. In: ICASSP. (1992)
4. M. Saghir, e.a.: Exploiting dual data-memory banks in digital signal processors. In: 7th Inter. Conf. on Arch. Supp. for Prog. Lang. and Oper. Sys. (1996)
5. Sudarsanam, A., Malik, S.: Simultaneous reference allocation in code generation for dual data memory bank asips. ACM Trans. on Design Auto. of Elec. Sys. (2000) 242–264
6. Garey, M.R., Johnson, D.S. In: Computers and intractability. Freeman (1979)
7. Jiao, L.C., Wang, L.: A novel genetic algorithm based on immunity. IEEE Trans. on Systems, Man and Cybernetics, Part A **30** (2000) 552–561
8. Yao, X. In: Evolutionary Computation: Theory and Applications. World Scientific, Singapore (1999)
9. Srinivas, M., Patnaik, L.M.: Adaptive probabilities of crossover and mutations in gas. IEEE Trans. on SMC (1994) 493–530
10. Zhang, J.S., et al.: The whole annealing genetic algorithms and their sufficient and necessary conditions of convergence. Science in China (1997) 151–164
11. V. Zivojnovic, e.a.: Dspstone: A dsp-oriented benchmarking methodology. In: the 5th Inter. Conf. on Sig. Proc. Apps. and Tech. (ICSPAT). (1994)

Bi-phase Encoded Waveform Design to Deal with the Range Ambiguities for Sparse Space-Based Radar Systems

Hai-hong Tao, Tao Su, and Gui-sheng Liao

State Key Lab of Radar Signal Processing, Xidian University,
Xi'an, P.R. China, 710071
{hhtao, sutao, gsliao}@xidian.edu.cn

Abstract. In order to mitigate the Range-Doppler ambiguities inherent in a sparse aperture, high pulse repetition frequency is adopted to resolve Doppler ambiguous and waveform approach exploits temporal diversity to resolve range ambiguities. In this paper, a novel GA with gradient-like reproduce is presented to optimize multiple bi-phase encoded waveforms, so their peak side-lobe and integrated side-lobe of auto-correlation and cross-correlation are all as lower as possible. The fitness function with adaptive scale gene corresponding to multiple constraint is used to overcome optimal trend. The simulation results are presented to show the performance and behavior of the algorithm proposed.

1 Introduction

The advantages of Sparse Space-based Radar Systems are numerous. First, it may be less expensive to launch several microsats than to launch a large satellite with the same overall antenna aperture. Manufacturing costs are also reduced through the benefits of mass production. In addition, a microsat constellation degrades gracefully as individual microsats fail, either as expected or prematurely, and the constellation can be reconfigured to optimize its configuration after a failure. Failure in a monolithic satellite, however, is catastrophic for the entire radar system. There are also disadvantages, however, to space-borne radar, the most significant being the tradeoff between sensor weight, size, and power. Other factors requiring large apertures are ambiguity and resolution. For sparse synthetic aperture radar (SAR), low cost lightweight radar payload development is necessary, the minimum antenna size is governed by the minimum SAR antenna area constraint, commonly 2 meters. Complying with this constraint ensures that Range-Doppler ambiguities are not illuminate.

There are a number of ways to deal with the ambiguities[1]. One way in the experiment is to limit the viewing geometry, so that unambiguous range/Doppler operation is possible. By viewing at high grazing angles, the illuminated spot size is minimized. A second way is to operate Doppler unambiguous but allow range ambiguities, and use a multi-PRF waveform to resolve the range ambiguities. This technique can be difficult to make work in a high target density environment however. Another way is to operate Doppler ambiguous and range unambiguous and let beamforming processing nulls the Doppler ambiguities. This approach requires additional degrees of freedom that are in short supply in the flight experiment[1]. A last way that is being investigated is the focus of some basic research in waveform design and signal processing.

The novel waveform approach presented in the paper exploits temporal diversity to resolve range ambiguities. This approach transmits a different waveform pulse-to-pulse. The number of different waveforms transmitted is the number of different ambiguous ranges that can be resolved. Since each waveform is different, the radar returns from different range bins that arrive at the same time at the radar receiver can be resolved due to the different echoed waveforms for each range. There have been previous attempts to achieve this goal, but due to the large cross-correlation side-lobes of the waveforms, it hasn't been very successful. By modifying the signal processing approach to the waveforms and designing the waveforms to be mathematically invertible, other signal processing approaches are possible that improve the integrated side-lobe issue. In the paper, bi-phase encoded signal is adopted as transmitter. On account of high resolution as high as 1m, the required signal band width is 150MHz. If the time duration is $1\ \mu s$, for example, the code length is 150, and the blur time is N, near optimal 150×N chirp codes were located in the search space. The search space for this pair is 2150×N possibilities! Clearly enumerate is infeasible, an automated method was required to search through the space of possible waveforms.

In the paper, we present a new waveform optimal design method based on Gradient-Genetic Algorithm (Gradient-GA). GA, inspired by the mechanics of natural selection, is one of the most powerful members of the class of stochastic search techniques. GA techniques are considered attractive since GA can handle problem constraints by embedding them into the chromosome coding and are techniques that are independent of the error surface, so they can be used to solve multimodal, nonlinear, non-convex, non-continuous or NP-complete problems[2]. The Conventional GA (CGA) is known as a powerful stochastic search technique which mimics the mechanisms of natural evolution, by operating on a population of potential solutions to find a global optimum. However, the process of 'breeding' solutions from successive populations may lead to significant computational loads, similar to the case with the optimal algorithm. An alternative is to combine the Gradient to solve the problem[3]. Since Gradient-GA requires smaller size of initial population and lower computational complexity, it is facile to implement the method in little time.

2 Signal Model

2.1 Doppler-Range Ambiguities and PRF Selection

For a SAR system, the azimuth resolution is determined by the antenna length. Reducing the antenna length results in a wide beamwidth, which is at the expense of azimuth resolution. The return echo signal is recorded whenever the platform moves a distance. The maximum cross range spatial sample separation required to process the measured signals without aliasing effects (azimuth ambiguities). For each azimuth sample, one pulse signal is transmitted by the radar and the echo recorded by the receiver[4]. The spatial separation of the samples is thus determined by the platform velocity and PRF as (1). However, the PRF also determines the maximum swath width, the higher the PRF, the smaller the swath:

$$PRF_{azi} \geq 2 \times v / La \tag{1}$$

$$PRF_{range} < c /(2 \times R \times \tan\theta \times \lambda / Wa) \tag{2}$$

where v is the satellitic motion velocity, c is the speed of light, λ is the signal wavelength, θ is the arrival angle, R is the slantrange between satellite and focus target of beam, La is the along-track aperture size and Wa is the cross-track aperture size of the antenna.

According to (1) and (2), two contradicting requirements have to be met when designing a SAR-system. For a given platform velocity a small aperture size requires a high pulse rate, which in turn results in a small ambiguous free swath width according to (2) [5]. The paper investigates an approach to overcome the above mentioned contradicting requirements in SAR systems, we select $PRF > PRF_{azi}$ to ensure Doppler unambiguous, transmit several temporal diversity bi-phase encoded waveform to resolve range ambiguities.

2.2 Bi-phase Encoded Signal Model

If the envelope of bi-phase encoded signal is rectangle, the complex envelope is shown as (3),

$$u(t) = \begin{cases} 1/\sqrt{P} \sum_{K=0}^{P-1} C_K v(t - K\Delta), & 0 < t < T \\ 0, & \text{others} \end{cases} \tag{3}$$

where C_K is the binary sequence, i.e. $C_K = +1$ or -1, Δ is the subpulse width, P is the code-length, $T = P\Delta$ is the duration of encoded signal[4]. Where

$$v(t) = \begin{cases} 1/\sqrt{\Delta}, & 0 < t < \Delta \\ 0, & \text{others} \end{cases} \tag{4}$$

2.3 Encode

Without loss of generality, if there are multiple range ambiguities, multiple temporal diversity transmit signals are needed to resolve multiple range ambiguities. For bi-phase code is a pseudo-random sequence, binary encoding is adopted in the paper.

$$V_i = \{C_i, f_i\} \tag{5}$$

where $C_i = a_1^i a_2^i \cdots a_N^i \cdots a_{n \times N}^i$ is the binary encoding, $a_1^i a_2^i \cdots a_N^i$ is corresponding to signal 1, the rest may be deduced by analogy. f_i is the fitness value of chromosome C_i. $P(k)$ is the kth population of structure $V_i(k)(1 \leq i \leq M)$, M is the population size.

$$P(k) = \{V_i(k)\} \quad i = 1 \cdots M \tag{6}$$

3 The Fitness Function with Adaptive Scale Gene

As a pulse compression signal, not only the Low peak side-lobes (PSL) of aperiodic auto-correlation and cross-correlation, but also cross-correlation energy must be taken into account. For given bi-phase code $C_1, C_2, \cdots C_n$, their aperiodic auto-correlation function[4,6] is

$$\chi_i(m) = \sum_{k=0}^{p-1-m} C_i(k) C_i(k+m) \tag{7}$$

corresponding aperiodic cross-correlation function is

$$\chi_{ij}(m) = \sum_{k=0}^{p-1-m} C_i(k) C_j(k+m) \tag{8}$$

So, the nonlinear programming about bi-phase encoded waveform optimize may be written as follows:

$$s.t. \begin{cases} Max(\sum_{i=1}^{n} auto\_PSL(i)) \\ min(\sum_{j=1}^{n}\sum_{i=1}^{n} cross\_PSL(ij)) \\ min(\sum_{i=1}^{n} auto\_ISL(i)) \\ min(\sum_{j=1}^{n}\sum_{i=1}^{n} cross\_ISL(ij)) \end{cases} \tag{9}$$

where $auto\_PSL$ is the auto-correlation peak sidelobe, $cross\_PSL$ is the cross-correlation integral sidelobe, $auto\_ISL$ is the auto-correlation integral side-lobe energy, $cross\_ISL$ is the cross-correlation integral energy,

$$auto\_PSL(i) = 20\lg\frac{\max_{|m|<\delta}(\chi_i(m))}{\max_{\delta<|m|}(\chi_i(m))}$$

$$cross\_PSL(i,j) = 20\lg\frac{\max_{|m|<\delta}(\chi_{ij}(m))}{\sqrt{\sum_{m=1}^{p-m-1}\chi_{ij}(m)\chi_{ij}^*(m) - (\max_{|m|<\delta}(\chi_{ij}(m)))^2/(p-m-2)}} \quad (10)$$

$$auto\_ISL(i) = \sum_{m=1}^{p-m-1}\chi_i(m)\chi_i^*(m) - (\max_{|m|<\delta}(\chi_i(m)))^2$$

$$cross\_ISL(i,j) = \sum_{m=1}^{p-m-1}\chi_{ij}(m)\chi_{ij}^*(m)$$

In the paper, penalty techniques transform the multi-constrained problem into an unconstrained problem by penalizing solutions.

$$f(C_1,C_2,\cdots C_n) = \max\begin{Bmatrix} w1*\sum_{i=1}^{n}auto\_PSL(i) + w2*\left[Con2 - \sum_{j=1}^{n}\sum_{i=1}^{n}cross\_PSL(ij)\right] + \\ w3*\left[Con3 - \sum_{i=1}^{n}auto\_ISL(i)\right] + w4*\left[Con4 - \sum_{j=1}^{n}\sum_{i=1}^{n}cross\_ISL(ij)\right] \end{Bmatrix} \quad (11)$$

where $Con = [Con2, Con3, Con4]$ is positive constant vector to make sure each restriction non- negativity, $W = [w_1, w_2, w_3, w_4]$ is adaptive scale of penalty value.

In the initial stage, the adaptive scale gene W and Con can be adjusted according to the fitness value of each constrain and the iteration number of genetic algorithms..

4 Gradient-GA for Waveform Design

Suppose $X(0)$ is an initial population, $X(k)$ is the kth population. So the procedure for waveform optimal design based on Gradient-GA is as **Fig. 1**.

A. Generating an initial population $X(0)$ randomly, and evaluate the fitness value according to (**11**), then $P(0)$ is obtained, where $W = W_0 = [1,1,1,1]$;

B. Select the best individual from $P(0)$, evaluate value of each quantity according to (**10**), and estimate magnitude Q1、Q2、Q3、Q4 of every restriction roughly, then obtained the difference of magnitude, so adaptively modified $Con2, Con3, Con4$ and $W = [w_1, w_2, w_3, w_4]$ according to optimize intention. According to $Con2, Con3, Con4$ and $W = [w_1, w_2, w_3, w_4]$, we can finish the fitness function (**11**) and computer individuals' fitness according to (**11**), so updating $P(0)$;

C. Reproduction Operator of Gradient-GA[3]

CGA generally employs a reproduction operator based on roulette wheel selection. If a small chromosome population is adopted for fast convergence, CGA becomes ineffective since, by the nature of the selection procedure, the population may lose its genetic diversity at an early stage. The Gradient-GA employs a gradient-based reproduction operator and the simple crossover and mutation operators of CGA. The new reproduction operator is reminiscent of hill climbing and gives the CGA its hybrid stochastic/deterministic nature. The operator effectively improves the average fitness of a population while preserving its genetic diversity.

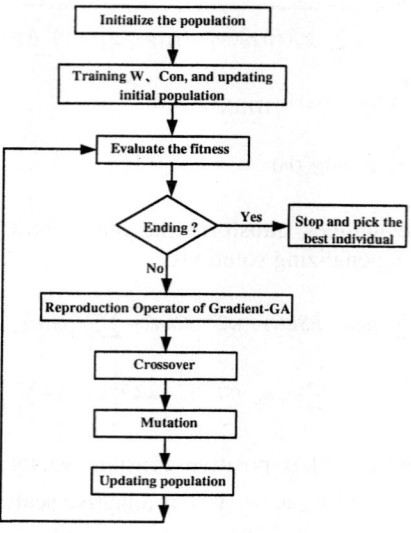

Fig. 1. The layout of Gradient-GA

New reproduction operator: The new reproduction operator is employed to overcome the drawbacks of the commonly adopted roulette wheel selection method. These drawbacks, include the loss of the fittest individual, excessive dominance of strong individuals and inability to explore new points in the search space.

Let $V^l = \{V \mid v_i^{(v)} \leq v \leq v_i^{(u)}\}$ be the search space, where $v_i^{(v)}$ and $v_j^{(v)}$ are the lower and upper bounds, respectively, of the jth component V of vector X and n is the dimension of V. The new reproduction operation involves the following three steps[3]:

Step1: The structures $X_j(k)(1 \leq j \leq M)$ in $X(k)$ are decoded into

$$V_j(k) = [v_{j1}(k)\cdots v_{ji}(k)\cdots v_{jn}(k)]^T \in V^l (1 \leq i \leq n) \qquad (12)$$

Step2: A new vector is computed as follows:

$$V_j(k+1) = V_j(k) + \eta_j \frac{\left[f_b(k) - f_j(k)\right]}{f_b(k)} \left[V_b(k) - V_j(k)\right] \quad (1 \leq j \leq M) \qquad (13)$$

where η_j is a positive coefficient. Note that the new point cannot lie outside the search space as it is limited by the corresponding upper or lower bound.

Step3: The N parameter vectors $V_j(k+1)$ $(1 \leq i \leq M)$ are encoded into structures $X_j(k+1)$ to form the mating pool.

The new reproduction operators assigns each individual chromosome in the current population a new parameter vector based on both the normalized fitness difference, the parameter difference between the individual and the best chromosome, which, according to (13), is preserved automatically. For successful operation, new parameter points must not attempt to grow outside the search space during reproduction. Choosing η_j between 0 and 2 ensures the stability of the reproduction operator.

For the current population, experiencing by applying the CGA approach with gradient-like reproduction operators to optimal design leads us to use a population of 8 individuals.

$$P\{T_s(X_j(k)) = Y_j(k)\} = \begin{cases} f(Y_j(k))/\sum_{X \in X(k)} f(X), & (Y_j(k)) \in X(k) \\ f(X_j(k))/\sum_{X \in X(k)} f(X), & (Y_j(k)) \notin X(k) \text{ and satisfied(13)} \\ 0, & \text{otherwise} \end{cases} \quad (14)$$

where $j = 1 \sim M$, only individuals having the best fitness remain unaltered. Then encode $X_j(k)$ into structure $Y_j(k)$ to form mating pool $Y(k)$.

D. Crossover

Single-point crossover with probability p_c ($0 < p_c \leq 1$) is given as follows[7,8]:

$$P\{T_c(Y_1^{(j)}, Y_2^{(j)}) = X_j'(k+1)\}$$
$$= \begin{cases} jp_c/n & , X_j'(k+1) \neq Y_1^{(j)} \boxplus X_j'(k+1) = AY_1^{(j)} + (I-A)Y_2^{(j)} \\ (1-p_c) + jp_c/n & , X_j'(k+1) = Y_1^{(j)} \\ 0 & , \text{otherwise} \end{cases} \quad (15)$$

where $j = j(Y_1^{(j)}, Y_2^{(j)}, X_j'(k+1))$ is the number of locus which $(Y_1^{(j)}, Y_2^{(j)})$ can move forward to $X_j'(k+1)$, l is the length of chromosome, crossover probability p_c is satisfied $0 < p_c \leq 1$, A is diagonal matrix with anterior r equals to one and the others are zeros, where r is the position of crossover point.

E. Mutation

$X'(k+1) = (X_1'(k+1), \cdots, X_M'(k+1))$ is transformed to $X(k+1) = (X_1(k+1), \cdots, X_M(k+1))$ by mutation with a probability equal to the mutation rate p_m [7,8].

$$P\{T_m(X_j'(k+1)) = X_j(k+1)\} = p_m^{d(X_j'(k+1), X_j(k+1))}(1-p_m)^{l-d(X_j'(k+1), X_j(k+1))} (j \leq M) \quad (16)$$

where $d\left(X'_j(k+1), X_j(k+1)\right) = \sum_{i=1}^{l}\left|a'_{ji} - a_{ji}\right|$ is the hamming distance between $X'_j(k+1)$ and $X_j(k+1)$.

F. Termination

After reaching an acceptable fitness in a number of generations, the genetic engine can be stopped and the GA finishes. This guarantees an overall lower complexity than the algorithm, which searches for the best population. If termination condition is not satisfied, go back to **C**.

From above procedure, we can obtain $\{X(k); k \geq 0\}$ from $X(0)$ as shown below,

$$X(k) = T(X(k-1)) = T_m \bullet T_c \bullet T_s(X(k-1)) \tag{17}$$

5 Simulation and Performance Analysis

The parameters for simulation: λ =0.03, v =7000m/s, La =2m, Wa =1m, R=979.06km , $\theta = 45°$, B_r=150MHz , $T = 1\mu S$. From(1),(2), $PRF_{azi} \geq 2*7482$(Hz) $PRF_{range} \leq 5107$. In the paper, $PRF = 15000$ Hz) , so Doppler unambiguous, and range ambiguities is three times, that is to say, $N = 3$, $P = 150$, $\Delta = T/P = 0.01\mu s$ from $B_r \times T = 150$. $M = 8$; $p_c = 0.6$, $p_m = 0.1$, the maximum generation is 1000。

Fig. 2 is the best fitness performance of Gradient–GA and CGA from 100 independent Monte Carlo experiments so far. From this figure, it can be seen that Gradient-GA can converge at optimal value with a small population size, but CGA converge at local optima quickly. Because the Gradient operator guides the population towards the best chromosome. Weak chromosome undergo more correction than strong chromosomes. Duplication of individuals is minimized because, from (**13**), only chromosomes having the same fitness as the best remain unaltered. This enables the reproduction operator to maintain genetic diversity in the population.

Table 1 is the optimal codes A、B、C searched by the presented algorithm. **Fig. 3** is their auto-correlation curves. **Fig. 4** is their cross-correlation curves. From **Fig. 3**, optimal codes have both low PSL, which is less than –15 decibels, and integrated sidelobe(ISL), which is less than –40 decibels, of auto-correlation (pulse compression). From **Fig. 4**, they also have a both low integrated energy, which is less than –40 decibels, and peak main-lobe in cross-correlation. **Fig. 5** and **Fig. 6** are weighted pulse compression performance figures, where **Fig. 5** is the result corresponding to 300 order filter, its PSL is less than –18 decibel. **Fig. 6** is the result corresponding to 600 order filter and its PSL is less than –23 decibels. The mismatched filters adopted in the paper is to minimize the PSL, this technique sees reference [9,10].

From **example**, optimal codes searched by the presented algorithm have both low PSL and ISL of auto-correlation, also have a both low integrated energy and peak mainlobe of cross-correlation. The PSL reduction achieved through the use of mismatch filters varies from about 5 to 10 decibel depending on the code and filter length used. The loss in processing gain is usually less than 0.6 decibel and main-lobe widen is fewer.

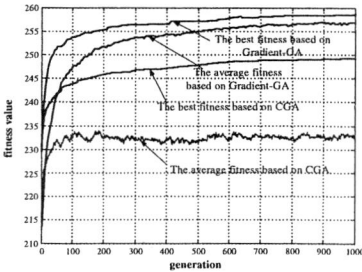

Fig. 2. Convergence curve of Gradient-GA and CGA

Table 1. Optimal code A,B,C based on Gradient-GA

码元 A	1001001010111000001110101101000011001111011011010101100000010010111011110001100010000011111101011001111100110011100110111000101100000101001011011 10
码元 B	1000111010010000010010110011110010101110110001111110111001001011000001110001101111001010011110100111001100110001000001101010010011010000100101001101 00
码元 C	0000100111010111011001000110101011110001110000100111010011000011111101100111110011001010011000111111101111000100011000011001001100100000000000101111010

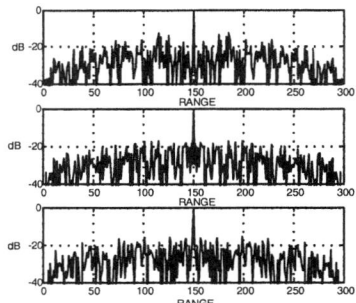

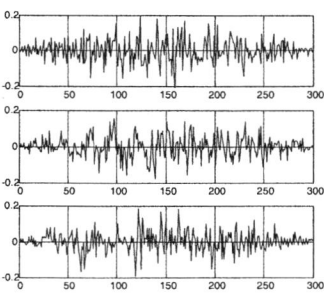

Fig. 3. Auto-correlation curves of optimal code A,B,C

Fig. 4. Cross-correlation curves of optimal code A,B,C

6 Conclusion

To operate Doppler unambiguous but allow range ambiguities, an optimal waveform is used to resolve the range ambiguities. The paper present a novel bi-phase code optimal algorithm based on Gradient-GA. So their PSL and ISL of auto-correlation and cross-correlation are all as lower as possible. The fitness function with adaptive scale gene corresponding to multiple constraints is used to overcome local optimal trend. The simulation results based on x-wave band sparse space-based radar were presented to show that the algorithm proposed is efficient and feasible.

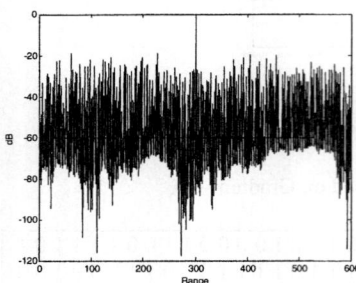

Fig. 5. Mismatch filter(300 order) performance analysis

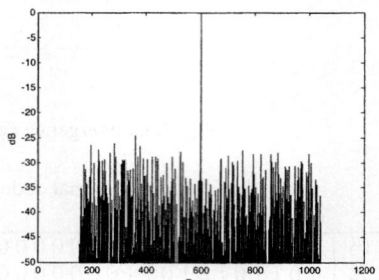

Fig. 6. Mismatch filter(600 order) performance analysis

References

1. Gamham J., Wainwright R., Bums R.: Enabling Research and Development for Flight Demonstration of Sparse Aperture Sensing. AIAA Space 2001-Conference and Exposition, Albuquerque, NM, 8 (2001) 143-147.
2. Holland J.H.: Adaptation in Natural and Artificial Systems. Ann Arbor, MI: Univ, MichiEAn Press (1975) 26-29.
3. Pham D.T., Jin G.: Genetic Algorithm Using Gradient-like Reproduction Operator. Electronics letters IEE 31st, Vol. 31 No.18, (1995) 1558-1559.
4. Skolnik M.I.: Radar Handbook (Second Edition) (In Chinese). Beijing: Publishing House of Electronics Industry. 7 (2003) 395-399.
5. Liu Y.T.: Radar Imaging Techniques. Harbin: Harbin industry university press. 10(1999) 166– 171.
6. Somaini U.: Binary Sequences with Good Autocorrelation and Cross Correlation Properties. IEEE Tranc. on AES, Vol. 11, No.6, (1975) 634-637.
7. Papoulis A., Pillai S.U.: *Probability, Random Variables and Stochastic Processes* (Fourth edition). The McGraw-Hill companies, Inc. (2002) 322-345.
8. Zhang W.X., Liang Y.: Mathematical Foundation of Genetic Algorithms. Xi'an: Xi'an Jiaotong University Press. 5(2000) 106-112.
9. Baden J.M., Cohen M.N.: Optimal Peak Sidelobe Filters for Biphase Pulse Compression. IEEE International Radar Conference. (1990) 249-252.
10. Goodman N.A., Stiles J.M.: An MMSE Filter for Range Sidelobe Reduction. In Proc. of the IEEE International Geoscience and Remote Sensing Symposium, Honolulu, Hawaii. (2000) 2365-2367.

Analytic Model for Network Viruses*

Lansheng Han[1], Hui Liu[2], and Baffour Kojo Asiedu[3]

[1] School of Computer Science and Technology,
Huazhong University of Science and Technology,Wuhan 430074, China
hanlansheng@hotmail.com
[2] School of Electrical and Electronic Engineering,
Hubei University of Technology, Wuhan 430068, China
[3] Msc. Computer Science and Technology Department,
Computer Science School of Computer Science Engineering, Ghana

Abstract. Most existing spreading models for network viruses are developed refereing to the epidemic models for biological viruses. However, Why most network viruses spread much slower than those models predicate? Why most network viruses still exist when they go beyond the threshold predicated by those models? Contrary to the prior models, the paper points out network viruses have different spreading features compared with biological viruses, such as the connectivity rate and cure rate are both functions of the time which are also key factors to affect the spreading of viruses. Based on which the paper constructs a more general epidemiological model for the network viruses. For several particular cases the paper presents the simulations of the connectivity rate and cure rate and find they are consistent well with the statistics of some real viruses. Thus the paper opens one path to modifying the traditional epidemic models.

1 Introduction

Network viruses constitute one of the major Internet security problems. However, currently most research has focused on detection and defense against network viruses. Little research has been pursued on modelling viruses' propagation or even to mention them. Though there are some papers in a relatively small number on the modelling viruses' spreading [1][2][3][4][5], much still remains unknown about the propagation characteristic of the network viruses. Kephart and White are among the first to propose epidemiology-based analytic models called homogenous models which assume that every individual has equal contact to everyone else in the population, and the rate of the infection is largely determined by the density of the infected population[1][2]. However, there is overwhelming evidence that real networks deviate from such homogeneity. Pastor-Satorras and Vespignani studied epidemic spread for power-law networks where the connectivity distribution is characterized as $P(k) = k^{-\tau}$ ($P(k)$ is the probability of

---

* Supported by National Natural Science Foundation of China(NO. 60403027) and also supported by Graduate Students Foundation(NO:X0333).

a node has k links) and developed an analytic model which depends critically on the assumption $\tau = 3$ [3][4], but it does not hold for the real networks[5][6]. Boguñá and Satorras studied epidemic spreading in correlated networks where the connectivity of a node is related to the connectivity of its neighbors[7]. However there is no conclusive evidence to support the type of correlation[8]. Zou and Towsley focused on the simulation of email viruses' spreading but did not present the analysis process for the spreading model[9].

In fact, all those models have similar basis: the connectivity frequency and the cure rate (or death rate) of the viruses are both assumed as relatively stable or satisfy some simple distributions which originate from the epidemiological models of the biological viruses[10]. However statistical observations of virus incidents in the real network indicate that all viruses that are able to pervade, spread much slower than those model predicate and affect just a small fraction of the total number of computers[11][12]. This striking contradiction with the theoretical prediction indicates that the view obtained so far with the modeling of network viruses' epidemics is very instructive but not completely adequate to represent the real phenomenon[13].

Hence we believe these contradictions have some root reasons: there are some epidemiological differences between network viruses and biological viruses.

First, the spreading of the biological viruses is by physical contact of the hosts. The spreading speed is determined by the mobility of the population and this mobility is relatively stable in a region. While the spreading of the network viruses is by the connectivity of the computer systems. This connectivity is not physical contact but a kind of logical contact[14]. The two computer systems in one connection are not restricted in a local region, and this logical connectivity is variable with time or even has periodicity.

Second, the carriers of biological viruses, such as a man or a woman has little difference from the others, so the biological model only takes the number the infected as its main object; while in network virus model, the carriers such as a computer system may be very different from the others. For example, in terms of spreading a virus, a big hot site is many times powerful as a personal computer.

Third, biological viruses can cause a host die, then end this spreading of the host, which is also one of reasons that cause the number of the infected decrease. But the network viruses never really cause the number of the infected decrease.

Four, the patients of biological virus once cured will get the immunity against the virus. While the infected computer, strictly speaking, can't get the immunity against the virus. This is to say, the same virus can infect the cured computer again.

It is these differences that make the network viruses have different spreading features compared with the biological viruses. So network viruses should have their own epidemiological model. As the above analysis informs, the key factor that influence the network viruses' spreading is the logic, dynamic and directed connectivity between two computer systems. If we take the connectivity rate as a basic characteristic that influences the viruses' spreading, it will be more accurate to construct the epidemiological model for network viruses. Fortunately this connectivity rate can be quantified, such as the click rate and the flow rate of the computer are both direct indication of the connectivity rate in a net.

This paper is organized as follows: Section 1 reviews the previous work in the field and points out the differences between network viruses' propagation and the biological viruses' propagation. Section 2 takes the connectivity rate as a key factor for the computer to spread viruses and constructs the epidemiological equation for the viruses. Section 3 presents the solution to the equation and discusses the deterministic influences of the variations of the connectivity rate and the cure rate on the spreading of viruses. Section 4 concludes the paper.

2 Constructing the Epidemiological Model

A single computer system on the network is looked as a node such as a PC or a site. A connection from node A to node B is looked as a directed edge from B to A which coincides the direction of viruses' spreading. We assume there are N nodes in a network in a given region. Then we get a dynamic directed graph $G(V, E(t))$, where V is the set of nodes and $E(t)$ is the set of edges which is also a function of time.

According to the protocol and the Paralleled ability of the current networks, we know each node can send a connecting request to at most one of the other nodes at time t. While one node can accept the connecting requests from more than one node. So we assume, in the directed graph $G(V, E(t))$ with N nodes, there are at most N edges at time t. Those edges can end at one or more than one node but they must start from distinct node. In fact this assumption tallies with the biological viruses' spreading. In biological model, one infected node can infect more than one uninfected nodes but one node can be infected by only one node at time t.

By the above analysis, the click rate is one of the most direct indications of the connectivity rate. One click corresponds one directed edge. Therefore, we let $c(t)$ denote the connectivity rate which is the rate of the number of directed edges at time t to N in a given net. α denotes the probability of infected node A infects uninfected node B once B clicks A. $I(t)$ denotes the number of the infected nodes at time t in the region. $\beta(t)$ denotes the cure rate at time t which is the rate of number of the cured nodes to the number of the infected nodes. In biological models, the cure rate is the average probability of an infected node to be successfully cured. $\beta(t)$ is determined by the virus and the medical skill. However in the network, once the antiviral software against the virus emerges, the probability of the infected node to be cured is almost 100%. So it is obvious that the cure rate of network virus is different from that of biological virus. Further more, the cure rate of network virus is also a function of the time. For example, when a new virus appears on the net $\beta(t) = 0$, when the antiviral software against the virus is developed $\beta(t) > 0$, if the spreading speed of the antiviral software is higher than the spreading speed of the virus, $\beta(t)$ will increase and finally tends to a constant $\beta(< 1)$. Thus $I(t)\beta(t)$ is the decreased number of infected nodes be cured at time t. Considering that current computer system doesn't possess the real immunity to most viruses, we let $N - I(t)$ denote the number of susceptible nodes which includes the cured nodes.

Now we begin with one infected node ν_i, let's look how it infects its neighbors, and then we will construct the epidemiological model for the network viruses.

From the above discussion, we know, at time t, ν_i can be clicked by at most the rest $N - 1$ nodes. As infection can only happen when uninfected node clicks the infected nodes, so among $c(t)(N - 1)$ nodes that are neighbors of ν_i, the rate of uninfected nodes is $(1 - I(t)/N)$. Then $c(t)(N - 1)(1 - I(t)/N)$ is the number of susceptible nodes that connect to ν_i at time t. Since one uninfected node that connects to one infected node has the probability of α to be infected, then $\alpha c(t)(N - 1)(1 - I(t)/N)$ is the number of nodes infected by ν_i at time t. For there are $I(t)$ infected nodes in the net at time t, so the increasing number of infected nodes at time t is $\alpha c(t)(N - 1)(1 - I(t)/N)I(t)$. As the decreasing number of infected nodes at time t is $\Delta I(t)\beta(t)$, so we get the epidemiological equation for the viruses:

$$\frac{dI(t)}{dt} = \alpha c(t)(N - 1)(1 - \frac{I(t)}{N})I(t) - \beta(t)I(t).$$

As N is a larger number $N \approx N - 1$, then the above equation can be simplified as:

$$\frac{dI(t)}{dt} = (N\alpha c(t) - \beta(t))I(t) - \alpha c(t)I^2(t). \tag{1}$$

3 Mathematically Analysis of the Solution to the Equation

According to separation of variables, the equation:

$$\frac{dI(t)}{dt} = C_1 I(t) - C_2 I^2(t), \text{(Where } C_1, C_2 \text{ are selected constants)}. \tag{2}$$

has the solution of the following form:

$$I(t) = \frac{C_1}{C_2 - C_0 e^{-C_1 t}}, \text{ (where } C_0 \text{ is a constant)}.$$

By the variation of parameters, we assume equation (1) has the solution of the following form:

$$I(t) = \frac{C_1}{C_2 - C_t e^{-C_1 t}}, \text{ (where } C_t \text{ is a function of t with relation to } C_1, C_2). \tag{3}$$

Let

$$I(t)|_{t=0} = I_0. \tag{4}$$

Substituting (3),(4) into (1) we get:

$$C_0(t) = e^{-\int_0^t (N\alpha c(s) - \beta(s))ds + C_1 t}(C_2 - \frac{C_1}{I_0} + p(t)),$$

where $p(t) = \int_0^t (\alpha c(s)(NC_2-C_1)-C_2\beta(s))e^{\int_0^s (N\alpha c(x)-\beta(x))dx}ds$. Then substituting the above form into (3), we get the solution to (1) with the initial value (4):

$$I(t) = \frac{C_1}{C_2 - e^{-\int_0^t N\alpha c(s)-\beta(s)ds}(C_2 - \frac{C_1}{I_0}p(t))}. \tag{5}$$

As there are many undetermined factors in $c(t), \beta(t)$, we can't present the complete accurate forms for them. But for several particular cases (which are also cases of special viruses), we can present the simulations of $c(t), \beta(t)$. However, as the form of $I(t)$ is still too complicated, in order to see how the variations of $c(t)$ and $\beta(t)$ influent the viruses' spreading clearly, we discuss their deterministic influences respectively.

Case 1: let $c(t) \equiv C, \beta(t) \equiv \beta$, (where C, β are both constants and $C > 0$). Then let $C_1 = N\alpha C - \beta, C_2 = \alpha C$, and take them into (5), we get:

$$I(t) = \frac{N - \frac{\beta}{\alpha C}}{1 - (1 - \frac{N}{I_0} + \frac{\beta}{I_0 \alpha C})e^{-(N\alpha C - \beta)t}}.$$

This solution is the same as Kephart and White has discussed[1], if $t \to \infty$ then $I(t) \to N - \beta/\alpha$, which is also consistent with their result. Here is no necessary to repeat it. But one point worth mentioning is that the solution being consistent with their experiment as Kephart and White said has little practical meaning for modern networks. The reason is that their experiment condition was just designed as $c(t) \equiv c, \beta(t) \equiv \beta$. As we know this is just an ideal condition not a practical one. However, considering the dangerous of network viruses on the real Internet, we can't take the Internet as our experiment. Fortunately, there are often new viruses appearing on the Internet. We can utilize the statistic of those viruses to verify our analysis.

Case 2: let $C(t) \equiv C$, $\beta(t)$ be a smoothing function of the time,

$$\beta(t) = \begin{cases} 0, & 0 \leq t \leq t_0; \\ \text{monotonous increasing function}, & t_0 < t \leq t_1; \\ \beta, & t > t_1. \end{cases}$$

Since the cure rate not only has relation with the particular virus, but also can be affected by many personal factors. So we simulate the variation of $\beta(t)$ in Fig.1(A). Since there are always some one who don't clean the virus for any kinds of reasons, we let the final constant $\beta < 1$.

Let $C_1 = NC, C_2 = C$, and bring them into (5), we get the solution to I(t):

$$I(t) = \frac{I_0}{\frac{I_0}{N} - (\frac{I_0}{N} - 1)e^{(\int_0^t \beta(s)ds - N\alpha C(t))} + \frac{I_0}{N}\int_0^t \beta(s)e^{(-N\alpha C(t-s) + \int_s^t \beta(x)dx)}ds}.$$

By the form of $I(t)$, we can numerically simulate the variation of $I(t)$ along with the variation of $\beta(t)$ as shown in Fig.1(B) which compares the variation of $I(t)$ with the statistic of particular virus named Gaobot.gen in USA (*from www.pandasoftware.com*). Gaobot.gen is a worm appearing on Sept. 19. 2003.

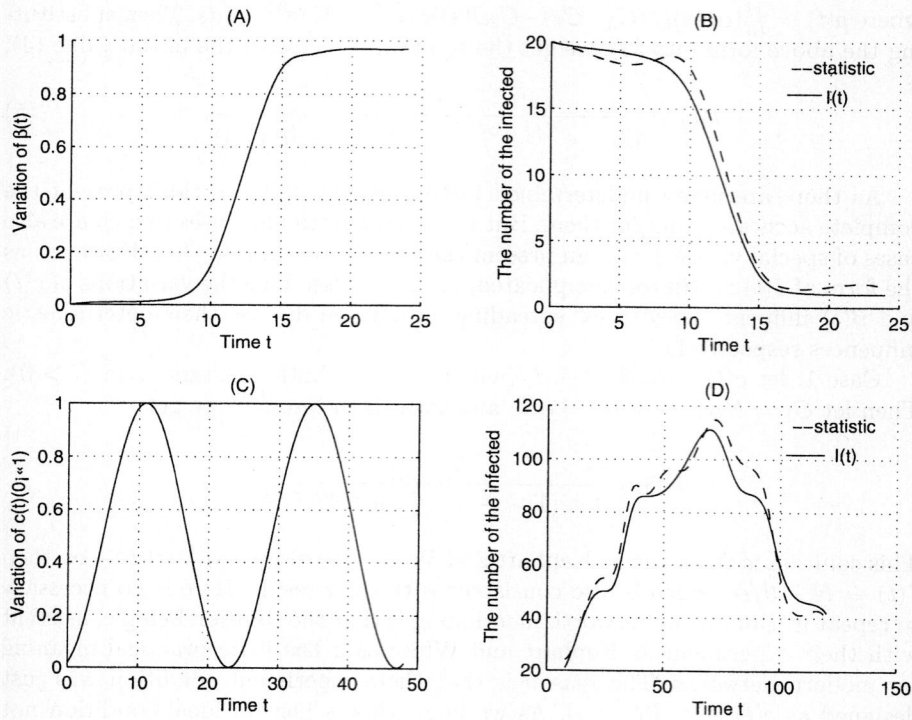

Fig. 1. Simulation and the statistic. (A) is the variation of $\beta(t)$; (B) is the simulation of $I(t)$ with $\beta(t)$ and the statistic of Gaobot.gen; (C) is the variation of $c(t)$; (D) is the simulation of $I(t)$ with $c(t)$ and the statistic of Briss.A

New tools against the virus were developed on May 17, 2004 and then widely used by most users. So it is obvious that the infection rate decrease sharply after that time. From the Figure, we can see the simulation of $I(t)$ fit perfectly the statistic of Gaobot.gen.

As we explain above, for some viruses, $\beta(t)$ tends to a constant $\beta < 1$, so in Fig.1(B) the $I(t)$ of those viruses also tends to a constant greater than 0. Which means those viruses still hide in some nodes. If those nodes can still connect to other nodes in the Internet, there is the probability for the viruses to spread again. However as the β is very high at that time, the viruses can only spread in a small scale instead of a large one. That is why some earlier viruses still exist on the Internet today, and continually disturb some local users but never break out again[11].

Case 3: Let $\beta(t) \equiv \beta$, $c(t) = \omega(1+\sin(\gamma t))$ (where $\omega < 1$). Here $c(t)$, a periodic function, is also a simulation from the practice. Although the variation of $c(t)$ has no direct relation with particular virus, it is still influenced by many personal factors. For example, $c(t)$ increases when people are on the job, while decreases when people are off the job. So in this case we can assume $\gamma = \frac{\pi}{12}$, which means the periodicity is 24 hours. Fig.1(C) is the numerically simulation of c(t).

Let $C_1 = N\alpha\omega - \beta, C_2 = \alpha\omega$, and bring them into (5) we get:

$$I(t) = \frac{N - \frac{\beta}{\alpha\omega}}{1 - q_1(t) + q_2(t)},$$

where

$$q_1(t) = (1 - \frac{N}{I_0} + \frac{\beta}{\alpha\omega I_0})e^{(\frac{12N\alpha\omega}{\pi}(\cos(\pi t/12)-1)-(N\omega-\beta)t)},$$

$$q_2(t) = \beta \int_0^t (\frac{\pi}{12}s)e^{(-(N\alpha\omega-\beta)(t-s)+\frac{12N\alpha\omega}{\pi}(\cos\frac{\pi}{12}t-\cos\frac{\pi}{12}s))}ds.$$

Fig. 1(D) is the variation simulation of $I(t)$ along with $c(t)$ and the statistic of a particular virus named Briss.A in North American appeared on May 24, 2004 (from www.pandasoftware.com). It is obvious that $I(t)$ does not increase in exponential liner way as the prior models predict but in exponential circularly way with the circular variation of $c(t)$ of the network. The statistic of virus Briss.A also shows a typical periodical increase. So the both fit well.

By the above analysis, we can easy to understand the problem asked by White: Why most viruses decline before the threshold as the traditional models predict? The reason is, in biological model, $\alpha C/\beta$ is a constant, but in modern real network $\alpha c(t)/\beta(t)$ is depend on the time. When a new virus appears on the net, It is very natural that most users will minimize their time spent on the net and will avoid the time when the click rate is very high. As the Fig.1(D) shows that if $c(t)$ decreases then the increasing speed of $I(t)$ will decline. Further more considering the $\beta(t)$ still increases as shown in Fig.1(A), then $I(t)$ will decrease much more time than biological model predicts.

4 Summary

Contrary to the prior models, our aim in this paper is to point out that connectivity rate and cure rate are both dynamic functions of the time. Then we developed a more general analytic model for viruses' propagation. As there are many undetermined factors, we don't anticipate presenting the complete accurate forms of the connectivity rate and cure rate, but emphasizing on the deterministic impacts of the both factors on the spreading of the viruses. To several particular cases of connectivity rate and cure rate, we present the simulations of the both and find they are consistent well with the statistics of real viruses. The paper opens one path to considering modifying the traditional models. If we want to catch the more accurate forms of $c(t)$ and $\beta(t)$, one efficient way, we think, is the classification on both the viruses and the type of the topology of networks.

References

1. Kephart, J. O., White, S. R.: Directed-graph Epidemiological Models of Computer Viruses. In Proceedings of the 1991 IEEE Computer Society Symposium on Research in Security and Privacy, IEEE, Oakland, California(1991)343-359
2. Kephart, J.O., White, S. R.: Measuring and Modeling Computer Virus Prevalence. In Proceedings of the 1993 IEEE Computer Society Symposium on Research in Security and Privacy, IEEE, Oakland, California(1993)2-15
3. Pastor-Satorras,R., Vespignani, A.: Epidemic Dynamics and Endemic States in Complex Networks. Physical Review E, 63:066117(2001)
4. Pastor-Satorras, R., Vespignani, A.: Epidemics and Immunization in Scale-free Networks. In: Bornholdt, S., Schuster, H. G.(eds): Handbook of Graphs and Networks: From the Genome to the Internet. Wiley-VCH, Berlin(2002)
5. Wang, C. J., Knight, C., Elder, M. C.: On Computer Viral Infection and the Effect of Immunization. In Proceedings of the 16th ACM Annual Computer Security Applications Conference, IEEE, Washington(2000)246-257
6. Kumar, S. R., Raghavan, P., Rajagopalan, S., Tomkins, A.: Trawling the Web for Emerging Cyber-communities. In: Computer Networks, Vol. 31(1999)1481-1493
7. Boguñá, M., Pastor-Satorras, R.: Epidemic Spreading in Correlated Complex Networks. Physical Review E, 66:047104(2002)
8. Newman, M. E. J., Forrest, S., Balthrop, J.: Email Networks and the Spread of Computer Viruses. Physical Review E, 66, 035101(R)(2002)
9. Cliff, C.Zou, Don Towsley, Gong, W.B.: Email Worm Modeling and Defense. In Proceeding of ICCCN'04, IEEE, Chicago(2004)
10. Bailey, N.(ed.): The Mathematical Theory of Infectious Diseases and Its Applications. Griffin, London(1975)
11. White, S.R.: Open Problems in Computer Virus Research. In: Virus Bulletin Conference, Munich, Germany(1998)
12. Chess, D.M.: The Future of Viruses on the Internet. In: Virus Bulletin International Conference, San Francisco, California(1997)
13. José, R.C.P., Betyna, F.N., Luiz, H.A.M.: Epidemiological Models Applied to Virues in Computer Networks. Journal of Computer Science, Vol.1(1)(2005)31-34
14. Jongyun, K., Scidhar, R., Sudarshan K. D.: Measurement and Analysis of Worm Propagation on Internet Network Topology. In Proceeding of ICCCN'04, IEEE, Chicago(2004)

Ant Colony Optimization Algorithms for Scheduling the Mixed Model Assembly Lines

Xin-yu Sun and Lin-yan Sun

School of management, the State Key Laboratory for Manufacturing System Engineering,
Xi'an Jiaotong University,710049, 8686716317, P. R. China
sunxy@ap88.com, lysun@xjtu.edu.cn, ylwang@xjtu.edu.cn

Abstract. Solving the mixed-model scheduling problem is the most important goal for Just-in-time production systems. But it is a difficult combinatorial optimization problem. This study presents a novel co-operative agents approach, Ant Colony Optimization algorithm (ACO) scheme, for solving the scheduling mixed-model assembly lines. The results show that the solution which ant algorithm produces is better than the one which Toyota's goal chasing algorithm, simulated annealing algorithm and genetic algorithm produce. Finally, this example may extend to a bigger scale, and the satisfied solutions, benchmark results and CPU time to generate a satisfied tour are given.

1 Introduction

Mixed model assembly lines are used in many manufacturing factories because they can meet the diversified demands of their customers without possessing a large amount of inventories. Since the sequencing problem is NP hard, it is essential to develop efficient approximation algorithms for large-scale problems to obtain a good sub-optimal solution.

2 Mixed Model Sequencing Problem

Mixed-model assembly lines are widely adopted in manufacturing industries [1], Sequencing for mixed models is recognized as an important work for improving the performance of an assembly line.

The study uses the Toyota's goal. The goal is to keep the constant usage of every part used in the assembly line, which is a good way of fitting the just-in-time (JIT) concept in Toyota production system. Toyota's goal for an assembly line with multiple workstations is [1]

$$Z_D = \min \sum_{j=1}^{D}\sum_{i=1}^{n}\sum_{p=1}^{m}(k\alpha_p - b_{ip} - \beta_{j-1,p})^2 x_{ji} \qquad (1)$$

3 Implementation of the ACO

3.1 Generation Scheduling Strategy by ACO

Now we give an example (Fig. 1) of search space defined in the ACO algorithm. The columns represent stages in a schedule. The rows represent the models that the ant can choose in a stage. The area of the circle represents the probability by which the ant choose model i. The area of circle changes during the optimization process. Finally, a satisfied solution is found [2].

For example, we have three models named A, B and C to be scheduled. In a production cycle, three model A's, two model B's, and one model C are needed. In other words, we need to produce six items in a production cycle. The columns represent the six stages and the rows represent three models that the ant can choose.

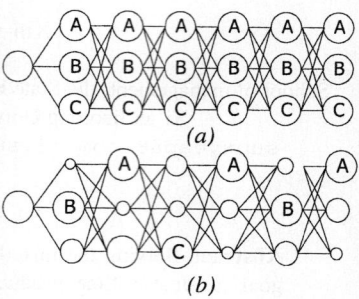

Fig. 1. An instance of search space for scheduling mixed-model in assembly line

The initial search state is described in Fig. 1a. The area of circle represents the possibility of choice that consists of local search value and pheromone trail. Fig. 1b describes the changed search space after many iterations. Finally, a possible satisfied solution is B-A-C-A-B-A.

3.2 General Framework of the ACO Algorithm [3][4]

In general, in the ACO algorithm an ant is defined to be a simple computational agent. Partial problem solutions are seen as *states*; each ant *moves* from a state ι to another one ψ, corresponding to a more complete partial solution.

(1) Computation of Attractiveness

The attractiveness η_{ij} of a move can be computed by means of the goal chasing method. This means that from a state ι to another one ψ, we choose the least increment of goal function. The local search procedure is a straightforward greedy method. Before starting the construction of a solution η_{ij} are randomly generated. When a solution is completed and we want to find the corresponding local optimum.

(2) Transition probabilities

One of the most difficult aspects to be considered in meta-heuristic algorithm is the trade-off between exploration and exploitation. To obtain good results, a system should prefer actions that has tried in the past and found to be effective in producing desirable solutions (exploitation); but to discover such actions, it has to try actions that it has not selected before (exploration). The ACO algorithm integrates a stagnation avoidance procedure to facilitate exploration and a move probability definition mechanism to determine the desirability of different moves.

(3) Trail update

After each iteration of the algorithm, that is, when all ants have completed a solution, trails are updated and the coefficient ρ must set $0 \le \rho < 1$ to avoid unlimited accumulation of trail.

4 Numerical Results

(1) Simple example

Now we use the problem defined in article [1]. In each experiment only one of the values was changed, except for α, which have been tested over different sets of values. All the tests have been carried out and were averaged over ten trials. The best value in the experiment is followed:

☆ $\rho = 0.9$ ☆ $\alpha = 0.2$ ☆ $Q = 20000$ ☆ $NC_{max} = 400$ ☆ n_ant=5

☆The value of the objective function is 2859.8

☆the sequences is C-A-D-E-B-A-D-E-A-C-A-B-E-D-A-C

Table 1. Computational results of ACO algorithms and benchmark with GCA, GA and SAA

The algorithm	The goal function	The percent that ant algorithm improved
Goal chasing algorithm	3293	13%
Genetic algorithm	3073	6%
Simulated annealing algorithm	3162	10%
ACO algorithms	2859.8	

Table 1 shows the comparative good performance of ACO algorithm. The results show that the solution, which the ant algorithm produces, is better than the one which Toyota's goal chasing algorithm, simulated annealing algorithm and the genetic algorithm produce. Fig. 2 shows the values of best-found tour at each cycle, and Fig. 3 shows the average value of the tour population at each cycle of same run.

Note how in the early cycles the ACO identifies good values that are subsequently refined in the rest of the run. Since the average value never equalled each other, we are assured that algorithm actively searches solutions, which differ from the best-so-far found. So the algorithm may find the better solution possibly. The search for better solutions is carried on in selected regions of search space determined by the trail resulting front preceding cycles.

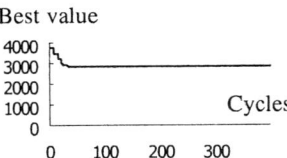

Fig. 2. Evolution of best tour. Typical run

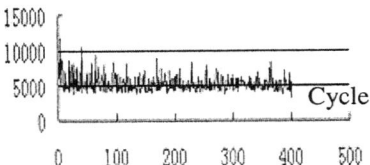

Fig. 3. Evolution of the average value of population's objective function. Typical run

(2) Extended example
Since the example we used is so small, we have studied extend examples using the ACO algorithm. In our experiment, P4 3.06G CPU, DDR 1G Memory, Window2000 Professional, the test of different scale problems is showed in table 2.

Definition:

    1: *Scale* in the paper, the scale refers to total demand in a production cycle.
    2: *n*-**scale problem** the scale is n for mixed model sequencing problem.
    3: *n*2* **scale problem solution** n is defined as *Scale*. We combine two feasible solutions into one solution for larger problem. We present the $n*2$ scale problem to benchmark the performance of ACO algorithm for the scheduling mixed model assembly lines. We test different scale of problem in order to validate the computation efficiency of ACO algorithm and learn the relation between CPU time and scale.

Table 2. ACO performance for bigger scheduling mixed-model assembly lines

The problem scale	Model					The goal function	The sequences	CPU time to generate a tour(s)
	A	B	C	D	E			
16	5	2	3	3	3	2859.8	C-A-D-E-B-A-D-E-A-C-A-B-E-D-A-C	1.2
16*2	10	4	6	6	6	1116479.3	C-A-D-E-B-A-D-E-A-C-A-B-E-D-A-C- C-A-D-E-B-A-D-E-A-C-A-B-E-D-A-C	
32						788783.4	E-A-E-B-E-E-A-C-E-B-A-E-A-C-A-C- A-C-C-A-C-A-B-A-A-B-D-D-D-D-D-D	3.1
32*2	20	8	12	12	12	19576747.6	C-A-D-E-B-A-D-E-A-C-A-B-E-D-A-C- C-A-D-E-B-A-D-E-A-C-A-B-E-D-A-C- C-A-D-E-B-A-D-E-A-C-A-B-E-D-A-C- C-A-D-E-B-A-D-E-A-C-A-B-E-D-A-C	
64						15087183.8	E-A-E-E-B-E-E-B-A-E-E-A-E-E-E-A- E-B-A-A-C-B-A-C-A-C-A-C-A-C-C-B- A-A-C-C-A-C-A-C-A-A-C-B-A-C-A-A- A-B-B-D-D-D-D-D-D-D-D-D-D-D-D	10.9

Acknowledgements

The authors express thanks to the NSFC (70433003) and IBM SUR project for the financial support.

References

1. ZHAO Wei, HAN Wen-xiu, LUO Yong-tai. Scheduling mixed-model assembly lines in JIT production systems. *Journal of Management Sciences in China*, 3(4): 23-28, 2000.
2. YOW-YUH LEU, LANCE A.MATHESON, LOREN PAUL REES. Sequencing mixed-model assembly lines with genetic algorithms. *Computers ind. Engng*, 30(4): 1027-1036, 1996.
3. Marco Dorigo, Eric Bonabeau, Guy Theraulaz. Ant algorithms and stigmergy, *Future Generation Computer Systems*, 16: 851–871, 2000.
4. I.K.Yu,Y.H.Song. A novel short-term generation scheduling technique of thermal units using ant colony search algorithms. *Electrical Power and Energy System*, 23: 471-479, 2001.

Adaptive and Robust Design for PID Controller Based on Ant System Algorithm

Guanzheng Tan, Qingdong Zeng, Shengjun He, and Guangchao Cai

School of Information Science and Engineering, Central South University,
Changsha 410083, Hunan Province, P. R. China
tgz@mail.csu.edu.cn

Abstract. In this paper, a novel optimal design method for PID controller is proposed based on the ant system (AS) algorithm. In this method, for a given control system with a PID controller, by taking the overshoot, settling time, and steady-state error of unit step response of the system as the performance indexes and using the AS algorithm, the optimal PID controller parameters K_p^*, T_i^*, and T_d^* can be obtained. The proposed method has excellent features, including easy implementation, good convergence property, and efficient tuning of PID controller parameters. The PID controller designed using this method is called the AS-PID controller. In order to verify the good performance of the AS-PID controller, four typical control systems were tested. The simulation results show that the proposed method is indeed adaptive and robust in quick search of the optimal PID controller parameters.

1 Introduction

The proportional-integral-derivative (PID) controller has been used in industry for many years because of its simpler structure and good robust performance. However, the performance of a PID controller fully depends on the tuning of its parameters. It has been a problem to tune properly these parameters because many industrial plants are often burdened with problems such as high order, time delays, and nonlinearities. About this problem, Ziegler and Nichols proposed a tuning formula for PID controller parameters [1]. But, using their formula the transient response of system often has a greater overshoot. Aiming at this drawback, Hang *et al.* proposed the refinements of the Ziegler-Nichols tuning formula [2]. Although the greater overshoot can be overcome using this formula, this method is not suitable to the devices with a greater phase-lag. Astrom and Hagglund proposed two tuning methods for PID controller parameters, which can ensure a control system has a given phase margin [3], [4]. Generally speaking, if a gain margin and a phase margin are used simultaneously to tune PID parameters, the tuned system will have a better control performance. Ho *et al.* proposed a tuning method for PID parameters based on a given gain margin and a given phase margin, but their method is not suitable to unstable objects [5].

Ant system (AS) algorithm was proposed by Dorigo *et al.*[6], [7]. It is a general-purpose heuristic algorithm. The main characteristics of AS algorithm are positive feedback search mechanism, distributed computation, and the use of a constructive greedy heuristic. So far, AS algorithm has been used successfully to solve many problems such as traveling salesman problem (TSP) [8], quadratic assignment problem [9], job-shop scheduling problem [10], discrete optimization problem [11], and so on.

This paper presents a new design method for PID controller based on the AS algorithm. The PID controller designed using this method is called the AS-PID controller. In the paper, we will demonstrate how to employ the AS algorithm to determine the optimal PID controller parameters and measure the adaptation and robustness of the proposed AS-PID controller by testing several typical control systems.

2 Description of PID Controller

The PID controller is a feedback controller. It is often employed to make a plant less sensitive to changes in the surrounding environment and small changes in the plant. Fig.1 shows a feedback control system that consists of a plant and a PID controller.

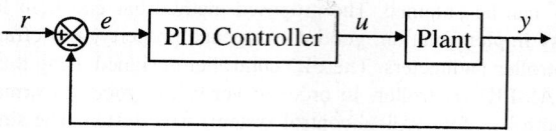

Fig. 1. PID control system

where r and y are the input and output of the system respectively, and u is the output generated by the PID controller. The expression of a conventional PID controller, with input $e(t)$ and output $u(t)$, is given by

$$u(t) = K_p \left\{ e(t) + \frac{1}{T_i} \int_0^t e(\tau)d\tau + T_d \frac{de(t)}{dt} \right\}, \tag{1}$$

where K_p is the proportional gain, T_i is the integral time constant, and T_d is the derivative time constant. In the discrete-time domain, the PID control law is expressed as:

$$u(k) = K_p e(k) + K_i \sum_{j=0}^{k} e(j) + K_d [e(k) - e(k-1)], \tag{2}$$

where $K_i = K_p T / T_i$, $K_d = K_p T_d / T$, and T is the sampling period.

The role of each separate part of a PID controller can be described as follows. The proportional part reduces the error responses of the system to disturbances, the integral part eliminates the steady-state error of the system, and the derivative part dampens the dynamic response and thereby improves the stability of the system. From the perspective of time, the proportional part estimates the system at present, the integral part takes the past into account, and the derivative part estimates what will happen in the future, which yields a much more stable control than the control with only one or two of these features.

In order to evaluating a PID controller, we need a suitable performance criterion. The typical performance criteria in the time domain include the overshoot σ, settling time t_s, and steady-state error e_{ss} of the system's unit step response. First three functions f_1, f_2, and f_3 are constructed using σ, t_s, and e_{ss}, which are given as:

$$f_1 = \sigma/\sigma_0 , \qquad (3)$$

$$f_2 = t_s/t_{s0} , \qquad (4)$$

$$f_3 = \begin{cases} e_{ss}/e_{ss0}, & if\ e_{ss} \neq 0 \\ 0, & if\ e_{ss} = 0 \end{cases}, \qquad (5)$$

where σ_0, t_{s0}, and e_{ss0} are the performance values obtained from the Ziegler-Nichols tuning formula [1, 2]. Then, the performance criterion of the system, F, is designed as:

$$F = \lambda_\sigma f_1 + \lambda_{ts} f_2 + \lambda_{ess} f_3 , \qquad (6)$$

where λ_σ, λ_{ts}, and λ_{ess} are three weighting coefficients. According to our experience, λ_σ, λ_{ts}, and λ_{ess} can be set respectively to 0.6, 0.2, and 0.2. The constraints on σ, t_s, and e_{ss} are specified as: $\sigma<\sigma_0$, $t_s<t_{s0}$, and $e_{ss}<e_{ss0}$.

Designing a PID controller means finding the optimal PID controller parameters K_p^*, T_i^*, and T_d^* so that the control system has the minimum value of F.

3 Optimal PID Controller Design Using AS Algorithm

There is a substance called *pheromone* in an ant's body. An ant can use this substance to communicate information with other ants. The movement feature of an ant colony can be described as follows. When an ant moves on the ground, it will lay pheromone in varying amount on its path. If another isolated ant that moves randomly encounters this path, the ant can detect it and decides with high probability to follow it. When the latter ant moves along the path formed by the former ant, the latter one will lays its own pheromone on the path, thus reinforcing the amount of pheromone on the path. This kind of path choosing method is adopted by each ant in the colony, so a positive feedback mechanism is formed, that is, the more the ants moving along some path, the more likely the coming ants follow this path. It is using this information communicating method that the ants can manage to establish paths with the shortest route from their living nest to feeding sources and back.

3.1 Generation of Nodes and Ant Paths

Take PID parameters K_p, T_i, and T_d as the optimized variables, and assume that the value of each of them has five valid digits. According to the ranges of their values in many practical applications, we assume that in the five digits of K_p there are two digits before decimal point and three digits after decimal point; in the five digits of T_i and T_d there is one digit before decimal point and four digits after decimal point.

In order to use the AS algorithm conveniently, we figure K_p, T_i, and T_d abstractly on plane O-XY. The method is drawing fifteen lines L_1, L_2, ..., L_{15}, which have equal length and equal separation and are perpendicular to axis X, as shown in Fig.2.

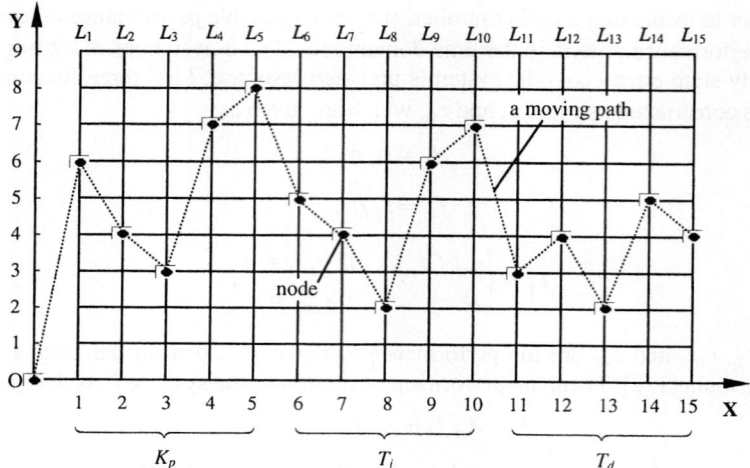

Fig. 2. Diagram of generating nodes and ant paths

In this figure, L_1–L_5, L_6–L_{10}, and L_{11}–L_{15} represent the first digit to the fifth digit of K_p, T_i, and T_d, respectively. The positions of these lines on axis **X** are represented by numbers 1–15 respectively. Then, we divide equally each of these lines into nine portions and thus ten nodes are generated on each line, as shown in Fig.2. The ten nodes of each line represent ten numbers 0–9 respectively, which are ten possible values of the digit corresponding to the line. On plane O-**XY** there are 15×10 nodes totally. We use symbol *node* $(x_i, y_{i,j})$ to denote a node, in which x_i is the **X** coordinate of line L_i ($i=1$–15, $x_i=1$–15) and $y_{i,j}$ is the **Y** coordinate of node j on line L_i ($j=0$–9). Each node represents a value that is equal to the **Y** coordinate of the node. For example, *node* (5, 8) indicates the value of the fifth digit of K_p is equal to 8.

Let an ant depart from the origin of O-**XY**. When it moves to any node of line L_{15}, it completes a tour. Its moving path is expressed by *Path*={O, *node* $(x_1, y_{1,j})$, *node* $(x_2, y_{2,j})$, ..., *node* $(x_{15}, y_{15,j})$}, where *node* $(x_i, y_{i,j})$ is on line L_i. Obviously, the values of K_p, T_i, and T_d represented by the path can be computed by the following formulas:

$$\begin{cases} K_p = y_{1,j} \times 10^1 + y_{2,j} \times 10^0 + y_{3,j} \times 10^{-1} + y_{4,j} \times 10^{-2} + y_{5,j} \times 10^{-3} \\ T_i = y_{6,j} \times 10^0 + y_{7,j} \times 10^{-1} + y_{8,j} \times 10^{-2} + y_{9,j} \times 10^{-3} + y_{10,j} \times 10^{-4} \\ T_d = y_{11,j} \times 10^0 + y_{12,j} \times 10^{-1} + y_{13,j} \times 10^{-2} + y_{14,j} \times 10^{-4} + y_{15,j} \times 10^{-4} \end{cases} \quad (7)$$

For example, a moving path of an ant is shown in Fig.2, the values of K_p, T_i, and T_d represented by the path are $K_p = 64.378$, $T_i = 5.4267$, and $T_d = 3.4254$.

3.2 Selection of Nodes and Ant Paths

Assume that from any node on line L_i to any node on the next line L_{i+1}, an ant has the same moving time, i.e., the moving time is not relevant to the distance between any two nodes on two adjacent lines. Thus, if all ants depart from the origin of O-**XY** at the same time, they will arrive on each line L_i ($i =1-15$) at the same time too, and finally arrive on terminal line L_{15} at the same time. To this point, they all complete a tour, and the AS algorithm completes an iteration.

Assume m represents the total number of ants. Let $\tau(x_i, y_{i,j}, t)$ represent the pheromone concentration at *node* $(x_i, y_{i,j})$ in iteration t (t is the iteration counter, $1 \le t \le t_{max}$, t_{max} is the maximum number of iterations). Assume that at time $t=0$ all of the nodes have the same pheromone concentration, i.e., $\tau(x_i, y_{i,j}, 0) = \tau_0$ (τ_0 is a small positive constant). In moving process, each ant k ($k=1-m$) will select one from the ten nodes of the next line to move to according to the pheromone concentration and visibility of each one of the ten nodes. Let $P_k(x_i, y_{i,j}, t)$ be the transition probability of ant k from any point of line L_{i-1} to *node* $(x_i, y_{i,j})$, it can be computed by

$$P_k(x_i, y_{i,j}, t) = \frac{\tau^\alpha(x_i, y_{i,j}, t)\eta^\beta(x_i, y_{i,j}, t)}{\sum_{j=0}^{9}\tau^\alpha(x_i, y_{i,j}, t)\eta^\beta(x_i, y_{i,j}, t)}, \qquad (8)$$

where $\eta(x_i, y_{i,j}, t)$ is the visibility of *node* $(x_i, y_{i,j})$ and defined as:

$$\eta(x_i, y_{i,j}, t) = \frac{10 - |y_{i,j} - y_{i,j}^*|}{10}, \qquad (9)$$

where the values of $y_{i,j}^*$ ($i=1-15$, $j=0-9$) are set in the following way : In the first iteration of the AS algorithm, the values of $y_{i,j}^*$ are set to the **Y** coordinates of the fifteen nodes which are obtained by mapping the values of PID parameters K_{p0}, T_{i0}, and T_{d0} onto Fig.2, where K_{p0}, T_{i0}, and T_{d0} are obtained from the Ziegler-Nichols tuning formula. In each of the following iterations, $y_{i,j}^*$ are set to the **Y** coordinates of the fifteen nodes which are obtained by mapping the values of PID parameters K_p^*, T_i^*, and T_d^* onto Fig.2, where K_p^*, T_i^*, and T_d^* are the PID parameters corresponding to the optimal traveling path generated in the previous iteration by the ants.

α and β in (8) represent respectively the relative importance of the pheromone concentration and visibility in transition probability $P_k(x_i, y_{i,j}, t)$, and they are set to 3.

3.3 Updating of Pheromone Concentration

Assume that at time $t=0$ all of the ants are at the origin of plane O-**XY**, then they will arrive at their respective terminal nodes on line L_{15} after fifteen moving steps. At this moment, the pheromone concentration of each node on O-**XY** needs to be updated according to the following formulas:

$$\tau(x_i, y_{i,j}, t+1) = \rho\tau(x_i, y_{i,j}, t) + \Delta\tau(x_i, y_{i,j}), \qquad (10)$$

$$\Delta\tau(x_i, y_{i,j}) = \sum_{k=1}^{m}\Delta\tau_k(x_i, y_{i,j}), \qquad (11)$$

where $0 < \rho < 1$ is the pheromone decay parameter; $\Delta\tau_k(x_i, y_{i,j})$ is the amount of pheromone laid at *node* $(x_i, y_{i,j})$ by ant k in the iteration just completed and computed by the following formula:

$$\Delta\tau_k(x_i, y_{i,j}) = \begin{cases} \dfrac{Q}{F_k}, & \text{if ant } k \text{ passed through } node\ (x_i, y_{i,j}) \\ & \text{in the iteration just completed} \\ 0, & \text{otherwise} \end{cases} \quad (12)$$

where F_k is the value of performance criterion of ant k in the iteration just completed and computed by formula (6); Q is a positive constant. Because the value of F_k is about 1, Q can be set to 0.1. Assume that at $t=0$, $\Delta\tau(x_i, y_{i,j})=0$.

3.4 Optimization Procedure for PID Controller Parameters

The AS algorithm for finding the optimal PID controller parameters K_p^*, T_i^*, and T_d^* can be summarized as follows.

Step 1: For a given control system with a PID controller, compute PID controller parameters K_{p0}, T_{i0}, and T_{d0} using the Ziegler-Nichols tuning formula, and compute the system's performance indexes σ_0, t_{s0}, and e_{ss0}.

Step 2: Define m (the number of ant), t_{max} (the maximum number of iterations), τ_0 (the initial pheromone concentration of each node), and ρ (the decay parameter); Set $\Delta\tau(x_i, y_{i,j})=0$; Define a one-dimensional array $Path_k$ with fifteen elements for each ant k ($k=1-m$), in which the **Y** coordinates of the fifteen nodes that ant k will pass through will be stored in order. $Path_k$ is used to represent the moving path of ant k.

Step 3: Set $t=1$ (t is the iteration counter); Then, place the m ants at the origin of plane O-**XY**.

Step 4: Set $i=1$.

Step 5: Compute the transition probability of each node on line L_i using formula (8); According to these probabilities, select one node from line L_i for each ant k ($k=1-m$) using the *Roulette Wheel Selection* method and move ant k to this node, then save the **Y** coordinate of the node into the ith element of $Path_k$.

Step 6: Set $i=i+1$. If $i\leq 15$, go to *Step 5*; Otherwise, go to *Step 7*.

Step 7: For each ant k ($k=1-m$), (a) according to its moving path, i.e., the array $Path_k$, compute the PID parameters K_p^k, T_i^k, and T_d^k using formula set (7); (b) execute a computer simulation for the control system using K_p^k, T_i^k, and T_d^k, and compute the system's performance indexes σ^k, t_s^k, and e_{ss}^k; (c) compute the performance criterion F_k using formula (6).

Then, find the optimal moving path of this iteration which has the minimum value of the performance criterion (i.e., $\min_k F_k$, $k=1, 2, \ldots, m$), and save the values of PID controller parameters corresponding to the path into K_p^*, T_i^*, and T_d^*.

Step 8: Update the pheromone concentration of each node in Fig.2 according to formulas (10)–(12); Then, set each element of $Path_k$ to zero, $k=1-m$.

Step 9: Set $t\leftarrow t+1$; If $t<t_{max}$ and all of the m ants do not make the same tour, place all of the m ants at the origin of O-**XY** and go to *Step 4*; If $t<t_{max}$ but all of the m ants make the same tour, or $t=t_{max}$, output the optimal moving path and its corresponding PID controller parameters K_p^*, T_i^*, and T_d^*. Then stop.

4 Computer Simulation Examples and Results

Four typical control systems were chosen to test and verify the adaptation and robustness of the AS algorithm and AS-PID controller. The transfer functions of the plants in the four control systems are given as follows.

Case 1 (two-order system):

$$G_1(s) = \frac{1}{s^2 + 1.6s + 1}; \qquad (13)$$

Case 2 (high-order system):

$$G_2(s) = \frac{1}{(1+s)(1+0.01s)(1+0.05s)(1+0.2s)}; \qquad (14)$$

Case 3 (time-delay system):

$$G_3(s) = \frac{2e^{-sL}}{1+Ts}, \quad L=1.0, \ T=5.0; \qquad (15)$$

Case 4 (high-order and time-delay system):

$$G_4(s) = \frac{e^{-sL}}{(1+s)(1+0.125s)(1+0.25s)(1+0.5s)}, \quad L=1.0. \qquad (16)$$

For each of the four study cases, simulation experiments were executed. In these experiments, the input of the system is a unit step signal. The parameters of the AS algorithm are set to $t_{max}=30$, $\rho=0.5$, and $m=10$. For the four cases, the optimal PID parameters of the AS-PID controller are shown in Table 1.

Table 1 also summarizes the performance indexes of unit step responses of the four cases in the time domain, including the overshoot σ, rise time t_r (defined as the time needed from 10% of the steady-state value to 90% of the value), settling time t_s (the allowed error $\Delta \leq 2\%$), and steady-state error e_{ss}. These performance indexes were obtained from the AS-PID method and the Z-N PID method respectively. From Table 1, we can find that for each of the four cases, using the proposed AS-PID controller, the overshoot σ and settling time t_s of the unit step response are reduced greatly compared with the Ziegler-Nichols method.

The unit step responses of the four control systems are shown in Fig.3–Fig.6. In these figures, the solid curves (AS) are the responses obtained from the proposed AS-PID controller, and the dotted curves (Z-N) are the responses obtained from the classical Ziegler-Nichols method.

Fig.7–Fig.10 display the convergence tendency of the performance criterion F of the four cases during the iteration process of the AS algorithm.

As can be seen, the AS-PID controller has a quick convergence rate for each of the four different cases (less than twelve iterations). This is because in evolutionary processes the AS algorithm does not perform some operations such as selection and

Table 1. PID parameters and performance indexes of the two PID control methods

Case	PID type	K_p	T_i	T_d	$\sigma(\%)$	t_r	t_s	e_{ss}
1	AS-PID	4.3110	1.5544	0.5202	1.91	0.3534	0.5572	0
	Z-N PID	3.5000	1.2000	0.3000	26.25	0.9227	4.8520	0
2	AS-PID	14.480	3.4135	0.1543	0.00	0.2817	0.6793	0
	Z-N PID	15.150	0.3142	0.0754	69.09	0.1562	1.8976	0
3	AS-PID	1.3625	5.8901	0.3610	0.67	2.7710	5.5883	0
	Z-N PID	2.5507	1.8605	0.4465	55.52	0.5939	8.9956	0
4	AS-PID	2.1185	2.3934	0.3412	5.59	1.0362	4.1886	0
	Z-N PID	3.0189	1.2964	0.3111	45.34	0.6834	5.2891	0

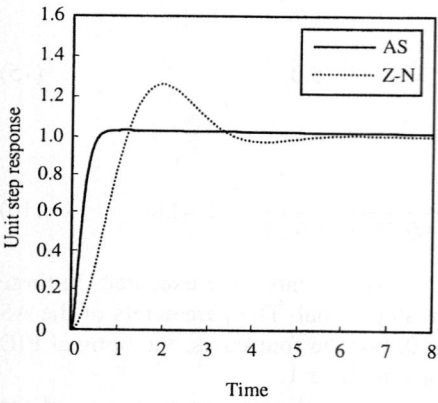

Fig. 3. The unit step response of Case 1   **Fig. 4.** The unit step response of Case 2

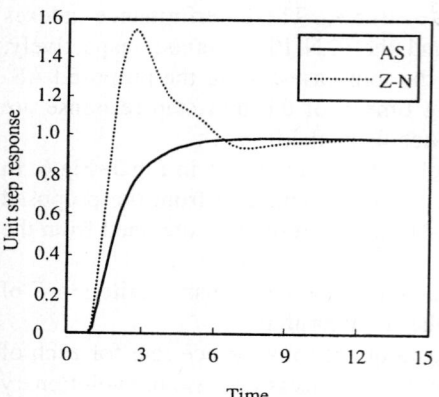 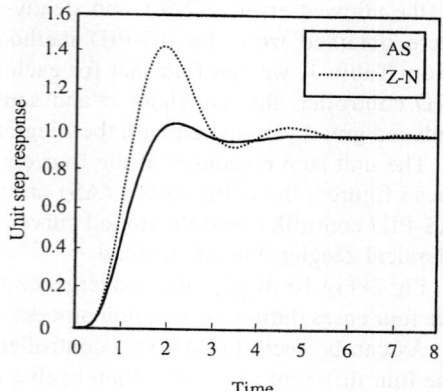

Fig. 5. The unit step response of Case 3   **Fig. 6.** The unit step response of Case 4

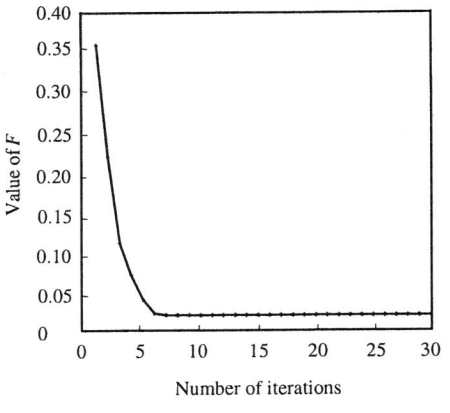
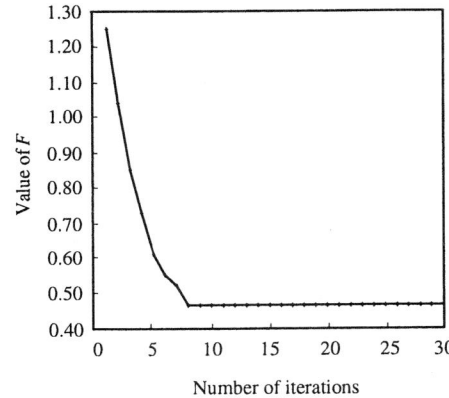

Fig. 7. Convergence of Case 1   **Fig. 8.** Convergence of Case 2

crossover, so it can save some computation time compared with other evolutionary computation methods, for example, genetic algorithms. Thus, we can conclude that the proposed AS-PID controller is capable of obtaining the high-quality solution quickly. In addition, from these figures we can find that for all of the four different cases, the performance criterion F can always converge to the minimum value, which verifies that the proposed AS algorithm has adaptive property and robust convergence property in solving the optimal design problem of PID controller.

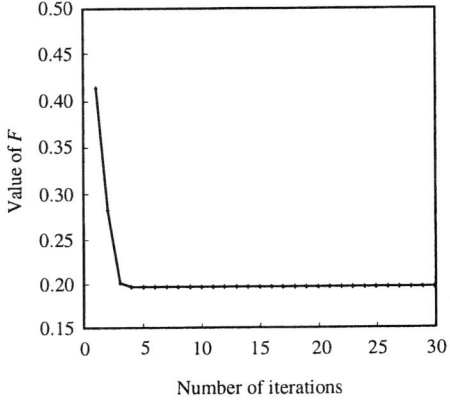
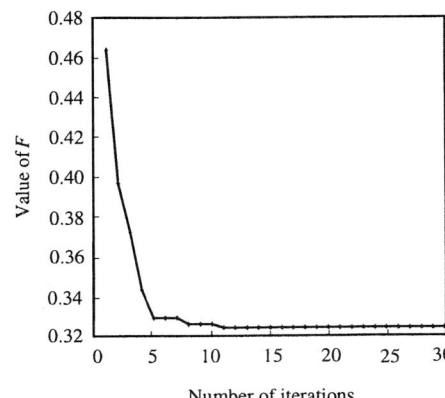

Fig. 9. Convergence of Case 3   **Fig. 10.** Convergence of Case 4

5 Conclusions

This paper presents a novel optimal design method for PID controller based on the ant system (AS) algorithm. The proposed method has excellent features, including easy implementation, good convergence property, and efficient searching for the optimal PID controller parameters. This method has been demonstrated to be a good method, which has adaptive property and robust stability for tuning the PID controller parameters when facing different control plants. The AS-PID controller has been verified to have better control performance

Acknowledgement

The authors gratefully acknowledge the financial support from the National Natural Science Foundation of China under Grant No.50275150 and the National Research Foundation for the Doctoral Program of Higher Education of China under Grant No. 20040533035.

References

1. Ziegler, J. G., Nichols, N. B.: Optimum Setting for Automatic Controllers. ASME Transactions (1942) 759-768
2. Hang, C. C., Astrom, K. J., and Ho, W. K.: Refinements of the Ziegler-Nichols Tuning Formula. IEE Proceedings of Control Theory and Applications, Series D, Vol. 138, (1991) 111-118
3. Astrom, K. J., Hagglund. T.: Automatic Tuning of Simple Regulators with Specifications on Phase and Amplitude Margins. Automatica, Vol. 20, No. 5, (1984) 645-651
4. Hagglund, T., Astrom, K. J.: Industrial Adaptive Controllers Based on Frequency Response Techniques. Automatica, Vol. 27, No. 4, (1991) 597-609
5. Ho, W., Hang, C. C., and Cao, L. S.: Tuning of PID Controllers Based on Gain and Phase Margin in Specifications. Proceedings of the 12th IFAC World Congress, Sydney, Australia, Vol. 5, (1993) 267-270
6. Colorni, A., Dorigo, M., Maniezzo, V.: Distributed Optimization by Ant Colonies. Proceedings of the First Europe Conference on Artificial Life, Paris, France, (1991) 134-
7. Dorigo, M., Maniezzo, V., Colorni, A.: Ant System: Optimization by a Colony of Cooperating Agents. IEEE Transactions on Systems, Man, and Cybernetics, Part B, Vol. 26, No. 1, (1996) 29-41
8. Dorigo, M., Gambardella, L. M.: Ant Colony system: a Cooperative Learning Approach to the Traveling Salesman Problem. IEEE Transactions on Evolutionary Computation, Vol. 1, No. 1, (1997) 53-66
9. Maniezzo, V., Colorni, A.: The Ant System Applied to the Quadratic Assignment Problem. IEEE Transactions on Knowledge Data Engineering, Vol. 11, No. 5, (1999) 769-778
10. Colorni, A., Dorigo, M., Maniezzo, V., Trubian, M.: Ant System for Job-Shop Scheduling. Belgian J. Oper. Res. Statist. Comput. Sci., Vol. 34, No.1, (1994) 34-53
11. Dorigo, M., Caro, G. Di., Gambardella, L. M.: Ant Algorithms for Discrete Optimization. Artificial Life, Vol. 5, No.2, (1999) 137-172

Job-Shop Scheduling Based on Multiagent Evolutionary Algorithm

Weicai Zhong, Jing Liu, and Licheng Jiao

Institute of Intelligent Information Processing, Xidian University,
Xi'an 710071, China
neouma@163.com

Abstract. With the intrinsic properties of job-shop scheduling problems (JSPs) in mind, we integrate the multiagent systems and evolutionary algorithms to form a new algorithm, Multiagent Evolutionary Algorithm for JSPs (MAEA-JSPs). In MAEA-JSPs, all agents live in a latticelike environment. Making use of the designed behaviors, MAEA-JSPs realizes the ability of agents to sense and act on the environment in which they live. During the process of interacting with the environment and the other agents, each agent increases energy as much as possible, so that MAEA-JSPs can find the optima. In the experiments, 59 benchmark JSPs are used, and good performance is obtained.

1 Introduction

Since modern manufacturing environments are very complex, making it very difficult and time-consuming for people to create good schedules, it is a great advantage to have the scheduling process performed automatically by a computer system. There has been a considerable research effort on scheduling, such as the methods based on EAs, multiagents, simulated annealing, neural networks, hybrid heuristic technique, fuzzy logic. The focus of this paper is on the job-shop scheduling problems (JSPs)[1].

Agent-based computation has been studied for several years in the field of distributed artificial intelligence[2, 3] and has been widely used in other branches of computer science[4-6]. In this paper, with the intrinsic properties of JSPs in mind, we integrate the multiagent systems and evolutionary algorithms (EAs) to form a new algorithm, Multiagent Evolutionary Algorithm for Job-shop Scheduling Problems (MAEA-JSPs). In MAEA-JSPs, all agents live in a latticelike environment. Making use of the designed behaviors, MAEA-JSPs realizes the ability of agents to sense and act on the environment in which they live. During the process of interacting with the environment and the other agents, each agent increases energy as much as possible, so that MAEA-JSPs can find the optima. Experimental results show that MAEA-JSPs provides good performance.

2 Multiagent Evolutionary Algorithm for Job-Shop Scheduling Problems

According to [3] and [5], an agent is a physical or virtual entity essentially having the following properties: (a) it is able to live and act in the environment; (b) it is able to sense the local environment; (c) it is driven by certain purposes and (d) it has some reactive behaviors. Multiagent systems are computational systems in which several agents interact or work together in order to achieve goals. As can be seen, the meaning of an agent is very comprehensive, and what an agent represents is different for different problems. In general, four elements should be defined when multiagent systems are used to solve problems. The first is the meaning and the purpose of each agent. The second is the environment in which all agents live. Since each agent has only local perceptivity, so the third is the local environment. The last is the behaviors that each agent can take to achieve the purpose.

2.1 Job-Shop Scheduling Problems

A JSP of size $n \times m$ consists of n jobs and m machines. For each job J_i, a sequence of m operations $O_i = (o_{i,1}, o_{i,2}, \ldots, o_{i,m})$ describing the processing order of the operations of J_i is given. Each operation $o_{i,j}$ is to be processed on a specific machine and has a processing time $\tau_{i,j}$. When the operations are processed each machine can process only one operation at a time, each job can only have one operation processed at a time, and no preemption can take place. A solution to a JSP is a schedule specifying when to process each of the operations, not violating any of the constraints.

One encoding method in common use for JSPs is permutation with repetition, where a schedule is described as a sequence of all $n \times m$ operations, and each operation in the sequence is described by the job-number. Thus, the search space $\mathbf{S}$ of a JSP consists of the elements satisfy the following conditions:

$$\forall P \in \mathbf{S},\ P = \langle P_1, P_2, \cdots, P_{n \times m} \rangle \text{ and}$$
$$(P(1) = m) \text{ and } (P(2) = m) \text{ and } \ldots \text{ and } (P(n) = m) \tag{1}$$

Where $P_i \in \{1, 2, \ldots, m\}$, $i=1, 2, \ldots, n \times m$, and $P(j)$, $j=1, 2, \ldots, n$ stand for the number of j in P. When transforming P into a schedule, P_i stands for $o_{j,k}$ if $P_i = j$ and the number of j among $P_1, P_2, \ldots, P_i$ is equal to k. The schedule is obtained by considering the operations in the order they occur in P and assigning the earliest allowable time to that operation. Such encoding method has the advantage that no infeasible solutions can be represented, and each element in $\mathbf{S}$ corresponds to a feasible schedule.

2.2 Definition of Agents

An agent used to solve JSPs is defined as follows:

Definition 1: A agent for JSPs, a, represents an element in the search space, with energy equal to

$$\forall a \in \mathbf{S},\ Energy(a) = -makespan(a) \tag{2}$$

where $makespan(a)$ stands for the time elapsed from the beginning of processing until the last job has finished according to the scheduling corresponding to a. The goal of each agent is to maximize the energy through agent behavior.

Since each agent must record some information, it is represented by the following structure:

```
Agent = Record
   P: P∈S;
   E: The energy of the Agent, E=Energy(P);
   SL: The flag for the self-learning behavior, which
       will be defined later. If SL is True, the self-
       learning behavior can be performed on the Agent,
       otherwise, cannot;
End.
```

In the following text, *Agent*(•) is used to represent the corresponding component in the above structure.

2.3 Environment of Agents

In order to realize the local perceptivity of agents, the environment is organized as a latticelike structure, which is similar to our previous work in [6].

Definition 2: All agents live in a latticelike environment, L, which is called an agent lattice. The size of L is $L_{size} \times L_{size}$, where L_{size} is an integer. Each agent is fixed on a lattice-point and can only interact with the neighbors. Suppose that the agent located at (i, j) is represented as $L_{i,j}$, $i, j=1,2,...,L_{size}$, then the neighbors of $L_{i,j}$, $Neighbors_{i,j}$, are defined as follows:

$$Neighbors_{i,j} = \{L_{i',j}, L_{i,j'}, L_{i'',j}, L_{i,j''}\} \quad (3)$$

where $i' = \begin{cases} i-1 & i \neq 1 \\ L_{size} & i = 1 \end{cases}$, $j' = \begin{cases} j-1 & j \neq 1 \\ L_{size} & j = 1 \end{cases}$,

$i'' = \begin{cases} i+1 & i \neq L_{size} \\ 1 & i = L_{size} \end{cases}$, $j'' = \begin{cases} j+1 & j \neq L_{size} \\ 1 & j = L_{size} \end{cases}$.

The agent lattice can be represented as the one in Fig.1. Each circle represents an agent, the data represent the position in the lattice, and two agents can interact with each other if and only if there is a line connecting them.

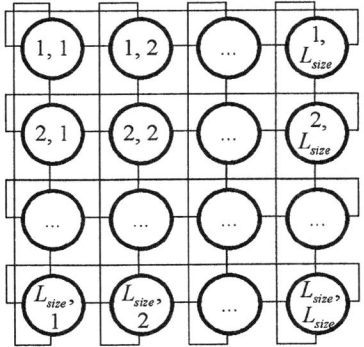

Fig. 1. The model of the agent lattice

2.4 Behaviors of Agents

The goal of an algorithm for JSPs is to find solutions by a computational cost as low as possible. So the computational cost can be considered as the resources of the environment in which all agents live. Since the resources are limited and the behaviors of the agents are driven by their purposes, an agent will compete with others to gain more resources. On the bases of this, two behaviors are designed for agents to realize their purposes, that is, the competitive behavior and the self-learning behavior.

Competitive behavior: In this behavior, the energy of an agent is compared with those of the neighbors. The agent can survive if the energy is maximum; otherwise, the agent must die, and the child of the one with maximum energy among the neighbors will take up the lattice-point.

Suppose that the competitive behavior is performed on the agent located at (i, j), $L_{i,j}$, and $Max_{i,j}$ is the agent with maximum energy among the neighbors of $L_{i,j}$, namely, $Max_{i,j} \in Neighbors_{i,j}$ and $\forall Agent \in Neighbors_{i,j}$, then $Agent(E) \leq Max_{i,j}(E)$. If $L_{i,j}(E) \leq Max_{i,j}(E)$, then $Max_{i,j}$ generates a child agent, $Child_{i,j}$, to replace $L_{i,j}$, and the method is shown in Algorithm 1; otherwise, $L_{i,j}$ is left untouched.

```
Algorithm 1 Competitive behavior
  Input:    Max_{i,j}:  Max_{i,j}(P) = ⟨m_1, m_2, ..., m_{n×m}⟩ ;
            p_c: A predefined parameter in the range of 0~1;
  Output:   Child_{i,j}: Child_{i,j}(P) = ⟨c_1, c_2, ..., c_{n×m}⟩ ;
Swap(x, y) exchanges the values of x and y. U(0, 1) is a uni-
form random number between 0 and 1. Random(n, i) is a random
integer among 1, 2, ..., n and is not equal to i. Min(i, j) is the
smaller one between i and j.
begin
  Child_{i,j}(P) := Max_{i,j}(P);  i := 1;
  repeat
    if (U(0, 1)<p_c) then
    begin
      l := Random(n, i);
      Swap(c_i, c_l);
    end;
    i := i+1;
  until (i>n);
  Child_{i,j}(SL) := True;
end.
```

In fact, $Child_{i,j}$ is generated by exchanging a small part of $Max_{i,j}$, and is equivalent to performing a local search around $Max_{i,j}$. The goal of the competitive behavior is to eliminate the agents with low energy, and give more chances to the potential agents.

Self-learning behavior: Agents have knowledge relating to the problems that they are designed to solve. As well-known, integrating local searches with EAs can improve the performance. Therefore, we design the self-learning behavior for agents by making use of local search techniques. Since a number in P occurs many times, the algorithm must be prevented from swapping two identical values. Let $P=\langle P_1, P_2, ..., P_{n \times m} \rangle$, o_{p_i} represents the operation corresponding to P_i, and M_{p_i} is the machine on which o_{p_i} is to be processed. Suppose that P_i and P_j ($P_i \neq P_j$ and $i<j$) is swapped and P' is obtained. Based on the method transforming P to a schedule, we can obtain that the two schedules corresponding to P and P' are identical if P_i and P_j satisfy (4).

$$\begin{cases} \forall P_k, \ i<k<j, \ \left(M_{P_i} \neq M_{P_k}\right) \text{ and } \left(P_k \neq P_i\right) \text{ and } \left(M_{P_k} \neq M_{P_i}\right) \\ \qquad\qquad \text{ and } \left(P_k \neq P_j\right) \text{ and } \left(M_{P_k} \neq M_{P_j}\right) \end{cases} \quad (4)$$

Suppose that this behavior is performed on $L_{i,j}$. The details are shown in Algorithm 2.

Algorithm 2 Self-learning behavior
Input: $L_{i,j}$: $L_{i,j}(P)=\langle P_1, P_2, ..., P_{n\times m}\rangle$;
Output: $L_{i,j}$;
begin
  repeat
    $Repeat := False$; $k := 1$; $Iteration := 1$;
    while ($k \leq n \times m$) **do**
    begin
      $Energy_{old} := L_{i,j}(E)$;
      $l := Random(n \times m, k)$, $P_k \neq P_l$, and P_k, P_l do not satisfy (35);
      $Swap(P_k, P_l)$; $Energy_{new} := L_{i,j}(E)$;
      if ($Energy_{new} < Energy_{old}$) **then** $Swap(P_k, P_l)$
      else begin
            if ($Energy_{new} > Energy_{old}$) **then** $Repeat := True$;
            $k := k+1$;
          end;
      if ($Iteration < n \times m - 1$) **then** $Iteration := Iteration + 1$
      else begin $Iteration := 1$; $k := k+1$;   **end;**
    end;
  until ($Repeat = True$);
  $L_{i,j}(SL) := False$;
end.

The goal of Algorithm 2 is to find a swap for the components in the permutation which violate constraints, such that the energy of $L_{i,j}$ is increased after the swap is performed. For a component, the algorithm iteratively performs a swap until no constraint is violated or the predefined iterative count, $Iteration = (n \times m - 1)$, is achieved. Then, the algorithm goes on to deal with the next component. $Iteration$ can prevent the algorithm from repeating infinitely. When the self-learning behavior has been performed on an agent, the probability that the energy of the agent can be increased by this behavior is very low, thus $L_{i,j}(SL)$ is set to $False$ in the last step.

2.5 Implementation of MAEA-JSPs

At each generation, the competitive behavior is performed on each agent first. As a result, the agents with low energy are cleaned out from the agent lattice so that there is more space developed for the agents with higher energy. Then, the self-learning behavior is performed according to the state of the agent. In order to reduce the computational cost, this behavior is only performed on the best agent in the current agent lattice. The process is performed iteratively until the quality of the solution satisfies the predefined conditions or the maximum computational cost is reached.

Algorithm 3 Multiagent evolutionary algorithm for job-shop scheduling problems
  Input: $Evaluation_{Max}$: The maximum number of evaluations
                for the energy;

L_{size}: The scale of the agent lattice;
p_c: The parameter used in the competitive behavior;
Output: A solution or an approximate solution for the JSP under consideration;
L^t represents the agent lattice in the tth generation. $Agent^t_{Best}$ is the best agent in $L^0, L^1, ..., L^t$, and $Agent^t_{tBest}$ is the best agent in L^t.
begin
  for $i:=1$ **to** L_{size} **do**
    for $j:=1$ **to** L_{size} **do**
  begin
    Generate a permutation randomly and assign it to $L^0_{i,j}(P)$;
    Compute $L^0_{i,j}(E)$;
    $L^0_{i,j}(SL) := True$;
  end;
  $Evaluations := L_{size} \times L_{size}$;
  Update $Agent^0_{Best}$; $t := 0$;
repeat
  for $i:=1$ **to** L_{size} **do**
    for $j:=1$ **to** L_{size} **do**
  begin
    if ($L^t_{i,j}$ wins in the competitive behavior) **then**
      $L^{t+1}_{i,j} := L^t_{i,j}$
    else $L^{t+1}_{i,j} := Child_{i,j}$
      (generated according to Algorithm 1);
    Compute $L^{t+1}_{i,j}(E)$;
    $Evaluations := Evaluations+1$;
  end;
  Update $Agent^{t+1}_{(t+1)Best}$;
  if $\left(Agent^{t+1}_{(t+1)Best}(SL) = True\right)$ **then**
    Perform the self-learning behavior on $Agent^{t+1}_{(t+1)Best}$;
  if ($Agent^{t+1}_{(t+1)Best}(E) < Agent^t_{Best}(E)$) **then**
  begin
    $Agent^{t+1}_{Best} := Agent^t_{Best}$;
    $Agent^{t+1}_{Random} := Agent^t_{Best}$ ($Agent^{t+1}_{Random}$ is randomly selected from L^t and is different from $Agent^{t+1}_{(t+1)Best}$);
  end

```
else  Agent_{Best}^{t+1} := Agent_{(t+1)Best}^{t+1} ;
t := t+1;
until  ( Agent_{Best}^{t+1}(E) satisfies the predefined conditions)
        or  (Evaluations ≥ Evaluation_{Max}) ;
end.
```

3 Experimental Studies

Three test suites[1] are used to investigate the performance of MAEA-JSPs, namely, FT[7], LA[8], and ORB[9], which have been widely used in the field of JSPs. FT consists of 3 problems, LA 40 problems, and ORB 10 problems. The optimal makespan, labeled as *Makespan**, of the 53 problems are known[10]. Therefore, to study the computational cost, the termination criterion of MAEA-JSPs is set to find the optimal makespan or run more than 5000 generations. L_{size} is set to 10. The experimental results averaged over 100 independent runs of MAEA-JSPs are shown in Table 1. They include the best (*Best*) and the average (*Aver*) makespan found, and the percentage of gap between *Aver* and *Makespan** (*Gap*),

$$Gap = \frac{\left(Aver - Makespan^*\right)}{Makespan^*} \times 100\% \tag{5}$$

The computational cost is represented by two forms, the average running times (*Times*) and the average number of evaluations (*Evals*). All experiments are executed on a 2.4-GHz Pentium IV PC with 1G RAM.

From Table 1 we can see that the best solutions for 45 out of 53 problems are equal to *Makespan**, and the ones for the other 8 problems are also very close to *Makespan**. For instance, those of LA24, LA27, LA40, and ORB02 are only larger 1 or 2 than *Makespan**. The average solutions for 21 out of 53 problems are equal to *Makespan**, that is to say, MAEA-JSPs finds the optimal makespan in all 100 runs for these problems. There are 7 problems, LA02, LA03, LA04, LA16, LA18, LA26, and ORB10, whose average solutions are very close to *Makespan**, and the *Gap* is smaller than 0.5%. For the other 25 problems, only the *Gap* of LA29 and LA38 are 4.33 and 3.88, respectively, and all remainder is smaller than 2.6%. The standard deviations for 43 out of 53 problems are smaller than 10, and only those of LA29 and LA38 are larger than 15. The running times of MAEA-JSPs are smaller than 1 second for 18 problems, between 1 to 10 seconds for 23 problems, and larger than 10 seconds for 19 problems, where the maximum is 60.67s for LA27.

Reference [1] indicates that a JSP can be considered hard if the number of operations is no smaller than 200 and $n≥15$, $m≥10$, $n<2.5m$. On the basis of this observation, LA26-LA30 and LA36-LA40, whose names are shown in boldface in Table 1, are more difficult than the other problems. For these 10 problems, MAEA-JSPs finds *Makespan** for 4 problems. In general, both the solution quality and the computational cost of MAEA-JSPs are appropriate.

---

[1] ftp://mscmga.ms.ic.ac.uk/pub/jobshop1.txt

Table 1. The experimental results of MAEA-JSPs

Names	n×m	Makespan*	Makespan			Computational cost	
			Best	Aver	Gap (%)	Times (s)	Evals
FT06	6×6	55	**55**	55	0	0.00	450
FT10	10×10	930	**930**	944.45	1.55	10.47	2 270 375
FT20	20×5	1165	**1165**	1178.89	1.19	13.56	3 106 852
LA01	10×5	666	**666**	666	0	0.00	1 631
LA02	10×5	655	**655**	655.39	0.06	0.78	296 570
LA03	10×5	597	**597**	598.86	0.31	1.12	409 782
LA04	10×5	590	**590**	591.41	0.24	1.75	635 362
LA05	10×5	593	**593**	593	0	0.00	262
LA06	15×5	926	**926**	926	0	0.00	349
LA07	15×5	890	**890**	890	0	0.00	1 540
LA08	15×5	863	**863**	863	0	0.00	2 519
LA09	15×5	951	**951**	951	0	0.00	802
LA10	15×5	958	**958**	958	0	0.00	316
LA11	20×5	1222	**1222**	1222	0	0.00	495
LA12	20×5	1039	**1039**	1039	0	0.00	865
LA13	20×5	1150	**1150**	1150	0	0.00	1 061
LA14	20×5	1292	**1292**	1292	0	0.00	321
LA15	20×5	1207	**1207**	1207	0	0.02	5 578
LA16	10×10	945	**945**	945.79	0.08	6.84	1 408 499
LA17	10×10	784	**784**	784	0	1.05	225 340
LA18	10×10	848	**848**	848.22	0.03	3.23	719 109
LA19	10×10	842	**842**	853.79	1.40	9.59	2 174 830
LA20	10×10	902	**902**	908.11	0.68	9.12	2 042 142
LA21	15×10	1046	**1046**	1068.11	2.11	25.64	4 153 326
LA22	15×10	927	**927**	940.88	1.50	25.69	4 110 514
LA23	15×10	1032	**1032**	1032	0	0.42	68 246
LA24	15×10	935	937	958.79	2.54	25.94	4 188 613
LA25	15×10	977	**977**	993.50	1.69	23.84	3 738 814
LA26	20×10	1218	**1218**	1219.15	0.09	17.07	1 939 943
LA27	20×10	1235	1236	1263.83	2.33	60.67	6 812 466
LA28	20×10	1216	**1216**	1225.55	0.79	55.28	6 351 364
LA29	20×10	1152	1167	1201.88	4.33	54.08	5 972 694
LA30	20×10	1355	**1355**	1355	0	66.59	727 852
LA31	30×10	1784	**1784**	1784	0	0.50	37 799
LA32	30×10	1850	**1850**	1850	0	0.98	79 068
LA33	30×10	1719	**1719**	1719	0	0.34	26 238
LA34	30×10	1721	**1721**	1721	0	2.96	228 581
LA35	30×10	1888	**1888**	1888	0	1.45	105 840
LA36	15×15	1268	1274	1295.49	2.17	48.88	4 992 731
LA37	15×15	1397	**1397**	1429.24	2.31	52.92	5 517 937
LA38	15×15	1196	1204	1242.42	3.88	56.71	5 956 429
LA39	15×15	1233	1239	1258.61	2.08	56.73	6 011 274
LA40	15×15	1222	1224	1247.06	2.05	54.99	5 770 028
ORB01	10×10	1059	**1059**	1084.28	2.39	10.38	2 253 621
ORB02	10×10	888	889	893.77	0.65	9.79	2 059 680
ORB03	10×10	1005	**1005**	1027.69	2.26	11.05	2 475 761
ORB04	10×10	1005	**1005**	1024.29	1.92	10.08	2 175 029
ORB05	10×10	887	**887**	893.70	0.76	9.91	2 120 907
ORB06	10×10	1010	**1010**	1026.90	1.67	11.16	2 470 842
ORB07	10×10	397	**397**	402.62	1.42	8.59	1 891 497
ORB08	10×10	899	**899**	910.89	1.32	8.47	1 826 795
ORB09	10×10	934	**934**	941.73	0.83	9.10	1 836 018
ORB10	10×10	944	**944**	945.70	0.18	4.52	1 015 080

4 Conclusion

In this paper, multiagent systems and evolutionary algorithms are combined to form a new algorithm to solve job-shop scheduling problems. MAEA-JSPs obtains good performance on three benchmark test suites, FT, LA, and ORB. All results show that it is of a high potential in solving complex and ill-defined problems to combine multiagent systems and EAs.

References

1. S. Jain, S. Meeran, "Deterministic job-shop scheduling: past, present and future," *European Journal of Operational Research*, 113, 1999, pp.390-434.
2. J. Ferber, *Multi-Agent Systems: An Introduction to Distributed Artificial Intelligence*. New York: Addison-Wesley, 1999.
3. J. Liu, *Autonomous Agents and Multi-Agent Systems: Explorations in Learning, Self-Organization, and Adaptive Computation*. Singapore: World Scientific, 2001.
4. J. Liu, Y. Y. Tang, and Y. C. Cao, "An evolutionary autonomous agents approach to image feature extraction," *IEEE Trans. Evol. Comput.*, vol.1, no.2, pp.141-158, 1997.
5. J. Liu, H. Jing, Y. Y. Tang, "Multi-agent oriented constraint satisfaction," *Artif. Intell.*, vol. 136, no. 1, 2002, pp.101-144.
6. W. Zhong, J. Liu, M. Xue, L. Jiao, "A multiagent genetic algorithm for global numerical optimization," *IEEE Trans. Syst., Man, and Cybern. B*, vol. 34, no. 2, 2004, pp.1128-1141.
7. Fisher, G. L. Thompson, "Probabilistic learning combinations of local job-shop scheduling rules," in *Industrial Scheduling*, Prentice-Hall, Englewood Cliffs, NJ, 1963, pp.225-251.
8. S. Lawrence, "Resource constrained project scheduling: An experimental investigation of heuristic scheduling techniques (Supplement)," *Graduate School Ind. Adm.*, Carnegie-Mellon Univ., Pittsburg, PA, 1984.
9. D. Applegate, W. Cook, "A computational study of the job-shop scheduling problem," *ORSA Journal on Computing*, 3(2), 1991, pp.149-156.
10. L. Wang, *"Shop Scheduling with Genetic algorithms,"* Tsinghua University Press, Beijing, China, 2003.

Texture Surface Inspection: An Artificial Immune Approach

Hong Zheng[1,2] and Li Pan[3]

[1] School of Electronic Information, Wuhan University, 129 Luoyu Road,
Wuahn, Hubei 430079, P.R. China
zhenghong@21cn.com
[2] National Key Lab for Novel Software Technology at Nanjin University,
Nanjin University, Nanjing, Jiangshu 210093, P.R. China
[3] School of Remote Sensing Information and Engineering, Wuhan University,
129 Luoyu Road, Wuahn, Hubei 430079, P.R. China
li.pan@126.com

Abstract. This paper presents a novel approach for visual inspection of textures. The approach applies the artificial immune theory to learning the filters for texture flaw detection, which are invariant to changes of texture orientations and scales. In this paper, defect textures and defect-free textures are regarded as non-self and self respectively, and texture filters are regarded as antibodies. The clonal selection based algorithm is presented to evolve antibodies. Experimental results on TILDA textile images were done to show the feasibility of the proposed method.

1 Introduction

Visual inspection is an important part of quality control in industry. Since the accuracy of human visual inspection declines with dull and endlessly routine jobs. Slow, expensive and erratic inspection is the result. Computer based visual inspection is obviously the alternative to the human inspector. This paper is concerned with the problem of computer inspection of texture surface. A major problem with the application of texture inspection to real problems is that textures in the real world are often not uniform, due to changes in orientation, scale or other visual appearance. How to extract robust texture features has become a key issue in the field of texture inspection. In order to solve the problem, this paper presents a new approach to automatically detect defects from texture images. This approach employs the clonal selection based mechanism inspired from the biological immune system to learn texture filters and segmentation thresholds. The detailed algorithm is described in this paper. This paper is organized as follows: Section 2 describes the learning algorithm for texture defect detection. Section 3 shows the experimental results and gives the conclusions.

2 Algorithms

The clonal selection is the theory used to explain how an immune response is mounted when a non-self antigenic pattern is recognized by a B-cell. The clonal selection algorithm (CSA) is proposed to fulfil the clonal selection processes[1]. The design of CSA mainly includes the definition of immunological terms and the design of immune evolutionary operations. In this paper, the immunological terms are defined in the following manner:

Antigen: any of training texture images.

Antibody: a float string encoded by filter parameters and a segmentation threshold. Fig.1 illustrates an antibody structure.

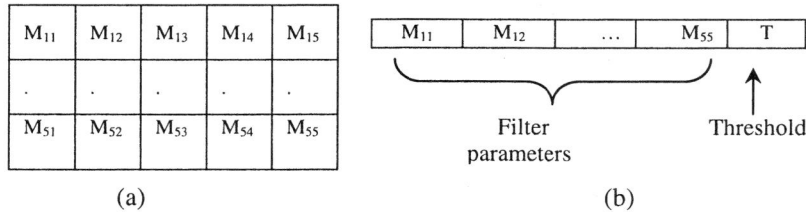

Fig. 1. Antibody encoding scheme.(a) a 5 by 5 filter architecture, $M_{ij} \in [-2,2]$ (b) an antibody architecture, $T \in [0,512]$

Affinity: the detection rate of an antibody. It is defined as :

$$p = \frac{N_c}{N_t} \times 100\% \qquad (1)$$

where N_c is the number of correctly detected images, and the N_t is the total number of trained images. The greater the value of p, the higher the antibody's affinity.

For each antibody, the procedure to detect texture images consists of following three steps.

1) Decode an antibody and get a filter and a threshold.
2) Convolve all training images by the filter. The 2D convolution of the image $I(i,j)$ and filter $A(i,j)$ with size $2\alpha+1$ by $2\alpha+1$ ($\alpha = 2$) is given by the relation

$$F(i, j) = A(i, j) * I(i, j) = \sum_{k=-a}^{a} \sum_{l=-a}^{a} A(k,l) I(i+k, j+l) \qquad (2)$$

3) Calculate the standard deviation of every convolved trained image. If the standard deviation value of an image is greater than the threshold, the image is recognized as a defective image. Otherwise, the image is a defect-free image.

The immune evolutionary operations are defined in the following manner:

Clone: This operation is to generate copies of every individual in an antibody population proportionally to its affinity with the antigen. The amount of clones of an antibody is given by

$$n_i = round\ (N \times \frac{f_i}{\sum_{i=1}^{N} f_i}) \qquad (3)$$

where N is the number of all individuals in an antibody population. f_i is the affinity value of the ith antibody.

Mutation: The mutation operation creates a new antibody by randomly changing one or more of the unit values in the antibody with a probability inversely proportional to their affinities. The mutation probability is given by

$$P_i = \frac{f_{max} - f_i}{f_{max} - f_{min}} \quad i = 1, 2, \ldots, N \tag{4}$$

where f_{max} is the maximum affinity value, and f_{min} is the minimum affinity value.

Reselection: This operation sorts all individuals in descending order, and replace **m** (**m<N**) individuals with the least affinity values with **m** new randomly generated individuals.

The whole learning algorithm is described as follows:

1) Randomly generate an antibody population (M) which represent a set of filters and segmentation thresholds;
2) Evaluate the affinity value of each antibody in the population with Eq. 1;
3) Generate clone copies of all individuals with Eq. 3 ;
4) Mutate all these copies with Eq. 4;
5) Sort all individuals in descending order, and replace n1 individuals with the least affinity values with n1 new randomly generated individuals.
6) Repeat Steps 2 to 5 until a given iteration time is met. In general, a fixed maximum iteration number is allowed as the termination condition. In this paper it is 50 according to our experimental experience.

After the optimal antibody is acquired, the antibody can be used to detect antigens. Firstly, according to Eq.2, convolve the test image by the learned filter. Secondly, calculate the standard deviation within a 2n+1 by 2n+1 (n=7) window at point(i,j). The standard deviation is defined as the texture feature TE at the point. Thirdly, compare the TE value at every point with the learned threshold. If the TE is greater than the threshold, the point belongs to a defect texture region. Otherwise, it belongs to a defect-free texture region. Finally, a post-processing based on morphology operations is employed to remove noise.

3 Experimental Results and Conclusions

The proposed approach was evaluated on the TILDA Textile Texture Database created at the University of Freiburg. In our experiment, two groups of textiles, c1 and c3, were considered. We resized each textile image by a factor 0.5. Each group split into two categories. Each category included 4 defect classes e_1-e_4 and a defect-free class e_0, and each class had 10 images.

In order to learn one defect filter and one segment threshold for each category textile, we collected 4 sub-images with size 41*41 from each class (e_0~e_4) of each category of each group as sample images. The experiments were carried out as follows:

1) *Training phase*: Obtain texture filter parameters and a segmentation threshold for each category through learning the trained samples using CSA.
2) *Detection phase*: Detect flaws from proposed textile images using obtained filters and thresholds. In order to remove noise, erosion operations are implemented on detected images to remove small areas. Fig. 2 shows some examples of different flaw detections, where highlight lines indicate the detected locations of flaws. It can be seen that, although the defect appearances on different textile surfaces are much different, they can be detected correctly by proposed method.

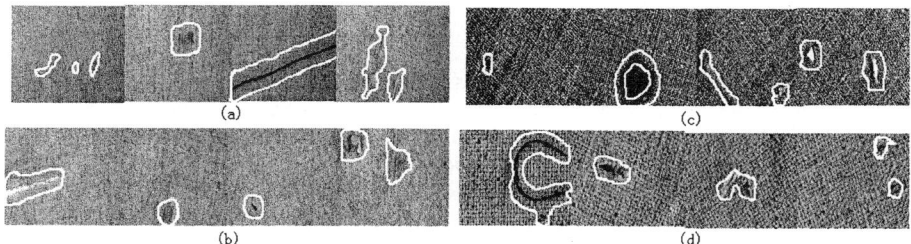

Fig. 2. Some detection results for category (a) c1r1 (b) c1r3 (c) c3r2 (d) c3r3

We also compared the learning behavior between CSA and standard genetic algorithms. We did 20 learning by CSA and GA respectively. The average generations of finding the optimal solution for CSA and GA were 9 and 20, respectively. This shows that CSA is easier to find the optimal solution than GA due to its diversity.

In this paper we have described a new approach for defect detection using learning techniques with the clonal selection principle. Comparing with some earlier investigations [2][3], the proposed method in this paper not only is able to detect slack-end and broken-pick flaws, but also use the same detection window size for different defect types. In addition, the proposed method employs only one optimized filter for texture detection, the whole processing is easily implemented by hardware. As a result, the proposed approach is suitable for industrial application.

It is seen by a survey that the AIS is not used widely to image applications. Although this paper has been devoted almost entirely to the textile inspection problem, this initial study shows its potential application in the field of visual inspection. We plan to further implement more properties of AIS for better results and exploit more applications for machine vision.

References

1. De Castro, L. N., Von Zuben, F. J.: The Clonal Selection Algorithm with Engineering Applications. Proc. of GECCO'00, (2000) 36-37
2. Mamic, G., Bennamoun, M.: Automatic Flaw Detection in Textiles Using a Neyman-Pearson Detector. Proceedings of International Conference on Pattern Recognition, 4 (2000) 767-770
3. Bodnarova, A., Bennamoun, M., Latham, S.J.: Textiles Flaw Detection Using Optimal Gabor Filter. Proceedings of International Conference on Pattern Recognition, 4 (2000) 799-802

Intelligent Mosaics Algorithm of Overlapping Images

Yan Zhang, Wenhui Li, Yu Meng, Haixu Chen, and Tong Wang

College of Computer Science and Technology, Key Laboratory of
Symbol Computation and Knowledge Engineering of the Ministry
of Education, Jilin University, Changchun, 130012 P.R. China
zhangyanjlu@yahoo.com.cn

Abstract. Panoramic Video which uses 360 degree panoramic image is a new approach for composing virtual environment. The panoramic images can be created by "stitching" together overlapping images taken with an ordinary camera. So image mosaics are very important in creating panorama. In this paper, we proposed an intelligent mosaics algorithm. We first use particle swarm optimization (PSO) to find a certain area which contains sufficient objective characters, then we use pattern matching method to search the matching patch in another image and adjust image; at last, the mosaic image is created by a multi-resolution method. Experimental results testy that this algorithm is able to seamlessly stitch two overlapping images automatically.

1 Introduction

Panoramic image is a method to make use of realistic images to get a full view panoramic space[1~3]. Users can use ordinary cameras to take a serial of images surrounding a scene[4]. When we create panoramic image, the first job of image mosaics is to exactly allocate the overlapping areas of two images. And the second one is to adjust the lightness, since the light intensity of two images from different points might be of great difference. Based on above two tasks, we propose a character-based solution for image adjusting, and we make use of particle swarm optimization[5] (PSO) to find an area which contains sufficient objective characters in one image and find corresponding area in another image using pattern matching, and then adjust these images. We apply multi-resolution techniques for image mosaics and finally achieve image automated seamless mosaics.

2 Optimized Characteristic Block Extraction Based on PSO

In the first image, if we can confirm area A, then we can easily get area B using pattern matching methods in the other image, according to image overlapping theory, taking acceptable range of error into consideration. The more objective characters we are searching in area A, the much difference is required between this area and surrounding areas, and the better. Distance L_2 is simplest and most frequently used distance function to compare the degree of similitude of two areas. For a certain area S, we can calculate four values of L_2 by comparing itself with its surrounding up, down, left and right four areas of the same size, denoted as f_1, f_2, f_3, f_4. The bigger of sum of f_1, f_2, f_3, f_4, the more difference between area S and its surrounding areas. We denote evaluation function of areas S as F.

For any area S in the right half of the first image, the bigger of value F, the easier we can find an area with sufficient information needed for matching searching. How to find an area S containing sufficient objective characters is a better problem and we just need a satisfied result. Therefore, we can use PSO[5] to searching for area S.

We randomly distributed 10 particles in the right half of the first image. The initial position is the coordinate of several pixels and we define an initial velocity of these particles. Each particle is moving in the solution space. We can find a matching area with certain characters, by adjusting the moving direction and velocity of particles using fitness function. Each particle can decide an area of 20*20, which is used to search for areas with multiobjective characters. Figure 1 demonstrated how to find area S with sufficient characters in one image using PSO algorithm.

Our PSO-based algorithms to search for characteristic areas can be described as follows:

i. Randomly distributing 10 particles in the right half of the first area, initializing the original location of each particle and its original velocity;
ii. Calculation fitness value of areas determined by each particle, using evaluation function F;
iii. For each particle, comparing its current fitness value and the fitness value of the best location it ever passed and updating;
iv. For each particle, comparing its current fitness value and the fitness value of the best location the whole particle swarm ever passed and updating;
v. Adjusting the velocity and location of particles;
vi. The algorithm ends if termination condition, which is enough good location and biggest number of time of iteration, is met. Current global optimized position is the result. Otherwise, go to (ii).

(a) (b)

Fig. 1. Optimized characteristic block extraction based on PSO

3 Multi-resolution Mosaic

If we simply mosaic two images together using PSO algorithm, there might be an obvious seam at the splicing tape, as shown in Fig.2. We can apply multi-resolution image mosaics to address this problem, in order to smooth the transition of the splicing area and get a high quality seamless image. In order to do so, we expand the original two images and apply multi-resolution analysis on them to get a serial of octave like images, and at last we mosaic them at the same resolution and combine the images after image mosaics. As a result, we can get a seamless and smooth image.

Fig. 2. An obvious seam image

3.1 Gaussian Pyramid Generation

We create a region image D, at the size of mosaic image. In the region, the centers found by PSO image mosaics algorithm is used as the boundary line. We fill white in the left side of the line and black in the right. Gaussian Pyramid is applied in the region image D.

The region image is represented initially by the level G_{D0}. This image becomes the bottom or zero level of the Gaussian pyramid. Gaussian Pyramid level 1 contains image G_{D1}, which is a reduced or low-pass filtered version of G_{D0}. Each value within level 1 is computed as a weighted average of values in level 0 within a 5-by-5 window. Each value within level 2, representing G_{D2}, is then obtained from values within level 1 by applying the same pattern of weights.

$$G_{D0}(i,j) = D(i,j)$$
$$G_{Dl}(i,j) = \sum_{m=-2}^{2}\sum_{n=-2}^{2} w(m,n) G_{D(l-1)}(2*i+m, 2*j+n) \quad (1)$$

Where, for levels $0 < l < N$ and nodes i, j, $0 \le i < C_l, 0 \le j < R_l$. In this paper N=4, C_l and R_l represent the horizontal width and vertical height in level 1 in the Gaussian Pyramid, and $w(m,n)$ is the generating kernel. The level-to-level averaging process is called REDUCE. We now define a function EXPAND as the reverse of REDUCE. Thus, EXPAND applied to array G_{Dl} of the Gaussian pyramid would yield an array G'_{Dl} which is the same size as $G_{D(l-1)}$.

$$G'_{Dl}(i,j) = EXPAND(G_{Dl}(i,j)) = \sum_{m=-2}^{2}\sum_{n=-2}^{2} w(m,n)G_{Dl}((i-m)/2,(j-m)/2) \quad (2)$$

Where, $0 < l < N, 0 \le i < C_{l-1}, 0 \le j < R_{l-1}$. When a Gaussian Pyramid is constructed, the Gaussian Pyramid vlue of each level in the region image D is recorded and is used to contrast the weight of Laplacian Pyramid for the mosaic image.

3.2 Laplacian Pyramid Generation

Two original images $I1$ and $I2$ Expand the size of the region image respectively, the extended part is filled by each original image. For the extended images $I1$ and $I2$, the Laplacian Pyramid of its *RGB* component chart is a sequence of error images $L_0, L_1 ... L_N$. Each is the difference between two levels of the Gaussian pyramid. They are Laplacian Pyramid of R channel for the extended images $I1$ and $I2$.

$$\begin{aligned} L_{IN} &= G_{IN} \\ L_{Il}(i,j) &= G_{Il}(i,j) - G_{I(l+1)}(i,j) \end{aligned} \quad (3)$$

For $0 \le l < N-1$. N is the total number of levels in Laplacian Pyramid and in this paper $N=4$.

3.3 Image Mosaic

The last images in image mosaics can be obtained by calculate the Laplacian Pyramid of its RGB system. We set the Laplacian Pyramid image in level l in each channel is L_{Ml}. We take the pixel value of G_{Dl} in level l in Gaussian Pyramid in the region image as a weight, based on which we can calculate the pixel value of L_{Ml} in its position by:

$$L_{Ml} = G_{Dl}(i,j)LI1(i,j) + (1 - G_{Dl}(i,j))LI2(i,j) \quad (4)$$

Where, *LI*1 is the Laplacian Pyramid in the current level of the expanded original image *I*1, *LI*2 is the Laplacian Pyramid in the current level of the expanded original image *I*2. *(i,j)* is the position of the pixel. *LI*1 and *LI*2 can be calculated using formula (3). Each *RGB* channel of the last mosaic image can be rebuilt by decomposed N-level multi-resolution image $L_{M0}, L_{M1},...,L_{M(N-1)}, L_{MN}$ ($L_{MN} = G_{MN}$) In our paper, $N=4$. i.e.,

$$M = L_{M0} + EXPAND(L_{M1} + EXPAND(...(L_{M(N-1)} + EXPAND(L_{MN})))) \quad (5)$$

After the rebuilt of each *RGB* channel image, we can calculate the *RGB* value and output the last resulting image, which is a clear and smooth seamless image. As shown in Fig.3.

Fig. 3. Multi-resolution mosaic image

4 Conclusion

In this paper, we proposed a new fast image mosaics algorithm based PSO multi-resolution mosaics algorithms. Compared with other image mosaics algorithms, our approach is straightforward and easy to implement. We first use PSO to find a certain area which contains sufficient objective characters, then we use pattern matching method to search the matching patch in another image and adjust image; at last, the mosaic image is created by a multi-resolution method. Experimental results testy that this algorithm is able to seamlessly stitch two overlapping images automatically. According to our experiments, our algorithm can easily solve the seam problem when mosaic two images. In our experiment on a PC, which is DELL 4100 PIII 1G, 256M memory, we selected 10 particles, the size of matching area is 20*20 and 4 level pyramid, it cost 2s~3s to mosaic two 300*230 pixels images.

References

1. Du W., Li H.: A novel panoramic representation for dynamic scenes. Chinese Journal of Computers. Vol. 25, No. 9. (2002) 968-975
2. Szliski R., Shum H. Y.: Creating full view panoramic image mosaics and environment maps. In: Computer Graphics Proceedings. Annual Conference Series. ACM SIGGRAPH. Los Angeles. California (1997) 251-258
3. Cai Y., Liu X. H., Wu E. H.: Image-based rendering a technology for virtual reality system. Journal of Software.Vol.8, No.10.(1997) 721-728
4. Fang X. Y., Pan Z.G., Xu D.: An improved algorithm for image mosaics. Journal of computer-aided design & computer graphics.Vol.15, No.11. (2003) 1362-1365
5. Kennedy J., Eberhart R C.: Particle swarm optimization. Proc. IEEE int'l conf. On neural networks. Vol.IV. IEEE, (1995) 1942-1948

Adaptive Simulated Annealing for Standard Cell Placement

Guofang Nan, Minqiang Li, Dan Lin, and Jisong Kou

Institute of System Engineering, Tianjin University,
300072, Tianjin, P R China
gfnan@tju.edu.cn
http://www.tju.edu.cn

Abstract. A standard cell placement algorithm based on adaptive simulated annealing is presented in this paper. Considering the characters of different circuits to be placed, adaptively initial temperature and adaptive searching region are added to traditional simulated annealing algorithm. At the same time, the punishment item in objective function and initial placement approach are improved for the standard cell placement problem. This algorithm is applied to test a set of benchmark circuits, and experiments reveal its advantages in placement results and time performance when compared with the traditional simulated annealing algorithm.

1 Introduction

Given an electrical circuit consisting of modules with predefined input and output terminals, we need to construct a layout indicating the positions of the modules, so that the estimated wirelength and the layout area are minimized.

Given a design with m cells denoted by $C = \{c_1, c_2, ..., c_m\}$, $E = \{e_1, e_2, ..., e_n\}$ represents the set of n nets. To each cell $c_i (1 \leq i \leq m)$, the coordination (x_i, y_i) is used to denote the lower left point of the cell. The design area is a rectangle one denoted by points $(0,0)$ and (X, Y). All the circuit modules are placed in k rows, denoted by $R = \{r_1, r_2, ..., r_k\}$, the main purpose is to get the positions of all modules such that total wirelength TWL of all nets is minimized [1].

$$TWL = \sum_{i=1}^{n} l_i \tag{1}$$

where l_i represents estimated wirelength of net i, n represents net number.

The placement problem has been proved to be NP hard, and therefore, it cannot be solved exactly in polynomial time. The traditional placement algorithm includes min-cut graph algorithm [2-3], force-directed algorithm [4], tabu search algorithm [5], genetic algorithm [6], and simulated annealing [7]. Especially, the simulated annealing algorithm was widely and successfully used in most of placement tools, but there are also some problems in traditional simulated annealing. Therefore, a standard cell placement algorithm based on adaptive simulated annealing is presented.

2 Problems to Be Improved

In standard cell placement, all cells are of the same height and different width, and each move or position exchange may cause cell overlap penalty, which makes the optimization process more difficult. Moreover, it also results in the row length control penalty. A lot of experiments show that too many penalties lead to difficulties in finding the best placement solution.

Table 1 lists Δc and probability of accepting inferior solution at different temperatures for the placement of three benchmark circuits, where Δc represents the average value change of object function for the first 100 perturbs, suppose that $\{\Delta c_1, \Delta c_2, ..., \Delta c_{100}\}$ represents the difference of the object function in the first 100 perturbations, Δc can be calculated by

$$\Delta c = \frac{\sum_{i=1}^{100} |\Delta c_i|}{100} \quad (2)$$

It is clearly shown from Table 1 that Δc varies greatly with different circuits at the same initial temperature denoted by T_0, probability of accepting inferior solution denoted by P also varies greatly with detailed circuit. It is necessary in the simulated annealing that probability of accepting inferior solution is 50% at the beginning, so initial temperature should be a different value for different circuits.

Table 1. Probability of accepting inferior solution at different temperatures for circuits

Circuit	T_0 ($\times 10^3$)	Δc	$e^{-\Delta c/T}$	P
Fract	1.5	1302	0.419	41.9%
	15	1365	0.913	91.3%
	500	1267	0.997	99.7%
Primary1	1.5	19026	0	0%
	15	19255	0.277	27.7%
	500	18128	0.964	96.4%
Biomed	1.5	418723	0	0%
	15	429156	0	0%
	500	415348	0.435	43.5%

Perturbations are limited to a region within a windows of height H_T and width W_T, two cells a and b coordinated at (x_a, y_a) and (x_b, y_b) are selected for interchange only if $|x_a - x_b| < W_T$ and $|y_a - y_b| < H_T$. H_T and W_T vary with temperature T. where $\{T_1, T_2, ...T_i, ...\}$ is temperature sequence in cooling process, the algorithm is terminated when $T_i < T_l$, T_l is the terminated temperature, here $T_l = 1$. the corresponding parameters $\{W_{T_1}, W_{T_2}, ...W_{T_i}, ...\}$ and $\{H_{T_1}, H_{T_2}, ...H_{T_i}, ...\}$ represent searching region.

$\alpha < 1$ is the cooling rate parameter, which is determined experimentally. It can be seen from many experiments that the temperature and searching region are reduced gradually, especially when the temperature is close to the terminated temperature, searching region is approximately zero, which makes invalid cell change and cell movement. Therefore, we adopt a kind of adaptive searching region.

3 Adaptive Simulated Annealing

Traditional initially placement method may cause overlaps between two or more cells. In this paper, overlaps are eliminated by a heuristic initial placement method, which is finished in two steps. First, the averaged cell number in each row is calculated according to total cell number and row number, then, these cells are randomly allocated to each row. It should be noted that there are no overlaps between cells. Second, the remaining cells are allocated one by one to the rows whose total length is the shortest.

When a cell is displaced or when two cells are swapped, it is possible that there is an overlap between cells. So, in order to eliminate overlap, we must update involved cells' coordinate timely, which can also simplify the objective function.

$$Cost = \sum_{i=1}^{n}(\alpha_i^H \times X_i + \alpha_i^V \times Y_i) + \omega \sum_{i=1}^{R}|L_A(i) - L_R(i)| \qquad (3)$$

where $Cost$ is objective function, α_i is the weight, X_i, Y_i is the horizontal and the vertical length of net i, ω is the weight of unevenness, R is the total row number, and $L_A(i), L_R(i)$ are the expected length and the real length of row i.

Probability of accepting inferior solutions should be 50%, so initial temperature is calculated by

$$e^{-\frac{\Delta c}{T}} = 0.5 \qquad (4)$$

With the decrease of the temperature, the searching region is reduced gradually. Especially when the temperature is close to the terminated temperature, the searching region shrinks to zero, which leads to most invalid cell exchange and cell movements operations. In order to solve this kind of problems, we divide the total annealing process into three phases. In the 100 perturbations from the beginning of the SA, the searching region is the whole placement plane. In the intermediate annealing process, cell exchanges or cell movements should be limited in a region. When the searching region becomes very small, the searching region is the whole placement plane.

The main purpose of a perturbation is to produce a new placement, including two cases: Move a single cell to a new location, say to a different row, or swap two cells and update their coordinates.

The annealing schedule is divided into three phases. Initially, the temperature is reduced rapidly. Intermediately, the temperature is reduced slowly, most of cell processing is done in this range. In the later phrase, the temperature is reduced rapidly again. So the annealing schedule is formulated as follows:

$$\alpha = \begin{cases} 0.8 & T > \frac{3}{4}T_0 \\ 0.95 & \frac{1}{4}T_0 \leq T \leq \frac{3}{4}T_0 \\ 0.8 & T < \frac{1}{4}T_0 \end{cases} \quad (5)$$

All of the cooling rate parameters are determined experimentally, and the algorithm is terminated when $T < T_l = 1$.

4 Experiments and Conclusions

In formula (3), $\alpha_i^H = 1, \alpha_i^V = 1$ $\omega = 6$, Some parameters mentioned above are used in adaptive simulated annealing (ASA) to test some benchmark circuits, and the results including estimated wirelength, chip size, row number, and computation time are listed in Table 2. Meanwhile, we listed some results achieved by simulated annealing (SA), which is used to make a comparison with the ASA.

Table 2. Comparison with two algorithms

Circuits	SA				ASA			
	Wirelength (μm)	Row length (μm)	Rows	Time (m)	Wirelength (μm)	Row length (μm)	Rows	Time (m)
Fract	46901	976	8	1.48	45732	976	8	1.5
Struct	530214	3477	29	18.3	506734	3480	29	16.5
Primary1	818366	3605	23	19.4	750926	3602	23	19.2

Compared with the traditional SA, the adaptive initial temperature and adaptive searching region are added in the ASA. Meanwhile, the punishment item in objective function is improved, which show its advantages in results and time performance.

Acknowledgements

This research was supported by the National Science Foundation of China (Grant No.70171002, No.70301005).

References

1. Bo Yao, Wenting Hou, Xianlong Hong, Yici Cai, FAME: A Fast Detailed Placement Algorithm for Standard Cell Layout Based on Mixed Min-cut and Enumeration, Chinese Journal of Semiconductors, (2000), 21(8): 744-753
2. Terai M, Takahashi K, Sato K, A new min-cut placement algorithm for timing assurance layout design meeting net length constrain, Design Automation Conference, (1990) 96-102

3. Saurabh Adya, Igor Markov, Villarrubia P G, Improving Min-cut Placement for VLSI Using Analytical Techniques, IBM ACAS Conference, (2003) 55-62
4. Quinn J R, Breuer M A, A Forced Directed Component Placement Procedure for Printed Circuit Boards, IEEE Trans. CAS, (1979) 26(6): 377-388
5. Suit S M, Youssef H, Barada H R, Al-Yamani A, A parallel tabu search algorithm for VLSI standard-cell placement, Circuits and Systems, 2000. Proceedings. ISCAS 2000 Geneva. The 2000 IEEE International Symposium on, (2000) 2: 581-584
6. Manikas T W, Mickle M H, A genetic algorithm for mixed macro and standard cell placement, Circuits and Systems, (2002) 2: 4-7
7. Grover L K, A new simulated annealing algorithm for standard cell placement, Proc Int. Conf. on CAD, (1986) 378-380

Application of Particle Swarm Optimization Algorithm on Robust PID Controller Tuning

Jun Zhao, Tianpeng Li, and Jixin Qian

Institute of systems engineering, Zhejiang University, Hangzhou, 310027, China
jzhao@iipc.zju.edu.cn

Abstract. The performance of the PID controller may deteriorate when the operating condition of a process fluctuates. A robust parameter tuning method to improve the PID controller performance under bounded model uncertainty is presented. First an enhanced performance criterion is proposed to reduce the overshoot and large control move. Then the robust tuning problem is formulated as a Min-Max optimization. Particle Swarm Optimization (PSO) is applied to solve the nonlinear, non-differentiable problem. Examples are given to demonstrate the effectiveness of the proposed method. Compared with other PID tuning methods, the result shows that better performance can be achieved with the model parameter fluctuation.

1 Introduction

Proportional-integral-derivative (PID) controllers are widely used in industrial process control system, for their simple structure, good robustness and easy implementation; on the other hand, the principle of PID controller is easier to understand than most other advanced controllers. Since Ziegler and Nichols proposed their first PID tuning method [1], a good insight into the PID controller parameter tuning has been widely studied with many approaches proposed [2-6]. In physical processes, uncertainties are ineluctably encountered in the control systems. The equipment ageing or change in process dynamics due to alterations of operation conditions causes fluctuations of the model parameters. Most current PID parameter tuning methods, however, design PID parameters according to single operation condition. Therefore, the performance of the resultant PID controller may be poor if the process operates in a different condition. Then, controllers need to be regularly retuned. To avoid tuning PID parameters frequently, a robust PID tuning method was proposed by R. Toscano [11], in which the optimal PID parameters tuning problem is formulated as a Min-Max numerical optimization, and a frequency domain cost function is used to evaluate the performance. But the control performance in time domain is not guaranteed.

Though Min-Max optimization is useful in robust PID controller design, the existing difficulty is that how to keep the outer layer objective function decreasing and the inner layer objective function increasing at the same time. Particle Swarm Optimization (PSO) [7],[8] is parallel evolutionary computation technique developed by Kennedy and Eberhart based on the social behavior metaphor. Generally, PSO is characterized as simple in concept, easy to implement, and computationally efficient. Unlike the other heuristic methods, PSO has flexible and well-balanced mechanism to enhance the global and local exploration abilities. Compared with other optimization algorithm such as GA, the PSO is more effective and economic for solving Min-Max optimization problem [12].

Our purpose is to propose a novel parameter robust tuning algorithm, with which the close-loop system can adapt to the fluctuation of model parameters. Once the PID parameters are determined, the close-loop system remains stable if the perturbation of process is within a preset range. In Section 2, a new performance evaluation criterion, which simultaneously suppresses large overshoot and control move, is proposed. The robust parameters tuning approach is formulated as Min-Max optimization problem. The robustness measures of close-loop system are also introduced. Section 3 presents the searching algorithm using PSO for Min-Max optimization problem. Two examples are given to demonstrate the effectiveness over some classic and latest developed design methods in Section 4.

2 Robust PID Controller Design

2.1 Performance Criterion of Control System

The PID feedback control system is shown in Fig. 1.

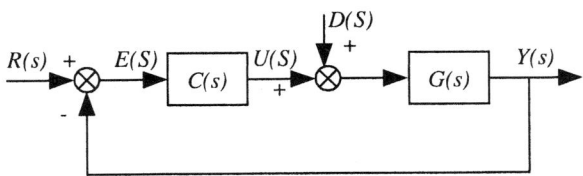

Fig. 1. Block diagram of the PID feedback control system

where $G(S)$ represents the transfer function of the real process. It is approximated as a first-order plus dead time model or a second-order plus dead-time model.

$$G(s) = \frac{K}{Ts+1} e^{-\tau s} \quad (1)$$

$$G(s) = \frac{K}{a_1 s^2 + a_2 s + 1} e^{-\tau s} \quad (2)$$

$C(S)$ is the transfer function of the PID controller. Note that the PID algorithm is composed of a standard PID algorithm followed a first order filter. This type of PID algorithm can reduce the impact of high-frequency disturbance.

$$C(s) = K_c \left(1 + \frac{1}{T_i s} + T_d s\right) \frac{1}{T_f s + 1} \quad (3)$$

The open-loop transfer function of the control system in Fig. 1 can be expressed as:

$$L(s) = C(s)G(s) \qquad (4)$$

The sensitivity function is defined as:

$$S(s) = \frac{1}{1+C(s)G(s)} = \frac{1}{1+L(s)} \qquad (5)$$

The complementary sensitivity function of the system is defined as:

$$T(s) = 1 - S(s) = \frac{C(s)G(s)}{1+C(s)G(s)} = \frac{1}{1+L(s)} \qquad (6)$$

The maximum sensitivity function and complementary sensitivity function are defined as:

$$M_s = \max_{\omega} |S(j\omega)| \qquad M_p = \max_{\omega} |T(j\omega)| \qquad (7)$$

The sensitivity function and complementary sensitivity function are the measures of robustness for the variations of real process to be controlled. Besides, the sensitivity function shows how the disturbances are influenced by feedback control system, and the complementary sensitivity function represents the first overshoot of the step response as well. A small M_s means that the system can stand larger variation of the process than a large M_s. M_p tells how the closed-loop system properties are influenced by variations in the process; a smaller M_p result in a more robust system with a smaller overshoot [13].

In optimal PID tuning, typical performance criterions to evaluate close-loop system response are the integral of squared error and time weighted error, such as ISE, IAE, ITAE, etc. Different performance index results in different PID parameters and different performance. Considering the PID tuning with ISE (Integral Squared Error) criterion always output large overshoot, which may cause product unqualified in real processes and thus undesirable, a new enhanced ISEWE (EISTWE) performance criterion is proposed to reduce the overshoot.

$$EISTWE = \int_0^\infty (t^n * e(t)^2 + q * \Delta u(t)^2) dt \qquad (8)$$

$$EISTWE_M = (1 + r*(a+b)) * EISTWE \qquad (9)$$

Where $e(t) = r(t) - y(t)$, $\Delta u(t)$ denotes the rate of controller output. a and b are shown in Fig.2. q and r are weight parameters. As a is the first overshoot of the unit step response of closed-loop system, a is related to the maximum value of complementary sensitivity function M_p; if a is large, then M_p is large. A small overshoot is required to obtain good robustness.

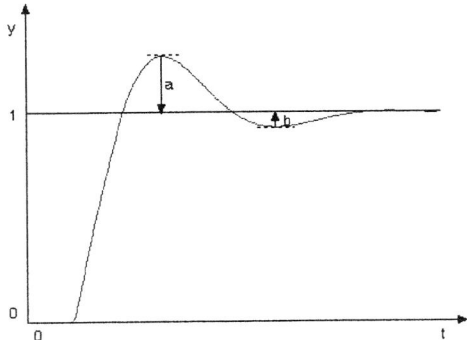

Fig. 2. Response of PID feedback control system

2.2 Min-Max Expression of Robust PID Tuning

The worst operating conditions may occur within the uncertainty boundary δ of model parameters. Considering the process models (1) and (2), suppose the magnitude of model uncertainty is bounded to less than a constant δ. In other words, the parameters in process model (1) may vary from $[K(1-\delta), T(1-\delta), \tau(1-\delta)]$ to $[K(1+\delta), T(1+\delta), \tau(1+\delta)]$. Min-Max criterion can guarantee that the eventual PID parameters is optimal for the worst operating conditions, at the same time, the robustness of the closed-loop system is ensured as the close-loop system is stable when the operating condition fluctuates within the preset range. The robust parameters tuning method of the PID controller can be described as:

$$\min_{P_c} \max_{P_m} EISTWE_M(P_c, P_m)$$
$$s.t. \ |\Delta u(t)| \leq \Delta u(t)_{max} \quad (10)$$
$$P_c \in S$$
$$P_m \in R$$

Where $P_c \underline{\Delta} [K_c, T_i, T_d, T_f]$ are the PID controller parameters, S is a close set defined by engineers to limit the gains of controller. $P_m \underline{\Delta} [K, T, \tau]$ are the model parameters for the process model (1). R is a close set which represents the variation range of the model parameters relating to the model uncertainty magnitude δ. $EISTWE_M$ is the performance criterion presented in formulas (8) and (9).

Since Min-Max optimization (10) is a nonlinear multi-objective problem, there is not any known analytical solution of this optimization problem. A Min-Max searching algorithm implemented by particle swarm optimizer is proposed for solving this complex optimization problem.

3 PSO for Min-Max Problem

In PSO algorithm, the system is initialized with a population of random solutions, which are called particles, and each potential solution is also assigned a randomized velocity. PSO relies on the exchange of information between particles, which are volume-less particles of the population called swarm, the whole swarm is considered as the neighborhood. Each particle adjusts its trajectory towards its best solution (fitness) that is achieved so far. This value is called *pbest*. Each particle also modifies its trajectory towards the best previous position attained by any member of its neighborhood. This value is called *gbest*. Each particle moves in the search space with an adaptive velocity.

Let D be the dimension of the search space. Then $x_i \underline{\Delta} [x_{i1}, x_{i2}, \cdots, x_{iD}]^T$ denotes the current position of ith the particle of the swarm, and $x_i^{pbest} \underline{\Delta} [x_{i1}^{pbest}, x_{i2}^{pbest}, \cdots, x_{iD}^{pbest}]^T$ denotes the best position that has ever visited; and $x^{gbest} \underline{\Delta} [x_1^{gbest}, x_2^{gbest}, \cdots, x_D^{gbest}]^T$ represents *gbest*, the best place obtained thus far by any particle in the population. The rate of the velocity for the ith particle is represented as $v_i \underline{\Delta} [v_{i1}, v_{i2}, \cdots, v_{iD}]^T$ and $V_i^{max} \underline{\Delta} [V_{i1}^{max}, V_{i2}^{max}, \cdots, V_{iD}^{max}]^T$ denotes the upper bound on the absolute value of the velocity the particle can move at each step. In PSO, the particles are manipulated according to the following equations:

$$v_{id} = w * v_{id} + c_1 * r_1 * (x_{id}^{pbest} - x_{id}) + c_2 * r_2 * (x^{gbest} - x_{id}) \quad (11)$$

$$v_{id} = \begin{cases} V_d^{max}, & v_{id} > V_d^{max} \\ -V_d^{max}, & v_{id} < -V_d^{max} \end{cases} \quad (12)$$

$$x_{id} = x_{id} + v_{id} \quad (13)$$

Where c_1 and c_2 are positive constants, represent the cognitive and social parameter respectively; r_1 and r_2 are random numbers uniformly distributed in the range [0,1]; w is inertia weight to balance the global and local search ability [9]. A large inertia weight facilitates a global search, while a small inertia weight facilitates a local search. By linearly decreasing the inertia weight from a relatively large value to a small one, the PSO tends to have more global search ability at the beginning of the run while having more local search ability near the end of the run.

The PSO algorithm for solving the Min-Max problem (10) can be expressed as:

Step1: Set swarm parameters such as population size P_C and P_G, c_1, c_2, w, V_i^{max}.
Step2: $k=0$, Initialize $P_C(0)$ and $P_G(0)$, then arbitrarily choose $x_{min} \subset P_C(0)$.
Step3: Initialize population $P_G(k)$. For each particle $y \subset P_G(k)$, execute the following two steps:

3.1): Let $-EISTWE_M(x_{min}, P_G(k))$ as objective function to update $P_G(k)$,

3.2): Let $y_{max} = gbest(P_G(k))$.

Step4: Initialize population $P_C(k)$. For each particle $x \subset P_C(k)$, execute the following two steps:

4.1): Let $EISTWE_M(P_C(k), y_{max})$ as objective function to update $P_C(k)$,

4.2): Let $x_{min} = gbest(P_C(k))$.

Step5: $k=k+1$

Step6: Repeat **Step3** to **Step5** if terminal conditions are not satisfied.

Setp7: $P_C(k)$ and $P_G(k)$ corresponding to minimum x_{min} and maximal y_{max} are the solution, and $P_C(k)$ is the final PID parameters.

4 Simulation and Discussion

4.1 Example 1

In this example, the effectiveness of the proposed tuning method is compared with two classic tuning methods, Ziegler- Nichols method [1] and ISTWE rule [10]. Consider the first-order plus dead-time process: $G_1(s) = \dfrac{0.8}{1.07s+1}e^{-2.1s}$, assuming that $\delta=0.4$. The robust PID parameters given by proposed tuning method and the PID values obtained by Ziegler- Nichols method and ISTWE rule are listed in Tab.1, and the robustness measurements of close loop system in normal condition ($\delta=0$) are also listed in Tab.1. It is observed that maximum sensitivity function M_s and complementary sensitivity function M_p of the proposed method are smaller than the others; phase margin Φ_m of Ziegler-Nichols method is larger than the proposed method, but the amplitude margin A_m of Ziegler-Nichols method is smaller.

Table 1. PID controller parameters and robustness measurements of process $G_1(s)$

Tuning Method	PID Controller Parameters				Measurements of Robustness			
	K_c	T_i	T_d	T_f	M_s	M_p	A_m	Φ_m
Proposed Method	0.4622	1.8094	0.5830	0.1115	1.3342	0.9995	4.1486	72.9008
Ziegler Nichols	0.7643	4.200	1.0570	0	2.4866	1.4866	1.6556	98.1844
ISTWE	0.2700	0.7000	0.7200	0	1.7705	1.1967	3.2983	50.0210

All PID controllers perform well in the normal condition. The unit step responses and load-disturbance responses are compared as shown in Fig.3. It shows that the response of Ziegler-Nichols method is slow. The fastest response is obtained from

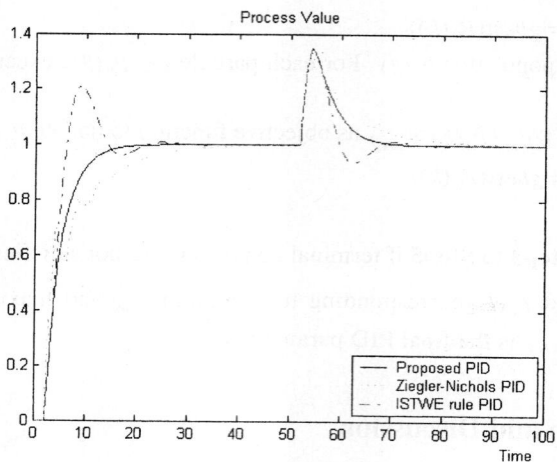

Fig. 3. Unit step response and load-disturbance response of process $G_1(s)$

ISTWE method, but with large overshoot. PID controller tuned by the proposed method has faster response and small overshoot. The result is owing to that the EISEWE performance criterion suppresses the large control action to reduce the overshoot, although PID parameters obtained through Min-Max search is not optimal in normal condition.

When the process-model mismatch is presented $\delta=0.4$, the transfer function of real process in this condition is $G_1'(s) = \dfrac{1.12}{1.498s+1} e^{-2.94s}$. Unit step response and load-disturbance response at this condition are shown in Fig.4. The responses of ISTWE method and Ziegler-Nichols method oscillate. But PID controller tuned by proposed method results in a stable response. This is owing to the fact that Min-Max search can guarantee the performance in the worst operating conditions.

4.2 Example 2

In this example, two latest developed tuning methods, Optimal Gain and Phase Margin Tuning (GPM-PID) method [5] and robust PI/PID controller design via numerical optimization method (R.Toscano method) [11], are employed to compare with the proposed tuning method.

Consider the second-order plus dead-time process: $G_2(s) = \dfrac{1}{s^2+2s+1} e^{-1.58s}$, assuming that $\delta=0.4$. The robust PID parameters given by the proposed tuning method and the PID parameters tuned by GPM-PID method and R.Toscano method are summarized in Tab.2, and robustness measurements of the close-loop system are also illustrated in Tab.2.

The unit step responses and load-disturbance responses of three PID controllers at normal condition $\delta=0$ are shown in Fig.5. The response of the proposed PID controller is a little slower than that of GPM-PID method and R.Toscano method, but the overshoot is much smaller.

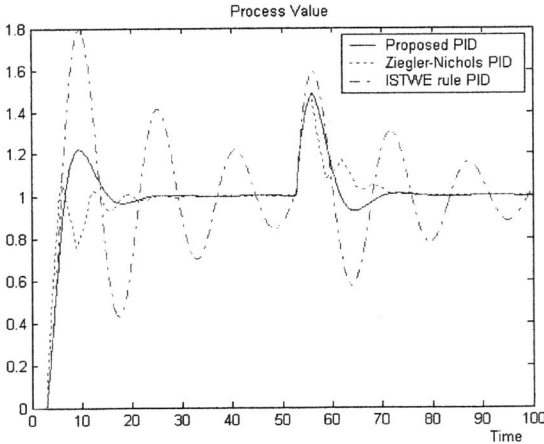

Fig. 4. Unit step response and load-disturbance response of process $G_1^{'}(s)$

Table 2. PID controller parameters and Measurements of robustness of process $G_2(s)$

Tuning Method	PID Controller Parameters				Measurements of Robustness			
	K_c	T_i	T_d	T_f	M_s	M_p	A_m	ϕ_m
Proposed Method	0.4173	1.9990	0.6831	0.1540	1.3251	0.9686	4.8160	69.8873
GPM-PID	0.6600	2.0000	0.5000	0	1.6268	1.0049	3.0123	60.1260
R.Toscano Method	0.7983	2.2718	0.5633	0	1.7062	1.0000	2.6412	61.9546

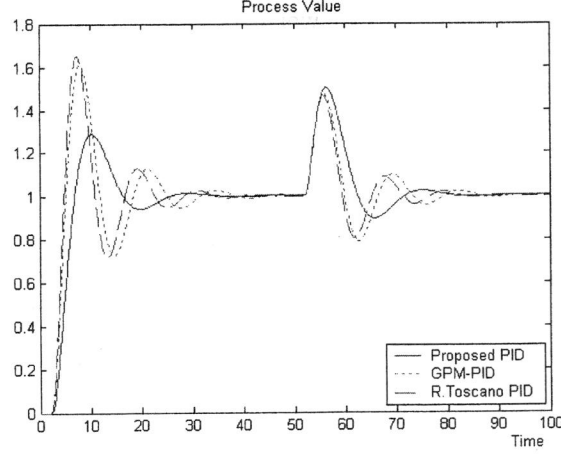

Fig. 5. Unit step response and load-disturbance response of process $G_2(s)$

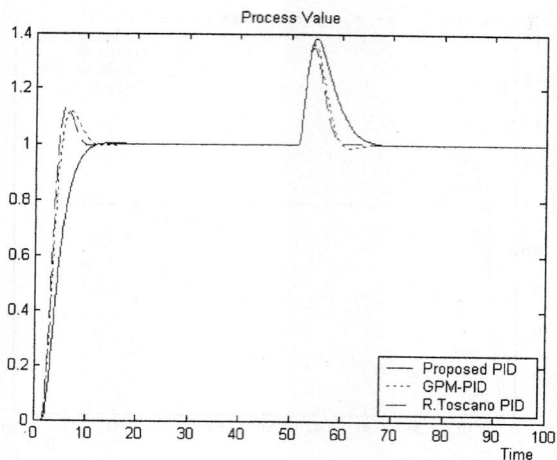

Fig. 6. Unit step response and load-disturbance response of process $G_2^{'}(s)$

When the process operates at the operating condition: $K=K(1+\delta)$, $a_1=a_1(1+\delta)$, $a_2=a_2(1+\delta)$, $\tau=\tau(1+\delta)$ and $\delta=0.4$. The transfer function $G_2^{'}(s) = \dfrac{1.4}{1.4s^2+2.8s+1}e^{-2.94s}$. Unit step response and load-disturbance response at this operating condition are shown in Fig.6. The performance of each controller is inferior to that at the normal condition $\delta=0$ because of the large model uncertainty. Both GPM-PID method and the R.Toscano method produce large overshoot and oscillation. As a contrast, small overshoot and stable performance is maintained by the proposed method at this operating condition.

Due to our design principles, the worst conditions have been considered and dealt with. When model parameter is precise, the proposed method has close result to the other PID design methods. When the plant model mismatch appears, PID tuned by our method still performs well, but those systems controlled by other PIDs usually output poor responses

5 Conclusions

In real process, the operating conditions are not constant and the model parameters may fluctuate. A robust parameter tuning method for PID controller is proposed via Min-Max optimization approach for bounded uncertainties in model parameters. An enhanced ISEWE performance criterion is presented to reduce the overshoot and large control move. A Min-Max searching algorithm implemented by particle swarm optimizer is presented. Simulations demonstrate that the algorithm is efficient with advantages over some classic and latest developed design methods.

Acknowledgement

The authors would like to gratefully acknowledge financial support from the China National Key Basic Research and Development Program under Grant 2002CB312200 and National High Technology Development Program under Grant 2004AA412050.

References

1. Ziegler, J.G., Nichols, N.B.: Optimum settings for automatic controllers. Trans. ASME, **64**(1942)759-768
2. Åström, K.J., Hägglund, T.: Automatic tuning of simple regulators with specification on phase and amplitude margins. Automatic, **20**(1984)645-651
3. Cohen, G.D., Coon, G.A.: Theoretical consideration for retarded controllers. Trans. ASME, **75**(1953)827-834
4. Zhuang, M., Atherton, D.P.: Automatic tuning of optimum PID controllers. Proceedings of IEE Proc Control Theory, **140**(1993)216-224
5. Ho, W.K., Lim, K.W., Xu, W.: Optimal Gain and Phase Margin Tuning for PID Controllers. Automatic, **34**(1998)1009-1014
6. Lee, Y., Park, S., Lee, M., Brosilow, C.: PID controller tuning for desired closed-loop response for SI/SO systems. AIChE J., **44**(1998)106-115
7. Kennedy, J., Eberhart, R.C.: Particle swarm optimization. Proc. IEEE Int. Conf. on Neural Networks, Perth, WA, Australia, (1995)1942-1948
8. Eberhart, R. C., Kennedy, J.: A new optimizer using particle swarm theory. Proc. the Sixth Int. Symposium on Micro Machine and Human Science, Nagoya, Japan, (1995)39-43
9. Shi, Y., Eberhart, R.C.: Parameter Selection in Particle Swarm Optimization. Proceedings of 7th Annual Conference on Evolution Computation, (1998)591-601
10. Liu, G.P., Daley, S.: Optimal-tuning PID controller design in the frequency domain with application to a rotary hydraulic system. Control Engineering Practice 7(1999)821-830
11. Toscano, R.: A simple robust PI/PID controller design via numerical optimization approach. Journal of Process Control, **15**(2005)81-88
12. Abido, M.A.: Optimal Power Flow Using Particle Swarm Optimization. Electrical Power and Energy Systems, **24** (2002)563-571
13. Michael, G., Limebeer, D. J. N.: Linear Robust Control. Prentice Hall, Englewood Cliffs, N.J.(1995)

A Natural Language Watermarking Based on Chinese Syntax*

Yuling Liu, Xingming Sun, and Yong Wu

School of Computer and Communication Hunan University, Changsha, China
yuling_liu@126.com, sunnudt@163.com, wydvdv@21cn.com

Abstract. A novel text watermarking algorithm is presented. It combines natural language watermarking and Chinese syntax based on BP neural networks. Since the watermarking signals are embedded into some Chinese syntactic structure rather than the appearance of text elements, the algorithm is totally based on the content that can prove to be very resilient. It will play an important role in protecting the security of Chinese documents over Internet.

1 Introduction

With the development of digitalization technology, it is indispensable to protect the copyright over the text documents. Although there are many text watermarking algorithms in recent years, but it is easy to remove it[1]. A better text watermarking approach is to use natural language watermarking [2,3,4] that Atallah et al. proposed. This paper describes a natural language watermarking based on Chinese syntax.

The organization of the paper is as follows: In Sect. 2, we will present a kind of natural language processing techniques of Chinese syntax based on Backpropagation (BP for short) neural networks [5]. A natural language (NL for short) watermarking based on Chinese syntax will be depicted in Sect. 3.The finally is the conclusions.

2 NLP Technique of Chinese Syntax

Natural Language Processing (NLP for short) aims to design algorithms that will analyze and understand natural language text automatically, such as machine translation, information retrieval and so on. In this section, we describe a Chinese syntax analysis system based on BP neural networks(see Fig. 1.).

Database adopts production rules to express the knowledge, which is standardized into binary rules and is coded to be stored in the neural networks. In general, the form of production rules is as follows:

---

* This paper is supported by National Natural Science Fundation of China (NSFC No.60373062), Hunan Provincial NaturalScience Fundation of China (HPNSFC No. 02JJYB012), Key0 Foundation of Science and Technology of Ministry of Education of China (No. 03092).

If $a_1 \wedge a_2 \cdots \wedge a_n$ then $b_1 \wedge b_2 \cdots \wedge b_n$

Standardize the above form to become binary form:

If a then $b_1 \wedge b_2$ or If a then $b_1 \wedge b_2$

We uses 106 pieces of Chinese language knowledge so that they will be represented with seven bits, for instance:

noun *encoded*:0000001, verb *encoded*:000 0010, Sub *encoded*:0011110
Pre *encoded*:0011111, Sub_Pre *encoded*:0100100, No_Sub_Pre *encoded*:0100101

Chinese syntax rules can be described as follows:

$S \rightarrow Sub\_Pre \vee No\_Sub\_Pre$ encoded : 0000000 $\rightarrow$ (0100100) $\vee$ (0100101)
$Sub\_Pre \rightarrow Sub \wedge Pre$ encoded : 0100100 $\rightarrow$ (0011110) $\vee$ (0011111)

Inference machine makes inference based on neural networks, which are BP neural networks grounded on Leverberg-Marquard algorithm. The learning algorithm of BP networks can depict in the following way:

$$\begin{cases} f(p^{k+1}) = \min_\alpha f(p^{(k)} + \alpha^{(k)} p(x^{(k)})) \\ p^{(k+1)} = p^{(x)} + \alpha^{(x)} s(p^{(k)}) \end{cases} \quad (1)$$

Where $p^{(k)}$ is a vector, which contains all the values of weights and thresholds; $s(p^{(k)})$ is the search direction of the vector space, which is composed by each p's weight; $\alpha^{(k)}$ is the teeny length of the pace of $f(p^{(k+1)})$ in the $s(p^{(k)})$ direction.

For example, if the sentence is "", the input would be: "n adv v n". The syntax inference tree is left out. Taking out the empty node, the syntax analysis tree will be as shown by Fig. 2.

3 A NL Watermarking Based on Chinese Syntax

3.1 Principle

In Chinese, a sentence might have several ways to describe without changing the meaning. So, our scheme is to embed the watermark by transforming the syntactic structure. In this mechanism, we intend to select all the sentences except the topic sentences to carry the watermark bits. To describe the principle clearly, some definitions and backgrounds should be presented formally at first.

$A = \{C \cup N \mid C$ is the set of all the topic sentences, and N is the set of all the non-topic sentences$\}$, i.e., A is the set of all the sentences in the text.

p denotes the secret key and it is a large prime. w denotes watermark bits, its length is λ. β denotes the number of watermark bits in each sentence. T_i denotes a corresponding tree that represents s_i syntactically. $B_i = D(T_i)$ denotes the corresponding binary string to each T_i. $B'_i = H(B_i)$, where H denotes a one-way hash function. d_i denotes the number of 0's in the bitwise XOR of B'_i and $H(p)$. S is the set of sentences to be watermarked, that is a list of the $s_i (i = 0, 1, \ldots, n-1)$ sorted according to their d_i values, r denotes s_i's rank in S.

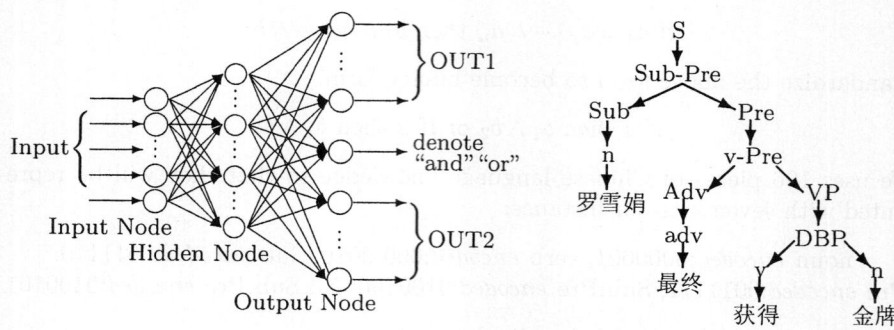

Fig. 1. Model of the BP   **Fig. 2.** Syntax Analysis Tree

Definition 1. *Syntactic transformation is meaning-preserving and near-meaning preserving text substitutions for NL watermarking. Three common syntactic transformations are as follows:*

1) Adjunct Movement, where an adjunct is like a prepositional phrase or adverbial phrase.
2) Passivization: Any sentence with a transitive verb can be passivized.
3) Insertion "transitional" phrases that has empty meaning, such as and so forth.

3.2 Algorithms

Embedding Algorithm :

```
program Embedding(A, w)
   begin
      get S from A, then generate B from S with D(Ti)
      select β value according to the comparison of n and λ
      sort the sentences of S
      for each sentence ∈ S do
         if it is able to be transformed, then
            the indicator bit is 1, embed the watermark
            by syntactic transformation
         else
            the indicator bit is 0, and that sentence are ignored
            during the watermark detecting time
         end-if
      end-for
   end
```

The technique to select β value according to the comparison of n and λ is very important for the robustness of the algorithm. There are two circumstances for it, which are as follows:

if $n \geq \lambda$ then $\beta = 2$(the first bit is an indicator bit)
else $\beta = \frac{\lambda}{n}$ or repeating the watermark $\frac{\lambda}{n}$ times.

As for generating B from N with $D(T_i)$, we will present the algorithm at once.

```
program Generating(N,p)
   begin
      Chinese syntax analysis to get Ti of each sentence in N
         for each Ti do
            give the nodes of Ti numbers
            replace every number i at a node by a bit: 1 if i+H(P)
            is a quadratic residue modulo p, 0 otherwise
            get a listing of bits
         end-for
   end
```

This algorithm is with regard to the technique of Chinese syntax analysis, which we have discussed in Sect. 2.

Watermark Detecting. Anyone with the secret prime p can generate the B_i of every sentence s_i, hence its B'_i and its rank in S. We simply read the watermark bits w out of each sentence having its indicator bit is 1.

4 Conclusions

With the development of natural language processing, the performance of which a computer can understand the meaning of a text correctly is getting better and better. Furthermore, natural language text watermarking technique will improve greatly in the future.

References

1. Maxemchuk, N. F.. Electronic Document Distribution. AT&T Technical Journal,1994.
2. M. Atallah, C. McDonough, S. Nirenburg, and V. Raskin. Natural Language Processing for Information Assurance and Security: An Overview and Implementations. Proceedings 9th ACM/SIGSAC New Security Paradigms Workshop, pp. 51-65, September, 2000.
3. M. Atallah, V. Raskin, M. C. Crogan, C. F. Hempelmann, et al. Natural language watermarking: Design, analysis, and a proof-of-concept implementation. Proceedings of the Fourth Information Hiding Workshop, LNCS 2137, 25-27 April 2001.
4. M. Atallah, V. Raskin, et al. Natural language watermarking and tamperproofing. Proceedings of the Fifth Information Hiding Workshop, LNCS 2578, 7-9 October 2002.
5. Yumei Wang, Xiaogang Ruan. Expert system of Chinese syntax analysis based on backpropagation networks. Journal of Kunming University of Science and Technology, 28(3)(2003).

A Steganographic Scheme in Digital Images Using Information of Neighboring Pixels

Young-Ran Park[1], Hyun-Ho Kang[2], Sang-Uk Shin[1], and Ki-Ryong Kwon[3]

[1] Department of Information Security, Pukyong National University, 599-1 Daeyeon-3Dong, Nam-Gu, Busan 608-737, Republic of Korea
podosongei@hanmail.net, shinsu@pknu.ac.kr
[2] Department of Computer Science, Pukyong National University, 599-1 Daeyeon-3Dong, Nam-Gu, Busan 608-737, Republic of Korea
hefitop@hanmail.net
[3] Department of Electronic and Computer Engineering, Pusan University of Foreign Studies, 55-1 Uam-Dong, Nam-Gu, Busan 608-738, Republic of Korea
krkwon@pufs.ac.kr

Abstract. In this paper, we propose a steganographic technique on images that provides high capacity of secret information as well as imperceptibility of stego image. Our method inserts secret data into every pixel of the image and decides the number of insertion bits using the difference value between two pixels adjacent to the target pixel. Therefore, the number of insertion bits in each pixel is dependent on whether the target pixel is included in an edge area or a smooth area. The experiment results show that the proposed method provides more efficient performance than that of the existing methods from the viewpoint of both the insertion amount and the visual measures.

1 Introduction

Image steganography is a secret communication technique used to transmit secret messages that have been embedded into an image. In image steganography, the original image and the embedded image are called the cover image and the stego image, respectively. The sender hides the secret message in a cover image that has no meaning, and then transmits the stego image to the receiver. In particular, the confidentiality, the amount of secret message to be inserted, and the imperceptibility of stego image should be considered in image steganography [1].

At present, insertion processing of secret information is employed on the special domain or the frequency domain. One of the common methods for inserting secret information into the spatial domain is the LSB (Least Significant Bits) substitution method [2]-[4].

Most images consist of edge and smooth areas. The human perceptibility has a property that it is not sensitive to some changes in the pixels of the edge areas, while it is sensitive to changes in the smooth areas. Not all pixels in the image can tolerate the changes of pixels without causing a recognizable difference to an observer, so the stego image has low quality when equally changing LSBs of all pixels. Hence, to make up for this weakness in the LSBs method, several methods in which the number of bits to be inserted in each pixel depends on the difference between neighboring pixels have been recently studied [5], [6].

The proposed method uses the difference value between two pixels adjacent to the target pixel. The difference value is used to decide the number of secret data bits to insert into a target pixel. The modular function is also used to improve the quality of the stego image. We experiment on various images to evaluate the efficiency of the proposed method, and as a result, our method is able to insert much more information than existing methods. Besides this, the quality of the image is improved as well.

The remainder of this paper is organized as follows. In Section 2, our scheme is described in detail. Experimental results will be shown in Section 3. Finally, concluding remarks are given in Section 4.

2 Proposed Method

Our method improves Thien's [4] method and Chang's [6] method. The results show that our method increases the amount of secret messages and produces an improved quality of stego image as well. To increase the capacity, our scheme decides the number of bits to be inserted into a target pixel by using the difference value between the other two pixels close to the target pixel. When inserting secret data into a target pixel, we used the modular operation to improve the quality of stego image. Therefore the proposed method is more effective than Chang's scheme because it not only provides a good quality stego image but also embeds more secret message.

2.1 The Data Embedding Procedure

Our method refers to two neighboring pixels to embed secret message into the target pixel. In the cover image, given a target pixel P_X with gray value g_x, let g_u and g_l be the gray values of its upper P_U pixel and left p_L pixel, respectively. The embedding procedure is performed following the steps below.

[Step 1] Calculate difference value d between the upper pixel and the left pixel in a given target pixel by

$$d = | g_u - g_l |. \tag{1}$$

By calculating the difference d between the upper and left pixel, we judge whether the target pixel is included in an edge area or a smooth area. This is why the number of bit n, inserted into the target pixel, is determined by value d. Also, because using the upper and left pixels that were already handled when calculating difference d the embedding and extracting process has the same value d, making it more accurate.

[Step 2] Calculate n that is the number of the insertion bits in a target pixel P_X from

$$n = \begin{cases} \lfloor \log_2 d \rfloor, & \text{if } d > 3 \text{ and } d = odd; \\ \lfloor \log_2 d \rfloor - 1, & \text{if } d > 3 \text{ and } d = even. \end{cases} \tag{2}$$

If the value of d is less or equal to 3, n in P_X is determined to be 1, otherwise n is the value from the result calculated by equation (2). We appropriately adjust n to enhance both the capacity and the imperceptibility.

[Step 3] Calculate a temporary value t_x from

$$t_x = b - (g_x \mod 2^n). \tag{3}$$

Where, b is the decimal representation of secret messages as the n bits.

[Step 4] To make the quality of the image higher, select the nearest value to the target pixel's value of the cover image by

$$t'_x = \begin{cases} t_x, & \text{if } (-\left\lfloor \dfrac{2^n-1}{2} \right\rfloor) \leq t_x \leq \left\lceil \dfrac{2^n-1}{2} \right\rceil; \\ t_x + 2^n, & \text{if } (-2^n+1) \leq t_x < (-\left\lfloor \dfrac{2^n-1}{2} \right\rfloor); \\ t_x - 2^n, & \text{if } \left\lceil \dfrac{2^n-1}{2} \right\rceil < t_x < 2^n. \end{cases} \tag{4}$$

[Step 5] Finally, we can get the new pixel value g^*_x for P_X using

$$g^*_x = g_x + t'_x. \tag{5}$$

An effectiveness of equation (3) and (4) has been proved already in Thien's method. We wish to refer to Thien's method [4], and Chan's method [7] about the more detailed proof. The stego image can be created after performing the insertion processing to all pixels except the first row and column in the cover image.

When the new value of pixel P_X is out of the range, it has to be adjusted by

$$g^*_x = \begin{cases} g^*_x + 2^n, & \text{if } g^*_x < 0; \\ g^*_x - 2^n, & \text{if } g^*_x > 255. \end{cases} \tag{6}$$

Thus we solved the problem that may occur when pixels exceed the boundary from 0 to 255.

2.2 The Data Extracting Procedure

The extracting speed of our method is faster than the Chang's method because the algorithm is much simpler.

[Step 1] Calculate the difference value d^* between the upper pixel P^*_U and the left pixel P^*_L in stego image by

$$d^* = |g^*_u - g^*_l|. \tag{7}$$

[Step 2] Calculate the value of n as the number of bits to be inserted pixel P^*_x by

$$n = \begin{cases} \lfloor \log_2 d^* \rfloor, & \text{if } d^* > 3 \text{ and } d^* = odd ; \\ \lfloor \log_2 d^* \rfloor -1, & \text{if } d^* > 3 \text{ and } d^* = even . \end{cases} \quad (8)$$

Where if the value of d^* is less of equal to 3, the value of n is 1, otherwise n is the value calculated in equation (8) as in the embedding procedure.

[Step 3] Finally, Calculating the value of b by $b = \mod(g^*_x, 2^n)$. The decimal value b is represented into the binary of n bits.

We can see the secret message inserted to the pixels after performing the extraction processing.

3 Experimental Results

This section presents experimental results and the discussion of analysis of its results. Several experiments were performed to evaluate the proposed method. Test images applied to the experiment are gray-scale images with size of 256 by 256. Figure 1 are the cover image, stego image of Chang's method, and stego image of our method respectively.

Table 1 compares the amount of insertion and PSNR (peak signal to noise ratio) for the Chang method and the proposed method respectively. In reference to Table 1, the

Fig. 1. Cover image Lena with size of 256 by 256 pixels (left), stego image of Chang's (middle), and stego image of the proposed method (right).

Table 1. Experimental results of Chang's and our method for the capacity and PSNR

Cover images	Capacity (bit)		PSNR (dB)	
	Chang's method	Our method	Chang's method	Our method
Lena	109,101	115,898	37.05	38.82
Sailboat	128,889	143,023	34.85	35.21
Baboon	176,588	179,255	32.36	34.33

proposed method has more embedded bits in a pixel, so the number of secret message in total is larger than the Chang's. Although the amount of bits inserted is larger, the PSNR of the proposed scheme is high. This is possible by using the property of the modular operation. When changing the value of a target pixel in the proposed scheme to insert the secret messages, we get a better quality of the stego image because our method selects the nearest value to the original pixel.

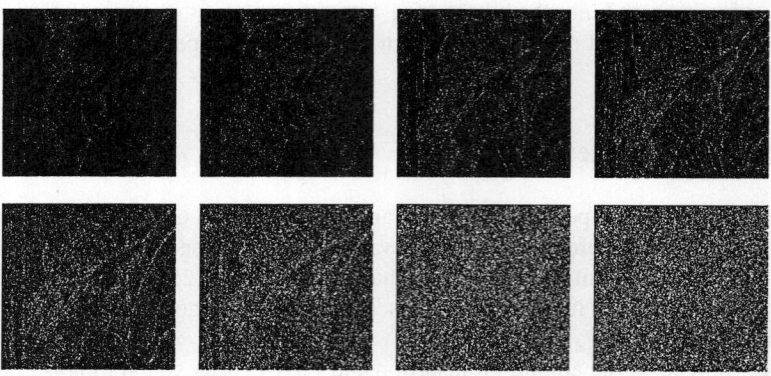

Fig. 2. The bit-planes from the result of the difference between the bit-planes of cover image and stego image in the Chang method: from MSB plane (top-left) to LSB plane (bottom-right).

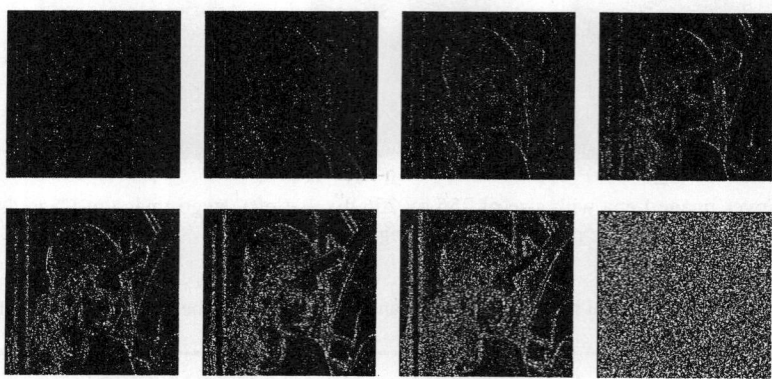

Fig. 3. The bit-planes from the result of the difference between the bit-plane of cover image and the bit-plane of stego image in the proposed method: from MSB plane (top-left) to LSB plane (bottom-right).

Figure 2 and Figure 3 are the bit-planes of difference respectively between the bit-planes of cover image and the bit-planes of stego images by the Chang method and the proposed method. In Figure 3, we can see that the proposed scheme embedded secret message into pixels containing the exact edge area. That is, our scheme embeds more amount of bit in the edge areas than the smooth areas.

4 Conclusions

In this paper, we proposed a method for image steganography using the difference value between neighboring pixels. In the proposed scheme, the number of insertion bit is dependent on each pixel according to whether the pixel is an edge area or smooth area. As we can see from Figure 3, that is, our method has judged the edge area and smooth area more accurately for each pixel and choose the number of the bits to be embedded. Also, the time of processing is short because our technique in embedding and the extracting algorithm is simple.

Especially, our scheme can improve the quality of stego images by using the modular operation and also the capacity of bit rate to be embedded. We have shown that our system is more effective than other methods by the experiments with the capacity and the imperceptibility.

Acknowledgements

This work was supported by grant No. (R01-2002-000-00589-0) from the Basic Research Program of the Korea Science & Engineering Foundation.

References

1. F. Johnson, Z. Duric and S. Jajodia, Information Hiding, Kluwer Academic Publishers, London, 2001.
2. W.N. Lie and L.C. Chang, "Data Hiding in Image with Adaptive Numbers of Least Significant Bit Based on the Human Visual System", International Conference on Image Processing, IEEE, Vol. 1, pp. 286-290, 1999.
3. R.Z. Wang and C.F. Lin, "Image Hiding by Optimal LSB Substitution and Genetic Algorithm", Pattern Recognition, ELSEVIER, Vol. 34, pp. 671-883, 2001.
4. C.C. Thien and J.C. Lin, "A Simple and High-Hiding Capacity Method for Hiding Digit-by-Digit Data in Images Based on Modulus Function", The Journal of The Pattern Recognition Society, PERGAMON, Vol. 36, pp. 2875-2881, June 2003.
5. D.C. Wu and W.H. Tsai, "A Steganographic Method for Images by Pixel-value Differencing", Pattern Recognition Letters, ELSEVIER, Vol. 24, pp. 1613-1626, 2003.
6. C.C. Chang and H.W. Tseng, "A Steganographic Method for Digital Images Using Side Match", Pattern Recognition Letters, ELSEVIER, Vol. 25, pp. 1431-1437, June 2004.
7. C.K. Chan and L.M. Cheng, "Hiding Data in Images by Simple LSB Substitution", The Journal of The Pattern Recognition Society, PERGAMON, Vol. 37, pp.469-474, 2004.

Noun-Verb Based Technique of Text Watermarking Using Recursive Decent Semantic Net Parsers*

Xingming Sun[1] and Alex Jessey Asiimwe[2]

[1] Zhuzhou Institute of Technology, Hunan University, Changsha, China
sunnudt@163.com
[2] Institute of Computer Science, Makerere University, 7062, Kampala, Uganda
asiimwealex@hotmail.com

Abstract. The proposed method of text watermarking by exploits nouns and verbs in a sentence parsed with a grammar parser while using semantic networks. Change is done on the structure of the sentence to generate nouns and verbs whose non terminals, away from the root sentence are used with random numbers to hide the watermark. The modifications, range from active to passive voices or use of linking verbs or using mid-sentence modifiers, terminal modifiers to combining modifiers.

Keywords: watermarking, semantic networks, nouns and verbs.

1 Introduction

Watermarking natural language has proven to be a difficult task because, understanding and processing of natural language itself is even more difficult to the Artificial Intelligence Community. Because of the complexity of natural language, this has motivated much of the research in natural language watermarking. Typically, the prior art natural language processing systems function in a manner analogous to the diagramming of sentences to determine the functions of the various words in the context in which they are used (noun, verb, etc.).

Other techniques proposed for watermarking multimedia documents include, use of frequency domain [4], inserting spelling, syntactic, punctuation or even content errors [2]. There is also a semantically based scheme, which hides data in the text-meaning representation (TMR) [1].

The remainder of this paper is organized as follows. Section 2, briefly reviews semantic networks. Section 3 discusses parsing using recursive decent parsers. Section 4 presents the embedding methodology and watermark extraction processes. Finally, Section 5 presents the conclusions.

---

* This paper is supported by National Natural Science Fundation of China (NSFC No.60373062), Hunan Provincial Natural Science Fundation of China (HPNSFC No. 02JJYB012), Key Foundation of Science and Technology of Ministry of Education of China (No. 03092).

2 Semantic Networks

A semantic network is a system for capturing, storing and transferring information that works much the same way as the human brain. Semantic networks can grow to extraordinary complexity, necessitating a sophisticated approach to knowledge visualization, balancing the need for simplicity with the full expressive power of the network[5]. Semantic networks are basically composed of, concepts(any ideas or thoughts that have meaning), relation(specific kinds of links or relationships between two concepts) and instances(concepts linked by a specific relation). Let n(t) be the number of nodes at time t. Starting with a

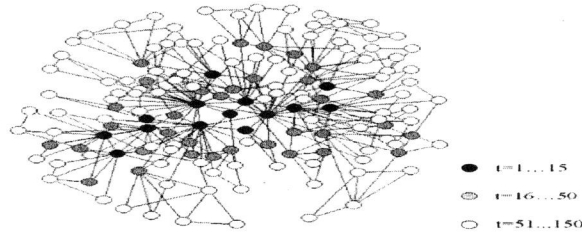

Fig. 1. Undirected growing network

small fully connected network of M nodes (M << n), at each time step, a new node with M links is added to the network that targets its connections to some neighborhood i(in accordance with the locality principle). Let the neighborhood of a node i be the set of neighbors H_i of node i including the node i itself. The probability $P_i(t)$, of choosing a neighborhood is based on neighborhood size and is given by:

$$p_i(t) = \frac{k_i(t)}{\sum_{i=1}^{n(t)} k_i(t)} \qquad (1)$$

where $k_i(t)$ is the degree of node i at time t. The connections of the new node are targeted towards nodes within the chosen neighborhood H_i. The probability $P_{ij}(t)$, of connecting to a node j in the neighborhood of node i is based on:

$$p_{ij}(t) = \frac{U_j}{\sum_{i \in H_i} U_j} \qquad (2)$$

If all utilities are equal, then it follows that:

$$p_{ij}(t) = \frac{1}{k_i(t)} \qquad (3)$$

A sentence is represented as a verb node, with various case links to node representing other participants in the action. In parsing a sentence, the program finds the verb and retrieves the case frames for that verb from its knowledge base and it binds the values of the agents, objects, etc. to the appropriate nodes in the case frame.

3 Recursive Decent Parsers

Consider the subset of English rules below [3];
{Sentence} →{Nounphrase}{Verbphrase}
{NounPhrase} →{NounPhrase}|{NounPhrase}{Prep_Phrase}
{VerbPhrase} →{VerbPhrase}|{VerbPhrase}{Prep_Phrase}
{Prep_Phrase} → {Prep} {NounPhrase}
{NounPhrase} →{Article}{Noun}
{VerbPhrase} →{Verb}|{Verb}{NounPhrase}
Parsing the above sentence "Sarah fixed the chair with glue"

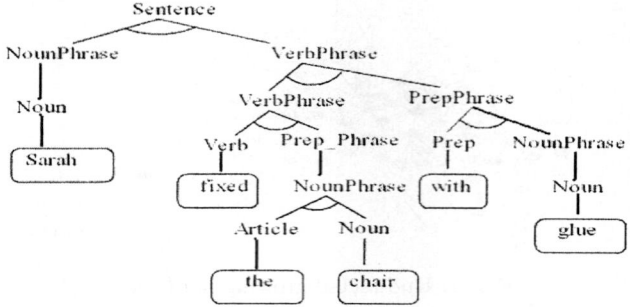

Fig. 2. The and/or parse tree for "Sarah fixed the chair with glue"

4 Watermark Embedding and Extraction

Encoding a single bit

Let the text to be watermarked consist of n sentences $S_1, S_2,.., S_n$. Let the watermark W consist of k bits $w_1, w_2,...,w_k$. xi denotes the number of nodes between the each terminal and the root in a sentence. $H(x_1x_2x_3..)$ - is the hashed value after concatenating the labels. M(S) denotes the marked sentences. Let Rn be the pseudo-random numbers, $Rn_1, Rn_2,..., Rn_k$.

```
generate n random numbers seeded with a secret key P
from 1 to n repeat the folllowing
parse sentence;
for each parsed sentence
   for each terminal
      start with leftmost terminal,count(non terminals
      between the terminal and the start variable);
      create a list L1 of labels;
      hash the concatenation the labels;
      if (H(x1x2x3.)+ Rn_i) mod k equals 0
         mark the sentence;
   end for;
```

```
      for each sentence next to M(S_i)
        start with rightmost terminal
        for each noun or verb terminal
        Count(non terminals from the root);
        Create a list L of labels;
        Concatenate(labels) to form a numeric figure NV(T);
        if(Rn_i + NV(T)) mod k is a quadratic residue
            return bit (rb)is equal to 1;
        else
            return bit (rb) is equal to 0;
        if (rbj==wj)
            proceed;
        else (modify);
        end for;
    end for;
end.
```

Watermark Extraction

The extraction process goes through the same steps like in watermark embedding, but only reads the returned bits. The detection algorithm is blind. It simply extracts W bits of information from the text, without requiring access to the original text or watermark to arrive at its decision. The watermark is a concatenation of the piecemeal bits from each selected sentence.

5 Conclusion

The consequences of neural network computing for natural language processing may be more convulsively revolutionary than anything imagined in the current technology. Therefore, the growth of intelligent systems in digital watermarking is not far from now, more specifically with natural language watermarking.
About author: Alex Jessey Asiimwe is going for a project in Hunan University.

References

1. Atallah, M. J., V. Raskin, M. Crogan, C. F. Hempelmann, F. Kerschbaum, D. Mohamed, and S. Naik,"Natural Language Watermarking: Design, Analysis, and a Proof-of-Concept Implementation". April 2001.
2. Benjamin B., S. Gomez and V. Bogarin. "Steganographic Watermarking for Documents", 34th Annual Hawaii International Conference on System Sciences (HICSS-34)-Volume 9, January, 2001.
3. George F Luger, "Structures and Strategies for Complex Problem Solving" Artificial Intelligence, Fourth Edition, 2002.
4. Huijuan Yang and Alex, C. Kot, "Text Document Authentication by Integrating Inter Character and Word Spaces Watermarking". IEEE International Conference on Multimedia and Expo. June 2004.
5. Sowa, John F., ed."Principles of Semantic Networks: Explorations in the Representation of Knowledge", Morgan Kaufmann Publishers, CA, 1991.

A Novel Watermarking Scheme Based on Independent Component Analysis

Haifeng Li, Shuxun Wang, Weiwei Song, and Quan Wen

Institute of Communication Engineering, Jilin University, Changchun 130025, China
lhfvip_2000@163.com

Abstract. A new blind watermarking algorithm is proposed in this paper. Our watermark embedding algorithm mainly exploits the important properties of Singular Value Decomposition (SVD). By means of Independent Component Analysis (ICA), the watermark is successfully extracted without the original image. Experiment results have shown that the proposed approach is robust against the common signal processing and geometric attacks.

1 Introduction

Digital watermarking provides a promising way of resolving copyright protection and information security problems by embedding a robust additional signal (watermark) into the digital multimedia. Most of recent work in watermarking can be grouped into two categories: spatial domain methods and frequency domain methods [1]. Furthermore, to achieve efficient trade-off between robustness and invisibility, some author proposed adjusting the strength according to the properties of the human vision system (HVS). The current means for the watermark detection is mainly applying some kinds of correlating detector to verify the presence of the watermark.

In this paper the proposed technique employs the properties of the Singular Value Decomposition (SVD) of a digital image. Independent Component Analysis (ICA), is introduced for watermark blind extraction. Simulation results show that ICA can perform watermark extraction perfectly without the original image.

2 Stability of ICA

Independent Component Analysis (ICA) is introduced to handle the Blind Source Separation (BSS) problems, given only the mixtures of unknown sources[2].

The linear ICA mixing model is written as

$$X = AS \tag{1}$$

where $S = [s_1, s_2, \cdots, s_n]^T$ are mutually independent source signals, $A = (a_{i,j}), i = 1,2,\cdots,m; j = 1,2,\cdots,n$ is the unknown mixing matrix, $X = [x_1, x_2, \cdots, x_m]^T$ is the observations.

For demixing process, we can obtain the independent component by:

$$Y = PX \qquad (2)$$

where the matrix P is the inverse of A., the vector $Y = [y_1, y_2, \cdots, y_m]^T$ is an estimate of the possibly scaled and permutated source vector S.

This paper applies the fast fixed-point ICA (FastICA) [3] originally proposed by A. Hyvärinen and E. Oja for the watermark extraction.

3 Watermarking Scheme

3.1 Watermark Embedded Algorithm

In brief, our watermark embedding algorithm mainly exploits the important properties of SVD. The original image is an $N \times N$ matrix I, $I \in C^{N \times N}$. A black-white image is used as a watermark. The key is also an image, reshaped from a pseudorandom sequence.

1. Perform singular value decomposition of the original image I.

$$I = USV^H \qquad (3)$$

2. Add a watermark W into the original image I, and perform singular value decomposition on the matrix $I + \alpha \cdot W$

$$I + \alpha \cdot W = U_W S_W V_W^H \qquad (4)$$

where α is a positive constant, which controls the strength of the watermark to be inserted.

3. Obtain the watermarked image I_W by multiplying U, S_W and V^H

$$I_W = U S_W V^H \qquad (5)$$

4. Create the key image K. By selecting a proper seed, a pseudorandom sequence of the length $L = N \times N$ is generated. Re-arranging the sequence into the matrix of size $N \times N$, the key image K is obtained

5. Obtain a copy of the original image I_K, which is used to identify the ownership of any copy of a watermarked image.

$$I_K = I + \beta \cdot K \qquad (6)$$

where β is also a positive constant controlling the strength of the embedded key image.

3.2 Watermark Extraction Scheme

ICA process is the core of the scheme accomplished by the FastICA [3] algorithm. The following step is used to extract the embedded watermark.

1. Compute the SVD of the watermarked image I_W' which may have suffered non-malicious or malicious attacks.

$$I' = U' S_W' V'^H \tag{7}$$

2. The first mixture signal D_1 is obtained by

$$D_1 = U_W S_W' V_W \tag{8}$$

3. The second mixture signal D_2 is equal to the copy of the original image I_K.

$$D_2 = I_K \tag{9}$$

4. Using the key image K and with the help of D_1 or D_2, the last mixture D_3 is generated by

$$D_3 = D_2 + \gamma_1 \cdot K + \gamma_2 \cdot D_1 \tag{10}$$

where γ_1, γ_2 are arbitrary real number. For simplicity, γ_2 is set to zero.

5. Re-arrange the above three mixtures into three row vectors $D_1(k), D_2(k), D_3(k)$. Input them to FastICA [3] algorithm and the watermark embedded in the original image can be extracted successfully.

4 Experimental Results and Discussions

A series of experiments have been carried out to demonstrate the effectiveness of the proposed watermarking scheme. .

The $PSNR$ of the watermarked image is 41.59 dB. From this $PSNR$, it can be seen that the objective quality of the watermarked image is quite good.

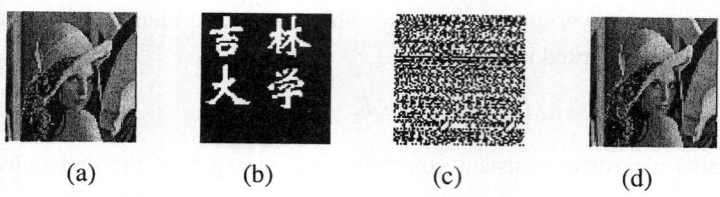

(a)　　　　　(b)　　　　　(c)　　　　　(d)

Fig. 1. (a) The original image (b)The watermark (c) The key image (d) The watermarked image

Fig. 2(a) shows the comparison results against JPEG compression. As is seen clearly, the proposed algorithm performs better than Dan Yu's method [4] in terms of robustness against JPEG compression.

Scaling is a common attack for the watermarked image. In Fig. 2(b) the performance of our algorithm compared to Dan Yu [4] shows that the proposed method is more robustness against scaling attacks.

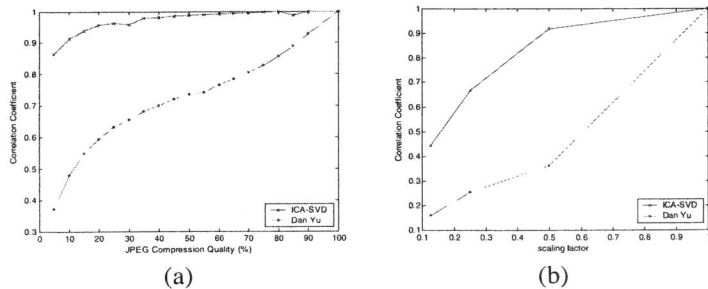

Fig. 2. (a) Results against JPEG compression (b) Results against scaling attacks

5 Conclusions

In this paper, a novel watermarking scheme based on ICA is proposed. A readable logo, is inserted to the original image. We applied ICA derived from BSS for blind extraction. The simulation results are encouraging in that the proposed algorithm can survive under most kinds of attacks.

References

1. F. Hartung, and Martin Kutter.: Multimedia watermarking techniques. Proceedings of the IEEE, Vol. 87, No. 7, (1999) 1079-1106
2. A. Hyvärinen, and E. Oja.: Independent component analysis: algorithm and applications. Neural Networks, Vol. 13, No. 4, (2000) 411-430
3. A. Hyvärinen, and E. Oja.: A fast fixed-point algorithm for independent component analysis. Neural Computation, Vol. 6, (1997) 1484-1492
4. Dan. Yu, F. Sattar, and K. K. Ma.: Watermark detection and extraction using independent component analysis methods. EURASIP journal on Applied Signal Processing, Vol.1, (2002) 92-104

On Sequence Synchronization Analysis Against Chaos Based Spread Spectrum Image Steganography

Guangjie Liu, Jinwei Wang, Yuewei Dai, and Zhiquan Wang

Department of Automation, Nanjing University of Science and
Technology, Nanjing, 210094, Jiangsu, P.R. China
guangj_liu@yahoo.com.cn

Abstract. In this paper, we propose the steganalysis based on sequence synchronization analysis against chaos based spread spectrum image steganography (CSSIS). This method uses the correlation between the estimated chaotic sequences in two stegoimages to buildup synchronization measure, which can effectively detect the presence of CSSIS. Based on the analysis, a more secure method is presented, which is constructed on key transmission channel (KTC). This improved method uses the stochastic modulation to realize the steganography. It avoids the sequences synchronization fault in CSSIS by randomly choosing the parameters of chaotic map, which is proved by the experimental results.

1 Introduction

Steganography is the art of hiding messages into host signals, which should not only satisfy the demand of imperceptibility and large payload but also keep the characteristics of cover objects unchanged, because any unnatural traces may arouse the steganalyzer's suspicion.

Lots of methods have been reported to realize data hiding in still image, such as the classical LSB [1], the spread-spectrum based methods [2,3],and the QIM based steganographic methods[5]. Hartung [5] first presented the idea to use the spread spectrum method to modulate message bits and add them into host signals. Marvel [2] used image restoration technique and error-control coding method to propose a spread spectrum based image steganography (SSIS). In [3] Satish gave a chaos based SSIS scheme which uses the chaotic map to generate noise sequence and encrypt the message bits.

2 Chaotic Sequence Synchronization Analysis

In a practical system, the keys used in CSSIS can not be changed frequently because the transmission of keys need more secure channel which mean more expensive than the transmission of the data. If two stegoimages can be acquired, the estimate of the embedded chaotic sequences can be obtained. Different from the natural noisy image introduced by image devices, the sequences in two stegoimages using the same keys may exhibit synchronization.

Different from the median-filter based image restoration technique used in [4], the two-dimensional Wiener filter is used to get the estimated cover image $\tilde{s}$. And then the estimated chaotic sequence can be obtained by $n = \tilde{s} - s$. If the message bit embedded in position i is "1", the practical chaotic signal should be n_i, else the practical chaotic signal is $-n_i$, so the estimate of chaotic sequence should be $|n|/\alpha$, where α is the scaling factor used in CSSIS.

Assuming the attacker can access two stegoimages s^1, s^2 with the same size, it is possible that the scaling factor used in the two stegoimage is different. Let the scaling factors are α_1, α_2 respectively. The estimate of the chaotic sequences should be $|n^1|/\alpha_1$ and $|n^1|/\alpha_1$ respectively. We define the correlation function as equation (1) to measure the synchronization degree

$$C(|n^1|,|n^2|) = \frac{\sum_i\sum_j (|n^1_{ij}|-mean(|n^1|))(|n^2_{ij}|-mean(|n^2|))}{\sqrt{\sum_i\sum_j (|n^1_{ij}|-mean(|n^1|))^2 \times \sum_i\sum_j (|n^2_{ij}|-mean(|n^2|))^2}} \quad (1)$$

It can be easily proved that $C(|n^1|-|n^2|)$ is equal to $C(|n^1|/\alpha_1|-|n^2|/\alpha_2|)$, so the scaling factor is unnecessary to be known to measure the correlation. Considering two stegoimages embedded with the same stegokeys, the estimate of the chaotic sequences should be synchronizing; hence the correlation must have bigger value. But this value is less than the theoretical value "1" because of the quantization process and the inaccurate restoration. Before steganalysis, the correlation between the images with the stochastic noises added can be estimated by a simple and slight permutation as equation (2).

$$P(n) = n', n'_i = n_{i-(-1)^i}, i = 1,...,L \quad (2)$$

where n'_i is the permuted value of n_i. To two synchronizing sequences, the permutation may cause the rapid decease of the correlation value. From experiments, the value $d = C(|n^1|, P(|n^2|)) - C(|n^1|, P(|n^2|))$ is found to obey the Gaussian distribution with mean being -1.0×10^{-5} and variance being 2.05×10^{-5}. So the value SYN can be defined as following equation to measure the synchronization degree between two estimated sequences.

$$SYN = syn(n^1, n^2) = \frac{C(|n^1|,|n^2|) - C(|n^1|, P(|n^2|))}{\sqrt{\text{maxvar}}} \quad (3)$$

where maxvar is set to be 3×10^{-5}. According to the analysis above, SYN should obey normal distribution. Let the threshold for the detection is ε, for two natural noisy images, the probability of $SYN > \varepsilon$ is equal to $1 - \Phi(\varepsilon)$, where the function Φ is the normal cumulative distribution function.

Based on 1000 pairs of gray images with size equal to 256×256, the chaotic sequence synchronization analysis method is tested. First, a series of stegoimages is created by CSSIS with scaling factor varying from 5 to 8 randomly, and then the SYN is calculated from two arbitrary stegoimages. The result is shown in Fig.1 (a). The mean value of SYN is 16.47.

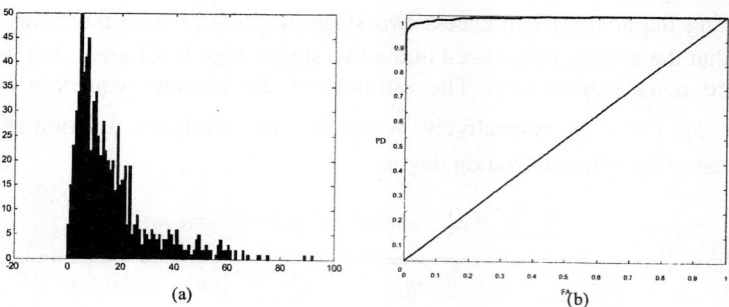

Fig. 1. (a) Distribution of SYN of 1000 pairs of stegoimages after CSSIS. (b) ROC for the synchronization analysis of CSSIS.

The ROC is shown in Fig.1 (b), with the average stegosignals power about 33(db), when the threshold ε is chosen equal to 5, the probability of false alarm is equal to 2.8×10^{-7} and the corresponding probability of detection is equal to 0.81. From the ROC, we can see CSSIS can be effective detected by the method based on chaotic sequence synchronization analysis proposed here.

Through randomly choosing setgokeys at each steganographic communication, the uniqueness of estimated sequence can be avoided. We divide the steganographical channel into the data transmission channel (DTC) based on CSSIS and the random key transmission channel (KTC) based on the stochastic modulation approach [10]. The former is used to transmit the message data, and the latter is used to transmit randomly chosen stegokeys. The experimental results are shown is Fig 2

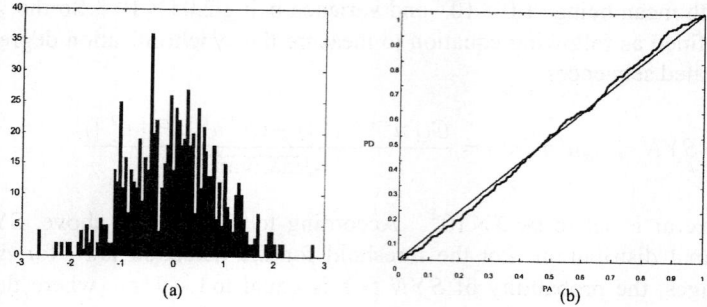

Fig. 2. (a) Distribution of SYN of 1000 pairs of stegoimages after CSSIS with KTC. (b) ROCfor the synchronization analysis of CSSIS with KTC.

From the results shown in the Fig. 2, the estimated sequences of two stegoimages are not correlative mutually, which resists the attack based on sequence synchronization analysis. In the current scheme, we use the parameter of logistic map as the input of KTC, but the interleaving key or the combination of these two keys can also be a proper choice.

3 Conclusions

In this paper, we give the steganalytic method to attack CSSIS, which is based on the chaotic sequence synchronization analysis. The method uses the common characters in two stegoimages as the start of analysis. Some extra experiments have proven that this method is also valid to analyze SSIS and stochastic modulation when the fixed stegokeys are used. To improve the security of CSSIS, we also present a KTC-based transmission scheme. It is obvious that the scheme can also be used to enhance the security of SSIS and stochastic modulation.

The steganalysis based on two stego-objects is different from the existing steganalytical methods which are all based on one stego-object. These can be called memoryless attack. The attack based on more than one stego-object like the presented method can be called memory attack. It needs further study, for example, that how to use the memory attack to analysis other steganographic methods, and how to ensure the security under memory attack.

Acknowledgement

This work was supported by the National Natural Science Foundation of China through the grant number 60374066, the Province Natural Science Foundation of China through the grant number BK2001054 and PhD Training Foundation of the Education Ministry of China through the grant number 20020288052.

References

1. Bender, W., Gruhl, D., Morimoto, N.: Techniques for data hiding. IBM System Journal, Vol. 35, no. 3/4, (1996) 131-336
2. Marvel,L.M., Boncelet, C.G., Retter C.T: Spread spectrum image steganography. IEEE Transactions on Image Processing, vol.8, No.8, Aug.(1999) 1075 -1083,.
3. Satish, K., Jayakar, T., Tobin, C., Madhavi, K., Murali, K.: Chaos Based Spread Spectrum Image Steganography, IEEE Transactions on Consumer Electronics, vol. 50, no.2, Mar. (2004) 578-590.
4. Chen, B., Wornell G.W.: Quantization index modulation: A Class.of provably Good Methods for Digital Watermarking and information Embedding, IEEE Transaction on Information Theory, vol. 47, no. 4, May (2001) 1423-1443
5. Hartung, F., Girod,B.: Watermarking of Uncompressed and Compressed Video, Signal Processing, vol. 66, no. 3 (Special issue on Watermarking), May (1998) 283-301,
6. Fridrich, J., Goljan M.: Digital Image Steganography Using Stochastic Modulation, In Proc. EI SPIE, Santa Clara, Jan. (2003) 191-202

Microstructure Evolution of the K4169 Superalloy Blade Based on Cellular Automaton Simulation

Xin Yan, Zhilong Zhao, Weidong Yan, and Lin Liu

Xin Yan, Ms., Northwestern Polytechnical University, Xi'an,
710072, P. R. China
goldnwpu@163.com
Zhilong Zhao, Prof., Northwestern Polytechnical University, Xi'an,
710072, P. R. China
zhaolong@nwpu.edu.cn

Abstract. A two-dimensional cellular automaton model has been developed to simulate the process of microstructure evolution of K4169 superalloy blade produced by investment casting. The dynamic process of grain-structure formation of the blade castings without chemical refiner or with refiner during solidification can be observed real-time on the computer. A CA model coupling micro-kinetics with macro-thermal transfer is adopted to calculate the feature of grain microstructure. The results show that the simulated grain structure is in good agreement with optical micrographs.

1 Introduction

The microstructure simulation of casting is an important technology to determine the reasonable proceeding parameters and control forming quality of castings. Cellular Automaton is one kind of probabilistic method [1]. Based on the physics mechanism of the nucleation and the grain growth kinetics theories, CA method has the actual physical meanings. Using CA method to simulate the microstructure evolution has already been one of the important research topics of material science, especially more challenge in complex alloys [2]. In this paper, we will discuss the CA mathematic models and simulate the microstructure evolution of K4169 superalloy blade during solidification.

2 Mathematical Models

2.1 Nucleation Model

The continuous nucleation model based on the Gaussian distribution is adopted. At undercooling ΔT, the nucleation density $n(\Delta T)$ is expressed as:

$$n(\Delta T) = \int_0^{\Delta T} \frac{dn}{d(\Delta T')} d(\Delta T') = \int_0^{\Delta T} \frac{n_{max}}{\sqrt{2\pi}\Delta T_\sigma} \exp\left[-\frac{(\Delta T' - \Delta T_N)^2}{2\Delta T_\sigma^2}\right] d(\Delta T') \quad (1)$$

where n_{max} is the maximum grain density; ΔT_N is the average nucleation undercooling, ΔT_σ is the standard deviation of continuous nucleation distribution.

2.2 Grain Growth Model

To simplify the calculation, the K4169 alloy system is divided into seven binary systems and the equivalent method is developed to get the liquidus slope m. Then the modified KGT [3] model is:

$$\begin{cases} \Delta T = \Delta T_C + \Delta T_R + \Delta T_T \\ \Omega = I_V(P_C) \\ R = 2\pi \left(\dfrac{\Gamma}{mG_C\xi - G} \right)^{1/2} \\ V = 2DP_C / R \end{cases} \quad (2)$$

where $\Delta T_C, \Delta T_R$ and ΔT_T are respectively the undercooling of the constitution, the curvature and the heat, Ω is the supersaturation degree of solute, P_C is the Peclet number of solute concentration, I_V is the Ivantson function, Γ is the Gibbs-Thompson coefficient, G_C is the solute concentration gradient, G is the temperature gradient, ξ is a function of P_C, D is the solute coefficient of diffusion in the liquid, R is the radius of dendrite tip, V is the growth velocity of dendrite.

2.3 The Calculation of Thermal Flow and Solidifying Latent Heat

During the solidification of the superalloy blade, the thermal flow Q_{ext} erived from the surface of blade to the mold is:

$$Q_{ext} = h \cdot \Delta T = h \cdot (T - T_m) \quad (3)$$

where h is the interfacial thermal conductive coefficient between the blade and the mold sell, T is the temperature diversity between the blade and the mold on the interface, T_m is the temperature of the mold sell. The enthalpy method is adopted to solve the latent heat, and the temperature diversity δT at a time-step Δt can be get:

$$\delta T = \frac{\Delta H + L \cdot \Delta f_s}{c_p} \quad (4)$$

where Δf_s is the variation of the fraction solid with a time-step Δt.

The grain density and the grain size at any solidification time can be gained by coupling the simulation of the grain organization and the temperature field.

3 The CA Model and Results of Simulation

To create the CA model, the section of blade is divided into a square lattice of regular cell. Von-Neumann neighborhood [4] is adopted and the neighborhood of each cell is given by its four neighbors along the north, south, east, and west directions. Thus, every cell has four ones which are called the first-nearest neighbors, and then outwards are the second-nearest neighbors, the third-nearest neighbors and so on.

The cellular state (solid or liquid) is defined by an index. The index of liquid cell is zero; of solid cell is a positive integer standing for the crystal directions which is selected randomly and given to the cell solidifying. The cells with different state index are indicated by different colors. At the beginning, each cell is attributed an initial temperature, which is uniform and above the liquidus of the alloy, and their index are zero. Subsequently the temperature descends, the nucleation and growth of crystal happened when the temperature becomes lower than the liquidus. The grain density of new nucleation is expressed as:

$$\delta n = n[\Delta T + \delta(\Delta T)] - n(\Delta T) \tag{5}$$

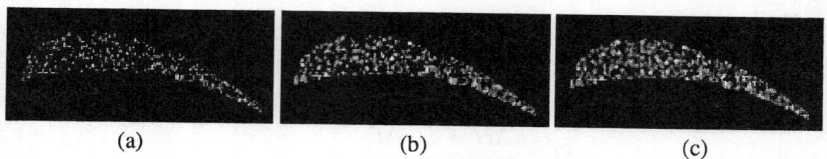

Fig. 1. Section micrographs simulated for the K4169 blade added chemical refiner at various solidifying time: (a) t=7.3s (b) t=7.55s (c) t=8.5s

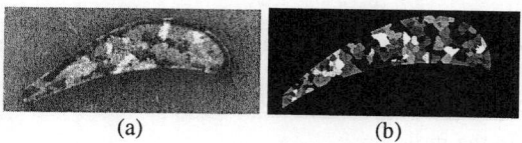

Fig. 2. The section of blade without chemical refiner: (a) Optical micrograph and (b) simulated grain structure

Fig. 3. Section micrographs simulated for the K4169 blade added chemical refiner at various solidifying time: (a) t=7.3s (b) t=7.55s (c) t=8.5s

Each newly formed nucleus grows like a small square with the growth kinetics. It will trap the neighbors if they are still liquid. These neighboring cells captured are given the same state index and filled with the same color as the parent cell. When the original nucleus is completely surrounded by solid neighbors, its growth is finished.

For the K4169 superalloy blade without chemical refiner and with chemical refiner, the process of the grain nucleation and growth are respectively shown in fig. 1 and fig. 3 and the section micrographs of simulated and optical grain structure of casting blades are respectively shown in fig. 2 and fig. 4.

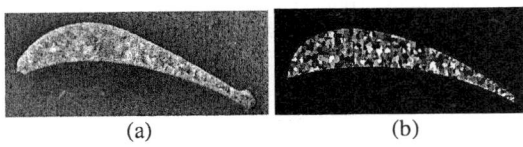

Fig. 4. The section of blade added chemical refiner: (a) Optical micrograph and (b) simulated grain structure

4 Conclusion

The process of microstructure evolution for K4169 superalloy blades produced by investment casting has been simulated with a cellular automaton model coupling micro-kinetics with macro-thermal transfer. The CA model bases on a sound physical background and it brings a valuable insight into the mechanisms of grain structure formation. The dynamic process of microstructure formation for the blade during solidification can be observed real-time on the computer and the microstructure at any time can be given. The simulated results show that the finally simulated grain structure for K4169 superalloy blade without chemical refiner or with chemical refiner is in good agreement with optical micrographs. An extension of CA model will be of great value in predicting and analyzing the grain structure qualitatively.

References

1. Rappaz M. and Gandin A. C., A 3D Cellular Automaton Algorithm for the Prediction of Dendritic Grain Growth, Acta Mater. (1997) 45, 2187-2195
2. Rappaz, M., Gandin, A.C., Probabilistic Modelling of Microstructure Formation in Solidification Process . Acta metall mater.(1993) 41(2) , 345-360
3. Rappaz, M., Thevoz, P., Solute Diffusion Model for Equiaxed Dendnlic Growth, Analylical Solution. Acta Metall.(1987) 35(12), 2929-2935
4. Numann ,J.V., Theroy of Self-reproducing Automata. Edited and completed by Burks A W, Univ of Illinois Press, Champaign, II .(1966)

Mobile Robot Navigation Based on Multisensory Fusion

Weimin Ge[1,2] and Zuoliang Cao[2]

[1] International Institute for Software Technology, United Nations University, Macao SAR
weimin@iist.unu.edu
[2] School of Mechanical Engineering, Tianjin University of Technology, Tianjin, China
zlcao@126.com

Abstract. Multisensory fusion is being increasing viewed as an important activity in the filed of mobile robot navigation and obstacle avoidance. The fusion of data from a variety of sensors makes the mobile robot more easily survival in a hostile environment. It takes advantage of the redundancy and reciprocity of multisensory data and increases the precision and reliability of inference and judgment for the mobile robot. This paper presents a method which employs fuzzy logic and neural networks to fuse data from several kinds of sensors. As a result, more exact navigation and quick obstacle avoidance can be achieved.

1 Introduction

With the development of modern industry, the mobile robot has found many applications in different areas. The mobile robot navigates in the environments based upon its different sensors perceiving its surroundings. In order to obtain more information, different kinds of sensors are employed to work as sensory organs, and fusion of these sensors is the key point for the mobile robot to achieve successful navigation. The TUT-1 mobile robot was developed to meet the research for multisensory fusion[1]. It consists of a multisensory module for sensing the environment. The multisensory module consists of three kinds of sensors, a CCD camera, a magnetic sensor and six ultrasonic sensors. The CCD camera is fixed on the front top of the mobile robot, capable of locating a specified magnetic strip. In the laboratory hallway, the mobile robot runs over the magnetic strip that is paved on the floor and depends on the equipped magnetic sensor to direct the vehicle to follow the strip collaborating with the CCD camera. The magnetic sensor is fixed underneath the front bottom of the mobile robot. On the front and both sides of the mobile robot, six ultrasonic sensors are installed to detect the distance from any obstacles and the hallway walls.

2 Multisensory Fusion Method

Fig. 1 shows how the multisensory data is fused[2]. After initialization, the CCD camera searches the magnetic strip, analyses the magnetic strip and decides the next three actions depending on the Nearest Neighbor method. If the action is to keep moving forward, then the magnetic sensor starts to track the magnetic strip and fuzzy controller is invoked. The function of fuzzy controller is to maintain the tracking precision, in addition it is necessary to keep the mobile robot precisely following the magnetic strip; if the action is to let the mobile robot turn left or right, then the ultrasonic sensors start to detect the environments based upon the Parallel Back Propagation Neural Network and the decisions can be made as follows: turn left a little bit, turn left, turn right a little bit and turn right. And then, CCD camera continues to detect the magnetic strip and a new data fusion cycle starts.

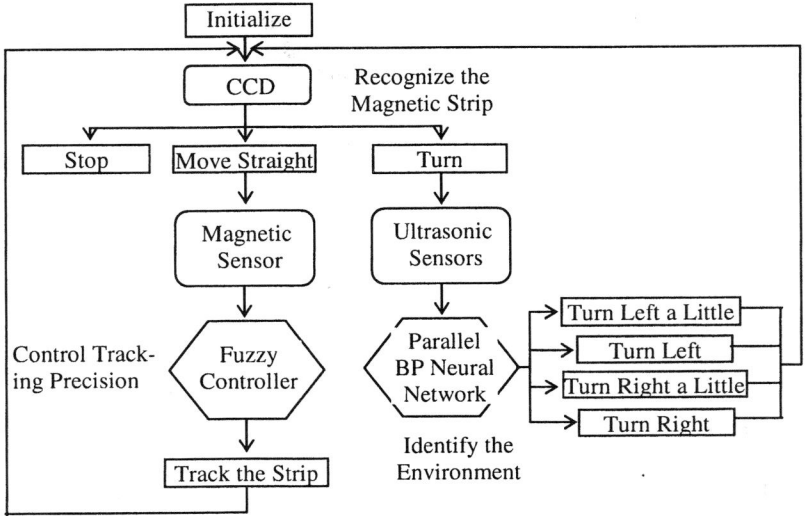

Fig. 1. Multisensory Fusion Flowchart

2.1 The Magnetic Strip Recognition

After searching the magnetic strip, the centerline of the magnetic strip can be founded, as shown in Figure 2. Recognition of each signal is as follows:

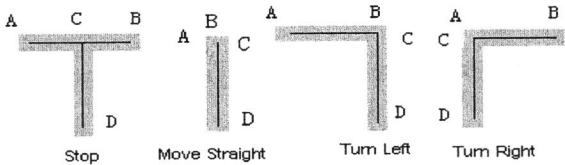

Fig. 2. Magnetic Strip

Suppose the two ends of the level magnetic strip are A and B, and the two ends of the vertical strip are C and D. The distance of three end is set as three elements of a characteristic vector: $x_1=|AC|$, $x_2=|BC|$, $x_3=|CD|$, and the difference of two arms' length of the level strip is set as another element: $x_4=|AC|-|BC|$. Now a four-dimensional vector $X=(x_1, x_2, x_3, x_4)$ has been set up.

At the same time, four standard models can be set up corresponding to four image signals: X0, X1, X2, X3. Let Xi = (xi0, xi1, xi2, xi3) where **i** = 0, 1, 2, 3. Then calculate the difference between the characteristic and all of the standard models, letting **di** = |X-Xi| for **i**=0,1,2,3. When **di** reaches the minimum, **i** is the result of the recognition.

2.2 The Fuzzy Controller Design

While the mobile robot is tracking the magnetic strip it is important to maintain the tracking precision. A 2-D fuzzy controller is developed to guide the mobile robot to track the magnetic strip when it is far enough from an obstacle and lead the mobile robot to navigate around the obstacle when it is too close to the obstacle[3].

When it is far enough from the obstacle, the mobile robot tracks the magnetic strip, and the inputs of the controller are **e** and **ce**. **e** is the input error variable, and **ce** is the derived change in error.

Let $e = \Delta x = (\Delta x_1 + \Delta x_2)/2$ and $ce = \theta$

Δx_1 and Δx_2 are the range errors detected by the magnetic sensor and the CCD camera respectively. θ is the angle between the magnetic strip and the mobile robot.

When it is too close to the obstacle the inputs of the controller are as follows:

$e = \Delta d = d - d_0$ and $ce = \varphi$

d is the distance between the mobile robot and the obstacle detected by the ultrasonic sensors, and φ is the angle between the obstacle and the mobile robot. For these two cases, the output variable of the controller is ΔU, the difference voltage between the left and right wheel motors.

2.2.1 Fazzification

Define a set [-8,8] as the input domain of **e**, and the fuzzy subset of **e** is

e=[LN, MN, SN, NZ, PZ, SP, MP, LP]

where LP: large positive; MP: medium positive; SP: small positive; PZ: positive zero; ZE: zero; NZ: negative zero; SN: small negative; MN: medium negative; LN: large negative.

And define [-6, 6] as the input domain of **ce** and the output domain **u**, and the fuzzy subset of **ce** is

ce=[LN, MN, SN, ZE, SP, MP, LP]

and the fuzzy subset of **u** is

u=[LN, MN, SN, ZE, SP, MP, LP].

2.2.2 Defuzzification

Based upon the Max-Min inference method, the true value of the control value **u** can be defuzzified as follows:

$$u = \frac{\sum_{k=1}^{13} u(\Delta uk) \Delta uk}{\sum_{k=1}^{13} u(\Delta uk)}$$

where $u_{\Delta U}$ (Δu_k) is the grade of membership of Δu_k subjection to the fuzzy subset of the control value ΔU_{ij}.

3 Experimental Work and Coclusion

In order to test the validation of the control methods, several experiments have been carried out and the result has been recorded, as shown in Fig. 3:

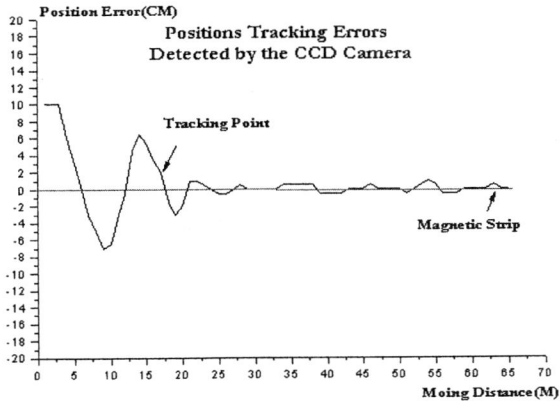

Fig. 3. The CCD Camera Records

The mobile robot is navigating along a hallway and both the CCD camera and the magnetic sensor record the tracking data and convert it into a curve. As shown in Fig.3, the position tracking errors detected by both the CCD camera and the magnetic sensors keep stable and are less than ±2 centimeters after the initializing period. It means this multisensory fusion method can be used to control a mobile robot in a constructed environment or a semi-constructed environment successfully.

References

1. W. Ge, Z. Cao, X. Peng: Web-Based Telerobotics System In Virtual Reality Environment, Proceedings of SPIE, Vol. 5267, SPIE (2003): 99-106
2. J. Hu: Research On The Technology for Multi-Sensor Date Fusion Based On AGV, M.S. Thesis of TUT, Tianjin, China (2002)
3. C. Ding: Mobile Robot's All Following Based On Neural Network and Fuzzy Control, M.S. Thesis of HUT, Tianjin, China (2001)

Self-surviving IT Systems

Hengming Zou[1] and Leilei Bao[2]

[1] Department of Computer Science and School of Software,
Shanghai Jiao Tong University, China
zou-hm@cs.sjtu.edu.cn
[2] Billion Star Business Research, China
mail@blnstar.com

Abstract. Human social and economic life is becoming increasingly dependent on computers and information technologies. Many important systems such as banking, tax filing, traffic control, and even military functions are now controlled by or receive data feed from computers. Hence, the protection of IT systems from natural and man-made disasters has taken on critical importance. This paper presents a framework for building self-surviving IT systems that can defend themselves against and survive natural and man-made disasters such as earthquake, flood, fire, virus, intrusion, or outright war. The work presented here is a partial result of an ongoing research project called *HERMES IT Shield* we are conducting at Shanghai Jiao Tong University, China.

1 Introduction

Human social and economic life is becoming increasingly dependent on computers and information technologies. Many important systems such as banking, tax filing, traffic control, and even military functions are now controlled by computers. Failure or service interruption of relevant IT systems often inflicts severe damages to property, business processes, or even human lives. Unfortunately, IT systems today face increasing threats from natural and man-made disasters such as earthquake, flood, fire, virus, intrusion, or outright war. Countless organizations world-wide have suffered financial, business, and even human life losses due to its IT systems being damaged by disasters.

Many techniques and methods have been proposed in the past two decades to deal with IT failures and disasters. These techniques and methods include but are not limited to virus/spam filtering [7,16], intrusion detection [20,11,2,19,9,14], data backup and recovery [13,3], distributed processes [18,4,6,15], replication [5], clustering [8,23], rollback and restart [10,1,12], redundant power supply, and disaster recovery [22,17]. Depending on the particular threat analysis, each organization may take one or more of the aforementioned measures at any given time to achieve its particular disaster defense objective. After 911, many organizations have endorsed disaster recovery as one of their main defense against unappealing events for their IT infrastructure in general and vital data centers in particular.

While many of the measures taken by organizations to deal with IT disasters are useful, and even very effective against particular types of disasters under particular circumstances, they all suffer the common drawbacks of restricted applicability, localized solutions, limited effectiveness, and constant manual intervention. Most of all, current techniques and solutions lack a coherent underpinning strategy or theory. Each technique or method may be effective to an extent for one type of disaster, but usually are not effective for other types of disasters. For example, a technique that is effective against intrusion may not be effective against fire or terrorist attacks. Hence, to defend an IT system against multiple types of disasters at the same time, one has to integrate multiple techniques and/or methods into one environment. This kind of approach means higher cost, more complex procedures, and less effectiveness. Sometimes, such integration is simply too difficult to perform all together.

With the advance in fields of pervasive computing and communications, mobile computing, distributed and grid computing, utility computing, etc., the erection of a protective shield around those new computing environments will be much more complex and challenging. Current disaster defense techniques will be over-stretched to handle the stress and intensity that are required to prevent or protect complex IT infrastructure from disaster-induced failures. Yet at the same time the capability to defend against and survive disasters is becoming a fundamental requirement for the success of any future viable IT solutions. Hence, it is imperative that we find a holistic, integrated solution to this problem.

This paper presents a framework for building self-surviving IT systems that can defend themselves against and survive multiple types or occurrences of disasters. The work represents a partial result of an ongoing research project called *HERMES IT Shield* we are conducting at Shanghai Jiao Tong University, China. The framework consists of seven sub-components with each performing a distinct yet interrelated function in an IT system's overall disaster-defense ability. Since each of the seven components is itself a comprehensive research subject and needs a full length paper to discuss, we opt not to go deep inside the mechanism of each subsystem. Rather, this paper only gives a description of the capabilities of each of the seven subsystems and shows how these subsystems work together to guarantee smooth operation, rapid recovery, limited loss, and harmless abruption for IT systems, even in the face of disasters.

The layout of the rest of the paper is as follows: next section defines relevant terms followed by the presentation of the self-surviving IT system framework in section 3. Section 4 describes the operation of a self-surviving IT system. Section 5 concludes the paper.

2 Terms and Definitions

Human being's natural intuition is to avoid disasters or escape from the impact of disasters. If disasters are not avoidable, then we try to limit the losses caused by disasters. The utmost goal in human being's disaster defense strategy is to preserve human life or as many human lives as we can.

A self-surviving IT system simulates human being's action when dealing with IT disasters. It first tries to neutralize the impact of the striking disaster (humanoid escapes unscathed). If the action fails, the system then tries to recover from the disaster impact (escapes with wound); if recovery action fails, then it tries to restrict the loss or damage to the part where disaster directly strikes (localizes disaster impact); if the restriction of disaster impact fails, then it brings the system down to a stable state (transforms all disasters into fail silent ones). Hence, we have the following definition:

Definition 1. *A self-surviving IT system is a system that can escape or mitigate the impact of striking disasters, or at the least prevent rolling disasters from occurring and transform all types of disasters into fail silent ones, all without human intervention.*

Specifically, a self-surviving IT system must possess the following four abilities: disaster preemption, disaster recovery, disaster locking, and harmless abruption. **Disaster preemption** is the ability of neutralizing the disaster and shielding users from any disaster impact. If disaster preemption is successful, IT system users will not feel any service interruption. **Disaster recovery** is the ability of recovering an IT system from service interruption caused by disasters. It is activated when disaster preemption fails or if the system decides that recovery is the best course of action in the first place.

Disaster locking blocks the spread of disaster impact and limits damages to the part where disasters directly strike. When activated, it separates the interlocking paths of disasters and prevents rolling disasters from occurring. It is used if either a disaster recovery action fails or the system determines that it is the best course of action. **Harmless abruption** brings an IT system into a reversible dormant state. It is used to foil any adversary attempt to take control of the system and prevent malicious transformation of disasters (i.e., prevent Byzantine failures). It is activated if either a disaster locking action fails or the system determines that it is the best course of action.

Let us introduce the following notations:
S : normal state of an IT system
D : striking disaster(s)
S_{DP} : disaster preemption state of the IT system
S_{DR} : disaster recovery state
S_{DL} : disaster locking state
S_{HA} : harmless abruption state

Then, a system is a self-surviving system if:
$$S + D \rightarrow S \vee S_{DP} \vee S_{DR} \vee S_{DL} \vee S_{HA}$$

Each of the four abilities of a self-surviving IT system we described above is based on one subject of research we have been conducting. The key technology for disaster preemption is software self-regeneration and wide-area fully active system replication. Our software self-regeneration mechanism can re-generate the damaged part of IT system software while the fully active system replication can absorb disaster impact without passing the effect to users. Used either alone or in conjunction, the two abilities enable an IT system to continue operation in the face of disasters.

Disaster recovery in this paper is a little bit different from the same term used by IT corporations today. The objective is the same in that it tries to recover an IT system from service interruption. The difference lies in the techniques used to achieve the objective. The technology underpinning our disaster recovery ability is our self-repairing virtual bus system and self-recursive multi-dimensional IT architecture. Self-repairing virtual bus can repair a file system on the fly and self-recursive multi-dimensional IT architecture can efficiently and automatically reconfigure and reconstitute itself when struck by disasters.

The underlying technology for disaster locking is our disaster stacking theory and fundamental theory of disasters. These two researches study the properties of disasters, the progression of disaster impact, the transformation of disasters, and the interrelations between different disasters or phases of the same disaster. By separating the interlocking path of disaster progression, we can limit disaster impact to the area where it directly hit and prevent rolling disasters from occurring.

Harmless abruption is based on our research in disaster determination and reversible self-collapse theory. Normally it is activated only if other disaster defense measurements have failed. But if a disaster is judged to be severe or if a judgement cannot be made, the system can activate harmless abruption in the first place to bring the system into a reversible dormant state. When disasters have passed or the situation is back under control, the self-surviving IT system can wake up and resume normal operation.

3 The Framework

Our self-surviving IT system framework is developed as a middleware that can be superimposed on a stand alone or network of computers. By installing and running the self-surviving software package on every node in the system, the entire networked system will collectively possess the ability to defend against and survive natural as well as man-made disasters. The number of active nodes in the system directly influences the level of disaster defense capability of the entire system. The more active nodes there are in the system, the more robustness the defense capability it possesses. But a minimum level capability of harmless abruption is guaranteed for any kind of configuration.

Structure wise, the framework is divided into modules with each module plays one distinct but essential role in the system's overall ability to defend against and survive disasters. In addition to the four disaster defense capabilities we discussed in the previous section, our framework also contains three additional modules that play other critical functions that are necessary for the normal operation of our self-surviving IT system framework.

Disaster prediction module is responsible for predicting disaster occurrence and providing early warning for the networked IT system. We have in another work developed a time-space ODE model that models the relationship existing between disasters and IT systems. The ODE model is further based on a priori estimates for a semi-linear elliptic system[21] and provides the capability of disaster prediction. A prototype based on the ODE model has been constructed and preliminary test result has shown that it is indeed able to predict the occurrence of disasters to an extent.

Impact analysis and determination module offers the system the ability of analyzing the consequence of approaching or striking disasters. Depending on the result of such analysis, the system can determine a best course of action in defending against and surviving the striking disaster(s). Specifically, our impact analysis and determination module must determine if a disaster is preemptable, recoverable, or lockable; and make such determination quickly. This work is based on our fundamental theory of disaster and independent state determination in distributed systems.

System metamorphosis module offers the system the ability of seamlessly switching operation states at any time. Depending on the dynamic analysis result of the impact analysis and determination module, system metamorphosis will direct the system to adapt a particular operation mode to deal with the approaching or striking disasters. This work is based on our cell-like state switch scheme and dynamic hybrid active-passive replication paradigm.

Fig.1 depicts the conceptual composition of our self-surviving IT system framework along with the state transition conditions.

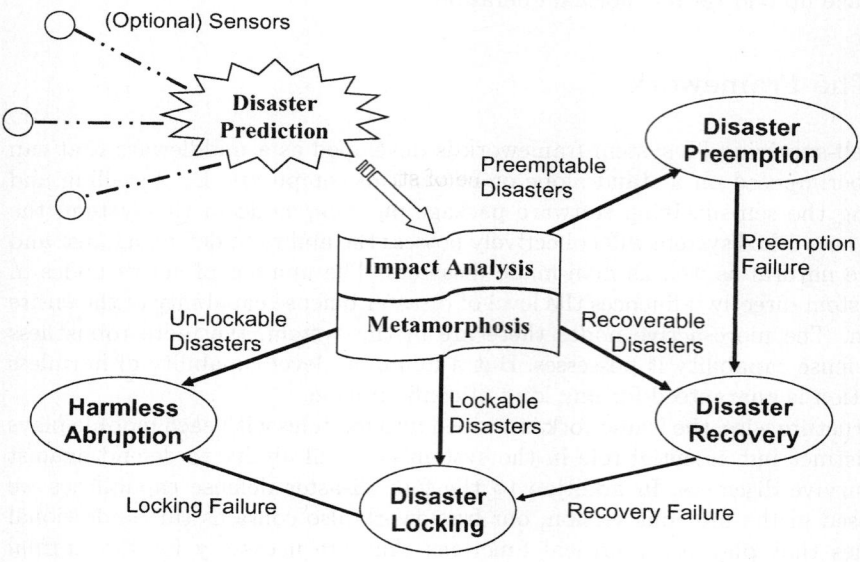

Fig. 1. Self-Surviving IT System Model

4 System Operation

As mentioned earlier, our self-surviving IT system model is a holistic integration of seven distinct yet inter-related subsystems. Each subsystem plays one important role in the functioning of the entire system. At any point of time, our self-surviving system operates in any one of the four possible states: disaster preemption state, disaster recovery state, disaster locking state, and disaster harmless abruption state. Based on the information obtained from the impact analysis and determination module and its own observation of system state changes, the system automatically switches operation states via metamorphosis to position itself for the approaching or striking disasters.

In the model depicted in Fig.1, the disaster prediction and early warning subsystem acts as the first line of defense against disasters and attacks. The function of this subsystem is to analyze the occurrence likelihood of disasters and attacks; and if possible, predict the timing and scale of disasters and attacks. This subsystem could and should utilize any available external sensors that might be deployed for the concerned IT infrastructure.

Impact analysis and determination is the centerpiece of our self-surviving IT system model. It gets input from the disaster prediction module as well as from its own observation of the state of system operation. It analyzes the possible impact of any approaching and occurring disaster and provides inputs to the system metamorphosis module which directs the system to switch operation modes to position for the incoming disasters. Our cell-like state switch scheme ensures that the switch of system operation state is seamless and leaves no noticeable trace to the outside clients.

Disaster preemption module gets activated if impact analysis module determines that the result of an incoming or occurring disaster can be preempted. Its role is to preempt the impact resulted from a disaster or attack, and shields users from the knowledge that such an event has ever happened. Thus, clients of such a system do not notice any trace of striking disasters.

Disaster recovery mode is switched on if impact analysis module determines that an incoming or occurring disaster is not preemptable but the entire system could recover from such a disaster. Its role is to recover the system after service interruption. It could also be triggered by a failure of a disaster preemption attempt. This failure trigger mechanism is critical for the system's self-awareness.

Disaster locking module gets involved when impact analysis module determines that our system could not recover from an incoming or occurring disaster. Its role is to lock the disaster to the part where it directly hits, and prevents spreading or rolling disasters. It can separate the interlocking paths of disasters and block disasters from rolling out of control. This mode can also be triggered by a failure in a disaster recovery attempt.

Harmless abruption is our last line of defense against disasters. It gets switched on if impact analysis module determines that an incoming or occurring disaster could not be locked or if a disaster locking attempt has failed. The role of harmless abruption is to preemptively bring the system to a safe state and shut down the operation; and consequently prevent the system from becoming malicious or be controlled by unfriendly forces. This mode is also switched on if the system is unable to make a determination regarding the approaching or striking disasters. After the disaster or attack is over, the self-surviving IT system could wake up from the dormant state and reactivate itself. This module can, however, under some extreme circumstances, irreversibly destroy the system.

5 Concluding Remarks

This paper presented a self-surviving IT system framework that aims to arm an IT system with the ability of defending itself against and surviving multiple types or occurrences of natural and man-made disasters. We have described the capabilities and underlying theoretical researches that anchor each of the seven sub-components of the self-surviving system, and explained how the modules work together to contribute to an IT system's overall self-surviving capability. Most of our researches have been validated by prototype experiments, and a full featured self-surviving IT system framework is currently under construction.

References

1. Special issue on advanced transaction models. *Data Engineering*, 14(1), March 1991.
2. T. Bass. Intrusion detection systems and multi-sensor data fusion. *Communication of ACM*, 43, No.3:99–105, April 2000.
3. P. A. Bernstein, V. Hadzilacos, and N. Goodman. *Concurrency Control and Recovery in Database Systems*. Addison-Wesley, Reading, MA, 1987.
4. K.P. Birman. The process group approach to reliable distributed computing. *Communications of the ACM*, 36(12):37–53, December 1993.
5. M. Chereque, D. Powell, P. Reynier, J-L. Richier, and J. Voiron. Active replication in delta-4. *Digest of Papers, 22nd International Symposium on Fault-Tolerant Computing*, 1992.
6. F. Cristian and C. Fetzer. The timed asynchronous distributed system model. In *Proc. Symposium of International Fault-Toleranct Computing*, June 1998.
7. G. Robert Malan Farnam Jahanian David Watson, Matthew Smart. Protocol scrubbing: network security through transparent flow modification. *IEEE/ACM Transactions on Networks*, 12, No. 2:261–273, 2004.
8. D. Dolev and D. Malki. The transis approach to high availability cluster communication. *Communications of the ACM*, 39(4):64–70, April 1996.
9. S. Elbaum and J. Munson. Intrusion detection through dynamic software measurement. *Proceedings of the Workshop on Intrusion Detection and Network Monitoring, Santa Clara, CA*, pages 41–50, 1999.
10. A.K. Elmagarmid, editor. *Database Transaction Models for Advanced Applications*. Morgan Kaufmann, 1993.
11. R. Lippmann et al. Evaluating intrusion detection systems: the 1998 darpa offline intrusion detection evaluation. *in Proceedings of DARPA Information Survivability Conference and Expositions*, pages 12–16, January 2000.
12. S. Jajodia and L. Kerschberg, editors. *Advanced Transaction Models and Architectures*. Kluwer Academic Publishers, 1997.

13. F. Jahanian K.G. Shin, G.Koob. Fault-tolerance in real-time systems. In *Panal Session in the Workshop on Real-Time Operating Systems and Software, Atlanta*, May 1991.
14. R. Maxion and K. Tan. Benchmarking anomaly-based detection systems. *in Proceedings of the International Conference on Dependable Systems and Networks, New York, NY*, pages 623–630, 2000.
15. R. Rajkumar, M. Gagliardi, and L. Sha. The real-time publisher/subscriber interprocess communication model for distributed real-time systems: Design and implementation. In *Proc. Real-Time Technology and Applications Symposium*, pages 66–75, May 1995.
16. W. Stallings. Network and inter-network security principles and practice. *Prentice Hall*, 1995.
17. Jon William Toigo. *Disaster Recovery Planning*. Prentice Hall, 2002.
18. J. Turek and D. Shasha. The many faces of consensus in distributed systems. *IEEE Transactions on Computers*, pages 8–17, June 1992.
19. S.J. Stolfo W. Lee and K.W.Mok. A data mining framework for building intrusion detection models. *in Proceedings of IEEE Symposium on Security and Privacy*, pages 113–119, 1999.
20. Y. Zhang Ye, N. and C. Borror. Robustness of the markov-chain model for cyber attack detection. *IEEE Trans. Reali*, 53, No.1:116–123, 2004.
21. Henghui Zou. a priori estimates for a semilinear elliptic system without variational structure and their applications. *Mathematische Annalen*, 323, No.3:713–735, 2002.
22. Hengming Zou. SRDF for server clusters. *Technical White Paper*, May 2001.
23. Hengming Zou. Use device/consistency group agent in cluster environment. *Technical White Paper*, August 2001.

PDE-Based Intrusion Forecast

Hengming Zou[1] and Henghui Zou[2]

[1] Shanghai Jiao Tong University, China
zou-hm@cs.sjtu.edu.cn
[2] University of Alabama at Birmingham, USA
hhzou@math.uab.edu

Abstract. Current techniques used to detect hacker intrusion are post-mortem in that they get into action only if someone or something is intruding, in other words, they are reactionary. This paper proposes a PDE-based intrusion forecast model that aims to forecast hacker intrusion before they actually occur.

1 The Hacker-Computer Model

A computer system could be viewed as a living entity to some extent: it can possess some basic ability to maintain operation and a set of capabilities to defend itself against hacker intrusion. These capabilities include (but are not limited to) the security feature of CPU, OS, and application software, a set of possible anti-intrusion measurements such as fire-wall and anti-virus software, and any data protection mechanism such as encryption and encoding. These capabilities are organized as layers of defense which any intrusion must penetrate to gain full control of the system. As each layer of defense is penetrated, the defensive capability of the computer system decreases correspondingly. When all defensive layers are penetrated, the computer system lays bare in front of hackers just like a prey lies defenselessly in front of a predator. Hence, the interaction and struggle between hackers and computer systems largely resembles the characteristics of that of the classic predator-prey phenomenon in ecology.

Having analyzed the nature of the relationship between hackers and computers, we can now introduce our hacker-computer model.

For a given computer system, we denote (Ω, F, P) the probability space of all its possible states (finitely many), where F is the s-algebra of all subsets of the state space Ω and P is the probability on Ω. Note that (Ω, F, P) is individualized in the sense that it associates with exactly one specific computer system. Throughout the rest of the paper, we consider only one fixed computer system, being called the computer. For the computer, let the function $u = u(\omega, t)$ represent the intensity of its anti-hacking defensive capability at time t and state ω. A system's anti-hacking defensive capabilities can include such things as its hacking detection ability, the robustness of any data protection mechanism, and the system's ability in launching a preset program to terminate hacker attacks.

Similarly, we consider for simplicity only one fixed hacker, being called the hacker. The hacker is not one person literally, but rather a category of objects that implement all of the cyber attacks on the computer. Let $v = v(\omega, t)$ be the intensity of all the attacks launched by the hacker. At a given time t, there can be multiple attacks and the intensity v is naturally understood to be the sum of the intensity of individual attacks. The intensity of attacks includes but is not limited to the level of attacks (such as against operating system layer, application layer, or middleware layer), the frequency and methods of attacks, and the damage caused by the attack, etc., against the computer system.

The derivatives of functions $u(\omega, t)$ and $v(\omega, t)$ with respect to time t are the rate of changes of u and of v respectively. For time $s, t \geq 0$, we shall assume that there is a family of transformations θ_t on Ω such that

1. $\theta_0 = \mathrm{id}_\Omega$;
2. $\theta_{s+t} = \theta_s \circ \theta_t$.

For a start state $\omega \in \Omega$, at time $t > 0$, it changes to the state $\theta_t \omega$. We propose the following stochastic differential equation model

$$\begin{aligned}
u' &= au - au^2/K - \phi(t_t(o), u, v), & t &> 0, \\
v' &= -bv + \psi(t_t(\emptyset), u, v), & t &> 0, \\
u(\omega, 0) &= u_0(\omega); \; v(\omega, 0) = v_0(\omega),
\end{aligned} \quad (1)$$

where $a, b, K > 0$ are constants, and ϕ and ψ are positive functions, to quantitatively study the hacker-computer relationship. (Non-stochastic) equation of type (1) has been widely used to model the classic predator-prey phenomenon in ecology, where v is the predator and u the prey. In our computer-hacker model, the hacker is considered predator and the computer considered prey. For obvious reasons we only consider non-negative u and v. The two subjects u and v constantly interact, with the hacker-intensity v preying exclusively on the computer anti-hacking-intensity u. The two non-negative functions $u_0(\omega)$ and $v_0(\omega)$, which depend on the state of the computer, are the initial profile of u and of v at $t = 0$.

2 Technical Rational

The non-negative function $u = u(\omega, t) \geq 0$ represents the intensity of the anti-hacking defensive ability of the specific computer's security system. The stronger the defensive ability is, the larger the value of $u(\omega, t)$ (at given time t and given state ω) will be. Similarly, the non-negative function $v = v(\omega, t) \geq 0$ represents the intensity of the hacker-attack on the computer system, and the stronger the attacks are, the larger the value of $v(\omega, t)$. It is assumed that the hacker and the computer system constantly interact each other, namely, it is assumed that v constantly attacks u (however, not all attacks cause noticeable damage to the computer system, though it may inflict some penetration into certain defensive layer, see also Section 4 on predication).

When the system is free of hacker attacks (i.e., $v(\omega, t) \equiv 0$), we assume that the intensity $u(\omega, t)$ grows exponentially initially (with a growth rate $a > 0$, proportional to $u(t)$ itself, i.e., $u' \approx au > 0$), meaning the computer system is invincible (this is a natural conclusion in the absence of hackers). The growth is damped by the negative term $-au^2/K$ when u becomes large. In fact, the computer's defensive ability cannot exceed the level of invincibility K, namely, $u(\omega, t) < K$ for all $t > 0$. The rational behind this growth assumption is that one is willing to constantly upgrade the computer's security system through measures such as operating system upgrade, application upgrade, installation and upgrade of anti-virus software, fire-wall installation and upgrade, installation of data protection mechanism such as encryption, encoding, and the enacting of secure network such as VPN, etc., which is to increase the value of u over the time. In the meantime, all upgrades of the computer are clearly limited at certain level (say, by resource, management, etc.). In the absence of the computer (i.e., $u(\omega,t) \equiv 0$), v sustains a so-called exponential decay (with a decay rate $b > 0$, proportional to $v(t)$ itself, i.e., $v' = -bv < 0$). The intensity v eventually dies out (Note: after an infinite period of time!), namely, $v(\omega, t) \to 0$ as $t \to \infty$. The decay of v is naturally attributed to the fact that the survival of the hacker (on the specific computer system) exclusively depends on the presence of the computer system. In reality, for our purpose of studies, we may safely rule out the possibility of disappearance of the computer (i.e., crash, etc.). Indeed, most corporate computer servers are up 24x7, and 365 days a year (almost all of the servers are running in clusters or other type of fault tolerant configuration such that the system would keep running at all times). If for some reason, the system suffers any interruption, it will be repaired and put back into service very soon. Computer system at banks, security exchange, and some government institutions are also kept running year-around and repaired promptly in case of any failure. It should be pointed out that in these cases, no stochastic process is involved.

Of course, the interesting case to us is when both u and v are present. The attacks on the computer system contribute a negative impact on the growth of u which, we shall refer to as "attack rate", causes u to decrease. This, mathematically, is reflected by the negative term $-\phi(\theta_t(\omega), u, v)$ in the first equation of (1). The stronger of v is, the severer the negative impact on the growth of u will be. On the other hand, we assume that the hacker would benefit from the attacks, contributing a positive impact on the growth of v which, we shall refer to as "hacking rate", makes v increase. For example, from a psychological point of view, hackers may become more interested in repeating attacks on the same computer after implementing an initial successful attack (i.e. penetration of certain defensive layers and the acquisition of partial data or control). This, similarly, is reflected by the positive term $\psi(\theta_t(\omega), u, v)$ in the second equation of (1) and the stronger of u is, the larger the positive impact on the growth of v will be. Note both the attack rate (degree of damage to the computer's defensive ability) and the hacking rate (degree of benefit to the hacker's attacking ability) depend on the success degree of the attack(s). This success degree is reflected by the state(s) of the computer, i.e, the stochastic term $\theta_t(\omega)$, and affects both the attack rate and the hacking rate positively. We use the levels of defensive layer as one measurement of the degree of attack success. As each defensive layer is penetrated, the success degree of the attack is increased by one degree. Of course, there could be other measurement for attack success such as the acquirement of confidential data and the control of a system. But our chosen measurement is adequate because we assume that when the defensive layers are penetrated, the attackers would steal data and progress to take control of the system.

A stochastic process comes into play when the hacker and the computer co-exist. The hacker randomly chooses when and where to attack, depending on many random factors. Therefore, hacker attacks are widely characterized as random events. In our model (1), a stochastic process θ_t is incorporated to reflect the random feature of hacking, see Section 3 for more details.

3 Determination of Key Quantities

The proper values of various quantities in (1) depend on the individual computer system. Specifically, they depend on the importance of the computer, its security system, and the pattern of the computer's past attacks. A better-maintained and securer computer should have larger values of a and b since it has stronger defensive ability and it is harder for the hacker to gain materially from the attack(s). Meanwhile, a more important or better-known computer system would have larger a but smaller b values since more hackers tend to attack more interesting computers and the management is more willing to upgrade more important computers' security. For example, the hacker may not be interested at all in attacking a home-computer unit with no importance, but show genuine interest to a bank's computer system. The two interaction functions ϕ and ψ shall also be determined essentially on the same accounts. In fact, the better the quality of the computer's security system (i.e., the stronger the intensity u), the smaller the functions ϕ and ψ are, which suggests that both ϕ and ψ are inversely proportional to u. On the other hand, the more important the computer system is (i.e., the stronger the intensity v), the larger the functions ϕ and ψ are, which suggests that both ϕ and ψ are proportional to v.

The initial profiles $u_0(\omega)$ and $v_0(\omega)$ will be determined at the initial time $t = 0$ (relative to other quantities). For example, by observing past hacking activities, we can establish a baseline as to what type of system equipment is adequate for the prevalent hacker attacks. Thus, a computer with the said resource and security measure can be set in correspondence with the said hacker intensity. However, we can at our discretion set the initial state without resorting to the use of those historical data. In such case, we define each type and level of security measure with a numerical value, then, according to the types and levels of the measurements a computer system is equipped, we can compute its initial u_0 state with the numerical values obtained. The hacker's initial state can be correspondingly set as a normalized value after the initial state of the computer is obtained. Because of the nature of our model, the setting of the hacker's initial state does not affect our ability to forecast the future trend of hacker attacks.

As mentioned before, the family of transformations θ_t is a stochastic process introduced to model the randomness of the hacker's attacks. In general, we assume $\theta_t(\omega) = \xi_t(\omega)$ is a nice stationary (memoryless, or the so-called Markov property) stochastic process in the sense that only the value of the perturbation at time t influences the system (it forgot what happened before time t). In other words, the computer with an initial state ω will have a (random) state $\xi_\tau(\omega)$ at time $\tau > 0$ and the states $\xi_t(\omega)$ ($t < \tau$) happened before τ have no effect to the state $\xi_\tau(\omega)$. There are many stochastic processes available for such uses. The choice of the process ξ_t shall depend on the specific computer and, in particular, its past history. For instance, one can employ the well-known Wiener process (continuous) or jump Markov process (discontinuous) for this purpose.

4 Forecast

Two types of forecast data are available. After determining the relevant quantities, we can employ (1) to compute the values of $u(\omega, t)$ and $v(\omega, t)$, and their derivatives $u'(\omega, t)$ and $v'(\omega, t)$, at any given time $t > 0$ and for a given initial state $\omega \in \Omega$. Using historical data of the specific computer, we can set thresholds for anti-hacking intensity $u(t)$ and hacker intensity $v(t)$ respectively. If at a given time t, the anti-hacking intensity $u(t)$ is below the threshold, the system will alert the inadequacy of the security system, which, consequently, needs to be upgraded. If at any time t the hacker intensity $v(t)$ is above the threshold, the system will alert excessive hacking-activities and corresponding counter-measures are required counter hacker-attacks. Similarly, we can set up a warning model based on the derivatives $u'(t)$ and $v'(t)$. A large (positive) $v'(t)$ (against a preset threshold) would indicate a sudden and large increase of the hacking-intensity level, which should triggers an alert. On the other hand, a large (negative) $u'(t)$ (against a preset threshold) would indicate a sudden and large decrease of the anti-hacking-intensity level, which should also triggers an alert.

After each alert and preferably upgrade, the parameters in (1) will be re-adjusted according to the changes made to the system and the time will be reset to zero. The thresholds can also be adjusted according to the feedback from the system operator and the analysis of the response that has been taken after each alert. Such procedure is to be repeated and another cycle begins.

Similarly, we can setup a forecast model based on the derivatives of $u(\omega, t)$ and $v(\omega, t)$. With the base data gathered either from experiments or from statistics observed during the uptime period of the computer, we can project the value of those functions at any point of time in the future. The value obtained this way is, mathematically, a forecast of hacker activities and defensive intensity of the computer at that point of time. Furthermore, we can apply integral to $v'(t)$ on any time frame in the future to obtain the aggregated intensity or activities for that future time period. The integral obtained this way would be a forecast of hacker activities in the time period where the integral is applied, and thus offers a clue to the future trend and activities of hackers regarding the computer.

Due to space limitation, the introduction, conclusion, and reference sections have been omitted from the paper.

A Solution to Ragged Dimension Problem in OLAP

Lin Yuan[1], Hengming Zou[1], and Zhanhuai Li[2]

[1] Shanghai Jiao Tong University, China
{yuanlin, zou-hm}@cs.sjtu.edu.cn
[2] Northwestern Polytechnical University, China
lizhh@nwpu.edu.cn

Abstract. One problem facing many existing OLAP (On-Line Analytical Process) systems is the so-called ragged dimensions. Ragged dimensions occur if the logical parents of some members in a dimension hierarchy are two or more levels apart. In other words, there exist empty holes in the dimension hierarchy. The problems caused by ragged dimension are two-fold. First, aggregation of measure data could be incorrect. Second, the pre-computation strategy, the most prevalent technique used to speed up query processing in current OLAP system, could be rendered invalid. This paper proposes a simple yet efficient solution to remedy the ragged dimension problem for existing OLAP systems.

1 Introduction

The objective of OLAP applications is to provide decision support through multidimensional analysis of the information stored in enterprise data warehouses. To achieve this goal, OLAP tools often employ multidimensional data models (MDM) for the presentation, analysis and visualization of enterprise data. The advantages of MDM are its natural structure and improved query performance. In a MDM, data is classified into two categories: measure and dimension. The former serves as the object to be analyzed and the latter is used to describe the former. Measures are modeled as points in a multidimensional space and organized as cubes. We call such a cube MD (multidimensional data set).

Unlike the linear dimensions in programming languages, dimensions in an OLAP system typically have hierarchies defined on them. These hierarchies represent different categories of measure data and play a dominant role in OLAP queries. Aggregate operations such as ROLLUP and DRILLDOWN, which enable users to view data at different levels of granularity, make sense only if there are dimension hierarchies with more than one level. However, current MDMs and most of the OLAP systems fall short in their ability to model the complex dimension hierarchies found in real-world applications. This problem is particularly acute in the case of ragged dimensions in which the distance between some members and their immediate parents is more than one level apart. Figure 1 shows a ragged dimension: there is no Province level for the city of Beijing because it is a municipality directly under the central government.

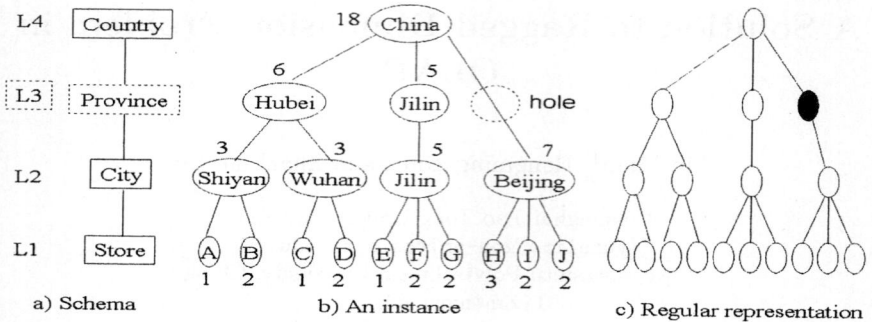

Fig. 1. Ragged dimension and its modeling

Ragged dimension poses two serious problems for MDMs and their implementations. First, the empty holes in the hierarchy violate the property of summarizability. Summarizability is a constraint over MDMs that requires dimension hierarchies to be complete. In other words, the mapping function between two adjacent levels in a hierarchy must be total. So a low-level member in a dimension belongs to a member one-level above. Violation of the summarization rule can lead to incorrect analytical results. For example, if we summarize the total sales to the Country level from Province level in Figure 1, the result will be 11 (=6+5) which is incorrect. The correct number is 18.

Second, ragged dimensions render the technique of pre-aggregation invalid. The most prevalent technique to accelerate multidimensional queries is to pre-aggregate and materialize the results of some MD. For example, computing and storing total sales at fine granularity identified by (Province, Day) enable fast answers to the queries for the total sales at coarse granularity identified by (Province, Month) or (Country, Month). But such techniques are rendered invalid by ragged dimensions. For example, in Figure 1, getting total sales for the Country level from Province level will produce the wrong result of 11. To get the correct answer, one has to calculate the result from the lower level of City or Store. This leads to more I/O and in-creased processing time. Thus, aggregation on ragged dimensions is inefficient.

This paper proposes a simple but efficient solution for the ragged dimension problem in OLAP systems. Our solution solves two problems: semantic correctness and efficiency of aggregation on ragged dimensions. The key point of our approach is to consider ragged dimension as a view defined over a special conventional dimension, in which empty holes are replaced by placeholders.

2 Extended Multidimensional Model

Regular dimension are described by schemas and instances. Each path from the lowest level to the highest level in a dimension is called a hierarchy. A dimension instance consists of a set of dimension members for each level and the mappings between these members. Let $LEVEL$ be a finite set of levels, $dom(L)$ be the corresponding set of dimension members, $HoldSet$ be the set of placeholders e_{hi}, we define regular dimensions as follows.

Definition 1. *Schema of regular dimension D is denoted by $DS = (DN, \{L_i\}, \leq_L)$, here DN is the dimension name, $\{L_i | i = 1, 2, \ldots, n\} \in LEVELS$, $\leq_L)$ is a partial order relation over with a unique bottom level L_{inf} and a unique top level ALL, satisfy $\forall L_i \in DS(L_{inf} \leq_L L_i \leq_L ALL)$.*

Definition 2. *A Regular dimension D is a 2-element tuple: $D = (DS, Rup)$, where Rup is a set of surjection functions: for each pair of levels $L1, L2 \in DS \wedge L_1 <_L L_2$ there exists a surjection function $Rup_{L1}^{L2} : dom(L_1) \to L_2$, here $<_L$ denotes the quasi-ordering relationship over Li.*

Definition 3. *Dimension operators **decendants**$(e_j, L_i) = \{e_i | Rup_{L_i}^{L_j}(e_i) = e_j \wedge e_j \in dom(L_j)\}$, where $L_i <_L L_j$ and $e_i \in dom(L_i)$.*

2.1 Ragged Dimension

In our extended data model, ragged dimension D_H can be considered a special view defined over a regular dimension $\tilde{D}_H$ in which the empty holes are replaced with placeholders. $\tilde{D}_H$ can be regarded as a physical expression of D_H, and is called regular expression of ragged dimension D_H. Figure 1 depicts a ragged dimension schema, its instance, and its regular representation.

In real applications, we can predict the position of the ragged levels in a dimension according to specific semantics. Our model supports correct data aggregation by keeping track of the levels that are ragged. This information can then be used to either prevent users from doing illegal actions on the data, or to warn the users that the result might be wrong.

Definition 4. *Schema of ragged dimension D_H is denoted by $DS = (DN, \{< L_i, B_{hole} >\}, \leq_L), i = 1, 2, \ldots, n$, where for each L_i, there exists a Boolean variable B_{hole}, denoted by $L_i.B_{hole}$, that marks the level that is allowed to be ragged.*

Definition 5. *Ragged dimension D_H can be projected to another regular dimension $\tilde{D}_H$ whose schema is $DS(\tilde{D}_H) = (\tilde{D}N, \{< \tilde{L}_i, B_{hole} >\}, \leq_L), i = 1, 2, \ldots, n$, where: if $L_i \in D_H \wedge L_i.B_{hole} = true$, then $dom(\tilde{L}_i) = dom(L_i) \wedge Holds_i$, in which $dom(L_i), Holds_i$ meets $Holds_i \subset HoldSet \wedge Holds_i \cap dom(L_i) = \emptyset$.*

2.2 Measure and Multidimensional Data Set

Definition 6. *Measure schema is denoted by $MS = (Mname, MT, O)$, where $Mname$ is the measure name; $MT = (idT, MVT)$ is the type of measure in which idT is the identification type, MVT is the type of measure value; O is a set of aggregation functions applied on MVT.*

Definition 7. *MS is a measure schema, and each measure cell is an object of type MT, and there exists a bijection function $rep : dom(MT) \leftrightarrow dom(idT)$, measure domain is denoted by $dom(M) \subseteq dom(MT)$.*

Definition 8. *The schema of n-dimensional data set is a 3-element tuple* $MDS = (DSset, G, MS)$, *where* $DSset = \{DS_i | 1 \leq i \leq n\}$ *is the set of dimension schema,* $G = <DS_1.L_1, \cdots, DS_i.L_i, \cdots, DS_n.L_n>$ *represents the granularity of n-dimensional data set, and MS is the measure schema.*

Definition 9. *Multidimensional Data Set MD over schema MDS is denoted by* $MD = (MDname, MDS, Dset, M, ML)$, *where* $Dset = \{D_1, \ldots, D_i, \ldots, D_n\}$ *is a set of dimension over DSset,* $ML = \{ml_i : dom(M) \rightarrow dom(L_i) | L_i \in G, 1 \leq i \leq n\}$, *and M is the measure over schema MS.*

3 Operations on Ragged Dimension

Now we define three types of query operations on ragged dimensions: *limit, rollup,* and *drilldown*. Among which rollup and drilldown are summary operations. Figure 2 depicts a schematic view of the query processing on ragged dimensions. After semantic check and query rewrite, queries against a ragged dimension D_H is transformed into queries against its corresponding regular representation $\tilde{D}_H$.

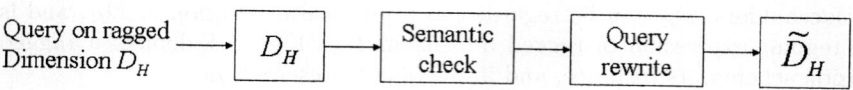

Fig. 2. Query processing on ragged dimension

Let $D_H.L_i \in G$ represents the granularity level on ragged dimension D_H of MD represented by $\tilde{D}_H$. The output of the operation is MD'.

Definition 10. *Limit Operation* $\sigma[P](MD) = MD'$, *where P is the limit predicate applied to MD, which can be expressed by production* $P \rightarrow P_M | P_{D_i, L_j}$ *and* $P \rightarrow (P_M | P_{D_i, L_j}) \wedge P$. *Here* P_M *is applied on measure,* P_{D_i, L_j} *is applied on level* L_j *of dimension* D_i. *Since the definition of* $\sigma[P_M](MD)$ *is trivial, we only define* $\sigma[P_{D_i, L_j}](MD)$. *Suppose* $DS_i.L_i$ *is the granularity level of MD on dimension* D_i, *the operation satisfy:* $L_i \leq_L L_j$. *Let:* $dom(L_i | P_{D_i, L_j}) = \cup_{e_j \in dom(L_j) \wedge P_{D_i, L_j}(e_j)} descendant(e_j, L_i)$,
$dom(M') = \{m \in dom(M) | \exists e_i \in dom(l_i)(ml_i(m) = e_i \wedge dom(L_i | P_{D_i, L_j}))\}$,
$ML' = \{(m', (e_1, e_2, \cdots, e_n)) \in ML | m' \in dom(M')\}$, *and* $MDS' = MDS$.

For ragged dimensions, the definition above will be revised as the following.

Definition 11. $\sigma[P](MD) = \sigma[P'](MD) = MD'$, $\sigma[P_{D_H, L_j}](MD) = \sigma[P_{\tilde{D}_H, \tilde{L}_j} \wedge \neg P_{Hold}(e) \wedge e \in dom(\tilde{L}_i)](MD) = MD''$

In Figure 2, semantic check will reveal that Province level is ragged. So the query will be rewritten and the holes are eliminated by an expended predicate formula.

Definition 12. Roll-up Operation $Rollup[G', Agg](MD) = MD'$, where G' is the granularity of MD', $Agg \in O$. The operation satisfy $L_i \leq_L L'_i, i = 1, 2, \cdots, n$, and at least there exists $L_j <_L L'_j$.

Again, the definition for ragged dimensions will be revised as the following.

Definition 13. $Rollup[G', Agg](MD) = Rollup[G', Agg](MD') = MD''$

Since rollup is summary operation, we need to make certain that such operation is valid. Suppose $E \in dom(L_i)$ is the set of dimension members that identifies the measure data of MD, then we have:
If $\exists e' \in dom(L'_i)(L'_i.Bool_{hole} \wedge P_{Hold}(e') \wedge e' = Rup_{L_i}^{L'_i}(e) \wedge e \in E)$ **then** current operation is invalid.
Else $Rollup[G', Agg](MD) = Rollup[G', Agg](MD') = MD''$

In the phase of query rewrite (Figure 2), the OLAP system will find a properly pre-computed aggregation MD (represented by $\tilde{D}_H$) to calculate the result. For example, if the MD represented by $Province$ (contains empty holes) is already pre-computed, the query will be rewritten as the following: $Rollup[<Country, day>, Sum]MD = Rollup[<Province, day>, sum]MD'$

Drill down operations is rewritten as rollup operations within our model. The only difference is that the rule for semantic check is changed to 'drilling down to empty holes is invalid.'

4 Related Work

There has been a substantial amount of work on the general topic of multidimensional data model (Blaschka [5], Vassiliadis [6]). But works on dimension hierar-chies have been rare. Among all those models, only Shoshani [7] and Jagadish [8] have touched upon the subject of complex dimension hierarchies.

Due to space limit, **detailed discussions of related work and relevant references are omitted.** Readers please contact the authors for detail.

5 Conclusion

This paper extended the conventional multidimensional data model for OLAP to support ragged dimensions. In order to avoid potentially erroneous computational result, our model places built-in constraints on multidimensional operations such that the correctness of aggregation semantics along ragged dimension hierarchies is assured. For system implementation, our model projects a ragged dimension onto a regular one and replaces empty holes with placeholders. Our approach ensures that the widely used pre-aggregation strategy in OLAP remain valid. In conclusion, our extended MDM is a simple but efficient remedy to the existing ragged dimension problem in OLAP systems.

A Convolutional Neural Network VLSI Architecture Using Sorting Model for Reducing Multiply-and-Accumulation Operations

Osamu Nomura[1,2], Takashi Morie[2], Masakazu Matsugu[1], and Atsushi Iwata[3]

[1] Canon Inc., Intelligent I/F Project, Atsugi, 243-0193, Japan
{nomura.osamu, matsugu.masakazu}@canon.co.jp
[2] Graduate School of Life Science and Systems Engineering,
Kyushu Institute of Technology, Kitakyushu, 808-0196, Japan
{nomura, morie}@brain.kyutech.ac.jp
[3] A-R-Tec Corporation, Higashi-Hiroshima, 739-0047 Japan
iwa@a-r-tech.jp

Abstract. Hierarchical convolutional neural networks are a well-known robust image-recognition model. In order to apply this model to robot vision or various intelligent real-time vision systems, its VLSI implementation is essential. This paper proposes a new algorithm for reducing multiply-and-accumulation operation by sorting neuron outputs by magnitude. We also propose a VLSI architecture based on this algorithm. We have designed and fabricated a sorting LSI by using a 0.35 μm CMOS process. We have verified successful sorting operations at 100 MHz clock cycle by circuit simulation.

1 Introduction

Processing models for object detection or recognition from natural images should tolerate pattern deformations and pattern position shifts. The convolutional neural network (CoNN) model with a hierarchical structure, which imitates the vision nerve system in the brain, has such functions [1,2,3,4,5]. The operations required for implementing CoNNs are 2-D convolutional mappings, which include a large number of multiplications by weights and nonlinear conversion as usual neural network models. Because they require huge computational power, in order to execute these operations in real-time and with low power consumption for intelligent applications such as robot vision, efficient VLSI implementation is required. So far, analog VLSI processors suitable for CoNNs were reported [6,7,8]. For the practical use, however, further improvement of CoNN VLSIs is required from the viewpoint of the operation speed.

In this paper, on the basis of our previous work [9], we propose a new algorithm that improves the operation speed by reducing the number of connection weighting operations; i.e. multiply-and-accumulation (MAC) operations. In this algorithm, neuron outputs are sorted by magnitude, and only neuron outputs whose ranking is higher than the predefined ranking are used for MAC operations. We also propose a VLSI architecture based on the proposed algorithm.

We have designed a sorting LSI by using a 0.35 μm CMOS process. Section 2 describes the CoNN model for object detection/recognition. We describes the new algorithm and VLSI architecture for CoNNs in Sec. 3 and Sec. 4, respectively. In Sec. 5, we present a sorting circuit and a designed sorting LSI. Finally, Sec. 6 presents our conclusion.

2 Hierarchical CoNN Model

The CoNN with a hierarchical structure for object detection/recognition is shown in Fig. 1. The first layer of the hierarchical structure only receives images. The following layers consist of two sub-layers: a feature detection (FD) layer and a feature pooling (FP) layer. Each layer includes some feature classes, each of which has neurons that respond the same image feature. The neurons are arranged in a 2-D array to maintain the feature position of the input image. Therefore, the feature class size is equal to the input image size, and each neuron corresponds to each pixel. All neurons receive the signals from the neurons in a predefined area near the same position of the previous layer, which is called a *receptive field*.

Figure 2 shows the principle of pattern detection using a CoNN. The FP neurons are used to achieve recognition tolerant to pattern deformation and position shifts. The FD neurons operate for integrating features. By the hierarchically repetitive structure, local simple features (e.g., line segments) in the input image are gradually assembled into complex features.

Operations between layers are 2-D convolutions, because all neurons belonging to a feature class have a receptive field with the same weight distribution. The receptive field of the FP neurons is on the same feature class of the previous FD layer. All neurons of the FP layer have the same positive-weight Gaussian-like distribution. The shifts of feature positions in the FD layers are tolerated in the FP layers by this convolution. On the other hand, the receptive fields of the FD neurons are on all feature classes of the previous FP layer. The weights of the FD neurons are obtained by training.

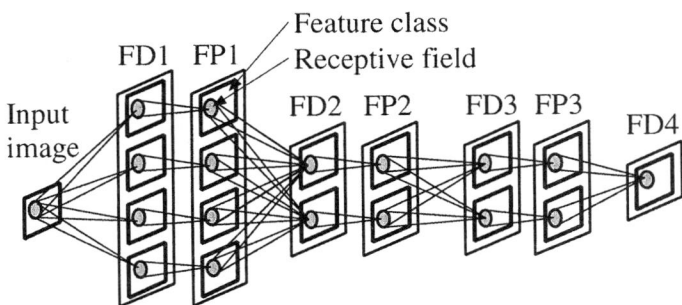

Fig. 1. Hierarchical CoNN model for object detection or recognition

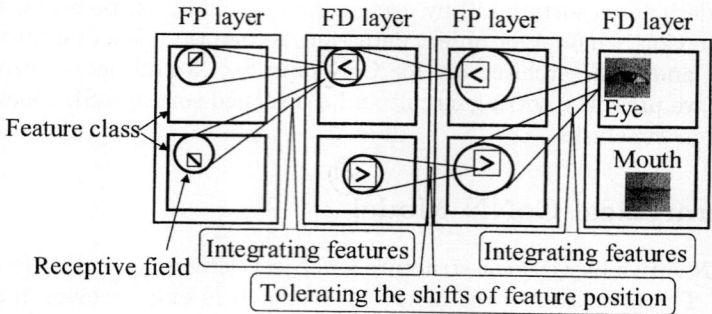

Fig. 2. Principle of pattern detection using a CoNN (an example of eye and mouth pattern detection)

3 Reduction of MAC Operations by Sorting

We found from numerical simulations of face detection from natural scene images that, in the layers of the latter stages, only a few neurons have significant output values and most neurons have very small values. Even if we omit MAC calculations with such negligible output values, it is expected that the calculation result is not so different from the exact one. In fact, we found from the numerical simulations of face detection that the detection accuracy hardly degrades by using such operation.

We therefore propose a new algorithm with a use of sorting for decreasing the number of MAC operations. In order to implement the algorithm effectively, we have already introduced the projection-field model instead of the conventional receptive-field model [9]. In the projection-field model, the postsynaptic neurons

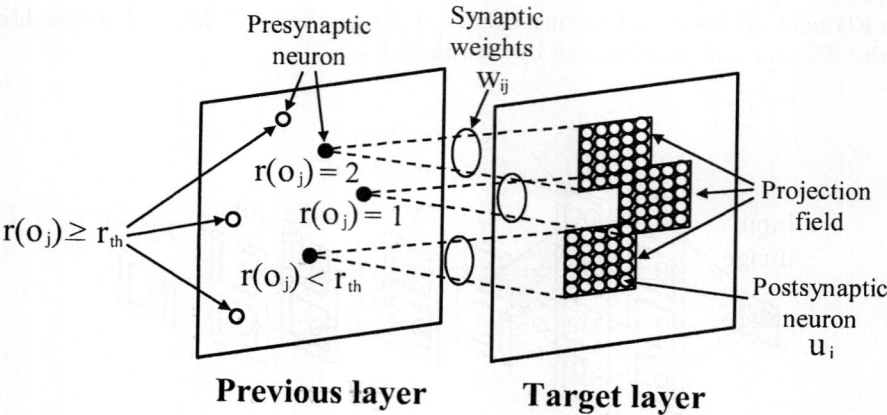

Fig. 3. Schematic for our sorting model

belonging to a projection field in the target layer receive an input from the corresponding presynaptic neuron of the previous layer.

Figure 3 explains the projection-field model with sorting, which we call a *sorting model*. It executes only MAC operations related to the presynaptic neuron output o_j with a ranking $r(o_j)$ higher than the predefined ranking threshold r_{th}. Internal potential u_i of a neuron in the target layer is given by

$$u_i = \sum_{j \in \mathcal{R}, r(o_j) < r_{th}} w_{ij} o_j, \tag{1}$$

where w_{ij} is the connection weight from presynaptic neuron j to postsynaptic neuron i, and $\mathcal{R}$ is the set of neurons belonging to the receptive field. Because the projection-field model is essentially equivalent to the receptive-field model in calculation of u_i, we use the receptive-field to specify j in Eq. (1).

4 New CoNN Architecture

We propose a new VLSI architecture for CoNNs based on the sorting model. Figure 4 shows the architecture, which implements a convolution for one feature-class. Calculation for the whole hierarchical structure is achieved by time-sharing

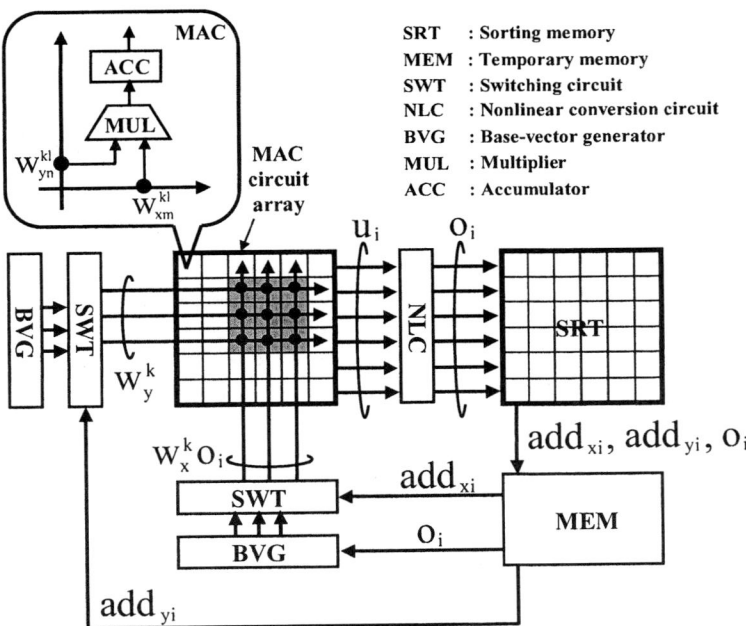

Fig. 4. CoNN architecture based on the sorting model

operations with repetitive use of this VLSI. The VLSI includes a MAC circuit array corresponding to the 2-D postsynaptic neuron array, a sorting circuit (SRT), a temporary memory (MEM), switching circuits (SWTs), a nonlinear conversion circuit (NLC) and base-vector generators (BVGs). The MAC circuit consists of a multiplier (MUL) and an accumulator (ACC).

For efficient calculation in the MAC circuit array, we have already introduced the synaptic weight decomposition approach [9]. Synaptic weight matrix $W(=\{w_{MN}\})$, which expresses an $M \times N$-pixel projection field, is decomposed into some products of base vectors $\boldsymbol{w}_x^k \equiv {}^t(w_{x1}^k, w_{x2}^k, \cdots, w_{xM}^k)$ and $\boldsymbol{w}_y^k \equiv {}^t(w_{y1}^k, w_{y2}^k, \cdots, w_{yN}^k)$;

$$W = \sum_{k=1}^{N_w} \boldsymbol{w}_x^k \cdot {}^t\boldsymbol{w}_y^k, \qquad (2)$$

where N_w is the number of decomposed products of the base vectors and ${}^t\boldsymbol{w}$ indicates a transposed vector. We can calculate the product of $\boldsymbol{w}_x^k$ and $\boldsymbol{w}_y^k$ for each k by N_w-step operations with the MAC circuit array. In general, $N_w > 1$ because weight matrix W does not have enough symmetry. We found from the numerical simulations of face detection that $N_w \sim 5$. On the other hand, in the conventional row- or column-parallel architecture [7,8], N-step operations are required for $N \times N$-pixel convolution. Because $N_w << N \ (\geq 20)$, our decomposition approach is much more efficient.

The operation of this circuit is as follows: (1) the MAC circuit calculates u_i by accumulation of all multiplication results, and outputs the MAC results to NLC; (2) NLC performs nonlinear conversion of the MAC results, and outputs the conversion results to SRT; (3) SRT outputs the value o_i according to ranking $r(o_i)$ higher than r_{th} and its addresses add_{xi}, add_{yi} one by one to MEM; (4) MEM stores these data temporarily, and outputs the value o_i to one BVG and addresses to SWTs at a next convolution calculation step; (5) BVGs output the pair of base vectors $\boldsymbol{w}_x^k$ and $\boldsymbol{w}_y^k o_i$ to SWTs; (6) SWTs output the pair of base vectors $\boldsymbol{w}_x^k$ and $\boldsymbol{w}_y^k o_i$ to the projection field of the MAC circuit array using the addresses add_{xi} and add_{yi}. By repeating the above sequence, the hierarchical CoNN operation is performed.

We estimated the performance of our VLSI processor based on the proposed architecture. As a performance measure we used GCOPS (Giga Convolutional Operations Per Second) defined in the previous work [9]. Here, we took into account the relative improvement of the convolutional operation performance by reduction of MAC operations by sorting, and calculated the performance P by using the following equation;

$$P = R_{size}^2 N_{MAC}/(R_{sort} N_w T_{MAC}), \qquad (3)$$

where R_{sort} is the ratio of the presynaptic neurons where $r(o_j) < r_{th}$ to the whole presynaptic neurons; $R_{sort} \approx 0.35$ from the numerical simulations, R_{size} is the size of the side of a square projection field, N_{MAC} is the number of operations for MAC (= 2 : a multiplication and an accumulation), and T_{MAC}

is the processing time for one MAC operation. The difference between GCOPS and GOPS (Giga Operations Per Second), which is a commonly-used measure in the digital signal processing, is division by N_w and R_{sort}. The reason why such additional factors are needed is that N_w-step operations are unnecessary if the weight decomposition approach is not used and that equivalent operations are performed at R_{sort} times the computational costs without sorting. If $T_{MAC} = $ 40 ns and $R_{size} = 81$, which seems achievable using the present VLSI technology, then $P \approx 187$ GCOPS. On the other hand, the performance of the conventional CoNN VLSIs was 10 GCOPS [6], 2 GCOPS [7,8] and 66 GCOPS [9]. Comparing these values, this estimation shows that our architecture will be able to achieve very high performance for CoNN operation.

5 Design of a Sorting Circuit

For implementing the proposed CoNN architecture, we designed a sorting circuit, which is one of the main components in our architecture. The sorting circuit is based on a content addressable memory (CAM). By repeating a search sequence of CAM in descending order of search data, the circuit performs sorting of the output values of the presynaptic neurons by magnitude.

Figure 5 shows the sorting circuit which includes $Q \times P$ processing elements (PEs) and flag-read circuits (FLAGREAD_X and FLAGREAD_Y). Each

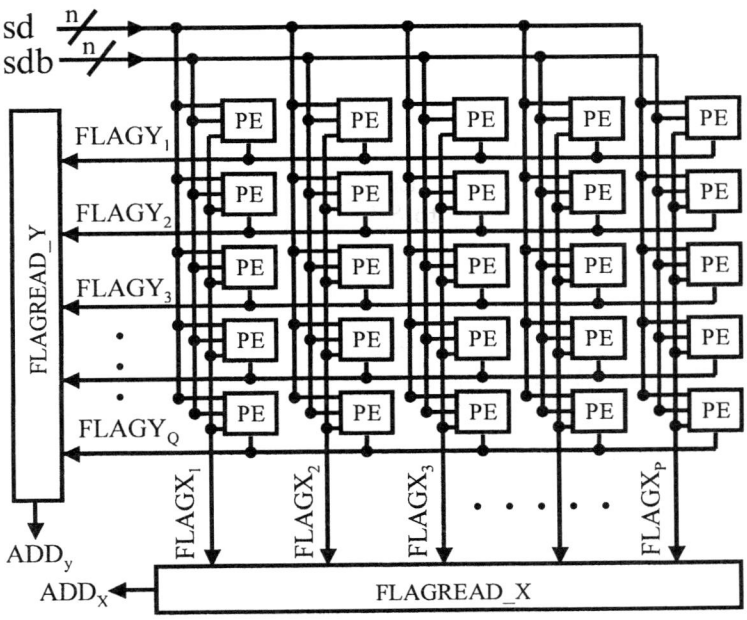

Fig. 5. Sorting circuit

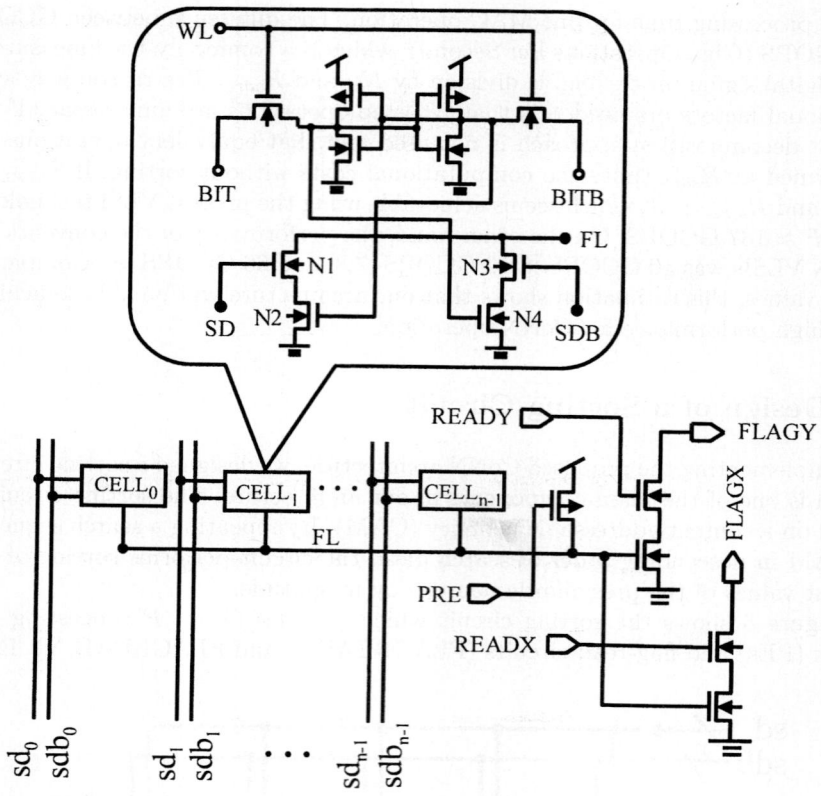

Fig. 6. n-bit processing element circuit of the sorting circuit

PE holds an output value of the corresponding presynaptic neuron, and wires $FLAGX_p$ ($p = 1, 2, \cdots, P$) and $FLAGY_q$ ($q = 1, 2, \cdots, Q$) are precharged at a high voltage. The operation of this circuit is as follows: (1) a searched n-bit data sd and its reverse data sdb are fed into all PEs; (2) only PEs whose storage data equals to the searched data discharge the connected wires, $FLAGX_p$ and $FLAGY_q$; (3) the FLAGREAD_X and the FLAGREAD_Y output the address data of the discharged wire, $FLAGX_p$ and $FLAGY_q$, one by one.

Figure 6 shows an n-bit PE circuit. Each PE includes n cell circuits (CELL$_0$ - CELL$_{n-1}$), four NMOS switches and one PMOS switch. Each cell circuit includes a SRAM cell with six transistors and four NMOS switches. The operation of the PE is as follows: (1) node FL is precharged at a high voltage by PRE; (2) a searched n-bit data sd_0 - sd_{n-1} and its reverse data sdb_0 - sdb_{n-1} are fed into nodes SD and SDB of each cell; (3) in each cell, the searched data is compared with the storage data by pairs of NMOS switches, $N1/N2$ and $N3/N4$, and

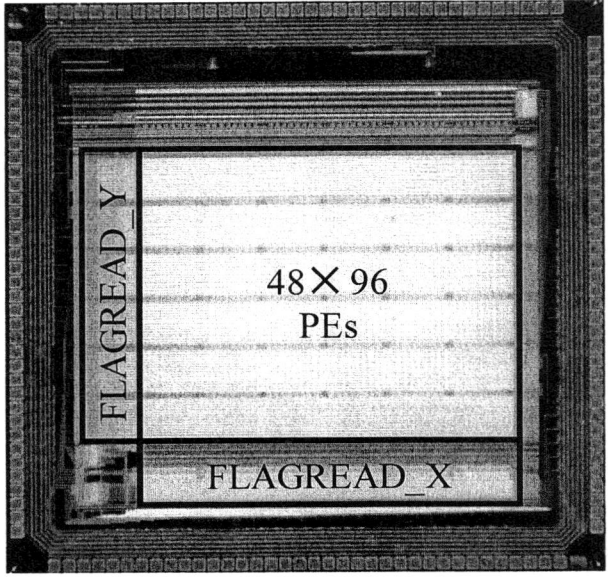

Fig. 7. Micro-photograph of the sorting LSI

only if both data are the same, the node FL keeps high voltage; (4) high voltage control signals are given at ports $READX$ and $READY$, and if node FL keeps high voltage, a matching flag (low voltage signal) is outputted to ports $FLAGX$ and $FLAGY$.

We designed a sorting LSI by using a 0.35 CMOS process as a proof of concept for our proposed architecture. A micro-photograph of this LSI is shown in Fig. 7. The die size is 4.9 mm sq., and the power supply voltage is 3.3 V. The LSI includes 48 × 96 PEs, each of which holds 6-bit data. For face position detection at video rate (30 fps), a sorting cycle should be 100 MHz. We verified successful sorting operations at 100 MHz clock cycle by circuit simulation, and therefore we can use this LSI for implementing our proposed VLSI architecture.

6 Conclusion

We proposed a new algorithm and VLSI architecture for CoNNs. Using a sorting procedure, we execute only MAC operations related to the postsynaptic neuron output whose ranking is higher than the predefined ranking. For the proposed VLSI architecture, we have designed and fabricated a sorting LSI by using a 0.35 μm CMOS process. We verified successful sorting operations at 100 MHz clock cycle by circuit simulation.

References

1. Fukushima, K., Miyake, S.: Neocognitron: A new algorithm for pattern recognition tolerant of deformations and shifts in position. Pattern Recognition **15** (1982) 455–469
2. Lawrence, S., Giles, C.L., Tsoi, A.C., Back, A.D.: Face recognition: A convolutional neural-network approach. IEEE Trans. Neural Networks **8** (1997) 98–113
3. Neubauer, C.: Evaluation of convolutional neural networks for visual recognition. IEEE Trans. Neural Networks **9** (1998) 685–696
4. Matsugu, M.: Hierarchical pulse-coupled neural network model with temporal coding and emergent feature binding mechanism. In: Proc. Int. Joint Conf. on Neural Networks (IJCNN). (2001) 802–807
5. Matsugu, M., Mori, K., Ishii, M., Mitarai, Y.: Convolutional spiking neural network model for robust face detection. In: Proc. Int. Conf. on Neural Information Processing (ICONIP). (2002) 660–664
6. Boser, B.E., Säckinger, E., Bromley, J., Cun, Y.L., Jackel, L.D.: An analog neural network processor with programmable topology. IEEE J. Solid-State Circuits **26** (1991) 2017–2025
7. Korekado, K., Morie, T., Nomura, O., Ando, H., Nakano, T., Matsugu, M., Iwata, A.: A convolutional neural network VLSI for image recognition using merged/mixed analog-digital architecture. In: 7th Int. Conf. on Knowledge-Based Intelligent Information and Engineering Systems (KES'2003). Volume II. Oxford (2003) 169–176
8. Korekado, K., Morie, T., Nomura, O., Ando, H., Nakano, T., Matsugu, M., Iwata, A.: A VLSI convolutional neural network for image recognition using merged/mixed analog-digital architecture. J. Intelligent & Fuzzy Systems **15** (2004) 173–179
9. Nomura, O., Morie, T., Korekado, K., Matsugu, M., Iwata, A.: A Convolutional Neural Network VLSI Architecture Using Thresholding and Weight Decomposition. In: 8th Int. Conf. on Knowledge-Based Intelligent Information and Engineering Systems (KES'2004). Volume I. (2004) 995–1001

A 32-Bit Binary Floating Point Neuro-chip

Keerthi Laal Kala and M.B. Srinivas

International Institute of Information Technology, Hyderabad, India
klkala@research.iiit.ac.in
srinivas@iiit.ac.in

Abstract. The need for high precision calculations in various scientific disciplines has led to development of systems with various solutions specific to the problem on hand. The complexity of such systems not withstanding, a generic solution could be the use of neural networks. To be able to leverage the best out of the neural network, hardware implementations are ideal as they give speed-up of several orders of magnitude over software simulations. A simple architecture for such a neuro-chip is proposed in this paper. The neuro-chip supports the current draft version of the IEEE-754 standard for floating-point arithmetic. The synthesis results indicate an estimated 84 MCUPS speed of operation.

1 Introduction

Neural networks have the ability to derive meaning from complicated or imprecise data and can be used to extract patterns and detect trends complex for humans or other computer techniques to recognize. This capability makes them suitable for solving problems in real world, where traditional techniques are unable to deliver optimal performance. A neural network is composed of a large number of highly interconnected processing elements, called neurons, working in parallel to solve a specific problem. These neurons are the building blocks of the network and are connected to each other by weighted edges, which determine the driving strength of each neuron with reference to the neuron at the other end of the connection. Thus, the output at each neuron is sum of the weighted inputs from other neurons that excite it. Digital hardware implementations of Neural Networks [1], until now have used different standards for the way in which the data is represented internally and the outputs presented to the external world. This paper proposes the use of the IEEE-754 standard for floating-point arithmetic throughout the implementation. The architecture is simple, yet tries to emulate the parallel computing processing power of neural networks.

2 Design and Implementation

A block diagram of the 32-bit floating point neuro-chip is shown in Fig 1. The architecture consists of a Neuron Processing Unit (NPU), one Control Logic Unit (CLU) and four Memory Units (MU). The neuro-chip is capable of modeling a network with 4 layers, including the output layer and with at most 8 neurons in each layer. Each neuron in the network can be connected to 4 neurons in the succeeding layer, limiting the number of inputs to each neuron to 4. The number of neurons and the number of layers in the neural network is limited only by the size of the on-chip memory. The number of layers in the neural network is given as a separate input to the neuro-chip. The inputs to the neuro-chip are 32-bit floating point input with guard, round and sticky bits, 2 bits for selecting the input line and 3 bits for the neuron are appended at the beginning. The extra 5 bits appended double as addresses for the input memory as well. The weights are also read in, before the neuro-chip is put into operation, with 2 bits extra appended for the corresponding layer, apart from 2 bits for the input line and 3 bits for the neuron. The first 7 bits double as addresses for the memory in this case. The number of layers in the network is also given as input to the neuro-chip. Figs. 2 and 3 show the input and the weight storage formats respectively. Once the weights have been obtained the neuro-chip is ready for operation and processing starts with the given data.

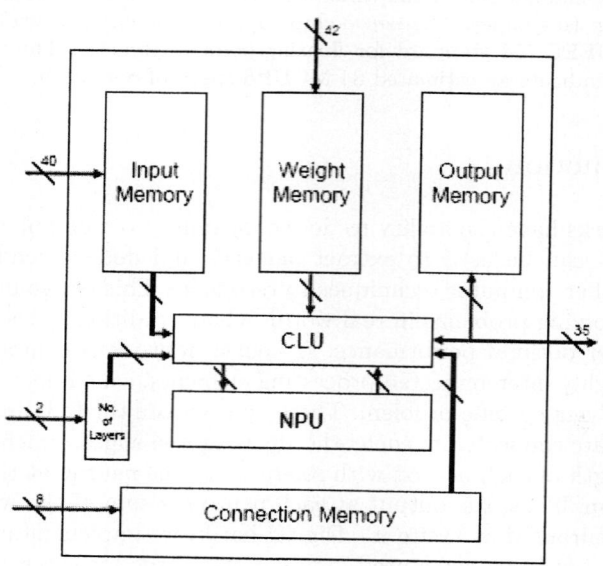

Fig. 1. Block Diagram of the Neuro-chip (32-FPNC)

3 neuron select bits	2 input line select bits	32bit floating point number	3 guard, round and sticky bits

40 bits wide

Fig. 2. 40-bit Input Format

2 layer selection bits	3 neuron select bits	2 input line select bits	32bit floating point number	3 guard, round and sticky bits

42 bits wide

Fig. 3. 42-bit Weight Format

2.1 Neural Processing Unit (NPU)

The NPU is the heart of the neuro-chip that consists of an array of neurons, four in this case. Each neuron independently calculates the weighted sum of all the inputs and the sum is then passed through a sigmoid activation function unit that applies the threshold function on the sum. Fig. 4 shows the block diagram of a neuron and each neuron is capable of receiving four weighted inputs. The multipliers shown in the figure are 32-bit floating point multipliers that are complaint with the IEEE-754 floating-point arithmetic standards. The unit takes in the input and the weight value, both 32-bit floating point numbers, and generates the product. The usage of guard, round and sticky bits and rounding and normalization after multiplication in compliance with the standards are built into each of the multiplier units. The result is passed onto the adder module, which is a tree structure of 32-bit floating point adders, generating a valid 32-bit floating point sum. This sum is then passed onto the sigmoid function activation unit, which then applies limiting function. The basic functionality of a neuron is thus simulated using this architecture. The most widely used limiting function is the sigmoid function which, as given by McClelland and Rumelhart [2], is represented by the equation:

$$f(x) = \frac{1}{1+e^x} \ . \tag{1}$$

An approximation to this function proposed in [2] is used here for generating the limiting function. The function used is given as:

$$f(x) = \frac{1}{2}\left(\frac{x}{1+|x|} + 1\right) \ . \tag{2}$$

This function is a simple polynomial which uses no transcendentals but approximates the sigmoid function with good precision that is suitable for a hardware implementation. It is the general characteristics of the sigmoid, not the precise equation, that is important for efficient functioning of the network. Fig. 5 shows a block diagram of this sigmoid activation function unit [3]. The circuit takes as its input a value x and generates the output $f(x)$. The functional units used by the circuit are:

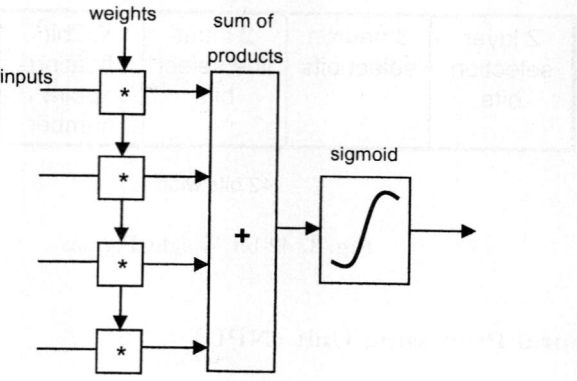

Fig. 4. Representation of a Neuron

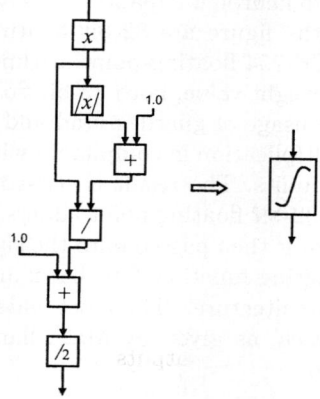

Fig. 5. The Sigmoid Activation Function

1. two adder circuits
2. one divider circuit
3. one absolute value generator circuit
4. one divide-by-two circuit

All these functional units are IEEE-754 floating-point standard compatible. The adder units are 32-bit adders [4] generating a normalized 32-bit result. The divide-by-two unit is a shifter, shifting the data right by 1-bit. The data is normalized after the shifting operation.

The NPU thus computes the output of four neurons at a time. The individual units in this stage are pipelined to achieve best delay results for each pass through one neuron. The divider and adder architectures used are optimal, giving low area utilization and greater throughput.

2.2 Control Logic Unit (CLU)

The Control Logic Unit (CLU) controls the flow of data into and out of the NPU. The CLU is responsible for retrieving data from the input and weight memories to pass onto the NPU and also to receive the data generated by the NPU to be stored in the output memory. It includes decoding mechanisms for addressing the data in the memories. The CLU incorporates logic to read in data from the weight memories and inputs to be indexed onto a neuron in the correct manner. Each neuron needs four input values and their corresponding weight values. After having generated outputs corresponding to the first (hidden) layer of the network, the CLU takes the data in the output memory and transmits the data as inputs to the NPU, along with the corresponding weights for generating the outputs of the output layer or another hidden layer. The cycle repeats for the next hidden layer until the output layer is encountered. The CLU keeps track of the current layer for which the outputs are being generated by the NPU. The number of layers in the neural network is given as a separate input to the neuro-chip.

2.3 Memory Units (MU)

The Memory Units (MU) store the input data, weight data, interconnections between neurons in the layers and the partial outputs generated by the NPU. All the data are 32-bit floating point numbers. There is a provision for storing 128 (32x4) weights corresponding to 32 neurons in the network. Each weight is indexed by 2 bits for the layer, 3 bits for identifying which neuron in the layer it refers to and finally 2 bits for the corresponding input direction for that particular neuron. The partial outputs are 32-bit floating point numbers which additionally have 2 bits for associating each with their layer and 3 bits for associating them with a particular neuron in that layer. The connection memory stores the interconnections between the neurons in different layers. A maximum of eight neurons can be present in any layer, so an 8-bit number for each neuron in i^{th} layer will define connections with neurons in the i-1th layer. The corresponding bits for connected neurons will be set to logic high. The CLU uses this information in routing the inputs and the corresponding weights. This technique ensures that correct inputs are given to the right neuron, as needed. The number of layers in the network is assumed not be beyond four. A maximum of 8 neurons in a single layer is considered, therefore, 4x8x8 bits of memory is needed for storing the interconnections.

3 Functioning of the Neuro-chip

The neuro-chip is capable of modeling a network with four layers, including the output layer and with at most eight neurons in each layer. Each neuron in the network can be connected to a maximum of four neurons in the succeeding layer. The network, thus, can have thirty two neurons as a whole.

The neuro-chip takes relevant number of passes to compute the outputs of the neurons for the output layer and then sums them to generate the final output. The neuro-chip initially computes the outputs of the first layer, reading inputs and corresponding weights. Once the process has been internally signaled completed, the output memory acts as input with the partial outputs acting as inputs now. The process repeats until it accounts for all the layers in the network. The final output, thus obtained, is placed on the output lines. Until then the neuro-chip is in busy state signaled by a busy bit.

Thus, the neuro-chip is capable of handling a variety of network architectures with good speeds of operation and high amount of precision. The usage of IEEE-754 complaint floating-point standard improves the accuracy and precision of the results very much.

4 Results of Simulation and Synthesis

The system has been synthesized with the help of Leonardo Spectrum^{TM} of Mentor Graphics and refined using Magma Blast^{TM} from Magma Design Automation. The best clock speed achieved was 20 MHz. At this speed the neuro-chip is capable of an average performance of 84 MCUPS (Connections Updated per Second).

5 Conclusions

The proposed architecture is capable of handling various network topologies that need high precision. The speed of operation of the neuro-chip is compared with various previous implementations (with lesser bit resolutions, though) as shown in the Table 1. The convergence of data with software simulations using MATLAB^{TM} is encouraging as the results are precise to the order of 6 to 10 digits in the mantissa part.

Table 1. Comparison with other NN Implementations [5]

Type	Name	Neurons	Speed($MCUPS$)
Digital	WSI	144	300
Digital	MANTRA1	40x40	133
Digital	HNC 100-NAP	100PU	64
Digital	32-FPNC	13	84
Hybrid	Neuroclassifier	6	21000

Acknowledgements

The authors wish to thank M/s Magma Design Automation (India) Pvt. Ltd., Bangalore for sponsoring Magma tool suite which has been used extensively in this work.

References

[1] Ayala J. L., Lomena A.G., Lopez Vallejo M., Fernandez A.: Design of a Pipelined Hardware Architecture for Real-Time Neural Network Computations IEEE Midwest Symposium on Circuits and Systems, Tulsa, Oklahoma, USA 2002
[2] McClelland J. L., Rumelhart D. E.: Explorations in Parallel Distributed Processing: A Handbook of Models, Programs and Exercises MIT Press 1988
[3] Steven A. Guccione, Mario J. Gonzalez: A Neural Network Implementation using Reconfigurable Architectures "More FPGAs", Will Moore and Wayne Luk, Abingdon EE & CS Books, Abingdon, England 1993 443-451
[4] John Thompson, Nandini Karra, Micheal J. Schulte: A 64-bit Decimal Floating-Point Adder. Proceedings of IEEE Computer Society Annual Symposium on Emerging Trends in VLSI Systems Design ISVLSI'04 2004
[5] Nordstrõm T., Svensson B.: Using and Designing Massively Parallel Computers for Artificial Neural Networks Journal of Parallel and Distributed Processing 1992 260-285

Improved Blocks for CMOS Analog Neuro-fuzzy Network

Weizhi Wang and Dongming Jin

Institute of Microelectronics,
Tsinghua University, 100084,
Beijing, China
wangwz02@mails.tsinghua.edu.cn
jdm-ime@tsinghua.edu.cn

Abstract. This paper proposes several improved CMOS analog circuits for neuro-fuzzy network, including Gaussian-like membership function circuit, minimization circuit, and a centroid algorithm defuzzier circuit without using division. A two-input/one-output neuro-fuzzy network composed of these circuits is implemented and testified for non-linear function approximating. HSPICE simulation results show that all the proposed circuits provide characteristics of high operation capacity, high speed, simple structures, and high precision. They are very suitable for rapid implementation of neuro-fuzzy networks.

1 Introduction

General researches on neuro-fuzzy systems mainly focus on the software implementations, which typically operate below K flips rate (flips stands for fuzzy logic inferences per second) [1]. It is not fast enough for many high-speed control problems such as automotive engines control [2]. Hardware systems using IC technology provide an alternative to overcome this drawback. Particularly, the analog domain is worth considering for these applications, providing parallel processing with a speed limited only by the delay of signals through the network so that it has intrinsically higher speed and lower power consumption than their digital counterparts [3]. And the non-linear characteristics of transistors are functionally apt to the implementations of non-linear processing of neuro-fuzzy systems, i.e. only a few transistors are needed for an analog functional block which is usually much less than that for a digital one [4].

In this paper, several improved analog voltage-mode functional blocks are proposed, composed of which a neuro-fuzzy network is designed and its validity is also proved by approximating a non-linear function. All the circuits can be fabricated with the CMOS single-poly scaled technologies, using MOS transistors as the only primitive circuit so as to be compatible with the conventional digital circuitry that may be needed to integrate together with the fuzzy circuitry for complex control tasks such as adaptive control. Finally, the related HSPICE simulation results (for 0.18μm CMOS mixed-signal technology provided by SMIC) are presented to illustrate performance of the proposed circuits.

2 Blocks of Mamdani Model Based Neuro-fuzzy Network

Referring to the Mamdani model based neuro-fuzzy network shown in Fig. 1, the catalog of functional blocks can be identified [5].

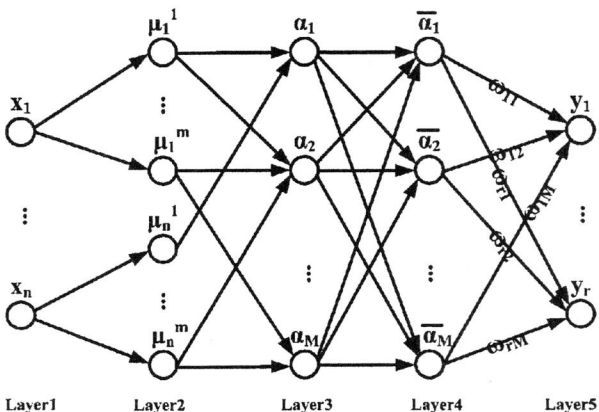

Fig. 1. Architecture of the general neuro-fuzzy network based on Mamdani model

- Gaussian membership function block for layer 2, whose input is voltage variable vector and output is the matrix of matching degrees.
- Minimization block for layer 3, which maps the matrix of matching degrees into the vector of firing rule activities.
- Defuzzier block for layer 4 and layer 5, generally using the centroid algorithm, calculating the average firing activity of its corresponding rule and aggregating the consequent outcome to obtain the inferred output.

2.1 Gaussian Membership Function Circuit

It's hard to implement the exact Gaussian shape membership function, as shown in Eq. (1), with CMOS circuits:

$$\mu(x) = e^{-\frac{(x-c)^2}{2\sigma^2}} \qquad (1)$$

where c is the mean of the Gaussian curve and is the breath. A bell-like function circuitry was introduced in [1]. Based on similar principle, an improved circuit of programmable Gaussian-like membership function circuit is designed in Fig. 2.

During V_{IN} increasing, the drain current of M2 I_{D2}, as well as I_{D5}, changes from zero to I_{SS}, assuming M1, M2, M5 and M6 are identical and I_1, I_2 are equal to I_{SS}. Output current I_{OUT} is always doubling the difference of the two drain currents I_{D2} and I_{D5}. When the transistors operating in the saturation region, from the square-law, I_{D2} and I_{D5} can be derived as Eq. (2). If reference voltage E_1 is set below E_2, I_{D2} would approach I_{SS}

ahead of I_{D5}, which imply that the waveform of I_{OUT} can be alike as Gaussian curve. So changing the values of the control voltages E_1 and E_2 can change the mean and breadth of the output Gaussian-like voltage curve, R and I_{SS} determining the amplitude. The input voltage is applied to the gates of M2 and M5, the W/L of which will decide the slope of each side of the Gaussian-like curve. Fig. 3 shows the HSPICE simulation result. In this simulation, W/L for all transistors are 7/3.5, and R is about 93k. The difference between control voltage E_1 and E_2 is fixed as 200mV, and the voltage of E_1 changes from –1V to 1V.

$$I_{OUT} = 2(I_{D2} - I_{D5}), \quad I_{Di} = \frac{I_{SS}}{2} \alpha_i \sqrt{2\beta_i - \alpha_i^2 \beta_i^2}$$

$$\alpha_i = \frac{|V_{IN} - V_{REFi}|}{V_{TH}}, \quad \beta_i = \frac{1}{2} \mu C_{ox} \frac{W V_{TH}^2}{L_i I_{SS}}, i = 2,5 \tag{2}$$

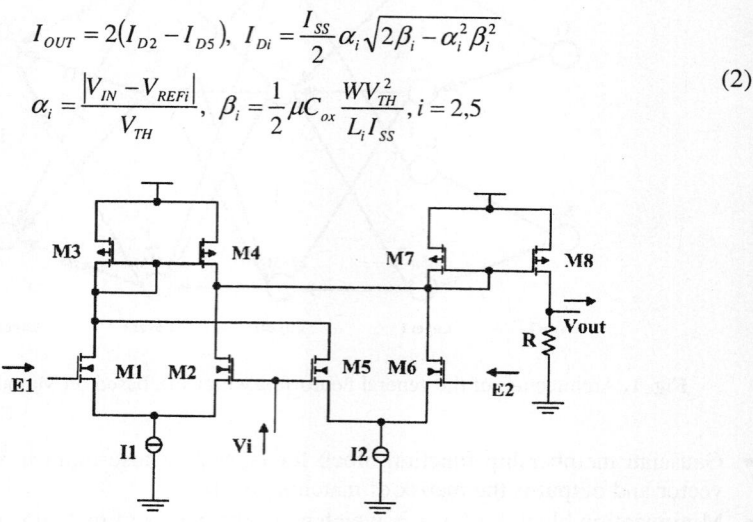

Fig. 2. Proposed Gaussian-like membership function circuit. M1-M8 are identical, E_1 is set below E_2, I_1 and I_2 are equal to I_{SS}.

2.2 Minimization Circuit

A simple design of minimization CMOS circuits can be realized by parallel PMOS source followers. However it suffers from limited input and output swing and also the output level shift. A high precision, high speed minimization circuit was introduced in [6]. Some extra compensation circuits need to be added to eliminate the output level shift and to enhance the input swing as well. The final schematic circuit diagram with two input voltages is presented in Fig. 4. M5 and M11 form the based voltage source follower minimization circuit; M6 is used to cancel the output level shift. M1-M4 forms a PMOS input amplifier so that the input voltage, i.e. the output of Gaussian membership function circuit, can be low to V_{SS}. And with the feedback M1-M6, or M6-M11, construct a unity gain buffer, making the output voltage just equal to the minimization input voltage. The proposed circuit can therefore perform in very large input range with little output level shift. This circuit can be easily expanded for more voltage inputs when similar circuit structures as M1-M5 are added. Fig. 5 shows the HSPICE simulation result of the minimization circuit with three input voltages. All the transistors are of the same sizes as 7/3.5.

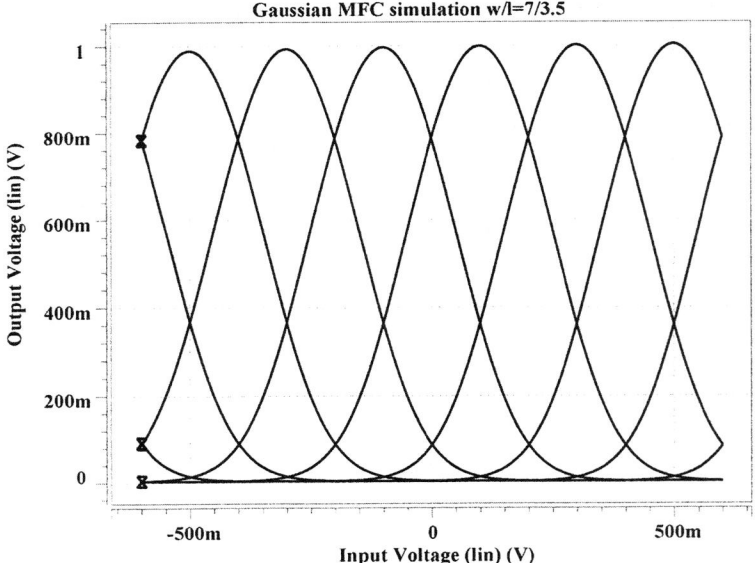

Fig. 3. An example of output voltage from proposed Gaussian-like membership function circuit with HSPICE simulation

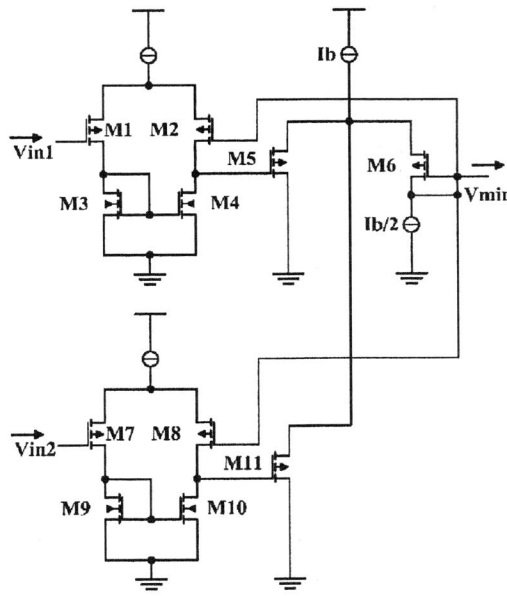

Fig. 4. Proposed minimization circuit with tow inputs, the tail currents are all equal to I_B and the drain current of M6 is always equal to $I_B/2$

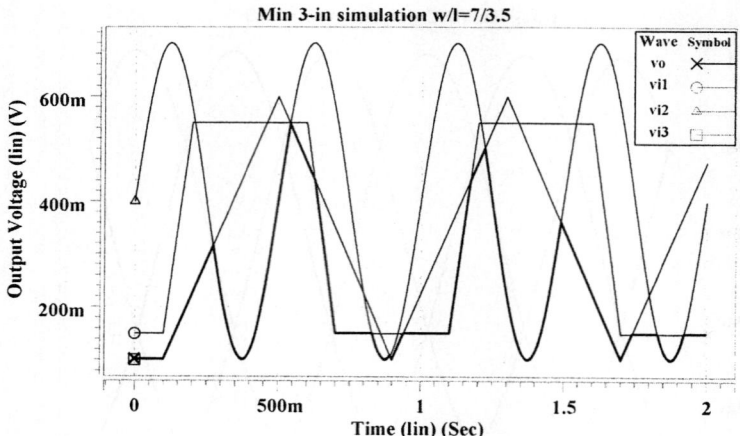

Fig. 5. HSPICE simulation result of an example of output voltage (V_O) from the proposed minimization circuit with three inputs (V_{IN1}, V_{IN2} and V_{IN3})

2.3 Defuzzier Circuit

The centroid algorithm (COA) is the most popular method for defuzzier. However, using analog dividers is impractical — analog dividers are troublesome in terms of time and area. Many of the reported fuzzy systems impose the condition that the denominator in expression added up to the value 1 to avoid the division or recur to the use of approximate normalization [1]. A convenient alternative uses parallel feedback OTAs to implement COA [7]. Unfortunately, those schemes are poor in transient response while consuming large area.

In this paper a simple defuzzier circuit is proposed, with which the COA is implemented without employing a division circuit or feedback loop. The main idea is based on parallel transconductances, as shown in Fig. 6.

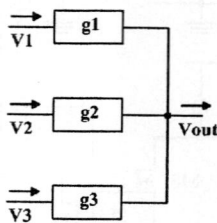

Fig. 6. Parallel transconductances circuit

The output voltage can be derived from:

$$\sum g_i (V_i - V_{OUT}) = I_{OUT} = 0 \qquad (3)$$

$$V_{OUT} = \frac{\sum g_i V_i}{\sum g_i} \qquad (4)$$

This means that the output voltage is the average value of the inputs. The contribution of each input to the output is weighted by the transconductance of g_i. Eq. (4) effectively provides a defuzzier output. Using a MOS transistor as a controllable g-element, noting that $g_{DS}=K(V_{GS}-V_{TH})$ when it operating in the deep triode region, if V_{TH} is cancelled the g_{DS} could be controlled by V_{GS} ($g_{DS}=KV_{GS}$) linearly. In Fig. 7, M3, as well as M6, acts as the controllable transconductance. M1 and M2, as well as M4 and M5, just act as a positive level shift circuit to cancel V_{TH} of M3 and M6. To eliminate body effect that would cause V_{TH} of M2 (M5) changing with the bulk potential, the bulk of M2 (M5) must connect to the source that is feasible for PMOS. Ignoring the impact of source potential, the output voltage is:

$$V_{OUT} \cong \frac{V_{IN1} \times V_1 + V_{IN2} \times V_2}{V_{IN1} + V_{IN2}} \qquad (5)$$

This circuit could also be expanded for more inputs normalization circuit when the same block as M1-M3 is added. The HSPICE simulation of three-input/one-output normalization circuit is performed. In this simulation, the weight voltages are fixed as: V_1=90mV, V_2=60mV, and V_3=20mV. And the control voltages (V_{IN1}, V_{IN2} and V_{IN3}) are summed to have waveforms shown in Fig. 8. When the weight voltages are set below 200mV, the output of the circuit would be under 200mV, so that the impact of source potential can be ignored versus V_{TH}, ensuring M3 (M6) operating in deep triode region as well. Fig. 9 shows the output waveforms of the proposed circuit compared with the ideal output. All the transistors have the same W/L as 7/3.5.

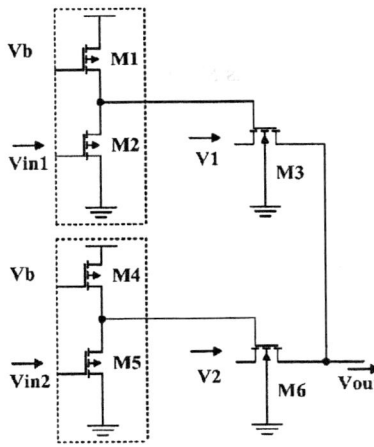

Fig. 7. Proposed COA simple-structure normalization circuit based on parallel transconductances

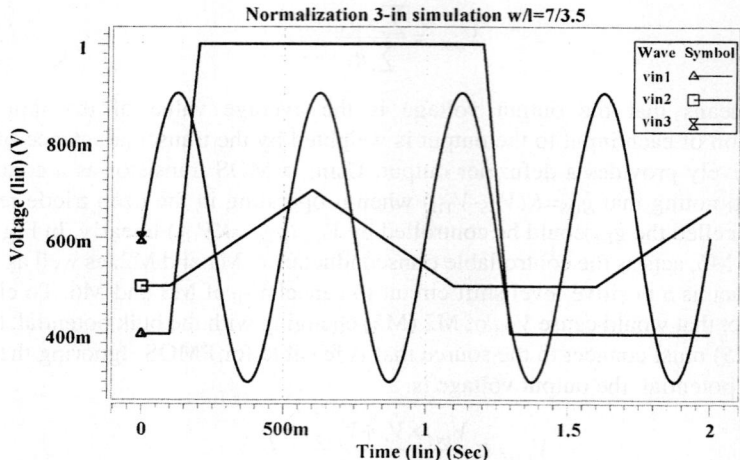

Fig. 8. Input voltages waveforms

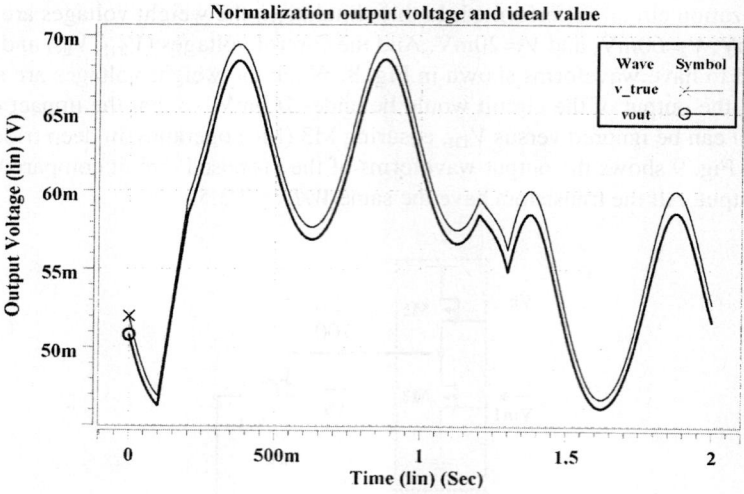

Fig. 9. HSPICE simulation output voltage (V_{OUT}) of defuzzier circuit compared with the ideal value (V_{TRUE})

3 Analog CMOS Implementation of Neuro-fuzzy Network

In this section, fuzzy functional blocks, which are described in the previous sections, are combined into a two-input/one-output neuro-fuzzy network with the block diagram as shown in Fig. 10.

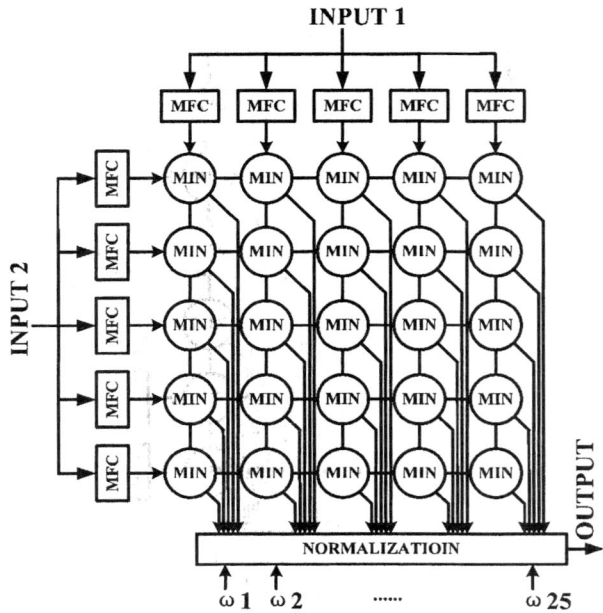

Fig. 10. Block diagram of two-input/one-output neuro-fuzzy network

Table 1. Parameters of neuro-fuzzy network (R=93kΩ and σ=0.25)

	E_1 /mV	E_2 /mV	$_i$/mV	c_i
MFC_1	-200	200	50	0
MFC_2	50	450	204	0.25
MFC_3	300	700	45	0.50
MFC_4	550	950	0	0.75
MFC_5	800	1200	169	1.00

Each input has five membership functions or linguistic terms. All membership functions have Gaussian-like shape. Parameters used for determining membership functions (voltage E_1 and E_2) are illustrated in Table I with corresponding means c_i of ideal Gaussian curves. Each R equals to 93kΩ. The breath σ of ideal Gaussian curves is 0.25.

The performance of this neuro-fuzzy network is testified as a function approximator. The approximated function is y=0.05sin(7x)+0.08 with only one variable, so one of the inputs of network must be set to V_{DD} and only five weights are needed. The values of weight ω_i are generated by Matlab, also illustrated in Table 1, applied to the neuro-fuzzy network. Fig. 11 shows the HSPICE simulation output voltage (V_{OUT}) compared with the ideal value (V_{TRUE}). Input voltage changes from 0 to 1V within 2sec. With a square wave input, the output response also shows a rise time of 200ns and a fall time of 65ns in 33.4mV~114mV. It corresponds to a speed of 5M flips including the defuzzier process. Since neuro-fuzzy inferences are performed in parallel before the defuzzier part, their inference speed does not depend on the number of fuzzy rules. This speed is in a good range for most control applications.

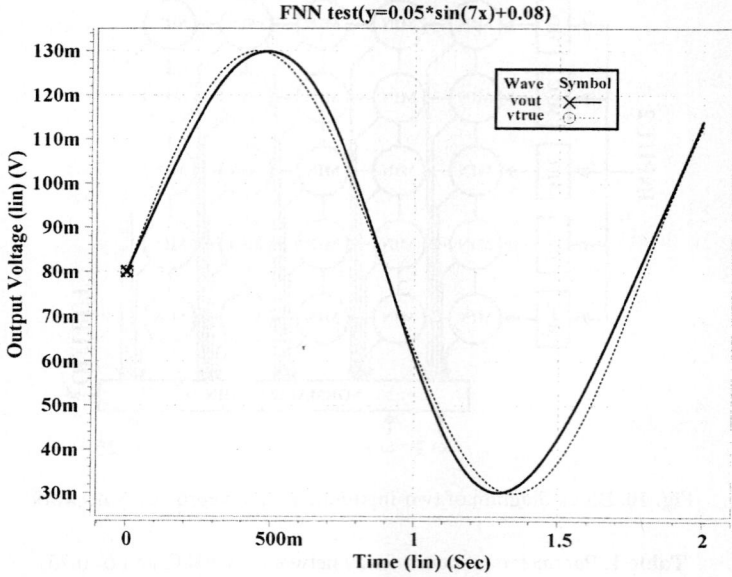

Fig. 11. HSPICE simulation result when proposed neuro-fuzzy network used to approximate a non-linear function $y=0.05\sin(7x)+0.08$

4 Conclusion

This paper proposed several improved voltage-mode CMOS analog circuits for neuro-fuzzy network. The simplicity as well as the programmability of these circuits permits increasing controller complexity, by adding rules and/or input with no extra design effort. A two-input/one-output neuro-fuzzy network is implemented and testified as non-linear function approximation. Adding software or hardware self-learning blocks, this system will be of much adaptation and practicality. Anyway, the proposed architecture provides characteristics of high operation capacity, simple structures, and high precision.

References

1. Fernando Vidal-Verdú, Manual Delgado-Restituto, Rafael Navas, and Angel Rodríguez-Vázquez: A Design Approach for Analog Neuro/Fuzzy Systems in CMOS Digital Technologies. Comput. Electr. Eng.. vol. 25 (1999) 309-337
2. Namakura K. et al.: Fuzzy Inference and Fuzzy Inference Processor. IEEE Micro. vol. 13 (1993) 37-48

3. Vittoz E. et al.: The Design of High-Performance Analog Circuits on Digital CMOS Chips. IEEE J. Solid-State Circuit. vol. 20 (1985) 657-665
4. Rajapakse, J.C., Wang, L.P. (Eds.): Neural Information Processing: Research and Development. Springer, Berlin (2004)
5. Haykin, S.: Neural Networks: A Comprehensive Foundation. Prentice Hall, New Jersey, 2nd ed. (1999)
6. Carvajal R.G., Ramirez-Angulo, and Martinez-Heredia J.: High-speed High-precision Min/Max Circuits in CMOS Technology. IEE Electron. Lett.. vol. 36 (2000) 697-699
7. Guo S., Peters L., and Surmann H.: Design and Application of an Analog Fuzzy Logic Controller. IEEE Trans. Fuzzy Syst.. vol. 5 (1996) 429-438

A Design on the Vector Processor of 2048point MDCT/IMDCT for MPEG-2 AAC

Dae-Sung Ku, Jung-Hyun Yun, and Jong-Bin Kim

Department of Electronics Engineering, Chosun University,
375 Seosuk-Dong, Dong-gu, Gwangju 501-759, Korea
vlsi@chosun.ac.kr

Abstract. High Quality CD, and DAT audio is very data intensive. Currently, the multi-channel technique is the preferred method of audio transmission. The MPEG(Moving Picture Experts Group) provides data compression technology for sound and image systems. The MPEG-2 AAC standard provides multi-channel 5.1 sound, using the same audio algorithm as MPEG-1, thus MPEG-2 audio both forward and backward compatible. The MDCT(Modified Discrete Cosine Transform)is a linear orthogonal lapped transform based on the concept of TDAC(Time Domain Aliasing Cancellation). In this paper, we propose an efficient algorithm for the optimization of the core in the audio part of the data transmission based on the MDCT/IMDCT(Inverse MDCT). This algorithm reduced the operating coefficient by overlapped area to bind. In the comparison of the original algorithm with the optimized algorithm that cosine coefficient reduced 0.5%, multiplies operating 0.098% and adds operating 0.58%. The proposed Algorithm was implemented using the C language then we designed hardware architecture of micro-programmed method it's applied to optimized algorithm. This processor was designed with the VHDL language and was synthesized using the design analyzer of SYNOPSYS, with rule checking by SADAS. This processor operates at a clock frequency of 20MHz and a voltage of 5V. Thus, the designed system can be used for systems based on other FPGA and ASIC.

1 Introduction

The technology to make an electronic communication information industry and market force came to be identical MPEG audio field. Currently, the most important technology in the field of multimedia is compression. The methods employed in audio compression, make use of the properties of the human central auditory nervous system. These method, which are based on the psychoacoustic model, utilize perceptual audio coding techniques that must not code above the limits of human perception [1]. MPEG-2 AAC(Advanced Audio Coding) is the most advanced coding scheme available for high quality audio coding. This AAC standard is the first codec system to fulfill the requirements of the ITU-R for 'indistinguishable' quality at data rates of 320 Kbits/sec for five full-bandwidth channel audio signals. The compression ratio of the AAC format is 1.4 times better than that of MPEG-1 Layer3 and the provides an audio signal that has CD tone quality at 96-128Kbits/sec, at a bitrate that is 30%

lower than that of MPEG-1 Layer3. MPEG-2 AAC is composed of Huffman coding, Quantization, scaling, MDCT, Gain control and Hybrid filter-bank. Among these different components, the most operational part is MDCT/IMDCT. MDCT technology removes the aliasing that is introduced during subband coding by means of the TDAC(Time Domain Aliasing Cancellation) method. MDCT involves time domain to frequency domain conversion, whereas reverse IMDCT involves frequency domain to time domain conversion [2,3]. MDCT has the advantage of removing the time domain aliasing by using windows that overlap by 50%. Fig 1. shows a block diagram of the MPEG/Audio encoder and decoder.

In this high-level representation, encoding closely parallels the process described above. The input audio stream passes through a psychoacoustic model that determines the signal-to-masking ratio of each subband. The bit or noise allocation block uses the signal-to-masking ratio to decide how to apportion the total number of code bits available for the quantization of the subband signals, so as to minimize the audibility of the quantization noise. Finally, the last block takes the representation of the quantized audio samples and formats the data into a decodable bit stream. The decoder simply reverses the formatting, then reconstructs the quantized subband values, and finally transforms the set of subband values into a time domain audio signal [4]. As specified by the MPEG requirements, ancillary data not necessarily related to the audio stream can also be fitted within the decoded bit stream.

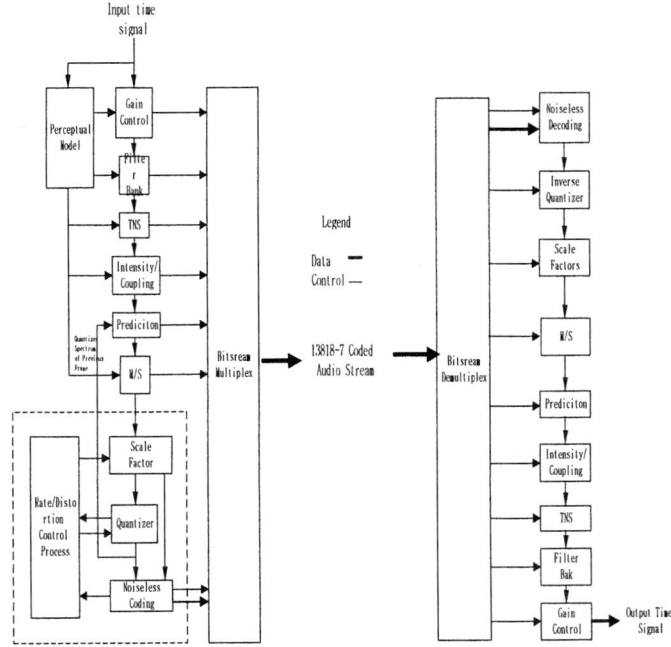

Fig. 1. MPEG-2 AAC Encoder and Decoder

This paper is organized as follows. In section 2, we describe the MDCT/IMDCT algorithm and its optimization. Section 3, we describe an efficient system design using the vector program method. Section 4, discuss the design implementation and experimental results. The results of the simulation and verifications are given in section 5, along with our conclusions.

2 MDCT/IMDCT

In this section, we briefly discuss the concept of the MDCT/IMDCT algorithm, as well as the architecture, operation and specifications based on this concept. The MDCT is a time domain data to frequency domain conversion algorithm, whereas the reverse IMDCT is a frequency data to time domain conversion algorithm. The MDCT combines critical sampling with the good frequency resolution provided by a sine window and the computational efficiency of a fast FFT like algorithm [5].

Typically 128 to 512 equally spaced bands are used. The MDCT also offers the possibility of changing the block length of the transform dynamically. For very dynamic input signals, a short block length keeps the quantization error local in time, while for quasi static signals a long block length provides good frequency resolution. The MDCT and IMDCT algorithms employ a technique called time-domain aliasing cancellation. The equation of the MDCT is

$$X(i,k) = 2 \cdot \sum_{n=0}^{N-1} x(i,n) \cos(\frac{2\pi}{N}(n+n_0)(k+\frac{1}{2}))$$
$$\text{for } 0 \leq k < \frac{N}{2} \quad (1)$$

The equation of the Inverse MDCT is

$$X(i,k) = \frac{2}{N} \cdot \sum_{n=0}^{\frac{N}{2}-1} x(i,k) \cos(\frac{2\pi}{N}(n+n_0)(k+\frac{1}{2}))$$
$$\text{for } 0 \leq k < N \quad (2)$$

Methods (1) and (2) are essentially the same, except for the length of the coefficient and the multiplexing factor 2, and 2/N, respectively, which are used after accumulating. Fig 2 shows the MDCT windows transition between the long and short block modes. The length of the short block is one third that of the long block. In the short block mode, three short blocks replace a single long block, so that the number of MDCT samples per frame of audio samples remains unchanged, regardless of the block size. For a given frame of audio samples, the MDCTs can all have the same block length (long or short) or a mixed-block mode. In the mixed-block mode, the MDCTs for the two lower frequency subbands have long blocks, while the MDCTs for the 30 upper subbands have short blocks. This mode provides better frequency resolution for the lower frequencies, where it is needed the most, without sacrificing the time resolution for the higher frequencies [6]. The switch between long and short blocks is not instantaneous however. A long block with s specialized long-to-short or short-to-long data window serves as the transition between the long and short block types. Because the MDCT processing of a subband signal provides better frequency resolution, it has poorer time resolution. The MDCT operates on 12 or 36 polyphase filter samples, so that the effective time window of the audio samples involved in this processing is 12 or 36 times larger [7]. The MDCT/IMDCT coefficients are selected in a lookup table according to the block type, long, long-short, short, or short-long. Similarly, the windows table corresponding to this block type is selected in order to improve the individual subband isolation, and we used the delay component of z^{-18} for the 50% overlapped windows in the time domain.

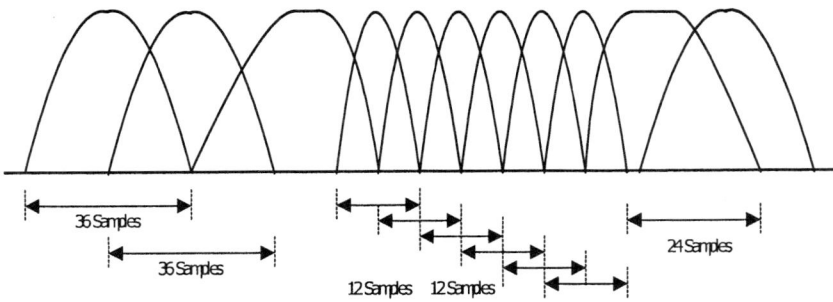

Fig. 2. The arrangement of overlapped MDCT windows

2.1 MDCT/IMDCT Algorithm Optimization

Several MDCT/IMDCT algorithms are known based on (1) and (2). Equation (1) applies to (2) of optimization. Equation (3) shows that Cosine coefficient applied to an exponential function.

$$\cos(\frac{2\pi}{N}(n+n_0)(k+\frac{1}{2})) = e^{j\frac{2\pi}{N}(n+n_0)(k+\frac{1}{2})}$$
$$= C_N^{(n+n_0)(k+\frac{1}{2})} \qquad (3)$$

$$e^{j\frac{2\pi}{N}} = C_N$$

Therefore, (3) can be represented by (4)

$$X(i,k) = 2 \cdot \sum_{n=0}^{N-1} x(i,n) C_n^{(n+n_0)(k+\frac{1}{2})}$$
$$= C_N^{n_0(k+\frac{1}{2})} \sum_{N=0}^{N-1} x(i,n) C_N^{n(k+\frac{1}{2})} \qquad (4)$$

(4) can be split into even and odd domains.

$$X(i,k) = C_N^{n_0(k+\frac{1}{2})} [\sum_{even} x(i,n) C_N^{n(k+\frac{1}{2})} + \sum_{odd} x(i,n) C_N^{n(k+\frac{1}{2})}]$$

$$= C_N^{n_0(k+\frac{1}{2})} [\sum_{r=0}^{(N/2)-1} x(i,2r) C_N^{2r(k+\frac{1}{2})} + \sum_{r=0}^{(N/2)-1} x(i,2r+1) C_N^{(2r+1)(k+\frac{1}{2})}] \quad (5)$$

$$= C_N^{n_0(k+\frac{1}{2})} [\sum_{r=0}^{(N/2)-1} x(i,2r) C_N^{2r(k+\frac{1}{2})} + C_N^{(k+\frac{1}{2})} \sum_{r=0}^{(N/2)-1} x(i,2r+1) C_N^{2r(k+\frac{1}{2})}]$$

Equation (5) is converted N point MDCT into an N/2 point MDCT.

$$X(i,k) = C_N^{n_0(k+\frac{1}{2})} [\sum_{r=0}^{(N/2)-1} x(i,2r) C_{N/2}^{r(k+\frac{1}{2})} + C_N^{(k+\frac{1}{2})} \sum_{r=0}^{(N/2)-1} x(i,2r+1) C_{N/2}^{r(k+\frac{1}{2})}] \quad (6)$$

Equation (6) can be split into even and odd areas.

$$E(i,k) = \sum_{r=0}^{(N/2)-1} x(i,2r) C_{N/2}^{r(k+\frac{1}{2})}$$

$$O(i,k) = \sum_{r=0}^{(N/2)-1} x(i,2r+1) C_{N/2}^{r(k+\frac{1}{2})} \quad (7)$$

$$X(i,k) = C_N^{n_0(k+\frac{1}{2})} [E(i,k) + C_N^{(k+\frac{1}{2})} O(i,k)]$$

A flowchart representing equation (7) is shown in Fig 3.

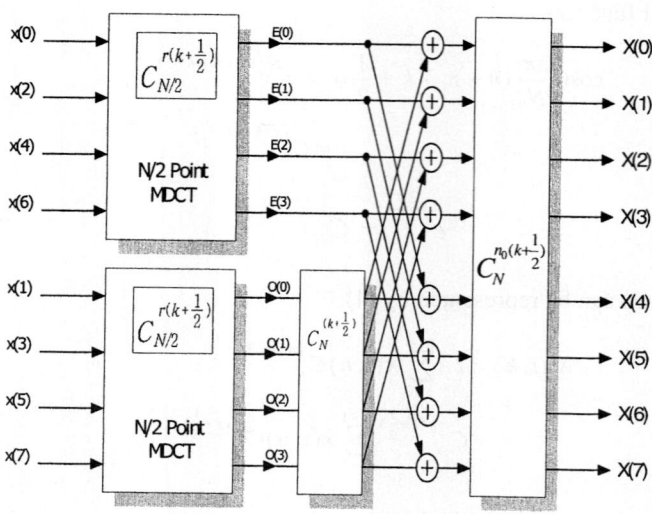

Fig. 3. N/2 point MDCT Flowchart

In order to use this method, we have to split each even and odd area that E(i,k) and O(i,k).

$$E(i,r) = \sum_{r=0}^{(N/2-1)} e(i,r) C_{N/2}^{r(k+\frac{1}{2})}$$

$$= \sum_{m=0}^{(N/4-1)} e(i,2m) C_{N/2}^{2m(k+\frac{1}{2})} + \sum_{m=0}^{(N/4-1)} e(i,2m+1) C_{N/2}^{(2m+1)(k+\frac{1}{2})}$$

$$= \sum_{m=0}^{(N/4-1)} e(i,2m) C_{N/4}^{m(k+\frac{1}{2})} + C_{N/2}^{(k+\frac{1}{2})} \sum_{m=0}^{(N/4-1)} e(i,2m+1) C_{N/4}^{m(k+\frac{1}{2})}$$

$$= G(i,k) + C_{N/2}^{k+\frac{1}{2}} H(i,k) \qquad (8)$$

$$G(i,k) = \sum_{m=0}^{(N/4)-1} e(i,2m) C_{N/4}^{m(k+\frac{1}{2})}$$

$$H(i,k) = \sum_{m=0}^{(N/4)-1} e(i,2m+1) C_{N/4}^{m(k+\frac{1}{2})}$$

Also, it is representative of an N/4 point MDCT when N/2 is odd.

$$O(i,k) = \sum_{r=0}^{(N/2)-1} x(i,2r+1) C_{N/2}^{r(k+\frac{1}{2})}$$

$$= \sum_{m=0}^{(N/4)-1} o(i,2m) C_{N/2}^{2m(k+\frac{1}{2})} + \sum_{m=0}^{(N/4)-1} o(i,2m+1) C_{N/2}^{(2m+1)(k+\frac{1}{2})} \qquad (9)$$

$$= \sum_{m=0}^{(N/4)-1} o(i,2m) C_{N/4}^{m(k+\frac{1}{2})} + C_{N/2}^{k+\frac{1}{2}} \sum_{m=0}^{(N/4)-1} o(2m+1) C_{N/4}^{m(k+\frac{1}{2})}$$

A flowchart representing equation (9) is shown in Fig 4.

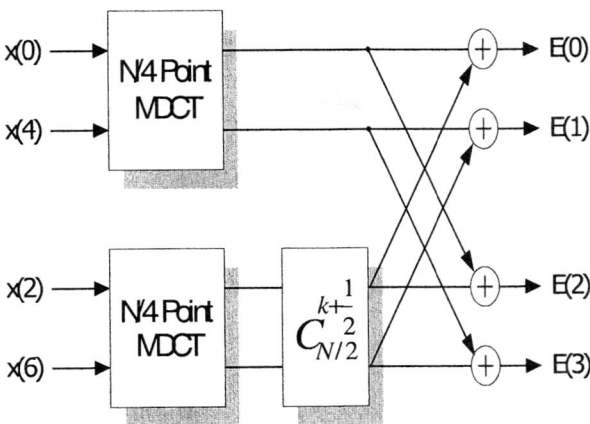

Fig. 4. N/4 point MDCT Flowchart

We used an N/4 point MDCT to express an N/8 point MDCT. The operation course like there, a minimum operation element a to be used multiplies the factor in the even domain of the 2 inputs and adds. The N/8 point MDCT is shown in Fig 5.

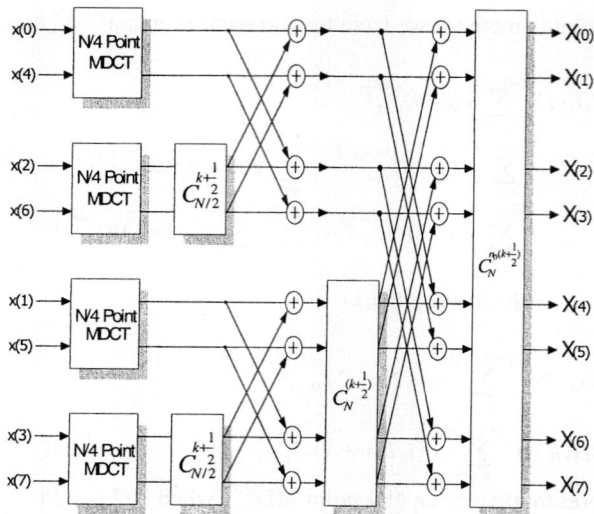

Fig. 5. N/8 point MDCT Flowchart

In the case of MPEG-2 AAC, performs on the maximum 2048 MDCT that necessary coefficient number is 2048, but used to this algorithm 10 memory words are necessary for the hardware implementation of $p = (\log_2 2048) - 1$. If N=2048 and, k=2068 in a 2048-point MDCT, then the total multiplexing is 10,400. Compared with the original algorithm, the number of operations is reduced by 400 times. The minimum operational flowchart is shown in Fig 6.

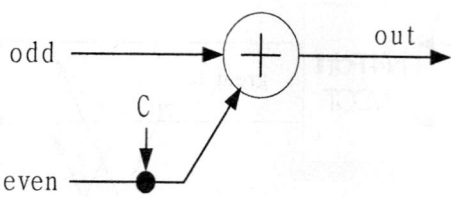

Fig. 6. The minimum operational elements of the MDCT

2.2 The Minimization of the MDCT/IMDCT Operation

In this paper, we reduced the number of coefficients required to bind the overlapping part of the MDCT/IMDCT operation. A normalization course is to find the rule in the course of the II paragraph as adapt to P-step in $N = 2^p$. That is the product operation p-step is $\log_2 N$. MDCT coefficients value of N block to represents $N/2^p$ point MDCT, because MDCT coefficients has p-step in $p = \log_2 N$. In this paper, the MDCT coefficients is necessary to cosine (256x), cosine(128x), cosine(64x), cosine(32x), cosine (16x), cosine(8x), cosine(4x), cosine(2x). Therefore, the first term coefficient value unconditional 2 number and number degree of next step need coefficient value. In the case of a 2048 point MDCT, the total number of coefficients is $\log_2 2048 = 11$. Consequently, 2048 points MDCT calculate in coefficient value of twelve numbers. Also, input sequence of each steps apply to inverse bit sequence as output of front step appear correct sequence.

Also the MDCT minimum operation element has accomplish N/2 of each steps. Therefore, the memory need for N/2. The coefficient quantity of necessary for the operation factor was reduced innovatively in the course such as this paragraph. The next executes the optimization about a cosine coefficient index K of the equation 1. A reduce of operation is able to K. A coefficient index is altered according to the change of K index, A degrade the operation quantity if it has the duplicate part if we are according to the change of K. A cycle about step p is 2p because cycle about p is $C_2^{(n+n_0)(k+\frac{1}{2})}$, $C_4^{(n+n_0)(k+\frac{1}{2})}$, $C_8^{(n+n_0)(k+\frac{1}{2})}$, ... $C_{2^n}^{(n+n_0)(k+\frac{1}{2})}$.

Every step is connected to the addition in Fig 3 and the equation 3 is remains cosine function as final result part use quantity part. The cycle is 2^{p-1}, because use a cycle attribute of cosine function exception symbol element. A table 1 expresses the output value according to an index factor.

3 System Design of Vector Program

The MDCT requires many cumulative operation relatively, about high precision 96dB is desired compared with an image data. Therefore, this system use floating point multiplier and adder to satisfy a precision 96dB about maximum 2048 point MDCT, multiplier has exponent 6bit and mantissa 24bit, and adder used floating-point addition which have exponent 6bit and mantissa 56bit to cumulative addition can do the chance of multiplication result. The exponent has dynamic range and mantissa designed a plan sufficiently great to reduce the error of mantissa operation. The mantissa of adder is 56bit. This is keep throw mantissa when cumulative addition is multiplication output from adder because do not use MAC specially.

In this paper, multiplier and adder designed a plan all pipeline to operation speed optimization. The Addition structure of used mantissa multiplication of pipeline radix-4 booth multiplier is desired adder which mantissa input bit width have double when parallel booth multiply. But in this paper, 24bit radix-4 booth multiplier is consisting of addition tree by 26bit adder, used last node 31bit adder of addition tree. Fig 7 shows that structure of 56bit floating point adder. In this paper, 56bit FP-Adder is used CSA (Carry Save Adder). The reason of CSA method uses that it is not consume pipeline stage.

Pre-normalizer assumes by floating point number to become barrel shifter inputting, pre/post normalizer used each 46bit barrel shifter. Vector instruction is defined micro-program instruction as a basis operation element which accomplishes with the multiplier to the adder.

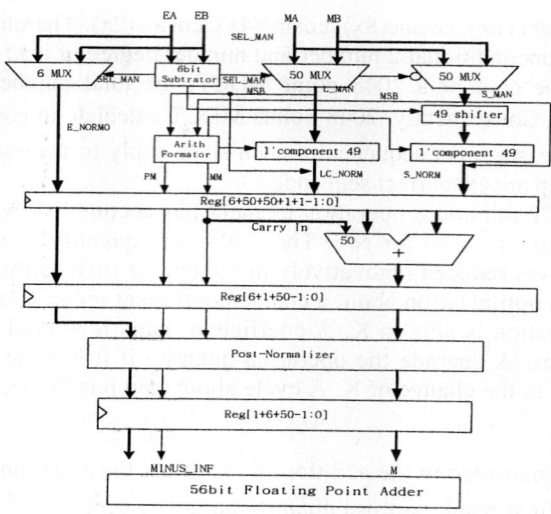

Fig. 7. The architecture of 56bit floating point adder

The vector controller of micro-program method is shown in Fig 8. The features of such structure, the operation that the user wants to accomplish as defined micro-program instruction of the best suited taking the hazard into account. We are based on the basis instruction make the application program operate, it's can display a processor performance of the best suited. This processor is able to implement flexible processor like software.

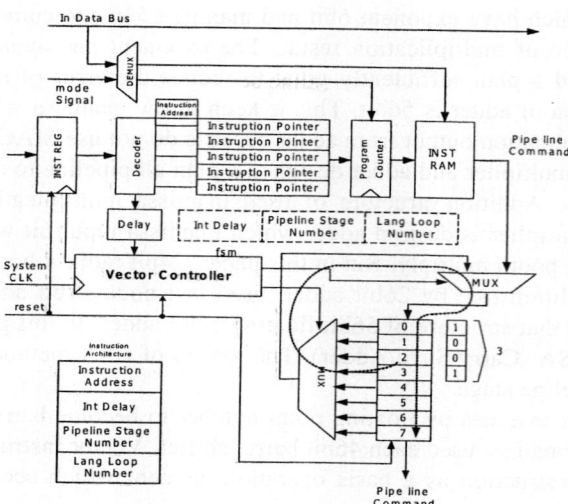

Fig. 8. Vector instruction controller

Total system is consists of FP-Adder, FP-multiplier, input/output buffer instead of Vector register, a hazard control programming delay controller, and Vector instruction controller of micro-program method. The Buffers to instead of the vector register is not overhead to operation because buffers operate outside Synchronous RAM by interface. The total structure of Vector-MDCT processor is shown in Fig 9.

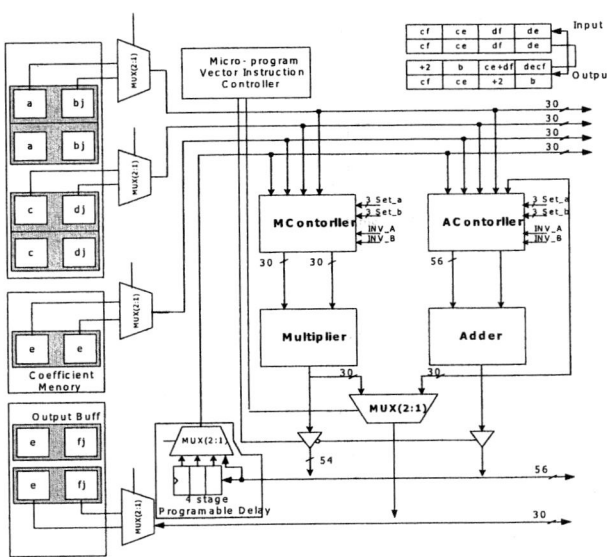

Fig. 9. Vector MDCT processor block diagram

The pipeline scheduling method of MDCT/IMDCT operation element is shown in Fig 10. The above scheduling is the pipeline scheduler that an operative removal the pipeline hazard used to MDCT/IMDCT.

ce	df	de	cf
-	ce+a	+df	de+b	+cf

	1	2	3	4	5	6	7	8	9	10	11	12
MR1	ce	df	de	cf								
MR2		ce	df	de	cf							
MR3			ce	df	de	cf						
TM1				ce	df	de	cf					
TM2					ce	df	de	cf				
TM3						ce	df	de	cf			
AR1						ce-df	de+cf	+a	+B			
AR2							ce-df	de+cf	+a	+B		
AR3								ce-df	de+cf	+a	+B	

Fig. 10. The scheduling of the operation elements

The FP-Adder and FP-Multiplier all input data is operates in rising edge and output result is falling edge. The hazard is controlled by program delay. The case which we multiply the complex number of 1unit with the complex number of 2unit and add to be the operation.

4 Design Implementation and Experimental Results

In this paper, the system to be implemented the user uses an outside ROM at an initialization and a defined a vector instructions. It was the low in the operate mode so that an application program which mixes this could be executed. The controller organized of an Instruction RAM, Instruction Pointer, Vector instructions ring buffer and Shifter. The MDCT input data and the value to express the output data of MDCT operation as shown in fig 11.

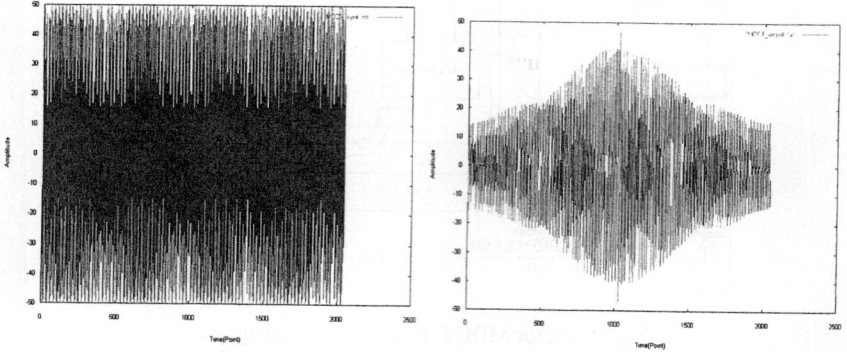

Fig. 11. The MDCT input and output data

We see a result waveform of the simulation confirmed the part to be overlapped on another up. The SHMOO test simulation result is shown in Fig 12.

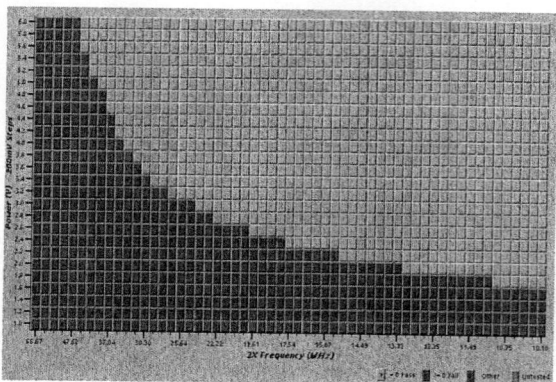

Fig. 12. The SHMOO test simulation result

In this paper, algorithm verification is used C language and data represents used the GNU-Plot. The synthesis of a gate level used the SYNOPSYS. Multiplier and adder perform on the independent operation. In this case, one clock cycle has two outputs. This processor operates at a clock frequency of 20 MHz and a voltage of 5V. The processor is designed with VHDL language and synthesis by design analyzer of synopsys, rule checked by SADAS. Verilog-XL of cadence performs on the functional and timing simulation, Pre/Post layout simulation. Thus, the designed system can be used for systems based on other FPGA and ASIC.

5 Conclusions

In this paper, the MDCT/IMDCT algorithm is an optimized of used MPEG-2 AAC and this processor is designed using vector program method. We optimize a standard algorithm so that the processing was possible to a 0.25% operation. I.e., we showed efficiency in the 0.098% of multiplication and 0.58% of addition compared with the optimization. 30bit FPU multiplier and 56bit FPU adder designed high precision and high speed to treat sufficiently until other operation of MPEG-2 AAC in designed process. In this paper, the core has general DSP architecture that consists of 40,000 gates. This processor able to process 2048-point MDCT/IMDCT of MPEG-2 AAC within 5000 cycle, TNS 38 tap filter of AAC within 10,000 cycle and 2048 FFT within 12,000 cycle. Designed system accomplished with pipeline method, a control unit design is very much to situation of designer because pipeline instruction and pipeline scheduling define user of all system.

Also, situation of user uses application program by exchange binary without development again application program by exchange instructions. The designed MDCT/IMDCT Vector processor is adapted to core of digital broadcasting.

References

1. 1. M. ITU-R Document TG10-2/3-E only, "Basic Audio Quality Requirements for Digital Audio Bit-Rate Reduction Systems for Broadcast Emission and Primary Distribution", 28 October 1991.
2. ISO/IEC JTC1/SC29/WG11 N1650, "IS 13818-7(MPEG-2 Advanced Audio Coding, AAC)" April 1997, p3.
3. "Presented at the 101st Convention 1996 November 8-11 Los Angeles, California", An Audio Engineering Society PREPRINT. P284.
4. Mark Kahrs, Karlheinz Brandenburg, "APPLICATIONS OF DIGITAL SIGNAL PROCESSING TO AUDIO AND ACOUSTICS", 1998 by Kluwer Academic Publishers.
5. T. Mochizuki, "Perfect Reconstruction Conditions for Adaptive Blocksize MDCT", Trans. IEICE, vol. E77-A, no. 5, pp.894-899. May 1994.
6. J. Princen, A. Jhonson, A. Bradely: "Subband/Transform Coding Using Filter Bank Designs Based on Time Domain Aliasing Cancellation", Proc. of the ICASSP 1987, pp. 2161 –2164.
7. Vijay K. Madisetti "VLSI digital signal processors An Introduction to Rapid Prototyping and Design Synthesis" *IEEE PRESS*.

Neuron Operation Using Controlled Chaotic Instabilities in Brillouin-Active Fiber Based Neural Network in Smart Structures

Yong-Kab Kim[1], Jinsu Kim[1], Soonja Lim[1], and Dong-Hyun Kim[2]

[1] School of Electrical Electronics & Information Engineering, Wonkwang University,
344-2. Sinyong-Dong, Iksan, Chon-Buk 570-749, Korea
ykim@wonkwang.ac.kr
http://www.forlab.wonwang.ac.kr
[2] Department of Mechanical Engineering, Wonkwang University,
344-2. Sinyong-Dong, Iksan, Chon-Buk 570-749, Korea
ncatcello@hanmail.net

Abstract. In this paper the neuron operation using stimulated Brillouin scattering (SBS) in optical fiber is described. The inherent optical feedback by the backscattered Stokes wave in optical fiber leads to instabilities in the form of optical chaos. At low power, the nature of the Brillouin instability can occur below threshold. At high power, the temporal evolution above SBS threshold is periodic and can become chaotic. Control of chaos induced transient instability in Brillouin-active fiber is experimentally implemented with Kerr nonlinearity having a non-instantaneous response in netowork systems. Controlling chaotic instabilities can lead to multistable periodic states; create optical logic '*on*' or high level "*1*" or '*off*, or low level "*0*". It can be used in neural networks. It can also lead, in principle, to large memory capacity.

1 Introduction

It is well known that optical fibers have potential usage in diverse fields [1] other than optical communications, such as expanding research in versatile fiber optic sensors. Our research has also focused on integrating fiber optic sensors with actuation materials to create a system that is capable of sensing, and controlling shape or orientation of the medium with respect to its environment, as a first step in creating a smart sensor structure. Specifically, we have focused on configuring and developing a Stimulated Brillouin Scattering (SBS) sensing system that behaves as a neural network, capable of learning by experience, predicting future reactions to environmental changes, and executions as prescribed.

Such a smart sensor system can potentially implement a massively parallel computational architecture with its attendant reduction in processing time while managing the complexity of the system, i.e. the sensing/actuation grid. Our SBS network would learn the correct "algorithms" by example during training and have the ability to generalize to untrained inputs after training is completed. The inputs to the network are the fiber optic sensor signal outputs, and the network outputs are the control signals for actuation controls. The true advantage of this system for application to smart sensor structures lies both in its capability to analyze complex sensor signal patterns and its speed in generating the appropriate control signal for the actuators. The key lies in the implementation of a neuron operation using SBS in optical fiber.

2 SBS Based Neuron

Nonlinear effects in optical fibers, specifically stimulated Brillouin scattering (SBS), has emerged as a versatile tool for the design of active optical devices for all-optic in-line switching, channel selection, amplification and oscillation, as well as in optical sensing, and optical communications[2], [3], [4]. The backward nature of SBS scattered light, with a frequency shift equal to that of the laser induced acoustic wave in the fiber (known as the Stokes or Brillouin shift), has long been viewed as an ultimate intrinsic loss mechanism in long haul fibers [5], [6]. The very backscattering nature of this nonlinear process and the existence of a threshold provide potential optical device functions, such as optical switching, arithmetic and neural functions.

An artificial neuron, used in neural network research, can be thought of as a device with multiple inputs and single or multiple outputs. The inputs to a neuron are weighted signals. The neuron adds the weighted signals, compares the result with a preset value, and activates if the sum exceeds threshold. In the nonlinear optical phenomenon, the system's combined weighted signals also produce an output if the weighted sum is greater than the threshold. A typical neuron is illustrated in Fig. 1.

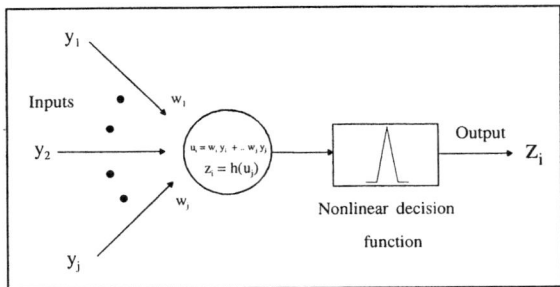

Fig. 1. A simplified multi-layered feedward neural network; the processing node between interconnects, where weighted sums are fed to a threshold decision-processing element

The system through SBS mixing combines weighted signals to produce an output if the weighted sum exceeds the threshold. The threshold decision is made by an individual neuron in conjunction with weighted inputs from other neurons.

A theoretical SBS based neural network, utilizing SBS threshold sensing with an embedded sensor is shown in Fig.2. [7]

The arithmetic building block of energy addition and subtraction (normally difficult to perform), as in Fig.2, can conceivably be accomplished by the SBS process, which involves energy transfer between waves. Thus, if two waves at a frequency difference equal to the Stokes downshift of the fiber propagate in the fiber in opposite directions, then energy is "subtracted" from the higher frequency wave and "added" to the lower frequency wave. If three waves are present in a fiber with equal Stokes shifts, then the wave at the middle frequency will receive energy from the higher frequency wave and lose energy to the lower frequency wave. Practical implementation of this scheme calls for all the waves to be generated by the same laser, since the Brillouin shifts are typically very small.

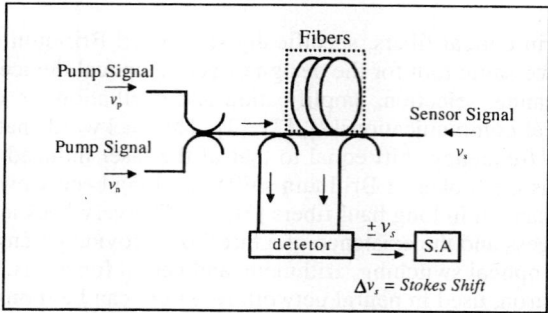

Fig. 2. SBS implementation of threshold logic

3 SBS Threshold Logic Theory

Since the Stokes shift is small, the wavelengths in each wave λ_p, λ_n, and λ_s are almost equal [7]. With these assumptions, the nonlinear coupled equation can be written as [6]

$$\frac{dI_p}{dz} = -\alpha I_p - g_B I_p I_s \tag{1}$$

$$-\frac{dI_s}{dz} = -\alpha I_s + g_B I_s I_p - g_B I_n Is \tag{2}$$

$$\frac{dI_n}{dz} = -\alpha I_n + g_B I_n Is \tag{3}$$

where I represents wave intensity of the pump "p", the backward Stokes wave "s" and the acoustic wave "n", and α and g_B are respectively the fiber attenuation coefficient and Brillouin gain coefficient for all the waves. In the basic optical neuron-type setup shown in Fig. 2, the input-output conditions of the waves are given as follows:

$$I_p(L) = I_p(0) e^{-\alpha L} \tag{4}$$

$$I_n(L) = I_n(0) e^{-\alpha L} \tag{5}$$

$$I_s(0) = I_s(L) e^{-\alpha L g_B L_{eff} \Delta I} \tag{6}$$

where $\Delta I = I_p(0) - I_n(0)$ and $I_p(0)$ is the pump transmission. If the net gain of the sensor signal is close to 0 dB, then $I_s(L) \approx I_s(0)$ so that $P_s(0) \approx P_s(L) \ll \alpha A_{eff}/g_b \leq p_p(0)$, where we have used $I = p/A_{eff}$, in which $A_{eff} = \pi r^2$ is the effective cross sectional area of the fiber, and p is the power. The ratio $\beta = P_s(L)/P_s(0)$ is on the order of 0.01 or less. Using pump power level for 0 dB gain, we can estimate the pump power value,

$$p_s(L) = 0.001 p_n(0) \qquad (7)$$

if $p_s = 1$ mw, the pump power $p_n(0)$ required will be 1W. The intensity level of each wave is set below the SBS threshold ($I_{th} = 21/g_b L_{eff}$) in order to avoid the generation of backward Stokes from spontaneous scattering. The stokes gain v_s versus total pump

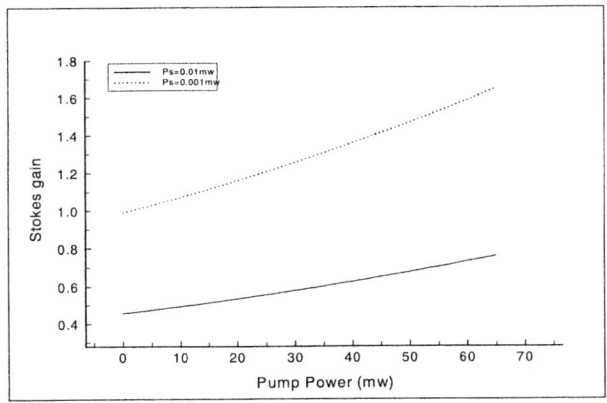

Fig. 3. Backward Stokes signal (vs) vs. pump power difference $p_p(0) - p_n(0)$

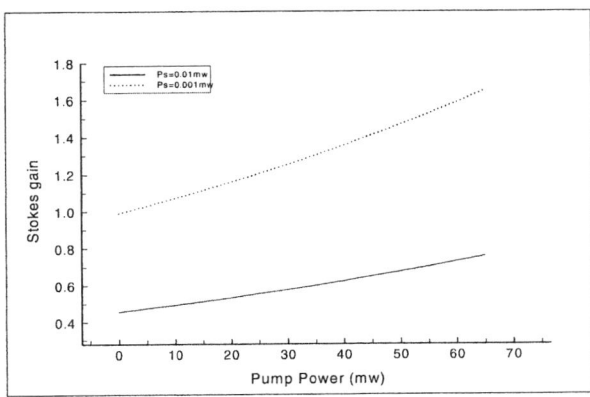

Fig. 4. Net gain of stokes signal vs. as a function of pump power. The change in stokes power is the reflected as change in the 0dB

power difference $p_p(0) - p_n(0)$ is shown in Fig.3. The gain can be converted to loss and vice versa, simply by changing the pump power levels. The output state of a neuron can be changed by changing one or both input pump intensities. The threshold of the neuron can be controlled by changing the power launched in the stokes signal as shown in the Fig.3.

Assuming $\alpha = 0.2$ *dB/km* at 1.03 *μm* and a fiber core diameter of 8*μm* by 3M. The net gain of stokes signal as a function of the pump power is shown in Fig.4, It shows a change in pump power as a change in the 0 *dB*(or 1.0) gain point. The threshold of the neuron can be controlled by changing the power launched in the Stokes signal. Thus different neurons can have different thresholds. For a single mode optical fiber, the threshold incident laser power required is on the order of 10 *mw* for 1*Km* fiber. Thus, the sensor power level should be ~10 *mw*, and the pump power level should be greater than 10 *mw*.

4 Controlling SBS Chaotic Instability

Conversion of SBS chaos induced instability to periodic effect is inspired by theory in nonlinear dynamics. The basic idea lies in the stabilization of unstable periodic orbits embedded within a chaotic attractor [8].

Since these orbits are very dense in such an attractor, a successful control may therefore serve as a generator of rich forms of periodic waves, thus turning the presence of chaos to advantage. The experimental setup for controlling SBS chaotic instability is shown in Figure 5.

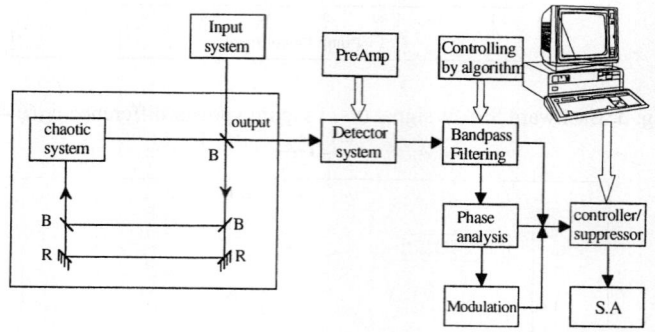

Fig. 5. Schematic diagram for controlling chaos induced instability in Brillouin-active fiber system. The optical implementation included a chaotic system configured in a fiber ring. R is the mirror reflectivity and B is beam splitter.

A stabilized *cw* probe laser operating at 1310 *nm* was used as a pump source for low scattering losses in the fiber, yielding a ≈13 *GHz* Brillouin scattering shift. We use a fiber length of 4.28 km *LITESPEC-G-ZEANQ*. Detection is also achieved with a 25*GHz IR* Photodetector Set (New Focus and an amplifier with 20*ps* impulse response) connected to a *HP* Oscilloscope. The temporal repetition rate of which corresponds to a pulse round-trip time in the fiber-ring taken to be less than 10 *nsec*.

The Brillouin pulse train amplitudes remain unstable, particularly just below pump threshold. When the observation is made using a long time scale (5µsec /division), the Brillouin output exhibits randomly distributed trains of periodic pulses. Partial stabilization of amplitude fluctuations is achieved as laser pump power approaches maximum value. These experimental features are shown in real time in Figure 6 (a) and (b).

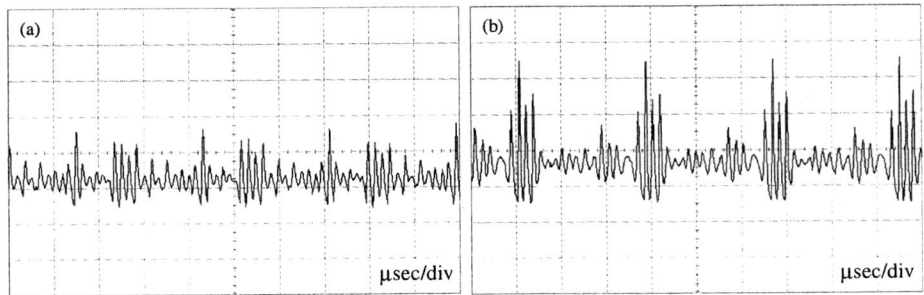

Fig. 6. Brillouin induced instabilities in function of time (5µsec/div) at threshold (a) and high above threshold (b)

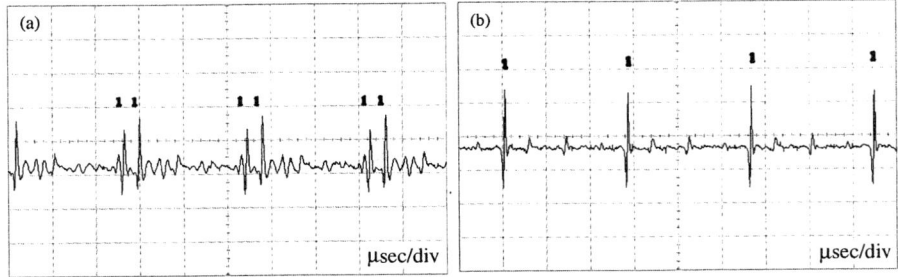

Fig. 7. Transiently controlled SBS chaos induced instabilities (5µsec/div) at threshold (a) and high above threshold (b). The examples of sequence of suppression are assigned by '0' and '1' symbols.

At low power, the Brillouin instability can occur below SBS threshold. This is much lower than the power required for normal Brillouin process, involving single pump power. The temporal evolution immediately above threshold is periodic and at lower intensities can become chaotic. We propose to employ continuous optical feedback for control in which coherent interference of the chaotic optical signal with itself, when delayed, can achieve signal differencing for feedback. If suppressing by attractor proves to control chaos then, suppressing under natural chaos can be exploited as a means of sensing structural chaos.

The examples of sequence of suppression are assigned by 'low level' and 'high level' states. Multi-stable periodic states, as shown in Figure 7 (a) and (b), can lead to logic '0' or '1' and can in principle create large memory capacity as input bit streams in TDM network systems. Its implementation still requires much engineering improvements, such as arriving at a spatial resolution that is comparable to the references or speckle, and suppression of its tendency to chaos.

5 Conclusions

Control of SBS chaos-induced transient instability in optical systems leads to logic '*on*' or '*off*' with multistable periodic states. It is theoretically possible to apply the multi-stability regimes as an optical memory device for encoding/decoding messages and complex data transmission in optical communications systems. It can also in principle create large memory capacity.

Acknowledgement

This paper was supported by Wonkwang University in 2004.

References

1. Grossman, B., Alavie, T., Ham, F., Franke, F., Thursby, M.: Fiber-optic sensor and smart structures research at Florida Institute of Technology. SPIE. **1170** (1989) 213-218.
2. Koyamada, Y., Sato, S., Nakamura, S., Sotobayashi, H., Chujo. W.: Simulating and Designing Brillouin Gain Spectrum in Single-Mode Fibers. J. of Lightwave Tech. 22(2) (2004) 631-639.
3. Bernini, R., Minardo, A., Zeni. L.: Stimulated Brillouin scattering frequency-domain analysis in a single-mode optical fiber for distributed sensing. Optics Letters. 29(17) (2004) 1977-1979.
4. Tanemura, T., Takyshima, Y., Kikuchi. K.: Narrowband optical filter, with a variable transmission spectrum, using stimulated Brillouin scattering in optical fiber. Opt. Lett. **27**(17) (2002) 1552-1554.
5. Cotter, D.: Stimulated Brillouin scattering in Monomode Optical Fiber. J. Opt. Com. **4** (1983) 10-19.
6. Agrawal, G, P.: Nonlinear Fiber Optics, 3rd, Academic press, London (2001).
7. Tariq, S., Habib, M, K.: Neural operation using stimulated Brillouin scattering in optical fiber. Opt. Eng. 37 (1998) 1823-1826.
8. Yong, K, Kim., Choon, B, Park.: Study of chaotic and instability effect of optical fiber using on the internet. SPIE. **5246** (2003) 648-655.

Parallel Genetic Algorithms on Programmable Graphics Hardware

Qizhi Yu[1], Chongcheng Chen[2], and Zhigeng Pan[1,2]

[1] College of Computer Science, Zhejiang University, Hangzhou 310027, P.R. China
qizhi.yu@gmail.com
[2] Spatial Information Research Center of Fujian Province,
Fuzhou University, Fuzhou 350002, P.R. China

Abstract. Parallel genetic algorithms are usually implemented on parallel machines or distributed systems. This paper describes how fine-grained parallel genetic algorithms can be mapped to programmable graphics hardware found in commodity PC. Our approach stores chromosomes and their fitness values in texture memory on graphics card. Both fitness evaluation and genetic operations are implemented entirely with fragment programs executed on graphics processing unit in parallel. We demonstrate the effectiveness of our approach by comparing it with compatible software implementation. The presented approach allows us benefit from the advantages of parallel genetic algorithms on low-cost platform.

1 Introduction

Genetic algorithms (GAs) are robust search algorithms inspired by the analogy of natural evolutionary processes [1]. They have demonstrated to be particularly successful in the optimization problems. As many GA solutions require a significant amount of computation time, a number of parallel genetic algorithms (PGAs) have been proposed in past decades [2][3]. These algorithms differ principally from the classical sequential genetic algorithm, but they seem to have even better optimization quality [4]. Previous proposed parallel implementations usually rely on parallel computers, distributed systems or specialized GA hardware which are not easily available to the common users. The goal of this paper is to implement PGA by utilizing graphics hardware found in PC.

The graphics processors (GPUs) on today's commodity video cards have evolved into an extremely powerful and flexible processor. Modern GPUs perform floating-point calculations much faster than today's CPUs [5]. Furthermore, instead of offering a fixed set of functions, current GPUs allow a large amount of programmability [6]. These desirable properties have attracted lots of research efforts to utilize GPUs for various non-graphics applications in recent years [7][8][9][10][11][12]. Previous research work has already shown that GPUs are especially adept at SIMD computation applied to grid data [9]. Therefore, we can envision that some type of parallel genetic algorithms should be a good fit for commodity programmable GPUs.

In this paper, we present a novel implementation of fine-grained parallel genetic algorithm on the GPU. Real-coded individuals of a population are represented as a set of 2D texture maps. We perform BLX-α crossover and non-uniform mutation by executing a fragment program on every pixel at each step in a SIMD-like fashion. Thus, when application related fitness evaluation is assumed to be implemented on GPU, the GA iterations can run entirely on GPU. We will demonstrate the effectiveness of GPU implementation by applying it to function optimization problem. Relative to software implementation, a speedup of about 15 times has been achieved with population size 512^2.

The rest of the paper is organized as follow: The subsequent section gives background of both genetic algorithms and graphics hardware to facilitate understanding of our implementation. In Section 3, we describe the proposed GPU-based implementation. Section 4 presents performance results, and the paper concludes with suggestions for future work in Section 5.

2 Background

2.1 Genetic Algorithms

A simple GA starts with a population of solutions encoded in one of many ways. The GA determines each string's strength based on an objective function and performs one or more of three genetic operators on certain strings in the population. As described in Golberg [13]: in general terms, a genetic algorithm consists of four parts.

1. Generate an initial population.
2. Select pair of individuals based on the fitness function.
3. Produce next generation from the selected pairs by applying pre-selected genetic operators.
4. If the termination condition is satisfied stop, else go to step 2.

The termination condition can be either:

1. No improvement in the solution after a certain number of generation.
2. The solution converges to a pre-determined threshold.

In real-code GA, a solution is directly represented as a vector of real-parameter decision variable [14]. This coding scheme is particularly natural when tackling optimization problems of parameters with variable in continuous domains.

It has long been noted that genetic algorithms are well suited for parallel execution. There are three main type of parallel GAs: master-slave, fine-grained, and coarse-grained [2]. In a master-slave model, there is a single population just as in sequential GA, but the evaluation of fitness is distributed among several processors. In a coarse-grained model, the GA population is divided into multiple subpopulations. Each subpopulation evolves independently, with only occasional exchanges of individuals between subpopulations. In a fine-grained model, individuals are commonly mapped onto a 2D lattice, with one individual per node. Selection and crossover are restricted to a small and overlapping neighborhood.

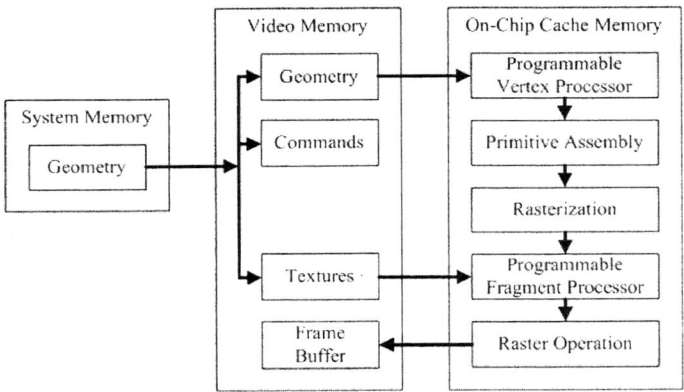

Fig. 1. The programmable graphics pipeline

2.2 Graphics Hardware

Graphics hardware is originally designed for accelerating rendering images. Figure 1 shows a simplified pipeline of modern programmable GPU. First, commands, textures, and vertex data are received from the host CPU through shared buffers in system memory or local frame-buffer memory. The vertex processor allow for a program to be applied to each vertex in the object, performing transformations and any other per-vertex operation the user specifies. Vertices are then grouped into primitives, which are point, lines, or triangles. Next, rasterization is the process of determining the set of pixels covered by a geometric primitive. After this, the results of rasterization stage, a set of fragments, are processed by a program which runs in the programmable fragment processor. Meanwhile, the programmable fragment processor also supports texturing operations which enable the processor to access a texture image using a set of texture coordinates. Finally, the raster operations stage performs a sequence of per-fragment operations immediately before updating the frame buffer.

Graphics cards hardware have features which help parallelism. A GPU contains a multiple number of pixel pipelines which process data in parallel (sixteen in our case). These pixel pipelines are each SIMD processing elements, carrying out operations typically on four color components in parallel [5].

3 A Real-Coded Parallel Genetic Algorithm on the GPU

3.1 Algorithm Overview

In this paper, we adopt the fine-grained parallel model suitable for SIMD implementation. A typical fine-grained parallel GA has been proposed and studied in [4]. We adopt a 2D toroidal grid as the spatial population structure where each grid point contains one individual. The neighborhood defined on the grid

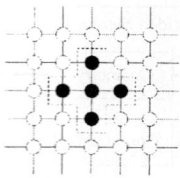

Fig. 2. Spatial population structure and neighborhood shape

always contains 5 individuals: the considered one plus the North, East, West, and South individuals (see Figure 2).

The crossover operator defines the procedure for generating a child from two parent genomes. For each individual, the best individual in its neighborhood will be selected as one of the parents, while the other one is itself.

Several crossover operators can be defined for real representation: averaging crossover, uniform crossover and blend crossover [14]. In this work, blend crossover is used. Let us assume that and are two chromosomes that have been selected to apply crossover to them. Blend crossover operator randomly selects a value for each offspring gene y_i, using a uniform distribution within the range:

$$[C_{\min} + \alpha \cdot I, C_{\max} - \alpha \cdot I]$$

where $C_{\min} = \min\{x_i^1, x_i^2\}$, $C_{\max} = \max\{x_i^1, x_i^2\}$, $I = C_{\max} - C_{\min}$, and α is the tunable parameter, the higher the value of α the more explorative the search.

Mutation operation is the final step of genetic operation. The role of mutation in GA is to restore lost or unexpected genetic material into a population to prevent the premature convergence of GA to a local result. Some of the commonly used mutation operators for real-coded GA are reviewed in [14]. In our approach, a non-uniform mutation [15] is adopted. If the operator is applied at generation step t and tmax is the maximum number of generations then the new value of the i-th gene in an individual will be:

$$y_i = \begin{cases} x_i + \delta \cdot (U_i - x_i) & \tau = 0 \\ x_i - \delta \cdot (x_i - L_i) & \tau = 1 \end{cases}$$

where τ is a random number taking value 0 or 1 with equal probability, L_i and U_i are the lower bound and upper bound of x_i, and

$$\delta = 1 - r^{(1-t/t_{\max})^b}$$

where r is a random number within the range $[0, 1]$ and b is a user defined parameter.

3.2 Representation of Population

In this section we describe the internal representation of population. If the GPU is to perform GA operators for us, the first thing we need to do is to represent

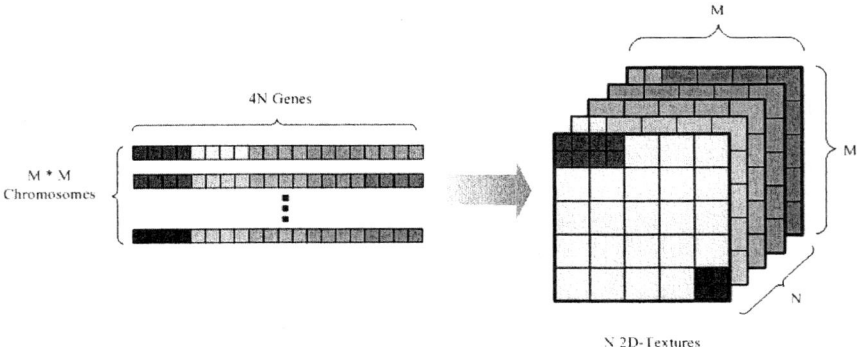

Fig. 3. The representation of chromosomes in a population as a set of 2D textures is shown

population data in a format that is accessible by the GPU. The general idea is to store population in a set of texture maps and to exploit fragment programs to implement genetic operators.

In our representation, the chromosome of each individual is sequentially divided into several segments which are distributed in a number of textures with the same position (see Figure 3). Every segment contains four genes packed into a single pixel's RGBA channels. We call those textures *population textures*. Another 2D texture map, called *fitness texture*, is used to hold the fitness scores of each individual in the population. The position of the fitness of a particular individual maps to the position of the individual in the population.

The proposed representation enables the efficient computation of genetic operators. It has several advantages: First, it naturally keeps 2D grid topology of the population described in Section 3.1. Second, for each individual, fragment programs of genetic operators only need lookup considered pixel or near neighborhood pixels in each texture map. Thus it keeps the memory footprint of each fragment as low as possible to efficiently utilize texture cache. Third, packing of four concessive genes in one texel makes use of the wide SIMD computations carried out by the GPU. Up to four times as many genes can be processed simultaneously.

3.3 Fitness Evaluation

It is important to emphasize that our framework is designed for solving problems whose fitness function can be implemented entirely in GPU. Only in this case can we avoid the bottleneck of reading population data from graphics hardware to system memory in each iteration of GA. On the other hand, executing fitness evaluation on GPU can take advantage of the GPU's parallel processing capabilities,

Implementation of fitness evaluation on GPU is application related. In some cases, such as solving function optimizer problems, fitness evaluation can be easily implemented in a single fragment program. For more complicated applications, we refer readers to a homepage of research on general purpose use of GPU (http://www.gpgpu.org). After the fragment program responsible for fitness evaluation has been executed, the fitness values are stored in fitness texture. This texture is then redisplayed in following rendering pass, and other fragment program is run to perform genetic operators.

3.4 Random Numbers Generator

As described above in Section 3.1, we can find random numbers are involved in both crossover and mutation operator. However, current graphics hardware does not provide the function for generating random numbers. We use the Linear Congruential Generator (LCG) to generate pseudo-random numbers [16]:

$$I_{j+1} = a \cdot I_j + c \pmod{m}$$

where m is called the modulus, and a and c are multiplier and the increment respectively. LCG can be implemented in a simple fragment program. We store a matrix of random numbers in a texture called *random texture*. It is updated once by the fragment program in each iteration of GA loop.

3.5 Genetic Operators

Selection, crossover and mutation operators described in Section 3.1 can be easily mapped to a single fragment program. The fragment program needs lookup *population textures*, *fitness texture* and *random texture* described in above sections. System parameters such as mutation probabilities and crossover probabilities etc. are passed to the fragment program by uniform parameters. We invoke the fragment program by rendering a screen-parallel quadrilateral. The result is written into a new population texture.

In our implementation, for a population represented by n population textures, n rendering passes have to be performed in every generation of GA. In each rendering pass, four genes of each chromosome are processed parallelly. This is possible because the crossover operator and mutation operator we used all can be performed on independent gene.

4 Experimental Results

Our performance results were measured using an AMD Athlon 2500+ CPU with 512M RAM and an NVidia GeForce 6800GT GPU. The GPU-based implementation was developed with Cg code [6]. We used the Colville minimization problem as benchmark. It is defined as:

$$f(\bar{x}) = 100(x_1^2 - x_2)^2 + (1 - x_1)^2 + 90(x_3^2 - x4)^2 + (1 - x_3)^2$$
$$+ 10.1((1 - x2)^2 + (1 - x_4)^2) + 19.8(x2 - 1)(x4 - 1)$$

Table 1. GA Parameters

Parameters	Value
Crossover Rate	1.0
Mutation Rate	0.05
Blend Crossover Parameter α	0.5
Non-uniform Mutation Parameter b	3

Table 2. Time cost and speed up for different GA module (500 generations)

Population Size	Genetic Operators			Fitness Evaluation		
	GPU(s)	CPU(s)	Speedup	GPU(s)	CPU(s)	Speedup
32^2	0.211	0.296	1.4x	0.044	0.013	0.3x
64^2	0.262	1.201	5.8x	0.046	0.062	1.4x
128^2	0.444	5.230	11.8x	0.074	0.587	7.9x
256^2	1.187	21.209	17.9x	0.176	2.725	15.4x
512^2	4.075	81.882	20.1x	0.602	10.299	17.1x

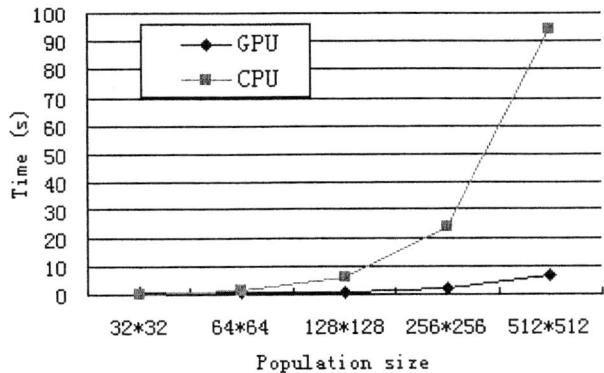

Fig. 4. The effects of population size on the run time (500 generations)

where $-18 \leq x_i \leq 10, i = 1,2,3,4$; with the global solution $(1,1,1,1)$ and $f(1,1,1,1) = 0$.

GPU-based implementation was compared with software implementation running on single CPU with different population size. GA parameters are shown in Table 1. Figure 4 shows GPU-based implementation is much faster than the software implementation. We see that speedup increases as we increase the population size. Table 2 shows performance improvement of the GPU-based implementation stems from both genetic operators and fitness evaluation. The results also show that when the population size is 32^2, fitness evaluation of GPU-based implementation is slower than that of software version. This happens because when the objective function is simple and meanwhile the population is small, the evaluation time is mainly consumed by the overhead of graphics pipeline.

5   Conclusion

In this work, we have presented a novel implementation of parallel genetic algorithms on commodity graphics hardware. Our approach gives a representation of population suitable for GPU processing. All genetic operators have been implemented on GPU. Tests on a function optimization problem show that the larger the population size is, the better speedup over the software implementation can be achieved. Our work has provided a promising platform for implementation of PGAs. Looking toward future, programmable GPUs are on a much faster performance growth than CPUs. They also have many other advantages: inexpensive, readily available, easily upgradeable, and compatible with various operating systems and hardware architectures.

There are still several constrains in our approach. For problems whose fitness function is not suitable for GPU implementation, the performance of our method will be seriously limited because of the bottleneck of transferring data between system memory and video memory in each GA loop. Another limitation is that commonly used binary encoding scheme of GAs seems hard to be implemented on the GPU because there is no bit-operator supported in current GPUs.

In the future, we will apply the presented approach in real-world problems such as GA-based image processing [17]. Another future work is further implementations of other variants of genetic algorithms. Using GPU cluster [18] to perform parallel genetic algorithms is also of interest.

Acknowlegement

This project is co-supported by 973 Program (No.2002CB312100) and Excellent Youth Teacher Program of MOE in China.

References

1. Holland, J.H.: Adaptation in Natural and Artificial Systems. MIT Press Cambridge, MA, USA (1992)
2. Tomassini, M.: A survey of parallel genetic algorithms. World Scientific **III** (1995) 87–118
3. Konfrst, Z.: Parallel genetic algorithms: advances, computing rends, applications and perspectives. In: Parallel and Distributed Processing Symposium. (2004) 162
4. Spiessens, P., Manderick, B.: A massively parallel genetic algorithms: Implementation and first analysis. In: Int. Conf. Genetic Algorithms, San Diego, Morgan Kaufmann Publishers (1991) 279–285
5. Fernando, R.: GPU Gems: Programming Techniques, Tips, and Tricks for Real-Time Graphics. Addison Wesley (2004)
6. Fermando, R., Kilgard, M.J.: The Cg Tutorial. Addision-Wesley (2003)

7. Thompson, C.J., Hahn, S., Oskin, M.: Using modern graphics architectures for general-purpose computing: a framework and analysiy. In: Internaltional Symposium on Microarchitecture, Istanbul, Turkey, IEEE Computer Society Press (2002) 306–317
8. Krger, J., Westermann, R.: Linear algebra operators for gpu implementation of numerical algorithms. ACM Transactions on Graphics **22** (2003) 908–916
9. Harris, M.J.: Real-Time Cloud Simulation and Rendering. Dissertaion, University of North Carolina at Chapel Hill (2003)
10. Bolz, J., Farmer, I., Grinspun, E., Schroder, P., Schrder, P.: Sparse matrix solvers on the gpu: Conjugate gradients and multigrid. ACM Transactions on Graphics **22** (2003) 917–924
11. Hillesland, K.E., Molinov, S., Grzeszczuk, R.: Nonlinear optimization framework for image-based modeling on programmable graphics hardware. ACM Transactions on Graphics **22** (2003) 925–934
12. Govindaraju, N.K., Lloyd, B., Wang, W., Lin, M., Manocha, D.: Fast computation of database operations using graphics processors. In: International Conference on Management of Data. (2004) 215–226
13. Goldberg, D.: Genetic Algorithms in Search Optimization and Machine Learning. Addison Wesley, New York (1989)
14. Raghuwanshi, M., Kakde, O.: Survey on multiobjective evolutionary and real coded genetic algorithms. In: The 8th Asia Pacific Symposium on Intelligent and Evolutionary Systems, Cairns, Australia (2004)
15. Michalewicz, Z.: Genetic Algorithms + Data Structures = Evolution Programs. 3rd edn. Springer (1996)
16. Press, W.H., Teukolsky, S.A., Vetterling, W.T., Flannery, B.P.: Numerical Recipes in C++: The Art of Scientific Computing. Cambridge University Press (2002)
17. Lukac, R., Plataniotis, K.N., Smolka, B., Venetsanopoulos, A.N.: Color image filtering and enhancement based on genetic algorithms. In: The 2004 IEEE International Symposium on Circuits and Systems. (2004)
18. Houston, M., Fatahalian, K., Sugerman, J., Buck, I., Hanrahan, P.: Parallel computation on a cluster of gpus. In Lastra, A., Lin, M., Manocha, D., eds.: ACM Workshop on General-Purpose Computing on Graphics Processors, Los Angeles, California (2004) 50

A Neuro-fuzzy Approach to Part Fitup Fault Control During Resistance Spot Welding Using Servo Gun

Y.S. Zhang and G.L Chen

School of Mechanical and Power Engineering,
Shanghai Jiao Tong University, Shanghai, 200030, China
{zhangyansong, glchen}@sjtu.edu.cn

Abstract. Resistance spot welding (RSW) is widely utilized as a joining technique for automobile industry. However, good weld quality control method has not yet been developed in plant environment when part fitup fault exists. This paper proposed a neuro-fuzzy algorithm to control weld quality by adjusting welding current. An experimental system was developed to measure electrode displacement curve. Accordingly based on electrode displacement curve optimal current for every cycle will be achieved under poor fitup fault condition. Results showed that proposed neuro-fuzzy system is suitable as a weld quality monitoring for resistance spot welding.

1 Introduction

Resistance spot welding (RSW) is a dominant sheet metal joining process in the automotive industry. Joint quality determines strength and durability of the automobile body. Although RSW is widely used, it is difficult to ensure the consistency of joint quality in real production. One major reason is that various faults often exist in production. These process faults affect the relationships between nugget size and input process variables (including current, force and time) and thus make defective welds. In an assembly process, it is desirable to control weld quality immediately by adjusting input variables when defective welds have been detected. Therefore, developing an intelligent control approach is a key issue to control the quality of the resistance spot welding process when fault happens.

In recent years investigation has been performed to understand the effects of fault conditions. Nagel and Lee [1] developed a process control system considering some fault conditions. Karagoulis[2]studied fifty-four plant variables and qualitatively concluded that several fault conditions will affect weld quality. Wei Li et al [3] developed a new two-stage, sliding-level experiment design and analysis procedure to study process fault conditions and suggested an optimal weld lobe to minimize their effects. Y Cho et al [4] further studied the effects of fault conditions for resistance spot welding of steel and aluminum alloys. However, none of them were set up to monitor and control weld quality when faults exist.

Electrode displacement, which gives good indication of thermal expansion, melting, and expulsion, has proven to be a particularly useful signal to monitor. It is believed that the amount of thermal expansion, melting, and expulsion can be corrected to the slope and magnitude of the displacement curve. A number of control systems have been developed based on maximum electrode displacement or its changing rates. [5-7]. Attempts are being made to apply fuzzy control algorithm, or artificial neural networks (ANN) et al to explain functional relationship between the process variables and weld quality. However, these algorithms are not industrially applicable because of the effects of fault conditions and the limit of conventional pneumatic welding machines. [8-12]

This paper develops a RSW experimental system using servo gun. Use part poor fitup fault an example to describe the real-time development of spot weld nugget size based on an electrode displacement curve when fault exists. Proposed a neuro-fuzzy inference system is applied to control of weld quality. Electrode displacement and electrode velocity are regards as input parameters of neuro-fuzzy inference system. An optimal current curve is achieved through neuro-fuzzy system to reduce the effects of part fitup fault on weld quality.

2 Electrode Displacement Curve for Monitoring Fitup Fault

Because of the current flow, heat will be generated and temperatures in the system will start to increase. Electrode displacement will rise due to thermal expansion caused by heat. It can be concluded that electrode displacement indicates the relative movement of the electrodes during the welding process. In this paper, the trace of relative electrode movement was measured by an OMRON laser displacement sensor. The displacement signal was fed into a low-pass filter for decreasing noise. Then the signal conditioning unit scales the signals to suitable voltage levels via an A/D converter in the computer. The data acquisition software used is National Instrument's Labview. An experimental data acquisition system including servo gun and sensor is shown in Fig.1-2. The measured signals of a whole welding cycle for a typical weld is shown in Fig 3.From the measured electrode displacement curves we could see that the electrodes will approach due to the electrode force, then the electrodes separate at a constant velocity because of thermal expansion of the sheet. Maximum expansion occurs when electric current is cut off. Finally the electrode displacement starts to fall owing to cooling. This curve has been verified to reflect the physical phenomenon occurring during the weld formation [6].

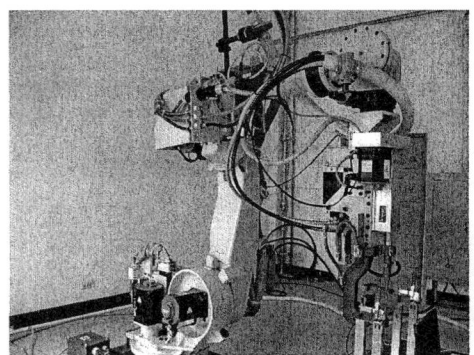 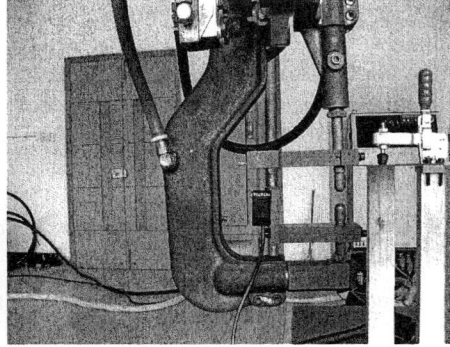

Fig. 1. Experimental system using servo gun   **Fig. 2.** Fixture for installing sensor

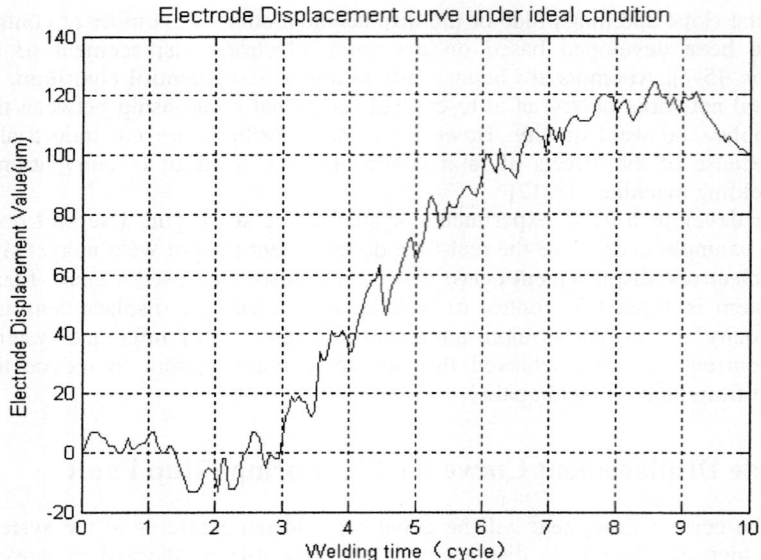

Fig. 3. Electrode displacement curve under idea condition

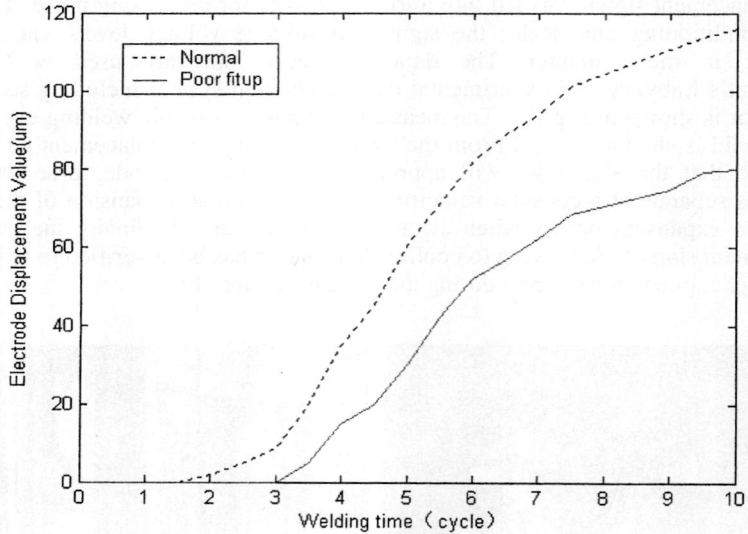

Fig. 4. Electrode displacement curve under poor fitup fault condition

When part poor fitup fault exists, electrode displacement curve shift the right as shown Fig.4. This is indicative of a smaller weld nugget being formed due to the small workpiece contact area at the initial stage of welding. Experimental results show that electrode displacement and electrode velocity values of the curve are well corrected with nugget size.

The above experiment results showed that electrode displacement curve could reflect the nugget formation during RSW. And Electrode displacement and electrode velocity not only can reflect growth of a spot weld nugget but also are two measurable output parameters based on electrode displacement curve. Thus, electrode displacement and electrode velocity values were selected as fuzzy input variables for a neuro-fuzzy inference system under the non-expulsion condition. Input variables are shown in Fig.5 [8]. When expulsion occurs, weld schedules were adjusted to meet welding quality demand according to electrode displacement signal.

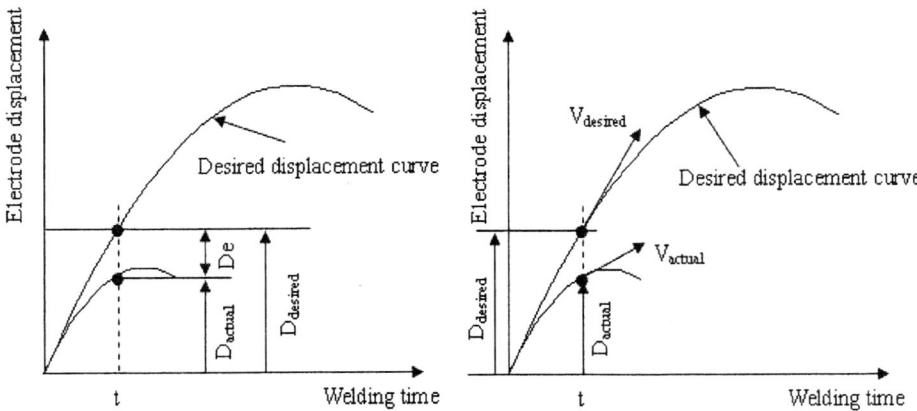

Fig. 5. Fuzzy input variables of neuro-fuzzy system[8]

3 Neuro-fuzzy Inference System

The neuro-fuzzy modeling has been used as a powerful tool which can facilitate the effective development of models. The combined use of the learning ability of neural networks and the representation ability of fuzzy systems can partially overcome vague and imprecise data related to a fuzzy system. The approach is especially useful for large complex and nonlinear systems, which cannot be represented reasonably as simple and unique. Thus, the approach is ideally suited to investigate the complex spot welding control problems.

Neuro-fuzzy models describe systems by mean of fuzzy if-then rules represented in a network structure; to which learning algorithms known from the area of ANN can be applied. They provide new directions in the application of on-line measurement to spot welding systems.

This paper proposed the neuro-fuzzy inference system with two input variables (electrode displacement and electrode velocity) and one output variable (weld current). The neuro-fuzzy scheme is shown is Fig.6. Firstly, the two inputs are codified into linguistic values by the set of Gaussian membership functions. The next step will calculate its respective activation degree to each rule. Lastly, the inference mechanism weights each conclusion value. The error signal between the inferred output value and the respective desired value is used by the gradient-descent method to adjust each rule conclusion.

The fuzzy inference system consists of three main blocks: membership functions selection, fuzzy rules, and conclusion value output. The following subsections represent the neural structure which is proposed here to map the fuzzy inference to ANN. This neuro-fuzzy scheme consists of three layers.

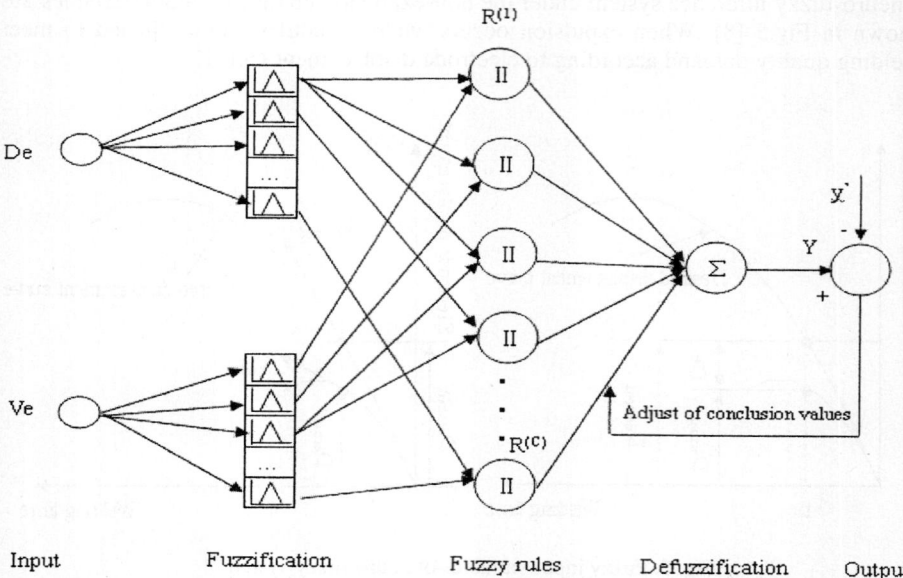

Fig. 6. The structure of neuro-fuzzy system

3.1 Membership Functions Selection

The first layer is composed of neurons with Gaussian activity functions which are determined by the centers c_j and the variances σ_j^2. Membership functions denoted by $\mu_{A_{ij}}(x_i)$ as we expressed in Equation (1). This layer performs the fuzzification of crisp network input values in that neuron.

$$\mu_{A_{ij}}(x_i) = a_{ij} e^{-\left(\frac{x_i - c_{ij}}{\sigma_{ij}}\right)^2} \tag{1}$$

3.2 Fuzzy Rules

The second layer represents the rule layer in which the logical operators are implemented and the antecedent's possibilities are aggregated. The most common neuro-fuzzy network is used to develop or adjust a fuzzy model in Mamdani form. A Mamdani fuzzy model consists of a set of fuzzy if-then rules in the following form:

R : IF (x_1 is A_1 and x_2 is A_2 and ... x_m is A_m) THEN (y is B);

Each if-then rule defines a fuzzy implication between antecedent and consequent. The reasoning process combines all rule contributions using the defuzzification formula in a weighted form.

3.3 Conclusion Value Output

The third layer performs the defuzzifications to achieve a crisp value of the variable. The output of the inference process so far is a fuzzy set, specifying a possibility distribution of control action. In the on-line control, a nonfuzzy (crisp) control action is usually required. This paper used defuzzification operator is center of area (COA). It generates the center of gravity of the possibility distribution of the inferred fuzzy output.

3.4 The Learning Mechanism

At the computational level, a fuzzy system can be seen as a layered network structure, similar to artificial neural networks of the RBF-type. In order to optimize parameters in a fuzzy system, gradient-descent training algorithms known from the area of neural networks can be applied [13-17].

The gradient-descent algorithm changes the conclusion values to minimize an objective function E usually expressed by equation (2). By changing the learning rate parameter and number of learning iterations executed by the algorithm each conclusion value was adjusted.

$$E = \frac{1}{2}[Y(x(k)) - y'(k)]^2 \qquad (2)$$

Where the value $y'(k)$ is the desired output value and $Y(x(k))$ is the inferred output value.

4 Result

When the metal parts are not completely matched fitup fault will arises. Electrode displacement curve will have a delay compared with ideal electrode displacement curve under nominal welding current. Fig.7 shows the simulated electrode displacement curve for poor fitup without control. When neuro-fuzzy control system is applied, an optimal current curve was achieved by making the actual electrode displacement close to the desired electrode displacement. Results are shown in Fig.8. This demonstrates that the proposed neuro-fuzzy system is able to compensate for the quality variations caused by part fitup fault conditions. And the results are similar to the FLC control results [8].

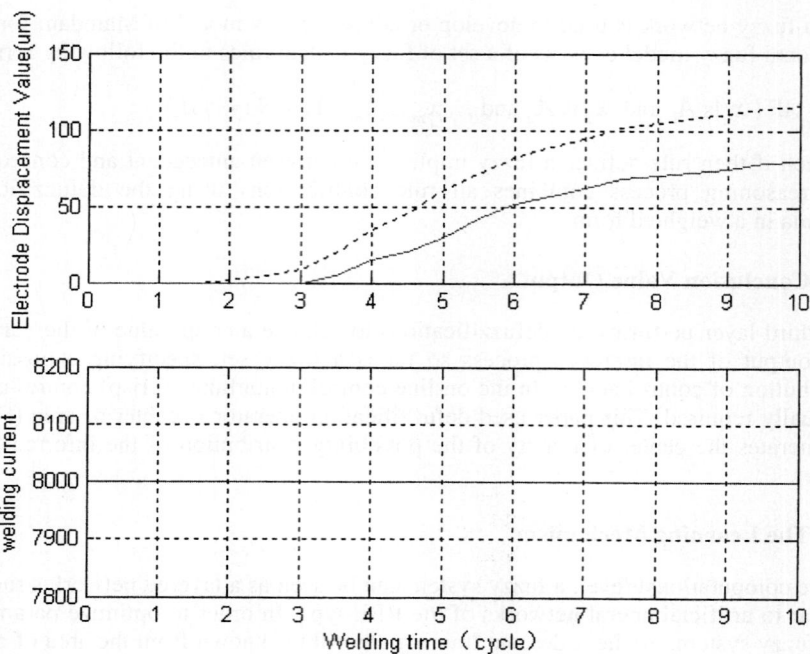

Fig. 7. Electrode displacement curve for poor fit-up without control

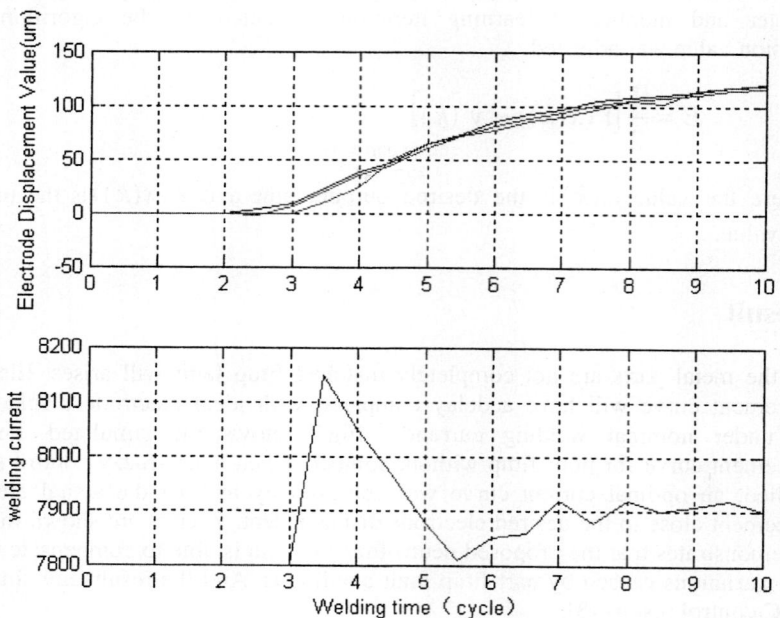

Fig. 8. Electrode displacement curve after neuro-fuzzy control

5 Conclusion

The neuro-fuzzy modeling and the learning mechanism can compensate for the quality variations caused by part fitup fault conditions in resistance spot welding. Good control can be achieved without a complex mathematical model compared to conventional controllers. Proposed neuro-fuzzy algorithm is suitable as a weld quality monitoring for resistance spot welding. We believe that emerging technologies as neuro-fuzzy systems have to be used together with genetic algorithms to produce more intelligent weld quality control systems.

References

1. Nagel, G, L., Lee, A., A new approach to spot welding feedback control, SAE Technical Paper, 1988, No.880371
2. Karagoulis, M., Nuts-and-Bolts approach to the control of resistance spot welding. Welding Journal, 1995, 73(7) : 27—31
3. Li, W., Shaowei Cheng, Hu, S.J., Statistical Investigation on Resistance Spot Welding Quality Using a Two-State, Sliding-Level Experiment, Journal of Manufacturing Science and Engineering-Transactions of The ASME, 2001,123(8): 513-520
4. Y Cho., S J Hu., W Li, Resistance spot welding of aluminum and steel: a comparative experimental study, Proceedings of the institution of mechanical engineers part B-Journal of Engineering Manufacture, 2003,217(7): 1355-1363
5. Tsai, C.L., Dai, W.L., Dickinson, D.W., and Papritan, J.C., Analysis and development of a real-time control methodology in resistance spot welding, Welding Research Supplement, 1991, 12: 339-351.
6. Cho,H.S., and Chun, D.W., A microprocessor-based electrode movement controller for spot weld quality assurance. IEEE Transactions on Industrial Electronics, 1985, 32(3):234-238.
7. Chang, H.S., Cho, Y.J., Choi, S.G., and Cho, H.S., A proportional-integral controller for resistance spot welding using nugget expansion, ASME Journal of Dynamic Systems, Measurement, and Control, 1989, 111: 332-336.
8. Robert W. Messler, Jr., Min Jou, An intelligent control system for resistance spot welding using a neural network and fuzzy logic, Conference Record-IAS Annual Meeting, 1995 :1757 ~ 1763
9. Jou, M, Experimental investigation of resistance spot welding for sheet metals used in automotive industry, JSME International Journal Series C-Mechanical Systems Machine Elements and Manufacturing, 2001,44(2): 544-552
10. Khoo,L.P. and Young, H.Y. A prototype fuzzy resistance spot welding system. International Journal of Production Research. 1995, 33(7), 2023-2036.
11. Dilthey, U. and Dickersbach, J. Application of neural networks for quality evaluation for resistance spot welds. ISIJ International, 1999, 39(10), 1061-1066.
12. S.R.Lee and Y.J.Choo., A quality assurance technique for resistance spot welding using a neuro-fuzzy algorithm, Journal of manufacturing systems, 2001: 320-328
13. Jang, S.R. ANFIS: Adaptive-network-based fuzzy inference systems. IEEE Transactions on Systems, Man & Cybernetics, 1993, 23(3), 665–685.

14. Kiguchi, K., Tanaka, T., Fukuda, T.: Neuro-fuzzy control of a robotic exoskeleton with EMG signals. IEEE Trans. Fuzzy Systems.12.(2004) 481-490
15. Wang, L.P., Frayman, Y.: A Dynamically-generated fuzzy neural network and its application to torsional vibration control of tandem cold rolling mill spindles. Engineering Applications of Artificial Intelligence 15 (2003) 541-550
16. Lin, C.-M., Hsu, C.-F.: Supervisory recurrent fuzzy neural network control of wing rock for slender delta wings. IEEE Trans. Fuzzy Systems, 12 (2004) 733-742
17. Frayman, Y., Wang, L.P.: A Dynamically-constructed fuzzy neural controller for direct model reference adaptive control of multi-input-multi-output nonlinear processes. Soft Computing, 6 (2002) 244-253

Automatic Separate Algorithm of Vein and Artery for Auto-segmentation Liver-Vessel from Abdominal MDCT Image Using Morphological Filtering

Chun-Ja Park[1], Eun-kyung Cho[2], Young-hee Kwon[2],
Moon-sung Park[3], and Jong-won Park[1]

[1] Chungnam National University, Dept of Information Communications Engineering,
305-764, 220 Gung-dong, Yuseong-gu, Daejeon, Korea
whtdeer@cnu.ac.kr, jwpark@crow.chungnam.ac.kr
[2] DaeDuk College, Department of Computer, Internet & Information,
305-715, 48 Jang-dong You-sung-gu Daejeon, Korea
{ekcho, yhkwon}@ddc.ac.kr
[3] ETRI, Postal Technology Research Center, 305-700,
161 Ga-jung-dong Yousunggu, Daejeon, Korea
mspark@etri.re.kr

Abstract. This study proposes the algorithm for segmentation liver and segmentation vessel inside the liver by using MDCT image. There are two main vessels in the liver. During the transplantation, it is important to decrease damage on the vessels and to raise the rate of success by providing medical doctors with the necessary incision rate of the liver and type of the vessels before operation. When transplanting, the size of donator's liver is important for the survival of both donator and receiver. For the survival of both, the donator should leave 35% of his/her own liver, and the receiver should get more than 40% of his/her own liver. By finding out distribution of essential vessels that determine the cutting part for the transplantation and by showing artery and vein separately from the several segmentation vessel image, we can find the liver vein, which is the most important criterion during the incision, and can progress the cutting of the liver from the liver vein. It can be of help to minimize the damage on the three thick vessels and their surrounding vessels, and to cut the liver according to the volume rate of the liver. Using the features that each vessel has circle type and stick type with many angles, segmentation liver through morphological filtering and segmentation liver vessel were performed. Then, the separation of artery and vein from other combined vessels, and its reconstruction was possible, and finally the 3Dimension vessel image was produced.

1 Background and Objective

The technology of medical image treatment is playing an important role not only for the understanding of inside the body, but for the decision of planning or method for treatment. In this process, the demanding for various additional information that can be helpful to the diagnosis activity is getting increased.

In Korea, about 10,000 liver cancer patients are being generated annually, and it is the third commonest cancer followed by stomach cancer and lung cancer. It takes up 11.3% among the total cancer outbreaks. According to the Annual Statistics Report on Causes of Death, average 23.1(male: 34.8 people, female: 11.3 people) out of 100,000 people died of liver cancer and it shows that Korea has the highest rate among OECD member states.

Liver is an essential organ to sustain life and in particular, its function is very complicated and diverse so there are no organs that can be substitutable to the liver. Thus, it is very hard to be recovered once it is damaged. For this reason, the most effective and sole treatment method for the recovery of liver is to receive liver from other people through transplantation.

Liver transplantation is to plant a new and normal liver after removing the whole abnormal liver, and this is a way to cure abnormalities of liver function such as liver cancer and hepatocirrhosis. In case that the patients with early liver cancer diagnosis receive transplantation, more than 85% of the patients show a complete recovery.

As the biggest organ in the body, liver has a strong reproduction power. Even though the 70% of the total liver is cut, it recovers its original form in two or three months. Liver is divided into left liver and right liver, and if one liver does not exist, the other liver grows large, and then forms left liver and right liver again. The size of left liver occupies 30~40% of the total liver and 60~70% for the right liver. The liver transplantation is broken down into two categories, which are the whole liver transplantation and part liver transplantation. The whole liver transplantation is getting the liver from a donor's dead body, and the part liver transplantation is getting the liver from a donor's dead body or living body. Since it is rare to receive organs from the donor who has a brain death in Korea, many patients are dying due to lacking of the necessary organs.

Lately, 'the part liver transplantation from living body', which takes part of liver away from a living person, is rising to the surface as a promising remedy for the liver patients.

In cutting the liver for the part liver transplantation, an operation should be done to guarantee both lives of donors and receivers. In case of liver transplantation from a living body, it is certainly more important of the donor's health than the receiver's, thus it has been an unwritten law to give the left liver, which is smaller, to the receiver and leave the right liver for the donor. But as the fact that giving right liver is also safe is approved, the right liver transplantation is getting increased. For the survival of donor, 0.8% of liver in his/her standard weight should be left in donor's body, and 0.8% of liver in his/her standard weight should be given to the receiver for the receiver's survival as well [1].

There are two main vessels, which are a liver artery and a portal vein. For the liver transplantation, accurate information about the distribution of liver vessel is very important to cut the liver, meeting to the right proportion. Therefore, the technology of image diagnosis using MDCT or MRI is playing a crucial role to determine a planning or method for treatment or operation, and it is also expected to be developed continuously in the future through medical image [2][3].

In this study, auto-segmentation liver artery and liver vein by using morphological filtering from MDCT image were performed in order to provide information of liver vessel, which is important during the liver transplantation.

2 Content

2.1 MDCT Image

The image in this thesis is a picture of normal liver, which is medicated by contrast media, saved with Dicom Version 3 format, and acquired in a hospital of Cheonbuk University.

Dicom Version 3 format is widely being used in PACS (Picture Archiving and Communication System) and it has a structure to contain patients, image, and information of medical doctors all together [3][4][5].

Table 1. Parameter of DICOM file

Classification	Name	Gender	Size	Thickness	Pixel spacing
Abnormal	K.M.D	F	512*512	1mm	0.7070312
Normal	U.Y.S	M	512*512	1mm	0.5859375
Normal	K.P.S	M	512*512	1mm	0.6328125

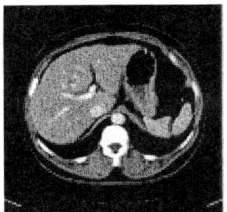 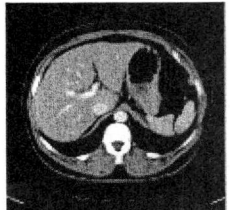

Fig. 1. (a) AccuLite view   (b) AccuLite bitmap transformation

2.2 Preprocessing

Most MRI machines and CT use DICOM (Digital Imaging Communications in Medicine) file in ACR/NEMA version 3.0 format as a standard form for the transmission, storage, and management of image(See Table1). But this format is not recognized or conducted by personal computer or workstation in general, so the preprocessing work is needed in order that personal computer or workstation can recognize or conduct this image. This preprocessing work was performed using AccuLite Version 3.1 program of AccuImage Diagnostics Inc. and bitmap file format was used for the transformed image(Fig. 1 (a), (b)).

2.3 Segmentation Liver Area

2.3.1 Algorithm for Auto-Segmentation of Liver Area

The brightness value of the normal liver, which is medicated by contrast media, ranges from 180-220, and surrounding tissues such as bones or vessels simultaneously exist in that scope. Only for the segmentation liver in the condition of removing surrounding tissues to the maximum, the algorithm was developed as follows (See Fig. 2) [6].

This algorithm uses morphological filtering to remove the surrounding tissues that has the same brightness value range as the liver or to remove noise where exists on the border of liver and its surrounding tissues [7].

In the first step, the surrounding tissues that has the same brightness value range as the liver was taken away using erosion, one of Morphological filtering, and at the same time, opening to take away noise where exists on the border of liver was repeatedly performed.

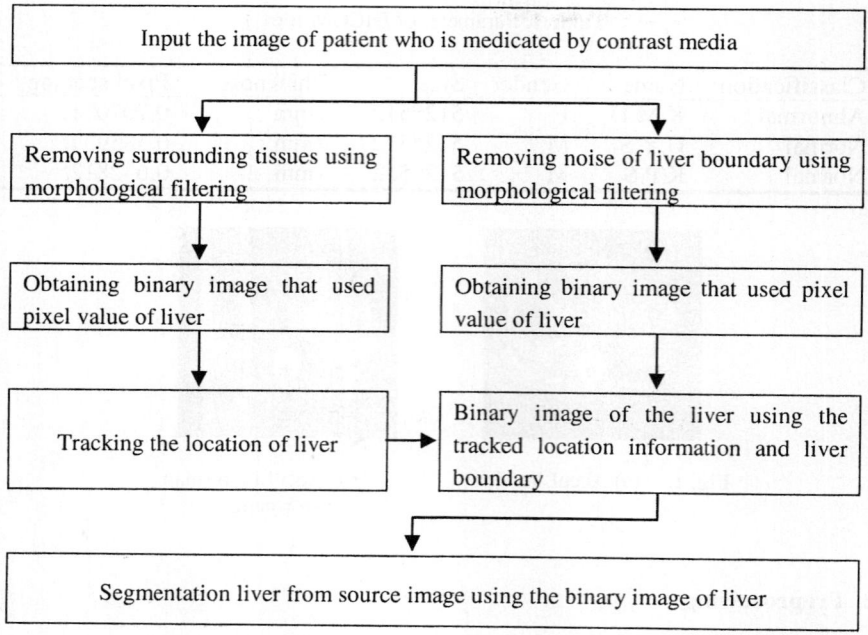

Fig. 2. Algorithm for auto-segmentation of liver area

In the second step, each result was transformed into binary image using the distribution of the brightness value of liver. The removal image of the surrounding tissues acquired through the first step is used to search for the location of the liver in the third step since the original border information of the liver is lost. Also, the image that removed noise on the border of liver is used to obtain border information of the liver in the same step. By using the acquired location and border information, the liver segmentation is possible from the source image in the fourth step.

2.3.2 Segmentation Liver Area

The area that has brightness value between 180 - 220 in histogram for auto-segmentation of the liver area, which is brighter than other organs due to the contrast media, was segmented (See Fig. 3).

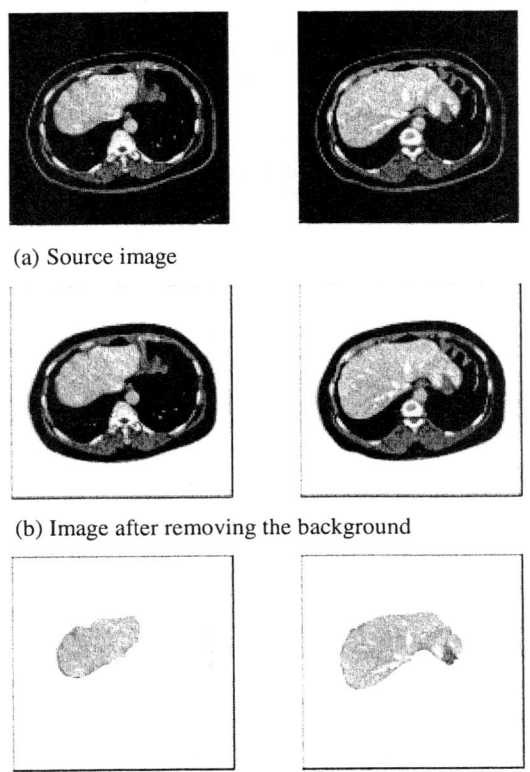

(a) Source image

(b) Image after removing the background

(c) Image after segmentation liver

Fig. 3. Image of auto-segmentation liver

2.4 Segmentation Liver Vessel

2.4.1 Algorithm for Segmentation Liver Vessel

The brightness value of normal liver, which was medicated by contrast media, ranges from 155 – 220, and in case of vessel inside the liver, it ranges from 220-255, which has higher brightness value due to the effect of contrast media. For the auto-segmentation liver vessel, the performance was done like Fig. 4.

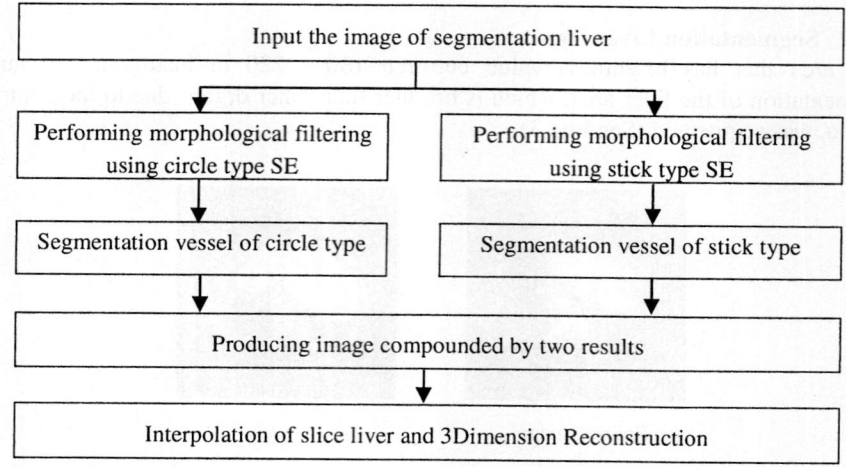

Fig. 4. Algorithm for auto-segmentation of liver vessel area

Fig. 5. Various SE types used for segmentation vessel

Morphological Filtering was performed using SE (Structuring Element), which has several kinds of type such as circle type and stick type with many angles as shown in Fig. 5, and auto-segmentation by each slice of vessel inside the liver was performed by compounding the two results. A circle type SE was made and used to find out circle type vessel that has more than a definite size among the pixels included into the distribution of brightness value of vessel. Also, a stick type SE was used to search for stick type vessel and each filtering was performed. Then, a new image by compounding the results from each slice of two images was constructed (See Fig. 6).

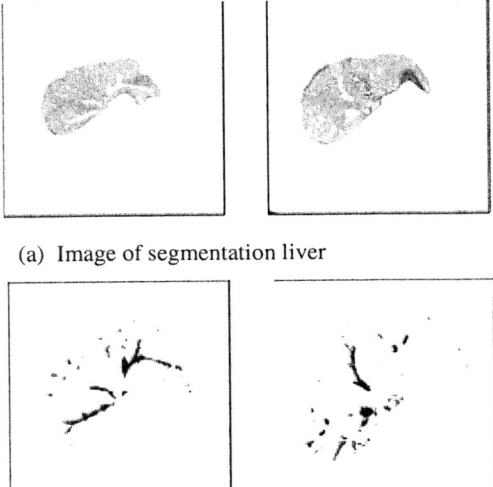

(a) Image of segmentation liver

(b) Image of auto-segmentation liver vessel

Fig. 6. Image of auto-segmentation vessel

2.4.2 3 Dimension Reconstruction of Vessel Area

The two dimensional results from each slice were reconstructed into 3 Dimension to see the result of segmentation vessel image more conveniently, which was acquired through auto-segmentation algorithm in the liver area.

It is necessary to go through preprocessing work to transform the segmentation image into binary image and to correct a rapid change between each slice of liver. This correction work is called Interpolation, and Volume Reconstructor function of Image J Plug-in, the program that National Institutes of Health USA distributes to the public, was used. For this, the image is corrected on the basis of VPS (width of each pixel), HPS (length of each pixel), and spacing between slices, and the 3 Dimension reconstruction program was made using Visualization Tool Kit of Kitware Inc. and Visual Studio of Microsoft. By using this program, the binary work is done and the image followed by Interpolation into 3 Dimension image is reconstructed as shown below in Fig. 7.

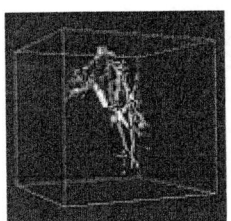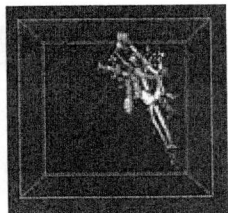

Fig. 7. 3 Dimension liver vessel

2.5 Separation of Artery and Vein of Liver Vessel

2.5.1 Finding the Start Point of Vein

There are several main vessels in the liver. The artery of liver delivers blood with affluent oxygen from heart to liver, portal vein carries nutrients, metabolic material and toxin needed for detoxication, and vein plays a role to bring the blood back to heart after consuming the oxygen. Using the information of exact vessel distribution of artery and vein, middle vein is found and the cutting angle is decided focusing on the line, which passes the thickest part of artery, perpendicularly with artery.

After calculating the volume of the incised part among the volume rate of liver along with the left line of middle vein, if the donator and receiver have volume as much as they want, it is good to cut it along with, and if it is not enough, cut it along with right line. Then, if the volume rate is appropriate for both, one can cut it.

For this work, it is necessary to show the location that each vessel passes inside the incised model of liver through 3 Dimension and to separate vein and artery vessel in order to minimize the damage on other vessels.

As the work for finding the start part of vein, the feature that the several vessels gathering together at the start part of vessel, which appears like a big and circular lump, is use, a big circle type SE is made, and the start point of slide that has the biggest point from each slide via Morphological filtering is found.

2.5.2 Finding the Connection Part of Vein Vessel

After finding out the location of slice, which has the start point and is not zero (0), by using the sum of slice pixel value, the overlapped pixel is found from the slice by taking AND, which has the start point with neighboring slices of both directions, and the pixels that has the shape of 8 directed connection within the front and back of slices are marked, centering on these overlapped pixel parts.

This work can be applied from its start point slice to all the slices of both directions in order, and it is performed to the start point conversely, curving like letter 'n' or 'u'. After founding out the connected part, segmentation of connected pixel value of the whole vein can be performed (See Fig. 8).

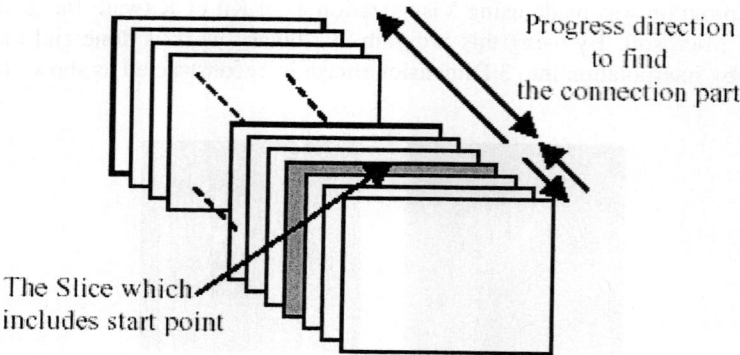

Fig. 8. The work to find out the connection part

The slices that have segmentation value from source image with vein and artery are taken away, stored, and the rest artery can be mapped out. After going through the Interpolation, the artery and vein are made by 3Dimension, and then the type of vein and artery are seen (See Fig. 9).

The vessel located on the middle of separated vein is the middle vein and a decision for the incision of liver is made focusing on this part.

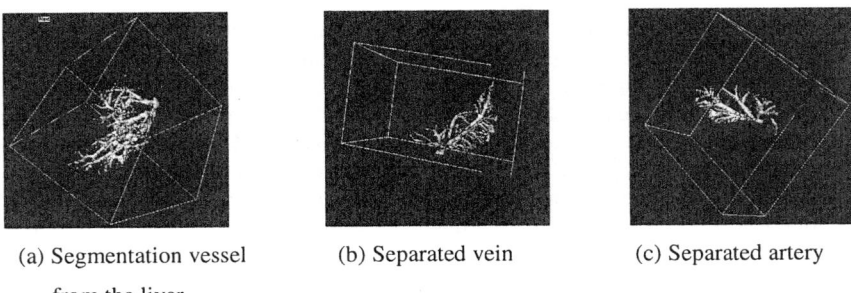

(a) Segmentation vessel from the liver   (b) Separated vein   (c) Separated artery

Fig. 9. Separation of liver vessel

3 Conclusions and Considerations

As the number of liver patients is increasing, promising remedies driven by the development of technology have been coming out. Thus, providing accurate and various information is essential for the high rate of success during the liver transplantation. Since everyone has a different liver in terms of size and shape, the accurate information is essential and the criteria of incision can make a great impact on the life-support of both donators and receivers. In this study, the accuracy of algorithm by comparing segmentation liver vessel with passive segmentation image from the MDCT image could be verified. To make a 3 Dimension image that is automatically incised, it was needed to find the middle vein, and to search for where the artery and its incision point is. For this, the work to separate vein and artery vessel was needed, the cutting part was found by slices through the angel where the middle vein meets artery vertically, and finally a line could be drawn from the separated image of vein and artery. Through this auto-segmentation, it was possible to show the information of vessel inside the liver to medical doctors more clearly and in detail. By doing this before operation, it is predictable whether the operation is successful or not, and the operation time can be shortened with the accurate information of the liver by proceeding the operation rapidly. It will give a sense of security and promote the rate of success.

This algorithm dealt with segmentation of image with MATLAB, and constructed segmentation image into 3Dimension using Image J and Visual Studio.

Based on this result, the research will be conducted in the future as well by doing several trials such as cutting the liver by slices along with the left side of middle vein on the basis of middle vein and artery from the image and auto measure the volume, or if the volume is not enough, it can be cut along with the right side to see inside. The result of this study will make a contribution to raise the rate of success during the liver transplantation by cutting each section and providing medical doctors with the location of the vessel of incised liver.

References

1. Organ Transplantation Center in Seoul Asan Medical Center : http://www.amc.seoul.kr.
2. National Cancer Center : Cancer Information Service http://ncc.re.kr
3. Annual Report on Causes of Death, Korea National Statistical Office : Annual mortality trends by leading causes of death in Korea (1990, 1995 & 2002)
4. Jae-Hoon L., Won-Sik P., Jung-Mo A., Sam-Soo K., Hwan J., Hyung-Sik C. : Analysis for Economical Efficiency of PACS, The Korean Society of PACS, Journal vol. 6 (2000) 9-18
5. NEMA draft doc. Digital Image and Communication in Medicine(DICOM)
6. Carlotto M. J. : Histogram Analysis Using a Scale-Space Approach, IEEE Transaction on PAMI (1987) 121-129
7. J.P. : Parker Algorithms fir Image Processing and Computer Vision, Wiley (1997) 69-115
8. Hyung-Kyung Y. : Segmentation Cerebrum from MR Image and Removal Calculation (2000)
9. Y.C. S., et al. : Partial volume Effects on Segmentation Matter from the Brain, Proceedings of the 4th Asia Conference on Medical Biological Engineering 210-213
10. Brun A. and Gustafson L. : Distribution of cerebral Degree Alzheimer's Disease, Arch. Psychiatry 223 (1976) 15-33
11. Shareef N. an d Wang D.L. : Segmentation of Medical Image LEGION, IEEE Transaction on Medical Image, Vol. (1999) 77-91
12. Suzuki H. and Toriwaki J. : Automatic Segmentation of Image by Knowledge Guided Thresholding, Computerize Image Graphics, vol. 15, No4 (1991) 223-240
13. S. W. Y., Y.C.S., J.S.C., S.M. Noh, K.S.S., J.W. P. : Segmentation of Liver and Spleen by using Lattice Estimation System in Abdominal CT Image, ITC-CSCC '99, Volume II (1999) 991-994

Run-Time Fuzzy Optimization of IEEE 802.11 Wireless LANs Performance

Young-Joong Kim and Myo-Taeg Lim

Department of Electrical Engineering, Korea University,
1, 5-ka, Anam-dong, Sungbuk-ku, Seoul 136-701, Korea
{kyjoong, mlim}@korea.ac.kr
http://cml.korea.ac.kr

Abstract. In this paper we focus on run-time optimization of the IEEE 802.11 protocol to improve its performance using a well-known fuzzy logic approach. Specifically, we derive the simple, and more accurate, approximation of the network contention level and the average size of contention window to maximize the theoretical throughput limit. In addition, we propose and evaluate a new distributed fuzzy contention control mechanism that is a modification of the asymptotically optimal backoff (AOB) mechanism using a fuzzy logic approach. The proposed mechanism can be used to extend the standard 802.11 access mechanism without requiring any additional hardware like the AOB mechanism. To verify efficiency of our mechanism, the performance of the IEEE 802.11 standard protocol with the AOB and the proposed mechanism are investigated through simulations.

1 Introduction

IEEE 802.11 is the standard for Wireless Local Area Networks (WLANs) promoted by the Institute of Electrical and Electronics Engineers. Wireless technologies in the LAN environment are becoming increasingly important and the IEEE 802.11 is the most mature technology to date [1], [2], [3]. In this paper we focus on the IEEE 802.11 WLAN presented in [4], [5]. Since a WLAN relies on a common transmission medium, the transmissions of the network stations must be coordinated by the medium access control Media Access Control (MAC) protocol. MAC protocols for LANs can be roughly categorized into random access (e.g., CSMA, CSMA/CA) and demand assignment (e.g., token ring). Due to the inherent flexibility of random access systems (e.g., random access allows unconstrained movement of mobile hosts) the IEEE 802.11 standard committee decided to adopt a random access CSMA-based scheme for WLANs. In this scheme there is no collision detection capability due to the WLANs inability to listen while sending, since there is usually just on antenna for both sending and receiving.

Some researchers have investigated the enhancement of the IEEE 802.11 MAC protocol to increase its performance when it is used in WLANs. Through a performance analysis, it has been studied the tuning of the standard's parameters [2], [3]. In [6], solutions have been proposed for achieving a more uniform distribution of the accesses.

Recently, other researchers have pointed out that the standard protocol can be very inefficient [7], [8], [9]. Specially, the average size of the contention window that maximizes the theoretical throughput limit was derived analytically, and it was shown that depending on the network configuration, the standard can operate very far from the theoretical throughput limit. In addition, an appropriate tuning of the backoff algorithm that can drive the IEEE 802.11 protocol close to the theoretical throughput limit was proposed by [9]. That is a distributed algorithm that enables each station to tune its backoff algorithm at run-time. To perform this tuning, a station must have exact knowledge of the network contention level; unfortunately, in a real case, a station cannot have exact knowledge of the network contention level (i.e., number of active stations and length of the message transmitted on the channel), but it, at most, can estimate it [10], [11].

Hence, a distributed mechanism for contention control in IEEE 802.11 WLANs was proposed and evaluated by [10], [11]. This mechanism, named *Asymptotically Optimal Backoff* (AOB), dynamically adapts the backoff window size to the current network contention level and guarantees that an IEEE 802.11 WLAN asymptotically achieves its optimal channel utilization for a large number of stations. The AOB mechanism measures the network contention level by using two simple estimates: the *slot utilization* S_U and the average size of transmitted frames. These estimates are simple and can be obtained by exploiting information that is already available in the standard protocol. AOB can be used to extend the standard IEEE 802.11 access mechanism without requiring any additional hardware. According to AOB mechanism, its control is based on the parameter, named *Probability of Transmission*, P_T, whose value depends on the S_U. However, this control is not effective for a small number of stations. Moreover, since the P_T depends on the ratio, $S\_U/S\_U_{optimal}$, so P_T is always small. Therefore, it always offers a little opportunity.

In this paper, we derive the simple, and more accurate, approximation of the network contention level and the average size of contention window to maximize the theoretical throughput limit, and we propose a new P_T formula using a well-known fuzzy logic approach. The fuzzy approach became the major field of researches in mathematics and control systems, since it was initiated by Lotfi A. Zadeh in 1965. Moreover, it can be very easy to design and worked very well for many problems [12], [13]. In addition, we propose and evaluate a new *distributed fuzzy contention control* (DFCC) mechanism using the proposed P_T formula.

The contents of this paper are as follows. In the section 2, we sketch the portions of the IEEE 802.11 standard and the AOB mechanism which are relevant for this paper. In the section 3, we derive the approximated theoretical throughput limit, and the proposed DFCC mechanism is proposed and evaluated. To verify our proposed mechanism, we make the steady-state analysis in the section 4. Finally, the section 5 gives our conclusions.

2 The AOB Mechanism for the IEEE 802.11 Protocol

2.1 IEEE 802.11

The IEEE 802.11 MAC protocol provides an access control that is asynchronous, time-bounded, and contention-free. The basic access method in the IEEE 802.11 MAC protocol is the *Distributed Coordination Function* (DCF) which is a *Carrier Sense Multiple Access with Collision Avoidance* (CSMA/CA) MAC protocol. A detailed description can be found in [4].

As long as the channel is sensed to be idle, a *Backoff Counter* (BC) is counted down every *Slot_Time*. A station can transmit when the BC reaches zero. The BC stops when a transmission is detected and continues to elapse when the channel is sensed to be idle again for more than a *Distributed Inter-Frame Space* (DIFS). The *Binary Exponential Backoff* described in [4], [14] is characterized by the expression giving the dependency of the CW_{Size} parameter by the number of *unsuccessful transmission attempts* (N_A) already performed for a given frame. It is defined that the first transmission attempt for a given frame is performed adopting CW_{Size} equal to the minimum value CW_{min}. After each unsuccessful (re)transmission of the same frame, the station doubles until it reaches the maximum value CW_{max} fixed by the standard, i.e., CW_{Size} had been defined as follows:

$$CW_{Size}(N\_A) = \min(CW_{max}, CW_{min} \cdot 2^{(N\_A-1)}). \qquad (1)$$

To reduce the probability of collision, the CW_{Size} is doubled for the new scheduling of the retransmission attempt, thus further reducing contention. However, by analyzing the behavior of the IEEE 802.11 DCF mechanism, it was shown that the channel utilization is negatively affected by the increase of the contention level [9], [10], [11]. This occurs because i) the increase in the CW_{Size} is obtained at the cost of a collision, ii) after a successful transmission, no memory of the actual contention level is maintained.

2.2 The AOB Mechanism

The drawbacks of the IEEE 802.11 backoff algorithm, explained in the previous section, indicate a direction for improving the performance of a random access scheme by exploiting the information on the current network congestion level that is already available at the MAC level. Specifically, the utilization rate of the slots called S_U presented in [10], [11] observed on the channel by each station is used as a simple and effective estimate of the channel congestion level. A simple and intuitive definition of the S_U is then given by:

$$S\_U = \frac{Num\_Busy\_Slot}{Num\_Available\_Slot} \qquad (2)$$

where Num_Busy_Slot is the number of slots in the *Backoff Interval* (BI) where one or more stations start a transmission attempt, and $Num\_Available\_Slot$ is the total number of slots available for transmission in the BI, i.e., the sum of idle and busy slots. In the IEEE 802.11 standard mechanism, every station performs a *Carrier Sensing* activity and thus, the S_U estimate is simple to obtain and no additional hardware is required [10], [11].

The current S_U estimate can be used by each station to evaluate the opportunity to either perform or defer the scheduled transmission attempt. When the probability of a successful transmission is low, it should defer its transmission attempt. This can be achieved in an IEEE 802.11 network by exploiting the AOB mechanism proposed in [11]. The AOB mechanism can be to dynamically tune the backoff window size to achieve the theoretical capacity limit of the IEEE 802.11 protocol. This mechanism is based on the P_T parameter which depends on the current contention level of the channel, i.e., SU and the function of q value, named *Asymptotic Contention Limit* $ACL(q) = M \cdot p_{min}(q)$. Here, M is the number of current stations. The heuristic formula of the P_T is as follows:

$$P\_T(ACL(q),\ S\_U,\ N\_A) = 1 - \min\left(1,\ \frac{S\_U}{ACL(q)}\right)^{N\_A} \tag{3}$$

and a detailed description can be found in [11].

This mechanism guarantees that the optimal channel utilization is asymptotically achieved for large M values. However, since the P_T depends on the rate, $S\_U/ACL(q)$, the P_T is always small. Therefore, it always offers a little opportunity. So, this control is not effective when the number of current stations is small in network, i.e., $M < 10$.

3 Run-Time Fuzzy Optimization of IEEE 802.11

We assume that the network is represented by the IEEE 802.11 p-persistent model defined in [8], [9], because it is a useful and simple tool for analytically estimating the protocol capacity. To simply, we assume that each station transmit messages whose lengths are a geometrically distributed with parameter q. In other words, the average message length, $\bar{m}$, is given by: $\bar{m} = t_{slot}/(1-q)$, where the length of slot is denoted with t_{slot}. The IEEE 802.11 maximum channel utilization can be closely approximated by adopting, in the standard protocol, a contention window whose average size is identified by the optimal p value, i.e., $E[CW] = 2/p_{min} - 1$.

3.1 Approximated Theoretical Throughput Limit

By the help of [9], we approximate p_{min} with the p value satisfying the following relationship:

$$E[Coll] \cdot E[N_c] = (E[N_c] + 1) \cdot E[Idle\_p] \tag{4}$$

where $E[Coll]$ is the average time the channel is busy due to a collision, $E[Idle\_p]$ is the average number of consecutive idle slots, and $E[N_c]$ is the average number of collisions in a virtual transmission time. The expressions in (4) are as follows:

$$E[N_c] = \frac{1-(1-p)^M}{Mp(1-p)^{M-1}} - 1 \qquad (5)$$

$$E[Coll] = l(q) \cdot t_{slot} \qquad (6)$$

$$E[Idle\_p] = \frac{(1-p)^M}{1-(1-p)^M} \cdot t_{slot} \qquad (7)$$

where

$$l(q) = \frac{1+2q}{1-q^2} . \qquad (8)$$

However, since this p_{min} derivation is too complex for our purpose, we use the Taylor series expansion. By applying Taylor series expansion, we have:

$$(1-p)^M \simeq 1 - Mp + \frac{M(M-1)p^2}{2} - \frac{M(M-1)(M-2)p^3}{6} \qquad (9)$$

$$Mp(1-p)^{M-1} \simeq Mp - M(M-1)p^2 + \frac{M(M-1)(M-2)p^3}{2} . \qquad (10)$$

By substituting (9), (10) in (5)-(7), and after some algebraic manipulations, we can obtain that the optimal p value is the solution of the following equation:

$$\{2l(q)-1\}M(M-1)(M-2)p^3 - 2\{l(q)-1\}M(M-1)p^2 - 6Mp + 6 = 0 \quad (11)$$

Moreover, for computational convenience, we alter $M(M-1)$, $M(M-1)(M-2)$ into M^2, M^3, respectively. (11) can be rewritten as follows:

$$\{2l(q)-1\}(Mp)^3 - 2\{l(q)-1\}(Mp)^2 - 6Mp + 6 = 0 . \qquad (12)$$

Table 1. Comparison of optimal p values

Methods	q value	Average payload size	p_{min}				
			$M=2$	$M=4$	$M=10$	$M=50$	$M=100$
Analytical estimate	0.50	2	0.379796	0.186354	0.074237	0.014835	0.007417
	0.75	4	0.294945	0.138190	0.053771	0.010622	0.005303
	0.90	10	0.206660	0.092635	0.035281	0.006897	0.003439
	0.98	50	0.103674	0.044290	0.016498	0.003192	0.001589
	0.99	100	0.075545	0.031870	0.011805	0.002278	0.001134
Asymptotic estimate	0.50	2	0.284365	0.142183	0.056873	0.011375	0.005687
	0.75	4	0.220974	0.110487	0.044195	0.008839	0.004419
	0.90	10	0.153367	0.076684	0.030673	0.006135	0.003067
	0.98	50	0.075371	0.037686	0.015074	0.003015	0.001507
	0.99	100	0.054541	0.027270	0.010908	0.002182	0.001091
Proposed estimate	0.50	2	0.420037	0.210019	0.084007	0.016801	0.008401
	0.75	4	0.281507	0.140754	0.056301	0.011260	0.005630
	0.90	10	0.176485	0.088243	0.035297	0.007059	0.003530
	0.98	50	0.079881	0.039940	0.015976	0.003195	0.001598
	0.99	100	0.056785	0.028393	0.011357	0.002271	0.001136

By using the approximated theoretical throughput limit $M \cdot p_{min}$ value that is the solution of (11), we can find that the maximum channel utilization is achieved when the q value is given. Furthermore, for a given average payload size, $M \cdot p_{min}$ is a quasi-constant value.

The comparative results are presented in Table 1. Analytical and asymptotic estimates of p_{min} value are obtained by the formulas reported in [9] and [11], respectively. Table 1 shows that the proposed estimate obtained by (12) is very closer to analytical estimate than the asymptotic estimate.

3.2 Distributed Fuzzy Contention Control Mechanism

In this paper, we propose a new P_T parameter using fuzzy logic approach and the heuristic formula is as follows:

$$P\_T(S\_U, N\_A, y) = \left(1 - S\_U^{N\_A}\right) \cdot y \tag{13}$$

where y is the output variable of the following fuzzy IF-THEN rules:

$$\begin{aligned}
Rule^{(1)} &: IF\ x_1\ is\ S\ and\ x_2\ is\ L,\ THEN\ y\ is\ VL \\
Rule^{(2)} &: IF\ x_1\ is\ S\ and\ x_2\ is\ M,\ THEN\ y\ is\ L \\
Rule^{(3)} &: IF\ x_1\ is\ S\ and\ x_2\ is\ S,\ THEN\ y\ is\ M \\
Rule^{(4)} &: IF\ x_1\ is\ M\ and\ x_2\ is\ L,\ THEN\ y\ is\ L \\
Rule^{(5)} &: IF\ x_1\ is\ M\ and\ x_2\ is\ M,\ THEN\ y\ is\ VM \\
Rule^{(6)} &: IF\ x_1\ is\ M\ and\ x_2\ is\ S,\ THEN\ y\ is\ S \\
Rule^{(7)} &: IF\ x_1\ is\ L\ and\ x_2\ is\ L,\ THEN\ y\ is\ M \\
Rule^{(8)} &: IF\ x_1\ is\ L\ and\ x_2\ is\ M,\ THEN\ y\ is\ S \\
Rule^{(9)} &: IF\ x_1\ is\ L\ and\ x_2\ is\ S,\ THEN\ y\ is\ VS
\end{aligned} \tag{14}$$

where x_1 is an input variable as the number of current stations M, x_2 is an input variable as the proposed estimate of p_{min}, the linguistic variables S, M, and L mean "small," "medium," and "large," respectively, and a hedge V means "very." Moreover, each proposed membership function is presented in Fig. 1.

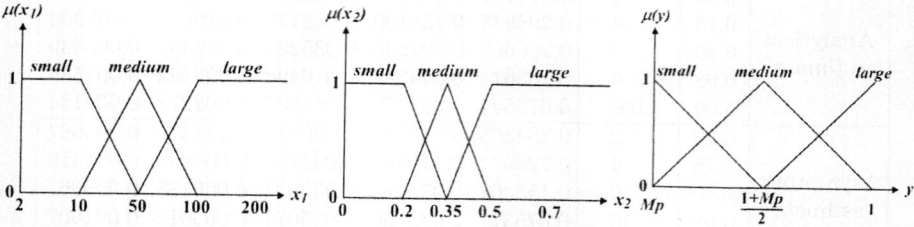

Fig. 1. (i) The number of current stations, x_1, as a linguistic variable that can take fuzzy sets "slow", "medium," and "fast" as M values in the left plot. (ii) The proposed estimate, x_2, as a linguistic variable that can take fuzzy sets "slow," "medium," and "fast" as p_{min} values in the center plot. (ii) The output of fuzzy rules, y, as a linguistic variable that can take fuzzy sets "slow," "medium," and "fast" as $[Mp_{min}, 1]$ values in the right plot.

The proposed P_T parameter can be used to evaluate the opportunity to perform a transmission on the shared channel. When the station decides to defer the transmission, it reschedules a new attempt, as in the case of a collision occurred. Specifically, the proposed algorithm adopted by each station is sketched in Algorithm 1.

Algorithm 1: Distributed fuzzy contention control mechanism
```
if (Backoff_Counter == 0) /* A slot for transmission is reached */
then
    calculate the S_U;
    calculate the M_p;
    obtain the y; /* y is the output of the fuzzy IF-THEN rules */
    calculate the P_T(S_U, N_A, y);
    if (Rand() < P_T(S_U, N_A, y))
    then
        BYPASS the transmission indication to the HW;
    else
        DEFER the transmission;
    if ((transmission deferred) or (collision occurred))
    then
        NOTIFY the collision occurred;
                        /* schedule a new retransmission */
        ...
```

The proposed mechanism can be used to extend the standard 802.11 access mechanism without requiring any additional hardware like AOB.

4 Steady-State Analysis of the DFCC Mechanism

In this section, to verify efficiency of our mechanism, the performance of the IEEE 802.11 standard protocol with AOB and proposed mechanism is investi-

Table 2. Physical parameters for simulations

Parameters	Values
Number of current stations (M)	2 to 200
CW_{min}	16
CW_{max}	1024
Channel transmission rate	2Mb/s
Payload size	Geometric distribution with q
Acknowledgement size	200 μ sec
Header size	136 μ sec
Slot Time (t_{slot})	50 μ sec
SIFS	28 μ sec
DIFS	128 μ sec
Propagation time	$< 1\ \mu$ sec

gated through simulations. The physical characteristics and parameter values of the investigated system are reported in Table 2. To analyze the DFCC behavior in a more realistic scenario, we assume that the message length distribution is bimodal. Specifically, we assume that "long messages" have an average length of 100 slots while "short messages" have an verage length of 2.5 slots, and a slot corresponds to 100 bits.

Fig. 2 and 3 show the protocol capacity of the IEEE 802.11 protocol with and without the additional mechanisms. In the Fig. 2 and 3, real lines (—) are the optimal analytical value and dotted lines (···) are the optimal estimate value of the IEEE 802.11 protocol, dash-dotted lines (- ·) are the channel utilization of the IEEE 802.11 protocol with the AOB mechanism, dashed lines (- -) are the channel utilization of the IEEE 802.11 protocol with the DFCC mechanism,

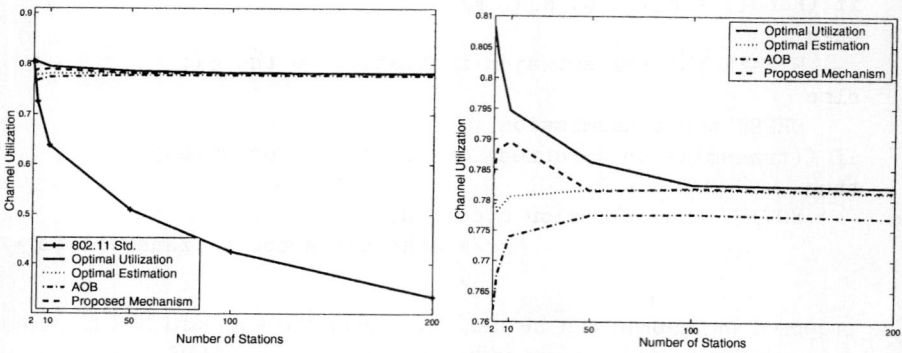

Fig. 2. (i) The left plot is the channel utilization of the IEEE 802.11 protocol with and without the additional mechanisms versus long messages. (ii) The right plot is the zooming version of the left plot.

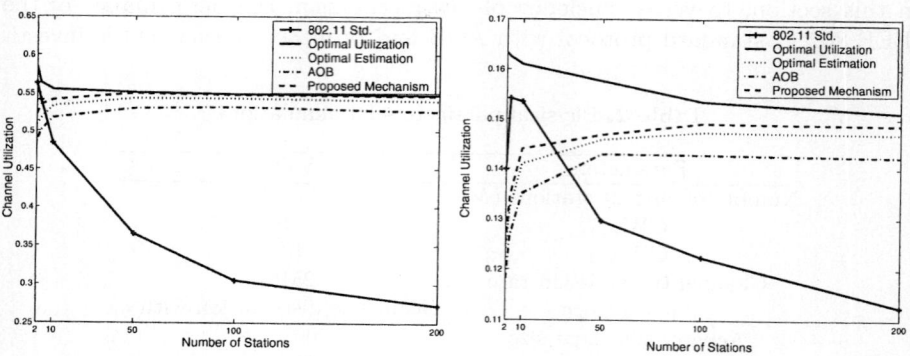

Fig. 3. (i) The left plot is the channel utilization of the IEEE 802.11 protocol with and without the additional mechanisms versus mixed traffic condition with $q = 0.2$. (ii) The right plot is the channel utilization of the IEEE 802.11 protocol with and without the additional mechanisms versus short messages.

and plus signed real lines (-+-) are the channel utilization of the standard IEEE 802.11 protocol. Simulation results indicate that the channel utilization with the DFCC mechanism is near-optimal and the DFCC mechanism is more effective than the AOB mechanism.

5 Conclusion

In this paper, the simple, and more accurate, approximation of the network contention level to maximize the theoretical throughput limit have been derived. Moreover, we have proposed and evaluated the DFCC mechanism, using a fuzzy logic approach, that can be applied to dynamically control the network contention level in an IEEE 802.11 network. This control is implemented through the computation in each station of the proposed *probability of transmission*. By simulation of the protocol capacity of the IEEE 802.11 protocol with and without the additional mechanisms, efficiency of the proposed DFCC mechanism is proven.

References

1. Bianchi, G., Fratta, L., Oliveri, M.: Performance Evaluation And Enhancement of The CSMA/CA MAC Protocol for 802.11 Wireless LANs. Proc. PIMRC. Taiwan, Oct. (1996) 392–396
2. Crow, B. P., Widjaja, I., Kim, J. G., Sakai, P. T.: IEEE 802.11 Wireless Local Area Networks. IEEE Commun. Mag., Sept. (1997) 116–126
3. Chhaya, H. S., Gupta, S.: Performance Modeling of Asynchronous Data Transfer Methods in The IEEE 802.11 MAC Protocol. ACM/Balzer Wireless Netw., Vol. 3. (1997) 217–234
4. IEEE Standard for Wireless LAN - Medium Access Control and Physical Layer Specification, P802.11. Nov. (1997)
5. Stallings, W.: Local & Metropolitan Area Networks. Englewood Cliffs, Prentice Hall (1996)
6. Weinmiller, J., Woesner, H., Ebert, P., Wolisz, A.: Analyzing and Tunning the Distributed Coordination Function in the IEEE 802.11 DFWMAC Draft Standard. Proc. Int. Workshop on Modelling, MASCOT (1996)
7. Cali, F., Conti, M., Gregori, E.: IEEE 802.11 Wireless LAN: Capacity Analysis and Protocol Enhancement. Proc. INFOCOM Conf., Mar./Apr. (1998) 142–149
8. Cali, F., Conti, M., Gregori, E.: Dynamic IEEE 802.11: Design, Modeling and Performance Evaluation. IEEE J. Selected Areas in Comm., Vol. 18(9). Sept. (2000) 1774–1786
9. Cali, F., Conti, M., Gregori, E.: Dynamic Tuning of The IEEE 802.11 Protocol to Achieve A Theoretical Throughput Limit. IEEE/ ACM Trans. Networking, Vol. 8(6). Dec. (2000) 785–799
10. Bononi, L., Conti, M., Donatiello, L.: Design And Performance Evaluation of A Distributed Contention Control (DCC) Mechanism for IEEE 802.11 Wireless Local Area Networks. J. Parallel And Distributed Computing, Vol. 60(4). Apr. 2000.

11. L. Bononi, M. Conti, and E. Gregori, *Runtime Optimization of IEEE 802.11 Wireless LANs Performance,* IEEE Trans. on Parallel and distributed Systems, Vol. 15(1). Jan. (2004) 66–80
12. Sugeno, M. and Nishida, M.: Fuzzy control of model car. Fuzzy Sets and Systems. (1985) 103–113
13. Wang L. X.: A Course in Fuzzy Systems and Control. Prentice-Hall Inc. (1997)
14. Hastad, J., Leighton, T., Rogoff, B.: Analysis of Backoff Protocols for Multiple Access Channels. SIAM J. Computing, Vol. 25(4). Aug. (1996) 740–774

TLCD Semi-active Control Methodology of Fuzzy Neural Network for Eccentric Buildings

Hong-Nan Li[1], Qiao Jin[1], Gangbing, Song[1,2], and Guo-Xin Wang[1]

[1] Department of Civil Engineering, Dalian University of Technology, Dalian 116024, China
hnli@dlut.edu.cn
[2] Department of Mechanical Engineering, University of Houston,
Houston 77204, USA

Abstract. In this paper, a semi-actively tuned liquid column damper (TLCD) based on fuzzy neural networks (FNN) is proposed to vibration control of irregular buildings excited by multi-dimensional earthquake ground motions. The fuzzy neural networks method takes advantage of both neural networks and fuzzy controls and has the unique combination of ability to learn via nonlinear mapping of neural nets and the capacity to integrate expert knowledge via fuzzy rules. The fuzzy neural networks based on Takagi-Sugeno model is adopted in this research to actively adjust the orifice opening-area of the TLCD. An eccentric building equipped with two TLCDs arranged in perpendicular directions is used as an object for suppressing vibrations induced by multi-dimensional earthquake ground motions. For numerical simulations, a state space representation of the building-TLCD system is derived. Numerical simulations demonstrate that TLCDs regulated by the fuzzy neural networks are effective in controlling both the translational and rotational seismic response of the eccentric building.

1 Introduction

Structural vibration control using neural networks and fuzzy theories has been conducted[1,2]. The main advantages of these intelligent methods is the relaxation of the requirement of an exact mathematical model. In addition, these methods can be applied to systems with nonlinearities, couplings and time varying parameters. Fuzzy control is thought as a technique of imitating man's thinking and does not require a mathematical model of the plant. Fuzzy control has the ability to approximate reasoning by utilizing experts' knowledge. However, this method lacks of both self-learning and self-adaptation in case of time-varying nonlinear systems. How to automatically generate or update the membership function and fuzzy rules are complicated problems. The neural networks technique has a powerful self-learning capability. From the modeling point of view, this technique is a typical black-box based method. After training, the input and output relationship of the neural networks is difficult to express. It is a challenge in control engineering to combine the advantage of the easy knowledge expression in fuzzy theory and the advantage of the

---

[1] Hong-Nan Li is a professor with the Dalian University of Technology.

strong self-learning capability in neural networks in order to improve the control system's learning and expressing capabilities.

Fuzzy neural network (FNN) is a relatively new development in intelligent control. Though it is a local approaching network, it is established based on the fuzzy system model in the sense that each node and parameter in the network have an obvious physical meaning. Hence, the initial values of these parameters could be determined based on the fuzzy or qualitative knowledge of the system, and the input-output relationship will quickly converge to the desired one by using the aforementioned learning algorithm. This is an advantage of FNN as compared with a pure neural networks method. Meanwhile, an FNN has the neural network structure and has the learning and parameter adaptation capabilities. Therefore it is better than a pure fuzzy logical system. A commonly used FNN is the one developed by Takagi-Sugeno[3]. This Takagi-Sugeno model based FNN has the advantage of computational efficiency and will be adopted in this research.

Tuned liquid column dampers (TLCD), basically a U-shape pipe with an orifice opening in the middle, was first proposed by Sakai et al.[8] and has been widely researched since then[4-7]. Recent years have seen an increasing number of researches in semi-active control of TLCD by actively adjusting the orifice opening-area. However, semi-active control of TLCD based on fuzzy neural networks intelligent control is rarely reported. In this paper, the Takagi-Sugeno model based fuzzy neural networks control is applied to semi-actively tuned liquid column dampers arranged in two perpendicular directions for suppressing both translational and rotational vibrations of an eccentric building subjected to multi-dimensional earthquake excitations. To help the control system design, this paper also briefly presents the theory of fuzzy neural network (FNN) based on the Takagi-Sugeno model (T-S model). The mathematical model of a multi-story eccentric structure-TLCD system in state space representation is derived. On the bases of control strategy, a semi-active control of vibration suppression of an eccentric building subjected to an earthquake excitation is established. Numerical examples are finally implemented by using FNN based on T-S model to verify the effectiveness of this method.

2 T-S Model-Based FNN in Structural Control

2.1 T-S Model-Based FNN

The T-S model based FNN is one kind of fuzzy neural networks in which the linear combination of input variables is the typical state of fuzzy criterions. This method was named as T-S fuzzy model that was presented by two Japanese researchers: Takagi and Sugeno[3]. The fuzzy networks consist of front and rear networks, which are utilized to match the former and later portions of fuzzy criterion, respectively.

2.2 Front Network

The front networks are composed of four layers. The first layer is the input that plays the role of transmitting the input value $x = [x_1 \ x_2 \cdots x_n]^T$ to the next layer as every node on this layer is connected to each component of input vector. The total number of nodes of this layer N_1 is equal to n.

The second layer has the function of calculating the membership function, μ_i^j. Every node on the second layer represents one linguistic variable,

$$\mu_i^j \triangleq \mu_{A_i^j}(x_i) \tag{1}$$

where $i = 1, 2, \cdots, n$ (n is the dimension of the inputs), and $j = 1, 2, \cdots, m_i$ (m_i is the total number of the linguistic variable x_i). For example, if the Gaussian bell-shape membership function is adopted, the membership function μ_i^j is given as follows,

$$\mu_i^j = e^{-\frac{(x_i - c_{ij})^2}{\sigma_{ij}^2}} \tag{2}$$

in which, c_{ij} and σ_{ij} are the center value and the width, respectively. The total number of nodes of this layer N_2 is computed based on,

$$N_2 = \sum_{i=1}^{n} m_i \tag{3}$$

The third layer has the role of matching the former portion of fuzzy criterion and calculating the degree of applicability of each criterion. Each node of this layer represents one fuzzy criterion.

$$\alpha_j = \min\{\mu_1^{i_1}, \mu_2^{i_2}, \cdots, \mu_n^{i_n}\} \tag{4}$$

or

$$\alpha_j = \mu_1^{i_1} \mu_2^{i_2} \cdots \mu_n^{i_n} \tag{5}$$

where $i_1 \in \{1, 2, \cdots, m_1\}$, $i_2 \in \{1, 2, \cdots, m_2\}$, $\cdots$, $i_n \in \{1, 2, \cdots, m_n\}$, $j = 1, 2, \cdots, m$, and $m = \prod_{i=1}^{n} m_i$. The total number of nodes of this layer N_3 is equal to m.

A larger value of membership function will appear only when the linguistic variables are near the inputs, otherwise the value will be much smaller (Gaussian membership function) or even close to zero (Triangular membership function). The value of the membership function will be treated as zero if it is close to zero. Therefore, only few outputs, αj, of nodes in this layer are nonzero and the most outputs are zero. This is quite similar to a local approaching function.

The fourth layer has the function of conducting normalization. The number of nodes of this layer is the same as that of the third layer, ie, $N_3 = m$. The normalization can be represented by,

$$\overline{\alpha}_j = \alpha_j \bigg/ \sum_{i=1}^{m} \alpha_i \qquad j = 1,2,\cdots,m \qquad (6)$$

2.3 Rear Networks

The rear networks comprise r parallel subnets with the same structure and each subnet generates an output.

The first layer of each subnet represents inputs. Each input is connected to every node of the second layer. The input value of the 0th node in the input layer is a constant 1, i.e., $x_0 = 1$. Its function is to provide the constant for the later portion of fuzzy criterion.

The second layer of each subnet has m nodes. Each node represents one criterion. The role of this layer is to compute the later portion of every criterion, i.e.

$$y_{ij} = p^i_{j0} + p^i_{j1} x_1 + \cdots + p^i_{jn} x_n = \sum_{k=0}^{n} p^i_{jk} x_k \qquad (i = 1,2,\cdots,r \qquad j = 1,2,\cdots,m) \qquad (7)$$

The third layer of each subnet represents system outputs, y_i, which is computed based on,

$$y_i = \sum_{j=1}^{m} \overline{\alpha}_j y_{ij} \qquad (i = 1,2,\cdots,r) \qquad (8)$$

where y_{ij} is the output of every node in the second layer, and $\overline{\alpha}_j$ denotes the weight of later portion of every criterion.

2.4 Learning Algorithm

Suppose that the total number of the linguistic variables is pre-determined, the main parameters to be identified through learning are the weights of the later network $p^k_{ji} (j = 1,2,\cdots,m; i = 0,1,\cdots,n; k = 1,2,\cdots,r)$ as well as the center value c_{ij} and width $\sigma_{ij} (i = 1,2,\cdots,m; j = 1,2,\cdots,m_i)$ of membership function of every node in the second layer in former network.

Assume the error cost function is

$$E = \frac{1}{2} \sum_{i=1}^{r} (y_{di} - y_i)^2 \qquad (9)$$

where y_{di} and y_i are the expected and actual outputs, respectively. The learning algorithm for p^k_{ji} is given as follows:

$$\frac{\partial E}{\partial p^k_{ji}} = \frac{\partial E}{\partial y_k} \frac{\partial y_k}{\partial y_{kj}} \frac{\partial y_{kj}}{\partial p^k_{ji}} = -(y_{dk} - y_k) \overline{\alpha}_j x_i \qquad (10)$$

$$p_{ji}^k(l+1) = p_{ji}^k(l) - \beta \frac{\partial E}{\partial p_{ji}^k} = p_{ji}^k(l) + \beta(y_{dk} - y_k)\overline{\alpha}_j x_i \qquad (11)$$

where $j = 1,2,\cdots,m$; $i = 0,1,\cdots,n$; $k = 1,2,\cdots,r$; and $\beta > 0$ is the learning rate. By assuming $y_{ij} = \omega_{ij}$, the results obtained earlier can be fully utilized, i.e.

$$\delta_i^{(5)} = y_{di} - y_i \qquad i = 1,2,\cdots,n \qquad (12)$$

$$\delta_j^{(4)} = \sum_{i=1}^r \delta_i^{(5)} y_{ij} \qquad (j = 1,2,\cdots,m) \qquad (13)$$

$$\delta_j^{(3)} = \delta_j^{(4)} \sum_{\substack{i=1 \\ j\neq 1}}^m \alpha_i \bigg/ \left(\sum_{i=1}^m \alpha_i\right)^2 \qquad (j = 1,2,\cdots,m) \qquad (14)$$

$$\delta_{ij}^{(2)} = \sum_{k=1}^m \delta_k^{(3)} S_{ij} e^{-\frac{(x_i - c_{ij})^2}{\sigma_{ij}^2}} \qquad (i = 1,2,\cdots,n; \quad j = 1,2,\cdots,m_i) \qquad (15)$$

$S_{ij} = 1$ when μ_i^j is the minimum of inputs at the node of the *kth* criterion and when the min calculation (Eq. 4) is adopted, otherwise $S_{ij} = 0$.

$S_{ij} = \prod_{\substack{j=1 \\ j\neq i}}^n \mu_j^i$ when μ_i^j is one of the inputs at the node of the kth criterion and when the multiplying calculation (Eq.5) is adopted, otherwise $S_{ij} = 0$. Finally, the following equations are derived as

$$\frac{\partial E}{\partial c_{ij}} = -\delta_{ij}^{(2)} \frac{2(x_i - c_{ij})}{\sigma_{ij}^2} \; ; \quad \frac{\partial E}{\partial \sigma_{ij}} = -\delta_{ij}^{(2)} \frac{2(x_i - c_{ij})^2}{\sigma_{ij}^3} \qquad (16)$$

$$c_{ij}(k+1) = c_{ij}(k) - \beta \frac{\partial E}{\partial c_{ij}} \; ; \quad \sigma_{ij}(k+1) = \sigma_{ij}(k) - \beta \frac{\partial E}{\partial \sigma_{ij}} \qquad (17)$$

where $\beta > 0$ is the learning rate. $i = 1,2,\cdots,n$, and $j = 1,2,\cdots,m_i$.

3 Equation of Motion for a Structure-TLCD System

The mechanical model of multi-story eccentric structure-TLCD system is shown in Fig.1[2], in which the O, S and M are the geometry, stiffness and mass centers; u, v and θ represent the floor displacements in x and y directions, and the angle around central axis; $\ddot{u}_g$, $\ddot{v}_g$ and $\ddot{\theta}_g$ designate the ground accelerations in x, y and θ directions.

The mass center is taken as the origin of uMv coordinate system. Assuming TLCDs installed on the top of structure along the x and y directions separately with (luh, lvh) and (lus, lvs) coordinates, the liquid displacements from the equilibrium position in the TLCDs are h and s.

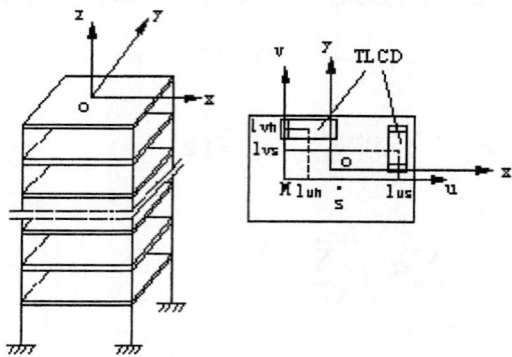

Fig. 1. Analytical model

Lay two TLCDs on the top of structure. The equation of motion for the structure-TLCD system excited by multi-dimensional earthquake ground motions could be derived as follows:

$$[M]\{\ddot{X}\}+[C]\{\dot{X}\}+[K]\{X\} = -[M][E]\{\ddot{X}_g\} \tag{18}$$

where $[M]$, $[C]$ and $[K]$ are the mass, damper and stiffness matrices, respectively. The $\{X\}$ is the displacement vector and $\{\ddot{X}_g\} = \{\ddot{u}_g \quad \ddot{v}_g \quad \ddot{\theta}_g\}$ is the vector of three dimensional ground motions. $[E]$ is the unit vector.

4 Control Strategy

Assume that the structure can be modeled as a single degree of freedom system with TLCD. Using the equivalency between the head loss during the half-cycle harmonic response in the U-type pipe and the energy consuming of a linear system, the equivalent damping ratio of TLCD can be obtained by [8]

$$\zeta_T = \frac{\kappa \omega_T^3 \xi_0}{3\omega_s \pi g} \tag{19}$$

where ε_0 is the amplitude of liquid movement when the liquid velocity relative to the U-shaped pipe is zero, and k represents the head loss coefficient of liquid. ω_r and w_s designate the vibrating frequencies of liquid in TCLD and the structure, respectively. The optimized damping value adopted here means that regulating the

TLCD damper to the optimum value can attain the optimized energy-consuming effect. Based on the previous studies [8]. The following basic assumptions are adopted in this paper: 1) the optimal control effect could be achieved if $\omega_s \approx \omega_T \approx \omega_s/\sqrt{1+\mu}$; 2) the mass ratio , μ , is barely affected by the structure; 3) the equivalent damping ratio, ζ_T, is barely affected by the structure; 4) the structural damping ratio, ζ_s, is very small and can be negnected. Thus, the circular modal frequency and modal damping ratio are:

$$\omega_{1,2} = \omega_a \left(1 \pm \frac{\operatorname{Im}\beta}{2}\right); \quad \zeta_{1,2} = (\zeta_T \pm \operatorname{Re}\beta)/2 \qquad (20)$$

The corresponding mode shape vector is

$$\begin{Bmatrix} \phi_x \\ \phi_\xi \end{Bmatrix}_{1,2} = \begin{Bmatrix} 1 \\ -i(\zeta_T \pm \beta)/(\mu\gamma) \end{Bmatrix} \qquad (21)$$

where $\omega_{1,2}$ and $\zeta_{1,2}$ represent the circular frequency and damping ratio of the 1st and 2nd modes. $\gamma = B/L$. $\beta = \sqrt{\zeta_T^2 - \mu\gamma^2}$. Im and Re are the imaginary part and the real part, respectively. Eq. (24) indicates that the two damping ratios can effectively play their roles only when the two damping ratios are equal. Otherwise, the damping ratio of the 2nd mode will play the dominant role. Therefore, the optimal damping ratio can be obtained by

$$\zeta_T^{opt} = \gamma\sqrt{\mu} \qquad (22)$$

Since the damping ratio, ζ_T, depends on the cell-opening ratio as well as the liquid head loss coefficient κ, the best effects of vibration reduction could be achieved by continuously regulating the value of κ to keep ζ_T optimal. In fact, the orifice opening area in the U-shape pipe needs to be quickly adjusted only when the velocity of liquid relative to the pipe reaches zero.

The control strategy used here focuses on reducing the vibration of the 2nd mode with low damping by reasonably choosing ζ_T via adjusting orifice-opening area. In this way, only the 1st mode, not the 2nd mode, will be excited. The modal-participation factor of the 1st mode is kept the largest. To realize this, the following condition should be satisfied:

$$\frac{\xi}{\dot{x}} = -\frac{\zeta_T + \beta}{\omega_a H \gamma} \qquad (23)$$

Within a short time interval after $\dot{\xi} = 0$, the structural response may be approximated by

$$\dot{x} = \operatorname{Re}[\dot{x}_0 e^{i\omega_a t}]; \quad \xi = \operatorname{Re}[\xi_0 e^{i\omega_a t}] \qquad (24)$$

where $\dot{x}_0$ is the structural velocity when the relative liquid velocity is equal to zero. Substituting Eq. (27) in Eq. (26), one can obtain

$$\xi_0 = -\frac{(\zeta_T + \beta)\dot{x}_0}{\mu \gamma \omega_a} \qquad (25)$$

With $\zeta_T \gg \gamma\sqrt{\mu}$ and ζ_T being non-negative, Eq. (28) may be further simplified to

$$\zeta_T = \left|\frac{\mu \gamma \omega_a \xi_0}{2\dot{x}_0}\right| \qquad (26)$$

Substitution of Eq. (29) into Eq.(26) yields

$$\kappa = \frac{3\omega_s \pi g}{2\omega_T^3}\left|\frac{\mu \gamma \omega_a}{\dot{x}_0}\right| \qquad (27)$$

5 Example of TLCD Semi-active Control

An eccentric structure is taken as the numerical simulation object. Its mass $m_s = 2.5 \times 10^6 \, Ns^2/m$. The inertia of floor to the mass center is J=5.1×105kg·m2. Its stiffness characterisctics are given as: kx=3.1×106N/m in the x direction, ky=4.6×106N/m in the y direction, and kt=3.27×108N·m/Rad in the torsion direction. The structural damping ratioζs=0.05 and eccentric distance ey=3m only in y direction. The inherent period in x direction Tx=5.64s. The TLCD parameters are: the mass ratio µ=0.01, =0.5, liquid length L=15.96m and cross-section area A=1.566m. The El Centro seismic record of USA in May 18, 1940 is used as the input in x direction.

The orifice-opening rate is continuously controlled by T-S model based FFN. Its essential principle is that the cell-opening area needs to be adjusted quickly when the relative liquid velocity in TLCD is zero. In this numerical simulation, the T-S model based FNN is selected, in which there is an unit in the input layer representing the structural velocity $\dot{x}_0$ when the relative velocity of liquid is zero and an unit in the output layer representing the orifice-opening ratio. The seismic response results of structure excited by the El-Centro wave with the theoretical analysis are used as the training sample. To make the FNN have a better generalized capability, the amplitude of El Centro wave is changed to different levels, 0.03g, 0.06g, 0.12g, 0.25g and 0.5g and their corresponding earthquake intensities are changed from V to IX. The network target error is chosen as 0.002. Thus, the training will stop if the error of the FNN is less than or equal to this value.

Fig. 2 shows the time history of orifice-opening ratio in TLCD under the excitation of the El Centro wave. For comparison purpose, the results of the case with a standard neural network controller is also presented in Fig. 2. This figure clearly reveals that the FNN has a better performance. The structural translational and rotational responses in three different cases of uncontrolled, passive control with the orifice fully open, and semi-active control, are shown in Fig. 3 and Fig.4, respectively. These two figures show that the semi-active control of TLCD with FNN achives the best seismic response reduction. The maximum values of vibration reduction using the passive and semi-active control methods are listed in Table 1.

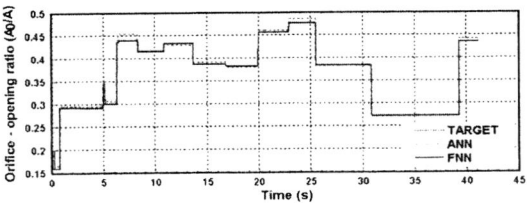

Fig. 2. Orifice-opening ratio versus time

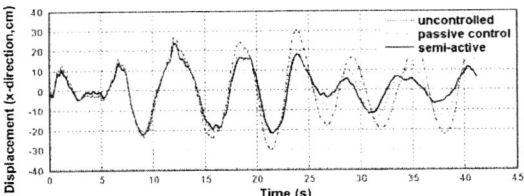

Fig. 3. Displacement time history of structural system

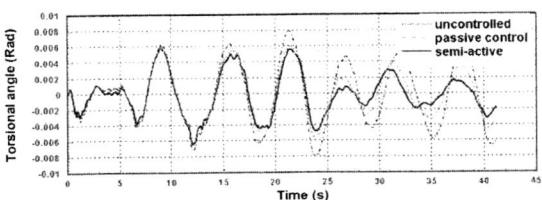

Fig. 4. Torsional angle time history of structural system

Table 1. Vibration reduction effect of TLCD

Orifice-opening ratio deviation (%)		2.54
Displacement reduction ratio (%)	Passive	26.13
	Semi-active	31.56
Rotational angle reduction ratio (%)	Passive	28.96
	Semi-active	33.47

6 Conclusions

The application of the T-S model based FNN in TLCD semi-active control has been studied in this paper. The conclusions can be summarized as follows:

1) Using the T-S model based FNN in the structural vibration control is not only feasible, but also effective.

2) Structural seismic response control using FNN can effectively solve some complex problems, such as non-linearity and structural coupling, and also make the online learning based structural control possible.
3) Structural semi-active control by regulating the orifice opening area in TLCD is simple, convenient and effective. This semi-active method is more effective than a pure passive control.

References

1. Yan Shi. Study on artificial neural net and fuzzy logical method in structural intelligent control, Ph.D dissertation, Dalian University of Technology (2000)
2. Li Hong-Nan, Huo Lin-Sheng, Yan Shi. Study on control of neural network semi-active TLCD to irregular buildings. earthquake engineering and engineering vibration **21** (2001) 135-141
3. Takagi.K and Sugeno.M. Fuzzy identification of systems and its application to modeling and control. IEEE Transactions on Systems, Man and Cybernetics **15** (1985) 116-132
4. T. BALENDRA, C. M.WANG and H. F. CHEONG, E!ectiveness of tuned liquid column dampers for vibration control of towers, Engineering Structures **17** (1995) 668-675
5. H. GAO,K. C. S.KWOK and B. SAMALI, Optimization of tuned liquid column dampers, Engineering Structures **19** (1997) 476-486
6. K. C. S. KWOK, Y. L.XU and B. SAMALI Computational Mechanics (Y. K. Cheung, J. H. W.Lee and A. Y. T. Leung, editors) (1991) 249-254. A. A. Balkema, Rotterdam, Control of wind-induced vibrations of tall structures by optimized tuned liquid column dampers
7. B. SAMALI,K. C. S.KWOK, S.PARSANEJAD and Y. L. XU, Vibration control of buildings by tuned liquid column dampers, Proceedings of the Second International Conference on Highrise Buildings, Nanjing, China (1992) 402-407
8. Abe N., Kimura S. and Fujino Y. Control Laws for Semi-Active Tuned Liquid Column Damper with Variable Orifice Openings. Proc. of 2nd international Workshop on Structural Control. Hong Kong (1996) 5-10

Use of Adaptive Learning Radial Basis Function Network in Real-Time Motion Tracking of a Robot Manipulator

Dongwon Kim[1], Sung-Hoe Huh[1], Sam-Jun Seo[2], and Gwi-Tae Park[1,*]

[1] Department of Electrical Engineering, Korea University, 1, 5-Ka Anam-Dong,
Seongbuk-Gu, Seoul 136-701, Korea
{upground, gtpark}@korea.ac.kr
[2] Department of Electrical & Electronic Engineering, Anyang University, 708-113,
Anyang 5dong, Manan-gu, Anyang-shi, Kyunggi-do, 430-714, Korea
ssj@anyang.ac.kr

Abstract. In this paper, real time motion tracking of a robot manipulator based on the adaptive learning radial basis function network is proposed. This method for adaptive learning needs little knowledge of the plant in the design processes. So the centers and widths of the employed radial basis function network (RBFN) as well as the weights are determined adaptively. With the help of the RBFN, motion tracking of the robot manipulator is implemented without knowing the information of the system in advance. Furthermore, identification error and the tuned parameters of the RBFN are guaranteed to be uniformly ultimately bounded in the sense of Lyapunov's stability criterion.

1 Introduction

Many kind of manipulator systems are widely used in various application fields, as the development of mechatronics and computer controlled systems. Especially, application of intelligent control techniques (fuzzy system, neural network, and fuzzy-neural network) to the modeling and control of robotic manipulators have received considerable attention [1]. In general, robot manipulators have to face various uncertainties in their dynamics such as payload parameters, friction, and disturbance. So it is difficult to establish an appropriate mathematical model for the design of a model-based control system. Therefore the real time motion tracking task to an environment and its dynamic behavior analysis are required.

Recently, many researches [2-5] have been applied both fuzzy system and neural networks for robot manipulators. It is known that fuzzy system is able to deal with human knowledge. Therefore, the precise mathematical models of the plant and the environment are not needed for designing the controller. However, there are some difficulties to design the fuzzy controller systematically. In addition once fuzzy rules and membership functions are decided, usually they will not be modified even if the controller is not perfect. In the other hand, it is known that neural networks have

---

* Corresponding author.

ability to learn from experiments and adapt to a new environment. Because of these abilities, this controller is especially effective in the case that the dynamics of the environment is unknown. But it is difficult to design a good neural network system without learning [6]. As another method, radial basis function network (RBFN) is one of the most promising because of its drastic identification performance with simple structure, fast computation time and higher adaptive performance.

In this paper, we employed a adaptive learning RBFN as an identifier of robot manipulator system. The adaptive RBFN has no need of an initialization and has the ability to change its own structure during learning procedure. The RBFN initially has only one node in the hidden layer, but during the learning process, the network creates new nodes, and annexes similar nodes if they are needed. This adaptive learning scheme [7-10] is combined with identification algorithm for uncertain nonlinear system. Learning algorithm also guarantees the stability of the whole network in the sense of Lyapunov. The variables that must be at least bounded are the identification error, weights, centers and widths of RBFs. The employed learning algorithm makes these variables be uniformly ultimately bounded, and the experimental implementation for the robot manipulator shows the performance and efficiency of the scheme.

2 Robot Manipulator and Its Experimental Environment

We consider a two-degree of freedom robot arm and its practical robot manipulator to be modeled in this paper. They are shown in Fig. 1.

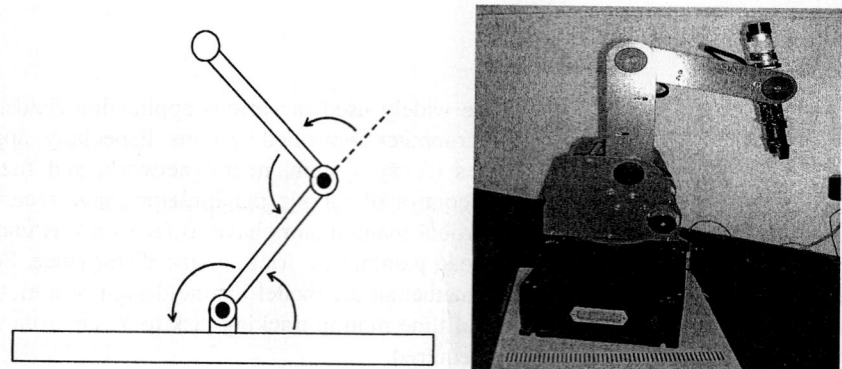

Fig. 1. Schematic diagram of the two links manipulator and its actual structure

The robot arm consists of two-link: the first one mounted on a rigid base by means of a frictionless hinges and the second mounted at the end of link one by means of a frictionless ball bearing. The two joints robot arm in the horizontal plane contains a personal computer, a D/A card, a decoder etc. The first and second link is individually driven by AC motor.

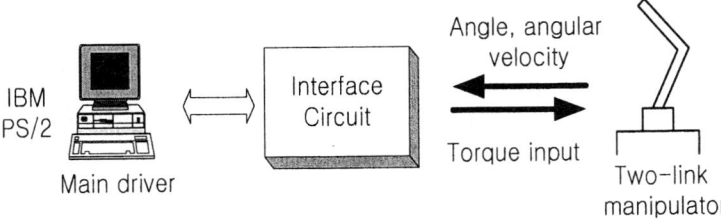

Fig. 2. Experimental setup for two joints robot arm

Since the pre-information about the robot manipulator is unknown, for the identification process, measuring procedure for real input-output vector is necessary. For that purpose, a simple experimental environment connecting to the manipulator is set up. Its block diagram is shown in Fig. 2. In this experimental system, IBM PS/2 compatible computer is used as a main driver which gives torque commands for driving the actuators on each link in manipulator. Because the main driver is digital system but the controlled manipulator is analogue one, the additional interface circuit is necessary. After the desired torque commands are to be engaged in the manipulator through the main driver and interface circuit, we can obtain the real input-output data of the identified robot manipulator.

3 Adaptive Learning of Radial Basis Function Network

3.1 General Description of the RBFN

RBFN is a three-layer neural networks structure. The employed structure of the RBFN is shown in Fig. 6. In RBFN, each hidden neuron computes the distance from its input to the neuron's central point, m, and applies the RBF to that distance, as shows in eq. (1)

$$\xi_i(x) = \phi(\|x - m_i\|^2 / \sigma_i^2) \tag{1}$$

where $\xi_i(x)$ is the output yielded by hidden neuron number i when input x is applied; ϕ is the RBF, m_i is the center of the ith hidden neuron, and σ_i is its radius.

The neurons of the output layer perform a weighted sum using the outputs of the hidden layer and the weights of the links that connect both output and hidden layer neurons

$$y_j(x) = \sum_{i=1}^{n} \theta_{ij} \xi_i(x) + h_{0j} \tag{2}$$

where $y_j(x)$ is the value yielded by output neuron number j when input x is applied: θ_{ij} is the weight of the links that connects hidden neuron number i and output neuron number j, h_{0j} is a bias for the output neuron, and finally, n is the number of hidden neurons.

3.2 Adaptive Learning Algorithm of the RBFN

In the conventional design procedure, we have to set the initial structure before starting the learning of the network. In particular, it is hard to specify this initial structure in advance due to the uncertain distribution of on-line incoming data. We approach this problem by using a adaptive RBFN inspired by the methods in [7-10].

Similarity measure
Suppose the μ_A and μ_B as the activation functions of neurons A and B, respectively.

$$\mu_A(x) = \exp\{-(x-m_1)^2 / \sigma_1^2\}$$
$$\mu_B(x) = \exp\{-(x-m_2)^2 / \sigma_2^2\} \tag{3}$$

And consider a criterion for the degree of similarity of two neurons, $S(\cdot, \cdot)$. Then, $S(\cdot, \cdot)$ takes the values in [0, 1], and the higher $S(A, B)$ is the more similar A and B are. Similarity is measured as follows,

$$S(A, B) = \frac{|A \cap B|}{|A \cup B|} = \frac{|A \cap B|}{\sigma_1 \sqrt{\pi} + \sigma_2 \sqrt{\pi} - |A \cap B|} \tag{4}$$

where

$$|A| + |B| = |A \cap B| + |A \cup B|,$$

$$|A \cap B| =$$
$$\frac{1}{2} \frac{h^2(m_2 - m_1 + \sqrt{\pi}(\sigma_1 + \sigma_2))}{\sqrt{\pi}(\sigma_1 + \sigma_2)} +$$
$$\frac{1}{2} \frac{h^2(m_2 - m_1 + \sqrt{\pi}(\sigma_1 - \sigma_2))}{\sqrt{\pi}(\sigma_2 - \sigma_1)} + \tag{5}$$
$$\frac{1}{2} \frac{h^2(m_2 - m_1 - \sqrt{\pi}(\sigma_1 - \sigma_2))}{\sqrt{\pi}(\sigma_1 - \sigma_2)}$$
$$h(x) = \max\{0, x\}$$

Creating a new neuron
The procedure for creating new neuron is described as follows.

Step 1: Get the input $\mathbf{x}(t)$ and calculate the ϕ vector shown in Fig. 3(a).

$$\phi = \begin{bmatrix} \phi_1 & \phi_2 & \cdots & \phi_{N(t)} \end{bmatrix}^T \tag{6}$$

where ϕ_q, $q = 1, 2, \cdots, N(t)$ is the output value of each hidden neuron.

Step 2: Find the unit J having the maximum response value shown in Fig. 3 (b).

$$\phi_J = \max_{q=1, N(t)} \phi_q \tag{7}$$

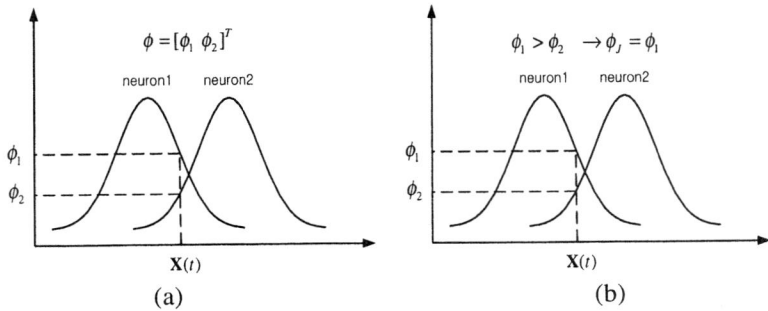

Fig. 3. Schematic representations of step 1 and 2

Step 3: Determine whether a new neuron is added or not according to the following criterion (refer to Fig. 4)

$$\begin{cases} if\ \phi_J \geq \overline{\phi} & \to \quad J \text{ is winner (Do nothing).} \\ if\ \phi_J < \overline{\phi} & \to \quad \text{Create a new unit.} \end{cases} \quad (8)$$

where $0 \leq \overline{\phi} < 1$ is a threshold value

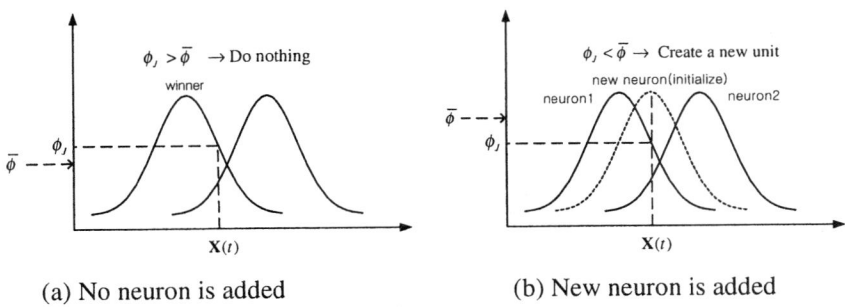

(a) No neuron is added   (b) New neuron is added

Fig. 4. Schematic representations of step 3

Step 4: Modify or initialize parameters.
1) If J th neuron is the winner (Do nothing),

$$n_J(t) = n_J(t-1)$$

$$\alpha_J(t) = \frac{1}{n_J(t)} \quad (9)$$

$$N(t) = N(t-1)$$

$$\mathbf{m}_J(t) = \mathbf{m}_J(t-1) + \alpha_J(t)\left[u(t) - \mathbf{m}_J(t-1)\right]$$

where α_J is the local gain

The local gain, α_J, governs the speed of the adaptive process for $\mathbf{m}_J$ and is inversely proportional to the active frequency, n_J, of the Jth unit up to the present time instant. The reason why we use this local gain is that it prevents the neurons from concentrating on the small area.

2) If a new neuron is created, we initialize parameters.

$$N(t^+) = N(t) + 1$$
$$\mathbf{m}_{N(t^+)} = \mathbf{x}(t)$$
$$\sigma_{N(t^+)} = \sigma_J \qquad (10)$$
$$\theta_{N(t^+)i} = 0, \quad i = 1,...,n$$

where t^+ indicates the time right after t.

Annexing two neurons
Step 5: Find the similarity set for annexation. Refer to Fig. 5 (a). If we have N(t) neuron at time instance t, the similarity set is

$$S_{annexation} = \{S(1,2), S(1,3), \cdots S(N(t)-1, N(t))\} \qquad (11)$$

where S(i, j) is the similarity between ith and jth neuron.

Step 6: In the similarity set, if there are elements which satisfy $S(i, j) > S_0$, ith and jth neuron are annexed. Refer to Fig. 5 (b). The annexed neuron has the center, slope and weight determined as

$$N(t^+) = N(t) - 1$$
$$\mathbf{m}_{annex}(t^+) = \frac{\mathbf{m}_i(t) + \mathbf{m}_j(t)}{2}$$
$$\sigma_{annex}(t^+) = \frac{\sigma_i(t) + \sigma_j(t)}{2} \qquad (12)$$
$$\theta_{annex,k}(t^+) = \frac{\theta_{ik}(t)\phi_i(t) + \theta_{jk}(t)\phi_j(t)}{\phi_{newi}(t^+)}, \quad k = 1,...,n$$

In step 4 and step 6, the new weight $\theta_{N(t^+)k}$ and $\theta_{annex,k}(t^+)$, $k = 1,...,n$ are set to have no effect on the output of the RBFN by creation or annexation, that is $\hat{y}(t) = \hat{y}(t^+)$. The RBFN gets to find proper structure with above procedures step 1-step 6 going on.

Learning procedure based on the Lyapunov stability
The input-output behavior of the system to be approximated is describe by

$$\dot{\mathbf{x}} = f(\mathbf{x}, \mathbf{u}) \qquad 13)$$

where $\mathbf{x} \in R^n$ is the state and $u \in R^m$ is the input of the system, and $f(\cdot)$ is an unknown nonlinear function.

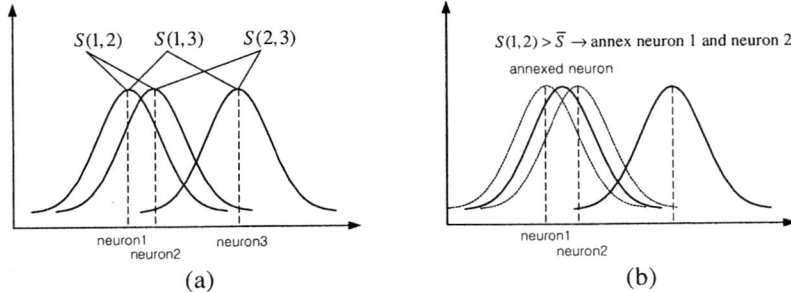

Fig. 5. Schematic representations of step 5 and 6

Let the eq. (13) rewrite using self-organizing RBFN eq. (1) including the reconstruction error of the network, ε :

$$\dot{\mathbf{x}} = -\mathbf{A}\mathbf{x} + \mathbf{A}\mathbf{x} + f(\mathbf{x}, \mathbf{u}) = \\ -\mathbf{A}\mathbf{x} + \boldsymbol{\theta}^{*T}\boldsymbol{\xi}(\mathbf{x}, \mathbf{u} | \mathbf{c}^*, \boldsymbol{\delta}^*) + \varepsilon \quad (14)$$

where $\xi = [\xi_1\ \xi_2, ..., \xi_{N(t)}]^T$, $c = [m_1^T\ m_2^T, ..., m_{N(t)}^T]^T$ and $\delta = [\sigma_1^T\ \sigma_2^T, ..., \sigma_{N(t)}^T]^T$ are the output of the hidden layer, center value and the width of the neurons, respectively, and A>0. In eq. (14), '*' means the optimal value of the parameters in the RBFN, and in normal cases, identified model of eq. (14) can be written as

$$\dot{\hat{\mathbf{x}}} = -\mathbf{A}\hat{\mathbf{x}} + \hat{\boldsymbol{\theta}}^T \boldsymbol{\xi}(\mathbf{x}, \mathbf{u} | \hat{\mathbf{c}}, \hat{\boldsymbol{\delta}}) \quad (15)$$

By using eq. (14) and eq. (15) the time derivative of error, $\dot{e}$, is derived as

$$\dot{e} = \dot{\hat{\mathbf{x}}} - \dot{\mathbf{x}} = -\mathbf{A}\dot{e} + \hat{\boldsymbol{\theta}}^T \hat{\xi} - \boldsymbol{\theta}^{*T}\xi^* - \varepsilon \\ = -\mathbf{A}e + \tilde{\boldsymbol{\theta}}^T \{\hat{\xi} - \dot{\hat{\xi}}\hat{\varphi}\} + \hat{\boldsymbol{\theta}}^T \dot{\hat{\xi}}\tilde{\varphi} + w(t) \quad (16)$$

where $w(t) = \tilde{\boldsymbol{\theta}}^T \dot{\hat{\xi}}\varphi^* - \boldsymbol{\theta}^{*T} O(\cdot) - \varepsilon$ and it is norm-bounded

Now, if the update laws for the parameters in the adaptive learning RBFN are determined as

$$\dot{\tilde{\boldsymbol{\theta}}} = \dot{\hat{\boldsymbol{\theta}}} = r_\theta [\dot{\hat{\xi}}\hat{\varphi}e^T\mathbf{P} - \hat{\xi}e^T\mathbf{P}] - \kappa r_\theta |e|\hat{\boldsymbol{\theta}} \\ \dot{\tilde{\varphi}} = \dot{\hat{\varphi}} = r_q[-e^T\mathbf{P}\hat{\boldsymbol{\theta}}^T\dot{\hat{\xi}}]^T - \kappa r_q |e|\hat{\varphi} \quad (17)$$

where κ is a positive constant at designer's disposal.

Then, the identification error e and the estimated parameters $\boldsymbol{\theta}$, φ in the RBF network are all uniformly ultimately bounded.

4 Experimental Results

The performance and capability of the adaptive learning RBFN will be demonstrated experimentally for robot manipulator system in this section. Any information and characteristics about the identified manipulator is not known, and the characteristics of the actuators for each link are also merging into the identification process.

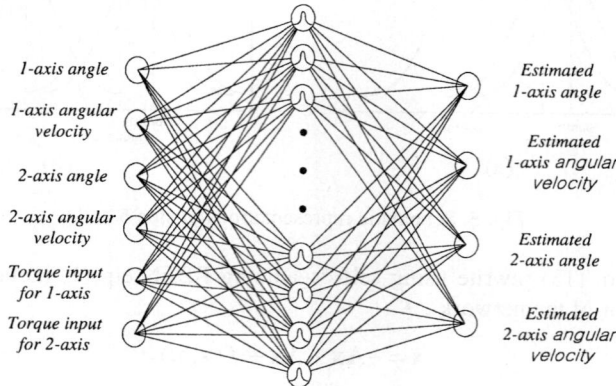

Fig. 6. Structure of the RBFN for robot manipulator

For the identification of the robot manipulator, the input vector of the adaptive RBFN consists of angle, angular velocity and torque input for each axis, and all of them are to be measured with experimental setup. The output vector is the estimated angle and angular velocity for each axis. This structure is shown in Fig. 6, and the initial value of the number of hidden neuron is one. However, as the learning phase is going on, the number of neurons in the hidden layer can be increased by the self-organizing mechanism.

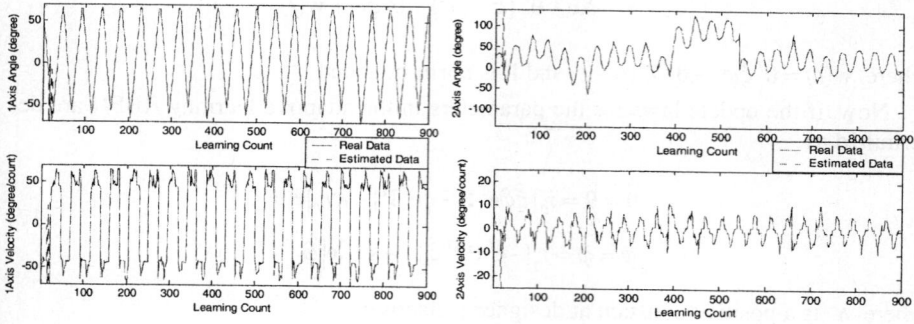

Fig. 7. Angle and angular velocities in 1-axis and 2-axis

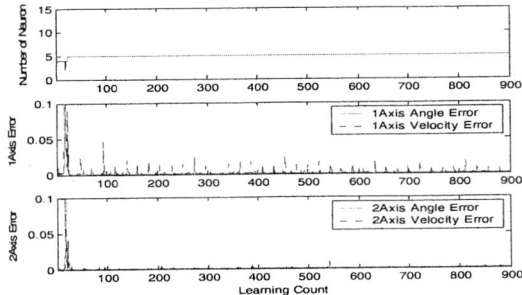

Fig. 8. Number of neurons and errors of angle and angular velocity of each axis

The design parameter of learning procedure are as follows: κ 5×10^{-7}, $\bar{\phi}$ in Step 3 0.750, S_0 in Step 5 0.980, total number of learning phase 900, initial number of neuron 1. Parameters of learning rate, r_θ and r_q are 7 and 0.06, respectively.

The experimental results are illustrated in Figs. 7-8. In these figures, the real (measured) and estimated values of angle and angular velocity of each axis, and their errors are presented. And the variation of the number of neurons in the hidden layer is also displayed.

4 Conclusions

In this paper modeling of robot manipulator using adaptive learning radial basis function network is implemented and experimentally verified. The RBFN creates and annexes neurons on-line and automatically during the identification procedure. And with the structure learning procedure, the centers and widths of RBFN as well as the weights are to be adaptively determined. If the input vector is too far away from the existent neurons, the new neuron will be created, and if the two neurons are too close each other, these neurons will be annexed. In this paper, we guaranteed the stability of the whole closed-loop system in the Lyapunov standpoint. The identification error and the learned parameters of the RBFN are also guaranteed to be uniformly ultimately bounded.

Acknowledgment

The authors thank the financial support of the KESRI and MOCIE. This work has been supported by KESRI(R-2003-B-485), which is funded by MOCIE(Ministry of commerce, industry and energy).

References

[1] Wai, R.J., Chen, P.C.: Intelligent Tracking Control for Robot Manipulator Including Actuator Dynamics via TSK-Type Fuzzy Neural Network. IEEE Trans. Fuzzy Syst. 12 (2004) 552-559
[2] Morris, A., Khemaissia, S.: Stable and fast neurocontroller for robot arm movement. IEE Proc.- Control Theory and Application. 142 (1996) 378-384

[3] Gurkan, E., Erkmen, I., Erkmen, A.M.: Two-way fuzzy adaptive identification and control of a flexible-joint robot arm. Inf. Sci. 145 (2003) 13-43
[4] Liu,M.: Decentralized control of robot manipulators: nonlinear and adaptive approaches. IEEE Trans Automatic Control. 44 (1999) 357-363
[5] Tayebi, A.: Adaptive iterative learning control for robot manipulators. Automatica. 40 (2004) 1195-1203
[6] Kiguchi, K., Fukuda, T.: Robot Manipulator Contact Force Control Application of Fuzz-Neural Network. Proc. IEEE Intl. Conf. Robotics and Automation. (1995) 875-880
[7] Nie, J., Linkens, D.A.: Learning control using fuzzified self-organizing radial basis function network. IEEE Trans Fuzzy Systems. 1 (1993) 280-287
[8] Lin, C.J., Lin, C.T., Lee, C.S.G.: Fuzzy adaptive learning network with on-line neural learning. Fuzzy Sets and Systems. 71 (1995) 25-45
[9] Sanner, R.M., Slotine, J.J.E.: Gaussian networks for direct adaptive control. IEEE Trans Neural Networks. 3 (1992) 837-863
[10] Schaal, S., Atkeson, C., Vijayakumar, S.: Real-time robot learning with locally weighted statistical learning. Proc. IEEE Intl. Conf. Robotics and Automation. 1 (2000) 288-293
[11] Panchapakesan, C.; Palaniswami, M.; Ralph, D.; Manzie, C.: Effects of moving the center's in an RBF network. IEEE Trans. Neural Networks 13 (2002) 1299 - 1307
[12] Fu, X.J., Wang, L.P.: Data dimensionality reduction with application to simplifying RBF network structure and improving classification performance. IEEE Trans. System, Man, Cybern, Part B Cybernetics 33 (2003) 399-409
[13] Bohte, S.M.; La Poutre, H.; Kok, J.N.: Unsupervised clustering with spiking neurons by sparse temporal coding and multilayer RBF networks. IEEE Trans. Neural Networks 13 (2002) 426 - 435
[14] Rajapakse, J.C., Wang, L.P. (Eds.): Neural Information Processing: Research and Development. Springer, Berlin (2004)

Obstacle Avoidance for Redundant Nonholonomic Mobile Modular Manipulators via Neural Fuzzy Approaches

Yangmin Li and Yugang Liu

Department of Electromechanical Engineering, Faculty of Science and Technology,
University of Macau, Av. Padre Tomás Pereira S.J., Taipa, Macao S.A.R., P.R. China
{ymli, ya27401}@umac.mo

Abstract. This paper addresses an obstacle avoidance issue for redundant nonholonomic mobile modular manipulators. On the basis of modular robot concept, an integrated dynamic modeling method is proposed, which takes both the mobile platform and the onboard modular manipulator as an integrated structure. A new obstacle avoidance algorithm is proposed which is mainly composed of two parts: a self-motion planner (SMP) and a robust adaptive neural fuzzy controller (RANFC). One important feature of this algorithm lies in that obstacles are avoided by online adjusting self-motions so that the end-effector task will not be affected unless the obstacles are just on the desired trajectory. The RANFC does not rely on exact aprior dynamic parameters and can suppress bounded external disturbance effectively. The effectiveness of the proposed algorithm is verified by simulations.

1 Introduction

In recent years, autonomous mobile manipulators have been paid extensively attention due to their wide applications. Compared with a conventional manipulator mounted on a fixed base, a mobile manipulator has much larger mobility in workspace. Modeling and control for redundant nonholonomic mobile modular manipulators are difficult to realize due to interactive motions, nonholonomic constraints and self-motions. Neural-fuzzy system has been widely used for robotic control due to its characteristics as universal approximators.

Obstacle avoidance for mobile platforms [1,2] and robotic manipulators [3,4] is realized easily in a sense in case of treating respectively, complexity will increase significantly if obstacle avoidance is performed for an assembled mobile modular manipulator. Several obstacle avoidance schemes have been proposed, such as the artificial potential field (APF) method [1], the vector field histogram (VFH) algorithm [2], and the redundancy resolution scheme [3]. To get over the local minima problem of the APF method, harmonic artificial potential function is devised [4]. As for investigations on modular robots or mobile manipulators, back propagation neural network has been used for vibration control of redundant modular manipulators [5]. An integrated task planning and a decoupled force/position control algorithm are proposed [6]. Regarding to researches on neural-fuzzy robotic control, a neural-fuzzy integrated controller is developed for mobile robot navigation and multi-robot convoying [7]. A robust adaptive generalized fuzzy-neural controller is presented for motion control of multi-link robotic manipulators [8].

Different from previous works in which the mobile platform and manipulator are modeled separately, the entire robot is modeled as an integrated structure in this paper. The redundancy of a redundant mobile manipulator is utilized to fulfil a task of obstacle avoidance by adjusting self-motions without changing end-effector's specified job. Furthermore, most obstacle avoidance algorithms are only concerned with tasks of the start and goal points. However, the algorithm proposed can ensure the motion tasks not be affected during the entire course of navigation. In addition, unlike the previous schemes, this algorithm considers obstacles not only in the motion plane of the mobile platform, but also in the entire 3-D operational space of the onboard modular manipulator.

This paper is arranged as follows. An integrated dynamic modeling method is proposed in Section 2. The obstacle avoidance algorithm is presented in Section 3. A simulation is carried out in Section 4. Conclusions are given in Section 5.

2 An Integrated Dynamic Modeling Method

In this paper, we analyze a 3-wheeled nonholonomic mobile modular manipulator, which is supposed to just move on a horizontal plane, as shown in Fig. 1. The coordinate systems are defined as follows: $O_B X_B Y_B Z_B$ forms an inertial base frame, and $O_m X_m Y_m Z_m$ is a frame fixed on the mobile platform. The origin of $O_m(x_m, y_m)$ is selected as the midpoint of the line segment connecting the two fixed-wheel centers. Y_m is along the line segment mentioned above. In Fig. 1(b), θ_i and r_i are the yaw angle and steering radius at the time interval $[t^i, t^{i+1}]$. ΔS_L, ΔS_R, and ΔS_m represent advance of the left wheel, the right wheel, and O_m respectively. ϕ_L and ϕ_R are rotating angles of the left and right front wheels, ϕ_r and β_r denote rotating angles of the castor wheel around its own axis and the fixed bar. d_m, r_f, l_G, l_r, d_r and r_r are all constants determined by physical structures.

Assume $\Delta t = t^{i+1} - t^i \to 0$, from Fig. 1(b)

$$\begin{cases} \dot{x}_m = \lim_{\Delta t \to 0} \left(\frac{\Delta x_m}{\Delta t}\right) = \frac{r_f \cdot C_m}{2} \cdot \left(\dot{\phi}_L + \dot{\phi}_R\right) \\ \dot{y}_m = \lim_{\Delta t \to 0} \left(\frac{\Delta y_m}{\Delta t}\right) = \frac{r_f \cdot S_m}{2} \cdot \left(\dot{\phi}_L + \dot{\phi}_R\right) \\ \dot{\phi}_m = \lim_{\Delta t \to 0} \left(\frac{\Delta \phi_m}{\Delta t}\right) = -\frac{r_f}{d_m} \cdot \left(\dot{\phi}_L - \dot{\phi}_R\right) \end{cases} \quad (1)$$

Where $S_m = \sin(\phi_m)$, $C_m = \cos(\phi_m)$.

In the same way, we have

$$\begin{cases} \dot{\phi}_r = \frac{C_{rm} \cdot \dot{x}_m + S_{rm} \cdot \dot{y}_m - l_r \cdot S_r \cdot \dot{\phi}_m}{r_r} \\ \dot{\beta}_r = \frac{S_{rm} \cdot \dot{x}_m - C_{rm} \cdot \dot{y}_m - (d_r - l_r \cdot C_r) \cdot \dot{\phi}_m}{d_r} \end{cases} \quad (2)$$

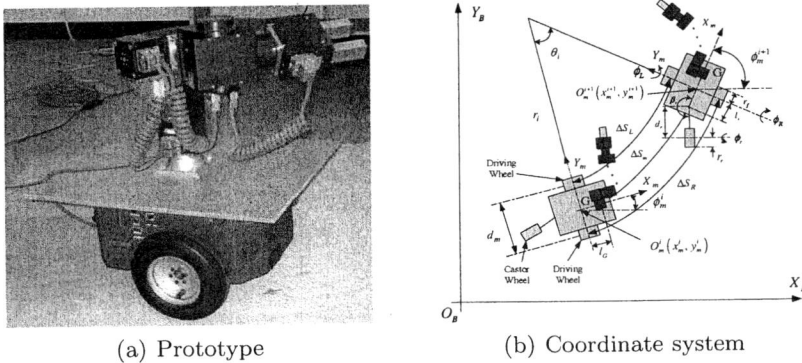

(a) Prototype (b) Coordinate system

Fig. 1. Prototype and coordinate system for a mobile modular manipulator

Where $S_{rm} = \sin(\beta_r + \phi_m), C_{rm} = \cos(\beta_r + \phi_m), S_r = \sin(\beta_r), C_r = \cos(\beta_r)$.

Define $\xi = [x_m \ y_m \ \phi_m \ \phi_r \ \beta_r \ \phi_L \ \phi_R]^T$, then from Eqs. 1 and 2, the nonholonomic constraints can be given by

$$A(\xi) \cdot S(\xi) = 0. \tag{3}$$

Where the matrices $A(\xi)$ and $S(\xi)$ can be detailed by

$$A = \begin{bmatrix} C_m & C_m & -S_m & C_{rm} & -S_{rm} \\ S_m & S_m & C_m & S_{rm} & C_{rm} \\ -\frac{d_m}{2} & \frac{d_m}{2} & 0 & -l_r S_r & k_r \\ 0 & 0 & 0 & -r_r & 0 \\ 0 & 0 & 0 & 0 & d_r \\ -r_f & 0 & 0 & 0 & 0 \\ 0 & -r_f & 0 & 0 & 0 \end{bmatrix}^T, \quad S = \begin{bmatrix} \frac{r_f \cdot C_m}{2} & \frac{r_f \cdot C_m}{2} \\ \frac{r_f \cdot S_m}{2} & \frac{r_f \cdot S_m}{2} \\ \frac{r_f}{d_m} & \frac{r_f}{d_m} \\ \frac{r_f(d_m C_r + 2l_r S_r)}{2d_m r_r} & \frac{r_f(d_m C_r - 2l_r S_r)}{2d_m r_r} \\ \frac{r_f(d_m S_r + 2k_r)}{2d_m d_r} & \frac{r_f(d_m S_r - 2k_r)}{2d_m d_r} \\ 1 & 0 \\ 0 & 1 \end{bmatrix}$$

(4)

Where $k_r = d_r - l_r C_r$.

According to modular robot concept, the mobile platform can be treated as a special module attached to the base of the modular manipulator. From Denavit-Hartenberg notation, transformation matrix of the ith module with respect to $O_B X_B Y_B Z_B$ can be derived, see [9] for details.

Let $\zeta = [\xi^T \ q_1 \ \cdots \ q_n]^T$, $q = [\phi_L \ \phi_R \ q_1 \ \cdots \ q_n]^T$, $x = [p_x \ p_y \ p_z]^T$, then

$$\dot{\zeta} = \begin{bmatrix} S & 0_{7 \times n} \\ 0_{n \times 2} & I_{n \times n} \end{bmatrix} \cdot \dot{q}, \quad \dot{x} = \frac{\partial x}{\partial q} \cdot \dot{q} = \frac{\partial x}{\partial \zeta} \cdot \frac{\partial \zeta}{\partial q} \cdot \dot{q} \tag{5}$$

In short $\dot{\zeta} = \overline{S} \cdot \dot{q}$, $\dot{x} = J \cdot \dot{q}$.

In this paper, as long as $n > 1$, the robot will be redundant, then from Eq. 5

$$\dot{q} = J^\dagger \cdot \dot{x} + (I_{n+2} - J^\dagger \cdot J) \cdot \dot{q}_s \tag{6}$$

Where $J^\dagger = J^T \cdot (J \cdot J^T)^{-1}$ is the Moore-Penrose generalized inverse of J, $\dot{q}_s \in \Re^{n+2}$ is an arbitrary vector.

Let $J_\aleph \in \Re^{(n+2) \times (n-1)}$ be a matrix with all its columns be the normalized bases of $\aleph(J)$, which is the null space of J. Then

$$J \cdot J_\aleph = 0_{3 \times (n-1)}, \quad J_\aleph^T \cdot J^\dagger = 0_{(n-1) \times 3},$$
$$J_\aleph^T \cdot J_\aleph = I_{(n-1)}, \quad J_\aleph \cdot J_\aleph^T = I_{n+2} - J^\dagger \cdot J. \quad (7)$$

Define $\dot{x}_\aleph = J_\aleph^T \cdot \dot{q}_s$, $x_E = \begin{bmatrix} x^T & | & x_\aleph^T \end{bmatrix}^T$, $J_E^\dagger = \begin{bmatrix} J^\dagger & | & J_\aleph \end{bmatrix}$. From Eqs. 6 and 7, we have

$$\dot{\zeta} = \bar{S} \cdot J_E^\dagger \cdot \dot{x}_E, \quad \ddot{\zeta} = \bar{S} \cdot J_E^\dagger \cdot \ddot{x}_E + \left(\dot{\bar{S}} \cdot J_E^\dagger - \bar{S} \cdot J^\dagger \cdot \dot{J}\right) \cdot \dot{x}_E \quad (8)$$

The constrained dynamics can be determined by [10]

$$M \cdot \ddot{\zeta} + V \cdot \dot{\zeta} + G = B \cdot \left(\tau + J^T \cdot F_{ext}\right) + C \cdot \lambda \quad (9)$$

Where $B = \begin{bmatrix} 0_{(n+2) \times 5} & I_{n+2} \end{bmatrix}^T$, $C = \begin{bmatrix} A & 0_{5 \times n} \end{bmatrix}^T$, F_{ext} is an external force vector, $\lambda = \begin{bmatrix} \lambda_1 & \cdots & \lambda_5 \end{bmatrix}^T$ are Lagrange multipliers, $\tau = \begin{bmatrix} \tau_L & \tau_R & \tau_1 \cdots \tau_n \end{bmatrix}^T$ are corresponding driving torques.

Substituting Eq. 8 into Eq. 9, and left multiplying $\left(J_E^\dagger\right)^T \cdot \bar{S}^T$, yields

$$\bar{M} \cdot \ddot{x}_E + \bar{V} \cdot \dot{x}_E + \bar{G} = \bar{\tau} \quad (10)$$

Where $\bar{M} = \left(J_E^\dagger\right)^T \bar{S}^T M \bar{S} J_E^\dagger$, $\bar{V} = \left(J_E^\dagger\right)^T \bar{S}^T (M \dot{\bar{S}} J_E^\dagger - M \bar{S} J^\dagger \dot{J} + V \bar{S} J_E^\dagger)$, $\bar{G} = \left(J_E^\dagger\right)^T \bar{S}^T G$, $\bar{\tau} = \left(J_E^\dagger\right)^T \bar{S}^T B \left(\tau + J^T F_{ext}\right)$; and $\left(J_E^\dagger\right)^T \bar{S}^T C \lambda = 0$ is eliminated.

Remark 1. The following properties hold for Eq. 10: 1) For any $r \in \Re^{n+2}$, $r^T \cdot \bar{M} \cdot r \geq 0$; 2) For any $r \in \Re^{n+2}$, $r^T \cdot (\dot{\bar{M}} - 2\bar{V}) \cdot r = 0$; 3) If J is full rank, $J_E = \left(J_E^\dagger\right)^{-1} = \begin{bmatrix} J^T & | & J_\aleph \end{bmatrix}^T$; 4) If J is full rank, $\bar{M}, \bar{V}, \bar{G} \in \ell_\infty$. Here $\ell_\infty = \{x(t) \in \Re^n : \|x\|_\infty < \infty\}$.

3 A New Obstacle Avoidance Algorithm

3.1 Problem Formulation

According to whether on the desired end-effector trajectory or not, obstacles can be divided into two kinds: the task-consistent one and the task-inconsistent one, see Fig. 2(a). The task-consistent obstacles can be avoided by on-line adjusting self-motions. However, the task-inconsistent obstacles can not be avoided without affecting end-effector executed tasks. One solution to avoid task-inconsistent obstacles is to regenerate the desired end-effector task, which belongs to the high-level decision making problem and is beyond the discussion of this paper. In this paper, only task-consistent obstacles are concerned and redundancy of the robot is supposed to be high enough to avoid obstacles just by adjusting self-motions. Obstacle avoidance is realized online, so the exact positions of obstacles need not be known in advance. Furthermore, the mobile modular manipulator is supposed to work in a unstructured environment and the obstacles can be detected by sonar, infrared, laser range finder, vision or some other sensors in a realtime manner.

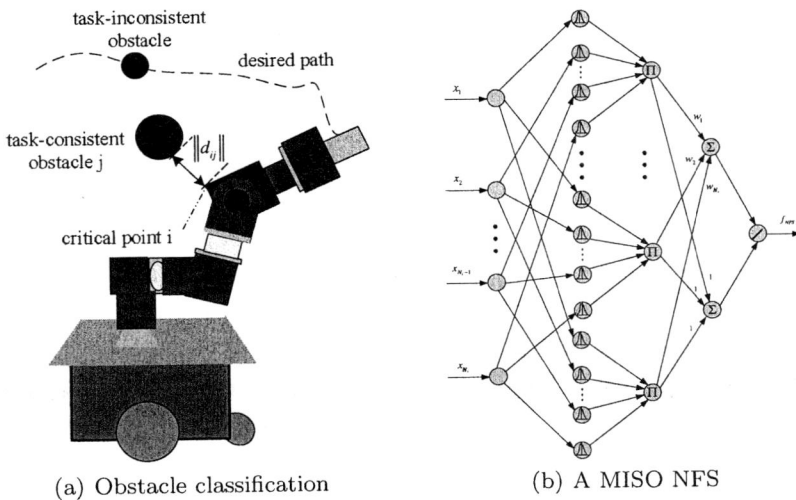

(a) Obstacle classification   (b) A MISO NFS

Fig. 2. Obstacle classification and a MISO neural-fuzzy system

3.2 Self-motion Planning

Let $x_{\aleph d}$, $\dot{x}_{\aleph d}$ and $\ddot{x}_{\aleph d}$ be the desired self-motions. Assume the system is far away from singularity and physical limits, then the self-motions can be used specially for obstacle avoidance.

If a point on the robot gets too close to an obstacle ($\|d_{ij}\| < d_c$), this point can be called a critical point, and d_c is called the cut-off distance. The artificial potential function for the ith critical point and the jth obstacle can be defined by

$$\phi_{ij}(q) = \begin{cases} \frac{1}{2} \cdot k_\phi \cdot \left(\frac{1}{\|d_{ij}\|} - \frac{1}{d_c} \right)^2, & \|d_{ij}\| < d_c \\ 0, & \|d_{ij}\| \geq d_c \end{cases} \quad (11)$$

Where $k_\phi > 0$ is a constant coefficient, $d_{ij} = x_{ci} - x_{oj}$ is the nearest distance between the ith critical point and the jth obstacle, as shown in Fig. 2(a). Here, $x_{ci} = [p_{cix}\ p_{ciy}\ p_{ciz}]^T$ and $x_{oj} = [p_{ojx}\ p_{ojy}\ p_{ojz}]^T$ are position vectors for the ith critical point and the jth obstacle with respect to $O_B X_B Y_B Z_B$.

To avoid obstacles in a realtime manner, the self-motions can be planned to optimize the following function:

$$\Phi(q) = \sum_{j=1}^{N_o} \sum_{i=1}^{N_c} \phi_{ij}(q) \quad (12)$$

Where N_o and N_c are the numbers of obstacles and critical points respectively. Then

$$\dot{q}_{sd} = -\frac{\partial \Phi(q)}{\partial q} = -\sum_{j=1}^{N_o}\sum_{i=1}^{N_c} \frac{\partial \phi_{ij}(q)}{\partial q} \tag{13}$$

Where $\frac{\partial \phi_{ij}(q)}{\partial q}$ can be derived from Eq. 12.

$$\frac{\partial \phi_{ij}(q)}{\partial q} = \begin{cases} -\left[k_\phi \cdot \left(\frac{1}{\|d_{ij}\|} - \frac{1}{d_c}\right) \cdot \frac{d_{ij}^T}{\|d_{ij}\|^3} \cdot \left(\frac{\partial x_{ci}}{\partial q^T} - \frac{\partial x_{oj}}{\partial q^T}\right)\right]^T, & \|d_{ij}\| < d_c \\ 0, & \|d_{ij}\| \geq d_c \end{cases} \tag{14}$$

Then, $x_{\aleph d}$, $\dot{x}_{\aleph d}$ and $\ddot{x}_{\aleph d}$ can be determined.

3.3 Robust Adaptive Neural-fuzzy Controller Design

Theorem 1. (Universal Approximation Theorem [12])
The multiple inputs single output (MISO) fuzzy logic system (FLS) with center average defuzzifier, product inference rule and singleton fuzzifier, and Gaussian membership function can uniformly approximate any nonlinear functions over a compact set $U \in \Re^n$ to any degree of accuracy.

If the FLS described above is realized by a neural network (NN), a neural fuzzy system (NFS) can be obtained as shown in Fig. 2(b). Output of this NFS is given by

$$f_{NFS} = \frac{\sum_{j=1}^{N_r}\left\{w_j \cdot \prod_{i=1}^{N_i}\left\{\exp\left[-\left(\frac{x_i - \varpi_{ji}}{\sigma_{ji}}\right)^2\right]\right\}\right\}}{\sum_{j=1}^{N_r}\left\{\prod_{i=1}^{N_i}\exp\left[-\left(\frac{x_i - \varpi_{ji}}{\sigma_{ji}}\right)^2\right]\right\}} \tag{15}$$

Where x_i is the ith input variable, w_j denotes the jth centroids for the output fuzzy sets, $i = 1, 2, \cdots, N_i, j = 1, 2, \cdots, N_r$, here N_i and N_r represent the number of input variables and rules respectively. ϖ_{ji} and σ_{ji} are the mean and standard derivation of the Gaussian membership functions accordingly.

Let x_d, $\dot{x}_d$ and $\ddot{x}_d$ be desired task-space position, velocity and acceleration. Define $x_{Ed} = [x_d^T \mid x_{\aleph d}^T]^T$, then the error system can be defined as

$$e(t) = x_E(t) - x_{Ed}(t), \; \dot{x}_s(t) = \dot{x}_{Ed}(t) - \Lambda \cdot e(t), \; s(t) = \dot{x}_E(t) - \dot{x}_s(t) \tag{16}$$

Where $s(t)$ is the tracking error measure, Λ is a constant positive definite matrix. Substituting Eq. 16 into 10, yields

$$\bar{M} \cdot \dot{s}(t) + \bar{V} \cdot s(t) + \bar{M} \cdot \ddot{x}_s(t) + \bar{V} \cdot \dot{x}_s(t) + \bar{G} = \bar{\tau} \tag{17}$$

Define $h(\zeta, \dot{\zeta}, \dot{x}_s, \ddot{x}_s) = \bar{M} \cdot \ddot{x}_s + \bar{V} \cdot \dot{x}_s + \bar{G}$. According to the universal approximation theorem mentioned above and *Remark*1, each element of h can be approximated by a MISO NFS as long as the Jacobian matrix J is full rank. Then

$h = h_{NFS} + \epsilon$. Here $h_{NFS} \in \Re^{n+2}$ are NFS approximates of h and ϵ are approximated errors, $h_{NFSk} = f_{NFS}(x_{in}, \varpi_k, \sigma_k, w_k)$, $\varpi_k, \sigma_k \in \Re^{N_r \times N_i}$, and $w_k \in \Re^{N_r}$ are adjustable parameter matrices for these NFS, $x_{in} = [\zeta^T \ \dot{q}^T \ x_{Ed}^T \ \dot{x}_{Ed}^T \ \ddot{x}_{Ed}^T]^T$ are corresponding inputs, $k = 1, 2, \cdots, n+2$.

Assume $x_{in} \in [\underline{x}_{in}, \bar{x}_{in}]$, $h \in [\underline{h}, \bar{h}]$, then the adjustable parameters can be initialized by

$$\varpi_{kji0} = \underline{x}_{ini} + j \cdot \frac{\bar{x}_{ini} - \underline{x}_{ini}}{N_r}, \quad \sigma_{kji0} = \frac{\bar{x}_{ini} - \underline{x}_{ini}}{N_r}, \quad w_{kji0} = \underline{h}_k + j \cdot \frac{\bar{h}_k - \underline{h}_k}{N_r} \quad (18)$$

Let $\hat{\varpi}_k$, $\hat{\sigma}_k$, and $\hat{w}_k$ be estimates of ϖ_k, σ_k and w_k respectively. Taking the Taylor series expansions of h_{NFSk} around $\hat{h}_{NFSk} = f_{NFS}(x_{in}, \hat{\varpi}_k, \hat{\sigma}_k, \hat{w}_k)$, yields

$$\tilde{h}_{NFSk} = \sum_{j=1}^{N_r} \left\{ \sum_{i=1}^{N_i} \left[\frac{\partial \hat{h}_{NFSk}}{\partial \varpi_{kji}} \cdot \tilde{\varpi}_{kji} + \frac{\partial \hat{h}_{NFSk}}{\partial \sigma_{kji}} \cdot \tilde{\sigma}_{kji} \right] + \frac{\partial \hat{h}_{NFSk}}{\partial w_{kj}} \cdot \tilde{w}_{kj} \right\} + h_{res} \quad (19)$$

Where $\tilde{h}_{NFSk} = h_{NFSk} - \hat{h}_{NFSk}$, $\tilde{\varpi}_{kji} = \varpi_{kji} - \hat{\varpi}_{kji}$, $\tilde{\sigma}_{kji} = \sigma_{kji} - \hat{\sigma}_{kji}$ and $\tilde{w}_{kj} = w_{kj} - \hat{w}_{kj}$; $h_{res} = \sum_{j=1}^{N_r} \left\{ \sum_{i=1}^{N_i} \left[O(\tilde{\varpi}_{kji}^2) + O(\tilde{\sigma}_{kji}^2) \right] + O(\tilde{w}_{kj}^2) \right\}$; here $O(\tilde{\varpi}_{kji}^2)$, $O(\tilde{\sigma}_{kji}^2)$, and $O(\tilde{w}_{kj}^2)$ are higher-order terms.

The RANFC is represented by

$$\tau = (\bar{S}^T B)^{-1} J_E^T \left\{ \hat{h}_{NFS} - K_\epsilon sgn(s) - K_P s(t) - K_I \int_0^t s(t) \, dt \right\} - J^T F_{ext} \quad (20)$$

Where $K_P > 0$, $K_I^T = K_I > 0$ are proportional and integral gain matrices, $K_\epsilon = diag\{k_{\epsilon 1} \ \cdots \ k_{\epsilon(n+2)}\}$ is the gain matrix for the robust term, with its elements determined by $k_{\epsilon k} \geq |\epsilon_k| + |h_{res}|$.

Substituting Eq. 20 into Eq. 17 and considering Eq. 10, yields the following error equation

$$\bar{M} \cdot \dot{s}(t) + \bar{V} \cdot s(t) + \epsilon + K_I \cdot \int_0^t s(t) \, dt + K_P \cdot s(t) + K_\epsilon \cdot sgn(s) + \tilde{h}_{NFS} = 0 \quad (21)$$

Theorem 2. *The closed-loop system in Eq. (21) is asymptotically stable under the adaptation laws given by Eq. (22). The error signals are convergent along with time, i.e., $e(t), \dot{e}(t) \to 0$, as $t \to +\infty$.*

$$\dot{\hat{\varpi}}_{kji} = -\Gamma_{\varpi_{kji}} s_k \frac{\partial \hat{h}_{NFSk}}{\partial \varpi_{kji}}, \dot{\hat{\sigma}}_{kji} = -\Gamma_{\sigma_{kji}} s_k \frac{\partial \hat{h}_{NFSk}}{\partial \sigma_{kji}}, \dot{\hat{w}}_{kj} = -\Gamma_{w_{kj}} s_k \frac{\partial \hat{h}_{NFSk}}{\partial w_{kj}}.$$
(22)

Where $\frac{\partial \hat{h}_{NFSk}}{\partial \varpi_{kji}}$, $\frac{\partial \hat{h}_{NFSk}}{\partial \sigma_{kji}}$, and $\frac{\partial \hat{h}_{NFSk}}{\partial w_{kj}}$ can be detailed by

$$\frac{\partial \hat{h}_{NFSk}}{\partial w_{kj}} = \frac{\prod_{i=1}^{N_i} \left\{ \exp\left[-\left(\frac{x_{ini} - \hat{\varpi}_{kji}}{\hat{\sigma}_{kji}}\right)^2\right] \right\}}{\sum_{j=1}^{N_r} \left\{ \prod_{i=1}^{N_i} \exp\left[-\left(\frac{x_{ini} - \hat{\varpi}_{kji}}{\hat{\sigma}_{kji}}\right)^2\right] \right\}}, \quad \frac{\partial \hat{h}_{NFSk}}{\partial \varpi_{kji}} = \frac{2(x_{ini} - \hat{\varpi}_{kji})(\hat{w}_{kj} - \hat{h}_{NFSk})}{\hat{\sigma}_{kji}^2} \frac{\partial \hat{h}_{NFSk}}{\partial w_{kj}}$$

$$\frac{\partial \hat{h}_{NFSk}}{\partial \sigma_{kji}} = \frac{(x_{ini} - \hat{\varpi}_{kji})}{\hat{\sigma}_{kji}} \cdot \frac{\partial \hat{h}_{NFSk}}{\partial \varpi_{kji}}$$
(23)

Proof. Considering the following Lyapunov candidate:

$$V_S = \tfrac{1}{2} \cdot s^T \cdot \bar{M} \cdot s + \tfrac{1}{2} \cdot \left[\int_0^t s(t)\,dt\right]^T \cdot K_I \cdot \left[\int_0^t s(t)\,dt\right]$$
$$+ \tfrac{1}{2} \cdot \sum_{k=1}^{n+2} \left\{ \sum_{j=1}^{N_r} \left[\sum_{i=1}^{N_i} \left(\frac{\tilde{\varpi}_{kji}^2}{\Gamma_{\varpi_{kji}}} + \frac{\tilde{\sigma}_{kji}^2}{\Gamma_{\sigma_{kji}}} \right) + \frac{\tilde{w}_{kj}^2}{\Gamma_{w_{kj}}} \right] \right\} \geq 0 \qquad (24)$$

The time derivative of Lyapunov candidate is

$$\dot{V}_S = s^T \cdot \left\{ \bar{M} \cdot \dot{s} + K_I \cdot \left[\int_0^t s(t)\,dt\right] \right\} + \frac{s^T \cdot \dot{\bar{M}} \cdot s}{2}$$
$$+ \sum_{k=1}^{n+2} \left\{ \sum_{j=1}^{N_r} \left[\sum_{i=1}^{N_i} \left(\frac{\tilde{\varpi}_{kji} \cdot \dot{\tilde{\varpi}}_{kji}}{\Gamma_{\varpi_{kji}}} + \frac{\tilde{\sigma}_{kji} \cdot \dot{\tilde{\sigma}}_{kji}}{\Gamma_{\sigma_{kji}}} \right) + \frac{\tilde{w}_{kj} \cdot \dot{\tilde{w}}_{kj}}{\Gamma_{w_{kj}}} \right] \right\} \qquad (25)$$

From Eq. 21, we have

$$s^T \cdot \left\{ \bar{M} \cdot \dot{s} + K_I \cdot \left[\int_0^t s(t)\,dt\right] \right\} = -s^T \cdot \bar{V} \cdot s$$
$$- s^T \cdot K_P \cdot s - s^T \cdot \left[\tilde{h}_{NFS} + k_\epsilon \cdot \mathrm{sgn}(s) + \epsilon \right] \qquad (26)$$

Notice that $\dot{\tilde{\varpi}}_{kji} = -\dot{\hat{\varpi}}_{kji}$, $\dot{\tilde{\sigma}}_{kji} = -\dot{\hat{\sigma}}_{kji}$, $\dot{\tilde{w}}_{kj} = -\dot{\hat{w}}_{kj}$. Substituting Eqs. 19, 22 and 26 into 25, and considering $k_{\epsilon k} \geq |\epsilon_k| + |h_{res}|$ at the same time, yields

$$\dot{V}_S \leq -s^T \cdot K_P \cdot s \leq 0 \qquad (27)$$

From Eqs. 24 and 27, V_S is a Lyapunov function. According to LaSalle's theorem, the system is asymptotically stable and $s \to 0$ as $t \to +\infty$. Define $\ell_p = \{x(t) \in \Re^n : \|x\|_p < \infty\}$. From Eqs. 24 and 27, $s(t) \in \ell_2$. According to Eq. 16, $e(t) \in \ell_2 \cap \ell_\infty, \dot{e}(t) \in \ell_2$, and $e(t) \to 0$, as $t \to +\infty$. Since $\dot{V}_S \leq 0$, $V_S \in \ell_\infty$, which implies that $\tilde{\varpi}_{kji}, \tilde{\sigma}_{kji}, \tilde{w}_{kj} \in \ell_\infty$, if the Jacobian is full rank, $h_{NFS} \in \ell_\infty$ and $\varpi_{kji}, \sigma_{kji}, w_{kj} \in \ell_\infty$, so, $\hat{\varpi}_{kji}, \hat{\sigma}_{kji}, \hat{w}_{kj} \in \ell_\infty$ and $\hat{h}_{NFS} \in \ell_\infty$. Considering that $h_{res} \in \ell_\infty$, so $K_\epsilon \in \ell_\infty$. Then, from Eq. 21, $\dot{s}(t) \in \ell_\infty$. Since $s(t) \in \ell_2$ and $\dot{s}(t) \in \ell_\infty$, $s(t) \to 0$ as $t \to +\infty$, which is followed by $\dot{e}(t) \to 0$. End of the proof.

4 Simulation Results

The simulation is performed on a real robot composed of a 3-wheeled mobile platform and a 4-DOF modular manipulator, as shown in Fig. 1(a). In order to verify the algorithm, the robot is required to follow a spacial trajectory in Fig. 3(a), which has been planned to ensure the robot far away form singularities or joint limits. Two ball-like task-consistent obstacles with radius of $0.2m$ are considered, one is on the motion plane of the mobile platform and the other is on the way of the modular manipulator as shown in Fig. 3(b).

The simulation time is selected as 20 seconds. Each element of h is approximated by a NFS. The gain matrices and constants are selected as follows: $K_P = diag\{100\}, K_I = diag\{10\}, K_\epsilon = diag\{50\}, \Gamma_{\varpi_{kji}} = 0.1, \Gamma_{\sigma_{kji}} =$

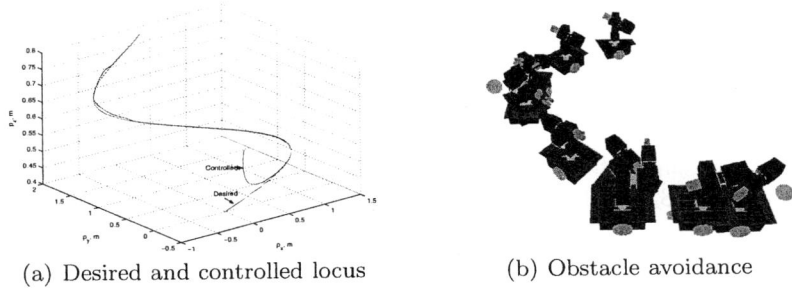

(a) Desired and controlled locus   (b) Obstacle avoidance

Fig. 3. Desired and control locus and obstacle avoidance

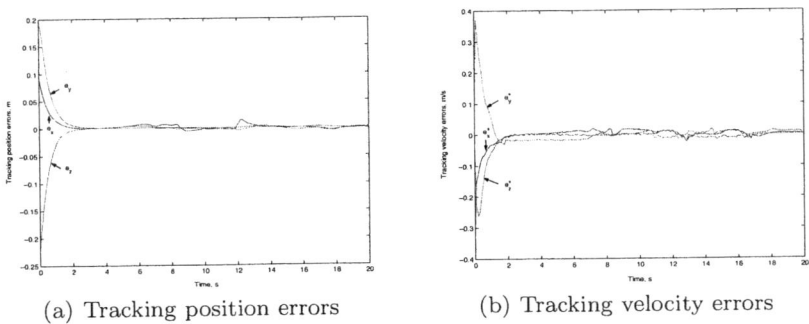

(a) Tracking position errors   (b) Tracking velocity errors

Fig. 4. Tracking position and velocity errors

$0.1, \Gamma_{w_{kj}} = 0.1, \Lambda = diag\{2.0\}$ and $N_r = 200$. The cut-off distance is selected as $d_c = 0.5m$, and the coefficient is determined by $k_\phi = 1.0$.

The desired and the controlled locus are shown in Fig. 3(a). Two obstacles are avoided by controlling self-motions of the mobile modular manipulator in Figure 3(b). The tracking position and velocity errors are given by Fig. 4. It can be observed that the proposed algorithm is effective in both avoiding obstacles and controlling the end-effector to follow a desired spacial trajectory simultaneously.

5 Conclusions

A mobile modular manipulator composed by a 3-wheeled nonholonomic mobile platform and a n-DOF onboard modular manipulator is investigated in this paper. Firstly, an integrated dynamic modeling method is presented. Secondly, a new obstacle avoidance algorithm using self-motions is proposed, which can avoid obstacles without affecting the end-effector planning task. Lastly, simulations are performed on a real mobile modular manipulator, which demonstrate that the proposed algorithm is effective. The dynamic modeling method and the obstacle avoidance algorithm proposed can be extended to study other kinds of mobile manipulators as well.

Acknowledgements

This work was supported by the Research Committee of University of Macau under grant RG082/04-05S/LYM/FST.

References

1. Ge, S. S. and Cui, Y. J.: New Potential Functions for Mobile Robot Path Planning. IEEE Trans. on Robotics and Automation. **16** (2000) 615–620
2. Borenstein, J. and Koren, Y.: The Vector Field Histogram-fast Obstacle Avoidance for Mobile Robots. IEEE Trans. on Robotics and Automation. **7** (1991) 278–288
3. Zhang, Y. N. and Wang, J.: Obstacle Avoidance for Kinematically Redundant Manipulators Using a Dual Neural Network. IEEE Trans. on System, Man, and Cybernetics-Part B: Cybernetics. **34** (2004) 752–759
4. Kim, J. O. and Khosla, P. K.: Real-Time Obstacle Avoidance Using Harmonic Potential Functions. IEEE Trans. on Robotics and Automation. **8** (1992) 338–349
5. Li, Y., Liu, Y., Liu, X. and Peng, Z.: Parameters Identification and Vibration Control in Modular Manipulators. IEEE/ASME Trans. Mechatronics. **9** (2004) 700–705
6. Tan, J., Xi, N. and Wang, Y.: Integrated Task Planning and Control for Mobile Manipulators. Int. Journal of Robotics Research. **22** (2003) 337–354
7. Ng, K. C. and Trivedi, M. M.: A Neuro-Fuzzy Controller for Mobile Robot Navigation and Multirobot Convoying. IEEE Trans. on Syst., Man, and Cybern.- Part B: Cybernetics. **28** (1998) 829–840
8. Er, M. J. and Gao, Y.: Robust Adaptive Control of Robot Manipulators Using Generalized Fuzzy Neural Networks. IEEE Trans. on Industrial Electronics. **50** (2003) 620–628
9. Li, Y. and Liu, Y.: Control of a Mobile Modular Manipulator Moving on a Slope. IEEE Int. Conf. on Mechatronics, Turkey (2004) 135–140
10. de Wit, C. C., Siciliano, B. and Bastin, G.: Theory of Robot Control. Springer-Verlag London Limited (1996)
11. Haykin, S.: Neural Networks: A Comprehensive Foundation. 2nd edition. Prentice-Hall, Inc. (1999)
12. Wang, L. X., Adaptive Fuzzy Systems and Control: Design and Stability Analysis, Prentice-Hall International, Inc., (1994).

Invasive Connectionist Evolution

Paulito P. Palmes and Shiro Usui

RIKEN Brain Science Institute,
2-1 Hirosawa, Wako, Saitama 351-0198 Japan
ppalmes@brain.riken.jp, usuishiro@riken.jp

Abstract. The typical automatic way to search for optimal neural network is to combine structure evolution by evolutionary computation and weight adaptation by backpropagation. In this model, since structure and weight optimizations are carried out by two different algorithms each using its own search space, every change in network topology during structure evolution requires relearning of the entire weights by backpropagation. Because of this inefficiency, we propose that the evolution of network structure and weights shall be purely stochastic and tightly integrated such that good weights and structures are not relearned but propagated from generation to generation. Since this model does not depend on gradient information, the entire process allows more flexibility in the implementation of its evolution and in the formulation of its fitness function. This study demonstrates how invasive connectionist evolution can easily be implemented using particle swarm optimization (PSO), evolutionary programming (EP), and differential evolution (DE) with good performances in cancer and glass classification tasks.

1 Introduction

Artificial Neural Network (ANN) has been a popular tool in many fields of study due to its general applicability to different problem domains that require intelligent processing such as classification, recognition, clustering, prediction, generalization, etc. The most popular algorithm in ANN learning is BP (backpropagation) which uses minimization of the error surface by gradient descent. Since BP is a local search algorithm, it has fast convergence but can easily be trapped to local optima. Moreover, choosing the optimal architecture for a particular problem remains to be an active area of research because of BP's tendency to overfit or underfit the training data due to its sensitivity to the choice of architecture.

A typical approach to help BP figure out the appropriate architecture is by evolving its structure. Many studies have been conducted how to carry out structure evolution by evolutionary computation. A comprehensive review of papers related to evolutionary neural networks can be found in [1]. Recent insights and techniques for effective evolution strategies are found in the papers of [2,3].

The most typical approach is non-invasive [4]. This type of evolution uses dual representation: one for stochastic or rule-based structure evolution and the other for gradient-based weight adaptation. While non-invasive evolution makes the hybridization process straightforward, there is no tight integration between its structure evolution and weight adaptation. Hence, every time its network structure evolves, there is a need for the relearning of the entire weights by BP. In a typical evolutionary model, optimal parameter values are not relearned but propagated to the succeeding generations. This is not possible, however, in a gradient-based weight adaptation.

One alternative approach we proposed belongs to the class of "invasive evolutionary model" [4] which relies on pure stochastic evolution of the network structure and weights. Invasive evolution uses a network representation where weights and structures are tightly integrated such that changes to the former bring corresponding changes to the latter, and vice-versa. It avoids relearning of good weights and structures by propagating them in the succeeding generations. Since invasive connectionist evolution uses direct representation and does not rely on fix rules or heuristics, it can easily utilize the evolution process of other evolutionary models such as particle swarm optimization (PSO) [5], differential evolution (DE) [6], and evolutionary programming (EP) [7].

Dynamic adaptation is important since fix rules or parameter values optimized for a particular problem domain become useless for another set of problem domain [8]. What is needed is to let the processes of mutation, crossover, adaptation, and selection filter the most appropriate set of rules, traits, and parameters to solve the problem under consideration. It is important, therefore, to avoid developing evolutionary systems that rely on fix rules or heuristics. We believe in the principle that a pure stochastic implementation with a proper adaptation strategies are important for a robust connectionist evolution.

2 Invasive Connectionist Model

ANN learning can be considered as a form of optimization with the main objective of finding the appropriate network structure and weights that has optimal generalization performance. Its performance is measured using quality function Q_{fit} which measures the distance of ANN's output $F(X, S, W)$ from the target output $T(X)$:

$$Q_{fit} = \|T(X_i), F(X_i, S_i, W_i)\|_\theta \tag{1}$$

where X, S, and W are the network's input, structure, and weights, respectively; and $\|x\|_\theta$ is a similarity metric or error function. The main objective is to evolve the appropriate structure and weights so that the output of the function F is as close as the output of the target T. The function F uses the typical feedforward computation commonly used in n-layered network:

$$o_i = F\left(\sum_j w_{ij}\right) \tag{2}$$

$$F(x) = \frac{1}{1 + e^{-x}} \tag{3}$$

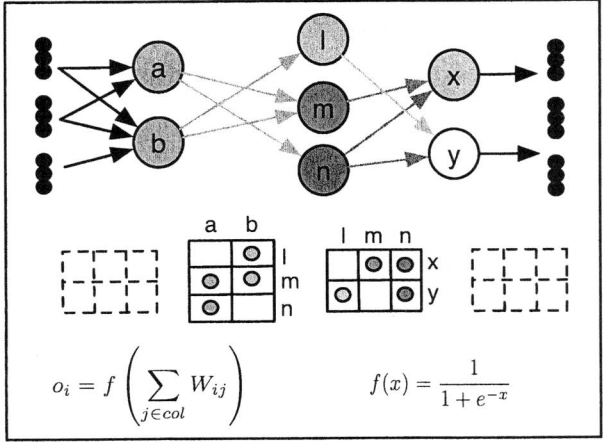

Fig. 1. Subnetwork Nodule

Figure 1 shows the invasive connectionist's building-block component which is composed of two weight marices. The first weight matrix contains the topology, strength of connections, and threshold values between the input and the hidden layer. Similarly, the second weight matrix describes the topology, threshold values, and connection strengths between the hidden layer and the output layer. While each nodule can be considered as a complete network capable of performing neural computation or learning, more complex structures can be easily created by combining several of these nodules to address more challenging problems in machine learning.

Figure 2 shows an example of a complex network formed by combining a population of nodules. Evolutionary operators such as mutation and crossover can independently operate on the weight matrices of each nodule to improve the fitness of the entire network. In the next section, we will discuss several ways to induce invasive evolution on swarm of networks using PSO, DE, and EP.

3 Invasive Connectionist Algorithm

Figure 3 shows a neural network swarm model. Each independent nodule optimizes its structure and weights through its interactions with other nodules in the neighborhood. In this example, the degree of overlapping is set to two. Hence, every network pair has 2 neighboring pairs.

This model can be reduced into the commonly used single population model by considering just one neighborhood. From the implementation point of view, multi-neighborhood representation is a generalization of the single neighborhood representation. This allows us to develop both single and multiple neighborhood

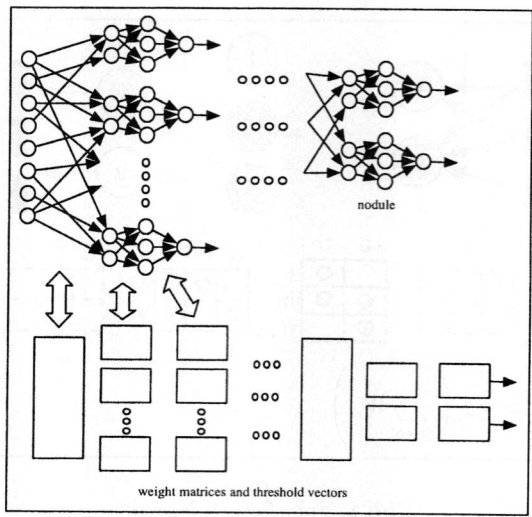

Fig. 2. Invasive Connectionist Model

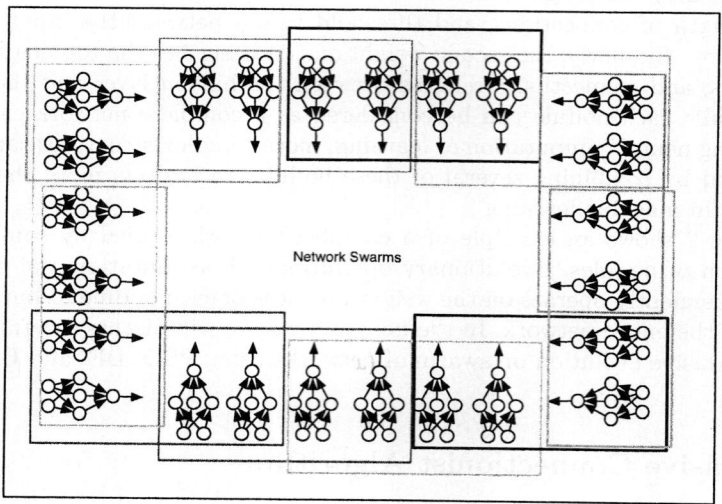

Fig. 3. Connectionist Swarm

approaches without changes to the representation of the base component network.

The invasive connectionist evolution algorithm is summarized in Fig. 4. For PSO implementation, the update of component's position relative to its best neighbor and personal best has the following formulation [9,5]:

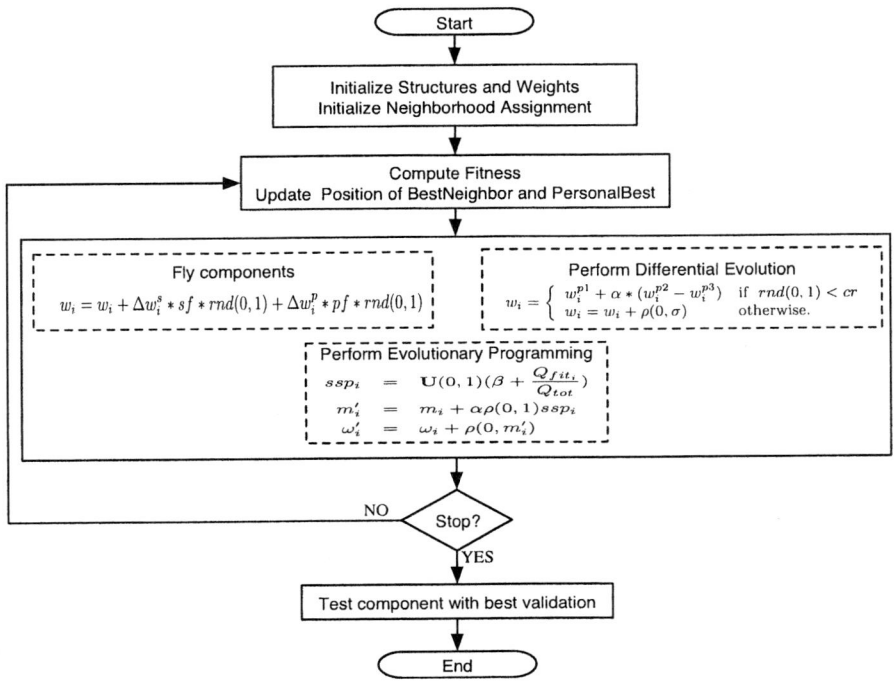

Fig. 4. Invasive Connectionist Algorithm

$$w_i = w_i + \Delta w_i^s * sf * \mathbf{U}(0,1) + \Delta w_i^p * if * \mathbf{U}(0,1) \qquad (4)$$

such that:

$$\Delta w_i^s = (w_i - w_i^s) \qquad (5)$$
$$\Delta w_i^p = (w_i - w_i^p) \qquad (6)$$

where $sf = 1.0$ and $if = 1.0$ refer to the component's sociability and individuality factors, respectively. More sociable components have higher sf over if and have greater tendency to converge towards the best component in their neighborhood. On the other hand, components with higher if over sf have greater tendency to converge towards their personal best. It is through the interactions of each component based on their sociability and individuality that allows the entire population to perform both local and global searching of the weight and structure spaces. All weights are randomly initialized between the range of -1 and 1.

The invasive connectionist model also supports the incorporation of other evolutionary approaches such as differential evolution (DE) [6] and evolutionary programming (EP) [7]. The DE and EP in the current implementation operate on the entire population although it can also be applied to each neighborhood. The feasibility of the latter scheme will be studied in the future.

The weight update of DE resembles roughly with that of the PSO. It randomly selects 3 neighbors $(p1, p2, p3)$ from the entire population as bases for changing the weights and structure of a component. Equation (7) is a modification of the DE implementation. There are two main operations, namely: exploitation and discovery. The exploitation part uses information from 3 randomly selected parents to form a new set of weights while the discovery part introduces new weights by gaussian perturbation:

$$w_i = \begin{cases} w_i^{p1} + \alpha * (w_i^{p2} - w_i^{p3}) & \text{if } \mathbf{U}(0,1) < cr \\ w_i + \rho(0, \sigma) & \text{otherwise.} \end{cases} \qquad (7)$$

where $cr = 0.99$ is the probability of exploitation and $1 - cr$ is the probability of discovery; $\mathbf{U}$ is a uniform distribution; ρ is the gaussian distribution with mean 0 and standard deviation σ; and α is a scaling factor.

Network initialization starts from zero weights and the only way for the components to have new weights is through the discovery operation in (7). The purpose of having the probability cr set to a value close to 1 is to give the population more time to exploit the existing weight space before dealing with the new weights slowly added by the discovery operation. Selection follows the standard DE policy where only new components with better fitness replace their corresponding parents.

EP implementation [4], on the other hand, uses uniform crossover, rank-based selection, and adaptation of the step size parameter (ssp) during mutation:

$$ssp_i = \mathbf{U}(0,1)(\beta + \frac{Q_{fit_i}}{Q_{tot}}) \qquad (8)$$

$$m_i' = m_i + \alpha\rho(0,1)ssp_i \qquad (9)$$

$$\omega_i' = \omega_i + \rho(0, m_i') \quad \text{if } \mathbf{U}(0,1) < mp \qquad (10)$$

where: $\alpha = 0.25$ and $\beta = 0.5$ are arbitrary constants that minimize the occurrences of too large and too weak mutations, respectively; Q_{fit} and Q_{tot} refer to the component's fitness and total fitness, respectively; $\mathbf{U}$ is the Uniform random function which minimizes large ssp occurrences; $mp = 0.01$ is the mutation probability; ρ is the gaussian; and ω refers to weights and threshold values.

The parameter m accumulates the net amount of changes in the mutation strength intensity over time. It is expected that those networks that survived in the later generation have the appropriate m that enabled them to adapt their structure and weights better than the other networks. EP implementation uses elitist replacement policy to avoid loosing the best traits found so far. The initial state of all networks start with no connection. This ensures that introduction of new connections and weights are carried out gradually by stochastic mutation.

All algorithms use the stopping criterion described in our previous papers [10,11,4]. It monitors the presence of overfitness using validation performance and stop training as soon as overfitness becomes apparent.

4 Simulations and Results

The quality or fitness function we used in this study considers two major criteria, namely: classification error and normalized mean-squared error:

$$Q_{fit} = \alpha * Q_{acc} + \beta * Q_{nmse} \qquad (11)$$

$$Q_{acc} = 100 * (1 - \frac{correct}{total}) \qquad (12)$$

$$Q_{nmse} = \frac{100}{NP} * \sum_{j=1}^{P}\sum_{i=1}^{N}(T_{ij} - O_{ij})^2 \qquad (13)$$

where: N and P refer to the number of samples and outputs, respectively; Q_{acc} is the percentage error in classification; Q_{nmse} is the percentage of normalized mean-squared error (NMSE); $\alpha = 0.7$ and $\beta = 0.3$ are user-defined constants used to control the strength of influence of their respective factors.

Simulation results include comparisons of the performances of four types of connectionist evolution, namely: connectionist EP (cEP), connectionist DE (cDE), connectionist PSO (cPSO), and connectionist PSO-DE (cPSO-DE).

These four variants were tested using cancer and glass classification tasks from the UCI repository [12]. The datasets from each task were copied from the experiments of Prechelt. They were divided into 50% training, 25% validation, and 25% testing [13]. Also, results from Prechelt's manually optimized pivot BP architecture were included for benchmarking purposes.

Table 1 summarizes the main features of the different variants. Analysis of variance (ANOVA) and Tukey's HSD test using $\alpha = 0.05$ level of significance were used for significance and multiple comparison testing.

Figure 5 shows the plots of means and standard deviations of the different variants in the cancer and glass problems, respectively. A line connecting two or more means indicates no significant difference within this group of means.

Result of the ANOVA for the cancer problem indicates no significant difference in the mean classification error among the five approaches. However, the ANOVA for the glass problem indicates significant difference in their performances. A closer analysis using Tukey HSD indicates that cEP has the best

Table 1. Main Features of Invasive Connectionist Variants

Features	cEP	cDE	cPSO	cPSO-DE
Population size	100	100	100	100
Hidden Units	20	20	20	20
Neighborhood size	1	1	10	10
Overlapping Size	0	0	5	5
No. of Neighborhoods	1	1	20	20
Classification	1-of-m classes using 1/0 output			
Selection	Rank-based	Std DE		Std DE
Replacement	Elitist	Std DE	N.A.	Std DE
Crossover	Uniform	Std DE		Std DE
Mutation	Gaussian	Gaussian		Gaussian

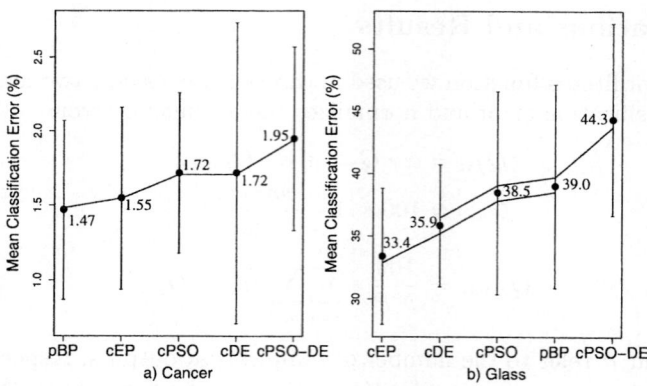

Fig. 5. Mean Classification Error Performance

performance. Its performance, however, is not significantly different from the performance of cPSO, cDE, and pBP.

5 Conclusion

All variants performed as good as the manually optimized BP architecture in spite of using a relatively large hidden layer (see Table 1). These two preliminary results demonstrated the feasibility of using invasive connectionist evolution. Furthermore, this study showed several advantages of invasive evolution such as high degree of flexibility in formulation and ease in implementation such that incorporating and combining other stochastic evolutionary techniques becomes trivial.

The swarm model of neural network is one way of combining several nodules to achieve complexity base on their collective behavior. This nodule organization has great potential to be used for expert ensembling. The idea is to have several swarms specializing on different parts of the solution space. Finding the best solution requires identifying which swarm will be used for evaluation. The degree of overlapping can be minimized to increase specialization or search localization of each swarm. This may provide better identification or discrimination in noisy classification or clustering tasks. This concept will be further investigated in the near future.

References

1. Yao, X.: Evolving artificial neural networks. Proceedings of the IEEE **87** (1999) 1423–1447
2. Mitchell, M.: An Introduction to Genetic Algorithms. MIT Press, Cambridge, MA (1998)
3. K.C.Tan, Lim, M., Yao, X., Wang, L., eds.: Recent Advances in Simulated Evolution and Learning, Singapore, World Scientific (2004)

4. Palmes, P., Hayasaka, T., Usui, S.: Mutation-based genetic neural network. IEEE Transactions on Neural Network **16** (2005)
5. Eberhart, R.C., Kennedy, J.: A new optimizer using particle swarm theory. In: Proceedings of the Sixth International Symposium on Micromachine and Human Science, Nagoya, Japan (1995) 39–43
6. Storn, R., Price, K.: Differential evolution - a simple and efficient heuristic for global optimization over continuous spaces. Journal of Global Optimization **11** (1997) 341–359
7. Fogel, D.: Evolutionary Computation. Toward a New Philosophy of Machine Intelligence. IEEE Press, Piscataway, NJ (1995)
8. Wolpert, D.H., Macready, W.G.: No free lunch theorems for optimization. IEEE Transactions on Evolutionary Computation **1** (1997) 67–82
9. Kennedy, J., Eberhart, R.C.: Particle swarm optimization. In: Proceedings of IEEE International Conference on Neural Network. Volume 8., Piscataway, NJ (1995) 1942–194
10. Palmes, P., Hayasaka, T., Usui, S.: Evolution and adaptation of neural networks. In: Proceedings of the International Joint Conference on Neural Networks, IJCNN. Volume II., Portland, Oregon, USA, IEEE Computer Society Press (2003) 397–404
11. Palmes, P., Hayasaka, T., Usui, S.: Sepa: Structure evolution and parameter adaptation. In Paz, E.C., ed.: Proceedings of the Genetic and Evolutionary Computation Conference. Volume 2., Chicago, Illinois, USA, Morgan Kaufmann (2003) 223
12. Murphy, P.M., Aha, D.W.: UCI Repository of machine learning databases. University of California, Department of Information and Computer Science, Irvine, CA (1994)
13. Prechelt, L.: Proben1–a set of neural network benchmark problems and benchmarking. Technical report, Fakultat fur Informatik, Univ. Karlsruhe, Karlsruhe, Germany (1994)

Applying Advanced Fuzzy Cellular Neural Network AFCNN to Segmentation of Serial CT Liver Images

Shitong Wang[1,2], Duan Fu[1], Min Xu[1], and Dewen Hu[3]

[1] School of Information, Southern Yangtze University, Wuxi, 214122, China
{wxwangst, fuduan008, wst_wxs}@yahoo.com.cn
[2] Department of Mechanical Eng. & Eng. Management,
City Univ. of HongKong, China
[3] College of Mechatronics and Automation, National University of Defense Technology, Changsha 410073, China
dewenhu@nudt.edu.cn

Abstract. In [1], a variant version of the fuzzy cellular neural network, called FCNN, is proposed to effectively segment microscopic white blood cell images. However, when applied to the segmentation of serial CT liver images, it does not work well. In this paper, FCNN is improved to be the novel neural network--Advanced Fuzzy Cellular Neural Network AFCNN. Just like FCNN, AFCNN still keeps its convergent property and global stability. When applied to segment serial CT liver images, AFCNN has the distinctive advantage over FCNN: it can keep boundary integrity better and have better recall accuracies such that the segmented images can approximate original liver images better.

1 Introduction

The approach of FCNN has been successfully employed in white blood cell detection [1,2]. However, when applied in the segmentation of serial CT liver images, the obtained results are unsatisfactory, due to serial CT liver image's specific characteristics [3,4]: (1) the boundaries of serial CT images are often uneven and even overlap a little with other organs such as human's spleen and gallbladder such that well-separated binary outputs of the corresponding boundaries can not be easily and accurately determined; (2) Since the liver regions occupy most of parts of CT liver images, both the fuzzy feed-forward and the feedback mechanisms in FCNN is uneasy to capture the information contained in comparatively small non-liver regions. Therefore, its improvement is required in segmenting serial CT liver images. In this paper, the novel fuzzy cellular neural network AFCNN, as the improved version of FCNN, is presented to address the above problems.

The remainder of this paper is organized as follows. In section 2, the framework of the novel fuzzy cellular neural network AFCNN is addressed. Experimental results are demonstrated in section 3 to verify AFCNN's effectiveness in segmenting serial CT liver images. Section 4 concludes this paper and addresses the future work.

2 Framework of the Novel Fuzzy Cellular Neural Network AFCNN

Here we first introduce the framework of the single-layer fuzzy cellular neural network FCNN [1], which has been successfully applied to segment white blood cell images. This locally connected network consists of $M \times N$ neurons. The output of a neuron is connected to all the inputs of every neuron in its $r \times r$ neighborhood, and similarly all the inputs of a neuron are only connected to the outputs of each neuron in its $r \times r$ neighborhood. Each neuron in this $M \times N$ FCNN performs in the following way:

The state equation of a cell c_{ij} is given by

$$C\frac{dx_{ij}}{dt} = -\frac{1}{R_x}x_{ij} + \sum_{c_u \in N_r(i,j)} A(i,j;k,l)y_{kl} + \sum_{c_u \in N_r(i,j)} B(i,j;k,l)u_{kl} + I_{ij}$$
$$+ \widetilde{\bigwedge_{c_u \in N_r(i,j)}} (A_{f\min}(i,j;k,l) + y_{kl}) + \widetilde{\bigvee_{c_u \in N_r(i,j)}} (A_{f\max}(i,j;k,l) + y_{kl})$$
$$+ \widetilde{\bigwedge_{c_u \in N_r(i,j)}} (B_{f\min}(i,j;k,l) + u_{kl}) + \widetilde{\bigvee_{c_u \in N_r(i,j)}} (B_{f\max}(i,j;k,l) + u_{kl}) \quad (1)$$

Input equation of C_{ij}: $u_{ij} = E_{ij}, 1 \le i \le M, 1 \le j \le N$ (2)

Output equation of C_{ij}: $y_{ij} = f(x_{ij}) = \frac{1}{2}(|x_{ij} + 1| - |x_{ij} - 1|)$ (3)

Constraint conditions: $|u_{ij}| \le 1, 1 \le i \le M, 1 \le j \le N$

$$A(i,j;k,l) = A(k,l;i,j), \quad A_{f\min}(i,j;k,l) = A_{f\min}(k,l;i,j),$$
$$A_{f\max}(i,j;k,l) = A_{f\max}(k,l;i,j), \quad 1 \le i \le M, 1 \le j \le N \quad (4)$$

Where $\widetilde{\wedge}, \widetilde{\vee}$ denote fuzzy AND and fuzzy OR respectively; u, x and y denote input variable, state variable and output variable, respectively; $A_{f\min}(k,l;i,j)$, $A_{f\max}(i,j;k,l)$, $B_{f\max}(i,j;k,l)$ and $B_{f\min}(i,j;k,l)$ are elements of the fuzzy feed-forward MAX template and the fuzzy feedback MIN templates, respectively; $A(i,j;k,l)$, $B(i,j;k,l)$ are elements of the feed-forward and feedback templates, respectively. In order to measure the influence of neighbor neurons on a neuron better, we introduce an input called *the fuzzy status* into FCNN state equation, and accordingly, the above FCNN model is reformulated as AFCNN. Its state equation:

$$C\frac{dx_{ij}}{dt} = -\frac{1}{R_x}x_{ij} + \sum_{c_u \in N_r(i,j)} A(i,j;k,l)y_{kl} + \sum_{c_u \in N_r(i,j)} B(i,j;k,l)u_{kl} + I_{ij}$$
$$+ \widetilde{\bigwedge_{c_u \in N_r(i,j)}} (F_{f\min}(i,j;k,l) + x_{kl}) + \widetilde{\bigvee_{c_u \in N_r(i,j)}} (F_{f\max}(i,j;k,l) + x_{kl}) \quad (5)$$

Input equation of C_{ij}: $u_{ij} = E_{ij}, 1 \le i \le M, 1 \le j \le N$ (6)

Output equation of C_{ij}: $y_{ij} = f(x_{ij}) = \frac{1}{2}(|x_{ij}+1|-|x_{ij}-1|)$ (7)

Constraint conditions: $|x_{ij}(0)| \leq 1, 1 \leq i \leq M, 1 \leq j \leq N$, $|u_{ij}| \leq 1, 1 \leq i \leq M, 1 \leq j \leq N$

$$A(i,j;k,l) = A(k,l;i,j), \quad F_{f\max}(i,j;k,l) = F_{f\max}(k,l;i,j),$$
$$F_{f\min}(i,j;k,l) = F_{f\min}(k,l;i,j), \quad 1 \leq i \leq M, 1 \leq j \leq N. \quad (8)$$

we can find that fuzzy feed-forward templates and the fuzzy feedback templates are replaced by the fuzzy status templates ($\widetilde{\bigwedge}_{c_{kl} \in N_r(i,j)}(F_{f\min}(i,j;k,l) + x_{kl}) + \widetilde{\bigvee}_{c_{kl} \in N_r(i,j)}(F_{f\max}(i,j;k,l) + x_{kl}))$, where $F_{f\max}(i,j;k,l)$, $F_{f\min}(i,j;k,l)$ denote the connected weights between neuron C_{ij} and C_{kl}, respectively. Thus, the entire template, which determines the connection between a neuron and its neighbors, consists of the $(2r+1)\times(2r+1)$ matrix $A, B, F_{f\min} F_{f\max}$. The symmetric matrixes are taken in the above template to meet the AFCNN's symmetric requirement.

When applying AFCNN to a $M \times N$ liver image, we should take $M \times N$ neurons in AFCNN in which each neuron corresponds to a pixel. Each neuron will change its state iteratively according to (5), until the entire AFCNN network converges. In other words, we transform one liver image into a dynamic system (i.e, AFCNN), and its state equations will continuously change towards the minimum energy until the final convergence is achieved. When handling the boundary of a liver region using the above AFCNN, we find that the corresponding fuzzy feed-forward and feedback templates cannot sufficiently utilize the information beyond the liver region, which will perhaps result in non- binary outputs and poor convergence in segmenting the boundary of a liver region. AFCNN has the obvious superiority over FCNN in keeping the boundary integrity. We will demonstrate AFCNN's power by our experimental results on the segmentation of serial CT liver images.

The global stability of the above AFCNN can be proved. We omit the concrete proofs here for the space sake. Its global stability assures that AFCNN has its binary output, which is very crucial for classification problems existing in image processing.

3 Experimental Studies

Based on the choice of the parameter templates in [1] and a lot of experiments on serial CT liver images, we take the following parameter templates of AFCNN in segmenting serial CT liver images:

$$A = \begin{bmatrix} 1/9 & 1/9 & 1/9 \\ 1/9 & 1/9 & 1/9 \\ 1/9 & 1/9 & 1/9 \end{bmatrix}, B = \begin{bmatrix} 1/9 & 1/9 & 1/9 \\ 1/9 & 1/9 & 1/9 \\ 1/9 & 1/9 & 1/9 \end{bmatrix}, F_{f\min} = \begin{bmatrix} 1/9 & 1/9 & 1/9 \\ 1/9 & 2/9 & 1/9 \\ 1/9 & 1/9 & 3/9 \end{bmatrix}, F_{f\max} = \begin{bmatrix} 1/9 & 1/9 & 1/9 \\ 1/9 & 2/9 & 1/9 \\ 1/9 & 1/9 & 5/9 \end{bmatrix}, R_x = 1,$$
$I = 0$, $u = X$, $x_0 =$ undefined, $y = Y$.

In order to state our experimental results fairly, we take 2 images from five serial CT image sequences to run the above AFCNN with fifty iterations. Fig.1 shows the segmented results using both FCNN and AFCNN. The two original liver images are shown in Fig.1(a). Fig.1 (b) and Fig.1(d) demonstrate the corresponding segmentation results for boundaries of livers in the liver images, using FCNN and AFCNN respectively. Fig.1(c) demonstrates the segmented liver images using FCNN. Fig.1(d) demonstrates the final segmented livers from 2 original liver images using AFCNN. Even in the complicated convex/concave parts of the boundaries, the segmented results by AFCNN are very acceptable.

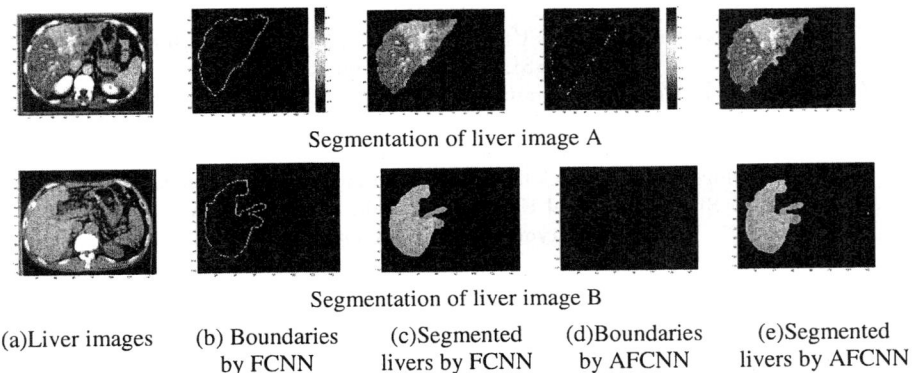

Segmentation of liver image A

Segmentation of liver image B

(a)Liver images   (b) Boundaries by FCNN   (c)Segmented livers by FCNN   (d)Boundaries by AFCNN   (e)Segmented livers by AFCNN

Fig. 1. Segmentations for 2 CT liver images

4 Conclusions and Future Work

An important feature of AFCNN is to introduce the concept of the fuzzy status into its framework. However, how to choose an appropriate parameter template in the fuzzy status still keeps an open problem. Moreover, another good study direction may perhaps be to integrate AFCNN together with current other liver image processing techniques [5]. We are expecting to report our research results along these study lines in near future.

References

1. Wang Shitong, Wang Min: A New Algorithm NDA Based on Fuzzy Cellular Neural Networks for White Blood Cell Detection [J], IEEE Trans. Information Technologies in Biomedicine (accepted with the revised version)
2. Fu Duan, Wang Shitong et al: Improved Fuzzy Cellular Neural Network IFCNN and Its Application in White Blood Cell Detection [J], Chinese J. Control and Decision (Accepted)
3. Yan Lirong, Hu Dewen et al: Image Segmentation of Serial CT liver Image Based on the Deformable Model [J], J. of SanXia University, (2002), 24(6): 529−532
4. W. L. Lee, K. S. Hsieh et al: A Study of Ultrasonic Liver Images Classification with Artificial Neural Networks Based on Fractal Geometry and Multiresolution Analysis, Biomedica Engineering-Applications, Basis & Communications, (2004), 16(2): 59-67
5. Wang Shitong, Lu Hongjun: On new fuzzy morphological associative memories, IEEE Trans. Fuzzy systems, (2004), 12(3): 316-323.

New Algorithms of Neural Fuzzy Relation Systems with Min-implication Composition*

Yanbin Luo[1], K. Palaniappan[2], and Yongming Li[3]

[1] National Laboratory of Industrial Control Technology, Institute of Modern Control Engineering, Zhejiang University, Hangzhou, 310027, China
luoyanbin008@yahoo.com.cn
[2] Department of Computer Engineering and Computer Science, University of Missouri-Columbia, MO 65211-2060, USA
palaniappank@missouri.edu
[3] Institute of Fuzzy Systems, College of Mathematics and Information Sciences, Shaanxi Normal University, Xi'an, 710062, China
liyongm@snnu.edu.cn

Abstract. Min-implication fuzzy relation equations based on Boolean-type implications can also be viewed as a way of implementing fuzzy associative memories with perfect recall. In this paper, fuzzy associative memories with perfect recall are constructed, and new on-line learning algorithms adapting the weights of its interconnections are incorporated into this neural network when the solution set of the fuzzy relation equation is non-empty. These weight matrices are actually the least solution matrix and all maximal solution matrices of the fuzzy relation equation, respectively. The complete solution set of min-implication fuzzy relation equation can be determined by the maximal solution set of this equation.

1 Introduction

In recent years, neural networks and fuzzy inference systems have been combined in different ways, and also have got successful applications in the field of pattern recognition systems, fuzzy control and knowledge-based systems [1,3,4,5,6]. The fuzzy associative memory network with max-min composition is first studied by Kosko [3]. Pedrycz has used neural networks for the resolution of max-min fuzzy relation equations (FREs) [1]. The neural network proposed in [1] converges with the aid of a learning algorithm to the maximum solution of $\sup -t$ FRE [5], when the solution set of the FRE is non-empty. Because fuzzy inference systems with min-implication composition (where the implication is any Boolean-type implication, which mainly contains R-implication, S-implication and Ql-implication) have good logic foundation [11], and approximate capability [9,10], and it is also shown that in most practical cases these FREs do have non-empty solution sets

---

* This work is supported by 973 program of China (Project No.2002CB312200), National Science Foundation of China (Project No.60474045), Zhejiang University Scientific Research Foundation for the Returned Overseas Scholars, Zhejiang Province Foundation for the Returned Overseas Scholars, and the SRF for ROCS, SEM.

[7,8]. Min-implication FREs can also be viewed as a way of implementing fuzzy associative memories (FAM) with perfect recall. So, neural fuzzy relation systems with min-implication composition are better applied into fuzzy modeling than those with sup $-t$ composition.

In this paper, we extend the neural network for implementing fuzzy relation systems based on sup $-t$ composition in [5] to min-implication composition. We suppose that the respective constructed FRE has a solution, and provide learning algorithms in order to find the least solution and all maximal solutions of the equation.

The structure of the rest of paper is organized as follows. In section 2, we give a brief review of Boolean-type implications, min-implication FREs and some solvable criteria for min-implication FREs based on Boolean-type implications. A type of neuron that implements min-implication composition FREs and new learning algorithms for solving the least solution and all maximal solutions of FREs are proposed in section 3. In section 4, some simulation results are presented and finally the conclusions are given in section 5.

2 Preliminaries

In this paper we assume that the universe of discourse is a finite set. Suppose that $X = \{x_1, x_2, \cdots, x_n\}$, $Y = \{y_1, y_2, \cdots, y_m\}$ and $N_n = \{1, 2, \cdots, n\}$, $N = \{0, 1, 2, \cdots, n, \cdots\}$. Let $F(X)$ denote the set of all of fuzzy sets in X, $A \in F(X)$, $B \in F(Y)$, $R \in F(X \times Y)$.

Because X and $X \times Y$ are finite, any element of $F(X)$ and $F(X \times Y)$ can be denoted by a vector and a $n \times m$ matrix, respectively.

For a min-implication FRE:

$$A \circ^\theta R = B. \tag{1}$$

where A, R and B are $n \times m$ matrix, $m \times k$ matrix and $n \times k$ matrix, respectively. Eq.(1) can be decomposed as a set of k simpler min-implication FREs:

$$A \circ^\theta \mathbf{r} = \mathbf{b}. \tag{2}$$

where $r_{m \times 1}$ and $b_{n \times 1}$ are the column vectors of R and B. Let $\zeta(A, \mathbf{b})$ be the solution set of the FRE of the form (2), i.e. $\zeta(A, \mathbf{b}) = \{\mathbf{r} : A \circ^\theta \mathbf{r} = \mathbf{b}\}$.

Let $a\hat{\otimes}^\theta b$ and $a\check{\otimes}^\theta b$ denote the maximal and the minimal, respectively, solution of the equation $a\theta x = b$ (if they exist).

Based on the above notations, the maximal solution operator (max-SO) $\hat{w}_\theta$ and the minimal solution operator (min-SO) $\check{w}_\theta$ are defined as follows:

$$\hat{w}_\theta(a, b) = \begin{cases} a\hat{\otimes}^\theta b, & a\theta 0 \leq b \\ 1, & \text{otherwise,} \end{cases} \tag{3}$$

$$\check{w}_\theta(a, b) = \begin{cases} a\check{\otimes}^\theta b, & a\theta 0 < b \\ 0, & \text{otherwise.} \end{cases} \tag{4}$$

For the convenience of denoting the maximal solution matrix, we define the following operator:

$$w_{max}(a,b) = \begin{cases} 1, a > b \\ b, \text{otherwise}. \end{cases} \quad (5)$$

Definition 1. *Let θ be a Boolean-type implication. θ is called a nice Boolean-type implication (NBoolean-type implication) if θ is continuous with respect to its second variable, i.e. $\forall a \in [0,1]$, the function $f(x) = a\theta x : [0,1] \to [0,1]$ is continuous.*

Let θ be an NBoolean-type implication. The mean-SM ($\bar{\Gamma}$), the min-SM ($\check{\Gamma}$) and the max-SM ($\hat{\Gamma}$) of Eq.(2) are defined in [7,8]. We extend the solvable criteria for any S-implication [7] and R-implication [8] to any Boolean-type implication and present them in the following propositions.

Proposition 1. *Let $A \circ^\theta r = b$ be a min-implication FRE of the form (2). If $\forall i \in N_n, \exists j \in N_m$, such that $b_i \in I(a_{ij})$, and $b_k \notin I(a_{kj})$, $\forall k \in N_n - \{i\}$, then $\zeta(A,b) \neq \emptyset$.*

Proposition 2. *Let θ be an NBoolean-type implication, $A \circ^\theta r = b$ be a min-implication FRE of the form (2). Then, $\zeta(A,b) \neq \emptyset$ iff (if and only if) $A \circ^\theta \inf \bar{\Gamma} = b$.*

Proposition 3. *Let θ be an NBoolean-type implication, $A \circ^\theta r = b$ be a min-implication FRE of the form (2), $t = \sup \check{\Gamma}$. Then, $\zeta(A,b) \neq \emptyset$ iff $A \circ^\theta t \leq b$, and t is the least solution.*

Proposition 4. *Let θ be an NBoolean-type implication, $A \circ^\theta r = b$ be a min-implication FRE of the form (2). The following statements are equivalent:*
(i) $\zeta(A,b) = \emptyset$;
(ii) $\exists j \in N_n$ such that $\hat{\Gamma}_{\cdot j} = 1$ and $b_j \neq 1$.

In the following, we propose new learning algorithms to obtain the least solution and all maximal solutions of the FRE of the form (1), respectively.

3 Min-implication Operator Networks and New Algorithms

3.1 A Type of Neuron That Implements Min-implication FREs

Let $D = \{(\mathbf{a}_j, \mathbf{b}_j), j \in N_n\}$ be a set of input-output data. Compositional fuzzy associative memories can be generalized to the finding of the fuzzy relation matrix R for which the following equation holds:

$$\mathbf{a}_j \circ^\theta R = \mathbf{b}_j, \quad j = 1, 2, \ldots, n \quad (6)$$

where θ is an NBoolean-type implication.

However, the matrix satisfying (6) doesn't always exist in most case. Even if it exists, the weight matrix satisfying (6) doesn't have to be a solution of the equation. The choice of training sets plays an important role in the generation of their connection weights. But, it is difficult to give ideal training sets D. Therefore, an effective method is to adjust the weights to matching the input-output pairs.

A type of compositional neuron that implements the union-intersection composition of fuzzy relation is proposed by G. B. Stamou and S. G. Tzafestas [5]. In the following, we propose a similar type of neuron for the min-implication composition.

The general structure of a conventional neuron can be shown in Fig.1. The equation that describes this kind of neuron is as follows:

$$y = g(u) = g(f(x)) = g(\sum_{j=1}^{n} w_i x_i + \theta), \qquad (7)$$

where θ is a threshold and w_i $(i = 1, 2, \ldots, n)$ are weights that can change on-line with the aid of a learning process.

The compositional neural has the same structure with the neuron of (7) (Fig.1), but it can be described by the equation:

$$y = g(S_{j \in N_n} t(x_i, w_i)), \qquad (8)$$

where S is a fuzzy union operator (an s-norm), t is a fuzzy intersection operator (a t-norm) and g is the activation function:

$$g(x) = \begin{cases} 0, & x \in (-\infty, 0) \\ x, & x \in [0, 1] \\ 1, & x \in (1, +\infty). \end{cases} \qquad (9)$$

The structure of this neural network is shown in Fig.2.

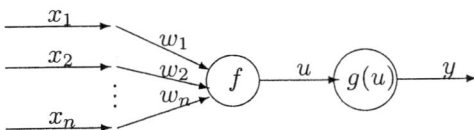

Fig. 1. The structure of the neuron

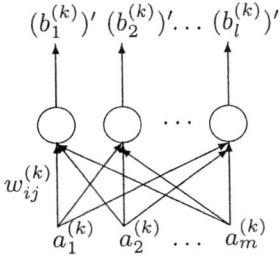

Fig. 2. The structure of the compositional neuron

The equality index proposed in [1] is defined by:

$[(b_i^{(k)})' \equiv b_i^{(k)}] = \frac{1}{2}[((b_i^{(k)})' \to b_i^{(k)}) \wedge (b_i^{(k)} \to (b_i^{(k)})') + ((\overline{b}_i^{(k)})' \to \overline{b}_i^{(k)}) \wedge (\overline{b}_i^{(k)} \to (\overline{b}_i^{(k)})')]$, where "$\to$" denotes the Łukasiwicz implication, the complement (negation) is linear, i.e. $\overline{b}_i^{(k)} = 1 - b_i^{(k)}$. Finally, we obtain the following expression for the equality index:

$$[(b_i^{(k)})' \equiv b_i^{(k)}] = \begin{cases} 1 + (b_i^{(k)})' - b_i^{(k)}, & (b_i^{(k)})' < b_i^{(k)} \\ 1 + b_i^{(k)} - (b_i^{(k)})', & (b_i^{(k)})' > b_i^{(k)} \\ 1, & (b_i^{(k)})' = b_i^{(k)} \end{cases} \quad (10)$$

The error is defined as follows:

$$E_i^{(k)} = 1 - [(b_i^{(k)})' \equiv b_i^{(k)}].$$

Our goal in learning processes is minimize the total error

$$E^{(k)} = \sum_i E_i^{(k)}. \quad (11)$$

Due to the decomposition of the FRE [7,8], the proposed algorithm converges independently for each neuron. For simplicity and without loss of generality, we only consider the single neuron case. The response of the neuron $(b^{(k)})'$ is given by

$$(b^{(k)})' = \inf_{i \in N_m} (a_i^{(k)} \theta w_i^{(k)}).$$

where $w_i^{(k)}$ ($i \in N_m$) are the weights of the neuron and the input $a_i^{(k)}$. In this case, the desired output is $b_i^{(k)}$.

3.2 The Learning Algorithm for Solving the Least Solution of the FRE

Based on the neuron network described by the Fig.2, we give the learning algorithm for solving the least solution of the FRE of the form (2) in the following:

Algorithm 1. Step 1. Initialize the weights as $\breve{w}_i^{(1)}(0) = 0$, $i \in N_m$, and give an error constant ϵ and the upper limit value of iteration μ.

Step 2. Input a pair of pattern $(\mathbf{a}_k, \mathbf{b}_k)$, $k \in N_n$, and let $v = 0$.

Step 3. The network on-line weights $\breve{w}_i^{(k)}$ ($i = 1, 2, \ldots, m$) are adjusted by the following algorithm

$$\breve{w}_i^{(k)}(v+1) = \breve{w}_i^{(k)}(v) + \Delta \breve{w}_i^{(k)}(v), \quad (12)$$

$$\Delta \breve{w}_i^{(k)}(v) = \alpha l_s, \quad (13)$$

$$l_s = \begin{cases} \alpha_1(\breve{w}_\theta(a_{ki}, b_k) - \breve{w}_i^{(k)}(v)), & \breve{w}_i^{(k)}(v) < \breve{w}_\theta(a_{ki}, b_k) \\ \alpha_2(\breve{w}_i^{(k)}(v) - \hat{w}_\theta(a_{ki}, b_k)), & \breve{w}_i^{(k)}(v) > \hat{w}_\theta(a_{ki}, b_k) \\ 0, & \text{otherwise,} \end{cases} \quad (14)$$

where $\widecheck{w}_\theta$ and $\widehat{w}_\theta$ are given by (3) and (4), $0 < \alpha \leq 1$ and $0 \leq \alpha_1, \alpha_2 \leq 1$ are learning rates.

Step 4. Compute the total error $E^{(k)}$.

Step 5. Return to Step 3 until $E^{(k)} < \epsilon$ or $v > \mu$, in this case, the last weights are denoted by $\widecheck{w}_j^{(k)}, j = 1, 2, \ldots, m$.

Step 6. If $k < n$, return to Step 2 with $k = k+1$ and $\widecheck{w}_j^{(k+1)}(0) = \widecheck{w}_j^{(k)}, j = 1, 2, \ldots, m$.

With this algorithm we obtain the following theorem.

Theorem 1. Let $D = \{(\mathbf{a}_j, \mathbf{b}_j), j \in N_n\}$ be a training set, where $\mathbf{a}_j$ and $\mathbf{b}_j$ are the jth column of the matrix A and B, respectively. The neuron network of Fig.2 with the learning algorithm described by (12),(13) and (14), converges (with $\epsilon = 0$) to the least solution of the FRE:

$$A \circ^\theta R = B$$

if $\zeta(A, B) \neq \emptyset$ and $\alpha = 1, \alpha_1 = 1, \alpha_2 = 0$.

Proof (of theorem). Without loss of generality, we will prove the Theorem only for one neuron. Since $\zeta(A, B) \neq \emptyset$, it is clear that $\zeta(A, \mathbf{b}) \neq \emptyset$. Then, from Proposition 4 we have that

$\hat{\Gamma}_{\cdot j} = 1$ implies $b_j = 1, \forall j \in N_n$.

From the definition of $\hat{\Gamma}$ we have that

$$\hat{\Gamma}_{ij} = w_{max}(\sup_{k \in N_n} \widecheck{\Gamma}_{ik}, \bar{\Gamma}_{ij}), \forall i \in N_m, \forall j \in N_n. \tag{15}$$

From (15), it is true that for any $j \in N_n$ there exists $i \in N_m$, such that

$$\hat{\Gamma}_{ij} = \bar{\Gamma}_{ij} \geq \sup_{k \in N_n} \widecheck{\Gamma}_{ik}.$$

Hence, from the definition of the solution matrices, we have

$$\widehat{w}_\theta(a_{ji}, b_j) \geq \sup_{k \in N_n} \widecheck{w}_\theta(a_{ki}, b_k). \tag{16}$$

From (16) it is true that $\forall j \in N_n, \exists i \in N_m$ such that $\forall v \in N$,

$$\widehat{w}_\theta(a_{ji}, b_j) \geq \widecheck{w}_i^{(j)}(v).$$

From (12)-(14), and $\alpha = \alpha_1 = 1, \alpha_2 = 0$, we have $\forall j \in N_n, \exists i \in N_m$ such that $\forall v \in N$,

$$\widecheck{w}_i^{(j)}(v+1) = \begin{cases} \widecheck{w}_\theta(a_{ji}, b_j), & \widecheck{w}_\theta(a_{ji}, b_j) \geq \widecheck{w}_i^{(j)}(v) \\ \widecheck{w}_i^{(j)}(v), & \text{otherwise,} \end{cases}$$

and $\{\widecheck{w}_i^{(j)}(v)\}(v \in N)$ is a upper bounded and monotonic increasing sequence. Thus, there exists $v_0 \in N$ such that $\forall v > v_0$, it is

$$\widecheck{w}_i^{(j)}(v) = \sup_{k \in N_n} \widecheck{w}_\theta(a_{ki}, b_k), i = 1, 2, \ldots, m.$$

Therefore, there exists $v_0 \in N$ such that $\forall v > v_0$, it is true that
$$\mathbf{a}_j \circ^\theta \widecheck{\mathbf{w}}^{(j)}(v) = b_j, \quad \forall j \in N_n. \qquad \square$$

3.3 The Learning Algorithm for Solving All Maximal Solutions of the FRE

From Algorithm 1 and Theorem 1, we can get the least solution $\mathbf{t} = \sup \check{\Gamma}$ of the FRE of the form (2). In the following, we give a learning algorithm for calculating all maximal solutions of the FRE. The structure of the single-layer neural network with compositional neurons is also illustrated in Fig.2. For simplicity and without loss of generality, we only consider the single neuron case.

The adaptation of the neural network is supported by the following algorithm.

Algorithm 2. Step 1. Initialize the weights as $\hat{w}_j^{(1)}(0) = 1, j \in N_m$, and give an error constant ϵ and the upper limit value of iteration μ.

Step 2. Input $(\mathbf{a}_k, b_k), k \in N_n$, then calculate $N(k)$, where $N(k) = \{j \in N_m : a_{kj}\theta t_j = b_k\}, t_j = \sup_i \check{w}_\theta(a_{ij}, b_i)$, and let $v = 0$.

Step 3. The weights $\hat{w}_j^{(k)}, j = 1, 2, \ldots, m$, are adjusted as follows

$$\hat{w}_j^{(k)}(v+1) = \hat{w}_j^{(k)}(v) - \Delta\hat{w}_j^{(k)}(v), \tag{17}$$

$$\Delta\hat{w}_j^{(k)}(v) = \eta l_s, \tag{18}$$

$$l_s = \begin{cases} \hat{w}_j^{(k)}(v) - (a_{kj}\hat{\otimes}b_k \wedge \hat{w}_j^{(k)}(v)), & j \in N(k) \\ 0, & \text{otherwise,} \end{cases} \tag{19}$$

$j = 1, 2, \ldots, m$.

Step 4. Compute the total error $E^{(k)}$.

Step 5. Return to Step 3 until $E^{(k)} < \epsilon$ or $v > \mu$, in this case, the last weights are denoted by $\hat{w}_j^{(k)}, j = 1, 2, \ldots, m$.

Step 6. If $k < n$, return to Step 2 with $k = k+1$ and $\hat{w}_j^{(k+1)}(0)) = \hat{w}_j^{(k)}, j = 1, 2, \ldots, m$.

Step 7. Calculate the set $E_t = \{f \in N_m : f \cap N(1) \cap N(2) \cap \cdots \cap N(n)$ contains at least one element$\}$. Let F be the subset of E_t including all the minimal elements of E_t. For any $f \in F$, adjust the elements of the weight vector $\hat{\mathbf{w}} = \{\hat{w}_1^{(n)}, \hat{w}_2^{(n)}, \ldots, \hat{w}_m^{(n)}\}$ as follows

$$\hat{w}_j^{(f)} = \begin{cases} \hat{w}_j^{(n)}, & j \in f \\ 1, & \text{otherwise,} \end{cases} \tag{20}$$

$j = 1, 2, \ldots, m$.

With the above algorithm we get the following theorem.

Theorem 2. *Let $D = \{(\mathbf{a}_j, b_j), j \in N_n\}$ be a training set, where $\mathbf{a}_j$ and b_j are the jth column of the matrix A and the vector $\mathbf{b}$, respectively. All the weight vectors $\hat{\mathbf{w}}^{(f)} = (\hat{w}_1^{(f)}, \hat{w}_2^{(f)}, \ldots, \hat{w}_m^{(f)}), \forall f \in F$, from Algorithm 2, converge (with $\epsilon = 0$) to all maximal solutions of the FRE:*

$$A \circ^\theta \mathbf{r} = \mathbf{b}$$

if $\zeta(A, \mathbf{b}) \neq \emptyset$ and $\eta = 1$.

Proof (of theorem). It is obvious that E_t is a finite poset under the subset inclusion from the definition of E_t. Then F is also finite and for any $f \in E_t$, there is $g \in F$ such that $g \subseteq f$ and the elements of F are not comparable with each other (in other words, the elements of F do not contain each other). In the following, we verify that $M = \{\hat{\mathbf{w}}^{(f)} : \forall f \in F\}$ satisfies the conditions of the theorem.

At first, we prove that $\hat{\mathbf{w}}^{(f)}, \forall f \in F$ all are solutions of the FRE of the form (2). If $b_i = 1$, then for any $j \in N(i), t_j = 1$. In this case, $a_{ij} = 0$ and $\hat{w}_j^{(f)} = 1$, and hence $\inf_j(a_{ij}\theta \hat{w}_j^{(f)}) = 1 = b_i$. If $b_i < 1$, then there exists $j_0 \in N_m$ such that $a_{ij_0}\theta t_{j_0} = b_i$, then $j_0 \in N(i)$. In this case, $\inf_j(a_{ij}\theta \hat{w}_j^{(f)}) \leq a_{ij_0}\theta \hat{w}_{j_0}^{(f)} = a_{ij_0}\theta \hat{w}_{j_0}^{(n)} = a_{ij_0}\theta(\inf\{a_{ij_0}\hat{\otimes}^\theta b_i : j_0 \in N(i)\}) \leq a_{ij_0}\theta(a_{ij_0}\hat{\otimes}^\theta b_i) = b_i$. On the other hand, since $j \in N(i)$, that is $a_{ij}\theta t_j = b_i$, then $a_{ij}\hat{\otimes}^\theta b_i \geq t_j$. Thus, $\hat{w}_j^{(f)} = \hat{w}_j^{(n)} = \inf\{a_{ij}\hat{\otimes}^\theta b_i : j \in N(i)\} \geq \inf\{t_j : j \in N(i)\} = t_j$. Then, $\inf_j(a_{ij}\theta \hat{w}_j^{(f)}) \geq \inf_j(a_{ij}\theta t_j) = b_i$. So, $\hat{\mathbf{w}}^{(f)} = (\hat{w}_1^{(f)}, \hat{w}_2^{(f)}, \ldots, \hat{w}_m^{(f)})$ is a solution.

Second, for $f_1, f_2 \in E_t$, if $f_1 \subseteq f_2$, then it is obvious that $\hat{\mathbf{w}}^{(f_1)} \geq \hat{\mathbf{w}}^{(f_2)}$ from the definition of $\hat{\mathbf{w}}^{(f)}$.

Third, for any $\mathbf{r} \in \zeta(A, \mathbf{b})$, we shall show that there exists a $f \in F$ such that $\mathbf{r} \leq \hat{\mathbf{w}}^{(f)}$. Let $N'(i) = \{j \in N_m : a_{ij}\theta r_j = b_i\}$, then $N'(i) \neq \emptyset$ and $N'(i) \subseteq N(i)$. Construct $E_r = \{f \subseteq N_m : \forall i \in N_n, f \cap N'(i)$ contains at least one element$\}$, then it is obvious that $E_r \subseteq E_t$. We show that $\mathbf{r} \leq \hat{\mathbf{w}}^{(f)}, \forall f \in E_r$, then there exists a $f \in F$ such that $\mathbf{r} \leq \hat{\mathbf{w}}^{(f)}$. For any $f \in E_r$, if $\forall j \in f$, then $\forall j \in N'(i), a_{ij}\theta r_j = b_i$. Then $r_j \leq a_{ij}\hat{\otimes}^\theta b_i$, hence, $r_j \leq \inf\{a_{ij}\hat{\otimes}^\theta b_i : j \in N(i)\} = \hat{w}_j^{(f)}$. Therefore, $\mathbf{r} \leq \hat{\mathbf{w}}^{(f)}, \forall f \in E_r$.

Finally, we show that $M = \{\hat{\mathbf{w}}^{(f)} : \forall f \in F\}$ is the set of maximal solutions of the FRE of the form (2). The left is only show that the elements of M are not comparable with each other. Since F is minimal, for any $f_1, f_2 \in F$, there are $j_1 \in f_1$ and $j_2 \in f_2$ such that $j_1 \notin f_2, j_2 \notin f_1$. In this case, the j_1th coordinate of $\hat{\mathbf{w}}^{(f_1)}$ is 1 and the j_2th coordinate of $\hat{\mathbf{w}}^{(f_2)}$ is 1, while the j_2th coordinate of $\hat{\mathbf{w}}^{(f_1)}$ and the j_1th coordinate of $\hat{\mathbf{w}}^{(f_2)}$ is not equal to 1. This implies that $\hat{\mathbf{w}}^{(f_1)}$ and $\hat{\mathbf{w}}^{(f_2)}$ are not comparable with each other. Thus, M is the maximal subset of $\zeta(A, \mathbf{b})$. □

4 Simulation Results

Example. The training set $D = \{(\mathbf{a}_j, b_j), j = 1, 2, 3, 4\}$ is as follows:

$$\begin{array}{ll} [0.7\ 0.8\ 0.7] & 0.3 \\ [0.4\ 0.7\ 0.6] & 0.5 \\ [0.3\ 0.1\ 0.3] & 0.7 \\ [0.2\ 0.1\ 0.1] & 0.8 \end{array}$$

Let θ be a Kleene-Dienes implication, i.e. $a\theta b = (1-a) \vee b, \forall a, b \in [0, 1]$.
Let the error constant $\epsilon = 0$ and the learning rate $\alpha = 1, \alpha_1 = 1, \alpha_2 = 0$. First initialize the weights $\breve{w}_j^{(1)}(0) = 0, j = 1, 2, 3, 4$. From the Algorithm 1, we

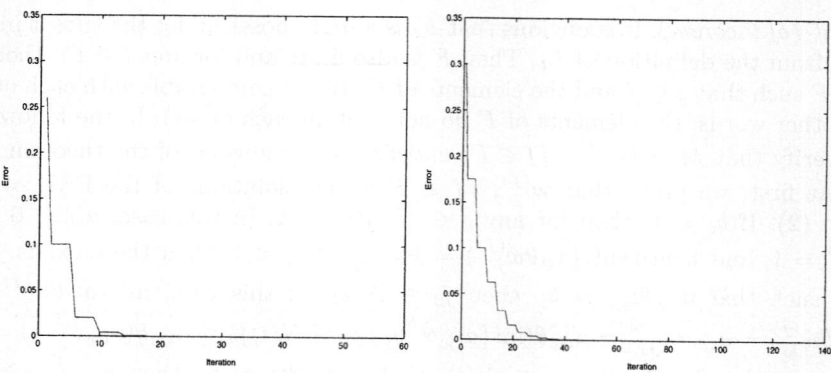

Fig. 3. The result of Algorithm 1 for initial conditions $\alpha = 0.8$(left) and $\alpha = 0.5$(right)

Table 1. The relation between α and iterations ($\epsilon = 1.0e - 10$)

α	Iterations
0.9	38
0.8	54
0.7	74
0.6	94
0.5	126

can get the following weight vector after 2 iterations:

$$\check{\mathbf{w}} = (0 \ \ 0.5 \ \ 0.5)^T,$$

that is, the least solution of the equation $A \circ^\theta R = b$, where

$$A = \begin{pmatrix} 0.7 \ 0.8 \ 0.7 \\ 0.4 \ 0.7 \ 0.6 \\ 0.3 \ 0.1 \ 0.3 \\ 0.2 \ 0.1 \ 0.1 \end{pmatrix}, \mathbf{b} = (0.3 \ \ 0.5 \ \ 0.7 \ \ 0.8)^T.$$

In the following, we calculate all maximal solutions of the above equation using Algorithm 2. First initialize the weights $\hat{w}_j^{(1)}(0) = 1, j = 1, 2, 3, 4$. Let the error constant $\epsilon = 0$ and the learning rate $\eta = 1$. After 4 iterations, we can get the adjusted weight vector is $\hat{\mathbf{w}}^{(4)} = (0.3 \ \ 0.5 \ \ 0.5)^T$, and $N(4) = \{1\}$. In this case, $E_t = \{\{1,2\}, \{1,2,3\}, \{1,3\}\}$, and then $F = \{\{1,2\}, \{1,3\}\}$. Thus, the adjusted weight vector is $\hat{\mathbf{w}}^{(f_1)} = (0.3 \ \ 0.5 \ \ 1)^T, \hat{\mathbf{w}}^{(f_2)} = (0.3 \ \ 1 \ \ 0.5)^T$, where $f_1 = \{1,2\}, f_2 = \{1,3\}$. Thus, the maximal solution set $M = \{(0.3 \ \ 0.5 \ \ 1)^T, (0.3 \ \ 1 \ \ 0.5)^T\}$.

Let $\alpha = 0.8(0.5)$ and using Algorithm 1 with $\epsilon = 1.0e - 10$ after 54 (126) iterations it converges to:

$$\check{\mathbf{w}} = (0 \ \ 0.5 \ \ 0.5)^T,$$

the change of the error is illustrated in Fig. 3.

These simulation results also illustrate that the last stable points of the network are good approximate solutions when the FRE has no solution.

5 Conclusions

In the present paper, we have studied the resolution problem of min-implication FREs based on neural network. Due to the relatively complement of neural networks and fuzzy inference systems, the adaptation ability of system paraments in fuzzy inference systems is greatly improved. Both the least solution and all maximial solutions are obtained by taking the proposed learning algorithms when the solution set of the FRE is nonempty, otherwise, the learning of the neural network converges to good approximate solutions. Finally, we demonstrate them in detail, and provide some simulation results to get the last stable points. The results of the present paper can be applied into fuzzy modeling.

References

1. Pedrycz, W.: Neurocomputation inrelational systems. IEEE Trans. Pattern Anal. Machine Intell. **3** (1991) 289-297
2. De Basets, B.: Analytical solution methods for fuzzy relational equations. In: D. Dubois, H. Prade (Eds.): Fundamentals of fuzzy sets. The handbooks of fuzzy sets series. vol. 1. Kluwer Academic Publishers, Dordrecht (2000) 291-340
3. Kosko, B.: Neural networks and fuzzy systems: a dynamical apporach to machine intelligence. Prentice-Hall, Englewood Cliffs, NJ (1992)
4. Li, X., Ruan, D. (Eds.): Novel neural algorithms based on fuzzy δ rules for solving fuzzy relation equations: Part I, Fuzzy Sets Syst. **90** (1997) 11-23
5. Stamou, G.B., Tzafestas, S.G. : Neural fuzzy relational systems with a new learning algorithm. Math. and comput. in simul. **51** (2000) 301-314
6. Satio, T., Mukaidono, M.: A learning algorithm for max-min network and its application to solve fuzzy relation equations. Proc. 2nd Internat. Conf. on fuzzy logic and neural networks, Izuka (1991) 184-187
7. Luo, Y., Li, Y.: Decomposition and resolution of min-implication fuzzy relation equations based on S-implications. Fuzzy Sets Syst. **148** (2004) 305-317
8. Luo, Y., Li, Y.: Decomposition and resolution of θ-Fuzzy relation equations based on R-implications. Fuzzy Syst. Math. **4** (2003) 81-87 (in Chinese)
9. Li, Y., Shi, Z., Li, Z.: Approximation theory of fuzzy systems based upon genuine many valued implications-SISO cases. Fuzzy Sets Syst. **130** (2002) 147-157
10. Li, Y., Shi, Z., Li, Z.: Approximation theory of fuzzy systems based upon genuine many valued implications-MIMO cases. Fuzzy Sets Syst. **130** (2002) 159-174
11. Wang, W.: On the logic foundation of fuzzy reasoning. Inform. Sci. **117** (1999) 47-88

Neural Networks Combination by Fuzzy Integral in Clinical Electromyography

Hongbo Xie, Hai Huang, and Zhizhong Wang

Department of Biomedical Engineering, Shanghai Jiao Tong University, Shanghai, 200030, PR of China
xiehb@sjtu.edu.cn

Abstract. Motor unit action potentials (MUAPs) recorded during routine electromyography (EMG) examination provide important information for the assessment of neuromuscular disorders, and the neural network based MUAPs classification system has been used to enhance the diagnosis accuracy. However, the conventional neural networks methods of MUAP diagnosis are mainly based on single feature set model, and the diagnosis accuracy of which is not always satisfactory. In order to utilize multiple feature sets to improve diagnosis accuracy, a hybrid decision support system based on fusion multiple neural networks outputs is presented. Back-propagation (BP) neural network is used as single diagnosis model in every feature set, i.e. i) time domain morphological measures, ii) frequency parameters, and iii) time-frequency domain wavelet transform feature set. Then these outputs are combined by fuzzy integral. More excellent diagnosis yield indicates the potential of the proposed multiple neural networks strategies for neuromuscular disorders diagnosis.

1 Introduction

The motor unit is the smallest functional unit of the muscle. At slight voluntary muscle contraction the motor unit action potential (MUAP) is recorded that reflects the electrical activity of a single anatomical motor unit, the procedure known as electromyography (EMG). The MUAP findings are used to detect and describe different neuromuscular disease [1]. With the development of quantitative EMG techniques, some automated decision making system of neuromuscular disorder diagnosis emerged. Andreassen and associates [2] employed a causal probabilistic network for assessment the EMG findings. Coatrieux and co-workers [3] applied clustering method for the automatic diagnosis of pathology based on the MUAPs records. Pattichis, et al. gave series research yields of neural networks classifying MUAPs for differentiation motor neuron disease and myopathy from normal [4]. The networks they used include back-propagation, the radial basis function network, and the self-organizing feature map network. The feature sets used as network input include time domain parameters, frequency domain parameters, AR coefficients, cepstral coefficients, wavelet transform coefficients. However, the problem is currently solved with not very satisfactory accuracy by using these single neural networks classifiers of different architectures and based on different sets of features for the MUAP is a complicated physiological electric action. In order to improve the accuracy of computer-aided MUAP diagnosis, new architecture of classifier or new feature extractor is still in considered by some researchers.

It is well known that in many situations combination the output of several neural networks leads to an improved classification result. This happens because each network makes errors on a different region of the input space. Till now, many methods to combine the outputs of several individual neural networks have been developed [5]. To our knowledge, few research are focused on MUAP diagnosis based on combination multiple neural networks [6]. The aim of this preliminary study is to explore the feasibility of developing a multiple neural networks decision support system for improving the diagnostic performance in computer-aid clinical electromyography. Fuzzy integral is adopted as the combination scheme, which considers the difference of performance of each network in combination.

The paper is organized as follows. Section 2 proposes and describes the multiple neural networks structure. Section 3 presents the fuzzy integral fusion method that considers the difference of performance of each network in combining the networks in detail. Section 4 describes MUAP feature sets used as neural networks inputs and Section 5 will covers the experimental results for the assessment of normal subjects (MYO) and subjects suffering with myopathy (MYO) and motor neuron disease (MND) with the fuzzy integral fusion method, and section 6 the concluding remarks.

2 Multiple Neural Networks Structure

A neural network can be considered as a mapping device between an input set and an output set. Mathematically, a neural network represents a function F that maps I into O; $F: I \rightarrow O$, or $y = f(x)$ where $y \in O$ and $x \rightarrow I$. Since the classification problem is a mapping from the feature space to some set of output classes, we can formalize the neural network, especially the back propagation neural network trained with the generalized delta rule, as a classifier.

Suppose that we have a neural network classifier with N neurons in the input layer, H neurons in the hidden layer, and K neurons in the output layer. Here, N is the number of input feature vector dimension, K is the number of classes, and H is an appropriately number. The network is fully connected between adjacent layers. Richard's research has revealed [7]: the outputs of the neural network are not just likelihoods or binary logical values near zero or one, instead, they are estimates of Bayesian a posteriori probabilities.

The operation of this network can be thought of as a nonlinear decision-making process. Considering the problem of assigning an input sample $X\{x_j : j = 1, \cdots N\}$ to one of the classes set $\{C_i : i = 1 \cdots K\}$. With a squared-error cost function, each output neuron estimates the probability $P(C_i | X)$ of belonging to this class by

$$P(C_i | X) \approx f\{\sum_{m=1}^{H} v_{im} f(\sum_{j=1}^{N} w_{mj} x_j)\} \qquad (1)$$

where w_{mj} is a weight between the jth input neuron and the mth hidden neuron, v_{im} is the weight from the mth hidden neuron to the ith class output, and f is a sigmoid function. The neuron having the maximum value is selected as the corresponding class. Because the outputs of neural networks are estimates of Bayesian a posteriori probabilities as mentioned earlier, the classification of an input X is actually based on a set of real value measurements

$$P(C_i | X) \quad 1 \leq i \leq K \tag{2}$$

They represent the probabilities that X comes from each of the C classes under the condition X. A network of a finite size, however, does not often load a particular mapping completely or it generalizes poorly. Increasing the size and number of hidden layers most often does not lead to improvements. The basic idea of multiple neural networks scheme is to develop M independently trained neural networks with relevant features, and to classify a given input pattern by obtaining a classification from each copy of the network and then utilizing combination methods to decide the collective classification. It means that M neural networks fusion problem is how to combine the value:

$$P(C_i | X) \quad 1 \leq i \leq K \quad 1 \leq k \leq M \tag{3}$$

A variety of combination schemes can be adopted such as unanimity, majority, Borda count, and so on [5]. But these schemes are not much available for measurement level combination. So, in this paper, combination scheme based on fuzzy integral is developed for the study of neuromuscular disorders classification.

3 The Combination Scheme Based on Fuzzy Integral Theory

3.1 The Fuzzy Integral Theory

A set function $g : 2^Y \to [0,1]$ with $g(\phi) = 0$, $g(Y) = 1$ and $g(A) < g(B)$ if $A \subset B$, is said a fuzzy measure. From this definition, Sugeno [8] introduced the so-called g_λ-fuzzy measure which comes with an additional property

$$g(A \cup B) = g(A) + g(B) + \lambda_g g(A) g(B) \tag{4}$$

for all $A, B \subset X$ and $A \cap B = \phi$, and for some $\lambda > -1$.

Let $Y = \{y_1, y_2, \cdots, y_n\}$ be a finite set and let $g^i = g(\{y_i\})$. The values g^i are called the densities of measure. λ is given by solving the equation

$$\lambda + 1 = \prod_{i=1}^{n} (1 + \lambda g^i) \tag{5}$$

where $\lambda \in (-1, +\infty)$ and $\lambda \neq 0$.

It affords that the measure of the union of two disjoint subsets can be computed from the component measures.

Let Y be a finite set and $h: Y \to [0,1]$ a fuzzy set of Y. The fuzzy integral over Y of the function h with respect to a fuzzy measure g is defined by

$$h(y) \circ g(\cdot) = \max_{E \subseteq Y}[\min(\min_{y \in E} h(y), g(E))]$$
$$= \max_{\alpha \in [0,1]}[\min(\alpha, g(F_\alpha))] \qquad (6)$$

where $F_\alpha = \{y \mid h(y) \geq \alpha\}$

When Y is a finite set, the calculation of the fuzzy integral is easily given. Let $Y = \{y_1, y_2, \cdots, y_n\}$ and $h: Y \to [0,1]$ be a function. Suppose $h(y_1) \geq h(y_2) \geq \cdots \geq h(y_n)$, (if not, Y is rearranged so that this relation holds). Then a fuzzy integral e, with respect to a fuzzy measure g over Y can be computed by

$$e = \max_{i=1}^{n}\{\min(h(y_i), g(A_i))\} \qquad (7)$$

where $A_i = \{y_1, y_2, \cdots, y_i\}$.

When g is a g_λ-fuzzy measure, the values of $g(A_i)$ can be calculated recursively as

$$g(A_1) = g(\{y_1\}) = g^1 \qquad (8)$$

$$g(A_i) = g^i + g(A_{i-1}) + \lambda g^i g(A_{i-1}) \qquad (9)$$

where $1 < i < n$

In terms of multiple evidences combination, a more explicit understanding over the fuzzy integral is given as following [9]:

When Y is a set of evidence sources, $h(y_i)$ could be interpreted as an evaluation of how certain we are about decision proposition of the evidence toward the final evaluation. If an evidence subset $A \subset Y$ is considered, $\min_{y \in A} h(y)$ may be regard as the most conservative evaluation that this subset gives about decision proposition. $g(A)$ indicates the degree of importance of the subset A toward the final evaluation. The fuzzy integral could be interpreted as searching for the maximal grade of agreement between the objective evidence and the expectation.

3.2 Combination Algorithm by Fuzzy Integral

Given K diagnosis propositions by $\Theta = \{A_1, A_2, \cdots, A_K\}$, $A_j = X \in C_j$, $\forall j \in \Lambda$, which respectively denote that the input sample X belongs to the category C_j. For the input sample X, M neural networks are considered and each of them will produce a confidence value for each class. These networks are represented by the integral set Y above. Those confidence values are represented by the function h about the decision proposition. On the other hand, the output of each network in corresponding feature domain will present an evidence about the final diagnosis evaluation. According to the meaning of Richard's results [7], the output, O_{ij}, ($i = 1, 2, \cdots$,

M; $j = 1, 2, \cdots K$) is just an appropriate evaluation that the evidence in domain i about proposition A_j. So, it is reasonable to take O_j^i as $h_j(x_i)$ [9].

The fuzzy density indicates the worth of various 'expert' for the diagnosis proposition. Therefore, we take the diagnosis accuracy of each network as this degree of importance, i.e. the fuzzy densities, $\{g^i : i = 1, 2, \cdots, M\}$, could be obtained by network test in various feature domains. Given the fuzzy densities, the parameter λ could be determined by Eq. (9).

Now, we can calculated the fuzzy integral e_j over Y of the functions, $\{h_j : j = 1, 2, \cdots, K\}$, with respect to the fuzzy densities, $\{g^i : i = 1, 2, \cdots, M\}$ by

$$e_j = \sum_{i=1}^{M} [\min(h_j(x_i), g(A_i))] \tag{10}$$

The overall confidence for the class is the fuzzy integral. The class with the largest integral value can be taken as the final diagnosis result.

4 MUAP Features Sets

In this study, the EMG signal is acquired from the biceps brachii muscle using a concentric needle electrode. The template matching method was used to identify twenty MUAPs recorded from the motor unit. Three various MUAP feature set parameters are considered as neural network inputs.

4.1 Time Domain Morphological Parameters

As shown in Figure.1, the features measured from each MUAP in time domain include [4, 10]:

Duration: *(Dur)*, beginning and ending of the MUAP are identified by sliding a measuring window of 3ms in length and 10uV in width;

Spike duration: (SpDur), measured from the first to the last positive peak;

Amplitude: *(Amp)*, maximum peak to peak measure of the MUAP;

Area: sum of the rectified MUAP integrated over the duration;

Spike area: *(SpArea)*, sum of the rectified MUAP integrated over the spike duration;

Phase: *(Ph)*, number of the baseline crossings that exceed $25\mu V$, plus one;

Turns: *(T)*, number of positive and negative peaks separated from the preceding and following peak by $25\mu V$.

4.2 Frequency Domain Parameters

The frequency parameters of MUAP are derived from its autoregressive (AR) model. The AR model of a signal is given by:

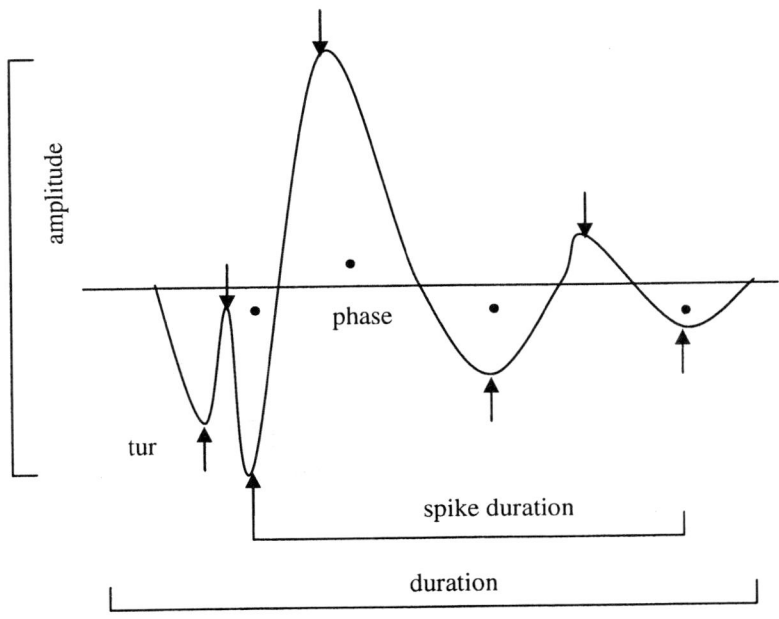

Fig. 1. MUAP morphological parameters

$$x(k) = \sum_{i=1}^{M} a_i x(k-i) + e(k) \qquad (11)$$

where $x(k)$ is the signal we want to model, a_i are the coefficients of the AR model signal, M is the order of the AR model of the signal, and $e(k)$ is the white noise. According to the Akaike's information criterion, $AR(12)$ model is usually used for MUAP processing [6]. Several techniques are available for estimating the parameters of an autoregressive random process. We use the Fast Transversal Filters (FTF) algorithm, which presents highly desirable characteristics in terms of numerical stability and time of convergence [11]. After the AR coefficients a_i of each MUAP are estimated, then it was normalized with its maximum power value. The following frequency domain spectral parameters are computed from the AR power spectrum curve [12].

Bandwidth (BW) is the difference of frequencies at the upper (F_2) and lower (F_1), 3dB points of the power spectrum and is given as:

$$BW = F_2 - F_1 \qquad (12)$$

Quality factor (Q) is the ratio of the dominant peak frequency F_0 divided by BW and is expressed as:

$$Q = \frac{F_0}{BW} \qquad (13)$$

Moments of order 0, 1 and 2: A moment M_j of order j is defined as given by Lindstrom and Petersen [9]:

$$M_j = \frac{2}{(2\pi)^{j+1}} \sum_{n=0}^{N-1} f(n)^j P_{AR}(f(n))$$ (14)

Median frequency (*FMED*) is the frequency at which the power spectrum is divided into two regions with equal power defined as:

$$\sum_{n=0}^{FMED} P_{AR}(f(n)) = \sum_{FMED}^{N-1} P_{AR}(f(n))$$ (15)

Maximum frequency (*FMAX*) is the frequency with the maximum power.

4.3 Time-Frequency Domain Wavelet Transform Energy Coefficients

The process of converting a signal from the time domain to the frequency domain is achieved conventionally with the Fourier transform (FT). Fourier transform does not provide enough information when used on non-stationary signals. FT determines only the frequency components of a signal, but not their location in time. In order to overcome this drawback, short time Fourier Transform (STFT), using a technique called windowing, was proposed. STFT maps the signal into a two-dimensional space of time and frequency using a single fixed window. Wavelet transform enables analysis with multiple window durations that allow for a coarse to fine multi-resolution perspective of the signal. Being able to dilate or compress the variable sized window region (wavelet), different features of the signal will be extracted in WT. It gives the information of the signal localized in both time and frequency domain. The wavelet transform of the signal $x(t)$ is defined as:

$$W(s,\tau) = \frac{1}{\sqrt{s}} \int x(t)\psi(\frac{t-\tau}{s})dt$$ (16)

where mother wavelet ψ is scaled by parameter s and translated by τ. The result of such decomposition is a series of detail coefficients d_j and approximation coefficients a_j. Here, the index j represents the decomposition level. In our study, Daubechies 4 mother wavelet is selected and the energy in each frequency band, i.e. d_1 to d_6 and a_6 is used as time-frequency domain feature set.

5 Experimental Results

There are total of 80 subjects corresponding to 3 situations, 20 normal, 30 suffering motor neuron disease (MND) and 30 myopathy (MYO), involving in the experiment. The data are recorded from the biceps brachii of each subject at Hua Shan Hospital, Shanghai. Three back-propagation neural networks are chosen as the single model classifier of corresponding feature set. For each single network, the average vector of 20 MUAPs per subject for each feature set is computed as input. The conjugate gradient method is used in training to improve the convergence [13]. The architecture of the networks is determined as follows:

1) NN1-network: 7×14×3 . The inputs are the aforementioned time domain morphological parameters' means of 20 MUAP per subject.
2) NN2-network: 7×14×3 . Frequency domain seven parameters.
3) NN3-network: 7×14×3 . Normalized percentage value of wavelet energy coefficients d_1 to d_6 and a_6

15 subjects of each category are extracted randomly to compose the training set. The mean value of there feature domain for the NOR, MND, and MYO groups of the train set are given in Table 1, Table 2, and Table 3. The others are used as testing set. In order to verify the effectiveness and robustness of the multiple neural networks diagnosis approach, bootstrap resample technique is used to obtain 6 different training and testing samples [14]. The output in each network of corresponding feature set presents an evidence about the final diagnosis evaluation. After training the three neural networks, we obtain the diagnosis performance of the various neural networks. The diagnosis accuracy of various feature parameters is shown in table 4. Then, utilizing the outputs and diagnosis accuracy of each neural network, the consensus diagnosis result could be calculated. The diagnosis yields based on fuzzy integral is also shown in Table 4.

Table 1. The mean value of morphological parameters for the train sets of three groups

	Duration ms	Spike Duration ms	Amplitude mV	Area mVms	Spike Area mVms	Phases	Turns
NOR	8.73	4.92	0.342	0.337	0.221	2.5	2.9
MND	12.27	6.25	0.568	0.758	0.475	4.1	4.5
MYO	6.58	3.96	0.301	0.223	0.149	2.6	3.3

Table 2. The mean value of frequency domain parameters for the train sets of three groups

	M_0 mV^2	M_1 $mV^2/s*10^3$	M_2 mV^2/s^2*10^6	FMED Hz	FMAX Hz	Bandwidth Hz	Quality factor
NOR	9.24	13.95	22.46	399	202	507	0.44
MND	14.97	8.92	12.84	305	197	388	0.80
MYO	27.15	26.01	40.28	622	423	778	0.66

Table 3. The mean value of normalized percentage wavelet energy distribution for the train sets of three groups

	d_1	d_2	d_3	d_4	d_5	d_6	a_6
NOR	0.52	1.75	5.95	26.7	18.4	17.7	28.9
MND	0.33	1.27	4.04	15.29	16.56	23.71	38.80
MYO	0.83	3.31	9.77	38.86	22.78	11.48	12.97

Table 4. MUAPs diagnosis results based on single network and multiple networks combination

Network	Accuracy (%)
Time domain neural network	72.38 ± 7.8
Frequency domain neural network	60.48 ± 10.6
Time-frequency domain neural network	65.24 ± 7.1
Multiple neural networks fusion	80.95 ± 7.2

6 Conclusions

The multiple neural networks consensus diagnosis based on fuzzy integral is investigated in this study for the assessment of MUAPs recorded from NOR, MND, and MYO subjects. When the single feature set and single neural network is used, the morphological feature gives the highest diagnostic yield, followed by time-frequency parameters. Frequency domain feature gives the worst classification performance. Compared to the above single domain single network method, the proposed multiple neural networks consensus diagnosis strategy based on fuzzy integral achieves high accurate and more reliable diagnosis result. This happens for the hybrid system utilizing the multiple source information of the initial data. Moreover, for the conventional majority vote combination scheme, the class label assigned to the sample is the one that is most represented in the set of the crisp class labels obtained from all networks. The deficiency is that all networks are treated equally. In fact, the recognition ability of each feature set in each network is not the same. The fuzzy integral is an improved combination scheme, which considers the difference of performance of each network in combination. Fuzzy density of each network is an important factor in the combination scheme. In the present work, we take the diagnosis accuracy of each network as fuzzy density. In order to obtain the optimal network architecture, new method to determine the fuzzy density should be considered in the future works.

Acknowledgements

This work is supported by the National Science Foundation numbered 60171006 of China.

References

1. Stalberg, E., Nandedkar, S.D., Sanders, D.B.: Quantitative Motor unit potential analysis. Clinical Neurophysiology. 13(1996) 401-422
2. Andreassen, S., Andreassen, S.K., Jensen, F. V.: MUNIN—An expert system for EMG. Electroence Clinical Neurophysiol. 66(1987) S4
3. Coatrieux, J.L., Toulouse, P., Rouvrais, B: Automatic classification of electromyographic signals. Electroence Clin Neurophysiol. 55(1983) 333-341
4. Pattichis, C. S., Elia, A.C.: Autoregressive and cepstral analyses of motor unit action potentials. Med Eng Physi. 21(1999) 405-419
5. Shipp, C.A., Kuncheva, L.I.: Relationships between combination methods and measures of diversity in combining classifiers. Information Fusion. 3(2002) 135-148
6. Christodoulou, C.I., Pattichis, C.S. Fincham, W.F.: A modular neural network decision support system in EMG diagnosis. Intelligence Systems. 8(1998) 99-143
7. Richard, M.D., Lippmann, R.P.: Neural network classifier estimate Bayesian a posteriori probabilities. Neural Computation. 3(1991) 461-483
8. Sugeno, M.: Fuzzy measures and fuzzy integrals: a survey. Fuzzy Automata and Decision Processes. Amsterdam. North Holland. (1977)
9. He, Y.Y., Chu, F.L., Zhong, B.L.: A study on group decision-make based fault multi-symptom- domain consensus diagnosis. Reliability Engineering & System Safety. 74(2001) 43-52
10. Stalberg, E., Andreassen, S., Falck, B.: Quantitative analysis of individual motor unit potentials: A proposition for standardized terminology and criteria for measurement. Clinl Neurophysiol. 3(1986) 313-348
11. Cioffi, J.M., Kailath, T.: Fast recursive least-squares traversal filters for adaptive filtering. IEEE Trans Acoust Speech Sig Process. 32(1984) 304-337
12. Lindsotrm, L., Petersen, I.: Power spectrum analysis of EMG signals and its application. In Desmedt, J.E., eds.: Computer-Aided Electromyography Prog Clin Neurophysiol. Basel, Karger. 10(1983) 1-51
13. Johansson, E.M., Dowla, F.U., Goodman, D.M.: Back propagation learning for multilayer feedforward neural networks using the conjugate gradient method. Int J Neural Systems 2 (1992) 291-301
14. Breiman, L.: Bagging predictors. Machine Learning. 24(1996) 123-140

Long-Term Prediction of Discharges in Manwan Hydropower Using Adaptive-Network-Based Fuzzy Inference Systems Models

Chun-Tian Cheng[1], Jian-Yi Lin[1], Ying-Guang Sun[1], and Kwokwing Chau[2]

[1] Institute of Hydroinformatics, Department of Civil Engineering,
Dalian University of Technology, Dalian, 116024, P.R. China
[2] Department of Civil and Structural Engineering, Hong Kong Polytechnic University,
Hunghom, Kowloon, Hong Kong, People's Republic of China
ctcheng@dlut.edu.cn

Abstract. Forecasting reservoir inflow is important to hydropower reservoir management and scheduling. An Adaptive-Network-based Fuzzy Inference System (ANFIS) is successfully developed to forecast the long-term discharges in Manwan Hydropower. Using the long-term observations of discharges of monthly river flow discharges during 1953-2003, different types of membership functions and antecedent input flows associated with ANFIS model are tested. When compared to the ANN model, the ANFIS model has shown a significant forecast improvement. The training and validation results show that the ANFIS model is an effective algorithm to forecast the long-term discharges in Manwan Hydropower. The ANFIS model is finally employed in the advanced water resource project of Yunnan Power Group.

1 Introduction

Accurate time and site-specific forecasts of streamflows and reservoir inflow are required for effective hydropower reservoir management and scheduling. In the past few decades, a wide range of hydrologic models has been proposed for this purpose. Conventionally, factor analysis and hydrological analysis methods such as historical evolution method, time series analysis, multiple linear regression method and so forth, are used to forecast the long-term discharges. Nowadays, time series analysis and multiple linear regression method are the two most commonly used methods. The time series analysis is based on the decomposition of various factors into trend and cycle. After 1970s, autoregressive moving-average (ARMA) models proposed by Box et al. [1] are also widely used. Since 1990s, artificial neural network (ANN) [2,3], based on the understanding of the brain and nervous systems, is gradually used in hydrological prediction. In this paper, the potential of the adaptive-network-based fuzzy inference system (ANFIS) [4-7], first developed by Jang (1993), in hydrological prediction will be discussed and evaluated. This approach has been tested and evaluated in the field of signal processing and related areas.

The past few years have witnessed a rapid growth in the number and variety of applications of fuzzy logic and fuzzy set theory, which were introduced by Zadeh

[22]. The applications range from consumer products such as cameras, washing machines, and microwave ovens to industrial process control, medical instrumentation, decision-support systems, and portfolio selection. An apparent recent trend relates to the use of fuzzy logic in combination with neurocomputing and genetic algorithms. In general, fuzzy logic, neurocomputing, and genetic algorithms might be viewed as principal constituents of soft computing. Among various combinations of methodologies in soft computing, the most interesting applications offer an appropriate combination of fuzzy logic and neurocomputing. It results in a hybrid system that operates on both linguistic descriptions of the variables and the numeric values through a parallel and fault tolerant architecture. This effective method, ANFIS, has been successfully applied to many problems such as prediction of workpiece surface roughness [8], pesticide prediction in ground water [9] and validation in financial time series [10]. Specially, the neuro-fuzzy system for modeling hydrological time series was presented by Nayak et al. [11].

2 Fuzzy Inference System

2.1 Fuzzy Rule-Based Models

The process of fuzzy inference involves membership functions, fuzzy logic operators, and if-then rules. Fuzzy inference systems (FIS) have been successfully applied in fields such as automatic control, data classification, decision analysis, expert systems, and computer vision. The basic structure of a FIS consists of three conceptual components: a rule base, which contains a selection of fuzzy rules; a database which defines the membership functions (MF) used in the fuzzy rules; and a reasoning mechanism, which performs the inference procedure upon the rules to derive an output (see Fig. 1). FIS implements a nonlinear mapping from its input space to the output space. This mapping is accomplished by a number of fuzzy if-then rules, each of which describes the local behavior of the mapping. The parameters of the if-then rules (referred to as antecedents or premises in fuzzy modeling) define a fuzzy region of the input space, and the output parameters (also termed consequents in fuzzy modeling) specify the

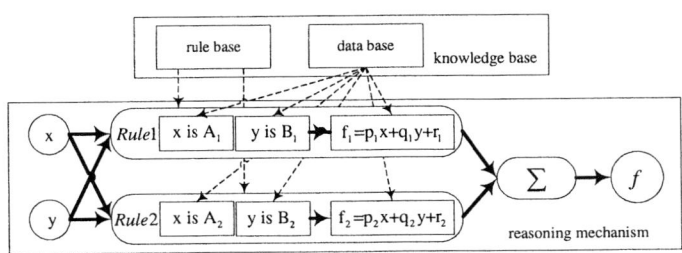

Fig. 1. Fuzzy inference system (first-order Sugeno)

corresponding output. There are three types of fuzzy inference systems in wide use: Mamdani-type [12], Sugeno-type [13-14] and Tsukamoto-type [15]. These three types of inference systems vary somewhat in the way outputs are determined.

2.2 Sugeno Models

The Sugeno model (or Takagi-Sugeno model) was proposed by Takagi and Sugeno [14]. A typical rule in a Sugeno fuzzy model has the form:
If x is A and y is B, then $z = f(x, y)$
where A and B are fuzzy sets of antecedent, and $z = f(x, y)$ is the precise function. Usually, $z = f(x, y)$ are polynomials of input variables x and y. In the first-order Sugeno model, the function $z = f(x, y)$ is a first-order polynomial of the input variables. For a zero-order Sugeno model, the output level z is a constant. For instance, consider that the FIS has two inputs x and y and one output z and, for the first-order Sugeno fuzzy model, a typical rule set with two fuzzy if-then rules can be expressed as:

Rule 1: If x is A_1 and y is B_1, then $f_1 = p_1 x + q_1 y + r_1$

Rule 2: If x is A_2 and y is B_2, then $f_2 = p_2 x + q_2 y + r_2$

Figure 2 illustrates the fuzzy reasoning mechanism for this Sugeno model to derive an output function (f) from a given input vector [x, y]. The Sugeno fuzzy inference system is computationally efficient and works well with linear techniques, optimization and adaptive techniques. It is extremely well suited to the task of developing a FIS using the framework of adaptive neural networks which is termed an ANFIS.

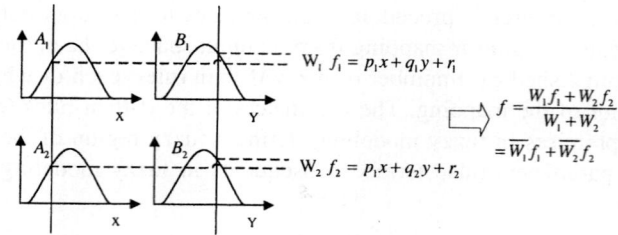

Fig. 2. First-order Sugeno fuzzy model

3 ANFIS

3.1 ANFIS Architecture

This neuro-fuzzy network is a five-layer feed forward network that uses neural network learning algorithms coupled with fuzzy reasoning to map an input space to an output space. The ANFIS architecture is shown in Figure 3, and an introduction of the model is as follows.

Layer 1: input nodes
Each node in this layer generates membership grades of an input variable. The node output $O_{1,i}$ is defined by:

$$O_{1,i} = \mu_{A_i}(x), \ i=1,2 \ \text{or} \ O_{1,i} = \mu_{B_{i-2}}(y), \ i=3,4 \tag{1}$$

where x (or y) is the input to the node; A_i (or B_{i-2}) is a fuzzy set associated with this node, characterized by the shape of the MFs in this node and can be any appropriate functions that are continuous and piecewise differentiable such as Gaussian, generalized bell shaped, trapezoidal shaped and triangular shaped functions. Assuming a generalized bell function as the MF, the output $O_{1,i}$ can be computed as,

$$\mu_A(x) = \frac{1}{1+|(x-c_i)/a_i|^{2b}} \tag{2}$$

where $\{a_i, b_i, c_i\}$ is the parameter set that changes the shapes of the MF with the maximum equal to 1 and the minimum equal to 0; and $\{a_i, b_i, c_i\}$ are called premise parameters.

Layer 2: rule nodes
Every node in this layer multiplies the incoming signals, denoted as Π, and the output $O_{2,i}$ that represents the firing strength of a rule, is computed as,

$$O_{2,i} = w_{A_i}(x)\mu_{B_i}(y), \ i=1,2 \tag{3}$$

Therefore, the outputs $O_{2,i}$ of this layer are the products of the corresponding degrees from layer 1.

Layer 3: average nodes
The node of this layer, labeled as N, computes the normalized firing strengths as,

$$O_{3,i} = \overline{w} = \frac{w_i}{w_1 + w_2}, \ i=1,2 \tag{4}$$

Layer 4: consequent nodes
Node i in this layer computes the contribution of the ith rule towards the model output, with the following node function:

$$O_{4,i} = \overline{w_i} f = \overline{w_i}(p_i + q_i + r_i) \tag{5}$$

where $\overline{w_i}$ is the output of layer 3 and $\{p_i, q_i, r_i\}$ is the consequent parameter set.

Layer 5: output nodes

The single node in this layer computes the overall output of the ANFIS as:

$$\text{overall output} = O_{5,1} = \sum \overline{w_i} f_i = \frac{\sum_i w_i f_i}{\sum_i w_i} \tag{6}$$

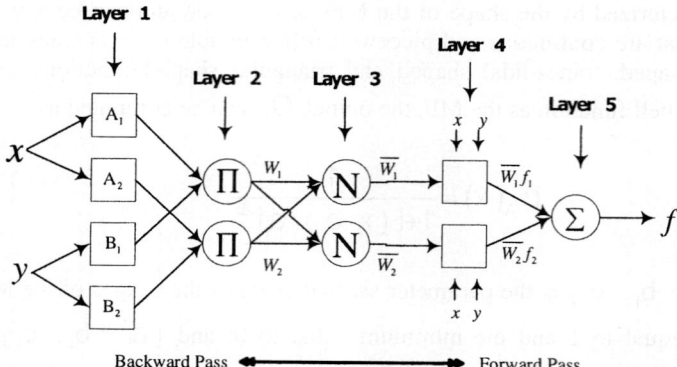

Fig. 3. ANFIS architecture

3.2 Hybrid Learning Algorithm

The ANFIS architecture consists of two parameter sets for optimization: the premise parameters $\{a_i, b_i, c_i\}$, which describe the shape of the MFs, and the consequent parameters $\{p_i, q_i, r_i\}$, which describe the overall output of the system. From the ANFIS architecture shown in Fig.3, it can be seen that when the values of the premise parameters are fixed, the overall output can be expressed as a linear combination of the consequent parameters. In symbols, the output f in Fig.3 can be rewritten as

$$f = \overline{w}_1 f_1 + \overline{w}_2 f_2 = (\overline{w}_1 x) p_1 + (\overline{w}_1 y) q_1 + (\overline{w}_1) r_1 + (\overline{w}_2 x) p_2 + (\overline{w}_2 y) q_2 + (\overline{w}_2) r_2 \tag{7}$$

which is linear in the consequent parameters $p_1, q_1, r_1, p_2, q_2, r_2$. Therefore, a hybrid learning algorithm combines the backpropagation gradient descent and the least squares estimate method, which outperforms the original backproagation algorithm [16]. The consequent parameters are updated first using the least squares algorithm and the antecedent parameters are then updated by back propagating the errors that still exist. Specifically, in the forward pass of the hybrid learning algorithm, node outputs go forward until layer 4 and the consequent parameters are identified by the least squares method. In the backward pass, the error signals propagate backward and the premise parameters are updated by gradient descent. Table 1 summarizes the activities in each pass. More details about the hybrid learning algorithm can be found in Jang and Sun [6].

4 Study Area and Data Used

The Manwan Hydropower in the Lancangjiang River is selected as the study site. The Lancangjiang River is a large river in Asia, which originates from the Qinghai-Tibet Plateau, penetrates Yunnan from northwest to the south and passes through the Laos, Burma, Thailand, Cambodia and Vietnam, ingresses into the South China Sea at last.

Table 1. Two passes in the hydrid learning procedure for ANFIS

	Forward pass	Backward pass
Premise parameters	Fixed	Gradient descent
Consequent parameters	Least-squares estimate	Fixed
Signals	Node outputs	Error signals

The river is about 4,500 km long and has a drainage area of 744,000 km^2. The Manwan Hydropower merges on the middle reaches of the Lancang River and at borders of Yunxian and Jingdong counties. The catchment area at the Manwan dam site is 114,500 km^2, the length above Manwan is 1,579 km, and the mean elevation is 4,000 km. The average yearly runoff is 1,230 cubic meters per at the dam site. Rainfall provides most of the runoff and snow melt accounts for 10%. Nearly 70% of the annual rainfall occurs from June to September.

The monthly flow data from January 1953 to December 2003 are studied. The data set from January 1953 to December 1998 is used for training whilst that from January 1999 to December 2003 is used for validation. In the modeling process, the data sets of river flow were normalized to the range between 0 and 1 as recommended by Masters [17].

5 Application of ANFIS to Flow Prediction in Manwan

5.1 Model Development and Testing

There are no fixed rules for developing an ANFIS, even though a general framework can be followed based on previous successful applications in engineering. The goal of an ANFIS is to generalize a relationship of the form of

$$Y = f(X^n) \tag{8}$$

where X^n is an n-dimensional input vector consisting of variables $x_1, \ldots, x_i, \ldots, x_n$, and Y is the output variable. In the flow modeling, values of x_i may be flow values with different time lags and the value of Y is generally the flow in the next period. However, the number of antecedent flow values that should be included in the vector X^n is not known a priori. An ANFIS model is constructed initially with one antecedent flow in the input vector. The input vector is then modified by successively adding flow at one more time lag, and a new ANFIS model is developed each time. With the increase of the input vectors adding from one to six, Six ANFIS models were developed as follows:

$$\text{Model n} \quad Q_t = f(Q_{t-1}, \ldots, Q_{t-n}) \quad n=1,\ldots,6 \qquad (9)$$

where Q_t corresponds to the river flow at time t. The model performance is examined by means of the following indices: (1) the coefficient of correlation (CORR) and (2) The root mean square error (RMSE).

5.2 Results and Discussions

Table 2 shows the performance indices of ANFIS form model 1 to model 6, which are developed in Section 5.1, using the Gaussian membership function and the trapezoidal membership function respectively. The membership function of every input parameter within the architecture can be divided into two areas, i.e. small and large areas. The results indicate that model 3, which consists of three antecedent flows in input, showed the highest CORR and minimum RMSE during validation regardless of the adoption of Gaussian membership function or trapezoidal membership function for the ANFIS. It is selected as the best-fit model for describing the flow of the Manwan Hydropower. To demonstrate the effect of choice of membership function on the model performance, the triangular membership function (TRIMF), the trapezoidal membership function (TRAPMF), the generalized bell membership function (GBELLMF), the Gaussian membership function (GAUSSMF), the Gaussian combination membership function (GAUSS2MF), the spline-based membership function (PIMF) and the sigmoidal membership function (DSGMF) for the ANFIS structure are tested using model 3, and the results are presented in Table 3. It is showed that, the TRAPMF performs the best with the highest CORR and minimum RMSE during validation, and the GBELLMF performs the worst.

Table 2. CORR and RMSE for different models

Model	GAUSSMF Training RMSE	CORR	Validation RMSE	CORR	TRAPMF Training RMSE	CORR	Validation RMSE	CORR
1	0.11843	0.78539	0.13043	0.77773	0.11889	0.78348	0.12958	0.78156
2	0.090325	0.88157	0.10475	0.86359	0.09186	0.87722	0.10694	0.85762
3	0.075927	0.91793	0.099208	0.87957	0.075795	0.91823	0.097094	0.88877
4	0.06605	0.93861	0.13718	0.78263	0.067406	0.93597	0.10266	0.87995
5	0.061604	0.9469	0.14105	0.78515	0.065892	0.939	0.16199	0.72977
6	0.058825	0.9518	0.41629	0.38461	0.060644	0.94868	0.27504	0.58358

5.3 Result Comparison with ANN Model

ANN model has been widely applied in flow prediction. The main advantage of the ANN approach over traditional methods is that it does not require information about the complex nature of the underlying process under consideration to be explicitly described in mathematical form. Hence, an ANN model is constructed using the same input parameters to the ANFIS model 3 to compare the performance of them in this case. A scaled conjugate gradient algorithm [18, 19] is employed for training, and the hidden neurons are optimized by trial and error. The final ANN architecture consists of 3 hidden neurons. In order to have the same basis of comparison, the same training and verification sets are used for both models. The performances of ANN and ANFIS during training period and validation period are respectively presented in Figure 4 and Figure 5, and the performance indices of them is showed in Table 4. It is demonstrated that, when employed for flow prediction in Manwan, ANFIS exhibits some advantages over ANN model. During validation, the correlation coefficient of ANFIS model is 0.88877, which is larger than its counterparts of ANN model (0.87766). Moreover, the RMSE of ANFIS model is 0.097094, which is much smaller than that of ANN model (0.099927).

Table 3. CORR and RMSE for model 3 with different MFs

MF	Training		Validation	
	RMSE	CORR	RMSE	CORR
TRIMF	0.079641	0.9093	0.097281	0.88339
TRAPMF	0.075795	0.91823	0.097094	0.88877
GBELLMF	0.075036	0.91993	0.10304	0.86983
GAUSSMF	0.075927	0.91793	0.099208	0.87957
GAUSS2MF	0.074961	0.9201	0.098256	0.88327
PIMF	0.075463	0.91898	0.98573	0.88652
DSGMF	0.07424	0.92169	0.99168	0.87999

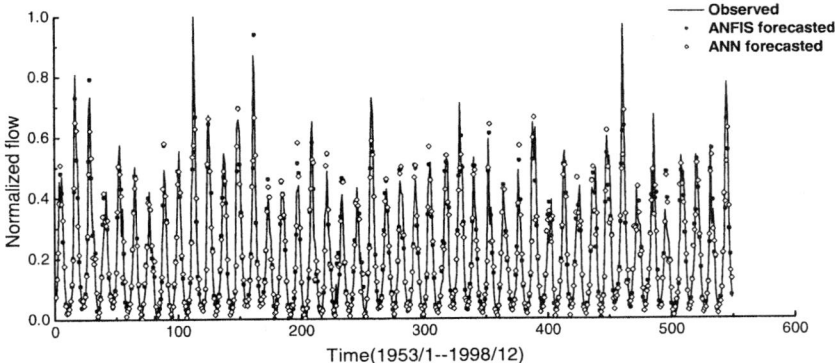

Fig. 4. ANFIS forecasted, ANN forecasted and observed flow during training period

Table 4. Performance indices of ANN and ANFIS models

	Training		Validation	
	RMSE	CORR	RMSE	CORR
ANFIS	0.075795	0.91823	0.097094	0.88877
ANN	0.080755	0.90662	0.099927	0.87766

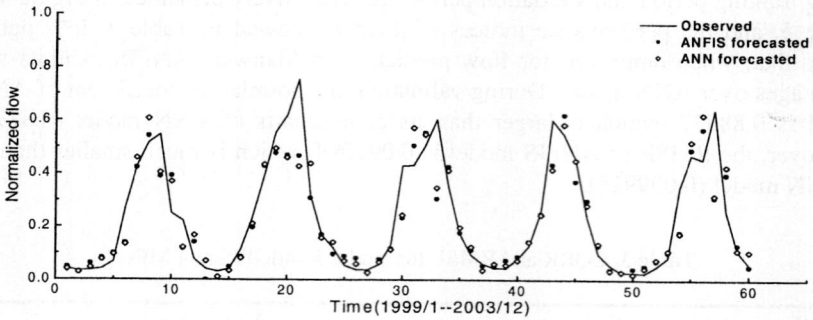

Fig. 5. ANFIS forecasted, ANN forecasted and observed flow during validation period

6 Conclusion

In this study, an ANFIS model is used to predict long-term flow discharges in Manwan based on historical records. Data from January 1953 to December 1998 and from January 1999 to December 2003 are used for training and validation in monthly flow predictions, respectively. The results indicate the ANFIS model can give good prediction performance. The correlation coefficients between the prediction values and the observational values are 0.88877 and 0.91823 for validation and training, respectively. The adoption of different membership functions for ANFIS show that the TRAPMF performs the best in long-term prediction of discharges in Manwan Hydropower consisting of three antecedent flows in input. It is found, through result comparison with an appropriate ANN model, that the ANFIS model is able to give more accurate prediction. This demonstrates its distinct capability and advantages in identifying hydrological time series comprising non-linear characteristics.

Acknowledgement

This research was supported by the National Natural Science Foundation of China (No.50479055) and the Internal Competitive Research Grant of Hong Kong Polytechnic University (G-T592).

References

1. Box, G.E.P., Jenkins, G.M: Time Series Analysis Forecasting and Control. Holden-Day, San Francisco, 1976
2. ASCE Task Committee: Artificial neural networks in hydrology-I: Preliminary concepts. Journal of Hydrologic Engineering, ASCE 5(2)(2000) 115-123
3. ASCE Task Committee: Artificial neural networks in hydrology-II: Hydrological applications. Journal of Hydrologic Engineering, ASCE 5(2)(2000) 124-137
4. Jang, J.-S. R.: Fuzzy Modeling Using Generalized Neural Networks and Kalman Filter Algorithm. Proc. of the Ninth National Conf. on Artificial Intelligence, (1991) 762-767
5. Jang, J.-S. R.: ANFIS: Adaptive-Network-based Fuzzy Inference Systems. IEEE Transactions on Systems, Man, and Cybernetics, 23(3)(1993) 665-685
6. Jang, J.-S. R. and C.-T. Sun: Neuro-fuzzy modeling and control. Proceedings of the IEEE, 83(3)(1995) 378-406
7. Jang, J.-S. R. and C.-T. Sun: Neuro-Fuzzy and Soft Computing. A Computational Approach to Learning and Machine Intelligence, 1997
8. Ship-Peng Lo: An adaptive-network based fuzzy inference system for prediction of workpiece surface roughness in end milling. Journal of Materials Processing Technology 142 (2003) 665–675
9. G.B. Sahooa, C. Raya , H.F. Wadeb: Pesticide prediction in ground water in North Carolina domestic wells using artificial neural networks. Ecological Modelling 183 (2005) 29–46
10. D.E. Koulouriotis, I.E. Diakoulakis, D.M. Emiris, C.D. Zopounidis: Development of dynamic cognitive networks as complex systems approximators: validation in financial time series. Applied Soft Computing 5 (2005) 157–179
11. P.C Nayak, K.P.Sudheer, D.M.Rangan and K.S.Ramasastri: A neuro-fuzzy computing technique for modeling hydrological times series. Journal of Hydrology 291(2004) 52-66
12. Mamdani, E.H. and S. Assilian: An experiment in linguistic synthesis with a fuzzy logic controller. International Journal of Man-Machine Studies, 7(1)(1975) 1-13
13. M.Sugeno and G.T.Kang: Structure identification of fuzzy model: fuzzy Sets and Systems, 28:15-33, 1988
14. T.Takagi and M.Sugeno: Fuzzy identification of systems and its applications to modeling and control. IEEE Transactions on Systems, Man, and Cysbernetics, 15(1985) 116-132
15. Y.Tsukamoto: An approach to fuzzy reasoning method. Advances in fuzzy set theory and applications, (1979) 137-149
16. Rumelhart, D.E., Hinton, G.E., Williams, R.J: Learning representations by back-propagating errors. Nature 323(1986) 533–536
17. Masters, T: Practical Neural Networks Recipes C++. Academic Press, San Diego, 1993.
18. Fitch, J.P., Lehman, S.K., Dowla, F.U., Lu, S.K., Johansson, E.M., Goodman, D.M.: Ship Wake Detection Procedure Using Conjugate Gradient Trained Artificial Neural Network. IEEE Transactions on Geosciences and Remote Sensing 9(5) (1991) 718-725
19. Moller MF: A Scaled conjugate gradient algorithm for fast supervised learning Neural Networks 6(1993) 523-533
20. Huang W, Foo S: Neural network modeling of salinity in Apalachicola River. Water Resources Research 31(2002) 2517-2530
21. Hilde Vernieuwe, Olga Georgieva, Bernard De Baets, Valentijn R.N. Pauwels,Niko E.C. Verhoest, Francois P. De Troch: Comparison of data-driven Takagi–Sugeno models of rainfall–discharge dynamics. Journal of Hydrology 302 (2005) 173–186
22. Zadeh, L.A: Fuzzy sets. Information and 8 (3)(1965) 338–353
23. Zadeh, L.A: Fuzzy Logic. Computer, 1(4) (1988) 83-93

Vector Controlled Permanent Magnet Synchronous Motor Drive with Adaptive Fuzzy Neural Network Controller

Xianqing Cao[1,2], Jianguang Zhu[1], and Renyuan Tang[1]

[1] Research Institute of Special Electric Machines, Shenyang University of Technology, Shenyang, China
qingxiancao2004@yahoo.com.cn
[2] Shenyang Institute of Chemical Technology, Shenyang, China

Abstract. This paper presents the implementation of adaptive fuzzy neural network controller (FNNC) for accurate speed control of a permanent magnet synchronous motor (PMSM). FNNC includes neural network controller (NC) and fuzzy logic controller (FC). It combines the capability of fuzzy reasoning in handling uncertain information and the capability of neural network in learning from processes. The initial weights and biases of the artificial neural network (ANN) are obtained by offline training method. Using the output of the fuzzy controller (FC), online training is carried out to update the weights and biases of the ANN. Several results of simulation are provided to demonstrate the effectiveness of the proposed FNNC under the occurrence of parameter variations and external disturbance.

1 Introduction

Permanent magnet synchronous motors (PMSMs) are receiving increased attention for drive applications because of their high torque to current ratio, large power to weight ratio, higher efficiency, and robustness [1]-[4]. Like any other ac machine, the PMSM is inherently nonlinear with its parameters varying, and possesses a multivariable coupled system with high-order complex dynamics. Fortunately, the utilization of vector control technique simplifies the motor modeling and the corresponding control scheme, the electromechanical torque of PMSM is generated proportionately to the product of stator current, resulting in equivalent performance characteristics of separately excited dc motor, which guarantees fast response [5]. So Vector control has been accepted as one of the most effective methods for the control of PMSM drives. However, for a high-performance drive system, not only a fast response is required, but also the ability of quick recovery of the speed from any disturbances and insensitivity to parameter variation is essential [6].

The speed controller used in PMSM drive system plays an important role to meet all the requires mentioned above. It should be enable the drive to follow any reference speed taking into account the effects of the load impact and parameter variations. Parameter-fixed, conventional controllers such as proportional integral (PI) controller have been widely used. For a long-run drive system, the performances of these controllers are unsatisfactory. Because the results obtained by the integral operation usually holds integral error brought with the unknown load dynamics, and other factors such as noise, temperature change, parameters variation, etc. So it is difficulty to choose the optimal parameters of the PI controller for the PMSM drive.

Nowadays, some adaptive controllers have been applied in both ac and dc motor drive. Such as model reference adaptive controller (MRAC) [7] and sliding model controller (SMC) [8], etc. all the types of controllers can improve the performance of the motor drive system. However, they are usually based on the parameters and structure of the system model. It will lead to complex computation when the system model is uncertainty. The artificial-neural-network (ANN) has received increased applications on the system modeling and control system. Because it has many advantageous features including efficient nonlinear mapping between inputs and outputs without an exact system model [6]. To replace the conventional controller, some persons put forward an approach of designing speed controller for PMSM drive through tuning the weights of the ANN on-line to meet the system's dynamic characteristics. Generally, in order to get the error to tune the weights of the ANN, they all adopt an other controller (such as MRAC) to generate a signal which compare with the output of the ANN. Inevitably, it will lead to the complex computation again, To overcome this difficulty, this paper present an approach of designing adaptive fuzzy neural network controller (FNNC) which adopts the fuzzy logic to the artificial-neural-network. FNNC combines the capability of fuzzy reasoning in handling uncertain information and the capability of neural network in learning from processes.

The proposed control scheme has been testified by simulation, the results indicate the PMSM drive with the adaptive fuzzy neural network controller will have the ability of quick recovery of the speed from any disturbances and parameters variation. Accordingly, the PMSM drive will have better dynamic performances and robustness.

2 Vector Control Model of the PMSM

The vector control technique was firstly proposed for induction motors, while it was applied to PMSM later. Its basic principle is to decouple the stator current to get direct axis (d-axis) and quadrature axis (q-axis) components. The vector control strategy is formulated in the synchronously rotating reference frame. An efficient control strategy of the vector control technique is to make the d-axis current i_d zero so that the torque becomes dependent only on q-axis current, which is similar to the control of a separately excited dc motor. With this control strategy, the motor model of the PMSM becomes simpler as can be described by the following equations [5]

$$pi_q = \left(v_q - R_s i_q - K_b \omega_r \right)/ L_q \tag{1}$$

$$p\omega_r = \left(T_e - T_L - B\omega_r \right)/ J \tag{2}$$

$$T_e = K_T i_q \tag{3}$$

Where v_q is the q-axis stator voltage, i_q is q-axis stator current, L_q is q-axis stator inductance, ω_r is rotor speed, R_s is stator resistance, p is differential operator, $K_b = P \Psi_m$ and $K_T = 3P \cdot \Psi_m$, J is the rotor inertia, B is the damping coefficient, T_e, T_L are the electromagnetic torque and the load torque.

The motor and load dynamics can be represented by [5]

$$T_e = T_L + Jp\omega_r + B\omega_r \tag{4}$$

$$T_L = K_1 \omega_r^2 + K_2 \omega_r + K_3 \tag{5}$$

Where K_1, K_2 and K_3 are constants. Now to make the control task easier, the equations of the PMSM can be expressed as a single input single output (SISO) system in continuous time domain by combining (1)-(5), giving [6]

$$LqJ \frac{d^2\omega_r(t)}{dt^2} + (R_s J + L_q B + K_2 L_q) \frac{d\omega_r(t)}{dt} + (R_s B + K_b K_T + K_2 R_s)\omega(t) + K_1 L_q \frac{d\omega_r^2(t)}{dt} + K_1 R_s \omega_r^2(t) + K_3 R_s - K_T v_q(t) = 0 \tag{6}$$

Accordingly, the discrete time model of the PMSM can be expressed by [5]

$$\omega_r(n+1) = \alpha \omega_r(n) + \beta \omega_r(n-1) + \gamma \omega_r^2(n) + \delta \omega_r^2(n-1) + \varepsilon v_q(n) + \vartheta \tag{7}$$

Where $\alpha, \beta, \gamma, \delta, \varepsilon, \vartheta$ are given in Appendix A.

Now in discrete form, the q-axis current can be expressed by [5]

$$i_q(n) = A_1 i_q(n-1) + B_1[\omega_r(n) - (\alpha + \frac{\varepsilon C_1}{B})\omega_r(n-1) - \beta \omega_r(n-2) - \gamma \omega_r^2(n) - \delta \omega_r^2(n-2) - \vartheta]/\varepsilon \tag{8}$$

Where A_1, B_1, C_1 are given in Appendix A. Equation (8) reveals the non-linear function between i_q and $_r$. The purpose of the ANN is to map the non-linear relationship between i_q and $_r$.

3 Structure of the FNNC for PMSM Drive

3.1 Structure of the ANN

The inverse dynamics of PMSM as described in equation (8) indicates the inputs and output of the ANN used in the control system. And the identification model in the form of a neural network controller (NC) can be given as

$$\hat{i_q}(n) = NC(i_q(n-1), \omega_r(n), \omega_r(n-1), \omega_r(n-2)) \tag{9}$$

The input vector $[i_q(n-1)\ \omega_r(n)\ \omega_r(n-1)\ \omega_r(n-2)]^T$ is comprised of the previous sample of q-axis current as well as the present and previous two samples of motor speed. This also fixes the numbers of neurons in the input and output layers. Numbers of the neurons in hidden layer are chosen by trial-and-error, keeping in mind that the smaller the numbers are, the better it is in term of both memory and time requirement to implement the ANN in motor control. For the present work, the structure of one hidden layer having three neurons gives satisfactory results. The proposed architecture of three-layer ANN is shown in Fig. 1. It includes $M=4$ input nodes, $N=3$ hidden-layer neurons, and $Q=1$ output nodes. W_1, b_1 are the weights matrix and biases vector between the input layer neurons and hidden layer neurons, W_2, b_2 are the weights matrices and biases vector between the hidden-layer neurons and output-layer neuron. The transfer function used in the hidden layer neurons and output layer neuron are tan-sigmoid f^h and pure-linear f^o, respectively. Giving

$$f^h(x) = \frac{1}{1-e^{-x}} \tag{10}$$

$$f^o(x) = x \tag{11}$$

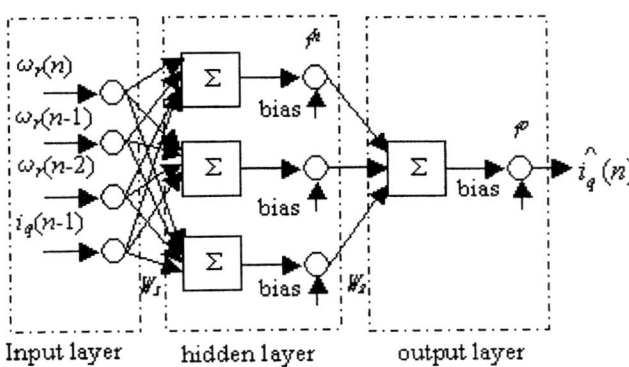

Fig. 1. Block diagram of the structure of the three-layer artificial-neural-network

Once the structure of the ANN is done, the initial weights and biases are obtained through the off-line training. The back-propagation training algorithm is used for this purpose which is based on the principle of minimization of a cost of the error between the outputs and the target. To get the satisfactory weights and biases, the training data should slid over the entire speeds and q-axis currents. Therefore, the simulation is carried out at random speed to obtain various q-axis current according to the relationship described in equation (7) and (8). Considering the mechanical limitation of the motor, the speed should be limited by the motor rated speed value. Supposing the load torque is a constant (T_L=0N·m), two sets of data are obtained. The input matrix is the size of 4×960. while the output vector is the size of 1×960. After the off-line training is well performed, the weights and biases are considered as the initial parameter set of the neural network controller for the online control of the PMSM drive.

The main goal of the control system is to track the reference speed by providing the appropriate q-axis current depending on the operating conditions. So it is necessary for the weights and biases to tune online. To do this work, the neural network error gradient must be evaluated online. In order to evaluate the error gradient, the system output error between desired output (i_q^*) and actual output (i_q) is necessary. In fact, the desired output (i_q^*) is unknown. So we can adopt the fuzzy logic to the ANN. using the desired speed and actual speed, we can get the q-axis current increment Δi_q to tune the weights and biases online.

3.2 Structure of the FC

A fuzzy logic rule with consequent part of the following form is adopted in the FNNC:

$$R_j : \text{IF } x_j \text{ is } A_1^j \text{ and } \cdots \text{and } x_n \text{ is } A_n^j \text{ THEN } y = B_j$$

Where x_j and y are the input and output variables, respectively, A_i^j is the linguistic term of the precondition part with membership function $u_{A_i^j}$, B_j is he linguistic term of the consequent part with membership function u_{B_j}, n is the number of input variables. In this work, the output is the q-axis current increment Δi_q, the number of the input variables is 2, giving

$$e_{s1} = \omega_r(n)^* - \omega_r(n) \tag{12}$$

$$e_{s2} = \omega_r(n-1) - \omega_r(n) \tag{13}$$

Where $\omega_r(n)^*$ is the reference speed at the present, $\omega_r(n)$, $\omega_r(n-1)$ are the actual speed at the present and previous sample interval, respectively.

The fuzzy membership functions of the input variables and output variable are shown in Fig. 2. And the corresponding fuzzy logic rule is shown in Tabel 1.

Table 1. Tabel of the fuzzy logic rule

e_{s2} \ e_{s1}	NB	NM	NS	ZO	PS	PM	PB
NB	PB	PB	PM	PM	PS	ZO	ZO
NM	PB	PB	PM	PS	PS	ZO	NS
NS	PM	PM	PM	PS	ZO	NS	NS
ZO	PM	PM	PS	ZO	NS	NM	NM
PS	PS	PS	ZO	NS	NS	NM	NM
PM	PS	ZO	NS	NM	NM	NM	NB
PB	ZO	ZO	NM	NM	NM	NB	NB

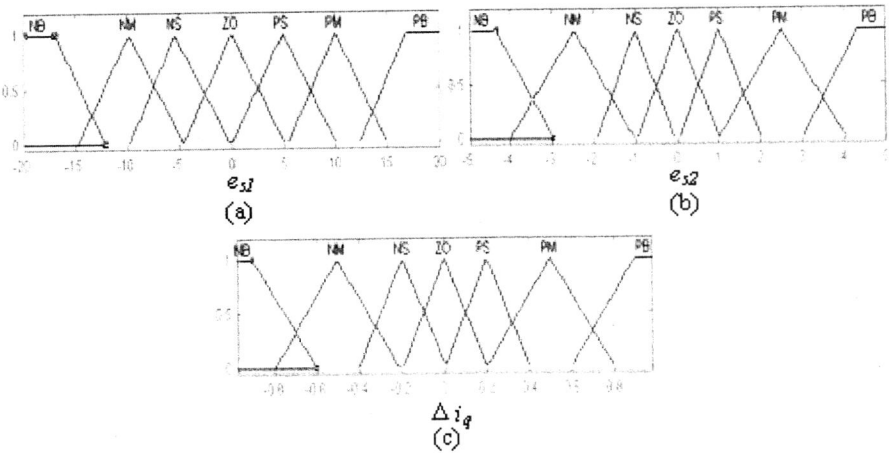

Fig. 2. The fuzzy membership functions of the input variables and output variable: (a) input variable e_{s1} (b) input variable e_{s2} (c) output variable Δi_q

In this work, the range of Δi_q is -0.96A~0.96A which is about 18% of the rating current. The same as e_{s2}, when e_{s1}<-20rad/sec and e_{s1}>20rad/sec, we consider e_{s1}=-20rad/sec and e_{s1}=20rad/sec, respectively. Using the reference speed and the actual speed, we can calculate e_{s1} and e_{s2}. Once the actual speed can not track the reference speed. We can tune the weights and biases of the ANN with the output of the *FC*.

3.3 Online Weights and Biases Updating

The error function is given by

$$e(n) = \frac{1}{2}\Delta i_q^2(n) \tag{14}$$

Using the error, we can update the weights and biases as follows.

The input and output of the *jth* neuron of the hidden layer is given by [6]

$$Y_j^h(n) = \sum_{i=1}^{N} W_{ij}^h(n) X_i(n) \tag{15}$$

$$O_j^h(n) = f^h(Y_j^h(n) + B_j^h(n)) \tag{16}$$

Where x_i is the output of the *ith* neuron of the input layer, W_{ij}^h is the weight between *ith* neuron of the input layer and *jth* neuron of the hidden layer, N is the number of neuron at the hidden layer, B_j^h is the bias of the *jth* neuron, f^h is the transfer function as shown in equation (10).

The input and output of the kth neuron of the output layer is given by [6]

$$Y_k^o(n) = \sum_{j=1}^{Q} W_{jk}^o(n) O_j^h(n) \tag{17}$$

$$O_k^o(n) = f^o(Y_{k'}^o(n) + B_k^o(n)) \tag{18}$$

Where W_{jk}^o is the weight between jth neuron of the hidden layer and kth neuron of the output layer, Q is the number of neuron at the hidden layer, B_k^o is the bias of the kth neuron.

Weights and biases of the hidden layer and output layer are up-dated as [6]

$$W_{ij}^h(n+1) = W_{ij}^h(n) + \eta \delta_j^h(n) X_i(n) \tag{19}$$

$$B_j^h(n+1) = B_j^h(n) + \eta \delta_j^h(n) \tag{20}$$

$$W_{jk}^o(n+1) = W_{jk}^o(n) + \eta \delta_k^o(n) O_j^h(n) \tag{21}$$

$$B_k^o(n+1) = B_k^o(n) + \eta \delta_k^o(n) \tag{22}$$

Where is the learning rate, δ_j^h and δ_k^o are the local gradient. Giving [6]

$$\delta_j^h(n) = \delta_k^o(n) W_{jk}^o(n) [1 - Y_j^h(n)]^2 \tag{23}$$

$$\delta_k^o(n) = e(n) \frac{\partial e(n)}{\partial O_k^o(n)} Y_k^o(n)(1 - Y_k^o(n)) O_j^h(n) \tag{24}$$

In real time implementation, error is derived from the fuzzy controller at each instant. When the actual speed can track the reference speed, the output of the fuzzy controller is zero, and the previous set of weights and biases is kept intact to compute the q-axis reference current. Otherwise, the weights and biases will be updated online as described above. And the structure of the FNNC is shown in Fig. 3.

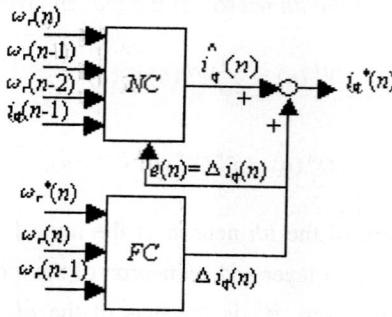

Fig. 3. Block diagram of the structure of the fuzzy neural network controller (FNNC)

4 Results of Simulation

A block diagram of the PMSM drive with the fuzzy neural network speed controller is shown in Fig. 4. And the availability is conformed by computer simulations. The simulation conditions including parameter variation and load disturbance are considered here

Case1: $\overline{J} = J, T_L = 0\text{N} \cdot \text{m}, \omega_r^* = 1000 \text{r/min}$

Case2: $\overline{J} = 2 \times J, T_L = 5\text{N} \cdot \text{m}, \omega_r^* = 1000 \text{r/min}$

Case3: $\overline{J} = J, T_L = 5\text{N} \cdot \text{m}$

Where $\overline{J}$ is the changed rotor inertia. For the FC, the membership functions and the fuzzy rule are shown in Fig. 2. and Tabel 1, as mentioned before. These were simulated in C language using the S-function of the MATLAB tool-box. For all the simulation conditions, the results of the reference speed ω_r^*, actual speed ω_r and the output of the NC (i_q) are given by Fig. 5, Fig. 6, and Fig. 7.

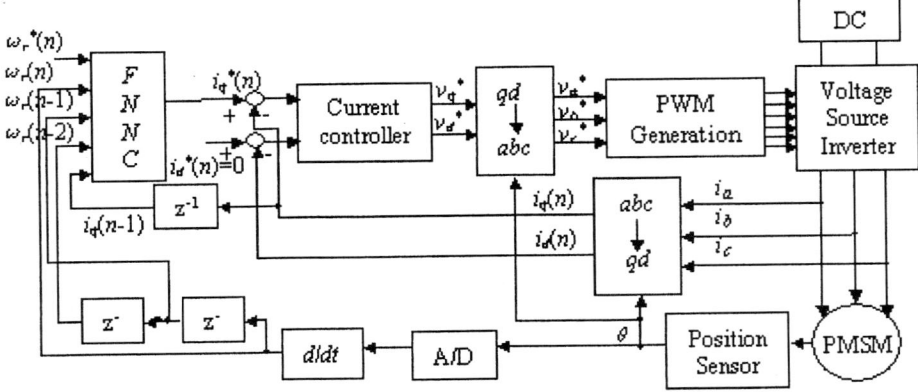

Fig. 4. Block diagram of PMSM drive with the proposed FNNC

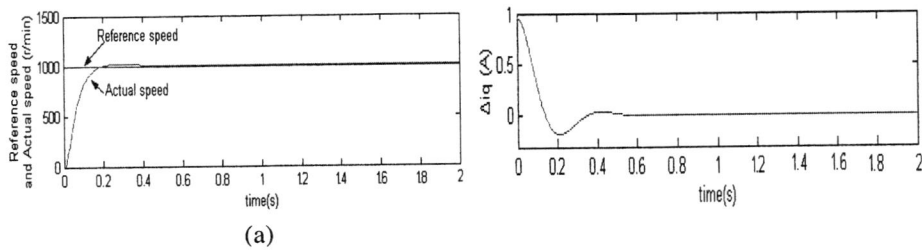

Fig. 5. Simulation results of the PMSM drive with the FNNC at case 2:(a) Track response (b) Control effort

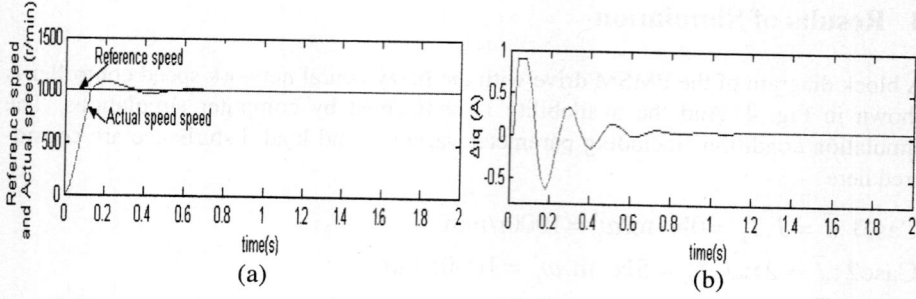

Fig. 6. Simulation results of the PMSM drive with the FNNC at case 2:(a) Track response (b) Control effort

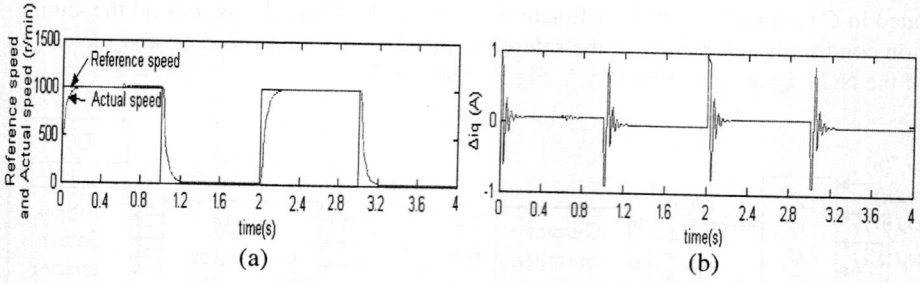

Fig. 7. Simulation results of the PMSM drive with the FNNC at case 3:(a) Track response (b) Control effort

Fig. 5 shows the simulation results of the constant speed (ω_r^*=1000r/min) operation in the case when the machine parameters are kept their original values, with which the ANN is trained offline. In this figure, the motor speed ω_r approximately follows the reference speed ω_r^*.

Fig. 6 shows the simulation results of the load change (T_L=0N·m→T_L=5N·m) and the machine parameter change (J=7.25e-3kg.m^2→J=2*7.25e-3kg.m^2). Because of these changes, the motor speed changes slightly, but the motor speed approximately tracks the reference speed after that.

At case 3, the reference speed follows a profile of 1000r/min-0r/min-1000r/min-0r/min, as depicted in Fig. 7. This figure shows the proposed control scheme is operated well even if at the instant of the reference speed changes.

5 Conclusion

In this paper, a vector control scheme with the fuzzy neural network controller (FNNC) for the PMSM has been presented. FNNC includes neural network controller (NC) and fuzzy logic controller (FC). It combines the capability of fuzzy reasoning in handling uncertain information and the capability of neural network in learning from processes. The structure of the proposed ANN is derived from the inverse dynamic model of the PMSM. The initial weights and biases of the artificial neural network (ANN) are obtained by offline training method. Using the output of the fuzzy controller (FC), online training is carried out to update the weights and biases of the ANN. The results of simulation have shown that the PMSM drive with the proposed FNNC has the merits of simple structure, robustness, accurate tracking performance, and parameter learning algorithms.

References

1. Faa-Jeng Lin, Chih-Hong Lin.: A Permanent-Magnet Synchronous Motor Servo Drive Using Self-Constructing Fuzzy Neural Network Controller. *IEEE Transactions on Energy Conversion*, Vol. 19. No. 1(2004)66-72
2. T. J. E.Miller.: Brushless Permanent Magnet and Reluctance Motor Drives. Oxford, U. K. Clarendon (1989)
3. Wen Lin. Sonng, Nesimi Ertugrul: Field-Weakening Performance of Interior Permanent-Magnet Motors. *IEEE Transactions on Industry Applications*, Vol. 38. No. 5(2002)1251-1258
4. Jung-Ik Ha, Toshihiro Sawa, Seung-Ki Sul: Sensorless Rotor Position Estimation of an Interior Permanent-Magnet Motor From Initial States. *IEEE Transactions on Industry Applications*, Vol. 39. No. 3(2003)761-767
5. Yang Yi,D. Mahinda Vilathgamuwa, M. A. Rahman: Implementation of an Artificial-Neural-Network-Based Real-Time Adaptive Controller for an Interior Permanent-Magnet Motor Drive. *IEEE Transactions on Energy Conversion*, Vol. 39. No. 1(2003)96-104
6. M. A. Rahman, St. John: On-line Adaptive Artificial Neural Network Based Vector Control of Permanent Magnet Synchronous Motor. *IEEE Transactions on Energy Conversion*, Vol. 13. No. 4(1998)311-318
7. H. Naitoh, S. Tadakuma: Microprocessor Based Adjustable Speed dc Motor Drives Using Model Reference Adaptive Control. *IEEE Transactions on Industry Applications*, Vol. 23. No. 2(1987)313-318
8. Y. Dote, R. G. Hoft: Microprocessor Based Sliding Mode Controller for dc Motor Drives. *IEEE/IAS Annual Meeting*(1980)641-645

Appendix A: Inverse Dynamic Constants

$D = L_q J + \Delta T(R_s J + L_q B + K_2 L_q);$

$\alpha = [2LqJ + \Delta T(R_s J + L_q B + K_2 L_q) - \Delta T_2(R_s B + K_T K_b + K_2 L_q)]/D;$

$\beta = -LqJ/D; \gamma = -[\Delta TK_1(L_q + R_s \Delta T)]/D; \delta = [\Delta TK_1 L_q]/D; \varepsilon = [K_T \Delta T^2]/D;$

$\vartheta = -[K_3 R_s \Delta T^2]/D; A_1 = 1 - \dfrac{R_s \Delta T}{L_q}; B_1 = \dfrac{\Delta T}{L_q}; C_1 = -\dfrac{\Delta T K_b}{L_q}.$

Where ΔT is the sampling interval.

Appendix B: PMSM Parameters

3kW, three-phase, 400V, 50Hz, $P=4$, $L_q=L_d=8.5e-3H$, $R_s=2.875$, $J=7.25e-3kg.m^2$, $_m=0.175Wb; B=0.8e-3(N·m)/rad/sec.$

Use of Fuzzy Neural Networks with Grey Relations in Fuzzy Rules Partition Optimization

Hui-Chen Chang[1] and Yau-Tarng Juang[2]

[1] Department of Electrical Engineering,
National Central University, Chung-Li, Taiwan and
Department of Electronics Engineering,
Ta Hwa Institute of Technology, Hsin-Chu, Taiwan
huichen@thit.edu.tw
[2] Department of Electrical Engineering, National Central University, Chung-Li, Taiwan
ytjuang@ee.ncu.edu.tw

Abstract. The objective of this paper is to use the back-propagation (BP) algorithm in conjunction with grey relations to find the optimal partitions of the consequent part in fuzzy neural networks (FNN). A BP algorithm with grey relational coefficient (GRC) is proposed in order to decrease the square errors of the FNN for acquiring the optimal partitions of the consequent part of fuzzy rules. From the simulation results, we find that the present method applied for fuzzy logic control of an inverted pendulum has better performance than that of the traditional BP algorithm.

1 Introduction

In the standard learning scheme for the BP algorithm, the weights of the network are iteratively updated according to the recursion

$$\mathbf{w}(t+1) = \mathbf{w}(t) + \eta \mathbf{d}(t) \qquad (1)$$

Where η is called the learning rate and the direction vector $\mathbf{d}(t)$ is the negative of the gradient of the output error function E

$$\mathbf{d} = -\nabla E(\mathbf{w}) \qquad (2)$$

Therefore, we consider that the BP algorithm takes into account the grey relation existing between the inputs and the connection weights propagating to the neuron in each training iteration of the network. Such a significant relation is called the grey relational coefficient (GRC)[1].

2 Background

2.1 The Structure of the Fuzzy Neural Networks

We adopt the following fuzzy rules whose consequent parts are assumed to be a linear combination of the fuzzy sets associated with an output linguistic variable. The idea of using a linear combination of fuzzy sets has been used in Nozaki et al. [2] where a linear combination of two fuzzy sets represents a consequent part.

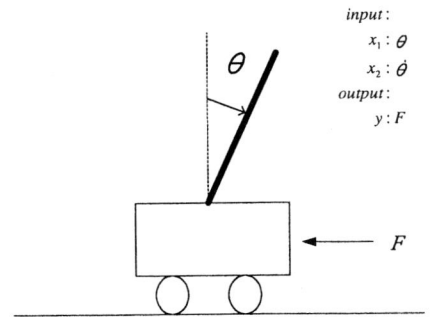

Fig. 1. An inverted pendulum system

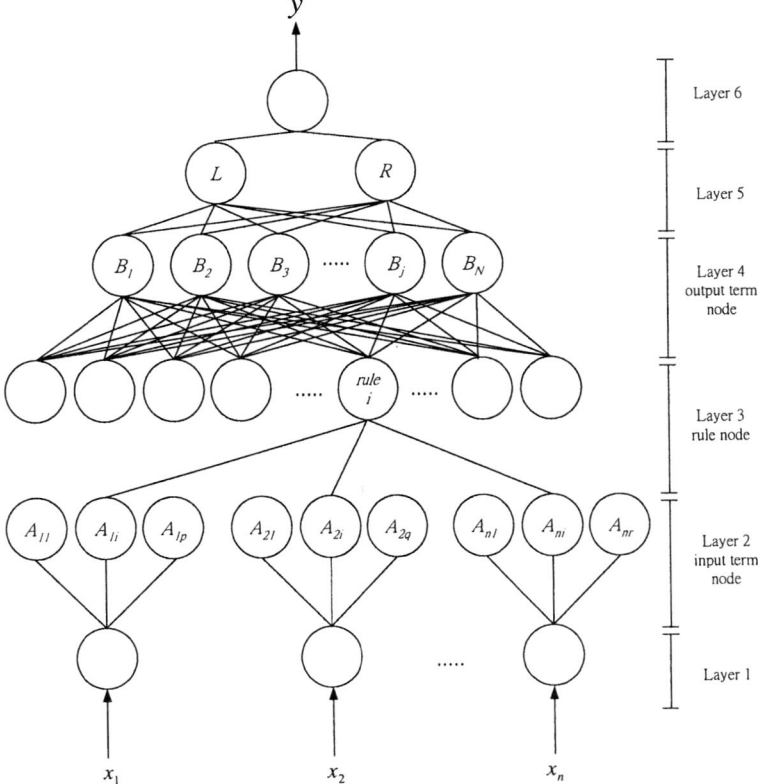

Fig. 2. Structure of fuzzy neural network

R_i: IF x_1 is A_{i1} AND...AND x_n is A_{in} THEN y_i is

$$\sum_{j=1}^{m} \omega_{ij} \cdot B_j, \quad 0 \leq \omega_{ij} \leq 1 \quad (3)$$

and where n is the number of inputs $x_1 \ldots x_n$, y_i denoting the ith rule output, B_j are the output fuzzy sets, m is the number of output partitions, $A_{i1} \ldots A_{in}$ are the labels of input fuzzy sets pertaining to the ith rule and ω_{ij} are the coefficients that form the consequent parameter set. These fuzzy rules are represented in a network which is a six-layer connective structure, as shown in Fig. 2, where the nodes in layer one are input nodes which represent input linguistic variables. The nodes in layer two are the input term nodes that stand for membership functions for the respective terms of the linguistic variables. The nodes in layer three are the rule nodes, which form the entire fuzzy rule base; layer three and layer four serve as the inference mechanism; the links of layer three define the preconditions of the fuzzy rule nodes, and the links of layer four define the consequent parts of the fuzzy rule nodes. Layer five has two nodes for the prearrangement of the defuzzification, and layer six is the last layer to perform the defuzzification. Thus, the output values f_i^k of the ith unit in the kth layer are given by:

Layer 1: $\quad f_i^1 = x_i$

Layer 2:
$$f_i^2 = \begin{cases} 0, & \text{if } f_i^1 < (c-L); \\ 1 - \dfrac{c - f_i^1}{L}, & \text{if } (c-L) \leq f_i^1 < c; \\ 1 - \dfrac{f_i^1 - c}{L}, & \text{if } c \leq f_i^1 < (c+R); \\ 0, & \text{if } (c+R) \leq f_i^1; \end{cases}$$

where c is the center of a triangle-shaped membership function; L and R are the span of left side and right side of the function, respectively.

Layer 3: $\quad f_i^3 = \min(f_1^2, f_2^2, \cdots, f_n^2)$
$\qquad\qquad\quad = \hat{\alpha}_i$

Layer 4:

$$f_j^4 = \sum_{i=1}^{n}(\omega_{ij}^4 \cdot \mu_{B_j}(y)) \cdot f_i^3 = \sum_{i=1}^{n}(\omega_{ij}^4 \cdot \mu_{B_j}(y)) \cdot \hat{\alpha}_i$$

where ω_{ij}^4 is a weight of link between the node i in layer 3 and the node j in layer 4.

Layer 5: the node on the left is

$$f_L^5 = \sum_{i=1}^{m} c_j \cdot f_i^4 = \sum_{j=1}^{m} c_j \cdot [\sum_{i=1}^{n} \omega_{ij}^4 \cdot \hat{\alpha}_i \cdot \mu_{B_j}(c_j)] = \sum_{j=1}^{m} c_j \cdot \sum_{i=1}^{n} \omega_{ij}^4 \cdot \hat{\alpha}_i$$

and the node on the right is $f_R^5 = \sum_{j=1}^{m} f_j^4 = \sum_{j=1}^{m}\sum_{i=1}^{n} \omega_{ij}^4 \cdot \hat{\alpha}_i$

Layer 6:

$$f^6 = \frac{f_L^5}{f_R^5} = \frac{\sum_{j=1}^{m} c_j \cdot \sum_{i=1}^{n} \omega_{ij}^4 \cdot \hat{\alpha}_i}{\sum_{j=1}^{m} \sum_{i=1}^{n} \omega_{ij}^4 \cdot \hat{\alpha}_i} = \frac{\sum_{i=1}^{n} \hat{\alpha}_i \cdot (\sum_{j=1}^{m} c_j \cdot \omega_{ij}^4)}{\sum_{i=1}^{n} \hat{\alpha}_i \cdot \sum_{j=1}^{m} \omega_{ij}^4}$$

2.2 Grey Relational Coefficient GRC

Grey relational analysis is a method that can find the relationships between one major sequence and other sequences in a given system [3]. The GRC ξ_{ij} can be computed as

$$\xi_{ij} = \frac{\Delta_{min} + \rho \Delta_{max}}{\Delta_{ij} + \rho \Delta_{max}} \qquad (4)$$

3 The BP Algorithm with GRC

To train the weights of layer 4 in the network, the learning algorithm of BP with GRC is used. This is also categorized as supervised learning that minimizes the mean-square error between the actual output and desired outputs of a network. The learning rule is:

$$\mathbf{w}(t+1) = \mathbf{w}(t) - \eta(\xi)^k \nabla E(\mathbf{w}) \qquad (5)$$

$$E = \frac{1}{2}[\hat{y}(t) - y(t)]^2 \qquad (6)$$

where $\hat{y}(t)$ is the desired output, $y(t)$ is the current output, k is a pre-specified positive real number, and ξ is the GRC between the inputs and the connection weights propagating to the neuron. The final GRC ξ is computed as the mean value of GRC ξ_j. The algorithm proceeds as follows: 1. Initialize the connection weights corresponding to each node in layer 4 randomly. 2. Present a training input/output pair through the network. 3. Compute ξ_j and ξ. 4. Update the new weights using Eq. (5). 5. Go to step 2 until the training iterations are finished. We can see that the learning rule of BP with GRC is not determined only by the learning rate and the gradient of the output error function.

4 Application to Inverted Pendulum System

The structure of an inverted pendulum is illustrated in Fig. 1. Four sets of training data (with initial starting states of +50, -50 +10 and -10 degrees) based on a set of fuzzy rules found in [2] are used to give training in the fuzzy rules. After the learning is completed, six sets of random initial starting states (+56, +36, +16, -4, -24, and -44 degrees) are chosen to test the fuzzy rules. The number of iterations is 1800, and the learning rate η is 0.0001. As a performance index of a fuzzy rule-based system, we use the summation of square errors between the desired output y_p and the inferred output $y(\mathbf{x}_p)$ for each input-output pair $(\mathbf{x}_p; y_p)$, and there are 200 input-output pairs for training data in this system:

$$PI = \sum_{p=1}^{m} \{y(\mathbf{x}_p) - y_p\}^2 / 2, \quad m=200. \quad (7)$$

The control rules are of the following form

$$R_i : \text{IF } x_1 \text{ is } A_{i1}, x_2 \text{ is } A_{i2} \quad \text{THEN } y \text{ is } \sum_{j=1}^{m} \omega_{ij} \cdot B_j \quad (8)$$

Table 1. PI of BP with GRC algorithm for different output fuzzy partitions with various k

k \ Partition	M=2	M=3	M=4	M=5	M=6
5	0.0501	0.0442	0.0443	0.0458	0.0544
6	0.0549	0.0467	0.0449	0.0522	0.0638
7	0.0591	0.0474	0.0577	0.0660	0.0990
8	0.0615	0.0525	0.0682	0.0842	0.1080
9	0.0642	0.0539	0.0734	0.1232	0.1639
10	0.0661	0.0808	0.1080	0.1302	0.1939
11	0.0677	0.0832	0.1234	0.1781	0.2606
12	0.0843	0.1191	0.1769	0.2691	0.3046
13	0.0850	0.1488	0.2449	0.3112	0.3910

Table 2. PI of BP with GRC algorithm for different output fuzzy partitions with various ρ

ρ \ Partition	M=2	M=3	M=4	M=5	M=6
0.2	0.1124	0.1973	0.3251	0.4577	0.6007
0.3	0.0763	0.0827	0.1446	0.2004	0.2405
0.4	0.0627	0.0555	0.0746	0.1119	0.1377
0.5	0.0554	0.0492	0.0523	0.0658	0.0976
0.6	0.0552	0.0480	0.0491	0.0538	0.0741
0.7	0.0497	0.0476	0.0438	0.0468	0.0679
0.8	0.0495	0.0459	0.0429	0.0437	0.0565

Table 3. The best result of the PI by BP with GRC and the classical BP

Partition Method	M=2	M=3	M=4	M=5	M=6
BP with GRC	0.0245	0.0221	0.0216	0.0227	0.0235
Classical BP	0.0311	0.0256	0.0314	0.0347	0.0255

Where the consequent part of each rule is modified to be a linear combination of the output fuzzy sets with weights ω_{ij}, where $i=1,2,\ldots,n$ (number of rules); and $j=1,2,\ldots,m$ (number of output partitions). Tables 1 and 2 summarize the average values of the performance index for different output fuzzy partitions through various k and ρ, respectively. From theses tables, we get the following results. (1) Large values of k lead to worse PI for different output fuzzy partitions. The minimum value of square errors (PI) is 0.0442 which occurs at M=3 and $k=5$. (2) Large values of ρ lead to better PI for different output fuzzy partitions. The minimum value of square errors is 0.0429 which occurs at M=4 and $\rho = 0.8$. Table 3 summarizes the best result of the PI by BP with GRC and the classical BP. From Table 3, we observe the following. (1) The performance of the BP with GRC is better than the classical BP for different output fuzzy partitions. (2) Large values of M (i.e., fine output fuzzy partitions) lead to better PI in the classical BP method, however, it is not the same situation in the BP with GRC method. The minimum value of square errors is 0.0216 which occurs at M=4.

5 Conclusions

This algorithm is developed by directly incorporating the grey relational coefficient (GRC) into the BP algorithm. Generally speaking, the square errors of proposed method are much smaller than that of the classical BP for an inverted pendulum system. Large values of M (i.e., fine output fuzzy partitions) do lead to a better performance index in the classical BP method, however, it does not produce same outcome as for the BP with GRC method, where the PI is smaller.

References

1. Deng, J. L. : Control problems of grey systems, Systems Control Lett. 1(5) (1982) 288-294.
2. Nozaki, K., Ishibuchi H. and Tanaka, H.:A simple but powerful heuristic method for generating fuzzy rules from numerical data, Fuzzy sets and Systems 86(1997) 251-270.
3. Huang, Y. P., Huang, C. H.: Real-valued genetic algorithms for fuzzy grey prediction system, Fuzzy Sets Systems 87(3) (1997) 265-276.

A Weighted Fuzzy Min-Max Neural Network and Its Application to Feature Analysis[*]

Ho-Joon Kim[1] and Hyun-Seung Yang[2]

[1] School of Computer Science and Electronic Engineering,
Handong University, Pohang, 791-708, Korea
hjkim@handong.edu
[2] Department of Computer Science, KAIST
Daejeon, 305-701, Korea
hsyang@cs.kaist.ac.kr

Abstract. In this paper, we present a modified fuzzy min-max neural network model and its application to feature analysis. In the model a hyperbox can be expanded without considering the hyperbox contraction process as well as the overlapping test. During the learning process, the feature distribution information is utilized to compensate the hyperbox distortion which may be caused by eliminating the overlapping area of hyperboxes in the contraction process. The weight updating scheme and the hyperbox expansion algorithm for the learning process are described. A feature analysis technique for pattern classification using the model is also presented. We define four kinds of relevance factors between features and pattern classes to analyze the saliency of the features in the learning data set.

1 Introduction

Many neuro-fuzzy methodologies for pattern classification and feature analysis have been proposed in the last decade[1-4]. Fuzzy Min-Max(FMM) neural network is a hyperbox-based pattern classification model[1-2]. In our previous work, a weighted fuzzy min-max(WFMM) neural network has been proposed[3]. The model employs a new activation function which has the weight value for each feature in a hyperbox. In this paper, we introduce an improved structure of the WFMM neural network and its application to feature analysis technique. We define four kinds of feature relevance measures to analyze the saliency of the features in the pattern classification problem. In the proposed model, the weight concept is added to reflect frequency factor of feature values. Since the weight factor effectively reflects the relationship between feature range and its distribution, the system can prevent undesirable performance degradation which may be caused by noisy patterns. Therefore the model can be used for the applications in which more robust and efficient classification performance is needed. The proposed feature relevance measures also can be utilized to select an optimal feature set for training. Through the experimental results using Iris data and Cleveland medical data[5], the usefulness of the proposed method is discussed.

---

[*] This research was supported by Brain Science and Engineering Research Program sponsored by Korean Ministry of Commerce, Industry and Energy.

2 A Weighted Fuzzy Min-Max Neural Network

As shown in Equation (1), the model employs a new activation function which has the weight value for each feature in a hyperbox

$$b_j(A_h) = \frac{1}{\sum_{i=1}^{n} w_{ji}} \cdot \sum_{i=1}^{n} w_{ji}[\max(0, 1-\max(0, \gamma_{jiv} \min(1, a_{hi}-v_{ji})))$$
$$+ \max(0, 1-\max(0, \gamma_{jiu} \min(1, u_{ji}-a_{hi})))-1.0] \quad (1)$$

In the equation, the w_{ji} is the connection weight between i-th feature and j-th hyperbox, n means the number of features in the test pattern, γ is the sensitivity parameter in the range [0, 1]. a_{ih} is the value of i-th feature of h-th input pattern. u_{ji} and v_{ji} mean the minimum and maximum value of dimension i of hyperbox b_j, respectively. The original FMM neural network classifier is built using hyperbox fuzzy sets. The learning process is performed by properly placing and adjusting hyperboxes and weights in the pattern space[2].

The learning algorithm consists of hyperbox creation, expansion and contraction processes. The weight value increases in proportion to the frequency factor for each feature in the expansion process. The contraction process is to eliminate overlaps between hyperboxes that represent different classes. However it is considered as an optional part of our model. We define a new contraction method including the weight updating scheme. To determine if the expansion created any overlap, a dimension by dimension comparison between hyperboxes is performed. We define new scheme of overlapping handling techniques for four cases of overlaps. The proposed model is capable of utilizing the feature distribution and the weight factor in the learning process as well as in the classification process. Consequently the proposed model can provide more robust performance of pattern classification when the training data set in a given problem include some noise patterns or unusual patterns.

3 Feature Analysis

One of the advantageous features of the proposed model is a feature analysis capability. We can analyze the relationships between the features and the given classes from the weight data. In this paper we define four kinds of relevance factors as follows:

$RF1(x_i, B_j)$: the relevance factor between a feature value x_i and a hyperbox B_j
$RF2(x_j, C_k)$: the relevance factor between a feature value x_j and class C_k
$RF3(X_i, C_k)$: the relevance factor between a feature type X_i and class C_k
$RF4(X_i)$: the saliency measure of feature X_i for the given problem

These four factors are defined as Equation (2), (3), (4) and (5), respectively. In the equations, constant N_B and N_k are the total number of hyperboxes and the number of hyperboxes that belong to class k, respectively.

$$RF1(x_i, B_j) = w_{ij} \quad (2)$$

$$RF2(x_i, C_k) = (\frac{1}{N_k} \sum_{B_j \in C_k} S(x_i, (u_{ji}, v_{ji})) \cdot w_{ij}$$
$$- \frac{1}{(N_B - N_k)} \sum_{B_j \notin C_k} S(x_i, (u_{ji}, v_{ji})) \cdot w_{ij}) / \sum_{B_j \in C_k} w_{ij} \quad (3)$$

$$RF3(X_i, C_k) = \frac{1}{L_i} \sum_{x_i \in X_i} RF2(x_i, C_k) \quad (4)$$

$$RF4(X_i) = \frac{1}{M} \sum_{j=1}^{M} RF3(X_i, C_j) \quad (5)$$

In Equation (3), S is a function which measures the similarity between two fuzzy intervals. In Equation (4), L_i is the number of feature values which belong to i-th feature. If the $RF2$ has a positive value, it means an excitatory relationship between the feature and the class. But a negative value of $RF2$ means an inhibitory relationship between them. A list of relevant features for a given class can be extracted using the $RF2$ for each feature. The $RF3$ shown in Equation (4) represents the degree of importance of a feature for classifying a given class. Therefore it can be utilized for feature selection or knowledge extraction process for pattern classification problems. The fourth measure, $RF4$, also can be defined in terms of the $RF3$ as shown in Equation (5). The $RF4$ means the saliency measure of a feature type for the given problem. We can utilize this information for the feature selection in designing process of the pattern classifier.

4 Experimental Results

We have developed a face detection model using the weighted FMM neural network for a real time robot vision system. In order to evaluate the proposed model and the feature analysis method, we have conducted the experiments using the Fisher's Iris data and the Cleveland medical data[5]. The Iris data set consists of 150 pattern cases in three classes (50 for each class) in which each pattern consists of four features. The Cleveland medical data consist of 297 pattern cases in five classes in which each pattern case has thirteen features. We have developed a hybrid neural network model for face detection by combining the proposed model with a convolutional neural network[4] which provides invariant feature extraction capability for distorted image patterns. From the feature analysis results using the proposed model, 1848 features extracted form the raw data have been reduced into 260 features without any performance degradation. For the Iris data and Cleveland medical data classifications, we have analyzed the relevance factors. Four kinds of analysis results have been generated as illustrated in Table 1. The table shows the relevance factors($RF2$) between feature values and target classes for the Iris patterns.

Table 1. Relevance factors(RF2) between feature values and target classes(Iris data)

Feature value	Target Class	RF2
F4 : (0.0, 0.13)	Setosa	0.312
F1: (0.03, 0.22)	Setosa	0.190
F3: (0.51, 0.65)	Versicolor	0.443
F2: (0.13, 0.54)	Versicolor	0.158
F3: (0.65, 0.78)	Virginica	0.272
F2: (0.21, 0.67)	Virginica	0.133

5 Conclusion

The proposed relevance measure $RF1$ makes it possible to eliminate the hyperbox contraction process since the measure represents different relevance values within overlapped hyperbox feature ranges. The other measures also can be utilized in designing an optimal structure of the classifier. For examples, $RF2$ and $RF3$ can be used for a knowledge extraction method, and the $RF4$ can be useful to select more relevant feature set for a given problem. The weighted FMM neural network model presented in this paper is capable of utilizing the feature distribution and the weight factors in the learning process as well as the classification process. We have applied the proposed model to a real-time face detection system in which there may be many unusual patterns or noise in the learning data set.

References

1. Simpson, P. K.: Fuzzy Min-Max Neural Networks Part 1: Classification. IEEE Transaction on Neural Networks, Vol.3. No.5. (1997) 776-786
2. Gabrys, B. and Bargiela A.: General Fuzzy Min-Max Neural Network for Clustering and Classification. IEEE Transaction on Neural Networks, Vol.11. No.3. (2000) 769-783
3. Kim, H. J., Ryu, T. W., Nguyen, T. T., Lim, J. S. and Gupta, S.: A Weighted Fuzzy Min-Max Neural Network for Pattern Classification and Feature Extraction. Proceeding of International Conference on Computational Science and Its Application, Part.4 (2004) 791-798
4. Garcia, C. and Delakis, M.: Convolutional Face Finder: A Neural Architecture for Fast and Robust Face Detection. IEEE Transaction on Pattern Analysis and Machine Intelligence, Vol.26. No.11. (2004) 1408-1423
5. Blake, C .L. and Merz, C. J.: UCI Repository of machine learning databases [http://www.ics.uci.edu/~mlearn/MLRepository.html]. Irvine, CA: University of California, Department of Information and Computer Science. (1998)

A Physiological Fuzzy Neural Network

Kwang-Baek Kim[1], Hae-Ryong Bea[2], and Chang-Suk Kim[3]

[1] Dept. of Computer Engineering,
Silla University,
Korea
gbkim@silla.ac.kr
[2] Dept. of Environmental Engineering,
Geyongju University,
Korea
baehr@kyongju.ac.kr
[3] Dept. of Computer Education,
Kongju National University,
Korea
csk@kongju.ac.kr

Abstract. In this paper, a physiological fuzzy neural network is proposed, which shows more improved learning time and convergence property than that of the conventional fuzzy neural network. First, we investigate the structure of physiological neurons of the nervous system and propose new neuron structure based on fuzzy logic. And by using the proposed fuzzy neuron structures, the model and learning algorithm of physiological fuzzy neural network are proposed. We applied the proposed algorithm to 3-bit parity problem. The experiment results showed that the proposed algorithm reduces the possibility of local minima more than the conventional single layer perceptron does, and improves the time and convergence for learning.

1 Introduction

We analysis the exciting neuron in the physiological structure and classify an inhibited neuron into a forward inhibitory neuron and a backward inhibitory neuron. And fuzzy logic has a merit of induction, and is composed of fuzzy set theory and fuzzy logic operation. There are fuzzy AND, fuzzy OR, and fuzzy NEGATION in the conventional fuzzy logic operations [1], [2]. The conventional perceptron, due to its use of unit step function was, highly sensitive to change in the weights, difficult to implement and could not learn from past data [3]. In this paper, we propose a new fuzzy neural network, a modification to the conventional fuzzy perceptron that replace the generalized delta rule using physiological neuron structure. Therefore, we define a proposition that a forward inhibitory neuron is fuzzy logical-AND organization and a backward inhibitory neuron is fuzzy logical-NEGATION organization. We define a fuzzy OR structure by analyzing excitatory neuron in the physiological neuron organization. The learning algorithms that combine the merits of fuzzy logic with the neural networks based on physiological organization are proposed in this paper. We applied the proposed algorithm to 3-bit parity problem.

2 A Physiological Fuzzy Neural Network

2.1 Physiological Neuron Structure

Physiological neuron organization structure is composed of excitatory neuron and inhibitory interneuron, which are each activated by agonistic neuron and inactivated by antagonistic neuron.

Agonistic neuron is the one that directs to forward and antagonistic neuron does to backward. Inhibition is classified into antagonistic inhibition, forward inhibition and backward inhibition. Antagonistic inhibition makes on inhibitory synapse through an interneuron, which control the antagonistic neuron. Forward inhibition is inhibited without previous excitation of an antagonistic neuron. Backward inhibition is inhibited backwards in case that an inhibited interneuron acts upon the cell, which activated itself [4].

2.2 A Physiological Learning Model

We defined a fuzzy OR structure by analyzing excitatory neuron in the physiological neuron organization. We also defined a fuzzy AND structure by classifying the inhibitory neuron structure as the forward inhibitory neuron structure and the backward inhibitory neuron structure. The interneuron is defined as fuzzy NEGATION. The proposed learning structure is shown in Fig. 1.

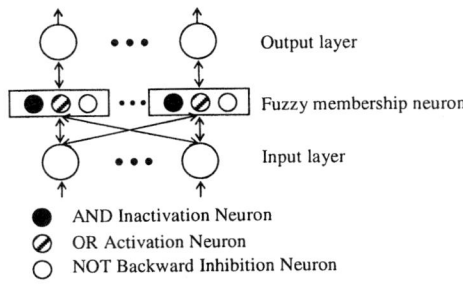

● AND Inactivation Neuron
⊘ OR Activation Neuron
○ NOT Backward Inhibition Neuron

Fig. 1. Physiological Learning Model

2.3 A Physiological Learning Algorithm

The learning steps are classified as the forward step and the backward step in the proposed neural fuzzy algorithm. In the forward steps, the actual output values are calculated through the fuzzy neuron membership function. The initial weight range is established by [5].

We use fuzzy logic operator Max & Min instead of sigmoid function. With these operators, Max operator can be used if target value is '1' or Min operator if '0'. In the backward steps, the weight is adjusted by dividing each neuron into excitatory neuron and inhibitory neuron in accordance with the fuzzy neuron membership function. The proposed algorithm as follows:

Step 1: Initialize Logic_value, Logic_weight, and Logic_mark
  Logic_weight : $W_{AND_{ji}} = 1, W_{OR_{ji}} = 1, W_{NT_{ji}} = 1$
  Logic_value : $V_{AND_{ji}} = 1/I, V_{OR_{ji}} = 1, V_{NT_{ji}} = -1$
  Logic_mark : $ON_{AND_{ji}^p} = 1, ON_{OR_{ji}^p} = 1, ON_{NT_{ji}^p} = 1$
  where $W_{AND_{ji}}$: forward inhibitory operation
       $W_{OR_{ji}}$: forward excitatory operation, $W_{NT_{ji}}$: backward inhibitory operation

Step 2: Read input pattern
Step 3: Select target bit j for input pattern
Step 4: Calculate and normalize Synapse_value from 0 to 1

$$Synapse_{ji} = Synapse_{ji} + \left(ON_{AND_{ji}^p} \times x_i^p \times V_{AND_{ji}} \times W_{AND_{ji}}\right) + \left(ON_{OR_{ji}^p} \times x_i^p \times V_{OR_{ji}} \times W_{OR_{ji}}\right)$$

  if $(Synapse_{ji} > 1.0)$ then $Synapse_{ji} = Synapse_{ji} + V_{NT_{ji}}$

Step 5: Determine Soma_value for output value
  if $\left(target_j^p = 1.0\right)$ then $Soma_j = \vee(Synapse_{ji})$
  if $\left(target_j^p = 0.0\right)$ then $Soma_j = \wedge(Synapse_{ji})$ where $1 \le p \le P$, P: Number of pattern
  $\vee$: Fuzzy MAX operation, $\wedge$: Fuzzy MIN operation

Step 6: Update Logic_weight and Logic_mark value
  if $\left(\left(W_{AND_{ji}} \le 1.0\right) \text{ and } \left(ON_{AND_{ji}^p} = 1\right)\right)$ then
    $W_{AND_{ji}} = W_{AND_{ji}} + \beta \times error_j \times \left(\left(x_i^p \times W_{AND_{ji}}\right)/insize\right)$, $ON_{AND_{ji}^p} = 1$
  if $\left(W_{AND_{ji}} > 1.0\right)$ then $W_{AND_{ji}} = W_{AND_{ji}} - 1.0$, $ON_{AND_{ji}^p} = 0$
  if $\left(\left(W_{OR_{ji}} \le 1.0\right) \text{ and } \left(ON_{OR_{ji}^p} = 1\right)\right)$ then
    $W_{OR_{ji}} = W_{OR_{ji}} + \beta \times error_j \times \left(x_i^p / insize\right)$, $ON_{OR_{ji}^p} = 1$
  if $\left(W_{OR_{ji}} > 1.0\right)$ then $W_{OR_{ji}} = W_{OR_{ji}} - 1.0$, $ON_{OR_{ji}^p} = 1$

  where β : Learning rate, insize : Gravity Center

Step 7: Repeat step 3, until it process all target bits
Step 8: Repeat step 2, until it process all input patterns

3 Experimental Results

It was implemented on the IBM/Pentium-III 550 MHz PC using Delphi tool. The testing data is the 3-bit parity using the benchmark in neural network. We fixed error criteria value to 0.05.

We set initial learning rate at 0.5 in our algorithm. In our proposed algorithm, we set up the range of initial weight at [0, 1] by [5].

Table 1 is the summary of learning results measured in terms of Epoch and TSS (Total Sum of Square). In our proposed algorithm, the network was converged on 3-bit parity. Therefore, it is known that the proposed algorithm guarantees the convergence.

Table 1. Learning results

3-bit parity	Physiological Learning Algorithm
Epoch Number	100
TSS	0.02745

4 Conclusions

The study and application of fusion fuzzy theory with logic and inference and neural network with learning ability have been actually achieving according to expansion of automatic system and information processing, etc.

We proposed the neural fuzzy learning algorithm on the theoretical basis of fuzzy logic and physiological neural network. The proposed network is able to extend the arbitrary layers and has high convergence in case of two layers or more. When we considered only the case of the single layer, the networks had the capability of the high speed learning process and the rapid processing on huge patterns. The proposed algorithm is the learning method which contains logic operations to imitate the structure of human brains. This algorithm combines the learning ability, which is the merit of artificial neural network, with the manipulation of human's obscure expression, which is the merit of fuzzy logic. And the proposed algorithm shows the possibility of the application to the real world besides benchmark test in neural network by single layer structure. In the future study, we will develop the novel fuzzy neuron learning and recognition algorithm and apply to the handwritten digit recognition.

References

1. Gupta, M. M, Qi, J.: On fuzzy Neuron Models. Proceedings of IJCNN, Vol.2 (1991) 431-435
2. Lin, C. T., Lee, C. S. G.: Neural network based fuzzy logic control and decision system. IEEE Trans. On Computer, Vol. C-40, No. 12 (1991) 1320-1336
3. Kim, K. B., Joo, Y. H., Cho, J. H.: An Enhanced Fuzzy Neural Network. Lecture Notes in Computer Science, LNCS 3320 (2004) 176-179
4. Kuffer, S. W., Nicholls, T. G., Martin, A. R.: Form Neuron to Brain: A Cell Approach to the function of Nervous System. 2nd ed. Sunderland, Mass. Sinauer (1984)
5. Kim, K. B., Seo, C. J., Yang, H. K.: A Biological Fuzzy Multilayer Perceptron Algorithm. International Journal of Maritime Information and Communication Sciences, Vol. 1, No. 3 (2003) 104-108

Cluster-Based Self-organizing Neuro-fuzzy System with Hybrid Learning Approach for Function Approximation

Chunshien Li[1], Kuo-Hsiang Cheng[1], Chih-Ming Chen[2], and Jin-Long Chen[1]

[1] Department of Electrical Engineering,
Chang Gung University, Tao-Yuan, 333, Taiwan, R.O.C
jamesli@mail.cgu.edu.tw
[2] Department of Electrical Engineering,
Northern Taiwan Institute of Science and Technology, Taipei, Taiwan, R.O.C

Abstract. A novel hybrid cluster-based self-organizing neuro-fuzzy system (HC-SONFS) is proposed for dynamic function approximation and prediction. With the mechanism of self-organization, fuzzy rules are generated in the form of clusters using the proposed self-organization method to achieve compact and sufficient system structure if the current structure of knowledge base is insufficient to satisfy the required performance. A hybrid learning algorithm combining the well-known random optimization (RO) and the least square estimation (LSE) is use for fast learning. An example of chaos time series for system identification and prediction is illustrated. Compared to other approaches, excellent performance of the proposed HC-SONFS is observed.

1 Introduction

Neuro-fuzzy approaches which possess the ability for system optimization of structure and parameter learning have arouse much interest and regarded as a branch of computation intelligence. Recently, the studies of system self-organization with the salient characteristics of self-adjustment, intelligent learning and adaptability, have become an emerging research field. In this paper, a hybrid cluster-based self-organizing neuro-fuzzy system (HC-SONFS) for function approximation is proposed to aim at fast learning convergence and system structure optimization with ease and efficiency. The Takagi-Sugeno (T-S) type of fuzzy rules is used in the paper.

$$\text{IF } (x_1 \text{ is } s_1^i(h_1(k))) \text{ and} \ldots \text{and } (x_M \text{ is } s_M^i(h_M(k)))$$
$$\text{THEN } z^i(k) = a_0^i + a_1^i h_1(k) + \ldots a_M^i h_M(k) \quad (1)$$

where x_j, $h_j(k)$, and a_j^i, $j= 1, 2,\ldots, M$ are the input linguistic variables, the crisp inputs at time k, and the consequent coefficients of the i-th rule, respectively. There are two phases which are system structure identification and parameter identification. A cluster-based rule structure is used for the neuro-fuzzy system. A hybrid RO-LSE learning algorithm is used for the parameter identification. The well-known RO algorithm [1-2] is for the premise fuzzy sets, and the LSE for the consequent parameters.

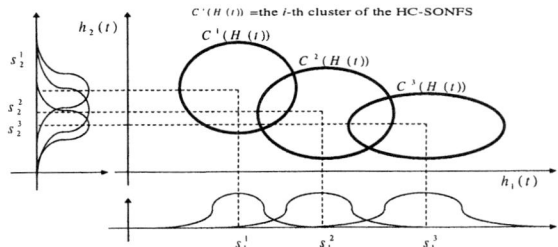

Fig. 1. The cluster-based fuzzy sets of HC-SONFS

Suppose that there are Ω rules in the rule base. The output of the HC- SONFS is given as

$$\hat{y}(k) = \sum_{i=1}^{\Omega} \beta^i(k) \times z^i(k) / \sum_{i=1}^{\Omega} \beta^i(k) = \sum \bar{\beta}^i(k) z^i(k) \qquad (2)$$

where $\beta^i(k) = C^i(H(k)) = \prod_{k=1}^{M} \exp(-(h_j(k) - m_j^i)^2 / (\varpi_j^i)^2)$, $\bar{\beta}^i(k)$ the normalized firing strength of the i-th fuzzy rule, and m_j^i and ϖ_j^i the spreads and means of Gaussian membership function of the j-th input variable. For the proposed HC-SONFS, the if-parts are corresponding to clusters, shown in Fig. 1. The antecedent parameter sets are collected as $\Sigma^i = \begin{bmatrix} m_1^i & m_2^i & \cdots & m_M^i \end{bmatrix}$ and $\Delta^i = \begin{bmatrix} \varpi_1^i & \varpi_2^i & \cdots & \varpi_M^i \end{bmatrix}$.

2 Self-organization Learning Processes of HC-SONFS

Suppose that the neuro-fuzzy system (NFS) possesses a few rules initially and that the current performance of NFS is not satisfied. The self-organization process of HC-SONFS includes two phases of the structure learning and the parameter learning. The structure learning is to find necessary rules covering the training data. The parameter learning is to concern with the parameters of the premise parts and the consequent parts. The proposed HC-SONFS can achieve the two tasks simultaneously. If an input training pattern is sufficiently covered by the current rule base, no new rule is generated; otherwise a new cluster is generated. The output of the HC-SONFS can be expressed as $\hat{y}(k) = f(W, H(k))$, where $W = \{\Sigma, \Delta, A\}$ is the parameter set of the system. Assume that there are N pairs of I/O training patterns, $\{(H(k), y(k)), k = 1, 2, ..., N\}$, where $H(k)=[h_1(k), h_2(k),..., h_M(k)]$. The error vector is given as $\vec{E}=[e(1), e(2), ..., e(N)]^T$, where $e(k) = y(k) - \hat{y}(k)$. The largest absolute error, $e_{max} = \max(|e(k)|, k = 1, 2, ..., N)$, is used in such a way that the input vector $H(\phi)$ is viewed as the position in the input space a potential fuzzy rule (cluster) should be generated. Denote that $\beta_{max} = \max(\beta^i(H(\phi)), i = 1, 2, ..., \Omega)$. If $\beta_{max} < T_1$ (a pre-given threshold) then $\Sigma_j^{(\Omega+1)} = h_j(\phi)$ and $\Delta_j^{(\Omega+1)} = T_2$ (pre-given width of new cluster) and $\Omega=\Omega+1$. The constant T_1 is designed as $T_1=T_1(0.95)^\Omega$ to avoid that the rules may increase rapidly. In hybrid way, the RO is used for training the premise parts of the HC-SONFS and the LSE for the consequent parts. The detail of the RO algorithm is given in [1-2]. With the firing strengths, the update of consequent parts is executed by LSE. The cost function is defined as $J(W) = \sum_{k=1}^{N} [y(k) - \tilde{y}(k)]^2$. The output of the HC-SONFS is expressed as $\vec{Y} = \overline{B}A$. The estimate of A is obtained as $\tilde{A} = inv(\overline{B}^T \overline{B})\overline{B}^T \vec{Y}$.

$$\vec{Y} = \begin{bmatrix} y(1) \\ y(2) \\ \vdots \\ y(N) \end{bmatrix} \quad \overline{B} = \begin{bmatrix} \overline{\Lambda}(1) \\ \overline{\Lambda}(2) \\ \vdots \\ \overline{\Lambda}(N) \end{bmatrix} = \begin{bmatrix} \Lambda^1(1) & \Lambda^2(1) & \cdots & \Lambda^\Omega(1) \\ \Lambda^1(2) & \Lambda^2(2) & \cdots & \Lambda^\Omega(2) \\ \vdots & \vdots & \ddots & \vdots \\ \Lambda^1(N) & \Lambda^2(N) & \cdots & \Lambda^\Omega(N) \end{bmatrix} \quad A = \begin{bmatrix} [a_0^1 & a_1^1 & \cdots & a_M^1]^T \\ [a_0^2 & a_1^2 & \cdots & a_M^2]^T \\ \vdots & \vdots & \ddots & \vdots \\ [a_0^\Omega & a_1^\Omega & \cdots & a_M^\Omega]^T \end{bmatrix} \quad (3)$$

where $\Lambda^i(k) = [\overline{\beta}^i(k) \quad \overline{\beta}^i(k)h_1(k) \quad \cdots \quad \overline{\beta}^i(k)h_M(k)]$. The recursive least squares estimation (RLSE) algorithm can also be used in sequential way.

3 Experimental Simulations

The approach is applied to the identification and prediction of the Mackey-Glass chaos time series [3] to test its feasibility and capability. It is given as $\dot{x}(t) = \dfrac{0.2x(t-\tau)}{1 + x^{10}(t-\tau)} - 0.1x(t)$, where $\tau=17$, and time step is given as 0.1. The initial

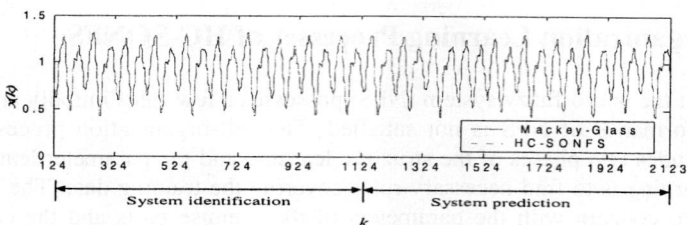

Fig. 2. Response performance of HC-SONFS for function approximation and prediction of the Mackey-Glass time series

Table 1. Comparison with other works

Method	RMSE$_{training}$	RMSE$_{testing}$	No. of rules
D-FNN[3]	0.0132	0.0131	5
RBF-AFS[4]	0.0158	0.0163	13
OLS[5]	0.0107	0.0128	21
Our method	0.0086	0.0089	3
Our method	0.0065	0.0066	4
Our method	0.0055	0.0056	5

conditions are given as $x(0)=1.2$, and $x(t)=0$ for $t<0$. In this experiment, the relationship of the I/O mapping by the HC-SONFS can be given as $x(k+P) = f(x(k), x(k-\Delta), ..., x(k-(D-1)\Delta))$ where $P = \Delta = 6$, and $D = 4$. The HC-SONFS estimates the advanced point $x(k+6)$ using $x(k-18)$, $x(k-12)$, $x(k-6)$ and $x(k)$. The input to the HC-SONFS is given as $H(k) = [x(k-18), x(k-12), x(k-6), x(k)]$ and $\hat{y}(k) = x(k+6)$. 2000 data pairs are obtained. The first 1000 data points from k =124 to 1123 are collected as the training patterns for supervisory HC-SONFS training. After training, the rest 1000 data points from k=1124 to 2123 are used for prediction purpose. The root mean square error (RMSE) is used as the performance index. Initially, there are 2 rules in HC-SONFS, and T_1 and T_2 for the cluster-generation are set to 0.01 and 1. After 80 training epochs, there are 5 rules in HC-SONFS. The response is given in Fig. 2, where the RMSE is converged to 0.0055 for identification and 0.0056 for prediction. The performance comparison to other works of D-FNN [3], RBF-AFS [4] and OLS [5] is given in Table I.

4 Conclusions

The proposed HC-SONFS has been successfully applied to nonlinear function approximation and prediction of Mackey-Glass time series. By the proposed approach, the knowledge base is machine-learned to capture the essence of input-output information. With the proposed RO-LSE hybrid algorithm, the system premise parameters are updated using RO and the consequent parameters using LSE. Through the experimental results and the performance comparison to other methods shown in Table 1, the distinguishing capability of the proposed HC-SONFS is shown.

References

1. C. Li and C. Y. Lee.: Self-organizing neuro-fuzzy system for control of unknown plants IEEE Trans. Fuzzy Syst. 11 no.1 (2003) 135-150
2. C. Li, R. Priemer and K.-H. Cheng. : Optimization by Random Search with Jumps. International Journal for Numerical Methods in Engineering. 60 (2004) 1301-1315
3. S. Wu and M. J. Er.:Dynamic Fuzzy Neural Networks-A Novel Approach to Function Approximation IEEE Trans. Syst. Man. Cybern., Part B: Cybernetics. 30 no.2 (2000) 358-364
4. K. B. Cho and B. H. Wang.: Radial basis function based adaptive fuzzy systems and their applications to system identification and prediction. Fuzzy Sets and Systems 83 (1996) 325-339
5. S. Chen, C. F. N. Cowan, and P. M. Grant.: Orthogonal least squares learning algorithm for radial basic function network. IEEE Trans. Neural Networks 2 (1991) 302-309

Fuzzy Output Support Vector Machines for Classification

Zongxia Xie, Qinghua Hu, and Daren Yu

Harbin Institute of Technology, Harbin, China, 150001
{xiezongxia, huqinghua, yudaren}@hcms.hit.edu.cn

Abstract. Support vector machines just use the sign of decision value to get the decision class but don't take its value into consideration. Compared with the support vector machines, the proposed machine not only gives the decision class, but also the membership to each class using the decision value. For SVMs are essentially a 2-class classifier, we first construct the fuzzy output SVMs for 2-class, then extend it to multi-class case. In multi-class case, the feature space is divided into three parts: absolutely classified region, unclassified region and positive margin region because of different accuracy in them. In different regions, the range of the value of membership is different. Through the membership, we can get the location information of the data, which can tell us the confidence of the decision. So this will be helpful for further decision and analysis. The experiments show that the performance of fuzzy output SVMs is almost the same as the one-to-one approach, but when the membership to two classes is comparative and less than 0.8, the second maximal membership can sometimes correspond to the real class.

1 Introduction

Support vector machines (SVMs) based on the statistical learning theory are developed by Vapnik [1, 2]. SVMs have better performance than other traditional learning machines and have been gained acceptance for a wide range of application [12], such as handwritten digit recognition, object recognition, speech recognition [2] and spatial data analysis [3].

Recently, fuzzy set theory has been introduced to support vector machines [11]. In 2001, Inoue etc. proposed a fuzzy SVM to solve the unclassified regions that exist when extending two-class classification to multi-class case [4]. The generalization ability of the fuzzy SVM is the same as or better than that of the SVM for pairwise classification [5, 6].Then, since the optimal hyperplane obtained by SVM depends on only a small part of the data points, it may become sensitive to noises or outliers in the training set. In 2003, to deal with this problem, another fuzzy SVM was proposed. It employed the fuzzy memberships to evaluate the importance of data points. This method can prevent some points from making narrower margin by setting lower fuzzy membership to the data points that are considered as noises or outliers with higher probability [7]. Subsequently, researchers paid much attention to automatically setting the fuzzy memberships of the training data points [8, 9]. In a word, the fuzzy membership function is introduced to treat data points with different importance.

In this paper, we propose a fuzzy output SVM, which not only gives the decision class of the data points, but also the location information in the feature space through the fuzzy membership. That is, we employ the membership function to treat the decision with different importance. This machine makes full use of the information of the decision value, which will be helpful for the further decision and analysis. For example, a datum lies near the separating hyperplane, whose membership to class 1 is 0.45, to class 2 is 0.55. In original SVM, it will be classified to class 2 absolutely. But it is not definite and the confidence of data points to a class in different places is different. Hence through the decision value, the fuzzy output SVMs can give users the confidence of data points to a class. When the datum can't be classified to any class with high confidence, it can remain the users to import more information for the further decision. By this way, a binary classifier is extended to a fuzzy classifier.

Because SVMs are originally designed for 2-class classification, firstly fuzzy output binary SVMs are proposed. Then we analyze the boundary of multi-class case in detail and partition the feature space into three different regions because of different accuracy in them. Finally, some numeric experiments show the method effective.

2 Two-Class Fuzzy Output SVMs

In this section, we first review the two-class classification model of the original SVMs, and then use the decision value to give the 2-class fuzzy output model. Due to the symmetry of separating plane to each class, we choose the sigmoid membership function to describe the confidence of the data point to a class. And the decision process of the fuzzy output SVMs for 2-class is given at the end of this section.

Consider the following two-category classification problem:

$$(x_1, y_1), (x_2, y_2), \cdots (x_i, y_i), \cdots, (x_l, y_l), x_i \in R^n, y_i \in \{-1, +1\},$$

where x_i is a training example and y_i the corresponding class. First, SVM maps x into a high dimensional space via a function ϕ, then in order to construct the optimal hyperplane $w \bullet \phi(x) + b = 0$, we have to solve:

$$\min \quad \phi(w, \varepsilon) = \frac{1}{2}(w \cdot w) + C \sum_{i=1}^{l} \varepsilon_i \qquad (1)$$
$$s.t. \quad y_i(w \cdot \phi(x_i) + b) - 1 + \varepsilon_i \geq 0 \quad 0 \leq i \leq l$$

where ε_i is the slack variable, the constant C determines the trade-off between $\frac{w \cdot w}{2}$ margin maximization and $\sum_{i=1}^{n} \varepsilon_i$ training error minimization. Then the hyperplane can generalize well according to SRM [1]. According to Karush-Kuhn-Tucker condition in optimization theory, optimization problem (1) is equivalent to

$$\min \quad \frac{1}{2}\sum_{i=1}^{l} a_i a_j y_i y_j K(x_i, x_j) - \sum_{i=1}^{l} a_i$$
$$s.t. \quad \sum_{i=1}^{l} a_i y_i = 0, a_i \geq 0, 0 \leq i \leq l \tag{2}$$

where $K(x_i, x_j) = \phi(x_i) \cdot \phi(x_j)$ is an inner product in the feature space which can map the data points into feature space without computing $\phi(x)$. Through the kernel trick, SVMs can deal with the classification in nonlinear case easily.

Through solving the optimization problem (2), we can obtain w and b of the separating plane $w \bullet \phi(x) + b = 0$. In original SVMs, we can also obtain the following decision function:

$$f(x, w, b) = \text{sgn}\{w \bullet \phi(x) + b\} = \text{sgn}\{\sum_{i=1}^{l} a_i y_i K(x_i, x) + b\},$$

which just uses the sign of the decision value $w \bullet \phi(x) + b$. If the decision value is positive, the unseen data x is classified to class 1; while if the decision value is negative, x will be classified to class 2. In order to use the decision value to compute the membership to each class, we can get that the decision value to each class is, respectively

$$D_1 = w_1 \bullet \phi(x) + b_1, \quad D_2 = w_2 \bullet \phi(x) + b_2,$$

where $w_1 = -w_2 = w$, $b_1 = -b_2 = b$. Notice that the decision value is a signed value. If D_1 is positive, x belongs to class 1, while D_2 must be negative. What is more, because the 2 classes have the same separating hyperplane, but just in the opposite side, we can get $D_1 = -D_2$.

In the case of no apriori information, the separating hyperplane lies in the right middle of the margin. Most of the training data lie out of the margin. And the data in the margin are punished in training. By this method, the separating hyperplane can get the maximal generalization ability. With a trained SVM, we can set the following conditions to class 1:

1) When the decision value is greater than 1, the data point is out of the margin. Correspondingly, it can be classified to class 1 with high confidence. Here we set the confidence of data that lie on the same hyperplane as the support vectors, whose decision value is equal to 1, as 0.8. And the confidence of the data to class 1 increases with the decision value.
2) If the decision value is between 0 and 1, the data point is within the margin, which has more probability to be misclassified. Hence it can be classified to class 1 with less confidence, we can set it between 0.8 and 0.5;
3) If the decision value is equal to 0, the data point is on the separating plane. It may have the same confidence to each class. We set the confidence of the data point to class 1 as 0.5.
4) Due to these features, we can employ the following kind of membership function to give the confidence of the data points to a class showing in Equation (3). And we change the decision function to

where

$$\arg\max_{i=1,2} \mu_i(x)$$

$$\mu_i = \frac{1}{1+e^{-A(D_i-c)}} \tag{3}$$

In order to satisfy the above conditions, we have $A=-\ln(0.25)$, $c=0$. The membership function to class 1 shows in figure 1:

1) The line in the middle denotes the separating hyperplane $w\bullet\phi(x)+b=0$. The membership of data lying on the hyperplane to the two classes is 0.5 respectively. Look at the data denoted by diamond;
2) Data denoted by circle lie on the same hyperplane as support vectors of class 1, which satisfy $D_1=w_1\bullet\phi(x)+b_1=1$. The membership of these to class 1 is 0.8, while Data denoted by square lie on the same hyperplane as support vectors of class 2, the membership of these to class 1 is 0.2;
3) With the increase of the decision value, the membership to class 1 is towards 1.

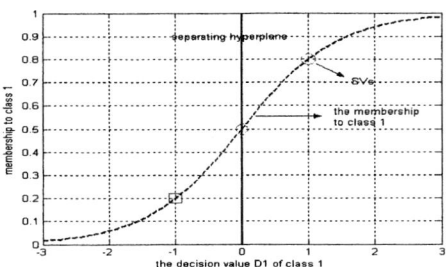

Fig. 1. The membership function to class 1

3 Multi-class Fuzzy Output SVMs

For SVMs are essentially a two-class classifier, some methods have been devised to extend SVMs to multi-class classification such as one-to-one, one-to-all and SVMDAG[10]. In this paper, we take one-to-one method to solve multi-class case. This method constructs SVMs between all pairs of classes and then uses a voting scheme to classify an unseen datum point. As for k-class classification, it needs to train $k(k-1)/2$ classifiers:

$$D_{ij}=w_{ij}\bullet x+b_{ij} \quad 0<i<j<k$$

where D_{ij} denotes the classifier for the i class and the j class. So we can get that $D_{ji}(x)=-D_{ij}(i\neq j)$ and we don't need to take the case of $i=j$ into consideration.

In [6], Shigeo Abe etc. point out that there exists unclassified region in one-to-one method and employ the membership function to solve this problem. In this paper, we use the same multi-hyperplane to construct the fuzzy output SVMs. But we separate the computing course of decision value to one class from that of membership. In order to get the similar membership to the 2-class case, firstly we analyze the boundary in detail. Three different regions are defined in the feature space showing in figure 2:

1) Absolutely classified region, in which $\forall i$ class, all $D_{ij} \geq 1$ except $j = i$;
2) Positive margin region, in which $\forall i$ class, all $0 < D_{ij} < 1$ except $j = i$;
3) Unclassified region, in which $\forall i$ class, all $D_{ij} \leq 0$ except $j = i$.

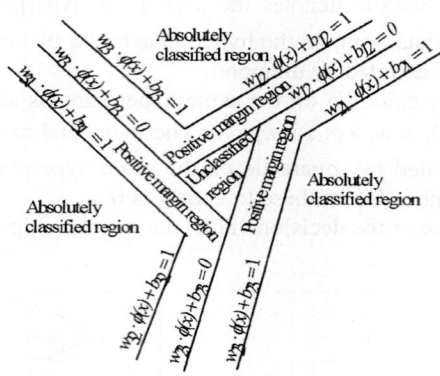

Fig. 2. The different regions in the feature space

Then we directly use the decision value $D_{ij}(x)$ of all the related classifiers to compute the decision value and the membership to each class. The decision process is as follows:

1) Computing the decision value of the i class: $D_i(x) = \min_{j=1,2,\cdots,n} D_{ij}(x)$. It means the decision value to this class depends on the nearest decision value of all the related classifiers to this class in the positive direction, while in the negative direction, it depends on the biggest absolute decision value of all the related classifiers.

2) Computing the membership to the i class:

$$\mu_i(x, w, b) = \frac{1}{1 + e^{-A(D_i(x)-c)}};$$

3) Decide the class of the unseen data: $\arg \max_{i=1,2,\cdots,n} \mu_i(x)$. When making the decision, we get the membership at the same time.

There are some features of the membership in different regions: the membership of the data in the absolutely classified region to the decision class is more than 0.8, to other classes is close to 0. In unclassified region, the membership to each class is between 0 and 0.5. The decision class is corresponding to the class that has the maximal membership. But sometimes the membership to another class is comparative to the maximal membership. In this case, the data may be really belongs to another class because the confidence of the decision class is small and comparative to another. The membership of the data in the positive margin region to their decision classes is between 0.5 and 0.8, to other classes are between 0 and 0.5. In this region, it has the same case as 2). When the membership of two classes is comparative, the class may be really belongs to one or another class. Although the decision class is corresponding to the maximal membership, sometimes the real class may be corresponding to the second maximal membership. Therefore, based memberships, we can get the location information of the data, which will be helpful for the further decision and analysis, especially when the comparative membership exists.

4 Experiment Results

We choose 8 datasets of UCI repository to show our method. The features of benchmark data are listed in Table 1.

Table 1. The features of benchmark data

No.	Data	Classes	Input	Train.	Test
1	zoo	7	16	67	34
2	breast	2	9	466	233
3	wdbc	2	30	379	190
4	cleve	5	13	202	101
5	Dermatology	6	34	245	121
6	ecoli	8	7	222	114
7	yeast	10	8	989	495
8	vowel	11	10	660	330

Table 2. The performance of the above method

No.	Data	1-1	FOut.	Abs.	Pos.	Unc.
1	zoo	88.24%	88.24%	100%	85.19%	NaN
2	breast	98.28%	98.28%	100%	63.64%	NaN
3	wdbc	93.16%	93.16%	95.95%	64.71%	NaN
4	cleve	59.41%	57.43%	78.18%	38.24%	16.67%
5	Der.	90.91%	91.74%	98.91%	68.99%	33.33%
6	ecoli	70.18%	70.18%	97.37%	57.33%	0.00%
7	yeast	51.72%	51.72%	61.82%	51.28%	18.18%
8	vowel	59.09%	57.27%	93.02%	58.11%	30.77%

We get the performance of one-to-one method (1-1), the fuzzy output method in all regions (FOut.), absolutely classified region (Abs.), positive margin region (Pos.) and unclassified region (Unc.) in table 2. It shows that:

1) The accuracies of 1-1 and FOut. are almost the same. Only in Cleve dataset, the former is better; in Dermatology dataset, the latter is better.

2) In different regions, the accuracy is different. In Abs., the accuracy is more than 80%, better than FOut; In Pos., the accuracy is less than FOut; And in Unc., the accuracy is very low, less than about 30%.

At last, we take part of the vowel dataset for instance, giving the output of fuzzy output SVMs. Look at the table 3. The accuracy of different regions varies very much.

Table 3. The number of data in three different regions

Regions	All	Absolutely.	Positive.	Unclassified.
Right/all	189/330	40/43	129/222	20/65
Accuracy	57.27%	93.02%	58.11%	30.77%

In table 4, a part of the vowel data is selected randomly to show the effect of fuzzy output in different regions.

1) Only 3 data in the absolutely classified region are classified to a wrong class. Look at No. 1, No.2 and NO.3 data. It is a regret the second maximal membership isn't corresponding to the real class. But the accuracy in this region is so high that we can accept the decision with high confidence.
2) Look at NO.4, No.5 and No.6 data. They are in positive margin region and classified to a wrong class. The real classes of No. 4 and No. 5 data are corresponding to the second maximal membership. And the maximal membership is comparative to the second maximal membership. Here memberships will be helpful.
3) Especially in the unclassified region, the accuracy is low to 30.77%. Look at NO.7 to No.10 data. They are classified to a wrong class. The real classes of these 4 data are corresponding to the second maximal membership. And the value of membership is less than 0.5.

Table 4. The fuzzy output of the vowel dataset. L. stands for the location of the data in the feature space. A. stands for absolutely classified region; P. stands for positive margin region; U. stands for Unclassified region; μ_i denotes the membership of the point to class i; D. denotes the decision class by the fuzzy output SVM; R. denotes the real class of the point.

No.	L.	μ_3	μ_4	μ_5	μ_6	μ_7	μ_8	μ_9	μ_{10}	μ_{11}	D.	R.
1	A.	0.00	0.00	0.17	0.01	0.83	0.04	0.07	0.00	0.01	7	8
2	A.	0.00	0.00	0.17	0.00	0.83	0.05	0.05	0.00	0.00	7	8
3	A.	0.00	0.03	0.03	0.04	0.82	0.05	0.17	0.01	0.10	7	11
4	P.	0.00	0.00	0.53	0.13	0.47	0.00	0.03	0.00	0.04	5	7
5	P.	0.00	0.00	0.67	0.13	0.33	0.00	0.01	0.00	0.03	5	7
6	P	0.00	0.04	0.00	0.01	0.65	0.04	0.12	0.04	0.04	7	11
7	U.	0.21	0.45	0.03	0.26	0.40	0.01	0.01	0.00	0.16	4	3
8	U.	0.00	0.18	0.49	0.48	0.05	0.00	0.01	0.00	0.24	5	6
9	U.	0.08	0.43	0.04	0.30	0.19	0.00	0.03	0.04	0.30	4	6
10	U.	0.00	0.00	0.49	0.19	0.31	0.01	0.07	0.00	0.12	5	7

For the above analysis, we can see that although the fuzzy output method gets almost the same performance with the one-to-one approach, the fuzzy method can give us more information to help for the further decision, especially for the data point in the positive margin region and the unclassified region. In different regions, the accuracy varies very much. Through memberships, we can deduce the confidence of the decision and tell us whether we need import more information to get the real decision.

5 Conclusion and Future Work

In this paper, a fuzzy output support vector machine is proposed, which gives the location information of an unseen datum. We define three different regions because of different accuracy in them. Fuzzy output SVMs make full use of the decision value and is helpful to the further decision and analysis, especially for the unseen data lying in the positive margin region and unclassified region.

References

1. V. N. Vapnik, Statistical Learning Theory, New York: John Wiley & Sons, 1998.
2. J.C. Burges, A Tutorial on Support Vector Machines for Pattern Recognition, Data Mining and Knowledge Discovery, Vol.2, pp.121-167, 1998
3. M. Kanevski, A. Pozdnukhov, S. Canu, and M. Maignan, Advanced Spatial Data Analysis and Modeling with Support Vector Machines, international Journal of Fuzzy Systems, Vol.4, No.1, pp.606-615, 2002
4. Takuya Inoue, Shigeo Abe. Fuzzy Support Vector Machines for Pattern Classification. In Proceedings of International Joint Conference on Neural Networks, 2001: 1449-1454
5. Shigeo Abe. Analysis of multiclass support vector machines. International Conference on Computational Intelligence for Modeling Control and Automation. 385-396, 2003.
6. Shigeo Abe, Takuya Inoue. Fuzzy support vector machines for multiclass problems. European symposium on Artificial Neural Networks. 24-26 April 2002, pp.113-118
7. C.-F.Lin, S.-D.Wang. Fuzzy support vector machines. IEEE Transaction on Neural Networks, Vol.13, No.2, pp.464-471, 2002
8. C.-F.Lin, S.-D. Wang. Training algorithms for fuzzy support vector machines with noisy data. IEEE XIII workshop on neural networks for signal processing, pp.517-526, 2003
9. Han-Pang Huang, Yi-Hung Liu. Fuzzy support vector machines for pattern recognition and data mining. International journal of fuzzy systems, Vol.4, No.3, 2002, pp.826-836
10. Hsu C-W, Lin C-J. A comparison of methods for multiclass support vector machines. IEEE Transaction on Neural Networks, 2002, 13(2): 415-425
11. Kecman, V.: Learning and Soft Computing, Support Vector machines, Neural Networks and Fuzzy Logic Models. The MIT Press, Cambridge, MA, 2001
12. Wang, L.P. (Ed.): Support Vector Machines: Theory and Application. Springer, Berlin Heidelberg New York, 2005

Credit Rating Analysis with AFS Fuzzy Logic*

Xiaodong Liu[1] and Wanquan Liu[2]

[1] Research Center of Information and Control, Dalian University of Technology,
Dalian, 116024, P.R. of China
xdliuros@hotmail.com
[2] Dept. of Computing, Curtin University of Technology,
Bentley, WA, 6102, Australia
wanquan@cs.curtin.edu.au

Abstract. In this paper, we propose a new machine learning approach based on AFS (Axiomatic Fuzzy Sets) fuzzy logic, in attempt to provide a better model with interpretability. First, we will concisely present the AFS theory. Second, we will propose new membership functions for fuzzy sets and their logic operations. Third, we will design a new machine learning algorithm based on the new membership functions and their logic operations. This algorithm has two advantages. One is that it can mimic the human reasoning comprehensively and offers a far more flexible and effective means for the study of large-scale intelligent systems. Another is its simplicity in implementation and mathematical beauty in fuzzy theory. Finally, a credit data example is used to illustrate its effectiveness.

1 Introduction

Credit rating has been extensively used by bond investors, debt issuers, and government as a surrogate measure of risk analysis. Company credit ratings are typically very costive, since they require professional agencies to invest large amount of time and human resources to perform deep analysis of the company's risk status based on various aspects ranging from strategic competitiveness to operational level details.

Substantial papers can be found in bond-rating prediction. We categorized the existing methods into statistical methods and machine learning methods. Statistical researchers utilized logistic regression analysis [1] and probability analysis [2,7]. These studies used different data sets and the prediction results were typically between 50% and 70%. Moody and Utans [8] used neural networks to predict 16 categories of S and P rating. Their model predicted the ratings of 36.2% correctly. They also tested the system with 5-class prediction and 3-class prediction and obtained prediction accuracies of 63.8% and 85.2%, respectively. Maher and Sen [9] compared the performance of neural networks on bond-rating

---

* This work is supported by the Natural Science Fund of China (60174014) and ARC Fellowship Scheme supported by Australian Research Council.

prediction with that of logistic regression. They used data from Moody's Annual Bond Record and Standard and Poor's Compustat financial data. The best performance they obtained was 70%. Kwon et al. [10] applied ordinal pairwise partitioning (OPP) approach to the back propagation neural networks. They used Korean bond-rating data and demonstrated that neural networks with OPP had the highest level of accuracy (71–73%), followed by conventional neural networks (66–67%) and multiple discriminant analysis (58–61%). Chaveesuk et al. [11] also compared back propagation neural network with radial basis function, learning vector quantization and logistic regression. Their study revealed that neural networks and logistic regression model produced the best performances with accuracy of 51.9% and 53.3%, respectively. Zan Huang,et al. [14] obtained prediction accuracy around 80% via SVM (support vector machine) methods for data from the United States and Taiwan markets.

In this paper, we study the machine learning by the AFS theory which is a different approach from the current fuzzy theories. In current fuzzy theories, the membership functions and the logic operations of the fuzzy sets are often given by personal intuition and independent of the original data. AFS fuzzy logic [3-5,12,13] is a new approach to study the mathematical structure and logical operations for fuzzy concepts. In AFS fuzzy logic, the membership functions and their logic operations are implemented by AFS structures and AFS algebra with the following advantages. 1. With a few simple concepts, we can express a great large number of complex fuzzy concepts and to implement their logic operations. 2. With AFS structure, one can give representations of the membership degrees for any fuzzy set.

2 AFS Fuzzy Logic

In this section, we explain AFS fuzzy theory with an example of the credit data which is from the database at University of California, Irvine, the credit-screening. Let X be the set of the 75 randomly selected training samples. For each $s = (s_1, s_2, ..., s_{18}) \in X, s_1 = 1, 0$ is the label of sample s i.e. if $s_1 = 1$, sample s is positive credit, otherwise is negative credit. s_i is the value of sample s on feature i, $i = 2, 3, ..., 18$. On each feature from s_1 to s_{12}, there are two simple concepts: $m1$: credit, $m44$: no-credit; $m2$: jobless, $m43$: no-jobless; $m3$: purchase, pc, $m42$: no purchase, pc; $m4$: purchase car, $m41$: no purchase car; $m5$: purchase stereo, $m40$: no purchase stereo; $m6$: purchase jewel, $m39$: no purchase jewel; $m7$: purchase medinstru, $m38$: no purchase medinstru; $m8$: purchase bike, $m37$: no purchase bike; $m9$: purchase furniture, $m36$: no purchase furniture; $m10$: male, $m35$: female; $m11$: unmarried, $m34$: married; $m12$: live in problematic region, $m33$: no live in problematic region; For feature s_{13} to s_{17}, each feature has four simple concepts {large, mid, no large, no mid}. $m13$: old, $m14$: average age, $m32$: no old, $m31$: no average age; $m15$: more deposit, $m16$: average deposit, $m30$: no more deposit, $m29$: no average deposit; $m17$: loan payment more, $m18$: loan payment average, $m28$: no loan payment more, $m27$: no loan payment average; $m19$: pay off loan more, $m20$: pay off loan average, $m26$: no pay off loan more,

$m25$:no pay off loan average; $m21$:number of years working more, $m22$: number of years working average, $m24$: no number of years working more, $m23$: no number of years working average. So there are total 44 simple concepts.

In order to study the essential nature of fuzzy concepts and fuzzy logic, let X, M be two sets, in general M is the set of crisp or fuzzy concepts on X, for example, in credit data, M ={m1, m2, ..., m44}, X is the set of 75 training samples. Let

$EM^* = \{\sum_{i \in I} A_i \mid A_i \subseteq M, i \in I, I$ is any no empty indexing set$\}$,
$EXM^* = \{\sum_{i \in I} a_i A_i \mid a_i \subseteq X, A_i \subseteq M, i \in I, I$ is any no empty indexing set$\}$.

In [3,5], an equivalence relation R is defined in EM^* and EXM^* respectively, and we always denote EM^*/R as EM and EXM^*/R is denoted as EXM. For two elements in EM (or in EXM), the semantic of them (or the membership degrees they represented) are equivalent if they have relation R.

For a fuzzy set ζ on universe of discourse X, any $x \in X$, either x belongs to ζ at some degree or does not belong to ζ at all, while for a crisp subset A of X, any $x \in X$, either x belongs to A or does not belong to A at all.

Based on this opinion, both a fuzzy set and a crisp subset on X can be represented by a binary relation R on X through comparing degrees of each pair of x, y belonging to the concept.

Definition 1. *Let ζ be any concept (fuzzy or crisp concept) on the universe of discourse X. R_ζ is called a binary relation (i.e. $R_\zeta \subset X \times X$) of ζ if R_ζ satisfies: $x, y \in X$, $(x, y) \in R_\zeta \Leftrightarrow x$ belongs to concept ζ at some degree and the degree of x belonging to ζ is larger than or equals to that of y, or x belongs to concept ζ at some degree and y does not at all.*

In practice, R_ζ can also be obtained by comparing the degrees of each pair x and y belonging to concept ζ through human intuitions. We will apply the binary relation representations of concepts to obtain the ordinary fuzzy sets or L-fuzzy sets representations for concepts. We should notice that $(x, x) \in R_\zeta$ indicates that x belongs to concept ζ at some degree and $(x, x) \notin R_\zeta$ implies that x does not belong to concept ζ at all.

Definition 2. [6] *Let X be a set and R be a binary relation on X. R is called a preference relation on X if 1. $\forall x \in X$, $(x, x) \in R$; 2. If $(x, y) \in R$, $(y, z) \in R$, then $(x, z) \in R$, $x, y, z \in X$; 3. For any $x, y \in X$, either $(x, y) \in R$ or $(y, x) \in R$.*

By Definition 1, one knows that for some concept ζ there exists $x \in X$ such that $(x; x) \notin R_\zeta$. Although preference relations are very simple and have very good mathematical properties, Condition 1 of Definition 2 is too strict to represent ordinary concepts.

Definition 3. *Let X be a set and R is a binary relation on X. R is called a sub-preference relation on X if for $x, y, z \in X$, $x \neq y$, R satisfies:1. If $(x, y) \in R$, then $(x, x) \in R$; 2. If $(x, x) \in R$ and $(y, y) \notin R$, then $(x, y) \in R$; 3. If (x, y),*

$(y, z) \in R$, then $(x, z) \in R$; 4. If $(x, x) \in R$ and $(y, y) \in R$, then either $(x, y) \in R$ or $(y, x) \in R$. A concept ζ is called a simple concept or simple attribute on X if R_ζ is a sub-preference relation, otherwise is called a complex concept or a complex attribute on X.

With any simple concept ζ, X is divided into three classes: $T_\zeta = \{x \in X | (x, y) \in R_\zeta, \forall y \in X\}$, $F_\zeta = \{x \in X | (x, x) \notin R_\zeta\}$, $M_\zeta = X - T_\zeta - F_\zeta$.

Definition 4. [3,5] *Let X, M be sets, 2^M be the power set of M, $\tau : X \times X \to 2^M$. (M, τ, X) is called an AFS structure if τ satisfies: AX1: $\forall (x_1, x_2) \in X \times X$, $\tau(x_1, x_2) \subseteq \tau(x_1, x_1)$; AX2: $\forall (x_1, x_2), (x_2, x_3) \in X \times X$, $\tau(x_1, x_2) \cap \tau(x_2, x_3) \subseteq \tau(x_1, x_3)$. X is called the universe of discourse, M is called the attribute set and τ is called the structure.*

We can verify that (M, τ, X) is an AFS structure if each $m \in M$, m is a simple concept and τ is defined as $\tau(x_i, x_j) = \{m | m \in M, (x_i, x_j) \in R_m\}$, $x_i, x_j \in X$. (M, τ, X) is the mathematical abstraction of the complicated relationships among objects in X under the attributes in M. This implies that the information contained in databases and human intuitions are transited to (M, τ, X) from which we can obtain the fuzzy sets and fuzzy logic operations.

Theorem 5. [3] *Let (M, τ, X) be an AFS structure. $x \in X$, $A \subseteq M$, we define the symbol: $\underline{A}(\{x\}) = \{y \mid y \in X, \tau(x, y) \supseteq A\}$. For any given $x \in X$, if we define a mapping $\phi_x(\sum_{i \in I} A_i) = \sum_{i \in I} \underline{A_i}(\{x\}) A_i \in EXM$, then ϕ_x is a homomorphism from lattice $(EM, \vee, \wedge)$ to lattice $(EXM, \vee, \wedge)$.*

By Theorem 5, we know that for any given concept $\zeta = \sum_{i \in I} A_i \in EM$, we get a mapping $\zeta : X \to EXM$. In this way, for each $\zeta \in EM$, ζ is L-fuzzy set on X and the membership degree of x ($x \in X$) belonging to fuzzy set ζ is $\sum_{i \in I} \underline{A_i}(\{x\}) A_i \in EXM$. Further, in [12,13], the logic operator $'$ (negation) is defined as: $(\sum_{i \in I} A_i)' = \wedge_{i \in I} (\vee_{a \in A_i} \{a'\})$. $(EM, \vee, \wedge, ')$ is called an AFS fuzzy logic systems.

3 Membership Functions Based on AFS Theory

Definition 6. *Let X be a set, S be a σ-algebra over X. $\rho : X \to R^+ = [0, \infty)$. $0 < \sum_{x \in X} \rho(x) < \infty$. For any $A \in S$, a measure m is defined as, $m(A) = \frac{\sum_{x \in A} \rho(x)}{\sum_{x \in X} \rho(x)}$.*

Definition 7. *Let X be a universe of discourse and M be a set of simple concepts, S be a σ-algebra over X, (M, τ, X) be an AFS structure. (M, τ, X, S) is called a semi-cognitive field. For each $a \in M$, m_a is the measure defined by Definition 6 with ρ_a as the weight function for simple concept a. If $\sum_{i \in I} a_i A_i \in EXM$ satisfying $a_i \in S, \forall i \in I$, we define $\| \sum_{i \in I} a_i A_i \| = \sup_{i \in I} (\prod_{a \in A_i} m_a(a_i)) \in [0, 1]$.*
For fuzzy concept $\sum_{i \in I} A_i \in EM$, if $\underline{A_i}(\{x\}) \in S, \forall i \in I$, then $\sum_{i \in I} A_i$ is called measurable in (M, τ, X, S) and we define the membership function of ordinary fuzzy set representing for fuzzy concept $\sum_{i \in I} A_i$ in semi-cognitive field (M, τ, X, S) as follows: $\forall x \in X$, $\mu_{\sum_{i \in I} A_i}(x) = \|(\sum_{i \in I} A_i)(x)\|$.

Proposition 8. Let (M, τ, X, S) be a semi-cognitive field. Then for $\alpha = \sum_{i \in I} a_i A_i$, $\beta = \sum_{j \in J} b_j B_j \in EXM$, $\zeta = \sum_{i \in I} A_i, \eta = \sum_{j \in J} B_j \in EM$, the followings hold: 1. If $\alpha = \beta$, satisfying $a_i, b_j \in S, \forall i \in I, \forall j \in J$, then $\|\alpha\| = \|\beta\|$. 2. If α, β, satisfying $a_i, b_j \in S, \forall i \in I, \forall j \in J$, then $\|\alpha \vee \beta\| = \max(\|\alpha\|, \|\beta\|)$, $\|\alpha \wedge \beta\| \leq \min(\|\alpha\|, \|\beta\|)$. 3. If $\zeta \geq \eta$, then for any $x \in X$, $\mu_{\sum_{i \in I} A_i}(x) \geq \mu_{\sum_{j \in J} B_j}(x)$.

4 Credit Rating Analysis with AFS Fuzzy Logic

Now, it is time for us to study machine learning algorithm based on AFS fuzzy logic. In the following, the membership functions are all defined by Definition 7. Let's analysis human how to learn a concept by some training samples (e.g. For the credit-screening data, each training sample has been shown that positive or negative credit). Let X be the set of the given training samples and F be all relative attributes (fuzzy or crisp) on X. $F \subseteq M$, where M is a set of simple concepts on X. Let P is the set of all training samples belonging to the given concept (e.g. for the credit-screening data, P is the set of all positive credit samples). For each $x \in P$, find a fuzzy set $\zeta_x \in (F)_{EI}$, the sub EI algebra generated by F, such that at the largest degree x belongs to ζ_x; For any $y \in X - P$, at smallest degree y belongs to ζ_x and for $z \in P, z \neq x$, at comparatively larger degree z belongs to ζ_x. In other words, x can be distinguished from any $y \in X - P$ by fuzzy set ζ_x at the greatest extent. Finally, fuzzy set $\zeta_P = \bigvee_{x \in P} \zeta_x$ is the fuzzy set in EM which approximates the concept. For each new pattern s, the degree of s belonging to the concept is estimated by $\mu_{\zeta_P}(s)$.

For the credit-screening data, since each simple concept $m \in M - \{m1, m44\}$, m is a concept related to the credit, hence any fuzzy set in $(\Lambda)_{EI}$ correlates the classification, where $\Lambda = \{\{m\} | m \in M - \{m1, m44\}\}$. There are more than $\sum_{i=1}^{42}(2^{C_n^i} - 1)$ different fuzzy sets in $(\Lambda)_{EI}$. To find ζ_x for each $x \in X$, it is impossible to check each fuzzy set in $(\Lambda)_{EI}$. Therefore we need to solve this problem in this paper.

Theorem 9. Let (M, τ, X, S) be a cognitive field. $\Lambda \subseteq M$, Λ is countable set. $\forall \gamma \in \Lambda$, γ is a measurable fuzzy set. For a given $x \in X$ and a given $\varepsilon > 0$, $\alpha \in \Lambda_x^\varepsilon$ which is the set of all molecular elements in $(\Lambda)_{EI}$ the degrees of x belonging to them are larger than ε, where $(\Lambda)_{EI}$ is the sub-EI algebra generated by the elements in Λ. let $\vartheta_\alpha^x = \{\beta \in (\Lambda)_{EI} \mid \beta \geq \alpha\}$. Then the followings hold: 1. ϑ_α^x is a sub-EI algebra of $(\Lambda)_{EI}$; 2. ϑ_α^x is an upper[5] set of $(\Lambda)_{EI}$ i.e. for $\beta \in (\Lambda)_{EI}$, if $\exists \gamma \in \vartheta_\alpha^x$, $\beta \geq \gamma$, then $\beta \in \vartheta_\alpha^x$; 3. $\mu_{\bigvee_{b \in \Lambda} b}(x) \geq \mu_{\bigwedge_{b \in \vartheta_\alpha^x} b}(x) \geq \mu_\alpha(x) \geq \mu_{\bigvee_{b \in \Lambda} b}(x) - \varepsilon$; 4. For $\eta \in (\Lambda)_{EI}$, if $\mu_\eta(x) > \mu_{\bigvee_{b \in \Lambda} b}(x) - \varepsilon$, then $\exists \alpha \in \Lambda_x^\varepsilon$, for any $y \in X$, $y \neq x$, $\mu_\eta(y) \geq \mu_{\bigwedge_{b \in \vartheta_\alpha^x} b}(y) \geq \mu_\alpha(y)$.

Now we can describe the learning algorithm as below:

Step1: Establish (M, τ, X, S) and ρ_m, for each $m \in M$ from the original data.
Step2: Select $\Lambda \subseteq M$, to design the classifier. $(\Lambda)_{EI}$ is the sub EI algebra generated by Λ.

Step 3: Given small positive numbers $\varepsilon > 0, \delta > 0$, for each $i = 1, 2, ...c$, find $\zeta_P \in (\Lambda)_{EI}$, such that $\zeta_P : \sum_{y \in P} \mu_{\zeta_{X_i}}(y) = \max_{\xi \in F_\varepsilon^\delta}\{\sum_{y \in P} \mu_\xi(y)\}$, where $E_\Lambda^\delta = \{\gamma | \gamma \in (\Lambda)_{EI}, \forall y \in X - P, \mu_\gamma(y) < \delta\}$, $F_\varepsilon^\delta = \{\xi | \xi \in E_\Lambda^\delta, \forall y \in X_i, \mu_\xi(y) \geq \mu_{\vee_{b \in \Lambda} b}(y) - \varepsilon\}$. ζ_P is the fuzzy set in EM which approximates the given concept. δ is a parameter to control the extent of fuzzy set ζ_P distinguishing $x \in P$ and $y \notin P$. ε is a parameter to control the degree of each training sample x ($x \in X_i$) belonging to ζ_P.

Step 4: For each testing sample s, we estimate the degree of s belonging to the fuzzy set ζ_P.

In this paper, we apply the proposed design method to study the classification problem for credit data. We have done 10 experiments, in each time randomly select 60% as training samples and 40% as testing samples. In the proposed algorithm, we set $\varepsilon = 0.3$, $\delta = 0.1$. By solving the optimization problem, we can obtain the credit description η_P. For any testing sample s, if $\mu_{\eta_P}(s) \geq 0.3$, then s is regarded as positive credit. We list the classification results in the table. One can see that the results here are comparable with the existing reported results.

Table 1. Table 1 Correct rate of 10 experiments

i-th experience	1	2	3	4	5	6	7	8	9	10
$\mu_{\eta_P}(s) \geq 0.3$	66%	72%	54%	72%	60%	70%	62%	60%	66%	50%

5 Conclusion

In this paper, with the framework of AFS theory, we propose a new algorithmic framework for determining fuzzy sets (membership functions) and their logic operations, where the membership functions and their logic operations are impersonally and automatically determined by a consistent algorithm from the original data. This approach is new in the following aspects: 1. The classification can be done directly from the training data without much human involvement; 2. The approach can mimic human thinking process. Its effectiveness has been proved via the credit data classification. Indeed, this new machine learning algorithm also can be regard as the knowledge representation of the training data and it can be used in other areas.

References

1. H.L. Ederington, Classification models and bond ratings, Financial Review 20 (4) (1985) 237–262.
2. J.A. Gentry, D.T. Whitford, P. Newbold, Predicting industrial bond ratings with a probit model and funds flow components, Financial Review 23 (3) (1988) 269–286.
3. Xiaodong Liu , The Fuzzy Theory Based on AFS Algebras and AFS Structure, Journal of Mathematical Analysis and Applications, vol. 217, pp. 459-478, 1998.

4. Xiaodong Liu , The Topology on AFS Algebra and AFS Structure, Journal of Mathematical Analysis and Applications, vol. 217, pp. 479-489, 1998.
5. Xiaodong Liu , The Fuzzy Sets and Systems Based on AFS Structure, EI Algebra and EII algebra, Fuzzy Sets and Systems, vol. 95, pp. 179-188, 1998.
6. Kim K. H. Boolean matrix Theory and Applications, Inc.: Marcel Dekker, 1982.
7. J.D. Jackson, J.W. Boyd, A statistical approach to modeling the behavior of bond raters, The Journal of Behavioral Economics 17 (3) (1988) 173– 193.
8. J. Moody, J. Utans, Architecture selection strategies for neural networks application to corporate bond rating, in: A. Refenes (Ed.), Neural Networks in the Capital Markets, Wiley, Chichester, 1995, pp. 277–300.
9. J.J. Maher, T.K. Sen, Predicting bond ratings using neural networks: a comparison with logistic regression, Intelligent Systems in Accounting, Finance and Management 6 (1997) pp.59– 72.
10. Y.S. Kwon, I.G. Han, K.C. Lee, Ordinal Pairwise Partitioning (OPP) approach to neural networks training in bond rating, Intelligent Systems in Accounting, Finance and Management 6 (1997) pp.23– 40.
11. R. Chaveesuk, C. Srivaree-Ratana, A.E. Smith, Alternative neural network approaches to corporate bond rating, Journal of Engineering Valuation and Cost Analysis 2 (2) (1999) pp.117– 131.
12. Liu Xiaodong, Zhang Qingling, AFS Fuzzy logic and its applications to fuzzy information processing, Dongbei Daxue Xuebao, (in Chinese) 2002, 23(4):321-323.
13. Liu Xiaodong, Witold Pedrycz and Zhang Qingling, Axiomatics Fuzzy sets logic, IEEE International Conference on Fuzzy Systems, vol1, pp 55-60, 2003.
14. Zan Huang, Hsinchun Chen, Chia-Jung Hsu, Wun-Hwa Chen, Soushan Wu, Credit rating analysis with support vector machines and neural networks: a market comparative study, Decision Support Systems 37 (2004) pp.543– 558.

A Neural-fuzzy Based Inferential Sensor for Improving the Control of Boilers in Space Heating Systems

Zaiyi Liao

Dept. of Architectural Science, Ryerson University, 350 Victoria Street, Toronto
Ontario, M5B 2K3, Canada
zliao@ryerson.ca

Abstract. Conventionally the boilers in space heating systems are controlled by open-loop control systems due to the absence of a practical method for measuring the overall thermal comfort level in the building. This paper describes a neural-fuzzy based inferential sensor that can be used to design close-loop boiler control schemes. Both simulation and experimental results show that the proposed technique results in significant energy saving and improvement on the control of thermal comfort in the built environment. The paper also describes the ongoing and future work.

1 Introduction

In the absence of an economic and technically reliable method for measuring the overall thermal comfort level in the building, the boilers in hydraulic space heating systems are normally controlled to maintain the temperature of either the supply or the return hot water within a predefined range [1]. As shown in Fig.1, an open-loop scheme is normally employed to determine the set-point of the water temperature. Considering that the purpose of such space heating systems is to control the air temperatures in the buildings rather than the water temperatures, it is essential to predefine the set-point schedule of the water temperature appropriately or to vary the set-point according to the changing operating conditions, such as the external climatic condition and the use of the buildings [2] [3]. It has been proved through the practice of the last several decades that it is extremely difficult, if not impossible, to determine the set-point of the water temperature such that the long-term energy performance of the space heating system is optimized [4] [5]. The overall energy efficiency of the entire heating system is significantly affected by temperature of hot water because it alters: (1) the operating energy efficiency of boilers (2) the energy loss through the distribution system and (3) the characteristics of the terminal devices, such as radiators and fan-coil units, and their controls. Generally, the lower the water temperature is, the higher the overall energy efficiency is [3] [6]. It is desirable to operate the heating system with as low water temperature as possible [6]. However, if the water temperature is too low, the heating capacity delivered to the terminal devices is insufficient, resulting in compromised thermal comfort in the building [2]. Therefore it is important to find out the optimal value of operating water temperature at which the energy efficiency is maximized while sufficient heating capacity is delivered to the end-users.

Fig. 1 shows that a feedback loop is needed to detect the overall level of thermal comfort in the building and to transfer this information to the water temperature scheduler that can in turn determine the optimal set-point of the water temperature. Liao and Arthur developed a physical-based inferential sensor that can estimate the average air temperature in the building based on the information available to conventional boiler controllers, including the boiler control signal, the external air temperature and the solar radiation [7]. A simplified physical model of multiple-zone space heating systems was developed and incorporated with conventional boiler control system to design a novel boiler control scheme, which is referred to as Inferential Control Scheme [1]. This control technique was investigated through simulations and experiment. They concluded that the overall performance of a heating system, no matter whether the terminal devices are controlled well or badly, can be improved significantly if a representative value of the room air temperature in the building can be obtained and the associated controllers can be tuned correctly [5][8]. However, the simulation and experimental study also showed that the physical sensor and the inferential control scheme are difficult to commissioned, a process through which all the relevant parameters are determined using short-term monitoring data [6][8]. This can be explained because the physical-model based inferential sensor intends to estimate the time-dependent value of the average air temperature in the building, which requires a very high level of accuracy for both the physical model and the values of the relevant parameters [6].

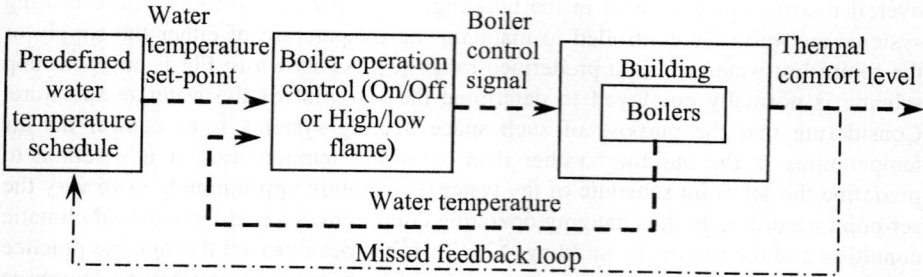

Fig. 1. A typical conventional boiler control scheme needs a feedback loop between the thermal comfort level in the building and the determination of the desired water temperature

It was reported that it is not necessary to determine the value of the optimal water temperature with high resolution in such inferential control schemes [6]. It is possible to achieve optimal long-term performance if the water temperature can be changed according to the heating load appropriately with a resolution of only 5 °C [6]. Therefore it seems unnecessary to maintain the high accuracy required by the physical-model based inferential sensor.

This paper presents the development of a neuro-fuzzy based inferential sensor, which estimates the level of the heating load in the building based on the same information used by the physical-model based inferential sensor, and an inferential sensor based boiler control scheme that optimize the long-term performance of space heating systems.

2 Methodology

This study has been conducted through surveys, simulation study and experimental study. Through the survey, typical heating systems used in current practice were identified. The survey was conducted in three ways:

- Walk-through audits and interviews with occupants
- Interviews with facility management companies
- Communication with relevant professional organisations, control system manufacturers, system integrators and designers.

The following information was collected through the survey:

- Boiler size and building information. This is to be used to estimate the design heating load.
- Control of the boiler and the heat emitters, including the commissioning, maintenance of the controllers.
- Room temperature. This is only carried out in a few buildings.
- Historical fuel consumption and cost over the last year, if available.
- Climatic data. This is collected from existing data resources.

The typical heating systems identified through the survey were in turn represented in a simulator of multiple-zone heating systems, which was developed and rigorously validated in a previous project [9]. The simulation models of the conventional boiler controllers were also developed and integrated with the simulator for use in the simulation study.

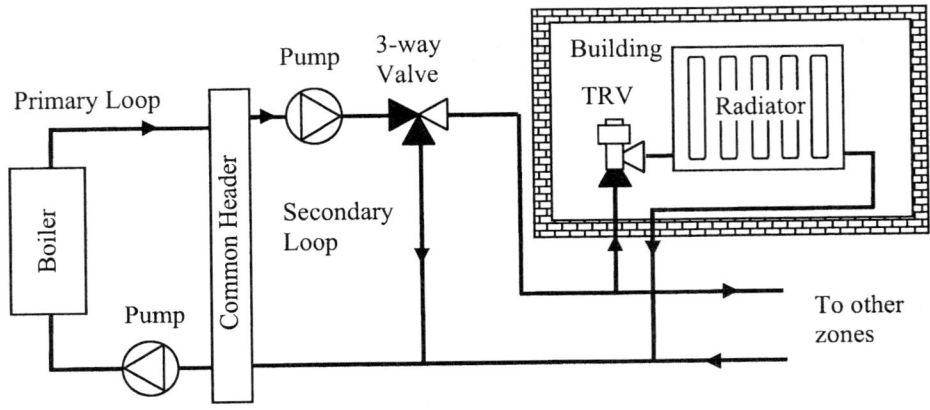

Fig. 2. A Multi-zone heating system

Fig. 2. shows the structure of a typical multiple-zone heating system. The simulator can have one single boiler or multiple boilers. Both condensing and non-condensing boiler [10] can be selected. Multiple zones can be built and each zone can have a different structure. The heat emitters are radiators, which may be uncontrolled or be controlled by Thermostat Radiator Valve (TRV). The climatic data used is Kew64 [11].

The simulator was used for the following tasks:

- To investigate the performance of conventional boiler controllers in the typical heating systems
- To carry out a sensitivity study in order to understand the influence of boiler controls on the overall performance of multi-zone heating systems.
- To design proposed inferential sensor and the integrated control scheme
- To assess the long-term control performance.

The inferential sensor and the integrated control scheme were first developed and assessed using the simulator and existed in the form of software and hence it is referred to as a "software sensor" and a "software controller". To test their performance in a real heating system, a hardware prototype sensor and controller were developed. The prototypes are based on microprocessor. To ensure that the software sensor and controller had been implemented properly, the prototypes were tested with the simulator first. Any discrepancy between the behavior of the software and the prototypes indicated a bug in the code of the prototypes. The prototypes were accordingly debugged until there is no discrepancy. Through this "Test-Modify" procedure, one can ensure that the control scheme to be tested in the field trial is the same as the one developed in the simulator. Once the implementation of the control scheme had been validated, it was installed in two different heating systems for the field trials: a multiple-zone heating system in an office building located in the UK and a residential house located in Toronto, Canada. The first field trial was carried out over two heating seasons in order to test the long-term performance. The second field trial was conducted throughout the heating season 2004/2005.

The field trials were focused on the accuracy of the inferential sensor only. The long-term control performance of the proposed control technique was only partially investigated. The ongoing research activities focus on this part.

3 Description of the Inferential Sensor

Before the proposed neuro-fuzzy based inferential sensor is described, the physical-model based inferential model [7] is summarized as follows:

There are three major inputs to the inferential sensor, including the external air temperature ($T_e(t)$), the energy intensity of the solar radiation ($Q_{sol}(t)$), and the energy power of the boiler ($Q_d(t)$) that is estimated from the control signal ($B(t)$). There is one output: the estimated value of the overall average air temperature in the building ($T_a(t)$). The relationship between these inputs and the output is governed by a set of first-order differential equations [7]. Figure 3 shows an electric analogue of the dynamic model. There are nine relevant parameters that need to be commissioned using short-term monitoring data before the inferential sensor can be used. These relevant parameters are: the total heat transfer coefficient (W/°C) between the air in the building and the interior surface of the external wall (K_2), between the interior surface and the exterior surface of the external wall (K_4), between the exterior surface of the external wall and the external air (K_5), and between the air in the building and the external air through light-weighted structures such as windows (K_3), the total thermal capacity (J/°C) of the indoor air (C_a), external wall (C_{e1} and C_{e2}), constant α and β, and the time constant of the boiler (τ_0). The Simplex optimization [12] was used to commission the inferential sensor based on a short-term monitoring data that contains the time-dependent value of all the inputs and the output. It is worth mentioning that the value of the output of the inferential sensor (T_a) is not available for long-term operation.

The results presented in [7] indicate that this physical-model based inferential sensor is capable of estimating the overall average air temperature in the building with a satisfactory level of accuracy if it is commissioned appropriately. However, if the quality of the data used for the commissioning is not good or the optimization process terminated at local extremes, the inferential sensor fails to function properly.

The neuro-fuzzy based inferential sensor has the same inputs that are used by the physical-model based inferential sensor. But it has a different output, which indicates the level of the heating load in the building (E_d) rather than the overall average air temperature in the building.

Fig. 4 shows a diagram of the proposed inferential sensor, which is based on an Adaptive Neural Fuzzy Interference System (ANFIS) [13]. The ANFIS is trained

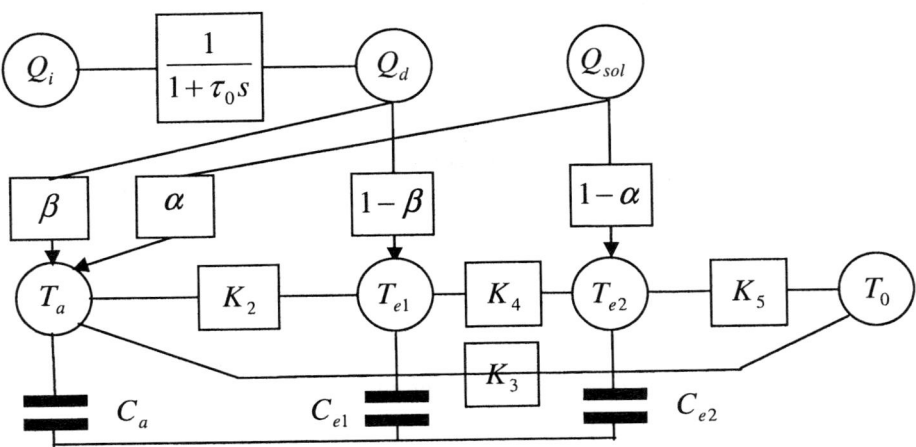

Fig. 3. An electronic analogue of the physical inferential model

using the same short-term monitoring data that was used to commission the physical-model based inferential sensor.

The output of the inferential sensor is used to vary the set-point of the hot water temperature as follows (1) When E_d is Low, the temperature of the hot water ranges from 55 °C to 65 °C; (2) When E_d is Medium, the temperature of the hot water ranges from 65 °C to 75 °C; (3) When E_d is High, the temperature of the hot water ranges from 75 °C to 85 °C

Thus the overall energy performance of the space heating system can be improved if the proposed inferential sensor can correctly predict the heating load based on the three inputs.

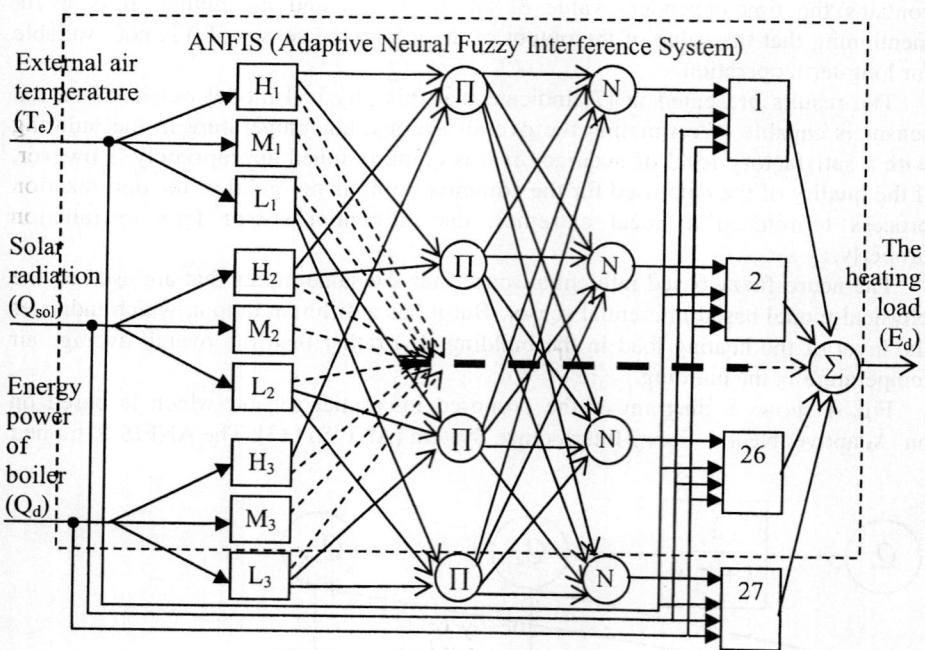

Fig. 4 Diagram of the proposed inferential sensor

4 Assessing the Performance of the Proposed Inferential Sensor

In the simulation studies, the simulator can produce the time-dependent values of the following variables that are used to assess the performance of the proposed inferential sensor (t is the time in seconds and i refers to the number of the thermal zones): (1) The total heating load: $E_h(t)$ in kW; (2) The air temperature in each of the thermal zones: $T_a(i, t)$ in °C; (3) The external air temperature: T_e in °C; (4) The solar radiation: Q_{sol} in W. The value of $E_h(t)$ is normalized by:

$$e(t) = \frac{E_d(t)}{E_{d\_max}} \tag{1}$$

where $E_{d\_max} = \max\limits_{t\in[t_1\ t_2]}(E_d(t))$ [t_1 t_2] is the heating period concerned.

Then e(t) represents the actual heating load of the heating system. The comparison between e(t) and the output of the inferential sensor ($E_d(t)$) indicates how accurate the inferential sensor is. In the field trial, the actual energy power of the boiler is monitored, resulting in an array of the heating capacity. In the meantime, the indoor thermal environment is being monitored. If the indoor thermal environment falls into the comfort range, the monitored heating capacity is regarded as the heating load (e˙(t)). This is compared with the output of the inferential sensor to identify the accuracy.

5 Simulation Study

The testing conditions are as follows: (1) The building was divided into 6 zones. The terminal devices are hot water radiators. The radiators in each of the thermal zones are simulated as a single heat emitter; (2) The air temperature set-point at the individual thermal zones is 20 °C during the occupancy period, i.e. from 09:00 to 18:00. Outside of the occupancy period the air temperature set-point was reduced to 17 °C; (3) The performance of the inferential sensor in two typical types of heating system has been studied. The first type is the heating systems with radiators well controlled by TRVs. The second is the heating system with radiators that are not controlled automatically; (4) A week of training data has been created using the simulator and has been used to train the ANFIS; (5) The sampling time is 30 minutes.

Fig. 5 shows a daily comparison between the actual heating load and the output of the inferential sensor in a heating system with radiators well controlled by TRVs. Fig. 6 shows the result obtained in a heating system with radiators that are not controlled automatically. These figures shows that the neuro-fuzzy based inferential sensor is able to accurately estimate the heating load of heating systems, no matter whether the heat emitters are controlled automatically or not, once it has been commissioned properly. Figure 5 and 6 show that the daily profile of the heating load in heating systems with the radiators controlled by TRVs fluctuates more dramatically than in the other type of heating system. This can be explained because the actual heating load is dominated by the external weather if the radiators are controlled properly. However the actual heating load is dominated by the indoor air temperature, which only exhibits a small range of variation, in heating systems with radiators that are not controlled automatically.

6 Experimental Study

The neuro-fuzzy based inferential sensor has been implemented in a microprocessor-based prototype, which has been tested in real heating systems through field trials.

Two test cases will be discussed here. Test case 1 was conducted in a commercial office building with one boiler that can be operated between 50% and 100% of the nominal heating capacity. The total floor area of this building is around 2000 m². There are 120 individual offices and three big lecture theatres. The heat emitters are radiators that are controlled by TRVs.

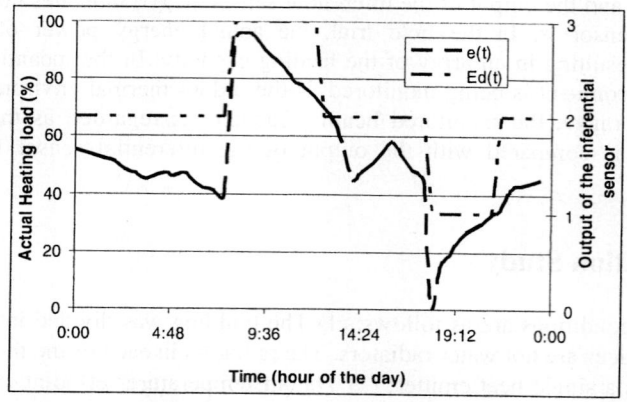

Fig. 5. Daily comparison between the actual heating load e(t) and the output of the inferential sensor $E_d(t)$ (in a heating system with radiators well controlled by TRVs)

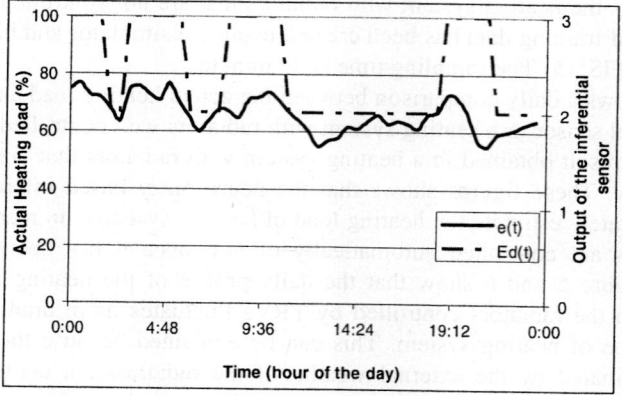

Fig. 6. Annual comparison between the actual heating load e(t) and the output of the inferential sensor Ed(t) (in a heating system with radiators well controlled by TRVs)

The test lasted for two consecutive heating seasons. The data logged in the first two weeks was selected to train the inferential sensor. Fig. 7 compares the actual heating load of the building with the output of the inferential sensor during a typical day. It shows that the neuro-fuzzy based inferential sensor accurately estimated the heating load of the building. An analysis on the data of the entire heating season revealed that during 96.5% of the heating period, the inferential sensor could accurately predict the level of the heating load.

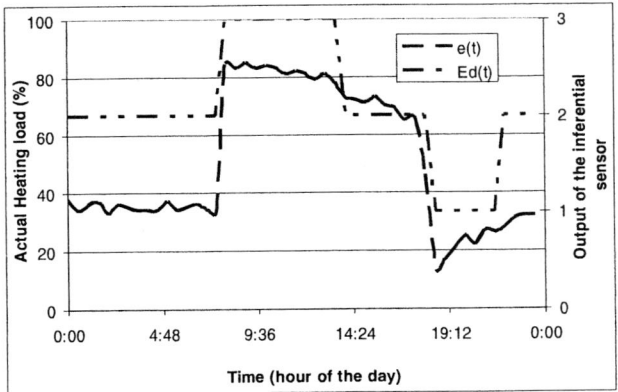

Fig. 7. Daily comparison between the actual heating load e(t) and the output of the inferential sensor Ed(t) (Test case 1)

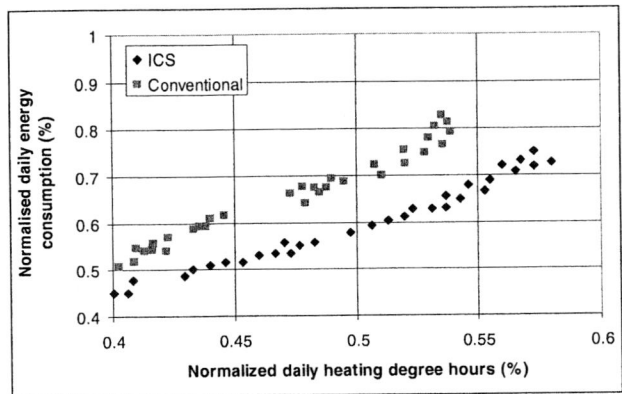

Fig. 8. The energy performance of the building when the heating system is controlled by the conventional controller and by the inferential sensor supported controller (Test case 2)

Test case 2 was conducted in a residential house located in Toronto. The total floor area of this house is about 250 m². The house is heated by a forced warm air heating system. A furnace is used to warm the air being circulated between the furnace and the individual rooms in the house. There 4 regular occupants living in the house. It was realized that the inferential sensor was designed initially for use in hydraulic space heating system. However, it is also applicable in forced warm air heating systems because both heating systems share the same heat transfer principles. In this test, the author was able to make a comparative study on the performance between the conventional control unit and the one supported by the inferential sensor. In this case, the output of the inferential sensor was used to determine the temperature of the supply air from the furnace. Fig. 8 compares the energy efficiency of the house when the heating system was controlled by the conventional controller and by the inferential sensor supported control system (ICS). The result shows that under the similar climatic conditions (represented by the normalized heating degree hours), the energy consumption is 12% lower when the heating system is controlled by the ICS controller than when it is controlled by the conventional controller. This is because the inferential sensor could accurately estimate the actual heating load of the building and the estimate was used to determine the optimal temperature for the supply air.

7 Conclusions and Future work

A neuro-fuzzy based inferential sensor can accurately estimate the heating load of a building based on the same information used by the physical-model based inferential sensor. The inferential sensor can be commissioned using short-term monitoring data. The inferential sensor is also applicable in forced warm air heating systems. When the inferential sensor is incorporated with the conventional heating controller, the overall performance of the building can be improved significantly.

Currently The following research activities being currently carried out include: (1) Investigating how the quality of the training data influences the long-term accuracy of the inferential sensor and the control performance of the inferential sensor supported controllers; (2) Studying whether the inferential sensor can be adapted to estimate other important control variables than can not be easily measured by conventional building automation system.

Acknowledgement

This paper is partially based on my PhD work carried out in the University of Oxford, which was financially supported by the Foundation of the Built Environment, the UK, and partially supported by the Faculty of Engineering and Applied Science, Ryerson University, Canada through the New Faculty Research Fund.

References

1. Z. Liao and A. L. Dexter (2003), An inferential control scheme for optimising the operation of boilers in multi-zone heating systems, Building Services Engineering Research and Technology, Vol.24, No.4, pp. 245~256
2. Z. Liao, A. L. Dexter, and M. Swainson (2004), On the control of heating systems in the UK, Buildings and Environment, Vol. 40 (3), pp. 343-351.
3. G. J. Levermore (1992), Building Management Systems − Application to Heating and Control, E & FN Spon, London, Glasgow, New York, Tokyo, Melbourne, Madras. ISBN 0-419-15290-3

4. BRECSU (1996), General Information Report No. 40: Heating systems and their control, Energy Efficiency Best Practice Programme, DETR, the UK.
5. Z. Liao and A. L. Dexter (2004), The potential for energy saving in heating systems through improving boiler controls, Energy and Buildings, Vol. 36(3), pp. 261-271.
6. Z. Liao (2004), An inferential control scheme for optimizing the control of boilers in multiple-zone heating systems, PhD Thesis, the University of Oxford.
7. Z. Liao and A. L. Dexter (2004), A simplified physical model for estimating the average air temperature in multi-zone heating systems, Buildings and Environment, Vol. 39(9), pp. 1009-1018
8. Z. Liao and A. L. Dexter (2005), An experimental study on an inferential control scheme for optimising the control of boilers in multi-zone heating systems, Energy and Buildings, Vol. 37(1), pp. 55-63
9. Liao Z and Parand F (2001), Controller Efficiency Improvement for Commercial and Industrial Gas and Oil Fired Boilers, Building Research Establishment (BRE), A CRAFT project, contract JOE-CT98-7010. 1999-2001.
10. Martin A J, Banyard C P (1998), Application guide AG7/98: library of system control strategies. The Building Services Research and Information Association (BSRIA), ISBN 0-86022 497.
11. Clarke J (2001), Energy simulation in building design (2nd Edition), Butterworth-Heinemann, ISBN 0750650826.
12. Spendley W, Hext G R, Himsworth F R (1963), Sequential application of simplex designs in optimization and evolutionary operation, Technometrics, 1962;4;441-61.
13. Jang S R, Sun C T, Mizutani E (1997), Neuro-Fuzzy and Soft Computing: a computational approach to learning and machine intelligence, Matlab Curriculum Series, Prentice Hall, ISBN 0-13-261066-3.

A Hybrid Neuro-fuzzy Approach for Spinal Force Evaluation in Manual Materials Handling Tasks

Yanfeng Hou[1], Jacek M. Zurada[1],
Waldemar Karwowski[2], and William S. Marras[3]

[1] Department of Electrical and Computer Engineering, University of Louisville,
y0hou002@louisville.edu
[2] Department of Industrial Engineering, University of Louisville,
karwowski@louisville.edu
[3] Biodynamics Laboratory, Institute for Ergonomics, The Ohio State University,
marras.1@osu.edu

Abstract. Evaluation of the spinal forces from kinematics data is very complicated because it involves the handling of relationship between kinematic variables and electromyography (EMG) responses, as well as the relationship between EMG responses and the forces. A recurrent fuzzy neural network (RFNN) model is proposed to establish the kinematics-EMG-force relationship and model the dynamics of muscular activities. The EMG signals are used as an intermediate output and are fed back to the input layer. Since the EMG signal is a direct reflection of muscular activities, the feedback of this model has a physical meaning. It expresses the dynamics of muscular activities in a straightforward way and takes advantage from the recurrent property. The trained model can then have the forces predicted directly from kinematic variables while bypassing the procedure of measuring EMG signals and avoiding the use of biomechanics model. A learning algorithm is derived for the RFNN.

1 Introduction

The loads on the lumbar spine during manual lifting are very useful in judging if such a task is risky. Studying the forces applied to the lumbar spine is fundamental to the understanding of low back injury [1]. Biomechanical models are often used to obtain the forces applied to the lumbar spine from the measured electromyographic responses of trunk muscles during the lifting motions. The EMG signals are measured because they directly reflect the muscular activities [2]. However, the measuring of EMG signals is costly and the use of biomechanical models is time consuming.

EMG signals are also related to the kinematic characteristics in the motion. The kinematic variables (with other auxiliary variables) can be used to evaluate the EMG signals generated in the muscles during the motion [8][9]. Thus we may be able to connect the spinal forces with kinematic variables through EMG signals. We want to develop a model that can express the kinematics-EMG-force relationship and predict forces on lumbar spine without the procedure of measuring EMG signals and the use of biomechanics model.

To Evaluate the dynamic forces on lumbar spine we build a recurrent fuzzy neural network model. There are several ways to provide feedback connections. In [13] and [14], the output of each membership function is fed back to itself to achieve the recurrent property. However, the fuzzy rules obtained from the model can not offer a clear understanding to the system. In the premise of the rules, the inputs are combined with the feedback of the outputs of their own membership functions. The rules become hard to understand and not meaningful in explaining the behavior of the system. The only function of the feedback is to add a memory element to the model.

In [15] and [16], the output of all rule nodes, the firing strength, is fed back. It serves as an internal variable. The rules generated by the model have a form like:

IF *the external variables* (at t) are A and *the internal variables* (at t) are B, THEN *the outputs* (at $t+1$) are C and the *internal variables* (at $t+1$) are D.

A, B, C, D are fuzzy sets in the above rule.

Although the internal variables play a role in the fuzzy rules and contribute to the model, it is not useful to us in understanding the system under consideration. What we attempt to know is the relationship between the input and output of the system.

In [17] and [18], the final output of the network is fed back to the input layer. In [17], the feedback is multiplied with the external inputs of the model. Thus, the inputs of the first layer becomes:

$$net_i^1 = \prod_o x_i^1 \cdot w_{oi} \cdot y_o^4(t-1) \qquad (1)$$

where x_i^1 is the external input; w_{oi} are the weights of the feedback connections; $y_o^4(t-1)$ is the output of the model at $t-1$; o is the number of outputs. As we can see, the rules obtained from the model also lose their clear physical meaning. In [18], the feedback of the outputs is not combined with other signals. It is fed to the input layer as regular input variables. However, the membership functions used for the feedback connections are of this form:

$$\mu = exp(-(w \cdot y_o^4(t-1))^2), \qquad (2)$$

where w denotes the weights of the feedback connections. Formula (2) is actually a Gaussian membership function centered at zero with one adjustable parameter of width. The advantages of doing so are that the network has less parameters and the update rules for the tuning parameters are easier to calculate. However, setting all the feedback membership functions' centers as a fixed value of zero may decrease the effectiveness of the feedback variables.

In our model, we use the EMG signals as an intermediate output and feed them back to the input layer. By doing that, more information (EMG) was provided to the model and the feedback of the intermediate output has a physical meaning (the direct relationship of EMG-force). This reflects the dynamics of the system in a clear and straightforward way. At the same time, the advantages of recurrent property is utilized. The rules generated from the model can be easily interpreted and can help us understand the muscular activities better.

2 Model Construction

We come up with a recurrent fuzzy neural network model which takes the kinematics data and EMG data at time t and evaluates the spinal forces and EMG signals at time $t + 1$. The EMG signals of ten trunk muscles are scaled and delayed before they are fed back to the input layer. The delay of EMG is used to represent the muscular activation dynamic properties. The interaction between muscles influences the EMG and the forces on the spine. By presenting the previous EMG to the input, we hope the modle can take such interaction into account. The proposed system structure is shown in Figure 1. As we can see

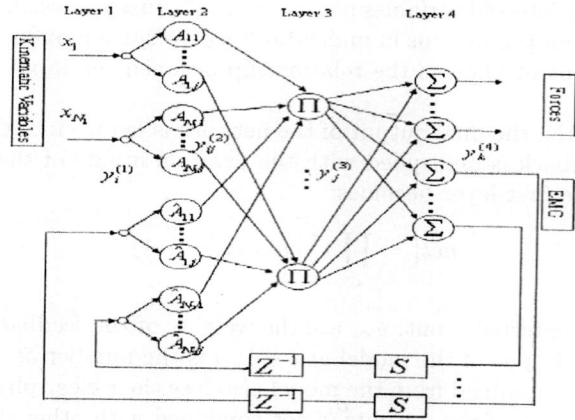

Fig. 1. The proposed recurrent fuzzy neural network structure (Z^{-1} is a unit delay operator and S is a scale operator)

in Figure 1, the direct physical relationships (kinematics-EMG and EMG-force) reside in the model. Three forces on the lumbar spine and ten EMG signals of trunk muscles are the model outputs. Twelve kinematic variables and ten EMG feedback signals are the model inputs.

The function of each layer in Figure 1 is described as follows:

Layer 1 is the input layer. It includes two parts. One is the kinematic variables and the other one is the feedback of EMG signals. They are passed to the second layer.

For external inputs,
$$y_i^{(1)} = x_i, \tag{3}$$

$i = 1, 2, ..., N_1$, where $N1$ stands for the twelve kinematic variables.

For the internal (feedback) inputs,
$$y_i^{(1)} = y_k^{(4)}(t-1) \tag{4}$$

$y_k^{(4)}(t-1)$ is the kth output of layer 4 at time $(t-1)$, denoting the EMG feedback. $i = N_1 + 1, N_1 + 2, ..., N$, and $N = N_1 + N_2$, where N_2 stands for the number of EMG feedback signals.

Layer 2 is the input fuzzification layer, which represents linguistic sets in antecedent fuzzy membership functions. Each neuron describes a membership function and encodes the center and width of membership functions. The output of this layer is the degree of membership of each input:

For external inputs, the following Gaussian membership function is used:
$$y_{ij}^{(2)} = exp(-(\frac{y_i^{(1)} - m_{ij}}{\sigma_{ij}})^2) \tag{5}$$

$i = 1, 2, ..., N_1$, $j = 1, 2, ..., M$, where M is the number of rules.

For the internal inputs, the following sigmoid membership function is used:
$$y_{ij}^{(2)} = exp(-(\frac{y_i^{(1)} - \hat{m}_{ij}}{\hat{\sigma}_{ij}})^2) \tag{6}$$

$i = N_1 + 1, N_1 + 2, ..., N$ and $j = 1, 2, ..., M$.

Layer 3 computes the firing strength. Nodes in this layer perform the product operation. The links establish the antecedent relation with an "AND" operation for each fuzzy set combination (both the external input and the feedback). The output of this layer is the firing strength of each fuzzy rule:

$$y_j^{(3)} = \prod_{i=1}^{M} y_{ij}^{(2)} = \prod_{i=1}^{N_1} exp(-(\frac{y_i^{(1)} - m_{ij}}{\sigma_{ij}})^2) \prod_{i=N_1+1}^{N} exp(-(\frac{y_i^{(1)} - \hat{m}_{ij}}{\hat{\sigma}_{ij}})^2) \tag{7}$$

where $j = 1, 2, ..., M$.

Layer 4 is the defuzzification layer. The output of this layer is the overall output:
$$y_k^{(4)} = \sum_{j=1}^{M} W_{jk} y_j^{(3)} (\sum_{j=1}^{M} y_j^{(3)})^{-1} \tag{8}$$

$k = 1, 2, ..., K$, where K is the number of outputs.

This is a fuzzy system model with learning capabilities. It uses a singleton to represent the output fuzzy set of each fuzzy rule. The product operator instead of minimum operator is used for the calculation of the firing strength because the calculation of the partial derivatives is easier for the product operator.

The rules generated for the above model are in such form: the jth rule:

IF $Kine_1(t)$ is μ_{1j} and ... and $Kine_{(N1)}(t)$ is $\mu_{(N1)j}$
and $EMG_1(t)$ is $\hat{\mu}_{1j}$ and ... and $EMG_{(N2)}(t)$ is $\hat{\mu}_{(N2)j}$
THEN $Force_1(t+1)$ is O_{1j} and ... and $Force_{K1}(t+1)$ is $O_{(K1)j}$
and $EMG_1(t+1)$ is Y_{1j} and ... and $EMG_{(N2)}(t+1)$ is $Y_{(N2)j}$

where μ_{ij} ($i = 1, 2, ..., N1; j = 1, 2, ..., M$) are fuzzy sets of $Kine_i$ (the ith kinematic variable). $\hat{\mu}_{ij}$ ($i = 1, 2, ..., N2; j = 1, 2, ..., M$) are fuzzy sets of EMG_i. O_{kj} ($k = 1, 2, ..., K1$) are the output singletons for forces. Y_{kj} ($k = 1, 2, ..., N2$) are the output singletons for EMG signals.

The forces predicted for time $t + 1$ depend on not only the inputs at time t, but also the predicted EMG at time t, which again depend on the previous inputs. This is a dynamic approach that can represent the dynamic properties of the forces better than a feedforward network.

The above rules represent the relationships between kinematic variables, EMG signals and forces. They can be decomposed into three subsets of fuzzy rules as follows.

The Kinematics-EMG relationship:
IF $Kine_1$ is μ_{1j} and ... and $Kine_{(N1)}$ is $\mu_{(N1)j}$
THEN EMG_1 is Y_{1j} and ... and $EMG_{(N2)}$ is $Y_{(N2)j}$

The EMG-Force relationship:
IF EMG_1 is $\hat{\mu}_{1j}$ and ... and $EMG_{(N2)}$ is $\hat{\mu}_{(N2)j}$
THEN $Force_1$ is O_{1j} and ... and $Force_{K1}$ is $O_{(K1)j}$

The Kinematics-Force relationship:
IF $Kine_1$ is μ_{1j} and ... and $Kine_{(N1)}$ is $\mu_{(N1)j}$
THEN $Force_1$ is O_{1j} and ... and $Force_{K1}$ is $O_{(K1)j}$

These Kinematics-EMG-Force relationships are knowledge we would like to find out.

2.1 Structure Adaptation and Parameter Tuning

During the training process, both the premise and the consequence parameters are tuned simultaneously. This approach involves two phases, structure adaptation and parameter tuning. The fuzzy rules are created and tuned based on the training data.

At first, the rule base contains only one rule defined by the first input-output data pair. Then Additional rules are created during the training process using other input-output pairs. When the new training pattern does not excite any of the existing fuzzy rules, a new fuzzy rule should be created. If the firing strength $S_u > \beta$, then the rule base is unchanged and perform the gradient training to match the new sample pair. If the firing strength $S_u < \beta$, then a new rule is created. β is a threshold defined as the least acceptable degree of excitation of the existing rule base. It is important that this predefined threshold should decay during the learning process. Otherwise new rules may continually be added to the model.

The free parameters (the membership functions of the external variables, the membership functions of the internal variables, and the weights of the consequence singleton) in the fuzzy inference mechanism are then tuned after new rules are created. Parameter tuning is carried out simultaneously with the structure adaptation. The ordered derivative [19] is used to derive the learning algorithm.

The error function to be minimized is

$$E(t+1) = \frac{1}{2}\sum_{k=1}^{K}\varepsilon(t+1)^2 = \frac{1}{2}\sum_{k=1}^{K}(d_k(t+1) - y_k^{(4)}(t+1))^2 \qquad (9)$$

where $d_k(t+1)$ is the target and $y_k^{(4)}(t+1)$ is the output of the model (the output of layer 4).

The update rule for the output singleton w_{kj} (the weights of the connections between layer 3 and layer 4) is

$$w_{kj}(t+1) = w_{kj}(t) - \eta \frac{\partial E(t+1)}{\partial w_{kj}} \qquad (10)$$

where

$$\frac{\partial E(t+1)}{\partial w_{kj}} = \frac{\partial E(t+1)}{\partial y_k^{(4)}}\frac{\partial y_k^{(4)}}{\partial w_{kj}} = \varepsilon(t+1)\frac{y_j^{(3)}}{\sum_{j=1}^{M} y_j^{(3)}} \qquad (11)$$

The centers of the membership functions of external variables are m_{ij}. The update rule is

$$m_{ij}(t+1) = m_{ij}(t) - \eta \frac{\partial E(t+1)}{\partial m_{ij}} \qquad (12)$$

where

$$\frac{\partial E(t+1)}{\partial m_{ij}} = \frac{\partial E(t+1)}{\partial y_j^{(3)}}\frac{\partial y_j^{(3)}}{\partial m_{ij}} = \sum_{k=1}^{K}\varepsilon(t+1) \cdot D \cdot \frac{\partial y_j^{(3)}}{\partial m_{ij}} \qquad (13)$$

in which D is defined as follows for notation simplicity

$$D = \frac{(w_{kj} - y_k^{(4)}(t+1))}{\sum_{j=1}^{M} y_j^{(3)}} \qquad (14)$$

From formula 7 we get

$$y_j^{(3)} = exp\left(-\sum_{i=1}^{N_1}\frac{(y_i^{(1)}(t) - m_{ij})^2}{\sigma_{ij}^2} - \sum_{i=N_1+1}^{N}\frac{(y_i^{(4)}(t) - \hat{m}_{ij})^2}{\hat{\sigma}_{ij}^2}\right) \qquad (15)$$

in which $y_i^{(4)}(t)$ again depends on m_{ij}.

Then the derivative can be written as

$$\frac{\partial y_j^{(3)}}{\partial m_{ij}} = y_j^{(3)} \left(A_1 - \sum_{i=N_1+1}^{N} B \cdot \frac{\partial y_j^{(4)}(t)}{\partial m_{ij}} \right) \qquad (16)$$

where A_1 and B are defined as

$$A_1 = \frac{2(y_i^{(1)}(t) - m_{ij})}{\sigma_{ij}^2} \qquad (17)$$

$$B = \frac{2(y_i^{(4)}(t) - \hat{m}_{ij})}{\hat{\sigma}_{ij}^2} \qquad (18)$$

Finally a recursive function is obtained for $\frac{\partial y_j^{(4)}}{\partial m_{ij}}$.

$$\frac{\partial y_j^{(4)}(t)}{\partial m_{ij}} = D \cdot y_j^{(3)} \cdot \left(A_1(t-1) - \sum_{i=N_1+1}^{N} B(t-1) \cdot \frac{\partial y_j^{(4)}(t-1)}{\partial m_{ij}} \right) \qquad (19)$$

The update rules for other parameters ($\sigma_{ij}, \hat{m}_{ij}, \hat{\sigma}_{ij}$) are omitted here. The initial values of $\frac{\partial y_j^{(4)}(t)}{\partial m_{ij}}, \frac{\partial y_j^{(4)}(t)}{\partial \sigma_{ij}}, \frac{\partial y_j^{(4)}(t)}{\partial \hat{m}_{ij}}$ and $\frac{\partial y_j^{(4)}(t)}{\partial \hat{\sigma}_{ij}}$ are set to zero.

All the parameters are tuned during the training process when new data pairs are presented to the network.

3   Simulations and Results

This section shows the results and the performance of the proposed model. We evaluated the performance of the proposed recurrent fuzzy neural network with two kinds of data. One is the sagittal symmetric motions, while the other one is unsymmetrical motions. To make the results comparable, similar task variables are selected for these two motions. Both motions are done with two hands and controlled placement. The lift frequency is 2 lifts/min; the weight of object is 25 lbs; the origin height is 60 cm; the origin distance is 45; the destination height is 105 cm; and the destination distance is 55 cm.

For the sagittal symmetric motions, 720 training patterns are used. The learning rate of the parameters of feedback connections ($\hat{m}_{ij}$ and $\hat{\sigma}_{ij}$) is $\hat{\eta} = 0.02$. The learning rate for other parameters (m_{ij}, σ_{ij} and w_{kj}) is $\eta = 0.01$. The initial threshold β for firing strength is set as 0.2.

As stated above, the learning rates for the parameters of external inputs (kinematic variables) and for the parameters of internal inputs (EMG feedback) are different. Since the initial values of parameters of internal inputs are small random values while the initial values of parameters of external inputs are good values with physical meaning, the convergence of the latter is faster than the convergence of the former. Figure 2 was obtained after 200 epoches. In this figure, both the forces and the EMG signals are predicted well, which means the

A Hybrid Neuro-fuzzy Approach for Spinal Force Evaluation 1223

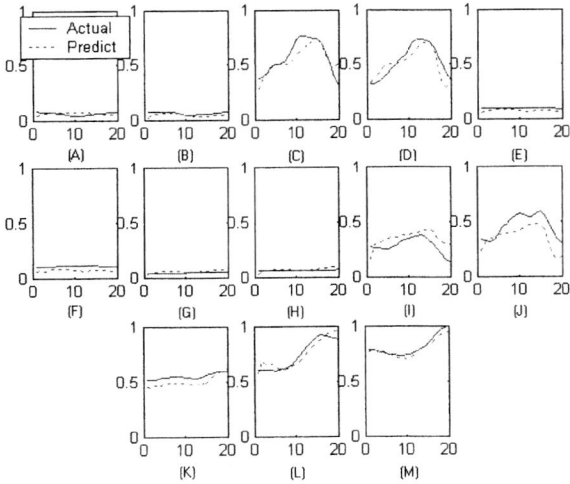

Fig. 2. Output after 200 training epoches (the first 10 are EMG signals, the last three are forces). (A) RLD, (B) LLD, (C) RES, (D) LES, (E) RRA, (F) LRA, (G) REO, (H) LEO, (I) RIO, (J) LIO, (K) Lateral shear force, (L) A-P shear force, and (M) spinal compression

parameters of both the external inputs and the feedback are well trained after 200 epoches.

The rules obtained are of the following form:

IF $Kine_1(t)$ is $\mu(0.443, 0.832)$ and $Kine_2(t)$ is $\mu(0.521, 1.334)$ and $Kine_3(t)$ is $\mu(0.714, 1.587)$ and $Kine_4(t)$ is $\mu(-1.654, 1.583)$ and $Kine_5(t)$ is $\mu(0.476, 1.011)$ and $Kine_6(t)$ is $\mu(-0.803, 1.486)$ and $Kine_7(t)$ is $\mu(-1.770, 2.118)$ and $Kine_8(t)$ is $\mu(0.746, 1.342)$ and $Kine_9(t)$ is $\mu(0.833, 1.535)$ and $Kine_{10}(t)$ is $\mu(0.493, 1.566)$ and $Kine_{11}(t)$ is $\mu(-0.017, 1.833)$ and $Kine_{12}(t)$ is $\mu(-0.387, 1.322)$

and $EMG_1(t)$ is $\mu(0.025, 1.258)$ and $EMG_2(t)$ is $\mu(0.025, 1.259)$ and $EMG_3(t)$ is $\mu(0.006, 0.992)$ and $EMG_4(t)$ is $\mu(0.005, 0.074)$ and $EMG_5(t)$ is $\mu(0.023, 1.249)$ and $EMG_6(t)$ is $\mu(0.025, 1.259)$ and $EMG_7(t)$ is $\mu(0.029, 1.263)$ and $EMG_8(t)$ is $\mu(0.019, 1.266)$ and $EMG_9(t)$ is $\mu(0.009, 0.805)$ and $EMG_{10}(t)$ is $\mu(0.104, 1.246)$

THEN $Force_1(t+1)$ is 0.443 and $Force_2(t+1)$ is 0.559 and $Force_3(t+1)$ is 0.758

and $EMG_1(t+1)$ is 0.033 and $EMG_2(t+1)$ is 0.120 and $EMG_3(t+1)$ is 0.267 and $EMG_4(t+1)$ is 0.318 and $EMG_5(t+1)$ is 0.055 and $EMG_6(t+1)$ is 0.057 and $EMG_7(t+1)$ is 0.061 and $EMG_8(t+1)$ is 0.044 and $EMG_9(t+1)$ is 0.218 and $EMG_{10}(t+1)$ is 0.102

We also can decompose the above fuzzy rule into three subsets as we did previously to understand the system better.

4 Conclusions

A spinal force prediction model was developed using a recurrent fuzzy neural network. The EMG feedback represents the muscular activation dynamics better. At the same time, it brings more information to the model and utilizes the advantages of recurrent properties. The model predicts forces directly from kinematics data, avoiding EMG measurements and the use of biomechanics model. EMG signals are obtained as byproduct. It can help us understand the relationships between kinematic variables and EMG signals and spinal forces. An adaptive learning algorithm is derived for the recurrent fuzzy neural network.

Acknowledgment

This study was conducted under a research grant on the "Development of a Neuro-Fuzzy System to Predict Spinal Loading as a Function of Multiple Dimensions of Risk", sponsored by the National Institute for Occupational Safety and Health (DHHS).

References

1. D.G. Lloyd, Besier, T.F., "An EMG-driven Musculoskeletal Model to Estimate Muscle Forces and Knee Joint Moments in Vivo", *Journal of Biomechanics*, 36 (2003), pp. 765–776.
2. P.A. Crosby, "Use of surface electromyogram as a measure of dynamic force in human limb muscles", *Med. and Biol. Eng. and Comput.*, vol. 16, 1978, pp. 519–524.
3. L. Wang, T.S. Buchanan, "Prediction of Joint Moments Using a Neural Network Model of Muscle Activations from EMG Signals", *IEEE Trans. on Neural Systems and Rehabilitation Engineering*, vol. 10, no. 1, Mar. 2002, pp. 30–37
4. J.J. Luh, G.C. Chang, C.K. Cheng, J.S. Lai, T.S. Kuo,, "Isokinetic elbow joint torques estimation form surface EMG and joint kinematic data: Using an artificial neural network model", *J. Electromyogr. Kinesiol.*, vol. l, no. 9, 1999, pp. 173-183.
5. M.M. Liu, W. Herzog, H. H. Savelberg, "Dynamic muscle force predictions from EMG: An artificial neural network approach", *J. Electromyogr. Kinesiol.*, vol. 9, 1999, pp. 391-400.
6. S.E. Hussein, M.H., Granat, "Intention detection using a neuro-fuzzy EMG classifier", *Engineering in Medicine and Biology Magazine, IEEE*, vol. 21, no. 6, Nov.-Dec. pp. 123–129
7. K. Kiguchi, T. Tanaka, T. Fukuda, "Neuro-fuzzy control of a robotic exoskeleton with EMG signals", *IEEE Transactions on Fuzzy Systems*, vol. 12, no. 4, Aug. 2004 pp. 481–490
8. Y. Hou, J.M. Zurada, W. Karwowski, "Prediction of EMG Signals of Trunk Muscles in Manual Lifting Using a Neural Network Model", *Proc. of the Int. Joint Conf. on Neural Networks*, Jul. 25-29, 2004, pp. 1935–1940
9. Y. Hou, J.M. Zurada, W. Karwowski, "Prediction of Dynamic Forces on Lumbar Joint Using a Recurrent Neural Network Model", *Proc. of the 2004 Int. Conf. on Machine Learning and Applications (ICMLA'04)*, Dec. 16-18, 2004, pp. 360-365

10. S. Wu and M. J. Er, "Dynamic fuzzy neural networks-a novel approach to function approximation," *IEEE Trans. on Systems, Man and Cybernetics* B, vol. 30, Apr. 2000, pp. 358-364.
11. S. Wu, M. J. Er, and Y. Gao, "A fast approach for automatic generation of fuzzy rules by generalized dynamic fuzzy neural networks," *IEEE Trans. on Fuzzy Systems*, vol. 9, Aug. 2001, pp. 578-594.
12. C.F. Juang and C.T. Lin, "An on-line self-constructing neural fuzzy inference network and its applications", *IEEE Trans. on Fuzzy Systems*, vol. 6, pp. 12-32, Feb. 1998.
13. C.H. Lee and C.C. Teng, "Identification and control of dynamic systems using recurrent fuzzy neural networks", *IEEE Trans. on Fuzzy Systems*, vol. 8 , no. 4 , Aug. 2000 pp. 349–366.
14. C.M. Lin and C.F. Hsu, "Supervisory recurrent fuzzy neural network control of wing rock for slender delta wings", *IEEE Trans. on Fuzzy Systems*, vol. 12 , no. 5 , Oct. 2004 pp. 733–742.
15. C.F. Juang, "A TSK-type recurrent fuzzy network for dynamic systems processing by neural network and genetic algorithms", *IEEE Trans. on Fuzzy Systems*, vol. 10 , no. 2 , Apr. 2002 pp. 155–170
16. F.J. Lin, R.J. Wai, "Hybrid control using recurrent fuzzy neural network for linear-induction motor servo drive", *IEEE Trans. on Fuzzy Systems*, vol. 9 , no. 1 , Jan. 2001 pp. 68–90.
17. F.J. Lin, R.J. Wai, C.M. Hong, "Hybrid supervisory control using recurrent fuzzy neural network for tracking periodic inputs", *IEEE Trans. on Neural Networks*, vol. 12 , no. 1 , Feb. 2001 pp. 102–115.
18. Y.C Wang, D. Zipser, "A learning algorithm for continually running recurrent neural networks", *Neural Comput.*, vol. 1 , no. 2 , 1989 pp. 270–280.
19. R.J. Williams, C.J Chien, C.C. Teng, "Direct adaptive iterative learning control of nonlinear systems using an output-recurrent fuzzy neural network", *IEEE Trans. on Systems, Man, and Sybernetics*, vol. 34 , no. 3 , Jun. 2004 pp. 1348–1359.
20. Y. Hou, J.M. Zurada, W. Karwowski, "Identification of Input Variables using Fuzzy Average with Fuzzy Cluster Distribution"; submitted to *IEEE Trans. on Fuzzy Systems*.
21. S. Auephanwiriyakul, J.M. Keller, "Analysis and efficient implementation of a linguistic fuzzy c-means"; *IEEE Trans. on Fuzzy Systems*, vol. 10 , no. 5 , Oct. 2002 pp. 563 - 582
22. W. Lee, W. Karwowski, W.S. Marras, D. Rodrick, "A neuro-fuzzy model for estimating electromyographical activity of trunk muscles due to manual lifting", *Ergonomics* 46 (1-3), JAN 15 2003, pp. 285-309

Medicine Composition Analysis Based on PCA and SVM

Chaoyong Wang, Chunguo Wu, and Yanchun Liang*

College of Computer Science and Technology, Jilin University,
Key Laboratory of Symbol Computation and Knowledge Engineering of Ministry of Education,
Changchun 130012, China
ycliang@jlu.edu.cn

Abstract. Medicine analysis becomes more and more important in production and life, especially, the composition analysis of medicines. Available data are often characterized by the data with small amount and high dimensionality. Support vector machine (SVM) is an ideal algorithm for dealing with this kind of data. This paper presents a combined method of principal component analysis (PCA) and least square support vector machine (LS-SVM) to deal with the work of medicine composition analysis. The proposed method is applied to practical problems. Experiments demonstrate the predominance of the proposed method on both running time and prediction precision.

1 Introduction

In the course of producing and selling medicines, it is an important issue to measure principal medicines constituents (namely concentration) correctly and quickly. This offers not only the reference basis for medicine analysis and quality control in the process of production but also the security to the consumers. In recent years, the near-infrared spectroscopy detection technique has been developed rapidly in the medicine composition analysis field. This technique utilizes the measurement of the reflection rate or absorption rate of samples at different wavelengths in near-infrared region to get NIR (near-infrared) spectrum (namely input samples) [1], later utilizes predictability model to carry on the measurement of the concentration of the medicines composition.

Support vector machine (SVM) is a powerful new tool for prediction. SVM possesses a solid foundation of the complete theory and outstanding learning performance [2]. Recently SVM has been successfully applied to a wide variety of domains such as function estimation and pattern recognition. Related work on SVMs has been developed [3, 4].

2 LS-SVM Algorithm

Recently, Suykens J.A.K proposed a modified vision of SVM algorithm called least square support vector machine (LS-SVM). LS-SVM employs least squares loss function instead of quadratic programming of the classical SVM approach. The following LS-SVM formulation

---

* Corresponding author.

$$\min_{w,e} J(w,e) = \frac{1}{2} w^T w + \frac{1}{2} \gamma \sum_{k=1}^{N} e_k^2, \qquad (1)$$

is subject to the equality constraints $y_k = w^T \varphi(x_k) + b + e_k$. The corresponding Lagrangian can be defined as

$$L(w,b,e,\alpha) = J(w,e) - \sum_{k=1}^{N} \alpha_k (w^T \varphi(x_k) + b + e_k - y_k), \qquad (2)$$

where α_k are Lagrangian multipliers. As shown in [5], the optimality condition leads to the following linear system:

$$\begin{bmatrix} 0 & \vec{1}^T \\ \vec{1} & \Omega + \gamma^{-1} I \end{bmatrix} \begin{bmatrix} b \\ \alpha \end{bmatrix} = \begin{bmatrix} 0 \\ y \end{bmatrix}, \qquad (3)$$

where $y = [y_1, \cdots, y_N]^T$, $\vec{1} = [1, \cdots, 1]^T$, $\alpha = [\alpha_1, \cdots, \alpha_N]^T$ and the Mercer condition $\Omega_{kl} = \varphi(x_k)^T \varphi(x_l) = K(x_k, x_l)$ $(k, l = 1, \cdots, N)$ is used.

The LS-SVM function estimation is then constructed as follows:

$$y(x) = \sum_{k=1}^{N} \alpha_k K(x, x_k) + b, \qquad (4)$$

where α and b can be obtained according to Eq.(3). The Gaussian function can be chosen as kernel function [6].

3 Prediction of the Component Contents of Medicines Based on LS-SVM

3.1 Collection of the Sample Data

Utilizing near-infrared detection technique to get NIR (near-infrared) spectrum, we obtained sample data with the spectrum ranging from 1100 to 2500nm. Because of the difference of concentration conditions, absorption rates to different wavelength are distinct. We take the spectrum corresponding to certain concentration as an input sample and the concentration of the medicines composition as an output. In this way we obtain a data set with 35 samples and 1401 dimensions.

3.2 Data Processing

Though SVM algorithm can effectively handle the problem with high dimension, the linear dependence between different variables of samples influences the precision and generalization of SVM algorithm. On the contrary, principal component analysis (PCA) can deal with the linear dependence between different variables effectively and reduce the dimensions of the input samples and strengthen the ability of SVM algorithm to approximate to a non-linear function.

PCA is mainly applied to solve multi-variable problems. One of the main difficulties lying in multi-variable questions is that there are strong dependences among variables. Thus the whole information of the data will be overlapped and it is difficult to get the concise law. PCA is used to study how to convert multi-variable problems into that with less comprehensive variables (principal components). The comprehensive variables are the linear combinations of original variables. They are mutual independent and reflect the information of original variables.

The basic rule of the principal component analysis can be formulated as follows. Let $X=(x_1,x_2,\cdots,x_n)^T$ be an m-dimension, normal and stochastic column vector. Now we will change X into a new stochastic vector $F = (F_1, F_2, \cdots, F_m)^T$ and don't lose the whole information of X. This is equivalent to solve a set of linear equations.

$$\begin{cases} F_1 = u_{11}x_1 + u_{12}x_2 + \cdots + u_{1m}x_m \\ F_2 = u_{21}x_1 + u_{22}x_2 + \cdots + u_{2m}x_m \\ \vdots \\ F_m = u_{m1}x_1 + u_{m2}x_2 + \cdots + u_{mm}x_m \end{cases} \text{ or } F = U^T X \quad (5)$$

where F_i $(i=1,2,\cdots,m)$ is referred to as the i th principal component. F_1 holds most information of the original variables, namely its variance is the biggest. It is linear independent with other F_i $(i = 2,3,\cdots,m)$. F_2 has the second biggest variance among all F_i $(i=1,2,\cdots,m)$ and also is independent with other F_i $(i=1,3,\cdots,m)$. The rest have the same cases. Because the data obtained using the near-infrared spectroscopy have too many attributes and these attributes are highly dependent, which make the prediction very difficult. The PCA technique is used here to reduce the sample attributes/dimensions, which is necessary to improve the prediction quality and raise the efficiency. After the processing using the PCA, the number of attributes/dimensions is reduced to 100 from the original 1401. The following numerical experiments are based on the processed data.

4 Numerical Implementations

First of all, we utilize the PCA to preprocess the data. The results obtained from PCA-processed data are compared with those obtained from original data. From Table 1 it can be seen that the advantage is obvious in running time for PCA-processed data. The results show that the use of the PCA technique can reduce the running time significantly almost without precision loss.

In order to reflect the advantages of LS-SVM algorithm itself, we have selected a data set that has 30 principal components which is attained through PCA to train and test relevant models. When 3 kinds of different training samples, parameter of LS-SVM algorithm, parameters and network structure of BP algorithm are not the same, we take better test result to compare through training repeatedly. As table 2 shows, it can be found that the test errors of LS-SVM compared with the BP algorithm for various data sets are superior obviously. This demonstrates LS-SVM algorithm has possessed good generalization. It can also be found that the precision of LS-SVMS algorithm is higher than BP algorithm on the same training and test data set; in the test error, the precision of LS-SVM algorithm compared with BP algorithm is higher the largest very nearly 5 percentage points, and in the training error, LS-SVM algorithm can be negligible approximately, but BP algorithm does not have so good performance. At the same time, it can be found that when the training set is changed, the generalization error of LS-SVM algorithm is smaller than BP algorithm. Namely it has been proved that the degree of dependence to the sample data of LS-SVM algorithm is smaller than BP algorithm.

Table 1. Result Comparison of Data Processed

Training sample #	Testing sample #	PCA LS-SVM		Standard LS-SVM	
		Test MSE	Training time (s)	Test MSE	Training time (s)
20	15	0.013560	3.12×10^{-3}	0.014342	11.53×10^{-2}
18	17	0.013900	2.66×10^{-3}	0.013863	9.89×10^{-2}
15	20	0.013875	2.18×10^{-3}	0.013721	8.29×10^{-2}

Table 2. Result Comparisons of LS-SVM and BP

Number of training samples	Number of testing samples	LS-SVM	BP
		Test MSE	Test MSE
15	20	0.014488	0.0621
20	15	0.011078	0.0564
25	10	0.012899	0.0334

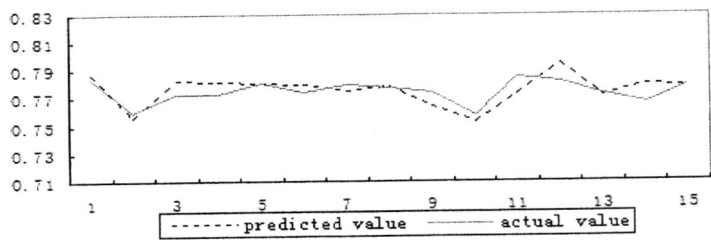

Fig. 1. Prediction using LS-SVM

Comparatively seeing from predicted value and actual value (Fig. 1 and Fig. 2), the result of LS-SVM algorithm is a lot better than BP algorithm. And then we can find out that LS-SVM algorithm has the stronger generalization performance and obvious advantages in predicting ability in the analysis of the medicines composition.

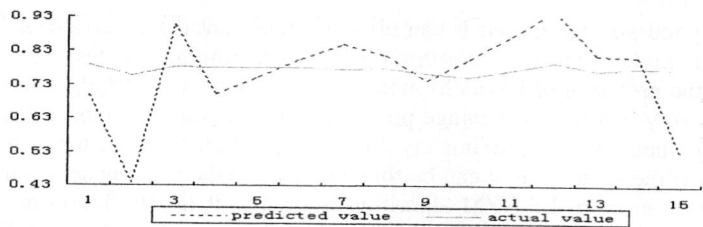

Fig. 2. Prediction using BP

5 Conclusions

Data used in the analysis of the medicine composition usually are characterized by small sample amount and high dimension. To deal with this kind of problems, a combined method of PCA and LS-SVM is proposed. PCA is used to process the raw data obtained by NIR and LS-SVM is used to analyze the processed data. The results of the simulated experiments demonstrate that compared with the traditional BP algorithm the proposed algorithm has obvious advantages on time efficiency and precision. The combination of the PCA and LS-SVM can be a good method for the problem of medicine composition analysis. But it remains a task to optimize our proposed method with smart mechanisms for parameter choice, in order to obtain the better results convincingly.

Acknowledgment

The authors are grateful to the support of the National Natural Science Foundation of China (60433020), the science-technology development project of Jilin Province of China (20030520), and the doctoral funds of the National Education Ministry of China (20030183060).

References

1. Laporte, M.F., Paquin, P.: Near-infrared Analysis of Fat, Protein, and Casein in Cow's Milk. Journal of agricultural and Food Chemistry 47 (1999) 2600–2605
2. Vapnik, V. N.: Statistical Learning Theory. John Wiley, New York (1998)
3. Kecman, V.: Learning and Soft Computing, Support Vector Machines. Neural Networks and Fuzzy Logic Models. The MIT Press, Cambridge (2001)
4. Wang, L.P. (Ed.): Support Vector Machines: Theory and Application. Springer-Verlag, Berlin Heidelberg New York (2005)
5. Suykens, J.A.K., Vandewalle, J.: Least Squares Support Vector Machine Classifiers. Neural Processing Letter 9 (1999) 293–300
6. Suykens, J.A.K., Vandewalle, J., De, M. B.: Optimal Control by Least Squares Support Vector Machines. Neural Networks 4 (2001) 23–35

Swarm Double-Tabu Search*

Wanhui Wen and Guangyuan Liu**

School of Electronic & Information Engineering,
Southwest China Normal University,
Chongqing 400715,
People's Republic of China
wenwanh@swnu.edu.cn, liugy@swnu.edu.cn

Abstract. In this work, a new heuristic algorithm, named Swarm Double-Tabu Search (SDTS), has been proposed. SDTS attempts to solve the problems of NP-hard combinatorial optimization effectively and efficiently. The particle swarm and the double-tabu strategies adopted in the SDTS algorithm have got excellent search result. Simulations on Traveling Salesman Problem (TSP) were performed, and the results compared to those obtained by neural network approaches were optimal or near optimal.

1 Introduction

Particle swarm optimization (PSO) is an evolutionary computation technique proposed by Kenney and Eberhart in 1995 [1]. It has been thought that the uniqueness of PSO lies in the dynamic interactions of the particles [2].

Tabu search is a meta-heuristic methodology proposed by F. Glover in 1986[3]. It has been widely applied to the solution of the NP-hard optimization problem over the past years. However, the quality of the final solution found by tabu search depends much on the quality of the initial solution, the intensification and diversification strategy in tabu search algorithm.

In our recent work, a new heuristic algorithm named Swarm Double-Tabu Search (SDTS) was developed on the basis of the particle swarm optimization and tabu search. SDTS adopts two strategies to ensure the effective and efficient search of the algorithm. One is the particle swarm strategy to eliminate the dependence of search result on initial solution, as well as enhance the ability of the algorithm to explore new search space. The other is the double-tabu strategy to guide thorough search in local space and avoid local optimum. Following the introduction, brief description about particle swarm optimization and tabu search can be found in section 2 and section 3. In section 4, the SDTS technique is presented in detail. The experimental data and conclusion are given in section 5 and section 6, respectively.

---

* Supported by Natural Science Fund (cstc-2004bb2083) of Chongqing and the Key Science & Technology Commission of Ministry of Education(104262).
** Corresponding author.

2 Particle Swarm Optimization

A swarm is a collection of particles. In literature [1], the PSO was presented in equations. However, it is uneasy to determine the proper values of those parameters in the equations. Regardless of this deficiency, the PSO has its benefit, that is, the search process of each particle is guided by two "bests", namely, the local best and the global best. These two "bests" can solve the problem of "explorers" and "settlers"[1].

3 Tabu Search

Tabu Search algorithm is a meta-heuristic algorithm to find the global optimum in optimization problems. It achieves this goal mainly by using a finite-size list of forbidden solutions derived from the recent history of the search. Nevertheless, for the reason of neighborhood structure, the quality of best solution found by TS depends on the quality of initial solution. Better initial solution always leads to better final solution, vice versa. Furthermore, effective strategy is needed to make thorough search in the local space and to avoid local optimum.

4 Swarm Double-Tabu Search (SDTS)

In SDTS, search can work in parallel way by a particle swarm, and each particle applies a double-tabu search method to look for solutions better than those found in the past.

The double-tabu strategy featured two tabu strategies, tight tabu and loose tabu. The best solution not in the tight tabu list is chosen as the candidate best of current iteration. Loose tabu strategy records the solutions free from tight tabu list, viz. the solutions whose forbidden periods in tight tabu list expired are recorded in the loose tabu list. When an above-mentioned candidate has been found in the loose tabu list, it means that cycle happened in the search process. If the cycle times become larger than a prearranged number, the selected candidate will be discarded, and a new randomly chosen solution in current neighborhood will replace the former one as the candidate best solution of current iteration. When the best solution of current iteration is determined, it will be recorded in the tight tabu list so that it will not be chosen as the candidate best of next iteration.

The best solutions found by the individual particles are the so-called *local bests*. Information of the best *local best* is exchanged among the particles and shared as the *global best* at certain time of the search process.

The skeleton of SDTS is given as follows.

Step 1: Initialize particle swarm. Randomly choose some solutions as the initial state of particle swarm. Then initialize the tabu lists of each particle, namely, the tight tabu list and loose tabu list.
Step 2: Perform double-tabu strategy in the search process of individual particles.
Step 2.1: Record current solution in the loose tabu list.
Step 2.2: Generate neighborhood of current solution.

Step 2.3: Find the best neighbor not in the tight tabu list to be a candidate best for current iteration.

Step 2.4: Compare the candidate found in step 2.3 to the solutions recorded in the loose tabu list. If more cycles than the predicted number happened, discard the candidate best, randomly select a non-tightly-tabued solution in the neighborhood to be the best solution of current iteration. Otherwise, the candidate found in step 2.3 becomes the best solution of current iteration.

Step 2.5: Record best solution of current iteration in the tight tabu list.

Step 2.6: If it's not the time for information exchange among particles, let the best solution of current iteration be current solution of next iteration and go to Step 2.1. Otherwise, go to Step 3.

Step 3: Compare the *local bests* found by individual particles. The best of these *local bests* becomes the *global best*.

Step 4: If the new *global best* is better than the past one, let one particle choose *global best* as its new initial solution, the others randomly select solutions in the neighborhood of the *global best* as their new initial solutions.

Step 5: Go back to Step 2.1 until the stop condition is satisfied.

In the above description of SDTS, the number of particles in the swarm, the neighborhood generation rule and the stop condition of the algorithm depend on the given optimization problem. The length of the tight tabu list is set to be a fixed number, but the length of loose tabu list could be an alterable one. The tabued object could be a solution or one character of the solution. It's time for information exchanging in the swarm if more cycles than the preset threshold happened in the search process of all or part of the particles.

5 Simulation

Since TSP is often regarded as the benchmark to verify the effectiveness and efficiency of a new algorithm, experiments applying SDTS to Traveling Salesman Problem (TSP) were carried out to demonstrate the performance of this new heuristic algorithm. Simulation for the problems of eil51 and KroA100 were performed under Matlab6.5 circumstance on a Dell workstation with 1.40GHz CPU and 2G RAM. Data of the simulation are given in Table 1.

According to literature [4], the major drawbacks of the Hopfield network when it is applied to some combinatorial problems, e.g. TSP, are invalidity of the obtained solutions, trial-and-error setting value process of the network parameters and low-computation efficiency, thus an improved neural network model called Columnar Competitive Model (CCM) was presented in this literature. Simulation result of a 48-city instance in literature [4] was cited in Table 2 to make a comparison between SDTS and CCM. In Table 2, k is a scaling parameter in CCM; d_{max} and d_{min} are the max and min distances between two cities, respectively; data corresponding to *valid*, *invalid* and *good* refer to simulation times which valid, invalid and good solutions were got; *Min* and *Ave* refer to the minimum and average route length.

Table 1. Parameters and experimental results of SDTS

TSP Instances	Known optimum	Tour length of the solution found by SDTS			Relative error of the worst	Epoch
		Best	Worst	Average		
eil51	426	426	438	429.92	1.70%	500
KroA100	21282	21282	21643	21401.22	2.35%	3500

Table 2. Performance of CCM for the 48-city example

k	Valid	Invalid	Good	Min	Ave
d_{max}	90	10	0	24.6860	32.7950
$d_{max}+d_{min}$	92	8	0	24.9204	33.8892
$2d_{max}-d_{min}$	100	0	0	35.9438	42.4797

From Table 1 and Table 2, it can be seen that SDTS didn't face the problem of invalid solution, and the worst solution obtained by SDTS is also a near-optimal solution. More detailed simulation results of neural network approaches are available in literature [4].

6 Conclusion

SDTS holds the soul of particle swarm optimization instead of its shell. By means of particle swarm parallel search and information exchanging among particles, SDTS depends little on the quality of the initial solution. Another reason for the effective search of SDTS is its double-tabu strategy. With the tight tabu and loose tabu strategies, SDTS has strong ability to search thoroughly in local space as well as escape the local optimum. According to the comparison between SDTS and CCM in literature [4], the SDTS in this work is good at finding high quality solutions and avoiding the problem of invalid solution.

References

1. J. Kennedy and R. C. Eberhart: Particle swarm optimization. Proceedings of IEEE International Conference on Neural Networks, Vol. IV, 1942-1948, Piscataway, NJ, Perth, Australia (1995)
2. Leandro Nunes de Castro: Immune, Swarm, and Evolutionary Algorithms. Proceedings of the 9th International Conference on Neural Information Processing, Vol. 3, 1464-1473, Piscataway, NJ, Singapore (2002)
3. F. Glover and M. Laguna: Tabu search. Kluwer Academic Publishers, Boston MA (1997)
4. Huajin Tang, Tan, K.C. and Zhang Yi: A columnar competitive model for solving combinatorial optimization problems. IEEE Transactions on Neural Networks, Vol. 15, Issue 6, 1568 – 1574, IEEE Neural Network Society (2004)

A Meta-heuristic Algorithm for the Strip Rectangular Packing Problem

Defu Zhang, Yanjuan Liu, Shengda Chen, and Xiaogang Xie

Department of Computer Science, Xiamen University, 361005, China
dfzhang@xmu.edu.cn

Abstract. A new meta-heuristic algorithm to find the minimum height for two-dimensional strip rectangular packing problem is presented. This algorithm is mainly based on the heuristic recursive strategy and simulated annealing algorithm. The computational results on a class of benchmark problems have shown that this algorithm not only finds shorter height than known meta-heuristic but also runs in shorter time.

1 Introduction

Packing problems have found many industrial applications, with different applications incorporating different constrains and objects. For example, in wood or glass industries, rectangular components have to be cut from large sheets of material. Newspapers paging, articles and advertisements are generally concerned with the guillotine packing of rectangular items from a page of fixed width and length. These applications have a similar logical structure and can be formalized as packing problems [1]. For more extensive and detailed descriptions of packing problems, the reader is referred to [1, 2, 3].

The focus of this paper is a new method for a two-dimensional strip rectangular packing problem, the objective of which is to find the minimum height. This problem belongs to a subset of classical cutting and packing problems and has been shown to be NP hard [4, 5]. Optimal algorithms for orthogonal two-dimension cutting were proposed in [6, 7]. However, they might not be practical for large problems. Some heuristic algorithms were developed by [8]. Hybrid algorithms combining genetic and deterministic methods for the orthogonal packing problem were proposed by [9, 10, 11]. An empirical investigation of meta-heuristic and heuristic algorithms of the strip rectangular packing problems was given by [12]. Many meta-heuristic approaches have been utilized to solve different packing problems, and these are usually hybridized algorithms combing simulated annealing (SA) or genetic method with heuristic method [12,13,14]. An effective quasi-human heuristic, Less Flexibility First, for solving the rectangular packing problems was presented by [15]. However, generally speaking, the known meta-heuristic algorithms are more time consuming and are not effective enough. Recently, some new models and algorithms were developed by [16, 17,18]. Especially, several new heuristic methods were presented by [19,20] and some promising results were obtained. SA is a general stochastic search algorithm for combinatorial optimization problems. In contrast to other local search algorithms, it provides more opportunities to escape from local minimum. SA has been widely used to solve packing problems [12, 21]. In this paper, we will present a rather effective meta-heuristic algorithm based on SA and heuristic recursive (HR) algorithm [19] for solving the orthogonal strip rectangular packing problem. The computational results on a class of benchmark problems show that this algorithm not only finds shorter height than known meta-heuristic but also runs in shorter time.

2 Mathematical Formulation of the Problem

Given a rectangular board of given width and a set of rectangles with arbitrary sizes, the strip packing problem of rectangles is to pack each rectangle on the board so that no two rectangles overlap and the used board height is minimized. This problem can also be stated as follows.

Given a rectangular board with given width W, and n rectangles with length l_i and width w_i, $1 \leq i \leq n$, take the origin of two dimensional Cartesian coordinate system at the bottom-left corner of the rectangular board, (x_L, h) denotes the top-left corner coordinates of the rectangular board and (x_R, y_R) denotes the bottom-right corner coordinates of this board (See Fig. 1). The aim of this problem is to find a solution composed of n sets of quadruples

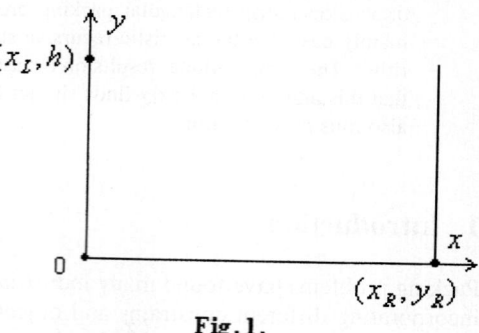

Fig. 1.

$$P = \{((x_{li}, y_{li}), (x_{ri}, y_{ri})) \mid 1 \leq i \leq n, x_{li} < x_{ri}, y_{li} > y_{ri}\},$$

where, (x_{li}, y_{li}) denotes the top-left corner coordinates of rectangle i, and (x_{ri}, y_{ri}) denotes the bottom-right corner coordinates of rectangle i. For all $1 \leq i \leq n$, the coordinates of rectangle i satisfies the following conditions:

(1) $x_{ri} - x_{li} = l_i \wedge y_{li} - y_{ri} = w_i$ or $x_{ri} - x_{li} = w_i \wedge y_{li} - y_{ri} = l_i$.

(2) For all $1 \leq j \leq n$, $j \neq i$, rectangle i and j cannot overlap, namely, $x_{ri} \leq x_{lj}$ or $x_{li} \geq x_{rj}$ or $y_{ri} \geq y_{lj}$ or $y_{li} \leq y_{rj}$.

(3) $x_L \leq x_{li} \leq x_R, x_L \leq x_{ri} \leq x_R$ and $y_R \leq y_{li} \leq h, y_R \leq y_{ri} \leq h$.

Such that the used board height h is minimized.

It is noted that the orthogonal rectangular packing problems denote the packing process has to ensure the edges of each rectangle are parallel to the $x-$ and $y-$ axes respectively, namely, all rectangles to be packed cannot be packed aslant.

3 A New Meta-heuristic Algorithm (SA+HR)

3.1 Heuristic Recursive Algorithm (HR)

HR is a new heuristic that has proven to be effective on the strip rectangular packing problems [19], it can be stated as follows:

(1) Put a rectangle into the space to be packed and divide the unpacked space into two subspaces (See Fig.2).
(2) Pack each subspace by packing them recursively. If the subspace sizes are small enough to only pack a rectangle, just pack this rectangle into the subspaces.
(3) Combine the solutions to the sub-problems into the solution to the strip rectangular packing problem.

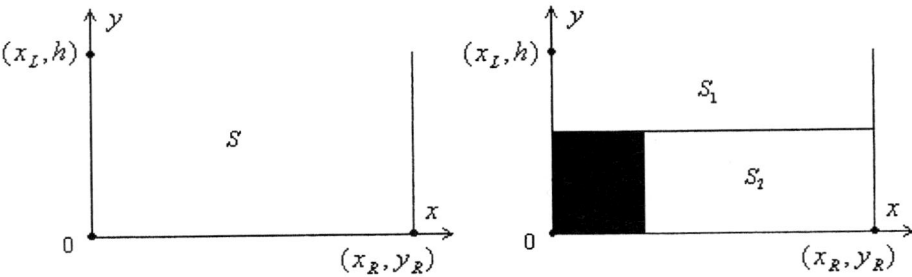

Fig. 2. Divide the unpacked space into two subspaces

Given a sequence X of rectangles, the heuristic recursive algorithm for packing X can be described as follows:

```
program HR( X )
   Repeat
      Select a rectangle from X and pack it into S according to heuristic strategy;
      Divide the unpacked space into the unbounded space S₁ and the bounded space S₂;
      Packing S₂ recursively until no rectangle can be packed into S₂;
      S = S₁ ;
   until all rectangles are packed
end.
```

For more detailed descriptions of HR, the interest reader can be referred to [19].

3.2 Simulated Annealing Algorithm

We have known that the quality of the layout obtained from the above placement algorithm (HR) depends on the sequence in which the rectangles are presented to the routine. So we must find a good sequence of the rectangles to produce a good solution. SA is a good search technique, so we'll use it to search a better solution in this paper.

SA is a stochastic heuristic algorithm which is used to solve combinatorial optimization problems. Simulated annealing optimization is similar to the annealing of metals. Different from other algorithms, SA uses a probability mechanism to control the process of jumping out of the local minimum. In the process of search, SA not only accepts better solutions, but also accepts worse solutions randomly with a certain probability. At high temperatures, the probability of accepting better solutions is relatively big. With the decrease of the temperature, the probability of accepting worse solutions also descends, and when the temperature closes in upon zero, SA no longer accepts any worse solution. These make SA have more chance to avoid getting trapped in a local minimum and avoid the limitation of other local search algorithms and the gradient algorithms.

Because of its merits above, SA has become an extremely popular method for solving large-sized and practical problems like job shop scheduling, timetabling, traveling salesman and packing problem [12, 13, 21]. However, for various reasons, like many other search algorithms, SA may get trapped in a local minimum or take a long time to find a reasonable solution. For these reasons, SA is often used as a part of a hybrid method.

3.3 A New Meta-heuristic Algorithm

It is noted that a sequence X of the rectangles to be packed can represent a feasible solution to packing problem. In addition, how to choose an initial solution may greatly influence the result of SA. So in this paper, we sort the rectangles by nonincreasing ordering of area size in the first place and obtain a better solution by the method of exchanging the position of two rectangles in the sequence, finally we use the better sequence obtained as the initial solution.

For each feasible solution X, we call the heuristic recursive function HR (X) to compute its evaluation value $E(X)$. A new feasible solution X_1 can be obtained by randomly exchanging the position of two rectangles in the sequence. When there are ten consecutive new solutions which are not accepted, the algorithm stops.

In detail, the new meta-heuristic algorithm that combines SA with HR can be stated as follows:

```
program SA+HR (Output)
   initial temperature T₀ , a ;
   Set the ordered sequence as initial solution X₀ ;
   Set the iterative times L at each temperature;
   While the number of consecutive new solutions which
are not accepted is less than 10
```

```
For i:=1 to L
    generate a new solution X₁ by randomly exchanging
the position of two rectangles in the sequence X₀;
    $E(X_0) := \text{HR}(X_0)$, $E(X_1) := \text{HR}(X_1)$;
    Compute $\Delta E := E(X_1) - E(X_0)$;
    if $\Delta E < 0$ then $X_0 := X_1$;
    else $X_0 := X_1$ with probability $\exp(-\Delta E/T)$;
$T_0 := a T_0$;
Return $X_0$
```

Since the performance of SA is significantly impacted by the choice of T_0, a etc., these parameters should be selected rationally. In this paper, we choose $T_0 = 0.5, a = 0.9, L = 20000$.

4 Computational Results

Performance of the new meta-heuristic algorithm (SA+HR) has been tested with seven different sized test instances ranging from 16 to 197 items [12]. The optimal solutions of these test instances are all known. In order to compare SA+HR with known meta-heuristic, two best meta-heuristic GA+BLF and SA+BLF in [12] are selected, they are run on a PC with a Pentium Pro 200 MHz processor and 65MB of RAM under Windows NT4.0 [12], so the relative distance of best solution to optimum height (RDBSOH) and the running time are directly taken from [12]. We also take HR in [19] for comparison; it was run on a DELL GX260 with a 2.4GHz CPU [19]. The results obtained from their realization of the GA+BLF, SA+BLF and HR are also given from [19]. DELL GX260 with a 2.4GHz CPU is about thirteen times faster than PC with a Pentium Pro 200 MHz processor, therefore we adjust the running time of GA+BLF, SA+BLF by dividing by 13. Our experiments were run on a Dell GX270 with a 3.0GHz CPU. Dell GX270 with a 3.0GHz CPU is about 1.25 times faster than DELL GX260 with a 2.4GHz CPU; therefore we adjust the running time of SA+HR by multiply 1.25. The computational results are reported in Tables 1 and 2.

On this test set, as shown in Table 1, RDBSOH of SA+HR ranges from 1.86% to 5% with the average RDBSOH 3.07%. The average RDBSOH of GA+BLF, SA+BLF and HR are 4.57, 4 and 3.97 respectively. The average RDBSOH of SA+HR is lower than that of GA+BLF, SA+BLF and HR. From Table 1, we can observe that RDBSOH of SA+HR is lower than that of GA+BLF and SA+BLF for all given instances. From Table 2, the computational speed of SA+HR is faster than that of GA+BLF, SA+BLF.

Table 1. RDBSOH of GA+BLF, SA+BLF, HR and SA+HR (%)

	C1	C2	C3	C4	C5	C6	C7	Average
GA+BLF	4	7	5	3	4	4	5	4.57
SA+BLF	4	6	5	3	3	3	4	4
HR	8.33	4.45	6.67	2.22	1.85	2.5	1.8	3.97
SA+HR	5	4.47	2.23	2.22	1.86	2.5	3.24	3.07

Table 2. Average running time of GA+BLF, SA+BLF, HR and SA+HR (s)

	C1	C2	C3	C4	C5	C6	C7	Average
GA+BLF	4.61	9.22	13.83	59.93	165.96	396.46	3581.97	604.57
SA+BLF	3.227	11.064	18.44	152.13	530.15	1761.02	19274.41	3107.2
HR	0	0	0.03	0.14	0.69	2.21	36.07	5.59
SA+HR	29.00	53.5	74	212.5	429.5	556.12	1661.00	430.75

5 Conclusion

In this paper we presented a new meta-heuristic algorithm for the strip rectangular packing problem. This algorithm can solve the rectangular packing problem effectively. Using data provided by other researchers in the field of cutting and packing, this new meta-heuristic algorithm (SA+HR) has produced better results than the GA+BLF and SA+BLF for all given instances and its average result is better than HR. As we can see, its average running time is also shorter than that of GA+BLF and SA+BLF. Many other areas of operations research, including paper industry, ship building industry, memory allocation and multiprocessor scheduling, share a similar logical structure to the problem in this paper. Therefore, the techniques proposed in this paper could be applied to these fields with the possible similar improvements in solution quality. Future work is to further improve the performance especially the running time of SA+HR and extend this algorithm for three-dimensional rectangular packing problems.

References

1. Andrea Lodi, Silvano Martello, Michele Monaci.: Two-dimensional packing problems: A survey. European Journal of Operational Research 141 (2002) 241–252
2. K.A. Dowsland, W.B. Dowsland.: Packing problems. European Journal of Operational Research 56 (1992) 2–14
3. David Pisinger.: Heuristics for the container loading problem. European Journal of Operational Research 141 (2002) 382–392
4. D.S. Hochbaum Wolfgang Maass.: Approximation schemes for covering and packing problems in image processing and VLSI. Journal of the Association for Computing Machinery 32 (1)(1985) 130–136

5. J. Leung, T. Tam, C.S. Wong, Gilbert Young, Francis Chin.: Packing squares into square. Journal of Parallel and Distributed Computing 10 (1990) 271–275
6. J.E. Beasley.: An exact two-dimensional non-guillotine cutting tree search procedure. Operations Research 33 (1985) 49–64
7. E. Hadjiconstantinou, N. Christofides.: An optimal algorithm for general orthogonal 2-D cutting problems. Technical report MS-91/2, Imperial College, London, UK
8. J.O. Berkey and P.Y. Wang.: Two-dimensional finite bin packing algorithms.: Journal of the Operational Research Society, 38 (1987) 423–429
9. S. Jakobs.: On genetic algorithms for the packing of polygons. European Journal of Operational Research 88 (1996) 165–181
10. D. Liu, H. Teng.: An improved BL-algorithm for genetic algorithm of the orthogonal packing of rectangles, European Journal of Operational Research 112 (1999) 413–419
11. C.H. Dagli, P. Poshyanonda.: New approaches to nesting rectangular patterns. Journal of Intelligent Manufacturing 8 (1997) 177–190
12. E.Hopper, B.C.H. Turton.: An empirical investigation of meta-heuristic and heuristic algorithms for a 2D packing problem, European Journal of Operational Research 128 (2001) 34–57
13. De-fu Zhang, An-Sheng Deng.: An effective hybrid algorithm for the problem of packing circles into a larger containing circle. Computers & Operations Research 32(8) (2005) 1941–1951
14. P. Ross, S. Schulenburg, J. Marín-Blázquez, and E. Hart.: Hyper-heuristics: learning to combine simple heuristics in bin-packing problems. Proceedings of the Genetic and Evolutionary Computation Conference. Morgan Kaufmann (2002) 942–948
15. Yu-Liang Wu, Wenqi Huang, Siu-chung Lau, C.K. Wong, Gilbert H. Young.: An effective quasi-human based heuristic for solving the rectangle packing problem. European Journal of Operational Research 141 (2002) 341–358
16. G. Belov. Problems.: Models and algorithms in one- and two-dimensional cutting. PhD thesis, Technischen Universitat Dresden, 2003. Http://www.math.tu-dresden.de/belov/publ/text030908_SUBMIT.pdf
17. Alberto Caprara, and Michele Monaci.: On the two-dimensional Knapsack Problem. Operations Research Letters 32 (2004) 5–14
18. S.P.Fekete, J.Schepers.: On higher-dimensional packing □: Exact algorithms. Operations Research, 2004. Technical Report ZPR 97-290. http://www.zaik.uni-koeln.de/~paper/preprints.html?show=zpr97290&preprint_session=9b657999e2faecfc37a9ce6acf104144
19. Defu Zhang, Yan Kang, Ansheng Deng.: A new heuristic recursive algorithm for the strip rectangular packing problem, to be published by Computers & Operations Research.
20. Defu Zhang, Ansheng Deng and Yan Kang.: A Hybrid Heuristic Algorithm for the Rectangular Packing Problem. Lecture Notes in Computer Science, Vol. 3514. Springer-Verlag, Berlin Heidelberg New York (2005) 783–791
21. Defu Zhang, Wenqi Huang.: A Simulated Annealing Algorithm for the Circles Packing Problem. Lecture Notes in Computer Science, Vol. 3036. Springer-Verlag, Berlin Heidelberg New York (2004) 206–214

Music Composition Using Genetic Algorithms (GA) and Multilayer Perceptrons (MLP)

Hüseyin Göksu[1], Paul Pigg[2], and Vikas Dixit[3]

[1] Süleyman Demirel University, Isparta, 32260, Turkey
goksu@sdu.edu.tr
[2] The Boeing Company, Seattle, Washington, USA
paul.pigg@boeing.com
[3] University of Missouri-Rolla, Rolla, Missouri, USA
vdry2@umr.edu

Abstract. In this work, authors have developed a system which is capable of composing songs using Genetic Algorithms (GA) to evolve melody and rhythm. Each GA uses two Multilayer Perceptron (MLP) type artificial neural networks (ANN) to judge for the fitness of individuals in the population. MLPs are forward and backward sliding-window predictors trained on melody and rhythm extracted from songs of different genres. Separately evolved rhythms and melodies are dynamically mixed to obtain verses, which are then mixed into whole songs.

1 Introduction

The problem of using computers to generate music has been researched for decades. The real problem is that musical results are not as quantifiable as other computational intelligence problems. Every person has different influences, tastes, and dislikes. For this reason, most research in this field is very scattered, with their only connection being in the common goal.

Genetic Algorithms, or GA, is a computational intelligence tool where a population of solutions is evolved with operators of mutation, crossover and selection given a fitness value [1]. Genetic Algorithms appear to be a widely used method for music generation. However, the problem often presents itself in finding a good fitness function. Some researchers choose to use humans as fitness function, but this is time-consuming, as the listener must hear and judge each individual melody in the population [1], [2], [3], [4].

A Multi-layer Perceptron, or MLP, is a feedforward ANN that is proven to be quite successful for its system identification and time series prediction ability [5], [6], [7].

2 Method

Because this is not meant to be an exercise in sound file format dissection, we decided to use a text format known as ABC for input and output. This format allows for the subtle complexities in music, while giving simplicity to the user in reading and understanding the music represented by the format. Tools for this format exist on the internet to allow conversion both ways between ABC and the standard MIDI format.

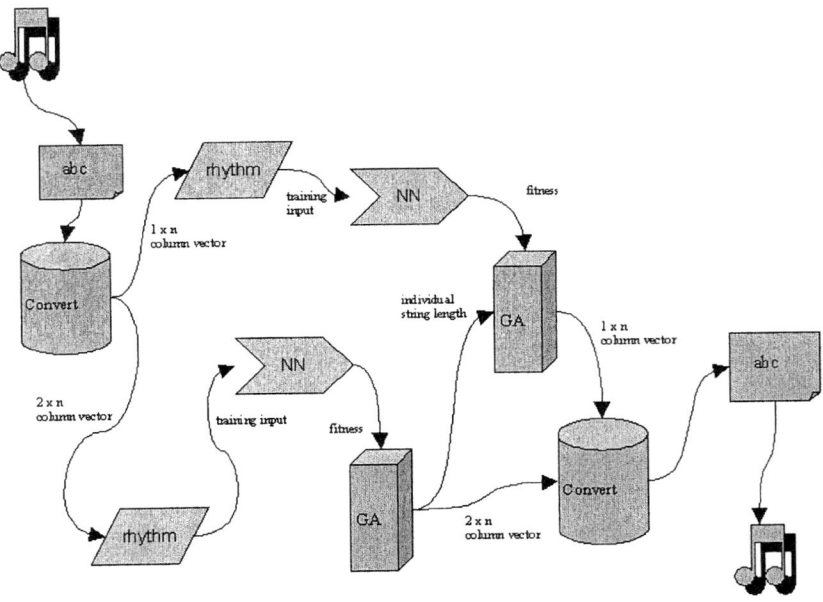

Fig. 1. Flow Chart of the Composition Process

Table 1. Numerical Notation for Melody

Note	Numerical Eq.	Note	Numerical Eq.
A	-3	D#	3
A#	-2	E	4
B	-1	F	5
C	0	F#	6
C#	1	G	7
D	2	G#	8

The Flow Chart of the Composition Process has been sketched in Figure 1. The melody and rhythm parsed from ABC files were converted to numerical values using Tables 1, 2. The rhythm consisted of an n × 2 vector of one integer variable containing the note length (over 32, i.e. 32 = 32/32 or a whole note), and one binary variable declaring the rhythm mark as either a rest or a note.

The melody consisted of an n × 1 vector, with the parameter containing the numerical value of a note. The melody is not confined to the single octave in Table 1 (with middle-C at 0), but rather spans the octaves of the input song.

Table 2. Numerical Notation for Rhythm

Parameter	Numerical Eq.
Length	1-32
Rests/Notes	0/1

2.1 The Multilayer Perceptrons

Sliding windows of size 8 are then used to train the MLP networks. Figure 2a and 2b shows example MLPs for learning rhythm and notes. For the rhythm, the MLP architecture consists of an input layer of 16 neurons (window size = 8, 2 inputs per rhythm mark) fed by the delayed sequence of rhythm marks, one hidden layer of 16 neurons and a two-neuron output layer aimed to give the predicted rhythm.

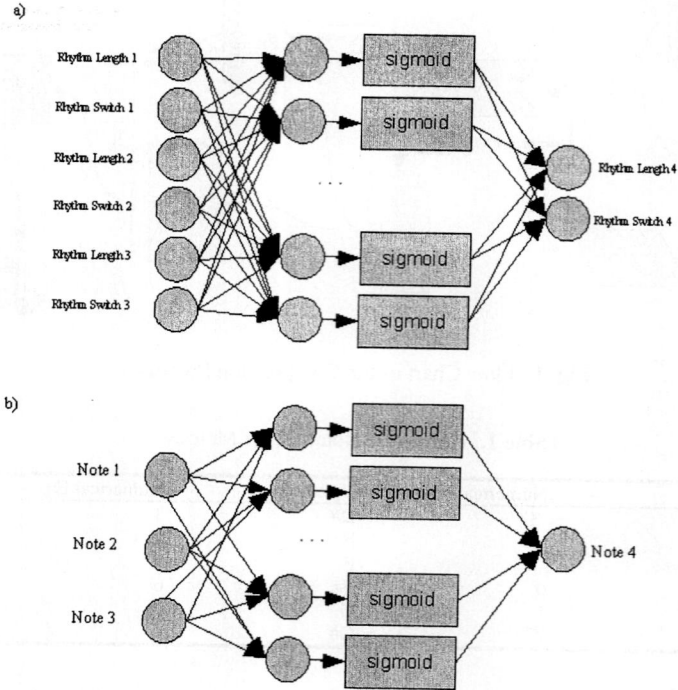

Fig. 2. MLPs for predicting a) Rhythm b) Notes. Window size: 3, round units are adders.

While the hidden layer neurons have tangential sigmoid transfer functions, the output layer has linear transfer function. The network is adaptively trained on rhythm sequences by Levenberg-Marquardt backpropagation, which can then be used as a fitness function for the sequences that the GA evolved, by one step predictions. A similar setup is used for the note-predicting ANNs, with the difference being in that notes require only one variable per note mark. In both cases, two MLPs are trained: one for forward predictions, and another for backward predictions.

2.2 Genetic Algorithms

For the rhythm, a length of 32 is given, and a population of 10 individuals is evolved. Selection used is Roulette Wheel Selection with ranking. Mutation is Gaussian. Fitness is the error percentage of the forward ANN predictor and the backward ANN predictor, combined with the error between the note percentage of the input song and the note percentage of the individual. Once the population is evolved for a set number of epochs, individuals are selected using the same selection method as above until a set number of song pieces are selected (in our work, 20).

For each separate rhythm that is selected, a population of notes is evolved using the same method as above, with the length of individuals given by the corresponding rhythm. In the case that an individual from the rhythm population is used more than once in the song, all corresponding notes are taken from the same population of notes, as in Figure 3. MATLAB was the computational environment during the work.

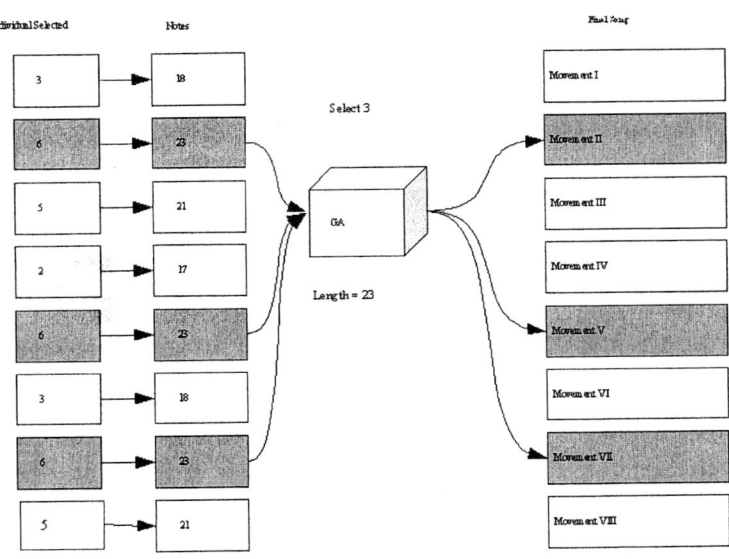

Fig. 3. Evolution of Notes. Same rhythm pieces used in different parts of the final song use notes from the same population

3 Results and Discussion

We found that the MLPs trained on rhythm generally converged faster than the MLPs trained on notes. This is likely due to the rhythm having a lower range of variables to deal with, and is often dependent upon the song's octave range, and the number of training patterns. For example, figure 5 shows the MSE plots of the neural networks for the Super Mario Theme Song. In contrast, the Beatles' Yesterday, which has a low number of training patterns and lower note values (the highest note in the song is the F below middle C), often did not converge well in the MLPs for predicting notes.

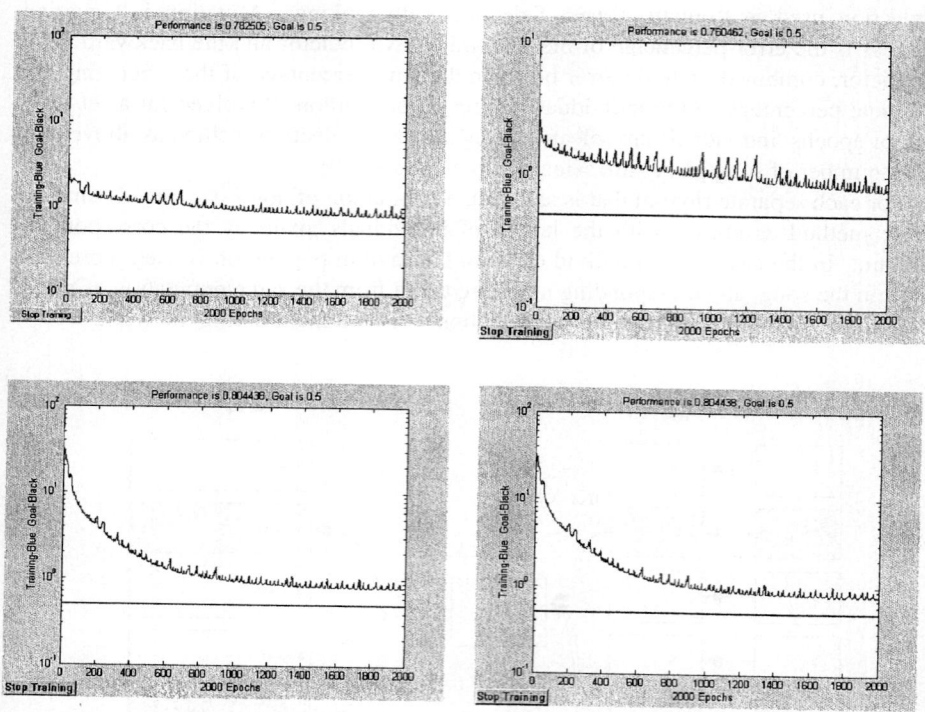

Fig. 4. Example of typical MSE-time graphs on the SMB Theme Song for a) forward rhythm predictor b) backward rhythm predictor c) forward note predictor d) backward note predictor

It is found that by evolving rhythm and notes separately using the above method, songs are often created with a high number of rests of long note-lengths. We attempted to counter this by including an error based on note-percentage (i.e., number of notes over number of rhythm marks), as well as an error based on rest length, in the fitness for rhythm. The results proved to be promising, given enough generations of evolution, as shown by the difference in number of rests between figures 7 and 8.

It is also found that by evolving a separate population for each separate rhythm selected in a song, the process takes a significant amount of time. This could be countered by evolving only one moderately-sized population for all notes in a song, with the length of individuals defined by the maximum number of notes of all rhythms.

The best way to describe the value of a music is to listen to it, or at the very least, view it. Figures 5, 6, and 7 show the song after 40 generations of evolution (for both rhythm and note GAs), after 100 generations, and after 500 generations. Comparing key components of the pieces visually, one can see that the less-evolved music is slightly more chaotic, i.e. there are more visible patterns in the higher-evolved music (though they are admittedly difficult to read with their current signature and formatting). Evolving for more generations should give more distinguishable music.

5 Conclusion

This overall work shows that evolving rhythm and melody for music using a GA and using MLP as a fitness judge is a promising tool for music composition. This tool can be used to generate practice exercises for musicians and can also be used as an inspirational tool for composers.

Acknowledgements

We would like to thank Dr. Ganesh Kumar Venayagamoorthy for his feedback.

References

1. Biles, J.A.: GenJam: A genetic algorithm for generating jazz solos. In: Proc. of the Int. Computer Music Conference (1994) 131-137
2. Bilotta, E., Pantano P.: In search of Musical Fitness on Consonance. Electronic Musicological Review, Vol 5, 3 (2000)
3. Marques, M., Oliveira, V., Vieira, S., Rosa, A.C.: Music Composition Using Genetic Evolutionary Algorithms. In: Proc. of 2000 IEEE-Congress on Evolut. Comput. (2000) 714-719
4. Wiggins, G.A., Papadopoulos, G., Phon-Amnuaisuk,S., Tucson, A.: Evolutionary Methods for Musical Composition. Int. J. of Computing Anticipatory Systems, Vol. 1 (1999)
5. Goksu, H., Wunsch, D.C.: Neural Networks applied to electromagnetic compatibility (EMC) simulations. Lecture Notes In Computer Science, 2714 (2003) 1057-1063
6. Goksu, H., Pommerenke, D. J., Wunsch, D. C. II.: FDTD data extrapolation using multilayer perceptron (MLP). In: Proc. of the IEEE Int. Symp. on EMC (2003) 735-737
7. Narendra, K., Parthasarathy, K.: Identification and control of dynamical systems using neural networks. IEEE Trans. Neural Networks, Vol. 78 (1990) 4-27

Appendix: Figures Showing the Composed Songs

Fig. 5. Music derived from the Super Mario Theme Song with 40 epochs of evolution

Music Composition Using Genetic Algorithms (GA) and Multilayer Perceptrons (MLP) 1249

Fig. 6. Music derived from the Super Mario Theme Song with 100 epochs of evolution

Fig. 7. Music derived from the Super Mario Theme Song with 500 epochs of evolution

On the Categorizing of Simply Separable Relations in Partial Four-Valued Logic*

Renren Liu, Zhiwei Gong, and Fen Xu

College of Information Engineering, Xiangtan University, Xiangtan, Hunan, 411105, China
renrenliu@hotmail.com

> **Abstract.** In completeness theories of multiple-valued logic, the characterization of Sheffer functions is an important problem, and the solution can be reduced to determining the minimal coverings of precomplete categories. It's well known that each precomplete set is a function set, $T(G_m)$, preserving the relation G_m, therefore, the categorizing of this relation has provided the determination of precomplete set's minimal covering with more convenient ways. In this paper, simply separable relations in partial four-valued logic are categorized by similar relation.

1 Introduction

The structure theory of multiple-valued logic functions is an important research field in multiple-valued logic theory.

Another important problem in multiple-valued logic completeness theory is the decision on Sheffer [1] functions, which depends on the deciding of the minimal covering of precomplete sets of all precomplete sets. For the partial multiple-valued logic function, the author has concisely decided the minimal covering of precomplete sets in 3-valued by using the similar relation among the precomplete sets [2]. In addition, the author proved that T_E, $P_K \cup \{*\}, L_P, L_{G_{4,2}}$ are included in the minimal covering for any k [3]. For the complexity of full symmetric function sets, simply separable function sets and regularly separable function sets, the problem has not been completely solved yet [4].

It's well known that each precomplete set is a function set, $T(G_m)$, preserving the relation G_m. The author has already proved that [5], if G_m is similar to G'_m, $T(G_m)$ and $T(G'_m)$ are either within or without the minimal covering. Therefore, the categorizing of this relation has provided the determination of precomplete set's minimal covering with more convenient ways. In this paper, simply separable relations in P_4^* are categorized by the similar relation.

---

* This work is supported by the National and Hunan Province Natural Science Foundation of China (60083001,60375021, 60433020, 03JJY3099).

2 Basic Definitions

Let $E_k = \{0, 1, 2, ..., k-1\}$, $k \geq 2$. The total and non-total k-valued logic functions over E_k are called *partial k-valued logic functions*. The set of all partial k-valued logic functions is denoted by P_k^*, and the set of all total k-valued logic functions is denoted by $P_k (\subset P_k^*)$, namely,

$$P_k = \{f(x_1, \cdots, x_n) \mid f : E_k^n \to E_k, \quad n \geq 1\}$$
$$P_k^* = \{f(x_1, \cdots, x_n) \mid f : E_k^n \to E_k \cup \{*\}, \quad n \geq 1\}$$

where $f(\alpha_1, \cdots, \alpha_n) = *$ means that f is undefined at point $(\alpha_1, \cdots, \alpha_n)$. We denote by $*$ the empty function that is undefined at every point.

A set of some m-tuples $<a_1, \cdots, a_m>, a_i \in E_k$ is called an m-ary relation over E_k, denoted by G_m. $\tilde{a}^1 = (a_1^1, \cdots, a_n^1), \cdots, \tilde{a}^m = (a_1^m, \cdots, a_n^m)$ are said to preserve the m-ary relation G_m if $<a_i^1, \cdots, a_i^m> \in G_m$, $i = 1, \cdots, n$. A function $f(x_1, \cdots, x_n)$ is said to preserve the m-ary relation G_m if for arbitrary $\tilde{a}^1, \cdots, \tilde{a}^m$ preserving G_m either $<f(\tilde{a}^1), \cdots, f(\tilde{a}^m)> \in G_m$ or one of $f(\tilde{a}^1), \cdots, f(\tilde{a}^m)$ is undefined. The set of all functions preserving G_m is denoted by $T(G_m)$. Hereafter we always assume $2 \leq m \leq k$.

G_m and G_m' are said to be similar if $|G_m| = |G_m'|$ and there is a one-one mapping $\sigma : E_k \to E_k$ such that

$$G_m' = \{<\sigma(a_1), \cdots, \sigma(a_m)> \mid <a_1, \cdots, a_m> \in G_m\}$$

Clearly, the similar relation defined above is equivalent relation. We denote by $G_m \stackrel{\sigma}{\sim} G_m'$ that G_m is similar to G_m' under one-one mapping σ. Let

$$G_m = \overline{G}_m \cup \overline{G}_m^{\sigma_1} \cup \cdots \cup \overline{G}_m^{\sigma_{h-1}}$$

where $\overline{G}_m = \{<a_1, \cdots, a_m> \mid a_i \neq a_j, i \neq j, i, j = 1, \cdots, m\}$,

$G_m^\sigma = \{<a_{\sigma(1)}, \cdots, a_{\sigma(m)}> \mid <a_1, \cdots, a_m> \in G_m\}$, and $H = \{e, \sigma_1, \cdots, \sigma_{h-1}\}$ is a subgroup of symmetric group $S_m = \{1, \cdots, m\}$. G_m is said to be simply separable if there is a direct partition on E_K:

$$E_K = A_1 + \cdots + A_m, \quad A_i \cap A_j = \emptyset, i \neq j, i, j = 1, \cdots, m \quad,$$

such that $a_i \in A_i, i = 1, \cdots, m$ for arbitrary $<a_1, \cdots, a_m> \in \overline{G}_m$. $T(G_m)$ is said to be a simply separable function set and denoted by $S_{l,m}$ if G_m is simply separable.

3 Main Results

When m=2, there are 83 binary simply separable relations such as $S_{1,2} = T(G_2)$, $G_2 = \overline{G_2} \cup \overline{G_2}^{\sigma_1} \cup \cdots \cup \overline{G_2}^{\sigma_{h-1}}$, where $H_1 = \{(1)\}$, $H_2 = \{(1),(12)\}$, and G_2 is as follows by similar relation:

i. The relations that only include one binary couple are as follows:

$\{<0,1>\} \overset{(12)}{\sim} \{<0,2>\} \overset{(23)}{\sim} \{<0,3>\} \overset{(01)(23)}{\sim} \{<1,2>\} \overset{(23)}{\sim} \{<1,3>\} \overset{(12)}{\sim} \{<2,3>\}$;

ii. The relations that include two binary couples are 4 categories as follows:

$\{<0,1>,<1,0>\} \overset{(12)}{\sim} \{<0,2>,<2,0>\} \overset{(23)}{\sim} \{<0,3>,<3,0>\} \overset{(01)(23)}{\sim} \{<1,2>,<2,1>\}$
$\overset{(23)}{\sim} \{<1,3>,<3,1>\} \overset{(12)}{\sim} \{<2,3>,<3,2>\}$;

$\{<0,1>,<0,2>\} \overset{(23)}{\sim} \{<0,1>,<0,3>\} \overset{(12)}{\sim} \{<0,2>,<0,3>\} \overset{(01)}{\sim} \{<1,2>,<1,3>\} \overset{(12)}{\sim} \{<2,1>,<2,3>\} \overset{(23)}{\sim} \{<3,1>,<3,2>\}$;

$\{<0,1>,<2,1>\} \overset{(23)}{\sim} \{<0,1>,<3,1>\} \overset{(123)}{\sim} \{<0,2>,<1,2>\} \overset{(13)}{\sim} \{<0,2>,<3,2>\} \overset{(123)}{\sim} \{<0,3>,<1,3>\} \overset{(12)}{\sim} \{<0,3>,<2,3>\}$;

$\{<0,1>,<3,2>\} \overset{(123)}{\sim} \{<0,2>,<1,3>\} \overset{(23)}{\sim} \{<0,3>,<1,2>\} \overset{(123)}{\sim} \{<0,1>,<2,3>\} \overset{(13)}{\sim} \{<0,3>,<2,1>\} \overset{(23)}{\sim} \{<0,2>,<3,1>\}$.

iii. The relations that include three binary couples are 2 Categories as follows:

$\{<0,2>,<0,3>,<1,2>\} \overset{(23)}{\sim} \{<0,2>,<0,3>,<1,3>\} \overset{(01)}{\sim} \{<0,3>,<1,2>,<1,3>\} \overset{(23)}{\sim} \{<0,2>,<1,2>,<1,3>\} \overset{(021)}{\sim} \{<0,1>,<0,3>,<2,1>\} \overset{(13)}{\sim} \{<0,1>,<0,3>,<2,3>\} \overset{(02)(13)}{\sim} \{<0,1>,<2,1>,<2,3>\} \overset{(13)}{\sim} \{<0,3>,<2,1>,<2,3>\} \overset{(0312)}{\sim} \{<0,1>,<0,2>,<3,1>\} \overset{(12)}{\sim} \{<0,1>,<0,2>,<3,2>\} \overset{(03)(12)}{\sim} \{<0,1>,<3,1>,<3,2>\} \overset{(12)}{\sim} \{<0,2>,<3,1>,<3,2>\}$;

$\{<0,1>,<0,2>,<0,3>\} \overset{(12)}{\sim} \{<1,0>,<1,2>,<1,3>\} \overset{(12)}{\sim} \{<2,0>,<2,1>,<2,3>\} \overset{(23)}{\sim} \{<3,0>,<3,1>,<3,2>\}$

iv. The relations that include four binary couples are 3 Categories as follows:

$\{<0,2>,<0,3>,<2,0>,<3,0>\} \overset{(02)(13)}{\sim} \{<0,2>,<1,2>,<2,0>,<2,1>\} \overset{(23)}{\sim} \{<0,3>,<1,3>,<3,0>,<3,1>\} \overset{(02)(13)}{\sim} \{<1,2>,<1,3>,<2,1>,<3,1>\} \overset{(021)}{\sim} \{<0,1>,<0,3>,<1,0>,<1,3>\} \overset{(01)(23)}{\sim} \{<0,1>,<2,1>,<1,0>,<1,2>\} \overset{(13)}{\sim} \{<0,3>,<2,3>,<3,0>,<3,2>\} \overset{(01)(23)}{\sim} \{<2,1>,<2,3>,<1,2>,<3,2>\} \overset{(032)}{\sim} \{<0,1>,<0,2>,<1,0>,<2,0>\} \overset{(01)(23)}{\sim} \{<0,1>,<3,1>,<1,0>,<1,3>\} \overset{(12)}{\sim} \{<0,2>,<3,2>,<2,0>,<2,3>\} \overset{(01)(23)}{\sim} \{<3,1>,<3,2>,<1,3>,<2,3>\}$;

$\{<0,2>,<0,3>,<1,2>,<1,3>\} \overset{(12)}{\sim} \{<0,1>,<0,3>,<2,1>,<2,3>\} \overset{(23)}{\sim} \{<0,1>,<0,2>,<3,1>,<3,2>\}$;

$\{<0,2>,<1,3>,<2,0>,<3,1>\} \overset{(12)}{\sim} \{<0,1>,<2,3>,<1,0>,<3,2>\} \overset{(13)}{\sim} \{<0,3>,<2,1>,<3,0>,<1,2>\}$.

v. The relations that include six binary couples are 2 Categories as follows:

$\{<0,2>,<0,3>,<1,2>,<2,0>,<3,0>,<2,1>\} \overset{(23)}{\sim} \{<0,2>,<0,3>,<1,3>,<2,0>,<3,0>,<3,1>\} \overset{(01)}{\sim} \{<0,3>,<1,2>,<1,3>,<3,0>,<2,1>,<3,1>\} \overset{(23)}{\sim} \{<0,2>,<1,2>,<1,3>,<2,0>,<2,1>,<3,1>\} \overset{(021)}{\sim} \{<0,1>,<0,3>,<2,1>,<1,0>,<3,0>,<1,2>\} \overset{(13)}{\sim} \{<0,1>,<0,3>,<2,3>,<1,0>,<3,0>,<3,2>\} \overset{(02)(13)}{\sim} \{<0,1>,<2,1>,<2,3>,<1,0>,<1,2>,<1,3>\} \overset{(13)}{\sim} \{<0,3>,<2,1>,<2,3>,<3,0>,<1,2>,<3,2>\} \overset{(0312)}{\sim} \{<0,1>,<0,2>,<3,1>,<1,0>,<2,0>,<1,3>\} \overset{(12)}{\sim} \{<0,1>,<0,2>,<3,2>,<1,0>,<2,0>,<2,3>\} \overset{(03)(12)}{\sim} \{<0,1>,<3,1>,<3,2>,<1,0>,<1,3>,<2,3>\} \overset{(12)}{\sim} \{<0,2>,<3,1>,<3,2>,<2,0>,<1,3>,<2,3>\}$;

$\{<0,1>,<0,2>,<0,3>,<1,0>,<2,0>,<3,0>\} \overset{(01)}{\sim} \{<1,0>,<1,2>,<1,3>,<0,1>,<2,1>,<3,1>\} \overset{(12)}{\sim} \{<2,0>,<2,1>,<2,3>,<0,2>,<1,2>,<3,2>\} \overset{(23)}{\sim} \{<3,0>,<3,1>,<3,2>,<0,3>,<1,3>,<2,3>\}$.

vi. The relations that include eight binary couples are as follows:

$\{<0,2>,<0,3>,<1,2>,<1,3>,<2,0>,<3,0>,<2,1>,<3,1>\} \overset{(12)}{\sim} \{<0,1>,<0,3>,<2,1>,<2,3>,<1,0>,<3,0>,<1,2>,<3,2>\} \overset{(23)}{\sim} \{<0,1>,<0,2>,<3,1>,<3,2>,<1,0>,<2,0>,<1,3>,<2,3>\}$.

When m=3, there are 60 triple simply separable relations such as $S_{1,3} = T(G_3)$, $G_3 = \overline{G_3} \cup \overline{G_3}^{\sigma_1} \cup \cdots \cup \overline{G_3}^{\sigma_{h-1}}$, where the subgroups are $H_1 = \{(1)\}$, $H_2 = \{(1),(23)\}$, $H_3 = \{(1),(12)\}$, $H_4 = \{(1),(13)\}$, $H_5 = \{(1),(123),(132)\}$, and $H_6 = \{(1),(23),(12),(13),(123),(132)\}$, G_3 is as follows:

i. The relations that only include one triple are as follows:

$\{<0,1,2>\} \overset{(23)}{\sim} \{<0,1,3>\} \overset{(12)}{\sim} \{<0,2,3>\} \overset{(01)}{\sim} \{<1,2,3>\}$;

ii. The relations that include two triple sequences are 6 Categories as follows:

$\{<0,1,2>,<0,2,1>\} \overset{(23)}{\sim} \{<0,1,3>,<0,3,1>\} \overset{(12)}{\sim} \{<0,2,3>,<0,3,2>\} \overset{(01)}{\sim} \{<1,2,3>,<1,3,2>\}$;

$\{<0,1,2>,<1,0,2>\} \overset{(23)}{\sim} \{<0,1,3>,<1,0,3>\} \overset{(12)}{\sim} \{<0,2,3>,<2,0,3>\} \overset{(01)}{\sim} \{<1,2,3>,<2,1,3>\}$;

$\{<0,1,2>,<2,1,0>\} \overset{(23)}{\sim} \{<0,1,3>,<3,1,0>\} \overset{(12)}{\sim} \{<0,2,3>,<3,2,0>\} \overset{(01)}{\sim} \{<1,2,3>,<3,2,1>\};$

$\{<0,1,2>,<0,1,3>\} \overset{(12)}{\sim} \{<0,2,1>,<0,2,3>\} \overset{(01)}{\sim} \{<1,2,0>,<1,2,3>\};$

$\{<0,1,3>,<0,2,3>\} \overset{(01)}{\sim} \{<1,0,3>,<1,2,3>\};$

$\{<0,2,3>,<1,2,3>\};$

iii. The relations that include three triple sequences are as follows:

$\{<0,1,2>,<2,0,1>,<1,2,0>\} \overset{(23)}{\sim} \{<0,1,3>,<3,0,1>,<1,3,0>\} \overset{(12)}{\sim} \{<0,2,3>,<3,0,2>,<2,3,0>\} \overset{(01)}{\sim} \{<1,2,3>,<3,1,2>,<2,3,1>\};$

iv. The relations that include four triple sequences are 9 Categories as follows:

$\{<0,1,2>,<0,1,3>,<0,2,1>,<0,3,1>\} \overset{(12)}{\sim} \{<0,2,1>,<0,2,3>,<0,1,2>,<0,3,2>\} \overset{(01)}{\sim} \{<1,2,0>,<1,2,3>,<1,0,2>,<1,3,2>\};$

$\{<0,1,2>,<0,1,3>,<1,0,2>,<1,0,3>\} \overset{(12)}{\sim} \{<0,2,1>,<0,2,3>,<2,0,1>,<2,0,3>\} \overset{(01)}{\sim} \{<1,2,0>,<1,2,3>,<0,1,2>,<2,1,3>\};$

$\{<0,1,2>,<0,1,3>,<2,1,0>,<3,1,0>\} \overset{(12)}{\sim} \{<0,2,1>,<0,2,3>,<1,0,2>,<3,2,0>\} \overset{(01)}{\sim} \{<1,2,0>,<1,2,3>,<0,2,1>,<3,2,1>\};$

$\{<0,1,3>,<0,2,3>,<0,3,1>,<0,3,2>\} \overset{(01)}{\sim} \{<1,0,3>,<1,2,3>,<1,3,0>,<1,3,2>\};$

$\{<0,1,3>,<0,2,3>,<1,0,3>,<2,0,3>\} \overset{(01)}{\sim} \{<1,0,3>,<1,2,3>,<0,1,3>,<2,1,3>\};$

$\{<0,1,3>,<0,2,3>,<3,1,0>,<3,2,0>\} \overset{(01)}{\sim} \{<1,0,3>,<1,2,3>,<3,0,1>,<3,2,1>\};$

$\{<0,2,3>,<1,2,3>,<0,3,2>,<1,3,2>.\};$

$\{<0,2,3>,<1,2,3>,<2,0,3>,<2,1,3>\};$

$\{<0,2,3>,<1,2,3>,<3,2,0>,<3,2,1>\}.$

v. The relations that include six triple sequences are 4 Categories as follows:

$\{<0,1,2>,<0,2,1>,<1,0,2>,<2,1,0>,<2,0,1>,<1,2,0>\} \overset{(23)}{\sim} \{<0,1,3>,<0,3,1>,<1,0,3>,<3,1,0>,<3,0,1>,<1,3,0>\} \overset{(12)}{\sim} \{<0,2,3>,<0,3,2>,<2,0,3>,<3,2,0>,<3,0,2>,<2,3,0>\} \overset{(01)}{\sim} \{<1,2,3>,<1,3,2>,<2,1,3>,<3,2,1>,<3,1,2>,<2,3,1>\};$

$\{<0,1,2>,<0,1,3>,<2,0,1>,<1,2,0>,<3,0,1>,<1,3,0>\} \overset{(12)}{\sim} \{<0,2,1>,<0,2,3>,<1,0,2>,<2,1,0>,<3,0,2>,<2,3,0>\} \overset{(01)}{\sim} \{<1,2,0>,<1,2,3>,<0,1,2>,<2,0,1>,<3,1,2>,<2,3,1>\};$

$\{<0,1,3>,<0,2,3>,<3,0,1>,<1,3,0>,<3,0,2>,<2,3,0>\} \overset{(01)}{\sim} \{<1,0,3>,<1,2,3>,<3,1,0>,<0,3,1>,<3,1,2>,<2,3,1>\};$

$\{<0,2,3>,<1,2,3>,<3,0,2>,<2,3,0>,<3,1,2>,<2,3,1>\};$

vi. The relations that include twelve triple sequences are 3 Categories as follows :

{<0,1,2>,<0,1,3>,<0,2,1>,<1,0,2>,<2,1,0>,<2,0,1>,<1,2,0>,<0,3,1>,<1,0,3>,<3,1,0>,<3,0,1>,<1,3,0>} $\overset{(12)}{\sim}$ {<0,1,2>,<0,2,3>,<0,2,1>,<1,0,2>,<2,1,0>,<2,0,1>,<1,2,0>,<0,3,2>,<2,0,3>,<3,2,0>,<3,0,2>,<2,3,0>} $\overset{(01)}{\sim}$ {<0,1,2>,<0,2,3>,<0,2,1>,<1,0,2>,<2,1,0>,<2,0,1>,<1,2,0>,<0,3,2>,<2,0,3>,<3,2,0>,<3,0,2>,<2,3,0>} $\overset{(01)}{\sim}$ {<0,1,2>,<1,2,3>,<0,2,1>,<1,0,2>,<2,1,0>,<2,0,1>,<1,2,0>,<1,3,2>,<2,1,3>,<3,2,1>,<3,1,2>,<2,3,1>};

{<0,1,3>,<0,2,3>,<0,3,1>,<1,0,3>,<3,1,0>,<3,0,1>,<1,3,0>,<0,3,2>,<2,0,3>,<3,2,0>,<3,0,2>,<2,3,0>} $\overset{(01)}{\sim}$ {<0,1,3>,<1,2,3>,<0,3,1>,<1,0,3>,<3,1,0>,<3,0,1>,<1,3,0>,<1,3,2>,<2,1,3>,<3,2,1>,<3,1,2>,<2,3,1>};

{<0,2,3>,<1,2,3>,<0,3,2>,<2,0,3>,<3,2,0>,<3,0,2>,<2,3,0>,<1,3,2>,<2,1,3>,<3,2,1>,<3,1,2>,<2,3,1>}.

References

1. Sheffer, H.M.: A Set of Five Independent Postulates for Boolean Algebras with Application to Logical Constants, Trans. Am. Math. Soc., 14, (1913) 481-488.
2. Renren Liu: The Minimal Covering of Precomplete Sets in Partial Three-Valued Logic, Natur. Sci. J. Xiangtan Univ., 13(2), (1991)158-165; MR92g:03035 03B50.
3. Renren Liu: Some Results on the Decision for Sheffer Functions in Partial K-Valued Logic, Multiple Valued Logic-An International Journal, 1 (1996) 253-269.
4. Renren Liu: Some Results on the Decision for Sheffer Functions in Partial K-Valued Logic, Proceedings of the 28th International Symposium on Multiple-Valued Logic (II), (1998) 77-81.
5. Renren Liu: Research on the Similarity among Precomplete Sets Preserving m-ary Relations in Partial K-Valued Logic, Proceedings of the 29th International Symposium on Multiple-Valued Logic, (1999) 77-81.

Equivalence of Classification and Regression Under Support Vector Machine Theory

Chunguo Wu[1,2], Yanchun Liang[1,*], Xiaowei Yang[3], and Zhifeng Hao[3]

[1] College of Computer Science and Technology, Jilin University,
Key Laboratory of Symbol Computation and Knowledge Engineering of Ministry of Education,
Changchun 130012, China
ycliang@jlu.edu.cn
[2] The Key Laboratory of Information Science & Engineering of Railway Ministry/
The Key Laboratory of Advanced Information Science and Network Technology of Beijing,
Beijing Jiaotong University, Beijing 100044, China
[3] Department of Applied Mathematics,
South China University of Technology,
Guangzhou 510640, China

Abstract. A novel classification method based on regression is proposed in this paper and then the equivalences of the classification and regression are demonstrated by using numerical experiments under the framework of support vector machine. The proposed algorithm implements the classification tasks by the way used in regression problems. It is more efficiently for multi-classification problems since it can classify all samples at a time. Numerical experiments show that the two classical machine learning problems (classification and regression) can be solved by the method conventionally used for the opposite problem and the proposed regression-based classification algorithm can classify all samples belonging to different categories concurrently with an agreeable precision.

1 Introduction

Pattern classification and function regression are two typical issues in machine learning fields. In short, we refer to pattern classification as classification and function regression as regression. To the best known of our knowledge, there aren't reported works presenting the equivalence between them. However, it's obvious that they have some potential common characteristics. After the statistical learning theory (SLT) was presented as a theoretical foundation of machine learning by Vapnik [1], the equivalence between classification and regression is more evident. Furthermore, the practical algorithms for the two kinds of problems are very similar [2]. The parallel formations of theories and similarities of practical algorithms inspire us to study the equivalence between the two kinds of primary problems in machine learning fields. In this paper, a classification method based on regression is proposed and the equivalence between the classification and regression is formulated using the least squares support vector machines [3~5].

---

* Corresponding author.

2 Formulations of Classification and Regression

Traditional classification includes two kinds of problems. One is binary-category classification and the other multi-category classification. The former refers to the problem with two categories, and the later to the problem with at least three categories. Suykens *et al* ascribes the binary-category classification to the following algebraic problem, name least squares support vector classification (LSVC):

$$\begin{bmatrix} 0 & -y^T \\ y & \Omega + C^{-1}I \end{bmatrix} \begin{bmatrix} b \\ \alpha \end{bmatrix} = \begin{bmatrix} 0 \\ \vec{1} \end{bmatrix}, \qquad (1)$$

where $\Omega_{ij} = y_i y_j \varphi(x_i, x_j)$, $\varphi(\cdot, \cdot)$ is the kernel function. α and b can be solved from Eq. (1). The classification function can be obtained as [5]

$$f(x) = \sum_{i=1}^{N} \alpha_i y_i \psi(x, x_i) + b. \qquad (2)$$

Traditionally, a multi-classification problem is handled via converting it to several binary classifications and then the converted problems is solved, instead of solving the original multi-classification problem.

Function regression using least squares support vector machine is ascribed to the following algebraic problem [4], name least squares support vector regression (LSVR):

$$\begin{bmatrix} 0 & \vec{1}^T \\ \vec{1} & \Omega + \gamma^{-1}I \end{bmatrix} \begin{bmatrix} b \\ \alpha \end{bmatrix} = \begin{bmatrix} 0 \\ y \end{bmatrix}, \qquad (3)$$

where $\Omega_{ij} = \varphi(x_i, x_j)$. After Eq. (9) is solved, the regression function takes the form as

$$y = f(x) = \sum_{i=1}^{N} \alpha_i \psi(x, x_i) + b. \qquad (4)$$

3 The Equivalence of Classification and Regression

Comparing conventional classification and regression, it can be seen that all of the differences resulted from the forms of constraint conditions. However, it should be pointed out that actually these differences are merely caused by artificial factors, but not inherent in the classification or the regression. Only for easy handling, researchers formulate their constraints in current different ways. Classification-based regression method proposed in [2] can be regarded as demonstration from regression to classification, where two classes of data are constructed from original regression data using a ε tolerance.

To present the equivalence from classification to regression, we propose a novel classification approach based on regression method. Comparing the training sets for pattern classification and function regression, $S_1 = \{(x_i, y_i) \mid x_i \in R^n, y_i \in L, i=1, 2, \ldots,$

N }, $S_2=\{(x_i, y_i) \mid x_i \in R^n, y_i \in R, i=1, 2, ..., N\}$, where $L=\{l_1, l_2, ... l_n\}$ is the label set and l_j ($j=1, 2, ..., n$) the label of the j-th category, it can be seen that $S_1 \subset S_2$. This observation motivates us to solve classification by the regression method. Hence, the regression function given by Eq. (4) still is valid for pattern classification. The proposed approach differs from that for pure pattern classification on judgment of category labels. Sample x is assigned the element of label set L, which has the smallest difference with $f(x)$, e.g.

$$j^* = \arg \min_{1 \leq j \leq n}\{|f(x) - l_j|\}. \tag{5}$$

4 Simulation Experiments

Two simulation experiments are given to demonstrate the feasibilies of the algorithms mentioned above. The first one is to regress the function $sin(x)$ ($0 \leq x \leq 4\pi$) by using LSSVC. The second one is to classify a multi-class instance (named as "Strip") generated randomly within a 40×20 2D square by using LSSVR. The running parameters for each instance are presented in table 1. For "Sine" instance both of the training and the testing correct rates are 100%. For "Strip" instance, the training correct rate is 100% and the testing correct rate is 99.6%. The detailed information about the simulation will be published on international journals soon.

Table 1. Parameters for each data set

Data names	Parameters		
	σ	C/γ	ε
Sine	10.0	1.0	0.01
Strip	800.0	3.0	NA

5 Conclusion and Discussion

A novel classification method is proposed in this paper, and then the dual equivalence between classification and regression is analyzed and demonstrated by using numerical experiments. The equivalence is of much importance for efficiency improvement in multi-classification problems, which enables one to classify all samples belonging to different categories at a time.

Acknowledgment

The authors are grateful to the support of the National Natural Science Foundation of China (60433020), the science-technology development project of Jilin Province of China (20030520) and the doctoral funds of the National Education Ministry of China (20030183060).

References

1. Vapnik, V.N.: Statistical Learning Theory. Springer-Verlag, New York (1998)
2. Tao, Q., Cao, J.D., Sun, D.M.: A Regression Method Based on The Support Vectors for Classification. Journal of Software 13 (2002) 1024-1028
3. Suykens, J.A.K., Gestel, T.V., Brabanter, J.D., Moor, B.D., Vandewalle, J.: Least Squares Support Vector Machines. World Scientific, Singapore (2002)
4. Suykens, J.A.K., Lukas, L., Wandewalle, J.: Sparse Approximation Using Least Squares Support Vector Machines. In: Proceedings of the IEEE International Symposium on Circuits and Systems (ISCAS 2000), Geneva, Switzerland (2000) 757-760
5. Suykens, J.A.K., Vandewalle, J.: Least Squares Support Vector Machine Classifiers. Neural Processing Letters 9 (1999) 293–300
6. Murphy, P.M., Aha, D.W.: UCI Repository of Machine Learning Database (1992) http://www.ics.uci.edu/~mlearn/MLRepository.html

Fuzzy Description of Topological Relations I: A Unified Fuzzy 9-Intersection Model

Shihong Du[1], Qiming Qin[1], Qiao Wang[2], and Bin Li[3]

[1] Institute of Remote Sensing and GIS, Peking University, Beijing 100871, China
dshgis@hotmail.com, qmqin@pku.edu.cn
[2] College of Geographic Information Science, Nanjing Normal University,
Nanjing 210097, China
wangqiao@zhb.gov.cn
[3] Department of Geography, Central Michigan University, Mount Pleasant,
Michigan 48859, USA
Bin.li@cmich.edu

Abstract. First, the impacts of uncertainty of position and attribute on topological relations and the disadvantages of qualitative methods in processing the uncertainty of topological relations are concluded. Second, based on the above point, the fuzzy membership functions for dividing topology space of spatial object and for describing uncertainty of topological relations are proposed. Finally, the fuzzy interior, exterior and boundary are defined according to those fuzzy membership functions, and then a fuzzy 9-intersection model that can describe the uncertainty is constructed. Since fuzzy 9-intersection model is based on fuzzy set, not two-value logic, the fuzzy 9-intersection model can describe the impacts of position and attribute of spatial data on topological relations, and the uncertainty of topological relations between fuzzy objects, relations between crisp objects and fuzzy objects, and relations between crisp objects in a united model.

1 Introduction

So far, there are two methods for modeling spatial phenomena in Geographical Information System (GIS): one is crisp method and another is fuzzy one. The crisp method assumes that the extent and the borders of spatial phenomena are precisely determined, homogenous, and universally recognized, while the fuzzy method models many spatial phenomena that do not have shape boundaries or whose boundaries can not be precisely determined [1]. The first kind of spatial phenomena often is modeled by crisp objects, such as crisp points, crisp lines and crisp regions, while the second can be represented as fuzzy objects.

Topological relations denote the unchanged characteristics under the topological transform, such as translation, rotation and scale. Its description is an attractive topic of spatial relations research, and also an important component of spatial Structure Query Language (SQL). Most existing methods for describing topological relations between crisp objects are qualitative, and refinement metrics are adopted to overcome the shortcomings. That is, qualitative methods can't describe the metric information of topological relations. On the one hand, as an extensively used method to describe topological relations, the 9-intersection model is a binary relation and based on crisp set theory, which only uses 0 and 1 to describe topological relations, so it can not deal with uncertainty of topological relations and their similarities. On the other hand, the uncertainty of spatial data (including position uncertainty of crisp objects and spatial extent fuzziness introduced by fuzzy objects) makes topological relations also uncertain. By far, three methods - such as qualitative, fuzzy and probability - are used to describe uncertainty of topological relations. However, as different methods are chose to describe the topological relations between crisp objects and the relations between fuzzy objects, it is possible to bring difficulties on spatial analysis about spatial relations, and to make information loss.

In this paper, the fuzzy set theory is introduced to deal with the uncertainty of topological relations. We focus our attention on a unified fuzzy 9-intesection model, which can describe the topological relations between crisp objects and relations between fuzzy objects in a uniform framework. Our contribution consists of: (i) the definition of membership functions for partitioning the topological space into three fuzzy sets: fuzzy interior, fuzzy boundary and fuzzy exterior; (ii) the development of a united fuzzy 9-intersection model that can describe uncertainty of topological relations introduced by position uncertainty and fuzzy objects.

Section 2 discusses the influence of position uncertainty and fuzzy objects on topological relations and reviews some related papers. The existing method for describing topological relations between crisp objects and relations between fuzzy objects are analyzed, and existent problems are pointed out in section 3. In section 4, we propose the membership functions for dividing a crisp object into three fuzzy parts: fuzzy interior, fuzzy boundary and fuzzy exterior, and constructs a fuzzy 9-intersection model to describe the uncertainty of topological relations. Finally, some advantages and disadvantages of the fuzzy 9-intersection model are pointed out in section 5.

2 Related Work

2.1 The Uncertainty of Spatial Data

Uncertainty in geographical information science mainly includes position uncertainty, attribute uncertainty, temporal uncertainty, logical consistency and data integrality, etc. In this paper, the two main uncertainties of spatial data will be discussed. The first is the position uncertainty which is not inherent in spatial phenomena, such as road, park and house, etc. but introduced by limitation of data capture systems and the constraints of the capacity of digital stores, etc. The second is fuzziness leaded by fuzzy objects, which is inherent in spatial phenomena, such as the intersection area between the city and the rural areas and the transition zone between various soil types. Because of the position uncertainty and fuzziness, the topological relations between road and park and the relations between road and intersection area is uncertain. Therefore, how to model the relations and to deal with the query, "find all roads which go across the intersection area of city and the rural area", still remains to be an unresolved problem. Because of the complexity of this problem, we only focus our attention on the basic theory and model, and the query is not preferred.

Position Uncertainty. Position uncertainty mainly denotes position variances between spatial position stored in GIS and real ones leaded by data production, representation and analysis, etc. that is, the position stored in GIS is not the real ones of phenomena, but distributes in a band with some probabilities. In general, the position uncertainty of a crisp point is measured by an error ellipse (Fig. 1a). The position uncertainty of a crisp line and a crisp region can be modeled by ε band model [3], which is a zone with fixed width along the line (Fig. 1b), or the boundary of the region (Fig. 1c). The error band model was proposed to process position uncertainty [4].

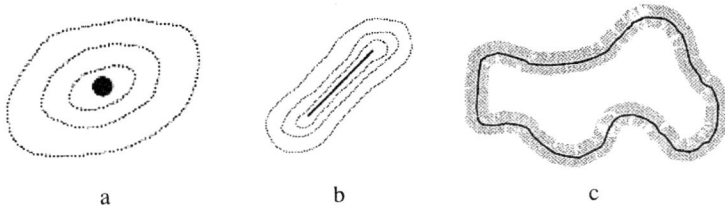

a   b   c

Fig. 1. Position uncertainty: (a) error ellipse for a crisp point, (b) -error band for a crisp line, (c) -error band for a crisp region [2]

Fuzzy Objects. Fuzzy objects show fuzziness of boundaries of spatial phenomena [5]. In a fuzzy object, each element have a membership degree indicating the extent that the element belong to the object, therefore each element can belong to many objects (classes) with different membership degree. Fuzzy objects can model fuzzy phenomena and resolve the shortcoming of crisp ones that each element only belongs to one object with maximum membership degree 1. Let $\mu(x,y)$ is the membership degree of an element belonging to an object, then for crisp objects, the domain of $\mu(x,y)$ is $\{0, 1\}$; while for fuzzy objects, it is $[0, 1]$. Cheng et al. proposed a way of extracting fuzzy objects from observations [6, 7]. Although fuzzy objects resolve the model of fuzzy phenomena, it brings difficulties on describing topological relations between fuzzy objects.

2.2 The Description of Topological Relations Between Crisp Objects

The 4- and 9-intersection models are based on the point-set topology. In 4-intersection model [8], a spatial object A is decomposed into two parts: the interior ($A°$) and the boundary (∂A). The topological relations between spatial object A and B is determined by a 2×2 matrix formed by intersection of two parts of A and B. In 9-intersection model [9], intersection of three sets - interior, boundary and exterior - forms a 3×3 matrix to distinguish topological relations.

In general, the intersection between two crisp sets has two states: non-empty (1) or empty (0), so 4-intersection model can describe 16 topological relations, while 9-intersection model 512. However, most of topological relations determined by 9-intersection model make no sense if considering the physical reality of 2D space. For example, there are only 8 significant topological relations between two crisp regions, 19 between crisp lines and crisp regions and 33 between two crisp lines.

Qualitative topological relations are binary in essence; therefore qualitative method is a crisp one. According to the criteria of uniqueness of representation of spatial relations, each qualitative relation between objects can be uniquely distinguished in the formulism, i.e., the possible relations are mutually exclusive [10]. As a result, qualitative one can not deal with the uncertainty of topological relations introduced by position uncertainty and fuzzy objects.

2.3 The Description of Topological Relations Between Uncertain Objects

The Influence of Position Uncertainty on Topological Relations. The error band model of position uncertainty, violating the definition of boundary in 9-intersection model based on the point-set topology, makes objects be not a crisp point set, but be an uncertain set. That is, a point does not only belong to only one set of the three. As 9-intesection model can not handle the influence of position uncertainty, the relations distinguished by the model are different with the real relations.

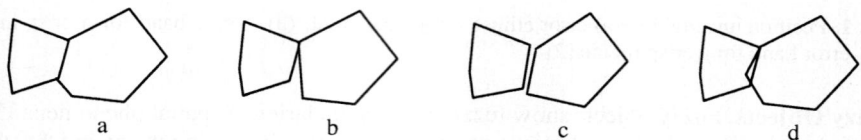

Fig. 2. Impact of position uncertainty on topological relations: (a) geometric graphic of topological relations; (b) meet; (c) disjoint; (d) overlap

The error band of position uncertainty makes the topological relation between crisp objects is not unique any more, but corresponds with many ones with different membership degrees. For example, the topological relation in Fig. 2a is *meet* according to the position stored in GIS, while it may be *meet* (Fig. 2b), *disjoint* (Fig. 2c) or *overlap* in real world(Fig. 2d). In addition, despite topological relations in Fig. 2a and 2b are same, they have different dimension of boundary intersection: the first is 1-dimension, while the second is 0-dimension. The other topological relations have similar problems.

The Influence of Fuzzy Objects on Topological Relations. The influence of fuzzy objects on topological relations lies in following three aspects: (1) each element in fuzzy objects partly belongs to several objects with different membership degrees, rather than strictly belong to one object or not. This makes it difficult to define the interior, boundary and exterior of fuzzy objects in term of the 9-intersection model; (2) the membership degree of each element and its distribution in space also have effect on topological relations between fuzzy objects, therefore fuzzy objects can't be regarded as a whole, but each element influence on topological relations should be considered; (3) fuzziness and position uncertainty of fuzzy objects exist simultaneously, and both of them limit description of topological relations. Existing methods, especially qualitative one, do not consider the influence of each element; therefore they can not describe the topological relations between fuzzy objects accurately.

2.4 Shortcomings of Existing Methods

If not considering the uncertainty of topological relations introduced by position and fuzzy objects, it is concluded that the qualitative method, such as 9-intersection model, is a successful and mature method. On the one hand, although the 9-intersection model has many advantages for modeling binary and composite topological relations between crisp objects, and has been applied to many fields, it cannot be directly used to handle with the uncertainty of topological relations. On the other hand, the existing methods for describing uncertainty are imperfect and inconsistent each other, especially inconsistent with 9-intersection model. As different methods are selected to model topological relations between crisp objects, relations between fuzzy objects and relations between uncertain objects (denoting crisp objects with position uncertainty), they possibly results in different resulting relations, which brings difficulties on application about topological relations. Accordingly, it is necessary to use a model to describe topological relations between fuzzy objects, relations between crisp objects, relations between uncertain objects and relations between uncertain objects and fuzzy objects in a uniform framework.

By expanding the 9-intersection model proposed by Egenhofer, a unified fuzzy 9-intersection model is created to represent topological relations between fuzzy objects, relations between uncertain objects and relations between fuzzy objects and uncertain objects based on fuzzy sets. In order to achieve it, following three problems about crisp 9-intersection model must be resolved:

(1) In the crisp 9-intersection model, a crisp method is adopted to divide topological space into crisp interior, boundary and exterior. Since there has no a smooth transition zone among three crisp parts, an element can be allowed strictly to belong to only one of the three sets, which results in the 9-intersection model can not handle with the influence of position uncertainty and fuzzy objects on topological relations. In order to consider the uncertainty, a unified fuzzy 9-intersection model should adopt a soft partition method to divide topological space into three fuzzy parts: fuzzy interior, boundary and exterior, and allow overlaps among them and partly membership between an element and the three fuzzy parts.

(2) In the crisp 9-intersection matrix, because each element is either empty (0) or non-empty (1), and non-overlap among three crisp parts, the topological relation between two objects only corresponds to a matrix, that is, the topology between two objects can only be represented by one topological relation. While position uncertainty and fuzzy objects make the topology between two objects is not unique any more. This means the topology may be represent by many relations with different membership degrees. Therefore, in the fuzzy 9-intersection matrix, the domain of each element is [0, 1], rather than {0, 1}, which makes the relation between the topology and the topological relations is a many-to-many mapping, rather than one-to-one.

(3) Each element of an uncertain object or a fuzzy object has different contributions on its topological relations, but the crisp 9-intersection model only regards them as a whole. The fuzzy 9-intersection model should take into account the contribution of each element to topological relations.

3 Fuzzy Description of Topological Relations

3.1 Fuzzy Set Theory

The fuzzy set theory is an extension of crisp set theory [11]. It overcomes the disadvantage of *bool* logic of the crisp one, makes that there has a smooth transition between the element inside and outside a set, and allows an element can partly belong to a set, rather than completely belong to or not.

Like the crisp set, the operators of fuzzy union (∪), fuzzy intersection (∩), fuzzy difference (-) and fuzzy complement (*C*) can be defined as formula (1 – 4) according to min - max principle.

$$\mu_{\tilde{A} \cup \tilde{B}}(x) = max(\mu_{\tilde{A}}(x), \mu_{\tilde{B}}(x)). \tag{1}$$

$$\mu_{\tilde{A} \cap \tilde{B}}(x) = min(\mu_{\tilde{A}}(x), \mu_{\tilde{B}}(x)). \tag{2}$$

$$\mu_{\tilde{A}^c}(x) = 1 - \mu_{\tilde{A}}(x). \tag{3}$$

$$\mu_{\tilde{A} - \tilde{B}}(x) = min(\mu_{\tilde{A}}(x), \mu_{\tilde{B}^c}(x)). \tag{4}$$

In formula (1 – 4), symbols $\tilde{A}$ and $\tilde{B}$ denote fuzzy set, and function $\mu_{\tilde{A} \cup \tilde{B}}(x)$, $\mu_{\tilde{A} \cap \tilde{B}}(x)$, $\mu_{\tilde{A}^c}(x)$ and $\mu_{\tilde{A} - \tilde{B}}(x)$ is the membership function of fuzzy union $\tilde{A} \cup \tilde{B}$, fuzzy intersection $\tilde{A} \cap \tilde{B}$, fuzzy complement $\tilde{A}^c$ and fuzzy difference $\tilde{A} - \tilde{B}$ respectively between fuzzy sets $\tilde{A}$ and $\tilde{B}$.

Let $\tilde{A}$ be a fuzzy set defined on domain U, then for an any real number $\alpha \in [0,1]$, the $A_\alpha = \{x | \mu_{\tilde{A}}(x) \geq \alpha, x \in U\}$ crisp set is called the α-cut set of $\tilde{A}$.

3.2 Formal Definitions of Topological Relations

Topological relations can be represented as a five-tuple $S\_Topologic(U, V, F, H, D)$. Symbol U stands for the set of spatial objects, V is the set of topological relations, F is the set of mapping functions, H is the functions set for partitioning topological space, D is the domain of functions in F and H. For an arbitrary topological relation $v_i \in V$, there always have a mapping function f_i in F correspondence with v_i. The function $f_i : U \times U \to D$ means membership degree between topology between any objects in U and v_i.

For crisp description of topological relations between regions, $V = \{disjoint, meet, overlap, cover, coveredBy, contain, inside, equal\}$, and each relation in V has a 9-intersection matrix. F is a set of binary functions, each function f_i in the set judges which matrix of topological relation in V is equal with the 9-intersection matrix between two regions, therefore the domain of function f_i is $\{0, 1\}$. The functions in H are defined in terms of interior point, exterior point and boundary point of point-set topology, so they are also crisp and their domains are $\{0, 1\}$.

For the fuzzy description of topological relations, the topological relation set is equal with that of crisp topological relations. There are three functions, $\tilde{h}_1(x, y)$, $\tilde{h}_2(x, y)$ and $\tilde{h}_3(x, y)$, defining the membership degree of any one point belonging to fuzzy interior, fuzzy exterior and fuzzy boundary, so their domains are [0, 1]. Function $\tilde{f}_i : U \times U \to [0,1]$ in F computes the membership degree that the topology between objects belongs to . v_i Therefore, the fuzzy description is to define the membership functions in H and F. Defining membership function $\tilde{f}_i$ is called fuzzy partition of topological space (section 3.3), and the ones in H is called fuzzy description of topological relations (section 3.4).

3.3 Fuzzy Partition of Topological Space

The key in fuzzy description of topological relations is expanding the crisp partition based on two-value logic to fuzzy partition. The fuzzy model uses fuzzy set to partition topological space and to define membership functions.

Fuzzy Partition of Topological Space for a Crisp Region. Since influenced of data uncertainty, the fuzzy boundary of a crisp region does not only denote the vector boundary, but is a buffer zone, which is a ($a \geq 0$) width and centered on the boundary of the region, expanding into exterior and taken from region's boundary into interior. The longer the distance from a point to the region's boundary is, the smaller membership degree that the point belongs to the region's boundary is; contrarily, the larger membership degree is.

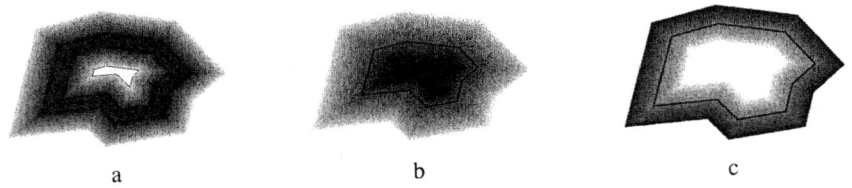

a　　　　　　　　　　b　　　　　　　　　　c

Fig. 3. Fuzzy partition of a crisp region: (a) fuzzy boundary; (b) fuzzy interior; (c) fuzzy exterior

The membership degree of a point belonging to the fuzzy boundary reaches maximum value 1 on the region's boundary (Fig. 3a). If the trapeziform function is selected to compute the membership degree of any point belonging to the fuzzy boundary, then the membership function of fuzzy boundary is defined by formula (6).

$$D(x,y) = \begin{cases} d(x,y) & (x,y) \in A^\circ \\ -d(x,y) & (x,y) \in A^- \\ 0 & (x,y) \in \partial A \end{cases} \quad (5)$$

$$\mu_{border}(x,y;a) = \begin{cases} 0 & D(x,y) \leq -a \\ \dfrac{D(x,y)+a}{a} & -a < D(x,y) < 0 \\ 1 & D(x,y) = 0 \\ \dfrac{a-D(x,y)}{a} & 0 < D(x,y) < a \\ 0 & D(x,y) \geq a \end{cases} \quad (6)$$

In the formula (5), the symbol $A°$, A^- and ∂A denotes the crisp interior, exterior and boundary of a region respectively in crisp 9-intersection model, and function $d(x, y)$ represents the minimum distance from a point (x, y) to the boundary.

As showed in Fig. 3b, the fuzzy interior of a crisp region does not denotes the space bounded by its vector boundary, but a buffer zone that has width a ($a \geq 0$) from the crisp exterior to the crisp interior. Those points whose $D(x,y)$ value to region's boundary is larger than or equals a have maximum membership degree 1, while the degrees of other points reduce from 1 to 0 gradually with the $D(x,y)$ value decreasing. The membership function of the fuzzy interior of a crisp region is:

$$\mu_{interior}(x, y; a) = \begin{cases} 0 & D(x, y) \leq 0 \\ \dfrac{D(x, y)}{a} & 0 < D(x, y) < a \\ 1 & D(x, y) \geq a \end{cases} \quad (7)$$

The membership function of the fuzzy exterior of a crisp region is:

$$\mu_{exterior}(x, y; a) = \begin{cases} 1 & D(x, y) \leq -a \\ \dfrac{D(x, y)}{-a} & 0 \geq D(x, y) > -a \\ 0 & D(x, y) > 0 \end{cases} \quad (8)$$

For convenience, the boundary of fuzzy interior with maximum degree is called interior boundary, while the boundary of fuzzy exterior with maximum degree is called exterior boundary. The interior boundary is a close curve by shrinking from the boundary, while the exterior boundary is the one by expanding into the exterior. Parameter a controls the width of fuzzy zone and its value can be equal to the width of error band.

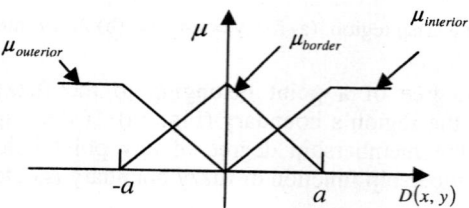

Fig. 4. Membership curves of fuzzy partition of a crisp region

Fuzzy Partition of Topological Space for a Crisp Line. Fuzzy partition of topological space for a crisp line is showed in Fig. 5, the fuzzy interior, fuzzy boundary and fuzzy exterior overlap each other. In addition, the fuzzy interior or fuzzy boundary is not a crisp line or a crisp point any more, but a buffer zone or a buffer circle with membership degree for each point. Any point can belong to fuzzy interior, fuzzy boundary or fuzzy exterior with different membership degree, rather than only belong to one of crisp interior, crisp boundary and crisp exterior.

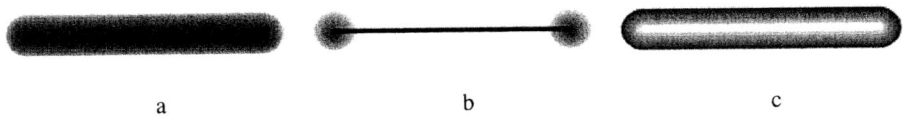

a b c

Fig. 5. Fuzzy partition of a crisp line: (a) fuzzy interior; (b) fuzzy boundary; (c) fuzzy exterior

Let a be a control parameter, and condition $a \geq 0$ holds, then the membership functions of the fuzzy interior, the fuzzy boundary and the fuzzy exterior are defined by formula (9 – 11), where function $d(x, y)$ means computing minimum distance from point (x, y) to the crisp interior of a crisp line; $d'(x, y)$ denote computing minimum distance from point (x, y) to the end-points of a crisp line.

$$\mu_{border}(x, y; a) = \begin{cases} 0 & d'(x, y) \geq a \\ \frac{a - d'(x, y)}{a} & d'(x, y) < a \end{cases} \quad (9)$$

$$\mu_{interior}(x, y; a) = \begin{cases} 0 & d(x, y) \geq a \\ \frac{a - d(x, y)}{a} & d(x, y) < a \end{cases} \quad (10)$$

$$\mu_{exterior}(x, y; a) = \begin{cases} 1 & d(x, y) \geq a \\ \frac{d(x, y)}{a} & d(x, y) < a \end{cases} \quad (11)$$

Fuzzy Partition of Topological Space for a Crisp Point. A crisp point can be partitioned into fuzzy interior and fuzzy exterior (Fig. 6). The fuzzy interior of a crisp point is a fuzzy circle zone, in which the membership degree that a point belongs to the fuzzy interior decreases from the center point of the zone to its boundary gradually, while the membership degree that a point belongs to the fuzzy exterior increases from the center point of the zone to its boundary.

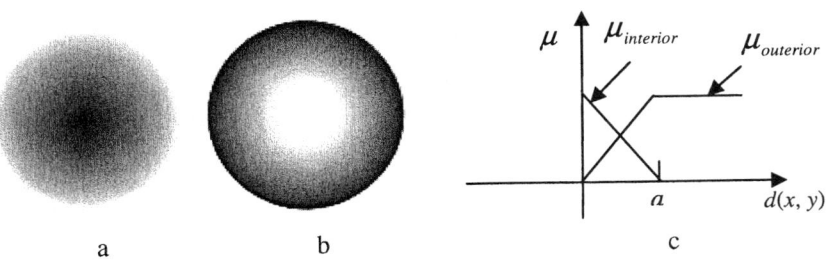

a b c

Fig. 6. Fuzzy partition of a crisp point: (a) fuzzy interior; (b) fuzzy exterior; (c) membership function curve

$$\mu_{interior}(x,y;a) = \begin{cases} 0 & d(x,y) \geq a \\ \dfrac{c-d(x,y)}{a} & d(x,y) < a \end{cases}. \tag{12}$$

$$\mu_{exterior}(x,y;a) = \begin{cases} 1 & d(x,y) \geq a \\ \dfrac{d(x,y)}{c} & d(x,y) < a \end{cases}. \tag{13}$$

The control parameter in formula (12) and (13) has same meanings with formula (9 – 11).

3.4 The Unified Fuzzy 9-Intersection Model

Fuzzy partition of topological space allows the fuzzy interior, fuzzy boundary and fuzzy exterior to overlap each other, and those points in common zone have different membership degree belonging to the three fuzzy parts whose width can be adjusted by the value of control parameters in membership functions. In fact, the three fuzzy parts formed by fuzzy partition of topological space can be regarded as three fuzzy sets, and each point with a membership degree in the three fuzzy sets.

For a crisp object, topological space can be partitioned into the fuzzy interior, fuzzy boundary and fuzzy exterior. In addition, both objects A and B impose two partitions on the topological space, which makes that any point can simultaneously belong to the three fuzzy parts of A and of B with different membership degree. As a result, there are 6 fuzzy sets: $\tilde{A}^\circ, \partial\tilde{A}, \tilde{A}^-, \tilde{B}^\circ, \partial\tilde{B}$ and $\tilde{B}^-$. Let symbol U_{AB} mean the plane space in which A and B are embedded, then the six fuzzy sets of crisp A and B are defined by formula (14 – 19).

$$\tilde{A}^\circ = \{\mu_{Ainterior}(x,y)|(x,y)\in U_{AB}\}. \tag{14}$$

$$\partial\tilde{A} = \{\mu_{Aborder}(x,y)|(x,y)\in U_{AB}\}. \tag{15}$$

$$\tilde{A}^- = \{\mu_{Aexterior}(x,y)|(x,y)\in U_{AB}\}. \tag{16}$$

$$\tilde{B}^\circ = \{\mu_{Binterior}(x,y)|(x,y)\in U_{AB}\}. \tag{17}$$

$$\partial\tilde{B} = \{\mu_{Bborder}(x,y)|(x,y)\in U_{AB}\}. \tag{18}$$

$$\tilde{B}^- = \{\mu_{Bexterior}(x,y)|(x,y)\in U_{AB}\}. \tag{19}$$

In formula (14 – 19), function $\mu_{Ainterior}(x,y)$ and $\mu_{Binterior}(x,y)$ is the membership function of the fuzzy interior defined according to crisp A and B respectively (control parameters are omitted), and other membership functions have similar meanings. According to definitions above, the crisp 9-intersection model can be expanded into the unified fuzzy 9-intersection model:

$$\tilde{I}(A,B) = \begin{pmatrix} \mu_{11} & \mu_{12} & \mu_{13} \\ \mu_{21} & \mu_{22} & \mu_{23} \\ \mu_{31} & \mu_{32} & \mu_{33} \end{pmatrix} = \begin{pmatrix} \sigma(\tilde{A}^\circ \cap \tilde{B}^\circ) & \sigma(\tilde{A}^\circ \cap \partial\tilde{B}) & \sigma(\tilde{A}^\circ \cap \tilde{B}^-) \\ \sigma(\partial\tilde{A} \cap \tilde{B}^\circ) & \sigma(\partial\tilde{A} \cap \partial\tilde{B}) & \sigma(\partial\tilde{A} \cap \tilde{B}^-) \\ \sigma(\tilde{A}^- \cap \tilde{B}^\circ) & \sigma(\tilde{A}^- \cap \partial\tilde{B}) & \sigma(\tilde{A}^- \cap \tilde{B}^-) \end{pmatrix} \tag{20}$$

Where $\tilde{I}(A,B)$ is denoted as fuzzy 9-intersection matrix, where σ means finding maximum membership degree from a fuzzy set. For example,

$$\sigma(\tilde{A}° \cap \tilde{B}°) = max_{(x,y) \in U_{AB}}(min(\mu_{Ainterior}(x,y), \mu_{Binterior}(x,y)))$$

The value of each element in the fuzzy 9-intersection model $\tilde{I}(A,B)$ is the maximum value of the intersection of two fuzzy sets. Because the three fuzzy sets are determined by the membership functions of partitioning topological space, the value of element in fuzzy 9-intersection matrix is also decided by the membership functions. If the fuzzy partition is degraded into a crisp one, then the six fuzzy sets: $\tilde{A}°$, $\partial\tilde{A}$, $\tilde{A}^-$, $\tilde{B}°$, $\partial\tilde{B}$ and $\tilde{B}^-$ also become six crisp sets. The degradation will be reached by adjusting value of the control parameters in membership functions.

3.5 Fuzzy Description of Topological Relations Between Fuzzy Objects

The topological relations cover three categories: topological relations between fuzzy objects (TRFF), relations between fuzzy objects and crisp objects (TRFC) and relations between crisp objects (TRCC). The fuzzy 9-intersection matrix of TRCC can be computed by formula (20). But the others must be based on the fuzzy partition of a fuzzy object.

Topological Relations between a Fuzzy Object and a Crisp Object. TRFC deals with topological relations between a fuzzy region and a crisp object, such as a crisp region, a crisp point and a crisp line. The fuzziness of TRFC depends on fuzzy partition of crisp objects and fuzzy objects. To describe TRFC, the crisp object is partitioned into three fuzzy sets, and the fuzziness of the fuzzy object should be also considered. Let $\tilde{A}$ be a fuzzy object, and B be a crisp one. α, β be any two real number in [0, 1] with $\alpha > 0.5$ and $0.5 > \beta \geq 0$. Let α- and β-cut set of fuzzy object $\tilde{A}$ be A_α and A_β respectively, then the crisp set A_α, $A_\beta - A_\alpha$ and $A_0 - A_\beta$ is the crisp interior, boundary and exterior of $\tilde{A}$ respectively (Fig. 7). The distance from any point to crisp boundary of $\tilde{A}$ is defined by formula (21).

$$D(x,y) = \min_{(x',y') \in A_\beta - A_\alpha}(d(x,y,x',y')) . \tag{21}$$

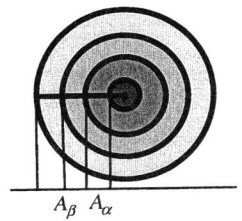

Fig. 7. Fuzzy partition of a fuzzy object

Membership function of fuzzy partition of $\tilde{A}$ is defined by replacing formula (5) with formula (21). The three fuzzy sets of $\tilde{A}$ can be determined by formula (22 - 24).

$$\tilde{A}^{\circ} = \tilde{A} . \tag{22}$$

$$\partial \tilde{A} = \left\{ \mu_{Aborder}(x,y) \big| (x,y) \in A_{\beta} - A_{\alpha} \right\} . \tag{23}$$

$$\tilde{A}^{-} = \tilde{A}^{c} . \tag{24}$$

First, according to formula (22 - 24), the three fuzzy sets of $\tilde{A}$ will be obtained. Second, the three fuzzy sets of B will be computed by formula (17) – (19). Finally, the fuzzy 9-intersection matrix of TRFC will be computed by formula (20).

Topological Relations between Fuzzy Objects. TRFF mainly deals with the topological relations between two fuzzy regions. The fuzziness of TRFF comes from the fuzziness of two fuzzy objects and that of fuzzy partition of topological space of fuzzy objects. Six fuzzy sets about two fuzzy objects $\tilde{A}$ and $\tilde{B}$ can be obtained by formula (22 - 24), and then the fuzzy 9-intersection matrix of TRFF will be identified by formula (20).

4 Conclusions

In this paper, a unified fuzzy 9-intersection model is proposed to describe the uncertainty of topological relations introduced by position uncertainty and fuzzy objects in a uniform framework. In comparison with existing method for describing topological relations, the fuzzy model has following advantages: (1) it can describe the uncertainty of objects and their topological relations in a uniform framework, where the fuzziness of fuzzy objects and position uncertainty of a crisp object is described by the membership functions, while the fuzzy 9-intersection model handles with the uncertainty of topological relations; (2) it can describe the topological relations among fuzzy objects and crisp objects in a uniform framework; (3) it is based on the fuzzy partition of topological space, and allows the three fuzzy sets to overlap each other, therefore the domain of each element is [0, 1] in fuzzy 9-intersection matrix, not {0, 1} any more; (4) the uncertainty of topological relations in fuzzy 9-intersection model is indicated by a membership degree.

Acknowledgments

The work described in this paper was substantially supported by grants from the China National Natural Science Foundation (No. 40271090) and by China Postdoctoral Science Foundation (No. 2004036029).

References

1. Schneider, M.: Uncertainty Management for Spatial Data in Databases: Fuzzy Spatial Data Types. In: Goos, G., Hartmanis, J., Leeuwen, J. V. (eds.): Advances in Spatial Databases. Lecture Notes in Computer Science, Vol. 1651. Springer-Verlag, Berlin Heidelberg New York (1999) 330–351.
2. Zhang, J. X., Du, D. S.: Field-Based Models for Positional and Attribute Uncertainty. Acta Geodaetica et Cartographica Sinica, 3 (1999) 244–249.

3. Perkal, J.: On epsilon Length. Bulletin de l'Academie Polonaise des Sciences, 4 (1956) 399–403.
4. Zhang, G. Y., Tulip, J.: An Algorithm for Avoidance of Sliver Polygons and Clusters of Points in Spatial Overlay. In: Proceedings of 4th Spatial Data Handling, (1990) 141–150.
5. Altman, D.: Fuzzy Set Theoretic Approaches for Handing Imprecision in Spatial Analysis. International Journal of Geographical Information Science, 3 (1994) 271–289.
6. Cheng, T., Molenaar, M., Bouloucos, T.: Identification of Fuzzy Objects from Field Observation Data. In: Hirtle, S. C., Frank, A. U. (eds.): Spatial Information Theory: A Theoretical Foundation for GIS. Lecture Notes in Computer Science, Vol. 1329. Springer-Verlag, Berlin Heidelberg New York (1997) 241–259.
7. Cheng, T., Molenaar M.: Objects with Fuzzy Spatial Extent. Photogrammetric Engineering and Remote Sensing, 7 (1999) 797–801.
8. Egenhofer, M., Franzosa, R.: Point-Set Topological Spatial Relations. International Journal of Geographical Information Systems, 2 (1991) 161–174.
9. Egenhofer, M. J., Herring, J.: Categorizing Binary Topological Relations between Regions, Lines and Points in Geographic Databases. Technical Report, Department of Surveying Engineering, University of Maine, Orono, ME., 1991.
10. Abdelmoty, A. I., Williams, M. H.: Approaches to the Representation of Qualitative Spatial Relationships for Geographic Databases. In: Molenaar, M., Hoop, S. D. (eds.): Advanced Geographic Data Modeling: Spatial Data Modeling and Query Language for 2D and 3D applications. Delft, The Netherlands (1994) 204–216.
11. Zadeh, L. A.: Fuzzy sets. Information and Control. 8 (1965) 338–353.

Fuzzy Description of Topological Relations II: Computation Methods and Examples

Shihong Du[1], Qiao Wang[2], Qiming Qin[1], and Yipeng Yang[2]

[1] Institute of Remote Sensing and GIS, Peking University, Beijing 100871, China
dshgis@hotmail.com, qmqin@pku.edu.cn
[2] College of Geographic Information Science, Nanjing Normal University,
Nanjing 210097, China
wangqiao@zhb.gov.cn

Abstract. The unified fuzzy 9-intersection model of topological relations can describe the uncertainty of topological relations introduced by the uncertainty of spatial data. In this article, first, the raster algorithm for computing fuzzy 9-intersection model is presented, and the vector algorithms for computing fuzzy 9-intersection model of point/point, point/line, point/region, line/line, line/region, region/region topological relations are also provided. Second, based on the software developed by us, the examples for computing fuzzy 9-intersection matrix between two crisp objects, between two fuzzy objects and between a crisp object and a fuzzy object are listed. The results and analysis show that the unified fuzzy 9-intersection model is effective to describe the uncertainty of topological relations.

1 Introduction

In the first paper, "Fuzzy Description of Topological Relations I: A Unified Fuzzy 9-Intersection Model", we present the main idea of our model. In this paper, we intend to bear out our model from algorithm and experiment, the main content includes: (i) the design of the raster and the vector algorithm to compute the fuzzy 9-intersection matrix; (ii) the implementation of the fuzzy 9-intersection matrix.

For convenience, in the following part of this paper, the formula (1 - 24) denotes the corresponding formula in the first paper.

2 Raster Method for Computing Fuzzy 9-Intersection Matrix

After identifying the membership functions and their control parameters, the fuzzy 9-intersection matrix and the three fuzzy sets of spatial objects can be computed by the membership functions of the fuzzy 9-intersection model. The raster method is computing membership degree of each point belonging to the three fuzzy sets, and then the fuzzy 9-intersection matrix can be worked out by formula (20). Because the vector space is continues, how to get discrete points is critical. Raster method computes membership degree in terms of following three principles: (1) if both object A and B are stored as raster format, then the center point of a raster are used to compute membership degree (fuzzy objects are stored as raster format); (2) if one of object A and B is a fuzzy object, the other is a crisp one, then the crisp one must be rasterized according to the raster's size of the fuzzy object to compute membership degree; (3) if both A and B are vector objects, then both of them must be rasterized according to a predefined size. The raster method approximates continuous space by discrete rasters, so the precision is limited by the raster's size. If the size is too large, the precision will be small; if the size is too small, the precision would be fine, but the compute speed would be slow. Therefore, except for fuzzy objects, the raster method is not a good option.

3 Vector Method for Computing Fuzzy 9-Intersection Matrix

Since the precision of raster method is smaller than vector one, and compute speed slower, the vector method can be adopted to compute membership degrees for vector objects. For convenience, the symbol μ_{11}, μ_{12}, μ_{13}, μ_{21}, μ_{22}, μ_{23}, μ_{31}, μ_{32} and μ_{33} denotes the value of corresponding element in the unified fuzzy 9-intersection matrix (formula 20) respectively. The following algorithm assumes that the controls parameters of point, line and polygon fuzzy partition are same.

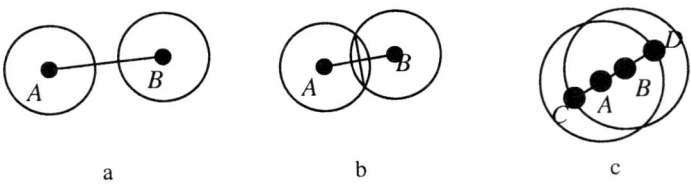

Fig. 1. Vector algorithm for computing point/point fuzzy topological relations

Because of a crisp point no fuzzy boundary, the 5 elements related to fuzzy boundary in fuzzy 9-intersection matrix make no sense, and only μ_{11}, μ_{13}, μ_{31} and μ_{33} make sense. The point/point topological relations fall into three categories: (i) Distance $(A, B) \geq 2a$ (Fig. 1a); (ii) $a \leq$ Distance $(A, B) < 2a$ (Fig. 1b); (iii) $0 \leq$ Distance $(A, B) < a$ (Fig. 1c), where Distance (A, B) represents the distance between A and B, and a denotes the control parameter in formula (12) and (13).

(1) No matter which one holds of the three conditions, the value of μ_{11} will be obtained by inputting into formula (12) the coordinates of center point between A and B, because the intersection between membership functions of fuzzy interior of A and B reaches maximum value at the center point.

(2) When (i) and (ii) holds, the value of μ_{13} and μ_{31} must be 1 (Fig. 1a and 1b); if (iii) holds, as showed in Fig. 1c, for computing μ_{13}, the coordinate of center point between A and C is input into formula (12), and for μ_{31} the coordinate of center point between B and D.

(3) μ_{33} is 1.0, because the intersection between fuzzy exteriors of two points always reaches 1.0.

Other algorithms for point/line, point/region, line/line, line/region and region/region are similar with point/point.

4 Fuzzy 9-Interesection Matrix

4.1 Fuzzy 9-Interesection Matrix Between Crisp Objects

Based on the membership functions and the vector algorithm above, provided the value of the control parameters in the membership functions are identified, the fuzzy 9-intersection matrix can be worked out. The values of control parameters can be equal to the width of error band, such as the ε-error band. In this paper, we just care about the width of error band, not the method to compute the width, therefore the values control parameters are set to 200 meter in following examples, and the scale of spatial data is 1: 250,000. As the parameters only control the width of the fuzzy parts, while not change the characteristics of membership functions, choosing a value 200 for the parameters does not limit the effect of our method.

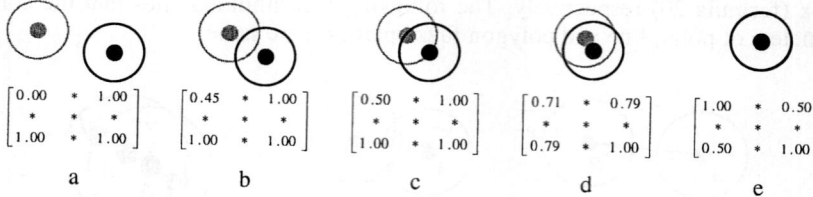

Fig. 2. Fuzzy 9-interesection matrix of point/point topological relations

The back object is denoted as point A and the gray object point B in Fig. 2, while the circle outside the points are boundary of their fuzzy zones. Symbol '*' means that the element in fuzzy 9-intersection matrix is insignificant (because crisp points have no fuzzy boundary). As showed in Fig. 2, when both two crisp points are outside the two fuzzy zones (Fig. 2a – 2c), μ_{31} and μ_{13} always are 1.0; when they are inside (Fig. 2d – 2e), with the distance between two crisp points decreasing, μ_{31} and μ_{13} decrease from 1.0 to 0.5, and μ_{11} increases from 0.0 to 1.0 at the same time. It must be pointed out that μ_{31} and μ_{13} in fuzzy 9-intersection matrix is 0.5, while they are 0 in crisp 9-intersection matrix when two crisp points are equal. According to theory of position uncertainty, the real positions of two identical points are distributed in an error band, which results in that those points in the error band belong to the fuzzy interior and the fuzzy exterior of a crisp point with different membership degree simultaneously. Accordingly, μ_{31} and μ_{13} is not 0.0 at the real positions, but 0.5 possibly, which is logical according to formula (20). This also indicates that the fuzzy 9-intersection model can describe the influences of position uncertainty on topological relations between two crisp points. By the way, like the crisp 9-intersection model, μ_{33} always is 1.0 in fuzzy 9-intersection matrix, which results from the infinite of fuzzy exterior of a crisp point.

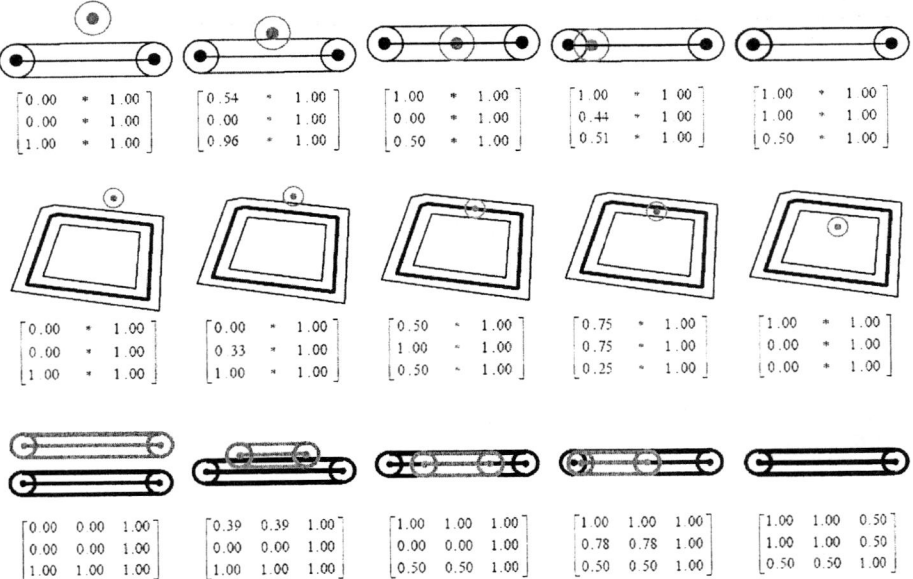

Fig. 3. Fuzzy matrix of point/line, point/region and line/line topological relations

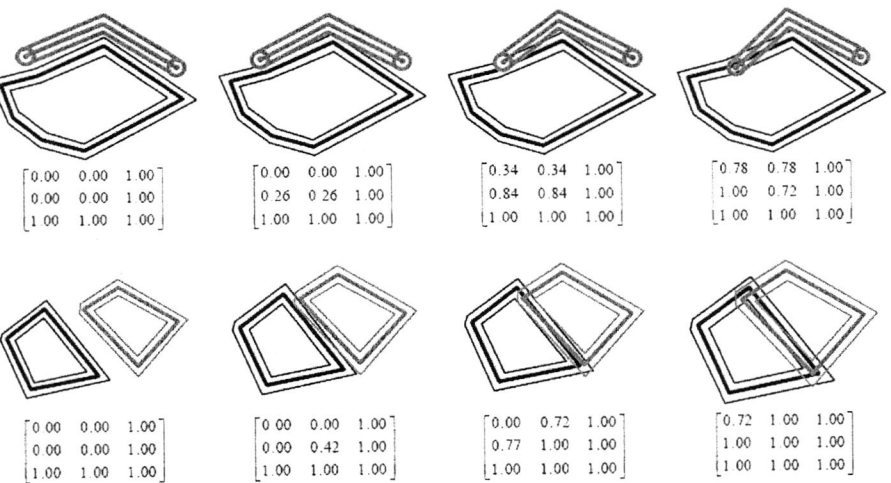

Fig. 4. Fuzzy matrix of line/region and region/region topological relations

The fuzzy matrices between a crisp point and a crisp line, between a crisp point and a crisp region, between two crisp lines are listed in Fig. 3; while Fig. 4 shows the fuzzy matrix between a crisp line and a crisp region and between two crisp regions. These fuzzy matrices in Fig.3 and Fig.4 have similar characteristics with those in Fig.2.

4.2 Fuzzy 9-Interesection Matrix Related Fuzzy Objects

Several examples of fuzzy 9-intersection matrix between a crisp point and a fuzzy region are listed in Fig. 5, where the fuzzy region is A, and crisp object is B. In the fuzzy 9-intersection matrix, when the point moves from the exterior of A to its core gradually, μ_{11} increases gradually, μ_{21} increases first and then decreases, and μ_{31} decreases.

Other examples between a crisp line and a fuzzy region, between a crisp region and a fuzzy region and between two fuzzy regions are listed in Fig. 6. These fuzzy 9-interesection matrices have similar characteristics with those in Fig. 5.

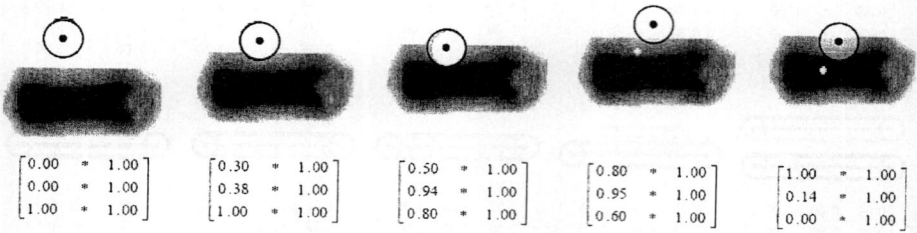

Fig. 5. Fuzzy matrix between a crisp point and a fuzzy region

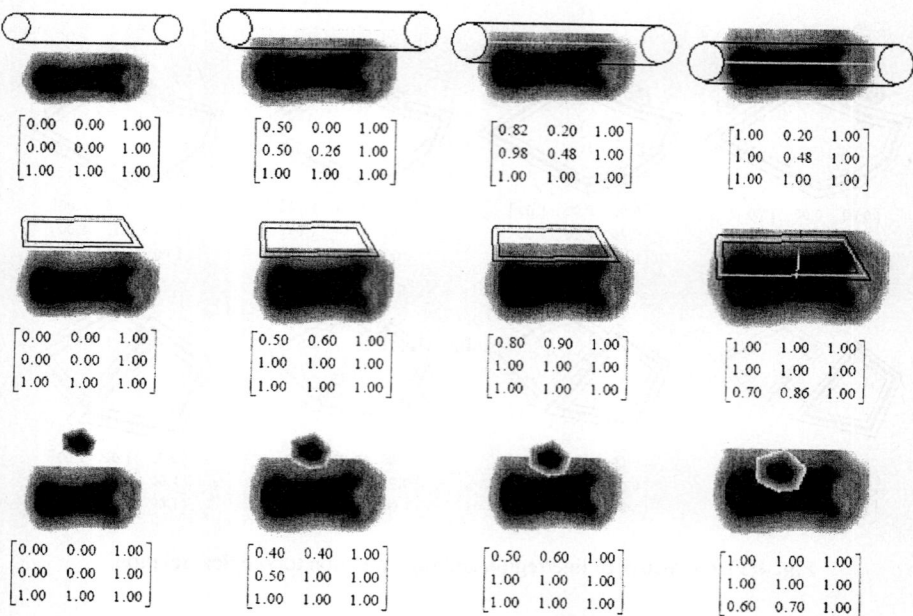

Fig. 6. Fuzzy matrix related fuzzy regions

5 Conclusions

(1) There are two the algorithms for computing fuzzy 9-intersection matrix: the raster and the vector. The vector one is more complex, but is more precise and faster than the raster one; while the raster is simpler, but its precision is limited by the resolution of raster, and slower than the vector one.

(2) Despite the trapeziform function is chose to partition topological space into three fuzzy parts, and the maximum and minimum operator are selected to implement fuzzy union and fuzzy intersection in the fuzzy 9-intersection matrix, the other function and operators of fuzzy union and intersection may be adopted [1]. However, in this situation, the vector algorithm proposed in this paper is not appropriate any more. In general, the trapeziform function and the operators of maximum and minimum can meet the need, and are helpful to process membership degree in posterior steps.

(3) The fuzzy description of topological relations violates the criterion of uniqueness of representation of topological relations [2], but this is logical, because the uniqueness criterion is proposed under no considering the uncertainty of topological relations, and only appropriate to evaluate the qualitative methods for describing topological relations. From the perspective of uncertainty of topological relations, the topological relation between two objects is not unique; therefore the result of fuzzy description is logical.

Acknowledgments

The work described in this paper was substantially supported by grants from the China National Natural Science Foundation (No. 40271090) and by China Postdoctoral Science Foundation (No. 2004036029).

References

1. Zimmermann, H. J.: Fuzzy Set Theory and Its Applications. Kluwer, Boston MA (1991).
2. Abdelmoty, A. I., Williams, M. H.: Approaches to the Representation of Qualitative Spatial Relationships for Geographic Databases. In: Molenaar, M., Hoop, S. D. (eds.): Advanced Geographic Data Modeling: Spatial Data Modeling and Query Language for 2D and 3D applications. Delft, The Netherlands (1994) 204–216.

Modeling and Cost Analysis of Nested Software Rejuvenation Policy

Jing You, Jian Xu, Xue-long Zhao, and Feng-yu Liu

Department of Computer, Nanjing University of Science and Technology,
Nanjing, China
{youjing00, senjianjoe, zhaoxuein}@163.com
liu.fengyu@126.com

Abstract. To counteract software aging, a new nested software rejuvenation policy is put forward in this paper. Comparing to the conventional periodic software rejuvenation policy, the nested policy takes into account the application-level and system-level rejuvenation simultaneously and executes N times application-level rejuvenation before system-level rejuvenation. If any application-level rejuvenation is not executed successfully, then the system has to be rebooted directly. Comparing the minimum average rejuvenation cost per year and the maximum system availability of the nested software rejuvenation policy with the conventional periodic software rejuvenation policy's, the results demonstrate that the new policy consumes less downtime and lower rejuvenation cost, and enhances software availability and reliability.

1 Introduction

During the past 20 years, the software performance has yielded tens of thousands fold improvement. However, the software complexity along with high-performance also brings high maintenance cost, even more than the acquisition cost of system. The cutthroat competition in IT industry requires the developers provide more perfect software and sooner update. Consequently it is impossible to perform the all-round test before throwing the software into market. Some "heisenbugs" and "aging-related bugs"[1] cannot be discovered and corrected in time. In addition, the modularization development of software also makes it difficult to maintenance. All these reasons increase the failure probability of system, and the software availability and reliability are encountering new challenge.

In general, the software reliability can reference the mean time to failure (MTTF) and the software availability can reference the ratio MTTF to the sum of MTTF and MTTR, where MTTR is the mean time to repair. In order to improve the availability and reliability of software, we can increase the MTTF or reduce the MTTR. However, whatever technology cannot postpone infinitely the failure time of system without degradation, thus more and more researchers began to focus on the technologies that can reduce MTTR, e.g. software rejuvenation[2-4], recursive restartability[5], and microreboot[6]. In this paper, a new nested software rejuvenation policy is proposed. This policy can reduce the rejuvenation cost further.

The rest of this paper is organized as follows. Section 2 discusses the previous related work to software rejuvenation and the novel aspects of the new policy. The nested software rejuvenation policy are elucidated in Section 3. Section 4 analyzes a case with two rejuvenation policies, and the results show that the nested policy indeed consumes less downtime and lower cost. Conclusions are discussed in section 5.

2 Related Work

Software aging is a very common phenomenon in a large system during the continuous running time. This phenomenon and some special reasons have been reported by Huang et al [2; 3]. Software aging degrades the performance of software and ultimately induces software to crash. To counteract software aging, a proactive technique called software rejuvenation has been proposed in [2]. It involves stopping the running software, "cleaning" its internal state (e.g., garbage collection, flushing operating system kernel tables, reinitializing internal data structures) and restarting it. When the system performance drops down to a certain extent, software rejuvenation can release the system resources and rejuvenate the system [2; 3; 7].

Software rejuvenation is different from the other two techniques that can reduce MTTR. Both recursive restartability[5] and microreboot[6] are reactive recovery to software failure. While software rejuvenation is a proactive fault management technique, which can rejuvenate the degenerative software before it encounters failure.

Conventional software rejuvenation is to perform a predetermined rejuvenation policy periodically without considering rejuvenation granularity [3; 8-12]. As a rule, fine-grained rejuvenation consumes less downtime and lower cost. Hong Y et al [13], Bao Y et al [14] and Xiea W et al [15] proposed the rejuvenation policies considering two different granularities. However, these policies are based on the values of performance parameters detected on-line, not based on the contributing degree of the applications to the performance degradation. We firstly ascertain the main contributor of all applications to the performance degradation, formulate the application-level and system-level rejuvenation, and then propose a new nested software rejuvenation policy.

3 Nested Software Rejuvenation Policy

Simply periodic rejuvenation can reduce rejuvenation cost to a certain degree. However, it consumes more rejuvenation cost than that we expect. In order to reduce the rejuvenation cost further, a nested software rejuvenation policy is put forward (Fig. 1). This policy embeds the application-level rejuvenations in the system-level rejuvenation. We must ascertain the main contributor of all applications to the performance degradation and the evaluating index of system performance.

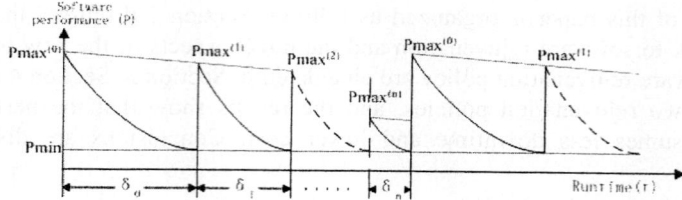

Fig. 1. When the evaluating index reaches the predetermined threshold (P_{min}), the system executes the application-level rejuvenation to the main contributor. Recurrently a serial of rejuvenation values of the evaluating index $\{P_{max}^{(1)}, P_{max}^{(2)}, \ldots, P_{max}^{(n)}\}$ and rejuvenation intervals $\{\delta_0, \delta_1, \ldots, \delta_n\}$ will be concluded. The two serials are degressive in order, which implies the application-level rejuvenation will be executed more and more frequently and the system will not work normally when the rejuvenation times (n) equals to the upper limit N, which causes least downtime (i.e. highest availability) or lowest rejuvenation cost. When n equals N, the system-level rejuvenation is executed, and the system performance rejuvenates to the initial value $P_{max}^{(0)}$, then a new cycle begins. If other software or hardware malfunctions do not happen, the system with this policy will run forever.

The whole rejuvenation process can be divided into $N+1$ sub-processes. However, not all application-level rejuvenations can be executed successfully. One reason is in the policy itself. Any rejuvenation can fail according to a certain probability because the policy is based on the stochastic rule of historical data of system resources. Another reason is the unpredictable hardware or software malfunctions because of the change of environment or situation.

If the system encounter failure when $n<N$, then the obligatory reboot of system will be necessary whatever state the system is being in. After the system-level rejuvenation or obligatory reboot, the system rejuvenates the optimal performance and the nested policy executes the next cycle.

4 Rejuvenation Case Analysis

One sub-process of the system failure and rejuvenation is modeled in Figure 2.

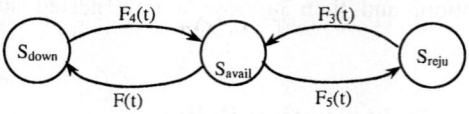

Fig. 2. S_{avail}, S_{down} and S_{reju} show respectively system available state, system failure state and system rejuvenation state. The curves with arrow denote the transitions from one state to another, and the labels at curves denote the distribution functions of system sojourn time in previous state.

Assuming that the sojourn times of system in states S_{avail}, S_{reju} and S_{down} have respectively general distributions $F(t)$, $F_3(t)$ and $F_4(t)$, and let $p(t)=F(t)$, then $p(t)$ is the failure probability of system staying in state S_{avail} at time t. The probability distribution $F_5(t)$ from state S_{avail} to state S_{reju} is a unit step function $U(t-\delta)$, where δ is the predetermined rejuvenation interval. Assuming the degradation course of software is a two-step behavior [1,3,4,8], the state S_{avail} contains two states S_{up} called system robust state and S_{prob} called system failure probable state. If the sojourn times of system in states S_{up} and S_{prob} have respectively general distributions $F_1(t)$ and $F_2(t)$, then $F(t)=F_1*F_2(t)$.

Define the transition probability $Q_{ij}(t)(i,j=0,\cdots,3, i\neq j)$, then its L-S transformation matrix is $Q_{ij}(s)=(q_{ij}(s))=\int_0^\infty e^{-st}dQ_{ij}(t)$. Set the serial numbers of three system states S_{avail}, S_{reju}, S_{dow} as 0, 1, 2, then

$$\begin{cases} q_{01}(s) = \int_0^\infty e^{-st}\overline{F}(t)dF_5(t) \\ q_{02}(s) = \int_0^\infty e^{-st}\overline{F}_5(t)dF(t) \\ q_{10}(s) = \int_0^\infty e^{-st}dF_3(t) \\ q_{20}(s) = \int_0^\infty e^{-st}dF_4(t) \end{cases}$$

The total probability with which the system is in the three states is $h(t)$, and its L-S transformation is

$$h(s) = (\overline{q}_{01}(s) - q_{02}(s)) + q_{01}(s)\overline{q}_{10}(s) + q_{02}(s)\overline{q}_{20}(s).$$

Define the transient probability from 0 to j ($j=1,2$) at time t ($t>0$) by $P_{0j}(t)(j=0,\cdots,3)$, and its L-S transformation is $p_{0j}(s) = \int_0^\infty e^{-st}dP_{0j}(t)$, then

$$\begin{cases} p_{00}(s) = (\overline{q}_{01}(s) - q_{02}(s))/h(s) \\ p_{01}(s) = q_{01}(s)\overline{q}_{10}(s)/h(s) \\ p_{02}(s) = q_{02}(s)\overline{q}_{20}(s)/h(s) \end{cases}$$

Note that the rule $\overline{\psi}(\bullet) = 1 - \psi(\bullet)$ meets all above equations.

Define that the rejuvenation cost per unit time is C_c, the repair cost per unit time after failure is C_r, and $C_r >> C_c$, then the expected rejuvenation cost per unit time in the steady-state becomes

$$C2 = \lim_{s\to 0}\{C_c p_{01}(s) + C_r p_{02}(s)\}$$

Based on the above assumptions, the system downtime (DT) and rejuvenation cost (C) per unit time can be calculated by

$$\begin{cases} DT = \dfrac{1}{ET}\left[r\times(1-p(\delta)) + R\times p(\delta)\right] \\ C = \dfrac{1}{ET}\left[r\times C_r(1-p(\delta)) + R\times C_f p(\delta)\right] \\ ET = r\times(1-p(\delta)) + R\times p(\delta) + \int_0^\delta(1-p(t))dt \\ p(t) = F_1(t)*F_2(t) \end{cases} \quad (1)$$

where ET is the expected rejuvenation timeperiod including the running time before rejuvenation and the expected time executing rejuvenation. r and R denote respectively the expected times executing scheduled and unscheduled rejuvenation and $R>r$. C_r and C_f denote the rejuvenation costs of scheduled and unscheduled rejuvenation respectively and $C_f >> C_r$. Moreover, r equals r_a (or r_s) when executing application-level (or system-level) rejuvenation and $r_s > r_a$. C_r equals C_a (or C_s) when executing application-level (or system-level) rejuvenation and $C_s > C_a$. δ can be calculated by the lowest cost $C_{min}(\delta)$ or the given-failure-probability $p=p(\delta)$.

To implement the nested rejuvenation policy, we must conclude the rejuvenation interval sequence $\{\delta_0, \delta_1, \ldots, \delta_N\}$ and the maximal times N of application-level rejuvenation. To facilitate the analysis, we assume the distribution functions $F_1(t)$, $F_2(t)$, $F_3(t)$ and $F_4(t)$ are exponential distributions with respective failure rate $\lambda_1(t)$, λ_2, $\lambda_{31} / \lambda_{32}$ and λ_4. λ_{31} (λ_{32}) denotes failure rate of application-level (system-level) rejuvenation. Due to software aging, $\lambda_1(t)$ is a monotone non-decreasing function. For different rejuvenation sub-processes, approximately, the sojourn time of system at state S_{up} can be regarded as exponential distribution with different failure rates λ_{1i} ($0 \leq i \leq N$), which can be obtained by

$$\begin{cases} \lambda_{10} = \lambda_1(0), & i = 0 \\ \lambda_{1i+1} = \lambda_1\left(\sum_{k=1}^{i}\left(\delta_{k-1} + i\frac{1}{\lambda_{31}}\right)\right), & 0 \leq i < N \end{cases} \quad (2)$$

The set of downtimes $\{DT_0, DT_1, \ldots DT_{n-1}, DT_n\}$ and rejuvenation costs $\{C_0, C_1, \ldots C_{n-1}, C_n\}$ can be calculated by Eqs. (1) and (2). The average downtime per year (EDT_n) and average rejuvenation cost per year EC_n can be computed by the following equation.

$$\begin{cases} EDT_n = \dfrac{\sum_{i=0}^{n-1} DT_i(\delta_i + \frac{1}{\lambda_{31}}) + DT_n(\delta_n + \frac{1}{\lambda_{32}})}{\sum_{i=0}^{n-1}(\delta_i + \frac{1}{\lambda_{31}}) + \delta_n + \frac{1}{\lambda_{32}}} \times 12 \times 30 \times 24, \; n \geq 0 \\[2ex] EC_n = \dfrac{\sum_{i=0}^{n-1} C_i(\delta_i + \frac{1}{\lambda_{31}}) + C_n(\delta_n + \frac{1}{\lambda_{32}})}{\sum_{i=0}^{n-1}(\delta_i + \frac{1}{\lambda_{31}}) + \delta_n + \frac{1}{\lambda_{32}}} \times 12 \times 30 \times 24, \; n \geq 0 \end{cases} \quad (3)$$

According to the minimum rejuvenation cost rule (Rule I), let $EC=Min\{EC_n\}$, then EC is the minimum rejuvenation cost, and the corresponding n is the maximum N_1 of application-level rejuvenation times. Similarly, according to the maximal availability rule (Rule II), let $EDT=Max\{EDT_n\}$, then EDT is the minimum downtime, and the corresponding n is the maximum N_2. Apparently, N_1 is not equal to N_2.

For the conventional periodic rejuvenation policy, the average rejuvenation cost per year EC' and the system downtime per year DT' can be solved as bellow:

$$\begin{cases} DT' = \dfrac{1}{ET'}\left[r_s \times (1-p(\delta)) + R \times p(\delta)\right] \times 12 \times 30 \times 24 \\ C' = \dfrac{1}{ET'}\left[r_s \times C_s (1-p(\delta)) + R \times C_f p(\delta)\right] \\ ET' = r_s \times (1-p(\delta)) + R \times p(\delta) + \int_0^\delta (1-p(t))dt \\ EC' = C' \times 12 \times 30 \times 24 \end{cases} \quad (4)$$

In this equation, r_s replaces r in Eq. (1) as the unique scheduled rejuvenation time because only system-level rejuvenation can be implemented at this policy.

5 Experiment and Results

In this subsection, we illustrate the superiority of nested software rejuvenation policy (Policy I) by comparing its minimum average rejuvenation cost per year and minimum average downtime with conventional periodic policy's (Policy II).

Extending the parameters of experiments in reference [2], the parameters of this case are listed in table 1.

Table 1. Known failure rates and rejuvenation costs. C_a, C_s and C_f denote the costs of application-level rejuvenation, system-level rejuvenation and system crash. $\lambda_1(t)$ is a monotone non-decreasing function. Assume $\lambda_1(t)=kt+1/240$, in which t is the total running time of system and $k>0$.

$\lambda_1(0)^{-1}$	240hrs	λ_4	0.2/hrs
λ_2^{-1}	2160hrs	C_f	$5000/hr
$\lambda_{31}, \lambda_{51}$	6/hrs	C_s	$1000/hr
$\lambda_{32}, \lambda_{52}$	3/hrs	C_a	$500/hr
slope of $\lambda_1(t)$		k	

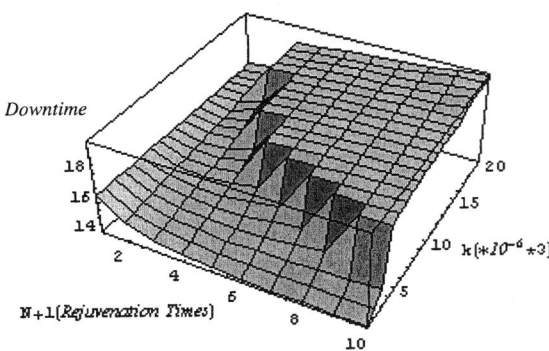

Fig. 3. The relation among the application-level rejuvenation times N, the slope k and the system downtime per year. (Policy I)

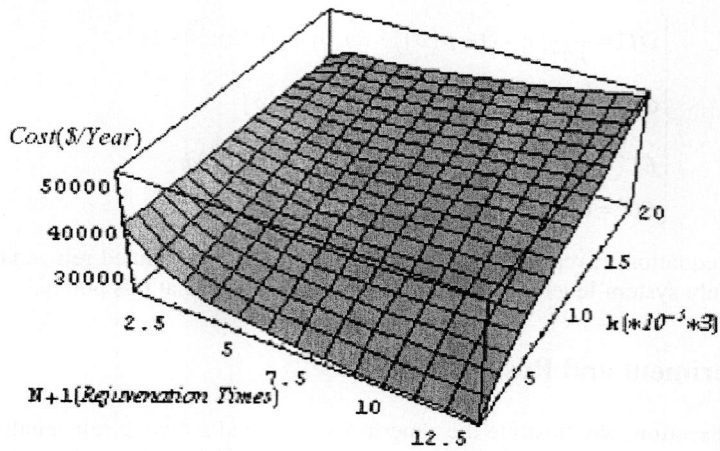

Fig. 4. The relation among the application-level rejuvenation times N, the slope k and the average rejuvenation cost per year. (Policy I)

After determining the slope k of $\lambda_1(t)$, the average downtime and average rejuvenation cost per year of system with nested policy for different application-level rejuvenation times can be solved. (Figs. 3 and 4)

In order to describe clearly the relation between the average rejuvenation costs per year for given slopes, we take sections to different slopes in Fig. 4. Figure 5 is sectional views of Figure 4 to different slopes.

The reason of the phenomena in Figs. 3, 4 and 5 is that the larger slope means all support applications consume more system resources, and then the rejuvenation intervals reduce, the downtimes increase, the average rejuvenation cost increases.

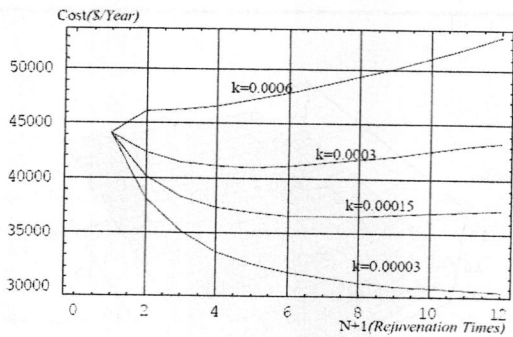

Fig. 5. The average rejuvenation costs per year to different slopes. It can be found that the relation function (EC_n) between the average rejuvenation cost per year and application-level rejuvenation times is concave, decreasing before increasing or monotone increasing for a given slope. The minimum average rejuvenation cost per year increases and the maximum application-level rejuvenation-times decreases with slope.

Given the failure rate $\lambda_l=1/240$, the average rejuvenation cost per year EC' and system downtime DT' of the conventional periodic software rejuvenation policy can be obtained by Eq. (4). The former equals identically $44032.9/year$ and the latter equals identically 16.4264 $hrs/year$.

To demonstrate the virtue of Policy I , we compare the minimum average rejuvenation cost per year of the two policies in Fig. 6.

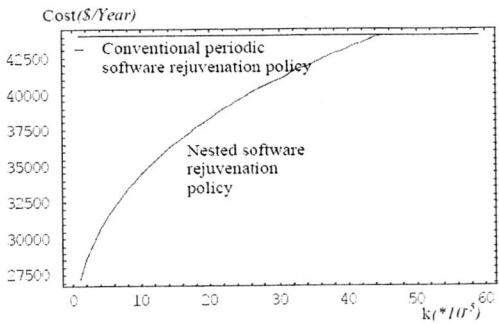

Fig. 6. Comparison of the minimum average rejuvenation costs per year between the two software rejuvenation policies. Note that the minimum average rejuvenation costs per year of Policy I are increasing with slope and there is a maximum when k is greater than or equal to 0.00045. The maximum is equal to $44032.9/year$, which is just the rejuvenation cost per year of Policy II.

The Comparison of the minimum system downtime per year between the two software rejuvenation policies is similar with figure 6. The system with Policy II encounter 16.4264 hrs downtime per year , which is the maximum downtime of the system with Policy I . Consequently Policy I consumes lower rejuvenation cost and provides higher availability, that is the system using Policy I can run more reliable than that using Policy II .

6 Conclusion

Commonly, there is a main contributing factor to performance degradation in a practical system. Therefore a new nested software rejuvenation policy is proposed in this paper, which contains the application-level and system-level rejuvenation simultaneously, specially emphasizes nesting. This policy reduces further the overhead incurred by software rejuvenation.

To demonstrate the superiority of nested rejuvenation policy to conventional periodic policy, we analyze a case in which each sub-process is a time-based rejuvenation and conclude the rejuvenation cost and system downtime for the two policies. Respectively, according to the rules of minimum rejuvenation cost and maximum availability, a series of minimum average downtime and rejuvenation costs per year to different slopes for the two policies are calculated and compared. The numerical results show that the nested policy consumes less downtime and lower cost, and enhances the software availability and reliability.

The nested policy described in this paper is a two-level rejuvenation. In practice, if we can ascertain the contributing degree of all applications, the nested rejuvenation policy can be extended to more level. In addition, the equations and results in this paper are only approximations of true values because the failure rate λ_{1i} in Eq. (2) is an approximation. Assuming $\lambda_1(t)$ is a monotone non-decreasing linear function with slope k, the deviation from real value is increasing with slope. So a more accurate solution is needed to develop in the further work.

References

1. Vaidyanathan, K., and Trivedi, K. S.: Extended Classification of Software Faults Based on Aging. *the IEEE Int'l. Symp. on Software Reliability Engineering, ISSRE 2001*, Hong Kong (2001)
2. Huang, Y., Kintala, C., Kolettis, N., and Fulton, N. D.: Software Rejuvenation: Analysis, Module and Applications. *Proc. of FTCS-25*, Pasadena, CA (1995)
3. Castelli, V., Harper, R. E., Heidelberger, P., Hunter, S. W., K.S.Trivedi, Vaidyanathan, K., and Zeggert, W. P.: Proactive Management of Software Aging. *IBM JRD*, Vol. 45. (2001) 311-332
4. Malek, M., Salfner, F., and Hoffmann, G. A.: Self-Rejuvenation - an Effective Way to High Availability. *Proceedings of SELF-STAR: International Workshop on Self-* Properties in Complex Information Systems*, Bertinoro, Italy (2004)
5. Candea, G., and Fox, A.: Recursive Restartability: Turning the Reboot Sledgehammer into a Scalpel. *8th Workshop on Hot Topics in Operating Systems*, Schloss Elmau, Germany (2001)
6. Candea, G., Kawamoto, S., Fujiki, Y., Friedman, G., and Fox, A.: Microreboot - A Technique for Cheap Recovery. *6th Symposium on Operating Systems Design and Implementation*, San Francisco, CA (2004)
7. International Business Machines. IBM Director Software Rejuvenation- White Paper. (2001)
8. Garg, S., Puliafito, A., and Trivedi, K. S.: Analysis of Software Rejuvenation using Markov Regenerative Stochastic Petri Net. *Proc. of ISSRE 1995*, Toulouse, France (1995)
9. Pfening, S., Garg, S., Puliafito, A., Telek, M., and Trivedi, K. S.: Optimal Software Rejuvenation for Tolerating Soft Failures. *Performance Evaluation*, Vol. 27/28. (1996) 491-506
10. Garg, S., Puliafito, A., Telek, M., and Trivedi, K. S.: Analysis of Preventive Maintenance in Transactions Based Software Systems. *IEEE Trans. on Computers*, Vol. 47. (1998) 96-107
11. Trivedi, K. S., Vaidyanathan, K., and Goseva-Popstojanova, K.: Modeling and Analysis of Software Aging and Rejuvenation. *Proceedings of the IEEE Annual Simulation Symposium* (2000)
12. Dohi, T., K.Goseva-Popstojanova, and K.S.Trivedi. Analysis of Software Cost Models with Rejuvenation. *Proc. 5th IEEE International Symposium on High Assurance Systems Engineering (HASE 2000)*, Albuquerque, New Mexico (2000)

13. Hong, Y., Chen, D., Li, L., and Trivedi, K.: Closed Loop Design for Software Rejuvenation. *Workshop on Self-Healing, Adaptive and self-MANaged Systems (SHAMAN)*, New York (2002)
14. Bao, Y., Sun, X., and Trivedi, K. S.: Adaptive Software Rejuvenation: Degradation Model and Rejuvenation Scheme. *2003 International Conference on Dependable Systems and Networks (DSN'03)*, San Francisco, California (2003)
15. Xiea, W., Hongb, Y., and Trivedi, K.: Analysis of a two-level software rejuvenation policy. *Reliability Engineering and System Safety*, Vol. 87. (2005) 13-22

A Fuzzy Multi-criteria Decision Making Model for the Selection of the Distribution Center

Hsuan-Shih Lee

Department of Shipping and Transportation Management,
Department of Computer Science, National Taiwan Ocean University,
Keelung 202, Taiwan, Republic of China

Abstract. The location selection of distribution is one of the most important decision issues for logistic managers. In order to encompass vagueness in decision data, a new fuzzy multiple criteria decision-making method is proposed to solve the distribution center selection problem under fuzzy environment. In the proposed method, the ratings of alternatives and the weights of the criteria are given in terms of linguistic variables which is in turns represented by triangular fuzzy numbers.

1 Introduction

In terms of logistical system design and administration, distribution center is a common problem encountered by logistic managers. During the last decade, seeking reduced transportation cost in the increased economic scale of production has shifted the focus to the selection of distribution center. A distribution center links suppliers (source) and consumers (demand). A distribution center selection problem is homomorphic to a plant location selection problem. Factors such as investment cost, climate condition, labor force quality and quantity, transportation availability may be considered in the selection of the plant location [4,18,19,20,22]. These factors can be classified into objective factors and subjective factors. Many precision-based methods for location selection have been developed. Mathematical programming is usually utilized to determine the optimal location of facilities [1,7,11]. Tompkins and White [22] introduced a method which used the preference theory to assign weights to subjective factors by making all possible pairwise comparisons between factors. Spohrer and Kmak [18] proposed a weight factor analysis method to integrate the quantitative data and qualitative ratings to choose a suitable plant location from numerous alternatives. All the methods stated above are based on the concept of accurate measure and crisp evaluation.

In the selection of a best distribution center, the values for the qualitative criteria are often imprecise. The desired value and importance weight of criteria are usually described in linguistic terms such as "very low", "medium", "high", "fair", and "very high". A distribution center selection problem can modeled as a multiple criteria decision making (MCDA) problem. In traditional MCDM, performance rating and weights are measured in crisp numbers [10,12,21]. Under many circumstances where performance rating and weights can not be given precisely, the fuzzy set theory is introduced to model the uncertainty of human judgements and such problems is known as fuzzy multiple criteria decision making (FMCDM). In FMCDM, performance ratings and weights are usually represented by fuzzy numbers. A FMCDM with m alternatives and n criteria can be modeled as follows:

$$D = \begin{bmatrix} \tilde{A}_{11} & \tilde{A}_{12} & \cdots & \tilde{A}_{1n} \\ \tilde{A}_{21} & \tilde{A}_{22} & \cdots & \tilde{A}_{2n} \\ \tilde{A}_{m1} & \tilde{A}_{m2} & \cdots & \tilde{A}_{mn} \end{bmatrix}$$

and

$$W = \begin{bmatrix} \tilde{W}_1 & \tilde{W}_2 & \cdots & \tilde{W}_n \end{bmatrix}$$

where $\tilde{A}_{ij}$ is the fuzzy number representing the performance of ith alternative under jth criterion and $\tilde{W}_j$ is the fuzzy number representing the weight of jth criterion.

In dealing with fuzzy numbers, aggregation of fuzzy numbers and ranking fuzzy number are some of the important issues in group decision. Methods of aggregation such as OAM can be found in [14]. Many methods for fuzzy ranking have been proposed [2,3,5,6,8,9,13,17,23,24]. They can be classified into two categories. The first category is based on defuzzification. Various methods of defuzzification have been proposed. In the first category, fuzzy numbers are defuzzified into crisp numbers or the so-called utilities in some literatures. The ranking are then done based on these crisp numbers. Though it is easy to compute, the main drawback of this type is that defuzzification tends to loss some information and thus is unable to grasp the sense of uncertainty. The other category is based on fuzzy preference relation. The advantage of this type is that uncertainties of fuzzy numbers are kept during ranking process. However, the fuzzy preference relations proposed thus far are too complex to compute. Yuan [24] has proposed criteria for measuring ranking method. Lee [13] has proposed a new fuzzy ranking method based on fuzzy preference relation satisfying all criteria proposed by Yuan. In [15], we extended the definition of fuzzy preference relation [16] and propose an extended fuzzy preference relation which satisfies additivity and is easy to compute. In this paper, we are going to propose a new method for FMCDM for the selection of distribution center.

2 Mathematical Preliminaries

Definition 1. *The α-cut of fuzzy set A, A^α, is the crisp set $A^\alpha = \{x \mid \mu_A(x) \geq \alpha\}$. The support of A is the crisp set $Supp(A) = \{x \mid \mu_A(x) > 0\}$. A is normal iff $sup_{x \in U} \mu_A(x) = 1$, where U is the universe set.*

Definition 2. *A fuzzy subset A of real number R is convex iff*

$$\mu_A(\lambda x + (1-\lambda)y) \geq (\mu_A(x) \wedge \mu_A(y)), \forall x, y \in R, \forall \lambda \in [0,1],$$

where $\wedge$ denotes the minimum operator.

Definition 3. *A is a fuzzy number iff A is a normal and convex fuzzy subset of R.*

Definition 4. *A triangular fuzzy number A is a fuzzy number with piecewise linear membership function μ_A defined by*

$$\mu_A(x) = \begin{cases} \frac{x-a_1}{a_2-a_1}, & a_1 \leq x \leq a_2, \\ \frac{a_3-x}{a_3-a_2}, & a_2 \leq x \leq a_3, \\ 0, & \text{otherwise}, \end{cases}$$

which can be denoted as a triplet (a_1, a_2, a_3).

Definition 5. *Let A and B be two fuzzy numbers. Let $\circ$ be a operation on real numbers, such as $+$, $-$, $*$, $\wedge$, $\vee$, etc. By extension principle, the extended operation $\circ$ on fuzzy numbers can be defined by*

$$\mu_{A \circ B}(z) = \sup_{x,y: z = x \circ y} \{\mu_A(x) \wedge \mu_B(y)\}. \tag{1}$$

Definition 6. *Let A be a fuzzy number. Then A_α^L and A_α^U are defined as $A_\alpha^L = \inf_{\mu_A(z) \geq \alpha}(z)$ and $A_\alpha^U = \sup_{\mu_A(z) \geq \alpha}(z)$ respectively.*

Definition 7. *A fuzzy preference relation R is a fuzzy subset of $\Re \times \Re$ with membership function $\mu_R(A, B)$ representing the degree of preference of fuzzy number A over fuzzy number B.*

1. *R is reciprocal iff $\mu_R(A, B) = 1 - \mu_R(B, A)$ for all fuzzy numbers A and B.*
2. *R is transitive iff $\mu_R(A, B) \geq \frac{1}{2}$ and $\mu_R(B, C) \geq \frac{1}{2} \Rightarrow \mu_R(A, C) \geq \frac{1}{2}$ for all fuzzy numbers A, B and C.*
3. *R is a fuzzy total ordering iff R is both reciprocal and transitive.*

If fuzzy numbers are compared based on fuzzy preference relations, then A is said to be greater than B iff $\mu_R(A, B) > \frac{1}{2}$.

Definition 8. *An extended fuzzy preference relation R is an extended fuzzy subset of $\Re \times \Re$ with membership function $-\infty \leq \mu_R(A, B) \leq \infty$ representing the degree of preference of fuzzy number A over fuzzy number B.*

1. *R is reciprocal iff $\mu_R(A, B) = -\mu_R(B, A)$ for all fuzzy numbers A and B.*
2. *R is transitive iff $\mu_R(A, B) \geq 0$ and $\mu_R(B, C) \geq 0 \Rightarrow \mu_R(A, C) \geq 0$ for all fuzzy numbers A, B and C.*
3. *R is additive iff $\mu_R(A, C) = \mu_R(A, B) + \mu_R(B, C)$*
4. *R is a total ordering iff R is both reciprocal, transitive and additive.*

If fuzzy numbers are compared based on extended fuzzy preference relations, then A is said to be greater than B iff $\mu_R(A, B) > 0$.

Our extended fuzzy preference relation is defined as follows.

Definition 9. *For any fuzzy number A, B, extended fuzzy preference relation $F(A, B)$ is defined by the membership function*

$$\mu_F(A, B) = \int_0^1 ((A - B)_\alpha^L + (A - B)_\alpha^U) d\alpha \qquad (2)$$

Lemma 1. *F is reciprocal, i.e.,*

$$\mu_F(B, A) = -\mu_F(A, B). \qquad (3)$$

Proof: Since $(A - B)_\alpha^L + (A - B)_\alpha^U = -((B - A)_\alpha^L + (B - A)_\alpha^U)$, we have $\mu_F(B, A) = -\mu_F(A, B)$. □

Lemma 2. *F is additive, i.e.,*

$$\mu_F(A, B) + \mu_F(B, C) = \mu_F(A, C) \qquad (4)$$

Proof:

$$\mu_F(A, B) + \mu_F(B, C)$$
$$= \int_0^1 ((A - B)_\alpha^L + (A - B)_\alpha^U) d\alpha + \int_0^1 ((B - C)_\alpha^L + (B - C)_\alpha^U) d\alpha$$
$$= \int_0^1 A_\alpha^L - B_\alpha^U + A_\alpha^U - B_\alpha^L + B_\alpha^L - C_\alpha^U + B_\alpha^U - C_\alpha^L d\alpha$$
$$= \int_0^1 ((A - C)_\alpha^L + (A - C)_\alpha^U) d\alpha. \qquad (5)$$

□

Lemma 3. *F is transitive, i.e.,*

$$\mu_F(A, B) \geq 0 \text{ and } \mu_F(B, C) \geq 0 \Rightarrow \mu_F(A, C) \geq 0. \qquad (6)$$

Proof: By lemma 2, we have $\mu_F(A, C) = \mu_F(A, B) + \mu_F(B, C)$. Since $\mu_F(A, B), \mu_F(B, C) \geq 0$, we have $\mu_F(A, c) \geq 0$. □

Lemma 4. *Let $A = (a_1, a_2, a_3)$ and $B = (b_1, b_2, b_3)$ be two triangular fuzzy numbers. $\mu_F(A, B) \geq 0$ iff*

$$a_1 + 2a_2 + a_3 - b_1 - 2b_2 - b_3 \geq 0 \qquad (7)$$

Proof: $\mu_F(A, B) \geq 0$ iff

$$\mu_F(A, B) = \int_0^1 (A - B)_\alpha^L + (A - B)_\alpha^U d\alpha = \frac{a_1 + 2a_2 + a_3 - b_1 - 2b_2 - b_3}{2} \geq 0. \qquad (8)$$

□

Definition 10. *Let $\geq$ be a binary relation on fuzzy numbers defined by*

$$A \geq B \text{ iff } \mu_F(A, B) \geq 0. \qquad (9)$$

Theorem 1. *$\geq$ is a total ordering relation.*

3 The Fuzzy Decision Making Method

To facilitate our method, define the preference function of one fuzzy number $\tilde{A}_{ij}$ over another number $\tilde{A}_{kj}$ as follows:

$$P(\tilde{A}_{ij}, \tilde{A}_{kj}) = \begin{cases} \mu_F(\tilde{A}_{ij}, \tilde{A}_{kj}) & \text{if } \mu_F(\tilde{A}_{ij}, \tilde{A}_{kj}) \geq 0 \\ 0 & \text{otherwise} \end{cases}$$

Let J be the set of benefit criteria and J' be the set of cost criteria where

$$J = \{1 \leq j \leq n \text{ and } j \text{ belongs to benefit criteria}\}$$

$$J' = \{1 \leq j \leq n \text{ and } j \text{ belongs to cost criteria}\},$$

and

$$J \cup J' = \{1, \ldots, n\}.$$

The strength matrix $S = (S_{ij})$ is given by letting

$$S_{ij} = \begin{cases} \sum_{k \neq i} P(\tilde{A}_{ij}, \tilde{A}_{kj}) & \text{if } j \in J \\ \sum_{k \neq i} P(\tilde{A}_{kj}, \tilde{A}_{ij}) & \text{if } j \in J'. \end{cases} \quad (10)$$

Similarly, the weakness matrix $I = (I_{ij})$ is given by letting

$$I_{ij} = \begin{cases} \sum_{k \neq i} P(\tilde{A}_{kj}, \tilde{A}_{ij}) & \text{if } j \in J \\ \sum_{k \neq i} P(\tilde{A}_{ij}, \tilde{A}_{kj}) & \text{if } j \in J'. \end{cases} \quad (11)$$

The fuzzy weighted strength matrix $\tilde{S} = (\tilde{S}_i)$ can be obtained by

$$\tilde{S}_i = \sum_j S_{ij} \tilde{W}_j \quad (12)$$

and the fuzzy weighted weakness matrix $\tilde{I} = (\tilde{I}_i)$ can be obtained by

$$\tilde{I}_i = \sum_j I_{ij} \tilde{W}_j, \quad (13)$$

where $1 \leq i \leq m$. Now we are ready to present our method for FMCDM.

Step 1: Identify the criteria for the selection of distribution selection.

Step 2: Aggregate the fuzzy decision matrices and fuzzy weight matrices given by decision makers and normalized the group fuzzy decision matrix. Let $D = (\tilde{A}_{ij})$ be the normalized group fuzzy decision matrix and $W = (\tilde{W}_j)$ be the weight matrix.

Step 3: Calculate the strength matrix by (10).

Step 4: Calculate the weakness matrix by (11).

Step 5: Calculate the fuzzy weighted strength indices by (12).

Step 6: Calculate the fuzzy weighted weakness indices by (13).

Step 7: Derive the strength index S_i from the fuzzy weighted strength and weakness indices by

$$S_i = \sum_{k \neq i} P(\tilde{S}_i, \tilde{S}_k) + \sum_{k \neq i} P(\tilde{I}_k, \tilde{I}_i) \qquad (14)$$

Step 8: Derive the weakness index I_I from the fuzzy weighted strength and weakness indices by

$$I_i = \sum_{k \neq i} P(\tilde{S}_k, \tilde{S}_i) + \sum_{k \neq i} P(\tilde{I}_i, \tilde{I}_k) \qquad (15)$$

Step 9: Aggregate the strength and weakness indices into total performance indices by

$$t_i = \frac{S_i}{S_i + I_i} \qquad (16)$$

Step 10: Rank alternatives by total performance indices t_i for $1 \leq i \leq m$.

4 Numerical Example

Suppose a company desires to select a suitable city for establishing a new distribution center. The evaluation is done by a committee of three decision-makers D_1, D_2, and D_3. After preliminary screening, there are three alternatives A_1, A_2, and A_3 under further evaluation. Assume the linguistic variables employed for weights and ratings are respectively shown in Table 1. The evaluation committee then undergoes the proposed evaluation procedure:

Step 1: Five selection criteria are identified:
    (1) investment cost (C_1),
    (2) expansion possibility (C_2),
    (3) availability of acquirement material (C_3),
    (4) human resource (C_4),
    (5) closeness to demand market (C_5).

Table 1. Linguistic variables for the importance weights of criteria and the ratings

Importance weights of criteria		Linguistic variables for the ratings	
Very low (VL)	(0,0,0.1)	Very poor (VP)	(0,0,1)
Low (L)	(0,0.1,0.3)	Poor (P)	(0,1,3)
Medium low (ML)	(0.1,0.3,0.5)	Medium poor (ML)	(1,3,5)
Medium (M)	(0.3,0.5,0.7)	Faire (F)	(3,5,7)
Medium high (MH)	(0.5,0.7,0.9)	Medium good (MG)	(5,7,9)
High (H)	(0.7,0.9,1.0)	Good (G)	(7,9,10)
Very high (VH)	(0.9,1.0,1.0)	Very good (VG)	(9,10,10)

Table 2. The importance weights of the criteria

	D_1	D_2	D_3
C_1	H	VH	VH
C_2	H	H	H
C_3	MH	H	MH
C_4	MH	MH	MH
C_5	H	H	H

Table 3. The fuzzy weights of the criteria

	C_1	C_2	C_3	C_4	C_5
Weight	(0.83,0.97,1)	(0.7,0.9,1)	(0.57,0.77,0.93)	(0.5,0.7,0.9)	(0.7,0.9,1)

Table 4. The ratings of alternatives given by decision makers

Criteria	Alternatives	D_1	D_2	D_3
C_1	A_1	6×10^6	8×10^6	7×10^6
	A_2	3×10^6	4×10^6	5×10^6
	A_3	4×10^6	5×10^6	6×10^6
C_2	A_1	G	VG	F
	A_2	VG	VG	VG
	A_1	MG	G	VG
C_3	A_1	F	G	G
	A_2	G	G	G
	A_1	G	MG	VG
C_4	A_1	VG	G	G
	A_2	G	G	G
	A_1	G	VG	VG
C_5	A_1	F	F	F
	A_2	G	F	G
	A_1	G	G	G

Table 5. The group fuzzy decision matrix

	C_1	C_2	C_3	C_4	C_5
A_1	7×10^6	(6.3,8,9)	(5.7,7.7,9)	(7.7,9.3,10)	(3,5,7)
A_2	4×10^6	(9,10,10)	(7,9,10)	(7,9,10)	(5.7,7.7,9)
A_3	5×10^6	(7,9,10)	(7,9,10)	(8.3,9.7,10)	(7,9,10)

The benefit criteria are C_2, C_3, C_4, and C_5. The cost criterion is C_1. The weights of the criteria are shown in Table 3.

Step 2: The ratings of alternatives given three decision makers are shown in Table 4. The group fuzzy decision matrix is obtained by averaging the ratings of three decision makers and is shown in Table 5. The group fuzzy decision matrix is normalized by dividing ratings with the largest value in the support

Table 6. The normalized group fuzzy decision matrix

	C_1	C_2	C_3	C_4	C_5
A_1	(1,1,1)	(0.62,0.8,0.9)	(0.57,0.77,0.9)	(0.77,0.93,1)	(0.3,0.5,0.7)
A_2	(0.57,0.57,0.57)	(0.9,1,1)	(0.7.0.9,1)	(0.7,0.9,1)	(0.57,0.77,0.9)
A_3	(0.71,0.71,0.71)	(0.7,0.87,0.97)	(0.7,0.87,0.97)	(0.83,0.97,1)	(0.7,0.9,1)

Table 7. The strength and weakness matrices

	strength					weakness				
	C_1	C_2	C_3	C_4	C_5	C_1	C_2	C_3	C_4	C_5
A_1	0	0	0	0.067	0	1.43	0.52	0.45	0.067	1.25
A_2	1.14	0.63	0.3	0	0.5	0	0	0	0.2	0.25
A_3	0.57	0.13	0.2	0.2	1	0.29	0.25	0.05	0	0

Note: For A_1: strength in C_4 is 0.067; weakness values: C_1=1.43, C_2=0.52, C_3=0.45, C_4=0.067, C_5=1.25.

Table 8. The fuzzy weighted strength indices and weakness indices of alternatives

	fuzzy weighted strength index		fuzzy weighted weakness index
A_1	(0.033,0.278,0.339)	A_1	(2.712,3.369,3.674)
A_2	(1.913,2.283,2.462)	A_2	(0.275,0.365,0.43)
A_3	(1.482,1.766,1.947)	A_3	(0.441,0.541,0.582)

Table 9. The strength and weakness indices of alternatives

	strength index		weakness index
A_1	0	A_1	18.376
A_2	11.176	A_2	0
A_3	8.526	A_3	1.325

of the fuzzy numbers in the same criterion. The normalized group fuzzy decision matrix is shown in Table 6.

Step 3: The strength matrix derived by (10) is shown in Table 7.

Step 4: The weakness matrix derived by (11) is shown in Table 7.

Step 5: The fuzzy weighted strength indices of alternatives derived by (12) are shown in Table 8.

Step 6: The fuzzy weighted weakness indices of alternatives derived by (13) are shown in Table 8.

Step 7: The strength indices of alternatives derived by (14) are shown in Table 9.

Step 8: The weakness indices of alternatives derived by (15) are shown in Table 9.

Step 9: The total performance indices aggregated by (16) are $A1:0, A2:1$, and $A3:0.866$.

Step 10: The rank of alternatives by total performance indices are $A1 : 3$, $A2 : 1$, and $A3 : 2$. Alternative 2 is the best distribution center.

5 Conclusions

In this paper, we have proposed a new fuzzy multiple criteria decision making (FMCDM) method for the problem of selecting distribution center under fuzzy environment. Our method enables decision makers to assess alternatives with linguistic variables so that vagueness can be encompassed in the assessment of distribution centers. Our method provides the strength index and the weakness index beside the overall performance index so that decision makers can assess distribution centers from different perspectives.

Acknowledgement

This research work was partially supported by the National Science Council of the Republic of China under grant No. NSC93-2416-H-019-004-.

References

1. C.H. Aikens, Facility location models for distribution planning, *European J. Poer. Res.* 22 (1985) 263-279.
2. S.M. Baas and H. Kwakernaak, Rating and ranking of multiple-aspect alternatives using fuzzy sets, *Automatica* 13 (1977) 47-58.
3. G. Bortolan and R. Degani, A review of some methods for ranking fuzzy subsets, *Fuzzy Sets and Systems* 15 (1985) 1-19.
4. D.J. Bowersox, D.J. Closs, *Logistical Management - The Integrated Supply Chain Process*, (McGraw-Hill, Singapore, 1996).
5. W. Chang, Ranking of fuzzy utilities with triangular membership functions, *Proc. Internat. Conf. on Policy Analysis and Information Systems* (1981) 263-272.
6. S. Chen, Ranking fuzzy numbers with maximizing set and minimizing set, *Fuzzy Sets and Systems* 17 (1985) 113-129.
7. M.D. Dahlberg, J.H. May, Linear programming for sitting of energy facilities, *J. Energy Eng.* (1908) 5-14.
8. M. Delgado, J.L. Verdegay and M.A. Vila, A procedure for ranking fuzzy numbers using fuzzy relations, *Fuzzy Sets and Systems* 26 (1988) 49-62.
9. D. Dubois and H. Prade, Ranking fuzzy numbers in the setting of possibility theory, *Inform. Sci.* 30 (1983) 183-224.
10. J.S. Dyer, P.C. Fishburn, R.E. Steuer, J. Wallenius, S. Zionts, Multiple criteria decision making, Multiattribute utility theory: The next ten years, *Management Sci.* 38 (5) (1992) 645-654.
11. J.E. Hodder, M.C. Dincer, A multifactor model for international plant location and financing under uncertainty, *Comput. & Oper. Res.* 13(5) (1986) 601-609.
12. C.L. Hwang, K. Yoon, *Multiple Attributes Decision Making Methods and Applications*, Springer, Berlin Heidelberg, 1981.

13. H.-S. Lee, A new fuzzy ranking method based on fuzzy preference relation, *2000 IEEE International Conference on Systems, Man And Cybernetics* (2001) 3416-3420.
14. H.-S. Lee, Optimal consensus of fuzzy opinions under group decision making environment, *Fuzzy Sets and Systems* 132 (2002) 303-315.
15. H.-S. Lee, An Extended Fuzzy Preference Relation for Comparison of Fuzzy Numbers, The 6h World Multi-Conference on Systemics, Cybernetics and Informatics, July 14-18, 2002, Orlando, USA, XI 76-79.
16. H.-S. Lee, On fuzzy preference relation in group decision making, *International Journal of Computer Mathematics* 82(2) (2005) 133-140.
17. K. Nakamura, Preference relations on a set of fuzzy utilities as a basis for decison making, *Fuzzy Sets and Systems 20*, 147-162 (1986).
18. G.A. Spohrer, T.R. Kmak, Qualitative analysis used in evaluating alternative plant location scenarios, *Indust. Eng.* (August 1984) 52-56.
19. W.J. Stevenson, *Production/Operations Management,* (Richard D. Irwin Inc., Illinois, 1993).
20. D.R. Sule, *Manufacturing Facility; Location, Planning and Design,* (PWS Publishing, Boston, 1994).
21. J. Teghem, Jr., C. Delhaye, P.L. Kunsch, An interactive decision support system (IDSS) for multicriteria decision aid, Math. Comput. Modeling 12:10/11 (1989) 1311-1320.
22. J.A. Tompkins, J.A. White, *Facilities Planning,* (Wiley, New York, 1984).
23. R.R. Yager, A procedure for ordering fuzzy subsets of the unit interval, *Inform. Sci.* 24 (1981) 143-161.
24. Y. Yuan, Criteria for evaluating fuzzy ranking methods, *Fuzzy Sets and Systems 44*, 139-157 (1991).

Refinement of Clustering Solutions Using a Multi-label Voting Algorithm for Neuro-fuzzy Ensembles

Shuai Zhang[1], Daniel Neagu[1], and Catalin Balescu[2]

[1] Department of Computing, University of Bradford,
Bradford, BD7 1DP, United Kingdom
{S.Zhang5, D.Neagu}@bradford.ac.uk
[2] Department of Painting, National University of Arts,
19 General Budisteanu, Bucharest, 70744, Romania
balescu@unarte.ro

Abstract. This paper proposes a new approach to further refine and validate clusters using a multi-label voting algorithm to identify and classify similar objects by neuro-fuzzy classifier ensembles. The algorithm uses predictions of neuro-fuzzy experts trained on provisional clusters of heterogeneous collections of data. The multi-label predictions of the modular ensemble of classifiers are further combined, using fuzzy aggregation techniques. The proposed refinement algorithm considers then the votes, triggered by the confirmation of the classifiers' expertise for voted labels, and updates the clustering solution. Experiments on a Visual Arts objects database of color features show better interpretations and performances of the clusters inferred by the proposed algorithm. Its results can be widely used in various classification and clustering applications.

1 Introduction

Many Machine Learning techniques are used for clustering and classification tasks in Data Mining [1]. Unfortunately, for applications with fluid or numerous classes' neighborhoods, one specific classifier cannot solve the whole problem of data classification. A multiple labeling classifier system is a powerful solution. The approach allows evaluation and integration of different models and experts' diversity requires more attention than selection of the best performing model. In our approach, the main objective in analyzing initial data is the identification and refinement of groups of objects with similar descriptive patterns. We propose an integrative approach based on neuro-fuzzy experts fusion to model heterogeneous sources of information. The hierarchical multi-labeling algorithm uses ensembles of neuro-fuzzy experts qualified in "easy-to-learn" domains by clustering methods. For further clusters refinement, these experts express their opinions on the confusing cases. The voting procedure proposes a refinement procedure, the fluid cases will be subsequently re-assigned to the most appropriate cluster. We emphasize some preliminary results of the proposed algorithm in Visual Arts Data Mining case study.

2 The Multi-label Voting Algorithm for Neuro-fuzzy Classifier Ensemble

2.1 The Neuro-fuzzy Classifier Ensemble

Each expert is implemented as a five-layer neuro-fuzzy network [2]. The neuro-fuzzy experts act as classifiers: the defuzzification strategy identifies the most significant output fuzzy set as the predicted class by mom. The goal of Neuro-Fuzzy Classifier Ensemble [2] (Fig. 1) is to model combinations of data and experts information to the corresponding output whose domain is a set of class labels $\{C_1, C_2, ..., C_L\}$.

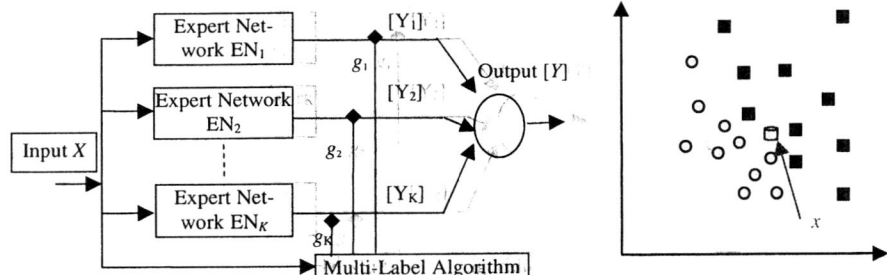

Fig. 1. The Neuro-Fuzzy Classifier Ensemble System architecture

Fig. 2. A confusion case refined by proposed multi-label algorithm

A set of diverse experts are then developed as strong learners with high accuracy predictions on its own domain. Each expert is generated by training a neuro-fuzzy classifier on each combination of k provisional clusters, where $k > L/2$. Consequently, for $K = C_L^k$ training disjunctive subsets, K individual experts are generated. Such a committee will identify not just the class, but also the most similar classes.

2.2 The Multi-label Algorithm for Neuro-fuzzy Classifier Ensembles

This approach validates initial clusters and also identifies similarities between groups of objects (Fig. 2). We propose an off-line stepwise algorithm: in step 1, a provisional list of classes is generated by an unsupervised training method. For each training set combination, during step 2, neuro-fuzzy experts are designed, trained and evaluated. For step 3, for every record presented to the neuro-fuzzy experts, the votes for each label are collected and a majority voting procedure is applied. The algorithm associates the Labels list with information on the most significant class, and number of experts' votes. The Labels list shows not only the prediction of the ensemble, but also information on correlations between the existing labels.

```
Inputs: a vector of attribute values for one instance
Output: the list Labels of estimations (indexed by the
number of votes) assigned to each instance
```

```
#Define initial L (not well bounded) clusters Cl,l=1..L
#Generate K=C_L^k, k>L/2, disjunctive unions of clusters
as expertise domains for neuro-fuzzy networks
#Design and train K neuro-fuzzy classifiers
For each new record i
  Votes_i[C1,C2,..,CL]=0
  #Count expert votes:
  For each expert j=1..K
      Votes_i[expert_j_output]++
  #Identify labels of ranked classes:
  Labels[i]=NIL (dynamic list of labels and votes)
  Remaining_votes=K
  While Remaining_votes>0
    Labels[i].addNewItem
    Labels[i].class=index_of_max(Votes_i)
    Labels[i].number_of_votes=max(Votes_i)
    Remaining_votes-=max(Votes_i)
    Votes_i[index_of_max]=0
  #Analyze Labels[i] for bias and majority voting
  If max(Labels[i].number_of_votes)<bias Then Outlier
  Else If (Labels[i].number_of_votes)<K/2 Then
      #Identify the most significant non-dominant
        multi-labels
      Else #Identify the dominant label and any
        subsequent non-dominant multi-labels
```

2.3 The Algorithm for Refinement of Clustering Solutions

The proposed algorithm to refine the initial unsupervised clustering consists on re-labeling the confusion cases by the number of votes of experts. For evaluation, the prediction accuracy of the multi-classifier system for the top label and the first two labels could be considered: the results are significant just for the first 2 top-ranked labels. The algorithm for Refinement of Clustering is showed below:

```
Inputs: for each training instance a vector of attrib-
ute values
Output: the experts ensemble and the list Labels of es-
timations assigned to each instance

Step1: Define initial L clusters Cl,l=1..L
Step2: Generate K=C_L^k, k>L/2, disjunctive unions of
clusters as expertise domains for neuro-fuzzy networks
Step3: Design and train K neuro-fuzzy classifiers
Step4: Identify the confusion cases applying the Multi-
label Voting algorithm
Step5: Re-label the cases according to experts votes
Step6: Re-design a new neuro-fuzzy classifiers ensemble
```

3 Visual Arts Data Mining: A Case Study

A main objective in analyzing Visual Arts data is the identification of groups of objects with similar descriptive patterns [3]. 1002 Visual Arts digital images are used for the experiment. Three normalized input variables are defined: W/B, R/B, Y/B clusterized into 5 provisional groups C1-C5 by unsupervised method (K-Means). We split data in three sets: training, test cases (for initial ensemble development) and validation cases (for testing the re-developed ensemble and clusters). A number of $10 = C_5^3$ diverse neuro-fuzzy experts are generated. The multi-label algorithm refines the initial clusters and re-distributes the mismatched components (Table 1). Consequently, we can define special relationships between colors, values, geometrical structure of drawing etc. The Ensemble predictions are nearer to the visual perception of colors distribution and have much better results than an individual global neuro-fuzzy network.

Table 1. Data distribution for initial clusters and for refined clusters

	C1	C2	C3	C4	C5
Initial Clusters	27%	39%	7%	7%	20%
Tuned Clusters	26%	40%	7%	5%	22%

4 Conclusions and Further Research

This paper proposes a novel refinement of clustering solutions by a multi-label voting algorithm to combine neuro-fuzzy experts as multi-classifier ensembles. The algorithm identifies class-wise similarities emphasized by individual classifiers to refine initial clusters for the confusion cases on the border between neighborhood classes. The algorithm emphasizes further similarities and shows robustness. The experiment shows significantly improvements for the quality of the clusters memberships compared to the average classification accuracy of any individual classifier. Moreover, the multi-label classification provides additional information on provisional classes based on similarities achieved by individual experts. Relationships between patterns are thus inferred. This study demonstrates that the multi-labeled combination of neuro-fuzzy networks allows a better analysis and interpretation of classification and refinement tasks for large data collections in the general framework of data mining.

References

1. Kuncheva, L.I.: Combining Classifiers: Soft Computing Solutions. In: S.K. Pal (ed.) Pattern Recognition: From Classical to Modern Approaches, World Scientific (2001) 427-452
2. Neagu, D. and Palade, V.: Modular neuro-fuzzy networks: an overview of explicit and implicit knowledge integration. In Procs 15 Int'l FLAIRS Conf, AAAI Press (2002) 277-281
3. Eakins, J.P.: Towards intelligent image retrieval. Pattern Recognition 35 (2002) 3-14

Comparison of Meta-heuristic Hybrid Approaches for Two Dimensional Non-guillotine Rectangular Cutting Problems

Alev Soke[1] and Zafer Bingul[2]

[1] Kocaeli University, Department of Electronics and Computer Edu.,
Umuttepe Campus, 41380, Kocaeli, Turkey
alevsoke@kou.edu.tr

[2] Kocaeli University, Department of Mechatronics Eng.,
Veziroglu Campus, 41300, Kocaeli, Turkey
zaferb@kou.edu.tr

Abstract. In this paper, six different approaches using genetic algorithms (GA) and/or simulated annealing (SA) with improved bottom left (I-BL) algorithm [1] were applied for solution of two dimensional non-guillotine cutting problems. As examples, test problems including 29 individual rectangular pieces were used [2]. Performances of hybrid approaches on solutions of cutting problems were compared. Due to combined global search feature of GA and local search feature of SA, the hybrid approach using GA and SA yields the best results for these problems.

1 Introduction

The cutting stock problem belongs to a special category of problems named "Cutting and Packing Problems". The objective of the cutting problems is to increase the usability of main object and thus to obtain the layout pattern that has minimum trim loss value. The trim loss is unused area in main object. A cutting pattern or a layout pattern represented by a permutation corresponds to the sequences in which the pieces are to place into main object [2]. In the area of cutting problems, it is very common to use hybrid approaches combining meta-heuristics with placement algorithms. GA and SA are the most widely applied meta-heuristic methods, which may work a set of solutions or a solution at each an iteration, for large combinatorial problems.

2 Solution Approaches

Two pure meta-heuristic approaches and four hybrid meta-heuristic approaches to an optimal solution of two dimensional non-guillotine rectangular cutting problems are developed in this study. The details of these approaches are given as follows:
 GA approach: In GA approach, pure GA was carried out with the best parameters (population size: 80, mutation rate: 0.7 and crossover technique: order based

crossover (OBX)) obtained in [4]. Also in this approach, 6 different crossover techniques (OBX, CX, OX, PMX, UX, and SJX) were examined to look at effects of crossover techniques on the solutions of the cutting problems.

SA approach: In SA approach, pure SA was applied with using the best parameters (cooling schedule: Lundy and Mees schedule, number of inner loop: 3, neighborhood move: swapping move, initial temperatures: between 0.1 and 0.8) obtained in [4].

1st hybrid meta-heuristic approach (GA-RMC): This approach is denoted by GA-RMC (genetic algorithms-random multiple crossover), because of applying random multiple crossover techniques. In this approach, best parameters obtained from GA approach are used. The steps in this algorithm are detailed as follows:

1. Randomly initialize a population and evaluate the fitness values of population.
2. Select chromosomes for reproduction as proportional with its fitness.
3. Apply six times crossover to the selected chromosomes according to ordered crossover permutation. The permutation includes six crossover techniques. It is generated randomly by selecting from among six different crossover techniques.
4. Evaluate the fitness values of the obtained population after crossover operation.
5. Apply the SA operator (Boltzman-type operator) to decide which of two of the current population and previous population according to mean fitness values.
6. Repeat above steps (3-5) up to number of inner loop. Then decrease the temperature as to predetermined cooling schedule.
7. Apply mutation operation to the obtained population.
8. Evaluate the fitness values of the new population. If the optimization criterion is reached, return the best solution. Otherwise, go to step 2.

2nd hybrid meta-heuristic approach (GA-MCNM): This approach is similar to GA-RMC approach but only difference is generation of crossover permutation. In this approach, crossover permutation is obtained using neighborhood move operator of SA (swapping move). This approach is denoted by GA-MCNM (genetic algorithms-multiple crossover with neighborhood move), because crossover permutation is formed with neighborhood move.

3rd hybrid meta-heuristic approach (ASAGA): This approach is different from previous two hybrid approaches. Mutation operator does not affect according to solutions obtained from GA approach on the solution of these problems [4]. Therefore SA algorithm, which is produced a neighbor solution for each chromosome in population, was used instead of mutation operator. This approach is known adaptive simulated annealing genetic algorithm (ASAGA) [5]. The steps of this algorithm are given as detailed in below:

1. Randomly initialize a population and evaluate the fitness values of population.
2. Select chromosomes for reproduction as proportional with its fitness.
3. Apply OBX technique to the selected chromosomes.
4. Evaluate the fitness values of the obtained population after crossover operation.
5. Apply neighborhood move to each chromosome in population to produce a neighbor solution and evaluate the new solutions.
6. Then apply the SA operator to decide which of two of the current population and previous population according to cost function value.

7. Repeat above steps (5-6) up to number of inner loop. Then decrease the temperature as to predetermined cooling schedule.
8. Evaluate the fitness values of the new population. If the optimization criterion is reached, return the best solution. Otherwise, go to step 2.

4th *hybrid meta-heuristic approach (GASA):* In the final approach, GA and SA were used separately on the solution of cutting problems. The iteration was repeated 1000 times. The pure GA was run with the best parameters obtained from [4] until 200 iterations. Then the best five chromosomes were selected from population obtained in GA. The pure SA was run with the best chromosomes during number of 800 iterations. The best SA parameters obtained from [4] are used. This approach is denoted by GASA (genetic algorithms-simulated annealing).

3 Experimental Results

Our test problems consisting of 29 individual rectangular pieces to place on a main object were employed to test the solution approaches [1]. The main object is limited with a size of 200x200 units. All of these problems were chosen with an optimal solution with zero trim loss.

Best results taken from all of these approaches are given in Fig 1. The values denote the minimum trim loss values obtained from the test problems. When the similar test problems in the literature were considered, it was appeared clearly that these trim loss values are within acceptable standards (from 0% to 8%) [2].

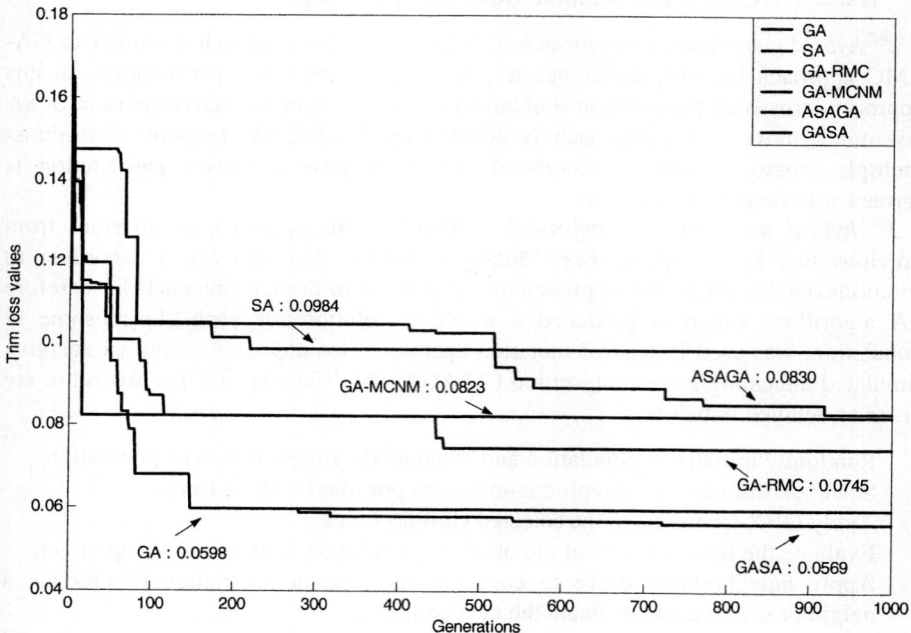

Fig. 1. Comparisons of the all approaches for 29 individual rectangular pieces

Fig. 1 shows the performances of the all approaches for 29 individual rectangular pieces. As can be seen in the figure, GASA approach performs the best in all of the algorithms for the every condition of generations. The trim loss value obtained from this approach is the best as compared to other algorithms since it is benefited from combined global search feature of GA and local search feature of SA in this approach. First 200 iterations of GASA approach are the same as pure GA approach. It is not appeared in the figure because their values are overlapped on pure GA approach. Since GA is global search techniques, they are poor at hill climbing. Therefore, as seen the figure, pure GA approach is poor to reach the optimal solution of the cutting problems. ASAGA approach has started to converge faster than other algorithms in the beginning of the iteration, but it has not continued this state. Nevertheless, the obtained results tend to improve generation-by-generation. SA does not search efficiently on the large search space, since it is local search algorithm. As seen the figure, SA approach did not escape from local minima. GA-RMC and GA-MCNM approaches converge to same trim loss value at approximately 450th iteration. But after 450th iteration, GA-MCNM approach keeps its state. A convergence characteristic of GA-MCNM approach is very good at the beginning but it does not realize to converge to minimum optimal solution at the last. Also, searching at the GA-RMC approach is not enough to reach the optimal solution for 1000 iterations.

4 Conclusions

In this study, 4 hybrid meta-heuristic approaches and 2 pure meta-heuristic approaches for solution of two dimensional non-guillotine rectangular cutting problems have compared to each other. Based on this, the best results are obtained from GASA approach. SA as a local search algorithm is good at fine-tuning and GA as a global search algorithm is good at large search spaces. In this approach, it is benefited from combined global search feature of GA and local search feature of SA.

References

1. Leung, T.W., Yung, C.H., Troutt, M.D.: Applications of Genetic Search and Simulated Annealing to The Two-Dimensional Non-Guillotine Cutting Stock Problem. Computers and Industrial Engineering, Vol.40. (2001) 201-214.
2. Hopper, E.: Two Dimensional Packing Utilizing Evolutionary Algorithms and Other Meta-Heuristic Methods, University of Wales, Cardiff School of Engineering, (2000) PhD. Thesis, London.
3. Liu, D. and Teng, H.: An Improved BL Algorithm for Genetic Algorithm of the Orthogonal Packing of Rectangles, European Journal of Operational Research, Vol.112 (1999) 413-420.
4. Soke, A., Bingul, Z.: Genetic Algorithm and Simulated Annealing Applied to Two Dimensional Non-Guillotine Rectangular Cutting Problems, Proceedings of the Eighth IASTED International Conference Artificial Intelligence and Soft Computing, September 1-3, 2004, Marbella, Spain.
5. Jeong, I.K., Lee, J.J.: Adaptive Simulated Annealing Genetic Algorithm for System Identification, Engineering Applications Artificial Intelligence, Vol. 9(5), (1996) 523-532.

A Hybrid Immune Evolutionary Computation Based on Immunity and Clonal Selection for Concurrent Mapping and Localization

Meiyi Li[1,2], Zixing Cai[1], Yuexiang Shi[1,2], and Pingan Gao[1,2]

[1] College of Information Science & Engineering,
Central South University,
Changsha China, 410083
meiy_li@yahoo.com.cn
[2] The College of Information Engineering,
Xiangtan University,
Xiangtan China, 411105

Abstract. This paper addresses the problem of Concurrent Mapping and Localization(CML) by means of a hybrid immune evolutionary computation based on immunity and clonal selection for a mobile robot. An immune operator, a vaccination operator, is designed in the algorithm. The experiment results of a real mobile robot show that the computational expensiveness of the algorithm in this paper is less than other algorithms and the maps obtained are very accurate.

1 Introduction

CML (Concurrent Mapping and Localization) can be described as that acquiring a map of an unknown environment with a moving robot, while simultaneously localizing the robot relative to this map[1].

The CML problem can be translated to a global optimization problem in which the objective is to search the space of possible robot maps. It is known that some new hybrid evolutionary computation[2-3] inspired by biologic principles like immune will largely increase the convergence rate and has great ability of global searching. Hence, this paper utilizes a hybrid evolution algorithm based on immune and vaccination to solve the CML problem.

In CML map ones often make the use of *occupancy grid* present by Moravec and Elfes[4], where a map is consisted of grids or cells. A occupancy grid is described as grid$[i][j]$, and every grid$[i][j]$ has a probability or belief occ$[i][j]$ which is occupied and a probability or belief emp$[i][j]$ which is free. The calculations of occ$[i][j]$ and emp$[i][j]$ depended on data from range-finder. Reliable degree of data from range-finder is not the same when the distance from the axels of range-finder varies, so usually the reliable degree of data from range-finder is relevant to the distance [5]. Then, the reliable degree of data from range-finder is projected to occ$[i][j]$ and emp$[i][j]$ by means of a sensor fusion approach like theories of evidence. In this paper Dempster-Shafer theory of evidence is employed and works as a method of sensor fusion.

2 A Hybrid Immune Evolutionary Algorithm for CML

2.1 Chromosome, Fitness Selection, Recombination and Immune Operators

A trajectory in CML can be defined as a vector $[T_1, T_2, ..., T_N]$, where $T_j=[d_j, \dot{e}_j]$, d_j and $\dot{e}_j$ are the relative distance and rotation traveled by the robot in one small step j, and there are N steps in total.

Each chromosome is encoded as a string of floating point numbers $[X_1, X_2, ..., X_N]$ corresponding to the correction factors applied to the recorded odometry data, where $X_j=[\Delta d_j, \Delta \dot{e}_j]$, and $-d_{max} < \Delta d_k < d_{max}$, $-\dot{e}_{max} < \Delta \dot{e}_k < +\dot{e}_{max}$, $k=1,2,...,N$. d_{max} and $\dot{e}_{max}$ are real positive integers.

The occupancy grid model is used to construct a map for each candidate solution, and three heuristics are combined to obtain a fitness value for each map:

$$f = \sum \min(1-occ[i][j], 1-emp[i][j]) + w_1 \sum \delta(i,j) + w_2 \sum \zeta(i,j) \quad (1)$$

where w_1 and w_2 are real numbers in (0,1), and if $occ[i][j]>0.5$, $\delta(i,j)=1$, else $\delta(i,j)=0$; If $emp[i][j]>0.5$, $\zeta(i,j)=1$, else $\zeta(i,j)=0$. In our experiments $w_1=0.2$ and $w_2=0.05$.

The selection operator based on probability proposed by Michalewicz[6] is used. In the implement of the algorithm parameter $q=0.4$.

Pairs of selected strings are then combined by crossover. Multiple crossover sites are used, so that the encoded values in the two mating strings are completely mixed up in the two strings produced. This is achieved by randomly choosing between the two parents at each site in the chromosome. Crossover is carried out with probability p_c.

The clonal selection operator at step (4) in later algorithm is that an individual will reproduce N_c children from which the best one will be selected to replaced the parent individual. In the implement of the algorithm below N_c is equal to 10. The clonal selection is carried out with probability p_m and children are reproduced with Gauss distribution of mean $=0$ and Std. Dev.$=1$.

A local exploration process, named as a vaccination operator, is constructed by means of the feature of parallel line segments, which can be described as follows:

(1) Both trajectories T_j and T_{j+1} are selected uniformly from an individual.

(2) Line segments are abstracted by means of some abstracting methods[7] from range-finder data at T_j and T_{j+1} respectively

(3) If there is no any line segment in range-finder data at either of T_j and T_{j+1}, the vaccination operator goes to end.

(4) Line segments extracted at T_j are $L_{j,k}$, and angles between $L_{j,k}$ and X axis under global coordinate system are $\hat{a}_{j,k}$.

(5) If some k and n are existed, and $|\hat{a}_{j,k} - \hat{a}_{j+1,n}| < \hat{a}_0$ is satisfied, where $\hat{a}_0$ is a positive real constant. $L_{j,k}$ and $L_{j+1,n}$ are regarded as a pair of parallel lines which are corrupted by noise; Else, the vaccination operator goes to end.

(6) Let $\hat{a} = (\hat{a}_{j,k} + \hat{a}_{j+1,n})/2$, and adjust the correction factors $\Delta \dot{e}_j$ and $\Delta \dot{e}_{j+1}$ such that both angles between line $L_{j,k} / L_{j+1,k}$ and X axis are equal to $\hat{a}$. After $\Delta \dot{e}_j$ and $\Delta \dot{e}_{j+1}$ are adjusted T_j and T_{j+1} are described as T'_j and T'_{j+1}.

If the correction factors $\Delta \dot{e}_j$ and $\Delta \dot{e}_{j+1}$ applied to the angle measurements at T_j and T_{j+1} are adjusted in the vaccination operator, an immune selection operator will be performed. The change of the correction factors $\Delta \dot{e}_j$ and $\Delta \dot{e}_{j+1}$ will make improvements of the consistency and compactness of the maps. Measure of improvements will be used to evaluate the performance of a vaccination operator. If the performance is improved, T_j and T_{j+1} are replaced with T'_j and T'_{j+1} in the individual in which the vaccination operator has been performed, Else, the operator of replacement will be done with probability[2]

2.2 Immune Hybrid Immune Evolutionary Algorithm

A hybrid immune evolutionary computation algorithm (HIECA) used in this paper is described as follows.

(1) choose an initial population, and calculate the fitness of each individual
  repeat {
  (2) perform selection
  (3) perform recombination with adaptive probability
  (4) perform clonal selection with adaptive probability
  (5) perform vaccination with probability p_I
  (6) perform immune selection
  (7) calculate the fitness of each individual
  (8) keep the best individual
  } until some stopping criterion applies

In implement of EC, if the best fitness values in the population are not improved in N_{gen} generations, the algorithm will go to the end, which is often the convergence critical. In this paper, let $N_{gen}=10$.

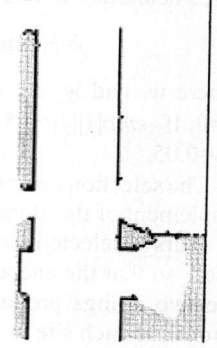

Fig. 1. A gridmap was gotten by means of our algorithm when the robot ran in our experiment Lab

3 Implementation of the Algorithm and Experiment Results

The algorithm was tested by an AmigoBOT mobile robot produced by ActivMedia Robotics, LLC with the addition of a SICK laser scanner at the Intelligence Control Lab of the Central South University in China. The odometer trace was divided into segments of about from 1 to 2 meters in length. For the environment of Fig. 1, there were 20 segments corresponding to the about 25 meters traveled by the robot. Because movable scope for robot is not large enough, all range-finder data are truncated such that the lengths of range-finder are less than 3 meters, which means that if $r_i>3$ in range-finder data $(r_i, \ddot{o}_i)$, $r_i=3$.

In our experiments $D_{max}=0.32$, $d_{max}=20$cm, $\dot{e}_{max}=10$, $\hat{a}_0=1$meters, integer $d_k \in$ [-20, 20], integer $\dot{e}_k \in$ [-10, 10]. In implement of the algorithm the population size is 50, $p_I=0.6$, p_c and p_m are calculated adaptively as in Ref. [8].
Both the algorithms proposed in this paper and in Ref. [9] run 5 times for the same test case (environment, trajectories, and range-finder data) in order to prove that the

algorithm in this paper outperforms other approaches based on evolutionary computation. Running results of both algorithms are list in Table 1, and a gridmap gained through the algorithm in this paper is shown in Fig. 1. Table 1 shows that the convergence rate is higher than the algorithms in Ref. [9]. To sum up, the algorithm proposed in this paper can increase the convergence rate of evolutionary computation for CML.

Table 1. Comparisons of running results for two algorithms

Algorithms	Mean number of fitness function evaluations	Mean value of best fitness values
Algorithm in this paper	28522.1	437.7
Algorithm in Ref.[9]	37925.6	438.8

4 Conclusions

A hybrid immune evolutionary computation for CML has bee proposed which is combined with feature of parallel line segments in range-finder data in order to increase the convergence rate of CML based on evolutionary computation. By means of experiments the algorithm proposed in this paper can improve the searching ability and adaptability, and greatly increase the convergence rate.

Acknowledgements

This work was supported in part by the National Natural Science Foundation of China (No. 60234030 and 60404021).

References

1. G. Dissanayake, P. Newman, S. Clark, H.F. Durrant-Whyte, and M Csorba. A solution to the simultaneous localisation and map building (SLAM) problem. Transactions of Robotics and Automation(2001)
2. Jiao L C, Wang L. A novel genetic algorithm based on immunity. IEEE Trans. Syst., Man, Cybern. A. (2000) 30(5) 552-561
3. De Castro L N,Vov Zuben F J. Learning and optimization using the clonal selection principle. IEEE Trans. Evolutionary Computation, (2002) 6(3): 239-251
4. Moravec H, Elfes A. High resolution maps from wide angle sonar. In: Proceedings of the IEEE International Conference on Robotics and Automation (ICRA'85), (1985) 116-121
5. Drumheller M. Mobile robot localization using sonar. IEEE Transactions on Pattern Analysis and Machine Intelligence, PAMI-9, (1987) 323-332
6. Michalewicz, Z.: Genetic Algorithms + Data Structures = Evolution Programs. 3rd edit. Springer-Verlag, Berlin Heidelberg New York (1996)
7. Siadat A, Kaske A, Klausman S. An optimized segmentation method for a 2d laser-scanner applied to mobile robot naviagation. In 3rd IFAC Symp. on Intelligent Components and Instuments for Control Applications, (1997) 153-158
8. Srinvas M, Patnai L M. Adaptive probabilities of crossover and mutation in genetic algorithms [J]. IEEE Trans.Syst.,Man,and Cybern,1994,24(4):656-666
9. Duckett T. A genetic algorithm for simultaneous localization and mapping. In: IEEE International Conference on Robotics and Automation, Taipei, Taiwan, (2003) 434-439

Author Index

Ahmad, Muhammad Bilal II-43
Akin, Erhan III-787
Alatas, Bilal III-787
Almeida, Gustavo Maia de III-313
Amin, Hesham H. I-456
An, Wensen I-546
Anh, Vo III-337
Aoki, Terumasa II-622
Araabi, Babak N. II-1250
Arita, Jun II-165
Asiedu, Baffour Kojo III-903
Asiimwe, Alex Jessey III-968
Aydin, Serkan III-703

Baba, Sapiyan I-893
Bae, Hyeon I-1160, II-564
Bae, SungMin II-530
Bai, JianCong III-74
Bai, Lin II-780
Baicher, Gurvinder S. III-877
Balescu, Catalin III-1300
Bao, Leilei III-988
Bao, Zhejing I-688
Barbosa, Helio J.C. II-941
Bea, Hae-Ryong III-1182
Belatreche, A. I-420
Bertoni, Alberto III-235
Bi, D. II-266, II-592
Bianco, Luca II-1155
Bin, Guang-yu I-1031, III-646
Bingul, Zafer III-1304
Bolat, Bülent I-110
Bonfim, Danilo Mattos I-1275
Borne, Pierre III-259
Bu, Nan II-165
Butun, Erhan II-204
Byun, Kwang-Sub II-85

Čada, Josef I-1234
Cai, Guangchao III-915
Cai, Jiamei I-1117
Cai, Yici III-181
Cai, Yunze I-51, I-528, I-582, II-175
Cai, Zhiping II-913

Cai, Zixing III-1308
Campadelli, Paola III-235
Cao, Chunhong I-783, II-139
Cao, Qixin III-535, III-723
Cao, Xianqing III-1162
Cao, Yijia II-895
Cao, Zuoliang III-984
Carvalho, Andre C.P.L.F. I-1189
Chai, Tianyou II-214
Chambers, J.A. I-199
Chang, Chia-Lan II-735
Chang, Chuan-Wei II-296
Chang, Hui-Chen III-1172
Chang, HuiYou III-74
Chang, Min Hyuk II-43
Chang, Pei-Chann I-364, II-983, III-205
Chang, Ping-Teng I-619
Chang, Ray-I I-1224
Chang, Yongmin I-850
Chau, Kwokwing III-1152
Chen, Chen-Tung I-619
Chen, Chih-Ming III-1186
Chen, Chongcheng III-1051
Chen, Chunlin II-686
Chen, Duo II-1269
Chen, G.L III-1060
Chen, Gang II-37, II-270
Chen, Guangzhu III-444
Chen, Guochu II-610, III-515
Chen, Haixu III-938
Chen, Hongjian II-1218
Chen, Huanwen III-384
Chen, Jiah-Shing II-735, III-798
Chen, Jin-Long III-1186
Chen, Jing II-539
Chen, Ke II-656
Chen, Liangzhou I-679
Chen, Ling II-1218, II-1239
Chen, Qian III-490
Chen, Qingzhan III-782
Chen, S. II-1122
Chen, Shengda III-1235
Chen, Shengyong I-332
Chen, Shi-Fu III-855

Chen, Shiming II-913
Chen, Shu-Heng III-612
Chen, Shuang I-101
Chen, Tianping I-245
Chen, Tieming I-1117
Chen, Xin III-628
Chen, Xinghuan III-57
Chen, Xuefeng II-324
Chen, Yan Qiu II-705, III-822, III-845
Chen, Yanmin I-947
Chen, Ying-Chun III-482
Chen, Yingchun II-1101
Chen, Yong II-890
Chen, Yun Wen II-705
Chen, Zehua II-945
Chen, Zhao-Qian II-55
Chen, Zhong II-1
Chen, Zong-Ming II-425
Chen, Zonghai II-686
Cheng, Chun-Tian III-453, III-1152
Cheng, Kuo-Hsiang III-1186
Cheng, Lixin I-470
Cheng, Yinglei III-215
Cheng, Zhihong III-444
Cheremushkin, Evgeny II-1202
Chi, Huisheng I-167
Chien, Shu-Yen II-296
Chiu, David II-306
Cho, Daehyeon I-536
Cho, Eun-kyung III-1069
Cho, Yeon-Jin I-1009
Cho, Yeun-Jin I-1002
Choi, Dong-Seong I-797
Choi, Jinsung II-552
Choi, Jonghwa I-1185, II-552
Choi, Wonil I-850
Chu, Ming-Hui II-296
Chu, Tianguang I-769
Chua, Ming-Hui II-296
Chun, Jong Hoon II-43
Chunjie, Yang I-696
Cong, Shuang I-773
Cooper, Leon N. I-71, I-554, I-877
Copper, J. I-1039
Corchado, Emilio I-778
Cui, Baotong I-1
Cui, Du-Wu II-1269, III-86
Cui, Zhihua III-255, III-467
Cukic, Bojan I-750

Dai, Hongwei III-332
Dai, Yuewei III-976
Damiance, Antonio P.G., Jr. I-1189
Dang, Chuangyin III-392
Dang, Yan I-956
Daoying, Pi I-696
de Carvalho, Luis A.V. II-941
de Castro, Leandro Nunes I-1275, I-1279
Demir, Ibrahim II-648
Deng, Fei-Qi I-1150
Deng, Weihong I-915
Ding, Hongkai I-119
Ding, Juling II-804
Ding, Lixin II-1049
Ding, Zhan I-835
Dixit, Vikas III-1242
Do, Tien Dung II-849
Dong, Chaojun I-340
Dong, Daoyi II-686
Dong, Jin-xiang III-48
Dong, Jingxin II-105
Dong, Jinxiang II-1229
Dong, Min I-397
Dong, Qiming II-185
Dong, Xiuming III-374
Du, Haifeng II-826, II-876, II-931, III-399
Du, Shihong III-1261, III-1274
Du, Wenli II-631
Du, Ying I-480
Du, Yuping III-592
Duan, Ganglong I-640

Ebecken, Nelson F.F. III-245
Egan, G.F. I-1057
Elena, José Manuel II-147
Engin, Seref N. II-648
Eom, Il Kyu II-400
Erfidan, Tarık II-204
Estevam, R. Hruschka Jr. III-245
Eto, Tsuyoshi I-439
Everly, R.D. I-1039

Fan, FuHua II-493
Fan, Hong I-476
Fan, Muhui II-592
Fan, Zhi-Gang II-396
Fang, Bin III-663
Fang, Yi II-135
Farkaš, Igor II-676

Feng, Chen I-793, I-1256
Feng, Chunbo III-698
Feng, Ding I-25
Feng, Du I-679
Feng, Guangzeng III-457
Feng, Guiyu I-209, I-675
Feng, Guorui I-720
Feng, Jiuchao II-332
Feng, Li III-374
Feng, Naiqin III-562
Feng, Xiao-Yue II-698
Figueredo, Grazziela P. II-941
Fong, Alvis C.M. II-849
Fontana, Federico II-1155
Freeman, Walter J. I-378
Freund, Lars II-1112
Fu, Chaojin I-664
Fu, Duan III-1128
Fu, Xiao II-627
Fu, Y.X. III-668
Fu, Zetian II-352
Fujii, Robert H. I-456
Fukumura, Naohiro I-313
Furutani, Hiroshi II-1025

Gao, Hai-Hua I-565, II-21, II-89
Gao, Pingan III-1308
Gao, Xieping I-358, I-783, II-139
Gao, Ying II-386
Ge, Weimin III-984
Ge, Yang III-553
Geem, Zong Woo III-741, III-751
Germen, Emin I-353
Glackin, B. I-420
Goebels, Andreas II-744
Goëffon, Adrien III-678
Göksu, Hüseyin II-618, III-1242
Gong, Dengcai II-602
Gong, Ling I-925
Gong, Maoguo I-449, II-826, III-399, III-768
Gong, Zhiwei III-1251
Górriz, J.M. III-863
Gou, Jin III-490
Gowri, S. III-361
Gu, Faji I-1052
Gu, Xingsheng II-880
Guan, Qiu I-332, II-795
Guan, Xinping II-75
Guan, Yi I-947

Guang, Cheng II-338
Guangli, Liu I-650
Günes, Salih II-830
Guo, Hongbo II-957
Guo, Huawei I-679
Guo, Jun I-915
Guo, Lei III-698
Guo, Ya-Jun III-28
Guo, Zhenhe II-867

Hakl, František I-1234
Ham, Fredric M. I-1100
Han, Cheon-woo I-797
Han, Dongil II-328
Han, Jianghong III-782
Han, Jong-Hye I-850
Han, Lansheng III-903
Han, Lu II-1105
Han, Ray P.S. III-269
Han, Soowhan I-1100
Hang, D. I-1057
Hao, Fei I-769
Hao, Jin-Kao III-678
Hao, Zhifeng III-137, III-1257
Harris, C.J. II-1122
Hayward, Serge I-1214
He, Han-gen II-1035
He, Jun II-1015, III-279, III-323
He, Lianlian III-636, III-668
He, Mi I-508
He, Pilian I-692
He, Shengjun III-915
He, Wenxiu III-782
He, Wuhong II-931
He, Xiaoguang I-187
He, Yinghao II-12
He, Yuguo III-434
He, Yunhui II-71
He, Yuyao I-273
He, Zhengjia II-324
He, Zhenya I-683
Heckman, C. I-1039
Herbert, Joseph I-129
Herrero, Álvaro I-778
Hlaváček, Marek I-1234
Ho, Daniel W.C. I-730
Hong, Chao-Fu III-11
Hong, Gye Hang II-710
Hong, Keongho I-789
Hong, Kwang-Seok I-1179

Hong, Qin   I-264
Hong, Sang Jeen   I-1113
Hong, Wei-Chiang   I-619, I-668
Hong, Xianlong   III-181
Hong, Yuan   II-1206
Hong, Zhang   I-499
Hooke, J.   I-1039
Hosoi, Satoshi   II-438
Hou, Chong   II-876
Hou, Cuiqin   III-768
Hou, Kunpeng   II-483
Hou, Yanfeng   III-1216
Hou, Yimin   III-873
Hou, Yunxian   II-352
Hou, Zeng-Guang   III-622
Hruschka, Eduardo R.   III-245
Hsu, Chi-I   III-812
Hsu, Hao-Hsuan   II-859
Hsu, Pei Lun   III-812
Hsu, Yuan Lin   III-812
Hu, Chunfeng   II-65
Hu, Chunhua   II-234
Hu, Dewen   I-101, I-209, I-675, I-700, III-1128
Hu, Guangshu   III-654
Hu, Hong   I-91, I-1039
Hu, Huaqiang   I-835
Hu, Jiani   I-915
Hu, Jianming   II-1089
Hu, Qiao   II-324
Hu, Qinghua   III-1190
Hu, Shigeng   I-740
Hu, Tao   II-352
Hu, Tingliang   II-234
Hu, Weisheng   III-102
Hu, Xiaomin   II-592
Hu, Zhi-kun   III-477
Hu, Zhonghui   I-528, II-175
Hua, Yong   II-12
Huang, Gaoming   I-683
Huang, Hai   III-772, III-1142
Huang, Han   III-137
Huang, Houkuan   III-323
Huang, Min   I-1
Huang, Wanping   III-289
Huang, Wentao   I-449, II-826
Huang, Xiyue   II-890
Huang, Xuemei   II-800
Huang, Xueyuan   II-913
Huang, Ya-Chi   III-612

Huang, Yan-Xin   II-698
Huang, Yu-Ying   I-668
Huh, Sung-Hoe   III-1099
Hui, Siu Cheung   II-849
Hui-zhong, Yang   I-25
Hwang, Changha   I-512, I-521, I-536, II-306
Hwang, Su-Young   I-797

Ibershoff, Joseph   II-1206
Ibrahim, Zuwairie   II-1174, II-1182
Ichikawa, Michinori   I-293
Im, Kwang Hyuk   II-530
Iwata, Atsushi   III-1006

Jaromczyk, Jerzy W.   II-1206
Jeon, In Ja   II-764, III-356
Jeon, Jun-Cheol   III-348
Jeong, Eunhwa   I-789
Jeong, EunSung   II-764
Jeong, Kee S.   I-818
Jeong, Ok-Ran   I-850
Ji, Guangrong   I-793, I-1256
Jia, Sen   II-391
Jian, Gong   II-338
Jiang, Chunhong   I-985
Jiang, Michael   I-750
Jiang, Minghu   I-1140
Jiang, Minghui   I-740
Jiang, Weijin   I-139, I-345
Jiang, Xiaoyue   III-215
Jiang, Yaping   II-800
Jiang, Zefei   I-608
Jianmin, Han   I-336
Jianying, Xie   I-44
Jiao, Licheng   I-449, II-780, II-826, II-839, II-876, II-905, II-931, III-366, III-399, III-768, III-925
Jie, Liu   I-254
Jin, Dongming   III-1022
Jin, Qiao   III-1089
Jin, Wuyin   I-390
Jin, Xiaogang   I-1209
Jin, Xiaoguang   II-584
Jin, Yaochu   II-1145
Jin, Yaohui   III-102
Jing, Guixia   II-376
Jing, Ling   I-217
Jiskra, Jan   III-841
Jiuzhen, Liang   I-336

Author Index

Jordan, R.   I-1039
Juang, Yau-Tarng   III-1172
Jun, Feng   I-33
Jun, Liu   I-44
Jun-an, Lu   I-254
Jung, In-Sung   I-888
Jung, Jo Nam   II-109
Jwo, Dah-Jing   II-425

Kala, Keerthi Laal   III-1015
Kang, Hyun-Ho   III-962
Kang, Jaeho   II-1259
Kang, Kyung-Woo   II-543
Kang, Lishan   II-1049
Kang, Yuan   II-296
Karwowski, Waldemar   III-1216
Kasai, Nobuyuki   II-1174
Katayama, Susumu   II-1025
Kato, Tsuyoshi   II-963
Katsaggelos, Aggelos K.   II-1192
Kaya, Mehmet Ali   II-618
Ke, Hengyu   II-210
Kel, Alexander   II-1202
Khajehpour, Pooyan   II-1250
Khalid, Marzuki   II-1182
Kikuchi, H.   III-684
Kim, Chang-Suk   III-1182
Kim, Dong-Hyun   III-1044
Kim, Dongwon   III-1099
Kim, DuckSool   II-714
Kim, Eun Ju   II-155
Kim, Hang-Joon   II-543
Kim, Ho-Joon   III-1178
Kim, Hyeoncheol   I-1002, I-1009
Kim, Hyun-jung   I-1247
Kim, Hyung-Bum   I-1027
Kim, Jinsu   III-1044
Kim, Jong-Bin   III-1032
Kim, Jong-Min   II-224
Kim, Ju Han   I-965
Kim, Kap Hwan   II-1259
Kim, Kee-Won   III-348
Kim, Kwang-Baek   I-237, III-1182
Kim, Myung Won   II-155
Kim, Nam H.   I-818
Kim, Pan-Koo   I-1027
Kim, Seong-Whan   II-451
Kim, Sun   II-636
Kim, Sung-il   I-797
Kim, Sungshin   I-1160, II-564

Kim, Tae Hyun   II-530
Kim, Tae Hyung   II-400
Kim, Won-sik   I-797
Kim, Woong Myung   I-760
Kim, Yong-Kab   III-1044
Kim, Yoo Shin   II-400
Kim, Young-Joong   III-1079
Knidel, Helder   I-1279
Kobayashi, Kunikazu   I-439
Kodaz, Halife   II-830
Kökçe, Ali   II-618
Kong, Min   I-15
Konovalova, Tatiana   II-1202
Kou, Jisong   III-37, III-943
Kouh, Jen-Shaing   I-1224
Kramer, Oliver   II-744
Krishnamurthy, E.V.   II-784
Ku, Dae-Sung   III-1032
Kuremoto, Takashi   I-439
Kwon, Ki-Ryong   III-962
Kwon, Young-hee   III-1069

Lai, Chien-Yuan   III-205
Lai, Kin Keung   I-382
Lai, Liang-Bin   I-1224
Lai, Yungang   III-782
Lam, Kin-man   II-7
Lan, Shu   I-33
Lee, Bu-Sung   II-1112
Lee, Byung C.   I-818
Lee, Chung K.   I-818
Lee, Dong-Un   I-237
Lee, Hak-Sung   II-328
Lee, Hsuan-Shih   III-1290
Lee, Hyon Soo   I-760
Lee, Jang Hee   II-710
Lee, Jay   III-535
Lee, Jongkeuk   I-1100
Lee, KangWoo   I-855
Lee, Kwangeui   I-1100
Lee, Myung-jin   I-797
Lee, Sang-Ho   I-965
Lee, Sun-young   I-797
Lee, Sungyoung   II-101
Lee, Woo-Gul   I-797
Lee, Yong Hwan   II-1259
Lee, Yunsik   I-1113
León, Carlos   II-147
Li, BiCheng   II-37
Li, Bin   III-1261

Li, Chun-lian II-1159, III-93
Li, Chunshien III-1186
Li, Fu-ming II-992
Li, G.Q. III-668
Li, Guang I-378, I-411, I-1052
Li, Guodong I-773
Li, Guoyou I-397
Li, Haifeng III-972
Li, Hejun II-185
Li, Hong I-952
Li, Hong-Nan III-1089
Li, Hua II-483
Li, Huiguang I-397
Li, Hui-Xian III-453
Li, Jianyu I-867
Li, Jing I-293, II-931
Li, Meiyi III-1308
Li, Ming I-209, I-675
Li, Minqiang III-37, III-171, III-185, III-808, III-943
Li, Na-na I-1047
Li, Qingyong I-903, III-496
Li, Ruonan III-654
Li, Shanbin II-242
Li, Shaoqian II-316
Li, Tao II-800, II-804
Li, Tianpeng III-948
Li, Wei I-995
Li, Wenhui III-938
Li, Wu-Jun II-55
Li, Xiao feng III-505
Li, Xiaobin II-922
Li, Xiaohong II-584
Li, Xiaoming III-808
Li, Xiu II-574
Li, Xu I-378, I-1121
Li, Xu-yong III-68
Li, Xue-yan I-1047
Li, Xuewei III-309
Li, Xuming II-468
Li, Xunming II-602
Li, Yangmin III-628, III-1109
Li, Ye II-175
Li, Yijun II-123
Li, Ying III-215
Li, Yinglu II-627
Li, Yongming III-1132
Li, Yuan I-1132
Li, Yuangui I-528, II-175
Li, Yuanyuan II-774
Li, Yunfeng II-119
Li, Zeng-Zhi III-602, III-883
Li, Zhanhuai III-1001
Li, Zhengxue I-720
Li, Zhishu III-444
Li, Zhong-Wei I-1132
Li, Zi-qiang II-1080
Li, Zongmin II-483
Lian, Hui-Cheng II-438
Liang, Min II-316
Liang, Yan-Chun II-698
Liang, Yanchun III-137, III-1226, III-1257
Liao, Benjamin Penyang III-798
Liao, Guisheng III-1, III-893
Liao, Shasha I-1140
Liao, Zaiyi III-1205
Liebman, M.N. I-1039
Lim, Dudy II-1112
Lim, Heuseok I-844
Lim, Karam I-797
Lim, Myo-Taeg III-1079
Lim, Sehun I-1270
Lim, Soonja III-1044
Lin, Chun-Cheng II-859
Lin, Dacheng I-903
Lin, Dan III-171, III-185, III-808, III-943
Lin, Jian-Yi III-1152
Lin, Jianning III-225
Lin, Mu-Hua III-11
Lin, Pan III-873
Lin, Qian I-390
Lin, Zuoquan I-825
Liu, AnFei II-37
Liu, Benyong I-660
Liu, Bin III-181
Liu, Chen-Hao I-364, II-983, III-205
Liu, Chongyang III-1
Liu, Dang-hui II-7
Liu, Ding II-922
Liu, Dong II-75
Liu, Fang II-780
Liu, Feng II-316
Liu, Feng-yu III-1280
Liu, Guangjie III-976
Liu, Guangyuan III-1231
Liu, Hongbing I-592
Liu, Hua-Yong III-28
Liu, Hui III-903

Liu, Ji II-863
Liu, Jing III-366, III-543, III-925
Liu, Juan III-636
Liu, Jun I-411
Liu, Li II-135
Liu, Lianggui III-457
Liu, Lin III-980
Liu, Ping II-185
Liu, Renren III-1251
Liu, San-yang II-1044
Liu, Shumei III-566
Liu, Wanquan I-1057, III-1198
Liu, Wenhuang II-574
Liu, Xiande II-1105
Liu, Xianghui II-913
Liu, Xiaodong III-1198
Liu, Xiaojie II-804
Liu, Xueliang II-376
Liu, Yan I-750
Liu, Yanjuan III-1235
Liu, Ye III-761
Liu, Yilin II-690
Liu, Yong I-149
Liu, Yongpan III-219
Liu, Yuan-Liang II-296
Liu, Yugang III-1109
Liu, Yuling III-958
Liu, Yutian III-449
Liu, Zhiyong I-340
Liu, Zhongshu III-772
Long, Dong-yun II-1159
Lou, Zhengguo I-411
Lou, Zhenguo I-378
Lu, Bao-Liang I-293, I-303, II-396, II-438
Lu, Bin II-826, III-399, III-768
Lu, Guihua III-129
Lu, Hongtao II-28
Lu, Huifang I-720
Lu, Jiang III-592
Lu, Jiwen I-640
Lu, Qi-Shao I-480, I-1199
Lu, Wenkai II-410
Lu, Yiyu II-584
Lucas, Caro II-1250
Luo, Bin II-55
Luo, H. III-684
Luo, Rong III-219
Luo, Siwei I-322, I-710, I-867
Luo, Yanbin III-1132

Lu-ping, Fang I-499
Lv, Qiang I-81

Ma, Longhua III-289
Ma, Xiaojiang II-81
Maeda, Michiharu I-283, II-361, II-415
Maguire, L.P I-420
Manca, Vincenzo II-1155
Mao, Keji III-782
Mao, Zong-yuan I-601
Marras, William S. III-1216
Matsugu, Masakazu III-1006
Matsuka, Toshihiko I-933
Matsuoka, Kiyotoshi II-274
Maul, Tomás I-893
Mayumi, Oyama-Higa I-811
McGinnity, T.M. I-420
Meng, Fan II-371
Meng, Hong-yun II-1044
Meng, Qingchun II-1005
Meng, Yu III-938
Miao, Gang II-81
Miao, Shouhong III-723
Miao, Tiejun I-811
Mills, Ashley II-666
Min, Zhao I-374
Miyajima, Hiromi I-283, II-361, II-415
Mohanasundaram, K.M. III-572
Monedero, Iñigo II-147
Montaño, Juan C. II-147
Morie, Takashi III-1006
Mozhiwen I-33
Mu, Weisong II-352
Muhammad, Mohd Saufee II-1182
Murthy, V.K. II-784

Nagao, Tomoharu III-566
Nakayama, Hirotaka III-409
Nam, Kichun I-844, I-850
Nam, Mi Young II-109
Nan, Guofang III-943
Narayanan, M. Rajaram III-361
Neagu, Daniel III-1300
Nepomuceno, Erivelton Geraldo III-313
Neskovic, Predrag I-71, I-554, I-877
Ng, Hee-Khiang II-1112
Nguyen, Duc-Hoai I-1113
Nguyen, Ha-Nam I-1017
Nhat, Vo Dinh Minh II-101
Nian, Rui I-793, I-1256

Nie, Weike II-839
Nie, Yinling II-839
Niu, Xiao-hui I-1047
Niu, Xiaoxiao I-592
Nomura, Osamu III-1006
Nowinski, Wieslaw L. I-1065

Obayashi, Masanao I-439
Oh, Heung-Bum I-1009
Ohn, Syng-Yup I-1017
Ohyama, Norifumi II-274
Ok, Sooyol II-714
Olhofer, Markus II-1145
Ong, Yew-Soon II-1112
Önkal-Engin, Güleda II-648
Ono, Osamu II-1174, II-1182
Ooshima, Masataka II-274
Ou, Ling II-814
Ou, Zongying II-119, III-688

Pai, Ping-Feng I-619, I-668
Palaniappan, K. III-1132
Palmes, Paulito P. III-1119
Pan, Chen II-135
Pan, Li III-934
Pan, Zhigeng III-1051
Pappalardo, Francesco III-161
Park, Chang-Hyun II-85
Park, Chun-Ja III-1069
Park, Dong-Chul I-1113, I-1266
Park, Gwi-Tae III-1099
Park, Hyun Jin II-451
Park, Hyun-Soo II-543
Park, Jaehyun I-1017
Park, Jong-An I-1027, II-43
Park, Jong-won III-1069
Park, Kinam I-844
Park, Kyu-Sik I-1017
Park, Kyungdo I-1247, II-636
Park, Moon-sung III-1069
Park, Sang Chan II-530
Park, Seoung-Kyu II-224
Park, Taesu I-1027
Park, Yongjin III-741
Park, Youn J. I-818
Park, Young-Ran III-962
Parsopoulos, K.E. III-582
Parvez, Shuja II-1112
Pei, Xiao-mei I-1031, III-646
Pei, Xiaomei II-376

Peng, Jing III-194
Peng, Tao II-690
Peng, Wei I-835
Peng, Wen II-1229
Peng, Xiao-qi III-477
Pi, Daoying I-688, I-706, I-716
Pi, Xiongjun I-1035, I-1043
Pigg, Paul III-1242
Polat, Kemal II-830
Posenato, Roberto III-235
Priesterjahn, Steffen II-744
Puntonet, C.G. III-863
Pyun, Jae Young II-43

Qi, Huan III-482
Qi, Ming II-51
Qian, Feng II-631
Qian, Jixin III-289, III-948
Qian, Yuntao II-391
Qin, Guoqiang III-592
Qin, Qiming III-1261, III-1274
Qin, Zheng II-756, III-592
Qin-ye, Tong I-499
Qiu, Jiang I-952
Qiu, Yuhui III-562
Qiu, Zulian I-340

Rameshkumar, K. III-572
Ravi, S. III-361
Ren, Quanmin II-81
Ren, Xinhua II-774
Rhee, Phill Kyu II-109, II-764, III-356
Richer, Jean-Michel III-678
Ríos, Sebastían A. II-622
Rocha e Silva, Valceres Vieira III-313
Rojas, F. III-863
Rong, Lili III-151
Ropero, Jorge II-147
Rowlands, Hefin III-877
Rubo, Zhang III-553
Ruizhi, Sun I-650
Ryu, Joung Woo II-155
Ryu, Kwang Ryel II-1259

Sadedin, Suzanne II-1131
Sahan, Seral II-830
Sáiz, José Manuel I-778
Sakamoto, Makoto II-1025
Sang, Enfang. I-199
Sasaki, S. III-684

Sendhoff, Bernhard   II-1112, II-1145
Sengupta, Biswa   I-429
Seo, Kyung-Sik   I-1027
Seo, Sam-Jun   III-1099
Seok, Kyung Ha   I-536
Shang, Fu hua   III-505
Shang, Jincheng   III-374
Shang, Lin   III-855
Shen, Hong-yuan   III-477
Shen, Lan-sun   I-975, II-7
Shen, Xisheng   I-470
Shen, Xueqin   I-692
Shen, Yi   I-740
Shen, Zhenyao   III-129
Shi, Feng   I-1047, III-636
Shi, Haixiang   I-1080
Shi, Jun   III-496
Shi, Lukui   I-692
Shi, Min   I-229
Shi, Wenkang   I-679
Shi, Xi   II-1089
Shi, Xiangquan   II-508
Shi, Yan-jun   II-1080
Shi, Yuexiang   III-1308
Shi, Zhiping   III-496
Shi, Zhongzhi   I-903, III-496
Shigei, Noritaka   II-361, II-415
Shi-hua, Luo   I-374
Shim, JeongYon   I-1170
Shim, Jooyong   I-512, I-521
Shin, Dongil   I-1185, II-552
Shin, Dongkyoo   I-1185, II-552
Shin, Jeong-Hoon   I-1179
Shin, Kyung-shik   I-1247, II-636
Shin, Sang-Uk   III-962
Shou-jue, Wang   I-264
Shriver, C.D.   I-1039
Sim, Kwee-Bo   I-237, II-85, III-713
Smutek, Daniel   III-841
So, Yeon-hee   I-797
Soh, W-S.   I-1057
Sohn, Insuk   II-306
Soke, Alev   III-1304
Somiari, R.   I-1039
Somiari, S.B.   I-1039
Song   III-1089
Song, Chonghui   II-214
Song, Gangbing   III-1089
Song, Hong   II-863, III-602
Song, Jingyan   II-1089

Song, Shiji   I-470
Song, Weiwei   III-972
Song, Xiao-yu   II-992
Song, Yexin   II-1101
Srinivas, M.B.   III-1015
Su, Guangda   I-985
Su, Juanhua   II-185
Su, Tao   III-893
Su, Tieming   III-688
Su, Xiao-hong   I-213
Suenaga, Masaya   I-283
Sun, Changping   I-397
Sun, Changyin   II-602
Sun, Jiancheng   I-573
Sun, Jigui   III-434
Sun, Jun   III-543
Sun, Lin-yan   III-911
Sun, Shiliang   II-652
Sun, Wei   II-190
Sun, Xin-yu   III-911
Sun, Xingming   III-958, III-968
Sun, Yanguang   I-546
Sun, Yi   II-12
Sun, Ying-Guang   III-1152
Sun, Youxian   I-688, I-706, I-716,
    II-242, II-292
Sun, Yu   II-1159, III-93
Sun, Zengqi   II-234, II-252,
    II-262, III-141
Sun, Zhengxing   I-655
Sun, Zonghai   II-292
Sung, HyunSeong   II-451
Sureerattanan, Nidapan   I-157
Sureerattanan, Songyot   I-157
Suresh, R.K.   III-572
Szeto, Kwok Yip   III-112

Takikawa, Erina   II-438
Tan, E.C.   I-975
Tan, Guanzheng   III-915
Tan, Min   III-622
Tan, Ying   II-476, II-493, II-501, II-867
Tang, Chang-jie   III-194
Tang, Deyou   II-1049
Tang, Enyi   I-655
Tang, Min   II-1229, III-48
Tang, Renyuan   III-1162
Tang, Xiaojun   I-806
Tang, Xiaowei   I-1052
Tang, Xusheng   III-688

Tang, Yinggan   II-75
Tang, Yiyuan   I-1052
Tang, Yuan Yan   III-663
Tang, Zhe   II-252
Tao, Hai-hong   III-893
Tao, Jun   III-761
Taylor, Meinwen   III-877
Temeltas, Hakan   III-703
Teng, Hong-fei   II-1080
Tesař, Ludvík   III-841
Thapa, Devinder   I-888
Tiño, Peter   II-666, II-676
Tian, Jie   I-187
Tian, Lian-fang   I-601
Tian, Shengfeng   III-323
Tian, Zheng   II-371
Ting, Ching-Jung   III-205
Toh, C.K.   III-525
Tong, Ruofeng   II-1229
Tong, Weimin   II-123
Tsaftaris, Sotirios A.   II-1192
Tseng, Chung-Li   III-741
Tsuboi, Yusei   II-1174
Tsuji, Toshio   II-165
Tu, Li   II-1218

Ueda, Satomi   II-1182
Uno, Yoji   I-313
Usui, Shiro   I-1074, III-1119

Valeev, Tagir   II-1202
Valenzuela, O.   III-863
van Noort, Danny   II-1206
Velásquez, Juan D.   II-622
Vera, Eduardo S.   II-622
Von Zuben, Fernando J.   I-1279
Vrahatis, M.N.   III-582

Wakaki, Keitaro   I-313
Wan, Jinming   III-332
Wan, Qiong   III-855
Wang, Ai-guo   III-93
Wang, Bin   II-410, III-822
Wang, Chao-Xue   II-1269, III-86
Wang, Chaoyong   III-1226
Wang, Chen   III-845
Wang, Chong-Jun   II-55
Wang, Dingsheng Luo Xinhao   I-167
Wang, Fang   III-562, III-622
Wang, G.L.   II-266

Wang, Gang   I-700
Wang, Gi-Nam   I-888
Wang, Guizeng   II-95
Wang, Guo-Xin   III-1089
Wang, Guoqiang   II-119
Wang, Hai   III-883
Wang, Hai-Xia   I-1199
Wang, Haijun   I-405
Wang, He-Jun   I-1150
Wang, Hong   III-171, III-185
Wang, Honggang   III-22
Wang, Hongguang   III-727
Wang, Hui   I-716, III-219
Wang, Jigang   I-71, I-554
Wang, Jinwei   III-976
Wang, Jun-nian   III-477
Wang, Le   I-378
Wang, Lei   II-839, III-86
Wang, Lifang   III-467
Wang, Ling   III-417, III-832
Wang, Lipo   I-1080
Wang, Long   I-769, III-424
Wang, Longhui   III-636
Wang, Lunwen   II-501
Wang, Nong   I-217
Wang, Qiao   III-1261, III-1274
Wang, Qing-Yun   I-1199
Wang, Qingquan   III-151
Wang, Rubin   I-490
Wang, Shan-Shan   III-482
Wang, Shi-min   I-480
Wang, Shitong   III-1128
Wang, Shouyang   I-382
Wang, Shuqing   II-270
Wang, Shuxun   III-972
Wang, Song   II-574
Wang, Tong   III-938
Wang, W.   I-199
Wang, Wanliang   I-332, II-795
Wang, Weihong   I-1209
Wang, Weizhi   III-1022
Wang, X.X.   II-1122
Wang, Xi-cheng   II-1159, III-93
Wang, Xiaodong   I-221
Wang, Xiaofan   II-283
Wang, Xiaolong   I-947
Wang, Xihuai   II-196
Wang, Xin   III-525
Wang, Xinfei   II-584
Wang, Xing-Yu   I-565, II-21, II-89

Wang, Xiufeng   II-978
Wang, Ya-dong   I-213
Wang, Yan   II-12, II-698
Wang, Yaonan   II-190
Wang, Yen-Nien   II-859
Wang, Yen-Wen   I-364, II-983, III-205
Wang, Yong   I-565
Wang, Yong-Xian   II-1164
Wang, Yongcheng   I-925
Wang, Yongqiang   II-292
Wang, Yuping   III-392
Wang, Zhanshan   I-61
Wang, Zheng-Hua   II-1164
Wang, Zhijie   I-476
Wang, Zhiquan   III-976
Wang, Zhizhong   III-1142
Wang, Zhu-Rong   II-1269, III-86
Wang, Zilei   I-1090
Wang, Ziqiang   II-727, II-822
Wanlin, Gao   I-650
Watanabe, Atsushi   II-274
Wei, Ding   II-338
Wei, Li   I-601
Wei, Xiaopeng   I-405
Wei, Yaobing   I-390
Wei, Yunbing   I-332
Wei, Zhi   II-592
Wei, Zhiqiang   II-1005
Weijun, Li   I-264
Weimer, Alexander   II-744
Weizhong, Guo   I-44
Wen, Quan   III-972
Wen, Wanhui   III-1231
Wen, Xiangjun   I-51, I-582
Woo, Kwang Bang   I-1160, II-564
Wu, Chunguo   III-137, III-1226, III-1257
Wu, Fangfang   I-608
Wu, Hao   III-417
Wu, Huizhong   III-225
Wu, Jianping   II-105
Wu, Kai-Gui   II-814
Wu, Lenan   II-468
Wu, Qing   I-692
Wu, Qingliang   III-761
Wu, QingXiang   I-420
Wu, Qiongshui   II-210
Wu, Tihua   I-397
Wu, Wei   I-720, III-772
Wu, Xiaoping   II-1101
Wu, Xihong   I-167

Wu, Yadong   III-332
Wu, Yan   III-1
Wu, Ying   I-390, I-508
Wu, Yiqiang   I-8
Wu, Yong   III-958
Wu, Yun   III-120
Wu, Zhong-Fu   II-814

Xi, Hongsheng   I-1090
Xia, Feng   II-242
Xiang, Zheng   I-573
Xiang-guan, Liu   I-374
Xiao, Fen   I-783, II-139
Xiao, Jian   I-101
Xiao, Jianmei   II-196
Xiao, Yunshi   I-119
Xiaolong, Deng   I-44
Xie, Gang   II-945
Xie, Guangming   III-424
Xie, Hongbo   III-1142
Xie, Jun   II-951
Xie, Keming   II-945, II-951, II-957
Xie, Li   I-386
Xie, Lijuan   III-384
Xie, Qihong   III-57
Xie, Sheng-Li   I-839
Xie, Shengli   I-229, II-386, II-442
Xie, Xiaogang   III-1235
Xie, Zongxia   III-1190
Xin-guang, Shao   I-25
Xiong, Shengwu   I-592
Xiong, Zhangliang   II-508
Xu, Bin   II-520
Xu, Chen   I-264
Xu, Chunlin   II-800
Xu, De   III-622
Xu, Fen   III-1251
Xu, Haixia   II-371
Xu, Jian   III-505, III-1280
Xu, Jianxue   I-508
Xu, Jin   I-1031, II-376, III-646
Xu, Jinhua   I-730
Xu, Junqin   III-299
Xu, Min   III-1128
Xu, Wenbo   III-543
Xu, Xiaoming   I-51, I-582, II-175
Xu, Xin   I-700, II-1035
Xu, Xinli   II-795
Xu, Xinying   II-945
Xu, Xiuling   I-221

Author Index

Xu, Yangsheng II-1089
Xu, Yubin III-22
Xu, Yuelei I-449
Xu, Yuhui I-139, I-345
Xu, Yusheng I-139, I-345
Xu, Zhenhao II-880
Xu, Zhiwei I-750
Xue, Juan III-68
Xue, Q. II-266
Xue, Xiangyang III-525
Xue, Xiaoping I-466

Yan, Gaowei II-951
Yan, Haifeng III-444
Yan, Shaoze III-632
Yan, Weidong III-980
Yan, Xiao-Ke I-1150
Yan, Xin III-980
Yan, Xiong III-181
Yang, Bo I-213
Yang, C.F. II-557
Yang, Chunyan II-214
Yang, Hai-Dong I-1150
Yang, Hsiao-Fang III-11
Yang, Huazhong III-219
Yang, Hui II-214
Yang, Hui-Hua I-565, II-21, II-89
Yang, Hwan-Seok II-224
Yang, Hyun-Seung III-1178
Yang, Jian I-322
Yang, Jiangang III-490
Yang, Jie II-95
Yang, Jing I-1132
Yang, Jun III-120
Yang, Jun-an II-461
Yang, Kongyu II-978
Yang, Li-ying II-756
Yang, Luxi I-683
Yang, Pin II-804
Yang, Qing II-442
Yang, Shun-Lin I-668
Yang, Shuzhong I-710
Yang, Wenlu I-1043
Yang, Xiaohua III-129
Yang, Xiaowei III-137, III-1257
Yang, Xin I-187
Yang, Xiyang I-225
Yang, Xuhua I-332
Yang, Yipeng III-1274
Yang, Yong III-873

Yang, YonQing I-15
Yang, Zheng Rong I-179
Yang, Zhifeng III-129
Yang, Zhixia I-217
Yang, Zhuo I-806
Yao, JingTao I-129
Yao, Shuzhen II-1049
Yao, Xin III-279
Yasuda, Hiroshi II-622
Yazhu, Qiu I-33
Ye, Bin II-895
Ye, Hao II-95
Ye, Jun II-1105
Ye, Mao II-557
Ye, Xiuzi I-835
Ye, Zhongfu II-461
Yi, Bian I-264
Yi, Yang III-74
Yibo, Zhang I-696
Yim, Hyungwook I-844
Yin, Bo II-1005
Yin, Changming III-384
Yin, Chao-wan II-992
Yin, Chuanhuan III-323
Yin, Jianping II-65, II-913
Yin, Junsong I-101
Yin, Ling I-1052
Yin, Xiao-chuan II-539
Yokoyama, Ryuichi III-313
Yoo, Kee-Young II-512, III-348
Yoo, Sun K. I-818
Yoon, Eun-Jun II-512
Yoon, Han-Ul III-713
Yoon, Hye-Sung I-965
Yoon, Mi-sun I-797
Yoon, Min III-409
You, Jing III-1280
You, Xinge III-663
Young, Natasha I-179
Youxian, Sun I-696
Yu, Changjie II-262
Yu, Daren III-1190
Yu, Fusheng I-225
Yu, Jin-shou I-81
Yu, Jinshou I-630, II-610, III-515, III-832
Yu, Lean I-382
Yu, Qizhi III-1051
Yu, Wei I-490
Yu, Xinjie II-1064, II-1072

Author Index

Yu, Zhenhua II-627
Yu, Zu-Guo III-337
Yuan, Chang-an III-194
Yuan, Hong I-952
Yuan, Lin I-199, III-1001
Yue, Jiguang I-119
Yun, Jung-Hyun III-1032
Yun, Sung-Hyun I-797
Yun, Yeboon III-409
Yusof, Azwina I-893
Yıldırım, Tülay I-110

Zeng, Jianchao III-22, III-255, III-467
Zeng, Libo II-210
Zeng, Qingdong III-915
Zeng, Sanyou II-1049
Zeng, Zhigang I-664
Zhan, Tao III-602, III-883
Zhang, Changjiang I-221
Zhang, Changshui II-652
Zhang, Chunfang II-1239
Zhang, Chunkai I-91
Zhang, Dan II-863, III-602, III-883
Zhang, Defu III-1235
Zhang, Dexian II-727, II-822
Zhang, Dongmo I-956
Zhang, Erhu I-640
Zhang, Feng III-873
Zhang, Gang II-957
Zhang, Guomin II-65
Zhang, Haoran I-221
Zhang, Hongbo II-210
Zhang, Huaguang I-61
Zhang, Huidang I-273
Zhang, Jian II-266, III-112
Zhang, Jiang III-309
Zhang, Jianming II-270
Zhang, Jian-Pei I-1132
Zhang, Jihui III-299
Zhang, Jing I-660, I-1052, III-194
Zhang, Jingjing III-102
Zhang, Jun I-358, I-783, II-139, II-592
Zhang, Lei III-535
Zhang, Ling II-501
Zhang, Liqing I-1043
Zhang, Lisha I-655
Zhang, Min II-476, III-668
Zhang, Qiang I-405
Zhang, Qing-Guo III-28
Zhang, Sanyuan I-835

Zhang, Shuai III-1300
Zhang, Shui-ping II-539
Zhang, Taiyi I-573
Zhang, Tao I-806
Zhang, Wei III-28
Zhang, Weidong I-528
Zhang, Wen III-449
Zhang, Wenquan I-8
Zhang, Xianfei II-37
Zhang, Xiangrong II-905
Zhang, XianMing II-1
Zhang, Xiao-hua II-1044
Zhang, Xiaoshuan II-352
Zhang, Xiufeng II-774
Zhang, Xuanping III-592
Zhang, Xudong III-654
Zhang, Y.S. III-1060
Zhang, Yan III-938
Zhang, Yanning III-215
Zhang, Yanxin II-283
Zhang, Ye I-8
Zhang, Yuanzhen II-483
Zhang, Yulei I-956
Zhang, Yuming III-723
Zhang, Yuntao I-925
Zhang, Z.Z. III-668
Zhang, Zhen-Hui II-1164
Zhang, Zhengwei II-95
Zhang, Zhijie I-952
Zhang, Zhousuo II-324
Zhao, Bin II-461
Zhao, Bo II-895
Zhao, Guoying I-740
Zhao, Hai I-303
Zhao, Hengping I-630
Zhao, Jian II-346
Zhao, Jieyu II-432
Zhao, Jin-cheng II-1159
Zhao, Jing II-557
Zhao, Jun III-948
Zhao, Keyou III-698
Zhao, Li II-71
Zhao, Liang I-1189
Zhao, Liping I-956
Zhao, Mingyang III-727
Zhao, Pengfei III-688
Zhao, Qiang III-632
Zhao, Qijun II-28
Zhao, Qin II-346
Zhao, Rongchun III-215

Zhao, Wencang   I-793, I-1256
Zhao, Xi   III-137
Zhao, Xinyu   I-825
Zhao, Xue-long   III-1280
Zhao, Yinliang   I-608
Zhao, Yu   I-1090, II-584
Zhao, Zhefeng   II-957
Zhao, Zhi-Hong   III-855
Zhao, Zhilong   III-980
Zhao, Zijiang   III-444
Zheng, ChongXun   I-1031, II-376, III-646, III-873
Zheng, Da-zhong   III-417
Zheng, Hong   II-210, III-934
Zheng, Ji   III-525
Zheng, Jin-hua   III-68
Zheng, Shiqin   II-978
Zheng, Yi   I-8
Zheng, Yisong   I-773
Zhexin, Cao   II-316
Zhi, Qiang   II-316
Zhong, Jiang   II-814
Zhong, Weicai   III-366, III-925
Zhong, Weimin   I-706
Zhong, Xiang-Ping   II-55
Zhou, Changjiu   II-252
Zhou, Chun-Guang   II-698
Zhou, Dongsheng   I-405
Zhou, Jian   III-120, III-684
Zhou, Jiping   III-727
Zhou, Li-Quan   III-337
Zhou, Lifang   III-289
Zhou, Ming-quan   II-346

Zhou, Qiang   III-181
Zhou, Shude   III-141
Zhou, Wen-Gang   II-698
Zhou, Xiaoyang   III-374
Zhou, Ying   II-814
Zhou, Yuanfeng   II-105
Zhou, Yuanpai   III-269
Zhou, Yuren   II-1015
Zhou, Zhi-Heng   I-839
Zhou, Zhong   III-772
Zhou, Zongtan   I-101, I-209, I-675
Zhu, Chengzhi   II-895
Zhu, Daqi   I-15
Zhu, En   II-65
Zhu, Jia   III-93
Zhu, Jianguang   III-1162
Zhu, Jihong   II-234, II-262
Zhu, Qingsheng   III-57
Zhu, Xinglong   III-727
Zhu, Xue-feng   I-995
Zhu, Yan-fei   I-601
Zhu, Yun-long   II-992
Zhu, Zheng-Zhou   II-814
Zhu, Zhengyu   III-57
Zi, Yanyang   II-324
Zou, Cairong   II-71
Zou, Henghui   III-996
Zou, Hengming   III-988, III-996, III-1001
Zou, Qi   I-867
Zribi, Nozha   III-259
Zuo, Wanli   II-690
Zuo, Wen-ming   II-51
Zurada, Jacek M.   III-1216

Lecture Notes in Computer Science

For information about Vols. 1–3537

please contact your bookseller or Springer

Vol. 3659: J.R. Rao, B. Sunar (Eds.), Cryptographic Hardware and Embedded Systems – CHES 2005. XIV, 458 pages. 2005.

Vol. 3654: S. Jajodia, D. Wijesekera (Eds.), Data and Applications Security XIX. X, 353 pages. 2005.

Vol. 3653: M. Abadi, L.d. Alfaro (Eds.), CONCUR 2005 – Concurrency Theory. XIV, 578 pages. 2005.

Vol. 3649: W.M.P. van der Aalst, B. Benatallah, F. Casati, F. Curbera (Eds.), Business Process Management. XII, 472 pages. 2005.

Vol. 3639: P. Godefroid (Ed.), Model Checking Software. XI, 289 pages. 2005.

Vol. 3638: A. Butz, B. Fisher, A. Krüger, P. Olivier (Eds.), Smart Graphics. XI, 269 pages. 2005.

Vol. 3636: M.J. Blesa, C. Blum, A. Roli, M. Sampels (Eds.), Hybrid Metaheuristics. XII, 155 pages. 2005.

Vol. 3634: L. Ong (Ed.), Computer Science Logic. XI, 567 pages. 2005.

Vol. 3633: C. Bauzer Medeiros, M. Egenhofer, E. Bertino (Eds.), Advances in Spatial and Temporal Databases. XIII, 433 pages. 2005.

Vol. 3632: R. Nieuwenhuis (Ed.), Automated Deduction – CADE-20. XIII, 459 pages. 2005. (Subseries LNAI).

Vol. 3627: C. Jacob, M.L. Pilat, P.J. Bentley, J. Timmis (Eds.), Artificial Immune Systems. XII, 500 pages. 2005.

Vol. 3626: B. Ganter, G. Stumme, R. Wille (Eds.), Formal Concept Analysis. X, 349 pages. 2005. (Subseries LNAI).

Vol. 3625: S. Kramer, B. Pfahringer (Eds.), Inductive Logic Programming. XIII, 427 pages. 2005. (Subseries LNAI).

Vol. 3624: C. Chekuri, K. Jansen, J.D.P. Rolim, L. Trevisan (Eds.), Approximation, Randomization and Combinatorial Optimization. XI, 495 pages. 2005.

Vol. 3623: M. Liśkiewicz, R. Reischuk (Eds.), Fundamentals of Computation Theory. XV, 576 pages. 2005.

Vol. 3621: V. Shoup (Ed.), Advances in Cryptology – CRYPTO 2005. XI, 568 pages. 2005.

Vol. 3620: H. Muñoz-Avila, F. Ricci (Eds.), Case-Based Reasoning Research and Development. XV, 654 pages. 2005. (Subseries LNAI).

Vol. 3619: X. Lu, W. Zhao (Eds.), Networking and Mobile Computing. XXIV, 1299 pages. 2005.

Vol. 3615: B. Ludäscher, L. Raschid (Eds.), Data Integration in the Life Sciences. XII, 344 pages. 2005. (Subseries LNBI).

Vol. 3614: L. Wang, Y. Jin (Eds.), Fuzzy Systems and Knowledge Discovery, Part II. XLI, 1314 pages. 2005. (Subseries LNAI).

Vol. 3613: L. Wang, Y. Jin (Eds.), Fuzzy Systems and Knowledge Discovery, Part I. XLI, 1334 pages. 2005. (Subseries LNAI).

Vol. 3612: L. Wang, K. Chen, Y. S. Ong (Eds.), Advances in Natural Computation, Part III. LXI, 1326 pages. 2005.

Vol. 3611: L. Wang, K. Chen, Y. S. Ong (Eds.), Advances in Natural Computation, Part II. LXI, 1292 pages. 2005.

Vol. 3610: L. Wang, K. Chen, Y. S. Ong (Eds.), Advances in Natural Computation, Part I. LXI, 1302 pages. 2005.

Vol. 3608: F. Dehne, A. López-Ortiz, J.-R. Sack (Eds.), Algorithms and Data Structures. XIV, 446 pages. 2005.

Vol. 3607: J.-D. Zucker, L. Saitta (Eds.), Abstraction, Reformulation and Approximation. XII, 376 pages. 2005. (Subseries LNAI).

Vol. 3606: V. Malyshkin (Ed.), Parallel Computing Technologies. XII, 470 pages. 2005.

Vol. 3603: J. Hurd, T. Melham (Eds.), Theorem Proving in Higher Order Logics. IX, 409 pages. 2005.

Vol. 3602: R. Eigenmann, Z. Li, S.P. Midkiff (Eds.), Languages and Compilers for High Performance Computing. IX, 486 pages. 2005.

Vol. 3599: U. Aßmann, M. Aksit, A. Rensink (Eds.), Model Driven Architecture. X, 235 pages. 2005.

Vol. 3598: H. Murakami, H. Nakashima, H. Tokuda, M. Yasumura, Ubiquitous Computing Systems. XIII, 275 pages. 2005.

Vol. 3597: S. Shimojo, S. Ichii, T.W. Ling, K.-H. Song (Eds.), Web and Communication Technologies and Internet-Related Social Issues - HSI 2005. XIX, 368 pages. 2005.

Vol. 3596: F. Dau, M.-L. Mugnier, G. Stumme (Eds.), Conceptual Structures: Common Semantics for Sharing Knowledge. XI, 467 pages. 2005. (Subseries LNAI).

Vol. 3595: L. Wang (Ed.), Computing and Combinatorics. XVI, 995 pages. 2005.

Vol. 3594: J.C. Setubal, S. Verjovski-Almeida (Eds.), Advances in Bioinformatics and Computational Biology. XIV, 258 pages. 2005. (Subseries LNBI).

Vol. 3593: V. Mařík, R. W. Brennan, M. Pěchouček (Eds.), Holonic and Multi-Agent Systems for Manufacturing. XI, 269 pages. 2005. (Subseries LNAI).

Vol. 3592: S. Katsikas, J. Lopez, G. Pernul (Eds.), Trust, Privacy and Security in Digital Business. XII, 332 pages. 2005.

Vol. 3591: M.A. Wimmer, R. Traunmüller, Å. Grönlund, K.V. Andersen (Eds.), Electronic Government. XIII, 317 pages. 2005.

Vol. 3590: K. Bauknecht, B. Pröll, H. Werthner (Eds.), E-Commerce and Web Technologies. XIV, 380 pages. 2005.

Vol. 3587: P. Perner, A. Imiya (Eds.), Machine Learning and Data Mining in Pattern Recognition. XVII, 695 pages. 2005. (Subseries LNAI).

Vol. 3586: A.P. Black (Ed.), ECOOP 2005 - Object-Oriented Programming. XVII, 631 pages. 2005.

Vol. 3584: X. Li, S. Wang, Z.Y. Dong (Eds.), Advanced Data Mining and Applications. XIX, 835 pages. 2005. (Subseries LNAI).

Vol. 3583: R.W. H. Lau, Q. Li, R. Cheung, W. Liu (Eds.), Advances in Web-Based Learning – ICWL 2005. XIV, 420 pages. 2005.

Vol. 3582: J. Fitzgerald, I.J. Hayes, A. Tarlecki (Eds.), FM 2005: Formal Methods. XIV, 558 pages. 2005.

Vol. 3581: S. Miksch, J. Hunter, E. Keravnou (Eds.), Artificial Intelligence in Medicine. XVII, 547 pages. 2005. (Subseries LNAI).

Vol. 3580: L. Caires, G.F. Italiano, L. Monteiro, C. Palamidessi, M. Yung (Eds.), Automata, Languages and Programming. XXV, 1477 pages. 2005.

Vol. 3579: D. Lowe, M. Gaedke (Eds.), Web Engineering. XXII, 633 pages. 2005.

Vol. 3578: M. Gallagher, J. Hogan, F. Maire (Eds.), Intelligent Data Engineering and Automated Learning - IDEAL 2005. XVI, 599 pages. 2005.

Vol. 3577: R. Falcone, S. Barber, J. Sabater-Mir, M.P. Singh (Eds.), Trusting Agents for Trusting Electronic Societies. VIII, 235 pages. 2005. (Subseries LNAI).

Vol. 3576: K. Etessami, S.K. Rajamani (Eds.), Computer Aided Verification. XV, 564 pages. 2005.

Vol. 3575: S. Wermter, G. Palm, M. Elshaw (Eds.), Biomimetic Neural Learning for Intelligent Robots. IX, 383 pages. 2005. (Subseries LNAI).

Vol. 3574: C. Boyd, J.M. González Nieto (Eds.), Information Security and Privacy. XIII, 586 pages. 2005.

Vol. 3573: S. Etalle (Ed.), Logic Based Program Synthesis and Transformation. VIII, 279 pages. 2005.

Vol. 3572: C. De Felice, A. Restivo (Eds.), Developments in Language Theory. XI, 409 pages. 2005.

Vol. 3571: L. Godo (Ed.), Symbolic and Quantitative Approaches to Reasoning with Uncertainty. XVI, 1028 pages. 2005. (Subseries LNAI).

Vol. 3570: A. S. Patrick, M. Yung (Eds.), Financial Cryptography and Data Security. XII, 376 pages. 2005.

Vol. 3569: F. Bacchus, T. Walsh (Eds.), Theory and Applications of Satisfiability Testing. XII, 492 pages. 2005.

Vol. 3568: W.-K. Leow, M.S. Lew, T.-S. Chua, W.-Y. Ma, L. Chaisorn, E.M. Bakker (Eds.), Image and Video Retrieval. XVII, 672 pages. 2005.

Vol. 3567: M. Jackson, D. Nelson, S. Stirk (Eds.), Database: Enterprise, Skills and Innovation. XII, 185 pages. 2005.

Vol. 3566: J.-P. Banâtre, P. Fradet, J.-L. Giavitto, O. Michel (Eds.), Unconventional Programming Paradigms. XI, 367 pages. 2005.

Vol. 3565: G.E. Christensen, M. Sonka (Eds.), Information Processing in Medical Imaging. XXI, 777 pages. 2005.

Vol. 3564: N. Eisinger, J. Małuszyński (Eds.), Reasoning Web. IX, 319 pages. 2005.

Vol. 3562: J. Mira, J.R. Álvarez (Eds.), Artificial Intelligence and Knowledge Engineering Applications: A Bioinspired Approach, Part II. XXIV, 636 pages. 2005.

Vol. 3561: J. Mira, J.R. Álvarez (Eds.), Mechanisms, Symbols, and Models Underlying Cognition, Part I. XXIV, 532 pages. 2005.

Vol. 3560: V.K. Prasanna, S. Iyengar, P.G. Spirakis, M. Welsh (Eds.), Distributed Computing in Sensor Systems. XV, 423 pages. 2005.

Vol. 3559: P. Auer, R. Meir (Eds.), Learning Theory. XI, 692 pages. 2005. (Subseries LNAI).

Vol. 3558: V. Torra, Y. Narukawa, S. Miyamoto (Eds.), Modeling Decisions for Artificial Intelligence. XII, 470 pages. 2005. (Subseries LNAI).

Vol. 3557: H. Gilbert, H. Handschuh (Eds.), Fast Software Encryption. XI, 443 pages. 2005.

Vol. 3556: H. Baumeister, M. Marchesi, M. Holcombe (Eds.), Extreme Programming and Agile Processes in Software Engineering. XIV, 332 pages. 2005.

Vol. 3555: T. Vardanega, A.J. Wellings (Eds.), Reliable Software Technology – Ada-Europe 2005. XV, 273 pages. 2005.

Vol. 3554: A. Dey, B. Kokinov, D. Leake, R. Turner (Eds.), Modeling and Using Context. XIV, 572 pages. 2005. (Subseries LNAI).

Vol. 3553: T.D. Hämäläinen, A.D. Pimentel, J. Takala, S. Vassiliadis (Eds.), Embedded Computer Systems: Architectures, Modeling, and Simulation. XV, 476 pages. 2005.

Vol. 3552: H. de Meer, N. Bhatti (Eds.), Quality of Service – IWQoS 2005. XVIII, 400 pages. 2005.

Vol. 3551: T. Härder, W. Lehner (Eds.), Data Management in a Connected World. XIX, 371 pages. 2005.

Vol. 3548: K. Julisch, C. Kruegel (Eds.), Intrusion and Malware Detection and Vulnerability Assessment. X, 241 pages. 2005.

Vol. 3547: F. Bomarius, S. Komi-Sirviö (Eds.), Product Focused Software Process Improvement. XIII, 588 pages. 2005.

Vol. 3546: T. Kanade, A. Jain, N.K. Ratha (Eds.), Audio- and Video-Based Biometric Person Authentication. XX, 1134 pages. 2005.

Vol. 3544: T. Higashino (Ed.), Principles of Distributed Systems. XII, 460 pages. 2005.

Vol. 3543: L. Kutvonen, N. Alonistioti (Eds.), Distributed Applications and Interoperable Systems. XI, 235 pages. 2005.

Vol. 3542: H.H. Hoos, D.G. Mitchell (Eds.), Theory and Applications of Satisfiability Testing. XIII, 393 pages. 2005.

Vol. 3541: N.C. Oza, R. Polikar, J. Kittler, F. Roli (Eds.), Multiple Classifier Systems. XII, 430 pages. 2005.

Vol. 3540: H. Kalviainen, J. Parkkinen, A. Kaarna (Eds.), Image Analysis. XXII, 1270 pages. 2005.

Vol. 3539: K. Morik, J.-F. Boulicaut, A. Siebes (Eds.), Local Pattern Detection. XI, 233 pages. 2005. (Subseries LNAI).

Vol. 3538: L. Ardissono, P. Brna, A. Mitrovic (Eds.), User Modeling 2005. XVI, 533 pages. 2005. (Subseries LNAI).